2.00

THE ILLUSTRATED ENCYCLOPEDIA OF AMERICAN COOKING

THE ILLUSTRATED ENCYCLOPEDIA OF AMERICAN COOKING

By the editors of FAVORITE RECIPES PRESS

THE SOUTHWESTERN CO., NASHVILLE, TENNESSEE

Library of Congress Cataloging in Publication Data
Main entry under title:
The Illustrated Encyclopedia of American Cooking.
Includes index.
1. Cookery, American – Dictionaries. I. Favorite Recipes Press. II. Title: American cooking.
TX715.I.32 1983 641.5'03'21 83-628
ISBN 0-87197-149-6

Introduction

In the *Illustrated Encyclopedia of American Cooking,* the excitement and diversity of American cuisine has been captured and brought to you in one easy-to-use volume. American cooking has always been uniquely varied. Part of its uniqueness comes from the almost infinite variety of foods available in America. Part comes from the influence of generations of newcomers from many nations, all of whom helped to create American cookery.

Here, in this volume, you will find more than 5,000 recipes for all the foods and dishes American families have made their own. They are recipes that women can feature on occasions when a homemaker's cooking is the measure of her effectiveness. The recipes in this encyclopedia are representative of every food dish served in American homes. They are not restricted to the usually prepared foods but include exotic specialties such as mangoes, lane cake, and sweetbreads.

Every recipe included in this encyclopedia has been edited so that the ingredients are listed in the order they will be used. Those ingredients that require such advance preparation as dicing, mincing and so on, are specified. It was felt that listing ingredients this way prevents a homemaker from getting halfway through preparing a recipe, then discovering she must stop to prepare an ingredient she needs. As a further aid to efficiency in preparing food, every recipe has been edited to use a minimum of pots and pans, bowls, and so on.

But the thousands of recipes in these pages are just one feature of this amazingly comprehensive volume. The recipes have been grouped by specific foods or dishes into more than 200 separate alphabetically-organized entries. Many of

these entries include detailed, up-to-date information with interesting facts about the origin or use of the food, its nutritional and caloric value, when it is available, and how to buy, store, prepare, and serve it.

Complementing these entries are 146 brilliant full-color photographs and 250 black-and-white ones to help you envision how a specific recipe might look when you serve it. And because we know that you expect more from a complete encyclopedia than information about foods, recipes, and illustrations, we have created special feature sections. Throughout this volume, these features explain the intricacies of many food-related subjects: how to use your microwave oven; how to make bread, cake, candy, and pastry; how to carve ham, beef, lamb, pork, and poultry; how to garnish every type of dish; how to set an attractive table for every occasion from the most casual breakfast to the most important formal dinner; how to can and preserve just-picked fruits and vegetables; how to prepare fondues and souffles; and how to choose the right wine for every occasion and every food.

Many of these special features are accompanied by charts that contain valuable information in an easy-to-read format. Other charts, too, are featured throughout the volume. Beginning with a chart describing the major varieties of apples and how to serve them, you'll discover charts that tell how to select and serve different cheeses; how to season with herbs and spices; the various cuts and ways of preparing beef, veal, poultry, lamb, and pork; why the various nutrients mentioned throughout the encyclopedia are important for growth and development; and the wine glasses to use with each course you serve.

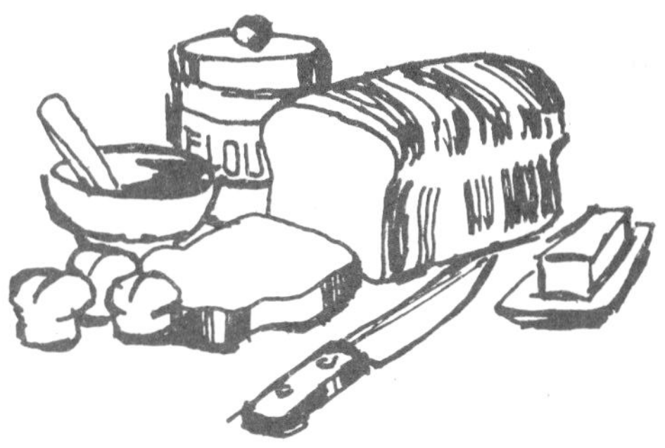

Best of all, every bit of this invaluable information has been organized so that you can find it in just seconds. It is contained in one handy, easy-to-use, alphabetized volume. To find the food or dish you are seeking, simply consult the cross-referenced index at the back of the book. For example, if you want to prepare a cake but don't know what kind, look under "Cake." If it's a chocolate cake recipe you want, look under either "Cake" or "Chocolate." You're certain to find just the recipe you want. At the top of each page is a key word to tell you just what information appears on that page. The individual entries have been cross-referenced, too, so that if information contained under one entry is relevant to another, you'll know about it. For instance, under the entries for both "Jam" and "Jelly", you'll find cross-referencing to "Canning and Preserving."

But the wonders of this encyclopedia don't stop with recipes, detailed information, colorful photographs, informative charts, and careful cross-referencing. To further help you, drawings were created especially to clarify difficult-to-understand points. One shows how to cut up a whole chicken, another how to prepare a lobster for cooking. Then, too, there are illustrations of unusual utensils such as bombe molds, spring form pans, and fondue equipment. The entire volume was designed to make it as easy as possible for you to become the best cook ever.

Browse now through the pages of your new *Illustrated Encyclopedia of American Cooking* and discover for yourself how one carefully compiled volume *can* give you all the information you'll ever need to provide your family and guests with excitingly varied, delicious dishes at every meal!

COOKING TECHNIQUES

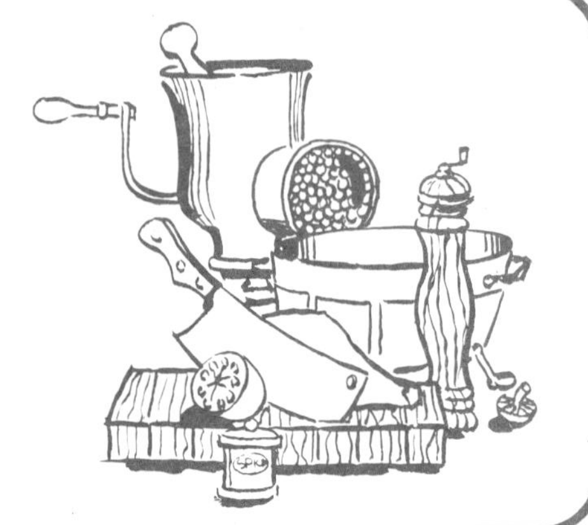

Bake – To cook by dry heat in an oven or under hot coals.

Baste – To moisten, especially meats, with melted butter, pan drippings, and so on during cooking.

Beat – To mix ingredients by vigorous stirring.

Blanch – To immerse, usually vegetables or fruit, briefly into boiling water so as to inactivate enzymes, loosen skins, or soak away excess salt.

Blend – To combine a number of ingredients so as to produce a mixture of uniform consistency.

Boil – To heat liquid until it bubbles; the boiling point for water is usually about 212 degrees.

Braise – To cook, especially meats, covered in a small amount of liquid or in steam.

Brew – To prepare a beverage by allowing boiling water to extract flavor and/or color from certain substances.

Broil – To cook by direct exposure to intense heat such as a flame or an electric heating unit.

Chill – To cool in the refrigerator or in cracked ice.

Cream – To blend butter, usually softened, with a granulated or crushed ingredient until the mixture is soft and creamy.

Curdle – To congeal milk with rennet or heat until solid lumps or curds are formed.

Cut-in – To disperse solid shortening into dry ingredients with a knife or pastry blender. The texture of the mixture should resemble coarse cracker meal.

Deep-fry – To cook in a deep pan or skillet containing hot cooking oil. Deep-fried foods are generally completely immersed in the hot oil.

Dice – To cut into small cubes about a quarter-inch in size.

Dissolve – To create a solution by thoroughly mixing a solid or granular substance with a liquid.

Dredge – To sprinkle with flour, bread crumbs, and so on to form a coating.

Ferment – To change the chemical composition of certain foods through the action of microorganisms. For example, yeast acts on malt to produce beer.

Fillet – To remove the bones from meat or fish.

Fold in – To blend a delicate, frothy mixture

into a heavier one preferably with a rubber spatula so that none of the lightness or volume is lost. The motion used is one of turning under and bringing up.

Fry – To cook in a pan or skillet containing hot cooking oil. The fat should not totally cover the food.

Glaze – To cover or coat with sauce, syrup, egg white, or a jellied substance. After applying, it hardens and becomes firm adding color and flavor.

Grate – To rub food against a rough, perforated utensil reducing the foods to slivers, chunks, curls, and so on.

Grill – To broil, usually on an open grating.

Grind – To cut, crush, or force through a chopper so as to produce small bits.

Jell – To become semisolid either through chilling or the addition of gelatin or pectin.

Julienne – To cut vegetables and fruit especially, into long thin strips.

Knead – To press, fold, and stretch dough until it is smooth and uniform.

Lard – To insert strips of fat or bacon into or on lean meat so as to keep it moist and juicy during cooking. Larding is an internal basting technique.

Leaven – To cause batters and doughs to rise usually by means of a chemical leavening agent. This process may occur before or during baking.

Marinate – To soak usually in a highly seasoned oil-acid solution so as to flavor and/or tenderize food.

Melt – To liquify solid foods by the action of heat.

Mince – To cut or chop into very small pieces.

Mix – To combine ingredients so as to distribute them uniformly.

Mold – To shape into a particular form. Gelatin and rice are two such molded foods.

Panbroil – To cook in a skillet or pan using no fat other than what is needed to prevent sticking.

Panfry – To cook in a skillet or pan containing only a small amount of fat.

Parboil – To partially cook in boiling water. Most parboiled foods require additional cooking.

Parch – To dry or roast slightly through exposure to intense heat.

Pit – To remove the hard inedible seed from peaches, plums, and so on.

Plank – To broil and serve on a board or wooden platter.

Plump – To soak fruits, usually dried, in liquid until they appear puffy and swollen.

Poach – To cook in a small amount of gently simmering liquid.

Preserve – To prevent food spoilage by pickling, salting, dehydrating, smoking, boiling in syrup, and so on. Preserved foods have excellent keeping qualities.

Puree – To reduce the pulp of cooked fruit and vegetables to a smooth and thick liquid by straining or blending.

Render – To melt animal fat.

Roast – (1) To cook by dry heat either in an oven or over hot coals; (2) To dry or parch by intense heat.

Saute – To cook in a skillet containing a small amount of hot cooking oil. Sauteed foods should never be immersed in the oil.

Scald — (1) To heat a liquid almost to the boiling point; (2) To soak usually vegetables or fruit in boiling water until the skins are loosened; see *blanch.*

Scallop — To bake with a sauce in a casserole. The food may either be mixed or layered with the sauce.

Score — To cut diagonally across in parallel lines, especially to cut meat.

Scramble — To cook and stir simultaneously.

Shirr — To crack eggs into individual buttered baking dishes and bake or broil them until the whites have set. Chopped meats or vegetables, cheese, cream, or bread crumbs may also be added.

Shred — To cut or shave food into slivers.

Shuck — To remove the husk from corn or the shell from oysters, clams, and so on.

Sieve — To pass dry and liquid ingredients through a closely meshed metal utensil so as to separate liquid from solid and fine from coarse.

Sift — To pass usually dry ingredients through a fine wire mesh so as to produce a uniform consistency.

Simmer — To cook in a liquid at or just below the boiling point.

Skewer — (1) To thread usually meat and vegetables onto a sharpened rod (as in shish kabob); (2) To fasten closed the opening of stuffed fowl with small pins.

Skim — To ladle or spoon off excess fat or skum from the surface of a liquid.

Smoke — To preserve or cook through continuous exposure to wood smoke for a long time.

Steam — To cook with water vapor either in a steamer, on a rack, or in a double boiler.

Sterilize — To cleanse and purify through exposure to intense heat.

Stew — To simmer usually meats and vegetables for a long time. Also used to tenderize meat.

Strain — To pass through a strainer, sieve, or cheesecloth so as to break down or remove solids or impurities.

Stuff — To fill or pack cavities especially those of meats, vegetables, and poultry.

Toast — To brown and crisp usually by means of direct heat.

Whip — To beat a mixture until air has been thoroughly incorporated and the mixture is light and frothy.

Wilt — To apply heat so as to cause dehydration and a droopy appearance.

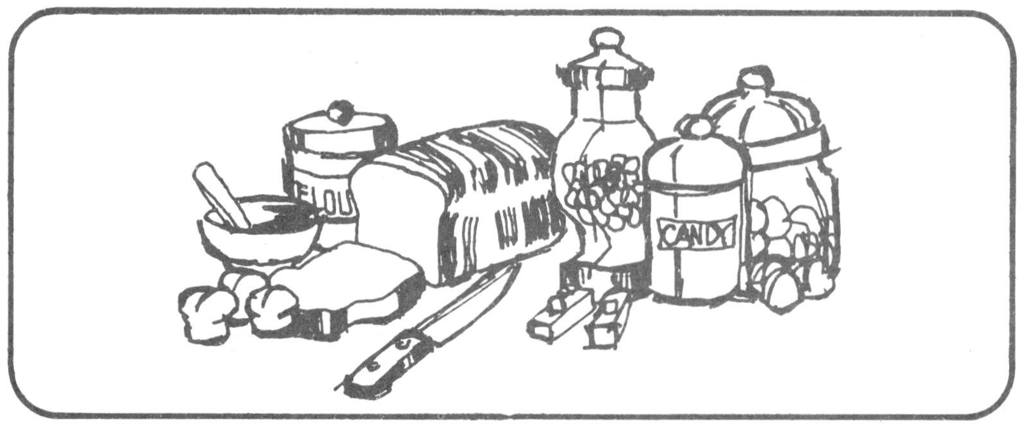

IN MEASURING, REMEMBER . . .

3 tsp. = 1 tbsp.
2 tbsp. = 1/8 c.
4 tbsp. = 1/4 c.
8 tbsp. = 1/2 c.
16 tbsp. = 1 c.
5 tbsp. + 1 tsp. = 1/3 c.
12 tbsp. = 3/4 c.
4 oz. = 1/2 c.
8 oz. = 1 c.
16 oz. = 1 lb.
1 oz. = 2 tbsp. fat or liquid
2 c. fat = 1 lb.

2 c. = 1 pt.
2 c. sugar = 1 lb.
5/8 c. = 1/2 c. + 2 tbsp.
7/8 c. = 3/4 c. + 2 tbsp.
1 oz. butter = 2 tbsp.
1 lb. butter = 2 c. or 4 sticks
2 pt. = 1 qt.
1 qt. = 4 c.
A few grains = less than 1/8 tsp.
Pinch = as much as can be taken between tip of finger and thumb
Speck = less than 1/8 tsp.

ABBREVIATIONS

Cup	c.
Tablespoon	tbsp.
Teaspoon	tsp.
Pound	lb.
Ounce	oz.
Package	pkg.
Gallon	gal.
Quart	qt.
Pint	pt.
Dozen	doz.
Large	lge.
Small	sm.

OVEN TEMPERATURES

Temperature Fahrenheit	Term
250-300	Slow
325	Moderately slow
350	Moderate
375	Moderately quick
400	Moderately hot
425-450	Hot
475-500	Extremely hot

WHEN YOU'RE MISSING AN INGREDIENT . . .

Substitute 1 teaspoon dried herbs for 1 tablespoon fresh herbs.
Try 1 cup minus 2 tablespoons all-purpose flour as a substitute for 1 cup cake flour.
Add 1/4 teaspoon baking soda and 1/2 cup buttermilk to equal 1 teaspoon baking powder. The buttermilk will replace 1/2 cup of the liquid indicated in the recipe.
Use 3 tablespoons dry cocoa plus 1 tablespoon butter or margarine instead of 1 square (1 ounce) unsweetened chocolate.
Make custard with 1 whole egg rather than 2 egg yolks.
Mix 1/2 cup evaporated milk with 1/2 cup water (or 1 cup reconstituted non-fat dry milk with 1 tablespoon butter) to replace 1 cup whole milk.
Make 1 cup of sour milk by letting stand for 5 minutes 1 tablespoon lemon juice or vinegar plus sweet milk to make 1 cup.
Substitute 1 package (2 teaspoons) active dry yeast for 1 cake compressed yeast.
Add 1 tablespoon instant minced onion, rehydrated, to replace 1 small fresh onion.
Substitute 1 tablespoon prepared mustard for 1 teaspoon dry mustard.
Use 1/8 teaspoon garlic powder instead of 1 small pressed clove of garlic.
Substitute 2 tablespoons of flour for 1 tablespoon of cornstarch to use as a thickening agent.
Mix 1/2 cup tomato sauce with 1/2 cup of water to make 1 cup tomato juice.
Make catsup or chili with 1 cup tomato sauce, 1/2 cup sugar and 2 tablespoons vinegar.

Abalone

Abalone meat is the foot flesh of a single-shelled mollusk. It has a clam-like flavor. In North America abalone is found in the waters off southern and Baja California. It is a low-fat source of thiamine and riboflavin. (3 1/2 ounces abalone = 98 calories)

AVAILABILITY: In the United States fresh abalone is available only in California. Frozen and canned abalone are available on a limited basis in specialty and oriental food stores.

PREPARATION: Canned or frozen meat is usually ready-to-cook. Fresh abalone meat is tough and must be thoroughly pounded before cooking. Dark meat is minced and used in appetizers or in soups, chowders, and sandwiches. Light meat is cut into cross-grain steaks and may be deep-fat fried, sauteed, or boiled as for any fish. Because it toughens, abalone should never be overcooked.

ABALONE COCKTAIL

1 can abalone
1 No. 303 can mixed vegetables
1 8-oz. can tomato sauce
2 fresh tomatoes, diced
5 green onions and tops, chopped
3 jalapeno peppers, chopped

Drain abalone; cut into 1-inch squares. Combine abalone, mixed vegetables, tomato sauce, diced tomatoes, onions and peppers in large covered jar. Refrigerate overnight. Serve in small bowls with saltine crackers.

ABALONE SOUP

1/4 lb. lean pork, sliced thin
1 tsp. soy sauce
1/2 tsp. sugar
1 tsp. cornstarch
1 tbsp. oil
1/2 tsp. pepper
2 thin slices fresh ginger
2 tsp. salt
4 med. fresh mushrooms
2 stalks celery
8 oz. canned abalone
1 green onion, chopped

Combine pork, soy sauce, sugar, cornstarch, 1 1/2 teaspoons oil and pepper in saucepan. Heat remaining oil in skillet. Fry ginger in oil. Add to pork mixture. Add salt and 6 cups boiling water. Slice mushrooms thinly; cut celery into diagonal slices. Add mushrooms and celery to pork mixture. Simmer, covered, for 10 minutes. Cut abalone into 1-inch square pieces. Add abalone to soup; simmer for 5 minutes and serve. Garnish with green onion.

Almond

Almonds, which are high in calories (12-15 dried, unblanched = 90 calories), are used to add flavor and eye appeal to many dishes.

AVAILABILITY: Available year-round, both shelled and unshelled.

STORING: Nuts in shell keep one year in cool, dry, dark place. Shelled nuts keep several months in tightly closed container in refrigerator or may be frozen.

PREPARATION: *Blanch*—Shell; cover with boiling water and let stand 3-5 minutes. Drain. Remove outer husk with fingers. Dry before using or storing. *Roast*—Place shelled nuts in single layer in pan. Glaze with oil or butter. Bake at 300 degrees 15-20 minutes, stirring often. To dry-roast, follow above method but omit oil or butter.

SERVING: Unroasted or unblanched, in dishes to be cooked. Toasted or roasted, in salads or uncooked desserts. Blanched, in vegetable, fish, or poultry dishes. May also be sugared, spiced, or salted for snacking.

ALMOND MERINGUE RING

12 shortbread cookies, finely rolled
1/4 lb. blanched almonds, finely ground
5 eggs, separated
1/4 tsp. salt
3/4 c. sugar
1/4 tsp. almond extract
1 tsp. unflavored gelatin
1/4 c. confectioners' sugar
1/4 tsp. vanilla
1/2 c. heavy cream, whipped

Combine cookie crumbs and almonds. Beat egg whites and salt until stiff but not dry; beat in sugar gradually until stiff peaks form. Fold in crumb mixture and almond extract. Pour into greased and floured 1 1/2-quart ring mold. Bake at 350 degrees for 30 minutes; cool for 10 minutes. Loosen side. Turn out on serving plate; cool. Soften gelatin in 2 tablespoons cold water; dissolve over boiling water. Beat egg yolks with confectioners' sugar until thick; beat in gelatin and vanilla gradually. Fold in whipped cream; chill until cool. Spoon sauce over almond ring. Garnish center of ring with fruit. Yield: 8 servings.

ALMOND HOLIDAY CAKE

Color photograph for this recipe on page 481.

3/4 c. butter
3/4 c. sugar
2 eggs
1/4 c. ground almonds
1 tsp. vanilla
1 1/2 c. flour
1 tsp. baking powder
3/8 c. cream
Bread crumbs
Whipped cream
Strawberries

Cream butter and sugar in bowl until fluffy. Add eggs, one at a time, beating well after each addition. Stir in almonds and vanilla. Sift flour with baking powder. Combine cream and 1/4 cup water; add to creamed mixture alternately with flour mixture. Sprinkle greased tube pan with bread crumbs; pour batter into pan. Bake at 325 to 350 degrees for about 45 minutes or until cake tests done. Cool cake for 10 minutes; remove from pan. Cool on wire rack. Cut cake in half crosswise; spread whipped cream between layers and on top of cake. Garnish with whole and halved strawberries.

ALMOND-CREAM CAKE

1/2 c. butter or margarine
1 1/2 c. sugar
4 egg whites
2 1/2 c. flour, sifted
2 tsp. baking powder
1 c. milk
1/2 tsp. almond flavoring

Cream butter and sugar together until fluffy. Add egg whites, mixing well. Sift flour and baking powder together; add to creamed mixture alternately with milk. Add almond flavoring. Spoon batter into 2 greased 9-inch layer cake pans. Bake at 350 degrees for 30 to 35 minutes or until cake tests done.

Filling

1 c. cream
3 egg yolks, beaten
2 tbsp. sugar
1 1/2 tsp. cornstarch
1/2 c. slivered blanched almonds

Blend cream and egg yolks together in saucepan. Combine sugar and cornstarch; add to cream mixture. Cook over low heat, stirring constantly, until thickened. Add almonds. Cool; spread filling between cake layers. May frost with white icing if desired. Garnish with halved almonds.

MARZIPAN

1 lb. almond paste
1/3 c. light corn syrup
1 tsp. vanilla
1 1/4 c. marshmallow creme
6 c. confectioners' sugar
Food coloring

Mix almond paste, corn syrup, vanilla and marshmallow creme until smooth; add confectioners' sugar, 1/2 cup at a time. Knead until smooth and blended. Form small balls of dough into various fruit shapes. Dilute desired colors of food coloring with water; paint fruits with small brush. Store in refrigerator or airtight container. Yield: 80 pieces.

ALMOND-BUTTER CRUNCH

1 c. butter
1 1/3 c. sugar
1 tbsp. corn syrup
1 c. coarsely chopped almonds, toasted
4 4 1/2-oz. bars milk chocolate, melted
1 c. finely chopped blanched almonds, toasted

Melt butter in large saucepan. Add sugar, corn syrup and 3 tablespoons water. Cook, stirring occasionally, to hard crack stage or 300 degrees on candy thermometer. Stir in coarsely chopped almonds quickly. Spread candy in ungreased 13 by 9 1/2 by 2-inch pan. Cool thoroughly. Turn out on waxed paper; spread half the chocolate over almond mixture. Sprinkle with half the finely chopped almonds. Cover with waxed paper; invert. Spread remaining chocolate over almond mixture. Sprinkle with remaining almonds. Chill until chocolate is firm; break into pieces.

ALMOND CREAM PIE

2/3 c. sugar
1/3 c. cake flour
Dash of salt
2 eggs, slightly beaten
1/2 c. rum
1 1/2 c. scalded milk
1 9-in. crumb pie shell, chilled
1/2 c. blanched almonds, toasted
1 c. whipping cream, whipped
1/2 c. shaved unsweetened chocolate

Sift sugar, flour and salt into double boiler. Stir in eggs and 3 tablespoons rum; blend thoroughly. Stir in milk and remaining rum gradually, almost drop by drop. Cook over hot water, stirring constantly, until mixture thickens. Cool. Sprinkle pie shell with almonds; pour in filling. Cover with whipped cream; garnish with shaved chocolate. Yield: 6-8 servings.

ALMOND CONGEALED DESSERT

1 env. unflavored gelatin
5 eggs, separated
Salt
1 c. sugar
1 tsp. almond extract
1/2 c. chopped blanched almonds
Green food coloring
Red food coloring
2 c. milk
1 tsp. vanilla

Soften gelatin in 1/4 cup cold water for 5 minutes; dissolve in 3/4 cup boiling water. Chill until mixture begins to thicken. Beat egg whites with 1/4 teaspoon salt until soft peaks form: add 3/4 cup sugar gradually. Beat until stiff peaks form. Add gelatin mixture, almond extract and 1/4 cup almonds. Beat until blended. Divide mixture into 3 parts; tint 1 part green and 1 part pink with food coloring. Leave 1 part untinted. Sprinkle remaining almonds over bottom of wet 2-quart mold; spread green layer over almonds. Top with white layer; then with pink layer. Chill until firm. Beat egg yolks with 1/2 cup milk, remaining sugar, vanilla and dash of salt; scald remaining milk. Stir egg volks into milk gradually; cook over hot water, stirring constantly, until mixture coats spoon. Chill. Unmold gelatin; serve with sauce. Yield: 6-8 servings.

Almond Gateau . . . Puffy pastry filled with ice cream and topped with crunchy almonds.

ALMOND GATEAU

1/2 c. butter
Pinch of salt
1 c. flour
4 eggs
1 1/2 c. whipping cream
1/4 c. powdered sugar
2 qt. cherry-vanilla ice cream
1/2 c. roasted slivered almonds

Combine 1 cup water, butter and salt in saucepan; bring to a boil. Add flour all at once. Cook over medium heat, stirring constantly, until mixture leaves side of pan and forms stiff ball. Remove from heat. Blend in eggs, one at a time, beating well after each addition, until mixture is smooth and shiny. Drop 12 tablespoons mixture 3 inches apart on ungreased cookie sheet. Mark 8-inch circle on separate cookie sheet. Place remaining puff mixture in pastry bag with large plain tip. Pipe mixture onto cookie sheet using marked circle as guide for inside diameter. Bake puffs and ring in 400-degree oven for 30 to 35 minutes or until golden brown and firm to the touch. Turn off heat; cool puffs and ring in oven with door ajar. Whip cream with sugar until stiff. Split puffs and ring crosswise. Fill lower half of each puff with ice cream; replace top. Place in refrigerator or freezer. Spoon remaining ice cream onto lower half of ring; replace top. Garnish top of ring with whipped cream; sprinkle with 2 or 3 tablespoons almonds. Combine remaining almonds and cream in bowl. Stack individual puffs in center of ring. Serve at once with whipped cream mixture.

ALMOND TRIFLE

1 c. milk
3 eggs, separated
3/4 c. sugar
Pinch of salt
1 tsp. vanilla
1/2 tsp. almond flavoring
1 1/2 tbsp. gelatin
1 qt. heavy cream, whipped
1 1/2 doz. ladyfingers

Combine milk, beaten egg yolks and sugar in saucepan. Cook over low heat, stirring constantly, until of custard consistency. Stir in salt and flavorings. Soften gelatin in 1/4 cup cold water; stir into hot custard. Cool. Fold in stiffly beaten egg whites and half the whipped cream. Split ladyfingers lengthwise. Line 9-inch tube pan with ladyfingers; pour custard over ladyfingers. Chill until set. Unmold on serving dish; frost with remaining whipped cream. Chill thoroughly. Garnish with maraschino cherries if desired.

ALMOND CUSTARD

Milk
1 1/2 c. sugar
6 egg yolks, beaten
1 1/2 tbsp. unflavored gelatin
2 c. whipping cream
1 tsp. vanilla
1 tsp. almond flavoring
Shaved almonds

Blend 3 cups milk and sugar together; add to egg yolks. Cook milk mixture in double boiler until mixture coats spoon. Dissolve gelatin in 6 tablespoons milk; stir into custard. Chill until custard begins to thicken. Whip remaining cream; add flavorings. Fold cream into partially set custard. Pour into shallow pan; chill until set. Sprinkle with almonds before serving. Yield: 16 servings.

ALMOND LACE COOKIES

3/4 c. finely ground unblanched almonds
1/2 c. butter
1/2 c. sugar
1 tbsp. flour
1 tbsp. cream
1 tbsp. milk

Combine all ingredients in small heavy pan; cook, stirring constantly, over low heat until butter melts. Drop from teaspoon 3 inches apart on greased and floured baking sheet. Bake at 350 degrees for about 5 minutes or until slightly brown and bubbly in center. Cool until edges are firm enough to lift with spatula; transfer to absorbent paper, turning upside down. Roll cookies immediately around handle of wooden spoon to shape into cones.

SUGARED ALMOND STICKS

2/3 c. unblanched almonds, ground
Sugar
1 c. sifted all-purpose flour
1/4 tsp. salt
1/2 c. butter
1 egg, separated
1/4 tsp. almond extract

Combine 2 tablespoons ground almonds with 2 tablespoons sugar. Set aside. Combine remaining almonds, flour, salt and remaining sugar in mixing bowl. Cut in butter until particles are fine. Add egg yolk and almond extract. Mix well to form dough; divide into 6 portions. Roll each portion out to 12-inch strip on lightly floured board. Place strips side by side; brush tops generously with slightly beaten egg white. Sprinkle with almond-sugar mixture. Cut across strips to make 1 1/2-inch pieces;

separate pieces. Place on ungreased baking sheet. Bake at 350 degrees for 14 to 18 minutes or until light golden brown. Yield: 4 dozen sticks.

ALMOND TRIANGLES

Color photograph for this recipe on page 489.

1/2 c. butter
1 c. sugar
6 tbsp. evaporated milk
3 eggs
1/2 tsp. salt
1 5/8 c. flour
Chopped almonds

Cream butter and sugar in bowl; stir in milk and 2 eggs. Add salt and flour; mix well. Chill overnight. Roll out on floured surface; cut in triangular shapes. Beat remaining egg; brush on triangles. Sprinkle with almonds. Place on greased cookie sheet. Bake at 375 degrees until golden brown.

ALMOND-ROCA COOKIES

1 c. butter
1/2 c. sugar
1/2 c. (packed) brown sugar
1 egg yolk
1 tsp. vanilla
2 c. sifted cake flour
1 9-oz. milk chocolate bar, melted
1/2 c. toasted sliced almonds

Cream butter, sugar and brown sugar until fluffy; beat in egg yolk and vanilla. Add flour; stir until blended. Spread batter evenly in ungreased 10 x 15-inch rimmed cookie sheet. Bake at 350 degrees for about 20 minutes or until golden. Remove from oven. Spread with chocolate; sprinkle with almonds. Cut in squares while still warm; chill until chocolate is firm. Yield: 4 dozen bars.

MARZIPAN BARS

1/2 c. butter
1/2 c. (packed) brown sugar
1 egg yolk
1 tsp. vanilla
1/2 tsp. soda
2 c. sifted all-purpose flour
1/4 tsp. salt
1/4 c. milk
1 c. red raspberry jelly
Almond Paste Filling

Cream butter; add brown sugar gradually. Beat in egg yolk and vanilla. Sift dry ingredients together; add sifted mixture and milk to creamed mixture alternately. Spread batter in greased 10 x 15 x 1-inch pan; cover with jelly. Spread Almond Paste Filling over jelly. Bake at 350 degrees for about 35 minutes. Cool. Top with almond-flavored powdered sugar glaze if desired. Cut into bars; serve.

Almond Paste Filling

8 oz. almond paste
1 egg white
1/2 c. sugar
1 tsp. vanilla
3 tbsp. softened butter
3 eggs

Cut almond paste into small pieces. Blend almond paste, egg white, sugar, vanilla and butter until smooth. Beat in eggs. Yield: 5 dozen.

ALMOND-CARAMEL CREAM

1 qt. vanilla ice cream
12 toasted macaroons, crushed
1 pt. whipping cream
1 box brown sugar
Toasted almonds, crushed

Freeze ice cream until hard; peel off carton. Place macaroon crumbs on waxed paper; roll ice cream in crumbs until well-coated. Wrap in foil. Return to freezer. Pour cream over brown sugar in saucepan; mix well. Cook for about 1 hour or until syrup coats spoon. Slice ice cream; pour sauce over slices. Top with almonds. Serve immediately. Yield: 6 to 7 servings.

FROZEN ALMOND CREAM

1 box vanilla wafers
1/2 c. butter or margarine
1 c. powdered sugar
2 eggs, beaten
2 c. cream, whipped
1 tsp. almond extract

Crush wafers; place half the crumbs in greased 8-inch square pan. Mix butter and sugar in double boiler; add eggs. Cook, stirring constantly, until thickened. Cool slightly. Pour half the whipped cream over crumb layer. Add almond extract to egg mixture; pour over cream layer. Cover with remaining cream. Sprinkle remaining crumbs over top. Freeze. Cut into squares. Yield: 6-9 servings.

FROZEN ALMOND DESSERT

3/4 c. sugar
2 1/2 tbsp. flour
2 eggs
3/4 c. light corn syrup
1 tbsp. vanilla
1 tsp. butter
1/3 c. milk
2 c. cream
1 tsp. almond flavoring
1/2 c. finely chopped blanched almonds
1/2 c. red candied cherries, chopped

Combine sugar and flour in double boiler; stir in eggs, 1/4 cup water and corn syrup. Cook, stirring constantly, until thickened. Add vanilla and butter; cool. Add milk, cream and almond flavoring. Pour into 2 refrigerator trays. Freeze to mushy stage. Beat in almonds and cherries. Freeze until firm.

Ambrosia

CLASSIC AMBROSIA

1 doz. oranges
1 sm. can crushed pineapple
1 fresh coconut, grated
1 c. sugar

Peel oranges; section and cut into small pieces. Add remaining ingredients. Chill well. Spoon into dessert dishes; top with cherries if desired. Yield: 12-15 servings.

BANANA AMBROSIA

1 6-oz. can frozen orange juice
3 med. apples
1 banana, thinly sliced
1 sm. can crushed pineapple
1 sm. box coconut
Sugar to taste

Prepare orange juice according to can directions; pour into punch bowl. Peel, core and coarsely grate apples; add apples and banana to juice. Add pineapple and coconut; sweeten with sugar. Serve immediately. Yield: 10 servings.

CHILLED MELON AMBROSIA

1/2 c. sugar
1/2 c. grape juice
4 tbsp. lemon juice
2 c. cantaloupe balls, chilled
2 c. watermelon balls, chilled
2 c. honeydew balls, chilled
Fresh grated coconut

Combine sugar, grape juice, lemon juice and 1 cup water in saucepan; boil for 1 minute. Cool; chill. Arrange melon balls in serving cups; pour juice mixture over fruit. Sprinkle with coconut. Garnish with red cherries and mint leaves. Yield: 8 servings.

FROZEN AMBROSIA

1/2 c. candied pineapple
1/2 c. maraschino cherries
1/4 c. cherry juice
1/2 c. sugar
1/3 c. water
3 egg whites, stiffly beaten
1/8 tsp. salt
1/2 pt. cream, whipped
1 tsp. vanilla
1 tbsp. lemon juice

Cut pineapple and cherries in small pieces. Add cherry juice; chill for several hours. Mix sugar and water; bring to a boil. Cook till syrup spins thread. Pour into egg whites slowly, beating constantly. Add salt; beat until cool. Fold in whipped cream; add vanilla and lemon juice. Add fruit mixture. Place in freezer container and freeze, using 3 parts ice and 1 part rock salt.

MOLDED AMBROSIA

1 c. graham cracker crumbs
1/4 c. melted butter or margarine
1 9-oz. can crushed pineapple
1 sm. package orange gelatin
1/3 c. sugar
1 c. sour cream
1/4 tsp. vanilla
1 c. diced orange segments
1/2 c. flaked coconut

Combine crumbs and butter; reserve 1/3 cup crumb mixture. Press remaining crumb mixture into 8 x 8 x 2-inch baking dish. Drain pineapple; reserve syrup. Dissolve gelatin and sugar in 1 cup hot water; stir in reserved syrup. Chill until partially set; add sour cream and vanilla. Whip until fluffy; fold in pineapple, orange and coconut. Pour over crumb mixture; sprinkle with reserved crumb mixture. Chill until firm; cut into squares. Yield: 9 servings.

MARSHMALLOW AMBROSIA

1 No. 3 can crushed pineapple
1 lb. miniature marshmallows
1 pt. whipping cream
1 c. chopped pecans
Sliced bananas

Pour pineapple over marshmallows; let stand overnight. Fold in whipped cream and pecans just before serving; do not stir. Top with sliced bananas if desired. Yield: 12 servings.

MELON BOAT AMBROSIA

1 cantaloupe
1 honeydew melon
Green seedless grapes
2 tbsp. honey
1 sm. can pineapple chunks, drained
Dash of lemon juice
Salt to taste

Cut melons in half lengthwise; remove seeds. Scoop out balls with melon scoop. Combine melon balls, honey, pineapple, lemon juice and salt; toss lightly. Serve in scooped out melon rinds. Sprinkle with grated coconut if desired Yield: 12 servings.

STRAWBERRY AND SOUR CREAM AMBROSIA

1 pt. strawberries
1 tbsp. sugar
1/4 lb. miniature marshmallows
1/4 c. shredded coconut
1 c. sour cream

Reserve 4 whole strawberries; quarter remaining strawberries. Mix sugar with quartered strawberries; let stand for 10 minutes. Fold sugar mixture, marshmallows and coconut into sour cream. Chill for 1 hour or longer. Pile lightly into sherbet glasses. Garnish with reserved whole strawberries. Yield: 4 servings.

GRAPE AMBROSIA

1/2 lb. green grapes
1/2 lb. Concord grapes
1/2 lb. red grapes
1 c. sour cream
1/2 c. honey
1/2 c. shredded coconut

Cut grapes in half; remove seeds. Place in individual cocktail dishes; top with sour cream. Drizzle honey over sour cream; sprinkle with coconut.

HEAVENLY AMBROSIA

2 c. cooked rice
1 c. drained crushed pineapple
1/2 c. coarsely chopped almonds or walnuts
1/3 c. sugar
1 c. heavy cream, whipped
12 to 16 marshmallows, cut up

Mix rice, pineapple, almonds and sugar; fold in whipped cream and marshmallows. Chill thoroughly. Garnish with fresh strawberries or raspberries. Yield: 6-8 servings.

TRADITIONAL AMBROSIA

3 lge. oranges
1 lb. seedless grapes
3 lge. red apples
5 bananas
1 sm. can mandarin oranges
1 can pineapple chunks
Sugar to taste
Lemon juice to taste
1 sm. package shredded coconut
1 pkg. miniature marshmallows
1 c. walnut or pecan halves
1 sm. jar red maraschino cherries
1 sm. jar green maraschino cherries

Peel and slice oranges, removing outer membrane and seeds. Halve grapes. Core and slice apples. Slice bananas. Drain canned fruits. Layer oranges, grapes, apples, bananas, canned orange segments and pineapple chunks in 3-quart glass serving bowl. Sprinkle each layer with sugar and lemon juice. Cover with coconut. Arrange marshmallows, walnuts and cherries on top in decorative pattern. Yield: 16-20 servings.

FLORIDA AMBROSIA

2 Florida grapefruit
3 Florida oranges
2 Florida tangerines
1/3 c. sugar
1/2 c. shredded coconut

Cut slice from top of each grapefruit; remove peel in strips from top to bottom, cutting deep enough to remove white membrane. Cut off slice from bottom of grapefruit. Remove all white membrane. Cut along side of each grapefruit, dividing membrane from outside to middle of core. Separate sections over bowl to retain juice. Cut peeling from orange as in paring an apple. Loosen sections as for grapefruit. Peel tangerines; cut sections in half and remove seeds. Turn half the fruit into serving dish; sprinkle with half the sugar and coconut. Repeat layers. Chill for at least 1 hour before serving. Yield: 8 servings.

Florida Ambrosia . . . Tender flakes of coconut sprinkled over tart citrus fruits.

Anchovy

ANCHOVY PUFFS

1/2 c. butter or margarine
1 3-oz. package cream cheese
1 c. flour
Anchovy paste

Combine butter and cream cheese; blend in flour. Chill dough thoroughly. Roll dough out thin; cut with 2-inch cookie cutter. Spread with anchovy paste; fold over. Seal edges with fork. Bake at 400 degrees for 10 minutes. May be made ahead and frozen before baking.

ANCHOVY SPREAD

3 3-oz. packages cream cheese
Cream
1/2 tube anchovy paste
1 tbsp. lemon juice
Dash of cayenne pepper
1 tsp. Worcestershire sauce
1 tsp. minced chives
1/4 bottle stuffed olives, chopped
1/4 tsp. paprika

Soften cream cheese with small amount of cream. Add anchovy paste, lemon juice, cayenne pepper, Worcestershire sauce, chives, olives and paprika; mix well. Serve on toast rounds or crackers.

ANCHOVY DIP

1 clove of garlic, minced
1/2 tsp. salt
1/2 tsp. freshly ground pepper
1/2 tsp. prepared mustard
1/3 c. chopped parsley
3 tbsp. chopped onion or chives
3 tbsp. vinegar
1 c. mayonnaise
1/2 c. sour cream
1 can anchovies, finely cut

Combine all ingredients, mixing well; chill for at least 2 hours. Stir dip; pour into serving bowl. Serve with fresh vegetables or chips.

CHEESY ANCHOVY DIP

1 8-oz. package cream cheese
1 tbsp. grated sharp cheese
1 tsp. anchovy paste
1 tbsp. evaporated milk
1 tbsp. Worcestershire sauce

Soften cream cheese at room temperature. Combine all ingredients; mix well.

PARTY ANCHOVY DIP

1/3 c. French dressing
1 8-oz. package cream cheese, softened
2 tbsp. catsup
1 tbsp. minced dried onions
1 tbsp. anchovy paste

Blend French dressing into cheese, a small amount at a time. Stir in remaining ingredients; mix well.

TANGY ANCHOVY CANAPÉS

10 anchovies
6 tbsp. chopped pecans
1 tbsp. chopped parsley
1/2 clove of garlic, minced
1 tbsp. anchovy oil
1 tsp. lemon juice
Toast rounds

Combine all ingredients except toast rounds; mix until well blended. Spread on toast rounds to serve.

ANCHOVY-BLEU CHEESE SALAD

1/4 head lettuce
1/2 head romaine
2 green onions, minced
2 anchovy fillets, cut up
2 tbsp. Dressing
Salt and pepper to taste
1 tbsp. crumbled bleu cheese
1 tbsp. crisp bacon, crushed

Tear lettuce and romaine into salad bowl. Add onions and anchovy fillets; toss lightly. Toss in Dressing; season with salt and pepper. Spoon onto salad plate; sprinkle with bleu cheese and bacon. Garnish with sprig of parsley, if desired. Yield: 1 serving.

Dressing

1/3 c. mayonnaise or salad dressing
2/3 c. sour cream

Combine ingredients; blend well.

CREAMY ANCHOVY SALAD

1 3/4-oz. can anchovy fillets, chopped fine
1/2 c. chopped ripe olives
1/8 tsp. garlic powder or 1 crushed clove of garlic
1/4 c. chopped parsley
1/3 c. chopped green onions
2/3 c. sour cream
1 c. mayonnaise
2 tbsp. lemon juice
1/4 c. tarragon vinegar
Romaine, iceberg and escarole

Combine anchovies, olives, garlic powder, parsley and onions in small mixing bowl. Stir in sour cream, mayonnaise, lemon juice and vinegar; mix well. Cover; chill for several hours. Tear greens into salad bowl. Pour in anchovy dressing; toss to coat greens. May be served as a dunk with crackers, chips or fresh vegetables. Yield: 2 3/4 cups.

ZESTY ANCHOVY SALAD

1 head romaine lettuce, broken into bite-sized pieces
8 ripe olives, chopped
8 1/2-in. cubes sharp cheese
1 carrot, cubed
2 stalks celery, cubed
1/2 c. wine vinegar
1/4 c. salad oil
2 bay leaves, crushed
1/4 tsp. celery seed
1 can anchovies

Combine lettuce, olives, cheese, carrot and celery in salad bowl. Shake vinegar, oil, bay leaves and celery seed together. Pour over lettuce mixture; toss to mix well. Serve in individual salad bowls; arrange 1 or 2 anchovies on top of each salad. Yield: 6 servings.

Angel Cake

A very light, soft, and delicate cake whose secret lies in a special blending of ingredients. **INGREDIENTS:** *Eggs*—Separate whites while eggs are cold; when whites are at room temperature, beat to stiff peaks. Underbeating causes coarsely textured cake, overbeating makes crust crack. *Sugar*—fine, superfine, or confectioners', as specified in recipe. Too much sugar either causes a sticky crust or makes the cake fall. *Flour*—Use only cake flour. *Cream of tartar*—Gives whiteness and softness to cake. *Never use* shortening or egg yolks.

BAKING: Use ungreased tube pan. Follow specified oven temperature exactly: a too-hot oven results in a tough cake, a too-cool one in shrinkage. Allow cake to cool completely in pan; if removed too soon, it collapses.

ALMOND ANGEL CAKE

1 c. sifted cake flour
1 1/2 c. sugar
12 egg whites
1 1/4 tsp. cream of tartar
1/4 tsp. salt
1 1/4 tsp. almond flavoring

Preheat oven to 375 degrees. Sift flour with 3/4 cups sugar 4 times. Beat egg whites with cream of tartar, salt and almond flavoring until soft peaks form. Add remaining sugar, 2 tablespoons at a time, beating well after each addition. Sift 1/4 cup flour over egg whites; fold in. Fold in remaining flour by fourths. Pour into ungreased 10-inch round tube pan. Bake for 35 to 40 minutes. Invert pan; cool cake. Frost as desired.

CHANTILLY CAKE

1 box angel food cake mix
3 c. whipping cream
1 c. drained crushed pineapple
1 c. miniature marshmallows
1 qt. fresh strawberries, slightly sweetened
1/2 tsp. vanilla
Butter (opt.)
1 c. coconut, toasted

Prepare and bake cake according to package directions; let cool thoroughly. Slice cake to form 3 layers. Whip 2 cups cream until stiff; fold in pineapple, marshmallows, strawberries and vanilla. Spread layers lightly with butter to prevent whipped cream filling from soaking into cake. Fill and stack layers; frost top of cake. Whip remaining cream until stiff; frost side of cake. Sprinkle top and side with coconut; chill for several hours before serving.

BURNT SUGAR ANGEL FOOD CAKE

1 1/2 c. egg whites
1 1/2 tsp. cream of tartar
2 c. brown sugar
2 tsp. vanilla
1 1/4 c. cake flour
1 tsp. salt

Beat egg whites until stiff but not dry; add cream of tartar. Add sugar gradually, beating constantly; stir in vanilla. Sift flour with salt; fold into egg white mixture. Turn into tube pan; place in cold oven. Bake at 325 degrees for 50 minutes to 1 hour. Invert pan; cool before removing from pan.

CHERRY ANGEL FOOD CAKE

1 c. cake flour
1 5/8 c. sugar
1 1/2 c. egg whites
1 1/2 tsp. cream of tartar
1/4 tsp. salt
1 1/2 tsp. vanilla
1/2 tsp. almond flavoring
1/2 c. chopped maraschino cherries

Preheat oven to 375 degrees. Combine flour and 7/8 cup sugar; set aside. Beat egg whites with cream of tartar and salt until foamy. Add remaining sugar slowly, beating constantly; beat until meringue holds stiff peaks. Fold in flavorings. Sprinkle flour mixture and cherries over egg whites; fold just until blended. Turn into ungreased tube pan; cut through batter gently to remove air pockets. Bake for 30 to 35 minutes. Invert on a funnel until cold. Remove from pan; frost with white fluffy icing, if desired.

TWENTY-FIVE MINUTE ANGEL FOOD CAKE

1 1/2 c. egg whites
1/2 tsp. salt
1 tsp. cream of tartar
1 1/2 c. sugar
1 1/4 c. cake flour, sifted
1 tsp. vanilla
1/4 tsp. lemon extract

Preheat oven to 400 degrees. Beat egg whites and salt until frothy. Add cream of tartar; beat until egg whites hold a soft peak. Add sugar slowly, beating constantly; beat until stiff peaks form. Fold in cake flour; add vanilla and lemon extract. Pour into angel food cake pan. Bake for 25 minutes. Invert to cool before removing from pan.

MOCK ANGEL FOOD CAKE

2 c. sugar
2 c. flour
1 c. boiling water
5 egg whites
1/2 tsp. cream of tartar
Pinch of salt
2 tsp. baking powder
1 tsp. vanilla
1/2 tsp. almond flavoring

Preheat oven to 350 degrees. Sift sugar and flour together 4 times. Add boiling water; mix thoroughly. Let flour mixture stand until cool. Beat egg whites until foamy. Add cream of tartar and salt; beat until stiff. Fold in flour mixture. Add baking powder, vanilla and almond flavoring; pour into 2 oiled and floured 9-inch layer cake pans. Bake for 25 minutes. Cool before removing from pans. Frost as desired.

SMALL ANGEL CAKE

7 egg whites, beaten slightly
1/2 tsp. baking powder
1 tsp. cream of tartar
7/8 c. sugar, sifted twice
3/4 c. cake flour, sifted twice
1 tsp. vanilla
1 tsp. almond flavoring

Combine egg whites, baking powder and cream of tartar; beat until stiff. Fold in sugar and flour; blend in flavorings. Pour into a medium size cake pan; place cake in cold oven. Bake at 350 degrees for 45 minutes. Cool before removing from pan.

COFFEE ANGEL FOOD CAKE

1 box angel food cake mix
6 tbsp. powdered instant coffee
1/2 c. softened butter
1/4 tsp. salt
2 1/2 c. sifted confectioners' sugar
3 tbsp. milk
1 tsp. vanilla

Prepare cake batter according to package directions; stir in 4 tablespoons coffee. Bake according to directions. Cool cake; place on serving plate. Cream butter, salt and sugar. Add milk, vanilla and remaining coffee; beat until light and fluffy. Spread on cooled cake.

STRAWBERRY TALL CAKE

1 15-oz. package angel food cake mix
1/3 c. port
1 1/2 c. heavy cream
1/4 c. sugar
2 pt. fresh California strawberries
2 tbsp. toasted slivered almonds

Prepare cake according to package directions; slice in half crosswise. Sprinkle each layer with 2 tablespoons port. Whip cream with sugar and remaining wine until stiff. Crush 1 cup strawberries; fold into cream mixture. Spread cream mixture over cake layers. Slice 1 cup strawberries onto 1 layer; top with remaining layer. Arrange remaining strawberries on cake. Sprinkle with almonds.

Strawberry Tall Cake . . . A light, airy, and delicious cake.

SUNTAN ANGEL FOOD CAKE

4 tbsp. cocoa
1 1/2 c. sugar
3/4 c. sifted cake flour
1 1/2 c. egg whites
1/4 tsp. salt
1 tsp. cream of tartar
1 tsp. vanilla

Preheat oven to 350 degrees. Sift cocoa with 1 cup sugar 2 times. Sift flour with remaining sugar 3 times. Beat egg whites until foamy. Add salt and cream of tartar; beat until whites hold peaks. Fold egg whites into cocoa mixture; fold in flour mixture. Blend in vanilla. Pour into ungreased tube pan. Bake for 1 hour and 10 minutes. Invert until cool; frost as desired.

Anise

ANISE HARDTACK CANDY

2 c. sugar
2 c. white corn syrup
15 drops of oil of anise
Red food coloring

Combine sugar, syrup and 1/4 cup water in saucepan. Boil to hard-crack stage. Boil 1 second longer. Add oil of anise and food coloring. Pour into greased pan; cool. Turn upside down on waxed paper; break into pieces.

ANISEED-CINNAMON COOKIES

3/4 c. sugar
1 1/2 c. shortening
1 tsp. aniseed
2 egg yolks, beaten
6 c. sifted flour
3 tsp. baking powder
1 tsp. salt
Cinnamon

Cream 3/4 cup sugar and shortening until light and fluffy. Add aniseed and egg yolks; beat for several seconds until well blended. Sift flour, baking powder and salt together; stir into sugar mixture. Add 1/2 cup water; knead until well mixed. Roll out; cut with cookie cutter. Combine desired amounts of cinnamon and additional sugar; sprinkle on cookies. Place on baking sheets. Bake in 350-degree oven for 12 minutes or until golden brown. Yield: 6 dozen servings.

ANISEED-CITRON BARS

3 eggs
1 1/4 c. sugar
3/4 c. oil
3 c. flour
1 tsp. aniseed
1 tsp. soda
1 c. chopped citron
1 c. raisins
1 c. chopped nuts

Beat eggs; blend in sugar and oil. Mix flour, aniseed, and soda together, reserving 1/2 cup flour. Add aniseed mixture to egg mixture. Coat citron, raisins and nuts with reserved flour. Blend into cookie dough. Roll out on greased 11 x 17-inch cookie sheet. Bake in 350-degree oven for 20 minutes. Cut into 1 1/4 x 3-inch diagonal bars.

ANISE DROP COOKIES

1 egg
1/2 c. sugar
Pinch of salt
1/2 c. flour
3/4 tsp. grated lemon rind
2 drops of oil of anise
1 tsp. aniseed

Beat egg until light. Sift sugar, salt and flour into mixing bowl; stir in lemon rind. Add egg, anise oil and aniseed; mix well. Drop by 1/2 teaspoonfuls onto greased cookie sheet 1 inch apart. Let stand at room temperature for 12 to 24 hours. Bake at 300 degrees for 20 to 25 minutes or until tops begin to brown lightly. Store in airtight containers. Yield: 2 1/2 dozen cookies.

ANISE REFRIGERATOR COOKIES

1 c. butter or margarine
2 c. (packed) brown sugar
2 eggs
1 tbsp. crushed aniseed
1 c. finely chopped nuts
2 1/2 tsp. baking powder
1/4 tsp. salt
3 1/2 c. flour

Cream butter and brown sugar until fluffy. Add eggs, one at a time, beating well after each addition. Stir in aniseed and nuts. Sift baking powder, salt and flour together; add to creamed mixture gradually, mixing well. Form 2 rolls about 1 3/4-inches thick; wrap in waxed paper. Chill. Slice thin. Place cookies on greased baking sheet. Bake at 350 degrees for 10 minutes.

ANISETTE COOKIES

2 c. sugar
1 c. butter, melted
4 tbsp. aniseed
4 tbsp. oil of anise
2 tsp. vanilla
2 c. chopped almonds
6 eggs
5 1/2 c. flour
1 tbsp. baking powder

Cream sugar and butter until fluffy. Stir in aniseed, oil of anise, vanilla, 2 tablespoons water and almonds. Add eggs, one at a time, beating well after each addition. Sift flour and baking powder; blend thoroughly with sugar mixture. Chill for 2 to 3 hours. Turn out on lightly floured board. Shape dough to form loaves 2-inches wide, 1/2-inch thick and the length of cookie sheet. Place 2 loaves at a time on greased cookie sheet. Bake in 375-degree oven for 20 minutes. Cool on cookie sheets. Cut in diagonal 1/2-inch thick slices. Place slices, cut sides down, close together on cookie sheet. Return to oven. Bake for 15 minutes or until lightly toasted. Store in airtight container. Yield: 9 dozen servings.

SPRINGERLE COOKIES

4 eggs
2 c. sugar
2 tbsp. butter
4 c. flour
2 pinches of cream of tartar
1 tbsp. crushed aniseed

Beat eggs until light; add sugar gradually, beating until thick and lemon-colored. Beat in butter. Add flour and cream of tartar gradually until dough is stiff. Roll to 1/4-inch thickness. Flour springerle press; press dough to make clear imprint. Cut and separate squares. Let dry in open for 24 hours. Sprinkle aniseed on greased cookie sheet. Place cookies over aniseed. Bake at 300 degrees for 20 to 25 minutes or until cookie bottoms are yellow. Store in air-tight container. Yield: 60 cookies.

ANISE-ALMOND LOAF

2 1/4 c. flour, sifted
2 tsp. baking powder
1/2 tsp. salt
1/2 c. soft butter
1 c. sugar
1 tsp. aniseed
1/2 tsp. almond extract
5 eggs
3/4 c. ground toasted almonds

Preheat oven to 350 degrees. Sift flour, baking powder and salt together twice. Cream butter and sugar until fluffy. Add aniseed and almond extract; blend well. Add eggs, one at a time, beating well after each addition. Add sifted dry ingredients; mix thoroughly. Fold in almonds. Spoon batter into greased and lightly floured 9 x 5 x 3-inch loaf pan. Bake for 1 hour.

ANISE BREAD

4 eggs
1 c. sugar
2 c. flour
1/4 c. aniseed

Cream 3 egg yolks and 1 whole egg with sugar until fluffy. Add flour, aniseed and egg whites. Spoon batter into loaf pan. Bake at 350 degrees until bread tests done; cool. Slice; toast on both sides in 450-degree oven.

ANISE-CHERRY BREAD

4 c. flour
8 tsp. baking powder
2 tsp. salt
1 c. sugar
2/3 c. vegetable shortening
3 eggs, well-beaten
2 c. milk
1 c. drained maraschino cherries
1/2 tsp. almond extract
1 tsp. aniseed

Mix flour with baking powder, salt and sugar; cut in shortening with 2 knives until mixture resembles cornmeal. Beat eggs and milk together. Add egg liquid to flour mixture all at once. Beat to blend dough well. Fold in cherries, almond extract and aniseed. Turn dough into large floured pan. Bake in 350-degree oven for 1 hour to 1 hour and 15 minutes. Yield: 10 servings.

ANISE HOLIDAY BREAD

1 c. milk
1/2 c. sugar
1/4 butter
2 tsp. salt
5 3/4 c. flour
1 pkg. yeast
2 eggs, beaten
1 tsp. grated lemon rind
1 tbsp. aniseed
1/2 c. white raisins
1/2 c. chopped blanched almonds

Scald milk; cool to lukewarm. Combine milk, sugar, butter and salt; stir in 1 cup flour. Dissolve yeast in 1/4 cup lukewarm water; stir into milk mixture, blending well. Add remaining flour and eggs alternately, mixing well. Blend in lemon rind, aniseed, raisins and almonds. Knead on lightly floured board until smooth. Place dough in greased bowl. Cover; let rise until doubled in bulk. Punch down; divide into 5 equal parts. Let rest for 10 minutes. Roll each portion into long strand. Place 3 strands on greased baking sheet; braid loosely, beginning in middle. Twist remaining strands on top. Let rise until almost doubled in bulk. Bake at 350 degrees for about 40 minutes.

Apple

Apples are excellent sources of Vitamin C and natural sugar yet are low in calories. (1 raw apple = 70 calories)

AVAILABILITY: Available year-round.

BUYING: Good quality fruit is fresh, firm, brightly colored, and free from any sign of disease or insects.

STORING: Keep either in a moisture-proof bag in a cold, well-ventilated area or in refrigerator. Best storage conditions are those with a temperature around 35 degrees and humidity between 85 to 90 percent.

PREPARATION: A versatile fruit, apples may be cooked or baked in pies, cakes, puddings, or other desserts as well as in stuffings. Raw apples are popular for salads and snacks. Cut apples turn brown when exposed to air. Dip them in lemon, orange, grapefruit, or pineapple juice to prevent discoloration.

SERVING: Tart, firm apples are preferred for baking and cooking while the sweeter ones are eaten or used raw in salads.

APPLE-LIME MOLDS

Color photograph for this recipe on page 307.

1 1/2 tbsp. unflavored gelatin
1/3 c. fresh lime juice
1/2 c. sugar
1/8 tsp. salt
1 tsp. grated lime peel
10 drops of green food coloring
2 med. red Delicious apples
1 c. whipping cream, whipped
Strawberries

Soften gelatin in lime juice. Heat 1 1/4 cups water with sugar and salt in saucepan to simmering. Add gelatin; stir until dissolved. Stir in lime peel and food coloring; chill until thickened. Pare and dice 1 apple. Fold whipped cream into gelatin mixture; fold in the diced apple. Spoon into individual molds; chill until firm. Cut remaining apple into thin slices. Unmold salads; garnish with apple slices, strawberries and mint sprigs, if desired. Yield: Seven 5-ounce molds.

APPLE AND BANANA SALAD

2 tbsp. cornstarch
1 c. milk
1 egg, beaten
3 tbsp. sugar
3 tbsp. vinegar
Pinch of salt
6 bananas, chopped
4 apples, chopped

Dissolve cornstarch in small amount of milk in saucepan. Add egg, sugar, vinegar, remaining milk and salt. Cook, stirring, over low heat until thickened; cool. Pour dressing over fruits; serve chilled. Yield: 10 servings.

APPLE-CELERY SALAD

4 c. chopped unpared apples
1 c. raisins
3 stalks celery, chopped
1/2 c. chopped nuts
1 c. miniature marshmallows
Salad dressing to taste

Combine all ingredients; chill and serve. Yield: 4 servings.

APPLE-NUT SALAD

1 3-oz. package wild cherry gelatin
2 apples, shredded
1/2 c. coarsely chopped nutmeats
Lettuce

Dissolve gelatin in 2 cups boiling water. Chill until thickened. Add apples and nutmeats; pour into mold or flat pan. Chill until firm. Cut into squares. Serve on lettuce. Yield: 6 servings.

AUTUMN'S GOLD APPLE SALAD

Color photograph for this recipe on page 318.

1 tsp. unflavored gelatin
1 3-oz. package lemon gelatin
1/2 c. sour cream
1/4 tsp. dry mustard
Lemon juice
1 tbsp. grated onion
1/4 tsp. salt
1 1/2 c. shredded Cheddar cheese
2 c. diced unpared golden Delicious apples
1/2 c. chopped green pepper
1 c. whipping cream, whipped
Salad greens
Unpared apple slices

Soften unflavored gelatin in 2 tablespoons cold water. Combine lemon gelatin and 1 cup boiling water in bowl; stir until gelatin is dissolved. Add softened gelatin; stir until dissolved. Add sour cream, mustard, 2 tablespoons lemon juice, onion and salt; beat with rotary beater until smooth. Chill until thickened. Fold in cheese, apples and green pepper and whipped cream. Spoon into wet mold; chill until firm. Unmold on salad greens; garnish with apple slices which have been dipped in lemon juice to prevent turning brown. Add additional shredded Cheddar cheese if desired. Yield: 8-10 servings.

FROZEN APPLE SALAD

1 sm. can crushed pineapple
2 eggs, beaten
1/2 c. sugar
Dash of salt
3 tbsp. lemon juice
2 c. finely chopped apple
1/2 c. finely chopped celery
1 c. cream, whipped

Drain pineapple; reserve juice. Add enough water to reserved juice to equal 1/2 cup liquid. Add eggs, sugar, salt and lemon juice. Cook over low heat until thick. Chill. Add apple, celery and pineapple; fold in whipped cream. Pour into large mold or individual molds; freeze. Garnish with unpeeled apples for added color. Yield: 12 servings.

FRESH APPLE SALAD

1 lge. mellow apple
1/3 c. shredded mild cheese
1/4 c. pecans
1 tbsp. salad dressing

Cut apple into small chunks. Place apple, cheese and pecans in small bowl; add salad dressing. Mix well; serve. Yield: 2 servings.

CREAMY GOLDEN WALDORF

Color photograph for this recipe on page 309.

1 6-oz. package lemon gelatin
1/4 tsp. salt
Lemon juice
3 med. golden Delicious apples
1/2 c. mayonnaise
1 c. heavy cream, whipped
1 c. finely chopped celery
1 c. finely chopped walnuts
Salad greens

Dissolve gelatin and salt in 2/3 cup hot water in bowl; stir in 2 tablespoons lemon juice. Chill until thickened. Pare 2 apples partially; core and dice. Skin will add color to salad. Core and cut remaining apple into thin slices; arrange, skin side down, around bottom of 8-cup mold. Sprinkle sliced and diced apples with lemon juice. Blend mayonnaise into thickened gelatin; fold in whipped cream. Fold in diced apples, celery and walnuts gently; spoon over apple slices in mold carefully. Chill until firm. Unmold on salad platter; garnish with greens. Yield: 10-12 servings.

STUFFED APPLES

Color photograph for this recipe on page 306.

4 apples
1/4 c. red cinnamon candies
3/4 c. sugar
1 c. mashed sweet potatoes
Pinch of salt
1/4 c. brown sugar
1/4 c. chopped pecans
4 marshmallows

Core apples; peel. Combine candies, sugar and 1/2 cup water in large saucepan. Cook over moderate heat for about 15 minutes or until sugar and candies are dissolved and syrup thickened. Place apples in syrup; simmer until apples are coated with syrup and partially cooked. Remove apples; place in baking dish. Reserve syrup. Combine sweet potatoes, salt, brown sugar and pecans. Stuff apples with sweet potato mixture; pour reserved syrup over top. Bake at

350 degrees for about 25 to 30 minutes or until tender, basting frequently. Place large marshmallow on top of each apple just before removing from oven; bake for about 5 minutes or until brown.

WALDORF SALAD

2 c. cubed unpeeled red apples
1/2 c. chopped pitted dates
1/2 c. chopped celery
1/2 c. mayonnaise or salad dressing
1/4 c. whipped cream

Combine apples, dates and celery in salad bowl. Blend mayonnaise and cream for dressing. Toss salad with dressing; serve on lettuce. Yield: 4 servings.

APPLE CRISP

1 c. oatmeal
1 c. flour
1 1/2 c. (packed) brown sugar
1 1/2 c. sugar
1 c. butter or margarine
6 c. sliced apples
Salt to taste
Cinnamon to taste

Combine oatmeal, flour, brown sugar, sugar and butter; blend together until crumbly. Place apples in 8 x 13-inch pan. Top with oatmeal mixture; sprinkle with salt and cinnamon. Bake at 350 degrees for 40 minutes. Yield: About 12 servings.

APPLE DESSERT

6 med. apples
Sugar
1/2 c. butter
3 c. bread crumbs

Core apples; pare and slice. Cook apples in saucepan in 1 cup water until tender; add 1/2 cup sugar. Combine butter, crumbs and 2 tablespoons sugar in skillet; cook, stirring, until crumbs are browned. Alternate layers of crumbs and apples in baking dish. Bake at 375 degrees for 20 to 25 minutes. Cool; serve with whipped cream. Yield: 6 servings.

APPLE-FRUIT KABOBS

1 can mandarin oranges, drained
1 1/2 c. diluted orange marmalade
4 apples
6 fresh apricots
12 dried prunes
6 green canned figs, drained

Drain oranges, reserving 2 tablespoons juice; add reserved juice to marmalade, mixing well. Core apples; slice each apple into 6 wedges. Arrange fruits on 6 kabob sticks. Dip in diluted marmalade. Place under broiler for 3 to 8 minutes. Serve hot. Yield: 6 servings.

APPLE ISLANDS

2 c. pared sliced apples
1/2 c. sugar
1/2 tsp. red food coloring
Cinnamon to taste
Nutmeg to taste
1/2 tsp. salt
1 1/2 c. biscuit mix
Butter or margarine

Place apples in greased casserole. Mix 1 cup water, sugar and food coloring in saucepan; bring to a boil. Pour sugar mixture over apples; sprinkle with cinnamon, nutmeg and salt. Prepare biscuit mix according to package directions; drop by spoonfuls onto apple mixture. Place small piece of butter on top of each biscuit island. Bake at 375 degrees until biscuits are golden. Serve warm with cream or ice cream. Yield: 6 servings.

BAKED APPLES WITH FIGS

6 fig newton cookies, quartered
1/3 c. orange juice
3 tbsp. light corn syrup
6 lge. tart apples, cored
1 c. sugar
1 tbsp. butter
1 tsp. grated orange rind

Combine cookies with orange juice and corn syrup; let stand for 10 minutes. Pare apples 1/4 of the way down; place in shallow, buttered 6 x 8-inch baking dish. Spoon cookie mixture into center of apples. Add sugar to 1/2 cup boiling water; stir until sugar is dissolved. Add butter and orange rind; pour over apples. Bake in 350-degree oven for 45 minutes to 1 hour or until apples are tender. Baste apples often while baking. Yield: 6 servings.

APPLE-ALMOND CAKE

1 1/2 c. sugar
3 c. flour
Margarine or butter
1/2 c. slivered almonds
1 egg
1/2 c. milk
2 tsp. almond flavoring
1/2 tsp. salt
1 tbsp. baking powder
3 c. sliced apples

Combine 1 cup sugar, 1 cup flour, 1/2 cup margarine and almonds. Blend together until crumbly. Beat egg lightly; add remaining sugar, milk, almond flavoring and 2 tablespoons margarine. Sift remaining flour, salt and baking powder together; fold into egg mixture. Pour into greased 9 x 12-inch pan. Arrange apple slices over batter; sprinkle apples with almond mixture. Bake at 375 degrees for 35 to 40 minutes. Serve warm or cold. Yield: 10-12 servings.

MOIST APPLE LOAF

4 c. diced or cubed apples
2 c. sugar
1 c. coarsely chopped nuts
3 c. flour
1/2 tsp. cinnamon
1/2 tsp. nutmeg
1/2 tsp. salt
2 tsp. soda
1 c. vegetable oil
1 tsp. vanilla
2 eggs, beaten

Mix apples, sugar and nuts together; let stand for 1 hour. Sift flour, cinnamon, nutmeg, salt and soda together; add to apple mixture alternately with oil, vanilla and eggs. Pour batter into tube pan. Bake at 350 degrees for 1 hour and 15 minutes. Wrap in aluminum foil to keep moist.

APPLE TAPIOCA

6 tart apples
1 c. sugar
1/2 tsp. salt
Cinnamon to taste
1 tbsp. butter
1/2 c. quick-cooking tapioca

Peel and slice apples; place in baking dish. Sprinkle apples with sugar, salt and cinnamon. Dot with butter. Prepare tapioca according to package directions; pour over apples. Bake at 350 degrees until apples are soft. Serve warm with whipped cream or ice cream. Yield: 6 servings.

APLETS CANDY

1 1/4 c. grated apple
2 tbsp. unflavored gelatin
2 c. sugar
1 tsp. lemon juice
1 tsp. vanilla
1 c. chopped nuts
1/2 c. confectioners' sugar
1 tbsp. cornstarch

Combine 1/2 cup grated apple and gelatin. Let stand for 10 minutes. Combine 3/4 cup grated apple, sugar and lemon juice. Bring to a boil; add gelatin mixture. Cook for 15 minutes. Cool. Add vanilla and nuts. Pour into oiled 8-inch square pan. Chill for 24 hours in refrigerator. Cut into squares. Combine confectioners' sugar and cornstarch. Roll squares in confectioners' sugar mixture.

CANDY APPLES

1 lb. vanilla caramels
6 crisp med. apples
Chopped walnuts

Combine caramels and 2 tablespoons water in double boiler. Cook, stirring, until caramels are melted and smooth. Stick wooden skewers into blossom ends of each apple; dip apples in syrup, turning until completely coated. Roll bottom half of each apple in chopped nuts at once. Place on waxed paper-covered cookie sheet. Chill until coating is firm. May add several drops of water to syrup if necessary. Yield: 6 candied apples.

CHILLED APPLE DESSERT

1 c. sugar
3 tbsp. lemon juice
2 tsp. vanilla
6 apples
1 c. heavy cream
1 tbsp. confectioners' sugar

Combine sugar, 1 cup water, lemon juice and 1 1/2 teaspoons vanilla in saucepan. Cook, stirring, over low heat until sugar is dissolved. Simmer for 5 minutes. May add drops of red food coloring if desired. Peel and core apples. Place in syrup. Cook over low heat until tender. Turn once or twice in syrup. Let cool. Remove to serving dish; chill well. Whip cream. Add confectioners' sugar and remaining vanilla. Serve with apples.

QUICK APPLE DUMPLINGS

2 c. biscuit mix
Soft butter or margarine
2 c. finely diced apples
Cinnamon to taste
Sugar
1/2 c. chopped nuts or raisins

Prepare biscuit mix according to package directions; roll out 1/2 inch thick on floured board. Spread with butter. Mix apples, cinnamon, sugar to taste and nuts. Spread over dough; roll up. Cut into 3/4-inch slices. Bring 3/4 cup sugar and 1/2 cup water to boiling point; pour syrup into muffin tins or baking dish. Place apple rolls over syrup. Bake at 450 degrees for 15 to 20 minutes. Yield: 6-8 servings.

APPLE DUMPLINGS

Color photograph for this recipe on page 494.

2 2/3 c. sifted flour
1 1/4 tsp. salt
1 c. shortening
1/2 c. red cinnamon candies
Confectioners' sugar
1/3 c. chopped pecans
1/4 tsp. nutmeg
6 med. tart apples
Cream

Mix flour and salt in bowl; cut in shortening until mixture resembles coarse cornmeal. Sprinkle with 6 1/2 tablespoons cold water; mix well. Divide into 6 equal parts. Roll each part out on floured surface to 7-inch square. Place cinnamon candies and 1/4 cup water in saucepan; cook, stirring constantly, until candies are melted. Add 1/3 cup confectioners' sugar, pecans and nutmeg. Peel and core apples. Place 1 apple on each pastry square; fill cavities with pecan mixture. Moisten edges of squares with cream. Bring opposite corners of pastry over apples; press together. Brush dumplings with cream; place on baking sheet. Bake at 400 degrees for about 35 minutes or until brown. Mix 2 cups confectioners' sugar with enough cream to just moisten. Spoon onto hot dumplings; garnish dumplings with cooked apple pieces.

GLAZED BAKED APPLES

4 lge. baking apples
Butter or margarine
1/2 c. seedless raisins
2 tbsp. grated lemon peel
1 tsp. cinnamon
1/2 c. sugar
1/2 c. red currant jelly

Core apples; pare 1/3 of the way down from stem. Place in baking dish. Combine 2 tablespoons butter, raisins, lemon peel and cinnamon; fill centers of apples with raisin mixture. Top each apple with 1/2 teaspoon butter. Combine 2/3 cup boiling water and sugar; pour over apples. Bake, covered, for 45 minutes to 1 hour or until tender, basting once or twice with syrup. Remove from oven. Melt jelly over low heat, stirring with fork. Spoon over apples. Place in broiler, 3 inches from source of heat; broil for 3 to 4 minutes or until glazed. Serve warm or cold with cream. Yield: 4 servings.

Apple Fondue . . . Tart, firm fruit is dipped in a luscious cheese and wine sauce.

APPLE FONDUE

1 3-oz. package cream cheese
3/4 c. grated Cheddar cheese
3/4 c. grated Swiss cheese
1 tbsp. flour
1/2 c. white wine
1/8 tsp. garlic salt
Dash of cayenne pepper

Pour 1 cup water into fondue base and position tray, rack and bowl. Cut cream cheese into cubes. Mix cheeses with flour. Plug unit into outlet. Pour the wine into fondue bowl and heat until bubbles rise to surface. Stir in cheeses, small amount at a time, and heat, stirring, until melted. Beat with fork to blend smoothly. Stir in garlic salt and cayenne pepper. Use wedges of fresh pears and apples for dippers. Yield: 1 1/2 cups.

EASY APPLE COBBLER

2 1/2 c. canned sliced pie apples
1 1/2 c. sugar
1 c. orange juice
3 tbsp. butter
3/4 c. flour
1/2 tsp. salt
1 tsp. baking powder
1/2 c. milk

Combine apples, 1 cup sugar, orange juice and 1 tablespoon butter in saucepan; bring to a boil. Combine remaining sugar, flour, salt and baking powder. Stir in milk and remaining melted butter separately. Pour batter into greased baking dish; add apple mixture. Bake at 350 to 400 degrees or until batter rises to top of dish. Yield: 6 servings.

APPLE-COCONUT CHIPS

1 egg, beaten
3/4 c. milk
1 tsp. nutmeg
1/2 tsp. salt
1 c. flour
1/4 tsp. baking powder
1/2 c. shredded coconut
6 green apples, sliced

Beat egg and milk until blended; stir in seasonings, flour, baking powder and coconut until smooth. Dip apple slices into batter; fry in deep fat at 400 degrees until brown. Yield: 6-8 servings.

APPLE FRITTERS

1 c. flour
Pinch of salt
1 egg
2/3 c. milk
4 med. cooking apples
Juice of 1 lemon
Sugar to taste

Sift flour and salt into bowl; add egg and half the milk. Beat until smooth. Add remaining milk, beating well. Let stand for 30 minutes. Pare and core apples; slice into 1/2-inch rings. Dip into batter, coating well. Fry in deep hot fat until golden brown. Drain on absorbent paper. Sprinkle with lemon juice and sugar. Yield: 4 servings.

BAKED STUFFED APPLES

6 lge. tart red apples, cored
1 c. chopped bananas
1 c. chopped cranberries
1 c. (packed) brown sugar
1 tsp. cinnamon
Chopped nuts
Whipped cream

Place apples in baking dish. Combine bananas, cranberries, sugar and cinnamon. Fill apples with banana mixture; cover with nuts. Bake in 375-degree oven until tender. Serve cold; top with whipped cream.

JAMAICAN APPLES

5/8 c. sugar
2 tsp. apricot jam
1 tbsp. rum flavoring
Lemon juice to taste
4 cooking apples
1/2 c. dates
2 c. chopped nuts

Combine sugar, 3/4 cup water and jam in saucepan; boil for several minutes or until syrupy. Stir in rum flavoring and lemon juice. Pare and core apples; stuff cavities with dates. Place apples in greased baking dish; pour syrup over apples. Sprinkle with nuts. Bake at 350 degrees for 40 to 45 minutes. Yield: 4 servings.

APPLE PAN DOWDY

8 lge. tart apples
1 c. sugar
1/2 tsp. cinnamon
1/2 tsp. grated nutmeg
3 tbsp. butter
1/2 c. flour
1/4 tsp. salt
1/4 c. shortening

Pare, core and slice apples into 2-quart casserole. Combine sugar, cinnamon and nutmeg; sprinkle over apples. Dot with butter. Sprinkle apple mixture with water. Blend flour, salt and shortening with pastry blender to consistency of small peas. Add 3 tablespoons water, several drops at a time, until dough forms ball and leaves side of bowl. Roll out on floured board to size and shape of baking dish; cut small slits in dough. Moisten edges of dish with water; press dough to edges to seal. Sprinkle with additional sugar and cinnamon. Bake at 425 degrees for 30 minutes. Remove from oven; break crust with spoon into 3-inch square pieces. Partially fold pieces into apple filling. Return to oven; bake at 350 degrees for 15 minutes longer or until apples are tender. Yield: 8 servings.

NEW ENGLAND APPLE PAN DOWDY

12 firm apples
2 1/4 c. flour
1/4 c. yellow cornmeal
1/2 tsp. salt
1 1/4 tsp. baking powder
1 c. milk
1/2 c. molasses
1/4 c. sugar

Pare and core apples; slice into 10 x 12 x 3-inch dish. Sift flour, cornmeal, salt and baking powder together; blend in milk. Roll crust 1/2 inch thick; place over apples. Bake in 350-degree oven for about 30 minutes or until apples are soft and crust is hard. Remove crust; cool. Sweeten apples with molasses and sugar. Break crust into small pieces; mix thoroughly with apple mixture. Chill. Serve in dessert dishes with cream. Yield: 12 servings.

APPLE BARS

2 1/2 c. flour
1 c. shortening
Sugar
1 tsp. salt
1 egg, separated
Milk
1 c. corn flakes
10 apples, sliced
1 tbsp. cinnamon
1 c. powdered sugar

Combine flour, shortening, 2 tablespoons sugar and salt; mix as for pie crust. Pour egg yolk into cup; add enough milk to equal 2/3 cup liquid. Stir milk mixture into dough. Roll out half the dough; fit on large cookie sheet. Sprinkle corn flakes over dough. Place apples over corn flakes. Mix 1 cup sugar and cinnamon; sprinkle over apples. Roll out remaining dough; place over apples for top crust. Pinch edges together firmly. Beat egg white until stiff; brush over top crust. Bake at 350 degrees for 1 hour. Combine powdered sugar and enough water to make of spreading consistency; spread icing over hot pastry. Yield: 24 servings.

APPLE WALNUT PASTRY

1 egg
2/3 c. sugar
2 tbsp. (heaping) flour
1/2 tsp. baking powder
1 tsp. vanilla
1/2 c. chopped walnuts
1 med. apple, chopped or grated

Beat egg; add sugar, beating until well mixed. Add flour and baking powder, mixing well. Stir in vanilla; fold in walnuts and apple. Place in 7 x 9-inch shallow pan. Bake in 350-degree oven for 30 minutes. Serve with ice cream or whipped cream if desired. May be frozen. Yield: 6 servings.

APPLE AND WALNUT PIZZA-GO-ROUND

2 sticks pie crust mix
8 med. juicy apples, pared
1 1/2 tbsp. lemon juice
Sugar
1 tsp. cinnamon
1/4 tsp. nutmeg
3/4 c. all-purpose flour
1/2 c. butter or margarine
3/4 c. chopped walnuts

Prepare pie crust mix according to package directions. Cut 15-inch circle of heavy-duty aluminum foil. Roll pastry on foil circle. Trim edge to fit. Place on pizza baking sheet. Core and slice apples. Overlap apple slices making circles, 1 inside the other, beginning 3/4-inch from edge of pastry. Sprinkle apples with lemon juice. Combine 1/3 cup sugar with spices; sprinkle over apples. Combine flour and 1/2 cup sugar. Cut in butter until crumbly; sprinkle over apple mixture. Turn up rim of pastry and foil; flute. Sprinkle walnuts over top. Bake in 450-degree oven for 20 to 25 minutes or until crust is brown and apples are tender. Serve warm with dash of cream topping or small wedges of cheese. Yield: 10 servings.

WAGON WHEEL APPLE PIE

2 sticks prepared pastry mix
1 c. shredded American cheese
1/2 c. golden raisins
1/2 c. chopped walnuts
2/3 c. (packed) brown sugar
1 tbsp. flour
1/2 tsp. cinnamon
1/4 tsp. mace
1/2 tsp. grated lemon peel
1/8 tsp. salt
5 Washington State apples
2 tbsp. lemon juice
1 tbsp. butter
Milk

Prepare pastry according to package directions, adding cheese and blending well. Combine raisins and walnuts in small bowl; set aside. Combine brown sugar, flour, cinnamon, mace, lemon peel and salt in separate bowl. Line 9-inch pie plate with half the cheese pastry; roll remaining half to 6 by 12-inch rectangle. Cut 10 1/2-inch strips. Pare apples; core and cut into thin slices. Arrange half the apples in pastry-lined pan; sprinkle with half the raisin mixture and half the sugar mixture. Repeat layers; sprinkle apples with lemon juice. Dot with butter. Twist pastry strips to make spoke-wheel top; finish edge by fluting with fingers. Brush strips with milk. Bake in 425-degree oven for 30 to 45 minutes or until tender and browned. Cover pie with foil if crust browns before apples are tender. Serve warm with whipped cream or ice cream if desired. Yield: One 9-inch pie.

APPLE DEEP-DISH PIE

1/2 recipe pie pastry
1 tbsp. flour
1 c. sugar
5 apples
2 tsp. butter
1/4 tsp. nutmeg

Roll out pie pastry to fit into deep dish; flute edges of pastry. Sprinkle flour and 1/4 cup sugar on pastry. Pare apples; quarter. Place in pastry shell, cut sides down. Cover with remaining sugar; dot with butter. Sprinkle with nutmeg. Bake in 350-degree oven for about 35 minutes or until apples are baked and syrup has formed. Yield: 6 servings.

APPLE-BUTTER PIE

1/2 c. sugar
2 eggs, beaten
1 1/2 tbsp. cornstarch
1 tsp. cinnamon
1/2 tsp. salt
1/2 c. apple butter
2 c. milk
1 unbaked 9-in. pie crust

Combine sugar, eggs, cornstarch, cinnamon, salt and apple butter; mix well. Add milk gradually; blend. Pour filling into pie crust. Bake at 350 degrees for 35 minutes. Yield: 6 servings.

Wagon Wheel Apple Pie . . . This ingeniously twisted pastry crowns a spicy apple filling.

OLD-FASHIONED FRIED APPLE TARTS

1 8-oz. package dried apples
Sugar to taste
1/2 c. shortening
2 c. sifted self-rising flour

Prepare apples according to package directions. Mash thoroughly; add sugar. Chill. Cut shortening into flour; add about 5 tablespoons cold water, mixing until pastry holds together. Knead until smooth. Roll into saucer-sized circles. Place small amount of apples in center of each circle; fold in half. Seal and trim edges. Fry in hot fat in skillet until lightly browned, turning once. Drain. Yield: 15-18 servings.

APPLE SPONGE

Sliced apples
2 tbsp. butter
1/4 c. sugar
1 egg
1/2 c. self-rising flour
Powdered sugar

Fill deep pie dish with enough apple slices to fill 3/4 full. Cream butter and sugar until fluffy; beat in egg. Add flour gently, mixing well. Spoon flour mixture over apples. Bake in 350-degree oven for 40 minutes or until brown. Sprinkle with powdered sugar. Serve with cream. Yield: 4 servings.

DEEP-DISH APPLE PIE

6 tart apples
1 c. (packed) brown sugar
1 c. cake flour
1/4 tsp. salt
1/8 tsp. nutmeg
1/2 c. butter

Pare apples; cut into slices. Place apple slices in deep, greased pie dish. Blend brown sugar, flour, salt and nutmeg together; cut in butter to coarse meal consistency. Sprinkle brown sugar mixture over apples. Bake at 325 degrees for 50 minutes. Serve with whipped cream or ice cream. Yield: 6-8 servings.

APPLE-PECAN PIE

2 c. flour
1/4 tsp. salt
2/3 c. shortening
1 c. pecan halves
2 tsp. cinnamon
3/4 c. (packed) brown sugar
6 med. apples, pared
2 tbsp. butter

Combine flour and salt; reserve 1/2 cup flour mixture. Blend reserved flour mixture with 1/4 cup water to form paste. Cut shortening into remaining flour mixture until of small pea consistency. Add paste mixture, blending only until dough leaves side of bowl. Roll pastry out into two 10-inch circles. Fit 1 circle into 9-inch pie pan. Trim edges. Arrange pecan halves in pastry shell. Combine cinnamon and brown sugar. Sprinkle half the cinnamon mixture over pecans. Slice apples over cinnamon mixture; sprinkle with remaining cinnamon mixture. Dot with butter. Top with remaining pastry, fluting edges together. Bake at 425 degrees for about 10 minutes; reduce oven temperature to 350 degrees. Bake for about 35 minutes longer or until done.

APPLE-CHEESE CRUMBLE PIE

1/2 c. sugar
1/2 c. (packed) brown sugar
1 tsp. ground cinnamon
1 pkg. pie crust mix
3 tbsp. butter
2 c. shredded Cheddar cheese
7 med. apples
1 tbsp. flour
1/2 tsp. nutmeg

Combine sugar, brown sugar, cinnamon and 1 cup pie crust mix. Cut in butter until crumbly; set aside. Mix half the cheese into remaining pie crust mix; stir in 3 tablespoons water, mixing lightly. Roll dough out on lightly-floured surface about 1-inch longer than 9-inch pie pan. Fit pastry into pie pan; flute

VARIETY	USES	CHARACTERISTIC
Delicious, Golden	Snacks, salads, sauces or pies	A crisp-textured, tangy-flavored apple that is yellow.
Delicious, Red	Snacks or cooking	A crisp-textured, sweet-flavored apple that is red.
Jonathan	Snacks or cooking	A smooth-textured, sweet-flavored apple that is red.
McIntosh	All-purpose	A tender-textured, rich and spicy flavored apple that is two-toned—green and red.
Rome Beauty	Cooking or baking	A firm-textured, mild apple that is red with yellow stripe-like markings.
Stayman	All-purpose	A semi-firm textured, richly flavored apple that is a deep red.
Winesap	All-purpose	A firm-textured, richly flavored tart apple that is a deep red.

edges with fork. Pare apples; core and slice. Spoon apples into pastry shell. Combine flour and nutmeg; sprinkle over apples. Cover apples with half the crumbly mixture; sprinkle with remaining cheese. Cover with remaining crumbly mixture. Bake at 375 degrees for 40 to 45 minutes or until apples are tender. Yield: 6 servings.

DELUXE APPLE PIE

3 tbsp. butter
1 c. brown sugar
1/2 c. pecan halves
2/3 c. shortening
2 c. flour
1 tsp. salt
Sliced apples
1 c. sugar
1 tsp. cinnamon

Melt butter; mix with brown sugar. Spread in 9-inch pie plate; press pecans on brown sugar mixture, flat sides up. Blend shortening into flour; add salt, mixing well. Add about 5 tablespoons cold water, blending until pastry leaves side of bowl. Roll half the pastry to fit pan. Fit pastry over brown sugar mixture. Fill crust with sliced apples; add sugar and cinnamon. Dot with additional butter. Roll out remaining pastry; arrange over apples, sealing edges. Bake in 375-degree oven until apples are tender. Turn out upside down. May be served with ice cream or plain. Yield: 6 servings.

OPEN-FACED APPLE PIE

6 c. sliced pared apples
1 unbaked 9-in. pie shell
1 1/3 c. sugar
3 tbsp. flour
3/4 tsp. salt
1/3 c. light cream
1/4 tsp. cinnamon

Arrange apples to fill pie shell. Combine sugar, flour and salt; add cream. Mix well. Cover apples with cream mixture. Sprinkle with cinnamon. Cover pie with aluminum foil. Bake at 375 degrees for 1 hour; remove foil. Bake for 30 minutes longer or until apples are tender. Yield: 6 servings.

PARADISE APPLE PIE

6 lge. apples
Cloves
Sugar
Lemon peel slivers
1 9-in. baked pie crust
1/2 pt. whipping cream, whipped
Chopped nuts

Core apples; stick 2 or 3 whole cloves into each apple. Fill cavities with sugar and lemon slivers. Bake at 400 degrees until apples are soft. Chill; remove skins and cloves. Blend apples with enough sugar to sweeten to taste. Fill pie shell with apple mixture; cover with whipped cream. Sprinkle with chopped nuts.

CLASSIC APPLE PIE

6 c. sliced apples
Pastry for 2-crust pie
3/4 c. sugar
2 tbsp. flour
1/4 tsp. each salt, nutmeg
1 tbsp. lemon juice
2 tbsp. butter
1 tsp. sugar

Place apple slices in pastry-lined pie pan. Sprinkle with next 5 ingredients; dot with butter. Cover with crust; cut vents. Brush with additional melted butter; sprinkle with sugar. Bake at 400 degrees for 45 minutes.

Photograph for this recipe on cover.

APPLE-RICE BETTY

1 c. cooked rice
1 1/3 c. apple juice
1/8 tsp. salt
2/3 c. (packed) brown sugar
1/2 c. raisins
1 1/3 c. diced apples
1 tbsp. butter
1 c. heavy cream

Combine all ingredients except butter and cream in saucepan. Bring to a boil. Cover; simmer for 5 to 10 minutes or until most of liquid is absorbed. Remove from heat; blend in butter until melted. Chill. Whip cream; fold in rice mixture. Garnish with additional whipped cream. Serve. Yield: 6-8 servings.

OZARK PUDDING

2 eggs
1 1/2 c. sugar
4 tbsp. flour
2 1/2 tsp. baking powder
1/4 tsp. salt
1 tsp. cinnamon
1/2 tsp. nutmeg
2 c. chopped apples
1 c. chopped nuts
2 tsp. vanilla

Beat eggs and sugar until smooth. Combine flour, baking powder, salt, and spices; blend into sugar mixture. Add apples, nuts and vanilla. Place in greased 10 x 6-inch pan. Bake in 350-degree oven for 35 minutes. Serve with sweetened whipped cream or ice cream. Yield: 8 servings.

TAFFY APPLE BLOSSOMS

1/2 c. light molasses
1/2 c. sugar
3 tbsp. lemon juice
6 tart apples
1 pt. vanilla ice cream

Combine molasses, sugar, 1/2 cup water and lemon juice in 10-inch skillet. Peel and core apples; bring molasses mixture to a boil. Add apples; reduce heat. Cover; simmer for 15 minutes. Remove cover; turn apples. Simmer for about 30 minutes or until tender. Chill. Cut apples 3/4 of the way down to form petals. Scoop out 6 small scoops of ice cream; place in freezing compartment. Place ice cream ball in center of each apple when ready to serve. Yield: 6 servings.

APPLE BROWN BREAD

1 c. raisins
2/3 c. dates
2/3 c. chopped apples
2 tsp. soda
1 c. sugar
1 tbsp. shortening
1 egg
1 tbsp. molasses
1 tsp. vanilla
2 1/2 c. flour

Combine raisins, dates, apples and 1 1/2 cups water in saucepan; bring to a boil. Remove from heat; add soda and let cool. Cream sugar and shortening until fluffy; beat in egg, mixing well. Add molasses and vanilla. Add apple mixture alternately with flour to molasses mixture. Spoon batter into loaf pan. Bake at 350 degrees for 1 hour. Yield: 25 servings.

BAKED APPLE MUFFINS

1 1/2 c. sifted flour
1 3/4 tsp. baking powder
1/2 tsp. salt
1/2 tsp. nutmeg
Sugar
1/3 c. shortening
1 egg, beaten
1/3 c. milk
1/2 c. grated apple
1 tsp. cinnamon
1/2 c. melted margarine

Sift flour, baking powder, salt, nutmeg and 1/2 cup sugar together; cut in shortening. Mix egg, milk and apple; add all at once to dry ingredients. Mix well. Fill greased muffin cups 2/3 full. Bake at 350 degrees for 25 to 30 minutes. Combine 1/3 cup sugar and cinnamon. Roll hot muffins in margarine; roll in sugar mixture. Serve warm. Yield: 12 muffins.

SPICED APPLE MUFFINS

2 c. flour
Sugar
4 tsp. baking powder
1/2 tsp. salt
Cinnamon
1 egg, beaten
1 c. milk
4 tbsp. melted butter
1 c. chopped apples

Sift flour, 1/2 cup sugar, baking powder, salt and 1/2 teaspoon cinnamon together. Combine egg, milk and melted butter. Add dry ingredients. Beat well; fold in apples. Drop batter by spoonfuls into greased muffin tins, filling 2/3 full. Combine 2 tablespoons sugar and 1/2 teaspoon cinnamon; sprinkle over muffin batter. Bake at 425 degrees for 15 to 18 minutes. Yield: 12 muffins.

Applesauce

APPLESAUCE SALAD

1 c. red hots
1 1/2 c. boiling water
1 box cherry gelatin
1 No. 303 can applesauce
1 sm. can crushed pineapple

Dissolve red hots in water; add gelatin, stirring to dissolve. Chill until partially congealed. Stir in applesauce and pineapple; refrigerate until set.

FROZEN APPLESAUCE SALAD

3 eggs, beaten
1/2 c. sugar
1/3 c. lemon juice
1/4 tsp. salt
1/2 c. crushed pineapple, drained and juice reserved
1/2 c. shredded carrots
1/2 c. chopped walnuts
1 c. diced celery
2 c. chilled canned applesauce
1 c. sour cream

Combine eggs, sugar, lemon juice, salt and reserved juice in saucepan; cook over low heat until thick, stirring constantly. Cool. Add pineapple, carrots, walnuts and celery; fold in applesauce and sour cream. Pour into two 1-quart ice cube trays or one 2-quart mold; freeze until firm. Let thaw slightly before serving. May be stored in freezer for 1 month. Yield: 8-10 servings.

APPLESAUCE-NUT BREAD

2 c. sifted flour
3/4 c. sugar
1 tsp. salt
2 tsp. baking powder
1/2 tsp. soda
1/2 tsp. cinnamon
1 c. chopped nuts
1 egg, beaten
1 c. thick applesauce
2 tbsp. melted shortening

Sift flour, sugar, salt, baking powder, soda and cinnamon together. Add nuts, egg, applesauce and shortening; stir until blended. Pour into greased loaf pan. Bake at 350 degrees for 1 hour.

GRILLED APPLESAUCE BREAKFAST

8 slices bread
1/2 c. butter or margarine
1 c. applesauce
4 tsp. sugar or cinnamon sugar
Powdered sugar

Heat grill to 375 degrees. Spread one side of bread slices with butter. Spread 4 tablespoons applesauce on unbuttered side of 4 slices. Sprinkle each with 1 teaspoon sugar. Cover with remaining slices of bread, buttered side up. Grill on both sides until golden brown. Cool for 10 minutes; dust with powdered sugar. Serve. Yield: 4 servings.

APPLESAUCE DESSERT WITH VANILLA SAUCE

2 c. zwieback or bread crumbs
4 tbsp. melted butter
1 1/3 c. applesauce
3 egg yolks, beaten
2 tbsp. sugar
1 c. cream
2 tsp. vanilla
3/4 c. whipping cream, whipped

Brown crumbs in melted butter in skillet. Line buttered 9-inch baking dish with crumbs. Arrange alternate layers of applesauce and remaining crumbs in baking dish, ending with crumbs. Bake in 375-degree oven for 25 to 35 minutes. Cool; invert onto serving plate. Combine egg yolks, sugar and cream in saucepan; cook over low heat until thick, stirring constantly. Remove from heat; stir in vanilla. Cool sauce. Fold in whipped cream; spoon over squares of apple dessert to serve. Yield: 6-8 servings.

APPLESAUCE PUDDING

3 c. sweetened applesauce
3 eggs, separated
1 tsp. grated lemon rind
1 1/2 tsp. vanilla
2 tsp. lemon juice
6 tbsp. sugar
1/8 tsp. salt

Place applesauce in bowl. Add egg yolks, lemon rind, 1/2 teaspoon vanilla and lemon juice; mix well. Beat egg whites until soft peaks form. Add sugar gradually, beating constantly; beat until stiff. Mix in salt and remaining vanilla. Pour applesauce mixture in baking dish; spread meringue on top. Place baking dish in pan of hot water. Bake at 300 degrees for 15 minutes. Serve immediately or chill and serve with cream. Yield: 6 servings.

APPLESAUCE DROP COOKIES

1/2 c. shortening
1 c. sugar
1 egg, beaten
2 1/2 c. flour
1 tsp. soda
1 tsp. cinnamon
1/4 tsp. cloves
1 tsp. salt
1 1/4 c. applesauce
1 c. raisins
1/2 c. chopped nuts

Cream shortening and sugar; stir in egg. Sift dry ingredients together; add to creamed mixture alternately with applesauce. Stir in raisins and nuts. Drop from teaspoon onto greased cookie sheet. Bake at 400 degrees for 15 minutes. Yield: 4 1/2 dozen cookies.

APPLESAUCE PUFFS

2 c. biscuit mix
Sugar
Cinnamon
1/2 c. applesauce
1/4 c. milk
1 slightly beaten egg
2 tbsp. cooking oil
2 tbsp. melted butter

Preheat oven to 400 degrees. Combine biscuit mix, 1/4 cup sugar and 1 teaspoon cinnamon. Add applesauce, milk, egg and cooking oil; beat vigorously for 30 seconds. Fill greased 2-inch muffin pans 2/3 full. Bake for 12 minutes or until golden. Cool slightly; remove from pans. Combine 1/4 cup sugar and 1/4 teaspoon cinnamon. Dip top of muffins in melted butter and then in sugar mixture. Yield: 24 muffins.

BAKED DANISH DELIGHT

2 c. lightly sweetened applesauce
1 1/3 c. ground blanched almonds
1/2 c. confectioners' sugar
3 eggs, separated

Spread applesauce in buttered 8 x 8 x 2-inch baking dish. Combine almonds with sugar. Beat in egg yolks, one at a time; fold in stiffly beaten egg whites. Spread over applesauce; set in shallow pan of hot water. Bake at 350 degrees for 15 minutes or until lightly browned. Serve warm with whipped cream. Yield: 6-8 servings.

APPLESAUCE CHOCOLATE CAKE

1/2 c. butter
1 c. sugar
1 egg
1 c. raisins
1/4 tsp. salt
1 tsp. cinnamon
1 3/4 c. flour
1 tsp. soda
2 tbsp. cocoa
1 c. hot applesauce
1/2 c. nuts

Cream butter; beat in sugar. Add egg; mix well. Stir in raisins. Sift dry ingredients together; stir into butter mixture. Stir in applesauce and nuts. Pour into greased loaf pan. Bake at 350 degrees for 1 hour.

APPLESAUCE CUPCAKES

1 c. sugar
1/2 c. shortening
1 egg
1 c. applesauce
1 1/2 c. sifted flour
1/3 c. cocoa
1 tsp. cinnamon
1/2 tsp. ground cloves
1/2 tsp. nutmeg
1/2 tsp. salt
1 tsp. soda
1 tsp. water

Cream sugar and shortening; add egg, mixing well. Stir in applesauce. Sift flour, cocoa, spices and salt together; add to applesauce mixture. Mix soda and water; add to batter. Pour into paper-lined cupcake tins. Bake at 350 degrees for 20 to 30 minutes or until toothpick inserted in cupcake comes out clean. Spread with peanut butter frosting, if desired. Yield: 12 servings.

FROSTED APPLESAUCE CAKE

1 1/2 c. applesauce
1/2 c. butter
1 c. (packed) brown sugar
1 c. raisins
1 tsp. cloves
1 tsp. cinnamon
1 tsp. nutmeg
1/4 tsp. salt
2 c. flour
2 tsp. soda
1 c. chopped nuts
2 c. confectioners' sugar
4 tbsp. hot milk
3 tbsp. melted butter
1/2 tsp. vanilla

Combine applesauce, butter, brown sugar and raisins in saucepan; heat until butter and sugar are dissolved. Let stand until cool. Sift spices, salt, flour and soda together; stir into applesauce mixture. Add nuts. Turn into greased 9 x 9-inch cake pan. Bake in 350-degree oven for 20 to 30 minutes. Mix remaining ingredients together until smooth; spread on warm cake.

FRUITED APPLESAUCE CAKE

3/4 c. butter
2 c. warm unsweetened applesauce
2 tsp. soda
1 c. sour milk
3 c. flour
2 c. sugar
1 tbsp. cocoa
1 tsp. cinnamon
1 tsp. cloves
1 tsp. nutmeg
1/2 tsp. salt
1 tsp. allspice
1 c. raisins
1 lb. mixed candied fruit
1/4 lb. candied cherries, halved
1 c. chopped nuts

Cream butter; add applesauce, mixing well. Dissolve soda in sour milk; add to applesauce mixture. Sift dry ingredients together; blend into applesauce mixture. Dredge fruits and nuts with additional flour; add to batter, stirring well. Turn into tube pan. Bake at 300 degrees for 2 hours and 30 minutes. Yield: 16 servings.

IRISH APPLESAUCE CAKE

3 c. sifted flour
3/4 c. sugar
3 egg yolks
1 c. butter
Grated rind of 1 lemon
2 c. applesauce
1/2 tsp. cinnamon
1/4 tsp. cloves

Mix flour, sugar, egg yolks, butter and rind together; divide into 2 equal parts. Press 1 part into well-greased pan. Mix applesauce and spices; spread over dough. Sprinkle remaining dough over applesauce. Bake at 350 degrees for 40 to 45 minutes. Top with whipped cream or lemon sauce. Yield: 12 servings.

GUMDROP-APPLESAUCE CAKE

1 c. butter
1 c. sugar
2 eggs
4 c. flour
1 tsp. salt
1 tsp. soda
1 tsp. cloves
1 tsp. cinnamon
1 1/2 c. applesauce
1 1/2 c. chopped nuts
3 c. raisins
1 1/2 lb. gumdrops

Cream butter and sugar; add eggs. Sift dry ingredients together; add to creamed mixture alternately with applesauce. Add nuts and raisins; blend well. Add gumdrops; mix well. Turn into two 3 x 7-inch loaf pans. Bake at 350 degrees for about 1 hour or until cake tests done.

TOPSY-TURVY APPLESAUCE CAKE

2 c. flour, sifted
1/2 tsp. salt
1 tsp. soda
1/2 tsp. cloves
1/2 tsp. nutmeg
1 tsp. cinnamon
1/2 c. shortening
1 1/4 c. sugar
2 eggs
2 1/3 c. applesauce
1/2 c. broken walnuts
3/4 c. raisins
1/3 c. cinnamon candies
1 3 1/2-oz. can flaked coconut
1/4 c. butter, softened

Sift flour, salt, soda and spices together. Blend shortening and 1 cup sugar with electric mixer. Add eggs; beat for 1 minute and 30 seconds. Add 1 cup applesauce, walnuts and raisins. Add flour mixture; beat for 1 minute and 30 seconds. Bring remaining applesauce to a boil; reduce heat. Add candies; stir until dissolved. Stir in remaining sugar and remaining ingredients. Pour into 9 x 13 x 2-inch pan; spread cake batter over icing. Bake at 350 degrees for 55 minutes. Cool for 10 minutes; invert on cake plate to remove. Yield: 16-24 servings.

APPLESAUCE GRAHAM DELIGHT

1 lb. box graham crackers, crushed
2 1-lb. cans applesauce
1 pt. whipping cream, whipped

Press crumbs about 1/4 inch thick in 9 1/4 x 13 x 2-inch dish to form crust. Spread layers of applesauce, whipped cream and remaining crumbs over crust; repeat layers until all ingredients are used. Cover with plastic wrap; refrigerate for at least 12 hours or overnight. Cut into squares to serve. Yield: 12 servings.

APPLESAUCE REFRIGERATOR DESSERT

Lemon juice
1 can sweetened condensed milk
2 egg whites, stiffly beaten
2 c. applesauce
Whole vanilla wafers
1 c. whipping cream, whipped

Combine 1/4 cup lemon juice with sweetened condensed milk. Fold egg whites into condensed milk mixture. Stir 2 tablespoons lemon juice into applesauce. Line 8 x 8 x 2-inch pan with waxed paper; place layer of wafers on bottom. Cover with 1/2 of the milk mixture and 1/2 of the applesauce mixture. Repeat layers; top with vanilla wafers. Chill for at least 12 hours. Invert onto serving plate; serve with whipped cream. Yield: 8 servings.

APPLESAUCE SNOW WITH CUSTARD SAUCE

1 tbsp. unflavored gelatin
3 tbsp. cinnamon candies
1 c. applesauce
2 tbsp. lemon juice
1/2 c. sugar
3 egg whites
Dash of salt
Custard Sauce

Soften gelatin in 1/4 cup cold water. Combine 1 cup boiling water, cinnamon candies and gelatin in saucepan; heat until candies are dissolved. Remove from heat; stir in applesauce, lemon juice and 1/4 cup sugar. Chill until slightly thickened. Beat egg whites and salt until soft peaks form. Beat in remaining sugar until stiff peaks form. Beat slightly thickened gelatin mixture until foamy; fold in egg whites. Pour into individual dishes or serving bowl; chill until firm. Serve with Custard Sauce.

Custard Sauce

3 egg yolks, slightly beaten
1/4 c. sugar
1/4 tsp. salt
2 c. scalded milk
1 tsp. vanilla

Combine egg yolks, sugar and salt in top of double boiler; add milk. Cook over boiling water, stirring constantly, for 15 to 20 minutes or until mixture coats metal spoon. Add vanilla. Cool.

EASY-FRIED TURNOVERS

1 pkg. refrigerator dinner rolls
Canned sweetened applesauce

Roll out each roll separately to about 1/8 to 1/4-inch thickness. Spoon 1 teaspoon applesauce into center of each roll. Fold over; press edges together to form crescents. Fry in 1/2 inch melted shortening until golden brown. Serve hot. Yield: 6-12 servings.

CRUSTLESS APPLESAUCE PIE

1 1/2 c. sifted flour
2 tsp. baking powder
1/2 tsp. salt
1/2 c. shortening
2/3 c. milk
Sugar
1 1/2 tsp. nutmeg
Melted butter
4 c. canned applesauce
2 tbsp. grated orange rind
1/4 c. orange juice
2 tbsp. quick-cooking tapioca

Combine flour, baking powder and salt; cut in shortening with pastry blender. Add enough milk to make a soft dough; form dough into 16 balls. Combine 1/3 cup sugar and nutmeg. Roll balls in melted butter, then in sugar mixture; set aside. Combine applesauce, sugar to taste, orange rind and juice; stir in tapioca. Pour into 10-inch pie plate; place dough balls around edge and in center of pie. Bake at 400 degrees for 25 to 30 minutes or until puffs are brown. Serve with ice cream, if desired.

FLAKY APPLE WREATH

1 c. butter or margarine
3 c. flour, sifted
1 egg
Light cream
Sugar
1/2 tsp. cinnamon
2 c. sweetened applesauce
Confectioners' sugar
3/4 c. whipping cream
1 tsp. vanilla

Cut butter into flour until of cornmeal consistency. Combine egg and enough cream to measure 1/2 cup liquid; mix well. Sprinkle over flour mixture; toss lightly until dough holds together. Divide into 4 equal parts; form into balls. Wrap balls in waxed paper; refrigerate until chilled. Roll out 1 ball at a time on floured surface to 1/2-inch thickness; cut circle around 9-inch inverted pie pan. Cut 3-inch round hole from center; reserve center dough. Place large circle of dough on ungreased baking sheet; prick generously. Combine 1/4 cup sugar and cinnamon; sprinkle 1 tablespoon mixture over pastry ring. Bake at 450 degrees for 8 to 10 minutes or until light brown. Cool ring; remove from pan. Repeat, using all dough. Cut small stars, hearts or other desired shapes from reserved centers; bake with fourth circle. Place 1 pastry ring on serving plate; spread with 1/3 of the applesauce. Repeat, stacking all circles; end with plain top circle. Sprinkle with confectioners' sugar. Whip cream until thick; fold in 3 tablespoons sugar and vanilla. Spoon into center of ring; decorate with baked pastry cut-outs. Slice into wedges to serve. Fill ring 1 hour or less before serving. Yield: 8 servings.

LIME-APPLESAUCE FLUFF PIE

2 1/2 c. applesauce
1 pkg. lime gelatin
1 c. sugar
2 tbsp. lemon juice
1 14 1/2-oz. can evaporated milk, whipped
2 9-in. graham cracker pie shells

Measure applesauce into saucepan; heat to boiling point. Add gelatin; stir until dissolved. Blend in sugar; chill until partially congealed. Add lemon juice to whipped milk; fold into applesauce mixture. Pour into pie shells; refrigerate for several hours before serving.

Apricot

As attractive to look at as it is delicious, the pale gold-orange apricot is an excellent source of Vitamins A and C and iron. The raw fruit is low in calories (3 medium apricots = 55 calories), but in dried or canned form, the calorie count increases significantly.

AVAILABILITY: Fresh apricots are available from late May to early September, with June and July the peak months. Canned and dried apricots are available year-round.

BUYING: Choose mature, firm, well-rounded fruit uniform in color. Immature fruit is greenish, hard, and slightly shriveled; overripe fruit is soft and mushy.

STORING: Fresh apricots are highly perishable. If bought fully ripe, they should be refrigerated. Immature fruit ripens if it is placed in a bag and the bag is then sealed and left in a warm room. Keep unopened bags of dried fruit in cupboard; once opened, the package should be tightly sealed and refrigerated.

SERVING: Apricots are versatile and can be used in salads, sherbets, souffles, and to highlight meat (particularly pork, lamb, and ham) and fish. Jam, syrup, and candy made from apricots are delicious.

APRICOT AND ALMOND SALAD

1 1-lb. package dried apricots
1 No. 2 can crushed pineapple
1 c. slivered almonds
1 lge. package orange gelatin
1 env. unflavored gelatin

Prepare apricots according to package directions. Drain and mash. Drain pineapple; reserve juice. Add pineapple and almonds to apricots. Prepare orange gelatin according to package directions using reserved juice as part of the liquid. Soften unflavored gelatin in 1/4 cup water; dissolve over hot water. Add to orange gelatin. Stir in apricot mixture. Pour into pan or individual molds; chill until firm. Serve with tart mayonnaise. Yield: 6 servings.

APRICOT-CHEESE SALAD

1 1-lb. can apricots
1/4 lb. Cheddar cheese, grated
1 c. chopped pecans
1/2 c. sugar
2 tbsp. flour
1 egg, slightly beaten

Drain apricots; reserve juice. Arrange apricots in large flat dish; cover with cheese. Sprinkle cheese with pecans. Combine reserved juice, sugar, flour and egg. Cook over medium heat, stirring constantly, until thickened. Pour over layered mixture. Chill thoroughly. Spoon onto lettuce for serving.

APRICOT SALAD

8 apricot halves, drained
Salad greens
2 tbsp. chopped celery
2 tbsp. chopped pecans
4 tbsp. salad dressing
4 tbsp. whipped cream
1/2 tsp. salt

Arrange apricots on salad greens in bowl. Combine celery and pecans; mix in salad dressing and whipped cream. Add salt; blend. Spoon dressing onto apricot halves. Yield: 4 servings.

Apricot Surprise Ring . . . A creamy-textured and mild-flavored salad delight.

APRICOT SURPRISE RING

1 1-lb. 4-oz. can apricot halves
1 3-oz. package orange gelatin
1/3 c. small curd cottage cheese
1 c. evaporated skimmed milk

Drain apricots, reserving syrup. Bring reserved syrup to boiling point in saucepan. Dissolve gelatin in syrup. Stir in 1/2 cup water; let mixture cool. Fill apricot halves with cottage cheese. Place halves together; arrange in bottom of 5 1/2-cup ring mold. Stir milk into gelatin mixture; pour over apricots. Chill until firm. Unmold; garnish with additional cottage cheese, mint sprigs and whole apricots. Yield: 6 servings.

APRICOT NECTAR SALAD

2 pkg. orange gelatin
3 c. apricot nectar
1 c. miniature marshmallows
1/2 c. sugar
2 tbsp. flour
1 egg, beaten
1/2 pt. cream, whipped
Shredded longhorn cheese

Dissolve gelatin in 2 cups boiling water; cool. Add 2 cups apricot nectar; chill until partially set. Add marshmallows; pour into 8 x 12-inch glass dish. Chill until firm. Mix sugar, flour and egg; cook until thickened, stirring constantly. Add remaining apricot nectar gradually; cool. Fold in whipped cream; spread over gelatin mixture. Sprinkle with cheese; chill for 6 to 8 hours. Serve on lettuce. Yield: 8-10 servings.

MOLDED APRICOT SALAD

1 12-oz. can apricot nectar
1 pkg. lemon gelatin
1/8 tsp. salt
2 tsp. horseradish
1 c. grated carrot
2 tbsp. lemon juice
1/2 c. slivered blanched almonds

Combine apricot nectar and 1/4 cup water in saucepan; bring to a boil. Add gelatin; stir until dissolved. Cool. Chill until partially congealed. Fold in remaining ingredients; pour into individual molds. Chill until firm. Serve on lettuce with mayonnaise. Yield: 6 servings.

APRICOT-CARAMEL COBBLER

1 1-lb. 14-oz. can unpeeled apricot halves
2 tsp. quick-cooking tapioca
Brown sugar
Butter or margarine
1 tbsp. lemon juice
1/2 c. sugar
1 1/2 c. flour
2 tsp. baking powder
1/2 c. milk
Cream

Combine apricots, tapioca, 1/3 cup packed brown sugar, 1 tablespoon butter and lemon juice. Boil, stirring constantly, until mixture becomes translucent. Pour into 2-quart baking dish. Combine sugar, flour and baking powder; cut in 2 tablespoons butter until mixture resembles coarse cornmeal. Add milk, stirring only until dry ingredients are dampened. Drop over apricot mixture around edge of baking dish. Bake at 425 degrees for 15 minutes. Mix 1/2 cup packed brown sugar and 1/4 cup water, boil for 1 minute. Spoon over apricot mixture. Bake for about 5 minutes longer; serve warm with cream. Yield: 6 servings.

APRICOT BARS

2/3 c. dried apricots
1/2 c. butter or margarine
1/4 c. sugar
1 1/3 c. flour
2 eggs
1 c. brown sugar
1/2 tsp. baking powder
1/4 tsp. salt
1/2 tsp. vanilla
1/2 c. chopped pecans
Confectioners' sugar

Preheat oven to 350 degrees. Cover apricots with water; boil for 10 minutes. Drain; cool. Chop apricots. Mix butter, sugar and 1 cup flour until crumbly; pack into greased 8 x 8 x 2-inch pan. Bake for 25 minutes. Beat eggs well; add brown sugar, beating until well mixed. Sift remaining flour, baking powder and salt; add to egg mixture. Mix well. Add vanilla, pecans and apricots; spread over baked layer. Bake for 30 minutes longer. Cool in pan. Cut into 1 x 2-inch bars; roll in confectioners' sugar. Yield: 32 bars.

APRICOT BETTY

3 c. canned apricot halves, drained
1 c. bread crumbs
1/4 c. brown sugar
1/4 c. margarine
1/2 tsp. mace
1/2 tsp. cinnamon
1/4 tsp. ginger
1/4 c. nonfat dry milk

Arrange apricots in baking dish. Combine crumbs and brown sugar; add margarine, blending well. Stir in spices and dry milk; mix well until crumbly. Sprinkle apricots with crumbly mixture. Bake at 375 degrees for 30 minutes. Serve warm with milk or cream if desired. Yield: 4-6 servings.

APRICOT NECTAR CAKE

1 pkg. yellow cake mix
1 pkg. apricot gelatin
1/2 c salad oil
Apricot nectar
6 eggs
2 c. powdered sugar

Mix cake mix and gelatin; add oil, 3/4 cup apricot nectar and eggs. Beat well. Pour batter into tube pan or bundt pan. Bake at 350 degrees for 1 hour or until cake tests done. Combine powdered sugar and 1/3 cup apricot nectar. Pour over warm cake.

APRICOT TARTS

All-purpose flour
2 tsp. salt
1 c. (heaping) shortening
1 1/4 c. sugar
2 c. milk, scalded
2 eggs, beaten
2 tsp. vanilla
1 pkg. apricots

Preheat oven to 400 degrees. Sift 3 cups flou. and 1 teaspoon salt into large bowl; cut in shortening until of coarse cornmeal consistency. Add 6 tablespoons cold water gradually, mixing just until dough leaves side of bowl. Roll out half the dough at a time; cut into 5-inch circles. Fit pastry circles into muffin tins; pinch edges. Prick dough with fork. Bake for about 25 minutes or until golden brown. Combine 1/2 cup sugar, 5 tablespoons flour and 1/2 teaspoon salt in double boiler. Stir in milk. Cook, stirring constantly, until thickened; remove from heat. Add small amount hot mixture to eggs, beating well. Return egg mixture to double boiler. Cook, stirring, for about 5 minutes longer. Remove from heat; stir in vanilla. Chill. Simmer apricots in water to cover in saucepan for about 1 hour; add remaining sugar and salt. Bring to a boil, stirring frequently. Remove from heat; chill. Spoon custard into tart shells; top with apricot mixture. Serve with whipped cream if desired. Serve immediately.

APRICOT VELVET

2 c. milk
2 tbsp. cornstarch
2/3 c. sugar
1/4 tsp. salt
3 eggs, separated
1 tsp. vanilla
2 c. sweetened cooked dried apricots

Scald milk in double boiler. Blend cornstarch, sugar and salt. Add to hot milk; cool slightly. Add small portion of milk mixture to beaten egg yolks, stirring constantly; stir egg yolk mixture into hot milk mixture. Cook, stirring until smooth and thickened. Remove from heat; add vanilla. Force apricots through colander or ricer; fold into custard. Fold in beaten egg whites. Turn into wet mold; chill. Serve with cream or whipped cream if desired. Yield: 6 servings.

APRICOT BALLS

1 lb. dried apricots, ground
1/4 c. lemon or orange juice
1/4 c. sugar
1 7-oz. package coconut
1 c. finely chopped pecans
Confectioners' sugar

Combine apricots, lemon juice, sugar, coconut and pecans; form into small balls. Add additional juice if necessary. Roll balls in confectioners' sugar.

APRICOT-COCONUT BALLS

3 c. ground apricots
1 can sweetened condensed milk
4 c. flaked coconut
Powdered sugar

Combine apricots, condensed milk and coconut; chill for several hours. Form into 1-inch balls; let stand for several hours. Store, loosely covered. Roll in powdered sugar just before serving. Yield: 70 balls.

APRICOTS SUPREME

6 boiled potatoes
1 1/2 c. flour
1 egg, beaten
Pinch of salt
16 ripe apricots
1/2 c. bread crumbs
3/4 tbsp. butter
Powdered sugar
Cinnamon

Press potatoes through ricer. Combine potatoes, flour, egg and salt to make stiff dough. Roll dough out on floured board; cut into 16 squares. Remove seeds from apricots; wrap each apricot in 1 square of dough. Drop into boiling water; cook for about 10 minutes or until apricots are soft. Remove from water. Brown bread crumbs in butter; roll apricots in crumbs. Combine powdered sugar and cinnamon; sprinkle over apricots to serve.

APRICOT-CHEESE DELIGHT

1 29-oz. can apricots
1 29-oz. can crushed pineapple
2 3-oz. packages orange gelatin
3/4 c. miniature marshmallows
1/2 c. sugar
2 tbsp. flour
1 egg, slightly beaten
2 tbsp. butter
1 c. whipped cream
1/2 c. grated cheese

Drain apricots and pineapple, reserving 2 cups combined juices. Cut apricots into small pieces. Chill fruits. Dissolve gelatin in 2 cups boiling water. Add 1 cup reserved juices to gelatin; reserve remaining juice for topping. Chill gelatin mixture until partially congealed. Fold in fruits and marshmallows. Pour into 11 x 7 x 2-inch pan. Chill until firm. Combine sugar and flour; blend in egg. Stir in juices gradually. Cook over low heat until thickened, stirring constantly. Remove from heat; stir in butter. Cool. Fold in whipped cream; spread over congealed layer. Top with cheese. Chill. May be served on lettuce. Yield: 8-10 servings.

APRICOT CREAM

3 4 3/4-oz. jars baby food apricots
2 tbsp. lemon juice
1/2 c. sugar
1 tbsp. unflavored gelatin
1 1/2 c. whipping cream, whipped
1 box ladyfingers

Mix apricots, lemon juice and sugar. Soften gelatin in 3 tablespoons cold water; dissolve over hot water. Combine gelatin and apricot mixture. Cool. Fold in cream. Pour over ladyfingers in dessert dishes. Chill until set. Yield: 6-12 servings.

APRICOT NECTAR DESSERT

1 sm. can crushed pineapple
2 pkg. orange gelatin
2 c. apricot nectar
6 oz. miniature marshmallows
1 egg, beaten
1/2 c. sugar
3 tsp. (heaping) flour
1 c. heavy cream, whipped

Drain pineapple; reserve juice. Add enough water to reserved juice to equal 1/2 cup liquid. Dissolve gelatin in 2 cups boiling water; add 1 1/2 cups apricot nectar and pineapple. Chill until partially set. Add marshmallows; pour into 13 x 9 x 2-inch pan. Chill for several hours or overnight, until set. Combine remaining apricot nectar and pineapple liquid in pan. Blend egg with sugar and flour; add to juice mixture. Cook over medium heat until thick, stirring constantly. Cool thoroughly. Fold in whipped cream; spread on top of gelatin. Chill until ready to serve. Yield: 16 servings.

DELICIOUS APRICOT DESSERT

1 lb. cream-filled wafers
2/3 c. soft butter
2 c. powdered sugar
2 eggs
1 c. nuts
1 No. 2 1/2 can apricots
1/2 pt. whipping cream, whipped

Grind wafers; press 2/3 of the crumbs in greased baking dish. Cream butter and sugar; add eggs, one at a time, beating well after each addition. Spread egg mixture over crumbs. Sprinkle with nuts. Drain and chop apricots; spread over nuts. Spread whipped cream over apricots. Sprinkle remaining crumbs over top. Refrigerate overnight. Yield: 8 servings.

APRICOT-TANGERINE MOLD

2 env. unflavored gelatin
1/2 c. sugar
1/4 tsp. salt
1 3/4 c. tangerine juice
1 12-oz. can apricot nectar
3 egg whites
1/2 c. cream, whipped
Lettuce

Combine gelatin, sugar, salt and tangerine juice in saucepan. Cook, stirring constantly, over medium heat until gelatin is dissolved. Stir in apricot nectar; chill until partially set. Add egg whites; beat until fluffy. Fold in whipped cream; pour into 6-cup mold. Chill until firm. Unmold on lettuce; garnish with tangerine sections and small pitted canned apricots. Yield: 10 servings.

APRICOT GLACÉ PIE

1 stick pie crust mix
1 1-lb. can apricot halves
1 1/2 tbsp. cornstarch
1 8-oz. package cream cheese
1 can sweetened condensed milk
1/3 c. lemon juice
1 tsp. vanilla
Whipped cream

Prepare pie crust mix according to package directions; pat into 9-inch pie pan. Bake as directed. Cool. Drain apricots; reserve juice. Add enough water to reserved juice to equal 1 cup liquid. Mix liquid and cornstarch; bring to a boil. Boil for 1 minute, stirring constantly; cool. Whip cream cheese until light and fluffy; beat in condensed milk gradually until blended. Blend in lemon juice and vanilla; pour filling into pie shell. Arrange apricot halves over filling; pour sauce over top. Chill for 2 hours or until firm. Graham cracker crust may be used if desired. Serve with whipped cream. Yield: 6 servings.

FROZEN APRICOT MOUSSE

1 lge. can apricots
Sugar to taste
1 env. unflavored gelatin
2 eggs, lightly beaten
1 pt. heavy cream, whipped

Drain apricots; reserve juice. Sieve apricots; add sugar. Soften gelatin in 1/4 cup cold water. Heat reserved apricot juice; stir in gelatin until dissolved. Cool well. Add eggs; fold in whipped cream and apricots. Pour into ice trays; freeze overnight.

APRICOT PIE

Sugar
1/4 c. melted butter
2 c. graham cracker crumbs
1 1/2 c. chopped dried apricots
1/4 tsp. salt
2 tbsp. cornstarch

Blend 1/4 cup sugar and butter in bowl; pour over crackers. Press cracker mixture into 8-inch pie pan; chill. Place apricots in saucepan with 1 1/2 cups water; cook until soft. Mix 1/3 cup sugar, salt and cornstarch together. Add 3 tablespoons liquid from apricots to cornstarch mixture. Return cornstarch mixture to apricots; bring to a boil. Cook for 3 minutes, stirring, until thickened. Cool. Spoon filling into pie shell. Top with whipped cream or ice cream if desired. Yield: 6 servings.

APRICOT BREAD

1 can apricot nectar
1 1/2 c. chopped dates
1/3 c. dried chopped apricots
1 tbsp. grated orange rind
2 3/4 c. flour
2 tsp. soda
1 tsp. salt
1 tbsp. shortening
1 c. sugar
1 egg, slightly beaten
1/3 c. cream
1/2 c. chopped nuts

Mix apricot nectar, dates and apricots together in saucepan. Simmer for 5 minutes. Add orange rind. Sift flour, soda and salt together; blend in shortening and sugar. Add to hot mixture. Add egg, cream and nuts; mix well. Pour into 4 greased and floured Number 2 cans, filling cans 2/3 full. Bake at 350 degrees for 50 minutes to 1 hour. Slide bread out of cans immediately; cool. Serve thinly sliced.

APRICOT-DATE AND NUT LOAF

15 dried apricots
1 7-oz. package pitted dates
1 c. raisins
1 tsp. soda
1 egg
3/4 c. sugar
1 1/2 c. sifted flour
1 tsp. vanilla
1 c. chopped walnuts

Chop apricots, dates and raisins; mix. Add soda to 1 cup boiling water; pour over fruit mixture. Let stand for 15 minutes. Beat egg; add sugar gradually. Add flour and fruit mixture alternately; stir in vanilla and walnuts. Spoon batter into greased 5 x 10-inch loaf pan. Bake at 350 degrees for 1 hour.

APRICOT-NUT ROLLS

1 tbsp. melted butter or margarine
1/4 c. butterscotch sundae sauce
1/3 c. apricot jam
3 tbsp. chopped pecans
12 brown and serve dinner rolls

Preheat oven to 400 degrees. Combine butter, butterscotch sauce and jam. Spread jam mixture evenly in ungreased pan. Sprinkle with pecans; place rolls in mixture with tops down. Bake for 15 minutes. Let stand for 2 minutes. Invert onto plate; serve immediately.

EASY APRICOT BREAD

1 box date bread mix
1 egg
1 c. chopped pecans
1 c. chopped dried apricots

Combine date bread mix, 1 cup water and egg; mix thoroughly. Add pecans and apricots. Blend well. Pour into greased and floured loaf pan. Bake at 350 degrees for 1 hour. Cool thoroughly in pan. Slice and serve. Yield: 15 to 20 servings.

Artichoke

There are two varieties: the globe–plump, green, and thick-leaved; and the Jerusalem, which resembles a firm but knotted potato. Both types of artichokes taste similar.

AVAILABILITY: *Globe*–year-round, with April and May peak months. *Jerusalem*–from October to May.

BUYING: *Globe*–Choose fresh, rounded, heavy, and compact artichoke with head that yields slightly to pressure and has visible hole in middle. Avoid those with discolored, spread-apart leaves. One artichoke serves 1-2 people. *Jerusalem*–Select firm, blemish- and mold-free specimens. One and one-half pounds serves 4.

STORING: *Globe*–Sprinkle with water, wrap in plastic; refrigerate. May also be frozen after cooking but freeze hearts separately from rest of vegetable. *Jerusaleum*–Refrigerate. Both types keep several days in refrigerator.

PREPARATION: *Globe*–Wash in cold running water, pluck off outer leaves. Cut 1 inch off top and trim stem so vegetable sits flat. Trim leaves. Tie securely with string to prevent leaves from loosening. Place base downward in boiling salted water to cover; add 1 tablespoon vinegar or 1 tablespoon each of salad oil and lemon juice for each quart water. Boil 20-45 minutes or until a leaf pulls out easily. *Jerusalem*–Wash, pare, and slice or leave whole. Cook covered in small amount of boiling salted water for about 20-30 minutes.

SERVING: *Globe*–May be served as an appetizer, garnish, vegetable, or main dish salad. *Jerusalem* – Serve as hot vegetable; goes with white fish, veal, lamb, meat loaf, ham and chicken.

(See VEGETABLES.)

ARTICHOKE BALLS

2 14-oz. cans artichoke hearts
1 box seasoned bread crumbs
2 tbsp. salad oil
2 eggs, beaten
2 tbsp. lemon juice
3 cloves of garlic, pressed
Grated Romano cheese

Drain and chop artichoke hearts; add bread crumbs, oil, eggs, lemon juice and garlic. Mix well; form into bite-sized balls. Roll balls in cheese; serve with wooden picks.

ARTICHOKE AND CHEESE PUFFS

12 baked patty shells
2 8-oz. packages cream cheese
3 tbsp. chopped chives
6 tbsp. softened butter
3 eggs, beaten
1 tsp. hot sauce
1 tbsp. Worcestershire sauce
12 cooked artichoke hearts

Preheat oven to 475 degrees. Place patty shells in shallow baking dish. Combine cream cheese, chives, butter, eggs and seasonings in medium bowl; beat until smooth and well blended. Spread half the cheese mixture in shells; top with artichoke hearts. Cover artichokes with remaining cheese mixture. Bake for 30 minutes or until cheese filling has puffed and is lightly browned. Yield: 12 servings.

ARTICHOKES AND HAM BITES

1 can artichoke hearts
1/2 c. garlic dressing
1 6-oz. package sliced ham

Drain and halve artichoke hearts; marinate in garlic dressing for 1 hour or longer. Slice ham into 1 1/2-inch strips. Drain artichoke halves well. Roll ham strip around each artichoke half; secure with wooden pick. Bake at 300 degrees for 10 minutes or until heated through.

ARTICHOKE HEARTS AND MARINATED MUSHROOMS

2 pkg. frozen artichoke hearts
2 lb. small mushrooms
1 bottle Italian salad dressing

Cook artichoke hearts according to package directions until just tender; drain. Slice mushrooms in half through stems. Combine mushrooms and artichoke hearts; cover with salad dressing. Refrigerate in covered dish for 4 to 8 hours, stirring occasionally. Drain before serving. Yield: 16-20 servings.

MARINATED ARTICHOKE HEARTS

1 pkg. frozen artichoke hearts
1 tsp. salt
1/2 tsp. cayenne pepper
1/4 tsp. dry mustard
3 tbsp. salad vinegar
1 tbsp. lemon juice
1 c. salad oil
3 cloves of garlic, minced
Dash of hot pepper sauce

Cook artichoke hearts according to package directions; drain. Combine remaining ingredients in glass jar; cover. Shake well. Pour over artichoke hearts; chill for several hours, spooning dressing over hearts several times. Drain. Serve with wooden picks. Hearts may be cut if too large.

ORLEANIAN ARTICHOKE APPETIZER

4 artichokes
1 3-oz. package cream cheese
4 oz. blue cheese
1 tsp. lemon juice
1/4 tsp. garlic puree
1 tbsp. vinegar
3 tbsp. sherry
Dash of hot sauce

Boil artichokes until tender. Place remaining ingredients in mixer bowl; beat at highest speed until smooth and creamy. Spoon sauce into 4 cocktail glasses; serve with artichokes. Yield: 4 servings.

PIQUANT ARTICHOKE APPETIZER

2 carrots, sliced
2 tbsp. olive oil
2 tbsp. lemon juice
1 sm. bay leaf
1 tsp. salt
1/8 tsp. garlic salt
1 pkg. frozen artichoke hearts

Combine carrots, olive oil, lemon juice, bay leaf, salt, garlic salt and 1/2 cup water in saucepan. Boil for 5 minutes. Add frozen artichoke hearts; boil for 5 to 10 minutes longer or until vegetables are tender. Chill artichoke hearts in seasoned liquid. Drain; serve as appetizer. Yield: 4 servings.

ARTICHOKES WITH AL PESTO BUTTER

Color photograph for this recipe on page 728.

6 artichokes
1/4 c. olive oil
2 tbsp. lemon juice
2 bay leaves
2 lge. cloves of garlic
Salt
Dash of pepper
1 c. softened butter
2 tbsp. finely chopped pine nuts
1 tsp. basil leaves
1/8 tsp. thyme leaves
1 c. chopped parsley

Trim stems from base of artichokes; cut 1-inch slice from top of each. Remove discolored leaves; snip off spike ends of leaves. Wash artichokes in cold water; drain. Tie each with twine to hold leaves in place. Combine 6 quarts water, olive oil, lemon juice, bay leaves, 1 split clove of garlic, 1 teaspoon salt and pepper in large cooking pot; bring to a boil. Place artichokes in boiling water; reduce heat. Simmer, covered, for 30 minutes or until tender. Drain well; remove twine. Whip butter until light and fluffy. Add pine nuts, remaining pressed clove of garlic, basil, 1/8 teaspoon salt and thyme; whip until well blended. Reserve 1 tablespoon parsley; stir remaining parsley into butter mixture. Turn into serving dish; sprinkle with reserved parsley. Serve with hot artichokes. Yield: 6 servings.

ARTICHOKES WITH DESERT SLAW

Color photograph for this recipe on page 315.

6 artichokes
2 tsp. salt
1 c. (packed) shredded carrots
1/3 c. chopped radishes
1 1/2 c. (packed) shredded red cabbage
1/4 c. sliced stuffed olives
1/4 c. chopped parsley
1/4 c. olive oil
2 tbsp. vinegar
Dash of pepper
1 tsp. sugar
1 clove of garlic, minced

Wash artichokes; cut stems off evenly at base so artichokes will stand. Remove small bottom leaves. Trim prickly tips off remaining leaves; cut about 1 inch off top of each artichoke. Stand artichokes upright in deep saucepan or Dutch oven. Add 1 1/2 teaspoons salt and 2 to 3 inches of boiling water; cover. Simmer for 35 to 45 minutes or until a leaf may be pulled off without effort, adding boiling water if needed. Turn artichokes upside down to drain. Spread leaves apart gently; remove choke from cavity with metal spoon. Chill. Combine carrots, radishes, cabbage, olives and parsley in large bowl. Blend remaining salt, oil, vinegar, pepper, sugar and garlic. Pour over cabbage mixture; toss lightly to blend. Cover; chill for several hours. Drain. Fill each artichoke with slaw; serve with mayonnaise.

ARTICHOKE-CUCUMBER SALAD

2 cans artichoke hearts, drained
2 sm. cucumbers, pared and sliced
3 tbsp. white vinegar
3 tbsp. oil
Salt and pepper

Combine artichoke hearts and cucumbers in bowl. Blend vinegar, oil, salt and pepper; pour over vegetables. Chill for 2 hours before serving. Yield: 6 servings.

ARTICHOKE DELIGHT SALAD

1 14-oz. can artichoke hearts
Romaine
2 tbsp. chopped chives
1/2 tsp. dry mustard
Salt and pepper to taste
Vinegar
Olive oil

Cut artichoke hearts into quarters; tear romaine into bite-sized pieces. Toss romaine, artichokes and chives together. Chill. Mix remaining ingredients, using 1 part vinegar to 2 parts oil. Add dressing to salad just before serving. Yield: 2-4 servings.

ARTICHOKES WITH OLIVES A LA GRECQUE

4 artichokes
1 1/4 tsp. salt
1 c. sliced pimento-stuffed olives
1 3-oz. can sliced mushrooms, drained
1/3 c. finely-chopped green pepper
1/4 c. chopped parsley
2 tbsp. finely-chopped celery
1 tbsp. capers
1 tbsp. chopped chives
2 tsp. chopped anchovy fillets
1/4 tsp. basil leaves
1/8 tsp. pepper
2/3 c. olive oil
1/3 c. lemon juice

Cut off artichoke stems at base; remove small bottom leaves. Trim tips of leaves; cut off about 1 inch from top of artichokes. Stand artichokes upright in deep saucepan. Add salt and 2 to 3 inches of boiling water. Cover; simmer for 35 to 45 minutes or until base can be pierced easily with fork. Turn artichokes upside-down to drain. Spread leaves apart gently; remove choke from center of artichokes with metal spoon. Chill. Combine remaining ingredients; mix well. Chill for several hours or overnight. Fill centers of artichokes with olive mixture with slotted spoon. Spoon remaining marinade over artichokes; chill for 30 minutes. Garnish with anchovy fillets if desired. Serve with any remaining marinade. Yield: 4 servings.

Artichokes with Olives a la Grecque . . . An authentic Greek-style delicacy fit for a party.

ARTICHOKE SALAD BOWL

1 pkg. frozen artichoke hearts
8 c. torn mixed salad greens
1/2 c. sliced radishes
1/2 c. herb-seasoned croutons
1/3 c. buttermilk
3 tbsp. mayonnaise
1/2 c. minced pared cucumber
1 tbsp. lemon juice
1/2 tsp. garlic salt
1/2 tsp. sugar
1/8 tsp. pepper

Cook artichoke hearts according to package directions; drain and chill. Place salad greens in a large bowl; arrange artichoke hearts and radish slices over top. Sprinkle with croutons. Blend buttermilk and mayonnaise until smooth; stir in cucumber, lemon juice, garlic salt, sugar and pepper. Drizzle half the dressing over salad; toss lightly to mix. Serve salad with remaining dressing.

ARTICHOKES VINAIGRETTE

12 artichokes
3 cloves of garlic
6 tbsp. olive oil
3 tsp. salt

Cut stems and prickly ends of leaves from artichokes. Stand artichokes in large skillet in 1 inch boiling water. Add garlic, oil and salt to water. Simmer, covered, for 20 to 30 minutes or until artichokes are tender. Drain artichokes; chill. Serve with Vinaigrette Sauce.

Vinaigrette Sauce

1 1/4 c. olive oil
5 tbsp. vinegar
Salt and freshly ground pepper to taste
2 tbsp. chopped capers
1 tbsp. chopped parsley
1 tbsp. chopped onion
1 hard-cooked egg, finely chopped
2 tbsp. sweet pickle relish

Combine all ingredients. Mix well. Serve with artichokes.

CHILLED ARTICHOKES WITH GARLIC MAYONNAISE

6 lge. artichokes
Lemon juice
1 tsp. salt
1 c. mayonnaise
1 clove of garlic, mashed
Paprika

Wash artichokes thoroughly; drain well. Slice off thorny tip one-third of the way down. Remove stem and small leaves around base; cut thorns from tips of outer leaves. Rub cut edges with lemon juice. Separate leaves slightly; scoop out fibrous center leaves and fuzzy core. Stand artichokes in 1 inch boiling salted water. Simmer, covered, for 30 minutes or until tender. Drain; chill, covered, for 1 hour or longer. Blend mayonnaise and garlic. Spoon into artichokes; sprinkle with paprika. Yield: 6 servings.

MARINATED ARTICHOKE SALAD

1/2 c. salad oil
1/3 c. vinegar
1 sm. onion, thinly sliced
1 tbsp. sugar
1 clove of garlic, crushed
1/4 tsp. celery seed
1/2 tsp. salt
1/2 tsp. pepper
1 pkg. artichoke hearts
1 4-oz. can pimentos

Combine oil, vinegar, 2 tablespoons water, onion, sugar, garlic and seasonings in medium saucepan; bring to a boil. Add artichoke hearts; cook according to package directions. Drain and chop pimentos; add to artichoke mixture. Chill in glass jar in refrigerator until serving time. Drain; serve on crisp salad greens. Yield: 6 servings.

ARTICHOKES IN CONSOMME

1 1/2 env. unflavored gelatin
2 cans beef consomme
1 tsp. (scant) Worcestershire sauce
Juice of 1 lemon
Salt to taste
1 can artichoke hearts

Soften gelatin in 1/4 cup cold water. Heat consomme in saucepan; add gelatin, stirring until dissolved. Cool. Add Worcestershire sauce, lemon juice and salt. Chill to consistency of unbeaten egg white. Cut artichoke hearts into halves or quarters; fold into gelatin mixture. Turn into ring mold or individual molds. Chill until firm. Serve on lettuce leaves topped with homemade mayonnaise if desired. Yield: 6 servings.

ARTICHOKE SALAD

1 qt. tomato juice
2 pkg. lemon gelatin
Juice of 1 lemon
1 c. chopped celery
1 med. onion, minced
1 lge. can artichoke hearts, halved
Worcestershire sauce to taste
Salt and pepper to taste

Heat tomato juice in saucepan; add gelatin, stirring until dissolved. Combine all ingredients; pour into individual molds. Chill until set. Yield: 8-10 servings.

ARTICHOKE SALAD MOLDS

1 env. unflavored gelatin
1 can beef consomme
1 can whole artichoke hearts
Lemon juice
Salt
Softened blue cheese
Mayonnaise

Soften gelatin in 1/4 cup cold water. Heat consomme in saucepan; dissolve gelatin in consomme. Fill individual molds 1/2 full of consomme mixture; chill until nearly firm. Insert 1 whole artichoke heart into each mold; season with lemon juice and salt. Pour remaining consomme mixture into molds until full. Chill until set. Unmold on lettuce leaves. Combine 1 part blue cheese to 2 parts mayonnaise. Serve dressing over congealed salads.

ARTICHOKE CASSEROLE

2 15-oz. cans artichoke hearts, drained
2 c. fresh bread crumbs
1 tsp. oregano
1/2 tsp. salt
1/2 tsp. pepper
1/4 c. oil

Place artichoke hearts in greased casserole. Mix remaining ingredients; spread over artichokes. Bake in 325-degree oven for 20 to 30 minutes or until golden. Yield: 10 servings.

ARTICHOKE HEARTS IN PARMESAN CUSTARD

2 9-oz. packages frozen artichoke hearts
1/2 c. canned tomatoes
1 tsp. salt
1/4 tsp. pepper
1/4 tsp. garlic salt
2 tsp. chopped parsley
1/2 c. grated Parmesan cheese
1/4 c. olive oil
6 eggs, beaten

Place frozen artichoke hearts in greased 2-quart casserole. Drain and chop tomatoes; pour over artichoke hearts. Sprinkle tomatoes with salt, pepper, garlic salt, parsley and cheese. Pour in 3/4 cup water and olive oil. Bake, covered, at 350 degrees for 1 hour. Pour eggs over artichokes; bake, uncovered, for 15 to 20 minutes longer or until eggs are set. Yield: 8 servings.

ARTICHOKE HEARTS AND PECANS

2 No. 2 cans artichoke hearts, drained
2 tbsp. butter
2 tbsp. flour
1 c. cream
Salt and pepper to taste
Hot sauce to taste
1/2 c. broken pecans
1/4 c. bread crumbs
2 tbsp. Parmesan cheese

Arrange artichoke hearts in small casserole. Blend butter and flour in saucepan; add cream. Cook, stirring constantly, until thickened. Season with salt, pepper and hot sauce. Pour sauce over artichoke hearts; add pecans. Sprinkle with bread crumbs and cheese. Bake at 300 degrees until bubbly. Yield: 6 servings.

ARTICHOKE BOTTOMS WITH TOMATOES

2 tbsp. butter
3 tbsp. chopped onion
1 1-lb. can tomatoes
1/2 tsp. salt
1/4 tsp. garlic powder
1/2 bay leaf
6 canned artichoke bottoms, drained

Melt butter in skillet; cook onion in butter tor 3 to 4 minutes. Drain and chop tomatoes. Add tomatoes, salt, garlic powder and bay leaf to onion mixture; cook for 10 minutes, stirring occasionally. Remove bay leaf. Place artichoke bottoms in baking dish; spoon tomato mixture over top. Bake in 400-degree oven for about 5 minutes. Yield: 6 servings.

CHEESY ARTICHOKE BAKE

1 pkg. frozen artichoke hearts
1 tbsp. dried minced onion
1 clove of garlic, crushed
1 tbsp. chopped parsley
1/2 c. dry bread crumbs
1 tsp. salt
Freshly ground pepper
1/4 c. olive oil
4 tbsp. grated Parmesan cheese

Cook artichokes in boiling salted water for 5 minutes; drain well. Place in buttered baking dish. Mix remaining ingredients; sprinkle over artichokes. Bake at 400 degrees for 20 minutes or until soft. Yield: 4 servings.

ARTICHOKE HEART HOT DISH

1 tbsp. minced onion
1/3 c. olive oil
1 tbsp. flour
2 carrots, sliced
1 bunch green onions, chopped
1 tsp. peppercorns
1 tsp. salt
1 tsp. dillweed
2 pkg. frozen artichoke hearts
Juice of 1/2 lemon

Saute onion in oil in skillet. Add flour, 1 cup boiling water, carrots and green onions. Cook for 10 to 15 minutes, stirring frequently. Add seasonings, artichoke hearts and lemon juice. Cook for 45 minutes or until vegetables are tender but not watery. Yield: 6 servings.

ARTICHOKE HEARTS IN LEMON BUTTER

1/2 c. minced onion
1/2 clove of garlic, pressed
2 tbsp. butter
2 15-oz. cans artichoke hearts, drained
3/4 c. chicken broth
3 tbsp. lemon juice
1 1/2 tsp. salt
1 tsp. oregano
1/4 tsp. grated lemon rind

Saute onion and garlic in butter in saucepan until transparent; add artichoke hearts and chicken broth. Season with lemon juice, salt, oregano and lemon rind. Simmer for 10 minutes or until artichokes are heated through. Serve. Yield: 6-8 servings.

ARTICHOKES WITH PARSLEY SAUCE

2 10-oz. packages frozen artichoke hearts
3 tbsp. butter
3 tbsp. flour
2 c. milk
1/2 tsp. salt
1/8 tsp. pepper
2 tbsp. minced parsley
Paprika

Cook artichoke hearts in saucepan according to package directions; drain and dice. Melt butter in skillet; stir in flour and milk gradually. Cook, stirring constantly, until thickened. Add salt and pepper; fold in parsley. Pour sauce over artichoke hearts. Heat thoroughly; sprinkle with paprika. Yield: 8 servings.

GOURMET ARTICHOKE HEARTS

1/2 c. cooking sherry
1/2 c. chicken broth
1 pkg. frozen artichoke hearts
2 tomatoes, cut into wedges
1 chopped onion
1/2 green pepper, sliced
Dash of thyme
Salt and pepper to taste

Combine all ingredients in saucepan; cover. Cook over medium heat for about 15 minutes or until done. Yield: 4 servings.

Artichokes Santa Cruz . . . Elegance characterizes this seafood-artichoke combination.

ARTICHOKES SANTA CRUZ

6 artichokes
Salt
1 6-oz. package frozen King crab meat
1/4 lb. fresh mushrooms, chopped
1/4 c. chopped green onion
2 tbsp. salad oil
1/2 c. chopped cucumber
1/2 lb. cooked shrimp, chopped
2 hard-cooked eggs, chopped
1/2 c. mayonnaise
1/2 c. sour cream
2 tbsp. chopped fresh dill
1/8 tsp. white pepper
2 tbsp. lemon juice

Cut off artichoke stems at base; remove small bottom leaves. Trim tips of leaves; cut off about 1 inch from top of artichokes. Stand artichokes upright in deep saucepan. Add 1 1/2 teaspoons salt and 2 to 3 inches boiling water. Cover; simmer for 35 to 45 minutes or until base can be pierced easily with fork. Turn artichokes upside-down to drain. Spread leaves apart gently; remove choke from center of artichokes with metal spoon. Chill. Thaw and chop crab meat. Saute mushrooms and onion in oil until tender but not browned. Combine mushroom mixture, cucumber, crab meat, shrimp, eggs, mayonnaise, sour cream, dill, 1 teaspoon salt, pepper and lemon juice in large bowl. Chill. Fill prepared artichokes with salad. Garnish with lemon wedges and parsley if desired. Yield: 6 servings.

ITALIAN-STYLE STUFFED ARTICHOKES

4 artichokes
1 1/2 c. soft bread crumbs
1 1/2 tsp. salt
1/4 tsp. pepper
3 tbsp. minced parsley
3/4 c. grated Parmesan cheese
1/4 c. hot beef bouillon
1 clove of garlic, sliced
1 tbsp. salad oil

Dip each artichoke upside down in warm water; cut off entire stem. Trim tips of petals; place in 3 cups boiling water in saucepan. Cook for 10 to 20 minutes or until partially done; drain. Press petals open. Combine bread crumbs, 1/2 teaspoon salt, pepper, parsley, cheese and bouillon. Stuff artichokes with bread crumb mixture. Place stuffed artichokes in casserole; add 1 inch water, remaining salt, and garlic. Sprinkle with oil. Bake at 350 degrees until tender. Yield: 4 servings.

Asparagus

For at least 2,000 years asparagus, a tender, edible shoot of a member of the lily family, has been widely cultivated as a luxury and gourmet food. It is an excellent source of Vitamin C and is very low in calories (2/3 cup or 6 canned spears = 20 calories).

AVAILABILITY: Sold by the bunch or pound from mid-February to late June; peak season is between April and June. Also available canned or frozen year-round.

BUYING: Choose crisp, rounded, smooth stalks with a rich green color and only a small length of light-colored, woody base. Tips should be compactly formed and tightly closed. Signs of aging include spread tips and angular or ridged shoots.

STORING: Asparagus is highly perishable and should be cooked as quickly as possible. It keeps in the refrigerator only 1-2 days. Wrap dampened toweling around the stem ends and keep in a tightly sealed container. May also be frozen.

PREPARATION: Scrub thoroughly with a vegetable brush. Scrape off small sandy scales. Snap off and discard woody bases. Prepare bundles of approximately 6 spears and stand upright in deep kettle of boiling salted water (1 1/2 teaspoons salt per quart water). Cover and cook 10-15 minutes or until tender. May also be cooked in skillet: lay spears flat in 1 inch boiling water; sprinkle with salt and pepper. Cover and cook 8-15 minutes until tender.

SERVING: Serve hot or cold as a separate course or a garnish for salads, eggs, fish, shellfish, meat, or poultry; in casseroles; on toast; or in souffles, sandwiches, omelets, or soups. Especially good cooked and chilled with a marinade and served as appetizer or vegetable. (See VEGETABLES.)

Rolled Pancake Supper . . . Asparagus spears wrapped in pancakes, a hearty one-dish meal.

ROLLED PANCAKE SUPPER

4 eggs, beaten
1 c. sieved cottage cheese
1/2 tsp. salt
1/3 c. sifted flour
1/3 c. instant nonfat dry milk
1 No. 2 can med. asparagus spears

Combine eggs and cottage cheese; add salt, flour, dry milk and 2 tablespoons water. Blend well. Drop 1/4 cup batter on hot greased griddle for each pancake. Bake on both sides until golden brown. Drain asparagus. Roll 3 or 4 stalks of asparagus up in each pancake; arrange in flat casserole.

Chipped Beef Sauce

1/2 stick butter
4 tbsp. flour
2/3 c. instant nonfat dry milk
Dash of pepper
2 2 1/2-oz. jars chipped beef
Parmesan cneese

Melt butter in saucepan; remove from heat and blend in flour until smooth. Combine dry milk, pepper and 2 cups water, blending well. Add milk mixture to flour mixture; stirring well. Cook over low heat, stirring constantly, until thickened. Add chipped beef to sauce. Pour sauce over pancake rolls; sprinkle with cheese. Bake at 350 degrees for 20 to 25 minutes. Yield: 8 pancake rolls.

ASPARAGUS FOLD-OVERS

20 bread slices
1 c. hollandaise sauce
1/2 c. Parmesan cheese
20 canned asparagus spears, drained

Remove crusts from bread slices. Roll slices flat; spread with hollandaise sauce. Sprinkle with cheese; fold each slice over asparagus spear. Secure with toothpick. Place on baking sheet. Bake at 400 degrees for 12 minutes. Yield: 20 servings.

CREAM OF ASPARAGUS SOUP

1 pkg. frozen asparagus, chopped
2 c. half and half
Pepper to taste
2 tbsp. butter

Cook asparagus according to package directions. Drain; reserve liquid. Place asparagus in blender container. Blend for 2 to 3 minutes. Pour in enough half and half to make cream soup consistency. Add portion of reserved liquid if stronger flavor is desired. Simmer, stirring, until heated through. Add pepper; dot with butter.

CREAMED ASPARAGUS ON CRACKERS

2 tbsp. butter
2 tbsp. flour
1 c. milk
1 sm. can asparagus
1/4 tsp. salt
Soda crackers

Melt butter in skillet; blend in flour. Add milk gradually; cook over low heat, stirring constantly, until thick. Drain asparagus; add salt and asparagus to white sauce. Serve over crackers. Asparagus liquid may be substituted for part of milk.

ASPARAGUS STICKS

1/4 tsp. celery salt
1/8 tsp. pepper
1 egg, beaten
1 pkg. frozen asparagus spears
1/2 c. bread crumbs

Combine 2 tablespoons water, celery salt, pepper and egg; mix well. Cook asparagus according to package directions; drain. Roll asparagus spears in half the bread crumbs; dip in egg mixture. Roll spears in remaining bread crumbs. Brown in hot fat for 5 minutes or until golden, turning occasionally. Yield: 4-5 servings.

ASPARAGUS AMANDINE

1/4 c. slivered blanched almonds
1/4 c. butter
1/4 tsp. salt
2 tsp. lemon juice
2 sm. cans chopped asparagus

Saute almonds in butter until golden, stirring occasionally; remove from heat. Add salt and lemon juice. Drain asparagus; heat in small saucepan. Remove from heat. Place in serving dish. Pour almond mixture over asparagus. Let stand for several minutes before serving. Yield: 4 servings.

ASPARAGUS BEARNAISE

2 pkg. frozen asparagus
1 1/2 tsp. monosodium glutamate
3 egg yolks
2 tbsp. lemon juice
1/4 tsp. minced onion
1/4 tsp. minced parsley
1/2 tsp. dried tarragon
Dash of cayenne pepper
1/2 c. butter

Cook asparagus according to package directions; drain. Sprinkle monosodium glutamate over asparagus. Combine egg yolks, lemon juice, onion, parsley, tarragon and cayenne pepper; beat well. Melt butter; blend into egg mixture, stirring constantly. Pour over hot asparagus; serve immediately. Yield: 8 servings.

ASPARAGUS-HAM ROLLS

2 cans asparagus spears
6 thin slices ham
4 tbsp. butter
4 tbsp. flour
1/4 tsp. salt
Pepper to taste
2 c. milk
1/2 lb. cheese, grated
6 slices toast

Drain asparagus spears; divide spears equally among ham slices. Roll ham around asparagus; place rolls, seam side down, on lightly greased baking sheet. Bake at 325 degrees until heated through. Melt butter in medium saucepan; blend in flour, salt, pepper and milk. Simmer, stirring constantly, until sauce is thickened. Stir in cheese. Place asparagus rolls on toast; top with cheese sauce. Yield: 6 servings.

ASPARAGUS HUNGARIAN

2 pkg. frozen asparagus spears
1/2 tsp. salt
1/4 tsp. pepper
2 tbsp. butter
1/4 c. bread crumbs
1 c. sour cream

Cook spears according to package directions; drain. Arrange in shallow casserole; sprinkle with salt and pepper. Dot with butter; cover with bread crumbs. Pour in sour cream gently. Bake in 350-degree oven for 15 to 20 minutes. Yield: 4 servings.

ASPARAGUS IN BLANKETS

24 fresh asparagus spears
2 c. prepared biscuit mix
2 tbsp. melted butter
1 2 1/2-oz. jar dried beef
Cheese sauce

Cook asparagus spears in 1 cup water; drain. Prepare biscuit mix according to package directions for rolled biscuits. Divide in half; roll into two 12-inch circles. Brush each circle with butter; cut circles into 6 wedges. Divide asparagus and dried beef into 12 equal portions; place crosswise on wide end of biscuit wedges. Roll; place on greased baking sheet. Bake at 450 degrees for 10 minutes. Serve with cheese sauce. Yield: 6 servings.

ASPARAGUS AU GRATIN

2 lb. asparagus spears
6 tbsp. melted butter
1/4 c. milk
1/4 tsp. salt
1/8 tsp. pepper
1/2 c. grated Parmesan cheese

Discard tough ends of asparagus; tie spears in bunch. Stand upright in deep saucepan. Add 2 cups boiling salted water. Steam for 15 minutes. Remove; drain and untie. Place in baking dish. Pour butter and milk over asparagus. Add salt and pepper; sprinkle with cheese. Bake at 425 degrees for 10 minutes or until cheese is browned. Yield: 4 servings.

ASPARAGUS WITH HAM

1 bunch fresh asparagus
3 tbsp. butter
3 tbsp. flour
1 1/2 c. milk
1 med. can deviled ham
6 slices toast
1/8 tsp. paprika

Cook asparagus in 1 cup boiling salted water until crisp-tender; drain. Melt butter; blend in flour. Add milk gradually; cook, stirring constantly, until thickened. Stir in ham. Arrange asparagus on toast; pour ham mixture over asparagus. Sprinkle with paprika.

ASPARAGUS VINAIGRETTE

1 tsp. sugar
1 1/2 tsp. salt
1/8 tsp. cayenne pepper
1/4 tsp. paprika
Several drops of garlic juice
1/3 c. vinegar
1 c. salad oil
3 tbsp. chopped green onion
4 tbsp. sweet pickle relish
2 tbsp. chopped parsley
4 tbsp. chopped green pepper
2 tbsp. chopped pimento
1 tbsp. capers
2 lge. cans asparagus, drained

Combine sugar, salt, cayenne pepper, paprika and garlic juice. Add vinegar and salad oil slowly, beating thoroughly. Add onion, relish, parsley, green pepper, pimento and capers to oil mixture. Pour sauce over asparagus. Marinate in refrigerator overnight. Yield: 4-6 servings.

ASPARAGUS WITH HOLLANDAISE SAUCE

2 lb. fresh asparagus
1 1/2 tsp. salt
2 egg yolks
1 tbsp. lemon juice
1/8 tsp. paprika
3 tbsp. butter
2 tbsp. flour
1/3 c. blanched almonds

Cook asparagus with 1 teaspoon salt in 1 cup boiling water until tender. Drain asparagus; keep warm. Combine egg yolks, 1 tablespoon cold water, lemon juice, remaining salt and paprika in top of double boiler; beat well. Melt butter in pan; blend in flour. Stir in 1 cup boiling water slowly; cook, stirring constantly, over low heat until thick. Pour over egg mixture, stirring constantly; cook until smooth. Pour sauce over asparagus; sprinkle with almonds. Yield: 6-8 servings.

ASPARAGUS WITH SHRIMP SAUCE

2 pkg. frozen asparagus
4 tbsp. milk
1 can frozen shrimp soup, thawed

Cook asparagus according to package directions; drain. Combine milk and soup in small saucepan; heat through. Pour over asparagus; serve. Yield: 6 servings.

ASPARAGUS ORIENTAL

2 to 3 lb. fresh asparagus
Salad oil
1/2 tsp. salt
1/2 tsp. monosodium glutamate
Pepper to taste
1/4 c. slivered almonds

Cut asparagus diagonally into thin 1 1/2-inch long slices. Place asparagus in hot oil in skillet; sprinkle salt, monosodium glutamate, pepper and almonds over asparagus. Cook, covered, over low heat for 4 to 5 minutes or until tender, shaking pan.

BROILED ASPARAGUS SANDWICH

6 slices toast
6 slices American cheese
24 cooked asparagus spears
6 lge. tomato slices
6 bacon slices, halved

Arrange toast on cookie sheet. Layer 1 cheese slice, 4 asparagus spears, 1 tomato slice and 1 bacon slice on each toast slice. Broil until bacon is crisp; serve hot. Yield: 6 servings.

ASPARAGUS GOURMET

1 lge. can asparagus
1 c. grated American cheese
1 c. bread crumbs
1/2 c. blanched almonds
2 c. white sauce

Drain asparagus; place in baking dish. Sprinkle cheese over asparagus. Add bread crumbs; sprinkle almonds over crumbs. Cover with white sauce. Bake at 350 degrees for 30 to 45 minutes. Yield: 4 servings.

ASPARAGUS LOAF

1 can asparagus tips
2 eggs, beaten
1 c. cracker crumbs
2 tbsp. melted butter
2 c. hot milk
1 tsp. grated onion
1 tsp. salt

Drain and chop asparagus. Add remaining ingredients; pour into greased casserole. Bake at 325 degrees for 45 minutes or until golden brown. Yield: 6-8 servings.

ASPARAGUS SOUFFLÉ

1 lb. fresh asparagus
4 tbsp. butter
4 tbsp. flour
1/2 c. milk
2 1/4 tsp. salt
Dash of pepper
4 eggs, separated

Cut asparagus into 1/4-inch pieces; simmer in 1 cup boiling water until tender. Drain; reserve 1/2 cup liquid. Melt butter; stir in flour. Combine milk and reserved asparagus liquid; add to flour mixture gradually. Cook, stirring constantly, until sauce is thickened. Add seasonings. Remove from heat. Beat egg yolks until thickened. Add small amount of sauce to egg yolks, stirring well. Combine egg yolks with mixture in saucepan; return to heat. Cook slowly, stirring constantly; mix with asparagus. Beat egg whites until stiff peaks form. Fold egg whites into asparagus mixture. Turn into buttered casserole; place in shallow pan containing water. Bake at 350 degrees for 1 hour or until knife inserted in center comes out clean.

Cheese Sauce

2 tbsp. butter
1/4 c. flour
1 1/2 c. hot milk
1/4 tsp. salt
Dash of pepper
4 tbsp. grated sharp Cheddar cheese

Melt butter; blend in flour. Add milk gradually. Cook, stirring, until thickened. Remove from heat. Add salt, pepper and cheese; stir until blended. Pour over souffle before serving. Yield: 6 servings.

Asparagus with Creamed Vegetable Sauce . . . A medley of flavored vegetables and sauce.

ASPARAGUS SHORTCAKE

1 pkg. refrigerator biscuits
1 can asparagus spears, drained
1 can cheese soup
French-fried onion rings

Preheat oven to 350 degrees. Arrange half the biscuits in greased 1-quart casserole; layer asparagus over biscuits. Top with remaining biscuits. Bake for 15 minutes. Spread with soup; top with onion rings. Bake for 10 minutes longer or until bubbly. Yield: 4-6 servings.

CRUNCHY ASPARAGUS CASSEROLE

1 sm. bag potato chips
2 hard-boiled eggs, sliced
1 sm. can asparagus tips
1 can cream of mushroom soup
1 c. grated cheese

Line casserole with potato chips; layer eggs over chips. Drain asparagus; reserve liquid. Combine 1/2 cup reserved liquid with soup to make thin sauce. Pour over eggs. Arrange asparagus over sauce; top with cheese. Bake in 350-degree oven for 20 minutes. Yield: 8 servings.

ASPARAGUS WITH CREAMED VEGETABLE SAUCE

2 sm. bunches asparagus
Butter
1 tbsp. lemon juice
12 sm. new potatoes
1/4 c. flour
1 1/2 tsp. salt
Dash of pepper
1/4 tsp. onion salt
2 c. milk
1 c. cooked peas
3/4 c. sliced cooked celery

Trim asparagus stalks, removing woody bases. Cook asparagus in covered saucepan in boiling salted water until tender. Drain; arrange in fan shape, stems together, on heated platter. Melt 1/3 cup butter in small pan over low heat; add lemon juice, mixing well. Pour butter mixture over asparagus. Peel 1/2-inch strip around center of each potato. Cook potatoes in boiling salted water until tender. Drain. Melt 1/2 stick butter in saucepan over low heat. Blend in flour and seasonings until smooth. Add milk gradually, stirring. Cook over low heat, stirring constantly, until thickened. Arrange hot potatoes across asparagus fan. Stir 3/4 of the peas and celery into cream sauce; pour over potatoes. Spoon remaining peas and celery over sauce. Yield: 4 servings.

ASPARAGUS PUDDING

3/4 c. cracker crumbs
Butter
1 14 1/2-oz. can asparagus, drained
1 c. grated American cheese
1 can mushroom soup
1/2 c. milk

1/4 tsp. nutmeg
1/2 c. chopped almonds
1 tsp. Worcestershire sauce
Salt to taste

Place 1/4 cup cracker crumbs in casserole; dot with 2 tablespoons butter. Add half the asparagus; add half the cheese. Add 1/4 cup crumbs; add remaining asparagus. Combine soup, milk, nutmeg and almonds in saucepan. Add 1 tablespoon butter, Worcestershire sauce and salt; heat, stirring, until blended. Pour over asparagus. Sprinkle with remaining cheese and crumbs. Bake at 350 degrees for 45 minutes. Yield: 4-5 servings.

CURRIED ASPARAGUS

2 1/2 lb. asparagus
2 1/2 tsp. salt
1/4 c. butter or margarine
3 tbsp. chopped green onion
1/4 tsp. curry powder
1/3 c. flour
2 c. milk
1/3 c. Romano cheese, grated

Discard tough ends of asparagus. Reserve 3 spears for garnish; cut remaining asparagus diagonally into 1/2-inch slices. Place in large shallow pan; add 2 teaspoons salt. Cover with water. Cook over high heat until water comes to a boil; reduce heat. Simmer for about 8 minutes or until crisp-tender; drain. Melt butter in saucepan; add onion, curry powder and remaining salt. Cook until bubbly. Add flour, stirring until blended. Add milk gradually. Cook over medium heat, stirring constantly, for about 10 minutes or until sauce is thickened. Add asparagus. Turn into shallow 1 1/2-quart baking dish; place reserved spears on top. Sprinkle with cheese. Bake in 425-degree oven for 15 minutes. One-third cup of the milk may be replaced by 1/3 cup white wine. Yield: 6 servings.

DRIED BEEF AND ASPARAGUS

2 pkg. dried beef
4 c. medium noodles
1 c. chopped celery
1 pkg. frozen cut asparagus
1/4 c. butter
1/2 c. flour
3 c. milk
1/2 lb. Cheddar cheese, grated
Bread crumbs

Fry dried beef in small amount of fat in skillet until crisp and curled. Cook noodles according to package directions; drain. Cook celery in 1/2 cup water until tender. Cook asparagus according to package directions or until almost tender. Melt butter; blend in flour. Add milk gradually. Cook, stirring constantly, until sauce is thickened. Stir in cheese; cook until melted. Drain celery and asparagus. Combine beef noodles, celery, asparagus and sauce mixture; stir well. Turn into buttered casserole. Refrigerate overnight. Top with crumbs. Bake at 350 degrees for 30 to 45 minutes or until bubbly. Yield: 8 servings.

ITALIAN-BAKED ASPARAGUS

4 tbsp. butter
1 lb. asparagus spears
3 tbsp. finely chopped onion
3 tbsp. finely chopped celery
2 tbsp. freshly grated Parmesan cheese
2 tbsp. freshly grated bread crumbs
4 canned Italian peeled tomatoes, diced
Salt and pepper to taste
Pinch of oregano
Pinch of thyme

Melt butter in rectangular baking dish; add asparagus. Sprinkle with onion, celery, cheese, bread crumbs and tomatoes. Season with salt, pepper, oregano and thyme. Bake, covered, at 375 degrees for 45 minutes or until tender. Yield: 4 servings.

LAYERED ASPARAGUS

1 can cream of chicken soup
1/2 c. milk
2 cans asparagus, drained
2 tsp. Italian dressing mix
2 hard-boiled eggs, chopped
3 slices toast, cubed

Combine soup and milk in small saucepan; heat through. Set aside to cool. Place asparagus in buttered casserole; sprinkle dressing mix over asparagus. Add eggs and toast cubes. Pour soup mixture over top. Bake in 350-degree oven for 1 hour. Yield: 6 servings.

TASTY ASPARAGUS CASSEROLE

1 can cream of mushroom soup
1 can mushrooms, drained
1/4 lb. Velveeta cheese, cubed
1/4 lb. sharp American cheese, cubed
1 pkg. frozen asparagus
10 shredded wheat wafers

Pour soup into saucepan; add mushrooms. Simmer until heated through; add cheeses, stirring until melted. Place asparagus in casserole; cover with soup mixture. Crush wafers; top casserole with crumbs. Bake at 350 degrees until bubbly. Garnish with hard-boiled egg slices. Yield: 4 servings.

CREAMED ASPARAGUS ON CHOW MEIN NOODLES

1/4 c. butter
1/4 c. flour
1 c. milk
1 c. chicken bouillon
6 hard-cooked eggs, quartered
1 tsp. minced onion
Salt to taste
1/2 tsp. marjoram
1/8 tsp. pepper
2 lb. fresh asparagus
1 3-oz. can chow mein noodles
12 strips crisp-fried bacon

Melt butter in small saucepan; blend in flour. Combine milk and bouillon; add to flour mixture gradually, stirring constantly until thickened. Add eggs, onion, salt, marjoram and pepper, stirring well. Heat through. Arrange asparagus over noodles in serving dish. Spoon egg mixture over asparagus. Crumble bacon over top. Yield: 6-8 servings.

TANGY ASPARAGUS CASSEROLE

2 cans asparagus spears, drained
1 carton sour cream
1 tbsp. prepared horseradish
1/2 c. bread crumbs
1/2 tsp. salt
Dash of pepper
Dash of garlic salt
2 tbsp. margarine

Arrange asparagus in casserole. Bake in 350-degree oven for 10 minutes. Combine sour cream and horseradish; spoon over asparagus. Combine bread crumbs and seasonings; brown in margarine. Sprinkle over casserole. Return to oven. Bake for 10 minutes longer or until heated through. Yield: 6 servings.

FANCY ASPARAGUS

1 lb. fresh asparagus
3 tbsp. oil
1/4 c. minced onion
1 5-oz. can mushrooms, drained
1/2 tsp. salt
Dash of pepper
1/4 c. light cream

Slice asparagus diagonally into 1 1/2-inch pieces. Combine oil and 1/2 cup water in large skillet; bring to a boil. Add asparagus, onion, mushrooms, salt and pepper. Cook, covered, for 8 to 10 minutes, or until tender, shaking skillet occasionally. Add cream; serve. Yield: 4-6 servings.

FRENCH-FRIED ASPARAGUS

2 tbsp. butter
3 tbsp. flour
1 c. milk
1/2 tsp. salt
1 No. 2 can asparagus tips
1 c. grated cheese
1 egg, beaten
1 1/2 c. fine bread crumbs
1 1/2 qt. cooking oil

Melt butter. Add flour; blend until smooth. Add milk gradually; cook, stirring constantly, until thick. Add salt. Drain asparagus. Dip in hot white sauce; roll in cheese. Chill until sauce sets. Dip in egg; roll in bread crumbs. Fry in oil at 375 degrees until brown. Yield: 4 servings.

GOLDENROD ASPARAGUS

1 No. 1 can asparagus
3 hard-cooked eggs
12 stuffed olives
2 c. medium white sauce
Buttered toast

Place asparagus in saucepan; heat thoroughly. Chop egg whites and olives; add to white sauce. Drain hot asparagus; arrange on toast. Cover with sauce mixture. Garnish with sieved egg yolks. Yield: 6 servings.

PEKING-STYLE ASPARAGUS

2 tbsp. oil
1/4 c. chicken stock
2 tbsp. soy sauce
1 tbsp. cornstarch
1 No. 2 can asparagus, drained

Combine oil, stock, 1/4 cup water, soy sauce and cornstarch in saucepan; heat, stirring constantly, until mixture comes to a boil. Add asparagus; heat thoroughly. Serve hot. Yield: 4-5 servings.

ASPARAGUS-EGG SALAD

1 pkg. frozen asparagus spears
2 hard-cooked eggs, sliced
1 tbsp. vinegar
1 tsp. grated onion
1 tsp. prepared mustard

Cook asparagus according to package directions; drain. Chill thoroughly. Place asparagus on salad plates; arrange egg slices over asparagus. Combine remaining ingredients. Sprinkle over asparagus. Yield: 4 servings.

ASPARAGUS SOUFFLÉ SALAD

1 pkg. frozen chopped asparagus
Pimento strips
1 env. unflavored gelatin
1 can cream of asparagus soup
1 tbsp. lemon juice
1/4 tsp. salt
1 8-oz. package cream cheese, softened
1 c. sour cream
1/2 c. chopped celery
Lettuce

Prepare asparagus according to package directions; drain. Arrange with pimento strips in well-greased mold. Soften gelatin in 1/4 cup cold water. Combine soup, lemon juice, salt and gelatin in saucepan. Heat, stirring until gelatin is dissolved. Beat in cream cheese and sour cream. Chill until partially set; fold in celery. Pour into mold; chill until firm. Unmold on lettuce. May garnish with slices of hard-cooked eggs.

CONGEALED ASPARAGUS SALAD

1/2 c. white vinegar
3/4 c. sugar
1 tsp. salt
2 env. unflavored gelatin
1/2 c. chopped pecans
2 pimentos, diced
1 c. chopped celery
1 tbsp. grated onion
1 med. can asparagus, cut in 1-in. pieces

Combine 1 cup water, vinegar, sugar and salt; simmer, stirring until sugar dissolves. Soften gelatin in 1/2 cup cold water; add to vinegar mixture. Stir until gelatin is dissolved. Cool until partially congealed. Stir in pecans, pimentos, celery, onion and drained asparagus. Pour into 8 individual molds; refrigerate until set. Yield: 8 servings.

Aspic

AVOCADO ASPIC

1 1/2 env. unflavored gelatin
1 c. fresh grapefruit juice
2 ripe avocados, mashed
1 tsp. Worcestershire sauce
2 tsp. minced onion
1/2 tsp. salt
1/2 c. mayonnaise

Soften gelatin in 1/2 cup cold water; dissolve in 1/2 cup boiling water. Add grapefruit juice; chill until partially set. Add remaining ingredients, beating with rotary beater until smooth. Pour into mold; chill until firm. Garnish with ripe olives. Yield: 8 servings.

CHEESE ASPIC

2 env. unflavored gelatin
2 cans consomme
4 tbsp. sherry
3 pkg. cream cheese
1/2 c. Roquefort cheese
1 tbsp. Worcestershire sauce
1/2 tsp. hot sauce

Soften gelatin in 1/2 cup cold water. Heat consomme in saucepan; add gelatin, stirring to dissolve. Add 2 tablespoons sherry; cool. Pour gelatin mixture 1 inch deep in lightly greased melon mold. Chill until firm. Blend remaining ingredients well; place in center of mold. Fill mold with remaining consomme mixture. Chill until set. Unmold. Serve with crackers or melba toast.

GRAPEFRUIT ASPIC

2 env. unflavored gelatin
3/4 c. sugar
3 lge. pink grapefruit
3 tbsp. lemon juice
1 avocado
3/4 c. chopped celery
1/2 c. slivered almonds

Soften gelatin in 1 cup cold water; dissolve in 1 cup boiling water. Add sugar; stir until dissolved. Section grapefruit, reserving juice. Add reserved juice and lemon juice to gelatin mixture. Chill until partially set. Peel avocado; cut into thin slices. Fold celery, grapefruit sections, almonds and avocado slices into thickened gelatin; pour into mold. Chill overnight. Unmold on lettuce; garnish with mayonnaise. Yield: 10-12 servings.

ASPIC-TOPPED CHICKEN

3 env. unflavored gelatin
3 1/2 c. cold tomato juice
1 1/4 tsp. salt
1/2 tsp. pepper
3 tbsp. lemon juice
3/4 c. cold chicken stock
3/4 c. mayonnaise
1 1/2 c. diced cooked chicken
3 tbsp. diced green pepper
1/2 c. diced celery

Soften 2 envelopes gelatin in 1 cup tomato juice in saucepan; heat, stirring constantly, until gelatin is dissolved. Remove from heat; stir in remaining tomato juice, 1/2 teaspoon salt, pepper and 2 tablespoons lemon juice. Pour half the mixture into two 5-cup ring molds; chill until firm. Soften remaining gelatin in chicken stock in saucepan; heat until dissolved. Remove from heat; add remaining salt and lemon juice. Cool. Stir in mayonnaise, chicken, green pepper and celery; pour over congealed layers. Chill until firm. Yield: 12 servings.

CHICKEN AND SOUR CREAM ASPIC

2 env. unflavored gelatin
2 1/2 c. chicken broth
2 tbsp. grated onion
1 tsp. salt
Dash of pepper
2 c. cooked diced chicken
1/2 c. toasted slivered almonds
1/2 c. sliced black olives
2 c. sour cream

Soften gelatin in 1 cup chicken broth. Place over low heat; stir until dissolved. Remove from heat; stir in remaining chicken broth, onion, salt and pepper. Chill to consistency of unbeaten egg white. Fold in chicken, almonds, olives and sour cream. Turn into 6-cup mold; chill until firm. Unmold on serving plate; garnish with salad greens. Yield: 8 servings.

CHICKEN IN ASPIC

2 env. unflavored gelatin
2 10 1/2-oz. cans consomme
1/2 tsp. salt
4 tbsp. lemon juice
2 c. diced cooked chicken
1 c. cooked mixed vegetables
1/2 c. chopped celery
4 tbsp. chopped green pepper
4 tbsp. chopped pimento
Crisp spinach leaves
Toasted almonds

Soften gelatin in 1 cup cold water in saucepan. Place over low heat; stir until dissolved. Remove from heat; add 1 cup water, consomme, salt and lemon juice. Chill to consistency of unbeaten egg white. Fold in chicken, mixed vegetables, celery, green pepper and pimento. Turn into 6-cup mold or individual molds; chill until firm. Unmold on spinach; top with almonds.

CORNED BEEF ASPIC

1 tbsp. unflavored gelatin
1 1/2 c. tomato juice
1/2 tsp. salt
1 tsp. lemon juice
1 12-oz. can corned beef, shredded
3 hard-cooked eggs, chopped
1/2 c. chopped cucumber
1 1/2 c. chopped celery
2 tbsp. chopped onion
1 c. mayonnaise

Soften gelatin in 1/4 cup cold water. Heat tomato juice in saucepan; add gelatin, stirring to dissolve. Add salt and lemon juice; chill until partially set. Fold in remaining ingredients; pour into 1 1/2-quart mold or loaf pan. Chill until firm. Yield: 6-8 servings.

VEAL IN ASPIC WITH SAUCE

1 4-lb. meaty veal knuckle
1 lge. onion, chopped
1 bunch celery tops, chopped
1 tbsp. salt
1 tbsp. unflavored gelatin
3 tsp. Worcestershire sauce
1 c. mayonnaise
2 hard-cooked eggs, chopped
1/2 c. chopped English walnuts
12 stuffed olives, sliced
1 tsp. grated onion
1/2 pt. heavy cream, whipped
2 c. diced celery

Cut veal knuckle into pieces. Combine veal, chopped onion, celery tops and salt in saucepan; cover with water. Cook over medium heat until veal is tender. Drain veal, reserving broth. Strain reserved broth. Remove meat from knuckle; grind. Soften gelatin in 1/4 cup cold water; dissolve over hot water. Stir gelatin mixture into 2 cups hot broth; add veal and Worcestershire sauce. Pour into mold; chill until set. Combine remaining ingredients; serve as sauce for aspic.

CRAB ASPIC

1 env. unflavored gelatin
1 3/4 c. tomato juice
1 tbsp. sugar
1/2 tsp. Worcestershire sauce
4 tbsp. lemon juice
1/2 lb. crab meat

Soften gelatin in 1/2 cup tomato juice in saucepan; heat gradually until gelatin is dissolved. Remove from heat; stir in remaining tomato juice, sugar, Worcestershire sauce and lemon juice. Chill to consistency of egg whites. Add crab meat; pour into mold. Chill until firm. Yield: 4-6 servings.

LOBSTER ASPIC

2 tbsp. unflavored gelatin
3/4 c. cold bouillon
1 c. hot bouillon
Juice of 1 lge. lemon
1/2 c. chili sauce
Salt to taste
1 lb. fresh cooked lobster meat
2 dill pickles, chopped
1 c. diced celery

Soften gelatin in cold bouillon; add hot bouillon. Stir until dissolved. Cool slightly; add lemon juice, chili sauce and salt. Chill until slightly thickened. Dice lobster meat; add pickles and celery. Fold lobster mixture into gelatin mixture. Pour into mold. Chill for several hours until set. Serve on lettuce leaves; garnish with mayonnaise. Yield: 4-6 servings.

SALMON ASPIC

1 env. unflavored gelatin
1/4 c. lemon juice
2 c. salad dressing
1 1-lb. can salmon
3 tbsp. minced onion
2 hard-cooked eggs, chopped
1/3 c. chopped stuffed olives
Russian dressing

Soften gelatin in 1/4 cup cold water; dissolve over hot water. Mix in lemon juice and salad dressing, blending until smooth; remove from heat. Drain and flake salmon; add onion, salmon, eggs and olives to gelatin mixture. Mix well. Pour into oiled 1 1/2-quart mold; chill until firm. Garnish with lettuce and cherry tomatoes if desired. Serve with Russian dressing. Yield: 6-8 servings.

SEAFOOD ASPIC

2 cans stewed tomatoes
Dash of Worcestershire sauce
2 tbsp. lemon juice
2 3-oz. packages lemon gelatin
1 can shrimp, drained
1 can crab, drained

Break up tomatoes with fork; add Worcestershire sauce and lemon juice. Add enough boiling water to equal 4 cups liquid. Pour into saucepan; bring to boiling point. Remove from heat; stir in gelatin until dissolved. Chill until partially congealed; fold in shrimp and crab. Pour into mold; chill until firm. Yield: 12 servings.

SHRIMP ASPIC RING

2 env. unflavored gelatin
2 c. tomato juice
1 beef bouillon cube
2 tsp. prepared horseradish
2 tsp. Worcestershire sauce
1 tsp. salt
1/2 tsp. celery salt
1 7-oz. bottle lemon-lime carbonated drink
1 lb. cooked shrimp

Soften gelatin in 1/2 cup cold water. Combine tomato juice and bouillon cube in saucepan; bring to boiling point. Stir in gelatin until dissolved. Add horseradish, Worcestershire sauce, salt and celery salt; cool slightly. Add carbonated drink. Pour half the mixture into 2-quart mold; chill until firm. Arrange shrimp on firm gelatin mixture; add remaining gelatin mixture. Chill until firm; garnish with additional shrimp if desired. Yield: 8-10 servings.

SHRIMP-AVOCADO ASPIC

1 env. unflavored gelatin
1/4 c. lemon juice
1 8-oz. can tomato sauce
1/2 tsp. Worcestershire sauce
1 c. chopped celery
Grated onion to taste
1 c. small cooked shrimp
1/2 c. sliced stuffed olives
1 avocado, sliced

Soften gelatin in lemon juice; dissolve in 3/4 cup boiling water. Stir in tomato sauce and Worcestershire sauce. Chill until thickened; fold in celery, onion, shrimp, olives and avocado. Pour into mold; refrigerate until firm. Yield: 6-8 servings.

TUNA ASPIC

2 3-oz. packages lemon gelatin
2 cans tuna
1 tbsp. lemon juice
1 c. mayonnaise
1/2 sm. onion, chopped
2 hard-cooked eggs, chopped
1 c. chopped celery
1/2 pt. whipping cream, whipped
2 c. tomato juice
Dash of salt

Dissolve 1 package gelatin in 1/2 cup hot water; add 1/2 cup cold water. Drain and flake tuna. Combine lemon juice, mayonnaise, onion, eggs, celery and tuna; add to gelatin mixture. Fold in whipped cream; pour into 8 x 8-inch pan. Chill until firm. Dissolve remaining gelatin in 1 cup hot tomato juice; add remaining cold tomato juice and salt. Cool; pour over congealed salad. Chill for 4 hours or overnight until set. Yield: 9 servings.

ASPIC CUBES IN GREEN SALAD

1 env. unflavored gelatin
1 tbsp. lemon juice
1/2 tsp. salt
1 8-oz. can tomato sauce
1 1/2 tbsp. vinegar
1/2 c. crumbled blue cheese
Dash of pepper
6 c. mixed salad greens
1/2 c. chopped watercress
1/4 c. sliced scallions
1/4 c. sliced olives
1 c. grapefruit sections
Garlic salad dressing

Soften gelatin in 1/4 cup cold water; dissolve in 3/4 cup boiling water. Add lemon juice, salt, tomato sauce, vinegar, blue cheese and pepper. Pour into 8-inch square pan; chill until set. Cut congealed gelatin mixture into 1/2-inch cubes. Combine salad greens, watercress, scallions, olives and grapefruit sections in salad bowl. Add salad dressing, tossing lightly. Serve in individual salad bowls topped with aspic cubes. Yield: 8 servings.

ARTICHOKE ASPIC

3 env. unflavored gelatin
2 cans tomato soup
1 can tomato juice
Seasoning salt
Red pepper
Worcestershire sauce
Juice of 1 lemon
2 tbsp. Durkee's dressing
3 stalks celery, minced
2 green onions, minced
1 sm. jar marinated artichokes, drained
Lettuce
6 hard-boiled eggs, sliced
Mayonnaise

Soften gelatin in 3/4 cup water. Combine soup, tomato juice and 1 juice can water in saucepan; bring to boiling point. Add gelatin; stir until dissolved. Cool. Add seasonings to taste, lemon juice and Durkee's dressing. Chill until partially set. Fold in celery, onions and artichokes; pour into individual molds. Chill until set. Arrange lettuce on serving plates. Unmold aspics on lettuce; garnish with egg slices and mayonnaise.

ASHEVILLE ASPIC

1 c. tomato soup
1/2 lb. cream cheese, whipped
2 tbsp. unflavored gelatin
1 c. mayonnaise
1 1/2 c. chopped celery
1 green pepper, chopped
1 sm. onion, chopped
1/4 tsp. salt
1 c. chopped pecans

Bring soup to boiling point in saucepan; add cream cheese, stirring until smooth. Soften gelatin in 1/2 cup cold water; add gelatin to soup mixture. Chill until thickened; add mayonnaise, vegetables and salt. Fold in pecans. Pour into individual wet molds; chill until set. Unmold on shredded lettuce.

BARBECUE ASPIC

1 env. unflavored gelatin
1 tbsp. lemon juice
1 8-oz. can tomato sauce
1 tsp. onion juice
1 1/2 tbsp. white vinegar
1/2 tsp. salt
Dash of pepper
1/2 c. cubed sharp Cheddar cheese

Soften gelatin in 1/4 cup cold water; dissolve in 1 cup boiling water. Add lemon juice, tomato sauce, onion juice, vinegar, salt and pepper. Chill until partially thickened. Place 6 or 8 cheese cubes in bottom of mold; spoon layer of gelatin over cheese. Repeat layers ending with gelatin mixture on top. Chill until firm. Yield: 8 servings.

QUICK TOMATO ASPIC

1 env. unflavored gelatin
1/2 c. cold tomato juice
1 1/4 c. hot tomato juice
1/4 tsp. salt
1/8 tsp. pepper
1 tbsp. lemon juice
Salad greens
Cottage cheese

Soften gelatin in cold juice; add hot juice, stirring until gelatin is dissolved. Add seasonings and lemon juice. Pour into molds; chill until firm. Unmold on salad greens. May top with cottage cheese if desired. Yield: 4 servings.

SOUP ASPIC

1 env. unflavored gelatin
1 tbsp. lemon juice
1 10-oz. can tomato soup
1/3 c. chopped celery
1/3 c. chopped green pepper
1/3 c. chopped onion
1 c. cottage cheese
1/2 c. mayonnaise or salad dressing

Soften gelatin in 1/4 cup cold water; dissolve in 1/2 cup boiling water. Stir in lemon juice and soup; chill until partially thickened. Fold in remaining ingredients; pour into mold. Chill until set. Yield: 8-10 servings.

TOMATO ASPIC IN CHEESE CRUST

1 c. finely crushed cheese crackers
1/4 c. melted butter
1 env. unflavored gelatin
1 8-oz. can tomato sauce
1 1/2 tbsp. vinegar
1/2 tsp. salt
Dash of pepper
1/2 c. chopped olives
1/4 c. sliced green onions

Combine crumbs and butter. Press firmly into 8-inch pie plate, building up sides. Bake at 375 degrees for 6 to 7 minutes; chill. Soften gelatin in 1/4 cup cold water; dissolve in 3/4 cup boiling water. Add tomato sauce, vinegar, seasonings, olives and onions; chill until partially thickened. Pour gelatin mixture into crust; chill until set. Cut into wedges to serve. Yield: 6 servings.

TOMATO ASPIC WITH CREAM CHEESE

2 env. unflavored gelatin
3 c. tomato juice
Dash of hot sauce
2 tsp. Worcestershire sauce
1 3-oz. package cream cheese
1/3 c. chopped onion
1 c. diced celery
3/4 c. chopped olives

Soften gelatin in 1/2 cup cold water. Bring tomato juice to a boil in saucepan; remove from heat. Add gelatin; stir until dissolved. Add hot sauce and Worcestershire sauce; chill until slightly thickened. Cut cream cheese into small pieces; fold cream cheese, onion, celery and olives into partially thickened gelatin. Pour into mold; chill until set.

Valentine Aspic . . . Warm your family's hearts with this lovingly prepared and festive salad.

VALENTINE ASPIC

3 1/2 c. tomato juice
2 env. unflavored gelatin
1/4 tsp. hot sauce
1/2 tsp. salt
1 tsp. sugar
1/4 c. lemon juice
1 tsp. Worcestershire sauce
8 bread slices
6 stuffed olives
1 3-oz. package cream cheese

Pour 1 cup tomato juice in saucepan; add gelatin. Let stand for about 5 minutes or until softened. Simmer gelatin mixture over low heat, stirring constantly, until gelatin is dissolved. Remove from heat; add remaining tomato juice, hot sauce, salt, sugar, lemon juice and Worcestershire sauce. Pour into 8 1/2-cup individual heart-shaped molds; chill until firm. Cut bread slices into heart shapes the same size as molds. Chop olives finely; add to cream cheese and blend well. Spread bread with cream cheese mixture. Unmold aspics on cream cheese-topped bread. Garnish with hot sauce-seasoned mayonnaise. Yield: 8 servings.

TOMATO ASPIC ON SLAW

1 env. unflavored gelatin
1 tbsp. lemon juice
1 8-oz. can tomato paste
2 tbsp. vinegar
Salt
Pepper
Celery seed
1 egg, beaten
1/4 tsp. mustard
1 tsp. sugar
1 tbsp. vinegar
3 c. green cabbage, shredded

Soften gelatin in 1/4 cup cold water; dissolve in 1 cup hot water. Add lemon juice, tomato paste, vinegar, 1/2 teaspoon salt, pepper and celery seed to taste. Pour into 6 individual molds; chill until set. Combine egg, 1/2 cup water, mustard, sugar, vinegar, dash of salt, pepper and celery seed to taste in saucepan. Cook over low heat, stirring constantly, until thickened. Cool. Toss cabbage with dressing. Arrange slaw on individual salad plates. Unmold aspics; place on slaw. Yield: 6 servings.

TOMATO ASPIC SALAD

2 env. unflavored gelatin
2 c. tomato juice
1 tbsp. vinegar
3/4 tsp. salt
Dash of garlic salt
Dash of celery salt
1/4 tsp. onion salt
2 tbsp. chopped green pepper
1/2 pt. cottage cheese
1/2 c. evaporated milk
1/3 c. mayonnaise
1 tbsp. lemon juice
1/2 c. diced celery
1/2 c. diced cucumber

Soften 1 package gelatin in 1/4 cup cold water. Bring tomato juice to boiling point in saucepan; dissolve softened gelatin in hot juice. Add vinegar, 1/4 teaspoon salt, garlic salt, celery salt and onion salt. Pour into oiled 2-quart salad mold. Chill until firm. Soften remaining gelatin in 1/4 cup cold water. Add 1/3 cup boiling water; stir until dissolved. Chill until partially thickened. Add green pepper, cottage cheese, milk, mayonnaise, lemon juice, remaining salt, celery and cucumber to partially thickened gelatin. Score top of firm tomato juice mixture with tines of fork lightly. Pour cheese mixture over tomato juice mixture. Chill until firm. Unmold. Garnish with greens and ripe olives. Yield: 8-10 servings.

Avocado

A green, pear-shaped fruit native to the tropical and subtropical Americas, the avocado is high in both nutrients and calories. An avocado contains protein, 14 basic minerals, and 11 vitamins. (1/2 an avocado = 150 calories)

AVAILABILITY: Available year-round.

BUYING: Avocados are never allowed to ripen on the tree. They mature either in the grocery store or in the consumers' homes. For immediate use, choose fruit that gives slightly under light pressure. Buy firm fruit if it will be stored a few days before using. Avoid buying very soft specimens. Avocados ripen naturally after 2-4 days if left at room temperature.

STORING: Fully ripe avocados can be stored in the refrigerator. Never freeze avocados, and always handle them carefully to avoid bruising.

PREPARATION: Cut the fruit in half lengthwise, working around the center seed. Twist slightly to separate; lift seed out. Pare skin. Fruit may be mashed, cut into desired shapes, or left in halves for stuffing. To prevent darkening, sprinkle the cut surfaces with fresh lime or lemon juice. Unused cut fruit may be wrapped in waxed paper or foil and stored in the refrigerator for a short time.

SERVING: Avocado halves can be filled with

hot foods; slices are popular in salads; mashed avocado is an ingredient in sandwich spreads or dips.

AVOCADO CREAM

Color photograph for this recipe on page 733.

2 ripe avocados
1/4 c. lime juice
1 c. heavy cream, whipped

Halve avocados lengthwise; twisting gently to separate halves. Insert sharp knife directly into seeds; twist to lift out. Peel and quarter avocados. Blend in electric blender with lime juice until smooth; fold into whipped cream. Place in bowl. May be served with tomato wedges and corn chips. 3 cups.

AVOCADO COCKTAIL

3 tbsp. lemon juice
3 avocados, pared and cubed
1 c. catsup
1 tsp. Worcestershire sauce
1 tsp. horseradish
1/2 tsp. salt

Pour lemon juice over avocados; stir to coat well. Drain avocados; reserve juice. Combine catsup, Worcestershire sauce, horseradish and salt with reserved juice. Arrange avocados in cocktail glasses; pour sauce over top. Chill and serve. Shrimp may be added, if desired.

AVOCADO-BACON SPREAD

4 slices bacon
1 avocado
1 tbsp. lemon juice
1 tbsp. mayonnaise
1/4 tsp. garlic salt

Fry bacon until crisp; drain. Crumble bacon. Pare, remove seed and mash avocado. Combine bacon, avocado, lemon juice, mayonnaise and garlic salt; blend well.

COTTAGE AVOCADO QUICKIE

1 med. avocado, mashed
1 1/2 c. cottage cheese
1/2 c. sour cream
2 tbsp. chopped pickle
1/4 c. crumbled bacon
1/2 tsp. salt
1 clove of garlic, crushed
1 tbsp. minced onion
2 dashes of hot sauce
1 tsp. lemon juice

Combine avocado, cottage cheese and sour cream. Add remaining ingredients. Mix well. Chill for 2 hours. Serve with potato, corn or tortilla chips. Yield: 2 1/2 cups.

GUACAMOLE DIP

2 ripe avocados, mashed
1/4 tsp. red wine vinegar
1 tsp. salad dressing
1/4 tsp. ground comino
1/4 tsp. chili powder
1/2 tomato, chopped
1 clove of garlic, crushed
Salt and pepper to taste
1 tbsp. grated onion
Juice of 1/2 lemon

Combine all ingredients in blender container; mix well. Chill; serve with corn chips.

CHILLED CREAM OF AVOCADO SOUP

4 tbsp. flour
4 1/4 c. chicken stock
2 med. avocados
1/2 c. cream, chilled
1/4 tsp. white pepper

Combine flour and 1/4 cup chicken stock; stir until smooth. Add to remaining chicken stock in large saucepan. Bring to a boil, stirring constantly; remove from heat. Peel; remove seed and puree avocados. Add to stock mixture; blend thoroughly. Chill. Stir in cream and pepper just before serving. Garnish with chopped chives, if desired. Yield: 6 servings.

JELLIED AVOCADO SOUP

1 ripe avocado
1 can jellied consomme
1 tbsp. lemon juice
Salt to taste
Dash of hot sauce
Sour cream

Peel, remove seed and puree avocado. Combine avocado with consomme, lemon juice, salt and hot sauce; blend thoroughly. Chill. Serve topped with sour cream; garnish with diced avocado, if desired. Yield: 3 servings.

QUICK AVOCADO SOUP

1 qt. seasoned chicken broth
2 avocados, sieved

Pour broth into saucepan; bring to a boil. Reduce heat; add avocados. Simmer, stirring constantly, until blended and heated through. Yield: 6-8 servings.

AVOCADO-CHEESE SALAD

1 oz. blue cheese, crumbled
1 c. French dressing
1 lge. avocado, sliced
Lettuce, shredded

Blend cheese and French dressing; add avocado and mix well. Refrigerate for at least 4 hours. Add avocado mixture to lettuce. Toss lightly. Yield: 8 servings.

AVOCADO CIRCLE SALAD

1 avocado
2 tbsp. lemon juice
Dash of salt
1/2 c. cottage cheese
1 tsp. grated onion
1/4 tsp. paprika
Lettuce
French dressing

Peel avocado; halve lengthwise and remove seed. Sprinkle avocado with lemon juice and salt. Mix cottage cheese, onion and paprika; fill avocado cavities with cottage cheese mixture. Place halves together. Chill. Slice crosswise. Serve on lettuce with French dressing. Yield: 4 servings.

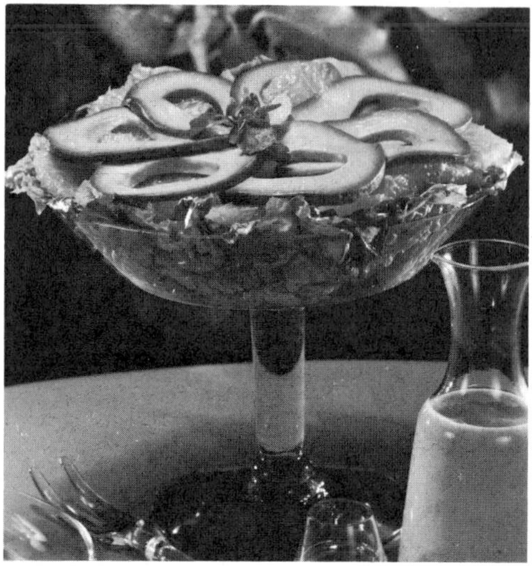

Orange and Avocado Salad . . . Freshness is captured in this chilled summer salad.

ORANGE AND AVOCADO SALAD

2 California avocados
3 fresh oranges
Iceberg lettuce leaves
3/4 c. mayonnaise
1/4 c. fresh orange juice
1/2 tsp. paprika
1/2 tsp. salt

Peel and pit avocados; cut into slices. Peel oranges, cut into slices, removing membrane and seeds. Arrange avocado and orange slices on lettuce leaves in 6 compotes. Combine remaining ingredients for dressing. Drizzle dressing over salads. Serve.

AVOCADO CITRUS SALAD

2 grapefruit
3 oranges
2 avocados
Lettuce
1/2 c. lemon juice
1/2 c. salad oil
1 tsp. salt
1/4 c. honey
1/4 c. red jelly or jam

Peel and section grapefruit and oranges. Peel and slice avocados lengthwise. Alternate grapefruit sections, orange sections and avocado slices on lettuce. Combine remaining ingredients; blend well. Serve dressing over salad. Yield: 6 servings.

AVOCADO-FRUIT SQUARES

1 lge. avocado, diced
2 tbsp. lemon juice
1 3-oz. package cream cheese, softened
2 tbsp. sugar
1/4 c. mayonnaise
1/4 tsp. salt
1 c. diced canned peaches
1/4 c. chopped maraschino cherries
1/2 c. whipping cream, whipped

Sprinkle avocado with 1 tablespoon lemon juice; set aside. Blend cream cheese, remaining lemon juice, sugar, mayonnaise and salt together. Stir in avocado and fruits; fold in whipped cream. Pour into refrigerator tray; freeze until firm. Let stand at room temperature for 15 minutes before serving; cut in squares. Garnish with cherries and avocado balls, if desired. Yield: 6 servings.

AVOCADO-EGG SALAD

6 hard-boiled eggs, chopped
2 avocados, chopped
1 chili pepper, minced
1 onion, minced
3 tbsp. chopped parsley
2 tbsp. vinegar
1 1/2 tsp. salt

Combine eggs, avocados, chili pepper, onion, parsley, vinegar and salt; blend until smooth. Chill. Serve on lettuce leaves; garnish with shrimp, if desired. Yield: 4 servings.

AVOCADO-VEGETABLE PLATTER

Color photograph for this recipe on page 306.

English peas
Sliced cucumber
Sliced string beans
Sliced California avocado
Cooked asparagus
Pimento-stuffed green olives
Oil and vinegar dressing

Arrange peas, cucumber, beans, avocado, asparagus and olives on serving platter. Serve with oil and vinegar dressing.

AVOCADO-RED CABBAGE SALAD

1 med. ripe avocado, diced
Lemon juice
4 c. shredded red cabbage
1/4 c. finely chopped onion
1 c. finely diced celery
1/4 tsp. salt
Dash of pepper
Roquefort Dressing
2 hard-cooked eggs, sliced

Marinate avocado in lemon juice; drain. Combine avocado, cabbage, onion, celery, salt and pepper lightly with Roquefort Dressing. Arrange in salad bowl; garnish with eggs.

Roquefort Dressing

1/4 lb. Roquefort cheese
1/4 tsp. salt
Dash of hot sauce
1 tsp. Worcestershire sauce
3 tbsp. tarragon vinegar
1/2 c. salad oil

Mash cheese; blend in salt, hot sauce, Worcestershire sauce and vinegar. Beat well. Add salad oil slowly; mix well.

AVOCADO AND SHRIMP SALAD

1/2 c. mayonnaise
1/3 c. sour cream
2 tbsp. lemon juice
1 tsp. salt
2 tbsp. capers
2 hard-cooked eggs, finely chopped
2 tbsp. chopped chives
Cocktail shrimp
Avocado wedges

Combine mayonnaise, sour cream, lemon juice, salt, capers, eggs and chives; blend well. Arrange shrimp and avocado on bed of lettuce. Serve with dressing. Yield: 6 servings.

AVOCADO WITH SHRIMP RÉMOULADE

1/4 c. tarragon vinegar
2 tbsp. horseradish mustard
1 tbsp. catsup
1 1/2 tsp. paprika
1/2 tsp. salt
1 1/4 tsp. cayenne pepper
1/2 c. salad oil
1/4 c. minced celery
1/4 c. minced green onions and tops
2 lb. cooked shrimp
4 med. avocados

Combine vinegar, mustard, catsup, paprika, salt and cayenne pepper in bowl. Add oil slowly, beating constantly. Stir in celery and onions. Pour over shrimp; refrigerate for 4 to 5 hours. Cut avocados in half and peel. Lift shrimp from sauce, reserving sauce. Arrange 6 shrimp on each avocado half. Serve with sauce. Yield: 8 servings.

AVOCADO SUPREME

3 tbsp. butter
3 tbsp. sugar
3 tbsp. catsup
3 tbsp. vinegar
3 tbsp. Worcestershire sauce
1 avocado

Combine first 5 ingredients in saucepan; heat. Halve avocado; remove seed. Fill cavity of each avocado half with hot sauce; serve immediately. Yield: 2 servings.

GOURMET AVOCADO SALAD

3 ripe avocados, chilled
1/3 c. light rum
2/3 c. salad oil
1/8 tsp. white pepper

Halve avocados; remove seeds. Beat rum, salad oil and pepper until slightly thickened. Serve avocado halves on bed of lettuce; fill cavities with dressing. Yield: 6 servings.

AVOCADO-CREAM MOLD

3 env. unflavored gelatin
2 c. pineapple juice
1/3 c. lemon juice
2 tsp. grated onion
2 1/2 tsp. seasoned salt
1 or 2 drops of hot sauce
3/4 c. salad dressing
2 avocados, mashed
1 c. sliced ripe olives
3/4 c. diced cucumber

Sprinkle gelatin on 1 cup pineapple juice in small saucepan. Let stand for 5 minutes. Simmer, stirring constantly, until gelatin is dissolved. Remove from heat; stir in remaining pineapple juice, lemon juice, onion, salt and hot sauce. Cool. Beat in salad dressing; chill until slightly thickened. Fold avocados, olives and cucumber into gelatin; pour into 5 or 6-cup mold. Chill until firm; garnish with ripe olives, if desired. Yield: 8 servings.

AVOCADO MOLD

2 env. unflavored gelatin
6 tbsp. lemon juice
1 1/2 tsp. grated onion
1 clove of garlic, minced
2 1/2 tsp. salt
Hot sauce to taste
3 c. sieved avocado
3/4 c. mayonnaise

Soften gelatin in 1/2 cup cold water; dissolve in 1 1/4 cup hot water. Blend in lemon juice, onion, garlic, salt and hot sauce; chill until slightly thickened. Add avocado and mayonnaise; pour into lightly oiled mold. Chill until firm. Yield: 8 servings.

AVOCADO AND GRAPEFRUIT SALAD

2 pkg. lemon gelatin
6 tbsp. lemon juice
Salt to taste
1/2 tsp. onion juice
Green food coloring
2 sm. packages cream cheese
1/2 c. mayonnaise
2 grapefruit
2 sm. avocados, sliced

Dissolve gelatin in 2 cups boiling water; add lemon juice, salt, onion juice and food coloring to tint as desired. Cool. Whip cream cheese; add mayonnaise. Mix well; add gelatin mixture. Peel and section grapefruit; remove membrane. Add avocados and grapefruit sections to cheese mixture. Spoon into mold. Chill until firm. Yield: 8-10 servings.

RIBBON AVOCADO SALAD

3 env. unflavored gelatin
2 3/4 tsp. salt
3 tbsp. lemon juice
Hot sauce to taste
1 1/2 c. sieved ripe avocados
1 or 2 drops of green food coloring
12 oz. cream cheese, softened
1/2 c. milk
2/3 c. mayonnaise
1/4 tsp. Worcestershire sauce
3 c. tomato juice
1/2 bay leaf
2 whole cloves
2 or 3 sprigs of parsley
2 stalks celery, chopped
Dash of cayenne pepper
1 1/2 tbsp. vinegar
1 1/2 tsp. grated onion

Soften 1 envelope gelatin in 1/4 cup cold water; add 1/2 cup boiling water. Stir in 1 teaspoon salt, lemon juice and hot sauce. Chill until thickened. Stir in avocados; add food coloring. Pour into 9 x 5 x 2 1/2-inch loaf pan; chill until firm. Soften 1 envelope gelatin in 1/4 cup cold water; dissolve over boiling water. Combine cream cheese with milk, blending well. Stir in 1 teaspoon salt, mayonnaise and Worcestershire sauce. Add dissolved gelatin; spread over avocado layer. Chill until firm. Mix tomato juice with bay leaf, cloves, parsley, celery, remaining salt and cayenne pepper in saucepan; simmer for 10 minutes. Strain. Soften remaining gelatin in 1/4 cup cold water. Add to hot tomato juice; add vinegar and onion. Chill until thickened; pour over cheese layer. Chill until firm. Remove from mold; garnish with tomato quarters and greens, if desired. Yield: 10-12 servings.

AVOCADO RING WITH STRAWBERRIES

2 3-oz. packages lime gelatin
1/2 tsp. salt
2 ripe avocados
2 tbsp. lemon juice
1/3 c. mayonnaise
2 1/2 c. sliced strawberries

Dissolve gelatin and salt in 2 cups hot water; add 1 1/2 cups cold water. Chill until slightly thickened. Peel, pit and mash avocados; cover with lemon juice. Stir avocados and mayonnaise into gelatin; blend well. Pour into 5-cup ring mold; chill until firm. Unmold ring onto salad greens; fill with strawberries.

Honey Cream Dressing

1/2 c. sour cream
1/2 c. mayonnaise
1 tbsp. honey
1/2 c. sliced strawberries

Combine all ingredients; blend well. Serve over salad.

AVOCADO SALAD MOLD WITH SHRIMP DRESSING

3 pkg. lime gelatin
2 avocados, diced
1/2 c. chopped nuts
1/2 c. diced celery
6 tbsp. minced pimento
1 c. mayonnaise
2 tbsp. lemon juice
1 1/2 tbsp. grated onion
2 cans med. shrimp, drained

Prepare gelatin according to package directions; chill until partially set. Fold in avocados, nuts, celery and 2 tablespoons pimento; pour into large ring mold. Refrigerate until firm. Combine mayonnaise, lemon juice and onion. Fold shrimp and remaining pimento into mayonnaise mixture; chill. Unmold salad; spoon shrimp mixture into center. Yield: 12 servings.

BAKED STUFFED AVOCADO

1/2 sm. onion, finely chopped
1/2 green pepper, finely chopped
Lemon juice
1/4 tsp. salt
Dash of cayenne pepper
1/4 tsp. dry mustard
1/2 c. mayonnaise
1 7-oz. can crab meat, drained
1 hard-boiled egg, finely chopped
2 med. avocados
2 slices bread, trimmed
2 tbsp. melted butter

Combine onion, green pepper, 1 tablespoon lemon juice, salt, pepper, mustard and mayonnaise. Blend in crab meat and egg. Cut avocados in half; remove seeds. Arrange avocado halves, cut side up, in shallow baking dish. Brush cut sides of avocados with lemon juice. Mound crab meat mixture on avocado halves. Crumble bread into bowl. Add melted butter; toss to coat crumbs well. Sprinkle crumbs over top of crab meat mixture. Bake at 350 degrees for 12 to 14 minutes or until bread crumbs are brown. Garnish with parsley. Yield: 4 servings.

CREAMY AVOCADO MOLD

3 env. unflavored gelatin
2 c. pineapple juice
1/3 c. lemon juice
2 tsp. grated onion
2 1/2 tsp. seasoned salt
2 drops of hot sauce
3/4 c. salad dressing
2 avocados, mashed
1 c. sliced ripe olives
3/4 c. diced cucumber

Soften gelatin in 1 cup pineapple juice. Simmer, stirring, until gelatin is dissolved. Remove from heat; add remaining pineapple juice, lemon juice, onion, salt and hot sauce. Cool. Beat in salad dressing until well blended. Chill until thickened. Fold in avocados, olives and cucumber; pour into 6-cup mold. Chill until firm. Unmold. Garnish with whole ripe olives. Yield: 8 servings.

AVOCADO BREAD

2 c. sifted flour
1/2 tsp. soda
1 c. chopped pecans
1/4 tsp. salt
3/4 c. sugar
1/2 tsp. baking powder
2 tbsp. shortening
1 egg, slightly beaten
1/2 c. mashed avocado
1/2 c. buttermilk

Combine flour, soda, pecans, salt, sugar and baking powder in large bowl. Blend shortening, egg and avocado with buttermilk. Add to flour mixture; stir just to moisten. Pour into greased loaf pan. Bake at 350 degrees for 1 hour. Yield: 15-18 servings.

CREAMY LIME-AVOCADO ICE CREAM

2 ripe California avocados
1/4 c. lime juice
1/2 c. honey
1/2 pt. whipping cream, whipped

Peel and pit avocados; place in blender container. Add lime juice and honey. Mix with blender until smooth. Fold into whipped cream. Spoon into freezer tray. Freeze for about 4 hours or until firm. Yield: About 1 quart.

Creamy Lime-Avocado Ice Cream . . . Sweet and citric harmonize uniquely in this ice cream.

AVOCADO SHERBET

1 c. apricot nectar
3/4 c. sugar
1/2 c. lemon juice
1/4 tsp. salt
2 lge. avocados
2 egg whites

Combine apricot nectar, sugar, lemon juice and salt with 3/4 cup water in saucepan. Bring to a boil; reduce heat. Simmer for 5 minutes; cool. Peel avocados; press through sieve. Add to apricot syrup. Pour into refrigerator trays; freeze until mushy. Beat egg whites until stiff peaks form. Place frozen mixture in chilled bowl; beat. Fold in egg whites. Return to freezer trays; freeze for 3 hours or until firm. Yield: 6 servings.

AVOCADO-PINEAPPLE SHERBET

Sugar
1 c. sieved avocado
1/2 c. lemon juice
1 c. pineapple juice
2 egg whites

Mix 1 cup sugar with 1 cup water in a saucepan; bring to a boil. Stir until sugar is dissolved; cool. Add avocado and fruit juices; mix thoroughly. Place in refrigerator tray; freeze until mushy. Beat egg whites until stiff peaks form. Beat 4 tablespoons sugar into egg whites. Place frozen mixture in chilled bowl; beat. Fold egg whites into mixture. Return to freezer trays. Freeze until firm. Yield: 8 servings.

Bacon

Bacon is an American favorite for breakfast, sandwiches, and as a cooking ingredient. It is the economy cut from the flank or side of a hog that is cured. Bacon provides some protein, minerals, and B vitamins. (2 slices bacon = about 100 calories) Canadian bacon is meat similar to bacon but cooked like ham. It is from the eye of a pork loin.

BUYING: Available in packages of 16-22 slices per pound; thick-sliced, 12 slices per pound; or in slabs. Look for firm white fat alternating with strips of pinkish-red lean. Too much fat causes shrinkage during cooking; too much lean, toughness. The lean round slices of Canadian bacon are available in 1/8-, 1/4-, and 1/2- inch slices; in rolls; or in cans.

STORING: Both bacon and Canadian bacon keep safely in refrigerator one week in original wrapper or in foil. Do not freeze.

PREPARATION: *To fry,* place slices in cold skillet and cook over moderate heat. Pour off excess fat as it accumulates. Cook 6-8 minutes; drain and serve. *To broil,* place on rack in broiler pan 3-5 inches away from medium heat. Cook 2 minutes on each side; drain and serve. *To bake,* cook in shallow pan at 400 degrees for 10 minutes. Do not turn. Drain and serve. Broil Canadian bacon 1/4-inch thick, 6-8 minutes; 1/2-inch thick, 8-10 minutes.

BACON ROLLS

1/2 loaf bread, cubed
1 med. onion, chopped
1 egg, slightly beaten
Salt and pepper to taste
1/4 lb. margarine, melted
Parsley flakes to taste
Bacon slices
1 can tomato sauce

Combine bread, onion, egg, salt, pepper and margarine; add parsley flakes. Mix well; form into medium balls. Wrap each ball with slice of bacon; fasten with wooden picks. Fry bacon rolls in skillet until almost done; add tomato sauce. Serve hot in chafing dish. Yield: 4 servings.

BACON-CURRY DIP

1/2 lb. bacon
1 8-oz. carton sour cream
1/3 c. chopped peanuts
2 tbsp. milk
1/2 tsp. curry powder

Fry bacon in skillet until crisp; drain and crumble. Combine bacon, sour cream, peanuts, milk and curry powder. Serve bacon dip with crackers or potato chips. Yield: 1 1/2 cups.

CRUNCHY BACON CHIP DIP

1/2 c. softened cream cheese
2 tsp. catsup
1 tsp. prepared mustard
Dash of ground ginger
1/4 c. sour cream
1/2 c. chopped cooked bacon
Potato chips or crackers

Combine cream cheese, catsup, mustard, ginger, sour cream and bacon. Blend well. Serve with chips or crackers. Yield: About 1 cup.

BACON IN CRUMBS

1 tbsp. Worcestershire sauce
1 tbsp. mustard
1 egg yolk
4 bacon strips
Fine bread crumbs

Beat Worcestershire sauce and mustard into egg yolk. Dip bacon strips into egg mixture; coat well. Roll in crumbs. Place on rack in broiler pan. Bake at 300 degrees for 20 minutes. Yield: 4 servings.

MUSHROOM-BACON TOAST

Bacon slices
1 loaf fresh sandwich bread
1 can cream of mushroom soup
Melted butter

Fry bacon until crisp; drain and crumble. Trim crusts from bread; cut each slice in half. Spread bread with soup; sprinkle with bacon. Roll up as for jelly roll; secure with wooden picks. Brush each roll with melted butter. Place in baking pan. Bake at 450 degrees until lightly browned. Serve hot.

BRUNCH BACON AND EGGS

1 lb. bacon
1/4 c. butter
1/4 c. flour
1 c. cream
1 c. milk
1/4 tsp. thyme
1/4 tsp. marjoram
1/4 tsp. basil
1 lb. Cheddar cheese, grated
18 hard-cooked eggs, thinly sliced
1/4 c. chopped parsley
Buttered crumbs

Fry bacon in skillet; drain and crumble. Melt butter in saucepan; stir in flour until smooth. Add cream and milk gradually, stirring constantly. Cook, stirring, until thickened. Add seasonings and cheese, stirring until cheese is melted. Arrange layers of eggs, bacon and white sauce in greased casserole, sprinkling each layer with parsley. Sprinkle with crumbs. Bake at 350 degrees for about 30 minutes. May be refrigerated overnight before baking if desired. Yield: 6-8 servings.

SUNDAY BRUNCH SPECIAL

8 strips of bacon
4 slices pineapple, drained
1 egg
1/2 c. milk
Salt and pepper
4 slices bread

Fry bacon until crisp in skillet; remove and drain. Saute pineapple slices in bacon grease until browned; remove from skillet. Beat egg; add milk, salt and pepper. Dip bread slices into egg mixture. Brown on both sides in bacon grease. Arrange pineapple on bread; top with bacon slices. Yield: 4 servings.

OPEN-FACED SANDWICHES

1 lb. bacon
1 lb. Old English cheese
4 tomatoes
2 tbsp. Worcestershire sauce
4 tbsp. salad dressing
Hamburger buns, halved

Dice bacon; fry in skillet until partially done. Drain. Chop cheese into small cubes; chop and drain tomatoes. Combine bacon, cheese, tomatoes, Worcestershire sauce and dressing in bowl. Place buns on baking sheet. Spoon bacon mixture over each bun. Broil until cheese melts and bacon is done.

BACON POWWOW SANDWICHES

1/2 lb. bacon
2 1/2 oz. dried beef, shredded
3/4 c. chili sauce
1/3 c. sweet pickle relish
6 buns
Butter
6 slices American cheese

Fry bacon in skillet; drain and crumble. Combine bacon, dried beef, chili sauce and relish. Split buns; spread with butter. Spoon bacon mixture on half the buns; cover with cheese. Top with remaining buns. Wrap in foil; place on baking sheet. Bake at 325 degrees for 25 minutes. Yield: 6 servings.

HOT BACON AND TOMATO SANDWICHES

1 lb. sliced bacon
5 lge. tomatoes, sliced
8 slices bread, toasted
1 can Cheddar cheese soup

Fry bacon in skillet until crisp; drain well. Place tomatoes and bacon on toast slices. Heat soup; pour over sandwiches. Serve sandwiches immediately. Yield: 8 sandwiches.

STUFFED BACON SLICES

2 1/2 c. soft bread crumbs
1 egg, beaten
Salt and pepper to taste
1/4 c. minced celery
2 tbsp. minced onion
15 bacon slices

Combine all ingredients except bacon. Place 1 heaping teaspoon mixture on 1 end of each bacon slice. Roll bacon around dressing; fasten with small skewers. Fry in pan, turning to cook evenly on all sides and basting with drippings. Yield: 4-5 servings.

CANADIAN BACON-BROWN SUGAR TREAT

2 lb. unsliced Canadian bacon
5/8 c. brown sugar
1/2 tsp. dry mustard
Unsweetened pineapple juice
Pineapple slices
1 tbsp. butter

Place bacon on baking sheet. Combine 1/2 cup sugar, mustard and 1/2 cup pineapple juice; spread over bacon. Bake at 325 degrees for 1 hour, basting at 15 minute intervals. Simmer pineapple slices in butter, remaining brown sugar and 1 tablespoon pineapple juice until brown. Place bacon on serving platter; garnish with pineapple slices. Yield: 8 servings.

CANADIAN BACON WITH ORANGE SAUCE

1 12-in. roll Canadian bacon
1 c. (packed) brown sugar
1 1/2 c. orange juice
1 tsp. dry mustard

Place bacon in baking pan. Bake at 350 degrees for 20 minutes per pound. Combine brown sugar, orange juice and mustard in saucepan; cook, stirring constantly, until slightly thickened. Pour sauce over bacon; bake for 30 minutes longer.

CANADIAN BACON WITH PEANUT BUTTER GLAZE

3 lb. Canadian bacon
3 tbsp. vinegar
3 tbsp. sugar
1/2 c. peanut butter
1/2 c. brown sugar
Whole cloves
1 c. peach syrup

Place bacon in pan of cold water; bring to a boil. Stir vinegar and sugar into boiling water; simmer for 1 hour. Place bacon in baking pan; coat with peanut butter and brown sugar. Insert cloves into bacon. Pour syrup over bacon. Bake at 350 degrees for 1 hour, basting occasionally with pan drippings. Yield: 6 servings.

CANADIAN BACON-TOMATO BAKE

1 1/2 lb. unsliced Canadian bacon
2 c. canned green lima beans
3 ripe tomatoes, halved
Salt and pepper

Place bacon in baking pan or roaster. Bake at 350 degrees for 30 to 35 minutes. Arrange lima beans on 1 side of bacon. Sprinkle tomatoes with salt and pepper; place, cut sides up, on other side of bacon. Bake for 20 minutes longer. Yield: 6 servings.

FRUIT-GLAZED BACON ROAST

5 lb. unsliced Canadian bacon
1/2 c. pineapple juice
1/2 c. pickled peach juice
1/2 c. pear juice
Canned pineapple slices
Brown sugar
Canned pear halves
Pickled peaches

Place Canadian bacon on rack in roasting pan. Combine juices; pour over bacon. Bake at 350 degrees for 1 hour, basting frequently with juices in pan. Cut bacon into 1/2-inch slices; arrange on large platter. Sprinkle pineapple slices with brown sugar. Place under broiler; broil until golden brown. Heat pears and peaches. Arrange pineapple and pear halves around bacon. Top each pineapple slice with a peach. Garnish with parsley if desired. Yield: 8-10 servings.

Baked Alaska

A regal dessert made trom cake and ice cream covered with delicately browned meringue. It was once called Alaska-Florida because of its contrasting cold and hot ingredients.

BASIC PREPARATION: Baked Alaska is baked on a heavy wooden board. Cover board with heavy paper and place 1-inch thick cake in center. Put hard-frozen ice cream on cake, making sure cake extends 3/4 inch beyond ice cream. Cover with meringue. Meringue *must* seal ice cream completely to prevent its melting. Bake at 400 degrees until delicately brown, about 3-4 minutes, or place under broiler for about 3 minutes. Slip onto chilled platter and serve.

ELEGANT RAINBOW ALASKA

1 1 lb. 1-oz. package pound cake mix
1 pt. strawberry ice cream
1 pt. vanilla ice cream
1 1/2 pt. pistachio ice cream
5 egg whites
1/4 tsp. cream of tartar
1/2 tsp. vanilla
2/3 c. sugar
Flaked coconut

Prepare pound cake according to package directions in two 8-inch round cake pans; cool. Line deep 1 1/2-quart bowl with aluminum foil, allowing 1-inch border to extend over edge of bowl. Soften strawberry ice cream; spread in bottom of bowl. Return to freezer until firm. Soften vanilla ice cream; pack on top of strawberry layer. Return to freezer until firm. Top with softened pistachio ice cream. Cover with foil. Press to smooth top. Freeze until firm. Place 1 cake layer on cookie sheet; wrap remaining layer in foil and freeze for future use. Preheat oven to 500 degrees. Combine egg whites, cream of tartar and vanilla; beat until soft peaks form. Add sugar gradually, beating until stiff peaks form. Remove foil from top of ice cream, invert onto cake layer, using foil border to lift. Cover completely with meringue quickly. Sprinkle with coconut. Bake immediately for 3 minutes or until brown. Yield: 10 servings.

Elegant Rainbow Alaska . . . A version of a classic dessert that will highlight special dinners.

BAKED PINEAPPLE ALASKA

1 pineapple
1/4 tsp. salt
3 egg whites
6 tbsp. sugar
Vanilla ice cream

Preheat oven to 550 degrees. Cut pineapple and crown in half lengthwise. Scoop out pineapple meat, leaving 1-inch shell. Cut meat coarsely; refrigerate. Chill pineapple halves. Add salt to egg whites; beat until frothy. Add sugar gradually; beat until stiff peaks are formed. Fill pineapple halves with ice cream; top with chopped pineapple. Spread meringue on top, sealing edges. Bake for 3 minutes or until meringue is golden and peaks are brown.

CANTALOUPE BAKED ALASKA

1 med. cantaloupe, chilled
4 scoops vanilla ice milk
2 tsp. sherry
2 egg whites
1/4 tsp. cream of tartar
2 tbsp. nonfat dry milk
Sugar to taste

Preheat oven to 500 degrees. Peel and seed cantaloupe; cut into 4 slices. Place on aluminum foil on cookie sheet. Place scoop of ice milk on each section. Make depression in each scoop of ice milk; pour 1/2 teaspoon sherry into each depression. Beat egg whites with cream of tartar until stiff peaks are formed; beat in milk powder and sugar. Cover each cantaloupe slice completely with meringue. Bake for 5 minutes or until meringue is browned. Yield: 4 servings.

CRUNCHY ALASKA

2 qt. vanilla ice cream
1 c. chopped peanuts
4 egg whites
1/2 tsp. cream of tartar
1/2 c. sugar

Preheat oven to 450 degrees. Soften ice cream slightly; mound on ovenproof platter. Press peanuts lightly into ice cream mound. Freeze until firm. Beat egg whites until stiff, adding cream of tartar and sugar. Spread meringue over ice cream mound. Bake for 5 minutes or until meringue is lightly browned. Yield: 8 servings.

ELEGANT BAKED ALASKA

2 pt. coffee ice cream, softened
1 pt. strawberry ice cream, softened
1/2 c. shortening
1/2 c. brown sugar
4 egg yolks
1 c. sifted flour
1/8 tsp. salt
2 tsp. baking powder
1/3 c. milk
1/2 tsp. vanilla
1 c. chopped nuts

Line 8-cup mold or mixing bowl with aluminum foil, leaving 1-inch overhang. Spread coffee ice cream evenly over bottom and up side of mold, leaving hollow for strawberry ice cream; fill with strawberry ice cream. Smooth flat with table knife. Freeze until firm. Cream shortening with brown sugar until fluffy; beat in egg yolks, one at a time, beating until well blended. Sift in dry ingredients alternately with milk; stir in vanilla and nuts. Place in greased and floured 9-inch pan. Bake at 350 degrees for 30 minutes or until top springs back when touched; cool for 5 minutes. Remove from pan; cool on rack. Place on double thick piece of aluminum foil on cookie sheet. Loosen molded ice cream by lifting up overhanging tabs of foil; invert onto center of cake. Peel off foil; trim cake layer to within 1/4 inch of ice cream mold. Freeze.

Meringue

4 egg whites
1/2 tsp. cream of tartar
1/2 c. sugar

Beat egg whites with cream of tartar until soft peaks form. Add sugar, 1 tablespoon at a time; beat until stiff peaks form. Spread over ice cream and cake, swirling in peaks to cover completely. Bake at 475 degrees for 3 to 4 minutes; serve immediately. Yield: 12 servings.

FLAMING BAKED ALASKA

Ice cream
4 dessert sponge cake cups
3 egg whites
1/4 tsp. cream of tartar
6 tbsp. sugar
2 oz. brandy

Place dips of ice cream in dessert cups; cover. Place in freezer for several hours or overnight. Beat egg whites and cream of tartar until frothy; add sugar gradually, beating until stiff peaks form. Cover each dessert cup completely with meringue. Place on brown paper-covered, dampened board. Return to freezer. Bake at 500 degrees for 2 minutes or until golden brown. Place cups on individual serving platters. Warm brandy gently at table; flame and spoon over Alaskas. Yield: 4 servings.

GRAPEFRUIT BAKED ALASKA

3 lge. grapefruit
Sugar
1/8 tsp. salt
3 egg whites
1/2 tsp. vanilla
1 pt. vanilla ice cream

Halve grapefruit; remove cores. Cut around each section, loosening fruit from membrane. Sprinkle lightly with sugar; chill. Preheat oven to 500 degrees. Add salt to egg whites; beat until foamy. Add 6 tablespoons sugar, beating until stiff and glossy. Add vanilla. Place 1 heaping spoonful ice cream in center of each grapefruit half; cover with meringue, sealing well around edges. Bake for about 1 minute or until lightly browned; serve at once. Yield: 6 servings.

INDIVIDUAL BAKED ALASKAS

Ladyfingers
1 egg white, stiffly beaten
1 tsp. sugar
Vanilla to taste
Vanilla ice cream

Split ladyfingers; place around sides and bottoms of 4 individual custard cups. Combine egg white, sugar and vanilla; beat until blended. Scoop ice cream into cups; cover with meringue, sealing edges well. Place cups on foil-lined cookie sheet. Bake at 325 degrees for 5 to 8 minutes or until lightly browned. Yield: 4 servings.

INDIVIDUAL BROWNIE ALASKAS

12 brownies
Vanilla ice cream
3 egg whites
6 tbsp. sugar
Vanilla to taste

Place brownies on dampened, brown paper-lined board. Arrange slice of ice cream on each brownie. Place in freezer. Beat egg whites until frothy; add sugar and vanilla gradually, beating until stiff peaks form. Cover brownies and ice cream with meringue. Bake at 450 degrees for 4 or 5 minutes or until meringue is lightly browned. Yield: 12 servings.

TRADITIONAL BAKED ALASKA

Patty shells
Ice cream
2 egg whites
4 tbsp. sugar
1/4 tsp. vanilla

Preheat oven to 450 degrees. Place patty shells on foil-lined cookie sheet; fill with ice cream. Freeze until firm. Beat egg whites until frothy; beat in sugar gradually. Beat until stiff peaks form. Add vanilla. Spread meringue over patty shells, sealing edges well. Bake for 5 minutes or until meringue is lightly browned. Serve immediately.

Banana

Imported from Central and South America and the West Indies, this "fruit of paradise" is available in red and yellow varieties and as plantains, bananas used only for cooking. Much of the nutritional value of bananas lies in the carbohydrate content (primarily sugar). They contain Vitamins A and C and all the B-group vitamins. (1 banana = 85 calories)

BUYING: Look for a not-quite-yellow color that indicates they are not yet fully ripe. Avoid soft, mushy fruit with blackened areas or mold.

STORING: Leave bananas on the stalk until ready to use. Not-yet-ripened fruit comes to full flavor at room temperature. When ripened, bananas may be stored in the refrigerator where skins turn black but the flavor of the fruit is not affected.

PREPARATION: May be eaten raw or sliced for salads or desserts. May also be cooked. Underripe bananas may be baked, broiled, sauteed, or fried and will come to full flavor during cooking. 2-3 medium-sized bananas = 1 pound = 2 cups sliced or 1 1/2 cups mashed.

BANANA CREAM SALAD

1 8-oz. package cream cheese
2 tbsp. mayonnaise
2 tbsp. lemon juice
1 tsp. salt
1/2 c. crushed pineapple
1/4 c. chopped maraschino cherries
3 med. bananas, sliced
1/2 c. chopped walnuts
3/4 c. heavy cream, whipped

Soften cream cheese. Combine cream cheese, mayonnaise, lemon juice and salt; beat until fluffy. Add fruits and walnuts; fold in whipped cream. Turn into molds; chill for 3 hours.

BANANA-NUT SALAD

1 egg
1 c. sugar
2 tbsp. flour
1/4 c. vinegar
3/4 c. water
2 tbsp. butter
8 bananas
1 c. finely chopped nuts
Lettuce

Beat egg lightly in top of double boiler; stir in sugar and flour. Add vinegar and water; cook, stirring, until thickened. Stir in butter; cool. Peel bananas; dip into cooked dressing. Roll in nuts; arrange on lettuce-lined salad plates.

FROZEN BANANA SALAD

1 No. 2 1/2 can crushed pineapple
2 c. miniature marshmallows
4 bananas, sliced
1 c. sliced strawberries
1 c. diced peaches
1/2 c. mayonnaise
1/2 c. whipped cream

Combine pineapple and marshmallows in saucepan; stir over low heat until marshmallows are melted. Add bananas; cool slightly. Add strawberries and peaches; fold in mayonnaise and whipped cream. Pour into mold; cover. Freeze until firm. Yield: 8 servings.

BANANA HOLIDAY BREAD

1/3 c. shortening
2/3 c. sugar
2 eggs, slightly beaten
1 3/4 c. sifted flour
2 3/4 tsp. baking powder
1/2 tsp. salt
1 c. mashed ripe bananas
1/2 c. coarsely chopped nuts
1/4 c. raisins
1 c. chopped candied fruits

Cream shortening; add sugar gradually. Beat until light and sugar is dissolved. Add eggs; beat until thick and lemon-colored. Sift flour, baking powder and salt together; add to egg mixture. Fold in bananas; blend well. Stir in nuts, raisins and fruits. Place shallow pan of water in bottom of oven. Spoon batter into greased loaf pan. Bake at 350 degrees for 1 hour and 10 minutes or until bread tests done. Cool bread in pan for 20 minutes; turn out to cool completely. May be frosted with white icing if desired.

BANANA BREAD

1/2 c. shortening
1 c. sugar
2 eggs, well beaten
1 tsp. soda
2 c. flour
1/4 tsp. salt
3 lge. bananas, mashed
1 tsp. vanilla

Combine shortening, sugar and eggs; blend well. Dissolve soda in 3 tablespoons hot water; mix with sugar mixture. Add 1 cup flour and salt; beat well. Add bananas, remaining flour and vanilla; mix until smooth. Pour into loaf pan. Bake at 375 degrees for 45 minutes.

BANANA-MINCEMEAT BREAD

1/4 c. butter
1/2 c. sugar
2 eggs
1 1/4 c. sifted flour
1 c. whole wheat flour
1/4 tsp. baking powder
1/2 tsp. salt
1 tsp. soda
1 c. mashed bananas
1 c. mincemeat, drained

Cream butter and sugar. Add eggs; beat well. Combine dry ingredients; add to sugar mixture alternately with bananas and mincemeat. Pour into buttered loaf pan. Bake at 325 degrees for 1 hour to 1 hour and 10 minutes. Cool.

BANANA DROP COOKIES

2/3 c. shortening
1 1/2 c. sugar
2 eggs
1 c. ripe mashed bananas
1 tsp. vanilla
2 1/2 c. flour
2 tsp. baking powder
1/4 tsp. soda
3/4 tsp. salt
1 tsp. cinnamon

Cream shortening and 1 cup sugar; beat in eggs, bananas and vanilla. Sift flour, baking powder, soda and salt together; blend into banana mixture. Combine remaining sugar and cinnamon. Drop cookie dough from teaspoon onto greased baking sheet; sprinkle with cinnamon sugar. Bake at 350 degrees for 12 minutes or until browned. Yield: 4 dozen.

BANANA JUMBOS

1 c. soft shortening
1 c. sugar
2 eggs
1 c. mashed ripe bananas
1/2 c. sour cream
1 tsp. vanilla
3 c. flour
1 1/2 tsp. soda
1/2 tsp. salt
1 c. chopped nuts

Cream shortening; add sugar gradually. Add eggs; beat well. Stir in bananas, sour cream and vanilla. Blend flour, soda and salt together. Stir into sugar mixture; beat well. Fold in nuts; chill for 1 hour. Drop by tablespoonfuls 2 inches apart onto lightly greased baking sheet. Bake at 375 degrees for 10 minutes or until lightly browned. Cool. Frost with favorite icing. Yield: 2 dozen cookies.

BANANA CHIFFON CAKE

2 c. flour
1 1/2 c. sugar
3 tsp. baking powder
1 tsp. salt
1/2 c. salad oil
7 egg yolks
1 ripe banana, mashed
1 tsp. vanilla
1 c. egg whites
1/2 tsp. cream of tartar

Preheat oven to 325 degrees. Sift flour, sugar, baking powder and salt together into large bowl; make well in center. Add oil, egg yolks, 3/4 cup water, banana and vanilla; beat well. Combine egg whites and cream of tartar in large bowl; whip until stiff peaks form. Add egg yolk mixture gradually; fold gently until blended. Pour into ungreased 10-inch tube pan. Bake for 55 minutes. Increase oven temperature to 350 degrees. Bake for 10 to 15 minutes longer. Invert pan. Remove cake when cool.

BANANA CREAM CAKE

2 c. sifted flour
1 1/3 c. sugar
1 1/2 tsp. baking powder
1 tsp. soda
1 tsp. salt
1/2 tsp. nutmeg
1/2 c. shortening, softened
1 c. mashed ripe bananas
1/4 c. milk
1 tsp. vanilla
2 eggs
1/2 c. finely chopped walnuts

Sift dry ingredients over shortening. Add bananas, milk and vanilla; mix until dry ingredients are moistened. Beat vigorously for 2 minutes. Add eggs; beat for 2 minutes longer. Stir in walnuts. Pour into greased and floured 9 x 9 x 2-inch pan. Bake at 350 degrees for 35 to 40 minutes or until cake tests done.

Sour Cream Frosting

1 c. sour cream
1/3 c. brown sugar
1/4 c. broken walnuts

Combine sour cream and brown sugar; spread over warm cake in pan. Sprinkle with walnuts. Bake at 350 degrees for 5 minutes or until frosting is set. Cut into squares. Garnish with sliced bananas. Yield: 12 servings.

BANANA-SPICE LAYER CAKE

2 1/2 c. sifted cake flour
2 1/2 tsp. baking powder
1/2 tsp. soda
3/4 tsp. salt
1/8 tsp. cloves
1 1/4 tsp. cinnamon
1/2 tsp. nutmeg
1/2 c. shortening
1 1/4 c. sugar
2 eggs
1 tsp. vanilla
1 1/2 c. mashed ripe bananas

Sift flour, baking powder, soda, salt, cloves, cinnamon and nutmeg together. Cream shortening. Add sugar gradually; beat until light and fluffy. Add eggs, one at a time, beating well after each addition; stir in vanilla. Add flour mixture alternately with bananas; beat well after each addition. Turn into 2 well-greased 9-inch cake pans. Bake at 375 degrees for 25 minutes or until cake tests done.

Banana-Butter Frosting

1/2 c. mashed ripe banana
1/2 tsp. lemon juice
1/4 c. butter
3 1/2 c. sifted confectioners' sugar

Combine banana and lemon juice. Cream butter; add sugar and banana mixture alternately. Beat until light and fluffy; frost cake.

BANANA-HONEY CAKE

1 c. honey
1 tsp. soda
1 c. rolled oats
3/4 c. butter, softened
1/2 c. sugar
2 eggs, beaten
1 c. mashed bananas
3/4 tsp. salt
1 1/2 c. sifted all-purpose flour
3/4 tsp. baking powder
2 3-oz. packages cream cheese
2 1/2 c. sifted confectioners' sugar

Preheat oven to 350 degrees. Bring honey to a boil in medium saucepan; add 1/2 teaspoon soda. Pour hot honey mixture over oats; stir and cover. Let stand for 10 minutes. Beat butter until creamy; add sugar gradually, beating until fluffy. Blend in eggs. Add oats mixture and bananas; beat until blended. Sift salt, flour, baking powder and remaining soda together. Add to creamed mixture, mixing well. Pour batter into 2 greased and waxed paper-lined 8-inch round cake pans. Bake for 30 to 35 minutes. Cool on wire rack for about 10 minutes. Remove from pans; cool. Soften cream cheese; beat until fluffy. Add confectioners' sugar gradually, beating until frosting is of spreading consistency. Spread between layers and over top of cake; refrigerate. Garnish with banana slices just before serving.

Banana-Honey Cake . . . A sweet blend of bananas and honey, with a creamy frosting.

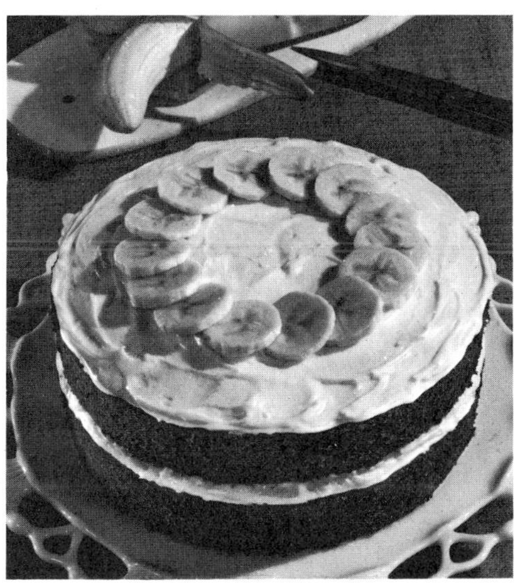

BANANA CUPCAKES

1/2 c. shortening
1 1/2 c. sugar
2 beaten eggs
2 c. flour
1/2 tsp. salt
1 tsp. baking powder
3/4 tsp. soda
1/4 c. sour milk
Mashed bananas
1 tsp. vanilla
1/3 c. butter
2 c. powdered sugar
1 tbsp. lemon juice

Cream shortening and sugar. Add eggs; beat well. Sift flour, salt, baking powder and soda together; add to creamed mixture alternately with sour milk, 1 cup bananas and vanilla. Fill greased cupcake pans half full. Bake at 375 degrees for 20 minutes. Cream butter and sugar; add 3 tablespoons bananas and lemon juice, mixing until smooth. Frost cupcakes. Yield: 2 1/2 dozen cupcakes.

BAKED BANANAS IN ORANGE JUICE

6 med. firm bananas
1 med. orange
2 tbsp. orange juice
2 tbsp. lemon juice
1/3 c. sugar
Dash of cinnamon
Dash of nutmeg

Preheat oven to 325 degrees. Peel bananas; peel and coarsely chop orange. Arrange bananas and orange in shallow baking dish. Combine juices, sugar, cinnamon and nutmeg; pour over fruit. Bake at 325 degrees for 25 to 30 minutes or until bananas are golden and tender. Serve hot. Yield: 6-8 servings.

BAKED BANANAS WITH VANILLA CREAM

6 green-tipped bananas
1 12-oz. jar apricot preserves
1/2 c. orange juice
1/4 c. golden rum
1/2 c. flaked coconut
1 pt. vanilla ice cream

Preheat oven to 375 degrees. Peel bananas; arrange in shallow baking dish. Heat preserves in small saucepan until melted. Remove from heat; stir in orange juice and rum. Pour over bananas; sprinkle with coconut. Bake, uncovered, for 20 minutes or until bananas are tender. Top bananas with ice cream. Yield: 6 servings.

BANANA-CRANBERRY PARFAIT

1 1-lb. can jellied cranberry sauce
3 tbsp. sugar
3 tbsp. orange juice
1 c. mashed ripe bananas
1 c. heavy cream, whipped

Mash cranberry sauce with fork. Dissolve sugar in orange juice; stir into cranberry sauce. Add bananas; mix well. Turn into freezer tray; freeze at coldest setting until partially frozen. Turn into chilled bowl; beat with rotary beater until smooth. Fold in whipped cream. Return to tray; freeze until firm. Yield: 4-6 servings.

FROZEN BANANA TREATS

6 sm. bananas
1 12-oz. package chocolate chips
1/2 c. crunchy peanut butter

Peel bananas; cut in half crosswise. Wrap bananas separately in plastic wrap; freeze until firm. Combine chocolate chips and peanut butter in top of double boiler; stir over hot water until chocolate chips are melted. Spread chocolate mixture on bananas; wrap in foil. Return to freezer.

BANANA DELIGHT

1 box strawberry gelatin
2 c. miniature marshmallows
3 lge. bananas, sliced
1 sm. can crushed pineapple, drained
1 c. whipped cream

Prepare gelatin according to package directions. Add marshmallows; stir constantly until dissolved. Chill until thickened. Fold in bananas, pineapple and whipped cream; chill until firm. Yield: 8-10 servings.

BANANA HAWAIIAN DELIGHT

1/2 pt. whipping cream
1 c. sour cream
2 tbsp. confectioners' sugar
6 firm bananas
1 8-oz. can flaked coconut

Whip cream until stiff; add sour cream and sugar. Whip until just blended. Cut bananas into 2-inch pieces. Dip into cream mixture; coat well. Roll in coconut; chill until ready to serve. Yield: 18 servings.

BANANA SPLIT DESSERT

7/8 c. butter
2 c. vanilla wafer crumbs
1 1/2 c. powdered sugar
2 eggs
1 c. whipping cream
1/4 c. sugar
2 tbsp. cocoa
1 banana, mashed
1 c. chopped nuts
1/4 c. sliced maraschino cherries

Melt 1/3 cup butter in saucepan. Mix crumbs with butter. Reserve 1/2 cup crumb mixture; spread remaining mixture in 9 x 13-inch pan. Freeze for 30 minutes. Cream remaining butter and powdered sugar. Add eggs, one at a time, beating well after each addition. Spread over wafer crust; return to freezer. Whip cream; add sugar and cocoa. Fold in banana, nuts and cherries; spread over egg mixture. Sprinkle with reserved crumbs; freeze for 12 to 24 hours before serving. Yield: 12 servings.

BANANA SCALLOPS

6 bananas
1 egg
1 tsp. salt
3/4 c. fine bread or corn flake crumbs

Peel bananas; cut crosswise into 3/4-inch thick pieces. Beat egg; add salt. Dip banana pieces in egg; drain. Roll in bread crumbs. Fry in hot fat for 2 minutes or until brown and tender. Yield: 6 servings.

FRIED BANANAS

6 ripe bananas
1 egg
3/4 c. milk
1/2 c. flour
1 tbsp. sugar
1/2 tsp. salt
Dry bread crumbs
Lemon juice

Peel and slice bananas in half lengthwise. Combine egg, milk, flour, sugar and salt. Dip banana halves into batter; roll in bread crumbs. Fry in shallow fat until golden brown; drain on absorbent paper. Sprinkle with lemon juice. Yield: 6-8 servings.

FRUIT KABOBS

1 c. grapefruit juice
1/2 c. honey
2 tbsp. kirsch
1 tsp. finely chopped fresh mint
6 canned peach halves
4 bananas
2 apples
1 fresh pineapple
2 grapefruit

Combine grapefruit juice, honey, kirsch and mint. Drain peach halves; cut in half. Peel bananas; cut in 2-inch pieces. Cut apples in wedges. Peel and dice pineapple. Section grapefruit. Combine fruits in shallow container; pour grapefruit juice marinade over fruits. Let stand at room temperature for 1 hour. Thread fruits on skewers. Broil for 5 minutes, brushing frequently with marinade. Yield: 6 servings.

OLD-FASHIONED BANANA PUDDING

1/3 c. cornstarch
1/2 tsp. salt
3/4 c. sugar
4 c. milk
1/4 c. butter
1 tsp. vanilla
3 doz. vanilla wafers
4 to 5 bananas, sliced

Combine cornstarch, salt and sugar with 1 cup milk. Scald remaining milk; add to cornstarch mixture. Stir over medium heat until thickened. Reduce heat; simmer for 10 minutes, stirring occasionally. Remove from heat; add butter and vanilla. Cool. Alternate layers of vanilla wafers, bananas and pudding in large shallow dish. Chill. May be topped with whipped cream. Yield: 6 servings.

JIFFY BANANA PUDDING

1 box vanilla pudding mix
48 vanilla wafers
6 bananas, sliced
2 egg whites
1/4 c. sugar
1 tsp. vanilla

Prepare pudding mix according to package directions. Arrange layer of whole wafers in baking dish; crumble remaining wafers. Layer bananas, pudding and crumbled wafers in baking dish until all are used. Beat egg whites until foamy. Add sugar and vanilla, beating until stiff peaks form. Spread meringue over pudding. Bake at 425 degrees until meringue is lightly browned. Yield: 6 servings.

HERBED PORK ROAST
Recipe On Page 694.

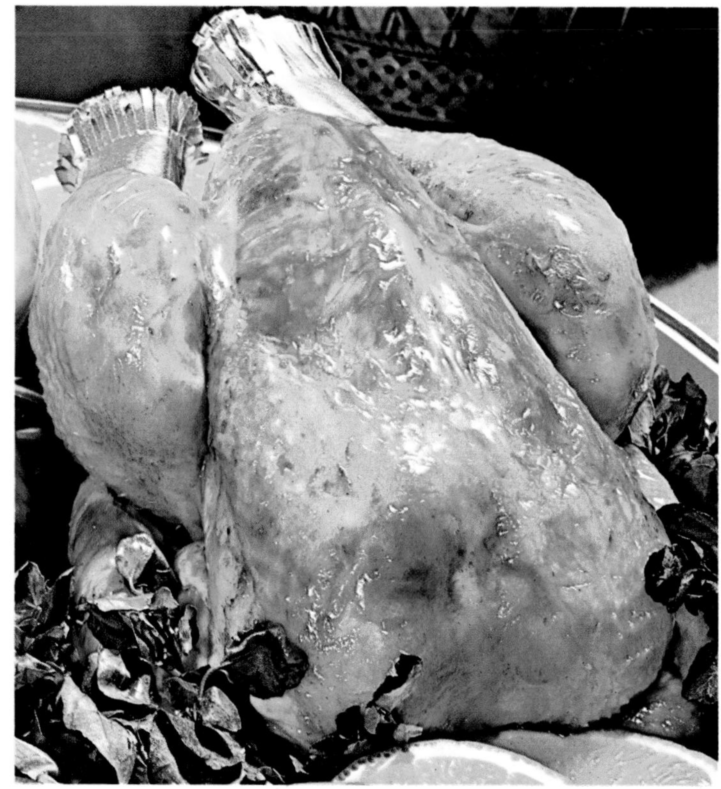

SCALLOP SHRIMP KABOBS
Recipe For This Photograph
On Page 809.

CHICKEN L'ORANGE
Recipe For This Photograph
On Page 245.

BEEF-STUFFED GREEN PEPPERS
Recipe For This Photograph On Page 662.

SUKIYAKI
Recipe For This Photograph On Page 119.

CALIFORNIA-STYLE LAMB CHOPS
Recipe For This Photograph On Page 516.

STUFFED PORK CHOPS
Recipe For This Photograph on Page 688.

GROUSTARK VENISON
Recipe For This Photograph on Page 421.

HERB AND WINE-MARINATED STEAK
Recipe For This Photograph On Page 116.

COD ROE PATTIES WITH SHRIMP SAUCE
Recipe For This Photograph On Page 288.

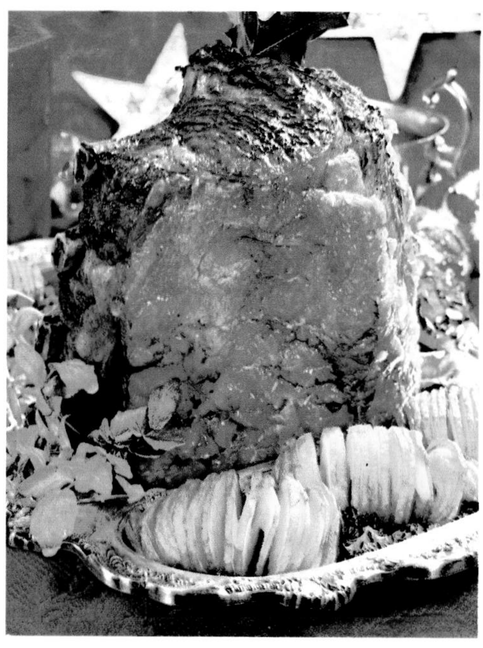

CHRISTMAS DAY ROAST OF BEEF
Recipe For This Photograph On Page 108.

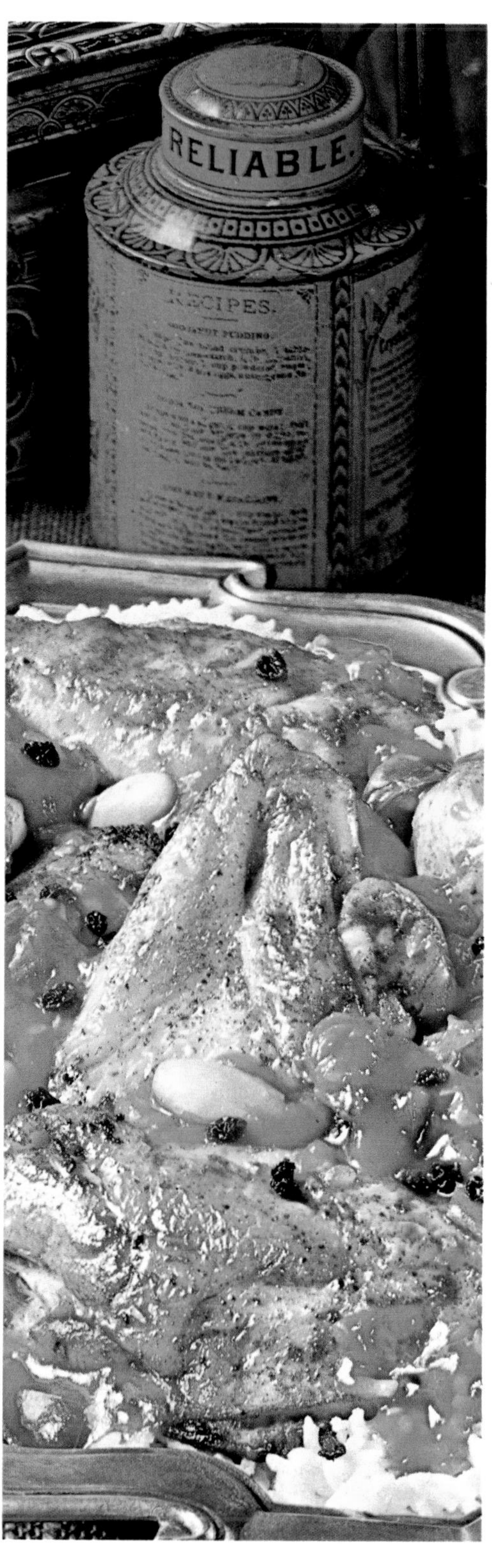

COUNTRY CAPTAIN
Recipe For This Photograph On Page 255.

GRILLED BURGERS
Recipe For This Photograph On Page 453.

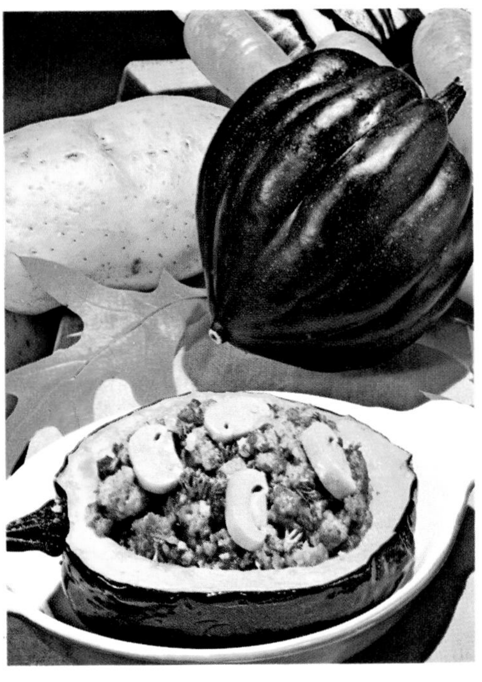

GROUND BEEF-FILLED SQUASH
Recipe For This Photograph On Page 844.

GLAZED HAM
Recipe For This Photograph On Page 475.

MACARONI WITH FRANKFURTER SAUCE
Recipe For This Photograph On Page 552.

MUSHROOMS AND EGGS IN CHEESE SAUCE
Recipe For This Photograph On Page 589.

ROCK LOBSTER APPETIZERS
Recipe For This Photograph On Page 539.

SHISH KABOB WITH RICE PILAF
Recipe For This Photograph On Page 518.

PRESIDENT'S BARBECUED CHICKEN
Recipe For This Photograph On Page 245.

BRAVO CORNED BEEF AND CORN BREAD
Recipe For This Photograph On Page 103.

BEST BARBECUED TURKEY
Recipe For This Photograph On Page 899.

MAIN DISH NOODLE PUDDING
Recipe For This Photograph On Page 595.

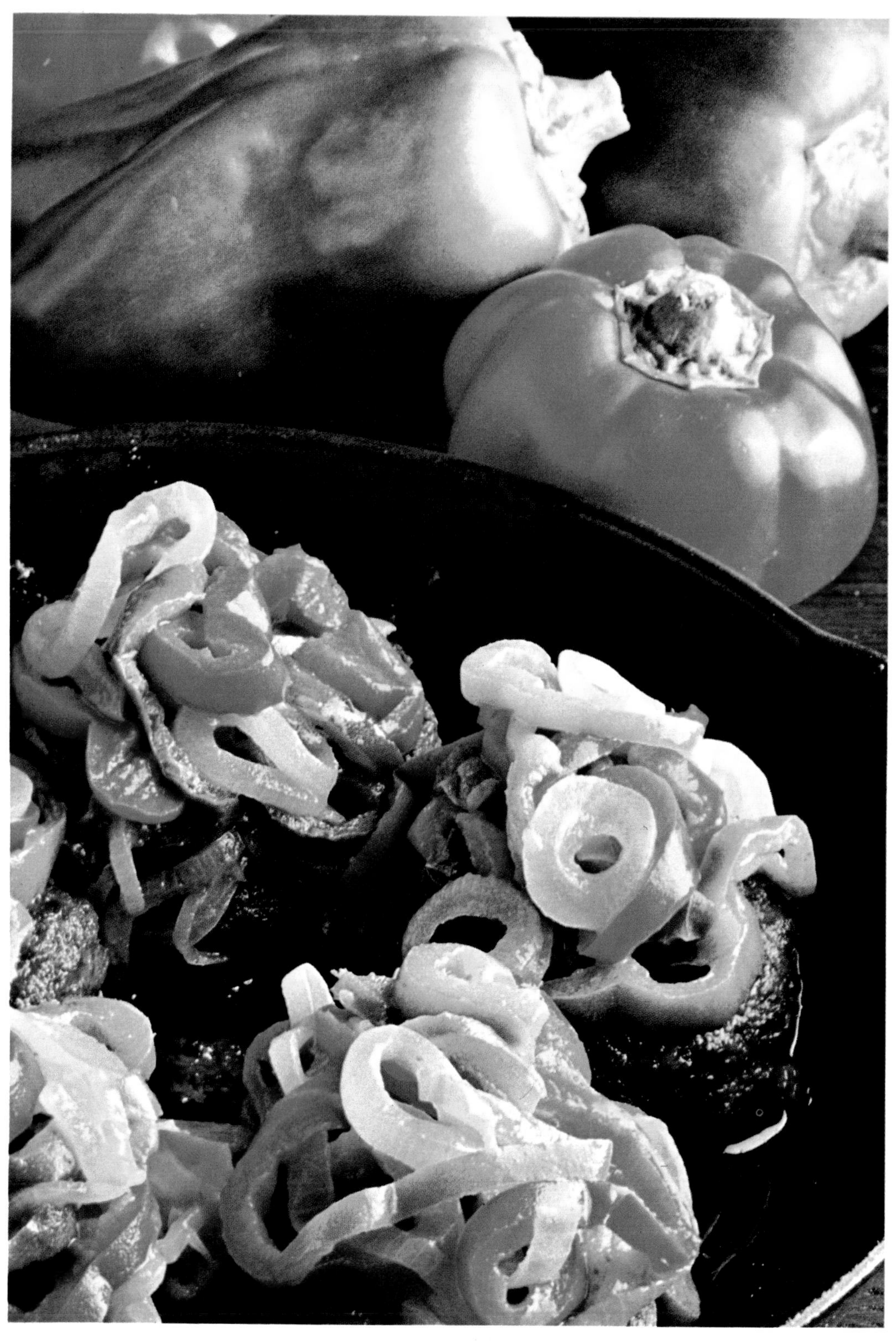

PEPPERED HAMBURGERS
Recipe For This Photograph On Page 453.

GRILLED CHICKEN WITH SPICED SAUCE
Recipe For This Photograph On Page 246.

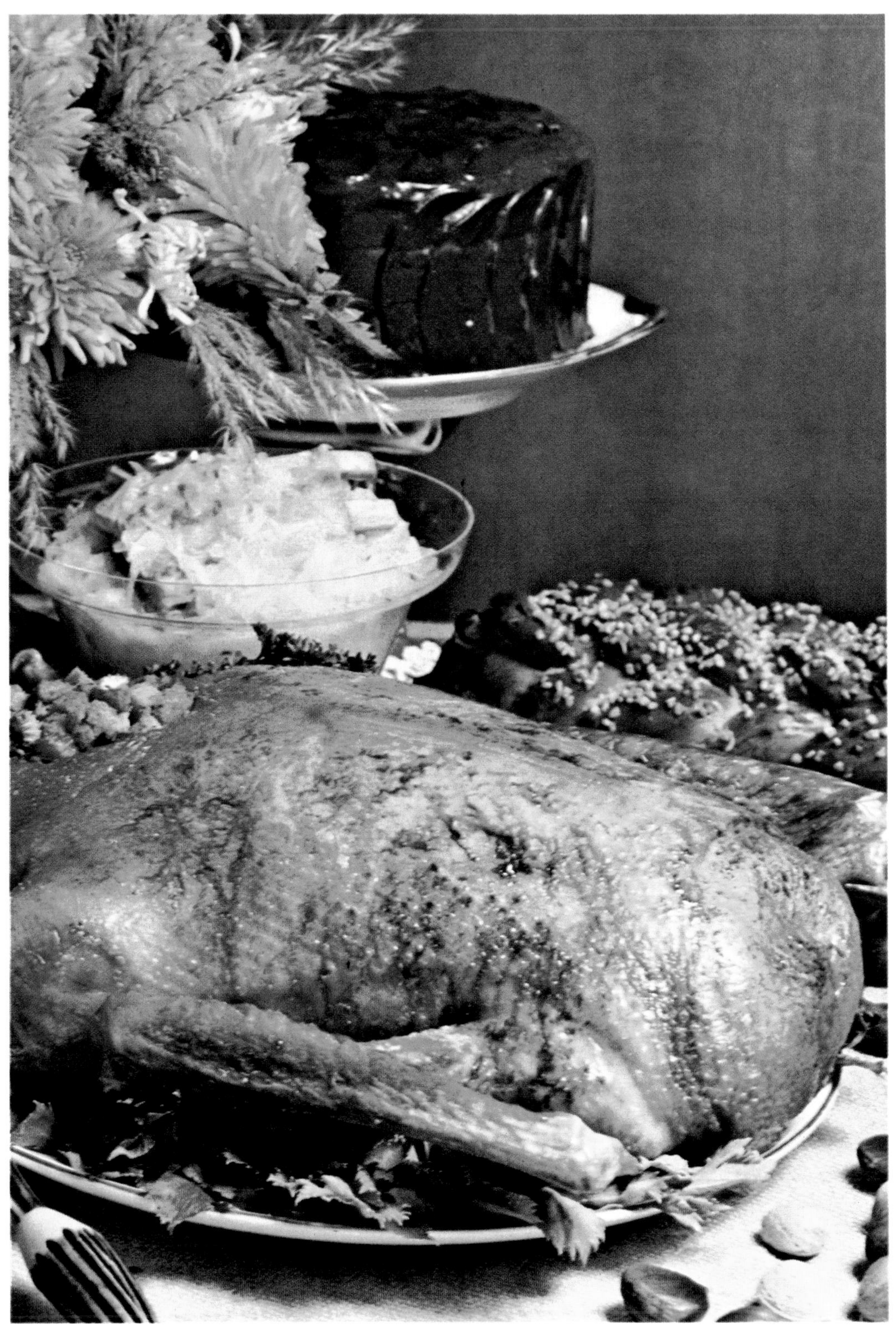

BAKED GOOSE
Recipe For This Photograph On Page 427.

VEAL CUTLET CORDON BLEU
Recipe For This Photograph On Page 906.

LAMB CHOP AND TOMATO BROIL
Recipe For This Photograph On Page 515.

STRIPED BASS A LA FEREZANA
Recipe For This Photograph On Page 84.

HUSBAND-PLEASER BANANA PUDDING

Sugar
1/3 c. flour
1 14-oz. can evaporated milk
3 eggs, separated
Dash of salt
2 tsp. vanilla
1/2 lb. vanilla wafers
4 bananas, sliced

Combine 1 cup sugar and flour in top of double boiler; blend in milk, a small amount at a time. Add 1 2/3 cups water; cook, stirring, to a boil. Beat egg yolks lightly; beat small amount of hot mixture into egg yolks. Add egg yolks to remaining hot mixture, stirring constantly. Add salt and 1 teaspoon vanilla; remove from heat. Cool custard for about 10 minutes. Layer half the wafers, half the bananas and half the custard in baking dish; repeat layers. Beat egg whites until foamy. Add 2 tablespoons sugar and remaining vanilla, beating until meringue is stiff and glossy. Spread meringue over pudding. Bake at 350 degrees until meringue is lightly browned. Yield: 6 servings.

BANANA-NUT PUDDING

1 c. sugar
2/3 c. flour
1 qt. milk
4 eggs, slightly beaten
2 tbsp. butter
1 tsp. vanilla
6 bananas, sliced
1 c. chopped dry roasted peanuts
Sweetened whipped cream (opt.)

Blend sugar with flour in heavy 2-quart saucepan. Add milk gradually; cook over medium heat until mixture thickens and comes to a boil, stirring constantly. Stir about 1/4 of the mixture into eggs; return egg mixture to pan. Cook over medium heat for 2 minutes longer, stirring constantly. Remove from heat. Add butter and vanilla; stir until butter is melted. Cover; let cool. Spoon half the pudding in 2-quart serving dish; arrange bananas over pudding. Sprinkle with half the peanuts. Top with remaining pudding; sprinkle with remaining peanuts. Garnish with whipped cream. Yield: 2 quarts.

BANANA-COCONUT CREAM PIE

Sugar
5 tbsp. flour
Salt
2 c. milk
3 egg yolks, beaten slightly
1 c. flaked coconut
2 1/4 tsp. vanilla
3 bananas
1 baked 9-in. pie shell
2 egg whites

Combine 4 tablespoons sugar, flour and 1/4 teaspoon salt in top of double boiler. Add milk and egg yolks; mix thoroughly. Cook over boiling water for 10 minutes, stirring constantly. Remove from heat. Add half the coconut and 1 1/4 teaspoons vanilla; cool. Slice 1 banana into pie shell; fill with coconut mixture. Slice 1 banana over filling. Beat egg whites in large bowl until frothy. Add 1/2 cup sugar gradually; beat until stiff peaks form. Add remaining vanilla and dash of salt. Pile meringue over filling; seal edges. Slice remaining banana in a circle over meringue; sprinkle with remaining coconut. Bake at 450 degrees until lightly browned. Yield: 6-8 servings.

SHRIMP STROGANOFF
Recipe For This Photograph
On Page 823.

ELEGANT BANANA PIE

1 env. unflavored gelatin
1/2 c. sugar
1/4 tsp. cinnamon
1 tsp. instant coffee powder
Dash of salt
3 eggs, separated
1 1/3 c. evaporated milk
1 tsp. vanilla
1 9-in. baked pastry shell
2 bananas, sliced
Whipped cream

Soften gelatin in 1/4 cup cold water. Combine sugar, cinnamon, coffee powder and salt in top of double boiler; add egg yolks and evaporated milk. Mix well. Cook, stirring constantly, until mixture coats spoon; remove from heat. Stir in gelatin and vanilla; refrigerate until partially set. Beat egg whites until stiff peaks form; fold into gelatin mixture. Spoon half the gelatin mixture into pastry shell; arrange bananas on top. Cover with remaining gelatin mixture. Refrigerate pie for several hours. Serve with whipped cream.

SUMMERTIME BANANA PIE

1 1/4 c. vanilla wafer crumbs
1/2 c. finely chopped walnuts
5 tbsp. butter, melted
1 c. milk
1 pkg. vanilla instant pudding mix
1 c. sour cream
2 bananas, sliced

Combine wafer crumbs, walnuts and butter; press crumb mixture firmly against bottom and side of 9-inch pie plate. Combine milk and pudding mix; beat for about 5 minutes with rotary beater. Fold sour cream into pudding. Arrange bananas in crumb crust; pour pudding over bananas. Chill for several hours before serving. Yield: 6-8 servings.

BANANA-RUM TORTE

Color photograph for this recipe on page 483.

3 lge. bananas
1 tbsp. lime juice
3 tbsp. dark rum
1 1/2 c. whipping cream
3 tbsp. sugar
1/2 tsp. instant coffee
2 baked 9-in. rum cake layers
8 Pepperidge Farm Pirouettes

Peel bananas; slice about 1/4 inch thick. Combine lime juice and 1 tablespoon rum; pour over banana slices. Beat whipping cream with sugar and coffee until soft peaks form. Beat in remaining rum; beat until stiff peaks form. Place cake layers together with half the cream and half the drained banana slices. Top with remaining cream; refrigerate for 30 minutes to 1 hour to mellow. Drain remaining banana slices; arrange on top. Place Pirouettes spoke-fashion on cream. One and 1/2 teaspoons rum extract may be substituted for rum.

BANANA CREAM TORTE

6 egg whites
1/2 tsp. cream of tartar
2 1/4 c. sugar
1 pt. heavy cream
1/2 tsp. vanilla
3 bananas

Beat egg whites and cream of tartar until frothy; add 1 3/4 cups sugar gradually; beat until stiff and glossy. Spread meringue in 2 waxed paper-lined 9-inch layer pans. Bake at 250 degrees for 1 hour. Turn oven off and allow meringues to cool in oven. Remove paper. Whip cream; add remaining sugar gradually. Stir in vanilla. Slice bananas and place on meringue. Top with remaining meringue and frost top and side with whipped cream. Refrigerate for several hours.

BANANA-NUT TORTE

1 c. graham cracker crumbs
1/2 c. shredded coconut
1/2 c. chopped pecans
4 egg whites
1 c. sugar
1/4 tsp. salt
1 tsp. vanilla
1 banana, sliced
Whipped cream
Slivered almonds
Maraschino cherries

Combine crumbs, coconut and pecans. Beat egg whites until soft peaks form. Add sugar gradually; beat until stiff peaks form. Add salt and vanilla. Fold in crumb mixture. Spread into greased and floured 9-inch cake pan. Bake for 30 minutes in 350-degree oven. Cool. Cover with banana slices. Frost with whipped cream; sprinkle with almonds and cherries.

Barley

BARLEY CASSEROLE

1 stick butter
3/4 c. barley
2 c. chicken broth
1 4-oz. can sliced mushrooms, drained
1 sm. onion, chopped
1/2 c. slivered almonds
1 sm. can minced pimento

Melt butter in heavy skillet; add barley, stirring constantly until golden brown. Add chicken broth, mushrooms and onion; bring to a boil. Pour into 1 1/2-quart casserole; cover. Bake at 350 degrees for 1 hour, stirring occasionally. Add almonds and pimento. Bake, uncovered, for 15 minutes longer Yield: 6 servings.

BARLEY SOUP

3/4 c. pearl barley
1 2-lb. beef soupbone
1/2 c. diced celery
1 c. diced carrots
1 c. diced potatoes
Salt to taste

Simmer barley in 2 cups water until tender. Cook soupbone in water to cover until meat leaves bone; remove from stock. Combine celery, carrots and potatoes in 1 quart beef stock; cook until tender. Cut beef into bite-sized pieces; add to celery mixture. Add barley and salt. Simmer for several minutes longer. Yield: 6 servings.

Bass

This popular game fish includes both sea and freshwater varieties. Both may be caught by sports fishermen or can be bought in supermarkets.

BUYING: *Sea bass* are available whole, drawn, dressed, in fillets, or in steaks. *Striped bass* are a kind of sea bass available whole or dressed but seldom in fillets or steaks. *Freshwater bass* include the small-mouthed, large-mouthed (black crappie), rock, and spotted bass. In buying bass, choose fish with bright, clear eyes, reddish-pink gills free from slime or odor, and firm, elastic flesh that springs back from a light touch. Allow 1 pound fresh whole or drawn fish per person or 1/3 pound fresh or frozen steak or fillets.

STORING: If feasible, bass should be cooked immediately. If it cannot be cooked, pack it in ice or store in the coldest part of the refrigerator overnight. Fish bought frozen may be kept that way until ready for use.

PREPARATION: Sea bass can be baked, broiled, boiled, steamed, sauteed, or fried; freshwater bass can be baked, broiled, fried, steamed, or sauteed. *Do not overcook.* Bass is done when the flesh turns cream color and flakes easily from the bone.

SERVING: Garnish with brightly colored foods–radishes, paprika, lemon wedges, pickles, watercress, or crisp, raw vegetables.

(See SEAFOOD.)

BAKED BASS

1 3 to 4 lb. bass
Salt
1 tbsp. lemon juice
1 1/2 c. bread cubes
1/4 tsp. pepper
1/2 tsp. thyme
1 tsp. monosodium glutamate
Melted butter
1 egg, slightly beaten
1/2 c. finely chopped onion

Rub dressed bass inside and outside with 1 teaspoon salt and lemon juice. Mix bread cubes, 1/2 teaspoon salt, pepper, thyme, monosodium glutamate, 3 tablespoons melted butter, egg and onion; stuff bass cavity. Fasten with skewers. Place in baking pan; brush with melted butter. Bake at 450 degrees for 15 minutes. Reduce oven temperature to 400 degrees; bake for 45 minutes longer. Garnish with parsley and lemon wedges. Yield: 6 servings.

BADISCHER BASS

4 bass fillets
Salt to taste
Lemon juice
1/3 c. sour cream
3 tbsp. grated horseradish
4 tbsp. grated cheese
Pepper to taste
Bread crumbs

Sprinkle fillets with salt and lemon juice; refrigerate for several hours. Drain. Place in buttered baking dish; sprinkle with additional lemon juice. Combine sour cream, horseradish, cheese and pepper; spread over bass. Sprinkle with bread crumbs. Bake at 350 degrees for 30 to 40 minutes. Yield: 4 servings.

BAKED BASS WITH CURRIED SAUCE

2 lb. bass fillets
1/2 c. mayonnaise
1/8 c. sour cream
4 tbsp. lemon juice
Salt to taste
Curry powder to taste
1 sm. jar mushrooms, drained
Butter
Green grapes

Place fillets in buttered casserole. Combine mayonnaise, sour cream, lemon juice, salt and curry powder; mix well. Saute mushrooms in small amount of butter; fold into mixture. Spread sauce over fillets; arrange grapes on top. Bake at 350 degrees for 20 minutes. Yield: 4 servings.

BAKED SEA BASS

2 tbsp. butter
2 lb. sea bass fillets
1 lge. sweet onion, sliced
2 or 3 ripe tomatoes, sliced
Salt and pepper
1/2 c. dry white wine
1 can cream of mushroom soup
Grated cheese

Preheat oven to 400 degrees. Add butter to shallow baking dish; place in oven to melt. Arrange bass in dish; cover with onion and tomatoes. Season with salt and pepper; add wine. Bake for 10 minutes. Drain off juices and reserve. Dilute mushroom soup with reserved juices. Cover with soup mixture; sprinkle cheese over top. Return to oven; bake for 20 minutes longer. Yield: 6 servings.

BAKED STUFFED BASS

2 slices bacon
2-lb. bass
Salad oil
1/4 tsp. pepper
1 tsp. salt
Flour
1 onion, chopped
1 c. dry bread crumbs
1 hard-cooked egg, diced
1 tbsp. butter
1 tsp. parsley, chopped
1/4 tsp. thyme
1 tsp. Worcestershire sauce
3 tbsp. chicken broth

Fry bacon until crisp; remove from pan. Rub bass on outside with oil, pepper, salt and flour. Saute onion in 2 tablespoons bacon fat in frying pan. Crumble bacon. Combine remaining ingredients and bacon; stir until moistened. Place dressing inside fish; close with skewers. Place fish in baking pan with small amount of water. Bake at 400 degrees for 30 minutes. Yield: 3-4 servings.

BARBECUED BASS

1 4-lb. bass
2 tbsp. salad oil
2 tbsp. vinegar
1/2 c. catsup
1/4 c. water
1/2 c. onion, finely diced
1 clove of garlic, minced
2 tsp. Worcestershire sauce
2 drops of hot sauce
1 tsp. salt
1/4 tsp. pepper
1/4 tsp. dry mustard
1/2 tsp. chili powder
1 6-oz. can broiled in butter mushrooms

Place bass on double sheet of heavy-duty foil; bring foil up around fish. Combine remaining ingredients; heat. Pour hot sauce over fish. Fold foil securely. Place on grill 4 inches above coals. Cook for 25 to 30 minutes or until fish flakes easily.

BEST BASS

6 bass fillets
1 c. milk
Salt and pepper to taste
Flour
1/2 c. lemon juice
Several drops of hot sauce
1/2 c. cooking oil
1 c. finely ground nuts

Soak fish in milk for at least 3 hours; remove. Sprinkle with salt and pepper; roll in flour. Drizzle lemon juice and hot sauce over fillets. Fry fish in hot cooking oil to a light brown. Sprinkle with nuts; serve. Yield: 6 servings.

BISHOP'S BASS

1 3 to 4-lb. sea bass
Salt and pepper to taste
2 c. toasted bread crumbs
1/2 c. chopped onion
1/2 c. chopped celery
1/4 c. melted butter
1/2 tsp. marjoram
1/2 c. raisins
3 strips bacon

Bone sea bass for stuffing; sprinkle cavity with salt and pepper. Combine crumbs, onion, celery, butter, marjoram and raisins; stuff sea bass. Secure edges. Place sea bass in greased baking pan; top with bacon. Bake at 375 degrees for 14 minutes per pound, basting with drippings. Remove to platter; keep warm.

Sauce

3 tbsp. shaved blanched almonds
1/4 c. butter or margarine
2 tbsp. lemon juice
2 tbsp. minced parsley

Brown almonds in butter; add lemon juice and parsley. Heat. Serve over fish; garnish with lime slices and parsley sprigs.

BROILED FRESHWATER BASS

4 freshwater bass
Paprika to taste
Salt and pepper to taste
4 tbsp. butter

Cut bass to make 8 fillets. Place in broiler pan, skin side up. Brown under broiler; turn fillets. Sprinkle with paprika, salt and pepper. Dot with butter. Cover bottom of pan with small amount of water. Continue broiling until fish flake easily.

Bass with Peppered Stuffing . . . The mild flavor of bass is complemented with a zesty stuffing.

BASS WITH PEPPERED STUFFING

1 5-lb. striped bass, dressed
Salt and pepper to taste
Butter
1/2 8-oz. package herb-seasoned stuffing mix
1/2 tsp. hot sauce
2 tbsp. chopped onion
3/4 c. diced celery with leaves
1 tbsp. chopped parsley
4 1/2 tsp. lime juice

Remove backbone from bass; sprinkle cut surfaces with salt and pepper. Melt half the butter called for in stuffing mix package directions in saucepan. Add 1/4 teaspoon hot sauce, onion, celery and 1 tablespoon parsley. Saute until onion is tender. Add half the liquid called for in stuffing mix package directions. Bring to a boil; stir into stuffing mix, blending well. Stuff bass with stuffing, place on baking sheet. Bake at 500 degrees for 10 minutes. Reduce oven temperature to 400 degrees. Bake for about 30 minutes longer or until bass flakes easily. Melt 4 tablespoons butter in saucepan; stir in lime juice, remaining hot sauce and parsley. Serve sauce with bass. May garnish bass with boiled potatoes and parsley sprigs if desired.

BROILED BASS WITH SAUCE

1/4 c. chopped onion
2 tbsp. chopped green pepper
2 tbsp. melted margarine
1 8-oz. can tomato sauce
1/4 c. lemon juice
1/4 c. dark corn syrup
1 tbsp. Worcestershire sauce
1 tsp. salt
1/4 tsp. garlic powder
1 tsp. pepper
2 lb. bass fillets

Saute onion and green pepper in margarine until tender. Stir in tomato sauce, lemon juice, corn syrup, Worcestershire sauce, salt, garlic powder and pepper; simmer for 5 minutes. Place fillets in shallow pan; pour sauce over fillets. Refrigerate for 30 minutes, turning once. Remove fish from marinade; place in baking pan. Broil 6 inches from heat for 8 to 10 minutes or until fish flakes easily with fork, basting occasionally with marinade. Yield: 6 servings.

DEEP-FRIED BASS

Shortening
1 c. cornmeal
1 c. flour
4 tbsp. salt
1 3 to 5-lb. bass, dressed

Place 3 to 4 inches shortening in deep fat fryer. Heat to 350 to 375 degrees. Combine cornmeal, flour and salt in paper sack. Cut fish in serving pieces. Place fish, several pieces at a time, in sack; shake until well coated. Shake off loose cornmeal. Place fish in heated shortening; do not crowd. Cook for 5 to 10 minutes or until brown. Remove with tongs; drain on paper towel. Serve hot with hush puppies, if desired. Yield: 6-8 servings.

POACHED BASS

1 bass
1/2 c. white vinegar
Salt
1 lge. onion, sliced
3 or 4 whole allspice
2 bay leaves
3/4 c. melted butter
Juice of 1 lemon

Place dressed fish in saucepan; cover with water. Add vinegar, 1 teaspoon salt, onion, allspice and bay leaves. Simmer for 20 to 30 minutes. Bring to a boil; cook for 5 to 8 minutes longer. Remove fish to platter; skin, bone and cut into serving pieces. Combine butter, lemon juice and salt to taste; pour over fish. Garnish with parsley.

SOUTHERN PAN-FRIED BASS

1 2 to 3-lb. bass
1 c. shortening
2 tbsp. salt
1/2 c. cornmeal

Cut fish into serving pieces. Heat shortening in frypan over medium heat. Mix salt and cornmeal; roll fish in cornmeal mixture. Place fish in frypan; fry for 3 minutes or until browned. Yield: 4 servings.

STRIPED BASS A LA FEREZANA

Color photograph for this recipe on page 79.

1/4 c. pine nuts
Butter
1/2 c. thinly sliced white leeks
1/4 lb. mushrooms, coarsely chopped
2 med. carrots, finely grated
1/2 c. raisins
1/2 chopped green pepper
1 c. chopped cooked shrimp
1/2 c. small whole pimento-stuffed olives
Salt and pepper
1 4-lb. striped bass, cleaned
3 tbsp. olive oil
1/2 c. brandy

Saute pine nuts in 1/4 cup butter in saucepan until lightly browned. Remove with slotted spoon; set aside. Saute leeks and mushrooms in same pan until tender but not browned. Add carrots, raisins and green pepper; cover. Cook over low heat for 5 minutes. Stir in shrimp and olives; season to taste with salt and pepper. Set aside. Place bass in large shallow roasting pan. Pour 3 tablespoons melted butter, oil and 1/4 cup brandy over bass; sprinkle with salt and pepper. Bake in 400-degree oven for 15 minutes. Arrange olive mixture next to bass; sprinkle with pine nuts. Heat remaining brandy; ignite and pour over olive mixture. Bake for 15 to 20 minutes longer or until fish flakes easily, basting occasionally. Serve with parsley potatoes. Yield: 4-6 servings.

Bavarian Cream

An egg custard recipe to which gelatin is added is the basis of Bavarian Cream. Gelatin is added to hold its shape. Whipped heavy cream and various flavors and/or extracts (fruit juices, liqueurs, chocolate, rum) are added to create the characteristic fluffy texture and delicate flavor. Thorough mixing of ingredients is essential in order to prevent a hardened or stiff product.

APRICOT BAVARIAN CREAM

1/2 c. sugar
1 env. unflavored gelatin
Pinch of salt
1 12-oz. can apricot nectar
3 tbsp. lemon juice
1 unbeaten egg white
1/2 c. heavy cream

Combine sugar, gelatin, salt and apricot nectar in top of double boiler. Heat, stirring, until gelatin is dissolved. Pour into small mixing bowl; add lemon juice. Cool to room temperature. Stir in egg white. Chill until partially set. Whip until soft peaks form. Whip cream until stiff; fold into gelatin mixture. Pour into 1-quart melon mold; chill until firm. Yield: 4-6 servings.

BERRY BAVARIAN CROWN

1 3-oz. package strawberry gelatin
2 10-oz. packages frozen strawberries
2 c. whipping cream, whipped
1 10-in. angel food cake
1 tbsp. cornstarch
3 drops of red food coloring
1 tsp. soft butter

Dissolve gelatin in 1 cup boiling water; add 1/2 cup cold water. Chill until gelatin is partially congealed. Thaw and drain strawberries, reserving 1 cup strawberry syrup. Whip gelatin until fluffy; fold in strawberries and whipped cream. Trim crust from cake; tear cake into small pieces. Alternate layers of gelatin mixture and cake pieces in 10-inch tube pan; chill until firm. Blend small amount of reserved strawberry syrup and cornstarch in saucepan. Add remaining reserved syrup; cook, stirring, until clear and thickened. Remove from heat; stir in food coloring and butter. Unmold dessert; drizzle sauce over top. Yield: 12 servings.

CREME DE MENTHE BAVARIAN

1 2/3 c. evaporated milk
2 env. unflavored gelatin
1/3 c. sugar
1/8 tsp. salt
2 eggs, slightly beaten
1/2 c. water
1/3 c. green creme de menthe
1 tbsp. lemon juice

Freeze 2/3 cup evaporated milk until partially frozen. Combine gelatin, sugar and salt in medium saucepan. Combine eggs, remaining milk and water. Stir into gelatin mixture gradually, blending well. Cook over low heat, stirring constantly, until gelatin is dissolved. Remove from heat. Cool quickly by placing pan in ice water and stirring frequently. Stir in creme de menthe; continue cooling in water until gelatin begins to thicken. Pour icy cold milk into small bowl of electric mixer; add lemon juice. Beat at high speed until milk is stiff and will hold a peak. Fold in gelatin mixture quickly but thoroughly. Turn into lightly oiled 5-cup mold. Chill for about 6 hours until set. Unmold on serving dish.

Easy Chocolate Sauce

1 6-oz. package chocolate chips
3/4 c. evaporated milk

Combine chocolate chips and milk in small saucepan. Place over low heat until chocolate is melted, stirring frequently to blend smoothly. Serve warm or cold over Bavarian cream.

Creme de Menthe Bavarian . . . A party dessert that blends chocolate and mint flavors.

PINEAPPLE BAVARIAN PIE

1 c. fine graham cracker crumbs
1/4 c. melted butter
1 20-oz. can crushed pineapple
1 tbsp. unflavored gelatin
1/4 c. sugar
1/4 tsp. salt
1 2/3 c. evaporated milk
2 tbsp. lemon juice

Mix crumbs and butter; press on bottom of 8-inch square pan. Chill. Drain pineapple, reserving 1/2 cup syrup. Pour reserved syrup into saucepan; add gelatin. Let stand for 5 minutes. Add sugar and salt. Stir over medium heat until gelatin and sugar are dissolved. Remove from heat. Stir in 1 cup milk; chill until slightly congealed. Beat until doubled in bulk. Beat in remaining milk and lemon juice. Fold in pineapple. Pour over chilled crumbs; smooth top. Chill until firm. Decorate with cherries. Yield: 8 servings.

EASY STRAWBERRY BAVARIAN

1 pkg. strawberry gelatin
1 6-oz. package frozen strawberries
1/2 pt. whipping cream

Dissolve gelatin in 1 cup boiling water; add frozen strawberries. Stir until strawberries are thawed; refrigerate until thick. Whip cream until stiff; fold gently into gelatin mixture. Pour into mold. Refrigerate for at least 2 hours before serving. Yield: 6-8 servings.

FRUITED BAVARIAN CREAM

1 1-lb. 1-oz. can fruit cocktail
1 3-oz. package strawberry gelatin
1 3-oz. package raspberry gelatin
1 env. dessert topping mix
1/4 c. chopped pecans

Drain fruit cocktail, reserving syrup. Add enough water to syrup to equal 2 cups liquid. Dissolve gelatins in 2 cups boiling water; stir in fruit cocktail liquid. Chill until almost firm. Prepare dessert topping mix according to package directions. Whip gelatins until fluffy; whip in dessert topping. Fold in fruit cocktail and pecans; pour into pan or mold. Refrigerate until ready to serve. Yield: 16 servings.

MAGIC BAVARIAN CREAM

1/2 c. evaporated milk
1 3-oz. package lime gelatin
2 tbsp. sugar
1 1/2 c. (packed) miniature marshmallows

Pour milk into electric mixer bowl; chill until icy. Dissolve gelatin and sugar in 1 cup boiling water; stir in 1 cup cold water. Chill gelatin until partially congealed. Whip milk until stiff. Whip gelatin until fluffy. Fold milk and marshmallows into gelatin. Pour into pan or mold; refrigerate until firm. Yield: 8 servings.

MOCHA BAVARIAN CREAM

1 tbsp. unflavored gelatin
1/4 c. cold water
1 c. confectioners' sugar
3 tbsp. strong coffee
6 egg yolks
2 c. heavy cream, whipped
1 tsp. rum flavoring
Toasted nuts

Soften gelatin in cold water; dissolve over boiling water. Add sugar and coffee. Beat egg yolks until light; beat in gelatin mixture. Fold in whipped cream and flavoring. Place in oiled ring mold; chill until firm. Invert onto serving dish; garnish with nuts. Yield: 8 servings.

ORANGE BAVARIAN CREAM

1 tbsp. gelatin
1/4 c. cold water
3/4 c. orange juice
2 tbsp. lemon juice
1/2 tsp. grated orange rind
1/3 c. sugar
1 egg white
1/4 tsp. salt
1/2 c. heavy cream, whipped

Soften gelatin in cold water. Combine orange juice, lemon juice, orange rind and half the sugar in saucepan. Heat, stirring, almost to a boil; dissolve gelatin in hot mixture. Chill gelatin mixture until partially thickened. Beat egg white until stiff, beating in salt and remaining sugar. Fold egg white and whipped cream into gelatin mixture; pour into 1-quart mold. Chill until firm. Yield: 4 servings.

PEACH BAVARIAN

1 1-lb. 13-oz. can sliced peaches
1 3-oz. package lemon gelatin
2 tbsp. sugar
Dash of salt
1 c. heavy cream, whipped

Drain peaches, reserving 1/2 cup syrup. Dissolve gelatin, sugar and salt in 1 cup boiling water; stir in reserved peach syrup. Pour about 1/4 cup gelatin mixture into 1-quart mold; arrange 8 peach slices in mold. Chill until almost firm. Chill remaining gelatin mixture until partially thickened. Dice remaining peaches; fold diced peaches and whipped cream into thickened gelatin mixture. Pour over peach layer in mold; refrigerate until firm. Yield: 8 servings.

PEPPERMINT BAVARIAN CREAM

1 1/2 env. unflavored gelatin
1/3 c. cold water
6 egg yolks
3/4 c. sugar
1/4 tsp. salt
1 1/2 c. milk
3/4 c. finely crushed peppermint candy
1/4 tsp. peppermint essence
Red food coloring
1 1/2 c. heavy cream, whipped

Soften gelatin in cold water. Beat egg yolks, sugar and salt together in top of double boiler. Heat milk and candy almost to a boil, stirring to dissolve candy. Beat hot milk gradually into egg yolk mixture. Heat, stirring, over hot water, until thickened. Do not allow to boil. Stir in gelatin until dissolved.

Cool; stir in peppermint essence and food coloring. Fold in whipped cream gently; pour into 6-cup mold. Chill for at least 4 hours or overnight. Unmold; decorate with candies. Serve with chocolate sauce. Yield: 10 servings.

CHOCOLATE-COCONUT BAVARIAN PIE

3 sq. unsweetened chocolate
2 tbsp. butter or margarine
Milk
2/3 c. sifted confectioners' sugar
2 1/2 c. grated coconut
1 env. unflavored gelatin
3 eggs, separated
1/2 c. sugar
1/4 tsp. salt
1 c. heavy cream, whipped
1 tsp. vanilla

Melt 2 squares chocolate and butter together in top of double boiler; stir to blend. Combine 2 tablespoons hot milk and confectioners' sugar; stir into chocolate mixture. Add 1 1/2 cups coconut; mix well. Press to bottom and side of greased 8-inch pie plate; refrigerate. Soften gelatin in 1/4 cup cold water. Beat egg yolks lightly in top of double boiler; stir in gelatin mixture, 1/4 cup sugar and 1 cup milk. Cook over hot water, stirring, until custard coats spoon. Refrigerate, stirring occasionally, until custard mounds when dropped from spoon; beat just until smooth. Beat egg whites with salt until soft peaks form; add remaining sugar, gradually, beating until stiff. Fold in custard mixture, whipped cream, vanilla and 1/2 cup coconut. Pour into crust, reserving about 1/3 of the filling mixture. Refrigerate pie and reserved filling until almost set; heap reserved filling on center of pie. Refrigerate until ready to serve. Let stand at room temperature for 15 minutes before serving. Grate remaining chocolate; garnish pie with chocolate and remaining coconut. Yield: 8 servings.

COCONUT BAVARIAN PIE

1 env. unflavored gelatin
1 c. milk
3 eggs, separated
1/2 c. sugar
1/4 tsp. salt
1 c. heavy cream, whipped
1 tsp. vanilla
1/2 c. shredded coconut
1 9-in. baked pie shell

Soften gelatin in 1/4 cup cold water. Scald milk in double boiler. Combine egg yolks and 1/4 cup sugar; stir in milk. Return to double boiler; cook over hot water until custard coats spoon. Stir in gelatin until dissolved; refrigerate until partially congealed. Beat egg whites with salt until soft peaks form; add remaining sugar gradually, beating until stiff. Fold custard mixture into egg white mixture; add whipped cream, vanilla and coconut. Pour into pie shell; refrigerate until set. Yield: 6-8 servings.

CREAMY CHOCOLATE BAVARIAN PIE

1 tbsp. unflavored gelatin
1 1/2 c. chocolate cookie crumbs
1/4 c. melted butter
3 eggs, separated
1/2 c. sugar
1/4 tsp. salt
1 c. milk, scalded
1 tsp. vanilla
1 c. heavy cream, whipped

Soften gelatin in 1/4 cup cold water. Combine cookie crumbs and butter; press mixture against side and bottom of 9-inch pie plate. Beat egg yolks lightly in top of double boiler; add sugar and salt. Stir in milk gradually; cook, stirring, until thickened. Dissolve gelatin in hot mixture; chill until partially congealed. Beat egg whites until stiff, beating in vanilla. Fold egg whites and whipped cream into gelatin mixture; spoon into crumb crust. Refrigerate until firm. Yield: 6 servings.

PINEAPPLE BAVARIAN CREAM

1 can crushed pineapple
1 tbsp. unflavored gelatin
1 c. sugar
1 pt. whipping cream, whipped

Drain pineapple, reserving syrup. Soften gelatin in half the pineapple syrup. Combine remaining pineapple syrup and sugar in saucepan; cook, stirring, until dissolved. Dissolve gelatin in hot mixture; chill until partially thickened. Fold pineapple and whipped cream into gelatin mixture. Pour into pan or mold; refrigerate until firm. Yield: 8-10 servings.

RICE BAVARIAN CREAM

2 env. unflavored gelatin
2 c. pineapple juice
1 c. sugar
1 env. dessert topping mix
1 1/2 c. cooked rice
1 tsp. vanilla
1/2 c. chopped maraschino cherries
1 c. chopped nuts
1 c. crushed pineapple, drained
1 c. miniature marshmallows

Soften gelatin in 1/2 cup cold water. Combine pineapple juice, sugar and 1 cup water in saucepan; bring to a boil. Dissolve gelatin in hot mixture; chill until almost firm. Prepare dessert topping mix according to package directions; fold in rice, vanilla, cherries, nuts, pineapple and marshmallows. Whip gelatin mixture until fluffy; fold into rice mixture. Pour into 13 x 9 x 2-inch dish; refrigerate until firm. Yield: 12-15 servings.

RUBY GLEAM BAVARIAN CREAM

1 pkg. strawberry gelatin
2 tbsp. sugar
1 env. dessert topping mix
1/2 c. chopped maraschino cherries

Dissolve gelatin and sugar in 1 cup boiling water. Stir in 1 cup cold water; chill until thick. Prepare dessert topping mix according to package directions. Whip gelatin until fluffy; whip in dessert topping. Fold in cherries; place in dessert dishes. Refrigerate until firm. Yield: 6 servings.

Beans

Beans were part of man's diet from the earliest times of land cultivation, but until foodstuffs were imported from the Americas no one in Europe had tasted kidney, lima, navy, or string beans. Today that has changed, and beans form an important part of the diet. They can be bought fresh, frozen, canned, or dried. There are many different types of beans and many of them can be bought as dried beans.

To prepare dried beans, first soften them. To soften, soak beans in water overnight or boil beans in water for 2 minutes and let sit for one hour. Allow 2 1/2-3 cups water per cup beans. Use in recipes according to instructions. Should some beans not soften in 2 minutes, add about 1/8 teaspoon baking soda per cup of water to compensate for the alkaline quality of some water.

In the following section, information and recipes are grouped into three major categories: String Beans, Lima Beans and Soybeans. (See VEGETABLES.)

STRING BEANS

These beans, either green or yellow in color, once had fibrous strings which gave them their name. Modern agriculture has developed stringless varieties, but the name persists. They are also known as green beans, wax or butter beans, snap beans, pole beans, or bush beans. String beans are an excellent source of Vitamins A and C, and they are a dieter's favorite. (1/2 cup string beans = 13 calories)

AVAILABILITY: Available fresh, frozen, or canned year-round. Peak of fresh bean season is from June to August.

BUYING: Look for clean, firm, crisp, well-shaped beans free from scars. Beans should snap readily when broken; if they don't, it is a sign of poor quality or overmaturity. If seeds inside bean pods are half-grown or larger, beans will be tough.

STORING: Fresh beans may be stored in a plastic bag in the vegetable crisper for 3-5 days. *To freeze* string beans, blanch by boiling for 3 minutes then cool in ice water, drain beans; place in freezer container; label. May be frozen up to 10 months.

PREPARATION: Wash beans. Snap off both ends. String the varieties that have strings. Beans may be cooked whole, French-style (cut lengthwise), julienne (cut on the diagonal) or in 1-inch pieces. Cook whole beans or 1-inch pieces 15-30 minutes; French or julienne beans should cook 10-20 minutes. Avoid overcooking.

STRING BEAN SOUP

1 1/2 qt. green string beans
1 sm. onion, diced
3 tbsp. shortening
4 tbsp. flour
Noodles

Cut beans into bite-sized pieces. Combine beans and onion in large kettle; cover with water. Cook until tender. Blend shortening and flour to a paste; brown in skillet. Pour 3 cups cold water into flour mixture gradually, stirring constantly. Cook, stirring, until thickened. Add thickened mixture to soup, blending well. Add noodles. Simmer until noodles are tender. Yield: 6 servings.

PENNSYLVANIA DUTCH GREEN BEAN SALAD

3 strips bacon
1 sm. onion, sliced
2 tsp. cornstarch
1/4 tsp. dry mustard
Salt to taste
1 No. 303 can cut green beans
1 tbsp. brown sugar
1 tbsp. vinegar
1 hard-cooked egg

Fry bacon in skillet until crisp; drain and crumble. Reserve 1 tablespoon bacon drippings in skillet; brown onion lightly. Stir in cornstarch, mustard and salt. Drain beans, reserving 1/2 cup liquid. Stir reserved liquid into skillet. Cook, stirring, until mixture boils. Blend in brown sugar and vinegar; add beans, heating thoroughly. Turn into serving dish; garnish with sliced egg. Crumble bacon over top. Yield: 4 servings.

MARINATED STRING BEANS

1/2 c. cider vinegar
1 1/2 tbsp. cooking oil
1/4 tsp. salt
1/4 tsp. pepper
1/2 c. sugar
1 No. 303 can sm. green beans
1 med. onion, thinly sliced

Blend vinegar, 1/4 cup cold water, oil, salt, pepper and sugar. Drain beans. Arrange layers of beans and onion in baking dish; pour marinade over layers. Cover; chill overnight. Yield: 6-8 servings.

GREEN BEANS ITALIANO SALAD

1 clove of garlic
1/2 tsp. salt
1/2 c. salad oil
1 sm. red onion, sliced
1/2 c. chopped dill pickles
1/4 c. vinegar
1/2 tsp. oregano leaves
1/2 tsp. ground rosemary
2 pkg. frozen green beans

Mash garlic in salt; add to oil. Combine all ingredients except beans in jar; cover and shake well. Cook beans according to package directions; drain. Place beans in serving dish; pour dressing over beans. Refrigerate for several hours before serving. May be served with crumbled bacon on top if desired. Yield: 6-8 servings.

CANNED BEANS

4 c. string beans
1 tbsp. salt
3 tbsp. vinegar

Combine beans, salt, vinegar and 3 cups water in kettle; bring to a boil. Boil for 7 minutes. Pack in hot sterilized jars; seal.

COUNTRY-STYLE GREEN BEANS

1/2 lb. bacon, diced
1 14-oz. package frozen green beans
2 sm. onions, chopped
2 tsp. salt
1 tsp. sugar
1/4 tsp. red pepper
1 lb. new potatoes, peeled

Partially cover bacon with water in large saucepan, boil for 20 minutes. Add beans, onions, salt, sugar and red pepper. Cover; cook for 15 minutes. Add potatoes; cook for about 15 minutes or until potatoes are tender. Serve in large vegetable dish. Yield: 6-8 servings.

DEVILED GREEN BEANS

1 med. onion, chopped
1 clove of garlic, minced
1/2 green pepper, chopped
2 canned pimentos, sliced
Butter
2 tsp. mustard
1 8-oz. can tomato sauce
1 c. shredded cheese
1 10-oz. package frozen green beans

Saute onion, garlic, green pepper and pimentos in small amount butter until onion is transparent. Stir in mustard, tomato sauce and cheese. Cook beans in small amount of salted water until just tender. Drain. Combine beans and sauce; turn into greased 1-quart casserole. Bake in 350-degree oven for 25 minutes. Yield: 4 servings.

ONION RING-BEAN CASSEROLE

1 1-lb. can cut Blue Lake green beans
1/4 lb. cooked ham
1 4 lb. Muenster cheese
1 can cream of mushroom soup
1 5 1/2-oz. package frozen French-fried onion rings

Drain beans. Cut ham and cheese into narrow 3/4-inch wedges. Combine beans, ham, cheese and soup in greased wide shallow 1 1/2-quart baking dish. Arrange onion rings in circle on top. Bake in 350-degree oven for 25 minutes or until bubbly. Yield: 4-5 servings.

Onion Ring-Bean Casserole . . . Beans, ham, cheese, mushrooms, and onion flavor this dish.

GARDEN GOOD GREEN BEANS

1 lb. fresh green beans
1 med. onion
3 tbsp. margarine
1/2 tsp. salt
Dash of pepper
1 chicken bouillon cube

Halve beans lengthwise, cut crosswise. Saute onion in margarine in saucepan until soft. Stir in beans; toss until well coated. Stir in seasonings, 1/4 cup water and bouillon cube, crushing bouillon with spoon until dissolved. Cover; cook for 10 minutes or until beans are crisp-tender. Yield: 4-6 servings.

GERMAN SWEET-SOUR BEANS

1 c. minced onion
Butter
1 tbsp. flour
1 1-lb. can green beans
1/4 c. vinegar
2 tbsp. sugar
1 tsp. salt
1/4 tsp. pepper
2 strips bacon

Saute onion in butter until transparent; stir in flour until smooth. Drain beans, reserving 1/2 cup bean liquid. Stir reserved bean liquid, 1/4 cup water and vinegar into onion mixture gradually. Cook, stirring, until smooth and slightly thickened. Add seasonings and beans; heat through. Fry bacon until crisp; drain and crumble. Sprinkle bacon over bean mixture. Yield: 4 servings.

GREEN BEAN CROQUETTES

2 tbsp. margarine
2 1/2 tbsp. flour
2/3 c. milk
1/2 tsp. salt
2 tsp. minced onion
1/4 tsp. Worcestershire sauce
1 No. 2 can cut green beans, drained
2 c. coarse whole wheat bread crumbs
3/4 c. fine whole wheat bread crumbs
1 egg

Melt margarine in small saucepan; blend in flour. Add milk gradually; cook, stirring constantly, until thick. Add salt, onion and Worcestershire sauce. Chop beans; add coarse bread crumbs and hot white sauce. Mix well. Chill. Shape mixture into croquettes, using 1 tablespoon for each. Roll in fine bread crumbs. Beat egg slightly with 2 tablespoons cold water. Dip croquettes into egg mixture. Roll again in fine crumbs. Fry in small amount of hot fat in skillet until browned. Serve with chili sauce, if desired. Yield: 5 servings.

GREEN BEAN LOAF

1 c. crushed saltine crackers
4 tbsp. melted butter
2 eggs, slightly beaten
2 c. warm milk
1/2 tsp. salt
Dash of pepper
2 tbsp. chopped onions
1 15 1/2-oz. can cut green beans
1 can tomato sauce

Line sides of greased 9 x 5-inch loaf pan with strip of buttered foil. Saute crackers in butter until golden brown. Combine eggs, milk, salt, pepper and onions. Drain beans; add beans, crackers and tomato sauce to egg mixture. Pour bean mixture into loaf pan. Bake in 350-degree oven for 1 hour or until inserted knife comes out clean. Cool for 5 minutes. Loosen around sides; unmold. Yield: 6 servings.

GREEN BEAN PUFF

4 c. cooked green beans, drained
1/4 c. diced celery
3/4 c. mayonnaise
1 tsp. mustard
1/4 tsp. salt
1 tsp. vinegar
1/4 c. milk
1 stiffly beaten egg white
1/4 tsp. paprika

Combine beans and celery in 5-cup casserole. Blend mayonnaise, mustard, salt, vinegar and milk. Fold egg white into mayonnaise mixture; pile lightly over beans. Sprinkle with paprika. Bake at 400 degrees for 15 minutes or until sauce puffs and browns and beans are thoroughly heated. Yield: 4 servings.

GREEN BEANS ALOHA

1 16-oz. can French-style green beans
1 8 3/4-oz. can pineapple chunks
2 tbsp. brown sugar
1 tbsp. cornstarch
1/2 tbsp. salt
2 tbsp. butter
3 tbsp. cider vinegar

Drain beans; reserve 1/3 cup liquid. Drain pineapple; reserve juice. Combine brown sugar, cornstarch, salt and butter in medium saucepan. Add reserved bean liquid, pineapple liquid and vinegar. Bring to a boil, stirring constantly. Cook for 3 minutes. Add beans and pineapple. Heat and serve.

GREEN BEANS BEARNAISE

6 pkg. frozen French-style green beans
3/4 c. melted butter or margarine
3 6-oz. cans evaporated milk
3 tbsp. vinegar
1 1/2 tsp. salt
1/2 tsp. thyme
1/2 tsp. tarragon
1 1/2 tsp. chopped parsley
1 tbsp. grated onion
9 egg yolks, slightly beaten
1 1/2 beef bouillon cubes

Cook green beans according to package directions; drain. Melt butter in double boiler; stir in milk, vinegar, salt, thyme, tarragon, parsley and onion. Stir constantly until smooth. Add 1 tablespoon boiling water and beat with rotary beater if mixture starts to curdle. Pour half the hot sauce into egg yolks, stirring constantly; return to remaining mixture in double boiler. Add bouillon cubes; cook until thick, stirring frequently. Serve sauce over hot beans. Yield: 24 servings.

GREEN BEANS WITH FRENCH-FRIED ONIONS

2 packages French-cut green beans
1 can cream of mushroom soup
1 3 1/2-oz. can French-fried onion rings

Cook beans according to package directions. Drain. Place half the beans in 1 1/2-quart casserole. Spread half the soup over beans. Arrange layer of half the onions. Add remaining beans, soup and onions. Bake at 350 degrees for about 30 minutes. Yield: 6-8 servings.

GREEN BEANS AU GRATIN

2 c. fresh beans
2 tbsp. butter
2 tbsp. flour
1/2 tsp. salt
Dash of pepper
Dash of paprika
1 c. evaporated milk
1/2 c. grated cheese

Cook beans in boiling salted water until tender; drain, reserving 1 cup bean stock. Melt butter in double boiler; blend in flour and seasonings. Stir until smooth and bubbling. Add reserved bean stock to milk; stir milk mixture into flour mixture gradually. Cook, stirring constantly, until smooth and thickened. Place beans in greased casserole; pour sauce over beans. Sprinkle with cheese. Bake at 350 degrees for 20 minutes. Yield: 6 servings.

GREEN BEANS WITH HERB BUTTER

1 lb. green beans
1/4 c. butter or margarine
3/4 c. minced onions
1 clove of garlic, minced
1/4 c. minced celery
2 tbsp. sesame seed
1/4 tsp. rosemary
1/4 tsp. dried basil
3/4 tsp. salt
1/4 c. chopped parsley

Cut beans crosswise into thin slices. Cook beans, covered, in 1/2 inch boiling, salted water for 15 minutes or until tender; drain. Melt butter in saucepan; add onions, garlic, celery and sesame seed. Saute for 5 minutes. Add remaining ingredients. Simmer, covered, for 10 minutes. Toss beans with sauce. Yield: 4 servings.

POLE BEANS WITH MUSTARD SAUCE

Color photograph for this recipe on page 318.

1 1/2 lb. fresh Florida pole beans
1/2 tsp. salt
1 3/4-oz. package white sauce mix
1 tbsp. prepared mustard
1/4 tsp. lemon juice
2 tbsp. diced pimento

Remove tips from pole beans; cut into 1-inch pieces. Bring 1 inch water and salt to boiling point in medium saucepan. Add beans; cook for 5 minutes. Reduce heat; cover. Simmer for 10 minutes or until beans are crisp-tender. Drain. Prepare sauce mix according to package directions. Add mustard and lemon juice; mix well. Stir in pimento. Place beans in serving bowl. Serve with sauce spooned over top. Yield: 6 servings.

GREEN BEANS IN TANGY SAUCE

3 slices bacon, diced
1 med. onion, sliced
3 tbsp. sugar
2 tsp. cornstarch
3 tbsp. tarragon vinegar
1/2 c. sherry
4 c. cooked green beans

Saute bacon and onion in skillet; add sugar, cornstarch, vinegar and sherry. Cook, stirring, until thickened. Pour sauce over hot beans; serve. Yield: 8 servings.

GREEN BEANS WITH WALNUT SAUCE

4 tbsp. butter
6 tbsp. flour
1 sm. bay leaf
2 c. chicken stock
1/4 lb. American cheese, diced
3 c. cooked green beans
1/4 c. chopped walnuts

Brown butter in saucepan over low heat; add flour and bay leaf. Stir until blended. Remove from heat; add stock gradually, stirring constantly. Return to heat. Cook, stirring, until smooth and thickened. Add cheese; stir until melted. Arrange beans in serving dish. Pour sauce over beans; sprinkle with walnuts. Yield: 6-8 servings.

PIQUANT GREEN BEANS

2 pkg. frozen green beans
1 c. chicken consomme
1 c. tomato puree
1 sm. onion, finely chopped
1/2 tsp. ground thyme

Cook beans in boiling salted water for about 5 minutes or until partially done. Drain. Add consomme, tomato puree, onion and thyme. Simmer for 20 minutes. Yield: 8 servings.

GREEN BEANS IN SOUR CREAM SAUCE

1 1/2 lb. green beans
1 med. onion, chopped
1 tsp. salt
2 tbsp. instant flour
2/3 c. sour cream
1 tsp. lemon juice
1 tbsp. minced parsley
1/8 tsp. pepper

Cut beans diagonally into 1-inch slices. Cook beans and onion with 1/2 teaspoon salt in 1 cup boiling water until tender. Drain, reserving 1/2 cup liqiud. Blend flour with sour cream, lemon juice and reserved liquid. Cook over low heat, stirring constantly, until sauce thickens. Stir in parsley, remaining salt and pepper; pour sauce over beans. Serve immediately.

SWISS-STYLE GREEN BEANS

2 No. 300 cans French-style green beans
4 tbsp. butter or margarine
2 tbsp. flour
1 tsp. salt
1 tsp. sugar
1/4 tsp. pepper
1/2 tsp. grated onion
1 c. sour cream
1/4 c. grated Swiss or Parmesan cheese
1 c. crushed corn flakes

Heat beans in bean liquid in saucepan; drain. Melt 2 tablespoons butter in saucepan over low heat; stir in flour and seasonings until smooth. Add onion. Add sour cream gradually, stirring constantly. Simmer until heated through. Add beans to sauce; mix well. Spoon bean mixture into greased baking dish; top with cheese and corn flakes. Bake at 400 degrees for 20 minutes. Yield: 4-6 servings.

SOUTHERN-STYLE FRESH POLE BEANS

1/4 lb. salt pork
1 lb. pole beans
3/4 tsp. salt
Fresh onion rings

Score salt pork; make crosswise cut through center down to rind. Cut 3 or 4 crosswise slashes. Place salt pork in kettle in 1/2 inch boiling water. Cover; cook for 35 minutes or until pork is tender. Remove tips from pole beans; cut into 1-inch pieces. Add beans and salt to pork mixture. Cover; cook for 20 minutes or until beans are just tender. Garnish with onion rings; serve. Yield: 6 servings.

SPANISH GREEN BEANS

2 lb. green beans
3 tbsp. olive oil
2 med. onions, chopped
Chopped parsley to taste
1 clove of garlic, pressed
1/4 lb. ham, chopped
1/4 lb. bacon, chopped
3 oz. white wine
Dash of nutmeg
Salt to taste
Pepper to taste

Cook beans in boiling salted water until tender; drain. Heat olive oil in large skillet; add onions, parsley, garlic, ham and bacon. Cook until ham and bacon are done; add wine, nutmeg, salt and pepper. Add beans and small amount of water if necesarry. Cover; simmer until heated through. Yield: 6 servings.

LIMA BEANS

Lima beans is the term applied to the seeds found inside lima bean pods. There are three major kinds of lima beans; Fordhook–large, thick beans; Baby–small, thin beans; and Green–the youngest of lima beans. Sometimes lima beans are referred to as butter beans. Lima beans are all an excellent source of protein. (1/2 cup lima beans = 75 calories)

AVAILABILITY: Frozen and canned available year-round. Fresh available July-November.

BUYING: In buying fresh lima beans, examine the bean in the pod. If it is flat, it is too young and has little flavor. If it is dried, the beans are too old and will have poor flavor. Look for plump beans with deep green shells that are hard to open. Two to three pounds of unshelled lima beans serve 6.

STORING: Lima beans whether shelled or unshelled should be stored, *without washing,* in the vegetable crisper. Use within 3 days. *To freeze* limas, first wash and shell the bean pods. (Do not wash lima beans after shelling.) Then scald (small and medium beans 3 minutes, larger ones 4 minutes). Chill, drain, package, and freeze for up to 10 months.

PREPARATION: Wash lima bean pods and shell. Simmer beans in covered pan in 1 inch boiling, salted water for about 20-30 minutes. Drain and serve.

SERVING: Serve as an appetizer with vinaigrette or curry sauce; as a vegetable side dish, especially with fried fish, ham, poultry, or pork; and in combination salads.

BUTTER BEANS IN SAUCE

4 egg yolks
1/2 c. butter or margarine
2 tbsp. grated onion
2 tbsp. tarragon vinegar
1/2 tsp. salt
1/2 tsp. pepper
1/2 c. water
1/2 tsp. beef flavoring
Cooked butter beans

Beat egg yolks lightly in top of double boiler; add butter, onion, vinegar, salt, pepper, water and beef flavoring. Cook, stirring constantly, for 15 minutes or until sauce is thickened. Pour sauce over hot beans; serve immediately.

DEVILED BUTTER BEANS

2 c. dried butter beans or lima beans
Salt and pepper to taste
1 tbsp. olive oil
1/4 c. chopped pimento
1/4 c. minced onion
1/4 c. chopped green pepper
1/4 c. crisp bacon
1 can deviled ham
1/2 c. grated cheese

Place beans in large kettle; add cold water to cover. Let stand overnight. Add salt, pepper and oil. Bring to a boil; cover kettle. Reduce heat; simmer until beans are almost tender. Add pimento, onion and green pepper; simmer, covered, until beans are tender. Add boiling water as needed. Stir in bacon, deviled ham and cheese just before serving. Yield: 6-8 servings.

ZESTY BUTTER BEANS

2 tbsp. chopped onion
2 tbsp. chopped green pepper
1 tbsp. butter
1 10 1/2-oz. can tomato soup
1/4 c. water
1 tbsp. brown sugar
1 tbsp. vinegar
1 tsp. mustard
2 1-lb. cans butter beans

Saute onion and green pepper in butter; stir in soup, water, brown sugar, vinegar and mustard. Bring mixture to a boil, stirring constantly. Drain beans; place in greased baking dish. Pour hot soup mixture over beans. Bake at 375 degrees for 45 minutes. Yield: 4-6 servings.

BAKED LIMA BEANS

1 lb. dried lima beans
1 tsp. salt
1 lge. onion, chopped
Bacon
1/4 c. corn syrup
1 lge. bottle catsup
1/8 tsp. pepper

Place beans in large kettle; add water to cover. Let stand overnight. Add salt and onion. Bring to a boil; cover kettle. Reduce heat; simmer until beans are tender, adding boiling water as needed. Chop 3 slices bacon; add chopped bacon, corn syrup, catsup and pepper to beans. Pour into large baking dish; arrange several slices bacon over top. Bake at 250 degrees for 2 hours and 30 minutes to 3 hours. Yield: 4 servings.

BARBECUED LIMA BEANS

4 1/2 c. dried baby lima beans
1/2 lb. salt pork or bacon, diced
1 c. chopped onions
1 1/4 tsp. minced garlic
3 tbsp. mustard
2 tsp. Worcestershire sauce
1/2 tsp. salt
2 tsp. chili powder
4 tsp. brown sugar
1/4 c. vinegar

Place beans in large heavy kettle; add 2 quarts water. Bring to a boil; cook for 2 minutes. Cover; let stand overnight. Bring to a boil again; reduce heat. Simmer, covered, for 40 minutes. Drain beans, reserving 2 cups liquid. Render salt pork in skillet. Saute onions and garlic in pork fat; stir mixture into beans. Add mustard, Worcestershire sauce, salt, chili powder, brown sugar and vinegar; stir in reserved liquid. Turn into greased baking dish. Bake at 350 degrees for 35 to 40 minutes.

DRIED LIMA BEANS

1 lb. dried lima beans
1 hambone
1 onion, diced
1 tbsp. salt
2 tbsp. bacon drippings
1/4 c. flour

Place beans, hambone, onion and salt in large heavy kettle. Add cold water to cover; bring to a boil. Reduce heat; cover kettle. Simmer until beans are tender, adding boiling water as needed. Heat bacon drippings in skillet. Blend in flour; cook, stirring constantly, until flour is browned. Remove hambone from kettle. Stir browned flour into beans; bring to a boil, stirring until bean liquid is thickened.

GREEN LIMAS A LA CREME

2 lb. green lima beans
Salt
1/2 tsp. minced onion
1/4 c. grated process American cheese
1 tbsp. butter or margarine
1/4 c. light cream
1/4 c. milk
Pepper to taste

Cook beans in saucepan in 1 inch boiling water with 1/2 teaspoon salt for 20 to 30 minutes or until done; drain. Add onion, cheese, butter, cream and milk. Toss lightly with fork over low heat until cheese is melted. Season with pepper and salt. Yield: 4 servings.

LIMA CASSEROLE

2 pkg. frozen green lima beans
1 can green chilies, chopped
1 can cream of mushroom soup
Grated sharp Cheddar cheese

Cook beans according to package directions; drain. Arrange layers of beans, chilies, soup and cheese in casserole, ending with cheese on top. Bake in 375-degree oven until cheese melts and mixture is bubbly. Yield: 6-8 servings.

LIMA-CELERY SCALLOP

2 c. fresh lima beans
2 c. sliced celery
4 tbsp. butter
4 tbsp. flour
1 tsp. salt
1/8 tsp. pepper
2 1/2 c. hot milk
1 c. grated American cheese
1/2 c. slivered almonds
1/2 c. buttered bread crumbs

Cook beans in boiling salted water until tender; drain. Cook celery in boiling salted water until partially done; drain. Melt butter in saucepan; add flour and seasonings. Blend well. Add milk gradually. Cook, stirring constantly, until thickened. Stir in cheese until melted. Arrange layers of beans, celery, almonds and cheese sauce in 1 1/2-quart casserole. Top with crumbs; chill well. Bake at 350 degrees for about 20 minutes or until crumbs are brown and casserole is bubbly. Yield: 8 servings.

LIMA-SOUR CREAM CASSEROLE

1/2 c. sliced onion
1 tbsp. minced parsley
2 tbsp. butter
2 tbsp. flour
1 tsp. salt
1/4 tsp. pepper
1/2 tsp. grated lemon peel
2 pkg. frozen green lima beans
1 c. sour cream
1/2 c. shredded American cheese
1/2 c. buttered bread crumbs

Saute onion and parsley in butter in skillet until onion is tender. Blend in flour, salt, pepper and lemon peel. Cook beans according to package directions; drain. Stir sour cream and lima beans into onion mixture. Heat, stirring gently. Turn into greased baking dish. Top with cheese and crumbs. Bake at 250 to 300 degrees until cheese is melted and crumbs are brown. Yield: 6 servings.

LIMAS MILANO

4 c. dried baby lima beans
Salt
2 1/2 c. chopped onions
1 1/2 c. chopped green peppers
1 clove of garlic, chopped
1/3 c. oil
2 c. chopped ripe olives
Grated Parmesan cheese
2 tsp. chili powder
2 6-oz. cans tomato paste

Soak beans in water overnight; drain. Simmer in salted water until tender; drain, reserving 2 cups liquid. Saute onions, green peppers and garlic in oil until tender; stir mixture into beans. Add reserved liquid, olives, 1/2 cup cheese, 2 teaspoons salt, chili powder and tomato paste. Turn into 4-quart casserole; sprinkle with cheese. Bake at 375 degrees for 30 minutes. Yield: 12 servings.

Lima Beans with Sour Cream . . . This hearty dish adds new flavor excitement to an old favorite.

LIMA BEANS WITH SOUR CREAM

1 lb. large dried lima beans
2 tsp. salt
1/3 c. margarine
1 c. dark corn syrup
1 med. onion, chopped
1 tsp. dry mustard
1 c. sour cream

Soak beans overnight in 2 1/2 quarts water and 1 teaspoon salt. Drain; rinse with hot water. Drain again. Melt margarine in large saucepan; add corn syrup, remaining salt and beans. Cover; simmer for about 1 hour or until beans are tender. Stir in onion, mustard and sour cream. Turn into 2 1/2-quart casserole; cover. Bake at 350 degrees for 1 hour. Yield: 6 servings.

LIMAS AU GRATIN

1 pkg. frozen baby lima beans
2 tbsp. milk
1/2 tsp. salt
1/8 tsp. pepper
Pat of butter
2 tbsp. grated Parmesan or Romano cheese

Thaw beans; place in foil pie plate. Add remaining ingredients. Cover with heavy-duty foil, crimping edges tightly. Grill over hot coals for 15 minutes, turning often. Yield: 2 servings.

LIMAS IN PEPPER BOATS

6 green peppers
1 med. onion, minced
1 No. 2 can strained tomatoes
1/8 tsp. cayenne pepper
1/2 tsp. salt
2 c. cooked lima beans
1 c. grated cheese
1/2 c. buttered cracker crumbs

Cut green peppers in half lengthwise; remove seeds. Boil in salted water for 5 minutes; drain. Brown onion in 2 tablespoons fat; add tomatoes, seasonings and beans. Simmer for 20 minutes. Remove from heat; add cheese. Fill green peppers with bean mixture; sprinkle with crumbs. Place in shallow pan in 1/2 inch hot water. Bake in 350-degree oven for 20 to 30 minutes.

SKILLET LIMA BEANS

2 tbsp. melted butter
1/2 lge. onion, diced
1/2 pimento, diced
2 tbsp. diced green pepper
3 c. cooked lima beans, drained
1 c. sour cream
Salt and pepper to taste

Melt butter in large skillet; add onion, pimento and green pepper. Saute until soft. Add beans; simmer for about 4 minutes or until heated through. Mix in sour cream, salt and pepper; simmer for 2 minutes longer. Serve. Yield: 8 servings.

SPANISH LIMAS

1 med. onion, chopped
1 green pepper, chopped
2 tbsp. butter or margarine
1 c. canned tomatoes
1 tsp. salt
1/4 tsp. pepper
1/8 tsp. cayenne pepper
1 tsp. Worcestershire sauce
2 c. canned lima beans, drained
1 1/2 c. grated process cheese

Saute onion and green pepper in butter until golden; add tomatoes. Simmer for 10 minutes. Add seasonings and beans. Alternate layers of bean mixture and cheese in greased 1-quart casserole. Bake in 350-degree oven for 30 minutes. Yield: 6 servings.

SOYBEANS

Soybeans are unique among beans in that they alone are a true meat substitute. They contain tremendous amounts of protein, a little sugar, virtually no starch, and are high in calcium and B vitamins. (1/2 cup soybeans = 75 calories)

AVAILABILITY: Fresh soybeans are seldom available except occasionally in late summer months in the regions where they are grown (Michigan, Illinois, Missouri, Iowa, Minnesota, Alabama, Mississippi). Dried soybeans and soy sauce are available year-round in specialty grocery and health food stores.

STORING: Dried soybeans keep on the kitchen shelf or in the freezer for one year. Soybean flour should be refrigerated and keeps for six months. Store soy sauce in the cupboard where it keeps almost indefinitely. **PREPARATION**: Before using dried soybeans in a recipe, let them soak overnight or boil them for 2 minutes and let sit one hour. Allow about six cups water per pound beans. Use soybean flour or soy sauce as directed in recipes.

COMPANY'S COMING SOYBEANS

2 c. dried soybeans
1 sm. ham hock
2 tbsp. sugar or molasses
1 lge. onion, diced
1/2 c. diced celery
3 bay leaves
Salt to taste

Soak beans overnight. Drain beans; place in large kettle. Add ham hock, sugar, onion, celery, bay leaves, salt and 6 cups cold water. Bring to a boil; cover kettle. Reduce heat; simmer for 3 hours or until beans are tender.

SOYBEAN CASSEROLE

1/4 c. diced salt pork
2 c. diced celery
2 tbsp. chopped onion
2 tbsp. chopped green pepper
6 tbsp. flour
1 tbsp. salt
2 c. milk
2 c. chopped cooked soybeans
1 c. buttered bread crumbs
1/2 tsp. paprika

Fry salt pork in skillet. Saute celery, onion and green pepper in pork drippings. Blend in flour and salt; add milk slowly. Cook to a boil, stirring constantly. Add beans; mix well. Turn into casserole. Cover with bread crumbs; sprinkle with paprika. Bake at 350 degrees for 30 minutes.

SOYBEAN LOAF

1 c. soybeans
1 onion, chopped
1 c. ground walnuts
1 c. toasted bread crumbs
1/2 c. cream
2 eggs, lightly beaten
1 tbsp. butter or oil
Salt to taste

Soak beans overnight. Drain beans; cover with fresh water. Bring to a boil; reduce heat. Simmer, covered, until beans are almost tender. Add onion; cook until onion is tender. Drain beans and onion well; mash until smooth. Stir in walnuts, bread crumbs, cream, eggs, butter and salt. Mix well; press into baking dish. Bake at 350 degrees for 45 minutes. Serve with tart jelly. Yield: 8 servings.

SUPER SOYBEAN SOUP

2 c. soybeans
7 c. water
Salt to taste
1 ham hock

Combine all ingredients in pressure cooker; cover. Cook at 10 pounds pressure for 30 minutes.

MISCELLANEOUS BEANS

BLACK BEAN DIP

1 can black bean soup
1 sm. package cream cheese
1/2 c. mayonnaise
Juice of 1 lemon
Dash of hot sauce
Dash of salt
1/2 tsp. garlic salt

Combine all ingredients in electric mixer bowl; let stand at room temperature for 1 hour. Beat at low speed of mixer until smooth and blended. Serve with chips and crackers.

BLACK BEAN SOUP

1 lb. black beans
2 tbsp. salt
5 cloves of garlic
1/2 tbsp. cumin
1/2 tbsp. oregano
2 tbsp. white vinegar
1/2 lb. onions, chopped
1/2 lb. green peppers, chopped
5/8 c. Spanish oil
1/2 c. rice, cooked

Soak beans in water to cover overnight. Add salt; bring to a boil. Reduce heat; cover. Simmer until beans are tender, adding boiling water as needed. Crush garlic, cumin and oregano in half the vinegar; stir into beans. Saute half the onions and green peppers in half the oil; add to beans. Simmer until ready to serve. Combine rice and remaining vinegar, oil and onion. Add 1 tablespoon rice mixture to each serving of soup. Yield: 6 servings.

FRIJOLES

1/2 lb. black beans
1 lge. onion, chopped
3 green peppers, chopped
1 clove of garlic, minced
1/2 c. olive oil
1 tbsp. salt
1 oz. whole bacon
1/4 lb. hambone
3 bay leaves
1/2 c. vinegar

Soak beans in 1 1/2 quarts water overnight. Fry onion, green peppers and garlic in olive oil until tender. Add onion mixture, salt, bacon, hambone and bay leaves to beans. Cook over low heat until beans are tender and liquid is thickened. Add vinegar; heat through. Yield: 4 servings.

EASY BAKED BEANS

1 qt. dry Great Northern beans
1 tsp. soda
1/2 bottle catsup
1 c. sugar
2 tbsp. prepared mustard
1 lge. onion, chopped
1 lb. salt pork

Place beans in large kettle; add cold water to cover. Let stand overnight. Add soda to beans; bring to a boil. Cook for 10 minutes. Drain beans; rinse with cold water. Cover with water; bring to a boil. Cook for 10 minutes. Drain beans, reserving cooking water. Place beans in bean pot. Mix catsup, sugar, mustard and onion; stir into beans. Score salt pork; add to pot. Bake, covered, at 300 degrees for 6 hours. Add reserved cooking water as needed. Yield: 8-10 servings.

Country-Style Cassoulet . . . This bean, meat, and duckling casserole came from France.

COUNTRY-STYLE CASSOULET

2 lb. dried navy beans
1/4 lb. salt pork, diced
1 c. chopped onion
1 10 1/2-oz. can tomato puree
2 carrots, sliced
4 cloves of garlic
2 lb. smoked pork butt, sliced
1 1/2 lb. Spanish-style sausage
1 4 3/4-oz. jar pimento-stuffed olives
1/2 tsp. pepper
Duckling giblets
1 4-lb. duckling
1 tsp. salt

Cover beans with water; soak overnight. Drain well. Cover beans with salted water in large pot; bring to a boil. Boil for 2 minutes. Let stand for 30 minutes. Fry salt pork in saucepan; add onion, tomato puree, carrots and garlic. Simmer for about 15 minutes or until onion is tender. Add onion mixture, pork butt, sausage, olives and pepper to beans; cover. Cook for 2 hours and 30 minutes to 3 hours, stirring occasionally, until beans are tender. Add giblets and salt to 1 cup boiling water in saucepan; cover and simmer until tender. Chop giblets; add giblets and stock to beans. Prick duckling with fork; place on rack. Bake at 350 degrees for 2 hours or until done. Remove duckling meat in slices. Alternate layers of bean mixture and duckling slices in casserole. Bake at 350 degrees for 1 to 2 hours, stirring occasionally. Yield: 8-10 servings.

BAKED BEANS WITH GUSTO

4 c. Great Northern beans
3 med. onions
2 tsp. salt
4 cloves
1/2 c. molasses
1 c. (packed) brown sugar
2 tsp. dry mustard
1 tsp. pepper
1/2 lb. salt pork, scored

Place beans in large saucepan; pour in enough cold water to cover. Bring to a boil; boil for 2 minutes. Remove from heat; let stand for 1 hour. Bring to a boil again. Add 1 onion and 1 teaspoon salt. Half cover pan; simmer beans for 30 minutes. Drain beans; discard onion and water. Stud remaining onions with cloves; place in 2 1/2-quart bean pot or heavy casserole with tight-fitting cover. Place beans in pot. Combine molasses, 3/4 cup brown sugar, mustard and remaining salt and pepper in bowl; stir in 2 cups water. Pour mixture over beans; push pork into beans. Cover tightly. Bake at 250 degrees for 4 hours and 30 minutes to 5 hours. Remove cover; sprinkle with remaining brown sugar. Bake for 30 minutes longer. Yield: 10-15 servings.

HOME-BAKED BEANS

1 lb. Great Northern beans
1 bay leaf
1 tsp. salt
1/2 tsp. dried thyme or savory
1 onion, sliced
1 tbsp. dry mustard
1/2 c. (packed) dark brown sugar
1 12-oz. bottle catsup
1/2 c. diced bacon

Wash beans; place in large kettle. Cover with water; bring to a boil. Remove from heat; let stand for 1 hour. Add bay leaf, salt and thyme; simmer, covered, until beans are tender. Add onion, mustard, brown sugar, catsup and bacon; mix well. Pour into large pan or bean pot; cover. Bake at 250 degrees for 4 to 6 hours. Stir beans occasionally; add boiling water as needed. Yield: 10-12 servings.

CREAMY KIDNEY BEAN SALAD

1 No. 2 can kidney beans, drained
1/4 c. diced celery
1 sm. onion, minced
2 hard-cooked eggs, diced
1/2 tsp. salt
1/8 tsp. pepper
1/4 c. sour cream
3 sweet pickles, chopped

Combine all ingredients; chill thoroughly. Serve on salad greens. May be garnished with grated cheese or sliced hard-cooked egg. Yield: 6 servings.

CREOLE RED BEANS

1 lb. red kidney beans
1/4 c. bacon drippings
1 lge. onion, minced
1 ham hock
1 sm. red pepper
2 bay leaves
2 sprigs of thyme
Salt to taste

Soak beans in water overnight. Heat bacon drippings in large heavy saucepan; cook onion in drippings until lightly browned. Drain beans; add to onion. Add ham hock, red pepper, bay leaves, thyme, salt and 4 cups cold water. Bring to a boil; cover saucepan. Reduce heat; simmer for 3 to 4 hours, stirring occasionally. Add boiling water as needed. Remove red pepper before serving. Yield: 6 servings.

GORDO'S BEANS

1 lb. pink beans
2 cloves of garlic
1 lge. onion, finely chopped
1/2 green pepper, finely chopped
1/4 lb. bacon, finely chopped
1 8-oz. can tomato sauce
Worcestershire sauce to taste
Hot sauce to taste
1/2 tsp. salt
1/2 tsp. pepper
2 tbsp. chili powder

Soak beans overnight; drain. Cover with 1 1/2 quarts boiling water; add garlic, onion, green pepper, bacon, tomato sauce, Worcestershire sauce and hot sauce. Cover; simmer for 2 hours. Uncover; simmer for 4 hours longer, stirring occasionally. Stir in salt, pepper and chili powder just before removing from heat. Yield: 10 servings.

GOURMET KIDNEY BEANS

3 sm. onions, chopped
1/2 green pepper, minced
1/4 c. chopped ham
Salad oil
1 sm. can tomato paste
1 c. red wine
2 cans kidney beans, drained
3 bacon strips

Saute onions, green pepper and ham in skillet in small amount of oil; add tomato paste and wine. Cook for 5 minutes; add beans. Pour into casserole; cover with bacon. Bake in 350-degree oven for 30 minutes. Yield: 6 servings.

KIDNEY BEAN CASSEROLE

1/4 lb. salt pork, diced
1 lb. dried kidney beans
Salt and pepper to taste
1 lge. onion, chopped
1 med. green pepper, chopped
1 c. grated Cheddar cheese
1 6-oz. can tomato paste
2 strips bacon

Render salt pork in large heavy kettle; pour off excess fat. Add beans and water to cover. Bring to a boil; cover kettle. Reduce heat; simmer until beans are tender. Add salt, pepper, onion, green pepper, cheese and tomato sauce to beans. Mix well; turn into baking dish. Place bacon over beans. Bake at 300 degrees until bacon is cooked. Yield: 8 servings.

KIDNEY BEAN LOAF

2 tbsp. chopped onions
2 tbsp. vegetable oil
4 c. cooked kidney beans
1 grated carrot
1 tbsp. chopped parsley
1/2 c. tomatoes
1 c. whole wheat crumbs
2 eggs, beaten
2 celery stalks, chopped
1 tsp. oregano
1 1/2 tsp. sweet basil
Tomato sauce to taste

Saute onions in oil in skillet until brown; add to beans. Add carrot, parsley, tomatoes, crumbs, eggs, celery, oregano and 1 tablespoon sweet basil. Mix well. Spoon into greased loaf pan. Bake at 350 degrees for 1 hour. Mix tomato sauce and remaining sweet basil. Serve with loaf.

NEW ORLEANS-STYLE RED BEANS

1 lb. dried red kidney beans
1 hambone
1 lb. ham, diced
1 lge. onion, chopped
1/2 c. chopped green pepper
1/2 c. chopped celery
1 clove of garlic, chopped
3 tbsp. tomato paste
Salt and pepper to taste
1 tbsp. minced parsley

Soak beans overnight. Drain and rinse beans. Place in large heavy kettle; add hambone, ham, onion, green pepper, celery, garlic, tomato paste, salt, pepper and parsley. Pour in 2 quarts cold water; bring to a boil. Reduce heat; cover kettle. Simmer for 4 hours or until beans are tender. Serve over rice. Yield: 6 servings.

BEAN SALAD

1 can French-style green beans
1 can yellow beans
1 can red beans
1 sm. onion, minced
1/2 c. chopped green pepper
Diced celery to taste
1/2 c. cider vinegar
1/2 c. salad oil
3/4 c. sugar
1 tsp. salt
1 tsp. pepper

Drain beans; combine vegetables in large bowl. Combine remaining ingredients; pour over vegetables, mixing well. Cover; refrigerate for several hours. Keeps well.

MIXED BEAN RAREBIT

1 1-lb. can red kidney beans
1 1-lb. can lima beans
4 slices bacon, chopped
1 med. onion, chopped
1 1-lb. can baked beans in tomato sauce
1/4 lb. American cheese, diced
1/2 c. brown sugar
1/4 c. catsup
2 tsp. Worcestershire sauce
Grated Parmesan cheese

Drain kidney beans and lima beans. Brown bacon and onion lightly in large skillet; remove from heat. Stir in beans, American cheese, brown sugar, catsup and Worcestershire sauce. Place in shallow baking dish; sprinkle with Parmesan cheese. Bake at 350 degrees for 30 minutes. Yield: 8 servings.

BROILED BEAN SANDWICHES

1 5-oz. can pork and beans
1/4 c. pickle relish
1/8 tsp. salt
1/2 tsp. mustard
6 slices bread
6 slices sharp cheese
6 slices bacon, halved

Combine beans, relish, salt and mustard. Place bread on baking sheet; top with bean mixture. Add cheese and bacon. Broil until bacon is crisp and cheese is melted. Yield: 6 servings.

BEAN LOAF

1 c. dried navy beans
1 c. soft bread crumbs
1 egg, beaten
1 tsp. salt
1/4 tsp. pepper
3 tbsp. melted butter
2 tbsp. minced onion

Soak beans in water overnight. Bring to a boil; reduce heat. Simmer, covered, until beans are tender. Drain beans well; mash until smooth. Combine beans, bread crumbs, egg, salt, pepper, butter and onion. Mix well; turn into greased bread pan. Bake at 350 degrees for 25 to 30 minutes. Unmold loaf onto serving platter. Serve with tomato sauce.

BEAN PATTIES

2 c. baked beans, drained
2 tbsp. finely chopped onion
3 tbsp. fine dry bread crumbs
3 tbsp. bacon drippings

Mash beans; mix with onion. Shape mixture into 4 patties; coat patties with crumbs. Brown on both sides in bacon drippings.

BEAN PORRIDGE

1 c. sliced carrots
1 c. sliced celery
1/2 c. sliced onion
1 c. sliced potatoes
2 tsp. salt
2 c. stewed tomatoes
4 c. cooked navy beans, pureed
1 bay leaf
1 tbsp. parsley
2 tbsp. chili sauce

Combine carrots, celery, onion, potatoes and salt in large kettle. Add 2 quarts water; bring to a boil. Reduce heat; cook until carrots are almost tender. Add tomatoes, beans, bay leaf, parsley and chili sauce. Mix well; simmer for 2 hours.

COMPANY BAKED BEANS

1 lb. navy beans
1/4 c. molasses
1/2 c. (packed) brown sugar
1 tsp. salt
1 tsp. dry mustard
2 tbsp. chopped onion
1/8 tsp. pepper
1/4 lb. salt pork or bacon, diced

Soak beans overnight in water to cover. Bring to a boil; reduce heat. Simmer, covered, for 1 hour. Add molasses, brown sugar, salt, mustard, onion and pepper. Turn into baking dish; scatter salt pork over top. Bake at 325 degrees for 4 to 5 hours. Yield: 6-8 servings.

OLD-TIME BAKED BEANS

2 c. dried navy beans
1 env. dry onion soup mix
1/2 c. dark molasses
2 tbsp. prepared mustard
1/2 c. (packed) dark brown sugar
1/4 lb. bulk bacon

Soak beans overnight. Rinse beans; cover with fresh water. Bring to a boil; cover. Reduce heat; simmer for 40 minutes. Add onion soup mix, molasses, mustard and brown sugar to beans; mix well. Turn mixture into 3-quart bean pot. Score bacon; add to bean pot. Cover. Bake at 300 degrees for 6 hours, stirring occasionally and adding boiling water as needed. Yield: 8-10 servings.

POTLUCK BAKED BEANS

2 c. navy beans
2 tsp. salt
1/2 c. catsup
1/3 c. (packed) brown sugar
1/4 c. diced bacon
2 tbsp. molasses
1 tsp. dry mustard
1 tbsp. diced onion
1/8 tsp. pepper

Place beans in large saucepan; add cold water to cover. Let stand overnight. Bring beans to a boil; reduce heat. Cover; cook for 30 minutes. Add remaining ingredients to beans; mix well. Turn into 2-quart casserole; cover. Bake at 325 degrees for 4 hours. Stir beans occasionally; add boiling water as needed. Yield: 6-8 servings.

SPECIAL BAKED BEANS

2 c. dried navy beans
1/2 lb. salt pork
6 sprigs of parsley
1 lge. onion
1 clove of garlic
1 green pepper
2 sweet red peppers
2 tbsp. maple syrup
6 tbsp. catsup

Soak beans overnight. Rinse salt pork with boiling water. Grind salt pork, parsley, onion, garlic, green pepper and red peppers with food chopper, using medium blade. Drain beans; place in kettle. Add salt pork mixture, syrup, catsup and cold water to cover. Bring to a boil; reduce heat. Simmer, covered, for 2 hours. Drain beans, reserving liquid. Place beans in bean pot; add enough reserved liquid to cover beans. Cover pot. Bake at 300 degrees for 1 hour and 30 minutes. Yield: 6 servings.

BAKED BEANS WITH MOLASSES

1/2 lb. Great Northern beans
1/2 lb. kidney beans
1 1/2 tsp. salt
1/4 tsp. pepper
1 tsp. dry mustard
1/2 c. molasses
1/2 lb. fat salt pork
1 sm. onion, chopped

Place beans in container in enough water to cover by 1 inch. Soak overnight. Combine beans and enough water to cover in 2-quart casserole. Place salt, pepper, mustard and molasses in measuring cup; add enough water to equal 1 cup liquid. Pour over beans. Slash salt pork at 1-inch intervals. Place salt pork and onion in center of beans; cover casserole. Bake at 250 degrees for about 6 hours, adding water if necessary.

BAKED BEANS BARBECUE

1/2 lb. dried pea beans
1 meaty hambone
1/2 bottle catsup
2 tbsp. molasses
1/2 tbsp. salt

Place beans in heavy saucepan; cover with cold water. Let stand overnight. Add hambone to beans; bring to a boil. Reduce heat; cover. Simmer until beans are tender. Remove hambone; cut ham from bone in small pieces. Return ham to beans; stir in catsup, molasses and salt. Turn into casserole. Bake at 350 degrees for 1 hour.

BOSTON BAKED BEANS

1 1/2 lb. pea beans
1 tsp. dry mustard
1/4 tsp. pepper
2 tsp. salt
3 med. onions, chopped
1/4 c. dark brown sugar
3/4 c. dark molasses
2 tbsp. cider vinegar
1/4 tsp. ground cinnamon
1/4 tsp. ground allspice
1 tsp. hickory-smoked salt
1/4 tsp. paprika
1/2 lb. salt pork, diced

Soak beans overnight in cold water. Bring to a boil; cook for 20 minutes. Drain; place in earthen crock or bean pot. Add remaining ingredients; cover with hot water. Bake, covered, at 250 degrees for 6 to 8 hours, adding boiling water as needed. Yield: 8-10 servings.

BOSTON-STYLE PEA BEANS

2 c. pea beans
1/4 lb. fat salt pork
1 onion
1 tsp. salt
1/2 c. light molasses
1/2 tsp. dry mustard
1 tbsp. sugar

Soak beans overnight. Drain beans; cover with fresh water. Bring to a boil; cover. Reduce heat; simmer until beans are tender. Drain beans, reserving cooking water. Rinse salt pork with boiling water. Cut 1/4-inch slice from pork; place in bean pot. Add onion and beans. Score rind of remaining pork; push pork into beans, leaving rind exposed. Bring 1 cup reserved cooking water to a boil; add salt, molasses, mustard and sugar. Pour hot mixture over beans; add enough remaining cooking water to cover beans. Cover bean pot. Bake at 300 degrees for 6 to 7 hours, adding boiling water as needed. Uncover; bake for 1 hour longer.

Baked Beans with Molasses . . . Molasses and beans, cooked all day, provide a hearty supper.

CRANBERRY BAKED BEANS

Color photograph for this recipe on page 317.

1 1/2 c. dried pea beans
1 1/2 tsp. salt
2 c. cranberry juice cocktail
1/3 c. chopped onion
2 tbsp. molasses
1 tsp. dry mustard
1/8 tsp. ginger
1/4 c. catsup
2 tbsp. (packed) dark brown sugar
1/4 lb. salt pork, sliced

Place beans, salt, cranberry juice and 2 cups water in saucepan; bring to a boil. Remove from heat; set aside for 1 hour. Cover; bring to a boil. Reduce heat; simmer until beans are tender, adding water if necessary. Drain, reserving bean liquid. Combine beans and remaining ingredients except salt pork; pour half the mixture into bean pot or 2-quart casserole. Top with half the salt pork. Repeat layers. Add 1 1/2 cups reserved bean liquid. Bake, covered, at 250 degrees for 5 to 7 hours. Uncover; bake for 1 hour longer, adding more reserved liquid if necessary to keep beans from drying. Yield: 6-8 servings.

GLORIFIED PINTO BEANS

1 1/2 c. pinto beans
2 oz. bacon
1 tsp. minced onion
1 green pepper, chopped
1 c. chili sauce or tomato sauce
1 tsp. sugar

Place beans in heavy kettle; add bacon and cold water to cover. Bring to a boil; cover kettle. Reduce heat; simmer until beans are tender. Add onion, green pepper, chili sauce and sugar; simmer for 30 minutes longer.

PINTO BEAN PIE

2 c. cooked pinto beans
2 c. sugar
2 tbsp. flour
1/2 c. margarine, melted
4 eggs
1 tsp. vanilla
1 tsp. nutmeg
2 8-in. unbaked pastry shells

Place beans in large mixing bowl; mash until smooth. Stir in sugar, flour and margarine; beat in eggs, one at a time. Add vanilla and nutmeg; mix well. Spoon bean mixture into pastry shells. Bake at 350 degrees for 35 minutes or until browned. Serve warm. Top with whipped cream or dessert topping, if desired.

Beef

Probably America's favorite meat, beef comes in a variety of cuts to suit every taste and budget. Beef is also a rich source of nutrients; it contains all 21 amino acids (protein building blocks) essential for growth and health maintenance as well as Vitamins A, B_6, B_{12}, thiamine, riboflavin, and niacin. Beef tends to be high in calories but the count can be reduced by carefully trimming off excess fat before cooking.

AVAILABILITY: Available year-round with slight peak in fall months.

BUYING: Allow 1/2 to 3/4 pound of bone-in beef or 1/3 to 1/2 pound boneless per person. Look for lean meat that is bright red and velvety in appearance and well-marbled with creamy fat. *Quality grading*—the U. S. Department of Agriculture inspects about 80 percent of beef marketed. Private packers usually grade their beef in accordance with USDA standards. *Prime* is the best beef but is generally available only to restaurants. *Choice* is the next best grade and is similar to prime but with less fat. *Good, Standard, Commercial, and Utility*, the lower grades, are considered less tender and of lower quality than Prime or Choice. *Tender cuts* include rib roasts (standing, rolled, or rib eye); tenderloin (roast or filet mignon steak); and porterhouse, sirloin, or T-bone steaks. *Less tender cuts* include rump roast, sirloin tip roast, arm or round bone chuck roast, blade bone chuck roast, and chuck, cube, flank, or round steaks. Also considered less tender are stew beef, corned beef (also sold as fresh brisket), and short ribs.

STORING: Rib roasts may be stored in the refrigerator 5-8 days; steaks, 3-5 days; pot roasts, 5-6 days; stew meat, 2 days; and corned beef, 7 days. All meat should be removed from its original store wrapper and re-wrapped loosely in plastic or waxed paper to allow free circulation of air. Store in the coldest part of the refrigerator. Beef may also be frozen: steaks, roasts, and stew beef keep for 6-8 months in a home freezer.

PREPARATION: The kind of beef you buy determines how it is to be prepared. Consult the chart that follows for recommended cooking methods and temperatures.

TIMETABLE FOR COOKING BEEF

CUT	ROASTED AT 300 F. OVEN TEMPERATURE		BROILED		BRAISED	COOKED IN LIQUID
	Meat Thermometer Reading Degrees F.	Time Minutes per lb.	Meat Thermometer Reading Degrees F.	Total Time Minutes	Total Time Hours	Total Time Hours
Standing Ribs	140 (rare)	18 to 20				
Standing Ribs	160 (medium)	22 to 25				
Standing Ribs	170 (well)	27 to 30				
Rolled Ribs	Same as above	Add 10 to 15				
Blade, 3rd to 5th Rib (high quality only)	150-170	25 to 30				
Rump (high quality only)	150-170	25 to 30				
Tenderloin	140-170	20 to 25				
Beef Loaf	160-170	25 to 30				
Steaks (1 inch)			140 (rare) 160 (medium)	15 to 20 20 to 30		
Steaks (1 1/2 inch)			140 (rare) 160 (medium)	25 to 35 35 to 50		
Steaks (2 inch)			140 (rare) 160 (medium)	30 to 40 50 to 70		
Beef Patties (1 inch)			140 (rare) 160 (medium)	12 to 15 18 to 20		
Pot-Roasts						
Arm or Blade					3 to 4	
Rump					3 to 4	
Swiss Steak					2 to 3	
Corned Beef						3 1/2 to 5
Fresh Beef					3 to 4	3 to 4
Stew						2 to 3

COACH HOUSE PLATTER

Color photograph for this recipe on page 308.

2 15-oz. cans red kidney beans
1 4-oz. can whole mushrooms
1 12-oz. can whole kernel corn
1 4-oz. can pimentos
1 1/2 c. diagonally sliced celery
2 tbsp. finely chopped onion
1/4 c. finely chopped parsley
2 tbsp. capers
1/2 tsp. salt
1/4 tsp. pepper
2/3 c. Cheddar and wine dressing
12 slices cold roast beef
Salad greens

Drain kidney beans, mushrooms, corn and pimentos; cut pimentos in strips. Combine celery, kidney beans, mushrooms, corn, onion, half the pimento strips, 2 tablespoons parsley and 1 tablespoon capers in mixing bowl. Sprinkle with salt and pepper. Add dressing; toss to mix well. Chill. Fold slices of roast beef; arrange along sides of serving platter. Place salad greens at ends of platter; spoon corn mixture in mound in center. Spoon additional dressing over corn mixture if desired. Garnish with remaining pimento strips, parsley and capers. Yield: 6 servings.

WESTERN HOSPITALITY CASSEROLE

3/4 c. flour
2 tsp. salt
4 lb. stew beef
1/2 c. oil
2 cloves of garlic, minced
1 6-oz. can tomato paste
1 1/4 c. dry red wine
1 tsp. thyme
2 bay leaves
2 4-oz. cans mushrooms
1 8-oz. package egg noodle bows
3 c. shredded Cheddar cheese

Combine flour and salt. Cut beef into 1-inch cubes. Dredge beef cubes with flour mixture. Brown in oil in Dutch oven over medium heat. Add garlic, tomato paste, wine, 3 cups of water, thyme and bay leaves; cover. Simmer for 1 hour and 30 minutes or until beef is tender. Remove bay leaves; stir in mushrooms. Cook noodles according to package directions; drain. Combine noodles and beef mixture; pour into two 12 x 8-inch baking dishes. Cover with foil. Bake at 350 degrees for 1 hour. Uncover; border with cheese. Bake for 15 minutes longer. Yield: 12 servings.

DRIED BEEF AND FRESH VEGETABLE SALAD

Color photograph for this recipe on page 313.

Leaf lettuce	*Swiss cheese strips*
Dried beef	*Fresh tomato wedges*
Fresh cucumber slices	*Watercress*
Hard-cooked egg slices	*Oil and vinegar dressing*
Fresh radish slices	

Place lettuce in salad bowl to cover bottom and side. Arrange dried beef, cucumber slices, egg slices, radish slices, cheese strips and tomato wedges in desired pattern on lettuce. Garnish with watercress; serve with dressing.

HEARTY BEEF FONDUE

Color photograph for this recipe on page 731.

Sirloin steak	*1 tbsp. finely chopped parsley*
Peanut oil	*1 tbsp. lemon juice*
3/4 c. peeled diced tomato	*3/4 tsp. salt*
1/3 c. finely diced green pepper	*1/4 tsp. pepper*
1/4 c. finely diced peeled cucumber	*1/2 tsp. sugar*
1/4 c. tomato paste	*1/4 tsp. paprika*
2 tbsp. finely chopped onion	*3/4 tsp. minced garlic*
	1 tsp. cornstarch

Trim all fat from steak; cut into 1-inch cubes. Dry steak; let stand at room temperature. Fill fondue pot 2/3 full with peanut oil. Heat on burner of stove to 425 degrees or until small piece of steak browns. Place pot oil on fondue stand in center of table over canned heat. Combine tomato, green pepper, cucumber, tomato paste, onion, parsley, lemon juice, 1 tablespoon peanut oil, salt, pepper, sugar, paprika and garlic in blender. Whirl just until the mixture is liquified. Stir in cornstarch; pour into saucepan. Heat, stirring, until mixture comes to a boil; reduce heat. Cook for 1 minute. Have each guest spear steak with long-handled fork and dip in oil. Cook steak cubes to desired doneness. Dip into hot sauce.

INTERNATIONAL FONDUE

Color photograph for this recipe on page 722.

Beef tenderloin	*Spareribs*
Leg of lamb	*4 c. corn oil*
Chicken breasts	

Cut beef tenderloin and lamb into 3/4-inch cubes. Bone chicken breast; skin and cut into cubes. Cut spareribs in 1 1/2-inch single-rib pieces; parboil. Pour oil into base of automatic fondue; position tray and rack. Plug unit into 120 volt outlet. Preheat oil for 10 to 15 minutes or until signal light goes on. Proper temperature for cooking is 375 degrees. Signal light will go on and off during cooking indicating proper temperature is automatically being maintained. Follow manufacturer's directions for cooking if your electric fondue pot differs from one pictured here. Provide each person with a plate for sauces, a fondue fork for cooking and a separate fork for eating. Each person spears and cooks choice of meat in hot corn oil to desired doneness, lets it drain briefly on rack, then, using dinner fork, dips cooked meat into desired sauce. Prepare 1 1/2 to 2 pounds of 2 to 4 different meats for 4 to 5 main dish servings or 12 appetizer servings.

Chinese Plum Sauce

1 c. plum preserves or jam	*2 tbsp. corn oil*
1/4 c. red wine vinegar	*1 tbsp. dry mustard*
	1/2 sm. clove of garlic, crushed

Mix all ingredients together in a bowl. Yield: 1 cup.

Oriental Sauce

1/2 c. mayonnaise	*1/4 c. chopped green onions*
1/4 c. sour cream	*1 tsp. ground ginger*
1 tbsp. soy sauce	

Mix all ingredients together in a bowl. Yield: 3/4 cup.

STEAK-BURGUNDY BAKE

1 1/2 to 2 lb. beefsteak	*1/2 tsp. salt*
8 oz. sliced mushrooms	*1/4 tsp. pepper*
1/4 c. chopped onion	*1/2 tsp. oregano*
1/4 c. chopped parsley	*1/4 tsp. sweet basil*
2 sm. cloves of garlic, chopped	*1/4 tsp. ground thyme*
2 tbsp. oil	*1 sm. bay leaf*
3/4 c. Burgundy	*5 cooked potatoes, mashed*
1 6-oz. can tomato paste	*1 egg*
	1 tbsp. grated Parmesan cheese

Cut beefsteak in thin strips; brown in small amount of fat. Saute mushrooms, onion, parsley and garlic in oil until tender; add steak. Mix Burgundy, tomato paste and 1/2 cup water; pour over steak mixture. Add seasonings; simmer for 25 minutes. Place in casserole. Mix potatoes, egg and cheese; shape into balls. Place on steak mixture. Bake at 375 degrees for 20 minutes. Yield: 4 servings.

BEEF TIPS VERONIQUE

2 lb. lean beef	*2 tbsp. chopped parsley*
1 tbsp. dry mustard	*3 c. cooked rice*
1 tbsp. honey	*1/2 c. seedless grapes*
1 tsp. salt	

Cut beef into 1-inch cubes; brown in small amount of fat in skillet. Add 1/4 cup water; simmer until tender. Remove beef from skillet to heated dish. Combine mustard, honey, salt and 1/2 cup water; add to pan drippings. Simmer to blend. Add parsley, rice and grapes; heat through. Serve rice mixture with beef. Yield: 6 servings.

CORNED BEEF BRISKET

1 6-lb. brisket of beef	*Salt*
	2 tbsp. saltpeter

1/2 c. (packed) brown sugar
1/2 c. minced pickling spice
Garlic
Pepper to taste
Paprika

Sprinkle beef liberally with salt; refrigerate overnight. Combine 1 quart lukewarm water, saltpeter, brown sugar, pickling spice, 1 cup salt and 2 minced cloves of garlic. Place beef in crock. Pour water mixture over beef, adding enough cold water to cover. Keep in cool place for 10 days, skimming occasionally. Wash beef well; cover with cold water. Add salt, pepper and garlic to taste. Simmer slowly for 3 hours. Cool beef in liquid. Remove beef from liquid; drain. Sprinkle with paprika. Serve hot or cold.

BRAVO CORNED BEEF AND CORN BREAD

Color photograph for this recipe on page 74.

1 egg
1/2 c. milk
1 10-oz. package corn bread mix
3/4 lb. corned beef, chopped
1 1-lb. can kidney beans
1 1-lb. can stewed tomatoes
1 tsp. salt
1/2 tsp. oregano
1/4 tsp. pepper
1 tsp. cornstarch
Parmesan cheese
Parsley sprigs

Preheat oven to 425 degrees. Place egg and milk in bag of corn bread mix. Squeeze upper part of bag to force air out; close top of bag by holding tightly between thumb and index finger. Place bag on table; mix, working bag vigorously with fingers, for about 40 seconds or until egg is completely blended. Squeeze bag to empty batter into ungreased aluminum pan contained in package. Bake for about 20 minutes. Brown corned beef in skillet in small amount of fat; drain off excess drippings. Drain kidney beans; add to corned beef. Add tomatoes, 1/4 cup water, salt, oregano and pepper; cook over medium heat for 20 minutes. Mix cornstarch with small amount of water; stir into corned beef mixture. Cook for about 5 minutes longer or until slightly thickened. Cut corn bread into 6 pieces. Split each piece horizontally; toast. Place 2 pieces of corn bread on each serving plate; spoon corned beef mixture over corn bread. Sprinkle with Parmesan cheese; garnish with parsley. Yield: 6 servings.

CORNED BEEF IN FOIL

2 oranges, sliced
2 med. onions, diced
4 stalks celery, chopped
2 cloves of garlic
2 tsp. dillseed
1 tsp. rosemary
12 whole cloves
1 6-in. cinnamon stick
2 bay leaves
1 3 to 4-lb. corned beef brisket

Combine all ingredients except beef; arrange half the mixture on large sheet of heavy-duty foil. Place beef on top; add remaining mixture to top of beef. Seal foil loosely; place in shallow pan. Bake in 325-degree oven for 3 to 4 hours or until beef is tender. Yield: 6-8 servings.

GLAZED CORNED BEEF

1 5 to 7-lb. corned beef
6 peppercorns
1 onion, sliced
4 whole cloves
1 stalk celery, chopped
1/3 c. (packed) brown sugar
1 tbsp. prepared mustard
1 tsp. bottled horseradish
1/3 c. catsup
3 tbsp. vinegar
2 tbsp. butter or margarine

Place beef in Dutch oven; cover with water. Add peppercorns, onion, cloves and celery. Simmer for 4 hours and 30 minutes to 5 hours or until almost tender. Remove from water; place in baking pan. Combine brown sugar, mustard, horseradish, catsup, vinegar and butter in saucepan. Stir over medium heat until blended and bubbly. Spoon part of sauce over beef. Bake in 350-degree oven for 30 minutes or until tender, basting frequently with remaining sauce. Yield: 8 servings.

BARBECUED HEART

1/2 beef heart
2 med. onions, shredded
2 tbsp. margarine
2 tbsp. brown sugar
1/4 c. vinegar
2 cloves of garlic, minced
2 tbsp. Worcestershire sauce
1/2 c. catsup
1 tsp. salt
1/4 tsp. pepper

Cut heart into 1/2-inch cubes; place in pressure cooker pan with 1 cup boiling water. Cook at 10 pounds pressure for 1 hour. Brown onions in margarine; stir in remaining ingredients. Simmer sauce for 45 minutes. Add heart; simmer for about 30 minutes longer. Serve on rice, noodles or toast. Three lamb or pork hearts may be substituted for beef heart. Yield: 6 servings.

STUFFED ROASTED BEEF HEART

1 beef heart
1/2 tbsp. chopped onion
1 tbsp. chopped celery
3 tbsp. melted butter
1 c. bread crumbs
1 tsp. salt
1/4 tsp. pepper
1 tsp. chopped parsley
2 tbsp. flour

Clean heart. Saute onion and celery in butter; add crumbs, seasonings, parsley and 2 tablespoons water. Fill heart; tie with string. Place in baking dish with 1 cup water. Bake, covered, at 350 degrees for 3 hours, basting occasionally. Remove heart from baking pan. Stir flour into pan juices; cook until gravy is thickened, stirring constantly. Add seasonings, if needed. Yield: 6 servings.

SIRLOIN KABOBS

6 bacon slices
3 lb. sirloin, cut in 1 1/2-in. cubes
1 lb. large mushroom caps
2 c. Italian dressing

Cut bacon into 1 1/2-inch squares. Thread skewers with sirloin, bacon and mushroom caps; repeat until skewers are full. Marinate in dressing for 2 to 3 hours at room temperature, turning frequently. Cook over charcoal grill to desired doneness.

EASY SHISH KABOB

1 4-lb. beef chuck or arm roast
1 pt. Italian dressing
Pepper to taste
Salt to taste
Monosodium glutamate
2 green peppers
6 sm. onions
1 pt. cherry tomatoes
1/2 pt. fresh mushrooms

Cut beef into 1-inch cubes; place in shallow casserole. Pour dressing over beef, coating well. Sprinkle with pepper, salt and monosodium glutamate. Marinate for 1 hour and 30 minutes. Cut green peppers and onions into wedges. Coat green peppers, onions, tomatoes and mushrooms with marinade sauce. Arrange beef and vegetables alternately on individual metal skewers. Grill for 15 to 20 minutes, turning once and basting with remaining marinade. Serve immediately.

ISLAND TERIYAKI

1 c. soy sauce
1/2 c. (packed) brown sugar
1/4 c. salad oil
2 tsp. ginger
1 tsp. monosodium glutamate
1/2 tsp. pepper
4 cloves of garlic, minced
1 3-lb. sirloin steak, 1-in. thick
Canned water chestnuts, drained

Combine soy sauce, brown sugar, oil, ginger, monosodium glutamate, pepper and garlic in deep bowl; mix well. Cut steak into thin slices. Add steak and water chestnuts to marinade; toss until coated. Marinate for 2 hours at room temperature. Thread steak strips on skewers accordion fashion alternately with water chestnuts. Broil for 5 to 6 minutes, over hot coals, turning frequently. Yield: 4 servings.

SHISH KABOBS

1 3-lb. beef sirloin tip roast
Seasoned meat tenderizer
3/4 c. Worcestershire sauce
2 tbsp. olive oil
3/4 c. soy sauce
1 lge. green pepper, cubed
1 can whole mushrooms
1 clove of garlic, minced
Oregano to taste
Salt to taste
Pepper to taste
1 sm. onion, chopped

Cut beef into 1-inch cubes; season with meat tenderizer. Let stand for 2 hours. Combine beef, Worcestershire sauce, olive oil, soy sauce, green pepper, mushrooms, garlic, oregano, salt, pepper and onion; refrigerate overnight. Place beef, mushrooms and green pepper alternately on skewers; broil until browned, basting with marinade. May be grilled over hot coals, if desired.

SKEWERED STEAK AND MUSHROOMS

1/2 c. Burgundy
1 tsp. Worcestershire sauce
1 clove of garlic
1/2 c. salad oil
2 tbsp. catsup
1 tsp. sugar
1/2 tsp. salt
1/2 tsp. monosodium glutamate
1 tbsp. vinegar
1/2 tsp. marjoram
1/2 tsp. rosemary
1 lb. sirloin steak
12 lge. fresh mushrooms

Mix Burgundy, Worcestershire sauce, garlic, oil, catsup, sugar, salt, monosodium glutamate, vinegar, marjoram and rosemary. Cut beef into 2-inch cubes. Marinate steak cubes and mushrooms in wine mixture for 2 hours. Drain; reserve marinade. Alternate beef cubes and mushrooms on skewers. Broil, turning on all sides; baste with remaining marinade frequently. Yield: 4 servings.

BAKED BEEF LIVER AND BACON

1 egg, slightly beaten
1/4 c. milk
4 slices liver
Flour
3/4 c. bread crumbs
Salt and pepper to taste
8 slices bacon

Combine egg and milk. Dredge liver in flour; dip into egg mixture. Roll in bread crumbs. Place in greased shallow pan; sprinkle with salt and pepper. Cover with bacon. Bake at 350 degrees for 20 minutes. Yield: 4 servings.

BRAISED LIVER WITH VEGETABLES

Flour
1 1/2 tsp. salt
1/8 tsp. pepper
1 lb. liver
4 tbsp. fat
6 potatoes, sliced 1 in. thick
2 carrots, diced
1 sm. onion, chopped
1 c. tomato juice
1 tbsp. lemon juice
1 tbsp. vinegar
2 tbsp. catsup

Mix 3 tablespoons flour, 3/4 teaspoon salt and pepper. Cut liver into 2-inch squares; dredge in seasoned flour. Brown in hot fat; remove liver from pan. Place potatoes, carrots and onion in pan; brown lightly. Add liver, tomato juice, 1 cup boiling water, remaining salt, lemon juice, vinegar and catsup; stir well. Simmer, covered, for 1 hour. Add small amount of flour to pan liquid to thicken for gravy if desired. Yield: 6 servings.

LIVER AND BACON LOAF

1 lb. beef liver
6 slices bacon
1 med. onion
1/4 c. finely chopped celery
1 c. coarsely crushed corn flakes
1 1/2 tsp. salt
1/8 tsp. pepper
1/4 tsp. marjoram
1/4 c. chili sauce
1 tbsp. flour
1 egg, lightly beaten

Place liver in saucepan with boiling water to cover. Simmer for 10 minutes. Drain, reserving 1 cup broth. Cut liver into pieces; grind liver, bacon and onion. Combine celery, crumbs, salt, pepper, marjoram and chili sauce; add to liver mixture. Add 1/4 cup water gradually to flour, blending until smooth. Add flour mixture to reserved broth gradually; simmer until thickened, stirring well. Add small amount broth mixture to egg, stirring constantly; stir egg mixture into broth mixture gradually. Cook until thickened, stirring constantly. Add to liver mixture, blending well. Pack into buttered 9 x 5 x 3-inch pan. Bake at 350 degrees for 1 hour.

LIVER DUMPLINGS

1 1/2 lb. liver
1 tbsp. butter
1 lge. onion, diced
8 c. bread crumbs
2 eggs, beaten
Salt and pepper to taste
1/2 c. flour
6 c. beef or chicken broth

Cook liver in small amount of water for 5 minutes. Remove from pan and grind. Melt butter in large skillet; saute onion and crumbs in butter. Combine liver and eggs; add to crumb mixture. Season with salt and pepper. Stir in flour. Pour broth in large saucepan; bring to boiling point. Drop liver mixture by spoonfuls into hot broth. Cook, covered, for 30 minutes, shaking frequently. Soup may be substituted for broth. Yield: 6-8 servings.

BEEF PIE

2 c. chopped cooked beef
3 c. thin gravy
1 lge. onion, chopped
1 c. sliced carrots
2 c. sliced potatoes
1/4 tsp. salt
Dash of pepper
1/4 tsp. minced onion
1/4 tsp. celery salt
1 recipe biscuit dough

Combine beef, gravy, chopped onion, carrots, potatoes, salt and pepper in saucepan; mix well. Bring to a boil; reduce heat and simmer for about 10 minutes, stirring occasionally. Pour into casserole. Add minced onion and celery salt to biscuit dough. Drop dough by spoonfuls onto beef mixture. Bake at 350 degrees for 35 minutes. Yield: 8 servings.

CHIPPED BEEF POTPIE

1 c. chopped onions
1 4-oz. package dried beef, diced
1/4 c. margarine
2 tbsp. flour
1/2 tsp. salt
1/4 tsp. pepper
2 c. thinly sliced carrots
2 c. thinly sliced potatoes
1 beef bouillon cube

Saute onions and beef in margarine; stir in flour and seasonings. Add carrots and potatoes. Dissolve bouillon cube in 2 cups hot water. Add to beef mixture; bring to a boil. Simmer, covered, for 5 minutes. Pour into 2-quart casserole.

Topping

1 c. flour
1/2 tsp. salt
1/2 c. shortening

Combine flour and salt; cut in shortening. Sprinkle 2 tablespoons water over mixture, mixing with fork until dough clings together. Roll out pastry on floured board to fit over casserole. Slash top to allow steam to escape. Bake at 425 degrees for 25 to 30 minutes.

CORNISH PASTY

1 1/2 lb. beef
1/8 lb. suet
1 lge. onion, finely diced
4 med. potatoes, finely diced
4 carrots or 1 rutabaga, diced
1 tsp. salt
1/4 tsp. pepper
Pastry for 2 two-crust pies

Cut beef into 1/2-inch cubes. Break suet into small pieces; combine with beef, vegetables and seasonings. Roll pastry into 4 rounds. Place 1/4 of the beef mixture on one side of each pastry round. Fold pastry over beef mixture; pinch edges together. Place on baking sheet. Bake at 350 degrees for 1 hour. Yield: 4 servings.

LITTLE MEAT PIES

1 lb. flank steak
6 oz. fresh pork
3 c. flour
1 tbsp. salt
1 c. lard
1 sm. rutabaga, grated
5 potatoes, diced
Salt and pepper to taste
2 tbsp. chopped suet
6 tbsp. minced onion

Cut steak and pork into 1-inch cubes. Sift flour and salt together into bowl; cut in lard until particles are size of small peas. Add 1 cup cold water, small amount at a time, tossing until dough clings together. Divide dough into 6 parts; roll to 9-inch circles on floured surface. Place 2 tablespoons rutabaga, 3/4 cup potatoes, 1/6 of the steak and 1 ounce pork on half of each dough circle; season with salt and pepper. Sprinkle with 1 teaspoon suet and 1 tablespoon onion. Fold dough over filling; seal edges. Place on baking sheet; slash to let steam escape. Bake at 400 degrees for 1 hour. Yield: 6 servings.

STEAK AND KIDNEY PIE

1 1/2 lb. stewing beef, diced
1 6-oz. kidney, sliced
1/2 lb. mushrooms, sliced
1 c. chopped onion
1/4 c. minced parsley
1/2 bay leaf, crumbled
1 tsp. salt
1 c. butter
3 c. sifted self-rising flour
1 c. milk

Place beef, kidney, mushrooms, onion, parsley, bay leaf and salt in baking dish; add 2 cups water. Cut butter into flour until of cornmeal consistency. Add milk; mix to form soft dough. Roll dough to about 1/8-inch thickness on floured surface. Place on top of beef mixture, sealing edges. Slash dough several times. Bake at 325 degrees for 1 hour and 45 minutes. Yield: 6 servings.

PRESSED BEEF

4 lb. beef shanks
6 whole cloves
1 med. onion, sliced
1 stick cinnamon
2 tsp. salt
1/4 tsp. pepper
1 tbsp. sage

Place beef in large saucepan; add water to cover. Stir in cloves, onion, cinnamon, salt and pepper. Simmer, covered, for 3 hours or until beef is tender. Remove beef from broth; reserve broth. Remove meat from bones; chop fine. Pack into 5 x 9-inch loaf pan. Strain reserved broth; add sage. Cook, reducing liquid to 1 cup; pour over beef. Chill until firm. Slice thin to serve. Yield: 12 servings.

BARBECUED BEEF BRISKET

1 5 to 6-lb. beef brisket
Bottled liquid smoke
Celery salt to taste
Garlic salt to taste
Onion salt to taste
Meat tenderizer
Salt and pepper to taste
1 tbsp. Worcestershire sauce
3/4 c. barbecue sauce
2 tbsp. flour

Rub brisket on all sides with liquid smoke. Sprinkle with celery salt, garlic salt, onion salt and meat tenderizer. Seal in aluminum foil; refrigerate overnight. Sprinkle both sides with salt, pepper and Worcestershire sauce. Place in baking pan. Bake, covered, at 275 degrees for 5 hours. Uncover; add barbecue sauce. Bake for 1 hour longer. Remove brisket from pan; skim fat from pan drippings. Combine flour and 1/4 cup water; stir gradually into pan dripping gravy to thicken. Add additional barbecue sauce to taste. Cool brisket for 1 hour; slice. Pour gravy over sliced meat or serve hot in separate dish. Yield: 8-10 servings.

PEPPERED BEEF SLICES

1 4-lb. boned beef brisket
1 tbsp. peppercorns, crushed
1 1/2 tsp. salt
1/8 tsp. allspice
2 tbsp. fine dry bread crumbs
1 tsp. garlic salt
1/4 c. chopped onion
3 tbsp. bacon fat

Pound beef flat; score on both sides. Combine peppercorns, salt, allspice, crumbs and garlic salt; sprinkle evenly over beef. Roll beef firmly; tie with cord. Saute onion lightly in fat in Dutch oven until transparent. Add beef roll; cover with boiling water. Simmer, covered, for 4 hours or until tender. Slice to serve. Yield: 10 servings.

BARBECUED POT ROAST

1 8-oz. can tomato sauce
1/2 c. beef broth
1 onion, chopped
Paprika to taste
Garlic powder to taste
Salt to taste
1 5-lb. pot roast
1/4 c. vinegar
1/4 c. catsup
2 tsp. Worcestershire sauce
1 tsp. mustard

Combine tomato sauce, beef broth and onion; season with paprika, garlic powder and salt. Place roast in refrigerator dish; add tomato sauce mixture. Refrigerate, covered, for about 12 hours or overnight. Remove roast from marinade, reserving marinade. Brown roast slowly in hot fat in Dutch oven. Add vinegar, catsup, Worcestershire sauce and mustard to reserved marinade; stir to blend. Pour over roast. Simmer, covered, for 2 hours and 30 minutes or until tender. Roast may be baked in 350-degree oven, if desired. Yield: 8 servings.

BAVARIAN POT ROAST

1 5-lb. chuck roast
1 tbsp. cinnamon
1 tbsp. vinegar
2 tsp. ginger
1 1/2 tsp. salt
1 1/2 c. apple juice
1 8-oz. can tomato sauce
1 med. onion, chopped
1 bay leaf
1/4 c. flour
1/4 c. sliced mushrooms

Brown roast on all sides in oil in Dutch oven. Combine cinnamon, vinegar, ginger and salt; add 1 cup water, apple juice, tomato sauce, onion and bay leaf. Place roast in Dutch oven; pour tomato sauce mixture over top. Simmer, covered, for 3 hours or until tender. Remove bay leaf. Combine flour and 1/2 cup water to make paste. Add to tomato mixture gradually, stirring constantly, until thickened. Add mushrooms to gravy. Serve gravy over roast slices. Yield: 8-12 servings.

BOEUF CHANDELIER

1 3-lb. arm roast
Salt and pepper to taste
1 tbsp. sugar
1 tsp. butter
1 tsp. oil
1/2 to 1 c. tomato or chili sauce
1 tsp. hot sauce
1/2 tsp. garlic salt
1 tsp. Worcestershire sauce
1 tbsp. (packed) brown sugar
1/2 tsp. curry powder
1/2 tsp. pepper
1/2 c. dry sherry
1/4 tsp. smoked salt

Rub roast with salt and pepper; sprinkle with sugar. Melt butter and oil in skillet. Place roast in skillet; brown, turning once. Remove roast; place in large foil-lined baking pan. Add remaining ingredients to drippings in skillet; bring to a boil. Pour mixture over roast; seal foil. Bake at 250 degrees for 3 hours or until tender. Yield: 6-8 servings.

DILL POT ROAST WITH CARROT GRAVY

6 tbsp. flour
3 tsp. salt
1/4 tsp. pepper
1 4-lb. chuck roast
3 tbsp. oil
1 med. onion, sliced
1 tsp. dillseed
2 tbsp. vinegar
1 c. grated carrots

Combine 4 tablespoons flour, salt and pepper; dredge roast in mixture. Brown roast on all sides in oil in Dutch oven. Drain off excess oil. Add onion, dillseed, vinegar and 1/2 cup water; simmer for 2 hours and 30 minutes. Add carrots; simmer for 1 hour longer. Remove roast. Mix remaining flour with 1/2 cup water; add to pan juices gradually. Cook, stirring constantly, until thickened. Serve gravy with roast. Yield: 6-8 servings.

GINGER BEEF

1 tsp. turmeric
2 tsp. ginger
2 tsp. salt
1 4-lb. beef pot roast
2 med. onions, chopped
2 cloves of garlic, minced
1 c. canned tomatoes
1 c. beef broth
2 dried red peppers, crushed

Combine turmeric, ginger and salt; rub roast with mixture. Brown roast in 2 tablespoons hot fat in heavy skillet. Place rack under roast in skillet; add remaining ingredients. Simmer, covered, for 3 hours and 30 minutes. Yield: 6 servings.

SHREDDED BARBECUED BEEF

1 3-lb. chuck roast
1 lge. onion, chopped
1 stalk celery, chopped
1 lge. green pepper, chopped
2 cloves of garlic
1 tsp. salt
2 c. catsup
2 tbsp. (packed) brown sugar
2 tbsp. vinegar
1 tsp. allspice
1 tsp. dry mustard
1/2 tsp. chili powder
3 drops of hot sauce
1 tsp. Worcestershire sauce
1 bay leaf
1/4 tsp. garlic salt
1/4 tsp. paprika

Place roast, onion, celery, green pepper and garlic in large kettle; add 1 1/2 quarts water. Cover; bring ro a boil. Reduce heat; cook for 4 hours. Remove roast, reserving 1 1/2 cups broth; cool. Shred roast; return to reserved broth. Stir in remaining ingredients. Cook, uncovered, for 1 hour, adding water as needed. Yield: 20 servings.

SPICED YORK POT ROAST

1 5-lb. beef roast
Salt and pepper to taste
1 med. onion, thinly sliced
1 sm. piece of horseradish root, grated
3 celery tops
1 carrot, thinly sliced
1 tsp. peppercorns
3 bay leaves
Red wine vinegar
Shortening
1 c. sour cream
1 egg, beaten

Rub beef with salt and pepper; place in crock. Add onion, horseradish, celery tops, carrot, peppercorns and bay leaves. Combine with equal amounts of vinegar and water; pour over beef to cover. Place crock in cold place; marinate beef for 2 to 3 days, turning occasionally. Drain; dry beef, reserving marinade. Melt shortening in skillet; brown beef on all sides. Place in roasting pan. Strain marinade; pour over beef. Bake, covered, at 350 degrees for about 3 hours or until tender. Remove beef; simmer pan juices until reduced by half. Combine sour cream and egg; add to pan juices gradually. Simmer, stirring constantly, for 5 minutes. Serve with roast. Yield: 10-12 servings.

SPICED AND FRUITED CHUCK ROAST

1 7-oz. bottle ginger ale
24 dried apricot halves
18 dried prunes, pitted
1/3 c. (packed) brown sugar
2 tsp. salt
1 tsp. cinnamon
1/2 tsp. mace
1 4 to 5-lb. beef chuck roast
2 tbsp. shortening
1 c. chopped onion

Preheat oven to 300 degrees. Combine ginger ale, apricots and prunes; set aside. Combine brown sugar, salt, cinnamon and mace; rub into both sides of beef. Melt shortening in heavy pan; brown beef slowly on both sides. Add onion, 1/2 cup water and any remaining sugar mixture. Bake, covered, for about 2 hours. Spoon fruit mixture over beef; bake for 30 minutes longer or until tender. Yield: 8 servings.

PEPPERED RIB EYE OF BEEF

1 5-lb. beef rib eye roast
1/2 c. coarsely ground pepper
1/2 tsp. ground cardamom seed
1 tbsp. tomato paste
1 c. soy sauce
1/2 tsp. garlic powder
1 tsp. paprika
3/4 c. vinegar
1 1/4 tbsp. cornstarch

Trim fat from beef. Sprinkle pepper and cardamom seed over beef; press in with heel of hand. Place beef in close-fitting dish. Mix tomato paste with soy sauce; add garlic powder, paprika and vinegar. Pour over beef; marinate overnight. Remove beef, reserving marinade; wrap tightly in foil. Place in pan; let stand at room temperature for 1 hour. Bake in 300-degree oven for about 1 hour and 30 minutes or until tender. Remove beef from oven. Combine 1 cup water, 1 cup pan juices, and small amount reserved marinade; pour into saucepan. Mix cornstarch with 1/4 cup water; stir into pan juice mixture. Cook, stirring constantly, until thickened. Slice beef thin; serve with gravy. Yield: 10 servings.

ROLLED RIB ROAST

1 5 lb. rolled rib roast
Salt
Pepper

Season roast with salt and pepper to taste. Place, fat side up, on rack in shallow pan. Insert meat thermometer in center of roast. Bake in 325-degree oven for about 2 hours or to 150 degrees on meat thermometer. Let roast stand for 20 minutes in warm place before carving. Serve with browned whole potatoes. Yield: 12 servings.

Rolled Rib Roast . . . The ultimate beef dish that pleases every member of the family.

ENGLISH ROAST BEEF AND YORKSHIRE PUDDING

Flour
6 tbsp. butter
1 tbsp. dry mustard
1 tsp. paprika
1/4 tsp. pepper
1 6-lb. standing rib roast
2 eggs, well-beaten
1 c. milk
1/4 tsp. salt

Place 1/4 cup flour in heavy skillet; brown over medium heat, stirring until lightly browned. Remove from heat. Cream butter; add browned flour, mustard, paprika and pepper. Blend well. Place roast, standing on bones, in roasting pan. Spread flour mixture over roast. Bake at 325 degrees to desired doneness. Combine eggs and milk; add 3 tablespoons drippings from roast. Add 1 cup sifted flour and salt; beat until smooth. Pour into greased cups. Bake at 450 degrees for 25 minutes or until well browned. Yield: 6 servings.

CHRISTMAS DAY STANDING RIB ROAST OF BEEF

Color photograph for this recipe on page 70.

1 standing 4-rib beef roast
Salt
Freshly ground pepper
1 crumbled bay leaf
6 med. potatoes
Cooking oil

Have butcher remove chine from roast and cut ribs short. Sprinkle with salt and pepper to taste and bay leaf. Insert meat thermometer so tip is in center of roast. Bake at 325 degrees until meat thermometer reads 120 degrees for rare, 140 degrees for medium rare or 150 degrees for well done. Remove from oven; cover. Let set for 20 minutes before carving. Peel potatoes; cut with spiral French cutter. Fill deep fat fryer about 1/3 full with oil; heat to 360 degrees on thermometer. Place potatoes in single layer in fryer basket. Lower into hot fat; cook until potatoes are tender but not brown. Remove from oil; drain well on paper towels. Keep at room temperature until almost serving time. Reheat oil to 375 degrees. Fry potatoes until golden brown. Drain; sprinkle with salt. Place on tray around roast; garnish with watercress.

STUFFED RIB ROAST

1/4 c. chopped onion
1 clove of garlic, minced
1 tbsp. (packed) brown sugar
1 tsp. salt
Dash of pepper
1 tsp. mustard
1 tsp. Worcestershire sauce
1 c. soft bread crumbs
1 3 to 4-lb. rolled rib roast
1 3-oz. can sliced mushrooms
2 tbsp. chopped stuffed green olives
1/2 c. shredded American cheese

Combine onion, garlic, brown sugar, salt, pepper, mustard, 1/4 cup water, Worcestershire sauce and bread crumbs. Unroll roast; spread with crumb mixture. Drain mushrooms; sprinkle mushrooms, olives and cheese over bread mixture. Roll roast up; tie securely. Fasten ends with skewers. Place on rack in shallow baking pan. Bake at 325 degrees to desired doneness. Yield: 9-12 servings.

ROAST RIB AU JUS

1 select prime standing rib roast
Salt and pepper to taste

Let roast stand at room temperature for 1 hour. Season with salt and pepper; place in baking pan. Bake, uncovered, at 350 degrees for 1 hour. Increase oven temperature to 375 degrees; bake for 40 minutes longer. Do not open oven door during baking. Remove roast; carve.

GOURMET BEEF ELEGANTE

1 3-lb. beef rump roast
Salt and pepper to taste
Monosodium glutamate
1 6-oz. can tomato paste
2 c. cold chicken stock
1 c. dry white wine
1/4 c. dry sherry
1 lge. onion
1 stalk celery, halved
1 bay leaf
1/2 tsp. oregano
2 tbsp. caraway seed, crushed
3 tbsp. flour
1/2 c. sour cream

Place beef in large bowl; sprinkle with salt, pepper and monosodium glutamate. Cover with tomato paste. Add chicken stock, wines, onion, celery, bay leaf and oregano. Marinate overnight, turning once. Remove beef from marinade; reserve marinade. Brown beef on all sides in Dutch oven; add marinade and caraway seed. Simmer until tender. Remove beef. Blend flour and 1 cup cold water. Add slowly to simmering liquid. Cook until thickened, stirring constantly. Remove onion, celery and bay leaf. Stir in sour cream slowly; blend well. Serve with beef. Yield: 4-6 servings.

BEEF SUPERIOR

1 3-lb. bottom round roast
Salt
1 med. onion, sliced
1/2 tsp. peppercorns
4 bay leaves
3 sprigs of parsley
3 celery tops
1 med. cabbage
3 tbsp. prepared horseradish
3 tsp. prepared mustard
Pepper to taste
3 tbsp. flour

Place roast in kettle; add water to cover. Add 2 teaspoons salt, onion, peppercorns, bay leaves, parsley and celery tops. Simmer, covered, for about 3 hours or until tender. Cut cabbage into 6 wedges; place around roast. Cook until cabbage is tender; remove roast and cabbage to platter. Strain broth, reserving 3 cups. Combine horseradish, mustard, salt and pepper and reserved broth. Bring mixture to a boil. Mix flour with small amount of water to make a paste; stir into broth mixture gradually. Cook, stirring constantly, until thick; serve over roast and cabbage.

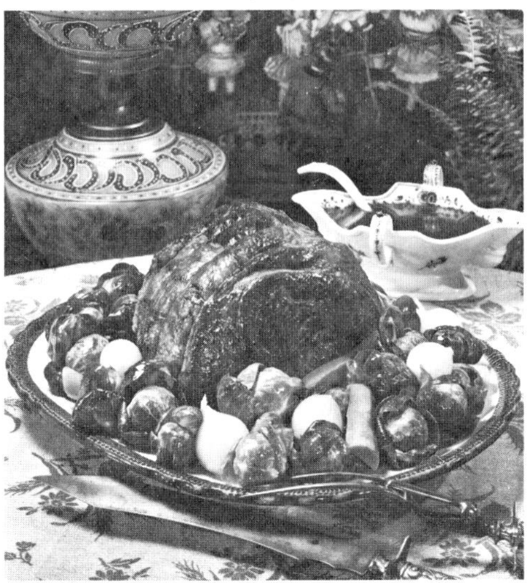

Rolled Shoulder Medley . . . A dish that blends the flavors of beef and Brussels sprouts.

ROLLED SHOULDER MEDLEY

1 4-lb. rolled boneless beef shoulder roast
1/4 c. flour
2 tbsp. salad oil
2 tsp. salt
1/8 tsp. pepper
1/4 tsp. thyme leaves
1/2 tsp. oregano leaves
1 bay leaf
2 beef bouillon cubes
1 c. red wine
6 med. carrots
1 lb. white onions, peeled
2 10-oz. packages frozen California Brussels sprouts

Roll roast in flour until coated on all sides. Heat oil in Dutch oven over medium heat; brown roast on all sides for about 15 to 20 minutes, turning as necessary. Add seasonings, bouillon, 1 cup water and wine. Cover tightly, simmer, turning occasionally for about 3 hours or until roast is tender. Pare carrots; cut into strips. Add carrots and onions to roast; cook for 25 minutes longer. Add Brussels sprouts; cook for about 15 minutes. Place roast in center of large heated serving platter; surround with vegetables. Cook pan drippings until reduced to desired consistency; remove bay leaf. Spoon fat off from surface of gravy. Spoon some gravy over roast and vegetables; serve remaining gravy in bowl. Yield: 6 servings.

BEEF TOURNEDOS

1 1-lb. beef tenderloin
10 fresh mushrooms, sliced
1/2 c. butter
1/2 c. cubed slab bacon
2 tbsp. Worcestershire sauce
2 beef bouillon cubes
2 tbsp. flour
1/3 c. Burgundy

Cut beef into bite-sized cubes. Saute mushrooms in butter in skillet for about 5 minutes. Remove mushrooms; pour butter from skillet and reserve. Brown bacon cubes slowly in skillet until brown and crisp. Remove bacon and grease from skillet; drain bacon. Wipe skillet lightly. Add reserved butter. Place beef in skillet; saute to desired degree of doneness, stirring occasionally. Add Worcestershire sauce, mushrooms and bacon. Combine 1 cup boiling water and bouillon cubes; stir until dissolved. Pour over beef mixture. Blend flour with Burgundy; stir into beef mixture. Cook, stirring, for about 4 minutes. Serve immediately with rice or noodles. Yield: 4 servings.

IMPERIAL TENDERLOIN

1 beef tenderloin
1/4 c. olive oil
1 clove of garlic
1 tbsp. Worcestershire sauce
4 oz. blue cheese
Butter
1 lb. mushroom caps
1 tsp. onion salt
1/2 tsp. caraway seed
Pepper to taste

Trim surface fat from beef. Brush with olive oil. Bake at 450 degrees for 45 to 60 minutes or until meat thermometer registers 140 degrees. Remove from oven. Mash garlic into Worcestershire sauce; combine with blue cheese and 1/2 cup butter. Spread over top of beef. Brown mushrooms in 2 tablespoons butter for 5 minutes. Add onion salt, caraway seed and pepper; toss. Serve immediately with beef. Yield: 8 servings.

ROAST BEEF TENDERLOIN

1 lge. beef tenderloin
1 clove of garlic, halved
Melted butter
Salt and pepper to taste
1 c. hot vegetable or meat stock
1 tbsp. cornstarch

Trim excess fat from beef; rub with garlic. Place on rack in baking pan. Brush with butter; sprinkle with salt and pepper. Pour vegetable stock in pan. Bake at 425 degrees for 30 minutes; reduce oven temperature to 300 degrees. Bake for 15 minutes per pound for rare, 20 minutes per pound for medium and 25 minutes per pound for well done. Baste every 15 minutes with butter. Remove beef; cool for 15 minutes before slicing. Stir cornstarch into small amount water; add to drippings gradually. Cook, stirring, until thickened. Serve with beef.

TENDERLOIN WITH MUSHROOM STUFFING

1 3-lb. beef tenderloin
1/4 c. butter
1/2 sm. onion, chopped
1 4-oz. can mushrooms
1 1/2 c. soft bread crumbs
1/2 c. diced celery
Salt and pepper to taste
4 slices bacon

Have tenderloin split and flattened at market. Melt butter in skillet; add onion and mushrooms, browning lightly. Add bread crumbs, celery and enough hot water to moisten. Season with salt and pepper; spread over half the beef. Bring second half over; fasten edges together. Season with salt and pepper; place on rack in baking pan. Arrange bacon over top. Bake at 350 degrees for 1 hour. Yield: 6 servings.

FILLET WELLINGTON

Butter
2 shallots, minced
1 1/2 lb. mushrooms, minced
1 tbsp. flour
2 tbsp. cream
2 tbsp. Madeira
1 tbsp. minced parsley
1/2 tsp. salt
1/8 tsp. pepper
1 4 1/2 to 5 1/2-lb. fillet of beef
2 tbsp. soy sauce
2 tbsp. Worcestershire sauce
1 recipe pie pastry
1 egg yolk

Melt 2 tablespoons butter in hot skillet; saute shallots with mushrooms until mushrooms are browned and moisture evaporates. Stir in flour. Reduce heat; add cream, Madeira, parsley, salt and pepper. Cook for 2 minutes, stirring constantly, until thickened; refrigerate. Let fillet stand to room temperature; sprinkle with soy sauce and Worcestershire sauce. Roll out 1/2 of the pastry into 16 x 9-inch rectangle. Pastry should be longer than fillet and more than twice as wide. Place dough on jelly roll pan; refrigerate. Spread fillet with 3 tablespoons butter; place in roasting pan. Bake at 400 degrees for 30 minutes. Remove from oven; set aside to cool for at least 1 hour or longer. Reserve pan drippings. Remove pastry and mushroom dressing from refrigerator. Spread mushroom mixture down center of pastry. Place fillet, top side down, on mushrooms. Fold dough to enclose fillet. Turn fillet onto jelly roll pan, seam side down. Make crisscross design over top with knife. Combine egg yolk and small amount of water. Brush fillet with egg mixture. Bake at 400 degrees for 35 minutes.

Wine Sauce Au Perigord

2 tbsp. chicken liver pate
1 sm. truffle, minced
1/2 c. port
1 tbsp. cornstarch
1 1/2 c. beef broth

Blend pate, truffle and port together. Mix cornstarch and 2 tablespoons water. Cook beef broth with reserved pan drippings for 3 to 5 minutes. Blend pate, cornstarch and broth mixtures, stirring constantly, until thickened. Place fillet on large oval platter; slice in 1/2-inch slices. Garnish with watercress. Spoon sauce over each slice to serve. Yield: 8-10 servings.

STUFFED CHATEAUBRIAND ROAST

1 4-lb. beef tenderloin
4 c. Chablis
1/2 c. butter, softened
1/2 c. brandy
1/4 tsp. thyme
1/2 bay leaf
1 med. onion, thinly sliced
1/2 lb. mushrooms, sliced

Marinate beef in Chablis for at least 12 hours. Combine butter, brandy, thyme, bay leaf, onion and mushrooms in saucepan; simmer until liquid is reduced by half. Cut lengthwise pocket in beef; fill with mushroom mixture. Tie or skewer opening together. Place in roasting pan. Bake, uncovered, in 325-degree oven for 45 minutes or until to desired degree of doneness. Serve with bearnaise sauce; garnish with watercress. Yield: 8 servings.

BARBECUED BEEF

1 3-lb. beef roast
2 tsp. pickling spice
1 lge. bottle catsup
2 green peppers, minced
1 lge. onion, minced
2 tsp. sugar
2 tsp. vinegar
1 tsp. dry mustard
1 tsp. salt

Place roast in shallow pan; seal with foil. Bake at 300 degrees for 2 hours. Pierce foil to let steam escape. Reserve pan juices. Chill roast. Tie pickling spice in small bag; combine with catsup, peppers, onion, 1/3 cup water, sugar, vinegar, mustard and salt. Simmer for 30 minutes, stirring frequently. Cut roast into cubes. Add reserved pan juices and roast; simmer until heated through. Serve in buns.

BARBECUED STEAK SANDWICHES

1/2 c. sliced onion
1/2 c. butter
1/2 tsp. salt
2 tbsp. Worcestershire sauce
2 tbsp. lemon juice
2 tbsp. sugar
1/2 tsp. oregano
2/3 c. catsup
1 c. canned applesauce
6 cube steaks
6 hamburger rolls, buttered

Saute onion in butter until lightly browned; stir in salt, Worcestershire sauce, lemon juice, sugar, oregano, catsup and applesauce. Mix thoroughly; pour sauce over steaks. Let stand for 15 minutes. Lift out steaks; arrange on grill 2 inches from hot coals. Broil for about 3 minutes on 1 side. Baste with sauce; cook on other side. Toast rolls on grill; place steaks on rolls. Top with remaining sauce. Yield: 6 servings.

CORNED BEEF POKIES

1 12-oz. can corned beef
2 tbsp. prepared mustard
1 tbsp. Worcestershire sauce
1 to 2 tsp. prepared horseradish
1/2 c. diced American cheese
6 hot dog rolls

Separate corned beef into small pieces. Combine with mustard, Worcestershire sauce, horseradish and cheese. Mix well; fill rolls with mixture. Wrap each roll individually in aluminum foil. Bake at 350 degrees for 20 minutes or until cheese melts. Yield: 6 servings.

GRILLED CORNED BEEF AND CHEESE SANDWICHES

1 12-oz. can corned beef, shredded
4 oz. sharp American cheese, diced
1/2 c. mayonnaise
2 tbsp. sweet pickle relish
1 tbsp. instant minced onion
8 hamburger buns, split and buttered

Mix corned beef, cheese, mayonnaise, relish and onion; spoon into buns. Wrap in heavy foil. Heat over medium coals for 12 to 15 minutes, turning several times. Yield: 8 servings.

CORNED BEEF SANDWICH

1 can corned beef, shredded
1 sm. carton sour cream
1/2 pkg. onion soup mix
2 tbsp. mayonnaise
1 loaf dark rye bread
Lettuce

Mix beef, sour cream, soup mix and mayonnaise, stirring well. Spread mixture on half the bread. Cover with lettuce; top with remaining bread. Yield: 8-10 servings.

REUBEN SANDWICH

12 slices pumpernickel bread
1/2 c. prepared mustard
6 slices Swiss cheese
6 tbsp. sauerkraut, drained
1/2 lb. sliced corned beef
Butter

Spread 6 slices bread with mustard; top with cheese, 1 tablespoon sauerkraut and corned beef. Cover with remaining bread. Spread butter on both sides of bread. Grill on both sides until hot and cheese is melted. Yield: 6 servings.

DRIED BEEF SANDWICH

1/2 lb. dried beef, shredded
8 hard-boiled eggs, chopped
1/2 c. salad dressing
1/4 c. chili sauce
1/4 c. catsup
2 tbsp. minced onion
Buns

Mix beef, eggs, dressing, chili sauce, catsup and onion. Spread on buns. Place under broiler or in oven until heated through. Yield: 18 sandwiches.

NIPPY BEEF SANDWICHES

1/2 c. finely shredded dried beef
1 3-oz. package cream cheese, softened
1 tbsp. horseradish
1 tbsp. minced onion
1 tbsp. salad dressing
Soft butter
12 whole wheat bread slices

Combine beef, cream cheese, horseradish, onion and salad dressing. Butter bread slices to edge. Divide beef mixture into 6 parts. Place 1 part on each of 6 bread slices, spreading to edges. Top with remaining bread slices; cut in half. Sandwiches freeze well. Yield: 6 servings.

GRILLED BEEF SANDWICHES

1 tbsp. onion soup mix
1 tbsp. horseradish
Dash of freshly ground pepper
6 tbsp. softened butter
8 slices white bread
8 thin slices cooked roast beef
4 slices American or Swiss cheese

Soften soup mix in 1 tablespoon water; stir. Add horseradish and pepper. Stir into butter; spread on both sides of each bread slice. Place 2 slices beef and 1 slice cheese on 4 slices bread; top with remaining bread. Brown on both sides on griddle until cheese begins to melt. Serve warm. Yield: 4 servings.

ITALIAN STEAK SANDWICHES

Butter
1 Bermuda onion, sliced
1 8-oz. can tomato sauce
1/8 tsp. salt
1/8 tsp. instant minced onion
1/2 tsp. oregano
Dash of pepper
Dash of garlic salt
1/2 tsp. Worcestershire sauce
1 1/4 lb. sandwich steaks
4 Italian rolls
Olive oil
2 med. dill pickles, sliced

Melt 2 tablespoons butter in skillet. Brown onion slices in butter slowly until tender. Combine tomato sauce, salt, minced onion, oregano, pepper and garlic salt in saucepan; bring to a boil. Stir in 1 teaspoon butter and Worcestershire sauce. Cover; reduce heat. Simmer for 10 minutes. Brown steaks on both sides in pan with onion. Slice rolls; sprinkle with olive oil. Place 2 tablespoons tomato mixture in each roll; add steak and onion. Top steak with remaining mixture. Garnish with pickle slices and additional oregano. Serve immediately. Yield: 4 servings.

BRAISED SHORT RIBS

3 lb. beef short ribs
Salt
3/4 c. long grain rice
1/2 c. chopped onion
1/2 c. chopped celery
1/4 c. chopped green pepper
2 tsp. beef gravy base
1 tsp. Worcestershire sauce
1/4 tsp. thyme
1/8 tsp. pepper

Cut ribs into serving pieces; brown, without added fat, on all sides in heavy skillet for about 10 to 15 minutes. Season with small amount of salt. Transfer to 3-quart casserole. Bake, covered, at 325 degrees for 1 hour. Combine rice, onion, celery, 2 tablespoons salt and green pepper with pan drippings in skillet; mix well. Cook until rice is lightly browned. Remove ribs from casserole; pour off fat. Spread rice mixture in casserole; top with ribs. Combine 2 1/4 cups water, gravy base, Worcestershire sauce, thyme and pepper in small saucepan; bring to a boil. Pour over ribs. Bake, covered, for 1 hour longer. Yield: 4-6 servings.

PICNIC SHORT RIBS

1 1/2 tsp. toasted sesame seed
2 1/2 lb. English cut short ribs
Unseasoned meat tenderizer
2 scallions, chopped
1 clove of garlic, crushed
1/8 tsp. monosodium glutamate
1/4 tsp. salt
Pepper to taste
1 tbsp. salad oil
1/2 c. soy sauce
1/4 c. sugar
1/4 c. sherry

Crush sesame seed. Cut short ribs with bones into 2-inch pieces; slash at 1/2-inch intervals lengthwise and crosswise. Rub with tenderizer; let stand for 1 hour. Combine remaining ingredients in deep bowl; mix well. Add short ribs; marinate for 30 minutes. Remove short ribs. Grill over hot coals until done. Yield: 5 servings.

CANTONESE SHORT RIBS

1 No. 2 1/2 can sliced pineapple
3 lb. short ribs
3 tbsp. shortening
1/3 c. soy sauce
Brown sugar
1 tsp. ginger
Melted butter

Drain pineapple, reserving juice. Add enough water to reserved juice to make 2 cups liquid. Brown ribs in shortening in roasting pan. Mix reserved pineapple liquid, soy sauce, 1 tablespoon brown sugar and ginger. Pour over ribs. Simmer for 3 hours or until tender. Brush pineapple slices with melted butter; sprinkle with brown sugar. Place under broiler to brown. Serve pineapple slices with ribs. Yield: 3-4 servings.

ROYAL BEEF RIBS

2 tbsp. instant minced onion
1 tbsp. (packed) brown sugar
1 tsp. monosodium glutamate
1 tbsp. mustard seed
2 tsp. paprika
1 tsp. crushed oregano
1 tsp. chili powder
1 tsp. cracked peppercorns
1/2 tsp. salt
1/2 tsp. ground cloves
1 bay leaf
1 clove of garlic, minced
1 c. catsup
1/2 c. water
1/4 c. olive or salad oil
1/4 c. tarragon vinegar
2 tbsp. wine vinegar
2 tbsp. Worcestershire sauce
2 or 3 drops of liquid smoke
4 to 5 lb. short ribs

Combine all ingredients except ribs in saucepan; stir well. Bring to a boil. Reduce heat; simmer for 20 to 25 minutes, stirring occasionally. Remove bav leaf. Sprinkle ribs with additional salt; place, bone side down, on grill away from coals. Add dampened hickory chips to coals. Grill for 3 hours. Baste with sauce. Cook for 30 minutes longer, basting frequently.

BOEUF BOURGUIGNONNE

5 lb. beef chuck
Flour
Butter
Olive oil
Salt and pepper to taste
2 oz. warm cognac
1/2 lb. bacon, diced
4 cloves of garlic, minced
2 carrots, chopped
2 leeks, chopped
4 med. onions, chopped
2 tbsp. chopped parsley
2 bay leaves
1 tsp. thyme
1 bottle Burgundy
2 lb. small onions, peeled
1 tbsp. sugar
1/2 c. red wine
2 lb. mushroom caps
2 tbsp. lemon juice

Cut beef into large cubes; roll in flour. Combine 1 cup butter and 1 cup olive oil in skillet; brown beef on all sides over high heat. Sprinkle with salt and pepper. Pour cognac over beef; ignite. Let stand until flames die. Transfer beef to casserole. Add bacon, garlic, carrots, leeks, chopped onions and parsley to skillet. Cook until bacon is crisp and vegetables lightly browned, stirring frequently. Transfer vegetables to casserole; add bay leaves, thyme, Burgundy

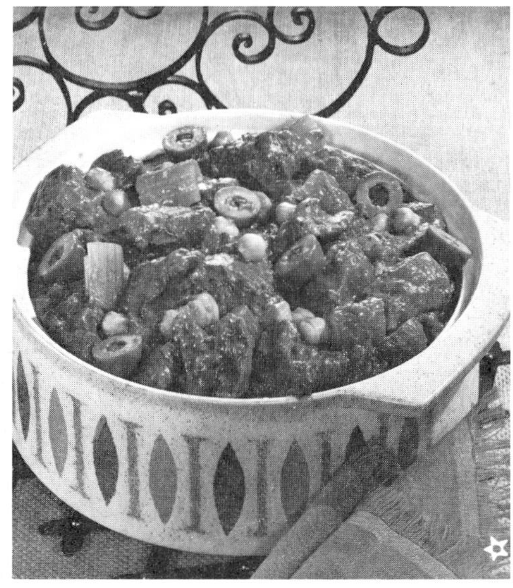

Beef Stew Espanole . . . A Mediterranean flavor is added to this hearty stew.

and enough water to cover. Bake in 350-degree oven for 1 hour and 30 minutes to 2 hours. Mix 1 tablespoon butter and 1 tablespoon flour; stir into beef mixture. Bake for 2 to 3 hours longer. Melt small amount of butter in skillet. Place whole onions in skillet; sprinkle with sugar. Saute whole onions until brown. Add red wine; cover. Bake for 15 minutes or until onions are almost tender. Saute mushroom caps in small amount of butter and olive oil until browned on one side. Sprinkle with 2 tablespoons lemon juice; brown on other side. Keep warm, uncovered. Add onions and one half the mushrooms to casserole; arrange remaining mushrooms on top. Sprinkle with additional parsley.

BEEF AND RIGATONI STEW

1 1/2 lb. lean beef
1 c. dried prunes
1/4 c. flour
3 tsp. salt
2 tbsp. salad oil
1 med. onion, coarsely chopped
1 clove of garlic, minced
1/4 tsp. pepper
1/2 tsp. oregano
4 drops of hot sauce
1 8-oz. can tomato sauce
1/2 1-lb. package rigatoni or lge. macaroni

Cut beef into 1 1/2-inch cubes. Cook prunes in 2 cups water for 5 minutes; drain. Cool; remove pits and set aside. Shake beef cubes, several at a time, in bag with flour and 1 teaspoon salt until coated. Brown beef in hot oil in deep 4-quart Dutch oven; add onion, garlic, remaining salt, pepper, oregano and hot sauce. Add tomato sauce and enough hot water to measure 1 inch above beef; stir well. Cover. Bake in 300-degree oven for 2 hours. Add rigatoni, prunes and enough hot water to cover beef mixture. Bake for 1 hour longer. Yield: 6 servings.

BEEF STEW ESPANOLE

3 tbsp. flour
1 1/2 tsp. salt
1/4 tsp. pepper
2 lb. boneless beef, cubed
3 tbsp. shortening
1 chopped onion
2 stalks of celery
1/2 c. stuffed green olives
1 16-oz. can garbanzo beans

Combine flour, salt and pepper. Dredge beef in seasoned flour. Brown beef in shortening in skillet; pour off drippings. Add 1 cup water; cover tightly. Simmer for 1 hour. Chop onion; cut celery into 1-inch pieces. Add onion and celery to beef. Cover; cook for 1 hour and 30 minutes to 2 hours or until beef is tender. Halve olives; drain beans. Add olives and beans to beef mixture. Cook just until heated through. Yield: 6 to 8 servings.

FLEMISH BEEF STEW

6 slices bacon
1 med. onion, sliced
2 lb. stew beef
Salt and pepper to taste
2 tbsp. flour
2 cans consomme
1 bay leaf
Pinch of thyme
Pinch of garlic salt
2 tsp. vinegar
1 tbsp. sugar

Fry bacon in skillet until crisp; remove from skillet. Crumble into 2-quart casserole. Fry onion in bacon drippings until tender. Remove; place over bacon. Brown beef in remaining pan drippings; add salt and pepper. Sprinkle beef with flour; stir well. Remove from heat; add consomme gradually, stirring constantly. Pour beef mixture over onion; add bay leaf, thyme, garlic salt, vinegar and sugar. Cover. Bake at 325 degrees for 1 hour and 30 minutes. Yield: 8 servings.

FAMILY BEEF STEW

1 1/2 lb. beef stew meat
1 1/2 c. diced celery
1 1/2 c. sliced carrots
1 lge. onion, sliced
4 med. potatoes, cubed
1 1/2 tsp. salt
Pepper to taste
1/4 tsp. monosodium glutamate
1 recipe biscuit dough

Cook beef in 3 cups water until almost tender. Add vegetables and seasonings. Cook over low heat until tender. Turn into baking dish; add monosodium glutamate, stirring well. Roll out biscuit dough on floured surface; cut into small biscuits. Place biscuits over stew. Bake at 450 degrees until biscuits are brown. Yield: 4-5 servings.

HUNGARIAN GOULASH

2 lb. beefsteak
Butter
1 lb. onions, sliced
2 tsp. paprika
1 c. stewed tomatoes
1 c. beef stock
1 clove of garlic, chopped
1 slice lemon peel, chopped
1/2 tsp. caraway seed
2 tbsp. flour
1 lb. noodles

Cut beefsteak into small pieces. Melt 1/4 cup butter in heavy pan; add beef steak and onions. Saute until onions are transparent. Add paprika and tomatoes. Combine beef stock, garlic, lemon peel and caraway seed; add to beefsteak mixture. Simmer for 45 minutes to 1 hour. Melt 2 tablespoons butter; add flour to make a paste. Add to beefsteak mixture gradually, stirring well. Cook until thickened. Cook noodles according to package directions; drain. Serve beefsteak mixture over noodles. Yield: 4-6 servings.

ANGOSTURA PEPPERPOT

2 eggs
Salt
1 1/2 c. all-purpose flour
1 1/2 lb. beef chuck, cubed
1 green pepper, chopped
1 onion, chopped
2 peeled potatoes, diced
1 tbsp. angostura bitters
2 10 1/2-oz. cans beef broth
Pepper

Beat eggs with 1/2 teaspoon salt until blended. Stir in enough flour to make soft paste. Knead dough on heavily floured board until smooth and elastic. Roll out paper thin; cut into 1 1/2 inch squares with sharp knife. Let noodles dry on a cloth for several hours. Cover beef with water; simmer, covered, for about 2 hours until beef is almost tender. Add remaining ingredients, except pepper, noodles and 2 cups of water. Cover; simmer for 15 minutes longer or until noodles and potatoes are tender. Season with salt and pepper to taste. Yield: 4 servings.

Angostura Pepperpot . . . Highlight beef, pepper, onion, and potato with a touch of bitters.

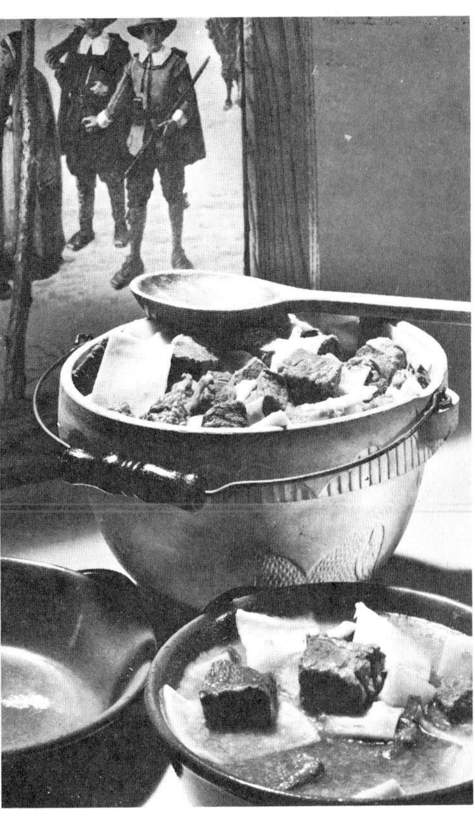

BARBECUED CHUCK STEAK

2 cloves of garlic, crushed
2 2-lb. chuck steaks
1/2 c. red wine

Rub garlic into both sides of steaks. Marinate steaks in wine at room temperature for at least 4 hours, turning occasionally. Place on broiler rack 4 inches from heat; broil for 6 minutes or longer on each side. Cut into thin diagonal slices. Yield: 4-6 servings.

PEPPER STEAK

1 1-lb. boneless chuck steak, 1/2 in. thick
1 tsp. unseasoned meat tenderizer
2 tbsp. salad oil
2 med. green peppers
2 tbsp. minced onion
1 clove of garlic, mashed
1/2 c. diagonally sliced celery
2 tbsp. cornstarch
1/2 c. beef stock or consomme
1 tsp. soy sauce
Salt and pepper to taste
Hot cooked rice

Cut steak into thin strips; sprinkle with meat tenderizer. Brown in oil in skillet. Cut green peppers into thin strips; add onion, garlic, green peppers and celery to steak. Saute for about 2 minutes or until vegetables are partially tender. Combine cornstarch, beef stock and soy sauce; add to steak mixture. Cook, stirring, until liquid is slightly thickened and begins to simmer. Add salt and pepper. Serve immediately over rice.

SWISS STEAK SUPREME

1/2 c. flour
2 tsp. salt
Pepper
1 chuck steak
2 cans tomato soup
1/4 tsp. garlic powder
2 bay leaves
1 1/2 tsp. basil
1 1/2 tsp. celery seed
1 1/2 tsp. parsley flakes
1 1/2 tsp. oregano
1 med. onion, chopped
2 tbsp. Worcestershire sauce
1 tbsp. soy sauce
1 c. mushroom pieces

Mix flour, salt and 1/4 teaspoon pepper; pound into steak. Brown steak in small amount of hot fat in Dutch oven. Combine soup, 1 1/2 teaspoons pepper and remaining ingredients; pour over steak. Cover. Bake at 350 degrees for 1 hour and 30 minutes. Yield: 6 servings.

CHARCOALED TERIYAKI STEAK

1 2-lb. flank steak
1/2 c. sugar
1 tsp. sesame seed
Dash of salt
1/2 c. soy sauce
1 tsp. vinegar
1 tsp. ginger
2 cloves of garlic, crushed

Trim steak, removing all fibers. Cut steak crosswise in medium thick slices. Mix sugar, sesame seed, salt, soy sauce, vinegar, ginger and garlic to make marinade. Place steak in marinade; let stand for at least 2 hours. Drain steak. Grill over hot coals to desired doneness. Serve on toasted buns, if desired. Yield: 8 servings.

DOWN THE CHIMNEY FLANK STEAK

1/4 c. wine vinegar
1/4 c. oil
1 tbsp. instant onion flakes
1/4 tsp. dried dill
1/8 tsp. garlic powder
1/2 tsp. salt
1/8 tsp. pepper
1 2-lb. flank steak
1 tbsp. cornstarch
1 1/2 tsp. sugar

Combine vinegar, oil, 1/4 cup water, onion flakes, dill, garlic powder, salt and pepper. Place steak in shallow glass dish. Pour vinegar mixture over steak. Cover; let stand for at least 2 hours. Drain steak; reserve marinade. Place steak on rack in broiling pan. Broil for about 5 minutes on one side and 4 minutes on other side for rare steak. Remove to heated serving platter. Combine cornstarch, sugar, 1/2 cup water and reserved marinade. Add to drippings in broiler pan. Cook, stirring constantly, until mixture comes to a boil and thickens. Cut thin diagonal slices of steak; top each slice with sauce. Yield: 6 servings.

MARINATED FLANK STEAK

1/4 c. soy sauce
3 tbsp. honey
2 tbsp. vinegar
1 1/2 tsp. garlic powder
1 1/2 tsp. ginger
3/4 c. salad oil
1 green onion, minced
1 1 1/2-lb. flank steak

Mix soy sauce, honey and vinegar; blend in garlic powder and ginger. Add oil and green onion. Place steak in shallow pan; cover with marinade. Let stand for at least 4 hours. Cook steak on grill for 5 minutes on each side for medium rare, basting occasionally with marinade. Yield: 4 servings.

STUFFED FLANK STEAK

Butter
1/2 c. chopped celery
1/2 tbsp. chopped parsley
1 tbsp. chopped onion
2 c. bread crumbs
1 tsp. savory seasoning
Salt and pepper to taste
1 1 1/2-lb. flank steak
Flour

Melt 1/4 cup butter in skillet; add celery, parsley and onion. Cook, stirring, for about 4 minutes. Combine celery mixture, crumbs and seasonings; mix stuffing lightly. Spread over steak; roll, jelly roll fashion. Tie securely. Brown steak roll in 2 tablespoons butter in Dutch oven; slip rack under steak roll. Bake at 350 degrees for 1 hour and 30 minutes. Transfer steak roll to serving platter. Mix small amount of flour and water to make a paste; stir into pan drippings. Add enough water gradually to make gravy. Cook, stirring constantly, until thickened. Serve with steak roll. Yield: 8 servings.

CHARCOAL-BROILED STEAK

2 rib steaks, 1 1/2 in. thick
Salt and pepper to taste
Butter

Place steaks on rack over glowing charcoal. Broil for 9 minutes; turn. Sprinkle with salt and pepper; broil for 9 minutes longer. Place steaks, seasoned side down, on hot platter; sprinkle with salt and pepper. Spread with butter. Yield: 4 servings.

FULL-FLAVORED STEAK

2 1/2 tbsp. brown sugar
1 1/2 tbsp. sugar
1 tbsp. ground ginger
1 clove of garlic, crushed
1/2 c. soy sauce
1 tbsp. tarragon vinegar
3 lb. rib steaks, 1 1/2 in. thick

Blend all ingredients except steaks. Place steaks in large shallow dish; pour sauce over top. Marinate for at least 30 minutes, basting frequently and turning once or twice. Remove steaks from marinade, reserving marinade. Place steaks on grill about 3 inches from coals. Grill for 6 minutes or until one side is browned, brushing frequently with marinade. Turn and grill other side for 6 minutes or until done. Serve immediately. Yield: 6 servings.

STEAK ORIENTAL

1 c. soy sauce
1/4 c. (packed) brown sugar
1 tbsp. ginger
4 rib steaks, 3/4 in. thick

Combine soy sauce, brown sugar and ginger. Marinate steaks for 1 hour and 30 minutes in mixture. Broil for 5 to 10 minutes in broiler, 2 inches from heat. Yield: 4 servings.

BEEF FILLET

4 beef fillets, 1 in. thick
Butter
1/4 tsp. rosemary
Salt and pepper to taste
2 1/2 tsp. Worcestershire sauce
1/2 tsp. mustard
2 tbsp. brandy (opt.)

Remove fat from beef. Melt 2 tablespoons butter in skillet; add rosemary. Brown butter lightly; add fillets. Cook over high heat for about 3 minutes on each side. Season with salt and pepper. Mix Worcestershire sauce, mustard and brandy. Pour brandy mixture into skillet, adding a small amount of butter, if needed. Cook fillets for 1 minute longer; turn once. Remove beef from sauce. Continue cooking sauce over high heat for 1 minute. Pour sauce over fillets; serve immediately. Yield: 4 servings.

FILET MIGNON

4 beef fillets, 1 in. thick
4 slices bacon
2 med. bananas, sliced
4 tbsp. butter
1 tsp. beef extract

Trim fillets; wrap bacon around fillets and secure with toothpick. Let stand for 20 minutes; broil until rare. Saute bananas in 2 tablespoons butter. Add 4 tablespoons boiling water, beef extract and remaining butter, stirring well. Arrange fillets and bananas on platter. Drizzle beef extract mixture over fillets and bananas to serve.

COMPANY STEAK

4 beef fillets, 1 in. thick
2 tbsp. cooking oil
2 tbsp. onion, finely chopped
8 lge. fresh mushrooms, sliced
1/2 c. red wine
2 tsp. tomato paste
Salt and pepper to taste
Juice of 1/2 lemon
1 tbsp. minced parsley

Brown fillets in oil; place in casserole. Combine onion, mushrooms, wine, 1/4 cup water, tomato paste, salt, pepper and lemon juice. Pour over fillets. Sprinkle with parsley. Bake at 350 degrees until tender. Yield: 4-6 servings.

BLUE CHEESE STEAK

1 4-lb. porterhouse steak
1/2 c. corn oil
1/4 c. blue cheese
1/2 c. lemon juice
1 tbsp. Worcestershire sauce

Score edge of fat side of steak; place in shallow pan. Combine oil, blue cheese, lemon juice and Worcestershire sauce. Beat well; pour over steak. Marinate overnight. Drain steak; reserve marinade. Place steak under broiler 6 inches from source of heat; broil 15 minutes on each side for rare or about 20 minutes on each side for well done. Brush steak with marinade every 5 minutes during cooking time. Yield: 6 servings.

STEAK SUBLIME

1 porterhouse steak, 2 in. thick
Seasoned salt and pepper to taste
1/4 lb. mushrooms, halved
1/4 c. butter
1/2 c. red wine
1 tbsp. instant minced onion
1 tbsp. minced parsley
1 tsp. lemon juice
1/4 tsp. salt

Preheat broiler. Sprinkle steak on both sides with seasoned salt and pepper. Broil for about 15 minutes on each side for rare steak. Saute mushrooms in butter until golden; add wine, onion, parsley, lemon juice and salt. Bring to a boil; simmer for 5 minutes. Serve steak on a warm platter; pour hot sauce over steak. Yield: 4 servings.

PAN-AMERICAN STEAK

1/2 c. butter
Juice of 2 limes
1 tsp. garlic powder
1/2 c. Burgundy
1 tbsp. Worcestershire sauce
1 tsp. soy sauce
1 tsp. monosodium glutamate
1 tsp. hot sauce
Salt and pepper to taste
1 3-lb. porterhouse steak, 2 in. thick

Combine butter, lime juice, garlic powder, Burgundy, Worcestershire sauce, soy sauce, monosodium glutamate, hot sauce, salt and pepper in saucepan. Simmer for 3 minutes. Pour over steak; marinate for at least 2 hours, turning steak every 15 minutes. Cook under broiler or over hickory chips and charcoal to desired degree of doneness. Baste frequently with marinade. Yield: 4 servings.

HERB AND WINE-MARINATED STEAK

Color photograph for this recipe on page 69.

1 2/3 c. Burgundy
1/2 c. salad oil
2 tbsp. instant minced onion
2 tsp. thyme leaves
3/4 tsp. instant minced garlic
2 tsp. salt
1/4 tsp. ground pepper
3 lb. round steak, 2 1/2 in. thick
1 7/8-oz. package brown gravy mix

Combine Burgundy, oil, onion, thyme, garlic, salt and pepper; mix well. Place steak in pan; pour Burgundy mixture over steak. Marinate for at least 18 hours in refrigerator, turning occasionally. Drain steak; reserve marinade. Grill steak over hot coals for 15 to 20 minutes on each side or to desired doneness. Strain reserved marinade; combine with 1 cup water and gravy mix in saucepan. Bring to boiling point, stirring constantly; cook until slightly thickened. Serve with steak. Garnish steak with canned peach halves pierced with whole cloves if desired. Yield: 6 servings.

BEEF PARMIGIANA

1 1 1/2-lb. round steak, 3/4 in. thick
1/3 c. grated Parmesan cheese
1/3 c. dry bread crumbs
1 egg, beaten
1/3 c. oil
1 med. onion, minced
1 tsp. salt
1/4 tsp. pepper
1/2 tsp. sugar
1/2 tsp. marjoram
1 6-oz. can tomato paste
1/2 lb. mozzarella cheese, sliced

Place beef between pieces of waxed paper on board; pound thin. Trim off gristle and excess fat; cut into 6 to 8 pieces. Mix Parmesan cheese and bread crumbs. Dip beef in egg; roll in Parmesan cheese mixture. Brown beef on both sides in oil in skillet. Arrange in shallow baking dish. Cook onion in pan drippings in skillet over low heat until soft; stir in salt, pepper, sugar, marjoram and tomato paste. Add 2 cups hot water gradually, stirring constantly. Cook for 5 minutes, scraping pan. Pour 2/3 of the sauce over beef. Top with cheese slices; top with remaining sauce. Bake at 350 degrees for 1 hour or until tender.

CHATEAUBRIAND

3 lb. round steak, 2 in. thick
Seasoned meat tenderizer
1/2 c. beef broth
1 c. dry white wine
1/2 c. butter
3 tsp. lemon juice
1/2 tsp. pepper
1/4 c. minced parsley
1/4 c. minced chives
1 4-oz. can sliced mushrooms, drained

Sprinkle steak with meat tenderizer. Pierce surface at 1-inch intervals with fork. Cover; refrigerate overnight. Cook steak on grill 6 inches from coals for 20 minutes on each side. Combine broth, wine, butter, lemon juice and pepper in saucepan. Bring to a boil; reduce heat. Simmer until butter is melted. Add parsley, chives and mushrooms. Carve steak across grain in diagonal slices. Serve with sauce. Yield: 6 servings.

PARSLEY STEAK ROLLS

1 can mushroom pieces, drained
1 onion, diced
3 tbsp. grated Parmesan cheese
Salt and pepper to taste
1 tbsp. parsley flakes
1 lge. round steak
1 tbsp. cornstarch
1 can beef broth

Place mushrooms, onion, cheese, salt, pepper and parsley over steak. Roll into large roll; tie securely. Brown in fat on all sides in ovenproof frypan. Drain off excess fat. Stir cornstarch in small amount of broth; add to remaining broth, stirring well. Pour over steak. Cover. Bake at 350 degrees for 1 hour. Yield: 6-8 servings.

ROUND STEAK SAUERBRATEN

1 1/2 lb. round steak, 1/2 in. thick
1 env. brown gravy mix
1 tbsp. instant minced onion
1 tbsp. (packed) brown sugar
2 tbsp. wine vinegar
1 tsp. Worcestershire sauce
1/4 tsp. ginger
1 bay leaf
1/2 tsp. salt
1/4 tsp. pepper
6 oz. noodles
Butter to taste

Cut steak in 1-inch squares. Brown in skillet in small amount of fat; remove from skillet. Combine gravy mix and 2 cups water in skillet; bring to a boil. Stir in onion, brown sugar, vinegar, Worcestershire sauce, ginger, bay leaf, salt, steak and pepper. Pour into 1 1/2-quart casserole; cover. Bake at 350 degrees for 1 hour and 30 minutes; remove bay leaf. Cook noodles according to package directions; drain. Add butter. Serve steak mixture over noodles. Yield: 5-6 servings.

SAUCY BEEF ROULADES CONTINENTAL

1 1 1/2-lb. round steak, 1/4 in. thick
1 1/2 c. herb-seasoned stuffing mix
1/4 c. finely chopped celery
1/4 c. minced onion
2 tbsp. shortening
1 10 3/4-oz. can tomato soup
1/8 tsp. oregano
1 sm. clove of garlic, minced

Pound steak; cut into 6 long pieces. Combine stuffing mix, celery and onion; place small amount on end of each steak piece. Roll up; fasten with skewers. Brown in shortening in skillet. Pour off fat; add soup, 1/2 cup water, oregano and garlic. Cover; simmer for 1 hour and 30 minutes or until tender, stirring occasionally. Arrange on platter; serve with whole green beans and white onions, if desired. Yield: 6 servings.

SAUCY SWISS STEAK

4 lb. tenderized round steak
Garlic salt
Pepper
Flour
Oil
1 bottle catsup
1 jar piccalilli
1 med. onion, chopped
1 sm. hot pepper, chopped
1 sm. can mushrooms

Cut steak into serving pieces; season generously with garlic salt and pepper. Roll steak in flour; brown in small amount of oil. Place steak in roaster. Combine catsup, piccalilli, onion, hot pepper, mushrooms and 6 cups water; pour over steak. Bake at 325 degrees for 1 hour. Yield: 8-10 servings.

STRIPS OF BEEF CASSEROLE

1 1-lb. round steak	*1 tbsp. sugar*
1/4 c. shortening	*1 1/2 tsp. salt*
1 1/2 c. chopped onions	*1/4 tsp. pepper*
2 tbsp. flour	*1/2 tsp. Worcestershire sauce*
1 c. canned tomatoes	*1 c. mushrooms*
1 6-oz. can tomato paste	*1 c. sour cream*

Cut steak into strips; brown in shortening in skillet. Add onions; cook until lightly brown. Stir in flour, 1 cup water and remaining ingredients except mushrooms and sour cream. Cover; simmer for 1 hour and 30 minutes, stirring occasionally. Add mushrooms and sour cream; simmer for 5 minutes longer. Spoon beef mixture into casserole.

Sour Cream Puffs

1 1/4 c. flour	*1/4 c. shortening*
2 tsp. baking powder	*3/4 c. sour cream*
1/2 tsp. salt	*Sesame seed*

Sift flour, baking powder and salt together; cut in shortening. Add sour cream; mix well. Pat dough out on floured surface to 1/2-inch thickness. Cut into 6 to 8 biscuits. Place biscuits over beef mixture; sprinkle with sesame seed. Bake at 425 degrees for 20 to 25 minutes. Yield: 6-8 servings.

SWISS STEAK

1 1/2 lb. round steak, 1 in. thick	*1 tsp. paprika*
1/2 c. flour	*1 lge. bay leaf*
1 10 1/2-oz. can consomme	*1/4 tsp. marjoram*
1/2 tsp. salt	*1/4 tsp. thyme*
1/8 tsp. ground cloves	*1 sm. onion, chopped*
	4 carrots, chopped
	1 c. sour cream

Trim fat from steak. Pound flour into steak; brown in small amount of fat in Dutch oven. Add consomme, salt and spices; cover. Simmer for 1 hour and 30 minutes. Add onion and carrots; cook for 1 hour and 30 minutes longer, adding water if necessary. Stir in sour cream. Yield: 4 servings.

SWISS VEGETABLE BAKE

1/4 c. flour	*4 med. potatoes, quartered*
1 1-lb. round steak, 1/2 in. thick	*Salt and pepper to taste*
Cooking oil	*1/4 tsp. parsley*
1 can onion soup	
4 med. carrots, diced	

Pound flour into steak; brown in small amount of oil. Place in casserole; add soup, 1/2 soup can water, carrots, potatoes, and seasonings. Bake, covered, for 1 hour at 350 degrees. Uncover; bake for 15 minutes longer. Top with parsley. Yield: 4 servings.

STEAK DELUXE

1 sirloin steak, 2 in. thick	*1 sm. bay leaf*
Flour	*1/2 clove of garlic*
Salt and pepper to taste	*1 tsp. Worcestershire sauce*
1 can cream of mushroom soup	*1/2 onion, sliced*

Cut steak into serving pieces; dredge in flour. Brown in skillet in hot fat on both sides. Place steak in large casserole; season with salt and pepper. Add soup, bay leaf, garlic, Worcestershire sauce, 2/3 cup water and onion to steak drippings in skillet. Bring to a boil; cook for several minutes to blend. Pour sauce over steak; cover. Place on lowest rack of oven. Bake at 325 degrees for 1 hour and 30 minutes or until tender. Yield: 6 servings.

OPEN FIRE SIRLOIN

1 sirloin steak, 2 1/2 in. thick	*1/2 c. melted butter*
Salt	*Sliced French bread*

Cover one side of steak thickly with salt. Turn quickly; place salted side directly onto hot coals. Cook for about 25 minutes for medium rare. Cover top side of steak thickly with salt; turn quickly onto coals. Cook for about 20 minutes longer. Slice into serving pieces. Dip steak into butter; place on bread.

STEAK WITH MUSHROOMS

1/2 c. butter	*1 tsp. Worcestershire sauce*
1 2-lb. sirloin steak, 1/4 in. thick	*2 tbsp. vinegar*
6 peppercorns	*1 4-oz. can mushrooms, drained*
1/4 c. chopped onion	

Melt butter in skillet; add steak, peppercorns and onion. Cook steak for about 1 minute on each side; remove to platter. Add Worcestershire sauce, vinegar and mushrooms to skillet; simmer for about 5 minutes, stirring constantly. Return steak to skillet; cook for 1 minute. Serve immediately. Yield: 4 servings.

STEAK SUPREME

1 4-lb. top sirloin steak, 2 in. thick	*1 c. Worcestershire sauce*
1 c. soy sauce	*Monosodium glutamate*
	Melted butter

Let steak stand at room temperature. Marinate steak in soy and Worcestershire sauces for at least 2 hours. Sprinkle with monosodium glutamate; let stand for 30 minutes before cooking. Place steak on hot grill; cook, turning once, for 9 minutes on each side. Brush with melted butter occasionally. Slice steak to 1/4-inch thickness. Yield: 12 servings.

STEAK DIANNE

1 2-lb. sirloin steak, boned
Freshly ground pepper to taste
Dry mustard to taste
1 tbsp. butter
4 med. mushrooms, sliced
1 bunch green onions, chopped
Worcestershire sauce to taste
Juice of 1 lemon

Cut steak into serving pieces; pound on both sides. Rub pepper and mustard over both sides of steak. Melt butter in electric frying pan at 200 degrees. Add steak; saute on both sides. Remove steak to heated platter; keep warm. Place mushrooms, onions, Worcestershire sauce and lemon juice in frying pan; saute until mushrooms and onions are cooked through. Pour sauce over steak; serve. Yield: 4 servings.

STEAK BITES

4 lb. sirloin steak
Seasoned meat tenderizer
1 clove of garlic, halved
1 c. cooking sherry
1/2 c. margarine
1 tbsp. dry mustard
1/2 tsp. garlic salt
1 tbsp. Worcestershire sauce
1/8 tsp. pepper
1/8 tsp. hot sauce
1 tbsp. liquid smoke
1 sm. can mushroom stems and liquid

Sprinkle sirloin with tenderizer; rub with garlic on both sides. Marinate in sherry for 1 hour, turning once; reserve marinade. Broil steak until medium-well done; cut into bite-sized pieces. Combine 1/3 cup marinade with remaining ingredients; pour over steak. Heat; serve in chafing dish. Yield: 5 servings.

SIRLOIN TIPS JARDINIERE

1 2-lb. beef sirloin tip, cubed
4 tbsp. flour
2 tbsp. salad oil
Salt and pepper to taste
Monosodium glutamate
1/2 c. chopped onion
1/2 c. chopped carrots
1/2 c. chopped celery
1/2 tsp. chopped garlic
1 tsp. paprika
1/4 tsp. cumin
1/4 tsp. Italian seasoning
2 4-oz. cans sliced mushrooms

Roll beef cubes in flour; brown in oil in skillet. Season with salt and pepper; sprinkle with monosodium glutamate. Cover with onion, carrots, celery and garlic; sprinkle with paprika, cumin and Italian seasoning. Drain mushrooms; spread over top. Add 1/4 cup water to skillet. Simmer, covered, for 45 minutes or until beef is tender. Serve over noodles or rice. Yield: 6 servings.

NEW YORK STRIP STEAK

3 lge. red onions, sliced
1 c. butter
4 tsp. salt
1/2 tsp. freshly ground pepper
4 tsp. dry mustard
4 tsp. Worcestershire sauce
4 tbsp. red table wine
1 6-lb. New York strip steak

Place half the onions on piece of wide foil. Dot onions with 1/2 cup butter. Add salt, pepper and mustard. Pour Worcestershire sauce over mixture. Pour 2 tablespoons wine on one side of steak; turn and add remaining wine. Place steak on top of butter and onions. Place remaining onions and butter over steak. Fold foil and seal edges. Seal in 2 more pieces of foil. Cook on grill for about 45 minutes. Remove steak from foil; place over charcoal for about 8 minutes on each side. Serve onions and juice in bowl. Yield: 6-8 servings.

BEEF STROGANOFF

3 lb. lean beef
1/2 c. flour
2 tsp. salt
1/4 tsp. pepper
1/4 c. butter
2 onions, sliced
1 lge. clove of garlic, minced
1 1/2 tbsp. Worcestershire sauce
1/4 c. catsup
1 8-oz. can button mushrooms
1 1/2 c. buttermilk

Cut beef into 1/2 by 2-inch strips about 1/4 inch thick. Combine flour, salt and pepper. Coat beef with flour mixture. Brown beef slowly in butter in Dutch oven. Add onion, garlic, Worcestershire sauce and catsup. Drain mushrooms; add enough water to mushroom juice to make 1 cup liquid. Add to beef mixture. Cover; simmer for about 2 hours or until tender, adding additional water as needed. Add mushrooms and buttermilk; cook over low heat only until heated through. Serve over cooked noodles or rice. Yield: 8-10 servings.

Beef Stroganoff . . . This dish can be prepared in advance to provide an elegant dinner.

SUKIYAKI

Color photograph for this recipe on page 66.

2 1/2 lb. prime sirloin
1 8-oz. can bamboo shoots
1 8 1/2-oz. can water chestnuts
2 c. thinly sliced carrots
2 c. thinly sliced celery
1 c. finely chopped onions
1 tbsp. sugar
1/4 c. soy sauce
1 c. beef broth
1 tbsp. angostura aromatic bitters

Cut fat from outer edge of sirloin; reserve. Freeze sirloin until hard; cut into 1 1/2-inch paper-thin strips. Drain bamboo shoots and water chestnuts; slice. Mix with carrots, celery and onions. Combine remaining ingredients in bowl. Dice reserved fat; fry in large skillet until crisp. Remove crisp pieces; add sirloin to hot fat. Cook over high heat until browned. Add celery mixture; stir well. Add broth mixture; cover. Simmer for 5 minutes or until vegetables are tender-crisp. Yield: 6 servings.

TERIYAKI STICKS

1 1/2 c. soy sauce
1/2 c. cooking oil
1 c. vinegar
1 c. (packed) brown sugar
1 tsp. salt
5 cloves of garlic, chopped
1 lge. onion, chopped
1/3 c. chopped fresh gingerroot
3 lb. boneless beef

Combine soy sauce, oil, vinegar, 1 cup water, brown sugar, salt, garlic, onion and gingerroot to make marinade. Cut beef into thin strips; thread strips accordion-style on bamboo skewers. Place skewers in shallow pan. Pour marinade over beef; let stand for 4 hours or longer, turning frequently. Broil beef strips over hot coals until tender, turning often.

BROILED T-BONE STEAK

1 T-bone steak, 1 1/2 to 2 in. thick
Salt to taste

Let steak stand at room temperature. Preheat oven and broiling pan. Sprinkle steak with salt; place on rack about 3 inches from source of heat. Broil until brown, turning once. Add salt to other side. Serve on heated platter immediately.

OVEN-BROILED T-BONE

1/2 c. margarine
2 tbsp. Worcestershire sauce
1 tbsp. prepared mustard
4 T-bone steaks
Salt and pepper to taste

Melt margarine; add Worcestershire sauce and mustard. Season steaks with salt and pepper; place on rack. Brush heavily with mustard mixture. Broil for 20 minutes on each side, turning once; baste with remaining mustard sauce. Yield: 4 servings.

Beets

Both the darkish-purple root and the brilliant green leaves of this colorful vegetable are edible. And both parts are rich in needed nutrients. Two-thirds cup cooked beets supply 33 percent of the minimum adult requirement of Vitamin C. One-half cup of the green leaves supplies Vitamins A and C as well as iron. (1 cup cooked beets = 70 calories; 1/2 cup beet greens = 15 calories)

AVAILABILITY: Roots are available year-round fresh, frozen, or canned. Peak months are June and July. Greens available during summer months with peak June-July.

BUYING: Choose young, firm, smooth, and blemish-free beets without soft, rough, or shriveled spots. Look for fresh greens with no sign of discoloration, ragged edges, or yellowed leaves.

STORING: Store in a plastic bag in a cool place, preferably a vegetable crisper. Greens should be used within 2 days; roots within 5 days. *To freeze* beets remove and discard leaves. Wash and scald in boiling water until tender. Chill; rub off skins; package and label; freeze. May be kept up to 6 months.

PREPARATION: *Roots*—Scrub thoroughly with brush; do not trim root but leave 2-inch stems above crown when leaves are trimmed. Place in boiling, salted water to cover; simmer; peel off or rub off skins. Tender young whole beets require 30-45 minutes; older, whole beets 45-90 minutes; sliced or diced beets, 15-25 minutes. *Greens*—Wash; put in small amount of boiling water (just enough to start wilting process). Cover and steam for 10-15 minutes , or until tender.

(See VEGETABLES.)

BEET RELISH

3 c. finely chopped canned beets
1 c. vinegar
6 1/2 c. sugar
2 tsp. prepared horseradish
1/4 tsp. cinnamon
1/4 tsp. allspice
1/4 tsp. cloves
1 bottle liquid fruit pectin

Drain beets well. Place in large saucepan; add vinegar, sugar, horseradish and spices. Mix well. Bring to a rolling boil over high heat; boil for 1 minute, stirring constantly. Remove from heat; stir in liquid pectin at once. Skim off foam. Pour into hot sterilized jars; seal at once. Yield: 4 pints.

BEETS A LA TOSCA

1 can whole sm. beets
Garlic salt to taste
1 clove of garlic, pressed
Wine vinegar

Drain beets well. Place in plastic refrigerator container; sprinkle with garlic salt. Add garlic; cover with vinegar. Leave at room temperature for 2 to 3 hours, stirring once or twice. Refrigerate for at least 1 day. Place beets in serving dish; serve with wooden picks. Will keep for 2 weeks in refrigerator.

SPICED PICKLED BEETS

24 sm. beets
1 pt. vinegar
2 tbsp. salt
1 1/4 c. sugar
1 3-in. long stick cinnamon
6 whole cloves
3 med. onions, sliced

Remove beet tops, leaving roots and 1-inch stem. Place beets in saucepan; cover with boiling water. Cook until beets are tender; drain, reserving 1 cup cooking liquid. Remove beet skins; slice. Combine reserved cooking liquid, vinegar, salt and sugar in kettle. Tie cinnamon and cloves in small cloth bag; place in kettle. Bring to a boil; add beets and onions. Reduce heat; simmer for 5 minutes. Remove spice bag. Simmer while quickly packing beets and onions into hot pint jars. Fill to 1/2 inch of jar tops. Adjust lids; process in boiling water bath for 30 minutes. Remove jars from canner; place on towel in warm dry place.

POLISH BEET SALAD

4 med. cooked beets
1/4 c. chopped walnuts
Juice of 1/2 lemon
1/2 tsp. salt
1 tbsp. sugar
1 tbsp. minced parsley
1 green onion, chopped

Slice beets thin; add remaining ingredients. Toss lightly with fork; chill before serving.

BEET AND PINEAPPLE SALAD

1 pkg. strawberry gelatin
1 pkg. raspberry gelatin
1 pkg. cherry gelatin
1 No. 303 can julienne beets
1 No. 2 can crushed pineapple
1/2 c. sweet pickle juice

Dissolve gelatins in 4 cups boiling water. Drain beets and pineapple, reserving juices. Add reserved juices and pickle juice to gelatin; chill until syrupy. Stir in beets and pineapple; pour into 3-quart mold. Chill until firm. Yield: 16-18 servings.

BEET AND PEANUT SALAD

2 c. peeled beets
2 c. salted peanuts
1 tsp. lemon juice
1/4 c. French dressing
2 tbsp. mayonnaise
Salt to taste

Grind beets and peanuts together, using coarse grinder blade. Combine beet mixture, lemon juice, French dressing, mayonnaise and salt. Toss lightly with fork; chill. Serve mounded on lettuce. Serve with additional mayonnaise, if desired. Yield: 6 servings.

BEET-COTTAGE CHEESE SALAD

1 can shoestring beets
1 carton chive cottage cheese
Lettuce leaves
6 tbsp. French dressing
4 hard-boiled eggs, chopped
Chopped parsley

Chill beets; drain. Spoon cottage cheese onto 6 lettuce-lined salad plates; top with beets. Pour 1 tablespoon French dressing over each salad. Garnish with eggs and parsley. Yield: 6 servings.

BEET-CABBAGE SOUFFLE

1 pkg. lemon gelatin
1/4 c. beet juice
1 tbsp. vinegar
1/2 c. mayonnaise
1/4 tsp. salt
Dash of pepper
1 c. shredded cabbage
1 tbsp. minced onion
1 c. diced beets, drained

Dissolve gelatin in 1 1/4 cups boiling water. Add beet juice, vinegar, mayonnaise, salt and pepper. Blend with rotary beater. Pour into refrigerator tray. Chill in freezing unit for 15 to 20 minutes or until firm about 1 inch from edge but soft in center. Whip with rotary beater until fluffy. Fold in cabbage, onion and beets; place in pan or mold. Refrigerate until firm. Yield: 4-6 servings.

MOLDED BEET SALAD

1 No. 2 can shoestring beets
1 pkg. lemon gelatin
1 1/2 tbsp. vinegar
1 tsp. salt
1 1/2 tbsp. grated onion
1/4 c. sliced stuffed olives
2 tbsp. horseradish
1 1/4 c. chopped celery
1/2 c. chopped nuts

Drain beets, reserving fluid. Add enough water to beef fluid to equal 1 1/2 cups liquid. Pour liqiud into saucepan; add gelatin, vinegar and salt. Heat, stirring, until gelatin is dissolved. Chill until partially congealed. Fold in onion, olives, horseradish, celery and nuts; pour into pan or mold. Refrigerate until firm. Yield: 6-8 servings.

HUNGARIAN BEET SALAD

1 No. 2 can sliced beets
1/2 c. vinegar
2 tbsp. sugar
1 1/2 tsp. salt
1 tsp. caraway seed
1/8 tsp. freshly ground pepper
2 tbsp. horseradish (opt.)

Drain beets; reserve 1/4 cup liquid. Place beets in 1-quart bowl. Mix reserved liquid with remaining ingredients; pour over beets. Cover; refrigerate for 2 days, stirring occasionally. Drain; serve with marinade. Yield: 4 servings.

BEET COMPOTE

4 lge. beets
1 c. canned applesauce
2 tbsp. butter
1/4 tsp. salt
1/4 tsp. nutmeg

Cook beets in lightly salted water until tender; drain. Remove skins; mash with potato masher. Stir in applesauce, butter, salt and nutmeg; heat through. One Number 303 can sliced beets may be substituted for fresh beets. Yield: 6 servings.

BAKED BEETS

7 tbsp. butter
4 tbsp. flour
1 c. water
1/4 tsp. salt
4 tbsp. brown sugar
3 tbsp. prepared horseradish
4 c. chopped cooked beets
1/3 c. dried bread crumbs

Melt 4 tablespoons butter in saucepan; blend in flour. Add water gradually, stirring; cook until thickened, stirring constantly. Add salt, sugar, horseradish and beets. Mix well; pour into greased baking dish. Cover with crumbs; dot with remaining butter. Bake at 350 degrees for 20 minutes or until crumbs are browned. Yield: 6 servings.

BEETS IN ORANGE SAUCE

2 tbsp. cornstarch or flour
2 tbsp. beet juice
1 c. orange juice
1/4 c. lemon juice
2 tbsp. vinegar
2 tbsp. sugar
1/2 tsp. salt
2 No. 2 cans baby beets, drained
1/4 c. butter
2 tbsp. grated orange rind

Mix cornstarch and beet juice. Combine orange juice, lemon juice and vinegar in saucepan; add cornstarch mixture. Cook until clear, stirring constantly; add sugar, salt and beets. Heat thoroughly; add butter and orange rind. Yield: 8 servings.

BEETS WITH PINEAPPLE

2 1-lb. cans sliced beets
1 13 1/2-oz. can pineapple chunks
1/2 c. water
1/3 c. cider vinegar
1 tbsp. cornstarch
1/2 tsp. salt
4 tbsp. brown sugar
1/8 tsp. ginger

Drain beets and pineapple, reserving pineapple syrup. Blend reserved pineapple syrup, water, vinegar, cornstarch, salt, sugar and ginger in saucepan; cook until thickened, stirring constantly. Add beets; heat to boiling point. Fold in pineapple chunks; heat through. Serve immediately. Yield: 8-10 servings.

BOILED BEETS AND GREENS

Beets with leaves
Salt to taste
Butter

Scrub beets well; cook in boiling water for 50 to 60 minutes or until tender. Cool; rub skins off beets. Season with salt and butter. Cut stems and large veins from leaves, removing damaged leaves. Wash leaves well; place in saucepan. Do not add water. Steam for 8 to 15 minutes or until tender. Season with salt and butter.

BEET CASSEROLE

16 med. fresh beets
1/4 c. sugar
3/4 tsp. salt
1/4 tsp. paprika
1 tbsp. lemon juice
3 tbsp. butter
1 tbsp. grated onion
1/3 c. water

Pare and slice beets; place in greased 7-inch baking dish. Add sugar, salt, paprika and lemon juice. Dot with butter and onion; add water. Cover. Bake in 400-degree oven for 30 minutes or until beets are tender, stirring twice. Yield: 8 servings.

CHRISTMAS BEETS

2 c. diced cooked beets
1/2 c. French dressing
1 c. sour cream, whipped
1/2 c. finely chopped green onions

Place hot beets in serving dish; pour French dressing over beets. Toss lightly. Top with sour cream; sprinkle with onions. Yield: 4-6 servings.

TANGY BEETS

2 tbsp. butter or margarine
2 tbsp. flour
1/2 tsp. salt
1 c. milk
3 tbsp. horseradish
3 c. diced cooked beets

Melt butter in saucepan; blend in flour and salt. Add milk gradually; cook until thickened, stirring constantly. Stir in horseradish. Pour over hot beets; serve immediately. Yield: 4-6 servings.

CREAMED BEETS

2 tbsp. vinegar
2 tbsp. butter
Salt and pepper to taste
1 tbsp. water
1/3 c. sour cream
12 sm. cooked or canned beets

Combine vinegar, butter, salt, pepper and water in saucepan; bring to a boil, stirring to melt butter. Add sour cream and beets; reduce heat. Simmer until beets are heated through. Serve immediately. Yield: 6 servings.

HARVARD BEETS WITH CLOVES

1 tbsp. cornstarch
1/2 c. sugar
1/2 tsp. salt
1/4 c. vinegar
1/4 c. water
3 whole cloves
3 c. sliced cooked beets
2 tbsp. butter or margarine

Blend cornstarch, sugar and salt in saucepan. Combine vinegar and water; stir slowly into cornstarch mixture. Cook over low heat, stirring constantly, until smooth and thickened. Add cloves and beets; let stand in warm place for 30 minutes. Remove cloves; add butter. Heat to serving temperature. Yield: 6 servings.

Golden Glory Beets . . . A Blend of pineapple chunks and beets in a sweet and sour sauce.

GOLDEN GLORY BEETS

1 13 1/2-oz. can pineapple chunks
1/3 c. vinegar
3 tbsp. brown sugar
2 1/2 tbsp. flour
1/2 tsp. seasoned salt
2 1-lb. cans sliced beets, drained

Drain pineapple, reserving syrup. Combine reserved syrup, 1/2 cup water and vinegar in saucepan. Blend brown sugar, flour and salt; add to pineapple liquid. Cook, stirring for about 10 minutes, until mixture boils and thickens. Add beets. Heat through. Add pineapple chunks; serve hot. Yield: 6-8 servings.

HARVARD BEETS

2 1-lb. cans diced beets
2/3 c. sugar
2 tbsp. cornstarch
1/2 c. white vinegar
3/4 tsp. salt
1/4 c. butter or margarine

Drain beets, reserving 1/2 cup liquid. Mix sugar and cornstarch in saucepan; blend in reserved beet liquid, vinegar and salt. Bring to a boil, stirring constantly. Reduce heat; simmer for 2 minutes. Add beets; simmer for 15 minutes longer. Stir in butter just before serving. Yield: 8 servings.

QUICK HARVARD BEETS

1/2 c. sugar
1/2 c. vinegar
1 tbsp. cornstarch
1 med. can sliced or diced beets
1 tbsp. butter

Mix sugar, vinegar and cornstarch in saucepan. Cook, stirring constantly, over medium heat for 5 minutes or until thickened. Add beets; let stand for 30 minutes. Bring to a boil. Remove from heat; add butter. Yield: 4 servings.

Beverages

There is a beverage to complement every occasion, mood, and kind of weather. There is after-dinner coffee for special company or breakfast cocoa for the family. There is festive holiday punch or tea for a quiet afternoon refresher. Then, too, there's steaming chocolate for a cold and rainy day or frosty lemonade when the temperature climbs. Beverages complete meals, provide a party atmosphere, or make for a midmorning snack—in fact, they do just about everything.

SERVING: When serving *hot tea,* include with

your tea service milk, sugar, lemon slices, and a small pitcher of hot water so that those people who prefer a milder flavor can dilute their tea. Provide cream and sugar with *hot coffee*. For *iced tea*, use tall glasses and long-handled spoons and serve sugar, lemon wedges, and mint sprigs. Accompany *iced coffee* with sugar and cream. Serve *hot chocolate* plain or topped with marshmallows or whipped cream in tall and narrow cups.

There are many ways to make *fruit drinks and punches* appealing. Freeze ice cubes from fruit juices or soft drinks, or create unusual cubes by freezing cherries, lemon slices, or mint sprigs in water in the ice cube tray. Lemon, lime, and orange slices make colorful fruit drink and punch garnishes, as do strawberries, cherries, and grapes.

HOLIDAY APPETIZER

3 cans consomme
1/4 c. chili sauce
1 tbsp. Worcestershire sauce

Combine all ingredients; heat to serving temperature. Strain into cups to serve.

TOMATO COCKTAIL

1 46-oz. can tomato juice
1/2 c. chopped celery
1 clove of garlic, chopped
1/2 med. green pepper, chopped
1 6-oz. can frozen lemonade
1 6-oz. can frozen orange juice
Pinch of salt

Combine tomato juice, celery, garlic and green pepper; let stand for 3 hours or overnight. Strain tomato juice; add lemonade, orange juice and salt. Mix well; chill before serving.

TOMATO JUICE

4 qt. chopped tomatoes
4 bay leaves
8 tsp. salt
6 whole cloves
1 tsp. paprika
8 onions, chopped
1/2 c. sugar

Combine all ingredients in large kettle; mix well. Bring to a boil, stirring constantly. Reduce heat; simmer for 1 hour, stirring frequently. Strain into pitcher; refrigerate until ready to serve.

BRAZILIAN CHOCOLATE

1/2 c. chocolate syrup
1/4 tsp. salt
1/4 tsp. cinnamon
2 tbsp. instant coffee
2 c. hot milk
Vanilla to taste

Combine chocolate syrup, salt, cinnamon and coffee in saucepan; stir in 1/4 cup hot water. Cook over medium heat until heated through. Add 1 1/2 cups hot water and milk; cook until heated through, stirring occasionally. Add vanilla; beat with rotary beater until foamy. Serve immediately. Yield: 6 servings.

FRENCH CHOCOLATE

2 1/2 oz. unsweetened chocolate
1/2 c. water
2/3 c. sugar
1/2 tsp. salt
1/2 c. heavy cream, whipped
1 qt. hot milk

Combine chocolate and water in saucepan; stir over low heat until chocolate is melted. Add sugar and salt; mix well. Bring to a boil. Reduce heat; simmer for 4 minutes. Cool to room temperature; fold in whipped cream. Place 1 rounded tablespoon chocolate mixture in each serving cup; fill cups with hot milk. Stir and serve immediately.

HOT CHOCOLATE MIX

8 qt. powdered milk
1 11-oz. jar non-dairy coffee creamer
1 1-lb. box chocolate drink mix
1 1-lb. box (scant) powdered sugar

Combine all ingredients, mixing well. Store in tightly covered container. Stir 1 tablespoon mix into each cup boiling water to serve.

COFFEE-CREAM PUNCH

3 qt. vanilla ice cream
2 qt. hot coffee
Nutmeg to taste

Place ice cream in punch bowl; pour coffee over ice cream. Stir until ice cream is partially melted; sprinkle with nutmeg. Yield: 16 servings.

COFFEE PUNCH

4 qt. strong coffee
1 qt. heavy cream
5 tbsp. sugar
5 tsp. vanilla
2 qt. vanilla ice cream

Chill coffee. Whip cream, adding sugar and vanilla. Spoon ice cream into large punch bowl; add whipped cream. Pour coffee over top; mix well. Serve in cups. Yield: 50-60 servings.

VIENNESE COFFEE

1/4 c. instant coffee
5 whole cloves
1 3-in. stick cinnamon
3 c. water
Crushed ice
Vanilla ice cream
Whipped cream
Ground cinnamon

Combine coffee, cloves, cinnamon and water in saucepan; bring to a boil. Remove from heat; let stand for 5 minutes. Strain and cool. Fill glasses 1/4 full with crushed ice; add 1 scoop ice cream. Add coffee; stir. Top with whipped cream; sprinkle with ground cinnamon. Serve with long spoon and straw. Yield: 4-6 servings.

Wassail Bowl . . . Bring in the holidays by serving this time-honored beverage.

WASSAIL BOWL

6 Constant Comment tea bags
1 bottle Madeira
1 c. sugar
3 eggs, separated
1/2 c. brandy
3 warm baked apples

Pour 3/4 cup boiling water over tea bags; steep for 5 minutes. Remove tea bags. Combine Madeira and sugar in saucepan; heat, stirring, until sugar dissolves. Pour tea into hot Madeira mixture; keep warm. Beat egg whites until stiff but not dry. Turn into punch bowl. Beat egg yolks until thick and yellow; fold into egg whites. Stir hot Madeira mixture into eggs gradually. Heat brandy; add to punch. Float apples in wassail bowl before serving. Yield: 2 quarts.

BANANA SHAKE

1 c. cold milk
1 banana, chopped
2 tsp. sugar
1 egg

Combine all ingredients in blender or electric mixer bowl. Beat until smooth and creamy.

CHERRY-CRANBERRY PUNCH

1 3-oz. package cherry gelatin
1 6-oz. can frozen lemonade
1 qt. cranberry juice cocktail
1 pt. ginger ale, chilled

Dissolve gelatin in 1 cup boiling water; stir in lemonade, cranberry juice cocktail and 3 cups cold water. Pour over ice in punch bowl; pour in ginger ale slowly. Yield: 25 servings.

CRANBERRY PUNCH

4 c. cranberry juice
2 c. unsweetened pineapple juice
1 c. lemon juice
8 7-oz. bottles ginger ale

Mix cranberry juice, pineapple juice and lemon juice in large punch bowl. Add ginger ale just before serving. Yield: 20 servings.

DEWBERRY FRAPPÉ

2 c. dewberry juice
1 qt. lemonade
Juice of 1 orange

Combine all ingredients; freeze until mushy. Spoon into small dessert glasses; garnish with fresh mint.

DIXIE SPARKLE

5 c. sugar
7 c. water
5 bananas, mashed
1 c. lemon juice
1 2/3 c. orange juice
Lemon-lime carbonated beverage

Combine sugar and water in saucepan. Bring to a boil, stirring to dissolve sugar. Cook for 5 minutes; cool to room temperature. Combine sugar syrup, bananas, lemon juice and orange juice. Pour into freezer container; freeze until mushy. Spoon mixture into 6 tall glasses; finish filling glasses with carbonated beverage.

FROSTY COOL OFF

2 c. sugar
4 c. water
1/2 c. bottled lemon juice
1/2 c. bottled lime juice
2 12-oz. bottles ginger ale

Combine sugar and water in saucepan; heat, stirring constantly, until sugar is dissolved. Bring to a boil; cook for about 5 minutes. Combine sugar syrup and fruit juices in punch bowl; add ginger ale just before serving. Float ice ring or ice cubes in punch. Yield: 25 servings.

GINGER PEACHY DRINK

1 1-lb. 4-oz. can peach halves
1/4 c. lime juice
1 qt. chilled ginger ale

Combine peaches and lime juice in blender container; cover. Process at high speed for 30 seconds. Pour mixture over ice cubes in 8 tall glasses; finish filling glasses with ginger ale.

MANY-FRUITED PUNCH

1 6-oz. can frozen orange juice
2 6-oz. cans frozen limeade
1 6-oz. can frozen lemonade
1 pt. cranberry juice
1 46-oz. can pineapple juice
3 c. cold water
2 qt. ginger ale
1 qt. club soda, chilled

Combine fruit juices and cold water in punch bowl. Add ginger ale and club soda just before serving. Float ice ring in punch. Yield: 40 servings.

HAWAIIAN LEMONADE

1 6-oz. can frozen lemonade
1 12-oz. can unsweetened pineapple juice, chilled
1 12-oz. can apricot nectar
1 bottle ginger ale, chilled
1 lemon, sliced

Dilute lemonade with 3/4 cup water; stir in apricot nectar and pineapple juice. Pour fruit juice mixture over ice cubes in 6 glasses. Fill glasses with ginger ale; garnish with lemon slices.

HAWAIIAN PUNCH

3 c. unsweetened pineapple juice
1 1/2 c. unsweetened orange juice
3/4 c. lemon juice
2 tbsp. liquid sweetener
2 qt. carbonated water, chilled

Combine juices and sweetener; chill. Add carbonated water just before serving. Garnish with lemon slices, pineapple spears and mint sprigs. Serve immediately.

Hawaiian Punch . . . The warmth and sweetness of the Islands are in this party-perfect punch.

OAHU FRAPPÉ

1/2 c. sugar
3/4 c. water
3/4 c. orange juice
1 1/2 c. unsweetened pineapple juice

Combine sugar and water in saucepan, stirring to dissolve sugar. Bring to a boil; cook for 5 minutes. Cool syrup to room temperature; add fruit juices. Freeze until mushy. Serve in chilled sherbet glasses. Yield: 6 servings.

ORANGEADE BASE

Grated rind and juice of 4 oranges
2 oz. citric acid
4 lb. sugar
Juice of 3 lemons

Combine orange rind, citric acid and sugar; add 2 quarts boiling water, stirring to dissolve sugar. Cool; add orange juice and lemon juice. Let stand for 24 hours. Strain into sterilized bottles; seal. Use 1/4 cup concentrate for each quart water to serve.

SUMMER CHAMPAGNE

3/4 c. sugar
1 c. water
1 c. canned grapefruit juice
1/2 c. canned pineapple juice
1 qt. chilled ginger ale

Mix sugar and water in saucepan; bring to a boil. Cook for 5 minutes; cool. Add fruit juices to syrup; chill. Add ginger ale just before serving. Pour into six 10-ounce glasses. Garnish with cherries, strawberries or pineapple chunks.

APRICOT FLIP

1/2 c. strained apricots
1 tsp. lemon juice
1 c. vanilla ice cream
3 c. ginger ale

Mix apricots and lemon juice well. Spoon mixture into 4 tall glasses. Add 4 tablespoons ice cream to each glass; pour in half the ginger ale. Stir; add remaining ginger ale. Serve immediately.

STRAWBERRY THICKSHAKES

Color photograph for this recipe on page 733.

2 pt. fresh California strawberries
1 qt. vanilla ice cream, softened

Reserve several strawberries for garnish; puree remaining strawberries in blender. Strain puree through double thickness of cheesecloth to remove seeds. Process puree and ice cream in blender until smooth. Place blender container in freezer for about 1 hour. Blend for several seconds until smooth before serving. Spoon into tall glasses; serve immediately with long spoons. Garnish with whole strawberries. Yield: 4 servings.

CHILDREN'S PARTY PUNCH

2 6-oz. cans pink lemonade
2 pt. vanilla ice cream
1 qt. milk
Red food coloring

Turn lemonade into punch bowl; add 1 pint ice cream. Beat until smooth. Tint milk with food coloring; stir into lemonade mixture. Scoop remaining ice cream into punch. Yield: 12 servings.

CRANBERRY COCKTAIL

1 pt. vanilla ice cream
1 qt. cranberry juice

Place ice cream in large pitcher; pour cranberry juice slowly over ice cream, beating well with wooden spoon. Mix until ice cream is melted and mixture is creamy. Refrigerate until ready to use. Yield: 8 servings.

CRANBERRY-LEMON FLOAT

2 c. ice water
1/3 c. sugar
1/3 c. lemon juice, chilled
1 pt. cranberry juice, chilled
1 pt. ginger ale, chilled
1 pt. lemon sherbet

Combine water, sugar, lemon juice and cranberry juice in small punch bowl; pour in ginger ale slowly. Top with small scoops of sherbet just before serving. Yield: 12 servings.

FROSTY FRUIT SHRUB

1 6-oz. can frozen pineapple juice
4 c. cold milk
Dash of salt
1 pt. orange sherbet

Partially thaw frozen juice; add remaining ingredients. Mix well. Yield: 12 servings.

ORANGE PARTY PUNCH

2 pkg. strawberry gelatin
1 1/2 c. sugar
1 can pineapple juice
1 can orange juice
1 c. lemon juice
2 qt. orange sherbet
1 bottle ginger ale

Dissolve gelatin and sugar in 2 cups boiling water; stir in 2 cups cold water and fruit juices. Chill until ready to serve. Spoon sherbet into punch bowl; pour gelatin mixture and ginger ale over sherbet. Yield: 40 servings.

HOT CINNAMON-SPICED WINE

Color photograph for this recipe on page 734.

1 c. sugar
2 sticks cinnamon
2 doz. cloves
1/2 lemon, sliced
4 c. hot unsweetened fruit juice
1 qt. red wine

Combine sugar, 1/2 cup water, spices and lemon in saucepan; boil for 5 minutes. Strain hot syrup; stir in fruit juice and wine. Keep warm but do not boil. Serve in individual mugs; garnish with lemon slices. Yield: 16 servings.

HOT CRANBERRY PUNCH

3/4 c. brown sugar
1 c. water
1/4 tsp. salt
1/4 tsp. nutmeg
2 sticks cinnamon
1/2 tsp. whole allspice
3/4 tsp. whole cloves
1 qt. pineapple juice
1 qt. cranberry juice cocktail
Juice of 1/2 lemon

Combine sugar, water, salt and spices in large saucepan; bring to a boil. Reduce heat; simmer for 8 minutes. Strain through several thicknesses of cheesecloth. Stir in pineapple juice, cranberry juice and lemon juice. Simmer for 5 minutes longer. Serve hot with cinnamon stick muddlers. Yield: 8 cups.

HOT HOLIDAY PUNCH

1 tbsp. allspice
1 tbsp. whole cloves
1 tbsp. nutmeg
1 tbsp. cinnamon
1 gal. apple cider
1 c. brown sugar
1 can frozen lemonade
1 can frozen orange juice

Tie spices in small cloth bag. Combine all ingredients in large kettle; simmer for 20 minutes. Yield: 16-18 servings.

HOT SPICED CIDER

1 tsp. whole cloves
1 3-in. stick cinnamon
1 tsp. whole allspice
1/2 gal. apple cider
1/2 c. brown sugar
1/4 tsp. salt

Tie spices in small cloth bag. Combine cider, brown sugar and salt in kettle; add spice bag. Cover; simmer for 20 minutes. Yield: 4-6 servings.

HOT SPICED GRAPE JUICE

2 sticks cinnamon
8 whole cloves
3/4 c. sugar
4 c. water
4 c. grape juice
2 c. orange juice
12 slices lemon

Tie spices in small cloth bag. Combine sugar and water in kettle, stirring to dissolve sugar. Add spice bag; bring to a boil. Cook for 10 minutes. Remove spice bag; add grape juice, orange juice and lemon slices. Reheat to serving temperature. Yield: 12 servings.

HOT SPICED PUNCH

1/4 c. whole cloves
3 c. water
1 c. sugar
1/2 gal. orange juice
1 46-oz. can pineapple juice

Combine cloves and water in saucepan. Bring to a boil; cook for about 10 minutes. Add sugar. Strain syrup into large kettle; add fruit juices. Heat to serving temperature. Yield: 20 servings.

SWEDISH BREW

1/2 tsp. ginger
1 stick cinnamon
1/2 tsp. whole cloves
4 1/2 qt. water
3 c. sugar
Juice of 1 doz. lemons
Juice of 8 oranges
1 can raspberry juice

Tie spices in small cloth bag. Combine water and sugar in large kettle; bring to a boil. Cook until syrupy; add spice bag. Let syrup stand for 8 minutes. Remove spice bag. Stir in fruit juices; reheat to serving temperature.

TEA PARTY PUNCH

3 c. sugar
4 qt. water
1 qt. apple juice
2 qt. cranberry juice
1 1/4 c. lemon juice
2 c. orange juice
2 c. strong black tea

Combine sugar and water in saucepan, stirring to dissolve sugar. Bring to a boil; cook for 5 minutes. Combine sugar syrup, fruit juices and tea in large container. Mix well; chill until ready to serve. Yield: 40 servings.

INSTANT SPICED TEA MIX

1/2 c. instant tea
2 c. orange-flavored instant breakfast drink
1 tsp. cinnamon
1/2 tsp. cloves
1 1/2 c. sugar
2 pkg. lemonade mix

Mix all ingredients; store in tightly covered container. Use 2 teaspoons mix to each cup of boiling water to serve. Yield: 30 servings.

ALMOND TEA

2 c. sugar
2 tbsp. grated lemon rind
2 c. strong tea
1 tsp. almond extract
1 tsp. vanilla
Juice of 3 lemons

Combine sugar, 2 cups water and lemon rind in saucepan; bring to a boil, stirring until sugar is dissolved. Add tea, almond extract, vanilla, lemon juice and enough water to equal 1 gallon liquid. Serve hot or cold. Yield: 16 servings.

Biscuits

Rich and buttery to the taste, flaky to the touch, with a smooth, browned top, biscuits are universal favorites any time of the day. There are two kinds of biscuits, those made with quick-acting leavening, such as baking powder or baking soda and sour milk, and those made with slower acting yeast.

BASIC PREPARATION: Prepare biscuits by mixing and kneading dough. Good biscuits are made by the proper measuring and cutting in of the shortening. So be sure to follow the amount of shortening specified in the recipe. Shortening should always be cut into the sifted dry ingredients with a pastry blender or with two knives held in a scissor-like fashion. The dough should be puffy and easy to roll out. It should never be handled too much. Cut with biscuit cutter or water glass dipped in flour. Bake in a hot oven for 12-15 minutes.

BAKING POWDER-HAM BISCUITS

2 c. sifted flour
3 tsp. baking powder
1 tsp. salt
1/4 c. shortening
7/8 c. milk
2/3 c. chopped cooked ham

Sift flour with baking powder and salt into bowl; cut in shortening to consistency of rice grains. Add milk and ham; mix just to blend ingredients. Turn onto lightly floured board; knead gently 5 to 6 times. Roll out to 1/2 to 3/4-inch thickness; cut with 2-inch biscuit cutter. Place on ungreased cookie sheet. Bake at 400 degrees for 12 to 15 minutes. Yield: 12-16 biscuits.

BEATEN BISCUITS

8 c. sifted flour
1/2 tsp. sugar
1 tsp. salt
1/4 tsp. soda
3/4 c. lard

Sift flour, sugar, salt and soda together. Cut in lard until of consistency of fine meal. Stir in 1 cup water; blend thoroughly. Place dough on wooden block; pound with hammer, turning frequently, for 20 to 30 minutes or until dough blisters and becomes satiny in texture. Roll dough to 1/3-inch thickness; cut with small biscuit cutter. Bake at 400 degrees for 25 minutes or until lightly browned. Yield: 6 dozen biscuits.

CORNMEAL BISCUITS

2/3 c. cornmeal
1 pt. milk
2 pkg. dry yeast
1/2 c. sugar
1/2 c. shortening
1 tsp. salt
3 eggs, beaten
6 c. flour

Combine cornmeal and milk in large saucepan; cook until of consistency of mush. Dissolve yeast in 1/2 cup warm water. Add sugar, shortening, salt, eggs, yeast and flour to cornmeal mixture. Blend until smooth. Turn out on floured board; knead for 8 to 10 minutes. Place in greased bowl to rise in warm place until doubled in bulk. Roll to desired thickness; cut with biscuit cutter. Place on greased cookie sheet to rise again. Bake at 350 degrees for 20 minutes.

BUTTER DIPS

1/3 c. butter
2 1/4 c. sifted flour
1 tbsp. sugar
3 1/2 tsp. baking powder
1 1/2 tsp. salt
1 c. milk

Preheat oven to 450 degrees. Melt butter in 13 x 9 1/2 x 2-inch pan. Sift dry ingredients into bowl; add milk, stirring slowly until dough just clings together. Turn out onto well-floured board. Knead lightly 10 times. Roll out 1/2 inch thick into 8 x 12-inch rectangle. Cut in half lengthwise; cut crosswise into 16 strips. Dip each strip on both sides in melted butter; place close together in 2 rows in pan. Bake for 15 to 20 minutes, until golden brown. Yield: 32 butter dips.

BUTTERMILK BISCUITS

1/3 c. shortening
1 tbsp. sugar
1 2/3 c. sifted flour
2 tsp. baking powder
1 1/2 tsp. salt
1/4 tsp. cream of tartar
1 c. buttermilk
1/2 tsp. soda

Cream shortening and sugar; sift flour, baking powder, salt and cream of tartar together. Blend buttermilk and soda. Add dry ingredients alternately with buttermilk mixture to creamed mixture. Blend well. Roll out on lightly floured board; cut with biscuit cutter. Place biscuits on baking sheet. Bake at 475 degrees for 10 minutes. Yield: 20 biscuits.

CHEESE BISCUITS

2 c. sifted flour
3 tsp. baking powder
1 tsp. salt
1/4 c. shortening
1/3 c. grated sharp cheese
3/4 c. milk

Combine flour, baking powder and salt in bowl. Cut in shortening until of consistency of cornmeal; stir in cheese. Add milk to flour-shortening mixture; blend just to combine ingredients. Roll out dough on floured surface; cut with biscuit cutter. Place on ungreased cookie sheet. Bake at 425 degrees for 12 to 15 minutes. Yield: 16-20 biscuits.

COTTAGE CHEESE BISCUITS

1 egg, lightly beaten
3 tbsp. milk
1 c. cottage cheese
2 c. flour
4 tsp. baking powder
1 tsp. salt
1/4 c. minced parsley
2 tbsp. melted butter

Preheat oven to 450 degrees. Combine egg, milk and cottage cheese thoroughly. Stir flour, baking powder, salt and parsley together; add to egg mixture, blending with fingertips. Add additional milk, one drop at a time, if necessary to hold dough together. Turn onto floured board; knead for 30 seconds. Pat out to 1/2-inch thickness; cut into 18 squares. Spread with butter. Place on greased baking sheet. Bake for 12 minutes or until lightly browned. Yield: 18 biscuits.

DROPPED BAKING POWDER BISCUITS

2 c. sifted flour
3 tsp. baking powder
1/2 tsp. salt
6 tbsp. shortening
1 c. milk

Sift flour, baking powder and salt together. Cut in shortening until of consistency of cornmeal. Scald milk; cool. Add milk; blend well. Drop by teaspoonfuls onto greased and lightly floured cookie sheet. Bake at 400 degrees until browned. Yield: 10 servings.

EASY BISCUITS

2 c. sifted flour
4 tsp. baking powder
1 tsp. salt
1 tsp. sugar
1/4 c. shortening
1 c. milk

Sift dry ingredients together; make well in center. Place shortening and milk in well. Mix until smooth. Pat out on generously floured board; turn once. Pat out; cut. Place on baking sheet. Bake at 450 degrees for 12 minutes. Yield: 6-8 servings.

EGG BISCUITS

2 c. flour
4 tsp. baking powder
1/2 tsp. cream of tartar
1/2 tsp. salt
2 tbsp. sugar
1/2 c. shortening
1 egg
2/3 c. milk

Mix dry ingredients; cut in shortening. Stir in egg and milk; turn onto floured board. Knead 10 times. Roll dough; cut with biscuit cutter. Place on ungreased baking sheet. Bake at 450 degrees for 10 to 15 minutes.

GRAHAM BISCUITS

1 1/2 c. graham flour
2 tsp. baking powder
2 tsp. sugar
1/8 tsp. soda
1 tsp. salt
2 1/2 tbsp. lard
1/4 c. milk

Sift flour, baking powder, sugar, soda and salt together. Cut in lard; add milk. Mix dough thoroughly. Place on floured surface. Roll dough to 1/3-inch thickness; cut with biscuit cutter. Place biscuits on ungreased baking sheet. Bake at 325 degrees until lightly browned.

ONION BISCUITS

1 sm. package biscuit mix
1 tsp. instant onion
1 tsp. dried parsley flakes
1/2 c. sauterne
Mayonnaise
3 tbsp. grated Parmesan cheese

Combine biscuit mix, onion and parsley; add sauterne and 1/4 cup mayonnaise. Stir to form soft dough. Turn out on floured board; roll to 1/2-inch thickness. Cut with small cutter; place on ungreased baking sheet. Blend 2 tablespoons mayonnaise with cheese; spread on biscuits. Bake at 450 degrees for 12 to 15 minutes.

SOURDOUGH BISCUITS

1/2 tsp. soda
3/4 c. Starter
2 c. prepared biscuit mix
Melted shortening

Dissolve soda in Starter; stir into biscuit mix. Place on floured board; knead lightly. Flatten with fingers into circle of 1-inch thickness; cut into 10 wedges. Dip each wedge in melted shortening. Place in 9 x 9-inch pan. Bake at 425 degrees for 12 to 15 minutes. Yield: 10 rolls.

Starter

1 env. yeast
2 med. potatoes, chopped
1 tbsp. sugar
1 tsp. salt
2 c. flour

Dissolve yeast in 1/2 cup warm water. Cook potatoes in 3 cups water until tender. Drain potatoes, reserving 2 cups water. Cool potato water to lukewarm; add yeast, sugar, salt, flour and potatoes. Mix well; cover. Let stand in warm place for 3 days; stir each day. Leftover Starter may be kept in refrigerator for later use.

SOUR MILK BISCUITS

3 c. flour
4 tsp. baking powder
1/8 tsp. soda
1 tsp. salt
1/2 c. shortening
1 1/2 c. sour milk
Melted butter

Sift dry ingredients; cut in shortening. Add sour milk. Turn out onto floured board; knead until stiff dough forms. Roll 1/2 inch thick; cut with biscuit cutter. Place on well-greased baking sheet; brush with butter. Bake at 450 degrees until golden brown. Yield: 2 dozen biscuits.

SOUTHERN SAUSAGE BISCUITS

1 10-oz. package sharp cheese
1 lb. bulk sausage
3 c. prepared biscuit mix

Grate cheese; let cheese and sausage stand at room temperature. Combine cheese, sausage and prepared biscuit mix; blend thoroughly. Shape into small balls. Place on ungreased baking sheet. Bake at 425 degrees for 10 to 12 minutes. Yield: 30 biscuits.

SWEET POTATO BISCUITS

2 c. flour
2/3 c. sugar
1 1/2 tsp. salt
2 tbsp. baking powder
1/4 c. shortening
2 c. mashed baked sweet potatoes
1/4 c. milk

Sift flour, sugar, salt and baking powder together; cut in shortening until mixture resembles cornmeal. Stir in sweet potatoes; add milk gradually to form soft dough. Turn onto lightly floured board. Knead lightly. Roll or pat 1/2 inch thick; cut with 2-inch biscuit cutter. Place on greased cookie sheet. Bake at 475 degrees for 12 to 15 minutes.

WHOLE WHEAT BISCUITS

1 1/2 c. flour
1/2 c. whole wheat flour
3 tsp. baking powder
1 tsp. salt
1/3 c. vegetable shortening
2/3 c. milk

Sift flours, baking powder and salt together into mixing bowl; cut in shortening until well blended. Add milk; stir until just blended. Turn out onto well-floured board; knead for several minutes. Roll to 1/2-inch thickness; cut with biscuit cutter. Place on baking sheet. Bake at 425 degrees for 15 minutes or until lightly browned. Yield: 16-18 biscuits.

Biscuit Tortoni

Biscuit tortoni or Bisque tortoni is a festive ice cream-like dessert made from rich, heavy cream. It is topped with colorful maraschino cherries, crushed wafers, macaroons, or crunchy, unsalted toasted almonds and served frozen in a pleated paper container.

ALMOND TORTONI

1 egg white
6 tbsp. sugar
1 tbsp. brown sugar
1 c. heavy cream
1 tsp. almond flavoring
2 tbsp. chopped coconut
2 tbsp. chopped almonds
Maraschino cherries

Beat egg white until frothy; beat in 2 tablespoons sugar and brown sugar gradually. Beat cream until stiff; beat in remaining sugar and almond flavoring. Fold in egg whites. Mix coconut and almonds; reserve half for topping. Add remaining coconut mixture to egg mixture. Spoon into paper cups; top with reserved coconut mixture. Garnish each cup with 1 maraschino cherry. Place cups in muffin tins; freeze for at least 3 hours.

ELEGANT TORTONI

2 eggs, separated
1/2 c. sugar
2 c. heavy cream
2 tbsp. instant coffee
2 tsp. vanilla
1/4 c. semisweet chocolate bits
1/2 c. minced nuts

Beat egg whites until stiff, adding 1/4 cup sugar gradually. Beat egg yolks lightly. Whip cream with remaining sugar and coffee; add egg yolks and vanilla. Fold in egg whites. Melt chocolate over hot water; cool slightly. Fold chocolate and nuts into egg white mixture. Spoon into paper cups. Freeze. Yield: 12-14 servings.

CHOCOLATE CHIP TORTONI

2 egg whites
1/4 c. sugar
1 c. whipping cream
1 tbsp. vanilla
2 tsp. butter
1 c. chocolate chips

Beat egg whites until foamy. Add sugar; beat until stiff. Beat cream until thick; add vanilla. Fold egg whites into cream. Place in freezer for 45 minutes. Melt butter and chocolate chips together; stir into whipped cream mixture. Spoon into paper cupcake liners; freeze until firm. Yield: 10 servings.

MACAROON TORTONI

2 eggs, separated
1/2 c. powdered sugar
2 tbsp. sherry
1/2 tsp. vanilla
1 c. heavy cream, whipped
Macaroon crumbs

Beat egg whites until stiff. Beat egg yolks and sugar until fluffy; stir in sherry and vanilla. Fold in egg whites and whipped cream gently. Stir in 1/2 cup macaroon crumbs. Turn into paper dessert cups; sprinkle lightly with macaroon crumbs. Freeze until firm. Yield: 8 servings.

MILANESE MARVEL

1 tbsp. gelatin
1/4 c. cold milk
2 eggs, separated
1/2 c. sugar
1 c. scalded milk
1 c. cream, whipped
1 tsp. vanilla
Pinch of salt
Almond macaroon crumbs

Soften gelatin in cold milk for 5 minutes. Beat egg yolks with sugar; add scalded milk. Cook over low heat until mixture coats spoon. Stir in gelatin until dissolved. Add stiffly beaten egg whites and whipped cream. Fold in vanilla and salt. Place in refrigerator tray or paper baking cups; freeze until firm. Sprinkle macaroon crumbs over top; serve with additional whipped cream and cherries. Yield: 10-12 servings.

RUM TORTONI

1/2 c. minced toasted almonds
1/2 c. shredded toasted coconut
1/2 c. seedless dark raisins
1 qt. vanilla ice cream
3 tsp. rum extract
Maraschino cherries

Combine almonds, coconut and raisins. Soften ice cream until of thin consistency. Stir in rum extract and almond mixture quickly. Spoon into paper cups in 2 1/2-inch muffin tins. Freeze slightly; top with cherries. Freeze until firm. Remove from freezer just before serving. Yield: 12-14 servings.

TORTONI SPLENDIDE

6 eggs, separated
3/4 c. sugar
1/2 tsp. almond flavoring
2 tbsp. maraschino cherry juice
1 pt. whipping cream, whipped
1/4 c. crunchy nut-like cereal nuggets
2 doz. macaroons, grated

Whip egg whites until stiff. Beat egg yolks until thick and creamy, beating in sugar gradually. Fold egg whites into egg yolks; add almond flavoring and cherry juice. Fold in whipped cream, cereal nuggets and 3/4 of the macaroon crumbs. Spoon into small paper cups; freeze until firm. Sprinkle with remaining macaroon crumbs just before serving. Yield: 12 servings.

Blackberry

These delectable juicy berries are the black or reddish-purple fruit of a prickly-stemmed bush. (1 cup fresh, unsweetened blackberries = 80 calories)

AVAILABILITY: Available on the market from May to August, with June the peak month.

BUYING: Choose large, plump, and dry blackberries with a glossy bright skin. They should be free of dirt and decay. Overripe berries are dull in color and soft and lifeless to the touch. Unripe berries have green off-color portions. Generally they are sold in pint or quart containers. A stained container indicates crushed fruit is inside.

STORING: Blackberries are extremely perishable and should be used within a day or two of purchase. Wash them before storing in the vegetable crisper. *To freeze* blackberries, wash in ice water and discard overripe or underripe berries before freezing.

SERVING: Use blackberries in jams, jellies, chutneys, cobblers, pies, tarts, muffins, and salads. If they become soft, prepare them in a simple sugar syrup for use as ice cream topping or cake sauce.

BLACKBERRY BREAD

4 c. blackberries
1 c. sugar
8 slices bread
1/2 c. soft butter

Cook blackberries over low heat until soft; stir in sugar. Spread bread with butter. Alternate layers of bread and blackberries in loaf pan, ending with blackberries. Chill until ready to serve. Slice; serve with whipped cream. Yield: 4-6 servings.

BLACKBERRY ICE

1 c. water
1 c. sugar
1 c. orange juice
2 c. blackberry juice

Mix water and sugar in saucepan; bring to a boil. Cool. Add orange juice and blackberry juice. Pour into ice cream freezer container; freeze according to freezer directions. Yield: 10-12 servings.

BLACKBERRY ICE CREAM

2 c. blackberry pulp
16 lge. marshmallows
1 tbsp. lemon juice
1 c. sugar
1/8 tsp. salt
1 1/2 c. whipped cream

Heat blackberry pulp in double boiler; add marshmallows, lemon juice, sugar and salt. Stir until marshmallows are melted. Chill; fold in whipped cream. Turn into pan or mold; freeze without stirring. Yield: 6-8 servings.

BLACKBERRY SALAD MOLD

1 pkg. grape gelatin
1 sm. can crushed pineapple
2 c. fresh blackberries
2 c. prepared dessert topping

Dissolve gelatin in 1 cup boiling water. Add 6 ice cubes; stir until ice is melted. Chill gelatin until syrupy. Drain pineapple; fold pineapple, blackberries, and dessert topping into gelatin. Turn into ring mold; refrigerate until firm. Yield: 6-8 servings.

BLACKBERRY CAKE

3 eggs
1 1/2 c. sugar
1 c. shortening
2 tsp. cinnamon
1 tsp. cloves
2 c. undrained blackberries
1 tsp. soda
3 1/2 c. flour
2 tsp. baking powder

Combine eggs, sugar, shortening, cinnamon and cloves in mixer bowl; beat until blended. Add blackberries, soda, flour and baking powder; beat well. Pour into 13 x 9 x 2-inch pan. Bake at 350 degrees for 40 minutes. Yield: 12 servings.

BLACKBERRY CAKE WITH HOT SAUCE

2 c. sugar
3/4 c. margarine
3 eggs
Flour
1 tsp. soda
1 tsp. cinnamon
1 tsp. cloves
1 tsp. allspice
1/2 c. sour milk
1 c. drained blackberries
1 c. blackberry juice

Cream 1 cup sugar and 1/2 cup margarine until light and fluffy. Beat in eggs. Sift 2 cups flour, soda and spices together; add to creamed mixture alternately with milk. Mix well; fold in blackberries. Turn batter into greased 13 x 9 x 2-inch pan. Bake at 350 degrees for 50 minutes or until cake tests done. Mix remaining sugar and 2 tablespoons flour in saucepan; stir in blackberry juice. Add remaining margarine. Cook over low heat, stirring constantly, until sauce is thickened. Pour hot sauce over warm cake. Yield: 12 servings.

BLACKBERRY JAM CAKE

1 c. butter
4 1/2 c. sugar
5 eggs
1 c. blackberry jam
3 c. flour
1 tsp. soda
1 tsp. nutmeg
1 tsp. cloves
2 tsp. cinnamon
1 tsp. allspice
1 c. buttermilk
1 c. chopped pecans
1 c. raisins
1 tsp. vanilla

Cream butter and 2 cups sugar until fluffy. Separate 3 eggs; beat egg yolks and remaining eggs into creamed mixture. Stir in jam. Sift flour, soda, nutmeg, cloves, cinnamon and allspice together. Add to jam mixture alternately with buttermilk; mix well. Stir in pecans and raisins. Spread batter in 2 greased and floured 9-inch layer pans. Bake at 350 degrees for 35 to 40 minutes or until cake tests done. Cool cake in pans for 10 minutes; turn onto racks to cool completely. Melt 1/2 cup sugar in heavy skillet. Combine remaining sugar and 1 cup water in saucepan. Boil rapidly to soft-ball stage; stir in melted sugar. Beat egg whites at high speed of electric mixer, pouring in sugar syrup in fine stream. Beat in vanilla. Spread frosting between layers and on top and side of cake.

BLACKBERRY DELIGHT

1/4 c. sugar
2 tbsp. cornstarch
Dash of salt
1 No. 2 can blackberries
1 tbsp. lemon juice
1 lb. marshmallows
1/2 c. milk
1 c. heavy cream
15 graham crackers
1/4 c. melted butter
1/2 c. chopped nuts

Mix sugar, cornstarch and salt in saucepan; add blackberries and lemon juice. Cook over low heat, stirring constantly, until thickened. Cool. Combine marshmallows and milk in saucepan; stir over low heat until marshmallows are melted. Cool. Whip cream until stiff; fold into marshmallow mixture. Roll graham crackers to fine crumbs; stir butter into crumbs. Sprinkle about 3/4 of the crumbs in 12 x 8 x 2-inch dish. Pour half the marshmallow mixture into dish; cover with blackberry mixture. Add remaining marshmallow mixture; sprinkle with remaining crumbs and nuts. Refrigerate for 24 hours before serving. Yield: 10 servings.

BLACKBERRY FLUFF

1/2 c. evaporated milk
1/2 c. sugar
1 env. unflavored gelatin
1 1/2 c. pureed blackberries

Chill milk, mixing bowl and rotary beater. Dissolve sugar in 1/2 cup boiling water. Soften gelatin in 2 tablespoons cold water; add to sugar mixture, stirring until dissolved. Chill until slightly thickened. Beat chilled milk with rotary beater until fluffy and tripled in volume. Add gelatin mixture; beat well. Fold in blackberries gently. Pour into dessert glasses; chill until ready to serve. Yield: 5 servings.

BLACKBERRY SUPREME

1 box vanilla wafers
1/2 c. butter or margarine
1 c. powdered sugar
2 eggs
1 can blackberry pie filling
1 c. heavy cream, whipped
1/4 c. chopped walnuts

Crush wafers to fine crumbs. Cream butter and sugar until fluffy; beat in eggs, one at a time. Spread 2/3 cup wafer crumbs evenly in 8-inch square pan; spread egg mixture evenly over crumbs in pan. Cover with pie filling; spread whipped cream over pie filling. Sprinkle with walnuts and remaining crumbs; refrigerate for 24 hours before serving. Yield: 9 servings.

CREAMY BLACKBERRY DESSERT

1/2 c. sugar
1/4 c. butter, melted
2 c. graham cracker crumbs
1 pkg. raspberry gelatin
2 c. ice cream
1 No. 2 can blackberry pie filling
1 tbsp. lemon juice

Combine sugar, butter and cracker crumbs. Reserve 1/4 cup crumb mixture. Press remaining crumb mixture against bottom of 8-inch square pan. Dissolve gelatin in 1 cup boiling water; add ice cream. Stir to melt ice cream. Chill until thickened; fold in pie filling and lemon juice. Turn into crumb-lined pan; top with reserved crumbs. Chill until firm. Yield: 9 servings.

FROSTED BLACKBERRY MOLD

2 6-oz. packages blackberry gelatin
1 sm. can crushed pineapple
1 can blackberries
1 8-oz. package cream cheese
1/2 c. sour cream
1/4 c. sugar
1 c. chopped pecans

Dissolve gelatin in 3 cups boiling water; stir in 3 cups cold water, pineapple and blackberries. Pour into large flat dish; chill until firm. Soften cream cheese; add sour cream and sugar. Spread cream cheese mixture over gelatin mixture; sprinkle with pecans. Refrigerate until ready to serve. Yield: 16 servings.

BLACKBERRY BUCKLE

1/2 c. butter
1 c. sugar
1 1/3 c. flour
1/2 tsp. cinnamon
1 egg
1 1/2 tsp. baking powder
1/8 tsp. salt
1/3 c. milk
1 tsp. vanilla
2 c. sweetened blackberries

Combine 1/4 cup butter, 1/2 cup sugar, 1/3 cup flour and cinnamon; mix until crumbly. Cream remaining butter and sugar well; beat in egg. Sift remaining flour, baking powder and salt together; add to creamed mixture alternately with milk. Stir in vanilla. Spread batter in greased and floured 7-inch pan. Scatter blackberries over batter; sprinkle crumb mixture over blackberries. Bake at 375 degrees for 45 minutes. Serve with whipped cream, if desired. Yield: 6 servings.

DELUXE BLACKBERRY COBBLER

1 c. flour
1 c. sugar
1/4 tsp. salt
2 tsp. baking powder
3/4 c. milk
1/2 c. melted butter
2 drops of almond extract
2 c. sweetened blackberries

Sift flour, sugar, salt and baking powder together; add milk. Mix to smooth batter; spread batter in baking dish. Pour butter evenly over batter. Stir almond extract into blackberries; spoon blackberries evenly over batter. Bake at 350 degrees for 45 to 50 minutes or until batter rises to top of dish and is brown. Yield: 6 servings.

EASY BLACKBERRY COBBLER

2 c. sugar
1/3 c. butter
2 c. flour
2 tsp. baking powder
1 tsp. salt
1 c. milk
2 c. blackberries
2 c. boiling water

Cream 1 cup sugar with butter; add flour, baking powder, salt and milk. Mix well; pour into 12 x 8 x 2-inch baking pan. Pour blackberries over batter; sprinkle remaining sugar over blackberries. Pour boiling water over top. Bake at 350 degrees for 50 minutes or until golden brown. Serve plain or with cream. Yield: 10-12 servings.

BLACKBERRY PUDDING

4 c. bread crumbs
2 eggs, beaten
1 qt. blackberries
1 tsp. nutmeg
1 tsp. cinnamon
4 c. sugar
1 tsp. vanilla
Milk

Preheat oven to 500 degrees. Combine bread crumbs, eggs, blackberries, nutmeg, cinnamon, sugar and vanilla. Add enough milk to make thin batter; pour batter into greased baking dish. Place pudding in oven. Reduce oven temperature to 350 degrees immediately. Bake for 2 hours. Yield: 8 servings.

BLACKBERRY MERINGUE PIE

3 eggs, separated
1 c. sour cream
1/4 c. melted butter
1 c. blackberry jam
1/2 c. sugar
Dash of salt
1 tbsp. cornstarch
1 9-in. unbaked pastry shell
14 marshmallows
1 tbsp. light cream

Beat egg yolks lightly; beat in sour cream, 3 tablespoons butter and jam. Mix sugar, salt and cornstarch; stir into jam mixture. Pour into pastry shell. Bake at 425 degrees for 30 minutes. Cool. Melt marshmallows in top of double boiler; stir in remaining butter and light cream. Cool. Beat egg whites until stiff; fold into marshmallow mixture. Spread meringue over pie. Bake at 350 degrees for 15 minutes or until meringue is browned. Yield: 6 servings.

BAKED BERRY PUDDING

1 No. 2 can blackberries
2 c. sifted flour
4 tsp. baking powder
1/2 tsp. salt
1/4 c. shortening
2/3 c. sugar
2 eggs
2 tbsp. lemon juice

Drain blackberries, reserving 3/4 cup juice. Sift flour, baking powder and salt together. Cream shortening and sugar until light and fluffy; beat in eggs. Add flour mixture alternately with reserved blackberry juice and lemon juice; beat until smooth. Fold in blackberries; turn into greased 11 x 7 x 2-inch baking dish. Bake at 350 degrees for 35 minutes. Increase oven temperature to 400 degrees; bake for 10 minutes longer. Serve warm or cold; top with a lemon sauce, if desired. Yield: 8 servings.

Black Bottom Pie

BLACK BOTTOM PIE

2 sq. unsweetened chocolate
1 env. unflavored gelatin
1/4 c. cold water
1 c. sugar
1 tbsp. cornstarch
Dash of salt
2 c. milk
4 eggs, separated
1 tsp. vanilla
1 baked pastry shell
1 tbsp. rum flavoring
1/8 tsp. cream of tartar
1 c. whipping cream

Melt chocolate. Soften gelatin in cold water. Mix 1/2 cup sugar, cornstarch and salt in pan. Stir in milk; cook over low heat, stirring constantly, until thickened. Beat egg yolks. Stir hot custard, slowly, into egg yolks. Add gelatin. Strain into 4-cup measure. Spoon 1 cup custard back into saucepan; blend in chocolate and vanilla. Pour chocolate mixture into pastry shell. Chill. Stir rum flavoring into remaining custard. Cool. Beat egg whites with cream of tartar; add remaining sugar. Fold egg whites into custard; spoon over chocolate mixture. Chill for 2 hours. Top with whipped cream. Yield: 6 servings.

Blintzes

Blintzes are similar in appearance to unleavened French crepes. They are filled either with cottage cheese, fruit, or meat mixtures. Blintzes are a staple of Jewish cookery. Cheese blintzes are still the most popular variety.

BASIC PREPARATION: Prepare simple batter of flour, water or milk, eggs, shortening, and salt. Pour enough blintze batter into a 5- or 6-inch greased skillet to make a thin pancake; cook until top is bubbly. Remove from pan to towel. Place measured amount of filling on one side of each blintze. Roll up like a jelly roll. Place seam side down in a greased skillet and fry until golden brown, turning once. Or, bake in a 425-degree oven until browned. Top with sour cream, applesauce, or jam.

BASIC BLINTZES

1/2 lb. dry cottage cheese
1 egg yolk
Sugar
1 c. flour
1/2 tsp. salt
2 eggs
1 1/2 c. milk
Butter

Combine cottage cheese, egg yolk and 1/3 cup sugar for filling. Mix flour, salt and 2 tablespoons sugar. Beat eggs well; add flour mixture alternately with milk. Beat until smooth. Butter 7-inch skillet; heat skillet. Pour just enough batter into skillet to cover bottom; tilt skillet to spread batter evenly. Cook until browned on both sides, turning once. Repeat until all batter is used. Place 1 tablespoon filling on each pancake; roll pancakes. Place in greased baking dish. Bake at 350 degrees for 15 minutes. Yield: 3 servings.

CINNAMON BLINTZES

9 eggs
2 c. flour
4 c. milk
Browned butter
Cinnamon sugar

Beat eggs well. Combine flour and milk; beat until smooth. Beat in eggs. Pour just enough batter into hot greased skillet to cover bottom of skillet. Tilt skillet to spread batter evenly and thinly. Brown cake on one side. Turn; brown other side. Repeat with remaining batter. Spread cakes with butter; sprinkle with cinnamon sugar. Roll cakes as for jelly roll; keep warm until ready to serve. Yield: 10 servings.

CHEESE-FILLED BLINTZES

1 c. flour
Pinch of salt
1 tsp. sugar
1/4 tsp. baking powder
4 eggs, separated
1 c. cream
Melted butter
Cheese Filling

Sift flour, salt, sugar and baking powder together. Combine beaten egg yolks and cream; beat in flour mixture. Fold in stiffly beaten egg whites and 1 teaspoon butter. Brush bottom of hot 7-inch frypan with butter. Pour in 2 tablespoons batter; tilt pan to spread batter evenly. Cook until edges are bubbly; turn. Cook for 2 minutes longer. Place on waxed paper. Repeat with remaining batter. Spread cakes with Cheese Filling; fold cakes over filling. Place in greased baking dish; pour any remaining Cheese Filling over cakes. Bake at 350 degrees until heated through. Serve warm; top with fresh berries, if desired.

Cheese Filling

1 tsp. butter
1/2 c. sugar
1 8-oz. package cream cheese
3 egg yolks
Pinch of salt
3 tbsp. sour cream

Cream butter and sugar; add remaining ingredients, mixing well.

COTTAGE CHEESE-FRUIT BLINTZES

3 eggs
1 c. creamed cottage cheese
2 tbsp. salad oil
1/4 c. sifted flour
1/4 tsp. salt
Butter
1/2 c. raspberry jam
Confectioners' sugar

Preheat griddle. Beat eggs; beat in cottage cheese and oil. Sift flour and salt together; add to cheese mixture. Beat only until blended. Grease griddle lightly with butter; drop batter from spoon onto griddle, making thin 4-inch cakes. Bake until lightly browned on both sides. Place 1 tablespoon jam in center of each cake; roll cakes around jam. Sprinkle with confectioners' sugar; serve immediately. Yield: 8 blintzes.

FLAMING BLINTZES

1/3 stick butter
1/2 c. flour
1 c. water
5 eggs
Salt to taste
1 lb. hoop cheese, grated
1 tbsp. sugar
2 tbsp. sour cream
1 can cherry pie filling
1 can crushed pineapple, drained
1/4 c. rum or kirsch

Melt butter. Sift flour into water; beat until smooth. Beat in 3 eggs, butter and salt. Pour just enough batter into hot, lightly greased skillet to cover bottom of skillet. Tilt skillet to spread batter evenly. Cook until underside of cake is browned and top is dry. Turn cake onto towel. Repeat with remaining batter. Combine cheese, remaining eggs, sugar and sour cream; spoon mixture into center of each cake. Fold in sides of cakes; roll cakes. Place in greased baking dish. Bake at 375 degrees for 1 hour, turning once. Combine cherry pie filling and pineapple in chafing dish; heat. Pour rum over cherry mixture; set aflame. Spoon over blintzes. Yield: 6 servings.

ISRAELI BLINTZES

1 1/2 c. creamed cottage cheese
1 1/2 tsp. salt
1 tbsp. sugar
3 eggs
1 c. flour
Shortening
Butter

Combine cottage cheese, 1/2 teaspoon salt and sugar; beat in 1 egg. Mix flour and remaining salt; beat in 1 cup cold water and remaining eggs. Batter should be smooth and thin. Brush hot skillet lightly with shortening; pour in just enough batter to cover bottom of skillet. Tilt skillet to spread batter evenly. Cook until underside is browned and top is dry. Turn cake onto towel. Repeat until all batter is used. Spoon cottage cheese filling onto browned side of each cake. Roll cakes as for jelly roll; place in baking pan. Dot heavily with butter. Bake at 400 degrees for 10 minutes. Dot with butter again; bake for 10 minutes longer. Serve hot; top with sour cream or cinnamon sugar. Yield: 6 servings.

RUSSIAN CHEESE BLINTZES

4 eggs, beaten
Small curd cottage cheese
Sour cream
1 c. flour
1 tbsp. sugar
1/2 tsp. salt
Strawberries

Mix eggs, 1 cup cottage cheese and 1 cup sour cream. Add flour, sugar and salt; stir until thick. Fry in 5-inch pancakes on griddle. Place 1 heaping teaspoon cottage cheese in center of each pancake. Roll up; top with sour cream and strawberries. Yield: 12 servings.

Blueberry

Blueberries are a staple of New England cookery. Modern homemakers appreciate their fine flavor and nutritional values. Blueberries supply Vitamins A and C yet are low in calories. (1/2 cup of blueberries = 42 calories)

AVAILABILITY: Fresh blueberries are available only from June to August but canned and frozen blueberries are available year-round.

BUYING: In buying fresh blueberries, look for firmly packed pint baskets full of plump, clean, and dry berries. A stained container is a sign that the fruit inside has been crushed.

STORING: Fresh unwashed blueberries can

be stored in the refrigerator for 10-12 days. If you plan to store them for such a length of time keep them in a colander to ensure free air circulation around the berries. If kept at room temperature, blueberries last only 2-3 days. *Do not wash blueberries until they are ready for use*—wet berries spoil quickly. *To freeze,* wash in ice water, drain, and place in freezer container with or without sugar syrup or dry sugar, allow 1/2-inch head space for expansion. They may be frozen for 6-8 months.

SERVING: Add to cakes, pancakes, sweet breads, or use in pies, tarts, or muffins. They are also delicious served as a dessert or breakfast fruit.

BLUEBERRY CONGEALED SALAD

1 6-oz. package black cherry gelatin
1 can blueberry pie filling
1 sm. can crushed pineapple
1/2 c. chopped nuts
1/2 pt. sour cream
2 3-oz. packages cream cheese, softened
1/2 c. sugar
1/2 tsp. vanilla

Dissolve gelatin in 1 1/2 cups boiling water; add 1 1/2 cups cold water. Chill until thickened. Fold in pie filling, pineapple and nuts. Pour into mold; chill until set. Unmold on serving platter. Blend sour cream, cream cheese, sugar and vanilla together; pour over salad.

BLUEBERRY SALAD WITH TOPPING

1 pkg. black raspberry gelatin
1/2 pkg. lemon gelatin
1 can blueberry pie filling
Grated rind of 1 lemon
2 tsp. lemon juice
4 tbsp. sugar
1/2 pt. sour cream
2 tsp. grated lemon rind
Dash of lemon flavoring

Mix 1 1/2 cups hot water and gelatins; stir until dissolved. Cool until syrupy; add pie filling, grated rind, lemon juice and half the sugar. Pour into large mold; chill until set. Combine remaining ingredients; mix well. Serve topping over salad. Yield: 6-8 servings.

BLUEBERRY WHIPPED CREAM SALAD

2 pkg. raspberry gelatin
1 No. 2 can blueberries
1 No. 2 can crushed pineapple
1 c. chopped pecans
1 c. whipped cream

Dissolve gelatin in 2 cups boiling water. Drain blueberries and pineapple, reserving juices. Add enough water to reserved juices to equal 2 cups liquid; add to gelatin mixture. Reserve 1 cup gelatin mixture; chill until partially set. Fold blueberries, pineapple and pecans into remaining gelatin mixture. Pour into mold. Chill until firm. Add reserved gelatin mixture to whipped cream; beat well. Spread over congealed blueberry mixture. Chill until firm. Yield: 10-12 servings.

PATRIOTIC SALAD

2 3-oz. packages raspberry gelatin
1 tsp. raspberry flavoring
1 env. unflavored gelatin
1 c. half and half
1 c. sugar
1 tsp. vanilla
1 8-oz. package cream cheese
1/2 c. chopped walnuts
1 16-oz. can blueberries
1/4 tsp. blueberry flavoring

Dissolve 1 package raspberry gelatin in 2 cups boiling water; stir in raspberry flavoring. Pour into 9 x 13-inch baking pan. Chill until firm. Soften unflavored gelatin in 1/2 cup cold water. Heat half and half with sugar; add unflavored gelatin, stirring to dissolve. Stir in vanilla; blend in cream cheese. Add walnuts. Cool to room temperature; pour over raspberry layer. Chill until firm. Dissolve remaining raspberry gelatin in 1 cup boiling water; stir in blueberries with juice and blueberry flavoring. Cool to room temperature. Pour over cream cheese layer. Chill until firm. Cut into squares to serve. Yield: 18 servings.

BLUEBERRY CAKE

1/2 c. butter or shortening
Sugar
2 eggs
2 1/2 c. flour
2 tsp. baking powder
Salt to taste
1/4 tsp. nutmeg
2/3 c. milk
1 1/2 c. blueberries

Cream butter, 1 1/2 cups sugar and eggs until fluffy. Sift flour, baking powder, salt and nutmeg together; add to creamed mixture alternately with milk. Fold in blueberries; spoon batter into 9 x 9 x 2-inch cake pan. Sprinkle with sugar. Bake in 400-degree oven for about 35 minutes until cake tests done.

BLUEBERRY CRUMB CAKE

2 c. sifted flour
1 1/2 c. sugar
2/3 c. butter
2 tsp. baking powder
1 tsp. salt
2 eggs, separated
1 c. milk
1 c. drained blueberries

Sift flour and sugar together into large mixer bowl; cut in butter until of small pea consistency. Reserve 3/4 cup flour mixture for topping. Add baking powder, salt, egg yolks and milk to remaining mixture in bowl; beat with electric mixer at low speed for 3 minutes. Beat egg whites until stiff but not dry; fold gently but thoroughly into batter. Spread in greased and lightly-floured 12 x 8 x 2-inch pan. Arrange blueberries over batter; sprinkle with reserved flour mixture. Bake in 350-degree oven for 40 to 50 minutes. Serve warm; top with whipped cream. Yield: 12 servings.

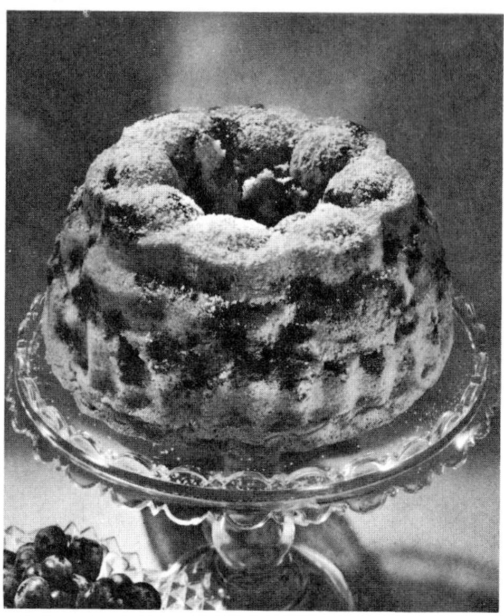

Blueberry-Maple Syrup Cake . . . Blueberries and maple syrup in an elegant molded cake.

BLUEBERRY-MAPLE SYRUP CAKE

1/3 c. butter
1/2 c. sugar
3 eggs
3/4 c. maple syrup
2 1/4 c. all-purpose flour
3 tsp. baking powder
1/2 c. milk
2 c. fresh or frozen blueberries
Confectioners' sugar

Preheat oven to 350 degrees. Cream butter and sugar until light and fluffy. Beat in eggs, one at a time, beating well after each addition. Stir in maple syrup. Sift flour and baking powder together. Beat in dry ingredients and milk alternately, beginning and ending with dry ingredients. Fold in blueberries. Pour batter into greased and floured 1 1/2 quart mold. Bake for 45 to 50 minutes or until top is richly browned. Unmold; cool on rack. Dust top with confectioners' sugar.

BLUEBERRY CUPCAKES

1/2 c. butter
1/2 c. sugar
3 eggs
2 c. flour
2 tsp. baking powder
1/2 tsp. salt
1 c. milk
3/4 c. fresh blueberries
Powdered sugar

Cream butter and sugar until fluffy; beat in eggs. Sift flour, baking powder and salt together. Beat flour mixture into creamed mixture alternately with milk. Fold in blueberries by hand. Spoon batter into greased muffin tins. Bake at 400 degrees for 20 minutes. Dust cakes with powdered sugar. Yield: 18 cakes.

BLUEBERRY-MARSHMALLOW DESSERT

2 c. graham cracker crumbs
1/3 c. melted butter
1 tbsp. sugar
1 pt. whipping cream
1 pkg. miniature marshmallows
1 1-lb. 5-oz. can blueberry pie filling

Mix cracker crumbs, butter and sugar; press 2/3 of the crumb mixture into bottom of 9 x 13-inch pan. Bake for 10 minutes in 350-degree oven. Whip cream; stir in marshmallows. Pour half the marshmallow mixture into crumb crust; spread pie filling over marshmallow mixture. Spread remaining marshmallow mixture over filling; sprinkle with remaining cracker crumbs. Refrigerate overnight. Serve with whipped cream, if desired. Yield: 18 servings.

BLUEBERRY PUDDING

11 graham crackers
1 c. sugar
1/4 c. melted butter
2 eggs
1 8-oz. package cream cheese
1/2 tsp. vanilla
1 can blueberry pie mix

Crush crackers; blend in 1/2 cup sugar and butter. Pat into greased 9 x 9-inch pan. Beat eggs; add cream cheese, beating until smooth. Add remaining sugar and vanilla; pour over crumb crust. Bake in 375-degree oven for 15 minutes. Cool. Pour blueberry pie mix over cream cheese mixture; refrigerate overnight. Serve with whipped cream, if desired. Yield: 6-8 servings.

PEACH AND BLUEBERRY CREAM PARFAITS

1/2 c. sugar
3 tbsp. cornstarch
1/4 tsp. salt
2 c. milk
2 eggs, slightly beaten
1 tsp. vanilla
1 c. sweetened, sliced fresh peaches
1 c. fresh blueberries

Mix sugar, cornstarch and salt in saucepan; stir in milk. Cook over low heat, stirring constantly, until thickened. Blend small amount of hot mixture into eggs; return to cooked mixture. Cook for 2 minutes longer over low heat, stirring constantly. Cool; blend in vanilla. Chill. Alternate layers of chilled cream pudding, peaches and blueberries in tall tumblers or parfait glasses. Repeat layers to fill glasses. Top with spoonful of pudding and 1 peach slice. Serve cold. Yield: 6 servings.

NEW ENGLAND-STYLE BLUEBERRIES

1 c. sugar
2 tsp. cinnamon
1 qt. blueberries
12 slices white bread
4 tbsp. butter

Combine sugar and cinnamon; stir in blueberries. Add 2 tablespoons water. Bring to a boil in saucepan; set aside. Remove crusts from bread; spread with butter. Cut bread into strips; line loaf pan with strips. Alternate layers of blueberry mixture and bread strips, ending with bread strips on top. Chill overnight; garnish with whipped cream. Yield: 6-8 servings.

BLUEBERRY BUCKLE

1/2 c. shortening
1 c. sugar
1 egg, beaten
2 1/2 c. flour
1/2 tsp. salt
2 1/2 tsp. baking powder
1/2 c. milk
1 c. drained blueberries
1/2 tsp. cinnamon
1/2 c. margarine

Cream shortening in bowl; add 1/2 cup sugar and egg. Mix well. Sift 2 cups flour with salt and baking powder; add to creamed mixture alternately with milk. Turn into greased 9-inch layer cake pan. Sprinkle blueberries over batter. Combine remaining sugar, remaining flour and cinnamon in small bowl; cut in margarine with pastry blender or 2 knives until crumbly. Sprinkle over blueberries. Bake in 350-degree oven for 40 to 45 minutes or until coffee cake tests done. Yield: 8 servings.

Peach and Blueberry Cream Parfaits . . . This dessert blends tart blueberries with sweet peaches.

BLUEBERRY COBBLER

Fresh blueberries
1 3/4 c. sugar
3 tbsp. butter
1 tsp. baking powder
1/4 tsp. salt
1/2 c. milk
1 c. sifted flour
1 tbsp. cornstarch

Cover bottom of 8-inch square pan with blueberries. Mix 3/4 cup sugar, butter, baking powder, salt, milk and flour together until crumbly; pour over blueberries. Mix remaining sugar and cornstarch; sprinkle over flour mixture. Pour 2/3 cup boiling water over top. Bake at 375 degrees for 45 minutes. Yield: 9 servings.

BLUEBERRY DREAM DESSERT

2 c. oats
Flour
1 c. (packed) brown sugar
3/4 c. butter, melted
2 c. blueberries
1/2 c. sugar
2 tbsp. lemon juice
1/8 tsp. salt

Mix oats, 1 cup flour and brown sugar. Stir in butter. Line 8-inch square pan with oat mixture, reserving 1/2 cup for topping. Blend 1 tablespoon flour and 3/4 cup water until smooth. Combine flour mixture, blueberries, sugar, lemon juice and salt in saucepan. Simmer for about 5 minutes. Remove from heat; pour into crust. Sprinkle with remaining crumb mixture. Bake in 350-degree oven for 45 minutes. Serve topped with whipped cream. Yield: 6-8 servings.

BLUEBERRY DUMPLINGS

2 1/2 c. fresh blueberries
Sugar
Salt
1 tbsp. lemon juice
1 c. all-purpose flour
2 tsp. baking powder
1 tbsp. butter
1/2 c. milk

Combine blueberries, 1/3 cup sugar, dash of salt and 1 cup water in saucepan; bring to boiling point. Reduce heat; cover and simmer for 5 minutes. Stir in lemon juice. Sift flour, baking powder, 1/4 teaspoon salt and 2 tablespoons sugar together; cut in butter until of coarse meal consistency. Add milk, all at once; stir only until flour mixture is dampened. Drop from tablespoon into simmering blueberry mixture. Cover tightly; cook over low heat for 10 minutes. Serve with cream. Yield: 6 servings.

BLUEBERRY PUDDING

1 pt. blueberries
3 c. sugar
2/3 c. shortening
2 eggs
1 tsp. vanilla
1 c. milk
2 c. flour
4 tsp. baking powder
1 tsp. salt

Combine blueberries, 2 cups sugar and 1/4 cup water in 5-quart saucepan. Combine shortening, remaining sugar, eggs and vanilla; beat well. Add milk, beating thoroughly. Sift flour, baking powder and salt. Add flour mixture to shortening mixture; beat well. Spread over blueberries in saucepan; cook over low heat for 2 hours. Serve hot with vanilla ice cream, if desired. Yield: 12 servings.

BLUEBERRY-BANANA PIE

2 baked 9-in. pie shells
2 bananas, sliced
3/4 c. sugar
1 8-oz. package cream cheese
1 env. dessert topping mix
1 can blueberry pie filling

Line pie shells with bananas. Cream sugar and cream cheese until fluffy. Prepare dessert topping mix according to package directions; add to cream cheese mixture, mixing well. Spread over bananas; spread pie filling on top. Refrigerate until firm. Yield: 12 servings.

BLUEBERRY-CREAM CHEESE TARTS

1 8-oz. package cream cheese
2 tbsp. milk
1 c. sugar
1 tsp. vanilla
1/2 tsp. almond extract
1/2 c. heavy cream, whipped
12 baked 2 1/2-in. tart shells
2 c. blueberries

Blend cream cheese and milk until soft; beat in sugar gradually. Add vanilla and almond extract; fold in whipped cream. Spoon filling into tart shells; top with blueberries. Refrigerate until ready to serve. May be garnished with additional whipped cream, if desired.

BLUEBERRY-PEACH PIE SUPREME

1 pt. blueberries
4 med. peaches, sliced
2 1/2 tbsp. tapioca
1 c. sugar
1/2 tsp. almond extract
Cinnamon to taste
1 c. flour
1/2 tsp. salt
1/2 tsp. baking powder
1/3 c. shortening

Combine fruits in bowl. Mix tapioca and sugar together; add to fruit. Add almond extract and cinnamon. Stir, mixing well. Let stand for 15 minutes. Mix flour, salt and baking powder together. Blend 2 tablespoons flour mixture with 2 tablespoons water; stir to paste consistency. Work shortening into remaining flour mixture; add paste, mixing thoroughly. Reserve 1-inch ball of dough. Roll remaining dough as for pie crust; line 9-inch pie plate with pastry. Pour fruit mixture into pie crust. Roll reserved dough into 6-inch circle. Cut into 6 pie-shaped wedges; arrange over fruit mixture. Sprinkle additional sugar and cinnamon over crust wedges. Bake in 425-degree oven for 15 minutes. Reduce oven temperature to 375 degrees; bake for about 20 minutes longer. Yield: 12 servings.

BLUEBERRY PIE DELUXE

4 c. fresh blueberries
1 c. sugar
3 tbsp. cornstarch
Juice of 1/2 lemon
1 c. heavy sweetened cream, whipped
1 baked 9-in. pie shell

Boil 1 cup blueberries with 1 cup water and sugar; strain, reserving liquid. Add cornstarch to reserved liquid; boil in saucepan, stirring, until thickened. Place remaining blueberries in large bowl; add lemon juice. Pour boiling mixture over blueberries; cool. Place whipped cream in pie shell; spoon in blueberry mixture. Chill for several hours. Yield: 8 servings.

BLUEBERRY-SOUR CREAM PIE

2 c. sour cream
1 c. sugar
1/4 c. sifted flour
1/2 tsp. salt
3/4 tsp. almond extract
2 eggs
1 unbaked 9-in. graham cracker pie shell
2 c. blackberry pie filling
1/2 c. whipping cream

Combine sour cream, sugar, flour, salt, almond extract and eggs; beat well. Pour filling into pie shell. Bake at 375 degrees for 30 minutes. Spread pie filling over sour cream layer; chill. Whip cream; spread over pie. Serve chilled. Yield: 6 servings.

Bombe

A sophisticated French dessert that combines different flavors of ice cream, sherbet, or ices in a frozen mold.

BASIC PREPARATION: Chill mold. With back of spoon line side 1 inch thick with ice cream, sherbet, or ice. Pack center with filling and cover with ice cream, sherbet, or ice. Adjust lid and freeze mold 3 hours in freezer or in ice and salt mixture (4 parts ice, 1 part salt). To remove bombe, wrap mold in hot cloth a few seconds, unseal lid, and invert mold onto chilled platter. Serve topped with whipped cream or accompany with dessert sauce.

BANANA BOMBE

3 c. whipping cream
3 bananas, sliced
1 tsp. vanilla
1/4 c. sugar
1 qt. chocolate ice cream

Whip cream until stiff; fold in bananas, vanilla and sugar. Soften ice cream enough to press against side of mold, covering mold completely. Fill mold with whipped cream mixture. Freeze until firm. Yield: 6-8 servings.

BOULE DE NEIGE

3/4 c. diced mixed candied fruits
1/4 c. white raisins
1/4 c. kirsch
1 qt. vanilla ice cream
Sweetened whipped cream

Soak candied fruits and raisins in kirsch for 1 hour, stirring frequently. Add ice cream; mix well. Pack into bombe mold; freeze until solid. Unmold onto chilled dish. Place whipped cream in pastry tube with fluted nozzle; make small rosettes over frozen mixture, completely covering ice cream. Garnish with holly or fresh flowers.

ELEGANT BOMBE

1 qt. chocolate ice cream
2 c. sugar
2/3 c. water
1/4 tsp. cream of tartar
8 egg yolks
2 c. whipping cream, whipped
Kahlua to taste

Line bombe mold with ice cream; freeze. Combine sugar, water and cream of tartar in saucepan. Bring to a boil; cook rapidly to 232 degrees on candy thermometer or until syrup spins a thread. Beat egg yolks until thick and pale; continue beating, adding syrup gradually. Cook over hot water, stirring constantly, until thick and smooth. Chill. Add whipped cream; flavor with Kahlua. Pour into mold; freeze. Yield: 6-8 servings.

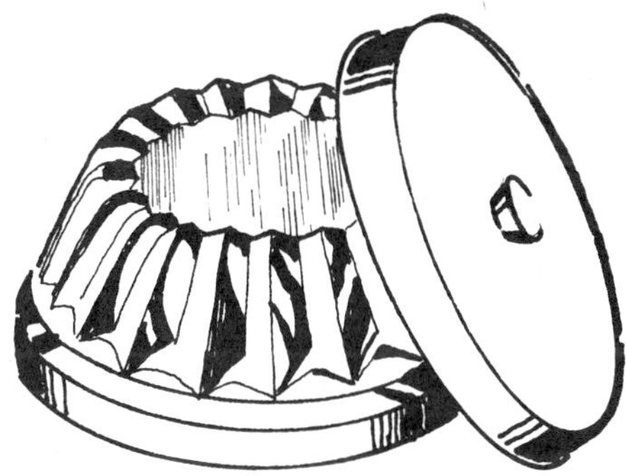

BOMBE MOLD

OUTSTANDING BOMBE

2 c. milk
1 1/4 c. sugar
5 egg yolks, beaten
1/2 tsp. vanilla
1/4 tsp. lemon juice
1/4 tsp. rum flavoring
2 c. heavy cream, whipped
1/2 c. chopped maraschino cherries
1/2 c. chopped green cherries
1/4 c. diced canned pineapple
1/4 c. grated orange peel
1 tbsp. grated lemon peel
1/2 c. chopped walnuts or pecans

Combine milk, 3/4 cup sugar, egg yolks, vanilla, lemon juice and rum flavoring in double boiler. Cook, stirring occasionally, until slightly thickened. Pour into refrigerator tray and freeze until almost firm. Combine whipped cream, remaining sugar, cherries, pineapple, orange peel, lemon peel and walnuts; mix well. Coat deep 2 1/2-quart mold with custard mixture. Spoon fruit mixture into mold. Freeze until firm. Yield: 6-8 servings.

Strawberry Cream Bombe . . . A delicious dessert certain to turn every meal into a special occasion.

STRAWBERRY CREAM BOMBE

2 pt. strawberry ice cream
2 egg yolks
Sugar
1 tbsp. lemon rind
2 tbsp. lemon juice
1 egg white
1 c. whipping cream, whipped

Chill 7-cup mold in freezer. Soften ice cream. Spread ice cream quickly as evenly as possible with back of spoon on inside of mold to make 1/2-inch thick shell lining. Return to freezer to harden. Beat egg yolks well in top of double boiler. Beat in 1/3 cup sugar, lemon rind, juice and 1 tablespoon cold water. Cook for about 10 minutes, stirring constantly, over rapidly boiling water until thickened. Cool thoroughly. Beat egg white until frothy in small mixing bowl. Beat in 2 tablespoons sugar gradually. Beat until stiff peaks form. Fold in lemon mixture and whipped cream. Pour into ice cream-lined mold. Freeze. Dip into warm water; turn out onto chilled plate. Garnish with fresh strawberry halves if desired.

RASPBERRY BOMBE

3 pt. red raspberry sherbet
2 pt. pink peppermint ice cream
1 c. whipping cream
3 tbsp. confectioners' sugar
Dash of salt
1/4 c. minced mixed candied fruits
1/4 c. chopped toasted almonds
1/2 tsp. rum flavoring

Chill 2 1/2-quart metal bombe mold or bowl in freezer. Stir sherbet just to soften; spread with chilled spoon in layer over bottom and side of mold. Freeze until firm. Stir ice cream until soft. Spread quickly over sherbet layer; freeze. Whip cream with sugar and salt; fold in fruits and almonds. Add flavoring; pile into center of mold. Smooth top; cover with foil. Freeze overnight. Rub mold with hot towel to loosen; peel off foil. Invert onto chilled plate. Yield: 8-12 servings.

SWEET CHERRY BOMBE

2 c. fresh dark sweet cherries
1/3 c. melted butter
1 1/2 c. graham cracker crumbs
1 tbsp. unflavored gelatin
1/4 c. cold water
2 c. scalded milk, cooled
1/2 c. sugar
1/8 tsp. salt
3 eggs, separated
1 tsp. vanilla
Whipped cream

Pit and halve 1 1/2 cups cherries; reserve remaining cherries for garnish. Mix butter and cracker crumbs; press around side and bottom of 1 1/2-quart bowl. Chill until firm. Soften gelatin in cold water. Combine gelatin and milk in top of double boiler; add sugar and salt. Cook, stirring, until gelatin and sugar are dissolved. Beat egg yolks lightly; stir in small amount of hot milk mixture. Return to boiler; cook, stirring, for 10 minutes or until slightly thickened. Chill until thickened. Fold in stiffly beaten egg whites, vanilla and cherries. Pour into prepared bowl; chill for 2 to 3 hours. Unmold; garnish with whipped cream and reserved cherries. Yield: 8 servings.

Bonbon

This bundle of sweetness is a type of candy. It is a small chocolate-cooked or fondant-covered candy with a soft center. The center varies.

PREPARATION: Bonbons are prepared in one of three ways. (1) The fondant, often containing fruit and nuts as well as flavoring and coloring, is shaped or cut into balls, cubes, patties, strips, or diamonds and allowed to dry. (2) Candies formed as described above are dipped in melted chocolate coating. (3) The fondant is melted and used to coat a filling of nuts or fruits.
(See CANDY.)

BILLIONAIRE BONBONS

1/2 lb. graham crackers
1 c. butter or margarine
1/2 c. peanut butter
1 lb. confectioners' sugar
1 c. chopped nuts
1 sm. can flaked coconut
1 tsp. vanilla
1 sm. bar paraffin
1 1/2 c. chocolate chips

Crush crackers to fine crumbs. Soften butter; cream butter and peanut butter. Blend in confectioners' sugar and cracker crumbs; add nuts, coconut and vanilla. Shape coconut mixture into small balls; chill well. Shave paraffin into top of double boiler; add chocolate chips. Stir over hot water until melted and smooth. Dip coconut balls into chocolate mixture; place on waxed paper-lined tray to dry.

BAKED BONBONS

1 lb. pitted dates
1/2 lb. walnuts
3 egg whites
3/4 c. sugar
1 tsp. vanilla
Food coloring

Grind dates and walnuts through food chopper twice. Shape into 72 balls. Beat egg whites until stiff. Add sugar gradually, beating until meringue stands in stiff peaks. Add vanilla and several drops of food coloring. Roll balls in meringue; place on greased cookie sheet, swirling top of each bonbon. Bake in 250-degree oven for 30 minutes. Store in airtight container.

BUTTERCREAM EGGS

Butter
1 8-oz. package cream cheese
3 boxes confectioners' sugar
1/2 lb. semisweet chocolate
1 2-in. square paraffin
1/4 tsp. vanilla

Cream 1 cup butter and cream cheese until light and fluffy; blend in confectioners' sugar, a small amount at a time. Shape mixture into small eggs; chill for at least 1 hour. Combine chocolate, paraffin, 1 tablespoon butter and vanilla in top of double boiler. Stir over hot water until melted and smooth. Dip eggs into chocolate mixture; arrange on waxed paper to harden. Yield: 90-100 eggs.

CANDY EGGS

1 fresh coconut, grated
1 egg
3 1/2 to 4 boxes powdered sugar
1 lb. unsweetened chocolate
2 oz. paraffin

Combine coconut and egg; knead in enough sugar to make stiff fondant. Shape fondant into eggs; place on baking sheet. Refrigerate overnight. Melt chocolate and paraffin together; dip eggs into chocolate mixture. Arrange eggs on greased baking sheet to dry.

CHEWY DIPS

2/3 c. peanut butter
1/4 c. margarine
2 c. powdered sugar
1/2 tsp. salt
1 c. chopped nuts
1 c. flaked coconut
12 maraschino cherries, chopped
3 1/2 tbsp. shaved paraffin
1 pkg. chocolate chips

Combine peanut butter, margarine, powdered sugar, salt, nuts, coconut and cherries; shape mixture into 1-inch balls. Combine paraffin and chocolate chips in double boiler; stir over hot water until melted. Dip balls in chocolate mixture; place on waxed paper to cool.

CREAMY BUTTER BALLS

3/4 c. margarine
3/4 c. peanut butter
1 1/2 lb. powdered sugar

2 c. rolled oats
2 tsp. vanilla
1 1/2 c. raisins
1 1/2 c. flaked coconut
1 c. chopped nuts
2 pkg. chocolate bits
1 bar paraffin

Soften margarine. Cream margarine and peanut butter together; blend in powdered sugar. Add oats, vanilla, raisins, coconut and nuts; knead with hands to mix. Shape mixture into 1-inch balls; chill for at least 1 hour. Combine chocolate bits and paraffin in top of double boiler; stir over hot water until melted. Dip candy balls into chocolate mixture; place on waxed paper to harden.

DELIGHTFULLY DIFFERENT BONBONS

1 1-lb. box confectioners' sugar
1 c. butter
1 c. crunchy peanut butter
2 pkg. butterscotch bits
2 tbsp. shaved paraffin

Sift confectioners' sugar. Soften butter. Combine butter and peanut butter; blend in sugar, a small amount at a time. Shape mixture into small balls; chill for several hours. Melt butterscotch bits and paraffin together in top of double boiler. Dip balls into butterscotch mixture; arrange on greased pan. Chill until coating is dry.

DOUBLE-NUT BALLS

2 tbsp. soft butter
1 c. peanut butter
1 c. powdered sugar
1 c. ground dates
1 c. ground nuts
1 1/2 c. semisweet chocolate bits
2 tbsp. shaved paraffin

Mix butter and peanut butter; blend in powdered sugar. Add dates and nuts; mix well. Shape mixture into 24 balls; chill for at least 1 hour. Melt chocolate bits and paraffin together in top of double boiler. Dip balls into chocolate mixture; arrange on waxed paper to dry.

KENTUCKY COLONELS

1/2 c. butter
2 lb. confectioners' sugar
3/4 c. bourbon whiskey
1 c. finely chopped pecans
6 oz. bitter chocolate
1/2 sq. paraffin

Cream butter and sugar together, adding whiskey gradually. Mix in pecans. Shape pecan mixture into 72 balls; chill until firm. Melt chocolate and paraffin together in top of double boiler. Dip pecan balls into chocolate mixture; place on waxed paper to cool. Store in refrigerator.

MARTHA WASHINGTON CANDY

1/2 c. butter
2 boxes confectioners' sugar
1 can sweetened condensed milk
4 tsp. bourbon
4 c. chopped pecans
1/2 lb. semisweet chocolate
1 box paraffin

Soften butter. Combine butter, sugar, condensed milk and bourbon; mix until smooth. Work pecans into sugar mixture; shape into 1-inch balls. Place candy balls on waxed paper-lined tray; chill until firm. Melt chocolate and paraffin together in double boiler. Dip candy balls into warm chocolate mixture; replace on tray to harden.

SKINNY DIPS

1/2 c. butter or margarine
2 lb. powdered sugar
1 15-oz. can sweetened condensed milk
4 c. finely chopped pecans
1 1/2 tsp. vanilla
1 12-oz. package semisweet chocolate
1/4 lb. paraffin

Cream butter, powdered sugar and condensed milk together. Add pecans and vanilla; mix well. Form into 1/2-inch balls; place on cookie sheets. Refrigerate overnight. Melt chocolate and paraffin together in double boiler. Dip balls into chocolate quickly to coat. Allow to dry.

CLASSIC BONBONS

2 c. finely chopped nuts
2 lb. confectioners' sugar
1 14-oz. package flaked coconut
1/4 lb. butter, melted
1 can sweetened condensed milk
1/4 lb. paraffin
1 12-oz. package chocolate chips

Combine nuts, sugar and coconut; add butter and milk. Mix well; chill. Form into balls; chill balls until firm. Melt paraffin and chocolate chips together in double boiler. Insert wooden picks into candy balls; dip into chocolate mixture. Place on waxed paper to harden.

TAFFY EGGS

2 c. sugar
1 c. brown sugar
1/2 c. water
1 c. evaporated milk
3 tbsp. dark corn syrup
1/8 tsp. salt
1/2 c. butter
2 c. finely chopped nuts
2 pkg. butterscotch bits
1 bar paraffin

Combine sugar, brown sugar, water, milk, corn syrup and salt in large saucepan. Cook over low heat, stirring, until sugar is dissolved. Increase heat to medium; cook to 240 degrees on candy thermometer or to soft-ball stage. Shave butter into electric mixer bowl; add nuts. Pour in hot candy mixture; beat at medium speed of mixer until fondant becomes too stiff for mixer. Turn onto greased surface; cool enough to handle. Knead fondant until smooth and creamy. Shape into 4 eggs; place on cake rack. Refrigerate for 24 hours. Melt butterscotch bits and paraffin together in top of double boiler. Dip fondant eggs into warm butterscotch mixture; replace on cake rack to drip. Refrigerate for at least 1 week to ripen. Coated eggs may be decorated with cake icing, if desired.

SURPRISE EASTER EGGS

Butter or margarine
1 lb. confectioners' sugar
1/3 c. mashed potato
1 tsp. vanilla
1 c. flaked coconut
8 oz. semisweet chocolate
1/3 bar paraffin

Combine 1/2 cup butter, confectioners' sugar, potato and vanilla. Add coconut; refrigerate for 3 hours. Shape into eggs; refrigerate eggs overnight. Combine chocolate, paraffin and 1 tablespoon butter in top of double boiler. Place over hot water, stirring, until melted and smooth; keep chocolate mixture warm. Dip eggs into chocolate mixture; arrange eggs on waxed paper to dry.

Borscht

BORSCHT

1 1-lb. soupbone with meat
1 onion, chopped
2 med. beets, coarsely grated
3 c. shredded cabbage
1 c. tomato juice
Salt and pepper to taste
1/2 c. sour cream
1 tbsp. dill

Cover soupbone with 10 cups water in kettle; simmer for at least 1 hour. Add onion and beets; simmer for 15 to 20 minutes longer or until beets are partially cooked. Add cabbage; cook until vegetables are tender. Stir in remaining ingredients. Let stand for several hours before serving. May be frozen.

SUMMERTIME BORSCHT

1 c. minced cooked beets
1 1/2 c. beet stock
3 cans consomme
1/4 c. lemon juice
Sour cream
Chopped chives

Combine beets, beet stock and consomme in saucepan; heat until blended, stirring constantly. Remove from heat; add lemon juice. Chill thoroughly. Stir well; serve in chilled bowls. Top with spoonfuls of sour cream; sprinkle with chives. Yield: 8 servings.

Boston Brown Bread

PILGRIM BREAD

1 c. sifted all-purpose flour
2 c. graham flour
1 tsp. salt
1/2 c. maple sugar
1 1/2 tsp. soda
2 c. buttermilk

Combine flour, graham flour, salt and sugar in mixing bowl. Stir soda into buttermilk; add to dry ingredients, mixing well. Pour into greased 9 x 5 x 3-inch pan. Bake at 350 degrees for 1 hour.

BOSTON BROWN BREAD

1 c. raisins
2 c. water
2 tsp. soda
1 tbsp. butter
1 tsp. salt
2 3/4 c. flour
1 tsp. baking powder
1 c. sugar
1/4 c. molasses
1 egg, beaten
1/2 c. chopped nuts

Combine raisins, water, soda, butter and salt in saucepan; bring to a boil. Cool. Sift flour, baking powder and sugar together; stir in raisin mixture. Add molasses, egg and nuts; mix well. Spoon batter into 4 greased number 2 cans. Bake at 325 degrees for 40 minutes or until bread tests done.

EASY BROWN BREAD

1 c. sifted flour
1/2 c. sugar
2 tsp. soda
1/2 tsp. salt
1 1/2 c. graham flour
3/4 c. evaporated milk
1/2 c. water
1 tbsp. vinegar
1 egg, beaten
1 c. dark molasses

Sift flour, sugar, soda and salt together into bowl; add graham flour. Mix milk and water; stir in vinegar. Add egg and molasses. Stir into dry ingredients; mix well. Pour batter into greased loaf pan. Bake at 325 degrees for 1 hour and 15 minutes or until bread tests done.

LOW-CALORIE BROWN BREAD

3 c. sour milk
1 tbsp. soda
1 egg
1/2 c. molasses
1 tsp. salt
3 c. graham flour
2 c. white flour

Mix all ingredients; place in loaf pan. Bake at 350 degrees for 30 minutes or until done. Yield: 1 loaf.

ROYAL HIBERNIAN BROWN BREAD

5 c. whole wheat flour
2 1/2 c. all-purpose flour
1/3 c. sugar
2 tsp. soda
1 tsp. salt
1 c. butter
2 eggs
2 1/4 c. sour milk or buttermilk

Combine flours, sugar, soda and salt in large bowl. Add butter; work by hand until mixture resembles fine bread crumbs. Beat eggs lightly; stir in milk. Make well in center of flour mixture; add egg mixture. Mix by hand to form stiff dough. Turn dough onto floured board; knead. Divide dough in half. Shape into 2 round loaves; place on greased baking sheet. Flatten tops of loaves; cut 1/2-inch deep cross in tops of loaves. Bake at 400 degrees for 45 minutes or until browned. Cool slightly; slice and serve. Yield: 16-20 servings.

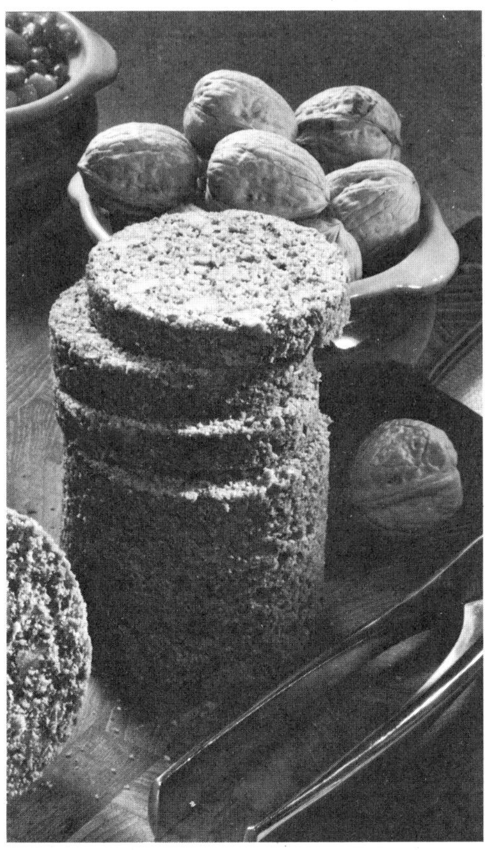

Boston Brown Bread . . . Make this easy recipe, and serve your family homemade bread.

BOSTON BROWN BREAD

1 1/4 c. sifted all-purpose flour
2 tsp. baking powder
3/4 tsp. soda
1 1/4 tsp. salt
1 1/4 c. graham flour
1 c. chopped California walnuts
1 egg
1/3 c. (packed) brown sugar
1/2 c. light molasses
3/4 c. buttermilk
3 tbsp. melted shortening

Sift all-purpose flour with baking powder, soda and salt. Stir in graham flour and walnuts. Beat egg lightly; beat in brown sugar, molasses, buttermilk and shortening. Stir into dry mixture just until all of the flour is moistened. Spoon into 3 greased 1-pound size cans. Bake at 350 degrees for 45 minutes or until bread tests done. Let stand for 10 minutes; turn out onto wire rack. Serve warm or cold. Yield: 3 small loaves.

QUICK BROWN BREAD

2 c. graham flour
1/2 c. flour
1 tsp. baking powder
1 tsp. soda
1 tsp. salt
1/4 c. melted shortening
1 1/2 c. sour milk
1/2 c. molasses

Sift flours, baking powder, soda and salt together. Add shortening, milk and molasses; mix well. Turn batter into greased loaf pan. Bake at 375 degrees for 50 minutes to 1 hour.

Boston Cream Pie

BOSTON CREAM PIE

1 1/4 c. sifted flour
1 tsp. baking powder
1/4 tsp. salt
3 eggs
1 2/3 c. sugar
2 1/2 c. milk
1 tbsp. butter
2 tbsp. cornstarch
1 tsp. vanilla
Confectioners' sugar

Sift 1 cup flour, baking powder and half the salt together. Separate 2 eggs; beat egg whites until stiff. Beat egg yolks until thick and lemon colored, beating in 1 cup sugar. Fold in flour mixture and egg whites. Heat 1/2 cup milk; melt butter in milk. Cool slightly; beat into batter. Turn batter into greased and floured 8-inch layer pan. Bake at 350 degrees for 25 to 30 minutes. Cool cake; split in half, making 2 layers. Mix cornstarch and remaining flour, sugar and salt in top of double boiler. Scald remaining milk; stir into cornstarch mixture. Cook, stirring frequently, for 10 minutes or until thick and smooth. Beat remaining egg lightly; beat in small amount of hot custard. Return to pan; cook, stirring, for 2 minutes longer. Add vanilla; cool. Spread custard between cake layers; sift confectioners' sugar over top of cake. Yield: 6 servings.

BOSTON CREAM PIE DELUXE

1 pkg. yellow cake mix
1 3/4 c. sugar
Salt
5 tbsp. cornstarch
3 1/2 c. milk
3 eggs
1 1/4 tsp. vanilla
5 tbsp. butter
3 sq. bitter chocolate
1/2 c. light cream

Prepare cake mix according to package directions. Spread batter in 2 greased 15 x 11 x 1-inch pans. Bake at 350 degrees until cake tests done. Cool cake in pans for 10 minutes; place on rack to cool. Combine 1 cup sugar, 1/4 teaspoon salt and cornstarch in saucepan; stir in milk. Cook over low heat until thickened, stirring constantly. Beat eggs lightly; stir about 1/2 cup hot custard into eggs. Return to pan; cook for 5 minutes longer. Stir in 1/2 teaspoon vanilla and 2 tablespoons butter. Cool custard, stirring occasionally. Place 1 cake layer on tray; spread with custard. Top with remaining layer. Melt chocolate in top of double boiler; stir in cream. Add remaining sugar and butter and dash of salt; cook, stirring, until smooth and blended. Add remaining vanilla; cool. Pour chocolate sauce over cake. Yield: 12 servings.

Easy Boston Cream Pie . . . Thrill your family with this easy-to-prepare version of a classic.

EASY BOSTON CREAM PIE

1/2 c. rolled oats
1/3 c. butter, softened
1/2 c. sugar
1/2 c. (packed) brown sugar
1 oz. unsweetened chocolate
1/2 tsp. vanilla
1 egg
1 c. sifted all-purpose flour
1/2 tsp. soda
1/4 tsp. salt
1 3 1/2-oz. package vanilla pudding and pie filling
1 1/2 c. milk
Confectioners' sugar

Pour 3/4 cup boiling water over oats; let stand for 20 minutes. Cream butter, sugar and brown sugar together until fluffy. Melt chocolate in double boiler; cool. Blend chocolate, vanilla and egg into creamed mixture. Add oats mixture, blending well. Sift flour, soda and salt together; stir into creamed mixture. Spoon batter into greased and floured 9-inch pie plate. Bake at 350 degrees for 25 to 30 minutes. Let stand for about 10 minutes. Remove from pie plate; cool on wire rack. Combine pudding mix and milk in saucepan. Cook over medium heat, stirring constantly, until mixture comes to a full boil. Cool. Place piece of waxed paper directly on pudding mixture while cooling. Remove paper when pudding is cooled. Stir well. Split cake horizontally; spread filling between layers. Garnish top with confectioners' sugar. Yield: 6 servings.

CREAM PIE WITH CUSTARD FILLING

2 c. flour
2 tsp. baking powder
1/2 tsp. salt
3 c. sugar
1/2 c. heavy cream
5 eggs
1 c. milk
1 tsp. vanilla
1/3 c. cornstarch
2 tbsp. butter
1 tbsp. lemon extract
1 c. boiling water
Powdered sugar

Sift flour, baking powder and salt together. Combine 2 cups sugar and cream; beat until fluffy. Beat in 2 eggs. Add flour mixture alternately with milk; mix well. Stir in vanilla; turn batter into 2 greased and floured 8-inch layer pans. Bake at 350 degrees for 40 to 45 minutes. Cool layers in pan for 10 minutes; cool on racks. Combine remaining sugar and cornstarch in top of double boiler; beat in remaining eggs. Add butter, lemon extract and boiling water. Cook, stirring frequently, until thickened. Cool custard and spread between cake layers. Dust top of cake with powdered sugar. Yield: 10 servings.

Bouillabaisse

Pronounced bool-yah-BAYS, this is a robustly flavored seafood stew. Supposedly it was first created when Marseilles fishermen tossed their day's inferior, unmarketable catch into a huge kettle and discovered the resulting flavor.

INGREDIENTS: The original French version includes twelve kinds of *fish* and *shellfish,* some of which are not obtainable outside Mediterranean areas. The American version may use haddock, sea bass, cod, whiting, eel—in fact, practically any fish available in the United States. Fish must, however, be firm-fleshed. American bouillabaisse may also include such shellfish as lobsters and mussels. The stew usually contains twice as much fish as shellfish. Quite often ingredients include *olive oil, garlic,* and *saffron;* and, *vegetables* such as tomatoes, leeks, and onions. Genuine bouillabaisse does *not* contain wine or liquor.

SERVING: Pour stew liquid over slices of bread on one platter; arrange seafood on second platter and serve. Or serve stew in a bowl with French bread, garlic bread, or croutons for a vigorous one-dish meal.

OLD-FASHIONED BOUILLABAISSE

1 doz. clams
1 lb. shrimp
1 lobster-tail
1 1-lb. package frozen flounder fillets
1 1-lb. package haddock fillets
1 c. chopped onions
1 c. thinly sliced leeks
2 tbsp. olive oil
1/2 c. dry white wine
1 tsp. salt
1/4 tsp. pepper
1 tsp. saffron
1 clove of garlic, crushed
1 19-oz. can tomatoes
1/4 c. butter
1 tsp. flour
2 tbsp. coarsely chopped parsley

Clean clams and shrimp; cut lobster-tail into large pieces. Thaw flounder and haddock fillets; cut into bite-sized pieces. Cook onions and leeks in oil in saucepan until onions are tender; stir in wine, salt, pepper, saffron, garlic and tomatoes. Simmer for 20 minutes. Melt butter in skillet; add seafood. Cover skillet; simmer for 15 minutes. Blend flour and 2 tablespoons water; stir into tomato mixture. Add seafood. Heat through. Sprinkle with parsley. Yield: 6 servings.

LOUISIANA BOUILLABAISSE

1 1-lb. lobster, cooked
2 doz. small hard-shelled clams
1/2 c. salad oil
1 lge. clove of garlic, minced
1 tsp. sage
1 tsp. thyme
1/8 tsp. saffron
2 bay leaves
1 tsp. salt
1 tsp. paprika
1/4 c. minced onion
1 stalk celery, finely chopped
2 lb. halibut fillets
1 lb. fresh shrimp
1 c. fresh crab meat
6 peeled tomatoes, cut up
1 c. sherry

Remove lobster meat from shell; cut into 2-inch pieces. Steam clams in 4 cups water in kettle until shells open; shuck. Reserve clam broth. Heat oil in Dutch oven. Combine garlic, seasonings, onion and celery. Arrange halibut, shellfish and tomatoes in Dutch oven, sprinkling with garlic mixture and sherry. Simmer for 10 minutes, stirring occasionally. Add reserved clam broth; simmer for 20 minutes. Yield: 10-12 servings.

WEST COAST BOUILLABAISSE

1 med. onion, chopped
1 clove of garlic, minced
1/2 c. chopped parsley
1 1-lb. 12-oz. can tomatoes
2 6-oz. cans tomato paste
Pinch of rosemary
1/2 tsp. salt
1/4 tsp. pepper
1 tsp. saffron
2 cracked crabs
2 lb. clams
1/2 lb. prawns
4 whitefish fillets
1/2 c. sherry

Combine onion, garlic, parsley, tomatoes, tomato paste, rosemary, and seasonings in 6-quart kettle. Simmer for 2 to 3 hours or until of sauce consistency. Arrange crabs, clams, prawns and fish in sauce; add sherry. Simmer for 20 minutes longer; serve. Yield: 4-6 servings.

SANDBRIDGE BEACH BOUILLABAISSE

2 lb. onions, minced
2 bunches celery, finely chopped
4 tbsp. bacon drippings
10 lb. peeled tomatoes
1/2 c. finely chopped parsley
Garlic salt to taste
Basil to taste
Worcestershire sauce to taste
Monosodium glutamate
Salt to taste
White pepper to taste
2 lb. small lobster-tails
2 lb. cocktail crab claws
5 lb. unshelled mussels
4 lb. whitefish fillets

Cook onions and celery until transparent in bacon drippings in large kettle. Add tomatoes and parsley; season with garlic salt, basil, Worcestershire sauce, monosodium glutamate, salt and pepper. Add 4 quarts water; bring to a boil. Add lobster-tails; cook for 10 minutes. Add remaining seafood; simmer for 10 minutes longer. Yield: 12 servings.

California Bouillabaisse . . . A zesty fish stew of halibut, shrimp, oysters, and seasonings.

CALIFORNIA BOUILLABAISSE

2 lb. halibut steak
1 carrot
1 bay leaf
2 tsp. salt
1/4 tsp. pepper
2 med. onions, sliced
3 tbsp. olive oil
1/4 c. flour
1 lb. peeled shrimp, deveined
1 c. oysters and liquor
1 1-lb. can tomatoes, cut up
1 tbsp. lemon juice
1 2/3 c. canned pitted California ripe olives
2 tbsp. chopped parsley

Cut halibut into large pieces, removing skin and bones. Combine carrot, 4 cups water, bay leaf, salt and pepper in saucepan; heat to boiling point. Add halibut; reduce heat. Simmer for 10 minutes. Remove halibut, carrot and bay leaf. Saute onions in oil until tender but not browned. Stir in flour. Strain stock; stir into onion mixture gradually. Cook, stirring constantly, until thickened. Add shrimp; simmer for 5 minutes. Add oysters with liquor, tomatoes, lemon juice, olives and halibut; heat together for 5 minutes. Add parsley just before serving. Yield: 3 quarts.

CAPE COD BOUILLABAISSE

1 lb. red snapper
1 lb. perch
1 lb. tail cod
1 1/2 lb. striped or sea bass
2 1/2 lb. mackerel
1 lb. eel
2 1 1/2-lb. lobsters
3 lge. leeks, chopped
2 med. onions, chopped
1 lge. carrot, chopped
1 lb. chopped tomatoes, seeded
2 cloves of garlic, crushed
1 tbsp. chopped parsley
1 tsp. saffron
1 bay leaf
Pinch of thyme
Pinch of fresh fennel tips
Dried rind of 1/2 orange
1 tbsp. salt
White pepper
1/2 c. olive oil
1 c. dry white wine
1 pt. clams with juice

Clean fish; cut into 1-inch slices. Remove heads from lobsters, remove nonedible sacs located behind heads. Split tails; remove intestinal veins. Cut lobsters in shells into 1-inch pieces. Place leeks, onions, carrot and tomatoes into large kettle; add herbs and seasonings. Place lobster, snapper, bass, mackerel and eel over vegetables. Pour in olive oil, wine and water to cover. Bring to a boil quickly; boil rapidly for 8 minutes. Add perch, cod and clams. Cook for 8 minutes longer. Serve in large soup bowls with French bread, if desired.

NEW ORLEANS BOUILLABAISSE

6 med. tomatoes, chopped
3 med. onions, diced
1 lge. carrot, chopped
1/4 c. olive oil
2 cloves of garlic, pressed
Pinch of thyme
2 bay leaves
2 tbsp. chopped parsley
1 tsp. saffron
Salt and pepper to taste
3 lb. Spanish mackerel fillets
1 lge. lobster, cut up
1 lb. peeled cleaned shrimp

Combine tomatoes, onions and carrot in large kettle; add olive oil and garlic. Cover with water; add thyme, bay leaves, parsley, saffron, salt and pepper. Bring to a boil; add fish fillets and lobster. Simmer for 8 to 10 minutes. Add shrimp; simmer for 8 to 10 minutes longer. Serve in large soup bowls over thick sliced toasted French bread, if desired. Yield: 6 servings.

Bouillon

BRACING BOUILLON

1 beef knuckle soupbone
2 tsp. salt
1/4 tsp. pepper
1 tsp. monosodium glutamate
1 No. 2 can tomatoes

Place soupbone in large pot; add 1 gallon water and seasonings. Bring to a boil; reduce heat. Simmer for 2 hours. Add tomatoes; simmer for 20 minutes. Strain and cool. Skim off fat. Reheat to serving temperature. Garnish with thin lemon slices. Yield: 6-8 servings.

CHILLED TOMATO BOUILLON

2 c. tomato juice
2 c. beef broth
1/2 tsp. salt
1/4 tsp. pepper
1/4 tsp. sugar
Whipped cream
Paprika

Combine tomato juice, beef broth, salt, pepper and sugar in saucepan. Bring to a boil; cook for 5 minutes. Pour into bouillon cups; chill until ready to serve. Garnish with whipped cream and paprika. Yield: 6 servings.

COAST BOUILLON

2 c. court bouillon
1 c. shredded cooked fish
2 tsp. grated onion
1/3 tsp. salt
1/4 tsp. pepper
1/2 tsp. Worcestershire sauce
3 drops of hot sauce
2 tbsp. lemon juice
Watercress

Combine all ingredients except watercress; chill until firm. Break up with fork. Serve in chilled bouillon cups; garnish with watercress. Yield: 4 servings.

DINNERTIME REFRESHER

4 c. tomato juice
1 c. water
1/2 c. sugar
1 c. minced celery
1 tbsp. salt
Pepper to taste
2 tbsp. Worcestershire sauce
2 tbsp. lemon juice

Combine tomato juice, water, sugar, celery, salt and pepper in saucepan; simmer until celery is tender. Strain through colander, forcing celery through. Return to saucepan; add Worcestershire sauce and lemon juice. Heat for 2 minutes; serve.

HOLIDAY BOUILLON

6 lb. meaty beef bones, cracked
4 qt. cold water
2 carrots, sliced
3 stalks celery and leaves, diced
2 onions, sliced
2 tbsp. chopped parsley
8 peppercorns
1 bay leaf
2 tsp. salt

Bake bones in 350-degree oven for 1 hour or until brown. Place bones in soup pot. Add remaining ingredients. Bring to a boil slowly; skim off foam. Cover; simmer for 3 hours or until liquid is reduced by half. Remove bones, meat and vegetables; strain broth through cheesecloth. Serve hot.

HOT BOUILLON

2 c. tomato juice
1 1/2 c. water
2 beef bouillon cubes
2 chicken bouillon cubes
1/2 tsp. Worcestershire sauce
1/4 tsp. salt
1/4 tsp. crushed red pepper
1/4 tsp. dried green onion flakes
1/4 tsp. monosodium glutamate
1 tsp. dried parsley flakes

Combine tomato juice, water and bouillon cubes in saucepan; heat, stirring, until bouillon cubes are dissolved. Add remaining ingredients; bring to a boil. Reduce heat; simmer for 30 minutes. Strain into bouillon cups; serve immediately. Yield: 4-6 servings.

ICED ORANGE BOUILLON

2 tbsp. unflavored gelatin
2 tbsp. water
3 c. orange juice
3/4 c. sugar
2 tbsp. lime or lemon juice
6 oranges, cut in half

Soak gelatin in water for 5 minutes. Heat 1 cup orange juice; stir in gelatin until dissolved. Stir in sugar; mix well. Add remaining orange juice and lime juice; chill until thickened. Beat with rotary beater several times during chilling process. Scoop out orange pulp; chop fine. Combine with gelatin mixture; beat until mixed. Serve in bouillon cups; garnish with orange sections and mint sprigs. Yield: 12 servings.

JELLIED BOUILLON

1 1/2 tbsp. unflavored gelatin
1/2 c. cold water
2 c. canned beef bouillon
1 c. canned chicken bouillon
1 onion, sliced
1 sm. bunch parsley
1/2 tsp. salt
Dash of pepper
1 hard-cooked egg, sliced

Soak gelatin in water for 5 minutes. Combine remaining ingredients except egg. Heat to a boil; reduce heat. Simmer for 10 minutes. Add gelatin; stir until dissolved. Let stand for 5 minutes; strain. Pour into bouillon cups; chill until firm. Draw fork through chilled mixture to break in small pieces. Place slice of egg in each cup. Garnish with lemon wedges and chopped chives, if desired. Yield: 6 servings.

Bran

BRAN CORN BREAD

1/2 c. shortening
1/2 c. sugar
2 eggs
1 1/2 c. whole bran cereal
1 c. milk
1 c. flour
1/2 c. yellow cornmeal
3 tsp. baking powder
1/2 tsp. salt

Cream shortening and sugar; beat in eggs. Stir in cereal and milk; let stand for 5 minutes. Sift flour, cornmeal, baking powder and salt together; stir into cereal mixture. Turn batter into greased 9-inch square pan. Bake at 375 degrees for 25 minutes or until bread tests done. Yield: 8 servings.

BRAN BROWN BREAD

1 c. whole bran cereal
1 c. sour milk or buttermilk
1/2 c. raisins
2 tbsp. molasses
1/4 c. sugar
1 c. flour
1 tsp. soda
1/4 tsp. salt

Combine cereal, sour milk, raisins, molasses and sugar. Sift flour, soda and salt together; add to bran mixture. Mix well; place in greased loaf pan. Bake at 375 degrees for 35 to 40 minutes.

FRUITED BRAN LOAF

3 c. packaged biscuit mix
1 c. whole bran cereal
1/2 c. sugar
2 eggs
1 1/2 c. milk
Grated rind of 1 orange
1/2 c. chopped nuts
1/2 c. chopped mixed candied fruits
1 1/2 c. fresh cranberries

Combine biscuit mix, cereal and sugar. Add eggs and milk; stir until dry ingredients are moistened. Fold in orange rind, nuts, candied fruits and cranberries; pour into greased 9 x 5 x 3-inch pan. Bake at 350 degrees for 1 hour and 10 minutes or until bread tests done. Remove from pan; cool on rack before slicing.

IRISH BRAN BREAD

4 1/3 c. sifted flour
3 tsp. soda
1 tsp. sugar
2 tsp. salt
1 2/3 c. crushed whole bran cereal
2 1/2 c. buttermilk

Sift flour, soda, sugar and salt together into mixing bowl; stir in cereal and buttermilk. Turn dough onto floured surface; knead lightly. Shape into loaf; place in greased 9 x 5 x 3-inch pan. Bake at 350 degrees for 1 hour.

MOIST BRAN BREAD

2 c. oven-toasted bran cereal
1 pkg. yeast
1 1/2 c. sieved applesauce
1/2 c. (packed) brown sugar
1 tsp. salt
2 tbsp. melted butter
8 1/4 c. sifted flour

Soak cereal in 1 1/2 cups boiling water for 30 minutes. Dissolve yeast in 1/3 cup warm water. Combine cereal mixture, yeast mixture, applesauce, brown sugar, salt and butter; mix well. Add 7 cups flour, blending in 1 cup at a time. Let rise for 1 hour or until doubled in bulk. Knead on board with remaining flour; shape into 2 loaves. Place in 2 greased 9 x 5 x 3-inch pans; let rise for 1 hour. Bake at 400 degrees for 30 minutes. Reduce heat to 350 degrees; bake for 30 minutes longer.

BRAN REFRIGERATOR MUFFINS

2 c. boiling water
2 c. bran flakes
1 1/4 c. butter or shortening
3 c. sugar
4 eggs
1 qt. buttermilk
5 c. flour
5 tsp. soda
1 tbsp. salt
2 c. chopped dried figs
4 c. whole bran cereal

Pour boiling water over bran flakes; let stand to soften bran. Cream butter and sugar; beat in eggs. Stir in buttermilk and bran flake mixture. Sift flour, soda and salt together; add to buttermilk mixture. Add figs and whole bran cereal; mix lightly. Spoon batter into greased muffin tins. Bake at 400 degrees for 20 minutes. Batter may be kept refrigerated for up to 1 month; bake as needed. Yield: 5 dozen muffins.

BRAN-RAISIN MUFFINS

1 c. whole bran cereal
1/2 c. milk
1/2 c. molasses
1 egg
1/4 c. cooking oil
1/2 c. raisins
1 c. sifted flour
2 1/2 tsp. baking powder
1/2 tsp. salt

Combine bran, milk and molasses; let stand until milk is almost absorbed. Add egg and oil; beat well. Stir in raisins. Sift flour, baking powder and salt together; add to bran mixture, stirring just until mixed. Spoon into 12 greased and floured muffin tin cups. Bake at 400 degrees for about 20 minutes.

OLD-FASHIONED BRAN MUFFINS

1 c. whole bran cereal
3/4 c. milk
1 egg
1/4 c. soft shortening
1 c. sifted flour
2 1/2 tsp. baking powder
1/2 tsp. salt
1/4 c. sugar

Combine cereal and milk; let stand until most of the moisture is taken up. Add egg and shortening; beat well. Sift flour, baking powder, salt and sugar together. Add to cereal mixture, stirring only until combined. Fill greased muffin pans 2/3 full. Bake at 400 degrees for about 25 minutes. Serve immediately.Yield: 9 muffins.

Old-Fashioned Bran Muffins . . . Start your morning right by serving these muffins at breakfast.

PINEAPPLE-BRAN MUFFINS

1/3 c. shortening
1/2 c. sugar
2 eggs
1/3 c. honey
1 8-oz. can crushed pineapple
1 1/3 c. bran
1 1/3 c. flour
2 tsp. soda
1/2 tsp. salt
1 c. milk

Cream shortening and sugar; beat in eggs. Stir in honey, pineapple and bran. Sift flour, soda and salt together; add to bran mixture alternately with milk. Mix lightly; spoon batter into oiled muffin cups. Bake at 350 degrees for 20 to 25 minutes. Yield: 18 small muffins.

BRAN CRESCENT ROLLS

1 c. shortening
1 c. boiling water
3/4 c. sugar
1 c. whole bran cereal
1 1/2 tsp. salt
2 pkg. yeast
1 c. lukewarm water
2 eggs, beaten
6 c. flour
Melted margarine

Combine shortening, boiling water, sugar, bran cereal and salt; cool. Dissolve yeast in lukewarm water; add to bran mixture. Stir in eggs; fold in flour. Roll out half the dough at a time to 1/2-inch thick circle. Cut into pie-shaped wedges; brush with margarine. Roll up, starting at wide end. Place on baking sheet; let rise for 1 hour and 30 minutes. Bake at 450 degrees for 12 minutes or until golden brown. Yield: 36 rolls.

BRAN DINNER BUNS

1 pkg. yeast
1 tsp. sugar
1 c. lukewarm water
1 c. boiling water
1 c. whole bran cereal
1/2 c. shortening
1/2 c. brown sugar
2 eggs
1/4 tsp. salt
5 c. sifted flour

Dissolve yeast and sugar in lukewarm water. Pour boiling water over cereal. Cream shortening and brown sugar; beat in eggs. Stir in yeast mixture, cereal mixture and salt. Add flour, mixing to a soft dough. Cover; let rise until doubled in bulk. Stir dough down; cover. Let rise until almost doubled in bulk. Shape dough into small buns; place in greased baking pan. Let rise again. Bake at 400 degrees for 20 to 25 minutes or until lightly browned.

BRAN PULL-APARTS

1/2 c. shortening
1/2 tsp. salt
1/3 c. sugar
1 egg, beaten
1/2 c. whole bran cereal
1 pkg. yeast
1 c. warm water
3 1/4 c. flour
Cooking oil

Mix shortening, salt and sugar; add egg and cereal. Dissolve yeast in warm water; add to shortening mixture. Stir in flour; knead lightly. Place in greased bowl; let rise for 1 hour and 30 minutes or until doubled in bulk. Knead lightly again. Form into small balls; roll in oil. Stack in greased tube pan; let rise for 1 hour and 30 minutes. Bake at 400 degrees for 30 minutes or until bread tests done. Yield: 8 servings.

Bread, Loaves

There are two divisions of breads; quick breads and yeast breads. Both are prepared with flour, salt, liquid, and a leavening agent and may include eggs, flavorings, fruits, nuts, and so forth. *Quick breads* are those that use baking powder, baking soda, air, sourdough, or steam for leavening. They are called quick because they do not require a prolonged period of rising before being cooked. In preparing quick breads, handle ingredients quickly and lightly. Do not knead unless recipe so specifies. *Yeast breads* rise through the action of yeast on other ingredients, especially flour. These breads almost always require at least one period of rising before being baked and many recipes specify kneading as well.

YEAST BREAD INGREDIENTS: *Yeast* is the leavening agent and is available in cakes or dry form. The latter is easier to store and keeps longer than cake yeast. Dry yeast is best dissolved in water that is warm but not hot to the touch; cake yeast dissolves best in water that feels slightly cool. The *liquid* in yeast breads is generally water but some milk may be used. Milk helps create tender, small-crumbed bread. The basic bread-making flour is enriched all-purpose and is often mixed with other flours. The usual proportion is 80 percent enriched white flour to 20 percent of other flours. *Salt* adds flavor and helps the rising process. Never mix salt directly with yeast–it will retard the rising action and may kill the yeast. Mix it with milk or other liquids before adding. *Shortening* and *sugar* are sometimes added. Shortening helps create a flaky crumb and aids in keeping bread from spoiling. Sugar provides immediate food for the yeast to react with. Other ingredients may include fruit or nuts–the usual proportion is 20 to 30 percent of the total volume.

METHODS OF PREPARATION: There are three basic methods used to prepare yeast breads. In the *sponge method,* yeast, water, and some of the flour are combined and allowed to sit overnight. The remaining ingredients are added the next day. The dough is kneaded and allowed to rise according to recipe directions. In the *straight or regular method,* yeast is combined with water. Then scalded milk, shortening, sugar, and salt are mixed separately and are combined with the yeast and water mixture, and flour is added. Kneading follows the mixing of the dough and there are usually two risings, one in the bowl and the other in the pan. The *batter method* utilizes the electric mixer to blend ingredients thoroughly. The batter is spooned into baking pans and allowed to rise before baking.

In mixing ingredients, blend them thoroughly. Part of the secret of successful bread making is to distribute ingredients evenly throughout every part of the baked product.

Kneading helps spread the gluten (that substance in flour which expands under the action of yeast) throughout the dough and to thoroughly blend the ingredients. Work with the heel of your hand—the muscle below your thumb and just above your wrist. Dough has been kneaded sufficiently when it is smooth and small bubbles appear under the surface. If you have doubts about the kneading being complete, cut the dough from top to bottom with a sharp knife. Bubbles along the cut surface indicate kneading is complete.

After kneading, grease a clean bowl with liquid shortening (it adheres more evenly than other shortenings to the dough's surface). Place dough in bowl, let rest for a minute, then turn over so that greased side is up. Cover bowl with clean cloth and set in warm place for rising.

Rising is a result of the interaction of gluten and yeast. It occurs best in a draftless place where the temperature is between 83 and 90 degrees. After the recipe's specified time for rising has elapsed, press two fingers into dough. If the dents remain, dough is ready for shaping.

To shape loaves, roll the amount of dough you need for one loaf into a ball and flatten it into a rectangle with your hand or a rolling pin, being careful to squeeze out as many gas bubbles as possible. Roll up dough into loaf shape, tucking in the ends. Place in greased pan, seam side down. Let rise again.

Baking follows rising in pans. When baking French or Vienna bread, place a shallow pan of boiling water on the bottom of the oven to help develop the hard crust characteristic of these breads.

You can determine doneness of any bread by tapping the crust: a hollow noise indicates that baking is completed. For a soft crust, brush tops of cooling loaves with melted butter and cover with a clean towel for several minutes. Cool bread thoroughly before cutting.

ANADAMA BREAD

1 1/2 c. water
1 tsp. salt
1/3 c. cornmeal
1/3 c. molasses
1 1/2 tbsp. shortening
1 pkg. yeast
1/4 c. lukewarm water
4 1/4 c. sifted flour

Bring water and salt to a boil; stir in cornmeal, molasses and shortening. Cool to lukewarm. Dissolve yeast in lukewarm water; stir into cornmeal mixture. Add flour; mix with spoon until stiff. Knead until smooth. Let rise in warm place for 1 hour and 30 minutes. Punch down; place in greased loaf pan. Let rise for 45 minutes or until doubled in bulk. Bake at 375 degrees for 40 to 45 minutes.

BATTER BREAD

1 pkg. dry yeast
1/2 c. warm water
1/4 tsp. ginger
3 tbsp. sugar
1 lge. can evaporated milk
2 tbsp. oil
1 tsp. salt
4 1/2 c. flour

Dissolve yeast in warm water in large mixing bowl; stir in ginger and 1 tablespoon sugar. Let stand in warm place until mixture begins to bubble. Add remaining sugar, milk, oil, salt and 3 cups flour; beat at medium speed of electric mixer until smooth. Work in remaining flour with spoon; knead lightly. Divide dough into 2 balls; place in 2 greased 1-pound coffee cans. Place plastic tops on cans; allow dough to rise until lids pop off. Bake at 350 degrees for 45 minutes. Cool in cans for 5 minutes. Bread may be frozen after baking; heat to serve.

COTTAGE BREAD

1 pkg. yeast
1 1/4 c. warm water
1 1/2 tbsp. sugar
1 1/4 tsp. salt
1 tbsp. soft shortening
4 c. cake flour

Dissolve yeast in 1/4 cup warm water. Combine sugar, salt, shortening, yeast mixture and remaining warm water in large bowl; add 2 cups flour. Beat until smooth. Add 1 3/4 cups flour; stir until dough cleans side of bowl. Turn onto floured board; knead until smooth. Place dough in greased bowl; cover. Let rise in warm place for 45 minutes to 1 hour. Turn onto floured board; shape into loaf. Place in greased loaf pan; cover. Let rise for 30 to 45 minutes. Make 5-inch slashes 1/4 inch deep on top of loaf; sift remaining flour over top. Bake at 400 degrees for 35 to 40 minutes. Cool on rack.

COTTAGE CHEESE BREAD

1 pkg. yeast
2 tbsp. melted butter
2 tbsp. sugar
1 tsp. salt
1/4 tsp. soda
1 egg
1 c. small curd cottage cheese
2 1/4 c. sifted flour

Dissolve yeast in 1/4 cup warm water. Combine butter, sugar, salt, soda, egg and cottage cheese with 1 1/4 cups flour. Blend well. Add remaining flour; mix thoroughly. Allow to rise in warm place for 1 hour. Stir down and place in greased 8-inch round casserole. Allow to rise for 1 hour longer. Bake at 350 degrees for 30 minutes. Brush with melted butter; sprinkle with salt.

COUNTY FAIR EGG BREAD

1/2 c. butter
2 tsp. salt
1/2 c. sugar
1 1/2 c. scalded milk
2 pkg. yeast
1/2 c. lukewarm water
2 eggs
9 c. sifted flour

Combine butter, salt and sugar in mixing bowl; stir in hot milk. Let stand until cooled. Dissolve yeast in lukewarm water; add to milk mixture. Beat in eggs. Add 3 cups flour; beat to a smooth sponge. Work in enough remaining flour to make soft, easily handled dough. Turn dough onto floured surface; knead until smooth and elastic. Place dough in greased bowl; cover. Let rise for 1 hour and 30 minutes or until doubled in bulk. Punch dough down; turn onto floured surface. Shape into 3 loaves; place in greased 8-inch loaf pans. Let rise until doubled in bulk again. Bake at 425 degrees for 10 minutes. Reduce oven temperature to 350 degrees; bake for 40 minutes longer.

FRENCH LOAVES

Color photograph for this recipe on page 722.

1 pkg. yeast
3/4 c. melted butter
2 c. lukewarm milk
1 tsp. salt
6 c. flour
1 egg, beaten

Place yeast in bowl. Mix the butter and milk. Pour over yeast; stir until dissolved. Add the salt and flour; mix until smooth. Let rise until doubled in bulk. Knead on floured board until smooth. Reserve 1 cup dough. Divide remaining dough in half; shape each half into an oblong loaf. Place on baking sheet. Divide reserved dough in half; shape each half into a roll the length of loaves. Twist; place each roll on a loaf. Let rise until doubled in bulk. Brush with egg. Bake in 350-degree oven for about 20 minutes.

EASY WHITE BREAD

6 1/2 to 7 c. flour
2 tbsp. sugar
1 tbsp. salt
2 pkg. yeast
1/2 c. softened margarine
2 c. hot water
Peanut oil

Mix 2 cups flour, sugar, salt and yeast in large bowl; add margarine and hot water. Beat for 2 minutes at medium speed of electric mixer. Add 1 cup flour; beat at high speed for 2 minutes, scraping bowl occasionally. Stir in enough remaining flour to make soft dough. Turn onto lightly floured board; knead for 10 minutes or until smooth and elastic. Cover with plastic wrap and towel; let rest for 20 minutes. Punch dough down. Divide in half on lightly floured board; shape into loaves. Place in 2 greased 9 x 5 x 3-inch pans. Brush with oil. Cover pans loosely with plastic wrap. Refrigerate for 2 to 24 hours. Remove from refrigerator; uncover dough carefully. Let stand for 10 minutes at room temperature. Puncture any gas bubbles with skewer. Bake in 400-degree oven for 30 to 40 minutes. Remove from pans; cool on wire racks.

HERB BREAD

1/2 c. margarine or butter
1/3 c. (packed) brown sugar
2 c. scalded milk
1 tbsp. salt
1/2 tsp. thyme
1 tsp. basil
1 tsp. caraway seed
2 pkg. yeast
1/2 c. warm water
8 c. (about) sifted flour

Brown margarine in saucepan; add brown sugar, milk, salt, thyme, basil and caraway seed. Cool to lukewarm. Dissolve yeast in warm water in large bowl; add milk mixture. Add enough flour gradually to make stiff dough. Knead on floured surface for 7 to 8 minutes. Place in greased bowl; cover. Let rise for 1 hour and 30 minutes. Punch dough down; let rise for 30 minutes. Shape into 2 loaves. Place in greased loaf pans; cover. Let rise in warm place for 45 minutes. Bake at 375 degrees for 35 to 40 minutes. Turn out on racks to cool.

HIGH PROTEIN BREAD

3 pkg. yeast
3/4 c. warm water
6 c. hot water
9 c. instant dry milk
6 tbsp. shortening
2 tbsp. salt
6 tbsp. sugar
19 1/2 c. flour

Soften yeast in warm water. Mix hot water, dry milk, shortening, salt and sugar in large bowl; cool to lukewarm. Stir in yeast; add flour, 2 cups at a time, mixing well after each addition. Turn dough onto floured board; knead until smooth. Place in greased bowl; cover. Let rise for 1 hour and 30 minutes or until doubled in bulk. Punch down; let rise until nearly doubled in bulk. Divide into 6 parts; shape into loaves. Place in greased pans; let rise again until doubled in bulk. Bake at 400 degrees for 45 minutes.

SALLY LUNN

1 pkg. yeast
1 c. warm milk
1/2 c. butter or margarine
1/3 c. sugar
3 eggs, beaten
4 c. flour
1 tsp. salt

Dissolve yeast in warm milk. Cream butter and sugar; add eggs. Sift flour and salt together; add to creamed mixture alternately with yeast mixture. Beat until smooth. Cover; let rise in warm place until doubled in bulk. Beat batter down; pour into greased pan or mold. Let rise until doubled in bulk. Bake at 350 degrees for 40 to 45 minutes. Yield: 12-16 servings.

HOMEMADE FRENCH BREAD

1 pkg. yeast
1 tbsp. sugar
2 tsp. salt
Sifted flour
Cornmeal

Dissolve yeast in 1 1/2 cups warm water in large bowl; stir in sugar and salt. Add 4 1/2 cups flour all at once; stir vigorously with wooden spoon. Dough will be stiff and sticky. Cover; let rise for 1 hour or until doubled in bulk. Turn half the dough onto floured board; sprinkle lightly with flour. Roll and stretch into 10 x 14-inch rectangle; roll up, starting at broad side. Pinch edge to seal. Shape with hands to 18-inch long tapering loaf. Sprinkle greased baking sheet lightly with cornmeal; arrange loaf on baking sheet. Repeat with remaining dough. Cut 3 or 4 shallow diagonal slashes in tops of loaves. Cover; let rise until doubled in bulk. Brush lightly with cold water. Bake at 425 degrees for 10 minutes. Reduce oven temperature to 325 degrees; brush loaves again with water. Bake for 40 minutes longer or until golden brown. Transfer loaves to rack to cool.

IRISH FRECKLE BREAD

Color photograph for this recipe on page 727.

4 3/4 to 5 3/4 c. unsifted flour
1/2 c. sugar
1 tsp. salt
2 pkg. dry yeast
1 c. potato water
1/2 c. margarine
2 eggs, at room temperature
1/4 c. warm mashed potatoes
1 c. seedless raisins

Mix 1 1/2 cups flour, sugar, salt and undissolved yeast thoroughly in large bowl. Combine potato water and margarine in saucepan; place over low heat until liquid is warm. Margarine does not need to melt. Add to dry ingredients gradually; beat for 2 minutes with electric mixer at medium speed, scraping bowl occasionally. Add eggs, potatoes and 1/2 cup flour; beat at high speed for 2 minutes, scraping bowl occasionally. Stir in raisins and enough remaining flour to make soft dough. Turn out onto lightly floured board; knead for 5 to 10 minutes or until smooth and elastic. Place in greased bowl, turning to grease top. Cover; let rise in warm place, free from draft, for about 1 hour and 15 minutes or until doubled in bulk. Punch down. Turn out onto a lightly floured board; divide into 4 equal pieces. Shape each piece into loaf about 8 1/2 inches long. Place 2 loaves, side by side, in each of 2 greased 8 1/2 x 4 1/2 x 2 1/2-inch loaf pans. Cover; let rise in warm place, free from draft, for about 1 hour or until doubled in bulk. Bake in 350-degree oven for about 35 minutes or until done. Remove from pans; cool on wire racks.

ITALIAN BREAD

1 pkg. yeast
2 c. lukewarm water
1 tbsp. salt
6 c. flour

Soften yeast in lukewarm water in large bowl; stir in salt. Add flour gradually, mixing well. Turn dough onto floured surface; knead for 15 minutes. Place in greased bowl; cover. Let rise for 2 hours or until doubled in bulk. Turn onto floured surface; knead for 5 minutes. Divide dough into 2 parts; cover. Let rest for 10 minutes. Shape dough into long tapering loaves; place on baking sheet. Let rise for 1 hour. Bake at 425 degrees for 10 minutes. Reduce oven temperature to 350 degrees; bake for 20 minutes longer.

NO-FAIL WHITE BREAD

3 pkg. yeast
1/3 c. lukewarm water
1/2 c. shortening
3/4 c. sugar
2 1/2 tbsp. salt
4 c. scalded milk
4 c. boiling water
25 c. (about) sifted flour

Soften yeast in lukewarm water. Combine shortening, sugar and salt in large bowl; add milk and boiling water. Cool to lukewarm; add yeast and about 7 cups flour. Beat to a smooth sponge. Work in enough remaining flour, 2 cups at a time, to make stiff dough. Turn onto floured surface; knead dough until smooth and elastic. Place in greased bowl; cover. Let rise until doubled in bulk. Punch dough down; shape into 8 loaves. Place in greased bread pans; let rise until almost doubled in bulk. Bake at 400 degrees for 30 minutes or until bread tests done.

NO-KNEAD BATTER BREAD

1 pkg. yeast
1/4 c. warm water
1/3 c. cooking oil
1 egg, beaten
1 c. milk
1 1/2 tsp. salt
3 tbsp. sugar
2 1/2 c. flour

Soften yeast in warm water in large mixing bowl; add oil, egg, milk, salt, sugar and flour. Mix well; spoon into greased bread pan. Shape top of loaf with floured hands; let rise until doubled in bulk. Bake at 375 degrees for 45 minutes or until bread tests done.

NORWEGIAN COUNTRY LOAVES

Photograph for this recipe on page 722.

2 pkg. yeast
2 3/4 c. lukewarm milk
Molasses
1 tsp. salt
1/4 c. melted margarine
4 1/2 c. sifted rye flour
3/4 c. whole wheat flour
4 1/2 c. (about) flour

Dissolve yeast in milk in large bowl; stir in 1 1/4 cups molasses, salt and margarine. Add rye flour and whole wheat flour gradually; mix well. Add enough flour for stiff dough; mix until smooth. Shape into 2 oblong loaves; place on greased baking sheets. Let rise until doubled in bulk. Dilute 2 tablespoons molasses with 1 tablespoon water; brush on loaves. Sprinkle with additional whole wheat flour. Bake at 350 degrees for about 45 minutes or until well browned. Wrap each loaf in a towel; cool.

PARMESAN CASSEROLE BREAD

1 pkg. dry yeast
1/4 c. milk, scalded
1 1/2 c. sifted all-purpose flour

1 tbsp. sugar (opt.)
1/2 tsp. salt
Butter
1 egg, beaten
1/2 c. grated Parmesan cheese
2 tbsp. chopped parsley

Soften yeast in 1/4 cup warm water. Cool milk to lukewarm. Sift flour, sugar and salt into mixing bowl; cut in 1/3 cup butter until mixture resembles cornmeal. Add egg, yeast and milk; beat well. Stir in cheese and parsley; turn into greased round casserole. Cover with damp cloth; let rise for about 40 minutes or until doubled in bulk. Dot with additional butter. Bake in 375-degree oven for 20 to 25 minutes.

QUICK-RISE BREAD

2 pkg. yeast
3/4 c. warm water
1 1/4 c. buttermilk
5 c. (about) flour
1/4 c. shortening
2 tbsp. sugar
2 tsp. baking powder
2 tsp. salt
Soft butter

Dissolve yeast in warm water in large electric mixer bowl. Add buttermilk, 2 1/2 cups flour, shortening, sugar, baking powder and salt. Blend for 30 seconds at low speed of mixer, scraping side and bottom of bowl. Beat for 2 minutes at medium speed. Stir in remaining flour by hand. Dough should be soft and slightly sticky. Turn dough onto heavily floured board; knead well. Roll dough to 18 x 9-inch rectangle. Roll up from short side as for jelly roll; press each end to seal. Fold ends under loaf. Place seam side down in greased bread pan; brush loaf lightly with butter. Let rise for 1 hour or until doubled in bulk. Bake at 375 degrees for 45 minutes or until bread tests done.

RUSSIAN BLACK BREAD

Color photograph for this recipe on page 727.

4 c. unsifted rye flour
3 c. unsifted flour
1 tsp. sugar
2 tsp. salt
2 c. whole bran cereal
2 tbsp. crushed caraway seed
2 tsp. instant coffee
2 tsp. onion powder
1/2 tsp. crushed fennel seed
2 pkg. dry yeast
1/4 c. vinegar
1/4 c. dark molasses
1 1-oz. square unsweetened chocolate
1/4 c. margarine
1 tsp. cornstarch

Combine rye flour and flour. Mix 2 1/3 cups flour mixture, sugar, salt, cereal, caraway seed, coffee, onion powder, fennel seed and undissolved yeast thoroughly in a large bowl. Combine 2 1/2 cups water, vinegar, molasses, chocolate and margarine in a saucepan; place over low heat until liquids are warm. Margarine and chocolate do not need to melt. Add to dry ingredients gradually; beat for 2 minutes at medium speed with electric mixer, scraping bowl occasionally. Add 1/2 cup flour mixture; beat at high speed 2 minutes, scraping bowl occasionally. Stir in enough remaining flour mixture to make soft dough. Turn out onto lightly floured board. Cover dough with bowl; let rest for 15 minutes. Knead for 10 to 15 minutes or until smooth and elastic. Dough may be sticky. Place in greased bowl, turning to grease top. Cover; let rise in warm place, free from draft, for about 1 hour or until doubled in bulk. Punch down. Turn out onto lightly floured board; divide dough in half. Shape each half into a ball about 5 inches in diameter. Place each ball in center of greased 8-inch round cake pan. Cover; let rise in warm place, free from draft, for about 1 hour or until doubled in bulk. Bake in 350-degree oven for 45 to 50 minutes or until bread tests done. Combine cornstarch and 1/2 cup cold water in a saucepan. Bring to a boil over medium heat, stirring constantly. Cook, stirring constantly, for 1 minute. Brush over tops of loaves. Return bread to oven; bake for 2 to 3 minutes longer or until glaze is set. Remove from pans; cool on wire racks.

RAISIN BREAD

Color photograph for this recipe on page 722.

2 pkg. yeast
1/4 c. melted butter
2 1/2 c. lukewarm milk
1/4 c. molasses
1 tsp. salt
5 3/4 c. graham flour
5 3/4 c. flour
1 c. raisins

Place yeast in large bowl. Mix butter, milk, 1 1/4 cups water and molasses. Pour over yeast; stir until dissolved. Add salt, flours and raisins; mix thoroughly. Place dough into 2 round greased casseroles; let rise until doubled in bulk. Bake in 350-degree oven for about 1 hour or until bread tests done. Wrap each loaf in a towel; cool.

SEEDED WHITE BREAD

Color photograph for this recipe on page 722.

5 1/2 to 6 1/2 c. unsifted flour
3 tbsp. sugar
2 tsp. salt
1 pkg. dry yeast
1/2 c. milk
3 tbsp. margarine
1 egg white, beaten
1 tbsp. poppy seed

Mix 2 cups flour, sugar, salt and yeast thoroughly in a large bowl. Combine 1 1/2 cups water, milk and margarine in saucepan; place over low heat until liquids are warm. Margarine does not need to melt. Add to dry ingredients gradually; beat for 2 minutes with electric mixer at medium speed, scraping bowl occasionally. Add 3/4 cup flour; beat at high speed for 2 minutes, scraping bowl occasionally. Stir in enough remaining flour to make soft dough. Turn out onto lightly floured board; knead for 8 to 10 minutes or until smooth and elastic. Place in greased bowl, turning to grease top; cover. Let rise in warm place, free from draft, for about 1 hour or until doubled in bulk. Punch down; turn out onto lightly floured board. Cover; let rest for 15 minutes. Roll into 16 x 9-inch rectangle; roll as for jelly roll, starting from 16-inch side. Pinch seam to seal; place in greased 10-inch tube pan, sealed edge down. Seal ends together firmly; press dough down to fully cover bottom of pan. Cover; let rise in warm place, free from draft, for about 1 hour or until doubled in bulk. Brush ring lightly with beaten egg white; sprinkle with poppy seed. Bake at 400 degrees for about 40 minutes or until bread tests done. Remove from pan; cool on wire rack.

SOURDOUGH BREAD

Color photograph for this recipe on page 732.

5 to 6 c. unsifted flour
3 tbsp. sugar
1 tsp. salt
1 pkg. dry yeast
1 c. milk
2 tbsp. margarine
1 1/2 c. Starter

Combine 1 cup flour, sugar, salt and undissolved yeast in large bowl. Combine milk and margarine in saucepan; place over low heat until liquid is warm. Margarine does not need to melt. Add to dry ingredients gradually; beat for 2 minutes with electric mixer, at medium speed, scraping bowl occasionally. Add Starter and 1 cup flour; beat at high speed for 2 minutes, scraping bowl occasionally. Stir in enough remaining flour to make soft dough. Turn out onto lightly floured board; knead for 8 to 10 minutes or until smooth and elastic. Place in greased bowl, turning to grease top. Cover; let rise in warm place, free from draft, for about 1 hour or until doubled in bulk. Punch down. Turn out onto lightly floured board; let rest for 15 minutes. Divide in half. Shape each half into loaf; place in 2 greased 9 x 5 x 3-inch loaf pans. Cover; let rise in warm place, free from draft, for about 1 hour or until doubled in bulk. Bake in 400-degree oven for about 30 minutes or until done. Remove from pans; cool on wire racks.

Starter

2 1/2 c. unsifted flour
Sugar
1 tbsp. salt
1 pkg. dry yeast

Combine 1 3/4 cups flour, 1 tablespoon sugar, salt and undissolved yeast in large bowl. Add 2 1/2 cups warm water gradually; beat for 2 minutes with electric mixer at medium speed, scraping bowl occasionally. Cover; let stand at room temperature for 4 days, stirring down daily. To reuse Starter, add remaining flour, 1 1/2 teaspoons sugar and 1 1/2 cups lukewarm water; beat for 1 minute with electric mixer at medium speed. Cover; let stand until ready to make bread again, stirring down daily.

CRACKED WHEAT BREAD

2 pkg. yeast
1 1/2 c. warm water
1 c. evaporated milk
2 1/2 c. honey
2 1/2 tsp. salt
2 tbsp. oil
7 c. flour
1 c. boiling water
1 c. cracked wheat
1/2 c. wheat germ
1 egg, beaten

Sprinkle yeast over 1/2 cup warm water in large bowl; let stand until yeast is softened. Stir in remaining warm water, milk, honey, salt, oil and 3 cups flour; beat until smooth. Cover; let stand in warm place for 20 minutes or until spongy. Pour boiling water over cracked wheat; let stand for 15 minutes. Stir cracked wheat and wheat germ into sponge; work in 3 cups flour with spoon. Cover; let rise for 1 hour and 30 minutes or until doubled in bulk. Spread remaining flour on board; turn dough onto flour. Knead dough until smooth and elastic, kneading in flour until dough is no longer sticky. Shape dough into 2 loaves; place in greased 9 x 5 x 3-inch pans. Cover; let rise for 45 minutes or until doubled in bulk. Brush tops of loaves with egg. Bake at 350 degrees for 45 minutes or until bread tests done.

SPICED CHEESE LOAVES

1 c. milk
2 tbsp. sugar
1 tbsp. salt
1 tbsp. margarine
1/4 tsp. cumin seed
6 c. unsifted flour
8 oz. sharp Cheddar cheese, grated
3 pkg. yeast

Scald milk; stir in sugar, salt, margarine and cumin seed. Pour into large mixing bowl; cool to lukewarm. Blend in 2 cups flour. Beat for 2 minutes at medium speed of electric mixer. Stir in cheese. Pour 1 1/2 cups lukewarm water into small warm bowl; sprinkle yeast over water, stirring to dissolve. Blend into milk mixture. Stir in enough additional flour to make soft dough with wooden spoon. Turn out onto lightly floured board. Knead for about 10 minutes or until smooth and elastic. Place dough in greased bowl, turning to grease top. Cover; let rise in warm place, free from draft, for about 45 minutes or until doubled in bulk. Punch dough down; turn out onto lightly floured board. Divide in half. Cover; let rest for 5 minutes. Shape each half into a ball; place balls in greased 8-inch round cake pans. Cover; let rise in warm place, free from draft, for about 30 minutes or until doubled in bulk. Bake at 400 degrees for about 45 minutes or until dark golden brown.

Spiced Cheese Loaves . . . Zesty breads rich with Cheddar are perfect for family meals.

OLD-FASHIONED WHOLE WHEAT BREAD

1 pkg. yeast
3/4 c. warm water
1 qt. milk
1 tbsp. salt
1 tbsp. sugar
7 c. whole wheat flour
Butter

Dissolve yeast in warm water. Heat milk to lukewarm; add yeast, salt and sugar. Stir in half the flour; blend well. Add enough remaining flour to make stiff dough. Knead on floured board until smooth. Place in bowl; cover. Let rise for 1 hour. Shape into 2 loaves; place in greased loaf pans. Let rise for 15 minutes. Bake at 350 degrees for 1 hour. Brush with butter.

Brioche

Brioche is an individual-size sweet roll prepared from a very light yeast dough that includes eggs and butter among its ingredients. It is usually baked in muffin tins.

BRIOCHES

Color photograph for this recipe on page 732.

1 pkg. yeast
1 3/4 c. flour
1 tsp. sugar
1/2 tsp. salt
3/4 c. butter
3 eggs, lightly beaten

Dissolve yeast in 3 tablespoons warm water. Combine flour, sugar and salt in bowl; cut in butter. Add eggs and yeast; mix until smooth. Drop by tablespoonfuls into greased and floured custard cups or large muffin cups, placing 3 tablespoonfuls in each. Let rise until doubled in bulk. Bake in 450-degree oven for about 8 minutes. Brush with water; serve warm.

HOLIDAY BRIOCHE

1/2 c. lukewarm milk
1 pkg. yeast
1/3 c. melted margarine
1 egg
2 egg yolks
1/4 c. sugar
1/4 tsp. salt
1 tbsp. Grand Marnier
2 1/4 c. all-purpose flour

Combine milk and yeast in 4-quart mixing bowl; let stand for 5 minutes. Stir well. Cool margarine; add to yeast mixture. Mix in egg, egg yolks, sugar and salt. Beat with wooden spoon until well-blended. Stir in Grand Marnier. Stir in 1 1/4 cups flour; beat for 10 minutes by hand or 3 minutes at high speed with electric mixer. Beat in remaining flour, mixing thoroughly. Cover bowl with loose cloth; let rise for 3 hours. Stir down; refrigerate overnight. Remove dough from refrigerator. Use small portion of dough to form twelve 1-inch balls; set aside. Place remaining dough in muffin tins, filling 1/3 full. Make deep indentation in each brioche; press reserved balls of dough in indentation. Let rise until doubled in bulk. Bake at 375 degrees for about 15 minutes.

PETITS BRIOCHES

1/2 c. butter
Sugar
1 tsp. salt
1/2 c. milk
1 pkg. yeast
4 eggs
3 1/2 c. unsifted flour

Cream butter in large mixing bowl; add 1/3 cup sugar and salt gradually, creaming until fluffy. Scald milk; cool to lukewarm. Dissolve yeast in 1/4 cup warm water. Add milk, yeast mixture, 3 eggs, 1 egg yolk and flour to yeast mixture. Beat vigorously with wooden spoon for 2 minutes. Cover; let rise in warm place for about 2 hours or until more than doubled in bulk. Stir dough down; beat for 2 minutes. Cover; place in refrigerator overnight. Punch dough down; turn out onto lightly floured board. Remove 1/4 of the dough; shape into 24 small balls. Shape remaining dough into 24 larger balls. Place larger balls in greased muffin tins; make deep indentation in center of each ball. Dampen slightly with cold water. Press small balls into each indentation. Let rise in warm place for about 50 minutes or until doubled in bulk. Combine 1 tablespoon sugar and remaining egg white; brush glaze over dough. Bake at 375 degrees for about 15 to 20 minutes. May remove small balls; scoop out part of the roll and fill with desired filling. Replace small ball; serve.

Broccoli

A relative of the cabbage, broccoli was introduced to American families over 200 years ago by Italian immigrants. It is rich in Vitamins A and C and contains lesser quantities of the B vitamins and of iron, calcium, and potassium. (2/3 cup broccoli = 26 calories)

AVAILABILITY: In plentiful supply during October and November and again from January through April.

BUYING: Look for compact bud clusters. Fresh broccoli may vary in color from dark green to deep sage green to purplish-green, depending upon the variety. Avoid tough, woody stalks but remember that the very base portion of even the freshest broccoli will be slightly woody. A pound of fresh broccoli serves 3-4 people; a 10-ounce package serves 2-3.

STORING: Cover fresh broccoli with foil or plastic wrap and seal tightly. Will keep 4-5 days in refrigerator. Cooked broccoli, stored in an airtight container, may be refrigerated for up to 4 days. *To freeze* broccoli, wash, peel, trim, and cut the stalks into 5-6 inch pieces. Boil for 3 minutes to blanch. Pack into freezer containers. May be frozen for up to 6 months.

PREPARATION: Edible portions are the tender young stalks and branches and the bud clusters of the head. Outer leaves are also edible and may be served raw in salads as well as cooked. When cooking broccoli, take precautions against the strong odor which may develop by (1) cooking a minimum of time and (2) removing the lid occasionally throughout cooking process to permit gases to escape. Trim stalks, then rinse. Place in about 1 inch boiling salted water, cover, cook until tender. (See VEGETABLES.)

BROCCOLI AND EGGS AU GRATIN

2 10-oz. packages frozen broccoli stalks
4 hard-cooked eggs
Butter
1/4 c. flour
1 1/2 tsp. salt
2 c. milk
1/2 tsp. Worcestershire sauce
1 c. shredded American cheese
1/4 c. fine bread crumbs

Cook broccoli according to package directions; drain. Quarter eggs lengthwise. Arrange broccoli in rows over bottom of greased 13 x 9 x 1 1/2-inch shallow baking dish. Top with rows of egg quarters. Melt 1/4 cup butter in saucepan over low heat; blend in flour and salt. Add milk, stirring constantly. Cook, stirring, until sauce is smooth and thickened. Add Worcestershire sauce and cheese, stirring just until cheese is melted. Pour sauce over eggs and broccoli. Melt 2 tablespoons butter in frypan. Add bread crumbs; brown lightly, stirring constantly. Sprinkle crumbs over sauce. Bake at 350 degrees for 20 to 25 minutes. Yield: 6 servings.

BROCCOLI ELEGANTE

2 10-oz. packages frozen cut broccoli
1/2 c. butter
3 egg yolks
2 tbsp. lemon juice
1/4 tsp. salt
1/4 tsp. onion salt
Dash of cayenne pepper

Cook broccoli according to package directions; drain and place in serving dish. Heat butter until bubbling. Place remaining ingredients except broccoli into blender container; cover. Blend at low speed until mixed; remove cover. Pour in bubbling butter in slow steady stream. Turn blender off immediately after all butter has been added. Serve over hot broccoli. Yield: 6 servings.

BROCCOLI FRY

1 bunch broccoli
1 clove of garlic, minced
2 tbsp. olive oil
Salt and pepper to taste

Trim broccoli; cook in boiling salted water for 10 minutes. Drain; rinse in cold water. Saute garlic in oil in skillet; remove garlic. Add broccoli; saute until tender. Season with salt and pepper; serve hot. Yield: 4 servings.

BROCCOLI WITH LINGUINE

3 cloves of garlic, minced
1/2 c. salad oil
2 tsp. salt
1/2 tsp. pepper
1 bunch broccoli

Broccoli and Eggs au Gratin . . . Broccoli and eggs are complemented by a rich cheese sauce.

1 8-oz. package linguine
1 3-oz. can chopped mushroom
1/2 c. grated Parmesan cheese

Combine garlic and oil in saucepan; cook over moderate heat. Add 1 quart water, salt and pepper; bring to a boil. Trim broccoli; cut into 1-inch pieces. Add to boiling water. Cook for 5 minutes. Add linguine and mushrooms with liquid; cook until barely tender and liquid is absorbed. Sprinkle with cheese; serve. Yield: 4 servings.

BROCCOLI RING

2 pkg. frozen chopped broccoli
1 clove of garlic, chopped
2 tbsp. butter
2 tbsp. flour
1 c. milk
4 eggs, separated

Cook broccoli with garlic according to package directions only until easily separated. Melt butter in skillet; stir in flour until smooth. Stir in milk gradually; cook, stirring constantly, until thickened. Cool. Add beaten egg yolks and broccoli. Fold in stiffly beaten egg whites; season to taste. Pour into greased and lightly floured ring mold; place in pan of hot water. Bake in 350-degree oven for 30 minutes or until knife inserted comes out clean. Yield: 8 servings.

BROCCOLI AND SHRIMP DELIGHT

1/4 c. chive cream cheese
1/4 c. milk
1 can frozen cream of shrimp soup
2 tbsp. lemon juice
1 10-oz. package frozen shrimp
2 10-oz. packages frozen broccoli spears
1/3 c. slivered almonds

Blend cream cheese and milk together. Thaw soup; combine cream cheese mixture and soup in saucepan. Cook over low heat, stirring, for about 10 minutes or until smooth and hot. Add lemon juice; cook for about 2 minutes longer. Thaw shrimp; add to sauce. Cook broccoli according to package directions; drain. Place broccoli in serving dish; pour sauce over broccoli. Garnish with almonds; serve. Yield: 6-8 servings.

BROCCOLI BAKE

2 pkg. frozen broccoli
1 c. grated Cheddar cheese
2/3 c. evaporated milk
1 can cream of mushroom soup
Onion rings

Cook broccoli according to package directions; drain. Arrange broccoli in casserole; sprinkle with cheese. Combine milk and soup, stirring well; pour over broccoli. Bake at 350 degrees for 25 minutes. Top with onion rings; bake for 10 minutes longer. Yield: 8 servings.

BROCCOLI AND GARLIC CHEESE

1 pkg. frozen broccoli
1/2 pkg. garlic cheese
2 tbsp. butter
1/2 can mushroom soup
1/2 c. buttered bread crumbs

Thaw broccoli until easily separated; place in greased baking dish. Mix cheese and butter; blend in soup. Pour sauce over broccoli. Sprinkle crumbs over sauce. Bake at 350 degrees for 30 minutes or until crumbs are brown.

BROCCOLI AND HAM CASSEROLE

1 10-oz. package chopped frozen broccoli
12 slices bread
3/4 lb. sliced sharp American cheese
2 c. diced cooked ham
6 eggs, lightly beaten
3 1/2 c. milk
2 tbsp. dry minced onion
1/2 tsp. salt
1/4 tsp. dry mustard

Cook broccoli according to package directions; drain. Cut bread with doughnut cutter; reserve holes and doughnuts. Tear remaining bread into bite-sized pieces; place in 13 x 9 x 2-inch pan. Arrange layers of cheese, broccoli and ham over bread; top with reserved doughnuts and holes. Combine remaining ingredients; pour over layers. Cover; refrigerate for 6 hours or overnight. Bake at 325 degrees for 55 minutes. Yield: 12 servings.

BROCCOLI WITH PARMESAN CRUST

3 10-oz. packages frozen chopped broccoli
2 cans cream of chicken soup
1/2 c. milk
1 1/2 tsp. salt
Pepper to taste
1 tbsp. lemon juice
1/4 c. potato flakes
1 tbsp. melted butter
1 tbsp. Parmesan cheese

Cook broccoli according to package directions; drain. Place in large shallow baking dish. Blend soup, milk, salt, pepper and lemon juice. Pour sauce over broccoli. Combine potato flakes, butter and cheese; sprinkle over broccoli. Bake at 350 degrees for 20 to 30 minutes or until topping is browned. Yield: 12 servings.

GLAZED BROCCOLI WITH ALMONDS

2 lb. broccoli
1 bouillon cube
4 tbsp. butter or margarine
4 tbsp. flour
1 c. cream
2 tbsp. sherry
2 tbsp. lemon juice
Pepper to taste
1/2 tsp. monosodium glutamate
1/4 c. grated Parmesan cheese
1/4 c. slivered toasted almonds

Trim and separate broccoli; cook in boiling salted water until just tender. Drain broccoli; arrange in shallow 8 x 12-inch casserole. Dissolve bouillon cube in 3/4 cup hot water. Melt butter; blend in flour. Stir in cream and bouillon mixture. Cook, stirring constantly, until smooth and thick. Add sherry, lemon juice, pepper and monosodium glutamate. Pour sauce over broccoli; sprinkle with cheese and almonds. Bake at 375 degrees for 20 minutes or until heated through. Yield: 6 servings.

BROCCOLI AND RICE

1 c. rice
1 onion, chopped
1 tbsp. oil
1/2 c. grated sharp Cheddar cheese
3/4 c. milk
1 tsp. salt
1 can cream of chicken soup
1 pkg. frozen chopped broccoli
Sliced mushrooms

Cook rice in 2 1/2 cups boiling salted water until tender. Brown onion in oil; add cheese, milk, salt and soup; heat, stirring, until cheese melts. Place rice in greased casserole. Cook broccoli according to package directions until partially done; drain. Arrange broccoli over rice. Pour soup mixture over broccoli mixture; top with mushrooms. Bake at 350 degrees for 30 minutes. Yield: 4-6 servings.

BROCCOLI IN SOUR CREAM

1 10-oz. package frozen chopped broccoli
1 tbsp. butter
1/4 c. sour cream
1/2 tsp. salt
1/8 tsp. pepper
3 tbsp. grated Parmesan cheese

Prepare broccoli according to package directions; cook until just tender. Drain. Combine broccoli, butter, sour cream, salt, pepper and cheese; mix well. Spoon broccoli mixture into small casserole; sprinkle with additional cheese. Bake at 350 degrees for 15 to 20 minutes. Yield: 4 servings.

CHEESY BROCCOLI CASSEROLE

1 8-oz. package cream cheese
1/2 c. grated Parmesan cheese
1 c. medium white sauce
2 pkg. broccoli
1 c. round buttery cracker crumbs

Soften cream cheese; blend with Parmesan cheese. Stir into hot white sauce until melted. Alternate layers of broccoli and cream cheese mixture in baking dish. Top with crumbs. Bake at 350 degrees for 30 minutes.

CRUSTY BROCCOLI

1 bunch broccoli, trimmed
1 c. medium white sauce
1/2 pkg. bread stuffing mix
1/2 c. grated Parmesan cheese

Cook broccoli for about 7 to 8 minutes in boiling salted water until partially done. Drain. Arrange broccoli in casserole. Pour white sauce over broccoli; top with stuffing mix and cheese. Bake at 325 degrees for about 30 minutes or until broccoli is tender. Yield: 4-6 servings.

QUICK BROCCOLI CASSEROLE

1 sm. diced onion
1/4 c. diced green pepper
2 tbsp. butter
3/4 c. cooked rice
1 sm. jar Cheez Whiz
1 sm. can evaporated milk
1 can cream of chicken soup
2 pkg. frozen chopped broccoli

Saute onion and green pepper in butter in skillet. Add rice, Cheez Whiz, milk and soup, stirring until Cheez Whiz is melted. Thaw broccoli; place in casserole. Spoon sauce over broccoli. Bake at 325 degrees for 30 minutes. Yield: 6 servings.

DEVILED BROCCOLI

2 pkg. frozen broccoli
1/4 lb. butter
2 tbsp. chili sauce
2 tbsp. Worcestershire sauce
2 tbsp. mustard

Prepare broccoli according to package directions; drain. Melt butter; add chili sauce, Worcestershire sauce and mustard, blending well. Pour sauce over broccoli just before serving. Yield: 8 servings.

GOLDENAISE BROCCOLI

2 hard-boiled egg yolks
2 pkg. frozen broccoli spears
1/2 c. mayonnaise
1 tbsp. lemon juice
1/2 tsp. onion salt
1/8 tsp. thyme

Sieve egg yolks. Prepare broccoli according to package directions. Combine mayonnaise, lemon juice, onion salt and thyme. Spoon over broccoli; sprinkle with egg yolks. Yield: 6-8 servings.

SURPRISE BROCCOLI MOLD

2 pkg. frozen broccoli
1 env. unflavored gelatin
1 can consomme
2 tbsp. minced onion
2 tbsp. lemon juice
1 c. mayonnaise
Salt and pepper to taste
2 hard-cooked eggs, finely chopped

Cook broccoli in 2 1/2 cups salted water for 20 minutes or until well done. Soften gelatin in 1/4 cup cold water. Dissolve gelatin in consomme in saucepan over low heat; cool. Combine onion, lemon juice, mayonnaise, salt and pepper with gelatin mixture; blend well. Fold broccoli and eggs into gelatin mixture. Pour into ring mold; chill until set. Yield: 6-8 servings.

Brownies

BLONDE BROWNIES

1 1/2 c. sifted flour
3/4 tsp. baking powder
1/4 tsp. soda
3/4 tsp. salt
1 c. chopped nuts
1/3 c. butter
1 1/2 c. (firmly packed) brown sugar
1 egg
1 1/2 tsp. vanilla
1 c. chocolate bits

Sift flour, baking powder, soda and salt together; stir in nuts. Melt butter in saucepan; stir in sugar. Beat in egg and vanilla; add flour mixture. Mix well; spread batter in greased 13 x 9 x 2-inch pan. Sprinkle chocolate bits over top. Bake at 350 degrees for 20 to 25 minutes. Cool; cut into bars.

CHOCOLATE-CREAM CHEESE BROWNIES

1/4 lb. sweet cooking chocolate
5 tbsp. butter
1 3-oz. package cream cheese
1 c. sugar
3 eggs
Flour
1 1/4 tsp. vanilla
1/4 tsp. salt
1/2 tsp. baking powder
1/2 c. chopped nuts
1/4 tsp. almond extract

Melt chocolate with 1 tablespoon butter; cool. Cream remaining butter and cream cheese; add 1/4 cup sugar gradually. Blend in 1 egg, 1 tablespoon flour and 1/4 teaspoon vanilla. Beat remaining eggs until thick; add remaining sugar, 1/2 cup flour, salt and baking powder. Blend in chocolate, nuts, remaining vanilla and almond extract. Measure 1 cup batter; reserve. Spread remaining batter in greased 9-inch square pan; top with cream cheese mixture. Drop reserved batter from tablespoon onto cheese mixture; swirl to marble. Bake at 350 degrees for 35 to 40 minutes. Cool and cut. Store in refrigerator. Yield: 20 brownies.

Fudge Brownies . . . Chocolaty rich and chewy, these are popular snack-time fare.

COUNTRY HOUSE BROWNIES

1/3 c. butter
1 c. brown sugar
1 egg
1/2 tsp. salt
3/4 c. sifted flour
1 tsp. baking powder
1/2 tsp. vanilla
1/2 c. coconut
1 6-oz. package chocolate chips
1/2 c. chopped nuts

Melt butter in saucepan; cool. Add brown sugar, egg, salt, flour, baking powder and vanilla. Mix well; add coconut, chocolate chips and nuts. Spread in greased 9-inch square pan. Bake at 350 degrees for 25 minutes. Yield: 12-16 servings.

FUDGE BROWNIES

2/3 c. sifted cake flour
1/2 tsp. baking powder
1/4 tsp. salt
2 eggs
1 c. sugar
1/4 c. corn oil
2 oz. unsweetened chocolate
1 tsp. vanilla
1/2 c. coarsely chopped nuts

Sift cake flour, baking powder and salt together; set aside. Beat eggs well in mixing bowl. Add sugar gradually, beating well. Mix in corn oil. Melt chocolate; add chocolate and vanilla to egg mixture. Stir in sifted dry ingredients and nuts, mixing well. Turn into greased 8-inch cake pan. Bake in 350-degree oven for about 35 minutes or until brownies test done. Cut into squares while warm. Yield: 16 brownies.

DIFFERENT BROWNIE BARS

2 c. fine graham cracker crumbs
1/2 c. chopped pecans
1/2 c. semisweet chocolate pieces
1/4 c. sugar
1/4 tsp. salt
1 c. skim milk
1 tbsp. confectioners sugar

Mix all ingredients except confectioners' sugar. Turn into lightly greased 9-inch square pan. Bake at 350 degrees for 30 minutes. Cut into bars while warm. Sprinkle with confectioners' sugar. Yield: 40 bars.

FROSTED BROWNIES

2 c. flour
2 c. sugar
1/2 tsp. salt
1 c. margarine
1/2 c. shortening
1 c. water
1/2 c. cocoa
Buttermilk
2 eggs, beaten
1 tsp. soda
2 tsp. vanilla
1 lb. confectioners' sugar

Mix flour, sugar and salt in bowl. Combine 1/2 cup margarine, shortening, water and 1/4 cup cocoa in saucepan; bring to a boil. Pour into flour mixture; add 1/2 cup buttermilk, eggs, soda and 1 teaspoon vanilla. Mix well; spread batter in greased 16 x 11 x 1-inch pan. Bake at 400 degrees for 20 minutes. Combine remaining margarine and cocoa in saucepan; add 1/3 cup buttermilk. Bring to a boil. Blend in confectioners' sugar and remaining vanilla; pour over warm brownies.

FUDGE SQUARES

Butter
1 c. (packed) brown sugar
3/4 c. self-rising flour
1/4 c. cocoa
2 tsp. vanilla
1 egg
1 c. shredded coconut
3/4 c. sweetened condensed milk
3 tbsp. milk
Powdered sugar

Melt 1/2 cup butter in saucepan; add brown sugar, flour, 2 tablespoons cocoa, 1 teaspoon vanilla and egg. Mix until smooth; spread batter in greased 8-inch square pan. Combine coconut and condensed milk; spread over batter. Bake at 350 degrees for 30 minutes. Combine 1 tablespoon butter and milk in saucepan; bring to a boil. Stir in remaining cocoa and vanilla; add enough powdered sugar to make of spreading consistency. Ice brownies while warm. Cool; cut into squares.

LAYERED FUDGE BARS

1/2 c. shortening
1 c. (packed) light brown sugar
1 egg
1 1/2 tsp. vanilla
3/4 c. flour
1/2 tsp. soda
3/4 tsp. salt
2 c. quick oats
1 6-oz. package chocolate chips
1 tbsp. butter
1 can sweetened condensed milk
1/2 c. chopped nuts

Cream shortening and sugar. Beat in egg and 1/2 teaspoon vanilla. Combine flour, soda and 1/4 teaspoon salt; add to creamed mixture. Stir in oats; reserve 1 cup oat mixture. Press remaining oat mixture against bottom of 10 x 7-inch pan. Combine chocolate chips, butter, condensed milk and remaining salt in top of double boiler. Stir over boiling water until chocolate chips are melted; add remaining vanilla and nuts. Spread over oat layer in pan; spread reserved oat mixture over top. Bake at 350 degrees for 25 minutes.

LAZY DAY BROWNIES

1 lge. box brownie mix
1 1/2 c. shredded coconut
1 1/2 c. chopped candied cherries

Prepare brownie mix according to package directions. Add coconut and cherries; mix well. Spread batter in greased 13 x 9 x 2-inch pan. Bake at 350 degrees for 35 minutes.

LOW-CAL FUDGE SQUARES

1/4 c. margarine or shortening
2 oz. unsweetened chocolate
1/4 c. liquid artificial sweetener
2 eggs, beaten
1 tsp. vanilla
1 1/2 c. package biscuit mix
1/2 c. chopped walnuts

Melt margarine and chocolate together; cool. Combine sweetener, eggs and vanilla; stir in biscuit mix, chocolate mixture and walnuts. Spread batter in greased 8-inch square pan. Bake at 325 degrees for 25 minutes. Cool; cut into squares.

MACAROON BROWNIES

1 lge. package brownie mix
1 pkg. macaroon mix

Prepare mixes separately, according to package directions. Spread half the brownie mix in greased 13 x 9-inch pan; cover with macaroon mix. Cover macaroon mix with remaining brownie mix. Bake at 350 degrees for 35 to 40 minutes.

MIRACLE BROWNIES

3/4 c. sifted flour
1 c. sugar
2 1/2 tbsp. cocoa
1/2 tsp. baking powder
3/4 tsp. salt
3/4 c. shortening
2 eggs
1 tsp. vanilla
1 tbsp. corn syrup
1 c. chopped nuts

Sift dry ingredients together into mixing bowl; add remaining ingredients except nuts. Beat at medium speed of electric mixer for 2 minutes; add nuts. Pour into greased 10 x 7-inch pan. Bake at 350 degrees for 25 minutes.

PEANUT BUTTER BROWNIES

1 c. brown sugar
1/3 c. sugar
3/4 c. shortening
1 c. peanut butter

2 eggs
2 tsp. vanilla
1/4 c. water
2 c. flour
1 tsp. baking powder
1 tsp. soda
3/4 tsp. salt

Cream sugars and shortening; add peanut butter, eggs, vanilla and water. Sift flour, baking powder, soda and salt together; add to peanut butter mixture. Spread in greased and floured 13 x 9 x 2-inch pan. Bake at 350 degrees for 25 to 30 minutes.

RAISIN BROWNIES

1/2 c. butter
2 sq. chocolate
1 c. sugar
2 eggs, well beaten
1 tsp. vanilla
1/2 c. flour
1/4 tsp. salt
1 c. chopped nuts
1 c. raisins

Preheat oven to 325 degrees. Melt butter and chocolate together. Add remaining ingredients in order listed. Spread batter in greased 9-inch square pan. Bake for 30 minutes. Cut into 18 squares while still warm.

RICH BROWNIES

4 eggs
2 c. sugar
1 c. sifted self-rising flour
1 c. chopped nuts
1 c. butter or margarine
3 sq. semisweet chocolate, melted

Beat eggs and sugar together; add flour and nuts. Stir in margarine and chocolate. Place batter in greased and floured 13 x 9-inch pan. Bake at 375 degrees for 35 minutes.

SPECIAL BROWNIES

1/2 c. margarine
3 tbsp. oil
7 tbsp. cocoa
1 c. water
2 c. flour
2 c. sugar
1 tsp. soda
1/2 c. buttermilk
1/4 tsp. salt
1/2 tsp. cinnamon
3 tsp. vanilla
2 eggs, beaten
1/2 c. chopped nuts
2 c. powdered sugar
2 tbsp. butter
2 tbsp. hot coffee

Combine margarine, oil, 4 tablespoons cocoa and water in saucepan; bring to a boil. Sift flour and sugar together; dissolve soda in buttermilk. Add to cocoa mixture; beat well. Add salt, cinnamon, 2 teaspoons vanilla, eggs and nuts; mix well. Pour batter into 15 x 11-inch cookie sheet. Bake at 400 degrees for 18 to 20 minutes. Combine powdered sugar, butter, remaining cocoa, remaining vanilla and coffee. Mix until smooth; frost brownies.

SPICE BROWNIES

1/2 c. sifted flour
1 tsp. baking powder
1/4 tsp. salt
1/4 tsp. allspice
1/4 tsp. nutmeg
1/2 tsp. cinnamon
1/4 c. margarine
1 c. (packed) brown sugar
1 egg
1/2 tsp. vanilla

Sift flour, baking powder, salt and spices together. Melt margarine over low heat; blend in sugar. Cool. Stir in egg, flour mixture and vanilla. Spread in greased and floured 8-inch square pan. Bake at 350 degrees for 30 minutes. Cool in pan for 10 minutes. Turn out; cut into squares.

SUNDAY BROWNIES

2 1/2 c. sugar
Margarine
4 eggs
1/4 tsp. salt
2 tsp. vanilla
1 1-lb. can chocolate syrup
1 c. flour
1/2 tsp. baking powder
1 c. chopped nuts
6 tbsp. milk
1/2 c. chocolate chips

Cream 1 cup sugar and 1 cup margarine until fluffy; beat in eggs, one at a time. Stir in salt, vanilla and chocolate syrup. Mix flour and baking powder; add flour mixture and nuts to chocolate mixture. Mix well; spread batter in greased 13 x 9 x 2-inch pan. Bake at 350 degrees for 30 minutes. Combine 6 tablespoons margarine, milk and remaining sugar in saucepan; bring to a boil. Add chocolate chips; remove from heat. Beat until chocolate chips are melted. Spread over brownies. Cool; cut into squares.

SURPRISE BROWNIES

1 1/2 c. flour
1/2 tsp. salt
1 c. chopped nuts
Margarine
1/2 c. cocoa
4 eggs
2 c. sugar
2 tsp. vanilla
1 lge. package miniature marshmallows
1 box powdered sugar
1/3 c. milk

Combine flour, salt and nuts. Melt 1 cup margarine in saucepan over low heat; blend in half the cocoa. Beat eggs until light; beat in sugar gradually. Stir in cocoa mixture and flour mixture. Add vanilla; mix well. Turn batter into greased 14 x 10 x 2-inch pan. Bake at 350 degrees for 35 to 40 minutes or until cake tests done. Turn oven off. Spread marshmallows evenly over hot cake. Let cake stand in oven until marshmallows are softened. Press marshmallows against cake, smoothing top. Cool cake. Soften 6 tablespoons margarine; blend in powdered sugar, remaining cocoa and milk. Frost brownies.

WAFFLE IRON BROWNIES

1/2 c. melted butter or margarine
1/4 c. cocoa
3/4 c. sugar
2 eggs, beaten
1 tbsp. water
1 1/4 c. flour
1/4 tsp. salt
2/3 c. chopped nuts
Powdered sugar

Blend butter and cocoa; stir in sugar, eggs and water. Add flour, salt and nuts; mix well. Drop from teaspoon onto heated waffle iron. Bake for about 1 minute and 30 seconds. Sprinkle with powdered sugar.

TRI-LEVEL BROWNIES

Flour
1/4 tsp. soda
1/2 tsp. salt
1 c. oats
1/2 c. (packed) brown sugar
3/4 c. butter
2 sq. unsweetened chocolate
3/4 c. sugar
1/4 tsp. baking powder
1 egg, beaten
1/4 c. milk
1 1/2 tsp. vanilla
1/2 c. chopped nuts
1 1/2 c. powdered sugar

Preheat oven to 350 degrees. Sift 1/2 cup flour, soda and 1/4 teaspoon salt together; add oats and brown sugar. Melt 6 tablespoons butter; stir into oat mixture. Press oat mixture into 10-inch square pan; bake for 10 minutes. Melt 4 tablespoons butter and 1 square chocolate together; stir in 2/3 cup flour, sugar, baking powder, remaining salt, egg, milk, 1/2 teaspoon vanilla and nuts. Mix well; pour batter over oat layer. Bake for 25 minutes; cool. Melt remaining butter and chocolate together; add powdered sugar and remaining vanilla. Mix until of spreading consistency, adding small amount of warm water, if needed. Frost brownies; cut into squares.

Brunswick Stew

From Brunswick County, Virginia, comes the popular hunter's stew of the same name. This stew was originally laden with succulent morsels of squirrel or rabbit, onions, corn, okra, lima beans, and tomatoes. However, the latter day version of Brunswick stew often substitutes chicken, pork or inner pork parts (or a combination of these meats) for the gamier ingredients. Simmering the meat until it has separated from the bone, blends flavors and creates the proper full-bodied taste and mushy texture.

BRUNSWICK STEW

1 6-lb. hen, disjointed
8 lb. potatoes, cubed
3 lb. onions, diced
2 No. 2 cans cream-style corn
4 No. 2 cans tomatoes
2 No. 2 cans green lima beans
2 cans tomato soup
Salt and pepper to taste

Simmer chicken in 4 quarts water until tender. Remove chicken from broth; reserve broth. Debone and dice chicken. Cook potatoes in water to cover until tender; drain and mash. Combine chicken, potatoes, onions and reserved broth in large kettle. Add corn, tomatoes, lima beans and soup to stew. Season with salt and pepper. Simmer, stirring occasionally, for 4 to 5 hours. Yield: 12 quarts.

EASY BRUNSWICK STEW

1 chicken, cut up
4 tbsp. flour
1/2 c. vegetable oil
1/2 c. chopped onion
3 c. canned tomatoes
1 1/2 tbsp. salt
1 tbsp. Worcestershire sauce
2 tsp. sugar
3 c. frozen corn
3 c. frozen lima beans

Shake chicken pieces in flour; saute in hot oil until brown. Add onion; cook until onion is transparent. Add tomatoes, 6 cups water, seasonings and sugar. Simmer until almost tender. Add corn and limas. Cook until vegetables are tender. Serve hot. Yield: 8 servings.

KENTUCKY BRUNSWICK STEW

1 lge. chicken
1 onion, chopped
4 lge. tomatoes
4 ears corn
4 biscuits, crumbled
Salt and pepper
1/2 c. butter

Simmer chicken and onion in water to cover until meat falls from bones. Remove chicken from broth. Debone chicken and shred meat; return to broth. Peel and chop tomatoes; cut corn from cob. Combine tomatoes, corn, biscuits, salt and pepper to taste and butter with chicken mixture. Simmer, stirring occasionally, until vegetables are tender and stew is thickened. Yield: 6 servings.

VIRGINIA BRUNSWICK STEW

1 fryer
1 squirrel
1 lge. onion, chopped fine
12 lge. tomatoes, chopped
3 c. butter beans
1/2 lb. butter
2 c. corn
2 c. chopped potatoes
1 tbsp. salt
1/2 tsp. pepper
1 tbsp. sugar

Disjoint fryer and squirrel; brown well in small amount of hot fat in skillet. Place in large kettle with 1 gallon water. Simmer until meat falls from bones. Remove bones; shred meat. Return meat to broth; add onion, tomatoes, butter beans and butter. Simmer, stirring occasionally, for 3 hours. Add corn, potatoes and seasonings. Simmer for 30 minutes longer.

Brussels Sprouts

A member of the cabbage family, Brussels sprouts have leaves that form small green heads (sprouts). They resemble miniature cabbages. Brussels sprouts are rich in Vitamin C (one serving provides nearly half the adult daily minimum requirement) calcium, iron, and riboflavin. (An average serving has less than 40 calories)

AVAILABILITY: Fresh Brussels sprouts are available during the fall until the end of the winter; peak months are October-December. Frozen Brussels sprouts are available year-round.

BUYING: Choose small to medium-sized sprouts that are bright green, firm, compact, and well-formed. Avoid sprouts with discolored leaves—an indication of inferior quality—or sprouts that are soft, open-leaved, or blemished. One pound of fresh Brussels sprouts yields 4 servings.

STORING: Brussels sprouts are highly perishable. After wrapping in clear plastic or a cellophane bag, store them no longer than 2 days in the refrigerator. *To freeze* Brussels sprouts, cut off stems and remove coarse outer leaves. Wash. Boil for 3-5 minutes (the longer time for larger sprouts) and chill in iced water for 5 minutes. Package in freezer container and freeze. One pound of Brussels sprouts yields one pint frozen vegetables. Use within 11 months.

PREPARATION: Cut off stems and remove wilted or discolored outer leaves. Wash under cold running water. Cook covered or uncovered in a small amount of boiling salted water until tender—10-15 minutes. Do not overcook—it destroys the fine, distinctive flavor.

SERVING: Serve as side dish vegetable, particularly with fish. Also used in salads, casseroles, and souffles. May also be served raw as an appetizer.

(See VEGETABLES.)

BRUSSELS SPROUTS AND CARROTS

2 pkg. frozen Brussels sprouts
4 carrots, sliced
1 tsp. salt
1 can cream of mushroom soup
1/2 c. grated cheese

Cook Brussels sprouts and carrots in 1/2 cup boiling salted water until tender. Add soup; heat through. Sprinkle with cheese. Toss lightly and serve immediately. Yield: 6-8 servings.

BRUSSELS SPROUTS IN CELERY SAUCE

2 qt. Brussels sprouts
1 1/4 tsp. salt
1 1/2 c. diced celery
2 c. milk
6 tbsp. butter
6 tbsp. flour
Dash of pepper

Cook Brussels sprouts in boiling water with 1 teaspoon salt until tender. Drain and keep warm. Cook celery in boiling water with remaining salt until tender. Drain celery, reserving 1 cup cooking water. Combine milk and reserved cooking water. Melt butter in saucepan; blend in flour. Add milk mixture gradually; cook, stirring constantly, until smooth and thickened. Stir in pepper and celery; pour over Brussels sprouts. Yield: 8 servings.

BRUSSELS SPROUTS WITH GRAPES

2 pkg. frozen Brussels sprouts
3/4 c. sour cream
1/2 c. slivered almonds
2/3 c. canned sliced mushrooms
1 c. seedless white grapes
1/4 c. chopped pimento
1 tsp. sugar
2 tsp. salt
1/2 tsp. pepper
3/4 c. grated American cheese
Paprika

Cook Brussels sprouts according to package directions; drain. Place in top of double boiler; add sour cream, almonds, mushrooms, grapes, pimento, sugar, salt and pepper. Heat for 7 minutes. Place in serving dish; sprinkle with cheese and paprika. Yield: 8-10 servings.

BRUSSELS SPROUTS POLONAISE

2 lb. Brussels sprouts
1/4 c. butter or margarine
1/4 c. fine dry bread crumbs
1 hard-cooked egg yolk, sieved
2 tbsp. minced parsley

Cut any large Brussels sprouts in half. Cook, uncovered, in boiling salted water for 12 to 15 minutes or until just tender. Drain. Place in serving dish; keep warm. Brown butter lightly in small saucepan; stir in bread crumbs, egg yolk and parsley. Spoon crumb mixture over Brussels sprouts; toss lightly. Yield: 6-8 servings.

SUNDAY BRUSSELS SPROUTS

Color photograph for this recipe on page 310.

1 qt. fresh Brussels sprouts
1 1/4 tsp. salt
3 tbsp. butter
1/8 tsp. pepper
Cheesed Noodle Ring

Trim Brussels sprouts; place in saucepan containing 1 inch boiling water and salt. Bring to a boil; cook for 5 minutes. Cover; cook for 15 minutes longer or until Brussels sprouts are crisp but tender. Drain. Add butter and pepper; toss lightly. Pile in center of Cheesed Noodle Ring.

Cheesed Noodle Ring

1 lb. noodles
1 tsp. salt
3 tbsp. butter
2 c. shredded cheese
1 1/2 tsp. Worcestershire sauce

Cook noodles in boiling salted water until tender; drain. Add butter to noodles; toss until butter has melted. Pour into greased ring mold. Place mold in pan of hot water. Bake at 350 degrees for 25 minutes. Unmold onto serving plate. Melt cheese; stir in Worcestershire sauce. Pour over noodle ring. Yield: 6 servings.

Brussels Sprouts Country Pie . . . Lend excitement to vegetables by preparing this pie.

BRUSSELS SPROUTS COUNTRY PIE

3 10-oz. packages frozen California Brussels sprouts
1/4 c. butter
1/4 c. all-purpose flour
1 tsp. salt
1 tsp. celery seed
1 tsp. dry mustard
1/4 tsp. pepper
2 c. milk
1/4 c. grated Parmesan cheese
1 1-lb. can whole onions

Cook Brussels sprouts according to package directions until just tender; drain. Melt butter in large saucepan. Combine flour with seasonings; blend into melted butter. Add milk gradually; stir over low heat until thickened. Blend in cheese until melted. Drain onions; add onions and Brussels sprouts to sauce. Cool.

Pastry

2 c. sifted flour
1 tsp. salt
1/2 c. grated Parmesan cheese
2/3 c. shortening
5 to 6 tbsp. cold water

Combine flour, salt and cheese; cut in shortening. Add water and blend lightly. Shape pastry into 2 balls; roll out between waxed paper into two 10 1/4-inch circles. Line 9-inch pie plate with one pastry circle; add Brussels sprouts filling. Top with remaining pastry circle; pinch and flute edges. May brush pastry with lightly beaten egg white if desired. Cut five 1 1/2-inch slits in top pastry. Bake in 425-degree oven for 30 minutes or until pastry is golden brown. Serve hot.

BRUSSELS SPROUTS IN WINE AND RAISINS

2/3 c. golden seedless raisins
2/3 c. dry white wine
4 10-oz. packages Brussels sprouts
1/2 tsp. salt
Dash of pepper
Dash of nutmeg
2 tbsp. butter

Combine raisins and wine; let stand for 1 hour. Cook Brussels sprouts according to package directions until almost tender; drain. Combine wine mixture, Brussels sprouts, seasonings and butter in saucepan. Cook over low heat for 5 minutes; serve with roast goose. Yield: 8 servings

BRUSSELS SPROUTS WITH TURNIPS

2 oz. salt pork
4 c. peeled sliced turnips
3/4 tsp. salt
3 tbsp. sugar
1 pkg. frozen Brussels sprouts
1 tbsp. butter
1/4 tsp. dry mustard
1/2 tsp. horseradish

Boil salt pork in 1 1/2 cups water for 20 minutes. Add turnips; reduce heat. Simmer for 30 minutes or until turnips are tender. Remove salt pork; drain turnips. Season turnips with salt and 2 1/2 tablespoons sugar. Turn into serving dish; keep warm. Cook Brussels sprouts according to package directions; drain. Season with butter, remaining sugar, mustard and horseradish; spoon over turnips. Yield: 6-8 servings.

BRUSSELS SPROUTS WITH WATER CHESTNUTS

2 tbsp. butter
2 tsp. flour
3/4 c. chicken broth
Salt
Pinch of white pepper
1/4 tsp. basil
3 lb. Brussels sprouts
1 c. sliced canned water chestnuts

Melt butter in small saucepan; blend in flour. Cook, stirring, for 1 minute; do not brown. Add chicken broth gradually; cook, stirring constantly, until thickened. Season sauce with 1/4 teaspoon salt, white pepper and basil; keep warm. Cook Brussels sprouts in boiling salted water until tender. Drain well; place in serving dish. Stir water chestnuts into sauce; pour over Brussels sprouts. Yield: 8 servings.

BRUSSELS SPROUTS WITH YAM FRILL

1/2 c. brown sugar
5 tbsp. butter, melted
3/4 c. orange juice
3 tbsp. grated orange peel
1/2 tsp. nutmeg
1/2 tsp. allspice
8 cooked yams, mashed
2 10-oz. packages frozen Brussels sprouts
1/4 tsp. white pepper

Blend sugar, 2 tablespoons butter, 1/4 cup orange juice, 2 tablespoons orange peel, 1/4 teaspoon nutmeg and 1/8 teaspoon allspice into yams; whip until light and fluffy. Heat to serving temperature; keep hot. Cook Brussels sprouts according to package directions; drain. Toss gently with remaining butter, orange juice, orange peel, nutmeg, allspice and white pepper. Turn onto warm serving dish; circle with yam mixture. Yield: 6-8 servings.

BAKED BRUSSELS SPROUTS

1 1-pt. box frozen Brussels sprouts
Salt
1/4 c. chopped green pepper
1 1/2 c. chopped celery
1 tbsp. margarine
1/2 c. milk
1/2 c. Cheddar cheese soup
3 drops of hot pepper sauce
1/2 tsp. Worcestershire sauce
Dash of pepper
1/2 c. bread crumbs

Cook Brussels sprouts in boiling salted water until tender; drain. Place in 1 1/2-quart casserole. Saute green pepper and celery in margarine; add milk, soup, hot sauce, Worcestershire sauce, 1/4 teaspoon salt and pepper. Bring to a boil; pour over Brussels sprouts. Top with bread crumbs. Bake at 400 degrees for 30 minutes. Yield: 6-8 servings.

FLAVORFUL BRUSSELS SPROUTS

2 boxes frozen Brussels sprouts
4 strips bacon
1 med. onion, chopped
1 pt. sour cream

Cook Brussels sprouts according to package directions; drain. Fry bacon until crisp; remove bacon from skillet. Sauce onion in bacon drippings; stir in sour cream. Pour sour cream mixture over Brussels sprouts. Place in casserole. Bake at 325 degrees for 30 minutes. Crumble bacon over top before serving. Yield: 8 servings.

BRUSSELS SPROUTS AU GRATIN

2 10-oz. packages frozen Brussels sprouts
1 c. boiling water
1 tsp. salt
1/2 c. grated sharp process cheese
1/4 c. butter or margarine
1/4 c. packaged seasoned dry bread crumbs
1/3 c. chopped walnuts

Cook Brussels sprouts in boiling, salted water for 5 minutes. Drain; turn into greased 1 1/2-quart casserole. Sprinkle with cheese. Melt butter in small pan; add bread crumbs and walnuts. Cook, stirring, until lightly browned. Sprinkle over Brussels sprouts. Bake at 400 degrees for 10 minutes. Yield: 6 servings.

COUNTRY SPROUTS

1 pt. Brussels sprouts
Salt to taste
1 tbsp. sugar
1 tbsp. cider vinegar
1 tsp. crushed dried tarragon

Halve Brussels sprouts lengthwise. Cook in boiling salted water for 12 minutes or until tender. Drain, reserving 1 tablespoon cooking water. Combine reserved cooking water, sugar, vinegar and tarragon; sprinkle over Brussels sprouts. Toss lightly; serve immediately. Yield: 4 servings.

DEVILED BRUSSELS SPROUTS

2 10-oz. packages frozen Brussels sprouts
1/3 c. butter or margarine
2 tsp. prepared mustard
1 tbsp. Worcestershire sauce
2 tbsp. chili sauce

Cook Brussels sprouts, covered, in small amount boiling salted water for 15 minutes or until tender; drain. Melt butter; stir in remaining ingredients. Pour over Brussels sprouts. Yield: 6 servings.

FRENCH SPROUTS

1 lb. chestnuts
1 qt. Brussels sprouts
1/4 c. melted butter or margarine

Cut gash in flat side of each chestnut; mix with small amount oil in pan. Bake at 350 degrees for 10 minutes. Remove shells and skins with sharp knife. Cook chestnuts and sprouts in small amount boiling salted water for 20 minutes or until sprouts are tender; drain. Add butter. Yield: 4 servings.

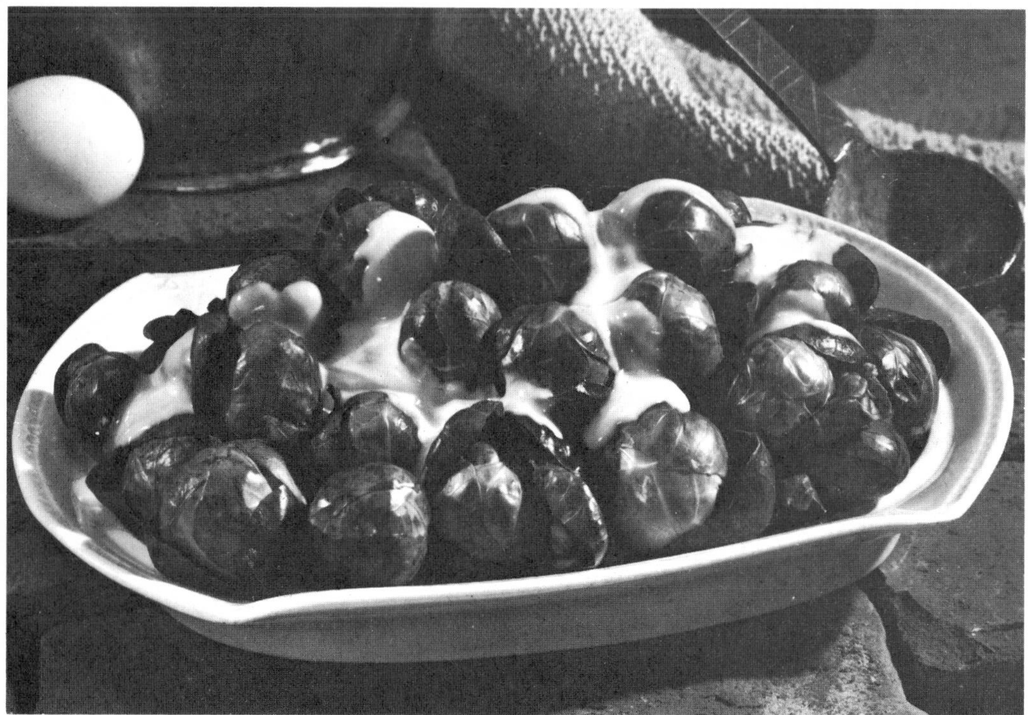

Brussels Sprouts with Hollandaise . . . An elegant dish perfect for a special dinner or buffet.

BRUSSELS SPROUTS WITH HOLLANDAISE

2 10-oz. packages frozen California Brussels sprouts
3 whole cloves
1/4 tsp. grated lemon peel
Dash of white pepper
3 egg yolks
1/4 tsp. salt
Dash of cayenne pepper
2 tbsp. lemon juice
1/2 c. butter, melted

Prepare Brussels sprouts according to package directions, cooking with cloves, lemon peel and white pepper until just tender. Drain; keep warm. Blend egg yolks, salt and cayenne pepper in electric blender for 5 seconds. Blend in lemon juice at low speed. Heat butter until bubbling; add hot butter gradually, blending until thick. Pour into heat-proof dish; keep warm over hot water, stirring occasionally. Serve over hot Brussels sprouts.

NUTMEG BRUSSELS SPROUTS

1 qt. fresh Brussels sprouts
1 1/4 tsp. salt
3 tbsp. butter
1 tsp. ground nutmeg
1/8 tsp. pepper

Place Brussels sprouts in saucepan containing 1 inch boiling water and salt; bring to a boil again. Cook for 5 minutes. Cover; cook for 15 minutes or until Brussels sprouts are tender. Drain. Add butter, nutmeg and pepper; toss lightly. Yield: 6 servings.

ROYAL BRUSSELS SPROUTS

2 10-oz. packages frozen Brussels sprouts
1 5-oz. can water chestnuts
2 tsp. salt
1 tsp. sugar
1/2 tsp. seasoned salt
1/2 c. minced parsley
1/4 c. butter

Halve larger sprouts. Drain and chop chestnuts, reserving fluid. Add enough water to chestnut fluid to equal 1 cup liquid. Pour liquid into saucepan; add salt, sugar, seasoned salt and parsley. Bring to a boil. Add sprouts. Cover; reduce heat. Simmer for 8 to 10 minutes. Drain; add chestnuts and butter. Toss lightly. Yield: 6-8 servings.

VINEYARD BRUSSELS SPROUTS

2 10-oz. packages frozen Brussels sprouts
1 1/2 tsp. salt
2 tsp. sugar
1/4 c. butter
Freshly ground pepper
1/4 clove of garlic, crushed
1 c. halved green grapes
2 tsp. honey

Cook Brussels sprouts for 2 minutes less than package instructions. Drain; add salt, sugar, 1 tablespoon butter, pepper and garlic. Combine remaining butter, grapes and honey in skillet; place over low heat until butter is bubbly. Add Brussels sprouts; toss gently. Serve immediately. Yield: 6-8 servings.

QUICK BRUSSELS SPROUTS

1 pkg. frozen Brussels sprouts
1 c. croutons
2 tbsp. melted butter
2 tbsp. minced parsley
1/2 tsp. salt
Grated Parmesan cheese

Cook Brussels sprouts according to package directions; drain well. Toss croutons with melted butter. Combine croutons, Brussels sprouts, parsley and salt; toss gently. Place in warm serving dish; sprinkle generously with cheese. Serve immediately. Yield: 4 servings.

Buttermilk

Rich-bodied and thick, buttermilk is the delicious and nourishing liquid that remains after butter is churned. The term is also applied to the culturally prepared milk product which is available commercially. Some buttermilks have butter granules added for flavor and eye appeal. Buttermilk contains all the food nutrients essential for health and well-being and is low in calories. (Generally, 8 ounces buttermilk = 90-112 calories)

AVAILABILITY: Available year-round.

STORING: Store immediately in the coldest part of the refrigerator. Cover or seal tightly as buttermilk easily absorbs odors and flavors from surrounding foods. Do not store more than 4 days—the longer the period of refrigeration, the greater the increase in acidity and the consequent loss of flavor. Freezing is not recommended because the whey separates from the milk solids. If you do freeze buttermilk, stir gently after thawing to recombine whey and solids.

SERVING: Chilled buttermilk is a delicious beverage. It is also used as an ingredient in many food recipes. Buttermilk can be substituted in any recipe that calls for sour milk.

BLUSHING BUTTERMILK

1/2 c. tomato juice
1/2 c. buttermilk
Dash of lemon juice

Combine tomato juice, buttermilk and lemon juice; blend thoroughly. Chill until ready to serve. Yield: 1 serving.

BUTTERMILK

1 c. nonfat dry milk
3 3/4 c. water
1/2 c. buttermilk
Pinch of salt

Mix milk with water; add buttermilk and salt. Stir well; cover and let stand at room temperature overnight. Stir until smooth; refrigerate until ready to serve. Yield: 4-5 servings.

COLD BUTTERMILK SOUP

2 egg yolks
1/3 c. sugar
1 qt. buttermilk
1 tsp. lemon juice
1 c. heavy cream, whipped
1 c. slivered almonds
Strawberry jam

Beat egg yolks until thick and lemon colored; add sugar, small amount at a time, beating well after each addition. Fold in buttermilk and lemon juice; chill. Garnish with whipped cream, almonds and strawberry jam. Yield: 6 servings.

DIETER'S CUCUMBER BUTTERMILK

2 cucumbers
1 qt. buttermilk
1 tbsp. chopped onion
1/4 c. snipped parsley
1 tsp. salt
Pepper to taste

Pare and remove seeds from cucumbers; grate cucumbers. Combine buttermilk, onion, parsley, salt and pepper with cucumbers; blend well. Chill, covered, until ready to serve. Yield: 4 servings.

BUTTERMILK-VEGETABLE MOLD

2 packages unflavored gelatin
4 tsp. vinegar
1/2 tsp. salt
2 c. buttermilk
1 c. grated carrots
1 c. diced celery
1 c. grated cucumber
Stuffed olive slices
8 cucumber slices
Cottage cheese

Soften gelatin in 1/2 cup cold water. Dissolve gelatin in 1 cup boiling water. Add vinegar, salt and buttermilk; mix well. Chill until partially set. Fold in carrots, celery and cucumber. Arrange olive and cucumber slices in bottom of 1-quart ring mold. Pour gelatin mixture carefully into mold. Chill until firm. Unmold; garnish with additional olive slices. Fill center with cottage cheese. Yield: 6-8 servings.

BUTTERMILK FRIED CAKES

2 c. sugar
2 eggs
3 tbsp. melted shortening
1 1/2 c. buttermilk
1 tsp. vanilla
1 tsp. soda
1 tsp. baking powder
1/2 tsp. salt
1/2 tsp. nutmeg
6 1/2 c. sifted flour

Beat sugar and eggs with shortening; add buttermilk and vanilla. Sift dry ingredients together. Add to sugar mixture; blend well. Roll dough to 1/4-inch thickness on floured board; cut into rounds. Fry in deep 375-degree fat for 3 minutes, turning once; drain on absorbent toweling. May be sprinkled with sugar if desired. Yield: 5 dozen cakes.

BUTTERMILK CAKE

1/2 c. shortening
1 1/2 c. sugar
2 eggs, well beaten
2 c. cake flour
1 tsp. soda
1 tsp. baking powder
1/8 tsp. salt
1 1/4 c. buttermilk
4 tbsp. grated orange rind
1/2 c. chopped nuts

Cream shortening and sugar. Add eggs; beat well. Sift dry ingredients together; add alternately with buttermilk. Add rind and nuts. Pour into greased loaf pan. Bake at 350 degrees for 45 minutes or until cake tests done. Remove from oven; prick top of cake with fork.

Glaze

2 1/2 c. confectioners' sugar
3 tbsp. butter, melted
1/3 c. orange juice

Combine confectioners' sugar, butter and orange juice; blend well. Spread glaze over cake.

BUTTERMILK MORSEL CAKE

Butter
1/2 c. graham cracker crumbs
1/2 c. chopped walnuts
1 6-oz. package chocolate morsels
2 c. sifted flour
1 tsp. soda
1 tsp. salt
Sugar
2 eggs
1 tsp. vanilla
1 1/4 c. buttermilk
1 c. heavy cream

Melt 1/3 cup butter; toss in crumbs. Stir in walnuts and 1/3 cup chocolate morsels. Melt remaining chocolate morsels. Combine flour, soda and salt. Cream 1/2 cup butter; add 1 1/2 cups sugar gradually. Cream well. Add eggs, one at a time, beating well after each addition. Blend in melted chocolate and vanilla. Add dry ingredients alternately with buttermilk; beat well. Turn into 2 greased and floured 9-inch cake pans. Sprinkle with crumb mixture. Bake at 375 degrees for 30 to 40 minutes. Cool. Beat cream with 2 tablespoons sugar until stiff peaks form. Spread filling between layers and around side of cake. Keep refrigerated.

BUTTERMILK WHITE CAKE

1/2 c. margarine
2 c. sugar
2 egg whites
2 3/4 c. cake flour
1/2 tsp. salt
1 3/4 c. buttermilk
1 tsp. soda
1 tsp. vanilla

Cream margarine; add sugar gradually. Add egg whites; blend well. Sift flour with salt. Combine buttermilk, soda and vanilla. Add flour mixture and buttermilk mixture alternately to sugar mixture. Pour into loaf pan. Bake at 350 degrees for 30 minutes or until cake tests done.

Icing

2 egg yolks, well beaten
2 tbsp. butter, melted
2 tbsp. thick cream
1 tsp. vanilla
Confectioners' sugar

Blend all ingredients, adding enough confectioners' sugar to make a spreading consistency.

LEMON-BUTTERMILK CAKE

1 c. shortening
1/2 c. butter
3 c. sugar
4 eggs
3 1/2 c. sifted flour
1/2 tsp. salt
1 c. buttermilk
1 tsp. lemon extract
1/2 tsp. soda
Juice and grated rind of 1 lemon

Cream shortening, butter and 2 1/2 cups sugar until fluffy. Beat in eggs, one at a time. Sift flour and salt together. Combine buttermilk and lemon extract. Add flour mixture to creamed mixture alternately with buttermilk mixture. Dissolve soda in 1 tablespoon hot water; stir into batter. Pour batter into greased and floured tube pan. Bake at 325 degrees for 1 hour and 15 minutes. Combine remaining sugar, lemon juice, lemon rind and 1/2 cup hot water in saucepan. Cook, stirring, until sugar is dissolved and syrup is clear. Pour hot syrup over hot cake. Yield: 20 servings.

BUTTERMILK CANDY

2 c. sugar
1 c. buttermilk
2 tbsp. light corn syrup
1 tsp. soda
1 stick butter or margarine
1 tsp. vanilla
Pinch of salt
1 c. chopped pecans

Combine sugar, buttermilk, syrup, soda and butter in large pan. Cook to soft-ball stage; remove from heat. Add vanilla and salt; beat well. Add pecans; drop from teaspoon onto waxed paper. Cool.

SUPERB BUTTERMILK CANDY

2 c. sugar
1 c. buttermilk
1 tsp. soda
1/4 tsp. salt
1 c. chopped nuts

Combine sugar, buttermilk, soda and salt. Bring to a boil, stirring constantly. Cook for about 7 minutes or to the soft-ball stage. Add nuts and beat until candy thickens. Pour onto waxed paper. Cut into squares. Yield: 2 pounds candy.

BUTTERMILK PIE WITH APRICOT GLAZE

1 can apricot halves
1 c. sugar
1/4 c. flour
1/2 tsp. salt
1/4 tsp. mace
1/4 tsp. cinnamon
2 c. buttermilk
3 eggs, well beaten
1 9-in. unbaked pie shell
4 tsp. cornstarch
1/3 c. orange marmalade

Drain apricots; reserve 1 cup juice. Combine sugar, flour, salt, mace and cinnamon with buttermilk in top of double boiler. Place over boiling water; cook, stirring constantly until mixture is smooth. Stir small amount of hot mixture into eggs; add egg mixture to hot mixture. Return to heat; cook, stirring constantly until thickened. Pour buttermilk mixture into pie shell. Bake at 325 degrees for 50 minutes or until filling is set. Remove from oven; cool. Mix 1/4 cup reserved syrup and cornstarch until smooth. Bring remaining syrup to a boil; add cornstarch mixture, stirring constantly. Cook until thickened. Remove from heat; blend in marmalade. Arrange apricot halves, cut side down, on top of pie. Cover with glaze. Serve with whipped cream, if desired. Yield: 6 servings.

MOCK BUTTERMILK PIE

1/2 stick butter
1 1/2 c. sugar
1/4 c. flour
1/4 tsp. salt
3 eggs
1/2 c. milk
1 tsp. vinegar
1 1/2 tsp. vanilla
1 unbaked pie shell

Cream butter with sugar, flour and salt. Add eggs, one at a time, beating well after each addition. Combine milk, vinegar and vanilla with creamed mixture. Pour into pie shell. Bake at 350 degrees for 45 minutes. Yield: 6-8 servings.

Butters

Flavored butters are classed as either compound or fruit butters. The former actually contain butter; the latter is a blend of fruit and sugar.

COMPOUND: Butter creamed with other ingredients or flavorings such as parsley, garlic, or honey. Compound butters make finishing touches for hors d'oeuvres and nutritious snack spreads. They also flavor meat and vegetable dishes. Refrigerate in closed jar until ready to use.

FRUIT: Wholesome spreads with a large fruit and small sugar content. Fruit butters may be apple, grape, plum, peach, and so on. To prepare: cook fruit until soft. Sieve and add sugar. Cook until smooth and thick.

APPLE BUTTER

1/2 c. bottled lemon juice
13 c. apple pulp
8 c. sugar
Dash of cinnamon
Dash of cloves

Mix all ingredients in large roaster. Bake, uncovered, at 350 degrees for 3 hours. Seal in hot sterilized jars.

BANANA BUTTER

3 c. ripe banana pulp
6 1/2 c. sugar
1/4 tsp. butter
Juice of 1 lemon
1 bottle pectin

Place pulp in preserving kettle; stir in sugar, butter and lemon juice. Mix well; bring to a boil, stirring constantly. Add pectin, stirring constantly; bring to a full rolling boil. Boil for 1 minute, stirring constantly from bottom of kettle to prevent sticking. Remove from heat; stir frequently for 8 minutes. Cool slightly; pour into hot sterilized jars. Seal with paraffin.

CINNAMON-APPLE BUTTER

3 qt. canned applesauce
10 c. sugar
1/2 c. vinegar
1 c. cinnamon candies

Combine all ingredients in large kettle; mix well. Simmer for 20 to 25 minutes or until candies dissolve and mixture is thick. Pour into hot jars; seal. Yield: 6 pints.

GRAPE BUTTER

1 pt. blue grapes
1 pt. sugar

Combine grapes and sugar in large saucepan. Bring to a boil, stirring occasionally. Boil rapidly for 20 minutes. Sieve. Seal in hot sterilized jars.

LEMON BUTTER

6 c. eggs
2 c. sugar
Juice of 3 lemons
Grated lemon rind
1/2 c. butter

Beat eggs and sugar until fluffy in top of double boiler. Add lemon juice and rind. Place over boiling water; cook, stirring, until thickened. Add butter; cool. Place in jar; store in refrigerator. Yield: 8 servings.

PEACH BUTTER

Fully ripe peaches
Sugar
Cinnamon to taste

Scald and pit peaches. Place in kettle, adding very small amount of water. Cook, stirring frequently, until mushy. Press peach pulp through sieve or food mill. Measure pulp into saucepan; add 1 cup sugar for each cup peach pulp. Simmer, stirring frequently, for 30 minutes; add cinnamon. Simmer, stirring, for 30 minutes longer or until thickened. Pour into hot sterilized jars; seal.

PEAR BUTTER

1/2 c. sugar
3 c. ground pears
1/2 tsp. cinnamon

Combine sugar and pears in saucepan. Cook, stirring, for 15 minutes. Add cinnamon; cook until thick, stirring frequently. Pour into hot sterilized 1-pint jar; seal.

TOMATO BUTTER

5 lb. peeled tomatoes, sliced
1 c. vinegar
3 c. sugar
1 sm. stick cinnamon
1/4 oz. gingerroot
1/2 tbsp. whole cloves

Combine tomatoes, vinegar and sugar in large kettle; mix well. Tie spices in small cloth bag; add to kettle. Cook, stirring constantly, until thickened. Pour into hot sterilized jars; seal.

WILD PLUM BUTTER

Wild plums
Water
Sugar

Place plums in large kettle. Cover with water; bring to a boil. Pour off water; add fresh water. Cook until skins pop, adding water as needed. Cook, stirring, until thickened. Press through a sieve; measure pulp into another kettle. Add 2 cups sugar for each cup pulp. Cook until thick; seal in hot sterilized jars.

Butterscotch

Almost as popular as chocolate, butterscotch is a sweet, smooth flavoring that is created when butter and brown sugar are combined under heat. It is a favorite flavor in cakes, cookies, puddings, pie fillings, frostings, sauces, and ice cream toppings.

BUTTERSCOTCH APPLES

6 med. apples
1 c. sugar
2 tbsp. flour
1 c. water
3 tbsp. butter
Pinch of salt
2 tsp. vanilla
Cinnamon to taste
12 marshmallows

Peel, core and halve apples; place in baking dish. Mix sugar, flour and water in saucepan; cook, stirring, until thickened. Add butter, salt and vanilla. Sprinkle apples with cinnamon; pour sauce over apples. Bake at 375 degrees until apples are tender. Place marshmallows on apples; bake until marshmallows are melted.

BUTTERSCOTCH MERINGUE PIE

1 c. (packed) brown sugar
1/2 c. flour
1/2 tsp. salt
2 c. milk, scalded
3 eggs, separated
3 tbsp. butter
1 tsp. vanilla
1 baked pastry shell
1/4 c. sugar

Combine brown sugar, flour and salt in top of double boiler; stir in milk gradually. Cook until thick, stirring constantly; remove from heat. Stir small amount of hot mixture into beaten egg yolks; return to hot mixture. Return boiler to heat; cook for 2 minutes longer, stirring constantly. Add butter and vanilla. Pour filling into pastry shell. Beat egg whites until stiff, beating in sugar gradually. Spread meringue over pie filling, sealing to edge of shell. Bake at 350 degrees for 12 minutes or until meringue is browned.

BAKED BUTTERSCOTCH PUDDING CAKE

Flour
1 1/2 tsp. baking powder
1/2 tsp. salt
1/4 c. margarine
1/3 c. sugar
2 eggs, separated
1 tsp. vanilla
1/2 c. milk
1 1/2 c. brown sugar
1 1/2 c. boiling water

Sift 1 cup flour, baking powder and salt together. Cream margarine and sugar until fluffy; beat in egg yolks and vanilla. Add flour mixture alternately with milk; mix well. Beat egg whites until stiff; fold into batter. Turn batter into greased 8-inch square pan. Mix brown sugar and 3 tablespoons flour; stir in boiling water. Pour mixture over batter; do not stir. Bake at 350 degrees for 1 hour. Serve warm. Yield: 4-6 servings.

BUTTERSCOTCH-NUT CAKE

6 eggs, separated
1 1/2 c. sugar
1/4 c. water
1 tsp. baking powder
2 tsp. vanilla
1 tsp. almond flavoring
2 c. graham cracker crumbs
1 c. chopped walnuts
1 pt. heavy cream
3 tbsp. powdered sugar

Line 13 x 10 x 2-inch pan with waxed paper. Beat egg yolks until lemon colored; beat in sugar, water, baking powder and flavorings. Beat egg whites to stiff peaks; fold in egg yolk mixture, cracker crumbs and walnuts. Pour into prepared pan. Bake at 325 degrees for 30 to 35 minutes. Cool for 10 minutes; peel off paper. Place on rack; cool. Whip cream and powdered sugar until stiff. Spread on cake; spoon sauce over whipped cream.

Sauce

1 tbsp. flour
1 c. (packed) brown sugar
1 egg, beaten
1/4 c. water
1/4 c. orange juice
1/4 c. butter
1 tsp. vanilla

Combine all ingredients in saucepan. Cook over low heat, stirring constantly, until thickened; cool.

FROSTED BUTTERSCOTCH CAKE

1 6-oz. package butterscotch pieces
1/2 c. boiling water
1 c. butter or margarine
2 c. sugar
4 eggs, separated
1 tsp. vanilla flavoring
2 1/2 c. sifted flour
1 tsp. soda

1/2 tsp. salt
1 c. buttermilk
Creamy Frosting

Melt butterscotch in boiling water; cool. Cream butter and sugar; beat in egg yolks, one at a time. Stir in butterscotch and vanilla. Sift flour, soda and salt together; add to butterscotch mixture alternately with buttermilk. Beat egg whites until stiff; fold into batter. Pour into greased and floured 10-inch tube pan. Bake at 350 degrees for 1 hour and 30 minutes. Cool for 10 minutes before removing from pan. Cool on rack; ice with Creamy Frosting.

Creamy Frosting

2 3/4 c. confectioners' sugar
1/2 tsp. salt
1 egg
1/4 c. maple syrup
1/2 c. butter
2 tsp. vanilla flavoring

Mix confectioners' sugar, salt and egg; blend in maple syrup. Add butter and vanilla. Mix until smooth and creamy.

ONE-BOWL BUTTERSCOTCH CAKE

2 c. sifted flour
1 tsp. salt
1 tbsp. baking powder
1 1/2 c. (packed) brown sugar
1/2 c. butter or margarine
1 c. milk
2 eggs
1 tsp. vanilla

Combine flour, salt, baking powder, brown sugar, butter and 2/3 cup milk in large electric mixer bowl. Beat at low speed of mixer until blended; beat at high speed for 2 minutes. Add remaining milk, eggs and vanilla; beat for 2 minutes longer. Turn into greased and floured 13 x 9 x 2-inch pan. Bake at 350 degrees for 30 to 35 minutes. Yield: 12 servings.

BUTTERSCOTCH CANDY

3 c. sugar
1 c. milk
1 tbsp. butter

Spread 1 cup sugar in heavy skillet; stir over low heat until sugar is melted and browned. Combine remaining sugar, milk and butter in saucepan; stir over low heat until sugar is dissolved and butter is melted. Increase heat; bring to a boil. Stir in melted sugar; cook to soft-ball stage. Beat vigorously until candy loses gloss; drop from teaspoon onto waxed paper to harden.

BUTTERSCOTCH PUDDING CANDY

1 pkg. butterscotch pudding mix
1 c. sugar
1 c. (packed) brown sugar
1/2 c. evaporated milk
1 tbsp. butter or margarine
1/2 c. chopped pecans

Combine all ingredients except pecans in saucepan; cook over low heat until sugar is dissolved. Increase heat; cook to soft-ball stage. Add pecans; stir until thickened. Drop by spoonfuls into 2-inch patties onto waxed paper; let stand until firm.

BUTTERSCOTCH YULE LOG

1 6-oz. package butterscotch bits
1/3 c. sweetened condensed milk
1/2 tsp. vanilla
1/3 c. chopped walnuts
1 egg white, lightly beaten
Walnut halves

Melt butterscotch bits over hot water. Remove from heat; stir in condensed milk and vanilla. Add chopped walnuts; mix well. Chill until firm enough to handle. Form into 12-inch roll on waxed paper; roll tightly to shape evenly. Unroll paper; score surface lengthwise with tines of fork. Brush with egg white. Press walnut halves into roll to cover completely. Reroll paper. Chill. Cut into 1/2-inch slices.

CREAMY BUTTERSCOTCH CANDY

2 c. marshmallow creme
1 6-oz. can evaporated milk
1/3 c. butter
1 3/4 c. sugar
1/4 tsp. salt
1 6-oz. package butterscotch chips
1 c. chopped English walnuts

Combine marshmallow creme, milk, butter, sugar and salt in heavy saucepan. Bring to a boil over medium heat, stirring constantly. Remove from heat; stir in butterscotch chips until melted. Add walnuts; pour into greased 8-inch square pan. Chill until firm; cut into 1-inch squares.

BUTTERSCOTCH FUDGE

2 6-oz. packages butterscotch morsels
1 14-oz. can sweetened condensed milk
16 marshmallows
1/2 c. peanut butter
1 tsp. vanilla
1/8 tsp. salt
Candied cherries, cut in quarters

Combine butterscotch morsels, milk and marshmallows in top of double boiler. Place over boiling water; stir occasionally, until melted and smooth. Remove from heat. Stir in peanut butter, vanilla and salt. Pour into greased 8-inch square pan. Chill until almost firm. Cut into squares; press cherry quarter on each square. Yield: About 2 1/4 pounds.

BUTTERSCOTCH-DATE COOKIES

3 c. flour
1 tsp. cream of tartar
1 tsp. soda
1/2 tsp. salt
2 c. (packed) brown sugar
3/4 c. butter
1 egg, beaten
1 tsp. vanilla
3 tbsp. cream
1 c. chopped dates
1 c. chopped nuts

Sift flour, cream of tartar, soda and salt together. Cream brown sugar and butter; beat in egg, vanilla and cream. Stir in flour mixture, dates and nuts; mix well. Shape cookie dough into 3 rolls; wrap in waxed paper. Chill until firm. Slice cookie dough into thin rounds; place on ungreased baking sheets. Bake at 375 degrees for about 8 minutes. Yield: 5 dozen cookies.

BUTTERSCOTCH COOKIES

Color photograph for this recipe on page 490.

1 6-oz. package butterscotch morsels
1 3-oz. package cream cheese, at room temperature
1/4 c. sugar
1 egg yolk
1/4 tsp. almond extract
1/2 tsp. salt
1 1/2 c. sifted all-purpose flour
1/2 c. semisweet chocolate morsels
1 tbsp. shortening

Melt butterscotch morsels in top of double boiler over hot, not boiling, water. Remove from water. Blend in cream cheese; stir in sugar. Beat in egg yolk. Add almond extract and salt. Blend in flour gradually. Pack into cookie press; press into desired shapes on ungreased baking sheet. Bake in 350-degree oven for 10 to 13 minutes. Remove at once from baking sheet; cool on rack. Melt chocolate morsels and shortening in top of double boiler over hot, not boiling, water; spoon chocolate mixture on cookies. Decorate with nuts, dragees, cinnamon candies, tinted coconut and glaceed fruit. Yield: 3-4 dozen.

BUTTERSCOTCH DROP COOKIES

1 tbsp. vinegar
1 tsp. vanilla
1 c. evaporated milk
2 1/2 c. flour
1 tsp. soda
1/2 tsp. baking powder
1/2 tsp. salt
2/3 c. butter or margarine
1 1/2 c. (packed) brown sugar
2 eggs
1 c. chopped nuts

Stir vinegar and vanilla into milk. Sift flour, soda, baking powder and salt together. Cream butter and sugar; beat in eggs. Stir in flour mixture alternately with milk mixture. Add nuts. Drop batter from teaspoon about 2 inches apart onto greased baking sheet. Bake at 350 degrees for 12 to 15 minutes. Lift onto rack to cool. Yield: 6 dozen cookies.

BUTTERSCOTCH SHORTBREAD BREAD

1 c. pastry flour
1/2 c. (packed) brown sugar
1/2 c. butter or margarine
2 eggs
1 tbsp. flour
1/2 tsp. baking powder
1/2 c. shredded coconut
1 6-oz. package butterscotch chips

Preheat oven to 350 degrees. Combine flour and 1/4 cup brown sugar; cut in butter. Press mixture firmly into 8-inch square pan. Bake for 15 minutes or until browned. Beat eggs, beating in remaining brown sugar. Add flour, baking powder, coconut and butterscotch pieces; mix well. Pour over baked shortbread. Bake for about 20 minutes. Cool; cut into squares.

BUTTERSCOTCH SNAPS

3 c. flour
3 c. brown sugar
1 1/2 tsp. soda
1 1/3 tsp. cream of tartar
1/2 c. melted butter
2 eggs, beaten

Sift flour, brown sugar, soda and cream of tartar together into bowl; stir in butter and eggs. Turn dough onto lightly floured surface; knead lightly. Shape into small rolls; wrap in waxed paper. Refrigerate overnight. Slice cookie dough in thin rounds; place on greased baking sheet. Bake at 350 degrees for about 12 minutes. Yield: 6-7 dozen cookies.

BUTTERSCOTCH HAYSTACKS

2 6-oz. packages butterscotch pieces
1 lge. can peanuts
1 lge. can chow mein noodles

Melt butterscotch pieces in top of double boiler over boiling water. Add peanuts and noodles; mix well. Drop by spoonfuls onto waxed paper; cool. Store candy in cool place.

STEAMED BUTTERSCOTCH BREAD PUDDING

4 slices buttered bread
1 c. (packed) dark brown sugar
1/2 c. raisins
2 eggs
2 c. milk
1 tsp. vanilla
1/4 tsp. salt

Butter 2-quart steamer or top of double boiler well. Cut bread into small uniform cubes. Place sugar in steamer; arrange bread on sugar. Sprinkle with raisins. Beat eggs; add milk, vanilla and salt. Pour over bread. Cover; steam for 1 hour and 30 minutes. Turn out carefully into large deep dish; serve warm. Yield: 4-6 servings.

QUICK BUTTERSCOTCH PUDDING

2 c. (packed) brown sugar
1 1/2 c. water
2 tbsp. butter
1 c. flour
1/2 c. sugar
1 tbsp. baking powder

Combine brown sugar, 1 cup water and butter in saucepan; bring to a boil, stirring to melt butter. Pour syrup into 8-inch square pan. Mix flour, sugar and baking powder; stir in remaining water. Pour flour mixture into syrup; do not stir. Bake at 350 degrees for 15 to 20 minutes. Serve pudding warm. Top with whipped cream or vanilla ice cream, if desired.

BUTTERSCOTCH PUDDING

1 c. (packed) dark brown sugar
2 tbsp. flour
1/4 tsp. salt
2 tbsp. butter
1 egg yolk
3 tbsp. water
1 c. milk

Combine all ingredients in saucepan; mix well. Cook over medium heat, stirring constantly, to a boil. Cool; pour into serving dishes. Chill and serve. Yield: 4 servings.

BUTTERSCOTCH REFRIGERATOR ROLLS

1 pkg. yeast
1/2 c. lukewarm water
1 c. mashed potatoes
2/3 c. shortening
1/2 c. sugar
1 tsp. salt
2 eggs
1 c. scalded milk, cooled
8 c. (about) sifted flour
Butter
Brown sugar
Chopped pecans

Soften yeast in lukewarm water. Combine potatoes, shortening, sugar, salt and eggs; mix well. Add yeast to milk; stir into potato mixture. Add enough flour to make stiff dough. Toss on floured board; knead well. Place in large bowl. Let rise until doubled in bulk. Knead lightly. Rub top with melted butter; place in container. Cover tightly; keep in refrigerator until ready to bake. Pinch off small pieces of dough; shape into balls. Place 1 teaspoon butter, 1 teaspoon brown sugar and 1 teaspoon pecans in each muffin cup; place dough in cups. Let rise for 1 hour and 30 minutes. Bake at 425 degrees for 25 minutes. Turn out while hot. Yield: 2 1/2 to 3 dozen rolls.

BUTTERSCOTCH STICKY BUNS

1/2 c. chopped nuts
2 10-oz. packages refrigerator biscuits
1/4 c. butter, melted
1/2 c. sugar
1 tsp. cinnamon
1 6-oz. package butterscotch flavored morsels
1/3 c. evaporated milk

Sprinkle nuts into greased 9-inch cake pan. Separate biscuits; dip on both sides in melted butter. Combine sugar and cinnamon; coat biscuits with cinnamon mixture. Overlap biscuits over nuts in pan. Bake in 400-degree oven for 30 to 35 minutes. Combine morsels and evaporated milk in small saucepan. Cook, stirring constantly, over medium heat until smooth and melted. Pour over hot biscuits. Let stand for 5 minutes. Turn out of pan onto plate; serve warm. Yield: 20 buns.

Butterscotch Sticky Buns . . . A sweet-tooth favorite that you'll want to serve often.

BUTTERSCOTCH CHEW BREAD

4 eggs
1 pkg. dark brown sugar
2 c. flour
2 tsp. baking powder
1 tsp. vanilla
2 c. coarsely chopped pecans

Mix eggs and sugar in double boiler; cook for 20 minutes. Cool to room temperature. Add flour, baking powder, vanilla and pecans. Pour into greased 11 x 16-inch pan. Place in 400-degree oven. Reduce oven temperature immediately to 325 degrees. Bake for 30 minutes. Cool in pan overnight. Cut into squares; serve with vanilla ice cream or sour cream. Yield: 24 servings.

EASY BUTTERSCOTCH BREAD

1 box brown sugar
3 tbsp. melted shortening
2 eggs
2 tsp. soda
1 tsp. salt
2 c. sour milk
4 c. flour
1/2 c. chopped nuts

Combine all ingredients in large electric mixer bowl; beat for 3 minutes at high speed of mixer. Pour batter into 2 greased and floured 8 x 4-inch pans. Bake at 325 degrees for 1 hour or until bread tests done. Turn onto racks to cool.

RAISED BUTTERSCOTCH BUNS

1/2 c. butter
3/4 c. brown sugar
2 tbsp. corn syrup
1/2 c. chopped pecans
1 pkg. yeast
3/4 c. warm water
1/4 c. sugar
1 tsp. salt
2 1/4 c. sifted flour
1 egg
1/4 c. soft shortening

Melt butter in 9-inch square pan. Mix in brown sugar, corn syrup and pecans. Dissolve yeast in warm water. Stir in sugar, salt and half the flour. Beat for 2 minutes or until mixture sheets off spoon. Add egg, shortening and remaining flour; beat until smooth. Drop from teaspoon evenly into brown sugar mixture. Cover; let rise in warm place for 30 minutes or until doubled in bulk. Bake at 375 degrees for 15 to 20 minutes. Invert onto serving plate immediately.

BUTTERSCOTCH BITES

1 c. brown sugar
1/2 c. melted butter
2 tbsp. hot water
Chopped nuts
2 pkg. dry yeast
1/2 c. warm water
3/4 c. lukewarm milk
1/2 c. shortening
2 eggs, beaten
3 1/4 c. flour

Combine brown sugar, butter and hot water. Place 1 1/2 teaspoons mixture in each of 24 muffin cups; sprinkle several nuts in each cup. Soften yeast in warm water. Combine milk, shortening, eggs, yeast and half the flour in electric mixer bowl. Beat at medium speed of mixer for 2 minutes. Add remaining flour; beat for 2 minutes longer. Drop 1 tablespoon batter into each muffin cup. Cover with waxed paper; let rise for 40 minutes. Bake at 375 degrees for 18 to 20 minutes. Invert onto baking sheet. Let stand for 5 minutes before removing from pan.

Cabbage

Cabbage belongs to a family of vegetables that includes kale, collards, cauliflower, broccoli, and Brussels sprouts. Both red and green cabbage are served in most American homes. Both are rich in Vitamin C, which can be preserved by cooking cabbage in very little water and for the least possible time. They are also both low in calories. (1 cup raw, shredded cabbage = 24 calories)

AVAILABILITY: Both red and green cabbage are available year-round. *Green cabbage* is available as *new or early* cabbage during the spring months and as *old* cabbage during all other months.

BUYING: Select new cabbages with firm heads, a heavy weight for their size, and crisp green outer leaves. Old cabbage has no outer leaves and lacks bright green color. Select heads that are not wilted, discolored, insect-damaged, bruised, or torn. Select red cabbage with compact heads, fresh-looking leaves, and dark red to purple color. Always avoid cabbages of any variety with yellow or withered leaves.

STORING: Moisten both red and green cabbages and wrap them in foil or plastic bags. Store in refrigerator vegetable crisper for a week to 10 days. Do not permit to dry out. *Cabbage may be frozen only after cooking. To freeze* cabbage, trim coarse outer leaves. Separate leaves or cut into medium shreds or thin wedges. Cook in boiling water 1 1/2 minutes; cool immediately by placing in ice water. Drain, pack in containers, leaving 1/2-inch space at top. Seal, label, date, and freeze.

PREPARATION: In preparing cabbage, plan on 1 pound green cabbage or 1-1/2 pound red cabbage to serve 4. The most common method of preparation is boiling. *To boil green cabbage,* wash the vegetable and discard any wilted outer leaves. Remove core; cut into wedges, quarters, or wide shreds. Cook covered, in a small amount of boiling water until tender. Allow about 5 minutes for shredded cabbage, 10-15 minutes for wedges or quarters. *To boil red cabbage,* proceed as described above for green cabbage, but (1) cook uncovered; (2) add two tablespoons vinegar or lemon juice to cooking water as a color preservative; and (3) allow longer cooking time. Wedges and quarters of red cabbage usually require 25 minutes to cook, shreds take slightly less time.

SERVING: Cooked cabbage may be served as a vegetable side dish, as sauerkraut, or scalloped or au gratin. Raw cabbage can be served in salads or slaws.

(See VEGETABLES.)

AUSTRIAN CABBAGE

1 sm. head cabbage
2 tbsp. butter
1/2 tsp. salt
1/4 tsp. paprika
1 sm. onion, minced
1 c. sour cream

Shred cabbage; saute lightly in butter. Add salt, paprika and onion. Place in greased baking dish; spread sour cream over cabbage mixture. Bake at 375 degrees for 20 minutes. Yield: 4 servings.

BIEROCKS

1 recipe yeast dough
1 onion, thinly sliced
1 2-lb. cabbage, shredded
1 lb. ground beef
1/2 tsp. pepper
1/2 tsp. salt

Let dough rise until doubled in bulk. Combine remaining ingredients in deep skillet; cook over medium heat until beef is done. Drain. Roll out dough 1/2 inch thick; cut into 6 squares, 6 inches wide. Place portion of beef mixture on each square; fold up edges. Seal; place in greased baking pan. Let rise until doubled in bulk. Bake at 300 degrees for 45 to 50 minutes. Serve hot or cold. Yield: 6 servings.

BAKED CABBAGE

1 med. cabbage, chopped
1 can mushroom soup
1 can French-fried onions

Steam cabbage in small amount of boiling, salted water for 10 minutes or until cabbage is crisp-tender; drain. Combine cabbage with mushroom soup in a greased 2-quart casserole. Bake at 350 degrees for 10 minutes. Top cabbage with onion rings. Bake for 10 minutes longer. Yield: 10-12 servings.

CABBAGE PIE

7 c. shredded cabbage
2 1/4 c. coarsely crumbled soda crackers
2 c. milk
1/4 c. butter
2 tsp. salt
1/2 tsp. pepper
1/2 tsp. celery seed

Preheat oven to 350 degrees. Arrange alternate layers of cabbage and crackers in a 1 1/2-quart casserole. Combine milk, butter, salt, pepper and celery seed in saucepan; bring to a boil. Pour milk mixture over cabbage mixture. Bake for 40 minutes or until lightly browned. Yield: 6-8 servings.

CABBAGE-NOODLE BAKE

1 sm. package noodles
1 med. cabbage
3 tbsp. salad oil
1 sm. onion, grated
Salt and pepper to taste

Prepare noodles according to package directions. Shred cabbage. Place oil and cabbage in large skillet; cook, stirring occasionally, over medium heat until cabbage is wilted and slightly browned. Add onion, salt and pepper. Combine cabbage mixture and noodles; mix well. Place in buttered casserole. Bake at 350 degrees for 25 minutes. Yield: 6 servings.

SCALLOPED CABBAGE

3 c. chopped cabbage
1 green pepper, finely chopped
1 sm. onion, minced
2 c. medium white sauce
1/2 c. bread crumbs
3 tbsp. melted butter

Combine cabbage, green pepper, onion and sauce; pour into well-greased baking dish. Combine crumbs and butter; sprinkle over cabbage mixture. Bake at 375 degrees for 20 to 30 minutes or until cabbage is tender.

RAISIN-CABBAGE ROLLS

3/4 c. California seedless raisins
1/2 lb. ground lean beef
1 c. cooked rice
1 tbsp. chopped onion
1 tsp. seasoned salt
1/4 tsp. dillweed
8 lge. outside cabbage leaves
1 10 1/2-oz. can beef broth
1/4 c. catsup
2 tsp. cider vinegar
2 tsp. cornstarch

Combine 1/2 cup raisins, beef, rice, onion, salt, dillweed and 2 tablespoons water. Pour boiling water on cabbage; let stand for 5 minutes. Drain; cut out thick portion at base of leaf. Spoon filling onto center of leaves. Fold sides in; roll up to enclose filling. Secure rolls with wooden picks. Place rolls in skillet with broth. Cover; simmer for 30 to 40 minutes or until tender. Remove rolls from skillet; keep warm. Add enough water to pan drippings to equal 3/4 cup liquid. Add catsup. Combine vinegar, cornstarch and remaining raisins. Add to pan drippings. Cook, stirring, until clear. Add cabbage rolls; heat for 5 minutes longer. Yield: 4 servings.

Raisin-Cabbage Rolls . . . Rice and ground beef in a tangy raisin sauce rolled in cabbage leaves.

CABBAGE-TOMATO-RICE CASSEROLE

4 c. shredded cabbage
3 1/2 c. chopped tomatoes
2 tsp. salt
1 tsp. sugar
1 tsp. minced onion
2 tbsp. melted butter
2 c. cooked rice
1/2 c. soft bread crumbs
2 tbsp. grated cheese

Steam cabbage in small amount of water until crisp-tender; drain. Combine tomatoes, salt, sugar, onion and 1 tablespoon butter in saucepan; cook for 5 minutes. Arrange cabbage, tomato mixture and rice in layers in casserole. Combine crumbs, remaining butter and cheese; sprinkle over top. Bake at 375 degrees for 45 minutes. Yield: 6-8 servings.

GLORIFIED CABBAGE

3 tbsp. butter
2 tbsp. flour
1 tsp. salt
Dash of pepper
1 tsp. dry mustard
1 1/3 c. milk
1 egg yolk, beaten
2 c. shredded cabbage
1 c. thinly sliced onions
1 c. shredded cheese
1 c. buttered bread crumbs

Melt butter in saucepan; add flour, salt, pepper and mustard. Cook, stirring constantly, until bubbly. Add milk gradually; cook, stirring, until thickened. Stir small amount of milk mixture into egg yolk; stir egg mixture into milk mixture in saucepan. Cook for 1 minute longer. Layer half the cabbage, onions, cheese and cream sauce in baking dish; repeat layers. Top with crumbs. Bake, covered, in 375-degree oven for 30 minutes. Remove cover; bake for 5 minutes longer. Yield: 4-6 servings.

SPICED CABBAGE CASSEROLE

1 med. cabbage, chopped
1 can cream of mushroom soup
1/4 tsp. onion seasoning
1/4 tsp. hickory smoked salt
1/4 tsp. barbecue spice
1/4 tsp. pepper
Salt to taste

Place cabbage in casserole. Mix soup with remaining ingredients; pour over cabbage. Bake in 300-degree oven for 1 hour. Yield: 4-6 servings.

CREAM CHEESE CABBAGE

5 c. shredded cabbage
1 3-oz. package cream cheese
1 tbsp. cream
2 tbsp. butter
Dash of pepper
1/4 tsp. celery seed
3/4 tsp. salt

Soak cabbage in ice water for 12 to 15 minutes; drain. Steam cabbage in small amount of salted boiling water for 4 to 5 minutes; drain. Mix cream cheese and cream; add to cabbage. Add butter, pepper, celery seed and salt; mix lightly. Serve immediately. Yield: 4 serving.

FRIED CABBAGE

1/4 lb. salt pork, cut into strips
1 med. cabbage, chopped
Salt and pepper to taste

Fry salt pork in saucepan until crisp; remove from pan. Combine cabbage, salt, pepper and 1/4 cup water in pork drippings. Simmer, covered, for 10 minutes or until cabbage is tender and begins to brown slightly. Stir occasionally. Yield: 6 servings.

GOURMET CABBAGE

1 lge. head cabbage, coarsely chopped
1/2 c. Chablis
1/2 c. chicken bouillon
1 tbsp. wine vinegar
2 tbsp. butter
1 tbsp. instant minced onion
1/4 tsp. dillweed
1/2 tsp. salt
Dash of pepper

Combine cabbage, Chablis, bouillon, vinegar, butter, onion, dillweed, salt and pepper in large saucepan. Simmer, covered, for 12 to 15 minutes. Yield: 4 servings.

PENNSYLVANIA RED CABBAGE

2 tbsp. bacon drippings
4 c. shredded red cabbage
2 c. chopped apples
1/4 c. vinegar
1/4 c. (packed) brown sugar
1 1/4 tsp. salt
1/2 tsp. caraway seed
Dash of pepper

Heat bacon drippings in large saucepan. Add cabbage, apples, vinegar, brown sugar, 1/4 cup water, salt, caraway seed and pepper. Simmer, covered, for 15 to 20 minutes, stirring occasionally. Yield: 5 servings.

CALIFORNIA CABBAGE MOLD

2 3-oz. packages lemon gelatin
1 1/2 tsp. celery seed
1 tsp. instant minced onion
1/2 tsp. salt
1/8 tsp. cayenne pepper
1 1/2 c. mayonnaise
6 c. shredded cabbage
1/2 c. diced orange sections

Dissolve gelatin in 1 cup boiling water. Stir in celery seed, onion, salt and cayenne pepper. Add 1 cup water; cool. Add mayonnaise; blend well. Chill until mixture is partially congealed. Fold in cabbage and orange sections; turn into lightly oiled 1 1/2-quart mold. Chill until firm. Yield: 6 servings.

CABBAGE SALAD

2 pkg. lemon gelatin
1 c. chopped apples
2 tbsp. lemon juice
3 c. shredded cabbage
1 c. chopped celery

Dissolve gelatin in 2 cups boiling water; add 1 3/4 cups cold water. Chill until partially set. Sprinkle apples with lemon juice. Combine apples, cabbage and celery with gelatin; chill until firm. Yield: 8-10 servings.

GARDEN SLAW

8 c. shredded cabbage
2 c. grated carrots
1 green pepper, slivered
1/2 c. chopped onion
1 env. unflavored gelatin
2/3 c. sugar
2/3 c. vinegar
2 tsp. celery seed
1 1/2 tsp. salt
1/4 tsp. pepper
2/3 c. salad oil

Mix cabbage, carrots, green pepper and onion. Sprinkle with 1/2 cup water; chill. Soften gelatin in 1/4 cup water. Mix sugar, vinegar, celery seed, salt and pepper in saucepan; bring to a boil. Stir in softened gelatin. Cool until slightly thickened; beat well. Beat in salad oil gradually. Drain vegetables; pour dressing over top. Toss lightly.Yield: 8 servings.

PERFECTION SALAD

2 env. unflavored gelatin
1/2 c. sugar
1 tsp. salt
1/2 c. vinegar
2 tbsp. lemon juice
2 c. finely chopped cabbage
1 c. finely chopped celery
1/4 c. finely chopped green pepper
1/4 c. diced pimento
1/3 c. stuffed green olives, sliced

Soften gelatin in 1/2 cup water. Combine softened gelatin, sugar, salt and 1 1/2 cups boiling water in bowl; stir until gelatin is dissolved. Add 1 cup water, vinegar and lemon juice; mix well. Chill until partially set. Add cabbage, celery, green pepper, pimento and olives; pour into loaf pan. Chill until firm. Garnish with carrot curls and ripe olives. Yield: 12-15 servings.

RED CABBAGE-ORANGE SALAD

1 sm. red cabbage
3 med. oranges
1/4 c. chopped chives
1/4 med. green pepper, slivered
Dash of salt
3/4 c. farm-style cottage cheese
1/4 c. orange juice

Shred cabbage; peel and section oranges. Combine cabbage, oranges, chives, green pepper, salt, cottage cheese and orange juice. Toss lightly. Serve on lettuce. Garnish with additional green pepper slivers and orange peel, if desired.

SAUCY CABBAGE WEDGES

1 2-lb. cabbage
1/3 c. mayonnaise
1/4 c. milk
4 tsp. vinegar
1 tsp. sugar
1/2 tsp. prepared mustard
Paprika

Cut cabbage into 8 wedges; cook in boiling salted water for 8 to 10 minutes; drain. Combine mayonnaise and milk in small saucepan; stir until smooth. Add vinegar, sugar and mustard; mix well. Simmer, stirring constantly, until well blended and heated through. Pour over cabbage; sprinkle with paprika. Yield: 8 servings.

STUFFED WHOLE CABBAGE

1 2-lb. cabbage
2 1/4 tsp. salt
1 c. finely chopped luncheon meat
1 c. shredded American cheese
1/4 c. finely chopped onion
3/4 c. bread crumbs
1 tbsp. milk
1/4 tsp. pepper
1 1/2 c. diced tomatoes
1 1/2 tbsp. melted butter

Place whole cabbage in kettle with 1 teaspoon salt and enough boiling water to cover; boil for 30 minutes or until crisp-tender. Remove from water; drain well. Slice off top; scoop out inside carefully, leaving 1 1/2-inch shell. Place shell in casserole. Shred enough cabbage center to measure 1 cup; combine shredded cabbage, meat, cheese, onion, 1/2 cup bread crumbs, milk, 1/2 teaspoon salt and pepper. Mix well; spoon into cabbage shell. Combine tomatoes, 3/4 cup water and remaining salt; pour into casserole around cabbage. Cover. Bake at 350 degrees for 1 hour. Combine remaining bread crumbs and butter. Remove casserole from oven; sprinkle with crumbs. Bake for 15 minutes longer or until crumbs are browned. Serve with pan drippings. Yield: 6 servings.

SCALLOPED CABBAGE WITH NUTMEG SAUCE

1 sm. head cabbage, coarsely shredded
2 tbsp. butter
2 tbsp. flour
1 1/2 c. milk
1/2 tsp. salt
Dash of pepper
Nutmeg
6 tbsp. grated Parmesan cheese
1 tbsp. lemon juice
1 1/2 c. cracker crumbs

Steam cabbage in small amount of boiling salted water until crisp-tender; drain. Melt butter in saucepan; stir in flour. Remove from heat; blend in milk gradually. Add salt, pepper and 1/4 teaspoon nutmeg; simmer until thickened, stirring constantly. Add 4 tablespoons cheese; stir until melted. Remove from heat; stir in lemon juice. Place 1/2 of the cabbage in greased baking dish; add 1/2 of the crumbs. Add remaining cabbage; add remaining crumbs. Pour sauce over crumbs; top with remaining cheese and sprinkle with nutmeg. Bake at 450 degrees for 10 minutes or until crumbs are browned. Yield: 6 servings.

SWEET AND SOUR CABBAGE

2 c. chopped cabbage
1 tbsp. butter
1/2 tsp. caraway seed
1/2 tsp. salt
1 tbsp. flour
1 tbsp. vinegar
2 tsp. sugar

Combine cabbage, butter, caraway seed, salt, flour and 1 cup water in saucepan. Simmer, covered, for 10 minutes or until cabbage is tender. Add vinegar and sugar; mix lightly. Yield: 4 servings.

Caesar Salad

Caesar Salad . . . A classic blend of greens, croutons, and anchovies.

CAESAR SALAD

1 clove of garlic, split
Olive oil
1 head romaine
1 head iceberg lettuce
2 c. herb-seasoned stuffing croutons
3/4 tsp. salt
1/2 tsp. pepper
1/4 tsp. dry mustard
1 tbsp. Worcestershire sauce
1/4 c. grated Parmesan cheese
1 egg
3 tbsp. lemon juice
1 2-oz. can anchovy fillets, drained

Place garlic in 1/3 cup olive oil; cover. Refrigerate for 1 hour. Tear salad greens into medium pieces in large salad bowl. Chill thoroughly for about 1 hour. Heat 2 tablespoons olive oil in frypan. Add croutons. Cook over moderate heat, stirring gently, until lightly browned and oil is absorbed. Set aside. Remove garlic from chilled oil; add salt, pepper, mustard and Worcestershire sauce. Sprinkle chilled greens with cheese. Pour seasoned oil over lettuce, tossing gently until leaves glisten. Coddle egg for 1 minute; add to salad, tossing gently until egg disappears. Add lemon juice. Sprinkle toasted croutons over salad; toss again. Serve immediately in chilled salad bowls; garnish with rolled anchovies. Yield: 8-10 servings.

CAESAR SALAD

1 clove of garlic
2 anchovies
Juice of 1/2 lemon
1 egg
1/2 c. olive oil
1 tbsp. cider vinegar
2 tbsp. wine vinegar
1/8 tsp. dry mustard
1/2 tsp. salt
1/8 tsp. freshly ground pepper
1/3 c. grated Parmesan cheese
2 lge. heads romaine
1 c. croutons

Mash garlic in wooden bowl; add anchovies. Mash anchovies. Add lemon juice. Warm egg in hot water; separate egg. Discard egg white; add egg yolk to bowl. Blend until thick and creamy. Add olive oil slowly, beating with spoon until blended. Add vinegars, mustard, salt, pepper and cheese. Break lettuce into bite-sized pieces; add to bowl. Toss salad well. Add croutons; toss lightly. Serve immediately. Yield: 6-8 servings.

ORIGINAL CAESAR SALAD

2 cloves of garlic, quartered
1 c. olive or salad oil
1 c. bread cubes
Grated Parmesan cheese
3 med. heads romaine lettuce
3 tbsp. wine vinegar
Juice of 1 lemon
2 eggs
Salt and pepper
Dash of Worcestershire sauce

Place garlic in olive oil; let stand for several days. Remove garlic. Spread bread cubes on cookie sheet. Pour small amount of garlic oil over bread cubes. Bake at 225 degrees for 2 hours. Sprinkle with cheese. Place in jar; refrigerate. Tear lettuce into pieces; place in chilled salad bowl. Sprinkle with remaining garlic oil, vinegar and lemon juice. Boil eggs for 1 minute. Break into salad; season with salt, pepper and Worcestershire sauce. Sprinkle with cheese. Toss until dressing is combined and leaves are well coated. Add croutons; toss lightly. Serve on chilled plates. Garnish with rolled anchovies if desired. Yield: 6 servings.

Cake

Cakes are of two basic types: Those made with shortening—the butter, pound, fruit, and chiffon cakes—and those made without shortening—the angel and sponge cakes. The first group are usually baked in round, square, or sheet pans; the second are almost always baked in tube pans.

INGREDIENTS: Before beginning to prepare a cake, assemble your ingredients. They should all be at room temperature (about 75 degrees).

Flour—Your recipe will specify the kind of flour to use. In cake recipes, the flour is always measured after sifting, unless otherwise specified. If you substitute regular flour for cake flour, allow one cup regular flour minus two tablespoons for every cup of cake flour.

Baking Powder—Most baking powders on the market today are double-action with rising beginning in the batter and continuing during the baking process. For each cup of flour, use 1/2 teaspoon double-action baking powder.

Shortening—Your recipe will specify the type of shortening to use: liquid, solid vegetable, or butter. If you substitute butter for other shortenings, reduce the amount of salt you use. Butter is usually presalted.

Eggs—Eggs are important to produce a fluffy-textured cake. If you must substitute egg size, use two large or four small eggs in place of every three medium ones. If a recipe calls for separated eggs, separate whites from yolks while eggs are still cold; let whites and yolks come to room temperature before using.

CAKE PANS: Unless the recipe specifies otherwise, cake pans should be thoroughly greased and floured. When preparing chocolate cake, flour the pans with unsweetened cocoa—it doesn't leave white edges on a dark cake.

Pans may be made of metal or glass. Medium weight metal pans with shiny upper surfaces and dulled lower ones produce a thin, heavily browned cake crust. Glass or enamel pans produce heavier, darker crusts. If using glass pans, reduce the oven temperature by 25 degrees.

Pan size is important. A recipe calling for two cups of flour should be baked in two 8-inch round pans that are 1 1/2 inches deep. A recipe calling for 2 1/3 to 3 cups of flour will bake best in two 9-inch round pans 1 1/2 to 2 inches deep or in two 8-inch square pans that are 2 inches deep.

Non-shortening cakes are usually baked in tube pans. These pans are not greased because the cakes rise by clinging to the ungreased sides of the pans.

METHODS OF PREPARATION: There are two methods used to make shortening-type cakes. One is the *creaming method,* in which shortening, sugar, eggs, and salt are creamed or blended together until they are light in color and smooth in texture. Then the dry ingredients and the liquid are added alternately and the entire mixture is blended until smooth. The other method, is often referred to as the *quick method.* In the quick method, shortening, the dry ingredients, and part of the liquid are mixed for two minutes. Then the eggs and remaining liquid are added, and the mixture is beaten for an additional two minutes.

Non-shortening cakes are usually prepared by beating the eggs thoroughly and adding the remaining ingredients in three or four parts.

BAKING: Preheat the oven before baking the cake. Fill cake pans one-half to two-thirds full. Before baking shortening-type cakes, rap the pans sharply with the bottom of your hand. This action releases air bubbles from the batter that could cause air pockets which might make the cake split when it is cooling. If you are baking a non-shortening cake, remove excess air by cutting through the batter with a spatula. Air must circulate around cake pans to maintain an even temperature. When placed in the oven, no pan should be directly over the other nor should pans touch each other or the wall of the oven. When the cake has cooked, let it cool. Shortening-type cakes cool on cake racks in their pans for about 10-15 minutes, then should be loosened, removed from pans by inverting on racks, and allowed to cool thoroughly. Non-shortening cakes should be inverted in their pans preferably with the tube placed over a funnel, and let stand until cold.

FINISHING: Cakes are usually frosted or iced and filled. They should be filled before being frosted or iced. An icing is a thin glaze that is usually uncooked. Frostings are thicker and more opaque and may be cooked. Brush all loose crumbs off the cake before frosting it. Cooked frostings should be cool enough not to soak into the cake. (See FROSTING.)

Cake, Basic

Basic White Cake is a shortening cake. It differs from other shortening-type cakes in that egg whites, not whole eggs, are among the ingredients. The whites contribute to this cake's pure, white color. The air beaten into the whites adds volume to the batter and lightness to the texture.

Many elaborate cakes such as the Lady Baltimore cake and wedding cake are based on the basic white cake recipe.

BASIC WHITE CAKE

2 c. sugar
1 c. butter
3 c. sifted cake flour
3 tsp. baking powder
1 c. milk
1/2 tsp. salt
1 tsp. vanilla
1 tsp. lemon flavoring
6 egg whites

Preheat oven to 375 degrees. Cream sugar and butter until fluffy. Combine flour and baking powder; add to creamed mixture alternately with milk. Beat well after each addition. Add salt and flavorings. Beat egg whites until stiff peaks form; fold into batter. Pour into 3 greased and floured cake pans. Bake for 25 to 30 minutes or until cake tests done.

BASIC YELLOW CAKE

11 egg yolks
1 1/2 c. sugar
Pinch of salt
1 tsp. baking powder
1 c. cold water
2 c. sifted cake flour
1 tsp. lemon flavoring

Beat egg yolks until thick and lemon colored; add sugar gradually, beating well after each addition. Add salt and baking powder; beat well. Add cold water and flour alternately, beating well after each addition. Add lemon flavoring. Pour batter into 3 greased and floured cake pans. Bake at 375 degrees for 30 minutes or until cake tests done.

SLICING BASIC CAKES

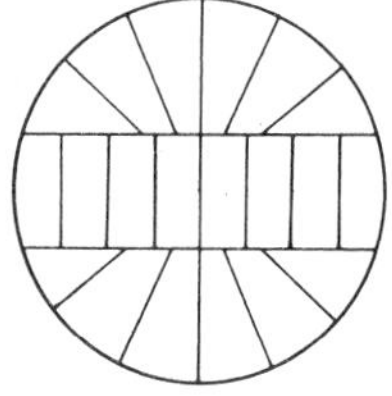

10-inch, 2-layer cake
Yield: 20 servings

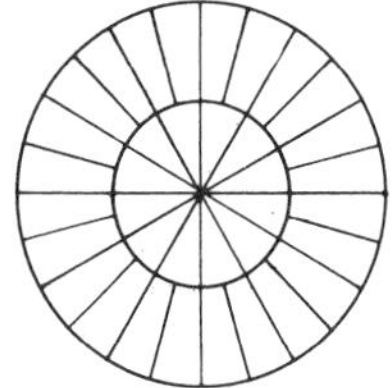

12-inch, 2-layer cake
Yield: 36 servings

Candy

There are many different types of candies. Some, such as *fudge, fondant, divinity,* and so on, are featured in entries throughout this volume. See these entries for information on preparing specific candies. One candy not described elsewhere is *brittle*. Brittles are prepared by incorporating air into a candy mixture that has been cooked to the hard crack stage; that is, a drop of the mixture when dropped toward cold water separates into hard threads that crack when pressed between the fingers and when the mixture registers 300-310 degrees on a candy thermometer. As the candy is poured onto a marble slab, it absorbs air, and that air forms pockets characteristic of brittles. After the candy has set into a hard sheet, it is broken into pieces by pounding it with a mallet.

CANDY-MAKING CHOCOLATE: Many candy recipes specify the use of candy-making chocolate. This chocolate is sold in blocks and must be tempered before being used. To temper chocolate, break it up in small pieces with an ice pick or awl and melt the pieces in the upper portion of a double boiler. Keep the water in the lower section between 140 and 150 degrees (nicely warm to the touch).

EQUIPMENT: Equipment necessary for candy-making includes: *a large kettle, a double boiler, a marble slab* about 30 inches square (available from most furniture manufacturers or marble quarries), and *a candy thermometer* to indicate temperatures of candies as they cook. The best kind of candy thermometer is made of copper and has a removable scale which makes it easy to clean after use. As a substitute for a candy thermometer, the cold water temperature test may be used. This is a test made by letting a drop of the candy fall into a dish of cold water. After it has fallen, the candy's texture ranges from soft ball to hard crack. By comparing its texture to the criteria outlined in the chart that follows, it is possible to determine the approximate temperature of the candy.

CANDY TESTS

TYPE OF CANDY	COLD WATER TEST	TEMPERATURE AT SEA LEVEL* (in degrees as measured on candy thermometer)
Fudge, fondant	Soft ball (flattens when picked up)	234-240
Caramels	Firm ball (holds shape unless pressed)	240-248
Divinity, taffy	Hard ball (holds shape but is still pliable)	250-268
Butterscotch, English toffee	Soft crack (separates into hard threads that are not brittle)	270-290
Brittles	Hard crack (separates into hard threads that crack when pressed between fingers)	300-310

*Subtract approximately two degrees for every 1,000 feet increase in altitude.

Canning

Canning is the process of preserving foods, particularly fruits and vegetables, in cans or jars for later use. There are two basic ways to can: in the water bath or in the pressure cooker. In the *water bath*, fruits and vegetables that have a high acid content are processed for preservation in boiling water. Food is packed into jars that are then put onto a rack and lowered into the canner, usually a large kettle. The canner is filled with water to cover the jar tops 1 or 2 inches without boiling over. Process time (specified in the charts that follow or in individual recipes) is counted from when the water boils. When the designated process time has elapsed, jars are removed from the canner. In the *pressure cooker*, vegetables with a low acid content are processed for preservation at temperatures higher than those obtainable in the water bath. These vegetables require higher processing temperatures than do high-acid vegetables in order to kill bacteria that could spoil the food. Jars are filled, placed on a rack, and lowered into the cooker as in the water bath method. Water is added according to the manufacturers' directions. The cooker is covered and a gauge is placed on the top, again, as the manufacturer directs. This gauge tells how many pounds of pressure is building up inside the cooker. At 10 pounds, the internal temperature is higher than 212 degrees–and will kill organisms that can't be killed by the water bath method.

CANNING VEGETABLES–BUYING: Select young, tender, fresh vegetables. The quality of the vegetables determines the flavor, color, and texture of the finished product.

PROCESSING: Vegetables may be processed raw pack or hot pack. In *raw pack* processing, there is no precooking unless blanching (dipping in boiling water) is specified under the recipe directions. Foods are cold when placed in jars. In *hot pack*, vegetables are partially cooked before being placed in jars and are hot.

PACKING: Be certain to leave head space when packing vegetables. Too much solid material in a jar reduces the amount of liquid it can hold and will retard the passage of the heat to the center. If heat does not reach the center during the canning process, organisms may not be killed and the product may spoil.

TIMETABLE FOR CANNING VEGETABLES

VEGETABLES	PREPARATION	WATER BATH (HRS.)	PRESSURE COOKER MINUTES PTS.	QTS.	PRESSURE LBS.
ASPARAGUS	Raw Pack – Wash, trim and pack raw	–	25	30	10
	Hot Pack – Wash, trim, boil 3 minutes Pack hot	3 hours	25	30	10
BEANS (String or Wax)	Raw Pack – Wash, string. Cut or leave whole. Pack	–	20	25	10
	Hot Pack – Wash, string. Cut or leave whole. Boil 3 minutes and pack	3 hours	20	25	10
BEANS, Lima	Raw Pack – Shell. Pack raw and loosely to 1 inch of top	–	40	50	10
	Hot Pack – Shell. Bring to boil Pack loosely	3 hours	40	50	10
BEETS	Hot Pack – Wash, leave roots and tops long. Boil 15 minutes. Skin. Pack	2 hours	25	40	10
CARROTS	Raw Pack – Wash, peel, slice or cube Pack raw		25	30	10
	Hot Pack – Wash, peel, slice or cube Bring to boil and pack	2 hours	25	30	10
	(Continued on next page)				

VEGETABLES	PREPARATION	WATER BATH (HRS.)	PRESSURE COOKER		
			MINUTES		PRESSURE
			PTS.	QTS.	LBS.
CORN (Whole Grain)	Raw Pack – Cut from cob. Pack raw and loosely	–	55	85	10
	Hot Pack – Cut from cob. Bring to boil Pack	3 1/2 hours	55	85	10
GREENS (All kinds)	Hot Pack – Wash, thoroughly. Steam or boil to wilt. Pack loosely	3 hours	45	70	10
PARSNIPS or TURNIPS	Raw Pack – Wash, peel, slice or cube Pack raw	–	20	25	10
	Hot Pack – Wash, peel, slice or cube Boil 3 minutes. Pack	1 1/2 hours	20	25	10
PEAS	Raw Pack – Shell, wash. Pack raw and loosely	–	40	40	10
	Hot Pack – Shell, wash. Bring to boil Pack loosely	3 hours	40	40	10
PEPPERS (Pimento)	Hot Pack – Place in moderate oven 6 to 8 minutes or in boiling water. Peel, stem, cut out seeds, flatten. Pack without liquid	40 min.	10	10	5
POTATOES, Irish	Raw Pack – Wash and scrape small new potatoes. Pack. Add boiling water	–	40	50	10

CANNING FRUITS–BUYING: Select only fruits that are uniformly ripened, firmly textured, and have good flavor to ensure a high quality yield in the finished product.

PROCESSING: Almost all fruits require peeling, halving, or sectioning and the addition of a darkening preventative before they are ready to be canned. Fruits may be processed in either the water bath or the pressure cooker. Processing times are shorter for fruits than for vegetables, especially in the water bath. The chart below gives directions for processing the most often canned fruits.

USE OF SYRUP: Most fruits and berries are canned in syrup. Sugar is used in making the syrup, not to prevent spoilage, but to bring out the flavor of the fruit and improve its texture.

PACKING: See method for packing under vegetables (above).

TIMETABLE FOR CANNING FRUITS

FRUITS	PREPARATION	WATER BATH (MIN.)	PRESSURE COOKER	
			MINUTES	PRESSURE
			QTS. PTS.	LBS.
APPLES	Wash, pare, core, cut in pieces. Boil 3 to 5 minutes in syrup. Pack. Add syrup or water	25	10	5
APRICOTS	Wash, halve and pit. Pack Add syrup or water	20	10	5
BERRIES (except Strawberries & Cranberries)	Wash, stem, pack. Add syrup or water	20	8	5

FRUITS	PREPARATION	WATER BATH (MIN.)	PRESSURE COOKER	
			MINUTES QTS. PTS.	PRESSURE LBS.
CHERRIES	Wash, stem, pit. Pack. Add syrup or water	20	10	5
FIGS	Boil in water 2 minutes. Use this water to make syrup. Boil 5 minutes in syrup Pack, add syrup	30	10	5
GRAPES	Wash, stem, pack. Add syrup or water	15	8	5
PEACHES	Peel, pack, add syrup, or boil 3 minutes in syrup. Pack. Add syrup	20	10	5
PEARS	Peel, halve, boil 3 to 5 minutes in syrup Pack. Add syrup	25	10	5
PINEAPPLE	Slice, peel, remove eyes and core. Boil in syrup 3 to 5 minutes. Pack. Add syrup	30	15	5
PLUMS	Wash, prick skins. Pack. Add syrup	20	10	5
RHUBARB	Wash, cut into pieces. Pack. Add syrup or bake until tender. Pack. Add syrup	10	5	5
TOMATOES	Scald 1/2 minute, cold dip, peel, core, quarter. Pack	35	10	5
TOMATO JUICE	Peel, quarter; simmer until soft. Put through fine sieve. Bring to boil. Pour in jars to 1/4 inch of top	10	–	–

Cantaloupe

MANALOPE FRUIT CUP

2 cantaloupes, scooped into balls
1 c. watermelon balls
2 sm. cans mandarin oranges

Combine all ingredients; chill for several hours. Spoon fruits from liquid into glass dishes. Yield: 4-6 servings.

MELON DELIGHT

1 cantaloupe
2 peaches
1/3 c. sugar
Juice of 1/2 lemon
1/2 tsp. salt
2 tbsp. rosewater

Cut melon in half; remove seeds and scoop out balls. Peel and slice peaches. Combine cantaloupe balls, peaches, sugar, lemon juice and salt. Chill for several hours. Add rosewater; spoon into serving dishes. Top each serving with small amount of crushed ice. Yield: 4 servings.

MELON BALL COCKTAIL

Cantaloupe balls
Honeydew melon balls
Watermelon balls
2 tbsp. strained lemon juice
2 tbsp. strained orange juice
2 tbsp. lime juice
1/3 c. water
2/3 c. sugar

Fill sherbet dishes with melon balls; chill. Mix fruit juices, water and sugar; chill. Spoon over melon balls before serving.

DELUXE CANTALOUPE SALAD

4 cantaloupes, quartered
2 slices pineapple, cut in wedges
24 watermelon balls
1 c. seedless grapes
24 orange segments
12 grapefruit segments
2 c. red raspberries
French dressing
1 pt. mint sherbet

Fill cantaloupe quarters with remaining fruits, arranging attractively. Reserve 16 raspberries. Pour small amount of dressing over fruits; chill. Add scoop of sherbet just before serving; top with reserved raspberries. Yield: 16 servings.

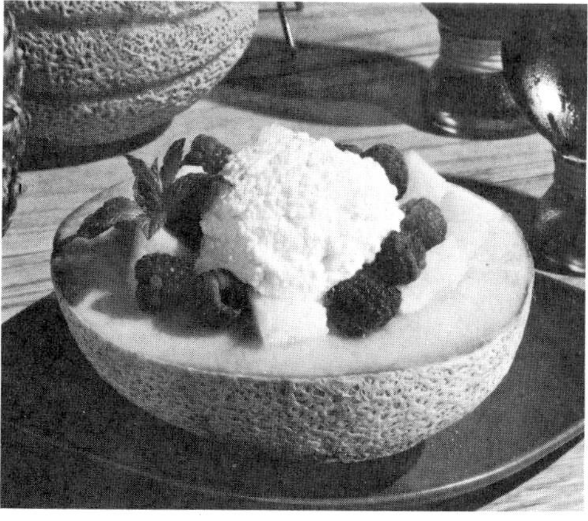

Fresh Cantaloupe Salad . . . A flavorful blend of low-calorie fruit and cottage cheese.

FRESH CANTALOUPE SALAD

3 fresh cantaloupe
2 c. cottage cheese
1 c. fresh raspberries
1 c. fresh pineapple wedges
Salad dressing

Chill cantaloupe. Cut in half lengthwise; scoop out seeds. Drain. Fill cavities with cottage cheese; surround cottage cheese with raspberries and pineapple wedges. Garnish with mint. Serve with salad dressing. Yield: 6 servings.

CANTALOUPE FRUIT SALAD

1 pkg. lime gelatin
1 1/2 c. ginger ale
1/2 c. halved white grapes
1 c. cantaloupe balls
2 fresh peaches, sliced
1/2 c. diced pineapple

Dissolve gelatin in 1/2 cup boiling water; cool. Add ginger ale and fruits. Pour into ring mold; chill until firm.

CANTALOUPE SALAD AND DRESSING

1 med. cantaloupe, peeled
Lettuce
3 oranges, peeled and sliced
3 fresh peaches, peeled and sliced
2 nectarines, peeled and sliced
5 slices pineapple
1 c. strawberries
White grapes
Yogurt Dressing

Slice cantaloupes crosswise into 5 rings. Use end pieces to make cantaloupe balls. Place rings on 5 lettuce-lined plates. Arrange orange, peach, nectarine and pineapple slices on top. Add strawberries and cantaloupe balls. Place small cluster of grapes by each ring. Serve with Yogurt Dressing.

Yogurt Dressing

1 c. yogurt
1/2 c. mayonnaise
1/2 c. blue cheese dressing

Combine all ingredients; beat until smooth. Chill until ready to serve.

CANTALOUPE-NUT BREAD

1/2 c. shortening
1 c. sugar
2 eggs
1 c. cooked cantaloupe
2 c. sifted flour
1 tsp. baking powder
1 tsp. soda
1/2 tsp. salt
1 tsp. pumpkin pie spice
1/2 c. chopped nuts
1/2 c. raisins

Cream shortening and sugar; beat in eggs. Stir in cantaloupe. Sift flour, baking powder, soda, salt and spice together; add to creamed mixture. Fold in nuts and raisins. Spread into greased and floured 9 x 5 x 3-inch pan. Bake at 325 degrees for 45 minutes.

CANTALOUPE PICKLE

3 1/2 lb. firm cantaloupe cubes
2 c. water
2 c. vinegar
3 1/2 c. sugar
Pinch of salt
1/2 tsp. oil of cinnamon
1/2 tsp. oil of cloves

Place cantaloupe cubes into medium crock. Combine remaining ingredients in saucepan; bring to a boil. Pour over cantaloupe; let stand overnight. Pour off syrup into saucepan; bring to a boil. Pour over cantaloupe; let stand overnight. Repeat procedure for 2 days. Heat cantaloupe and syrup together; bring to a boil. Pour into sterilized jars; seal.

CANTALOUPE WITH BLUEBERRY-WINE SAUCE

1/2 c. sugar
1 tbsp. cornstarch
3 thin slices lemon
3/4 c. port wine
2 c. blueberries
Vanilla ice cream
Peeled cantaloupe rings

Combine sugar, cornstarch, lemon and wine in small saucepan; simmer for 5 minutes or until clear. Remove lemon; add blueberries. Chill. Spoon ice cream into cantaloupe rings; top with blueberry sauce. Yield: 6-8 servings.

CANTALOUPE MARLOW

1/3 c. milk
20 marshmallows
1 1/2 c. ground cantaloupe
1/8 tsp. salt
1/4 c. ground maraschino cherries
1 c. whipping cream

Combine milk and marshmallows in saucepan; cover. Cook over low heat for 10 minutes or until marshmallows are melted. Cool; add cantaloupe, salt and cherries. Chill in freezer until mixture begins to thicken. Whip cream; fold into cantaloupe mixture. Pour into refrigerator tray; cover. Freeze until firm.

FROZEN CANTALOUPE

2 c. sugar
4 c. water
6 med. cantaloupe

Mix sugar and water in saucepan; cook until syrupy. Cool syrup; chill. Peel cantaloupe; remove seeds and fibers. Cut pulp into bite-sized pieces or scoop into balls. Pack into freezer cartons; shake down well. Cover with chilled syrup, leaving 1 inch headspace. Freeze immediately. Serve slightly frozen.

AUSTRIAN CANTALOUPE

1/2 c. brandy
1/4 lb. confectioners' sugar
Juice of 1 lemon
1 cantaloupe, peeled and cubed
1/2 pt. whipping cream
1 tsp. sugar
6 maraschino cherries
6 sprigs of mint

Mix brandy, confectioners' sugar and lemon juice; pour over cantaloupe. Cover tightly; refrigerate for at least 2 hours. Whip cream until stiff, adding sugar. Stir cantaloupe mixture lightly; spoon into dessert dishes. Top with whipped cream; garnish with cherries and mint.

CANTALOUPE SUPREME

2 c. strawberries
1 c. sugar
2 tsp. cornstarch
2 tbsp. butter
3 drops of red food coloring
2 tsp. lemon juice
4 c. small cantaloupe balls
1/2 pt. whipping cream, whipped

Combine strawberries, sugar, cornstarch, butter and food coloring in heavy saucepan; cook, stirring constantly, until thickened. Add lemon juice. Place cantaloupe balls in large buttered mold. Pour strawberry mixture over cantaloupe balls. Chill for 4 hours before serving. Decorate with whipped cream. Yield: 6-8 servings.

CANTALOUPE CHIFFON PIE

1 3-oz. package lemon gelatin
2 tbsp. lemon juice
1 c. whipping cream
1/4 c. sifted powdered sugar
1/4 tsp. pumpkin pie spice
2 c. diced cantaloupe
1 9-in. baked crumb crust

Dissolve gelatin in 1 cup boiling water; stir in lemon juice. Chill until partially congealed. Whip cream until stiff, beating in powdered sugar and spice. Whip gelatin until fluffy; fold in whipped cream and cantaloupe. Turn into crumb crust; chill until firm. Yield: 6-8 servings.

CANTALOUPE PIE

1 stick pie crust mix
1/4 c. toasted slivered almonds
2 tbsp. boiling water
2 c. milk
1 pkg. vanilla pudding mix
2 c. small cantaloupe balls
Toasted coconut

Combine pie crust mix and almonds. Stir in boiling water until pastry loses stickiness and comes away from side of bowl. Form into ball; roll on floured board to fit 9-inch pie plate. Place in plate; crimp edge. Prick surface with fork. Bake at 400 degrees for 10 to 12 minutes or until golden brown. Cool. Combine milk and pudding mix in saucepan. Cook over medium heat, stirring constantly, until mixture thickens. Cool for several minutes. Add cantaloupe balls; pour into pie shell. Chill. Sprinkle with coconut. Yield: 8 servings.

CANTALOUPE-ORANGE PIE

4 eggs, separated
1 c. sugar
1/2 tsp. salt
1 tbsp. lemon juice
1 tbsp. grated lemon peel
1/2 c. orange juice
1 pkg. orange gelatin
1/4 tsp. cream of tartar
1 1/2 c. diced cantaloupe, drained
1 10-in. baked pastry shell or crumb crust
1 c. whipping cream, whipped

Beat egg yolks, lightly in top of double boiler; add 1/2 cup sugar, salt, lemon juice and lemon peel. Cook until mixture coats spoon, stirring frequently; remove from heat. Bring orange juice to a boil; dissolve gelatin in orange juice. Stir gelatin into egg yolk mixture; cool. Beat egg whites and cream of tartar until stiff; beat in remaining sugar gradually. Fold in gelatin mixture; add cantaloupe. Pile into pastry shell; top with whipped cream. Chill for at least 4 hours. Yield: 8 servings.

Capon

(See CHICKEN and POULTRY.)

CAPON AND AVOCADO

1 6-lb. capon, quartered
1 qt. water
1 med. onion, chopped
2 to 3 stalks celery
1 1/2 tsp. salt
1/4 tsp. pepper
Butter
3 tbsp. flour
1 c. light cream
1/2 c. grated sharp cheese
Pinch of rosemary
Pinch of basil
Dash of hot sauce
1/2 lb. mushrooms, sliced
2 ripe avocados, diced
1/2 c. toasted slivered almonds

Place capon in large Dutch oven; add water, onion, celery, 1 teaspoon salt and pepper. Simmer until capon is tender; remove from broth. Cool. Remove meat from bones, except wings and neck; return bones, skin, neck and wings to broth. Simmer for 30 minutes. Strain stock; reserve and cool. Skim off excess fat. Melt 2 tablespoons butter in saucepan; blend in flour. Stir in 1 cup reserved stock and cream; cook, stirring, until thickened. Add cheese, remaining salt, rosemary, basil and hot sauce. Saute mushrooms in small amount butter. Place capon and mushrooms in casserole; pour sauce over top. Cover. Bake, at 350 degrees for 25 minutes. Add avocados. Bake for 10 minutes longer or until avocados are heated through. Sprinkle with almonds. Yield: 8 servings.

CAPON EUGENE

Butter
4 sm. capons
Salt and pepper to taste
Pinch of crushed rosemary
Pinch of crushed basil
4 slices ham
1/2 lb. mushrooms, sliced
1/2 c. sherry
1 c. light cream

Melt about 1/4 inch butter in heavy skillet over medium heat. Sprinkle capons with seasonings. Brown capons in butter on all sides. Cover skillet; reduce heat. Steam until capons are tender. Uncover; increase heat to medium. Cook capons on all sides long enough to crisp skin again. Remove to serving platter; keep warm. Fry ham lightly in skillet drippings; add to serving platter. Saute mushrooms in same skillet, adding butter as needed. Remove mushrooms from skillet. Stir sherry into skillet drippings, scraping any browned bits from bottom of skillet. Simmer for 5 minutes. Blend in cream; simmer for 5 minutes longer. Add mushrooms to sauce; heat through. Spoon sauce over capons and ham.

CAPON AND RICE

2 c. uncooked rice
10 sm. white onions
1 5 to 6-lb. capon
1/2 c. butter

Place rice and onions in large roasting pan; cover with water. Place capon on rack over rice; dot capon and rice with butter. Bake at 350 degrees for 2 hours or until done, adding hot water as needed. Yield: 6 servings.

Caramel

Caramel is a descriptive term for either a golden brown syrup or a chewy candy. The syrup is also known as burnt sugar. It is used as coloring, flavoring, or coating for desserts. **PREPARATION**: *For Syrup*—Melt granulated or brown sugar over low heat until golden brown in color. (NOTE: If sugar becomes dark brown from overheating, flavor will be bitter. Proper regulation of temperature is vital to the preparation of both caramel syrup and candy.) *For Candy*—Use brown or granulated sugar; corn or maple syrup; milk or cream; and butter. (Coffee, chocolate, raisins, and nuts are often added.) Cook ingredients over low heat until characteristic golden color develops. Be sure to follow temperature instructions on specific recipe. Cool in a *lightly* greased cooling pan to prevent globules of grease from clinging to candy. As candy hardens, score into bite-sized cubes. When thoroughly cooled, cut, remove from pan, and wrap each cube.

(See CANDY.)

CARAMEL CAKE

2 c. flour
1 c. cornstarch
1 tsp. cream of tartar
1 c. butter
2 c. sugar
4 eggs, separated
1 tsp. soda
1 c. buttermilk
1 1/2 tsp. vanilla
2 c. (packed) brown sugar
1/2 c. cream

Sift flour, cornstarch and cream of tartar together. Cream 1/2 cup butter and sugar until fluffy; beat in egg yolks. Stir soda into buttermilk. Add flour mixture to creamed mixture alternately with buttermilk. Stir in 1 teaspoon vanilla. Beat egg whites until stiff; fold into batter. Turn batter into lightly greased 13 x 9 x 2-inch pan. Bake at 350 degrees for 50 minutes to 1 hour or until cake tests done. Mix remaining butter, brown sugar, cream and remaining vanilla; spread over cake. Place cake under broiler until topping is melted and bubbly.

CARAMEL CAKE RING

3 tbsp. butter, melted
1 tbsp. warm water
1/3 c. (packed) brown sugar
2/3 c. toasted coconut
1 sm. package white cake mix

Combine butter, warm water and brown sugar; spread in bottom of greased 9-inch mold. Sprinkle coconut into mold. Prepare cake mix according to package directions; pour batter into mold. Bake at 350 degrees for 25 to 30 minutes or until cake tests done. Loosen cake from pan around edge; invert onto plate. Let stand for 1 minute; remove mold. Cool cake. Fill center of cake with fresh fruits and whipped cream or ice cream, if desired. Yield: 8 servings.

BLACK WALNUT CARAMELS

1 c. sugar
7/8 c. dark corn syrup
1 c. cream
1/2 c. butter
1/2 tsp. vanilla
1/2 c. chopped black walnuts

Combine sugar, corn syrup, 1/2 cup cream and butter in heavy saucepan; bring to a boil. Stir in remaining cream slowly; candy should remain at a boil. Cook to firm-ball stage. Remove from heat. Add vanilla and black walnuts; turn into greased shallow pan. Cool. Cut into cubes; wrap separately in waxed paper.

BUTTER CARAMELS

1 c. sugar
1 c. light corn syrup
1 c. light cream
1/4 c. butter
1 c. chopped pecans
1 tsp. vanilla

Combine sugar, syrup, cream and butter in large heavy saucepan. Cook over medium heat, stirring occasionally, until mixture begins to caramelize. Reduce heat; cook, stirring constantly, to 244 degrees on candy thermometer or firm-ball stage. Remove from heat; stir in pecans and vanilla. Spread in greased 8-inch square pan; cool. Cut into squares.

CARAMEL CHEWS

1 c. corn flakes	*1 c. chopped pecans*
1 c. oven-toasted rice cereal	*36 vanilla caramels*
1 c. flaked coconut	*3 tbsp. light cream*

Combine corn flakes, rice cereal, coconut and pecans in bowl. Place caramels and cream in top of double boiler; stir over hot water until caramels are melted. Pour over cereal mixture; mix with greased spoon. Drop from spoon onto waxed paper; cool.

CHRISTMAS CARAMELS

2 c. sugar	*1 2/3 c. evaporated milk*
1 c. butter	*4 tsp. vanilla*
1 3/4 c. light corn syrup	*1 c. finely chopped nutmeats*

Combine sugar, butter, corn syrup and milk in large saucepan. Cook over high heat, stirring frequently, for about 5 minutes or to 210 degrees on candy thermometer. Reduce heat to medium; continue cooking, stirring constantly to firm-ball stage or 244 degrees on candy thermometer. Remove from heat immediately. Add vanilla and nutmeats; stir quickly to blend. Pour mixture into greased 9-inch square pan. Chill thoroughly. Turn candy out onto wooden cutting board; cut into small squares with sharp knife. Wrap each square individually in heavy waxed paper. Yield: 3 lb. candy.

Christmas Caramels . . . Delicious candies perfect for holiday parties or gift-giving.

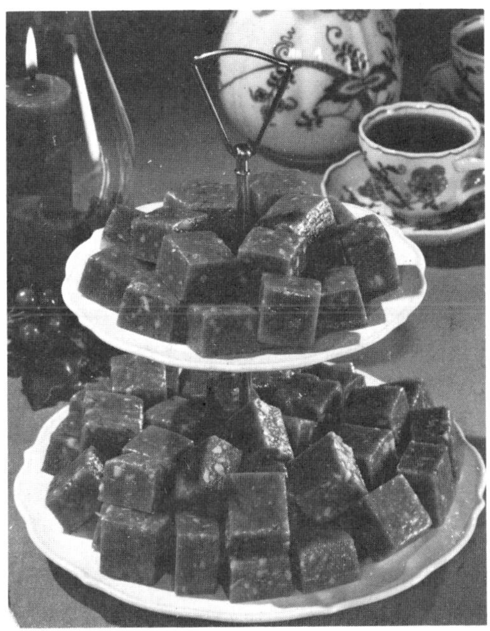

GRANDMA'S CARAMEL CANDY

2 c. sugar	*1 2/3 c. evaporated milk*
Pinch of salt	*1 tsp. vanilla*
1/2 c. butter	*1 1/2 c. chopped Brazil nuts*
2 c. light corn syrup	

Combine sugar, salt, butter and corn syrup in heavy saucepan. Bring to a boil over low heat, stirring constantly. Add milk slowly; candy should remain at a boil. Cook, without stirring, to 244 degrees on candy thermometer or firm-ball stage. Stir in vanilla and nuts; pour into greased shallow pan. Cool; cut into squares.

VANILLA CARAMELS

2 c. sugar	*1/2 tsp. salt*
2 c. light corn syrup	*1 13-oz. can evaporated milk*
1/2 c. butter or margarine	*2 tsp. vanilla*

Combine sugar, corn syrup, butter and salt in heavy 3-quart saucepan. Bring to a boil, stirring constantly. Stir in milk, 1/4 cup at a time. Cook, stirring constantly, to 265 degrees on candy thermometer or hard-ball stage. Remove from heat; add vanilla. Pour candy into greased 8-inch square pan. Cool; cut into small squares. Wrap each square in plastic wrap. Yield: 2 1/2 pounds.

CARAMEL-NUT DELIGHT

3 eggs, separated	*1/2 tsp. salt*
2 1/4 c. sugar	*1/2 c. hot strong coffee*
1 c. fine graham cracker crumbs	*1/4 c. evaporated milk*
3/4 c. finely chopped nuts	*Vanilla ice cream*

Preheat oven to 325 degrees. Beat egg whites until stiff but not dry. Beat egg yolks until thick and lemon colored, beating in 1 cup sugar. Fold egg whites, cracker crumbs, nuts and 1/4 teaspoon salt into egg yolk mixture. Spread in greased and floured 9-inch pie plate. Bake for 35 to 40 minutes; cool in pan. Spread remaining sugar in heavy saucepan; stir over medium heat until sugar is melted and golden brown. Add coffee slowly, stirring constantly. Mixture will boil up. Cook for 5 minutes or to smooth syrup. Cool for about 3 minutes. Add milk and remaining salt gradually, beating vigorously. Cut dessert into wedges; top with ice cream and sauce.

CARAMEL SUNDAES

3 tbsp. butter	*1/2 c. light cream*
1 c. (packed) brown sugar	*4 bananas, sliced*
	Ice cream
1/2 tsp. cinnamon	*Toasted coconut*

Melt butter in saucepan; add brown sugar and cinnamon. Stir over low heat until sugar is melted. Remove from heat; stir in cream. Return to low heat; drop in bananas. Serve hot over ice cream; sprinkle with toasted coconut.

CARAMEL-TOPPED BREAD PUDDING

2 eggs, beaten
1/3 c. sugar
1/4 tsp. salt
2 c. milk
1/2 tsp. vanilla
3 slices stale bread, cut in cubes
1/3 c. raisins
1/3 c. (packed) brown sugar
1 tbsp. soft butter
1 tbsp. cream
1/3 c. chopped nuts

Beat eggs with sugar and salt; add milk and vanilla. Stir in bread cubes and raisins. Place in 8-inch square pan. Place pan in container of water. Bake in 350-degree oven for 1 hour or until firm. Combine brown sugar, butter, cream and nuts; spread over pudding. Bake until topping is bubbly. Serve warm.

CARAMEL CUTS

1 1/2 c. flour
2 tsp. baking powder
1/2 tsp. salt
1/2 c. butter
2 eggs, beaten
2 c. (packed) light brown sugar
1 tsp. vanilla
1 c. chopped pecans

Sift flour, baking powder and salt together. Melt butter in saucepan; stir in eggs, sugar, vanilla and flour mixture. Add pecans; spread batter in greased 12 x 7 x 2-inch pan. Bake at 350 degrees for 30 minutes. Cut into 18 bars; cool on rack.

CARAMEL-NUT SQUARES

1 1/2 c. flour
1 tsp. baking powder
1/4 tsp. salt
1/2 c. butter or margarine
1 c. sugar
2 eggs, separated
2 tsp. vanilla
1 c. chopped nuts
1 c. (packed) brown sugar

Sift flour, baking powder and salt together. Cream butter and sugar; beat in egg yolks and 1 teaspoon vanilla. Stir in flour mixture and nuts; spread in greased and waxed paper-lined 13 x 9 x 2-inch pan. Beat egg whites until stiff, beating in brown sugar and remaining vanilla. Spread meringue over batter. Bake at 375 degrees for 45 minutes. Cool; cut into squares.

UNBAKED CARAMEL COOKIES

2 c. sugar
3/4 c. butter or margarine
1 6-oz. can evaporated milk
1 4-oz. package instant butterscotch pudding mix
3 1/2 c. quick oats

Combine sugar, butter and milk in large saucepan. Bring to a boil, stirring frequently. Remove from heat; add pudding mix and oats. Mix well; cool for 15 minutes. Drop from teaspoon onto waxed paper-lined tray.

CRISP CARAMEL COOKIES

3 c. flour
1/2 tsp. salt
1 tsp. soda
1 1/4 c. soft butter
1 c. (packed) brown sugar
1 c. sugar
2 eggs
3/4 c. chopped nuts

Sift flour, salt and soda together. Cream butter and sugars well; beat in eggs. Add flour mixture and nuts; mix well. Shape dough into small rolls; wrap in waxed paper. Freeze dough until ready to bake. Cut dough into 1/8-inch slices; place on baking sheet. Bake at 400 degrees for 8 to 10 minutes.

BAKED CARAMEL CUSTARD

1 c. (packed) brown sugar
3 eggs
1/4 c. sugar
1/8 tsp. salt
2 c. milk, scalded
1 tsp. rum flavoring

Spread brown sugar in baking dish. Beat eggs until light, beating in sugar and salt. Stir in milk slowly; add rum flavoring. Pour over brown sugar. Place baking dish in pan of hot water. Bake at 350 degrees until firm. Invert onto platter. Yield: 5 servings.

FRENCH CUSTARD

1 1/4 c. sugar
4 eggs
1 tsp. vanilla
3 c. scalded milk

Heat 1/2 cup sugar in heavy skillet until melted and browned. Pour into 6 custard cups. Beat eggs with remaining sugar and vanilla. Add hot milk, beating constantly. Fill custard cups with mixture; place cups in pan of hot water. Bake at 350 degrees for 30 minutes or until set. Chill for several hours. Yield: 6 servings.

CARAMEL CANDY PIE

18 graham crackers
1/4 c. sugar
1/4 c. melted butter or margarine
1 tbsp. unflavored gelatin
1/4 c. cold water
28 light caramel candies
3/4 c. milk
1/2 pt. heavy cream
1 c. chopped nuts
1 tsp. vanilla

Crush graham crackers to fine crumbs; add sugar and butter. Press crumb mixture against bottom and side of 8 or 9-inch pie plate. Bake at 375 degrees for 8 minutes; cool. Soften gelatin in cold water. Combine candies and milk in top of double boiler; stir over boiling water until candies are melted. Dissolve gelatin in hot mixture; cool. Whip cream until stiff; fold whipped cream, nuts and vanilla into caramel mixture. Turn into crumb crust; chill for several hours before serving. Yield: 6-8 servings.

CARAMEL CREAM PIE

2 1/4 c. sugar
1/4 c. flour
5 eggs, separated
2 c. milk
1/4 c. butter
1 tsp. vanilla
2 9-in. baked pie shells
1/4 c. slivered toasted almonds

Spread 2 cups sugar in heavy skillet; stir over low heat until sugar is melted and browned. Cool slightly. Blend flour into sugar. Beat eggs yolks; stir in milk. Add to flour mixture, stirring. Cook over low heat, stirring constantly, until thickened. Add butter and vanilla; cool to room temperature. Beat egg whites until foamy; add remaining sugar gradually, beating until stiff and glossy. Pour filling into pie shells; spread meringue over filling. Sprinkle with almonds. Bake at 350 degrees until meringue is lightly browned. Yield: 12 servings.

Carrot

The bright orange carrot is a root vegetable. Both the root and the green tops are considered edible portions; usually only the roots are served. Carrots contain carotene, a chemical compound that the body converts to Vitamin A. (1 raw carrot = 20 calories)

AVAILABILITY: Available canned, frozen, or fresh year-round, with January-June the most abundant period for fresh carrots.

BUYING: Fresh carrots are sold with or without tops in bundles or in plastic bags. Select fresh carrots that are firm, well-shaped, and smooth. The brighter the color, the more carotene a carrot contains. Wilted, soft, or shriveled carrots will be tasteless. Large plump carrots with cracked surfaces are fibrous and will have poor flavor.

STORING: Fresh carrots may be stored from one to three weeks in the refrigerator vegetable crisper. Before storing, remove and discard tops; rinse root in cold running water. Wrap in foil, waxed paper, or plastic bags. *To freeze* carrots, remove tops and wash. Scrape with vegetable scraper. Leave small carrots whole, dice larger ones or cut them lengthwise. Scald for 3 1/2 minutes; cool in ice water. Drain and package, leaving 1 inch space at top. Seal, label, date, and freeze. Use within 1 year.

PREPARATION: Carrots are most often cooked by boiling. Allow 1-1 1/2 pounds to serve 4 people. Scrape thin skin off with vegetable scraper. Leave carrots whole, dice, or slice them. Place in 1 inch boiling salted water. Cook covered. Whole carrots cook in 15-20 minutes, diced or sliced carrots in 10-20 minutes. Drain and serve.

SERVING: Cooked carrots are most often served as a vegetable side dish. They may be scalloped, glazed, or used in casseroles. Raw carrots are often used in salads and slaws or as an appetizer.

(See VEGETABLES.)

CARROTS WITH ARTICHOKE HEARTS

1 pkg. frozen artichoke hearts
1 1/2 lb. carrots, sliced
Butter
1/2 lb. mushrooms, quartered
1 tbsp. olive oil
Salt to taste
Freshly ground pepper to taste
2 tbsp. minced green onion
1/3 c. beef bouillon
2 tbsp. minced parsley

Cook artichoke hearts according to package directions; drain. Braise carrots lightly in small amount of butter. Saute mushrooms in oil and 1 1/2 tablespoons butter until brown; season with salt and pepper. Combine green onion, artichoke hearts and mushrooms in saucepan; cook, stirring, for at least 2 minutes over moderately high heat. Fold carrots into artichoke mixture; add bouillon. Cover; cook slowly for at least 4 minutes or until bouillon is almost evaporated. Season to taste. Spoon vegetables into hot serving dish; sprinkle with parsley. Yield: 6 servings.

CARROTS IN COGNAC

1 c. butter
3 dozen small carrots
Dash of salt
1 tsp. sugar
1/3 c. cognac

Melt butter in baking dish; add carrots, salt and sugar. Sprinkle with cognac; cover. Bake in 350-degree oven for 1 hour or until carrots are tender but not brown. Yield: 6 servings.

CARROT CROQUETTES

4 c. cooked carrots
1/2 tsp. salt
1/2 tsp. nutmeg
1 egg, beaten
2 tbsp. butter, melted
1 c. dry bread crumbs
Sprigs of parsley

Press carrots through coarse sieve; add salt, nutmeg, egg and butter, mixing thoroughly. Form mixture into carrot shapes; roll in crumbs. Chill for several hours or longer. Fry in hot deep fat until browned; drain on paper towels. Tuck 1 sprig of parsley in each top. Serve immediately. Yield: 8 servings

CARROTS LYONNAISE

6 med. carrots
1 chicken bouillon cube
4 tbsp. butter
3 med. onions, sliced
1 tbsp. flour
1/4 tsp. salt
Dash of pepper
Sugar

Cut carrots into 3 by 1/4-inch strips. Dissolve bouillon cube in 1/2 cup boiling water. Add carrots; cook, covered, for 10 minutes. Melt butter in skillet; add onions. Cook, covered, for 15 minutes, stirring occasionally. Combine flour, salt and pepper; stir in 3/4 cup water gradually. Bring to a boil. Add carrots and chicken stock; simmer about 10 minutes or until tender. Add pinch of sugar before serving. Yield: 6 servings.

CARROTS ELEGANTE

1 lb. carrots
1/4 c. butter
1/2 tsp. salt
2 tsp. sugar
1/2 tsp. celery seed
1/4 c. orange juice

Slice carrots into thin rounds. Melt butter in large saucepan; stir in salt, sugar, celery seed and carrots. Cover. Simmer, stirring frequently, for 10 minutes. Stir in orange juice; cook for 5 minutes longer or until carrots are crisp-tender. Spoon into heated serving bowl; garnish with fresh chopped parsley. Yield: 4 servings.

CARROT COLESLAW

2 c. finely chopped cabbage
2 c. shredded carrots
2 tsp. minced onion
1/4 c. chopped green pepper
1 tsp. salt
1/4 tsp. pepper
3/4 c. sour cream
2 tbsp. vinegar
1 tbsp. sugar
1 3-oz. package cream cheese, softened

Combine cabbage, carrots, onion, green pepper, salt and pepper. Blend sour cream, vinegar, sugar and cream cheese. Toss sour cream mixture with cabbage mixture. Serve chilled. Yield: 6 servings.

Candied Carrots and Grapes . . . A party-perfect side dish that is easy-to-prepare.

CARROTS IN ORANGE SAUCE WITH ALMONDS

10 to 12 carrots
1/2 c. slivered almonds
1 tbsp. butter
1 1/2 tbsp. (packed) brown sugar
2 tsp. cornstarch
1/4 tsp. salt
1/8 tsp. cinnamon
1/8 tsp. nutmeg
1 c. orange juice
1 tsp. grated orange rind

Cut carrots into strips; place in saucepan in water to cover. Bring to a boil; reduce heat. Simmer until tender. Saute almonds in butter in skillet for 5 minutes; remove from pan. Set aside. Combine brown sugar, cornstarch, salt, cinnamon and nutmeg; add orange juice and rind. Cook, stirring constantly, until thickened and clear. Add almonds. Serve over hot carrots. Yield: 6 servings.

CARROT-NUT MOLD

1 6-oz. package orange gelatin
1 c. sour cream
2 c. grated carrots
1 13 1/2-oz. can crushed pineapple
1/2 c. chopped walnuts
Salad greens

Combine 2 cups hot water and gelatin; stir until gelatin is dissolved. Add gelatin mixture to sour cream gradually, stirring until blended. Chill until partially thickened. Fold in carrots, pineapple and walnuts. Turn into greased 2-quart mold; chill for about 4 hours or until firm. Unmold on salad greens; garnish

with carrot curls and walnut halves. Yield: 12 servings.

CARROT-FRUIT SALAD

1 pkg. orange or lemon gelatin
2 carrots, grated
1 No. 2 can crushed pineapple

Dissolve gelatin in 1 cup boiling water; cool. Add carrots and pineapple. Pour into oiled mold; refrigerate for 2 hours or longer. Unmold; place on large salad plate. Garnish with lettuce leaves. Yield: 6-8 servings.

HOT CARROT SALAD

6 carrots, coarsely grated
4 tbsp. minced onion
4 tbsp. minced celery
1 tbsp. butter
1 tsp. sugar
1/2 tsp. salt

Place carrots, onion, celery, butter, 1/4 cup water, sugar and salt in skillet. Cook, covered, over medium heat for 10 minutes. Serve hot. Yield: 4-6 servings.

RELISHED CARROTS

1/2 c. cider vinegar
1/2 c. salad oil
3/4 c. sugar
1 can whole baby carrots
1 tbsp. chopped pimento
1/2 c. green pickle relish

Mix vinegar, salad oil and sugar in saucepan; bring to a boil. Remove from heat. Add carrots; refrigerate overnight. Drain. Add pimento and pickle relish; serve. Yield: 6 servings.

SAVORY CARROT STICKS

6 med. carrots
1/2 c. chopped onion
3 tbsp. vegetable margarine
1/4 tsp. rosemary
Salt and pepper to taste
Parsley, minced

Cut carrots into 2-inch sticks. Place carrot sticks in top of double boiler; add onion, margarine and rosemary. Cover; cook over boiling water for 30 minutes or until crunchy. Season with salt and pepper. Sprinkle with minced parsley. Yield: 4 servings.

CANDIED CARROTS AND GRAPES

1/4 c. butter
2 tsp. cornstarch
1/3 c. honey
1 tsp. lemon juice
1/8 tsp. cinnamon
3 c. cooked sliced carrots
1 c. green grapes, halved

Melt butter in small saucepan; blend in cornstarch. Add honey, lemon juice and cinnamon. Cook, stirring constantly, until mixture boils. Add glaze to carrots and grapes; stirring to mix. Serve immediately. Yield: 6-8 servings.

BAKED CARROTS

4 c. mashed cooked carrots
1 c. bread crumbs
1 tbsp. minced onion
3 tbsp. melted shortening
1/4 tsp. pepper
1 tsp. salt
1/4 c. grated cheese

Combine carrots, crumbs, onion, shortening, pepper and salt. Turn into greased baking dish; sprinkle with cheese. Bake at 350 degrees for 15 to 20 minutes. Yield: 6-8 servings.

BUFFET CHEESE-SCALLOPED CARROTS

12 med. carrots, sliced
1 sm. onion, minced
1/4 c. butter or margarine
1/4 c. flour
1 tsp. salt
1/4 tsp. dry mustard
2 c. milk
1/8 tsp. pepper
1/4 tsp. celery seed
1/2 lb. sharp American cheese, sliced
3 c. buttered cracker crumbs

Cook carrots in boiling salted water until tender; drain. Saute onion in butter in skillet for at least 2 minutes. Combine flour, salt, mustard and milk. Stir into onion in skillet. Cook, stirring constantly, until mixture is smooth and thickened. Add pepper and celery seed. Arrange carrots and cheese, alternately, in greased 2-quart casserole, ending with carrots. Pour sauce over carrots; top with crumbs. Bake at 350 degrees for 25 minutes. Yield: 8 servings.

CANDIED CARROTS

1/4 c. margarine
1/4 c. jellied cranberry sauce
2 tbsp. sugar
1/2 tsp. salt
2 No. 303 cans sliced carrots

Combine margarine, cranberry sauce, sugar and salt in skillet; simmer until cranberry sauce melts. Drain carrots. Add carrots to cranberry mixture, stirring well. Place in baking dish. Bake at 350 degrees for 10 minutes. Yield: 6 servings.

CARROT-APPLE CASSEROLE

8 med. apples, sliced
4 carrots, sliced
1/2 tsp. salt
4 tbsp. butter

Place apples and carrots in alternate layers in well-greased baking dish; sprinkle each layer with salt. Dot with butter. Bake, covered, in 350-degree oven for 45 minutes. Yield: 6 servings.

CARROT CASSEROLE

3 c. diced carrots
12 saltines, crumbled
2 tsp. minced onion
2 tbsp. butter
1/2 tsp. pepper
1/4 c. grated cheese

Cook carrots in boiling water to cover; drain. Reserve 2/3 cup carrot liquid. Mash carrots; add saltines, onion, butter and pepper stirring well. Place in casserole; pour over carrot liquid. Sprinkle with cheese. Bake in 375-degree oven until cheese melts. Yield: 4-5 servings.

CARROT-CAULIFLOWER CASSEROLE

2 pkg. frozen cauliflower
6 med. carrots, sliced
1 can mushroom soup
1/3 c. milk
Sliced American cheese
Salt and pepper to taste
Butter

Cook cauliflower according to package directions; drain. Place carrots in small amount of boiling salted water; cook until tender and drain. Arrange cauliflower and carrots in buttered shallow casserole. Combine soup and milk; pour over vegetables. Cover with cheese; sprinkle with salt and pepper. Dot with butter. Bake in 350-degree oven for 1 hour. Yield: 4-6 servings.

CARROT CUSTARD

2 c. cooked carrots, mashed
2 eggs, beaten
1 c. cracker crumbs
1 1/2 c. milk
1 c. shredded cheese
4 tbsp. butter
1/2 tsp. salt
2 slices bacon

Combine carrots, eggs, crumbs, milk, cheese, butter and salt; stir well. Pour into 1 1/2-quart greased casserole; arrange bacon over top. Bake at 350 degrees for 30 to 45 minutes. Yield: 6 servings.

CARROT DELIGHT

2 c. mashed cooked carrots
1 c. milk
1 c. cracker crumbs
1/2 c. grated sharp cheese
1/4 c. grated onion
1/3 c. soft butter
1 tsp. salt
1/4 tsp. pepper
1/8 tsp. red pepper
3 eggs, beaten

Combine carrots, milk, crumbs, cheese, onion, butter, salt, pepper and red pepper; mix well. Fold eggs into carrot mixture. Pour into well-oiled 1 1/2-quart ring mold. Bake in 350-degree oven for 30 minutes. Turn out onto hot platter; fill center with buttered green peas, if desired. Garnish with sprigs of parsley. Yield: 8 servings.

CARROT LOAF

1 1/2 c. ground carrots
1 c. peanuts, ground
2 c. cooked rice
1 egg
2 tbsp. onion juice
1/2 tsp. mustard
1/2 tsp. salt
2 bacon slices
2 tbsp. chopped green pepper

Combine carrots, peanuts, rice, egg, onion juice, mustard and salt, mixing well. Fry bacon in skillet until crisp; drain. Crumble bacon finely. Add bacon and green pepper to carrot mixture, stirring well. Place in greased 1 1/2-quart loaf pan. Bake at 350 degrees for 1 hour. Yield: 8 servings.

PIQUANT CARROT RING

2 c. mashed cooked carrots
3 eggs
1 tsp. chopped onion
1 tsp. salt
Dash of red pepper
1 c. milk

Combine carrots, eggs, onion, salt, pepper and milk; mix well. Pour into greased mold. Place in pan of water. Bake at 375 degrees for 35 minutes. Unmold on serving platter. Center of ring may be filled with creamed peas or lima beans. Yield: 8 servings.

COPPER PENNIES

2 lb. carrots, thinly sliced
1 sm. green pepper, chopped
1 med. onion, chopped
1 10 3/4-oz. can tomato soup
1/2 c. cooking oil
1 c. sugar
3/4 c. vinegar
1 tsp. prepared mustard
1 tsp. Worcestershire sauce
Salt and pepper to taste

Cook carrots in small amount of salted water for about 7 minutes. Cool and drain. Place layer of carrots, green pepper and onion in 1 1/2-quart casserole. Combine tomato soup, oil, sugar, vinegar, mustard, Worcestershire sauce, salt and pepper; beat until well blended. Pour over carrots. Cover with plastic wrap. Refrigerate for several hours or until flavors are blended. Bake in 375-degree oven until bubbly. Yield: 12-14 servings.

SCALLOPED CARROTS

12 med. carrots, sliced
1/4 c. butter
1 onion, minced
1/4 c. flour
1 tsp. salt
1/4 tsp. dry mustard
1/4 tsp. celery salt
2 1/2 c. milk
1/2 lb. sharp cheese, grated
3 c. buttered bread crumbs

Cook carrots in boiling salted water to cover until tender; drain. Melt butter in saucepan; add onion. Blend in flour, salt, mustard and celery salt. Add milk gradually; cook, stirring constantly, until sauce is thickened. Arrange alternate layers of carrots and cheese in greased baking dish, ending with carrots. Pour sauce over top; sprinkle with crumbs. Bake at 350 degrees for at least 35 minutes or until bubbly. Yield: 8 servings.

SWEDISH CARROT RING

1 c. bread crumbs
1/2 c. melted shortening
1 tsp. salt
1/2 tsp. sugar
1 1/2 c. milk
1/8 tsp. almond flavoring
3 c. cooked carrots, grated
4 eggs, beaten
Cooked peas

Combine crumbs, shortening, salt, sugar, milk and almond flavoring. Let stand for several minutes. Stir carrots and eggs into crumb mixture. Pour into greased ring mold; set in pan of water. Bake at 325 degrees for 45 minutes or until knife inserted in center comes out clean. Unmold; fill center with peas. Yield: 6-8 servings.

COMPANY CARROTS

1 lb. carrots, sliced
1 tbsp. butter
2 tbsp. orange marmalade

Combine carrots, butter and marmalade; add enough water to cover. Simmer until tender.

ZESTY CARROTS

12 med. carrots
4 tbsp. grated onion
1 1/2 tsp. horseradish
1 c. mayonnaise
1 tsp. salt
1/2 tsp. pepper
Buttered crumbs
Paprika

Slice carrots diagonally; cook in boiling salted water to cover until tender. Drain, reserving 1/2 cup liquid. Place carrots in baking dish. Combine reserved liquid, onion, horseradish, mayonnaise, salt and pepper; pour over carrots. Top with crumbs; sprinkle with paprika lightly. Bake at 375 degrees for at least 15 minutes. Yield: 6-8 servings.

CARROT CAKE

2 c. sugar
4 eggs, beaten
2 c. sifted flour
2 tsp. soda
3/4 tbsp. salt
2 tsp. cinnamon
1 1/2 c. cooking oil
1 c. chopped pecans
2 c. coarsely grated carrots

Add sugar to eggs gradually, stirring well. Combine flour, soda, salt and cinnamon; reserve small amount of flour. Add flour mixture and oil to egg mixture, alternately, beginning and ending with flour. Dredge pecans with reserved flour. Fold in pecans and carrots. Pour batter into greased waxed paper-lined layer cake pans. Bake at 350 degrees for 30 to 40 minutes. Remove cake pans from oven; cool cake in pans for 10 minutes. Turn onto racks to cool thoroughly.

Filling

2 8-oz. packages cream cheese
2 tsp. vanilla
1/2 c. butter
1 3/4 c. powdered sugar, sifted
1 1/2 c. chopped pecans

Mix cheese, vanilla, butter and powdered sugar. Add pecans; mix well. Spread between layers and on top of cake. Yield: 20 servings.

CARROT-PINEAPPLE CAKE

2 c. flour
2 tsp. baking powder
1 1/2 tsp. soda
1 tsp. salt
1 1/2 c. oil
2 c. sugar
4 eggs
2 c. grated carrots
1 sm. can crushed pineapple
1/2 c. chopped nuts
2 tsp. vanilla

Sift dry ingredients together; blend in oil, sugar and eggs. Beat until well blended. Mix in carrots, pineapple, nuts and vanilla. Pour into two greased and floured 8 or 9-inch round pans. Bake at 350 degrees for 35 to 40 minutes. Cool layers for 10 minutes in pans. Remove to racks; cool thoroughly.

Filling

3 1/2 c. powdered sugar, sifted
1/2 c. butter, softened
1 tsp. vanilla
1 3-oz. package cream cheese

Blend powdered sugar with butter, vanilla and cream cheese. Spread between layers and on top of cake; let frosting drizzle down side of cake.

CARROT-ORANGE COOKIES

1 c. mashed cooked carrots
1 c. shortening
1 c. sugar
1 egg
1 tsp. vanilla
1 tsp. lemon flavoring
2 c. sifted flour
2 tsp. baking powder
3/4 c. chopped nuts
Powdered sugar
Juice of 1 orange

Combine carrots, shortening and sugar, mixing until smooth; add egg, vanilla and lemon flavoring. Mix flour, baking powder and nuts; add to egg mixture. Drop from teaspoon onto greased cookie sheet. Bake in 350-degree oven for 12 to 15 minutes. Blend powdered sugar with enough orange juice to make icing. Spread icing on cooled cookies.

HERBED CARROTS WITH GREEN GRAPES

1 1/2 lb. carrots
1/2 tsp. salt
1 tsp. basil
1/2 c. butter
1 sm. clove of garlic, crushed
1/2 tsp. thyme
1/4 tsp. celery salt
1 c. seedless grapes
1 tbsp. lemon juice
1/8 tsp. salt
Dash of pepper

Cut carrots into 3 x 1/4-inch strips; place carrots in saucepan. Add salt, basil and boiling water to cover. Cook, covered, for at least 12 minutes or until carrots are crisp-tender. Melt butter; add garlic, thyme and celery salt. Set aside. Remove carrots from heat; add grapes. Let stand, covered, for about 2 minutes; drain. Stir lemon juice into butter and herb mixture; pour over carrots. Sprinkle with salt and pepper; toss mixture gently. Serve immediately.

MINTED GLAZED CARROTS

12 sm. carrots
1/4 c. butter
1/2 c. sugar
2 tbsp. fresh chopped mint

Cook carrots in boiling salted water until tender; drain. Melt butter in small saucepan; add sugar, stirring until blended. Place hot carrots in skillet; pour butter mixture over carrots. Cook until carrots are glazed but not brown. Sprinkle with chopped mint before serving. Canned baby carrots may be substituted for fresh carrots. Yield: 6 servings.

SUNSHINE CARROTS

5 med. carrots
1 tbsp. sugar
1 tsp. cornstarch
1/4 tsp. salt
1/4 tsp. ginger
1/4 c. orange juice
2 tbsp. butter

Cut carrots in slices, 1 inch thick; place in boiling salted water. Cover; cook for about 20 minutes or until tender. Drain. Combine sugar, cornstarch, salt and ginger in small saucepan. Add orange juice; mix well. Cook, stirring constantly, until mixture is thickened and bubbly; cook for 1 minute. Stir butter into orange juice mixture; pour over hot carrots, tossing to coat evenly. Yield: 4 servings.

Carving

Carving is an art that homemakers across America take pride in mastering. The instructions and illustrations that follow show the art of carving beef, pork, ham, lamb, chicken, and turkey. By following these instructions, you can be certain that the slices of meat you place on the table will be as good to look at as they are to eat.

STANDING RIB ROAST

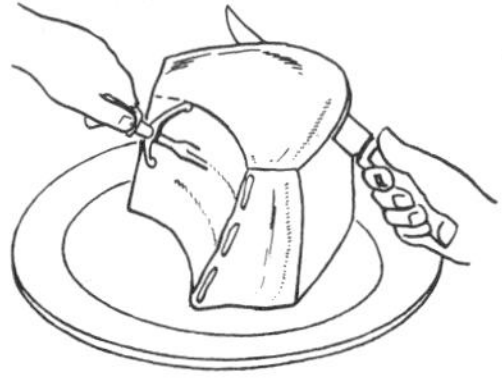

1. Place the roast on the platter with the largest end down to form a solid base. Insert the fork between the two top ribs. Starting across on the fat side, carve across the grain to the rib bone.

2. Use the tip of the knife to cut along the rib bone to loosen the slice. Be sure to keep close to the bone, to make the largest servings possible.

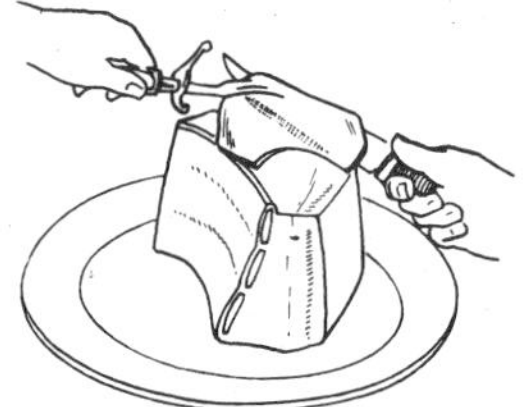

3. Slide the knife back under the slice, and steadying it with the fork, lift the slice to the side of the platter. If the platter is not large enough, place the slices on a heated platter close by.

ROLLED RIB ROAST

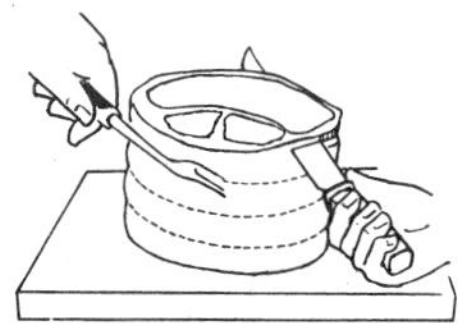

1. Do not remove the cords from the roast before carving. Insert the fork into the left side of the roast about one or two inches below the top. Start slicing across the meat grain from the right side toward the fork.

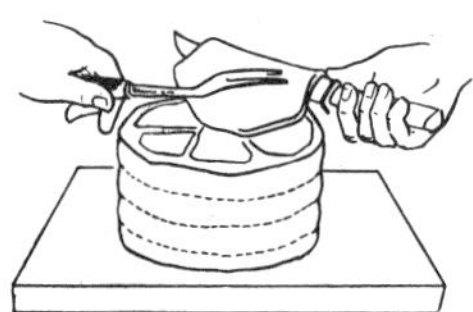

2. Make the first slice fairly thick to get a level surface. Use the knife and fork to lift each slice to the side of the platter. Move the fork lower in the meat for each slice and sever the cords as they are reached.

PICNIC SHOULDER

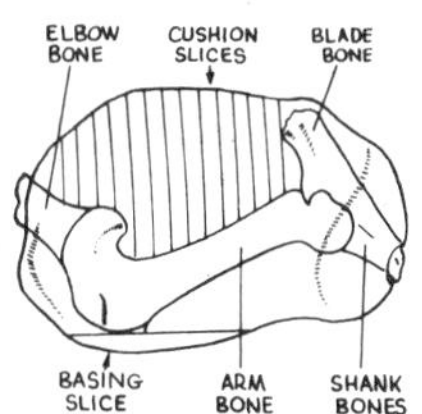

1. This diagram is your road map for carving attractive servings from a pork picnic shoulder. It may be a baked smoked picnic or a roasted fresh picnic—the method of carving is the same.

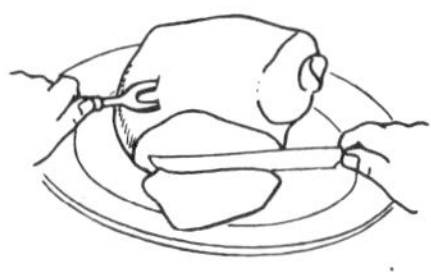

2. Place picnic on platter with fat side up and shank to carver's right. Use fork to anchor picnic, then remove a lengthwise slice from side opposite elbow bone.

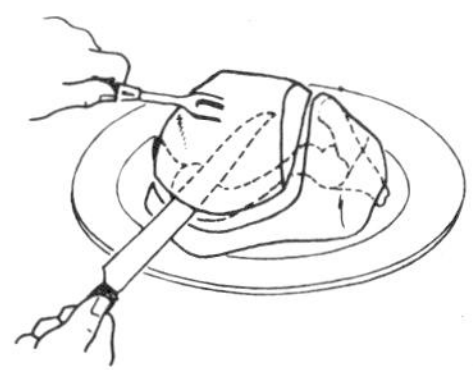

3. From the blade bone, cut down to the arm bone. Then turn the knife and cut all along the arm bone. The boneless arm meat will separate from the bones in one piece.

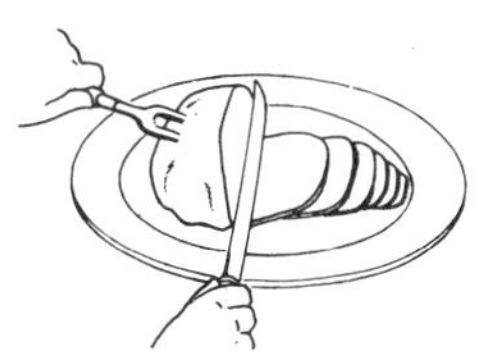

4. Carve boneless arm meat by making perpendicular slices from top side of meat down to platter. It is advisable to carve on a wooden board or a platter with a wooden insert.

WHOLE HAM

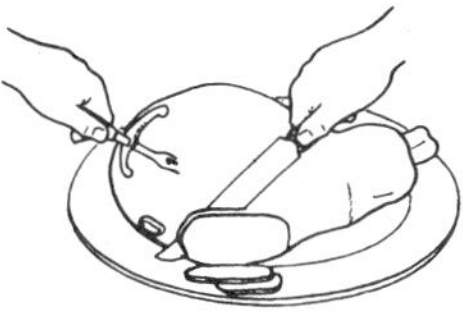

1. Place the ham on a platter with decorated side up and the shank to the carver's right. Remove several slices from the thinnest side to form a solid base on which to set the ham.

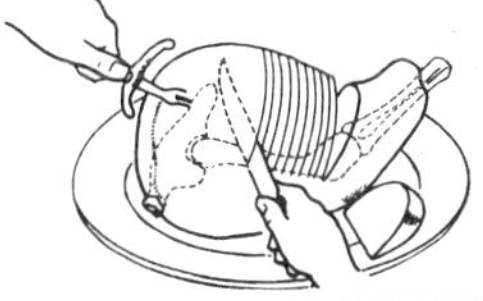

2. Turn the ham on its base. Starting at the shank end, cut a small wedge and remove; then carve perpendicular to the leg bone as shown in the illustration.

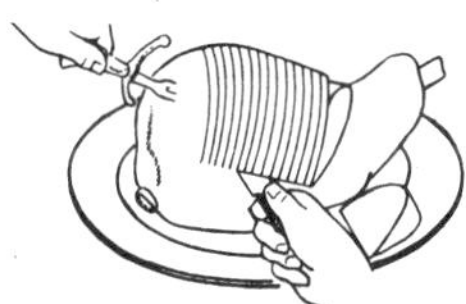

3. Release slices by cutting under them and along the leg bone, starting at the shank end. For additional servings, turn ham over and make slices to the bone; release and serve.

ROAST LEG OF LAMB	
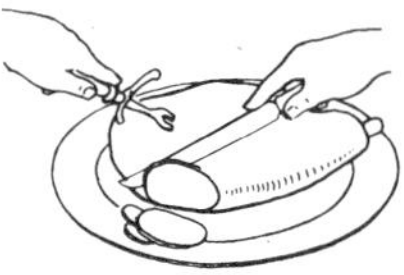	1. Place the roast on the platter with the shank to the carver's right and the thinnest section on the near side. From this thin section, remove two or three lengthwise slices to form a base.
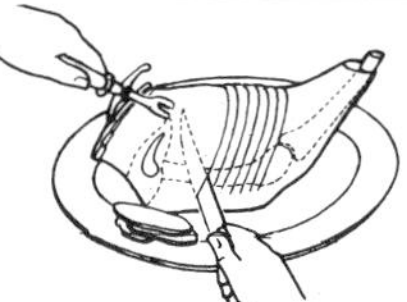	2. Turn the roast up on the base and starting at the shank end, make slices perpendicular to the leg bone as shown in the illustration.
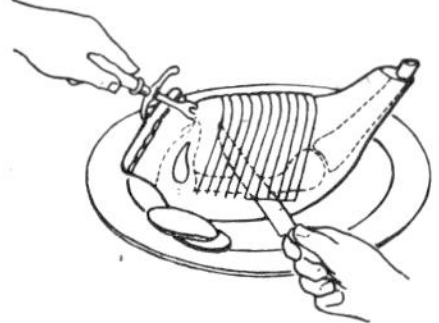	3. After reaching the aitchbone, loosen the slices by cutting under them, following the top of the leg bone. Remove slices to platter and then serve.

CHICKEN AND TURKEY	
	1. To remove leg, hold the drumstick firmly with fingers, pulling gently away from the body. At the same time, cut skin between leg and body.
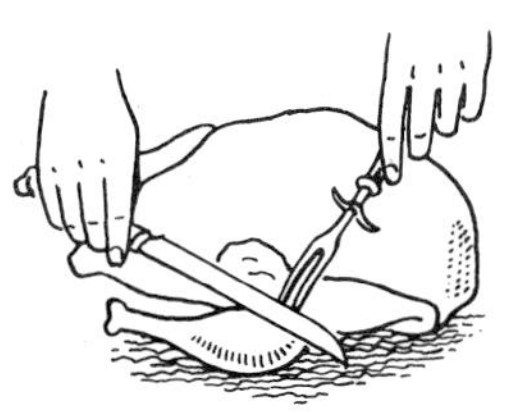	2. Press leg away from body with flat side of knife. Then cut through joint joining leg to backbone and skin on the back. If the "oyster," a choice oyster-shaped piece lying in the spoon-shaped section of the backbone, was not removed with the thigh, remove it at this point. Separate drumstick and thigh by cutting down through the joint.
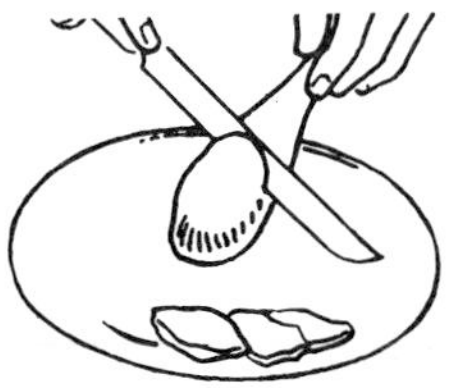	3. Slice drumstick meat. Hold drumstick upright at a convenient angle to plate and cut down, turning drumstick to get uniform slices. Chicken drumsticks and thighs are usually served without slicing.

4. Slice thigh meat. Hold thigh tightly on plate with a fork. Cut slices of meat parallel to the bone.

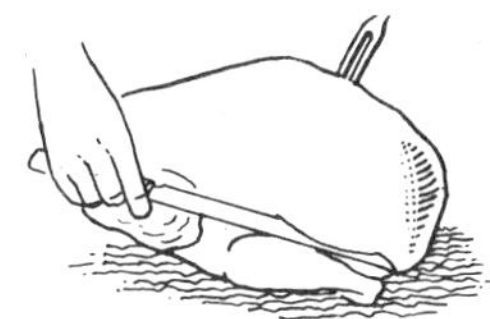

5. Cut into white meat parallel to wing. Make a cut deep into the breast until the knife reaches the body frame, parallel to and as close to the wing as possible.

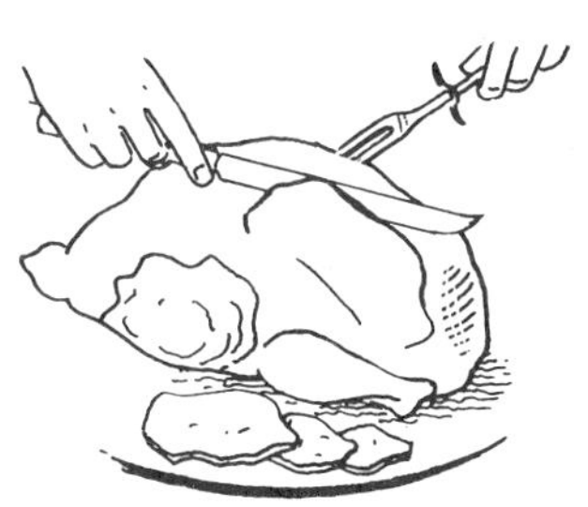

6. Slice white meat. Beginning at front, starting halfway up the breast, cut thin slices of white meat down to the cut made parallel to the wing. The slices will fall away from the bird as they are cut to this line. Continue carving for first servings. Additional meat may be carved as needed.

Cashew

BAKED CASHEWS

3 1/2 c. cashews
2 egg whites
1 c. sugar
Dash of salt
1/2 c. butter

Preheat oven to 325 degrees. Spread cashews in 15 x 10 x 1-inch pan; toast lightly. Cool. Beat egg whites until stiff peaks form, beating in sugar and salt; fold in cashews. Melt butter in same pan; spread cashew mixture in pan. Bake for 30 minutes, stirring 3 or 4 times. Cashews should be coated with meringue and all butter absorbed.

CASHEW SCRAMBLE

1 lb. margarine
1/2 c. bacon grease
1 1/2 tsp. garlic salt
Savory salt to taste
Celery salt to taste
2 tbsp. Worcestershire sauce
2 tsp. hot sauce
1 box puffed corn cereal
1 box puffed oat cereal
1 box bite-sized toasted rice cereal
2 cans peanuts
3 cans cashews
1 sm. box pretzel sticks

Preheat oven to 250 degrees. Melt margarine and bacon grease in large roaster; stir in garlic salt, savory salt, celery salt, Worcestershire sauce and hot sauce. Add cereals, nuts and pretzels; mix well. Bake for about 2 hours, stirring frequently. Store tightly covered.

CASHEW BRITTLE

1 1/2 c. sugar
1/2 c. corn syrup
2 tbsp. butter
1 c. broken cashew nuts
1 tsp. soda
1/2 tsp. vanilla

Combine sugar and corn syrup in heavy saucepan; stir in 2/3 cup water. Stir over low heat until sugar is dissolved. Increase heat; cook to 270 degrees on candy thermometer or soft-crack stage. Remove from heat; stir in butter and nuts. Dissolve soda in 1 teaspoon water. Return candy to heat; stir in vanilla and soda. Stir vigorously until foaming subsides. Turn candy into heavily greased shallow pan or platter; press as thin as possible. Cool; break into pieces.

Catfish

Catfish is a term applied to a large group of varied fish abundant in the lakes and streams of the Great Lakes area and in the Mississippi River and its tributaries. Principal North American types of catfish include the *bullhead,* up to one pound in size and the most common catfish; the *blue;* and the *flathead.* (3 1/2 ounces raw catfish = 100 calories)

AVAILABILITY: Catfish is available year-round primarily in inland areas. It is seldom available in coastal markets.

BUYING: Catfish are sold whole, or dressed. Look for fresh fish with firm, elastic flesh; a fresh, mild odor; bright, clear, slightly protruding eyes; red gills free from slime; and glistening skin with good color.
STORING: Refrigerate fresh catfish or keep them on ice. Catfish should be cooked immediately. *To freeze* catfish wrap whole fish in moistureproof and vaporproof paper. To save freezer space you can remove backbone, head, and tail. Store 1 to 3 months.
PREPARATION: Skin catfish before preparing by drawing a knife around the fish behind the gills and stripping off the skin. Cook by sauteeing, pan-frying, deep-frying, or poaching. Catfish heads are often used to prepare soup.
(See SEAFOOD.)

CATFISH MULLDOWN

2 lb. catfish
1/2 lb. bacon
3 onions
4 potatoes
Salt and pepper to taste

Cut catfish into 2-inch pieces. Reserve 2 slices bacon; chop remaining bacon. Peel onions and potatoes; cut into 1/4-inch slices. Render chopped bacon in 3-quart iron pot. Layer catfish, onions and potatoes in pot; sprinkle layers with salt and pepper. Arrange reserved bacon over top; cover pot tightly. Simmer until potatoes are tender and catfish is done. Yield: 6 servings.

DOWN EAST CATFISH STEW

1 1/2 lb. dressed catfish
3 onions, minced
6 potatoes, chopped
1/2 c. butter
Salt and pepper to taste
1 c. light cream

Steam fish in 1 1/2 cups water until done. Remove fish from broth; cool. Strain and reserve broth. Remove bones from fish; flake fish. Combine broth and onions in kettle; bring to a boil. Reduce heat; simmer for 10 minutes. Add potatoes, butter, fish, salt and pepper. Cook, stirring constantly, until potatoes are tender and stew is thick. Remove from heat. Stir in cream; serve immediately. Yield: 6-8 servings.

RED CATFISH STEW

3 lb. dressed catfish
2 slices bacon, diced
1 c. canned whole kernel corn
1 c. tomato juice
1/4 c. minced onion
Salt and pepper to taste

Place catfish, bacon and water to cover in kettle. Remove catfish; reserve broth. Cool catfish; remove bones and flake meat. Strain broth; return to kettle. Add corn, tomato juice, onion, salt and pepper. Cook over low heat, stirring constantly, until thickened. Yield: 4-6 servings.

BAKED CATFISH DINNER

2 catfish fillets
1 tsp. salt
1/2 tsp. pepper
2 tsp. onion powder
1 c. peas and carrots
1/2 c. tomato juice
1 env. vegetable bouillon mix

Place fish in single layer in greased baking dish; sprinkle with salt, pepper and onion powder. Scatter peas and carrots over fish. Mix tomato juice and bouillon mix; pour over top. Bake at 400 degrees for 20 minutes or until fish tests done. Yield: 2 servings.

BAKED CATFISH FILLETS WITH EGG AND ONION SAUCE

1 lb. catfish fillets
1 onion, thinly sliced
1/2 c. evaporated milk
3/4 tsp. salt
1/8 tsp. pepper
1 tbsp. cornstarch
1 hard-cooked egg, sieved
1 tbsp. butter
2 drops of vanilla

Preheat oven to 400 degrees. Cut fish into serving pieces; arrange in shallow baking dish. Arrange onion around fish. Dilute milk with 1/2 cup water; pour over fish. Bake for 25 minutes. Lift fish carefully to warm serving dish; keep warm. Strain broth from baking dish into saucepan; add salt and pepper. Blend cornstarch to a paste with small amount of cold water; stir into broth. Cook over low heat, stirring constantly, until thickened. Stir in egg, butter and vanilla; pour over fish. Serve immediately. Yield: 4 servings.

CREOLE CATFISH FILLETS

1 lb. catfish fillets
1/4 c. flour
1/2 tsp. salt
1/4 tsp. paprika
2 tbsp. minced onion
1/2 c. chili sauce
1/2 c. boiling water
1 tbsp. minced parsley
2 tbsp. melted butter

Sprinkle catfish with flour, salt and paprika. Place in shallow greased baking pan. Combine remaining ingredients; pour over catfish. Bake at 350 degrees for 20 minutes, basting frequently. Turn catfish; bake for 15 minutes longer, basting frequently.

FLAKED CATFISH SOUFFLE

2 eggs, separated
2 c. milk
2 tbsp. instant tapioca
1 1/2 tsp. salt
Dash of pepper
1 1/2 tsp. grated onion
1/2 c. minced celery
2 c. flaked cooked catfish
2 tbsp. chopped parsley
1/2 c. crushed corn flakes

Mix egg yolks and small amount of milk in saucepan; add remaining milk, tapioca, salt, pepper, onion and celery. Mix well. Cook over medium heat, stirring constantly, until mixture comes to a boil; remove from heat. Fold in catfish and parsley. Beat egg whites until stiff peaks form. Fold in catfish mixture; spoon into greased 1 1/2-quart casserole. Sprinkle with corn flake crumbs. Bake at 350 degrees for 50 minutes or until firm. Yield: 4 servings.

Cajun Catfish . . . Succulent catfish prepared in palate-tingling fashion with salad dressing.

CAJUN CATFISH

6 skinned, dressed catfish
1/2 c. tomato sauce
2 3/4-oz. packages cheese-garlic salad dressing
2 tbsp. melted fat
2 tbsp. chopped parsley
2 tbsp. grated Parmesan cheese

Dry catfish well. Combine remaining ingredients except cheese. Brush catfish inside and out with sauce. Place in greased 13 x 9 x 2-inch baking dish. Brush with remaining sauce; sprinkle with cheese. Let stand for 30 minutes. Bake in 350-degree oven for 25 to 35 minutes or until fish flakes easily. Remove from oven. Place about 3 inches from source of heat in broiler. Broil for 1 to 2 minutes or until crisp and lightly browned. Garnish with watercress and lemon slices. Yield: 6 servings.

CREAMY CATFISH

1 4-lb. catfish
1 2/3 c. evaporated milk
1/4 c. butter
1/4 c. cornstarch
Salt and pepper to taste
4 c. chopped cooked potatoes

Steam catfish until done. Remove bones; flake meat. Combine milk and butter in saucepan; heat, stirring, until butter is melted. Mix cornstarch to a paste with small amount of cold water. Stir paste into hot milk; cook, stirring constantly, until thickened. Add salt and pepper; fold in catfish and potatoes. Heat through. Serve immediately. Yield: 8-10 servings.

CAPTAIN'S DELIGHT

1/2 c. oil
1 can chicken broth
1/2 c. margarine
2 tbsp. brown sugar
1/4 bottle steak sauce
Juice of 1 lemon
1 4-lb. dressed catfish

Combine oil and broth in saucepan. Boil rapidly until reduced by one-third; stir in margarine, brown sugar, steak sauce and lemon juice. Cut several slashes in both sides of fish; place in shallow baking pan. Pour sauce over fish. Broil under low heat until fish is browned on both sides and tests done. Baste frequently with sauce. Yield: 6 servings.

BARBECUED CATFISH

6 med. catfish
1 tsp. Worcestershire sauce
1/8 tsp. paprika
1/2 c. salad oil
1/4 c. white vinegar
1/4 c. catsup
2 tbsp. sugar
1/4 tsp. salt
1/4 tsp. pepper

Clean, skin and fillet catfish. Combine remaining ingredients for sauce; mix well. Brush catfish with sauce; place on well-greased grill 3 to 4 inches above hot coals. Cook for 5 minutes on each side or until easily flaked, brushing frequently with sauce. Yield: 6 servings.

BATTERED CATFISH

1 can shortening
2 eggs, beaten
1 c. milk
Salt and pepper
12 lb. catfish, cut into steaks
Cornmeal

Melt shortening in deep heavy kettle. Mix eggs and milk. Season catfish with salt and pepper. Dip into milk mixture; roll in cornmeal. Drop into hot shortening. Fry until brown, turning once. Drain on absorbent paper. Serve hot with hush puppies, if desired. Yield: 12 servings.

FISH CHIPS

1 c. flour
1 tsp. baking powder
Salt
2 eggs, beaten
2/3 c. milk
1 tbsp. butter, melted
1 pkg. frozen catfish
Lemon juice
Dash of pepper

Sift flour, baking powder and 1/2 teaspoon salt together. Combine eggs, milk and butter; add to flour mixture. Beat until smooth. Cut fish into small pieces; sprinkle with lemon juice, pepper and salt to taste. Dip fish in batter. Fry in deep fat until golden brown. Yield: 6 servings.

FRIED CATFISH

Catfish
Salt and pepper to taste
Crumbs
1 egg, beaten
1 tbsp. flour
1 c. milk or cream
2 green peppers, chopped
6 sour pickles, chopped

Cut fish into small serving pieces. Season fish with salt and pepper. Dip in crumbs; brush with egg. Dip in crumbs again. Fry in deep shortening until browned; drain on brown paper. Dip 1 1/2 tablespoons hot shortening from kettle into saucepan. Blend in flour; stir in milk gradually. Cook, stirring constantly, until smooth and thickened. Cool; stir in green pepper and pickles. Serve over fish.

PATIO CATFISH

6 lb. catfish
2 eggs, beaten
1/2 c. milk
1 pkg. fish frying mix
Shortening

Cut fish into serving pieces. Combine eggs and milk. Dip fish into egg mixture; roll in frying mix. Fry in about 1 inch hot shortening until golden brown on both sides. Yield: 8-10 servings.

POLYNESIAN CATFISH

2 lb. skinned filleted catfish
1/4 c. soy sauce
1/2 c. flour
1/2 c. cornstarch
1 tbsp. baking powder
1 tsp. salt
1/4 tsp. pepper
1 c. water
1 egg, beaten

Cut fish into 2 x 1-inch strips; place in shallow pan. Drizzle with soy sauce; let stand for 30 minutes, turning once. Sift flour, cornstarch, baking powder, salt and pepper together. Combine water and egg; blend into flour mixture. Dip fish strips into batter. Fry in deep fat at 350 degrees for 5 to 6 minutes or until browned. Drain on absorbent paper. Pour Pineapple Sauce onto platter; arrange fish in sauce. Serve with rice. Yield: 6 servings.

Pineapple Sauce

1 sm. can pineapple chunks
2 tbsp. cornstarch
1/4 c. cold water

Turn pineapple and juice into saucepan; heat through. Dissolve cornstarch in water. Add to pineapple gradually; cook until thickened, stirring constantly.

SOUTH GEORGIA CATFISH AND SWAMP GRAVY

2 tbsp. salt
3 lb. dressed catfish
Cornmeal
3 c. diced potatoes
1 c. diced onions
1 No. 2 can tomatoes
1 can tomato juice
1 tsp. pepper

Sprinkle 1 1/2 tablespoons salt over fish; coat in 1 cup cornmeal. Fry in deep fat until golden brown; drain on paper towels. Drain all but 1/2 cup fat from pan; stir in 1 tablespoon cornmeal. Add potatoes and onions; cover. Cook until potatoes are tender. Stir in tomatoes, tomato juice, remaining salt and pepper. Cook, stirring, until thickened.

Catsup

Also known as *catchup* or *ketchup,* catsup is a spicy, especially thick sauce. It is used as an accompaniment to meat, fish, and other main dishes. It is also used as an ingredient in preparing these foods. The most common catsup is tomato-based.

AUTHENTIC TOMATO CATSUP

1 gal. chopped ripe tomatoes
2 tbsp. salt
2 c. sugar
2 sm. red peppers, finely chopped
1 tbsp. dry mustard
1 tsp. ground cloves
1 tsp. cinnamon
1 1/2 tsp. white pepper
1/4 c. paprika
2 c. white vinegar

Place tomatoes in large heavy kettle. Bring to a boil, stirring constantly. Reduce heat; simmer until tomatoes are soft. Sieve tomatoes; return puree to kettle. Stir in salt, sugar, red peppers, mustard, cloves, cinnamon, white pepper and paprika. Mix well; stir to a boil. Reduce heat; simmer for 1 hour. Add vinegar; simmer until thickened, stirring frequently. Pour into hot sterilized jars; seal.

BASIC TOMATO CATSUP

20 lb. ripe tomatoes
6 med. onions
4 med. sweet red peppers
2 c. vinegar
1 1/2 c. sugar
2 tbsp. salt
1/4 c. paprika
2 tsp. celery seed
1 tsp. whole allspice
1 tsp. whole cloves
3 oz. stick cinnamon

Peel tomatoes; chop into large kettle. Peel and chop onions. Chop red peppers. Add onions and red peppers to tomatoes. Bring to a boil, stirring constantly. Reduce heat; simmer until vegetables are soft. Press vegetables through a sieve; return puree to kettle.

Stir in vinegar, sugar, salt and paprika. Tie celery seed, allspice, cloves and cinnamon in small cloth bag; add to kettle. Bring to a boil, stirring; reduce heat. Simmer until thickened, stirring frequently. Pour into hot sterilized jars; seal. Yield: 4 pints.

OLD-TIME CATSUP

3 qt. chopped ripe tomatoes
2 c. chopped onions
1 c. vinegar
2 c. sugar
1 tbsp. salt
1 sm. hot pepper, chopped

Combine all ingredients in large kettle; mix well. Bring to a boil, stirring constantly. Reduce heat; simmer for 1 hour or until thickened, stirring frequently. Pour into hot sterilized jars; seal. Yield: 2 pints.

REAL RED CATSUP

2 gal. tomato juice
1/2 c. salt
2 onions, chopped
3 c. vinegar
1/4 tsp. oil of cloves
1/4 tsp. (scant) oil of cinnamon
8 c. sugar
6 tbsp. cornstarch

Combine tomato juice, salt, onions, vinegar, oil of cloves and oil of cinnamon in large kettle. Bring to a boil. Reduce heat; simmer until volume is reduced by 1/3. Mix sugar and cornstarch; stir into catsup. Cook, stirring, until thickened. Pour into hot sterilized jars; seal. Yield: 8-10 pints.

CHILI SAUCE

18 lge. ripe tomatoes
6 lge. onions
2 tsp. salt
1/2 tsp. cloves
1/2 tsp. allspice
1 tsp. cinnamon
1 tsp. nutmeg
1 1/2 c. vinegar
4 c. sugar

Peel and chop tomatoes and onions. Place in large heavy kettle; stir in remaining ingredients. Stir mixture to a boil. Reduce heat; simmer for 3 hours or until thickened. Pour into hot sterilized jars; seal.

QUICK AND EASY CHILI SAUCE

1/2 bushel ripe tomatoes
1/2 c. mixed pickling spices
1 c. white vinegar
2 c. sugar
2 tbsp. salt
Pepper to taste
2 c. chopped onions
1 c. chopped celery
1 c. chopped green peppers

Scald and skin tomatoes. Chop tomatoes into large heavy kettle. Stir to a boil. Reduce heat; simmer until tomatoes are soft. Cool; press tomatoes through sieve. Return puree to kettle. Tie pickling spices in small cloth bag; add to kettle. Add vinegar, sugar, salt, pepper, onions, celery and green peppers. Stir mixture to a boil. Reduce heat; simmer until thickened, stirring frequently. Pour sauce into sterilized 1-gallon jar; leave spice bag in sauce. Seal and cool. Keep refrigerated.

HOT CHILI SAUCE

1 gal. ripe tomatoes
2/3 c. chopped onion
1 1/2 c. sugar
1 tsp. nutmeg
3/4 tsp. hot sauce
1/2 tsp. curry powder
5 tsp. salt
2 tsp. ginger
1 tsp. cinnamon
1 tsp. dry mustard
2 c. vinegar

Peel and core tomatoes. Grind tomatoes and onion through food chopper; place in large heavy kettle. Add remaining ingredients. Cook, stirring, to a boil. Reduce heat; simmer for 2 hours or until thickened, stirring frequently. Pour into sterilized 1-pint jars; seal. Yield: 3 pints.

SPICY CHILI SAUCE

1/4 c. pickling spices
1 gal. ripe tomatoes
1/2 c. finely chopped sweet red pepper
1/2 c. finely chopped onion
1 c. brown sugar
2 c. white vinegar
2 tbsp. salt
1/2 tsp. cayenne pepper

Tie pickling spices in small cloth bag. Scald and peel tomatoes. Chop tomatoes into large kettle; bring to a boil. Simmer until tomatoes are soft; mash tomatoes with potato masher. Add red pepper, onion, sugar, vinegar, salt and cayenne pepper. Mix well; add spice bag. Bring to a boil, stirring constantly. Reduce heat; simmer until thickened, stirring frequently. Pour into hot sterilized jars; seal. Process for 15 minutes in hot water bath.

Cauliflower

A member of the cabbage family, cauliflower is a low-calorie source of Vitamin C and iron. (3 1/2 ounces = 30 calories)

AVAILABILITY: Available year-round with the largest supplies appearing from September to January, and the peak season in October and November.

BUYING: Look for firm, compact heads with creamy white flowerets and fresh green outer leaves. Quality is not affected if small leaves grow through the head. Avoid cauliflower with yellowed leaves; with an open, loose, or spread head; spotted, speckled, or bruised flowerets; or smudging.

STORING: Wash, wrap tightly, and keep in vegetable crisper for up to 5 days. Cooked cauliflower keeps 4 days if sealed tightly. *To freeze cauliflower,* remove core and outer leaves; separate into flowerets. Soak in salted water 1/2 hour; rinse. Scald in boiling water 4 minutes; chill in ice water. Pack tightly into container, leaving 1/2-inch space at top.

Label, date, and freeze. Store in the home freezer for 11 months or in the refrigerator freezer compartment for 1 month.

PREPARATION: Cauliflower, cooked, is most often boiled although it may also be baked au gratin in a casserole, pureed, or sauteed. To boil, wash cauliflower under cold running water; cut off core and tough outer leaves. Leave the head intact or cut it into small pieces. Place in one inch of boiling salted water with lemon juice or vinegar (to preserve white color). Do not cover. Allow water to return to boiling. Cook 8-15 minutes for small pieces or 20-30 minutes for whole heads.

SERVING: It can be served as a vegetable with seasoning or incorporated into soups or salads.

(See VEGETABLES.)

APPETIZER COLD FLOWER

1 head cauliflower
1 tbsp. vinegar
1 bottle Italian salad dressing

Break cauliflower into flowerets; spread in shallow dish. Combine vinegar and salad dressing; pour over cauliflower. Cover; refrigerate overnight. Serve cold.

CRISP CAULIFLOWER SALAD

1 cauliflower, shredded
2 stalks celery, minced
Salt and pepper to taste
Mayonnaise
Lettuce

Combine cauliflower and celery; sprinkle with salt and pepper. Stir in enough mayonnaise to moisten; spoon onto lettuce-lined salad plates. Yield: 6 servings.

COMPANY SALAD

1 med. head cauliflower
1 tbsp. salt
2/3 c. salad oil
1/2 c. cider vinegar
1 tbsp. sugar
1/2 tsp. oregano
1/4 tsp. basil
1/4 tsp. rosemary
1 clove of garlic, split
1 sm. red onion, thinly sliced
1/2 c. finely chopped dill pickles

Boil cauliflower with salt for 3 to 5 minutes. Drain. Separate into flowerets. Combine oil, vinegar, sugar, oregano, basil, rosemary and garlic. Mix well; pour over warm cauliflower. Add onion and dill pickles. Toss well; chill in refrigerator. Serve in bowl or on greens as salads. Frozen cauliflower may be used if not overcooked. Yield: 6-8 servings.

DOUBLE CHEESE CAULIFLOWER

1 lge. head cauliflower
Salt
Butter
3 tbsp. flour
1 1/2 c. milk
2 tbsp. Parmesan cheese
1 tbsp. lemon juice
Dash of pepper
2 egg yolks, beaten
1/2 c. toasted bread crumbs
1/2 c. grated American cheese

Boil cauliflower in salted water to cover for about 15 minutes or until tender. Melt 3 tablespoons butter in small saucepan; blend in flour. Add milk; cook until smooth and thickened, stirring constantly. Add Parmesan cheese, lemon juice, 1/2 teaspoon salt and pepper; blend well. Add small amount of sauce to egg yolks; stir back into sauce in pan. Divide cauliflower into flowerets; place in buttered 1 1/2-quart casserole. Cover with sauce; sprinkle with crumbs and American cheese. Pour 1/4 cup melted butter over top. Bake at 350 degrees for 30 minutes or until brown. Yield: 6 servings.

CRISPY-TOPPED CAULIFLOWER CASSEROLE

1 lge. head cauliflower
1/4 c. butter or margarine
1/4 c. flour
1 c. milk
1/2 c. white wine
1/2 green pepper, finely chopped
1/4 c. chopped onion
1/2 c. shredded blanched almonds
Salt and pepper to taste
1/4 c. grated Cheddar cheese
1/2 can French-fried onion rings

Separate cauliflower into flowerets; drop into boiling water. Cook for 15 minutes or just until tender. Melt butter in small saucepan; blend in flour. Add milk, wine, green pepper, onion and 1/2 cup water. Cook, stirring constantly, until thickened. Add almonds, salt and pepper. Drain cauliflower carefully; place in greased baking dish. Pour sauce over cauliflower; sprinkle with cheese. Bake at 375 degrees for 15 minutes. Sprinkle with onion rings; bake for 5 minutes longer. Yield: 6 servings.

CAULIFLOWER SOUFFLE

1 lge. cauliflower
Salt to taste
1/3 c. butter
2 tbsp. flour
1 c. milk
3 eggs, separated
3 tbsp. grated Parmesan cheese
Pepper to taste
Paprika

Cook cauliflower in boiling salted water until tender. Separate into flowerets; remove most of stem. Place cauliflower in baking dish. Melt butter in small saucepan; blend in flour. Add milk slowly; cook, stirring, until thickened. Remove from heat; beat in egg yolks. Cool. Fold in stiffly beaten egg whites, cheese, pepper and paprika. Pour over cauliflower. Bake at 350 degrees for 30 to 45 minutes. Yield: 4-6 servings.

CAULIFLOWER SUPREME

1 head cauliflower
Salt
1/2 lb. mushrooms, sliced
1/4 c. diced green pepper
1/3 c. butter
1/4 c. flour
2 c. milk
6 slices Velveeta cheese
Dash of paprika
Buttered bread crumbs

Separate cauliflower into flowerets. Cook covered in boiling salted water for 12 minutes or until just tender. Brown mushrooms and green pepper lightly in butter; blend in flour. Add milk slowly. Cook, stirring constantly, until thick. Stir in 1 teaspoon salt. Place half the cauliflower in 1 1/2-quart casserole. Cover with half the cheese; add half the sauce. Repeat layers; sprinkle with paprika. Bake at 350 degrees for 15 to 20 minutes. Sprinkle with crumbs. Yield: 6 servings.

CHEESE-CROWNED CAULIFLOWER

1 cauliflower
Salt
1/4 c. mayonnaise
1 tbsp. prepared mustard
1/2 c. grated cheese

Place whole cauliflower in saucepan; cover with boiling salted water. Cook until tender; drain well. Place in shallow baking dish. Combine mayonnaise, mustard, 1/4 teaspoon salt and cheese; spread on cauliflower. Bake at 400 degrees for 10 to 15 minutes. Yield: 6 servings.

DILLY CAULIFLOWER

1 cauliflower
Salt
1/4 c. butter or margarine
1/4 c. flour
2 c. milk
1/2 lb. sharp Cheddar cheese, shredded
1/2 tsp. dillseed
1/8 tsp. pepper
1 c. toasted bread crumbs

Break cauliflower into flowerets. Drop into saucepan of boiling salted water. Reduce heat; simmer for about 15 minutes. Drain well. Melt butter in small saucepan over low heat; blend in flour. Add milk slowly, stirring. Cook, stirring constantly, until thickened. Melt cheese in hot sauce; stir in dillseed, 1/2 teaspoon salt and pepper. Layer cauliflower and sauce in 2-quart casserole, ending with sauce. Top with bread crumbs. Bake at 350 degrees for 20 minutes. Yield: 6 servings.

NOVA SCOTIAN CAULIFLOWER

1 lge. cauliflower
1 pkg. frozen lima beans
1 pkg. frozen peas
1 c. chopped fresh mushrooms
1 sm. onion, minced
1/4 c. butter
2 1/2 tbsp. flour
1 c. milk
1/2 tsp. salt
1/4 tsp. pepper
1/4 c. minced parsley
1/2 c. grated cheese

Separate cauliflower into flowerets; cook in boiling water just until tender. Drain well. Cook lima beans and peas separately according to package directions; drain. Saute mushrooms and onion in butter in skillet for 5 minutes; remove from skillet. Stir flour into skillet drippings. Add milk; cook over medium heat until light and creamy, stirring constantly. Add salt, pepper and parsley; simmer for several minutes or until blended. Stir mushroom mixture and cheese into hot sauce. Spread lima beans in casserole; top with cauliflower. Spread peas over cauliflower; pour sauce over top. Bake at 350 degrees until vegetables are heated through and sauce is bubbly.

MAIN DISH CAULIFLOWER

1 head cauliflower
Salt
6 tbsp. butter or margarine
1/4 c. flour
1 1/2 c. milk
1/2 lb. sharp Cheddar cheese, diced
1 c. chopped cooked ham
1 c. soft bread crumbs

Break cauliflower into flowerets. Cook in boiling salted water just until tender. Drain and place in 2-quart casserole. Melt 1/4 cup butter in small saucepan; blend in flour. Add milk slowly, stirring constantly. Cook over low heat, stirring, until thickened; add cheese. Scatter ham over cauliflower; pour cheese sauce over top. Melt remaining butter; mix in crumbs. Spread over casserole. Bake at 350 degrees for 30 minutes. Yield: 6 servings.

SAVORY VEGETABLE CASSEROLE

1 10-oz. box frozen cauliflower
1 10-oz. box frozen broccoli spears
2 tbsp. butter
1 1/2 tbsp. flour
1/4 tsp. salt
1/4 tsp. seasoned salt
1/4 tsp. pepper
1/8 tsp. monosodium glutamate
2 c. hot milk
1 tsp. grated onion
1/4 c. chopped pimento
3/4 c. grated Cheddar cheese
1/2 c. cracker crumbs
Paprika

Cook cauliflower and broccoli separately according to package directions; drain well. Melt butter in small saucepan; blend in flour, salt, seasoned salt, pepper and monosodium glutamate. Stir in milk slowly; cook, stirring constantly, until thickened. Add onion, pimento and cheese, stirring to melt cheese. Layer cauliflower, broccoli and sauce in baking dish; cover with cracker crumbs. Sprinkle with paprika. Bake at 350 degrees until vegetables are heated through and sauce is bubbly.

ITALIAN CAULIFLOWER

1 cauliflower
1/2 tsp. salt
1/2 c. grated Parmesan cheese
1/2 c. olive oil
1/2 c. fine Italian bread crumbs

Break cauliflower into flowerets. Cook in boiling salted water until tender; drain well. Place cauliflower in casserole; sprinkle with cheese and oil. Cover. Bake at 325 degrees for 15 minutes. Sprinkle with bread crumbs; bake, uncovered, until crumbs are browned. Yield: 4 servings.

DEEP-FRIED CAULIFLOWER

1 egg, lightly beaten
1 tbsp. oil
1 c. milk
1 c. sifted flour
Salt
1 cauliflower

Combine egg, oil and milk; add to flour gradually. Add 1/4 teaspoon salt; beat with rotary beater until smooth. Divide cauliflower into flowerets; cook in boiling salted water until tender. Drain well. Dip flowerets in batter; fry in 375-degree deep fat until lightly browned. Yield: 4-6 servings.

Spiced Cauliflower . . . Cauliflower takes on an exciting taste in this seasoned dish.

SPICED CAULIFLOWER

1 tbsp. shortening
2 tbsp. finely chopped onion
1 sm. garlic clove, crushed
1/4 tsp. ground ginger
1/4 tsp. turmeric
2 whole cloves
1 head cauliflower
1/2 tsp. salt
1/2 c. sour cream
1/4 c. toasted slivered almonds

Melt shortening in electric skillet at 320 degrees. Add onion, garlic, ginger, turmeric, and cloves. Stir together and simmer. Break head of cauliflower into separate flowerets. Cut flowerets lengthwise into bite-sized pieces; add to spice mixture. Cover; shake until pieces are coated. Add 2 tablespoons water and salt. Steam at 320 degrees until tender; shaking pan frequently. Add additional water if needed. Toss cauliflower with sour cream. Place in serving bowl; garnish with almond slivers. Yield: 4 servings.

CAULIFLOWER FRITTERS

1 lge. head cauliflower
2 c. self-rising flour
1/4 c. lukewarm water
1 egg
2 tbsp. olive oil
2 tsp. tarragon vinegar
Dash of pepper
1 onion, chopped
1 tsp. chopped parsley
Garlic salt

Break cauliflower into flowerets. Cook for about 8 minutes in boiling salted water; drain. Combine flour, lukewarm water, egg and 1 tablespoon olive oil; mix well. Let batter stand for 1 hour. Mix remaining oil, vinegar, 1/4 teaspoon salt and pepper; stir in onion and parsley. Spread cauliflower in shallow dish; pour marinade over cauliflower. Let stand for 30 minutes. Drain cauliflower; dip into batter. Fry in deep hot fat until golden brown. Drain on paper towels; sprinkle with garlic salt.

CAULIFLOWER PATTIES

1 cauliflower
1 1/4 c. bread crumbs
1/2 c. grated Parmesan cheese
1 tsp. minced parsley
1/4 tsp. garlic salt
Salt and pepper
2 eggs, beaten
Cooking oil

Separate cauliflower into flowerets; cook in boiling water until tender. Turn into colander; drain well. Crumble cauliflower in small pieces; add bread crumbs, cheese, parsley, garlic salt, salt, pepper and eggs. Shape into small patties. Fry in hot oil in skillet for about 20 minutes or until browned on both sides. Yield: 4-6 servings.

CAULIFLOWERETS

1 cauliflower
1 egg
1 tbsp. milk
3/4 c. dry bread crumbs
1/4 c. grated Parmesan cheese
Salt and pepper
Pinch of oregano
Cooking oil

Separate cauliflower into flowerets. Cook in boiling water until almost tender; drain well. Beat egg and milk together. Mix bread crumbs, cheese and seasonings. Dip cauliflower into crumb mixture, then in egg mixture. Dip again in crumb mixture. Deep fry in hot oil until browned; drain on paper towels. Yield: 4 servings.

FRIED CAULIFLOWER WITH CHEESE SAUCE

1 lge. cauliflower
1 tsp. salt
Cooking oil
2 eggs, beaten
1 c. bread or cracker crumbs
1/4 c. butter
3 tbsp. flour
2/3 c. chicken broth
1 c. milk
Dash of aromatic bitters
1/2 c. heavy cream, whipped
Grated Parmesan cheese to taste

Separate cauliflower into flowerets. Simmer, covered, in salted water for 20 minutes or until tender. Drain. Heat cooking oil in deep fryer to 400 degrees. Dip each piece of cauliflower into eggs, then into crumbs. Fry until brown and crisp on outside. Melt butter in saucepan over low heat; blend in flour. Stir in broth, milk and bitters. Cook, stirring constantly until thick; fold in whipped cream. Sprinkle with cheese; cover. Remove from heat. Allow cheese to melt. Stir; pour over hot cauliflower. Yield: 4 servings.

CAULIFLOWER IN BEEF SAUCE

2 pkg. frozen cauliflower
2 cans cream of mushroom soup
1/2 lb. process cheese, diced
1 tbsp. lemon juice
1/4 lb. dried beef

Cook cauliflower according to package directions; drain well. Stir soup over low heat until smooth and bubbly. Add cheese, stirring until cheese is melted. Fold in lemon juice and shredded beef. Turn cauliflower into serving dish; pour sauce over cauliflower. Yield: 6 servings.

SAUTEED CAULIFLOWER

1 med. cauliflower
Salt
1 egg, beaten
1/4 c. butter or margarine
Dash of pepper

Trim cauliflower; separate into small flowerets. Cook in boiling salted water for 3 to 5 minutes. Drain; dip into egg. Saute in butter in heavy skillet until golden. Turn into heated shallow bowl; sprinkle lightly with salt and pepper. Yield: 6 servings.

CAULIFLOWER WITH ALMOND BUTTER

1 sm. cauliflower
Salt
1/4 c. slivered almonds
3 tbsp. butter

Cook cauliflower in boiling salted water for 10 minutes or until tender; drain. Saute almonds in butter until lightly browned. Place cauliflower in serving dish; pour butter and almonds over top. Yield: 4 servings.

CAULIFLOWER HOLLANDAISE

1 lge. head cauliflower
Salt
2 eggs, separated
2 tbsp. heavy cream
1/2 tsp. sugar
1/2 tsp. monosodium glutamate
2 1/2 tbsp. lemon juice
1/4 c. butter
Paprika

Separate cauliflower into flowerets. Cook, covered, in 1 inch lightly salted boiling water for 10 minutes or until tender. Drain well; keep warm. Beat egg yolks with cream in top of double boiler until thickened and light colored. Beat in 1/2 teaspoon salt, sugar, monosodium glutamate and 1/4 teaspoon paprika. Place over hot water. Beat in lemon juice gradually with wire whisk. Cook, beating constantly, until mixture is consistency of heavy cream. Remove from heat; leave over hot water. Add butter, 1/2 teaspoon at a time, beating until butter is melted. Remove from hot water. Beat egg whites just until soft peaks form. Fold into lemon mixture. Mound cauliflower in heated serving dish. Top with sauce; sprinkle with paprika. Yield: 6 servings.

CAULIFLOWER WITH POPPY SEED SAUCE

1 lge. head cauliflower
3/4 tsp. salt
1 1/2 tbsp. margarine
1 1/2 tbsp. flour
1/2 tsp. prepared mustard
2 tbsp. poppy seed
1 c. milk
Dash of pepper

Separate cauliflower into flowerets; cook in boiling salted water until just tender. Drain well; place in heated shallow bowl. Melt margarine in small saucepan; remove from heat. Beat in flour, mustard and poppy seed; stir in about 3 tablespoons milk. Return to heat; stir in remaining milk slowly. Cook, stirring, until thickened. Add remaining salt and pepper; pour over cauliflower. Serve immediately. Yield: 6 servings.

CAULIFLOWER-TOMATO PARMESAN

1 med. cauliflower
1 1/2 tsp. salt
1 tsp. lemon juice
1 sm. clove of garlic, minced
2 tbsp. oil
1 tomato, cut in thin wedges
1 tsp. chopped parsley
2 tbsp. grated Parmesan cheese

Separate cauliflower into flowerets. Place in saucepan; barely cover with water. Add 1 teaspoon salt and lemon juice. Cover. Cook for 10 minutes or until just tender; drain. Saute garlic in oil until browned in large skillet; add cauliflower. Saute lightly. Add remaining salt and tomato wedges; cover. Simmer for 3 minutes or until tomatoes are softened slightly. Serve sprinkled with parsley and cheese. Yield: 4-5 servings.

CHOUFLEUR POLONAISE

1 lge. cauliflower
Salt to taste
5 tbsp. butter
2 tbsp. chopped onion
1 sm. clove of garlic, pressed
1 tbsp. chopped parsley
2 tbsp. bread crumbs
1 hard-boiled egg, finely chopped

Separate cauliflower into flowerets; place in saucepan. Add salt and water to cover; bring to a boil. Reduce heat; simmer until cauliflower is just tender. Drain cauliflower; arrange in shallow serving bowl. Melt 3 tablespoons butter in small skillet; add onion. Cook for 1 minute. Add garlic; cook until onion is tender. Stir in parsley, bread crumbs and egg; add remaining butter. Pour over cauliflower; turn cauliflower in sauce carefully, coating well. Yield: 6 servings.

CAULIFLOWER WITH WATER CHESTNUTS

1 med. cauliflower
1 sliced can mushrooms
3 tbsp. oil
6 water chestnuts, quartered
1/4 c. bouillon
1 tbsp. sherry
2 tbsp. soy sauce
2 tbsp. cornstarch

Separate cauliflower into flowerets; pour 2 cups boiling water over cauliflower. Let stand for 5 minutes; drain. Drain mushrooms, reserving 1/2 cup liquid. Saute mushrooms lightly in oil; add water chestnuts, reserved mushroom liquid bouillon, sherry, soy sauce and cornstarch. Cook for about 3 minutes, stirring constantly. Add cauliflower; heat through. Yield: 4-6 servings.

CREAMED GRATED CAULIFLOWER

1 cauliflower
1/2 tsp. salt
2 tbsp. butter
3 tbsp. cream
Paprika to taste
1 tbsp. minced parsley

Let cauliflower stand in cold water until crisp; drain. Shred cauliflower with coarse shredder. Place in skillet; sprinkle with salt. Add 1/3 cup hot water; cover tightly. Cook for 5 to 7 minutes or until just tender. Do not drain. Add butter and cream, tossing with fork. Turn into serving dish; sprinkle with paprika and parsley. Yield: 4 servings.

CRUNCHY CAULIFLOWER

1 lge. cauliflower
Salt
1/4 c. butter
1/4 c. flour
2 1/2 c. milk
1/2 tsp. pepper
1 c. grated yellow cheese
12 slices fried bacon, crumbled

Trim cauliflower; soak, head down, in cold salted water for 20 minutes. Place in large amount of boiling salted water. Cook, uncovered, for 15 minutes or until tender; drain. Melt butter in double boiler; blend in flour. Add milk, 1 teaspoon salt and pepper. Cook, stirring frequently, until thickened. Melt cheese in hot sauce. Arrange cauliflower in serving dish; pour sauce over cauliflower. Top with bacon. Yield: 8 servings.

EASILY ELEGANT CAULIFLOWER

1 head cauliflower
Salt
1 can frozen cream of shrimp soup
1/2 c. sour cream
1/4 c. toasted slivered almonds

Break cauliflower into flowerets. Cook, covered, in small amount of boiling salted water for 12 minutes or until tender. Drain well. Place in heated serving dish; keep warm. Thaw soup; place in small saucepan. Stir over low heat until smooth; add sour cream and salt to taste. Cook, stirring, until heated through. Add almonds to sauce; pour over cauliflower. Yield: 4-6 servings.

KEY WEST GOLD CAULIFLOWER

1 lge. cauliflower
1/4 c. butter
1/4 c. flour
2 c. milk
1 med. onion, grated
Salt and pepper to taste
1/2 c. grated Parmesan cheese
2 lb. cooked shrimp

Place whole cauliflower in kettle; add boiling water to cover. Cook until tender; keep warm. Melt butter in saucepan; blend in flour. Stir in milk slowly; cook over low heat, stirring constantly, until thickened. Stir in onion, salt, pepper and cheese. Remove from heat; fold in shrimp. Drain cauliflower well; place on large platter. Pour sauce over cauliflower; garnish with parsley. Serve immediately. Yield: 6 servings.

Caviar

Caviar is sieved, lightly pressed, and salted fish eggs or, roe. It is a highly prized delicacy. True caviar is made from sturgeon roe and is gray. The finest kind of caviar has large eggs and minimal quantities of salt. It is imported from Iran and the Soviet Union. Less expensive kinds are made from the roe of fish other than sturgeon, such as red caviar from salmon and gray caviar from whitefish. (1 tablespoon caviar = 80 calories)

BUYING: True caviar is available in refrigerated tins. Less expensive kinds are available in vacuum-packed tins.

STORING: Refrigerate true caviar at 30 degrees until ready to use. Store unopened vacuum-packed tins at room temperature. *Never freeze caviar.*

SERVING: For an inimitable hors d'oeuvre, serve caviar in original container in bowl surrounded by crushed ice or in a bowl placed within a larger, ice-filled bowl. Traditional accompaniments for caviar are toast or dark bread, chopped raw onions, chopped egg whites, chopped egg yolks, sour cream, and lemon. Caviar canapes and open-faced sandwiches are also favorite appetizers.

CAVIAR PUFFS

2 tbsp. margarine
1/4 c. flour
1/4 tsp. salt
1 egg
3 tbsp. sour cream
1 4-oz. jar red caviar, drained

Preheat oven to 400 degrees. Place 1/4 cup water and margarine in saucepan; bring to a boil. Add flour and salt; cook, stirring, until batter forms small ball. Remove from heat; cool. Add egg; mix well. Drop from teaspoon onto cookie sheet 1 inch apart. Bake for 30 minutes or until puffed and golden. Remove from pan; cool on rack. Cut off top. Fill with 1 teaspoon sour cream; top with caviar.

CAVIAR-STUFFED EGGS

4 hard-cooked eggs
2 tbsp. mayonnaise
1 tbsp. lemon juice
2 tsp. minced onion
1/4 tsp. freshly ground pepper
2 tbsp. lumpfish caviar

Halve eggs lengthwise. Remove yolks; mash. Combine mayonnaise, lemon juice, onion and pepper. Add to mashed yolks; stir in caviar gently. Refrigerate for about 6 hours. Wrap egg white halves in plastic wrap; refrigerate. Fill egg whites with egg yolk mixture. Yield: 8 appetizers.

CAVIAR WEDGES

1 round loaf pumpernickel bread
1 3-oz. package cream cheese, softened
2 tbsp. mayonnaise
1 tsp. onion juice
6 hard-cooked eggs
1 sm. jar red caviar
1 sm. jar black caviar

Cut 1-inch thick slice from the center of bread loaf. Combine cream cheese, mayonnaise and onion juice, blending until smooth. Spread evenly on bread slice. Halve eggs; separate yolks from whites. Sieve yolks and whites coarsely into separate bowls. Drain caviars thoroughly. Spoon black caviar around edge of bread slice. Add circle of sieved egg yolks. Place red caviar in circle touching yolks; add sieved egg whites to center. Cover with plastic wrap. Cut in narrow wedges to serve. Yield: 12 servings.

MOLDED CAVIAR

3/4 tsp. unflavored gelatin
1/4 c. milk
4 oz. cream cheese
1 tbsp. mayonnaise
1 tbsp. sour cream
1/4 tsp. lemon juice
1/8 tsp. onion powder
1/8 tsp. dillweed
1/8 tsp. salt
1/8 tsp. Worcestershire sauce
2 oz. black caviar, drained

Combine gelatin and milk in saucepan; stir over low heat until gelatin is dissolved. Add cream cheese; blend thoroughly and cool. Stir in mayonnaise, sour cream, lemon juice, onion powder, dillweed, salt, Worcestershire sauce and caviar. Pour into mold; chill for several hours. Remove from mold to serving plate. Serve with small melba toast rounds.

SCANDINAVIAN CAVIAR DIP

3 tbsp. caviar
2 tbsp. minced onion
1/2 c. whipping cream, whipped
Sliced hard-cooked eggs
Sm. toast rounds

Fold caviar and onion into whipped cream. Mound caviar mixture in center of platter; garnish with sliced eggs. Serve with toast rounds. Yield: 1 1/2 cups.

AVOCADO HALF SHELLS WITH CAVIAR

2 ripe California avocados
Lemon juice
4 tbsp. black caviar

Cut avocados lengthwise, twisting gently to separate halves. Insert sharp knife directly into seeds and twist gently to lift out. Brush cut surfaces with lemon juice. Spoon caviar into cavities. Arrange half shells on ice; garnish with hard-boiled chopped egg if desired. Yield: 4 servings.

Avocado Half Shells with Caviar . . . An elegant dish that lends flavor to a special event.

RED CAVIAR SAUCE WITH SHRIMP AND VEGETABLES

1 c. mayonnaise
1 tbsp. lemon juice
1 tbsp. grated onion
1 sm. jar red caviar
Cooked shrimp
Broccoli spears
Cucumber spears
Green onions
Green pepper strips

Combine mayonnaise, lemon juice, grated onion and caviar; mix gently. Spoon sauce into bowl; chill. Arrange shrimp and vegetables on platter around bowl of sauce; chill until ready to serve. Yield: 6 servings.

Celery

Celery is a vegetable developed hundreds of years ago from a wild herb. The leaves, stalk, and heart of celery are edible. It is a low-calorie source of Vitamins A and C plus calcium. (1 large celery stalk = 5 calories)
AVAILABILITY: It is available year-round with little seasonal variation in supply.
BUYING: Celery is sold in bunches with leaves attached or trimmed. Select celery with fresh leaves and firm, brittle stalks of medium length and thickness. Avoid celery that is cracked, bruised, loosened from the heart, excessively soft or hard, or stringy in appearance. Do not buy celery with brown or black discoloration on either stalks or leaves.
STORING: Wash celery; wrap in foil or plastic; store in vegetable crisper or on refrigerator shelf for up to one week. Cooked celery may be refrigerated for up to 5 days.
PREPARATION: One medium bunch celery yields 4-6 servings. *Raw celery* can be left whole or cut into desired lengths, slices, strips, or curls. To revive wilted celery, lay stalks in a bowl of icy water for a few minutes. *To boil celery*, separate and trim root, dice or slice. Place in small amount of boiling, salted water. Cover and cook 15-20 minutes. Drain, season, and serve.
(See VEGETABLES.)

HAM-STUFFED CELERY

2 tbsp. mayonnaise
1 tbsp. grated American cheese
1 tsp. finely chopped sweet pickle
1 c. ground cooked ham
1/2 tsp. prepared horseradish
Celery

Mix all ingredients except celery. Cut celery stalks into 2-inch lengths; fill with ham mixture. Chill. Yield: 24 appetizers.

HOT CELERY CANAPES

1 3-oz. package cream cheese
1/4 c. celery soup
1 c. ground salami
Toast or crackers

Mash cream cheese; blend in soup. Add salami; mix well. Spread mixture on toast; heat under broiler until browned. Yield: 20 canapes.

SHRIMP-STUFFED CELERY

1 bunch celery
1 c. minced cooked shrimp
2/3 c. mayonnaise
2 tsp. lemon juice
1 tbsp. chili sauce
Dash of cayenne pepper
1 tsp. onion salt

Cut celery into 3-inch pieces. Combine shrimp, mayonnaise, lemon juice, chili sauce, cayenne pepper and onion salt. Stuff celery with shrimp mixture; chill for several hours.

WALDORF BOATS

1 c. minced apples
1/2 c. minced walnuts
2 tbsp. minced raisins
1 tsp. lemon juice
1/3 c. mayonnaise
16 3-in. pieces of celery

Combine apples, walnuts and raisins; stir in lemon juice and mayonnaise. Spoon into celery; chill.

CELERY-RICE SOUP

1 1/2 c. chopped celery and leaves
1/4 c. rice
1 sm. onion, chopped
1 1/2 tsp. salt
Dash of pepper
1 1/2 c. milk
1 tbsp. butter

Combine celery, rice, onion, salt, pepper and 3 1/2 cups water in saucepan; bring to a boil. Reduce heat; simmer for 20 minutes or until rice is tender. Add milk and butter; heat until butter is melted. Serve immediately.

CREAM OF CELERY SOUP

5 c. minced celery and leaves
2 c. chicken stock
1 slice onion
2 tbsp. butter
3 tbsp. flour
2 c. milk
1 c. cream
Salt and pepper to taste

Combine celery, chicken stock and 2 cups boiling water in saucepan; simmer until celery is tender. Saute onion in butter; blend in flour. Stir in milk; cook, stirring, until thick. Add celery mixture and cream; season with salt and pepper. Process in electric blender until smooth. Reheat to serve.

CELERY-BEAN SPROUT SALAD

1 can bean sprouts
3 c. thinly sliced celery
2 1/2 tbsp. olive oil
1 1/2 tbsp. soy sauce
3/4 tsp. salt
Dash of white pepper
2 tsp. lemon juice
1/2 tsp. minced onion

Pour bean sprouts into colander; drain overnight in refrigerator. Combine bean sprouts and remaining ingredients in bowl; toss lightly. Serve chilled. Yield: 6 servings.

CELERY PINWHEEL SALAD

1 bunch celery
1 pkg. cream cheese, softened
1 tsp. tarragon vinegar
1/2 c. mayonnaise
1/4 c. diced cucumber
1 tbsp. chopped green pepper
1/4 tsp. salt
Dash of pepper
Lettuce

Separate celery into stalks; fill stalks with cream cheese. Reassemble stalks to original shape; tie to hold firm. Chill for several hours. Combine vinegar, mayonnaise, cucumber, green pepper, salt and pepper for dressing. Slice celery; arrange on lettuce-lined plates. Spoon dressing over celery.

CELERY ROOT SALAD

1 lge. celery root
1 onion, finely chopped
2 tbsp. olive oil
2 tbsp. fresh lemon juice
Salt and pepper to taste
1/2 tsp. sugar
1 c. (about) mayonnaise
Lettuce

Place celery root in deep kettle; cover with water. Boil for 45 minutes or until easily pierced with fork. Drain and chill. Peel celery root; dice coarsely. Add onion, oil, lemon juice, salt, pepper and sugar; mix well. Moisten with mayonnaise; refrigerate for 2 to 3 hours before serving. Serve on lettuce.

HOLIDAY CELERY SLAW

1 tsp. salt
1 1/2 tsp. sugar
1/8 tsp. pepper
Dash of paprika
1/3 c. salad oil
2 tbsp. vinegar
1/4 c. cream
2 c. thinly sliced celery
2 tbsp. slivered pimento
Salad greens
Green pepper rings

Combine salt, sugar, pepper, paprika, oil and vinegar. Beat with rotary beater until blended. Add cream; beat until smooth. Marinate celery in dressing for several minutes. Add pimento; toss. Place greens in salad bowl; pile celery mixture in center. Garnish with green pepper rings. Yield: 6 servings.

BAKED CELERY

3 slices lean bacon, chopped
1 onion, thinly sliced
2 tbsp. minced parsley
1 sm. clove of garlic, crushed
8 med. stalks celery
1 c. beef consomme
1/4 c. fine soft bread crumbs
3 tbsp. melted butter

Place bacon, onion, parsley and garlic in greased shallow baking dish; arrange celery on top. Add consomme; cover. Bake at 325 degrees for 1 hour or until celery is tender. Saute bread crumbs in butter; sprinkle over celery. Bake for 10 minutes longer. Yield: 4 servings.

BAKED CELERY AND MUSHROOMS

3 c. sliced celery
Salt
3 tbsp. butter
2 tbsp. minced onion
3 tbsp. flour
1 3-oz. can broiled mushrooms
2/3 c. milk
1/8 tsp. pepper
2 oz. sliced American cheese
1/4 c. buttered bread crumbs

Cook celery in small amount of boiling salted water until almost tender; drain. Melt butter in saucepan; add onion. Cook onion for about 1 minute; blend in flour. Add mushrooms and milk. Cook over low heat, stirring constantly, until thickened. Add 1/2 teaspoon salt and pepper; fold in celery. Turn into casserole; cover with cheese. Sprinkle with bread crumbs. Bake at 325 degrees for 20 to 25 minutes. Yield: 4-6 servings.

CREAMED CELERY CASSEROLE

1/4 c. butter
1 c. slivered almonds
3 c. diced celery
2 tbsp. flour
1/2 c. light cream
1/8 tsp. pepper
1 c. boiling chicken broth
3 tbsp. grated Parmesan cheese

Heat 2 tablespoons butter in large skillet until frothy; add almonds and celery. Cover; cook for 15 to 20 minutes, stirring occasionally. Add remaining butter; blend in flour. Cook for 1 minute, stirring. Add cream, pepper and broth all at once, stirring to blend. Increase heat to moderate. Cook, stirring constantly, until thickened and bubbly. Spoon into 1-quart casserole; sprinkle with cheese. Place under broiler until cheese is brown. Yield: 4 servings.

CREOLE-BAKED CELERY

1/4 c. chopped onion
3 tbsp. butter
2 c. canned tomatoes
1/2 clove of garlic, chopped
Salt to taste
1 c. chopped ripe olives
1/2 tsp. chili powder
1/4 c. cornstarch
1/2 c. grated American cheese
3 c. cooked sliced celery
1/2 c. buttered bread crumbs

Saute onion in butter until lightly browned; add tomatoes, garlic, salt and olives. Bring to a boil. Reduce heat; simmer for 5 minutes. Mix chili powder and cornstarch with small amount of cold water; add to tomato mixture. Cook, stirring, until thick; blend in cheese. Place celery in baking dish; add tomato mixture. Sprinkle crumbs over top. Bake at 375 degrees for 30 minutes or until brown. Yield: 6 servings.

FRENCH-BRAISED CELERY

2 c. 1-in. pieces of celery
4 sprigs of parsley
4 slices onion
1/2 c. bouillon
1 tsp. salt
1/4 tsp. pepper
2 strips bacon, diced
Buttered bread crumbs

Place celery, parsley, onion and bouillon in casserole; sprinkle with salt, pepper and bacon. Cover. Bake at 375 degrees for 30 minutes. Sprinkle with bread crumbs. Bake, uncovered, for 10 minutes longer or until crumbs are browned. Yield: 4 servings.

EXOTIC CELERY

4 c. 1-in. slices celery
Salt
1 5-oz. can water chestnuts
1 can celery soup
1 can chicken soup
1/4 c. chopped pimento
1/2 c. bread crumbs
1/4 c. toasted slivered almonds
2 tbsp. melted butter
Dash of curry powder

Cook celery in small amount of salted water for 8 minutes; drain well. Drain and slice chestnuts. Mix soups; stir in celery, chestnuts and pimento. Turn into 1 1/2-quart casserole. Combine bread crumbs, almonds, butter and curry powder; toss to mix. Spread over casserole. Bake at 350 degrees for 35 minutes. Yield: 6 servings.

HOLIDAY CELERY AU GRATIN

2 tbsp. butter
2 tbsp. flour
1 c. chicken stock
1/4 c. light cream
2 c. chopped celery
Salt
1/4 c. chopped almonds
1/2 tsp. pepper
1 c. grated American cheese
1 c. buttered bread crumbs

Melt butter in saucepan; blend in flour until smooth. Add stock and cream gradually. Cook, stirring constantly, until thickened. Cook celery until partially tender in boiling salted water; drain well. Fold celery and almonds into sauce; add 1 teaspoon salt and pepper. Pour into greased 8-inch square pan; top with cheese and crumbs. Bake at 350 degrees for 15 to 20 minutes. Yield: 4-6 servings.

RUSSIAN CELERY BAKE

1 bunch celery
Salt
3 tbsp. butter
1 tbsp. flour
Dash of pepper
1 c. light cream
1 3-oz. package cream cheese
1/2 c. toasted slivered almonds

Remove heavy outer ribs of celery; cut remaining celery diagonally into 1/4-inch pieces. Cook celery in boiling, salted water for 5 minutes or until tender but crisp; drain well. Melt butter in small saucepan; blend in flour, 1/2 teaspoon salt and pepper. Add cream slowly. Cook over low heat, stirring constantly, until smooth and thickened. Melt cream cheese in sauce. Place celery in 1 1/2-quart greased casserole. Pour sauce over celery; sprinkle almonds on top. Bake at 325 degrees for 20 to 25 minutes. Yield: 4-5 servings.

Avery Island Celery . . . Peas, celery, and a richly seasoned sauce harmonize in this dish.

AVERY ISLAND CELERY

4 tbsp. butter
1 med. onion, chopped
1 1-lb. 3-oz. can tomatoes
1/2 tsp. hot sauce
1 tsp. salt
1/4 tsp. sugar
1/4 tsp. leaf thyme
4 c. diagonally cut celery
1 10-oz. package frozen peas, thawed

Melt butter in large skillet; add onion and saute lightly. Drain tomatoes; reserve liquid. Add reserved tomato liquid, hot sauce, salt, sugar and thyme to onion mixture; bring to a boil. Stir in celery and peas. Cover; boil for 5 minutes or until barely tender. Chop tomatoes; add to celery mixture. Heat through. Turn into serving dish; serve. Yield: 6 servings.

SCALLOPED CELERY

3 c. sliced celery
1 c. chopped green peppers
1/4 c. chopped onion
2/3 c. cream of celery soup
Salt and pepper
1/4 c. cracker crumbs

Combine vegetables in saucepan; add water just to cover. Simmer until celery is tender-crisp; drain well. Stir soup and seasonings into vegetables; turn into greased 1-quart casserole. Top with cracker crumbs. Bake at 350 degrees until heated through.

CELERY AMANDINE

1/3 c. blanched whole almonds
2 tbsp. butter
4 c. diagonally sliced celery
1 chicken bouillon cube, crumbled
1 tbsp. instant minced onion
1 tsp. monosodium glutamate
1/2 tsp. sugar
1/8 tsp. garlic powder
1/8 tsp. ground ginger

Saute almonds in butter in saucepan until lightly browned; add celery, bouillon cube, onion, monosodium glutamate, sugar, garlic powder and ginger. Mix well; cover. Cook, stirring occasionally, for 10 minutes or until celery is tender. Yield: 5 servings.

CELERY-MUSHROOM TOSS

3 c. 1/4-in. slices celery
1 c. chicken broth
1/2 lb. fresh mushrooms, sliced
1/2 c. butter
1/4 tsp. pepper
1 tsp. soy sauce
1/2 c. toasted slivered almonds

Simmer celery in chicken broth until tender; drain and keep warm. Saute mushrooms in butter until just tender; season with pepper and soy sauce. Combine mushrooms, celery and almonds in serving dish. Toss lightly; serve immediately. Yield: 6-8 servings.

CELERY-PECAN RING

1 c. fine dry bread crumbs
1 1/2 c. ground celery
2 tbsp. minced parsley
1/4 c. ground pecans
1 tbsp. minced green pepper
1 tsp. minced onion
3 eggs, beaten
3 tbsp. melted butter
1 1/2 tsp. salt
Pepper to taste
1 1/2 c. milk

Combine all ingredients; blend well. Press lightly into greased 5-cup ring mold. Let stand for 30 minutes. Place mold in pan containing hot water. Bake in 350-degree oven for 1 hour. Let stand in hot water for 10 minutes. Unmold. Fill center with creamed sweetbreads, mushrooms, chicken or seafood. Yield: 8 servings.

ORIENTAL CELERY SAUTE

1 4-oz. can sliced mushrooms
1 5-oz. can water chestnuts
2 tbsp. butter
2 c. sliced celery
1/2 c. diagonally sliced green onions
1 tsp. seasoned salt
1/4 tsp. seasoned pepper

Drain mushrooms and water chestnuts; slice water chestnuts. Melt butter in skillet. Add celery, green onions, mushrooms, water chestnuts and seasonings. Cook, stirring, for 2 minutes or until celery is tender-crisp. Yield: 4 servings.

Chard

CHARD WITH SOUR CREAM SAUCE

3 lb. chard
1 c. sour cream
1 pkg. onion soup mix
1/2 c. chopped walnuts

Remove stalks and coarse ribs from chard; chop coarsely. Cook, covered, in boiling salted water for 5 minutes or until tender; drain well. Blend sour cream and soup mix thoroughly. Combine with chard in 1 1/2-quart greased casserole; sprinkle walnuts over top. Bake at 325 degrees for 20 minutes or until heated through.

SCALLOPED CHARD

4 c. chard
1 c. butter, melted
3/4 c. cracker crumbs
1/3 c. chopped onion
1 can cream of mushroom soup
2 eggs, well beaten
1/4 c. buttered crumbs

Remove thick ribs from chard; chop leaves coarsely. Cook in boiling salted water for 3 to 5 minutes or until tender; drain well. Add butter, cracker crumbs, onion, soup and eggs; mix well. Pour into 7 x 12-inch baking dish; sprinkle with buttered crumbs. Bake in 350-degree oven for 30 minutes.

STEAMED CHARD

1 lb. chard
1 tbsp. butter
1 clove of garlic, minced
2 tbsp. olive oil
Salt and pepper

Wash chard leaves thoroughly; remove coarse ribs. Remove excess water; chop coarsely. Heat butter, garlic and olive oil in skillet; add chard. Bring to a boil, covered; reduce heat. Simmer for 5 to 6 minutes or until leaves are tender; salt and pepper to taste. Serve hot.

SWEET AND SOUR CHARD

1 lb. chard
3 slices bacon
2 tbsp. flour
Dash of salt
1/2 c. vinegar
1/2 c. sugar

Remove stalks and coarse ribs from chard; tear into small pieces. Wash chard thoroughly; drain well. Fry bacon in skillet until crisp; drain. Add flour to bacon drippings; stir until smooth and lightly browned. Combine salt, vinegar and sugar with 1/2 cup water; add to flour mixture. Simmer, stirring constantly, until smooth and thickened. Crumble bacon; add to sauce. Pour sauce over chard; toss lightly.

Charlotte

Charlotte is a term used to describe a decorative molded dessert made with ladyfingers or cake and Bavarian or whipped cream, and gelatin.

PREPARATION: The best-known Charlotte is *Charlotte Russe,* which is prepared by lining a mold with ladyfingers or thin cake and filling it with a rich cream mixture such as custard or Bavarian cream. It is chilled before being served.

CHARLOTTE RUSSE

12 ladyfingers
2 env. unflavored gelatin
1 c. sugar
1/4 tsp. salt
4 eggs, separated
2 1/2 c. milk
2 tbsp. brandy
1/3 c. chopped maraschino cherries
1/4 c. chopped nuts
2 c. whipped cream

Split ladyfingers; cut off ends to stand upright. Place around side of 8-inch springform pan. Mix gelatin, 1/2 cup sugar and salt together in 2-quart saucepan. Beat egg yolks and milk together; add to gelatin mixture. Place over low heat for about 6 minutes, stirring constantly, until gelatin is dissolved. Remove from heat; add brandy. Chill until mixture mounds slightly when dropped from spoon. Beat egg whites until stiff but not dry. Add remaining sugar gradually; beat until stiff peaks form. Fold in gelatin mixture, cherries, nuts and whipped cream. Turn into prepared pan; chill until firm. Release spring; remove side of mold carefully. Garnish with additional whipped cream, shaved chocolate, chopped nuts and pieces of maraschino cherries. Yield: 12 servings.

Charlotte Russe . . . The most famous of all Charlottes, loved for its smooth richness.

CHARLOTTE SUPREME

4 eggs, separated
1/2 c. sugar
2 c. milk, scalded
1 pkg. unflavored gelatin
1 tsp. vanilla
2 c. whipping cream, whipped
1 doz. almond macaroons, crumbled

Beat egg yolks until thick and frothy; add sugar gradually, blending thoroughly. Add to milk, stirring constantly, until slightly thickened. Soften gelatin in 1/4 cup water; dissolve gelatin in hot milk mixture. Cool. Beat egg whites until stiff peaks form. Add vanilla to gelatin mixture; fold in egg whites. Fold whipped cream into egg white mixture. Refrigerate until partially set; stir in macaroons. Refrigerate, covered, until set. Yield: 15-18 servings.

SHERRY CHARLOTTE

2 env. unflavored gelatin
4 c. whipping cream
1 c. sugar
1/4 tsp. salt
1 tsp. vanilla
1/2 c. sherry
4 egg whites, stiffly beaten

Soften gelatin in 1/2 cup cold water; place over hot water until gelatin is melted. Whip cream until stiff peaks form. Add sugar; stir until dissolved. Add salt, gelatin, vanilla and sherry; mix well. Fold in egg whites; pour into mold. Refrigerate until set. May be made 24 hours before serving. Yield: 8 servings.

SPRINGFORM PAN

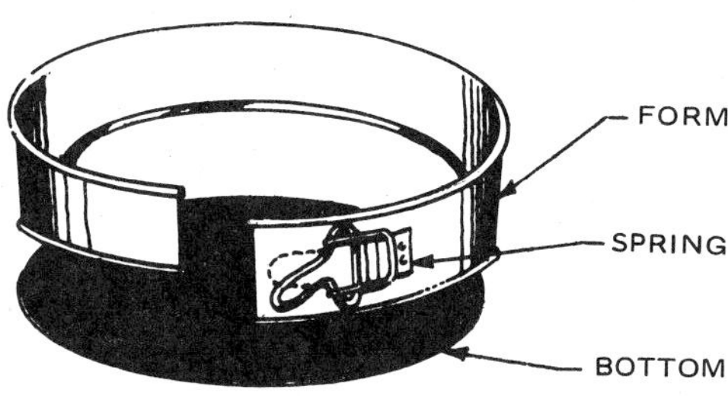

A springform pan is ideal for charlottes and other delicate desserts. The dessert is unmolded by releasing a spring at the side of the pan, thus overcoming any need to handle these easily-broken sweets.

SPRINGTIME CHARLOTTE

1 pkg. cherry gelatin
1 pt. vanilla ice cream
1/2 tsp. almond flavoring
1 pkg. ladyfingers, halved

Dissolve gelatin in 1/2 cup boiling water. Add vanilla ice cream; blend. Add almond flavoring. Line parfait glasses with ladyfingers. Pour gelatin mixture slowly into glasses; chill until set. Yield: 6 servings.

CHOCOLATE CHARLOTTE RUSSE

1 tbsp. unflavored gelatin
3 1-oz. squares unsweetened chocolate
4 eggs, separated
3/4 c. sugar
1 tsp. vanilla
Dash of salt
1/2 tsp. cream of tartar
1/2 c. heavy cream, whipped
1/2 c. chopped walnuts
18 ladyfingers

Soften gelatin in 2 tablespoons cold water. Melt chocolate in 1/2 cup water over low heat, stirring constantly; remove from heat. Add softened gelatin to chocolate; stir to dissolve. Beat egg yolks until thick and lemon colored; beat in 1/2 cup sugar gradually. Add vanilla and dash of salt; stir in chocolate mixture gradually. Cool; stir until smooth. Beat egg whites and cream of tartar until soft peaks form; add remaining sugar gradually, beating until stiff peaks form. Fold egg whites into chocolate mixture; fold in whipped cream and walnuts. Set aside ten ladyfingers for center layer. Line bottom of 8-inch springform pan with ladyfingers, cutting to fit; line side by standing ladyfingers, cutting to fit. Fill with half the chocolate mixture; add reserved ladyfingers, making layer. Top with chocolate mixture; chill 8 hours or overnight. Yield: 8-10 servings.

LEMON CHARLOTTE RUSSE

1 env. unflavored gelatin
1/2 c. fresh lemon juice
4 eggs, separated
1 1/2 c. sugar
1/8 tsp. salt
3 tbsp. butter
1 1/2 tsp. grated lemon peel
1 tsp. vanilla
Ladyfingers
Whipped cream

Soften gelatin in lemon juice. Combine egg yolks, 1 cup sugar and salt; beat until thickened. Combine egg yolk mixture, gelatin mixture and butter in top of double boiler. Cook over simmering water, stirring constantly with wooden spoon, for 10 minutes or until thickened. Stir in lemon peel and vanilla. Cool until mixture is partially set. Line bottom and side of 9-inch springform pan with ladyfingers. Beat egg whites until soft peaks form. Add remaining sugar gradually, beating until stiff. Fold egg whites and 1 cup whipped cream into lemon mixture. Turn into prepared pan. Refrigerate until firm; unmold onto serving platter. Garnish with whipped cream. Yield: 10 servings.

PISTACHIO CHARLOTTE RUSSE

1/2 c. semisweet chocolate pieces
1 tbsp. shortening
8 ladyfingers, split and halved
1/2 c. chopped pistachio nuts
1 tbsp. unflavored gelatin
1 c. milk
2 eggs, separated
1/2 c. sugar
1 tsp. grated lemon rind
1/4 c. lemon juice
1 c. whipping cream, whipped

Melt chocolate pieces and shortening together in double boiler; remove from heat. Dip rounded side and 1 end of each ladyfinger into chocolate; coat with nuts. Stand, chocolate end up, around edge of 9-inch springform pan. Place any remaining ladyfingers on bottom. Chill. Soften gelatin in 1/4 cup milk. Beat egg yolks; stir in remaining milk. Combine gelatin, 1/4 cup sugar and egg yolk mixture in double boiler. Cook over simmering water, stirring constantly, for about 6 minutes or until mixture coats spoon. Remove from heat; strain into large bowl. Chill until partially set. Stir in lemon rind and juice. Whip egg whites until foamy; beat in remaining sugar, one tablespoon at a time, until soft peaks form. Fold egg whites and whipped cream into gelatin mixture; pour into ladyfinger-lined pan. Chill for 3 hours or until firm. Yield: 8 servings.

MAPLE CHARLOTTE

2 c. milk
1 tbsp. unflavored gelatin
3 eggs, separated
Dash of salt
1 c. maple syrup

Pour milk into double boiler. Soften gelatin in 1/4 cup water. Sprinkle gelatin over milk; bring to a boil, stirring until gelatin dissolves. Beat egg yolks with salt. Stir in half the milk mixture slowly. Return to double boiler; cook over simmering water until mixture coats spoon. Remove from heat. Stir in syrup; cool until partially thickened. Whip syrup mixture until light and frothy. Beat egg whites until stiff peaks form; beat into maple mixture. Pour into mold; chill until firm. Serve with whipped cream.

NEAPOLITAN CHARLOTTE RUSSE

2 1/2 tbsp. unflavored gelatin
3 c. milk
1 1/2 c. sugar
4 eggs
4 c. whipping cream, whipped
2 tbsp. chocolate syrup
3 drops of red food coloring
1/4 c. chopped maraschino cherries
Ladyfingers

Dissolve gelatin in 1/2 cup water. Combine milk, sugar and eggs, mixing well. Cook milk mixture, stirring constantly, over medium heat until thickened. Add gelatin mixture; stir until dissolved. Cool until partially set. Fold in whipped cream. Divide mixture into 3 parts; set 1 part aside. Add chocolate syrup to second part; add food coloring and cherries to third part. Line mold with ladyfingers; pour each part into mold separately to make 3 layers. Refrigerate until set. Yield: 12 servings.

PRINCESS CHARLOTTE PUDDING

1 package unflavored gelatin
1/2 c. sugar
1 tbsp. cornstarch
2 eggs, slightly beaten
2 c. milk
Dash of salt
1/2 pt. whipping cream, whipped
1 tsp. vanilla
1/4 c. slivered almonds

Soften gelatin in 2 tablespoons water; let stand. Combine sugar and cornstarch; add to eggs. Stir in milk thoroughly. Simmer until thick, stirring constantly. Add salt and gelatin mixture; cool. Fold in whipped cream and flavoring; add almonds. Pour into individual molds; chill until set. Serve topped with crushed fresh raspberries. Yield: 8-9 servings.

ORANGE CHARLOTTE

1 1/3 tbsp. unflavored gelatin
1 c. sugar
3 tbsp. lemon juice
1 c. orange juice and pulp
3 egg whites
2 c. whipping cream, whipped

Soften gelatin in 1/3 cup cold water; add to 1/3 cup boiling water, stirring until dissolved. Combine sugar, lemon juice, orange juice and pulp. Add to gelatin mixture. Chill in pan of ice water until partially set. Beat with wire spoon or whisk until frothy. Beat egg whites until stiff peaks form; fold into orange juice mixture. Fold in whipped cream; chill until set. Garnish with orange sections or orange slices. Yield: 8 servings.

STRAWBERRY CHARLOTTE RUSSE

8 double ladyfingers
2 3-oz. packages strawberry gelatin
1 1/2 c. crushed strawberries
1 tbsp. lemon juice
1/2 c. sugar
Dash of salt
2 c. heavy cream, whipped

Place 3-inch strip of waxed paper around 8-inch springform mold pan. Split ladyfingers; arrange around edge of pan inside waxed paper. Combine gelatin and 2 cups boiling water; stir until dissolved. Add strawberries, lemon juice, sugar and salt; chill mixture until of consistency of unbeaten egg whites. Fold in whipped cream; spoon carefully into ladyfinger-lined pan. Chill at least 5 hours. Remove from mold; serve on large plate. Garnish with additional cream and whole strawberries. May be made in deep 2 1/2-quart casserole. Yield: 8 servings.

Cheese

Cheese, the most ancient of manufactured foods, is a highly nutritious concentrated form of milk. In the United States, most cheeses are made from cows' milk although goats' or ewes' milk is also used. Cheese contains a great deal of protein.

AVAILABILITY: It is available year-round.

BUYING: Consult the chart that follows to determine which type of cheese is best for your purpose.

STORING: Cheese refrigerates well but must be stored in an airtight container. Hard cheeses keep several weeks; if they begin to dry out, wrap them in cloths dampened with water or vinegar. Soft, unripened cheeses (cream, cottage) sour quickly and should be used as soon as possible after purchasing. Hard or semihard cheeses may be frozen, but only in small portions of 1 pound or less. *To freeze* cheese, first place in container or wrap in moisture- and vapor- proof paper. Soft cheeses crumble if frozen.

PREPARATION: Cheese served as a dessert or an appetizer should be at room temperature. Many hard cheeses are grated for inclusion in soups, salads, salad dressings, main dishes, and so on. One pound cheese yields 2 cups shredded or grated cheese.

Choosing Cheeses

There are three major classes of cheese: natural, pasteurized process, and pasteurized process cheese foods and spreads. *Natural cheese* is produced by souring milk and thereby coagulating part of the milk, called the curd, separating it from the more watery part of milk, the whey. Cheese is generally made from milk's curd. *Pasteurized process cheese* is a blend of fresh and aged natural cheeses that have been shredded, mixed, and heated (pasteurized). *Pasteurized process cheese foods and spreads* are prepared similarly to process cheeses but they may contain either nonfat dry milk or whey solids and water and have a reduced cheese content. Both pasteurized process cheese and process cheese foods and spreads are considered to lack the flavor of natural cheese. While process cheeses are handy for sandwiches and snacks, natural cheese gives better flavor in cooking and for appetizers or desserts.

Natural cheeses are grouped as soft, semihard, or hard. Except for cottage and cream cheeses, most soft and semihard cheeses are not usually recommended for cooking. Under heat they lose flavor, becoming tough or gummy. Most soft and semihard cheeses are most often served as appetizers on cheese trays or as desserts with or without fruits. Hard cheeses are excellent for cooking.

Some soft natural cheeses are sold unripened. Others are mold- or bacteria-ripened. Mold-ripened cheeses have a characteristic blue or green marbling through them and a sharp odor and flavor. Semihard natural cheeses are mostly bacteria-ripened, and hard natural cheeses are all bacteria-ripened.

NATURAL CHEESE	CHARACTERISTICS AND USES
Bel Paese	A soft cheese often used in cooking to replace mozzarella. Although it is an Italian cheese, there is a very good American version bearing the same name that is made in Wisconsin.
Blue	A crumbly and sharp-flavored soft dessert cheese that is white and contains blue mold. French blue cheese is referred to as "bleu cheese."
Brick	A pale-gold, semihard American cheese that slices easily. It is stronger-flavored than Cheddar, although not as strong as Limburger, and is used in cooking or in sandwiches and for snacks.
Brie	A soft, creamy dessert cheese ranked as one of the world's great cheeses. It should be served at room temperature. At room temperature, good Brie is almost always runny.
Camembert	A soft, creamy, rich dessert cheese that is another of the world's great cheeses. Camembert that is shrunken in appearance or smells like ammonia is past its prime.
Cheddar	A variety of hard cheese that is the most popular American cheese. Cheddar is sold as mild, mellow, or sharp cheese. Mild has aged 2-3 months; mellow from 6-9 months; and sharp, from 12-15 months. Excellent for eating or cooking.
Coon	A hard cheese produced primarily in New York State. Similar in flavor to Cheddar, coon cheese has a characteristic black cheesecloth covering and is eaten as is or used in cooking.
Cottage	The large or small drained curd of soured whole or skimmed milk. One of the few soft cheeses suitable for cooking.

NATURAL CHEESE	CHARACTERISTICS AND USES
Cream	An unripened American soft cheese that is popular for desserts. Like cottage cheese, cream cheese is a soft cheese suitable for cooking.
Edam	A mild, semihard cheese. It was originally Dutch cheese that now has several American versions. It has a bright red exterior rind and pale gold interior. Edam is primarily an eating cheese.
Emmentaler	A mild-flavored hard Swiss cheese used in preparing fondues and in other cooking.
Gorgonzola	A white and blue-veined Italian pressed cheese that may range from soft (very young) to semihard (aged). It is used in cooking, for desserts, or in sandwiches. An American gorgonzola is made in Wisconsin.
Gouda	Like gorgonzola, the mild-flavored gouda cheese becomes firmer with age. It was originally a Dutch cheese, that now has several American versions. Gouda is a popular dessert cheese.
Gruyère	A sharply-flavored Swiss hard cheese popular for fondues. It melts easily and is one of the best cooking cheeses.
Liederkranz	One of the soft American dessert cheeses, produced in Ohio. It has a strong odor and flavor.
Limburger	A semisoft, strong-smelling and sharply-flavored dessert or appetizer cheese that is almost runny in texture.
Monterey	Also known as Monterey Jack, this California cheese is of two types: a semihard cheese and a hard cheese. Both are good cooking cheeses.
Mozzarella	A semisoft white cheese popular in Italian dishes. There are American versions but they lack the flavor of the Italian varieties.

NATURAL CHEESE	CHARACTERISTICS AND USES
Parmesan	A staple hard cheese of Italian cookery. American Parmesans, sold already grated, have only a fraction of the flavor of the original, ungrated cheese.
Pot Cheese	A cottage cheese without the addition of cream or milk that most commercial cottage cheeses contain. Pot cheese is used in cooking.
Provolone	An Italian hard cheese that has a smoky flavor and is used primarily for appetizers or sandwiches. The American version has little of the flavor of the Italian cheese.
Ricotta	An Italian cottage-type cheese. American cottage cheese can be substituted in almost every recipe calling for ricotta.
Romano	A very hard Italian cheese grated like Parmesan and used for cooking. There is also an American Romano.
Roquefort	A soft dessert cheese that is white with a characteristic blue veining. The veining comes from the penicillin mold that gives this cheese its sharp flavor.
Swiss	The common United States term for any of the Emmentaler or Gruyere cheeses. Used in cooking. (Not to be confused with the process cheese of the same name.)
Vermont Cheddar	One of the finest American Cheddar cheeses.
Vermont Sage	Vermont Cheddar to which chopped or dried sage was added before aging.
Wisconsin Longhorn	A medium-sharp Cheddar cheese molded into a long, thin shape. It is an excellent cooking and eating cheese.

CHEESE MOUSSE

2 tsp. unflavored gelatin
2 c. sour cream
2 tsp. Italian salad dressing mix
1/4 c. crumbled bleu cheese
1 c. small curd cottage cheese

Soften gelatin in 1/4 cup cold water. Place over boiling water; stir until gelatin dissolves. Stir gelatin into sour cream; add dressing mix, bleu cheese and cottage cheese. Beat until well blended. Pour into 3 1/2-cup ring mold or small loaf pan; chill until firm. Unmold. Garnish with parsley and carrot curls.

APPETIZER PIE

1 8-oz. package cream cheese
2 tbsp. milk
1 pkg. dried beef, shredded
2 tbsp. instant minced onion
2 tbsp. minced green pepper
1/8 tsp. pepper
1/2 c. sour cream
1/4 c. coarsely chopped nuts

Have cream cheese at room temperature. Blend cheese with milk; stir in beef, onion, green pepper, pepper and sour cream. Blend well. Spoon into 8-inch glass pie plate or small shallow baking dish. Sprinkle with nuts. Bake at 350 degrees for 15 minutes. Serve hot with assorted crackers.

GOURMET CHEESE MOUSSE

1 tbsp. unflavored gelatin
1/4 c. cold water
1 3-oz. package Roquefort cheese
1 4-oz. package Camembert cheese
1 tsp. Worcestershire sauce
1 c. sour cream

Soften gelatin in 1/4 cup cold water; dissolve over hot water. Crumble Roquefort cheese; blend with Camembert cheese. Beat in gelatin, Worcestershire sauce and sour cream; spoon into mold. Chill until firm. Unmold. Garnish with parsley. Serve with crackers.

AUSTRIAN CHEESE ROLL

1 8-oz. package cream cheese
1/4 c. butter or margarine
1 tbsp. drained capers
4 anchovy fillets, chopped
1 tbsp. chopped chives
1/2 tsp. Worcestershire sauce
Dash of hot sauce
1 tsp. paprika
1/2 tsp. dry mustard
1/2 c. chopped nuts
1/4 c. chopped parsley

Allow cream cheese to soften at room temperature. Blend cheese with butter. Add capers, anchovies, chives, Worcestershire sauce, hot sauce, paprika and dry mustard to cheese mixture. Blend thoroughly. Chill mixture until firm enough to shape into roll. Roll in plastic wrap; refrigerate for 2 to 4 hours. Mix nuts and parsley; roll cheese roll in nut mixture. Serve immediately.

BRANDIED CHEESE BALLS

1 lb. sharp cheese
3 tbsp. mayonnaise
2 oz. brandy
1/4 tsp. bitters
Salt to taste
1/4 tsp. red pepper

Grind cheese. Cream cheese thoroughly with remaining ingredients. Chill for at least 2 hours. Roll into small balls; sprinkle with paprika. Top with sprig of green if desired. Store in refrigerator until ready to use.

CHEESE LOG

2 c. crumbled bleu cheese
2 c. grated Cheddar cheese
1/4 c. melted butter
2 to 3 tbsp. cream cheese
Hot sauce
Worcestershire sauce
Chopped salted nuts

Blend bleu cheese and Cheddar cheese with melted butter. Thin with cream cheese to desired consistency. Season to taste with hot sauce and Worcestershire sauce. Roll cheese mixture into log using waxed paper. Refrigerate, covered, overnight. Let stand at room temperature until surface is slightly softened. Roll in chopped salted nuts.

CHEESE AND SAUSAGE ROLLS

16 sausage links
16 slices bread
4 tbsp. butter
1 c. shredded American cheese

Cook sausage; drain. Cut crusts from bread; roll flat. Mix butter and cheese, spread on bread. Roll sausage in each slice. Bake on greased baking sheet at 400 degrees for 10 to 12 minutes. Slice and serve with wooden picks. Yield: 40 servings.

CHEESE-OLIVE ROLLS

1/2 lb. blue cheese
1/2 lb. cream cheese
1/4 c. butter
1 tbsp. minced chives
1 tbsp. brandy
1/2 c. minced ripe olives
1/4 tsp. salt
1 c. chopped toasted almonds
Chopped watercress

Combine blue cheese, cream cheese and butter; blend thoroughly. Stir in chives, brandy, olives and salt. Form mixture into 2 rolls. Chill for 2 to 3 hours. Cover with almonds and watercress; chill until ready to serve.

CHILI-CHEESE ROLL

1 8-oz. package Velveeta cheese
1 8-oz. package Cheddar cheese
1 3-oz. package cream cheese
3 tbsp. mayonnaise
Red pepper to taste
Salt to taste
3/4 c. finely chopped nuts
1 clove of garlic, minced
1/2 tsp. onion powder
1/2 c. chopped pimento
Chili powder
Paprika

Have cheeses at room temperature; blend thoroughly. Add mayonnaise, red pepper, salt, nuts, garlic, onion powder and chopped pimento; mix well. Shape into 2 rolls. Roll in chili powder and paprika; wrap in waxed paper. Chill for 24 hours before serving. Slice into thin slices; serve on crackers. Yield: 20 servings.

CHEESEWAGER

8 oz. cream cheese
8 oz. braunschweiger
1 tbsp. minced onion
1 tsp. Worcestershire sauce
1 tsp. lemon juice
1 tbsp. Russian dressing
Chopped parsley

Combine cheese and braunschweiger; blend thoroughly. Add onion, Worcestershire sauce, lemon juice and dressing; mix well. Shape into ball; roll in parsley. Chill for several hours. Serve on party rye bread or crackers.

CLAM-CHEESE LOG

2 7 1/2-oz. cans minced clams
1 lb. Cheddar cheese, grated
2 3-oz. packages cream cheese
3/4 tsp. hot sauce
1/4 c. butter
2 tsp. Worcestershire sauce
1 tsp. grated onion
6 tbsp. chopped parsley
1/2 c. finely chopped nuts

Drain clams. Combine clams, cheeses, hot sauce, butter, Worcestershire sauce and onion in mixer bowl; blend well. Mix in 3 tablespoons parsley. Shape mixture into ball; chill for at least 3 hours. Shape mixture into 1 or 2 logs. Combine remaining parsley and nuts; roll logs in parsley mixture. Chill for several hours or overnight. Serve on bread rounds or crackers.

FROSTED CHEESE BALL

1 lb. cream cheese
1 lb. Cheddar cheese, grated
1/4 lb. smoked cheese, grated
1 tsp. onion salt
1/4 tsp. garlic salt
1 tbsp. prepared mustard
Milk
2 tbsp. prepared horseradish
Chopped cashew nuts
Chopped parsley

Reserve 1 cup cream cheese. Combine remaining cream cheese, Cheddar cheese and smoked cheese in large mixer bowl; add onion salt, garlic salt and mustard. Beat until thoroughly blended; add milk until of desired consistency. Shape cheese mixture into ball; chill. Soften reserved cream cheese; add horseradish. Spread mixture over cheese ball; garnish with nuts and parsley. Refrigerate for at least 2 hours before serving. Cheese ball may be frozen.

PARTY CHEESE BALLS

3 tsp. snipped parsley
2 3-oz. wedges blue cheese
2 5-oz. jars Cheddar cheese spread
4 3-oz. packages cream cheese
1 c. ground pecans
1 tbsp. Worcestershire sauce

Combine parsley with cheeses, pecans and Worcestershire sauce; blend thoroughly. Shape into balls. Chill for several hours.

ROQUEFORT CHEESE BALLS

1 lb. Roquefort cheese
1/2 lb. cream cheese
1/4 lb. unsalted butter
Hot sauce to taste

Let all ingredients stand at room temperature. Cream Roquefort cheese until smooth . Add cream cheese and butter; blend thoroughly. Add hot sauce; shape into small balls. Roll in chopped nuts or chopped parsley, if desired; refrigerate until ready to use. Let stand at room temperature for about 20 minutes before serving.

SESAME CHEESE BALL

1/4 c. sesame seed
2 tbsp. instant onion
1 tsp. instant bouillon
2 tbsp. lemon juice
1/2 lb. sharp cheese
2 tbsp. mayonnaise
1 tbsp. catsup
1 tsp. Worcestershire sauce
1 tsp. dry mustard

Toast sesame seed in 350-degree oven for 15 minutes or until lightly browned. Dissolve onion and instant bouillon in lemon juice. Grate cheese. Combine cheese with lemon juice, mayonnaise, catsup, Worcestershire sauce and mustard. Shape into ball; roll in sesame seed. Chill for several hours.

SWISS CHEESE BALLS

1/3 stick butter
2 tbsp. flour
1/2 c. hot milk
1/2 lb. Swiss cheese, grated
Salt to taste
Pepper to taste
Nutmeg to taste
2 egg yolks

Melt butter in pan; stir in flour. Add milk, stirring vigorously. Add cheese, salt, pepper and nutmeg; mix well. Stir in egg yolks. Pour into baking dish. Bake at 300 degrees for 10 minutes. Remove from oven; cool in refrigerator. Form into balls. Roll in additional flour. Fry in deep fat until brown. Yield: 30-40 balls.

CHEESE-CRAB SPECIAL

1 8-oz. package cream cheese
1/4 c. light cream
2 tsp. lemon juice
1 1/2 tsp. Worcestershire sauce
1 clove of garlic, minced
Dash of salt and pepper
1 can crab meat

Allow cheese to soften at room temperature. Blend cream cheese and cream thoroughly. Add lemon juice, Worcestershire sauce, garlic, salt and pepper. Drain crab; remove any pieces of shell. Shred meat. Stir into cream cheese mixture. Chill. Yield: 1 1/2 cups dip.

A TRIO OF CHEESE DIPS

Color photograph for this recipe on page 733.

1 1/2 c. grated Cheddar cheese
Mayonnaise
3 tbsp. chopped pimento
3/4 c. Cheddar cheese spread
1/3 c. sour cream
1 1/2 c. shredded Monterey Jack cheese
1/8 tsp. salt
1/8 tsp. dillweed
3 Washington red Delicious apples
2 tbsp. lemon juice

Blend Cheddar cheese, 1/2 cup mayonnaise and pimento in a bowl. Mix Cheddar cheese spread and 3 tablespoons mayonnaise in separate bowl. Blend sour cream, Monterey Jack cheese, salt and dillweed in another bowl. Make diagonal cuts near top of each apple, each knife stroke at right angles to the preceding one, and cut just to center of apples. Lift off top; hollow apple, using melon ball cutter. Mix lemon juice with 2 tablespoons water; dip apple cups in lemon mixture. Drain well. Tops may be dipped in lemon mixture and used as a decorative float in punch. Place each dip in an apple. Place apples on a tray; garnish with mint.

BLEU CHEESE DIP

2 8-oz. packages cream cheese
1 3-oz. package bleu cheese
Garlic salt
Onion salt
Worcestershire sauce
Light cream

Allow cheeses to soften at room temperature. Blend cheeses thoroughly. Add garlic salt, onion salt and Worcestershire sauce to taste. Add light cream until of desired consistency. Chill until ready to use. Serve with crisp cauliflower, carrot sticks or corn chips. Yield: 12 servings.

CHEESE-PECAN DIP

3 eggs
2 tbsp. sugar
3 tbsp. vinegar
1 8-oz. package cream cheese
1/4 c. green pepper, grated
1 sm. onion, grated
1/2 c. chopped pecans

Beat eggs well; add sugar and vinegar. Cook over boiling water until thickened; cool slightly. Beat in cheese; fold in green pepper, onion and pecans. Chill for 2 hours or until ready to use.

CHEESE-VEGETABLE DIP

1 8-oz. package cream cheese
1 4-oz. package blue cheese
2 tbsp. minced green pepper
4 tbsp. minced onion
4 tbsp. minced celery
2 tbsp. chopped pimento
Dash of hot sauce
1 tsp. Worcestershire sauce
Mayonnaise

Let cheeses soften at room temperature; blend well. Combine green pepper, onion, celery, pimento, hot sauce and Worcestershire sauce with cheeses. Thin with mayonnaise to desired consistency. Chill for several hours. Yield: 2 1/2 cups.

CHEESE-PISTACHIO DIP

1 8-oz. package cream cheese
3 tbsp. crumbled blue cheese
1/2 c. light cream
1 tbsp. lemon juice
1/2 c. chopped salted pistachio nuts

Blend cream cheese and blue cheese thoroughly. Stir in cream; add lemon juice and nuts. Chill. Yield: 1 1/2 cups.

HOT CHILI CON QUESO

2 lge. onions, minced
Butter
3 cloves of garlic, minced
2 cans tomatoes, drained
6 jalapenos, minced
2 lb. Velveeta cheese, cubed
2 tsp. chili powder
1/2 tsp. pepper

Saute onions in small amount of butter until clear. Combine onions and remaining ingredients in double boiler over low heat. Stir constantly until cheese is melted. Serve hot in chafing dish with taco chips or corn chips.

SPICY CHEESE DIP FOR VEGETABLES

1 c. mayonnaise
4 tsp. mustard
4 tsp. dry mustard
1 1/2 c. cottage cheese
2 tsp. lemon juice
4 tsp. horseradish

Combine all ingredients; blend well. Chill. Serve with carrot sticks, celery sticks, green pepper strips and cauliflower strips.

CHEESE DOLLARS

1/2 c. butter
3 oz. sharp Cheddar cheese, grated
1 c. flour
1/8 tsp. red pepper
1/4 tsp. salt

Cream butter and cheese together; add remaining ingredients. Shape into 1 1/2-inch roll; wrap in foil. Chill well. Slice 1/8 inch thick. Place on baking sheet. Bake at 400 degrees for 6 minutes. Yield: 36 canapes.

CHEESE STRAWS

2 c. grated sharp cheese
2 c. flour
1 c. melted butter
4 eggs, beaten

Mix cheese, flour and butter well; stir in eggs. Roll on floured surface,; cut into 1/2 x 3-inch strips. Place on baking sheet. Bake at 375 degrees until brown. Yield: 8 dozen.

MARVELOUS CHEESE STRAWS

1 stick butter, melted
1 lb. sharp cheese, grated
1 1/2 tsp. salt
1/2 tsp. cayenne pepper
2 c. flour

Pour butter over cheese; let stand until cheese reaches room temperature. Sift salt, cayenne and flour together; add to cheese mixture. Blend thoroughly. Press through cookie press, using flat saw blade, in 4-inch strips onto baking sheet. Bake at 325 degrees for about 20 minutes; do not brown. Cool.

PASHKA

Color photograph for this recipe on page 489.

1 1/2 c. cottage cheese
1/2 c. unsalted margarine
1 3-oz. package cream cheese
1/2 c. sugar
1/2 c. chopped blanched almonds
1/2 c. seedless raisins
1/2 c. mixed candied fruit
1/2 tsp. vanilla

Wash cottage cheese; drain well to remove excess moisture. Cream margarine in bowl until fluffy. Add cottage cheese and cream cheese; beat until smooth. Press through strainer; stir in remaining ingredients. Line large strainer with clean cloth; turn cheese mixture into strainer. Place saucer, then a weight, such as 1-pound box of salt, on top. Let drain for 6 hours. Pack cheese mixture into 6 greased custard cups or individual molds; chill. Unmold; garnish with additional candied fruit.

GOUDA PARTY SPREAD

8 oz. Gouda cheese
1/4 c. sour cream
1/2 tsp. prepared mustard
1/4 tsp. Worcestershire sauce
Dash of hot sauce
1/8 tsp. garlic salt
1 tbsp. pickle relish
1 tbsp. minced green pepper
1 tbsp. minced pimento
3 oz. dried beef, chopped

Cut thin slice from top of Gouda shell; scoop out cheese, leaving shell intact. Allow cheese to come to room temperature. Combine cheese, sour cream, mustard, Worcestershire sauce, hot sauce and garlic salt; beat until smooth. Add pickle relish, green pepper, pimento and beef; blend well. Fill reserved shell with cheese mixture. Serve on bed of greens with assorted crackers or potato chips.

CHEESE PUFFS

1 lb. sharp Cheddar cheese, grated
1 lb. Swiss cheese, grated
1 sm. clove of garlic, mashed
1 tsp. dry mustard
1 to 1 1/4 tsp. salt
2 tsp. Worcestershire sauce
1/8 tsp. hot sauce
1 can beer
Toast triangles or rounds

Blend cheeses thoroughly. Combine cheeses, garlic, mustard, salt, Worcestershire sauce and hot sauce with beer; mix well. Spread on toast. Brown lightly under broiler. Serve hot.

FETA CHEESE TURNOVERS

1 lb. feta cheese, crumbled
5 tbsp. grated Parmesan cheese
2 eggs
Pepper to taste
1/2 lb. phyllo
Melted butter

Mix cheeses, eggs and pepper together. Stack several sheets phyllo, brushing each sheet with butter. Cut sheets in 4-inch squares. Spread half of 1 side of each square with cheese filling; fold unspread half over filling. Press edges firmly together; brush with butter. Place on baking sheet. Bake at 375 degrees for 20 to 30 minutes or until browned. Serve hot.

SURPRISE CHEESE PUFFS

1 lb. sharp Cheddar cheese, shredded
1/2 lb. butter
1 tsp. Worcestershire sauce
1 tsp. onion juice
1/2 tsp. hot sauce
1 lge. loaf unsliced sandwich bread

Allow cheese to soften for 1 hour. Blend cheese and butter thoroughly. Add Worcestershire sauce, onion juice and hot sauce; blend well. Remove all crusts from bread; cut into 1-inch cubes. Spread top and sides of cubes with cheese mixture. Place on cookie sheet carefully so cubes do not touch; stack with waxed paper between layers. Place in freezer until frozen; store in plastic bags in freezer until needed. Place desired amount of cubes on baking sheet. Bake in preheated 375-degree oven for 10 to 12 minutes or until corners are golden. Serve at once. Yield: 80-100 pieces.

CHEESE-EGG PIES

Bacon
2 partially baked 8-in. pie shells
1 c. grated Swiss cheese
3 eggs, slightly beaten
2 c. milk
Salt to taste
Pepper to taste
Nutmeg to taste
1 tbsp. melted butter

Fry and crumble enough bacon to cover bottoms of pie shells; add cheese. Combine eggs, milk, salt, pepper, nutmeg and butter. Pour into pie shells. Bake at 375 degrees for 25 to 30 minutes or until filling is set. Yield: 8-10 servings.

CHEESE PIE

2 8-oz. packages cream cheese
3/4 c. sugar
3 eggs
2 tsp. vanilla
1 graham cracker pie crust
1 pt. sour cream

Have cheese at room temperature. Cream cheese thoroughly. Add 1/2 cup sugar gradually; mix well. Add eggs, one at a time, beating well after each addition. Stir in vanilla. Pour into crust. Bake at 300 degrees for 45 minutes or until firm. Cool for 20 minutes. Mix sour cream, remaining sugar and vanilla well. Spread over cooled pie. Refrigerate overnight.

QUICHE AU ROQUEFORT

3 oz. Roquefort cheese
2 3-oz. packages cream cheese
2 tbsp. softened butter
3 tbsp. whipping cream
2 eggs
Salt and white pepper
Cayenne pepper to taste
1/2 tbsp. minced chives
1 8-in. pastry shell, partially cooked

Preheat oven to 375 degrees. Blend cheeses, butter and cream thoroughly. Add eggs; beat well. Season with salt, white pepper and cayenne pepper. Stir in chives; pour filling into pastry shell. Bake for 25 to 30 minutes or until quiche has puffed and top has browned. Cottage cheese may be substituted for cream cheese. Yield: 4-6 servings.

SHRIMP QUICHE

1 2-oz. can mushrooms, drained
2 tbsp. butter
1 c. grated Swiss cheese
1/4 c. grated Parmesan cheese
1 tbsp. flour
1 9-in. baked pie shell
1 5-oz. can shrimp, drained
2 c. cream
3 eggs, slightly beaten
1/2 tsp. seasoned salt
1/4 tsp. pepper

Saute mushrooms in 1 tablespoon butter until golden. Mix cheeses and flour; sprinkle half the mixture into pie shell. Add half the mushrooms and half the shrimp; repeat layers. Stir cream into eggs; add salt and pepper. Pour over shrimp mixture. Brown remaining butter; pour over top. Bake at 375 degrees for 25 to 30 minutes or until filling is set. Remove from oven; let stand for 10 minutes before serving. Yield: 6 servings.

CHEESE SOUFFLÉ

4 tbsp. butter
4 tbsp. flour
1/4 tsp. mustard
1/4 tsp. salt
1/8 tsp. pepper
1 c. milk
1 c. shredded sharp cheese
3 eggs, separated
1/4 tsp. cream of tartar
1 recipe shrimp sauce

Melt butter; stir in flour, mustard, salt and pepper. Add milk gradually, stirring constantly. Stir in cheese; remove from heat. Blend in well-beaten egg yolks. Beat egg whites with cream of tartar until stiff peaks form; fold into cheese mixture. Pour into 1 1/2-quart souffle dish. Form crown by running tip of knife through souffle mixture 1 inch from edge of dish. Set dish in pan of water. Bake at 350 degrees for 50 to 60 minutes or until puffed and golden. Serve immediately with shrimp sauce. Yield: 4 servings.

CHEESE STRATA

3/4 lb. sharp cheese
12 slices bread, crusts removed
1 pkg. chopped broccoli, cooked
2 c. finely diced ham
6 eggs, slightly beaten
3 1/2 c. milk
2 tbsp. instant minced onion
1/2 tsp. salt
1/4 tsp. dry mustard
Shredded cheese

Cut cheese into thin slices. Cut 12 doughnuts and holes from bread; set aside. Fit remaining scraps of bread into 13 x 9 x 2-inch baking dish. Place layer of cheese over bread; add layer of broccoli and a layer of ham. Arrange bread doughnuts and holes on top. Combine eggs, milk, onion, salt and mustard; pour over bread. Cover; refrigerate for at least 6 hours or overnight. Bake in 325-degree oven for 50 minutes. Sprinkle with shredded cheese. Bake for 5 minutes longer. Let stand for 10 minutes; cut into squares. Yield: 12 servings.

CHEESE TOAST

2 c. grated Cheddar cheese
1 tbsp. butter, melted
1 egg
2 tbsp. cream
1/2 tsp. Worcestershire sauce
Dash of hot sauce
1/2 tsp. dry mustard
Salt and pepper to taste
Small buttered toast rounds

Combine cheese, butter, egg, cream and seasonings; blend well. Spread cheese mixture on toast rounds; place on baking sheet. Bake at 400 degrees until golden brown. Yield: 40-50 servings.

CHEDDAR CASSEROLE

4 eggs
3 c. milk
2 c. grated Cheddar cheese
2 c. soft bread crumbs
1 tbsp. Worcestershire sauce
1 tsp. salt
Dash of pepper

Combine all ingredients. Pour into 1 1/2-quart greased casserole; set casserole in pan containing 1 inch hot water. Bake at 350 degrees until firm. Garnish with parsley if desired. Yield: 4-6 servings.

CREAM CHEESE PASTRY

1/2 lb. soft cream cheese
1 c. soft margarine
1/4 tsp. salt
2 c. sifted flour

Have cheese at room temperature. Cream cheese, margarine and salt; blend in flour. Refrigerate for several hours before using. Roll out on floured board; cut into small circles. May be filled as desired. Fold dough over filling; seal edges. Bake on ungreased cookie sheets at 350 degrees for 10 to 12 minutes or until lightly browned. Yield: 5 dozen.

EASY CHEESE BREAD

2 1/2 c. prepared biscuit mix
1 c. shredded sharp cheese
2 tsp. poppy seed
1 egg, beaten
1 c. milk

Combine biscuit mix, cheese and poppy seed; add egg and milk. Beat vigorously for 1 minute. Turn into well-greased loaf pan; sprinkle with additional poppy seed. Bake at 350 degrees for 50 minutes or until bread tests done. Remove from pan; cool on rack.

CHEESE SOUP

1 med. onion, sliced
1 c. chopped celery
2 tbsp. butter
1/2 c. flour
1/2 tsp. dry mustard
2 bouillon cubes
1 carrot, diced
1 qt. milk
1 1/2 c. shredded American cheese
1/2 c. cooked peas
Salt and pepper to taste

Saute onion and celery in butter in large saucepan for about 5 minutes. Stir in flour and mustard; remove from heat. Dissolve bouillon cubes in 2 cups hot water. Add bouillon and carrot to onion mixture; bring to a boil, stirring constantly. Simmer, covered, for 15 minutes or until vegetables are tender. Add milk; heat almost to boiling. Add 1 1/4 cups cheese and peas. Simmer, stirring, until cheese melts. Add salt and pepper; garnish with remaining cheese. Serve with croutons. Yield: 4 servings.

CREAM OF CHEESE SOUP

1/3 c. finely diced onion
4 tbsp. butter
4 tbsp. flour
1 tsp. Worcestershire sauce
2 chicken bouillon cubes
4 c. milk, scalded
1/2 c. diced cooked carrots
1 tsp. celery seed
1 c. diced cooked chicken
1 1/2 c. grated American cheese
Salt and pepper
2 tbsp. minced parsley

Saute onion in butter in large saucepan until tender. Blend in flour and Worcestershire sauce. Dissolve bouillon cubes in milk; add to flour mixture gradually. Simmer, stirring constantly, until thickened. Add carrots, celery seed, chicken and cheese; simmer, stirring, until cheese is melted. Add salt and pepper. Pour into warm soup bowls; garnish with parsley. Yield: 6-8 servings.

NEWPORT CHEESE SOUP

2 tbsp. butter
8 tbsp. flour
1/2 lb. Cheddar cheese, diced
3 c. chicken broth
2 c. milk, scalded
1 thin slice onion
1 c. warm cream
Salt and pepper

Melt butter in saucepan over low heat. Stir in flour and cheese; add broth gradually, stirring constantly. Add milk and onion; simmer until thickened. Strain; simmer liquid for 10 minutes, stirring constantly. Stir in cream, salt and pepper. Sprinkle with freshly cut parsley, if desired. Yield: 8 servings.

SAVORY CHEESE SOUP

1/4 c. butter
2 tsp. chopped onion
1 lb. cubed process cheese
4 c. milk
1/4 tsp. salt
1/2 tsp. dry mustard
1/4 tsp. paprika

Melt butter in top of double boiler. Add onions; cook until tender. Add cheese and milk; heat, stirring occasionally, until cheese melts. Add salt, mustard and paprika. Garnish with chopped parsley before serving. Yield: 4-6 servings.

CHEESE DREAMS

3 English muffins
Butter
6 slices crisp bacon
6 tomato slices
6 thin slices cheese

Split and butter muffins; broil until golden. Cut bacon slices in half. Top each muffin half with 1 tomato slice, 2 bacon halves and 1 cheese slice. Broil 5 inches from heat until cheese melts. Serve at once.

BAKED CHEESE SANDWICHES

8 bread slices
4 slices sharp cheese
2 eggs, beaten
2 c. milk
1/2 tsp. salt
1/8 tsp. pepper
1/4 tsp. dry mustard

Arrange 4 bread slices in greased baking dish; cover with cheese slices. Top cheese slices with remaining bread slices. Combine eggs, milk, salt, pepper and mustard; blend well. Pour over sandwiches; chill until milk mixture is absorbed. Bake in 350-degree oven for 30 minutes or until puffed and lightly browned. Serve hot with creamed mushroom or vegetable sauce.

CHILI-CHEESE BUNS

1/4 lb. dried beef, chopped
6 tbsp. chili sauce
6 sandwich buns, split
6 slices American cheese

Cover beef with 1/2 cup hot water for 2 minutes; drain well. Combine beef with chili sauce; mix well. Spread beef mixture over half of each bun; broil 2 to 3 inches from source of heat for 5 to 6 minutes. Top beef mixture with cheese slices; return to broiler with remaining bun halves. Broil for 1 to 2 minutes or until cheese melts and buns are toasted.

GRILLED CHEESE SANDWICH

4 sandwich buns
1/4 lb. grated cheese
1 tbsp. finely chopped onion
1/3 c. chopped sweet pickle
1 hard-cooked egg
1/4 tsp. Worcestershire sauce
1/8 tsp. salt
1/4 c. mayonnaise

Split buns; toast lightly. Combine all remaining ingredients; spread on buns. Broil until cheese is melted and lightly browned. Serve at once.

SWISS SANDWICH PUFFS

1/2 c. mayonnaise
1/4 c. chopped onion
2 tbsp. snipped parsley
32 sm. rye bread slices
1 pkg. Swiss cheese, sliced

Combine mayonnaise, onion and parsley; spread on rye slices. Top each with 1/4 slice Swiss cheese. Broil for 2 to 3 minutes. Yield: 32 servings.

CHEESE SANDWICH SPREAD

1 lb. Cheddar cheese
12 med. sweet pickles
1 sm. jar pimentos
1 c. salad dressing

Grate cheese; chop pickles and pimentos finely. Combine cheese, pickles and pimentos with salad dressing; mix well. Chill until ready to use.

GRUYÈRE CHEESE TARTLETS

4 pastry shells
3 tbsp. butter
2 c. chopped onions
2-oz. process Gruyère cheese, sliced
1 egg
1 c. heavy cream
1/2 tsp. salt
1/4 tsp. pepper

Bake pastry shells in 450-degree oven for 7 minutes. Melt butter in large skillet over low heat. Add onions; saute until tender and transparent. Arrange layer of onions in bottom of each pastry shell; cover with sliced cheese. Top with another layer of onions. Combine egg, cream, salt and pepper; beat thoroughly. Pour equal amounts of egg mixture into each shell. Bake in 425-degree oven for about 15 minutes or until golden brown on top. Garnish with fried onion rings and watercress if desired. Yield: 4 servings.

Gruyère Cheese Tartlets . . . A delicious pastry versatile enough for every occasion.

CHEESE BALL SALAD

1 8-oz. package cream cheese
1/4 c. minced green pepper
2 tbsp. mayonnaise
Walnuts
Lettuce

Have cream cheese at room temperature. Blend cheese and pepper with mayonnaise. Roll into small balls. Press 1/2 walnut into top of each ball. Place 5 balls on each lettuce leaf. Garnish with mayonnaise if desired. Yield: 8 servings.

COTTAGE CHEESE TOSSED SALAD

1 carton cottage cheese
1 med. tomato, chopped
1 med. green pepper, chopped
2 stalks celery, chopped
4 radishes, sliced
1 sm. onion, chopped
1 carrot, diced
2 tbsp. salad dressing
Salt and pepper to taste

Combine all ingredients in bowl; toss lightly. Chill; serve on lettuce if desired. Yield: 6 servings.

SUNDIAL CHEESE-FRUIT PLATTER

Color photograph for this recipe on page 731.

2 Washington red Delicious apples
Watercress
1 3-oz. triangle pkg. imported Roquefort cheese
1 8-oz. package old-fashioned Cheddar cheese
1 6-oz. package pasteurized process Gruyère cheese
2 sm. bananas
2 Anjou pears
1/2 c. lemon juice
8 slices pasteurized process American cheese

Place an apple on watercress in center of 12-inch plate. Cut the Roquefort, Cheddar and Gruyere cheese into 1/2-inch cubes. Insert picks in cheese cubes; spear into center of apple. Peel bananas; cut diagonally into 2-inch lengths. Core remaining apple and pears; cut into thick slices. Dip all fruits in lemon juice to prevent discoloration. Arrange banana lengths, spoke fashion, around center apple. Alternate apple and pear slices in circle around bananas. Cut American cheese slices in half diagonally. Curve into half circles; place between grouped apple and pear slices. Serve with desired dressing.

CHEESE FONDUE SAVANT

Color photograph for this recipe on page 721.

1/2 stick butter
3 tbsp. flour
1 1/2 c. milk
1 can Cheddar cheese soup
8 slices American cheese, cubed
Minced garlic to taste
Minced onion to taste
Seasoned salt to taste
Cauliflowerets
Rolled pepperoni
Sauteed mushroom buttons

Melt butter in fondue pot; stir in flour. Add milk gradually; cook, stirring, until thickened. Add soup, cheese, garlic, onion and salt. Cook over low heat, stirring frequently, until cheese is melted. Place pot on stand over low flame. Place cauliflowerets, pepperoni slices and mushroom buttons on fondue forks; dip into fondue.

CAMEMBERT MOUSSE

1 env. unflavored gelatin
3 oz. Camembert cheese
4 oz. Roquefort cheese
1 egg, separated
1 tsp. Worcestershire sauce
1/2 c. heavy cream, whipped

Soften gelatin in 1/4 cup cold water; dissolve over hot water. Have cheeses at room temperature. Blend cheeses thoroughly. Add egg yolk, Worcestershire sauce and gelatin to cheese mixture; beat until smooth. Beat egg white until stiff peaks form. Fold egg white and cream into cheese mixture. Pour into mold. Chill until firm.

CHEESE MOLD

1 carton cream-style cottage cheese
2 3-oz. packages cream cheese
1 env. unflavored gelatin
1/4 tsp. salt
1 c. seedless green grapes
1/2 c. broken pecans
2 tbsp. chopped chives
1 c. heavy cream, whipped

Have cheeses at room temperature; blend thoroughly. Soften gelatin in 1/4 cup cold water; dissolve over boiling water. Add salt; stir into cheese mixture. Add grapes, pecans and chives; fold in cream. Spoon into individual molds or 1-quart mold. Chill for 4 to 6 hours.

CHEESE-PIMENTO SALAD

1 pkg. lemon gelatin
1/2 tsp. vinegar
1/2 tsp. salt
1/2 c. mayonnaise
1/2 c. milk
1/4 tsp. paprika
1 tsp. chopped onion
1/2 c. grated cheese
1/3 c. chopped pimento

Dissolve gelatin in 1 1/2 cups boiling water; stir in vinegar and salt. Chill until partially set. Blend mayonnaise with milk, paprika and onion; combine with gelatin mixture. Add cheese and pimento. Pour into ring mold. Chill until firm.

COTTAGE CHEESE MOLD

1 env. unflavored gelatin
3/4 c. milk
2 c. cream-style cottage cheese
1/2 tsp. salt
2 tsp. grated onion
1 c. diced celery
1/2 c. diced green pepper

Soften gelatin in 1/4 cup milk; dissolve in 1/2 cup hot milk. Blend in cottage cheese, salt, onion, celery and green pepper. Turn into 1 large mold or individual molds. Chill until firm. Serve on lettuce leaves; garnish with tomato wedges and mayonnaise. Yield: 6 servings.

COTTAGE CHEESE RING

1 pkg. lemon gelatin
2 c. cottage cheese
1 c. mayonnaise
2 tbsp. horseradish
1/2 c. whipped cream
Pinch of salt

Dissolve gelatin in 1 cup boiling water; chill until slightly thickened. Fold in remaining ingredients; pour into ring mold. Chill until firm.

GREEN CHEESE RING

1 3-oz. package cream cheese
2 c. cottage cheese
1 tbsp. unflavored gelatin
1/2 tbsp. grated onion
1/2 c. mayonnaise
1/2 tbsp. lemon juice
Cayenne pepper to taste
Salt to taste
2 tbsp. chopped green pepper
Green food coloring

Have cream cheese at room temperature. Beat cottage cheese until smooth; beat in cream cheese. Soften gelatin in 1/4 cup cold water; dissolve over hot water. Blend gelatin, onion, mayonnaise, juice, cayenne pepper, salt and green pepper with cheese mixture. Tint with food coloring as desired. Pour into ring mold; chill until firm.

Puerto Rican Dressing

1/4 c. powdered sugar
1 tbsp. steak sauce
1/4 c. tarragon wine vinegar
1/2 tsp. grated onion
Paprika to taste
1 tbsp. lemon juice
1 tsp. Worcestershire sauce
1/3 c. catsup
1 tsp. salt
1/2 c. salad oil

Combine all ingredients except oil in jar; blend thoroughly. Add oil; shake well. Serve with Green Cheese Ring.

ROQUEFORT PINEAPPLE SALAD RING

2 env. unflavored gelatin
1 No. 2 can crushed pineapple
1 tbsp. sugar
6 tbsp. lime juice
1 pkg. cream cheese
1/4 lb. bleu cheese
1 c. heavy whipping cream
1/2 tsp. grated lime rind
2 cans sm. shrimp, drained
Green food coloring

Soften gelatin in 1/2 cup water. Drain pineapple; reserve syrup. Combine reserved syrup with enough water to measure 1 cup liquid in a saucepan. Bring to a boil; dissolve gelatin in hot liquid. Stir in sugar and juice. Chill until partially set. Have cheeses at room temperature; blend cheeses thoroughly. Whip cream until stiff peaks form. Add gelatin mixture gradually to cheese mixture; blend until smooth. Fold in pineapple, lime rind and whipped cream. Add shrimp. Tint with food coloring as desired. Chill until firm.

WELSH RAREBIT

1/2 lb. cheese, grated
1/2 tsp. dry mustard
1/2 tsp. salt
Cayenne pepper to taste
2 tsp. butter
1/4 c. cream
1 egg, beaten
Dry toast or wafers

Place cheese in chafing dish or double boiler. Combine seasonings; sprinkle over cheese. Add butter and cream. Stir until smooth. Add egg to mixture. Simmer, stirring constantly, for 1 minute. Serve at once on toast slices. Yield: 4 servings.

Cottage Cheese Ring . . . A cheese and sour cream mold that surrounds fresh fruit.

COTTAGE CHEESE RING

2 c. cottage cheese
1 c. sour cream
1 tsp. grated lemon rind
1 env. unflavored gelatin
3 tbsp. lemon juice
3 tbsp. sugar
1/2 tsp. salt
Salad greens
2 c. mixed fresh fruit

Blend cottage cheese, sour cream and lemon rind together; set aside. Sprinkle gelatin over 3 tablespoons water and lemon juice in saucepan to soften; dissolve over low heat. Stir in sugar and salt; remove from heat. Add to cottage cheese mixture, combining thoroughly. Turn into wet ring mold; chill until firm. Turn out onto salad greens; fill center with fresh fruit. Yield: 6 servings.

ROQUEFORT SALAD RING

3 pkg. cream cheese
1 c. Roquefort cheese
6 tbsp. milk
1 tsp. lemon juice
1 tsp. salt
1 tsp. paprika
1 tsp. white pepper
3 tbsp. gelatin
2 c. heavy cream

Have cheeses at room temperature. Blend cheeses with milk, lemon juice and seasonings; beat until smooth. Soften gelatin in 1/2 cup water; dissolve over hot water. Stir gelatin into cheese mixture. Whip cream until stiff peaks form; fold into gelatin mixture. Pour mixture into large ring mold. Chill until firm. Garnish with fruits. Serve with mayonnaise thinned with pineapple juice.

Cheesecake

Cheesecake is a creamy, smooth, mellow, and very popular dessert.

INGREDIENTS: Principal ingredients may include pot cheese, dry curd cheese, farmer's cheese, cream cheese, or cottage cheese as well as eggs and milk, cream, or sour cream. Cheesecake may also contain such flavorings as fruit juices, fruit rinds, or nuts. Toppings may include pineapple, strawberries, blueberries, or cherries.

PREPARATION: If prepared with gelatin, place cake in refrigerator until firm. Cheesecakes without gelatin are baked in a very slow oven for length of time recipe specifies or until set in center. Allow cake to cool in oven with door open before removing. Chill thoroughly before serving.

STORING: Cheesecake should be refrigerated since both cheese and eggs, main ingredients of this dessert, are highly susceptible to bacterial contamination at room temperature.

APPLESAUCE CHEESECAKE

1 2/3 c. evaporated milk
1 pkg. lemon gelatin
1 c. sugar
1 8-oz. package cream cheese
1 tsp. vanilla
2 c. applesauce
1 c. gingersnap crumbs
2 tbsp. (packed) brown sugar
1/4 c. margarine

Chill milk in freezer tray until ice forms on edges. Pour 3/4 cup boiling water into gelatin; stir until dissolved. Combine sugar and cream cheese in mixing bowl; blend until smooth. Add vanilla, applesauce and gelatin; beat until well blended. Whip milk; add to applesauce mixture. Place mixing bowl in larger bowl of ice; whip for 12 minutes. Combine crumbs, brown sugar and margarine; line springform pan with gingersnap mixture. Pour applesauce mixture into pan. Refrigerate for 5 hours.

BANANA CHEESECAKE

1 pkg. pineapple gelatin
1 8-oz. package cream cheese
1 c. sugar
1 tsp. vanilla
2 bananas, mashed
1 c. graham cracker crumbs
3 tbsp. butter, melted
1 14-oz. can evaporated milk, chilled
3 tbsp. lemon juice

Dissolve gelatin in 1 cup boiling water; cool. Combine cream cheese, sugar and vanilla in mixing bowl, blending well. Add bananas to cream cheese mixture; beat until fluffy. Add gelatin to banana mixture gradually; blend thoroughly. Chill until thickened, stirring occasionally. Mix graham cracker crumbs and butter thoroughly. Press half the mixture evenly onto bottom of 12 x 7-inch baking dish. Whip evaporated milk until thickened; add lemon juice. Beat milk mixture until stiff peaks form. Beat gelatin mixture slightly; fold into whipped milk mixture. Turn into crumb-lined dish; sprinkle remaining crumbs over top. Cover with plastic wrap; chill until set. Yield: 12 servings.

CHEESECAKE WITH BLACK CHERRIES

1 1/2 c. graham cracker crumbs
1/4 c. sugar
1/4 c. chopped almonds
1/4 c. butter, melted
1/4 tsp. salt

Combine crumbs, sugar, almonds, butter and salt; mix well. Press in bottom and onto side of greased 10 1/2-inch springform pan. Chill.

Filling

3 8-oz. packages cream cheese, softened
1 1/4 c. sugar
1 tsp. salt
1/4 c. sifted flour
5 eggs, separated
2 1/2 tbsp. lemon juice
1/4 tsp. nutmeg
1 tsp. vanilla
1/2 tsp. almond flavoring
1 c. sour cream
1 c. canned black cherries, drained

Preheat oven to 325 degrees. Combine cream cheese, 1 cup sugar and salt; mix well. Add flour and egg yolks to cream cheese mixture; beat thoroughly. Blend lemon juice, nutmeg, vanilla, almond flavoring and sour cream together; stir into egg yolk mixture. Beat egg whites with remaining sugar until stiff peaks form; fold into cheese mixture. Pour into crumb crust. Bake for 1 hour and 15 minutes. Cool in oven for 1 hour. Remove from oven; cool on rack. Chill. Place cherries in center to serve. Yield: 18 servings.

CHERRY-GLAZED CHEESECAKE

1/2 c. graham cracker crumbs
1 tbsp. softened corn oil margarine
7 1/2 tsp. liquid sweetener
3 eggs, separated
2 8-oz. packages cream cheese
1 tbsp. sugar
1/2 tsp. vanilla
1/4 tsp. cinnamon
1 lge. can black cherries, pitted
1 tbsp. cornstarch
Several drops of red food coloring

Preheat oven to 325 degrees. Combine crumbs, margarine and 1/2 teaspoon liquid sweetener, mixing well; press mixture against sides of small springform pan. Place egg yolks, cream cheese, 6 teaspoons liquid sweetener, sugar, vanilla and cinnamon in blender. Blend until mixture is smooth; pour into bowl. Beat egg whites until stiff peaks form; fold into cheese mixture. Pour into prepared pan. Bake for 15 minutes. Increase temperature to 450 degrees. Bake for 5 minutes longer. Cool. Drain cherries, reserving juice. Add enough water to reserved juice to make 1 cup liquid; mix in cornstarch, blending thoroughly. Place cornstarch liquid in saucepan; cook over medium heat until thickened slightly. Add 1 teaspoon liquid sweetener and food coloring. Remove from heat; mix thoroughly. Arrange cherries on top of cheesecake. Spoon on glaze. Refrigerate for at least 2 hours. Yield: 8 servings.

GERMAN CHEESECAKE

1 1/2 c. graham cracker crumbs
Sugar
1/2 tsp. cinnamon
2 tbsp. butter
4 eggs, separated
Vanilla
1 tsp. lemon juice
4 3-oz. packages cream cheese, softened
1 c. sour cream

Blend crumbs, 1 tablespoon sugar, cinnamon and butter together. Press into 9-inch pie plate, using slightly smaller plate to press mixture. Add egg yolks, 1/2 cup sugar, 1 teaspoon vanilla and lemon juice to smoothly beaten cream cheese. Beat egg whites until stiff peaks form. Fold egg whites into cheese mixture. Turn into crust. Bake at 375 degrees for 25 minutes. Cool. Combine 1 teaspoon vanilla, sour cream and 3 tablespoons sugar; spread over cooled cake. Return to oven. Bake for 5 minutes longer.

BLUEBERRY CHEESECAKE

1 3/4 c. graham cracker crumbs
1/2 c. powdered sugar
1/2 c. melted butter
2 eggs
1 c. sugar
1 8-oz. package cream cheese
Juice of 1/2 lemon
1 22-oz. can blueberry pie filling

Combine crumbs, powdered sugar and butter, mixing well; press into buttered 9 x 13-inch pan. Blend eggs, sugar and cream cheese together thoroughly; spread over crust. Bake at 300 degrees for 25 minutes. Cool slightly. Mix lemon juice and pie filling; pour over cheesecake. Chill. Yield: 12 servings.

GLAZED LEMON-CREAM CHEESECAKE

2 1/2 c. graham cracker crumbs
1 3/4 c. sugar
1/2 c. soft butter
3 8-oz. packages cream cheese, softened
3 tbsp. grated lemon peel
3 tbsp. flour
4 eggs
1/2 c. lemon juice

Combine crumbs, 1/4 cup sugar and butter; mix well. Press into bottom and on sides of greased 12 x 8-inch baking dish. Combine cream cheese, lemon peel, 1 1/2 cups sugar and flour; beat with mixer at medium speed until smooth and blended. Beat in eggs, one at a time; stir in lemon juice. Pour into crust. Bake at 350 degrees for 35 to 40 minutes or until center is firm. Cool on wire rack. Refrigerate for 4 hours or longer. Lightly score filling in half crosswise. Mark each half diagonally, making two crosses, 8 sections in all. Spoon glazes over alternate sections, making a pattern. Use Pineapple Glaze for 3 sections, Blueberry Glaze for 3 sections and Strawberry Glaze for 2 sections. Refrigerate for 1 hour; cut into squares to serve.

Pineapple Glaze

1 tbsp. sugar
2 tsp. cornstarch
1 8 3/4-oz. can crushed pineapple

Combine sugar and cornstarch in small saucepan; stir in pineapple. Bring to a boil over medium heat, stirring constantly; cook for 1 minute. Cool.

Blueberry Glaze

1 12-oz. package frozen blueberries, thawed
1 tbsp. sugar
2 tsp. cornstarch

Drain blueberries, reserving liquid. Combine liquid and enough water to make 1/2 cup liquid. Combine sugar and cornstarch in saucepan. Stir in liquid. Bring to a boil over medium heat, stirring constantly for 1 minute. Remove from heat; cool slightly. Stir in blueberries. Cool thoroughly.

Strawberry Glaze

1 10-oz. package frozen strawberry halves, thawed
1 tbsp. sugar
2 tsp. cornstarch

Drain strawberries; reserve juice. Add enough water to reserved juice to make 1/2 cup liquid. Combine sugar and cornstarch in saucepan; stir in liquid. Bring to a boil over medium heat, stirring constantly; cook for 1 minute. Remove from heat; cool slightly. Stir in strawberries. Cool thoroughly.

EASY LEMON CHEESECAKE

1 1/2 c. graham cracker crumbs
Sugar
1/3 c. melted margarine
1 1/2 c. cream-style cottage cheese
Milk
1 4-oz. package lemon pie filling mix
1 env. unflavored gelatin
1 c. crushed pineapple
2 egg whites

Combine crumbs, 2 tablespoons sugar and margarine, mixing well; press onto bottom and sides of 9 x 12-inch cake pan. Drain cottage cheese if moist; reserve cottage cheese liquid. Add enough milk to cottage cheese liquid to make 2 1/4 cups liquid. Beat cottage cheese until fluffy. Combine pie filling mix and gelatin; prepare mix according to package directions, using milk mixture for water. Stir pineapple and cottage cheese into pie filling mixture. Beat egg whites until soft peaks form; add 1/2 cup sugar, beating until stiff peaks form. Fold egg whites into pie filling mixture; pour into prepared pan. Chill for several hours. Garnish with fresh strawberries. Yield: 12 servings.

HOLIDAY CHEESECAKE

1 1/2 c. graham cracker crumbs
1 1/3 c. sugar
1 tsp. cinnamon
1/2 c. butter, softened
2 tbsp. unflavored gelatin
2 eggs, separated
1/2 c. milk
1 tsp. salt
1 tbsp. grated lemon peel
2 c. small curd cream-style cottage cheese
1/2 c. lemon juice
2 tsp. vanilla
1 c. heavy cream

Combine crumbs, 1/3 cup sugar and cinnamon in bowl; blend butter and crumb mixture together thoroughly. Press 1/2 of the crumb mixture into bottom of 9-inch springform pan. Soften gelatin in 1/4 cup cold water. Beat egg yolks slightly. Combine egg yolks, milk, remaining sugar and salt in double boiler; cook over hot water, stirring constantly, until mixture coats metal spoon. Remove from heat. Dissolve gelatin in egg yolk mixture; add lemon peel. Cool; beat well. Mix cottage cheese, lemon juice and vanilla together; add to gelatin mixture, stirring well. Fold cream into gelatin mixture. Whip egg whites until stiff peaks form; fold into cream mixture. Pour into prepared pan; sprinkle with remaining crumb mixture. Chill overnight. Garnish with candied fruits. Yield: 12 servings.

LEMON CHEESECAKE WITH RASPBERRY TOPPING

1 3/4 c. graham cracker crumbs
1/4 c. butter
1 1/4 c. sugar
1 pkg. lemon gelatin
3 tbsp. lemon juice

1 8-oz. package cream cheese
1 tsp. vanilla
1 can evaporated milk, chilled
1 pkg. raspberry Danish dessert mix
1 pkg. frozen raspberries

Combine crumbs, butter and 1/4 cup sugar, mixing well; press into 9 x 13-inch baking dish. Bake at 375 degrees for 7 minutes. Dissolve gelatin in 1 cup boiling water; add lemon juice. Chill until partially set; whip until light. Combine cream cheese, remaining sugar and vanilla, beating well; combine with lemon mixture. Whip evaporated milk; fold into cream cheese mixture. Pour into crumb-lined pan. Cook dessert mix with 1 cup water until thickened; add frozen raspberries. Stir until thawed; spread on cheesecake. Chill in refrigerator; cut in squares. Yield: 12 servings.

LOW-CALORIE CHEESECAKE

2 env. unflavored gelatin
1 c. reconstituted nonfat dry milk
4 eggs, separated
Artificial sweetener equivalent to 1 1/4 c. sugar
1/4 tsp. salt
1 tsp. grated lemon rind
1 tsp. grated orange rind
1 tbsp. lemon juice
1 1/2 tsp. vanilla
1/2 tsp. almond flavoring
3 c. creamed cottage cheese
1/2 tsp. cream of tartar
1/3 c. graham cracker crumbs
1/8 tsp. cinnamon
1/8 tsp. nutmeg

Sprinkle gelatin over milk in top of double boiler; add egg yolks. Stir until thoroughly blended. Place over hot water; stir constantly for about 5 minutes or until gelatin dissolves and mixture thickens slightly. Remove from heat; stir in sweetener, salt, rinds, lemon juice, vanilla and almond flavoring. Beat cottage cheese at high speed with mixer for at least 4 minutes or until smooth; stir into gelatin mixture. Chill, stirring occasionally, until mixture mounds slightly when dropped from spoon. Beat egg whites and cream of tartar until stiff peaks form; fold into gelatin mixture. Combine crumbs, cinnamon and nutmeg, mixing well. Sprinkle about half the crumb mixture over bottom of 8 or 9-inch springform pan. Pour gelatin mixture into pan; sprinkle with remaining crumb mixture. Chill until firm. Remove from pan to large plate for serving. Yield: 12 servings.

MANDARIN CHEESECAKE

1 c. graham cracker crumbs
2 1/4 c. sugar
1/4 c. butter, melted
5 8-oz. packages cream cheese
6 eggs
1/2 c. heavy cream
1 tsp. lemon flavoring
1/4 c. flour
1/4 tsp. salt
1 11-oz. can Mandarin orange slices
1 sm. jar apple jelly, melted

Combine crumbs, 1/4 cup sugar and butter, mixing well; press onto bottom of greased 9-inch springform pan. Beat cheese until fluffy. Add eggs, one at a time, to cheese; beat well after each addition. Combine cream and lemon flavoring; blend into cheese mixture thoroughly. Mix remaining sugar, flour and salt together; add to cheese mixture, beating until smooth. Pour into crumb-lined pan. Bake at 475 degrees for 15 minutes; reduce heat to 250 degrees. Bake for 1 hour and 15 minutes longer. Remove from oven; cool. Drain orange slices; arrange slices over top of cake. Spoon jelly over oranges slices; refrigerate. Yield: 12 servings.

PEACHY CHEESECAKE

2/3 c. graham cracker crumbs
5/8 c. sugar
1/4 c. butter, melted
2 3-oz. packages peach gelatin
2 tbsp. lemon juice
1 8-oz. package cream cheese
1 6-oz. can evaporated milk, chilled
1 1/2 c. diced sweetened peaches

Combine crumbs and 2 tablespoons sugar, mixing well; stir in butter. Press crumb mixture into bottom of springform pan. Dissolve gelatin in 2 cups boiling water; stir 1 cup cold water and lemon juice into gelatin mixture. Chill until partially set. Blend remaining sugar and cream cheese until light and fluffy; beat in milk. Whip gelatin mixture until light and fluffy; fold into cream cheese mixture. Chill until partially set. Drain peaches; fold into cheese mixture. Pour into crust-lined pan; chill until firm. Unmold to serve. Yield: 8-10 servings.

PECAN CHEESECAKE

1 12-oz. box vanilla wafers, crushed
1/2 c. melted butter
1 c. sugar
1 env. unflavored gelatin
1 c. milk
1 8-oz. package cream cheese
1 1/2 tsp. vanilla
1/2 c. whipping cream
1/2 c. chopped pecans

Combine crumbs and butter, mixing well; press into 13 x 9-inch pan. Combine 1/2 cup sugar and gelatin; stir in milk. Place over low heat, stirring until gelatin dissolves. Chill until mixture begins to thicken. Beat cream cheese, remaining sugar and vanilla; blend in gelatin mixture. Whip cream until stiff peaks form; fold into cream cheese mixture. Add pecans, stirring lightly. Pour into crumb-lined pan. Chill for at least 8 hours. Yield: 12 servings.

PINEAPPLE CHEESECAKE

1 1/2 c. graham cracker crumbs
1 c. drained crushed pineapple
1 c. sugar
3 8-oz. packages cream cheese, softened
4 eggs
1 tsp. vanilla
2 c. sour cream

Press crumbs into bottom of large angel food cake pan. Top with crushed pineapple. Combine sugar, cream cheese, eggs, vanilla and sour cream, blending well. Pour cream cheese mixture over pineapple. Bake at 350 degrees for 1 hour.

Refrigerator Cheesecake . . . A classic dessert popular for its smooth texture and good taste.

REFRIGERATOR CHEESECAKE

1 c. graham cracker crumbs
Sugar
1/4 c. softened butter
2 env. gelatin
2 eggs, separated
1 c. milk
1/4 tsp. salt
2 tbsp. grated lemon rind
3 c. creamed cottage cheese
1 tbsp. lemon juice
1 c. heavy cream, whipped

Blend cracker crumbs, 2 tablespoons sugar and butter together. Press firmly into even layer on bottom of springform pan. Chill. Soften gelatin in 1/2 cup water. Beat egg yolks slightly in top of double boiler. Add 1 cup sugar, milk and salt. Cook, stirring over hot water until mixture thickens. Stir in gelatin; remove from heat. Combine lemon rind, cottage cheese and lemon juice; stir in gelatin mixture. Refrigerate until mixture mounds slightly when dropped from spoon. Beat egg whites until frothy. Beat in 1/4 cup sugar gradually until mixture forms stiff peaks. Fold into cottage cheese mixture; fold in whipped cream. Pour into prepared pan. Refrigerate until firm. Remove from pan; place on serving dish.

Glaze

1/4 c. fresh crushed strawberries
1/2 c. sugar
1 tbsp. cornstarch
1 tsp. lemon juice
Whole strawberries, halved

Simmer crushed strawberries in 1/4 cup water for 3 minutes. Strain juice from berries. Combine sugar and cornstarch in saucepan. Blend in strawberry juice and lemon juice. Cook, stirring until mixture thickens and boils for 1 minute. Cool. Arrange halved berries on top of cake. Spoon thin layer of glaze over strawberries. Yield: 12 servings.

RICOTTA CHEESECAKE

1 pkg. vanilla pudding mix
Sugar
1 c. milk
1 lb. ricotta cheese
4 eggs, separated
1 tsp. lemon juice
1/4 tsp. salt
2 tsp. vanilla
1/2 c. heavy cream, whipped
3/4 c. crushed graham crackers
2 tbsp. melted butter

Mix pudding mix with 3/4 cup sugar and milk; cook, stirring until thickened. Cover; cool. Combine ricotta cheese, egg yolks, lemon juice, salt and vanilla; beat thoroughly. Stir pudding mix into cheese mixture, blending well. Beat egg whites until stiff peaks form; fold into pudding mixture. Fold in whipped cream. Mix cracker crumbs, 1 teaspoon sugar and butter; press into cake pan. Pour in whipped cream mixture. Bake at 425 degrees for about 30 minutes or until set. Yield: 7-10 servings.

NUT CRUST CHEESECAKE

1 3/4 c. chocolate wafer crumbs
1/2 c. butter, melted
1/4 c. finely chopped walnuts

Combine crumbs, walnuts and butter, mixing well. Reserve 3 tablespoons of mixture; press remaining crumb mixture onto bottom and side of 9-inch springform pan.

Filling

3 eggs, beaten
2 8-oz packages cream cheese, softened
1 c. sugar
1/4 tsp. salt
2 tsp. vanilla
1/2 tsp. almond flavoring
3 c. sour cream

Combine eggs, cream cheese, sugar, salt and flavorings in bowl; beat until smooth. Blend in sour cream; pour cheese mixture into prepared pan. Sprinkle with reserved crumb mixture. Bake at 375 degrees for 35 minutes or until set. Chill for at least 5 hours. Yield: 10 servings.

ROYAL CHEESECAKE

1 box zwieback, crushed
1/2 c. margarine, melted
1 1/4 c. sugar
1 tsp. cinnamon
2 8-oz. packages cream cheese
3 c. cottage cheese
Juice and grated rind of 1 lemon
1 tsp. vanilla
1/8 tsp. salt
1/4 c. sifted flour
1 c. half and half
4 eggs, beaten

Combine zwieback crumbs, margarine, 1/4 cup sugar and cinnamon, mixing well; reserve 1/4 of crumb mixture. Press remaining crumb mixture into 9-inch round pan. Press cream cheese and cottage cheese through sieve; add lemon juice and rind, vanilla and salt. Mix well. Add remaining sugar; stir thoroughly. Beat in flour; stir in half and half. Add eggs to mixture; beat well. Pour into crumb crust; sprinkle reserved crumb mixture on top. Bake at 350 degrees for 1 hour. Open oven door. Let cake set in oven for 1 hour. Chill. Yield: 10 servings.

STRAWBERRY CHEESECAKE

2 pkg. frozen strawberries, thawed
2 env. unflavored gelatin
1 1/2 c. sugar
1 1/2 tsp. salt
2 eggs, beaten
2 tsp. vanilla
2 tsp. grated lemon peel
1 tbsp. lemon juice
6 drops of red food coloring
3 8-oz. packages cream cheese, softened
1 c. heavy cream
1 14-oz. can crushed pineapple
1 graham cracker crust recipe

Drain strawberries; reserve juice. Blend gelatin, sugar and salt together in double boiler; stir in reserved juice and eggs. Place over boiling water; cook for 5 minutes, stirring occasionally. Remove from heat; stir in vanilla, lemon peel, lemon juice and food coloring. Beat cream cheese until fluffy; add gelatin mixture to cheese gradually, beating after each addition until smooth and blended. Whip cream until soft peaks form; fold into cheese mixture. Drain pineapple. Fold pineapple and strawberries into cheese mixture. Press graham cracker mixture into 9-inch springform pan. Pour mixture into pan. Place in refrigerator overnight.

TROPICAL LIME CHEESECAKE

1 c. shredded coconut
2 tbsp. flour
2 tbsp. melted margarine
1 env. unflavored gelatin
3 eggs, separated
3/4 c. sugar
2 8-oz. packages cream cheese
1/4 c. lime juice
1 tsp. grated lime rind
Green food coloring
1 c. whipping cream, whipped

Mix coconut, flour and margarine; press onto bottom of 9-inch springform pan. Bake at 350 degrees for at least 15 minutes. Soften gelatin in 1/4 cup cold water. Mix egg yolks, 3/4 cup water and sugar in saucepan; cook, stirring, over medium heat for 5 minutes. Add gelatin; stir until dissolved. Soften cream cheese; add gelatin mixture gradually, mixing until blended. Stir lime juice and rind into gelatin mixture; tint with several drops of food coloring. Beat egg whites until stiff peaks form. Fold cream and egg whites into lime mixture. Pour over crust. Chill until firm. Garnish with additional grated lime rind. Yield: 10-12 servings.

Cherry

A cherry is a stone fruit, consisting of a single seed surrounded by a stone that is encased in fleshy, edible tissue. There are three types of cherries available on the market: sweet, sour, and duke. Cherries contain some vitamins and minerals. (1 cup fresh cherries = 65 calories)

AVAILABILITY: *Sweet cherries* are marketed fresh from May until August, and are also available canned or as maraschino cherries year-round. *Sour cherries* are usually available year-round in canned or frozen form, but may sometimes be obtained fresh from June to August. *Duke cherries* are almost always bleached, pitted, and soaked in sugar syrup and available bottled.

BUYING: Choose fresh cherries that are plump, bright and well-colored, and firm. Overripe fruit will be soft, dull in color, and shriveled. Immature fruit is small, hard, and light in color. Avoid cherries with small brown spots, bruises, mold, or decay.

STORING: Long periods of storage are not recommended. Cherries with stems attached keep better than those without stems.

PREPARATION: *Sour cherries* are generally used in cooking pies, cakes, tarts, jam, or sauces. *Sweet cherries* are delicious stewed, spiced, brandied, or served fresh. From 1 quart stemmed cherries, plan to obtain 3-4 cups stemmed and pitted fruit or 2 cups juice.

CHERRY-CREAM DIP

1 3-oz. package cream cheese
2 tbsp. mayonnaise
2 tbsp. maraschino cherry juice
1 tbsp. milk
2 tsp. lemon juice
1 2-oz. package dessert topping mix
1 tbsp. finely chopped maraschino cherries
Red food coloring

Have cream cheese at room temperature. Combine cream cheese, mayonnaise, cherry juice, milk and lemon juice; beat until smooth. Prepare topping mix according to package directions; fold into cream cheese mixture. Stir in cherries; chill. Whip chilled mixture until fluffy; spoon into bowl. Drop 1 drop of red food coloring on top; swirl in. Serve with fresh apple slices or desired fruit.

CHERRY-NUT MOLD

1 8-oz. package cream cheese
1 16-oz. can red sour pitted cherries
Dr. Pepper
1 c. sugar
2 3-oz. packages cherry gelatin
1 c. chopped celery
1 c. chopped pecans
1 c. sliced stuffed olives

Dice cream cheese. Drain cherries, reserving syrup; add enough Dr. Pepper to cherry syrup to equal 2 cups liquid. Pour liquid into saucepan; add sugar and gelatin. Stir over low heat until mixture is heated and gelatin is dissolved. Chill until thickened; fold in cherries, cream cheese, celery, pecans and olives. Pour into pan or mold; refrigerate overnight.

MARASCHINO CHERRY SPREAD

1 3-oz. package cream cheese
2 tbsp. cherry syrup
10 maraschino cherries, minced

Soften cream cheese with cherry syrup; stir in cherries. Serve immediately with crackers. Yield: 20-24 servings.

BRANDIED CHERRY SALAD

1 lb. Bing cherries, pitted
1 c. brandy
1 pkg. black cherry gelatin
1 c. blanched almonds

Marinate cherries in brandy overnight. Drain cherries; reserve brandy. Add enough water to reserved brandy to measure 1 cup liquid. Dissolve gelatin in 1 cup boiling water; combine with brandy mixture. Pour gelatin mixture into 1-quart mold; chill until partially set. Fold in cherries and almonds; chill until firm.

CHERRY-PORT SALAD

1 No. 2 can pitted Bing cherries
1 pkg. black cherry gelatin
Pinch of salt
1 c. port
1/2 c. slivered almonds
1 c. mayonnaise
1 c. heavy cream
1 tbsp. sugar
1 tbsp. tarragon vinegar
Pinch of cayenne pepper

Drain cherries; reserve juice. Add enough water to reserved juice to measure 1 cup liquid. Pour into saucepan; bring to a boil. Remove from heat; stir in gelatin until dissolved. Add salt and port; chill until partially set. Fold in cherries and almonds. Pour into mold; chill until firm. Combine mayonnaise, cream, sugar, vinegar and cayenne pepper; blend well. Chill until ready to use. Serve as dressing for salad.

CHERRY SPARKLE

1 1-lb. 4-oz. can Bing cherries
1 1-lb. 4-oz. can crushed pineapple
2 pkg. black cherry gelatin
2 6 1/2-oz. bottles cola beverage

Drain cherries. Drain pineapple, reserving syrup. Add enough water to pineapple syrup to equal 2 cups liquid. Pour liquid into saucepan; bring to a boil. Stir in gelatin until dissolved; add cola beverage. Chill gelatin until thickened; fold in fruits. Turn into mold or pan; chill until firm. Yield: 20 servings.

CHERRY SALAD SUPREME

1 can Bing cherries
2 pkg. black cherry gelatin
1 3-oz. package cream cheese
Chopped pecans
Seeded white grapes
1/2 c. sugar
2 tbsp. flour
1 egg, slightly beaten
1 c. pineapple juice
2 tbsp. margarine
1 pkg. dessert topping mix

Drain cherries; reserve juice. Add enough water to reserved juice to measure 2 cups liquid. Dissolve gelatin in 1 cup boiling water; add to reserved juice mixture. Chill until partially set. Shape cream cheese into small balls; roll in pecans. Fold cherries, grapes and cream cheese balls into gelatin. Pour into mold; chill until firm. Combine sugar, flour, egg and pineapple juice in saucepan; cook, stirring constantly, until smooth and thickened. Stir in margarine; cool. Prepare dessert topping mix according to package directions. Combine with egg mixture. Pour over gelatin carefully. Chill until firm.

DARK SWEET CHERRY SALAD

1 No. 303 can dark sweet cherries
1 pkg. cherry gelatin
1 c. sour cream
1/4 c. pecans

Drain cherries; reserve juice. Add enough water to reserved juice to measure 1 cup liquid. Pour into saucepan; bring to a boil. Remove from heat. Add gelatin; stir until gelatin is dissolved. Chill until partially set. Add sour cream; blend thoroughly. Stir in cherries and nuts. Pour into mold; chill until firm.

LEMON-CHERRY SALAD

1 pkg. lemon gelatin
1 sm. jar Maraschino cherries
2 tbsp. lemon juice
1/2 tsp. salt
1/2 c. diced apples
1/2 c. chopped celery
1/2 c. chopped nuts

Dissolve gelatin in 1 cup boiling water. Drain cherries; reserve juice. Add enough water to reserved juice to measure 1 cup liquid; add to gelatin mixture. Stir in lemon juice and salt; chill until partially set. Fold in apples, cherries, celery and nuts; chill until firm.

SPICED BLACK CHERRY RING

1 No. 2 can pitted black cherries
2 tsp. mixed pickling spice
1 3-oz. package orange gelatin
1/3 c. lemon juice
3/4 c. chopped nuts

Drain cherries; reserve juice. Add enough water to reserved juice to measure 1 3/4 cups liquid; pour into saucepan. Add pickling spice to liquid; bring to a boil. Remove from heat; let stand for 5 minutes. Strain liquid; stir in gelatin until dissolved. Stir in lemon juice; chill until partially set. Fold in cherries and nuts. Pour into lightly oiled ring mold or individual molds; chill until firm.

STUFFED CHERRY SALAD

1 can pitted dark sweet Bing cherries
1 pkg. lime gelatin
Cream cheese

Drain cherries; reserve juice. Add enough water to reserved juice to measure 2 cups liquid. Pour into saucepan; bring to a boil. Remove from heat; stir in gelatin until dissolved. Chill until partially set. Have cream cheese at room temperature; cream until fluffy. Stuff cherries with cream cheese. Fold cherries into gelatin. Chill until firm.

CHERRY CAKE

2 c. butter
2 c. sugar
6 eggs, separated
1 tbsp. lemon extract
4 c. flour
1 tsp. baking powder
1 lb. white raisins
1/2 lb. maraschino cherries
4 c. chopped pecans

Cream butter and sugar; add lightly beaten egg yolks and lemon extract. Sift flour and baking powder together. Dredge fruits and pecans with 1/2 cup flour mixture. Stir remaining flour mixture into creamed mixture. Fold floured fruits and stiffly beaten egg whites into batter. Place in tube pan. Bake at 350 degrees for 1 hour and 10 minutes or until cake tests done.

CHERRY DUMP CAKE

1 can pineapple tidbits, drained
1 can cherry pie filling
1 sm. box white cake mix
1/2 c. quick-cooking oats
1/2 c. chopped pecans
1 stick butter, melted

Spread pineapple in small ungreased cake pan; spread pie filling over pineapple. Sprinkle cake mix over pie filling; sprinkle oats and pecans over cake mix. Pour butter evenly over top. Bake at 325 degrees for 1 hour.

CHERRY HOLIDAY CAKES

2 lb. red candied cherries
6 oz. crystallized ginger
3 c. chopped walnuts
2/3 c. orange juice
3 c. flour
1 tbsp. baking powder
1 tsp. salt
1 1/2 tsp. ground coriander
1 c. butter or margarine
1 c. sugar
6 eggs, separated

Cut cherries and ginger fine, using kitchen shears. Combine cherries, ginger and walnuts in bowl; stir in orange juice. Mix flour, baking powder, salt and coriander. Cream butter and 1/2 cup sugar until light; beat in egg yolks, one at a time. Stir in cherry mixture and flour mixture. Beat egg whites until stiff, beating in remaining sugar. Fold egg whites into cake batter. Spoon batter into greased small loaf pans or fluted molds. Bake at 350 degrees for 1 hour or until cakes test done. Cool cakes in pans for 10 minutes; turn onto racks. Frost with a confectioners' sugar icing, if desired.

CHERRY LOAF CAKE

2 c. sifted flour
1/4 tsp. soda
2 tsp. baking powder
1/2 tsp. salt
1 c. (firmly packed) brown sugar
1/3 c. butter or margarine
1 egg
3/4 c. milk
1/4 c. maraschino cherry syrup
1/2 c. chopped maraschino cherries
1/2 c. chopped nuts

Sift flour, soda, baking powder and salt together. Cream sugar and butter; beat in egg. Stir in flour mixture alternately with milk and cherry syrup. Fold in cherries and nuts; turn into greased loaf pan. Bake at 325 degrees for 1 hour.

CHERRY LOG

1 c. sifted flour
1 tsp. baking powder
1/2 tsp. salt
3 eggs
1 c. sugar
1 tsp. vanilla
1/3 c. hot water
2 tbsp. confectioners' sugar
1 can cherry pie filling
Whipped cream

Sift flour, baking powder and salt together. Break eggs into large electric mixer bowl. Beat at high speed until lemon colored. Add sugar, 1 tablespoon at a time, beating constantly. Add vanilla. Set mixer on slow speed; add flour mixture, beating only enough to blend. Add hot water; beat until smooth. Spread in greased waxed paper-lined jelly roll pan. Bake at 375 degrees for 12 to 14 minutes. Turn onto towel sprinkled with confectioners' sugar. Remove waxed paper; roll up, using towel. Cool on rack. Unroll; spread evenly with part of the pie filling. Reroll cake around pie filling; spread remaining pie filling over top of roll. Chill. Slice roll to serve, spooning up any pie filling that drops from top of roll. Serve topped with whipped cream. Yield: 6-8 servings.

CHERRY UPSIDE-DOWN CAKE

2 No. 2 cans pitted cherries
1 1/2 c. sugar
2 tsp. cinnamon
1 pkg. cherry cake mix

Drain cherries, reserving liquid. Mix cherries, sugar and cinnamon in bowl. Line bottom of 12 x 9 x 2-inch pan with waxed paper; grease sides. Spread cherry mixture in pan. Prepare cake mix according to package directions, using cherry liquid as part of required liquid. Pour over cherry mixture. Bake at 350 degrees for 40 minutes. Invert immediately onto large platter. Peel off waxed paper gently.

TIPSY CHERRY PARSON

Color photograph for this recipe on page 484.

2 pkg. dessert topping mix
1 c. cold milk
1 c. powdered sugar
1 8-oz. package cream cheese
1 baked angel food cake
Slivered toasted almonds
Slivered maraschino cherries

Combine dessert topping mix and milk in mixing bowl; beat well. Add powdered sugar gradually. Soften cream cheese; beat into topping mixture, small amount at a time. Cut cake into 3 layers. Place 1 layer on cake plate; spread with layer of topping mixture. Repeat with remaining cake and part of the topping mixture. Frost top and sides with remaining topping mixture; decorate sides with almonds and cherries. Refrigerate until chilled. Garnish with whole stemmed cherries.

SAUCED CHERRY CAKE

2 c. sugar
1/3 c. shortening
2 eggs
1 1/2 tsp. baking powder
3/4 tsp. salt
1/2 tsp. soda
2 1/4 c. flour
1 c. milk
1 No. 2 can sour cherries
1/2 c. nuts
2 tbsp. cornstarch
1/4 tsp. almond flavoring
Red food coloring

Cream 1 1/2 cups sugar with shortening; beat in eggs. Combine baking powder, 1/2 teaspoon salt, soda and flour. Add flour mixture to sugar mixture; blend well. Add milk gradually; beat until smooth. Drain cherries; reserve 3/4 cup juice. Fold in cherries and nuts. Place in greased and floured 13 x 9-inch baking pan. Bake at 375 degrees for 35 to 40 minutes or until cake tests done. Remove from oven; cool on rack. Combine remaining sugar, cornstarch, remaining salt and almond flavoring with 1 cup water and reserved juice. Cook, stirring constantly, over medium heat until clear and thickened. Tint with food coloring as desired. Serve sauce over cake.

CHERRY HOLIDAY BALLS

2 eggs, well beaten
1 c. sugar
1 c. chopped nuts
1 c. chopped dates
1/2 c. flaked coconut
1/2 tsp. almond extract
1/2 tsp. vanilla
Dash of salt
36 candied cherries
Confectioners' sugar

Combine eggs, sugar, nuts, dates, coconut, almond extract, vanilla and salt. Place in greased 8-inch square pan. Bake at 350 degrees for 30 minutes, stirring mixture at 10-minute intervals. Remove from oven; stir well. Cool; shape around cherries. Roll in confectioners' sugar.

FRUIT FANCIES

3 c. sugar
1 c. light corn syrup
1 1/2 c. light cream
1 tsp. vanilla
1 c. whole pecans
1 c. halved Brazil nuts
1 c. coarsely chopped walnuts
1 c. chopped candied pineapple
1 c. chopped candied cherries

Combine sugar, corn syrup and cream in saucepan; mix. Cook to soft-ball stage. Remove from heat; beat until thick and almost cool. Add vanilla, nuts and fruits, beating slowly. Turn into buttered 1 1/2-quart loaf pan. Chill for several hours. Cut into finger-length pieces.

QUICK CHERRY BALLS

1/2 c. margarine
1 1/2 c. confectioners' sugar
1 1/2 c. flaked coconut
1/2 tsp. almond or rum flavoring
1 tbsp. milk
18 stemmed maraschino cherries
Graham cracker crumbs

Cream margarine and sugar; add coconut. Blend in flavoring and milk. Shape about 1 teaspoon coconut mixture around each cherry. Roll in cracker crumbs; chill. Balls keep well if refrigerated.

CANDIED CHERRY SNAPS

1 c. butter
1 c. sifted powdered sugar
1 egg
1 tsp. vanilla
2 1/4 c. sifted flour
1 c. pecan halves
1 c. halved red candied cherries
1 c. halved green candied cherries

Cream butter, adding powdered sugar gradually. Blend in egg and vanilla; add flour. Mix well; stir in pecan halves and cherries. Chill dough for 1 hour; divide into thirds. Shape into 12-inch long rolls; wrap in waxed paper. Chill for at least 3 hours or place in freezer for 2 hours. Cut into 1/8-inch thick slices; place on ungreased cookie sheet. Bake at 325 degrees for 13 to 15 minutes or until edges are lightly browned. Yield: 7 dozen cookies.

CHERRY-CHEESE TURNOVERS

1 c. grated cheese
1 stick butter, softened
2 c. flour
1/8 tsp. salt
1 c. dark sweet canned cherries, drained

Blend cheese with butter, flour and salt; roll out dough. Cut into 2-inch squares. Place 1 tablespoon cherries in center of each square; fold over corners to seal. Place on cookie sheet. Bake at 375 degrees until lightly browned.

FRUITCAKE MACAROONS

Color photograph for this recipe on page 487.

1 lb. red candied cherries
1 lb. green candied cherries
1 lb. dates, chopped
2 c. chopped walnuts
2 cans flaked coconut
1 can sweetened condensed milk
1 tsp. vanilla

Chop cherries. Combine fruits, walnuts and coconut; mix well. Stir in milk and vanilla. Drop from teaspoon onto heavily greased cookie sheet. Bake at 375 degrees for 15 minutes. Yield: 48 cookies.

CHERRY-NUT DELIGHT

1 c. walnuts
1 1/4 c. flour
1/2 c. brown sugar
1/2 c. butter
1/2 c. flaked coconut
1/3 c. sugar
1 8-oz. package cream cheese
1 egg
1 tsp. vanilla
1 can cherry pie filling

Chop 1/2 cup walnuts coarsely; reserve for topping. Chop remaining walnuts fine. Combine flour, brown sugar and butter; blend to fine crumbs. Add coconut and finely chopped walnuts; mix well. Reserve 1/2 cup mixture. Pack remaining flour mixture into 9 x 13 x 2-inch greased baking pan. Bake for 12 to 15 minutes in 350-degree oven until edges are light brown. Mix sugar and cream cheese; stir in egg and vanilla. Beat until smooth. Spread over hot baked layer; bake for 10 minutes longer. Remove from oven; spread with cherry filling. Sprinkle with reserved walnuts and crumb mixture. Bake for 15 minutes longer; cool. Top with whipped cream or ice cream, if desired.

CHERRY-PECAN FANCIES

3/4 c. shortening
1 egg
1 tsp. vanilla
1 c. (packed) brown sugar
1/4 c. maraschino cherries, chopped
1/2 c. chopped nuts
2 c. sifted flour
1/2 tsp. soda
1/2 tsp. salt
1/2 tsp. cream of tartar

Combine shortening, egg, vanilla and brown sugar in mixing bowl; add cherries and nuts. Sift dry ingredients; add gradually to brown sugar mixture. Blend thoroughly. Shape into rolls; wrap in waxed paper. Chill until firm. Cut into 1/8-inch slices; place on ungreased baking sheet. Bake at 400 degrees for 6 to 8 minutes. Cool 1 to 2 minutes before removing from pan. May freeze dough wrapped in foil. Yield: 5 dozen cookies.

CHERRY SURPRISE BALLS

1 c. butter or margarine
Powdered sugar
2 c. cake flour
1 tsp. vanilla
1/2 c. chopped pecans
1 lb. candied cherries

Cream butter and 1/2 cup powdered sugar. Add flour and vanilla; mix well. Stir in pecans. Chill dough for several hours. Mold dough around cherries, covering completely. Place on ungreased cookie sheet. Bake at 375 degrees for 20 minutes. Roll warm balls in powdered sugar; place on rack to cool.

ROYAL CHERRY BARS

1 can sour cherries
1 1/4 c. oatmeal
1 1/2 c. flour
1 c. (packed) brown sugar
1 tsp. soda
1/2 tsp. salt
2/3 c. butter or margarine
1/2 c. sugar
1 1/2 tbsp. cornstarch

Drain cherries, reserving syrup. Combine oatmeal, flour, brown sugar, soda and salt; cut in butter until mixture is crumbly. Press half the crumb mixture evenly into greased 13 x 9 x 2-inch pan. Blend sugar and cornstarch in saucepan; stir in reserved cherry syrup. Cook over low heat until thick and clear, stirring constantly. Add cherries; cool. Spread cherry mixture over crumb mixture in pan; cover with remaining crumb mixture. Bake at 350 degrees for 20 to 25 minutes. Cool; cut into bars. Yield: 8-10 servings.

CHERRY CHIFFON

1 sm. can evaporated milk
1 pkg. cherry gelatin
1 tsp. lemon juice

Chill milk until very cold. Dissolve gelatin in 1 cup boiling water; chill until syrupy. Whip milk until slightly stiff; add lemon juice. Whip until stiff. Whip gelatin until light and frothy; fold in whipped milk. Pour into cups or molds; chill until firm. Yield: 4 servings.

CHERRY ANGEL DREAM

1 angel food cake
1 3-oz. package instant vanilla pudding mix
1 1/2 c. milk
1 c. sour cream
1 can cherry pie filling

Cut cake into 1-inch cubes. Place half the cake cubes in 13 x 9-inch cake pan. Combine pudding mix and milk; beat until smooth and slightly thickened. Blend in sour cream. Pour half the pudding mixture over cake cubes; spoon half the pie filling over pudding mixture. Repeat layers; smooth top with spatula. Refrigerate for several hours or overnight before serving. Yield: 12 servings.

COLD CHERRY SOUFFLÉ

2/3 c. chopped red maraschino cherries
1/2 c. orange juice
2 env. unflavored gelatin
Sugar
1/4 tsp. salt
8 eggs, separated
1 c. milk
2 c. heavy cream, whipped

Blend cherries with orange juice in electric blender; set aside. Mix gelatin, 2/3 cup sugar and salt in top of double boiler. Beat in egg yolks until light. Stir in milk and 1/2 cup water gradually. Cook over boiling water for about 10 minutes, stirring constantly, until slightly thickened and gelatin is dissolved. Add cherry mixture. Chill until slightly thickened. Beat egg whites until foamy. Add 1/2 cup sugar gradually, beating until stiff peaks form. Fold egg whites and whipped cream into gelatin mixture. Turn into 1 1/2-quart souffle dish with aluminum foil collar. Chill until firm. Remove collar; garnish with whole maraschino cherries and whipped cream. Yield: 10-12 servings.

Cold Cherry Soufflé. . . An elegant dessert souffle that doesn't mind waiting to be served.

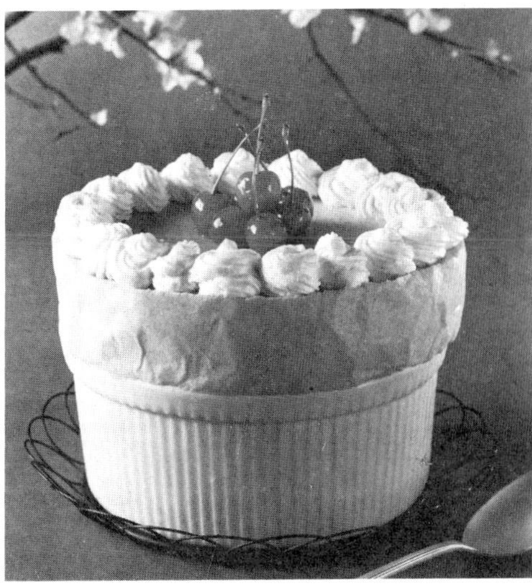

CHERRY FLUFF

1 8-oz. jar maraschino cherries
1 pkg. cherry gelatin
1 pkg. strawberry gelatin
Dash of salt
1 c. chopped pecans
Whipped cream

Drain and chop cherries, reserving syrup. Add enough water to syrup to equal 2 cups liquid. Pour liquid into saucepan; bring to a boil. Stir in gelatins and salt until dissolved; add 2 cups cold water. Refrigerate until partially thickened; whip until fluffy. Add cherries and pecans; fold in 4 cups whipped cream. Spoon into 12 to 15 dessert dishes; refrigerate until firm. Top with whipped cream to serve.

CHERRY-NUT SPONGE

1 pkg. vanilla wafers
1 env. unflavored gelatin
1 c. cold water
6 eggs, separated
6 tbsp. sugar
1 c. undrained maraschino cherries
1 c. chopped nuts
Whipped cream

Crush wafers to fine crumbs. Soften gelatin in cold water. Beat egg yolks in top of double boiler; beat in sugar. Stir in gelatin. Cook, stirring constantly, until gelatin is dissolved and mixture is thickened. Fold in wafer crumbs, cherries and nuts; cool. Beat egg whites until stiff; fold into sponge mixture. Turn into large bowl; refrigerate until set. Serve with whipped cream.

CORDIAL CHERRIES

1 No. 2 can sour cherries
3/4 c. heavy cream
3/4 c. sugar
1/2 tsp. vanilla
1 1/2 c. cooked rice
Cherry cordial or liqueur
2 tsp. lemon juice
1 tsp. cornstarch

Drain cherries; reserve juice. Whip cream until almost stiff. Beat in 1/2 cup sugar and vanilla; fold in rice. Chill well. Fold in cherries; spoon into sherbet glasses. Chill until ready to serve. Combine reserved cherry juice and enough cordial to make 1 cup liquid; pour into saucepan. Add remaining sugar, lemon juice and cornstarch. Simmer until slightly thickened; cool. Pour over cherry mixture. Yield: 8 servings.

CHERRY-CINNAMON FLOAT

2 1-lb. cans pitted tart red cherries
1/2 tsp. cinnamon
1/2 tsp. nutmeg
1/2 c. sugar
3 tbsp. cornstarch
1/2 tsp. red food coloring
4 tsp. lemon juice
1 9 1/2-oz. package refrigerator cinnamon rolls

Preheat oven to 375 degrees. Drain cherries, reserving syrup. Mix cinnamon, nutmeg, sugar and cornstarch in saucepan; add food coloring, lemon juice and cherry syrup. Bring to a boil, stirring constantly. Add cherries; pour into 1 1/2-quart casserole. Arrange cinnamon rolls around top. Bake for 20 minutes. Spread icing from roll package over rolls. Serve warm with whipped cream, if desired. Yield: 8 servings.

CHERRY FREEZE

1 15-oz. can sweetened condensed milk
1/4 c. lemon juice
1 can cherry pie filling
1 sm. can crushed pineapple
1/4 tsp. vanilla
2 c. whipped cream

Mix all ingredients; pour into 9 x 5 x 3-inch pan. Cover with aluminum foil. Freeze for 24 hours before serving. Yield: 18 servings.

CHERRIES JUBILEE

1 1/2 qt. vanilla ice cream
1 jar currant jelly
2 cans pitted Bing cherries
1/2 c. brandy

Shape ice cream into balls; wrap. Place in freezer for at least 2 hours. Place in bowl just before serving. Melt jelly in chafing dish over direct heat, stirring gently; add cherries. Heat slowly, stirring constantly, until simmering; pour brandy into center of cherries. Do not stir. Heat until warmed; light with match. Spoon flaming cherries over ice cream. One-half cup lemon extract and 10 sugar cubes may be substituted for brandy. Pour extract into cup; soak sugar cubes. Place cubes on cherries in chafing dish; light with match. Yield: 8 servings.

COUNTRY CHERRY CREAM

Color photograph for this recipe on page 494.

1 8-oz. jar red maraschino cherries
4 c. sour cream
1 c. sugar
1 3 1/2-oz. can flaked coconut
1/2 c. red currant jelly
1/4 tsp. grated lemon peel
2 tbsp. lemon juice

Drain cherries, reserving syrup. Add enough water to reserved syrup to equal 1/2 cup liquid. Chop cherries. Combine 1/3 cup cherries with sour cream, sugar and coconut; mix well. Pour into 1-quart souffle dish; freeze until firm. Combine cherry syrup mixture and jelly in saucepan, stirring over medium heat until jelly is melted. Add remaining cherries, lemon peel and juice; chill. Serve sauce with cherry cream. Yield: 8-10 servings.

CHERRY-NUT ICE CREAM

1 8-oz. jar maraschino cherries
4 eggs
1 1/2 c. sugar
Milk
1 2/3 c. evaporated milk
1 pt. whipping cream
1 1/2 c. chopped salted pecans

Drain and dice cherries, reserving cherry syrup. Beat eggs and sugar together in saucepan; stir in 1 1/3 cups milk and evaporated milk. Cook over low heat, stirring constantly, until slightly thickened. Cool. Whip cream until stiff; fold whipped cream, cherries, cherry syrup and pecans into cooked custard. Pour into 1-gallon freezer can; add enough milk to fill can to within 1 1/2 inches of top. Freeze according to freezer manufacturer's directions.

FROZEN CHERRY CREAM

2 eggs
1/2 c. sugar
1/2 tsp. salt
1 1/2 c. milk
1 tsp. vanilla
1 tsp. almond extract
1 1/2 c. chopped sweet dark cherries
1 c. heavy cream, whipped
1/2 c. toasted flaked coconut

Beat eggs until thick and light; beat in sugar gradually. Stir in salt and milk. Pour into freezing tray; freeze until almost firm. Turn into chilled bowl; add flavorings. Beat until smooth. Work quickly; mixture should not thaw completely. Fold in cherries and whipped cream. Return to tray; sprinkle with coconut. Freeze until firm. Yield: 6 servings.

FROZEN CHERRY DESSERT

1 c. chopped candied cherries
Brandy
1 qt. vanilla ice cream
1/4 c. rum

Cover cherries with brandy; soak for several hours. Drain. Let ice cream stand until softened; blend in cherries and rum. Freeze in individual sherbet glasses. Garnish with mint leaves. Yield: 10-12 servings.

CHERRY ROLL

3 c. sour cherries
2 c. flour
Sugar
3 tsp. baking powder
1 tsp. salt
6 tbsp. shortening
2/3 c. milk
3 tbsp. butter
1/4 tsp. cinnamon

Drain cherries, reserving syrup. Sift flour, 2 tablespoons sugar, baking powder and salt together into bowl. Cut in shortening; stir in milk. Roll dough to 12 x 6-inch rectangle. Mix 1/2 cup sugar, 1 tablespoon butter and cherries; spread over dough. Roll dough as for jelly roll; cut in 8 slices. Add enough water to reserved cherry syrup to equal 2 cups liquid. Mix cinnamon and 1/2 cup sugar in saucepan; stir in cherry liquid. Bring to a boil; add remaining butter. Pour syrup into baking pan; arrange cherry roll slices in pan. Bake at 450 degrees for 15 minutes. Yield: 8 servings.

CHERRY-RHUBARB COBBLER

1 16-oz. package frozen rhubarb
2 tbsp. quick tapioca
Sugar
3/4 tsp. salt
1 17-oz. can pitted tart cherries
2 tbsp. butter
1 1/2 c. sifted flour
2 tsp. baking powder
1/2 c. shortening
1/2 c. milk
Confectioners' sugar

Thaw rhubarb; drain. Mix tapioca, 1 cup sugar, 1/4 teaspoon salt, cherries and rhubarb in saucepan. Bring to a boil, stirring constantly. Pour into greased 11 x 7 x 2-inch pan; dot with butter. Sift flour and baking powder with 2 tablespoons sugar and remaining salt; cut in shortening. Add milk gradually; stir until dough is formed. Turn dough onto lightly floured board; knead for 30 seconds. Roll dough to fit pan. Arrange dough over filling; cut steam vents. Bake at 425 degrees for 20 to 25 minutes. Sprinkle with confectioners' sugar; serve with cream, if desired.

CHERRY COBBLER

1 No. 2 can pitted tart red cherries
3/4 c. sugar
1 tbsp. tapioca
6 tbsp. butter
1 c. flour
1 1/2 tsp. baking powder
1/4 tsp. salt
1/4 c. milk
1 egg, slightly beaten

Combine cherries, 1/2 cup sugar and tapioca; cook, stirring constantly, until mixture is clear and thickened. Add 2 tablespoons butter; pour into 10 x 6-inch baking dish. Combine flour, 1 tablespoon sugar, baking powder and salt; cut in remaining butter. Blend milk and egg; add to dry ingredients. Drop dough by spoonfuls over hot fruit. Sprinkle with remaining sugar. Bake at 400 degrees for 20 minutes.

CHERRY TARTS

2 16-oz. cans sour cherries
1 1/2 c. sugar
1/2 tsp. salt
1/4 c. cornstarch
1 1/3 c. grape juice
1 tsp. red food coloring
1 tsp. almond extract
1 tbsp. lemon juice
2 tbsp. butter or margarine
Pastry for 2-crust pie
Whipped cream or vanilla ice cream

Drain cherries well. Mix sugar, salt and cornstarch in saucepan. Blend in grape juice, cherries and food coloring slowly. Cook over medium heat, stirring, until thick. Remove from heat; add almond extract, lemon juice and butter. Cool. Roll pastry out; cut into rounds large enough to cover inverted muffin tins. Press gently onto tins; prick with fork. Bake at 450 degrees for about 8 minutes or until delicately browned. Cool slightly. Fill with cherry mixture. Cover with whipped cream. Yield: 12 servings.

CHERRY TRIANGLES

2/3 c. milk, scalded
1 pkg. yeast
1 1/4 c. butter
2 1/2 c. sifted flour
4 egg yolks, lightly beaten
2 cans cherry pie filling
1/2 tsp. vanilla
2 tbsp. cream
1 1/2 c. confectioners' sugar
3/4 c. chopped nuts

Cool milk to lukewarm; add yeast. Cut 1 cup butter into flour; add yeast mixture and egg yolks. Turn onto floured surface; knead 10 times. Divide dough in half. Roll half the dough to fit ungreased 18 x 12 x 1-inch jelly roll pan. Spread pie filling over dough. Roll remaining dough; fit over top. Pinch edges of dough together gently. Let rise for 15 minutes. Bake at 350 degrees for 45 to 55 minutes. Cream remaining butter, vanilla and cream; add sugar, beating until blended. Spread frosting over partially cooled mixture; sprinkle with nuts. Cool; cut into 3-inch squares. Cut each square diagonally. Yield: 48 triangles.

CHERRY-FILLED TASTIES

2 c. sour cherries	*3 1/2 c. sifted flour*
1 c. cherry juice	*1/2 tsp. soda*
Butter or margarine	*1/2 tsp. salt*
2 1/3 c. sugar	*1 tsp. vanilla*
1/4 c. cornstarch	*1 egg*
1 tsp. almond extract	*2 tbsp. vinegar*
Several drops of red food coloring	*1/4 c. milk*

Combine cherries, juice, 2 tablespoons butter, 1 1/3 cups sugar and cornstarch in saucepan; cook over medium heat, stirring until thickened. Cool. Add almond extract and food coloring. Sift flour, soda and salt together. Cream 1/2 cup butter, remaining sugar and vanilla together. Beat in egg; add flour mixture alternately with vinegar and milk. Chill. Roll dough thin. Cut into 1 3/4-inch squares. Place half the squares on cookie sheet. Place 1 teaspoon cherry mixture in center of each. Cut small design from center of each remaining square; place over cherry-topped squares. Press edges together with fork. Bake at 375 degrees for 12 minutes. Yield: 6 dozen.

DOUBLE CHERRY FRITTERS

1 c. flour	*1 egg, beaten*
1 1/2 tsp. baking powder	*1/3 c. milk*
2 tbsp. confectioners' sugar	*1/2 c. chopped maraschino cherries*
1/4 tsp. salt	*Cherry Sauce*

Sift flour, baking powder, sugar and salt together into bowl; stir in egg and milk. Beat until smooth; fold in cherries. Drop batter by spoonfuls into hot fat. Cook until golden brown. Drain on paper towels. Serve with Cherry Sauce.

Cherry Sauce

1/3 c. sugar	*2/3 c. boiling water*
1 tbsp. cornstarch	*1/4 c. minced maraschino cherries*
1/2 c. maraschino cherry syrup	*1/2 tbsp. butter*

Mix sugar and cornstarch in saucepan; stir in cherry syrup and boiling water. Bring to a boil, stirring constantly. Cook for 5 minutes. Remove from heat; stir in cherries and butter.

CHERRY PIZZA DOLCE

2 c. packaged biscuit mix	*1/4 c. red maraschino cherry syrup*
2 tbsp. sugar	*1/4 c. apricot jam*
1/2 c. milk	*3 tbsp. cherry brandy*
3 tbsp. butter, melted	*1 c. red maraschino cherries*
1 1-lb. can apricot halves	*1/4 c. walnut halves*
1 tbsp. cornstarch	*1/2 c. green maraschino cherries*
1/4 tsp. allspice	*1 8 3/4-oz. can pineapple tidbits, drained*
1/8 tsp. cinnamon	
1 tsp. grated lemon peel	

Blend biscuit mix and sugar together; stir in milk and butter. Knead dough gently 10 times on lightly-floured surface. Pat out on bottom and side of 12-inch pizza pan. Prick with fork. Bake in 450-degree oven for 10 to 15 minutes or until golden

Cherry Pizza Dolce . . . Pizza, a longtime favorite, becomes a tasty dessert.

brown. Drain apricots, reserving 1/2 cup syrup. Mix cornstarch with spices and lemon peel in saucepan; stir in cherry syrup and reserved apricot syrup. Cook, stirring until thickened and clear. Add jam; stir over low heat until melted. Remove from heat; add brandy. Arrange circles of red cherries, walnuts, apricots and green cherries, beginning at outer edge of pizza. Fill center with pineapple tidbits. Pour glaze evenly over fruit. Chill and serve. May top each serving with scoop of ice cream if desired. Yield: 8 servings.

CHERRY CHIFFON PIE

1 16-oz. can cherry pie filling
3 tbsp. brandy
2 env. whipped topping mix
1 9-in. baked pie shell

Combine pie filling and brandy in bowl; let stand for 30 minutes. Prepare topping mix according to package directions. Reserve 1 cup topping for garnish. Fold remaining topping into pie filling. Pile filling into pastry shell; chill. Garnish with reserved topping. Yield: 8 servings.

CHERRY PIE SUPREME

2/3 c. sugar
3 tbsp. cornstarch
1/4 tsp. salt
2 c. milk
2 eggs, lightly beaten
2 tbsp. butter
1 tsp. vanilla
2 oz. semisweet chocolate, melted
1 8-in. baked pastry shell
1 16-oz. can pitted dark sweet cherries
1/2 c. whipping cream, whipped

Combine sugar, cornstarch and salt in saucepan; stir in milk gradually. Cook, stirring, until bubbly. Cook for 2 minutes longer. Stir small amount of hot mixture into eggs; return to hot mixture. Cook for 2 minutes longer. Remove from heat; add butter and vanilla. Stir 1/2 cup vanilla mixture into chocolate; spread in pastry shell. Cover surface of remaining vanilla mixture with waxed paper; cool for 30 minutes. Drain and halve cherries. Arrange cherry halves, cut side down, on chocolate layer reserving 8 or 10 halves. Spread remaining vanilla mixture over cherries; chill. Spoon whipped cream over pie; top with reserved cherry halves. Yield: 6-8 servings.

CLOUD-TOP CHERRY PIE

2/3 c. evaporated milk
1 can red tart cherries
3/4 c. sugar
2 tbsp. cornstarch
Lemon juice
Few drops of red food coloring
1 3-oz. package cream cheese
1/2 tsp. almond extract
1 9-in. baked pie shell
Toasted slivered almonds

Pour evaporated milk into refrigerator tray; place in freezer until ice crystals form around edges. Chill small electric mixer bowl and beaters in freezer. Drain cherries, reserving syrup; add enough water to syrup to equal 1 cup liquid. Mix 1/2 cup sugar and cornstarch in saucepan; stir in cherry liquid. Cook over medium heat, stirring constantly, to a boil. Cook for 1 minute; remove from heat. Stir in cherries, 1 teaspoon lemon juice and food coloring; cool. Mix cream cheese and 2 tablespoons lemon juice until smooth. Pour evaporated milk into chilled bowl; add remaining sugar and almond extract. Beat at high speed of electric mixer until stiff; beat in cream cheese mixture at medium speed. Turn cherry filling into pie shell; spoon whipped milk mixture over filling. Chill pie for 3 hours before serving. Sprinkle with almonds.

OLD-FASHIONED CHERRY PIE

2 1-lb. cans pitted sour cherries
3 tbsp. flour
3 tbsp. cornstarch
1 1/2 c. sugar
1/2 tsp. salt
Pastry for 2-crust pie

Drain cherries, reserving 3/4 cup syrup. Mix flour, cornstarch, sugar and salt in saucepan; stir in reserved cherry syrup. Cook over medium heat, stirring constantly until thickened. Divide pastry in half; roll each half to fit 9-inch pie plate. Fit half the pastry into plate; add cherries. Pour hot mixture over cherries; fit remaining pastry over top. Seal edges; cut steam vents. Bake at 425 degrees for 40 to 45 minutes. Yield: 6-8 servings.

SWEET CHERRY PIE

1 1-lb. can pitted dark sweet cherries
1 3-oz. package cherry gelatin
1 pt. vanilla ice cream
1 tsp. lemon juice
3 tbsp. red Burgundy
1 baked 8-in. pastry shell
Whipped cream

Drain cherries, reserving syrup; quarter cherries. Add enough water to cherry syrup to make 1 cup liquid. Pour liquid into saucepan. Bring to a boil; dissolve gelatin in boiling liquid. Add ice cream by spoonfuls, stirring until ice cream is melted. Blend in lemon juice and Burgundy; chill until thickened. Fold in cherries; spoon into pastry shell. Chill until firm. Garnish with whipped cream. Yield: 6-8 servings.

MARTHA WASHINGTON PUDDING

1 No. 2 can pie cherries
Sugar
2 tbsp. quick tapioca
2 eggs, separated
1/4 tsp. cream of tartar
Dash of salt
1/2 c. sifted cake flour

Pour cherries into saucepan; crush. Add 3/4 cup sugar and tapioca. Bring to a boil over medium heat, stirring constantly. Reduce heat; simmer for 5 minutes, stirring constantly. Pour into 1 1/2-quart casserole. Combine egg whites, cream of tartar and salt in bowl; beat until stiff. Beat egg yolks until thick and light, beating in 1/3 cup sugar. Fold into egg whites; fold in flour. Pour over cherry mixture. Bake at 325 degrees for 45 minutes. Yield: 6 servings.

CHERRY COTTAGE PUDDING

3/4 c. sugar
1/4 c. shortening
1 egg
1 1/2 c. flour
2 tsp. baking powder
1/2 tsp. salt
1/2 c. milk
2 1/2 c. sour pitted cherries, drained
1/2 tsp. almond extract
1/2 c. chopped walnuts
Cherry Sauce

Cream sugar and shortening until fluffy. Beat in egg. Sift flour, baking powder and salt together; add to creamed mixture alternately with milk. Fold in cherries, almond extract and walnuts; pour into greased 8-inch square pan. Bake at 375 degrees for 45 minutes. Cut into squares; serve with Cherry Sauce.

Cherry Sauce

3/4 c. sugar
2 tbsp. cornstarch
1/2 tsp. salt
1 c. cherry juice
1/2 c. water
1/4 tsp. almond extract

Mix sugar, cornstarch and salt in saucepan. Stir in cherry juice, water and almond extract. Cook, stirring constantly, until thickened.

CHERRY-NUT DESSERT BREAD

1 8-oz. bottle maraschino cherries
3/4 c. butter or margarine
1 c. sugar
2 eggs
2 c. sifted flour
1/2 tsp. salt
1 tsp. baking powder
1/2 c. halved nuts
1 tsp. vanilla

Drain cherries, reserving syrup; add enough water to cherry syrup to equal 1 cup liquid. Cream butter and sugar; beat in eggs. Sift flour, salt and baking powder together; add to creamed mixture alternately with cherry liquid. Mix lightly; add nuts, cherries and vanilla, stirring only until mixed. Place in greased loaf pan. Bake at 350 degrees for 1 hour.

CHERRY TEA RING

1 pkg. yeast
1/4 c. warm water
3/4 c. lukewarm milk
1/4 c. sugar
1 tsp. salt
1 egg
1/4 c. shortening
4 c. (about) sifted flour
Soft butter
1/2 c. brown sugar
1/2 c. chopped pecans
1 1/2 c. drained cherries

Dissolve yeast in warm water in large bowl; add milk, sugar, salt, egg, shortening and 2 cups flour. Mix until smooth. Add enough flour to make soft easily handled dough. Knead until smooth. Place in greased bowl; cover. Let rise for 1 hour and 30 minutes or until doubled in bulk. Punch down; let rise for 30 minutes or until doubled again. Roll dough into 15 x 9-inch rectangle; spread with butter. Mix 1/2 cup flour, brown sugar, pecans and cherries; sprinkle over dough. Roll up tightly; seal edges. Place sealed edge down in ring on lightly greased baking sheet. Pinch ends together. Make cuts with scissors 2/3 through ring at 1-inch intervals; turn sections on sides. Let rise for 30 minutes or until doubled in bulk. Bake at 375 degrees for 25 minutes. Top with powdered sugar icing, if desired. Yield: 8-10 servings.

Chess Pie

DARK CHESS PIE

1 c. sugar
3 tbsp. cornmeal
3 tbsp. cocoa
3 eggs, well beaten
1/2 c. melted margarine
1/2 c. light corn syrup
1 tsp. vanilla
1 9-in. unbaked pie shell

Mix sugar, cornmeal and cocoa. Combine eggs, margarine, corn syrup and vanilla; add to sugar mixture. Stir until smooth; pour into pie shell. Bake at 350 degrees for 45 minutes or until filling tests done.

INDIVIDUAL CHESS PIES

1 recipe pie pastry
1 c. butter
1 c. sugar
3 eggs
1 c. chopped raisins
1 c. chopped walnuts
1 tsp. vanilla

Line 18 muffin tin cups with pastry. Cream butter and 7/8 cup sugar; beat in 2 eggs and 1 egg yolk. Stir in raisins, walnuts and vanilla; spoon into pastry-lined cups. Bake at 350 degrees for 25 minutes. Beat remaining egg white until stiff, beating in remaining sugar. Spoon small amount of meringue onto each tart; bake until meringue is lightly browned.

LEMON CHESS PIE

2 c. sugar
1 tbsp. cornmeal
2 tbsp. flour
2 tbsp. cornstarch
4 eggs, beaten
1/4 c. milk
1/4 c. lemon juice
1/2 c. melted butter
3 tbsp. grated lemon rind
1 9-in. unbaked pie shell

Combine sugar, cornmeal, flour and cornstarch; stir in eggs. Add milk, lemon juice, butter and lemon rind; mix well. Pour into pie shell. Bake at 400 degrees for 10 minutes. Reduce oven temperature to 350 degrees; bake for 30 minutes longer or until filling is firm and lightly browned.

OLD-FASHIONED CHESS PIE

2 c. sugar
2 tbsp. (heaping) flour
1 tbsp. (heaping) cornmeal
1/2 c. butter, melted
3 eggs, beaten
1/2 c. buttermilk
2 tsp. vanilla
1 10-in. unbaked pie shell

Mix sugar, flour and cornmeal; stir in butter, eggs, buttermilk and vanilla. Mix well; pour into pie shell. Bake at 425 degrees for 10 minutes. Reduce oven temperature to 325 degrees; bake for 30 minutes longer. Cover pie with foil, if necessary, to prevent burning. Yield: 6-8 servings.

Chicken

Chicken is a versatile food appreciated for its mild flavor and adaptability to a number of preparation methods. It is high in protein, niacin, and iron. Chicken is available year-round, but certain types have seasonal peaks.

AVAILABILITY: *Broiler-fryers* are available year-round with peak from May to September. *Roasters* are especially abundant from September to January. *Stewing* chickens are abundantly available from October to January. Cut up chickens and rolled chicken roasts are available year-round.

BUYING: Nearly all chicken sold today is examined and rated Grade A by government inspectors. Under the latest legislation, chicken-packing plants are continuously inspected. Whatever type chicken you desire choose one with a good fatty layer, which indicates tender meat. They should also have short legs, plump bodies, and unbruised skins.

STORING: Ready-to-cook whole chicken keeps in the refrigerator for 2-3 days; cut up chicken keeps 2 days. Giblets and liver should be used within 24 hours. To store, remove store wrapping, wash chicken, separate giblets and liver, and wrap chicken, liver, and giblets loosely in plastic wrap or foil. *To freeze* chicken, remove all wrapping and rinse under cold running water. Pat dry and wrap tightly in foil, transparent paper, or freezer wrap. Whole chickens may be frozen up to 1 year; cut up chicken for 6 months. Never freeze stuffed chicken. To store cooked chicken, remove stuffing and cooked meat. Cooked chicken with liquid may be refrigerated for 2 days or frozen for 6 months. Cooked poultry without liquid keeps in the refrigerator for 2 days and in the freezer for 1 month.

PREPARATION: Chicken may be roasted, grilled, broiled, fried, braised, or stewed. Follow recipe instructions.

SERVING: Chicken is served as a main dish by itself or in casseroles, in salads, as appetizers, or in sandwiches.

(See CARVING and POULTRY.)

CHICKEN NUGGETS

2 sm. whole chicken breasts
1/2 c. corn flake crumbs
1 tsp. salt
1/4 tsp. pepper
1/4 c. melted butter

Skin and bone chicken; cut into 1-inch chunks. Combine corn flake crumbs, salt and pepper. Dip chicken into butter; roll in crumb mixture. Arrange chicken in single layer on foil-lined baking sheet. Bake at 400 degrees for 30 minutes. Serve hot or cold.

CHICKEN-NUT PUFFS

1 c. chicken broth
1/2 c. salad oil
2 tsp. seasoned salt
1/8 tsp. cayenne pepper
1 tsp. celery seed
2 tsp. Worcestershire sauce
1 tbsp. parsley flakes
1 c. flour
4 eggs
1 1/2 c. minced cooked chicken
1/3 c. chopped toasted almonds

Combine chicken broth, oil, seasoned salt, cayenne pepper, celery seed, Worcestershire sauce and parsley flakes in saucepan; bring to a boil. Add flour; cook over low heat, stirring rapidly, until mixture leaves side of pan and forms smooth compact ball. Remove from heat; beat in eggs, one at a time. Beat with spoon until shiny; stir in chicken and almonds. Drop by 1/2 teaspoonfuls onto greased baking sheet. Bake at 450 degrees for 10 to 15 minutes. Serve hot. Yield: 20-25 servings.

CHOPPED CHICKEN LIVER SPREAD

1 lb. chicken livers
2 tbsp. butter
2 cloves of garlic
Salt to taste
4 hard-cooked eggs
1 med. onion
Pepper to taste

Brown chicken livers slowly in butter with garlic. Discard garlic. Sprinkle chicken livers with salt; cool. Quarter eggs and onion; grind chicken livers, eggs and onions through food chopper. Mix well; season with salt and pepper. Refrigerate for several hours. Serve with assorted crackers.

JET-SET CHICKEN FONDUE

Color photograph for this recipe on page 725.

Chicken wings
Oil
Peeled shrimp, deveined
Beef cubes

Parboil chicken wings; remove tips. Fill fondue pot 1/2 full with oil; heat to 375 degrees. Place pot on stand over high flame. Place chicken wings, shrimp and beef cubes on fondue forks; cook in oil to desired doneness.

Fondue Sauce

2 tbsp. corn oil
1 clove of garlic, minced
1/2 c. catsup
1/2 c. minced onion
2 tbsp. cider vinegar
1 tsp. salt
1 tsp. dry mustard
1 tsp. brown sugar
1/2 tsp. hot sauce

Mix all ingredients in small saucepan; bring to a boil over medium heat. Place in a bowl. Dip desired meat into sauce.

CHICKEN PUFFS

1 c. water
1 1/4 tsp. salt
1 c. butter or margarine
1 c. flour
4 eggs
1 1/2 c. diced celery
3 c. chopped cooked chicken
3 hard-cooked eggs, chopped
2 sweet pickles, chopped
Mayonnaise

Bring water and 1/4 teaspoon salt to a rolling boil; add butter. Stir until butter is melted. Add flour all at once; cook, stirring constantly, until mixture forms smooth ball. Remove from heat; beat in eggs, one at a time. Drop dough by small spoonfuls onto greased baking sheet, shaping dough into mounds. Bake at 450 degrees for 15 minutes. Reduce oven temperature to 325 degrees; bake for 20 minutes longer. Cool puffs on wire racks. Combine celery, chicken, hard-cooked eggs, pickles and remaining salt; moisten with mayonnaise. Cut tops from puffs; fill with chicken salad.

CHICKEN FINGER LOGS

1 3-oz. package cream cheese
2 c. ground cooked chicken
Chicken broth
1 loaf sliced bread
Butter or margarine

Soften cream cheese; add chicken and enough broth to make of spreading consistency. Trim crusts from bread; roll each slice thin with rolling pin. Spread bread with butter and chicken mixture; roll as for jelly roll. Place on baking sheet. Bake at 400 degrees until browned. Serve hot.

HOT CHICKEN CANAPES

1 can boned chicken
1/4 tsp. paprika
1 tsp. prepared mustard
1/2 tsp. Worcestershire sauce
3 drops of hot sauce
3 tbsp. sherry
1/2 c. mayonnaise
Small toast rounds or crackers

Drain chicken; chop fine. Mix chicken, seasonings, sherry and mayonnaise; pile onto toast rounds. Broil until bubbly.

INDIAN CHICKEN BALLS

1/2 lb. cream cheese
2 tbsp. mayonnaise
1 c. chopped cooked chicken
1 c. chopped blanched almonds
1 tbsp. chopped chutney
1/2 tsp. salt
1 tbsp. curry powder
1/2 grated coconut

Blend cream cheese and mayonnaise; add chicken, almonds, chutney, salt and curry powder. Shape into walnut-sized balls; roll in coconut. Chill for several hours before serving.

LIVER PATE

1 tbsp. flour
1/2 tsp. paprika
1/2 tsp. powdered rosemary
1 tsp. garlic salt
1 lb. chicken livers
1/4 c. butter
3/4 c. dry vermouth

Combine flour and seasonings; dredge chicken livers in flour mixture. Melt butter in skillet; saute chicken livers until golden. Add 1/2 cup vermouth. Cover; simmer until chicken livers are tender. Add remaining vermouth; cool. Process mixture in blender until smooth. Spoon into dish; refrigerate for several hours before serving. Serve with assorted crackers. Yield: 2 cups.

CHICKEN NIBBLERS

2 lb. chicken wings
1 sm. onion
2 stalks celery
1 tsp. salt
1/4 tsp. pepper
2 tbsp. honey
1 c. flour
2 c. shortening

Place chicken wings, onion, celery, salt and pepper in saucepan; add water to cover. Cook for 30 minutes; cool. Disjoint wings, discarding tips; cool. Combine 6 tablespoons water and honey. Dip wing pieces into water mixture; roll in flour. Let stand for at least 2 hours. Heat shortening in skillet; fry wing pieces until brown. Yield: 4 servings.

TASTY CHICKEN CANAPES

2 cans chicken spread
1 tbsp. minced onion
1 tbsp. diced pimento
Mayonnaise
Assorted crackers
Sliced stuffed olives

Combine chicken spread, onion and pimento; moisten with mayonnaise. Spread chicken mixture on crackers; top with olives.

BAKED CHICKEN SALAD

2 c. chopped cooked chicken
4 hard-boiled eggs, chopped
2 c. diced celery
1/2 c. chopped toasted almonds
1/2 tsp. salt
2 tbsp. grated onion
2 tbsp. lemon juice
1 c. mayonnaise
1 c. crushed potato chips
1/2 c. grated cheese

Combine chicken, eggs, celery, almonds, salt, onion and lemon juice in bowl; fold in mayonnaise. Turn into greased casserole; top with potato chips and cheese. Bake at 450 degrees for about 12 minutes or until salad is bubbly and cheese is melted. Yield: 6 servings.

CHICKEN SALAD WITH BACON

Color photograph for this recipe on page 315.

1 sm. head iceberg lettuce
1 sm. red pepper
1 cucumber
1 c. small whole mushrooms
2 c. cooked chicken pieces
2 hard-boiled eggs, quartered
4 slices crispy fried bacon
2 tbsp. wine vinegar
6 tbsp. salad oil
Salt to taste
1/4 c. mashed Roquefort cheese

Tear lettuce into large pieces; place in salad bowl. Cut red pepper into small chunks. Chop cucumber coarsely. Add red pepper, cucumber, mushrooms and chicken to lettuce; toss lightly. Garnish salad with eggs and bacon. Blend remaining ingredients together; serve with salad.

CHINESE CHICKEN SALAD

3 c. diced cooked chicken
1 can bean sprouts, well drained
2 c. finely chopped celery
1/2 c. thinly sliced water chestnuts
1/2 c. chopped green pepper
Salt and pepper to taste
1/4 c. French dressing
Mayonnaise
Lettuce
Sliced stuffed olives

Combine chicken, bean sprouts, celery, chestnuts, green pepper, salt and pepper in large bowl. Pour French dressing over salad; mix lightly. Chill for several hours. Add just enough mayonnaise to moisten; toss lightly. Spoon onto lettuce-lined plate; garnish with olives. Yield: 4 servings.

CHICKEN SALAD IN CRANBERRY RING

2 c. cranberry juice
2 pkg. cherry or lemon gelatin
1 c. ginger ale
2 c. diced cooked chicken
1 1/2 c. cooked rice
1 c. sliced celery
1 c. cooked peas
1 tsp. salt
1/2 tsp. curry powder
1/2 c. French dressing
1/2 c. sour cream
Lettuce

Combine 1 cup water and cranberry juice in saucepan; bring to a boil. Add gelatin; stir until dissolved. Add ginger ale; pour into 1 1/2-quart ring mold. Chill until firm. Combine chicken, rice, celery and peas in bowl; chill. Mix salt, curry powder, French dressing and sour cream; fold into chicken mixture. Unmold cranberry ring onto platter of lettuce; spoon salad into ring.

MOLDED CHICKEN SALAD

1 env. unflavored gelatin
1/4 c. cold water
3/4 c. mayonnaise
1/4 c. chicken broth
2 c. minced cooked chicken
1/2 c. minced celery
1/4 c. minced pimento

Soften gelatin in cold water in top of double boiler. Stir over boiling water until gelatin is dissolved. Blend mayonnaise and chicken broth into gelatin; add chicken, celery and pimento. Turn into pan or salad molds. Refrigerate until firm. Yield: 6 servings.

SOUTH SEAS SALAD

1 green pepper, minced
1 onion, minced
1/8 tsp. hot sauce
Juice of 1 lemon
1 coconut, grated
3 c. minced cooked chicken

Combine all ingredients in bowl; mix well. Cover; refrigerate for at least 3 hours before serving. Yield: 6 servings.

CHICKEN CONDIMENT SALAD

2/3 c. chopped toasted California walnuts
2 c. cubed cooked chicken
1/4 c. finely chopped celery
2 tbsp. chopped green onion
2 tbsp. chopped raisins
2 tbsp. chopped chutney
1/4 c. mayonnaise
1/4 tsp. salt
2 tsp. lemon juice
Crisp lettuce
4 slices tomato
4 slices pineapple
Toasted walnut halves

Combine walnuts, chicken, celery and onion. Stir raisins, chutney, mayonnaise, salt and lemon juice together. Fold into chicken mixture. Arrange lettuce on 4 individual chilled salad plates. Arrange tomato slices on lettuce; top with pineapple slice. Spoon chicken salad over each pineapple slice. Garnish with toasted walnut halves. Serve with additional mayonnaise if desired. Yield: 4 servings.

Chicken Condiment Salad . . . A chicken and walnut salad tops tomato halves and pineapple.

ORIENTAL CHICKEN SALAD

1 sm. can mandarin oranges
3 c. chopped cooked chicken
1 c. chopped celery
Salt and pepper
1/8 tsp. ginger
1 tsp. soy sauce
Mayonnaise
2 c. chow mein noodles

Drain oranges well. Combine oranges, chicken and celery in bowl; sprinkle with salt, pepper, ginger and soy sauce. Moisten to taste with mayonnaise; chill for several hours. Spread 1/2 cup noodles in 4 salad bowls; spoon salad over noodles.

WAIKIKI CHICKEN SALAD

1 3/4 c. pineapple chunks
3 c. chopped cooked chicken
2 c. diced celery
2 tbsp. diced pimento
1/4 c. toasted slivered almonds
1 c. mayonnaise
3/4 tsp. salt
Grated rind and juice of 1 lime

Drain pineapple. Combine pineapple, chicken, celery, pimento and almonds in large bowl; chill. Blend mayonnaise, salt, lime rind and juice. Pour over salad just before serving; toss lightly.

TOSSED CHICKEN SALAD

3 1/2 c. diced cooked chicken
1 lge. onion, thinly sliced
1 sm. head lettuce, shredded
3 tomatoes
1/2 c. olive oil
1/4 c. tarragon vinegar
1 tsp. salt
1/2 tsp. pepper

Combine chicken, onion and lettuce in salad bowl. Peel tomatoes; cut into thin wedges. Arrange tomatoes on salad. Mix oil, vinegar, salt and pepper; pour over salad. Toss lightly; serve immediately. Yield: 6 servings.

CHICKEN-BACON SANDWICHES

3 c. minced cooked chicken
2 c. minced celery
3 hard-boiled eggs, chopped
Salt and pepper
1 c. crumbled cooked bacon
1/3 c. chopped sweet pickles
Mayonnaise
White bread slices
Whole wheat bread slices
Shedded lettuce

Combine chicken, celery, eggs, salt, pepper, bacon and pickles; moisten with mayonnaise. Trim crusts from bread. Spread chicken mixture on white bread slices; add lettuce. Top with whole wheat bread; press down lightly. Cut sandwiches in half diagonally.

COUNTRY CHICKEN SANDWICHES

1 stewing chicken
1/2 tsp. monosodium glutamate
2 tsp. salt
Dash of pepper
1 doz. buttered buns

Place chicken in large kettle. Cover with boiling water; bring to a rapid boil. Reduce heat; simmer for 3 hours or until tender. Drain; reserve broth. Cool chicken. Cut chicken from bones in small pieces. Combine chicken, broth and seasonings in bowl; chill. Drain chicken; fill buns. Wrap in foil. Bake at 300 degrees until heated through. Yield: 12 sandwiches.

HEARTY BAKED SANDWICHES

1 c. diced cooked chicken
3/4 c. diced celery
1/4 c. chopped walnuts
1/2 tsp. minced onion
1 tbsp. lemon juice
1/4 tsp. salt
1/4 c. mayonnaise
4 slices bread
1/2 c. crushed potato chips

Preheat oven to 425 degrees. Combine chicken, celery, walnuts, onion, lemon juice, salt and mayonnaise. Place bread on cookie sheet; toast on 1 side. Turn bread; spread chicken mixture on untoasted side. Sprinkle with potato chips. Bake for 12 minutes. Yield: 4 servings.

HOT OPEN-FACED CHICKEN SANDWICHES

1 5-oz. can boned chicken
1 can mushroom soup
1 pkg. hamburger buns

Preheat broiler to 350 degrees. Turn chicken into bowl; shred with fork. Stir soup into chicken. Split buns; place on baking sheet. Spread chicken mixture on buns. Broil for 15 minutes or until bubbly and lightly browned. Yield: 8 servings.

HOMEMADE CHICKEN-NOODLE SOUP

1 frying chicken, disjointed
1 carrot, diced
1 stalk celery, diced
1 onion, diced
3 peppercorns
2 beef bouillon cubes
1 tbsp. salt
Juice of 1/2 lemon
1 pkg. fine noodles

Place chicken in large kettle; add carrot, celery, onion, peppercorns, bouillon cubes, salt, lemon juice and 2 quarts cold water. Bring to a boil; reduce heat. Cover; simmer until chicken is tender. Break noodles into 1-inch pieces; add to broth. Cook for 15 minutes longer or until noodles are done. Yield: 6 servings.

CHICKEN-CORN SOUP

1 c. canned corn
1/2 c. minced celery
1 c. minced cooked chicken
4 c. chicken broth
2 c. hot milk
2 egg yolks, lightly beaten
2 tbsp. butter
Salt and pepper to taste

Heat corn; force through coarse sieve. Combine celery, chicken and broth in saucepan; bring to a boil. Reduce heat; cover. Simmer for 15 minutes. Stir hot milk into egg yolks gradually; add to soup mixture. Cook for 2 minutes, stirring constantly. Add butter, salt and pepper. Serve with croutons. Yield: 8 servings.

CHICKEN-POTATO SOUP

2 tbsp. margarine
1 tbsp. minced onion
1 can clear chicken broth
1 can boned chicken
3 potatoes, chopped
1/4 c. evaporated milk

Melt margarine in deep saucepan. Add onion; cook until onion is tender but not brown. Add chicken broth, chicken and potatoes; cover. Cook for 25 minutes or until potatoes are tender. Add milk. Mash 1 or 2 pieces potato with spoon; stir well. Yield: 3 servings.

CREAMY CHICKEN SOUP

6 tbsp. butter or margarine
1/3 c. flour
3 c. chicken broth
1/2 c. milk
1/2 c. light cream
1 c. finely chopped cooked chicken
Dash of pepper

Melt butter in saucepan; blend in flour. Stir in chicken broth, milk and cream. Cook over low heat, stirring constantly, until thickened and boiling. Add chicken and pepper; return to a boil. Serve immediately. Yield: 4 servings.

Arroz Con Pollo . . . A chicken casserole that is a popular Spanish dish, will delight your family.

ITALIAN CHICKEN-NOODLE SOUP

1 env. dry chicken-noodle soup mix
3 c. water
1/2 c. canned tomatoes
1/4 tsp. oregano

Combine soup mix and water in saucepan; bring to a boil. Reduce heat; cover loosely. Simmer for 7 minutes, stirring occasionally. Add tomatoes and oregano; heat through. Yield: 4 servings.

ARROZ CON POLLO

1 broiling chicken, disjointed
1 tsp. monosodium glutamate
1 1/2 tsp. salt
1/2 tsp. paprika
1/4 c. olive oil
1 med. onion, chopped
1 20-oz. can tomatoes
1 1-lb. can peas
2 bouillon cubes
1/4 tsp. saffron
1 1/2 c. rice

Sprinkle chicken with monosodium glutamate, 1 teaspoon salt and paprika. Brown in hot oil in skillet. Remove chicken to baking dish with tight-fitting lid. Add onion to skillet; cook until tender. Drain juice from tomatoes and peas; reserve. Add enough water to reserved juice to make 3 cups liquid. Stir liquid into skillet, scraping brown particles from bottom of pan. Add bouillon cubes, saffron and remaining salt. Bring to a boil. Pour over chicken. Sprinkle rice around chicken, stirring to moisten. Add tomatoes. Cover tightly. Bake in 350-degree oven for 25 minutes. Uncover; toss rice. Add peas; cover. Bake for 10 minutes longer. Yield: 6 servings.

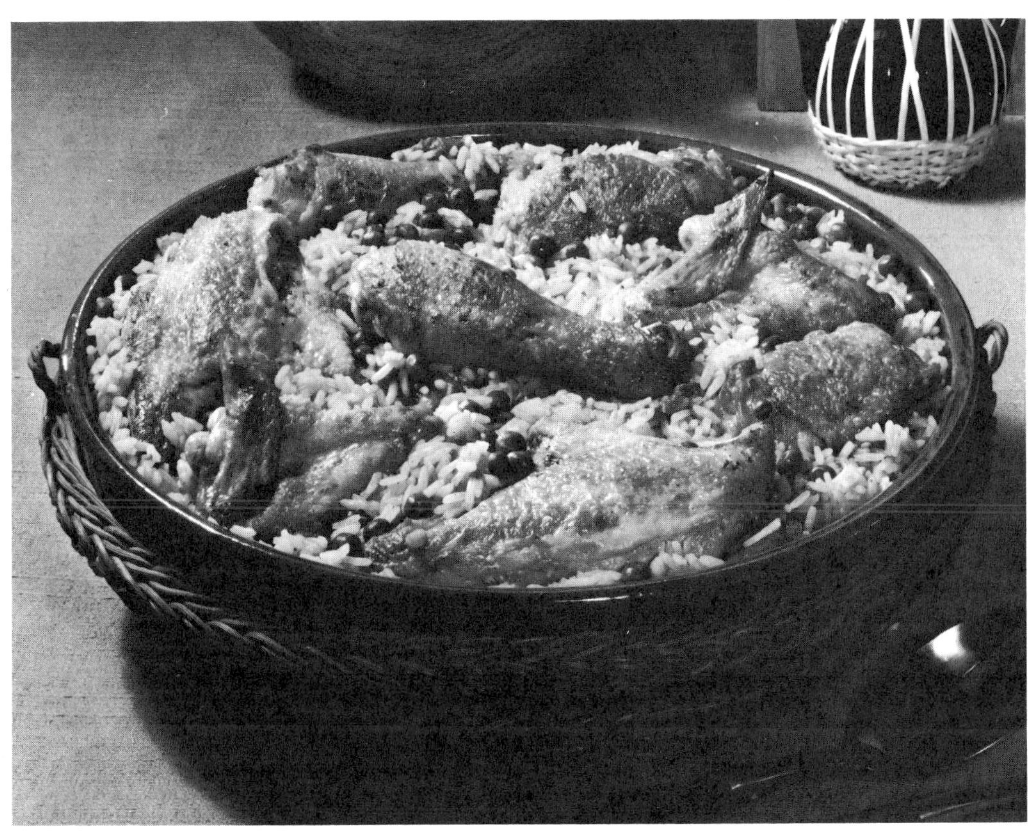

CHICKEN CACCIATORE

1 c. cooking sherry
2 cloves of garlic, chopped
1 3 1/2-lb. chicken, disjointed
Salt and pepper
Flour
2 c. minced onions
1 1/2 c. minced green peppers
1/2 tsp. white pepper
1 1/2 tsp. curry powder
1 1/2 tsp. powdered thyme
1 No. 303 can tomatoes
1 tsp. chopped parsley
Rice ring
1 c. sliced toasted almonds

Mix sherry and 1 clove of garlic; add chicken. Marinate in refrigerator for 2 hours. Drain; reserve marinade. Season chicken with salt and pepper; roll in flour. Fry in hot oil until golden brown; place in roasting pan. Combine onions, green peppers and remaining garlic; saute in 1/4 cup oil until tender. Stir in 1 teaspoon salt, white pepper, curry powder, thyme, tomatoes, parsley and reserved marinade; heat through. Pour over chicken; cover. Bake at 350 degrees for 40 minutes or until tender. Place chicken in center of 9-inch rice ring; cover with sauce. Sprinkle almonds over top. Yield: 6 servings.

CHICKEN DIVAN

1 10-oz. package frozen broccoli spears
2 c. diced cooked chicken
1 can cream of chicken soup
1/3 c. milk
1/2 c. shredded Cheddar cheese

Cook broccoli according to package directions; drain. Arrange broccoli in shallow baking dish; top with chicken. Blend soup and milk; pour over top. Sprinkle with cheese. Bake at 450 degrees for 10 minutes or until lightly browned. Yield: 4 servings.

CHICKEN FLORENTINE

2 pkg. frozen spinach
Butter
3 tbsp. flour
1 c. milk
1/2 c. cream
Salt and pepper
1/4 tsp. nutmeg
12 slices cooked chicken
Grated Parmesan cheese

Cook spinach according to package directions; drain well, pressing out as much moisture as possible. Melt 3 tablespoons butter in saucepan; blend in flour. Add milk and cream slowly. Cook over low heat, stirring constantly, until smooth and thickened. Season sauce with salt, pepper and nutmeg. Combine spinach and 1/2 cup sauce in saucepan; heat through gently. Spoon spinach into baking dish; arrange chicken over spinach. Stir about 3 tablespoons cheese into remaining sauce; pour over chicken. Sprinkle lightly with cheese; dot with butter. Broil until top is lightly browned. Yield: 6 servings.

CHICKEN ORIENTAL

1 5-lb. chicken, disjointed
1/2 c. soy sauce
1/4 c. honey
1 clove of garlic, minced
1/4 tsp. ginger
1/2 tsp. dry mustard
1/2 c. thinly sliced green onions

Arrange chicken, skin side down, in single layer in baking dish; cover. Bake at 350 degrees for 2 hours. Combine soy sauce, honey, garlic, ginger and mustard. Drain most of the drippings from baking pan; turn chicken. Spoon sauce over chicken. Cover; bake for 40 minutes longer. Uncover; bake until chicken is browned. Sprinkle chicken with onions; serve hot. Yield: 8 servings.

CHICKEN PEPE

1 pkg. tortillas
Oil
2 c. chopped cooked chicken
1 can cream of chicken soup
1/2 c. milk
1 can chopped green chilies
1/2 c. chopped onion
12 oz. Cheddar cheese, grated

Fry tortillas quickly in hot oil in skillet until soft. Combine chicken, soup, milk and chilies. Place layer of tortillas in greased 13 x 9 x 2-inch pan. Layer chicken mixture, onion, cheese and remaining tortillas in pan, ending with cheese. Bake at 350 degrees until heated through. Yield: 8 servings.

CHICKEN TONAK

1/2 c. butter or margarine
2 2-lb. chickens, disjointed
1 lge. onion, sliced
1/2 c. tomato juice
1/2 c. sherry
1 tbsp. paprika
1 tsp. salt
Pepper to taste

Heat butter in large skillet; brown chicken well on all sides. Transfer chicken to baking dish. Saute onion in skillet drippings; stir in 1 cup water, tomato juice, sherry, paprika, salt and pepper. Mix well; bring to a boil. Pour over chicken. Bake, uncovered, at 400 degrees for 1 hour and 15 minutes, turning chicken several times.

COQ AU VIN

1 sprig of parsley
1/2 tsp. peppercorns
1 bay leaf
1 sprig of thyme
1 clove of garlic, crushed
1/3 c. flour
1 tsp. salt
1/4 tsp. pepper
2 frying chickens, disjointed
1/4 c. butter
1 tbsp. salad oil
1/4 c. cognac
2 1/2 c. Burgundy
6 sm. whole onions
1/2 lb. mushroom cups

Tie parsley, peppercorns, bay leaf, thyme and garlic in small cloth bag. Combine flour, salt and pepper; dredge chicken in seasoned flour. Heat butter and oil in skillet; brown chicken on all sides. Heat cognac; pour over chicken. Ignite; let flame subside. Arrange chicken in large baking dish; add herb bag. Add 1 cup hot water to skillet dripping; stir to loosen browned bits. Remove from heat; stir in Burgundy. Pour over chicken; cover baking dish. Bake at 325 degrees for 30 minutes. Saute onions and mushrooms in small amount additional butter. Add to chicken. Bake, covered, for 2 hours longer. Remove herb bag; arrange chicken and vegetables in serving dish. Thicken sauce if desired and serve over chicken. Yield: 8 servings.

ROAST CHICKEN IN A BAG

1 5-lb. roasting chicken
1 lemon, halved
1/4 c. butter, softened
1 1/2 tsp. salt
1/2 tsp. pepper
Paprika
1/2 c. cooking oil
1 recipe stuffing

Rub chicken inside and out with lemon. Combine butter, salt and pepper. Rub chicken with butter mixture, coating back lightly and coating breast and thighs heavily. Sprinkle with paprika; chill. Pour oil into brown paper bag; shake until bag is well oiled. Place bag in baking pan. Stuff chicken lightly with stuffing. Place chicken in oiled bag, breast side up. Twist end of bag shut; tie with cord or wire. Bake at 325 degrees for 4 hours. Do not open bag while baking.

CHICKEN STUFFED WITH RICE

3/4 c. cream of mushroom soup
1 c. chicken broth
1 c. instant rice
Salt to taste
1/4 c. butter or margarine
2 3-lb. chickens
2 tbsp. thinly slivered orange peel
1/4 c. orange juice
1/2 c. light corn syrup
1/4 tsp. ginger
1/2 tsp. monosodium glutamate

Combine soup, chicken broth, rice, salt and butter in saucepan; cover. Cook according to package directions for rice; let stand for 15 minutes. Stuff chickens loosely with part of the rice mixture; place in shallow roasting pan. Bake at 350 degrees for 1 hour. Spoon remaining rice mixture around chickens; bake for 30 minutes. Combine orange peel, orange juice, corn syrup, ginger and monosodium glutamate; brush on chickens. Bake for 15 minutes longer; let chickens stand for about 15 minutes before carving.

HERBED ROAST CHICKEN

1 2 1/2 to 3-lb. chicken
2 carrots, sliced
Thyme
Salt
Butter
3 slices bacon
Paprika
1/2 c. beef bouillon
1/4 c. water
Juice of 1 lemon

Prepare chicken for baking. Combine carrots, 1 teaspoon thyme, 1/2 teaspoon salt and 1 tablespoon butter; stuff chicken with carrot mixture. Tie legs and wings to body; place in shallow roasting pan. Place bacon over breast. Dot chicken with butter; sprinkle with salt, paprika and thyme. Bake at 450 degrees for 15 minutes or until lightly browned. Reduce oven temperature to 350 degrees; bake for 1 hour and 45 minutes longer. Mix bouillon and water; spoon over chicken every 15 minutes while baking. Place chicken on hot platter. Add lemon juice to drippings. Scrape up browned bits in pan, stirring well. Heat; season to taste. Serve gravy with chicken. Yield: 3-4 servings.

CHICKEN L'ORANGE

Color photograph for this recipe on page 66.

2 fryers
Salt
6 oranges
3 sprigs of tarragon
1 garlic clove, cut in half
1/4 c. sugar
1/4 c. red wine vinegar
2 c. chicken stock
4 peppercorns
1 tbsp. cornstarch
Watercress

Sprinkle cavity of each chicken with 1/2 teaspoon salt; hook wing tips into back. Remove peel of 1 orange with vegetable peeler. Cut peel into long strips; reserve for sauce. Squeeze juice from 4 oranges; reserve juice for sauce. Cut 2 of the squeezed oranges into small chunks. Fill each chicken cavity with orange chunks and 1 sprig of tarragon. Tie legs together with string; tie legs and tail together. Rub each chicken with garlic; place chickens in shallow roasting pan. Bake in 375-degree oven for 30 minutes per pound. Stir sugar and vinegar together in saucepan; bring to boiling point, stirring until sugar is dissolved. Reduce heat; simmer for about 5 minutes or until thickened. Add chicken stock, remaining tarragon, peppercorns and s taste; bring to a boil. Reduce heat; simmer for a 10 minutes. Add reserved orange juice. Strain s into bowl; add reserved orange peel. Baste chickens frequently with sauce during last 30 minutes of baking. Remove chickens from pan onto heated serving platter; remove string and cavity filling. Stir small amount of water into cornstarch; stir into remaining orange sauce in saucepan. Cook, stirring constantly, until clear and thickened. Garnish chickens with slices of remaining oranges and watercress; serve with sauce. Yield: 8 servings.

PRESIDENT'S BARBECUED CHICKEN

Color photograph for this recipe on page 74.

1 c. butter
3/4 c. lemon juice
2 tsp. garlic salt
2 tbsp. paprika
2 tsp. dried leaf oregano
4 fryers, halved
3 tsp. salt
1/2 tsp. pepper

Melt butter in small saucepan; stir in lemon juice, garlic salt, paprika and oregano. Place chickens in shallow dish; sprinkle with salt and pepper. Pour marinade over chickens; cover. Marinate for 3 to 4 hours at room temperature, turning occasionally. Drain, reserving marinade. Place chicken, skin side up, on grill set 3 to 6 inches from charcoal briquets that have reached light gray ash stage. Brush generously with reserved marinade. Cook for 45 minutes to 1 hour and 15 minutes or until tender, turning and brushing with marinade occasionally. Leg should twist easily out of thigh joint and pieces should feel tender when probed with fork when chicken is done. Yield: 8 servings.

BARBECUED CHICKEN

1 frying chicken, disjointed
Seasoned flour
1 lge. onion, sliced
1/2 clove of garlic, minced
1/4 c. catsup
2 tbsp. Worcestershire sauce
1 1/4 tsp. salt
1 lemon, thinly sliced
1/2 tbsp. sugar
1/2 tbsp. butter
Dash of pepper
1/3 c. vinegar
1 can tomato soup
1 c. water

Dredge chicken in seasoned flour; brown in hot fat. Mix remaining ingredients; pour into baking pan. Add chicken. Bake at 350 degrees for 1 hour or until chicken is tender, basting occasionally. Yield: 4 servings.

CHICKEN ON A GRILL

1 broiling chicken, disjointed
5 tbsp. A-1 sauce
1 8-oz. can tomato sauce
2 tbsp. brown sugar
2 tbsp. salad oil
1 c. melted butter

Place chicken in baking pan; cover. Bake at 350 degrees for 30 minutes. Mix A-1 sauce, tomato sauce, brown sugar and oil. Place hot chicken on charcoal grill; cook until almost done, turning and basting with butter. Cook for 10 minutes longer, basting with tomato sauce mixture. Yield: 4 servings.

BARBECUED CHICKEN-LITTLE LEGS

Color photograph for this recipe on page 723.

3 lb. chicken wings
1/2 c. salad oil
1/2 c. lemon juice
1 clove of garlic, crushed
1 tsp. salt
1/8 tsp. pepper
1/2 c. chopped pimento-stuffed olives

Cut wings at both joints; discard tips. Combine disjointed wing pieces with remaining ingredients. Marinate for several hours or overnight in refrigerator, stirring occasionally. Arrange wing pieces on rack in shallow roasting pan. Bake in 450-degree oven for 35 to 45 minutes or until crisp and browned. Spoon marinade over wings several times during baking time.

OUTDOOR-BARBECUED CHICKEN

3/4 c. chopped onion
1/2 c. cooking oil
3/4 c. catsup
3/4 c. water
3 tbsp. Worcestershire sauce
2 tsp. salt
1/2 tsp. pepper
1/3 c. lemon juice
3 tbsp. sugar
2 tbsp. prepared mustard
2 1 1/2-lb. chickens, split

Cook onion in oil until soft; add remaining ingredients except chickens. Simmer for 15 minutes. Brush sauce on both sides of chickens. Place chickens on grill, skin side up, 6 to 8 inches from coals. Cook for 20 minutes, brushing with sauce frequently; turn. Cook until chickens are tender. Serve with remaining sauce. Yield: 4 servings.

GRILLED CHICKEN WITH SPICED SAUCE

Color photograph for this recipe on page 77.

1 broiler chicken
Salt and pepper to taste
2 tbsp. butter
1 tbsp. soy sauce
Juice of 1/2 lemon

Rub chicken with salt and pepper; place on rack in broiler pan. Broil about 5 inches from source of heat until chicken is tender. Melt butter in saucepan; add soy sauce and lemon juice. Bring to a boil. Add about 1/2 cup water; bring to a boil again. Arrange chicken on heated platter. Garnish with green pepper rings if desired. Serve sauce over chicken or in sauceboat.

PAPER BAG-BARBECUED CHICKEN

1/4 c. catsup
1/4 c. white vinegar
1/4 c. Worcestershire sauce
1/4 c. lemon juice
1 tbsp. chili powder
1 tbsp. mustard
1 tbsp. salt
1 tbsp. paprika
1/3 c. water
Dash of pepper
1/4 c. butter
2 frying chickens, disjointed

Combine all ingredients except chicken in saucepan; stir over low heat until butter is melted. Place chicken in large brown paper bag; pour sauce in bag. Roll top of bag down; secure with paper clips. Place in large pan or roaster; cover. Bake at 500 degrees for 15 minutes. Reduce oven temperature to 350 degrees; bake for 1 hour and 15 minutes longer.

BRAISED CHICKEN

1 broiling chicken, halved
Salt and pepper to taste
Celery salt
Onion salt
Garlic salt
1/4 c. butter or margarine
Juice of 1 lemon
1/2 tsp. Worcestershire sauce
1/4 c. water

Season chicken with salt and pepper. Sprinkle generously with celery salt; sprinkle lightly with onion salt and garlic salt. Melt butter in heavy skillet; brown chicken slowly on both sides. Add lemon juice, Worcestershire sauce and water; cover tightly. Simmer for 45 minutes or until chicken is tender. Yield: 2 servings.

CHICKEN INDIENNE

4 broiling chickens, split
Salt and pepper to taste
Butter
1 c. salad oil
6 tbsp. vinegar
2 sm. cloves of garlic, minced
1 c. minced Indian chutney

Season chicken with salt and pepper; rub with softened butter. Place, skin side down, in broiler pan. Combine oil, vinegar, garlic and chutney. Broil chicken for 8 minutes, basting with melted butter and chutney mixture. Turn chicken; broil until golden brown. Turn oven control to bake position;

set temperature to 300 degrees. Bake chicken until tender, basting frequently. Yield: 8 servings.

CHICKEN KABOBS

10 to 12 chicken breasts
1/2 c. soy sauce
2/3 c. salad oil
1/4 c. sugar
2 tbsp. sherry
1/2 tsp. monosodium glutamate
1 clove of garlic, minced
3 green peppers, cut into sq.
2 3-oz. cans whole mushrooms
1 No. 303 can pineapple chunks

Remove bones from chicken; cut chicken in 1-inch squares. Combine soy sauce, salad oil, sugar, sherry, monosodium glutamate and garlic; add chicken. Marinate for about 1 hour. Drain; reserve marinade. Alternate chicken, green peppers, mushrooms and pineapple on miniature skewers; brush with reserved marinade. Broil about 4 inches from heat for 20 to 25 minutes, brushing with marinade and turning frequently. Yield: 15 servings.

GOLDEN-BROILED CHICKEN

3 tbsp. butter
1 2-lb. chicken, disjointed
1 1/2 tsp. salt
1/4 c. honey
1/4 c. prepared mustard
1 tbsp. lemon juice

Melt butter in foil-lined 13 x 9 x 2-inch pan. Place chicken in butter, skin side down; sprinkle with 1/2 teaspoon salt. Blend remaining salt, honey, mustard and lemon juice. Brush half the honey mixture on chicken. Bake at 350 degrees for 30 minutes. Turn chicken; brush with remaining honey mixture. Bake for 30 minutes longer or until tender. Yield: 4 servings.

CHICKEN A LA KING

1/4 c. butter
3 tbsp. flour
1/2 tsp. salt
1/8 tsp. pepper
1 c. chicken broth
1 c. light cream
2 c. chopped cooked chicken
1/4 c. chopped pimento

Melt butter in heavy 2-quart saucepan; stir in flour, salt and pepper. Remove from heat; stir in chicken broth gradually. Add cream. Cook, stirring constantly, until thickened. Add chicken and pimento. Heat to serving temperature; serve immediately over toast or in patty shells.

CHICKEN ADOBO

1 lb. chicken thighs
1 lb. pork
1 clove of garlic
1/8 tsp. pepper
1/4 c. vinegar
1 bay leaf
1 c. broth or water
2 tbsp. salad oil

Cut chicken and pork into small pieces; place in saucepan. Add garlic, pepper, vinegar, bay leaf and broth. Simmer until chicken and pork are tender. Remove chicken and pork from broth with slotted spoon; drain on paper towels. Heat oil in heavy skillet; brown chicken and pork well. Strain broth into skillet; simmer until broth is almost evaporated. Serve over rice, if desired.

CHICKEN BREASTS SUPREME

1 4-oz. package dried beef
3 chicken breasts
3 slices bacon, halved
1 can cream of mushroom soup
1 c. sour cream

Rinse dried beef to remove salt; place in 9 x 13-inch baking dish. Bone, skin and halve chicken breasts. Place chicken over beef; place bacon on chicken. Bake, uncovered, at 350 degrees for 30 minutes. Combine soup and sour cream in saucepan; stir over low heat until blended. Pour soup mixture over chicken; bake for 45 minutes to 1 hour longer.

CHICKEN JUBILEE

1 2 1/2 to 3-lb. chicken
2 med. onions, chopped
1 clove of garlic, chopped
1 lge. green pepper, chopped
3 tbsp. butter
1 No. 2 can tomatoes
1 tsp. salt
1 tsp. pepper
1 tsp. thyme
1 tsp. curry powder
1/2 c. currants
1/4 lb. chopped toasted almonds

Disjoint chicken; place in kettle. Add water to cover; bring to a boil. Reduce heat; cover and simmer until chicken is tender. Reserve chicken broth; cut chicken from bones in small pieces. Saute onions, garlic and green pepper in butter in large saucepan. Add reserved broth, tomatoes and seasonings; bring to a boil. Reduce heat; simmer for 40 minutes, stirring occasionally. Add chicken and currants; simmer until heated through. Turn into serving dish; sprinkle with almonds. Serve with rice or wild rice. Yield: 8 servings.

CHICKEN KIEV

3 12 to 14-oz. chicken breasts
Salt and pepper to taste
1/4 c. minced onion
3 tbsp. minced parsley
1 1/4 c. butter
2 eggs, lightly beaten
3 tbsp. milk
1/3 c. flour
1 c. fine dry bread crumbs

Bone and halve chicken breasts. Place each piece of chicken between 2 sheets of waxed paper; pound with flat side of meat mallet until thin. Sprinkle each side with salt and pepper. Saute onion and parsley in 2 tablespoons butter. Place 2 tablespoons butter and part of the onion mixture in center of each piece of chicken. Tuck in short ends; fold long ends over. Secure with wooden picks. Mix eggs and milk. Roll chicken in flour; dip into egg mixture. Roll in bread crumbs. Dip into egg mixture and roll in bread crumbs again. Melt remaining butter in skillet. Add chicken, seam side down; fry for about 7 minutes. Turn; fry for about 7 minutes longer. Place skillet in oven. Bake at 500 degrees for 10 minutes. Remove picks; serve immediately.

CHICKEN CHOW MEIN

3 tbsp. butter
2 tbsp. minced onion
1/2 lb. lean pork, diced
2 1/2 tbsp. flour
2 1/2 c. chicken stock
3/4 c. diced celery
2 1/2 c. diced cooked chicken
3/4 c. canned mushrooms
2 tbsp. soy sauce
3/4 c. slivered blanched almonds

Melt butter in large skillet over low heat. Add onion, cook for 2 minutes. Add pork; cook until pork is browned on all sides. Blend in flour; stir in chicken stock. Add celery, chicken and mushrooms; simmer for about 15 minutes. Add soy sauce and almonds. Serve over crisp noodles. Yield: 10 servings.

CHICKEN DIJON

2 tbsp. butter
1 3-lb. chicken, quartered
2 c. dry white wine
1/4 tsp. dried tarragon
Pinch of thyme
1 bay leaf
1/4 tsp. salt
1/4 tsp. pepper
2 egg yolks, beaten
2 tbsp. sour cream
2 tbsp. Dijon mustard
Pinch of cayenne pepper

Melt butter in frypan; add chicken. Cook until browned well on all sides. Add wine, tarragon, thyme, bay leaf, salt and pepper. Bring to a boil. Cover; simmer for 45 minutes or until chicken is tender. Remove chicken to heated serving dish; keep warm. Discard bay leaf. Blend sauce with egg yolks; add sour cream, mustard and cayenne pepper. Heat through, stirring constantly; do not boil. Pour over chicken. Yield: 4 servings.

CHICKEN PAPRIKA

Flour
1 tsp. salt
1/4 tsp. pepper
2 3-lb. chickens, disjointed
2 tbsp. cooking oil
1 lge. onion, thinly sliced
3 tbsp. paprika
2 c. sour cream

Combine 1 cup flour, salt and pepper; dredge chicken in seasoned flour. Heat oil in Dutch oven; brown chicken in oil. Add onion, paprika and 1 1/2 cups water; cover. Simmer for about 30 minutes. Blend in sour cream; thicken with 1 tablespoon flour. Simmer until heated through. Serve on buttered noodles. Yield: 6-8 servings.

CHICKEN WITH LEMON SAUCE

2 frying chickens, disjointed
6 c. water
1 onion, sliced
4 celery tops, chopped
2 bay leaves
2 tsp. monosodium glutamate
2 tsp. salt
1/2 tsp. peppercorns
1/4 c. butter
1/4 c. flour
3 egg yolks
1/4 c. lemon juice
1/2 c. finely chopped parsley

Place chicken in kettle; add water, onion, celery tops, bay leaves, monosodium glutamate, salt and peppercorns. Cover tightly; bring to a boil. Reduce heat; simmer for 1 hour or until chicken is tender. Place chicken on serving platter; keep warm. Strain and reserve 3 cups broth. Melt butter in saucepan; blend in flour. Add reserved broth gradually. Cook, stirring constantly, until thickened and bubbly. Beat egg yolks with lemon juice; add small amount of hot sauce to egg yolks, stirring well. Add egg yolk mixture to sauce, stirring rapidly. Cook until mixture returns to a boil. Remove from heat; stir in parsley. Spoon half the sauce over chicken. Pour remaining sauce into serving bowl. Yield: 8 servings.

CREAMED CHICKEN IN PATTY SHELLS

40 lb. chicken breasts and leg quarters
Salt
2 c. butter or margarine
2 c. flour
4 c. milk
6 cans cream of mushroom soup
2 cans evaporated milk
Salt and pepper to taste
2 4-oz. jars pimentos
Patty shells

Cook chicken in salted water until tender. Remove chicken from broth; reserve broth. Cool chicken; cut meat from bones in bite-sized pieces. Melt butter in large saucepan; remove from heat. Blend in flour until smooth. Add milk slowly; stir in soup, evaporated milk and 4 cups broth. Season with salt and pepper. Cook over low heat, stirring constantly, until thickened. Drain and chop pimentos. Add pimentos and chicken to sauce; thin with broth, if necessary. Cook until heated through. Serve in patty shells.

CHICKEN CROQUETTES

2 tbsp. butter
2 tbsp. flour
1/4 tsp. salt
1 c. milk
2 c. diced cooked chicken
1/2 tsp. lemon juice
Pinch of sage
1 egg
1 tbsp. water
2 c. bread crumbs
Cooking oil

Melt butter in saucepan; blend in flour and salt. Stir in milk slowly; cook over medium heat, stirring constantly, until thick. Refrigerate for at least 2 hours. Add chicken, lemon juice and sage. Shape into croquettes. Beat egg and water together. Dip croquettes into egg mixture; roll in crumbs. Fry in hot oil until golden brown. Yield: 6 servings.

CHICKEN CUTLETS

1 1/2 c. ground uncooked chicken
Salt and pepper to taste
1/4 tsp. nutmeg
3/4 c. butter, melted
1/2 c. flour
1 egg
1 tsp. oil
1 tbsp. water
2 c. fresh bread crumbs

Mix chicken, salt, pepper, nutmeg and 5 tablespoons butter. Chill for several hours. Spread flour on sheet of waxed paper. Beat egg lightly in shallow container; add oil and water. Shape chicken mixture into 8 patties. Dip patties into flour then into egg mixture. Coat with bread crumbs. Heat remaining butter in large skillet; brown patties slowly on both sides.

CHICKEN WITH STUFFING

1 pkg. stuffing mix
3 c. chopped cooked chicken
1/2 c. butter
1/2 c. flour
1/4 tsp. salt
1/4 tsp. pepper
4 c. chicken broth
6 eggs, lightly beaten
1 can mushroom soup
1/4 c. milk
1 c. sour cream
1/4 c. chopped pimento

Prepare stuffing mix according to package directions. Spread stuffing in 12 x 9 x 1-inch baking pan; cover with chicken. Melt butter in saucepan; blend in flour and seasonings. Add broth; cook, stirring, until thickened. Stir small amount of broth mixture into eggs; add eggs to remaining broth mixture. Mix well; pour over chicken. Bake at 325 degrees for 40 to 45 minutes. Let stand for 5 minutes; cut in squares. Combine soup, milk, cream and pimento in saucepan; cook over low heat, stirring constantly, until heated through. Serve over chicken squares. Yield: 8-12 servings.

CHICKEN AND DRESSING

1 5-lb. chicken
1/3 c. butter
1/4 c. minced onion
4 c. dry bread crumbs
1/2 c. chopped celery
3 1/2 tsp. salt
1/2 tsp. pepper
1 tsp. poultry seasoning
3/4 c. flour
1 c. buttered crumbs

Place chicken in large kettle; add 6 cups water. Cover; bring to a boil. Reduce heat; simmer until chicken is tender. Remove chicken from broth. Reserve 4 1/2 cups broth. Chill until fat hardens; reserve 1/2 cup fat. Remove chicken from bones; cut in chunks. Melt butter in heavy pan; add onion. Cook until yellow. Add half the dry bread crumbs; cook, stirring, until lightly browned. Turn into bowl; add celery, 2 teaspoons salt, 1/4 teaspoon pepper, poultry seasoning and remaining dry bread crumbs. Melt reserved chicken fat in heavy pan; blend in flour, remaining salt and remaining pepper. Cook until bubbly; remove from heat. Add reserved broth all at once; cook over medium heat, stirring constantly, until thick. Spread chicken in 13 x 9 1/2 x 2-inch pan. Top with dry bread crumb mixture; pour broth mixture over top. Spread with buttered crumbs. Bake at 350 degrees for 35 minutes. Yield: 8 servings.

SCALLOPED CHICKEN

1 5-lb. chicken
Salt
3/4 c. flour
1 loaf dry bread
1/2 tsp. pepper
1 tbsp. leaf sage
2 c. diced onions
3 c. diced celery
2 eggs, beaten
1 can cream of mushroom soup
Corn flake crumbs

Place chicken in large kettle; add 2 quarts water and salt to taste. Simmer until chicken falls from bones. Reserve 4 cups broth; chill broth until fat is hardened. Remove and reserve fat. Cut chicken into bite-sized pieces; grind skin. Heat 1/2 cup chicken fat in saucepan; blend in flour. Add 2 1/2 cups reserved broth slowly. Cook over low heat, stirring constantly, until smooth. Add chicken to sauce. Crumble bread into large bowl; add 2 teaspoons salt, pepper, sage, ground chicken skin, 1/3 cup chicken fat, onions, celery, eggs and soup. Mix well; spread in large baking pan. Pour chicken and sauce over top; sprinkle with cornflake crumbs. Bake at 350 degrees for 1 hour. Yield: 12 servings.

STEWED CHICKEN AND RAISIN DUMPLINGS

2 stalks celery
1 carrot
1 onion
1 4-lb. stewing chicken, disjointed
2 tsp. salt
1/4 c. biscuit mix
Raisin-Cheese Dumplings

Cut celery and carrot into 1-inch pieces; peel onion. Place chicken in large kettle; add celery, carrot, onion, salt and 1 quart boiling water. Cover; cook over low heat for 2 to 3 hours or until tender. Skim off excess fat. Drop Raisin-Cheese Dumplings by spoonfuls onto chicken pieces. Cook for 10 minutes. Cover; steam for 10 minutes without removing cover. Remove chicken and dumplings from stock; place in heated serving dish. Combine biscuit mix and 1/2 cup water; add to stock, stirring until thickened. Pour gravy over chicken and dumplings. Yield: 6-8 servings.

Raisin-Cheese Dumplings

1/2 c. dark seedless raisins
2 c. biscuit mix
1/2 c. grated American cheese
3/4 c. milk

Combine raisins, biscuit mix and cheese; add milk, stirring to make soft dough.

Stewed Chicken and Raisin Dumplings . . . A soup tureen with stew and raisin-cheese dumplings.

STUPENDOUS CHICKEN AND DUMPLINGS

1 3-lb. chicken, disjointed
Salt and pepper to taste
2 tbsp. butter or margarine
1/2 c. water
1 c. sliced onions
1 tsp. poultry seasoning
1 can cream of chicken soup
1 2/3 c. milk
1 10-oz. package frozen mixed vegetables
1 c. prepared biscuit mix

Sprinkle chicken with salt and pepper; brown in butter in large heavy pan. Add water, onions and poultry seasoning; cover. Simmer for 30 minutes. Stir in soup and 1 1/2 cups milk; add vegetables. Bring to a boil; cover. Reduce heat; simmer for 10 minutes, stirring occasionally. Combine biscuit mix and remaining milk; drop from spoon into stew. Cook for 10 minutes. Cover; cook for 10 minutes longer. Yield: 4 servings.

FILIPINO CHICKEN

1/4 c. soy sauce
1/4 c. vinegar
1 tbsp. light corn syrup
Garlic salt to taste
Salt to taste
1 frying chicken, disjointed

Combine soy sauce, vinegar, corn syrup, garlic salt and salt. Place chicken in heavy saucepan; pour soy sauce mixture over chicken. Cover; simmer for 40 minutes or until chicken is tender. Serve hot or cold.

BUTTERMILK-FRIED CHICKEN

1 1/2 c. buttermilk
1 1/2 tsp. summer savory
1/2 tsp. pepper
2 1 1/2-lb. chickens, disjointed
1 c. flour
1 1/2 tsp. salt
1 tsp. monosodium glutamate
1 1/2 tsp. paprika
Shortening
Butter

Mix buttermilk, savory and 1/4 teaspoon pepper in large shallow dish; add chicken. Cover; marinate for 1 hour, turning chicken occasionally. Combine flour, salt, remaining pepper, monosodium glutamate and paprika; coat chicken with flour mixture. Place chicken on waxed paper; let stand for 30 minutes. Fry chicken slowly in mixture of shortening and butter until golden brown. Yield: 6 servings.

COUNTRY-FRIED CHICKEN AND GRAVY

1 frying chicken
1 c. flour
Salt
3/4 c. cooking oil
1/2 c. evaporated milk

Disjoint chicken; remove skin. Combine flour and 1 teaspoon salt in plastic bag; shake chicken in bag. Reserve any remaining flour. Heat oil in heavy skillet; brown chicken slowly on all sides. Cover skillet; reduce heat. Cook until chicken is tender. Remove chicken from skillet. Blend reserved flour into skillet drippings; add milk and enough water to make thick gravy. Cook, stirring constantly, until smooth. Season to taste with salt; serve with chicken. Yield: 4 servings.

EASY SKILLET CHICKEN

1 egg
1 c. milk
1 c. flour
1 tsp. salt
1/4 tsp. pepper
1 3-lb. chicken, cut up
Oil
Butter

Beat egg and milk together. Mix flour, salt and pepper. Dip chicken into egg mixture; roll in flour mixture. Brown chicken well in mixture of oil and butter in heavy skillet. Pour off skillet drippings; return chicken to skillet. Add 1/2 cup boiling water; cover. Cook over low heat for 45 minutes or until chicken is tender.

OVEN-FRIED CHICKEN IMPERIAL

2 c. bread or corn flake crumbs
3/4 c. grated Parmesan cheese
1/4 c. chopped parsley
1 clove of garlic, crushed
2 tsp. salt
1/8 tsp. pepper
1 frying chicken, disjointed
1/2 c. melted butter

Preheat oven to 350 degrees. Combine crumbs, cheese, parsley, garlic, salt and pepper. Dip chicken into butter; roll in crumb mixture, coating well. Arrange chicken in single layer in shallow baking dish; pour any remaining butter over chicken. Bake for 1 hour or until tender. Yield: 4 servings.

CHICKEN TERIYAKI

4 boned chicken breasts, skinned
1 9-oz. can sliced pineapple
1/4 c. teriyaki sauce
2 tsp. honey
2 tsp. brown sugar
2 tsp. butter
1 tsp. cooking oil
1 tsp. cornstarch

Place chicken in baking dish. Drain pineapple; reserve syrup. Combine pineapple syrup, teriyaki sauce, honey and brown sugar. Pour over chicken. Refrigerate for 2 hours. Drain chicken; reserve marinade. Melt 1 teaspoon butter in skillet; add oil. Brown chicken; place in baking dish. Blend reserved marinade and cornstarch in saucepan; add remaining butter. Bring to a boil; pour over chicken. Cover. Bake at 350 degrees for 15 minutes. Place pineapple over chicken; baste with pan liquid. Bake, uncovered, for 5 minutes longer or until glazed. Yield: 4 servings.

CRANBERRY-GLAZED CHICKEN

1 3-lb. chicken, disjointed
Salt and pepper to taste
1/4 c. butter or margarine
1 sm. can jellied cranberry sauce
1 1/2 tbsp. lemon juice
2 tbsp. soy sauce

Preheat oven to 350 degrees. Sprinkle chicken with salt and pepper. Combine butter, cranberry sauce, lemon juice and soy sauce in shallow baking pan. Place in oven until butter and cranberry sauce are melted; stir to blend. Arrange chicken in baking pan; cover. Bake for 1 hour and 15 minutes or until chicken is tender. Baste chicken frequently with sauce in pan.

GOURMET CHICKEN BREASTS

4 whole chicken breasts, boned
1/3 c. crumbled blue cheese
3 tbsp. sliced green onions
Melted butter or margarine
Salt and pepper
1 1-lb. 1-oz. can fruit cocktail
1 1/2 tbsp. cornstarch
2 tsp. prepared mustard
2 bouillon cubes
1/4 c. chopped parsley
1 tbsp. lemon juice

Cut chicken breasts in half. Place skin side down; sprinkle with cheese and onions. Roll up; fasten with metal pins. Place in shallow baking pan. Brush with butter; sprinkle with salt and pepper. Bake at 325 degrees for 1 hour and 15 minutes or until tender. Drain fruit cocktail, reserving syrup. Add enough water to reserved syrup to equal 1 cup liquid. Place 2 tablespoons butter in saucepan; stir in cornstarch. Heat until bubbly; stir in mustard, bouillon cubes and fruit liquid. Cook, stirring, until bouillon cubes are dissolved and mixture is thickened. Add fruit cocktail, parsley and lemon juice; heat through. Remove pins from chicken; arrange on platter. Stir 2 tablespoons pan drippings into fruit mixture. Spoon part of fruit mixture over chicken; pour remaining fruit mixture into serving bowl. Yield: 8 servings.

PERSIAN CHICKEN

1 16-oz. can sliced peaches
1/4 c. lemon juice
2 tbsp. melted butter or margarine
6 chicken breast halves
Salt and pepper to taste
1 can mandarin oranges

Puree peaches in blender or press through sieve. Combine peaches, peach syrup, lemon juice and butter. Arrange chicken on rack in broiler pan; sprinkle with salt and pepper. Broil chicken about 6 inches from source of heat for 30 minutes or until tender. Baste chicken with peach glaze at 5-minute intervals; turn chicken once during cooking. Combine remaining peach glaze and oranges in saucepan. Bring to a boil; pour over chicken.

HACIENDA CHICKEN

3 tbsp. butter or margarine
1/2 c. chopped onion
1 16-oz. can tomatoes
1 c. water
1/2 c. chopped green pepper
1 2 1/2-oz. can sliced mushrooms
1 tbsp. chopped parsley
1 tsp. paprika
1 tbsp. salt
1/4 tsp. pepper
1 stewing chicken, disjointed
1 c. rice
1/2 c. sliced green olives

Melt butter in heavy skillet or kettle. Add onion; cook until lightly browned. Add tomatoes, water, green pepper, mushrooms, parsley, paprika, salt and pepper. Arrange chicken in skillet. Cover; bring to a boil. Reduce heat; simmer for 1 hour. Add rice and olives. Cook for 1 hour longer or until rice is done and chicken is tender. Yield: 6 servings.

HUNGARIAN CHICKEN FRICASSEE

2 frying chickens
Salt and pepper to taste
1/2 c. butter or margarine
2 onions, finely chopped
2 tomatoes, finely chopped
2 tsp. paprika
1/8 tsp. soda
3 c. light cream

Disjoint chickens; sprinkle with salt and pepper. Melt butter in heavy saucepan or Dutch oven over low heat. Spread onions in pan; add chicken. Cover; cook for 10 minutes. Add tomatoes and paprika; mix gently. Simmer, covered, for 10 minutes. Stir soda into cream; pour over chicken. Simmer, covered, for about 30 minutes longer or until chicken is tender. Arrange chicken on serving platter; strain sauce over chicken. Yield: 8 servings.

CHICKEN LIVERS BAKED WITH RICE

3/4 lb. chicken livers
Salt and pepper to taste
Flour
1/4 c. butter or margarine
3 tbsp. minced onion
3 tbsp. finely chopped celery
1 c. rice
2 c. chicken broth
1 tsp. minced parsley

Sprinkle livers with salt and pepper; shake in small amount of flour in paper bag. Brown in butter in skillet; place in 6-cup casserole. Saute onion, celery and rice in skillet drippings until lightly browned. Add chicken broth; stir well. Add parsley; pour over livers. Cover. Bake at 350 degrees for 30 minutes or until rice is tender and liquid is absorbed; add salt, if needed.

LIVERS CHAMPIGNON

1 lb. chicken livers, halved
1/2 c. flour
1/4 c. corn oil
1/4 c. butter or margarine
2 scallions, minced
1 green pepper, minced
1 tomato, diced
1 tsp. salt
1/4 tsp. celery salt
Dash of pepper
1 sm. can sliced mushrooms

Dredge livers in flour. Heat oil in skillet over low heat; saute livers until brown. Remove livers from skillet; melt butter in skillet. Add scallions and green pepper; cook, stirring constantly, for 5 minutes or until brown around edges. Add tomato; simmer for 1 minute. Add 1/4 cup hot water; simmer until green pepper is tender. Return livers to skillet. Add 1 1/2 cups hot water, seasonings and mushrooms; cook until heated through.

CHICKEN LIVERS AND GIZZARDS SAUTE

1 1/2 lb. chicken livers and gizzards
Salt
1/4 c. butter
1/4 c. flour
2 tsp. bottled meat sauce

Cut livers and gizzards into halves. Boil gizzards in salted water for 30 minutes or until tender. Drain, reserving 2 cups broth. Fry livers in butter in skillet until lightly browned. Remove livers. Stir flour into skillet drippings; add gizzards and reserved broth, stirring constantly. Add 1 teaspoon salt, meat sauce and livers; heat through. Serve on toast or over rice. Yield: 6-8 servings.

CHICKEN LIVER CASSEROLE

1 6-oz. box long grain and wild rice mix
1/2 lb. chicken livers
Butter
2 6-oz. jars button mushrooms
3 c. chicken broth

Cook rice according to package directions. Saute chicken livers in butter. Arrange layers of rice, chicken livers and mushrooms in 2-quart casserole; add 2 cups broth. Bake at 350 degrees for 30 minutes, adding remaining broth as necessary to keep rice moist. Yield: 8 servings.

CHICKEN LIVER-OLIVE PATE

Color photograph for this recipe on page 723.

1/4 c. chopped shallots
1 1/4 c. butter
2 lb. chicken livers
1/3 c. Madeira
1/2 tsp. salt
1/8 tsp. nutmeg
1/8 tsp. pepper
Dash of thyme leaves
1/2 c. heavy cream
3/4 c. chopped pimento-stuffed olives
Sliced pimento-stuffed olives

Saute shallots in 1/4 cup butter in large skillet until crisp-tender but not browned. Remove shallots with slotted spoon. Set aside. Saute chicken livers in skillet, several at a time, until lightly browned, adding additional butter if needed. Remove livers. Pour Madeira into skillet; add seasonings. Bring to a boil, stirring, to loosen browned bits in skillet. Combine half the livers, shallots, Madeira mixture and cream in blender container; blend until smooth. Repeat, blending remaining half. Melt remaining butter; blend into liver mixture with chopped olives. Turn into pate mold or serving dish; chill for several hours or overnight. Make diagonal cuts on top of pate; garnish with sliced olives in center of each diamond.

CHICKEN LIVERS PORTUGAL

5 tbsp. butter or margarine
1 clove of garlic, minced
2 tbsp. minced onion
6 tbsp. flour
1 c. beef broth
1/2 tsp. salt
Dash of pepper
1 lb. chicken livers
2 tbsp. sweet Madeira or Marsala

Melt 3 tablespoons butter in heavy saucepan or skillet. Add garlic and onion; cook until tender but not brown. Blend in 2 tablespoons flour. Add beef broth; cook, stirring, until smooth and thickened. Combine remaining flour, salt and pepper; dredge livers in flour mixture. Brown livers in remaining butter over high heat; stir into sauce. Add Madeira; heat through. Serve over wild rice, if desired.

SPANISH-STYLE CHICKEN LIVERS

1 lb. chicken livers
Salt
1/2 c. butter
1/2 c. minced onion
1/2 c. rice
1/2 tsp. saffron
2 c. chicken broth
1/2 c. grated Parmesan cheese
Dash of pepper

Cook livers in boiling salted water until tender. Drain and chop livers. Melt butter in heavy saucepan; saute onion lightly. Add rice; cook, stirring, until rice is golden brown. Dissolve saffron in small amount of broth; stir into rice mixture. Add remaining broth; simmer for 30 minutes. Add 1/4 cup cheese, livers, salt to taste and pepper. Simmer, stirring, for 15 minutes. Turn into greased casserole; sprinkle with remaining cheese. Bake at 350 degrees until browned. Yield: 4-6 servings.

BAKED CHICKEN STROGANOFF

1/4 c. flour
1 tsp. salt
1/8 tsp. pepper
1 3-lb. chicken, disjointed
3 tbsp. butter or margarine
1 med. onion, chopped
1 clove of garlic, mashed
3 tbsp. lemon juice
1 c. chicken broth
2 4-oz. cans mushrooms
8 oz. medium noodles
1 c. sour cream
1/4 tsp. paprika

Combine flour, salt and pepper; roll chicken in flour mixture. Brown chicken slowly in butter in skillet; transfer to baking dish. Add onion and garlic to skillet drippings; stir in lemon juice, chicken broth and mushrooms. Simmer for about 5 minutes; pour over chicken. Cover baking dish. Bake at 350 degrees for 30 minutes. Break noodles into 1-inch pieces; cook according to package directions. Drain noodles. Remove chicken from baking dish; keep warm. Add noodles to sauce in baking dish; cover. Bake for 15 minutes longer. Stir sour cream and paprika into noodle mixture. Turn into serving dish; top with chicken. Yield: 4 servings.

CREOLE CHICKEN

2 c. diced cooked chicken
1 c. cooked macaroni
1 c. diced celery
1 tbsp. chopped red pepper
1 tbsp. chopped green pepper
2 tbsp. chopped parsley
1 1/2 c. chicken broth
3 eggs
1 tbsp. flour
1 c. cream or milk

Mix chicken, macaroni, celery, red pepper, green pepper and parsley; moisten with chicken broth. Beat eggs; stir in flour and cream. Fold into chicken mixture; turn into baking dish. Bake at 350 degrees for 45 minutes. Yield: 4 servings.

EASY CHICKEN TETRAZZINI

1 chicken
8 oz. spaghetti
1 can cream of mushroom soup
1/2 c. milk
2 tbsp. chopped pimento
1 sm. can mushroom pieces
1/2 c. shredded Cheddar cheese
Salt and pepper to taste
Grated Parmesan cheese

Place chicken in large kettle; add about 2 quarts cold water. Bring to a boil. Reduce heat; simmer until chicken is tender. Take chicken from broth, reserving broth. Cut chicken from bones in small pieces. Cook spaghetti in reserved broth until tender; drain well. Blend soup and milk in saucepan; add chicken, pimento and mushrooms. Heat through. Layer spaghetti, chicken mixture and Cheddar cheese in casserole, sprinkling each layer with salt and pepper. Top with Parmesan cheese; cover. Bake at 350 degrees for 30 to 35 minutes.

PATIO CHICKEN SKILLET

2 chicken breasts, halved
1/4 c. butter
4 tsp. seasoned salt
1/4 tsp. crushed thyme
Ground pepper
1 med. green pepper, diced
1 sm. onion, chopped
1/4 tsp. hot sauce
8 oz. egg noodles
1 can cream of celery soup
1/2 c. sliced ripe olives

Brown chicken on both sides in butter in large skillet; sprinkle with 2 teaspoons seasoned salt, thyme and pepper to taste. Cover; cook over low heat for 30 minutes or until tender. Remove chicken from skillet. Mix green pepper, onion, hot sauce, 1 quart water, remaining seasoned salt and 1/8 teaspoon pepper with pan drippings in skillet. Bring to a boil. Add noodles gradually; cover. Cook over low heat for 20 minutes, stirring occasionally, until noodles are tender. Stir in soup, olives and additional water if needed. Add chicken; heat through. Yield: 4 servings.

Patio Chicken Skillet . . . Sauce, noodles, and herb-flavored chicken provide a zesty meal.

BATTER-TOPPED CHICKEN PIE

1 5-lb. chicken with giblets
Salt
3 tbsp. melted butter
2 1/4 c. flour
Pepper
2 c. milk
2 tsp. baking powder
2 tbsp. lard
1 egg, beaten

Place chicken and giblets in large kettle; add 2 teaspoons salt and 2 quarts water. Bring to a boil; reduce heat. Cover; simmer until chicken is tender. Remove chicken and giblets from broth; reserve about 5 1/2 cups broth. Chill broth until fat is hardened. Remove and reserve 3 tablespoons fat. Cut chicken fron bones. Chop giblets. Melt butter and reserved chicken fat in saucepan; blend in 1/4 cup flour. Stir in 2 cups reserved broth and 1 cup milk slowly. Add remaining reserved broth; season to taste with salt and pepper. Cook, stirring, until bubbly. Fold in chicken and giblets; turn into greased 3-quart casserole. Sift remaining flour, 1/2 teaspoon salt and baking powder together into bowl; cut in lard. Combine remaining milk and egg; stir into flour mixture. Spread batter over chicken mixture. Bake at 425 degrees for 20 minutes or until topping is browned.

BISCUIT-TOPPED CHICKEN PIE

3 c. chopped cooked chicken
4 hard-cooked eggs, sliced
Salt to taste
1/4 tsp. pepper
2 2/3 c. chicken broth
1 can cream of mushroom soup
1 recipe biscuit dough

Preheat oven to 425 degrees. Place chicken in baking dish; cover with sliced eggs. Sprinkle with salt and pepper. Mix broth and soup; pour over chicken. Cut dough into rounds with biscuit cutter; arrange over chicken. Bake for 30 minutes; serve hot. Yield: 6-10 servings.

MEXICAN CHICKEN PIE

3 c. chopped cooked chicken
1 clove of garlic, crushed
1 12-oz. can whole kernel corn with green peppers
1 12-oz. can tomato paste
1 1/4 c. water
1 tbsp. chili powder
1 1/2 tsp. salt
1/2 tsp. sugar
1/4 tsp. pepper
3/4 c. cornmeal
1 tbsp. flour
1 1/2 tsp. baking powder
1 egg
1/3 c. milk
1 tbsp. melted margarine

Preheat oven to 400 degrees. Combine chicken, garlic, corn, tomato paste, water, chili powder, 1 teaspoon salt, sugar and pepper in large skillet. Simmer for 15 minutes or until heated; place in 1 1/2-quart casserole. Sift cornmeal, flour, baking powder and remaining salt together into bowl. Add egg, milk and margarine; beat until smooth. Pour over chicken mixture. Bake for 20 to 25 minutes. Serve hot. Yield: 5-6 servings.

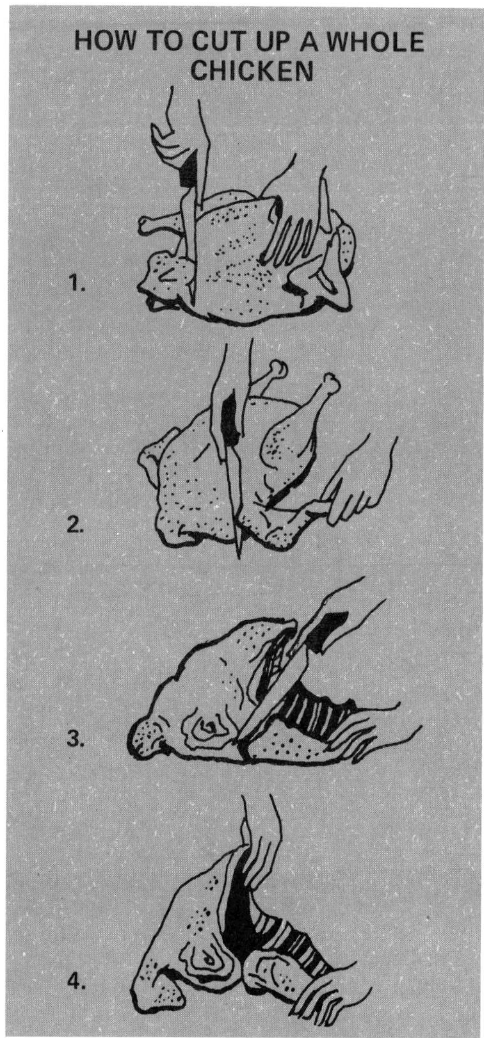

1. Place the chicken breast-up on a cutting surface. Cut off the tail from the base of the chicken's backbone.
2. Cut through the wing skin, joint, and flesh. Set wing aside. Repeat for other wing. Remove legs by pressing them down and outward until the joint cracks. (If the chicken is old, the joint may have to be cut with a knife.)
3. Separate backbone from breasts by cutting as shown in illustration (above).
4. Pry backbone from breast. Breasts may be left whole, broken in 2-4 pieces, or boned.

POULET AU PORTO

6 tbsp. butter
1 frying chicken, disjointed
Salt and pepper to taste
1/2 c. white port
1/2 lb. mushrooms, sliced
1/3 c. heavy cream

Melt butter in heavy skillet over low heat. Brown chicken slowly on all sides. Cover; simmer for 10 minutes or until chicken is tender. Season chicken with salt and pepper; add port and mushrooms. Simmer, covered, for about 15 minutes longer. Transfer chicken to warm serving dish. Stir cream slowly into skillet drippings. Mix well; pour over chicken. Yield: 4 servings.

BAKED ARROZ CON POLLO

2 frying chickens, disjointed
Salt to taste
3/4 c. olive oil
1 med. onion, diced
2 cloves of garlic, minced
1 sm. green pepper, diced
1/2 c. canned tomatoes
4 c. chicken broth
1 bay leaf
1 10-oz. package yellow rice mix

Season chickens with salt; brown in oil in skillet. Remove chicken from skillet. Saute onion, garlic and green pepper in skillet drippings. Add tomatoes, salt, broth and bay leaf. Bring to a boil. Spread rice in casserole; spoon broth mixture over rice, stirring well. Place chicken on top. Bake at 350 degrees for 1 hour. Garnish with pimento, if desired. Yield: 6-8 servings.

CHICKEN AMANDINE

1 sm. onion, minced
6 tbsp. butter
1/2 tsp. curry powder
Dash of paprika
6 tbsp. flour
1 can cream of chicken soup
2 c. milk
1/2 lb. Cheddar cheese, grated
2 c. diced cooked chicken
1 c. blanched slivered almonds, toasted
1 c. cooked rice
1 8-oz. can sliced mushrooms
Buttered crumbs

Saute onion in butter; blend in curry powder, paprika and flour. Blend soup and milk; stir into flour mixture. Cook over low heat, stirring constantly, until smooth and thickened. Add cheese, stirring until melted; fold in chicken, almonds, rice and mushrooms, mixing lightly. Pour into greased oblong baking dish; top with crumbs. Cover. Bake at 325 degrees for 20 minutes. Uncover; bake for 25 minutes longer. Yield: 8-10 servings.

CHICKEN BAKED IN RICE

1 frying chicken, disjointed
Salt and pepper to taste
1 c. rice
1 pkg. dry onion soup mix
2 1/2 c. water
1/2 c. margarine

Season chicken with salt and pepper. Combine rice, soup mix, salt and water in baking dish. Arrange chicken over rice; dot with margarine. Cover. Bake at 350 degrees for 1 hour and 15 minutes. Yield: 4-6 servings.

COUNTRY CAPTAIN

Color photograph for this recipe on page 70.

1 frying chicken
1 tsp. salt
1/4 tsp. pepper
1/4 c. butter
1 med. onion, chopped
1 sm. green pepper, chopped
1 clove of garlic, crushed
2 tsp. curry powder
1/2 tsp. leaf thyme
1 1-lb. can stewed tomatoes
1/4 c. currants
Hot cooked rice
Toasted blanched almonds
Chutney

Cut chicken into serving pieces; sprinkle with salt and pepper. Heat butter in large skillet. Add chicken; brown on all sides. Remove chicken from skillet. Add onion, green pepper, garlic, curry powder and thyme to skillet; cook until onion is tender but not brown. Add tomatoes, currants and chicken; cover. Cook for 20 to 30 minutes or until chicken is tender. Serve over rice with almonds and chutney. Yield: 4 servings.

MINI-ROLLS PARMIGIANA

8 boned broiler-fryer chicken thighs
1/2 tsp. salt
1 tsp. instant minced onion
1 tsp. parsley flakes
4 oz. mozzarella cheese
8 oz. spaghetti
1 15-oz. can tomato sauce
1/2 tsp. dried basil
1/2 tsp. dried oregano
Grated Parmesan cheese

Place thighs, skin sides down, on cutting board. Sprinkle with salt, onion and parsley flakes. Cut mozzarella cheese into 2 1/2 x 1/2 x 3/4-inch pieces. Place piece of cheese on each boned thigh; fold sides over cheese. Fasten with skewers. Place thighs, skewered sides down, in foil-lined shallow baking pan. Bake in 400-degree oven for 40 minutes. Cook spaghetti according to package directions; drain. Combine tomato sauce, basil and oregano in small saucepan; heat well. Place rolls on cooked spaghetti on serving platter. Pour tomato sauce over top. Sprinkle with grated cheese. Garnish with chopped parsley. Yield: 4 servings.

Mini-Rolls Parmigiana . . . Cheese-filled chicken thighs topped with tomato sauce.

SIMPLIFIED PAELLA

3 tbsp. olive oil
8 pieces of chicken
2 1/2 c. chicken broth
1 clove of garlic, minced
1/2 tsp. saffron
1 tsp. salt
1 c. rice
1 lb. shrimp, shelled and deveined
1 10-oz. package frozen peas
2 pimentos, cut into wide strips

Pour oil into electric skillet; set temperature control at 325 degrees. Arrange chicken, skin side down, in skillet; cover. Cook for 15 minutes. Combine chicken broth, garlic, saffron, salt and rice. Turn chicken; pour rice mixture around chicken. Scrape off any rice that falls on chicken. Reduce temperature to 250 degrees; cover. Cook for 20 minutes. Add shrimp, peas and pimentos; cover. Cook for 15 minutes longer. Turn off heat; let stand, covered, for 20 to 30 minutes before serving. Yield: 8 servings.

TASTY CHICKEN IN CREAM

4 half chicken breasts
3 tbsp. butter or oil
1/3 c. chopped onion
1 sm. clove of garlic, minced
3/4 c. chicken broth
3/4 c. light cream
1 1/2 tsp. salt
1/8 tsp. pepper
2 tsp. Worcestershire sauce
3 tbsp. flour
1 c. water

Brown chicken well in butter in skillet; transfer to baking pan. Combine onion, garlic, chicken broth, cream and seasonings in saucepan; heat through. Pour mixture over chicken; cover pan. Bake at 300 degrees for 2 hours. Uncover; bake for 15 to 20 minutes longer. Remove chicken from pan; keep warm. Blend flour and water into pan drippings; pour over chicken. Serve with wild rice. Yield: 4 servings.

YORKSHIRE CHICKEN

1 1/3 c. flour
1 tbsp. salt
1 1/2 tsp. sage
1/4 tsp. pepper
1 frying chicken, disjointed
1/4 c. oil
1 tsp. baking powder
1 1/2 c. milk
1/4 c. melted butter
3 eggs, well beaten
1/4 c. chopped parsley

Combine 1/3 cup flour, 2 teaspoons salt, sage and pepper in plastic bag. Shake chicken in bag to coat with flour. Brown chicken well in oil; transfer to baking dish. Sift remaining flour, remaining salt and baking powder together. Mix milk, butter and eggs; add to flour mixture. Stir until smooth; add parsley. Pour batter over chicken. Bake at 350 degrees for 1 hour. Yield: 4-6 servings.

Chili

Chili is a dried pod of red pepper. It is a hot pepper that is frequently pickled and served as a relish. When ground it is known as a hot seasoning called cayenne pepper. It is also the name for (1) a popular spice blend called *chili powder* and (2) a ground beef and red kidney bean dish known as *chili con carne.*

CHILI POWDER: This is generally a mixture of ground red peppers, chili peppers, cumin seed, ground oregano, powdered garlic, salt, and sometimes includes ground cloves, ground allspice, and powdered onion. It is used as a seasoning in shellfish and oyster cocktail sauces, boiled and scrambled egg dishes, gravies, and stews.

CHILI CON CARNE: Literally translated it means chili with meat. This popular American dish originated in the Southwest. Principal ingredients are usually ground beef, chili powder or minced chilies, tomatoes or tomato sauce, and red kidney beans.

TOUCHDOWN CHILI DIP

1 onion, chopped
1 green pepper, chopped
2 tbsp. butter, melted
1 can chili without beans
1 can cream of mushroom soup
3/4 lb. cubed sharp Cheddar cheese
Corn chips

Saute onion and green pepper in butter until onion is clear. Stir in chili and soup; blend. Add cheese; place over medium heat, stirring until melted. Pour into chafing dish; serve with corn chips. Yield: 12 servings.

CHILI-FRITO CASSEROLE

1 can chili
1 sm. onion, grated
1 pkg. corn chips, crushed
1/4 lb. grated cheese

Place chili in casserole; sprinkle with onion. Add corn chips; sprinkle cheese over top. Bake at 375 degrees for 20 minutes. Yield: 6 servings.

SOUTH OF THE BORDER CASSEROLE

1 6-oz. package egg noodles
1/2 c. chopped onion
1 1/2 lb. ground beef
1 tbsp. oil
1 tbsp. flour
Dash of pepper
1/2 tsp. salt
1 tsp. garlic salt
1/4 tsp. oregano
2 1/2 tsp. chili powder
1 c. evaporated milk
1 8-oz. can tomato sauce
1/2 c. chopped ripe olives
2 tbsp. grated Parmesan cheese

Cook noodles according to package directions; drain. Place 2/3 of the noodles in casserole. Brown onion and beef in skillet in oil over medium heat; drain excess fat. Stir in flour, pepper, salt, garlic salt, oregano, chili powder and milk; mix well. Add tomato sauce and olives to beef mixture, stirring well; blend over low heat. Pour over noodles in casserole; top with remaining noodles. Press noodles into mixture slightly; sprinkle with Parmesan cheese. Bake at 350 degrees for about 30 minutes. Yield: 6 servings.

CHALUPA LOAF

1 lb. ground beef
3 tbsp. oil
2 tbsp. chili powder
1/3 c. chopped onion
1 12-oz. can evaporated milk
1 8-oz. can tomato sauce
1 tsp. salt
1 doz. tortillas
1 lb. grated Cheddar cheese

Brown beef in oil in large skillet. Add chili powder and onion; simmer until onion is tender. Add milk, tomato sauce and salt. Simmer until mixture is blended. Cut tortillas in strips. Alternate layers of tortillas, beef mixture and cheese in baking dish. Bake at 300 degrees for about 40 minutes. Yield: 8 servings.

BORDER CHILI

2 lb. coarsely ground beef
1 minced clove of garlic
1/4 c. chopped onion
1/4 c. shortening
1/4 tsp. cumin seed
1/4 tsp. oregano
1 tsp. salt
1/4 tsp. red pepper
1/4 c. chili powder
2 tbsp. flour

Saute beef, garlic and onion in shortening until pink color disappears. Toast cumin seed and oregano in 300-degree oven for 15 minutes; crush. Add cumin seed, oregano, salt, red pepper and chili powder to beef. Simmer until beef is tender. Add boiling water as necessary. Mix flour with water to make paste; add to chili mixture gradually, stirring until thickened. Simmer for 10 minutes longer. Yield: 6-8 servings.

CHILI CON CARNE

1 med. onion, chopped
1 1/2 lb. lean ground beef
2 tbsp. oil
1 1-lb. can tomatoes
1 8-oz. can seasoned tomato sauce
1 c. catsup
1 1-lb. can kidney beans
1 1/2 tbsp. chili powder
1 1/2 tsp. salt
1 bay leaf
Dash of ground red pepper

Brown onion and beef in oil in heavy 4-quart saucepan. Add tomatoes, tomato sauce, catsup, beans, chili powder, salt, bay leaf and red pepper; stir well. Simmer, covered, for 1 hour and 30 minutes. Add water as necessary. Yield: 6 servings.

Chili Pie . . . Chili, beans, cheese, peppers and onions combine in a hearty main-dish pie.

CHILI PIE

2 green peppers
1 4-oz. package Cheddar cheese, shredded
1 unbaked 9-in. pastry shell
1 15 1/2-oz. can chili with beans
4 eggs, slightly beaten
1/4 c. milk
1 tsp. instant onion

Cut green peppers into five 1-inch rings; remove seeds. Parboil for 5 minutes in salted water; drain. Sprinkle cheese over bottom of pastry shell. Place pepper rings over cheese. Spoon chili into pepper rings. Combine eggs, milk and instant onion; pour around pepper rings. Bake in 375-degree oven for 35 minutes or until set. Yield: 5 servings.

CHILI FOR THE CROWD

1/2 lb. dried pinto beans
1 14 1/2-oz. can tomato puree
3 1/2 c. tomatoes
2 c. chopped onion
2 c. chopped green pepper
2 tbsp. oil
1/4 c. minced parsley
3 lb. ground beef chuck
1/3 c. chili powder
1 tbsp. salt
1 tsp. pepper
1 tsp. cumin
1 tsp. monosodium glutamate

Place beans and 4 cups water in 4-quart saucepan. Cover; bring to a boil. Cook for 5 minutes; remove from heat. Cover; let stand for 1 hour. Bring beans to a boil; cook, covered, for 1 hour and 30 minutes. Add puree and tomatoes. Simmer for 5 minutes. Saute onion and green pepper in oil; drain excess fat. Combine onion mixture, parsley, beef, chili powder, salt, pepper, cumin and monosodium glutamate. Simmer for 10 minutes. Combine beef mixture with beans. Cover; simmer for 45 minutes. Uncover; simmer for 30 minutes longer. Remove excess fat. Serve hot with corn chips. Yield: 4 quarts.

CHILI BEEF PIE

1 lb. ground round steak
1 c. chopped onions
1 tbsp. margarine, melted
2 tsp. chili powder
1 tsp. cumin
1 c. shredded carrots
1 tsp. salt
1/4 tsp. pepper
1/2 tsp. sugar
1/4 c. catsup
1 c. drained kidney beans
Pastry for 2-crust pie
1 tbsp. milk

Saute steak and onions in margarine in large skillet until steak loses red color. Add chili powder, cumin, carrots, salt, pepper, sugar and catsup. Simmer for 20 minutes. Add kidney beans. Pour into prepared pie crust. Top with pastry. Seal; crimp edges. Cut slits in top; brush with milk. Bake at 400 degrees for 30 minutes. Let stand several minutes before serving. Yield: 6 servings.

CHILI MAC

1 8-oz. package elbow macaroni
1 lb. ground beef
1 med. onion, minced
1 tsp. chili powder
1 tsp. salt
1 1-lb. can kidney beans
1 c. Cheddar cheese, shredded

Cook macaroni according to package directions; drain and set aside. Brush large skillet with small amount of fat; add ground beef and onion. Cook until browned. Add macaroni, 1 cup water, chili powder, salt and kidney beans. Cover; simmer for 15 minutes, stirring occasionally. Top with cheese; place over low heat until cheese melts. Yield: 4-6 servings.

OLD-FASHIONED CHILI CON CARNE

2 lb. ground beef
Garlic salt to taste
Salt and pepper
1 c. diced celery with leaves
3 No. 303 cans tomatoes
2 6-oz. cans tomato paste
2 tbsp. sugar
1 lb. pinto beans, cooked
1 can pitted ripe olives, quartered
Dash of oregano
1/2 c. finely chopped parsley
1 tbsp. Worcestershire sauce
3 tbsp. chili powder
Cayenne pepper to taste (opt.)
Hot sauce to taste (opt.)

Combine ground beef with garlic salt and salt and pepper to taste; place in hot, deep iron kettle. Add celery; cook mixture until browned, stirring constantly. Cover; simmer for about 10 minutes, stirring occasionally. Add tomatoes, tomato paste, sugar, 1 tablespoon salt, 1 teaspoon pepper, beans, olives, oregano, parsley and Worcestershire sauce; simmer for about 10 minutes. Add chili powder, cayenne pepper and hot sauce, stirring well. Refrigerate overnight. Reheat to serve. May be frozen. Yield: 4 quarts.

CHILI MEATBALLS

1 1/3 lb. ground beef
1/2 c. evaporated milk
1/2 c. bread crumbs
2 tbsp. chopped onion
1 3/4 tsp. salt
2 tbsp. flour
1 tsp. chili powder
2 tbsp. shortening
1 No. 2 can tomatoes
2 tsp. sugar

Combine ground beef, milk, bread crumbs, onion and 1 teaspoon salt, mixing lightly. Shape mixture into 12 meatballs. Mix flour and chili powder together; roll meatballs in flour mixture. Brown meatballs in hot shortening in large skillet; blend in any remaining flour mixture. Stir in tomatoes, remaining salt and sugar; bring to a boil. Simmer for 25 minutes. Stir mixture frequently, turning meatballs gently. Serve over cooked noodles or spaghetti. Yield: 4-6 servings.

ELK CHILI

1 lge. onion, sliced
1 med. green pepper, chopped
1 lb. elk, ground
3 tbsp. shortening
1 No. 2 1/2 can tomatoes
2 1/2 tsp. salt
1/8 tsp. paprika
1/8 tsp. cayenne pepper
3 whole cloves
1 bay leaf
2 tbsp. chili powder
1 No. 2 can kidney beans

Brown onion, green pepper and elk in shortening. Add tomatoes, salt, paprika, cayenne pepper, cloves, bay leaf and chili powder. Simmer for 2 hours, adding water as necessary. Add beans; cook for about 10 minutes longer. Yield: 6 servings.

OPEN-FACED CHILI SQUARES

1 lb. ground beef
1 tbsp. chili powder
4 tsp. onion soup mix
Dash of hot sauce
1/4 c. catsup
12 slices bread, toasted
Chili sauce
Parsley sprigs

Brown ground beef in small amount of fat in skillet. Add chili powder, onion soup mix, hot sauce and catsup to beef; cook until mixture is of spreading consistency. Spoon onto hot toast. Place slices on cookie sheet. Bake in 450-degree oven for 10 minutes. Cut each slice in half; garnish with dash of chili sauce and sprig of parsley. Serve as open-faced sandwiches. Yield: 6 servings.

MILD CHILI

1 sm. piece of suet
1 lb. ground beef chuck, ground twice
1 lge. onion, chopped fine
1 clove of garlic, crushed
Salt and pepper to taste
1 tbsp. Worcestershire sauce
1 can New Orleans-style kidney beans
1 tbsp. chili powder

Render suet in large heavy skillet. Place beef, onion and garlic in fat; cook until browned. Add 1 cup water to beef mixture; cook until of desired doneness. Add salt, pepper, Worcestershire sauce and beans. Simmer for about 10 minutes. Add chili powder; cook 5 minutes longer. Yield: 4-6 servings.

HOMEMADE CHILI

2 lb. ground beef chuck
1/2 onion, chopped
1 1/2 c. catsup
2 sm. cloves of garlic
2 lge. cans hot chili beans
Dash of red pepper
1/2 tsp. chili powder

Cook beef in large skillet until gray; pour off fat. Add onion; cook for 5 minutes. Add catsup, garlic, beans, seasonings and 1 bean can water. Simmer for about 1 hour and 30 minutes. Yield: 6 servings.

ROSY CHILI SOUP

1/2 lb. ground beef
2 tbsp. chopped onion
1 tsp. chili powder
1/2 tsp. salt
1 tbsp. butter
1 sm. can tomato soup
1 can beef soup

Combine beef, onion, chili powder and salt. Shape into 12 small balls. Melt butter in saucepan. Add meatballs; saute until browned. Add soups and 1 1/2 soup cans water; bring to a boil. Cook, stirring frequently, until well blended. Yield: 4 servings.

VENISON CHILI

1 1/2 lb. bacon
2 1/2 lb. ground venison
8 c. kidney beans
1 tbsp. chili powder
1 1/2 tsp. pepper
1 tbsp. salt
4 c. chopped onions
4 No. 3 cans tomatoes
1/2 tsp. cumin

Cut bacon into small pieces; fry in skillet until crisp. Add venison; cook until browned. Combine beans, chili powder, pepper, salt, onions, tomatoes and cumin. Add venison and enough water to cover; stir well. Simmer for 2 hours. Yield: 20 servings.

Chocolate

Chocolate, probably America's favorite flavoring, is produced from the beans of the tropical cacao tree. It has both fat and carbohydrate content and provides quick surges of energy. (1 oz. bar sweetened milk chocolate = 150 calories; 1 tablespoon chocolate syrup = 50 calories; 3 1/2 ounces unsweetened chocolate, semisweet chocolate, or sweet chocolate = approximately 500 calories)

BUYING: Chocolate can be bought in many forms: *as unsweetened or bitter chocolate* used for baking and cooking; *semisweet chocolate* for candy-making, frostings, and sauces; *semisweet morsels; sweet chocolate,* also called German chocolate; *milk chocolate;* and *cocoa.*

STORING: Store chocolate in a cool, dry

place. Wrapped chocolate keeps 1 year in the refrigerator or cupboard. When chocolate has become too warm, a harmless grayish film of fat covers the surface. Chocolate is no longer edible when the wrapper has become oily.

BUTTERMILK FUDGE CAKE

4 oz. chocolate
3 c. sugar
1 c. margarine
4 eggs
2 tsp. soda
3 c. flour
1 1/2 c. buttermilk
2 tsp. vanilla

Break chocolate in 1 cup boiling water. Set aside to melt. Cream sugar and margarine; add eggs, one at a time, beating well after each addition. Stir chocolate mixture until smooth; add to egg mixture. Sift soda with flour; add dry ingredients alternately with buttermilk to chocolate mixture. Add vanilla; pour into 4 well-greased and floured 8-inch cake pans. Bake at 350 degrees for 35 minutes or until cake tests done. Frost as desired.

CHOCOLATE FUDGE CAKE

1 stick margarine
1 c. sugar
4 eggs
1 1-lb. can chocolate syrup
1 c. sifted flour
1 tsp. baking powder
1 tsp. vanilla
1 c. chopped walnuts
1/2 pt. heavy cream, whipped
1 tsp. instant coffee
1 tbsp. honey

Cream margarine and sugar until fluffy. Beat in eggs, one at a time. Add 1/2 cup chocolate syrup. Sift flour with baking powder; stir into sugar mixture. Add remaining chocolate syrup, vanilla and walnuts; mix well. Pour into greased 9 x 12-inch loaf pan or a 1 1/2-quart tube pan. Bake at 350 degrees for 35 to 40 minutes; cool. Mix whipped cream, instant coffee and honey; spread on cake.

CHOCOLATE SHEATH CAKE

2 c. flour
2 c. sugar
1 stick butter
1/2 c. salad oil
4 tbsp. cocoa
1 c. buttermilk
2 eggs, beaten
1 tsp. soda
1 tsp. vanilla

Sift flour and sugar into large bowl. Combine butter, oil, cocoa and 1 cup water in saucepan; bring to a boil. Pour over flour mixture; beat well. Add remaining ingredients; mix thoroughly. Pour into oblong pan. Bake at 400 degrees for 20 minutes. Remove from pan.

Icing

4 tbsp. cocoa
1 stick butter
6 tbsp. cream
1 box confectioners' sugar
1 c. chopped pecans

Combine cocoa, butter and cream in saucepan; bring to a boil. Pour over confectioners' sugar, stirring constantly. Add pecans; beat well. Pour over hot cake.

CHOCOLATE TOFFEE BAR CAKE

2 c. (packed) brown sugar
2 c. flour
1/2 c. butter
1/2 tsp. salt
1 tsp. soda
1 egg
1 c. milk
1 tsp. vanilla
6 chocolate-covered toffee bars
1/2 c. chopped pecans

Mix brown sugar and flour thoroughly; cut in butter until of consistency of coarse meal. Reserve 1 cup mixture; add salt and soda to remaining mixture. Blend in egg, milk and vanilla; beat well. Pour into well-greased 9 x 13-inch baking dish. Chop toffee bars coarsely. Sprinkle batter with reserved mixture, nuts and toffee bars. Bake at 350 degrees for 35 minutes.

CHOCOLATE VELVET CAKE

Color photograph for this recipe on page 483.

1 6-oz. package semisweet chocolate morsels
2 1/4 c. sifted flour
1 tsp. soda
3/4 tsp. salt
1 3/4 c. sugar
3/4 c. softened butter
1 tsp. vanilla
3 eggs

Combine chocolate morsels and 1/4 cup water in saucepan; stir over low heat until chocolate is melted and smooth. Remove from heat. Sift flour, soda and salt together; set aside. Combine sugar, butter and vanilla in bowl; beat until blended. Add eggs, one at a time, beating well after each addition. Blend in melted chocolate mixture. Stir in flour mixture alternately with 1 cup water. Pour batter into 2 greased and floured 9-inch layer cake pans. Bake in 375-degree oven for 30 to 35 minutes. Cool.

Chocolate Velvet Frosting

1 6-oz. package semisweet chocolate morsels
3 tbsp. butter
1/4 c. milk
1 tsp. vanilla
1/4 tsp. salt
3 c. sifted confectioners' sugar

Melt chocolate morsels and butter over hot, not boiling, water. Remove from heat. Add milk, vanilla and salt; mix until well blended. Beat in confectioners' sugar gradually. Fill and frost cake. Garnish with chopped walnuts.

CONTINENTAL CAKE

1 c. chopped dates
1/2 lb. margarine
1 tsp. soda
1/2 tsp. salt
3 tbsp. cocoa
1 1/2 c. flour
2 eggs, lightly beaten
1 c. sugar
1 tsp. vanilla
1/2 c. chopped nuts
1/2 c. chocolate chips
1 c. (packed) brown sugar

Combine dates with 1 cup boiling water. Stir in margarine, soda, salt, cocoa and flour; mix thoroughly. Blend in eggs, sugar and vanilla. Pour batter into well-greased 13 x 9-inch pan. Combine nuts, chocolate chips and brown sugar; sprinkle over batter. Bake at 350 degrees for 40 minutes or until cake tests done.

DEVIL'S FOOD CAKE

1 c. butter
6 oz. baking chocolate
2 c. sugar
5 eggs, separated
1/2 c. light brown sugar
1 tsp. soda
1 tbsp. vanilla
1 c. buttermilk
3 c. cake flour
1 tsp. baking powder
1/4 tsp. salt

Cream butter well. Melt chocolate over hot water; add chocolate to butter. Add sugar; cream until sugar is dissolved. Beat egg yolks well. Add yolks and brown sugar to creamed mixture. Dissolve soda in 1/2 cup water. Combine soda water, vanilla and buttermilk. Sift flour, baking powder and salt. Add buttermilk mixture to creamed mixture alternately with dry ingredients, beginning and ending with dry ingredients. Beat egg whites until stiff peaks form; fold into cake mixture. Pour into three 9-inch layer pans. Bake at 350 degrees for 30 to 35 minutes or until cake tests done. Cool on racks. Spread with Seven-Minute frosting or chocolate frosting.

GERMAN CHOCOLATE CAKE

2 1/2 c. sifted cake flour
1 tsp. soda
Pinch of salt
1 pkg. sweet cooking chocolate
1 c. butter
2 c. sugar
4 eggs, separated
1 tsp. vanilla
1 c. buttermilk

Sift flour, soda and salt together. Melt chocolate in 1/2 cup boiling water. Cool. Line 3 greased 8 or 9-inch pans with waxed paper. Cream butter and sugar until light and fluffy; add egg yolks, one at a time, beating after each addition. Stir vanilla into chocolate mixture; add to creamed mixture. Add flour mixture alternately with buttermilk, beating well after each addition. Beat egg whites until stiff peaks form. Fold in egg whites; turn into prepared pans. Bake at 350 degrees for 30 to 40 minutes. Remove from pans; cool on racks.

Coconut-Pecan Frosting

1 c. evaporated milk
1 c. sugar
3 egg yolks
1/4 lb. margarine
1 tsp. vanilla
1 1/3 c. coconut
1 c. chopped pecans

Combine milk, sugar, egg yolks, margarine and vanilla in saucepan. Cook, stirring, over medium heat for about 12 minutes or until thickened. Add coconut and pecans. Beat until frosting is cool and of spreading consistency. Spread between layers and over top and side of cake.

LINCOLN LOG

1 c. sifted flour
1 tsp. baking powder
1/4 tsp. salt
1/4 c. cocoa
3 eggs
1 c. sugar
1 tsp. vanilla
Confectioners' sugar
1 c. whipped cream
1 1-oz. square bitter chocolate
1 tsp. butter

Sift flour, baking powder, salt and cocoa together. Beat eggs until thick; beat in sugar gradually. Blend in 1/3 cup water slowly. Add flour mixture and vanilla, mixing until blended. Spread batter in waxed paper-lined 15 1/2 x 10 1/2 x 1-inch pan. Bake at 375 degrees for 12 to 15 minutes. Loosen edges of cake from pan; invert onto towel sprinkled with confectioners' sugar. Remove paper; trim edges of cake. Roll cake and towel together; cool. Unroll cake; remove towel. Spread cake with whipped cream. Reroll cake; refrigerate. Melt chocolate and butter together over hot water. Add 1 cup confectioners' sugar and 2 tablespoons boiling water; beat until smooth. Frost roll.

RED VELVET CAKE

1 1/2 c. sugar
1/2 c. shortening
2 eggs
2 1/2 c. cake flour
1 c. buttermilk
2 oz. red food coloring
2 tbsp. cocoa
1 tsp. salt
1 1/2 tsp. vanilla
1 tsp. soda
1 tbsp. vinegar

Cream sugar, shortening and eggs; stir in flour and buttermilk. Mix food coloring, cocoa, salt and vanilla; stir into flour mixture. Dissolve soda in vinegar; stir into chocolate mixture. Place in 3 greased layer pans. Bake at 350 degrees for 25 minutes; cool.

Filling

5 tbsp. flour
1 c. milk
1 tsp. vanilla
1/2 c. butter
1 c. sugar

Mix flour and milk; cook over low heat, stirring constantly, until thickened. Cool completely; add vanilla. Cream butter and sugar until fluffy; add flour mixture gradually. Beat until fluffy. Spread between layers.

Brown Sugar Ten-Minute Frosting

1 1/2 c. (packed) brown sugar
2 egg whites
Pinch of salt
1/2 tsp. vanilla

Combine brown sugar, egg whites and salt with 6 tablespoons water; place over boiling water. Beat for 5 minutes; remove from heat. Beat for 3 minutes. Add vanilla; place over cold water. Beat for 2 minutes longer. Frost top and side of cake. Yield: 16-20 servings.

CHOCOLATE CUPCAKES

1 8-oz. package cream cheese
1 egg
Sugar
1 tsp. salt
2 tbsp. vanilla
1 sm. package chocolate chips
1 1/2 c. flour
1 tsp. soda
1/4 c. cocoa
1 c. cold water
1/3 c. salad oil
1 tbsp. vinegar
1/2 c. chopped nuts

Soften cream cheese. Combine cream cheese, egg, 1/3 cup sugar, 1/2 teaspoon salt and 1 tablespoon vanilla; beat well. Stir in chocolate chips. Sift 1 cup sugar, flour, soda, cocoa and remaining salt together; stir in cold water, oil, vinegar and remaining vanilla. Spoon into 24 greased and floured muffin cups; top with spoonfuls of cream cheese mixture. Blend nuts and 2 teaspoons sugar; sprinkle over tops. Bake at 350 degrees for 35 minutes.

VIENNA SPECKLED CAKE

7 egg yolks
1 1/2 c. confectioners' sugar
2 oz. bitter chocolate, grated
1 c. ground almonds
5 egg whites, stiffly beaten
Chocolate Cream Frosting

Cream egg yolks and sugar until light; fold in chocolate, almonds and egg whites. Pour into 2 buttered and floured 9-inch layer pans. Bake at 300 degrees for 45 minutes or until cake tests done. Fill and frost with Chocolate Cream Frosting.

Chocolate Cream Frosting

5 oz. unsalted butter
1 c. confectioners' sugar
2 eggs
2 oz. bitter chocolate, melted
1 tsp. vanilla

Cream butter and confectioners' sugar until fluffy; add eggs, chocolate and vanilla. Beat with mixer at high speed until thickened.

CHOCOLATE BUTTER-NUT CRUNCH

1 c. sugar
1/2 tsp. salt
1/4 c. water
1/2 c. butter or margarine
1 1/2 c. walnuts, finely chopped
2 6-oz. package semisweet chocolate pieces, melted

Combine sugar, salt, water and butter; bring to a boil. Cook to soft-crack stage or 285 degrees on candy thermometer. Add 1/2 cup nuts. Pour onto well-greased cookie sheet; cool. Spread with 1/2 cup melted chocolate; sprinkle with 1/2 cup nuts. Turn; spread with remaining chocolate and remaining nuts. Break into pieces.

CHOCOLATE CANDY

12 oz. semisweet chocolate bits
Dash of salt
1 tsp. vanilla
1 can sweetened condensed milk
1 c. chopped nuts

Melt chocolate in double boiler; remove pan from water. Add salt and vanilla to chocolate; stir well. Add milk; mix well. Add nuts. Drop by teaspoonfuls onto waxed paper; cool.

CHOCOLATE-COVERED PEANUT CLUSTERS

7 to 8 oz. semisweet chocolate
1/2 lb. roasted Spanish peanuts

Melt chocolate in bowl over hot water; remove from heat. Add peanuts; stir well. Drop from teaspoon onto waxed paper. Refrigerate for 12 hours; store candy in a cool place.

DELICIOUS CHOCOLATE CANDY

1/4 pkg. paraffin
1 pkg. sweet cooking chocolate
2 pkg. butterscotch morsels
1 c. toasted pecans

Melt paraffin in double boiler; add chocolate. Stir mixture until smooth. Add morsels, 1 package at a time, stirring constantly until smooth; remove from heat. Chop pecans; add to chocolate mixture and blend well. Drop by teaspoonfuls on waxed paper.

TEXAS MILLIONAIRES

1 c. (packed) brown sugar
1 c. sugar
1 c. light corn syrup
2 sticks margarine
1 tsp. vanilla
2 c. canned evaporated milk
1 lb. pecan halves
12 oz. sweet chocolate
1/4 lb. paraffin

Combine sugars, syrup, margarine, vanilla and 1 cup milk in saucepan; stir well. Bring to a boil, stirring constantly; add remaining milk gradually. Cook to soft-ball stage; add pecans. Pour into a large buttered pan; refrigerate overnight. Cut into squares. Melt chocolate and paraffin over hot water. Dip squares into hot mixture and place on waxed paper.

CHOCOLATE-MINT DESSERT

2 sq. chocolate
1/2 c. butter
1 c. confectioners' sugar
3 eggs, separated
1/2 c. walnuts
1 1/2 c. vanilla wafer crumbs
1/4 lb. peppermint stick candy
10 marshmallows, cut fine
1/2 c. pecans, chopped
3/4 c. heavy cream, whipped

Melt chocolate over hot water. Cream butter and sugar thoroughly; beat in egg yolks. Add chocolate and walnuts; blend well. Beat egg whites until stiff peaks form; fold into chocolate mixture. Layer 1/2 cup wafer crumbs in oblong dish; pour chocolate mixture over crumbs. Chill until firm. Crush peppermint candy coarsely. Combine candy, marshmallows, pecans and cream with 1/2 cup wafer crumbs. Spread peppermint mixture over chocolate mixture; top with remaining wafer crumbs. Chill for 24 hours.

CHOCOLATE MOUSSE

1/2 c. semisweet chocolate chips
3 eggs, separated
1 tsp. vanilla
1/2 tsp. salt
2 tbsp. sugar
1/2 c. chopped pecans

Melt chocolate over hot water. Beat egg yolks slightly; add vanilla and salt. Blend into chocolate. Beat whites until soft peaks form. Beat in sugar for 30 seconds. Fold in chocolate until well blended. Add nuts; spoon into sherbet dishes. Chill; top with whipped topping and chocolate shavings. Yield: 4 servings.

CHOCOLATE FINNISH CAKE

Color photograph for this recipe on page 493.

1 pkg. sweet cooking chocolate
1/2 c. shortening
2 sticks butter
3 c. sugar
5 eggs
1 tsp. lemon flavoring
1 tsp. vanilla
3 c. flour
1 tsp. baking powder
1/2 tsp. salt
1 c. milk
1 c. chopped almonds
Vanilla ice cream
Apricot halves
Sliced toasted almonds
Chocolate curls

Melt chocolate over hot water. Cream shortening and butter in large mixing bowl. Add sugar gradually; cream well. Add eggs, one at a time, beating well after each addition. Stir in flavorings. Sift flour, baking powder and salt together; add to sugar mixture alternately with milk. Stir in chopped almonds; pour into large greased ring mold or bundt pan. Bake at 350 degrees for 1 hour and 15 minutes. Cool for 10 minutes; remove from mold. Cool. Place on cake plate. Fill center of cake with ice cream. Garnish with apricots, sliced almonds and chocolate curls.

CHOCOLATE ICEBOX CAKE

3/4 lb. sweet chocolate
6 eggs, separated
3 tbsp. sugar
3 tbsp. water
3 tbsp. Cointreau
Ladyfingers
1 c. cream sherry
Slivered almonds
1 c. heavy cream, whipped
Maraschino cherries

Melt chocolate in top of double boiler. Beat egg yolks until thick and lemony. Add sugar, water, Cointreau and egg yolks to chocolate. Cook slowly, stirring constantly, until thickened and smooth. Cool. Beat egg whites until stiff peaks form; fold into chocolate mixture. Line sides and bottom of medium springform pan with split ladyfingers, placing flat side against pan. Moisten ladyfingers with sherry. Pour in half the chocolate filling; sprinkle with slivered almonds. Add another layer of ladyfingers, flat side down; moisten with sherry. Add remaining chocolate filling; sprinkle with slivered almonds. Cover with ladyfingers, flat side down; moisten with sherry. Refrigerate for at least 12 hours. Remove springform, leaving cake on bottom of pan. Cover top of cake with whipped cream; garnish with maraschino cherries or slivered almonds. Ladyfingers should not be soggy. Whipped cream may be sweetened and flavored with vanilla.

CHOCOLATE-PINEAPPLE PARFAIT

Color photograph for this recipe on page 486.

1 pkg. chocolate pudding mix
1 No. 2 can crushed pineapple

Prepare pudding mix according to package directions. Fill parfait glasses 1/2 full with pudding; place in leaning position in refrigerator until set. Drain pineapple; chill. Fill parfait glasses with pineapple. Add dollop of whipped cream to each glass; top with grapes.

CHOCOLATE SPONGE

4 eggs, separated
1 c. sugar
2 sq. chocolate, melted
1 1/2 tsp. gelatin

Beat egg yolks until light; add sugar gradually. Beat until thick and lemony; add chocolate. Soften gelatin in 1 tablespoon cold water; dissolve in 5 tablespoons boiling water. Add gelatin mixture to chocolate mixture; blend thoroughly. Beat egg whites until stiff peaks form; fold into chocolate mixture. Pour into mold; chill until firm. Serve with whipped cream, if desired.

FONDANT AU CHOCOLAT

3 sq. chocolate
2 tbsp. strong coffee
2/3 c. confectioners' sugar
1 c. butter
3 eggs, separated

Melt chocolate with coffee and 1/3 cup sugar in double boiler over hot water. Cream butter; add egg yolks and remaining sugar. Beat well. Add chocolate mixture. Beat egg whites until stiff peaks form; fold into chocolate mixture. Rinse 1-quart mold with cold water. Pour in fondant. Refrigerate for at least 6 hours or overnight. Dip mold in hot water for a few seconds; unmold fondant. Serve with vanilla custard sauce or whipped cream. Yield: 6 servings.

FRENCH CHOCOLATE CREAM

5 sq. unsweetened chocolate
3/4 c. butter
1 1/2 c. sugar
1 tsp. vanilla
1 1/2 tsp. instant coffee
2 egg yolks
1 c. instant mashed potatoes
1/4 tsp. salt
2 tbsp. rum

Melt chocolate over hot water. Cream butter and sugar thoroughly; blend in vanilla and coffee. Beat egg yolks until light; add to sugar mixture. Add chocolate; beat well. Combine potatoes and salt with 1 cup boiling water; whip for 1 minute. Blend potatoes with chocolate mixture thoroughly; stir in rum. Pour into waxed paper-lined 8 x 4 x 3-inch loaf pan. Chill, covered, for 8 hours or until firm. Serve sliced thin, topped with whipped cream. Will freeze well.

CHOCOLATE CRINKLE COOKIES

4 oz. unsweetened chocolate
1/2 c. corn oil
2 c. sugar
4 eggs
2 tsp. vanilla
1/2 tsp. salt
2 c. sifted flour
2 tsp. baking powder
1 c. confectioners' sugar

Melt chocolate over hot water; combine with oil and sugar. Beat in eggs, one at a time, beating well after each addition; stir in vanilla, salt, flour and baking powder. Chill for several hours or overnight. Drop dough by teaspoonfuls into confectioners' sugar; roll dough into balls in sugar. Arrange balls 2 inches apart on greased baking sheet. Bake at 350 degrees for 10 to 12 minutes. Yield: 4 1/2 dozen cookies.

CHOCOLATE RUM CREME

6 egg yolks
1 c. (scant) sugar
1 tbsp. gelatin
1 pt. heavy cream, whipped
3/4 to 1 c. dark rum
1 oz. no-melt baking chocolate
Grated bitter chocolate

Beat egg yolks well; add sugar. Soften gelatin in 1/2 cup water; bring to a boil, stirring constantly. Add to egg yolk mixture, stirring constantly. Fold in whipped cream, rum and chocolate. Pour into sherbet glasses and refrigerate until set. Sprinkle tops with grated chocolate. Yield: 12 servings.

CHOCO-WALNUT DROPS

1 c. shortening
2 c. (packed) dark brown sugar
1 tsp. cinnamon
1/2 tsp. nutmeg
2 eggs
2 c. sifted all-purpose flour
1 1/2 tsp. baking powder
1 1/2 tsp. salt
1/2 c. sour cream
1 c. quick-cooking oats
1 16-oz. package semisweet chocolate morsels
1 1/2 c. chopped California walnuts
1 c. raisins

Cream shortening, brown sugar and spices together until fluffy. Beat in eggs, one at a time, beating well after each addition. Resift flour with baking powder and salt. Add to shortening mixture alternately with sour cream. Stir in oats. Add chocolate morsels, walnuts and raisins. Drop by spoonfuls onto lightly greased cookie sheet. Bake at 350 degrees for 15 minutes or until lightly browned. Remove from baking sheet; cool on cookie rack. Yield: 8 dozen cookies.

Choco-Walnut Drops . . . A crisp, nut-filled cookie that's the perfect cookie jar filler.

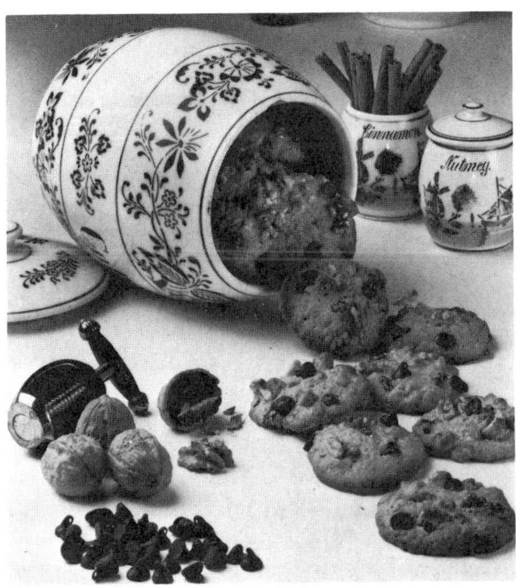

CHOCOLATE BUTTERSWEETS

1/2 c. butter
1/2 c. confectioners' sugar
1/4 tsp. salt
1 tsp. vanilla
1 to 1 1/4 c. flour

Cream butter; add sugar, salt and vanilla. Mix well; add flour gradually. Stir until well blended. Shape into small balls; place on ungreased cookie sheet. Press hole in center of each. Bake at 350 degrees for 12 to 15 minutes or until lightly browned.

Filling

1 3-oz. package cream cheese
1 c. confectioners' sugar
2 tbsp. flour
1 tsp. vanilla
1/2 c. chopped walnuts
1/2 c. flaked coconut

Soften cream cheese; blend in sugar, flour and vanilla. Add walnuts and coconut. Fill cookies while warm; cool.

Chocolate Frosting

1/2 c. chocolate morsels
2 tbsp. butter
1/2 c. confectioners' sugar, sifted

Melt chocolate morsels and butter in 2 tablespoons water over low heat, stirring occasionally. Add sugar; beat until smooth. Frost each cookie with about 1 teaspoon frosting. Yield: 3 dozen.

CHOCOLATE BALLS

Color photograph for this recipe on page 492.

3/4 c. margarine
3/4 c. confectioners' sugar
2 c. rolled oats
3 tbsp. cocoa
1 tsp. vanilla

Cream margarine with sugar; stir in oats, cocoa and vanilla. Shape into balls. May be rolled in sugar, flaked coconut, roasted almonds or crumbled corn flakes. Refrigerate until chilled.

CHOCOLATE-MINT STICKS

3 1-oz. squares unsweetened chocolate
Butter
2 eggs
1 c. sugar
1 tsp. peppermint extract
1/2 c. sifted flour
Dash of salt
1/2 c. chopped almonds
1 c. sifted confectioners' sugar
1 tbsp. cream

Melt 2 squares chocolate and 1/2 cup butter over hot water. Beat eggs until frothy; stir in sugar, chocolate mixture and 1/4 teaspoon peppermint extract. Add flour, salt and almonds; mix thoroughly. Pour into greased 9-inch square pan. Bake at 350 degrees for 20 to 25 minutes. Cool. Work 2 tablespoons soft butter into confectioners' sugar; add cream and remaining peppermint extract. Stir until smooth. Spread over cake; refrigerate cake. Melt remaining chocolate and remaining butter over hot water. Mix thoroughly. Dribble over chilled filling. Cut in strips. Yield: 48 sticks.

CHOCOLATE BARS

1 c. shortening
1/2 c. sugar
1 1/2 c. (packed) brown sugar
3 eggs, separated
2 c. flour
1/4 tsp. salt
1/4 tsp. soda
1 tbsp. vanilla
1 c. chocolate chips
1 c. chopped nuts

Cream shortening with sugar and 1/2 cup brown sugar until fluffy. Beat egg yolks with 1 tablespoon water. Add to sugar mixture; blend thoroughly. Combine flour, salt and soda; blend into egg mixture. Stir in vanilla. Press dough into large, shallow baking pan; sprinkle with chocolate chips. Beat egg whites until soft peaks form; add remaining brown sugar gradually. Beat until glossy. Spread over chocolate chips; sprinkle meringue with nuts. Bake in 350-degree oven for 25 minutes. Yield: 2 dozen bars.

CHOCOLATE DELIGHT BARS

Butter
1 egg yolk
1 1/4 c. sifted flour
Sugar
1 tsp. baking powder
2 c. chocolate pieces
2 eggs
Melted butter
2 tsp. vanilla
2 c. finely cut nuts

Beat 1/2 cup butter with 1 egg yolk and 2 tablespoon water. Sift flour, 1 teaspoon sugar and baking powder. Stir into butter mixture. Press into greased 13 x 9 x 2-inch pan. Bake for 10 minutes at 350 degrees. Sprinkle with chocolate pieces immediately; return to oven for 1 minute. Remove from oven; spread chocolate over top. Beat 2 eggs until thick; beat in 3/4 cup sugar. Stir in 6 tablespoons melted butter and vanilla. Add nuts; spread over chocolate. Bake at 350 degrees for 30 to 35 minutes. Cut in 1 1/2-inch squares. Yield: 4 dozen squares.

CHOCOLATE TIGER BARS

7/8 c. flour
1 c. sugar
1/2 tsp. soda
1/2 tsp. salt
3 eggs
1/3 c. buttermilk
1/2 tsp. vanilla
1/3 c. butter
2 6-oz. packages unsweetened chocolate chips
2 3-oz. packages cream cheese
1/2 tsp. grated orange rind

Combine 3/4 cup flour, 3/4 cup sugar, soda, salt, 1 egg, buttermilk and vanilla in mixing bowl; beat until light. Combine 1/4 cup butter and chocolate in saucepan; melt over low heat. Add chocolate mixture to batter; beat well. Pour into 9-inch square pan. Combine remaining flour, sugar, eggs and butter with cream cheese and orange rind in mixing bowl; beat until light and creamy. Pour cheese mixture over chocolate batter. Swirl knife blade through batter to obtain marble effect. Bake at 350 degrees for 40 to 45 minutes. Cool; cut into bars. Yield: Twenty 1-inch squares.

CHOCOLATE KISSES

2 egg whites
1/8 tsp. salt
1/8 tsp. cream of tartar
1/2 c. sugar
1 c. chocolate pieces
1/4 tsp. peppermint extract

Beat egg whites until foamy. Add salt and cream of tartar; beat until stiff peaks form. Add sugar, two tablespoons at a time; beat until glossy. Fold in chocolate pieces and peppermint extract. Drop dough by rounded teaspoonfuls onto baking sheets covered with heavy ungreased paper. Bake at 300 degrees for 25 minutes. Cool before removing from paper. Yield: 2 1/2 dozen cookies.

CHOCOLATE-CHEESE DROP COOKIES

1 1/2 c. sugar
1/2 c. butter
1/2 c. shortening
1 3-oz. package cream cheese
1 egg, beaten
2 tbsp. milk
1 tsp. vanilla
1/2 tsp. salt
2 1-oz. squares unsweetened chocolate
2 1/4 c. flour
1 1/2 tsp. baking powder
1/2 c. finely chopped walnuts
Walnut halves

Cream sugar, butter, shortening and cream cheese. Mix in egg, milk, vanilla and salt. Melt chocolate over hot water; stir into batter. Sift flour and baking powder; add gradually to chocolate mixture. Stir in chopped nuts. Drop from teaspoon onto greased baking sheet. Place walnut half on each cookie. Bake at 350 degrees for 12 minutes. Yield: 6 dozen cookies.

CHOCOLATE-MARSHMALLOW COOKIES

2 c. sugar
1 c. milk
2 sq. unsweetened chocolate
1 tbsp. butter
1 tsp. vanilla
16 marshmallows
2 1/2 c. graham cracker crumbs
1 c. chopped nuts

Combine sugar, milk and chocolate in saucepan; cook, stirring constantly, to soft-ball stage. Stir in butter and vanilla. Add cut-up marshmallows, crumbs and nuts; blend until smooth. Drop by spoonfuls onto waxed paper; cool. Yield: 24 cookies.

CHOCOLATE-NUT PUFFS

2 egg whites
1/2 tsp. salt
1/2 c. sugar
1/2 tsp. vanilla
1/2 tsp. vinegar
1 c. semisweet chocolate chips
3/4 c. nuts, chopped

Preheat oven to 350 degrees. Beat egg whites with salt until soft peaks form; add sugar gradually. Beat until stiff peaks form; blend in vanilla and vinegar. Melt chocolate chips over hot water; fold chocolate and nuts into egg whites. Drop from teaspoon onto greased cookie sheet. Bake for about 10 minutes. Yield: 24 cookies.

ONE-MINUTE COOKIES

2 c. sugar
1/2 c. cocoa
1/2 c. milk
1 stick margarine

2 1/2 to 3 c. quick cooking oats
1 tsp. vanilla

Combine sugar, cocoa, milk and margarine in saucepan; bring to a boil. Boil, stirring constantly, for 2 to 3 minutes; pour over oats. Add vanilla. Drop from teaspoon onto waxed paper. Yield: 2 dozen cookies.

NO-BAKE CHOCOLATE COOKIES

1/2 c. milk
1/2 c. butter
1/2 c. cocoa
2 c. sugar
1/2 c. peanut butter
1/2 c. coconut
1 tsp. vanilla
3 c. quick cooking oats

Combine milk, butter, cocoa and sugar; bring to a rolling boil. Remove from heat; blend in peanut butter, coconut, vanilla and oats. Drop from a teaspoon onto waxed paper. Cool.

CHOCOLATE FONDUE

2 tbsp. honey
1/2 c. light cream
1 9-oz. bar milk chocolate, broken
1/4 c. finely chopped pecans
1 tsp. vanilla

Heat honey and cream in fondue pot; stir in chocolate. Heat, stirring constantly, until chocolate is melted. Stir in pecans and vanilla. Serve with cake fingers or squares, fruit or marshmallows dipped into fondue.

CHOCOLATE-MARSHMALLOW FONDUE

Color photograph for this recipe on page 730.

1/8 tsp. cinnamon
1 tsp. sugar
3/4 c. heavy cream
12 oz. sweet chocolate
1/2 c. miniature marshmallows
2 tbsp. brandy

Mix cinnamon and sugar in 2-cup fondue pot; blend in cream. Add chocolate; cook over low heat, stirring frequently, until chocolate melts and mixture is smooth. Add marshmallows; stir until melted. Stir in brandy. Place fondue pot on stand over low heat. Place stemmed red maraschino cherries, chunks of ripe fruit, chunks of pound cake or angel food cake on fondue forks; dip into fondue.

SWISS CHOCOLATE FONDUE

5 3 3/4-oz. bars milk chocolate
1 c. heavy cream
Apple slices
Pineapple chunks
Strawberries
Banana Chunks
Pear slices
Maraschino cherries
Toasted pound cake fingers

Break chocolate into chafing dish; add cream. Stir constantly until smooth. Keep hot. Arrange fruit and pound cake fingers on platter. Serve with fondue.

CHOCOLATE BAR-ICE CREAM DESSERT

10 almond chocolate bars
1 c. margarine
6 eggs, separated
1 c. powdered sugar
1 c. nutmeats
5 c. crushed vanilla wafers
1/2 gal. ice cream, softened

Melt chocolate bars and margarine in saucepan. Cool. Beat egg yolks until thick and lemony. Combine chocolate mixture with egg yolks. Simmer, stirring constantly, until smooth and thickened. Add powdered sugar and nuts; cool. Beat egg whites until stiff peaks form. Combine egg whites with chocolate mixture. Line 17 x 11 x 2-inch pan with 4 cups vanilla wafer crumbs. Cover with ice cream; pour on chocolate mixture. Cut through several places to mix. Sprinkle top with remaining wafer crumbs. Freeze. Yield: 24 servings.

FROZEN CHOCOLATE

1 c. butter or margarine
2 c. confectioners' sugar, sifted
4 sq. chocolate, melted
4 eggs
1/4 to 1 tsp. peppermint flavoring
1 to 2 tsp. vanilla
1 c. crushed chocolate wafers

Cream butter. Add sugar; beat until light and fluffy. Add chocolate; blend well. Add eggs, one at a time, beating well after each addition. Blend in flavorings. Spread half the crumbs in bottom of 10 x 6-inch pan or in 18 cupcake liners in muffin tins. Spoon in chocolate mixture; top with remaining crumbs. Freeze for at least 4 hours. Garnish each serving with whipped cream and cherry. Yield: 6-8 servings.

CHOCOLATE CHIP ICE CREAM

6 eggs
1 3/4 c. sugar
2 tbsp. vanilla
1/2 tsp. salt
1 pt. whipping cream
1 lge. can evaporated milk
Milk
2 sq. baking chocolate

Beat eggs until light; add sugar. Beat until thick and lemony. Add vanilla, salt, cream, evaporated milk and about 2 cups milk. Beat well. Melt chocolate in top of double boiler. Add chocolate slowly to milk mixture. This will result in tiny chips of chocolate. Pour in freezer container; fill 2/3 full with milk. Freeze according to freezer directions. Yield: 1 gallon.

FRENCH CHOCOLATE ICE CREAM

1/4 c. sugar
1/3 c. water
1 6-oz. package semisweet chocolate
3 egg yolks
1 1/2 c. heavy cream, whipped

Combine sugar and water in small saucepan. Bring to a boil and boil rapidly for 3 minutes. Place chocolate in blender container; add hot sugar mixture. Cover; blend on high speed for 20 seconds or until chocolate sauce is smooth. Add egg yolks; stir to combine. Cover; blend on high speed for 10 seconds. Fold chocolate mixture into whipped cream. Spoon into refrigerator tray or 1-quart container. Cover with waxed paper; freeze. This needs no stirring; will not form ice crystals. Yield: 1 quart.

Mocha Ice Cream Pie... Rich chocolate sauce and crust complement coffee ice cream.

MOCHA ICE CREAM PIE

1 1/2 c. finely crushed chocolate wafers
1 stick butter, melted
1 qt. coffee ice cream

Mix chocolate crumbs and melted butter thoroughly; press into bottom and side of 9-inch pie pan. Chill. Spoon ice cream into chilled crust.

Chocolate Sauce

1/2 stick butter
2 sq. unsweetened chocolate
1 1/2 c. sugar
1/8 tsp. salt
3/4 c. heavy cream
1/2 tsp. vanilla

Melt butter and chocolate over low heat. Add sugar gradually, blending well. Mixture will be thick and dry. Add salt; stir in cream gradually. Cook for 5 to 6 minutes to dissolve sugar. Remove from heat; add vanilla. Pour sauce over ice cream; serve. Yield: about 2 cups.

CHOCOLATE MINT ICE CREAM

1 pkg. chocolate pudding mix
1/4 c. sugar
2 c. milk
1/4 tsp. peppermint extract
1 c. heavy cream, whipped

Combine pudding mix, sugar and milk. Bring to boil; cook, stirring constantly, until thickened. Stir in peppermint extract; cool. Chill in freezer tray for 30 minutes. Return to bowl; fold in whipped cream. Freeze for 1 hour. Return to bowl; beat until smooth. Return to tray; freeze until firm.

CHOCOLATE ANGEL PIE

3 egg whites
Dash of salt
1/8 tsp. cream of tartar
1/4 c. sifted sugar
3/4 c. ground blanched almonds
1 tsp. almond extract
1/4 lb. sweet chocolate chips
3 tbsp. coffee
1 tbsp. cognac
1 c. heavy cream

Beat egg whites until foamy. Add salt and cream of tartar; beat until soft peaks form. Beat in sugar, one spoonful at a time, until stiff peaks form. Fold in almonds and extract. Line bottom and side of a 9-inch buttered pie pan with meringue. Bake at 275 degrees for 45 minutes; cool. Melt chocolate in coffee in double boiler. Add cognac; stir until smooth. Whip cream; fold into chocolate mixture. Pour into pie shell. Chill for 3 hours or until ready to serve.

CHOCOLATE CHIFFON PIE

3 sq. unsweetened chocolate
2 1/2 c. milk
Sugar
1/2 c. cornstarch
1/2 tsp. salt
2 tbsp. butter
3 eggs, separated
1 tsp. vanilla
1 baked 9-inch pie shell

Melt chocolate in milk in top of double boiler. Beat for 1 minute or until blended. Sift 1 1/3 cups sugar, cornstarch and salt together. Add small amount of chocolate mixture; stir until smooth. Return to double boiler. Add butter; stir constantly until thickened. Cook for 10 minutes longer, stirring occasionally. Beat egg yolks slightly. Pour small amount hot mixture over egg yolks; stir vigorously. Return to double boiler and cook, stirring constantly, until thickened. Remove from heat; add vanilla. Cool. Pour filling into pie shell. Beat egg whites until soft peaks form. Add 6 tablespoons sugar gradually; beat until glossy. Pile meringue lightly on filling. Bake in 325-degree oven for 20 minutes or until lightly browned. Yield: 6 servings.

SOUTHERN CHOCOLATE-PECAN PIE

Color photograph for this recipe on page 484.

1 4-oz. package sweet cooking chocolate
1/4 c. butter
1 2/3 c. evaporated milk
1 1/2 c. sugar
3 tbsp. cornstarch
1/8 tsp. salt
2 eggs
1 tsp. vanilla
1 unbaked 10-in. pie shell
1 1/3 c. flaked coconut
1/2 c. chopped pecans

Mix chocolate with butter in saucepan. Place over low heat, stirring constantly, until blended. Remove from heat; blend in evaporated milk gradually. Mix sugar, cornstarch and salt in a bowl. Beat in eggs and vanilla. Blend in chocolate mixture gradually; pour into pie shell. Combine coconut and pecans; sprinkle over filling. Bake at 375 degrees for 45 to 50 minutes or until puffed and browned. Cover loosely with aluminum foil during last 15 minutes of baking if topping browns too quickly. Cool for at least 4 hours. Filling will set while cooling. Garnish with dollops of prepared whipped topping if desired. Yield: 10-12 servings.

CHOCOLATE CREAM PIE

2 sq. unsweetened chocolate
1 1/2 c. sugar
3 tbsp. cornstarch
1/2 tsp. salt
3 c. milk
3 egg yolks, lightly beaten
1 tbsp. butter
1 1/2 tsp. vanilla
1 9-in. baked pie shell

Shave chocolate into strips. Mix sugar, cornstarch, chocolate and salt in saucepan; stir in milk gradually. Cook over medium heat; stirring constantly, until mixture thickens and comes to a boil. Boil for 1 minute; remove from heat. Stir half the hot mixture into egg yolks; blend egg yolk mixture into hot mixture remaining in saucepan. Boil for 1 minute longer, stirring constantly. Remove from heat. Blend in butter and vanilla; pour immediately into pie shell. Chill for 2 hours. Garnish with whipped cream.

CHOCOLATE-PEPPERMINT CREAM PIE

2/3 c. soft butter
1 c. sugar
2 oz. unsweetened chocolate
2 oz. semisweet chocolate
3 eggs, lightly beaten
1/4 tsp. peppermint extract
1 9-in. graham cracker crust
1 c. heavy cream
1 tbsp. confectioners' sugar

Cream butter and sugar in mixer at high speed for 10 minutes or until fluffy. Melt chocolates; cool to lukewarm. Add to butter mixture; blend in eggs and flavoring. Pour into crust; chill for 8 hours or overnight. Whip cream with confectioners' sugar. Spoon over pie.

CHOCOLATE REFRIGERATOR PIE

4 egg whites
1/4 tsp. cream of tartar
1 1/2 c. sugar
2 egg yolks
1/8 tsp. salt
2 tbsp. flour
1 c. milk
1 sq. chocolate
1 c. whipping cream
Finely chopped nuts

Beat egg whites and cream of tartar until stiff peaks form. Add 1 cup sugar; beat until glossy. Spread meringue in greased and floured 10-inch pie pan. Bake at 275 degrees for 20 minutes; increase temperature to 350 degrees for 40 minutes. Cool thoroughly. Combine egg yolks, salt, remaining sugar, flour, milk and chocolate in double boiler. Cook, stirring constantly, over hot water, until smooth and thickened. Whip cream; spread thin layer of whipped cream over crust. Spread chocolate filling over whipped cream. Add remaining whipped cream; sprinkle with nuts. Chill for 10 to 12 hours.

CHOCOLATE-RUM PIE

1 recipe 2-crust pie pastry
1/4 c. finely chopped nuts
1 tbsp. rum
1 pkg. chocolate whipped dessert mix
1 pkg. frozen dessert topping mix
Shaved chocolate

Line 6 tart pans with pastry. Bake at 400 degrees until golden brown; cool. Prepare whipped dessert mix according to package directions; add nuts and rum. Pour into cooled tart shells; chill in refrigerator. Serve with dessert topping mix; garnish with shaved chocolate. Yield: 6 servings.

CHOCOLATE PASTRY TORTE

2 4-oz. packages sweet baking chocolate
1/2 c. sugar
1 1/2 tsp. instant coffee
2 tsp. vanilla
2 sticks pie crust
2 c. whipping cream

Combine chocolate, sugar, 1/2 cup water and coffee in saucepan. Cook over low heat until smooth, stirring constantly. Add vanilla; cool to room temperature. Blend 3/4 cup chocolate mixture into pie crust; divide into 6 equal parts. Press each part over bottom of inverted 8-inch cake pan to within 1/2 inch of edge. Bake at 425 degrees for 5 minutes. Lift off carefully. Cool. Whip cream until stiff peaks form; fold in remaining chocolate mixture. Stack crusts on plate, spreading cream mixture over each layer and on top. Chill for 8 hours or overnight. Garnish as desired. Yield: 12 servings.

CHOCOLATE STEAMED PUDDING

1/3 c. butter
1 c. sugar
1 egg, beaten
2 c. flour
4 tsp. baking powder
1/2 tsp. salt
1 c. milk
3 sq. baking chocolate
1 tsp. vanilla

Cream butter; add sugar gradually. Mix well; add egg. Sift flour, baking powder and salt together; stir into creamed mixture alternately with milk. Melt chocolate; add vanilla. Fold into pudding. Turn into buttered 2-quart pudding mold. Steam, covered, for about 1 hour and 30 minutes. Serve with hard sauce. Yield: 8 servings.

HOT FUDGE PUDDING

1 c. sifted flour
2 tsp. baking powder
1/4 tsp. salt
1/4 c. sugar
Cocoa
1/2 c. milk
2 tbsp. shortening, melted
1 c. chopped nuts
1 c. (packed) brown sugar

Sift flour, baking powder, salt, sugar and 2 tablespoons cocoa together; stir in milk and shortening. Mix until smooth; add nuts. Spread mixture into square baking pan. Sprinkle with brown sugar mixed with 4 tablespoons cocoa. Pour 1 3/4 cup hot water evenly over batter. Bake at 350 degrees for 40 to 45 minutes. Cut into squares; serve topped with any remaining sauce.

CHOCOLATE PUDDING

2 c. sugar
4 tbsp. cocoa
5 1/2 tbsp. flour
3 1/2 c. milk
2 tbsp. butter
2 tsp. vanilla

Combine sugar, cocoa and flour in 2-quart saucepan. Add milk slowly, stirring to mix well. Cook over medium heat, stirring constantly, until mixture comes to a boil. Cook, stirring, until smooth and thickened. Stir in butter and vanilla. Pour into custard cups; chill until firm. Top with whipped cream if desired. Yield: 6 servings.

POT DE CREME

2/3 c. milk
1 6-oz. package chocolate chips
1 egg
2 tbsp. sugar
1 tsp. vanilla
1/8 tsp. salt

Scald milk. Place remaining ingredients in blender container; add hot milk. Blend on low speed for 1 minute. Pour into 6 pot de creme serving dishes. Chill for several hours. Garnish each serving with a teaspoon of whipped topping. Yield: 6 servings.

CHOCOLATE SOUFFLE

4 eggs
3/4 c. sugar
1/4 tsp. salt
1/3 c. melted butter
1 tsp. brandy
1 c. heavy cream, whipped
3 tbsp. butter
3 tbsp. flour
1 c. milk
2 sq. unsweetened chocolate
1 tsp. vanilla

Beat 1 egg until light and lemony; add 1/4 cup sugar and 1/8 teaspoon salt. Add melted butter to egg mixture, beating constantly; stir in brandy. Fold in whipped cream. Chill until ready to use. Melt butter in top of double boiler; blend in flour. Add milk gradually; bring to a boil, stirring constantly. Melt chocolate over hot water. Combine chocolate with 3 tablespoons hot water. Add chocolate mixture, remaining flour and salt to butter mixture; blend well. Cool thoroughly; add vanilla. Separate remaining eggs. Beat egg yolks until thick and lemony; stir into chocolate mixture. Beat egg whites until stiff peaks form. Fold into chocolate mixture. Pour into ungreased souffle dish. Form crown by running tip of knife through souffle mixture 1 inch from edge of dish. Place dish in pan of hot water. Bake at 325 degrees for 50 to 60 minutes. Remove from oven. Serve immediately with brandy sauce.

BLACK FOREST WALNUT TORTE

14 eggs
2 c. sugar
12 oz. walnuts, ground
1/2 tsp. vanilla
1/2 lb. unsalted butter
1/2 lb. milk chocolate, melted

Preheat oven to 325 degrees. Separate 12 eggs. Place egg yolks and 1 1/2 cups sugar in small mixer bowl; beat for 15 minutes until thickened and lemon colored. Add walnuts and vanilla. Beat egg whites until stiff peaks form; fold into yolk mixture. Pour batter into 3 springform pans or 9-inch cake pans with scraper. Bake for 1 hour or until cake tests done. Remove pans from oven; invert onto cake racks until cool. Remove cake from pans. Place butter, chocolate and remaining sugar in small bowl; beat until blended. Add remaining eggs; beat until of spreading consistency. Spread on tops of layers and on sides; assemble cake. Sprinkle top with additional ground walnuts. Yield: 10 servings.

CHOCOLATE TORTE

4 oz. unsweetened chocolate
5 eggs
3/4 c. sugar
6 tbsp. cake flour
1/4 tsp. salt
1/2 tsp. baking powder
1 tsp. vanilla
Powdered sugar
1 c. heavy cream, whipped
3 tbsp. butter

Melt chocolate. Beat 4 egg whites until stiff, adding sugar gradually; fold in 4 well- beaten egg yolks. Sift flour with salt and baking powder; fold into egg white mixture. Fold in half the melted chocolate and vanilla. Spread thinly in waxed paper-lined 11 x 16-inch pan. Bake at 400 degrees for 15 minutes. Sprinkle cloth evenly with powdered sugar. Turn out cake on prepared cloth; trim edges. Remove paper; let cool. Cut in quarters. Spread 3 quarters with whipped cream; stack. Top with plain layer. Combine remaining chocolate, 1/2 cup powdered sugar and 1 tablespoon hot water in double boiler; blend well. Add remaining egg; beat well. Beat in butter. Spread on top and sides of layers. Yield: 8 to 12 servings.

Chop Suey

Chop suey is a Chinese-American dish supposedly created in the 1800's in San Francisco.

INGREDIENTS: Chop suey usually consists of cooked shredded beef, pork, or chicken and a variety of oriental vegetables including bean sprouts, bamboo shoots, and Chinese cabbage.

SERVING: Heap chop suey in mounds in center of hot platter. Surround with plain boiled rice and accompany with soy sauce.

BEEF CHOP SUEY

1 1/2 lb. beef, diced
1/4 c. oil
2 tbsp. soy sauce
Salt and freshly ground pepper to taste
3 c. sliced celery
2 lge. onions, chopped
1 tbsp. molasses
2 c. beef bouillon
2 c. canned bean sprouts, drained
3 tbsp. cornstarch
6 c. cooked rice

Fry beef in oil over high heat for 3 minutes, stirring constantly. Stir in soy sauce, salt and pepper. Remove beef from pan; keep hot. Add celery, onions, molasses and bouillon to remaining oil in pan. Bring to a boil; cook for 10 minutes, stirring frequently. Add bean sprouts. Cook for 3 minutes. Return beef to mixture in skillet. Mix cornstarch and 1/4 cup water; stir into beef mixture. Cook until thickened, stirring constantly. Serve with rice. Yield: 6 servings.

WEST COAST CHOP SUEY

1 lb. round steak, cut in thin strips
2 tbsp. salad oil
1 1/2 c. sliced fresh mushrooms
1 1/2 c. diagonally sliced celery
1 c. coarsely diced green pepper
1/2 c. coarsely diced green onion
1 can beef broth
2 tbsp. soy sauce
2 tbsp. cornstarch

Brown steak in oil in skillet; add mushrooms, celery, green pepper, onion, broth and soy sauce. Cover; cook for 20 minutes over low heat or until steak is tender, stirring occasionally. Blend cornstarch and 1/2 cup water; stir into steak mixture. Cook, stirring constantly, until thickened; serve with rice. Yield: 4 servings.

VEGETABLE BEEF CHOP SUEY

1/2 lb. string beans
2 med. carrots
3 sm. pods of okra
1 bunch green onions
3 stalks celery
1/2 lb. cauliflower
1/4 lb. beef, thinly sliced
1 onion, chopped
3 tbsp. cornstarch
1/2 tbsp. sugar
Soy sauce to taste
Salt and pepper to taste

Cut beans, carrots, okra, green onions, celery and cauliflower into thin slices. Bring 2 cups water to a boil in large saucepan; add sliced vegetables. Return to a boil; drain. Brown beef with onion in small amount of fat in large skillet. Add 3 cups water; bring to a boil. Mix cornstarch, sugar and 1/2 cup water; stir into beef mixture. Cook until thickened; add vegetables, soy sauce, salt and pepper. Simmer until heated through. Yield: 4 servings.

QUICK CHICKEN CHOP SUEY

1 c. chopped celery
2 med. onions, chopped
3 tbsp. butter
1 sm. can pimento, chopped
2 cans chicken with rice soup
2 cans cream of mushroom soup
1 1/2 cans chicken broth
1 med. can mushrooms
1 c. uncooked rice or instant rice
2 whole chicken breasts, cooked, boned and diced
Slivered almonds, toasted

Saute celery and onions in butter in skillet until onions are transparent but not brown. Combine pimento, soups, broth, mushrooms, rice and chicken. Place in greased 9 x 13-inch pan. Bake at 350 degrees for 2 hours. Sprinkle almonds over each serving. Yield: 7-8 servings.

CANTON CHOP SUEY

1/4 lb. bacon slices
1/2 lb. pork, chopped
1/2 lb. beef, chopped
Flour
1 can bean sprouts
1 can mushrooms
2 c. chopped celery
2 c. chopped green pepper
2 c. chopped onion
3 tbsp. soy sauce
2 tbsp. bead molasses

Saute bacon in skillet until crisp. Remove from skillet; set aside. Dredge chopped meats in small amount of flour; sear in bacon fat. Add 1 cup water to meats; simmer for 15 minutes. Add bean sprouts, mushrooms, celery, green pepper, onion, soy sauce and molasses. Simmer until meats are tender. Crumble bacon; add to mixture. Serve over rice.

CHICKEN CHOP SUEY

1 c. chopped onion
1 c. chopped celery
1/4 c. butter
1 can bean sprouts
2 c. cooked chicken
1 c. mushrooms
1 tbsp. brown sauce
2 tbsp. soy sauce
2 tbsp. cornstarch
2 c. cooked rice
1 can chow mein noodles

Saute onion and celery in butter until slightly browned; add 1 cup water. Simmer mixture for 20 minutes. Add bean sprouts, chicken, mushrooms, brown sauce and soy sauce. Mix cornstarch with 2 tablespoons water; stir into bean sprout mixture. Simmer for 20 minutes longer. Serve over cooked rice; sprinkle chow mein noodles over the top for garnish. Yield: 8 servings.

SHANGHAI CHOP SUEY

1 1/2 lb. fresh pork, cubed
1 lb. lean veal, cubed
6 lge. onions, sliced
2 lge. stalks celery, diced
2 tbsp. molasses
2 cans mushrooms
1 can bean sprouts
1 can Chinese vegetables
1 c. rice
1 can chow mein noodles

Place pork and veal cubes in skillet; brown in fat. Brown onions with cubes until tender. Place in large kettle; add enough water to partially cover. Add celery, molasses, mushrooms, bean sprouts, Chinese vegetables and rice; mix lightly. Simmer until cubes are tender. Serve with noodles.

PORK CHOP SUEY

1 med. onion, thinly sliced
1 green pepper, cut in slivers
1 1/2 c. sliced celery
2 tart apples, chopped
1 c. chicken broth
1 c. cooked and diced lean pork
Soy sauce to taste
Salt to taste
1 tbsp. cornstarch

Brown onion and green pepper in about 2 tablespoons fat. Stir in celery and apples. Add chicken broth. Cover; cook for 5 minutes. Add pork; season with soy sauce and salt. Mix cornstarch with 2 tablespoons water; stir into pork mixture. Cook until thickened, stirring constantly. Serve over rice or chow mein noodles. Yield: 4 servings.

EASY CHOP SUEY

3 lb. beef
3 lb. pork
2 onions, chopped
1 c. chopped celery
3 cans chop suey vegetables
1 1/2 c. brown gravy molasses
1/2 c. soy sauce
1/2 c. cornstarch
Cooked rice

Cut beef and pork into bite-sized pieces. Combine beef, pork, onion and celery; place small amount of fat in saucepan. Add meats mixture; cook, stirring, until lightly browned. Add chop suey vegetables and 3 vegetable cans water; simmer for about 2 hours. Stir in molasses and soy sauce. Blend cornstarch with 1 cup cold water; stir into meats mixture in saucepan. Cook, stirring, until thickened. Serve over rice. Yield: 16 servings.

SKILLET CHOP SUEY

1 lge. onion
3 stalks celery
1 green pepper
1/2 lb. fresh mushrooms
1 5-oz. can water chestnuts, drained
1/4 lb. snow peas
1 1-lb. can bean sprouts
1/2 lb. lean pork
2 tbsp. oil
1/2 tsp. salt
1 tbsp. cornstarch
1/2 c. meat broth
2 tbsp. soy sauce

Cut onion, celery and green pepper into thick slices; combine in bowl. Chop mushrooms and water chestnuts coarsely; break off tips of snow peas. Drain bean sprouts. Combine mushrooms, water chestnuts and snow peas in separate bowl. Cut pork into thin strips; brown quickly in oil in skillet, stirring constantly until pink color disappears. Sprinkle with salt. Add onion, celery and green pepper to pork; cook about 3 minutes, stirring until vegetables are crisp-tender. Add mushrooms, water chestnuts, snow peas and bean sprouts to pork mixture. Mix cornstarch with broth and soy sauce; add to mixture in skillet. Cook, stirring gently, until liquid is thickened slightly and vegetables look glossy. Serve with rice. Yield: 6 servings.

Chowder

A chowder is a thick hearty soup usually prepared with seafood. The soup originated in coastal France where fishermen and their families would prepare huge stews to celebrate a bountiful catch. These stews were prepared in *chaudieres*, or cauldrons—hence, the name chowder.

INGREDIENTS: Basic chowder ingredients may include gentle spices like thyme, salt pork or bacon, onion, and milk or tomatoes. In addition to traditional seafood chowders, the most famous of which is clam, there are vegetable, meat, and combined vegetable-and-meat chowders.

CLAM CHOWDER

1/8 lb. salt pork
2 lge. onions, ground
2 qt. clams
1/2 c. cornmeal
4 lge. potatoes

Fry salt pork in skillet until browned; add onions. Saute onions until tender. Place clams in brine solution to cover; sprinkle with cornmeal. Let stand for about 12 hours. Steam clams in small amount of fresh water until shells open. Reserve clam stock. Remove clams from shells; grind. Combine clams and reserved stock in large kettle; add about 1 quart water. Grind 1 potato; cube remaining potatoes. Add potatoes, salt pork and onions to chowder; bring to a boil, stirring constantly. Reduce heat; simmer for about 30 minutes, stirring frequently.

EASY CLAM CHOWDER

2 slices bacon, chopped
1 med. onion, chopped
1 can frozen cream of potato soup
Milk
1 7-oz. can clams, drained
Dash of pepper
Butter

Fry bacon and onion until onion is tender but not brown. Prepare soup with milk according to can directions. Combine soup, clams, onion, bacon and pepper in saucepan. Simmer for 12 minutes. Serve with pat of butter floating on top. Yield: 4 servings.

MANHATTAN CLAM CHOWDER

3 slices bacon, finely diced
1 1/2 tsp. salt
1 c. diced onions
1 c. diced celery
2 c. diced potatoes
1 c. canned tomatoes
1/2 tsp. pepper
1 lge. can minced clams
1 tbsp. flour
2 tbsp. butter

Fry bacon in Dutch oven until golden brown. Add 4 cups boiling water; simmer for 5 minutes. Add salt, onions and celery. Simmer for 20 minutes. Add potatoes, tomatoes and pepper. Simmer for 20 minutes longer. Add clams and juice. Cook for 10 minutes. Combine flour and butter, blending well. Stir into small amount of chowder mixture. Return flour mixture to Dutch oven, stirring constantly, until chowder is thickened. Simmer for several minutes before serving.

CORN CHOWDER

8 slices bacon, minced
1 sm. onion, sliced
2 17-oz. can cream-style corn
2 c. cubed cooked potatoes
2/3 c. evaporated milk
1 tsp. salt
1/4 tsp. garlic salt
1 1/2 c. cubed American cheese

Saute bacon in large pan until crisp; reserve 1/4 cup bacon drippings in pan. Add onion; saute until limp. Add corn, potatoes, milk, 2 1/2 cups hot water and seasonings. Simmer until hot. Place cheese cubes in soup just before serving. Yield: 6 servings.

NEW ENGLAND CORN CHOWDER

3 slices salt pork, cut into cubes
1 med. onion, sliced
4 med. potatoes, sliced
6 lge. soda crackers
2 c. milk
2 c. fresh or canned corn, cooked
1 tsp. salt
1/4 tsp. pepper

Brown salt pork in large saucepan. Add onion; cook until tender and lightly browned. Add potatoes and 2 cups water; cook until potatoes are tender. Soak crackers in milk; add to potato mixture. Add corn, salt and pepper; heat to boiling. Yield: 4 servings.

MEATBALL CHOWDER

2 lb. ground beef
2 tsp. seasoned salt
1/2 tsp. pepper
2 eggs, slightly beaten
1/4 c. finely chopped parsley
1/4 c. cracker crumbs
2 tbsp. milk
3 tbsp. flour
1 tbsp. oil
4 onions, chopped
6 c. tomato juice
6 beef bouillon cubes
4 c. sliced celery
3 c. diced potatoes
4 c. diced carrots
1/4 c. long grain rice
1 tbsp. sugar
2 tsp. salt
2 bay leaves
1/2 tsp. marjoram
1 12-oz. can Mexicorn

Combine beef, salt, pepper, eggs, parsley, cracker crumbs and milk; mix well. Shape into 40 small balls. Coat balls with flour; brown in oil in 10-quart kettle. Add 6 cups water and remaining ingredients except Mexicorn. Bring to a boil; cover. Reduce heat; simmer for 20 minutes. Add corn; simmer for 10 minutes longer.

HAM CHOWDER

1 hambone
1 sm. onion, chopped
1 stalk celery
1 qt. diced potatoes
3 tbsp. parsley
3 tbsp. butter
3 tbsp. flour
1 qt. milk
Salt and pepper
2 slices stale bread, cubed
1/4 c. ham drippings

Place hambone, onion, celery, and 1 quart water in kettle; cover. Bring to a boil gradually; reduce heat. Simmer for 1 hour. Remove hambone; trim off meat. Dice meat; add to stock. Add potatoes and half the parsley; boil gently for 20 minutes or until potatoes are tender. Melt butter in skillet; blend in flour. Add milk; cook, stirring constantly, until thickened. Add to stock; season to taste. Saute bread in hot ham drippings until crisp. Garnish chowder with bread cubes and remaining parsley. Yield: 6-8 servings.

LIMA BEAN-HAM CHOWDER

1 1/2 c. large dried lima beans
1 meaty ham hock
1 1/2 tsp. salt
1/2 c. chopped green pepper
1 lge. onion, chopped
Butter
1 1/2 c. cream-style corn
2 c. scalded milk

Soak beans overnight in 1 quart water; add ham hock. Simmer for 1 hour and 30 minutes or until beans are tender. Remove ham hock from beans; shred meat. Drain beans, reserving 1 cup liquid. Mash beans; add salt. Saute green pepper and onion in butter. Mix beans, ham and reserved bean liquid; stir in corn and milk. Heat through gently. Do not boil. Serve sprinkled with paprika, if desired. Yield: 4-6 servings.

SAUSAGE-BEAN CHOWDER

1 lb. pork sausage
2 1-lb. cans kidney beans
1 1 lb. 13-oz. can tomatoes
1 lge. onion, chopped
1 bay leaf
1 1/2 tsp. seasoned salt
1/2 tsp. garlic salt
1/2 tsp. thyme
1/8 tsp. pepper
1/2 green pepper, chopped
1 c. diced potatoes

Cook sausage in skillet; drain well. Combine beans, tomatoes, 1 quart water, onion, bay leaf and seasonings in large kettle; add sausage. Simmer, covered, for 1 hour. Add green pepper and potatoes. Cook, covered, for 30 minutes. Remove bay leaf before serving. Yield: 8 servings.

TURKEY-CORN CHOWDER

4 med. sliced onions
8 tbsp. butter
5 med. sliced potatoes
2 stalks celery, sliced
4 tsp. salt
1/2 tsp. pepper
1 chicken bouillon cube
5 c. milk
2 cans whole kernel corn
1/4 tsp. dried thyme
1 c. light cream
1 No. 303 can cream-style corn
1 1/2 tsp. paprika
3 c. cut-up roast turkey
Parsley

Saute onions in 4 tablespoons butter in large kettle, stirring frequently. Add potatoes, celery, salt, pepper, 2 cups water and bouillon cube; cover. Cook for 15 minutes or until vegetables are tender. Add milk, whole kernel corn, thyme, cream, cream-style corn, paprika and turkey. Heat through. Dot with remaining butter; snip parsley over top. Yield: 8-10 servings.

FRESHWATER FISH CHOWDER

2 lb. freshwater fish
4 tsp. salt
1/2 lb. salt pork
2 lb. onions
2 lb. potatoes, diced
1/4 c. butter
1 lge. can tomato soup
Worcestershire sauce to taste
1/2 tsp. pepper

Combine fish, salt and 1 gallon of water in large kettle. Simmer until fish flakes easily. Remove fish; strain and reserve stock. Grind salt pork and onions through coarse grinder. Boil in reserved fish stock for 45 minutes. Remove bones and skin from fish; cool. Add potatoes to fish stock; cook for 20 minutes. Add butter, soup, Worcestershire sauce, pepper and additional water if necessary. Add fish slowly, stirring to prevent sticking. Simmer until ready to serve. Yield: 10 to 12 servings.

SUWANNEE RIVER CATFISH CHOWDER

20 lb. large catfish, cleaned
20 lb. potatoes, cubed
4 1-lb. cans tomatoes
2 8-oz. cans tomato sauce
10 lb. onions, chopped
4 sticks butter
10 bay leaves
2 tbsp. thyme
4 tbsp. seafood seasoning
1/2 c. Worcestershire sauce
Salt and pepper to taste

Place catfish in water to cover in large kettle. Simmer until fish flakes easily. Add potatoes; cook until tender. Add remaining ingredients; simmer for 2 hours longer, stirring frequently. Yield: 40 servings.

TUNA CHOWDER

1 can cream of celery soup
1 1-lb. can stewed tomatoes
1 tbsp. instant minced onions
1 7-oz. can tuna, drained

Combine celery soup and tomatoes in 1 3/4-quart saucepan; add onion and tuna. Heat to serving temperature over medium heat. May be topped with grated Parmesan cheese. Yield: 3 servings.

Fish Chowder . . . Haddock, herbs, potatoes, and carrots are featured in a rich soup.

HADDOCK CHOWDER

12 lge. potatoes, cubed
1 lb. bacon
5 lge. onions, diced
2 lb. haddock fillets
3 cans evaporated milk
Salt and pepper to taste

Partially cover potatoes with water in large saucepan; simmer until tender. Cut bacon into 1-inch pieces; brown bacon and onions in skillet. Add bacon mixture to potatoes. Cut haddock into 2-inch pieces; arrange over potato mixture. Do not stir. Simmer until haddock flakes easily; pour milk over haddock. Stir gently. Heat through; add salt and pepper. Let stand for several hours; reheat and serve. Yield: 8 servings.

FISH CHOWDER

1/4 c. butter
1 c. thinly sliced onion
1 c. cubed potato
1 c. sliced carrot
2 tsp. salt
1/8 tsp. pepper
1 1-lb. package frozen haddock
3 c. milk
1/2 tsp. leaf rosemary
1/4 tsp. leaf thyme
1 c. light cream
2 tbsp. flour

Melt butter; add onion, potato, carrot, 1 cup water, 1 teaspoon salt and pepper. Cover; simmer for about 15 minutes or until carrot is almost tender. Thaw haddock; cut into 1-inch cubes. Add haddock, milk, herbs and remaining salt; heat to simmering. Cook until haddock flakes easily. Blend cream and flour together; add to chowder, heating thoroughly. Yield: 8-10 servings.

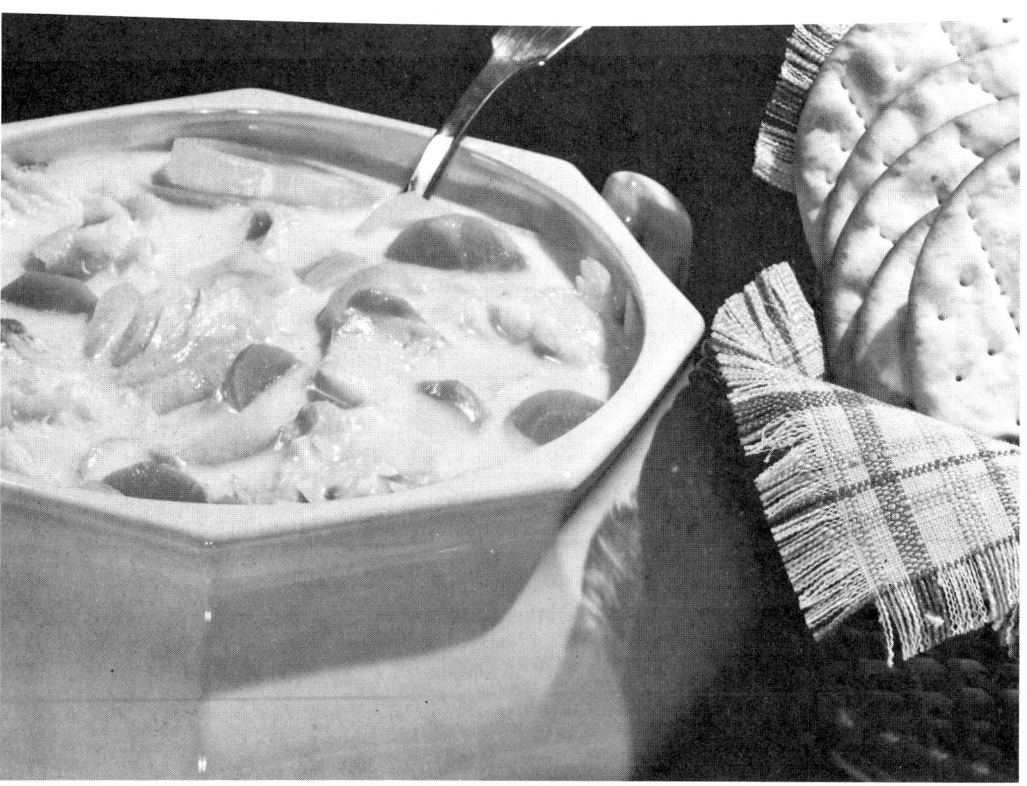

MAINE FISH CHOWDER

1 lb. haddock fillets
3 med. potatoes, diced
1 onion, finely chopped
Salt and pepper to taste
1 tsp. parsley flakes
4 slices cooked bacon, crumbled
1 tbsp. butter
3 c. milk
1 can cream-style corn

Simmer haddock in large pan in small amount of water until just tender; break gently with fork. Remove skin. Cook potatoes until almost done in small amount of water; add to haddock. Saute onion in bacon drippings; add to haddock mixture. Add salt, pepper and parsley to haddock and potatoes. Add bacon and butter to chowder. Add milk and corn; bring to a boil. Remove from heat; serve immediately. Yield: 4 servings.

SEAFOOD CHOWDER

12 slices bacon, diced
1 c. chopped onion
1 c. chopped celery
1/2 lemon, thinly sliced
2 No. 2 cans tomatoes
1 clove of garlic
1/4 c. catsup
1/4 tsp. curry powder
2 tsp. salt
1/8 tsp. hot sauce
1 tbsp. Worcestershire sauce
1 lb. scallops, cleaned
1 lb. shrimp, cleaned
1 lb. haddock
2/3 c. sherry
4 tbsp. butter

Cook bacon until brown. Add onion and celery; cook, covered, for 5 minutes. Add lemon, 1 quart water, tomatoes, garlic, catsup, curry powder, salt, hot sauce and Worcestershire sauce. Reduce heat; cook over low heat for 30 minutes. Add scallops and shrimp; simmer for 20 minutes. Cut haddock into 1-inch pieces; add to chowder. Add sherry and butter; cook for 10 minutes longer. Let stand overnight; reheat and serve. Yield: 8-10 servings.

Chutney

This term is applied to a group of sweet or sour relishes that originated in India and are often served as a condiment for curried dishes. **INGREDIENTS**: Chutney is made from a fruit base that varies; and raisins and dates are added. Seasonings include spices such as garlic and chilies; sugar; onions; and vinegar. There are many kinds of chutney including apple, peach, pineapple, mango, and tomato.
PREPARATION: Following recipe instructions, combine ingredients in saucepan. Cook until soft; cool; pack in jars. It should have the consistency of jam.
SERVING: In addition to being a spicy condiment for curries, chutney can be served with meat, poultry, and vegetable dishes and with stews.

APPLE CHUTNEY

3 lb. apples
1 lb. onions
1 lb. tomatoes
1 lb. yellow raisins
1/4 lb. crystallized ginger
1/4 lb. almonds
1 lb. brown sugar
1 tsp. ground ginger
2 tsp. dry mustard
1 tsp. salt
1/4 tsp. cayenne pepper
1 qt. white vinegar

Peel and chop apples, onions and tomatoes. Chop raisins, crystallized ginger and almonds. Combine brown sugar, ground ginger, mustard, salt, cayenne pepper and vinegar with fruits, vegetables, ginger and almonds in large kettle. Blend thoroughly. Bring to a boil; reduce heat. Simmer for 3 hours. Seal in sterilized jars.

HOT APPLE CHUTNEY

1 c. seedless raisins
1 c. currants
15 hot peppers
16 to 18 c. green apples
1 c. chopped preserved ginger
1 c. chopped onion
5 cloves of garlic, minced
3 tbsp. salt
2 c. vinegar
7 c. brown sugar

Grind raisins, currants and peppers; pare and chop apples. Combine raisins, currants and peppers with ginger, onion, garlic, salt, vinegar, sugar and 1 cup water in large kettle. Bring to a boil; boil for 45 minutes. Add apples; reduce heat. Simmer for 1 hour and 30 minutes or until fruit is transparent. Seal in sterilized jars. Yield: 12 pints.

CRANBERRY CHUTNEY

2 c. sugar
2 c. water
1 lb. fresh cranberries
1 c. cooking apples
1 c. raisins
1 c. chopped celery
2 tsp. ground ginger

Combine sugar and water in saucepan. Bring to a boil; boil for 3 to 5 minutes. Add cranberries. Bring to a boil; cook until skins of berries pop. Cool mixture. Core and chop apples. Combine raisins, apples, celery and ginger with cranberry mixture. Refrigerate until served. Yield: 4 cups.

ENGLISH CHUTNEY

1 1/2 lb. apples
1 1/2 lb. onions
1 1/2 lb. green tomatoes
1/2 lb. seedless raisins
1/2 lb. prunes
1 qt. vinegar
1 lb. sugar
2 oz. salt
1 oz. ground ginger
1/4 oz. cayenne pepper
1/2 oz. nutmeg
2 oz. mustard seed

Core and peel apples. Chop apples, onions, tomatoes, raisins and prunes coarsely. Combine fruits and vegetables with vinegar and seasonings. Simmer, stirring occasionally, for 4 hours. Yield: 4 quarts.

HAWAIIAN CHUTNEY

4 c. crushed canned pineapple
2 c. chopped seedless golden raisins
1/2 c. (packed) brown sugar
3 tbsp. white vinegar
1 tsp. salt
1/2 c. sugar
1/4 tsp. ground ginger
1/8 tsp. cayenne pepper
3/4 tsp. ground allspice
1/4 tsp. ground cloves
1/4 tsp. cinnamon
Few drops hot sauce
1/2 c. chopped almonds

Combine pineapple, raisins, brown sugar, vinegar and salt in large saucepan. Combine sugar, ginger, cayenne pepper, allspice, cloves, cinnamon and hot sauce in a small bowl. Stir spice mixture into pineapple mixture; simmer, stirring constantly, for 40 minutes or until mixture becomes clear. Remove from heat; add almonds. Pour into hot sterilized pint jars; seal at once. Yield: 3 pints.

MANGO CHUTNEY

25 mangos, peeled and sliced
2/3 tsp. nutmeg
2/3 tsp. cloves
1 1/2 tsp. allspice
2/3 tsp. ginger
1 1/4 qt. vinegar
4 lb. brown sugar
1/8 c. chopped chili peppers
1 clove garlic, minced
1/2 lge. onion, chopped
1/4 c. chopped gingerroot
1/4 lb. currants
1/4 lb. seedless raisins
1/4 c. preserved ginger, chopped

Peel and slice mangos. Combine nutmeg, cloves, allspice and ginger with vinegar and sugar in large saucepan; mix well. Add peppers, garlic, onion and gingerroot; bring to a boil. Boil for 10 minutes. Add currants, raisins and preserved ginger; boil for 15 minutes longer. Add mangos; simmer, stirring occasionally, for 30 minutes longer. Seal in sterilized jars.

MUSHROOM CHUTNEY

6 oz. canned mushrooms
2 c. peeled diced apples
1 c. raisins
1/2 c. chopped green pepper
1/2 c. chopped onion
1/2 c. crystallized ginger
1 c. (packed) brown sugar
1/4 c. vinegar
1/4 tsp. salt
1/8 tsp. cinnamon
1/8 tsp. nutmeg
1/8 tsp. cloves

Drain mushrooms; chop. Combine all ingredients in 2-quart saucepan. Bring to a boil; reduce heat. Simmer, covered, for 30 minutes. Remove cover; simmer for 15 minutes longer. Pack in sterilized jars. Yield: 2 pints.

PEACH CHUTNEY

10 c. firm peaches
1 c. walnuts
1 c. pecans
1 c. seedless raisins
6 to 8 hot peppers
1 c. chopped onion
1 c. currants
2 lemons, thinly sliced
5 cloves of garlic, minced
1 c. vinegar
7 c. sugar
1 tbsp. ginger
3 tbsp. salt
1 tbsp. cloves
1 tbsp. cinnamon
1 tbsp. paprika

Peel and slice peaches; chop walnuts, pecans, raisins and peppers coarsely. Combine peaches, walnuts and pecans; set aside. Combine onion, raisins, peppers, currants, lemons and garlic with vinegar, sugar and spices in large kettle. Bring to a boil; simmer for 1 hour. Add peaches and nuts. Simmer, stirring frequently, for 1 hour longer. Seal in sterilized jars.

PEAR CHUTNEY

6 c. chopped pears
1 1/2 c. raisins
1 onion, chopped
4 stalks celery, chopped
3 tbsp. salt
1 1/2 c. (packed) brown sugar
1 tsp. mustard
1/2 tsp. turmeric
1 qt. vinegar

Combine pears, raisins, onion, celery, salt, brown sugar and spices in large saucepan; add vinegar. Simmer for 45 minutes. Seal in sterilized jars. Yield: 5 pints.

PEAR-CANTALOUPE CHUTNEY

4 fresh Bartlett pears
4 c. cantaloupe, diced
1/2 c. pitted sliced dates
1/2 c. chopped onion
2 tbsp. chopped preserved ginger
2 tbsp. slivered lemon rind
1 c. cider vinegar
1 c. (packed) brown sugar
1 tsp. salt
6 drops hot sauce
1/2 c. chopped green pepper

Peel and core pears; slice lengthwise. Combine pears, cantaloupe, dates, onion, ginger and lemon rind with vinegar, brown sugar, salt and hot sauce. Bring to a boil; reduce heat. Simmer, stirring occasionally, for 40 minutes or until thickened. Add green pepper; simmer for 5 minutes longer. Seal in sterilized jars. Yield: 2 pints.

PEAR-TOMATO CHUTNEY

1 No. 2 can Bartlett pears
1 No. 2 can tomatoes
1 green pepper, coarsely chopped
1 med. onion, coarsely chopped
1 c. sugar
1/2 c. cider vinegar
1 tsp. salt
1/2 tsp. ginger
1/2 tsp. dry mustard
1/8 tsp. cayenne pepper
1 can pimento, coarsely chopped

Drain pears and tomatoes. Combine all ingredients except pimento in large saucepan. Bring to a boil; reduce heat. Simmer, stirring occasionally, for 1 hour. Break pears into pieces; add pimento. Simmer for 3 minutes longer. Seal in sterilized jars.

DIFFERENT TOMATO CHUTNEY

2 lb. apples
2 lb. tomatoes
4 med. onions
2 c. cider vinegar
2 tsp. salt
3 3/4 c. sugar

1/4 c. orange marmalade
2 tbsp. mixed pickling spices

Peel and core apples and tomatoes; chop apples, tomatoes and onions coarsely. Combine apples, tomatoes and onions in large saucepan. Add vinegar, salt, sugar and marmalade; mix well. Place pickling spices in cheesecloth bag; add to tomato mixture. Bring to a boil; reduce heat. Simmer, stirring frequently, for 1 hour and 30 minutes or until thickened. Discard spice bag. Seal in sterilized jars. Yield: 4 pints.

Cinnamon

Cinnamon is a pungently sweet aromatic spice produced from the dried bark of an evergreen tree. Most cinnamon sold in the United States is imported from Indonesia and Indo-China.

AVAILABILITY: Cinnamon is available year-round ground and in sticks.

USES: *Ground cinnamon* is widely used in baking. It also flavors fruits, vegetables, and meat dishes and is combined with sugar for cinnamon-and-sugar toppings. *Stick cinnamon* is used in seasoning stewed and preserved fruits, pickles, relishes, and hot and cold beverages.

STORING: Cinnamon should be stored in an airtight container to prevent flavor loss. Keep it in a dry place away from heat which also robs it of its flavor.

CINNAMON NUTS

3 c. nuts
1 c. sugar
1 tsp. cinnamon
1 tbsp. vanilla

Combine nuts, sugar, cinnamon and 5 tablespoons water in small saucepan. Cook over low heat until mixture spins a thread when dropped from teaspoon. Add vanilla. Turn onto buttered cookie sheet; separate nuts while cooling. Yield: 12 servings.

CINNAMON BARS

2 tbsp. margarine
3/4 c. sugar
2 1/4 c. flour
2 tsp. baking powder
Pinch of salt
1 c. milk
Melted butter
1 c. (packed) brown sugar
2 tsp. cinnamon
Nuts (opt.)

Cream margarine and sugar. Sift flour, baking powder and salt together; add to sugar mixture alternately with milk. Place in 8 x 8-inch buttered pan; spread top with melted butter. Combine brown sugar and cinnamon. Sprinkle brown sugar mixture and nuts over batter. Bake in 350-degree oven for 30 minutes. Cut into bars.

SWEET AND SPICY WHEELS

1/3 c. margarine
Sugar Smacks
1/4 c. sugar
1 tbsp. cinnamon

Melt margarine in heavy skillet. Add cereal; brown lightly. Remove from heat. Combine sugar and cinnamon; add to cereal. Stir well; spread onto waxed paper. Cool thoroughly.

CINNAMON DIAMONDS

1 c. butter
1 c. (packed) brown sugar
1 egg, separated
1/2 tsp. vanilla
2 c. sifted flour
1 tsp. cinnamon
3/4 c. chopped walnuts

Cream butter and sugar together until light; beat in egg yolk and vanilla. Sift flour and cinnamon together; stir into creamed mixture. Beat egg white lightly. Place dough in ungreased 15 1/2 x 10 1/2 x 1-inch baking pan; brush with egg white. Sprinkle with walnuts, pressing into surface lightly. Bake at 350 degrees for about 20 minutes. Cut into diamond shape while warm. Yield: 4 dozen.

CINNAMON STICKS

1 c. flour
1 c. sugar
2 tsp. cinnamon
3/4 c. margarine
1 egg, separated
1/2 tsp. vanilla
1 c. chopped pecans

Sift flour, sugar and cinnamon together. Add margarine, egg yolk and vanilla; mix well. Spread mixture 1/4 inch thick on cookie sheet. Beat egg white until light. Brush top with egg white; sprinkle with pecans. Bake at 325 degrees for 30 minutes. Cool for 10 minutes; cut into sticks.

CINNAMON KNOTS

2 pkg. yeast
Sugar
1/2 c. shortening
2 tsp. salt
2 c. hot milk
9 c. flour
3 eggs, beaten
2 tbsp. cinnamon
Butter, melted

Dissolve yeast in 1 1/2 cups lukewarm water; add 1 teaspoon sugar. Cream shortening, 1 cup sugar and salt together. Add milk and 3 cups flour; stir. Add eggs and yeast mixture; beat well. Add enough remaining flour to make a soft dough; let rise until doubled in bulk. Punch down; let rise until doubled in bulk. Mix 1 cup sugar and cinnamon together. Roll out dough, cutting into 3-inch strips; tie in knots. Dip knots into butter; coat with sugar mixture. Let rise until doubled in bulk. Bake at 350 degrees for 15 minutes or until brown. Yield: 36 knots.

Raisin-Whirl Sweet Rolls . . . Delight everyone at breakfast when you serve these flavor-filled rolls.

CINNAMON-NUT CRESCENTS

1 pkg. yeast
1 c. sugar
1 tsp. salt
2 tbsp. shortening
3 1/4 to 3 1/2 c. sifted flour
1 egg
Softened butter
3 tsp. cinnamon
Powdered sugar icing
1/2 c. chopped nuts

Dissolve yeast in 1 cup warm water; add 1/4 cup sugar, salt, shortening and half the flour. Beat thoroughly for 2 minutes; add egg, mixing well. Beat in remaining flour gradually until smooth. Cover with damp cloth; refrigerate until ready for use. Punch dough down occasionally. Divide dough into thirds. Roll each piece into a 12-inch circle on lightly floured board. Spread with butter. Mix remaining sugar and cinnamon; sprinkle over circles. Cut each circle into 8 wedges. Stretch wide end; roll up. Place on greased cookie sheets; let rise for about 1 hour. Bake in 400-degree oven for about 20 minutes. Cool. Frost with powdered sugar icing; sprinkle with nuts. Yield: 24 crescents.

QUICK CINNAMON ROLLS

1/4 c. sugar
1 tsp. cinnamon
2 tbsp. melted butter
1 pkg. refrigerator biscuits

Mix sugar and cinnamon together. Dip each biscuit into melted butter. Coat with cinnamon mixture. Place in pan. Bake according to package directions. Remove from oven; loosen rolls immediately. Yield: 10 rolls.

RAISIN-WHIRL SWEET ROLLS

2 pkg. yeast
3/4 c. milk, scalded
1/3 c. sugar
2 tsp. salt
1/3 c. butter
1 egg
4 1/2 c. sifted flour
1 c. rolled oats
Melted butter
1 c. brown sugar
2 tsp. cinnamon
1/2 c. raisins

Dissolve yeast in 1/2 cup warm water. Pour scalded milk over sugar, salt and butter; stir occasionally until butter melts. Cool to lukewarm. Stir in egg and 1 cup flour. Add yeast and oats. Stir in enough flour to make soft dough. Turn out on lightly floured board; knead for about 10 minutes or until smooth and satiny. Round dough into ball; place in greased bowl. Brush dough lightly with melted butter. Cover; let rise for about 1 hour in warm place until doubled in bulk. Combine brown sugar, cinnamon and raisins; set aside. Punch dough down; cover. Let rest for 10 minutes. Divide dough in half. Roll 1 half out to form 12 by 9-inch rectangle. Brush with melted butter. Sprinkle with half the cinnamon mixture. Roll up as for jelly roll; cut into twelve 1-inch slices. Arrange in greased 9-inch round baking pan. Repeat with remaining dough. Brush rolls with melted butter; cover. Let rise for about 45 minutes in warm place, until nearly doubled in bulk. Bake at 375 degrees for about 25 minutes. Invert on wire racks immediately.

CINNAMON ROLLS

2 pkg. yeast
3/4 c. sugar
2 tsp. salt
1/2 c. margarine
2 c. hot milk
6 c. sifted flour
2 eggs, beaten
2 tsp. cinnamon

Melted butter
1/2 c. raisins
1/2 c. chopped nuts
Powdered sugar icing

Soften yeast in 1/2 cup warm water. Add 1/4 cup sugar, salt, margarine and milk; stir until margarine is melted. Cool mixture to lukewarm. Beat in 3 cups flour; stir in eggs and yeast mixture, beating well. Add remaining flour, stirring thoroughly. Dough should be sticky. Let stand for 10 minutes; knead until smooth and satiny. Place in greased bowl, turning once; cover. Let rise in warm place until doubled in bulk. Punch down; divide into halves. Let stand for 10 minutes. Roll out on floured board. Combine cinnamon and remaining sugar. Spread dough halves with melted butter; sprinkle with cinnamon mixture, raisins and nuts. Roll dough jelly roll fashion; cut into 1-inch slices. Place in greased pan. Bake at 350 degrees for about 25 minutes. Frost with powdered sugar icing. Yield: 48 rolls.

CINNAMON STRIPS

2/3 c. hot milk
Sugar
1 1/2 tsp. salt
3/8 c. shortening
1 cake yeast
3 eggs, beaten
4 1/2 c. flour
1/2 c. melted margarine
4 tsp. cinnamon
Powdered sugar icing

Stir milk into 1/2 cup sugar, salt and shortening. Cool mixture to lukewarm. Combine 2/3 cup lukewarm water, 2 tablespoons sugar and yeast in bowl, stirring to mix. Let stand until dissolved; stir in milk mixture. Add eggs; stir in 3 cups flour, beating until smooth. Add remaining flour. Turn onto floured board; knead until smooth and elastic. Place dough in greased bowl; grease top of dough. Cover; set over hot water. Let rise until doubled in bulk. Punch down; place on floured board. Divide into halves. Roll each half to 15 x 15 1/2-inch rectangle; brush with margarine. Mix 1 1/2 cups sugar and cinnamon. Sprinkle 1/3 of the sugar mixture on 1/3 of the dough; fold dough over sugar mixture. Spread margarine over; add sugar mixture to remaining dough. Fold dough over other side; cut into 1-inch strips. Place strips 1 1/2 inches apart on greased cookie sheets. Bake at 400 degrees for about 20 minutes. Drizzle with powdered sugar icing. Yield: 4 1/2 dozen.

NO-KNEAD CINNAMON ROLLS

4 1/2 c. flour
1 5/8 c. sugar
1 tsp. salt
1/2 c. margarine
1 c. milk
2 pkg. yeast
3 eggs, beaten
1/4 c. soft butter
4 tsp. cinnamon

Sift flour, 1/2 cup sugar and salt together into large bowl. Melt margarine in small saucepan; add milk. Place over low heat until mixture is lukewarm. Dissolve yeast and 2 tablespoons sugar in 1/2 cup warm water; add milk mixture, eggs and flour mixture. Beat until smooth. Dough will be sticky. Grease dough; cover. Let rise until doubled in bulk. Punch dough down; let rise until doubled in bulk. Punch dough down a second time; let rise until doubled in bulk. Divide dough into 2 parts. Roll out into rectangles; spread with 2 tablespoons butter. Mix 1/2 cup sugar and 2 teaspoons cinnamon; sprinkle over rectangles. Roll jelly roll fashion; cut into 1-inch slices. Place in greased 11 x 15-inch pan. Let rise for about 40 minutes. Bake in 350-degree oven for about 25 minutes. Yield: 2 dozen.

PINWHEELS

2 c. prepared biscuit mix
2/3 c. milk
4 tbsp. melted butter
1 c. (packed) brown sugar
2 tsp. cinnamon

Prepare biscuit mix with milk according to package directions for rolled biscuits; knead dough on floured board for several minutes. Roll dough into large rectangle, 1/4 inch thick; spread with butter. Combine brown sugar and cinnamon. Sprinkle about 3/4 cup brown sugar mixture over dough. Grease muffin pan; sprinkle remaining brown sugar mixture in each cup. Roll dough, jelly roll fashion; slice into 12 biscuits. Place, cut side down, in muffin cups on brown sugar. Bake at 400 degrees for at least 10 minutes. Turn out of pan onto waxed paper immediately. Serve hot. Yield: 12 servings.

CINNAMON SWIRL LOAF

1 pkg. yeast
2 c. hot milk
1/2 c. shortening
1 1/4 c. sugar
2 tsp. salt
7 1/2 to 8 c. sifted flour
2 eggs, slightly beaten
1 1/2 tbsp. cinnamon

Soften yeast in 1/4 cup warm water. Combine milk, shortening, 1/2 cup sugar and salt. Add 3 cups flour; mix well. Stir in yeast mixture and eggs; beat well. Add enough remaining flour to make soft dough. Turn onto lightly floured surface. Knead until smooth. Place in lightly greased bowl, turning once. Cover; let rise for about 2 hours or until doubled in bulk. Punch down. Divide dough into halves. Cover; let stand for 10 minutes. Roll into two 15 x 7-inch rectangles about 1/2 inch thick. Mix remaining sugar and cinnamon together; sprinkle over dough. Sprinkle 1 teaspoon water over each rectangle. Roll each, jelly roll fashion, beginning with narrow side; seal edge. Place rolls, sealed edge down, in greased loaf pans. Let rise until doubled in bulk. Bake at 350 degrees for 35 to 40 minutes. Cover with foil if crust browns too quickly. Turn out of pans; cool on rack. Yield: 2 loaves.

CINNAMON SURPRISES

1 king-sized loaf bread
1 c. melted butter
Cinnamon sugar to taste

Remove crusts from bread slices; cut each slice into 3 strips. Dip each strip into butter; sprinkle generously with cinnamon sugar. Place on cookie sheet. Bake at 350 degrees for 10 minutes. Yield: About 2 dozen.

CINNAMON-PECAN RING

1 c. lukewarm milk
1 c. sugar
1 tsp. salt
1/4 c. soft shortening
1 pkg. yeast
1 egg
3 1/2 to 3 3/4 c. sifted flour
1 tsp. cinnamon
1/4 c. corn syrup
Melted butter
1 c. chopped pecans

Combine milk, 1/4 cup sugar, salt, shortening and yeast. Mix until dissolved. Stir in egg. Add flour gradually until dough is handled easily. Turn onto lightly floured board; knead until smooth and elastic. Place in greased bowl; cover. Let rise until doubled in bulk or for about 2 hours. Punch down; knead lightly. Let rise for 45 minutes. Combine remaining sugar and cinnamon. Pour corn syrup into greased 9-inch tube pan. Shape dough into balls the size of a walnut; dip into melted butter and into cinnamon mixture. Place in pan in layers. Sprinkle each layer with pecans. Let rise for 45 minutes. Bake at 375 degrees for 35 to 40 minutes.

CINNAMON RING

1 c. sugar
1 tsp. salt
1/2 c. margarine
1 c. hot milk
3 to 3 1/2 c. flour
1 pkg. yeast
2 eggs, lightly beaten
Melted margarine
1 tbsp. cinnamon
1/2 c. chopped walnuts

Place 1/4 cup sugar, salt and margarine in large mixing bowl. Pour in hot milk; stir until margarine melts. Add 1 cup flour; blend with mixer. Add yeast and 1 cup flour, stirring well; add eggs. Add remaining flour gradually, mixing well. Let rise in warm place until doubled in bulk; punch down. Refrigerate for 1 hour. Roll dough in melted margarine. Mix remaining sugar, cinnamon and walnuts together on waxed paper. Roll dough in sugar mixture; fit into greased tube pan. Bake at 350 degrees for 35 to 40 minutes. Yield: 12 servings.

CINNAMON TWISTS

1 c. sour cream
3 tbsp. sugar
1/8 tsp. soda
1/8 tsp. salt
1 pkg. yeast
1 lge. egg
2 tbsp. soft shortening
3 c. sifted flour
2 tbsp. soft butter
Cinnamon sugar

Place sour cream in large saucepan; heat to lukewarm. Remove from heat. Add sugar, soda, salt and yeast, stirring until dissolved. Add egg, shortening and flour; mix well. Turn dough onto floured board. Fold over several times until smooth; roll out into 24 x 6-inch rectangle. Spread dough with butter; sprinkle half the dough with cinnamon sugar. Fold over; cut into twenty-four 1-inch strips. Hold strips at both ends; twist in opposite directions. Place on greased baking sheet 2 inches apart. Press both ends of twists to baking sheet. Cover; let rise for about 1 hour or until light. Bake at 375 degrees for at least 12 minutes. Twists may be frosted, if desired. Serve warm. Yield: 2 dozen.

Clam

Clams are a shellfish available in a wide range of varieties including over 30 Pacific types. Atlantic clams include soft-shelled steamers, abundant north of Cape Cod, and hard-shelled (quahog) clams found south of the Cape. All clams are fat-free and high in protein. (4 medium raw clams = 65 calories; 3 ounces canned clams = 45 calories)

AVAILABILITY: Whole or minced clams, bottled clam juice, and fresh clams available year-round.

BUYING: In buying fresh clams, choose large hard-shelled varieties for chowders and smaller ones for serving raw. Look for fresh clams with tightly-closed shells.

STORING: Most fresh clams must be prepared immediately. However, quahogs can be refrigerated several weeks. Cooked clams keep two days in refrigerator. Unopened cans of clams keep one year in cupboard; opened cans keep in refrigerator, covered, for one day.

PREPARATION: To prepare clams for serving raw, scrub with brush. Insert tip of knife between edges of shell. Pry open. Preserve juice. To steam clams, allow 1 quart per person. Scrub clams and place in kettle in 1/2 inch boiling salted water. Cover and steam over low heat 10 minutes or until shells open.

SERVING: Serve raw clam meat with juice on half-shell atop crushed ice. Accompany with sauce or lemon wedges. Serve steamed clams hot, with butter and strained broth from cooking kettle. To eat steamed clams, lift from shells by neck and remove skin.

(See SEAFOOD.)

CLAM DIP

1 clove of garlic
1 8-oz. package cream cheese
1 8-oz. package ricotta cheese
1 1/2 tsp. Worcestershire sauce
1/4 c. clam broth
1/2 c. canned minced clams
1/4 tsp. angostura bitters
2 tsp. lemon juice
1/2 tsp. salt
Dash of freshly ground pepper

Rub wooden serving bowl with garlic. Blend cream cheese and ricotta cheese together in bowl until smooth. Add remaining ingredients, mixing well. Serve with crackers or potato chips. Yield: About 3 cups.

BROILED CLAM SNACK

1 can drained minced clams
1/2 c. mayonnaise
1/2 c. grated Parmesan cheese
1 tbsp. grated onion
2 tbsp. sweet pickle relish
1 tsp. Worcestershire sauce
French bread squares
Paprika

Combine clams, mayonnaise, cheese, onion, relish and Worcestershire sauce; mix well. Spread clam mixture over bread squares. Broil until lightly toasted and heated through. Sprinkle with paprika; serve immediately.

CLAM PUFFS

1 8-oz. package cream cheese
1 7-oz. can minced clams
1/4 tsp. salt
2 tsp. fresh, lemon juice
1 tbsp. grated onion
1 tbsp. Worcestershire sauce
1 egg white, stiffly beaten
Toast rounds

Soften cream cheese; beat until smooth. Drain clams. Combine cream cheese, clams, salt, lemon juice, onion and Worcestershire sauce. Fold in egg white carefully. Spoon clam mixture onto toast rounds. Bake at 450 degrees for 3 minutes; serve immediately. Yield: 36 puffs.

Clam Tart . . . Feature a popular seafood in this delicious main-dish pie.

CLAM BALLS

3 cans minced clams
3 stalks celery, minced
1 onion, ground
Salt and pepper
6 hard-cooked eggs, diced
1/2 lb. moist bread crumbs

Drain clams; reserve 2 cups broth. Combine celery, onion and 1 1/2 cups clam broth in saucepan; simmer until vegetables are tender. Add clams, salt and pepper to vegetable mixture; simmer for about 10 minutes. Add eggs, remaining broth and bread crumbs, mixing well. Shape clam mixture into 2-inch balls. Chill well. Fry in deep hot fat until browned; serve immediately with wooden picks.

CLAM TART

1 unbaked 9-in pie shell
1 tbsp. melted butter
1 7 1/2-oz. can minced clams
1 c. instant nonfat dry milk powder
3 eggs
1 tbsp. grated onion
1/2 tsp. seasoned salt
1/4 tsp. crushed thyme
Dash of pepper
Grated Parmesan cheese
Chopped parsley

Brush pie shell with butter; chill in freezer for 5 minutes. Drain clams, reserving juice; add enough water to equal 2 cups liquid. Pour into bowl. Stir in dry milk; beat in eggs, onion and seasonings. Add clams; pour into pie shell. Bake in 425-degree oven for 15 minutes. Reduce oven temperature to 300 degrees; bake for 15 minutes longer. Sprinkle with cheese; bake for 15 minutes longer or until knife inserted in center comes out clean. Garnish with parsley. Serve hot.

CLAM SANDWICHES

1/4 lb. butter
1 sm. box Velveeta cheese
Dash of Worcestershire sauce
1 can minced clams, drained
Hard rolls, split

Combine butter, cheese, Worcestershire sauce and clams in double boiler; cook, stirring, until butter and cheese are melted. Cool. Spread clam mixture on rolls. Broil until cheese mixture bubbles and rolls are toasted. Serve immediately.

CLAMBURGERS

1 c. chopped clams
1 egg, beaten
1 tbsp. lemon juice
1 tbsp. chopped parsley
1 tbsp. grated onion
1/2 tsp. salt
Dash of pepper
1/2 c. dry bread crumbs
6 buns, split and buttered

Combine clams, egg, lemon juice, parsley, onion and seasonings, mixing well. Shape into 6 flat cakes. Roll in crumbs. Fry cakes in deep hot fat until lightly browned on both sides. Heat buns; place cakes on half the buns. Top with remaining buns. Yield: 6 servings.

BAKED CLAMS

2 med. cans minced clams, drained
1 c. seasoned bread crumbs
1 tbsp. oregano
1/4 lb. melted butter
1/4 c. grated Romano cheese
Paprika

Combine clams, bread crumbs, oregano, butter and cheese, blending well. Spoon clam mixture into individual clam shells; sprinkle with paprika. Bake at 350 degrees for about 25 minutes.

BAKED CLAMS WITH MUSHROOM SAUCE

1/2 c. minced onion
1/2 c. chopped mushrooms
1/4 c. butter
3 c. minced clams
1/4 tsp. paprika
1/2 tsp. salt
1/3 c. chopped parsley
1 1/2 c. medium white sauce
Buttered bread crumbs

Saute onion and mushrooms in butter until lightly browned; add clams. Simmer for 5 minutes. Combine seasonings and white sauce; add clam mixture. Pour into greased casserole; sprinkle with crumbs. Bake at 375 degrees for 20 to 25 minutes. Yield: 6 servings.

BAKED STUFFED CLAMS

2 cans minced clams
Milk
1 c. crushed round buttery crackers
1 tbsp. butter
1/2 tsp. parsley flakes
1 tbsp. flour
1/4 tsp. poultry seasoning
1/2 tsp. salt
1/8 tsp. pepper
Buttered crumbs

Drain clams; reserve juice. Add enough milk to reserved clam juice to equal 2 cups liquid. Place clams in bowl; stir in crackers. Melt butter; blend in parsley flakes, flour, poultry seasoning, salt and pepper. Add clam juice mixture; cook, stirring, until thickened. Add clam mixture. Fill individual greased ramekins or 4-inch clam dishes; sprinkle with crumbs and additional parsley flakes. Garnish with paprika. Bake at 350 degrees for 15 minutes. May be served with lemon juice if desired. Yield: 6 servings.

CHEESY CLAM CASSEROLE

1/2 c. butter
3/4 c. toasted bread crumbs
3/4 c. cracker crumbs
1 tsp. salt
1 tsp. (scant) pepper
1 tsp. paprika
2 cans minced clams, drained
1/2 c. chopped parsley
1 lge. onion, minced
1/2 c. heavy cream
Grated Parmesan cheese

Melt butter in skillet; add bread crumbs and cracker crumbs. Add seasonings; stir until crumbs are well coated. Mix clams, parsley, onion and 1 cup crumb mixture. Turn into greased casserole. Sprinkle with remaining crumb mixture; dot with additional butter. Pour cream over top. Bake at 375 degrees for 25 minutes or until bubbly and browned. Sprinkle with cheese. Yield: 4 servings.

CLAM CASSEROLE

2 cans minced clams, drained
30 saltines, crushed
1/4 lb. melted butter
1 c. milk
1 can mushroom soup
2 eggs, beaten
Crushed corn flakes

Combine clams and saltines; stir in butter, milk, soup and eggs. Turn into baking dish. Top with corn flakes. Place baking dish in pan of water. Bake at 350 degrees for 1 hour. Yield: 8 servings.

DEVILED CLAMS

2 med. onions, chopped
2 tbsp. butter
4 tomatoes, chopped
2 doz. large clams, chopped
Salt and pepper to taste
Cracker crumbs
2 eggs, beaten

Saute onions in butter in skillet until golden brown. Add tomatoes, clams, 1 cup water, salt and pepper. Simmer for 2 minutes; add enough cracker crumbs to thicken mixture. Cook for 5 minutes; remove from heat. Cool. Add eggs; mix well. Fill clam shells with clam mixture; sprinkle with crumbs. Dot with additional butter. Bake at 375 degrees until brown. Yield: 12 servings.

LONG ISLAND-STUFFED CLAMS

1 tsp. powdered garlic
1 tbsp. diced onion
1 tsp. chopped parsley
Oregano to taste
1/2 c. Italian bread crumbs
2 tbsp. olive oil
1 can minced clams with liquid
Salt to taste
Parmesan cheese
Paprika

Saute garlic, onion, parsley, oregano and crumbs in oil in frypan for about 2 minutes or until onion begins to brown. Add clams and salt. Spoon into clam shells; sprinkle lightly with additional crumbs and cheese. Place on baking sheet. Bake in 375-degree oven for 25 to 30 minutes or until crusty on top. Sprinkle lightly with paprika. Yield: 24 servings.

PUGET SOUND CLAM SOUFFLÉ

5 cans minced clams
1 pt. milk
Fine cracker crumbs
2 eggs, beaten
Salt and pepper to taste
Lean bacon slices

Combine clams and milk; stir in crumbs until mixture is thickened. Add eggs and seasonings. Spoon clam mixture into greased casserole. Arrange bacon slices on top. Bake at 350 degrees for about 45 minutes to 1 hour or until firm. Yield: 4 servings.

CLAM QUICHE LORRAINE

2 cans minced clams
1 recipe 1-crust pie pastry
6 slices bacon
3 tbsp. minced onion
4 eggs, beaten
1 c. milk
Salt and pepper to taste

Drain clams, reserving 1 cup clam liquid. Place clams in pastry-lined 9-inch pie plate. Cook bacon slices; drain and crumble over clams. Saute onion in bacon drippings until golden brown; sprinkle over bacon. Combine eggs, milk and reserved clam liquid, beating until blended. Add seasonings; pour milk mixture over clam mixture. Bake at 375 degrees for 40 minutes or until knife inserted in center comes out clean. Yield: 6 servings.

CLAM AND CORN SPECIALTY

1 can minced clams
Milk
3 eggs, beaten
1 tbsp. minced onion
2 tbsp. chopped pimentos
1/2 tsp. salt
Dash of pepper
1 c. cream-style corn
1/2 c. cracker crumbs
1 tbsp. melted butter

Drain clams, reserving liquid. Combine clam liquid and enough milk to equal 1 cup liquid. Blend eggs into clam liquid; stir in clams. Add remaining ingredients; turn into greased casserole. Bake at 375 degrees for 45 minutes or until firm. Yield: 6 servings.

CLAM AND EGGPLANT CASSEROLE

3 tbsp. butter
1/4 c. flour
1/2 tsp. salt
1/4 tsp. pepper
1 tbsp. grated onion
1/2 c. clam juice
1/2 c. milk
1 lge. eggplant
1 egg, beaten
1/2 c. minced clams
1/3 c. chopped celery
1/4 c. chopped stuffed olives
Bread crumbs
4 strips bacon, cooked
Chopped parsley

Melt butter in skillet; stir in flour until smooth. Add seasonings and onion. Add clam juice and milk gradually, stirring constantly. Cook over low heat, stirring, until thickened. Cool. Peel eggplant; cut into small pieces. Simmer in water to cover until tender. Drain. Add egg to cooled white sauce, blending well. Stir in clams, eggplant, celery and olives. Spoon clam mixture into greased 2-quart casserole. Sprinkle with bread crumbs; dot with additional butter. Bake at 350 degrees for about 50 minutes. Crumble bacon over top; garnish with parsley.

CLAM AND POTATO CASSEROLE

2 6-oz. cans minced clams
6 med. potatoes
1 sm. onion, minced
8 tbsp. flour
Salt
Pepper
6 tbsp. butter or margarine
2 c. milk

Drain clams; reserve liquid. Peel potatoes; cut into thin slices. Arrange layer of potatoes in greased casserole. Add half the clams, onion and flour. Sprinkle with salt and pepper; dot with 2 tablespoons butter. Repeat layers of potatoes and clams. Cover with remaining potatoes, butter, salt and pepper. Combine reserved clam liquid and milk; pour over clam mixture. Bake at 350 degrees for 1 hour and 15 minutes or until potatoes are done. Yield: 8 servings.

CLAMS AU GRATIN

1 pt. cooked ground clams
Milk
1/2 c. melted butter
1 c. cooked shell macaroni
1 c. soft bread crumbs
1 c. grated sharp Cheddar cheese
1 tsp. salt
Dash of pepper
3 eggs, beaten

Drain clams, reserving liquid; add enough milk to reserved clam liquid to equal 1 1/2 cups liquid. Combine butter, macaroni, crumbs, cheese, seasonings, clams and clam liquid; mix well. Blend in eggs. Spoon into greased 2-quart casserole. Bake at 350 degrees for 45 minutes. Yield: 6-8 servings.

CLAM SPAGHETTI

2 cans minced clams
1 4-oz. can mushrooms
2 tbsp. olive oil
1 clove of garlic, minced
1/2 tsp. freshly ground pepper
2 cans cream of mushroom soup
2 tbsp. chopped parsley
1/4 tsp. paprika
Salt to taste
1 lb. spaghetti
Butter

Drain clams and mushrooms; reserve juices. Heat oil in large skillet; add garlic. Cook, stirring constantly, for about 30 seconds. Add reserved juices and pepper; boil for about 5 minutes or until liquid is reduced. Add clams and mushrooms; boil for 3 minutes, stirring frequently. Add soup, parsley and paprika; simmer for 30 minutes, stirring sauce occasionally to prevent sticking. Add salt and additional pepper if needed. Prepare spaghetti according to package directions; drain. Toss with small amount of butter. Serve sauce over spaghetti. Yield: 4 servings.

White Clam Sauce with Spaghetti . . . Bring new excitement to spaghetti with this sauce.

WHITE CLAM SAUCE WITH SPAGHETTI

2 doz. cherrystone clams
1/2 c. chopped onion
3 cloves of garlic, minced
1/4 c. chopped parsley
1/4 c. olive oil
Salt
Dash of white pepper
8 oz. spaghetti

Cook clams, covered, in large pot in small amount of water just until shells open. Drain clams, reserving 1 1/2 cups broth. Remove clams from shells; chop. Saute onion, garlic and parsley in skillet in hot oil; add clams, reserved broth, 1/2 teaspoon salt and pepper. Boil for 1 minute. Add 1 tablespoon salt to 3 quarts rapidly boiling water in large pot. Add spaghetti gradually so that water continues to boil. Cook, stirring occasionally, until spaghetti is tender. Drain in colander. Serve with clam sauce.

CLAM CAKES

5 cans minced clams
1 tsp. baking powder
1/2 tsp. salt
2 c. flour
2 eggs, beaten
1 c. milk

Drain clams, reserving 1/2 cup clam liquid. Sift dry ingredients together. Add dry ingredients to clams alternately with eggs and milk. Stir in reserved clam liquid, mixing well. Drop clam mixture by spoonfuls into deep hot fat. Fry until golden brown. May add cracker crumbs to clam mixture before frying if desired.

CLAMS CREOLE

1/2 c. chopped green pepper
1/2 c. chopped onion
2 tbsp. butter
24 littleneck clams and juice
1/2 tbsp. flour
Juice of 1/2 lemon
1 tbsp. pimento
1 tbsp. cream
Paprika

Saute green pepper and onion in 1 tablespoon butter. Add clams with juice. Bring to boiling point. Mix flour with remaining butter. Stir into clam mixture. Add lemon juice and pimento; simmer for 5 minutes, stirring. Add cream and sprinkle with paprika just before serving. Serve on toast. Yield: 4-6 servings.

RICED CLAMS FLAMENCO

40 fresh med. butter clams, in shells
Salt
1/2 c. cornmeal
1 med. Bermuda onion, chopped
1 celery heart, minced
1 green pepper, chopped
3/4 lb. butter
1 carrot, grated
1 sweet red pepper, chopped
6 c. chicken stock
1/2 tsp. chili powder
1/2 tsp. curry powder
1/8 tsp. powdered thyme
1 tbsp. sugar
1/4 tsp. pepper
1/8 tsp. garlic powder
1/8 tsp. cumin powder
1 lb. long grain rice
4 sprigs of finely chopped parsley

Cover clams with cold brine of 1/3 cup salt for each gallon of water; sprinkle with cornmeal. Let stand for 12 hours. Rinse with fresh water. Saute onion, celery and green pepper in 1/4 pound butter, stirring constantly; do not brown. Combine onion mixture, carrot, red pepper and chicken stock in large pan; boil for 5 minutes. Add 1 teaspoon salt and remaining seasonings. Stir in rice; simmer for 20 minutes. Add clams, pressing down into rice. Add water if liquid is absorbed. Simmer for 10 to 15 minutes. Melt remaining butter; add parsley. Stir butter mixture into rice. Clams will open, filling with rice mixture. Yield: 8 servings.

CLAM-MUSHROOM APPETIZERS

1 can minced clams
1/2 lb. cottage cheese
1/2 sm. onion, grated
Dash of garlic salt
1 tsp. Worcestershire sauce
1 tsp. celery salt
Mushroom caps

Drain clams well, reserving 1 tablespoon liquid. Place clams and cottage cheese in blender container; blend. Add onion, garlic salt, Worcestershire sauce, celery salt and reserved clam juice; blend until smooth. Fill mushroom caps; broil for several minutes.

Coconut

The round, hard-shelled coconut provides firm, white meat and sweet, clear liquid. The meat and liquid are used for flavoring desserts and main dishes. Coconut is high in fats. (2 tablespoons fresh coconut = 40 calories)

AVAILABILITY: Fresh coconuts are available year-round and are especially plentiful from September to December. Coconut is also available year-round dry or moist, sweetened or unsweetened, in cans and packages.

BUYING: Choose compact, heavy coconuts

full of liquid (shake nut to check for sound of liquid). Coconut without liquid has spoiled. Small rings or eyes, at one end of coconut, should not be wet or moldy.

STORING: Store fresh, uncracked coconut at room temperature up to 6 months. Fresh meat, grated or in pieces, and fresh liquid (covered) keep 1 week in refrigerator. Dried meat in unopened package or can keeps 6 months in cupboard. Opened packages or cans keep 1 month in refrigerator. Cover before refrigerating.

PREPARATION: Follow recipe directions. From 1 medium coconut, plan on obtaining 1 cup milk. To shell coconut, pierce eyes with ice pick, and drain liquid. Place in freezer 1 hour or in 350-degree oven 20 minutes. Remove and shatter shell by rapping sharply with hammer or cleaver. Pry meat from pieces of shell.

COCONUT CAKE

1 c. butter
5 c. sugar
3 1/2 c. flour
3 1/2 tsp. baking powder
1 c. milk
11 egg whites
1 1/2 tsp. vanilla
1 1/2 tsp. lemon extract
2 tsp. vinegar
1/2 tsp. cream of tartar
1 1/2 c. grated coconut

Cream butter; add 2 cups sugar gradually. Combine flour and baking powder; add to creamed mixture alternately with milk. Beat 8 egg whites until stiff peaks form. Fold into creamed mixture; add 1/2 teaspoon vanilla and 1/2 teaspoon lemon extract. Pour batter into 3 greased and floured 9-inch layer pans. Bake at 375 degrees for 30 to 35 minutes or until cake tests done. Cool layers on racks. Combine remaining sugar, vinegar and 1 cup water in saucepan. Cook until mixture spins thread. Beat remaining egg whites with cream of tartar until stiff peaks form. Add sugar mixture gradually; beat until glossy. Add remaining vanilla and lemon extract; mix well. Stir in coconut. Spread icing between layers and on top and side of cake.

FRESH COCONUT CAKE

1 c. shortening
2 c. sugar
1 tsp. vanilla
3 c. sifted flour
3 tsp. baking powder
1 tsp. salt
1/2 c. milk
1/2 c. coconut milk
1 c. grated fresh coconut
6 egg whites, beaten stiff

Cream shortening and sugar until fluffy; stir in vanilla. Combine flour, baking powder and salt; add creamed mixture alternately with milk and coconut milk. Stir in coconut; fold in egg whites. Turn into 2 greased paper-lined layer cake pans. Bake at 365 degrees for 25 minutes. Cool in pans for 10 minutes. Turn out onto wire rack.

Coconut Icing

Sugar
1/4 c. coconut milk
1/4 tsp. salt
1/2 tsp. cream of tartar
2 egg whites
1 tsp. vanilla
2 c. grated fresh coconut

Add 1 teaspoon sugar to coconut milk; spoon over cake layers. Combine 1 cup sugar, salt, cream of tartar, egg whites, 3 tablespoons water and vanilla in top of double boiler. Cook for 7 minutes, beating constantly at high speed. Stir in 1 1/2 cups coconut. Frost between layers and over cake; sprinkle cake with remaining coconut.

COCONUT-APRICOT BALLS

1 1/2 c. dried apricots, ground
2 c. shredded coconut
2/3 c. sweetened condensed milk
Confectioners' sugar

Combine apricots and coconut. Add milk; blend well. Shape into balls. Place small amount of confectioners' sugar in small plastic bag; shake balls in sugar. Refrigerate until firm. Yield: About 32 balls.

COCONUT CREAMS

2 3-oz. packages cream cheese
2 tsp. liquid sweetener
1 tsp. grated orange rind
1/2 c. shredded coconut, toasted

Have cheese at room temperature; cream well. Add sweetener and orange rind; mix thoroughly. Form into 24 balls about 1 inch in diameter; roll in toasted coconut. Chill. Yield: 24 servings.

CHOCOLATE-DIPPED COCONUT BALLS

2 lb. confectioners' sugar
1/4 lb. butter, melted
1 can sweetened condensed milk
2 c. grated coconut
1 12-oz. package chocolate chips
1 bar paraffin

Combine sugar, butter, milk and coconut; mix well. Shape mixture into balls; freeze. Melt chocolate chips and paraffin in double boiler over hot water; dip frozen balls in hot chocolate mixture. Yield: 120 balls.

COCONUT SQUARES

2 c. sugar
2 tbsp. butter
1/2 c. milk
1 c. shredded coconut
1 tsp. vanilla

Combine sugar, butter and milk in saucepan. Simmer, stirring constantly, to soft-ball stage or 238 degrees on candy thermometer. Remove from heat; stir in coconut and vanilla. Beat until creamy; pour into greased 9-inch pan. Allow to stand for 30 minutes. Cut into squares.

COCONUT-FRUIT BALLS

1 c. dried prunes
1 c. dried apricots
2 c. golden raisins
1 1/2 c. chopped nuts
2 c. sugar
1/2 c. light corn syrup
1/2 tsp. vanilla
1/4 tsp. salt
Finely grated coconut

Grind prunes, apricots and raisins; combine with nuts. Blend sugar, corn syrup and 1/2 cup water in saucepan. Bring to a boil, stirring constantly, until sugar is dissolved. Cook to soft-ball stage or 238 degrees on candy thermometer. Remove from heat; cool for 10 minutes. Beat until creamy; stir in vanilla and salt. Combine quickly with prune mixture; mix well. Press into waxed paper-lined 9-inch pan; let stand for 2 to 3 hours. Turn candy out of pan; remove paper. Pinch off 3/4-inch pieces; form into balls. Roll balls in coconut.

COCONUT-LEMON BALLS

1 pkg. lemon sauce mix
2 1/2 c. graham cracker crumbs
1 c. chopped dates
1 c. chopped pecans or walnuts
6 c. miniature marshmallows
1/2 c. sweetened condensed milk
4 to 5 c. flaked coconut

Prepare lemon sauce mix according to package directions, using only 1/4 cup water. Cool thoroughly. Combine crumbs, dates, pecans and marshmallows in large bowl. Fold milk into lemon sauce; pour over crumb mixture. Mix well. Drop by teaspoonfuls into coconut; roll to cover. Refrigerate. Marshmallows may be colored and coconut may be toasted or tinted. Yield: 60-70 balls.

COCONUT BARS

18 graham wafers
1 c. brown sugar
Margarine or butter
Milk
1 c. graham wafer crumbs
1 c. walnuts, chopped
1 c. coconut
10 maraschino cherries, cut up
1 c. confectioners' sugar
1/2 tsp. vanilla
1/2 oz. unsweetened chocolate

Place graham wafers in buttered 8 x 12-inch pan. Combine brown sugar, 1/2 cup margarine and 1/2 cup milk; bring to boiling point. Remove from heat; let cool. Add crumbs, walnuts, coconut and cherries. Spread over wafers. Blend 2 tablespoons margarine, 1 tablespoon milk, confectioners' sugar and vanilla; spread over top of cherry mixture. Melt chocolate; drizzle over top. Let stand overnight; cut into bars. Yield: 25 servings.

HAWAIIAN COCONUT BARS

1/2 c. butter
1 c. flour
1/2 c. brown sugar

Cream all ingredients; pat into bottom of an ungreased 11 x 7 x 1 1/2-inch pan. Bake at 350 degrees for 15 minutes. Cool.

Filling

2 eggs
1 c. brown sugar
1 tsp. vanilla
2 tbsp. flour
Dash of salt
1 tsp. baking powder
1 1/2 c. coconut
1 c. chopped macadamia nuts

Cream eggs, sugar and vanilla. Blend in remaining ingredients. Pour over crust. Return to oven; bake for 20 minutes longer. Cool.

Frosting

1 1/2 c. confectioners' sugar
2 tbsp. butter
2 tbsp. orange juice
1 tsp. lemon juice

Blend all ingredients thoroughly. Spread over cooled Filling. Cut in bars. Yield: 2 dozen bars.

COCONUT SQUARES

1/2 c. soft butter
1/2 c. (packed) light brown sugar
1 c. sifted all-purpose flour

Cream butter and sugar until light and fluffy. Add flour; mix well. Pat into greased 13 x 9 x 2-inch pan. Bake for 12 minutes at 375 degrees.

Topping

2 eggs, slightly beaten
1/2 tsp. salt
1 tsp. vanilla
1 can flaked coconut
1 c. chopped nuts
3 to 4 tbsp. flour
1 c. (packed) light brown sugar

Blend all ingredients well; spread evenly over baked mixture. Bake for 20 minutes at 375 degrees. Cut into squares; cool in pan.

COCONUT BALLS

1 c. sugar
1 1/2 c. dates, chopped
1/4 tsp. salt
5 tbsp. margarine
2 eggs
Oven-toasted rice cereal
Coconut

Combine sugar, dates, salt, margarine and eggs in saucepan; cook, stirring constantly, until thickened. Add 2 1/2 cups cereal and 1 cup coconut; stir well. Shape into balls. Roll in coconut and cereal; place on waxed paper. Yield: 24-30 cookies.

COCONUT TOPS

Color photograph for this recipe on page 483.

6 tbsp. evaporated milk
3 c. flaked coconut
5/8 c. sugar
1 egg, beaten
Flour

Mix milk, coconut, sugar and egg in mixing bowl. Shape into small balls; place balls on greased baking sheet sprinkled with flour. Bake at 375 degrees for 12 to 15 minutes or until golden brown. Yield: 2 1/2 dozen.

COCONUT-ORANGE BALLS

1 sm. box vanilla wafers
1 4-oz. can shredded coconut
1 c. powdered sugar
1/2 c. orange juice concentrate

Crush vanilla wafers. Combine all ingredients; mix thoroughly with fork. Chill for 1 hour. Shape into 1-inch balls. Roll in additional powdered sugar. Yield: 24 balls.

COCONUT GUMDROP COOKIES

1 c. brown sugar
1 c. sugar
1 c. shortening
2 c. flour
1/4 tsp. salt
1 tsp. soda
1 tsp. baking powder
2 eggs, well beaten
1 c. shredded coconut
1 c. oatmeal
1 c. gumdrops, finely chopped
1 tsp. vanilla

Cream sugars and shortening together. Sift flour, salt, soda and baking powder together. Add dry ingredients and eggs to creamed mixture alternately. Add coconut, oatmeal, gumdrops and vanilla. Form into 1/2-inch balls; place on cookie sheet. Press balls flat with fork. Bake at 350 degrees for 10 minutes or until delicately browned.

COCONUT MACAROONS

3 egg whites
1 c. sugar
2 tbsp. flour
1/8 tsp. salt
1 tsp. vanilla
1 1/2 c. grated coconut

Beat egg whites until stiff peaks form. Add sugar gradually; beat until glossy. Fold in flour, salt, vanilla and coconut. Line baking sheets with greased heavy brown paper. Drop coconut mixture by teaspoonfuls onto paper. Bake at 350 degrees for 20 minutes. Yield: 2 dozen.

CRUNCHY COCONUT MACAROONS

2 egg whites
1 c. sugar
1 c. coconut
1 1/2 c. corn flakes, slightly crushed
1 tsp. vanilla

Beat egg whites until stiff peaks form. Add sugar gradually; beat until glossy. Add coconut, corn flakes and vanilla. Line baking sheets with greased heavy brown paper. Drop coconut mixture by teaspoonfuls onto paper. Bake at 350 degrees for 20 minutes. Yield: 30 cookies.

COCONUT PIE

3 eggs
1 1/2 c. sugar
1 stick butter, melted
1 tbsp. vinegar
1 tsp. vanilla
1 can flaked coconut
1 unbaked 9-in. pastry shell

Beat eggs and sugar until fluffy; add butter, vinegar and vanilla. Beat well. Stir in coconut; pour into pastry shell. Bake in 350-degree oven for 1 hour.

COCONUT CHIFFON PIE

1 env. unflavored gelatin
1 1/2 c. milk
1 c. sugar
4 tbsp. flour
1/2 tsp. salt
3/4 tsp. vanilla
1/4 tsp. almond extract
1/2 c. heavy cream, whipped
1 1/4 c. flaked coconut
3 egg whites
Pinch of cream of tartar
1 baked 9-in. pie shell

Soften gelatin in 1/4 cup water. Combine milk, 1/2 cup sugar, flour and salt; simmer, stirring constantly, until mixture comes to a boil. Boil for 1 minute; remove from heat. Add gelatin; stir until dissolved. Chill until partially set; beat until smooth. Blend in vanilla and almond extract. Fold in whipped cream and 1 cup coconut gently. Beat egg whites until stiff peaks form; add remaining sugar and cream of tartar. Fold into gelatin mixture; pour into pie shell. Sprinkle with remaining coconut. Chill for at least 2 hours or until set.

COCONUT-ORANGE PIE

3 eggs
1 1/2 c. sugar
1/2 stick butter, melted
1 orange, grated rind and pulp
2 c. coconut
3 tbsp. milk
1 tsp. vanilla
1 9-in. unbaked pie shell

Beat eggs well; add sugar gradually, beating until thick and lemony. Stir in butter, orange rind and pulp, coconut, milk and vanilla; pour into crust. Bake at 325 degrees for 30 minutes or until filling is set.

Meringue

2 tbsp. sugar
1 tbsp. cornstarch
3 egg whites
1/2 tsp. vanilla
1/8 tsp. salt

Blend sugar and cornstarch with 1/2 cup water in saucepan. Simmer, stirring constantly, until thickened; cool. Beat egg whites until stiff peaks form; add vanilla and salt. Blend sugar mixture into egg whites gradually; beat until glossy. Pile meringue on pie. Bake at 350 degrees for 10 minutes or until lightly browned.

COCONUT CUSTARD PIE

2 1/2 c. milk
4 eggs
1/2 c. sugar
1/4 tsp. salt
1 tsp. vanilla
1 can flaked coconut
1 unbaked 9-in. pastry shell
1/4 c. brown sugar
2 tbsp. soft butter

Scald milk. Beat eggs with sugar, salt and vanilla. Stir in milk slowly; mix well. Reserve 1/2 cup coconut. Combine remaining coconut with egg mixture. Pour into pastry shell. Bake at 400 degrees for 25 to 30 minutes or until custard tests done. Combine reserved coconut, brown sugar and butter; sprinkle over pie. Broil 4 inches from source of heat for 3 minutes or until browned.

FRESH COCONUT PIE

1 c. sugar
1/2 c. cornstarch
1/4 tsp. salt
3 c. hot milk
3 egg yolks, beaten
1 tsp. vanilla
1/2 tsp. almond extract
2 c. grated fresh coconut
1 9-in. baked pie shell
1 c. heavy cream, whipped

Combine sugar, cornstarch and salt in saucepan; stir in milk gradually until smooth. Bring to a boil; boil for 2 minutes. Remove from heat; stir small amount of hot mixture into egg yolks. Return to hot mixture in saucepan. Cook over low heat, stirring constantly, for 5 minutes, until mixture boils and is thick enough to mound from spoon. Turn into bowl; stir in vanilla, almond extract and half the coconut. Place waxed paper over filling; refrigerate for 1 hour. Turn into pie shell; refrigerate for 3 hours. Spread whipped cream over filling; top with remaining coconut.

QUICK COCONUT PIE

1/4 c. butter
4 eggs
1 3/4 c. sugar
1/2 c. flour
1 tsp. vanilla
2 1/2 c. milk
7 oz. coconut

Melt butter in 2 pie pans. Beat eggs lightly; beat in sugar, flour and vanilla. Stir in milk and coconut; pour into pie pans. Bake at 350 degrees for 45 minutes or until filling is set.

BAKED COCONUT CUSTARD

1 c. sugar
1 1/2 tbsp. cornstarch
2 tbsp. butter
3 eggs, lightly beaten
1 lge. can evaporated milk
1 tsp. vanilla
1 can flaked coconut

Combine sugar and cornstarch; add butter. Cream well; add eggs, milk and vanilla. Mix well; fold in coconut. Pour into greased and floured 9-inch pan. Bake at 350 degrees for 30 minutes. Yield: 6 servings.

COCONUT-CARAMEL PUDDING

7 tbsp. (heaping) sifted flour
4 c. sugar
1/2 tsp. salt
4 eggs
2 4-oz. cans dry coconut
2 c. nuts, chopped

Mix flour, 3 cups sugar and salt. Beat eggs lightly; add to sugar mixture. Mix well. Brown remaining sugar. Add 1 quart boiling water gradually; blend thoroughly. Remove from heat; add egg mixture. Return to heat; simmer, stirring constantly, until thickened. Mix well; remove from heat. Stir in coconut and nuts. Cool. Serve with whipped cream. Yield: 14 servings.

COCONUT-CREAM PUDDING

1 c. flour
1/4 c. brown sugar
1/2 c. butter
1/2 c. chopped nuts
2 pkg. instant coconut cream pudding mix
1 c. whipped cream

Mix first 4 ingredients together; pat into 9 x 13-inch pan. Bake 12 minutes in a 350-degree oven. Cool completely; crumble and pat back into pan. Prepare pudding according to package directions. Fold in whipped cream; pour over crust. Refrigerate; serve with whipped cream and cherry garnish, if desired. Yield: 12 servings.

COCONUT-ORANGE CUSTARD

4 egg yolks, well beaten
4 tbsp. sugar
1 tbsp. flour
Pinch of salt
1 c. milk, scalded
1 tsp. vanilla
1 c. heavy cream, whipped
Fresh orange sections
Fresh grated coconut

Combine egg yolks with sugar, flour and salt. Add milk; mix well. Place in double boiler over boiling water; cook, stirring constantly, until thickened. Cool; add vanilla. Alternate sauce and whipped cream with layers of orange sections and coconut in parfait glasses.

COCONUT NESTS WITH STRAWBERRIES

1 8-oz. package cream cheese
1/2 c. sugar
2 tsp. milk
1 tsp. vanilla
2 pkg. dessert sponge cups
1 can flaked coconut
1 qt. fresh strawberries

Have cream cheese at room temperature. Beat cream cheese with sugar, milk and vanilla until smooth. Remove small amount of center from each dessert cup; frost cups with cream cheese mixture. Sprinkle with coconut. Spoon strawberries into cups at serving time. Yield: 8 servings.

COCONUT MOUSSE

2 pkg. unflavored gelatin
2 c. milk
1/2 c. sugar
1/2 tsp. almond flavoring
1/2 can shredded coconut
1 c. heavy cream
Strawberries

Soften gelatin in 1 1/2 cups water; dissolve over hot water. Combine milk and sugar in saucepan; bring to a boil, stirring until sugar is dissolved. Blend in gelatin. Remove from heat; add almond flavoring and coconut. Mix well; cool. Chill until partially set. Whip cream; fold into gelatin mixture. Pour into ring mold; chill until set. Unmold; fill center with strawberries.

Sauce

1 c. sugar
1 c. (packed) brown sugar
1/4 lb. butter
1 c. heavy cream

Combine sugars, butter and cream in top of double boiler; cook over boiling water until creamy and smooth. Serve warm over mousse and berries.

SNOWFLAKE PUDDING

1 c. sugar
1 pkg. gelatin
1/2 tsp. salt
1 1/4 c. milk
1 tsp. vanilla
1 3-oz. can flaked coconut
2 c. cream, whipped

Combine sugar, gelatin, salt, and milk in saucepan. Cook, stirring constantly, over medium heat until smooth and thickened. Chill. Add vanilla; fold in coconut and cream. Chill for 4 hours or until ready to use. Top with Crimson Sauce.

Crimson Sauce

1 10-oz. package frozen raspberries
1 1/2 tbsp. cornstarch
1/2 c. red currant jelly

Thaw and crush raspberries. Combine with cornstarch; add jelly. Bring to boiling; cook, stirring constantly, until mixture is clear and thickened slightly. Strain and chill. Yield: 8 servings.

COCONUT SNOWBALLS WITH CHERRY SAUCE

5 c. sour pitted cherries
1 c. sugar
1/4 c. cornstarch
1/8 tsp. salt
2 tsp. lemon juice
Few drops of red food coloring
1 qt. vanilla ice cream
1 c. shredded coconut

Drain cherries, reserving syrup. Add enough water to syrup to equal 2 cups liquid. Combine sugar, cornstarch and salt in saucepan; stir in cherry liquid gradually. Simmer, stirring constantly, until thickened and clear. Add lemon juice, cherries and food coloring; blend well. Scoop ice cream into 8 balls; roll in coconut. Serve with cherry sauce.

FROZEN COCONUT DELIGHT

1/2 c. butter, melted
2 1/2 c. oven-toasted rice cereal
1 c. chopped pecans
1 c. flaked coconut
1/2 c. brown sugar
1/2 gal. butter brickle ice cream

Combine butter, cereal, pecans and coconut; mix well. Place under broiler; stir until crisp. Add brown sugar, stirring to dissolve. Reserve 1/3 of the mixture; press remaining mixture into shallow oblong pan. Cool. Arrange slices of ice cream over crust; sprinkle with reserved mixture. Freeze until ready to serve. Yield: 12 servings.

SNOWBALLS

1 sm. can crushed pineapple
1 stick butter
1 c. sugar
3 eggs, separated
Vanilla wafers
1 c. heavy cream
Vanilla to taste
Coconut
Candied cherries

Drain pineapple thoroughly. Cream butter with sugar until fluffy. Beat egg yolks until thick and lemony. Beat egg whites until stiff peaks form. Combine egg yolks and pineapple with sugar mixture; blend well. Fold egg whites into mixture. Spread filling over 2 vanilla wafers. Stack wafers; place third wafer on top. Repeat procedure until all filling is used. Chill overnight. Whip cream; add vanilla to taste. Frost each stack; cover with coconut. Garnish with cherries. Refrigerate until ready to serve. May be frozen. Yield: 25 snowballs.

Cod

Cod is a fish native to both the Atlantic and Pacific. It was once so important to the New England economy that Bostonians erected a wooden codfish in their State House. Cod is a good source of protein, iron, calcium, and B vitamins. (3 1/2 ounces dried, salted cod = 130 calories)

AVAILABILITY: Fresh cod is available year-round with the best supply from September to December.

BUYING: Fresh cod is sold whole, drawn, dressed, or in steaks and fillets. *Frozen cod* fillets are also available. *Salt cod* is sold in slabs and is also available boneless, flaked, or shredded in packages or jars. *Prepared codfish cakes* are sold in cans.

STORING: If well wrapped, fresh cod can be refrigerated for 2 days. Codfish may be frozen 3 weeks in a refrigerator freezer compartment or 9 months in a home freezer. Store unopened jars or salt cod or codfish cakes in cool, dry place.

PREPARATION: Fresh codfish may be baked, broiled, poached, or prepared in casseroles. *To prepare salt cod*, soak for several hours in at least two changes of water to remove salt. Poach, fry, or use to prepare codfish cakes.

BROILED COD WITH SOUFFLÉ SAUCE

2 1/2 lb. cod fillets
Salt
Pepper to taste
1/2 c. mayonnaise
1/4 c. pickle relish
2 tbsp. parsley
1 tbsp. lemon juice
Dash of cayenne pepper
2 egg whites, stiffly beaten

Sprinkle cod with salt and pepper to taste. Place in lightly greased shallow baking pan. Mix mayonnaise, pickle relish, parsley, lemon juice, 1/4 teaspoon salt and cayenne pepper; fold in egg whites. Broil cod 2 inches from source of heat for 6 to 10 minutes or until fillets are partially done. Spread mayonnaise mixture over fillets; broil for 3 to 5 minutes longer or until puffed and lightly browned. Serve at once. Yield: 6 servings.

Mexicali Cod . . . Tuna and cod combine with seasonings in this zesty baked dish.

MEXICALI COD

1/3 c. yellow cornmeal
1/3 c. chopped onion
1/2 c. chopped celery
1/4 c. butter
2 tbsp. chopped parsley
1 tbsp. grated orange peel
2 6 1/2-oz. cans chunk-style tuna, drained
2 tbsp. dark brown sugar
1 tsp. salt
1/8 tsp. pepper
1 lb. cod fillets
1/2 c. sliced pimento-stuffed olives
1/4 c. toasted slivered almonds
1/3 c. dry white wine

Mix cornmeal with 1/2 cup water. Bring 1 cup water to a boil in saucepan. Stir in cornmeal mixture; bring to a boil, stirring constantly. Simmer, covered, for 10 minutes. Saute onion and celery in butter until crisp-tender. Combine cooked cornmeal mixture, onion mixture, parsley, orange peel, tuna, sugar, salt and pepper in mixing bowl; mix well. Place cod fillets in bottom of 1 1/2-quart rectangular baking dish; spoon tuna mixture on top. Sprinkle with olives and almonds. Pour wine over top. Bake in 350-degree oven for 25 to 30 minutes.

COD ROE PATTIES WITH SHRIMP SAUCE

Color photograph for this recipe on page 70.

1 can cod roe
1 egg, slightly beaten
Bread crumbs
2 tbsp. butter
1 can frozen shrimp soup

Open cod roe can at both ends; press roe onto plate. Cut roe in 1-inch slices; dip each slice in egg, then in bread crumbs. Fry in butter in skillet until golden brown; place on platter. Heat soup in saucepan over low heat until heated through, stirring frequently. Spread over roe patties. Garnish with dill sprigs and lemon wedges.

CREAMED COD ON WAFFLES

Color photograph for this recipe on page 728.

6 tbsp. butter
1/2 c. chopped onion
2 1/3 c. flour
3 3/4 c. milk
1 1/4 tsp. salt
1/4 tsp. chervil
3/4 c. Florida grapefruit juice
2 c. flaked cooked cod
1/2 c. light cream
3 tsp. baking powder
2 tbsp. sugar
3 eggs
1/2 c. shortening, melted

Melt butter in heavy saucepan over low heat. Add onion; cook for about 3 minutes, stirring frequently. Add 1/3 cup flour slowly, stirring until smooth. Stir in 2 cups milk gradually. Sprinkle with 1/2 teaspoon salt and chervil; bring to a simmer, stirring constantly. Do not boil. Add grapefruit juice and cod; cook until cod is heated through. Remove from heat; stir in cream. Keep warm. Sift remaining flour, baking powder, remaining salt and sugar. Separate eggs. Beat egg whites until stiff. Beat egg yolks in a bowl; stir in remaining milk and shortening. Add flour mixture; beat with rotary beater until smooth. Fold in egg whites. Pour 1/2 cup batter for each waffle into hot waffle iron. Bake until golden brown. Serve with creamed cod. Sprinkle with paprika if desired.

BAKED COD LOAF

1 1/2 lb. cod fillets
1 1/2 c. diced potatoes
2 onions, thin-sliced
3 tbsp. butter
2 tsp. lemon juice
1 tsp. dry mustard
Salt and pepper to taste

Soak cod fillets in cold water for 3 hours. Simmer cod fillets and potatoes in water to cover in saucepan for about 20 minutes; drain. Mash well with potato masher. Saute onion slices in butter in skillet until transparent. Combine cod mixture, onion slices, lemon juice, mustard, salt and pepper in greased casserole. Bake at 400 degrees for 25 minutes. May serve with cream sauce if desired. Yield: 5 servings.

BAKED COD SUPREME

1 sm. onion, minced
1 clove of garlic, pressed
1 tbsp. butter
2 lb. cod fillets
Salt and pepper to taste
1/2 c. sour cream
Chopped parsley to taste

Saute onion and garlic in butter until lightly browned; remove garlic. Place onion in shallow casserole; place cod fillets over onion. Season with salt and pepper. Mix sour cream and parsley; spread over fillets. Bake at 350 degrees for 15 to 20 minutes or until cod flakes easily. Yield: 3-6 servings.

COD FILLET IN SHRIMP SAUCE

1 can frozen cream of shrimp soup
1 fillet of cod
Bread crumbs
Grated cheese
Butter

Thaw soup. Arrange cod fillet in greased casserole; spoon soup over fillet. Sprinkle with crumbs and cheese; dot with butter. Bake at 350 degrees for about 35 minutes.

CODFISH BALLS

1 c. flaked salt cod
2 c. diced potatoes
1 egg, slightly beaten
Dash of paprika
1 tsp. melted butter
Pepper to taste
Celery salt to taste

Soak cod overnight in water. Cook cod and potatoes in covered pan in boiling water until well done. Drain well; mash thoroughly. Add remaining ingredients; beat until light and fluffy. Chill; form in balls. Fry in deep fat until golden brown. Drain on absorbent paper.

COD WITH SOUR CREAM

1/4 c. chopped onion
1/4 c. chopped celery
1/4 c. butter
1 chicken bouillon cube
1/8 tsp. poultry seasoning
1 1/4 tsp. salt
1/8 tsp. pepper
1 egg, slightly beaten
5 c. bread cubes
1 lb. cod fillets
1 tbsp. flour
1 c. sour cream
1 tsp. lemon juice
Paprika

Saute onion and celery in butter in saucepan; add 2 cups water. Cook until vegetables are tender. Add bouillon, poultry seasoning, 1 teaspoon salt and pepper. Combine egg and bread cubes; mix well. Spread bread mixture in 13 x 9-inch glass baking dish. Spoon onion mixture over bread mixture. Separate fillets; arrange on stuffing. Mix flour, sour cream, lemon juice and remaining salt; spread over fillets. Bake at 350 degrees for about 1 hour. Sprinkle with paprika. Yield: 6 servings.

COD IN TOMATO SAUCE

3 tbsp. chopped onion
2 tbsp. butter
2 tbsp. olive oil
2 c. mashed fresh tomatoes
1 clove of garlic, chopped
1 carrot, sliced
1 pkg. frozen cod fillets
Salt and pepper to taste
Lemon juice

Saute onion in butter and oil. Add tomatoes, garlic, carrot and 1 cup water. Cook until carrot is tender. Thaw cod slightly; cut into 8 squares. Add cod to tomato mixture; season. Simmer until cod flakes easily, basting occasionally with pan juices. Sprinkle with lemon juice; serve.

COD IN WHITE SAUCE

1-lb. frozen cod fillets
1/4 c. butter
2 c. milk
1 c. dry white wine
3 tbsp. chopped fresh parsley
Salt and pepper
1/4 c. flour
1 15 1/2-oz. can asparagus spears
2 4-oz. cans button mushrooms
1 c. cooked shrimp

Thaw cod fillets; cut into bite-sized pieces. Combine butter, milk, wine, parsley, salt and pepper in large saucepan; bring to boiling point gradually. Reduce heat. Mix flour with 1/2 cup cold water; add to wine mixture. Cook, stirring constantly, until thickened. Add cod; simmer for 15 minutes. Drain asparagus and mushrooms; add shrimp, asparagus and mushrooms to sauce. Heat through. Yield: 4-6 servings.

NEW ENGLAND CODFISH DINNER

1 1/2 salted cod
1/4 lb. salt pork, diced
6 potatoes
12 sm. beets
6 onions
2 hard-cooked eggs, diced
1 1/2 c. hot white sauce

Cut cod into serving portions. Soak in cold water for 2 to 3 hours; drain. Cover cod with water; bring to boil. Drain. Fry salt pork in skillet until brown. Cook potatoes, beets and onions separately until tender. Arrange cod on hot platter. Add eggs to white sauce; spread over cod. Garnish with salt pork. Arrange vegetables around cod. Yield: 6 servings.

SALT COD DINNER

1/2 lb. dried salt cod
4 med. potatoes
1 c. white sauce
1/8 tsp. pepper
1 tbsp. butter

Cut cod into bite-sized pieces; cover with cold water. Let stand for 10 minutes. Drain; rinse cod well. Peel potatoes; cut into eighths. Combine potatoes and cod in saucepan; cover with cold water. Cook for 20 minutes or until potatoes are done. Drain; add white sauce and pepper. Dot with butter. Yield: 4 servings.

CREAMED COD CASSEROLE

1 c. flaked salted codfish
2 tbsp. butter
2 tbsp. flour
1/4 tsp. salt
1/4 tsp. pepper
1 c. milk
3 c. mashed potatoes
1 beaten egg

Cover cod with cold water; let stand overnight. Simmer until water looks milky; drain. Melt butter; blend in flour, salt and pepper. Add milk; cook, stirring constantly, until thickened. Remove from heat; add cod. Line 1 1/2-quart casserole with half the potatoes; add cod mixture. Spread remaining potatoes on top. Brush potatoes with egg. Bake at 350 degrees for 30 minutes or until browned. Yield: 4 servings.

CURRIED COD

2 lb. frozen cod fillets
2 lge. onions, chopped
1 clove of garlic, minced
2 tbsp. butter
3 med. apples
1 6-oz. can tomato paste
2 tsp. salt
1 tsp. curry powder
1/8 tsp. pepper

Partially thaw cod fillets; cut into serving pieces. Arrange cod in 6-cup shallow baking dish. Saute onions and garlic in butter until soft. Peel and quarter apples. Add apples, tomato paste, 3/4 cup water, salt, curry powder and pepper to onion mixture. Bring to a boil, stirring constantly. Spoon apple mixture over cod. Bake at 350 degrees for 1 hour and 15 minutes or until cod flakes easily. Yield: 6 servings.

Coffee

Grown in the tropical regions of South America, the coffee plant produces coffee beans, which, when roasted, ground, and brewed, become a flavorful, non-caloric beverage that is often used as a flavoring. Because coffee contains caffein, a recognized heart stimulant, it may contribute to nervous upset and its use is restricted for certain people.

BUYING: *Whole roasted beans* are sold to be ground immediately before using. *Ground roasted beans* are available in several forms: regular or percolator grind for all percolators; drip grind for drip and vacuum models; fine grind for some vacuum-style models. *Instant coffee* (powdered and freeze-dried) is also available.

STORING: Vacuum- or bag-packed coffee retains its freshness for 1 week, with a gradual loss of flavor thereafter. Instant coffee, stored in a tightly sealed jar, will keep for 6 to 8 months.

PREPARATION: Select quality coffee in grind preferred. Rinse the coffeemaker to remove any residual coffee oil and fill with fresh, cold water to at least 3/4 capacity. Use 2 level tablespoons (1 standard measure) to 6 ounces water or vary the measurement to achieve desired strength. *Nonautomatic percolators*: Heat water to boiling point; percolate slowly for 6 to 8 minutes. *Automatic percolators*: Follow the manufacturer's instructions. *Drip*: Measure drip grind into the filter, fill upper container with boiling water, and place over filter. When water has dripped through, coffee is ready. *Vacuum method*: Heat water in lower bowl. Measure coffee into filter and place into upper bowl. When water rises, remove coffeemaker from heat and allow coffee to return to lower bowl before serving.

A clean coffeemaker is vital to prepare good coffee. *To clean coffeemaker*, wash thoroughly with hot, soapy water and rinse well. Regularly fill coffeemaker with water and add 1 teaspoon baking soda. Run the solution through one cycle. This process will remove any coffee or soap residue left in the pot.

COFFEE CARNIVAL

4 tbsp. instant tapioca
1/4 tsp. salt
1/3 c. seedless raisins (opt.)
2 c. hot coffee
1/2 c. sugar
1 tsp. vanilla
1 c. whipped cream

Combine tapioca, salt, raisins and coffee in double boiler; cook for 15 minutes over hot water. Stir in sugar; chill. Add vanilla; fold in whipped cream. Garnish with additional whipped cream, if desired. Yield: 6 servings.

COFFEE-CREAM CAKE

1 pkg. chiffon cake mix
3 tbsp. cornstarch
2/3 c. sugar
3 c. milk
1 lemon rind
3 egg yolks, slightly beaten
1 tsp. vanilla
1/4 c. white rum
1 1/2 c. cold coffee
Whipped cream

Prepare cake mix according to package directions in 10-inch tube pan. Cool. Combine cornstarch, sugar and milk in saucepan; add lemon rind and egg yolks. Blend well. Cook over low heat, stirring constantly, until mixture thickens. Remove from heat; remove lemon rind. Add vanilla, mixing thoroughly; cool. Cut cake into 4 layers. Combine rum and coffee; sprinkle on each side of cake layers. Fill between layers with egg mixture. Top cake with whipped cream; refrigerate for 2 hours before serving. Yield: 12 servings.

COFFEE-CREAM ROYALE

1 c. strong hot coffee
32 marshmallows, cut up
1 c. heavy cream, whipped
Chopped nuts (opt.)

Bring coffee to a boil; remove from heat. Dissolve marshmallows in hot coffee; cool. Stir coffee mixture; fold in whipped cream. Place in refrigerator; chill thoroughly. Spoon into sherbet dishes to serve. Top with nuts. Yield: 6-8 servings.

COFFEE-ICEBOX PIE

1 1/2 to 2 doz. ladyfingers
1 tbsp. unflavored gelatin
1/4 c. brandy
2 eggs, separated
1 1/4 c. milk
2 tsp. instant coffee powder
1/2 tsp. salt
3/4 c. sugar
1 tsp. vanilla
1/4 tsp. cream of tartar
1 c. heavy cream, whipped
1 c. chopped walnuts

Split ladyfingers; arrange over bottom and side of buttered 9-inch pie pan, flat side down, to make crust. Soften gelatin in brandy. Beat egg yolks. Combine milk, coffee powder, salt, 1/2 cup sugar, vanilla and egg yolks in top of double boiler. Cook over hot water for about 10 minutes or until mixture thickens slightly. Add gelatin mixture, stirring until dissolved; remove from heat. Chill until mixture is partially set. Beat egg whites with remaining sugar and cream of tartar until stiff peaks form; fold into gelatin mixture. Fold in whipped cream and 3/4 cup walnuts. Mound filling in ladyfinger crust. Garnish top with remaining walnuts. Chill until firm. Yield: 6-8 servings.

COFFEE-MALLOW WITH CHERRY SAUCE

32 lge. marshmallows
1 c. hot strong coffee
2 c. heavy cream, whipped
1 tsp. vanilla
2 1-lb. cans dark pitted cherries in heavy syrup
2 tbsp. cornstarch
Brandy to taste (opt.)

Combine marshmallows and coffee in top of double boiler. Cook over simmering water until marshmallows are melted; stir frequently. Cool to room temperature or until lukewarm. Blend whipped cream and vanilla into coffee mixture. Stir coffee mixture thoroughly to uniform color. Pour into mold; chill for several hours or overnight. Drain syrup from cherries; pour into saucepan. Set cherries aside. Blend cornstarch and syrup together; cook over moderate heat, stirring, until thickened. Add brandy and cherries. Unmold dessert on large plate; spoon cherry sauce around mold to serve. Yield: 12 servings.

FROZEN CREAMS

2 egg whites
1/8 tsp. salt
3/4 c. sugar
3 tbsp. instant coffee powder
2 c. heavy cream
1/2 c. sliced almonds, toasted
3 tbsp. bourbon

Beat egg whites until stiff peaks form; add salt, 1/4 cup sugar and coffee gradually. Whip cream; add 1/2 cup sugar gradually. Fold into egg white mixture. Add almonds, reserving a few for topping. Mix in bourbon. Line 2 muffin tins with paper muffin cups. Fill cups with mixture. Sprinkle with reserved almonds; freeze. Yield: 12 servings.

COFFEE-WHIPPED CREAM TORTE

4 tsp. instant coffee
1 1/3 c. sugar
4 c. whipping cream
2 10-in. angel food cake loaves
1 1/2 c. crushed toffee

Combine coffee, sugar and cream; refrigerate for at least 1 hour before whipping. Whip cream mixture until stiff peaks form. Split cakes into 3 layers each; spread whipped mixture between layers and over top and sides. Sprinkle crushed toffee over top. Chill. Yield: 8-10 servings.

DELICIOSA COFFEE DESSERT

1/2 c. butter
1 c. sugar
4 eggs
1 c. chopped pecans
1/4 c. cold coffee
2 c. vanilla wafer crumbs

Combine butter and sugar; cream thoroughly. Add eggs, one at a time, beating for about 5 minutes after each addition. Add pecans and coffee to sugar mixture, mixing well. Line 1 1/2-quart loaf pan with waxed paper. Alternate layers of crumbs and coffee mixture, beginning and ending with crumbs. Refrigerate for at least 24 hours before serving. Yield: 7-8 servings.

COFFEE FRAPPÉ

3 tbsp. sugar
8 c. strong coffee
2 c. heavy cream, whipped
1 tsp. vanilla
1 tbsp. brandy

Dissolve sugar in hot coffee; chill. Fold in whipped cream. Add vanilla and brandy, stirring lightly; freeze. Serve in parfait glasses topped with whipped cream and crumbled macaroons, if desired. Yield: 8 servings.

FROZEN CHOCO-COFFEE PIE

1 1/2 c. chocolate wafer crumbs
1/4 c. sugar
1/3 c. melted butter
1 qt. coffee ice cream
1 c. heavy cream, whipped

Combine chocolate crumbs, sugar and butter, mixing thoroughly. Press into bottom and side of 9-inch pie plate. Bake at 400 degrees for 5 minutes. Cool thoroughly. Soften ice cream slightly; pack into pie shell. Spread whipped cream over ice cream. Freeze. One-fourth cup crumb shell mixture may be reserved and sprinkled on top of pie before freezing. Remove pie from freezer for about 20 minutes before serving to soften slightly. Yield: 6-8 servings.

COFFEE ICE CREAM

6 tbsp. instant coffee
3 c. milk
2 eggs
1 1/2 c. sugar
2 tbsp. arrowroot
2 c. cream, whipped

Combine coffee and milk; bring to a boil. Remove from heat; strain through cheesecloth. Beat eggs, sugar and arrowroot together; stir in milk mixture. Cook in double boiler until mixture thickens. Remove from heat; cool. Add cream; pour into freezing tray. Freeze. Yield: 2 quarts ice cream.

MINI-COFFEE CHILLED SOUFFLÉS

2 env. unflavored gelatin
1 c. sugar
1/4 c. instant coffee powder
1/4 tsp. salt
4 eggs, separated
2 1/2 c. milk
1 tsp. vanilla
2 c. heavy cream, whipped
1/2 c. finely chopped walnuts

Combine gelatin, 1/2 cup sugar, coffee powder and salt in 2 1/2-quart saucepan. Beat egg yolks with milk; add to gelatin mixture. Stir over low heat for about 10 to 12 minutes or until gelatin dissolves and mixture thickens slightly. Remove from heat; add vanilla. Chill, stirring occasionally, until mixture mounds slightly when dropped from spoon. Place double strip of aluminum foil around tops of 4 or 6-ounce goblets, demitasse cups or stemmed dessert glasses, extending 1 inch above rim. Beat egg whites until stiff peaks form. Add remaining sugar gradually. Beat until stiff; fold in gelatin mixture. Fold in whipped cream and walnuts. Spoon into prepared goblets; chill until firm. Remove foil. Garnish with chopped walnuts, if desired. Yield: 8-12 servings.

Coffee Cake

Coffee cakes are as varied as are individual tastes. Whether large or small, plain or fancy, these sweet breads are enjoyed as breakfast, tea, or snack time pastries. There are two kinds of coffee cakes. Those made with quick-acting leavening, such as baking powder or baking soda, and those made with slower acting yeast. The yeast-raised varieties appear in imaginative shapes – rings, braids, or (if individual-sized cakes) horns, pinwheels, bowties, or crescents. Quick-raised coffee cakes are generally baked in loaf or cake pans.

BASIC INGREDIENTS: Coffee cakes usually contain flour, salt, sugar, shortening, liquid, and leavening. Follow specific recipe for preparation. To create golden-colored crumb in any coffee cake, you can add a dash of saffron to the batter. Coffee cakes may be filled with raisins, apples, blueberries, peaches; candied fruit or citron; jams or preserves; mild cheeses; nuts; and spices. Toppings, too, vary. Coffee cakes can be topped with a dusting of confectioners' sugar; sugared crumbs; or even elaborate fruit glazes or icings.

STORING: Quick-raised coffee cakes do not store well and are best served immediately after baking. Yeast coffee cakes store and reheat well. The flavor of any fruit and nut coffee cake mellows during storage.

ALMOND COFFEE CAKE

1 1/2 c. sugar
1/2 c. butter
2 eggs
1 c. sour cream
2 c. flour
1/8 tsp. salt
1 tsp. soda
1 1/2 tsp. baking powder
1 can almond paste
1 tsp. vanilla
1 c. chopped pecans
1 1/2 tsp. cinnamon

Cream 1 cup sugar, butter, eggs and sour cream. Add flour, salt, soda and baking powder; mix well. Blend in almond paste and vanilla. Pour into greased tube pan. Mix remaining sugar, pecans and cinnamon to make topping. Add topping to cake batter; mix with batter slightly. Bake at 375 degrees for 45 minutes. Yield: 10 servings.

APPLE-RAISIN COFFEE CAKE

Sugar
1/4 c. shortening
1 egg
1/2 c. milk
1 1/2 c. sifted flour
2 tsp. baking powder
1/2 tsp. salt
1/2 c. seedless raisins
1 c. sliced apples
1 tsp. cinnamon

Mix 3/4 cup sugar, shortening and egg together; stir in milk. Sift flour, baking powder and salt together; add flour mixture and raisins to milk mixture, stirring well. Spread batter in greased and floured 9 x 9-inch pan. Arrange apple slices on top of batter, pressing in slightly. Mix cinnamon and 2 tablespoons sugar; sprinkle over apple slices. Bake in 375-degree oven for about 35 minutes. Serve warm. Yield: 9 servings.

APRICOT JAM STRUDEL

1 c. butter
2 c. flour
1/2 tsp. salt
1 c. sour cream
1 1/2 c. apricot jam
1/2 c. white raisins
1 c. shredded coconut
2/3 c. chopped walnuts
Powdered sugar

Cut butter into flour and salt until mixture resembles coarse meal. Blend in sour cream. Refrigerate overnight. Bring to room temperature. Cut dough into thirds; roll each part to 10 x 15-inch rectangle. Mix jam, raisins, coconut and walnuts; spread rectangle with jam mixture. Roll jelly roll fashion. Place rolls on lightly greased cookie sheet. Bake at 350 degrees for 1 hour or until golden brown. Cool for

10 minutes on rack. Cut into 1-inch slices; sift powdered sugar over slices. Yield: 3 dozen.

BANANA KUCHEN

1/4 c. shortening
3/4 c. sugar
1 egg
1 med. banana, mashed
1/4 c. milk
1 1/2 c. sifted flour
2 tsp. baking powder
1/2 tsp. salt
1/3 c. (packed) brown sugar
1/3 c. chopped walnuts
1/2 tsp. cinnamon

Cream shortening and sugar. Add egg, banana and milk; beat until smooth. Sift flour, baking powder and salt together; stir into banana mixture. Spread in greased 11 x 7-inch pan. Combine brown sugar, walnuts and cinnamon; sprinkle over banana mixture. Bake at 375 degrees for about 30 minutes. May be frozen, if desired.

BLUEBERRY COFFEE CAKE

3/4 c. sugar
1/4 c. butter
1 egg
2 c. flour
2 tsp. baking powder
1/2 tsp. salt
1/2 c. milk
2 1/2 c. blueberries, drained

Combine sugar, butter and egg in mixing bowl; cream well. Sift flour, baking powder and salt together; add alternately to creamed mixture with milk. Beat well; blend in blueberries. Spread dough in greased 8 x 10-inch pan.

Topping

1/2 c. sugar
1/3 c. flour
1/2 tsp. salt
3 tbsp. soft butter

Combine sugar, flour, salt and butter; mix well. Sprinkle over top of cake. Bake at 375 degrees for about 25 minutes. Yield: 8 servings.

BLUEBERRY-COCONUT COFFEE CAKE

2 c. flour
1 c. sugar
3 tsp. baking powder
1/4 tsp. salt
1/2 c. shortening
2 eggs, beaten
1 c. milk
1 1/2 c. blueberries
1 1/3 c. coconut

Sift flour, sugar, baking powder and salt together into bowl; cut in shortening. Combine eggs and milk; stir into flour mixture. Fold in blueberries. Divide batter between 2 greased 9-inch layer cake pans. Sprinkle coconut over tops. Bake at 375 degrees for 25 minutes.

BUTTERCREAM COFFEE CAKE

2 pkg. yeast
1 c. warm milk
1/2 c. sugar
2 eggs, beaten
1 tsp. salt
1/4 c. butter
4 to 5 c. flour
Melted butter
Butter frosting

Dissolve yeast in 1/2 cup lukewarm water. Add milk, sugar, eggs, salt, butter and enough flour to make easily handled dough; mix well. Knead until smooth; place in greased bowl. Cover. Let rise until doubled in bulk. Punch down; divide into 3 parts. Roll into 1/2-inch thick rectangles; brush heavily with melted butter. Fold each rectangle in half, buttered sides together; place on baking sheet. Let rise until doubled in bulk. Bake at 375 degrees for about 25 minutes. Spread with butter frosting.

BRAIDED FRUIT BREAD

1 1/4 c. hot milk
1/4 c. shortening
1/3 c. sugar
1 tsp. salt
1 pkg. yeast
2 eggs, beaten
4 1/4 c. flour
1 1/2 tsp. cinnamon
1 6-oz. jar candied cherries, halved
1/2 c. white raisins
1/2 c. chopped walnuts
Confectioners' Sugar Frosting
Walnut halves

Combine milk, shortening, sugar and salt; cool to lukewarm. Add yeast; stir until dissolved. Add eggs. Sift flour with cinnamon; add to yeast mixture. Mix to soft dough; add cherries, raisins and chopped walnuts. Knead lightly until smooth and elastic. Place in greased bowl; cover with damp cloth. Let rise until doubled in bulk; divide dough in halves. Roll each half into 1/2-inch rectangle; cut each rectangle lengthwise into 3 strips. Braid 3 strips, making loaf; place on greased baking sheet. Let rise until doubled in bulk. Bake at 350 degrees for 30 minutes. Glaze loaves with Confectioners' Sugar Frosting while still warm. Decorate with walnut halves.

Confectioners' Sugar Frosting

1 c. confectioners' sugar
2 tbsp. milk
1/4 tsp. vanilla

Combine confectioners' sugar, milk and vanilla; blend well.

CANDY CANE COFFEE CAKE

1 pkg. yeast
1/4 c. melted butter
1/4 c. sugar
1 tsp. salt
1/3 c. instant nonfat dry milk powder
1 egg
3 1/2 c. sifted flour
1/2 c. chopped dates
1/2 c. chopped walnuts
1/2 c. strawberry preserves

Dissolve yeast in 1/4 cup lukewarm water. Add butter, sugar, salt, 3/4 cup water, milk powder, egg and 2 cups flour; beat well. Add remaining flour gradually. Turn onto floured surface; knead until smooth. Place in greased bowl; cover. Let rise until doubled in bulk. Punch down; divide into 3 parts. Cover; let stand for 10 minutes. Roll each part into 15 x 6-inch rectangle. Make 2-inch cuts from outer edges of the 15-inch sides at 1-inch intervals. Combine dates, walnuts and preserves; spread 1/3 of the mixture down center of each rectangle. Fold strips from each side alternately over filling. Place on greased baking sheet. Cover; let rise until doubled in bulk. Bake in 350-degree oven for about 15 minutes. Yield: 3 coffee cakes.

Cherry-Pecan Coffee Cake . . . A delicious cake just right to serve at mealtime or for snacks.

CHERRY-PECAN COFFEE CAKE

1/3 c. sugar
1/3 c. butter, softened
1/2 tsp. salt
3/4 c. evaporated milk
1 pkg. active dry yeast
2 eggs, beaten
1 c. chopped candied cherries
1/2 c. chopped pecans
4 1/2 c. sifted flour

Preheat oven to 375 degrees. Combine sugar, butter and salt in large mixing bowl. Add 1/2 cup boiling water, stirring to melt butter. Add milk. Sprinkle yeast over 1/4 cup warm water in cup; stir to dissolve. Add to butter mixture. Stir in eggs, cherries and pecans. Add flour, 1 cup at a time, beating until smooth after each addition. Cover; let rise at room temperature for about 1 hour and 30 minutes or until doubled in bulk. Punch batter down; beat for 2 minutes with large spoon. Turn into greased 10-inch tube pan; spread evenly. Cover; let rise for about 45 minutes or until doubled in bulk. Bake for 50 to 55 minutes or until lightly browned. Remove from pan immediately; cool on wire rack.

Icing

2/3 c. confectioners' sugar
1 tbsp. evaporated milk
1/2 tsp. vanilla

Combine all ingredients; spoon over coffeecake. Garnish with candied cherry halves and pecan halves if desired.

CHERRY-APPLE BRUNCH BREAD

2 c. flour
1 tsp. salt
2 1/2 tsp. baking powder
1 c. sugar
1 egg, slightly beaten
1 tbsp. grated orange rind
Orange juice
Melted butter
3/4 c. milk
1 tsp. vanilla
2 1/2 c. grated apples
1/4 c. (packed) brown sugar
1 tsp. cinnamon
10 maraschino cherries, diced

Sift flour, salt and baking powder together; stir in sugar. Add egg, orange rind, 1/4 cup orange juice, 1/4 cup butter, milk and vanilla. Mix until flour is moistened. Spread batter in greased 13 x 9-inch pan. Mix apples, brown sugar, cinnamon, 1 tablespoon orange juice, 2 tablespoons butter and cherries; spoon mixture over batter. Bake at 400 degrees for 30 to 40 minutes.

CHOCOLATE CHIP COFFEE RING

1 pkg. yeast
1 3/4 c. sifted flour
1/2 c. milk
4 tbsp. butter
3 tbsp. sugar
1/2 tsp. salt
1 egg
1/2 c. semisweet chocolate pieces
Confectioners' sugar icing

Combine yeast and 1 1/4 cups flour in large mixing bowl. Mix milk, butter, sugar and salt; place over low heat until butter is melted, stirring occasionally. Add milk mixture to flour mixture; add egg. Beat with electric mixer at low speed for 30 seconds, scraping side of bowl. Beat for 3 minutes at high speed. Stir in remaining flour with spoon. Add chocolate pieces; mix well. Place in well-greased 4 1/2-cup ring mold; cover. Let rise in warm place for about 1 hour or until doubled in bulk. Bake at 400 degrees for about 15 minutes. Remove from pan; drizzle with confectioners' sugar icing while warm.

CHRISTMAS STOLLEN

2 pkg. yeast
1 lb. raisins
1 lb. currants
1 1/2 c. butter, melted
11 c. flour
3/4 c. sugar
1/2 tsp. salt
1/2 tsp. cinnamon
1/2 tsp. mace
2 c. milk
6 eggs
3 tbsp. lemon juice
1 tsp. grated lemon peel
3 tbsp. cognac
1/4 lb. chopped blanched almonds
1/2 lb. finely chopped citron
1/2 c. confectioners' sugar

Dissolve yeast in 1/2 cup lukewarm water. Combine raisins and currants; cover with boiling water. Let stand for 5 minutes. Drain raisin mixture. Rinse well; drain thoroughly. Sift flour, sugar, salt and spices together into large bowl; add milk, eggs, 1 1/4 cups melted butter, lemon juice, lemon peel, 1 tablespoon cognac and yeast mixture. Stir mixture thoroughly. Add almonds, citron, raisins and currants; mix well. Knead dough on board until well blended. Cover; let stand in warm place for 12 hours. Turn dough onto lightly floured surface. Knead lightly; divide into 2 parts. Shape each part into crescent; place on greased cookie sheet. Cover; let rise until doubled in bulk. Bake at 350 degrees for 1 hour. Add remaining butter and cognac and confectioners' sugar. Mix until smooth. Frost loaves. Yield: 30 servings.

CINNAMON-FILLED COFFEE CAKE

1/2 c. margarine
1 c. sugar
3 eggs
1 tsp. vanilla
1 c. sour cream
2 c. flour
1 tsp. baking powder
1 tsp. soda

Cream margarine; add sugar, beating well. Stir in eggs. Add vanilla and sour cream; stir well. Combine flour, baking powder and soda; mix with egg mixture.

Filling

1/2 c. ground nuts
3/4 c. (packed) brown sugar
2 tbsp. flour
2 tbsp. butter
1 tbsp. cinnamon

Mix nuts, brown sugar, flour, butter and cinnamon together until mixture is crumbly; place layer of batter and layer of crumbs in greased angel food cake pan. Bake at 350 degrees for about 1 hour.

COFFEE BRAIDS

2 c. hot milk
Sugar
1/2 c. butter
3 eggs
1/2 tsp. salt
1/4 tsp. finely ground cardamom seed
1 1/2 pkg. yeast
7 to 8 c. flour
3/4 c. hot coffee

Place milk in large bowl; add 1 cup sugar, stirring until dissolved. Add butter; stir until melted. Let mixture stand until cool. Beat eggs until frothy. Add salt and cardamom seed; stir until mixed thoroughly. Add milk mixture; beat well. Dissolve yeast in 1/4 cup lukewarm water; stir into milk mixture. Add 5 cups flour; stir until mixed thoroughly. Add 1 1/2 to 2 cups flour, a little at a time; mix in thoroughly. Dough should be slightly sticky. Cover board with remaining flour; knead dough for 5 minutes. Place dough in greased bowl; cover with greased waxed paper and towel. Let rise for 2 hours, until doubled in bulk. Cut dough into 12 pieces; roll each piece into 12 x 1-inch rope. Braid 3 ropes together, making 4 loaves; seal ends firmly. Place on 2 greased cookie sheets; let rise about 1 hour and 30 minutes or until doubled in bulk. Bake at 375 degrees for 25 minutes. Combine 1/2 cup sugar and hot coffee; stir until sugar dissolves. Remove braids from oven; brush tops with coffee mixture. Sprinkle tops with sugar; return to oven. Bake for about 15 minutes longer. Remove from oven; cool on wire racks.

COTTAGE CHEESE STOLLEN

3 1/2 c. flour
4 tsp. baking powder
1/2 tsp. salt
2 c. raisins
1/2 c. chopped blanched almonds
2 eggs
3/4 c. sugar
2 tbsp. rum
Milk
Grated rind of 1/2 lemon
Butter
8 oz. cottage cheese
1 1/2 c. powdered sugar
1/4 tsp. almond flavoring

Sift flour, baking powder and salt together; stir in raisins and almonds. Beat eggs well; beat in sugar, rum, 1/4 cup milk and lemon rind. Cream 1/2 cup butter and cottage cheese together; stir into flour mixture and egg mixture alternately. Turn dough onto baking sheet; shape into loaf or ring. Bake at 350 degrees for 1 hour and 15 minutes. Combine powdered sugar, 2 tablespoons butter, 1 tablespoon milk and almond flavoring. Mix until of spreading consistency; ice warm bread with mixture. Garnish with cherries and nuts. Yield: 8 servings.

CRUNCHY COFFEE CAKE

1 1/2 c. sifted flour
2 tsp. baking powder
1/4 tsp. salt
1/4 c. shortening
Sugar
1 tsp. vanilla
1 egg
1/2 c. milk
2 c. small dry bread cubes
2 tbsp. melted butter
3/4 tsp. cinnamon
1/2 c. chopped nuts
1/2 c. sour cream

Sift flour, baking powder and salt together. Cream shortening, 3/4 cup sugar and vanilla; beat in egg until fluffy. Add flour mixture alternately with milk. Place in greased 11 x 7-inch pan. Toss bread cubes with butter. Mix cinnamon and 2 tablespoons sugar; sprinkle over bread cubes. Add nuts and sour cream; spread over cake batter. Bake at 350 degrees for 30 minutes. Yield: 8 servings.

FILLED COFFEE CAKE

1/4 c. butter
1 c. sugar
2 eggs, separated
2 tsp. baking powder
1 tsp. salt
1/2 c. milk
1 1/2 c. flour
1 tsp. vanilla

Cream butter and sugar together until fluffy; add egg yolks, blending well. Add baking powder, salt, milk, flour and vanilla. Beat egg whites until stiff; fold into flour mixture.

Filling

1 tbsp. flour
1/2 c. (packed) brown sugar
1 tsp. cinnamon
1 tbsp. butter
1/2 c. pecans
1 c. chopped dates

Combine flour, brown sugar, cinnamon, butter, pecans and dates. Fill greased 7 x 11-inch pan 2/3 full with batter. Pour filling over mixture; add remaining batter. Bake at 350 degrees for 45 minutes.

FRESH APPLE COFFEE CAKE

1 egg, beaten
1/2 c. milk
1/4 c. vegetable oil
1 c. grated tart apple
1 1/2 c. flour
1/2 c. sugar
2 tsp. baking powder
1/2 tsp. salt
1 tsp. cinnamon
1/3 c. (packed) brown sugar
1/3 c. chopped pecans

Combine egg, milk, oil and apple; mix well. Add flour, sugar, baking powder, salt and 1/2 teaspoon cinnamon; blend thoroughly. Stir until flour is moistened; do not overmix. Spread batter in 9 x 9-inch baking pan. Combine brown sugar and pecans; sprinkle over batter. Bake at 375 degrees for about 35 minutes. Yield: 9 servings.

GEORGIA PEACH COFFEE CAKE

2 pkg. yeast
Sugar
Butter
1/2 c. hot milk
2 tsp. salt
3 eggs
5 to 5 1/2 c. flour
2 tsp. cinnamon
1 c. chopped pecans
1 c. peach preserves
1 c. sifted powdered sugar
1 tsp. vanilla
3 tsp. milk

Soften yeast in 1/2 cup warm water. Combine 1 cup sugar, 1/2 cup butter, milk and salt; stir until butter is melted. Cool to lukewarm; blend in eggs and yeast mixture. Add flour gradually to form stiff dough; knead for about 5 minutes or until smooth. Place in greased bowl; cover. Let rise in warm place for 1 hour and 30 minutes. Combine 3 tablespoons sugar, cinnamon and pecans. Roll out half the dough to 20 x 10-inch rectangle. Spread with 1 tablespoon softened butter and 1/4 cup preserves. Sprinkle with half the cinnamon mixture; roll jelly roll fashion starting with 20-inch side. Seal edge and ends; shape in ring. Slash 1/3 through dough down center of ring. Repeat process with remaining dough; place on baking sheet. Let rise in warm place for 30 minutes; spoon 1/4 cup preserves down center of each circle. Bake at 350 degrees for about 25 minutes. Combine powdered sugar, vanilla and milk; spread over coffee cake.

HONEY-BUTTER COFFEE CAKE

1/2 c. butter
1/2 c. honey
1/4 c. maraschino cherry halves
1/2 c. pecan halves
2 cans refrigerator buttermilk biscuits

Melt butter in 9 or 10-inch skillet; stir in honey, cherries and pecans. Separate biscuits; place, overlapping, on honey mixture. Bake at 350 degrees for about 35 minutes or until browned; invert onto serving plate. Yield: 10 servings.

MERINGUE COFFEE CAKE

2/3 c. butter
1/2 c. milk
2 1/2 c. flour
3/4 tsp. salt
Sugar
2 pkg. yeast
3 eggs, separated
1/2 c. chopped nuts
1 tsp. cinnamon

Place butter and milk over low heat until butter is melted; cool. Sift flour, salt and 2 tablespoons sugar together. Dissolve yeast in 1/4 cup water; add butter mixture, flour mixture and 2 egg yolks. Beat until well blended; cover. Refrigerate overnight. Divide into 2 equal parts; roll each part out to 12 x 20-inch rectangle. Beat egg whites until frothy; continue to beat until stiff, adding 1 cup sugar gradually. Spread over dough; sprinkle with mixture of nuts and cinnamon. Roll jelly roll fashion; place on baking sheet. Bake at 350 degrees for 45 minutes. Yield: 20 slices.

KOLACHES

2 pkg. yeast
2 c. lukewarm milk
1/2 c. sugar
1 tsp. salt
Butter
6 to 7 c. flour
2 eggs, beaten
Poppy seed

Dissolve yeast in 1/2 cup lukewarm water. Mix milk, sugar and salt; stir until dissolved. Add 1 1/2 cups melted butter and 2 cups flour; beat well. Add eggs and yeast mixture; blend well. Let rise until spongy and bubbly. Add enough remaining flour to make soft dough. Grease with butter; let rise until doubled in bulk. Punch down; let rise until doubled in bulk. Roll out to 1/2-inch thickness; cut with biscuit cutter. Place on greased baking sheet, leaving space between each. Let rise until doubled in bulk. Press small hole in center of each circle; fill with poppy seed. Bake in 425-degree oven for 12 minutes or until light brown; sprinkle with chopped nuts or powdered sugar while hot, if desired. Yield: 5-6 dozen.

MINCEMEAT COFFEE RING

2 c. flour
3/4 c. sugar
2 1/2 tsp. baking powder
1/2 tsp. salt
1/3 c. shortening
1 egg, slightly beaten
1/2 c. milk
3/4 c. moist mincemeat
1 recipe powdered sugar icing

Sift flour, sugar, baking powder and salt together; cut in shortening until mixture resembles coarse meal. Combine egg, milk and mincemeat; add to dry ingredients. Mix until flour is dampened. Pour into greased 9-inch ring mold. Bake at 375 degrees for about 35 minutes. Frost warm coffee ring with powdered sugar icing.

ORANGE COFFEE CAKE

1 sm. can frozen orange juice concentrate, thawed
2 c. flour
1 1/3 c. sugar
1 tsp. soda
1 tsp. salt
1/2 c. shortening
1/2 c. milk
2 eggs
1 c. raisins (opt.)
Chopped walnuts (opt.)
1 tsp. cinnamon

Combine half the orange juice, flour, 1 cup sugar, soda, salt, shortening, milk and eggs in mixing bowl; blend. Beat for 3 minutes with mixer at medium speed. Add raisins and 1/3 cup walnuts; mix well. Pour into greased and flour 13 x 9-inch pan. Bake at 350 degrees for 35 minutes. Drizzle with remaining orange concentrate. Mix remaining sugar, 1/4 cup walnuts and cinnamon; sprinkle over coffee cake.

PECAN BREAKFAST BREAD

2 cans refrigerator crescent dinner rolls
2 tbsp. soft butter
1/2 c. sugar
2 tsp. cinnamon
1/4 c. chopped pecans

Unroll crescent rolls; separate into 16 triangles. Spread each triangle with butter. Combine sugar, cinnamon and pecans; sprinkle over triangles. Roll each triangle, starting from wide end and rolling to opposite point. Place rolls, point side down, in greased 9 x 5-inch pan, forming 2 layers of 8 rolls each. Bake at

375 degrees for about 40 minutes or until golden brown. Remove from pan; place right side up.

Topping

2 tbsp. honey
1/4 c. confectioners' sugar
2 tbsp. butter
1 tsp. vanilla
1/4 c. pecan halves

Combine honey, confectioners' sugar, butter and vanilla in saucepan; bring to a boil, stirring constantly. Stir in pecans; cool slightly. Drizzle over bread.

POTICA

2 pkg. yeast
1 1/2 c. hot milk
1/2 c. sugar
1/2 c. butter
2 eggs, beaten
8 c. flour
1 1/2 tsp. salt
Filling

Soften yeast in 1 1/2 cups lukewarm water. Combine milk, sugar and butter in large bowl; cool mixture to lukewarm. Stir in eggs and yeast mixture. Add flour and salt; mix until dough is no longer sticky. Let rise until doubled in bulk. Roll dough to 1/8-inch thickness; spread with Filling. Roll jelly roll fashion. Divide roll; place in 2 greased loaf pans. Let rise for 30 minutes. Bake at 350 degrees for 1 hour.

Filling

1/2 c. milk
1 c. honey
2 lb. finely chopped walnuts
1 c. sugar
1 c. melted butter
1 tsp. cinnamon
2 egg whites, beaten

Combine milk, honey, walnuts, sugar, butter and cinnamon; mix well. Fold in egg whites.

STREUSEL-GLAZED COFFEE CAKE

2 pkg. yeast
Milk
Butter
1/2 tsp. salt
1 2 5/8-oz. package egg custard mix
3 1/2 to 4 c. flour
1/2 c. sugar
1 tsp. cinnamon
2 c. confectioners' sugar

Soften yeast in 1/4 cup warm water. Simmer 1 cup milk until heated through. Combine milk, 1/4 cup butter, salt and custard mix; stir until blended. Cool to lukewarm; add yeast and 3 to 3 1/2 cups flour. Mix well; cover. Let rise in warm place for at least 45 minutes or until light and doubled in bulk. Combine 1/2 cup flour, sugar and cinnamon in small bowl; cut in 1/4 cup butter until mixture resembles coarse crumbs. Knead dough 12 times on lightly floured surface; spread in greased 13 x 9-inch pan. Cover; let rise for 30 minutes. Sprinkle with crumb mixture. Bake at 400 degrees for about 18 minutes. Melt 1 tablespoon butter; add confectioners' sugar and 2 tablespoons milk. Mix until smooth. Glaze cake while warm.

RICH WALNUT COFFEE CAKE

Flour
2 tsp. baking powder
3/4 c. sugar
1/4 c. shortening
1/2 c. milk
1 tsp. vanilla
2 eggs
2 tbsp. butter
1/2 c. (packed) brown sugar
1 c. chopped walnuts
1 tsp. cinnamon

Combine 1 1/2 cups flour, baking powder, sugar, shortening, milk and vanilla; blend with mixer. Beat for 2 minutes; add eggs. Beat for 2 minutes longer. Mix butter, brown sugar, walnuts, 1 tablespoon flour and cinnamon thoroughly. Spread half the cake mixture in well-greased and floured 9 1/2-inch square pan; sprinkle half the walnut mixture on top. Add remaining batter; sprinkle remaining walnut mixture on top. Bake at 350 degrees for 30 minutes. Yield: 8-12 servings.

SOUR CREAM COFFEE CAKE

3 c. flour
2 tsp. soda
1 tsp. baking powder
1 c. butter
2 c. sugar
3 eggs
1 c. sour cream
Juice of 1 lemon
1 tsp. vanilla
1 c. chopped nuts
1 tsp. cinnamon

Sift flour with soda and baking powder. Cream butter with 1 cup sugar; add eggs, one at a time, beating well. Add flour mixture to creamed mixture alternately with sour cream, beating at low speed with electric mixer. Add lemon juice and vanilla. Pour half the batter into greased and floured 13 x 9 x 2-inch pan. Combine remaining sugar with nuts and cinnamon; sprinkle half the mixture over batter. Spoon on remaining batter carefully; sprinkle remaining sugar mixture on top. Bake at 375 degrees for 45 minutes.

FRESH POTATO-FRUIT COFFEE CAKE

Color photograph for this recipe on page 729.

1 pkg. dry yeast
1 c. scalded milk
1/2 c. shortening
1 c. fresh hot mashed potatoes
Sugar
2 tsp. salt
2 lge. eggs, lightly beaten
8 1/2 c. (about) sifted flour
6 tbsp. melted butter
1 c. diced mixed glaceed fruits
3/4 tsp. ground cinnamon
1 lge. egg white

Sprinkle yeast over 1/2 cup warm water; stir until dissolved. Mix milk, shortening, potatoes, 1/3 cup sugar and salt in large bowl; cool to lukewarm. Add yeast and eggs, blending well. Add 1 1/2 cups flour; mix well. Cover; let rise in warm place for about 1 hour or until bubbly. Stir in enough remaining flour to make stiff dough. Turn onto lightly floured board; knead until smooth and elastic. Place in lightly greased bowl; turn to grease surface. Cover; refrigerate overnight. Roll out onto lightly floured board to 1-inch thickness. Cut with a 2-inch biscuit cutter. Dip each round into melted butter, then into glaceed fruits. Combine 3/4 cup sugar and cinnamon; dip rounds in cinnamon mixture. Stand rounds up in 2 greased and lightly floured 8-inch ring molds. Sprinkle with any remaining fruits. Beat egg white until foamy; brush on cakes. Let rise in warm place for about 1 hour or until doubled in bulk. Bake in a 350-degree oven for 35 minutes. Serve warm.

Prune-Filled Coffee Cake . . . The blending of lemon, prune, and walnuts gives this cake flavor.

PRUNE-FILLED COFFEE CAKE

1 c. dried prunes
1/2 tsp. cinnamon
Butter
Sugar
1/2 c. chopped walnuts
3 eggs
2 tbsp. lemon rind
3 c. sifted flour
3 tsp. baking powder
1 tsp. soda
1 c. evaporated milk
1 tbsp. lemon juice
Confectioners' sugar icing

Preheat oven to 375 degrees. Pour enough hot water over prunes to cover; let stand for 5 minutes. Drain and chop. Combine prunes, cinnamon, 3 tablespoons melted butter, 2 tablespoons sugar and walnuts. Set aside. Cream 1/2 cup butter in large electric mixer bowl. Add 1 cup sugar gradually beating well. Add eggs, one at a time, beating well after each addition. Add lemon rind. Sift flour, baking powder and soda together. Combine milk and lemon juice. Add flour mixture and milk mixture alternately to butter mixture, beating to blend after each addition. Turn 1/2 of the batter into greased 10-inch tube pan. Spread prune mixture evenly over batter. Top with remaining batter. Bake for 1 hour; cool. Remove from pan. Drizzle with icing; garnish with walnut halves.

SUGARPLUM RING

1 pkg. yeast
1/2 c. hot milk
Sugar
1/3 c. shortening
1 tsp. salt
4 c. sifted flour
2 eggs, beaten
1/4 c. melted butter
1 tsp. cinnamon
1/2 c. whole blanched almonds
1/2 c. whole candied red cherries
1/2 c. dark corn syrup

Soften yeast in 1/4 cup warm water. Combine milk, 1/3 cup sugar, shortening and salt in large bowl; cool to lukewarm. Stir in 1 cup flour; beat well. Add yeast mixture and eggs. Add enough remaining flour to make soft dough. Mix thoroughly; place in greased bowl, turning to grease surface. Cover; let rise for 2 hours or until doubled in bulk. Punch down; let stand for 10 minutes. Divide dough into 4 parts. Cut each part into 10 pieces; shape into balls. Dip balls into butter. Combine 3/4 cup sugar and cinnamon; roll balls in mixture. Arrange 1/3 of the balls in greased 10-inch tube pan. Sprinkle 1/3 of the almonds and cherries around balls. Repeat procedure twice. Mix corn syrup with remaining butter and sugar mixture; drizzle over top. Cover; let rise in warm place for 1 hour or until doubled in bulk. Bake at 350 degrees for 35 minutes. Cool for 5 minutes. Invert pan. Serve ring on large platter.

SAFFRON COFFEE RING

Color photograph for this recipe on page 724.

1 c. margarine
1/2 c. sugar
2 eggs
1/2 c. chopped raisins
1 1/4 c. milk
1/2 tsp. saffron
3 1/4 c. sifted flour
4 tsp. baking powder
1/4 c. chopped almonds

Cream margarine with sugar in a bowl. Add 1 egg, raisins and milk; mix well. Dissolve saffron in 1 tablespoon hot water; stir into egg mixture. Add flour and baking powder, mixing well. Shape into roll. Place on greased baking sheet; shape into ring. Beat remaining egg; brush on ring. Sprinkle with almonds and additional sugar. Bake in 450-degree oven for 10 to 15 minutes.

Conserve

Conserves usually consist of fruits and nuts gelled with pectin. They are similar to soft, spreadable jams or sweet, chunky marmalades. When preparing conserves, be sure to add the nutmeats *after cooking* to prevent the nuts' kernels from toughening. Serve as an accompaniment to meats and poultry or in place of jams and jellies with breads.

APRICOT CONSERVE

1/4 lb. dried apricots
1 No. 1 can crushed pineapple
1/4 c. raisins
Juice and grated rind of 1/2 lemon
1/2 c. chopped pecans
1 1/2 c. sugar

Soak apricots in 1 3/4 cups water according to package directions. Cook over low heat until soft and tender; mash to a pulp. Drain pineapple, reserving juice. Add enough water to reserved juice to equal 1/4 cup liquid. Combine apricots, pineapple, raisins, lemon juice and rind in saucepan; add pineapple liquid, pecans and sugar. Cook for about 15 to 20 minutes, stirring frequently. Pour into hot sterilized jars; seal.

APRICOT-ORANGE CONSERVE

1 1/2 c. orange juice
3 1/2 c. canned apricots
1/2 c. shredded orange peel
2 tbsp. lemon juice
3 1/2 c. sugar
1/2 c. chopped nuts

Combine orange juice, apricots, peel, lemon juice and sugar in large kettle; cook until thick, stirring constantly. Add nuts; stir well. Remove from heat. Cool for 5 minutes, stirring and skimming. Pour into hot sterilized jars; seal.

HEAVENLY APRICOT CONSERVE

2 qt. apricots
2 oranges
Juice of 1 lemon
1 No. 2 1/2 can crushed pineapple
Sugar to taste

Halve and pit apricots; peel oranges and cut into thin slices. Combine lemon juice, apricots, oranges and pineapple in saucepan. Cook over low heat for 15 minutes or until clear, stirring constantly. Add sugar; cook for about 30 minutes longer or until thickened to desired consistency. Pour into hot sterilized jars; seal.

CANTALOUPE AND PEACH CONSERVE

2 c. diced peaches
2 c. diced cantaloupe
2 lemons, ground
3 c. sugar
3/4 c. broken walnuts

Combine peaches, cantaloupe, lemons and sugar in saucepan. Bring to boiling point, stirring until sugar is dissolved. Boil over medium heat until thick; add walnuts. Pour into hot sterilized jars; seal.

CRANBERRY CONSERVE

1 lge. navel orange
1 lb. fresh cranberries
3 c. sugar
2/3 c. seeded raisins
1/8 tsp. salt
2/3 c. chopped walnuts

Quarter orange; remove seeds. Process through food grinder. Place orange in 6-quart kettle; add 2 cups water. Bring to a boil; reduce heat and simmer for about 15 minutes or until tender. Add cranberries, sugar, raisins and salt to orange mixture; bring to a boil, stirring, until sugar is dissolved. Boil rapidly for 8 to 10 minutes or until thick, stirring frequently. Add walnuts; cook for 5 minutes longer. Spoon into hot sterilized jars, filling to within 1/2 inch of top. Seal. Yield: Five 8-ounce jars.

DELICIOUS PEACH CONSERVE

6 c. sliced fresh peaches
3 c. white seedless grapes, halved
2 c. peeled diced red plums
2 c. diced pineapple
2 pared lemons, diced and seeded
1 c. orange juice
9 c. sugar

Combine all ingredients in large kettle; let stand for several hours or overnight. Cook until thickened. Pour into hot sterilized jars; seal. Yield: 7 pints.

PEACH-APPLE CONSERVE

6 c. finely chopped peaches
6 c. sugar
4 c. finely chopped apples

Combine peaches, sugar, apples and 1 1/2 cups water in kettle; stir well. Cook over medium heat, stirring constantly, until of honey consistency. Pour into sterilized jars and seal. Yield: 3-4 jars.

PEACH CONSERVE

4 lb. ripe freestone peaches
1 sm. jar maraschino cherries
1/2 c. frozen orange juice
Juice of 2 lemons
1 No. 2 1/2 can crushed pineapple
6 c. sugar
1 pkg. fruit pectin

Skin peaches; slice. Drain cherries; chop coarsely. Combine all ingredients in large kettle; cook for about 15 minutes or until thickened. Let stand for 5 minutes. Pour into hot sterilized jars; seal. Yield: 10 jars.

Ginger-Peach Conserve . . . This spicy blend of foods can accompany many main dishes.

GINGER-PEACH CONSERVE

1/4 c. sugar
1/2 tsp. ground cinnamon
1 12-oz. package frozen sliced peaches
1/2 c. coarsely chopped walnuts
2 tbsp. minced crystallized ginger
1/4 c. maraschino cherries

Combine sugar and cinnamon in small bowl. Thaw peaches. Drain juice from peaches; add to cinnamon mixture. Stir until sugar is dissolved. Pour cinnamon mixture over peaches. Add walnuts, ginger and cherries. Mix well. Chill until ready to serve. Yield: 2 1/2 cups.

SPICED MELON BALLS

2 12-oz. packages frozen melon balls
1/4 c. (packed) light brown sugar
1/4 c. cider vinegar
6 whole cloves
1 cinnamon stick

Thaw melon balls; drain juice from balls. Combine melon juice, brown sugar, vinegar, cloves and cinnamon in saucepan; simmer for 5 minutes. Pour hot syrup over melon balls. Let stand until cool; chill until ready to serve. Yield: 3 cups.

STRAWBERRY-RHUBARB MEDLEY

1 1-lb. package frozen whole strawberries
1 1-lb. package frozen rhubarb
Cornstarch
1/2 c. slivered blanched almonds
1 tsp. grated lemon rind

Thaw strawberries and rhubarb; drain off juice. Measure juice; add 1 1/2 tablespoons cornstarch for every cup of juice. Cook over low heat in saucepan, stirring constantly, until smooth and thick. Stir in almonds and lemon rind; cool slightly. Fold in strawberries and rhubarb carefully. Chill until ready to serve. Yield: 3 cups.

SPICED PEACH SLICES

2 12-oz. packages frozen sliced peaches
2 cinnamon sticks
1 tbsp. whole cloves
1/4 c. cider vinegar
1/3 c. seedless raisins

Thaw peaches; drain off juice. Combine peach juice, spices, vinegar and raisins in saucepan. Simmer for 5 minutes. Pour hot syrup over sliced peaches. Let stand until cool; chill until ready to serve. Yield: 3 cups.

MINTED GRAPEFRUIT SECTIONS

1/8 tsp. mint extract
2 13 1/2-oz. cans frozen grapefruit sections
2 tbsp. chopped fresh mint
Green vegetable coloring

Add mint extract to grapefruit sections; add fresh mint and enough green coloring to tint delicate green. Chill until ready to serve. Yield: 3 1/2 cups.

PEACH DELIGHT CONSERVE

18 ripe peaches
3 oranges
1 3-lb. 4-oz. can crushed pineapple
Sugar
1 c. chopped maraschino cherries

Peel peaches and 2 oranges; remove seeds. Quarter and seed remaining unpeeled orange. Grind peaches and oranges through food chopper, using fine blade. Add pineapple with juice. Add 1 1/2 cups sugar for each cup fruit mixture; mix well. Cook in large kettle until mixture sheets from spoon. Stir in cherries. Pour into hot sterilized jars; seal.

PEACH-ORANGE CONSERVE

1 orange
7 c. peeled chopped peaches
5 c. sugar
1/2 tsp. ginger
1/4 tsp. salt
2/3 c. sliced blanched almonds

Quarter orange; cut into thin slices. Combine orange and peaches in kettle; boil for 20 minutes. Stir in sugar, ginger and salt; cook until thick. Stir in almonds. Pour into hot sterilized jars; seal.

PEAR CONSERVES

18 pears
1 14-oz. can pineapple, drained
Juice and grated rind of 2 oranges
Sugar
1 3-oz. bottle maraschino cherries, chopped

Peel pears; chop coarsely. Add pineapple, orange juice, grated rind and 3/4 cup sugar for each cup of pulp. Cook over low heat in large kettle until thick. Chop cherries; add to pear mixture. Bring to a boil. Pour into hot sterilized jars; seal.

TART PEAR CONSERVE

3 c. peeled sliced pears
2 1/2 c. sugar
1 c. seedless raisins
1 orange
1 lemon
1 c. chopped nuts

Combine pears and sugar; let stand overnight. Add raisins. Squeeze juice from orange and lemon; chop orange rind. Add juices, rind and nuts to pear mixture. Pour into large saucepan. Cook for 30 to 35 minutes or until thick. Pour into sterilized jars; seal while hot. Yield: 2 pints.

PINEAPPLE CONSERVE

1 qt. chopped pineapple pulp
Pulp and grated rind of 2 oranges
Pulp and grated rind of 1 lemon
3 c. sugar

Cook pineapple with juice in kettle until tender; add oranges, lemon and sugar. Boil until thick. Pour into sterilized jars; seal.

PINECOT CONSERVE

1 lb. dried apricots
3 temple oranges
3 c. sugar
1 No. 2 can crushed pineapple

Cover apricots with water; cook until tender. Mash apricots to pulp, reserving cooking water. Grate orange rinds; grind orange pulp. Combine all ingredients; pour into 12 x 12-inch shallow glass baking pan. Bake at 350 degrees until mixture thickens and bubbles. Pour into hot sterilized jars; seal. Yield: 5 pints.

PLUM CONSERVE

3 lb. sliced damson plums
1 1/2 lb. sugar
1 lemon, thinly sliced
1 lb. seeded raisins
1 orange, thinly sliced
1 c. chopped walnuts

Combine plums, sugar, lemon, raisins and orange in large saucepan; add small amount of water. Cook until thick and clear; add walnuts. Pour into hot sterilized jars; seal. Yield: 4 pints.

SAND PLUM CONSERVE

8 c. seeded sand plums
4 tbsp. lemon juice
1 1/2 tsp. grated lemon rind
1 c. seedless raisins
6 c. sugar
1 c. chopped black walnuts

Chop plums. Combine plums, lemon juice, lemon rind, raisins and sugar in saucepan, mixing well. Cook over low heat, stirring, until thick. Blanch walnuts; drain. Add walnuts to plum mixture. Pour plum mixture into sterilized jars; seal. Yield: 5 pints.

TUTTI-FRUTTI CONSERVE

3 c. chopped pears
1 lge. seeded orange, chopped
3/4 c. drained crushed pineapple
1/2 c. chopped maraschino cherries
1/2 c. lemon juice
1/2 c. chopped nuts
1 c. coconut
1 pkg. powdered pectin
5 c. sugar

Combine pears, orange, pineapple, cherries, lemon juice, nuts and coconut in kettle; stir in pectin. Bring to a boil, stirring constantly. Add sugar, stirring well; bring to a rolling boil. Cook for 1 minute, stirring constantly. Remove from heat; skim and stir for 5 minutes. Pour into hot sterilized jars; seal.

Consommé

Consomme is a clear soup that is actually the skimmed stock in which meat or poultry bones have been cooked. There are two types: white consomme which is made from chicken or veal bones and brown consomme which is made from beef or ham bones. Consomme is an excellent source of protein, calcium, iron, riboflavin, and niacin. (1 cup consomme = 10 calories)

PREPARATION: Simmer bones in covered kettle with water and herbs, or bouquet garni, for several hours. Strain and refrigerate broth. Skim top layer of firm fat which forms.

STORING: Consomme, covered, keeps in refrigerator 3 days or in frozen foods compartment 2 1/2 months.

SERVING: Serve hot or chilled as first course soup. Garnish with lemon slices, cucumber slices, or parsley.

BEEF CONSOMMÉ

3 lb. soupbones and suet
1 head cabbage, shredded
1 stalk celery, chopped
3 to 4 lge. onions, chopped
1 bunch carrots, chopped
1 lb. okra, sliced
1 lb. green beans, sliced
1 lb. turnips, chopped
3 to 4 lb. tomatoes, chopped

Combine all ingredients in large kettle; cover with water. Simmer for 6 to 8 hours. Strain broth. Cool broth; skim off fat. Refrigerate until ready to serve.

JELLIED CONSOMMÉ

2 c. consomme
3 tbsp. lemon juice
1/2 tsp. Worcestershire sauce
Dash of cayenne
1 hard-cooked egg yolk, sieved

Bring consomme to a boil; add lemon juice, Worcestershire sauce and cayenne. Pour into shallow dish; chill until firm. Cut into small cubes; serve in chilled bouillon cups. Sprinkle egg yolk over top of jelled mixture. Yield: 6 servings.

MADRILENE WITH SHERRY

2 env. unflavored gelatin
2 c. tomato juice
2 c. chicken stock
1 tsp. grated onion
1/4 c. dry sherry
Salt and pepper to taste

Soften gelatin in 1/2 cup tomato juice. Combine remaining ingredients; bring to a boil. Simmer for 5 minutes; stir in gelatin mixture. Pour into shallow pan. Chill until firm. Cut into cubes; serve in chilled bouillon cups. Yield: 6 servings.

POT AU FEU

3 lb. beef brisket
1 lge. marrow bone
5 carrots
3 turnips
1 onion
3 cloves
1 bunch parsley
2 leeks
1 sm. bay leaf
1 tsp. sugar
Salt and pepper to taste

Place beef, bone and 6 cups cold water in large kettle; slowly bring to a boil and skim. Add 1 cup cold water; bring to a boil slowly and skim again. Pare and halve carrots and turnips; stud onion with 3 cloves. Add carrots, turnips, onion, parsley, leeks, bay leaf and sugar to beef broth. Season with salt and pepper. Simmer, covered, for 4 to 5 hours or until meat is tender. Strain broth. Yield: 6 servings.

TOMATO CONSOMMÉ

4 beef bouillon cubes
Celery leaves
1 med. onion, sliced
1/4 c. chopped parsley
1 tsp. salt
1/2 tsp. basil
2 bay leaves
1 46-oz. can tomato juice

Combine bouillon cubes, celery leaves, onion, parsley, salt, basil and bay leaves with 2 cups water in a large saucepan. Bring to a boil; simmer 15 minutes. Stir in tomato juice; simmer 5 minutes longer or until hot. Strain broth.

VEAL CONSOMMÉ

4 lb. veal soupbones
2 sm. carrots, chopped
1 onion, chopped
2 stalks celery with leaves, chopped
2 sprigs of parsley
6 to 8 white peppercorns
2 tsp. salt

Combine all ingredients with 4 quarts water in soup kettle. Bring to a boil slowly; skim broth. Simmer, covered, for 3 hours or until liquid is reduced by half. Remove bones; strain broth through cheesecloth. Cool and refrigerate.

VEAL-CHICKEN CONSOMMÉ

3 lb. veal knuckle
Necks and wings of 2 chickens
1 tbsp. salt
1/4 tsp. peppercorns
3 stalks celery
2 bay leaves
2 sprigs of thyme
2 cloves
1 onion
Dash of cayenne pepper
6 tbsp. minced pimento
6 tbsp. minced green pepper

Combine knuckle and chicken with 3 quarts water, salt, peppercorns, celery, bay leaves, thyme, cloves, onion and cayenne pepper in soup kettle. Bring to a boil; skim. Simmer, covered, for 4 hours. Strain through double thickness of cheesecloth; chill until firm. Break up with fork; serve in chilled bouillon cups. Garnish with pimento and green pepper. Yield: 2 quarts.

VEGETABLE CONSOMMÉ

1 tbsp. butter
1 c. carrot strips
1/2 c. turnip strips
1/2 c. shredded cabbage
1/4 c. chopped leek
1/2 c. chopped celery
1/4 c. chopped onion
Salt and pepper to taste
1 tsp. sugar
4 chicken bouillon cubes

Melt butter in medium saucepan; add vegetables, seasonings and sugar. Cover; cook over low heat for about 5 minutes or until vegetables are tender. Dissolve bouillon cubes in 1 quart boiling water. Add cooked vegetables. Simmer for 30 minutes. Strain broth. Yield: 6 servings.

Corn

Corn is a cereal or grain plant, the seeds or kernels of which are cooked as a vegetable. It is high in calcium, iron, and Vitamins A and C. (1 ear, cooked corn = 65 calories)

AVAILABILITY: Fresh corn is available year-round with peak supplies coming in July and August. Canned corn is available year-round as whole kernels, cream-style, or with other vegetables. Frozen corn on the cob, whole kernel, or with other vegetables is also available year-round.

BUYING: Choose fresh corn ears wrapped in crisp green husks that are well filled with firm, plump, milky kernels. Avoid ears with shrunken, soft, or excessively large or firm kernels and dry, yellowed husks.

STORING: Fresh corn should be cooked

within hours of having been picked. The sugar in corn begins to change to starch after that time. This causes the corn to change in flavor and texture. *To freeze* corn, husk freshly picked ears, remove silk, trim ends. Scald in covered pan, cool in water or ice, drain. Cut kernels from ears or leave whole, package, label, date, and freeze. Fresh frozen corn keeps 1 month in refrigerator's freezer compartment or 1 year in home freezer. Store unopened cans of corn in cupboard for up to 3 years. Opened, covered cans keep in refrigerator 3 days.

PREPARATION: Fresh corn is most often boiled. To boil corn, remove husks and silk. Wash, and either cut kernels from cobs or leave ears whole. Place corn in unsalted water to cover and cook until water reaches a boil. (See VEGETABLES.)

CORN AND MUSHROOMS

1 can buttered corn
1 8-oz. can mushrooms
Salt and pepper to taste
Butter

Place corn and mushrooms in saucepan; simmer for several minutes. Drain. Add salt and pepper to taste; place in serving dish. Top with square of butter. Yield: 6 servings.

CORN WITH CREAM CHEESE

1/4 c. milk
1 3-oz. package cream cheese
1 tbsp. butter
1/2 tsp. salt
1/8 tsp. pepper
2 12-oz. cans whole kernel corn

Combine milk, cream cheese, butter, salt and pepper in saucepan; cook over low heat, stirring constantly, until blended. Drain corn well; stir into cream cheese mixture, heating through. Serve immediately. Three cups cooked frozen corn may be substituted for canned corn. Yield: 6 servings.

FRESH CORN SOUP

1/4 c. minced onion
1/4 c. butter
1 tbsp. lemon juice
1/2 tsp. dry mustard
1 tsp. salt
1 tsp. sugar
Freshly ground pepper to taste
2 c. fresh corn
2 c. chicken stock
2 c. light cream
Dash of hot sauce

Saute onion in butter until transparent; stir in lemon juice, mustard, salt, sugar and pepper. Add corn and chicken stock. Bring to a boil; cover. Simmer for about 10 minutes. Add cream and hot sauce; mix well. Simmer until heated through; do not boil. Yield: 6-8 servings.

CORN SOUP

1 1/2 c. cream-style corn
1 c. meat broth
2 1/2 c. milk
1 tsp. salt
1/4 tsp. sugar
1/2 tsp. minced onion
1 1/2 tbsp. quick-cooking tapioca
1 1/2 tbsp. butter

Cook corn in meat broth for 10 minutes; press through sieve. Combine corn mixture with milk, salt, sugar, onion and tapioca in saucepan; bring to a boil, stirring constantly. Add butter; serve immediately. Garnish with chopped parsley. Yield: 4-6 servings.

BAKED CORN

1 No. 2 can cream-style corn
2 tbsp. flour
1 tbsp. melted butter
1 tsp. salt
2 eggs, well beaten
1/2 c. chopped green pepper
1 2-oz. jar pimento, chopped
1 c. grated sharp cheese
1/4 c. milk

Combine all ingredients in order given; mix well. Pour into greased 1-quart baking dish. Bake in 350-degree oven for about 50 minutes. Yield: 4-6 servings.

BAKED CORN IN CASSEROLE

1 No. 2 can cream-style corn
1 12-oz. can whole kernel corn
1/2 c. grated onion
1/2 c. chopped green pepper
2 pimentos, chopped
2/3 c. milk
1 egg, well beaten
1 c. cracker crumbs
1 c. grated American cheese
1/4 c. melted butter
2 tbsp. sugar
Black and red pepper to taste
Salt to taste

Combine all ingredients; mix well. Pour into buttered 2-quart casserole. Bake at 350 degrees for 1 hour. Yield: 8 servings.

BAKED VANILLA CORN

1 1/2 tbsp. cornstarch
1/4 c. sugar
2 c. lukewarm milk
3 eggs
1/4 tsp. salt
1 tsp. vanilla
1 can cream-style corn

Mix cornstarch and sugar in bowl; stir in several tablespoons milk to make a paste. Add eggs, beating well. Add remaining milk, salt, vanilla and corn; stir well. Place in baking dish. Bake at 350 degrees for 45 minutes. Yield: 6-8 servings.

BAKED WHOLE KERNEL CORN

1 pkg. frozen whole kernel corn
1/4 c. heavy cream
2 tbsp. milk
1 tbsp. butter
1 tsp. salt
1/4 tsp. pepper

Thaw corn partially; break apart with fork. Combine all ingredients in small casserole. Bake at 375 degrees for about 40 minutes, stirring occasionally. Yield: 5 servings.

BAKED CORN CUSTARD WITH CHEESE

2 green onions, minced
3 tbsp. butter
3 tbsp. flour
1/2 tsp. salt
2 c. milk
1 c. grated cheese
1 tsp. sugar
2 tbsp. minced pimento
1/2 tsp. marjoram
2 eggs, slightly beaten
2 No. 2 cans whole kernel corn
1/2 c. bread crumbs
Paprika

Saute onions in butter; blend in flour and salt. Add milk slowly, stirring constantly; cook over medium heat until thickened. Blend in cheese; add sugar, pimento and marjoram. Add eggs; blend well. Drain corn; stir into cheese sauce until well mixed. Pour into shallow 2-quart casserole. Sprinkle with crumbs; dust with paprika lightly. Bake at 350 degrees for 35 minutes. Yield: 8 servings.

BAKED CORN FONDUE

1 1/2 c. hot milk
1 1/2 c. soft bread crumbs
1 17-oz. can cream-style corn
2 c. shredded cheese
1/8 tsp. salt
1/8 tsp. pepper
3 eggs, separated

Preheat oven to 325 degrees. Combine milk, crumbs, corn, cheese and seasonings. Beat egg yolks; stir into corn mixture. Beat egg whites until stiff peaks form. Fold in egg whites; pour into ungreased 1 1/2-quart casserole. Bake for about 1 hour or until golden brown. Yield: 4-6 servings.

BOSTON-STYLE BAKED CORN

1 tsp. dry mustard
1/2 tsp. salt
2 tbsp. (packed) brown sugar
1 c. catsup
1 sm. onion, diced
2 12-oz. cans whole kernel corn, drained
2 to 3 slices bacon, diced

Preheat oven to 350 degrees. Combine mustard, salt, brown sugar and catsup. Add onion and corn; mix well. Pour into greased 1 1/2-quart casserole. Top with bacon. Bake for 40 minutes or until bacon is crisp. Yield: 6-8 servings.

CHRISTMAS CORN

2 c. corn
2 tbsp. minced red pepper
2 tbsp. minced green pepper
1 1/2 tbsp. flour
Salt and pepper to taste
1 c. milk
3 slices bacon

Combine corn, red pepper, green pepper, flour, salt and pepper; pour into 1 1/2-quart casserole. Add milk. Broil bacon until almost crisp; arrange over corn mixture. Bake in 350-degree oven for about 30 minutes. Yield: 4-6 servings.

CONFETTI CORN

2 No. 303 cans corn
2 eggs, well beaten
1 sm. jar pimento, chopped
3 tbsp. butter, melted
Salt and pepper
1 can onion rings

Mix corn with eggs, pimento and butter; season with salt and pepper. Place in greased casserole; cover with onion rings. Bake at 350 degrees for about 35 minutes. Yield: 6 servings.

CORN FAIRFAX

1/4 c. minced onion
1/4 c. chopped celery
1/2 c. butter, melted
1 can whole kernel corn
2/3 c. cooked string beans
1 1/2 c. milk
1 tbsp. flour
2 eggs, beaten
2/3 c. grated cheese
2/3 c. bread crumbs

Mix onion and celery; add to 1/4 cup butter. Simmer for 5 minutes. Add corn and beans; simmer for 5 minutes. Combine milk and flour; stir into corn mixture. Simmer for 4 minutes longer. Add eggs, stirring well; remove from heat. Pour into greased 1-quart casserole. Combine remaining butter with cheese and bread crumbs; spread over casserole. Bake at 375 degrees for 15 minutes or until browned. Yield: 8 servings.

CORN POTLUCK

3 hot dog buns
1 4-oz. can sliced mushrooms
9 lean bacon slices
2 cans cream-style corn
1 c. milk
3/4 tsp. salt
1/2 tsp. chili powder
1 c. grated Cheddar cheese

Crumble buns into medium fine crumbs. Drain mushrooms. Fry bacon. Remove from pan before crisp; drain well. Mince 6 slices; reserve 3 slices. Mix minced bacon with corn and milk. Stir in crumbs, salt, chili powder, cheese and mushrooms; mix well. Turn into casserole. Bake in 350-degree oven for 40 minutes or until puffed and creamy. Garnish with reserved bacon slices. Bake for 10 minutes longer. Yield: 8 servings.

SOUTHERN CORN PUDDING

Color photograph for this recipe on page 308.

2 c. fresh corn, cut from cob
2 tsp. sugar
1 1/2 tsp. salt
1/8 tsp. ground pepper
3 eggs, lightly beaten
2 tbsp. butter
2 c. milk

Preheat oven to 350 degrees. Combine corn, sugar, salt and pepper. Add eggs; mix well. Add butter to milk; heat until butter is melted. Blend with corn and egg mixture. Turn into greased 1-quart casserole. Place in pan of hot water. Bake for 1 hour or until knife inserted in center comes out clean. Garnish with fresh parsley. Yield: 6 servings.

CREAMED VEGETABLE SOUP
Recipe On Page 829.

MUSHROOM APPETIZER
Recipe For This Photograph On Page 587.

AVOCADO VEGETABLE PLATTER
Recipe For This Photograph On Page 54.

STUFFED APPLES
Recipe For This Photograph On Page 22.

APPLE-LIME MOLDS
Recipe For This Photograph On Page 21.

CREAMY GOLDEN WALDORF
Recipe For This Photograph On Page 22.

COACH HOUSE PLATTER
Recipe For This Photograph On Page 101.

SOUTHERN CORN PUDDING
Recipe For This Photograph On Page 304.

FRESH STUFFED TOMATOES
Recipe For This Photograph On Page 877.

SUNDAY BRUSSELS SPROUTS
Recipe For This Photograph On Page 163.

STUFFED BELL PEPPERS
Recipe For This Photograph On Page 661.

BOUNTIFUL VEGETABLE PLATTER
Recipe For This Photograph On Page 610.

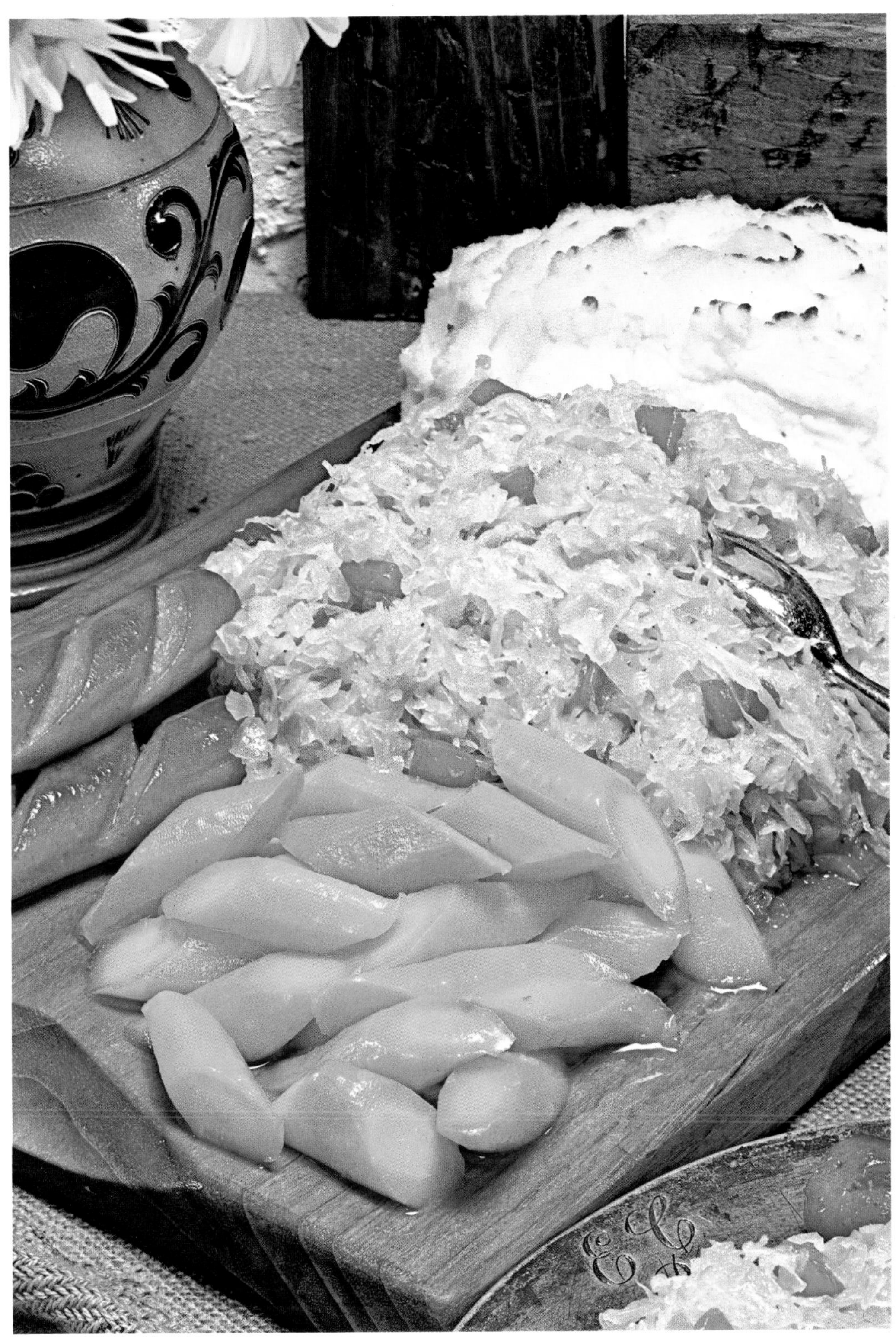

PLANKED KRAUT DINNER
Recipe For This Photograph On Page 801.

AL FRESCO OLIVE SALAD
Recipe For This Photograph On Page 604.

FRUITED RICE SALAD
Recipe For This Photograph On Page 757.

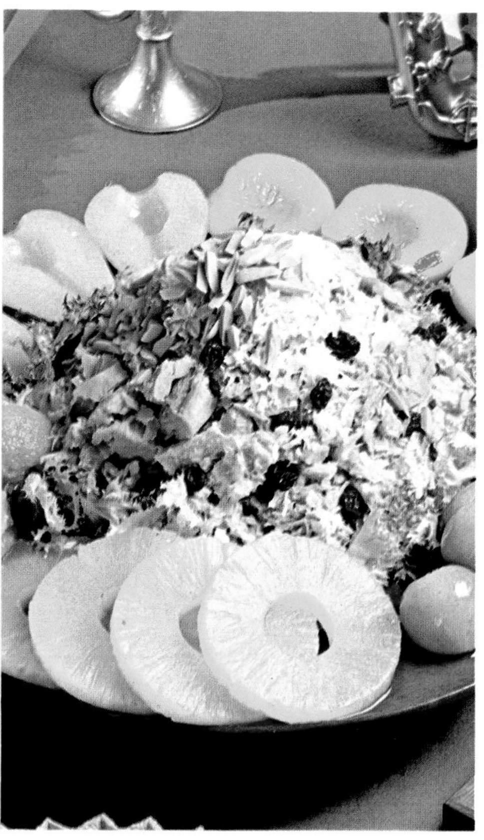

TUNA POLYNESIAN PLATTER
Recipe For This Photograph On Page 891.

DRIED BEEF AND FRESH VEGETABLE SALAD
Recipe For This Photograph On Page 102.

HASHED BROWN POTATOES
Recipe For This Photograph On Page 703.

POTATOES AU GRATIN
Recipe For This Photograph On Page 703.

WHIPPED POTATOES PAPRIKA
Recipe For This Photograph On Page 703.

BOILED POTATOES WITH CHEESE SAUCE
Recipe For This Photograph On Page 704.

CHICKEN SALAD WITH BACON
Recipe For This Photograph On Page 241.

SAUERKRAUT WITH APPLES
Recipe For This Photograph On Page 800.

ARTICHOKES WITH DESERT SLAW
Recipe For This Photograph On Page 38.

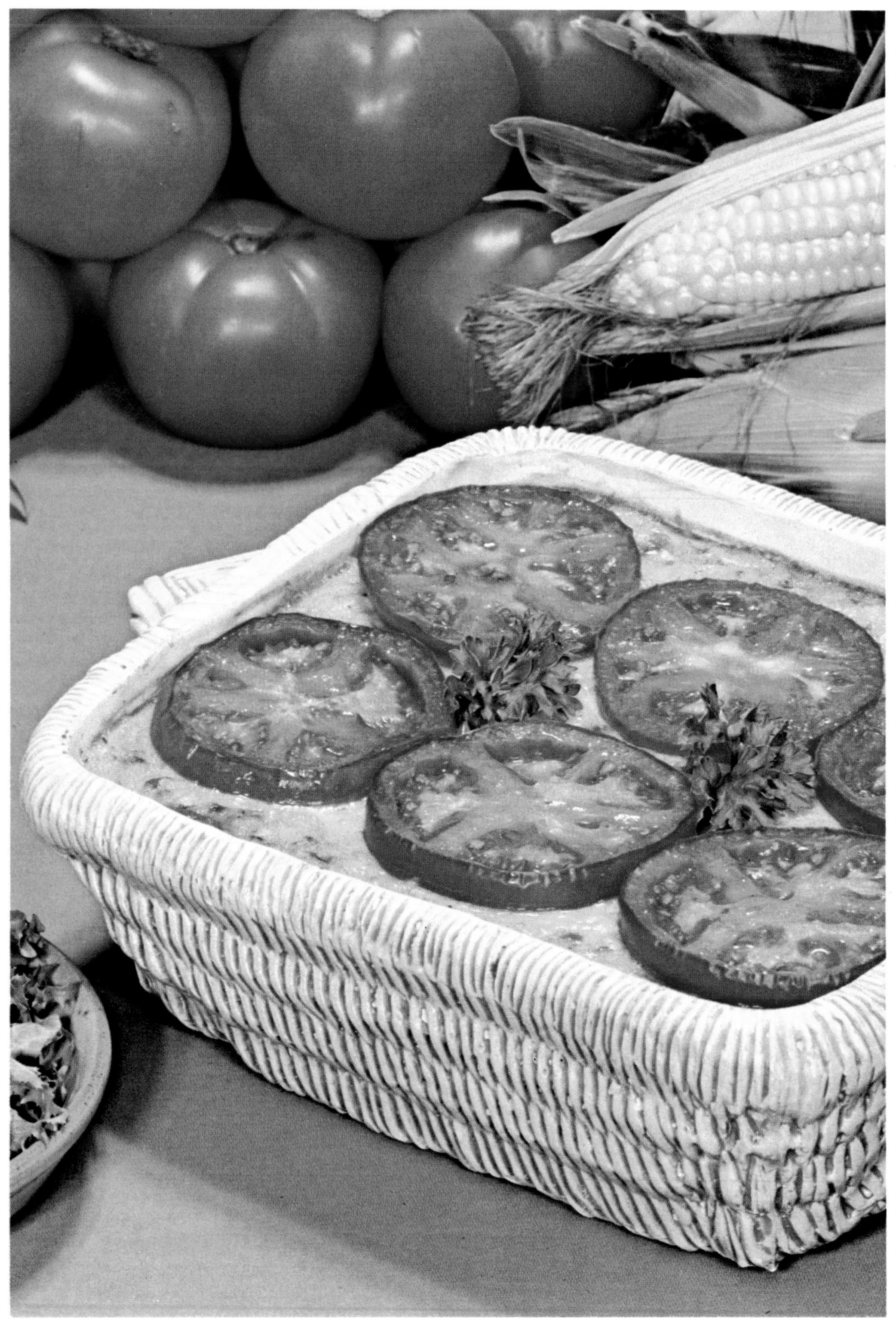

FRESH TOMATO CASSEROLE
Recipe For This Photograph On Page 880.

CRANBERRY BAKED BEANS
Recipe For This Photograph On Page 99.

ORANGE AND AVOCADO SALAD
Recipe For This Photograph On Page 613.

CRAB SALAD
Recipe For This Photograph On Page 332.

POLE BEANS WITH MUSTARD SAUCE
Recipe For This Photograph On Page 91.

AUTUMN'S GOLD APPLE SALAD
Recipe For This Photograph On Page 22.

CORN PIE

2 onions, chopped
Cooking oil
1 lb. ground beef
3 tbsp. flour
Salt and pepper to taste
2 hard-boiled eggs, sliced
6 c. fresh corn
Milk
1/4 tsp. oregano
Sugar

Fry onions in small amount of oil. Add ground beef; sprinkle with flour. Cook slowly until beef is brown. Add small amount boiling water; simmer until done. Remove from heat; add salt and pepper. Place beef mixture in casserole; arrange egg slices over top. Cook corn in oil over low heat, adding enough milk to prevent burning or sticking. Season with salt, pepper and oregano. Spread corn mixture over beef; sprinkle with sugar. Bake in 350-degree oven until browned. Serve hot. Yield: 6 servings.

CORN PUDDING

4 ears of corn
4 eggs
2 c. milk
1 tsp. salt
1 tsp. sugar
2 tbsp. shortening

Remove corn from cobs. Place all ingredients in blender; mix well. Pour into greased 1 1/2-quart casserole. Bake at 400 degrees for at least 45 minutes. Yield: 6 servings.

CORN-BREAD PUDDING

2 c. soft bread cubes
1 1/2 c. milk
2 eggs, beaten
Salt and pepper
1 No. 303 can cream-style corn
1 tsp. sugar

Combine all ingredients; let stand for several minutes. Pour into buttered casserole. Bake at 325 degrees for 1 hour or until firm.

CORN AND COTTAGE CHEESE

2 eggs
1 1/2 c. creamed cottage cheese
1/2 c. milk
3 tbsp. flour
1 16-oz. can whole kernel corn
1 1/2 tsp. salt
Dash of pepper
1 tbsp. sugar
1/4 c. shredded Cheddar cheese
Paprika

Beat eggs slightly; add cottage cheese, mixing well. Blend 1/4 cup milk with flour to make paste. Drain corn. Add flour mixture, remaining milk, corn, salt, pepper and sugar to egg mixture; blend. Pour into shallow 1 1/2-quart baking dish. Bake at 350 degrees for 20 minutes. Remove from oven. Stir well; sprinkle with cheese. Return to oven. Bake for 10 minutes longer. Sprinkle with paprika before serving. Yield: 6 servings.

STUFFED BAKED MUSHROOMS IN TOMATOES

Recipe On Page 880.

CORN AND OYSTER CASSEROLE

2 eggs
1/2 c. cream
1 sm. can oysters and liquid
1 tbsp. melted butter
1 No. 2 can cream-style corn
1 c. buttered cracker crumbs

Beat eggs until thick; add cream, oysters, butter, corn and 1/2 cup cracker crumbs. Stir mixture, blending well. Pour into buttered 1-quart baking dish. Sprinkle remaining cracker crumbs on top. Bake at 350 degrees for 30 minutes. Yield: 4-6 servings.

CORN SOUFFLÉ

2 eggs, separated
Milk
2 tbsp. flour
2 tbsp. sugar
2 tbsp. melted butter
1 can white cream-style corn

Beat egg yolks; add enough milk to make 3/4 cup liquid. Stir in flour, sugar, butter and corn. Beat egg whites until stiff peaks form; fold into corn mixture. Spoon into buttered 1-quart casserole. Bake at 350 degrees for 1 hour. Serve immediately. Yield: 6-8 servings.

CORN IN SOUR CREAM

3 strips bacon
2 cans whole kernel corn
1/2 tsp. salt
1 c. sour cream

Fry bacon in skillet until crisp. Remove bacon; drain. Pour bacon drippings from skillet, reserving 2 tablespoons drippings. Return reserved drippings to skillet; stir in corn. Add salt and sour cream; mix well. Crumble bacon over top; simmer until heated through. Serve immediately. Yield: 8 servings.

CREAMY CORN CUSTARD

5 eggs
3 c. milk
2 pkg. frozen corn, thawed
Salt and pepper to taste
Butter

Beat eggs slightly; add milk gradually. Beat well; add corn, salt and pepper. Spoon into buttered dish; dot with butter. Bake in 375-degree oven for 50 minutes. Yield: 10 servings.

CRUNCHY CORN

1 3 1/2-oz. can onion rings
1/2 c. chopped green pepper
1 tsp. butter
1 1-lb. can cream-style corn
2 tsp. chopped pimento
1 egg, slightly beaten

Crush onion rings. Saute green pepper in butter until soft. Add corn, pimento, egg and 1/2 of the onion ring crumbs; pour into 1 1/2-quart casserole. Bake at 350 degrees for 25 minutes or until firm. Sprinkle remaining onion ring crumbs on top; bake for 5 minutes longer. Yield: 6 servings.

GOLDEN HOLIDAY CORN

1 2/3 c. canned corn
2 c. cooked rice
2 1/2 c. grated carrots
1 1/4 c. grated cheese
2 eggs, well beaten
1/4 c. milk
1 tbsp. instant minced onion
1 tbsp. melted butter
1 tsp. salt
1/8 tsp. pepper

Combine all ingredients; mix well. Place in greased baking dish; cover. Bake at 325 degrees for 45 minutes. Yield: 6 servings.

INDIAN CORN

2 slices bacon, diced
1 lge. onion, minced
2 1-lb. cans cream-style corn
1 egg, well beaten
2 tbsp. flour
1 tbsp. sugar
1/4 c. milk

Brown bacon and onion in skillet. Add corn to egg; stir into onion mixture. Blend flour, sugar and milk; stir into corn mixture. Pour into buttered casserole. Bake at 350 degrees for about 1 hour or until set. Yield: 8 servings.

SAVORY CORN

3 slices bacon
1 No. 303 can whole kernel corn, drained
1/2 c. sour cream
1 tsp. onion flakes
Salt and pepper to taste
Paprika

Fry bacon until crisp; crumble. Drain fat from skillet; add corn. Stir in bacon and sour cream; season with onion flakes, salt and pepper. Simmer until heated through, stirring gently; sprinkle with paprika before serving. Yield: 3-4 servings.

SCALLOPED CORN

1 16-oz. can cream-style corn
1/4 c. chopped onion
1 tsp. salt
2 tbsp. butter
2 eggs, beaten
1 c. milk
1/2 c. chopped celery (opt.)
2/3 c. shredded American cheese (opt.)
1/4 tsp. paprika (opt.)
1 c. cracker crumbs

Combine all ingredients, adding cracker crumbs last. Pour into 1 1/2-quart casserole. Bake in 350-degree oven until knife inserted comes out clean. Yield: 4-6 servings.

SCALLOPED CORN WITH CRACKER TOPPING

1 No. 303 can cream-style corn
1 egg
Pinch of salt
Pinch of pepper
8 tbsp. cracker crumbs
1 c. milk
4 tbsp. butter

Mix corn, egg, salt, pepper and half the cracker crumbs, blending well; turn into 2-quart casserole. Pour milk over casserole. Spread remaining cracker crumbs over top; dot with butter. Bake at 350 degrees for 1 hour. Yield: 6 servings.

SCALLOPED CORN WITH OATMEAL

1 can cream-style corn
1/4 c. cream
1/4 c. quick-cooking oats

Blend corn, cream and oats in casserole. Bake at 350 degrees for about 45 minutes. Yield: 6 servings.

SCALLOPED CORN WITH PEPPERS AND PIMENTO

1 1/2 c. whole kernel corn
Evaporated milk
2 tbsp. butter
2 tbsp. flour
1 tsp. salt
1/4 tsp. pepper
1/2 tsp. monosodium glutamate
1 tsp. celery salt
3 tbsp. chopped green pepper
2 tbsp. chopped pimento
2 eggs, beaten
1/2 c. buttered bread crumbs

Drain corn; reserve liquid. Add enough evaporated milk to reserved corn liquid to make 1 cup liquid. Melt butter in saucepan over low heat; add flour, salt, pepper, monosodium glutamate and celery salt. Cook, stirring constantly, until smooth. Add evaporated milk mixture gradually; cook until thickened, stirring constantly. Add corn, green pepper, pimento and eggs, stirring well; pour into buttered baking dish. Sprinkle with bread crumbs; place in shallow pan of water. Bake in 350-degree oven for about 50 minutes. Yield: 6 servings.

WINTER CORN

1 1/2 c. chopped celery
2 c. canned whole kernel corn
1/2 c. minced ripe olives
1/2 c. minced green pepper
1/2 tsp. salt
1/2 tsp. pepper
1/4 c. butter
1/2 c. milk
1/4 c. dry bread crumbs

Cook celery in small amount of water until tender-crisp; drain well. Layer corn, celery, olives and green pepper in greased 2-quart casserole; sprinkle each layer with salt and pepper. Dot with half the butter. Pour in milk. Spread crumbs over top; dot with remaining butter. Bake at 350 degrees for 45 minutes. Yield: 6-8 servings.

BARBECUED CORN

8 ears of corn
1/4 c. barbecue sauce
1/2 c. butter, melted

Remove husks from corn. Blend barbecue sauce and butter; spread generously over corn. Wrap each ear of corn securely in heavy-duty aluminum foil. Cook over hot coals for about 20 minutes, turning several times. Yield: 8 servings.

CORN ON THE COALS

6 ears of corn, unhusked
Salt to taste
Butter

Soak corn in water for 2 hours. Place over hot charcoal; roast until husks are browned. Husk; serve with salt and butter.

PEANUT BUTTER-GRILLED CORN

Corn on the cob
Peanut butter
Bacon slices

Husk corn. Spread lightly with peanut butter; wrap corn in bacon. Fasten bacon with toothpick. Cook over hot coals for 10 minutes or until tender.

CORN FRITTERS

1/2 c. milk
1 c. corn
1 1/2 c. flour
1 tsp. salt
2 tsp. baking powder
1 tbsp. melted shortening
2 eggs, beaten

Mix milk and corn. Sift flour, salt and baking powder together; add to corn mixture. Add shortening and eggs; beat well. Drop from tablespoon into hot deep fat; fry at 375 degrees until golden and crisp. Yield: 4-6 servings.

FROZEN CORN-ON-THE-COB

20 ears of corn

Bring 4 quarts water to a boil; place 10 ears in water for 2 minutes. Remove immediately; place in ice water. Drain. Repeat process for remaining corn. Wrap in freezer paper. Place in freezer.

FROZEN CORN

4 c. corn
2 tsp. sugar
1/2 tsp. salt
Butter
Pepper to taste

Place corn in plastic freezing containers. Mix 2 cups water, sugar and salt; stir until dissolved. Cover corn with sugar mixture. Freeze. Thaw corn partially; cook for 6 minutes. Add butter to taste and pepper.

CORN PATTIES

2 eggs, separated
1 1/2 c. whole kernel corn
2 tsp. flour
2 tsp. cream
2 tsp. soft margarine
1/2 tsp. salt
Dash of pepper

Beat egg yolks. Combine corn, flour, cream, 1 teaspoon margarine, salt and pepper. Stir egg yolks into mixture. Beat egg whites until stiff peaks form. Fold into corn mixture. Grease griddle with remaining margarine. Drop corn mixture from tablespoon onto hot griddle; cook until brown on each side, turning once. Yield: 6 servings.

CORN-PEPPER SAUTÉ WITH PEANUTS

2 tbsp. margarine
2 tbsp. minced onion
1 12-oz. can whole kernel corn, drained
1 tbsp. chopped hot peppers
1/4 tsp. salt
1/2 c. cocktail peanuts

Melt margarine in small saucepan; saute onion until tender. Add corn, hot peppers and salt; heat thoroughly. Toss in peanuts; serve immediately. Yield: 4-5 servings.

Corn-Pepper Sauté with Peanuts . . . The crunchiness of peanuts lends contrast to this dish.

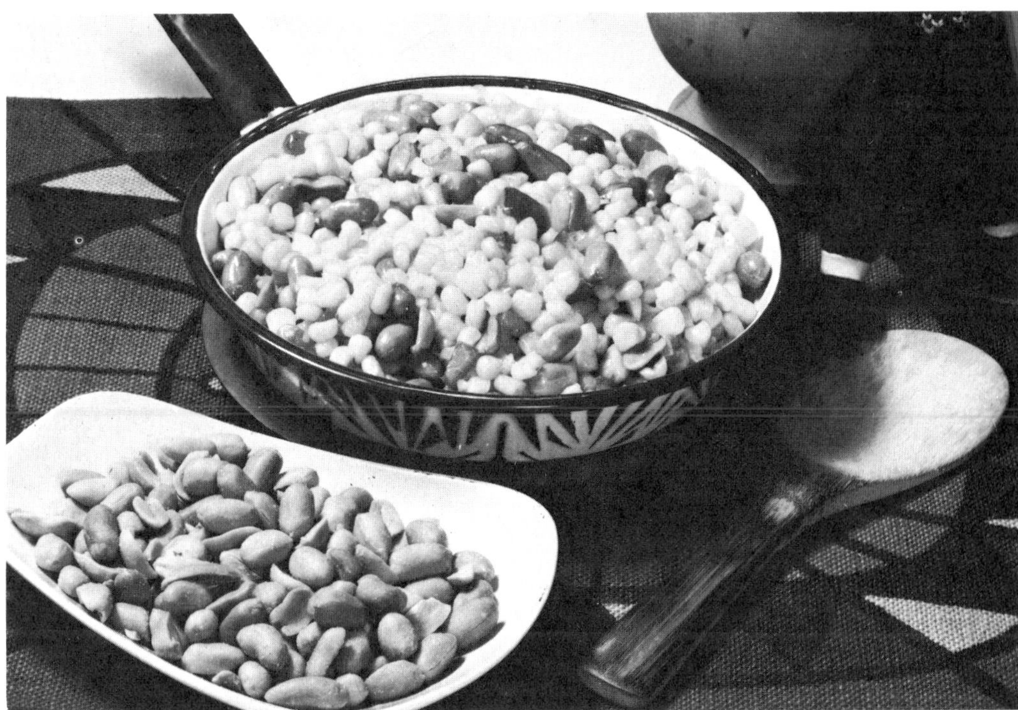

Corn Bread

Made from white or yellow cornmeal, corn bread is loved in many different regions of the United States. A few regional corn breads are New England journey or johnny-cakes and Southern spoon bread and hush puppies. All corn breads are either quick breads – made with baking powder or baking soda – or those made with slower acting yeast.

BASIC PREPARATION. Ingredients for *quick corn breads* include cornmeal, leavening, flour, liquid, shortening, eggs, salt, and sometimes sugar. They can be baked in a square pan, stick pan, muffin pan, casserole dish, or skillet. Or they can be fried in small cakes in a skillet or on a griddle. Ingredients for *yeast corn breads* include cornmeal, yeast, flour, liquid, shortening, eggs, salt, and sometimes sugar. Mixed batter is generally kneaded until smooth and elastic. It is then allowed to rise either once or twice, as the recipe specifies, before being baked in loaf pans. For a crisp crust on baked corn breads, preheat the greased baking pan in hot oven before adding batter. After baking if you want a browner crust, brush top with butter and place bread, still in pan, under broiler for about 1 minute.

BUTTERMILK CORN BREAD

1/4 c. flour
1/2 tsp. soda
1/2 tsp. salt
1 c. cornmeal
1 egg
1 c. buttermilk
4 tbsp. melted shortening

Sift flour, soda and salt; stir in cornmeal. Combine egg and buttermilk; add shortening. Pour into dry ingredients; stir just until mixed. Turn into hot 8-inch square pan. Bake in 400-degree oven for about 30 minutes.

CHEESE CORN BREAD

2 c. cornmeal
2 tbsp. sugar
2 eggs
1 c. milk
1/4 c. salad oil
1/2 tsp. dry mustard
1 c. shredded Cheddar cheese
1/2 c. thinly sliced green pepper
3 slices bacon, fried and crumbled

Stir cornmeal and sugar together; blend eggs, milk and oil. Add liquid all at once to cornmeal mixture, stirring until smooth. Pour into greased 9 x 1 1/2-inch round baking pan. Combine mustard and cheese; sprinkle over batter. Top with green pepper and crumbled bacon. Bake at 425 degrees for 20 minutes.

CHILI CORN BREAD

3 slices bacon
1 c. all-purpose flour
1 c. yellow cornmeal
2 tbsp. sugar
4 tsp. baking powder
1/2 tsp. salt
1 egg
1 c. milk
1/4 c. soft shortening
1 15 1/2-oz. can chili
1 c. shredded Cheddar cheese

Fry bacon until crisp; crumble. Sift flour with cornmeal, sugar, baking powder and salt into bowl. Make well in center; add egg, milk and shortening. Stir just until blended; stir in bacon. Spoon 2/3 of the batter into hot well-greased round baking dish; spread evenly. Pour chili into center; spoon remaining batter around edge. Bake at 400 degrees for 20 to 25 minutes. Sprinkle top with cheese; bake for 1 minute longer or until cheese melts.

CRACKLING CORN BREAD

2 tbsp. flour
1 1/2 c. cornmeal
1/2 tsp. sugar
1/2 tsp. salt
3 tsp. baking powder
1 egg, well beaten
1 1/4 c. milk
1 1/2 c. cracklings

Combine flour, meal, sugar, salt and baking powder in bowl; add egg and milk. Stir just to moisten dry ingredients. Add cracklings. Bake in hot well-greased shallow pan at 450 degrees for 20 minutes. Yield: 6 servings.

GOLDEN CORN BREAD

1 c. cornmeal
1 c. sifted flour
1/4 c. sugar
1/2 tsp. salt
4 tsp. baking powder
1 egg
1 c. milk
1/4 c. soft shortening

Sift cornmeal, flour, sugar, salt and baking powder into bowl; add egg, milk and shortening. Stir until just blended. Pour into hot well-greased 8-inch square pan or muffin pans. Bake for 20 to 25 minutes at 425 degrees.

JALAPENO CORN BREAD

1 c. yellow cornmeal
1 c. milk
1/2 c. salad oil
2 eggs
1 No. 2 can cream-style corn
1/2 tsp. baking powder
1/2 tsp. salt
1 lge. onion, grated
1 lb. longhorn cheese, grated
Finely chopped jalapeno peppers

Mix cornmeal, milk, oil, eggs, corn, baking powder and salt together; pour half the batter into greased 9-inch square pan. Sprinkle onion, cheese and peppers over mixture; pour in remaining batter. Bake for 1 hour at 350 degrees.

PEPPERCORN BREAD

1/2 c. sifted flour
2 tsp. baking powder
1 tsp. salt
1 tsp. sugar
1 c. cornmeal
2 eggs, well-beaten

3/4 c. milk
3 tbsp. oil
1/4 c. peppercorns

Sift flour, baking powder, salt, sugar and cornmeal into bowl. Combine eggs, milk and oil. Pour into dry ingredients; stir just to moisten. Add peppercorns; pour into hot greased corn stick pans. Bake at 400 degrees for about 30 minutes or until golden. Yield: 1 dozen corn sticks.

PINEAPPLE CORN BREAD

2 c. sifted flour
5 tsp. baking powder
1/4 tsp. soda
1 1/2 tsp. salt
1/2 c. sugar
1 c. yellow cornmeal
1 egg, slightly beaten
1 c. milk
3/4 c. crushed pineapple, drained
1/4 c. melted shortening

Sift flour, baking powder, soda, salt, sugar and cornmeal into bowl. Combine egg, milk, pineapple and shortening. Pour into dry mixture; stir just to moisten. Pour into greased 8-inch pan. Bake in 350-degree oven about 50 minutes. Cut into squares; serve hot.

FRIED CORN BREAD CAKES

1 c. white cornmeal
1/2 c. self-rising flour
1 tsp. salt

Sift cornmeal, flour and salt together into bowl. Stir in enough boiling water to make mixture consistency of dough. Scoop out lump about size of golfball while dough is still hot; roll and flatten in wet palm. Cake should be biscuit-shaped. Repeat procedure for remaining dough. Fry corn bread cakes to a golden brown on both sides over medium heat in well-greased skillet, adding oil as needed.

SOUTHERN CORNMEAL MUFFINS

3 c. self-rising cornmeal
1 c. self-rising flour
1 tsp. sugar
1 tsp. salt
1/2 c. cooking oil
1 to 1 1/2 c. buttermilk

Combine first 5 ingredients; mix in buttermilk until consistency of pancake batter. Fill hot well-greased muffin tins 1/2 full. Bake at 450 degrees for 20 minutes or until browned. Yield: 12 muffins.

SKILLET CORN BREAD

2 c. yellow cornmeal
1 c. flour
1 tbsp. baking powder
1 1/2 tsp. salt
2 tbsp. sugar
2 beaten eggs
1 to 2 c. milk
2 tbsp. cooking oil

Combine first 6 ingredients; stir in enough milk to make thick batter. Heat oil in skillet; pour into batter. Mix. Pour batter into skillet. Cook over medium heat; turn to brown both sides.

CHEDDAR SPOON BREAD

2 c. milk
1/2 c. cornmeal
1 c. shredded Cheddar cheese
1/3 c. butter
1 tbsp. sugar
1 tsp. salt
1/2 tsp. fines herbes
2 eggs, well beaten

Scald milk; add cornmeal slowly, stirring constantly. Cook over low heat, stirring, until thick, 5 to 10 minutes. Add cheese, butter, sugar, salt and fines herbes; stir until cheese and butter are melted. Stir in eggs; pour into 1-quart baking dish. Bake in 350-degree oven for about 35 minutes or until firm; serve immediately.

SPOON BREAD

3 c. milk
1 c. white cornmeal
1 tsp. melted butter
1 tsp. sugar
1 tsp. salt
3 eggs, separated

Scald milk in double boiler; add cornmeal gradually. Cook for 5 minutes, stirring until smooth. Cool slightly; add butter, sugar and salt. Beat egg yolks until thick and lemony; beat egg whites until stiff peaks form. Add egg yolks to cornmeal mixture; blend well. Fold in egg whites. Bake in greased baking dish at 350 degrees for about 45 minutes. Serve immediately.

SPOON BREAD SPUD MUFFINS

1 tbsp. butter
Salt
Instant mashed potatoes for 2 servings
2 eggs
3/4 c. milk
1 c. cornmeal
1 tsp. baking powder
4 slices cooked bacon, crumbled

Bring 3/4 cup water, butter and 1/2 teaspoon salt to boiling point in saucepan. Stir in instant mashed potatoes; beat until well mixed. Add eggs, one at a time, beating well after each addition. Beat in milk. Combine cornmeal, baking powder and 1/2 teaspoon salt; stir into potato mixture. Spoon cornmeal mixture into eight greased 2 3/4-inch muffin cups. Top with crumbled bacon. Bake at 400 degrees for 20 minutes. Yield: 8 servings.

Spoon Bread Spud Muffins . . . A classic bread that's as easy to prepare as one-two-three.

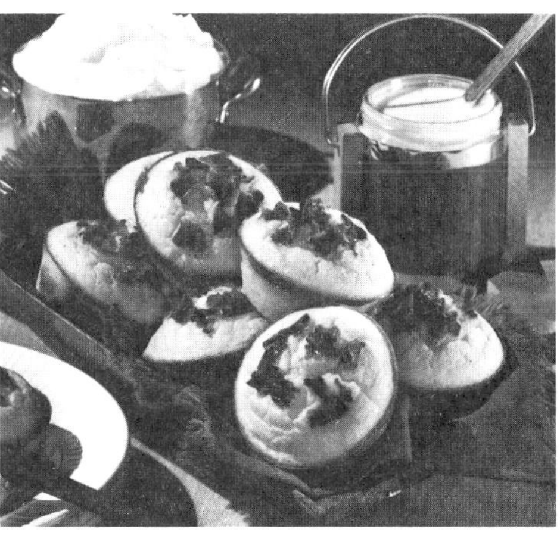

YEAST CORN BREAD

1 c. milk
2 tbsp. sugar
2 tsp. salt
1/2 c. shortening
2 pkg. yeast
2 eggs, beaten
3 1/2 c. flour
1 3/4 c. cornmeal

Scald milk; stir in sugar, salt and shortening. Cool to lukewarm. Dissolve yeast in 1/2 cup warm water in large bowl; stir in milk mixture, eggs, flour and cornmeal. Stir until blended. Turn into 2 greased loaf pans. Let rise for about 1 hour. Bake at 375 degrees for 30 to 35 minutes.

Cornish Hens

A small and compact white-meat member of the poultry family, the Cornish hen, or Rock Cornish hen is a specialized breed of fowl that weights 1/2 to 1 1/4 pounds. Like other poultry, it is a wholesome, low-calorie protein food and a source of both vitamins (riboflavin, thiamine, niacin) and minerals (phosphorus, calcium, iron).

AVAILABILITY: Available year-round.

BUYING: Whole Cornish hens are marketed frozen, either stuffed with wild rice dressing or unstuffed with only the giblets in the stomach cavity.

STORING: Keep Cornish hens frozen, preferably at temperatures of 0 degrees or lower, until ready to cook. (Higher temperatures and temperature fluctuations impair quality.) Store in refrigerator freezer compartment 4 to 5 weeks, in home freezer 6 months.

PREPARATION: To prepare stuffed hens for cooking follow package instructions. Allow unstuffed hens to thaw completely before preparing. Popular stuffings are cooked wild rice or bread and fruit stuffings. Cornish hens are most often roasted. They may also be broiled or fried. *To roast* – Roast at constant temperature of 325 degrees allowing 20 minutes per pound. (Add 5 minutes per pound for stuffed hen.) Or begin roasting by searing hen at 450 degrees for 15 to 20 minutes; reduce temperature to 325 degrees and bake until cooked. (Count searing time in total.) For both roasting methods, internal temperature should register 190 degrees. When roasting is nearly complete, you may want to glaze your Cornish hen. Follow specific recipe instructions. One small hen usually provides one serving. (See POULTRY.)

BAKED ROCK CORNISH GAME HEN

2 1-lb. Cornish hens with livers
1/4 c. finely chopped onion
2 tbsp. finely chopped mushrooms
1/2 c. finely chopped ham
1 c. butter, melted
2 c. bread crumbs
1/2 tsp. salt
1/4 tsp. pepper
1/2 tsp. poultry seasoning
1 egg, lightly beaten
1 tsp. chopped parsley
4 slices bacon
1/2 c. white wine

Chop livers. Saute livers, onion, mushrooms and ham in 1/2 cup butter; turn into large bowl. Cool. Add crumbs, seasonings, egg and parsley; mix well. Stuff hens with dressing mixture. Secure neck and body openings; tie wings in place. Crisscross bacon strips on breasts of hens. Place on baking rack. Bake at 400 degrees for 1 hour, basting frequently with remaining butter and wine. Serve on bed of seasoned wild rice. Yield: 2 servings.

BUTTER-BASTED CORNISH HENS

3/4 c. chopped onion
1 3/4 c. melted butter
4 1/2 c. cooked wild rice
2/3 c. chopped toasted almonds
Salt
1/2 tsp. thyme
8 Cornish hens
1/4 tsp. pepper
1/2 c. bourbon
1/2 c. currant jelly, melted

Saute onion in 1/4 cup butter. Combine onion, rice, almonds, salt to taste, thyme and 1/2 cup butter. Mix well. Stuff hens with rice mixture; place in shallow baking pan. Mix 1 1/2 teaspoons salt, pepper and 1/2 cup butter; pour over hens. Bake at 425 degrees for 20 minutes, basting 3 times with bourbon and remaining butter. Reduce oven temperature to 350 degrees. Turn hens in pan; pour jelly over hens. Bake for 30 minutes, basting every 15 minutes. Turn hens again; baste with pan drippings. Bake for 15 minutes longer. Add liquid as needed.

CORNISH HEN WITH PARSLEY SAUCE

1/4 c. flour
4 tsp. salt
1 tsp. pepper
3 Cornish hens, halved
6 tbsp. butter
Pinch of marjoram
Pinch of thyme
Pinch of sage
3/4 tsp. chili powder
3/4 tsp. paprika
2 tbsp. sherry
1 c. chopped parsley

Combine flour, salt and pepper in paper bag. Shake hens in flour mixture to coat evenly. Melt butter in heavy skillet or Dutch oven. Stir in marjoram, thyme, sage, chili powder and paprika. Heat butter mixture until bubbly; add hens. Brown evenly on all sides. Cover skillet tightly; cook over low heat until hens are tender. Arrange hens on heated platter. Add sherry to skillet, stirring to loosen brown particles. Add parsley; cook for 2 minutes. Pour sauce over hens. Yield: 6 servings.

CORNISH HENS WITH SPECIAL SAUCE

1/2 c. butter
1/2 c. cooking sherry
1/2 jar currant jelly
Juice of 1 lemon

1 tbsp. salt	*1 tsp. paprika*
1 tsp. dry mustard	*4 Cornish hens*

Melt butter in saucepan; add sherry. Bring to a boil. Blend in jelly, lemon juice, salt, mustard and paprika; boil for 5 minutes. Cool. Brush hens with sauce; place in roasting pan. Cover. Bake at 350 degrees for 1 hour and 30 minutes, basting often with remaining sauce.

CORNISH HENS FLAMBÉ

1/4 lb. bulk sausage	*Brandy*
1 med. onion, finely chopped	*1/4 c. bread crumbs*
3 lge. mushrooms, thinly sliced	*6 1-lb. Rock Cornish hens*
1 c. cooked wild rice	*Melted butter*
Salt	*Paprika to taste*
Pepper to taste	*1/4 c. Burgundy*
Poultry seasoning to taste	*1/4 c. sugar*
	Cornstarch
	1 No. 2 1/2 can black Bing cherries

Cook sausage in large skillet, breaking up with fork. Drain off excess fat. Add 1/4 cup water, onion and mushrooms; simmer until onion is tender. Add rice, salt to taste, pepper and poultry seasoning. Stir in 1 tablespoon brandy. Add bread crumbs, mixing well. Fill hen cavities with stuffing; brush with melted butter. Season hens with salt to taste, pepper and paprika; place in baking pan. Bake at 300 degrees for 1 hour and 30 minutes. Place hens in chafing dish. Combine 1 cup water, Burgundy, sugar and 1/4 teaspoon salt in saucepan; bring to a boil. Add enough cornstarch to thicken slightly. Cook, stirring constantly, until sauce is slightly thickened. Drain cherries; stir into sauce. Pour cherry sauce over hens in chafing dish. Pour 1/2 ounce warm brandy over sauce. Ignite and serve.

CORNISH HENS WITH WILD RICE DRESSING

1/2 c. wild rice	*2 tbsp. chopped pimento*
1 4-oz. can sliced mushrooms	*4 1-lb. Cornish hens*
1 sm. onion, chopped	*2 tsp. salt*
1/2 c. diced celery	
1/2 c. butter	

Bring 1 1/2 cups water to a boil; add rice. Cook for 40 minutes or until rice is tender. Saute mushrooms, onion and celery lightly in 1/4 cup butter. Combine rice, mushroom mixture and pimento. Rub cavities of hens with salt; fill lightly with dressing. Close openings with skewers; tie wings in place. Place hens, breast side up, on rack in roasting pan. Brush with remaining butter. Bake at 350 degrees for about 1 hour and 30 minutes, basting frequently with drippings. Yield: 4 servings.

FESTIVE ROCK CORNISH HEN

1/4 c. dry vermouth	*1/2 tsp. salt*
1/4 c. salad oil	*1 clove of garlic, crushed*
1 tsp. crumbled bay leaf	*4 Rock Cornish hens*

Combine vermouth, oil, bay leaf, salt and garlic; let stand for 1 hour. Remove garlic; brush marinade over hens. Let stand for 3 hours. Place in baking pan. Bake at 375 degrees for 1 hour or until hens are tender and browned.

GRILLED CORNISH HENS

1/4 c. salad oil	*2 tsp. soy sauce*
1/2 c. frozen orange juice	*1 clove of garlic, crushed*
1/2 c. meat or giblet stock	*1 tsp. salt*
2 tbsp. lemon juice	*1/2 tsp. ginger*
	4 Rock Cornish hens

Combine oil, orange juice, meat stock, lemon juice, soy sauce, garlic, salt and ginger. Pour mixture over hens; marinate for at least 1 hour. Remove hens from marinade, reserving marinade. Tie wings and legs to bodies of hens; balance hens on spit. Cook for about 1 hour, brushing occasionally with reserved marinade.

KENTUCKY CORNISH HENS

8 1-lb. frozen Rock Cornish hens	*1 1/2 c. dry wine*
1 box fresh mushrooms	*2 tbsp. chopped parsley*
Butter or margarine	*1 bay leaf*
Salt and pepper	*1/2 tsp. crumbled basil*
Beau Monde seasoning	*1/2 tsp. thyme*
1/4 c. flour	*2 tbsp. cornstarch*
1 sm. onion, chopped	*1/4 c. cold water*
1 14-oz. can chicken broth	

Thaw hens. Slice mushrooms; saute in small amount of butter. Sprinkle inside of hens with salt, pepper and Beau Monde seasoning; coat outside lightly with flour. Brown in 5 tablespoons butter in large frypan; place hens in large roasting pan. Saute onion in pan drippings until soft; stir in broth, wine, parsley, bay leaf, basil, thyme, 1/2 teaspoon salt and 1/4 teaspoon pepper. Pour into roasting pan. Bake, covered, at 350 degrees oven for 1 hour or until hens are tender. Lift hens from pan with wide spatula; keep warm. Blend cornstarch and water to smooth paste; stir into liquid in roasting pan. Cook, stirring constantly, until gravy thickens; boil for 3 minutes. Remove bay leaf. Add mushrooms. Serve with hens. Yield: 8 servings.

ORIENTAL GAME HENS

1 1/4 c. white wine	*1 c. brown sugar*
1 1/4 c. soy sauce	*4 sm. Cornish game hens*
2 tsp. ground fresh gingerroot	

Combine wine, soy sauce, gingerroot and brown sugar for marinade. Marinate hens for 3 hours, turning occasionally. Place hens on rotisserie spit; cook until tender and brown, basting frequently with marinade.

ROCK CORNISH HENS WITH ONION-RICE STUFFING

1 c. rice
2/3 c. chopped celery
Butter or margarine
2 tbsp. parsley flakes
1 3/4 tsp. onion salt
1/4 tsp. pepper
1 can French-fried onion rings
3 Rock Cornish hens
Salt to taste

Cook rice according to package directions. Saute celery in 6 tablespoons butter. Combine rice, celery, parsley flakes, onion salt, pepper and onion rings; toss to mix. Sprinkle hens with salt; stuff with rice mixture. Secure neck and body openings; place in roasting pan. Brush generously with butter. Bake at 325 degrees for 1 hour and 30 minutes or until tender. Baste as needed with melted butter.

ROCK CORNISH HENS WITH ORANGE RICE

1/4 c. shortening, melted
2 tsp. bottled browning sauce
2 Rock Cornish hens, split
1/4 c. butter
1/4 c. minced onion
1 6-oz. can sliced mushrooms
1 5-oz. can water chestnuts
1/2 c. white wine
1 bouillon cube
3 tbsp. cornstarch
1 c. butter
1/2 c. chopped celery
1 c. mandarin oranges, drained
2 c. cooked rice

Mix shortening and browning sauce. Brush hens with shortening mixture. Place in broiling pan. Broil for 10 minutes on each side. Melt butter in saucepan; add onion. Simmer for 3 minutes. Drain mushrooms and water chestnuts, reserving liquid. Slice water chestnuts. Add wine and enough water to reserved liquid to equal 2 cups fluid. Pour into saucepan; bring to a boil. Stir in bouillon cube. Mix cornstarch with 1/4 cup water. Stir into saucepan; cook until sauce is transparent. Add water chestnuts and mushrooms. Place hens in large skillet; pour sauce over hens. Simmer for 30 minutes or until cooked through. Melt margarine in saucepan; cook celery until tender but not brown. Add oranges and rice. Serve with hens.

STUFFED CORNISH GAME HENS

4 Cornish hens with giblets
Salt
2 tbsp. butter
2 cornmeal muffins
1 slice bread
8 saltine crackers
3/4 c. cooked rice
1/4 c. chopped celery
1/4 c. chopped pecans
1 tbsp. chopped onion
1 tsp. poultry seasoning
1 egg, beaten

Place giblets in saucepan; add 2 cups water, 1/2 teaspoon salt and butter. Cover; cook over medium heat for 45 minutes. Reserve 1/2 cup stock. Chop giblets. Crumble muffins, bread and crackers into large bowl; add reserved stock, giblets, rice, celery, pecans, onion, poultry seasoning, salt to taste and egg. Mix well; stuff hens with mixture. Wrap hens separately in aluminum foil; place on baking sheet. Bake at 375 degrees for 1 hour. Fold foil back; bake for 10 minutes longer to brown hens.

Cornish Hens with Spicy Stuffing . . . Tender white meat contrasts with a spice-rich stuffing.

CORNISH HENS WITH SPICY STUFFING

3 1/2 c. stale bread crumbs
1/2 c. chopped sweet mixed pickles
1/2 c. diced dried figs
1 egg, slightly beaten
1/4 tsp. salt
1/8 tsp. poultry seasoning
1/2 c. chopped celery
1/4 c. butter
4 frozen 1-lb. cornish hens, thawed

Mix bread crumbs, pickles, figs, egg, salt and poultry seasoning together in bowl. Saute celery in butter for 1 minute; add to bread mixture, tossing well. Thaw hens; stuff with stuffing. Truss hens; arrange on spit. Roast hens on rotisserie for 1 hour or until tender and browned, brushing occasionally with additional melted butter. Serve with additional sweet mixed pickles. Yield: 4 servings.

Court Bouillon

Court bouillon is the liquid in which fish are poached. Fish that have flavor of their own, such as bass and snapper, should be poached in water and salt. Other fish that lack distinctive flavor, such as halibut, cod, and other white fish, need a stronger bouillon. For these fish, use equal portions of milk and water with a little salt.

COURT BOUILLON

2 onions, sliced
1 lge. carrot, sliced
2 celery stalks, chopped
2 bay leaves
Tarragon to taste
Dill to taste
Thyme to taste
Savory to taste
1 tbsp. salt
1/8 tsp. pepper
1 5-lb. haddock, filleted

Place onions, carrot, celery, herbs and seasonings in large kettle in 2 quarts water. Simmer for 10 minutes. Place haddock in cheesecloth bag; lower into court bouillon. Simmer until tender; remove haddock and discard bag. Serve. Yield: 6 to 8 cups.

COURT BOUILLON FOR TROUT

3 lge. stalks celery, chopped
1 thinly sliced carrot
5 sprigs of parsley, chopped
3 bay leaves
4 whole cloves
3 lemon slices
2 tbsp. vinegar
1 4 lb. trout, filleted

Pour 2 quarts cold water into large kettle. Add all remaining ingredients except trout. Bring to a boil; simmer for 5 to 10 minutes. Cut trout into pieces; add to mixture. Simmer until tender. Strain. Yield: 6 to 8 cups.

Poached Lobster-Tails in Court Bouillon . . . A party-perfect dish certain to bring compliments.

HALIBUT COURT BOUILLON

2 tbsp. salt
1/2 c. vinegar
1 tbsp. peppercorns
3 bay leaves
6 cloves
2 sliced carrots
2 sliced onions
4 stalks celery, sliced
2 sprigs of parsley
4 halibut steaks

Combine 2 quarts water and remaining ingredients except halibut in large kettle. Simmer for about 10 to 15 minutes. Place halibut in cheesecloth bag; lower into simmering mixture. Poach until tender. Remove halibut; discard bag. Serve.

POACHED LOBSTER-TAILS IN COURT BOUILLON

6 4-oz. South African rock lobster-tails
6 c. water
2 tsp. salt
1 lge. onion, diced
4 carrots, sliced
1/2 tsp. thyme
1 bay leaf
6 peppercorns
1 sm. bunch parsley

Thaw lobster-tails. Cut away thin underside membrane. Remove meat from shells in 1 piece; refrigerate. Rinse empty shells; place in bottom of large kettle. Add remaining ingredients. Bring to a boil; skim off foam. Reduce heat; simmer for 30 minutes. Strain through fine sieve. Place clear broth in separate pan deep enough to cover lobster-tails; bring to a boil. Add whole lobster-tails; poach gently for 5 minutes. Remove lobster-tails from bouillon; serve piping hot on platter. Yield: 6 servings.

Crab

Crabs are hard- or soft-shelled fish that come in many varieties. A few of the common varieties include the either hard- or soft-shelled Atlantic and Gulf blue; the New England rock crab; the Pacific Dungeness crab; and the Alaskan king crab. Crabs are an excellent source of protein, calcium, iron, and niacin and contain traces of thiamine and riboflavin. (3 ounces crabmeat = 90 calories)

AVAILABILITY: Softshell *Atlantic and Gulf blue crabs* are sold fresh in coastal markets during spring and summer months. The hard-shell type are sold year-round in coastal markets as fresh crab and throughout the country as canned crabmeat. *New England rock crabs*, with their brownish colored meat, are available canned year-round. *Pacific Dungeness crabs* (which resemble hard-shelled Atlantic and Gulf blues but are four times larger) are frozen and shipped year-round. *Alaskan king crab meat* is flown fresh from Alaska to specialty markets and is also available year-round frozen or canned.

BUYING: Almost all fresh crabs are already boiled by dealer. Crabs should be red and free from unpleasant odor. The exception is soft-shell crabs, sold live.

STORING: Cook fresh crabs immediately; chill and use within 1 day. Unopened cans of crabmeat keep 1 year in cupboard. Opened cans should be covered and kept in refrigerator only 1 day. Frozen crab meat keeps 1 month in refrigerator's frozen foods compartment or 6 months in home freezer.

PREPARATION: Allow 1 pound crab meat or 3-pound whole crab for 4 people. *Hard-shelled crabs* – Plunge in boiling sea water, salted water, or a mild-flavored bouillon. Cover and boil 8 minutes per pound of crab. Cool. Discard back and spongy material under shell. Remove stomach shell to obtain meat. Crack claws, remove meat. Crabs may be served whole with melted butter and lemon. *Soft-shelled crabs* – Remove spongy white gills. Place crab on back, remove stomach shell. Wash, drain, and cook as recipe directs.

CRAB BISQUE

1 can tomato soup
1 can green pea soup
1 can beef bouillon
1 c. crab meat
1 c. milk
3 tbsp. sherry
1 can water chestnuts, sliced

Blend soups and bouillon with mixer; pour into double boiler, stirring over low heat until heated through. Add crab meat, milk, sherry and chestnuts; blend into soup mixture. Cook until flavors are blended. Yield: 4-6 servings.

CRAB COCKTAIL FRITTERS

1 c. prepared biscuit mix
1/2 c. milk
1 egg, slightly beaten
1/2 tsp. salt
1/8 tsp. pepper
1 tsp. instant minced onion
Hot sauce to taste
1 7 3/4-oz. can crab meat

Combine biscuit mix with milk, egg, salt, pepper, onion, hot sauce and crab meat, blending well. Drop batter from teaspoon into deep fat heated to 375 degrees. Fry until golden brown. Serve on picks with bowls of cocktail sauce, soy sauce or tartar sauce for dipping. Yield: 24 fritters.

CRAB MEAT-BACON ROLLS

1/2 c. tomato juice
1 beaten egg
1 c. dry bread crumbs
Dash of pepper
1/2 tsp. chopped parsley
1/2 tsp. chopped celery leaves
1 6 1/2-oz. can crab meat
12 slices bacon, cut in half

Mix tomato juice and egg; add crumbs, pepper, parsley, celery leaves and crab meat. Mix thoroughly; shape into 24 finger-length rolls. Wrap each roll with bacon; fasten with toothpick. Broil, turning frequently, until brown. Yield: 2 dozen.

CRAB MEAT CANAPÉS

1 8-oz. package cream cheese, softened
1 tbsp. cream-style horseradish
1/2 tsp. lemon juice
1/4 tsp. onion salt
Dash of pepper
Dash of garlic salt
1 6 1/2-oz. can flaked crab meat
1 c. peeled chopped cucumbers
4 individual French bread loaves
Margarine
Parsley

Combine cream cheese, horseradish, lemon juice and seasonings; mix until well blended. Stir in crab meat and cucumbers. Split bread loaves lengthwise; spread each half with margarine. Top with crab meat mixture; sprinkle with parsley. Cut diagonally into fourths. Yield: 32 servings.

SNAPPY CRAB DIP

1 6 1/2-oz. can flaked crab meat
1/2 c. sour cream
1/2 tsp. hot sauce
1 tsp. lemon juice
1/4 tsp. prepared horseradish
1/2 tsp. seasoning salt
1/2 c. shrimp, chopped

Combine all ingredients, tossing thoroughly. Serve as dip with chips or assorted crackers.

SWISS CRAB BITES

1 7 1/2-oz. can crab meat
1 tbsp. chopped chives
1 c. shredded Swiss cheese
1/2 c. mayonnaise
1 tsp. lemon juice
1/4 tsp. curry powder
1 12-count pkg. flake-style rolls
5 oz. slivered almonds, chopped fine

Combine crab meat, chives, cheese, mayonnaise, lemon juice and curry powder; mix well. Separate each roll into 3 sections; place on ungreased baking sheet. Spoon crab meat mixture on each section; top with small amount of almonds. Bake at 400 degrees for at least 10 minutes or until golden. Yield: 36 servings.

ZESTY CRAB MEAT SPREAD

1/2 c. chili sauce
1/2 c. mayonnaise
1 clove of garlic, crushed
1/2 tsp. dry mustard
1 tbsp. prepared horseradish
1 tbsp. Worcestershire sauce
1/8 tsp. hot sauce
1/2 tsp. salt
Dash of monosodium glutamate
1 hard-cooked egg, finely chopped
1 c. crab meat, flaked

Combine all ingredients; marinate for at least 3 hours. Use as cocktail spread with crackers.

CRAB MEAT ROLLS

2 c. lukewarm milk
1/2 c. sugar
2 tsp. salt
2 cakes yeast
2 eggs
1/2 c. soft shortening
7 to 7 1/2 c. flour
Melted butter
2 cans crab meat
1 c. finely diced celery
1/2 c. salad dressing
Chopped crisp lettuce
Chopped tomatoes

Mix milk, sugar and salt; crumble in yeast. Stir in eggs, shortening and flour until blended thoroughly. Allow dough to rise until doubled in bulk; punch down. Roll dough to 1/4-inch thickness; cut with biscuit cutter. Brush with melted butter; fold in center. Place close together in pan; allow to rise until doubled in bulk. Bake at 425 degrees for about 20 minutes. Mix crab meat, celery and salad dressing. Serve in warm rolls, adding lettuce and tomatoes. Yield: 48 rolls.

CRAB MEAT SANDWICH

1 c. crab meat
1/2 c. shredded sharp cheese
1/4 c. chopped celery
2 tbsp. pickle relish
2 tbsp. chopped green onion
1 hard-cooked egg, chopped
3 tbsp. salad dressing
1/2 tsp. lemon juice
1/2 tsp. prepared horseradish
10 slices bread
5 tomato slices
Salt and pepper
Butter

Combine crab meat, cheese, celery, relish, onion, egg, salad dressing, lemon juice and horseradish. Spread crab meat mixture on 5 slices of bread. Add tomato slices; season with salt and pepper. Top with remaining bread. Butter top of bread; place on griddle, turning once, until golden brown. Yield: 5 servings.

HOT CRAB SALAD BOATS

1 lb. lump crab meat
1 c. diced celery
1 c. canned peas
1/4 lb. process Swiss cheese, cubed
1/4 c. chopped parsley
3/4 c. mayonnaise
6 long hero rolls
1/4 c. butter, melted
Lemon wedges
Ripe Olives

Combine crab meat, celery, peas, cheese and parsley in bowl; fold in mayonnaise. Cut a slice from top of each roll; cut out middle with sharp knife to make boat-shaped shell. Brush inside of roll shells with melted butter. Fill with crab meat mixture; wrap each separately in foil. Bake at 400 degrees for 15 minutes. Thread lemon wedge and 2 ripe olives on wooden picks; serve with each boat. Yield: 6 servings.

CRAB LOUIS

1 c. mayonnaise
1/2 c. chili sauce
2 tbsp. lemon juice
1 tbsp. Worcestershire sauce
Dash of angostura bitters
Dash of hot sauce
1/4 tsp. onion powder
1 lb. crab meat
Salad greens
4 to 6 hard-cooked eggs, sliced
4 tomatoes, cut in wedges
2 lemons, cut in wedges

Combine mayonnaise, chili sauce, lemon juice, Worcestershire sauce, bitters, hot sauce and onion powder. Mix thoroughly; refrigerate. Mound crab meat on salad greens in large bowl or individual salad bowls. Garnish with eggs, tomatoes and lemon. Top with mayonnaise mixture. Yield: 6-8 servings.

CREAM-CRAB MEAT SALAD

1 tsp. mustard
1/2 tsp. salt
1 tbsp. flour
1 tbsp. sugar
1 tbsp. butter
3 tbsp. lemon juice
1 egg
1/2 c. half and half
1 tbsp. gelatin
2 c. crab meat
1 c. finely cut celery
2 c. cream, whipped

Combine mustard, salt, flour, sugar, butter, lemon juice, egg and half and half. Cook over low heat until thickened. Soften gelatin in 1/4 cup cold water; stir into mustard mixture. Cool. Add crab meat and celery. Chill until partially set. Fold in whipped cream. Place in large mold. Chill until firm. Garnish with stuffed eggs and olives, if desired.

CRAB SALAD

Color photograph for this recipe on page 318.

1 sm. head iceberg lettuce
1 sm. green pepper
1 sm. red pepper
1 lb. crab meat
2 tomatoes, chopped
4 green onions, sliced
Italian dressing

Tear lettuce into bite-sized pieces. Cut green pepper and red pepper into chunks. Place crab meat, lettuce, tomatoes, green and red peppers and onions in bowl; toss lightly. Serve on individual plates with dressing. Yield: 4 servings.

MOLDED CRAB MEAT COCKTAIL SALAD

1 env. unflavored gelatin
3 tbsp. lemon juice
1 c. crab meat, flaked
1/2 c. chili sauce
1/2 c. mayonnaise
2 hard-boiled eggs, diced
1/2 c. diced celery

Soften gelatin in 1/4 cup cold water; dissolve over hot water. Stir in lemon juice; add crab meat, chili sauce, mayonnaise, eggs and celery. Mix well. Pour into 1 large mold or 6 individual molds; chill until firm.

Sauce

1 cucumber, chopped
1/2 c. mayonnaise
1/4 c. cream

Mix all ingredients; serve with salad. Green peppers and pimentos may be added, if desired. Yield: 6 servings.

CRAB FOO YUNG

1/2 tsp. hot sauce
6 eggs
1 c. drained bean sprouts
1 7-oz. can crab
4 scallions, thinly sliced
2 tbsp. salad oil

Crab Foo Young . . . A popular Chinese favorite served with its own sweet and sour sauce.

Combine hot sauce and eggs; beat lightly with fork. Stir in bean sprouts, crab meat and scallions. Heat 2 teaspoons oil in skillet. Add 1/4 of the egg mixture; cook until lightly browned on both sides. Repeat until 4 cakes are cooked. Stack cakes on heated serving platter.

Sweet And Sour Sauce

2 tsp. sugar
1 1/2 tsp. cornstarch
2 tsp. vinegar
1 tbsp. soy sauce
1/4 tsp. hot sauce

Combine sugar, cornstarch, vinegar, soy sauce and hot sauce in saucepan. Stir in 3/4 cup cold water; cook over low heat, stirring until thickened. Serve sauce with crab cakes. May serve with hot rice if desired.

ALMOND-CRAB TETRAZZINI

2 tbsp. butter
2 tbsp. flour
1/2 tsp. paprika
1/2 tsp. salt
1/8 tsp. pepper
1 c. half and half
1 tsp. instant minced onion
1 egg yolk, beaten
2 tbsp. sherry
1/2 c. sour cream
1/2 lb. crab meat
2 tsp. lemon juice
1/3 c. finely chopped almonds
Hot cooked spaghetti

Melt butter over low heat; stir in flour, paprika, salt, pepper, half and half and onion. Cook, stirring constantly, until sauce comes to a boil. Remove from heat. Stir in egg yolk, sherry and sour cream. Return to stove; stir in crab meat gently until heated through. Add lemon juice and half the almonds. Fill four or six heated, individual casseroles with spaghetti halfway to top; spoon crab meat mixture over spaghetti. Sprinkle with remaining almonds.

CRAB MEAT MORNAY

1/2 c. butter
1 sm. bunch green onions, chopped
1/2 c. finely chopped parsley
2 tbsp. flour
2 c. half and half
2 c. grated Swiss cheese
1 tbsp. sherry flavoring
Red pepper and salt to taste
1 lb. white crab meat

Melt butter in heavy pan; saute onions and parsley in butter. Blend in flour, half and half and cheese; cook until cheese is melted. Add sherry flavoring, pepper and salt; fold in crab meat. Serve on melba toast or in patty shells; may be served in chafing dish.

CRAB NEWBURG

4 tbsp. melted butter
3 tbsp. flour
1/2 tsp. salt
1/2 tsp. paprika
Dash of cayenne pepper
1 1/2 c. coffee cream
3 egg yolks, beaten
1 lb. backfin crab meat
3 tbsp. sherry
Toast points

Melt butter; blend in flour, salt, paprika and cayenne pepper. Add cream gradually; cook until thickened and smooth, stirring constantly. Stir small amount of hot sauce into egg yolks; add to remaining sauce, stirring constantly. Add crab meat; simmer, heating through. Remove from heat; stir in sherry slowly. Serve on toast points. Yield: 4 servings.

BAKED CRAB MEAT

3 c. fresh bread crumbs
1/4 c. melted butter
1/2 lb. crab meat
1 c. mayonnaise
3 hard-boiled eggs, chopped
1/4 c. milk
1 tbsp. chopped onion
1 tsp. Worcestershire sauce
1 tsp. chopped parsley
1 tbsp. chopped pimento

Combine bread crumbs and butter, tossing thoroughly; set aside. Mix all remaining ingredients together; place in greased casserole. Cover with bread crumb mixture. Bake in 350-degree oven for 30 minutes. Yield: 4 servings.

BAKED CRAB MEAT IN SHELLS

2 c. soft bread crumbs
1/2 c. milk
1 lb. fresh or frozen lump crab meat
4 hard-boiled eggs, grated
Salt and pepper
1 tbsp. Worcestershire sauce
Red pepper to taste
1 can mushrooms, sliced
Butter

Reserve small amount of bread crumbs for topping. Soak remaining bread crumbs in milk, beating until smooth; mix with crab meat, eggs, salt, pepper, Worcestershire sauce, red pepper, and mushrooms. Stuff crab shells with mixture. Sprinkle tops with crumbs; dot with butter. Bake at 350 degrees for 30 minutes.

CRAB IMPERIAL

3 lb. flaked crab meat
1 green pepper, finely grated
1 tsp. dry mustard
1 tsp. salt
1/2 tsp. white pepper
Rosemary
1/3 bottle capers, drained
2 eggs, beaten
1 c. mayonnaise
Paprika

Combine crab meat, green pepper, mustard, salt, white pepper, rosemary, capers, eggs and mayonnaise; mix well. Place in casserole; dot with additional mayonnaise. Sprinkle with paprika. Bake at 350 degrees for about 28 minutes. Yield: 6 servings.

CRAB MEAT AU GRATIN

2 c. crab meat
2 tbsp. butter, melted
1 tbsp. cornstarch
1 c. cream
1 egg yolk
Salt to taste
1/2 c. grated Parmesan cheese
1/2 c. grated American cheese
Paprika

Add crab meat to butter; saute for 3 minutes. Mix cornstarch with cream and egg yolk; add to crab meat. Cook until thickened; season with salt. Pour into buttered casserole; sprinkle with cheeses and paprika. Bake at 350 degrees until cheeses melt. Yield: 2-4 servings.

CRAB MEAT GOURMET

7 tbsp. melted butter
3 tbsp. flour
1 1/3 c. milk
1/4 tsp. salt
1/4 tsp. dry mustard
1/8 tsp. paprika
1/2 tsp. minced parsley
1 chopped hard-cooked egg
1 1/2 c. cubed soft bread
1 tbsp. sherry
1 1/2 c. crab meat

Combine 3 tablespoons butter and flour in saucepan, stirring until blended; add milk. Cook until thickened, stirring constantly. Add salt, mustard, paprika, parsley, egg, 1/2 cup bread cubes, sherry and crab meat. Stir until blended. Pour into buttered shells. Top with mixture of remaining bread cubes and butter. Bake in 350-degree oven for 25 minutes. Yield: 6 servings.

COMPANY CRAB BAKE

Butter
2 tbsp. flour
1 c. milk
1 tsp. salt
1 sm. onion, finely chopped
1 c. chopped celery
1/2 sm. green pepper, finely chopped
1 lb. crab meat
2 hard-boiled eggs, chopped
2 c. bread crumbs

Place 2 tablespoons butter and flour in double boiler, over simmering water, stirring until blended. Add milk gradually, stirring constantly, until well blended. Add salt. Saute onion, celery and green pepper in a small amount of additional butter; add to milk mixture with crab meat and eggs. Place layer of crab mixture in 8-inch deep casserole; sprinkle with bread crumbs. Repeat layers, dotting top layer of bread crumbs with additional butter. Bake at 350 degrees for 40 minutes. Yield: 8 servings.

DEVILED CRABS

1 lb. white crab meat
1 lb. crab claw meat
1 recipe white sauce
8 hard-boiled eggs, finely mashed
Bread crumbs
3 stalks celery, finely chopped
1 lge. onion, grated
3 tbsp. catsup
Juice of 1 lemon
3 tbsp. Worcestershire sauce
1 tsp. red pepper
1 tsp. black pepper
Salt to taste
12 crab shells
Butter

Add crab meats to white sauce; add eggs, 1 cup bread crumbs, celery, onion, catsup, lemon juice, Worcestershire sauce, red and black pepper and salt. Blend well; stuff into shells. Sprinkle top with additional bread crumbs; dot with butter. Bake at 450 degrees until brown. Yield: 12-14 servings.

CRAB SUPREME

1/2 c. butter
1 green pepper, chopped
2 lb. crab meat
1 c. toasted bread crumbs
1/2 c. mayonnaise
2 eggs
2 tbsp. Worcestershire sauce
1 tbsp. dry mustard
Salt to taste
Pepper to taste

Melt butter; add green pepper. Saute until tender-crisp. Mix with crab meat, bread crumbs, mayonnaise, eggs, Worcestershire sauce, dry mustard, salt and pepper, stirring until blended. Place in casserole; pour 1/4 cup water over mixture. Bake at 350 degrees for 30 minutes. Stir during baking to prevent sticking. Yield: 8 servings.

SCALLOPED CRAB MEAT

1/2 c. seedless raisins
2 hard-cooked eggs, sliced
3 tbsp. chopped pimento
1/2 tsp. salt
1/8 tsp. pepper
1/4 tsp. paprika
2 c. medium white sauce
1 1/2 c. crab meat
1/2 c. buttered crumbs

Wash raisins in hot water; drain. Add raisins, eggs, pimento, salt, pepper and paprika to white sauce. Fold in crab meat. Pour into 1-quart baking dish; cover with crumbs. Bake in 350-degree oven for 30 minutes or until browned. Yield: 6 servings.

ALASKAN LASAGNA

2 6-oz. packages frozen Alaska King crab, thawed and drained
2 8-oz. cans tomato sauce
1 tbsp. chopped parsley
1/4 c. chopped green onions
1/2 tsp. seasoned salt
1 8-oz. package lasagna noodles, cooked and drained
8 oz. mozzarella cheese, sliced
2 c. ricotta or cottage cheese
1/4 c. grated Parmesan cheese

Combine crab meat in large skillet with tomato sauce, parsley, onions and seasoned salt. Simmer for 10 minutes. Spread half the noodles in 2 1/2-quart shallow baking dish. Cover with half the crab meat mixture. Add half the mozzarella slices. Repeat procedure. Spread with ricotta; sprinkle with Parmesan cheese. Bake at 375 degrees for about 30 minutes. Let stand for 10 minutes; cut into servings. Yield: 8 servings.

AVOCADO-CRAB MEAT DELIGHT

2 avocados, diced
1 c. fresh spinach, chopped
1 sm. onion, grated
1 can cream of chicken soup
1/2 c. milk
2 6 1/2-oz. cans crab meat
1 c. crushed potato chips
4 slices bacon, cooked crisp

Grease 7 1/2 x 11 1/2-inch baking dish. Place avocados in dish; sprinkle with spinach and onion. Place soup and milk in saucepan; simmer until heated through. Add crab meat. Pour over spinach and avocado. Sprinkle with potato chips. Fry bacon until crisp; crumble over potato chips. Bake at 450 degrees for 10 minutes. Yield: 8 servings.

BAKED CRAB SUPREME

1 lge. ripe avocado
Lemon juice
1 tbsp. finely minced shallots
1 tsp. butter
1 c. Chablis
1 c. sour cream
1 tsp. horseradish
Salt and white pepper to taste
1 1/2 lb. frozen crab meat
1 lb. frozen scallops
Chopped parsley

Dice avocado; brush with lemon juice. Saute shallots in butter. Stir in Chablis; add sour cream, horseradish, avocado, salt and white pepper. Place over low heat until heated through; add crab meat and scallops. Place in buttered casserole. Bake at 350 degrees for 20 minutes; sprinkle with parsley. Yield: 4 servings.

BUFFET CRAB

2 c. crab meat
Lemon juice
2 tbsp. butter, melted
2 tbsp. Worcestershire sauce
Pinch of dry mustard
1 1/2 oz. sherry
Herb-seasoned dressing mix

Flake crab meat in bowl; cover with lemon juice. Toss lightly; marinate at least 2 hours. Combine butter, Worcestershire sauce, mustard and sherry. Add dressing; mix until dressing is moist. Drain crab meat. Place crab meat and dressing mixture in layers in greased 1-quart casserole; cover. Bake in 375-degree oven for about 50 minutes. Freezes well.

CRAB MEAT CASSEROLE

6 tbsp. butter
2 tbsp. finely chopped onion
1/2 c. finely chopped celery
3 tbsp. flour
3/4 tsp. salt
2 c. half and half
4 tbsp. sherry
1 egg, beaten
1/4 tsp. hot sauce
3 c. crab meat
2 tbsp. chopped parsley
1 1/2 c. fine bread cubes

Heat 4 tablespoons butter in saucepan. Add onion and celery; saute until onion is tender but not brown. Blend in flour and salt; add half and half and sherry gradually. Cook, stirring constantly, until mixture thickens and comes to a boil. Remove from heat; add small amount of sauce to egg gradually, stirring rapidly. Return egg mixture to sauce; mix well. Add hot sauce, crab meat and parsley. Turn into 6 individual shells or casseroles. Melt remaining butter in skillet; add bread cubes, tossing well. Sprinkle over crab mixture. Bake in 350-degree oven for 20 minutes. Garnish each serving with lemon twist and sprig of parsley. Yield: 6 servings.

CRAB MEAT DELICIOUS

1/2 c. butter	2 cans crab meat, rinsed
1/2 lb. pimento cheese, shredded	4 oz. noodles, cooked
1 c. half and half	Nutmeg (opt.)

Melt butter and pimento cheese in top of double boiler. Add half and half; stir to blend. Drain crab meat. Add crab meat and noodles; stir until well blended. Turn into greased casserole; sprinkle with nutmeg. Bake at 350 degrees for 30 minutes. Yield: 6 servings.

CRAB-RICE CASSEROLE

1 can cream of celery soup	2 tbsp. chopped pimento
1/2 c. sour cream	1/4 tsp. salt
3/4 c. milk	Dash of pepper
1 7-oz. can crab meat	2 c. cooked rice
2 tbsp. chopped parsley	2 tbsp. buttered bread crumbs

Blend soup and sour cream; stir in milk. Add crab meat, parsley, pimento, salt, pepper and rice. Pour into shallow baking dish. Top with bread crumbs. Bake at 350 degrees for 30 minutes. Yield: 6 servings.

CRAB MEAT TETRAZZINI

3 tbsp. butter, melted	1 10 1/2-oz. can tomato soup
1 sm. onion, grated	1 18-oz. can tomato juice
1/4 c. chopped green pepper	2 10-oz. packages frozen crab meat
1 lb. fresh mushrooms, sliced	1 8-oz. package spaghetti, cooked
Salt and pepper	2 c. medium sharp grated cheese

Crab Meat Casserole . . . A main dish that combines succulent crab meat with a rich sauce.

Combine butter, onion, green pepper and mushrooms in skillet. Saute for 5 minutes. Add soup, juice, crab meat, spaghetti, salt, pepper and 1 1/2 cups cheese. Blend well. Pour into a greased 13 x 9-inch casserole; sprinkle remaining cheese over top. Bake in 350-degree oven for about 45 minutes or until heated thoroughly and browned. Yield: 8 servings.

CRAB-SHRIMP CASSEROLE

1 can frozen shrimp soup, thawed	1/2 c. mayonnaise
2/3 c. milk	2 c. noodles
1/4 c. medium sharp grated Cheddar cheese	1 7 or 8-oz. can crab meat
	1 sm. box frozen onion rings

Mix soup and milk in large kettle. Simmer until heated through. Add cheese, mayonnaise, noodles and crab meat. Mix well; place in flat, greased 8 x 12-inch casserole. Cover with foil. Bake at 350 degrees for about 30 minutes. Remove foil; cover with onion rings. Bake for at least 10 minutes longer. Yield: 5-6 servings.

NORTHWESTERN KING CRAB AND WILD RICE

1/2 lb. long grain and wild rice mix	2 cans sliced mushrooms
1 can golden mushroom soup	1 1/2 lb. frozen King crab meat, thawed
1/2 c. cream	1 c. grated cheese

Cook rice according to package directions. Dilute soup with cream; add mushrooms, stirring well. Layer rice, crab meat, soup mixture and cheese. Repeat procedure, ending with cheese. Bake, covered, at 350 degrees for 30 minutes. Uncover to brown cheese lightly. Yield: 8 servings.

Cranberry

Native to North America, the tart cranberry was first cultivated in the 1800's. Cranberries are now grown for commercial purposes primarily in Massachusetts (especially Cape Cod) and Wisconsin. They are a good source of Vitamin C, and small amounts of Vitamins A and B_1 (thiamine) and some minerals (calcium, iron, phosphorus). (3 1/2 ounces raw cranberries = 46 calories)

AVAILABILITY: Cranberries are harvested from September through November. They are available fresh from late September to January with peak month in November. Available year-round frozen, in cellophane bags or window packages and year-round canned (jellied and whole berries). Processed sauces, relishes, jellies, juices marketed extensively year-round.

BUYING: Choose fresh cranberries that are plump, firm, lustrous, and well-colored. The dark red variety is sweeter and smaller than bright red kind. Avoid shrunken, soft, dull, moist, or sticky berries.

STORING: Fresh, unwashed berries either covered or in original package can be refrigerated up to one month. Store unopened cans in cupboard 1 year; opened, covered cans in refrigerator 1 month. *To freeze* cranberries, either place original cellophane bag or window package in freezer until ready to use. Or, rinse fresh berries, pack in freezer container and freeze in refrigerator's frozen foods compartment for 2 1/2 months or in freezer for 1 year.

SERVING: Traditionally cranberries are used in sauce. They are also used in breads, muffins, cakes, pies, sherbets, ices, puddings, and jellied salads. Their high pectin (jellying substance) content makes cranberries popular in jams and jellies. They can be used to garnish meats and salads or served as a juice.

CRANBERRY COCKTAIL

1 pt. pineapple sherbet
2 c. cranberry juice cocktail, chilled
1 c. ginger ale, chilled

Scoop sherbet into 6 dessert glasses. Combine cranberry juice cocktail and ginger ale; pour over sherbet. Serve immediately.

CRANBERRY FLUFF SALAD

2 c. ground cranberries
3/4 c. miniature marshmallows
3/4 c. sugar
1/2 c. unpared diced apples
1/2 c. seedless green grapes
1/2 c. chopped walnuts
1/4 tsp. salt
2 c. whipped cream
Pineapple slices
Lettuce

Combine cranberries, marshmallows and sugar; cover. Refrigerate overnight. Add apples, grapes, walnuts and salt; fold in whipped cream. Chill until ready to serve. Spoon onto pineapple slices in lettuce cups. Yield: 8-10 servings.

FROZEN CRANBERRY SALAD

1 sm. can crushed pineapple
6 oz. cream cheese
2 tbsp. sugar
2 tbsp. mayonnaise
1 lge. can cranberry sauce
1/2 c. chopped nuts
2 c. prepared dessert topping

Drain pineapple. Soften cream cheese, beating in sugar and mayonnaise. Add cranberry sauce, pineapple and nuts; fold in dessert topping. Pour into loaf pan. Freeze for at least 12 hours before serving. Yield: 8-10 servings.

FROZEN CRANBERRY ROUNDS

1 1-lb. can jellied cranberry sauce
1/2 pt. sour cream
1/4 c. chopped nuts
1 No. 2 can crushed pineapple

Turn cranberry sauce into bowl; reserve can. Beat cranberry sauce until mushy. Combine sour cream and nuts. Drain pineapple well; reserve pineapple can. Stir pineapple into cranberry sauce; add sour cream and nuts. Clean reserved cans; grease insides lightly. Turn cranberry mixture into cans; cover tightly with foil. Freeze until firm. Let cans stand at room temperature for several minutes. Cut bottoms from cans; push salad from cans. Cut in slices to serve. Yield: 12-16 servings.

CONGEALED CRANBERRY DESSERT

2 c. fresh cranberries
1 c. sugar
2 cinnamon sticks
8 whole cloves
2 c. port
2 env. unflavored gelatin
1/3 c. lemon juice
1 1-lb. can peach slices
Sweetened whipped cream

Combine cranberries, 1 cup water, sugar and spices in saucepan. Bring to a boil. Lower heat; simmer for 5 minutes. Cool. Remove cinnamon sticks and cloves. Add port. Combine gelatin and lemon juice in saucepan; let stand for 5 minutes. Place saucepan over low heat; stir until gelatin is dissolved. Combine gelatin and cranberry mixture; chill until slightly

Congealed Cranberry Dessert . . . Cranberry and peaches mix to flavor this delicious iced dessert.

thickened. Drain peaches; fold into cranberry mixture. Pour into 1 1/2-quart mold; chill until firm. Unmold. Garnish with whipped cream and additional peach slices.

OVERNIGHT CRANBERRY SALAD

1 c. water
2 c. sugar
1 qt. cranberries
2 c. diced marshmallows
2 apples, diced
3 bananas, sliced
3 c. orange sections
1/2 c. chopped pecans

Combine water and sugar in saucepan; bring to a boil. Cook until syrupy. Add cranberries; cook until cranberry skins pop. Remove from heat; cover. Let stand for 10 minutes. Uncover; cook for 5 minutes longer. Cool cranberry mixture; stir in marshmallows, fruits and pecans. Pour into salad bowl; refrigerate for 24 hours before serving. Yield: 14 servings.

CRANBERRY COMPANY SALAD

1 pkg. unflavored gelatin
2 tbsp. sugar
1/4 tsp. salt
1/2 c. mayonnaise
1 tbsp. lemon juice
1 tsp. grated lemon rind
1 1-lb. can whole cranberry sauce
2 apples, peeled and diced
1/2 c. chopped walnuts

Combine gelatin, sugar and salt in saucepan; add 1 cup water. Cook, stirring constantly, until gelatin is dissolved. Remove from heat. Add mayonnaise, lemon juice and lemon rind; blend with rotary beater. Pour into refrigerator tray; place in freezer for 10 to 15 minutes or until mixture is firm about 1 inch from edge. Spoon into mixing bowl; beat until fluffy. Fold in cranberry sauce, apples and walnuts. Place in 4-cup mold; chill until firm.

CRANBERRY-APPLE SALAD

1 c. sugar
1/2 lb. cranberries
1/2 c. apple juice
1 pkg. wild cherry gelatin
15 marshmallows, chopped
1 apple, chopped
1 1/2 oranges, chopped
1 tbsp. finely chopped orange peel
Chopped nuts

Combine sugar, 1/2 cup water and cranberries in saucepan; bring to a boil. Cook until cranberry skins pop. Add apple juice; return to a boil. Dissolve gelatin in hot mixture. Add marshmallows; stir until marshmallows are melted. Chill until thickened; fold in apple, oranges and orange peel. Turn into pan or mold; sprinkle with nuts. Chill until firm. Yield: 12 servings.

CRANBERRY-FRUIT SALAD

1 tbsp. unflavored gelatin
1/3 c. sugar
1/4 c. lemon juice
1 14-oz. jar cranberry-orange relish
1 c. diced apples

Soften gelatin in 1/4 cup cold water. Dissolve gelatin and sugar in 1 cup boiling water; add lemon juice. Chill until thickened; fold in relish and apples. Turn into 1-quart mold; chill until firm. Yield: 6-8 servings.

FROSTED CRANBERRY SALAD

2 3-oz. packages raspberry gelatin
1 c. port
1 No. 2 can crushed pineapple, undrained
1 can whole cranberry sauce
1/2 c. chopped nuts
1 c. finely chopped celery
1 lge. package cream cheese
Mayonnaise

Dissolve gelatin in 2 cups boiling water; cool to room temperature. Add port to gelatin; chill until thickened. Stir in pineapple, cranberry sauce, nuts and celery; turn into lightly greased mold. Chill until firm. Soften cream cheese; blend in enough mayonnaise to make of spreading consistency. Unmold salad; spread with cream cheese mixture. Keep refrigerated until ready to serve.

LAYERED CRANBERRY SALAD

2 3-oz. packages orange gelatin
3 tbsp. sugar
1 tbsp. lemon juice
1 pkg. frozen cranberry-orange relish
1/3 c. cranberry juice
2 c. cottage cheese
1 c. chopped celery
1/2 c. chopped walnuts
1/4 tsp. salt
1 c. sour cream

Dissolve 1 package gelatin in 1 cup boiling water; stir in sugar, 2 teaspoons lemon juice and relish. Turn into mold; chill until firm. Pour cranberry juice into saucepan; bring to a boil. Dissolve remaining gelatin in hot cranberry juice; add cottage cheese, celery, walnuts remaining lemon juice and salt. Fold in sour cream; pour over firm gelatin. Chill until firm.

CRANBERRY-APPLESAUCE SALAD

1 6-oz. package raspberry gelatin
1 can cranberry sauce
1 c. applesauce

Dissolve gelatin in 2 cups boiling water; add cranberry sauce and 1 cup cold water. Chill until thickened; stir in applesauce. Pour into mold; chill until firm. Yield: 12 servings.

CRANBERRY-FRUIT LOAF

1 pkg. pound cake mix
1/2 tsp. cinnamon
1/2 tsp. mace
1 c. coarsely chopped cranberries
1/2 c. diced mixed candied fruits
1 tsp. grated orange rind

Prepare cake mix according to package directions, adding cinnamon and mace. Fold cranberries, candied fruits and orange rind into batter. Turn into greased and floured 8-inch tube pan. Bake at 325 degrees for 1 hour and 20 minutes or until cake tests done. Cool in pan for 10 minutes; turn onto rack to cool completely.

CRANBERRY CAKE

3 eggs, separated
2 c. sugar
1/2 c. boiling water
1 c. sifted flour
2 tsp. baking powder
Pinch of salt
1/2 lb. cranberries
1/2 c. butter
1 c. light cream
Light rum to taste

Beat egg yolks and 1 cup sugar with rotary beater until light; add boiling water. Sift flour, baking powder and salt together; add to egg yolk mixture. Beat until smooth. Add cranberries. Beat egg whites until stiff; fold into batter. Turn into greased and floured 8-inch square pan. Bake at 375 degrees for 35 to 40 minutes. Combine butter, cream and remaining sugar in saucepan. Bring to a boil over low heat, stirring until smooth. Remove from heat; add rum. Cut cake into 8 squares; serve hot sauce over cake.

CRANBERRY-NUT CAKE

1 c. shortening
1 1/2 c. sugar
4 eggs
3 c. sifted flour
2 1/2 tsp. baking powder
1/2 tsp. salt
1/2 c. milk
1 c. chopped pecans
2 1/2 c. chopped cranberries
1/4 c. water
1 tbsp. lemon juice
1/4 c. soft butter
4 c. sifted confectioners' sugar

Cream shortening and sugar; beat in eggs, one at a time. Sift flour, baking powder and salt together; add to creamed mixture alternately with milk. Fold in pecans and 2 cups cranberries. Spread batter in greased and floured 10-inch tube pan. Bake at 350 degrees for 1 hour and 20 minutes. Cool cake in pan for 10 minutes. Turn onto rack; cool completely. Combine remaining cranberries and water in saucepan. Cook, stirring occasionally, for 5 minutes or until cranberries pop. Cool; stir in lemon juice. Cream butter, adding confectioners' sugar alternately with cranberry mixture. Frost cake. Yield: 12 servings.

CRANBERRY-ORANGE CUPCAKES

2 c. biscuit mix
6 tbsp. sugar
1/4 tsp. allspice
2 eggs
1 1/4 tsp. orange flavoring
2/3 c. milk
1/2 c. whole cranberry sauce
1/3 c. melted butter or margarine

Combine biscuit mix, sugar and allspice in mixing bowl. Beat eggs lightly; stir in orange flavoring and milk. Add to dry ingredients; mix lightly. Add cranberry sauce and butter. Spoon batter into greased muffin tins. Bake at 400 degrees for 18 minutes or until muffins test done.

CRANBERRY SOUFFLE

1 pkg. red gelatin
1/2 pt. heavy cream
1 1/2 c. sugar
1 lb. cranberries, ground
1 c. drained crushed pineapple
5 oz. miniature marshmallows

Dissolve gelatin in 1 1/4 cups boiling water; chill until thickened. Whip cream until stiff, beating in sugar gradually. Fold whipped cream, cranberries, pineapple and marshmallows into gelatin. Turn into 2-quart mold; refrigerate until firm. Yield: 10-12 servings.

DESSERT CRANBERRIES

1 qt. fresh cranberries
4 qt. water
1 1/2 c. sugar
1 1/4 c. (about) cornstarch

Combine cranberries and water in large enamel or stainless steel saucepan. Bring to a boil. Reduce heat; simmer for 10 minutes, stirring frequently. Add sugar; simmer for 10 minutes longer or until cranberries pop. Remove from heat; stir in cornstarch gradually. Chill until thickened.

FROSTED CRANBERRY SQUARES

1 13 1/2-oz. can crushed pineapple
2 3-oz. packages lemon gelatin
1 7-oz. bottle ginger ale
1 1-lb. can jellied cranberry sauce
1 8-oz. package cream cheese
1 2-oz. package dessert topping mix
1/2 c. chopped pecans
1 tbsp. butter or margarine

Drain pineapple, reserving syrup. Add enough water to pineapple syrup to equal 1 cup liquid. Bring liquid to a boil; stir in gelatin until dissolved. Cool to room temperature. Add ginger ale; chill until thickened. Crush cranberry sauce with fork; add pineapple. Stir mixture into gelatin; turn into 9-inch square pan. Chill until firm. Soften cream cheese. Prepare dessert topping mix according to package directions; beat in cream cheese. Spread over gelatin. Spread pecans in shallow pan; add butter. Bake at 350 degrees for 10 minutes or until pecans are lightly toasted. Sprinkle pecans over cream cheese mixture. Chill dessert until ready to serve; cut into 9 squares.

CRANBERRY HOLIDAY FREEZE

2 3-oz. packages cherry gelatin
2 c. sour cream
1 1-lb. can whole cranberry sauce

Dissolve gelatin in 2 cups boiling water; chill until thickened. Beat in sour cream and cranberry sauce; turn into 2-quart mold or pan. Freeze until firm.

CRANBERRY ICE

2 c. cranberries
1 c. sugar
1 c. ginger ale

Cook cranberries in 1 cup water until skins pop. Force cranberries through sieve; stir sugar into puree. Cool to room temperature; add ginger ale. Pour into refrigerator tray; chill until mushy. Turn mixture into bowl; beat until fluffy. Return to tray; freeze until firm. Yield: 8 servings.

CRANBERRY FREEZE

2 c. cranberry juice
3 tbsp. frozen orange juice
1 pt. vanilla ice cream

Place all ingredients in blender container in order listed; cover. Process at high speed until smooth and frothy. Pour into freezer container; freeze until firm. Yield: 6 servings.

FROZEN CRANBERRY CREME

32 lge. marshmallows
1 pt. cranberry juice
2 tbsp. lemon juice

Set control of refrigerator freezing compartment at coldest setting. Combine marshmallows and 1/4 cup cranberry juice in saucepan; stir over low heat, until marshmallows are about 3/4 melted. Remove from heat; stir until smooth and fluffy. Cool; add remaining cranberry juice and lemon juice. Turn into freezing tray. Freeze until mushy. Turn into bowl; beat until smooth. Freeze until firm. Yield: 6-8 servings.

CRANBERRY-APPLE CRISP

1 c. sugar
1 c. water
2 c. fresh cranberries
2 c. chopped apples
1 c. quick oats
1/2 c. brown sugar
1/3 c. flour
1/2 tsp. salt
1/4 c. butter
1/2 c. chopped nuts

Combine sugar and water in saucepan; boil for 5 minutes. Add cranberries; cook for 5 minutes or until skins pop. Remove from heat; add apples. Pour into greased 8-inch square baking dish. Mix oats, brown sugar, flour and salt together; cut in butter. Add nuts; spread over cranberry mixture. Bake at 350 degrees for 35 minutes. Serve with whipped cream or ice cream if desired. Yield: 6-8 servings.

CRANBERRY CRUNCH

1 c. sugar
1 tbsp. cornstarch
1/2 c. water
1 tsp. vanilla
Dash of salt
2 c. fresh cranberries
1/2 c. raisins
1 c. oats
1 c. brown sugar
1/2 c. flour
1/3 c. butter

Mix sugar, cornstarch, water, vanilla and salt in saucepan. Stir in cranberries and raisins; bring to a boil over medium heat. Reduce heat; simmer for 5 minutes. Cool slightly. Mix oats, brown sugar and flour; cut in butter until crumbly. Sprinkle half the crumb mixture in greased pan. Add cranberry mixture; top with remaining crumb mixture. Bake at 350 degrees for 45 minutes.

CRANBERRY SURPRISE

1 c. cranberries
Sugar
1/4 c. chopped nuts
1 egg
1/2 c. flour
1/2 tsp. baking powder
1/2 c. melted butter or margarine

Spread cranberries in heavily greased 8-inch pie plate; sprinkle with 1/3 cup sugar and nuts. Beat egg until light, beating in 1/2 cup sugar. Add flour, baking powder and butter; mix until smooth. Pour batter into pie plate. Bake at 325 degrees for 45 minutes. Yield: 6-8 servings.

CRANBERRY-CHEESE PIE

8 oz. cream cheese
Sugar
1 1/2 tbsp. flour
1/8 tsp. salt
1 1/4 tsp. grated lemon rind
1/4 tsp. grated orange rind
3 eggs
1 egg white
2 tbsp. milk
1/4 tsp. vanilla
1 9-in. baked pie shell
1 1-lb. can whole cranberry sauce
1 tbsp. cornstarch
1 tsp. lemon juice

Soften cream cheese; beat until fluffy. Mix 1 cup sugar, flour, salt, 1/4 teaspoon lemon rind and orange rind; stir into cream cheese. Beat in eggs, egg white, milk and vanilla; turn into pie shell. Bake at 450 degrees for 7 minutes. Reduce oven temperature to 200 degrees; bake for 20 minutes longer. Combine cranberry sauce, 2 tablespoons sugar, cornstarch, lemon juice and remaining lemon rind in saucepan. Cook over low heat, stirring constantly, until thickened. Cool cranberry mixture; spread over cream cheese filling. Chill pie until ready to serve. Yield: 6-8 servings.

CRANBERRY HARVEST PIE

Pastry for 2-crust pie
1 1/2 c. sugar
1/3 c. flour
1 c. shredded sharp Cheddar cheese
1/2 tsp. nutmeg
3 c. chopped peeled apples
3 c. ground cranberries

Roll half the pastry to fit 9-inch pie plate. Combine sugar, flour, cheese, nutmeg, apples and cranberries; mix lightly. Spoon mixture into pastry-lined plate. Roll remaining pastry; fit over pie. Seal and flute edge; cut steam vents. Bake at 425 degrees for 35 to 40 minutes or until browned. Cool before cutting. Yield: 6-8 servings.

CRANBERRY DELIGHT PIE

1/2 lb. marshmallows
1/2 c. milk
3/4 c. ground cranberries
1 tbsp. grated orange rind
1 c. whipping cream
1 baked pie shell

Combine marshmallows and milk in top of double boiler; stir over hot water until marshmallows are melted. Chill to consistency of whipped cream. Drain cranberries. Fold cranberries and orange rind into marshmallow mixture; chill until thickened. Whip cream until stiff; fold into cranberry mixture. Turn into pie shell; chill for at least 2 hours before serving.

QUICK STEAMED CRANBERRY PUDDING

1 1/4 c. cranberries
1 1/2 c. prepared biscuit mix
1/2 c. dark corn syrup
1/2 c. warm water
2 tsp. soda

Combine cranberries and biscuit mix in bowl. Mix corn syrup, warm water and soda; stir into cranberry mixture. Turn into greased and floured 1-quart mold; cover tightly. Steam for 2 hours and 30 minutes to 3 hours. Serve hot with a lemon sauce or hot sauce. Yield: 8 servings.

STEAMED CRANBERRY PUDDING

Color photograph for this recipe on page 487.

6 tbsp. butter
3/4 c. sugar
2 eggs
2 1/4 c. sifted all-purpose flour
1/4 tsp. salt
2 1/2 tsp. baking powder
1/2 c. milk
2 c. cranberries
1/2 c. chopped pecans

Cream butter and sugar in large mixing bowl; add eggs, one at a time, beating well after each addition. Sift flour, salt and baking powder together; add to creamed mixture alternately with milk. Stir in cranberries and pecans. Turn into 6-cup greased mold; cover with foil. Press foil tightly around edges; secure with rubber band or string. Place mold on rack in kettle; pour enough water into kettle to come halfway up on mold. Bring water to a boil; cover tightly. Reduce heat to simmer. Steam for 1 hour and 30 minutes to 2 hours or until pudding is done. Let stand for 10 minutes; unmold.

Eggnog Dessert Sauce

1 c. butter
1 1/2 c. sugar
1 c. eggnog
1/2 tsp. rum extract

Combine butter, sugar and eggnog in saucepan. Cook over low heat, stirring occasionally, until heated through. Stir in rum extract. Serve sauce with pudding. Yield: 10-12 servings.

HOLIDAY BAKED PUDDING

2 c. flour
2 c. sugar
2 tsp. baking powder
1/2 tsp. salt
2 c. whole cranberries
1 c. milk
Melted butter
3/4 c. cream

Sift flour, 1 cup sugar, baking powder and salt together into bowl. Add cranberries, milk and 3 tablespoons butter; mix well. Turn into 8-inch square pan. Bake at 375 degrees for 1 hour. Mix 1/2 cup butter, remaining sugar and cream in saucepan; bring to a boil over high heat. Reduce heat to low; cook for 10 minutes. Spoon warm sauce over dessert. Yield: 8 servings.

OLD NEW ENGLAND PUDDING

1 1/2 c. sugar
1 c. flour
1 1/2 tsp. baking powder
1/2 tsp. salt
1/2 c. milk
1 c. cranberries
Butter
1/2 c. cream
1 tsp. vanilla

Mix 1/2 cup sugar, flour, baking powder and 1/4 teaspoon salt; stir in milk, cranberries and 1 1/2 tablespoons melted butter. Spread batter in greased 8-inch square pan. Bake at 375 degrees for 30 minutes. Combine remaining sugar, remaining salt, 1/2 cup butter, cream and vanilla in top of double boiler. Cook for about 15 minutes or until smooth and thickened. Serve hot sauce over pudding. Yield: 6-8 servings.

CHOPPED CRANBERRY PUDDING

3 1/2 c. flour
1 1/2 tsp. soda
1/2 c. butter
1 c. sugar
2 eggs
1 1/2 c. milk
1 1/2 c. chopped cranberries
1/2 tsp. vanilla

Sift flour and soda together. Cream butter and sugar; beat in eggs. Add flour mixture alternately with 1/2 cup milk; fold in cranberries. Turn into greased mold. Steam for 2 hours. Pour remaining milk into saucepan; add vanilla. Heat through gently. Unmold pudding; pour hot milk over pudding. Yield: 8-10 servings.

CAPE COD CRANBERRY BREAD

1 orange
1 1/2 c. coarsely chopped cranberries
1 c. sugar
1 egg, beaten
2 c. flour
1 1/2 tsp. baking powder
1 tsp. salt
1/2 tsp. soda
1/4 c. butter
1/2 c. chopped nuts

Cut orange into eighths; discard seeds. Grind through fine blade of food chopper. Add enough boiling water to orange to equal 1 cup liquid. Combine cranberries, sugar, egg and orange liquid in bowl. Sift flour, baking powder, salt and soda together; cut in butter with pastry blender until mixture resembles cornmeal. Pour in cranberry mixture; mix lightly. Fold in nuts; spoon batter into greased 9 x 5 x 3-inch pan. Let stand for 20 minutes. Bake at 350 degrees for 55 minutes to 1 hour.

TRADITIONAL CRANBERRY BREAD

4 c. flour
2 c. sugar
1 tsp. salt
1 tsp. soda
1 tbsp. baking powder
2 eggs, lightly beaten
1 c. orange juice
1/4 c. hot water
1/4 c. melted butter
1 tbsp. grated orange rind
2 c. chopped cranberries
3/4 c. chopped nuts

Combine flour, sugar, salt, soda and baking powder in bowl. Mix eggs, orange juice, hot water, butter and orange rind; stir into flour mixture. Fold in cranberries and nuts; spoon batter into 2 greased loaf pans. Bake at 325 degrees for 1 hour and 10 minutes. Remove from pans; cool on rack.

Cranberry-Cheese Bread . . . Cheddar cheese highlights the flavor of this tangy bread.

CRANBERRY-CHEESE BREAD

2 c. fresh cranberries
2 c. sifted all-purpose flour
1 tbsp. baking powder
1/2 tsp. salt
1 c. sugar
1/2 c. coarsely chopped pecans
1 c. milk
1 egg, slightly beaten
Grated rind of 1 orange
1/4 c. butter, melted
1 1/2 c. shredded Cheddar cheese

Preheat oven to 350 degrees. Halve cranberries; set aside. Sift flour, baking powder, salt and sugar together. Add cranberries and pecans to dry ingredients, coating well. Combine milk, egg, orange rind and melted butter; add to dry ingredients alternately with cheese. Stir just to moisten ingredients. Pour into 9 x 5 x 3-inch greased loaf pan; spread evenly, making corners and sides slightly higher than center. Bake for 1 hour or until bread tests done. Cool for 10 minutes; turn out of pan. Bread slices easier if stored overnight.

CRANBERRY-FRUIT LOAF

Color photograph for this recipe on page 731.

3 c. biscuit mix
1 c. whole bran cereal
1/2 c. sugar
2 eggs
1 1/2 c. milk
Grated rind of 1 orange
1/2 c. chopped nuts
1/2 c. mixed candied fruits
1 1/2 c. fresh cranberries

Combine biscuit mix, cereal and sugar. Add eggs and milk; stir until dry ingredients are moistened. Fold in orange rind, nuts, candied fruits and cranberries; pour into greased 9 x 5 x 3-inch loaf pan. Bake at 350 degrees for 1 hour and 10 minutes or until bread tests done. Remove from pan; cool on rack before slicing.

Crayfish

CRAYFISH PIE

1 onion, minced
2 stalks celery, minced
2 tbsp. margarine
1 lb. peeled crayfish tails
1/2 tsp. cornstarch
Salt and pepper to taste
2 tbsp. chopped green onions
Pastry for 2-crust pie

Saute onion and celery in margarine until tender. Add crayfish tails and 1/2 cup water. Simmer, covered, until crayfish tails are tender. Mix cornstarch with 1/4 cup water; stir into crayfish mixture. Simmer, stirring constantly, until thickened. Add seasonings and green onions. Remove from heat; cool. Line 6 individual pie pans with 2/3 of the pastry. Divide remaining pastry into 6 parts; roll thin for top crusts. Pour filling into pastry-lined pans; cover. Seal edges and slash top crusts. Bake at 425 degrees for 20 minutes or until lightly browned.

MINCED CRAYFISH

1 doz. crayfish
2 tbsp. bacon drippings
2 tbsp. olive oil
2 med. onions, chopped
1 sweet pepper, chopped
3 cloves garlic, minced
2 bay leaves
1 can tomato sauce
1/2 can tomato paste
Salt and pepper to taste

Boil crayfish until shells turn pink. Remove shells and chop crayfish. Pour bacon drippings and olive oil in frying pan; add onions, pepper, garlic and bay leaves. Saute lightly until tender. Add chopped crayfish; simmer, stirring frequently, for 10 minutes. Add tomato sauce, tomato paste, salt and pepper to taste. Simmer for 20 minutes longer. Serve over rice. Yield: 8-10 servings.

Cream Puffs

Cream puffs are round French pastry shells that are either filled with cheese, meat, or seafood or with whipped cream or custard.

BASIC PREPARATION: The pastry shell is made from a dough of flour, boiling water, butter, and eggs. The eggs cause the dough to swell during cooking. To prevent soggy, uncooked centers caused by steam trapped inside, puncture puffs after baking and replace in oven to dry. Larger puffs may be split open after baking. To fill puffs, cut off tops, removing any soggy or soft dough. Fill as specified in recipe and replace tops.

SERVING. Sprinkle sweet-filled puffs with confectioners' sugar for a dessert. Serve tiny cheese, meat, or seafood puffs as hors d'oeuvres.

BUTTERSCOTCH CREAM PUFFS

1/2 c. butter
1 c. boiling water
1 c. flour
1/2 tsp. salt
4 eggs

Add butter to water; bring to a boil. Add flour and salt; cook, stirring vigorously, until mixture leaves side of pan. Remove from heat; cool 1 minute. Add eggs, one at a time, beating after each addition. Drop by teaspoonfuls 2 inches apart on greased baking sheet. Bake in a 450-degree oven 10 minutes. Reduce heat to 400 degrees; bake for 25 minutes. Cool. Split and fill with cream filling. Top with sauce.

Filling

1 c. sugar
1/2 c. flour
1/8 tsp. salt
3 eggs, beaten
3 c. milk
1 1/2 tsp. vanilla
1 c. cream, whipped

Combine first 4 ingredients in top of double boiler; add milk gradually, stirring constantly. Cook, stirring constantly, until thickened. Cool; add vanilla and cream.

Butterscotch Sauce

1 c. brown sugar
1/4 c. milk
2 tbsp. white corn syrup
3 tbsp. butter

Combine all ingredients in saucepan. Bring to a boil, stirring constantly; simmer for 3 minutes. Yield: 20 cream puffs.

BASIC CREAM PUFFS

1/2 c. shortening
1 c. all-purpose flour
1/4 tsp. salt
5 eggs

Melt shortening in 1 cup boiling water. Add flour and salt all at once. Stir vigorously until mixture forms ball. Add eggs, one at a time, beating well after each addition until mixture is smooth. Drop by tablespoonfuls onto greased cookie sheet. Bake in 450-degree oven for 20 minutes. Reduce heat to 350 degrees; continue baking for 20 minutes longer. Cool; fill with desired cream pie filling, whipped cream or ice cream. Yield: 12 servings.

CHERRY-CREAM PUFFS

1 pkg. cream puff mix
1 1-lb. can pitted sweet cherries
2 tbsp. cornstarch
1/4 c. sugar
1 1/2 tbsp. lemon juice
1/4 tsp. red food coloring
1/2 c. whipping cream

Prepare cream puff mix according to package directions. Drain cherries; reserve syrup. Mix cornstarch with sugar; add reserved cherry syrup. Cook over low heat, stirring constantly, until thick and clear. Add lemon juice and red food coloring; chill. Whip cream until stiff peaks form; fold into cornstarch mixture. Fold in cherries. Fill cream puffs; garnish with additional whipped cream or powdered sugar. Yield: 8 puffs.

QUICK CHERRY CREAM PUFFS

1 stick pie crust mix
2/3 c. boiling water
2 eggs
1 1-lb. 5-oz. can cherry pie filling

Crumble pie crust into medium saucepan; add 2/3 cup boiling water. Cook, stirring vigorously till pastry forms ball and leaves side of pan. Cook for 1 minute over low heat, stirring constantly. Add eggs, one at a time; beat with mixer at low speed for one minute after each addition. Drop about 3 tablespoonfuls mixture onto greased baking sheet for each cream puff. Bake in 425-degree oven for 15 minutes; reduce temperature to 350 degrees. Continue baking till cream puffs are dry and golden brown. Remove from baking sheet; cool. Cut off tops; remove excess webbing. Fill cream puffs; reserve 1/2 cup pie filling. Top puffs with reserved filling. May be garnished with whipped cream, if desired.

Cream Puffs . . . Crisp-crusted pastries just waiting to be piled with your favorite filling.

CREAM PUFFS

1/2 c. butter
1 c. sifted flour
4 eggs

Bring butter and 1 cup water to boiling point. Add flour all at once; cook, stirring, until mixture leaves side of pan and forms a ball. Remove from heat; cool slightly. Add eggs, one at a time, beating well after each addition. Drop from tablespoon 3 inches apart on baking sheet. Bake in 425-degree oven for 30 to 35 minutes or until golden brown. Remove from oven; cut a slit in side of each puff. Return to oven for about 2 to 3 minutes. Cool on wire rack. Fill with desired filling. Yield: 6-8 cream puffs.

CREAM PUFFS WITH CHOCOLATE SAUCE

1/2 tsp. salt
1/2 c. butter
1 c. flour
4 eggs
Ice cream
1 c. sugar
1/2 c. cocoa
1/2 c. light corn syrup
1 c. milk
1/2 c. cream
1/2 tsp. vanilla

Combine 1 cup boiling water, 1/4 teaspoon salt and butter in saucepan; heat until butter melts and mixture boils. Add flour, all at once; stir vigorously until mixture leaves side of pan. Remove from heat; cool slightly. Add eggs, one at a time, beating vigorously after each addition. Place heaping tablespoonfuls mixture, 2 inches apart, on well-greased baking sheet. Bake at 450 degrees for 20 minutes. Reduce temperature to 325 degrees; bake for 20 minutes longer. Remove from pan with spatula; cool. Cut off bottoms of puffs. Fill tops with ice cream; replace bottoms. Wrap in foil; freeze until ready to use. Mix sugar, remaining salt and cocoa in saucepan. Stir in syrup; add milk and cream. Bring to a boil, stirring constantly; boil until candy thermometer reads 230 degrees or until mixture forms soft ball in cold water. Remove from heat; add vanilla. Serve warm over puffs. Yield: 10 servings.

CREAM PUFFS WITH CREAM FILLING

1/4 c. butter
Dash of salt
1/2 c. sifted flour
2 eggs, slightly beaten
3 tbsp. sugar
3/4 c. heavy cream, whipped
1 tsp. vanilla
1/2 c. confectioners' sugar

Combine butter, 1/2 cup water and salt. Bring to a boil. Remove from heat. Immediately add all flour; stir until mixture forms ball. Add eggs gradually; beat until smooth. Drop by tablespoonfuls onto a greased cookie sheet. Bake at 450 degrees for 10 minutes; decrease heat to 350 degrees. Bake 15 minutes longer. Cool; cut off tops. Fill with mixture of sugar, whipped cream and vanilla. Replace tops; sprinkle with confectioners' sugar. Yield: 6 puffs.

CREAM PUFFS WITH CUSTARD CREAM FILLING

1 stick margarine
Sifted flour
2 1/4 tsp. salt
4 eggs
1/2 c. sugar
3 tbsp. cornstarch
2 c. milk
1 egg yolk
1/2 c. heavy cream
1 tsp. vanilla

Bring 1 cup water and margarine to a boil; add 1 cup flour and 1/4 teaspoon salt all at once. Stir until mixture forms stiff ball; remove from heat. Beat in eggs, one at a time, until mixture is smooth and blended. Drop by tablespoonfuls onto greased cookie sheet. Bake at 375 degrees for 25 to 30 minutes. Turn oven off; leave puffs in oven to dry. Blend sugar, cornstarch, 2 tablespoons flour and remaining salt in saucepan; stir in milk. Bring to a boil; reduce heat. Cook, stirring constantly, until thickened. Beat egg yolk; stir in small amount of hot custard. Return yolk mixture to saucepan. Cook, stirring constantly, until blended; remove from heat. Chill; whip cream until soft peaks form. Fold cream and vanilla into custard. Slit puffs; fill with cream mixture.

CREAM PUFFS WITH VANILLA CREAM FILLING

1/4 c. butter
1/2 c. flour
2 eggs
Cream Filling

Add butter to 1/2 cup water; heat until butter melts. Fold in flour all at once; stir vigorously until ball forms in center of pan. Remove from heat; let stand for 5 minutes. Add eggs, one at a time, beating well after each addition. Drop by spoonfuls onto greased cookie sheet. Bake at 375 degrees for 40 minutes or until beads of moisture on puffs disappear. Cool and split. Fill puffs with Cream Filling.

Cream Filling

1 c. sugar
1/2 c. flour
1/4 tsp. salt
3 egg yolks, beaten
3 c. milk
2 tbsp. butter
1 tsp. vanilla

Combine first 4 ingredients in top of double boiler; add milk gradually, stirring constantly. Cook, stirring constantly, until thickened. Remove from heat; add butter and vanilla.

ST. JOSEPH'S CREAM PUFFS

1/4 lb. butter
1 c. flour
1/4 tsp. salt
4 eggs
Sugar
3 tbsp. grated orange rind
1 tbsp. grated lemon rind
2 lb. ricotta cheese
1/4 c. grated sweet chocolate
4 tsp. almond extract
Milk
18 maraschino cherries

Combine 1 cup water and butter in saucepan; bring to a boil. Add flour and salt; stir until mixture leaves side of pan. Remove from heat; cool. Add eggs, one at a time, beating well after each addition. Add 1 tablespoon sugar, 1 tablespoon orange rind and lemon rind; mix well. Drop by tablespoonfuls, 3 inches apart, on greased baking sheet. Bake for 10 minutes in 400-degree oven. Reduce oven temperature to 350 degrees; bake for 30 minutes longer. Remove from oven; slit immediately to allow steam to escape. Combine cheese, chocolate, almond extract and remaining orange rind; sweeten to taste. Blend in enough milk to make of custard consistency. Fill puffs with mixture; top with cherries. Yield: 18 puffs.

Crêpes

Crepes, thin, fragile pancakes that originated in France, have a flour and egg base. They are often rolled around a sweet filling and served as dessert. Well known *Crepes Suzettes* are sweetened in orange sauce, folded, doused with liqueur, and set aflame for a spectacular meal finale. They are also folded around a meat, cheese, or vegetable filling and served as an hors d'oeuvre or entree.
PREPARATION: Prepare batter as recipe specifies. Check the consistency of your batter on first crepe you remove from the pan: if the crepe is too thick, add milk to the batter; if it's too thin, add flour to the batter, if too dry, add butter to the batter. Be sure to rebutter the pan before cooking each crepe.
STORING: Crepes can be reheated. Wrap in waxed paper to prevent drying until ready to reheat. Or, they can be wrapped and frozen. Thaw completely before separating crepes.

ALMOND CRÊPES

1/3 c. sifted flour
1 tbsp. sugar
Dash of salt
1 egg
1 egg yolk
3/4 c. milk
1 tbsp. butter, melted

Sift flour, sugar and salt together into mixing bowl. Add remaining ingredients; beat with rotary beater until smooth. Refrigerate for several hours or until thick. Heat heavy greased 6-inch skillet until drop of water sizzles on surface. Pour in 2 tablespoons batter. Lift skillet off heat; tilt from side to side until batter covers bottom evenly. Return to heat; cook for 1 minute and 30 seconds or until underside of crepe is lightly browned. Invert skillet over paper towels; remove crepe. Repeat until all batter is used.

Almond Cream Filling

1 c. sugar
1/4 c. flour
1 c. milk
2 eggs
2 egg yolks
3 tbsp. butter
2 tsp. vanilla
1/2 tsp. almond extract
1/2 c. ground toasted blanched almonds

Combine sugar and flour in saucepan; add milk. Cook, stirring, until thick. Cook, stirring constantly for about 1 minute longer. Beat eggs and yolks slightly. Stir small amount of hot mixture into eggs; return to hot mixture. Bring to a boil, stirring; remove from heat. Stir in remaining ingredients. Cool to room temperature. Spread about 2 tablespoons filling on unbrowned side of each crepe. Roll up as for jelly roll. Place, folded side down, in greased 13 x 9 x 2-inch baking dish. Brush crepes with additional melted butter. Bake at 350 degrees for about 25 minutes or until hot. May sprinkle with grated unsweetened chocolate and sift confectioners' sugar over crepes if desired. Yield: 5 servings.

BAKED CHEESE CRÊPES

3 eggs
Sugar
1/2 tsp. salt
1 c. milk
1 1/4 c. flour
Butter
1 lb. riced cottage cheese
Rind of 1 lemon
1 pt. sour cream
2 egg yolks

Beat eggs; add 2 tablespoons sugar and salt. Stir in milk and flour alternately until smooth. Melt 1/2 tablespoon butter in 8-inch frying pan. Pour in 1/4 cup batter. Tilt pan until batter covers bottom of pan. Bake until crepe is lightly browned and dry; turn crepe. Bake remaining side. Repeat until all batter is used, adding butter to skillet as needed. Stack crepes on serving dish. Mix cottage cheese, 1/2 cup sugar and lemon rind; spread 1 tablespoon mixture on each crepe. Roll up as for jelly roll; place in layers in 9 x 12-inch dish. Mix sour cream, egg yolks and 1/4 cup sugar. Pour over top of crepes. Bake in 350-degree oven for 45 minutes. Serve hot. Yield: 6 servings.

CRÊPES SUZETTE

1 c. milk
1 c. flour
1 egg
1/2 tsp. salt
1/2 tbsp. salad oil
Cognac
Butter
Sugar
1 tbsp. confectioners' sugar
Juice of 1 orange
8 oz. orange liqueur
1 tbsp. grated orange peel
1 tsp. grated lemon peel

Combine milk, 1/2 cup water and flour; beat until smooth. Add egg, salt, salad oil and 1/2 tablespoon cognac; beat until velvety. Refrigerate overnight. Melt just enough butter in small frying pan to cover bottom of pan; pour in 1 serving spoon batter for each crepe. Crepes should be thin. Cook until crepes are lightly browned on both sides. Sprinkle sugar lightly between crepes. Melt 1/2 stick butter in chafing dish over hot fire. Add confectioners' sugar and orange juice; boil vigorously until sugar is completely dissolved. Add orange liqueur, orange and lemon peels; bring mixture to a boil again. Place 1 crepe at a time in chafing dish; turn over. Fold twice. Slide crepes to edge of pan; repeat with remaining crepes. Add 8 ounces cognac to liquid in chafing dish; bring to boil and ignite. Ladle flaming mixture over crepes; continue to ladle until flame is gone. Serve on warm plates, spooning hot sauce over each crepe. Yield: 6-8 servings.

CURACAO CRÊPES

2 tbsp. butter
1 c. sifted flour
1/4 c. sugar
1/4 tsp. salt
3 eggs, beaten
1 c. milk
1 tsp. grated orange peel
1 tsp. curacao
1/4 tsp. vanilla

Melt butter in 6-inch skillet. Sift flour, sugar and salt together. Combine eggs and milk, beating well; stir in butter, grated peel, curacao and vanilla. Combine egg mixture and dry ingredients; beat with rotary beater until smooth. Pour just enough batter into heated skillet to cover bottom. Tilt skillet to spread batter thinly and evenly. Cook each crepe over medium heat until lightly browned on bottom and firm to touch on top. Loosen edges with spatula; turn and brown remaining side. Serve crepes with additional melted butter. Batter may be prepared hours in advance, stored in a cool place and crepes cooked just before serving. Crepes may be cooked in advance and kept warm in oven.

FEATHERWEIGHT CRÊPES

3/4 c. skim milk cottage cheese
1/4 c. flour
1/4 tsp. salt
1/3 c. instant nonfat dry milk powder
3 eggs, separated

Combine cottage cheese, flour, salt, milk powder and 1/4 cup water; beat in egg yolks until smooth and blended. Fold in stiffly beaten egg whites. Drop by spoonfuls on lightly greased hot griddle. Bake until golden brown on each side. Roll up as for jelly roll; place in serving dish.

Sauce

1 1/2 c. orange juice
1 tsp. liquid artificial sweetener
2 tbsp. cornstarch
Dash of salt
Orange sections

Combine all ingredients except orange sections in saucepan. Cook, stirring, over low heat until thickened. Add orange sections. Serve sauce over crepes. Yield: 6 servings.

Crêpes á la Reine . . . Main dish chicken-filled pancakes fit for a queen.

CRÊPES A' LA REINE

3 tbsp. butter
1 4-oz. can sliced mushrooms, drained
1 tsp. instant minced onion
Flour
1 2/3 c. evaporated milk
1/3 c. chicken broth
Salt
Pepper
Nutmeg
2 tsp. chopped chives
3 tbsp. dry sherry
2 c. diced cooked chicken
3 eggs, well beaten

Melt butter in medium saucepan; add mushrooms and onion. Saute until mushrooms are lightly browned. Blend in 3 tablespoons flour; stir in 2/3 cup evaporated milk and chicken broth, gradually. Cook, stirring over medium heat until thickened. Season to taste with salt, pepper and nutmeg. Blend in chives, sherry and chicken. Cover and chill. Mix 3/4 cup flour with 1/2 teaspoon salt. Mix remaining evaporated milk with 1/2 cup water. Add flour mixture alternately with liquid to beaten eggs, blending until smooth. Pour 1/4 cup batter onto lightly greased hot griddle. Batter will be thin. Repeat to make 12 pancakes. Brown each of the pancakes on one side only, removing from griddle when upper surface looks bubbly and slightly dry. Place pancakes, browned sides down, on a towel to cool. Preheat oven to 350 degrees. Divide chilled filling mixture into 12 portions; place portion on uncooked side of each pancake. Roll each pancake up as for jelly roll. Place pancakes, seam sides down, in greased baking dish. Cover tightly. Bake for 20 minutes or until heated through. May transfer to chafing dish if desired.

Sauce Supreme

2 tbsp. butter
2 tbsp. flour
1/2 c. chicken broth
1 c. evaporated milk
Salt and pepper to taste

Melt butter in small saucepan; blend in flour until smooth. Add chicken broth and milk gradually. Cook, stirring, over medium heat until thickened. Season with salt and pepper. Pour hot sauce over crepes; serve.

ORANGE CRÊPES

3 eggs
2 egg yolks
1/2 c. milk
1/2 c. Florida orange juice
2 tbsp. salad oil
1 c. all-purpose flour
3/4 tsp. salt
1 tbsp. sugar
1 tsp. grated orange rind

Beat eggs and egg yolks together. Add remaining ingredients; beat until smooth. Let stand at room temperature for at least 1 hour. Brush hot 7 or 8-inch skillet lightly with oil. Add 2 tablespoons batter to skillet; turn and tip skillet so mixture covers bottom evenly. Batter will set immediately into thin lacey pancake. Cook for about 15 to 20 seconds, until lightly browned. Loosen with spatula; flip over. Brown remaining side; turn crepe out onto foil or waxed paper. Repeat with remaining batter.

Orange Sauce

1/2 c. soft butter
1/2 c. confectioners' sugar
1 tbsp. grated orange rind
3 tbsp. orange liqueur
1/3 c. Florida orange juice
1 c. Florida orange sections

Cream butter with sugar and orange rind. Blend in orange liqueur gradually. Spread about 1/2 teaspoon of the orange mixture over side of crepe that was browned last. Roll up crepes with orange mixture inside. Place remaining orange mixture and orange juice in large skillet or chafing dish. Heat until bubbly. Add crepes; heat through, spooning sauce over crepes. Add orange sections; heat for 2 to 3 minutes longer. Yield: 6 servings.

CRÊPES WITH PINEAPPLE FILLING

1 c. flour
Pinch of salt
1 tbsp. sugar
4 eggs, lightly beaten
2 c. milk
2 tbsp. butter, melted

Sift flour and salt together. Combine sugar and eggs. Beat in milk; stir into flour mixture. Beat until smooth; blend in butter. Refrigerate for 1 hour. Mixture should be consistency of heavy cream. Heat 5-inch skillet or crepe pan. Ladle 1 1/2 tablespoons of batter into pan, tilting and rotating pan to allow mixture to cover bottom of pan. Bake for 1 minute, or until edges are lightly browned. Bake remaining side. Place crepes on towel. Repeat until all batter is used. Spread crepes on towel-covered cookie sheet with toweling between layers. Cover.

Pineapple Filling

2 c. sweetened fresh pineapple chunks
1/2 tsp. apricot jam
Melted butter
Powdered sugar

Spread pineapple pieces, apricot jam and butter on each crepe; roll up as for jelly roll. Place crepes on ovenproof platter; sprinkle with butter and powdered sugar. Place under broiler until sugar is lightly browned. May serve with whipped cream and sprinkle with cinnamon if desired.

NEW ORLEANS CRÊPES

2 eggs
1 1/2 c. milk
Grated rind of 1/2 lemon
1/4 tsp. salt
1 tbsp. powdered sugar
1 c. cake flour
1 c. champagne
12 lumps sugar
Juice and grated rind of 1 orange
1/2 c. melted butter

Beat eggs until light and lemon colored; stir in milk, lemon rind and salt gradually. Sift powdered sugar with flour; beat milk mixture into flour gradually. Drop batter from large tablespoon on hot greased grill. Batter should be thin enough to spread easily. Bake until golden brown on underside; turn and brown remaining side. Pour champagne into chafing dish; heat. Crush lumps of sugar in orange juice; add to champagne. Add orange rind and butter. Cover; cook until thick. Dip crepes into sauce; roll cup as for jelly roll. Sprinkle with additional powdered sugar. Serve immediately. Yield: 8 servings.

STRAWBERRY CRÊPES

1 c. cake flour
1/2 tsp. salt
Powdered sugar
3 eggs
3/4 c. milk
5 tbsp. melted butter
2 pkg. frozen strawberries, thawed

Sift flour, salt and 2 tablespoons powdered sugar together. Beat eggs until light; add milk, mixing well. Add butter. Pour in enough batter to cover bottom of 8-inch hot greased frying pan. Brown crepes on both sides. Repeat until all batter is used. Spoon strawberries onto each crepe; roll up as for jelly roll. Sprinkle crepes with powdered sugar; garnish with whole unstemmed strawberries.

Cucumber

Cucumbers, members of the gourd family, consist primarily of water and thus have low food value. (1 raw, pared cucumber = 30 calories)

AVAILABILITY: Available fresh year-round. Most plentiful from April to August; least plentiful from December to March.

BUYING: Choose firm, bright green, well-shaped cucumbers. Whitish coloring at tips and seams does not mean inferior quality. Avoid withered, yellowed, puffy cucumbers or those with sunken areas or soft ends.

SERVING: The large-sized variety of cucumber is usually eaten raw (peeled or unpeeled); the small-sized variety is generally served pickled.

(See PICKLE and VEGETABLES.)

CRISP CUCUMBER SLICES

2 tbsp. sugar
1 tsp. salt
1/8 tsp. white pepper
1/4 tsp. monosodium glutamate
1 tsp. celery seed
1/4 c. cider vinegar
1 tbsp. lemon juice
1 cucumber
1/4 c. coarsely chopped onion
2 tbsp. chopped parsley

Mix sugar, salt, pepper, monosodium glutamate, celery seed, vinegar and lemon juice in bowl; blend well. Score cucumber by drawing tines of fork lengthwise over entire surface; cut into 1/4-inch thick slices. Add to vinegar mixture with onion and parsley; toss to coat evenly. Chill for 3 hours, stirring several times. Yield: 4 servings.

MARINATED CUCUMBERS

1 lge. cucumber
1 tsp. salt
3 tbsp. sugar
1/3 c. vinegar
1/2 tsp. celery seed
Several thin slices onion

Slice cucumber paper thin. Sprinkle with salt and sugar; add vinegar and celery seed. Mix thoroughly; fold in onions. Chill until ready to serve.

CUCUMBERS IN SOUR CREAM

2 cucumbers, sliced
Salt water
1 sm. onion
Vinegar
1/2 carton sour cream
2 sprigs of fresh dillweed

Soak cucumbers in salt water in refrigerator for 30 minutes; drain well. Rinse quickly; drain. Chop onion finely; add to cucumbers. Marinate in vinegar for 10 to 15 minutes; drain well. Fold in sour cream. Chop dillweed; sprinkle with dill. Yield: 6 servings.

CUCUMBER DIP

1 med. cucumber
1/2 pt. sour cream
1 8-oz. package cream cheese, softened
1 tsp. vinegar
2 tsp. celery salt
2 tbsp. chopped chives

Peel cucumber; chop fine. Mix sour cream and cream cheese; add vinegar, celery salt and chives. Fold in cucumber. Chill.

CUCUMBER ROYAL

3 cucumbers
1 pt. sour cream
4 tsp. horseradish
1 tbsp. paprika
1 tbsp. minced chives
1 tsp. salt
1 tsp. tarragon
1/4 tsp. garlic salt
Pepper to taste

Peel cucumbers; cut into strips. Combine all ingredients except cucumbers in bowl; mix well. Chill. Place cucumbers in ice water; refrigerate until ready to serve. Drain cucumbers well. Serve dip in bowl; arrange cucumbers around dip.

SUMMER CUCUMBER DIP

1 med. onion, diced
1 med. cucumber, sliced
1 lb. creamed cottage cheese
Salt to taste

Place onion in blender. Blend on low speed for 30 to 40 seconds; add cucumber. Blend on low speed until fine. Add cottage cheese and salt; blend at medium speed for 1 to 2 minutes. Chill until serving time. Serve with carrot and celery sticks or assorted crackers and chips.

STUFFED CUCUMBER RINGS

2 med. cucumbers
1/2 tsp. seasoned salt
1/4 tsp. onion salt
1 tbsp. lemon juice
1 1/2 tsp. Worcestershire sauce
1/8 tsp. garlic powder
2 3-oz. packages cream cheese, softened
Paprika
Chopped parsley

Peel and remove centers of cucumbers with apple corer. Combine seasoned salt, onion salt, juice, Worcestershire sauce, garlic powder and cream cheese; blend well. Stuff cavities of cucumbers with cream cheese mixture. Chill in refrigerator until firm; slice thinly. Sprinkle paprika and parsley over cucumber rings.

CUCUMBER ROUNDS

1 8-oz. package cream cheese
2 tbsp. mayonnaise
1/2 env. Italian dressing mix
Dash of hot sauce
40 slices bread
40 slices unpeeled cucumber

Have cream cheese at room temperature. Combine cheese, mayonnaise, dressing mix and hot sauce. Cut bread size of cucumber slices. Spread cheese mixture on bread; top with cucumber slices. Garnish with paprika and parsley.

CREAM OF CUCUMBER SOUP

4 cucumbers
1 c. chopped celery
2 tbsp. chopped onion
1 tbsp. chopped green pepper
4 c. milk
4 tbsp. butter, melted
4 tbsp. flour
1 tsp. salt
Dash of pepper
1 c. cream

Pare and finely chop cucumbers; place in double boiler. Add celery, onion, green pepper and milk to cucumbers; blend well. Cook for 20 minutes or until cucumbers are tender. Combine butter, flour, salt and pepper; add to cucumber mixture gradually. Cook for 10 minutes, stirring until thickened. Press mixture through sieve. Add cream; heat. Garnish with parsley. Yield: 6 servings.

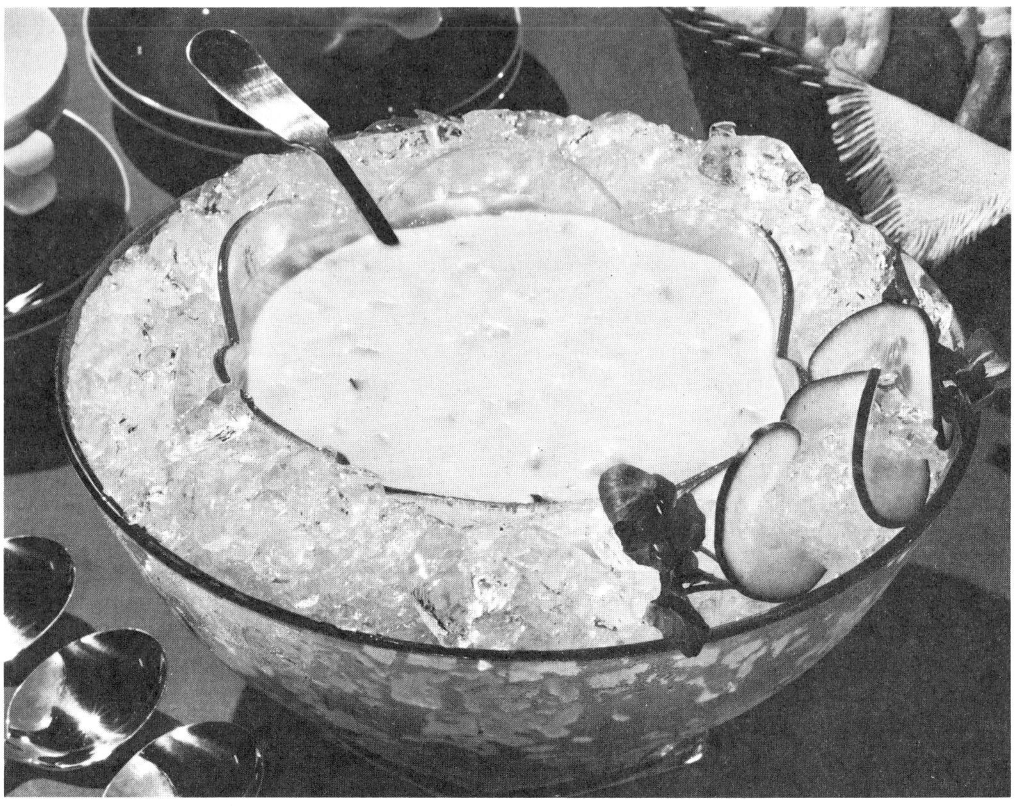

Chilled Cucumber Soup . . . A mild-flavored and icy-cold soup ideal for summertime meals.

CHILLED CUCUMBER SOUP

2 tbsp. minced onion
1/4 c. butter
1/4 c. flour
1 tsp. salt
3 c. milk
1 c. light cream
3 lge. cucumbers, diced

Saute onion in butter in saucepan over low heat until transparent but not brown. Blend in flour and salt. Add milk and cream, stirring constantly. Cook, stirring, until sauce is smooth and thickened. Add cucumbers to soup; puree in blender. Chill well. Serve in chilled bowls set in ice; garnish with thin slices of additional unpared cucumber. Yield: 6 servings.

CUCUMBER SOUR CREAM SOUP

4 lge. cucumbers
2 chicken bouillon cubes
4 stalks green onions, diced
1 tsp. salt
White pepper to taste
1 c. sour cream
Milk

Pare and dice cucumbers. Dissolve bouillon cubes in 2 cups boiling water in saucepan; add cucumbers and green onions to bouillon. Simmer until vegetables are tender; cool. Puree in blender; add seasonings and sour cream. Blend mixture at low speed; add milk until of desired consistency. Chill for several hours or until ready to use. Yield: 4-6 servings.

EASY CUCUMBER SOUP

1/2 c. sliced onion
1/2 c. diced potatoes
2 c. sliced cucumbers
1/4 tsp. dry mustard
Salt and pepper
2 c. chicken broth
Parsley to taste
1 c. milk

Combine all ingredients except milk in saucepan; cook for 10 minutes. Pour into blender; add milk. Blend until smooth; chill. Yield: 4 servings.

CUCUMBER AND COTTAGE CHEESE RING

1 3-oz. package lemon gelatin
1 lge. cucumber
1 sm. onion, grated
1 pt. cottage cheese
1/2 c. chopped celery
1/2 c. chopped blanched almonds
1/2 tsp. salt
1 tbsp. vinegar
1 c. salad dressing

Dissolve gelatin in 1 cup hot water. Pare and finely dice cucumber. Combine cucumber, onion, cottage cheese, celery, almonds, salt and vinegar with salad dressing. Add gelatin mixture to cucumber mixture; blend well. Pour into 1 1/2-quart ring mold. Refrigerate overnight.

COOL CUCUMBER MOLD

1 pkg. lime gelatin
2 sm. packages cream cheese
1 tsp. lemon juice
Pinch of salt
1/2 c. chopped nuts
1/2 c. chopped celery
1/2 c. chopped cucumbers

Dissolve gelatin in 1 1/2 cups boiling water; cool. Have cottage cheese at room temperature. Combine cottage cheese, lemon juice, salt, nuts, celery and cucumbers; blend well. Add gelatin mixture to cottage cheese mixture; blend thoroughly. Pour into mold; chill until firm.

CUCUMBER-CREAM MOLD

5 med. cucumbers
French dressing
2 tbsp. lemon juice
2 env. unflavored gelatin
1 1/2 tsp. salt
1/4 tsp. pepper
1 c. mayonnaise
2 tsp. Worcestershire sauce
1 c. heavy cream

Pare, seed and slice cucumbers; reserve several slices cucumber. Marinate reserved cucumber in French dressing overnight. Simmer remaining cucumber in lemon juice and small amount of water until tender; drain well. Soften gelatin in 1/4 cup water; dissolve over hot water. Puree cucumbers in blender. Combine puree with salt, pepper, mayonnaise, Worcestershire sauce and gelatin; chill until partially set. Whip cream until soft peaks form; fold into cucumber mixture. Tint to desired color with food coloring. Pour mixture into mold; chill until firm. Unmold; garnish with marinated cucumber slices.

STUFFED CUCUMBER SALAD

3 med. cucumbers
1/2 c. pimento cheese, softened
Crisp lettuce leaves
Salad Dressing

Pare cucumbers; halve lengthwise. Remove seeds and pulp; discard. Fill cucumber cavities with pimento cheese; press halves together. Roll cucumbers tightly in foil; chill until ready to use. Slice cucumbers into rounds; arrange on lettuce leaves. Serve with Salad Dressing.

Salad Dressing

1/3 c. white vinegar
1/3 c. salad oil
3 tsp. sugar
3/4 tsp. salt
Dash of dry mustard
Dash of pepper
1 tsp. paprika
1 tsp. lemon juice

Combine all ingredients in jar; cover. Shake well; chill. Shake well before serving.

CUCUMBER SANDWICHES

2 cucumbers, peeled
1 tsp. onion juice
Salt and pepper
1/3 c. mayonnaise
Buttered whole wheat slices

Remove cucumber seeds; chop cucumbers finely. Drain thoroughly. Add onion juice, seasonings and mayonnaise to cucumber pulp. Spread between bread slices.

BAKED STUFFED CUCUMBERS

3 med. cucumbers
1 c. baked salmon
1/2 c. white sauce
1/3 c. chopped celery
1 tbsp. chopped parsley
1 tbsp. chopped green pepper
1 tbsp. chopped onion

Pare cucumbers; slice in half lengthwise. Remove seeds and pulp; discard. Bring cucumbers to boil in saucepan in small amount of salted water; boil for 5 minutes. Drain well. Combine salmon, white sauce, celery, parsley, green pepper and onion; fill cucumber cavities with mixture. Arrange cucumbers in greased shallow baking dish. Bake at 400 degrees for 30 minutes.

BATTER-FRIED CUCUMBERS

1/2 c. flour
Salt
1 egg, beaten
1/2 c. chicken stock
12 sm. cucumbers

Mix flour with a pinch of salt, egg and chicken stock to make a batter. Cut off tips of cucumbers; dip into batter. Drop into deep 360-degree fat; fry until crisp and golden. Serve hot with sour cream and a sprinkle of fresh dill or parsley. Yield: 4 servings.

BRAISED CUCUMBERS

2 lge. cucumbers
1 cube chicken bouillon
1/4 c. hot water
1 tbsp. butter

Pare cucumbers and cut into 1-inch slices. Dissolve bouillon cube in 1/4 cup hot water in saucepan; add butter. Add cucumbers to bouillon. Simmer, covered, for 10 minutes or until cucumbers are tender. Drain; serve immediately. Yield: 2-3 servings.

BREADED CUCUMBERS

2 lge. cucumbers
1 egg, beaten
2 tbsp. cream
1 tsp. thyme
Cracker meal
Dash of salt
Dash of pepper
Butter

Pare cucumbers; slice into 8 pieces each. Combine egg, cream and thyme; dip cucumber pieces into mixture. Combine cracker meal and seasonings; roll cucumbers in cracker meal mixture. Fry in butter or dot with butter and broil; turn to brown all sides. Yield: 4-6 servings.

CREAMED CUCUMBERS

2 lge. cucumbers
3 tbsp. butter
3 tbsp. flour
1 1/2 c. milk
1/4 c. chopped parsley
Paprika

Pare and split cucumbers lengthwise. Remove seeds; dice cucumbers. Bring to a boil in small amount of salted water. Simmer, covered, for 15 minutes; drain well. Melt butter in top of double boiler; stir in flour. Add milk gradually; cook over boiling water, stirring constantly, until thickened. Combine drained cucumbers and sauce; add parsley. Sprinkle paprika over top. Yield: 4 servings.

Cucumbers with Herbs . . . A dieter's delight, low-calorie cucumbers with herb seasoning.

CUCUMBERS WITH HERBS

2 tbsp. oil
1 tsp. salt
2 cucumbers, thinly sliced
1 garlic clove, crushed
1/2 tsp. hot sauce
2 tbsp. chopped fresh thyme

Heat oil with salt in skillet; add cucumbers and garlic. Saute over medium heat for about 3 minutes, stirring. Combine 2 tablespoons water and hot sauce. Pour hot sauce mixture over cucumbers; sprinkle with thyme. Cover. Cook, shaking skillet occasionally for about 2 minutes. Serve immediately. Yield: 4 servings.

CARROT-STUFFED CUCUMBERS

4 lge. cucumbers
1 c. bread crumbs
1/2 c. butter
1 med. onion, finely chopped
4 med. carrots, cooked
1 green pepper
1/4 lb. chopped pecans
1/2 tsp. salt
1 tsp. Worcestershire sauce
Dash of hot sauce

Pare cucumbers and slice in half lengthwise; remove seeds and pulp. Brown 1/2 cup bread crumbs in 1/4 cup butter in skillet; set aside. Melt remaining butter in skillet; saute onion in butter until golden. Add carrots, green pepper, pecans, seasonings and remaining crumbs; heat through. Pack cucumber cavities lightly with carrot mixture; top with reserved crumbs. Bake at 350 degrees for 25 minutes. Sprinkle lightly with Parmesan cheese, if desired. Yield: 8 servings.

CUCUMBER CASSEROLE

2 lge. cucumbers
1/2 c. flour
1 tsp. salt
1/4 tsp. pepper
1/4 c. melted butter
1 1/2 tsp. Worcestershire sauce
1/2 c. sour cream
1/2 c. crushed potato chips

Peel and quarter cucumbers. Combine flour, salt and pepper; roll cucumber in flour mixture. Place in baking dish and pour melted butter over top. Add Worcestershire sauce, a drop at a time, over each piece of cucumber. Spread sour cream over all. Sprinkle with crushed potato chips. Bake at 350 degrees for 25 minutes, until golden and fork tender. Yield: 4 servings.

CUCUMBER PATTIES

2 lge. cucumbers
1 egg, beaten
Flour
Salt and pepper to taste

Pare and quarter cucumbers; remove seeds. Place cucumbers in small amount of water in saucepan. Bring to a boil; simmer until tender. Drain cucumbers well; mash. Combine cucumbers with egg and enough flour to make a thick batter. Add seasonings. Drop by spoonfuls into hot deep fat; fry until golden, turning once to brown both sides.

CUCUMBER-TOMATO CASSEROLE

4 lge. cucumbers
1/4 c. chopped onion
1/4 c. chopped parsley
1/2 c. margarine
1 1/2 c. bread crumbs
2 c. canned tomatoes
1 tsp. salt
1/8 tsp. pepper

Pare and slice cucumbers. Saute onion and parsley in margarine; add crumbs, tomatoes, salt and pepper. Simmer, covered, for 5 minutes. Layer cucumber slices and tomato mixture in shallow greased baking dish. Bake at 350 degrees for 1 hour or until cucumbers are tender. Yield: 4-6 servings.

Currant

A currant is either a fresh fruit similar to the gooseberry or a small, seedless dried grape that tastes more sour than does the raisin. *Fresh currants* are usually cooked in jams or jellies. See section on *Jellies* for more information about fresh currants. *Dried* currants are used in cakes, sweet breads, and cookies, either alone or in combination with raisins and other fruit. They contain carbohydrates, calcium, phosphorus, and iron. (1 tablespoon dried currants = 26 calories)

AVAILABILITY: Black and white dried currants are available year-round. They are usually sold in boxes.

STORING: Keep unopened box on kitchen shelf for 6 months. Store contents of opened box in airtight container in cool, dark place, preferably the refrigerator, for 6 months.

PREPARATION: Plumping currants before baking enhances the appearance of the finished product. To plump, soak in liquid 10 to 15 minutes; drain well before proceeding with recipe. Or wash currants briefly, drain, spread out in flat baking pan; cover and heat in 350-degree oven until plump. To chop currants easily, dust with a bit of flour and heat scissors or knife blade before chopping.

BOILED CURRANT CAKE

2 c. currants
2 c. sugar
1 tsp. salt
2 tsp. soda
1 tsp. nutmeg
1 c. oil
2 tsp. vanilla
4 c. flour
1 1/2 c. chopped nuts
1/2 c. frozen orange juice, thawed
1 c. (packed) brown sugar
1/2 c. butter
1 c. shredded coconut

Cover currants with water in saucepan; bring to a boil. Cook for 15 minutes; cool. Drain currants, reserving liquid. Add enough water to reserved currant liquid to equal 2 cups. Combine sugar, salt, soda and nutmeg; add oil, vanilla, reserved liquid and flour. Add currants and 1 cup nuts. Spoon batter into 8 x 13-inch pan. Bake at 325 degrees for 1 hour. Combine orange juice, brown sugar and butter in saucepan; cook, stirring, until sugar is dissolved. Add coconut and remaining nuts; pour over cake. Broil until brown.

CURRANT FRUIT CAKE

2 c. sifted flour
1/4 tsp. soda
1 tsp. cream of tartar
1/4 tsp. salt
1/4 tsp. allspice
1/4 tsp. cloves
1/4 tsp. mace
1/4 tsp. nutmeg
1 tsp. cinnamon
2/3 c. currants
2/3 c. raisins
1/2 c. chopped dried figs
1/3 c. candied citrus peel
Grated rind of 1/2 lemon
1/2 c. butter
1 1/2 c. (packed) dark brown sugar
1 egg
1 egg yolk
1/2 c. flat beer

Sift dry ingredients together; add fruits, candied peel and lemon rind. Mix until fruits and peels are well-coated. Beat butter and sugar with electric beater until creamy. Add egg and egg yolk. Beat until light. Add beer; beat in well. Fold beer mixture into fruit mixture until just blended. Spoon into greased and floured 9 x 5 x 3-inch pan. Bake in 350-degree oven for about 1 hour and 15 minutes or until cake tests done. Remove from oven; let stand for 5 minutes. Loosen edges with dull knife. Turn out onto waxed paper-covered cake rack. Cool. Cake may be topped with hard sauce if desired.

CURRANT EVENT CAKE

1 c. flour
1/3 c. shortening
1/4 tsp. salt
2 c. currants
1/4 c. sugar
1/4 tsp. lemon juice
1 tbsp. cornstarch

Combine flour, shortening, salt and 2 1/2 tablespoons cold water; mix as for pie pastry. Roll out. Line 8-inch square pan with pastry. Cover currants with water in saucepan; cook until tender. Add sugar and lemon juice; blend in cornstarch. Cook over low heat, stirring constantly, until thickened. Set aside.

Cake Batter

1/2 c. butter
1 c. sugar
2 eggs
1 tsp. vanilla
1 1/2 c. flour
2 1/2 tsp. baking powder
1/2 tsp. salt
3/4 c. milk

Cream butter and sugar until fluffy; add eggs, one at a time, beating well after each addition. Stir in vanilla. Sift flour, baking powder and salt together. Add dry ingredients and milk to creamed mixture alternately. Beat well. Spoon currant filling into pie crust; cover with batter. Bake at 375 degrees for about 30 to 35 minutes or until cake tests done. Cool; frost with icing if desired.

BOILED CURRANT BARS

1 c. currants
1 tsp. soda
1/2 c. shortening
1 c. sugar
2 eggs
1 tsp. cinnamon
1/2 tsp. nutmeg
1/2 tsp. allspice
1 tsp. baking powder
2 c. flour
1 recipe powdered sugar frosting

Place currants in water to cover in saucepan; boil for about 5 minutes. Drain, reserving 1 cup liquid. Cool. Dissolve soda in warm reserved liquid. Cream shortening and sugar until fluffy; add eggs, one at a time, beating well after each addition. Sift spices, baking powder and flour together. Add dry ingredients and soda liquid to creamed mixture alternately, mixing well. Stir in currants. Spoon batter into jelly roll pan. Bake at 350 degrees for 20 minutes. Ice with frosting. Cut into bars; serve.

CURRANT SQUARES

1 box currants
1 tbsp. flour
1/2 c. sugar
1 tsp. cinnamon
Juice of 1/2 lemon
1 recipe 2-crust pie pastry
Confectioners' sugar

Combine currants, flour, sugar, 1 cup water, cinnamon and lemon juice in saucepan. Cook over low heat, stirring, until thick. Roll pastry out on floured surface; divide in half. Roll each half to fit 16 x 11 x 1-inch jelly roll pan. Place pastry half in pan; spread with currant mixture. Cover with remaining pastry half, pressing pastry edges together. Bake at 325 degrees for 30 to 35 minutes; cool. Sift confectioners' sugar over top; cut into squares. Yield: 24 squares.

CURRANT TRIANGLES

3 c. flour
2 tsp. baking powder
1 c. brown sugar
1 c. margarine
1 c. milk
1 egg, separated
1 c. currants

Sift flour and baking powder together. Cream brown sugar with margarine until fluffy. Add sugar mixture and milk to dry ingredients, blending well. Fold in stiffly beaten egg white and currants. Roll dough out to 1/2-inch thickness; spread with beaten egg yolk. Cut into triangles; place triangles on cookie sheet. Bake at 350 degrees until golden brown. Yield: 2 dozen triangles.

SPICY CURRANT COOKIES

3 1/4 c. flour
2 tsp. baking powder
1/2 tsp. nutmeg
3/4 c. sugar
1 tsp. salt
1/2 c. shortening
1/2 c. butter
1/3 c. milk
2 eggs, beaten
1 c. currants

Sift flour, baking powder, nutmeg, sugar and salt together into mixing bowl. Cut in shortening and butter until of fine consistency. Add milk and eggs, beating well. Stir in currants. Dough should be stiff. Roll dough out on floured surface to 1/4-inch thickness; cut with cookie cutter. Bake in electric skillet at 400 degrees until golden and puffy on both sides.

CURRANT-PECAN PIE

1 c. flour
1/2 tsp. salt
1/2 c. margarine
2 eggs, beaten
3/4 c. chopped pecans
1 tbsp. vinegar
1 tsp. vanilla
1 c. sugar
1/2 c. chopped currants
Dash of cinnamon
1/4 c. butter, melted

Combine flour and salt in mixing bowl; cut in margarine until of fine consistency. Add 2 tablespoons ice water, blending quickly. Roll pastry out on floured surface; fit into 9-inch pie pan. Combine eggs, pecans, vinegar, vanilla, sugar, currants, cinnamon and melted butter. Pour filling into pie shell. Bake at 400 degrees for 10 minutes; reduce oven temperature to 350 degrees. Bake for 20 minutes longer. Yield: 6-8 servings.

CURRANT TARTS

1 11-oz. box currants
1 recipe pastry for 2-crust pie
2 eggs, beaten
1 tbsp. butter
2 c. (packed) brown sugar
1 tsp. vanilla
1 c. chopped walnuts

Cover currants with boiling water; set aside. Divide pastry into 24 equal parts; roll each part into 4-inch circle. Line 24 miniature tart or small muffin cups with pastry. Drain currants; mix with remaining ingredients. Fill shells. Bake at 350 degrees for 30 minutes. Serve warm. May be served with whipped topping. Yield: 2 dozen tarts.

FRENCH CURRANT CREAM PIE

1 c. currants
1 c. sugar
1 tbsp. flour
1 c. sour cream
2 eggs, separated
1/2 tsp. cinnamon
1 tsp. soda
1/4 tsp. salt
1 baked 9-in. pie shell
1/4 tsp. cream of tartar

Mix currants, 3/4 cup sugar and flour in 2-quart saucepan. Add sour cream and beaten egg yolks. Add cinnamon, soda and salt. Cook over medium heat until thick, stirring occasionally. Pour filling into pie shell. Beat egg whites until frothy; add cream of tartar and remaining sugar. Beat until stiff peaks form. Spread meringue over pie. Bake at 425 degrees for 5 minutes.

STEAMED WELSH PUDDING

1 1/2 c. sifted flour
1 c. sugar
1 tsp. salt
1 tsp. nutmeg
1 tsp. allspice
1 tsp. cinnamon
1/2 tsp. cloves
1 tsp. soda
1 c. finely chopped suet
1 c. grated carrots
1 c. grated potatoes
1 c. currants

Mix flour, sugar, salt, spices and soda; add suet. Mix well. Add remaining ingredients. Spoon into greased coffee tins, filling 2/3 full. Steam in double boiler for 2 hours and 30 minutes. Yield: 6 servings.

CURRANT ROLL-UPS

1 c. flour
1/2 tsp. baking powder
1 tbsp. sugar
1/4 tsp. salt
2 eggs, beaten
2 c. milk
1 tbsp. melted butter
Dried currants
Confectioners' sugar

Sift flour, baking powder, sugar and salt together. Beat eggs with milk thoroughly. Add egg mixture and butter to dry ingredients, mixing well. Batter will be thin. Pour batter into 4 circles on hot greased griddle; sprinkle with currants. Bake until lightly browned on both sides. Remove to heated platter; sprinkle with confectioners' sugar. Roll up as for jelly roll; serve hot. Yield: 4 servings.

CURRANT TEA RING

1 c. milk
2 pkg. yeast
Sugar
7 c. sifted flour
6 tbsp. butter, softened
3 eggs
1/2 tsp. salt
Brown sugar
3/4 c. currants
Cinnamon
1 recipe powdered sugar icing

Scald milk; cool to lukewarm. Combine 1 cup lukewarm water and milk in mixing bowl; dissolve yeast and 1 tablespoon sugar in milk mixture. Beat in 3 cups flour gradually until smooth. Cream butter well; beat in eggs, one at a time, until fluffy. Add egg mixture to dough. Add remaining flour, salt and 1/4 cup sugar gradually, mixing well. Place dough on floured board; knead well. Place in greased bowl; cover. Let rise for 2 hours. Roll dough out into 1/4-inch thick oblong shape; brush with additional melted butter. Sprinkle with brown sugar, currants and cinnamon. Roll up lengthwise; shape into circle in large greased cookie sheet. Bake at 350 degrees for about 20 minutes or until golden brown. Frost with icing while warm.

Curry

Curry is a term that describes: (1) *a powder* ground from turmeric and varying combinations of spices and herbs such as cayenne, coriander, and cumin, (2) *a sauce* with either a white sauce base or a brown sauce base, seasoned primarily with curry powder; and (3) *a meat, poultry, seafood, vegetable, fruit, or egg dish* flavored with curry powder.

PREPARATION: *Curry powder* is made by grinding various whole spices in a blender or spice grinder and then mixing them with already ground spices. Or, spices that are already individually ground are blended together in a bowl and bottled for future use. *Curry sauce* is generally made by simmering such ingredients as flour, shortening, liquid, curry powder, and other seasonings in a skillet over low heat to desired consistency. *Curry dishes* are prepared in many ways, in many utensils, and over many kinds of heat; follow specific recipe directions. There are some general suggestions for preparing curry dishes you might find helpful. They are: (1) When recipe specifies onions and garlic, chop finely. When cooking onions, do not allow them to brown; cook only until soft. (2) When recipe specifies coconut, use fresh coconut rather than canned or packaged coconut. (3) Never thicken a curry dish with flour: if consistency is too thin, add coconut milk, cow's milk, or dried coconut, or cook without lid to permit evaporation.

SERVING: *Curry powder* – Sprinkle over vegetables, soups and chowders, salted nuts, mayonnaise, French dressing, scrambled or deviled eggs, baked or sauteed fruits. *Curry sauce* – Pour over hard-boiled eggs or cooked fish. *Curry dishes* – Serve with rice and condiments such as chutney, grapes, pickles, raisins, chopped green peppers, shredded coconut, salted nuts, chopped onions, chopped hard-boiled eggs.

CURRY DIP

1 c. mayonnaise
1/2 c. sour cream
1 tsp. salt
1/2 c. chopped parsley
1 tbsp. chopped chives
1 tbsp. grated onion
1/2 tsp. curry powder
1 tbsp. capers
1/2 tbsp. lemon juice
4 tsp. paprika
1/2 tsp. Worcestershire sauce

Combine all ingredients; mix well. Serve with fresh vegetables.

CURRIED FRUITS

1 No. 2 can peach halves
1 No. 2 can sliced pineapple
1 No. 2 can pear halves
1/2 c. butter or margarine
3/4 c. brown sugar
1 tbsp. cornstarch
1 tsp. curry powder

Drain fruits; place in greased casserole. Melt butter; blend in sugar, cornstarch and curry powder. Spoon curry mixture over fruits. Bake at 325 degrees for 45 minutes. Yield: 8 servings.

CURRIED CHICKEN PÂTÉ

1 lb. chicken livers
6 tbsp. rendered chicken fat
1 tbsp. curry powder
Freshly ground pepper to taste
Salt to taste
Pinch of dried basil
Pinch of dried thyme
Pinch of dried marjoram
Pinch of dried cardamom
4 oz. dry vermouth
1 tsp. dry sherry
2 tbsp. sweet sherry
3 tbsp. sour cream

Cut livers into small pieces. Fry in fat in skillet for 15 minutes, mashing constantly with fork. Reduce heat; mix in seasonings and spices. Remove from heat; add vermouth and sherries. Mash to fine paste; stir in sour cream. Place in crock; cover. Refrigerate for at least 3 days. Serve on crackers or small toast rounds. Yield: 6-8 servings.

CURRIED NUTS

2 tbsp. oil
2 c. walnuts
1 tsp. salt
1/2 tsp. curry powder
Pinch of sugar
1/4 tsp. garlic powder

Heat oil in skillet; add walnuts. Cook slowly, stirring constantly, for 7 minutes or until walnuts are golden and crisp. Turn onto paper towels. Combine salt, curry powder, sugar and garlic powder. Sprinkle over walnuts. Cool walnuts; store in tightly covered container.

CURRIED CHICKEN SALAD

2 env. unflavored gelatin
1 10 1/2-oz. can beef broth
1 c. mayonnaise or salad dressing
2 tsp. curry powder
2 tbsp. chopped onion
1 tsp. salt
2 tbsp. lemon juice
2 tbsp. chopped pimento
1 c. diced celery
2 c. diced cooked chicken

Soften gelatin in 1 cup cold water in saucepan; stir over moderate heat until gelatin is dissolved. Remove from heat; stir in broth, mayonnaise, curry powder, onion, salt and lemon juice. Beat until smooth. Chill until thickened, stirring occasionally. Add pimento, celery and chicken. Pour into pan; chill until firm. Yield: 4 servings.

CURRIED GREEN SALAD

1/2 tsp. beef gravy base
1/4 c. hot water
1 c. mayonnaise or salad dressing
1 clove of garlic, minced
1 tbsp. curry powder
1/4 tsp. Worcestershire sauce
8 drops of hot sauce
4 c. torn fresh spinach
6 c. torn mixed salad greens
1/4 c. sliced radishes
1 1-lb. can artichoke hearts, chilled

Mix gravy base and hot water; stir into mayonnaise. Add garlic, curry powder, Worcestershire sauce and hot sauce; chill for several hours or overnight. Combine spinach, mixed greens and radishes in bowl. Drain artichoke hearts; cut in half. Add to salad; pour dressing over top. Toss to mix; serve immediately. Yield: 8 servings.

CURRIED SHRIMP SALAD

4 c. hot cooked rice
1/4 c. French dressing
3/4 c. mayonnaise
2 tbsp. minced onion
1/2 tsp. curry powder
1/2 tsp. salt
1/4 tsp. white pepper
3 drops of hot sauce
1/2 tsp. dry mustard
1 c. diced celery
1 1/2 c. cooked peas
2 cans shrimp
Lettuce

Combine rice and French dressing; cool to room temperature. Mix mayonnaise, onion and seasonings. Place celery and peas in large mixing bowl; pour in mayonnaise mixture. Add rice mixture; toss lightly with fork. Chill salad well. Drain and chill shrimp. Add shrimp to salad just before serving. Turn salad into lettuce-lined bowl. Garnish with tomato wedges. Yield: 8 servings.

CURRIED SHRIMP AND SAFFRON RICE

1/4 c. butter
1/3 c. flour
1 tsp. salt
3 tsp. curry powder
1 c. chicken broth
2 tbsp. instant minced onion
1 tsp. lemon juice
2 c. milk
2 lb. cooked shrimp

Melt butter in large skillet; stir in flour, salt and curry powder. Cook over low heat until bubbly. Remove from heat; stir in chicken broth and onion. Cook, stirring constantly, until mixture thickens. Add lemon juice, milk and shrimp. Heat through.

Curried Shrimp and Saffron Rice . . . This palate-tingling dish brings excitement to dining tables.

Saffron Rice

1 c. rice
1/4 tsp. saffron

Prepare rice according to package directions, adding saffron to water. Serve hot rice with curry. Serve curry with desired accompaniments, such as French-fried onion rings, fried bacon bits, raisins and chutney.

BEEF CURRY

1 lb. beef round
1 tbsp. flour
1 tsp. salt
1/8 tsp. pepper
1/4 c. oil
2 c. sliced onions
1/2 clove of garlic, minced
1 tsp. curry powder
1 bouillon cube
1 c. boiling water
1/2 c. tomato juice

Cut beef into small cubes. Mix flour, salt and pepper; roll beef in seasoned flour. Heat 2 tablespoons oil in skillet; brown beef cubes on all sides. Add remaining oil, onions and garlic; cook until onions are wilted. Sprinkle with curry powder; add bouillon cube and water. Simmer until beef cubes are tender. Add tomato juice; heat through. Yield: 4 servings.

CURRIED MEATBALLS

1 lb. ground beef
2 tbsp. butter
3 onions, sliced
1 tbsp. curry powder
4 tsp. flour
4 c. tomato juice
1 tsp. salt
1/4 tsp. pepper

Shape ground beef into balls. Melt butter in skillet; add onions. Cook slowly until onions are soft but not brown. Add curry powder. Place meatballs in skillet; cook over high heat for 15 minutes. Stir in flour; add tomato juice, salt and pepper. Simmer for 15 minutes. Serve over rice with chutney. Yield: 4 servings.

CURRIED PHEASANT

1 pheasant
Salt
1 can sliced mushrooms
1 tbsp. butter
1/2 tsp. curry powder
1 can cream of celery soup
Dash of seasoned salt
Dash of pepper
1/2 c. white wine

Disjoint pheasant; place in saucepan. Add salted water to cover; bring to a boil. Reduce heat; simmer until pheasant is tender. Drain pheasant; place in single layer in shallow baking dish. Cover with mushrooms. Melt butter in skillet; blend in curry powder. Add soup, seasoned salt, pepper and wine; pour over pheasant. Bake at 350 degrees until liquid is almost evaporated.

LAZY CURRY

2 lb. stew veal
Cooking oil
3 tbsp. curry powder
2 c. rice
2 pkg. frozen mixed vegetables
1 tbsp. salt
2 tbsp. instant minced onion
2 chicken bouillon cubes
5 c. boiling water

Cut veal in 3/4-inch pieces; brown in small amount of oil in frypan. Stir in curry powder. Place rice, mixed vegetables, salt, onion, bouillon cubes and veal in oiled 2-quart casserole; mix well. Pour water over top; cover. Bake at 350 degrees for 1 hour or until liquid is absorbed. Let stand for 10 minutes before serving. Yield: 8 servings.

CURRY-CHICKEN DIVAN

3 chicken breasts
1/2 c. chopped celery
1/2 c. chopped carrots
1/2 c. sliced onion
1 tsp. salt
1/4 tsp. pepper
2 No. 303 cans French-cut green beans
2/3 c. mayonnaise
1/3 c. evaporated milk
1 can cream of chicken soup
1/2 c. grated American cheese
1 tsp. lemon juice
1 tsp. curry powder
1/2 c. dry bread crumbs
1 tbsp. soft butter or margarine

Combine chicken, celery, carrots, onion, salt and pepper in saucepan; add water to cover. Simmer for 1 hour or until chicken is tender; cool. Cut chicken from bones in small pieces. Strain and reserve broth for future use. Place half the green beans in 13 x 9 x 2-inch baking dish; place half the chicken on beans. Combine mayonnaise, milk, soup, cheese, lemon juice and curry powder; pour half the soup mixture over chicken. Add remaining beans and chicken; top with remaining soup mixture. Mix crumbs and butter; spread over top. Bake at 350 degrees for 25 to 30 minutes. Yield: 6-8 servings.

CURRIED LOBSTER CASSEROLE

1 med. onion, minced
1/4 c. minced green pepper
1 c. sliced fresh mushrooms
1 can cream of mushroom soup
1 1/2 tsp. curry powder
Salt and pepper to taste
1 tbsp. minced parsley
1 1/2 c. chopped cooked lobster

Combine onion, green pepper, mushrooms and 1 cup water in saucepan. Cook for 15 minutes. Stir in soup and seasonings; simmer, stirring, until smooth. Fold in parsley and lobster; turn into casserole. Bake at 325 degrees for 10 minutes, stirring occasionally. Yield: 6 servings.

CURRIED TUNA PILAF

1 7-oz. can tuna
1/2 c. cooked rice
2 hard-boiled eggs, chopped
1 tsp. chopped parsley
1 green pepper, chopped
1 onion, finely chopped
1 can cream of mushroom soup
1/2 tsp. curry powder
1/2 c. milk
1 tbsp. lemon juice
Buttered bread crumbs

Drain and flake tuna. Combine rice, eggs, parsley, green pepper and onion; fold in tuna gently. Heat soup in saucepan; dissolve curry powder in soup. Add milk and lemon juice; stir into tuna mixture. Pour into greased casserole; cover with crumbs. Bake at 350 degrees for 1 hour. Yield: 6 servings.

CURRIED TUNA SQUARES

1 6-oz. can chunk-style tuna
4 c. crushed corn flakes
2 c. cooked rice
1 tbsp. finely chopped onion
1 tbsp. lemon juice
1/2 tsp. curry powder
1/2 tsp. salt
1/4 tsp. pepper
2 eggs, beaten
3/4 c. milk
2 tbsp. melted butter

Drain and flake tuna. Combine 3/4 cup corn flakes, rice, onion, lemon juice, seasonings, eggs, milk and tuna; spread in greased 10 x 6-inch baking pan. Mix remaining corn flakes and butter; sprinkle over tuna mixture. Bake at 350 degrees for 20 minutes. Cut into squares. Garnish with lemon wedges, if desired. Yield: 6 servings.

TURKEY CURRY IN AVOCADOS

1 tbsp. butter
1/2 tsp. curry powder
1/2 tsp. salt
1 10 1/2-oz. can white sauce
1 tbsp. instant minced onion
1 tbsp. lemon juice
2 c. diced cooked turkey
2 med. avocados
1 tbsp. toasted sesame seed

Melt butter in saucepan. Add curry powder; cook for 2 minutes. Add salt, white sauce, onion and lemon juice; stir until heated through. Add turkey; bring to a boil. Peel avocados; cut in half lengthwise. Remove seeds; place in shallow baking dish, cut side up. Spoon turkey mixture into avocados. Bake at 300 degrees for 10 minutes. Sprinkle with sesame seed before serving. Yield: 4 servings.

CURRIED ASPARAGUS

2 1/2 lb. asparagus
Boiling salted water
1/4 c. butter or margarine
3 tbsp. chopped green onions
1/4 tsp. curry powder
1/2 tsp. salt
1/3 c. flour
2 c. milk
1/3 c. grated Romano cheese

Reserve 3 asparagus spears for garnish; cut remaining asparagus diagonally into 1/2-inch pieces. Place in large shallow pan; cover with boiling salted water. Cook over high heat until water resumes boiling; reduce heat. Simmer for 8 minutes or until asparagus is tender but crisp; drain well. Melt butter in saucepan; add onions, curry powder, 1/2 teaspoon salt. Cook over low heat until onions are tender. Blend in flour; add milk gradually. Cook over medium heat, stirring, for 10 minutes or until sauce is thickened. Add asparagus. Turn into shallow 1 1/2-quart baking dish; place reserved asparagus spears on top. Sprinkle with cheese. Bake at 425 degrees for 15 minutes. Yield: 6 servings.

CURRIED TOMATOES

2 lge. cans tomatoes
2 1/2 c. coarse soda cracker crumbs
2 tbsp. instant minced onion
1/2 tsp. curry powder
1 tsp. dried basil
Salt and pepper
1/4 c. sugar

Partially drain tomatoes. Combine tomatoes, cracker crumbs, seasonings and sugar; turn into greased 2-quart casserole. Bake at 350 degrees for 1 hour. Yield: 8 servings.

CURRIED LIMA BEAN CASSEROLE

3 c. dried lima beans, cooked
1 can pepperpot soup
1 can cream of mushroom soup
1 lge. can mushrooms
1 tbsp. Worcestershire sauce
1 tbsp. curry powder
1/4 tsp. mace
10 whole cloves
4 slices bacon

Place beans in large casserole. Combine soups, mushrooms and seasonings; stir into beans. Fry bacon until brown and crisp; crumble. Add bacon and drippings to beans; cover tightly. Bake at 350 degrees for 30 minutes. Yield: 8 servings.

CHICKEN CURRY

5 onions, sliced
5 tbsp. butter
3/4 c. flour
4 c. hot chicken stock
Juice of 1/2 lemon
1 slice lemon
1 1/2 c. heavy cream
1 tbsp. curry powder
3 c. chopped cooked chicken
Salt and pepper to taste

Saute onions in butter until soft. Stir in flour; cook over low heat until onions are golden. Add chicken stock slowly; stir in lemon juice and lemon slice. Simmer for 20 minutes. Add cream. Make paste of curry powder and small amount of water; add to cream mixture. Stir in chicken, salt and pepper; heat through. Serve with rice and condiments of chutney, peanuts, coconut, bacon, parsley, egg and raisins. Yield: 8 servings.

CURRIED CHICKEN AMANDINE

12 chicken breasts, halved
Seasoned flour
2 cloves of garlic
4 med. onions, chopped
2 green peppers, finely chopped
2 No. 2 cans tomatoes
1 tsp. salt
1/2 tsp. pepper
1 tsp. curry powder
1/2 tsp. thyme
Dash of cayenne pepper
2 oz. toasted blanched almonds

Roll chicken in seasoned flour. Fry in deep fat until golden brown. Place in Dutch oven; add 1/2 cup hot water. Cover; place over low heat. Steam for about 15 minutes. Cook garlic, onions and green peppers in small amount of fat until lightly browned. Add 1/2 cup water; cook for 15 minutes. Stir in tomatoes, salt, pepper, curry powder, thyme and cayenne pepper; cook until heated through. Pour over chicken;

cook for 1 hour or until chicken is tender. Add almonds. Garnish with parsley if desired. Yield: 12 servings.

CURRIED VENISON

2 lb. venison
1/2 clove of garlic
1 bouillon cube
1 med. onion, chopped
1 1/4 c. water
1 tsp. curry powder
1 8-oz. can tomato sauce

Cut venison into small cubes; brown in 2 tablespoons fat. Add remaining ingredients; simmer for 2 hours or until venison is tender. Serve with rice. Yield: 6 servings.

MOOSE CURRY

1/2 clove of garlic, minced
2 c. sliced onions
1/4 c. shortening
1 tbsp. flour
1 1/8 tsp. salt
1/8 tsp. pepper
1 lb. moose round steak
1 tsp. curry powder
1 c. beef bouillon
1/2 c. tomato juice

Brown garlic and onions in shortening in heavy skillet. Combine flour, salt and pepper. Cut steak into 3/4-inch cubes; dredge in seasoned flour. Brown steak in skillet with onion mixture. Add curry powder, bouillon and tomato juice. Simmer until steak is tender. Serve over rice with assorted condiments. Yield: 6 servings.

HAWAIIAN SHRIMP CURRY

2 c. grated coconut
1/2 c. minced onion
3 tbsp. butter
3 tbsp. flour
1 tbsp. curry powder
1 tsp. salt
1/2 tsp. sugar
1 tsp. chopped gingerroot
2 c. milk
3 c. cooked shrimp

Place coconut in fine strainer suspended over bowl. Pour 1 cup boiling water over coconut; allow to drip through strainer. Pour same water over coconut several times until water is white and milky. Discard coconut. Cook onion in butter in heavy pan until tender; stir in flour, curry powder, salt, sugar and gingerroot. Add milk and coconut water; cook, stirring frequently, until smooth and thick. Add shrimp; heat to serving temperature.

FAR EAST CURRY

2 tbsp. butter
3 onions, chopped
2 tbsp. flour
1 tbsp. curry powder
2 c. stock
1 c. milk
2 hard-boiled eggs
1 c. diced cooked lamb
Salt and pepper to taste
Cayenne pepper to taste
Cooked rice

Melt butter in saucepan; add onions. Cook over low heat, stirring, until onions are tender and browned. Blend in flour and curry powder; add stock slowly. Stir in milk; cook, stirring constantly, until smooth and thickened. Cut eggs into small wedges; fold eggs and lamb into sauce. Add salt, pepper and cayenne pepper. Spread hot rice into ring on large platter; pour lamb mixture into center of platter. Serve with curry accompaniments.

CURRIED LAMB

2 tbsp. butter
1 med. onion, diced
1/2 c. diced green pepper
1/2 c. sliced mushrooms
1/2 c. sliced celery
Curry powder to taste
1 can cream of mushroom soup
1/2 c. hot milk
2 c. diced cooked lamb

Melt butter in saucepan over low heat; add onion, green pepper, mushrooms and celery. Cook, stirring, until celery is tender. Blend in curry powder; stir in soup, milk and lamb. Simmer, stirring, until heated through. Serve over noodles or rice. Yield: 4-6 servings.

LAMB BOMBAY

2 lb. boneless lamb
1/4 c. oil
1/2 med. onion, diced
1 sm. peeled apple, finely diced
1/4 c. diced celery
1/2 c. flour
2 tsp. curry powder
3 c. chicken broth
1 1/2 tsp. salt
1 c. sliced mushrooms

Cut lamb into 1-inch cubes. Brown in oil on all sides; add onion, apple and celery. Cover; cook over low heat for 15 minutes. Blend in flour and curry powder; stir in broth and salt. Cover; cook for 1 hour and 15 minutes or until lamb is tender. Add mushrooms; cook for 15 minutes longer. Serve over rice. Yield: 6 servings.

LAMB CURRY

3 c. lean lamb cubes
1 stick cinnamon
2 bay leaves
1/4 c. butter or margarine, melted
2 onions, sliced
1 lge. peeled green apple, sliced
1/4 c. flour
1/2 tsp. curry powder
1/2 tsp. salt
1/8 tsp. pepper
Juice and grated rind of 1/2 lemon
1/2 c. raisins
2 whole cloves

Place lamb in large skillet; add 4 cups hot water, cinnamon and bay leaves. Simmer until lamb is tender. Discard cinnamon stick and bay leaves; remove lamb. Strain and reserve pan liquid. Melt butter in skillet; add onions and apple. Cook, stirring, until onions are tender. Combine flour, curry powder, salt and pepper; add to onion mixture. Stir in reserved liquid slowly. Bring to a boil; add lemon juice, lemon rind, raisins, cloves and lamb. Reduce heat; simmer until heated through. Serve over rice. Yield: 6 servings.

Dandelion

DANDELION SALAD

2 oz. slab bacon
2 tbsp. vinegar
Salt and pepper to taste
Paprika to taste
1 tbsp. chopped onion
2 eggs, beaten
1 qt. tender dandelion leaves

Slice bacon. Combine bacon and 2 tablespoons water in frypan; cook until bacon is crisp. Remove bacon; reserve. Cool bacon drippings; stir in vinegar, salt, pepper, paprika, onion and eggs. Arrange dandelion leaves in salad bowl; crumble reserved bacon over top. Pour egg mixture over salad; toss gently.

PENNSYLVANIA DUTCH SALAD

3 c. (packed) tender dandelion greens
4 thick slices bacon, chopped
1/2 c. salad dressing
1 egg, beaten
1 tsp. salt
1 tbsp. flour
2 tbsp. sugar
1/4 c. vinegar
1 c. water
2 hard-cooked eggs, sliced

Place greens in salad bowl. Fry bacon until crisp; crumble. Pour bacon and drippings over greens. Blend salad dressing, egg, salt, flour, sugar, vinegar and water in skillet; cook, stirring, until smooth and thickened. Pour hot mixture over greens; mix well. Garnish with sliced eggs, serve immediately. Yield: 6 servings.

DANDELION BLOSSOMS

2 tbsp. powdered milk
1 tbsp. baking powder
1/2 c. flour
Pinch of salt
1 egg, beaten
1/4 c. milk
16 lge. fresh dandelion blossoms

Mix powdered milk, baking powder, flour and salt; stir in egg and milk. Dip dandelion blossoms into batter. Fry in deep hot fat until golden. Yield: 4 servings.

SAUTÉED DANDELIONS

2 lb. fresh dandelion greens
1/4 c. olive oil
2 cloves of garlic, chopped
Salt and pepper

Chop greens. Heat oil and garlic in saucepan. Add greens, salt and pepper. Cook for 12 minutes or until greens are tender. Serve very hot. Yield: 4 servings.

SCALLOPED DANDELIONS

2 tbsp. bacon drippings
2 tbsp. flour
3/4 c. water
2 c. milk
1 tbsp. vinegar
3/4 tsp. salt
2 tsp. sugar
1 c. (firmly packed) dandelions, chopped
1/4 c. minced onion
2 hard-boiled eggs, sliced

Heat bacon drippings in skillet; blend in flour. Cook, stirring, until flour is lightly browned. Add water, milk, vinegar, salt and sugar; cook, stirring, until smooth and thickened. Remove from heat; fold in dandelions, onion and eggs. Serve immediately. Yield: 6 servings.

Date

Dates, the sweet fruit of the date palm have been long-prized as a staple food in the deserts of the Middle East and northern Africa. The United States imports dates primarily from Iraq. Domestic dates are grown in southern California and Arizona. Dates are tree-ripened, picked, and dried before being marketed. They are high in sugar, protein, calcium, iron, and Vitamin A. Dried pitted dates are high in calories. (3 average-sized dates = 100 calories)

AVAILABILITY: Dates are available year-round in packages (pitted or unpitted) and in bulk (unpitted only). Also available diced and in pieces.

BUYING: Look for whole dates that are golden brown, plump, lustrous, and smooth.

STORING: Dates keep several months in a closed container in the refrigerator or other cool, dry places.

PREPARATION: To pit dates, slit fruit lengthwise with paring knife and lift out pit. To cut dates, use kitchen shears dipped in water to prevent sticking.

SERVING: Dates are used in breads, muffins, cookies, cakes, salads, or candies. They are also pitted and stuffed. One pound dates = 2 1/2 cups pitted or 3 cups chopped.

CREAMY DATE SALAD

1 can pineapple chunks
1 lb. cream cheese
1/3 c. mayonnaise
1 c. chopped dates
1/2 c. halved maraschino cherries
1 c. coarsely chopped nuts

Drain pineapple, reserving 1/3 cup syrup. Soften cream cheese. Combine cream cheese, mayonnaise and reserved pineapple syrup; beat until smooth and fluffy. Add dates, cherries and pineapple; refrigerate overnight. Add nuts just before serving. Yield: 8-10 servings.

DATE-CABBAGE SALAD

3 lge. leaves Chinese cabbage
1 apple, diced
12 dates, sliced
1/4 c. sliced Brazil nuts
2 tbsp. sugar
Pinch of salt
1 tbsp. lemon juice
1 tbsp. salad oil

Trim cabbage leaves; tear into small pieces. Combine cabbage, apple, dates and nuts in bowl; sprinkle with sugar and salt. Add lemon juice and oil; toss to mix. Serve chilled. Yield: 4 servings.

FLUFFY DATE SALAD

1/2 c. chopped dates
1 can drained pineapple chunks
2 c. tiny marshmallows
1/2 c. coarsely chopped nuts
2 c. whipped cream

Combine dates, pineapple, marshmallows and nuts; fold in whipped cream. Turn salad into glass serving bowl; chill for 1 hour before serving. Yield: 6 servings.

FROZEN DATE SOUFFLÉ

8 oz. cream cheese
1/4 c. maple-blended syrup
1 tbsp. lemon juice
1 banana, mashed
1/2 c. chopped pecans
1 c. drained crushed pineapple
1/2 c. finely chopped dates
2 c. whipped cream

Soften cream cheese; beat in syrup, lemon juice and banana. Stir in pecans, pineapple and dates; fold in whipped cream. Spoon salad into freezer container; cover. Freeze until firm. Yield: 9-12 servings.

DARK DATE CAKE

1 c. chopped dates
1 1/4 c. hot water
1 tsp. soda
1 1/2 c. flour
1 1/2 c. sugar
2 eggs, beaten
3/4 c. butter
1 tsp. vanilla
1/2 tsp. salt
1 pkg. chocolate pieces

Combine dates, hot water and soda. Mix flour, 1 cup sugar, eggs, butter, vanilla and salt in mixing bowl; add date mixture. Beat well. Pour into greased and floured 12 x 8 x 2-inch pan; sprinkle with chocolate pieces and remaining sugar. Bake at 350 degrees for 1 hour. Serve warm with ice cream, if desired.

DOUBLE-DATE CAKE

1 lb. pitted dates, chopped
1 c. butter
2 c. sugar
1 tsp. vanilla
1 egg, beaten
1 2/3 c. sifted flour
1 tsp. soda
1/4 tsp. salt
1 c. chopped pecans

Combine half the dates, 1/2 cup butter, 1 cup sugar, vanilla and 1 cup boiling water in heavy saucepan. Cook, stirring, for 10 minutes or until thickened. Cool date mixture; beat in egg. Stir in flour, soda, salt and 1/2 cup pecans. Spread batter in greased paper-lined 8-inch square pan. Bake at 350 degrees for 1 hour or until cake tests done. Combine remaining dates, butter and sugar in saucepan; add 1 cup boiling water. Cook, stirring, for 20 minutes. Add remaining pecans; cool to lukewarm. Spread over warm cake. Yield: 8-10 servings.

DATE SPICE CAKE

1 c. buttermilk
1 c. diced dates
2 c. sifted all-purpose flour
1/2 tsp. salt
1 tsp. soda
1 tsp. cinnamon
1/2 tsp. nutmeg
1/4 tsp. cloves
1/2 c. butter
1 1/2 c. (packed) brown sugar
2 eggs

Pour buttermilk over dates; let stand. Sift flour, salt, soda and spices together. Cream butter and sugar together until light and fluffy. Add eggs, one at a time, beating well after each addition. Add dry ingredients alternately with date mixture, beating until smooth after each addition. Turn into greased and floured 9-inch square pan. Bake in 350-degree oven for 40 to 45 minutes or until cake tests done.

Frosting

1/2 c. (2/3 stick) soft butter
1/4 c. light cream
2/3 c. (packed) brown sugar
1/2 c. chopped nuts

Combine butter, cream, brown sugar and nuts; spread over warm cake. Place under broiler until mixture bubbles and browns lightly.

Date Spice Cake . . . A delicious mixture of dates and spices, topped with a rich nut-filled frosting.

DATE-NUT CAKE

2 tsp. soda
1 c. boiling water
1 pkg. dates, chopped
1 c. sugar
1/2 c. shortening
2 eggs, beaten
1 tsp. vanilla
1 c. chopped nuts
2 c. sifted flour

Stir soda into boiling water; pour over dates. Cream sugar and shortening; add eggs and vanilla. Combine nuts and flour; add to creamed mixture alternately with date mixture. Pour into greased square cake pan. Bake at 350 degrees for 35 to 45 minutes. Serve topped with whipped cream or ice cream, if desired.

SPICY DATE CAKE

1 1/2 c. sugar
1 c. salad oil
3 eggs
2 c. sifted flour
1 tsp. soda
1 tsp. salt
1 tsp. nutmeg
1 tsp. cinnamon
1 tsp. allspice
1 c. buttermilk
1 c. chopped nuts
1 c. chopped dates
1 tsp. vanilla

Combine sugar, oil and eggs; beat until smooth and creamy. Sift flour, soda, salt and spices together; add to sugar mixture alternately with buttermilk. Stir in nuts, dates and vanilla. Pour batter into greased and floured 13 x 9 x 2-inch pan. Bake at 300 degrees for 55 minutes to 1 hour. Yield: 12-14 servings.

ARABIAN DATE CANDY

Sugar
1/2 c. milk
1 pkg. dates, chopped
1 bottle lime juice

Combine 1 1/2 cups sugar and milk in saucepan; stir over low heat until sugar is dissolved. Add dates; cook to soft-ball stage. Turn candy onto cold damp towel; roll towel around candy. Refrigerate for several hours. Shape candy into balls. Dip into lime juice; roll in sugar.

DATE BALLS

1 lb. dates, chopped
1 c. brown sugar
1/4 c. butter
1 egg, beaten
1/2 c. chopped nuts
2 c. oven-toasted rice cereal
1 tsp. vanilla
Dash of salt
Shredded coconut

Combine dates, brown sugar, butter and egg in top of double boiler; cook, stirring, until thick. Stir in nuts, cereal, vanilla and salt; cool enough to handle. Shape date mixture into balls; roll in coconut. Chill before serving.

DATE CANDY SLICES

2 c. sugar
1 c. milk
1/4 c. butter
1 c. chopped dates
1 c. chopped nuts
1 c. shredded coconut

Combine sugar, milk and butter in heavy saucepan. Cook to soft-ball stage. Add dates; cook, stirring, until thickened. Remove from heat; add nuts and coconut. Stir until of the consistency of soft cookie dough. Turn onto cloth dipped in cold water; form into two rolls about 1 1/2 inches in diameter. Cool; cut in slices. Wrap in waxed paper; store in refrigerator. Candy freezes well.

DATE LOAF

3 c. sugar
1 1/2 c. milk
1 1/2 tbsp. butter
1/2 lb. dates, chopped
4 c. chopped pecans
1 lb. pecan halves

Combine sugar, milk and butter in heavy saucepan; stir over low heat until blended. Increase heat; cook to firm-ball stage. Add dates; reduce heat. Simmer, stirring constantly, until dates are dissolved. Beat until lukewarm; stir in chopped pecans. Dampen 24-inch square cloth; place over thick pad of paper towels. Spread pecan halves on cloth; pour candy down center of cloth. Bring both sides of cloth over candy, pressing pecans deeply into candy. Roll candy smoothly in cloth; chill for several hours. Slice to serve.

DATE-NUT CHEWS

1/3 c. butter
1/2 c. sugar
1 1/4 c. finely chopped dates
2 c. oven-toasted rice cereal
1/2 c. chopped nuts

Combine butter, sugar and dates in saucepan; cook, stirring constantly, until thick. Cool date mixture; stir in cereal. Shape into 1 1/2-inch balls; roll in nuts.

DATE ICEBOX COOKIES

1 lb. dates, chopped
1 1/2 c. sugar
1/2 c. water
1/2 c. butter or margarine
1 c. brown sugar
3 eggs
4 c. flour
2 tsp. soda
Pinch of salt
1 tsp. vanilla

Combine dates, 1/2 cup sugar and water in saucepan; cook until thick. Cool. Cream butter, remaining sugar and brown sugar; beat in eggs. Sift in flour, soda and salt; add vanilla. Roll dough 1/2 inch thick; spread with date mixture. Roll as for jelly roll; wrap in waxed paper. Refrigerate overnight. Slice thin; place on baking sheet. Bake at 375 degrees for 8 to 10 minutes.

DATE-NUT SQUARES

6 oz. dates, chopped
3/4 c. sugar
1 tsp. vanilla
1 1/2 c. brown sugar
1 1/2 c. sifted flour
1 1/2 c. oats
1/2 tsp. soda
1/2 tsp. salt
1 c. melted butter or margarine
1/2 c. chopped nuts

Combine dates, sugar, vanilla and 3/4 cup water in saucepan; cook until thickened. Cool. Mix brown sugar, flour, oats, soda and salt; stir in butter and nuts. Press half the brown sugar mixture evenly in 12 x 8 x 2-inch pan; pour in date filling. Spread remaining brown sugar mixture over filling; press lightly with fingers. Bake at 350 degrees for about 40 minutes. Cool in pan; cut into squares.

HOLIDATES

1 1/4 c. sifted flour
3/4 tsp. soda
1/2 tsp. salt
1 c. chopped dates
3/4 c. sugar
1/2 c. shortening
1 tbsp. grated lemon rind
6 oz. semisweet chocolate morsels
2 eggs
1 c. coarsely chopped nuts

Sift flour, soda and salt together. Combine dates, sugar, shortening, 1/2 cup water and lemon rind in saucepan. Cook, stirring constantly, until dates soften. Remove from heat; stir in chocolate morsels. Beat in eggs; add flour mixture alternately with 1 cup water. Stir in nuts. Pour into greased 15 x 10 x 1-inch pan. Bake at 350 degrees for 25 minutes. Cool. Spread with a lemon glaze if desired. Cut into 2 x 1-inch bars. Yield: 6 dozen.

POLKA DATERS

1 1/4 c. chopped dates
1 c. hot water
1 c. soft butter
1 1/4 c. sugar
2 eggs
1 3/4 c. flour
1 1/2 tsp. soda
1 tsp. vanilla
2/3 c. chocolate chips
1/2 c. chopped nuts

Combine dates and hot water in saucepan; cook over low heat until dates are soft. Cool. Combine butter, sugar and eggs; beat until creamy. Stir in flour and soda gradually. Add date mixture, vanilla and 1/2 of the chocolate chips. Spread batter in greased pan; top with remaining chocolate chips and nuts. Bake at 350 degrees for 30 minutes. Cool; cut into bars.

SUGARED DATE SQUARES

1 1/4 c. sifted flour
1 tsp. baking powder
1/2 tsp. salt
1 c. chopped dates
3/4 c. sugar
1/2 c. shortening
1/2 c. water
1 tsp. vanilla
6 oz. chocolate pieces
2 eggs
1/4 c. milk
1 c. chopped walnuts
Powdered sugar

Sift flour, baking powder and salt together. Combine dates, sugar, shortening, water and vanilla in saucepan; simmer until dates are soft. Remove from heat; add chocolate pieces. Stir until melted; beat in eggs. Stir in flour mixture alternately with milk; add walnuts. Spread batter in greased and floured 13 x 9 x 2-inch pan. Bake at 350 degrees for 20 to 25 minutes. Cool in pan; cut into squares. Roll in powdered sugar.

DATE-NUT PUDDING

1 c. chopped dates
1 tsp. soda
5 tbsp. butter
1 c. sugar
1 egg
Flour
1 tbsp. vanilla
1/2 c. chopped nuts
1 1/2 c. brown sugar
2 tbsp. cornstarch

Combine dates and soda in bowl; pour in 1 cup boiling water. Cool. Combine 1 tablespoon butter, sugar and egg; beat until smooth. Stir in 1 cup flour, date mixture, 1 teaspoon vanilla and nuts. Spread batter in greased 9-inch square pan. Bake at 350 degrees for 45 minutes. Mix brown sugar, cornstarch and 2 tablespoons flour in top of double boiler; stir in 3 cups water slowly. Add remaining butter and vanilla; cook, stirring, until thickened and clear. Serve sauce over pudding. Yield: 12-15 servings.

SKILLET DATE PUDDING

1/4 c. butter or margarine
2 1/4 c. brown sugar
1 c. flour
1 tsp. baking powder
1/4 tsp. salt
2 tbsp. shortening
1 egg
1/3 c. milk
1/4 tsp. vanilla
1/2 c. chopped dates

Combine butter, 2 cups brown sugar and 1 1/2 cups water in electric skillet; heat to 225 degrees. Sift flour, baking powder and salt together. Cream shortening and remaining brown sugar; beat in egg. Add flour mixture alternately with milk; stir in vanilla and dates. Drop batter from tablespoon into hot brown sugar mixture; cover skillet. Cook for 25 minutes. Serve pudding warm; spoon hot syrup over pudding. Top with whipped cream, if desired. Yield: 4-6 servings.

STEAMED DATE BREAD

1 c. whole wheat flour
3/4 c. flour
3/4 c. white cornmeal
1 tbsp. baking powder
1/2 tsp. salt
1 c. milk
3/4 c. molasses
2 tbsp. melted shortening
1 c. chopped dates

Combine whole wheat flour, flour, cornmeal, baking powder and salt; stir in milk, molasses and shortening. Fold in dates. Spoon batter into greased and floured round 1 1/2-quart can; cover can. Place can in deep kettle; add enough boiling water to come within 1 inch of top of can. Cover kettle; boil for 1 hour and 30 minutes, adding boiling water as needed to maintain proper level. Cool bread to room temperature in can; turn onto rack. Yield: 15 servings.

DATE-APRICOT PIE

1 1-lb. 14-oz. can apricots
1 c. chopped dates
1 unbaked pie shell
1/4 c. sugar
2 tbsp. instant tapioca
1/2 tsp. cinnamon
1 tsp. grated lemon rind
1/2 c. quick oats
1/2 c. (firmly packed) brown sugar
1/3 c. flour
1/3 c. melted butter

Drain apricots, reserving 1/2 cup syrup. Chop apricots. Place dates and apricots in pie shell. Combine sugar, tapioca, cinnamon, lemon rind and reserved apricot syrup. Pour over fruits. Mix oats, brown sugar, flour and butter; spread over filling. Bake at 400 degrees for 45 minutes. Cover pie with foil; bake for 15 minutes longer.

DATE CRISP

1/2 c. sugar
2 tbsp. milk
1 egg, beaten
1/3 c. sifted flour
1/2 tsp. salt
1 tsp. baking powder
1 c. chopped walnuts
1 c. chopped dates

Combine sugar, milk, egg, flour, salt and baking powder; beat well. Add walnuts and dates; spread batter in greased 13 x 9 x 2-inch pan. Bake at 350 degrees for 20 to 25 minutes. Serve with whipped cream. Yield: 8 servings.

DATE-NUT CRUNCH

2 eggs, separated
1 egg yolk
1/2 lb. powdered sugar
1 tsp. baking powder
2 tbsp. bread crumbs
1/2 c. chopped walnuts
2 c. chopped dates
1 tsp. vanilla
2 c. whipped cream

Beat egg yolks until thick and light, beating in powdered sugar. Add baking powder, bread crumbs, walnuts, dates and vanilla. Beat egg whites until stiff; fold into date mixture. Spread in heavily greased shallow pan. Bake at 375 degrees for 20 minutes. Cool. Cut into squares; serve topped with whipped cream. Yield: 8 servings.

Dill

DILL DIP

1 c. sour cream
1/3 c. mayonnaise
3/4 tbsp. green onion, chopped
1 tsp. dillweed
1 tbsp. parsley
1 tsp. Beau Monde seasoning
Seasoned salt to taste
Salt to taste

Combine all ingredients; blend well. Chill until ready to serve.

STUFFED DILLS

1 3-oz. package cream cheese
1 tbsp. Worcestershire sauce
2 tbsp. salad dressing
1/2 c. chopped walnuts
3 lge. dill pickles, cored

Blend cream cheese, Worcestershire sauce and salad dressing until smooth; add walnuts. Stuff pickles. Chill for 1 hour or until cheese is firm. Cut into 1/4-inch slices.

DILL RING

1 env. unflavored gelatin
4 eggs
2 tbsp. dillweed
1/2 tsp. salt
1 c. vinegar
1 c. heavy cream, whipped

Soften gelatin in 1/4 cup water. Beat eggs until thick and lemony. Pour eggs over gelatin in double boiler; add dillweed, salt and vinegar. Cook, stirring constantly, over hot water until thickened; cool. Fold in whipped cream. Pour into ring mold; chill for several hours or until ready to use.

DILL PICKLE SALAD

1 pkg. lemon gelatin
1 sm. can crushed pineapple, drained
2 tbsp. chopped pimento
1/4 c. chopped dill pickle
1/4 c. chopped pecans

Prepare gelatin according to package directions. Chill until partially thickened. Blend pineapple, pimento, dill pickle and pecans in gelatin mixture. Pour into mold; chill until firm.

TOMATO-DILL MOLD

2 env. unflavored gelatin
1 1/2 c. tomato juice
2 tbsp. lemon juice
1/2 c. chili sauce
1 tsp. Worcestershire sauce
1/4 tsp. hot sauce
1 tbsp. dried dill leaf
1 pt. sour cream

Sprinkle gelatin over tomato juice in pan. Place over moderate heat; stir constantly until gelatin is dissolved. Remove from heat; stir in lemon juice, chili sauce, Worcestershire sauce, hot sauce and dill. Cool; stir in sour cream. Beat until smooth. Turn into 5-cup mold; chill until firm. Unmold; garnish with sprigs of dill, if desired.

DILLY BREAD

1 pkg. yeast
1 c. creamed cottage cheese
2 tbsp. sugar
1 tbsp. minced onion
2 tsp. dillseed
1 tsp. salt
1/4 tsp. soda
1 egg
2 1/4 to 2 1/2 c. flour
1 tbsp. butter

Soften yeast in 1/4 cup warm water. Heat cottage cheese until lukewarm. Combine cottage cheese, sugar, onion, dillseed, salt, soda, egg and yeast in mixing bowl; add enough flour to form stiff dough, beating well after each addition. Cover; let rise in warm place for 1 hour or until light and doubled in bulk. Stir down; turn into well-buttered 8-inch round 1 1/2 to 2-quart casserole. Let rise in warm place until doubled in bulk. Bake at 350 degrees for 45 to 50 minutes. Cool for 5 minutes; remove from casserole. Brush with butter; sprinkle with additional salt.

MONKEY-DILL BREAD

1 c. milk
1 1/2 pkg. yeast
4 tbsp. sugar
1 tsp. salt
Melted butter
3 1/2 c. sifted flour
1 1/2 tbsp. dillweed
1 tbsp. dillseed

Scald milk; cool to lukewarm. Dissolve yeast in milk; stir in sugar, salt, 1/2 cup butter, flour, dillweed and dillseed. Beat well; cover. Let rise for 1 hour or until doubled in bulk. Punch down; roll out on a lightly floured board to 1/4-inch thickness. Cut into diamond shapes about 2 1/2 inches long. Dip each piece in melted butter; arrange in layers in 9-inch ring mold. Let rise for 1 hour or until doubled in bulk. Bake at 400 degrees for 30 minutes or until golden brown.

SAVORY SUPPER BREAD

1/2 c. chopped onion
1 egg, beaten
1/2 c. milk
1 1/2 c. biscuit mix
1 c. grated sharp American cheese
1 tbsp. dillseed
2 tbsp. melted butter

Saute onion in small amount of fat until tender and lightly browned. Combine egg and milk; add to biscuit mix and stir only until dry ingredients are moistened. Add onion and half the cheese. Spread in greased 8 x 1 1/2-inch round or 8-inch square pan. Sprinkle top with remaining cheese and dillseed; drizzle with melted butter. Bake at 400 degrees for 20 to 25 minutes.

DILLED MAYONNAISE ROLLS

1 c. self-rising flour
2 tbsp. mayonnaise
1/2 c. sweet milk
2 tbsp. dillseed

Combine flour, mayonnaise and milk; blend well. Stir in dillseed. Drop by spoonfuls into small well-greased muffin cups. Bake at 450 degrees until lightly browned. Yield: 8.

SOUR CREAM-DILL ROLLS

3/4 c. sour cream
2 tbsp. sugar
1 tsp. salt
2 tbsp. soft shortening
1 pkg. yeast
2 1/4 c. flour
1 egg
1 1/2 tbsp. dillseed

Mix sour cream, sugar, salt and shortening in saucepan. Bring just to a boil; cool to lukewarm. Dissolve yeast in 1/4 cup warm water. Stir in sour cream mixture and half of flour; beat until smooth. Add remaining flour, egg and dillseed; beat until smooth. Cover; let rise in warm place about 30 minutes, until doubled in bulk. Stir down batter. Spoon into well-greased cups; fill half full. Let rise in warm place 20 to 30 minutes. Bake at 400 degrees for 15 to 20 minutes. Yield: 12 buns.

Divinity

Divinity is the name for a very sweet, soft candy or fudge. It is usually made from white or brown sugar, whipped whites of eggs, corn syrup, water, salt, and flavoring. If brown sugar is used instead of white sugar, the candy is called *Sea Foam*. If the basic ingredients are not cooked but beaten until spreading consistency is reached, the mixture can be used as a frosting. Some recipes for Divinity candy specify ingredients such as peppermint, cinnamon, chocolate, or candied fruits for flavor variation, or food coloring for color variation.

PREPARATION: All ingredients except the flavoring and egg whites are cooked in a saucepan to hard-ball stage (that is, a drop of syrup forms a hard ball when dropped in very cold water) and when it registers from 250 to 268 degrees on a candy thermometer. Syrup is then poured over stiffly beaten egg whites. Flavoring is added. The mixture is beaten with an electric mixer or by hand until it loses its gloss and forms soft peaks. The candy is then dropped from a spoon onto greased waxed paper to harden. Or it is allowed to harden in a buttered pan and cut into squares. Some hints to follow in making Divinity are: (1) If candy becomes stiff while beating with electric mixer, beat by hand with wooden spoon. (2) If candy begins to harden in bowl before you finish dropping it onto waxed paper, add a few drops of hot water.

SERVING: Top pieces of drop candy with nut half or candied cherry. Top pan candy with chocolate pieces, flaked coconut, or chopped nuts.

(See CANDY.)

BRAZIL NUT DIVINITY

3 c. sugar
3/4 c. dark corn syrup
1 c. water
1/8 tsp. salt
2 egg whites
1 c. chopped Brazil nuts
1/2 tsp. vanilla

Combine sugar, corn syrup, water and salt in heavy saucepan; stir to a boil. Cook to hard-ball stage. Beat egg whites at high speed of electric mixer until soft peaks form. Pour hot syrup into egg whites in thin stream, beating until candy loses gloss. Add nuts and vanilla; beat by hand until candy holds shape. Drop from teaspoon onto waxed paper; cool.

CAN'T FAIL DIVINITY

1 1/2 c. sugar
1/3 c. water
Pinch of salt
1 pt. marshmallow creme
1/2 c. chopped nuts
1 tsp. vanilla

Combine sugar, water and salt in saucepan; bring to a boil. Cook to hard-ball stage. Place marshmallow creme in mixer bowl; beat in hot syrup slowly until candy holds shape. Fold in nuts and vanilla. Drop from teaspoon onto waxed paper or buttered plate.

ALMOND DIVINITY SQUARES

2 egg whites
4 c. sugar
2/3 c. light corn syrup
1 c. water
Dash of salt
1 tsp. vanilla
1/2 tsp. almond extract
3/4 c. chopped walnuts

Place egg whites in electric mixer bowl; let stand until of room temperature. Combine sugar, corn syrup, water and salt in heavy saucepan; cover. Bring to a boil; uncover. Cook to 265 degrees on candy thermometer or hard-ball stage. Beat egg whites at high speed of mixer until stiff but not dry. Add hot syrup to egg whites in fine stream, beating constantly. Beat until candy loses gloss; beat in vanilla and almond extract. Stir in walnuts by hand; pour candy into heavily greased shallow pan. Mark into squares; cool. Cut candy with wet knife.

BLACK RASPBERRY FLUFF

3 c. sugar
3/4 c. water
3/4 c. light corn syrup
2 egg whites
1 3-oz. package black raspberry gelatin
1 c. chopped nuts
1/2 c. coconut

Combine sugar, water and corn syrup in heavy pan; bring to a boil, stirring constantly. Reduce heat; cook, stirring occasionally, to hard-ball stage. Beat egg whites until fluffy; add gelatin gradually, beating until mixture forms peaks. Pour hot syrup in thin stream into egg whites, beating constantly. Beat until candy loses gloss and holds shape. Fold in nuts and coconut. Pour into greased 9-inch square pan; cool. Cut into small squares with wet knife.

BROWN SUGAR DIVINITY

3 c. (packed) brown sugar
1/2 c. light corn syrup
2/3 c. water
2 egg whites
1/8 tsp. salt
1 c. chopped nuts
1 tsp. vanilla

Mix brown sugar, corn syrup and water in saucepan; cook to hard-ball stage. Combine egg whites and salt in electric mixer bowl; beat for 3 minutes at high speed. Pour hot syrup slowly into egg whites, beating constantly until candy loses gloss. Add nuts and vanilla; beat until candy holds shape. Drop from teaspoon onto greased platter.

COCONUT DIVINITY

3 c. sugar
3/4 c. light corn syrup
3/4 c. hot water
1/4 tsp. salt
2 egg whites
3 tbsp. red fruit gelatin
1 tsp. vanilla
1 c. flaked coconut

Grease side of heavy pan; combine sugar, syrup, hot water and salt in pan. Stir to a boil. Cook, without stirring, to hard-ball stage. Beat egg whites to soft peaks; add gelatin, beating to stiff peaks. Pour hot syrup into egg whites in thin stream, beating constantly. Beat until candy begins to hold shape; add vanilla and coconut. Mix well; spoon into mounds on greased platter. Cool.

CHOCOLATE RIPPLE DIVINITY

2 egg whites
2 c. sugar
1/2 c. light corn syrup
1/8 tsp. salt
1/2 tsp. vanilla
2 tsp. angostura bitters
1 6-oz. package semisweet chocolate bits

Place egg whites in mixing bowl; let stand at room temperature. Combine sugar, syrup, 1/2 cup water and salt in heavy saucepan. Bring to a boil; cover. Cook for 3 minutes. Uncover; cook, without stirring, until small amount of mixture dropped in cold water forms a hard ball or to 265 degrees on candy thermometer. Beat egg whites until stiff but not dry. Pour hot syrup over egg whites slowly, beating constantly. Add vanilla and bitters. Melt chocolate over boiling water; stir into candy just enough to marbleize. Drop by spoonfuls onto greased waxed paper. May be frozen. Yield: 2 dozen.

Chocolate Ripple Divinity . . . Perfect for snacking, this candy is marbled with rich chocolate.

CHRISTMAS DIVINITY

2 1/2 c. sugar
1/3 c. water
1/2 c. light corn syrup
2 egg whites
1/2 pkg. fruit-flavored gelatin
3/4 c. chopped nuts

Combine sugar, water and corn syrup in heavy saucepan; cook, stirring, to hard-ball stage. Beat egg whites until soft peaks form; beat in gelatin. Pour syrup over egg whites in thin stream, beating constantly. Beat until candy is stiff and glossy; stir in nuts. Drop from spoon onto waxed paper; cool.

CREAMY DATE DIVINITY

2 1/2 c. sugar
1/2 c. water
1/2 c. light corn syrup
2 egg whites
1 c. chopped dates
1/2 c. chopped nuts

Combine sugar, water and corn syrup in saucepan; bring to a boil. Cook to hard-ball stage. Beat egg whites until soft peaks form; add half the hot syrup to egg whites slowly, beating constantly. Return remaining syrup to heat; cook to soft-crack stage. Pour into egg white mixture, beating until creamy. Stir in dates and nuts; turn into greased pan. Cool.

DIVINITY DELIGHT

3 c. sugar
3/4 c. water
3/4 c. light corn syrup
2 egg whites
1 env. unflavored gelatin
1 c. chopped pecans
1/2 c. tinted shredded coconut

Mix sugar, water and corn syrup in heavy saucepan; stir to a boil over high heat. Reduce heat to medium; cook, stirring occasionally, to hard-ball stage. Beat egg whites until foamy; add gelatin, beating until egg whites hold soft peaks. Pour hot syrup into egg whites slowly, beating constantly. Beat until candy loses gloss; fold in pecans and coconut. Drop from spoon onto waxed paper; cool.

LEMON DIVINITY

5 c. sugar
1 c. light corn syrup
1 c. boiling water
4 egg whites
Pinch of salt
1 tsp. lemon flavoring
1 tsp. vanilla
Few drops of yellow food coloring

Combine sugar, corn syrup and boiling water in saucepan; stir to a boil. Cook to soft-ball stage. Beat egg whites and salt to soft peaks; beat 1 cup hot syrup into egg whites slowly. Add lemon flavoring, vanilla and food coloring. Return remaining syrup to heat; cook to soft-crack stage. Add to egg white mixture slowly, beating until candy loses gloss. Drop from spoon onto waxed paper; cool.

PEANUT BUTTER DIVINITY

3 c. sugar
1 c. light corn syrup
1 c. water
Dash of salt
3 egg whites
1 c. peanut butter

Combine sugar, corn syrup, water and salt in heavy saucepan over medium heat; stir to a boil. Cover pan; reduce heat. Cook for 3 minutes. Uncover pan; increase heat to medium. Cook until syrup spins a thread. Beat egg whites until stiff. Pour half the syrup into egg whites in fine stream, beating constantly. Return remaining syrup to heat; cook to firm-ball stage. Pour syrup into egg white mixture, beating until creamy. Pour candy onto heavily greased waxed paper; let stand until firm. Dampen hands with cold water; pat candy until about 3/4 inch thick. Spread peanut butter over candy. Roll as for jelly roll; cut in slices.

PEANUT DIVINITY

3 c. sugar
2/3 c. water
2/3 c. light corn syrup
3 egg whites
1 tsp. vanilla
1/2 c. peanut butter
1 c. ground salted peanuts

Mix sugar, water and corn syrup in deep heavy saucepan; bring to a boil. Cook to hard-ball stage. Beat egg whites to soft peaks; add hot syrup in thin stream, beating until stiff. Beat in vanilla, peanut butter and peanuts; spread in greased cookie sheet. Cool; cut into squares.

PERFECT DIVINITY

2 c. sugar
1/2 c. light corn syrup
1/2 c. hot water
1/4 tsp. salt
2 egg whites
1 tsp. vanilla
1/2 c. chopped nuts

Combine sugar, corn syrup, hot water and salt in 2-quart saucepan. Cook to boil, stirring constantly. Cook, without stirring, to hard-ball stage. Wipe crystals from side of pan with fork wrapped in damp cloth. Remove from heat. Beat egg whites until stiff. Pour hot syrup slowly over egg whites, beating constantly. Add vanilla; beat until candy forms soft peaks and begins to lose gloss. Add nuts; drop by teaspoonfuls onto waxed paper.

RAINBOW DIVINITY PUFFS

2 c. sugar
1/2 c. light corn syrup
1/2 c. water
Dash of salt
2 egg whites
1 tsp. vanilla
Red food coloring
Green food coloring

Combine sugar, corn syrup, water and salt in heavy saucepan. Cook, stirring to a boil. Cook, without stirring, to hard-ball stage. Beat 1 egg white to soft peaks; beat in half the hot syrup slowly. Add 1/2 teaspoon vanilla and enough red food coloring to tint pink; beat until stiff enough to hold soft peaks. Beat remaining egg white to soft peaks; beat in remaining syrup slowly. Add remaining vanilla; tint pale green. Beat until candy is stiff enough to hold soft peaks. Fold green candy into pink candy, making streaked effect. Drop from spoon onto greased cookie sheet; swirl tops of mounds to form peaks.

SHAMROCK DIVINITY

3 c. sugar
3/4 c. light corn syrup
3/4 c. hot water
1/4 tsp. salt
2 egg whites
1/2 3-oz. package lime gelatin
1 tsp. vanilla
3/4 c. green-tinted coconut

Grease side of heavy 2-quart saucepan; combine sugar, corn syrup, water and salt in saucepan. Cook, stirring, to a boil. Cook to hard-ball stage without stirring. Beat egg whites to soft peaks; add gelatin gradually, beating to stiff peaks. Beat in vanilla. Pour hot syrup slowly over egg whites, beating until candy holds soft peaks. Drop from teaspoon onto waxed paper. Sprinkle with coconut.

STRAWBERRY DIVINITY

3 c. sugar
3/4 c. light corn syrup
3/4 c. water
2 egg whites
1 3-oz. package strawberry gelatin
1 c. chopped nuts
1/2 c. flaked coconut

Combine sugar, corn syrup and water in heavy saucepan; bring to a boil, stirring constantly. Reduce heat; cook, stirring occasionally, to hard-ball stage. Beat egg whites until fluffy; add gelatin slowly, beating to firm peaks. Pour hot syrup slowly into egg whites, beating constantly. Beat until candy loses gloss and holds shape; fold in nuts and coconut. Drop from spoon onto waxed paper; cool.

Doughnuts

Doughnuts and their close relatives, crullers, are small cakes made from leavened and sweetened dough that is deep fried. The dough is usually prepared from flour, eggs, sugar, milk, shortening, and leavening (either baking powder or yeast). (1 baking powder doughnut = 200 calories; 1 yeast doughnut = 168)

BASIC PREPARATION: All ingredients should be at room temperature. Combine ingredients according to recipe. Mix until dough is soft yet stiff enough to be handled. Chill. Dough for yeast doughnuts must be kneaded and allowed to rise until doubled in bulk before it can be chilled. Be sure to place kneaded dough in a greased bowl, turning to grease entire surface before rising. When both types of dough are thoroughly chilled, roll out to thickness specified in recipe. Roll dough out on lightly floured surface. Cut with floured doughnut cutter or twist into cruller shape. Piece remaining scraps of dough together and recut. Allow baking powder doughnuts to dry 10 to 15 minutes after cutting, yeast doughnuts to double in bulk. As doughnuts dry or rise, heat fat in large kettle to specified recipe temperature. Dip spoon into hot fat, scoop up doughnut, and slide quickly into kettle. Repeat for each doughnut. Do not crowd the kettle. Cook doughnuts until brown, about 2-3 minutes, turning once. Remove from kettle and drain.

SERVING: Doughnuts can be served in many ways. Glazes can be spread thinly on cooling doughnuts; or they can be dusted with powdered, spiced, or flavored sugar. Doughnuts can be filled, too. To fill, make a small slit in side of doughnut and spoon such fillings as jelly, jam, custard, or whipped cream into the slit.

ANGEL FOOD DOUGHNUTS

1/2 c. sour cream
1/2 c. buttermilk
1 c. sugar
2 eggs
1 tsp. vanilla
4 1/2 c. sifted flour
1/2 tsp. nutmeg
1/2 tsp. soda
2 tsp. baking powder
1/2 tsp. salt

Combine sour cream, buttermilk, sugar, eggs and vanilla in large bowl; beat until smooth. Sift flour, nutmeg, soda, baking powder and salt together; add to sour cream mixture. Turn about 1/3 of the dough at a time onto floured surface; roll 1/3 inch thick. Cut with floured cutter. Fry in hot deep fat for 3 minutes, turning once. Drain on paper towels.

GERMAN DROP DOUGHNUTS

2 c. flour
1/2 c. sugar
2 tsp. baking powder
1/2 tsp. salt
1 tsp. cinnamon
1 egg
1/2 c. applesauce
1/2 c. milk
1 1/2 tbsp. melted shortening

Sift flour, sugar, baking powder, salt and cinnamon together. Beat egg; add applesauce and milk. Add egg mixture to dry ingredients, mixing well. Stir in shortening. Drop batter from teaspoon into hot deep fat; fry until golden brown, turning once. Drain on absorbent paper.

DUTCH APPLE DOUGHNUTS

1/4 c. warm water
1 pkg. yeast
1 c. sugar
3 tbsp. shortening
1 c. scalded milk
1 tsp. nutmeg
Salt to taste
2 eggs, beaten
5 c. flour
Raisins
Diced citron
Diced apples

Pour warm water into large bowl; stir in yeast and 1 tablespoon sugar. Melt shortening in hot milk; cool. Add milk mixture, 3/4 cup sugar, nutmeg, salt and eggs to yeast; stir in enough flour to make soft dough. Turn dough onto lightly floured surface; knead until smooth and elastic. Place dough in greased bowl; cover. Let rise for 1 hour or until doubled in bulk. Punch dough down; turn onto lightly floured surface. Round up into a ball; cover. Let rest for 10 minutes. Shape dough into egg-sized balls, tucking 2 raisins, 2 pieces citron and 1 piece apple into each ball. Place balls on greased cookie sheet; cover. Let rise for 45 minutes. Lift from cookie sheet with floured spatula; drop into hot deep fat. Fry until brown. Drain; roll in remaining sugar.

SPICY BUTTERNUT BALLS

3 1/2 c. flour
4 tsp. baking powder
1/2 tsp. soda
1 tsp. salt
3/4 c. sugar
1/2 c. minced nuts
2 eggs
3 tbsp. melted butter
1/4 c. milk
1 c. apple butter
Cinnamon sugar

Sift flour, baking powder, soda, salt and sugar together into mixing bowl; add nuts. Beat eggs lightly; beat in butter, milk and apple butter. Stir into flour mixture, mixing lightly. Drop dough from teaspoon into hot deep fat; fry until brown. Drain; roll in cinnamon sugar.

CALAS

1/2 c. rice
1 pkg. yeast
3 eggs
1 1/2 c. flour
Sugar
1/2 tsp. salt
1/2 tsp. nutmeg

Combine rice and 3 cups water in saucepan. Cook until rice is soft and water is absorbed; cool. Soften yeast in 1/4 cup warm water; stir into rice. Cover; refrigerate overnight. Beat eggs; stir into rice mixture. Add flour, 1/2 cup sugar, salt and nutmeg; let rise for 15 minutes. Stir dough down; drop from spoon into hot deep fat. Cook until browned on both sides. Drain; sprinkle with sugar.

CHOCOLATE CRULLERS

3 1/2 c. flour
1 tsp. salt
2 tsp. baking powder
1 tsp. cinnamon
2 eggs
1 c. sugar
1 tbsp. melted shortening
1 1/2 oz. chocolate, melted
1 tsp. vanilla
1 c. milk
Powdered sugar

Sift flour, salt, baking powder and cinnamon together. Beat eggs well, adding sugar gradually. Beat in shortening, chocolate and vanilla; add flour mixture alternately with milk. Drop dough from tablespoon into hot deep fat; fry for about 4 minutes. Drain on paper towels; roll in powdered sugar.

CHOCOLATE DOUGHNUTS

4 1/2 c. flour
4 1/2 tsp. baking powder
1 tsp. salt
1/2 tsp. cinnamon
5 tbsp. cocoa
2 tbsp. shortening
1 c. sugar
2 eggs
1 c. milk
1 tsp. vanilla

Sift flour, baking powder, salt, cinnamon and cocoa together. Cream shortening; add sugar, beating until light and fluffy. Beat in eggs; add flour mixture alternately with milk and vanilla. Chill dough for 30 minutes. Turn onto floured surface; roll out thin. Cut with doughnut cutter; let rest for 20 minutes. Fry in deep hot fat for about 4 minutes.

CINNAMON TWISTS

3 eggs
1 c. sugar
1 c. milk
3 1/2 c. flour
4 tsp. (rounded) baking powder
1 tsp. salt
1/2 tsp. cinnamon
3 tbsp. melted butter
1 tsp. vanilla
Cinnamon sugar

Beat eggs well, beating in sugar gradually; stir in milk. Sift flour, baking powder, salt and cinnamon together; stir into egg mixture. Add butter and vanilla; mix well. Turn dough onto floured board; knead lightly. Pat dough to thin rectangle; cut into 3 x 1 1 1/2-inch strips. Cut slit in center of each strip; pull one end of strip through slit. Let twists rest for about 5 minutes. Fry twists, 4 or 5 at a time, in deep hot fat until golden. Drain on paper towels; roll in cinnamon sugar. Yield: 3 dozen twists.

DIMPLED DOUGHNUTS

1 1-lb. can red tart cherries
1 1/3 c. sifted flour
1/3 c. sugar
2 tsp. baking powder
1/4 tsp. salt
1 egg, lightly beaten
1/2 c. milk
1 tbsp. cooking oil
1 tsp. vanilla
1 1/2 c. sifted confectioners' sugar

Drain cherries, reserving 6 tablespoons syrup. Sift flour, sugar, baking powder and salt together into mixing bowl. Combine egg, milk, oil and vanilla; add to flour mixture. Mix only until blended; stir in cherries. Drop batter from spoon into hot deep fat; fry for 3 minutes, turning once. Drain. Combine confectioners' sugar and reserved cherry syrup; dip hot doughnuts in mixture.

DOUGHNUT RAISIN BALLS

4 c. sifted flour
3 1/2 tsp. baking powder
1/2 tsp. salt
1 tsp. cinnamon
1/2 tsp. nutmeg
1/4 c. shortening
1 c. sugar
2 eggs
1 c. milk
1 c. chopped raisins
Powdered sugar

Sift 3 cups flour, baking powder, salt and spices together. Cream shortening and sugar; beat in eggs. Add flour mixture alternately with milk; mix until smooth. Fold in raisins; add enough remaining flour to make easily handled dough. Shape dough into small balls with floured hands. Fry in hot deep fat until brown. Drain on paper towels; cool. Roll in powdered sugar.

FASTNACHTS

1 1/2 c. milk
1/4 c. light molasses
1 tsp. salt
1/4 c. butter or margarine
1 pkg. yeast
1/2 c. warm water
1 egg
4 1/2 c. sifted flour
Cooking oil
Sugar

Scald milk; add molasses, salt and butter. Stir to melt butter; cool to lukewarm. Soften yeast in warm water in large bowl; add milk mixture, egg and 2 1/2 cups flour. Beat to a smooth soft dough. Cover; let rise until doubled in bulk. Spread remaining flour on board; turn dough onto board. Knead dough, working in enough flour to stiffen. Shape into ball; cover with bowl. Let rest for 10 minutes. Roll dough, half at a time, to 1/2-inch thick rectangle. Cut with 3-inch doughnut cutter; cover with towel. Let rise until doubled in bulk. Fry doughnuts, 3 or 4 at a time, in hot deep oil until brown on both sides. Drain on absorbent paper; roll in sugar.

FRENCH MARKET DOUGHNUTS

1/4 c. shortening
1/2 c. sugar
1 tsp. salt
1 c. boiling water
1 c. evaporated milk
1 pkg. yeast
1/2 c. lukewarm water
2 eggs
7 c. sifted flour
Cooking oil
Confectioners' sugar

Combine shortening, sugar and salt in mixing bowl; add boiling water, stirring to melt shortening. Add milk; cool to lukewarm. Soften yeast in lukewarm water. Beat eggs; add eggs, yeast and 4 cups flour to milk mixture. Beat until smooth; work in remaining flour. Turn dough onto lightly floured board; knead only until smooth. Place dough in greased bowl; cover. Refrigerate for 2 hours or up to 5 days. Roll about 1/4 of the dough at a time to 1/16-inch thick rectangle. Cut in small squares or triangles; let rise until light. Fry in hot deep oil until brown. Shake in bag with confectioners' sugar; serve hot.

GLAZED CRULLERS

2 1/2 c. flour
2 tsp. baking powder
1/2 tsp. salt
3 eggs
3/4 c. sugar
1/4 c. softened butter
1 tsp. vanilla
1 c. confectioners' sugar

Sift flour, baking powder and salt together. Beat eggs with electric mixer at medium speed until light, beating in sugar gradually. Add butter and vanilla; beat for 3 minutes. Stir in flour mixture with fork. Dough will be soft. Shape dough into finger-sized pieces with floured hands. Drop into hot deep fat; fry until brown. Drain on absorbent paper. Combine confectioners' sugar with enough warm water to make thin glaze; dip warm crullers into glaze.

GOLDEN CAKE DOUGHNUTS

3 1/2 c. flour
1 tsp. baking powder
1 tsp. soda
1/2 tsp. salt
1 tsp. nutmeg
2 eggs
1 1/4 c. sugar
2 tbsp. melted butter
1 tsp. vanilla
1 c. sour milk

Sift flour, baking powder, soda, salt and nutmeg together. Combine eggs, sugar, butter and vanilla in electric mixer bowl; beat at medium speed until fluffy. Beat in 2 cups flour mixture and milk alternately. Stir in remaining flour with spoon. Cover dough; refrigerate for at least 2 hours. Turn dough onto floured surface; roll to 1/4-inch thick rectangle. Cut with floured doughnut cutter. Fry in hot deep fat until golden brown. Drain on absorbent paper.

GRANDMOTHER'S DOUGHNUTS

6 3/4 c. flour
1 1/2 tsp. salt
2 tbsp. baking powder
1 1/2 tsp. soda
1 1/2 tsp. nutmeg
3 eggs
1 1/2 c. sugar
3 tbsp. oil
1 1/2 c. mashed potatoes
1 1/2 c. sour milk

Sift flour, salt, baking powder, soda and nutmeg together. Beat eggs until light, adding sugar gradually. Add oil, potatoes and milk; mix well. Stir in flour mixture; chill dough for about 1 hour. Turn dough onto lightly floured board; roll thin. Cut with doughnut cutter. Fry in hot deep fat until brown. Drain on paper towels.

MALASADAS

4 c. flour
1 tsp. salt
1 c. sugar
2 pkg. yeast
2 c. warm milk
8 eggs
Honey

Sift flour, salt and sugar together. Soften yeast in 1 cup milk in large mixing bowl; add 2 cups flour mixture gradually, beating until smooth. Beat in eggs, one at a time; add remaining flour alternately with remaining milk. Cover; let rise until doubled in bulk. Stir dough down; drop by tablespoons into hot deep fat. Fry until golden brown. Drain on absorbent paper. Dip into warm honey; serve immediately.

MOLASSES DOUGHNUTS

2 c. sifted flour
2 tsp. baking powder
1/2 tsp. soda
1 tsp. salt
1 tsp. cinnamon
1 tsp. ginger
1/2 tsp. ground cloves
1 egg
2/3 c. milk
Cooking oil
1/3 c. unsulphured molasses
Confectioners' sugar

Sift flour, baking powder, soda, salt and spices together. Add egg, milk, 1/4 cup oil and molasses; mix well. Pour 2 inches oil in skillet; heat to 365 degrees. Drop batter from teaspoon into hot oil; cook for 2 minutes, turning once. Drain on absorbent paper. Sprinkle with confectioners' sugar.

NEW ENGLAND CRULLERS

3 1/2 c. flour
3 tsp. baking powder
1/2 tsp. salt
2 tbsp. nutmeg

1/4 c. shortening	*1 c. milk*
1 c. sugar	*Powdered sugar*
2 eggs	

Sift flour, baking powder, salt and nutmeg together. Cream shortening and sugar until light; beat in eggs. Add flour mixture alternately with milk. Turn dough onto lightly floured surface. Knead lightly; roll 1/2 inch thick. Cut into 8 x 3/4-inch strips; fold each strip. Twist; press ends together firmly. Fry in deep hot fat for about 3 minutes, turning once. Drain; roll in powdered sugar. Yield: 2 dozen.

NUT PUFFS

1 c. buttermilk	*1 pkg. yeast*
1/2 c. sugar	*2 eggs*
1/4 c. shortening	*1/2 c. finely chopped walnuts*
1 tsp. salt	*1 tbsp. vinegar*
1/2 tsp. soda	
3 1/2 c. flour	

Heat buttermilk to lukewarm. Combine sugar, shortening, salt and soda in large bowl; stir in buttermilk. Add 1 cup flour and yeast; beat until smooth. Beat in eggs; add walnuts and remaining flour. Cover; let rise for 1 hour and 30 minutes. Punch dough down; let rest for 30 minutes. Drop dough from teaspoon into hot deep fat containing vinegar. Fry for 4 to 5 minutes.

DROP DOUGHNUTS

2 c. sifted flour	*1/2 c. sugar*
2 1/2 tsp. baking powder	*2 eggs*
1/2 tsp. salt	*1 tbsp. grated orange rind*
2 tbsp. soft shortening	*1/2 c. orange juice*

Mix flour, baking powder and salt. Blend shortening and sugar; beat in eggs and orange rind. Add flour mixture alternately with orange juice. Drop dough from teaspoon into hot deep fat; fry until golden brown. Drain on absorbent paper.

ORANGE-COATED CRULLERS

1 pkg. yeast	*1/4 c. butter*
1/4 c. warm water	*1 egg*
1 c. sugar	*4 c. flour*
1 tsp. salt	*1 tbsp. grated orange rind*
1 c. milk	

Soften yeast in warm water in large mixer bowl; stir in 1/4 cup sugar and salt. Scald milk; melt butter in hot milk. Cool to lukewarm. Add milk mixture, egg and 1 cup flour to yeast mixture; beat at low speed of mixer until blended. Add 1 1/2 cups flour; beat until smooth. Stir in remaining flour with spoon. Turn dough onto floured surface; knead until smooth and elastic. Place dough in greased bowl; cover. Let rise until doubled in bulk. Punch dough down; turn onto floured surface. Round dough up into smooth ball; pat out. Cut into 24 pieces; shape each piece to 12 x 3/4-inch roll. Fold rolls in half; pinch ends together. Twist rolls tightly. Cover; let rise for about 45 minutes. Fry in hot deep fat until golden brown. Drain on paper towels. Mix remaining sugar and orange rind; roll twists in mixture.

SPICY ORANGE DOUGHNUTS

4 c. flour	*3 eggs*
1/4 tsp. cinnamon	*1 1/4 c. sugar*
1 1/2 tsp. nutmeg	*3/4 c. sour cream*
2 tsp. baking powder	*1 1/2 tbsp. shortening*
1 tsp. soda	*Juice and grated rind of 1 orange*
1/2 tsp. salt	

Sift flour, cinnamon, nutmeg, baking powder, soda and salt together. Beat eggs well, beating in sugar gradually. Add sour cream, shortening, orange juice, orange rind and flour mixture; mix well. Turn dough onto floured surface; roll about 1/2 inch thick. Cut with doughnut cutter. Fry in hot deep oil until brown on both sides. Drain on paper towels.

ORANGE DOUGHNUT PUFFS

2 eggs	*2 tsp. grated orange rind*
1 1/2 c. sugar	*6 c. sifted flour*
1 2/3 c. evaporated milk	*1/2 tsp. salt*
2 tbsp. lemon juice	*2 tsp. soda*
1/3 c. fresh orange juice	*Sifted confectioners' sugar*

Beat eggs until light in medium mixing bowl. Beat in sugar gradually. Add milk, lemon juice, orange juice and rind, mixing well. Sift flour with salt and soda. Add to liquid mixture gradually, blending just until dry ingredients are dampened. Do not over-mix. Use 2 teaspoons to lift small amounts of batter from bowl; push batter into deep 370-degree fat in skillet. Fry for 4 to 5 minutes or until golden brown. Lift onto absorbent paper to drain. Cool; sprinkle with confectioners' sugar. Yield: about 6 dozen doughnut puffs.

Orange Doughnut Puffs . . . Easy-to-prepare tidbits a popular fare at breakfast or for snacks.

RAISED DOUGHNUTS

2 pkg. yeast
1/2 c. sugar
1/4 c. lukewarm water
1/2 c. shortening
2 tsp. salt
1 c. milk
2 eggs
5 c. flour
Confectioners' sugar glaze

Dissolve yeast and 1 teaspoon sugar in lukewarm water; let stand until bubbly. Combine shortening, remaining sugar and salt in mixing bowl. Scald milk; pour over shortening mixture. Stir to dissolve shortening; cool to lukewarm. Beat eggs; add eggs and yeast to shortening mixture. Stir in flour, one cup at a time. Turn dough onto floured surface; roll to 1/2-inch thick rectangle. Cut with doughnut cutter; let rise until light. Fry in hot deep oil until brown. Drain on paper towels; brush with glaze.

SOPAPILLAS

1/2 c. sugar
1 tsp. salt
2 tbsp. corn oil
1 egg, beaten
1 pkg. yeast
6 c. (about) flour

Combine sugar, salt and oil; pour in 2 cups boiling water. Cool to lukewarm. Stir in egg and yeast. Add enough flour to make easily handled dough. Turn dough onto floured surface; knead until smooth. Place in greased bowl; cover. Let rise in warm place until doubled in bulk. Punch dough down; turn onto floured surface. Knead lightly; roll 1/4 inch thick. Cut into diamonds or triangles. Fry in hot deep fat for 2 to 3 minutes or until browned on both sides. Remove with tongs; drain on paper towels. Serve with jam or honey. Yield: 20-30 servings.

TEA DOUGHNUTS

1 1/2 c. flour
1/4 tsp. salt
2 tsp. baking powder
1/2 tsp. cinnamon
1/4 tsp. nutmeg
1 egg
1/2 c. sugar
1 tbsp. melted butter
1/2 c. milk
1 tsp. vanilla
Grated rind of 1 lemon

Combine flour, salt, baking powder and spices. Beat egg; stir in sugar and butter. Add flour mixture alternately with milk; mix until smooth. Fold in vanilla and lemon rind. Drop dough from teaspoon into hot deep fat; fry for about 5 minutes or until brown.

TIPSY DOUGHNUTS

5 egg yolks
1/2 tsp. salt
3 tbsp. sugar
1 tbsp. brandy or cognac
5 tbsp. sour cream
2 1/2 c. cake flour
Powdered sugar

Combine egg yolks and salt in mixer bowl; beat at high speed of mixer until thick. Beat in sugar and brandy. Add sour cream and flour; beat by hand until blended. Turn dough onto floured surface; knead until smooth. Cut dough in half; roll as thin as possible. Cut into 2 x 4-inch strips. Make slit in center of each strip; pull one end of strip through slit. Fry in hot deep fat until light brown on both sides. Drain on absorbent paper; sprinkle with powdered sugar.

Dressings

Dressings are well-seasoned, starch-based mixtures, sometimes known also as stuffings. They are flavorful accompaniments to poultry, fish, boned and rolled meats (lamb, pork, and veal shoulder roasts), and vegetables. Dressing can either be baked in a pan, arranged in alternate layers with food being cooked; or it can be baked to fill a pocket or opening of food. Dressings, when used to stuff a food, prevent natural food juices from escaping while preserving the original shape of a roast or piece of food. Dress rich meats and seafood with simple or fruit dressings. Dress ducks and geese with orange, apple, or prune dressings to cut and absorb grease. Plain, lean meats require richer stuffings.

AVAILABILITY: Dressing breads and certain combinations of dressing ingredients requiring only the addition of liquid are available year-round.

PREPARATION: To prepare a stuffing allow 1 cup dressing per pound meat or fish. Use a dressing immediately; *never* prepare dressing before you need it because of the high amount of bacterial activity present in uncooked dressing. Because dressings absorb juices and therefore expand in volume, fill cavities lightly. If onions, shallots, or garlic are used in a dressing, saute them before combining with bread and liquid. Dressing mixtures may include precooked sausage or pork, herbs, oysters, clams, mushrooms, chestnuts and/or anchovies.

STORING: Prepared dressings may be stored 2-3 days in refrigerator. Always remove stuffing from a cavity before storing. Dressings do not freeze well.

(See POULTRY.)

BACON-MUSHROOM FISH DRESSING

6 strips bacon, diced
1/2 c. sliced mushrooms
2 c. stale bread cubes
1 tbsp. grated onion
2 tbsp. lemon juice
1 tbsp. parsley
1 tsp. sage
1 c. diced cooked shrimp
1/2 tsp. salt
1/8 tsp. pepper
1 egg, beaten

Cook bacon in large skillet until partially crisp; drain. Saute mushrooms in bacon drippings in skillet; stir in bacon and bread crumbs. Brown bread slightly, tossing lightly. Remove from heat. Stir in onion, lemon juice, parsley, sage, shrimp, seasonings and egg.

DRESSING FOR SALMON

1 1/2 c. minced onion
2 c. diced celery
1/2 c. butter, melted
2 c. chopped stuffed olives
2 2/3 c. cooked rice
1/2 tsp. salt
1/2 tsp. pepper
1/2 tsp. sage
1/2 tsp. thyme

Saute onion and celery in butter in skillet until tender. Add remaining ingredients; mix well. Yield: Dressing for 6-8 pound salmon.

TART VEGETABLE STUFFING FOR SALMON

3/4 c. ground carrots
3/4 c. ground onions
1/2 c. chopped celery
2 c. soft bread crumbs
1/4 c. melted butter
1 tsp. salt
2 tbsp. lemon juice

Combine all ingredients, mixing well. Yield: Dressing for 1 large salmon.

APPLE-RAISIN STUFFING FOR PORK

6 pared apples, diced
1 c. raisins
1 tsp. cinnamon
1/8 tsp. nutmeg
1 tsp. salt
12 slices dry bread, cubed
1/4 c. sugar
1 tsp. seasoning salt

Combine apples, raisins, cinnamon, nutmeg, salt, bread cubes, sugar and seasoning salt. Blend in enough hot water to moisten well.

ALL-TIME POULTRY DRESSING

Chopped turkey giblets
1/2 lb. ground beef
1 med. onion, chopped
4 c. bread cubes
4 celery stalks, chopped
1 tsp. salt
1 tsp. pepper
1/2 tsp. thyme
1 tsp. garlic powder
1 tsp. monosodium glutamate
1/2 tsp. sage
Chopped parsley leaves

Saute giblets, beef and onion in skillet until giblets and beef are done and onion is tender. Drain. Combine giblet mixture, bread and celery in large mixing bowl; add seasonings and parsley. Stir in about 3/4 cup boiling water. Yield: Dressing for 10-14 pound turkey.

CORN BREAD-SAUSAGE DRESSING

1 1/2 lb. bulk sausage
4 onions, chopped
1 stalk celery, chopped
6 c. soft white bread crumbs
1 tbsp. salt
2 tsp. poultry seasoning
1 tbsp. herb seasonings (opt.)
2 tbsp. steak sauce
2 eggs, slightly beaten
1 c. chicken broth
6 c. crumbled corn bread

Cook sausage in large skillet over medium heat, breaking up with fork. Remove sausage to mixing bowl, reserving 1/2 cup drippings in skillet. Saute onions and celery in reserved drippings for about 5 minutes or until tender. Add sauteed mixture to sausage; add remaining ingredients, mixing well. Yield: Dressing for 12-14 pound turkey.

CORN BREAD STUFFING

1 c. minced onion
1 c. minced celery
1/4 c. minced parsley
1/2 c. margarine
5 c. corn bread crumbs
3 c. soft bread crumbs
1 c. chopped pecans
1 1/4 tsp. salt
1/4 tsp. pepper
1 tsp. sage
1/2 tsp. thyme
1/2 c. cooking sherry

Saute onion, celery and parsley in margarine for about 5 minutes or until tender. Add remaining ingredients, mixing well. Yield: 9 cups.

DRESSING FOR TURKEY

1 c. raisins
1 c. chopped onion
1 c. chopped celery
3/4 c. turkey fat
3 c. diced crustless bread
1 tsp. salt
1 tsp. pepper
1/2 c. sugar
1/2 c. turkey stock
1/2 c. olive liquid
2 tbsp. vinegar
1 1/2 c. pitted ripe olives

Soak raisins in water to cover until plump. Drain. Saute onion and celery in turkey fat in large Dutch oven. Toss bread lightly in sauteed mixture. Add seasonings, sugar, stock, olive liquid, vinegar and olives. Stir in raisins.

EGGPLANT DRESSING FOR TURKEY

1 pared eggplant, diced
1/2 c. chopped onion
1/2 c. chopped celery
Butter
1 pkg. herb-seasoned stuffing mix
1 tsp. poultry seasoning
1 tsp. salt
1/2 tsp. pepper
2 eggs, beaten

Cook eggplant in salted water until tender; drain well. Saute onion and celery in butter until tender. Combine eggplant, sauteed mixture, stuffing mix, seasonings and eggs. Yield: Dressing for 10-12 pound turkey.

POTATO DRESSING FOR POULTRY

1 c. diced celery
1/2 c. diced onion
2 c. bread cubes
4 tbsp. margarine
3 eggs, beaten
Chopped parsley sprigs
2 c. mashed potatoes

Simmer celery and onion in 1/4 cup water until tender. Brown bread cubes in margarine in skillet. Fold eggs and parsley into potatoes; stir in celery mixture and bread cubes. Spoon into greased casserole; cover. Bake at 350 degrees for 30 minutes; uncover. Bake for 15 minutes longer. Yield: 6 servings.

POTATO DRESSING FOR TURKEY

2 c. mashed potatoes
1 1/4 c. dry bread crumbs
1/4 c. butter, melted
1 egg, beaten
1 tsp. poultry seasoning
1 tsp. salt
1 tsp. sage
Pepper to taste
1 onion, finely chopped
1 c. chopped celery
Ground giblets

Combine all ingredients, mixing well. Yield: Dressing for 10 to 12-pound turkey.

OLD-FASHIONED DRESSING FOR TURKEY

7 c. chopped onions
9 c. diced celery
2 c. butter
25 slices bread
1 tbsp. nutmeg
1/2 tsp. monosodium glutamate
1 1/2 tbsp. salt
1/2 tsp. pepper
2 tsp. poultry seasoning
4 eggs, slightly beaten

Saute onions and celery in butter until tender. Toast bread in oven until dry and golden brown; soak in cold water until soft. Squeeze dry. Tear bread into small pieces; place in bowl. Add onions, celery and butter. Combine seasonings; add to bread mixture. Add eggs, mixing well. Stuff turkey with dressing. Place any remaining dressing in greased casserole. Cover. Bake at 325 degrees for 30 minutes.

OYSTER DRESSING FOR TURKEY

6 tbsp. margarine
6 tbsp. oil or shortening
1 1/2 c. chopped onion
1 1/2 c. chopped celery
8 slices bread, cubed
3 tbsp. minced parsley
Salt to taste
Pepper to taste
3/4 tsp. thyme
3/4 tsp. sage
3/4 tsp. marjoram
3/4 tsp. oregano
1 1/2 c. chopped oysters
2 eggs, beaten

Combine margarine and oil in skillet; saute onion and celery until tender. Soak bread in cold water; squeeze dry. Add bread, parsley, seasonings, oysters and eggs to sauteed mixture. Cook, stirring, over low heat until bread is lightly browned. Yield: Dressing for 8 to 10-pound turkey.

WILD RICE STUFFING FOR FOWL

1 3-oz. can sliced mushrooms
Butter
1 can beef broth
2 onions, chopped
1/2 c. wild rice
1 c. long grain rice
2 tbsp. snipped parsley

Drain mushrooms, reserving liquid. Broil mushrooms in butter in skillet. Combine reserved mushroom liquid and beef broth; add enough water to equal 2 cups liquid. Bring broth mixture and onions to boiling point in saucepan. Add wild rice; reduce heat. Cover; simmer for 20 minutes. Add long grain rice; return to boiling point. Cover; simmer for 20 minutes or until rice is done. Add mushrooms and 2 tablespoons butter; heat briefly. Stir in parsley. Yield: 6-8 servings.

RICE PARMESAN STUFFING FOR TURKEY

3 med. onions, diced
3 stalks of celery, diced
1 stick butter
1 tsp. salt
1/2 tsp. pepper
1 1/2 c. rice
2 eggs, beaten lightly
2 tbsp. sweet basil
2 tbsp. parsley
1 tsp. garlic salt
1/2 c. grated Parmesan cheese

Saute onions and celery in butter in covered skillet until tender. Add salt and pepper. Prepare rice according to package directions. Combine sauteed mixture, rice, eggs, basil, parsley, garlic salt and cheese, mixing well. Yield: Dressing for 10 pound turkey.

SAVORY DRESSING FOR FOWL

Giblets
6 c. toasted bread cubes
1/4 c. minced parsley
1/4 c. chopped onion
1/4 c. chopped celery
1 tsp. salt
1/2 tsp. pepper
1 1/2 tsp. sage
1/2 c. milk
1 egg, beaten

Cook giblets in water to cover until tender. Drain and chop giblets, reserving 3/4 cup stock. Combine bread cubes, parsley, onion, celery and seasonings; add milk, egg, giblets and reserved giblet stock. Chill for 1 hour to blend flavors. Yield: Dressing for 5-6 pound turkey.

TURKEY DRESSING WITH MUSHROOMS

1 c. chopped onion
1 c. diced celery with leaves
1/2 c. butter
1/2 tsp. hot sauce
1/2 tsp. poultry seasoning
Salt
8 c. bread cubes
2 tbsp. chopped parsley
1/2 c. sliced mushrooms, drained
1/4 c. dry white wine
1/2 c. chopped pecans

Saute onion and celery in butter until tender; add seasonings. Pour sauteed mixture over bread; add parsley, mushrooms, wine and pecans, tossing dressing lightly. Yield: Dressing for 12 pound turkey.

WATER CHESTNUT DRESSING

1 c. yellow cornmeal
1 c. buttermilk
1 egg, slightly beaten
2 tsp. baking powder
1 tsp. soda
1 tsp. salt
1 tbsp. sugar
10 slices bread
15 crackers
6 hard-cooked eggs, chopped
5 c. broth
1 can water chestnuts, diced
1 tsp. rubbed sage
Pepper to taste

Combine cornmeal, buttermilk, egg, baking powder, soda, salt and sugar. Spoon mixture into greased pan. Bake at 450 degrees for about 30 minutes or until done. Brown bread slices and crackers in oven; crumble with corn bread. Add eggs, broth, water chestnuts, sage and pepper. Place in baking pan. Bake at 400 degrees for 20 minutes. Yield: 12 servings.

Duck

DUCKS WITH ORANGES IN CASSEROLE

2 young ducks
6 sm. carrots, sliced
1 pkg. frozen peas
3 sm. onions, sliced
1 c. canned lima beans
2 tbsp. flour
Juice and rind of 4 oranges
1 glass currant jelly
1/4 c. cranberry juice
1 tsp. salt
1/8 tsp. pepper
3 c. mashed potatoes
6 slices bacon
1/4 tsp. paprika
1/4 c. chopped parsley

Cut ducks into serving pieces; brown in frying pan in small amount melted fat, reserving drippings in pan. Place carrots, peas, onions and lima beans in 10 x 15-inch roasting pan with 1 cup water. Place browned duck pieces over vegetables; cover. Bake at 375 degrees for 1 hour. Combine flour, juice of oranges and grated rind, reserving some of rind for topping, jelly, cranberry juice, salt and pepper. Thin with small amount of liquid from ducks and vegetables. Season with additional salt, if desired. Simmer orange juice mixture until well blended. Spread duck pieces with mashed potatoes. Cut bacon slices into halves. Top potatoes with 2 halves of bacon. Sprinkle with paprika, reserved orange rind and chopped parsley. Return to oven. Bake at 475 degrees until bacon is crisp.

GLAZED DUCKLING WITH PINEAPPLE-ORANGE SAUCE

1 13 1/2-oz. can pineapple chunks
2 tbsp. chopped preserved ginger
2 tbsp. preserved ginger syrup
1/3 c. light corn syrup
1/3 c. sugar
1 tbsp. grated orange rind
1/3 c. orange juice
3 tbsp. lemon juice
1 tbsp. chopped fresh mint (opt.)
1 4 1/2 to 5-lb. frozen duckling, thawed
1/2 tsp. salt
1 c. diced orange sections
2 tsp. cornstarch

Drain pineapple, reserving juice. Combine pineapple juice, preserved ginger, ginger syrup, corn syrup, sugar, orange rind, orange and lemon juice. Simmer for 10 minutes; add mint. Set aside. Sprinkle neck and body cavities of duckling with salt. Skewer neck skin to back. Tie wings against breast. Tie legs together loosely, looping cord around tail. Bake at 325 degrees for 3 hours or until meat on drumstick is tender. Baste with pineapple glaze several times during last 30 minutes of cooking. Add pineapple chunks and orange sections to remaining glaze. Blend in cornstarch. Cook until thickened and clear. Serve with duckling. Yield: 4 servings.

WILD DUCK A LA FAUVETTE

2 wild ducks, halved
2 tbsp. butter, melted
2 tbsp. sherry
2 tbsp. tomato paste
2 tbsp. flour
1 1/2 c. bouillon
1/2 c. dry red wine
1 tsp. salt
1/4 tsp. pepper
1/2 lb. mushrooms, sliced
1 bay leaf
2 c. cooked wild rice, molded

Place ducks in butter in Dutch oven; cook, turning often, until dark brown. Pour sherry over ducks; remove ducks. Stir sherry with pan drippings; add tomato paste. Add flour gradually, stirring well; add bouillon and red wine, stirring briskly. Bring to a boil; return ducks to sauce. Add salt, pepper, mushrooms and bay leaf. Cover; cook over low heat until tender or for about 2 hours. Remove ducks; keep warm. Strain sauce; skim off fat. Return sauce to stove; reheat. Place rice molds between duck halves; spoon sauce over ducks. Garnish with spiced apples. Yield: 4 servings.

ROAST WATER FOWL

2 1 1/4-lb. wild ducks, cleaned
1 onion, chopped
1 garlic clove, minced
2 tbsp. unsalted butter
1 tsp. paprika
1/2 tsp. salt
1/4 tsp. hot sauce
1 lb. sliced bacon
4 c. cooked wild rice

Rub duck cavities with onion and garlic. Combine butter, paprika, salt and hot sauce; rub into duck skins. Truss legs together. Wrap ducks in cheesecloth; place, breasts down, on rack in greased shallow pan. Bake at 325 degrees for 1 hour, basting occasionally. Turn ducks over; remove cheesecloth. Cover ducks with bacon strips. Bake for about 1 hour longer. Serve ducks on platter of wild rice; garnish with spiced crab apples. Yield: 4 servings.

Roast Water Fowl . . . Wild ducks basted with garlic, onion, butter, and hot sauce, then baked.

ROAST WILD DUCK

1 wild duck	*1 or 2 apples*
Salt and pepper to taste	*1 or 2 onions*
	1 recipe dressing

Rub cavity of duck with salt and pepper. Quarter apples and onions; fill cavity. Brush small amount of fat on outside of duck; place in baking pan. Bake at 350 degrees for about 2 hours. Remove from oven. Discard apples and onions; place dressing around duck. Return to oven. Bake until drumsticks will twist out of joint. Yield: 1-2 servings.

ROAST WILD DUCK AND RICE STUFFING

2 c. wild rice	*1/4 c. melted margarine*
1/2 c. butter	*2 tsp. grated onion*
2 tsp. salt	*1 wild duck*
1/2 tsp. pepper	*Salad oil*
1/2 tsp. sage	*Bacon slices (opt.)*
1/4 tsp. thyme	

Cover rice with warm water. Soak for 1 hour; drain. Bring 4 cups water to a boil in top of double boiler; add rice, butter and salt. Cook, covered, for 2 hours. Drain; fluff rice by shaking pan over low heat for 10 minutes. Add pepper, sage, thyme, margarine and onion to rice. Rub inside of duck with salt. Fill with rice stuffing. Rub outside of duck with small amount of salad oil; lay bacon slices over breast, if desired. Place in roasting pan. Bake at 325 degrees until tender and browned. Baste with pan drippings occasionally during baking.

Dumplings

Dumplings are small pieces of dough usually made from a flour base. There are two types of dumplings, those simmered with soups and stews and those crusts of dough filled with fruit and baked or steamed for dessert. Dumplings used in soups and stews should be light and fluffy, moist on the outside and dry and flaky on the inside. In some recipes, bread crumbs or cereals replace flour. Herbed or potato dumplings may be served with pot roasts or casseroles.

PREPARATION: *Soup and Stew Dumplings*—Prepare dough according to specific recipe. Drop by spoonfuls into bubbling chicken or meat broth. Simmer slowly, uncovered, 10 minutes; cover and simmer 10 minutes more. Dough will drop from spoon easily if spoon is first dipped in liquid and dough is slipped off with rubber spatula. *Fruit-filled Dessert Dumplings*—Prepare dough according to specific recipe. Roll out 1/8 inch thick. Cut into squares. Place fruit on squares and bring opposite ends of dough over fruit to cover it. Ends should overlap. Cook according to recipe.

BREAD DUMPLINGS

1 lb. loaf bread	*1 egg*
1/4 c. salad oil	*1 tsp. salt*
3/4 c. milk	

Remove crusts from bread; cube. Combine oil, milk, egg and salt; pour over bread cubes. Knead mixture. Shape portions of kneaded mixture into 8 small loaves. Wrap each loaf tightly in aluminum foil, sealing edges to make waterproof. Chill well. Drop wrapped loaves in boiling water; cook for 45 minutes. Remove foil; serve with gravy.

CHEESE AND POTATO DUMPLINGS

2 lb. potatoes	*1 c. flour*
1 egg	*Nutmeg to taste*
1 1/2 tsp. salt	*1/4 lb. butter, melted*
1/2 c. cottage cheese	

Peel potatoes; boil until tender. Mash; cool. Add egg, salt, cheese, flour and nutmeg; mix well. Knead lightly until smooth. Shape into long thick roll; cut into 1-inch pieces. Roll into dumplings. Cook in rapidly boiling salted water until dumplings rise to surface; simmer for 5 to 7 minutes longer or until cooked through. Drain; pour butter over dumplings.

CRACKER DUMPLINGS

3 slices white bread	*1/4 tsp. garlic salt*
1 c. milk	*1/4 tsp. onion salt*
1/2 lb. saltine crackers, rolled fine	*3 eggs*
	1 tbsp. butter
	Flour

Tear bread into small pieces. Soak bread in milk; add cracker crumbs, salts, eggs and butter. Blend until mixture will hold shape. Form into six or eight cylinders 1 inch in diameter. Roll in flour until lightly coated. Drop into boiling salted water; cook, covered, for 20 minutes. Drain well. Garnish with parsley flakes. Serve with pork, veal or chicken.

CREAM OF WHEAT DUMPLINGS

1 egg, separated	*1 c. finely minced chicken livers*
2 tbsp. butter, softened	*1/4 tsp. pepper*
3 tsp. cream of wheat	*2 to 3 sprigs of parsley, chopped*
1 tsp. flour	

Combine egg yolk, butter, cream of wheat and flour; mix well. Beat egg white until stiff peaks form. Add egg white; fold in remaining ingredients. Roll out; cut into small strips. Let stand for 5 to 10 minutes. May be dropped into hot broth, soup or stew. Simmer, covered, for 10 minutes.

Country Dumpling Dinner . . . A hearty main dish of spareribs, sauerkraut, and dumplings.

COUNTRY DUMPLING DINNER

4 lb. spareribs
Salt and pepper
2 tbsp. shortening
1 1-lb. 11-oz. can sauerkraut
1 tsp. caraway seed
1 1/4 c. evaporated milk
1/4 c. instant potatoes
1 egg, slightly beaten
1 1/2 c. sifted flour
1 tbsp. baking powder

Cut ribs into serving portions; season with salt and pepper to taste. Melt shortening in large kettle. Add ribs; cook until lightly browned on all sides. Add 1 quart water, 1 teaspoon salt and 1/4 teaspoon pepper. Bring to a boil; cover. Reduce heat; simmer for 1 hour. Add sauerkraut and caraway seed. Simmer for 30 minutes longer. Mix 1/2 cup water and 1/2 cup evaporated milk in medium saucepan. Bring to a boil; stir in instant potatoes. Remove from heat; beat in egg and remaining milk. Sift flour, 1 teaspoon salt and baking powder together. Add to potato mixture, stirring to blend well. Drop dumplings by tablespoonfuls onto boiling sauerkraut. Cook over moderate heat for 5 minutes. Cover; cook for 10 minutes longer. Serve immediately. Yield: 6 servings.

EASY DROP DUMPLINGS FOR STEW

1 c. sifted flour
1 1/2 tsp. baking powder
1/2 tsp. salt
1 tbsp. vegetable shortening
1/2 c. milk

Sift flour with baking powder and salt. Cut in shortening until mixture is of cornmeal consistency. Add milk; mix lightly until soft dough is formed. Drop from teaspoon into boiling stew. Cover tightly; cook without removing cover for 12 minutes.

LIVER DUMPLINGS

4 slices dry bread
1 lb. beef liver, ground
1 lge. onion, finely chopped
1 egg
1/2 tsp. salt
1/2 tsp. pepper
1/2 tsp. nutmeg
1/2 tsp. thyme
4 tbsp. bread crumbs
4 tbsp. flour
3/4 stick butter

Soak bread in water. Squeeze dry; crumble into bowl. Combine liver, onion, egg, seasonings, crumbs and flour with bread; blend thoroughly. Dip spoon into kettle of boiling salted water; spoon dumplings into water. More bread crumbs may be added if mixture seems too soft. Cook for 3 minutes; remove with slotted spoon. Brown butter; pour over dumplings.

BOHEMIAN LIVER DUMPLINGS

1 clove garlic, mashed
1/2 tsp. salt
1 c. calf liver, ground
4 eggs, beaten
2 c. cracker crumbs

Combine garlic, salt, liver and eggs; add cracker crumbs gradually to form soft dough. Drop dough from teaspoon onto floured board. Roll dough in flour gently to form balls 1 inch in diameter. Drop dumplings carefully into boiling broth; boil for 15 to 20 minutes.

NEVER-FAIL DUMPLINGS

2 c. sifted flour
3 tsp. baking powder
1/2 tsp. salt
1 tbsp. shortening
3/4 c. milk
Meat stock or chicken broth

Sift flour with baking powder and salt; cut in shortening. Add milk to make a drop batter. Drop by spoonfuls into boiling stock. Simmer, covered tightly, for 10 minutes. Serve at once.

POTATO-BREAD DUMPLINGS

8 med. potatoes
1/2 c. flour
2 eggs, slightly beaten
1 1/2 tsp. salt
1 slice bread
1 tbsp. minced onion
2 tbsp. butter

Steam potatoes until tender; peel. Rice potatoes; refrigerate, uncovered, overnight. Combine flour, eggs and salt with potatoes; mix well. Remove crusts from bread; cut into small cubes. Brown onion and bread cubes in butter. Roll 1 spoonful potato mixture around small amount of bread mixture. Repeat procedure until both mixtures are used. Drop dumplings into boiling water in large kettle; boil for 20 minutes or until cooked through. Drain; serve at once.

RICH POTATO DUMPLINGS

2 eggs, slightly beaten
3 c. cooked riced potatoes
1 tsp. salt
2 c. sifted flour
1 c. melted butter

Combine eggs and potatoes; mix well. Add salt to flour; blend into potato mixture. Form into 1 1/2-inch roll; cut into 1-inch pieces. Drop dumplings into boiling water gradually ; boil, covered, for 15 to 20 minutes or until cooked through. Drain; roll in butter. Yield: 5-6 servings.

RAISED DUMPLINGS

1 pkg. yeast
3/4 c. milk
2 tsp. salt
2 eggs, beaten
4 c. sifted flour
5 slices bread
Butter
5 qt. boiling broth

Dissolve yeast in 1/4 cup warm water. Scald milk; cool to lukewarm. Add salt and eggs to milk; combine with yeast. Add flour to milk mixture gradually; beat thoroughly until dough is smooth and elastic. Spread bread with butter; toast lightly. Cut bread into cubes; fold into dough. Place dough in greased bowl and set in warm place to rise until doubled in bulk. Shape into balls 1 inch in diameter; let rise again until doubled in bulk. Drop gently into broth and cook about 30 minutes.

SPAETZLE

3 c. flour
1 tsp. salt
Dash of nutmeg
Dash of paprika
4 eggs
Melted butter

Combine flour, salt, nutmeg and paprika in bowl. Add eggs and 3/4 cup water; beat until smooth. Place 3/4 cup mixture on dampened cutting board; smooth until thin. Cut off small strips with wet knife; drop into large kettle of boiling salted water. Cook for about 5 minutes or until tender. Lift out; place in dish. Pour butter over strips. Repeat procedure until all dough is used; serve with goulash, sauerbraten or soup. Yield: 4-6 servings.

STEAMED DUMPLINGS

1 pkg. yeast
1 tsp. sugar
4 tbsp. butter
1 egg
3/4 c. lukewarm milk
1 tsp. salt
1/4 tsp. ground nutmeg
3 1/2 c. flour

Dissolve yeast and sugar in 1/4 cup lukewarm water. Melt butter; cool. Beat egg in large mixing bowl; beat in butter. Add milk, salt, nutmeg, and yeast mixture to egg mixture. Add flour, 1/2 cup at a time, beating well after each addition. Place on lightly floured surface; knead for about 10 minutes. Place in greased bowl; cover. Let rise in warm place for 1 hour or until doubled in bulk. Punch down; knead for 3 to 4 minutes. Shape dough into twelve 1 1/2-inch balls. Spread damp towel over rack in large roasting pan; arrange dumplings on towel 2 inches apart. Add enough water to pan to come within 1 inch of rack. Bring to a boil over high heat; cover. Reduce heat; steam dumplings for 20 minutes or until firm to touch. Serve hot.

STRIP DUMPLINGS

1 1/2 c. flour
1 egg, beaten
3 tbsp. shortening
1/2 tsp. salt
Chicken broth
1 hard-cooked egg, finely chopped

Combine flour, egg, shortening, salt and 5 tablespoons water; mix well to form soft dough. Divide into three parts. Roll out paper thin; let dough dry for 20 minutes. Cut in small strips; drop in boiling broth. Cook dumplings for 10 to 15 minutes or until tender. Add hard-cooked egg; stir lightly.

QUICK APPLE DUMPLINGS

2 c. prepared biscuit mix
Soft butter
2 c. finely diced apples
1 tsp. cinnamon
1 1/4 c. sugar
1/2 c. nuts

Prepare biscuit mix according to package directions for dumplings. Roll dough 1/2 inch thick; spread with butter. Combine apples, cinnamon, 1/2 cup sugar and nuts. Spread over dough; roll up. Cut roll into 3/4-inch slices. Combine remaining sugar with 1/2 cup water; bring to a boil. Simmer, stirring constantly, until sugar is dissolved. Pour syrup into well-greased baking dish. Arrange apple rolls over syrup. Bake at 450 degrees for 15 to 20 minutes. Yield: 6-8 servings.

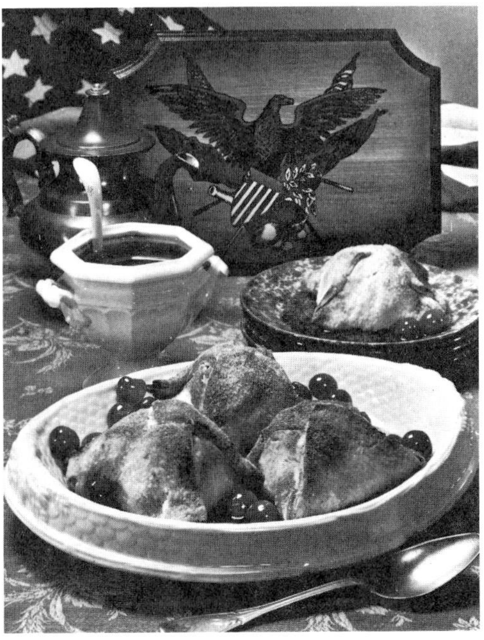

Cherry-Apple Dumplings . . . Fresh apples are stuffed with a cherry-walnut mixture and baked.

CHERRY-APPLE DUMPLINGS

2 2/3 c. sifted all-purpose flour
1 1/4 tsp. salt
1 c. vegetable shortening
1 8-oz. jar red maraschino cherries
3/4 tsp. cinnamon
1/3 c. (packed) light brown sugar
1/3 c. finely chopped walnuts
6 med. tart apples
Cream
Sugar

Combine flour and salt in bowl. Cut in shortening until of pea consistency. Sprinkle with 6 1/2 tablespoons water; toss with fork. Shape into ball. Roll pastry out on lightly floured surface to 14 x 21-inch rectangle. Cut into six 7-inch squares. Drain cherries, reserving 1/4 cup syrup. Chop half the cherries coarsely; drain on paper towels. Reserve remaining cherries. Combine chopped cherries, 1/4 teaspoon cinnamon, brown sugar and walnuts. Pare and core apples. Place 1 apple on each pastry square. Fill apple cavities with chopped cherry mixture. Moisten edges of squares with cream. Bring opposite points of pastry up over apples; press points together. Brush dumplings with cream. Blend 2 tablespoons sugar with remaining cinnamon; sprinkle over pastry. Place dumplings on ungreased baking sheet. Bake in 400-degree oven for about 30 to 35 minutes or until lightly browned. Spread 1 cup sugar evenly over bottom of large saucepan. Place over low heat and allow to stand undisturbed until sugar melts and forms light golden brown liquid. Bring 3/4 cup water and reserved cherry syrup to a boil. Add boiling mixture to caramelized sugar gradually. Stir until sugar dissolves and clear thick syrup is formed. Add reserved whole cherries. Serve sauce over dumplings. Yield: 6 servings.

APPLE-HONEY DUMPLINGS

6 med. apples
2 c. sifted flour
1 1/2 tsp. baking powder
1/2 tsp. salt
1/2 c. shortening
1/3 c. milk
1 tbsp. butter
6 tbsp. honey
1 tbsp. lemon juice
1/4 tsp. salt

Pare and core apples. Sift flour with baking powder and salt; cut in shortening. Add milk, mixing until soft dough is formed. Roll dough into 12 x 8-inch rectangle; cut into six squares. Place an apple in each square. Combine butter, honey, lemon juice and salt; blend well. Fill apple centers with mixture. Moisten edges of dough with cold water. Bring four corners of dough on top of apple; press edges firmly together. Place in greased 10 x 10 x 2-inch pan.

Honeysauce

3/4 c. honey
2 tbsp. butter
2 tbsp. shortening
1/4 tsp. salt
1/4 tsp. cinnamon
1/4 tsp. nutmeg

Combine honey, butter, shortening and salt with 1 1/2 cups water. Bring to a boil; boil for 5 minutes. Pour over dumplings. Sprinkle with cinnamon and nutmeg. Bake at 400 degrees for 30 to 35 minutes. Yield: 6 servings.

BLUEBERRY DUMPLINGS

2 1/2 c. blueberries
Sugar
Salt
1 tbsp. lemon juice
1 c. all-purpose flour
2 tsp. baking powder
1 tbsp. butter
1/2 c. milk

Mix blueberries, 1/3 cup sugar, dash of salt and 1 cup water in medium saucepan; bring to a boil. Simmer, covered, for 5 minutes; add lemon juice. Sift flour, 2 tablespoons sugar, baking powder and 1/4 teaspoon salt together; cut in butter till consistency of coarse meal. Add milk all at once; stir just until flour is dampened. Drop from tablespoon into simmering blueberry mixture. Cover tightly; cook over low heat for 10 minutes without removing cover. Yield: 6 servings.

CHERRY DUMPLINGS

1 can pitted sour cherries
Sugar
1 c. flour
2 tsp. baking powder
1/4 tsp. salt
1/2 c. milk
1/2 pt. whipping cream

Bring cherries and 1 cup sugar to a boil. Sift flour, baking powder and salt into bowl; add milk to make stiff dough. Drop from tablespoon into boiling cherries; cover tightly. Simmer for 10 minutes. Whip cream with 2 teaspoons sugar. Serve dumplings warm with whipped cream.

PLUM DUMPLINGS

1 pkg. yeast
Sugar
3 tbsp. shortening
1 1/4 c. milk
1 egg, beaten
Pinch of salt
6 c. flour
1 lge. can purple plums
1 1/2 sticks margarine, melted
Cinnamon

Combine yeast, 1/4 cup warm water and 1 teaspoon sugar in large cup. Add shortening and 1 cup sugar to milk; scald. Cool to lukewarm; add egg and salt. Stir yeast mixture into milk mixture in large bowl; add flour gradually to form a soft dough. Work in additional flour, if needed. Let rise in warm place until doubled in bulk. Pit plums; cover each plum completely with dough. Roll each dumpling in margarine. Arrange in greased baking dish, seam side down. Sprinkle with cinnamon and additional sugar. Let rise for 30 minutes. Bake at 425 degrees for 15 to 20 minutes or until lightly browned.

Éclairs

An eclair is a light and flaky pastry of French origin. It is similar to the cream puff and prepared from the same ingredients. (See *CREAM PUFF.*) Unlike the cream puff, it is oblong rather than round in shape.

PREPARATION: Eclairs are made from rich pastry dough, filled with whipped cream, ice cream, or custard, and iced with vanilla, chocolate, or coffee glaze. To fill pastry after baking, cut off tops with sharp knife. Remove any soggy or soft dough from the inside. Fill and replace tops. Chill and serve.

CHOCOLATE-FILLED ÉCLAIRS

1/4 c. butter
1/2 c. boiling water
1/2 c. sifted flour
1/4 tsp. salt
2 eggs
1 c. heavy cream
1/4 c. sugar
1 tbsp. cocoa
Confectioners' sugar

Preheat oven to 450 degrees. Combine butter and boiling water in saucepan over medium heat. Add flour and salt all at once, stirring vigorously with spoon until dough leaves side of pan in smooth mass. Remove from heat; beat in eggs, one at a time. Beat until smooth and stiff. Form dough into oblong shapes with wet spoon or cake decorator 3 inches apart on greased cookie sheet. Bake for 20 minutes. Reduce oven temperature to 350 degrees. Bake for 10 minutes longer or until golden brown. Cool on wire rack. Whip cream until stiff, beating in sugar and cocoa gradually. Split eclairs; fill with whipped cream. Sprinkle with confectioners' sugar.

ELEGANT EGGNOG ÉCLAIRS

1/2 c. water
1/4 c. butter
1/8 tsp. salt
1/2 c. sifted flour
2 eggs
2 1/2 tbsp. cornstarch
2 c. eggnog
1 tbsp. rum

Combine water, butter and salt in saucepan; bring to a boil. Add flour all at once, stirring until dough forms a ball. Beat in eggs, one at a time. Beat until dough is stiff and glossy. Drop dough from tablespoon onto greased baking sheet; shape dough into 4-inch long mounds. Bake at 400 degrees for 30 minutes. Remove to rack; slice off tops. Remove any moist dough; cool. Blend cornstarch and eggnog in saucepan. Cook over medium heat, stirring constantly, until thickened. Remove from heat; cool for about 10 minutes, stirring occasionally. Stir in rum; chill until firm. Fill eclairs with custard; drizzle with a chocolate or butterscotch sauce.

LEMON ÉCLAIRS

1 c. water
6 tbsp. butter
1 tsp. sugar
Dash of salt
Dash of nutmeg
1 c. sifted flour
4 eggs
1 pkg. lemon pudding mix
1/2 c. confectioners' sugar
Lemon juice

Combine water, butter, sugar, salt and nutmeg in saucepan; bring to a boil. Add flour all at once, stirring until dough clears side of pan. Beat in eggs, one at a time. Drop dough from spoon onto greased baking sheet; shape into oblongs. Bake at 425 degrees for 25 minutes. Cut small slit in side of each eclair; return to oven. Turn off heat; leave oven door open. Let eclairs dry for 10 minutes. Place on rack; cool enough to handle. Cut off tops; pull out any moist dough with fork. Prepare pudding mix according to package directions; chill until firm. Fill eclairs with pudding. Mix confectioners' sugar with enough lemon juice to make thin glaze; drizzle over eclairs.

PATE A CHOUX

3/4 c. flour
1/4 tsp. soda
1/4 tsp. salt
1 tbsp. sugar
1/4 c. butter or margarine
2 eggs
1 pkg. vanilla pudding mix
1 c. instant chocolate drink mix

Mix flour and soda. Combine salt, sugar, butter and 1 cup water in saucepan; bring to a boil. Remove from heat; add flour mixture all at once. Stir until dough forms a ball; beat in eggs, one at a time. Drop dough from teaspoon onto greased cookie sheet; shape into 2 x 1-inch oblong. Bake at 400 degrees for 30 minutes. Cool on rack. Prepare pudding mix according to package directions; chill until firm. Split eclairs; fill with pudding. Combine drink mix and 1 1/2 tablespoons hot water; spread over tops of eclairs.

Egg

Digestible and versatile eggs are good sources of protein, vitamins A and D, thiamine, riboflavin, and niacin. (1 large egg = 80 calories)

BUYING: Eggs are inspected before sale. Federal-State services grade eggs and establish weight requirements for each grade. The grades include: US grade AA or fresh fancy quality; US grade A; and, US grade B. Egg sizes include: Jumbo–30 ozs.; Extra large–27 ozs.; Large–24 ozs.; Medium–21 ozs.; Small–18 ozs.; and Peewee–15 ozs. The grade of an egg and the color of its shell do not affect food value.

STORING: Keep eggs *clean, cold,* and *covered.* Clean by wiping being careful to preserve thin, protective seal on eggshell. Store in refrigerator large end up. Cover stored eggs to prevent moisture loss and odor absorption. Maximum refrigerator storage time is 3 weeks; although 1 week is recommended. Keep separated eggs in refrigerator 2 days. Place yolks in container with small amount of cold water, seal; place whites in container, seal.

PREPARATION: Methods of preparation include boiling, poaching, frying, and scrambling. Accurate timing and low to moderate heat prevent rubbery, tasteless, dried out yolks.

STUFFED EGGS CURRY

1 doz. eggs, hard boiled
1 c. mayonnaise
1 tsp. chicken-seasoned stock base
1/4 tsp. white pepper
1/4 tsp. instant onion powder
1 tsp. curry powder
1/2 tsp. salt
1 c. minced cooked chicken

Slice cap off eggs 1/4 of the way down crosswise. Remove yolks; mash or force through a sieve. Add mayonnaise, stock base, pepper, onion powder, curry powder, salt and chicken. Mix well. Refill egg whites, piling yolk mixture high. Cap with smaller portion of white. Garnish each egg with rolled anchovies, sliced olives, capers, pimento, red or green onion and parsley. Caps may be tinted with food coloring and secured with colored toothpicks if desired. Yield: 12 servings.

Stuffed Eggs Curry . . . Hard-cooked eggs take on flavor excitement with a curry-based stuffing.

BRUNCH EGG CASSEROLE

2 c. croutons
1 c. shredded Cheddar cheese
4 eggs
2 c. milk
1/2 tsp. salt
1/2 tsp. prepared mustard
1/8 tsp. onion powder
Dash of pepper
4 slices cooked bacon

Combine croutons and cheese in greased 10 x 6 x 2-inch baking dish. Beat eggs; add milk and seasonings. Pour over crouton mixture in casserole. Crumble bacon over top. Bake at 325 degrees 1 hour or until eggs are set. Garnish with bacon curls if desired. Yield: 6 servings.

CREAMED DEVILED EGGS

12 hard-boiled eggs
1 tsp. salt
1/4 tsp. pepper
1/4 tsp. paprika
2 c. white sauce
1/2 c. buttered bread crumbs
1/4 c. grated cheese

Cut eggs in half lengthwise; remove yolks. Mash yolks with seasonings; stir in enough white sauce to moisten. Refill egg whites; press halves together. Place in casserole; cover with remaining white sauce. Combine bread crumbs and cheese; sprinkle over top. Bake at 400 degrees for 20 minutes or until brown. Yield: 6 servings.

EGG SALAD SANDWICHES

6 hard-cooked eggs, finely chopped
6 tbsp. minced celery
3 tbsp. sweet pickle relish
3 tbsp. minced parsley
1/2 tsp. dry mustard
Salt and pepper to taste
1/4 c. (about) mayonnaise
4 slices crisp bacon, crumbled
12 slices bread

Combine eggs, celery, pickle relish, parsley, dry mustard, salt and pepper in mixing bowl; moisten with mayonnaise. Chill until ready to serve. Stir in bacon. Spread egg mixture on half the bread; top with remaining bread.

PICKLED EGGS

12 hard-cooked eggs
1 tsp. whole cloves
2 tbsp. sliced gingerroot
1 tsp. peppercorns
3 c. cider vinegar
1 1/2 c. water
1 1/2 tsp. salt

Place eggs in large screw-top jar. Tie cloves, gingerroot and peppercorns in small cloth bag. Combine vinegar, water and salt in saucepan; add spice bag. Bring to a boil; cook for 10 minutes. Remove spice bag; chill vinegar mixture. Pour vinegar mixture over eggs; seal jar. Let stand for 2 days before serving.

MOLDED EGG SALAD

1 env. unflavored gelatin
1 tsp. salt
2 tsp. lemon juice
1/4 tsp. Worcestershire sauce
Dash of pepper
Mayonnaise
1 tsp. minced onion
1/4 c. minced celery
1/4 c. minced green pepper
1/4 c. minced pimento
4 hard-cooked eggs, chopped

Soften gelatin in 1/2 cup cold water; dissolve over low heat. Add salt, lemon juice, Worcestershire sauce and pepper. Cool. Stir in 3/4 cup mayonnaise, onion, celery, green pepper, pimento and eggs. Turn into mold; chill until firm. Garnish with celery tops; serve with mayonnaise. Yield: 6-8 servings.

MEXICAN EGG SANDWICH FILLING

6 hard-cooked eggs, finely chopped
10 stuffed green olives, minced
1/2 green pepper, minced
1/4 tsp. prepared mustard
1 tsp. sweet pickle liquid
1/4 c. minced celery
1/2 c. (about) mayonnaise
Salt and pepper to taste
1/2 tsp. paprika

Combine all ingredients; mix well. Yield: 4 servings.

DEVILED EGG CASSEROLE

6 hard-boiled eggs
2 tsp. prepared mustard
1 c. sour cream
1/4 tsp. salt
2 tbsp. butter
1/2 c. chopped green pepper
1/3 c. chopped onion
1/4 c. chopped pimento
1 can cream of mushroom soup
1/2 c. shredded Cheddar cheese

Halve eggs lengthwise; remove yolks. Mash yolks, mustard, 3 tablespoons sour cream and salt together. Fill egg whites with yolk mixture. Melt butter in large skillet; saute green pepper and onion until tender. Remove from heat; stir in pimento, soup and remaining sour cream. Place 1/2 of the soup mixture in 1 1/2-quart shallow baking dish; arrange eggs, cut side up, in single layer in dish. Pour remaining soup mixture over eggs; sprinkle with cheese. Bake at 350 degrees for 20 minutes or until heated through. Casserole may be prepared in advance and refrigerated.

EASTER SUPPER DISH

2 pkg. frozen peas
1 3-oz. can mushroom pieces
12 saltine crackers, crushed
3 tbsp. butter, melted
6 hard-boiled eggs
Sour cream
2 tsp. minced onion
1/2 tsp. salt
1/8 tsp. pepper
1/4 tsp. dry mustard
2 cans cream of mushroom soup
1/4 c. milk

Cook peas according to package directions; drain. Drain and chop mushrooms. Mix cracker crumbs and butter. Place peas in 11 x 8 x 2-inch baking dish; sprinkle with half the mushrooms. Halve eggs lengthwise; remove yolks. Mash yolks with remaining mushrooms, 2 tablespoons sour cream, onion, salt, pepper and mustard. Fill egg whites with yolk mixture; arrange eggs on peas. Blend soup, milk and 1/3 cup sour cream in saucepan; bring to a boil, stirring occasionally. Pour over eggs; sprinkle with buttered cracker crumbs. Bake at 350 degrees for 20 minutes.

EGG AND CHIPS

2 c. crushed potato chips
6 hard-cooked eggs, sliced
1 can cream of mushroom soup
1/2 c. milk
2 tbsp. finely chopped onion
Salt and pepper to taste

Preheat oven to 400 degrees. Spread 1 cup potato chips in 1-quart greased casserole; add eggs. Blend soup, milk and onion; season with salt and pepper. Pour over eggs; sprinkle with remaining potato chips. Bake for 25 minutes, until bubbly. Yield: 6 servings.

EGGS CHIMOY

1/2 lb. mushrooms, chopped
1 1/2 tbsp. minced chives
1 tbsp. minced onion
1/4 c. butter
12 hard-cooked eggs
1 1/2 tbsp. catsup
1 tsp. minced parsley
1 tsp. minced tarragon
4 c. medium white sauce
3 tbsp. grated Parmesan cheese
3/4 c. fine bread crumbs

Saute mushrooms, chives and onion in 2 tablespoons butter. Halve eggs lengthwise. Mash or sieve egg yolks; add mushroom mixture, catsup, parsley and tarragon. Mix well; spoon mixture into egg whites. Arrange eggs in casserole; pour white sauce over eggs. Sprinkle with cheese. Melt remaining butter; stir in bread crumbs. Spread bread crumbs over casserole. Bake at 300 degrees for 25 minutes or until heated through. Casserole may be prepared in advance. Cover; refrigerate until ready to bake. Yield: 6 servings.

EGG AND BACON CASSEROLE

8 slices bacon, diced
2 tbsp. butter
2 tbsp. flour
1 c. milk
1 tsp. Worcestershire sauce
1/2 tsp. salt
1/2 tsp. pepper
Dash of garlic salt
3 eggs, hard boiled
4-oz. egg noodles, cooked
1 4-oz. package shredded Cheddar cheese

Fry bacon pieces until crisp; drain on paper toweling. Melt butter in heavy saucepan; blend flour until smooth. Add 1/2 cup cold milk, mixing well; add 1/2 cup hot milk, Worcestershire sauce, salt, pepper and garlic salt. Mix well. Cook, stirring, over low heat until slightly thickened. Slice eggs. Arrange layers of eggs, noodles, cheese and white sauce in bottom of casserole, ending with bacon on top. Bake in 350-degree oven for 30 minutes. Serve immediately. Yield: 6-8 servings.

Egg and Bacon Casserole . . . Bacon, eggs, noodles, and cheese mingle in this hearty dish.

EGGS AU GRATIN

12 hard-boiled eggs
1/2 c. finely chopped pecans
1/2 c. chopped olives
Mayonnaise
Salt and pepper to taste
Cayenne pepper to taste
2 c. thin white sauce
1 c. grated sharp cheese
Crumbled corn flakes

Cut eggs in half lengthwise; remove yolks. Mash yolks; add pecans and olives. Stir in enough mayonnaise to moisten; season with salt, pepper and cayenne pepper. Fill egg whites with yolk mixture; place in shallow casserole. Cover with white sauce; sprinkle with cheese and crumbs. Bake at 300 degrees for 30 minutes or until heated through. Yield: 8 servings.

SUPPER EGGS

3 green onions and tops
3 slices boiled ham
Few sprigs of parsley
6 hard-boiled eggs
1/4 c. melted butter
1 tsp. A-1 sauce
1 tsp. prepared mustard
3 c. rich white sauce
1 c. grated cheese

Grind green onions, ham and parsley together. Cut eggs lengthwise; remove yolks. Grate egg yolks; add butter, A-1 sauce, mustard and ham mixture. Spoon into egg whites; arrange in greased baking dish. Pour white sauce over eggs; sprinkle with cheese. Bake at 350 degrees until heated through. Yield: 6 servings.

CREAMED EGGS

1/3 c. butter or margarine
1/2 c. chopped celery
1/4 c. chopped green pepper
1/3 c. flour
1 1/2 tsp. salt
3 c. milk
6 hard-cooked eggs, sliced
2 tbsp. chopped pimento

Melt butter in saucepan; add celery and green pepper. Cook slowly until vegetables are tender. Blend in flour and salt. Add milk; cook, stirring constantly, until thickened. Add eggs and pimento; heat. Serve on hot buttered toast points or biscuits. Yield: 4-6 servings.

EGGS POACHED IN TOMATO SAUCE

1/4 c. olive oil
1 onion, minced
2 1/2 c. canned tomatoes
1 tbsp. chopped parsley
Pinch of dried red pepper flakes
Salt to taste
6 eggs

Heat oil in 10-inch skillet; saute onion in oil until transparent. Add tomatoes, parsley, pepper flakes and salt; mix well. Cover; simmer for about 25 minutes. Break eggs into sauce, spacing apart. Cover; simmer until eggs are set.

EGGS IN TOAST CUPS

6 slices bread
Butter or margarine
6 eggs
Salt and pepper

Preheat oven to 325 degrees. Trim crusts from bread; brush both sides of bread with melted butter. Fit into custard cups or large muffin tins. Bake for 15 minutes. Break eggs into toast cups. Season with salt and pepper; dot with butter. Cover with foil. Bake for about 15 minutes or until eggs are set. Loosen toast from sides of cups with spatula. Serve hot.

EGGS SAINT-GERMAIN

1 tbsp. butter
1 tsp. flour
1 c. cream
Salt and pepper to taste
Hot puree of green peas
4 eggs
2 tbsp. grated Swiss cheese

Melt butter in small saucepan over low heat; blend in flour. Add cream, salt and pepper; cook, stirring, until smooth and blended. Spread 1/2-inch layer of puree in shallow baking dish. Poach eggs; arrange eggs in puree. Pour sauce over eggs; sprinkle with cheese. Broil only until top is glazed.

BOILED EGG CUSTARD

3 eggs
1 c. sugar
2 tsp. cornstarch
1 qt. milk
2 tsp. vanilla

Beat eggs until creamy in mixing bowl; add sugar and cornstarch gradually, beating after each addition until smooth. Combine egg mixture and milk in heavy saucepan; cook over medium heat, stirring frequently. Bring to a boil; turn heat off. Stir until thickened. Cool. Stir in vanilla. Chill.

EGG CIRCLES

2/3 c. (packed) brown sugar
1/3 c. finely chopped nuts
2 tsp. cinnamon
2 c. butter
1/2 c. sugar
4 c. flour
1/2 tsp. salt
1/2 c. rum
6 hard-boiled egg yolks, grated
1 egg, beaten

Mix brown sugar, nuts and cinnamon. Cream butter and sugar; work in flour and salt. Add rum and grated egg yolks; mix well. Turn dough onto floured surface; roll thin. Cut into small circles, removing centers as for doughnuts. Place on baking sheet; brush with beaten egg. Sprinkle with brown sugar mixture. Bake at 350 degrees for 12 minutes or until brown.

EGG CUSTARD PIE

2 egg yolks
1 egg
3 c. milk
4 tbsp. sugar
1/8 tsp. salt
1 tsp. vanilla
1 unbaked pie shell
Nutmeg to taste

Beat egg yolks and egg together; add milk, sugar, salt and vanilla. Mix well. Pour into pie shell; sprinkle with nutmeg. Bake in 450-degree oven for 10 minutes. Reduce oven temperature to 325 degrees. Bake for about 30 minutes longer. Custard is done when knife blade inserted in center comes out clean. Cool for 5 to 10 minutes.

Meringue

3 egg whites
1/8 tsp. cream of tartar
Pinch of salt
6 tbsp. sugar

Beat whites slightly. Add cream of tartar and salt; beat until frothy. Add sugar, one tablespoon at a time, beating after each addition until egg whites are stiff. Spoon over custard. Bake for about 20 minutes or until meringue is light brown. Yield: 5 servings.

BLENDER EGG CUSTARD PIE

1 13-oz. can evaporated milk
1 c. sugar
3 tbsp. flour
3 eggs
3 tbsp. butter or margarine
1/2 tsp. vanilla
Nutmeg

Preheat oven to 325 degrees. Combine milk, sugar, flour, eggs, butter and vanilla in blender container. Cover; blend at medium speed for about 30 seconds. Pour into heavily greased and floured 10-inch pie plate; sprinkle with nutmeg. Bake for about 45 minutes or until firm. Crust forms on bottom.

Eggnog

Eggnog, an extremely digestible beverage, is usually prepared with milk or cream, beaten eggs, sugar, and flavoring. It is traditionally served at Christmas time. Because eggnog has a high fat content, it contains more calories than whole milk. Yet the combined nutrients of the milk and eggs (calcium, Vitamin A, protein, riboflavin, niacin, and thiamine) make it an extremely healthful food. (1 5-ounce glass = 200 calories)

AVAILABILITY: Commercially prepared eggnog is usually available at the dairy section of supermarkets from Thanksgiving through New Year's Day.

PREPARATION: Chill mixing bowls, punch bowls, and serving cups. Use only the freshest ingredients that have been thoroughly chilled. Follow the directions specified in the recipe. Brandy, rum, or whiskey may be added to taste after beating.

SERVING: Eggnog is usually sprinkled with nutmeg or cinnamon and served well-chilled. To maintain the icy temperature of the drink, set the serving bowl in a bed of crushed ice.

APPLE EGGNOG

5 eggs, well beaten
2/3 c. honey
1 46-oz. can apple juice

Beat eggs well; blend with honey and juice. Chill well before serving. Yield: 15-20 servings.

HOT APPLE CIDER EGGNOG

1 c. apple cider
1/2 c. sugar
1/2 tsp. salt
1/4 tsp. cinnamon
1/8 tsp. nutmeg
2 eggs, separated
3 c. hot milk
1/2 c. whipping cream, whipped

Combine cider, sugar, salt, cinnamon, nutmeg and egg yolks. Mix in blender until sugar is dissolved. Add milk to mixture slowly. Beat egg whites until stiff peaks form. Pour milk mixture slowly over egg whites; fold together. Serve hot topped with whipped cream. Yield: 1 quart.

CHRISTMAS EGGNOG

4 eggs, separated
1 1/3 c. sweetened condensed milk
4 c. milk
1/4 tsp. salt
1 tsp. vanilla
Rum flavoring to taste

Beat egg yolks until thick; mix in condensed milk and milk gradually. Blend in salt and vanilla. Beat egg whites until stiff peaks form. Fold in egg whites and rum flavoring. Pour into chilled punch bowl. Garnish with sprinkling of nutmeg and whipped cream, if desired.

COFFEE EGGNOG

1/2 gal. ice milk
2 c. hot coffee
1 bottle bourbon
Nutmeg

Place ice milk in punch bowl; pour coffee over ice milk. Add bourbon and several ice cubes. Stir until ice is melted. Sprinkle nutmeg over top. Yield: 24 servings.

CRANBERRY EGGNOG

6 eggs, beaten
2 c. heavy cream, whipped
3/4 c. sugar
4 c. cranberry juice

Combine eggs and whipped cream; fold in sugar. Stir in cranberry juice; serve. Yield: 12 servings.

EGGNOG SUPREME

12 eggs, separated
1 1/2 c. sugar
1 qt. apple brandy
2 qt. milk
1 pt. light cream
1 pt. heavy cream
Nutmeg

Blend egg yolks with sugar. Add brandy. Add milk and light cream, blending well. Beat egg whites until soft peaks form. Whip heavy cream until fluffy. Fold egg whites and whipped cream into yolk mixture. Chill. Sprinkle with nutmeg to serve. Yield: 40 servings.

Eggnog . . . This rich eggnog is perfect for holiday entertaining or for a late evening snack.

EGGNOG

4 eggs, slightly beaten
1/2 c. sugar
1/4 tsp. salt
3 c. scalded milk
2 tsp. vanilla
1/2 tsp. almond extract
3 c. cold milk
1 c. whipping cream, whipped

Combine eggs, sugar and salt in top of double boiler. Stir scalded milk in gradually; mix well. Cook over boiling water until mixture thinly coats metal spoon. Remove from heat; cool. Stir in flavorings; cover. Refrigerate until ready to serve. Beat chilled custard until smooth and frothy. Stir in cold milk; spoon into punch bowl. Whip cream; drop by spoonfuls onto eggnog. Yield: 14 half-cup servings.

FROSTED EGGNOG

8 eggs, well beaten
3/4 c. sugar
1/2 tsp. salt
2 qt. milk
1 c. whipping cream
1 tsp. vanilla

Blend eggs, sugar and salt. Add milk gradually; mix thoroughly. Chill. Whip cream; fold in vanilla. Blend sugar mixture and whipped cream before serving. Top with additional whipped cream. Yield: 3 quarts.

GEORGETOWN EGGNOG

6 eggs, separated
1 c. sugar
1 pt. whiskey
1 qt. heavy whipping cream

Beat egg yolks until light; add 2/3 cup sugar, beating until thick and lemon colored. Add whiskey slowly, beating constantly; set aside. Beat egg whites until stiff but not dry; add remaining sugar, beating until glossy. Fold whiskey mixture into egg white mixture gently. Whip cream; fold into eggnog mixture. Chill. Yield: 10 servings.

HOLIDAY EGGNOG

3/4 c. sugar
3 eggs, separated
Salt
4 c. hot milk
1/2 tsp. vanilla
Freshly ground nutmeg

Beat 1/2 cup sugar and egg yolks; add 1/4 teaspoon salt. Stir into milk slowly. Cook in double boiler until mixture coats silver spoon, stirring constantly. Place in pan of cold water to cool. Beat egg whites and dash of salt until stiff peaks form. Add remaining sugar. Add egg white mixture and vanilla to milk mixture. Chill for 4 hours. Spoon lightly in punch cups; sprinkle with nutmeg. Yield: 6-8 servings.

HOT EGGNOG

12 eggs, separated
1 tsp. cream of tartar
3 1/2 c. powdered sugar, sifted
1/2 pt. whipping cream
1/2 tsp. vanilla
Nutmeg

Whip egg whites until stiff peaks form; add cream of tartar, beating well. Beat egg yolks until thick; add powdered sugar. Beat thoroughly. Whip cream until stiff peaks form. Fold egg whites into egg yolk mixture; fold in whipped cream and vanilla. Fill insulated cups 2/3 full. Add hot water to within 1/2 inch of top of cups . Sprinkle with nutmeg; stir. Yield: 30 servings.

INSTANT EGGNOG

1 4 1/2-oz. package instant vanilla pudding mix
1/3 c. sugar
1 tsp. vanilla
6 c. milk
2 eggs, separated
Nutmeg

Combine pudding mix, sugar, vanilla, milk and egg yolks in large mixing bowl; beat well. Beat egg whites until stiff peaks form. Fold in egg whites. Chill thoroughly. Pour into punch cups; top each with dash of nutmeg. Yield: 8 cups.

MOLASSES NOG

2 c. evaporated milk
Salt to taste
2 to 3 tbsp. light molasses
Dash of nutmeg, ginger or cinnamon

Combine milk, 2 cups ice water, salt and molasses, stirring well. Pour into glasses; sprinkle with nutmeg. Yield: 5 servings.

OLD FAMILY EGGNOG

6 eggs, beaten well
6 tbsp. clover honey
2 c. milk
4 oz. brandy

Beat eggs and honey at high speed with electric mixer until light; add milk and brandy. Beat at low speed until mixed. Pour into container. Cover; refrigerate overnight. Yield: 6 servings.

ORANGE EGGNOG

1/4 c. sugar
1/4 tsp. cinnamon
1/4 tsp. cloves
1/4 tsp. ginger
6 eggs, beaten
2 qt. chilled orange juice
1/2 c. lemon juice
1 qt. vanilla ice cream
1 qt. ginger ale
Nutmeg

Combine sugar and spices; beat into eggs. Stir in juices. Cut ice cream into small cubes; place in punch bowl. Pour orange juice mixture over ice cream; add ginger ale. Sprinkle with nutmeg. Yield: 20-25 servings.

PEPPERMINT EGGNOG PUNCH

1 qt. peppermint ice cream
1 qt. eggnog mix
1 lge. bottle lemon-lime carbonated drink
24 sm. candy canes

Mix ice cream, eggnog mix and carbonated drink together in punch bowl. Do not blend in ice cream thoroughly. Serve with a candy cane for stirring. Yield: 24 servings.

SOUTHERN PERFECT EGGNOG

6 eggs, separated
3/4 c. sugar
2 c. heavy cream
2 c. milk
2 c. brandy
1 oz. rum
Grated nutmeg

Beat yolks with 1/2 cup sugar until thick and lemon colored. Beat egg whites, adding remaining sugar gradually, until stiff peaks form. Fold egg whites into beaten yolks. Stir cream and milk into egg mixture. Add brandy and rum; stir thoroughly. Sprinkle nutmeg over each serving; chill. Yield: 5 pints.

STRAWBERRY EGGNOG

1 pkg. strawberry powdered drink mix
2 eggs, well beaten
3/4 c. sugar
3 c. milk

Prepare drink mix according to package directions; pour into large pitcher. Combine eggs, sugar, milk and 1 cup ice water; mix well. Combine mixtures; mix well. May serve topped with whipped cream or eggnog ice cream; sprinkle with nutmeg, if desired. Yield: 6 servings.

SOUTHERN-STYLE EGGNOG

12 eggs, separated
1 c. sugar
1 tsp. salt
2 tsp. vanilla
1 tbsp. nutmeg
2 c. bourbon
2 oz. rum
1/2 c. powdered sugar
4 c. heavy cream
4 c. milk

Beat egg yolks until creamy; beat in sugar, salt, vanilla and nutmeg. Beat in bourbon and rum slowly. Whip egg whites until stiff peaks form, beating in powdered sugar. Add cream and milk to yolk mixture; fold in egg whites. Refrigerate for several hours before serving. Yield: 20 servings.

Eggplant

Eggplant is a purple egg-shaped fruit that is commonly used as a vegetable. It is a good source of Vitamin B_1 and riboflavin and has a high water content. (2 slices raw eggplant = 20 calories)

AVAILABILITY: Eggplant is available year-round but is in greatest abundance from July-September.

BUYING: Choose heavy, firm, uniformly dark, glossy, pear-shaped eggplant. Avoid wilted, soft, or dull-skinned specimens. Dark brown spots indicate decay.

STORING: Use eggplant as soon as possible. Cooked eggplant may be refrigerated, covered, 4 days. *To freeze* eggplant, pare and slice into 1/2-inch pieces or dice. Blanch in boiling water 4 minutes or steam 5 minutes. Chill in mixture of 1 quart ice water and 1 tablespoon citric acid. Drain, package, and freeze. Eggplant can be frozen 2 1/2 months in refrigerator's frozen foods compartment or 1 year in home freezer.

PREPARATION: Eggplant may be baked, boiled, or fried. *To boil,* pare (if skin is tough) and slice, cube or cut into strips. Place in 1/2 inch boiling salted water. Cover and cook 12 minutes. *To fry,* pare (if necessary) and cut in 1/2 inch slices. Dip in egg-milk mixture and then in bread crumbs or flour. Cook in hot oil in frying pan over moderate heat 3 minutes or until tender and browned.

SERVING: Serve as a vegetable side dish with tomato or chili sauce, grated cheese, oregano, dill, marjoram, chives, or parsley. Or serve as an appetizer or in main-dish casseroles.

EGGPLANT-SOUR CREAM ACCOMPANIMENT

1 sm. eggplant
3 tbsp. butter, melted
1/4 tsp. chili powder
1/4 tsp. garlic salt
1 c. sour cream

Peel eggplant; cut into 1/2-inch cubes. Saute in butter in skillet until soft and golden brown. Remove from heat. Add chili powder and garlic salt to sour cream; pour over eggplant. Mix well; chill before serving.

MARINATED EGGPLANT

1 eggplant
1 bottle French dressing
1 clove of garlic, minced
1 carton sour cream with minced chives

Peel eggplant; cut into 3/4-inch slices. Combine French dressing and garlic; marinate eggplant for 1 hour. Drain. Place eggplant slices in baking dish. Bake at 450 degrees for 20 minutes. Remove from oven; spread with sour cream. Bake for 5 minutes longer; serve warm.

BAKED EGGPLANT

1 med. peeled eggplant, cubed
1 tbsp. diced onion
2 tbsp. butter
Salt and pepper
1 egg
1/2 c. milk
8 saltine crackers, crumbled

Cook eggplant with onion in saucepan until tender; drain. Season with butter, salt and pepper; place in greased baking dish. Blend egg and milk together. Sprinkle crackers over casserole; pour egg mixture over crackers. Bake at 350 degrees until bubbly and brown. Yield: 4-6 servings.

EASY EGGPLANT CASSEROLE

1 lge. eggplant, pared
1 egg, beaten
1 lge. onion, chopped
1 tsp. salt
1/2 tsp. garlic salt
Pepper to taste
1 tbsp. Worcestershire sauce
2 tbsp. bacon drippings
1 c. bread crumbs
1 c. grated cheese

Dice eggplant; cook in boiling salted water until tender. Drain and mash. Combine eggplant, egg, onion, salt, garlic salt, pepper and Worcestershire sauce. Melt bacon drippings in casserole; arrange layers of eggplant, crumbs and 3/4 cup cheese in drippings. Bake at 350 degrees for about 20 minutes. Sprinkle top with remaining cheese; bake for about 10 minutes longer. Yield: 6 servings.

EGGPLANT CASSEROLE WITH CHEESE SAUCE

1 peeled eggplant, diced
1/4 c. butter, melted
1/4 c. flour
1/2 tsp. cayenne pepper
1/4 tsp. salt
1 c. milk
1/2 lb. sharp cheese, grated
Bread crumbs
Butter

Boil eggplant in salted water until partially cooked; drain well. Melt butter in double boiler; stir in flour until smooth. Add seasonings. Stir in milk gradually. Cook, stirring constantly, until thickened. Remove from heat; add cheese, stirring until melted. Place eggplant in casserole; cover with cheese sauce. Top with bread crumbs; dot with butter. Bake at 350 degrees for about 20 minutes or until heated through. Yield: 6-8 servings.

EGGPLANT-CORN CASSEROLE

1/2 c. finely chopped onion
2 tbsp. butter
1 lge. eggplant
1 c. whole kernel corn
1/2 c. tomato soup
1 1/2 tsp. salt
Dash of pepper
1/2 c. soft bread crumbs

Saute onion in butter until tender. Peel eggplant; dice. Cook eggplant in boiling salted water until tender; drain well and mash. Combine onion mixture, eggplant, corn, soup and seasonings in greased casserole. Cover with crumbs; dot with additional butter. Bake at 400 degrees for 20 to 25 minutes. Yield: 6 servings.

EGGPLANT-TOMATO CASSEROLE

4 lge. tomatoes, peeled
1 med. eggplant
1 lb. chorizo, sliced
1 tsp. salt
1/2 c. olive oil
1 med. onion, chopped
1 1/2 c. rice
2 med. green peppers, chopped
1/4 c. chopped parsley
1/4 tsp. thyme leaves
1/8 tsp. pepper
3 c. chicken bouillon
3 c. cut-up cooked chicken
1/2 c. sliced pimento-stuffed olives
1/2 c. whole pimento-stuffed olives
3-oz. Gruyere cheese, grated

Chop 2 tomatoes; slice remaining tomatoes. Cut eggplant into slices. Brown chorizo in large skillet; drain on paper towels. Sprinkle eggplant with salt; fry in 1/3 cup oil in skillet. Remove eggplant; drain. Combine remaining oil, chopped tomatoes, onion and rice in same skillet; saute for 2 minutes. Mix in chorizo, green peppers, parsley, thyme, pepper and bouillon. Cover; simmer for 20 minutes or until rice is tender, stirring occasionally. Stir in chicken and sliced olives. Turn into 3 1/2-quart ovenproof serving dish. Overlap eggplant and tomato slices around edge

Eggplant-Tomato Casserole . . . Bring the flavor of Spain to your table with this savory casserole.

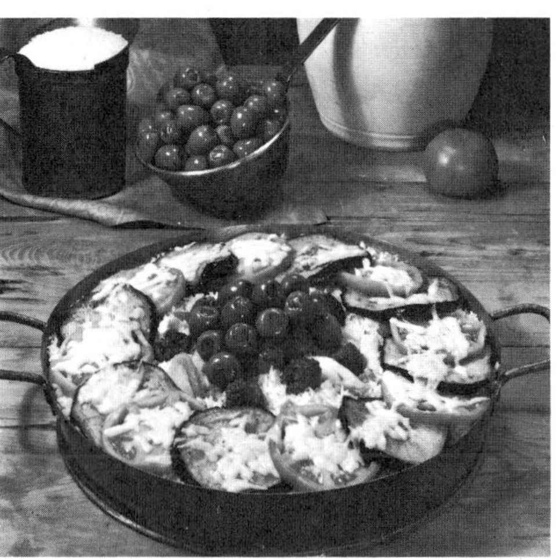

of dish. Place whole olives in center. Sprinkle cheese over tomato and eggplant slices. Broil 6 inches from source of heat for 4 minutes or until cheese melts and browns lightly.

EGGPLANT CREOLE

1 med. peeled eggplant, cubed
3 tbsp. butter
3 tbsp. flour
3 lge. tomatoes
1 sm. green pepper, chopped
1 sm. onion, chopped
1 tbsp. brown sugar
1 tsp. salt
1/2 bay leaf
2 cloves
Bread crumbs
Grated Cheddar cheese

Cook eggplant in boiling water for 10 minutes or until tender; drain. Place in greased 1 1/2-quart casserole. Melt butter; blend in flour. Peel and chop tomatoes; add to butter mixture. Add green pepper, onion, brown sugar, salt, bay leaf and cloves. Cook for 5 minutes; pour over eggplant. Top with bread crumbs and cheese. Bake at 350 degrees for about 30 minutes. Yield: 4-5 servings.

EGGPLANT AND MINCED CLAMS

1 med. eggplant
1 7-oz. can minced clams
3 eggs, beaten
1 1/2 c. bread crumbs
4 tbsp. melted butter

Peel and cube eggplant; boil in salted water until tender. Drain. Drain clams; add clams and eggs to eggplant. Mix bread crumbs with butter. Add 1/2 cup crumbs to eggplant mixture. Place in baking dish; top with remaining crumbs. Bake in 350-degree oven for 45 minutes. Yield: 4 servings.

EGGPLANT PARMIGIANA

1 lge. eggplant
Salt
4 tbsp. butter
1 lb. ground beef
2 tbsp. chopped parsley
1/2 c. chopped onion
1/4 tsp. pepper
1 tsp. salt
4 med. peeled tomatoes, sliced
1/4 c. grated Parmesan cheese
3 slices mozzarella cheese

Cut eggplant into 12 slices; sprinkle with salt. Let stand for 5 minutes; pat dry. Saute slices in butter until golden brown; drain on paper towel. Brown beef in skillet; stir in parsley, onion, pepper, salt and tomatoes. Cook for about 10 minutes. Arrange half the eggplant slices in shallow casserole; add tomato sauce. Top with remaining eggplant slices. Cover with Parmesan and mozzarella cheese. Bake at 350 degrees for 30 minutes. Yield: 6 servings.

EGGPLANT WITH SOUR CREAM

1 lge. peeled eggplant, cubed
2 tbsp. butter
2 tbsp. beef stock base
1 1/2 tsp. Italian seasoning
1 c. sour cream
1 tbsp. instant dried onions
1/2 tsp. salt
1/4 tsp. pepper
1/4 c. bread crumbs
2 tbsp. grated Parmesan cheese

Saute eggplant in butter for 5 minutes or until slightly tender. Combine 1/2 cup hot water, beef stock base and Italian seasoning; pour over eggplant. Simmer, covered, until eggplant is tender and liquid has evaporated. Spoon eggplant mixture into flat baking dish. Combine sour cream, onions, salt and pepper; pour over eggplant. Sprinkle with crumbs and cheese. Bake at 350 degrees for 20 to 25 minutes or until heated through and browned. Yield: 6 servings.

GREEK MOUSSAKA

1 lge. eggplant
1/2 c. shortening
1 1/2 c. sliced onions
3/4 lb. chopped beef
1 16-oz. can whole tomatoes
3 tbsp. chopped parsley
3 tsp. salt
1/2 tsp. oregano
1/4 tsp. pepper
3 tbsp. butter
2 tbsp. flour
2 c. milk
1 egg, beaten
1 c. grated Cheddar cheese

Peel eggplant; cut into 1/2-inch slices. Melt 1 tablespoon shortening in large skillet over moderate heat; brown eggplant on both sides. Add remaining shortening; cook onions until tender but not browned. Add beef; cook until browned. Add tomatoes, parsley, 2 teaspoons salt, oregano and pepper. Simmer for 15 minutes. Remove from heat. Melt butter in pan over low heat, stirring occasionally. Add flour; mix well. Pour in milk all at once; stir constantly over moderate heat until thickened. Add remaining salt; remove from heat. Arrange layers of eggplant slices, beef mixture and white sauce in greased 2-quart casserole, ending with eggplant slices on top. Pour egg over eggplant slices; sprinkle with grated cheese. Bake in 350-degree oven for 40 minutes or until golden brown. Yield: 6 servings.

ITALIAN EGGPLANT BAKE

1 med. peeled eggplant, cubed
1 lge. onion, sliced
1 med. green pepper, sliced
1 sm. clove of garlic, minced
1 tsp. crushed oregano
Butter
1 can tomato soup
1/4 tsp. salt
1 slice bread, cubed
Grated cheese

Cook eggplant in boiling salted water for 3 minutes; drain. Place in 10 x 6 x 2-inch casserole. Saute onion, green pepper, half the garlic and oregano in butter until tender; add soup, 1 cup water and salt. Heat; pour over eggplant. Bake at 350 degrees for 45 minutes, stirring frequently. Remove from oven; increase oven temperature to 425 degrees. Melt 2 tablespoons butter in skillet; add remaining garlic. Mix in bread cubes lightly. Cook over low heat, stirring constantly, until bread is crisp and lightly browned. Sprinkle croutons and cheese over eggplant mixture. Bake for 15 minutes longer.

SAVORY EGGPLANT CASSEROLE

1 med. eggplant, cooked and mashed
1 egg, beaten
1 c. bread crumbs
1 tsp. sage
1 tsp. parsley flakes
1 tsp. oregano
1/2 tsp. pepper
1 tsp. salt
2 tbsp. chopped onion
1/2 c. grated cheese

Peel eggplant; dice. Cook in boiling salted water until tender; drain and mash. Combine eggplant, egg, bread crumbs, seasonings, onion and cheese. Spoon eggplant mixture into 1 1/2-quart casserole. Bake at 325 degrees for 25 to 30 minutes. Yield: 6-8 servings.

SPANISH EGGPLANT

1 lge. peeled eggplant, cubed
1/2 c. chopped onion
2 tbsp. butter
2 c. tomato pulp and juice
1/4 tsp. garlic salt
4 green chilies, chopped
1/2 tsp. salt
Dash of pepper
2 eggs, beaten
1/2 c. buttered bread crumbs

Boil eggplant in salted water until tender; drain. Saute onion in butter; add tomatoes, garlic salt, chilies, salt and pepper. Simmer for 5 minutes; stir into eggplant. Cool; add eggs. Pour into greased casserole; top with crumbs. Bake at 350 degrees for 20 minutes. Yield: 4 servings.

EGGPLANT AND OYSTERS

1 lge. eggplant
1 c. flour
2 eggs, beaten
2 tbsp. butter, melted
8 fresh oysters
8 slices mozzarella cheese

Preheat broiler. Peel eggplant; cut into eight 3/4-inch thick slices. Coat eggplant slices with flour on both sides. Dip into eggs. Coat with flour again. Saute eggplant on both sides in butter in skillet until lightly browned. Arrange eggplant slices on oven-proof serving dish. Saute oysters in pan drippings in skillet for about 2 minutes on each side. Place 1 oyster on each eggplant slice; cover each oyster with slice of cheese. Broil until cheese is melted and bubbly. Yield: 8 servings.

EGGPLANT BALLS

1 lge. peeled eggplant, sliced
2 eggs, beaten
Pepper to taste
Biscuit mix
Oil

Cook eggplant in boiling salted water until tender; drain. Mash eggplant; add eggs and pepper. Stir in enough biscuit mix to make soft dough. Drop by spoonfuls into deep hot oil. Fry until evenly browned. Drain on paper towel; serve hot.

FRENCH-FRIED EGGPLANT

1 med. eggplant
1 tbsp. salt
1 egg, beaten
Cornmeal
Oil

Peel eggplant; cut into 1/2-inch strips. Place eggplant strips in salted water to cover; soak for 30 minutes. Drain well. Dip strips into egg; roll in cornmeal. Fry in deep hot oil in skillet until lightly browned; drain on paper toweling. Serve immediately.

EGGPLANT FRITTERS

2 eggs, beaten
1 c. buttermilk
1 tsp. salt
1/2 tsp. soda
2 tsp. baking powder
1 1/2 c. flour
4 tbsp. cornmeal
1 med. peeled eggplant, cubed
Oil

Combine eggs, buttermilk and dry ingredients, mixing well. Fold eggplant cubes into batter. Drop by large spoonfuls into hot deep oil in skillet. Fry until lightly browned on both sides. Drain well on paper toweling; serve immediately.

FRIED EGGPLANT

1 eggplant
1 egg, beaten
Flour
Oil

Peel eggplant; cut into thin slices. Soak eggplant in salted water for 10 minutes. Dip eggplant into egg; roll in flour. Fry in deep hot oil in skillet until lightly browned. Drain; serve hot.

EGGPLANT-ALMOND SOUFFLÉ

2 peeled eggplant, cubed
2 tbsp. butter
1/2 c. bread crumbs
1/2 c. milk
1/4 tsp. salt
1/4 tsp. pepper
1/4 tsp. nutmeg
1 onion, grated
3 eggs, separated
1/2 c. sauteed mushrooms
2 tbsp. buttered crumbs
2 tbsp. shredded toasted almonds

Cook eggplant in boiling salted water until tender; drain and mash. Add butter, bread crumbs and milk. Season with salt, pepper and nutmeg. Stir in onion and beaten egg yolks; cool. Fold in stiffly beaten egg whites and mushrooms. Spoon eggplant mixture into greased baking dish. Sprinkle with buttered crumbs and almonds. Bake at 400 degrees for 30 minutes. Yield: 10 servings.

EGGPLANT SOUFFLÉ

1 med. peeled eggplant, cubed
2 tbsp. melted butter
2 tbsp. flour
1 c. milk
1 c. grated American cheese
2 tsp. chopped onion
3/4 c. soft bread crumbs
1 tbsp. catsup
1 tsp. salt
1/8 tsp. pepper
Dash of cayenne pepper
2 eggs, separated

Cook eggplant in boiling salted water until tender; drain and mash. Melt butter in skillet; stir in flour until smooth. Add milk gradually, stirring. Cook over low heat, stirring constantly, until thickened. Combine cream sauce, eggplant, cheese, onion, bread crumbs, catsup, seasonings and beaten egg yolks. Fold in stiffly beaten egg whites. Turn into greased casserole. Bake at 375 degrees for about 45 minutes or until firm in center. Serve at once. Yield: 6 servings.

TEXAS EGGPLANT

1 eggplant
2 eggs, beaten
Cornmeal
Oil
Salt and pepper to taste

Peel eggplant; cut into thin slices. Dip eggplant slices into eggs; coat with cornmeal. Brown in hot oil at medium temperature on both sides until brown. Add salt and pepper. Garnish with lemon wedges.

MEXICANO-STUFFED EGGPLANT

1 2-lb. eggplant
6 tbsp. butter
1/4 tsp. minced garlic
1/2 c. diced celery
1/2 c. coarsely shredded carrots
1/4 c. chopped onion
1/2 tsp. salt
3/4 tsp. chili powder
1/2 tsp. oregano leaves
1/3 c. sliced stuffed olives
1 c. toasted croutons
1/2 c. chopped tomatoes

Cut lengthwise slice from one side of eggplant. Parboil for 25 minutes in salted water in saucepan. Drain and cool. Scoop out pulp to within 1/4 inch of the skin with grapefruit knife; cut pulp into cubes. Melt butter in medium skillet. Add garlic, celery, carrots and onion; saute until onions are transparent. Blend in seasonings, olives, croutons and tomatoes. Spoon stuffing into eggplant shell. Place in greased baking dish. Bake in preheated 400-degree oven for 20 minutes. Yield: 6 servings.

Mexicano-Stuffed Eggplant . . . Eggplant stuffed with carrots, olives, tomatoes, and seasonings.

CHILI-STUFFED EGGPLANT

1 eggplant
1/4 c. chopped onion
2 tbsp. butter
1 lb. cooked shrimp
1/4 c. dry bread crumbs
1 egg yolk
1 tsp. salt
1/4 tsp. ground black pepper
2 tsp. chili powder
1 tbsp. chopped parsley
1/2 c. soft bread crumbs

Cut eggplant in half lengthwise; parboil for 15 minutes. Scoop out pulp to within 1/2 inch of skin. Chop pulp fine. Saute onion in 1 tablespoon butter; mix with chopped eggplant. Chop shrimp; add to eggplant mixture. Blend in dry bread crumbs, egg yolk, salt, pepper, chili powder and parsley. Fill eggplant shells with filling. Melt remaining butter; toss soft bread crumbs in melted butter. Sprinkle over eggplant. Bake in 400-degree oven for 20 to 30 minutes or until crumbs are brown. Yield: 6 servings.

BAKED EGGPLANT PALERMO

2 lge. firm eggplants
2 4 1/2-oz. cans artichoke hearts
2 4-oz. cans mushrooms
1/2 tsp. garlic powder
1/2 c. butter
1 1/2 tsp. oregano
1 tsp. sweet basil
2 tbsp. minced onion
1 tsp. salt
2 sm. green peppers, chopped
2 sm. fresh tomatoes, chopped
1 c. Parmesan cheese

Cut eggplants in half lengthwise; scoop pulp out, leaving 1/2-inch thickness in shells. Reserve pulp. Dice reserved pulp; set aside. Parboil eggplant shells in boiling salted water until just tender; drain. Place shells in baking dish, cut sides up. Drain artichoke hearts and mushrooms. Cut artichoke hearts into halves. Saute mushrooms and garlic powder in butter. Add diced eggplant; saute until golden. Stir in oregano, basil, onion, salt, green peppers, tomatoes and artichoke hearts; simmer for 3 to 4 minutes or until heated through. Stir in 3/4 cup cheese. Spoon filling into eggplant shells; top with remaining cheese. Bake at 350 degrees for 20 minutes or until cheese is brown. Yield: 4 servings.

SHRIMP-STUFFED EGGPLANT

2 sm. eggplant
1 egg, beaten
1/2 lb. cooked shrimp, chopped
3/4 c. bread crumbs
2 cloves of garlic, minced
1 tbsp. chopped parsley
Salt and pepper
1 onion, minced
1/4 stick butter
Grated American cheese

Boil eggplant until just tender; halve lengthwise. Drain. Remove pulp leaving 1/2-inch thick shells. Blend eggplant pulp with egg, shrimp, bread crumbs, garlic and parsley. Season with salt and pepper to taste. Brown onion lightly in 1 tablespoon butter; add eggplant mixture. Simmer for 10 minutes. Stuff shells with shrimp filling; sprinkle with cheese. Place 1/2 teaspoon butter on each half. Place under broiler until lightly browned. Yield: 4 servings.

Endive

BELGIAN ENDIVE SALAD

4 heads endive
4 tbsp. olive oil
1 tbsp. wine vinegar
1/2 tsp. salt
1/8 tsp. freshly ground pepper
Dijon mustard

Separate endive leaves; rinse well. Chill until ready to use. Combine olive oil, vinegar, salt, pepper and mustard; mix thoroughly. Arrange leaves in salad bowl; coat well with dressing just before serving.

ENDIVE SALAD

1/2 c. salad oil
1/2 c. vinegar
1/2 c. sugar
Dash of pepper
1 tsp. salt
1 tsp. garlic salt
Paprika
1/2 head endive
1 chopped cabbage
2 grated carrots

Combine oil, vinegar and seasonings in a jar; blend thoroughly. Arrange endive, cabbage and carrots in salad bowl; toss lightly with dressing just before serving.

SALADE JACQUES

1 head endive
1/3 c. raisins
1/3 c. walnuts
1/3 c. halved Greek olives
1/3 c. diced Cheddar cheese
1/3 c. peeled chopped apple
1/3 c. chopped salami
1 tbsp. minced onion
1/2 c. olive oil
1/4 c. vinegar
1/2 tsp. dry mustard
1/2 tsp. Worcestershire sauce
Salt and pepper to taste

Remove tough outer leaves from endive; tear remaining leaves into bite-sized pieces into salad bowl. Add raisins, walnuts, olives, cheese, apple and salami to endive; toss well. Combine remaining ingredients in jar; blend thoroughly. Add dressing to salad; toss well to coat all ingredients. Serve immediately.

ENDIVE-ESCAROLE SALAD

1/4 head endive
1/4 head escarole
1 clove of garlic, cut
1 tbsp. vinegar
1 tbsp. safflower oil
1 tbsp. minced onions
1/2 tsp. honey
1/2 tsp. salt
1/2 tsp. pepper

Slice endive and escarole finely. Rub salad bowl with garlic; arrange greens in bowl. Combine vinegar, oil, onions, honey, salt and pepper; mix well. Pour over salad greens; toss well. Serve immediately.

HOT ENDIVE SALAD

1 lge. head endive
4 slices bacon
1 tbsp. (heaping) flour
1 egg
1/2 c. vinegar
1/2 c. sugar
Salt and pepper

Tear endive into bite-sized pieces. Chop bacon; fry until crisp in medium skillet. Blend flour, egg, vinegar and sugar with 1/2 cup water; add to bacon. Simmer, stirring constantly, until mixture is smooth and thickened; add water, if needed. Season with salt and pepper; pour over endive. Serve immediately. Yield: 6 servings.

Fig

Figs are plump, sweet, exotic fruits that are tree-ripened and sun-dried for the maximum concentration of natural sugar and nutrients. All figs (fresh or dried) are rich in riboflavin, thiamine, phosphorus, and calcium; dried figs, in particular, are sources of quick food energy and iron. (1 dried fig = 60 calories)

AVAILABILITY: Figs are marketed fresh, dried, canned in water or syrup, and candied. *Fresh figs* are available from June through October. *Dried figs* are available after the summer drying season which lasts from July to September. *Canned figs* are available year-round. *Candied figs* are available at Christmas.

BUYING: Select *fresh figs* that are unbruised, fully ripe, and fairly soft. Color and size depend on the variety. *Dried figs* are mechanically graded for size (Extra Fancy, Fancy, Extra Choice, Choice) and sold in packages, on strings, and in cans.

STORING: *Fresh figs* are highly perishable. They should be stored in the refrigerator and used within 2 to 3 days. *Dried figs* should remain in a tightly covered container in a cool place. They will keep on the kitchen shelf for 6 to 8 months. *Canned figs* (unopened) will keep on the kitchen shelf for 1 year. The contents of an opened can should be transferred to a covered container and refrigerated. Use within 4 to 5 days. *To freeze* figs, choose good fresh specimens. Sort them, wash, and cut off stems. Peel if desired. Pack figs in syrup or unsweetened liquid allowing 1/2-inch head space.

SERVING: *Fresh figs* can be served with cream and sugar. *Dried figs* are especially tasty in puddings. Figs are used extensively in such baked goods as fig bars, cakes, cookies, and pies.

CANDIED FIGS

3 lb. figs
2 c. sugar
1 c. water
Juice of 1 lemon
2 lb. nuts, chopped
1 tbsp. aniseed

Cut figs into quarters. Combine sugar, water and lemon juice in saucepan. Bring to a boil; cook until syrupy. Add figs; reduce heat. Cook, stirring constantly, until thick. Stir in nuts and aniseed; heat through. Spoon into hot sterilized jars; seal.

FIG-FILLED LADY BALTIMORE CAKE

2/3 c. butter
1 3/4 c. sugar
3 c. sifted flour
3 1/2 tsp. baking powder
3/4 tsp. salt
1 c. milk
4 egg whites, stiffly beaten
2 tsp. vanilla

Fig-filled Lady Baltimore Cake . . . A beautiful cake topped with a rich chopped fruit frosting.

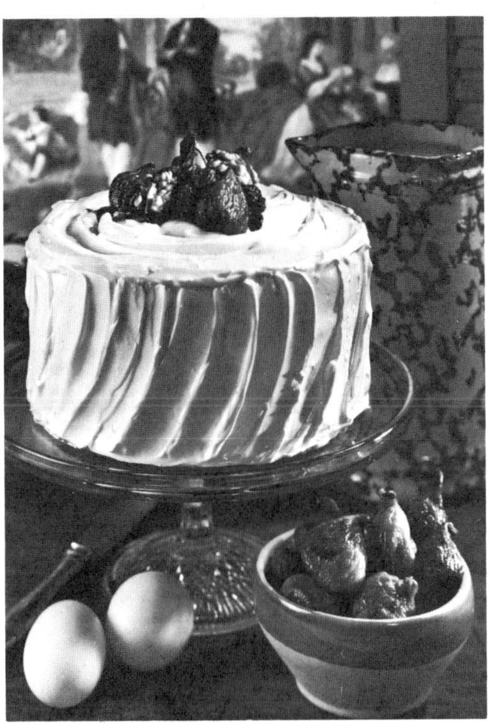

Beat butter and sugar until light and fluffy. Sift flour, baking powder and salt together. Blend milk and 1/3 cup water together. Add flour mixture and milk mixture to creamed ingredients alternately. Beat well. Fold in egg whites and vanilla. Spoon batter into 3 greased and floured 8-inch layer cake pans. Bake at 350 degrees for 30 minutes or until cake tests done. Cool in pans for 10 minutes; turn out on cake racks. Cool completely.

Fig Filling

1 1/2 c. sugar
1/8 tsp. cream of tartar
2 tbsp. light corn syrup
1/4 tsp. salt
3 egg whites
1 tsp. vanilla
1 c. chopped dried figs
1/2 c. chopped dark seedless raisins
1/2 c. chopped walnuts

Combine sugar, cream of tartar, 1/2 cup water, corn syrup and salt in 1-quart saucepan. Heat, stirring constantly, until sugar dissolves. Cover pan; cook syrup for 3 minutes or until steam has washed down any sugar crystals on side of pan. Uncover; cook without stirring, to 242-244 degrees on candy thermometer or to medium-firm ball stage. Beat egg whites in small bowl in electric mixer until stiff peaks form. Pour hot syrup in thin stream into egg whites, beating constantly. Add vanilla; beat until frosting is stiff enough to spread on cake. Mix 1/3 of the frosting with figs, raisins and walnuts; spread on 2 cake layers. Stack layers with unfrosted layer on top. Frost top and side of cake with remaining frosting. Garnish with figs, raisins and walnuts.

FIG CAKE

1 pt. fig preserves
1 box yellow cake mix
3 eggs
1/2 c. oil
1 1/2 c. chopped pecans

Pour fig preserves into blender; cover. Process until figs are chopped. Place cake mix in bowl; blend in amount of water called for in package directions. Add figs, eggs, oil and pecans; beat for 2 minutes. Pour into greased and floured tube pan. Bake at 350 degrees for 45 minutes or until cake tests done.

MAZUREK

2 c. flour
2 c. sugar
1/4 tsp. salt
1/2 c. butter, softened
3 eggs
3 tbsp. cream
1/2 lb. raisins, chopped
1/2 lb. dates, chopped
1/2 lb. figs, chopped
1/4 lb. nuts, chopped
Juice of 1 lemon
Juice of 1 orange

Sift flour, 1 cup sugar and salt together; cut in butter. Beat 1 egg with cream; stir into flour mixture. Spread dough in greased 16 x 10 x 1-inch pan. Bake at 350 degrees for about 30 minutes. Beat remaining eggs and remaining sugar together; add fruits and nuts. Stir in fruit juices; spread over baked pastry. Bake for 15 minutes longer. Cool; cut into bars.

FIG BARS

1/2 c. flour
1/2 tsp. baking powder
1/4 tsp. salt
1 1/2 c. diced figs
1 c. coarsely chopped nuts
2 eggs
1 c. (packed) dark brown sugar
1/4 c. salad oil
1 tsp. vanilla

Mix flour, baking powder and salt; add figs and nuts. Beat eggs well, beating in sugar, oil and vanilla. Stir into flour mixture; mix well. Spread batter evenly in greased and floured 13 x 9-inch pan. Bake at 350 degrees for 25 to 30 minutes. Cool slightly; cut into bars.

FIG AND PEAR FILLING

7 lb. pears
1 lb. figs
4 lb. sugar

Peel and core pears. Grind pears and figs through food chopper. Combine pears, figs and sugar in heavy kettle. Cook, stirring frequently, until thickened. Spoon into sterilized jars; seal with paraffin.

FIGS AFLAME

1 lge. can Kadota figs
1 tsp. arrowroot or cornstarch
2 thin slices lemon
Brandy
1/2 pt. cream
Lemon wafers

Drain figs; pour syrup into chafing dish. Add arrowroot; stir until thickened. Add figs, lemon and 2 tablespoons brandy; heat through. Heat 1/4 cup brandy; ignite. Pour over figs, coating each well. Serve at once with cream and lemon wafers. Yield: 4 servings.

FIG-STUFFED BAKED APPLES

6 fig bars, quartered
1/3 c. orange juice
3 tbsp. light corn syrup
6 lge. tart apples
1 c. sugar
1/2 c. boiling water
1 tbsp. butter
1 tsp. grated orange rind

Combine fig bars, orange juice and corn syrup; let stand for 10 minutes. Core apples; pare 1/4 of the way down. Place in greased shallow baking dish. Spoon fig mixture into center of apples. Dissolve sugar in boiling water; add butter and orange rind. Pour over apples. Bake at 350 degrees for 50 minutes or until apples are tender, basting frequently. Yield: 6 servings.

CUCCIDATE

1 lb. dried figs
1 lb. dates
1/2 lb. raisins
2 c. chopped nuts
2 tbsp. cinnamon
1 tsp. pepper
1/2 c. honey
1/4 c. orange juice
8 c. flour
2 tbsp. baking powder
1 tsp. salt
3 eggs
1 c. sugar
1 tsp. vanilla
2 1/2 c. shortening
1 c. milk

Combine figs, dates and raisins in kettle; add water to cover. Bring to a boil; reduce heat. Cover and simmer for 5 minutes. Drain fruit mixture, reserving 1 cup cooking water. Grind fruits and nuts through food chopper, using fine blade. Combine fruits, nuts, cinnamon, pepper, honey and orange juice; work in enough reserved cooking water to soften. Sift flour, baking powder and salt together. Combine eggs, sugar, vanilla and shortening in large electric mixer bowl; beat at medium speed until creamy. Turn mixer control to low speed; add flour mixture and milk alternately until dough is too stiff for mixer to beat. Stir in remaining flour mixture and milk with spoon. Turn dough onto lightly floured surface; roll thin. Cut dough into 3-inch squares; place about 1 tablespoon fruit filling in center of each piece of dough. Fold dough over filling; seal edges. Place on greased baking sheet. Bake at 350 degrees for 10 minutes or until lightly browned. Cool on rack.

FIG-FILLED PASTRY

1 pkg. figs, ground
1 1/4 c. sugar
3 c. flour
1 tsp. lemon extract
2 tsp. cream of tartar
1 tsp. soda
1/2 tsp. nutmeg
1/2 c. shortening
1 egg
1/2 c. milk

Mix figs, 1/4 cup sugar, 2 tablespoons flour and lemon extract in saucepan; cook until thick. Sift remaining flour, cream of tartar, soda and nutmeg together. Cream shortening and remaining sugar; beat in egg. Add flour mixture alternately with milk. Stir to make easily handled dough. Divide dough in 2 parts; roll each part to fit cookie sheet. Place half the dough on cookie sheet; spread with fig filling. Cover filling with remaining dough. Seal edges; cut steam vents. Bake at 350 degrees for 15 to 20 minutes.

FRESH FIG PIE

Pastry for 2-crust 9-in. pie
Sugar
2 tbsp. flour
Pinch of salt
2 c. sliced figs, drained
1 tbsp. lemon juice
1 tbsp. slivered lemon peel
Butter
Milk

Roll pastry thin; fit half the pastry into pie pan. Mix 2/3 cup sugar, flour and salt; sprinkle half the flour mixture evenly in pastry-lined pan. Arrange figs in pan; sprinkle figs with lemon juice, lemon peel and remaining flour mixture. Dot generously with butter; fit remaining pastry over pie. Seal edges and brush with milk; cut steam vents. Bake at 375 degrees for 15 minutes. Reduce oven temperature to 350 degrees; bake for about 30 minutes longer.

MOLASSES-FIG PUDDING

3 c. flour
1 tsp. baking powder
1 tsp. soda
1 tsp. cream of tartar
2 tsp. cloves
1 tsp. salt
1 egg
1 1/2 c. milk
1 c. molasses
6 oz. figs, chopped
1 c. chopped suet

1 c. chopped raisins
1/2 c. chopped nuts
1 c. sugar
1 tbsp. butter
1 tbsp. sherry

Reserve 1 tablespoon flour. Sift remaining flour, baking powder, soda, cream of tartar, cloves and salt together into large bowl. Beat egg; stir in milk and molasses. Add to flour mixture; mix well. Add figs, suet, raisins and nuts. Turn into 2-quart mold. Steam for 3 hours. Cool pudding in mold. Mix sugar and reserved flour in saucepan; stir in water. Cook over medium heat, stirring constantly, until smooth and thick. Stir in butter and sherry. Serve hot sauce over pudding.

AROMATIC FIG PUDDING

2 1-lb. 1-oz. cans Kodota figs
2 env. unflavored gelatin
Rind and juice of 1 lge. lemon
2 c. sour cream
2 tsp. angostura bitters
1/2 c. finely chopped nuts
3 eggs, separated

Drain figs, reserving 1 1/2 cups juice. Quarter figs. Soften gelatin in reserved fig juice for 5 minutes. Stir gelatin mixture over low heat in saucepan until dissolved. Combine lemon rind and juice, figs, sour cream, bitters, nuts and beaten egg yolks. Stir in gelatin mixture gradually; blend well. Cool to room temperature. Beat egg whites until stiff; fold into fig mixture. Pour into 2-quart mold; chill until firm. Dip quickly into warm water; unmold on serving dish. Serve cold. Garnish with additional whole canned figs if desired.

Aromatic Fig Pudding . . . This molded pudding blends lemon and fig flavors with a hint of nuts.

CHRISTMAS FIG PUDDING

1/2 lb. bread crumbs
2/3 c. sugar
4 tsp. baking powder
1/2 tsp. cinnamon
1/2 c. chopped nuts
2 lb. dried figs chopped
1/2 lb. suet, diced
1/4 c. milk
4 eggs

Combine crumbs, sugar, baking powder and cinnamon in large bowl; add nuts, figs and suet. Beat milk and eggs together; stir into crumb mixture. Turn batter into greased mold; cover. Let stand for 1 hour. Steam for about 4 hours. Serve with a hard sauce or hot lemon sauce.

RICH FIG PUDDING

7 eggs, separated
1 c. sugar
3/4 lb. bread crumbs
1/2 lb. dried figs, chopped
1/2 c. butter, melted
1/2 tsp. allspice
1/2 tsp. vanilla
2 tbsp. brandy

Beat egg yolks until light, beating in sugar gradually. Beat egg whites until stiff; fold into egg yolk mixture. Add bread crumbs, figs, butter, allspice, vanilla and brandy; mix lightly. Turn into greased 2-quart mold; cover. Steam for about 4 hours. Serve with hard sauce.

FIG BREAD

1 c. dried figs
3 1/2 c. sifted flour
3/4 c. sugar
1 tsp. salt
4 tsp. baking powder
3 tbsp. shortening
1 tsp. grated orange rind
1 egg
1 1/2 c. milk

Preheat oven to 375 degrees. Cover figs with boiling water; let stand for 10 minutes. Drain and dry figs; cut into thin slices. Sift flour, sugar, salt and baking powder together; cut in shortening until mixture resembles coarse cornmeal. Mix orange rind, egg and milk; add to dry ingredients. Stir until just blended; stir in figs. Pour into greased and paper-lined 9 x 5 x 3-inch pan. Bake for about 1 hour or until browned.

Filberts

A filbert is a round, mild-flavored, thick-shelled nut that is drier than the almond and walnut. The term "filbert" is often used interchangeably with "hazelnut." Filberts are a concentrated form of fat and protein. (1 filbert = 8 calories)

AVAILABILITY: Available year-round from Oregon and Washington and through European import.

BUYING: Filberts are usually sold in pound cellophane bags of nuts in the shell or nut meats. Look for smooth shells without cracks or holes. Nut should be well-filled and when shaken, kernel should not rattle. If possible check for plump and crisp kernels.

STORING: Store nuts in shell in cool, dry, dark place. Refrigerate kernels in air-tight container 3 to 4 months. Or freeze kernels in plastic bag in refrigerator's freezer for 1/2 year or home freezer for 1 year.

PREPARATION: *To shell*—Use nutcracker and remove whole kernel. 2 1/4 pounds in shell or 1 pound shelled = 3 1/2 cups shelled. *To slice or chop*—Use sharp knife and cutting board. *To grate*—Use food grater. *To grind*—Use nut grinder. Or place kernels in electric blender and run at high speed until kernels are finely ground. Use a meat grinder for butters and pastes. 1 cup whole kernels = approximately 1 1/3 cups ground kernels. *To blanch*—Pour boiling water over kernels. For large quantities, let stand 1 minute at most. Drain. Run under cold water to prevent further heating. Drain again. Rub off skins. *To toast*—Spread kernels in shallow pan. Bake in preheated oven at 400 degrees approximately 10 minutes, stirring occasionally. Add 1 teaspoon salt per 1 cup kernels. *To skillet roast*—Heat 2 teaspoons cooking oil in skillet over low heat. Add kernels and 1 teaspoon salt per 1 cup kernels. Stir constantly till heated. Drain. *To deep-fat fry*—Measure 1 quart cooking oil per 1/2 pound unblanched kernels. Heat oil to 300 degrees in deep-fat frying kettle. Place nuts in deep sieve. Lower into hot fat. Cook about 6 minutes, until kernels brown. Drain. Sprinkle with salt.

SERVING: *Whole filberts*—Eat plain, toasted, roasted, or deep-fat fried for snacks and with cocktails. *Chopped, grated, or ground filberts*—Use in candies, cakes, cookies, tortes, souffles. *Sliced*—Use to garnish salads, meats, fish, game.

FILBERT CAKE ROLL

6 eggs, separated
1 c. sugar
1 tsp. baking powder
1 c. wheat germ
1/2 c. grated filberts
1 1/2 c. heavy cream
1/4 tsp. vanilla
Confectioners' sugar

Beat egg whites until stiff. Beat egg yolks until thick, gradually adding 3/4 cup sugar. Combine baking powder, wheat germ and filberts; fold into egg yolk mixture. Fold in egg whites; spread in waxed paper-lined 15 x 10 x 1-inch pan. Bake at 350 degrees for 20 minutes. Cover with damp cloth; refrigerate for 2 hours. Turn cake onto cloth; remove waxed paper. Beat cream until stiff, beating in remaining sugar and vanilla. Spread whipped cream on cake. Roll cake gently from narrow end; refrigerate until ready to serve. Sprinkle with confectioners' sugar before serving.

SWEET NUT CAKE

6 eggs, separated
2 1/2 c. sugar
1/2 c. toasted bread crumbs
1 c. ground filberts
1 1/2 c. water
1/4 tsp. cinnamon
Juice of 1/2 lemon

Beat egg whites until stiff. Beat egg yolks with 1 cup sugar; fold in egg whites. Add bread crumbs and filberts; pour batter into lightly greased 8-inch square pan. Bake at 325 degrees for 35 minutes or until golden brown. Combine remaining sugar, water, cinnamon and lemon juice in saucepan; cook over low heat until syrupy. Cut warm cake into diamonds; pour hot syrup over cake. Yield: 8 servings.

FILBERT BRITTLE

2 c. sugar
1 c. butter
1 c. coarsely chopped filberts

Combine sugar and butter in skillet; cook over low heat, stirring constantly with fork until golden brown. Add filberts; cook until filberts crackle and syrup begins to bubble. Pour immediately onto cookie sheet, spreading with fork. Break into pieces by tapping bottom of pan. Yield: 1 pound.

FILBERT BARS

1/2 c. shortening
3/4 c. powdered sugar
2 eggs, separated
1 tsp. vanilla
1 c. sifted flour
1/4 tsp. salt
2/3 c. raspberry jam
1/4 tsp. nutmeg
1/2 c. sugar
3/4 c. filberts

Preheat oven to 350 degrees. Cream shortening, powdered sugar, egg yolks and vanilla until fluffy; blend in flour and salt. Press mixture into 13 x 9 x 2-inch pan. Bake for 15 minutes. Cool for 10 minutes. Spread jam over baked pastry. Beat egg whites until frothy; add nutmeg and sugar gradually, beating until stiff peaks form. Fold in filberts; spread over jam. Bake for 25 minutes. Cool and cut into bars.

FILBERT-COCONUT BARS

2/3 c. butter or margarine
1 1/2 c. (packed) brown sugar
1 3/4 c. sifted flour
1 c. chopped filberts
2 c. coconut
1/4 tsp. salt
3 eggs

Preheat oven to 325 degrees. Cream butter and 3/4 cup brown sugar; stir in 1 1/2 cups flour. Pat mixture in 13 x 9 x 2-inch pan. Bake for 20 minutes. Combine remaining brown sugar, filberts, coconut and salt. Beat eggs lightly; stir into filbert mixture. Spread over baked layer; bake for 25 minutes. Cut into bars; cool in pan.

HAZELNUSS TORTE

1 1/2 c. confectioners' sugar
6 egg yolks
2 tbsp. orange juice
2 tbsp. bread crumbs
Grated rind of 1 orange
8 egg whites
3 c. ground filberts
1/2 c. orange marmalade
2/3 c. chocolate chips
3 tbsp. butter or margarine
Whole filberts
1 c. whipped cream

Cream confectioners' sugar and egg yolks; stir in orange juice, bread crumbs and orange rind. Beat egg whites until stiff; fold egg whites and ground filberts into egg yolk mixture. Turn batter into greased and floured springform pan. Bake at 325 degrees for 40 minutes or until torte tests done. Cool torte; split into 2 layers. Spread 1 layer with marmalade; top with remaining layer. Melt chocolate chips and butter together in top of double boiler. Frost torte with chocolate mixture; garnish with whole filberts and whipped creamed. Refrigerate until ready to serve.

NUT-FILLED TORTE

1/2 c. sugar
8 eggs, separated
1/3 c. fine bread crumbs
2 1/3 c. ground filberts
1 tbsp. baking powder
1/2 tsp. salt
1 tsp. vanilla
3 tbsp. strong coffee
1 c. butter
1/2 c. confectioners' sugar
Chocolate frosting

Beat sugar and egg yolks together until light and creamy; add bread crumbs, 1/3 cup filberts, baking powder, salt and vanilla. Mix well. Beat egg whites until stiff; fold into batter. Turn into 3 greased and floured 9-inch layer pans. Bake at 350 degrees for 30 minutes. Remove layers from pans; cool. Combine remaining filberts and coffee in saucepan; cook over medium heat for 10 minutes, stirring constantly. Cool. Cream butter and confectioners' sugar; blend in coffee mixture. Spread between layers. Cover top and side of torte with chocolate frosting.

RUSSIAN TORTE

1/2 lb. shelled filberts, ground
8 eggs, separated
1 1/2 c. sugar
1/2 c. bread crumbs
Grated rind of 1/2 lemon
Juice of 1 lemon
1 tsp. vanilla
1 c. tart apricot jam
1 c. heavy cream, whipped

Reserve 2 tablespoons filberts. Beat egg whites until stiff. Beat egg yolks until thick and light, beating in sugar gradually. Add bread crumbs, lemon rind, lemon juice and vanilla; fold in egg whites. Spread batter in 2 greased and floured waxed paper-lined layer pans. Bake at 325 degrees for 30 minutes. Turn layers onto racks; cool. Spread jam between layers and on top of torte. Garnish top of torte with part of the whipped cream; frost side with remaining whipped cream. Refrigerate until ready to serve.

SNOW-TOPPED TORTE

7 eggs, separated
3/4 c. powdered sugar
1/8 tsp. cinnamon
1 tsp. lemon juice
Grated rind of 1/2 lemon
1/2 c. dry bread crumbs
1 c. ground filberts
1/4 tsp. salt
Sweetened whipped cream

Beat egg yolks and powdered sugar together until light; fold in cinnamon, lemon juice, lemon rind, bread crumbs and filberts. Beat egg whites and salt until stiff but not dry; fold into batter. Pour into 3 greased and waxed paper-lined 9-inch layer pans. Bake at 350 degrees for 30 minutes. Remove layers from pan; cool. Wrap well; let stand for 24 hours. Spread whipped cream between layers and on top of torte.

FILBERT MOUSSE

2 env. unflavored gelatin
2 1/4 c. milk
6 eggs, separated
1 c. sugar
2 tbsp. cognac
1 tsp. vanilla
1 1/2 c. ground toasted filberts
1 c. heavy cream, whipped

Soften gelatin in 1/3 cup water. Heat milk in medium heavy saucepan; stir in gelatin until dissolved. Beat egg yolks and sugar until light and fluffy; stir into hot milk gradually. Cook over low heat, stirring constantly, until mixture thickens and coats metal spoon. Do not boil. Remove from heat; stir in cognac, vanilla and ground filberts. Chill until thickened. Beat egg whites until stiff but not dry. Fold into filbert mixture with whipped cream. Pour into 5-cup souffle dish with 4-inch collar of waxed paper around dish. Chill until set. Remove collar. Garnish side of mousse with additional toasted chopped filberts if desired. Yield: 8 servings.

Filbert Mousse . . . An eye-pleasing dessert perfect for ladies' luncheons or dinner parties.

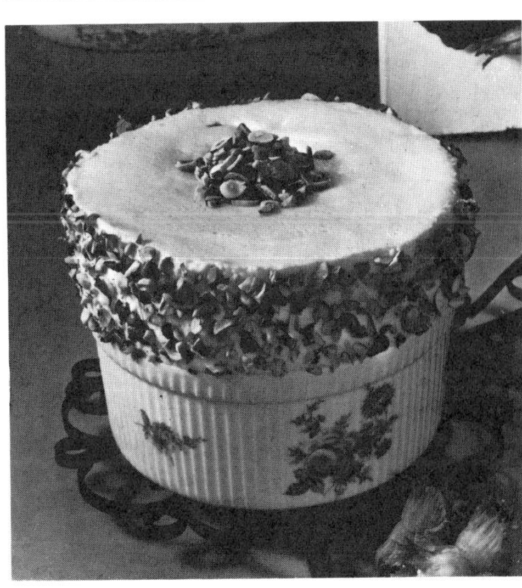

Floating Island Custard

FLUFFY FLOATING ISLAND

3 eggs, separated
Sugar
2 c. hot milk
1/8 tsp. salt
1/2 tsp. vanilla

Beat egg whites until stiff peaks form. Combine 6 tablespoons sugar and egg whites. Pour milk into double boiler; simmer until heated through. Drop egg white mixture into hot milk by spoonfuls. Cook for about 2 minutes or until firm. Place meringues in large bowl. Beat egg yolks until light and fluffy. Combine egg yolks, 1/4 cup sugar, salt and vanilla; add warm milk gradually, stirring constantly. Cook until thickened. Pour milk mixture into bowl; meringues will rise to top. Chill thoroughly before serving. Yield: 6 servings.

Flounder

Flounder is an oval-shaped, white-fleshed flatfish. It is often misnamed sole—which, in fact is a more delicate-fleshed flatfish imported from Europe. Summer and winter flounder abound in the Atlantic; Gulf flounder in the Gulf of Mexico; and starry flounder in America's northwestern waters. Flounder is high in protein and B vitamins. (5 ounces baked flounder = 155 calories)

AVAILABILITY: Fresh flounder is available year-round in coastal areas, usually in fillets (lengthwise cuts from sides). Frozen and packaged flounder is available nationwide year-round either whole or in fillets.

BUYING: Look for whole fresh fish that has bright, clear, bulging eyes; reddish pink gills, tight shiny scales; firm, elastic flesh; and fresh odor. Avoid fresh flounder that is soft or flabby.

STORING: Refrigerate whole flounder, wrapped, for 1 day. Flounder may be frozen. Store fresh frozen fish in refrigerator's frozen foods compartment 2 weeks, in freezer 1 year. Commercially frozen fish keeps in frozen foods compartment 2 months, in freezer for 1 year. Never refreeze flounder after thawing.

PREPARATION: Frozen flounder should be thawed in refrigerator. Both fresh and thawed fish should be washed in cold water. Flounder may be fried, broiled, baked, poached, or steamed. If broiled, it would be basted with melted fat. If baked, place bacon on top of fish.

SERVING: Flounder is often served with tomato, lemon, or egg sauce or with parsley garnishes.

(See SEAFOOD.)

ATHENAEUS-STYLE FLOUNDER

Parsley sprigs
1 bay leaf, crushed
1 sm. onion, sliced
3 lb. flounder fillets
1/2 c. olive oil
1 c. dry white wine
1/4 tsp. cumin
1 1/4 tsp. salt
1 beef bouillon cube

Line shallow baking dish with aluminum foil. Place parsley sprigs, bay leaf and onion over foil; place flounder steaks on onion mixture. Combine olive oil, wine, cumin and salt; pour over flounder. Crumble bouillon cube; scatter over steaks. Bake, covered, at 350 degrees for 40 minutes to 1 hour or until fish flakes easily. Yield: 8-10 servings.

Caper Sauce

2 sprigs of parsley
1 garlic clove, minced
1 tbsp. prepared mustard
2 to 3 tbsp. olive oil
Salt to taste
Vinegar to taste
1 tbsp. well-drained capers

Chop parsley fine; add garlic and mustard. Beat in olive oil gradually. Combine salt and vinegar with oil mixture; beat until smooth. Fold in capers; serve with flounder fillets.

BAKED FLOUNDER WITH LEMON-MUSHROOM SAUCE

2 pkg. frozen flounder fillets, thawed
1 can cream of mushroom soup
1/2 c. cream
1 can whole mushrooms
1 onion, chopped
2 tbsp. lemon juice
1 tbsp. paprika
1 bay leaf
1/2 tsp. salt
1/4 tsp. oregano
1/8 tsp. pepper
1/4 c. sherry
Buttered bread crumbs

Arrange flounder in greased shallow baking dish. Combine cream of mushroom soup with cream in saucepan; blend well. Add mushrooms, onion, lemon juice, paprika, bay leaf, salt, oregano, pepper and sherry. Simmer, stirring constantly, for 10 minutes. Pour sauce over flounder; top with crumbs. Bake at 375 degrees for 45 minutes or until fish flakes easily. Yield: 6 servings.

FLOUNDER AMANDINE

6 flounder fillets
1/2 c. butter, melted
1/2 c. lemon juice
2 tsp. salt
Dash of pepper
2 tsp. paprika
1/2 c. blanched almonds, slivered

Arrange flounder in well-greased baking dish. Combine butter, lemon juice, salt, pepper and paprika; pour over fish. Sprinkle with almonds. Bake at 350 degrees for 20 minutes or until fish flakes easily. Place in broiler for 2 to 3 minutes or until lightly browned.

FLOUNDER IN CHEESE SAUCE

3 tbsp. flour
3/4 tsp. salt
1/8 tsp. nutmeg
1/2 tsp. dry mustard
2 tbsp. butter
1 c. hot milk
3/4 tsp. lemon juice
1/2 c. shredded cheese
2 lb. flounder fillets

Combine flour, salt, nutmeg and mustard with butter in saucepan over low heat; stir in milk gradually. Simmer, stirring constantly, until sauce is thickened. Blend in lemon juice and cheese; stir until cheese is melted. Arrange fillets in shallow baking dish; pour sauce over fillets. Bake at 375 degrees for 45 minutes. Yield: 6 servings.

FLOUNDER AT ITS EASIEST

1 lb. flounder fillets
1 can celery soup
1/2 c. grated cheese

Arrange fillets in well-greased shallow baking dish. Spread soup over fillets; top with cheese. Bake at 350 degrees for 20 minutes or until fish flakes easily.

FLOUNDER AU GRATIN

1 1/2 lb. flounder fillets
1 tsp. salt
1/2 tsp. pepper
3 tbsp. lemon juice
3 tbsp. butter
2 egg yolks, beaten
2 c. medium white sauce
2 tbsp. grated cheese

Arrange fillets in shallow baking dish; sprinkle with salt, pepper and lemon juice. Dot with 1 tablespoon butter. Bake, covered, at 350 degrees for 20 minutes or until fish flakes. Combine remaining butter and egg yolks with white sauce. Pour sauce over fillets; sprinkle with cheese. Broil for 2 minutes or until lightly browned. Yield: 4-5 servings.

FLOUNDER ON A BED OF MUSHROOMS

1 lb. fresh white mushrooms, sliced
1 onion, chopped
2 sprigs of parsley, chopped
Salt and white pepper to taste
6 lge. flounder fillets
1 c. dry white wine
1 c. bouillon
Juice of 1 lemon
1/2 c. butter
2 tbsp. flour
1/2 c. heavy cream
1 egg yolk, slightly beaten

Place half the mushrooms in a shallow buttered pan. Add half the onion, half the parsley, salt and pepper. Arrange fillets over the onion. Add remaining mushrooms, onion, parsley and seasonings. Add wine, bouillon and lemon juice; dot with 1/4 cup butter. Bake, covered, at 350 degrees for 10 minutes or until liquid boils. Remove cover; bake for 10 minutes longer. Drain liquid into saucepan; simmer until quantity is reduced by half. Blend remaining butter with flour; add to liquid gradually. Simmer, stirring constantly, until sauce is thickened. Combine cream with egg yolk; blend into sauce thoroughly. Pour sauce over fillets; broil for 2 to 3 minutes or until lightly browned.

FLOUNDER IN SHRIMP SAUCE

2 lb. flounder fillets
2 cans frozen cream of shrimp soup
45 round buttery crackers, crushed
1 stick butter, melted
1 tsp. garlic juice
1 tsp. onion juice
1 tbsp. Worcestershire sauce

Place flounder in buttered baking dish; cover with soup. Bake at 350 degrees for about 15 minutes. Mix crumbs, butter, garlic juice, onion juice and Worcestershire sauce; pour over flounder. Bake for 10 minutes longer. Yield: 8 servings.

FLOUNDER IN WHITE WINE

1 lb. flounder fillets
1/3 c. minced onion
1/2 c. white wine
1 4-oz. can chopped mushrooms
Dash of salt
Coarsely ground black pepper
Paprika
1/2 tsp. curry powder

Arrange fillets in shallow, buttered baking dish; sprinkle with onion. Add wine, mushrooms and seasonings. Bake at 350 degrees for 30 minutes or until fish flakes easily.

BAKED STUFFED FLOUNDER

1 1/2 lb. shrimp
Salt and black pepper to taste
Cayenne pepper to taste
2 bay leaves
1/2 c. cooking oil
1/2 c. chopped celery
1 c. chopped onion
2 cloves of garlic, minced
1/2 lb. crab meat
3 stale buns soaked in water
4 eggs
1/2 c. bread crumbs
1/2 c. green onion tops
1/2 c. chopped parsley
4 med. flounder
Drawn butter or garlic butter

Place shrimp in large saucepan; add water to cover. Add salt, black pepper, cayenne pepper and bay leaves; bring to a boil. Remove from heat; let stand for 10 minutes. Peel and devein shrimp; set aside. Place oil, celery, onion and garlic in heavy saucepan; cook over medium heat until onions are transparent. Chop shrimp; add to onion mixture. Add crab meat, buns and 2 eggs; mix well. Add 2 egg whites, mixing thoroughly. Beat 2 egg yolks; combine with bread crumbs, green onion tops and additional salt, black pepper and cayenne pepper, stirring mixture well. Split flounders lengthwise, removing backbone; stuff with crab meat mixture. Brush tops of flounder with egg yolk mixture. Broil for about 15 minutes on each side. Remove from broiler. Brush with drawn butter; return to broiler to brown.

FLOUNDER STUFFED WITH SHRIMP

1 lge. onion, chopped
2 tbsp. butter
1 lb. shrimp, shelled and deveined
1 sm. can mushrooms
2 tbsp. snipped parsley
6 flounder fillets
Salt and pepper to taste
2 cans mushroom soup
Grated cheese

Saute onion in butter in medium skillet; add shrimp, mushrooms and parsley. Cook, stirring occasionally, for 10 minutes. Sprinkle fillets with salt and pepper; spoon shrimp mixture onto 1 end of fillets. Roll up fillets; secure edges. Place in well-greased baking dish. Combine mushroom soup with 1/4 cup water; pour over fillets. Sprinkle with cheese. Bake in 400-degree oven for 30 minutes.

STUFFED FLOUNDER

2 lb. flounder
Lemon juice
Parsley
1 onion
1 clove of garlic
1 sm. green pepper
Butter
3 slices toast
2 eggs, beaten
Salt and pepper to taste
1 1/2 c. crab meat
Parmesan cheese
Paprika

Dress flounder; slit deep pocket in one side. Sprinkle cavity with lemon juice and parsley; let stand for 1 hour. Mince onion, garlic and green pepper; saute in butter in saucepan until tender. Cut toast into small cubes; combine with onion mixture. Add eggs, salt, pepper and crab meat to bread mixture; blend well. Remove parsley from cavity; stuff with crab meat dressing. Secure edges; sprinkle with Parmesan cheese and paprika. Bake at 375 degrees for 1 hour or until fish flakes easily.

STUFFED FLOUNDER FILLETS

2 tbsp. flour
Salt
1 tbsp. mustard
1/2 tsp. Worcestershire sauce
3 1/2 tsp. lemon juice
Dash of pepper
Dash of hot sauce
6 tbsp. melted butter
2/3 c. milk
2 c. crab meat
8 fillets of flounder

Stir flour, salt, mustard, Worcestershire sauce, 1/2 teaspoon lemon juice, pepper and hot sauce into butter. Add milk gradually; simmer, stirring constantly, until thickened. Stir in crab. Arrange 4 flounder fillets in greased shallow pan; spread each with 1/4 of the crab mixture. Top with remaining fillets; brush with butter and remaining juice. Bake at 350 degrees for 25 minutes.

CASSEROLE OF FILLET OF FLOUNDER

2 1/2 lb. spinach
1 1/2 lb. flounder fillets
2 tbsp. finely chopped onion
Salt and pepper to taste
4 1/2 tbsp. butter
3 1/2 tbsp. flour
2 c. milk
White pepper to taste
12 whole cooked shrimp
1/4 c. grated sharp cheese

Cook spinach in small amount of boiling, salted water until just tender. Drain thoroughly; chop. Spread in greased 1 1/2-quart casserole. Place fillets on spinach; sprinkle onion over fillets. Season with salt and pepper. Melt butter; stir in flour. Add milk slowly; cook, stirring constantly, until thickened. Add salt and white pepper as desired; pour over onion. Arrange shrimp over top; sprinkle with cheese. Bake for 20 minutes in 400-degree oven. Yield: 4 servings.

BAKED FLOUNDER WITH VEGETABLES

1 3 to 4-lb. flounder
Salt
6 med. potatoes, sliced
2 med. onions, sliced
Pepper
4 tbsp. butter, melted
3 slices bacon

Sprinkle flounder and cavity with 1 1/2 teaspoons salt; place in greased baking dish. Arrange potatoes and onions around flounder; sprinkle vegetables with additional salt and pepper. Pour 1/2 cup water over flounder; brush top with butter. Top flounder with bacon. Bake at 350 degrees for 30 to 35 minutes or until potatoes are tender and fish flakes easily; baste occasionally with pan juices.

BATTER-FRIED FLOUNDER

1 c. flour
2 tbsp. baking powder
Salt to taste
1 egg, separated
2 lb. boneless flounder

Sift flour, baking powder and salt into bowl. Drop egg yolk in center; add 1/2 cup lukewarm water and 1 tablespoon melted fat. Mix well. Fold in beaten egg white. Dip flounder into batter. Fry at 365 degrees for about 6 minutes.

OVEN-FRIED FLOUNDER WITH ALMOND BUTTER

1 tbsp. salt
1 c. milk
6 flounder fillets
1 c. fine dry bread crumbs
Melted butter
Lemon juice
1/2 c. chopped blanched almonds

Combine salt and milk; dip fish into milk mixture. Roll in bread crumbs; place in baking dish. Drizzle melted butter over fish. Bake at 500 degrees for about 15 minutes, turning once. Sprinkle lemon juice over fish. Brown almonds in 6 tablespoons butter; serve with fish. Yield: 6 servings.

SOUTHERN PAN-FRIED FLOUNDER

1 2 to 3-lb. flounder
1 c. shortening
2 tbsp. salt
1/2 c. cornmeal

Cut fish into serving pieces. Place shortening in frypan over medium heat. Mix salt and cornmeal; roll fish in cornmeal mixture. Drop into frypan; fry for 3 minutes or until delicately browned. Yield: 4 servings.

FLOUNDER FILLETS IN WINE SAUCE

2 lb. fillets of flounder
Salt and pepper to taste
3 tbsp. butter
2/3 c. dry white wine
Juice of 1 lemon
1 tbsp. flour
1 egg yolk

Arrange fillets in pan in single layer; sprinkle with salt and pepper. Add 2 tablespoons butter, wine, 1/3 cup water and lemon juice. Bring to a boil; reduce heat. Simmer, covered, for 15 minutes. Remove fillets to heated platter; keep warm. Melt remaining butter; add flour. Combine flour mixture with wine stock gradually. Simmer, stirring constantly until sauce is thickened. Stir a small amount of hot mixture into egg yolk; return egg mixture to wine sauce. Season to taste; blend well. Strain sauce; pour over fish. Serve immediately.

FLOUNDER WITH LEMON SAUCE

3 lb. flounder
2 tsp. salt
3 tbsp. butter
2 onions, sliced fine
1/2 tsp. pepper
1/2 tsp. powdered ginger
Dash of mace
1/3 c. lemon juice
2 tbsp. grated lemon rind
2 tbsp. flour
2 eggs, beaten
1/2 tsp. saffron
2 tbsp. snipped parsley

Cut flounder into 6 thick slices; sprinkle with salt. Saute onions in butter in saucepan for 5 minutes. Add flounder slices; brown lightly, turning once. Sprinkle pepper, ginger and mace over flounder; add 2 cups water. Simmer, covered, for 30 minutes; stir in lemon juice and rind. Combine flour, eggs, saffron and parsley; beat well. Add 1/2 cup fish stock to egg mixture gradually, beating constantly. Return to saucepan; simmer, stirring constantly, until mixture is thickened. Remove flounder to hot platter; pour sauce over flounder. Serve immediately.

Fondant

A soft, creamy confection made of sugar that is used to coat nuts and fruits, to stuff dates and prunes, and to ice small cakes. Fondant is also used as the center of dipped bonbons.

PREPARATION: Heat sugar and water slowly in saucepan while stirring. When sugar dissolves *completely*, add specified recipe acidic substance (cream of tartar, corn syrup, glucose, or lemon juice). Quickly bring mixture to boil, washing down crystals on pan sides with fork wrapped in damp cloth. *Do not stir at any time.* Boil until syrup reaches soft-ball stage (when a drop of syrup dropped in very cold water forms a soft ball that flattens when removed from water) and when it registers from 234 to 240 degrees on a candy thermometer. Remove fondant from heat and pour on platters. Let stand until lukewarm. Add flavoring and coloring (depending on recipe). Knead batch until creamy and smooth. Place in tightly covered jar and allow to mellow several days at room temperature. To use as centers of bonbons, shape by hand or push into molds. To use as confection coating, melt fondant in top of double boiler.

(See CANDY.)

BASIC FONDANT

2 c. sugar
1/8 tsp. cream of tartar
2 tbsp. light corn syrup

Place 2/3 cup water, sugar, cream of tartar and corn syrup in heavy small saucepan over low heat; stir mixture gently until sugar is dissolved. Avoid splashing on sides of saucepan above level of mixture. Cover; bring to a boil, cooking gently for about 3 minutes. Do not stir. Remove cover; continue cooking gently to 238 degrees on candy thermometer. Remove from heat; pour onto a large wet platter. Do not scrape syrup from saucepan; cool to lukewarm. Stir until syrup changes to creamy white mass; knead until smooth and creamy. Disregard small lumps. Store, covered, at room temperature. Let stand for 2 days before using. Yield: 1/2 pound fondant.

THREE-FLAVOR FONDANT

1/2 c. butter
1/3 c. light corn syrup
1/2 tsp. salt
1 tsp. vanilla extract
4 1/2 c. confectioners' sugar
Yellow food coloring
1/2 tsp. lemon flavoring
Green food coloring
1/2 tsp. peppermint flavoring
1/2 tsp. almond flavoring
Walnuts, pecans or almonds

Combine butter, corn syrup, salt, vanilla and confectioners' sugar in large bowl. Mix with hands until well blended. Divide fondant into 3 parts, placing each part in small bowls. Add yellow food coloring and lemon flavoring to first part; mix green food coloring and peppermint flavoring into second part. Add almond flavoring to third part. Knead mixtures in each bowl making uniform color or marbleized effect. Mix in additional confectioners' sugar if mixture is sticky. Shape mixture into balls. Press nut halves into center of each ball, if desired. Yield: 8 dozen.

CHOCOLATE FONDANT

1/2 c. margarine
2 c. chopped pecans
2 boxes confectioners' sugar
1 can sweetened condensed milk
1 3 1/2-oz. can coconut
1 12-oz. package semisweet chocolate chips
1/4 lb. paraffin

Melt margarine; pour over pecans. Let stand for about 15 minutes. Sift sugar. Add milk; cream together thoroughly. Add coconut and pecans; mix well. Shape mixture into small balls. Place on waxed paper; refrigerate. Melt chocolate chips and paraffin in top of double boiler over hot water. Dip each ball, using toothpick, into chocolate until coated. Place on waxed paper.

CREAM FONDANT

3 c. sugar
1/2 tsp. cream of tartar
1/2 tsp. salt
1/4 c. orange juice
3 c. pecan halves

Combine sugar, 1 1/3 cups water, cream of tartar and salt; stir well. Cook over medium heat until sugar mixture forms soft ball. Do not stir. Cool; add juice and pecans. Beat until creamy and mixture holds shape; drop by spoonfuls onto waxed paper.

MINT FONDANT

4 c. sugar
1/8 tsp. cream of tartar
6 tsp. light corn syrup
Mint flavoring

Pour 2 cups water in saucepan; add sugar, cream of tartar, corn syrup and mint flavoring in order given. Bring to a boil, without stirring, to 236 degrees on candy thermometer. Pour onto wet platter; cool. Beat with spatula or wooden spoon until thick and white. Knead, if necessary. Store in covered container for at least 12 hours. Fondant may be stored for several months without refrigeration. Soften fondant over warm water. Food coloring may be added, if desired. Pour into molds or drop from teaspoon onto waxed paper.

PEANUT BUTTER FONDANT

2 c. sugar
2 tbsp. light corn syrup
1 tsp. vanilla
Peanut butter

Mix sugar, 1 1/4 cups water and corn syrup in saucepan; cook to 238 degrees on candy thermometer. Remove crystals from side of pan; pour mixture onto chilled platter. Cool to 100 degrees on candy thermometer; add vanilla. Beat until white and creamy; knead. Roll out; spread with peanut butter. Roll jelly roll fashion; slice.

SMOOTH FONDANT

Color photograph for this recipe on page 495.

1/3 c. margarine
1/3 c. light corn syrup
1 tsp. vanilla
1/2 tsp. salt
1 lb. confectioners' sugar
Pitted dates
Sugar

Blend margarine, corn syrup, vanilla and salt in large mixing bowl. Add confectioners' sugar all at once; mix well. Turn out onto board; knead until mixture is well blended and smooth. Store in cool place. Shape fondant into small finger-shaped rolls; stuff into dates. Roll in sugar.

Fondue

The word "fondue" comes from the French word *fondre,* meaning to melt. The original fondue was developed in Switzerland from hardened bread and cheese. An enterprising cook discovered that hard cheese melted under heat and that when pieces of stale bread were dipped into the melted cheese, the combination was delicious–thus fondue was created.

EQUIPMENT: A *fondue pot* is a must for making fondue. There are three types of fondue pots. Two are earthenware and the other is metal. Cheese fondues are prepared in round, heavy pottery dishes with wide mouths and a heavy handle. A smaller version of this same dish is used to prepare dessert fondues. The metal fondue pot is wider at the bottom than at the top. It is deeper than the larger earthenware pot and is used to prepare meat, seafood, and vegetable fondues that are cooked in hot oil. The metal can tolerate the 360 degrees of heat needed to keep the oil hot, without cracking, as would an earthenware pot. The shape of the metal pot keeps oils from spattering as foods cook. Choose earthenware or metal fondue pots that are well-balanced and have sturdy frames and trays. (See illustration below.) One pot is sufficient to serve 4 people.

The heat source for fondue pots depends on the kind of fondue being prepared. Cheese, meat, seafood, and vegetable fondues need more intense heat than do dessert fondues. For the latter, choose a *candle warmer.* (Dessert fondues are usually prepared on a stove over very low heat and poured into a fondue pot. The only heat source needed is one of sufficient strength to keep the dessert warm.) For all other fondues, choose from alcohol lamps, canned heat, or electricity.

There are two types of *alcohol lamps,*

both illustrated below. One has a bottom compartment that holds alcohol with a wick that is raised and lowered by turning a screw. The other has cotton wool in its base. Alcohol is poured over the cotton, ignited, and the degree of heat is controlled by a cover that opens and closes vents on the side of the lamp. When using either of these two lamps, never fill it more than half full. One tablespoon of alcohol gives about 12 minutes cooking time. Denatured alcohol is the best to use.

Canned heat fits into special lamps that come with fondue pots or can be purchased separately. The degree of heat is controlled by a vented cover similar to that on the alcohol lamp. A 2 5/8-ounce can burns for 50-60 minutes; a 7-ounce can burns 4 hours.

Electric fondue pots are available. To use, simply follow manufacturer's directions.

In addition to pots and heat sources, other important equipment for fondue making are *fondue forks* that often have wooden ends to prevent heat conduction and divided *fondue plates* with compartments for several sauces or accompaniments. The plates are available in a number of materials, but traditionally, fondue plates are made of wood.

TYPES: The classic fondue is *cheese,* and it is usually prepared with either Emmentaler or Gruyere cheese or a combination of both. Both cheeses are Swiss—Emmentaler is very mild and Gruyere is stronger. The proportion of the one to the other determines the mildness or strong flavor of your fondue. Cheese for a fondue should be diced or shredded but never grated as grated cheese will lump. Be certain to use only the cheese specified in your recipe since only certain cheeses can be used in fondue. Cheese is usually melted in a light, dry, sparkling white wine. The Swiss prefer Neuchatel, but Rhine, Reisling, or Chablis will do as well. Wine is heated until bubbles form around the edges and on the bottom of the pot. Cheese is added a handful at a time, and the mixture is stirred constantly with a wooden spoon. When all the cheese has melted, the fondue is flavored with Kirsch or brandy, or nutmeg and freshly ground pepper. Crusty pieces of bread are speared with a fondue fork and dipped into the cheese. Each place setting for cheese fondue should include a wooden plate with pieces of bread, a fondue fork, a dinner plate, and a dinner fork.

Fondue Bourguignonne, consists of pieces of meat or seafood speared on a fork and cooked in a pot of hot cooking oil. Some people prefer a mixture of peanut oil and butter while others use coconut oil, salad oil, or olive oil. The latter smokes quickly and can be hard to use. The meat for these fondues is usually beef. Tenderloin, sirloin, or porterhouse are the preferred cuts although other cuts may be used if they are first tenderized. Veal is apt to be tough unless cut from the tenderloin. If pork is used, caution those present to cook it thoroughly. Allow 5-7 ounces of meat per person. The most popular seafood fondue is shrimp—allow about 2 pounds raw, shelled shrimp for 4 people. Each place setting for fondue Bourguignonne should have a bowl filled with the meat or seafood to be cooked, a dinner plate, a fondue fork, and a dinner fork.

A *dessert fondue* usually consists of a sauce that may be chocolate, butterscotch, fruit, or almost any dessert-type flavor. Pieces of fruit, cake, doughnuts—anything that can be speared with a fondue fork and will harmonize with the sauce—are dipped into the sauce and eaten.

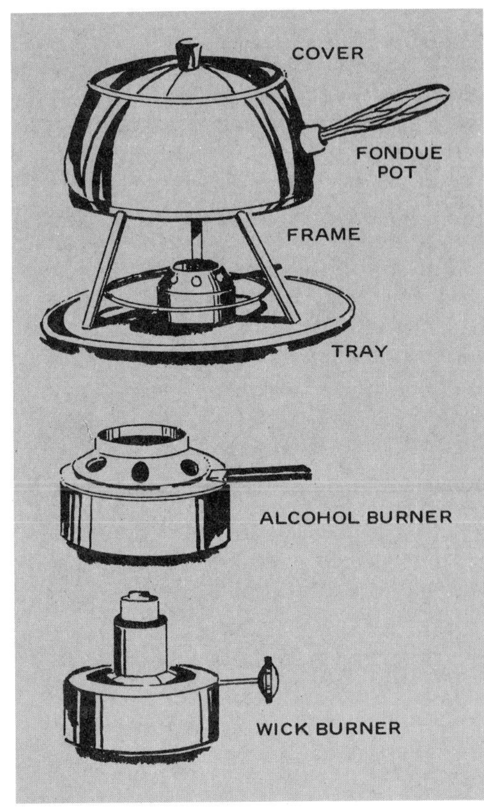

Frankfurters

A frankfurter is a type of sausage made from beef, pork, veal, or a combination of any of these three. The sausage meat is cured, chopped, seasoned, stuffed into casing, smoked, and cooked. Frankfurters contain protein, some of the B vitamins, iron, and calcium. (2 6-inch all beef frankfurters = 250 calories)

AVAILABILITY: Year-round in packages, jars, and cans.

BUYING: Look for a Federal inspection seal on packages, jars, and cans. Read labels for ingredients. Labels may read "All Meat," "All Beef," and/or "Skinless." "All Meat" indicates that the frankfurters are made from beef, pork, veal, or a combination using any of these three without the addition of cereal fillers. "All Beef" indicates beef content exclusively. "Skinless" means that the casing has been removed after processing and before packaging. Frankfurters can be bought in various sizes–6-inch, 12-inch, or bite-size.

STORING: Refrigerate packaged frankfurters in original package or wrapped in waxed paper up to one week. Store unopened cans and jars on kitchen shelf up to 1 year.

PREPARATION: *To boil*–Place in saucepan. Cover with boiling water, and heat 5 to 10 minutes, depending on size of frankfurters. *To Broil*–make about 5 diagonal cuts, 1/4 inch deep, on frankfurters. Brush with oil. Place on broiler pan. Cook 3 to 4 inches away from heat, turn once. *To pan-fry*–Heat shortening in skillet to coat. Slowly simmer whole frankfurters or frankfurters slashed lengthwise until they are browned and heated through, turning several times. *To charcoal-grill*–Place frankfurters 5 inches away from hot coals. Grill 3 to 6 minutes on each side.

SERVING: Serve with baked beans, sauerkraut, or chili sauce. Can be prepared in many ways for appetizers and sandwiches. Can be used in soups, salads, and casseroles.

FLAMING FRANKS

1/4 c. brown sugar
1/4 c. cornstarch
1/4 c. vinegar
1/4 c. orange marmalade
1 c. pineapple juice
1 lge. can pineapple tidbits, undrained
10 franks, quartered
1 c. peeled orange sections
8 maraschino cherries
1/2 c. Cointreau

Combine brown sugar, cornstarch, vinegar and marmalade in saucepan; add pineapple juice and pineapple. Cook, stirring, until thickened. Turn into chafing dish; add franks, orange sections and cherries. Heat through. Pour Cointreau over top. Ignite and serve. Yield: 4-5 servings.

FRANK KABOBS

1/3 c. (packed) brown sugar
1/2 tsp. nutmeg
2 tbsp. orange juice
6 tbsp. melted butter
4 onions
4 apples
1 lb. frankfurters
2 apple slices

Combine brown sugar, nutmeg, orange juice and butter for basting sauce. Parboil onions; cut in thick slices. Cut apples in thick slices. Cut frankfurters into 1-inch pieces. Thread frankfurters, onions and apples on cocktail skewers. Broil over low coals until frankfurters are heated through, brushing frequently with sauce.

HIBACHI FRANKS

1 8-oz. can crushed pineapple
1 lge. onion, finely chopped
2 tbsp. oil
1/4 c. brown sugar
1 tbsp. prepared mustard
1 tbsp. Worcestershire sauce
2 tbsp. vinegar
2 tbsp. dry mustard
Dash of salt
Dash of paprika
1/2 c. heavy cream, whipped
Canned cocktail frankfurters
Pineapple chunks

Drain pineapple, reserving 1/2 cup syrup. Cook onion in oil until soft. Add pineapple, reserved pineapple syrup, brown sugar, mustard, Worcestershire sauce and vinegar. Bring to a boil; reduce heat. Simmer for about 10 minutes. Keep warm over hibachi. Mix dry mustard and enough water to make thin paste; fold mustard, salt and paprika into whipped cream. Serve mustard sauce at room temperature. Spear cocktail franks and pineapple with toothpicks; grill over hibachi. Dip into mustard sauce.

SMOKY DOGS

1/4 c. vinegar
1/2 c. water
1 tbsp. lemon juice
2 tbsp. chopped onion
1/4 c. butter
2 tbsp. sugar
1 tbsp. prepared mustard
1 1/2 tsp. salt
1/2 tsp. pepper
1/4 tsp. cayenne pepper
1/2 c. catsup
2 tbsp. Worcestershire sauce
1 1/2 tsp. liquid smoke
1 lb. wieners

Combine vinegar, water, lemon juice, onion, butter, sugar, mustard, salt, pepper and cayenne pepper in top of double boiler; simmer, uncovered, for 20 minutes. Add catsup, Worcestershire sauce and liquid smoke; bring to a boil. Cut each wiener into 6 pieces; add to sauce. Cover; cook for 4 hours, stirring occasionally. Serve in chafing dish.

SWEET AND SOUR WIENER BITES

3/4 c. prepared mustard
1 c. currant jelly
1 lb. frankfurters

Mix mustard and jelly in chafing dish or double boiler. Slice frankfurters diagonally into bite-sized pieces. Add to sauce; heat through.

STUFFED DOGS

1/2 c. potato chip crumbs
1 c. grated American cheese
3 tbsp. chopped onion
1 tsp. Worcestershire sauce
1/4 c. tomato sauce
10 wieners

Combine potato chip crumbs, cheese, onion, Worcestershire sauce and tomato sauce; mix well. Split wieners almost through; fill wieners with cheese mixture. Place on baking sheet. Bake at 350 degrees for 20 minutes. Cut each wiener into 5 or 6 pieces. Serve hot.

SMALL FRYS

2 15-oz. cans tomato sauce
1/2 c. brown sugar
2 tbsp. Worcestershire sauce
1 tbsp. garlic salt
1/2 c. vinegar
1 tbsp. teriyaki sauce
2 lb. wieners

Combine tomato sauce, brown sugar, Worcestershire sauce, garlic salt, vinegar and teriyaki sauce in saucepan; mix well. Cut wieners into 1/2-inch pieces; add to sauce mixture. Simmer for about 25 minutes. Turn into chafing dish to keep warm. Serve with cocktail picks.

HOT DOG SANDWICH

8 wieners
1 can bean and bacon soup
1/2 c. catsup
1/3 c. water
8 hot dog buns

Cook wieners according to package directions; drain. Combine soup, catsup and water in saucepan; mix well. Simmer until heated through. Spread soup mixture on buns; add wieners.

CHEESE AND BACON FRANKS

1 c. grated American cheese
2 tbsp. butter
1 tbsp. prepared mustard
6 frankfurters
6 frankfurter rolls
Butter or margarine
6 strips dill pickle
6 slices cooked bacon

Combine cheese, butter and mustard. Split frankfurters almost through; fill with cheese mixture. Split rolls; spread with butter. Place frankfurters in rolls; arrange in shallow baking pan. Tuck pickle and bacon in rolls. Bake at 400 degrees for 10 minutes.

Mexican Round Dogs on Sauerkraut . . . Tortillas with zesty hot dogs, corn, and peppers.

MEXICAN ROUND DOGS ON SAUERKRAUT

1 med. onion, chopped
1 tbsp. butter
4 c. drained sauerkraut
1 10 1/4-oz. can marinara sauce
8 frozen tortillas
Salad oil
8 green pepper rings
8 frankfurters
1 8-oz. can whole kernel corn

Saute onion in butter in saucepan until golden. Add sauerkraut and marinara sauce; mix well. Cover; cook over low heat for 30 minutes. Fry tortillas in 1 inch hot oil in skillet until crisp; drain on paper towels. Fry green pepper rings for 1 minute; drain. Cut 10 slits in each frankfurter, taking care not to cut all the way through. Brown on both sides in skillet. Frankfurters will curl into rings. Spoon some sauerkraut mixture on each tortilla on serving platter. Place frankfurter circles on sauerkraut. Top each circle with green pepper ring. Heat corn in saucepan; drain. Spoon corn into green pepper rings. Serve. May reheat in 350-degree oven for 10 minutes if desired. Yield: 8 servings.

HOT DOG SURPRISE

1 lb. ground beef
1 tsp. salt
Dash of pepper
1/3 c. evaporated milk
3 frankfurters, split lengthwise
6 buttered toasted wiener buns

Combine ground beef, salt, pepper and milk; shape into six 5-inch rolls. Place in baking pan. Press 1 frankfurter half into each beef roll. Broil 3 inches from source of heat for 8 to 10 minutes, turning once. Place in buns. Garnish with mustard and sliced pickles.

FABULOUS FRANK SANDWICHES

6 frankfurters, finely chopped
1/2 c. grated sharp cheese
2 hard-cooked eggs, chopped
2 tbsp. chopped pickles
3 tbsp. catsup
1 tsp. prepared mustard
2 tbsp. salad oil
1/4 tsp. salt
8 frankfurter buns, split

Combine frankfurters, cheese, eggs, pickles, catsup, mustard, oil and salt; mix lightly. Fill buns with frankfurter mixture; wrap each bun in foil, twisting ends securely. Place on baking sheet. Bake at 350 degrees for 10 minutes. Serve hot.

PATIO SPECIAL

2 c. ground wieners
1/3 c. grated cheese
2 hard-cooked eggs, chopped
3 tbsp. chili sauce
2 tbsp. pickle relish
1 tsp. prepared mustard
1/2 tsp. garlic salt
Wiener buns

Combine wieners, cheese, eggs, chili sauce, pickle relish, mustard and salt. Split buns almost through; spread wiener mixture in buns. Wrap buns separately in foil. Place on grill over low coals; cook until heated through, turning frequently. Serve warm.

CHILI ROLLS

8 frankfurters, thinly sliced
2 1/2 c. chopped onions
1 tbsp. salad oil
1 tsp. chili powder
3 8-oz. cans tomato sauce
1 1-lb. can red kidney beans
1/4 tsp. salt
2 pkg. refrigerator biscuits
1 c. chili sauce
1 c. grated Cheddar cheese

Saute frankfurters and 1/2 cup onion in oil in skillet until onion is soft. Stir in chili powder, 1 can tomato sauce, beans and salt; simmer for 15 minutes. Separate biscuits; roll each to 5-inch rounds on lightly floured board. Fry biscuits over low heat for 2 minutes or until tops are bubbly and undersides flecked with brown. Turn; fry for about 2 minutes longer. Spread biscuits with frankfurter filling; roll up. Place seam-side down in double row in greased 13 x 9 x 2-inch baking pan. Combine remaining tomato sauce, chili sauce and remaining onions; spoon evenly over biscuit rolls. Sprinkle with cheese. Bake at 350 degrees for 30 minutes.

CREOLE CASSEROLE

3/4 c. rice
1 1/2 c. sliced onions
3 tbsp. butter or margarine
3 1/2 c. tomatoes
1 1/2 tsp. salt
1/4 c. diced green pepper
2 whole cloves
1 bay leaf
1 tsp. sugar
8 frankfurters, sliced

Cook rice according to package directions. Saute onions in butter until transparent. Add tomatoes, salt, green pepper, cloves, bay leaf and sugar; simmer for 20 minutes. Remove bay leaf and cloves; stir in rice. Layer rice mixture and frankfurters in casserole; cover. Bake at 325 degrees for 45 minutes. Uncover; bake for 15 minutes longer.

CROWN CASSEROLE

2 slices bacon
1/2 c. chopped onion
1 can cream of mushroom soup
1/2 c. water
1/2 tsp. salt
Dash of pepper
3 c. sliced cooked potatoes
1 c. cooked cut green beans
1/2 lb. frankfurters

Cook bacon; remove from skillet and crumble. Saute onion in bacon drippings; stir in soup, water, salt and pepper. Add potatoes and beans; pour into 1 1/2-quart casserole. Halve and split frankfurters. Stand frankfurters around edge of casserole. Bake at 350 degrees for 30 minutes. Top with bacon.

FRANKFURTER-NOODLE CASSEROLE

1 2/3 c. evaporated milk
1/2 tsp. salt
2 c. grated cheese
4 c. cooked noodles
2 c. sliced wieners

Scald milk; add salt and cheese. Stir until cheese is melted. Combine noodles and wieners in greased 1-quart casserole; cover with cheese sauce. Bake at 350 degrees for 30 to 40 minutes.

FRANKFURTER-POTATO CASSEROLE

4 frankfurters
4 c. thinly sliced cooked potatoes
1 1/2 tsp. salt
Dash of pepper
1/3 c. salad oil
3 tbsp. vinegar
1 1/2 c. cooked green beans
1/4 c. thinly sliced onion

Cook frankfurters in boiling water to cover for 7 to 8 minutes; drain and slice. Combine potatoes, seasonings, oil and vinegar. Place beans in greased 1 1/2-quart casserole. Layer potato mixture, onion and frankfurters over beans; cover. Bake at 400 degrees for 35 to 40 minutes.

FRANKFURTER-TOMATO CASSEROLE

1 med. onion, chopped
1/4 c. butter
1/4 c. flour
3 c. stewed tomatoes
1 tbsp. catsup
1 tsp. salt
1/4 tsp. pepper
8 frankfurters

Saute onion in butter in saucepan; blend in flour. Add tomatoes; cook until thickened, stirring constantly. Add catsup, salt and pepper. Split frankfurters lengthwise; arrange, cut side down, in greased casserole. Pour tomato sauce over frankfurters. Bake at 350 degrees for 25 to 35 minutes.

SUMMER CASSEROLE

10 wieners
1 green pepper, chopped
1 onion, chopped
2 tbsp. butter
2 c. soft bread crumbs

2 lge. cans pork and beans
1/2 lb. process cheese, grated

Cut wieners into thin slices. Saute green pepper and onion in butter; stir in bread crumbs, beans, wieners and cheese. Place in 4-quart casserole; cover. Bake at 325 degrees for 1 hour.

SUNDAY SUPPER CASSEROLE

1/4 c. shortening
1/2 c. chopped onion
1/4 c. flour
1 tsp. salt
2 c. milk
1 tbsp. mustard
1/4 lb. shredded American cheese
6 wieners
3 c. sliced potatoes

Melt shortening in saucepan; add onion. Cook until onion is tender. Stir in flour and salt; add milk gradually. Cook over low heat, stirring constantly, until thickened. Remove from heat; stir in mustard and cheese. Slice wieners thin. Layer potatoes, wieners and cheese sauce in greased 2-quart casserole until all are used, ending with cheese sauce. Bake at 325 degrees for 1 hour and 30 minutes.

QUICKIE CASSEROLE

10 wieners, split
10 strips cheese
10 slices bacon
1 lge. can sauerkraut

Stuff wieners with cheese strips. Wrap with bacon; secure bacon with picks. Spread sauerkraut in casserole; place wieners on sauerkraut. Bake at 350 degrees for 30 minutes.

FRANKFURTER-FRUIT POT

3/4 c. chopped onion
6 tbsp. butter
3 1/2 c. sauerkraut with juice
1 11-oz. package mixed dried fruit
12 frankfurters
1 1/2 tbsp. (packed) dark brown sugar
1 1/2 tsp. caraway seed
Dash of freshly ground pepper
2 tsp. bottled steak sauce
2 1/4 c. apple juice
1 1/2 tbsp. cornstarch

Saute onion in butter in Dutch oven until tender, stirring occasionally. Add sauerkraut; cook for several minutes. Trim any cores from dried fruit if necessary; cut large pieces of fruit in half. Add fruit to sauerkraut mixture. Cut frankfurters into thirds; add frankfurters, brown sugar, seasonings, steak sauce and apple juice to sauerkraut mixture. Cover; cook for 30 minutes or until fruit is tender, stirring occasionally. Drain about 2 cups liquid from sauerkraut mixture. Place sauerkraut mixture in serving dish; cover and keep warm. Return liquid to Dutch oven. Blend 2 tablespoons cold water with cornstarch. Stir into liquid. Cook, stirring constantly, until mixture boils for 2 minutes. Serve as sauce with sauerkraut mixture. Yield: 8 servings.

Frankfurter-Fruit Pot . . . Dried fruit and apple juice lend unusual flavor to this main dish.

GERMAN WIENER BAKE

1 lb. wieners
2 1-lb. cans pork and beans
1/4 c. chili sauce
1 1-lb. can sauerkraut
1/2 tsp. chopped dill

Slice 5 wieners. Combine sliced wieners, beans and chili sauce; place in 1 1/2-quart casserole. Drain sauerkraut; place in casserole. Sprinkle with dill. Bake at 325 degrees for 30 minutes. Top with whole wieners; bake for 15 minutes longer. Yield: 5 servings.

WESTERN FRANKFURTER BAKE

1 lb. frankfurters
1 head lettuce
2 c. cold water
1 tsp. salt
1 c. cornmeal
1 egg, lightly beaten
1 c. grated Cheddar cheese
1/2 c. minced celery
1/2 c. minced onion
1 tbsp. butter or margarine
1 8-oz. can tomato sauce
1/2 tsp. oregano

Cut frankfurters into 1-inch pieces. Shred lettuce. Combine water and salt in saucepan over low heat. Stir in cornmeal; cook until thickened, stirring constantly. Remove from heat; stir small amount of hot cornmeal mixture into egg. Return to remaining cornmeal mixture; fold in 1/2 cup cheese, stirring until melted. Line greased 1 1/2-quart casserole with cornmeal mixture, using wet spoon to push mixture against sides. Bake at 350 degrees 15 minutes. Saute celery and onion in butter until tender; add frankfurters, tomato sauce and oregano. Bring to a boil. Layer frankfurter mixture and lettuce in baked shell; sprinkle with remaining cheese. Broil until cheese melts. Serve immediately.

PIZZA DOGS

8 hot dog rolls
8 wieners
2 c. shredded American cheese
1 c. tomato paste
1 1/2 tsp. sugar
1/2 tsp. oregano
3/4 tsp. garlic salt

Split rolls; toast lightly. Cut wieners into thin circles. Mix cheese, tomato paste, sugar, oregano and salt; spread on rolls. Overlap wiener circles on cheese spread. Broil for 5 minutes.

Freezing Foods

Freezing is the process of preserving foods at temperatures below 32 degrees. There are two basic freezing units, the refrigerator freezer compartment and the home freezer. *Refrigerator freezer compartments* are units attached to refrigerators. The temperature in these units is below 32 degrees but seldom below zero degree. For this reason, frozen foods are kept in freezer compartments for less time than they are in home freezers. *Home freezers* are upright or chest units that maintain temperatures at below zero degree.

PROCESSING: Throughout this encyclopedia, directions for preparing specific foods for freezing are given under the separate entries for those foods. However, some foods may be processed for freezing that contain sauce or are part of casserole dishes. Before you process such foods for freezing there are some things you should know. They are as follows: *Cheese* does not freeze well and should be added to a dish only after the dish is thawed. *Hard-cooked egg yolks* should be diced or sieved before freezing. They become tough when frozen unless they are first diced or put through a sieve. *Fats* become rancid after two months freezing time has elapsed. *Mayonnaise* sometimes separates during freezing. Its original consistency can be restored by stirring during the thawing process. *Meats* that have been frozen may be thawed, cooked, and refrozen without affecting their flavor. But very small pieces of meat tend to dry out if frozen. *Noodles, spaghetti,* and *macaroni* that have been cooked lose flavor if frozen and thawed. *Potatoes* seldom freeze well—they break down when thawed and become mushy. Add them to a dish after thawing. *Sauces* with cheese or milk in their ingredients tend to curdle if they are frozen and reheated; thickened sauces tend to become thicker; always avoid freezing egg-based sauces. *Seasonings* undergo considerable changes during freezing. Parsley and chives may become soggy after thawing; onion and salt become considerably diminished in flavor as do most herbs; garlic and clove become unpleasantly strong; curry develops a musty flavor. As a general rule, do not include any seasonings in foods or dishes being frozen; add them after the thawing process is complete.

PACKAGING: *Preformed containers*—There are half-pint, pint, quart, and half-gallon containers made of material specifically designed to prevent moisture and vapors from escaping. In using these containers, allow the head space designated under each food entry. If none is specified or there is no entry, allow 1 1/2-inch head space. This space permits food to expand under freezing without stretching or bursting the packaging. *Do-it-yourself* wrapping—It is also possible to wrap foods for freezing without special containers. Use aluminum foil or special laminated papers. Wrap using the lock-seal method. That is, place food in the center of a large piece of foil or paper. Bring the ends together and fold them into an interlocking seam. Fold the paper down tightly against the food. Turn the package over so that this seam is against your working surface. Turn the package so that one of the open ends is near your body and the other one faces away from you. Pleat-fold the end nearest you, and fold it over again before pressing it against the package. Holding the closed end tightly against you, gradually force air out of the open end of the package. If air is left in packaged food, it draws on the moisture and juices of that food to form an exterior frost. The frost gives off the odor of the food it covers. Several such frosts on different foods may cause a mingling of flavors and radical alterations in the taste of the thawed products. For that reason, moistureproof, vaporproof wrappings are essential. Fold the remaining open end. Seal with special freezer tape or a sealing iron; label and date the package.

STORING: Food freezes more rapidly if it is placed near or touches the walls of the home freezer or freezing compartment. Never overload a freezer by putting several packages of unfrozen food into it at once. Leave plenty of room for the air to circulate around the packages of freezing foods. The quicker foods freeze, the better their flavor when thawed.

Frogs' Legs

LOUISIANA FROGS' LEGS

1 c. flour
Salt and pepper
12 lge. frogs' legs

Preheat deep fat to 238 degrees. Combine flour, salt and pepper in bag. Place frogs' legs in bag; shake, coating well. Remove frogs' legs; shake off excess flour. Drop into deep hot fat; fry until golden brown. Drain. Serve immediately. Yield: 6 servings.

FRIED FROGS' LEGS

8 frogs' legs
1 sm. onion, sliced
2 cloves of garlic, minced
1 c. vinegar
Salt
1 slice lemon
1 c. flour
1 egg, beaten
1/4 tsp. red pepper
1/2 c. milk

Place frogs' legs in layer in shallow baking dish; spread onion and garlic over top. Cover with vinegar. Let stand for 2 hours; drain. Place frogs' legs in water to cover, bringing to a boil; add 1 tablespoon salt and lemon. Cook for 20 minutes. Remove from heat; drain. Combine 1 teaspoon salt, flour, egg, red pepper and milk, mixing thoroughly to make batter. Dip frogs' legs into batter. Fry in hot deep fat until golden brown. Yield: 4 servings.

Frosting

A frosting is a sweet, decorative spread for cakes, cupcakes, cookies, and pastry. Its close relative is the filling, used to add content, flavor, and color between cake layers. A frosting is usually made from ingredients such as sugar, butter, egg whites, and liquid. Flavoring and coloring vary according to individual recipes. A frosting is distinguished from an icing in that a frosting may be cooked (ingredients are exposed to a heat source) or uncooked ingredients are blended together without the addition of heat). An icing is a thinner, uncooked glaze.

PREPARATION: The two most common cooked frostings are boiled frostings and 7-minute frostings. In *boiled frostings*, a sugar and water syrup is cooked in a saucepan to a certain temperature. It is then beaten slowly into whipped egg whites until smooth. A *7-minute frosting* is made in the top part of a double boiler over boiling water. The recipe's specified ingredients are beaten until stiff peaks form. Uncooked frostings are generally made by the gradual addition of confectioners' sugar to a creamed butter mixture. The mixture is then beaten to spreading consistency. Some frostings are prepared in the above method, without cooking, but are then spread on the cake and baked with it. They are called *baked frostings.* Or, they may be prepared without cooking, spread on the cake, and then broiled briefly until bubbly. These frostings are known as *broiled frostings. To color frostings*—Place a small amount of frosting in a cup. Add enough food coloring to create a bright color. Blend the colored frosting into the uncolored frosting, a little at a time until the desired color is obtained. A delicately tinted frosting is more appealing than a brightly colored frosting.

MEASUREMENTS: Prepare the following amounts of frosting for the size cake layers indicated:

Frosting	Cake Size
3/4 cup	1 9-inch round layer
1 1/2 cups	2 9-inch round layers
2 1/4 cups	3 9-inch round layers
1 - 1 1/2 cups	9 1/2 x 5 1/2 x 3-inch loaf pan
2 - 2 1/2 cups	16 x 5 x 4-inch loaf pan
1 - 1 1/4 cups	16 large or 24 small cupcakes
1 1/3 cups	10 x 15-inch sheet cake
2 cups	10 x 15-inch roll

APPLICATION: To apply cooked or uncooked frosting to a two-layer cake, brush loose crumbs from thoroughly cooled layers. Place one layer, top-side-down, on plate. With spatula, spread frosting to edges of cake. Place second layer, top-side-up, on top of first layer so that bottoms of layers are together. Frost sides with up and down strokes. Frost top, applying in rough strokes or creating peaks, swirls, or ridges as desired. While decorating cake, prevent frosting in bowl from forming crust by covering bowl with damp cloth. If the frosting is of thick consistency, it can be spread most evenly and easily if you occasionally dip the spatula in hot water while frosting cake. To keep the serving plate clean when applying frosting, lay several strips of strong paper on working area. Place cake on top of strips so that paper extends beyond cake. Frost cake, lift by strip ends, and place on serving platter. Pull out strips or tear off ends. You can add crushed candies, nuts, or tinted coconut to the top of a frosted cake. Or, press thinly sliced gumdrops into the frosting to create patterns.

ALWAYS-PERFECT ICING

1 egg white
1 c. sugar
1 tsp. light corn syrup
2 tbsp. cold water
1/4 tsp. salt
1/2 tsp. vanilla or other flavoring

Mix egg white, sugar, corn syrup and 2 tablespoons cold water in top of double boiler; place over boiling water. Beat until mixture holds shape. Add salt; beat until of spreading consistency. Stir in vanilla; spread top of cake with icing. Double this recipe if sides of cake are to be iced.

APRICOT FROSTING

1/2 c. soft butter
1 c. sugar
1 egg
1 No. 2 1/2 can pitted apricots

Cream butter and sugar until smooth; add egg, blending well. Drain apricots; peel and mash. Add butter mixture to apricots. Yield: Frosts two 9-inch layer cakes or 1 oblong cake.

BAKERY ICING

1 c. shortening
1/4 c. margarine
1 lb. confectioners' sugar
1/4 tsp. vanilla
1/2 sm. can evaporated milk

Blend shortening, margarine, confectioners' sugar and vanilla together thoroughly; add milk to mixture until of spreading consistency. May be stored in refrigerator for about a week, if desired.

BANANA ICING

1/2 c. butter
1 box confectioners' sugar
2 bananas, mashed
1 c. nuts

Cream butter; add sugar until mixture is of the consistency of whipped cream. Fold in bananas and nuts. A little lemon juice may be added, if desired.

BROWN SUGAR FROSTING

1 c. (packed) brown sugar
1 egg white
1 tsp. vanilla

Place sugar, egg white and 4 tablespoons cold water in top of double boiler; place over boiling water. Beat with electric mixer until thickened and stiff peaks form. Remove from heat; stir in vanilla.

BUTTER CREAM FROSTING

1 lb. powdered sugar
1/2 c. egg yolks
1 1/4 c. butter
1/4 c. cornstarch
1 tsp. almond flavoring

Sift 3/4 of the powdered sugar into double boiler. Place over hot water; add egg yolks, blending with sugar. Keep mixture lukewarm. Remove pan from water; beat until mixture is light and fluffy. Cool. Cream butter, cornstarch and remaining powdered sugar until foamy. Add flavoring; blend thoroughly. Add egg mixture to butter mixture gradually; do not overmix. Frost top and sides of cake. Chill for several minutes to set icing.

BUTTERY FUDGE ICING

3 tbsp. cocoa
2 c. sugar
2 tbsp. light corn syrup
2/3 c. milk
1/2 c. margarine

Mix cocoa with sugar; add corn syrup and milk. Bring to a boil; cook for about 12 minutes, stirring constantly. Continue cooking until mixture forms medium-hard ball when tested in cold water. Pour mixture into mixing bowl. Add margarine and vanilla. Beat at high speed with mixer until mixture turns satiny. Spread on top and side of cake. Yield: Icing for one 3-layer cake.

CARAMEL ICING

3 c. (packed) brown sugar
1 tbsp. butter
1 tsp. vanilla
Cream

Place sugar and 1 cup water in saucepan; bring to a boil or until mixture reaches 230 degrees on candy thermometer, until syrup spins a thread. Add butter and vanilla; remove from heat. Cool thoroughly; beat until thick and creamy. Thin mixture with cream until of spreading consistency.

CHOCOLATE GLAZE FROSTING

1/4 c. cocoa
2 tbsp. shortening
2 tbsp. light corn syrup
2 c. confectioners' sugar
1/4 tsp. vanilla

Combine cocoa, 3 tablespoons water, shortening and corn syrup in medium saucepan. Stir over low heat until shortening melts and mixture is smooth. Remove from heat; beat in sugar and vanilla. Pour over top of cake allowing to drizzle over sides. Blend in 1 tablespoon water if mixture does not pour easily.

ROCKY ROAD FROSTING

1 6-oz. package semisweet chocolate morsels
1/4 c. butter
2 1/2 c. sifted confectioners' sugar
3 tbsp. scalded milk
1 tsp. vanilla
1 egg
1 c. chopped California walnuts
1 1/2 c. miniature marshmallows

Rocky Road Frosting . . . Chocolate bits, nuts, and marshmallows give this frosting its texture.

Melt chocolate over hot, not boiling, water. Combine butter, sugar, milk and vanilla in mixing bowl; beat in egg. Add chocolate, stirring until blended. Stir in walnuts and marshmallows. Yield: Frosting for two 8 or 9-inch layer cakes.

QUICK CARAMEL FROSTING

1/2 c. butter
1 c. (packed) brown sugar
1/4 c. milk
1 3/4 to 2 c. confectioners' sugar

Melt butter in 8-inch skillet; add brown sugar. Cook over low heat, stirring constantly, for 2 minutes. Add milk; stir until mixture comes to a boil. Remove from heat; cool. Add confectioners' sugar gradually; beat well with spoon after each addition, until thick enough to spread. Yield: Frosting for 9-inch square cake or two 8-inch layers.

CHOCOLATE FLUFF ICING

4 tbsp. butter
1 1/2 c. sifted confectioners' sugar
1 tsp. vanilla
3 sq. unsweetened chocolate, melted
1/4 tsp. salt
2 egg whites

Cream butter; add 3/4 cup sugar. Blend well. Add vanilla, chocolate and salt. Beat egg whites until stiff but not dry. Add remaining sugar, small amount at a time, beating after each addition until blended. Beat until mixture forms stiff peaks. Fold into chocolate mixture gently. Yield: Icing for 2-layer cake or one 13 x 9-inch sheet cake.

FUDGE ICING

2 c. sugar
2 tbsp. cocoa
1 c. whipping cream
2 tbsp. light syrup
Dash of salt
1 tbsp. butter
1 tsp. vanilla

Mix sugar, cocoa, whipping cream, syrup and salt together in saucepan. Let stand for at least 20 minutes, stirring occasionally. Place over medium heat, stirring occasionally. Cook until soft ball forms in water. Add butter and vanilla. Remove from heat; beat until of spreading consistency.

LEMON FROSTING

2 3/4 c. confectioners' sugar
1/2 tsp. salt
1 egg
1 tbsp. light corn syrup
1/2 c. shortening
1 tsp. vanilla
1 tsp. lemon extract
1 tbsp. lemon juice
1 tsp. grated lemon peel

Combine confectioners' sugar, salt and egg; blend in syrup. Add shortening, vanilla, lemon extract, juice and peel; mix until smooth and creamy. Add more sugar to thicken or enough water to thin frosting until of spreading consistency.

CREAM CHEESE ICING

3 3-oz. packages cream cheese, softened
1 egg, beaten
1 1/2 tsp. vanilla
Dash of salt
2 lb. sifted confectioners' sugar

Combine cream cheese, egg, vanilla and salt; beat until fluffy. Add sugar; beat thoroughly. Yield: Frosting for three 8-inch layers.

LEMON CHEESE FILLING

6 eggs, well beaten
2 c. sugar
1/2 c. lemon juice
1/4 c. butter

Combine all ingredients; cook in double boiler until thick, stirring frequently. Use as filling for layer cakes. Yield: 2 cups.

ORANGE FLUFF FROSTING

1/2 c. orange juice
1 1/2 tbsp. lemon juice
3/4 c. sugar
Dash of salt
3 tbsp. flour
1 egg, beaten
2 tbsp. butter, melted
Grated rind of 1/2 orange
1 c. cream, whipped

Combine juices, sugar, salt, flour and egg in top of double boiler; cook until thickened. Remove from heat; add butter and orange rind. Cool; fold in whipped cream. Spread filling between layers and on top and sides of cake. Refrigerate at least 12 hours before serving.

PINEAPPLE CREAM FROSTING

1/2 c. butter
1 lb. confectioners' sugar
1 tsp. vanilla
1 8-oz. package cream cheese
3 to 4 tbsp. crushed pineapple, drained

Combine butter, confectioners' sugar, vanilla and cream cheese. Beat until fluffy with electric mixer. Fold in pineapple; spread over cake.

MAPLE FROSTING

1/2 c. sugar
1/2 c. maple sugar
1/2 c. half and half
1 c. chopped walnuts

Dissolve sugar and maple sugar in cream over low heat; bring to a boil. Boil until mixture forms soft ball in cold water. Remove from heat; beat until cool. Add walnuts; spread on cake. Yield: Frosting for two layers or medium square cake.

MARSHMALLOW FROSTING

1 c. sugar
1 egg white, beaten stiff
1/2 tsp. vanilla
1 c. miniature marshmallows

Combine sugar and 1/4 cup water; bring to a boil, cooking to 238 degrees on candy thermometer. Pour mixture over egg white, beating constantly. Add vanilla; beat until about thick enough to spread. Add marshmallows; beat until well blended. Spread on top and side of 2-layer cake.

PENUCHE FROSTING

1/2 c. butter
1 c. (packed) light brown sugar
1/4 c. milk
1 3/4 to 2 c. confectioners' sugar, sifted

Melt butter in saucepan; add sugar. Bring to a boil; cook for 2 minutes, stirring constantly; add milk. Bring back to a boil; remove from heat. Cool to lukewarm. Beat in confectioners' sugar until of spreading consistency.

SEVEN-MINUTE FROSTING

1 1/2 c. sugar
1/4 tsp. salt
1 tbsp. corn syrup
2 egg whites
1 tsp. vanilla

Combine sugar, salt, syrup and egg whites in top of double boiler; stir. Add 4 1/2 tablespoons water. Place over boiling water for 7 minutes, beating constantly. Remove from heat; add vanilla. Beat thoroughly with rotary beater or electric mixer on high speed until icing stands in stiff peaks.

STRAWBERRY ICING

2 egg whites
1 c. sugar
Dash of salt
1 pkg. frozen strawberries, drained

Place egg whites, sugar, salt and strawberries in top of double boiler; beat for 1 minute with rotary beater over boiling water. Remove from heat; beat with electric mixer until of spreading consistency or about 5 minutes. Yield: Frosting for two 9-inch layers.

SEAFOAM FROSTING

1 1/2 c. (packed) brown sugar
2 egg whites
2 tbsp. light corn syrup
1/4 tsp. salt
1 tsp. vanilla

Combine all ingredients and 1/4 cup water in double boiler; beat until blended. Cook, beating constantly with electric mixer, for 5 minutes or until firm peaks form; remove from heat. Frost layer or loaf cake.

Fruitcake

Fruitcakes are rich cakes composed mainly of fruits and nuts with just enough batter to bind the ingredients. The fruits are usually dried, candied, or crystallized, the nuts coarsely chopped. There are two main types of holiday-festive fruitcake: the *white or golden fruitcake* that is prepared from a lightly spiced batter containing white sugar and light fruit; and the *dark fruitcake* that acquires its characteristic color from brown sugar or molasses and dark spices such as cinnamon, allspice, nutmeg, and cloves.

INGREDIENTS: Most fruitcakes contain as their principal ingredients a variety of fruits and nuts such as dates, candied pineapple and cherries, citron, apricots, figs, raisins, currants, coconut, almonds, pecans, and walnuts. They are usually based on a cake batter and sometimes include spices (as in dark fruitcakes).

PREPARATION: The following suggestions may be helpful in preparing any of the fruitcake recipes listed in this section.To cut sticky fruits more easily, dip knife blade or scissors into boiling water often. To prevent dried fruits' absorbing moisture from the cake, soak them briefly in boiling water before mixing. Loaf or tube pans and shortening or coffee cans produce attractive baked fruitcakes. A sweet and shiny glaze may be applied to the fruitcake either before or after baking. Fruitcakes are baked in a very slow oven for about 1 1/2 to 2 1/2 hours to allow the heat to penetrate the heavy mixture. After baking, cool fruitcake completely in baking pan.

STORING: Wrap fruitcake in brandy or wine-soaked cheesecloth, then in moisture- and vaporproof paper or airtight container. Or, place an apple or orange peel in airtight container with fruitcake to provide a constant source of moisture. Fruitcakes, stored in a cool, dark place, will keep several months. If frozen in the appropriate wrapping (see above), they will keep for 10 to 12 months.

SERVING: Do not serve freshly baked fruitcake. Store fruitcake at least one week before serving to allow the flavors to blend and mellow. Chill before serving to facilitate even slicing.

APPLESAUCE FRUITCAKES

1/2 c. butter
1 c. sugar
1 c. unsweetened applesauce
2 c. flour
1 tsp. soda
1 tsp. cinnamon
1/2 tsp. cloves
1/2 c. chopped nuts
1 c. candied fruit
1 c. raisins

Cream butter; add sugar and applesauce gradually. Sift flour with soda and spices; add to creamed mixture. Stir in nuts, candied fruit and raisins. Pour into 2 greased and floured cake pans. Bake at 350 degrees for 40 minutes; cool. Wrap cakes in brandy-soaked cheesecloth; cover with foil.

CARROT FRUITCAKE

3 c. sifted flour
3 tsp. baking powder
2 tsp. cinnamon
2 tsp. soda
1 tsp. salt
1 1/2 c. salad oil
2 c. sugar
4 eggs
3 c. finely grated carrots
1 c. chopped mixed candied fruits
1 c. chopped pitted dates
1 c. raisins
1 1/2 c. coarsely chopped nuts

Sift flour, baking powder, cinnamon, soda and salt together; set aside. Combine salad oil and sugar; mix well. Add eggs one at a time, beating well after each addition until light and fluffy. Add dry ingredients gradually, mixing until smooth. Add carrots, candied fruits, dates, raisins and nuts. Mix well. Spoon batter into greased 10-inch tube pan. Bake at 350 degrees for 1 hour and 30 minutes or until cake tests done.

CAROLERS' FRUITCAKES

1 lb. candied red cherries
1/2 lb. candied green cherries
1 lb. candied pineapple
4 c. flour
2 c. sugar
1 c. butter
4 eggs
1/4 tsp. salt
1 tsp. baking powder
3/4 c. milk
3/4 c. whiskey
1 c. chopped pecans
1 can flaked coconut

Chop candied ingredients; dredge with 1 cup flour. Cream sugar and butter until fluffy; beat in eggs, one at a time, beating well after each addition. Add remaining flour, salt and baking powder; stir in milk and whiskey. Fold in floured fruits, pecans and coconut. Pack batter into 3 greased, brown paper-lined 8 x 4 x 3-inch pans. Bake at 300 degrees for 2 hours or until cakes test done. Remove from pans. Cool; remove paper. Yield: 25 servings.

COCONUT FRUITCAKE

1 c. butter
2 c. light brown sugar
4 eggs
3 c. sifted flour
1 tsp. baking powder
1/2 tsp. salt
1 1/2 c. chopped candied cherries
1 c. raisins
1 1/2 c. chopped candied pineapple
3/4 c. chopped citron
1 1/2 c. blanched almonds, chopped
3 c. shredded coconut
1 c. orange juice

Preheat oven to 275 degrees. Line greased 10-inch tube pan or two 9 x 5 x 2 1/2-inch loaf pans with heavy brown or waxed paper; grease again. Cream butter and sugar until light and fluffy; add eggs, one at a time, beating well after each addition. Sift flour, baking powder and salt together. Combine fruits, almonds and coconut in large mixing bowl. Sift flour mixture over fruit mixture; blend until all fruit is coated with flour. Stir fruit mixture into creamed mixture alternately with orange juice beginning and ending with fruit mixture; pour into pan. Bake for 3 to 4 hours or until cake tests done. Remove from oven; cool. Wrap in foil or plastic wrap to store.

Christmas Fruitcake . . . A traditional holiday fruit-laden cake that's just right for gift-giving.

CHRISTMAS FRUITCAKE

2 c. sifted all-purpose flour
1 tsp baking powder
1/2 tsp. salt
2/3 c. butter
1 c. sugar
3 eggs
1 tbsp. grated orange rind
2 tsp. grated lemon rind
1/2 c. orange juice
2 c. pecan halves
2 8-oz. jars mixed candied fruits
1 6 1/2-oz. jar whole red candied cherries
1 c. dried apricots, quartered
1 c. seedless raisins

Sift flour, baking powder and salt together. Cream butter; add sugar, creaming until fluffy. Beat in eggs, one at a time, beating well after each addition. Add grated fruit rinds. Add sifted dry ingredients alternately with orange juice; mix well. Stir in pecan halves. Chop mixed candied fruits; add to batter. Stir in whole cherries, apricots and raisins. Pack batter into greased and paper-lined 9 x 5 x 3-inch loaf pan. Bake in 250-degree oven for about 3 hours or until cake tests done. Cool. Remove from pan. Garnish with whole candied cherries and candied pineapple halves. Wrap cake in foil to keep moist. May glaze top of cake if desired.

GUMDROP FRUITCAKE

4 c. flour
1/4 tsp. salt
1 tsp. cinnamon
1/4 tsp. nutmeg
1/4 tsp. cloves
1 lb. raisins
2 lb. gumdrops, chopped
1 c. butter
2 c. sugar
2 eggs
1 1/2 c. applesauce
1 tsp. soda
1 tsp. vanilla
1 c. pecans

Sift flour with salt and spices; dredge raisins and gumdrops with small amount of flour mixture. Cream butter and sugar; add eggs, one at a time, beating well after each addition. Add remaining flour mixture alternately with applesauce. Combine soda, 1 tablespoon hot water and vanilla, stirring until soda is dissolved. Add to batter, mixing well. Mix in raisins, gumdrops and pecans. Spoon batter into 3 foil-lined loaf pans. Bake at 325 degrees for 2 hours. Store in tightly covered container. Do not use black gumdrops in cake.

HONEY FRUITCAKE

2 c. dried prunes
1 c. dried apricots
1 c. seedless raisins
1 c. slivered blanched almonds
1 c. coarsely chopped walnuts
1 lb. diced mixed candied fruits
1 c. shortening
1 c. honey
4 eggs
2 c. sifted all-purpose flour
1 tsp. salt
1 tsp. baking powder
1 tsp. cinnamon
1/2 tsp. allspice
1/4 tsp. cloves
1/4 tsp. mace

Cover prunes and apricots with boiling water; let stand for 10 minutes. Drain and cool. Remove pits from prunes; chop prunes and apricots. Combine dried fruits, nuts and candied fruits. Cream shortening and honey together; add eggs, one at a time, beating well after each addition. Sift flour, salt, baking powder and spices together; blend into creamed mixture. Pour batter over fruits and nuts; mix thoroughly. Line 8-inch tube pan with 2 thicknesses of greased brown paper and 1 thickness of greased waxed paper. Turn batter into pans. Place shallow pan of hot water in bottom of oven. Bake at 250 degrees for 3 hours and 30 minutes or until cake tests done. Decorate cake with nuts and honey-glazed fruit if desired. Yield: One 5 1/2-pound cake.

JAPANESE FRUITCAKE

1 lb. pecans
1/2 lb. candied cherries
1/2 lb. candied pineapple
1/4 lb. candied orange peel
1 tsp. cloves
1 tsp. cinnamon
1 tsp. allspice
1/2 lb. chopped dates
1/2 lb. white raisins
1 c. butter
6 c. sugar
4 c. flour
1 tsp. baking powder
1 c. pineapple juice
8 egg whites
Juice and grated peel of 3 lemons
Juice and grated peel of 2 lge. oranges
1/4 c. cornstarch
1 lge. coconut, grated

Chop pecans, cherries, pineapple and candied orange peel. Combine half the pecans, cherries, pineapple and candied orange peel. Mix remaining pecans, spices, dates and raisins together. Cream butter and 2 cups sugar. Sift flour and baking powder together; add to creamed mixture alternately with pineapple juice. Fold in stiffly beaten egg whites. Divide batter into 2 parts. Stir pecan-candied fruit mixture into half the batter; spread in 2 layer pans. Stir pecan-spice mixture into remaining batter; spread in 2 layer pans. Bake layers at 325 degrees for 25 minutes. Place lemon juice, grated lemon peel, orange juice, grated orange peel and remaining sugar in large pan; stir in 2 cups water. Bring to a boil, stirring. Mix cornstarch and enough water to make paste. Stir paste into cooked mixture, small amount at a time. Cook, stirring, until thickened. Remove from heat; stir in coconut. Cool filling. Spread cake layers with filling; stack layers. Spread top and sides of cake with filling.

LAST-MINUTE FRUITCAKES

1 c. butter
2 c. sugar
3 eggs, well beaten
1 c. buttermilk
1 tsp. soda
1 c. blackberry jam
1 c. chopped pecans
1 c. chopped raisins
1 c. grated coconut
3 c. flour

Cream butter and sugar until fluffy; add eggs, mixing well. Combine buttermilk and soda, stirring until soda is dissolved. Add to creamed mixture. Add blackberry jam, pecans, raisins and coconut, mixing thoroughly. Stir in flour. Pour into three 9-inch, greased brown paper-lined layer pans. Bake at 350 degrees for 25 to 30 minutes. Cool.

Frosting

2 c. sugar
4 tbsp. flour
1 c. butter
1 1/2 c. milk

Combine all ingredients in saucepan, mixing well. Cook over low heat, stirring, until thick. Beat until creamy. Frost between layers and top and sides of cake.

LIGHT FRUITCAKE

1/2 lb. candied pineapple
1/2 lb. candied cherries
1 lb. mixed candied fruit
1 lb. pitted dates
1 1/2 lb. nuts
1 1/2 lb. white raisins
2 c. butter
2 c. sugar
12 eggs, well beaten
1 tsp. almond extract
1 tbsp. vanilla
2 tsp. lemon extract
4 1/2 c. flour
2 tsp. baking powder
1/2 tsp. salt
1/2 c. whiskey
1/2 c. cherry preserves
1/2 c. apricot preserves

Prepare pans by lining with 2 or 3 thicknesses of well-greased heavy brown paper; add layer of waxed paper. Chop candied fruits, dates and nuts coarsely. Mix fruits and nuts; set aside. Cream butter and sugar; add eggs, almond extract, vanilla and lemon extract. Reserve 1 1/2 cups of flour. Sift remaining flour, baking powder and salt together; add to creamed mixture alternately with whiskey and preserves. Mix well. Dredge fruits and nuts with reserved flour; add to creamed mixture, mixing well. Pour into prepared pans, packing well. Bake in 250-degree oven until cakes test done. Cool; remove paper. Wrap cakes in brandy-soaked cheesecloth; store in cool place in covered container. Yield: 10 servings.

OLD-FASHIONED PORK FRUITCAKE

1 pt. hot coffee
1 lb. fat salt pork, ground
1 c. molasses
1 1/2 tsp. soda
3 eggs, slightly beaten
2 c. sugar
1 lb. raisins
1 lb. currants
1/2 lb. chopped citron
1/4 lb. orange and lemon peel, chopped
1 c. chopped nuts
1/2 tsp. nutmeg
1 tsp. cinnamon
1 tsp. cloves
5 c. flour

Pour hot coffee over salt pork; cool. Add molasses. Dissolve soda in about 1/4 cup cold water; add to pork mixture. Add eggs, sugar, fruits, peels and nuts. Mix in dry ingredients. Pour into 2 large or 3 small loaf pans. Bake at 300 degrees for 1 hour and 30 minutes.

POOR MAN'S FRUITCAKE

1 c. sugar
1 c. coffee
1/2 c. shortening
1/2 tsp. salt
1 tsp. cloves
1 tsp. cinnamon
1/2 tsp. mace
1 c. chopped dates
1 c. chopped citron
1 tsp. soda
2 c. flour

Combine sugar, coffee, shortening, salt, cloves, cinnamon, mace, dates and citron in saucepan; boil for 3 minutes. Cool to lukewarm. Dissolve soda in 2 tablespoons warm water; add flour and soda mixture to batter, beating well. Beat together hard. Bake in 9-inch pan 1 hour at 350 to 375 degrees. Yield: 10-12 servings.

LEMON-PECAN FRUITCAKE

1 box brown sugar
1 lb. margarine
6 eggs, separated
4 c. flour
1 tsp. baking powder
1 bottle lemon extract
1 qt. chopped pecans
1/2 lb. candied pineapple, chopped
1/2 lb. candied cherries, chopped

Cream brown sugar and margarine together until fluffy. Add beaten egg yolks; mix well. Combine 2 cups flour and baking powder; add to creamed mixture. Add lemon extract. Coat pecans, pineapple and cherries with remaining flour; add to creamed mixture. Fold in stiffly beaten egg whites. Cover. Let stand overnight. Spoon batter into greased tube pan. Bake at 250 degrees for 1 hour and 30 minutes. Yield: 20 servings.

WHISKEY CAKE

1 lb. red candied cherries
1/2 lb. golden raisins
1 pt. whiskey
3/4 lb. butter
1 c. (packed) brown sugar
2 c. sugar
6 eggs, separated
5 c. sifted flour
2 tsp. nutmeg
1 tsp. baking powder
4 c. pecan halves

Cut cherries into halves. Soak cherries and raisins in whiskey overnight. Cream butter, brown sugar and sugar until fluffy; add egg yolks, beating well. Add whiskey mixture and flour, reserving small amount of flour. Add nutmeg and baking powder. Fold in stiffly beaten egg whites. Roll pecans in reserved flour; add to batter. Turn into large greased paper-lined tube pan. Bake at 250 degrees for 3 hours or until cake tests done. Cool. Stuff center with cheesecloth soaked in additional whiskey. Wrap in heavy waxed paper. Store in covered container in refrigerator or freezer. Yield: 24 servings.

Fudge

Fudge is a creamy, smooth confection. It may be eaten as it is or used as the center of a coated bonbon. (3 1/2 ounces of fudge without nuts = 400 calories; 3 1/2 ounces fudge with nuts = 426 calories)

INGREDIENTS: The simplest fudge is prepared from milk, granulated sugar, light corn syrup, butter or margarine, vanilla, and salt. Though usually added, nuts are optional. Corn syrup, cream of tartar, or honey may be used to help create the characteristic creaminess. Evaporated milk may also be used to help create a smooth texture. Other flavorful ingredients, often added to the basic recipe are unsweetened chocolate, honey, peanut butter, chocolate chips, coffee, coconut, raisins, candied fruit, and crushed mints. Penuche is a type of fudge that is based on brown sugar instead of white granulated sugar.

PREPARATION: Combine ingredients and cook as directed in recipe. Fudge is usually cooked to the soft-ball stage (that is, a drop of the mixture forms a soft, pliable ball when dropped into very cold water), and when it registers from 234 to 240 degrees on a candy thermometer. Cool mixture to lukewarm and add remaining ingredients. The candy is then beaten until it loses its sheen. Do not beat the fudge until it is lukewarm or the candy will be sugary and grainy. Too little beating will also yield a granular product. When a small amount dropped from a spoon holds its shape, the mixture is appropriately thick and creamy in consistency. Pour fudge into buttered cooling pan, score into desired shapes before it hardens. Cool or chill until firm, then cut. To prepare fudge as centers for dipping, follow above directions. After cooling to lukewarm, beat mixture until thick; knead and shape.

STORING: Maintain the freshness of fudge for several weeks by wrapping it in waxed paper, plastic wrap, or aluminum foil and storing it in a tightly covered container in a cool dry place.

(See CANDY.)

BLACK WALNUT FUDGE

1 c. buttermilk
1 tsp. baking powder
2 c. sugar
2 tbsp. light corn syrup
1/2 c. butter
Vanilla to taste
3/4 c. chopped black walnuts

Mix buttermilk and baking powder together; set aside. Mix sugar and syrup together in large saucepan. Add buttermilk mixture to sugar mixture. Cook for about 25 minutes or until mixture forms hard ball in cold water. Remove from heat; let stand several minutes. Add butter, vanilla and walnuts; beat until thickened and no longer glossy. Pour onto buttered platter. Cool; cut into squares. Yield: 25 pieces.

BOSTON CREAM FUDGE

1 c. light corn syrup
3 c. sugar
1 c. cream
1 c. chopped pecans
1 tsp. vanilla
3 sq. unsweetened chocolate
1 tsp. butter

Combine syrup, sugar and cream in saucepan. Bring mixture to a boil; cook until mixture forms soft ball. Remove from heat; cool to just warm. Beat mixture until white and smooth. Beat in nuts and vanilla.

Pour into buttered 8-inch pan. Cool. Melt chocolate over warm water. Add butter. Pour chocolate over top of fudge. Let stand for several days. Cut into slices.

BROWN SUGAR FUDGE

1 c. (packed) light brown sugar
1 c. sugar
3/4 c. milk
1 tbsp. butter
1 tsp. vanilla
1/2 c. chopped walnuts

Combine sugars and milk in saucepan; cook over medium heat to soft-ball stage, stirring occasionally. Remove from heat; add butter and vanilla. Cool in pan of cold water; beat until thick. Add nuts; pour into greased 9-inch square pan. Refrigerate until set. Cut in squares. Yield: 36 squares.

BUTTERMILK FUDGE

2 c. sugar
1/2 c. buttermilk
1/2 c. light corn syrup
1/4 tsp. soda
1/4 tsp. salt
1 tbsp. cocoa
1 tbsp. butter
1/2 c. chopped nuts
1 tsp. vanilla

Mix sugar, buttermilk, syrup, soda, salt, cocoa and butter in saucepan. Cook to soft-ball stage. Cool; add nuts and vanilla. Beat until creamy. Pour onto buttered platter when candy loses gloss. Mark into squares.

BUTTERSCOTCH-PECAN FUDGE

1 pkg. butterscotch pudding mix
1/2 c. (packed) brown sugar
1/2 c. evaporated milk
1 c. sugar
1 1/2 c. chopped pecans
1 tbsp. butter
1 tsp. vanilla

Combine pudding mix, brown sugar, milk, sugar, pecans, butter and vanilla in saucepan. Bring to a boil; cook, for 5 minutes, stirring constantly. Remove from heat; beat until cool. Pour into buttered pan. Cut into squares.

CHOCOLATE FUDGE

2 sq. unsweetened chocolate
3/4 c. milk
2 c. sugar
Dash of salt
2 tbsp. butter
1 tsp. vanilla

Place chocolate and milk in heavy saucepan. Cook, stirring, over low heat until mixture is smooth and thickened slightly. Add sugar and salt. Stir over medium heat until sugar is dissolved; bring mixture to a boil. Cook, without stirring, until soft-ball stage. Remove from heat. Add butter and vanilla. Cool to lukewarm. Beat until mixture begins to lose gloss and holds shape. Turn immediately into buttered 8 x 4-inch pan. Cool; cut in squares. Yield: 18 pieces.

QUICK CHOCOLATE FUDGE

1/4 c. corn oil margarine
3-oz. unsweetened chocolate
1 lb. confectioners' sugar
1/3 c. instant nonfat dry milk powder
1/2 c. dark corn syrup
1 tsp. vanilla
1/2 c. chopped nuts

Melt margarine and chocolate in top of 2-quart double boiler over boiling water. Sift confectioners' sugar and dry milk powder together; set aside. Stir corn syrup, 1 tablespoon water and vanilla into chocolate mixture. Blend in sifted dry ingredients in 2 additions, stirring until mixture is blended and smooth. Remove from boiling water. Mix in nuts. Turn into greased 8-inch square pan. Cool. Cut into squares. Omit chocolate and water; use light corn syrup and increase vanilla to 2 teaspoons for bland fudge. Yield: 1 3/4 pounds.

Quick Chocolate Fudge . . . It's as easy as 1-2-3 to prepare this sweet tooth favorite.

CHOCOLATE FUDGE WITH CHERRIES

4 c. sugar
1/4 c. butter
1 can evaporated milk
3 pkg. chocolate pieces
1 pt. marshmallow creme
1 c. chopped nuts
1/2 c. candied cherries, halved

Combine sugar, butter and milk; bring to a boil over medium heat, stirring gently. Boil for 5 minutes. Add chocolate pieces, marshmallow creme, nuts and cherries; stir until blended thoroughly. Pour into two large pans; refrigerate overnight.

CHOCOLATE BUTTER FUDGE

3 c. sugar
1 env. plain gelatin
1/3 c. light corn syrup
1 c. butter
3 sq. chocolate
1 c. milk
2 tsp. vanilla
1 c. chopped nuts

Place sugar, gelatin, syrup, butter, chocolate and milk in heavy saucepan. Cook over medium low heat until candy forms soft ball in cold water. Add vanilla; cook for 15 minutes longer. Beat until of spreading consistency; add nuts. Pour into buttered pan. Cool; cut into squares.

MAGIC FRENCH FUDGE

1 12-oz. package semisweet chocolate pieces
3/4 c. sweetened condensed milk
Pinch of salt
1 tsp. vanilla
1/2 c. ground nuts (opt.)

Place chocolate pieces in top of double boiler. Melt over rapidly boiling water, stirring several times. Remove from heat; add condensed milk, salt, vanilla and nuts. Stir until just smooth. Turn into 8 x 8-inch waxed paper-lined pan; press to 1-inch thickness. Chill until firm or for about 2 hours. Remove from pan; cut into serving pieces. Store in airtight container. Yield: 1 pound.

HONEY FUDGE

2 c. sugar
3/4 c. milk
1/4 c. cream
1 sq. chocolate
1/4 c. honey
3 tbsp. butter
1 tsp. vanilla
1 c. nuts

Combine sugar, milk, cream and chocolate in saucepan. Bring to a boil; cook for 5 minutes. Add honey and butter; cook until mixture forms soft ball. Cool. Beat until thick. Add vanilla and nuts. Pour into buttered pan. Cut into squares. Yield: 8 servings.

MAPLE SUGAR FUDGE

2 c. maple syrup
1 tbsp. light corn syrup
3/4 c. half and half
1 tsp. vanilla
3/4 c. walnuts, coarsely chopped

Combine syrups and half and half in saucepan; bring to a boil over low heat, stirring constantly. Continue cooking without stirring to soft-ball stage. Remove from heat; cool to lukewarm. Beat until mixture is thickened and loses gloss. Add vanilla and nuts; pour immediately into buttered 8-inch square pan. Cool; cut into squares.

MEXICAN FUDGE

1 c. milk
3 c. sugar
1 c. pecans
1 tsp. vanilla

Combine milk and 2 cups sugar in saucepan; stir well. Bring to a boil; cook for 15 minutes. Place remaining sugar in iron skillet. Melt, stirring constantly; add to milk mixture. Add pecans and vanilla; stir until of spreading consistency. Pour onto buttered plate. Yield: 25 servings.

OPERA FUDGE

2 c. sugar
2/3 c. milk
2 tbsp. light corn syrup
1/4 tsp. salt
2 tbsp. butter
1 tsp. almond flavoring

Combine sugar, milk, corn syrup and salt in saucepan. Stir over medium heat until sugar dissolves. Cook to 234 degrees on candy thermometer or soft-ball stage. Remove from heat. Add butter; cool to lukewarm, without stirring. Add almond flavoring; beat until thickened and no longer glossy. Pour into buttered 8 or 9-inch square pan. Cool; cut into squares. Yield: 36 pieces.

PEANUT BUTTER FUDGE

1/3 c. butter, softened
1/2 c. light corn syrup
3/4 c. peanut butter
1/2 tsp. salt
1 tsp. vanilla
3 1/2 c. confectioners' sugar, sifted
3/4 c. chopped nuts

Blend butter into corn syrup; stir in peanut butter, salt and vanilla. Mix until creamy. Stir in confectioners' sugar. Turn candy onto pastry board; knead with hands until blended and smooth. Add nuts gradually, pressing and kneading into dough. Press candy into greased 8-inch square pan. Chill for 1 hour; cut into squares. Yield: 2 pounds.

PEPPERMINT FUDGE

2 tbsp. butter
1/2 tsp. salt
3/4 lb. marshmallows
1 6-oz. package chocolate pieces
1/2 tsp. vanilla
1/4 tsp. peppermint flavoring
1 c. chopped walnuts

Melt butter over low heat. Add 4 teaspoons water, salt and marshmallows; melt marshmallows, stirring frequently. Remove from heat; add chocolate, stirring until melted. Add vanilla and peppermint flavoring; beat until thick. Add nuts; mix well. Pour into greased pan; cool. Cut into squares.

PINEAPPLE FUDGE

2 c. sugar
1 c. brown sugar
1/2 c. half and half
1 lge. can crushed pineapple, drained
2 tbsp. butter
2 tsp. ginger
2 tsp. vanilla
1 c. walnuts, broken

Combine sugars, half and half and pineapple; cook, stirring occasionally, to soft-ball stage or to 236 degrees on candy thermometer. Remove from heat. Add butter, ginger and vanilla. Cool to room temperature, without stirring, until lukewarm. Beat until mixture loses gloss. Add nuts. Pour into buttered 8 x 8-inch pan. Score candy into squares. Press walnut half on each square. Cut when firm.

SHERRY FUDGE

1 6-oz. package semisweet chocolate pieces
2 tbsp. butter
1/4 c. sherry
1 egg yolk
3 1/2 c. powdered sugar, sifted
1 c. nuts, chopped
1 tsp. vanilla (opt.)

Melt chocolate and butter in sherry over hot, not boiling water. Add egg yolk to sifted sugar. Add chocolate mixture to sugar mixture; stir thoroughly. Add additional sherry, if necessary. Add nuts and vanilla. Spread in 8 x 8-inch buttered pan; refrigerate. Yield: 12 servings.

Game

Game is the term applied to wild birds or animals hunted for sport or for food. Game animals are not commercially available. But if you are a skillful hunter and have adequate freezing facilities, you can enjoy the unique flavor of game year-round. (See also GAME BIRDS.)

KINDS: The two main categories of game animals are small game and large game. *Small game* include such animals as the beaver, an inhabitant of American streams that has moist, dark flesh which smells and tastes like turkey; the opossum, an inhabitant of southeastern United States whose cooked meat is made tender by well-distributed natural fat; the rabbit, a favorite small game animal which has mildly-flavored and fine-grained meat; the raccoon, found near American ponds and streams which has delicious dark, somewhat coarse flesh; and the squirrel, popular throughout America for its firm, lean meat. *Large game* include animals such as the bear and members of the deer family.

PREPARATION: Both large and small game animals may be marinated 24 hours before cooking to remove gamy flavor. Generally all older game, large or small, requires marination and long, moist cooking; and is used in stews. *For small game*—Clean and skin as soon as possible. Remove all scent glands. Cut off head, feet, and tail. Cure in cool place by suspending from hook approximately 4 days. When ready to cook, lard according to recipe. Small game may be roasted, broiled, braised, fried, or stewed. See specific recipe directions. *For large game*—Bear—Clean immediately and cure for several days. When ready to cook, remove all fat. Do not lard. Broil or roast according to specific recipe directions. Do not undercook bear, treat it like pork leaving no traces of pink in the meat. Deer—Clean immediately. Cure young animal 1 week and older animal 3 weeks. Remove fat. Lard and cook according to specific recipe directions. Do not overcook venison because it dries out quickly.

FREEZING: To freeze all kinds of game, wrap small portions of flesh. Place in airtight container. Freeze up to 6 months at 0 degrees or below.

ANTELOPE STROGANOFF

1 lb. lean antelope meat
2 tbsp. butter, melted
1 1/2 c. diced onions
1 can cream of chicken soup
1 4-oz. can mushrooms
1 tsp. salt
4 c. hot cooked rice

Cut antelope meat into 1/2-inch cubes. Melt butter in skillet; saute meat and onions. Add soup, mushrooms with juice and salt. Cover; simmer for 1 hour. Serve over rice. Yield: 5 servings.

BRAISED ANTELOPE

3 lb. antelope, round steaks
Salt and pepper to taste
Flour
1/3 c. suet
3 tbsp. chopped onion
2 c. diced potatoes
3 c. diced carrots
1 can tomatoes

Season steaks with salt and pepper; coat with flour on both sides. Melt suet in heavy kettle; sear steaks well. Cover steaks with 1/2 cup water. Simmer until steaks are tender. Add vegetables; cook until tender, adding additional water if necessary.

BARBECUED BEAR

1 3-lb. bear roast
Salt and pepper
1 clove of garlic, crushed
2 tbsp. brown sugar
1 tbsp. paprika
1 tsp. dry mustard
1/4 tsp. chili powder
1/8 tsp. cayenne pepper
2 tbsp. Worcestershire sauce
1/4 c. vinegar
1 c. tomato juice
1/4 c. catsup

Place roast in small roaster. Season to taste with salt and pepper; rub with garlic. Bake at 350 degrees for 1 hour or until well done. Cut into thin slices. Combine 1 teaspoon salt, brown sugar, seasonings, vinegar, tomato juice, catsup and 1/2 cup water in heavy skillet. Simmer for 15 minutes. Add meat; simmer for 1 hour or until roast is tender.

ROAST BEAVER

1 sm. beaver
Bacon drippings
Salt and pepper
2 med. onions, sliced
2 tbsp. flour
1 bay leaf
Pinch of chervil

Skin and clean beaver, removing kernels in small of back, under forelegs and between rib and shoulder. Trim off excess fat. Dress as for rabbit. Brown beaver in bacon drippings in Dutch oven, adding salt and pepper to taste. Add onions. Bake at 350 degrees for 2 hours and 30 minutes to 3 hours or until tender. Remove beaver. Blend flour and 1/2 cup water together. Add flour mixture and bay leaf to pan drippings. Cook over low heat, stirring constantly, until gravy is thickened. Remove bay leaf; add chervil. Serve gravy over beaver. Yield: 8 servings.

COUNTRY-STYLE GROUNDHOG

1 groundhog
1/2 c. flour
1/4 tsp. salt
1/4 tsp. pepper
1/4 tsp. soda
1/4 c. cooking oil
1/2 tsp. sugar

Dress groundhog as for rabbit, removing the small sacs in the back and under the forearm. Soak groundhog overnight in salted water to remove wild flavor. Combine flour, salt, pepper and soda; rub into groundhog pieces. Brown groundhog in hot oil in skillet; sprinkle with sugar. Reduce heat; add 1/2 cup water. Cover; simmer for about 30 minutes or until tender. Remove cover; cook for 10 minutes longer.

BARBECUED ELK

1 3-lb. elk roast
1 c. catsup
1 tbsp. salt
2 tsp. Worcestershire sauce
1/4 c. vinegar
1 tbsp. butter
1/8 tsp. cinnamon
2 slices lemon
1 onion, thinly sliced
1/8 tsp. allspice

Sear roast in Dutch oven. Combine remaining ingredients in saucepan; bring to a boil, stirring. Simmer for 10 minutes. Cover roast with sauce. Bake at 350 degrees for 1 hour and 30 minutes to 2 hours, turning occasionally. Yield: 6-10 servings.

BRAISED ELK SWISS STEAK

2 elk round steaks
1 c. flour
1 pkg. dry onion soup mix
1 beef bouillon cube
1/4 c. flour
Salt and pepper

Remove all bone and fat from steaks; pound flour thoroughly into steaks. Quarter each steak; fry in fat in skillet until lightly browned on each side. Mix onion soup mix with 1 cup water; pour over steaks. Cover; simmer for 15 to 20 minutes. Remove steaks from skillet. Dissolve bouillon cube in 1 cup water; add to pan drippings. Mix 1/2 cup water with flour. Add flour mixture to stock gradually, stirring constantly until thickened. Season to taste. Cook for 5 minutes longer. Yield: 8 servings.

ELK-NOODLE STEW

1 egg yolk, beaten
1 tbsp. cream
Salt
1/8 tsp. baking powder
Flour
2 lb. elk meat, diced
3 onions, diced
1 bunch celery, diced
Pepper
2 cans mixed vegetables, drained
1 can tomatoes
2 c. finely chopped cabbage
2 potatoes, diced
2 slices bacon, diced
2 bay leaves
3 tbsp. chili sauce

Beat egg yolk and cream together; add 1/8 teaspoon salt and baking powder. Blend in enough flour to make stiff dough. Roll dough out thinly; cut into strips of desired length and width. Let dry for several hours. Saute elk meat and onions in large kettle until elk meat is browned. Add 1 gallon cold water to elk mixture. Add celery, salt to taste and pepper. Simmer for 2 hours or until meat is tender, adding water if necessary. Stir in vegetables, bacon and bay leaves. Cook for about 45 minutes longer. Add noodles; cook for 20 minutes or until noodles are tender. Add chili sauce just before serving.

MOOSE FONDUE WITH SAUCE

3 lb. moose steak
3 c. salad oil

Bring steak to room temperature; cut into 1-inch cubes. Pour oil into fondue pot; heat to 375 to 425 degrees. Place steak cubes on fondue fork; cook in oil for 10 to 30 seconds. Cool; dip into desired sauce.

Tomato Sauce

1 8-oz. can tomato sauce
2 tbsp. brown sugar
1/2 c. bottled steak sauce
2 tbsp. salad oil

Combine all ingredients; heat through.

Peanut Sauce

1/2 c. chunk-style peanut butter
2 tbsp. soy sauce
1 tsp. sugar
2 drops of hot sauce
1 clove of garlic, minced
1/2 c. water

Combine all ingredients; mix until smooth. Heat through.

Anchovy Butter

1 2-oz. can anchovies, drained
1/2 c. softened butter
2 tbsp. olive oil
1/2 tsp. paprika
Pinch of pepper

Combine all ingredients; beat with mixer until smooth. Yield: 6-8 servings.

MOOSE ROAST

1 6-lb. moose roast
Mustard to taste
1/2 c. flour
Salt and pepper
Garlic salt to taste
Margarine

Trim all fat from roast. Place roast on aluminum foil; spread with mustard. Sprinkle with flour, salt, pepper and garlic salt. Dot with margarine. Seal foil tightly. Place in roasting pan. Bake at 400 degrees for 3 hours or until tender.

MOOSE STROGANOFF

2 lb. moose meat
1/2 c. flour
Salt and pepper
Cayenne pepper to taste
6 tbsp. butter
1 onion, chopped
1 clove of garlic, chopped
2 bouillon cubes
1 can mushrooms
1 tsp. Worcestershire sauce
1 bay leaf
1 can cream of mushroom soup
1/2 pt. sour cream

Cut moose meat into 1-inch cubes. Combine flour, salt, pepper and cayenne pepper. Coat moose meat with flour mixture. Melt half the butter in skillet; brown moose meat evenly. Remove meat from skillet. Melt remaining butter in pan drippings; saute onion and garlic. Return meat to skillet. Add remaining ingredients except sour cream. Simmer for 15 minutes. Add sour cream; heat through. Serve with hot rice if desired.

MOOSE SWISS STEAK

3 tbsp. flour
1 tsp. paprika
1/2 tsp. salt
1 4-lb. moose top round steak
3 tbsp. shortening
1 1-lb. can pineapple slices
1 env. dry onion soup mix
1 tbsp. cornstarch

Combine flour, paprika and salt; rub into steak. Brown steak in shortening in ovenproof skillet. Drain syrup from pineapple; add enough water to syrup to make 1 1/2 cups liquid. Add onion soup mix to liquid. Pour over steak; cover. Bake at 375 degrees for 1 hour and 30 minutes or until steak is tender. Place pineapple over steak. Combine cornstarch with small amount of hot liquid from skillet; return to remaining hot liquid. Simmer, stirring until clear and thick. Garnish steak with green pepper and tomato wedges if desired.

OPOSSUM WITH SWEET POTATOES

1 opossum
Salt to taste
Pepper to taste
6 red peppers, chopped
4 lge. sweet potatoes

Skin and clean opossum, removing small sacs from small of back and under forelegs. Place opossum in 4 cups water in saucepan; add salt, pepper and red peppers. Simmer until pan liquid is reduced by half. Pare and slice sweet potatoes. Combine opossum with pan liquid and potatoes in baking pan. Bake at 350 degrees for about 1 hour or until opossum is tender, basting occasionally.

HASENPFEFFER

1 rabbit, dressed
2 c. vinegar
1 onion, sliced
2 tsp. salt
1/2 tsp. pepper
1 tsp. cloves
1 tbsp. bay leaves

Disjoint rabbit; place in large jar or crock. Combine 2 cups water and remaining ingredients; pour over rabbit. Let marinate in cool place for 48 hours. Remove rabbit from marinade, reserving 1 cup marinade. Brown rabbit evenly in hot grease in skillet. Add reserved marinade. Cover; simmer for 1 hour or until rabbit is tender. May thicken gravy with small amount of flour if desired. Yield: 4 servings.

RABBIT STEW

1 rabbit, dressed
3 tbsp. shortening
1 onion, finely chopped
1/4 c. chopped celery
2 tbsp. tomato paste
1/2 c. dry white wine
1 tsp. mixed spices
1 clove of garlic, minced
Salt and pepper to taste
2 tsp. vinegar

Disjoint rabbit; brown in shortening in skillet. Add onion, celery, tomato paste, wine and seasonings. Simmer for 1 hour or until rabbit is tender. Add vinegar; simmer for 5 minutes longer. Yield: 4 servings.

SWEET AND SOUR RABBIT

1 2 1/2-lb. rabbit, dressed
3/4 c. flour
Salt and pepper
2 tbsp. cooking oil
1 c. pineapple juice
1/4 c. vinegar
1 c. pineapple chunks
1 green pepper, sliced
1 1/2 tbsp. cornstarch
1/4 c. sugar

Disjoint rabbit. Combine flour, salt and pepper to taste; dredge rabbit in flour mixture. Brown rabbit evenly in hot oil in skillet. Add pineapple juice, vinegar and 1/2 teaspoon salt. Cover; simmer for 40 minutes or until rabbit is tender. Add pineapple chunks and green pepper. Cook until green pepper is tender. Combine cornstarch and sugar; add 1/2 cup water. Stir cornstarch mixture into rabbit mixture gradually. Cook, stirring constantly, for 5 minutes or until thickened. Yield: 6 servings.

SQUIRREL WITH RICE

1 1-in. square salt pork
2 squirrels, cut up
2 qt. water
1 c. rice
1/4 c. catsup
1/2 onion, sliced
Salt and pepper to taste

Dice salt pork; saute in large saucepan until brown. Add squirrel pieces; brown lightly. Add 2 quarts water; simmer until squirrels are tender, adding additional water if needed. Add rice, catsup, onion and seasonings. Cook over low heat, stirring frequently, until rice is tender.

BARBECUED VENISON

1 onion, chopped
5 stalks celery, chopped
1/4 c. butter
1 c. catsup
1/8 tsp. Worcestershire sauce
2 tbsp. prepared mustard
1 lb. cooked venison, finely chopped
Salt and pepper to taste

Saute onion and celery in butter in heavy skillet until tender. Stir in catsup, Worcestershire sauce, mustard, venison, salt and pepper. Simmer until thickened, stirring frequently.

VENISON MEATBALLS

2 slices rye bread
2 slices bread
2/3 c. milk
2 tsp. baking powder
1 1/2 lb. ground venison
1/3 c. chopped onion
1 tsp. salt
1/2 tsp. seasoning salt
1 can cream of mushroom soup
1 2/3 c. evaporated milk
1 c. crushed potato chips

Crumble bread slices coarsely; combine with milk and baking powder in mixing bowl. Let stand for 5 minutes. Add venison, onion, salt and seasoning salt to bread mixture; mix well. Shape into balls. Brown in small amount of fat in skillet; stir to brown on all sides. Place meatballs in baking dish. Combine soup with milk; blend well. Pour soup mixture over meatballs; top with potato chips. Bake at 350 degrees for 45 minutes.

VENISON AND RICE

1 green pepper, chopped
1 onion, chopped
1 clove of garlic, minced
3 tbsp. butter
1 1/2 lb. ground venison
2 tbsp. flour
1 tsp. salt
1/4 tsp. pepper
3 c. canned tomatoes
2 c. cooked rice

Saute green pepper, onion and garlic in butter in deep skillet until onion is transparent. Add venison; cook until venison is brown, stirring to break venison in small pieces. Sprinkle in flour; add salt, pepper and tomatoes. Mix well; simmer until blended and heated through. Serve over rice.

ROAST VENISON

1 4 to 5-lb. venison roast
Salt and pepper to taste
1 pod of red pepper, minced
1/2 c. vinegar
1 c. beef bouillon
2 onions, sliced
8 med. potatoes
8 carrots

Brown venison in small amount of hot fat in Dutch oven; turn to brown all sides. Sprinkle venison with salt and pepper; add red pepper, vinegar, bouillon and onions. Bake, covered, at 350 degrees for 1 hour and 30 minutes. Pare and halve potatoes and carrots. Add potatoes and carrots to venison. Bake, covered, for 30 minutes longer.

VENISON ROLLED ROAST

1/4 lb. salt pork
6 lb. boned shoulder venison
1/4 c. flour
2 tsp. salt
1/8 tsp. pepper
1/2 c. salad oil
1 tbsp. vinegar
1/2 c. diced celery
1 c. minced onion
1 carrot, sliced
1 tart apple, sliced
1 tbsp. lemon juice

Cut salt pork into strips; arrange strips down center of venison. Roll venison jelly roll fashion; tie securely. Combine flour, salt and pepper; rub into venison. Brown venison on all sides in hot oil in Dutch oven; place venison on rack in Dutch oven. Combine 1/2 cup water with vinegar; pour over venison. Simmer, covered, for 2 hours; add remaining ingredients. Simmer, covered, for 1 hour longer or until venison is tender. Serve with pan gravy if desired.

VENISON SAUERBRATEN

2 c. cider vinegar
2 c. red wine
1/2 c. olive oil
1 lemon, thinly sliced
1/2 tsp. ground allspice
1/2 tsp. ground cloves
3 peppercorns
1 clove of garlic, crushed
2 onions, sliced
1/4 c. brown sugar
1 tsp. salt
7 lb. venison rump
1/4 c. flour
1/2 pt. sour cream

Combine vinegar, wine and olive oil with 1 quart water; mix well. Add lemon, allspice, cloves, peppercorns, garlic, onions, brown sugar and salt to vinegar mixture; blend thoroughly. Place venison in deep bowl; pour marinade over venison. Refrigerate, covered, for 3 days; turn venison occasionally. Remove venison from marinade; reserve marinade. Brown venison on all sides in small amount of fat in Dutch oven; add 1 cup marinade. Bake at 325 degrees for 3 hours to 3 hours and 30 minutes or until venison is tender. Baste occasionally with pan juices; add reserved marinade as needed. Remove venison from Dutch oven; keep warm. Combine remaining marinade with pan drippings. Blend flour with 1/4 cup water; add to marinade mixture. Simmer, stirring constantly, until thickened. Stir in sour cream just before serving.

BAKED VENISON STEAKS

2 lb. small venison steaks	*2 cans cream of mushroom soup*
1/4 c. margarine	*1 1/3 c. water*
Salt and pepper to taste	*2 lge. onions, sliced*

Brown steaks in margarine in skillet; sprinkle with salt and pepper. Blend soup and water until smooth. Arrange layer of steaks in greased baking dish; add layer of onions. Add half the soup. Repeat layers, ending with soup. Bake, covered, at 350 degrees for 30 to 40 minutes or until steaks are tender.

VENISON IN SOUR CREAM

2 lb. venison steak	*1 bay leaf*
1 clove of garlic, minced	*8 peppercorns*
1 c. diced celery	*1 tsp. salt*
1 c. diced carrots	*1/4 c. butter*
1/2 c. minced onion	*1/4 c. flour*
1 c. tart fruit juice	*1 c. sour cream*
	1/4 tsp. pepper

Cut venison into 2-inch pieces. Saute venison and garlic in hot fat in heavy skillet; stir to brown venison on all sides. Spoon venison into 2-quart casserole. Saute celery, carrots and onion in remaining fat in skillet for 2 minutes; add 2 cups water, fruit juice, bay leaf, peppercorns and salt. Blend well; pour mixture over venison. Bake, covered, at 300 degrees for 45 minutes to 1 hour or until venison is tender. Remove from oven; drain liquid from casserole. Melt butter in skillet; stir in flour. Add venison liquid gradually; simmer, stirring constantly, until thickened. Add sour cream and additional salt and pepper if needed; blend well. Bring sauce just to a boil; pour over venison and vegetables in casserole. Serve immediately.

VENISON STEAK CASSEROLE

8 slices bacon	*1 bay leaf, crumbled*
6 potatoes, thinly sliced	*1/4 tsp. sweet basil*
6 onions, thinly sliced	*1 thick venison steak*
Salt and pepper to taste	*1/4 tsp. thyme*
	2 c. Burgundy
	1 10-oz. can beef consomme

Place half the bacon in large casserole; cover with layer of potatoes and layer of onions. Season each layer with salt and pepper; add bay leaf and basil. Place steak on vegetables; sprinkle with salt, pepper and thyme. Repeat layers of potatoes and onions; place remaining bacon on top. Add Burgundy and consomme; cover tightly. Bake at 350 degrees for 2 hours or until venison is tender. Liquid may be drained and thickened for gravy.

GROUSTARK VENISON

Color photograph for this recipe on page 69.

1 6-lb. leg of venison	*2 med. onions, quartered*
Salt to taste	*2 med. carrots, sliced*
2 c. dry red wine	
4 sprigs of parsley	*3 lb. small potatoes*
2 bay leaves	*White pepper to taste*
10 peppercorns	*Snipped parsley to taste*
4 whole cloves	*2 10-oz. packages frozen Brussels sprouts, thawed*
Dash of thyme	*1/4 c. chopped walnuts*
6 strips salt pork	
3/4 c. melted butter	
2 tbsp. flour	
1 c. beef broth	

Season venison with salt; place in shallow pan. Combine wine, onions, carrots, parsley, bay leaves, peppercorns, cloves and thyme. Pour over venison. Refrigerate for 24 hours, turning occasionally. Remove venison from marinade; strain, reserving marinade. Place venison on rack in shallow baking pan; place salt pork across venison. Bake in 450-degree oven for 25 minutes. Reduce oven temperature to 325 degrees; bake for about 2 hours longer or until venison is medium rare, basting frequently with half the reserved marinade. Remove venison to hot platter. Combine remaining marinade with pan drippings in saucepan; bring to a boil. Blend 2 tablespoons butter with flour; stir into marinade. Stir in broth slowly; cook, stirring constantly, until mixture comes to a boil. Cook for 1 minute longer. Peel potatoes; cut in half. Cook in boiling, salted water for 15 to 20 minutes or until tender. Drain and toss with 6 tablespoons butter, white pepper, salt and parsley. Saute Brussels sprouts in remaining butter for 10 minutes. Add walnuts; cook for 5 minutes. Arrange potatoes and Brussels sprouts around venison; serve with gravy. Yield: 6-8 servings.

Game Birds

The term game birds refers to wild, edible fowl that is both high in protein and low in fat. Game birds are not commercially available. But if you are a skillful hunter and have adequate freezing facilities, you can enjoy the unique flavor of game birds year-round.

KINDS: There are two main categories of game birds: upland fowl and waterfowl. *Upland fowl* are usually dry-plucked rather than scalded, and never skinned. They include: *quail*, a small, migratory game bird often known as a partridge that usually weighs less than 1/2 pound; *grouse* a game bird prized for its clean eating habits and consequent mild, wild flavor; *wild turkey*, an exceptionally swift and wary game bird with a wild, not gamy, flavor; *dove* and *squab*, small members of the pigeon family, and *pigeon*, all dark meat delicacies; and *pheasant*, a white meat game bird with a very mild flavor. (The pheasant hen is usually plumper and more tender

than the pheasant cock.) *Waterfowl* are very lean and, because they exist mainly on a diet of fish and marsh greens, their flavor is quite gamy and very often fishy. Like upland fowl, their feathers are dry-plucked. Included in this category are: *duck;* and *goose.*
(See DUCK and GOOSE for specific recipes.)
STORING: After curing (see below) game birds may either be cooked immediately or frozen. *To freeze* game birds–Wrap cured birds in moisture- and vapor-proof paper and freeze at 0 degrees until ready to use. Thaw frozen birds in the refrigerator rather than at room temperature. After thawing cook at once. Do not refreeze.
PREPARATION: Most game birds must be cured in a cool dry place before they are processed for storing or cooking. To cure game–Suspend it from a hook for a time specified by the type of game, to permit aging and tenderizing. In general, younger birds are hung for a few days, older birds for a week or more. When roasting game birds, you may want to fill the stomach cavity either with a bread-based dressing or with some celery, an apple, or an onion to absorb some of the gamy taste. If the bird is completely stuffed, add a few more minutes per pound to the total cooking time. Because all game birds are lean, they require larding (fastening bacon strips across the breast) and frequent basting. To prepare upland fowl follow specific recipe directions. The size and age of the bird usually determines the appropriate cooking method. Generally smaller, younger birds can be sauteed, broiled, roasted, or spit-roasted while older and larger birds are braised or stewed. Game birds are best if they are cooked until tender, not until the meat falls away from the bone. (See POULTRY.)

DOVE AND WILD RICE DRESSING

Flour
Salt and pepper to taste
Paprika to taste
12 to 16 dove breasts
Shortening
1/2 c. wild rice
1 sm. onion, chopped
Giblets (opt.)
1/2 tsp. sage
1/4 lb. sausage
1/2 c. wine

Combine flour, salt, pepper and paprika in paper bag. Add dove breasts; shake. Brown in shortening. Remove; place dove in circle in casserole. Wash rice; add to 2 cups boiling water. Cook, covered, until water is absorbed. Saute onion, giblets and sage with sausage. Add onion mixture to rice; cook for 2 minutes. Place rice mixture in center of dove breasts. Combine wine and 3/4 cup water; pour over dove breasts and rice. Cover. Bake in 350-degree oven for about 1 hour. Yield: 4-6 servings.

DOVE IN SOUR CREAM

6 to 12 dove
Salt and pepper to taste
Flour
Cooking oil
3 or 4 slices bacon
Poultry stock
1 c. sour cream

Dry dove thoroughly; season with salt and pepper. Dredge with flour; brown lightly in small amount of oil in skillet. Place bacon in baking dish; place dove on bacon. Add enough stock to avoid sticking; cover. Bake in 350-degree oven for about 50 minutes. Pour sour cream over dove; bake for 10 minutes.

DOVE BREASTS

12 to 18 dove breasts
1 med. onion, diced
1 can cream of mushroom soup
1/4 to 1/2 c. sherry
Pinch of oregano
Pinch of crushed rosemary
Salt and pepper to taste
1/2 pt. sour cream

Place dove breasts, meaty side down, in 15 x 12-inch baking dish. Do not overcrowd. Saute onion in small amount of fat in skillet. Mix onion, soup, sherry, herbs, salt and pepper. Pour over dove breasts; cover baking dish lightly with foil. Bake at 325 degrees for 1 hour, turning occasionally. Add sour cream; stir. Bake for about 20 minutes longer. Yield: 6 servings.

DOVE IN WINE AND MUSHROOMS

12 dove
1 dried red pepper
Salt to taste
Butter
Juice of 1 lemon
Worcestershire sauce
1 1/2 c. sherry
4 sm. cans button mushrooms
1/2 c. flour
Buttered toast

Open dove down backs, leaving breasts whole. Place dove in pan. Steam, covered, in small amount of water for 20 minutes. Place, breast side down, in roasting pan. Place small piece of dried hot pepper, salt and 1 tablespoon butter on each dove. Mix lemon juice, 1 tablespoon Worcestershire sauce and 1 cup sherry; add to dove. Bake in 300-degree oven for 1 hour or until tender, adding small amounts of boiling water as needed to keep from sticking. Remove drippings from pan; reserve. Drain mushrooms; reserve juice. Melt 1/2 cup butter; add flour. Cook until flour is browned. Add reserved pan drippings, reserved mushroom juice and remaining sherry. Add enough water to make 4 cups sauce. Season with red pepper, salt and Worcestershire sauce to taste. Cook, stirring constantly, until thickened. Stir in mushrooms. Pour over dove. Serve over buttered toast. Yield: 12 servings.

CHARCOALED DOVE

1/2 c. margarine, melted
1 c. vinegar
1 pod red pepper, chopped
20 to 30 dove

Combine margarine, vinegar and red pepper. Dip dove in sauce. Cook over hot coals, basting occasionally, until tender.

Paper Bag Grouse with Brussels Sprouts . . . Grouse is stuffed with mushrooms and walnuts.

PAPER BAG GROUSE WITH BRUSSELS SPROUTS

6 grouse with giblets
2 cloves of garlic, halved
10 tbsp. butter
3/4 c. chopped onion
1/2 lb. mushrooms, sliced
3/4 c. Madeira
1/2 c. chopped walnuts
1 tsp. salt
1/4 tsp. rosemary leaves
Dash of pepper
Shortening
2/3 c. chicken bouillon
2 10-oz. packages frozen California Brussels sprouts

Chop giblets. Brown garlic in 6 tablespoons butter in skillet; remove garlic. Saute onion and giblets for about 10 minutes in garlic butter; add mushrooms, 1/2 cup Madeira, walnuts and seasonings. Cook until mushrooms are tender and liquid is reduced. Spoon stuffing into grouse; truss. Dot each grouse with 1 teaspoon butter. Place grouse in small brown paper bags; fold over ends. Brush paper bags with shortening on all sides. Place in shallow roasting pan. Bake in 400-degree oven for 10 minutes; reduce oven temperature to 350 degrees. Bake for 1 hour and 15 minutes longer. Bring bouillon and remaining wine to a boil in saucepan; add Brussels sprouts, cooking just until tender. Drain; toss in remaining butter. Serve with grouse.

ROAST GROUSE

3 grouse
6 slices bacon
1/4 tsp. pepper
1/2 tsp. seasoned salt
1/2 tsp. paprika
Celery leaves
3 tsp. butter
1 c. sherry (opt.)
1 c. orange juice (opt.)

Preheat oven to 375 degrees. Rub pepper, seasoned salt and paprika inside grouse and over exterior. Cover grouse breasts with bacon slices. Fill each grouse with celery leaves; add 1 teaspoon butter per grouse to cavities. Bake at 325 degrees for about 25 minutes per pound or until tender. Combine sherry and orange juice; baste, if desired. Yield: 6 servings.

GUINEA HENS WITH ORANGE SAUCE

2 guinea hens
Salt and pepper to taste
4 tbsp. butter
2 oranges
1 tbsp. shredded orange rind
1 bouillon cube
1/2 c. white wine

Cut guinea hens into serving pieces; season with salt and pepper. Brown in butter in ovenproof skillet. Peel and quarter oranges. Add orange quarters and rind to mixture in skillet. Dissolve bouillon cube in 1/2 cup hot water. Combine bouillon and wine; add to guinea hen mixture. Cover. Bake at 300 degrees for 2 hours. Serve with sauce over wild or white rice. Yield: 4-6 servings.

HUNTSMAN-STYLED PARTRIDGE

2 or 3 young partridge
Seasoned flour
7 oz. brandy or rum
1 sm. onion, diced
2 carrots, cut into sticks
1 tsp. poultry seasoning
1 c. canned consomme
1 can mushrooms with juice

Cut partridge into serving pieces. Dredge with seasoned flour; brown well in skillet in hot fat. Pour brandy over partridge and ignite; add onion, carrots and poultry seasoning when flame has died down. Stir gently to blend with partridge, scraping up browned bits from pan. Add consomme and mushrooms. Cover; simmer for 45 minutes or until partridge are tender. Yield: 4-6 servings.

PHEASANT IN CREAM

1 pheasant
Milk
Salt and pepper to taste
Flour
3 tbsp. butter
1 pt. cream
1/4 c. chopped onion
1 tbsp. lemon juice

Cut pheasant into serving pieces; let stand for 30 minutes in enough milk to cover. Season pheasant with salt and pepper; dredge with flour. Place in skillet in hot butter; fry over medium heat until browned. Combine cream, onion and lemon juice; pour over pheasant. Simmer for about 45 minutes or until tender. Yield: 4 or 6 servings.

QUAIL COOKED IN SHERRY

6 quail
Salt
Flour
3/4 c. sherry
3 tbsp. Worcestershire sauce
1/3 c. lemon juice

Season quail with salt; dredge with flour. Brown in small amount of fat. Remove; place in casserole. Combine sherry, Worcestershire sauce and lemon juice; pour over quail. Cover. Bake at 350 degrees for 1 hour. Yield: 6 servings.

HOT QUAIL PIE

3 med. quail
Salt and pepper to taste
1 sm. onion, chopped
2 tbsp. margarine
3 tbsp. flour
Hot sauce to taste
1 tsp. bottled browning sauce
1 c. cooked diced carrots
1 sm. can green peas, drained
1 recipe buttermilk biscuits

Cook quail in 4 cups water with salt and pepper until tender. Drain; reserve liquid. Remove quail from bones; place in reserved liquid. Saute onion in margarine until tender. Add flour; stir well. Add quail mixture, hot sauce and browning sauce; cook over low heat until thickened. Add carrots and peas; pour into deep baking dish. Place biscuits on top. Bake in 375-degree oven for about 30 minutes; serve hot. Yield: 4 servings.

QUAIL WHITFIELD

6 dressed quail
Salt and pepper to taste
6 strips bacon
1/2 c. melted butter
3 tbsp. flour
2 beef bouillon cubes
1/2 c. lemon juice
Toast points

Preheat broiler. Season each quail with salt and pepper; wrap with bacon, covering completely. Secure with toothpicks; place on rack under broiler. Broil for 20 minutes, basting frequently with butter. Remove quail to heated platter; keep warm with tent of foil. Remove rack from broiler pan; place pan with drippings over medium heat. Add flour; brown, stirring constantly. Dissolve bouillon cubes in 2 cups water; add to roux, stirring constantly until blended. Bring to a boil; add lemon juice, stirring until thickened. Place quail on toast points; pour sauce over top. Serve with wild rice mixture, if desired. Yield: 6 servings.

STUFFED BAKED QUAIL

2 c. dry bread crumbs
1 egg
1 tbsp. chopped onion
2 tbsp. chopped pecans (opt.)
2 tbsp. sliced ripe olives (opt.)
2 tbsp. finely chopped celery
1/4 c. cream of chicken soup
1/4 tsp. salt
1/8 tsp. pepper
1/4 tsp. sage or poultry seasoning
1 tbsp. melted butter
4 quail
Shortening

Mix all ingredients except quail and shortening to make dressing; add small amount of water, if needed. Center each quail on square of foil, breast side up; stuff each with 1/4 of the dressing. Rub small amount of shortening over breasts; seal foil. Place in baking pan. Bake in 350-degree oven for 1 hour or until tender. Yield: 4 servings.

ROASTED SQUAB

4 squab and giblets
Salt and pepper
Butter
2 c. dry bread cubes
1 1/2 tbsp. chopped onion
1/8 tsp. poultry seasoning
Sage to taste
Hot broth

Rub inside of each squab with salt and pepper to taste. Brown giblets in 1/4 cup butter; combine with bread cubes, onion, 1/2 teaspoon salt, 1/8 teaspoon pepper, poultry seasoning, sage, 2 1/2 tablespoons melted butter and enough hot broth to moisten. Stuff squab with mixture. Rub outsides with butter. Place squab, breast sides up, on rack in shallow pan. Bake at 350 degrees for about 1 hour or until tender. Yield: 4 servings.

ENGLISH WOOD PIGEON

4 skinned pigeons, split
Cooking oil
1 can onion soup
6 green onions, chopped
1/4 c. margarine
1 4-oz. can mushrooms
Chopped parsley to taste
Seasoned salt to taste
Pepper to taste
Garlic salt to taste

Brown pigeons in 3/4 inch cooking oil; remove from skillet. Place pigeons in Dutch oven with soup. Saute onions in margarine; pour into soup. Add mushrooms, parsley and seasonings. Simmer, covered, for about 35 minutes or until tender. Serve over wild rice, if desired. Yield: 4 servings.

Garnishing

Garnishing is the art of decorating foods before serving them. A garnish adds color and, if it is edible, adds flavor, too. For instance, add a whole, peeled tomato to vegetable soup, and it will float like an island in the center of the soup bowl, adding both color and flavor.

Soups may be garnished with chopped herbs or a thin lemon or cucumber slice. Garnish fish with lemon slices or fruit sections. To add even more color to fruit garnishes, dip the skin edge of the fruit pieces into parsley or paprika.

Vegetables are often garnished with tiny onions, mushrooms, almonds, or pieces of hard-cooked eggs. Meat platters can be garnished with broiled fruit—apples for pork, peaches for chicken, oranges with duck, and so on. Vegetables, too, can be used to garnish meats. Small onions or tomatoes are particularly effective meat garnishes.

EASY GARNISHES: One of the most often used garnishes is a simple bunch of parsley attractively arranged around meat, vegetable, or salad platters. But there are other, equally eye-catching garnishes you can create with imagination and a sharp paring knife. Directions for some of these follow.

RADISH ROSE

Using a sharp knife, cut off the radish root. Leave some of the stem and roots, if desired. Scallop around the edge of the radish in rows from the stem to the root end. Place in ice water. Do not try to separate or spread the petals as the ice water will cause them to "bloom" naturally.

CARROT CURLS

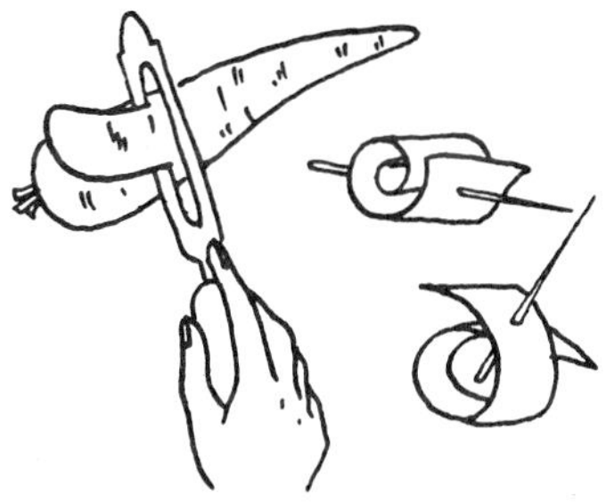

Scrape raw carrots to remove tough outer skin. Use potato peeler to make thin strips down the length of the carrot. Roll up strips, secure with toothpicks, and place in ice water until crisp and curled.

CELERY CURLS

Cut celery stalks into short pieces. Slice ends lengthwise. Both ends may be cut if desired. Place cut celery into ice water. The water will cause the cut ends to curl.

ONION RINGS

Thinly slice Bermuda or Spanish onion crosswise. Separate into thin rings and crisp in ice water until ready to serve.

PEPPER RINGS

Thinly slice a crisp green pepper crosswise. Remove seeds and white membrane. Crisp rings in ice water until ready to serve.

Ginger

Ginger is an exotic spice that is obtained from a sun-bleached root. It has a penetrating smell and a spicy-sweet flavor that is known as "gingerin".

AVAILABILITY: Ginger is in year-round supply in the United States through import from Jamaica, Africa, and India.

BUYING: Ginger is processed and sold in a variety of forms: *cracked ginger* which is small, slivered pieces of the tan-colored gingerroot; *ground ginger,* the most common form, which is a popular cooking spice of light tan color; and *crystallized* or *preserved gingers,* which are confections, not spices.

STORING: Like all other spices, ginger will retain its potency if stored in a cool, dry place.

USES: Processed forms of ginger are used in numerous products. One of the largest ginger-based commodities is ginger ale. For medicinal purposes ginger is a long-recognized digestive stimulant. Cracked ginger is an ingredient in many preserves and in the spice blend known as Mixed Pickling Spice. Ground ginger is a prominent addition to some curry powders; many baked products; soups; and meat, poultry, vegetable, and cheese dishes.

GINGER DIP

5 8-oz. packages cream cheese
3 c. crushed pineapple, drained
1/2 c. lemon juice
3 tsp. ground ginger
3 3-oz. cans flaked coconut
3 6-oz. cans chopped pecans

Soften cream cheese; add remaining ingredients. Mix well; chill.

ORIENTAL GINGER DIP

1 c. mayonnaise
1 c. sour cream
1/4 c. chopped onion
1/4 c. minced parsley
1/4 c. water chestnuts, chopped
2 tbsp. chopped candied ginger
2 cloves of garlic, minced
1 tbsp. soy sauce
Dash of salt

Combine mayonnaise and sour cream. Add remaining ingredients; mix thoroughly. Garnish with ginger pieces. Yield: 2 cups.

CHINESE FORTUNE COOKIES

2 eggs
3/4 c. powdered sugar
1/2 c. sifted flour
1/4 tsp. salt
1/4 tsp. ginger
1/4 c. melted butter

Beat eggs; add powdered sugar, beating thoroughly. Mix in remaining ingredients. Drop batter by spoonfuls onto greased and floured cookie sheet, about 3 inches apart. Spread each to thin 2 1/2-inch round. Bake at 300 degrees for about 12 minutes. Leave cookies in warm oven. Remove, one at a time, working rapidly before cookies harden. Fold each cookie in half over pencil, pinching ends together. Remove pencil; let cookie cool on rack. Before serving, insert fortunes or proverbs, written on small strips of paper, in each cookie. Yield: 24 cookies.

CRACKLE TOP GINGER COOKIES

1 c. shortening
2 c. (packed) brown sugar
1 egg, well beaten
1 c. unsulphured molasses
4 c. sifted flour
1/2 tsp. salt
2 tsp. soda
2 tsp. ginger
1 tsp. vanilla
1 tsp. lemon extract
Sugar

Cream shortening and brown sugar thoroughly; blend in egg and molasses. Beat until light and fluffy. Sift flour, salt, soda and ginger together. Blend dry ingredients gradually into creamed mixture. Dough should be soft but not sticky. Add vanilla and lemon extract. Chill for about 4 hours or until dough can be handled easily. Dust hands with flour; shape dough into balls about 1 1/2 inches in diameter. Place on greased cookie sheet. Bake in 350-degree oven for about 15 minutes or until brown. Sprinkle with sugar; remove from cookie sheet. Yield: 30 cookies.

FROSTED GINGER CREAMS

1/2 c. shortening
1/2 c. sugar
1 egg
1 tsp. ginger
1/2 tsp. cloves
1 tsp. cinnamon
1/2 tsp. salt
2 tsp. soda
1/2 c. sour milk
1 c. molasses
3 c. (about) flour
Powdered sugar frosting

Cream shortening and sugar; add egg, mixing well. Add spices and salt. Combine soda with milk; add to creamed mixture. Add molasses and flour to make soft batter. Drop by teaspoonfuls on greased cookie sheet. Bake at 350 degrees until brown. Spread thin powdered sugar frosting on warm cookies. Yield: 4 dozen.

GINGER DROP COOKIES

1 c. shortening
1 c. sugar
1 egg
1 c. molasses
1 tsp. soda
1 tsp. salt
1 tsp. ginger
5 c. flour
Confectioners' sugar icing

Cream shortening and sugar; add egg, beating well. Add molasses. Dissolve soda in 1 cup hot water; add alternately with salt, ginger and flour to egg mixture. Drop by rounded teaspoonfuls on ungreased cookie sheet. Bake at 375 degrees for about 15 minutes. Frost with confectioners' sugar icing while warm. Yield: 4-5 dozen.

GINGERSNAPS

3/4 c. shortening
3/4 c. (packed) brown sugar
1 egg
3/4 c. molasses
3 c. sifted flour
1/4 tsp. salt
2 tsp. soda
1/2 tsp. cloves
1 tsp. cinnamon
1 tsp. ginger
Sugar

Cream shortening and brown sugar. Add egg and molasses; beat well. Sift flour with salt, soda and spices; add to molasses mixture. Mix well. Chill. Form into small balls; roll in sugar. Place 2 inches apart on cookie sheet. Bake in 375-degree oven for 10 minutes. Yield: 9-10 dozen.

EASY GINGERBREAD

1 1/2 c. flour
1 tsp. soda
1 1/4 tsp. ginger
1 1/4 tsp. cinnamon
1/2 c. shortening
1/2 c. (packed) brown sugar
1 egg, beaten
1/2 c. molasses
1/2 c. cold tea

Sift flour, soda and spices together. Cream shortening and brown sugar together well; beat in egg and molasses. Add tea and flour mixture to creamed mixture alternately; mix well. Pour batter into greased 9-inch square pan. Bake in 350-degree oven for 30 minutes. Serve hot with whipped cream, ice cream or applesauce, if desired. Yield: 6 servings.

PARTY GINGERBREAD

4 c. sifted all-purpose flour
1 3/4 tsp. salt
2 1/2 tsp. baking powder
1 1/4 tsp. ginger
1 1/4 tsp. cloves
1 1/4 tsp. cinnamon
1 1/4 c. shortening
1 1/4 c. sugar
1 3/4 tsp. soda
1 1/4 c. unsulphured molasses
2 eggs
1 1/4 c. buttermilk

Sift flour, salt, baking powder and spices together. Cream shortening, sugar and soda; blend in molasses. Stir in 1/2 cup flour mixture. Beat in eggs, one at a time, beating well after each addition. Add buttermilk alternately with remaining flour mixture. Beat for 30 seconds. Turn into greased and floured baking pan. Bake in 350-degree oven for 50 minutes. Cool; cut into squares. Top with whipped cream and applesauce if desired.

Party Gingerbread . . . Dress up this dark, rich gingerbread with applesauce and whipped cream.

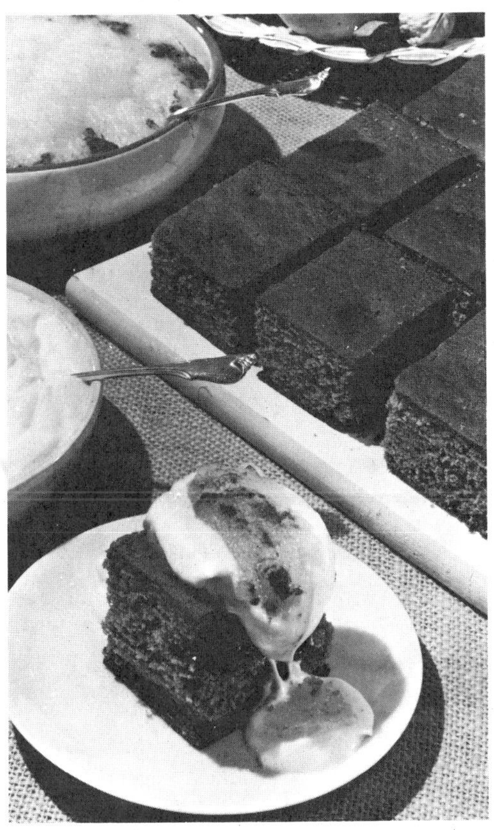

IRISH GINGERBREAD

2 1/2 c. sifted flour
1 tsp. soda
1/2 tsp. salt
1 tsp. cinnamon
1 tsp. ginger
3/4 c. sugar
2 eggs, slightly beaten
1 c. buttermilk
1/2 c. melted shortening
1/2 c. molasses

Sift flour, soda, salt, cinnamon and ginger into mixing bowl. Add sugar. Combine eggs, buttermilk, shortening and molasses. Add egg mixture to dry ingredients all at once; beat for 3 minutes. Pour into well-greased and lightly floured 9 x 9-inch pan. Bake at 375 degrees for about 40 minutes until gingerbread springs back when touched lightly in center. Serve warm. Yield: 12 servings.

GINGER MUFFINS

1/2 c. shortening
1/2 c. sugar
1 egg
1 c. molasses
3 c. flour
1 1/2 tsp. soda
1/2 tsp. salt
1 tsp. cinnamon
1 tsp. ginger
1/2 tsp. cloves

Cream shortening and sugar. Beat in egg; stir in molasses. Sift dry ingredients together; stir into molasses mixture. Add 1 cup hot water gradually; beat until smooth. Fill greased muffin pans 2/3 full. Bake at 375 degrees for about 25 minutes. Yield: 2 dozen.

GINGER SHERBET

1 6-oz. can frozen limeade concentrate
1 1/2 c. sour cream
Green food coloring
3 egg whites, stiffly beaten
1/4 c. finely chopped candied ginger

Let limeade stand until thawed. Blend sour cream, limeade and enough food coloring to make desired color. Fold sour cream mixture into egg whites. Blend in ginger. Pour into freezer tray; freeze. Yield: 4-6 servings.

Goose

BAKED GOOSE

Color photograph for this recipe on page 78.

1 8-lb. goose with giblets
Salt
2 c. browned bread cubes
1 onion, chopped
2 tbsp. fat
1/4 tsp. sage
Pinch of pepper
2 c. chopped celery

Rub goose cavity with salt. Cook giblets in salted water; cool and chop. Combine giblets, bread cubes, onion, fat, sage, salt to taste, pepper and celery; stuff goose with dressing. Secure goose with skewers; place in baking pan. Bake for 15 minutes at 500 degrees. Reduce oven temperature to 350 degrees; bake for about 3 hours longer or until tender.

GOOSE STUFFED WITH SAUERKRAUT

1 goose
1 lge. can sauerkraut
1 potato, grated
Salt and pepper to taste

Place goose on rack in baking pan. Bake at 400 degrees for 20 minutes. Combine sauerkraut and potato in saucepan; bring to a boil. Reduce heat; simmer for 20 minutes. Sprinkle cavity of goose with salt and pepper; stuff with sauerkraut mixture. Reduce oven temperature to 300 degrees; bake for 3 hours and 30 minutes or until drumstick moves easily.

ROAST GOOSE

1/2 c. chopped onion
1/4 c. butter
4 c. dry bread cubes
1 tsp. salt
1/2 tsp. pepper
2 eggs
1 lb. sausage
1 6 to 10-lb. goose

Saute onion in butter. Soak bread in water; squeeze out excess moisture. Combine onion, bread, salt, pepper, eggs and sausage; mix well. Stuff goose with mixture. Place in roasting pan, breast-side down, in 3 inches of boiling water. Bake, covered, at 350 degrees for 1 hour. Drain off water. Bake, back-side down, basting occasionally, for 2 hours longer or until drumstick moves easily. Yield: 8 servings.

ROAST GOOSE WITH BAKED APPLE

2 c. bread crumbs
1 onion, chopped
1/4 tsp. sage
1 tsp. salt
Pinch of pepper
1 8-lb. goose
6 to 8 apples
1/4 c. (packed) brown sugar
3 sweet potatoes, mashed

Combine bread crumbs, onion, 2 tablespoons fat, sage, salt and pepper; mix well. Cook giblets until tender; chop. Combine giblets with dressing mixture. Stuff goose with dressing; lace opening closed with string. Place goose on rack in roasting pan. Roast at 500 degrees for 15 minutes. Reduce heat to 350 degrees; roast for 3 hours longer or until drumstick moves easily. Wash and core apples; sprinkle with brown sugar. Stuff with seasoned sweet potatoes; bake until tender. Serve with goose.

WILD GOOSE WITH WILD RICE

1 wild goose
1 onion
1 carrot
1 apple
1 c. wild rice
Salt and pepper to taste
1/4 tbsp. sage
1/4 c. melted butter
3 tbsp. chopped celery
2 tbsp. chopped onion
Chopped green pepper to taste
Chopped pimento to taste
1 can consomme

Cover goose with salted water; let stand overnight. Drain goose; place onion, carrot and apple in cavity. Place goose in electric roaster; add 1 inch hot water. Roast, covered, at 325 degrees for 2 hours. Cook rice according to package directions; drain. Stir in seasonings, butter, celery, chopped onion, green pepper and pimento. Remove goose from roaster; take onion, carrot and celery from cavity. Stuff goose with rice mixture; return to roaster. Combine consomme and 3/4 cup water; pour over goose. Roast, covered, for 2 hours longer; baste goose occasionally with pan liquid.

HOLIDAY GOOSE AND SAUERKRAUT STUFFING

1 lge. onion, chopped
1 tbsp. butter
6 1/2 c. drained sauerkraut
1 1/2 c. grated potatoes
1 med. pared apple, diced
1 sm. carrot, grated
2 tsp. caraway seed
1/2 tsp. salt
1/4 tsp. pepper
1/2 c. dry white wine
1 12 lb. goose
1/2 c. honey
1/2 tsp. bottled browning sauce

Saute onion in butter in large skillet until golden. Add sauerkraut, potatoes, apple, carrot, seasonings

Holiday Goose and Sauerkraut Stuffing, Brussels Sprouts in Wine/Raisins, Orange-Filbert Noodles.

and wine. Cook over medium heat for 5 minutes, stirring constantly. Stuff goose cavity with stuffing; truss. Place goose on rack in shallow roasting pan. Bake in 325-degree oven for 4 hours. Blend honey with browning sauce; brush on goose. Bake for 30 minutes longer or until goose is glazed. Yield: 8 servings.

Graham

Graham is a type of flour, or fine meal, ground from wheat grain. Graham flour is also called whole wheat flour because it is ground from the entire wheat kernel—bran, germ, and endosperm. It retains the vitamins and minerals of the bran and germ that white flour—ground only from the endosperm or interior of the wheat kernel—loses in its milling process. Graham flour contains protein, B vitamins, iron, phosphorus, fat, and starch. (1 cup graham flour = 408 calories)

AVAILABILITY: Graham flour is available year-round in some local retail stores and many health food stores. Usually sold in 2-pound and 5-pound bags.

STORING: Store graham flour at room temperature in tightly covered container.

USES: Graham flour is used in the commercial production of whole wheat bread and graham crackers. It is also used to prepare home-baked yeast and quick breads, biscuits, muffins, and griddle cakes.

PREPARATION: Used alone in home-baked goods, graham flour does not create a light-textured product. It is usually combined with equal amounts of white flour. Yeast breads made from graham flour are generally not kneaded. The dough can be mixed and allowed to rise just once in the pan.

PILGRIM GRAHAM BREAD

1 c. sifted flour
2 c. graham flour
1 tsp. salt
1/2 c. maple sugar
1 1/2 tsp. soda
2 c. buttermilk

Combine flour, graham flour, salt and sugar in large bowl; stir well with spoon. Stir soda into buttermilk; add to dry ingredients, mixing well. Pour into greased 9 x 5 x 3-inch pan. Bake at 350 degrees for 1 hour.

HONEY-GRAHAM BREAD

2 pkg. yeast
1 3/4 c. lukewarm milk
1/4 c. shortening, softened
1/2 c. honey
1 tbsp. salt
3 3/4 c. graham flour
2 1/2 c. flour

Soften yeast in 1/2 cup warm water. Combine milk, honey and salt in large bowl; add yeast mixture. Beat in shortening and 1 cup graham flour well; add remaining flour. Mix until dough leaves side of bowl. Turn out onto floured board; knead until dough is smooth, elastic and no longer sticky. Place in greased bowl; cover. Let rise in warm place for about 1 hour or until doubled in bulk. Punch down. Let rise a second time until doubled in bulk. Punch down. Shape into 2 loaves; place in 9 x 5 x 3-inch loaf pans. Bake at 375 degrees for about 45 minutes. Yield: 2 loaves.

GRAHAM-BUTTERSCOTCH CAKE

1/2 c. shortening
1 c. sugar
3 eggs, separated
1/2 tsp. vanilla
1/4 c. sifted flour
1 1/2 tsp. baking powder
1/4 tsp. salt
2 c. graham cracker crumbs
3/4 c. milk
1/2 c. chopped pecans
Butterscotch Frosting

Cream shortening and sugar thoroughly; add egg yolks, one at a time, beating well after each addition. Add vanilla. Sift flour, baking powder and salt together. Beat into creamed mixture alternately with graham cracker crumbs and milk. Stir in nuts. Beat egg whites until stiff peaks form. Fold egg whites into crumb mixture. Pour batter into 2 waxed paper-lined 8-inch cake pans. Bake at 350 degrees for 30 minutes. Remove from oven. Cool in pan for 10 minutes; remove to cake racks. Fill layers with Butterscotch Frosting; frost top and side of cake with remaining frosting.

Butterscotch Frosting

1 c. milk
1 pkg. butterscotch pudding mix
1/2 c. shortening
1/2 c. butter
1 c. sugar
1 tsp. vanilla

Combine milk and pudding mix. Blend well; cook over low heat until thick, stirring constantly. Let stand until cool. Cream shortening with butter, sugar and vanilla until well blended. Add pudding to creamed mixture; beat until light and fluffy.

GRAHAM CRACKER-CURRANT CAKE

1 1/2 c. sugar
4 eggs, separated
2 c. graham cracker crumbs
1 1/2 tsp. baking powder
1 c. chopped walnuts
Red currant jelly
Whipped cream, sweetened

Mix sugar with egg yolks. Add crumbs and baking powder; mix well. Add 1 teaspoon water and nuts. Beat egg whites until stiff peaks form. Fold into crumb mixture. Pour into two 8-inch foil-lined cake pans. Bake at 350 degrees for 25 minutes. Turn cake out of pan; remove foil. Cool to lukewarm. Fill layers with red currant jelly; frost top and side of cake with sweetened whipped cream. Refrigerate for at least 24 hours. Yield: 10 servings.

HAWAIIAN GRAHAM CRACKER CAKE

1/3 c. butter
1 c. sugar
2 eggs
3 c. graham cracker crumbs
1 c. milk
1 1/2 c. coconut
1/2 c. chopped pecans
2 tsp. baking powder
Pineapple Topping

Cream butter and sugar together; add eggs. Beat until fluffy. Add crumbs, milk, coconut, nuts and baking powder, blending well. Pour into greased 9 x 12-inch cake pan. Bake in 350-degree oven for 25 minutes. Remove cake from oven; let stand for 10 minutes. Invert on cake plate; cool thoroughly. Spread with Pineapple Topping.

Pineapple Topping

3 egg yolks
1 c. sugar
1 tbsp. flour
1 c. milk
1/2 c. margarine
1 2-lb. can crushed pineapple

Combine all ingredients in saucepan, mixing well; cook until thickened, stirring constantly. Cool.

HONEY GRAHAM COOKIES

24 honey graham crackers
1 c. (packed) light brown sugar
1 c. butter
1 c. finely chopped pecans
6 solid chocolate candy bars

Line 10 x 15-inch cookie sheet with graham crackers. Combine brown sugar and butter; place in saucepan over low heat, stirring to melt. Bring butter mixture to a boil; cook for 2 minutes. Remove from heat; add pecans, mixing well. Pour over top of graham crackers. Bake at 350 degrees for 10 minutes. Do not overbake. Remove from oven. Lay candy bars over graham crackers when bubbles go down. Let melt; spread candy with back of spoon. Cut into squares while warm. Spread on waxed paper to cool.

REFRIGERATOR GRAHAM COOKIES

28 graham crackers, crushed
1 c. chopped dates
1/2 pkg. miniature marshmallows
1 c. chopped nuts
1 can sweetened condensed milk
Shredded coconut

Mix all ingredients, except coconut, stirring well; form into small balls. Mixture will be sticky. Roll balls in shredded coconut. Refrigerate overnight. Yield: 4-5 dozen.

FANCY GRAHAM CRACKER DESSERT

1 1/2 c. graham cracker crumbs
1 c. butter, melted
4 egg whites
1/2 tsp. cream of tartar
Pinch of salt
1 c. sugar
1 c. heavy cream
2 tsp. powdered sugar
1 can coconut
1 sm. can crushed pineapple with juice

Mix cracker crumbs and butter; pat into 9 x 13-inch pan. Beat egg whites until frothy; add cream of tartar and salt. Add sugar to egg whites gradually, beating until stiff peaks form. Spread over crumb mixture. Bake at 300 degrees for 30 minutes; cool. Whip cream, adding powdered sugar. Add half the coconut and pineapple. Spread over meringue mixture; top with remaining coconut. Refrigerate for 24 hours. Yield: 9 servings.

GRAHAM CRACKER DREAM SQUARES

20 graham crackers
2 c. butter
1 c. sugar
1/3 c. milk
1 egg, slightly beaten
1 c. grated coconut
1 c. chopped nuts
1 c. graham cracker crumbs
2 c. confectioners' sugar
Cream

Place layer of crackers in 9 x 13-inch pan. Combine 1 cup butter, sugar, milk and egg in saucepan. Cook, stirring constantly, until mixture comes to a boil. Add coconut, nuts and crumbs, stirring well; remove from heat. Pour crumb mixture over crackers. Refrigerate for at least 1 hour. Place layer of crackers over chilled mixture. Combine remaining butter and confectioners' sugar, blending well. Add small amount of cream until mixture is of spreading consistency. Top cracker layer with confectioners' sugar mixture. Cut into small bars. Yield: 32 bars.

GRAHAM TORTE

Color photograph for this recipe on page 491.

1 2/3 c. graham cracker crumbs
1 c. chopped walnuts
1 tsp. cinnamon
1/2 tsp. salt
1/2 tsp. ginger
1/4 tsp. allspice
1/2 tsp. baking powder
1/2 c. butter
1/4 c. sugar
4 eggs, separated
1/2 c. milk
1 pt. heavy cream
3 tbsp. confectioners' sugar
1 1/2 c. canned applesauce
Shaved sweet chocolate
Maraschino cherries

Combine first 7 ingredients. Cream butter in bowl. Add sugar gradually; beat until light and fluffy. Add egg yolks; mix thoroughly. Add crumb mixture alternately with milk. Beat egg whites until stiff but not dry; fold into sugar mixture. Pour into 2 waxed paper-lined and greased 8-inch cake pans. Bake in 325-degree oven for 30 to 35 minutes. Cool; remove from pans. Cool on wire racks. Whip cream until stiff; fold in confectioners' sugar. Split cake layers in half crosswise. Spread applesauce between cut sides of each layer. Arrange 1 filled layer on cake plate; spread with 3/4 of the whipped cream. Top with remaining filled layer. Place remaining whipped cream in pastry tube; pipe around edge and in center of cake. Garnish with chocolate and cherries.

GRAHAM CRACKER CRUST

1 1/2 c. graham cracker crumbs
1/2 c. sugar
1/2 c. butter, melted

Combine all ingredients, mixing well. Press mixture into greased 9-inch pie pan, forming even layer. Crust may be chilled until ready to use. Bake at 375 degrees for 8 minutes. Yield: One 9-inch pie crust.

SPICE GRAHAM CRACKER PIE

3 eggs, beaten
1/2 c. chopped pecans
1 c. sugar
1 c. graham cracker crumbs
1/8 tsp. nutmeg
1/8 tsp. cinnamon
1 c. heavy cream, whipped

Combine all ingredients except cream, mixing well. Place in greased pie pan. Bake at 350 degrees for 20 minutes. Top with whipped cream.

GRAHAM MERINGUE PIE

1 c. sugar
3 eggs, separated
1 c. graham cracker crumbs
1/2 c. chopped nuts
1 tsp. almond extract
1 tsp. vanilla
1 pt. butter pecan ice cream

Beat 1/2 cup sugar into egg yolks; add crumbs, nuts and flavorings. Beat egg whites with remaining sugar until stiff peaks form. Fold crumb mixture into egg whites. Pour into buttered pie plate. Bake at 350 degrees for 25 minutes. Turn oven off. Let pie stand in oven overnight with door closed. Top cooled pie with butter pecan ice cream before serving. Yield: 6-8 servings.

GRAHAM-RUM PIE

1 c. fine graham cracker crumbs
1 c. sugar
1 1/2 tsp. cinnamon
1/4 tsp. nutmeg
1/8 tsp. salt
1 1/2 tbsp. butter or margarine
1 egg white, slightly beaten
1 tbsp. unflavored gelatin
3 egg yolks, slightly beaten
1 c. hot milk
1/4 c. rum
2 c. heavy cream, whipped
Shaved chocolate

Combine cracker crumbs, 1/4 cup sugar, spices and salt; blend in butter well. Stir in egg white. Press mixture into greased 9-inch pie plate. Bake at 350 degrees for 5 minutes. Cool. Soften gelatin in 1/4 cup cold water. Mix egg yolks, 1/2 cup sugar and milk in double boiler. Cook, stirring constantly, over simmering water until custard coats spoon. Do not boil. Add gelatin to hot custard, stirring until dissolved. Cool, stirring occasionally. Add rum; mix well. Chill, stirring occasionally until slightly congealed. Beat egg whites until stiff peaks form; add remaining sugar gradually. Beat only until blended. Fold egg whites into cold custard, blending well. Add whipped cream; fold gently into mixture. Pour filling into pie shell; chill for at least 3 hours. Top with additional whipped cream and chocolate. Yield: 8 servings.

GRAHAM CRACKER-NUT PUDDING

1 c. sugar
3/8 c. soft butter
2 eggs, well beaten
1 c. milk
2 c. graham cracker crumbs
4 tsp. baking powder
1/2 c. chopped nuts
1 c. heavy cream, whipped

Combine all ingredients except cream in order given; blend well. Pour into greased 8 x 8-inch pan. Bake at about 350 degrees for 30 minutes. Serve topped with whipped cream. Yield: 8 servings.

GRAHAM CRACKER PUDDING

1/2 c. melted butter
1/2 c. (packed) brown sugar
1 tsp. cinnamon
2 c. graham crackers, crushed
2 tbsp. flour
7/8 c. sugar
3 eggs, separated
2 c. milk
1 tbsp. vanilla
Pinch of salt

Combine butter, brown sugar, cinnamon and cracker crumbs; mix thoroughly. Line 8 x 9-inch pan with half the mixture. Mix flour with 1/2 cup sugar; add egg yolks and milk, stirring well. Pour into double boiler; cook until thickened. Add vanilla just before removing from stove. Spread egg mixture over crumbs. Beat egg whites until stiff peaks form; add remaining sugar and pinch of salt gradually while beating. Pour over custard, sprinkling remaining crumbs on top. Bake at 325 degrees for 30 minutes. Serve with whipped cream.

Grape

Grapes are juicy, vine-ripened berries that grow in clusters. In the United States there are two varieties of domestic grapes: the European and the American. Originally imported from Europe, the European strains now thrive exclusively in California. They are larger and sweeter than the American varieties with thick skins that adhere to the flesh. The American varieties grown elsewhere in the country, are characterized by a fairly thick skin that slips easily from the flesh. European varieties are predominatly used as *table grapes* (Thompson Seedless, Emperor, Tokay, and Red and White Malaga); *wine grapes* (White Muscat); and *raisin grapes* (Thompson Seedless). True American varieties, like the Concord, are used primarily in unfermented grape juice, jams, and jellies. (1 cup European-type grapes = 100 calories; 1 cup American-type grapes = 70 calories)

AVAILABILITY: The season for grapes lasts from June through March. Peak months (depending on the variety) are August through October, after which the supply comes from storage.

BUYING: Look for grapes that are fresh, smooth, plump, and uniformly sized. Color should be characteristic of the variety. Be sure that the fruit is firmly attached to the stem by gently shaking the bunch; stems should be green and pliable.

STORING: Grapes are highly perishable. They should be stored uncovered and unwashed in the refrigerator. Use within 3 to 5 days. Some of the European varieties may keep for longer periods because of their firmer flesh. *To freeze*—Package grapes with syrup. Fruit to be used for juice or jelly may be frozen without sweetening. Always leave head space in container.

PREPARATION: Enjoy grapes as a fresh, raw fruit or in jams, jellies, baked products, or salads. To seed—Split grape lengthwise, slightly off center. All the seeds will usually be in the larger part and can then be flicked out with a knife.

FRESH GRAPE WALDORF SALAD

1 1/2 c. diced unpeeled apples
1 c. Thompson seedless grapes
1 c. diced fresh celery
1/2 c. chopped walnuts
1/2 c. mayonnaise
2 tbsp. fresh lemon juice
Lettuce

Combine apples, grapes, celery, walnuts, mayonnaise and lemon juice; toss lightly. Serve on lettuce; garnish with additional grapes if desired. Yield: 6 servings.

Fresh Grape Waldorf Salad . . . Crunchy walnuts, fruits, and celery mingle in this great lunch salad.

FROSTED GRAPES

1 egg white
Grapes
Sugar

Beat egg white slightly. Brush clusters of grapes with egg white; sprinkle with sugar. Let dry on wire racks; arrange on plate or platter.

FROZEN GRAPE SALAD

1 lge. package cream cheese
2 tbsp. salad dressing
2 tbsp. pineapple topping
1 pkg. miniature marshmallows
1 sm. can crushed pineapple
2 c. red grapes, halved and seeded
1/2 pt. whipping cream, whipped

Mix cream cheese, salad dressing and topping, blending well; set aside. Combine marshmallows, pineapple and grapes in large bowl. Fold cream cheese mixture into marshmallow mixture. Fold in whipped cream. Pour into freezer trays; freeze until ready to serve.

GRAPE-ALMOND SALAD

1 env. unflavored gelatin
1 can crushed pineapple
1 pkg. lemon gelatin
1 1/2 c. seedless grapes
2 c. sour cream
1 c. chopped almonds

Soften gelatin in 1/4 cup cold water. Drain pineapple, reserving juice; add enough water to reserved juice to equal 2 cups. Bring juice mixture to a boil; pour over lemon gelatin. Stir until lemon gelatin is dissolved; add unflavored gelatin mixture. Stir until dissolved; cool. Stir in pineapple, grapes, sour cream and almonds. Pour into mold; refrigerate until set.

GRAPE AND BLACK CHERRY SALAD

1 sm. can frozen grape juice
1 No. 2 can pitted black sweet cherries
2 pkg. black cherry gelatin
3/4 c. broken pecan halves

Prepare grape juice according to can directions. Drain cherries, reserving juice; add cherry juice to grape juice. Add enough water to make 4 cups liquid. Bring 2 cups liquid to a boil; add to gelatin, stirring until gelatin dissolves. Add remaining liquid; chill until thickened. Stir in cherries and pecans; chill until set. Yield: 6 servings.

GRAPE AND PEAR SALAD

8 fresh or canned pear halves, drained
8 chicory leaves
2 tbsp. cream

1 8-oz. package cream cheese
2 lb. seedless grapes

Place 1 pear half, cut side down, on each chicory leaf. Mix cream and cream cheese; spread thick layer over pear halves. Slice grapes in half. Press grapes, cut side down, on pear halves, covering pear halves. Arrange 1 piece grape stem in large end of each pear half, if desired.

GRAPE RING

2 pkg. grape gelatin
1 6-oz. can frozen grape juice
1 No. 2 can crushed pineapple
1/2 c. chopped nuts
1 c. whipped cream
1/2 c. pimento cheese spread
5 tbsp. marshmallow creme

Dissolve gelatin in 2 cups boiling water. Stir in frozen grape juice and pineapple. Chill until thickened slightly; add nuts. Pour into ring mold; refrigerate until firm. Add whipped cream to cheese spread and marshmallow creme; beat thoroughly. Unmold grape ring; fill center with cream filling.

GREEN GRAPE DESSERT SALAD

2 eggs
1/2 c. sugar
2 tbsp. flour
3/4 c. orange juice
Juice of 1 lemon
1 c. heavy cream, whipped
3 c. green grapes
1 No. 2 can pineapple chunks, drained
1 10 1/2-oz. package tiny marshmallows
1/2 c. chopped nuts

Combine eggs, sugar, flour, orange and lemon juices in double boiler. Cook over simmering water until thickened; cool. Fold whipped cream into cooled mixture. Fold remaining ingredients into dressing; cover. Chill for 8 hours or overnight. Yield: 8-10 servings.

MOLDED GRAPE SUPREME

1 env. unflavored gelatin
1/2 c. sugar
Dash of salt
1 6-oz. can frozen grape juice
3 tbsp. lemon juice
3/4 c. seedless grapes, halved
2 med. bananas, diced
1/4 c. chopped nuts

Soften gelatin in 1/4 cup cold water. Add 1 cup boiling water, sugar and salt to gelatin mixture; stir until dissolved. Stir in grape juice and lemon juice, mixing well. Refrigerate until partially set. Fold in fruits and nuts. Pour into 1-quart mold. Refrigerate until firm. Yield: 6 servings.

GOURMET GRAPES

5 c. green grapes
1/4 c. brown sugar
1/2 pt. sour cream

Drain grapes well. Blend brown sugar and sour cream; fold in dry grapes. Place in sherbet dishes; chill for several hours. Yield: 6-8 servings.

SPICED GRAPE MOLD

1 16-oz. can spiced seedless grapes
2 pkg. lime gelatin
3 tbsp. lime juice
Strawberries
Powdered sugar

Drain and chill grapes. Dissolve gelatin in 2 cups hot water. Add 1 1/2 cups ice water and lime juice. Chill until thickened slightly. Fold in grapes. Pour into a 5-cup ring mold. Chill until firm. Fill center of mold with strawberries dusted with powdered sugar. May use dressing of whipped cream and mayonnaise.

TOKAY SALAD

1/4 c. sugar
1/2 tsp. vanilla
1 c. cream, whipped
1 1/2 lb. Tokay grapes, halved and seeded
1/3 c. miniature marshmallows
3 bananas, sliced
6 tbsp. malted cereal granules

Mix sugar, vanilla and whipped cream. Stir in remaining ingredients except cereal; pour into mold. Chill; sprinkle with cereal just before serving. Yield: 8 servings.

PERFECTION FRUIT SALAD

2 lb. white grapes
2 No. 303 cans pineapple
1 lb. blanched almonds
1 lb. marshmallows
Juice of 2 lemons
4 egg yolks
2 c. milk
2 c. sugar
1 c. heavy cream, whipped

Combine fruits, almonds and marshmallows; place half the mixture in large bowl. Pour juice of 1 lemon over fruits. Add remaining fruits and lemon juice. Let stand until ready to use. Combine egg yolks, milk and sugar; bring to a boil. Cool; fold in whipped cream. Pour cream mixture over fruit mixture. Let stand overnight.

GRAPE CUP

1 pt. heavy cream
20 lge. marshmallows
1/2 c. grape juice
1 pkg. frozen black cherries, thawed

Whip heavy cream until stiff. Melt marshmallows in top of double boiler; blend in grape juice. Cool until syrupy. Combine marshmallow mixture with whipped cream; blend well. Pour into dessert dishes; top with cherries. Chill for at least 2 hours. Yield: 6 servings.

GRAPE ICE CREAM

40 marshmallows
2 c. grape juice
1 pt. heavy cream, whipped

Melt marshmallows in top of double boiler; blend in grape juice. Remove from heat; cool until syrupy. Add cream; mix well. Pour into freezer tray; freeze until partially set. Remove from freezer; stir well. Return to freezer; chill until firm.

GRECIAN GRAPE PUDDING

3 c. sugar
1 c. honey
2 cinnamon sticks
1 c. butter
2 1/2 c. cream of wheat
1/2 c. chopped toasted almonds
1 c. hot milk
1/4 tsp. almond extract
1/2 tsp. allspice
2 c. Tokay grapes

Combine sugar, honey, 3 cups water and cinnamon sticks in saucepan; simmer for 15 minutes or until syrupy. Set aside. Combine butter, cream of wheat and almonds in large heavy saucepan; saute over low heat until golden, stirring constantly. Add milk, almond extract, allspice and 2 cups of honey syrup; cook until liquid is absorbed, stirring constantly. Spoon into buttered 5-cup mold; chill. Simmer remaining syrup until reduced to about 1 1/2 cups; remove cinnamon sticks. Cool syrup. Halve and seed grapes; add to syrup. Unmold pudding on platter; Serve with grape mixture. Yield: 12-15 servings.

KREM

3 tbsp. sugar
2 tbsp. cornstarch
2 c. grape juice
Cinnamon

Combine sugar, cornstarch and 3 tablespoons water, blending well. Bring grape juice to a boil; add sugar mixture, stirring constantly. Cook for about 2 minutes or until thick and clear; pour into individual dessert dishes. Sprinkle cinnamon over top of grape mixture. Chill until ready to serve. Yield: 6 servings.

QUICK GRAPE COBBLER

1/4 c. margarine
1 1/4 c. sugar
1/2 c. flour
1/2 tsp. salt
1 tsp. baking powder
2 c. grape juice, unsweetened

Combine margarine, 1/2 cup sugar, flour, salt and baking powder in baking dish; blend well, using pastry blender. Combine grape juice and remaining sugar in saucepan, stirring well; bring to a boil. Pour over mixture in baking dish. Bake at 350 degrees until crust rises to top and browns. Yield: 4 servings.

CONCORD GRAPE PIE

1 1/2 qt. grapes
1 1/2 c. sugar
3 tbsp. quick-cooking tapioca
1 tsp. butter
1/8 tsp. salt
1/2 c. chopped pecans
1 recipe 2-crust pie pastry

Slip grape skins from pulp, reserving skins. Place pulp in saucepan; bring to simmering stage. Remove from heat; sieve to remove seeds. Add enough pulp to skins to make 3 1/2 cups after settling. Combine sugar, tapioca, butter, salt and pecans; mix well. Add to grape mixture, stirring thoroughly. Pour into pastry-lined 9-inch pie pan. Cover with pastry. Bake at 425 degrees for 15 minutes; reduce heat to 400 degrees. Bake for 30 minutes longer or until brown.

SCUPPERNONG PIE

2 eggs
1 1/2 c. sugar
3 tbsp. flour
2 tbsp. butter
2 c. canned grapes and syrup
1 recipe 2-crust pie pastry

Beat eggs slightly; add sugar, flour and butter. Beat until well mixed. Slash grapes; remove seeds. Stir grapes into egg mixture with syrup, mixing well. Pour into pastry-lined 9-inch pie plate; cover with top crust. Bake at 425 degrees for 10 minutes. Reduce heat to 375 degrees. Bake for 35 minutes longer.

GRAPE-CREAM CHEESE MOLD

3 env. unflavored gelatin
2 c. grape juice
1/2 c. sugar
1/3 c. orange juice
1 tsp. lemon juice
3 3-oz. packages cream cheese
3/4 c. light cream
1/4 tsp. salt

Soften 2 envelopes gelatin in 3/4 cup cold grape juice for about 5 minutes. Heat remaining grape juice to scalding. Add softened gelatin; stir until dissolved. Stir in sugar, orange juice and lemon juice; stir until sugar is dissolved. Fill 8 individual molds 1/2 full with grape mixture. Chill until firm. Soften cream cheese at room temperature. Soften remaining gelatin in 1/4 cup cold water for about 5 minutes. Pour 1/4 cup hot water over gelatin; stir until dissolved. Beat cream cheese until smooth and fluffy; stir in cream gradually. Stir in salt and gelatin; mix well. Pour cream cheese mixture over set grape layer. Return to refrigerator; chill until firm. Unmold; serve on grape leaves. Garnish with fresh grapes if desired. Yield: 8 servings.

Grape-Cream Cheese Mold . . . Top this layered dessert with fresh grapes for extra eye appeal.

Grapefruit

BROILED GRAPEFRUIT

1 grapefruit, halved
1 tbsp. brown sugar

Cut around each grapefruit section; remove center. Sprinkle sugar over each grapefruit half. Broil until sugar is melted and edge of grapefruit half is browned lightly. Serve immediately.

GRAPEFRUIT A LA SHRIMP

Grapefruit halves
Sm. shrimp
Sliced celery
Coarsely chopped pecans
Mayonnaise

Scoop out sections of grapefruit halves; remove membrane and seeds. Return sections to shells. Mix shrimp, celery, pecans and mayonnaise until just moistened. Top grapefruit sections with shrimp mixture. Serve cold or broiled, if desired.

ISLAND GRAPEFRUIT APPETIZER

2 grapefruit
1/2 c. rum
2 tsp. sugar
2 tsp. chopped mint
Orange segments
Cherries

Halve grapefruit, cutting in scallop pattern. Section grapefruit, removing membrane; reserve shells. Place half the grapefruit sections, rum, sugar and mint in blender container. Blend at high speed until liquefied. Arrange remaining grapefruit sections and orange segments in reserved grapefruit shells; pour blended mixture over top. Garnish with cherries. Chill and serve. Yield: 4 servings.

FROZEN GRAPEFRUIT SALAD

1 8-oz. package cream cheese
1 c. sour cream
1/4 tsp. salt
1/2 c. sugar
1 avocado, diced
2 c. grapefruit sections
1 c. halved seedless white grapes
1/2 c. chopped pecans
Salad greens

Soften cream cheese; blend in sour cream. Add salt and sugar; stir until blended thoroughly. Add avocado, grapefruit, grapes and pecans, tossing lightly. Pour into 5 x 9-inch loaf pan; cover. Freeze until firm. Slice; serve on salad greens. Yield: 8 servings.

GRAPEFRUIT IN SHELLS

2 grapefruit
2 3-oz. packages lemon gelatin
1 tbsp. flour
3 tbsp. sugar
1 egg yolk, beaten
Juice of 1 lemon
1/3 c. pineapple juice
4 marshmallows
1/2 c. cream, whipped
1/3 c. chopped nuts

Halve grapefruit. Scoop out pulp and juice; reserve. Remove membrane, leaving smooth shell. Dissolve gelatin in 3/4 cup boiling water. Stir in 3 1/4 cups grapefruit pulp and juice; pour into grapefruit shells. Chill until set. Combine flour, sugar, egg yolk, lemon and pineapple juices in double boiler; cook over simmering water until thickened, stirring constantly. Add marshmallows; stir until melted. Cool; fold in whipped cream and nuts. Serve over gelatin in shells. Yield: 4 servings.

GRAPEFRUIT SALAD

3 c. canned grapefruit sections
2 env. unflavored gelatin
1/4 c. sugar
1/2 c. chopped dates
1/2 c. chopped nuts
1/4 tsp. salt
1 4-oz. package cream cheese, softened
Mayonnaise

Drain grapefruit sections; reserve juice. Add enough water to reserved juice to equal 3 cups. Soften gelatin in reserved juice mixture; pour in 1/2 cup boiling water, stirring until gelatin is dissolved. Add sugar, dates, grapefruit sections, nuts and salt, mixing well. Pour into mold; chill until firm. Mix cream cheese with enough mayonnaise to moisten; spread over gelatin mixture. Chill before serving. Yield: 6 servings.

LEMON-GRAPEFRUIT SALAD

2 pkg. lemon gelatin
3/8 c. lemon juice
Salt to taste
1/2 c. mayonnaise
2 sm. packages cream cheese, whipped
2 grapefruit

Dissolve gelatin in 2 cups boiling water. Add lemon juice and salt; let cool. Add mayonnaise to cream cheese. Mix well. Add gelatin mixture. Peel and section grapefruit. Fold grapefruit sections into gelatin mixture; pour into mold. Chill until firm. Yield: 9-10 servings.

PIQUANT GRAPEFRUIT SALAD

2 c. grapefruit sections
Dry vermouth
6 heads Bibb lettuce
Paprika to taste
French dressing
Chopped chives

Place grapefruit sections in bowl, adding enough vermouth to cover; marinate in refrigerator for at least 12 hours. Spread lettuce open; cut out centers, leaving hollow. Fill with grapefruit sections; sprinkle with paprika. Serve with French dressing and chives. Yield: 6 servings.

TOSSED GRAPEFRUIT SALAD

Canned or fresh grapefruit sections
Lettuce
Italian salad dressing

Drain grapefruit. Break lettuce into bite-sized pieces. Toss lettuce and grapefruit together. Chill until ready to serve; toss with just enough dressing to coat grapefruit sections and lettuce before serving.

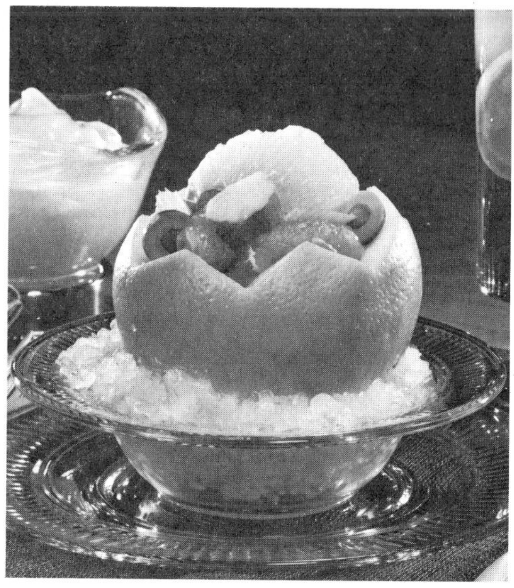

Fresh Grapefruit Appetizer . . . Easy-to-fill hollowed grapefruit with crabmeat, olives, and celery.

FRESH GRAPEFRUIT APPETIZERS

3 med. California grapefruit, chilled
3/4 lb. cooked crab meat
1/2 c. sliced celery
1/4 c. sliced pimento-stuffed olives
1 c. mayonnaise
1 tsp. Worcestershire sauce

Cut grapefruit in half crosswise with sharp knife; cut around each section to loosen from membrane. Remove sections with spoon carefully; drain well. Scrape remaining membrane from shells, leaving shells clean and intact. Drain crab meat well. Combine grapefruit sections, crab meat, celery and olives; spoon into grapefruit shells. Chill well. Combine mayonnaise and Worcestershire sauce; spoon over each serving. Serve on bed of crushed ice if desired. Yield: 6 servings.

FRENCH GRAPEFRUIT SOUFFLÉ

3 tbsp. butter
3 tbsp. flour
1 c. milk
4 eggs, separated
4 tbsp. sugar
1/4 tsp. salt
1/4 tsp. nutmeg
1/2 tsp. vanilla
1 c. canned grapefruit sections

Melt butter in saucepan; stir in flour. Add milk gradually, stirring constantly; cook until thick. Beat egg yolks with sugar and salt until thickened. Add small amount of sauce to egg yolk mixture, stirring constantly; stir egg mixture into sauce gradually, stirring constantly. Cool. Beat egg whites until stiff peaks form. Fold egg whites, nutmeg and vanilla into cooled mixture. Dice grapefruit sections; place in 2-quart casserole. Pour egg mixture over grapefruit. Place in pan of hot water. Bake at 325 degrees for about 40 minutes. Yield: 4 servings.

FROZEN GRAPEFRUIT CREAM

1/2 env. unflavored gelatin
1 18-oz. can grapefruit juice
2 eggs, separated
1/2 tsp. salt
2 tsp. artificial liquid sweetener
2 tsp. vanilla
1/2 tsp. nutmeg
1/3 c. evaporated milk
Yellow food coloring

Soften gelatin in 1/2 cup grapefruit juice in double boiler. Beat egg yolks until fluffy. Stir egg yolks and salt into gelatin mixture. Cook over hot water, stirring constantly, until gelatin is dissolved and mixture is thickened slightly. Remove from heat. Blend in remaining grapefruit juice, liquid sweetener, vanilla, nutmeg and evaporated milk. Add several drops of food coloring. Chill until mixture mounds slightly when dropped from spoon. Beat egg whites until stiff peaks form; fold into grapefruit juice mixture. Pour into refrigerator tray. Freeze, stirring occasionally. Pour into mixing bowl; beat with electric mixer. Return to tray; freeze until firm. Yield: 6 servings.

GRAPEFRUIT SUPREME

3 lge. grapefruit
Sugar
1/8 tsp. salt
3 egg whites
1/2 tsp. vanilla
1 pt. vanilla ice cream

Halve grapefruit; remove core. Cut around each section, loosening fruit from membrane. Sprinkle with sugar; chill. Preheat oven to 500 degrees. Add salt to egg whites; beat until foamy. Add 6 tablespoons sugar to egg whites gradually, beating until stiff and glossy; add vanilla. Remove grapefruit halves from refrigerator; place heaping spoonful of ice cream in center of each half. Cover with meringue. Place in oven for about 1 minute or until browned lightly. Serve at once. Yield: 6 servings.

GRAPEFRUIT CAKE

1 1/2 c. sugar
1 tbsp. finely grated grapefruit rind
1/2 tsp. finely grated lemon rind
3/4 c. butter
3 eggs
1/2 c. grapefruit juice
3 c. cake flour
3/4 tsp. salt
3 1/2 tsp. baking powder
1/4 tsp. soda

Place sugar, grated rinds and butter in mixing bowl; cream until light and fluffy. Add eggs, one at a time, beating well after each addition. Combine grapefruit juice and 1/2 cup water. Stir juice mixture into egg mixture. Sift cake flour with salt, baking powder and soda. Mix dry ingredients into juice mixture just enough at a time to blend. Mix after each addition lightly. Pour batter into two greased 9-inch layer cake pans. Bake at 375 degrees for 30 minutes or until cake is browned. Let cakes cool in pans for about 10 minutes; invert on wire racks. Cool.

Fluffy Grapefruit-Cheese Frosting

3 3-oz. packages cream cheese, softened
1 tbsp. butter, softened
4 tsp. finely grated grapefruit rind

1 tsp. finely grated lemon rind
1 tsp. finely grated orange rind
1/4 tsp. vanilla
4 c. confectioners' sugar
Sections from 2 grapefruit and 2 oranges

Cream cheese, butter, rinds and vanilla until fluffy. Beat in sugar, a little at a time, until fluffy and of spreading consistency. Spread thin layer of frosting between layers. Frost top and side of cake, swirling frosting. Garnish, alternating grapefruit and orange sections around top of cake and with clusters of fruit at base. Yield: 8 servings.

GRAPEFRUIT FLUFF

1 1-lb. can grapefruit sections
1 env. unflavored gelatin
1/4 c. sugar
1/4 c. lemon juice
2 1/2 c. whipped instant dry milk
14 vanilla wafers

Drain grapefruit sections; reserve syrup. Blend gelatin, sugar and 1/2 cup grapefruit syrup; simmer until dissolved, stirring constantly. Remove from heat; stir in lemon juice. Chill until thickened, stirring occasionally. Fold gelatin mixture into whipped milk. Spoon half the mixture into 9-inch pie plate; place vanilla wafers around edge of pie plate. Spoon grapefruit sections over gelatin mixture; cover with remaining gelatin. Chill until firm. Yield: 6 servings.

GRAPEFRUIT ICE

2 c. sugar
1/2 c. lemon juice
1 can grapefruit sections

Place sugar and 4 cups water in saucepan; bring to a boil, stirring constantly. Remove from heat; cool. Add lemon juice and grapefruit sections to cooled mixture; pour into freezer container. Freeze. Break up mixture with fork before serving. Yield: 16-18 servings.

GRAPEFRUIT-MINT COCKTAIL

4 med. grapefruit, halved
3 oz. mint jelly
1/2 c. sugar

Section grapefruit. Melt mint jelly in double boiler; beat until smooth. Bring 1 cup water to a boil; add sugar. Cook jelly mixture for 5 minutes. Add sugar mixture, stirring well, to mint jelly. Chill. Arrange 6 to 8 grapefruit sections in sherbet dish; pour mint mixture over grapefruit sections. Yield: 10-12 servings.

GRAPEFRUIT PIE

1 1/4 c. grapefruit juice
1 1/4 c. sugar
3 tbsp. cornstarch
2 eggs, separated
1/4 tsp. salt
1 baked 9-in. pie crust

Combine 1 cup grapefruit juice, 1/2 cup water and 1 cup sugar in saucepan; bring to a boil. Mix cornstarch and remaining grapefruit juice; pour into sugar mixture, stirring constantly until blended and thickened. Remove from heat. Beat egg yolks. Add small amount of hot mixture to yolks, stirring constantly; stir egg mixture into grapefruit juice mixture gradually. Cook until thickened, stirring constantly. Pour into pie shell; cool slightly. Beat egg whites, adding salt and remaining sugar gradually, until stiff peaks form. Cover pie filling with egg white mixture. Bake at 350 degrees for about 15 minutes or until brown.

GRAPEFRUIT SLUSH

1 1/2 c. sugar
1 46-oz. can grapefruit juice
Green food coloring
Mint flavoring

Combine sugar and 3 cups water, stirring well. Bring to a boil; cook for several minutes. Add grapefruit juice; mix well. Tint mixture with green food coloring; add several drops of mint flavoring. Pour into freezing tray; freeze to a slush. Yield: 16 servings.

Green Chili Pepper

FRIED GREEN CHILIES

Cheddar cheese
1 No. 2 1/2 can green chili peppers
1 egg, beaten
Cornmeal

Slice cheese into 1 1/2 x 1/2-inch strips. Drain peppers thoroughly. Slash peppers on one side; remove seeds. Insert cheese strip into each pepper. Dip peppers into egg; roll in cornmeal. Fry in small amount of fat until lightly browned on all sides; drain on absorbent towels.

GREEN CHILI DIP

1 8-oz. package cream cheese
1/2 c. sour cream
1/2 c. salad dressing
5 tbsp. chopped green chilies
4 tbsp. minced onion
Dash of salt

Have cream cheese at room temperature. Blend cheese with sour cream and salad dressing; mix well. Stir in chilies, onion and salt. Chill overnight.

CHILI RAREBIT DIP

1/4 c. margarine
1/2 c. chopped celery
1/2 c. chopped green pepper
2 tbsp. chopped onion
1 clove of garlic, minced
1/4 c. flour
1/2 tsp. salt
1 c. milk
1 1/2 c. cubed American cheese
1 10-oz. can tomatoes with chilies
4 jalapeno peppers, chopped

Melt margarine over low heat. Add celery, green pepper, onion and garlic; saute until tender. Stir in flour and salt. Add milk; cook, stirring constantly, until thickened. Add cheese; stir until melted. Stir in tomatoes and jalapenos. May be served warm or chilled. Yield: 1 quart.

GREEN CHILI-ENCHILADA CASSEROLE

1 doz. tortillas
1/2 c. shortening
2 c. chopped onion
2 c. grated Cheddar cheese
1/4 c. chopped green chilies
2 cans enchilada sauce

Dip tortillas in hot shortening to soften; drain on absorbent towels. Layer tortillas with onion and cheese in shallow baking dish; top with green chilies. Pour enchilada sauce over green chilies. Bake at 350 degrees for 30 minutes.

CHILI VERDE

1 sm. onion, chopped
1 clove of garlic, minced
1/2 c. salad oil
1 c. bouillon
2 c. tomatoes
1/2 c. chopped green chilies
Flour
12 tortillas
3 c. shredded Jack cheese

Saute onion and garlic in 2 tablespoons oil in saucepan until tender. Add bouillon, tomatoes and chilies; simmer for 10 minutes. Blend small amount of flour and water until smooth paste; stir into sauce. Heat remaining shortening in skillet. Dip tortillas in hot shortening just to soften; drain on absorbent toweling. Layer tortillas, sauce and cheese in casserole, ending with cheese. Bake at 350 degrees for 25 minutes. Garnish with ripe olives and sliced green onion.

CHILES RELLENOS

3 1/2 green chilies
1 lb. beef tips
1/4 c. chopped onion
2 tbsp. shortening
3/4 c. chopped pecans
3/4 c. raisins
Salt
1/4 tsp. chili powder
Flour
6 eggs, separated
1/2 onion, thinly sliced
2 tbsp. butter
1 8-oz. can tomato sauce
1 tsp. sugar

Chiles Rellenos... Batter-fried green peppers stuffed with a zippy beef mixture.

Remove tops and seeds from 3 peppers; cut peppers in half lengthwise. Cook in boiling salted water in saucepan for 8 to 10 minutes or until tender. Drain peppers; cool and peel. Cut beef tips into 1/2-inch cubes. Saute beef and chopped onion in shortening until lightly browned. Add pecans, raisins, 1/2 teaspoon salt and chili powder. Spoon beef mixture into pepper halves. Roll peppers in flour, coating well. Beat egg whites until stiff but not dry. Add 3 tablespoons flour and 1/2 teaspoon salt to egg yolks; beat until thick and lemon colored. Fold egg whites into egg yolk mixture. Drop egg mixture by 1/2 cupfuls into shallow hot fat in skillet, spreading to make circles slightly longer than peppers. Cook until egg mixture begins to set. Arrange pepper halves in circles; cover each pepper half with remaining batter. Cook until underside is browned; turn and brown remaining side. Slice remaining pepper; saute sliced pepper and sliced onion in butter. Remove pepper and onion from skillet. Add 1 1/2 tablespoons flour to pan drippings, blending until smooth. Add tomato sauce and 1 cup water. Cook, stirring constantly until thickened. Add sugar and 1/2 teaspoon salt. Add cooked peppers and onion. Place Chiles Rellenos in serving dish; spoon hot sauce over top. Serve immediately.

Grits

Grits is usually wheat or corn ground more coarsely than for flour or meal. It can also be ground from buckwheat, rye, oats, rice, and so on. The most popular kind is made from corn and called "hominy grits". Served at breakfast with fried ham, hominy grits is a regional favorite in the South. Grits is high in B vitamins, iron, and protein. (One cup cooked grits = 154 calories)

BUYING: Hominy grits is available in retail grocery stores in cans or packages. Instant or quick cook grits are also available. Grits made from grains other than corn are sometimes available in health-food stores.

PREPARATION: One pound grits yields approximately 2 1/2 cups. To boil hominy grits, stir 1 cup grits into 4 cups boiling salted water. Cover and cook over low heat 20-25 minutes, stirring often. Leftover cooked grits can be baked, fried, sauteed, or used in cheese or fish dishes.

SERVING: Hominy grits can be boiled and served with milk as a breakfast cereal, or boiled and served with butter or gravy as an accompaniment to meat, poultry, or game.

BAKED GRITS AND CHEESE

1 1/2 c. grits
3 eggs
3 tsp. savory salt
2 tsp. salt
1 tsp. paprika
Dash of hot sauce
1 lb. sharp cheese, grated
1/2 c. butter

Stir grits gradually into 6 cups boiling water; cook until thickened. Beat eggs until thickened; beat in seasonings. Add small amount of hot grits to egg mixture, stirring constantly. Stir egg mixture into remaining grits gradually; add cheese and butter. Mix well; pour into greased casserole. Bake at 350 degrees for 45 minutes. Yield: 6 servings.

BAKED MUSHROOM GRITS

1 c. quick-cooking grits
1/4 c. butter
2 eggs
2 tbsp. milk
1 c. grated cheese
1/2 can mushroom soup
Paprika to taste

Cook grits according to package directions. Add butter. Beat eggs and milk together slightly; add to grits mixture. Fold in grated cheese, reserving enough for topping. Add soup; stir mixture thoroughly. Pour mixture into buttered casserole. Sprinkle reserved cheese over top. Sprinkle with paprika lightly. Bake in 350-degree oven until firm.

CHEESE GRITS

2 c. grits
1 tsp. salt
1/2 c. margarine
1 8-oz. package sharp cheese, grated
2 eggs, beaten
1 sm. jar Cheez Whiz
1 sm. onion, grated
1/8 tsp. cayenne pepper
1/8 tsp. garlic powder
Paprika to taste

Preheat oven to 350 degrees. Add grits and salt to 7 1/2 cups boiling water gradually; cook until thickened. Add remaining ingredients except paprika. Pour grits mixture into oiled casserole; sprinkle with paprika. Bake for 30 minutes or until bubbly. Yield: 20 servings.

EASY CHEESE GRITS

1/2 c. grits
1 tsp. salt
4 eggs
2 tbsp. milk
1 c. grated mild cheese

Pour 1 1/2 cups water into double boiler; bring to a boil. Add grits and salt gradually; cook over boiling water until blended well. Cover; continue cooking for 25 minutes longer, stirring occasionally. Beat eggs with milk; add cheese. Add cheese mixture to grits mixture. Stir over low heat until eggs are cooked and cheese melted. Serve immediately. Yield: 3 servings.

Gala Grits Bavarian . . . A creamy chilled dessert of grits, lemon, almonds, and strawberries.

GALA GRITS BAVARIAN

1/2 c. quick-cooking grits
1/2 tsp. salt
1 tbsp. butter
3 c. milk
1 env. unflavored gelatin
1/2 c. sugar
3/4 tsp. grated lemon peel
1 tsp. grated orange peel
1 tsp. vanilla
1/2 c. coarsely chopped toasted blanched almonds
1 c. whipping cream
1 pt. sweetened whole strawberries

Combine grits, salt, butter and milk in saucepan. Bring to a boil, stirring occasionally. Simmer for about 10 minutes or until thickened, stirring frequently. Soften gelatin in 1/2 cup cold water. Add gelatin, sugar, lemon peel, orange peel and vanilla to grits mixture. Stir until gelatin and sugar are dissolved. Remove from heat; let stand for about 30 minutes or until lukewarm. Stir in almonds. Beat cream until stiff; fold into grits mixture. Pour into 1 1/2-quart wet mold. Chill until firm. Reserve 9 whole strawberries to garnish mold. Crush remaining strawberries. Unmold on serving dish; garnish with whole strawberries. Slice to serve; top each serving with crushed strawberries.

WEST TEXAS-STYLE GRITS

2 c. hot cooked grits
2 c. sharp cheese, grated
1/2 c. butter
2 cloves of garlic, minced
2 eggs, well beaten
1 sm. can green chilies, minced

Mix all ingredients together; place over low heat, stirring until cheese and butter are melted. Pour into greased casserole. Bake at 300 degrees for 1 hour. Yield: 8-10 servings.

GARLIC GRITS

1/2 c. milk
1 tsp. salt
1 c. quick-cooking grits
1/2 c. margarine
2 eggs, beaten
2/3 pkg. garlic cheese, finely diced
2 to 3 c. corn flakes, crushed
1/4 c. butter, melted

Combine 1 1/2 cups boiling water, milk, salt, grits, margarine, eggs and half the cheese in casserole; stir over low heat until cheese melts. Top with corn flakes. Pour butter over corn flakes; sprinkle with remaining cheese. Cook in 350-degree oven for 45 minutes. Yield: 6 servings.

GOURMET GRITS

4 c. milk, scalded
Butter
1 tsp. salt
1 c. grits
1 1/3 c. grated Swiss cheese
1/2 c. Parmesan cheese, grated

Pour milk in double boiler. Stir in 1/4 cup butter, salt and grits. Cook for about 10 minutes or to thick mush over simmering water, stirring constantly. Beat with electric mixer for 5 minutes. Pour into flat pan; chill. Slice; place in casserole in overlapping layers. Melt 1/3 cup butter; spoon over grits. Sprinkle cheeses over top. Bake at 400 degrees for about 30 minutes.

JALAPENO CHEESE GRITS

2 c. quick-cooking grits
2 qt. boiling water
1/2 c. butter
1 roll jalapeno cheese
1 8-oz. package Velveeta cheese, diced
1 sm. onion, grated
4 eggs, well beaten

Stir grits into 2 quarts boiling water gradually; add butter, cheeses and onion. Stir until cheeses and butter melt. Fold eggs into mixture. Pour into large well-greased casserole. Bake at 300 degrees for 1 hour or until mixture is set. Yield: 12 servings.

MEXICAN GRITS

1 c. quick-cooking grits
2 sm. jalapeno peppers
1/2 c. margarine
3/4 lb. grated American cheese
1 1/2 tbsp. Worcestershire sauce
1 clove of garlic, chopped
Dash of hot sauce
2 eggs, separated

Cook grits according to package directions. Remove jalapeno pepper seeds; mince peppers. Add margarine, cheese, Worcestershire sauce, garlic, hot sauce, peppers and egg yolks. Mix well; cool. Beat egg whites until stiff peaks form; fold into grits mixture. Pour into buttered casserole. Bake at 400 degrees for about 40 minutes. Yield: 4-6 servings.

SOUTHERN GRITS CASSEROLE

4 c. milk
3/4 c. butter
1 pkg. Gruyere cheese, diced
1 c. grits
1/3 c. grated Parmesan cheese
1 tsp. salt
1/8 tsp. pepper

Bring milk to a boil in large saucepan; add 1/4 cup butter and Gruyere cheese. Stir until butter and cheese are melted; add grits, salt and pepper gradually; cook, stirring constantly, until thickened. Remove from heat; beat hard for 5 minutes. Pour into casserole; cool. Melt remaining butter; pour over grits. Sprinkle with Parmesan cheese. Bake in 400-degree oven for 30 minutes. Yield: 8-10 servings.

Ground Beef

Ground beef, is most often prepared by grinding the least popular beef cuts—brisket, plate, or shank beef. Like all beef, it contains all 21 amino acids the body needs for growth and maintenance of body tissues. In addition, ground beef is a good source of Vitamin B and vitamins in the B group. (1 3 1/2-ounce ground beef patty = 285 calories)

AVAILABILITY: Ground beef is available year-round.

BUYING: Freshness is the most important quality in ground beef. Look for the bluish-red color that is a mark of fresh preparation. If possible, ask the butcher to grind the meat while you wait. Ground beef comes in many grades, the lowest of which is *hamburger.* It may contain up to 30 percent fat. *Regular ground beef,* often sold simply as ground beef, contains only 20 to 25 percent fat. *Ground chuck* contains 15-25 percent fat. *Ground round* is ground steak that has been ground and is so lean (containing 11 percent fat) that you may have to ask for a little ground beef suet to be added. *Ground sirloin* is another low-fat ground beef and also needs fat added. Always avoid buying ground beef that has been frozen and then thawed for sale because you have no way of knowing how old the ground meat was when it was frozen.

STORING: Handle ground beef as little as possible because it is easily contaminated. Loosen the wrapping and store in the coldest part of the refrigerator. The maximum safe storage time for ground beef is 2 days. *To freeze* ground beef, wrap immediately in vapor- and moisture-proof paper and place in freezer. If allowed to stand in refrigerator before being frozen, ground beef may begin to spoil. Ground beef may be frozen up to 2 weeks in the frozen foods compartment of the refrigerator or up to 4 months in a home freezer.

PREPARATION: Follow recipe directions to prepare ground beef. It may be broiled, baked, fried, or sauteed but is never cooked by moist-heat methods.

(See BEEF.)

BURGUNDY MEATBALLS

1 lb. ground beef chuck
1 c. bread crumbs
1 c. onions, chopped
3/4 tsp. cornstarch
1/2 tsp. salt
1/2 tsp. nutmeg
1 egg, well beaten
3/4 c. light cream
Flour
1 c. Burgundy
2 beef bouillon cubes
1 1/2 tsp. sugar

Combine beef, crumbs, onions, cornstarch, salt, nutmeg, egg and cream. Shape into small balls; roll in flour. Brown meatballs in hot fat in skillet. Combine Burgundy, bouillon cubes, sugar and 1 1/2 cups water in saucepan; simmer, stirring constantly, until smooth and blended. Add meatballs to sauce; simmer for 30 minutes. Serve in chafing dish.

CHINESE EGG ROLLS

1 lb. ground beef
1/4 c. butter
4 c. shredded cabbage
1/2 c. diced celery
1/4 c. soy sauce
Sugar
1/2 c. minced onions
2 c. bean sprouts
2 tsp. salt
Sifted flour
2 tbsp. cornstarch
1 egg

Brown beef in butter in skillet; add cabbage, celery, soy sauce, 2 tablespoons sugar, onions, bean sprouts and 1 teaspoon salt. Cook for 5 minutes; drain. Let stand until cool. Sift 2 cups flour, remaining salt and cornstarch together. Beat egg and 1 teaspoon sugar together; stir into dry ingredients. Blend 2 cups water into mixture gradually; beat until batter is smooth. Grease 6-inch skillet lightly with small amount of oil. Pour about 4 tablespoons batter into pan; tilt pan to spread batter over entire surface. Cook until edges pull away from side; gently turn with fingers. Remove from pan; spoon about 1 tablespoon ground beef filling in center. Fold edges together. Stir 1 tablespoon flour and 2 tablespoons water together. Seal edges of rolls with flour mixture. Fry rolls in deep fat until browned. Spread sparingly with hot mustard to serve. Yield: 30-40 egg rolls.

GINGER MEATBALLS

2 cans consomme
10 gingersnaps, crushed
4 tsp. (packed) brown sugar
1 1/2 tsp. lemon juice
3 lb. ground beef
Chopped onion to taste
Minced parsley to taste
1/2 c. bread crumbs
2 eggs
Salt and pepper to taste
1 sm. potato, grated

Combine consomme, gingersnaps, brown sugar and lemon juice in saucepan; simmer, stirring until smooth and blended. Combine remaining ingredients; shape into small balls. Drop into sauce; simmer, covered, for 30 minutes.

MEATBALLS IN GRAPE SAUCE

2 lb. ground beef
2 eggs, slightly beaten
1/2 c. bread crumbs
Salt and pepper
Garlic salt to taste
1 bottle chili sauce
1/2 c. grape jelly
2 tbsp. lemon juice

Combine ground beef, eggs, bread crumbs, salt, pepper and garlic salt with 1/2 cup water; blend well. Shape into small balls; brown in hot fat in skillet. Drain on absorbent toweling. Combine chili sauce, jelly and lemon juice in saucepan; simmer, stirring constantly, until smooth and well blended. Add meatballs to sauce; simmer for 5 to 10 minutes or until balls are heated through. Serve in chafing dish.

MEATBALLS IN HOT CHEESE SAUCE

1 1/2 lb. ground beef
1 1/2 c. soft bread crumbs
1 egg
1 1/4 tsp. seasoned salt
1/2 tsp. oregano
1/4 tsp. pepper
1 7-oz. bottle lemon-lime carbonated beverage
1 can cheese soup
1 tsp. Worcestershire sauce

Preheat oven to 400 degrees. Combine beef, crumbs, egg, salt, oregano, pepper and 1/2 cup carbonated beverage. Mix thoroughly. Form into small balls. Place in shallow baking pan. Bake for 15 minutes or until browned and thoroughly cooked. Combine soup, Worcestershire sauce and remaining carbonated beverage in saucepan; blend well. Combine meatballs and sauce; simmer until heated through. Serve in chafing dish with rye bread rounds.

PIQUANT MEATBALLS

1 1/2 lb. lean pork, ground
1 lb. ground beef
1 c. bread crumbs
1/2 c. finely ground almonds
2 eggs, beaten
2 cloves of garlic, minced
Soy sauce
2 tsp. salt
Dash of hot sauce
Nutmeg to taste
Cornstarch
1 lge. can pineapple chunks
2 c. vinegar
1 1/2 c. sugar

Combine pork, beef, crumbs and almonds; mix lightly. Add eggs, garlic, 2 tablespoons soy sauce, salt, hot sauce and nutmeg to pork mixture; blend well. Shape into walnut-sized balls; roll in cornstarch. Fry in hot fat in skillet for 10 minutes or until lightly browned. Drain pineapple; reserve juice. Combine 4 tablespoons cornstarch with 1 cup reserved juice; blend well. Combine 1/2 cup soy sauce, vinegar and sugar in saucepan over low heat; stir in cornstarch mixture. Simmer, stirring constantly, until sauce is clear and thickened. Add pineapple; simmer for 10 minutes. Add sauce to meatballs; stir gently to blend. Serve in chafing dish.

SHERRIED BEEF NUGGETS

1 lb. ground beef
1/2 c. corn flake crumbs
1 1/2 c. evaporated skim milk
1/4 c. minced onion
1/4 c. chili sauce
1 tsp. salt
2 1/2 tsp. Worcestershire sauce
2 tbsp. flour
2 tbsp. shortening
1 can cream of mushroom soup
1 tbsp. sherry

Combine beef, crumbs, 1/2 cup milk, onion, chili sauce, salt and 1 teaspoon Worcestershire sauce in 2-quart bowl. Shape into small balls. Roll in flour. Brown meatballs in shortening in skillet; drain on absorbent toweling. Drain off excess fat from skillet; return to heat. Combine remaining milk and Worcestershire sauce with soup and sherry over low heat in skillet; blend well. Add meatballs; simmer until meatballs are heated through. Serve in chafing dish.

SPICY TOMATO MEATBALLS

1 lb. ground beef
1/2 lb. ground pork
1/2 c. minced onions
3/4 c. fine dry bread crumbs
1 tbsp. minced parsley
Salt
Pepper
1 egg
1 tsp. Worcestershire sauce
1/2 c. milk
1 1/2 c. catsup
1/2 c. white vinegar
2 tbsp. (packed) brown sugar
Red pepper

Combine beef, pork, onions and crumbs with parsley, 1 1/2 teaspoons salt and 1/8 teaspoon pepper; mix lightly. Blend egg, Worcestershire sauce and milk into beef mixture; shape into small balls. Brown meatballs in skillet in small amount of hot fat; simmer, stirring occasionally, for 15 minutes. Combine catsup, vinegar, brown sugar, 1/8 teaspoon salt and pepper and red pepper to taste. Pour catsup mixture over meatballs; simmer, covered, for 15 to 20 minutes. Serve in chafing dish.

SWEDISH MEATBALLS

1 1/2 lb. ground round steak
1 egg
1/2 c. milk
1 1/2 slices bread, finely crumbled
2 tbsp. dried onion flakes
1 1/2 tsp. salt
1 1/2 tsp. sugar
1/2 tsp. paprika
1/2 tsp. allspice
1/4 tsp. nutmeg
1 tsp. dry mustard
1/2 tsp. marjoram
1/2 tsp. thyme
1 tsp. monosodium glutamate
1/4 tsp. pepper
2 c. beef bouillon
1/4 tsp. garlic powder
1 tsp. dillweed
1 c. sour cream

Combine ground round steak, egg, milk, crumbs, onion, salt and sugar with spices; mix lightly. Shape into small balls; brown in skillet in small amount of hot fat. Mix bouillon, garlic powder and dillweed; pour over meatballs. Simmer, covered, for 30 minutes; add additional bouillon, if needed. Stir in sour cream; simmer until sauce is just heated through. Serve in chafing dish.

SWEET AND SOUR BEEF BALLS

1 1/2 lb. ground beef
2 eggs
3 tbsp. flour
1/2 tsp. salt
Cracked pepper
3/4 c. salad oil
9 slices pineapple, diced
1 sm. can bamboo shoots
1 1/2 c. chicken bouillon
3 lge. green peppers, diced
1 tsp. monosodium glutamate
3/4 c. pineapple juice
3/4 c. sugar
1 tsp. ginger
3/4 c. vinegar
2 tbsp. cornstarch
2 tbsp. soy sauce

Shape ground beef into walnut-sized balls. Combine eggs, flour, salt and pepper; dip meatballs into flour mixture. Fry in hot oil in skillet until browned; remove meatballs. Keep warm. Drain off all but 1 tablespoonful fat; add pineapple. Cook, covered, over medium heat for 10 minutes. Rinse bamboo shoots thoroughly; drain. Combine pineapple, bamboo shoots, bouillon, green peppers, monosodium glutamate and pineapple juice with sugar, ginger and vinegar; blend thoroughly. Add cornstarch to soy sauce; stir until smooth. Add cornstarch mixture to pineapple mixture; cook, stirring constantly, until sauce comes to a boil and is thickened. Add meatballs; simmer for 15 minutes. Serve in chafing dish.

ALUMINUM FOIL STEW

15 potatoes, peeled
5 carrots, peeled
3 onions, peeled
1 1/2 lb. ground beef
Salt and pepper

Slice potatoes, carrots and onions; place in large bowl. Cover with water. Grease squares of foil. Shape beef into patties; place one on each square of foil. Drain vegetables thoroughly. Top ground beef with vegetables; season with salt and pepper. Fold foil; seal well. Place on outdoor grill. Cook for 30 minutes; turn foil package over. Cook until beef and vegetables are tender.

BEEFBURGER SOUP

1 beef bouillon cube
1 c. tomato juice
1 c. shredded cabbage
1/4 c. chopped onion
1/4 c. chopped green pepper
1/2 c. chopped celery
Pepper to taste
Seasoned salt to taste
Dash of monosodium glutamate
Worcestershire sauce to taste
1/2 lb. ground beef chuck

Bring 2 cups water to a boil in saucepan; add bouillon cube, stirring until dissolved. Add tomato juice, vegetables, seasonings, monosodium glutamate and Worcestershire sauce; simmer for 12 minutes. Break off small pieces of beef; pinch each piece together to prevent crumbling. Add to tomato juice mixture. Simmer for 10 minutes. Vegetables will be slightly crunchy. Yield: 3-4 servings.

HEARTY HAMBURGER SOUP

1 med. onion, coarsely chopped
3 tbsp. butter, melted
1 1/2 lb. ground beef

1 No. 2 1/2 can tomatoes
3 10 1/2-oz. cans beef bouillon
4 med. carrots, quartered
1 bay leaf
4 celery tops, chopped
6 sprigs of parsley
1/2 tsp. thyme
10 peppercorns
1 tbsp. salt

Saute onion in butter in large skillet until transparent. Add ground beef, cooking slightly. Stir in remaining ingredients and 2 cans water; cook, covered, over low heat for 45 minutes. Top with toast rounds; sprinkle with Parmesan cheese. Yield: 6-8 servings.

MEATBALLS WITH PEA SOUP

1 1/4 c. split peas
1/4 c. rice
3 med. onions, chopped
1 tsp. thyme
1/2 lb. ground beef
2 beef bouillon cubes
Salt and pepper

Combine peas, rice, 1 cup onions and thyme with 2 quarts water; cook for 1 hour or until peas and rice are tender. Shape beef into small balls; brown in skillet. Remove from skillet; set aside. Cook remaining onion in beef drippings for 10 minutes or until tender. Add meatballs and onion to rice mixture. Add bouillon cubes; stir gently until dissolved. Season to taste.

MINESTRONE-HAMBURGER SOUP

1 lb. ground beef
1 c. chopped onions
1 c. cubed potatoes
1 c. sliced carrots
1/2 c. sliced celery
1 c. shredded cabbage
1 No. 2 can tomatoes
1/4 c. rice
1 sm. bay leaf, crushed
1/2 tsp. dried thyme
1/4 tsp. dried basil
5 tsp. salt
1/8 tsp. pepper
Grated cheese

Brown beef and onions in small amount of fat in skillet; add potatoes, carrots, celery, cabbage and tomatoes. Bring to a boil; add rice gradually. Add bay leaf, thyme, basil, salt, pepper and 1 1/2 quarts water; cover. Simmer for 1 hour. Sprinkle servings with cheese. Yield: 6 servings.

TOMATO MEATBALL SOUP

1 lb. ground beef
1/2 c. cracker crumbs
1 egg, beaten
2 tbsp. milk
1 tsp. dried onion flakes
1/2 tsp. salt
1/4 tsp. pepper
1/4 c. salad oil
1 can stewed tomatoes
1 can tomato sauce
1 pkg. dry onion soup mix
1 tbsp. sugar
1 can mixed vegetables

Combine beef, cracker crumbs, egg, milk, onion and seasonings; mix well. Shape in 1 1/2-inch balls. Brown meatballs in oil in heavy skillet; drain. Combine tomatoes, tomato sauce, 1 cup water, onion soup mix and sugar in large saucepan; add vegetables and meatballs. Stir well; bring to a boil. Cover; simmer for 15 minutes.

SPICY HAMBURGER SOUP

1 1/2 lb. ground beef
1 lge. onion, chopped
4 lge. potatoes, cubed
4 carrots, sliced
1/2 head cabbage, shredded
4 c. tomatoes
1/2 bay leaf
1/4 tsp. thyme
Salt and pepper to taste
1/4 c. rice

Saute ground beef and onion in small amount of fat in Dutch oven; drain off fat. Add 4 cups water, potatoes, carrots, cabbage, tomatoes, bay leaf, thyme, salt and pepper. Bring to a boil; add rice. Reduce heat; cover. Simmer for 2 hours. Add water as needed during first 30 minutes. Yield: 4-5 servings.

BARBECUE FOR A CROWD

15 lb. ground beef
3 lb. onions, chopped
1 1/2 bottles catsup
1/2 c. prepared mustard
5 cans chicken gumbo soup
10 cans tomato soup
1 c. chopped celery

Mix ground beef, onions, catsup, mustard, soups and celery. Place in large kettle; simmer for at least 2 hours. Serve on buns.

BARBECUED HAMBURGERS

5 lb. ground beef
5 green peppers, chopped
5 onions, chopped
2 c. chopped celery
2 bottles catsup
1 c. (packed) brown sugar
1 c. mustard
1/2 c. Worcestershire sauce
2 1/2 tsp. chili powder
Salt and pepper to taste

Brown beef, green peppers, onions and celery in large kettle; add remaining ingredients. Stir mixture; blend well. Simmer for 1 hour; serve on split buns. May be frozen. Yield: 50 servings.

GRILLED HAMBURGER STEAK

1 round French bread loaf
1/2 tsp. prepared mustard
1/2 tsp. chili powder
1/2 c. soft butter
3 lb. ground beef chuck
2 tsp. seasoned salt
1/2 c. minced green onions and tops
2 tbsp. chili sauce
1 tbsp. soy sauce
1 cucumber
1 tomato

Cut bread in halves crosswise. Blend mustard, chili powder and butter; spread over cut sides of bread. Combine ground beef, seasoned salt, green onions, chili sauce and soy sauce; blend well. Form beef mixture into 2 patties slightly larger than cut side of bread. Place bread, crust down, on grill away from hottest coals to heat slowly. Grill patties on one side until browned; turn patties. Place bread on patties. Cook until patties are browned and tender. Arrange on platter. Cut cucumber and tomato into halves; slice thinly. Arrange on patties. Cut each round into 5 wedges to serve.

BEEF-EGG SCRAMBLE

1/4 lb. ground beef
1/4 c. chopped onions
2 tbsp. chopped green pepper
Salt and pepper to taste
3 eggs

Brown ground beef, onions and green pepper in about 1 tablespoon hot fat; add salt and pepper. Beat eggs with 1 1/2 tablespoons water. Pour over beef mixture; simmer, stirring, until eggs are set. Serve on buttered buns with catsup, if desired. Yield: 4-6 servings.

OPEN-FACED ENGLISH BURGERS

1/2 c. garlic dressing
2 lb. ground beef
6 English muffins
Seasoning salt to taste

Mix garlic dressing and ground beef; shape into 12 patties. Broil 4 to 6 inches from source of heat until browned on one side. Place patties on muffin halves, browned side down; sprinkle with seasoning salt. Broil until muffins and beef patties are browned. Sprinkle patties with Parmesan cheese while broiling or allow slices Swiss or Cheddar cheese to melt on patties just before serving, if desired.

CHOW MEIN BURGERS

1 lb. ground beef
1/2 c. chopped onions
1 1-lb. can chop suey vegetables, drained
3 tbsp. soy sauce
2 tbsp. cornstarch
8 split hamburger buns, toasted
1/3 can chow mein noodles

Combine ground beef and onions in skillet; cook until tender. Add vegetables. Mix 1/3 cup water, soy sauce and cornstarch; stir into beef mixture. Cook, stirring constantly, until thickened. Spoon onto bottom halves of buns; sprinkle with chow mein noodles. Cover with bun tops. Yield: 8 servings.

SANDWICH LOAF ITALIANO

1 lb. ground beef
1/3 c. Parmesan cheese
1/4 c. chopped onions
1 6-oz. can tomato paste
1 tsp. salt
1/2 tsp. oregano
1/8 tsp. pepper
1/4 c. chopped ripe olives
1 French bread loaf
10 tomato slices
5 Cheddar cheese slices

Combine beef, Parmesan cheese, onions, tomato paste, salt, oregano, pepper and olives. Cut loaf in half lengthwise. Spread beef mixture on loaf. Broil 5 inches from source of heat for 10 to 12 minutes; top with tomato slices. Cut cheese slices diagonally; place over tomato slices. Broil until cheese is melted and bubbly.

SLOPPY JOES

2 lb. ground beef
1 c. chopped onions
1 c. tomato sauce
2 tbsp. prepared mustard
Salt and pepper to taste
1 tsp. chili powder
Worcestershire sauce to taste

Brown ground beef and onions in small amount of fat. Cook until onions are transparent. Add salt, pepper, tomato sauce, 1/2 cup water, mustard, chili powder and Worcestershire sauce. Simmer for at least 15 minutes. Serve on buns. Yield: 8-10 servings.

PEPPY SLOPPY JOES

5 lb. ground beef
5 med. onions, chopped
1 sm. bunch celery, chopped
Butter
1 sm. can tomato paste
1 bottle barbecue sauce
1/3 c. tomato catsup
4 tsp. dry mustard
4 tbsp. Worcestershire sauce
Salt and pepper to taste
1/3 c. vinegar
1/3 c. (packed) brown sugar

Place ground beef in skillet; fry until partially cooked. Saute onions and celery in small amount of butter. Add remaining ingredients and ground beef. Cook over medium heat, stirring frequently, until ground beef is cooked sufficiently. Serve over buns. Yield: 25 servings.

STROGANOFF BURGERS

2 lb. ground beef
1/3 c. chopped onion
1/3 c. catsup
3 tbsp. prepared mustard
1 tsp. salt
1 12-oz. carton sour cream

Brown ground beef in skillet. Add onion; brown slightly. Add catsup, mustard, salt and sour cream; mix well. Simmer, covered, for 20 minutes. Serve on heated buns. Yield: 12 servings.

STUFFED WHOPPER BURGERS

2 lb. ground beef
1 tsp. salt
Pepper to taste
1 tbsp. Worcestershire sauce
1 egg
American cheese slices
1 onion, sliced
Mustard relish
Barbecue sauce

Combine beef, seasonings, Worcestershire sauce and egg; form into thin patties. Place slice of cheese, slice of onion and 1 teaspoon mustard relish on half the patties. Top with remaining patties; seal edges well. Cook on outdoor grill, basting with barbecue sauce. Yield: 6-8 servings.

BAKED STUFFED RIGATONI

Salt
8-oz. rigatoni
2 tbsp. shortening
3/4 c. chopped onion
1 clove of garlic, minced
2 lb. ground beef
2 eggs, beaten
1/2 c. dry bread crumbs
3 tbsp. chopped parsley
Pepper
Tomato Sauce

Add 1 tablespoon salt to 3 quarts rapidly boiling water in large saucepan. Add rigatoni gradually so that water continues to boil. Cook, stirring occasionally, until tender. Drain in colander; rinse with cold water. Drain again. Spread rigatoni out on tray. Melt shortening in large skillet; add onion and garlic. Cook over medium heat until golden. Add ground beef; cook, stirring constantly and breaking up with fork, just until lightly browned. Pour off excess fat from skillet. Remove beef mixture from heat; cool slightly. Blend in eggs, bread crumbs and parsley. Season to taste with salt and pepper. Stuff rigatoni with beef mixture. Arrange stuffed rigatoni in shallow greased 3-quart casserole. Pour Tomato Sauce over rigatoni. Bake in 350-degree oven for 30 minutes, spooning sauce over top occasionally. Serve with grated Parmesan cheese if desired.

Tomato Sauce

5 slices diced bacon
3/4 c. chopped onion
3/4 c. chopped celery
3/4 c. finely diced carrot
2 28-oz. cans tomatoes
2 cans beef broth
3/4 tsp. salt
1/2 tsp. sugar
8 parsley sprigs
2 cloves of garlic, crushed
1/2 tsp. thyme leaves
1 bay leaf

Cook bacon in large saucepan for about 2 minutes. Add onion, celery, and carrot. Cook until vegetables are tender. Stir in tomatoes, beef broth, seasonings and 2 cups water. Simmer for 2 hours, stirring occasionally. May add small amount of water if sauce becomes too thick. Strain sauce through a sieve; add enough water to make 6 cups sauce.

Baked Stuffed Rigatoni . . . Beef-stuffed pasta topped with a spicy, vegetable-rich tomato sauce.

BEEF SOUFFLÉ

2 lb. ground beef
2 tbsp. minced parsley
1 tsp. salt
Dash of pepper
2 tbsp. minced green onions
1 c. thick cream sauce
3 eggs, separated

Saute beef in 1 tablespoon fat until cooked thoroughly; add parsley, salt, pepper and onions. Stir in cream sauce. Beat egg yolks until thick and yellow; add to beef mixture. Beat egg whites until stiff peaks form; fold into beef mixture. Pour into baking dish; set in pan of water. Bake at 350 degrees for 45 minutes. Yield: 6-8 servings.

BARBECUED HAMBURGER STACKS

1 1/2 lb. ground beef
Salt
Pepper
3 c. soft bread cubes
1/4 c. hot milk
1 egg, beaten
1/4 c. melted shortening
1/8 tsp. marjoram
2 tbsp. chopped onion

Combine ground beef, 1/2 teaspoon salt and 1/4 teaspoon pepper; mix lightly. Shape into 10 patties. Blend bread cubes with milk, egg, shortening, 1/4 teaspoon salt, marjoram and onion; shape mixture into 5 patties. Place 5 beef patties in greased shallow baking dish; top each with bread patty. Cover with remaining beef patties.

Lemon Barbecue Sauce

1/4 c. salad oil
2 tbsp. chopped onion
1/4 c. minced celery
1/4 c. lemon juice
1/4 c. tomato puree
1 tbsp. Worcestershire sauce
1 clove of garlic, minced
2 tbsp. (packed) brown sugar
1/2 tsp. salt
1/4 tsp. pepper

Place oil in skillet; add onion and celery. Saute until tender over medium heat. Add remaining ingredients; simmer for 10 minutes. Pour over hamburger patties. Bake patties at 325 degrees for 30 minutes. Baste with sauce occasionally. Yield: 5 servings.

BEEF SUPREME

1 tsp. shortening
1 lb. ground beef
1 can tomatoes
1 8-oz. can tomato sauce
2 tsp. salt
2 tsp. sugar
2 cloves of garlic, crushed
1 5-oz. package egg noodles
1 c. sour cream
1 3-oz. package cream cheese
6 green onions and tops, chopped
1 c. grated cheese

Melt shortening in skillet; add beef. Cook until lightly browned; break up pieces with fork. Drain off fat; add tomatoes, tomato sauce, salt, sugar and garlic. Simmer for about 10 minutes. Cook noodles according to package directions; drain. Blend sour cream, cream cheese and onions into beef mixture. Pour small amount of beef mixture into greased casserole; cover with layer of noodles and grated cheese. Repeat layers; top with beef sauce. Bake in 350-degree oven for 35 minutes. Yield: 6-8 servings.

CASHEW-BEEF CASSEROLE

1 lge. package noodles
1 lge. onion, chopped
2 tbsp. butter
1 1/2 lb. ground beef
1 can cream of mushroom soup
1 soup can milk
Salt and pepper to taste
1 c. grated cheese
Stuffed olives
Cashews
1 can chow mein noodles

Cook noodles according to package directions; drain. Saute onion in butter in large skillet; add ground beef. Brown slightly. Combine ground beef mixture, soup, milk, cooked noodles, salt, pepper and cheese; mix well. Turn half the ground beef mixture into casserole. Slice olives over top; cover with remaining ground beef mixture. Bake at 350 degrees for 45 minutes. Sprinkle with cashews and chow mein noodles. Reduce oven temperature to 275 degrees. Bake for 15 minutes longer. Yield: 6-8 servings.

GROUND BEEF AND ALMOND CASSEROLE

2 lb. ground beef
1 tsp. salt
2 c. chopped celery
1/4 c. chopped green pepper
1/4 c. chopped onions
1/4 c. chopped pimento
1 can mushrooms
1 can mushroom soup
1/4 c. soy sauce
1 6-oz. package noodles, cooked
1 c. sour cream
1/2 c. sliced almonds

Saute ground beef in 2 tablespoons fat in saucepan; add salt, celery, green pepper, onions, pimento, mushrooms, soup and soy sauce. Stir well; simmer, covered, for 30 minutes. Mix noodles and sour cream; stir into beef mixture. Place in casserole; top with almonds. Bake at 325 degrees for 30 minutes. Yield: 12 servings.

GROUND BEEF AND ZUCCHINI CASSEROLE

6 med. zucchini
1 lb. ground beef
1 med. onion, chopped
1 No. 2 1/2 can tomatoes
1 8-oz. can tomato sauce
1 6-oz. can tomato paste
1 sm. green pepper, chopped
1 c. grated sharp Cheddar cheese
1/2 c. pitted ripe olives
1/2 tsp. salt
1/4 tsp. garlic salt
1/8 tsp. oregano
Grated Parmesan cheese

Cut zucchini into 1/2-inch slices. Saute beef and onion in 1 tablespoon fat in large skillet; add zucchini, tomatoes, tomato sauce, tomato paste, green pepper, Cheddar cheese, olives, salt, garlic salt and oregano. Simmer for 10 minutes; place in 8 x 12-inch pan. Sprinkle with Parmesan cheese generously. Bake at 350 degrees for 1 hour or until thickened and browned. Yield: 8 servings.

GROUND BEEF CASSEROLE

1 lb. ground beef
1 c. chopped celery
1 c. chopped onions
1 can cream of chicken soup
1 can mushroom soup
1/2 c. rice
1/4 c. soy sauce
1 can chow mein noodles

Brown ground beef, celery and onions in 1 tablespoon fat. Add soups, 1 1/2 cups hot water, rice and soy sauce; simmer for 30 minutes. Pour into greased 1 1/2-quart casserole. Bake, covered, at 350 degrees for 20 minutes. Uncover; sprinkle chow mein noodles on top. Bake for 15 minutes longer. Yield: 8 servings.

HOLIDAY BUFFET

1/2 c. chopped onions
1/4 c. diced green pepper
2 tbsp. butter
1 1/4 lb. ground beef
1 can tomato soup
1/2 c. catsup
Salt and pepper to taste
1/3 c. milk
2 3-oz. packages cream cheese
2 tsp. lemon juice
1/4 tsp. garlic salt
1 tsp. Worcestershire sauce
1 8-oz. package noodles
1/2 c. grated Cheddar cheese

Cook onions and green pepper in butter in large skillet until onions are transparent. Add beef; stir until browned. Add soup, catsup, salt and pepper; simmer for 8 minutes, stirring occasionally. Blend milk, cream cheese and lemon juice; add garlic salt and Worcestershire sauce. Cook noodles according to package directions; drain. Add cream cheese mixture to noodles. Spread noodle mixture in 8 x 12-inch baking dish. Pour beef sauce on top; sprinkle with cheese. Bake in 350-degree oven for 30 minutes. Yield: 8 servings.

JOHNNY MARZETTI

2 lge. onions, chopped
2 tbsp. butter, melted
1 1/2 lb. ground beef
1 c. tomato paste
2 4-oz. cans sliced mushrooms
1 c. diced celery
1 green pepper, diced
1 tsp. vinegar
Salt and pepper to taste
1/4 lb. sharp process cheese, diced
1 8-oz. package noodles

Cook onions in butter in large skillet until soft; add ground beef. Brown. Stir in tomato paste, mushrooms, 1 1/2 cups water, celery, green pepper, vinegar, salt, pepper and cheese. Simmer tomato paste mixture for 15 minutes. Cook noodles according to package directions; drain. Mix with sauce. Turn into baking dish. Bake, covered, at 350 degrees for 1 hour. Yield: 6-8 servings.

LASAGNA

3/4 lb. ground beef
1/4 lb. bulk sausage
1 sm. onion, minced
1/2 clove of garlic, chopped
1 sm. can mushroom pieces
1 bay leaf
1 tsp. salt
1/2 tsp. pepper
1 tsp. mixed Italian spices
2 sm. cans tomato paste
1 pkg. lasagna
1 carton ricotta cheese
12 oz. sliced mozzarella cheese
Grated Parmesan cheese

Brown ground beef, sausage and onion in skillet; pour off excess fat. Add garlic, mushroom pieces, bay leaf, salt, pepper, spices and tomato paste. Rinse each tomato paste can with 3 tablespoons water; stir into meat mixture. Simmer for 45 minutes, stirring occasionally. Cook lasagna according to package directions. Alternate layers of lasagna, meat sauce, ricotta, mozzarella and Parmesan cheeses in greased oblong baking dish. Repeat layers. Bake in 325-degree oven for 45 minutes.

MEATBALLS AND SCALLOPED POTATOES

1 lge. can evaporated milk
1 egg, slightly beaten
1 1/2 lb. ground beef
1/2 c. cracker crumbs
1 1/2 tsp. salt
1/8 tsp. pepper
1 tsp. dry mustard
1/4 c. chopped onions
1/2 c. diced green pepper
6 c. thinly sliced potatoes
1 can cream of celery soup
Chili sauce

Combine 2/3 cup milk, egg, beef, crumbs, seasonings, dry mustard, onions and green pepper; blend well. Shape into balls. Cook potatoes in boiling water to cover for 8 minutes or until partially tender; drain. Spread potatoes in 2 baking dishes. Combine remaining milk with soup; pour over potatoes. Arrange meatballs on top. Brush with chili sauce. Bake at 350 degrees for 45 minutes.

TEXAS HASH

1 lge. onion, chopped
1 green pepper, chopped
2 tbsp. shortening
1 lb. ground beef
2 c. tomato juice
1/2 c. rice
1/2 tsp. chili powder
1 tsp. salt
1 tsp. pepper

Saute onion and pepper in shortening in large skillet. Add ground beef; brown well. Add tomato juice, rice, chili powder and seasonings; stir well. Pour into casserole; cover. Bake at 375 degrees for 45 minutes. Yield: 4 servings.

SUPER LASAGNA

1 8-oz. package lasagna
1 1/2 lb. ground beef
1/2 tsp. olive oil
1/4 c. chopped onions
1 clove of garlic, crushed
2 6-oz. cans tomato paste
2 c. tomato sauce with mushrooms
1 tsp. salt
1/2 tsp. oregano
1 bay leaf
1 tsp. dried crushed sweet basil
1 tsp. dried parsley flakes
1/4 tsp. pepper
2 c. creamed cottage cheese
1 egg, well beaten
2 8-oz. packages mozzarella cheese

Cook lasagna according to package directions; drain. Brown beef in large skillet in oil with onions and garlic. Add tomato paste, tomato sauce, 1/2 teaspoon salt, oregano, bay leaf, basil, parsley, 1/8 teaspoon pepper and 1 1/2 cups water; simmer for 1 hour. Combine cottage cheese, egg, remaining salt and remaining pepper. Grate mozzarella cheese. Arrange layers of noodles, cottage cheese mixture, beef mixture and cheese in 12 x 8-inch baking dish, ending with cheese on top. Bake at 350 degrees for 30 minutes. Remove from oven; let stand for 15 minutes before serving. Yield: 6-8 servings.

ORIENTAL BEEF

1 1/2 lb. ground beef
1 c. chopped celery
1 c. chopped onions
1 sm. can mushrooms
1 sm. can water chestnuts, sliced
1 sm. can bamboo shoots, drained
1/3 c. soy sauce
1 bouillon cube
3/4 c. rice

Brown ground beef; drain. Mix in celery, onions, mushrooms, water chestnuts, bamboo shoots and soy sauce. Dissolve bouillon cube in 2 cups hot water; stir into ground beef mixture. Stir in rice; place in casserole. Bake, covered, at 350 degrees for 1 hour; stir mixture occasionally. Yield: 6-8 servings.

TAGLIARINI

1 onion, thinly sliced
1/4 c. cooking oil
Garlic salt to taste
1 sm. can tomato sauce
1 lb. ground beef
1 can mushrooms
1 c. whole kernel corn
1 4-oz. package cooked noodles
Grated cheese

Brown onion in oil; add garlic salt, tomato sauce, beef, mushrooms, corn and noodles. Stir mixture gently; turn into casserole. Bake at 350 degrees until bubbly. Sprinkle with cheese. Bake for 5 minutes longer. Yield: 8 servings.

UPSIDE-DOWN HAMBURGER DISH

2 1/2 c. macaroni
1/2 c. diced onions
3 tbsp. margarine
1 lb. ground beef
1 8-oz. can tomato sauce
1 tsp. salt
1/4 tsp. pepper
1 3-oz. package grated cheese
3 eggs, beaten
3/4 c. milk

Cook macaroni according to package directions; drain. Saute onions in margarine until tender. Add ground beef; brown well. Stir in tomato sauce, salt and pepper; simmer for several minutes. Spread in greased 2-quart casserole. Mix cheese with macaroni; spoon over ground beef mixture, packing firmly. Mix eggs with milk; pour over macaroni. Bake at 350 degrees for 1 hour and 30 minutes or until golden brown. Let stand for 15 minutes before serving. Yield: 6-8 servings.

CHEESE BEEFBURGERS

1 lb. ground beef
2/3 c. milk
1/3 c. oats
2 tbsp. chopped onion
1 tsp. salt
1/8 tsp. pepper
4 slices American cheese
4 slices bacon

Combine ground beef, milk, oats, onion, salt and pepper; form into eight patties. Cover 4 patties with cheese slices; top with remaining patties. Seal edges; wrap each patty with bacon slice. Secure bacon with wooden pick. Broil over hot coals, 4 inches from source of heat, for 5 to 7 minutes; turn. Broil for 5 minutes longer or until of desired doneness.

Classic Lasagna . . . An Italian dish made of layers of tomato sauce, pasta, and cheese.

BARBECUED BEEF-POTATO PATTIES

1 1/2 lb. ground beef
2 1/2 c. grated potatoes
Chopped onions to taste
6 tbsp. chopped green pepper
2 1/4 tsp. salt
1/2 tsp. (scant) pepper
3 tbsp. diced dill pickle
1/2 c. dill pickle juice
2/3 c. catsup
2 drops of hot sauce
2 tsp. Worcestershire sauce

Combine ground beef, potatoes, onions, green pepper, 1 3/4 teaspoons salt and pepper; shape into patties. Combine dill pickle, pickle juice, catsup, hot sauce, Worcestershire sauce and remaining salt in saucepan; simmer for 5 minutes. Broil patties over hot coals, 4 to 5 inches from source of heat, for 5 to 7 minutes; turn. Brush patties with sauce; broil for 5 minutes longer or until of desired doneness. Serve with remaining sauce.

GROUND BEEF SHISH KABOB

Sassafras sticks
1 lb. ground beef
1 c. corn flakes crushed
1 egg
1 1/2 tsp. salt
1 tbsp. Worcestershire sauce
1/8 tsp. pepper

Cut 6 sassafras sticks 1 inch in diameter and about 30 inches long. Peel off bark 4 to 6 inches from one end. Combine all ingredients in bowl. Divide into 6 portions; press each portion on sassafras stick. Broil over hot coals, turning frequently, until of desired doneness.

CLASSIC LASAGNE

1 med. onion, chopped
2 cloves of garlic, crushed
4 tbsp. olive oil
1 1-ib. 12-oz. can tomatoes
2 6-oz. cans tomato paste
Salt
1/2 tsp. basil leaves
1/2 tsp. oregano leaves
1/8 tsp. crushed red pepper
1 lb. ground beef chuck
1/2 lb. ground lean pork
1/4 c. chopped parsley
2 eggs
1/2 c. fine dry bread crumbs
Freshly grated Parmesan cheese
1/8 tsp. pepper
1 lb. curly edge lasagne
1 lb. ricotta cheese
1/2 lb. mozzarella cheese, sliced

Saute onion and garlic in saucepan in 2 tablespoons oil until lightly browned. Add tomatoes, tomato paste, 1/2 cup water, 1/2 teaspoon salt, herbs and red pepper. Simmer, covered, for 1 hour. Combine beef, pork, parsley, eggs, bread crumbs, 2 tablespoons Parmesan cheese, pepper and 1/2 teaspoon salt. Shape into 1/2-inch meatballs. Saute in remaining oil until browned; add to sauce. Simmer for 15 minutes. Add 2 tablespoons salt to 6 quarts rapidly boiling water in large saucepan. Add lasagne gradually so that water continues to boil. Cook, stirring occasionally, until tender. Drain in colander. Arrange layers of lasagne, meatball mixture, ricotta and Parmesan cheeses in large greased casserole. Top with mozzarella cheese. Bake at 375 degrees for about 25 minutes.

GRILLED BEEF PATTIES WITH SAVORY SAUCE

1 lb. ground beef
Salt and pepper to taste
3 tbsp. salad oil
1 tsp. vinegar
2 tbsp. prepared mustard
1 tbsp. Worcestershire sauce
Dash of hot sauce
1 tsp. sugar
1 clove of garlic, minced
1 sm. onion, chopped

Combine ground beef, seasonings and 1/2 cup water; form in patties. Combine remaining ingredients in saucepan; simmer for 5 minutes. Broil patties over hot coals, 3 inches from source of heat, for 5 minutes; turn. Spread sauce over patties; broil for 5 minutes longer or until of desired doneness.

GRILLED PATTIES WITH CRANBERRY-OLIVE SAUCE

2 lb. ground beef
2 tsp. salt
1/2 tsp. pepper
1 c. whole cranberry sauce
1/4 c. sliced stuffed olives
1/4 c. thinly sliced celery
1 tsp. lemon juice
1 tsp. chopped onion

Combine beef, salt and pepper; shape into 8 patties. Place patties on grill over glowing coals, about 3 inches from heat. Grill for about 10 minutes; turn. Grill for 5 minutes longer or until of desired doneness. Combine remaining ingredients; simmer, stirring occasionally, until sauce is heated through. Serve over patties. Yield: 8 servings.

HAWAIIAN BEEFBURGERS

1 lb. ground beef
1/2 tsp. salt
1 onion, chopped fine
1/2 c. soy sauce
1 sm. clove of garlic, minced
1/2 tsp. ground ginger

Combine beef, salt and onion; shape into 6 patties. Combine soy sauce, garlic and ginger; pour over patties. Marinate patties in sauce for at least 30 minutes. Remove from sauce; broil, over hot coals 4 to 5 inches from source of heat, for 5 to 7 minutes on each side.

HOBO DINNER

2/3 c. ground beef
Salt and pepper to taste
2 tbsp. chopped onion
1 carrot, cut into strips
1 sm. onion
1 sm. potato, quartered
1/2 ear corn
1/4 c. chopped ripe olives

Combine beef with salt, pepper and chopped onion; pat to fit bottom of small coffee can. Place carrot strips, onion, potato and corn over beef; sprinkle with salt, pepper and olives. Cover; cook over medium hot coals for 50 minutes. Yield: 1 serving.

MOCK FILET MIGNON

1 lb. ground beef
1 tbsp. Worcestershire sauce
1 tsp. dried minced onion
1/4 c. catsup
1 tsp. garlic juice
Salt and pepper to taste
4 slices bacon

Combine ground beef, Worcestershire sauce, onion, catsup, garlic juice, salt and pepper; shape into 4 patties. Wrap slice of bacon around each patty; secure with wooden pick. Broil over hot coals, 4 to 5 inches from source of heat, for 7 minutes on each side or until of desired doneness.

PICNIC KABOBS

1 1/2 lb. ground beef
1 c. oats
1 egg, beaten
1 tsp. salt
1 tbsp. Worcestershire sauce
1/4 c. tomato sauce
24 med. stuffed olives
4 med. tomatoes
2 green peppers
8 sm. whole cooked potatoes
8 button mushrooms
Barbecue sauce

Combine ground beef, oats, egg, salt, Worcestershire sauce and tomato sauce. Shape small amount of ground beef mixture around each olive. Cut tomatoes and green peppers into eighths; seed peppers. Alternate 3 meatballs, 2 tomato wedges, 2 green pepper pieces, 1 potato and 1 mushroom on eight 12-inch metal skewers; brush with barbecue sauce. Broil kabobs over coals, 6 inches from source of heat, for 8 to 10 minutes; turn and baste frequently with barbecue sauce.

SPECIAL BEEFBURGERS

1 lb. ground beef
Salt and pepper to taste
1 sm. onion, diced
3 oz. bleu cheese, crumbled
1 tomato, sliced

Combine ground beef with salt and pepper; shape into 4 patties 6 inches in diameter. Divide onion, cheese and tomato equally between 2 patties; season with additional salt and pepper. Cover with remaining patties; seal edges. Broil over hot coals, 4 to 5 inches from source of heat, for 6 to 8 minutes; turn. Broil for 5 minutes longer or until of desired doneness.

CHEESE-STUFFED MEAT LOAF

1 8-oz. package sliced process American cheese
2 eggs, slightly beaten
2 lb. ground beef
1 c. milk
1 c. rolled oats
3/4 c. chopped onion
2 tbsp. minced green pepper
2 tsp. salt
1/4 tsp. pepper
1 tbsp. prepared mustard
1 tsp. prepared horseradish

Cut cheese slices in half diagonally; reserve half the cheese triangles. Chop remaining cheese slices finely. Combine chopped cheese, eggs, ground beef, milk, oats, onion, green pepper and seasonings. Mix well. Press beef mixture into greased loaf pan. Invert pan onto foil-covered shallow baking pan; remove loaf from pan. Fold foil up around meat loaf to hold juices. Bake at 375 degrees for about 1 hour or until beef is done. Remove foil from around meat loaf; overlap reserved cheese slices on top of loaf. Return to oven just long enough for cheese to melt. Place meat loaf on heated serving dish; garnish with peach halves and sprigs of watercress. Yield: 8 servings.

Cheese-Stuffed Meat Loaf... Stuff ever-popular meat loaf with a seasoned cheese mixture.

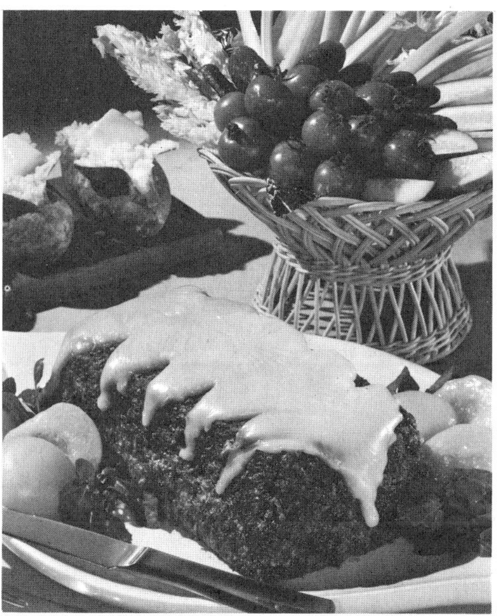

BACON-DILL MEAT LOAF

2 lb. ground beef chuck
6 slices crisp bacon, chopped
3/4 c. minced onions
1/4 c. chopped dill pickle
2 c. soft bread crumbs
2 eggs, slightly beaten
2 tbsp. horseradish
2 1/2 tsp. salt
1 tsp. dry mustard
1/4 c. milk
3/4 c. catsup

Combine all ingredients except 1/2 cup catsup. Form into loaf; top with remaining catsup. Bake at 350 degrees for 50 minutes.

CHEESY MEAT LOAF

1 lb. ground beef
2 c. soft bread crumbs
1/4 c. chopped onions
1 tsp. salt
1/2 tsp. celery salt
1/4 tsp. pepper
3/4 c. grated cheese
3/4 c. tomato juice
2 eggs, slightly beaten

Combine all ingredients; mix well. Shape into loaf in baking pan. Bake in 350-degree oven for 1 hour.

COUNTRY MEAT LOAF

4 bread slices
2 med. onions, minced
2 tbsp. butter
1 1/2 lb. ground beef chuck
1/2 tsp. salt
1/4 tsp. pepper
1 egg, beaten
2 tbsp. mustard
1 c. cubed Cheddar cheese
1 can tomato soup

Trim crusts from bread slices. Soften bread in small amount of water. Saute onions in butter lightly. Combine beef, bread, onions, salt, pepper, egg and mustard; mix well. Shape half the beef mixture into flat loaf; top with cheese. Shape remaining beef mixture into flat loaf; place over cheese. Mold loaf; seal edges. Place in baking dish; pour soup over loaf. Bake, covered, at 350 degrees for 1 hour. Bake, uncovered, for 15 to 20 minutes longer or until browned.

FROSTED MEAT LOAF

2 lb. ground beef
1/2 c. French dressing
1/2 c. dry bread crumbs
1/2 c. chopped onions
3 eggs
1 tsp. salt
1/4 tsp. pepper
2 c. mashed potatoes
1/2 c. salad dressing

Mix ground beef, French dressing, crumbs, onions, 2 eggs, salt and pepper. Shape into loaf; place in shallow baking dish. Bake at 350 degrees for 1 hour. Place on baking sheet. Beat remaining egg; add potatoes and salad dressing; mix well. Frost loaf with potato mixture. Broil until lightly browned. Garnish with mushrooms, pimento and parsley.

MEAT LOAF SUPREME

4 lb. ground beef
2 eggs, slightly beaten
1/8 tsp. curry powder
1 tbsp. salt
1 tsp. pepper
1 can vegetable soup
1/2 c. corn flake crumbs
1/8 tsp. garlic salt
1 tsp. dried parsley flakes
1/4 c. wine
1/2 c. chili sauce

Combine all ingredients except wine and chili sauce. Form into loaf; place in roaster with 3/4 cup water. Combine wine and chili sauce; pour over loaf. Bake at 350 degrees for 2 hours or to desired doneness.

MEAT LOAF WITH CHEESE STUFFING

3 lb. ground beef
3 c. soft bread crumbs
1 c. minced onions
1/2 c. minced green pepper
4 eggs, slightly beaten
3 tbsp. horseradish
1 tbsp. salt
2 tbsp. prepared mustard
1/4 c. evaporated milk
1/4 c. catsup
1 16-oz. package sharp cheese slices
Minced parsley to taste

Preheat oven to 400 degrees. Mix ground beef, crumbs, onions and green pepper lightly into eggs. Add remaining ingredients except cheese and parsley; mix lightly. Divide mixture into three parts; pat 1 part into large loaf pan. Cover with overlapping cheese slices. Spread with second part of ground beef mixture. Add layer of cheese slices. Spread with remaining ground beef mixture. Invert loaf onto jelly roll pan. Bake for 45 minutes. Crumble 2 cheese slices over top. Bake for 5 minutes longer. Cool for 15 minutes before serving. Garnish with parsley.

MEAT LOAF WITH SWEET-SOUR SAUCE

1 1/2 lb. ground beef
1 egg, beaten
2 c. bread crumbs
1 can tomato sauce
1 med. onion, chopped
1 tsp. salt
1/4 tsp. pepper
1 tbsp. vinegar
3 tbsp. (packed) brown sugar
3 tsp. mustard
1 tbsp. Worcestershire sauce

Combine ground beef, egg, crumbs, 1/2 can tomato sauce, onion, salt and pepper; mix well. Place in loaf pan. Mix all remaining ingredients and 1 cup water; pour over meat loaf. Bake in 375-degree oven for 1 hour and 10 minutes.

RIPE OLIVE MEAT LOAF

1 med. head cabbage
1 No. 1 can pitted ripe olives
1 1/2 lb. ground beef
1/4 c. minced onions
1 3/4 tsp. salt
1 beaten egg
1/4 tsp. pepper
1/2 c. soft bread crumbs
1/4 c. milk
1 1/2 tsp. caraway seed
1/4 tsp. thyme
1 tbsp. flour
1 tbsp. melted butter
1 bouillon cube
1/3 c. white wine

Core cabbage; tear leaves apart. Cover leaves with boiling water to wilt. Drain; line bottom and sides of greased loaf pan with cabbage leaves. Chop olives; reserve 1/4 cup. Mix olives, ground beef, onions, salt, egg, pepper, crumbs, milk, caraway seed and thyme; blend thoroughly. Spread half the beef mixture in pan; add layer of cabbage leaves. Cover with remaining beef. Top with cabbage leaves. Bake, covered, at 350 degrees for 1 hour and 30 minutes. Drain off pan drippings; add enough water to measure 2/3 cup. Blend flour with butter; stir liquid mixture into flour gradually. Add bouillon cube and wine; cook, stirring constantly, until thickened slightly. Add reserved olives. Serve wine sauce over sliced loaf.

SPICY GLAZED MEAT LOAF

1 1/2 lb. ground beef
3/4 c. gingersnap crumbs
1/2 c. chopped onions
2 eggs
2/3 c. evaporated milk
1 1/2 tsp. salt
1/2 tsp. cinnamon
1/2 c. peach preserves

Combine beef, gingersnap crumbs, onions, eggs, evaporated milk, salt and cinnamon; mix well. Turn into 1 1/2-quart loaf pan. Bake at 350 degrees for 1 hour. Drain off drippings. Cool for 5 minutes in pan; unmold. Mix preserves and 1/4 cup water in saucepan; cook, stirring constantly, over low heat until thick and smooth. Spread glaze over top of loaf. Garnish loaf with peach slices, maraschino cherries and parsley.

SUNDAY DINNER MEAT LOAF

1/2 med. onion, chopped
2 tbsp. bacon drippings
1 egg
1 tbsp. Worcestershire sauce
1/4 c. milk
2 lb. ground beef chuck
1/3 c. herb-seasoned stuffing mix
1/2 tsp. salt
2 tbsp. Dijon mustard
2 tbsp. catsup

Saute onion in bacon drippings until golden; drain. Combine egg, Worcestershire sauce and milk; beat slightly. Place onion, egg mixture and beef in large mixing bowl; add stuffing mix, salt, mustard and catsup. Mix well; place in 9 x 5-inch loaf pan. Pat into smooth loaf. Bake at 350 degrees for 1 hour or until browned and cooked through.

APPLE BEEF BALLS

1 lb. ground beef
1 c. dry bread crumbs
1 c. grated apples
1 1/2 tsp. salt
1/2 tsp. pepper
2 eggs, beaten
1 c. tomato juice

Combine ground beef, bread crumbs, apples, salt and pepper with eggs; mix lightly. Shape into balls; saute in skillet in small amount of hot fat until browned. Place meatballs in baking dish; add tomato juice. Bake, covered, at 375 degrees for 1 hour. Yield: 4 servings.

Buttermilk Meatballs . . . Meat appetizers served in their own buttermilk-mustard sauce.

BUTTERMILK MEATBALLS

1 lb. ground beef
3/4 c. milk
1/2 c. fine dry bread crumbs
1/4 c. finely chopped onion
1 1/2 tsp. salt
1/8 tsp. pepper
1/4 c. butter
2 tbsp. flour
2 tsp. sugar
2 c. buttermilk
2 tbsp. prepared mustard

Combine ground beef, milk, crumbs, onion, 1 teaspoon salt and pepper. Shape into 16 balls. Brown well on all sides in 2 tablespoons butter. Remove meatballs from pan. Add remaining butter. Blend in flour, sugar and remaining salt. Add buttermilk and mustard; cook, stirring constantly, until thickened. Return meatballs to sauce. Cover; simmer for about 20 minutes or until meatballs are done. Yield: 4-6 servings.

BAKED BURGER KABOBS

4 carrots
1 green pepper
4 sm. onions
1 lb. ground beef
1 egg, beaten
1/4 c. dry bread crumbs
Salt and pepper to taste
2 slices bacon, quartered
2 8-oz. cans tomato sauce
2 tsp. Worcestershire sauce
1 clove of garlic, crushed

Slice carrots into 1 1/2-inch pieces; cut green pepper into 1 1/2-inch squares. Simmer carrots, green pepper and onions in saucepan for 10 minutes or until just tender; drain. Mix ground beef, egg, crumbs, salt and pepper; shape into 12 balls. Thread carrots, onions, meatballs, green pepper and bacon onto 4 skewers; sprinkle with salt and pepper. Place in 11 x 7 x 2-inch pan. Bake at 400 degrees for 15 minutes or until lightly browned; turn skewers occasionally to brown evenly. Mix tomato sauce, 1/2 cup water, Worcestershire sauce and garlic; pour over kabobs. Bake at 350 degrees for 30 minutes. Serve on rice topped with sauce from pan. Yield: 4 servings.

HAWAIIAN MEATBALLS

2 lb. ground beef chuck
2 eggs
1 chopped onion
1 tsp. garlic salt
1 tsp. salt
Flour
2 tbsp. melted shortening
1/4 tsp. ginger
6 tbsp. (packed) brown sugar
1/4 tsp. dry mustard
1/2 tsp. onion salt
1 10-oz. can crushed pineapple
6 tbsp. catsup
1/4 c. vinegar
2 tbsp. cornstarch
2 tbsp. soy sauce

Combine beef, eggs, onion, 1/2 teaspoon garlic salt and 1/2 teaspoon salt. Shape into 15 balls. Roll meatballs in flour; brown in shortening in skillet. Drain on absorbent toweling. Combine remaining garlic salt and salt with ginger, brown sugar, mustard and onion salt; blend with pineapple, catsup, vinegar and 1 cup water in skillet. Mix cornstarch with soy sauce; stir into pineapple mixture. Simmer, stirring constantly, until sauce is clear and thickened; add meatballs. Simmer for 20 minutes. Yield: 6-8 servings.

MEATBALLS IN BUTTERMILK SAUCE

1 1/2 lb. ground beef
1 sm. onion, minced
3 tbsp. chopped green pepper
1/3 c. sliced celery
1 c. cooked rice
1 tsp. salt
1/2 tsp. pepper
1 egg
1 can cream of mushroom soup
1 soup can buttermilk
1 can mushroom stems and pieces

Combine ground beef, onion, green pepper, celery, rice, salt and pepper with egg; mix lightly. Shape mixture into 12 balls; saute in skillet in small amount of hot fat until well browned. Place meatballs in greased 2-quart baking dish. Combine soup, buttermilk and mushrooms in skillet; simmer, stirring constantly, until smooth and blended. Pour sauce over meatballs. Bake, covered, at 350 degrees for 1 hour. Yield: 6 servings.

MEATBALLS IN DILL SAUCE

2 lb. ground beef
2 med. onions, ground
1 egg
1 tsp. salt
1/4 tsp. pepper
1/2 tsp. Italian seasoning
Cracker meal
1 can mushroom soup
1 pt. fresh mushrooms, sliced
1 c. sour cream
1/2 c. dry white wine
2 sprigs of dill, chopped

Combine beef, onions, egg and seasonings; shape into small balls. Dip balls in cracker meal; brown in skillet in small amount of hot fat. Place in 2-quart baking dish. Blend soup with mushrooms, 2/3 cup sour cream and wine. Bake at 350 degrees for 30 minutes. Remove from oven; spoon remaining sour cream and dill over top. Yield: 8 servings.

MEATBALLS SUPREME

2 lb. ground beef chuck
1 c. quick-cooking oats

1 1/2 tsp. salt
1/4 tsp. pepper
1 c. tomato juice
2 eggs, beaten
1 can tomato soup
1 can cream of mushroom soup
1/4 c. milk
1/2 tsp. dried onion flakes
1/2 tsp. crushed oregano
1 can sliced mushrooms, drained

Combine ground chuck, oats, salt, pepper and tomato juice; mix lightly. Add eggs to ground chuck mixture; blend well. Shape into 1 1/2-inch balls; brown in skillet in small amount of hot fat. Place meatballs in greased 3-quart baking dish. Combine soups, milk, onion, oregano and mushrooms in skillet; simmer, stirring constantly, until blended and heated through. Pour sauce over meatballs. Bake, covered, at 325 degrees, for 1 hour. Serve over rice or noodles.

PARMESAN MEATBALLS

1/2 c. soft bread crumbs
1/2 c. grated Parmesan cheese
1 egg, slightly beaten
1/2 c. milk
1 tbsp. minced onion
1 tsp. monosodium glutamate
Salt and pepper to taste
1 lb. ground round steak
1/4 c. flour
1 c. beef bouillon
1 4-oz. can sliced mushrooms

Combine crumbs, cheese, egg, milk, onion, monosodium glutamate, salt and pepper with ground steak; shape into balls. Place meatballs in shallow greased baking pan. Bake at 350 degrees until browned. Remove meatballs from pan. Blend flour into pan drippings; add bouillon and mushrooms. Stir until smooth and blended; add meatballs to sauce. Bake, covered, at 350 degrees for 30 minutes. Serve over rice. Yield: 5-6 servings.

PORCUPINE MEATBALLS

1 lb. ground beef
1/2 c. rice
1/2 med. onion, chopped
1/4 tsp. salt
Pepper to taste
1 can tomato soup

Combine ground beef, rice and onion with salt and pepper; shape into 6 balls. Arrange meatballs in greased baking dish; cover with soup. Bake in 350-degree oven for 30 minutes. Yield: 6 servings.

SAUERBRATEN MEATBALLS

1 lb. ground beef
1/4 c. fine dry bread crumbs
2/3 c. chopped onions
1 1/2 tsp. salt
Dash of pepper
2/3 c. evaporated milk
2 tbsp. butter
2 tbsp. vinegar
2 tbsp. catsup
1 tbsp. (packed) brown sugar
8 peppercorns
1 bay leaf, crushed
1/3 c. raisins
6 gingersnaps, crushed

Combine beef, bread crumbs, onions, 1 teaspoon salt, pepper and milk; shape into balls. Brown meatballs in skillet in butter. Combine vinegar, catsup, brown sugar, peppercorns, bay leaf, raisins and gingersnaps with 1 cup water; mix well. Pour sauce over meatballs. Bring to a boil, stirring constantly; reduce heat. Simmer, covered, for 15 minutes. Stir gently; simmer, covered, for 15 minutes longer. Yield: 6 servings.

SKILLET LUAU

1 lb. ground beef
1 egg, beaten
1/4 c. dry bread crumbs
1/2 tsp. salt
1/4 tsp. ginger
1/4 c. flour
1 No. 2 can pineapple chunks
3 tbsp. (packed) brown sugar
3/4 tsp. cornstarch
1/4 c. vinegar
1 tbsp. soy sauce
2 green peppers, cut into strips

Mix beef with egg, crumbs, salt and ginger; form into 16 balls. Dredge balls in flour; brown in 3 tablespoons fat in large frying pan. Remove meatballs from pan. Drain pineapple, reserving syrup; add water to syrup to make 1 cup liquid. Stir syrup mixture into pan drippings. Mix brown sugar with cornstarch, vinegar and soy sauce. Add to syrup mixture. Cook, stirring constantly, until sauce is thickened and clear. Arrange meatballs, pineapple chunks and pepper strips separately in pan; stir each gently to coat with sauce. Cover; simmer for 10 minutes or until green pepper is crisp-tender. Serve with hot buttered noodles, if desired. Yield: 4 servings.

GRILLED BURGERS

Color photograph for this recipe on page 71.

1 env. dry onion soup mix
2 lb. ground beef
10 hamburger buns, toasted
Fresh lettuce
10 hamburger buns, toasted
10 slices fresh tomato
Large fresh onion rings

Combine 1/4 cup water and soup mix, blending well. Stir in ground beef until well mixed. Shape into 10 patties; place on grill over hot charcoal. Cook to desired doneness. Arrange lettuce on bottom halves of buns. Place patties on lettuce; add tomato slices and onion rings to each bun. Add bun tops; serve immediately.

PEPPERED HAMBURGERS

Color photograph for this recipe on page 76.

1 1/4 lb. ground beef
1 1/2 tsp. salt
1 tsp. paprika
1/2 tsp. pepper
1 egg yolk
6 tbsp. cola beverage
3/4 tbsp. flour
1 onion, sliced
1 green pepper, cut in rings
1 red pepper, cut in rings
Butter

Combine ground beef, salt, paprika, pepper, egg yolk, cola beverage and flour; mix well. Chill for about 1 hour. Saute onion, green and red peppers in small amount of butter in skillet until soft; remove and set aside. Shape beef mixture into thick patties; cook in skillet until done and browned. Top with onion mixture; serve.

BEEF UPSIDE-DOWN PIE

1 1/2 c. flour
3 tsp. baking powder
1 tsp. salt
1 tsp. paprika
1 tsp. celery salt
1/4 tsp. pepper
5 tbsp. shortening
3/4 c. milk
1/4 c. sliced onion
1 lb. ground beef
1 can tomato soup

Sift dry ingredients; blend in 3 tablespoons shortening. Add milk, stirring gently, until mixed thoroughly. Melt remaining shortening in frying pan. Add onion; cook until transparent. Add beef, browning lightly; stir in tomato soup. Bring beef mixture to a boil; simmer for several minutes. Place beef mixture in 9-inch cake pan; spread dough over beef mixture. Bake at 475 degrees for 20 minutes. Turn out onto large plate. Cut into wedges.

CHEESE CRUST BEEF PIE

1 1/2 lb. ground beef
2 tbsp. diced green pepper
1 3/4 tsp. salt
1/8 tsp. garlic powder
1/4 tsp. pepper
1 1/4 c. flour
3 c. tomato juice
2/3 c. diced celery
2 tsp. Worcestershire sauce
1/3 c. shortening
1/3 c. grated sharp cheese

Brown ground beef and green pepper lightly in 10-inch skillet; drain off excess fat. Add 1 1/2 teaspoons salt, garlic powder and pepper. Mix in 1/4 cup flour; add tomato juice, stirring constantly. Add celery and Worcestershire sauce; simmer for 15 minutes. Pour into 9 x 2-inch baking dish. Cut shortening into remaining flour and salt. Add cheese; mix well. Add 1/4 cup water, stirring with fork until dough holds together. Roll out on floured waxed paper. Place crust over top of beef mixture. Bake at 425 degrees for 30 minutes.

CHILEAN FRIED EMPANADAS

Paprika to taste
1 lb. ground beef
2 tbsp. chopped onion
Flour
1/2 c. broth
Salt
Pepper
1 hard-cooked egg, chopped
3 tbsp. shortening, melted
1/2 tbsp. vinegar

Blend paprika into beef. Saute in skillet until brown. Add onion. Stir in 1 tablespoon flour and broth; mix well. Cook, stirring constantly, over medium heat until thickened. Season with salt and pepper to taste. Remove from heat; add egg. Measure 4 cups flour into mixing bowl; season with 1 teaspoon salt. Add 3 tablespoons water, shortening and vinegar, blending well. Knead dough; roll out on floured surface. Cut into 2 1/2-inch rounds. Place spoonfuls of beef mixture on 1 side of rounds. Fold over; seal edges with fork. Fry in deep hot fat until lightly browned.

CORN BREAD TAMALE PIE

1 lb. ground beef
1 med. onion, chopped
1 can tomato soup
3/4 tsp. salt
1 tbsp. chili powder
1 c. whole kernel corn, drained
1/2 c. chopped green pepper
3/4 c. cornmeal
1 tbsp. flour
1 tbsp. sugar
1 1/2 tsp. baking powder
1 egg, beaten
1/3 c. milk
1 tbsp. oil

Saute beef and onion in small amount of fat in skillet until browned. Add soup, 1/4 teaspoon salt, chili powder, corn and green pepper; simmer for 15 minutes. Pour into greased 2-quart casserole. Combine cornmeal, flour, sugar, remaining salt, baking powder, egg, milk and oil. Stir until just moistened. Spread cornmeal mixture over beef mixture. Bake at 425 degrees for about 25 minutes or until browned.

CORNISH PASTIES

4 c. flour
1 c. lard
Salt
1 1/2 lb. chopped beef
1/2 lb. chopped pork
8 med. potatoes, diced
1 c. diced rutabagas
2 med. onions, chopped
Pepper

Mix flour, lard and 1 1/2 teaspoons salt together with pastry blender; add 8 tablespoons water or enough to form soft dough. Divide dough into 6 portions; roll out on floured board into 10-inch circles. Combine beef, pork, potatoes, rutabagas and onions; season with salt and pepper to taste. Place 1/6 of the beef mixture on 1/2 of each circle. Fold dough over; crimp edges. Make slot in each pastry. Place on cookie sheet. Bake in 350-degree oven for 1 hour.

COUNTRY BEEF PIE

2 8-oz. cans tomato sauce
1/2 c. bread crumbs
1 lb. ground beef
1/4 c. chopped onion
1/4 c. chopped green pepper
2 tsp. salt
1/8 tsp. oregano
1/8 tsp. pepper
1 1/3 c. packaged precooked rice
1 c. Cheddar cheese, grated

Combine 1/2 can tomato sauce, crumbs, ground beef, onion, green pepper, 1 1/2 teaspoons salt, oregano and pepper; mix well. Pat mixture in greased 9-inch pie plate; pinch 1-inch edges and flute. Set aside. Combine rice, remaining tomato sauce, remaining salt, 1 cup water and 1/4 cup cheese. Spoon rice mixture into beef shell. Cover with foil. Bake in 350-degree oven for 25 minutes. Remove cover; sprinkle top with remaining cheese. Return to oven. Bake, uncovered, for 10 to 15 minutes.

CREOLE MEAT PIES

1 lb. ground beef
Salt and pepper
Red pepper to taste
1/2 c. onion, chopped
1 clove of garlic, minced
1/2 c. chopped green onion tops
1/2 c. chopped parsley
4 c. flour
1/2 tsp. soda
2 tsp. baking powder
1/2 c. shortening
1 egg
1 c. milk

Combine ground beef, salt and pepper to taste, red pepper, onion, garlic, green onion and parsley with 1 teaspoon water. Simmer, stirring occasionally, until beef is lightly browned and onion is tender. Sift flour, soda and baking powder together; cut in shortening until of consistency of coarse meal. Stir in egg and milk; work dough until smooth and firm. Divide dough into 1 1/2-inch balls; roll each ball to 1/8-inch thickness. Place spoonful of meat on each circle. Fold dough over beef mixture; seal edges. Fry in deep fat until lightly browned. Drain on absorbent toweling.

HAMBURGER PIE

1 recipe 2-crust 9-in. pie pastry
1 lb. ground beef
1/2 tsp. poultry seasoning
2 tsp. salt
1/4 tsp. pepper
1 tbsp. Worcestershire sauce
3 tbsp. catsup
1 tsp. prepared mustard
2 med. potatoes, sliced
2 med. onions, chopped
1/4 c. butter
1 can brown gravy with mushrooms

Fit half the pastry into pie pan. Combine beef, poultry seasoning, salt, pepper and Worcestershire sauce with catsup and mustard. Spoon into pastry-lined pan. Fry potatoes and onions in butter until potatoes are soft and onions lightly browned; stir gravy into potato mixture. Pour over beef mixture. Fit remaining pastry over pie. Seal edges; cut steam vents. Bake at 375 degrees for 1 hour and 15 minutes.

HAMBURGER-CHEESE PIE

1 pkg. pastry mix
1/2 c. grated Cheddar cheese
1/2 tsp. paprika
Dash of cayenne pepper
1 1/2 lb. ground beef
1 sm. onion, minced
1 1/2 c. dry bread cubes
1 can beef bouillon
1/2 tsp. salt
1/2 tsp. pepper
1/4 tsp. thyme
1/4 tsp. marjoram
2 tsp. Worcestershire sauce

Prepare pastry mix according to package directions; add cheese, paprika and cayenne pepper. Roll out half the pastry on lightly floured board; fit into 9-inch pie pan. Cook beef and onion in skillet until beef is lightly browned; stir to break beef into small pieces. Mix bread cubes and bouillon; let stand for several minutes. Add beef mixture, salt, pepper, thyme, marjoram and Worcestershire sauce; blend well. Pour into pastry-lined pan. Roll remaining pastry and place over filling. Crimp edges; cut steam vents. Bake in 375-degree oven for 45 minutes or until crust is lightly browned. Yield: 6 servings.

LITTLE MEAT PIES

2 c. flour
Salt
2 tbsp. baking powder
4 tbsp. (scant) shortening
2 egg yolks
1/2 lb. ground beef
1 sm. onion, chopped
1 clove of garlic, crushed
1 green pepper, chopped
2 hard-cooked eggs, chopped
1/4 c. raisins
2 tbsp. tomato paste
Pepper

Combine flour, 1 teaspoon salt and baking powder. Cut shortening into dry ingredients; add egg yolks and enough water to moisten. Roll out 1/8 inch thick; cut into 3-inch circles. Saute beef, onion, garlic and pepper in fat until beef is tender. Cool; add eggs, raisins and tomato paste. Season with salt and pepper to taste. Spoon small amount of beef mixture onto each pastry half; fold over. Crimp edges with fork. Fry in deep fat until brown. Serve hot.

MEXICALI MEAT PIE

6 slices bacon
1 lb. ground beef
1 c. drained whole kernel corn
1/4 c. minced green pepper
1/4 c. minced onion
Cornmeal
Oregano
1/2 tsp. chili powder
1 tsp. salt
1/8 tsp. pepper
1 8-oz. can tomato sauce
1 c. flour
1 egg
1/4 c. milk
1/2 tsp. dry mustard
1/2 tsp. Worcestershire sauce
1 1/2 c. shredded Cheddar cheese
4 stuffed olives, sliced

Fry bacon until crisp; break into large pieces. Chill 1/3 cup bacon drippings until firm. Brown beef in large skillet; drain. Stir in corn, green pepper, onion, 1/4 cup cornmeal, 1/2 teaspoon oregano, chili powder, 1/2 teaspoon salt, pepper and tomato sauce. Combine flour, 1/8 teaspoon oregano and 2 tablespoons cornmeal; cut in chilled drippings until mixture resembles small peas. Sprinkle with 3 to 4 tablespoons cold water; stir with fork until ingredients hold together. Form into ball; roll out on floured surface to circle 1 1/2 inches larger than inverted 9-inch pie pan. Fit into pan. Fold edge to form standing rim; flute. Fill with beef mixture. Bake at 425 degrees for 25 minutes. Combine egg, milk, remaining salt, mustard, Worcestershire sauce and cheese. Spread over pie; top with bacon and olives. Bake for 5 minutes longer or until cheese melts. Let stand for 10 minutes. Serve with tomato sauce, if desired.

MOCK SHEPHERD'S PIE

1 med. onion, chopped
1 lb. ground beef
1 tsp. salt
1/4 tsp. pepper
1 No. 2 can cut green beans
1 can tomato soup
5 med. potatoes, cooked
1/2 c. warm milk
1 egg, beaten
Paprika

Brown onion in skillet in small amount of hot fat; add beef, salt and pepper. Cook until browned. Drain beans; add to beef mixture with soup. Pour into greased 2-quart casserole. Mash potatoes; add milk and egg. Add additional salt and pepper to taste. Spoon in mounds over beef mixture. Sprinkle paprika over top. Bake at 350 degrees for 30 minutes.

MEAT AND BISCUIT SQUARES

1 lb. ground beef
1/2 c. chopped onion
1 c. grated American cheese
2 eggs
1/4 tsp. hot sauce
2 1/2 tsp. salt
2 tbsp. chopped parsley
2 c. sifted flour
3 tsp. baking powder
1/2 c. shortening
1 c. milk

Saute ground beef and onion in skillet until lightly browned; stir occasionally. Remove from heat; cool. Combine beef mixture with cheese, 1 egg, hot sauce, 1 1/2 teaspoons salt and parsley; blend lightly. Sift flour, baking powder and remaining salt together; cut in shortening to consistency of coarse meal. Add remaining egg and milk; mix lightly. Turn dough out onto lightly floured board; knead 15 to 20 times. Divide dough in half; spread half the dough into 9-inch square pan. Spread beef mixture over dough; cover with remaining dough. Brush top crust with additional egg yolk. Bake at 400 degrees for 30 minutes or until crust is lightly browned. Serve, cut into squares, topped with mushroom sauce.

BEEF IN A BLANKET

1 lb. ground beef
1 tsp. minced onion
Salt and pepper
2 c. prepared biscuit mix
Milk
Butter, melted
1 can mushroom soup
1 sm. can peas

Brown ground beef and onion in small amount of fat in skillet. Sprinkle beef with salt and pepper; break up with fork. Combine biscuit mix and 2/3 cup milk; stir to blend. Roll out on floured board 1/4 inch thick. Drain excess fat from beef. Spread mixture evenly over dough. Roll up jelly roll fashion; moisten edges of dough with small amount of water. Seal edges securely. Brush top with butter. Bake at 450 degrees for 10 minutes. Mix soup, 1/3 soup can milk and peas; place over medium heat until heated through. Slice meat roll; serve with soup mixture. Yield: 6 servings.

BEEF ROULADES

1 c. sifted flour
1 tbsp. sugar
Dash of salt
3 eggs, beaten
1 c. milk
4 tbsp. butter, melted
Filling
1/2 c. dry sherry
1/2 c. Parmesan cheese, grated
16 thin slices mozzarella cheese
Paprika to taste

Sift dry ingredients together. Stir in eggs and milk. Add 2 tablespoons butter; mix well. Set aside for 2 hours. Pour thin layer of batter into hot greased skillet. Brown; turn pancake. Cook on each side for 1 minute. Repeat procedure until all batter is used. Spread Filling on pancakes; roll up. Place in greased baking dish. Sprinkle with sherry and Parmesan cheese. Place 2 mozzarella cheese slices on each roll; sprinkle with paprika and remaining butter. Bake at 400 degrees for 5 minutes or until cheese is melted. Yield: 6 servings.

Filling

1 4-oz. can mushroom stems and pieces
1 lb. ground beef
1 med. onion, minced
2 tbsp. butter, melted
1/2 tsp. salt
Dash of pepper
1 tsp. dry mustard
2 cloves of garlic, minced
1/2 c. catsup
1 tbsp. Worcestershire sauce
2 c. sharp Cheddar cheese
1 tsp. oregano
1 tsp. parsley
1 tsp. rosemary
1 bay leaf, crumbled
1/2 c. Parmesan cheese, grated

Drain mushrooms. Brown beef, onion and mushrooms in butter; add salt, pepper, mustard and garlic. Simmer for 5 minutes; add catsup and Worcestershire sauce. Crumble Cheddar cheese coarsely. Combine herbs, Cheddar cheese and 1/2 cup Parmesan cheese; add to beef mixture. Cover; simmer until cheese is partially melted. Remove from heat.

BEEF ROLL

3 doz. grape leaves
1/4 c. rice
1 lb. ground beef
Chopped parsley to taste
1/3 green pepper, diced
Chopped mint to taste
Pinch of sweet basil
1 sm. can tomatoes
Salt and pepper to taste
Lemon juice

Cut stems from leaves; soak leaves in enough boiling water to wilt. Mix rice with beef. Add parsley, green pepper, mint, basil, tomatoes, salt and pepper; blend well. Place small amount of mixture on grape leaf; roll leaf to cover mixture. Place several leaves in pan to cover bottom. Arrange rolls side by side in pan. Press rolls down firmly; add water to cover. Sprinkle small amount of lemon juice over rolls. Simmer, covered, for 1 hour. Serve with yogurt. Yield: 8 servings.

BULGARIAN GRAPE LEAF ROLLS

3 doz. grape leaves
Butter
2 lge. onions, minced
1 lb. ground beef
Salt and pepper to taste
1 egg
1/2 c. rice
Minced parsley to taste
2 c. canned tomatoes
1 beef bouillon cube
1 tsp. minced dillweed
Grated rind of 1/2 lemon
1 tbsp. butter
1 tbsp. flour
1 c. beef bouillon
Juice of 1 lemon
1/2 c. sour cream

Pour enough boiling water over grape leaves to wilt; rinse in cold water. Melt 2 tablespoons butter in skillet; saute onions until browned slightly. Add ground beef; cook for 5 minutes. Add salt, pepper, egg, rice and parsley; mix thoroughly. Fill leaves, folding each leaf over filling. Drain tomatoes; reserve liquid. Place liquid in saucepan over medium heat until heated through. Dissolve bouillon cube in tomato liquid. Chop tomato pulp; add pulp, additional parsley, dillweed and lemon rind to bouillon mixture. Mix well. Spoon small amount of tomato mixture into 2-quart casserole; arrange rolls in layers. Add tomato sauce between layers. Bake, covered, at 325 degrees for 45 minutes. Combine 1 tablespoon butter and flour; add bouillon, gradually, stirring constantly, to make gravy. Remove roll mixture from oven; stir in gravy. Return to oven. Bake for 15 minutes longer. Squeeze lemon juice over rolls; top with sour cream to serve. Yield: 6-8 servings.

DOUBLE CHEESE MEAT ROLL

1 1/2 lb. ground beef
1 egg
3/4 c. cracker crumbs
1/2 c. chopped onions
2 8-oz. cans tomato sauce with cheese
1 tsp. salt
1/2 tsp. oregano
1/8 tsp. pepper
2 c. shredded mozzarella cheese

Combine beef, egg, cracker crumbs, onions, 1/3 cup tomato sauce, salt, oregano and pepper. Mix well; shape into flat rectangle on waxed paper. Sprinkle cheese evenly over meat mixture. Roll up jelly roll fashion; press ends to seal. Bake at 350 degrees for 1 hour; drain off excess fat. Pour remaining tomato sauce over roll. Bake for 15 minutes longer. Yield: 4-6 servings.

HAMBURGER PINWHEELS

1 lb. ground beef
1/4 c. chili sauce
3/4 tsp. dry mustard
1 tsp. vinegar
Onion salt to taste
Pepper to taste
Paprika
1 recipe biscuit dough
1 c. milk
1/2 c. diced process cheese
1 tsp. salt
Dash of garlic salt

Mix ground beef, chili sauce, 1/4 teaspoon dry mustard, vinegar, onion salt, pepper and paprika to taste thoroughly. Roll dough into 1/2-inch thick oblong. Spread beef mixture over dough; roll lengthwise jelly roll fashion. Cut into 1 1/2-inch slices; place slices in greased pan. Bake in 425-degree oven for 30 minutes. Pour milk into double boiler; bring to a boil. Remove from heat immediately. Add cheese; stir until melted. Add salt, remaining dry mustard, 1/4 teaspoon paprika and garlic salt; pour over pinwheels.

MOZZARELLA MEAT WHIRL

1 1/2 lb. ground beef
1/2 c. soft bread crumbs
1 egg, slightly beaten
1 tbsp. mustard
1/8 tsp. pepper
3 tsp. salt
6 oz. mozzarella cheese, sliced
1 tsp. dried parsley flakes
3/4 c. catsup
1 tbsp. Worcestershire sauce

Mix ground beef, bread crumbs, egg, mustard, pepper and salt; pat into 10 x 14-inch rectangle on waxed paper. Place cheese slices on beef mixture; sprinkle with parsley. Roll jelly roll fashion; start at short end and lift paper with 1 hand. Press ends to seal. Transfer to shallow baking dish, seam side down. Combine catsup, 3/4 cup water and Worcestershire sauce; pour over beef. Bake at 375 degrees for 1 hour and 10 minutes, basting frequently; serve with sauce. Yield: 8 servings.

EASY STROGANOFF

1 lb. ground beef chuck
1 sm. onion, chopped
3 c. noodles
2 tsp. Worcestershire sauce
2 tsp. celery salt
1 tsp. salt
Freshly ground pepper to taste
3 c. canned tomato juice
1 c. sour cream
Minced parsley to taste

Brown beef and onion in 2 tablespoons fat in deep skillet, stirring occasionally. Place beef in greased casserole. Arrange noodles over beef. Stir Worcestershire sauce, celery salt, salt and pepper into tomato juice; pour over noodles. Simmer, covered, for 25 minutes or until noodles are tender, stirring occasionally. Stir in sour cream. Sprinkle with parsley before serving. Yield: 6 servings.

BEEF AND DUMPLINGS IN SOUR CREAM

1 lb. ground beef
1 sm. onion, chopped
1 8-oz. package dumplings
3 c. tomato juice
2 tsp. salt
Dash of pepper
2 tsp. Worcestershire sauce
1 c. sour cream
Parmesan cheese, grated
Paprika to taste

Brown ground beef and onion in 2 tablespoons hot fat in heavy saucepan. Place dumplings in layer over ground beef mixture. Mix remaining ingredients except sour cream, cheese and paprika; pour over dumplings. Bring to a boil. Simmer, covered, for 40 minutes or until dumplings are tender. Stir in sour cream. Bring to a boil; remove from heat immediately. Turn into serving dish; sprinkle with cheese and paprika. Yield: 4 servings.

CHINESE GROUND BEEF

1 1/2 lb. ground beef
Salt and pepper
1 lge. onion, chopped
3 c. celery, chopped
1 can water chestnuts
1 can chop suey vegetables
1 can mushrooms
1 can bean sprouts, drained
1 tbsp. molasses
1 tbsp. cornstarch
Soy sauce to taste
Crisp chow mein noodles
Cooked rice

Brown beef with salt, pepper, onion and celery. Cook, covered, for about 5 minutes. Drain water chestnuts; cut into thin slices. Add chop suey vegetables, mushrooms, bean sprouts and water chestnuts; bring to a boil. Mix molasses, cornstarch and 2 cups water; blend well. Stir molasses mixture into beef mixture gradually; cook, stirring constantly, until thickened. Add soy sauce; serve over noodles and rice. Yield: 6 servings.

GOULASH

1 lb. ground beef
1 med. onion, chopped
1 7-oz. package macaroni
1 tsp. salt
1/4 tsp. pepper
1 can tomato sauce
1/2 lb. cheese, grated
1 tsp. chili powder

Brown ground beef in 1 tablespoon fat in large heavy pan. Add onion; cook until transparent. Cook macaroni according to package directions; drain. Add to ground beef mixture. Stir in remaining ingredients. Simmer, covered, until cheese is melted. Yield: 6 servings.

GOULASH FOR A GANG

5 lb. ground beef
1 doz. onions, sliced
8 c. chopped tomatoes
2 green peppers, chopped
3 tbsp. salt
4 tbsp. chili powder
Cayenne pepper to taste
Pepper to taste
Cumin to taste
2 lb. pinto beans, cooked

Brown beef in large kettle. Saute onions in small amount of fat in skillet until transparent; add to beef. Add tomatoes and green peppers to beef mixture. Blend in salt, chili powder, cayenne pepper, pepper and cumin; simmer for 30 minutes. Stir beans into mixture. Yield: 20 servings.

LAZY DAY STROGANOFF

1/4 c. butter
1 lb. ground beef
1/2 c. minced onions
1 clove of garlic, minced
2 tbsp. flour
1 1/2 tsp. salt
1/4 tsp. pepper
1/4 tsp. paprika
1/4 tsp. monosodium glutamate
1 can cream of chicken soup
1 c. sour cream
1 lge. can mushrooms
2 tbsp. minced parsley

Melt butter in skillet; add beef, onions and garlic. Brown well; pour off excess fat. Stir in flour, salt, pepper, paprika and monosodium glutamate. Combine soup and sour cream in bowl; blend thoroughly. Add soup mixture and mushrooms to beef mixture. Place over medium heat until heated through; add parsley. Serve over noodles or rice. Yield: 6-8 servings.

MEXICAN DELIGHT

1 lb. ground beef
1 sm. onion, chopped
1 green pepper, chopped
4 lge. stalks celery, sliced
2 tbsp. flour
3/4 c. catsup
2 tbsp. chili powder
Salt to taste
1 lge. bag corn chips
1/2 lb. grated Cheddar cheese
1 sm. can chopped olives
1 avocado, diced
2 c. shredded lettuce
3 tomatoes, chopped

Crumble beef into large skillet; brown over medium heat. Drain excess fat from beef; add 1/2 cup water, onion, green pepper and celery. Mix flour with small amount of water, stirring until blended; add to beef mixture, stirring constantly, until thickened. Stir in catsup. Add chili powder and salt. Stir well; simmer until celery is tender. Spoon onto plates over layer of corn chips. Sprinkle cheese over top; let cheese melt slightly. Top with spoonfuls of chopped olives, avocado, lettuce and tomatoes. Yield: 4 servings.

Gumbo

A gumbo is a savory soup or stew that is usually thickened with unripe okra seed pods. It is made from meat, poultry, game, fish, or shellfish and vegetables and seasonings. Gumbo is a Creole specialty that grew out of French, Spanish, and African influences on Louisiana cuisine. Often the meat, poultry, game, fish, or shellfish used in preparing the gumbo determines its name, for example, crab gumbo, chicken gumbo, or duck gumbo. Gumbo is sometimes thickened and flavored with file powder, which is the ground leaves of the sassafras tree. If used, be sure to add the file at the end of cooking time to prevent stringiness.

SERVING: Fill a large bowl half full with gumbo. Pile boiled rice onto one side. Serve as a main course.

BEEF GUMBO SOUP

4 lb. 2-in. thick cross-cut beef shanks
2 tbsp. lard
2 tbsp. salt
1 onion, quartered
6 carrots, sliced
1 c. diced potato
1/2 c. chopped celery
6 green onions, sliced

Beef Gumbo Soup . . . A beef-based soup thickened with okra and made with eight vegetables.

1 16-oz. can tomatoes
1 10-oz. package frozen lima beans
1 9-oz. package frozen cut green beans
1 16-oz. can whole kernel corn
1/4 head cabbage, sliced
1 16-oz. can okra, drained

Brown beef shanks in lard in Dutch oven. Pour off drippings; add salt, 2 quarts water and onion. Cover tightly; simmer for 2 hours and 30 minutes. Add carrots, potato, celery and green onions. Cook for 30 minutes longer. Add tomatoes, lima beans, green beans, corn and cabbage; simmer for about 20 to 30 minutes or until vegetables are tender. Add okra; heat through and serve. Yield: 5 quarts.

BAKED CHICKEN GUMBO

1 3-lb. chicken, disjointed
1 tsp. salt
1 tsp. pepper
3/4 c. flour
1/2 c. shortening
1 sm. onion, chopped
4 c. sliced okra
1/4 c. chopped green pepper
1 1/2 c. cooked tomatoes
1 1/2 c. cooked rice

Sprinkle chicken with salt and pepper. Dredge with flour. Melt shortening in large skillet; cook chicken until brown. Remove chicken; place in 12 x 14-inch baking pan. Brown onion in remaining fat in skillet. Add okra and green pepper; simmer for 5 minutes. Pour over chicken; add tomatoes and 3 cups boiling water. Bake in 300-degree oven for 1 hour or until chicken is tender; add rice just before serving. Yield: 6-8 servings.

BAYOU SEAFOOD GUMBO

1 lb. chicken backs
Cooking oil
2 c. flour
1 lb. ham, chopped
1 bunch celery, chopped
1 lb. okra, chopped
1 c. chopped parsley
1 bunch shallots, chopped
3 cloves of garlic, chopped
2 lge. green peppers, chopped
2 sm. cans tomato paste
1 qt. oysters
2 lb. shrimp, deveined
1 1-lb. package frozen crab meat
1 tbsp. gumbo file

Place chicken parts in Dutch oven; cover with water. Bring to a boil; cook until tender. Cool; remove meat from bones, reserving stock. Bring 1 cup cooking oil to a boil; add flour gradually, stirring constantly. Cook until brown. Place 1 tablespoon cooking oil in large skillet over medium heat; add ham. Simmer for about 5 minutes. Place celery, okra, parsley, shallots, garlic, green peppers and ham in large Dutch oven; add reserved stock, tomato paste and enough water to fill pan 3/4 full. Bring to a boil; simmer for 1 hour. Add chicken, oysters, shrimp and crab meat; simmer for 30 minutes, stirring occasionally. Add gumbo file; simmer for 10 minutes, stirring occasionally. May be frozen.

CREAMY CREOLE GUMBO

1 10-oz. package frozen okra, thawed
2 tbsp. butter
1/2 c. onions, sliced
1/4 c. chopped green pepper
2 tbsp. flour
1 3/4 tsp. salt
1/4 tsp. pepper
1/2 tsp. thyme
1/8 tsp. hot sauce
1 c. crab meat
1 c. canned shrimp
1 1-lb. can tomatoes
2 c. milk

Cut okra into 1/2-inch pieces; set aside. Melt butter in saucepan; add onions and green pepper. Saute until tender. Blend flour, salt, pepper, thyme and hot sauce to form smooth paste. Stir in crab meat, shrimp, okra and tomatoes. Bring mixture to a boil. Reduce heat; cover, simmering for about 25 minutes. Stir in milk gradually; cook, stirring occasionally, over medium heat until heated through. Serve immediately. Yield: 4-6 servings.

CREOLE GUMBO

2 tbsp. flour
1 c. chopped onion
1/4 c. chopped parsley
2 cloves of garlic, minced
1 No. 2 can tomatoes
1 can okra
3 lb. deveined shrimp
3 c. chicken stock
4 bay leaves
Pinch of thyme
Salt and pepper to taste
1 c. cooked cubed chicken
1 c. cooked cubed ham
2 tbsp. gumbo file
Cooked rice

Brown flour in 2 tablespoons fat in skillet until dark; add onion, parsley and garlic. Saute onion mixture until tender; pour into deep kettle. Simmer tomatoes and okra together for several minutes; add to onion mixture. Add shrimp, chicken stock, bay leaves and thyme; season with salt and pepper. Simmer gumbo for 1 hour and 10 minutes. Stir in chicken and ham; simmer for 20 minutes longer. Add gumbo file; serve immediately over rice.

SEAFOOD GUMBO

1 6-in. slice salt pork
1/2 pkg. okra, sliced
1 onion, chopped
2 tbsp. flour
1 doz. oysters and liquor
2 c. canned tomatoes
2 sprigs of parsley
1 tsp. salt
1 bay leaf
1/2 tsp. garlic salt
Dash of pepper
Dash of cayenne pepper
1 can crab meat
1 lb. shrimp, deveined
1 tbsp. file

Fry salt pork in skillet until crisp. Remove from skillet; chop and set aside. Saute okra in pan drippings. Add onion; saute until tender, stirring constantly. Push vegetables to side of skillet; add flour, cooking until browned. Drain oysters, reserving liquor. Mix onion and okra into flour; add tomatoes, oyster liquor and 1 1/2 quarts boiling water gradually, stirring constantly until smooth. Add seasonings; stir well. Simmer for 1 hour. Add salt pork, crab meat and shrimp; simmer for several minutes longer. Add oysters; simmer for 13 minutes. Add file; cook for 2 minutes longer. Yield: 6 servings.

GULF GUMBO

1/2 c. butter
2 10-oz. packages frozen okra, thawed
1/2 c. minced onion
1/2 c. minced green pepper
1/2 tsp. minced garlic
2 tbsp. flour
4 c. chicken stock
6 sprigs of parsley
1 lge. bay leaf
2 c. coarsely chopped fresh tomatoes
1/2 tsp. thyme
2 tsp. salt
Freshly ground pepper to taste
1 lb. small shrimp, deveined
1/2 lb. lump crab meat
16 oysters
2 tsp. lemon juice
2 tsp. Worcestershire sauce
1/4 tsp. hot sauce
2 c. hot rice (opt.)

Melt 1/4 cup butter in large frying pan over moderate heat. Cut okra into thin slices; add to skillet, stirring constantly until okra is tender. Melt remaining butter in heavy 3-quart Dutch oven over moderate heat. Add onion, green pepper and garlic; cook for about 5 minutes or until onion is transparent. Stir in flour; cook for about 3 minutes longer, stirring constantly. Pour in chicken stock; stir with whisk to dissolve flour. Tie sprigs of parsley and bay leaf together with cord. Add okra, tomatoes, parsley and bay leaf, thyme, salt and pepper. Bring to a boil; reduce heat. Simmer, partially covered, for 30 minutes. Add shrimp; simmer for 5 minutes. Add crab meat and oysters; simmer for about 3 minutes or until oysters curl around edges and crab meat is heated through. Stir in lemon juice, Worcestershire sauce and hot sauce. Serve gumbo over rice. Yield: 8-10 servings.

LOBSTER GUMBO

3 tbsp. butter
1 onion, chopped
1 clove of garlic
1/2 c. chopped celery
1 lb. cooked lobster
1 No. 2 can tomatoes
1/2 lb. okra, sliced
1/2 bay leaf
Salt to taste
1/2 tsp. pepper
3 c. hot cooked rice

Melt butter in deep kettle; saute onion, garlic and celery in butter for 10 minutes. Remove garlic; add lobster, tomatoes, okra, bay leaf, salt and pepper. Stir; add 1 quart boiling water, stirring constantly. Cover; bring to a boil gradually. Simmer for 40 minutes longer. Spoon hot gumbo over rice. Serve at once.

LOUISIANA SEAFOOD GUMBO

2 tbsp. flour
2 tbsp. shortening
4 onions, chopped
6 stalks celery, chopped
1 bay leaf
2 cloves of garlic, chopped
Pinch of thyme
2 lb. shrimp, deveined
1 pt. oysters and liquid
2 c. crab meat
2 tbsp. file
Rice, cooked (opt.)

Brown flour in hot shortening in Dutch oven; stir until smooth. Saute onions and celery in roux for 15 minutes. Add 1 quart boiling water, bay leaf, garlic and thyme; simmer for 2 hours. Add shrimp; cook for 10 minutes. Mix in oysters and liquid and crab meat; cook for 10 minutes longer. Add file; serve over hot, cooked rice, if desired. Yield: 8 servings.

OYSTER AND CHICKEN GUMBO

1 lge. hen, disjointed
3/4 c. shortening
2/3 c. flour
2 lge. onions, chopped
2 tsp. salt
1/2 tsp. black pepper
1/4 tsp. red pepper
2 tsp. gumbo file
2 doz. oysters
Cooked rice
3 green onion tops, chopped
1/4 c. chopped parsley

Skin hen pieces; brown in 1/4 cup shortening in large Dutch oven. Remove from pan; drain and set aside. Brown flour in remaining shortening, stirring constantly, until darkened. Add onions; cook until tender. Add hen, 3 quarts water and seasonings; cook until hen is tender. Add oysters; cook for 3 minutes or until edges curl. Add onion tops and parsley before serving. Serve over rice. Yield: 8 servings.

SHRIMP AND CRAB GUMBO

8 slices bacon
1 pkg. frozen okra, sliced
1 lge. onion, chopped
1 green pepper, chopped
1/3 c. chopped parsley
1 c. tomato sauce
1 tsp. salt
1/4 tsp. pepper
6 cooked crabs, cleaned
1 lb. cooked shrimp, cleaned
1 tbsp. gumbo file
Steamed rice

Mince bacon; brown in 6-quart kettle over medium heat. Remove bacon from kettle; reserve. Brown okra in bacon drippings; add bacon, onion, green pepper, parsley, tomato sauce, salt, pepper and 4 cups water. Simmer for 1 hour. Add crabs and shrimp; simmer for 1 hour longer. Stir file into gumbo. Serve over rice. Yield: 6 servings.

SPICY SHRIMP GUMBO

2 onions, sliced
1/2 green pepper, thinly sliced
1/4 c. butter
2 tbsp. flour
1 1-lb. can tomatoes
1 6-oz. can tomato paste
1 1-lb. can okra
1/8 tsp. ground cloves
1/2 tsp. chili powder
Pinch of dried basil
1 bay leaf
1 1/2 tbsp. salt
1/4 tsp. pepper
1 1/2 lb. deveined shrimp
3 c. cooked rice
1/4 c. minced parsley

Saute onions and green pepper in butter in large kettle; blend in flour. Cook over low heat, stirring constantly, until mixture is bubbly and vegetables are tender. Remove from heat; add remaining ingredients except shrimp, rice and parsley. Simmer for 45 minutes. Add shrimp just before serving. Simmer, covered, for 5 minutes or until shrimp are pink and tender. Toss rice and parsley together. Serve gumbo in soup plates over rice and parsley. Yield: 8 servings.

SHRIMP GUMBO

1/4 c. butter
2 tbsp. flour
1 8-oz. can okra
1 8-oz. can tomatoes
1/2 c. chopped celery
1/4 c. chopped green pepper
1 clove of garlic, chopped
1 onion, chopped
1 red pepper
Salt and pepper to taste
2 lb. shrimp, deveined
1/4 tsp. marjoram
Pinch of thyme
Pinch of sage

Melt 2 tablespoons butter in large Dutch oven; stir flour into butter. Add enough water to make a gravy. Saute okra in remaining butter in small skillet. Add okra, tomatoes, celery, green pepper, garlic, onion, red pepper, salt, pepper and shrimp to gravy. Cover with 2 cups water; simmer for 1 hour. Remove red pepper; add marjoram, thyme and sage. Simmer for 30 minutes longer. Serve with steamed rice. Yield: 4-6 servings.

SAVORY SHRIMP GUMBO

3/4 c. flour
7/8 c. (about) bacon drippings
2 med. onions, chopped
1 med. green pepper, chopped
4 stalks celery, chopped
2 tomatoes, diced
2 1/2 lb. shrimp, deveined
1 tbsp. salt
1 tsp. pepper
1/2 tsp. cayenne pepper
1/4 tsp. thyme
3 bay leaves

Brown flour in bacon drippings in large Dutch oven, stirring constantly. Add onions, green pepper and celery; simmer, covered, for 5 minutes. Add tomatoes and shrimp; simmer, covered, until shrimp turn pink. Add seasonings, thyme, bay leaves and 3 quarts hot water; simmer for about 3 hours, stirring occasionally. Serve over rice. Yield: 6 servings.

TURKEY GUMBO

4 c. chopped turkey
2 16-oz. cans chicken broth
1 c. chopped celery
1/2 c. rice
1 c. chopped onions
1 10-oz. package frozen cut okra
1 can tomatoes
Salt and pepper to taste

Combine turkey and broth; bring to a boil in Dutch oven. Add celery, rice and onions; cook for 15 minutes. Add remaining ingredients; cook until okra is tender.

WILD DUCK GUMBO

1 c. flour
1 c. bacon drippings
1 lge. onion, chopped
2 cloves of garlic, chopped
2 wild duck, disjointed
1 tbsp. red pepper
Cayenne pepper
Pepper and salt to taste
Green onion tops, chopped
Chopped parsley
1 pt. oysters
Gumbo file

Brown flour in bacon drippings in Dutch oven, blending well. Cook until flour is rich brown. Add onion and garlic; saute until tender. Season duck well with red pepper and cayenne pepper; cook in onion mixture for about 5 minutes. Add 2 quarts warm water; simmer for about 2 hours. Season with pepper and salt. Add small amount of onion tops and parsley and oysters; simmer for about 30 minutes. Add gumbo file to taste. Serve over cooked rice.

Haddock

Haddock is a fish related to the cod but distinguished from cod by a black lateral line and spots above the side fins. Haddock has lean, white, tender flesh and is plentiful in Atlantic waters. It is high in protein and low in fat. (3 ounces breaded, fried haddock = 140 calories)

AVAILABILITY: Whole, fresh haddock is available year-round near the Atlantic coast. Elsewhere it is marketed in fresh or frozen fillets. Peak season is May to February. It is also sold smoked as Finnan Haddie.

BUYING: When buying whole fresh haddock, look for clear, bulging eyes; firm, elastic flesh; and good color. Avoid fish with a strong odor.

STORING: Wrap fresh haddock in moisture-proof paper or place in covered dish and refrigerate 1-2 days. Keep frozen fish in freezer or refrigerator's frozen foods compartment until ready to use. Once thawed, fish should never be refrozen. Refrigerate smoked haddock.

PREPARATION: Allow 1/3 pound fillets or one pound whole fish per person. Fresh or frozen haddock can be steamed, poached, stuffed and baked, broiled, boiled, fried, sauteed, or cooked in sauce or chowder. *Smoked haddock* is best steamed and should be cooked whole.

SERVING: Garnish haddock with brightly colored foods – paprika, parsley, lemon wedges, pickles, or crisp raw vegetables. Serve haddock with Yorkshire Pudding, dressing, pineapple, or sauce.

(See SEAFOOD.)

Haddock Macaroni Stew . . . Celery, green beans, and carrots add color and flavor to this stew.

HADDOCK-MACARONI STEW

1 c. thinly sliced celery
1/3 c. thinly sliced onion
1/4 c. butter
1 1-lb. package frozen haddock fillets
2 tsp. salt
1/2 tsp. monosodium glutamate
1/4 tsp. pepper
1/4 tsp. leaf thyme
1/4.tsp. leaf marjoram
1 sm. clove of garlic, crushed
1 bay leaf
1 1-lb. can cut green beans
1 1-lb. can sliced carrots
8 oz. elbow macaroni
2 c. milk

Saute celery and onion in butter for about 2 minutes or until crisp-tender. Partially thaw haddock; cut in 1-inch cubes. Add haddock and seasonings to sauteed mixture. Drain bean and carrot liquids; add enough water to equal 1 1/2 quarts liquid. Add liquid to haddock mixture. Simmer for 15 minutes; bring to a boil. Add macaroni gradually. Boil for 10 minutes or until macaroni is tender. Add vegetables and milk; heat to serving temperature.

HADDOCK SALAD

1 1/2 lb. haddock fillets
2 sm. carrots
1 stalk celery
1 sm. onion
1/2 green pepper
3/4 c. mayonnaise
1/4 c. catsup
3 sweet pickles, chopped
2 tbsp. pickle juice
Salt and pepper to taste

Steam haddock; flake. Chop carrots, celery, onion and green pepper finely; combine with haddock. Blend mayonnaise, catsup, pickles, juice, salt and pepper thoroughly. Pour over haddock mixture; toss lightly. Chill for several hours before serving.

ALMOND-BAKED FISH

2 onions
1/2 c. finely chopped almonds
2 tbsp. oil
2 tbsp. minced parsley
1 bouillon cube
1 tbsp. lemon juice
1 bay leaf
6 peppercorns
Thyme to taste
2 lb. frozen haddock fillets, thawed

Mince 1 onion; combine with almonds, oil and parsley. Dissolve bouillon cube in 2 tablespoons boiling water; add to almond mixture. Blend mixture thoroughly; place in saucepan. Simmer for 5 minutes; remove from heat. Stir lemon juice into mixture. Slice remaining onion. Place onion slices, bay leaf, peppercorns and thyme in shallow greased baking dish. Arrange haddock over onion mixture; spread with almond mixture. Bake at 375 degrees for 35 minutes. Yield: 6 servings.

BAKED HADDOCK FILLETS

2 lb. haddock fillets
1 onion, chopped
2 tbsp. butter
1 tbsp. flour
1 tsp. salt
1 tsp. pepper
1 c. cream
Paprika to taste

Cut haddock fillets into serving pieces; place in greased baking dish. Saute onion in butter until tender; blend in flour, salt and pepper. Add cream gradually, stirring constantly until thickened; pour over haddock. Sprinkle with paprika. Bake at 350 degrees for 30 minutes. Yield: 4 servings.

CHEESE HADDOCK

3 lb. haddock fillets
2 cans Cheddar cheese soup
1 sm. can evaporated milk
1/2 c. milk
1 egg, beaten
Cracker crumbs
1/2 c. melted butter
Paprika

Cut fillets into 2-inch pieces; place on greased baking sheet. Combine soup, evaporated milk, milk and egg; blend well. Pour soup mixture over haddock. Top with crumbs; drizzle with butter. Sprinkle paprika over top. Bake in 350-degree oven for 15 minutes or until haddock flakes easily.

FILLET OF HADDOCK

1 lb. frozen haddock fillets
1 can tomato soup
1/2 tsp. salt
15 whole cloves

Thaw haddock partially. Spoon 1/4 can soup into 8 x 8-inch buttered baking dish; add layer of haddock. Sprinkle with salt. Add remaining soup. Press cloves between fillets. Bake at 325 degrees for 30 minutes or until fish flakes easily. Yield: 5 servings.

HADDOCK BAKE

2 lb. frozen haddock fillets
1 can frozen cream of shrimp soup, thawed
1/4 c. butter, melted
1/2 tsp. grated onion
1/2 tsp. Worcestershire sauce
1/4 tsp. garlic salt
1 1/4 c. round buttery cracker crumbs

Thaw fillets partially; place in greased 13 x 9 x 2-inch baking dish. Spread soup over fillets. Bake at 375 degrees for 20 minutes. Combine butter, onion, Worcestershire sauce and garlic salt; mix with crumbs. Sprinkle crumb mixture over fish. Bake for 10 minutes longer. Garnish with parsley and lemon slices. Yield: 6-8 servings.

HADDOCK-CHEESE BAKE

1 1-lb. haddock
3 slices bread, cubed
2 sm. onions, minced
1 1/2 c. cottage cheese
1 egg
1 tsp. salt
Dash of pepper
Butter

Preheat oven to 450 degrees. Skin fish; place in oblong shallow baking dish. Combine bread cubes, onions, cottage cheese, egg, salt and pepper; blend well. Spread mixture over top and sides of fish. Dot with butter generously. Bake for 30 minutes or until crust is golden brown.

HADDOCK IN SHELLS

2 pkg. frozen haddock, thawed
Butter
8 slices bread, trimmed
1 tsp. lemon juice
1 tsp. garlic juice
1 1/2 tsp. onion juice
Dash of Worcestershire sauce
2 c. nondairy coffee creamer
1 tsp. dry mustard
1 tbsp. sugar
Buttered bread crumbs

Place haddock in shallow baking pan; dot with butter. Bake at 375 degrees for 15 minutes or until haddock flakes easily. Remove from oven. Cut bread slices into cubes. Flake haddock; combine cubed bread, lemon juice, garlic juice, onion juice, Worcestershire sauce, coffee creamer, mustard and sugar with haddock. Mix well. Cover; refrigerate for at least 2 hours. Stir mixture; place in 10 greased serving shells. Cover with bread crumbs; press crumbs into haddock mixture. Bake for 20 minutes at 375 degrees.

HADDOCK NEWBURG

3 lb. haddock, dressed
2 tbsp. butter
2 tbsp. flour
1 c. milk
2 tbsp. sherry
3/4 lb. Cheddar cheese, grated
3/4 tsp. salt
Dash of hot sauce
Buttered bread crumbs

Skin haddock; steam, covered, on rack in large shallow pan over boiling water for 20 minutes or until fish flakes easily. Break haddock into bite-sized pieces into greased casserole. Combine butter and flour in saucepan; blend well. Add milk gradually; simmer, stirring constantly, until smooth and thickened. Fold in sherry, cheese, salt and hot sauce; blend thoroughly. Pour sauce over fish; sprinkle with crumbs. Bake at 300 degrees for 30 minutes or until heated through.

HADDOCK RAREBIT

1 4-lb. haddock fillet
1/2 c. flour
2 tsp. dry mustard
1/2 tsp. salt
2 c. milk
2 c. shredded cheese
1 tbsp. butter

Place haddock in buttered baking pan. Sift flour, mustard and salt together. Add milk to flour mixture gradually; mix well, until smooth. Cook, stirring constantly, until thickened. Add cheese and butter; stir until blended. Pour over fish. Bake at 350 degrees for 30 minutes. Place on warm platter carefully; surround with broiled tomatoes, if desired. Yield: 6 servings.

HADDOCK SEVILLE

1 lb. haddock fillets
1 tbsp. minced onion
1 tsp. salt
1/4 tsp. pepper
1/2 tsp. nutmeg
1/8 tsp. cayenne pepper
1/4 c. sliced mushrooms
1/2 tbsp. bottled browning sauce
1 tbsp. sherry
2 sm. tomatoes, sliced
2 tbsp. minced shallots
1/2 c. bread crumbs
Butter

Place haddock in greased 12 x 8 x 2-inch baking dish; top with onion. Sprinkle with salt, pepper, nutmeg and cayenne pepper. Combine mushrooms, browning sauce and sherry; pour over haddock. Top with tomatoes and shallots. Sprinkle with bread crumbs; dot with butter. Bake in 400-degree oven for 25 minutes. Yield: 4 servings.

HADDOCK WITH YORKSHIRE PUDDING

3 lb. haddock
1/2 tsp. pepper
2 tsp. salt
4 thin slices salt pork
2 med. chopped onions
1 1/2 c. flour
2 tsp. baking powder
1 tbsp. shortening
1 1/2 c. milk

Place haddock in shallow baking pan; sprinkle with pepper and 1 teaspoon salt. Top haddock with salt pork strips and small amount of water. Bake at 400 degrees for 20 minutes; baste occasionally with pan drippings. Add onions; bake for 10 minutes longer. Combine flour, baking powder, shortening, remaining salt and 5 to 6 tablespoons water to make a dough; drop by spoonfuls around fish. Bake for 20 minutes longer or until pudding tests done. Remove fish and pudding, keep warm. Add flour to pan drippings; blend until smooth. Add milk gradually; simmer, stirring constantly, until thickened. Serve sauce over fish.

HADDOCK SURPRISE

1 1/2 lb. haddock fillets
1 c. saltine cracker crumbs
Butter
Salt and pepper to taste
1/2 green pepper, thinly sliced in rings
4 oz. sliced American cheese
2 c. milk

Alternate layers of haddock and 1/2 cup crumbs in buttered casserole; dot with butter. Add salt, pepper, green pepper rings and cheese slices. Sprinkle remaining crumbs on top. Dot with additional butter; sprinkle with additional salt and pepper. Pour milk into casserole. Bake at 350 degrees for 1 hour. Yield: 4-6 servings.

HADDOCK WITH DRESSING

3 tbsp. butter
1/4 c. chopped onion
1/2 c. chopped celery
2 c. packaged herb-seasoned stuffing mix
2 lb. haddock fillets, seasoned
Cheddar cheese strips
1 can mushroom soup
1 c. milk

Preheat oven to 350 degrees. Melt butter in skillet; add onion and celery. Cook until transparent. Combine stuffing mix and 1/2 cup hot water. Mix onion with stuffing mixture; set aside. Place layer of fillets, skin side down, in greased pan. Spread stuffing mixture over fillets; top with remaining fillets. Cover with cheese strips. Combine mushroom soup and milk; pour into pan. Bake for 45 minutes. Yield: 4-6 servings.

HADDOCK WITH INDIAN SAUCE

1 1/2 lb. haddock fillets
1 tbsp. butter
1 tbsp. flour
1 can tomato soup
2 tbsp. vinegar
1 green pepper, sliced
1 med. onion, sliced

Preheat oven to 375 degrees. Arrange fillets in 1 1/2-quart casserole. Combine butter and flour in saucepan; blend over low heat. Add soup; cook, stirring constantly, until thickened. Remove from heat; add vinegar, green pepper and onion. Return to heat; simmer for 2 minutes. Pour sauce over fillets. Bake for 45 minutes.

HADDOCK WITH PARMESAN STUFFING

6 c. soft bread crumbs
1 tbsp. minced onion
1/2 tsp. oregano
1/3 c. grated Parmesan cheese
3/4 c. condensed tomato soup
1/4 c. margarine, melted
6 haddock fillets
1/4 tsp. paprika

Mix bread crumbs, onion, oregano and cheese. Add soup; blend. Add 3 tablespoons margarine into mixture. Place the stuffing in baking pan; arrange fillets on top. Add paprika to remaining margarine; brush fillets with mixture. Bake in 350-degree oven until fish flakes easily. Yield: 6 servings.

HADDOCK WITH PINEAPPLE

1 c. drained pineapple chunks
2 c. flaked cooked haddock
6 tbsp. cream
1/2 tsp. salt
1/8 tsp. pepper
1 c. mashed potatoes
1 egg, beaten
2 tbsp. milk
1/8 tsp. paprika
1/4 c. grated Cheddar cheese

Arrange pineapple in buttered casserole. Combine fish, cream, salt and pepper; mix well. Spread over pineapple. Combine potatoes, egg, milk and paprika; beat until fluffy. Spread over fish. Bake at 375 degrees for 20 minutes. Sprinkle with cheese. Bake for 5 minutes longer or until cheese is melted. Yield: 4 servings.

STUFFED HADDOCK FILLET

2 haddock fillets
Salt to taste
Pepper to taste
2 c. canned tomatoes
1 sm. bay leaf
3 c. soft bread crumbs
1 tbsp. butter

Place 1 fillet in shallow pan; sprinkle with salt and pepper. Cook tomatoes and bay leaf for 5 minutes in small saucepan; add salt and pepper. Combine crumbs and butter; reserve 1/2 cup crumb mixture. Add crumb mixture to tomato mixture; stir gently. Spread tomato stuffing mixture over fillet in pan; place remaining fillet over stuffing. Sprinkle with reserved crumb mixture. Bake at 375 degrees for 30 minutes. Yield: 6 servings.

EPICUREAN FINNAN HADDIE

2 lb. smoked haddock
1 tbsp. finely chopped onion
2 tbsp. finely chopped green pepper
2 tbsp. butter
1 tsp. salt
1/2 tsp. paprika
Dash of cayenne pepper
4 tbsp. flour
2 c. light cream
2 tbsp. finely chopped pimento

Soak haddock in cold water for 1 hour; drain. Cover with water in skillet; simmer for 30 minutes. Drain well; flake. Cook onion and green pepper in butter for 5 minutes or until tender. Add salt, paprika, cayenne pepper and flour; stir until blended. Add cream gradually; cook, stirring constantly, until thickened. Add haddock and pimento; simmer until heated through. Serve over toast or in potato nests.

FINNAN HADDIE CASSEROLE

1 1/2 lb. smoked haddock
1 pkg. wide egg noodles
1/2 c. milk
1 can Cheddar cheese soup
1 pkg. frozen peas
Salt and pepper
Buttered Bread Crumbs

Poach haddock in liquid to cover for 15 minutes. Drain haddock carefully; reserve liquid. Remove bones from haddock; flake into bite-sized pieces.

Prepare noodles according to package directions; drain well. Combine noodles, milk and soup in casserole; blend well. Fold in haddock; add reserved liquid to desired consistency. Bake at 350 degrees for 20 minutes; stir in peas. Season with salt and pepper; top with crumbs. Bake for 20 minutes longer.

BATTER-FRIED HADDOCK

1 c. flour
2 tbsp. baking powder
Salt to taste
1 egg, separated
1 tbsp. melted butter
2 lb. halibut fillet

Sift flour, baking powder and salt into bowl. Drop egg yolk in center; add 1/2 cup lukewarm water and butter. Mix well. Beat egg white until stiff peaks form; fold into flour mixture. Dip fish into batter. Fry in hot fat at 365 degrees for 4 to 6 minutes.

PAN-FRIED HADDOCK FILLETS

1 lb. haddock fillets
1/4 c. shortening
1/3 c. milk
1 tbsp. mustard
1 tsp. seasoning salt
1/3 c. fine dry cracker crumbs
1 tsp. paprika
1/8 tsp. pepper
Golden Tartar Sauce

Cut haddock into serving pieces. Heat shortening in large skillet. Combine milk and mustard in small mixing bowl. Mix salt, cracker crumbs, paprika and pepper together. Dip pieces of haddock into milk mixture; roll in crumb mixture. Fry in hot shortening for 8 to 10 minutes or until pieces are browned and cooked through. Place on heated serving platter; garnish with parsley sprigs, lemon and cucumber slices. Serve with Golden Tartar Sauce.

Golden Tartar Sauce

1/3 c. mayonnaise
1 tbsp. mustard
3 tbsp. finely diced celery
1 tbsp. finely diced dill pickle
1 tbsp. diced pimento
1 tbsp. finely diced green pepper
2 tsp. instant minced onion

Mix mayonnaise, mustard, celery, pickle, pimento, green pepper and onion together in a bowl. Chill well.

DEEP-FRIED HADDOCK FILLETS

2 lb. shortening
1 lb. haddock fillets
Salt to taste
1/2 c. flour
1 egg, slightly beaten
Fine bread crumbs

Melt shortening in deep fat fryer at 370 degrees. Season fillets with salt; roll in flour. Beat egg with 1 tablespoon water. Dip fillets into egg mixture; coat well with bread crumbs. Fry in hot shortening until golden brown; drain well.

OVEN-FRIED HADDOCK

1 tbsp. salt
1 c. milk
6 haddock fillets
1 c. fine dry bread crumbs
Melted butter

Combine salt and milk; dip fish in milk mixture. Roll in bread crumbs; place in greased shallow baking dish. Drizzle melted butter over fish. Bake at 500 degrees for 10 to 15 minutes, turning once. Sprinkle lemon juice over fish, if desired.

Pan-Fried Haddock Fillets . . . Garnish this seasoned fish dish with lemon slices and tartar sauce.

HADDOCK PUFFS

1 lb. haddock
1 egg, beaten
2/3 c. milk
3/4 c. flour
1/2 tsp. baking powder
1/2 tsp. salt

Cut haddock into bite-sized pieces. Combine egg with milk; stir in flour, baking powder and salt. Dip haddock into batter. Fry in 350-degree deep fat until golden brown. Yield: 6 servings.

CRISP-FRIED HADDOCK

2 to 3 lb. haddock fillets
1 c. shortening
2 tbsp. salt
1/2 c. cornmeal

Cut fillets into serving pieces. Heat shortening in skillet over medium heat. Mix salt and cornmeal; roll fish in cornmeal mixture. Fry in hot shortening for 3 minutes or until delicately browned.

HADDOCK LOAF

1 1-lb. cooked haddock fillet
1 c. soft bread crumbs
2 eggs, well beaten
Milk
1/3 c. heavy cream
Onion salt to taste
Salt and pepper
1 1/2 tbsp. butter
1 1/2 tbsp. flour
1/4 c. half and half
1/2 c. cooked lobster

Flake haddock; mix with bread crumbs. Combine eggs with 2/3 cup milk, heavy cream, onion salt and salt and pepper to taste; blend well. Fold egg mixture into haddock mixture. Turn into well-greased loaf pan; place pan in shallow pan of hot water. Bake at 350 degrees for 30 minutes or until knife inserted in center comes out clean. Melt butter in saucepan; blend in flour. Add 1/2 cup milk and half and half; simmer, stirring constantly, until thickened. Stir in lobster, additional salt and pepper; serve with fish loaf.

POACHED HADDOCK

1 4-lb. haddock, dressed
1/2 c. vinegar
1/2 c. melted butter
1/4 c. minced parsley
1/4 tsp. pepper

Wrap haddock completely in cheesecloth; secure cheesecloth well. Place haddock in shallow pan; add boiling salted water just to cover haddock. Add vinegar; bring to a boil. Reduce heat; simmer, covered, for 30 minutes. Remove haddock from liquid; place on heated platter. Remove cheesecloth carefully; keep haddock warm. Combine butter, parsley and pepper; pour over haddock.

Halibut

Halibut is the largest of the flatfish, sometimes weighing 100 pounds. It is prized for its firm white flesh and lack of small bones. The chicken halibut weighing under ten pounds, is especially delicate in flavor. Halibut is rich in protein and Vitamins A and D. (3 1/2 ounces halibut = 120 calories)

AVAILABILITY: Halibut is available year-round, fresh or frozen. It is usually sold in steaks but is also marketed dressed or in fillets.

BUYING: Look for steaks and fillets with firm flesh and no traces of browning or drying out around edges. If steaks and fillets are sold wrapped, the package should be moisture- and vaporproof and airtight. In buying dressed fish, look for firm, elastic flesh and shiny skin with unfaded color.

STORING: Wrap fresh fish in moistureproof paper or place in tightly covered dish; refrigerate 1-2 days. Place frozen fish in home freezer or refrigerator's frozen foods compartment until ready to use.

PREPARATION: Follow recipe directions. Halibut can be baked, broiled, steamed, boiled, or fried.

(See SEAFOOD.)

HAWAIIAN HALIBUT SALAD

4 c. cubed cooked halibut
1/2 c. diced celery
1/2 c. toasted almond halves
1/4 c. diced green pepper
1 c. canned pineapple chunks, drained
3/4 c. mayonnaise
1 1/2 tsp. curry powder
2 tbsp. shredded coconut

Combine halibut with celery, almonds, green pepper and pineapple. Blend mayonnaise with curry powder; toss with halibut mixture. Sprinkle with shredded coconut; chill before serving. Yield: 6 servings.

BAKED HALIBUT

1 can frozen cream of shrimp soup
1 1/2 lb. halibut fillets
1/2 c. dried bread crumbs
Paprika

Thaw soup. Arrange halibut fillets in buttered baking dish. Spread soup over halibut; cover with crumbs. Sprinkle paprika over top. Bake at 350 degrees for 30 minutes or until flaked easily. Yield: 4 servings.

CREAMY ONION HALIBUT

1 c. bread crumbs
2 tsp. chopped parsley
3 tbsp. grated Romano cheese
1/2 tsp. paprika
1/4 tsp. monosodium glutamate
6 halibut steaks
1/2 c. creamy onion salad dressing

Combine crumbs, parsley, cheese, paprika, monosodium glutamate. Dip steaks into salad dressing. Roll in crumb mixture; place in buttered baking dish. Bake at 500 degrees for 15 minutes or until fish flakes easily. Garnish with lemon slices. Yield: 6 servings.

CRUSTY-BAKED HALIBUT

1/2 c. butter
2 lb. halibut fillet
Salt and pepper
10 to 12 saltines

Melt 2 tablespoons butter in baking dish. Sprinkle fillets with salt and pepper on both sides; arrange fillets in single layer in baking dish. Melt remaining butter in small saucepan; break crackers into butter. Stir broken saltines into butter thoroughly to make a paste. Spread saltine paste over fillets. Bake in 375-degree oven for 40 minutes, or until fish flakes easily. Yield: 6 servings.

CHEESE-BAKED HALIBUT

2 lb. halibut steaks
1 tbsp. tarragon vinegar
Salt and pepper to taste
1/4 tsp. basil
1/3 c. fine dry bread crumbs
1 c. grated Cheddar cheese
1/4 c. melted butter

Arrange halibut steaks in greased baking dish; sprinkle with vinegar, salt, pepper, and basil. Bake at 375 degrees for 20 minutes. Remove from oven. Combine bread crumbs and cheese; spread over steaks. Sprinkle with melted butter. Return to oven; bake for 10 minutes longer or until halibut flakes easily. Place on heated serving platter; garnish with parsley. Yield: 6 servings.

Cheese-Baked Halibut . . . Top halibut steaks with a cheese-and crumb mixture.

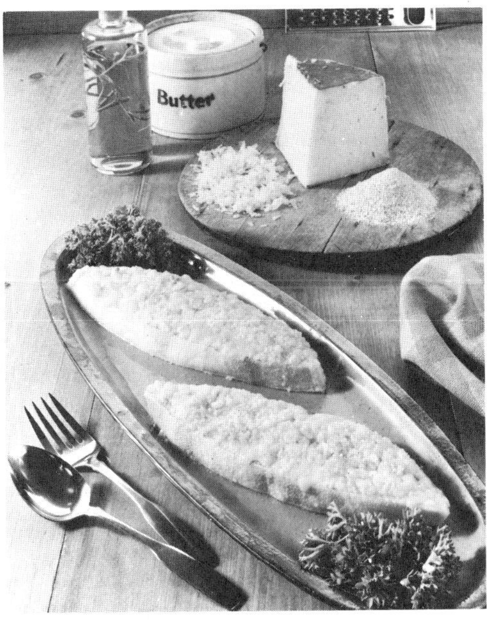

GOURMET HALIBUT WITH OYSTER SAUCE

1 1/2 to 2 lb. halibut
1/3 c. butter
1/2 pt. oysters
1/2 c. white wine
1 1/2 tbsp. flour
1/4 c. cream
1/4 tsp. salt
Cayenne pepper to taste
1/3 c. coarse cracker crumbs

Place halibut in skillet with 2 tablespoons butter; sear over low heat until halibut turns white. Place in baking dish. Cook oysters in pan drippings with wine for 3 minutes. Drain; reserve liquid. Place oysters on halibut. Melt 2 tablespoons butter in saucepan; blend in flour. Combine reserved liquid and cream. Stir into flour mixture gradually. Simmer, stirring constantly, until thickened; add seasonings. Pour sauce evenly over oysters. Melt remaining butter; stir in cracker crumbs. Spread over sauce. Bake in 400-degree oven for 20 minutes. Yield: 4 servings.

HALIBUT CREOLE

1 1/2 lb. halibut slices
Salt and pepper to taste
Tomato slices
Chopped green pepper
Chopped onion
1/3 c. melted butter

Place halibut slices in buttered baking dish; sprinkle with salt and pepper. Place 1 tomato slice on each halibut slice; top with 1/2 teaspoon green pepper and 1/2 teaspoon onion. Bake at 350 degrees for 40 to 45 minutes; baste with butter.

HALIBUT FILLETS ELEGANTE

1 can frozen cream of shrimp soup
1 1-lb. package frozen halibut fillets, thawed
Freshly ground pepper to taste
2 tbsp. butter
1/4 c. grated Parmesan cheese
Paprika to taste
1 lge. can Chinese noodles

Let soup stand until thawed. Arrange fillets in buttered 9-inch pie plate; sprinkle with pepper. Dot with butter. Spread soup over fillets; sprinkle with cheese and paprika. Bake at 400 degrees for 25 minutes. Arrange over Chinese noodles. Garnish with quartered lemons.

HALIBUT STEAKS

2 lb. halibut steaks
Salad oil
1 tsp. salt
1/4 tsp. pepper
1 c. sliced onions
1 c. cracker crumbs
2 tsp. marjoram
1 1/2 c. light cream

Wipe halibut with damp cloth; rub with small amount of salad oil. Place in baking dish; sprinkle with salt and pepper. Cook onions in small amount of fat until transparent; add crumbs and marjoram. Blend onion mixture thoroughly. Spread onion mixture over halibut; pour cream over fish and in baking dish. Bake at 375 degrees for 30 minutes. Yield: 4 servings.

HALIBUT FILLETS IN WINE

2 12-oz. packages frozen halibut fillets
1 c. butter, melted
1 tbsp. lemon juice
2 tbsp. white wine
1/4 tsp. paprika
1/2 tsp. parsley flakes
1/4 tsp. curry powder

Thaw halibut fillets; dry on absorbent paper. Combine butter, lemon juice, wine, paprika, parsley flakes and curry powder. Place fillets in 8 x 8 x 1 1/2-inch pan. Baste with butter mixture generously. Bake at 350 degrees for 15 minutes or until fish flakes easily. Baste fillets several times with butter mixture while baking. Pour off liquid from pan into any remaining butter mixture. Broil halibut for 5 minutes or until lightly brown. Remove from broiler; pour butter mixture over halibut.

HALIBUT IN TOMATOES

3 tbsp. butter
3 tbsp. flour
2 c. stewed tomatoes
1 tsp. sugar
1/4 tsp. rosemary
1/2 tsp. salt
Dash of pepper
2 lb. halibut steak
1 onion slice

Melt butter in saucepan. Add flour; blend well. Add tomatoes, sugar, rosemary, salt and pepper, stirring constantly, until thickened. Wipe halibut with damp cloth; place in baking dish with onion slice on top. Pour half the sauce over halibut. Bake in 350-degree oven for 40 minutes, basting occasionally with sauce in dish. Pour remaining sauce around halibut to serve. Garnish with parsley and olives, if desired. Yield: 6 servings.

HALIBUT NEW ORLEANS

1/4 c. butter
1 clove of garlic, minced
1/2 c. minced onions
1 can mushrooms, drained
2 tbsp. flour
2 1/2 c. tomatoes
2 tbsp. vinegar
1 tbsp. Worcestershire sauce
1 tsp. salt
1/8 tsp. pepper
1/4 tsp. thyme
1 pkg. frozen lima beans
1 1/2 lb. halibut steak, 1 in. thick

Preheat skillet. Melt butter; add garlic, onions and mushrooms. Saute for 5 minutes. Add flour; blend well. Combine tomatoes, vinegar, Worcestershire sauce, salt, pepper and thyme; add to flour mixture, stirring constantly. Bring to a boil; add beans. Cook for 5 minutes or until beans are separated. Add halibut; cover with sauce. Simmer, covered, for 30 minutes or until halibut is flaky. Yield: 4-5 servings.

HALIBUT STEAKS PARMESAN

2 lb. halibut steak
Juice of 1 lemon
2 tbsp. butter
2 tbsp. flour
1/2 tsp. nutmeg
1/2 tsp. paprika
1/2 tsp. salt
1/2 tsp. pepper
1 8-oz. can mushrooms
Milk
1/2 c. Parmesan cheese, grated

Place steaks in greased pan. Sprinkle lemon juice over steaks. Melt butter in saucepan. Stir in flour; blend well. Add nutmeg, paprika, salt and pepper. Drain mushrooms; reserve liquid. Add enough milk to reserved mushroom liquid to measure 1 cup. Add liquid to flour mixture gradually. Return to heat; cook, stirring constantly, until thickened. Pour sauce over steaks; sprinkle with mushrooms and cheese. Bake at 350 degrees for 30 minutes. Yield: 4 servings.

HALIBUT WITH CURRY SAUCE

2 lb. halibut fillets
2 1/2 oz. lime juice
4 tbsp. butter
1 lge. onion, diced
1 clove of garlic, diced
4 tbsp. flour
2 tbsp. curry powder
1/4 tsp. dry mustard
1/4 tsp. thyme
1/4 tsp. marjoram
1/2 tsp. salt
1/4 tsp. white pepper
Rind of 1/2 lemon
1 lge. ripe banana, sliced
1 lge. green apple, diced
3 stalks celery, diced
2 c. chicken broth
2 c. sauterne
2 whole cloves
2 bay leaves

Pat fillets dry with absorbent paper. Marinate for 30 minutes in lime juice. Melt butter in large heavy skillet; add onion and garlic. Saute until golden brown. Mix flour, curry powder, mustard, thyme, marjoram, salt and white pepper. Cut rind into thin strips. Combine rind and all remaining ingredients; add to curry mixture. Stir thoroughly. Add mixture to onion mixture in skillet; bring to a boil. Simmer for 10 minutes. Remove fish fillets from marinade; place in greased baking pan. Bake at 400 degrees for 10 minutes. Add curry sauce. Bake for 10 minutes longer. Remove bay leaves and cloves. Serve over unsalted, cooked rice with chutney, salted peanuts, crisp bacon chips and shredded coconut, if desired. Yield: 6-8 servings.

HALIBUT WITH VEGETABLES

2 lge. carrots, finely chopped
2 onions, minced
1 c. finely diced celery
2 lb. halibut
1 tbsp. lemon juice
1/4 tsp. pepper
1 tbsp. flour

Cook vegetables in 1 1/2 cups boiling water for 20 minutes. Drain; reserve 1 cup liquid. Brown halibut in small amount of fat in skillet. Place in greased baking pan; pour lemon juice over halibut. Sprinkle with pepper. Cover halibut with cooked vegetables; add reserved liquid. Bake at 350 degrees for 1 hour. Remove halibut to platter; arrange vegetables around halibut. Blend flour and 2 tablespoons water; mix with liquid in baking pan, stirring constantly, until thickened. Pour over halibut and vegetables to serve. Yield: 4 servings.

HALIBUT WALNUT

1 1/2 lb. halibut steak
Juice of 1 lemon
Salt and pepper

1/4 c. chopped walnuts
1/3 c. grated sharp cheese
2 tbsp. milk

Place halibut in buttered baking dish; sprinkle with lemon juice, salt and pepper. Mix walnuts with cheese and milk; season with salt and pepper. Sprinkle over halibut. Bake in 400-degree oven for 20 minutes. Yield: 4 servings.

HERBED HALIBUT BAKE

2 tbsp. butter
1 2-lb. halibut steak, 1 in. thick
1 can sliced mushrooms
1 1/2 c. sour cream
2 tbsp. flour
1 tsp. salt
1/8 tsp. pepper
1/2 tsp. savory
1/2 tsp. tarragon
Paprika to taste
Lemon slices
Chopped parsley

Preheat oven to 350 degrees. Melt butter in large casserole. Arrange halibut in casserole. Drain mushrooms; reserve liquid. Combine sour cream, flour, mushrooms, 3 tablespoons reserved mushroom liquid, salt, pepper, savory and tarragon; mix well. Spoon mixture over halibut; sprinkle with paprika. Bake for 30 minutes. Dip lemon slices into chopped parsley; arrange over baked mixture before serving. Yield: 8 servings.

NEW ENGLAND BAKED HALIBUT

Salt pork, thinly sliced
1 halibut
3 tbsp. butter
3 tbsp. flour
1/2 c. buttered cracker crumbs

Arrange several slices salt pork in 8 x 8-inch pan; place halibut over salt pork. Cream butter and flour; blend well. Spread over halibut. Sprinkle with crumbs; arrange several slices salt pork over halibut. Cover with buttered brown paper. Bake at 375 degrees for 50 minutes. Remove paper; bake until browned.

SCALLOPED HALIBUT

1 c. butter
1 c. flour
6 c. milk
1 lge. can mushrooms
Salt to taste
Celery salt to taste
Worcestershire sauce
1 bay leaf
1 sm. onion, diced
5 lb. cooked flaked halibut
Buttered crumbs

Combine butter and flour in saucepan over low heat; add milk gradually. Stir constantly until smooth and thickened. Add mushrooms, salt, celery salt, Worcestershire sauce, bay leaf and onion; blend well. Add halibut to sauce; mix gently. Spread into large greased baking dish; top with crumbs. Bake at 350 degrees for 45 minutes. Yield: 20 servings.

HALIBUT PATTIES IN CREAM SAUCE

1 1/2 lb. halibut
2 tbsp. flour
2 eggs
1 c. milk
1/2 tsp. nutmeg
Salt to taste
2 c. cream sauce
Chopped parsley to taste
Paprika to taste

Cut halibut into pieces; grind. Add flour; mix well. Beat in eggs, one at a time. Add milk, nutmeg and salt; mix well. Shape halibut mixture into rounded patties. Fry in small amount of fat until browned. Place in shallow casserole; pour cream sauce over patties. Sprinkle with parsley and paprika. Bake at 325 degrees for 30 minutes. Yield: 6 servings.

HALIBUT CAKES

1/4 lb. pork with fat
1 1/2 lb. halibut fillets, chopped
1 can water chestnuts
1 tbsp. candied ginger
3 tbsp. soy sauce
1/3 c. cornstarch
1 c. blanched almonds
1 tbsp. vegetable oil
3/4 c. canned pineapple juice
1/2 c. vinegar
1/2 c. sugar
1/3 c. chopped onion
1/3 c. chopped green pepper
1/3 c. pineapple chunks, drained

Grind pork; mix with halibut. Drain chestnuts. Chop chestnuts and ginger; add to halibut mixture. Blend 2 tablespoons soy sauce and 2 tablespoons cornstarch. Stir into halibut mixture thoroughly. Chop almonds; add to mixture with oil. Shape mixture into small cakes. Fry at 375 degrees in deep fat for 3 minutes. Combine juice, vinegar, remaining soy sauce and 2 tablespoons water. Bring juice mixture to a boil. Blend remaining cornstarch and sugar with 2 tablespoons water. Stir into juice mixture; cook, stirring constantly, until sauce is clear and thick. Stir in vegetables and pineapple. Pour sauce over halibut cakes.

HALIBUT CASSEROLE

2 lb. cooked halibut, flaked
1 tbsp. chopped onion
1 tsp. Worcestershire sauce
2 tbsp. butter
2 tbsp. flour
Pinch of salt
Pinch of pepper
1 1/2 c. milk
3 c. hot seasoned potatoes
1/2 c. grated cheese

Place halibut in greased 2-quart casserole; sprinkle with onion and Worcestershire sauce. Melt butter in saucepan; blend in flour and seasonings. Add milk gradually. Cook, stirring constantly, until thickened and smooth. Pour sauce over halibut; top with potatoes and cheese. Bake at 375 degrees for 25 minutes. Yield: 6 servings.

ITALIAN BAKED HALIBUT

1 c. chopped onions
3 lb. thick halibut fillets
1 c. chopped celery
1/2 c. chopped parsley
Salt and pepper
1/3 c. cooking oil
6 med. potatoes, peeled
2 cans tomato sauce

Sprinkle 1/2 cup onions in baking pan; place fillets over onions. Cover with remaining onions, celery, parsley, salt and pepper. Add enough water to cover fish; pour in oil. Arrange potatoes around fillets; turn potatoes to coat with liquid. Pour tomato sauce over mixture in casserole. Bake at 350 degrees for 1 hour or until fillets and potatoes are tender. Yield: 6 servings.

DEEP-FRIED FISH

Pancake flour
1 egg, beaten
1 bottle lemon-lime carbonated drink
1 lb. package frozen halibut fillets, thawed

Mix 1 cup pancake flour and egg; add enough carbonated drink to make thin batter. Roll fish in dry pancake flour; let stand for 20 minutes. Dip into batter. Heat deep fat to 375 to 400 degrees; cook halibut in fat for 3 to 4 minutes or until brown.

MARINATED FRIED HALIBUT

4 halibut steaks
1 can beer
1 egg
1/4 tsp. salt
1/8 tsp. pepper
1/2 c. fine dry bread crumbs
1/4 c. melted butter

Marinate halibut in beer for at least 30 minutes. Beat egg with salt, pepper and 1 tablespoon water in shallow bowl. Drain halibut. Dip in egg mixture; roll in crumbs. Spread on waxed paper; place in refrigerator to chill thoroughly. Arrange halibut in shallow greased baking dish; pour butter over top. Bake at 500 degrees for 12 minutes or until fish flakes easily. Yield: 4 servings.

OVEN-FRIED HALIBUT

1 tsp. salt
1/8 tsp. pepper
1 egg, beaten
1 tbsp. milk
4 halibut fillets
Cracker meal
Melted butter

Preheat oven to 350 degrees. Combine salt, pepper, egg and milk. Dip fillets in milk mixture; dredge in cracker meal. Place fillets in greased pan; brush with butter. Bake for 25 minutes. Yield: 4 servings.

PAN-FRIED HALIBUT

3 lb. halibut, salted
1/2 c. flour
1 egg
4 tbsp. milk
2 c. fine dry bread crumbs
Salt to taste

Roll halibut in flour. Combine egg and milk; beat well. Dip halibut in egg mixture. Combine crumbs and salt; coat halibut with bread crumbs. Fry in large skillet in deep hot fat for 15 minutes. Yield: 6 servings.

SOUTHERN PAN-FRIED FISH

2 to 3 lb. halibut
1 c. shortening
2 tbsp. salt
1/2 c. cornmeal

Cut halibut into serving pieces. Heat shortening in skillet over medium heat. Mix salt and cornmeal; roll fish in cornmeal mixture. Place in hot shortening in skillet; fry for 3 minutes or until delicately browned. Yield: 4 servings.

HALIBUT PUDDING

1/2 lemon, sliced
1 onion, minced
Salt to taste
1 bay leaf
1 whole allspice
1 1/2 lb. halibut
3/4 c. butter
Flour
2 c. milk
1 tsp. pepper
2 tsp. onion juice
4 eggs, separated
3 egg yolks
1 tsp. lemon juice
Cayenne pepper to taste
1/2 tsp. flour
2 tbsp. capers

Combine 4 cups boiling water, lemon, onion, salt, bay leaf and allspice; simmer halibut in liquid for 30 minutes. Remove halibut from liquid; reserve liquid. Remove skin and bones from halibut; flake. Melt 5/8 cup butter in saucepan; stir in 5/8 cup flour gradually. Add milk, pepper and onion juice gradually to flour mixture, stirring constantly, over low heat until thickened. Let cool. Stir 4 well-beaten egg yolks and halibut into cream sauce. Beat egg whites until stiff peaks form; fold into sauce. Pour into buttered ring mold; place in pan of hot water. Bake at 325 degrees for 45 minutes. Combine remaining egg yolks, butter, lemon juice, salt, cayenne pepper and 1/2 teaspoon flour; add 3/4 cup reserved liquid and capers. Pour over pudding. Yield: 7-8 servings.

MATELOTE

2 lb. halibut steaks
1 carrot, sliced
1 onion, minced
2 cloves of garlic, halved
1 tsp. salt
1/4 tsp. pepper
2 c. red wine
3 tbsp. brandy
3 tbsp. butter, melted
2 tbsp. flour

Dry halibut steaks with absorbent paper; place in skillet. Add carrot, onion, garlic, salt, pepper and wine; bring to a boil. Bring brandy to a boil in small saucepan; ignite. Pour brandy over halibut. Cover pan when flame dies; simmer halibut for 20 minutes. Remove to warm serving dish; keep hot. Strain remaining skillet mixture; reserve cooking liquid. Blend butter and flour in small skillet. Simmer, stirring constantly, until mixture is bubbly. Remove from heat; stir in reserved cooking liquid gradually. Cook over high heat, stirring constantly, until sauce thickens. Cook for 2 minutes longer; pour sauce over halibut. Serve with croutons browned in garlic butter, if desired. Yield: 4 servings.

Ham

A ham is a cut of pork from a hog's thigh. Portions of the hog's shoulder are often marketed under the names *shoulder hams* and *picnic hams.* Although these are not "true" hams cut from the thigh, they are similar in flavor and in preparation method. In this encyclopedia, shoulder and picnic hams are included under "ham". Most hams sold in America are mildly cured; many are smoked for a rich, mellow flavor. Ham is high in protein, iron, phosphorus, calcium, and B vitamins. (3 oz. lean and fat meat = 290 calories)

AVAILABILITY: Ham is available year-round wrapped in cellophane, prepackaged, or canned. Ham may be sold whole; cut into the butt half, the thicker, upper part of the thigh; cut into the shank half, the thinner, lower part of the thigh; or cut into slices.

BUYING: Read the label on the wrapper, package, or can. The label tells you the kind of ham packaged and how to cook it. Hams may be sold as: *fully cooked*—completely cooked and ready-to-eat or may be reheated; *ready-to-eat*—no cooking necessary but flavor improved by cooking; and as *cook before eating*—must cook ham before eating. Canned hams are ready to eat but may be reheated.

STORING: Refrigerate (in original wrapper) uncooked, whole hams and uncooked, whole picnics 2 weeks; uncooked half hams 1 week; cooked whole picnics 1 week; sliced ham 3 days. Refrigerate unopened canned hams and canned picnics until ready to use. Refrigerate opened cans and use meat within a few days. Freezing is not recommended for cured ham because the fat of salted meat becomes rancid if frozen.

PREPARATION: Uncooked hams may be baked for full flavor or may be cooked in water for a milder flavor. *To bake uncooked hams*—Season with salt and pepper if desired. Place ham, fat side up, on rack in open roasting pan. Insert thermometer into center of thickest part. Do not cover and use no water. Do not baste. Bake in slow oven until done. After baking, pour off drippings and remove rind. Score and glaze ham if desired. *To score*—Cut fat, 1/4-inch deep, to make diamond shapes. *To glaze*—Spread glaze evenly over scored ham. Bake ham in hot oven 15 to 20 minutes, until glaze forms brown coating. Some suggested easy glazes are: 1 cup brown sugar and 2 tablespoons flour; 1 cup brown sugar and 1 tablespoon dry mustard; 1 cup honey; 1/2 cup orange, peach, or apricot marmalade; 3/4 cup crushed pineapple and 1 cup brown sugar; 1 cup cranberry or currant jelly. *To water-cook uncooked ham*—Place ham in large pot and cover with water. When water boils, reduce heat. Simmer until thoroughly cooked; medium ham, 18 to 20 minutes per pound; picnic ham 35 to 45 minutes per pound; *To broil precooked ham slices*—Preheat broiler. Slash edges of ham fat to prevent curling. Place ham slices on broiler rack. Place in oven so that ham is 3 inches from heat. Cook 5 to 10 minutes on each side, depending on thickness of slices. *To pan-broil or pan-fry cooked ham slices*—Rub skillet lightly with fat. Place thin ham slices in skillet. Cook slowly until brown, 5 to 10 minutes depending on thickness of slices. Turn and brown other side. *To heat cooked hams*—Heat uncovered in slow oven about 10 minutes per pound, or to an internal temperature of 130 degrees on a meat thermometer.

(See PORK and CARVING.)

CRANBERRY-HAM ROLL-UPS

1 c. jellied cranberry sauce
1 tsp. grated onion
1/4 c. chopped celery
1 c. coarse saltine crumbs
12 slices boiled ham

Combine cranberry sauce, onion, celery and crumbs; blend well. Spread 1 tablespoonful on each ham slice 1 inch from edge; roll up. Chill. Slice each roll into thirds.

CREAMY DIP

1 8-oz. package cream cheese
1/2 c. ground ham
1 tsp. lemon juice
1 tsp. minced onion
1/3 c. chili sauce

Combine all ingredients; blend well. Serve at room temperature with chips or crackers.

DEVILED HAM DIP

1 1-lb. carton cottage cheese
1 sm. can deviled ham
1/2 env. dry onion soup mix

Process cottage cheese in blender until smooth. Turn into bowl; stir in remaining ingredients. Serve with corn chips.

FROSTED SANDWICH LOAF

8 slices bread
8 slices whole wheat bread
Butter
1 recipe ham salad
1 recipe egg salad
2 8-oz. packages cream cheese
4 to 5 tbsp. milk

Trim crusts from bread. Slices should be uniform. Butter 1 side of each slice. Arrange 4 slices wheat bread, buttered side up, on serving platter; spread with ham salad. Top with 4 slices white bread; spread with egg salad. Spread remaining wheat bread with ham salad; place, salad side down, on egg salad. Spread top with egg salad; cover with remaining white bread. Keep stacks even. Cover loaf with slightly damp cloth; weigh with folded heavy towel. Chill for 1 hour. Beat cream cheese with milk until smooth and fluffy. Frost loaf; chill for 2 hours. Cut into 12 slices.

HAM BALLS

1/2 c. ground cooked ham
6 hard-cooked eggs, chopped
1 tbsp. minced chives
Pepper to taste
1/4 c. mayonnaise
1 1/3 c. chopped walnuts

Combine ham, eggs, chives, pepper, mayonnaise and 2/3 cup walnuts. Mix well; shape into small balls. Roll balls in remaining walnuts; chill.

HAM-STUFFED CHERRY TOMATOES

1 pt. cherry tomatoes
2 2 1/2-oz. cans deviled ham
2 tbsp. sour cream
2 tbsp. horseradish

Slice tops from tomatoes; remove pulp. Drain shells upside down on paper towels. Combine ham, cream and horseradish; fill tomatoes. Refrigerate. Garnish with parsley.

HOT HAM BOUCHEES

2 tbsp. butter
1 peeled tomato, thinly sliced
2 tbsp. finely chopped green onion
1/2 c. finely chopped ham
2 eggs, slightly beaten
30 sm. bread rounds
Parmesan cheese

Melt butter in large frying pan; saute tomato for 5 minutes. Add onion, ham and eggs; cook over low heat, stirring, until thickened. Cool. Heap ham mixture on bread rounds; sprinkle with Parmesan cheese. Broil until lightly browned. Serve immediately.

MINIATURE CREAM PUFFS

6 tbsp. butter
3/4 c. sifted flour
3 eggs
4 tbsp. minced green pepper
1 c. ground ham
2 tsp. prepared mustard
4 tbsp. mayonnaise
2 tbsp. minced onion

Bring butter and 3/4 cup water to a boil. Reduce heat; add flour all at once, stirring rapidly. Cook, stirring constantly, until mixture thickens and leaves side of pan. Remove from heat. Add eggs, one at a time, beating well after each addition. Beat until mixture is glossy. Drop from teaspoon onto ungreased baking sheets. Bake at 425 degrees for 20 to 30 minutes or until lightly browned. Cool. Combine remaining ingredients. Refrigerate. Fill cream puffs just before serving. Yield: 4 1/2 dozen.

PARTY SANDWICH LOAF

4 hard-cooked eggs, minced
1/2 tsp. curry powder
Mayonnaise
1 c. ground cooked ham
1/2 c. minced celery
2 ripe avocados, mashed
2 tbsp. tart French dressing
1 sm. round loaf Italian bread
Softened butter or margarine
2 tomatoes, thinly sliced
8 oz. cream cheese
Cream
Sliced stuffed olives
Sprigs of parsley

Mix eggs, curry powder and enough mayonnaise to moisten. Combine ham and celery; moisten with additional mayonnaise. Blend avocados and French dressing. Cut bread into 4 slices; spread each slice with butter. Spread bottom slice with ham mixture; top with second slice bread. Spread with egg mixture; cover with tomatoes. Top with third slice; spread with avocado mixture. Replace top bread slice. Cream cheese; stir in cream until fluffy and of spreading consistency. Beat until smooth; frost loaf. Garnish with olives and parsley; cut in wedges to serve.

FRENCH-TOASTED HAM AND CHEESE

6 thin slices ham
6 thin slices cheese
12 thin slices bread
3 eggs, beaten
1/2 c. milk
1/4 tsp. salt
Butter

Make 6 sandwiches of ham, cheese and bread. Mix eggs, milk and salt in flat dish; dip each sandwich into egg mixture, coating completely. Saute sandwiches slowly in butter in skillet on both sides until heated through and golden brown.

MEXICAN-STYLE HAM AND CHEESE IN BUN

Ground ham
1 lb. Cheddar cheese, grated
1 clove of garlic, minced
1 can green chili peppers, chopped
2 sm. onions, grated
1/2 c. salad dressing
1 can chopped olives
1 can tomato sauce
2 tbsp. vinegar
Frankfurter buns

Mix first 9 ingredients in order given; stuff buns with mixture. Wrap buns in foil. Bake at 350 degrees for 30 minutes. Sandwiches may be made ahead and frozen. Bake when ready to serve.

HAM SOUP WITH DUMPLINGS

3 med. potatoes, diced
6 c. ham broth
1 c. diced cooked ham
1 egg, beaten
1 tbsp. milk
1 c. flour
Salt and pepper

Cook potatoes in ham broth until tender; add ham. Combine egg and milk; add flour to make stiff dough. Roll on floured surface; cut in 1-inch squares. Drop into boiling ham broth; cook, covered, for 10 minutes. Add salt and pepper to taste. Add boiling water if necessary.

HAM SUPPER SOUP

1 hambone
1 1/2 c. dried split peas
1 1/2 c. cubed carrots
1/2 c. chopped onion
1 1/2 c. cubed potatoes
1/2 c. chopped celery

Cover hambone with 2 quarts water in large kettle; simmer, covered, for 1 hour and 30 minutes. Add peas, carrots and onion; simmer for 1 hour longer. Add potatoes and celery. Remove bone; cut off meat. Return meat to kettle; simmer for 15 to 20 minutes longer.

HEARTY HAM AND VEGETABLE SOUP

2 c. navy beans
2 tsp. soda
1 meaty hambone
2 c. diced potatoes
2 c. diced carrots
Peas, corn, or onion to taste

Cook beans with soda in 3 cups water; drain. Bring to a boil in clear water twice; drain each time. Cook beans with hambone in 2 quarts water in large kettle until beans are tender; remove hambone from broth. Cut meat from bone in bite-sized pieces. Place potatoes and carrots in broth; cook for 10 minutes longer. Add remaining vegetables as desired; cook for 10 minutes longer. Return ham to soup; add water, if necessary. Bring to a boil; serve. Soup freezes well.

VEGETABLE-HAM SOUP

1 meaty hambone
1 sm. onion, sliced
1/2 c. chopped celery
Parsley to taste
1/2 tsp. salt
1/8 tsp. freshly ground pepper
4 carrots, diced
4 potatoes, cubed
1 can tomato sauce
1/2 c. noodles
1 c. frozen mixed vegetables

Cover hambone with 3 quarts water in large kettle; bring slowly to a boil. Add onion, celery, parsley, salt and pepper; reduce heat. Simmer, covered, for 1 hour. Add carrots and potatoes; simmer, covered, for 15 minutes longer. Remove hambone; cool. Stir tomato sauce into broth. Cut meat from bone in bite-sized pieces; return to broth. Add noodles and frozen vegetables; simmer for 30 minutes longer or until noodles and vegetables are tender.

BUFFET HAM RING

1 can tomato soup
2 tbsp. unflavored gelatin
1 3-oz. package cream cheese
2 tbsp. lemon juice
1 tbsp. grated onion
1/2 c. mayonnaise
2 tbsp. prepared mustard
2 c. cooked ground ham

Combine soup and 3/4 cup water; heat through. Remove from heat. Soften gelatin in 1/2 cup cold water; stir into soup mixture. Add cream cheese. Beat until smooth; cool. Add lemon juice, onion, mayonnaise, mustard and ham. Rinse ring mold with cold water; pour in ham mixture. Chill for 3 to 4 hours. Unmold on salad leaves; garnish with hard-cooked eggs and stuffed olives.

FROZEN HAM SALAD

1 tbsp. unflavored gelatin
4 tbsp. mayonnaise
2 tbsp. horseradish
2 c. ground ham
10 ripe olives, minced
2 c. heavy cream, whipped

Soften gelatin in 1/4 cup cold water; dissolve in 1/4 cup boiling water. Add mayonnaise, horseradish, ham and olives; fold in cream. Pour into refrigerator tray; freeze for 3 to 4 hours. Serve on lettuce. Garnish with mayonnaise and additional olives if desired.

PARTY HAM RING

1 env. unflavored gelatin
1 c. sour cream
1/2 c. mayonnaise
3 tbsp. vinegar
1/4 tsp. salt
Pepper to taste
1 1/2 c. diced cooked ham
1 c. sliced celery
1/4 c. chopped parsley
3 tbsp. chopped green onion

Soften gelatin in 1/4 cup water in saucepan; bring to a boil. Blend in sour cream, mayonnaise, vinegar, salt and pepper. Chill until thickened; whip until fluffy. Fold in remaining ingredients; pour into 5 1/2-cup ring mold. Chill until firm.

HAM AND EGG SALAD

6 hard-cooked eggs
1 1/2 c. diced cooked ham
1/2 c. diced celery
1/2 c. sliced gherkins
1/3 c. mayonnaise
2 tbsp. mustard
1 tbsp. lemon juice
Salt and pepper to taste

Dice eggs coarsely; add ham, celery and gherkins. Blend mayonnaise, mustard and lemon juice; add to ham mixture, tossing lightly. Season with salt and pepper. Chill.

HAM-PINEAPPLE SALAD

2 c. ham strips
1 sm. can pineapple chunks, drained
1 1/2 c. cooked rice
1/2 c. chopped celery
1/4 c. mayonnaise
1/2 c. slivered almonds
2 tbsp. French dressing
1 tsp. instant minced onion

Combine all ingredients; toss lightly until well coated. Serve on lettuce leaves.

CURRIED HAM

1 1/2 c. lemon juice
1 green pepper, finely chopped
1 c. finely chopped onions
1/2 c. finely chopped parsley
Dash of hot pepper sauce
1 tbsp. Worcestershire sauce
2 tsp. sugar
2 tsp. curry powder
1 6-lb. boneless ham

Combine all ingredients except ham; mix well. Marinate ham in sauce for at least 6 hours or overnight; turn ham occasionally. Place ham on rack in baking pan. Strain marinade; reserve. Bake at 300 degrees for 4 hours or until ham is tender, basting frequently with marinade. Garnish as desired.

BAKED COUNTRY HAM

1 country ham
2 c. brown sugar
1 tbsp. mustard
Sweet pickle juice
Whole cloves

Trim mold from ham; soak ham overnight in cold water. Seal in brown paper bag; place in roaster. Bake in 260-degree oven for 30 minutes per pound. Remove ham from bag. Remove rind; score fat. Combine brown sugar, mustard and enough juice to make a thick paste. Spread over ham; stud with cloves. Brown at 450 degrees.

HAM BAKED IN WINE

1/2 tbsp. chopped parsley
1/2 tbsp. garlic powder
1 tbsp. dry mustard
6 tbsp. brown sugar
1/2 tsp. thyme
1/2 tsp. marjoram
1 tsp. ground cloves
1/4 c. herb wine vinegar
1 bay leaf
1 ham
1 1/2 c. white wine

Combine all ingredients except bay leaf, ham and wine; mix to a smooth paste. Place bay leaf in bottom of pan; place ham on top bay leaf. Spread paste over ham. Pour wine around ham. Bake at 300 degrees for 15 minutes per pound of ham; baste frequently with pan juices.

HONEY-HAM PIQUANTE

1 10-lb. ham
6 whole cloves
1/2 c. cider vinegar
2 c. pickled peach juice
1 c. honey
1 c. brown sugar
1 c. diced oranges
1 c. diced pineapple
1 c. white grapes, seeded

Remove rind from ham; score fat. Place ham, fat side up, in roaster. Insert cloves in ham. Combine vinegar and peach juice; pour over ham. Spread ham with honey; sprinkle with brown sugar. Bake at 300 degrees for 1 hour. Bake, covered, for 2 hours; baste frequently with pan liquid. Add fruits; bake for 1 hour longer or until ham is tender. Serve sliced ham with fruit sauce.

HAM WITH APRICOT-PECAN STUFFING

1 10 to 12-lb. whole cooked ham
1 1/2 c. coarsely chopped dried apricots
1 c. finely chopped pecans
1 8 1/2-oz. can crushed pineapple
1/4 tsp. dried thyme
1 12-oz. can apricot nectar
1/2 tsp. allspice
1/2 c. honey

Bone ham; prepare cavity for stuffing by removing about 1/2 pound lean ham. Grind 1 cup ham. Combine ground ham, apricots, pecans, pineapple and thyme; mix well. Spoon into cavity in ham. Cover end with foil; skewer in place. Place in baking dish. Pour apricot nectar over ham; sprinkle with allspice. Cover tightly with foil. Bake at 325 degrees for 2 hours. Remove foil; spread half the honey over ham. Bake for 30 minutes longer. Brush with remaining honey; bake for 30 minutes longer or until golden brown and glazed.

HAM WITH CORN BREAD STUFFING

1 14 to 15-lb. ham
2 pkg. corn bread mix
6 tbsp. margarine
1 1/2 c. chopped celery
1 c. chopped onion
1 1/2 c. orange juice
1 egg, beaten
Seasoned salt
3/4 c. light corn syrup
2 tsp. soy sauce
1 11-oz. can mandarin oranges, drained

Bone ham; leave pocket for stuffing. Prepare and bake corn bread mix according to package directions. Cool; crumble into large bowl. Melt margarine in skillet; saute celery and onion. Add to bread crumbs; stir in 3/4 cup orange juice, egg and 1 teaspoon seasoned salt. Sprinkle ham inside and out with seasoned salt. Stuff pocket with dressing; cover opening with foil. Place in baking pan. Bake at 325 degrees for 2 hours. Combine remaining orange juice, corn syrup and soy sauce. Score ham; brush with sauce. Reduce oven temperature to 300 degrees; bake ham for 3 hours and 30 minutes to 4 hours longer, basting frequently with sauce. Let ham stand for 10 minutes; remove foil. Place on platter; garnish with oranges.

BAKED HAM

1 12-lb. ham
1 c. (packed) brown sugar
1 tbsp. dry mustard
1/2 c. spiced fruit juice
Whole cloves

Preheat oven to 350 degrees. Insert meat thermometer into center of ham. Bake until meat thermometer registers 130 degrees. Remove rind; score fat. Combine brown sugar, mustard and fruit juice; spread over ham. Insert cloves in scored ham fat. Return to oven for 15 to 20 minutes or until ham is glazed.

Baked Ham . . . A southern-style meal of clove-studded and glazed ham with candied yams.

STUFFED HAM SUPREME

1 lb. saltine crackers, crumbled
1 loaf sliced bread
3 med. onions, minced
1/2 lb. suet, ground
2 tbsp. sugar
1/2 c. minced celery
1 tbsp. mustard seed
2 tbsp. dry mustard
1/4 c. snipped parsley
1 9-oz. jar sweet pickle relish
4 eggs, well beaten
1/2 tsp. hot sauce
1 1/2 c. cider vinegar
1 10 to 12-lb. boneless cooked ham
1/2 c. apricot preserves, melted

Combine fine cracker crumbs and bread in large bowl; add onions, suet, sugar, celery, mustard seed, dry mustard, parsley and relish. Stir in eggs, hot sauce and vinegar. Place ham in large roasting pan. Make lengthwise cut through top center of ham halfway; spread halves apart. Fill cut with part of crumb mixture; pat remaining crumb mixture over top of ham. Bake, uncovered, in 350-degree oven for 1 hour. Brush crust with melted apricot preserves. Bake for 15 minutes longer. Cool. Refrigerate ham for 2 days before serving.

GLAZED HAM

Color photograph for this recipe on page 71.

1 10-lb. ham
Whole cloves
2 c. pickled peach juice
1/2 c. cider vinegar
1 c. honey
1 c. (packed) brown sugar

Remove rind from ham, leaving thin layer of fat. Score fat; stud with cloves. Place ham, fat side up, in roaster. Blend peach juice and vinegar; pour over ham. Spread honey over top; sprinkle with brown sugar. Bake at 300 degrees for 1 hour. Cover; bake for 3 hours longer or until ham is tender, basting frequently. Serve with cooked yams and apples.

HAM AND PINEAPPLE

6 baked sweet potatoes
Butter
Salt and pepper to taste
Pinch of nutmeg
Milk
1 No. 2 can pineapple chunks
2 c. cubed cooked ham
1/2 c. chopped green pepper
2 tbsp. (packed) brown sugar
1 tbsp. cornstarch
2 tbsp. vinegar

Mash sweet potatoes with 1 tablespoon butter, salt, pepper, nutmeg and milk. Drain pineapple; reserve liquid. Saute ham in 2 tablespoons butter; add green pepper and pineapple. Cook for 2 to 3 minutes; stir in brown sugar and cornstarch. Add 3/4 cup reserved liquid and vinegar; cook, stirring constantly, until thickened. Pour into 9-inch pie plate; drop potatoes by spoonfuls on top. Bake in 400-degree oven until bubbling hot.

HAM WITH POTATO DRESSING

1 12 to 14-lb. ham
2 c. diced boiled potatoes
3 c. corn bread crumbs
1 onion, chopped
4 hard-boiled eggs, chopped
1/2 tsp. salt
1 tsp. pepper
Sage to taste

Place ham in large kettle; cover with water. Bring to a boil. Reduce heat; simmer for 3 to 4 hours or until tender. Drain ham; reserve 1 quart broth. Place ham in large roaster. Bake at 350 degrees until browned. Combine potatoes, corn bread crumbs, onion, eggs and seasonings in large bowl; stir in reserved ham broth. Spoon into baking dish. Bake at 350 degrees for 30 minutes or until lightly browned.

HAM-EGG CASSEROLE

3 tbsp. butter
3 tbsp. flour
1 c. milk
1 c. ground cooked ham
1/4 c. grated carrots
1/8 c. minced celery
1 tbsp. parsley flakes
Dash of salt
3 eggs, separated

Melt butter in saucepan; stir in flour until smooth. Add milk gradually, stirring constantly until smooth and thickened. Add ham, carrots, celery, parsley and salt to sauce. Beat egg yolks slightly. Add small amount of sauce to yolks; stir well. Return mixture to sauce; blend until smooth. Beat egg whites until stiff peaks form; fold into ham mixture. Spoon mixture into ungreased 1 1/2-quart baking dish. Place dish in shallow pan of water. Bake at 300 degrees for 1 hour.

HAM-APPLE CASSEROLE

3 c. ground cooked ham
1/2 tsp. dry mustard
1 tbsp. grated onion
1 egg
1/2 c. milk
1 c. bread crumbs
2 med. apples
1/4 c. (packed) brown sugar
2 tbsp. butter

Combine ham, mustard, onion, egg, milk and crumbs; place in greased baking dish. Peel, core and slice apples 1/2 inch thick; arrange slices to overlap on top of mixture around edge of dish. Sprinkle with brown sugar; dot with butter. Bake at 375 degrees for 40 minutes or until apples are browned and tender.

HAM AND SWISS PUFF

2 c. ground cooked ham
2 c. grated Swiss cheese
1/2 c. mayonnaise
1 tsp. mustard
12 slices bread toasted
6 eggs
2 1/4 c. milk

Combine ham and cheese in medium bowl; blend in mayonnaise and mustard. Spread mixture on 6 toast slices; top with remaining toast to make sandwiches. Cut each sandwich diagonally into quarters; stand, crust edge down, in 13 x 9 x 2-inch buttered baking dish. Beat eggs slightly with milk in medium bowl; pour over sandwiches. Cover; chill for at least 4 hours or overnight. Bake at 325 degrees for 35 minutes or until custard sets. Cut between sandwiches to serve.

Ham Kabobs and Rice Salad . . . An elegant main dish of ham and honeydew melon balls.

HAM KABOBS AND RICE SALAD

1 1 1/2-lb. can smoked ham
Honeydew balls
1/4 c. tarragon vinegar
1/4 c. salad oil
1 tbsp. lemon juice
1/2 tsp. salt
1/2 tsp. dry mustard
Dash of pepper
6 c. cooked cold rice
1/4 c. minced parsley

Cut ham into 1-inch cubes. Alternate ham cubes and melon balls on bamboo skewers. Combine vinegar, oil, lemon juice and seasonings in jar with tight-fitting lid. Shake thoroughly until blended. Chill. Spoon rice into serving dish; sprinkle with parsley. Pour dressing over rice, tossing lightly. Arrange ham kabobs over rice; serve. Yield: 6 servings.

CHERRY-CROWNED HAM LOAF

1 1/2 c. rye bread crumbs
1/2 c. milk
1 lb. ground ham
1 lb. ground pork
2 tbsp. chopped onion
1/3 c. snipped parsley
1 tsp. mustard
2 eggs, beaten
1 16-oz. can pitted sour cherries
4 tsp. cornstarch
2 tbsp. sugar
1/4 tsp. salt
1/8 tsp. cinnamon
1/8 tsp. nutmeg
1/4 tsp. red food coloring

Combine bread crumbs and milk in large bowl; add ham, pork, onion, parsley, mustard and eggs. Mix well; pack into 1 1/2-quart round baking dish. Bake for 1 hour at 325 to 350 degrees. Drain cherries; reserve syrup. Add enough water to syrup to measure 1 cup liquid. Place liquid in saucepan; stir in cornstarch, sugar, salt, cinnamon and nutmeg. Cook over medium heat, stirring constantly, until thickened and clear; add cherries and food coloring. Cook until heated through. Pour drippings from baking dish. Unmold ham loaf on platter. Top with small amount of cherry sauce. Serve with remaining sauce.

HAM LOGS WITH RAISIN SAUCE

1 lb. ground ham
1/2 lb. ground pork
3/4 c. milk
1/2 c. oats
1 egg
2 tsp. horseradish
1/2 tsp. salt
Dash of pepper
1 tbsp. cornstarch
2 tbsp. lemon juice
2 tbsp. vinegar
1/2 c. (packed) brown sugar
1/2 c. seedless raisins

Combine ham, pork, milk, oats, egg, horseradish, salt and pepper. Shape into six or seven logs. Place in baking dish. Blend cornstarch and 3/4 cup cold water in saucepan; add remaining ingredients. Cook, stirring constantly, until mixture comes to a boil; pour over ham logs. Bake at 350 degrees for 35 to 40 minutes.

POLYNESIAN HAM CUBES

1 11-oz. can mandarin oranges
1 13 1/2-oz. can pineapple chunks
2 tbsp. cornstarch
1/4 tsp. cinnamon
2 tsp. soy sauce
1/4 tsp. ground ginger
2 tsp. chopped onion
2 tbsp. chopped green pepper
1 lb. cooked ham, cubed
1 c. sliced cooked celery

Drain oranges and pineapple; reserve liquids. Add enough water to measure 2 cups. Combine cornstarch and cinnamon in saucepan; add fruit liquid, soy sauce, ginger, onion and green pepper. Cook, stirring constantly, until thickened. Add ham, fruits and celery. Simmer until heated through. Serve over rice.

BARBECUED HAM SLICES

1 c. brown sugar
3 tbsp. catsup
1 tbsp. soy sauce
1 tsp. dry mustard
2 tbsp. green pepper flakes
1 c. crushed pineapple
1 1/2 tbsp. cornstarch
3/4 to 1-in. thick ready-to-eat ham slices

Combine 1 cup water and brown sugar in saucepan. Add catsup, soy sauce, mustard, pepper flakes and pineapple. Bring to a boil; simmer for 10 minutes. Dissolve cornstarch in 1/4 cup cold water; add to sauce. Cook, stirring, until sauce is clear and thickened. Cook ham on grill over hot coals for about 8 minutes; baste frequently with sauce. Serve with additional sauce.

FAVORITE HAM STEAKS

1/4 c. butter
1 c. chopped onion
1 1/3 c. mincemeat
1/4 c. lemon juice
2 1-in. thick ham steaks

Melt butter in large skillet; add onion. Cook until golden brown; stir in mincemeat, lemon juice and 1/4 cup water. Bring just to a boil. Slash fat on steaks; place 1 steak in 13 x 9 x 2-inch baking dish. Spread with 1/2 of the sauce. Top with remaining steak; spread with remaining sauce. Bake at 325 degrees for 1 hour and 15 minutes.

OLD VIRGINIA HAM WITH RED-EYE GRAVY

1 lge. 1/2-in. thick ham slice
1/8 tsp. salt
1/2 c. strong coffee

Slash fat on edge of ham in several places. Place ham in hot skillet; brown quickly on one side. Turn; brown lightly on other side. Simmer, covered, for 15 minutes or until tender. Remove from pan; place on heated platter. Sprinkle salt in hot skillet; add coffee. Boil for 2 minutes. Pour over ham. Serve with biscuits. Yield: 4 servings.

HAM COOKED IN OPEN FIRE

4 1-in. thick slices cooked ham
2 fresh tomatoes
Salt and pepper
4 tbsp. margarine
1/2 c. grated Parmesan cheese

Place ham on 4 pieces of foil. Cut tomatoes into 1/4-inch thick slices. Cover ham with tomatoes. Add seasonings and margarine; seal foil. Place on bed of hot coals; cook for 30 minutes or until ham is heated through. Sprinkle each serving with cheese just before serving.

HARVEST HAM SAUCE

2/3 c. apple butter
1 tbsp. grated orange rind
1 1-in. thick ham slice

Combine apple butter and grated orange rind. Place ham on rack in roasting pan. Spread apple butter mixture on top surface of ham. Bake at 300 degrees for 1 hour.

Herbs & Spices

Herbs and spices add greatly to the seasoning or flavoring of almost any dish. *Spices* are vegetable substances from plants containing woody tissue. Spices are dried before they are sold; many are available in both whole and powdered form. Whole spices ground immediately before use are more powerful than are those powdered before sale. *Herbs* are parts of seed plants that do not contain woody tissue. They are available fresh, dried, or powdered. Freshly-picked and crushed herbs have the best flavor; dried herbs are four times as powerful as fresh ones; powdered herbs are twice as powerful as dried ones or eight times stronger than fresh ones.

STORING: Dried and powdered herbs and powdered spices should be stored in a cool, dark place as their flavors change if they are exposed to extremes in temperature or to sunshine. Seeds, such as caraway or celery, should be stored in the refrigerator to prevent their becoming rancid. Fresh herbs should be checked periodically as they may lose flavor over long periods of time. Consult the table that follows to determine which herbs and spices will best complement the foods you are preparing. As a general rule, only one dish in any single meal should be seasoned with herbs or spices.

HERB OR SPICE	CHARACTERISTICS AND USES
Allspice	A spice native to the Americas that tastes like a blend of cloves, cinnamon, and nutmeg. Available whole or powdered. Use in meat broths; pickling liquids; gravies; fruit cakes and pies; sweet yellow vegetables and tomatoes.
Basil	A delicate fragrant herb especially popular in French and Italian cookery. Available in leaf form. Use in tomato-based dishes; veal, beef, pork, lamb, and seafood; peas, string beans, potatoes, and spinach.
Bay leaf	A spice that is the aromatic leaf of the laurel tree. It is a staple seasoning in Mediterranean cookery. Available whole. Use in stews and with meats, potatoes, soups, sauces, and fish. Remove leaf before serving foods.
Caraway seed	The hard, brown seed from a plant of the parsley family. This spice is available whole. Use in rye breads and other baked goods; with pork, sauerkraut, soups, meats, and stews.
Celery seed	An herb that is the fruit of wild celery. Available whole or as celery salt. Use with fish; in soups, stews, juices, salads, and sauerkraut.
Chervil	A member of the parsley family and a fines herbes of French cookery. Available whole. Use in salads, sauces, omelets, and soups.
Chive	A herbaceous member of the onion family, chive has a mild, piquant flavor. Available whole, dried, or freeze-dried. Use in almost any salad, vegetable, meat dish; in soups, stews, gravies, and combination dishes.
Cinnamon	(See CINNAMON.)
Cloves	A sharply-flavored spice once so precious that wars were fought over it. Available powdered or whole. Use whole cloves to stud ham and pork, in pickling, and in syrups and stews. Use powdered cloves in baked goods and desserts; on boiled beets, sweet potatoes, onions, and winter squash.
Dill	A strong-flavored herb that belongs to the parsley family. Available as dillseed or dillweed. Use seed in pickles, meats, fish, sauces, salads, and sauerkraut. Use weed in salads, sandwiches, and appetizer mixtures. Use sparingly.
Ginger	(See GINGER.)
Marjoram	An herb closely related to oregano and a member of the mint family. Leaves are available whole or ground. Use with lima beans, peas, green beans; lamb, mutton, poultry; and in Italian cookery.
Mustard	A spice that in its powdered form has no aroma but when mixed with water, grape juice, or other liquid takes on a pungent aroma and sharp flavor. Available as prepared mustard and in powdered and whole forms. Use with meat, fish, poultry; in sauces, salad dressings, cheese, and egg dishes; with boiled beets, cabbage and sauerkraut; in pickling.
Nutmeg	(See NUTMEG.)
Oregano	A member of the mint family, this herb is also called "wild marjoram." Available whole and ground. Use in preparing pizza and other Italian-style dishes; with meats, fish, cheese, and eggs; and tomatoes, zucchini, and green beans.
Parsley	An herb popular for garnishing as well as for seasoning and one that is a rich source of iron. Available whole, dried, and in dehydrated flakes. Use with almost any food from appetizers to main dishes.
Pepper	Both black and white pepper are spices that come from dried pepper berries. White

HERB OR SPICE	CHARACTERISTICS AND USES
	pepper is available ground. Use in light colored foods where black pepper flecks would detract from the food's attractiveness. Black pepper is available whole, ground, or coarsely ground. Use with almost every food, including spicy baked goods where a hint of pepper highlights other seasonings.
Poppy seed	(See POPPY SEED.)
Rosemary	A delicately flavored and sweet smelling herb from the mint family. Available only in whole form. Use with lamb, chicken, seafood; eggplant, turnips, cauliflower, green beans, beets, squash; and citrus fruit. Use with restraint; mix with thyme for particularly good flavor.
Saffron	(See SAFFRON.)
Sage	(See SAGE.)
Sesame seed	(See SEASAME SEED.)
Tarragon	An herb that has a faint hint of licorice about it. Available only in whole form. Use in vinegars or salad dressings; chicken and seafood; sauces and salads.
Thyme	A sweet-smelling herb that is a member of the mint family. Available whole or ground. Use in chowders and stuffings; seafood and creamed dishes; with onions, celery, asparagus, green beans, eggplant, and tomatoes.

Herring

Herring are small, bony food fish that contain twice the calcium of milk. They inhabit both fresh and salt waters. Freshwater or *lake herring* are lean fish (weighing up to 2 pounds) that abound in the Great Lakes. *Sea herring* have a higher fat content and weigh only about 1/2 pound. Caught primarily in the icy waters of the North Atlantic and North Pacific, they are perhaps the most numerous fish in the sea.

AVAILABILITY: Herring are available year-round in a variety of forms.

BUYING: Fresh lake and sea herring are marketed whole, drawn, and in fillets. Young sea herring are packaged mainly in cans and in that form are known as *sardines.* Adult sea herring are processed and sold in one of the following ways: brine-packed or pickled; salted; smoked; or kippered. Kippered herring is split and salted immediately after it is caught, then smoked. These fish are also known as *kippers.* Lightly kippered herring are known as *bloaters.* They are larger, fatter herring. Often in preparing bloaters, the salting stage is eliminated.

STORING: Fresh herring may be refrigerated 2 days or may be frozen for future use. Kippers will remain edible for several months without refrigeration. Bloaters are quite perishable and are usually eaten after curing.

PREPARATION: Fresh herring may be grilled, sauteed, fried, baked or stewed. Brine-packed, salted, and smoked herring usually require freshening in several changes of cold water and/or milk. Kippered herring and bloaters rarely need freshening because less salt is used in their curing.

SERVING: Salted, pickled, and smoked herring are excellent served as cold appetizers or in salads. Kippered herring is a popular breakfast accompaniment to scrambled eggs.

(See SARDINES and SEAFOOD.)

EASY PICKLED HERRING

2 salt herring
Vinegar
1 tbsp. sugar
Dash of pepper
1 lge. onion, sliced

Remove skin and bones from herring; cut into 2-inch pieces. Soak in cold water for 5 hours; change water frequently. Drain. Heat enough vinegar to cover herring; add sugar and pepper. Cool. Place herring and onion slices in bowl; pour vinegar mixture over. Let stand for several hours before serving.

HERRING IN SOUR CREAM

8 pickled herring fillets
Juice of 1 lemon
2 tart apples, peeled and sliced
2 med. onions, cut into rings
1 c. sauterne
1 bouillon cube
1 pt. sour cream

Marinate fillets in lemon juice. Combine apples, onions, wine and bouillon cube in saucepan; bring to a boil. Remove from heat; cover. Cool. Pour apple mixture over fillets; stir in sour cream. Chill in refrigerator until ready to serve.

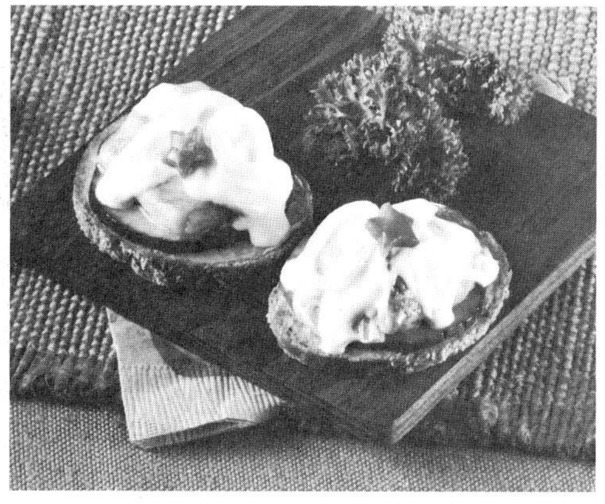

Busy Day Herring Canapes . . . Canned herring in sour cream atop rye slices are tasty canapes.

BUSY DAY HERRING CANAPES

1 lge. cucumber
1 8-oz. loaf party rye bread
2 tbsp. butter, softened
1 12-oz. jar herring in sour cream
Paprika

Score cucumber by running sharp-tined fork down length of cucumber from end to end. Cut crosswise into thin slices. Place in 3 cups salted ice water; let stand for 30 minutes to crisp. Drain on absorbent paper. Spread bread with butter. Overlap 2 slices cucumber on each slice of bread. Top cucumber with 1 large or 2 small pieces of herring. Sprinkle with paprika. Garnish with pimento stars if desired. Yield: About 24 canapes.

LEMON PICKLED HERRING

12 salt herring
2 lemons, sliced
6 lge. onions, sliced
12 bay leaves
2 tbsp. peppercorns
2 tbsp. mustard seed
1 1/2 c. vinegar

Soak herring in cold water overnight. Bone herring; cut into pieces. Alternate layers of herring, lemon, onions, bay leaves, peppercorns and mustard seed in glass jar. Pour vinegar over top layers. Place weight on herring mixture to let brine cover mixture. Refrigerate for 1 week.

PICKLED SALT HERRING

2 lge. salt herring
2 c. vinegar
1/4 c. sugar
1/4 c. chopped onions
5 peppercorns, crushed
20 allspice, crushed
2 sprigs of dillweed
1 onion, sliced
Chopped dillweed

Soak herring in cold water overnight; remove skin. Bone herring; dry carefully. Slice diagonally into 1/2-inch pieces. Arrange in serving dish. Mix 1/4 cup water and all remaining ingredients except sliced onion and chopped dillweed in saucepan. Bring to a boil; simmer for 5 minutes. Cool. Strain vinegar mixture; pour over herring. Top with sliced onion and chopped dillweed; cover. Refrigerate for three days.

HERRING SANDWICH

Thin bread slice, buttered
Lettuce leaf
4 pickled herring rolls
3 tbsp. sour cream

Cover bread slice with lettuce; arrange herring over lettuce. Top with cream. Garnish with sliced hard-cooked egg and chopped chives.

CREAMY HERRING SALAD

1 1/2 lb. salt herring
2 med. cooked potatoes, diced
4 cold cooked beets, cubed
3 to 4 apples, cubed
1 tbsp. minced onion
2 tbsp. vinegar
1 tbsp. sugar
1/4 tsp. white pepper
1/2 c. heavy cream, whipped

Soak herring overnight in water to cover. Remove bone and skin from herring; cut into cubes. Combine herring, potatoes, beets, apples, onion, vinegar, sugar and pepper; toss lightly. Chill in refrigerator. Fold in cream just before serving. Garnish with sieved hard-cooked eggs, if desired. Yield: 8-10 servings.

DANISH HERRING SALAD

2 lge. salt herring
2 tart apples, diced
2 cooked beets, diced
Shredded lettuce
7 sm. cooked potatoes, diced
3 tbsp. vinegar
2 tbsp. olive oil

Remove skin and bones from herring; cut into small pieces. Add apples, beets, shredded lettuce and potatoes; mix well. Add vinegar and olive oil; toss lightly. Serve garnished with eggs, onions and pickles.

GOURMET HERRING SALAD

5 sm. potatoes, cooked and cooled
5 sm. apples, cored and peeled
1 sour pickle
2 sweet pickles
1 can beets, drained
2 jars herring in cream
3 sm. onions
5 hard-cooked eggs
1 lb. cooked veal
3 stalks celery
1 bottle capers
1/2 tsp. prepared mustard
4 tbsp. olive oil
Salt and pepper to taste
Salad dressing

Dice potatoes, apples, pickles, beets, herring, onions, eggs, veal and celery. Add all remaining ingredients except salad dressing; toss thoroughly. Add enough salad dressing to moisten; mix gently. Refrigerate for 2 days, stirring occasionally. Yield: 12-16 servings.

ALMOND HOLIDAY CAKE
Recipe On Page 13.

PEACHY PARFAITS
Recipe For This Photograph On Page 634.

KULICH
Recipe For This Photograph On Page 860.

POPPY SEED CHIFFON CAKE
Recipe For This Photograph On Page 683.

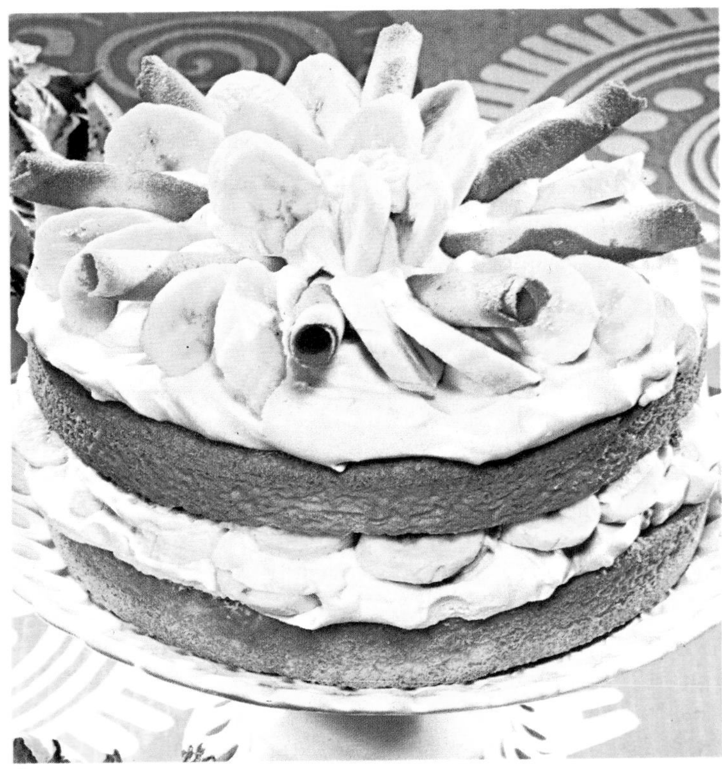

BANANA-RUM TORTE
Recipe For This Photograph On Page 81.

CHOCOLATE VELVET CAKE
Recipe For This Photograph On Page 259.

COCONUT TOPS
Recipe For This Photograph On Page 284.

SALLY LUNN
Recipe For This Photograph On Page 849.

TIPSY CHERRY PARSON
Recipe For This Photograph On Page 231.

SOUTHERN CHOCOLATE-PECAN PIE
Recipe For This Photograph On Page 266.

PUMPKIN CHIFFON PIE
Recipe For This Photograph On Page 718.

ORANGE FROMAGE
Recipe For This Photograph On Page 615.

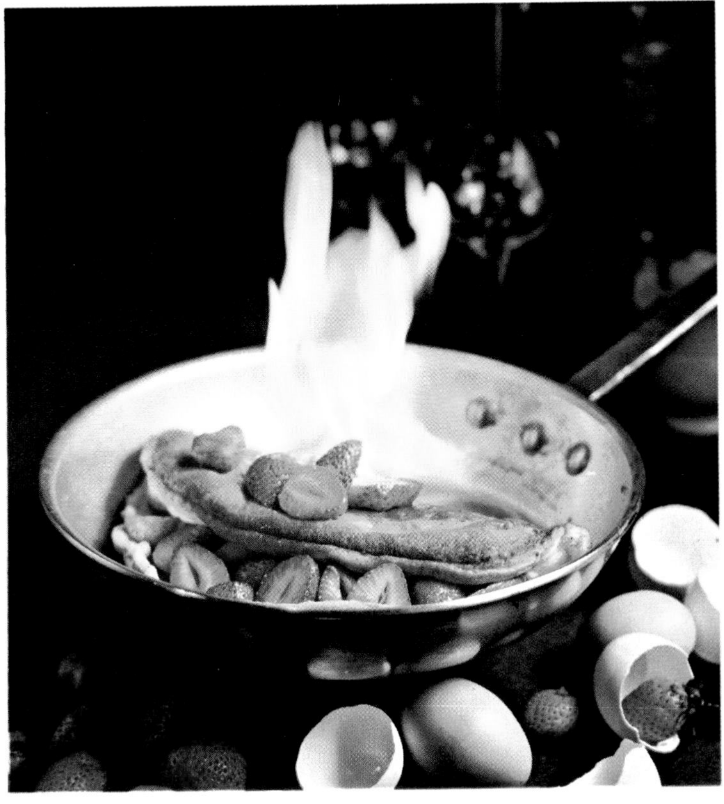

FLAMING STRAWBERRY OMELET
Recipe For This Photograph On Page 606.

STEAMED CRANBERRY PUDDING
Recipe For This Photograph On Page 340.

FRUITCAKE MACAROONS
Recipe For This Photograph On Page 232.

SUGA
SALT

TEMPTING PEANUT BRITTLE
Recipe For This Photograph On Page 641.

ALMOND TRIANGLES
Recipe For This Photograph On Page 15.

PASHKA
Recipe For This Photograph On Page 219.

LACE COOKIES
Recipe For This Photograph On Page 599.

BUTTERSCOTCH COOKIES
Recipe For This Photograph on Page 172.

BUTTERSCOTCH FUDGE
Recipe For This Photograph On Page 171.

KRIS KRINGLES
Recipe For This Photograph On Page 760.

ANIMAL SUGAR COOKIES
Recipe For This Photograph On Page 856.

PINEAPPLE-RAISIN COOKIES
Recipe For This Photograph On Page 674.

CREME DE MENTHE PIE
Recipe For This Photograph On Page 579.

STRAWBERRY BREAD PUDDING
Recipe For This Photograph On Page 853.

GRAHAM TORTE
Recipe For This Photograph On Page 430.

CHOCOLATE FINNISH CAKE
Recipe For This Photograph On Page 262.

OAT COOKIES
Recipe For This Photograph On Page 600.

CHOCOLATE BALLS
Recipe For This Photograph On Page 263.

NUTMEG COOKIES
Recipe For This Photograph On Page 597.

COUNTRY CHERRY CREAM
Recipe For This Photograph On Page 234.

SUGAR COOKIES
Recipe For This Photograph On Page 856.

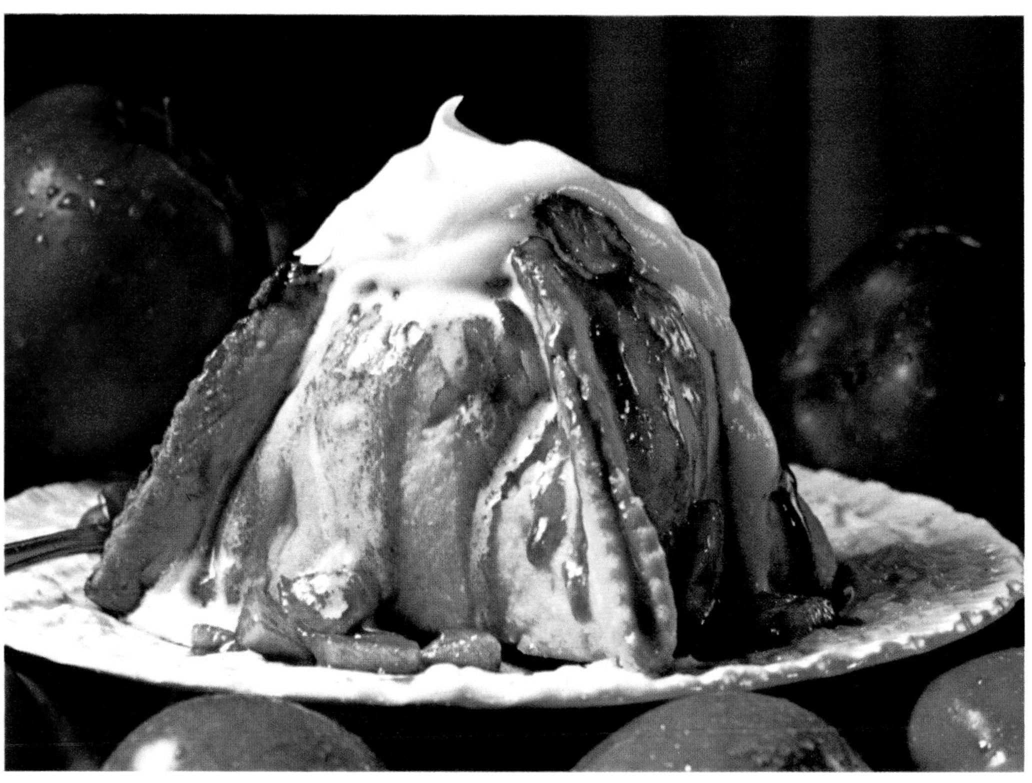

APPLE DUMPLINGS
Recipe For This Photograph On Page 24.

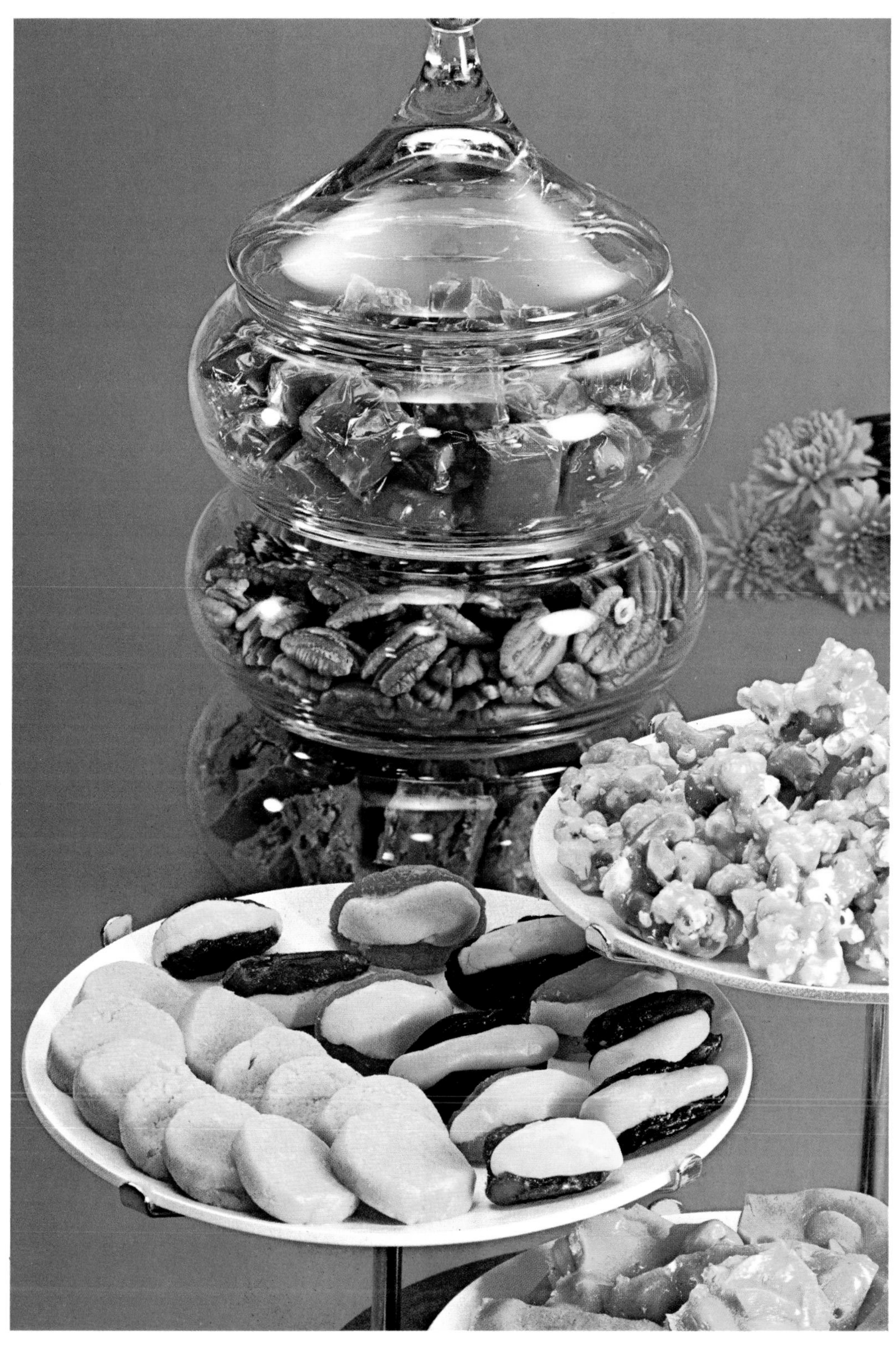

FONDANT, PEANUT BUTTER-COCONUT ROLL, CARAMEL POPCORN, AND PEANUT BRITTLE

Recipes For This Photograph On Pages 400, 641 and 682.

HEARTY HERRING SALAD

1 med. salt herring
1 c. diced cooked beets
1 sm. onion, diced
1 c. diced cooked potatoes
1 c. diced cooked carrots

Soak herring in cold water. Remove skin and large bones; dice. Add all remaining ingredients; toss lightly. Chill for several hours. Freshly ground pepper and vinegar may be added to taste. Yield: 4 servings.

HERRING SALAD WITH SOUR CREAM

1/2 c. coarsely chopped onion
1 tbsp. herring juice
1 c. pickled herring pieces
1 c. diced celery
1 c. diced apples
1 tbsp. sugar
1/2 c. sour cream

Marinate onion in herring juice. Combine herring, celery, apples, sugar, sour cream, onion and herring juice; toss thoroughly. Let stand at least 1 hour before serving.

SCANDINAVIAN HERRING SALAD

2 lge. salt herring
2 c. canned beets, cubed
2 c. cold boiled potatoes, diced
1/2 c. onions, finely chopped
1 c. apple, peeled, cubed
1/2 c. diced dill pickle
1/2 c. chopped walnuts
1 c. mayonnaise
1 tsp. prepared mustard
Salt to taste
1/2 tsp. pepper
5 tbsp. vinegar
1/2 tsp. sugar
1/2 c. sour cream
Red food coloring

Soak herring in cold water for at least 5 hours. Change water every hour. Skin herring; cut into small pieces. Combine herring, beets, potatoes, onions, apple, pickle and walnuts; toss thoroughly. Combine remaining ingredients; add to herring mixture. Toss lightly; chill in refrigerator overnight. Add mixture of additional mayonnaise and sour cream to moisten, if necessary.

HERRING-POTATO SCALLOP

3 salt herring
10 med. potatoes, sliced
2 onions, sliced
2 c. evaporated milk
6 whole allspice

Soak herring in cold water overnight. Cut herring into small pieces. Place layer of potatoes in casserole; add onions and herring. Top with remaining potatoes. Mix milk and 1 cup water; pour over top. Sprinkle with allspice. Bake at 375 degrees for 1 hour and 30 minutes or until potatoes are tender. Yield: 6 servings.

LEMON FRUIT PIE
Recipe On Page 530.

Hominy

HOMINY STEW

3 lb. pork shoulder chunks
6 c. canned hominy
1 sm. onion
3 tbsp. chili powder
1/2 tsp. oregano
1 clove of garlic, minced
Salt

Bring pork to a boil in 6 cups water; simmer until tender. Add hominy, onion, chili powder, oregano and garlic to pork and broth; salt to taste. Stir mixture thoroughly. Simmer hominy mixture for 30 minutes longer. Yield: 12 servings.

DELICIOUS HOMINY BAKE

1 can cream of mushroom soup
1/4 tsp. red pepper
1/2 tsp. pepper
1 tsp. celery seed
1 tsp. Worcestershire sauce
1 tsp. salt
2 No. 3 cans hominy, drained
1 c. buttered bread crumbs
1/2 c. slivered almonds

Combine soup, red pepper, pepper, celery seed, Worcestershire sauce and salt; place over medium heat until mixture is heated through. Place hominy in greased baking dish; pour soup mixture over hominy. Top with bread crumbs and almonds. Bake at 300 degrees for 15 minutes. Yield: 12 servings.

HOMINY AND TOMATOES

1 lge. onion, minced
2 tbsp. oil
1 lge. can tomatoes, drained
Chili powder to taste
Sugar to taste
Monosodium glutamate to taste
1 lge. can yellow hominy, drained
1 1/4 c. grated sharp Cheddar cheese

Cook onion in oil in skillet until browned lightly. Add tomatoes, chili powder, sugar and monosodium glutamate. Simmer, stirring frequently, for 30 minutes or until just a small amount of liquid remains. Add hominy; heat through. Remove mixture from heat; stir in cheese. Yield: 4-6 servings.

HOMINY AU GRATIN

2 1-lb. cans hominy, drained
2 c. diced pimento
1/2 c. diced onions
1/4 c. butter
2 c. milk
2 c. grated cheese
2 tsp. salt
4 tbsp. flour

Combine hominy, pimento and onions in greased baking dish. Combine butter, milk, cheese, salt and flour in saucepan; cook, stirring constantly, over low heat until cheese is melted. Pour over hominy mixture. Bake at 350 degrees for 20 minutes. Yield: 4-6 servings.

HOMINY CHILI

1 lge. can hominy, drained
2 tbsp. bacon drippings
1 2-oz. jar pimentos, chopped
Salt and pepper
1 can plain chili
1/4 c. grated cheese
1 c. coarsely chopped onions
Sliced olives

Saute hominy in bacon drippings for several minutes. Add pimentos, salt and pepper. Place hominy in greased baking dish. Heat chili in skillet; stir well. Sprinkle layer of grated cheese and onions over hominy; pour chili over. Add second layer of cheese and onions. Top with sliced olives. Bake in 350-degree oven for 20 minutes or until heated through. Yield: 4-6 servings.

HOMINY LUNCHEON DISH

3/4 lb. ground beef
1/4 c. minced onion
1/2 tsp. paprika
1 tsp. chili powder
1/2 tsp. sugar
1 tbsp. yellow cornmeal
1 tsp. salt
2 c. canned tomatoes
1 No. 2 1/2 can hominy, drained
1 c. grated Cheddar cheese

Brown beef and onion in skillet; add paprika, chili powder, sugar, cornmeal and salt. Add tomatoes to beef mixture; stir well. Simmer for several minutes. Place hominy in greased casserole; pour mixture over. Top with grated cheese. Bake at 350 degrees until cheese is melted and browned slightly. Yield: 6-8 servings.

HOMINY WITH GREEN CHILIES

1 onion, chopped
1 can green chilies, chopped
2 cloves of garlic, chopped
2 1-lb. cans hominy, drained
1/2 tsp. cumin
Salt and pepper to taste
1/2 pt. sour cream
1 c. grated sharp Cheddar cheese

Saute onion in 2 tablespoons fat until tender; add chilies, garlic, hominy, cumin, salt and pepper. Place in saucepan over medium heat until heated through. Add sour cream; fold in cheese. Pour into greased casserole. Bake at 350 degrees for 20 minutes or until bubbly. Yield: 6 servings.

Honey

Honey is an extra-sweet, thick liquid manufactured by honeybees from the nectars of flowers and stored in honeycombs. It is a quick food source of heat and energy because it consists primarily of two *natural* sugars (dextrose and fructose). Enzymes that aid in digestion, and quantities of iron, riboflavin, and Vitamin C make honey not merely a sweetener but also a nutritious food. (1 tablespoon honey = 59 calories)

AVAILABILITY: Honey is available year-round in supermarkets and health food stores.

BUYING: Purchase honey in cans or jars either with the honeycomb or as a thick, clear liquid. In general, the whiter the comb, the more flavorful and wholesome the honey. For an all-purpose sweetening substitute (as in coffee, tea, and chocolate), select a mild clover honey with a fairly neutral flavor.

STORING: Honey requires no refrigeration and is properly stored in a cool, dry place. Freezing does not alter the flavor of honey, though it may hasten granulation. To reliquify crystallized honey, set container in a pan or bowl of warm water.

USES: In cakes and bread doughs, honey enhances the keeping quality; the chewy texture; the brown color; and the uniformity of the mixture. (Note: The use of dark honey for baking is not recommended as the flavor may be disagreeably strong.) Honey can also be used in jams, jellies, and candies. When honey is used, a high temperature is usually required for gelling to occur.

PREPARATION: In most recipes that specify sugar, substitute honey in the following measured amounts: for breads, rolls, and general cooking–1 cup honey = 1 cup sugar; for cakes and cookies–7/8 cup honey = 1 cup sugar; reduce any other liquid specified in a recipe by 3 tablespoons for each cup of honey substituted.

SERVING: For ease in serving, pour a small portion of honey into a drip proof pitcher. Place the pitcher in a bowl or saucepan of warm water for 10 minutes. Heat liquifies the honey so that it pours more easily.

HONEY NUTS

3 c. powdered sugar
3 tsp. cinnamon
1 1/2 tsp. nutmeg
1 1/2 tsp. allspice
1 egg white
2 tbsp. honey
1/8 tsp. salt
3/4 lb. nut halves

Sift sugar and spices three times. Spread half the mixture in 1/4-inch layer on baking sheet. Beat egg white. honey and salt together until mixed thoroughly. Add nut halves; stir until coated well. Place nuts on sugar mixture one at a time; cover with remaining sugar mixture. Bake at 225 degrees for 1 hour and 30 minutes. Remove nuts; brush off excess sugar. Cool; store in covered jar. Yield: 1 pound.

CLOVER HONEY

60 white clover blooms
40 red clover blooms
5 lb. sugar
1 tsp. powdered alum
3 double pink roses

Remove all green parts from blooms; set blooms aside. Combine sugar, 3 cups water and alum; stir well. Bring sugar mixture to a boil; cook for 20 minutes or until of the consistency of thick syrup. Remove from heat. Remove petals from roses. Add blooms and rose petals to syrup; cover. Let stand for 25 minutes. Strain through cheesecloth; place in hot sterilized jars. Seal.

PEAR HONEY

3 lb. firm ripe pears, peeled
1 c. crushed pineapple
5 c. sugar
Red and yellow food coloring

Core and slice pears; grind pears. Combine pears, pineapple and sugar; bring to a boil. Simmer for 20 minutes or until thick, stirring frequently. Stir in several drops of red and yellow food coloring. Ladle into hot, sterilized glasses. Cover with 1/8 inch melted paraffin. Yield: 6-ounce glasses.

HONEY-BANANA MOLD

1 3-oz. package orange gelatin
2 med. ripe bananas
1/2 c. honey
3 tbsp. lemon juice
2/3 c. evaporated milk

Dissolve gelatin in 1 cup boiling water; cool. Mash bananas in large bowl of electric mixer at medium speed. Blend in honey, lemon juice and gelatin. Chill until thickened. Chill milk until icy crystals form; beat at low speed into gelatin mixture gradually. Turn to high speed; beat until mixture doubles in volume and becomes thick. Turn into lightly oiled 5-cup mold. Chill for about 3 hours or until set. Unmold on lettuce on serving dish; garnish with orange slices and maraschino cherries. Yield: 6 servings.

Honey-Banana Mold . . . This fluffy chilled fruit salad is a cool addition to any summertime menu.

HONEY ROLLS

2 c. scalded milk
1/2 c. shortening
1/3 c. sugar
Salt
2 cakes yeast
6 c. flour
2 eggs
1 egg white
1 c. powdered sugar
1/2 c. margarine
2 tbsp. honey

Combine milk, shortening, sugar and 1 tablespoon salt; mix well. Cool to lukewarm. Soften yeast in 1/4 cup lukewarm water; add to lukewarm mix. Add 1/2 of the flour; beat until smooth. Beat 2 eggs; add to flour mixture. Stir dough well. Add remaining flour to make soft dough; knead until smooth. Let rise until doubled in bulk. Divide dough in half; roll each half into 1/2-inch thick rectangle. Beat egg white, powdered sugar, margarine, honey and pinch of salt together until fluffy. Spread dough with honey mixture. Roll jelly roll fashion; cut into slices. Place in greased muffin tins; let rise until doubled in bulk. Bake at 375 degrees for 20 minutes or until brown. Yield: 36 rolls.

HONEY CRESCENTS

1 1/2 c. salad oil
Frozen orange juice concentrate
1/3 c. sugar
1 1/2 tsp. grated orange peel
3 1/2 c. sifted flour
1 tsp. cinnamon
3/4 tsp. baking powder
3/4 tsp. soda
1/4 tsp. salt
1/4 tsp. cloves
1/4 tsp. nutmeg
1 1/4 c. chopped pecans
3/4 c. honey

Combine salad oil, 3/4 cup orange juice concentrate, sugar and orange peel. Sift dry ingredients; add to orange juice mixture. Stir in 3/4 cup pecans; mix thoroughly. Shape dough into crescents. Bake at 350 degrees for 18 minutes or until browned lightly. Cool. Combine honey and 3 tablespoons orange juice concentrate; drizzle over crescents. Sprinkle with remaining pecans. Yield: 3 1/2 dozen.

DUTCH HONEY BREAD

1 1-lb. package brown sugar
1/4 c. honey
1 1/2 c. milk
4 c. flour
1 tsp. salt
1 tsp. baking powder
1 tsp. soda
1 tsp. nutmeg
1/2 tsp. cinnamon
1/2 tsp. ginger
1/2 tsp. cloves

Combine sugar, honey and milk; mix thoroughly. Sift dry ingredients together; add to sugar mixture. Blend mixtures thoroughly. Pour into two paper-lined and greased loaf pans. Bake at 300 degrees for 1 hour or until firm. Yield: 20 servings.

EASY HONEY BREAD

1 1/2 c. milk
1 1/2 tsp. salt
Sugar
1/4 c. shortening
1/2 c. honey
1 tsp. sugar
1 pkg. dry yeast
5 c. (or more) flour

Scald milk. Add salt, 2 tablespoons sugar and shortening; let stand until cool. Add honey to 1/3 cup warm water; dissolve 1 teaspoon sugar and yeast in honey mixture. Let stand for 20 minutes or until cool. Add yeast mixture to milk mixture. Beat in 3 cups flour; add remaining flour. Knead until smooth; let rise until doubled in bulk. Punch down; shape into loaves. Bake at 400 degrees for 15 minutes; reduce heat to 350 degrees. Bake for 35 minutes longer. Yield: 2 loaves.

EGYPTIAN BREAD

10 slices white bread, crusts removed
1 lb. honey

Soak bread in honey for at least 30 minutes. Place slices in buttered baking dish; layer each evenly over top of one another. Bake in 300-degree oven for 25 minutes. Cool; chill in refrigerator. Serve with cream over top. Yield: 6-8 servings.

GRECIAN HONEY CAKE

1 1/4 c. sugar
1 c. honey
1 tsp. lemon juice
3/4 c. butter
3 eggs
1 c. flour, sifted
1 1/2 tsp. baking powder
1/4 tsp. salt
1/2 tsp. cinnamon
Dash of nutmeg
1/4 c. milk
1/2 tsp. grated orange rind
1 c. chopped walnuts

Combine 1/2 cup sugar, honey and 3/4 cup water; mix thoroughly. Simmer for 5 minutes; skim top. Stir in lemon juice; cook for 2 minutes longer. Set mixture aside to cool. Cream butter and remaining sugar. Add eggs, one at a time; beat well after each addition. Sift flour, baking powder, salt, cinnamon and nutmeg together; add to batter. Stir in milk and orange rind. Mix well; stir in walnuts. Pour into greased and floured 8 x 8 x 2-inch pan. Bake at 350 degrees for 30 minutes. Cut into diamond shapes in pan while hot. Pour syrup over top; let stand until ready to serve. Yield: 12 servings.

HONEY-ORANGE BREAD

2 c. flour
1/4 tsp. salt
1/2 tsp. soda
1/2 c. butter
1/2 c. honey
1/4 c. milk
1 egg
2 tbsp. grated orange peel
1 c. diced orange pulp
2/3 c. diced dates
1/2 c. chopped nuts

Sift flour, salt and soda. Blend butter, honey, milk and egg; mix well. Add flour mixture, orange peel, orange pulp, dates and nuts to honey mixture; mix well. Pour into greased loaf pan. Bake at 325 degrees for 45 minutes to 1 hour.

SOUTHERN HONEY CAKE

1 c. sugar
3 eggs
1 c. salad oil
1 c. honey
2 1/2 c. sifted flour
1 tsp. baking powder
1 tsp. salt
2 tsp. cinnamon
1/2 tsp. allspice
1/4 c. pineapple juice
3/4 tsp. soda
1 tsp. vanilla
1/2 c. chopped pecans

Combine sugar, eggs, oil and honey; blend thoroughly. Beat mixture until thick. Combine dry ingredients; sift 3 times. Combine pineapple juice and 1/4 cup water; bring to boil. Stir in soda. Add juice mixture alternately with dry ingredients to egg mixture. Stir in vanilla and pecans. Pour into lightly greased waxed paper-lined 10-inch tube pan. Bake at 325 degrees for 1 hour and 15 minutes. Remove from oven; let cool in pan on rack.

HONEY-BUTTER BALLS

1 1/2 c. instant non-fat dry milk
1 c. honey
1 c. peanut butter
1 can coconut
1 c. wheat cereal flakes

Combine dry milk, honey and peanut butter in mixing bowl; stir until mixed thoroughly. Shape in long rolls. Combine coconut and flakes; mix on waxed paper. Coat rolls in coconut mixture. Shape into balls; chill before serving.

HONEY CONFECTIONS

2 pkg. vanilla wafers, crushed
1/2 c. honey
1/2 c. brandy
1/3 c. light rum
1 c. chopped walnuts

Combine all ingredients; mix thoroughly. Shape into small balls; roll in powdered sugar. Place in canister, covered tightly, for one week. Yield: 3 dozen.

HONEY SQUARES

2 c. sugar
3/4 c. milk
1/4 c. cream
1 sq. chocolate
1/4 c. honey
3 tbsp. butter
1 tsp. vanilla
1 c. nuts

Combine sugar, milk, cream and chocolate in saucepan; bring to a boil. Cook for 5 minutes. Add honey and butter; cook until mixture forms soft ball in cold water. Cool. Beat until thick; stir in vanilla and nuts. Pour into buttered pan. Cut into squares. Yield: 8 servings.

HONEY-DATE BARS

5 tbsp. flour
1/2 c. sugar
1/8 tsp. salt
1 tsp. baking powder
1 c. chopped dates
1 c. chopped pecans
1/4 c. honey
1 tsp. vanilla
3 eggs
Powdered sugar

Sift flour, sugar, salt and baking powder together. Combine dates and pecans; sift flour mixture over.

Add honey, vanilla and eggs; stir until mixed. Pour into greased 11 1/4 x 7 1/2-inch pan. Bake at 325 degrees for 45 minutes. Cool in pan. Cut in bars; roll in powdered sugar. Yield: 24 cookies.

HONEY STRIPS

5 eggs
3/4 c. sugar
1/4 c. honey
1/2 c. sifted flour
2 tbsp. confectioners' sugar

Preheat oven to 350 degrees. Combine eggs, sugar and honey in mixing bowl; beat until thickened. Add flour; beat in thoroughly. Pour batter into greased 9 x 12-inch pan. Bake in 350-degree oven for 45 minutes; stir cake with spoon after first 15 minutes of baking time. Bake until cake tests done. Cool cake in pan. Dust with confectioners' sugar; cut into strips to serve.

HONEY-LEMON SQUARES

1 lge. can evaporated milk
1 3-oz. package lemon gelatin
1/3 c. honey
1/8 tsp. salt
3 tbsp. lemon juice
Grated rind of 1 lemon
2 1/2 c. vanilla water crumbs

Chill evaporated milk overnight. Dissolve gelatin in 1 1/4 cups boiling water. Add honey, salt, lemon juice and rind; stir to blend. Chill until mixture is partially set. Whip milk until stiff peaks form; add gelatin mixture. Spread half the crumbs in 10 x 13 1/2-inch pan; pour lemon mixture over. Top with remaining crumbs. Chill for 3 hours. Cut into squares to serve. Yield: 15-18 servings.

Honeydew

STUFFED HONEYDEWS

3 honeydew melons
1 c. watermelon balls
1 c. cantaloupe balls
1 c. honeydew balls
1 c. pineapple chunks
1 c. fresh or mandarin orange slices
1 1/2 c. rose wine

Cut 1 inch off top each melon; scoop out seeds. Combine fruits; fill melons with fruit mixture. Pour 1/2 cup wine into each melon; replace tops. Chill for 2 to 3 hours. Cut melons into halves; serve. Yield: 6 servings.

FROSTY MELON SALAD

1 pkg. raspberry gelatin
3/4 c. fruit juice
1 med. honeydew melon
1 c. drained raspberries
3 3-oz. packages cream cheese
1 tbsp. milk

Dissolve gelatin in 1 cup hot water; add fruit juice. Chill until thickened. Peel melon, leaving whole. Cut slice from one end; scoop out seeds. Drain melon well; place upright in bowl. Fold raspberries into gelatin mixture; fill melon. Replace top slice, fastening with toothpicks. Chill. Combine cream cheese and milk; beat until smooth and fluffy. Cut thin slice from underside of melon to make firm base; place on plate. Spread cream cheese mixture over entire melon. Cut into slices.

HONEYDEW SPARKLE

1 pkg. lime gelatin
1/2 c. whipped cream
3 tbsp. sugar
1 c. seedless grapes
1/2 c. chopped celery
1 c. honeydew balls

Dissolve gelatin in 1 cup boiling water; chill till partially set. Combine whipped cream and sugar; fold into gelatin. Add grapes, celery and melon balls; pour mixture into 3-cup mold. Chill until firm.

HONEYDEW SURPRISE

1 pkg. lime gelatin
1 c. chunk pineapple, drained
1 c. mandarin oranges
1 honeydew melon
Salad greens
Cottage cheese
French dressing

Dissolve gelatin in 1 cup boiling water; chill until partially set. Fold in pineapple and oranges. Peel melon; cut slice from one end. Remove seeds. Fill melon center with gelatin mixture. Wrap in plastic wrap; refrigerate until firm. Slice; serve on bed of greens. Spoon cottage cheese on top. Serve with French dressing.

MELON-MINT MOLD

1 pkg. lemon gelatin
2 or 3 sprigs of fresh mint
2 tbsp. lemon juice
1/2 c. mayonnaise
1/2 tsp. salt
1 c. diced honeydew melon
1 c. diced cantaloupe
1/4 c. toasted blanched almonds, slivered

Dissolve gelatin in 1 cup hot water; add mint sprigs. Stir until gelatin is dissolved; steep for 5 minutes. Remove mint; add 1/2 cup cold water, lemon juice, mayonnaise and salt. Blend well. Pour into refrigerator tray; quick-chill in freezer for 15 to 20 minutes or until firm about 1 inch from edge. Beat until fluffy. Fold in remaining ingredients. Chill until firm.

MINTED MELON BALLS

1 c. sugar
4 mint leaves
4 tbsp. lemon juice
2 c. cantaloupe balls
2 c. watermelon balls
2 c. honeydew melon balls

Combine 2 cups water, sugar and mint leaves in saucepan; mix well. Bring to a boil; boil for 2 minutes. Remove from heat; strain. Stir in lemon juice; chill syrup. Arrange balls in chilled dessert cups; pour syrup over tops. Yield: 8 servings.

Western Melon Dessert . . . An easy-to-prepare cream cheese coated fruit dessert.

WESTERN MELON DESSERT

Fresh fruits
1 lge. honeydew melon
1 8-oz. package cream cheese

Chill fresh fruits. Peel melon, cutting off small slice at one end to expose center cavity. Remove seeds; drain. Spread outer surface of melon, with exception of cut end, with softened cream cheese. Place on cookie sheet; refrigerate until ready to serve. Cut larger pieces of fruit into bite-sized pieces. Place frosted melon on serving plate; fill center with fresh fruit. Arrange remaining fruit to surround melon. Slice melon crosswise; top each serving with fruit. Yield: 6-8 servings.

Horseradish

ZIPPY DIP FOR SEAFOOD

1 c. chili sauce
1 tbsp. horseradish
Dash of hot sauce
Lemon juice to taste

Blend all ingredients thoroughly; chill well before serving.

HORSERADISH CHIP DIP

1 8-oz. package cream cheese
3 tbsp. milk
2 tbsp. horseradish
1/4 tsp. Worcestershire sauce
Salt and pepper to taste

Have cream cheese at room temperature. Combine cheese with milk, horseradish, Worcestershire sauce, salt and pepper; blend well. Chill until ready to serve.

HORSERADISH-LEMON MOLD

1 pkg. lemon gelatin
2 tbsp. fresh lemon juice
1 c. heavy cream, whipped
1/3 c. horseradish

Dissolve gelatin in 1 cup boiling water; add lemon juice. Cool until partially set. Beat lightly; fold in whipped cream and horseradish. Pour into mold. Chill until firm.

HORSERADISH-RELISH SALAD

1 pkg. lemon gelatin
1 tbsp. lemon juice
1/4 c. horseradish
1 tbsp. minced green pepper
2 lge. green peppers

Dissolve gelatin in 3/4 cup boiling water; add lemon juice. Chill until partially set; fold in horseradish and minced green pepper. Cut thin slice from tops of green peppers; remove membrane and seeds. Pour gelatin mixture into green peppers; chill until firm. Cut into thin slices; serve on lettuce with French dressing, if desired.

Hush Puppies

Small, round, crisp hush puppies are a type of corn bread that originated in the South. They are usually prepared from cornmeal, liquid, salt, baking powder, finely chopped onion, and sometimes egg. The ingredients are mixed together to make a workable dough. The dough is shaped into small balls or oblong cakes which are then fried until well-browned. They are drained and served hot to accompany fried fish or other main dishes.

Hush puppies derive their intriguing name from an old-time southern activity. At fish fries, Southerners would quiet their hungry, whining dogs by throwing them scraps of fried cornmeal batter. At the same time, they admonished the dogs with the words, "Hush, puppy."

BUTTERMILK HUSH PUPPIES

1 1/2 c. cornmeal
1/2 c. flour
4 chopped green onions
1 egg
1/8 tsp. salt
2 tbsp. baking powder
1/2 tsp. soda
1 c. buttermilk
4 tbsp. melted bacon drippings

Mix all ingredients; drop by spoonfuls into hot deep oil in heavy iron skillet. Fry until golden brown.

EASY HUSH PUPPIES

2 c. cornmeal	*1 c. milk*
1/2 c. flour	*2 well-beaten eggs*
1 tsp. baking powder	*1 lge. onion, chopped*
1 tsp. salt	*1 tbsp. lard, melted*

Mix first 4 ingredients; add milk, eggs and onion. Stir in lard. Drop by spoonfuls into hot deep fat in which fish has been cooked. Fry until brown.

DEEP SOUTH HUSH PUPPIES

2 c. cornmeal	*2 tbsp. finely chopped parsley*
1 tsp. salt	*6 drops of hot sauce*
1 tbsp. shortening	
1 tsp. minced onion	

Mix cornmeal, salt and shortening; add 2 cups boiling water. Stir in onion, parsley and hot sauce. Shape into small ovals. Fry in hot deep fat until golden brown. Drain on absorbent towels.

Jam

Jam is a sweet and smooth spread, filling, or condiment made from sugar and chopped, crushed, or ground fruit. It is less firm than jelly, but evenly distributed pieces of fruit in jam make it thicker than jelly.

INGREDIENTS: All jams are made from fresh, frozen, canned, or dried *fruit* and beet or cane *sugar.* Berries and soft fruits like peaches and apricots make especially excellent jams. Some recipes specify the addition of liquid or powdered *commercial pectin*—a thickening substance—and/or *acid* such as lemon juice, depending on the type of fruit used and the flavor and consistency of jam desired.

PROCESSING: There are 3 methods for processing jam: the short boil; the long boil; and the no-cook. To process by the *short boil method*—A commercial pectin is used. Ingredients are combined according to instructions on pectin package. The mixture is brought to a boil and cooked about 1 minute. The jam is removed from the heat and canned, sealed, labeled, and stored. By the *long boil method*—No commercial pectin is used. Usually fruit and sugar are heated slowly in a saucepan until sugar dissolves. The mixture is quickly brought to a boil and allowed to cook until the jellying point is reached. *To test for doneness or jellying point* you can use one of the 3 following tests: (1) Bring water in saucepan to boil, noting temperature of boiling point with candy thermometer. Add 9 degrees to this temperature to determine temperature of jellying point (221 degrees at sea level). Test doneness of jam with candy thermometer. (2) Dip spoon in jam mixture while it cooks. When two drops of syrup run together and slide off spoon as one drop, the mixture is done. (3) Place small amount of jam mixture on plate. Put plate in refrigerator. If mixture sets in a few minutes, jam is done. Remove jam mixture in saucepan from heat while applying the latter test. To prevent fruit from rising to top of cooked jams processed by short- or long-boil methods, remove jam from heat when done. Stir at frequent intervals for 5 minutes. Skim off surface foam before each stirring. By the *no-cook method*—A commercial pectin is used and the fruit is uncooked. Usually sugar and fruit are combined in a bowl and allowed to stand until sugar dissolves. Commercial pectin is combined with water and acid (if specified in recipe). The fruit mixture and the pectin mixture are then combined and the resulting jam is canned, sealed, labeled, and stored.

PACKING: Before preparing jam, wash canning glasses or jars and lids in hot, soapy water. Rinse. Scald them in boiling water about 10 minutes. Keep hot until ready to pack jam. Melt paraffin over boiling water in top of double boiler. Pour jam into canning glasses or jars, leaving 1/8 to 1/2 inch head space. Cover with 1/8-inch thick sheet of paraffin. Prick air bubbles in paraffin to prevent imperfect sealing. Seal with metal lids or paper covers, following manufacturers' instructions. Label and date.

STORING: Store glasses or jars of cooked jam in a cool, dark, dry place. If stored in a warm place, jam expands, breaks the seal, and runs over the side of the glass or jar. Jam loses its color and flavor the longer it is stored so use as soon as possible. Store uncooked jam in refrigerator or in the freezer.

(See CANNING.)

APRICOT JAM

10 c. sugar
8 c. ground apricots
1 c. crushed pineapple
1/2 c. lemon juice

Mix sugar and fruits; refrigerate overnight. Bring to a rolling boil; boil for 8 minutes. Add lemon juice; boil for 2 minutes longer. Seal in sterilized jars. Yield: 8 pints.

BANANA JAM

6 c. mashed bananas
1 pkg. powdered pectin
3 c. sugar
2 pkg. strawberry gelatin

Bring 1 1/2 cups water and bananas to a boil, stirring constantly. Add pectin; continue boiling for 5 minutes. Add sugar and gelatin; bring to a rolling boil. Remove from heat; skim. Pour into sterilized jars; seal with paraffin.

BEET JAM

4 lb. beets, ground
3 lb. sugar
Juice and grated rind of 3 lemons
2 oz. fresh gingerroot
1/2 lb. almonds, chopped

Combine beets and just enough water to cover; cook slowly until tender. Add sugar, lemon juice and rind and gingerroot; cook for at least 1 hour or until thickened and clear. Add almonds. Pour into sterilized jars; seal with paraffin.

BLUEBERRY JAM

6 c. ripe blueberries
2 tbsp. lemon juice
1 box powdered pectin
4 c. sugar

Crush blueberries. Measure four cups; place in 6-quart saucepan. Add water to make 4 cups if necessary. Add lemon juice and pectin; mix well. Bring mixture to a hard boil, stirring constantly. Add sugar all at once; bring to a rolling boil. Boil hard for 1 minute; stirring constantly. Remove from heat; skim off foam with metal spoon. Stir and skim for 5 minutes. Pour into hot sterilized glasses; seal with paraffin. Yield: Eight 6-ounce glasses.

SPICED BLUEBERRY JAM

4 1/2 c. blueberries
1/2 tsp. cinnamon
1/2 tsp. cloves
7 c. sugar
Grated rind and juice of 1 lemon
1 bottle pectin

Simmer blueberries, cinnamon, cloves, sugar, lemon rind and juice for 5 minutes; remove from heat. Add pectin; stir and skim. Spoon into hot sterilized jars; seal. Yield: 1 1/2 pints.

BLUE PLUM JAM

3 lb. blue plums
1 box frozen raspberries
5 c. sugar

Seed and chop plums; combine with raspberries and sugar. Boil slowly till thickened. Seal in sterilized jars.

BLACKBERRY JAM

1 qt. mashed blackberries
1 qt. sugar

Cook blackberries for 20 minutes; add sugar. Bring to a rolling boil; cook for 20 minutes longer, stirring frequently. Remove from heat; skim. Pour into hot sterilized jars; seal with paraffin.

CANTALOUPE JAM

2 to 3 cantaloupes, diced
2 oranges, ground
1 lemon, ground
1 lge. can crushed pineapple
4 c. sugar
1/2 c. chopped almonds

Combine cantaloupe, oranges, lemon, pineapple and sugar. Bring to a boil; boil until thickened. Remove from heat. Skim; add almonds. Pour into sterilized jars; seal with paraffin.

CHERRY-PINEAPPLE JAM

1 can crushed pineapple
Juice of 2 lemons
7 1/2 c. sugar
1 9-oz. jar maraschino cherries
1 bottle liquid pectin
Red food coloring

Combine pineapple, lemon juice and sugar. Drain cherries; reserve juice. Add enough water to juice to measure 3/4 cup. Chop cherries; add with juice to pineapple mixture. Bring to a boil, stirring constantly; boil for 2 minutes. Remove from heat; add pectin and food coloring as desired. Stir and skim for 5 minutes. Pack into hot sterilized jars; seal. Yield: 2 1/2 pints.

CHOKECHERRY JAM

Chokecherries
1 pkg. powdered pectin
5 c. sugar

Grind chokecherries; cover with boiling water. Let stand overnight. Strain through cheesecloth; reserve juice. Mix 3 1/2 cups juice and pectin; bring to a boil. Add sugar. Bring to a rolling boil; boil for 1 minute. Skim; pour into sterilized jars. Seal with paraffin.

CARROT JAM

4 c. ground carrots
3 c. orange juice
1 c. crushed pineapple
2 pkg. powdered pectin
10 c. sugar

Boil carrots in orange juice until tender; add pineapple. Add pectin; bring to a rolling boil. Add sugar; boil for 5 minutes longer, stirring constantly. Skim; pour into sterilized jelly glasses. Seal with paraffin.

CRANBERRY-BANANA JAM

3 c. fresh cranberries
2 c. mashed bananas
7 c. sugar
1/2 bottle liquid pectin

Combine cranberries and 1 1/2 cups water in saucepan; bring to a boil. Reduce heat; simmer for 10 minutes. Stir in bananas and sugar. Return to a boil; cook for 1 minute. Remove from heat; add pectin. Spoon into sterilized jars; seal with paraffin.

CRANBERRY-STRAWBERRY JAM

2 c. cranberries
2 pkg. frozen strawberries, thawed
5 1/2 c. sugar
1 pkg. powdered pectin

Grind cranberries; combine with strawberries in large saucepan. Add sugar and pectin; mix well. Bring to a full rolling boil; boil hard for 1 minute, stirring constantly. Remove from heat; skim off foam with metal spoon. Stir and skim for 5 minutes. Pour into sterilized jars; seal with paraffin. Yield: Ten 8-ounce jars.

UNCOOKED CRANBERRY JAM

1 lb. cranberries
4 c. sugar
1 pkg. powdered pectin

Chop cranberries fine; add enough water to measure 2 cups liquid, if necessary. Combine cranberries with sugar; let stand for 30 minutes. Stir pectin into 1 cup water. Bring to a boil; boil rapidly for 1 minute. Remove from heat. Add cranberry mixture; stir for 2 minutes. Pour into sterilized jelly glasses; cover. Let stand at room temperature overnight or until jelled. Seal. Store in refrigerator or freezer. Yield: 5 cups.

DELICIOUS CONCORD GRAPE JAM

4 c. stemmed grapes
3 c. sugar

Mix grapes and sugar; bring to a boil. Boil for 20 minutes. Press mixture through sieve; pour into sterilized glasses. Seal with paraffin while hot. Yield: 4-5 glasses.

FIG JAM

2 qt. figs
4 c. sugar

Remove stems from figs; peel. Combine figs and sugar; mash. Cook to jelly-like consistency, or to 222 degrees on candy thermometer. Pack in hot sterilized jars; seal with paraffin.

EASY FIG JAM

3 c. mashed figs
3 c. sugar
2 pkg. strawberry gelatin

Combine all ingredients; let stand for 30 minutes. Bring slowly to a boil; cook, stirring, for 5 minutes. Seal in sterilized containers. Yield: 2-3 pints.

GREEN PEPPER JAM

12 med.-sized green peppers, seeded
7 c. sugar
1 1/2 c. vinegar
1 tsp. turmeric
1 pkg. powdered pectin

Grind peppers finely. Pour 2 cups peppers and half the juice into 6-quart kettle. Add sugar, vinegar and turmeric. Bring to a boil; add pectin. Bring to a rolling boil; boil hard, stirring constantly, for 1 minute. Remove from heat; let stand for 5 minutes. Pour into sterilized jars; seal. Yield: Ten 6-ounce jars.

ORANGE-RHUBARB JAM

5 c. rhubarb, diced
1 lb. candy orange slices, diced
5 c. sugar
1 pkg. orange gelatin

Combine rhubarb and orange slices in saucepan; add 1/2 cup water. Bring to a boil; stir until candy is partially dissolved. Add sugar and gelatin. Cook for 25 minutes or until thickened. Pour into sterilized jars; seal with paraffin. Yield: 4 pints.

PEACH JAM

4 lb. peaches
Sugar
1 3-in. cinnamon stick

Peel, pit and crush peaches; add 1/2 cup water. Bring to a boil in large kettle; cook, stirring, for 10 minutes. Measure peach mixture; add 3/4 cup sugar for each cup peach mixture. Add cinnamon stick. Bring to a boil; cook until thickened. Skim and stir frequently. Remove cinnamon stick; pour into hot sterilized jars. Seal with paraffin. Yield: 3 1/2 pints.

ROSY MELBA PEACH JAM

1 1/2 lb. ripe peaches
1/4 c. lemon juice
2 c. red raspberries
7 c. sugar
1 bottle liquid fruit pectin
1 tsp. almond extract

Peel, pit and crush peaches. Measure 2 cups peaches; add 2 tablespoons lemon juice. Stir gently; let stand. Crush berries; add remaining lemon juice. Combine peaches and berries with sugar in heavy kettle; mix well. Bring to a full rolling boil, stirring constantly; boil for 1 minute. Remove from heat; add pectin. Stir and skim for several minutes; add extract. Pour into hot sterilized glasses. Seal with paraffin. Yield: Eight 1/2-pint glasses.

PEAR-PEACH JAM

1 1/2 lb. pears
1 1/2 lb. peaches
4 1/2 c. sugar
1 pkg. powdered fruit pectin

Pare, core and finely chop pears; pare, pit and finely chop peaches. Combine pears and peaches in kettle; bring to a rolling boil, stirring constantly. Boil for 1 minute. Add sugar; boil for 1 minute longer, stirring until sugar is dissolved. Stir in pectin. Remove from heat; skim. Seal with hot paraffin.

PINEAPPLE-RHUBARB SPREAD

4 c. diced rhubarb
1 sm. can crushed pineapple
4 c. sugar
1 box strawberry gelatin

Mix first 3 ingredients in kettle; boil for 15 minutes, stirring constantly. Add gelatin; cook for 3 minutes longer, stirring constantly. Pour into hot sterilized jars; seal.

QUICK AND EASY RASPBERRY JAM

3 c. raspberries
3 c. sugar

Place berries in kettle; bring to a boil. Boil for 1 minute. Add sugar; bring to a boil again. Boil for 3 minutes. Remove from heat; beat with mixer for 4 minutes at medium speed. Pour into jelly glasses; seal with paraffin.

FRESH STRAWBERRY JAM

4 pt. fresh strawberries
4 1/2 c. sugar

Hull and crush strawberries in large saucepan. Stir in sugar. Cook over low heat, stirring constantly, until sugar dissolves. Cook for about 2 hours to 2 hours and 30 minutes, stirring occasionally, until thick. Skim as necessary. Pour hot jam into sterilized jars. Dip jars into boiling water; seal at once. Yield: About 4 1/2 cups.

Fresh Strawberry Jam . . . Jam, laden with bits of strawberries, can be a personalized holiday gift.

RED RASPBERRY JAM

3 12-oz. packages frozen red raspberries
5 c. sugar
1/2 bottle liquid pectin

Thaw raspberries; combine with sugar. Stir; let stand until sugar dissolves. Add pectin and 3/4 cup water. Stir for 3 minutes. Bring to a boil; boil for 1 minute. Pour into jars; seal with paraffin.

FREEZER STRAWBERRY JAM

2 c. fresh strawberries
4 c. sugar
1 pkg. pectin
2 tbsp. lemon juice

Mash strawberries; stir in sugar. Dissolve pectin in 1 cup water; boil for 1 minute. Add lemon juice. Pour over strawberries and sugar. Mix well. Place in containers; let stand overnight to dissolve sugar. Freeze.

STRAWBERRY JAM

1 qt. strawberries
5 c. sugar

Boil strawberries for 3 minutes; add 3 cups sugar. Stir; boil for 3 minutes longer. Add remaining sugar; boil for 3 minutes longer. Let stand in stone jar for 3 days; stir each day. Pour into hot sterilized jars; cover with paraffin. Seal.

LEMON-TOMATO JAM

3 c. peeled, chopped tomatoes
Sliced lemon
3 c. sugar
1 pkg. lemon gelatin

Combine tomatoes, lemon slices and sugar in saucepan; bring to a boil. Reduce heat; simmer for 15 minutes. Remove from heat; stir in gelatin until dissolved. Pour into sterilized jars; refrigerate.

RED TOMATO JAM

4 c. tomatoes
1/2 slice lemon
4 c. sugar

Scald tomatoes; peel. Squeeze out as many seeds and as much juice as possible. Measure 4 cups tomatoes into kettle. Add lemon and 1 cup sugar; boil for 5 minutes. Add 1 cup sugar; boil for 3 minutes. Add remaining sugar; boil for 20 minutes. Pour hot liquid into sterilized containers; seal.

Jambalaya

BAYOU JAMBALAYA

2 tbsp. butter
2 onions, chopped
1 tbsp. flour
1 No. 1 can tomatoes
1 green pepper, chopped
1 clove of garlic, chopped
1 tbsp. chopped parsley
Salt and pepper
1 c. rice

1/4 tsp. thyme
1 bay leaf
2 c. chopped cooked ham
2 c. cooked shrimp
2 c. oysters and liquid

Melt butter in skillet; add onions. Cook over low heat until browned. Add flour gradually; stir until mixture is browned lightly. Add 2 cups water; cook, stirring constantly, until smooth and thickened. Add tomatoes, green pepper, garlic, parsley, salt, pepper, rice and herbs; cover. Place over low heat; simmer 45 minutes or until rice is tender and small amount of liquid remains. Add ham, shrimp and oysters with liquid; cover. Simmer until edges of oysters are curled. Yield: 6 servings.

CHICKEN JAMBALAYA

1 c. chopped onion
1 c. chopped green pepper
2 cloves of garlic, minced
2 tbsp. salad oil
1 c. cooked diced ham
12 sm. pork sausages
1 c. cooked diced chicken
1 No. 2 can tomatoes
1 c. rice
1 1/2 c. chicken broth
1/2 tsp. thyme
1 tsp. salt
1 tbsp. chopped parsley

Add onion, green pepper and garlic to hot oil in skillet; cook over low heat, stirring frequently, until tender. Stir in meats; cook for 5 minutes. Add all remaining ingredients; place in greased casserole. Bake, covered, at 350 degrees for 1 hour. Yield: 8 servings.

SHRIMP JAMBALAYA

2 green peppers, chopped
1 med. onion, chopped
1/4 c. butter
2 cloves of garlic, minced
3/4 c. chopped mushrooms
1 c. canned tomatoes
2 doz. cooked shrimp, deveined
1 oz. sherry
Salt and pepper to taste
1 tsp. gumbo file

Saute green peppers and onion in butter until tender; add garlic. Stir in mushrooms, tomatoes and shrimp; simmer for 10 minutes. Add sherry, salt and pepper; mix well. Stir in file just before serving. Serve over cooked rice. Yield: 4 servings.

VENISON JAMBALAYA

1 onion, chopped
1 green pepper, chopped
3 tbsp. butter
1 tsp. garlic powder
1 qt. canned tomatoes
Salt and pepper to taste
1 1/2 c. chopped cooked venison
1 c. uncooked rice

Saute onion and green pepper in butter until tender. Add garlic powder, tomatoes, salt, pepper and venison; blend well. Stir in rice; simmer for 20 minutes.

Rock Lobster Jambalaya . . . Lobster creole-style with onions, peppers, tomatoes and rice.

ROCK LOBSTER JAMBALAYA

3 8-oz. packages frozen South African rock lobster-tails
2 tbsp. olive oil
2 med. onions, sliced
1 minced green pepper
2 1-lb. cans tomatoes
4 tsp. salt
1/4 tsp. basil
1 bay leaf
1 c. rice
2 tbsp. minced parsley
Hot sauce to taste

Prepare lobster-tails according to package directions. Cut away underside membrane; remove meat from shells. Cut into bite-sized pieces. Heat olive oil in Dutch oven. Add onions and green pepper; saute for 1 minute. Add tomatoes, 4 cups water, salt, basil and bay leaf. Simmer for 30 minutes. Add rice; cook until rice is tender. Add lobster-tails, parsley and hot sauce; bring to a boil. Serve in soup plates. Yield: 8 servings.

SPECIAL JAMBALAYA

2 lb. shrimp, deveined
Salt and pepper to taste
1 tbsp. flour
1 green pepper, minced
6 scallions, minced
4 stalks celery, finely diced
2 doz. oysters
1 1/2 c. diced cooked ham
1 c. diced cooked chicken
6 c. cooked rice

Cover shrimp with cold water. Season with salt and pepper. Cook for 5 minutes or until shrimp are tender; drain, reserving stock. Melt 3 tablespoons fat in pan; stir in flour until mixture is blended. Add 3/4 cup hot reserved stock, vegetables and oysters; simmer for several minutes or until vegetables are tender. Add shrimp, ham, chicken and rice. Stir until heated through. Garnish with parsley, hearts of celery, radishes and scallions. Yield: 8-10 servings.

DELICIOUS JAMBALAYA

3 tbsp. butter
1/2 c. chopped onions
1/2 c. chopped green onions
3/4 c. chopped green pepper
1/2 c. chopped celery
1/4 lb. cooked ham, diced
2 cloves of garlic, minced
2 c. chicken broth
3 lge. tomatoes, chopped
1/4 c. chopped parsley
1/2 tsp. salt
1/8 tsp. pepper
1/4 tsp. thyme
1 bay leaf
1/8 tsp. cayenne pepper
1 c. rice
3 4 1/2-oz. cans shrimp

Melt butter in large heavy skillet over low heat. Stir in onions and green onions, 1/2 cup green pepper, celery, ham and garlic; cook over medium heat for 5 minutes or until onions are tender. Stir in broth, tomatoes, parsley, salt, pepper, thyme, bay leaf and cayenne pepper; cover. Bring tomato mixture to a boil. Add rice gradually, stirring constantly. Simmer, covered, for 20 minutes or until rice is tender. Mix in shrimp and remaining green pepper; simmer, covered, for 5 minutes longer. Yield: 6-8 servings.

WILD RICE JAMBALAYA

1/2 c. wild rice, washed
1/2 c. rice
2 c. chopped celery
1 8-oz. can mushrooms
1/4 c. chopped onions
1/4 lb. ground pork
1/2 lb. ground veal
1/4 c. shortening
3 tbsp. soy sauce
1 can mushroom soup

Combine wild rice and 2 1/4 cups boiling water; simmer, covered, for 20 minutes. Add rice; bring to a boil. Reduce heat; cover. Cook for 20 minutes longer. Saute celery, mushrooms, onions and meats in shortening. Combine celery mixture and rice mixture; add soy sauce, soup and 3/4 cup water. Place in greased 2-quart casserole. Bake, covered, at 350 degrees for 2 hours. Yield: 8 servings.

Jelly

Fruit jellies are clear, semisolid gelatinous foods. They retain the characteristic color and flavor of the fruit from which they are prepared. They are smooth in texture yet firm enough to hold their shape when unmolded.
INGREDIENTS: All jellies contain *fruit juice* that is extracted by boiling the fresh fruit; and *sugar* to enhance the flavor and aid in the formation and preservation of the jelly. Some jellies may use liquid or powdered *commercial pectin,* a natural thickening substance; and/or *acid* such as lemon juice, to enhance the flavor and to aid in setting. The addition of pectin and/or acid usually depends on the type and maturity of the fruit specified in the recipe. Underripe fruit usually contains sufficient natural pectin and acid so that additional quantities of these ingredients are unnecessary.
PROCESSING: Follow instructions given below for preparing jellies without added pectin. (For recipes using commercial pectin, follow the pectin manufacturers' detailed instructions.) Select a combination of ripe and underripe fruit to achieve full flavor and color as well as the proper balance of pectin and acid. Wash all fruit in cold, running water. *To extract juice from fruit*—Measure fruit into heavy enamel or stainless steel saucepan. Crush bottom layer to provide sufficient liquid to prevent sticking. Begin cooking over low heat, stirring occasionally, until more moisture is drawn from the fruit. Increase heat to moderate and continue cooking until fruit is soft and has begun to lose its color. Pour mixture into damp jelly bag. Allow juice to drip through into container below; do not squeeze. *To prepare jelly*—Measure strained fruit juice into saucepan (as specified in recipe); simmer. Add sugar to simmering fruit juice. Stir to dissolve. Cook to the point of jellying, skimming as necessary. Begin to test juice about 10 minutes after sugar is added. *To test jelly*—Dip large spoon into boiling syrup. Lift spoon so that syrup runs over the side. When the drops of syrup merge and break from the spoon in a sheet, leaving the spoon clean, the jelly is ready. This "sheeting stage" registers from 220 to 222 degrees on a candy thermometer.
PACKING: Scald jelly glasses in boiling water for 10 to 15 minutes; drain and place on tray. Prepare paraffin according to instructions on label. Pour jelly into glasses to within 1/2 inch of top. Prick air bubbles with a pin. After jelly has set, cover with 1/8 inch melted paraffin (about 1 tablespoon). Allow jelly to cool thoroughly before screwing lids on tightly.
SERVING: Like jams, jellies can appear at any meal as spreads and condiments. Or, they can be sweet fillings for baked goods.
(See CANNING.)

BEET JELLY

3 lb. fresh beets
2/3 c. lemon juice
6 c. sugar
1 1/2 pkg. powdered pectin

Cook beets in water to cover; drain. Reserve 4 cups beet liquid. Combine reserved liquid with lemon juice in saucepan; bring to a rolling boil for 5 minutes. Add sugar; boil for 2 minutes longer. Add pectin; boil for 1 minute. Remove from heat; skim. Pour into sterilized jelly glasses; seal with paraffin.

CARROT JELLY

4 c. carrots, ground
3 c. orange juice
2 c. crushed pineapple
10 c. sugar
2 c. powdered pectin

Boil carrots with orange juice until soft; add pineapple. Pour half the mixture into large kettle. Add 5 cups sugar; bring to a rolling boil. Boil, stirring constantly, for 5 minutes. Add 1 cup pectin; bring to a rolling boil for 1 minute. Remove from heat; skim. Pour into sterilized jars; seal with paraffin. Repeat procedure.

CHRISTMAS APPLE JELLY

1 qt. canned apple juice
5 1/2 c. sugar
5 drops of red food coloring
1 pkg. powdered pectin

Combine juice and sugar in large saucepan; bring to a boil, stirring constantly until sugar is dissolved. Boil for 2 minutes. Add food coloring and pectin; bring to a rolling boil for 1/2 minute. Remove from heat; skim. Pour into hot sterilized jars; seal with paraffin. Yield: 7 half pints.

CINNAMON CANDY JELLY

5 1/2 c. sugar
1/2 lb. cinnamon candies
1 bottle liquid pectin

Mix sugar, 3 cups water and candies in large saucepan; bring to a boil. Boil, stirring constantly, until candies are melted. Add pectin; bring to a boil. Boil rapidly for 1 minute; skim. Pour into sterilized jelly glasses. Seal with paraffin.

CORNCOB JELLY

12 red corncobs, broken
3 c. sugar
1 pkg. powdered pectin

Boil corncobs in 6 cups water for 30 minutes; cool. Strain; add enough water to measure 3 cups, if necessary. Combine liquid with sugar; bring to a boil. Boil for 3 minutes; stir in pectin. Bring to a rolling boil for 1 minute. Remove from heat; skim. Pour into sterilized jars; seal with paraffin.

CRANBERRY JELLY

3 1/2 c. cranberry juice cocktail
4 c. sugar
1 pkg. powdered pectin
1/4 c. lemon juice

Combine cranberry juice and sugar in large kettle; bring to a full rolling boil. Stir in pectin; bring to a boil again. Boil for 1 minute, stirring constantly. Remove from heat; stir in lemon juice. Skim. Pour into hot sterilized jars; seal with paraffin. Yield: Six 1/2-pint jars.

CRANBERRY WINE JELLY

3 c. cranberry juice cocktail
7 c. sugar
1/4 tsp. cinnamon
1/4 tsp. cloves
1 c. red port wine
1 bottle liquid pectin

Combine cranberry juice cocktail, sugar and spices in large kettle; mix well. Bring to a rolling boil; boil for 1 minute, stirring constantly. Stir in wine and pectin; boil for 1 minute. Skim; pour into hot sterilized jelly glasses. Seal with paraffin. Yield: 8 glasses.

FIG JELLY

3 lb. half-ripe figs
3 lb. sugar
2 lge. lemons, sliced

Wash figs; remove stems. Bring sugar and 2 cups water to a boil in large kettle; stir until sugar is dissolved. Add figs and lemons; bring to a rolling boil for 30 minutes. Remove from heat; strain mixture through jelly bag. Return liquid to kettle; bring to a rolling boil. Boil for 5 minutes or until jelly sheets from spoon. Skim. Pour into hot sterilized jars; seal with paraffin.

FRUIT JELLY

2 c. apple juice
1 c. cherry juice
1 c. red raspberry juice
5 c. sugar
1 pkg. powdered pectin

Combine juices in large kettle; bring to a rolling boil. Add sugar; stir until dissolved. Boil until jelly sheets from spoon; stir in pectin. Boil for 1/2 minute. Remove from heat; skim. Pour into hot sterilized jars; seal with paraffin.

CONCORD GRAPE JELLY

3 1/2 lb. ripe Concord grapes
6 c. sugar
1 pkg. powdered pectin

Stem grapes; crush thoroughly in kettle. Add 1 1/2 cups water; bring to a boil. Simmer, covered, for 10 minutes; remove from heat. Strain through jelly bag. Combine 5 cups juice with sugar in large kettle; bring to a rolling boil, stirring constantly, until sugar is dissolved. Boil for 1 minute. Stir in pectin; boil for 1 minute, stirring constantly. Remove from heat; skim. Pour into hot sterilized jars; seal with paraffin.

GRAPE-BEET JELLY

4 c. beet juice
5 c. sugar
2 pkg. grape drink mix
1 box powdered pectin

Combine beet juice and sugar; bring to a boil. Add sugar mixture and powdered drink mix; bring to a rolling boil. Boil for 2 minutes; add pectin. Boil for 1 minute longer. Remove from heat; skim. Pour into hot sterilized glasses; seal with paraffin.

GRAPE JELLY

1 pt. bottled grape juice
3 1/2 c. sugar
1 pkg. powdered pectin

Combine grape juice with 1 cup water in large kettle; bring to a rolling boil, stirring constantly. Add sugar; bring to a rolling boil, stirring constantly. Boil for 1 minute. Add pectin; boil for 1 minute longer. Remove from heat; skim. Pour into hot sterilized jars; seal with paraffin.

GRAPE JUICE JELLY

6 1/2 c. sugar
3 6-oz. cans frozen grape juice
2 1/2 c. water
1 bottle liquid pectin

Combine sugar, grape juice and water in large kettle; bring to a rolling boil, stirring constantly. Boil for 1 minute; add pectin. Boil, stirring constantly, for 1 minute longer. Pour into hot sterilized jars; seal with paraffin. Yield: Twelve 6-ounce glasses.

GRAPEFRUIT JELLY

2 grapefruit
3 c. sugar

Peel, section and seed grapefruit; grind. Measure pulp; add 3 cups water to each cup pulp. Blend thoroughly; refrigerate overnight. Pour pulp into large kettle; simmer for 20 to 30 minutes. Strain through jelly bag. Pour 3 cups liquid into kettle; add sugar. Bring to a boil, stirring constantly, until sugar is dissolved and mixture reaches soft-ball stage. Pour into hot sterilized jars; seal with paraffin.

HONEY JELLY

3 c. honey
1/2 bottle pectin

Combine honey with 1 cup water; bring to a boil. Boil for 1 minute; add pectin. Bring to a rolling boil; boil for 1/2 minute. Remove from heat. Pour into sterilized jars; seal with paraffin.

MINT JELLY

1 1/2 c. (packed) fresh mint leaves
Green food coloring
4 c. sugar
1 pkg. powdered pectin

Pick and wash fresh mint leaves carefully; bring to a boil with 3 1/4 cups water. Steep, covered, for at least 10 minutes. Strain through double cheesecloth; measure 3 cups mint infusion. Add a few drops green food coloring to desired tint. Combine mint liquid and sugar in large kettle; bring to a boil, stirring constantly, until sugar is dissolved. Boil for 1 minute; add pectin. Boil, stirring constantly, for 1 minute longer. Remove from heat; skim. Pour into hot sterilized jars; seal with paraffin.

PEACH JELLY

3 1/2 lb. ripe peaches
4 1/2 c. sugar
Powdered pectin

Cut up and pit peaches; do not peel. Crush in large kettle. Add 1 cup water; bring to a boil. Reduce heat; simmer, covered, for 10 minutes. Strain through jelly bag. Combine 4 1/2 cups peach juice with sugar; bring to a rolling boil, stirring constantly until sugar is dissolved. Boil for 1 minute; stir in pectin. Bring to rolling boil; boil for 1 minute, stirring constantly. Remove from heat; skim. Pour into sterilized jars; seal with paraffin.

STRAWBERRY JELLY

3 qt. fresh strawberries
5 c. sugar
1 box powdered fruit pectin

Hull and crush strawberries; pour crushed berries into jelly bag over deep bowl. Let juice drip through bag. Juice should measure about 3 1/2 cups. Pour strawberry juice into kettle; bring to a rolling boil. Add sugar. Cook, stirring, until mixture returns to a fast boil. Add pectin; boil for exactly 60 seconds. Remove kettle from heat. Skim off foam quickly; pour jelly to within 1/2-inch of top of sterilized glasses. Seal while hot. Jelly may be tinted with red food coloring if desired.

RASPBERRY JELLY

Raspberries
Sugar

Wash raspberries; drain thoroughly. Crush raspberries in large kettle; bring to a boil. Reduce heat; simmer, covered, for 10 minutes. Strain juice through jelly bag. Measure 1 1/2 cups sugar for each cup juice into kettle; bring to a rolling boil, stirring constantly until sugar is dissolved. Boil for 2 minutes or until syrup sheets from spoon. Pour into hot sterilized jars; seal with paraffin.

RED CURRANT JELLY

3 1/2 qt. red currants
7 c. sugar
1 pkg. powdered pectin

Crush currants in large kettle; add 1 1/2 cups water. Bring to a boil; reduce heat. Simmer, covered, for 10 minutes. Strain through jelly bag. Combine 6 1/2 cups juice with sugar in kettle; bring to a rolling boil, stirring constantly until sugar is dissolved. Boil for 1 minute; add pectin. Boil, stirring constantly, for 1 minute longer. Remove from heat; skim. Pour into hot sterilized jars; seal with paraffin.

ROSEHIP JELLY

Wild rosehips
Pectin

Wash rosehips; cut off small leaves and blemishes. Cut in halves. Add 1 pint water for each quart of rosehips; boil until tender. Strain through jelly bag. Prepare according to pectin package directions for berry jelly. Pour into sterilized jars; seal with paraffin.

Strawberry Jelly . . . The clearness of this jelly is matched by its luscious sweet flavor.

Jelly Roll

JELLY ROLL CLASSIC

3 eggs, separated
1 1/2 c. sugar
1 tsp. orange juice
1 tbsp. grated orange rind
1 1/2 c. flour
1 1/2 tsp. baking powder
1/4 tsp salt
Confectioners' sugar
Jelly or jam

Beat egg yolks until thick and lemony; add sugar, juice and rind gradually. Add 1/2 cup hot water, stirring constantly. Sift flour, baking powder and salt; fold into egg mixture. Beat egg whites until stiff peaks form; fold into egg mixture. Line 10 x 15-inch jelly roll pan with greased waxed paper. Pour batter into pan. Bake at 375 degrees for 12 minutes or until cake tests done. Loosen edges of cake from pan; turn onto towel sprinkled with confectioners' sugar. Remove paper carefully; trim edges of cake. Roll cake and towel from narrow end immediately; cool on wire rack. Unroll cake; spread with jelly. Reroll; sprinkle with additional confectioners' sugar.

Kale

Kale is a green vegetable that is a member of the cabbage family. It is characterized by loose, spreading, curled leaves that do not form a head. Kale is an excellent source of Vitamin A and calcium. (1 cup cooked kale = 45 calories)

AVAILABILITY: Fresh kale is available year-round; some canned and frozen kale is also marketed.

BUYING: Look for fresh kale with young, tender leaves bright green in color and free from blemishes. Allow 2 1/2 pounds to serve 4 people.

STORING: Rinse kale in cold water and drain well to remove any sand. Wrap in plastic or in a cloth and store in the vegetable crisper. Use within two days.

PREPARATION: Before cooking kale, cut off the roots, any damaged leaves, and cut out the middle rib portion. Cook according to recipe or for 10-15 minutes in a small amount of water.

KALE LOAF

1/4 c. celery leaves
3 tbsp. butter
1 tbsp. flour
1/4 c. vegetable stock
1 1/2 c. cooked chopped kale
1 egg beaten
3/4 c. cooked diced carrots
1 1/2 c. cooked rice
1 tbsp. salt
2 slices bacon

Saute celery leaves in butter; add flour, vegetable stock, kale, egg, carrots, rice and salt. Blend mixture thoroughly. Shape into loaf; lay bacon across top. Bake at 400 degrees for 30 minutes. Yield: 8 servings.

SOUTHERN-STYLE KALE

2 c. cooked kale
1 tsp. butter
Salt and pepper to taste
3 slices bacon
3 hard-boiled eggs, halved
Paprika to taste

Mix kale with butter, salt and pepper; place in serving bowl. Fry bacon until crisp; drain. Crumble bacon over kale; top with eggs. Sprinkle with paprika. Yield: 4 servings.

Lamb

Lamb is the tender meat from young sheep under 2 years old. What is commonly marketed as lamb is an animal from 5 months to 1 year of age. *Milk finished lamb* ranges from 3 to 5 months; *yearlings* from 1 to 2 years; and mutton from 1 1/2 to 2 years or older. Lamb contains all 21 amino acids as well as minerals (iron, phosphorus, magnesium) and vitamins (thiamine, riboflavin, niacin). (3 1/2 ounces of lamb = 258 calories)

AVAILABILITY: Depending on the demand in a region, lamb is supplied either year-round or mainly during the early autumn and spring. Only a small amount of mutton is marketed in the United States.

BUYING: Allow 1/2 to 3/4 pound of bone-in lamb or 1/3 to 1/2 pound boneless lamb per person. Lamb is covered with a thin, clear, brittle membrane known as the *fell.* It is usually removed from chops but left on roasts. Beneath this paper-like covering is a layer of firm, white fat. Depending on the age of the animal, the lean ranges from pinkish to red in color with a fine grained and velvety texture.

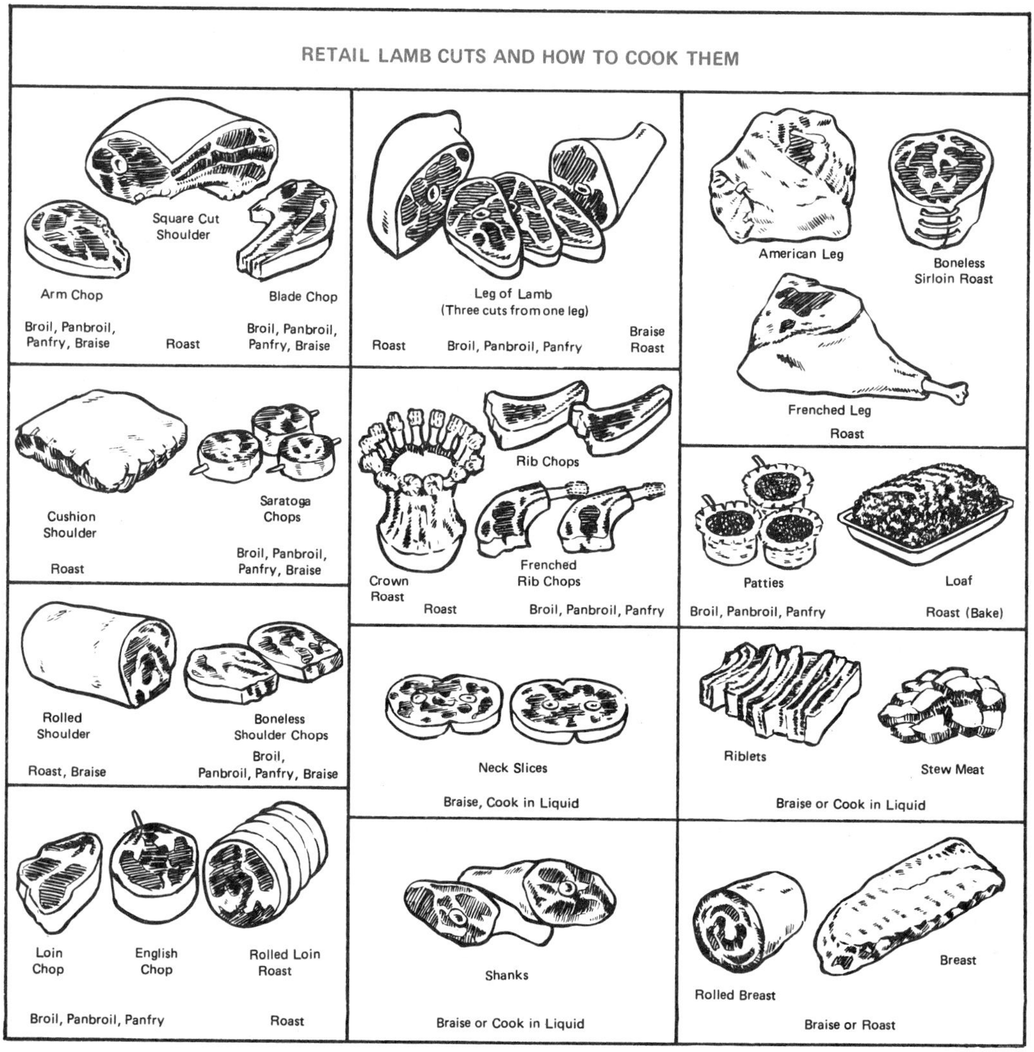

RETAIL LAMB CUTS AND HOW TO COOK THEM

Arm Chop — Broil, Panbroil, Panfry, Braise
Square Cut Shoulder — Roast
Blade Chop — Broil, Panbroil, Panfry, Braise

Leg of Lamb (Three cuts from one leg) — Roast; Broil, Panbroil, Panfry; Braise, Roast

American Leg
Boneless Sirloin Roast
Frenched Leg
Roast

Cushion Shoulder — Roast
Saratoga Chops — Broil, Panbroil, Panfry, Braise

Crown Roast — Roast
Rib Chops
Frenched Rib Chops — Broil, Panbroil, Panfry

Patties — Broil, Panbroil, Panfry
Loaf — Roast (Bake)

Rolled Shoulder — Roast, Braise
Boneless Shoulder Chops — Broil, Panbroil, Panfry, Braise

Neck Slices — Braise, Cook in Liquid

Riblets
Stew Meat
Braise or Cook in Liquid

Loin Chop
English Chop
Broil, Panbroil, Panfry
Rolled Loin Roast — Roast

Shanks — Braise or Cook in Liquid

Rolled Breast
Breast
Braise or Roast

TIMETABLE FOR COOKING LAMB

CUT	ROASTED AT 300 F. OVEN TEMPERATURE		BROILED	BRAISED	COOKED IN LIQUID
	Meat Thermometer Reading Degrees F.	Time Minutes per lb.	Time Minutes	Total Time Hours	Time Hours
Leg	175 to 180	30 to 35			
Shoulder (Whole)	175 to 180	30 to 35			
Rolled	175 to 180	40 to 45			
Cushion	175 to 180	30 to 35			
Breast (Stuffed)				1 1/2 to 2	
Rolled	175 to 180	30 to 35		1 1/2 to 2	
Lamb Loaf	175 to 180	30 to 35			
Chops (1 inch)	175 to 180	30 to 35	12		
Chops (1 1/2 inch)			18		
Chops (2 inch)			22		
Lamb Patties (1 inch)			15 to 18		
Neck Slices				1	
Shanks				1 1/2	
Stew					1 1/2 to 2
Panbroiling requires approximately one-half the time of broiling.					

It should be well-marbled with streaks of fat. *Quality Grading*—the U. S. Department of Agriculture inspects and grades lamb exactly as they do for beef: Prime, Choice, Good, Standard, Commercial and Utility. (See BEEF for thorough explanation of grades.) Because lamb is meat from a young animal, most cuts are quite tender. *Tender cuts* include leg, loin, shoulder and rib roasts; steak, loin, rib and shoulder chops. *Less tender cuts* are those from the breast and shank sections.

STORING: Remove fresh lamb from its original wrapper and re-wrap loosely in waxed paper to allow free circulation of air. Or loosen prepackaged wrapping. Store in coldest part of the refrigerator. Use within 3 days. Ground lamb and variety cuts keep only 24 hours in the refrigerator. For longer storage, plan on freezing the latter. *To freeze* lamb—wrap in moisture- and vapor-proof paper. Store large cuts in home freezer for 6 to 9 months; ground lamb and variety cuts for 3 to 4 months.

PREPARATION: Most lamb cuts can be cooked by dry heat methods (broiling, roasting, panbroiling, and grilling). Low temperatures are recommended for best results. Large cuts are usually roasted, steaks and chops broiled, panbroiled, and grilled, and less tender cuts braised.

SERVING: Lamb is best served either piping hot or cold, not lukewarm. Mint leaves or jelly provide a flavorful garnish.

(See CARVING.)

FRENCH RAGOUT

2 lb. lamb, cut in 1-in. cubes
1/4 c. flour
1 8-oz. bottle French dressing
1 c. small onions
1 c. sliced carrots
1 c. sliced mushrooms
2 c. hot mashed potatoes

Dredge lamb in flour; saute in 1/4 cup French dressing in skillet until browned. Add remaining dressing and 1/2 cup water; cook, covered, for 1 hour or until lamb is tender. Add onions and carrots; cook for 30 minutes longer or until vegetables are tender. Add mushrooms; pour into 2-quart casserole. Spoon potatoes around edge. Bake at 450 degrees for 10 minutes or until browned. Yield: 6 servings.

TASTY LAMB STEW

Flour
Salt and pepper to taste
3 lb. lamb stew meat
1 c. sliced carrots
1 c. sliced celery
1 c. chopped onions
2 c. string beans
4 c. cubed potatoes
2 tbsp. dried celery leaves
1/2 tsp. thyme
1/2 tsp. marjoram

Combine flour and salt and pepper. Dredge lamb in seasoned flour; brown in 3 tablespoons hot fat in large skillet. Add water to cover; simmer for 1 hour and 30 minutes. Add all remaining ingredients; simmer for 30 minutes longer. Blend 2 tablespoons flour and 1/4 cup water; add to lamb mixture gradually, stirring constantly, until thickened. Yield: 8 servings.

GLORIOUS LAMB STEW

Salt and pepper to taste
2 lb. lamb, cubed
1 clove of garlic, crushed
2 tbsp. flour
2 tbsp. tomato paste
4 carrots
2 slices onion
Leaves of 3 stalks of celery
1 bay leaf
Sprigs of parsley
4 med. mushrooms, sliced
10 sm. onions
1 tsp. sugar
5 med. potatoes, quartered
3 tbsp. sherry
1 c. cooked peas

Place fat in skillet over high heat. Salt and pepper lamb cubes; brown in hot fat evenly on all sides. Drain fat from pan; reserve. Reduce heat; add garlic to lamb in skillet. Sprinkle flour over lamb and garlic; cook, stirring, until blended well. Add 2 cups water and tomato paste to lamb mixture, blending well; bring to a boil. Pour mixture into 3-quart casserole. Dice 1 carrot; tie onion slices, carrot, celery leaves, bay leaf and parsley in cloth bag. Add to casserole. Bake, covered, at 325 degrees for 30 minutes; remove bag. Heat reserved fat in skillet; cook mushrooms gently for 3 minutes. Remove from skillet. Cut remaining carrots into quarters; add to skillet with onions. Sprinkle sugar over carrots and onions; cook until glazed. Add mushrooms, glazed vegetables and potatoes to lamb mixture. Bake, covered, for 1 hour longer or until lamb and vegetables are tender. Pour in sherry and peas just before serving. Serve with chopped parsley, if desired. Yield: 6 servings.

LAMB RAGOUT WITH DUMPLINGS

1 2-lb. lamb shoulder
Lamb fat
1 med. onion, chopped
1/2 c. diced celery
1 bay leaf
2 tsp. salt
1/2 tsp. marjoram
Dash of garlic salt
Dash of sweet basil
Dash of rosemary
6 sm. white onions
6 sm. carrots
2 tsp. cornstarch
6 tbsp. milk
1 c. prepared biscuit mix
1 tsp. curry powder

Cut lamb into 2-inch pieces. Brown in lamb fat in heavy pan. Remove lamb. Add onion and celery; cook for 3 minutes. Pour off fat. Return lamb to pan. Add 2 cups water, bay leaf, salt, marjoram, garlic salt, basil and rosemary. Simmer for 1 hour. Add onions and carrots. Simmer for 30 minutes longer. Mix cornstarch with small amount of cold water; stir into pan liquid gradually, stirring constantly until thickened. Stir milk into biscuit mix; add curry powder, mixing well. Drop by tablespoonfuls onto hot lamb mixture. Steam, tightly covered, for 10 minutes. Yield: 6 servings.

LAMB-STRING BEAN STEW

2 lb. lamb stew meat
1 lge. onion, chopped
3 tbsp. cooking oil
2 cans tomato sauce
2 No. 303 cans cut string beans

Brown stew meat and onion in oil in large skillet; cook until lamb is tender. Stir in tomato sauce; simmer for 30 minutes. Drain 1 can string beans; add to lamb mixture. Add remaining string beans with liquid. Simmer for 30 minutes longer. Serve over hot steamed rice. Yield: 6 servings.

PEASANT STEW

1 1/2 lb. lamb shoulder, cut in 1 1/2-in. cubes
1/2 c. Italian dressing
2 tbsp. shortening
1 env. onion soup mix
1 c. thinly sliced carrots
1/2 lb. green beans, cut up
1/2 c. sliced celery
2 tbsp. flour

Marinate lamb in dressing overnight in refrigerator. Drain lamb; reserve marinade. Heat shortening in heavy saucepan; saute lamb for 10 minutes, browning well. Drain off fat; stir in 2 1/2 cups water, reserved marinade and onion soup mix. Simmer, covered, 45 minutes or until tender. Add vegetables; simmer until vegetables are tender. Combine flour and 1/4 cup water; add broth, stirring constantly, until thickened. Yield: 6 servings.

SHERRIED LAMB STEW

3 lb. lamb stew meat
2 tbsp. oil
6 carrots, cut in 2-in. pieces
4 onions, quartered
2 cloves of garlic, minced
1 7-oz. can tomato sauce
1 c. sherry
1 tsp. salt
1/4 tsp. pepper
1/2 tsp. basil
1/2 tsp. rosemary
1/2 tsp. oregano
4 potatoes, quartered
2 tbsp. flour

Trim fat off lamb; brown in oil in skillet. Add all remaining ingredients except potatoes and flour. Simmer for 1 hour and 30 minutes. Add potatoes; simmer for 30 minutes longer or until potatoes are tender. Blend flour and 2 tablespoons water to make a paste; add to stew, stirring constantly, until thickened and smooth. Yield: 4-6 servings.

LAMB IN MINT JELLY

1/2 c. chopped mint leaves
2 tbsp. sugar
4 tbsp. white vinegar
2 tbsp. gelatin
1 tsp. salt
1/4 tsp. pepper
8 sm. tomatoes
2 sm. onions, thinly sliced
4 sm. cucumbers, sliced
3 c. diced cooked lamb
1/2 c. grated beets

Chop mint leaves; add 1/2 cup boiling water and sugar. Let stand for 30 minutes to cool. Add vinegar to cooled mint mixture. Soften gelatin in mint mixture; combine gelatin mixture and 1 1/2 cups boiling water. Stir to dissolve gelatin thoroughly. Add salt and pepper, blending well; cool to room temperature. Remove mint leaves. Arrange tomatoes in large mold. Dip onions and 1/2 cup cucumbers in gelatin mixture; press to sides of mold. Arrange layers of lamb alternately with beets and remaining cucumbers; add gelatin mixture to each layer to cover. Chill in refrigerator overnight; unmold on lettuce. Garnish with additional tomato and pickles, if desired. Yield: 6 servings.

BAKED LAMB CHOPS

4 shoulder lamb chops, 1/4 in. thick
Salt and pepper to taste
1/4 c. melted butter
1/4 c. chopped parsley
1/4 c. chopped chives

Arrange chops in shallow baking dish. Sprinkle with salt and pepper. Combine all remaining ingredients; mix well. Pour over lamb. Bake at 350 degrees for 30 minutes. Yield: 4 servings.

BARBECUED LAMB CHOPS

6 shoulder lamb chops
1 med. onion, sliced
1 1/2 tsp. ginger
1 1/2 tsp. dry mustard
1 tsp. salt
1/4 tsp. pepper
1/4 tsp. garlic salt
3 tbsp. chili sauce
3 tbsp. salad oil
1 1/2 tbsp. vinegar
1 tbsp. Worcestershire sauce

Place lamb chops and onion slices in shallow baking pan. Combine all remaining ingredients; pour over chops. Bake at 350 degrees for 40 minutes or until of desired doneness, basting occasionally. Yield: 4-6 servings.

ENGLISH LAMB CHOPS

1 tsp. salt
1/4 tsp. pepper
4 tbsp. corn oil
6 lamb chops
1 tbsp. butter
2 tbsp. flour
1 c. milk
1 tsp. Worcestershire sauce
1 c. soft bread crumbs
1/4 c. grated cheese

Combine salt, pepper and oil; marinate chops in mixture for 30 minutes. Combine butter, flour, milk and Worcestershire sauce; place mixture over low heat, stirring constantly, until thickened and smooth. Broil chops 4 inches from source of heat for 5 minutes on one side. Turn; spread uncooked side with white sauce. Combine crumbs and cheese; sprinkle over sauce. Place chops in baking dish. Bake at 350 degrees for 20 minutes. Garnish with parsley. Yield: 6 servings.

LAMB CHOP AND TOMATO BROIL WITH HORSERADISH SAUCE

Color photograph for this recipe on page 79.

6 1-inch thick loin lamb chops
3 med. tomatoes, halved
1/4 c. butter, melted
1/2 tsp. salt
1/8 tsp. pepper
12 sm. boiled potatoes
Chopped parsley
3 tbsp. drained horseradish
1 c. sour cream

Place lamb chops and tomato halves on rack in shallow pan. Broil 4 to 6 inches from source of heat for 8 to 12 minutes or to desired degree of doneness, turning once. Combine butter, salt and pepper; brush chops and tomatoes frequently with butter mixture. Peel potatoes; brown lightly in additional butter in skillet. Arrange chops, tomatoes and potatoes on heated platter; sprinkle tomatoes with parsley. Blend horseradish with sour cream. Season to taste with additional salt. Serve sauce with lamb chop dish.

LAMB CHOPS IN MARINADE

1/2 tsp. marjoram
1/2 tsp. salt
1/4 tsp. pepper
1 clove of garlic, minced
1/4 tsp. paprika
2 tbsp. vegetable oil
4 to 6 1-in. thick loin lamb chops

Blend marjoram, salt, pepper, garlic and paprika together; add oil. Cover lamb chops with marinade; let stand at room temperature for 1 to 3 hours. Broil to desired doneness, basting with marinade. Yield: 2-3 servings.

ROCKY MOUNTAIN LAMB RIBLETS

1 12-oz. bottle hot catsup
1/2 c. orange juice
1/4 c. chopped parsley
1/4 tsp. celery seed
1/4 tsp. rosemary leaves
3 lb. lamb riblets

Combine catsup, orange juice, parsley, celery seed and rosemary. Pour over lamb; marinate overnight. Remove lamb to large skillet; reserve marinade. Brown lamb thoroughly. Arrange lamb in baking dish; cover with reserved marinade. Cover. Bake in 375-degree oven for 35 to 40 minutes or until tender.

Rocky Mountain Lamb Riblets . . . Lamb steeped and baked in a seasoned marinade.

CALIFORNIA-STYLE LAMB CHOPS

Color photograph for this recipe on page 68.

6 lamb shoulder chops, 1 in. thick
1 tbsp. salad oil
1/4 c. sliced onion
2 1-lb. 14-oz. cans yellow cling peach halves
1 tsp. grated lime peel
1/4 c. lime juice
1 tbsp. honey
1 1/2 tsp. salt
1 tsp. monosodium glutamate
1/2 tsp. ginger
1/4 tsp. dry mustard
1 3-in. cinnamon stick
1 tbsp. cornstarch
12 to 16 whole strawberries

Brown lamb chops in oil in large skillet. Remove chops; drain, reserving 1/2 tablespoon drippings in skillet. Add onion to reserved drippings; saute until tender. Add chops. Drain peaches; reserve syrup. Mix 3/4 cup reserved peach syrup, lime peel, lime juice, honey, salt, monosodium glutamate, ginger, mustard and cinnamon stick; pour over chops. Simmer, covered, for 40 to 45 minutes or until chops are fork-tender. Remove lamb chops to serving dish; keep hot. Blend cornstarch with 1 tablespoon reserved peach syrup. Stir into simmering sauce in skillet; cook for 30 seconds, stirring constantly. Add peaches, cut sides up; top each peach half with a strawberry. Cover; heat for 2 to 5 minutes or until heated through. Remove peaches to serving dish with lamb; pour sauce over top. Garnish with watercress. Yield: 6 servings.

GOURMET LAMB CHOPS

8 rib lamb chops
1/2 c. Burgundy
1 clove of garlic, crushed
1/2 tsp. salt
1/2 tsp. onion powder
1/8 tsp. pepper
1/2 c. grated Parmesan cheese
2 tbsp. chopped parsley

Wipe chops with damp paper towels. Combine Burgundy, garlic, salt, onion powder and pepper. Place chops in single layer in marinade. Let stand at room temperature for 1 hour and 30 minutes, turning chops several times; drain. Broil chops 4 inches from source of heat for 10 minutes on one side. Broil on other side for 6 minutes or until of desired doneness. Combine cheese and parsley. Place chops on heated platter. Top each chop with small amount of cheese mixture. Yield: 8 servings.

MANDARIN LAMB CHOPS

8 lamb chops, 1/2 in. thick
2 tbsp. cooking oil
1 11-oz. can mandarin oranges
1 9-oz. jar red currant jelly
4 tsp. cornstarch
1 tsp. salt
1/2 c. light raisins

Brown chops on both sides in oil in large skillet. Remove from pan; drain oil from pan. Drain oranges; reserve liquid. Blend reserved liquid and jelly. Place jelly mixture over low heat, stirring until melted. Combine cornstarch with 1/2 cup water; blend into jelly mixture, stirring until smooth. Cook, stirring constantly, until clear; stir in salt. Return chops to sauce. Simmer, covered, until chops are tender. Add raisins and oranges; place over medium heat, stirring occasionally, until heated through. Serve with hot rice. Yield: 4 servings.

ORIENTAL LAMB CHOPS

1/2 c. dried apricots
1/2 c. dried prunes
2 tbsp. navy beans
6 lamb chops
1 tbsp. butter
Salt to taste
1/2 c. chopped walnuts
1 1/2 tsp. curry powder
1/2 lime, sliced

Soak apricots, prunes and beans separately in water to cover for several hours. Brown chops in butter; add 1/2 cup water. Simmer for 15 minutes. Add salt, dried fruits, beans and nuts; stir well. Place chop mixture in casserole. Bake at 350 degrees for 1 hour. Remove from oven; stir in curry powder and lime. Return to oven. Bake for 30 minutes longer. Serve with rice. Yield: 4 servings.

YORKSHIRE LAMB HOT POT

6 lamb chops
3 1/2 tbsp. butter
12 sm. white onions
12 sm. potatoes
1/2 tsp. salt
1/8 tsp. pepper
2 tbsp. flour
1/2 c. sherry
1/2 tsp. minced parsley

Brown chops in 1 1/2 tablespoons butter; add onions, potatoes, 4 cups water, salt and pepper. Simmer, covered, for 30 minutes or until vegetables are tender. Arrange chops, onions and potatoes on hot platter. Blend flour and 2 tablespoons water. Add to pan liquid, stirring constantly, over high heat until thickened. Add remaining butter and sherry, stirring well. Serve with lamb. Sprinkle servings with parsley. Yield: 6 servings.

ENGLISH-STYLE LAMB CURRY

1/4 c. chopped onion
1/4 c. chopped apple
1/4 c. butter
2 1/2 tbsp. flour
Pinch of salt
1 c. chicken broth
1 c. half and half
1 lb. cooked lamb, chopped
1 1/2 tsp. curry powder

Saute onion and apple in butter in heavy skillet; blend in flour and salt. Add chicken broth and half and half gradually, stirring constantly, until smooth and thickened. Stir in lamb and curry powder; simmer, covered, for 15 minutes. Serve over mound of rice. Yield: 4 servings.

HAWAIIAN LAMB CURRY

4 lb. lamb, cubed
Butter
3 tbsp. curry powder
2 pieces fresh gingerroot
2/3 c. diced celery
1 med. onion, chopped
1 1/3 c. flour
1 2/3 c. evaporated milk
Salt and pepper to taste
2 c. coconut milk

Saute lamb in butter in heavy skillet. Add curry powder and gingerroot; stir well. Pour off fat; add celery, onion and enough water to cover. Cook for 1 hour or until tender. Blend flour and evaporated milk; add to lamb mixture with salt and pepper. Add additional curry powder if needed. Add coconut milk; place over low heat until heated through. Do not boil. Remove gingerroot. Serve over rice with mango chutney, chives, peanuts, crushed bacon, chopped ham, chopped hard-cooked eggs, shredded coconut, lime rind and fresh pineapple spears. Yield: 12 servings.

LAMB-BROCCOLI BAKE

1 10-oz. package frozen broccoli spears, cooked and drained
6 slices Swiss cheese
8 thin slices cooked lamb
2 tbsp. flour
1 c. milk
1 tbsp. mustard with horseradish
1/2 tsp. salt
Dash of pepper
Dash of Worcestershire sauce

Arrange broccoli in bottom of 1 1/2-quart baking dish. Top with 2 slices cheese and 4 slices lamb. Repeat layers, ending with cheese on top. Melt butter in small saucepan; stir in flour quickly. Add milk gradually, stirring constantly, until sauce thickens. Stir in remaining ingredients; pour over lamb dish. Bake, covered, at 350 degrees for 20 minutes. Garnish with parsley or paprika. Yield: 4 servings.

ENGLISH HOT POT

2 c. diced cooked lamb
2 onions, sliced
3 med. potatoes, sliced
1 10-oz. can peas
3 tbsp. dry sherry
1 7-oz. can mushrooms, drained
1 c. leftover gravy
Paprika to taste

Place lamb, onions, potatoes and peas in alternate layers in greased 2-quart baking dish; combine sherry, mushrooms and gravy. Pour sherry mixture over top. Sprinkle with paprika. Bake, covered, at 350 degrees for 1 hour and 15 minutes. Uncover. Bake for 15 minutes longer. Yield: 6 servings.

LAMB-VEGETABLE KABOBS

1 bouillon cube
1/4 c. chopped mint
2 tbsp. wine vinegar
1 tsp. sugar
1 1 1/2-lb. lamb
2 tomatoes, quartered
8 sm. white onions
Salt and pepper to taste

Combine 1/2 cup water, bouillon cube and mint in saucepan; bring to a boil. Cook for 5 minutes. Stir in vinegar and sugar. Cut lamb into 1-inch cubes; marinate lamb in vinegar mixture for 1 hour. Drain lamb; reserve marinade. Alternate lamb cubes, tomatoes and onions on four long skewers. Place on rack in broiler pan. Season with salt and pepper. Broil about 3 inches from source of heat for 20 minutes. Brown on all sides. Baste frequently with remaining mint marinade. Yield: 4 servings.

LAMB KABOBS ON KASHA

2 lb. boned lamb
4 sm. green peppers
12 sm. white onions, parboiled
1/2 c. salad oil
1/4 c. lemon juice
2 cloves of garlic, crushed
1 tbsp. salt
1/2 tsp. freshly ground pepper
6 bay leaves, halved
16 cherry tomatoes

Cut lamb into 1 1/2-inch cubes. Cut green peppers in half; remove seeds. Parboil onions. Combine oil, lemon juice, garlic, salt, pepper and bay leaves. Pour over lamb; marinate for 4 to 5 hours in refrigerator. Alternate lamb cubes and bay leaves on skewers; brush with marinade. Place on baking sheet. Broil 4 to 5 inches from source of heat for 7 to 8 minutes on each side or to desired doneness. Arrange vegetables on separate skewers, allowing 1 pepper, 3 onions and 4 tomatoes per serving. Brush with marinade; broil for 2 to 3 minutes on each side.

Kasha

3 tbsp. minced scallions
1/4 c. finely chopped celery
Butter
1 egg, slightly beaten
1 1/2 c. buckwheat groats
4 c. boiling beef stock
1 1/2 tsp. salt

Saute scallions and celery in 2 tablespoons butter in saucepan. Combine beaten egg and groats; add to sauteed vegetables. Pour beef stock into groat mixture. Cover; simmer until all liquid is absorbed. Stir in salt and 6 tablespoons butter. Spoon groat mixture onto serving platter. Sprinkle with 2 tablespoons additional chopped scallions. Arrange lamb and vegetables on skewers over Kasha. Yield: 4 servings.

Lamb Kabobs on Kasha . . . Bring an Eastern flavor to your meal with this well-seasoned dish.

AMERICAN KABOBS

3/4 c. vinegar
2 bay leaves
1 tsp. salt
1 tsp. sugar
1 1/2 lb. lamb shoulder, cubed
3 tomatoes, cut in sixths
18 sm. mushrooms
6 slices bacon, cut in thirds

Combine vinegar, 3/4 cup water, bay leaves, salt and sugar in small saucepan. Bring to a boil; simmer for 5 minutes. Cool. Pour over lamb cubes in large bowl; marinate for 24 hours. Drain; reserve marinade. Arrange lamb, tomato wedges, mushrooms and bacon slices alternately on 6 skewers. Place in shallow pan. Broil for 15 minutes, 3 to 4 inches from source of heat, turning frequently. Baste with reserved marinade. Yield: 6 servings.

SKEWERED LAMB

1 leg of lamb
1 can tomato paste
1/4 c. white wine vinegar
1 sm. bunch parsley, chopped
1 clove of garlic
1/2 tsp. cinnamon
1 tsp. curry powder
1 tsp. salt
1/2 tsp. pepper
1/4 c. olive oil
Cherry tomatoes
Green pepper cubes
Mushrooms

Cut lamb into 1-inch cubes. Combine tomato paste, vinegar, parsley, garlic, cinnamon, curry powder, salt, pepper and oil in deep bowl. Marinate lamb in sauce for 24 hours or longer. Drain lamb; reserve sauce. Arrange lamb cubes, tomatoes, green pepper and mushrooms alternately on long skewers. Broil 3 or 4 inches from source of heat to desired doneness; baste with sauce. Yield: 6-8 servings.

TURKISH LAMB KABOBS

1/2 c. olive oil
1/4 c. lime juice
1 tsp. dry mustard
1/4 tsp. thyme
1 bay leaf
1/8 tsp. basil
1/8 tsp. rosemary
1/2 tsp. salt
1/8 tsp. pepper
1 med. onion, chopped
2 lb. lamb shoulder or rump
2 onions, sliced 1/4 in. thick
1 6-oz. can mushroom caps
1 green pepper, sliced in rings

Blend oil, lime juice, mustard, thyme, bay leaf, basil, rosemary, salt, pepper and onion in bowl. Cut lamb into 1 1/2-inch cubes. Add lamb cubes to onion mixture; marinate for 5 hours or overnight. Drain. Alternate lamb cubes on skewers with onion slices, mushrooms and pepper rings; repeat, ending with lamb cubes. Preheat broiler. Place kabobs on rack 3 inches from source of heat. Broil for 20 minutes, turning once. Serve with rice pilaf. Yield: 6 servings.

SHISH KABOB WITH RICE PILAF

Color photograph for this recipe on page 73.

1/4 c. tarragon vinegar
1/2 c. dry white wine
2 tbsp. salad oil
1 clove of garlic, minced
2 tbsp. mixed pickling spice
1/4 tsp. crushed rosemary
2 lb. boned lamb shoulder
1 green pepper
2 firm tomatoes, quartered
8 med. mushrooms
1/4 c. butter
1 c. rice
2 tbsp. minced onion
2 c. chicken broth

Combine vinegar, wine, oil, garlic, pickling spice and rosemary; mix well. Cut lamb in 1 1/2-inch cubes; place in bowl. Pour vinegar mixture over lamb; marinate in refrigerator for several hours or overnight. Drain lamb; reserve marinade. Cut green pepper in 1 1/2-inch squares. Alternate cubes of lamb, green pepper, tomatoes and mushrooms on 4 large skewers; brush with reserved marinade. Place on rack in broiler pan. Broil 3 to 4 inches from heat for 8 to 10 minutes on each side. Melt butter in saucepan; add rice and onion. Cook, stirring constantly, until rice is lightly browned. Add chicken broth; cover saucepan. Simmer for 20 to 25 minutes or until all liquid is absorbed and rice is tender. Place in serving dish; place kabobs on rice. Yield: 4 servings.

LAMB CROQUETTES

2 egg yolks, beaten
1/3 c. half and half
2 c. finely chopped cooked lamb
2 tbsp. minced parsley
1/2 tsp. lemon juice
1 hard-cooked egg yolk, mashed
1 c. cooked peas, sieved
Salt and pepper to taste
1 tbsp. butter, melted

Beat egg yolks with half and half; add all remaining ingredients except butter. Shape into croquettes; brush with butter. Place croquettes on greased baking sheet. Bake at 425 degrees for 15 minutes or until brown. Yield: 5-6 servings.

LAMB IN RAMEKINS

3 c. cubed cooked lamb
1 tbsp. bacon fat
1 12-oz. bottle beer
1 bay leaf
Sliced onion to taste
1 sprig of parsley
1/4 tsp. salt
1 can mushroom soup
1 can mushrooms, drained

Brown lamb cubes in bacon fat lightly; add beer, bay leaf, onion, parsley and salt. Simmer for 30 minutes. Drain, reserving 1/2 cup liquid. Spoon lamb mixture into 4 ramekins. Blend soup with reserved liquid; pour over lamb mixture. Top with mushrooms. Bake in 350-degree oven for 15 minutes. Yield: 4 servings.

LAMB KIDNEYS IN WINE

20 lamb kidneys
4 tbsp. butter
Salt and pepper
1 tbsp. Worcestershire sauce
1 c. red wine
2 tbsp. cornstarch
1/4 c. sour cream
Cooked buttered rice

Slice kidneys in half lengthwise; cut out fat with scissors. Brown in butter in heavy skillet. Salt and pepper to taste. Add Worcestershire sauce and wine; simmer for 15 to 20 minutes. Blend cornstarch and

1/2 cup water; add gradually to simmering kidneys, stirring constantly, until thickened. Add sour cream, blending well. Serve with rice. Yield: 4-6 servings.

LAMB TURNOVERS

1 clove of garlic, minced
1/4 c. bacon drippings
3 tbsp. flour
1/2 tsp. salt
1 c. milk
1/2 c. minced green pepper
1 1/2 c. diced cooked lamb
1 recipe pie pastry
1 can mushroom soup
1/2 tsp. Worcestershire sauce
Pepper to taste

Brown garlic in bacon drippings; add flour and salt, blending until smooth. Add milk gradually; cook over low heat until thickened. Remove from heat. Add green pepper and lamb; cool. Cut pastry into 5-inch rounds. Place 1/3 cup lamb mixture on each round. Fold over; crimp edges together well. Place on baking sheet. Bake at 425 degrees for 30 to 40 minutes. Mix all remaining ingredients; bring to a boil. Remove from heat; pour over turnovers to serve.

LAMB-VEGETABLE DISH

4 shoulder lamb chops, 1 in. thick
2 tbsp. flour
4 carrots, diced
2 1/2 c. string beans
3 potatoes, diced
1 med. onion, sliced
Salt and pepper to taste
2 c. bread dressing

Dredge chops in flour. Fry in 2 tablespoons fat until browned well and just tender. Place vegetables in square baking dish; pour 1/2 cup water and pan juices over vegetables. Season with salt and pepper. Place lamb over vegetables in single layer. Spoon dressing on top. Bake, covered with foil, in 350-degree oven for 1 hour. Bake for 15 minutes longer, uncovered, until browned.

PARTY PERFECT LAMB LOAF

2 3-oz. cans chopped mushrooms
2 tbsp. chopped onion
2 tbsp. butter
1/3 c. finely chopped cooked ham
1/4 c. fine dry bread crumbs
1/2 tsp. salt
1/4 tsp. pepper
2 tbsp. dry sherry
2 lb. lean ground lamb

Drain mushrooms, reserving liquid. Saute onion in butter until tender in large skillet; add reserved mushroom liquid. Add mushrooms. Simmer until liquid is reduced to 1 tablespoonful. Remove from heat; add ham, crumbs, salt, pepper and sherry. Divide lamb into three parts. Alternate layers of lamb and mushroom mixture in 9 x 5 x 3-inch loaf pan, ending with lamb. Bake at 350 degrees for 1 hour and 15 minutes. Drain off drippings. Yield: 6 servings.

GRILLED LAMB PARISIENNE

1 7-lb. leg of lamb, boned
1/2 c. salad oil
1/4 c. lemon juice
1 tsp. salt
1/4 tsp. pepper
1 tsp. oregano
1/2 tsp. basil
2 bay leaves
2 cloves of garlic

Wipe lamb with damp paper towels. Combine remaining ingredients in jar with tight-fitting lid; shake vigorously. Place lamb in large baking dish; pour marinade over lamb. Refrigerate, covered, for 12 hours to overnight, turning occasionally. Secure lamb on rotisserie spit. Grill for 2 hours or until done, basting frequently with marinade.

CROWN OF LAMB ROAST

1 crown of lamb roast
Salt
Pepper
2 tsp. instant dried minced onion
1 c. chopped celery
3 c. dry bread crumbs
3 c. chopped apple
3/8 c. butter
1/2 c. pignolia nuts
1/2 tsp. ginger
1 tsp. marjoram
Bacon

Preheat oven to 350 degrees. Rub roast with salt and pepper to taste. Saute onion, celery, bread crumbs and apple in butter in skillet; add nuts, 1/2 teaspoon salt, 1/8 teaspoon pepper, ginger and marjoram. Mix lightly. Fill roast with apple mixture. Wrap bacon around rib ends to prevent charring. Bake for 35 minutes per pound. Remove from oven; replace bacon with paper frills. Allow 2 ribs per serving.

CRANBERRY-LEMON GLAZED LAMB

1 4-lb. leg of lamb
Salt to taste
1 1-lb. can whole cranberry sauce
1/4 c. lemon juice
1 tbsp. grated lemon rind
3/4 tsp. rosemary

Sprinkle lamb with salt; place on rack in roasting pan. Bake at 300 degrees for 2 hours. Combine all remaining ingredients; mix well. Spread sauce over lamb. Bake, basting occasionally, for 1 hour and 30 minutes or until meat thermometer registers 175 degrees. Yield: 6 servings.

LAMB WITH APRICOT STUFFING

1 1/3 c. packaged precooked rice
1 1/3 c. sliced dried apricots
2/3 c. chopped celery
1/4 c. chopped parsley
2 tsp. salt
1/4 tsp. pepper
1/2 tsp. minced dried onion flakes
1/2 tsp. rosemary
1 c. chicken bouillon
1 5-lb. boned leg of lamb

Combine rice, apricots, celery, parsley, seasonings, onion flakes, rosemary and bouillon; let stand for 10 minutes. Stuff lamb with half the mixture; enclose remaining stuffing in foil. Secure lamb with string and skewers. Place on rack in shallow roasting pan. Bake at 325 degrees for 3 hours or until meat thermometer registers 175 degrees. Bake foil-wrapped stuffing for 1 hour. Serve lamb on platter with extra stuffing. Prepare gravy, if desired. Yield: 8-10 servings.

CUMBERLAND LAMB ROAST

1 leg of lamb
1 tsp. salt
1 tsp. dry mustard
1/2 tsp. ginger
5 thin slices lemon, halved
2/3 c. currant jelly
1 tbsp. lemon juice

Trim excess fat from lamb. Combine salt, mustard and ginger; rub lamb well with mixture. Place on rack in roasting pan, rounded side up. Bake at 325 degrees for 2 hours. Remove from oven. Arrange lemon slices with wooden picks, petal fashion, on side of lamb. Combine jelly and lemon juice; spread over lamb. Return to oven. Bake for 1 hour longer. Gravy may be made from pan drippings, if desired. Yield: 12 servings.

LAMB ROAST L'ORANGE

1 leg of lamb
1 tsp. rosemary
Salt
1 clove of garlic,
2 c. orange juice
1 tbsp. cornstarch

Rub lamb with rosemary; salt lightly. Pierce lamb; insert garlic in lamb. Bake at 325 degrees for 30 minutes per pound. Baste with orange juice occasionally. Let pan liquid brown between bastings. Remove lamb from oven; place on heated platter. Remove fat from pan drippings; add salt to taste. Blend cornstarch and 2 tablespoons water; add to pan drippings. Cook, stirring constantly, until thickened. Serve sauce over lamb. Yield: 8 servings.

LEG OF LAMB NEAPOLITAN

1 5-lb. leg of lamb
2 tsp. salt
1 tsp. oregano
1 med. green pepper, chopped
4 med. onions, chopped
1 clove of garlic, crushed
1 lge. can tomatoes

Sprinkle lamb with salt and oregano; place on rack in shallow roasting pan. Bake at 325 degrees for 1 hour and 30 minutes; drain off drippings. Combine green pepper, onions, garlic and tomatoes; baste lamb with small amount of tomato mixture. Bake for 1 hour longer or to 175 degrees on meat thermometer, basting occasionally. Thin sauce with small amount of water, if necessary. Serve lamb with sauce. Yield: 6-8 servings.

PINEAPPLE-LAMB ISLANDER

1 4-lb. boned leg of lamb
1 lge. can pineapple slices, quartered
1/4 c. lemon juice
1/4 c. wine vinegar
1/4 c. catsup
1/2 c. sauterne
3 tbsp. cooking oil
2 tsp. seasoned salt
1 tbsp. prepared mustard
1/2 tsp. oregano
2 sprigs of mint, bruised
2 cloves of garlic, halved
12 sm. canned onions
12 sm. plum tomatoes

Trim fat from lamb; cut lamb into 1 1/2-inch cubes. Drain pineapple; reserve 1/2 cup syrup. Combine reserved pineapple syrup with lemon juice, vinegar, catsup, sauterne, oil, salt, mustard and oregano. Add mint and garlic; combine with vinegar mixture thoroughly. Stir vinegar mixture into lamb; refrigerate, covered, for several hours or overnight. Remove mint and garlic. Thread 4 lamb cubes on each skewer. Grill over hot coals until lamb is brown on outside and faintly pink inside. Brush with marinade frequently, turning often. Thread pineapple on end of skewer, just before lamb is of desired doneness. Grill for several minutes, until pineapple is heated through and browned. Thread onions and tomatoes on separate skewers; grill, brushing with marinade, until heated and lightly brown. Yield: 6 servings.

SPIT-ROASTED LAMB

1/3 c. butter
1/2 lb. calf liver
2 c. soft bread crumbs
1/4 c. raisins
1 egg, slightly beaten
1 clove of garlic, minced
1/4 c. minced parsley
Salt
1/4 tsp. thyme
1/4 tsp. pepper
1 6-lb. leg of lamb, boned
Paprika to taste
Chopped mint leaves
Salad oil

Melt 2 tablespoons butter in skillet. Add liver; saute on both sides lightly or until just browned. Remove from pan; mince well. Melt remaining butter; combine with liver, bread crumbs, raisins, egg, garlic, parsley, 1/2 teaspoon salt, thyme and pepper. Lay boned lamb, skin side down, on flat surface. Spread stuffing over lamb; close opening securely. Rub lamb with salt to taste, paprika and mint leaves. Rub with oil. Place on spit; grill 4 inches from source of heat for 1 hour and 30 minutes or until tender.

GLAZED LEG OF LAMB

1 leg of lamb
Salt and pepper to taste
1/2 c. dry sherry
1/2 c. currant jelly
1/2 c. catsup
1/2 tsp. marjoram leaves
Parsley
Lemon wedges

Glazed Leg of Lamb . . . For an Easter dinner with a difference, feature springtime lamb.

Sprinkle lamb with salt and pepper; place on rack in shallow roasting pan. Bake in 325-degree oven for 30 to 35 minutes per pound or until meat thermometer registers 175 degrees for medium doneness. Combine sherry, jelly, catsup and marjoram in small saucepan; heat, stirring, until jelly melts. Brush on lamb occasionally during last 1 hour and 30 minutes of baking time. Heat remaining sauce; serve with lamb. Garnish with parsley and lemon wedges.

LAMB ARABIENNE

1 pkg. wild and long grain rice
1 4-lb. shoulder of lamb, boned
1 lge. can apricot halves and syrup
Parsley

Preheat oven to 425 degrees. Cook rice according to package directions. Stuff cavity in lamb with rice. Secure opening in lamb with skewers; place in roasting pan. Bake for 30 minutes or until fat is browned and crisp. Remove lamb from oven; reduce heat to 350 degrees. Drain off excess fat. Pour apricots and syrup over lamb. Bake, covered, for 2 hours longer or until tender. Bake, uncovered, for several minutes longer, basting with syrup and pan drippings until crisp and glazed on top. Serve surrounded with apricots. Garnish with parsley.

LAMB WITH VEGETABLE STUFFING

1 med. onion, diced
1/2 c. chopped celery
3 tbsp. chopped green pepper
3/4 c. grated carrot
2 c. soft bread crumbs
3 1/4 tsp. salt
3/8 tsp. pepper
1/2 tsp. thyme
1/4 tsp. paprika
1/4 c. butter, melted
1 4-lb. lamb shoulder
8 med. potatoes, pared

Combine onion, celery, green pepper, carrot, crumbs, 1 1/4 teaspoons salt, 1/8 teaspoon pepper, thyme, paprika and butter; mix thoroughly. Cut pocket in end of lamb; fill pocket with stuffing mixture. Fasten with skewers, or tie with string; brush with additional melted butter. Season with 2 teaspoons remaining salt and remaining pepper. Bake at 350 degrees for 2 hours. Bring 2 cups water to a boil; add potatoes. Cook for 10 minutes; arrange around roast in pan. Bake potatoes and lamb for 1 hour longer or until tender. Turn potatoes occasionally; baste with pan drippings.

ROAST LAMB ITALIENNE

1 5-lb. shoulder of lamb
Salt and pepper to taste
Garlic salt to taste
1 tsp. oregano
1 sm. can tomato sauce
1 c. consomme

Brown lamb well in small amount of fat on all sides in heavy Dutch oven. Salt and pepper lamb; sprinkle with garlic salt and oregano. Add tomato sauce and consomme. Reduce heat; simmer, covered, for 2 hours and 30 minutes or until tender, turning lamb frequently. Remove lamb to platter. Make gravy from pan drippings, if desired. Yield: 4 servings.

STUFFED SHOULDER OF LAMB

1 4-lb. lamb shoulder, boned
2 bay leaves, crushed
1 green pepper, finely chopped
1 onion, minced
1 1/2 c. quartered tomatoes
1 tsp. salt
1 c. cooked rice

Cut pocket in lamb for stuffing. Melt small amount of fat in skillet; add bay leaves, green pepper and onion. Cook until tender. Add tomatoes and salt; cook for 5 minutes. Stir in rice. Fill pocket of lamb with rice stuffing; close opening securely. Place on rack, fat side up, in roasting pan. Bake in 325-degree oven for 2 hours and 30 minutes or to 182 degrees on meat thermometer. Make gravy with pan drippings, if desired.

TEXAS-STYLE LAMB ROAST

1 6-lb. lamb shoulder, trimmed
3 cloves of garlic
Salt and pepper to taste
1/2 c. flour
1 tsp. crushed rosemary
2 c. white wine
12 sm. onions
12 sm. potatoes
3 med. carrots, cut in 1-in. pieces
3 stalks celery, cut in 1-in. pieces

Pierce lamb; insert garlic. Combine salt, pepper and flour; dredge lamb in mixture. Combine rosemary and wine; marinate lamb in wine mixture for 3 hours. Place vegetables in roasting pan; place lamb over vegetables, skin side up. Pour marinade over lamb. Add water to marinade to cover pan bottom, if necessary. Preheat oven to 375 degrees. Bake, covered, until fork-tender, or for 2 hours, basting twice. Remove from oven; bone lamb. Return to oven; brown lightly. Make gravy from pan drippings, if desired. Yield: 6 servings.

STUFFED BREAST OF LAMB

1 3-lb. breast of lamb
4 c. stale bread
3 tbsp. chopped onion
1/4 c. melted butter
1/4 c. chopped celery
1/2 tsp. sage
1 tsp. salt
1/4 tsp. pepper

Cut pocket in end of lamb breast. Combine remaining ingredients; mix lightly. Place stuffing in pocket of lamb. Place in baking dish in cold oven. Bake at 375 degrees for 2 hours and 30 minutes. Yield: 46 servings.

BRAISED LAMB SHANK

4 lamb shanks
Flour
Salt and pepper to taste
1/4 tsp. thyme
1/2 tsp. rosemary
1 c. diced carrots
1 c. diced potatoes
1/4 c. diced celery
1 med. onion, chopped

Crack bones in shanks; dredge shanks with flour. Brown well in hot fat in large skillet. Add seasonings and 2 cups hot water. Simmer, covered, for 1 hour and 30 minutes. Add vegetables. Cook for 30 minutes longer or until vegetables are tender. Yield: 4 servings.

LITTLE POT ROASTS

1/4 c. all-purpose flour
1 tbsp. paprika
4 lamb shanks, fat removed
1/4 c. butter
1 clove of garlic
1/4 c. currant jelly
3 tsp. salt
2 c. diced white turnips
2 pkg. frozen lima beans, thawed
1 c. half and half
1/8 tsp. pepper

Combine flour and paprika; coat shanks on all sides with mixture. Heat butter in Dutch oven; saute garlic until golden. Remove garlic. Place shanks in skillet; cook until browned well. Add 2 tablespoons water, jelly and 2 teaspoons salt. Simmer, covered, for 45 minutes or until shanks are just tender. Place turnips and limas on top of shanks. Cook, covered, for 30 minutes. Remove vegetables and shanks to heated platter. Stir half and half, remaining salt and pepper into pan juices. Bring to a boil; remove from heat immediately. Pour over shanks and vegetables. Garnish with parsley. Yield: 4 servings.

THRIFTY LAMB PIE

2 c. diced cooked lamb
1 c. diced potatoes
1 onion, finely chopped
1/3 c. diced green pepper
2/3 c. diced celery
2/3 c. canned tomatoes, drained
1/2 tsp. sugar
1 1/2 tsp. salt
2 c. lamb stock
1 recipe biscuit dough

Combine all ingredients except dough; bring to a boil. Simmer for 15 minutes or until vegetables are crisp-tender. Place mixture in 1 1/2-quart baking dish. Prepare biscuit dough; roll 1/2 inch thick. Place 1-inch strip around top of baking dish. Cut remaining dough into rounds; place over pie. Bake at 400 degrees for 20 minutes. Yield: 4 servings.

Lane Cake

A Lane Cake is a white layer cake. It is usually filled with a mixture of egg yolks, pecans, coconut, candied fruit, raisins, and other ingredients as specified by individual recipes. It is frosted with a cooked frosting. (See CAKE.)

SOUTHERN LANE CAKE

3 1/4 c. sifted flour
3 1/2 tsp. baking powder
1/2 tsp. salt
1 c. butter
2 c. sugar
1 tsp. vanilla
1 c. milk
8 egg whites, stiffly beaten

Preheat oven to 375 degrees. Sift flour with baking powder and salt. Cream butter and sugar until light and fluffy; add vanilla. Beat in flour mixture and milk alternately. Fold egg whites into batter gently. Grease bottoms of four 9-inch layer pans; line with waxed paper. Pour batter equally into pans. Bake for 15 to 20 minutes. Cool.

Filling

8 egg yolks, slightly beaten
1 1/4 c. sugar
1/2 c. butter
1 c. chopped pecans
1/3 c. whiskey
1 c. chopped candied cherries
1 c. grated fresh coconut
1 c. chopped seeded raisins

Combine egg yolks, sugar and butter in saucepan. Cook over low heat for about 5 minutes, stirring constantly, until slightly thickened. Add remaining ingredients; cool. Spread between cake layers.

Frosting

2 1/2 c. sugar
1/8 tsp. salt
1/3 c. dark corn syrup
2/3 c. water
2 egg whites
1 tsp. vanilla

Combine sugar, salt, corn syrup and water in saucepan. Cook over low heat, stirring constantly, until sugar dissolves. Bring to a boil without stirring. Beat egg whites until foamy. Add 3 tablespoons syrup mixture; beat until stiff peaks form. Cook remaining syrup to 240 degrees on candy thermometer; pour slowly over egg whites, beating constantly. Beat until frosting begins to lose gloss and hold shape. Add vanilla. Spread over top and side of cake.

Leek

LEEK PIE

2 c. sifted flour
1 tsp. salt
1/4 tsp. white pepper
1/2 c. miniature shredded wheat biscuits
2/3 c. shortening
3 to 4 young leeks
Butter, melted
2 c. cottage cheese
2 tbsp. cornstarch
2 eggs

Preheat oven to 450 degrees. Sift flour, 1/2 teaspoon salt and 1/8 teaspoon white pepper together; crush shredded wheat biscuits. Combine 1/4 cup crushed cereal with flour mixture. Blend shortening into dry ingredients until mixture resembles coarse cornmeal. Add small amount of water at a time. Toss lightly until mixture begins to form a stiff dough; knead into smooth ball. Allow dough to rest for 10 minutes. Roll out on floured board 1 inch larger than 9-inch pie pan; place in pie pan. Bake for 20 to 25 minutes or until lightly browned. Trim leeks within 2 inches white portion; wash. Cut into 1/4-inch pieces to measure 3 cups. Saute leeks in 3 tablespoons butter until tender. Mix cottage cheese, cornstarch, remaining salt and pepper in saucepan. Heat through, stirring constantly over low heat until smooth. Beat eggs until thick and lemon colored. Add small amount of cottage cheese mixture to eggs; mix well. Add egg mixture to remaining cottage cheese mixture; cook, stirring constantly, until thickened. Mix leeks with sauce; pour into pie shell. Toss crushed cereal with 1 teaspoon butter; sprinkle over pie. Bake for 10 minutes or until heated through and topping is crisp.

LEEKS AU GRATIN

2 bunches leeks	*Pepper*
1 tsp. salt	*1/2 c. grated cheese*

Wash and trim leeks. Cook in boiling, salted water to cover for 15 minutes or until tender; drain. Arrange in buttered baking dish; sprinkle with pepper and cheese. Heat under broiler until cheese is melted.

SAUTÉED LEEKS

2 lb. fresh leeks	*1 lge. fresh tomato, diced*
2 lge. onions, chopped	*1 tsp. salt*
1/2 c. olive oil	*1/4 tsp. white pepper*
3 med. carrots, sliced	

Wash leeks thoroughly; discard dark green tops. Slice leeks into 2-inch sections. Soak in cold water; drain. Saute chopped onions in olive oil in saucepan for 15 minutes or until transparent; add carrots, tomato, leeks, salt and pepper. Add enough boiling water to just cover vegetables. Steam, covered, for 1 hour or until leeks are tender.

Lemon

The tangy yellow lemon is an oval-shaped citrus fruit that grows on an evergreen found in warm climates. California and Arizona produce America's fresh lemon supply. Lemons for processing come from Florida. Lemons contain Vitamins A and C, carbohydrate, calcium, and phosphorus. (One medium fresh lemon = 20 calories; 1 cup fresh, bottled, or canned lemon juice = 60 calories)

AVAILABILITY: Lemons are marketed fresh year-round with the greatest supplies available June through August. They are also available as bottled and canned lemon juice and as canned, frozen lemonade concentrate. Processed rind oil is sold in bottles as lemon extract.

BUYING: Select firm, heavy, deep yellow fresh lemons with fine-textured skin. Light or greenish-yellow color indicates undesirable acidity. Avoid shriveled, tough, or spongy fruit.

STORING: Store fresh lemons in cool, dry, dark place or refrigerator. They keep up to two weeks in refrigerator.

PREPARATION: Cut lemon with sharp knife on cutting board to make slices or wedges. To preserve appearance before serving, keep pieces in container covered with a damp cloth. To make juice, roll whole fruit on hard surface, gently pressing with palm of hand as you roll. Slice in half crosswise. Press each half firmly on juicer to extract juice. To grate lemon peel, grate the colored portion of the rind with food grater. Do not grate bitter white portion underneath rind.

SERVING: Lemon slices or wedges are used to garnish meats, poultry, seafood, soups, salads, and beverages. Lemon peel is used in candied fruit peel recipes. Grated lemon peel is used in baked products, meats, stuffings, soups, sauces, icings, and desserts. Fresh or commercial lemon juice is served in many ways. Sprinkle over meats, poultry, seafood, fruits, and vegetables. Add to beverages. Use in flavored butters, cakes, pies, cookies, custards, sherbets, sauces, and icings. Use as an anti-darkening agent for many sliced fruits. Add it to cooking water to keep poached eggs firm and to meat and poultry marinades to help tenderize the meats. Rub fish inside and out with lemon juice before cooking to reduce odors.

CANDIED LEMON PEEL

Lemon peel	*1/3 c. light corn syrup*
1 tbsp. salt	
Sugar	

Cut peel into halves or quarters. Add salt to 1 quart water; add peel. Let stand overnight. Drain; wash thoroughly. Place peel in saucepan; add water to cover. Simmer, changing water several times, until no bitter taste remains and peel is tender. Drain; cut in strips. Combine 2 cups sugar, 1 cup water and corn syrup in saucepan; cook to 234 degrees on candy thermometer or until syrup forms thread when dropped from spoon. Add peel. Simmer until peel is transparent; drain. Roll peel in sugar. Allow peel to dry well before packing for storage.

LEMON SOUP

2 qt. water	*4 eggs*
1 lemon, sliced	*1/2 c. cream*
1 lb. ground beef	*Salt and pepper to taste*
1 lb. ground pork	*2 tbsp. cornstarch*
1 c. cornmeal	

Bring 2 quarts water to a boil; add lemon. Mix beef, pork, cornmeal, eggs, cream, salt and pepper; shape into small balls. Drop mixture from spoon into boiling lemon mixture; simmer for 1 hour and 30 minutes or until meatballs are tender. Blend cornstarch and 2 tablespoons water; add to soup gradually, stirring constantly until thickened. Cook for 5 minutes longer. Yield: 6-8 servings.

STUFFED LEMONS

Lemons	*1 pt. grenadine*
2 c. vinegar	*2 c. ground dried figs*
6 c. sugar	*2 c. ground raisins*
1 c. lemon juice	*2 c. ground nuts*
2 4-in. pieces of cinnamon bark	*1/2 c. maraschino cherries, ground*
4 tbsp. red food coloring	*Maraschino cherry halves*

Cut small holes in ends of lemons. Remove pulp; discard. Place lemon shells in saucepan; add water to cover. Bring lemon mixture to a boil. Simmer for 15 minutes. Drain. Cover with water; return to a boil. Cook for 10 minutes. Drain; repeat process. Combine vinegar, sugar, 1 cup water, lemon juice, cinnamon, food coloring and grenadine; add lemon shells. Simmer lemon mixture for 30 minutes or until tender. Remove lemon shells; reserve syrup. Combine figs, raisins, nuts and cherries; blend well. Stuff lemons with ground mixture; seal ends with maraschino cherry halves. Pack in sterilized jars; fill jar with reserved syrup. Seal. Process in water bath for 15 minutes. Slice with sharp knife. Serve with meat or fowl.

CRUNCHY LEMON SALAD

1 sm. package lemon gelatin	*1/2 c. diced apples*
1 c. maraschino cherry juice	*1/2 c. maraschino cherries*
2 tbsp. lemon juice	*1/2 c. chopped celery*
1/2 tsp. salt	*1/2 c. chopped nuts*

Combine gelatin, 1 cup hot water, cherry and lemon juices and salt; cool. Stir in apples, cherries, celery and nuts; chill until firm. Yield: 6-8 servings.

LEMONADE FRUIT SALAD

1 lge. can fruit cocktail	*1/2 c. chopped nuts*
1 3-oz. package lemon gelatin	*1/2 c. mayonnaise*
1 6-oz. can frozen lemonade	*1/2 c. sour cream*
	1 tbsp. lemon juice
	1 tbsp. orange juice
	2 tsp. sugar

Drain fruit cocktail, reserving syrup; add enough water to syrup to make 1 cup liquid. Pour into saucepan; bring to a boil. Remove water from heat. Add gelatin; stir until dissolved. Add lemonade; chill until partially thickened. Stir in fruit cocktail and nuts; pour into mold. Chill until firm. Combine all remaining ingredients; blend until smooth. Serve mayonnaise mixture over salad.

LEMON-CREAM SALAD

2 3-oz. packages lemon gelatin	*1 8 1/2-oz. can crushed pineapple, drained*
6 oz. cream cheese	*1 c. heavy cream, whipped*
1 tsp. salt	
1 c. chopped nuts	
1 c. chopped celery	

Dissolve gelatin in 3 3/4 cups hot water; cool. Blend cream cheese and salt; blend into gelatin. Add nuts, celery and pineapple; fold in whipped cream. Pour into mold; chill until firm. Yield: 12 servings.

GLAZED LEMON BREAD

1/4 c. butter	*2 1/2 tsp. baking powder*
Sugar	*1 tsp. salt*
2 eggs	*3/4 c. milk*
2 tsp. grated lemon peel	*1/2 c. chopped walnuts*
2 c. sifted flour	*2 tsp. lemon juice*

Preheat oven to 350 degrees. Cream butter and 3/4 cup sugar until light and fluffy. Add eggs and lemon peel; beat well. Sift flour, baking powder and salt together; add to creamed mixture alternately with milk, beating until smooth after each addition. Stir in walnuts; pour into greased 8 1/2 x 4 1/2 x 2 1/2-inch loaf pan. Bake for 50 to 55 minutes or until bread tests done. Cool in pan for 10 minutes. Mix lemon juice and 2 tablespoons sugar; spoon over bread. Remove from pan; cool completely before slicing. Yield: 1 loaf.

LEMON-PECAN BREAD

1 c. sugar	*1/2 tsp. salt*
1 c. butter	*1 c. chopped pecans*
3 eggs	*1 c. white raisins*
2 tbsp. lemon extract	*1 tsp. grated lemon peel*
2 c. sifted flour	
1/2 tsp. baking powder	

Preheat oven to 400 degrees. Cream sugar and butter until fluffy; add eggs, one at a time, beating well after each addition. Add lemon extract. Sift flour, baking powder and salt together; add to egg mixture, stirring until blended. Add pecans, raisins and lemon peel; pour into greased loaf pan. Bake for 10 minutes. Lower temperature to 350 degrees. Bake for 1 hour longer. Yield: 8 servings.

LEMON TEA BREAD

3/8 c. butter	*1/2 c. milk*
1 1/3 c. sugar	*Rind of 1 lemon, grated*
2 eggs	*1/2 c. coconut*
1 1/2 c. flour	*Juice of 1 lemon*
1 tsp. salt	
1 tsp. baking powder	

Preheat oven to 350 degrees. Cream butter and 1 cup sugar well. Add eggs; beat until blended well. Sift flour, salt and baking powder together; add alternately with milk to creamed mixture, beating thoroughly. Stir in rind and coconut. Pour into greased loaf pan. Bake for 1 hour or until loaf tests done. Remove from oven; turn out onto platter. Mix lemon juice with remaining sugar; spoon over hot bread. Let juice run down sides; cool.

DANISH LEMON CAKE

1 3-oz. package lemon gelatin	*1 pkg. yellow cake mix*
3/4 c. cooking oil	*4 eggs*
	1 tbsp. lemon extract

1 c. powdered sugar
4 tbsp. lemon juice
2 tbsp. melted butter

Preheat oven to 350 degrees. Dissolve gelatin in 3/4 cup boiling water; cool. Add oil and cake mix, blending thoroughly. Add eggs, one at a time, mixing well. Add lemon extract. Pour batter in greased and floured tube pan. Bake for 50 minutes or until cake tests done. Remove cake from pan while warm. Combine all remaining ingredients. Punch holes in warm cake with wooden pick; cover with sugar mixture. Yield: 12 servings.

LEMON-BUTTERMILK CAKE

1 c. shortening
1/2 c. butter or margarine
3 c. sugar
4 eggs
3 1/2 c. sifted flour
1/2 tsp. salt
1 c. buttermilk
1 tsp. lemon extract
1/2 tsp. soda
Juice and grated rind of 1 lemon

Preheat oven to 325 degrees. Cream shortening, butter and 2 1/2 cups sugar until fluffy. Beat in eggs, one at a time. Sift flour and salt together. Combine buttermilk and lemon extract. Add flour mixture to creamed mixture alternately with buttermilk mixture. Dissolve soda in 1 tablespoon hot water; stir into batter. Pour batter into greased and floured tube pan. Bake for 1 hour and 15 minutes. Combine remaining sugar, lemon juice, lemon rind and 1/2 cup hot water in saucepan. Cook, stirring, until sugar is dissolved and syrup is clear. Pour hot syrup over hot cake. Yield: 20 servings.

LEMON CHIFFON CAKE

2 c. sifted flour
1 1/2 c. sugar
3 tsp. baking powder
1 1/4 tsp. salt
1/2 c. salad oil
7 egg yolks
2 tsp. vanilla
2 tsp. grated lemon rind
1 c. egg whites
1/2 tsp. cream of tartar
3 tbsp. butter
3 c. sifted powdered sugar
1/2 c. drained crushed pineapple

Preheat oven to 325 degrees. Sift flour, sugar, baking powder and 1 teaspoon salt into bowl; make well in center. Add oil, egg yolks, 3/4 cup cold water, vanilla and lemon rind; beat until smooth. Beat egg whites and cream of tartar until stiff peaks form. Do not underbeat. Pour egg yolk mixture gradually over egg whites; fold gently until just blended. Do not overmix. Pour into ungreased large tube pan. Bake for 55 minutes. Increase heat to 350 degrees. Bake for 10 to 15 minutes longer. Cream butter, remaining salt and 1/2 cup sugar; add remaining sugar and pineapple. Beat until creamy; spread between layers and over cake. Yield: 14-16 servings.

LEMON-CREAM SHERBET CAKE

4 eggs, separated
1/4 tsp. salt
1/8 tsp. cream of tartar
2 1/8 c. sugar
2 tbsp. water
1 tsp. vanilla
1/2 tsp. lemon juice
1 c. sifted cake flour
2 c. milk
1 1/2 tbsp. lemon rind
1/2 c. lemon juice
2 egg whites
1 c. heavy cream

Preheat oven to 325 degrees. Beat egg whites until foamy; add salt and cream of tartar. Beat until stiff peaks form, adding 1/2 cup sugar gradually. Mix egg yolks with 1/2 cup sugar, water, vanilla and lemon juice; beat until thick and lemon colored. Fold into egg whites; fold in flour gradually. Pour into 2 ungreased 9-inch round layer pans. Bake for 30 to 35 minutes. Invert pans on rack; cool. Remove cake from pans. Dissolve 1 cup sugar in milk. Add lemon rind and lemon juice, stirring constantly. Pour into 2 refrigerator trays; freeze for 1 hour and 30 minutes or until mushy. Beat 2 egg whites until stiff peaks form, adding remaining sugar slowly. Whip cream until stiff; add to frozen mixture. Add egg whites; blend well. Pack into 9-inch round cake pan; freeze for 2 hours or until firm. Unmold lemon sherbet; place between cake layers. Serve immediately.

LEMON CHEESE CAKE

1 c. butter
2 c. sugar
3 1/3 c. sifted flour
2 tsp. baking powder
1/8 tsp. salt
1 c. milk
1 tsp. vanilla
8 egg whites

Preheat oven to 325 degrees. Cream butter and sugar together until light and fluffy. Sift dry ingredients together. Add flour mixture, milk and vanilla to creamed mixture gradually, beating after each addition. Fold in stiffly beaten egg whites. Spoon batter into 3 greased and floured 9-inch layer cake pans. Bake until cake tests done. Cool layers thoroughly; remove from pans.

Filling

8 egg yolks, beaten
1 c. lemon juice
3 tbsp. flour
2 1/2 c. sugar
1/4 lb. butter

Beat all ingredients and 1/2 cup hot water together well in double boiler. Cook, stirring constantly, over boiling water until of spreading consistency. Spread between layers of cake. Yield: 10-12 servings.

LEMON CAKE SUPREME

1 pkg. lemon supreme cake mix
1 c. apricot nectar
2/3 c. oil
1/2 c. sugar
1 pkg. lemon gelatin
4 eggs
1 c. powdered sugar
Juice of 2 lemons

Preheat oven to 325 degrees. Combine cake mix, apricot nectar, oil, sugar and gelatin in mixing bowl; mix well. Add eggs, one at a time, beating well after each addition. Pour into 10 x 13 x 2-inch pan or tube cake pan. Bake for 1 hour. Combine remaining ingredients for glaze. Punch holes in cake with pick; pour glaze over cake while hot.

SUNSHINE LEMON ROLL

1 c. flour
1 tsp. baking powder
1/4 tsp. salt
3 lge. eggs
1 c. sugar
1/4 c. water
1 tsp. vanilla
Confectioners' sugar
1 pkg. lemon pie filling
1 pkg. dessert topping mix
Lemon Glaze
1 c. coconut

Preheat oven to 375 degrees. Sift flour, baking powder and salt; set aside. Have eggs at room temperature. Beat eggs in large mixer bowl for 10 minutes or until light and lemony. Add sugar gradually, beating constantly. Blend in water and vanilla in thin steady stream. Fold in dry ingredients, a small amount at a time; blend until batter is smooth. Pour batter into greased, waxed paper-lined 15 1/2 x 10 1/2 x 1-inch jelly roll pan. Bake for 12 to 15 minutes or until cake tests done. Loosen cake edges from pan; turn out on towel sprinkled with confectioners' sugar. Remove paper carefully; trim off crusty edges. Roll cake and towel from narrow end; cool on wire rack. Prepare pie filling according to package directions; chill. Whip dessert topping mix according to package directions; fold into pie filling. Unroll cake; remove towel. Spread with lemon filling; reroll. Frost with Lemon Glaze; sprinkle with coconut.

Lemon Glaze

3/4 c. sugar
2 tbsp. cornstarch
1/4 tsp. salt
2 tbsp. lemon rind
1 tbsp. butter
1/3 c. lemon juice

Combine sugar, cornstarch and salt with 3/4 cup water in saucepan; mix well. Bring to a rolling boil; boil for 1 minute, stirring constantly. Remove from heat. Add lemon rind and butter; stir in lemon juice gradually. Cool thoroughly.

DAIQUIRI MOLD

2 env. unflavored gelatin
2 c. sugar
1/8 tsp. salt
6 eggs, separated
1 c. lemon juice
2/3 c. white rum
2 c. heavy cream, whipped

Combine gelatin 1 1/2 cups sugar and salt in saucepan. Beat egg yolks, 1/2 cup water and lemon juice together until blended well; stir into gelatin mixture gradually. Place over low heat, stirring constantly, until mixture thickens slightly and gelatin dissolves. Do not boil. Stir in rum; chill in refrigerator, stirring occasionally, until mixture mounds slightly when dropped from spoon. Beat egg whites in large bowl until soft peaks form; beat in remaining sugar gradually. Continue to beat until stiff peaks form; fold gelatin mixture into egg whites. Fold cream into mixture; turn into 10-cup shallow mold. Chill until firm. Unmold.

LEMON CHIFFON REFRIGERATOR CAKE

1/2 lb. vanilla wafers, crushed
1 1/4 c. sugar
Juice of 2 lemons
Grated rind of 1 lemon
1/2 c. soft butter
8 eggs, separated
1 tbsp. unflavored gelatin
Whipped cream

Combine vanilla wafers and butter; blend well. Press on bottom and sides of 12 3/4 x 9 x 2-inch pan, reserving small amount for topping. Beat egg yolks until thickened; add 1 cup sugar, lemon juice and grated rind. Cook in double boiler until thick. Soften gelatin in 1/4 cup cold water; dissolve over boiling water. Cool slightly; stir into egg yolk mixture. Beat egg whites until stiff peaks form; add remaining sugar gradually. Fold in lemon mixture. Pour over crumb crust. Chill for 8 hours or overnight. Serve with whipped cream; sprinkle with reserved crumbs. Yield: 10-12 servings.

ICE CREAM LEMON CAKE

3/4 c. sifted all-purpose flour
1 tsp. baking powder
1/2 tsp. salt
4 eggs, separated
3/4 c. sugar
1 6-oz. can frozen lemonade
Confectioners' sugar
2 pt. vanilla ice cream, softened
1 c. whipping cream

Sift flour, baking powder and salt together. Beat egg yolks until thick and lemon colored. Add 1/2 cup sugar gradually, beating until thick. Beat in 1/3 cup lemonade concentrate. Add dry ingredients; stir carefully until blended. Beat egg whites until frothy. Add remaining sugar gradually; beat until egg whites are stiff and glossy. Fold into batter. Spread batter evenly into greased and waxed paper-lined jelly roll pan. Bake in 375-degree oven for about 12 minutes or until cake tests done. Turn out onto towel dusted with confectioners' sugar. Remove waxed paper; trim off edges lengthwise. Roll cake up in towel; cool on rack. Unroll cake; spread with ice cream. Roll up as for jelly roll. Place in freezer to harden. Combine whipping cream and remaining lemonade concentrate; beat until cream forms soft peaks. Spread over ice cream roll. Store in freezer for at least 1 hour before serving. Yield: 8-10 servings.

LEMON CUSTARD MOLD

1 6-oz. can frozen orange juice concentrate
2 3-oz. packages orange gelatin
1 No. 2 can crushed pineapple
1 3-oz. package lemon pie filling mix
2 eggs, slightly beaten
1/3 c. sugar
1 c. sour cream

Break orange juice concentrate into chunks. Dissolve gelatin in 1 3/4 cups boiling water; add pineapple and orange concentrate. Stir until juice is blended. Pour into 9 x 13 x 2-inch pan; refrigerate until firm. Combine pie filling mix with eggs, sugar and 1/2 cup cold water; add 1 1/4 cups cold water. Cook over medium heat, stirring constantly, until mixture comes to a full boil and is thick. Cool, stirring occasionally. Add sour cream; spread over gelatin mixture. Chill thoroughly until set. Yield: 12 servings.

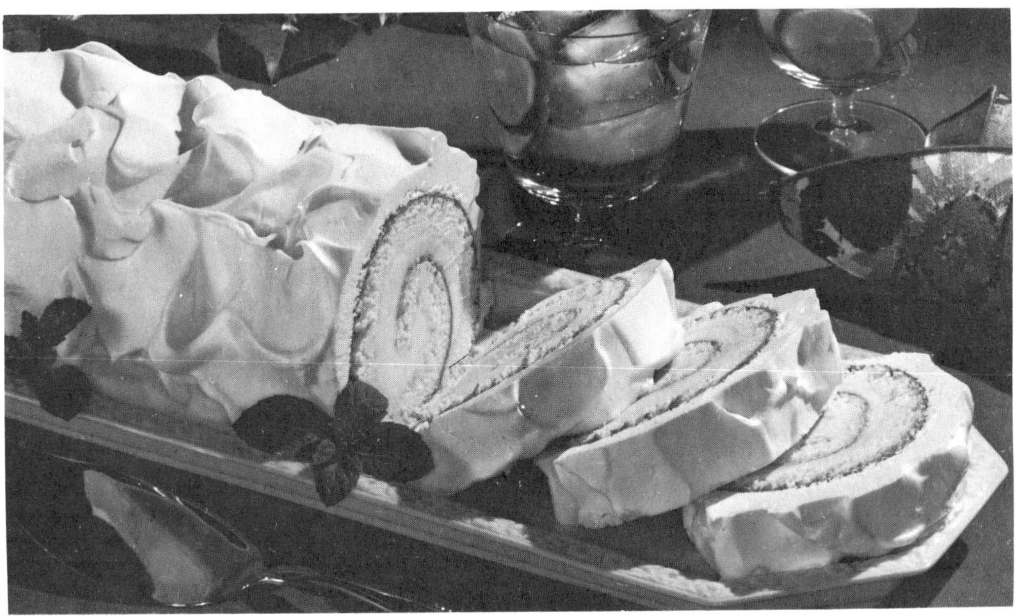

Ice Cream Lemon Cake . . . Serve this creamy frozen cake with iced tea as a summer dessert.

LEMON-COCONUT DESSERT

1 1/4 c. flour
1 1/4 c. coconut
1 1/2 c. sugar
3 soda crackers, crushed
Butter
2 tbsp. cornstarch
Juice and grated rind of 1 lemon
1 egg

Mix flour, coconut, 1 cup sugar and crumbs; cut in 3/4 cup butter. Pat half the mixture into 9 x 9-inch cake pan. Mix remaining sugar, 1 teaspoon butter, cornstarch, lemon juice and rind and egg; add 2 1/2 cups boiling water. Stir mixture thoroughly. Pour lemon mixture over crumb mixture. Sprinkle remaining crumb mixture evenly over filling. Bake at 350 degrees for 20 minutes or until lightly browned.

LEMON ICEBOX DESSERT

6 eggs, separated
1/4 tsp. salt
1/4 tsp. cream of tartar
1/4 tsp. vinegar
3 c. sugar
1 tsp. vanilla
Juice and grated rind of 2 lemons
1 pt. whipping cream
1 c. chopped walnuts

Beat egg whites slightly to blend; add salt, cream of tartar and vinegar. Add 2 cups sugar gradually, beating constantly. Beat until stiff peaks form; add vanilla. Spread meringue in buttered 14 1/2 x 11-inch pan, leaving depression in center. Bake at 300 degrees for 1 hour. Cool thoroughly. Combine egg yolks, remaining sugar, lemon juice and rind in double boiler; cook, stirring constantly, until thick and clear. Cool. Whip cream until thick. Spread half the cream on meringue; add lemon mixture. Top with remaining cream; sprinkle walnuts over top. Refrigerate for 24 hours. Yield: 15 servings.

LEMON SQUARES

1 lge. can evaporated milk, chilled
1 pkg. lemon gelatin
1/3 c. honey
1/8 tsp. salt
3 tbsp. lemon juice
Grated rind of 1 lemon
2 1/2 c. vanilla wafer crumbs

Chill bowl, beaters and 3-quart shallow cake pan. Pour milk in chilled bowl; beat with electric mixer until stiff peaks form. Dissolve gelatin in 1 1/4 cups boiling water; add honey, salt, juice and rind. Blend well; chill until partially set. Remove from refrigerator; beat until frothy. Stir in milk. Spread half the crumbs in chilled cake pan; pour in gelatin mixture. Top with remaining crumbs. Chill for 3 hours or overnight. Serve with whipped cream topping, if desired. Yield: 12-16 squares.

ROYAL ALMOND MOLD

1 pkg. lemon gelatin
2 tbsp. sugar
1/4 tsp. salt
1 c. heavy cream, whipped
1 tsp. almond extract
6 dry macaroons, crushed
9 marshmallows, chopped
3 tbsp. chopped candied cherries

Dissolve gelatin, sugar and salt in 1 cup boiling water; add 1/2 cup cold water. Chill until partially set. Whip gelatin until frothy. Combine whipped cream and almond extract; fold into gelatin mixture. Stir in macaroons, marshmallows and cherries; pour into mold. Chill until firm. Unmold; garnish with additional cherries. Yield: 6-8 servings.

LEMON LADYFINGER DESSERT

1 c. pineapple juice
1 pkg. lemon gelatin
6 eggs, separated
1 c. sugar
1/4 c. rum
Juice of 1 med. lemon
1 c. heavy cream, whipped
2 doz. ladyfingers

Bring pineapple juice to a boil; dissolve gelatin. Cool to room temperature. Cream egg yolks and sugar; add gelatin mixture. Add rum and lemon juice. Beat egg whites until stiff; add whipped cream. Blend gelatin mixture and egg white mixture together. Line 8-inch springform pan with ladyfingers. Spoon filling into pan. Chill for 24 hours. Yield: 8 servings.

LEMON BONBON COOKIES

Butter
1 1/3 c. sifted confectioners' sugar
3/4 c. cornstarch
1 1/4 c. sifted flour
1/2 c. finely chopped pecans
2 tbsp. lemon juice

Cream 1 cup butter and 1/3 cup sugar until light and fluffy. Add cornstarch and flour; mix well. Chill until dough is easy to handle; shape into 1-inch balls. Scatter pecans on waxed paper or foil; place balls of dough on top. Flatten with floured bottom of tumbler. Place cookies on cookie sheet, nut side down, with spatula. Bake in 350-degree oven for 12 to 15 minutes. Cool. Combine 1 teaspoon butter, remaining sugar and lemon juice; mix until of spreading consistency. Frost cooled cookies with lemon mixture. Yield: 2 1/2 dozen.

LEMON SOURS

3/4 c. flour
1/3 c. butter
2 eggs
1 c. (packed) brown sugar
3/4 c. coconut
1/2 c. nuts, chopped
1/8 tsp. baking powder
1 1/2 tbsp. lemon juice
1/2 tsp. grated lemon rind
1 c. confectioners' sugar

Combine flour and butter; blend until mixture resembles fine crumbs. Sprinkle evenly in 11 x 7-inch baking pan. Bake at 350 degrees for 10 minutes. Beat eggs; add brown sugar, coconut, nuts and baking powder. Mix thoroughly; spread over flour mixture. Bake for 20 minutes longer. Mix lemon juice, lemon rind and confectioners' sugar, blending well. Spread over top. Cool; cut into squares. Yield: 24 squares.

TART LEMON DROPS

2 c. sifted flour
3 tsp. baking powder
3/4 tsp. salt
1 tbsp. grated lemon rind
1/2 c. shortening
1 c. sugar
1 egg
1/4 c. lemon juice

Sift flour, baking powder and salt together. Combine lemon rind and shortening; add sugar gradually, creaming well. Add egg, lemon juice and 1/4 cup cold water; beat well. Add dry ingredients; mix thoroughly. Drop level tablespoonfuls of dough onto greased cookie sheet. Bake at 400 degrees for 8 minutes. Cool thoroughly before storing. Yield: 5 dozen cookies.

LEMON CUPS

3 eggs, separated
1/2 c. lemon juice
2/3 c. sugar
1/4 tsp. salt
1 tsp. vanilla
1 tsp. grated lemon rind
1 c. heavy cream, whipped
1/2 c. vanilla wafer crumbs
6 maraschino cherries, halved

Beat egg yolks until thick and light; pour into double boiler. Add lemon juice, sugar and salt; beat well. Cook over hot water until custard coats spoon. Add vanilla and rind. Chill. Beat egg whites until stiff peaks form; fold into lemon mixture. Fold whipped cream into lemon mixture. Sprinkle 1 teaspoon of vanilla wafer crumbs into 12 paper-lined muffin cups; fill with lemon mixture. Sprinkle top with crumbs; top with cherry halves. Freeze. Yield: 12 servings.

LEMON ANGEL RING

1 9-in. angel food cake
1 No. 2 can lemon pie filling
1/2 pt. heavy cream, whipped
1/4 c. crushed lemon candy drops

Line 9-inch tube pan with waxed paper. Remove brown crusts from cake; tear into bite-sized pieces. Fold lemon pie filling into whipped cream; fold in candy lightly. Alternate layers of lemon mixture and cake in prepared pan, beginning and ending with lemon mixture. Cover. Refrigerate overnight. Unmold on serving dish. Swirl additional whipped cream over top; sprinkle with additional chopped candy. Yield: 10-12 servings.

Lemon Angel Ring . . . Lemon filling and angel cake chunks alternate in this chilled dessert.

LEMONADE LOAF

1 10 x 4 x 2-in. loaf angel food cake
1 qt. vanilla ice cream
1 6-oz. can frozen pink lemonade concentrate
1 c. heavy cream, whipped

Slice cake lengthwise in 3 even layers. Stir ice cream to soften. Zigzag lemonade concentrate through ice cream until marbled, using spoon; spread between cake layers. Freeze. Spread top and sides of loaf with whipped cream 1 hour before serving. Return to freezer. Yield: 8-10 servings.

LEMON CUSTARD

3 eggs, separated
1/4 c. lemon juice
1/2 c. sugar
1/4 tsp. salt
1 tsp. grated lemon rind
1 tsp. vanilla
1 c. heavy cream, whipped
1/2 c. vanilla wafer crumbs

Beat egg yolks until thick and frothy. Combine yolks, lemon juice, sugar and salt in double boiler. Cook over hot water, stirring constantly, until custard coats spoon; chill. Stir in rind and vanilla. Beat egg whites until stiff peaks form; fold egg whites and whipped cream into custard. Sprinkle vanilla wafer crumbs in individual serving dishes; spoon in filling. Freeze. Remove from freezer 10 minutes before serving. Yield: 8 servings.

LEMON ICE

3/4 c. light corn syrup
1 c. sugar
1/4 tsp. salt
1 tbsp. grated lemon rind
2/3 c. lemon juice
Yellow food coloring

Combine 2 1/2 cups water, corn syrup, sugar, salt and lemon rind in saucepan. Cook, stirring constantly, over low heat until sugar is dissolved. Bring to a boil; cook for 5 minutes without stirring. Cool. Add lemon juice; strain syrup to remove lemon rind. Add several drops of food coloring, blending well. Pour into refrigerator tray; freeze until firm. Remove to chilled bowl. Break into lumps; beat until light and creamy. Return to refrigerator tray; freeze until firm.

LEMON SHERBET

Juice of 6 lemons
2 lemons, sliced paper-thin
1 1/2 pt. sugar
1/2 gal. milk

Mix all ingredients except milk together. Let stand for several hours. Add milk; pour into electric or crank freezer. Freeze until firm.

LEMON ICE CREAM

1 c. heavy cream
1 egg
1 1/2 c. sugar
1/3 c. lemon juice
2 tsp. grated lemon peel
1/8 tsp. salt
1 1/2 c. milk

Combine cream and egg in large bowl; beat with electric mixer until blended well. Add sugar gradually; beat mixture until stiff peaks form. Beat in lemon juice, lemon peel and salt; stir in milk. Pour into large refrigerator tray or 8-inch square pan. Cover with foil. Freeze for 5 hours. Yield: 6-9 servings.

MAGIC ICEBOX CAKE

1 c. graham cracker crumbs
3/8 c. sugar
3 tbsp. butter, melted
2 eggs, separated
1 can sweetened condensed milk
1 tbsp. lemon rind
1/2 c. lemon juice
1/4 tsp. almond extract

Combine crumbs, 2 tablespoons sugar and butter thoroughly. Press 1 cup mixture on bottom and sides of buttered refrigerator tray; chill. Beat egg yolks until thick; add milk. Add rind, juice and almond extract; stir until thick. Beat egg whites until stiff peaks form; add remaining sugar gradually. Beat until stiff peaks form; fold into milk mixture. Pour into tray. Top with remaining crumbs. Freeze until firm.

LEMON FREEZE

1 lb. cream-filled chocolate cookies
Juice of 2 lemons
2 cans sweetened condensed milk
2 c. heavy cream

Crush cookies; spread half the crumbs in 13 x 9-inch cake pan. Stir lemon juice into condensed milk gradually; do not beat. Stir until mixture begins to thicken. Fold in whipped cream. Pour over cookie crumbs; top with remaining crumbs. Yield: 12 servings.

LEMON-COCONUT BALLS

1 pkg. lemon sauce mix
2 1/2 c. graham cracker crumbs
1 c. chopped dates
1 c. chopped pecans
6 c. miniature marshmallows
1/2 c. sweetened condensed milk
4 to 5 c. flaked coconut

Prepare lemon sauce mix according to package directions, using only 1/4 cup water. Cool thoroughly. Combine graham cracker crumbs, dates, pecans and marshmallows in large bowl. Fold milk into lemon sauce; pour over crumb mixture. Mix well. Drop by teaspoonfuls into coconut; roll to cover. Chill until hardened. Yield: 60-70 balls.

LEMON CHESS PIE

2 c. sugar
1 tbsp. cornmeal
1 tbsp. flour
4 eggs, slightly beaten
1/4 c. milk
1/4 c. melted butter
1/4 c. lemon juice
Grated rind of 1 lemon
1 unbaked pie shell

Combine sugar, cornmeal and flour; add eggs, one at a time. Add milk, butter, lemon juice and rind; pour into pie shell. Bake at 375 degrees for 45 minutes. Yield: 8 servings.

LEMON-FRUIT PIE

Color photograph for this recipe on page 496.

2 3 1/4-oz. packages lemon pie filling mix
1 1/4 c. sugar
1 1/2 c. orange juice
4 eggs, separated
1 1/2 c. pineapple juice
1 2/3 c. graham cracker crumbs
1/4 c. softened butter
1/2 c. shredded coconut

Mix lemon pie filling mix with 1/2 cup sugar and 1/2 cup orange juice in saucepan. Add egg yolks; blend well. Add remaining orange juice and pineapple juice. Cook, stirring constantly, over medium heat for 5 to 7 minutes or until thickened; cool. Mix graham cracker crumbs, butter and 1/4 cup sugar; press into 9-inch pie plate. Bake at 375 degrees for 8 minutes; cool. Pour filling into crust. Beat egg whites until stiff but not dry, adding remaining sugar gradually. Pile meringue over filling; seal to edge of crust. Sprinkle coconut on top. Bake at 500 degrees for 4 to 5 minutes. Chill for 2 to 3 hours. Yield: 6-8 servings.

LEMON MERINGUE PIE

1 1/2 c. sugar
1/3 c. cornstarch
3 egg yolks, slightly beaten
3 tbsp. butter
1/4 c. lemon juice
1 tbsp. grated lemon rind
1 baked 9-in. pie shell
1 recipe meringue

Combine sugar and cornstarch in saucepan; stir in 1 1/2 cups water gradually. Cook over medium heat, stirring constantly, until mixture is bubbly and thickened. Cook for 1 minute. Stir half the hot mixture into egg yolks; blend egg yolks into hot mixture. Cook for 1 minute longer, stirring constantly. Remove from heat; stir until smooth. Blend in butter, lemon juice and rind; pour into pie shell. Cover with meringue. Bake at 400 degrees for 8 to 10 minutes or until meringue is light brown. Yield: 6-8 servings.

LEMON SPONGE PIE

Flour
1/2 tsp. salt
3/8 c. cooking oil
1 c. sugar
3 tbsp. butter
2 eggs, separated
Grated rind and juice of 1 lemon
1 c. milk

Sift 1 cup flour and salt together; add oil, cutting in with fork or pastry blender. Add enough ice water to hold ingredients together. Knead lightly; roll out on lightly floured board. Place in pie pan; flute edge of pastry. Beat sugar, butter and egg yolks together; add 3 tablespoons flour, lemon rind and juice. Mix well. Add milk. Beat egg whites until stiff peaks form; fold into lemon mixture. Pour into pie shell; place in oven. Bake at 400 degrees for 15 minutes. Reduce oven temperature to 350 degrees; bake for 30 minutes longer.

BAKED LEMON PUDDING

1 1/2 c. sugar
1/2 c. sifted flour
1/2 tsp. baking powder
1/4 tsp. salt
3 eggs, separated
2 tsp. grated lemon rind
1/4 c. lemon juice
2 tbsp. melted butter
1 1/2 c. milk

Sift sugar with flour, baking powder and salt. Beat egg yolks until light; add lemon rind and juice, butter and milk. Mix well with spoon. Stir in dry ingredients. beat until smooth with electric beater at high speed. Beat egg whites; fold into mixture. Pour into well-oiled 2-quart casserole. Place casserole in pan of warm water. Bake at 375 degrees for 45 minutes. Yield: 4-6 servings.

COLD LEMON SOUFFLÉ

2 env. unflavored gelatin
1 1/3 c. sugar
1/2 tsp. salt
8 eggs, separated
1 c. lemon juice
1 tbsp. grated lemon rind

Fold waxed paper into several 3-inch wide thicknesses long enough to go around 10-cup souffle dish with generous overlap. Attach to dish with sealing tape, leaving 1 inch of paper around dish to make collar 2 inches high. Mix gelatin, 2/3 cup sugar and salt together in top of double boiler. Combine slightly beaten egg yolks, lemon juice and 1/2 cup water; add to gelatin mixture. Cook over boiling water for about 6 minutes, stirring until gelatin dissolves and mixture thickens. Add lemon rind. Chill until mixture mounds slightly when dropped from

Cold Lemon Soufflé . . . Gelatin helps this light and cool dessert hold its attractive shape.

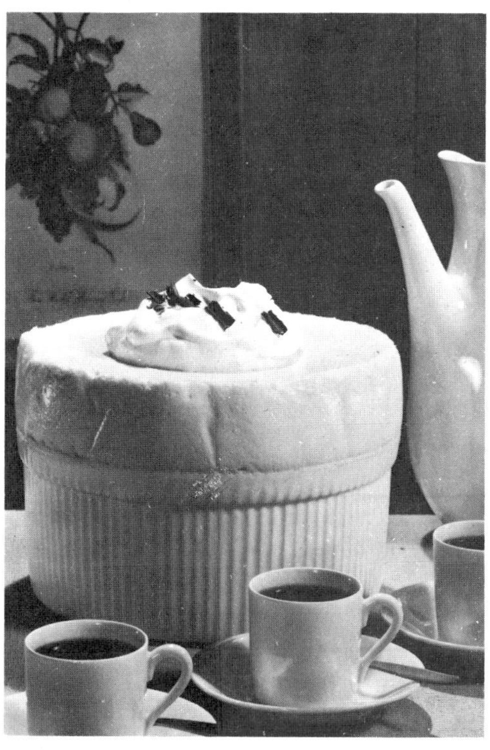

spoon. Beat egg whites until stiff but not dry. Add remaining sugar gradually; beat until stiff. Fold in gelatin mixture. Turn into prepared dish. Chill until firm. Remove paper collar carefully; serve. Garnish with whipped cream and shaved chocolate on top if desired. Yield: 8-10 servings.

LEMON BREAD PUDDING

2 c. soft bread crumbs
Juice of 2 lemons
2 eggs, separated
3/4 c. sugar
1/4 c. cooking oil
Pinch of salt
1/4 c. sugar

Combine crumbs, juice, 1/2 cup water and egg yolks with sugar and cooking oil; mix well. Pour mixture into buttered baking dish. Bake at 350 degrees for 25 minutes. Beat egg whites until stiff peaks form; add salt and sugar gradually. Beat mixture thoroughly until stiff peaks form. Remove pudding from oven; spread meringue over top. Return to oven. Bake meringue at 350 degrees for 15 minutes. Yield: 6-8 servings.

LEMON CREAM

1 pkg. lemon pie filling mix
1/4 c. lemon juice
1 c. heavy cream, whipped
1 c. drained fruit cocktail
1 1/2 c. miniature marshmallows

Prepare mix according to package directions; add lemon juice, stirring well. Fold in whipped cream; stir in fruit cocktail and marshmallows gently. Chill in refrigerator. Yield: 6-8 servings.

LIGHT LEMON TARTS

4 eggs, beaten well
1 c. sugar
1/4 c. butter, melted
Pinch of salt
Juice and grated rind of 2 lge. lemons
1 recipe pie pastry

Combine eggs, sugar, butter, salt, lemon juice and rind; mix well. Line twelve tart shells with pastry; fill with lemon mixture. Bake at 425 degrees for 25 to 30 minutes. Yield: 12 servings.

LEMONY TARTS

3 c. sifted flour
1 1/2 tsp. salt
1 c. shortening
Grated rind of 2 med. lemons
1/2 c. lemon juice
2 c. sugar
1 c. butter
4 eggs, well beaten

Sift flour and salt together; cut in shortening until mixture is coarse. Sprinkle 6 tablespoons cold water over mixture; mix thoroughly until smooth dough is formed. Roll out on floured surface to 1/8-inch thickness. Cut into 2 1/2-inch rounds; fit into greased muffin pans. Prick dough with fork. Bake at 450 degrees for 10 minutes or until golden brown; cool. Combine lemon rind, lemon juice and sugar in double boiler; add butter. Heat over boiling water, stirring, until butter is melted. Add small amount of hot mixture to eggs, stirring vigorously. Return egg mixture to double boiler, stirring well. Cook, stirring constantly, for 15 minutes or until smooth and thickened. Cool thoroughly. Spoon filling into cooled tart shells. Yield: 4 dozen tarts.

Lentils

Lentils are the seeds of plants belonging to the pea family. They are a good source of protein. Most often sold dried, lentils should be soaked in water before using as recipe specifies.
(See BEANS.)

LENTIL SOUP

1 c. lentils
1 qt. ham stock
1/4 c. minced celery
1/4 c. minced onion
1/4 c. grated carrot
3 cloves

Soak lentils overnight. Drain lentils; add ham stock and 1 quart cold water. Bring to a boil; cover. Reduce heat; simmer for 30 minutes. Add celery, onion and carrot; simmer for 1 hour. Add cloves; simmer for 1 hour and 30 minutes longer. Yield: 6-8 servings.

SAUCY LENTILS

1 lb. dried lentils
1 tbsp. butter
1 tbsp. chopped onion
2 tbsp. flour
1 15-oz. can tomato sauce

Bring 3 cups water to a boil in heavy kettle. Add lentils; cover. Reduce heat to medium; cook for 45 minutes or until lentils are tender. Melt butter in small saucepan; saute onion in butter. Blend in flour; cook, stirring, until browned. Stir in 1/2 cup water and tomato sauce; bring to a boil. Combine lentils and tomato sauce mixture; turn into greased casserole. Bake at 350 degrees for 30 minutes. Yield: 8-10 servings.

Lettuce

Lettuce is a leafy green vegetable that has many different varieties. Its mild-flavored leaves are commonly used in salads. Lettuce contains Vitamins A and C and calcium. (2 large or 4 small leaves = 5 calories)

KINDS: There are 4 primary types of lettuce: crisphead, butterhead, romaine (or cos), and leaf. *Iceberg* is the most commonly marketed variety of crisphead lettuce. Iceberg has a firm, compact, heavy head and crisp leaves. Its loose outer leaves are medium green; inner leaves are paler green. Iceberg has a sweet, mild flavor. *Boston* and *Bibb* lettuce are the popular varieties of butterhead. Boston lettuce has a soft head and inner leaves that feel oily. Boston lettuce has outer leaves that are dark green and inner leaves that are almost white. Bibb lettuce has a small, cup-shaped head. Its loose, succulent leaves are rich green on the outside and whitish-green near the core. *Romaine* (or cos) lettuce has a tall, elongated head and stiff, slightly coarse leaves. Its exterior leaves are greenish-white. Romaine is more pungently flavored than other lettuce. *Leaf* lettuce has loose, light green or dark green leaves and no "head." Its flavor is sweet and delicate.

AVAILABILITY: All kinds of lettuce are marketed year-round with some seasonal variation. Greatest supply from May to August. Least supply January to March. In some areas, *Bibb* and *leaf* lettuce may fluctuate.

BUYING: *Iceberg*–Choose firm, well-shaped head with clean, crisp leaves. Avoid lettuce with excessive outer leaves. *Boston*–Choose lettuce with fresh, clean, soft-textured leaves. *Bibb*–Choose lettuce with tender, soft-textured leaves. *Romaine*–Choose well-trimmed, full head with blemish-free leaves. *Leaf*–Choose lettuce with soft, tender leaves. Avoid any lettuce with decay, discoloration, or "tipburn" (small, ragged brown areas on inner leaves). Avoid wilted lettuce.

STORING: Wash and dry lettuce (see below). Wrap in plastic bag and place in vegetable crisper or refrigerator. *Iceberg* and *Romaine* keep about 1 week. *Boston* keeps only 1 to 2 days. Other types keep a few days. If lettuce is to be used within a few hours, wrap loosely in absorbent paper and chill in refrigerator until crisp. Do not freeze lettuce.

PREPARATION: *Iceberg*–Discard discolored or wilted outer leaves. Core with knife. Or, pound bottom of head on wooden board and twist out loosened core. Wash, cored-side-up, under cold running water. *Bibb* and other kinds–Separate leaves and wash individually. Place leaves in colander to drip dry. Or, allow cold water to run through head. Invert head.

SERVING: Tear most raw lettuce for use in salads or in sandwiches. Slice or shred Iceberg. May also be cooked; see specific recipe.

BIBB LETTUCE WITH CRUMBLED BACON

3 heads Bibb lettuce
6 slices bacon
Garlic salt
2 hard-boiled eggs, mashed
Italian dressing

Break lettuce into bite-sized pieces. Fry bacon until crisp; drain on paper toweling. Crumble. Rub salad bowl with garlic salt; shake out excess salt. Place lettuce, bacon and eggs in bowl; toss to mix. Serve with Italian dressing.

DRESSED LETTUCE

1 tsp. salt
2 1/2 tbsp. sugar
1 tsp. mustard
2 tbsp. cream
2 tbsp. vinegar
1/2 c. salad dressing
1 head lettuce, coarsely chopped
1 onion, minced
1/2 c. cheese, grated

Mix salt, sugar, mustard and cream. Add vinegar and salad dressing; stir until smooth. Arrange lettuce, onion and cheese in salad bowl; add dressing. Toss lightly.

EGG-LETTUCE SALAD

1/2 lb. sliced bacon
1 head lettuce, torn
4 hard-boiled eggs, sliced
1 c. sour cream
1 tbsp. mayonnaise
1 tbsp. minced onion
1/4 tsp. garlic powder
1/4 tsp. salt
Pepper to taste
Dillseed

Dice and fry bacon until crisp; drain. Combine lettuce, eggs and bacon in salad bowl; chill, covered, until ready to serve. Combine sour cream and mayonnaise; stir in onion, garlic powder, salt and pepper. Pour mixture over salad just before serving; toss lightly. Sprinkle with dillseed.

HOT LETTUCE SALAD

4 slices bacon
1 tbsp. sugar
1 tbsp. vinegar
2 tsp. India relish
1 head lettuce
1 hard-cooked egg, chopped

Fry bacon until crisp; drain. Crumble bacon. Drain bacon drippings; reserve 2 tablespoons drippings. Combine sugar, vinegar and India relish with reserved drippings in skillet; bring to a boil. Remove from heat. Tear lettuce into bite-sized pieces; toss with bacon and egg. Pour hot vinegar mixture over lettuce; toss lightly. Serve immediately.

BOUQUET SALAD

1 clove of garlic
1 head crisp lettuce
3 tomatoes, diced
3 hard-cooked eggs, sliced
1 sm. cucumber, sliced
1/2 green pepper, sliced
6 to 8 radishes, sliced
1 carrot, slivered
3 stalks celery, chopped
2 slices Swiss cheese, slivered
5 strips crisp bacon, crumbled
1/2 c. chopped olives
French dressing
Salt and pepper

Rub wooden salad bowl with cut garlic clove. Tear lettuce into bite-sized pieces. Combine lettuce with remaining vegetables; add cheese, bacon and olives. Toss with dressing just before serving; season with salt and pepper.

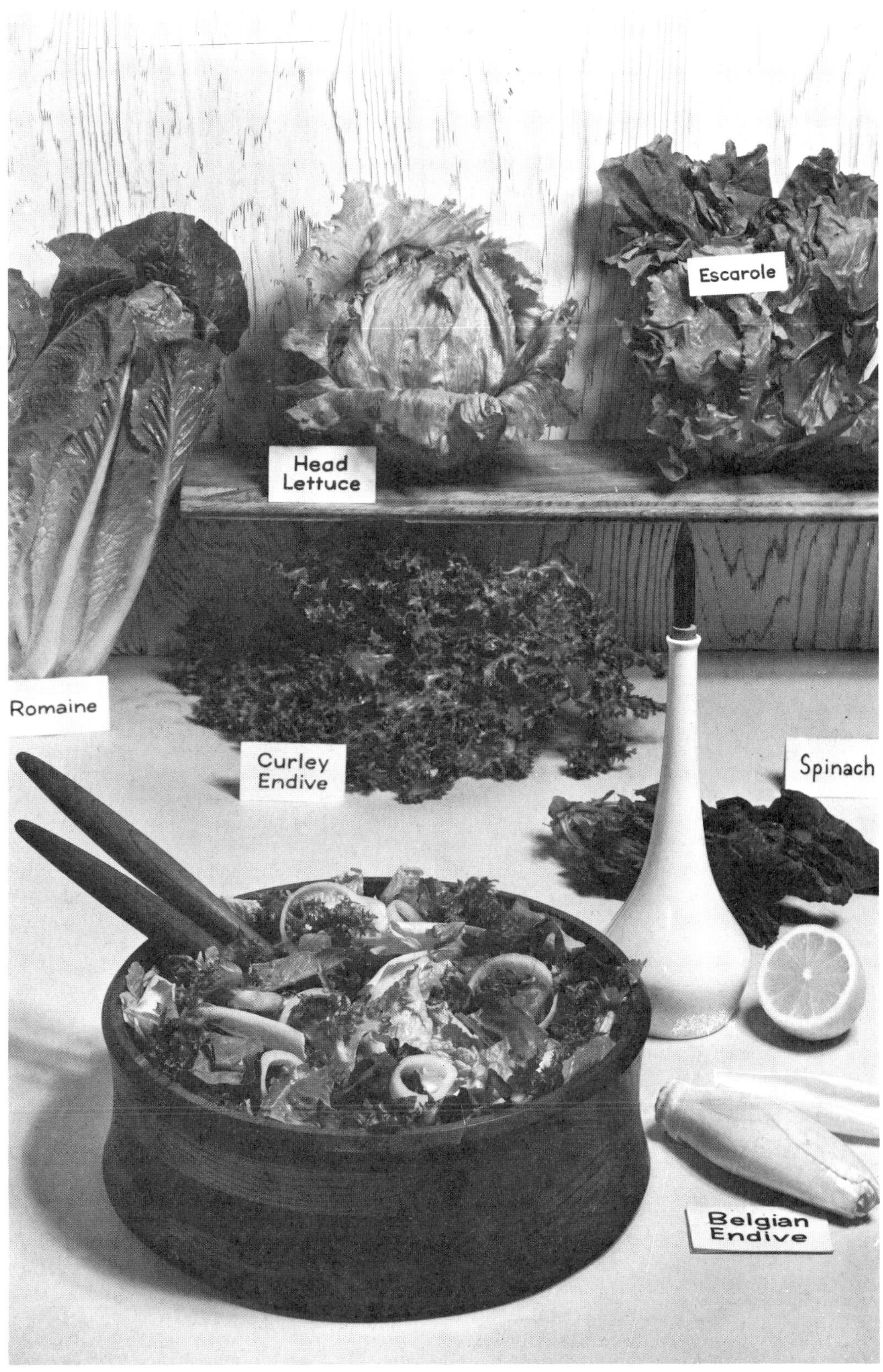
Escarole
Head
Lettuce
Romaine
Curley
Endive
Spinach
Belgian
Endive

PENNSYLVANIA DUTCH COLD LETTUCE

1 med. head lettuce
1/4 c. sugar
2 tbsp. mayonnaise
1 1/2 tbsp. cream
1/4 c. vinegar
Salt to taste

Tear lettuce into bite-sized pieces. Mix sugar and mayonnaise; blend in cream, vinegar and salt. Just before serving pour dressing over lettuce; toss lightly.

STUFFED ICEBERG LETTUCE

1 sm. head iceberg lettuce
1/2 lb. bleu cheese
1 3-oz. package cream cheese
2 tbsp. milk
1 tbsp. chopped chives
1 pimento, chopped
French dressing

Hollow out center of lettuce, leaving a 1-inch shell. Cream cheeses with milk until smooth; blend in chives and pimento. Fill lettuce cavity with cheese mixture; cover with foil. Refrigerate until cheese is firm. Just before serving, cut lettuce into 3/4-inch slices. Serve with French dressing.

VEGETABLE-STUFFED LETTUCE

1 lge. head lettuce
6 oz. cream cheese
1 tbsp. minced green pepper
2 tbsp. minced chives
2 tbsp. grated carrot
3 tbsp. finely diced tomato
1/2 tsp. salt
1/8 tsp. pepper

Remove loose outer lettuce leaves; remove core and heart. Cream cheese with vegetables and seasonings; pack tightly in lettuce cavity. Wrap in foil; chill until ready to serve. Cut head into quarters; serve with French dressing.

EASY TOSSED SALAD

1 c. lettuce, torn in small pieces
1/2 c. shredded cabbage
1/4 c. diced green pepper
1/4 c. chopped pickles
1 tomato, diced
1 apple, minced
1/4 c. diced carrot
Salad dressing
1 tbsp. sugar
Salt to taste

Combine lettuce with remaining ingredients; toss lightly.

SPRING SALAD BOWL

1 head leaf lettuce
1/2 bunch watercress
1 1/2 c. small spinach leaves
24 carrot curls
4 green onions, chopped
12 ripe pitted olives
12 toasted blanched almonds
Italian dressing

Tear lettuce into bite-sized pieces; chop watercress coarsely. Combine lettuce, watercress and spinach in salad bowl; add carrot curls and onions. Stuff olives with almonds; add to salad. Toss lightly with Italian dressing just before serving.

THREE-WAY SALAD

1 head lettuce
6 carrots, chopped
1 cucumber, chopped
1 tomato, sliced
1 c. croutons
3 stalks celery, diced
1 sm. onion, chopped
2 hard cooked eggs, chopped
2 6-oz. cans shrimp
3/4 c. dressing
1/2 c. Cheddar cheese, grated

Tear lettuce into bite-sized pieces; combine with vegetables, eggs and shrimp. Toss with dressing just before serving. Sprinkle with cheese.

WILTED LETTUCE AND EGG SALAD

4 slices bacon
1 sm. onion, chopped
1/4 c. vinegar
1 head lettuce
3 hard-cooked eggs, chopped
Bread cubes
Garlic salt

Fry bacon until crisp; drain, reserving drippings. Saute onion in bacon drippings until golden; add vinegar. Bring to a boil; reduce heat. Simmer. Tear lettuce into bite-sized pieces; combine with eggs and bacon. Season with salt and pepper. Saute bread cubes in small amount of bacon drippings until crisp and brown. Sprinkle with garlic salt. Pour hot vinegar mixture over lettuce; toss lightly. Sprinkle top with bread cubes; serve immediately.

DUTCH LETTUCE

1 head lettuce
1/2 c. diced bacon
2 hard-cooked eggs, chopped
2 sm. onions, chopped
4 boiled potatoes, mashed
1/3 c. vinegar
1 tbsp. sugar
1 tsp. salt

Separate lettuce in leaves; place in cold water. Refrigerate for 1 hour or longer; drain well. Cook bacon until crisp. Drain; reserve drippings. Place alternate layers of lettuce, bacon, eggs, onions and potatoes in serving dish. Add vinegar, sugar and salt to reserved bacon drippings; bring to a boil. Pour over lettuce mixture; serve immediately.

Lime

The small greenish-yellow lime is a citrus fruit that flourishes in tropical and semitropical climate. There are two varieties of limes: Key limes from Mexico and larger limes called either Persian or Tahitian that are grown in Florida. Limes are lemon-like but have a higher acid content and are rich in calcium, carbohydrates, and Vitamins A and C. (1 cup lime juice, fresh or canned = 65 calories)

AVAILABILITY: Limes are available year-round with peak supplies from June through

August. Canned lime juice and frozen limeade concentrate are also marketed.

BUYING: Look for firm limes that are heavy for their size. Freshness is indicated by a well-developed greenish-yellow skin color and a pale green flesh. The skin should be free from purplish-brown or water-soaked spots. Persian (or Tahitian) limes are the most common variety available. The Mexican Key limes have flesh that is uncharacteristically yellow when ripe.

STORING: Like lemons, limes should be kept, uncovered, in a cold room or the refrigerator. There they will remain fresh for 1 to 2 weeks or longer.

USES: Limes may be used interchangably with lemons even though their flavor is considerably more tart. If limes are substituted for lemons in sweet recipes, more sugar may be required. (For a more detailed explanation see LEMONS.)

SERVING: Limes are also served like lemons.

COLORADO DELIGHT SALAD

1 3-oz. package cream cheese
1 pkg. lime gelatin
1 c. chopped pecans
2 c. drained fruit cocktail
15 marshmallows, diced
1 c. whipped cream

Combine cheese and gelatin; add 1 cup boiling water gradually. Stir until smooth and blended; chill until partially set. Add pecans, fruit cocktail and marshmallows. Fold in cream; chill until firm.

EMERALD SALAD MOLD

1 3-oz. package lime gelatin
1 9-oz. can crushed pineapple
1/2 c. mayonnaise
1 c. creamy cottage cheese
1/2 c. whipped cream
1 c. chopped nuts
1/2 tbsp. horseradish

Dissolve gelatin in 1 cup boiling water. Drain pineapple; reserve juice. Add reserved juice to gelatin mixture; chill until partially set. Beat until frothy; fold in remaining ingredients. Chill until firm.

FROSTED LIME SALAD

1 pkg. lime gelatin
1 lge. can crushed pineapple, drained
1 tbsp. pimento, chopped
1/3 c. chopped nuts
1/2 c. diced celery, finely cut
1 c. small curd cottage cheese
1 3-oz. package cream cheese
1 tbsp. mayonnaise
1 tsp. lemon juice
Dash of paprika

Dissolve gelatin in 1 cup boiling water; cool until partially set. Add pineapple, pimento, nuts, celery and cottage cheese. Pour into mold; chill until firm. Unmold. Blend cream cheese, mayonnaise and lemon juice together; spread over gelatin mixture. Sprinkle with paprika.

LIME-APPLESAUCE MOLD

2 cans applesauce
2 pkg. lime gelatin
1 c. diced celery
1 c. chopped nuts
1 sm. jar pimentos, drained
2 bottles lemon-lime carbonated drink

Heat applesauce; dissolve gelatin in applesauce. Chill until partially set; add remaining ingredients. Pour into mold. Chill until firm.

LIME-CREAM CHEESE MOLD

1/4 lb. marshmallows
1 c. milk
1 pkg. lime gelatin
1 8-oz. package cream cheese
1 pkg. dessert topping mix
2/3 c. mayonnaise
1 No. 2 can crushed pineapple

Melt marshmallows in milk in top of double boiler. Pour over gelatin; stir until dissolved. Beat in cream cheese; chill until partially set. Prepare dessert topping mix according to package directions. Blend into gelatin mixture. Add mayonnaise and pineapple. Pour into mold; chill until firm.

LIME-MARSHMALLOW MOLD

1 pkg. lime gelatin
1 sm. package cream cheese
1/2 c. pineapple juice
1/3 c. chopped pecans
6 maraschino cherries, chopped
1 c. miniature marshmallows

Dissolve gelatin in 1 cup boiling water; fold cream cheese into gelatin. Blend in pineapple juice and 1/2 cup cold water; chill until partially set. Whip gelatin mixture; fold in remaining ingredients. Pour into mold; chill until firm.

LIME RIBBON DELIGHT

1 pkg. white cake mix
1 3-oz. package lime gelatin
1/2 c. fruit juice
1/2 c. drained crushed pineapple
1/4 c. chopped nuts
1/4 tsp. lemon juice
1 c. whipping cream
1/4 c. confectioners' sugar

Prepare cake mix according to package directions, making 2 round 9-inch layers. Cool layers; remove from pan. Dissolve gelatin in 1 cup hot water; stir in fruit juice. Chill until partially set; add pineapple, nuts and lemon juice. Place 2 strips aluminum foil across bottom of each layer pan, letting strips extend over edge. Replace cake layers in pans, placing 1 layer upside down and the other right side up. Spoon gelatin mixture over layers; chill until firm. Whip cream until stiff peaks form; beat in confectioners' sugar. Lift cake layers out of pans with foil strips. Stack layers, gelatin side up. Frost side with whipped cream. Refrigerate until ready to serve.

LIME-PINEAPPLE RING

1 pkg. lime gelatin
1/2 c. cottage cheese
1/2 c. maraschino cherries, sliced
1/2 c. chopped walnuts
1 c. crushed pineapple
1 c. whipped cream

Dissolve gelatin in 1 cup boiling water; add cottage cheese. Chill until partially set; fold in remaining ingredients. Pour into ring mold; chill until firm.

LIME SNOWFLAKE DESSERT

1/4 c. lime juice
1/2 c. sugar
3 eggs, separated
1/2 c. chopped nuts
1 c. heavy cream, whipped
1 c. graham cracker crumbs

Combine lime juice and sugar in saucepan; heat, stirring, until sugar is dissolved. Bring to a boil. Beat egg yolks lightly; stir small amount of hot mixture into egg yolks. Return to hot mixture; reduce heat and cook, stirring constantly, until custard is thickened. Chill custard. Whip egg whites until stiff peaks form; fold egg whites, nuts and whipped cream into custard. Spread half the cracker crumbs in greased 8-inch square pan; pour custard into pan. Spread remaining cracker crumbs over custard. Refrigerate for at least 4 hours before serving.

KEY LIME SHERBET

1 pkg. Key lime pie filling mix
3/4 c. sugar
2 eggs, separated

Combine pie mix and 1/2 cup sugar in saucepan. Beat egg yolks slightly. Combine 2 1/2 cups water and egg yolks; stir into pie filling mixture gradually. Cook over medium heat, stirring constantly, until mixture comes to a boil; break flavor capsule. Mix well. Remove from heat; cool. Beat egg whites until foamy; add remaining sugar gradually. Beat until soft peaks form. Add lime mixture slowly to egg whites. Pour into freezer tray; freeze until ready to serve.

LIME FREEZE

3 eggs, separated
1/2 c. sugar
Grated rind and juice of 1 lime
2 tbsp. lemon juice
Green food coloring
1 c. heavy cream, whipped
Green gumdrop slivers

Combine egg yolks, sugar, lime rind, lime juice and lemon juice in top of double boiler; cook over hot water, stirring constantly, until slightly thickened. Cool. Add food coloring to desired tint. Beat egg whites until stiff peaks form; fold stiffly beaten egg whites, whipped cream and gumdrop slivers into lime mixture. Pour into large refrigerator tray; freeze until firm. Cover with foil; keep frozen until ready to serve.

KEY LIME PIE

1 c. vanilla wafer crumbs
1/4 c. butter
1/2 c. chopped pecans
3 eggs, separated
1/2 c. lime juice
1 tsp. grated lime rind
1 can sweetened condensed milk
3 drops of green food coloring
1/4 tsp. cream of tartar
6 tsp. sugar

Mix crumbs, butter and pecans thoroughly; reserve small amount for topping. Press remaining mixture on bottom and side of 8-inch pie pan; chill for 20 minutes. Beat egg yolks. Add lime juice, grated rind, milk and food coloring; mix well. Pour into pie shell. Beat egg whites until frothy; add cream of tartar. Beat until stiff; add sugar gradually. Pile on pie lightly; seal edge. Sprinkle with reserved crumb mixture. Bake at 425 degrees for 4 minutes or until lightly browned.

FROZEN LIME PIE

1 env. unflavored gelatin
3/4 c. sugar
1/8 tsp. salt
1 c. milk
1/3 c. fresh lime juice
1 1/2 tsp. grated lime rind
Green food coloring
1 c. whipping cream, whipped
1 egg white
1 9-in. crumb crust

Combine gelatin, sugar and salt; add milk. Heat in saucepan just until gelatin and sugar are dissolved. Chill until mixture begins to thicken. Add lime juice, rind and desired amount of food coloring. Fold in whipped cream. Beat egg white until soft peaks form; fold into gelatin mixture. Pile into crumb crust. Freeze. Serve with additional whipped cream if desired.

Frozen Lime Pie . . . A crumb crust contrasts with the creamy texture of this delicious pie.

LIME GELATIN CAKE

1 pkg. white cake mix
1 pkg. lime gelatin
4 tsp. mint flavoring
1/3 c. salad oil
4 eggs, separated
1 c. powdered sugar
1/4 c. milk

Combine cake mix, gelatin, mint flavoring and salad oil with 1 cup water; add egg yolks. Beat well. Beat egg whites until stiff peaks form. Fold egg whites into batter; pour into greased and floured tube pan. Bake for 1 hour at 325 degrees. Mix remaining ingredients for glaze; pour over hot cake.

LIMEADE PIE

1 6-oz. can frozen limeade
1 c. sugar
1/4 c. cornstarch
4 eggs, separated
1 tbsp. butter
Green food coloring
1 baked 9 in. pastry shell

Thaw limeade. Mix 1/2 cup sugar and cornstarch. Beat egg yolks; add cornstarch mixture and limeade. Bring 1 cup water to a boil over low heat; add butter. Stir egg yolk mixture into water gradually, stirring constantly until thickened. Remove from heat; add food coloring to desired tint. Beat egg whites until frothy; beat in remaining sugar, a small amount at a time, until stiff peaks form. Fold half the meringue into cooked filling; pour into pastry shell. Top with remaining meringue. Bake at 350 degrees until meringue is lightly browned.

LIME CHIFFON PIE

1 tbsp. unflavored gelatin
4 eggs, separated
1 c. sugar
1/2 c. lime juice
1/2 tsp. salt
1 tsp. grated lime rind
1 baked 9-in. pastry shell
1 c. whipped cream
Grated chocolate

Soften gelatin in 1/4 cup cold water. Beat egg yolks in top of double boiler until thick and lemon colored; add 1/2 cup sugar, lime juice and salt. Cook, stirring, until smooth and thickened; stir in gelatin until dissolved. Add lime rind; chill until custard begins to thicken. Beat egg whites until stiff peaks form; beat in remaining sugar. Fold egg whites into custard. Mound into pastry shell; cover with whipped cream. Garnish with chocolate. Refrigerate until ready to serve.

LIME PARFAIT PIE

1 6-oz. package lime gelatin
1 tsp. shredded lime peel
1/3 c. lime juice
1 qt. vanilla ice cream
1 baked 10-in. pastry shell
Whipped cream
Maraschino cherries

Dissolve gelatin in 2 cups boiling water; stir in lime peel and lime juice. Add ice cream by spoonfuls, stirring until melted. Chill mixture until partially thickened. Pour into pastry shell; chill until firm. Top with whipped cream; garnish with cherries.

Linzer Torte

LINZER TORTE

1/3 c. milk
1 3/4 c. unsifted flour
1 c. ground almonds
1/4 c. sugar
1 tsp. lemon peel
3/4 tsp. salt
1/4 c. margarine
1 pkg. yeast
1 egg, slightly beaten
3/4 c. grape jam

Scald milk; cool to lukewarm. Combine flour, almonds, sugar, lemon peel and salt in large bowl. Cut in margarine with pastry blender to coarse meal consistency. Pour 1/4 cup lukewarm water into small warm bowl; sprinkle yeast over water. Stir until dissolved. Stir lukewarm milk, yeast mixture and egg into flour mixture. Mix until blended. Cover tightly with aluminum foil. Refrigerate for 2 hours or overnight. Reserve and refrigerate 1/4 of the chilled dough. Pat remaining dough evenly over bottom and 3/4 inch up side of 9-inch ungreased springform pan. Spread jam over bottom of dough. Pat out reserved dough into 6 x 9-inch rectangle; cut into eight 3/4-inch strips. Arrange strips to form lattice on top of preserves. Fasten lattice strips to dough around side of pan by pressing lightly. Refrigerate for 1 hour. Bake in 325-degree oven for about 40 minutes or until done. Remove rim of pan; cool. Garnish outer rim of torte with whipped cream if desired.

Linzer Torte . . . Almond-flavored pastry contrasts deliciously with a tart jam filling.

Lobster

Lobsters are saltwater crustaceans whose flesh are popular fare throughout America. The *Northern lobster* or "homard" inhabits the cold waters from Labrador to North Carolina and is found chiefly along the coasts of Maine and Massachusetts. It is a dark, mottled, blue-green color and contains two large pincer claws. The clawless *Spiny* or *Rock lobster* or "langouste" dwells in the warm waters off Mexico, Southern California, and South Africa. Smooth, spotty, reddish-orange shells characterize the Mexican and South African varieties, while rough, spotless, maroon shells mark the South African. Lobster is high in protein, iodine, and calcium. (1 average lobster = 120 calories; 1 large African lobster-tail = 150)

AVAILABILITY: Lobsters are available year-round. Whole *Northern lobsters* can be bought fresh, cooked in the shell, or frozen. Only the tail meat of *Spiny* or *Rock lobster* is marketed. The tails are frozen before shipping. *Cooked lobster meat* is available canned, frozen, or iced.

BUYING: For *Northern lobsters*—Look for fresh, alert, and active specimens whose tails snap back and forth under their bodies when they are handled. Females, considered finer in flavor, have soft, leathery, fin-like appendages on the underside where the head and tail meet. Preboiled lobster meat should have a bright red shell, a fresh seashore odor, and a curled tail that rolls back under the body when pulled. Common market sizes for fresh Northern lobsters are: 3/4 to 1 pound = "chickens"; 1 1/4 pounds = "quarters"; 1 1/2 to 2 1/4 pounds = large; 2 1/2 pounds and over = jumbo. For *Spiny* or *Rock lobsters*—Buy only frozen tails with clean white meat and no accompanying odor. Market sizes range from 2 to 10 ounces.

STORING: For *Northern lobsters*—Keep live in the refrigerator in salt or sea water or wrapped in a moistened cloth. Make sure that the claws are either wedged shut with wood or held together by thick rubber bands. Prepare before lobsters become slack. *To freeze* Northern lobsters—Boil, cool, and split lobsters. (See description of splitting below.) Put two halves together again to form whole lobster. Wrap in moisture- and vapor-proof paper and freeze. Or remove cooked meat from the tail and claws, pack in cellophane-lined cartons, leave 1/2 inch head space and freeze. For *Spiny* or *Rock lobsters*—Keep frozen until ready to use; thaw in refrigerator and use immediately.

PREPARATION: *Northern lobsters* are always split *before* broiling and *after* boiling. Split by inserting the knife point at the junction of the head and tail. Cut in half lengthwise, through only the hard upper shell. Lie the lobster flat with the meat exposed. Remove and discard the small stomach sac (known as the lady), the spongy lungs, and the black intestinal vein that runs the length of the meat. Do not discard the green liver, or tomalley, and the pink roe, or coral, (from the female) since both are tasty delicacies. Crack the claws with a hammer or nut cracker.) *To broil* – Place split lobster flesh side up on pan. Sprinkle with bread crumbs, brush with melted butter and place in broiler. Cook lobster from 20 to 30 minutes, depending on the size, basting occasionally. *To boil*—Place live lobster in pot filled with cold water. Bring water to a boil and continue cooking 20 to 30 minutes, depending on the size of the lobster. When the lobster is cooked, plunge it into cold water and drain. Split immediately before serving (see instructions above). Use a stainless steel or silver knife when cutting cooked lobster; a steel blade may discolor the meat. 1/2 large or 1 small lobster serves 1 person. For *Spiny* or *Rock lobsters*—Split lobster by inserting knife point at the end opposite the fin. Cut in half lengthwise as for Northern lobster. Remove intestinal vein. *To broil*—Follow directions for Northern lobsters. Rock lobsters are seldom boiled. An average serving is about 8 ounces of tail meat.

SERVING: Place settings when eating whole lobster generally include the following implements: Fingerbowls, bibs, napkins, nutcrackers, and seafood forks. An extra bowl or dish in which to discard the shells is also helpful. Serve broiled (both types) or boiled lobsters hot with drawn butter and lemon, or cold with mayonnaise or any other cold sauce. Pieces of lobster meat may be used in specialty entrees, chowders, and stews; or in salads or appetizers.

(See SEAFOOD.)

ROCK LOBSTER APPETIZERS

Color photograph for this recipe on page 72.

12 2-oz. frozen rock lobster-tails
6 tbsp. butter
6 tbsp. flour
1 1/2 c. light cream
1 tsp. grated lemon rind
1 tsp. paprika
2 eggs, separated
Salt and pepper to taste
1/2 c. grated Cheddar cheese

Drop frozen rock lobster-tails into boiling, salted water; bring to a boil. Drain lobster- tails immediately; drench with cold water. Remove underside membraine with scissors; pull out meat. Dice meat, reserving shells. Melt butter in saucepan; stir in flour. Stir in cream gradually; add lemon rind and paprika. Cook, stirring constantly, until thickened. Beat in egg yolks quickly; add salt and pepper. Add lobster meat to half the sauce; spoon into reserved shells. Place in cookie pan. Heat remaining sauce; stir in cheese until melted. Cool slightly; fold in stiffly beaten egg whites. Spoon over filled lobster shells. Bake in 350-degree oven for 25 to 30 minutes or until puffed and brown. Place in chafing dish and keep warm. Yield: 6 servings.

CALIFORNIA LOBSTER COCKTAIL

2 grapefruit
1 c. chopped cooked lobster
3 tbsp. orange juice
1/4 c. catsup
1/4 c. mayonnaise

Halve grapefruit; remove pulp. Cut grapefruit pulp into small pieces. Snip out membrane with scissors; notch edges of grapefruit shells. Combine lobster and grapefruit. Blend remaining ingredients for dressing; stir into lobster mixture. Spoon into grapefruit shells; chill. Yield: 4 servings.

LOBSTER COCKTAIL

4 tbsp. chili sauce
2 tbsp. lemon juice
8 drops of hot sauce
3 tbsp. finely chopped celery
1 tsp. Worcestershire sauce
3/4 tsp. salt
1 sm. can lobster, flaked

Combine chili sauce, lemon juice, hot sauce, celery, Worcestershire sauce and salt; mix thoroughly. Add lobster, tossing well. Chill thoroughly; serve in cocktail glasses. Yield: 4-6 servings.

LOBSTER RUMAKI

Cooked lobster, cut into 1 1/2-in. pieces
Water chestnuts, sliced
Salad oil
Soy sauce
Bacon slices, partially cooked

Split center of each piece of lobster; insert thin slice of water chestnut. Brush well with oil and soy sauce. Wrap in bacon; secure with wooden pick. Broil until bacon is crisp.

PARTY LOBSTER-BEEF KABOBS

3 9-oz. packages frozen lobster-tails
3/4 lb. 1-in. thick round steak
1/4 c. salad oil
1/4 c. wine vinegar
2 tbsp. lemon juice
1/4 c. tomato juice
1/2 tsp. garlic powder
1/8 tsp. pepper
1/2 tsp. salt
Dash of cayenne pepper
Unseasoned meat tenderizer

Thaw lobster-tails. Trim away undersides of shells with scissors. Remove meat; cut into bite-sized pieces. Slice steak into 1/4-inch strips; cut crosswise into 1-inch pieces. Place lobster and steak in shallow dish. Combine all remaining ingredients except tenderizer in jar with tight-fitting lid; shake well. Pour over lobster and steak; marinate in refrigerator for 2 hours. Drain, reserving marinade; separate steak from lobster. Sprinkle steak with tenderizer. Thread lobster and steak alternately on 12 small skewers or hibachi sticks; brush with reserved marinade. Place cake rack over grill. Arrange kabobs on rack. Grill 5 inches from source of heat for 6 to 7 minutes, turning occasionally and brushing with marinade. Kabobs may be broiled in oven 4 inches from source of heat for 15 minutes, turning occasionally and brushing with marinade. Yield: 12 servings.

LOBSTERBURGERS

2 lobster-tails
1/4 c. chopped celery
1 tsp. prepared mustard
1/4 tsp. salt
Dash of pepper
3 tbsp. mayonnaise
4 sandwich rolls
4 slices American cheese

Place lobster-tails in boiling water to cover; cook until tender. Remove lobster from shell. Cut into small pieces. Mix lobster, celery, mustard, salt, pepper and mayonnaise. Split rolls; place cut side up on cookie sheet. Spread bottom half with lobster mixture; place cheese slice on other half. Broil 3 inches from source of heat until cheese bubbles. Top with bun half; serve immediately. Yield: 4 servings.

ELEGANT LOBSTER-TAIL SALAD

6 4-oz. packages frozen lobster-tails
2 lb. white potatoes
1/2 c. minced onion
1 tsp. salt
1/4 tsp. white pepper
1 1/2 c. mayonnaise
1/4 c. heavy cream

Drop frozen lobster-tails into boiling salted water; bring to a boil. Reduce heat; simmer for 7 minutes. Drain; rinse with ice water. Cut away thin underside membrane; remove lobster from shell. Chill in refrigerator. Place potatoes in large kettle; cover with water. Bring to a boil; cook until tender. Drain; peel while warm. Cut in cubes. Add onion, salt and pepper to potatoes. Mix mayonnaise with cream until smooth. Pour over potatoes and onion. Cool slightly; chill in refrigerator. Cut chilled lobster-tails into bite-sized pieces; add to potato mixture. Toss until well blended. Yield: 6-8 servings.

Macaroni-Lobster Salad . . . Blend shell macaroni and lobster chunks with a piquant dressing.

MACARONI-LOBSTER SALAD

Salt
8-oz. shell macaroni
3 c. diced cooked lobster
1 c. sliced celery
1 c. diced cucumber
1/2 c. mayonnaise
3 tbsp. lemon juice
2 tbsp. capers
1/4 tsp. dry mustard
1/4 tsp. hot sauce
1/2 c. sour cream
Chicory leaves

Add 1 tablespoon salt to 3 quarts rapidly boiling water in large saucepan. Add macaroni gradually so that water continues to boil. Cook, stirring occasionally, until tender. Drain in colander. Rinse with cold water; drain again. Combine macaroni, lobster, celery, cucumber, mayonnaise, lemon juice, capers, 1 teaspoon salt, mustard and hot sauce. Chill until serving time. Stir in sour cream; serve on crisp chicory leaves.

LOBSTER-MELON SALAD WITH PUFFS

1/2 c. mayonnaise
1/4 c. sour cream
2 tbsp. minced parsley
2 tbsp. chopped green onion
1 tbsp. tarragon vinegar
1 tbsp. lemon juice
1 sm. clove of garlic, crushed
1/4 tsp. salt
Pepper
2 5 1/2-oz. cans lobster, drained
2 c. cantaloupe balls
3/4 c. self-rising cornmeal
3/4 c. self-rising flour
1/2 c. butter
4 eggs

Blend mayonnaise, sour cream, parsley, onion, vinegar, lemon juice, garlic, salt and pepper. Stir in lobster; refrigerate. Just before serving, fold in melon balls. Mix cornmeal and flour. Bring 1 cup water and butter to a boil in small saucepan. Stir until butter melts. Add dry ingredients all at once. Reduce heat; cook, stirring constantly, until mixture is smooth and forms ball. Remove from heat; cool slightly. Add eggs, one at a time, beating well after each addition. Drop batter from tablespoon onto baking sheet to make 10 shells. Bake at 350 degrees for 35 minutes or until firm to touch. Cool on wire rack. Cut tops off shells; remove soft interiors. Divide lobster salad among shells. Refrigerate until ready to serve.

LOBSTER ASPIC PARISIENNE

3 env. unflavored gelatin
2 cans bouillon, heated

2 tbsp. lemon juice
2 tsp. Worcestershire sauce
1 1/2 lb. cooked lobster
1 1/2 c. cooked peas
1 c. diced cooked carrots
1 1/2 c. diced cooked potatoes
2 tsp. salt
2/3 c. mayonnaise

Soften gelatin in 1 1/3 cups cold water; dissolve in bouillon. Add lemon juice and Worcestershire sauce. Chill until thick. Pour 1 cup gelatin mixture into 4-cup mold. Arrange several large pieces of lobster, red side down, in gelatin mixture. Chill until set. Dice remaining lobster; combine with peas, carrots, potatoes, salt and mayonnaise, tossing lightly. Stir in remaining gelatin mixture. Pour potato mixture over firm gelatin. Chill until firm. Unmold onto lettuce; garnish with wedges of tomato, hard-cooked eggs, ripe olives and lemon wedges, if desired. Yield: 8-10 servings.

LOBSTER MOLD

3 env. gelatin
4 chicken bouillon cubes
1 c. mayonnaise
2 dashes of hot sauce
1/4 c. lemon juice
2 tbsp. grated onion
1 tsp. paprika
3/4 c. heavy cream, whipped
4 c. cooked lobster, diced
1/2 c. chopped celery
1/2 c. drained capers

Soften gelatin in 1/2 cup water. Add bouillon cubes; heat, stirring, until dissolved. Cool. Add mayonnaise, hot sauce, lemon juice, grated onion and paprika. Chill until mixture begins to thicken; fold in whipped cream, lobster, chopped celery and capers. Place in 6-cup ring mold; refrigerate until set. Unmold on lettuce.

LOBSTER MOUSSE

3 3-oz. packages cream cheese
1 can tomato soup
2 tbsp. gelatin
2 tbsp. chopped green onion
1/2 c. chopped green pepper
3/4 c. chopped celery
1 1/2 c. chopped lobster
1 c. mayonnaise
Salt and pepper to taste
Hot sauce to taste
Worcestershire sauce to taste

Combine cheese and soup in saucepan; place over low heat, stirring until smooth. Soften gelatin in 1 cup cold water; dissolve in cheese mixture. Chill until partially set. Stir in green onion, green pepper, celery and lobster. Add mayonnaise, salt, pepper, hot sauce and Worcestershire sauce. Pour into 2-quart fish mold; chill until firm. Unmold on serving plate; keep chilled until ready to serve.

LOBSTER SALAD

2 eggs, beaten
1 tbsp. mustard
1/2 tsp. pepper
1/2 tsp. cayenne pepper
1 tbsp. olive oil
1 c. vinegar
1 tbsp. butter
1/2 tsp. salt
5 hard-cooked eggs
1 can lobster, chopped

Combine all ingredients except hard-cooked eggs and lobster; place over low heat. Cook, stirring constantly, until thickened. Cool. Chop egg whites; mash egg yolks. Combine with lobster and dressing; toss lightly. Yield: 6 servings.

LOBSTER SALAD DELUXE

1 c. shell macaroni
1/2 c. mayonnaise
1/2 c. sour cream
1 tbsp. diced pimento
1/2 c. milk
2 tbsp. minced green pepper
1 tbsp. sweet pickle relish
1 tsp. celery seed
1/4 c. finely cut celery
2 chopped green onions and tops
8 oz. cooked lobster, cubed
3/4 c. Cheddar cheese, diced

Cook macaroni according to package directions. Stir mayonnaise, sour cream, pimento, milk, green pepper, relish, celery seed, celery and green onions together. Mix with lobster and macaroni; add cheese. Chill; serve on lettuce leaf garnished with radish and tomato. Yield: 6 servings.

LOBSTER SALAD IN PINEAPPLE SHELLS

1 ripe pineapple
2 c. sour cream
2 tbsp. lemon juice
1 tsp. salt
1/2 c. chopped green mango chutney
1 tbsp. curry powder
4 c. chopped cooked lobster
1 c. sliced pimento-stuffed olives
1/2 c. toasted almonds

Cut pineapple in half lengthwise, leaving crown on pineapple. Remove pineapple in wedges, leaving 1/2-inch shell. Remove core; dice pineapple into 1 1/2-inch wedges. Blend sour cream, lemon juice, salt, chutney and curry powder; toss with lobster, sliced olives and pineapple wedges lightly. Heap into pineapple shells; sprinkle with almonds. Yield: 6 servings.

LOBSTER SALAD WITH MAYONNAISE

Cooked lobster meat
Chopped celery
Lettuce leaves
Lobster claws
Hard-cooked eggs, sliced
Capers
1/2 tsp. dry mustard
1 tsp. salt
2 tsp. sugar
1/8 tsp. pepper
2 egg yolks
1 1/2 c. olive oil
2 tbsp. vinegar

Cut lobster into bite-sized pieces; add celery. Arrange on lettuce; surround with lobster claws, eggs and capers. Chill. Mix mustard, salt, sugar and pepper. Add egg yolks; beat well. Add oil gradually; beat vigorously after each addition. Beat until stiff. Add vinegar; blend well. Serve over salad.

BARBECUED LOBSTER

Cooked lobster, cut into 1 1/2-in. pieces
Barbecue sauce

Marinate lobster in barbecue sauce to cover for several hours. Thread pieces on skewers. Broil 3 inches from source of heat until browned lightly.

BAKED MAINE LOBSTER

4 live lobsters
16 crackers, crushed
1/4 c. melted butter
1/4 c. milk
Sherry
Dash of Worcestershire sauce
Garlic salt to taste
Salt and pepper to taste

Place lobsters on backs; cross large claws, holding firmly. Cut quickly through entire length of body and tail, beginning at point between large claws. Remove craw and veins; leave tomalley in lobsters or mix with dressing. Mix crumbs with butter and milk. Moisten to desired consistency with sherry; season with Worcestershire sauce, garlic salt, salt and pepper. Stuff lobsters with mixture; pour additional butter over dressing. Sprinkle with Parmesan cheese, if desired. Bake at 450 degrees for 20 minutes. Yield: 4 servings.

SAUCY LOBSTER GRILL

6 rock lobster-tails
1 clove of garlic, mashed
Juice of 1 lemon
1 c. tomato juice
1/2 c. butter

Cut through middle of lobster shell with sharp knife; cut through flesh but not underside membrane. Grasp tail in both hands; open flat, exposing meaty sections. Combine remaining ingredients in saucepan; simmer until butter is melted. Place lobster, fleshy side down, on grill over 5 inches from source of heat. Cook for 5 minutes. Turn lobster; brush well with sauce. Cook until flesh is opaque, brushing several times with sauce. Brush with sauce just before serving.

SOUTH AFRICAN ROCK LOBSTER-TAILS

1/4 c. butter
1 c. rice
3 c. chicken broth
1/2 tsp. crumbled saffron threads
12 rock lobster-tails
1 10-oz. package frozen peas
Salt
Paprika

Melt butter in skillet; saute rice until golden. Add chicken broth and saffron; cover tightly. Simmer for 20 minutes. Drop lobster-tails into boiling salted water. Cook only until water reboils. Drain; drench with cold water. Cut away underside membrane; pull out meat in one piece. Add lobster meat and peas to rice. Add additional chicken broth if necessary to prevent sticking. Cover; simmer for 10 minutes or until peas are cooked. Season to taste with salt and paprika. Yield: 4-6 servings.

South African Rock Lobster-Tails . . . Green peas and saffron rice mingle with lobster-tails.

GINGER-BARBECUED ROCK LOBSTER

6 rock lobster-tails
1 1/2 c. salad oil
1/2 c. lemon juice
3 tbsp. soy sauce
3 tbsp. honey
1/2 tsp. ginger
2 tsp. angostura bitters

Cut underside membrane of lobster-tails around edge; remove. Grasp lobster-tails in both hands; bend backward toward shell sides to crack. Insert skewers to prevent curling. Combine all remaining ingredients for sauce; beat until blended. Place lobster-tails in shallow pan; pour sauce over lobster-tails. Let stand at room temperature for 1 hour. Drain; reserve marinade. Arrange lobster-tails on grill 5 inches from source of heat, flesh side down; cook for 5 minutes. Turn; brush with sauce. Cook for 3 to 5 minutes longer. Brush with sauce just before serving. Yield: 6 servings.

LOBSTER-TAILS WITH BUTTER SAUCE

Lobster-tails, 1/2 lb. each
Melted butter
2 tbsp. flour
1/4 tsp. pepper
1 1/2 tsp. lemon juice
Yellow food coloring

Slit undershells of tails lengthwise with scissors; bend backwards to crack shells. Brush melted butter on slit sides. Grill, shell side down, 6 inches from source of heat for 15 minutes. Brush slit sides with butter. Turn; grill for 3 minutes longer or until tender and opaque. Melt 1/4 cup butter in saucepan; stir in flour gradually. Add pepper, lemon juice and 1 cup hot water; bring to a boil, stirring constantly. Cook for 5 minutes, stirring occasionally. Remove from heat; stir in 1/4 cup butter. Tint with food coloring. Serve in individual cups for dipping lobster.

CANTONESE-STYLE LOBSTER

1 clove of garlic
3 tbsp. vegetable oil
1/4 lb. cooked pork, minced
1 tsp. salt
1/4 tsp. pepper
1 tsp. sugar
1 tbsp. cornstarch
2 c. cooked lobster, diced
2 c. hot chicken broth
2 eggs, beaten

Brown garlic in oil in skillet. Combine pork, salt, pepper, sugar and 1/2 teaspoon cornstarch. Add to garlic; stir for 1 minute. Add lobster; stir for 1 minute longer. Pour in hot broth, stirring constantly, until blended. Simmer, covered, for 10 minutes. Mix remaining cornstarch with enough cold water to make a paste. Add to broth mixture, stirring constantly, until thickened. Blend in eggs; cook, stirring constantly, until mixture is bubbly. Yield: 2-4 servings.

CREAMED LOBSTER

1 c. cream
1/4 c. milk
2 c. cooked diced lobster
1/4 tsp. mustard
Dash of onion juice
1/2 c. soft bread crumbs
1 tbsp. butter
1 egg, well beaten
1 tsp. lemon juice
Salt and pepper to taste
Cracker crumbs
Paprika

Mix cream and milk in double boiler; heat until hot. Add all remaining ingredients except cracker crumbs and paprika; cook until thickened, stirring frequently. Place in casserole. Top with cracker crumbs; sprinkle with paprika. Bake at 350 degrees for 20 minutes. Yield: 8 servings.

CREAMED LOBSTER AND RICE

1/4 c. butter
1/2 c. catsup
2 c. cooked rice
3/4 lb. lobster, diced
1 c. heavy cream

Melt butter in double boiler; add catsup and rice. Blend; cook for 20 minutes. Add lobster and cream, blending well. Serve with toast points. Yield: 4 servings.

DEVILED LOBSTER

2 c. diced cooked lobster
1 c. soft bread crumbs
1 hard-cooked egg, finely chopped
2 tsp. lemon juice
1 tbsp. butter
1 tbsp. flour
1 c. milk
1/2 tsp. salt
Dash of cayenne pepper
1/2 tsp. anchovy paste

Combine lobster, half the bread crumbs, egg and lemon juice. Melt butter in saucepan; blend in flour. Stir in milk gradually; cook until thickened, stirring constantly. Season with salt, cayenne pepper and anchovy paste. Combine sauce and lobster mixture; spoon into greased scallop shells or ramekins. Top with remaining crumbs. Bake at 375 degrees for about 15 minutes. Yield: 6 servings.

LOBSTER A LA KING

3 tbsp. butter
3 tbsp. flour
Salt to taste
1/4 tsp. paprika
1/2 c. milk
1 c. cooked peas
1 tbsp. chopped green pepper
2 tbsp. chopped pimento
1 c. flaked lobster
2 egg yolks, beaten

Melt butter; add flour, salt and paprika. Mix well. Add milk gradually; cook until smooth and thick, stirring constantly. Add peas, green pepper, pimento and lobster; cook for 3 minutes. Add egg yolks; cook for 1 minute longer. Serve on toast. Yield: 6 servings.

LOBSTER A L'AMERICAINE

1 3-lb. live lobster
1/4 c. cooking oil
2 tbsp. butter
1/4 c. chopped onion
1 can tomato paste
1/2 tsp. thyme
1/2 bay leaf
Dash of cayenne pepper
1 c. white wine

Insert knife between body and tail shells of lobster to sever spinal cord. Make deep, sharp cut lengthwise through back of body and tail. Separate halves; remove black line and stomach. Reserve liver and coral. Remove claws; reserve. Place oil and butter in 10-inch skillet. Cook lobster until shell turns red. Remove meat from shells; set aside. Cook onion in skillet over low heat until transparent; add tomato paste, thyme, bay leaf, cayenne pepper and wine. Cook, covered, over medium heat for 5 minutes. Add reserved liver and coral. Cook, stirring constantly, until sauce thickens. Add lobster. Cook over low heat until heated through. Garnish with claws. Yield: 6-8 servings.

LOBSTER AND BROCCOLI MORNAY

5 tbsp. flour
1/4 c. butter, melted
1 c. milk
1 c. heavy cream
1 c. Gruyere cheese, grated
Salt and pepper to taste
2 tbsp. dry sherry
1 bunch broccoli, cooked
1 lb. cooked lobster
1/4 c. grated Parmesan cheese
Buttered bread crumbs

Stir flour into butter in saucepan; add milk and cream gradually. Cook over medium heat until mixture thickens, stirring constantly. Add Gruyere cheese; heat until cheese melts. Stir in seasonings and sherry. Separate broccoli flowerets. Arrange broccoli and lobster in baking dish; pour on sauce. Top with Parmesan cheese and crumbs. Bake in 400-degree oven for 15 to 20 minutes. Yield: 4 servings.

LOBSTER AND MUSHROOMS FRICASSEE

Salt
1 2-lb. lobster
3/4 lb. mushrooms, coarsely sliced
1/4 c. butter
Onion juice to taste
1/4 c. flour
2 tbsp. sherry
1 1/2 c. milk
Paprika to taste

Combine 4 inches water and 3 tablespoons salt in large kettle; bring to a boil. Plunge live lobster into kettle head down, holding claws. Cover. Cook for 15 to 18 minutes. Drain; cool in colander. Cut from tip of tail to head. Remove head and small sac, being careful not to break sac. Crack claws; remove intestinal vein from body. Remove all meat; cut into bite-sized pieces. Saute mushrooms in large skillet in butter and onion juice until just tender; stir in flour, blending well. Add sherry and milk gradually, stirring constantly until thickened. Add lobster; season with salt to taste, paprika and additional sherry. Do not boil; heat through. Serve in patty shells, over hot cooked rice or with mashed potatoes. Yield: 6 servings.

PARTS OF A LOBSTER

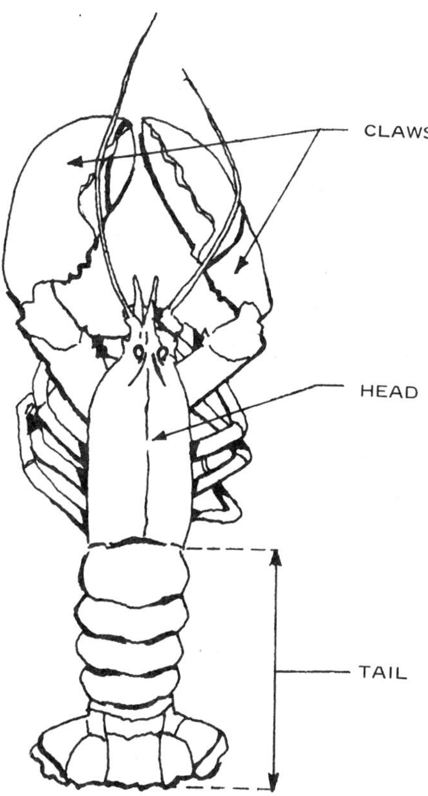

HOW TO SPLIT A LOBSTER

LOBSTER NEWBURG SUPREME

1 1/2 lb. cooked lobster
Butter
1/4 c. brandy
1 c. heavy cream
3 egg yolks
Seasonings to taste

Cut lobster in large pieces. Cook lobster in small amount of butter for 5 minutes over low heat. Add brandy; ignite. Blend cream and egg yolks in double boiler. Cook, stirring until mixture coats spoon; add lobster and seasonings. Serve hot in toast cups, patty shells or over rice.

LOBSTER-NOODLE CASSEROLE

3/4 lb. noodles, cooked
1 lb. mushrooms
Butter
Salt to taste
2 lb. cooked lobster, diced
1/2 c. sherry
1 tsp. lemon juice
3/4 c. flour
3 c. milk
1 c. cream
12 round buttery crackers

Rinse noodles; drain. Saute mushrooms in butter; season with salt. Remove mushrooms; reserve drippings. Combine lobster, 2 tablespoons butter, sherry and lemon juice in double boiler; heat, stirring, but do not boil. Combine reserved drippings and enough butter to make 3/4 cup butter mixture; turn into saucepan. Place butter mixture over low heat; blend in flour. Add milk; cook, stirring, until thickened. Season with salt. Stir in cream; bring sauce to a boil. Reduce heat; simmer for 5 minutes. Add mushrooms and lobster mixture; stir until blended. Season with salt, if needed. Arrange 3 alternate layers of noodles and lobster sauce in buttered 4-quart casserole. Crush crackers. Melt 3 tablespoons butter; blend in crumbs. Sprinkle on casserole. Bake, uncovered, at 350 degrees for 30 to 40 minutes. Yield: 12 servings.

LOBSTER-TAILS THERMIDOR

6 1-lb. frozen lobster-tails
5/8 c. melted butter
1 c. sliced fresh mushrooms
4 tbsp. flour
1 tsp. dry mustard
Dash of nutmeg
Dash of cayenne pepper
1 tsp. salt
1 c. milk
1 c. half and half
2 egg yolks, slightly beaten
1 tsp. lemon juice
2 tbsp. sherry
1/2 c. fine bread crumbs
2 tbsp. grated Parmesan cheese

Place lobster-tails in boiling water to cover; bring to a boil. Cook until tender; drain. Remove lobster meat; dice. Reserve shells; cut in half. Pour 1/4 cup butter in saucepan. Add mushrooms; saute until lightly browned. Blend in flour; mix in mustard, nutmeg, cayenne pepper and salt. Add milk and half and half gradually; cook, stirring constantly, until thick. Stir small amount of hot mixture into egg yolks, stirring constantly; return yolk mixture to sauce, stirring gradually. Cook until thickened, stirring constantly. Stir in lemon juice, sherry and lobster meat; spoon into reserved shells. Combine crumbs, cheese and remaining butter; sprinkle over lobster mixture. Place on cookie sheet. Bake at 400 degrees for 15 minutes. Yield: 4-6 servings.

LOBSTER SQUARES

3 tbsp. flour
3 tbsp. butter, melted
1 1/2 c. cream
1/4 tsp. nutmeg
1 tsp. salt
Dash of cayenne pepper
2 tsp. lemon juice
5 tbsp. sherry
1/2 tsp. hot mustard
Sliced mushrooms
1/2 c. grated cheese
3 c. cooked lobster, diced
1 c. soft bread crumbs
2 eggs, beaten

Combine flour and butter in saucepan over medium heat; stir well. Add cream gradually, stirring constantly, until thickened. Add nutmeg, salt, cayenne pepper, lemon juice, sherry and mustard; blend thoroughly. Add mushrooms and cheese to white sauce. Combine lobster, crumbs and eggs; mix into white sauce. Pour mixture into well-greased casserole. Bake at 350 degrees until firm. Cut in squares to serve. Yield: 6 servings.

LOBSTER SUPREME

1/2 c. margarine
1/2 c. flour
2 c. canned chicken stock
1 c. cream
2 3-oz. packages pimento cream cheese
1/2 c. sherry
Dash of salt and pepper
4 c. canned lobster
1 can mushrooms, drained
Hot cooked rice

Melt margarine; stir in flour. Add chicken stock and cream. Cook, stirring constantly, until mixture is bubbly and thickened. Add cheese and sherry; stir over low heat until cheese melts. Season with salt and pepper; add lobster and mushrooms. Heat gently until hot. Serve over rice. Yield: 6 servings.

LOBSTER WITH MUSTARD DRESSING

5 hard-cooked eggs
1 can lobster, drained
2 eggs, beaten
1 tsp. mustard
1/2 tsp. pepper
1/2 tsp. olive oil
1 c. vinegar
2 tbsp. butter
1/8 tsp. salt

Cut eggs in half. Mash egg yolks; mix with lobster. Chop egg whites; add to lobster mixture. Place all remaining ingredients in saucepan. Cook until thickened, stirring constantly; cool. Pour over lobster mixture. Yield: 4-5 servings.

STUFFED LOBSTER SUPREME

4 pkg. frozen rock lobster-tails
Melted butter
4 tbsp. flour
1 tsp. salt
1 tsp. paprika
Dash of cayenne pepper
2 c. half and half
2 tbsp. lemon juice
1/4 c. cracker crumbs
1/4 c. grated Parmesan cheese

Cook lobster-tails according to package directions; drain. Cut lobster from shells with scissors; dice. Reserve shells. Saute lobster in 1/2 cup butter in large skillet for 3 minutes. Remove from heat; blend in flour, salt, paprika and cayenne pepper. Stir in half and half gradually; cook, stirring constantly, until mixture thickens and is bubbly. Stir in lemon juice. Spoon filling into reserved shells. Combine crumbs, cheese and 1 tablespoon butter. Sprinkle tops lightly with crumb mixture. Place in shallow baking pan. Bake in 450-degree oven for 10 minutes or until tops are golden. Yield: 8 servings.

ROCK LOBSTER WITH PARSLEY BUTTER

16 2-oz. frozen rock lobster-tails
1 c. butter
1 tsp. paprika
2 tbsp. chopped parsley
2 bay leaves

Drop lobster-tails into boiling salted water to cover. Bring water to a boil; cook for 2 minutes. Drain immediately; rinse with cold water. Cut away underside membrane with kitchen shears. Remove lobster; cut in crosswise slices. Keep warm. Place butter, paprika, parsley and bay leaves in saucepan over low heat until butter is melted. Remove bay leaves. Pour butter mixture over lobster pieces. Serve with lemon slices. Yield: 8 servings.

BAKED STUFFED LOBSTER

12 crackers, crushed
1 can minced clams and liquid
2 tbsp. Worcestershire sauce
1/2 tsp. celery salt
1/4 tsp. pepper
Melted butter
1 can clam juice
Fresh lobster
Grated cheese
Paprika

Combine crackers, clams and liquid, Worcestershire sauce, celery salt, pepper, 1/4 cup butter and clam juice. Immerse live lobster in boiling water; remove. Cut body from head to tip of tail, splitting open. Remove intestinal vein. Fill lobster with clam mixture; place in broiler pan. Sprinkle with cheese and paprika. Brush with butter. Pour 1/4 cup water in pan. Place in oven on top rack. Bake at 425 degrees for 20 minutes.

SHERRIED LOBSTER-TAILS

4 6-oz. frozen lobster-tails
1/4 c. butter
2 onions, chopped
1 sm. clove of garlic, minced
1 sm. can mushrooms
1 tbsp. flour
3/4 c. sherry
1 tsp. paprika
1 tsp. salt
1/4 tsp. pepper
1/2 c. grated Parmesan cheese

Cook lobster-tails in boiling water for 15 minutes; cool. Remove lobster from shells, reserving shells. Cut into cubes. Melt 2 tablespoons butter in heavy skillet; add onions, garlic and mushrooms. Cook over low heat for 5 minutes. Sprinkle with flour; add sherry gradually. Cook for 5 minutes longer, stirring constantly. Add lobster, paprika, salt and pepper. Cook, covered, over low heat for 10 minutes. Place lobster shells in shallow baking pan; spoon lobster mixture into shells. Sprinkle with cheese; dot with remaining butter. Bake at 400 degrees for 10 minutes. Yield: 4 servings.

Luncheon Meats

LIVER SAUSAGE-NUT BALL

1 lb. liver sausage
1 8-oz. package cream cheese
1/4 c. mayonnaise
1/2 c. chopped dill pickle
Dash of hot sauce
1 tsp. Worcestershire sauce
1/4 tsp. garlic salt
1/4 c. chopped onion
1/2 c. chopped salted peanuts

Blend liver sausage and cream cheese; add remaining ingredients except peanuts. Form into ball; roll in peanuts. Chill until ready to serve.

PIQUANTE SPREAD

1 can luncheon meat, ground
1/2 c. chopped celery
1/2 c. chopped sweet pickle
2 hard-boiled eggs, chopped
1/4 c. chopped onion
1 tbsp. mustard
1/4 c. salad dressing
1 tsp. wine vinegar
1 tsp. salt
1 tsp. pepper

Combine luncheon meat with celery, pickle, eggs and onion. Blend mustard, salad dressing and vinegar; add to luncheon meat mixture. Season with salt and pepper.

VIENNA PICK-UPS

Vienna sausage
Barbecue sauce
Crushed corn chips

Dip individual Vienna sausages into barbecue sauce. Insert wooden pick into end of sausage; roll in corn chips. Place on broiler pan. Broil until hot; serve immediately.

BARBECUED SANDWICHES

2 tbsp. vinegar
1/2 tsp. paprika
1/2 tsp. dry mustard
2 tbsp. brown sugar
2 tbsp. jelly
1/2 bottle catsup
1 lb. luncheon meat, chopped
Hamburger buns

Combine all ingredients except meat and buns in saucepan; bring to boil. Add meat; simmer, covered, for 5 minutes. Serve hot on buns.

HOT BOLOGNA SANDWICHES

1/2 lb. bologna, chopped
1/2 c. diced Cheddar cheese
1/2 c. chopped stuffed olives
3 tbsp. mayonnaise
2 hard-boiled eggs, chopped
1/2 c. catsup
1 sm. onion, chopped
Frankfurter buns

Combine all ingredients except buns; let stand for 30 minutes. Fill buns; wrap in foil. Bake at 400 degrees for 15 minutes.

BRAUNSCHWEIGER-CHEDDAR SANDWICH

1/2 lb. braunschweiger
1/2 c. chopped celery
2 tbsp. chili sauce
4 slices rye bread, toasted
1/2 c. sharp Cheddar cheese, grated

Have braunschweiger at room temperature; combine with celery and chili sauce. Spread on toast. Place on baking sheet; top with cheese. Broil for 3 minutes or until cheese is melted.

JIFFY-BROILED PIZZAS

1 can luncheon meat
3 tbsp. mustard
8 slices bread
8 slices cheese
1/2 tsp. garlic powder
1 8-oz. can tomato sauce
1 tsp. salt
1/2 tsp. pepper
1/2 tsp. oregano

Cut luncheon meat into 8 slices; spread each slice of meat with mustard. Toast bread on one side. Place slice of meat on each untoasted side of bread; top with slice of cheese. Combine remaining ingredients; bring to a boil. Broil pizzas until cheese is melted; spoon sauce over pizzas.

SANDWICH LOAF

1 loaf French bread
Hickory-flavored catsup
Salami slices
Bologna slices
Sliced cheese

Cut bread into 1-inch slices almost to bottom crust. Brush between slices with catsup. Layer salami, bologna and cheese between slices. Wrap loaf in foil. Bake at 350 degrees for 10 to 15 minutes, or until heated through.

OPEN-FACED HOT SANDWICHES

1 12-oz. can diced luncheon meat
1/2 lb. diced Velveeta cheese
2 tbsp. chopped onion
2 tbsp. chopped green pepper
1 can cream of mushroom soup
Frankfurter buns

Combine luncheon meat, cheese, onion, green pepper and soup; blend well. Split buns; spread with meat mixture. Broil until cheese is melted and top is lightly browned.

CRISPY LUNCHEON SLICES

1/2 c. corn flake crumbs
2 tbsp. (packed) brown sugar
1/8 tsp. ground cloves
1 12-oz. can luncheon meat
2 tbsp. prepared mustard

Combine crumbs with brown sugar and cloves. Cut luncheon meat crosswise into 8 slices. Spread both sides of slices with mustard; coat generously with crumb mixture. Place in greased baking dish. Bake at 350 degrees for 20 to 30 minutes.

QUICK PIZZAS

1 sm. can pizza sauce
6 hamburger buns, split
1 pkg. pepperoni, sliced thin
1 6-oz. package sliced mozzarella cheese

Spread pizza sauce on cut side of buns. Place 6 pepperoni slices on each bun; cover with cheese. Broil for 5 minutes or until cheese melts.

BAKED LUNCHEON MEAT

1 can luncheon meat
Whole cloves
1/4 c. brown sugar
2 tbsp. prepared mustard

Place luncheon meat in shallow baking dish. Score meat; stud with cloves. Blend brown sugar with mustard; spread over meat. Bake at 325 degrees for 20 minutes; baste occasionally with pan juices.

GLAZED LUNCHEON BAKE

2 cans luncheon meat
2 cans sweet potatoes
3 tbsp. melted butter
1 12-oz. glass orange marmalade

Cut each loaf of meat into fourths about three-fourths through. Place loaves in a buttered 13 x 9 x 2 1/2-inch baking pan. Slice potatoes; place potatoes between slices of meat and around loaves. Brush meat and potatoes well with melted butter. Spread orange marmalade over top. Bake at 400 degrees for 20 minutes.

LUNCHEON LOAF

1 can luncheon meat
12 round buttery crackers
1/2 lb. Cheddar cheese
1 egg
1 1/2 c. milk

Grind meat, crackers and cheese; blend well. Beat egg and milk together; add to meat mixture. Place in greased loaf pan. Bake in 350-degree oven for 35 minutes.

OVEN BARBECUE

1 can luncheon meat
1 sm. can tomato sauce
1/4 c. water
2 tbsp. brown sugar
1 tbsp. finely grated onion
1/4 tsp. Worcestershire sauce

Slice meat lengthwise. Place in greased shallow baking dish. Combine remaining ingredients; pour over meat. Bake at 400 degrees for 30 minutes; baste occasionally.

SAUCY BAKE WITH MUSHROOM SAUCE

1 can luncheon meat
1/2 can cream of mushroom soup
3 tbsp. grated Parmesan cheese

Place luncheon meat in shallow baking pan. Combine soup with 1/4 cup water. Add cheese; stir until smooth. Pour over luncheon meat. Bake at 375 degrees for 30 minutes.

SWEET AND SOUR LUNCHEON MEAT

1 12-oz. can luncheon meat, ground
1/4 lb. cheese, ground
1/2 c. oats
1 egg, beaten
1 tbsp. (packed) brown sugar
1 tbsp. cornstarch
1 c. pineapple chunks
1 tbsp. vinegar
1/4 tsp. ginger

Combine meat, cheese, oats and egg in bowl; form into eight balls. Place meatballs in shallow baking pan. Bake at 400 degrees for 20 minutes. Blend brown sugar and cornstarch into small amount of fat in skillet; add 1 cup water gradually. Simmer, stirring constantly, until sauce is smooth and thickened; add pineapple, vinegar and ginger. Simmer, stirring constantly, until heated through. Drain off excess fat from meatballs; pour sauce over meatballs. Bake for 10 minutes longer.

BOLOGNA CUPS

2 tbsp. butter
2 tbsp. flour
1 c. milk
Salt and pepper
1 10-oz. package frozen peas, cooked
8 thin slices bologna

Melt butter in saucepan; blend in flour and milk gradually. Simmer, stirring constantly, until sauce is smooth and thickened. Season with salt and pepper; add peas. Simmer, covered, until heated through. Saute bologna in small amount of hot fat until edges curl and form cups. Fill meat cups with creamed peas.

BOLOGNA CASSEROLE

2 c. cubed potatoes
1 1/2 c. bologna
6 tbsp. flour
1/2 tsp. salt
1/4 tsp. pepper
2 tbsp. butter
2 c. milk

Place potatoes in casserole; cover with bologna. Sprinkle with flour, salt and pepper; dot with butter. Pour milk over bologna. Bake at 350 degrees for 1 hour.

CASSEROLE FOR A CROWD

1 lge. onion, chopped
1 lb. butter
1 c. flour
2 1/2 to 3 qt. milk
2 lb. Cheddar cheese, grated
1 1/2 15-oz. boxes instant rice
6 12-oz. cans luncheon meat
10 1/2 oz. potato chips, crushed

Saute onion in butter in large skillet; stir in flour. Add milk gradually; simmer, stirring constantly, until smooth and thickened. Add cheese; simmer stirring, until cheese is melted. Cook rice according to package directions; cut meat in small cubes. Combine all ingredients including liquid surrounding luncheon meat except potato chips. Place in casseroles; top with potato chips. Bake at 350 degrees for 30 minutes or until heated through.

Yule-Morn Yummies . . . Luncheon meat, peaches, crab apples and eggs blend for a brunch.

YULE-MORN YUMMIES

2 12 oz. cans luncheon meat
6 round hard rolls
12 eggs
1 1-lb. 13-oz. can cling peach halves
2 tbsp. brown sugar
6 sliced crab apples

Cut each piece of luncheon meat into 6 slices. Grease 6 small shallow casseroles. Cut rolls in half; place bottom halves in casseroles. Top each roll half with 2 slices of meat. Break 1 egg into sauce dish; slip carefully into one casserole around roll; repeat, placing 2 eggs in each casserole. Bake at 350 degrees for 15 minutes; remove from oven. Drain peach halves, reserving syrup. Combine 2 tablespoons reserved syrup with brown sugar; spoon over meat. Top each stack of meat with remaining roll halves. Arrange peach halves and crab apples on 6 wooden skewers; stick one in each roll. Bake for 5 to 7 minutes longer or until fruit is hot. Yield: 6 servings.

BUSY BEE LUNCH

4 c. potatoes, cubed
2 cans luncheon meat, cubed
2 med. onions, sliced
1 c. chopped green pepper
1 can tomato soup
1/8 tsp. pepper

Combine all ingredients; blend well. Place in casserole. Bake, covered, at 325 degrees for 35 to 45 minutes.

DINNER-IN-A-DISH

1 can sweet potatoes
1 No. 2 can sliced apples
1 can luncheon meat, sliced
1/4 c. (packed) brown sugar
1/2 tsp. cinnamon
1/2 tsp. thyme

Slice sweet potatoes in half lengthwise; layer with apples in 2-quart baking dish. Arrange slices of luncheon meat over top; sprinkle with brown sugar, cinnamon and thyme. Bake at 400 degrees for 25 minutes.

WAGON WHEEL PIE

1/2 c. chopped onion
2 tbsp. butter
1 can luncheon meat
1 1/2 pkg. frozen mixed vegetables
1/2 c. grated Cheddar cheese
1 c. evaporated milk
2 eggs, beaten
2 tbsp. flour
1/2 tsp. salt
1/4 tsp. paprika
1 pastry shell, unbaked

Steam onion in butter in covered saucepan for 10 minutes. Cut meat into 1/4-inch slices; reserve 5 slices. Cut remaining slices into bite-sized pieces. Partially cook frozen vegetables; drain. Combine vegetables, cheese, milk, eggs, flour, salt and paprika. Pour into pastry shell. Cut reserved meat into halves diagonally. Arrange on top of filling. Bake at 400 degrees for 35 to 40 minutes. Cool for 10 minutes before serving.

DIFFERENT STRATA

2 eggs, beaten
2 c. milk
1 can luncheon meat, diced
4 slices dry bread, cubed
1 c. grated sharp cheese
1 tsp. prepared mustard

Combine eggs and milk. Combine egg mixture with remaining ingredients in casserole. Bake at 350 degrees for 45 minutes.

HURRY UP CASSEROLE

1 can luncheon meat
1/2 c. chopped onion
2 tbsp. margarine
1 can cream of celery soup
1/2 tsp. prepared mustard
1/4 c. salad dressing
1/8 tsp. pepper
1 tbsp. chopped parsley
3 c. sliced cooked potatoes

Cut luncheon meat into strips; saute meat and onion in margarine in skillet. Simmer until onion is tender; stir in remaining ingredients. Simmer, covered, until heated through. Garnish with sliced hard-cooked egg and additional parsley, if desired.

PANTRY SHELF SPECIAL

1 can sweet potatoes
1 can luncheon meat
1 sm. can pineapple slices
1/4 c. brown sugar
1 tbsp. cornstarch
1/4 tsp. salt
1/4 c. cooking sherry wine
2 tbsp. butter

Slice potatoes; arrange in 10 x 6 x 2-inch baking dish. Cut luncheon meat into slices; place on top of potatoes. Place pineapple slices on top of meat. Combine syrup, sugar and cornstarch in saucepan;

simmer, stirring constantly, for 2 to 3 minutes or until thickened and clear. Add salt, sherry and butter; blend well. Pour over pineapple. Bake in 375-degree oven for 40 minutes.

PENNSYLVANIA KNOCKBOCKLE

1 can mushroom stems and pieces
1 lge. green pepper, cut in strips
2 lge. onions, sliced
2 tbsp. butter
1 1-lb. can mixed vegetables
2 8-oz. cans spaghetti sauce with mushrooms
1 12-oz. can luncheon meat, cut in bite-sized pieces

Drain mushrooms. Saute green pepper, onions and mushrooms in butter in large skillet until tender. Combine remaining ingredients with 1/4 cup water; bring to a boil. Place in 2-quart casserole. Bake at 425 degrees until heated through.

SALAMI-SPAGHETTI DINNER

1/4 c. margarine
1 1/2 tsp. salt
1/8 tsp. pepper
1/2 tsp. dry mustard
1/4 c. flour
1 tsp. Worcestershire sauce
2 c. milk
1 tbsp. minced onion
1 1/2 c. diced salami
1 c. grated American cheese
1/2 c. sweet pickle relish
6 oz. spaghetti

Melt margarine in saucepan; stir in salt, pepper, mustard, flour and Worcestershire until smooth. Add milk gradually; stir until thickened. Fold in remaining ingredients except spaghetti. Cook spaghetti according to package directions; drain. Add spaghetti to sauce; pour into well-greased 2-quart casserole. Bake at 350 degrees for 25 minutes. Top with additional grated cheese.

CASSEROLE SURPRISE FRUIT SALAD

1 can fruit salad
2 tsp. cornstarch
2 tsp. lemon juice
2 tsp. horseradish (opt.)
1 can luncheon meat

Combine fruit salad, cornstarch, lemon juice and horseradish; cook over low heat until thickened. Arrange luncheon meat in baking dish; cover with sauce. Bake in 350-degree oven for 30 minutes.

EASY CHOW MEIN

1 can luncheon meat, cubed
1 c. chopped onion
1 c. diced celery
1/2 tsp. salt
Dash of pepper
1 No. 2 can bean sprouts
2 tbsp. cornstarch
2 tsp. soy sauce
1 tsp. sugar

Saute meat and onion in small amount of hot fat in skillet until onion is tender; add celery, salt, pepper and 3/4 cup water. Simmer, covered, for 5 minutes. Drain bean sprouts; rinse well. Add bean sprouts to meat mixture. Blend cornstarch, soy sauce and sugar with 1/3 cup water; stir into meat mixture. Simmer, stirring constantly, until sauce is clear and thickened.

LUNCHEON MEAT BARBECUE

1 8-oz. can tomato sauce
1/4 c. brown sugar
3 tbsp. vinegar
1 tsp. dry mustard
1 tsp. onion flakes
1 tsp. chili powder
1 12-oz. can luncheon meat
1 1-lb. can sliced peaches

Combine tomato sauce, brown sugar, vinegar, mustard, onion flakes and chili powder in skillet; simmer for 5 minutes. Cut luncheon meat into 9 slices, cutting almost through to bottom of loaf. Place 1 peach slice into each cut. Place meat in tomato sauce; add remaining peaches. Simmer, covered, for 10 minutes; baste meat occasionally.

KING-SIZE KABOBS

2 12-oz. cans luncheon meat
2 med. green peppers, halved
4 sm. onions, halved
2 c. wine vinegar
1 c. salad oil
1/2 c. lemon juice
4 tsp. thyme
2 bay leaves
2 cloves of garlic, minced
1/2 tsp. hot sauce

Cut luncheon meat in half. Place meat, green peppers and onions in baking dish. Combine vinegar, oil, lemon juice and seasonings; pour over meat and vegetables. Marinate for 2 to 3 hours, turning occasionally. Thread meat, pepper and onion on long skewers. Broil 4 to 5 inches from source of heat for 15 minutes; brush with marinade. Turn; cook for about 15 minutes longer. Yield: 4 servings.

King-Size Kabobs . . . Skewered luncheon meat, onions, and peppers are marinated in herbs.

HOT ECONOMY LUNCH

1 lb. bologna
4 med. potatoes
1 lge. onion, chopped
2 whole allspice

Cut bologna and potatoes into 1/2-inch cubes; brown in large skillet in small amount of fat. Add onion and allspice; simmer, covered, for 15 minutes or until potatoes are tender.

SPEEDY KABOBS

1 can luncheon meat
2 green peppers
1 can pineapple chunks
1 sm. can ripe olives
1 8-oz. can tomato sauce
1/4 c. chopped green onions
1/4 c. butter
1 tsp. Worcestershire sauce
1 tsp. monosodium glutamate
1/2 tsp. salt
2 med. tomatoes, quartered

Cut luncheon meat into 12 cubes; cut green peppers into 12 squares. Drain pineapple; reserve 1/2 cup syrup. Alternate meat, green pepper, ripe olives and pineapple chunks on four skewers. Combine remaining ingredients except tomatoes; simmer for 15 minutes. Brush ingredients on skewers with mixture. Broil 5 to 6 inches from heat for 8 to 9 minutes or until lightly browned. Turn and place tomatoes on skewers. Brush with sauce mixture. Broil for 4 to 5 minutes longer. Serve immediately with remaining sauce.

Macaroni

Macaroni is a type of pasta or flour paste. It is marketed in various shapes and sizes. Elbow macaroni, short tubes bent slightly at the middle, and shell macaroni are two shapes that are used often. Most macaroni sold is enriched to meet federal standards. Enriched macaroni contains protein, carbohydrate, calcium, iron, and niacin. (1 cup cooked macaroni = 155 calories)

AVAILABILITY: Sold year-round in retail grocery stores in boxes and cellophane packages.

STORING: Store packages of macaroni on cupboard shelf until ready to use.

PREPARATION: Cook as near to serving time as possible. 1 pound = 5 cups uncooked = 12 cups cooked. Use a kettle large enough to hold desired quantity without boiling over—about three times the volume of the boiled macaroni. For each 8 ounces macaroni, bring to boil 2 quarts water and 2 teaspoons salt. You may add 1 tablespoon fat to boiling water to keep macaroni from clumping together. Slowly add macaroni to boiling water so that boiling does not stop. Leave kettle uncovered. Keep the boil active. If macaroni should stick to bottom of kettle while cooking, stir gently with wooden spoon. Cook until tender but firm and chewy. *Do not overcook.* Overcooked macaroni is soft and unappetizing. *To test for doneness*—Press a piece of macaroni on side of kettle with fork or spoon. It will break easily and cleanly when done. Macaroni to be used in combination dishes requiring further cooking should be slightly undercooked. If macaroni is to be served later, moisten with milk, bouillon, tomato juice, or butter to keep from drying out. Before serving drain well in colander.

SERVING: Serve with butter and grated Parmesan cheese for a main-dish accompaniment. Use in salads, soups, casseroles, and combination dishes such as macaroni and cheese.

GERMAN MACARONI SALAD

3/4 c. elbow macaroni
1/4 lb. liverwurst, chopped
1/2 c. chopped sweet pickles
1/2 c. sliced celery
1/3 c. mayonnaise
2 tbsp. chili sauce
3/4 tsp. salt

Cook macaroni according to package directions; drain. Combine macaroni, liverwurst, pickles and celery in bowl. Mix mayonnaise, chili sauce and salt; stir into macaroni mixture. Chill salad for about 3 hours before serving. Yield: 4-6 servings.

GOUDA-MACARONI SALAD

1 7-oz. package shell macaroni
1 sm. Gouda cheese, diced
1/2 c. chopped celery
3 hard-cooked eggs, diced
1/4 c. chopped green pepper
3 tbsp. pickle relish
2 tbsp. chopped pimento
1 c. sour cream
1 1/2 tsp. prepared mustard
1/2 tsp. sugar
1/2 tsp. salt
Dash of pepper
Lettuce

Cook macaroni according to package directions; drain. Combine macaroni, cheese, celery, eggs, green pepper, relish and pimento. Blend sour cream, mustard, sugar, salt and pepper; pour over macaroni mixture. Toss to mix; spoon onto lettuce-lined salad plates. Yield: 6-8 servings.

DANISH MACARONI SALAD

1 c. whipping cream
8 oz. cream cheese
1 tbsp. sugar
3 tbsp. vinegar
2 tbsp. horseradish
4 c. cooked macaroni

Whip cream until stiff. Soften cream cheese; beat into whipped cream. Add sugar, vinegar and horseradish; fold in macaroni. Chill for at least 2 hours before serving. Yield: 8-10 servings.

DOUBLE MACARONI SALAD

4 strips bacon
1 can bean sprouts
1 c. elbow macaroni
1 c. shell macaroni
Salt
1 c. chopped celery
1/2 c. salad olives
4 hard-boiled eggs, chopped
Dash of pepper
Bottled Italian dressing

Fry bacon until crisp; drain and crumble. Drain bean sprouts. Cook macaroni in boiling salted water for about 12 minutes; drain. Combine macaroni, celery, olives, eggs and bean sprouts; season to taste with salt. Add pepper and enough dressing to moisten. Chill until ready to serve. Sprinkle with bacon before serving. Yield: 10 servings.

HEARTY MACARONI SALAD

1/2 c. macaroni
1/4 lb. luncheon meat
1/2 c. canned green peas
1/2 c. chopped celery
1/4 lb. Cheddar cheese, chopped
1 tbsp. chopped onion
1 tbsp. minced parsley
1/4 c. chopped green pepper
Salt and pepper to taste
1/3 c. mayonnaise
1 hard-cooked egg, sliced

Cook macaroni until tender; drain. Combine macaroni, luncheon meat, peas, celery, cheese, onion, parsley and green pepper in bowl. Add salt, pepper and mayonnaise; toss lightly. Chill until ready to serve. Garnish with egg.

HOLIDAY MACARONI SALAD

7 c. cooked salad macaroni
2 1/2 c. chopped cooked ham
6 hard-boiled eggs, chopped
1/4 c. minced sweet pickles
5 green onions, thinly sliced
1/4 c. minced green pepper
1 c. mayonnaise
Salt and pepper to taste
Paprika to taste

Combine all ingredients in large bowl; mix well. Chill for several hours before serving. Yield: 8-10 servings.

HOT MACARONI SALAD

4 strips bacon
1/4 lb. elbow macaroni
1/2 c. diced celery
1/4 c. chopped green pepper
3/4 c. chopped pickles
1/4 c. chopped onion
1 tsp. salt
1/8 tsp. pepper
1 tsp. sugar
2 tbsp. chili sauce
1/2 tsp. Worcestershire sauce
1/4 c. mayonnaise

Chop bacon; fry until crisp. Drain well. Cook macaroni according to package directions; drain. Rinse with boiling water. Combine macaroni, bacon, celery, green pepper, pickles and onion; sprinkle with salt, pepper and sugar. Mix chili sauce, Worcestershire sauce and mayonnaise; stir into macaroni mixture. Serve immediately. Yield: 8 servings.

MACARONI AND CHEESE SALAD

3 oz. macaroni
1 12-oz. can chopped ham
1 c. chopped Cheddar cheese
1/2 c. diagonally sliced celery
1/3 c. chopped green pepper
1/4 c. sliced green onions
2 tbsp. chopped pimento
1/4 c. drained pickle relish
1/2 c. mayonnaise
1 tbsp. prepared mustard
1/4 tsp. salt

Cook macaroni according to package directions; drain and cool. Cut ham into thin strips. Combine macaroni, ham, cheese, celery, green pepper, green onions, pimento and pickle relish. Blend mayonnaise, mustard and salt; add to ham mixture. Toss lightly. Yield: 6 servings.

MARINATED MACARONI SALAD

3 c. macaroni
2/3 tsp. sugar
Dash of salt
1/4 tsp. dry mustard
1/2 tsp. paprika
1/4 c. salad oil
2 tbsp. lemon juice
2 tbsp. vinegar
1 onion, chopped
1 c. diced celery
1 c. chopped green pepper
1/4 c. chopped black olives
1/4 c. chopped pimento
4 hard-cooked eggs, chopped
Mayonnaise

Cook macaroni according to package directions; drain. Rinse with cold water. Place macaroni in large bowl; add sugar, salt, mustard, paprika, oil, lemon juice and vinegar. Cover; refrigerate overnight. Drain macaroni; add onion, celery, green pepper, olives, pimento and eggs. Moisten to taste with mayonnaise; toss to mix. Yield: 20 servings.

SWEET AND SOUR MACARONI SALAD

3/4 lb. macaroni
1/4 c. mayonnaise or salad dressing
1/4 c. vinegar
3 tbsp. sugar
Salt to taste
2 tbsp. water
1/2 c. chopped green pepper
1/2 c. chopped onion
1/2 c. shredded carrots

Cook macaroni according to package directions; drain well. Mix mayonnaise, vinegar, sugar, salt and water. Combine macaroni, green pepper, onion and carrots in bowl; add mayonnaise mixture. Toss well; chill for at least 2 hours before serving. Yield: 10-12 servings.

MACARONI WITH FRANKFURTER SAUCE

Color photograph for this recipe on page 73.

1 tbsp. salad oil
12 frankfurters
1 c. chopped onions
2 cloves of garlic, crushed
2 6-oz. cans tomato paste
2 beef bouillon cubes
Salt
1/8 tsp. crushed red pepper
1 tsp. crushed basil leaves
3 c. elbow macaroni

Heat oil in large skillet over medium heat. Cut frankfurters crosswise in 1/4-inch slices; brown in oil. Remove frankfurters with slotted spoon; drain on paper toweling. Saute onions and garlic in same skillet until tender. Stir in tomato paste, 3 cups water, bouillon cubes, 3/4 teaspoon salt, red pepper and basil. Bring to a boil, stirring constantly; cover. Simmer for 30 minutes. Add frankfurters; simmer for about 15 minutes longer. Add 1 1/2 tablespoons salt to 5 quarts boiling water; add macaroni gradually so that water continues to boil. Cook, stirring occasionally, until tender; drain in colander. Place macaroni in hot serving dish; top with frankfurter sauce. Garnish with parsley if desired. Yield: 6 servings.

MACARONI MARVEL

Salt
1 c. elbow macaroni
1/4 c. butter
1 c. soft bread crumbs
1 1/2 c. milk, scalded

Macaroni Marvel . . . Pimento and parsley bring eye appeal to macaroni and cheese.

1 pimento, minced
1 tbsp. chopped parsley
1 tbsp. chopped onion
1/8 tsp. pepper
Dash of paprika
3 eggs, beaten
1 1/2 c. grated Cheddar cheese
2 strips fried bacon, crumbled

Add 1 1/2 teaspoons salt to 1 1/2 quarts rapidly boiling water in Dutch oven. Add macaroni gradually so that water continues to boil. Cook, stirring occasionally, until tender. Drain in colander. Return macaroni to Dutch oven; add butter, tossing until butter melts. Add 1 teaspoon salt and remaining ingredients except bacon; mix well. Turn into 2-quart casserole. Bake in 350-degree oven for 40 to 45 minutes. Garnish with bacon.

CALIFORNIA MACARONI AND CHEESE

6 oz. elbow macaroni
4 strips bacon, diced
3 tbsp. flour
1 tsp. salt
Dash of pepper
1 1/2 c. milk
2 c. diced American cheese
Buttered cracker crumbs

Cook macaroni in boiling water until tender; drain and rinse. Brown bacon lightly in skillet; stir in flour, salt and pepper. Add milk; cook until sauce is thickened, stirring constantly. Add cheese; stir until cheese is melted. Fold in macaroni. Turn into 1 1/2-quart casserole; top with cracker crumbs. Bake at 350 degrees for 25 minutes. Yield: 4-6 servings.

CORN-MACARONI CASSEROLE

1 8-oz. package elbow macaroni
1 can cream-style corn
8 slices bacon

Cook macaroni according to package directions; drain. Combine macaroni and corn. Arrange half the bacon in casserole; pour in macaroni mixture. Top with remaining bacon. Bake at 350 degrees for 25 to 30 minutes. Yield: 4-6 servings.

DELUXE MACARONI

5 tsp. salt
1 1/2 c. elbow macaroni
3 c. milk
1/3 c. butter
2 c. soft bread crumbs
1/2 c. chopped pimento
3 c. grated process cheese
1/3 c. chopped parsley
1/2 c. chopped onion
1/4 tsp. pepper
6 eggs, beaten

Bring 3 quarts water to a rolling boil; add 4 teaspoons salt and macaroni. Cook for about 7 minutes. Drain macaroni; rinse with hot water. Combine milk and butter in saucepan; cook over low heat until milk is scalded. Stir in bread crumbs, pimento, cheese, parsley, onion, remaining salt and pepper; fold in eggs and macaroni. Turn into large greased baking dish. Bake at 350 degrees for 1 hour or until firm. Yield: 8 servings.

GLORIFIED MACARONI

1 1/2 c. macaroni
1 med. onion, chopped
1 tbsp. chopped green pepper

1/2 c. chopped celery
3 tbsp. butter or margarine
1 can tomato soup
1 tbsp. Worcestershire sauce
1/2 tsp. salt
1 c. diced cheese

Cook macaroni according to package directions; drain. Saute onion, green pepper and celery in butter until onion is soft and golden. Combine macaroni, soup, onion mixture, Worcestershire sauce, salt and cheese; turn into greased casserole. Bake at 400 degrees for 20 minutes. Yield: 6 servings.

DEVILED MACARONI

1/2 lb. elbow macaroni
1 can cream of mushroom soup
1/4 c. milk
1 c. grated sharp cheese
1/4 c. diced pimento
1 tsp. onion salt
1/4 tsp. pepper
2 tsp. prepared mustard
4 hard-boiled eggs, sliced
1/4 c. dry bread crumbs
2 tbsp. melted butter

Cook macaroni according to package directions; drain. Combine macaroni, soup, milk, cheese, pimento, onion salt, pepper and mustard. Spoon half the macaroni mixture into greased casserole; arrange 3 eggs on macaroni mixture. Spoon in remaining macaroni mixture. Mix bread crumbs and butter; spread over top. Bake at 350 degrees for 40 minutes. Serve garnished with remaining egg. Yield: 6 servings.

EASY MACARONI AND CHEESE

1 8-oz. package elbow macaroni
1 can cream of celery soup
3/4 c. milk
1 lb. sharp Cheddar cheese, coarsely grated
3/4 c. dry bread crumbs

Preheat oven to 350 degrees. Cook macaroni according to package directions, omitting salt. Drain macaroni; place in greased 2-quart casserole. Stir in soup, milk and all but 1/4 cup cheese. Mix well. Combine remaining cheese and bread crumbs; spread over macaroni mixture. Bake for 20 minutes or until bubbly and lightly browned. Yield: 4 servings.

ITALIAN MACARONI

8 oz. elbow macaroni
2 cloves of garlic, minced
1 sm. onion, minced
2 tbsp. olive oil
1 8-oz. can tomato sauce
1 19-oz. can tomatoes
1 1/2 tsp. salt
1/4 tsp. pepper
1 1/2 tsp. oregano
1 sm. carton cottage cheese
1/2 lb. mozzarella cheese, thinly sliced
1/2 c. grated Parmesan cheese

Cook macaroni according to package directions; drain. Brown garlic and onion in oil in heavy saucepan; stir in tomato sauce, tomatoes, salt, pepper and oregano. Cover; simmer for about 20 minutes, stirring frequently. Layer macaroni, cottage cheese, tomato sauce and mozzarella cheese in greased 3-quart casserole, making 2 layers each. Spread Parmesan cheese over top. Bake at 375 degrees for about 25 minutes. Yield: 6-8 servings.

MACARONI AND BLUE CHEESE CASSEROLE

2 slices bacon
8 oz. macaroni
1 can mushroom soup
1/2 can evaporated milk
1 c. crumbled blue cheese
1/4 tsp. salt
Buttered bread crumbs

Fry bacon until crisp; drain and crumble. Cook macaroni according to package directions; drain. Combine soup, milk, cheese and salt in saucepan; heat, stirring, until cheese is melted. Stir in bacon and macaroni; turn into greased casserole. Cover top with bread crumbs. Bake at 350 degrees for 25 to 30 minutes.

MACARONI WITH MIXED VEGETABLES

1 10-oz. package frozen mixed vegetables
2 c. macaroni
1/2 c. milk
1 can cream of celery soup
Salt to taste
1 c. grated cheese

Cook vegetables and macaroni separately according to package directions; drain. Combine milk and soup in saucepan; cook over low heat, stirring, until smooth and heated through. Combine macaroni, vegetables, soup mixture and salt; pour into greased 2-quart baking dish. Spread cheese over top. Bake at 400 degrees for 15 minutes or until cheese is melted. Yield: 6-8 servings.

POPULAR PASTA

3/4 lb. elbow macaroni
2 eggs
1/4 c. butter or margarine
1/4 c. flour
2 1/2 c. milk
1/2 c. sour cream
1 carton cottage cheese
1 tsp. oregano
1 tbsp. chopped parsley
Salt and pepper to taste
1/4 lb. mozzarella cheese, sliced
1/4 c. grated Parmesan cheese
1/4 c. dry bread crumbs

Cook macaroni according to package directions; drain. Beat 1 egg lightly. Melt butter in saucepan; blend in flour. Stir in milk and sour cream gradually. Cook over medium heat, stirring constantly, until thickened. Pour small amount of hot sauce into beaten egg; mix well. Return to remaining sauce; cook for 1 minute longer. Stir sauce into macaroni. Beat remaining egg into cottage cheese; add oregano, parsley, salt and pepper. Spoon half the macaroni mixture into greased baking dish; top with cottage cheese mixture and mozzarella cheese. Spoon in remaining macaroni mixture. Mix Parmesan cheese and bread crumbs; sprinkle over top. Bake at 350 degrees for 35 to 40 minutes. Yield: 6 servings.

MACARONI MOUSSE

1 c. macaroni
1/2 c. butter
1 c. scalded milk
3 eggs, separated
1 c. bread crumbs
1 c. grated cheese
1 tsp. grated onion
1/2 green pepper, chopped

Cook macaroni according to package directions; drain. Melt butter in hot milk; cool. Beat egg yolks; add milk mixture. Combine macaroni, milk mixture, bread crumbs, cheese, onion and green pepper. Beat egg whites until stiff; fold into macaroni mixture. Spoon into greased 2-quart casserole. Place casserole in pan of hot water. Bake at 350 degrees for 30 minutes or until firm.

MACARONI WITH MUSHROOMS

8 oz. macaroni
1 can mushroom soup
1 sm. can mushrooms
1 c. mayonnaise
1 lb. cheese, grated
1/4 c. chopped onion
1/4 c. chopped green pepper
1/4 c. chopped pimento
1 tsp. salt
3 tbsp. butter
2/3 c. cracker crumbs

Cook macaroni according to package directions; drain. Combine macaroni, soup, mushrooms, mayonnaise, cheese, onion, green pepper, pimento and salt. Mix well; turn into greased baking dish. Melt butter; stir in cracker crumbs. Spread cracker crumbs over macaroni mixture. Bake at 375 degrees for 25 to 30 minutes.

TANGY MACARONI AND CHEESE

1/2 lb. elbow macaroni
1/2 lb. bacon
1 onion, chopped
1 8-oz. can tomato sauce
1/4 lb. process cheese, shredded
2 c. applesauce
1/4 tsp. curry powder
1/8 tsp. dry mustard
1/2 tsp. Worcestershire sauce
Salt and pepper to taste

Prepare macaroni according to package directions; drain. Fry bacon in skillet until crisp. Drain bacon; crumble all but 4 slices. Pour most of the bacon drippings from skillet; saute onion in remaining drippings. Stir in tomato sauce, cheese, applesauce, crumbled bacon, seasonings and macaroni. Turn into 2-quart casserole. Bake at 350 degrees for 20 minutes. Arrange sliced bacon over casserole; bake for 5 minutes longer. Yield: 4 servings.

DELICIOUS MACARONI LOAF

1 c. bread crumbs
1 c. diced cheese
2 c. cooked macaroni
2 c. milk
3 eggs, beaten
1 sm. green pepper, chopped
1 sm. onion, chopped
2 tbsp. parsley flakes
3 tbsp. melted butter
Salt and pepper to taste
Paprika

Combine all ingredients except paprika; mix well. Turn into greased loaf pan; sprinkle with paprika. Bake at 350 degrees for 45 minutes or until firm. Yield: 12 servings.

MACARONI LOAF WITH SAUCE

1 1/3 c. elbow macaroni
3 eggs, separated
1 2/3 c. warm milk
2 tbsp. melted butter
3 tbsp. minced parsley
3 tbsp. chopped stuffed olives
2 tsp. minced onion
1/2 tsp. salt
Pepper to taste
1 c. grated American cheese
2/3 c. soft bread crumbs
1 can cream of mushroom soup

Cook macaroni according to package directions; drain and rinse. Beat egg yolks until light; beat in 1 cup milk and butter. Add macaroni, parsley, olives, onion, salt, pepper, cheese and bread crumbs; mix well. Turn into greased 9 x 5 x 3-inch pan. Bake at 325 degrees for 1 hour. Combine soup and remaining milk in saucepan; cook over low heat, stirring, until blended and heated through. Invert macaroni loaf onto platter; serve with soup mixture.

Mackerel

Mackerel is a richly flavored, oily-fleshed edible fish found in temperate Atlantic and Pacific waters. Its color is metallic blue, which changes immediately to iridescent green when the fish is caught. Most mackerel are 8 inches to 14 inches long. The young, smaller-sized fish are called "blinkers" or "tinkers." Mackerel has high quality protein and a large fat content. (3 ounces broiled mackerel = 200 calories; 3 ounces canned mackerel = 155 calories)

AVAILABILITY: Fresh mackerel is available year-round whole and in steaks and fillets. Best supply is in the summer months. Mackerel is sold year-round frozen (fillets), canned, salted, pickled, and smoked.

BUYING: Choose fresh whole fish with red gills and bright, protruding eyes. Flesh should be stiff and iridescent. Avoid limp fish, which may be spoiled and indigestible.

STORING: *Fresh fish*—Cover with plastic wrap or aluminum foil. Place in coldest part of refrigerator where temperature is between 35 and 40 degrees. Use within 1-2 days. *Commercially frozen fish*—Freeze at 0 degrees or below in home freezer or refrigerator's freezer until ready to use. *Canned fish*—Store up to 1 year in a cool, dry place. *Pickled, salted, and smoked fish*—Refrigerate several weeks. *To freeze* fresh whole mackerel—Cut off head and tail to save freezer space if desired. Wrap individual fish in moistureproof and vaporproof paper. Seal and label. Freeze at 0 degrees or below up to 6 weeks.

PREPARATION: Thaw frozen fish in refrigerator, 24 hours for each 1 pound package. For quicker thawing, place wrapped package under cold running water. Never thaw fish at room temperature or in warm water. Mackerel can be broiled, boiled, baked, poached, panfried, or grilled as specific recipe directs. *Salted mackerel* may be steamed, broiled, boiled, or fried, according to specific recipe directions. Salted mackerel must be freshened 24 hours before being cooked. To freshen, place fish, meat side down on rack in large bowl. Cover with cold water. Change water often. Salt will drop away from fish into bottom of bowl. If fish is to be broiled or fried, use milk instead of water.

SERVING: Serve plain with melted butter, lemon wedges, or sauce. Paprika and parsley make colorful garnishes. Use in salads, chilled molds, and soups.

(See SEAFOOD.)

MACKEREL MOLD

2 1-lb. cans mackerel
4 hard-cooked eggs, chopped
8 oz. cream cheese
1/2 c. butter
2 tbsp. lemon juice
Dash of hot sauce
1 c. chopped celery
1 c. chopped green pepper
2 tbsp. grated onion
Pimento
Olives

Drain mackerel. Combine mackerel, eggs, cream cheese, butter, lemon juice, hot sauce, celery, green pepper and onion; mix well. Pack mackerel mixture into 6-cup fish mold; chill for 3 hours. Loosen edge of mold with knife; invert onto platter. Place hot damp towel on mold until mold can be easily removed. Decorate mackerel mixture with pimento strips for scales and tail and olive slices for eyes. Yield: 6 servings.

MACKEREL SOUP

1 tall can mackerel
1 c. water
3 c. milk
1 tbsp. butter
1 tsp. salt
1/2 tsp. pepper

Turn mackerel into 2-quart saucepan; break into chunks with fork. Add water, milk, butter, salt and pepper. Place over medium heat; cook to serving temperature, stirring frequently. Yield: 6 servings.

MACKEREL SALAD

1 can mackerel
3 cooked potatoes, mashed
3 hard-boiled eggs, chopped
2 c. cracker crumbs
1/2 c. vinegar
1 onion, minced
Dash of sugar

Drain mackerel. Combine mackerel, potatoes, eggs and cracker crumbs in bowl; mix until smooth. Stir in vinegar, onion and sugar. Chill for 2 to 3 hours before serving.

BAKED MACKEREL

Mayonnaise
1 1/2 lb. mackerel fillets
Salt to taste
Melted butter
Paprika

Line shallow pan with foil; coat with mayonnaise. Place mackerel on foil, skin side down. Sprinkle with salt; spread with mayonnaise. Pour butter over mackerel; sprinkle with paprika. Bake at 425 degrees for 15 to 20 minutes. Yield: 4 servings.

FLAMING MACKEREL MEDITERRANEAN

1 4-lb. mackerel
2 tbsp. lemon juice
Salt
Dash of pepper
2 c. red wine
1 onion, sliced
2 cloves of garlic, mashed
4 peppercorns
1 clove
2 bay leaves
Dash of thyme
2 tbsp. chopped parsley
Lemon slices
1/4 c. brandy

Rub mackerel cavity with lemon juice, salt to taste and pepper. Combine wine, onion, garlic, 1 teaspoon salt, peppercorns, clove, bay leaves, thyme and parsley in glass or enamel bowl. Add mackerel; refrigerate for 3 hours or overnight. Place mackerel in baking dish. Strain marinade over mackerel. Bake at 350 degrees for 30 to 40 minutes or until mackerel flakes easily when tested with fork. Arrange mackerel on heatproof platter; garnish with lemon slices. Heat brandy in small saucepan until warm. Remove from heat; ignite. Pour flaming brandy over mackerel just before serving. Yield: 8 servings.

KING MACKEREL STEAKS SUPREME

2 lb. king mackerel steaks
1 egg
1 1/2 c. salad oil
Juice of 1 lemon
1/4 c. vinegar
1 1/2 tsp. salt
1 tbsp. Worcestershire sauce
Dash of hot sauce
1 tbsp. fish garni
1/2 tsp. pepper
1 onion, thinly sliced

Arrange mackerel in single layer in shallow baking dish. Combine egg and oil in electric blender; process until thick. Add lemon juice, vinegar, salt, Worcestershire sauce, hot sauce, fish garni and pepper. Process until mixed; pour over mackerel. Let stand for 30 minutes. Arrange onion over mackerel. Bake at 400 degrees for 25 minutes.

NEW ENGLAND BAKED MACKEREL

2 lb. mackerel fillets
3/4 to 1 c. milk
2 tbsp. butter
Salt and pepper to taste

Arrange mackerel in greased baking dish. Cover with milk; dot with butter. Sprinkle with salt and pepper. Bake at 350 degrees for 20 to 25 minutes.

Barbecued Spanish Mackerel . . . A quick-and-easy dish with hickory-flavored barbecue sauce.

BARBECUED SPANISH MACKEREL

2 lb. Spanish mackerel fillets
3/4 c. cocktail vegetable juice
1/2 c. hickory-flavored barbecue sauce
1/2 tsp. salt

Place fillets in single layer, skin side down, in greased 13 x 9 x 2-inch baking dish. Combine remaining ingredients. Pour over fillets. Bake in 350-degree oven for 25 to 30 minutes or until fish flakes easily. Garnish with lemon wedges and watercress. Yield: 6 servings.

MAQUEREAU AU VIN BLANC

1 tbsp. oil
Butter
2 onions, sliced
1 c. dry white wine
2 bouillon cubes
2 tbsp. flour
Salt and pepper to taste
1 can sliced mushrooms, drained
2 1/2 lb. mackerel fillets
1/2 c. bread crumbs
Juice of 1 lemon

Heat oil and 2 tablespoons butter in saucepan; add onions. Saute onions lightly; pour in wine. Cook rapidly until liquid is reduced by three-fourths. Dissolve bouillon cubes in 2 cups boiling water; stir into onion mixture. Mix flour and 2 tablespoons butter until crumbly; add to onion mixture. Cook, stirring, until sauce is thickened. Add salt, pepper and mushrooms; cook for 3 minutes longer. Pour half the sauce into baking dish; arrange mackerel in dish. Pour remaining sauce over mackerel. Sprinkle with bread crumbs and lemon juice; dot with butter. Bake at 375 degrees for 35 to 40 minutes. Yield: 6 servings.

BROILED MACKEREL

1 mackerel fillet
Salt and pepper to taste
Lemon juice to taste
Mayonnaise

Fashion small boat-shaped container from aluminum foil; place mackerel in container. Sprinkle with salt, pepper and lemon juice; coat generously with mayonnaise. Broil about 8 inches from source of heat for 8 to 10 minutes.

GLORIFIED MACKEREL

1 1-lb. mackerel fillet
1/2 c. cooking sauterne
1/2 tsp. celery salt
1/2 tsp. onion salt
1/2 tsp. Worcestershire sauce
1/2 tsp. salt
Self-rising flour
Bacon drippings
Cooking oil

Cut mackerel into 1-inch pieces. Mix sauterne, celery salt, onion salt, Worcestershire sauce and salt; add mackerel. Let stand for 20 minutes. Flour mackerel lightly. Heat equal parts bacon drippings and oil in deep fryer. Fry mackerel until brown. Serve immediately. Yield: 6 servings.

Mango

A mango is the fruit of an evergreen tree that grows in Florida and California. Mangoes are in season from May through August. They are red or yellow in color and have an acidic flavor. They are usually eaten ripe, although unripe mangoes are often pickled or preserved.

FLORIDA MANGO CAKE

1/2 c. shortening
3/4 c. sugar
2 eggs
1 c. mashed mango
2 c. flour
1 1/2 c. confectioners' sugar
1 tsp. butter
Milk
1/2 c. chopped walnuts

Cream shortening and sugar; beat in eggs. Add mango and flour; mix well. Spoon batter into loaf pan. Bake at 350 degrees until cake tests done. Combine confectioners' sugar and butter; add enough milk to make of spreading consistency. Stir in walnuts; spread over top of cake. Yield: 10 servings.

HAWAIIAN AMBROSIA

1 pineapple
3 papayas
4 mangoes
6 bananas
1/2 c. light honey
1/2 c. kirsch

Peel and chop fruits. Combine fruits in large bowl; pour in honey. Mix lightly. Cover; refrigerate until ready to serve. Add kirsch just before serving. Yield: 8 servings.

MANGO BROWN BETTY

3 lge. mangoes, sliced
1 c. malted cereal granules
Juice and grated rind of 1/2 lemon
1/4 c. (packed) brown sugar
1 tbsp. butter
1/2 c. water

Layer half the mangoes in greased baking dish; cover with 1/2 cup cereal. Add lemon juice and lemon rind. Layer in remaining mangoes; cover with remaining cereal and brown sugar. Dot with butter; pour water over top. Bake at 375 degrees for 30 minutes. Yield: 6 servings.

MANGO PIE

5 ripe mangoes, sliced
1 10-in. unbaked pie shell
1 c. sugar
3 tbsp. cornstarch
1/8 tsp. salt
1/2 tsp. cinnamon
1/4 tsp. nutmeg
1 egg, lightly beaten
1 c. heavy cream
1 1/4 tsp. vanilla
4 tsp. butter
1/2 c. coarsely chopped walnuts

Place mangoes in pie shell. Mix sugar, cornstarch, salt and spices. Blend egg, cream and vanilla; add sugar mixture gradually. Mix well; pour over mangoes. Dot with butter; sprinkle with walnuts. Bake at 450 degrees for 10 minutes. Reduce oven temperature to 350 degrees; bake for 55 minutes longer. Serve with ice cream. Yield: 6-8 servings.

Maple

Maple is an intensely sweet flavoring extracted and made from the sap of maple trees. The sap is boiled down either to a thick maple syrup or to a solid maple sugar. By federal regulations, maple syrup contains 35 percent maple sap. Maple-flavored syrup, widely available in retail markets, is neither as rich nor as sweet as its genuine counterpart. Because of its exceptional sweetness, maple sugar is used most often for flavoring.

AVAILABILITY: *Maple syrup* and *maple sugar* are available year-round, with a slight peak during the spring months when maple trees are tapped (known as "sugaring off") for the sap.

BUYING: *Maple syrup* is sold in bottles or cans, *maple sugar* in decorative shapes as candies or in blocks of varying weights. Though many specialty food stores stock these commodities, they are not generally marketed in all areas of the country.

STORING: Keep *maple syrup* covered in a cool, dry place; refrigeration is recommended. To reliquify crystallized maple syrup, set bottle or can in bowl of hot water. Store *maple sugar* in its original moistureproof and vaporproof wrapper in a cool, dry place. Both have excellent keeping qualities.

PREPARATION: For *maple syrup*—Use maple syrup whenever sweetening is required. For general cooking, allow 3/4 cup maple syrup for 1 cup granulated sugar. The same equivalent measurements apply to baking although the other liquid specified in the recipe should be reduced by 3 tablespoons for each cup of syrup substituted. 1 pint maple syrup has the identical sweetening power of 1 pound maple sugar. For *maple sugar*—Grate or pare off amount needed before combining with other ingredients. Maple sugar is unusually sweet and should be used sparingly. Allow 1/2 cup maple sugar for 1 cup granulated sugar.

SERVING: Maple syrup is a popular topping for pancakes, waffles, and so on. The flavor of maple can add a sugary goodness to cakes, pies, cookies, candies, custards, doughnuts, and many frozen desserts.

MAPLE-NUT ROLL

6 eggs, separated
3/4 c. sugar
Pinch of salt
1 tsp. baking powder
1 1/2 c. ground pecans
Confectioners' sugar
3/4 c. maple syrup
2 egg whites

Beat egg yolks until thick and lemon colored; add sugar gradually. Add salt, baking powder and ground nuts. Beat egg whites until stiff peaks form; fold egg whites into nut mixture. Grease a 15 1/2 x 10 1/2 x 1-inch pan; line the bottom with greased waxed paper. Spread mixture in pan; bake at 350 degrees for 15 minutes or until golden brown. Turn out on towel dusted with confectioners' sugar. Remove paper carefully; trim edges of cake. Roll cake up in towel jelly roll fashion; cool on wire rack. Cook maple syrup until it reaches soft-ball stage or 238 degrees on candy thermometer. Beat egg whites until soft peaks form. Pour in hot syrup gradually, continuing to beat until filling is thick and glossy. Unroll the cake; spread with filling and roll up jelly roll fashion. Chill until ready to serve.

MAPLE SUGAR CAKE

1 c. maple sugar
1/2 c. shortening
1 egg
2 c. flour
1/2 tsp. soda
2 tsp. baking powder
1 tsp. salt
1 1/2 tsp. cinnamon
1/2 tsp. cloves
1 c. buttermilk
1/2 c. raisins

Cream sugar and shortening until fluffy; beat in egg. Combine dry ingredients; add dry ingredients alternately with buttermilk to creamed mixture. Fold in raisins. Spoon batter into greased loaf pan. Bake at 350 degrees for 30 minutes. Yield: 12 servings.

MAPLE DIPPERS

2 lb. powdered sugar
1/2 c. melted butter
1 lge. package flaked coconut
1 can sweetened condensed milk
2 c. chopped walnuts
2 pkg. butterscotch pieces
3/4 cake paraffin
1/4 tsp. maple flavoring

Combine sugar, butter, coconut, milk and walnuts. Shape into small logs or patties. Melt butterscotch pieces and paraffin together; add maple flavoring. Dip each log or patty into butterscotch mixture with fork until well coated. Place on waxed paper to harden.

MAPLE-CHOCOLATE CREAMS

1 c. margarine
10 c. powdered sugar
1 c. sweetened condensed milk
1 tsp. maple flavoring
1 1/2 c. chopped pecans
1 12-oz. package chocolate pieces
1/4 lb. paraffin

Combine all ingredients except chocolate and paraffin; shape into balls. Chill for at least 1 hour. Melt chocolate with paraffin. Dip balls into chocolate; place on rack to harden.

MAPLE-CREAM TORTE

1 pkg. angel food cake mix
1 c. heavy cream
1/2 c. sifted powdered sugar
1/3 c. sour cream
1/4 tsp. maple flavoring
1/2 c. diced peaches, drained
1/4 c. chopped pecans

Prepare cake mix according to package directions. Cool; remove from pan. Split cake into 3 layers. Beat cream with sugar, sour cream and flavoring until thickened. Fold in peaches and pecans. Fill between layers and top of cake with cream filling. Chill until serving time. Yield: 10-12 servings.

MAPLE FLUFF

2 tbsp. unflavored gelatin
1 pt. cream
2 eggs, separated
1 c. maple syrup
1/2 c. shredded coconut
1/2 tsp. salt
1/2 tsp. almond flavoring

Soften gelatin in 1/4 cup cold water. Heat cream over hot water in double boiler. Pour over slightly beaten egg yolks gradually. Return mixture to double boiler; cook for 5 minutes or until slightly thickened, stirring constantly. Remove from heat; stir in softened gelatin. Add maple syrup; cool. Add coconut, salt and almond flavoring. Beat egg whites until stiff; fold into mixture. Pour into individual molds; chill until firm. Garnish with sweetened whipped cream; sprinkle with toasted coconut if desired. Yield: 8 servings.

MAPLE MOLD

2 c. (packed) brown sugar
1 tbsp. unflavored gelatin
4 egg whites, stiffly beaten

Combine brown sugar and 1/2 cup water; cook until mixture spins a thread. Soften gelatin in 1/2 cup cold water; add to hot sugar mixture. Cool for 15 to 20 minutes. Fold into egg whites. Pour into lightly greased ring mold; chill for several hours or overnight, until firm. May serve with sweetened whipped cream piled in center.

MAPLE MOUSSE

2 env. unflavored gelatin
1 c. milk
1 c. maple syrup

1 pt. heavy cream, whipped
1 c. chopped nuts
1/2 lb. vanilla wafers, crumbled

Dissolve gelatin in 1/4 cup cold water. Bring milk to boiling point; stir in gelatin until dissolved. Pour in syrup; chill until slightly thickened. Add whipped cream and nuts. Place half the crumbs in casserole; pour in maple mixture. Cover with remaining wafer crumbs. Chill until set. Yield: 12-16 servings.

MAPLE-PECAN MOLD

1 env. unflavored gelatin
2 c. (packed) maple sugar
2 egg whites, stiffly beaten
1 c. chopped pecans

Soak gelatin in 1/2 cup cold water for 5 minutes. Place sugar and 1/2 cup hot water in saucepan. Bring to a boil; boil for 10 minutes. Pour syrup over gelatin gradually. Chill until slightly thickened. Add egg whites and nuts. Turn into molds. Chill until set. Serve with whipped cream if desired. Yield: 6 servings.

MAPLE SPONGE

2 c. (packed) brown sugar
1 tbsp. unflavored gelatin
1/2 c. broken walnuts
2 eggs, separated
3 tbsp. sugar
2 tbsp. cornstarch
2 c. milk
1 tsp. vanilla
1/4 tsp. salt

Boil brown sugar and 1 1/2 cups water together for 10 minutes. Soften gelatin in 1/2 cup cold water; add to hot brown sugar mixture, stirring until dissolved. Add walnuts. Chill until firm. Break congealed mixture into pieces with fork; fold into stiffly beaten egg whites. Combine sugar, cornstarch, milk, vanilla and salt in double boiler. Cook over boiling water until custard coats spoon, stirring constantly. Cool. Spoon egg white mixture into 6 dessert cups. Top each serving with custard.

MAPLE MUNCHIES

1 1/2 c. flour
1 tsp. salt
1 tsp. baking powder
3 eggs
1 1/2 c. sugar
1 c. melted shortening
1 tsp. maple flavoring
1 c. walnuts
1 c. raisins
Confectioners' sugar

Sift flour, salt and baking powder together. Beat eggs; add sugar gradually, beating well. Add shortening and flour mixture gradually, mixing well. Stir in flavoring, walnuts and raisins. Spoon batter into baking pan. Bake at 350 degrees for about 25 minutes. Let stand for 5 minutes. Cut into squares; roll in confectioners' sugar. Cool well before storing. Yield: 1 dozen squares.

MAPLE-NUT DROPS

3 1/4 c. flour
1 tsp. baking powder
1 tsp. soda
1 tsp. salt
1/2 c. butter
1/2 c. shortening
3 eggs, slightly beaten
1 c. maple syrup
1/4 tsp. maple flavoring
1 c. chopped dates
1 c. chopped pecans

Sift flour, baking powder, soda and salt together. Cream butter and shortening together; add eggs, maple syrup and maple flavoring. Blend in dry ingredients, mixing well. Add 1/4 cup boiling water; mix well. Stir in dates and pecans. Chill for at least 1 hour. Drop by spoonfuls onto greased cookie sheet. Bake at 350 degrees for about 15 minutes. Cool. Yield: About 4 1/2 dozen.

Frosting

1/4 c. butter
2 tsp. cream
1 tsp. vanilla
1 tbsp. maple syrup
2 c. sifted powdered sugar

Melt butter in saucepan; add cream, vanilla and syrup. Mix well. Blend in sugar; beat until smooth. Frost cookies.

MAPLE PRALINE COOKIES

2/3 c. shortening
2/3 c. (packed) brown sugar
1 egg
1/2 tsp. maple flavoring
1/4 c. milk
1 3/4 c. sifted flour
1/4 tsp. salt
1/4 tsp. soda
2 c. oven-toasted rice cereal

Cream shortening and sugar; beat in egg. Add maple flavoring and milk. Mix flour, salt and soda; add to creamed mixture. Beat well. Add cereal. Drop batter 2 inches apart on greased cookie sheet by heaping teaspoonfuls. Flatten cookies with moistened, sugared glass. Bake in 375-degree oven for 8 to 10 minutes. Do not overbake. Yield: 3 dozen.

MAPLE SUGAR COOKIES

2 1/2 c. sifted cake flour
1 tsp. salt
2 1/2 tsp. baking powder
1/2 c. shortening
1 c. maple sugar, sifted
2 eggs, beaten
1/2 tsp. lemon extract
1 tbsp. milk

Sift flour, salt and baking powder together. Cream shortening; add maple sugar, creaming well. Add eggs, lemon extract, milk and dry ingredients; mix well. Chill for about 30 minutes. Roll out 1/4 inch thick; sprinkle with additional maple sugar. Cut with cookie cutter; place on greased baking sheet. Bake at 350 degrees for about 15 minutes. Yield: 3 dozen.

MAPLE-WALNUT BARS

1 egg
1/2 c. sugar
1/3 c. melted shortening
1/2 c. flour
1/4 tsp. salt
1/4 tsp. baking powder
1 c. chopped walnuts
1/4 c. raisins
1 tsp. maple flavoring

Beat egg. Add sugar and shortening, creaming well. Sift flour, salt and baking powder together; add to creamed mixture. Add walnuts, raisins and flavoring. Turn into pan. Bake at 350 degrees for 30 minutes. Cool slightly; cut into squares.

MAPLE-NUT ICE CREAM

6 eggs, separated
2 1/2 c. (packed) brown sugar
6 c. cream
6 c. milk
1 c. crushed walnuts
1 tbsp. maple flavoring

Beat egg yolks, sugar, cream and milk together. Fold in stiffly beaten egg whites. Mix in walnuts and flavoring. Pour into 1-gallon freezing container. Freeze until firm. Yield: 1 gallon ice cream.

MAPLE PARFAIT

3/4 c. maple syrup
3 eggs, separated
Salt
1 1/2 c. whipping cream, whipped
1 tsp. vanilla

Heat syrup in double boiler. Add syrup to beaten egg yolks gradually; return to double boiler. Cook, beating, until mixture is thick and light. Pour into stiffly beaten egg whites. Chill thoroughly. Add salt, whipped cream and vanilla. Mix thoroughly; pour into freezing container. Freeze, without stirring, until firm. Yield: 8-10 servings.

MAPLE CHIFFON PIE

1 tbsp. unflavored gelatin
1/2 c. milk
1/2 c. dark corn syrup
1/8 tsp. salt
2 eggs, separated
1/3 c. chopped walnuts
1 tsp. vanilla
1 c. heavy cream, whipped
1 9-in. baked pie shell

Soften gelatin in 1/2 cup cold water; set aside. Combine milk, corn syrup and salt in top of double boiler. Heat to scalding; add small amount of corn syrup mixture to beaten egg yolks. Stir into remaining corn syrup mixture. Cook over hot water, stirring constantly, until mixture coats spoon. Remove from heat; add gelatin, stirring until dissolved. Chill until partially set. Fold walnuts and vanilla into 3/4 cup whipped cream. Beat egg whites until stiff. Fold into whipped cream mixture. Fold into gelatin mixture. Pour into pie shell; chill until set. Garnish with remaining whipped cream.

MAPLE-COCONUT PIE

1 c. flaked coconut
1 unbaked 9-in. pie shell
1/3 c. butter
1/2 c. sugar
3 eggs, well beaten
1 c. maple syrup
1/2 tsp. vanilla

Sprinkle coconut over pie shell. Cream butter and sugar until fluffy; add remaining ingredients. Mix well; pour filling into pie shell. Bake at 425 degrees for 10 minutes. Reduce oven temperature to 350 degrees; bake for 15-20 minutes longer.

MAPLE CREAM PIE

1 1/2 c. milk
3/4 c. maple syrup
2 tbsp. cornstarch
1 egg
1/4 c. sugar
Dash of salt
1 baked 9-in. pie shell
1 c. heavy cream, whipped

Scald milk in double boiler. Combine syrup, cornstarch, egg, sugar and salt; add to scalded mixture. Heat, stirring constantly, until mixture thickens. Remove from heat; pour into pie shell. Chill. Top with whipped cream. Yield: 6 servings.

MAPLE SUGAR PIE

1 1/2 c. maple syrup
3 tbsp. butter
1 c. evaporated milk
2 tbsp. flour
1/4 tsp. salt
1 egg, beaten
1 recipe 2-crust pie pastry

Boil syrup in saucepan until reduced to about 1 cup; add butter. Combine milk, flour, salt and egg; add to syrup. Cool. Line pie pan with half the rolled out pastry. Pour filling into pie pan; cover with top crust. Bake at 350 degrees for 30 minutes or until crust is browned. Yield: 5-6 servings.

MAPLE SYRUP PIE

1 egg
1 c. dark corn syrup
1 tbsp. flour
1 recipe 2-crust pie pastry

Beat egg with corn syrup and flour. Line 8-inch pie pan with half the rolled out pastry. Pour filling into pastry-lined pie plate. Cover with top crust. Bake at 400 degrees for 45 minutes or until browned. Yield: 6 servings.

VERMONT MAPLE CHIFFON PIE

1 tbsp. gelatin
1/2 c. milk
1/2 c. maple syrup
1/8 tsp. salt
2 eggs, separated
1 c. heavy cream
3/4 c. chopped nuts
1 tsp. vanilla
1 baked 9-in. pie shell

Soften gelatin in 1/4 cup water. Combine milk, maple syrup and salt in double boiler. Cook, stirring constantly until bubbling. Pour hot syrup over beaten egg yolks beating constantly. Cook in double boiler until thickened, stirring constantly. Add gelatin; stir until dissolved. Chill until partially thickened. Whip cream until stiff; fold in nuts and vanilla. Fold whipped cream and stiffly beaten egg whites into custard. Fill pie shell; garnish with additional whipped cream. Chill.

MAPLE-COFFEE TRIFLE

1 c. milk
3 egg yolks
1/4 tsp. salt
Maple syrup
1 white cake
1/2 c. strong coffee
1/2 tsp. vanilla
1/2 c. sweetened cream, whipped
Strawberries

Scald milk in double boiler; stir into egg yolks gradually, stirring well. Add salt and 1/2 cup syrup. Cook in double boiler over hot water, stirring constantly, for about 10 minutes or until custard coats spoon. Remove from heat; cool to room temperature. Cut cake to line bottom and side of serving bowl. Combine coffee, 1 1/2 tablespoons syrup and vanilla;

pour over cake. Let stand for 15 minutes; pour custard over cake. Chill for at least 2 hours. Garnish with whipped cream and strawberries. Yield: 8 servings.

MAPLE-CREAM PUDDING

1 c. flour
2 tsp. baking powder
1/4 tsp. salt
1/4 c. sugar
2 tbsp. butter
1 egg
1/2 c. milk
1 c. maple syrup
Whipped cream

Sift flour, baking powder, salt and sugar together. Cream butter; beat in egg. Add dry ingredients and milk alternately to creamed mixture. Bring syrup to boiling point in saucepan. Pour into greased 8-inch square baking pan. Pour batter over syrup. Bake at 350 degrees for 30 to 35 minutes. Serve hot; garnish with whipped cream. Yield: 5-6 servings.

MAPLE-WALNUT PUDDING

2 c. milk
1 c. maple syrup
2 tbsp. cornstarch
1/4 tsp. salt
2 eggs
1/2 c. chopped walnuts
1 c. cream, whipped

Scald 1 3/4 cups milk with maple syrup in top of double boiler. Combine remaining milk with cornstarch and salt; add to hot mixture gradually. Stir until mixture thickens. Beat eggs; add to syrup mixture, gradually, stirring briskly. Cook, stirring, for 5 minutes longer. Pour into serving dish; sprinkle with chopped walnuts while pudding is still hot. Chill; cover with cream and serve.

Marble Cake

CHOCOLATE MARBLE BUNDKUCHEN

2 sq. chocolate
3 c. flour
2 tsp. baking powder
1/4 tsp. salt
1 c. butter
2 c. sugar
4 eggs
1 c. milk
1/4 tsp. cinnamon
2 tsp. vanilla

Melt chocolate in 3 tablespoons water; blend well. Sift flour, baking powder and salt. Cream butter and sugar; beat until light and fluffy. Add eggs, one at a time, beating well after each addition. Add flour mixture and milk alternately; beat until smooth. Place one-third of dough in small bowl; add cool melted chocolate, cinnamon and vanilla. Blend well. Pour alternate layers of batter in buttered 10-inch tube pan or bundt mold; begin and end with white batter. Bake at 350 degrees for 45 minutes to 1 hour. Cool for 10 minutes in pan. Remove from pan; cool completely on rack. Drizzle with powdered sugar frosting or sprinkle with powdered sugar.

MARBLE BROWNIE CAKE

1 stick margarine
2 c. sugar
4 eggs
2 c. sifted flour
1 c. chopped nuts
1 tsp. vanilla
2 sq. melted chocolate

Cream margarine and sugar; add eggs one at a time, beating well after each addition. Sift flour over nuts; add to creamed mixture with vanilla. Pour batter into 9 x 9 x 2-inch greased floured pan. Drop chocolate by spoonfuls over batter. Bake at 300 degrees for 15 minutes; reduce heat to 325 degrees. Bake for 15 minutes longer. Remove from oven; cool on rack. Ice with fudge frosting, if desired.

MARBLE SPICE CAKE

1 c. butter
3 c. sugar
4 3/4 c. flour
2 tsp. baking powder
1 tsp. salt
1 c. milk
1 tsp. vanilla
6 eggs
1/2 c. molasses
1/2 tsp. soda
1 1/2 tsp. cinnamon
1/2 tsp. ginger
1 tsp. cloves
1 tsp. allspice
1 tsp. nutmeg

Cream 1/2 cup butter and 1 1/2 cups sugar thoroughly. Combine 2 1/2 cups flour, 1/2 teaspoon baking powder and 1/2 teaspoon salt. Add flour mixture to creamed mixture alternately with 1/2 cup milk; add vanilla. Beat 5 egg whites until stiff peaks form; fold into flour mixture. Combine molasses and soda in saucepan; bring to a boil. Remove from heat; cool. Cream remaining butter and sugar thoroughly. Sift remaining flour, salt, baking powder and spices together. Add remaining milk alternately with dry ingredients to creamed mixture; add cooled molasses. Beat 5 egg yolks and remaining egg until thick and lemony; stir into molasses mixture. Blend thoroughly. Spoon portion of white batter into greased 10-inch tube pan; alternate with dark batter until all batter is used. Bake at 350 degrees until cake begins to rise. Increase temperature to 375 degrees. Bake for about 1 hour longer or until cake tester comes out clean. Cool on rack.

Marinades

A marinade is a spiced pickling or steeping solution made from a mixture of ingredients such as salad oil, soy sauce, wine or vinegar, and seasonings. Meat, poultry, seafood, and vegetables are often soaked in a marinade to absorb its flavor. The acidic ingredients of the marinade also help tenderize tough food fibers. Any marinade should be suited to the kind of food to be soaked.

PREPARATION: A marinade may be hot or cold, cooked or uncooked. A cooked marinade is usually prepared in advance and chilled or cooled to room temperature before use. Mix marinades in a glass or stainless steel dish, since most marinades are acidic. Combine ingredients in dish according to specific recipe instructions. Use a wooden spoon to stir acid-based marinades. Place food in marinade, and marinate for time specified in recipe. The food might marinate for minutes or overnight. Some foods may be refrigerated while they marinate. Foods may be removed from marinade before being cooked and basted with the marinade while cooking. Roasts may be cooked in their marinades. Some seafoods may be served in their marinades. Don't discard a marinade. Strain and refrigerate it for future use. Many marinades can be converted into flavorful sauces.

BEEFSTEAK MARINADE

1/4 c. salad oil
1/4 c. dry vermouth
1/4 c. soy sauce
1 tsp. prepared mustard
1/2 tsp. dry mustard
1 clove of garlic, minced
1/4 tsp. pepper
1/2 tsp. salt
2 tsp. Worcestershire sauce

Combine all marinade ingredients in electric blender container. Cover; process for about 2 minutes. Pour marinade over steak; let stand at room temperature for about 4 hours. Remove steak from marinade before cooking. Marinade may be used for basting sauce when cooking steak or reserved for other uses.

JAPANESE MARINADE FOR STEAKS

1/4 c. soy sauce
1/4 c. water
1/4 c. oil
2 tsp. ginger
1 1/2 tbsp. sugar

Combine all marinade ingredients well; pour over steaks. Marinate steaks at room temperature for 2 hours. Marinade may be used to steam sliced onions and mushrooms to accompany steaks.

LEMON-HONEY MARINADE FOR POT ROAST

1/2 lemon, sliced
2 bay leaves
2 tbsp. honey
1 c. tomato juice
1/2 tsp. dry mustard
1 tsp. parsley flakes
1/2 tsp. celery seed
1 tbsp. Worcestershire sauce
1 clove of garlic
1 c. beef bouillon
2 tsp. salt
6 peppercorns

Combine all marinade ingredients in Dutch oven or roasting pan; bring to a boil. Reduce heat; simmer for 10 minutes. Cool marinade to room temperature. Place pot roast in marinade; let stand for 1 hour, turning roast frequently. Cook roast in marinade.

MARINADE FOR BEEF CUBES

1 1/2 c. salad oil
1/3 c. lemon juice
3/4 c. soy sauce
1/4 c. Worcestershire sauce
2 tbsp. dry mustard
Salt to taste
1 tbsp. minced green pepper
1/2 c. wine vinegar
1 1/2 tsp. dried parsley flakes
2 cloves of garlic, crushed

Combine all ingredients; mix well. Marinate beef cubes in mixture for 2 to 3 hours before cooking. Marinade may be strained and refrigerated for future use.

MARINADE FOR CHARCOAL-GRILLED STEAK

2 8-oz. cans tomato sauce
1/2 c. cooking sherry
1/2 c. oil
1/2 tsp. tarragon
Garlic salt to taste
Pepper to taste

Combine tomato sauce, sherry, oil and seasonings; pour into shallow container. Add steak; cover. Marinate in refrigerator for 8 to 12 hours. Baste steak with marinade when cooking.

MARINADE FOR FLANK STEAK

1 c. salad oil
1/2 c. vinegar
2 tsp. Worcestershire sauce
1 tsp. salt
1/4 tsp. pepper
Dash of cayenne pepper
Dash of hot sauce
2 tsp. dry mustard
1 clove of garlic, split

Place all ingredients in jar; cover. Shake well; remove garlic. Pour marinade over flank steak; refrigerate for at least 3 hours. Broil flank steak to desired doneness. Reserve marinade for future use.

MARINADE FOR SKEWERED STEAK AND MUSHROOMS

1 c. Burgundy
2 tsp. Worcestershire sauce
1 tsp. monosodium glutamate
2 cloves of garlic, crushed
1 c. salad oil
1 tsp. salt
1/4 c. catsup
2 tsp. sugar
2 tbsp. vinegar
1 tsp. marjoram
1 tsp. rosemary

Combine all ingredients. Pour marinade over steak and mushrooms; marinate at room temperature for 2 hours. Use marinade as basting sauce when cooking steak and mushrooms.

MARINADE FOR STEAK STRIPS

1/2 c. oil
1 c. catsup
1 1/2 tsp. hot sauce
1 1/2 tsp. soy sauce
1 clove of garlic,
3/4 tsp. sugar
1 tbsp. minced onion
Salt and pepper to taste

Combine all marinade ingredients in bowl; add steak strips. Cover; marinate in refrigerator overnight. Remove steak strips from marinade before cooking.

MIRACLE MARINADE

1 1/2 c. salad oil
3/4 c. soy sauce
1/4 c. Worcestershire sauce
2 tbsp. dry mustard
2 1/4 tsp. salt
1 tbsp. pepper
1 1/2 tbsp. parsley flakes
1/3 c. lemon juice
1/2 c. wine vinegar

Combine oil, soy sauce and Worcestershire sauce in blender container; cover. Process for about 30 seconds. Add mustard, salt, pepper, parsley flakes, lemon juice and vinegar; process for about 30 seconds longer. Place beef in shallow container; pour marinade over beef. Cover; marinate in refrigerator for 24 hours. Remove beef from marinade before cooking.

SPECIAL MARINADE

1 can onion soup
1 can beef broth
1 can pineapple juice
1 tbsp. Worcestershire sauce
Juice of 1 lemon
1 lge. bottle soy sauce
1 tsp. dry mustard
Garlic salt to taste

Combine all ingredients in large saucepan; bring to a boil. Reduce heat; simmer for 5 minutes. Cool marinade to room temperature. Submerge steak in marinade; let stand for 4 to 6 hours. Remove steak from marinade before cooking.

TARRAGON MARINADE FOR SIRLOIN STEAK

1 lge. yellow onion, sliced
1 lemon, cut
5 cloves of garlic, split
1 bay leaf
1/2 tsp. dry mustard
1/2 tsp. salt
1/2 tsp. pepper
1 c. oil
3 tbsp. tarragon vinegar
1/2 c. dry red wine

Line shallow glass baking dish with about 3/4 of the onion slices. Squeeze lemon juice over onion; add 4 cloves of garlic, bay leaf, mustard, salt and pepper. Pour in oil, vinegar and wine. Lay steak in marinade; spread remaining onion slices on steak. Squeeze juice of remaining garlic over top. Marinate steak at room temperature for 2 to 4 hours. Remove steak from marinade before cooking. Onion slices in marinade may be drained and served with steak.

TERIYAKI MARINADE FOR STEAK

1/2 c. soy sauce
1/2 c. sake or whiskey
1 1-in. piece of fresh gingerroot, minced
1/4 c. catsup
1 tbsp. prepared mustard
1 tsp. Worcestershire sauce
1/4 c. (packed) brown sugar

Combine all marinade ingredients; add steak. Let stand at room temperature for several hours. Remove steak from marinade before cooking. Marinade may be used as basting sauce when cooking steak.

MARINADE FOR GRILLED CHICKEN

2 c. Worcestershire sauce
1 c. oil
1 c. white vinegar
1 c. wine vinegar
1 tsp. garlic powder
1/4 c. liquid smoke
1 tbsp. monosodium glutamate
3 pkg. dry Italian dressing mix
2 lemons, thinly sliced
1 tbsp. salt
1/2 tbsp. pepper

Combine all marinade ingredients in large shallow container; add chicken. Marinate at room temperature for 4 hours or in refrigerator for 8 to 12 hours. Use marinade as basting sauce when grilling chicken. Remove lemon from any remaining marinade and refrigerate for future use.

MARINADE FOR PHEASANT

1 c. corn oil
1 clove of garlic, minced
3/4 tsp. pepper
2 tsp. salt
2 tsp. ginger
1 7-oz. bottle lemon-lime carbonated beverage

Combine oil, garlic, pepper, salt, ginger and carbonated beverage in bowl; add pheasant. Cover; marinade at room temperature for 4 to 6 hours. Cook pheasant with marinade.

SIMMERED MARINADE FOR CHICKEN

1/2 c. white wine
1/2 c. hot water
1 tbsp. oil
1 tbsp. butter
1/2 tsp. thyme
1/4 tsp. rosemary
1/2 tsp. marjoram
1/2 tsp. salt
1/4 tsp. pepper

Combine all marinade ingredients in saucepan; cover. Simmer for about 10 minutes. Cool to room temperature. Add chicken to marinade; let stand for about 2 hours. Use marinade as basting sauce when cooking chicken.

MARINADE FOR ROASTED LEG OF LAMB

1/4 c. olive oil
2 tbsp. lemon juice
1 med. onion, chopped
1/4 c. chopped parsley
1 tsp. salt
1/2 tsp. pepper
1 tsp. marjoram
1 tsp. thyme
1 tsp. caraway seed
1 clove of garlic, minced

Combine oil, lemon juice, onion, parsley, salt, pepper, marjoram, thyme, caraway seed and garlic. Rub marinade over surface of lamb. Wrap lamb in foil; refrigerate for 12 to 14 hours before cooking.

SHISH KABOB MARINADE

2 sm. onions, sliced
1 tbsp. olive oil
1/2 c. sherry
1 tsp. salt
Pepper to taste
1 tsp. cumin

Combine all ingredients; pour over lamb. Toss to coat all pieces thoroughly. Cover; refrigerate overnight. Toss again; allow lamb cubes to remain in marinade until ready to place on skewers.

SOY SAUCE MARINADE FOR LAMB CHOPS

1 c. soy sauce
2 cloves of garlic
1 c. salad oil
1/2 c. honey

Place soy sauce, garlic, oil and honey in electric blender container. Cover; process until garlic is finely chopped. Pour marinade over lamb chops. Cover; marinate in refrigerator overnight. Remove chops from marinade before cooking. Marinade may be refrigerated for future use.

WINE MARINADE FOR SHISH KABOBS

1 clove of garlic, minced
1 onion, chopped
1/2 c. olive oil
1/2 c. red wine
1/4 c. wine vinegar
1/2 tsp. ground pepper
1 tsp. crushed oregano
1 tsp. salt
1/4 c. chopped parsley

Combine garlic, onion, olive oil, wine, vinegar, pepper, oregano, salt and parsley. Pour over lamb cubes; marinate overnight.

SEAFOOD MARINADE

1/2 c. oil
1/3 c. vinegar
1/2 c. catsup
1/2 c. tart fruit juice
1/4 c. minced onion
1 tsp. hot sauce
2 tsp. salt
1 tsp. chili powder
1/4 tsp. oregano

Combine all marinade ingredients in saucepan; bring to a boil. Reduce heat; simmer for 10 minutes. Pour hot marinade over cooked seafood. Cool to room temperature. Chill in refrigerator for several hours. Serve seafood in marinade.

SHRIMP MARINADE

Juice of 1 lemon
1/3 c. chili sauce
6 1/2 oz. salad oil
Dash of bay leaf powder
1/2 tsp. seasoned salt

Combine lemon juice, chili sauce, oil, bay leaf powder and seasoned salt in electric blender container. Cover; process until mixed. Layer cooked shrimp and sliced onions in shallow container; pour in marinade. Cover; marinate in refrigerator for 24 hours, stirring occasionally.

KABOB MARINADE

1 1/2 c. salad oil
3/4 c. soy sauce
1/4 c. Worcestershire sauce
2 tbsp. dry mustard
1 tbsp. freshly ground pepper
2 1/4 tsp..salt
1/2 c. wine vinegar
1 1/2 tsp. dried parsley flakes
2 cloves of garlic, crushed
1/3 c. lemon juice

Combine all marinade ingredients. Add kabob meats and vegetables; let stand for about 2 hours. Use marinade for basting sauce when grilling kabobs.

Marmalade

Marmalade is a sweet preserve used as a spread, filling, or condiment. It is generally made by boiling sugar and fruit pulp and usually the shredded, sliced, chopped, or ground fruit rind. Sometimes commercial pectin is added. Citrus fruit, especially oranges, are popularly used in making marmalade, although many other kinds of fruit may be used. Marmalade is clearer and firmer than jam. The *ingredients, method of canning,* and *storage* for marmalade are the same as those for jam. The *processing of marmalade* is the same as for jam except for the preparation of the fruit.
(See CANNING and JAM.)

CARROT MARMALADE

2 c. ground carrots
Juice and ground rind of 1 lemon
Juice and ground rind of 1 orange
Sugar

Mix carrots, lemon rind and orange rind; stir in 4 cups water. Boil for 30 minutes. Measure carrot mixture; add lemon juice, orange juice and sugar to equal carrot mixture. Simmer, stirring frequently, until glazed and thick. Pour into sterilized jars; seal with melted paraffin.

GOLDEN MARMALADE

1 lb. dried apricots, cut up
1/2 c. lemon juice
1 1-lb. 4-oz. can crushed pineapple
8 c. sugar

Combine apricots, lemon juice, pineapple, and sugar with 4 cups water; blend well. Cook over medium heat, stirring frequently, for 25 minutes or until mixture comes to a rolling boil. Boil rapidly for 35 minutes or until syrup is clear and thickened. Ladle into hot sterilized jars; seal with paraffin. Yield: Twelve 8-ounce glasses.

FRESH GRAPEFRUIT MARMALADE

2 lge. grapefruit
4 lge. oranges
2 lge. lemons
10 c. sugar
3 pieces gingerroot
1 tbsp. vanilla

Cut grapefruit, oranges and lemons in thin slices; remove seeds. Cut each slice into 1/4-inch strips. Place fruit in deep kettle or saucepan; add water to cover. Bring to boiling point; drain. Repeat twice. Add 4 cups cold water; bring to a boil. Reduce heat; simmer for 1 hour and 30 minutes or until fruit is tender. Add sugar and gingerroot. Cook over low heat, stirring frequently, for about 2 hours and 30 minutes or until thickened; add vanilla. Spoon into sterilized jars; seal immediately. Yield: About 12 half-pints.

LIME MARMALADE

6 limes
3 lemons
Sugar

Chop limes and lemons into small pieces; remove seeds. Measure fruits into large kettle; add water to triple amount of fruit mixture. Soak for 12 hours. Simmer for 20 minutes; let stand for 12 hours. Measure mixture; return to kettle. Add 3/4 cup sugar for every cup of fruit mixture. Cook, stirring frequently until syrup sheets from spoon. Pour into sterilized jars; seal with melted paraffin. Yield: 3 jelly glasses.

MARASCHINO CHERRY MARMALADE

Juice of 1 lemon
6 c. sugar
2 c. crushed pineapple
1 1/2 c. maraschino cherries
1 pkg. fruit pectin

Combine lemon juice with 1/2 cup water; bring to a boil, stirring constantly. Add remaining ingredients except pectin; bring to a boil. Boil, stirring constantly, for 2 minutes or until syrup sheets from spoon; stir in pectin. Skim. Ladle into hot sterilized glasses; seal with paraffin.

Fresh Grapefruit Marmalade . . . Add new flavor to biscuits by topping them with marmalade.

MYSTERY MARMALADE

2 c. finely chopped cucumbers
4 c. sugar
1/2 c. lime juice
2 tbsp. grated lime rind
Green food coloring
1/2 c. fruit pectin

Combine cucumbers, sugar, lime juice and lime rind in large saucepan; mix well. Add food coloring to desired tint. Bring to a rolling boil over high heat; boil, stirring constantly, for 1 minute. Remove from heat; stir in pectin. Stir and skim for 5 minutes. Ladle into hot sterilized glasses; seal with paraffin. Yield: 5 glasses.

PEACH-ORANGE MARMALADE

2 qt. ripe peaches
3/4 c. sliced orange peel
2 tbsp. lemon juice
1 1/2 c. chopped orange pulp
5 c. sugar

Peel and pit peaches; chop coarsely. Combine peaches, orange peel, lemon juice, orange pulp and sugar in large kettle; bring to a boil, stirring constantly, over low heat until sugar is dissolved. Boil rapidly, stirring frequently, for 20 minutes or until mixture is clear and thickened. Pour into hot sterilized jars; seal with paraffin. Yield: Eight 8-ounce jars.

PEAR AMBER MARMALADE

2 oranges
9 c. diced peeled pears
2 c. pared diced peaches
2 c. canned crushed pineapple
Sugar
1/4 c. lemon juice
1 8-oz. bottle maraschino cherries, thinly sliced

Peel oranges; reserve rind. Combine reserved rind with 1 quart water; boil for 5 minutes. Drain; repeat process. Drain; discard liquid. Grind oranges and rind. Peel and core pears; chop coarsely. Peel and pit peaches; chop coarsely. Drain pineapple. Combine fruits; measure into large kettle. Add 1/2 cup sugar for each cup fruit mixture. Add lemon juice; mix well. Bring to a rolling boil; cook, stirring occasionally, for 40 minutes or until just thickened. Add cherries; cook for 5 minutes longer. Pour into sterilized jars; seal with paraffin.

PLUM MARMALADE

1 qt. plums
4 c. sugar
1 lb. raisins, ground
2 oranges, ground
1/4 lb. walnuts, cut into fine pieces

Combine plums, sugar, raisins and oranges in large saucepan. Bring to a rolling boil; cook, stirring frequently, for 20 minutes. Cool; add walnuts. Pour into sterilized jars; seal with paraffin.

PRUNE MARMALADE

1 lb. dried prunes
1/2 c. vinegar
1 1/2 c. sugar
1/2 tsp. cloves
1/2 tsp. cinnamon

Soak prunes in water to cover; simmer for 1 hour. Drain; reserve liquid. Remove pits; chop prunes coarsely. Combine with reserved liquid, vinegar, sugar and spices in saucepan. Simmer, stirring frequently, until thickened. Pour into sterilized jars and seal with paraffin. Yield: 2 pints.

RASPBERRY MARMALADE

2 med. oranges
2 med. lemons
1 c. water
1/8 tsp. soda
1 qt. ripe raspberries, crushed
7 c. sugar
1 bottle fruit pectin

Cut peeling from oranges and lemons in thin strips; leave as much membrane on fruits as possible. Grind peelings; add 1 cup water and soda. Bring to a boil; reduce heat. Simmer, covered, for 10 minutes. Remove membrane and seeds from oranges and lemons; add pulp to peeling. Simmer, covered, for 20 minutes; stir in raspberries. Measure 4 cups fruit mixture into large saucepan; add sugar. Mix well. Bring to a rolling boil, stirring constantly; boil for 1 minute. Remove from heat; stir in pectin. Cool for 5 minutes; stir and skim. Pour into 11 sterilized glasses; seal with melted paraffin.

RHUBARB MARMALADE

2 lb. diced rhubarb
2 lb. sugar
Juice and ground rind of 1 orange
Juice and ground rind of 1/2 lemon
Paraffin

Combine rhubarb and sugar in large glass bowl; let stand overnight. Add juices and rinds to rhubarb mixture in enamel kettle; mix well. Simmer, stirring frequently, for 1 hour and 30 minutes or until mixture is thickened. Pour into sterilized jars; seal with melted paraffin.

RIPE TOMATO MARMALADE

1/2 peck ripe tomatoes
3 oranges
Juice of 2 lemons
8 c. sugar
1 lb. chopped walnuts

Cook tomatoes partially; drain partially. Chop oranges coarsely; remove seeds. Combine tomatoes, oranges, lemon juice and sugar. Bring to a boil over low heat. Simmer, stirring frequently, until mixture is thickened. Remove from heat; add walnuts. Pour into hot sterilized jars; seal with paraffin.

STRAWBERRY-RHUBARB MARMALADE

5 c. diced rhubarb
1 qt. strawberries
2 c. sugar

Combine fruits and sugar in kettle; let stand until sugar is moistened by fruit juices. Bring to a boil over low heat; simmer, stirring frequently, for 20 minutes or until mixture sheets from spoon. Pour into hot sterilized 8-ounce jars. Seal with melted paraffin. Yield: 8-10 glasses.

ZUCCHINI-GINGER MARMALADE

6 c. thinly sliced peeled zucchini
1 13 1/2-oz. can crushed pineapple
Juice of 2 lemons
1 tsp. grated lemon peel
5 c. sugar
2 tbsp. minced crystallized ginger
1 pkg. powdered fruit pectin

Place zucchini in large kettle. Drain pineapple well. Add pineapple, lemon juice and peel to zucchini; bring to a boil. Reduce heat; simmer for 15 minutes, until squash is crisp-tender. Stir in sugar and ginger; bring to a full rolling boil. Boil, stirring constantly, for 1 minute. Remove from heat; stir in pectin. Skim. Ladle into hot sterilized jars; seal with hot paraffin. Yield: Five 1/2-pint jars.

Mayonnaise

Mayonnaise is a rich, smooth, and creamy sauce or salad dressing usually made from egg yolks, oil, vinegar or lemon juice, and seasonings. Some recipes specify fruit juice, cream, minced egg white, pimento, or similar ingredients for flavor variation. Mayonnaise may be uncooked or cooked. Uncooked mayonnaise may be hand-beaten or made in the blender. Mayonnaise contains fat, Vitamin A, and calcium. (1 tablespoon = 110 calories)

PREPARATION: For *uncooked, hand-beaten* mayonnaise—Eggs, oil, bowl, and beater should be at room temperature. Warm oil slightly if it has been refrigerated. Rinse bowl in hot water and dry. Combine and beat ingredients according to specific recipe instructions. Bottle mayonnaise and refrigerate. For *uncooked, blender* mayonnaise—Combine and blend ingredients in electric blender according to specific recipe instructions. Use whole eggs rather than egg yolks. Mixture will have greater volume and fluffier texture than hand-beaten mayonnaise. For *cooked* mayonnaise—Combine ingredients in top of double boiler over boiling water. Cook according to recipe until sauce is smooth and thick. *To color mayonnaise* for salad dressings add beet juice, raspberry juice, cooked beet puree, or lobster paste for red mayonnaise. Add cooked spinach puree, chopped fresh spinach, minced parsley, or concentrated boiled artichoke liquor for green mayonnaise.

STORING: Refrigerate mayonnaise and foods containing mayonnaise in closed containers. Freezing mayonnaise and mayonnaise combinations is not recommended.

SERVING: Serve as a sauce for shellfish and vegetables. Use as a salad dressing, sandwich spread, or base for other sauces.

CURRIED MAYONNAISE

1 egg
1/2 tsp. curry powder
1/2 tsp. salt
1 clove of garlic, minced
2 tbsp. lemon juice
1/2 c. olive oil
1/2 c. salad oil

Place egg, curry powder, salt, garlic, lemon juice and 1/4 cup oil in blender container; blend on low speed for just a few seconds. Add remaining oil in a slow stream, blending on lowest speed until smooth and thickened. Chill until ready to use.

EASY BLENDER MAYONNAISE

1 egg
1/2 tsp. dry mustard
1 tsp. salt
2 tbsp. lemon juice
1/4 c. salad oil
3/4 c. sour cream

Combine first 5 ingredients in blender container; blend thoroughly. Fold in sour cream. Refrigerate until ready to use.

ONE-MINUTE MAYONNAISE

1 c. salad oil
1 tbsp. vinegar
1 tbsp. lemon juice
1 egg
1/2 tsp. salt
1/8 tsp. paprika
1/4 tsp. dry mustard
Dash of cayenne

Pour 1/4 cup oil into blender container; add vinegar, lemon juice, egg and seasonings. Cover; blend for 5 seconds. Remove cover while blender is running; add remaining oil in steady stream. Turn off blender immediately after adding oil. Yield: 1 1/2 cups.

CREAM MAYONNAISE

2 eggs, well beaten
1/2 c. sugar
1/2 tsp. salt
Pinch of cayenne pepper
1/4 tsp. dry mustard
1/2 c. vinegar
1/2 c. cream

Combine all ingredients in top of double boiler over boiling water. Cook, stirring constantly, until smooth and thickened. Cool; refrigerate until ready to use.

FRUIT MAYONNAISE

2 eggs
1/2 c. sugar
1/4 c. lemon juice
1/4 c. pineapple juice
1 1/2 c. heavy cream

Beat eggs until thick and lemony. Combine eggs, sugar, lemon juice and pineapple juice in top of double boiler; cook over boiling water, stirring constantly, until smooth and thickened. Chill. Just before serving, whip cream until soft peaks form; fold into dressing. Yield: 3 cups.

LEMON MAYONNAISE

1 c. flour
3 tsp. salt
3 tsp. sugar
3 tsp. mustard
3 eggs
1/3 c. vinegar
1/3 c. lemon juice
3 c. oil

Combine flour, salt, sugar and mustard in top of double boiler; mix well. Add 3 cups water gradually; place over boiling water. Cook, stirring constantly, until mixture begins to thicken. Cook, covered, for 10 minutes. Cool to lukewarm; pour into large bowl. Add eggs, vinegar, lemon juice and oil; beat until light and creamy. Yield: 2 quarts.

SMOOTH DRESSING

1/4 c. cornstarch
1 egg
2 tbsp. sugar
2 tsp. prepared mustard
1 tsp. salt
Dash of cayenne pepper
1/4 c. vinegar
1 c. salad oil
1/4 tsp. paprika

Combine cornstarch with 1 1/2 cups water in saucepan. Simmer, stirring constantly until mixture is clear. Remove from heat. Combine egg, sugar, mustard, salt, cayenne pepper, vinegar, salad oil and paprika in deep bowl; add cornstarch mixture gradually. Beat at medium speed for 5 minutes or until smooth and well blended. Cool. Store in refrigerator.

DIET MAYONNAISE

2 egg yolks
1/4 tsp. paprika
Dash of cayenne pepper
1 tsp. salt
1/2 tsp. dry mustard
2 tbsp. vinegar
2 c. corn oil
2 tbsp. lemon juice

Have egg yolks at room temperature. Combine dry ingredients with egg yolks; blend well. Add vinegar; mix well. Add oil, 1 teaspoon at a time, beating with mixer at high speed, until 1/4 cup has been added. Add remaining oil in increasing amounts, alternating last 1/2 cup with lemon juice. Add an extra tablespoon of lemon juice to vary the flavor, if desired. Refrigerate.

MAGIC MAYONNAISE

2/3 c. sweetened condensed milk
1/4 c. vinegar
1/4 c. salad oil
1 egg yolk
1/2 tsp. salt
Dash of pepper
1 tsp. dry mustard

Place all ingredients in pint jar; cover tightly. Shake vigorously for 2 minutes. Chill for about 1 hour before serving. Yield: 1 pint.

SIMPLE MAYONNAISE

2 egg yolks
1 c. salad oil
Juice of 1 lemon

Beat egg yolks until lemon colored. Continue to beat, adding salad oil, one drop at a time. Add lemon juice gradually, beating constantly. Store in a covered container in refrigerator. Yield: 1 cup.

Meringue

Meringue is a delicate mixture of egg whites, cream of tartar, sugar, flavorings and/or extracts that is baked until it is lightly browned, firm, and dry. It is used as a topping for pies, cakes, and so on. The egg whites are beaten until stiff, never dry, and combined with the cream of tartar and sugar. These last two ingredients help to stabilize the fragile mixture. Meringue can also be formed into shells and baked to be filled with fruit, jams, and so on.

STORING: Cooked and cooled meringues may be stored in a tightly closed container for several weeks. *To freeze* meringues–Gently wrap in clear plastic, then in foil. Freeze. Use within 1 month. To thaw, remove foil wrapping and allow meringues to stand at room temperature for 6 hours.

PREPARATION: Meringue is affected by humidity so plan to prepare it on a dry day. Have all utensils spotlessly free of grease. Allow egg whites to come to room temperature before beginning preparation. Follow specific recipe directions for combining ingredients. The following information will help you to make flawless meringue every time. *To apply* meringue topping–Spread lightly over surface from the edges of the pastry or baking dish to the middle. Make sure that it adheres at all points or the meringue will shrink during baking. For individual servings, drop the meringue by spoonfuls onto a shiny, ungreased cookie sheet or foil-lined pan. *To bake* meringue–Bake in a slow oven to minimize the amount of shrinkage of the protein contained in egg whites. For pies, tarts, and puddings, bake meringue in a 325- to 350-degree oven for 12 to 18 minutes, depending on the thickness. For kisses or shells, bake meringue in a 250- to 275-degree oven for 40 to 60 minutes depending on the size. *To cool* meringue–Place in warm spot after baking to avoid shrinkage.

USES: Meringue adds a lovely finishing touch to puddings or pies. As decorative shells, they surround such fruits as cherries, blueberries, and strawberries. Chewy cookies, filled with nuts, dates, and coconut and known as kisses, can also be made from meringue.

CHERRY-BERRY ON A CLOUD

6 egg whites
1/4 tsp. salt
1/2 tsp. cream of tartar
2 3/4 c. sugar
2 3-oz. packages cream cheese
1 tsp. vanilla
2 c. whipped cream
2 c. miniature marshmallows
1 can cherry pie filling
1 tsp. lemon juice
2 c. sliced frozen strawberries with juice

Beat egg whites, salt and cream of tartar until frothy. Add 1 3/4 cups sugar, 1 tablespoon at a time; beat until stiff peaks form. Spread meringue in greased 13 x 9 x 2-inch pan. Bake at 275 degrees for 1 hour. Turn oven off; leave meringue in oven until cold. Mix cream cheese, remaining sugar and vanilla. Fold in whipped cream and marshmallows. Spread over meringue; refrigerate for 12 hours. Cut into serving pieces. Mix pie filling, lemon juice and strawberries. Top serving pieces just before serving with fruit mixture. Yield: 12 servings.

COFFEE MERINGUES GLACE

2 egg whites
1/2 tsp. lemon juice
2/3 c. sugar
1 lge. can evaporated milk
1 12-oz. package semi-sweet chocolate pieces
1 qt. coffee ice cream

Combine egg whites and lemon juice; beat until egg whites form soft peaks. Add sugar gradually, beating well after each addition. Beat until stiff and glossy. Shape meringue into 6 circles on lightly buttered baking sheet. Build up edge to 1/2 inch with back of spoon, leaving 1/4-inch base. Bake at 275 degrees for 25 minutes. Turn off heat; leave meringue shells in oven until cooled thoroughly. Combine milk and chocolate; melt over low heat, stirring until well blended. Cool; chill. Mound ice cream in meringue shell. Pour sauce over ice cream; serve immediately. Yield: 6 servings.

CHEWY COOKIES

3 egg whites
1 c. sugar
1 c. chopped dates
1 c. chopped nuts
1 tbsp. vanilla

Place egg whites and sugar in double boiler; beat over medium heat until stiff peaks form. Remove from heat; add dates, nuts and vanilla. Drop from teaspoon onto greased cookie sheet. Bake at 325 degrees for 15 minutes on high rack. Yield: 4 dozen.

CLASSIC MERINGUE COOKIES

1/8 tsp. salt
1/2 tsp. vinegar
1/4 tsp. vanilla
3 egg whites
1 c. sugar

Add salt, vinegar and vanilla to egg whites. Beat until egg whites form stiff peaks. Add sugar, 1 tablespoon at a time, until stiff and glossy. Drop from tablespoon onto ungreased cookie sheet. Bake at 350 degrees for 50 minutes. Yield: 12 servings.

COCONUT KISSES

3 egg whites
Dash of salt
1 c. sugar
1/2 tsp. vanilla
2 c. corn flakes
1 1/4 c. coconut
1/2 c. chopped pecans
1/2 pkg. chocolate bits, melted

Beat egg whites and salt until foamy; add sugar gradually, beating constantly until stiff peaks form. Fold in vanilla, corn flakes, coconut and pecans gently. Drop from teaspoon onto well-greased cookie sheet. Bake at 350 degrees for 18 to 20 minutes. Remove to cooling rack. Swirl chocolate spiral over kisses. Yield: 42 cookies.

MARGUERITES

2 egg whites
1 c. sugar
Pinch of salt
1 c. chopped nuts
1 c. corn flakes

Preheat oven to 400 degrees. Beat egg whites until soft peaks form; add sugar gradually, beating until stiff peaks form. Add salt; fold in nuts and corn flakes. Drop from teaspoon onto well-greased cookie sheet. Place in oven; turn off heat. Leave until oven is cool. Yield: 40 cookies.

MERINGUE DROPS

2 egg whites
1/2 tsp. salt
1/2 tsp. vanilla
1 c. powdered sugar
1 6-oz. package butterscotch chips
1 c. flaked coconut
2 c. corn flakes

Combine egg whites, salt and vanilla; beat until stiff peaks form, but not dry. Beat in sugar until stiff and satiny. Fold in all remaining ingredients. Drop from teaspoon onto greased cookie sheet. Bake at 350 degrees for 20 minutes. Yield: 3 dozen.

MERINGUE SPICE COOKIES

1/4 c. shortening
1/2 c. (packed) brown sugar
1 egg, separated
3/4 c. sifted cake flour
1/4 tsp. soda
1/4 tsp. baking powder
1/4 tsp. cloves
1/4 tsp. cinnamon
1/8 tsp. salt
2 tbsp. sugar
1/4 c. buttermilk
2 tbsp. finely chopped walnuts

Beat shortening until fluffy and creamy. Add brown sugar gradually; beat until light. Add egg yolk; mix well. Sift together all dry ingredients except sugar; add alternately with buttermilk to creamed mixture. Stir until smooth. Pour into greased 8 x 8 x 2-inch pan. Beat egg white with sugar until stiff peaks form; spread over batter. Sprinkle with walnuts. Bake at 350 degrees for 25 minutes. Cool for 10 minutes in pan; cut into 2-inch squares. Remove from pan immediately. Cool on wire racks. Yield: 16 servings.

MERINGUE SQUARES

1/3 c. butter
1/3 c. sugar
2 eggs, separated
1 tsp. vanilla
1 c. sifted flour
1 tsp. baking powder
1 c. (packed) brown sugar
1 c. chopped nuts

Cream butter and sugar thoroughly. Beat egg yolks until light and frothy. Add yolks and vanilla to creamed mixture. Combine flour and baking powder; stir into yolk mixture. Mixture will be very dry. Flatten as thin as possible on greased cookie sheet. Beat egg whites until stiff peaks form; add brown sugar and nuts. Spread over first mixture. Bake at 350 degrees for 20 minutes. Cut into squares to serve. Yield: 10 servings.

PECAN KISSES

1 c. (packed) brown sugar
1 egg white, stiffly beaten
2 c. pecan halves

Add sugar to egg white; beat at low speed with electric mixer until stiff peaks form. Stir in pecans; drop from teaspoon onto greased and floured baking sheet. Bake for 25 minutes at 250 degrees.

PEPPERMINT KISSES

2 egg whites
2/3 c. sugar
1/4 tsp. salt
1/2 tsp. vanilla
2 tbsp. crushed peppermint candy
1/2 c. chocolate bits

Beat egg whites until stiff peaks form; add sugar gradually, beating well after each addition. Fold in salt, vanilla, candy and chocolate bits. Drop from teaspoon onto lightly greased cookie sheet. Bake at 275 degrees for 25 to 30 minutes. Yield: 3 dozen.

FAMILY FAVORITES

5 egg whites
1/4 tsp. salt
1/2 tsp. cream of tartar
1 1/2 c. sugar
1 tsp. vanilla
1/2 pt. cream

Preheat oven to 450 degrees. Beat egg whites and salt until foamy. Add cream of tartar; beat until stiff peaks form. Beat in 1 1/4 cups sugar, 1 tablespoon at a time; beat for 20 minutes. Add vanilla. Place in greased 8 x 8-inch pan. Place in oven; turn off heat. Leave meringue in oven overnight; do not open door. Whip cream and remaining sugar until stiff peaks form; spread over meringue. Refrigerate until serving time. Garnish with frozen berries or ice cream. Yield: 9 servings.

FILLED KISSES

3 egg whites
1/2 tsp. vinegar
1 c. sugar
1/2 tsp. vanilla
1 c. whipping cream
1/2 tsp. instant coffee
Powdered sugar to taste

Beat egg whites and vinegar at high speed with electric mixer until stiff peaks form. Add sugar gradually, beating constantly; add vanilla, beating at high speed until sugar dissolves. Cover cookie sheet with brown paper; spoon mixture onto paper, allowing space for doubling in size. Bake at 325 degrees for 45 minutes. Remove from paper immediately to cool. Whip cream until stiff peaks form; stir in coffee and powdered sugar. Lift off top of meringue with spoon; fill with whipped cream. Replace tops; refrigerate. Yield: 6 meringues.

FORGOTTEN MERINGUES

6 egg whites
1/2 tsp. cream of tartar
2 c. sugar
Ice cream

Preheat oven to 400 degrees. Beat egg whites with cream of tartar. Beat in sugar gradually until stiff peaks form and mixture is glossy. Drop from spoon in mounds or form Christmas tree or Easter egg shapes. Make center hollows with back of spoon. Place in oven; turn off oven. Let stand overnight in oven. Fill with ice cream to serve; top with sauce, if desired.

MERINGUE CHANTILLY

8 egg whites
1/4 tsp. salt
1/4 tsp. cream of tartar
2 c. sugar
1 tsp. vanilla
2 c. heavy cream, whipped and sweetened to taste with powdered sugar

Have egg whites at room temperature. Grease and flour 2 large baking sheets lightly; line with waxed paper. Pencil 9-inch circle twice on each sheet. Beat egg whites until frothy; add salt and cream of tartar, beating thoroughly. Add sugar, 1 tablespoon at a time, beating constantly. Add vanilla; beat until stiff and glossy but not dry. Divide meringue into 4 parts. Fill pastry bag with meringue. Press out a pencil-thick strip of meringue around rim of each circle. Make lattice by pressing 4 strips of meringue horizontally and 4 vertically across circle, touching meringue rim. Bake at 225 degrees for 45 minutes or until firm and dry. Cool circles slightly; remove from paper while warm. Divide whipped cream into 2 parts. Place 1 lattice on serving dish; spread lightly with whipped cream. Top with second layer. Repeat until all layers are used; do not spread whipped cream on last layer. Fill pastry bag with remaining whipped cream. Pipe decorative swirls on side and rosettes around top. Fill lattice cavities with strawberries. Refrigerate until serving time. Yield: 8 servings.

ANGEL PIE

4 eggs, separated
1/4 tsp. cream of tartar
1 1/2 c. sugar
3 tbsp. lemon juice
2 tsp. grated lemon rind
1 1/2 c. whipped cream

Beat egg whites and cream of tartar until stiff peaks form; add sugar gradually, beating well. Spread in greased 9-inch glass pie pan. Bake at 275 degrees for 20 minutes. Increase oven temperature to 300 degrees; bake for 40 minutes longer. Combine egg yolks, sugar, lemon juice and rind; cool, stirring frequently, until mixture is thickened. Spread meringue shell with 1 cup whipped cream; add custard filling. Top with remaining whipped cream. Chill overnight. Yield: 6-8 servings.

COCONUT-BUTTERSCOTCH PIE

4 egg whites
Dash of salt
1 c. sugar
1 tsp. vanilla
1/2 c. coconut
1/2 c. chopped pecans
1 c. graham cracker crumbs

Beat egg whites with salt until stiff peaks form; add sugar gradually. Add vanilla; fold in coconut, pecans and crumbs. Place in pie pan. Bake at 350 degrees for 30 minutes.

Sauce

1 c. scalded evaporated milk
1 c. (packed) brown sugar
1/2 c. sugar
1 tbsp. flour
1 egg, beaten

Mix all ingredients together in saucepan; cook for 5 minutes. Cool. Pour Sauce over meringue crust to serve. Top with vanilla ice cream, if desired.

FRENCH BLUEBERRY PIE

3 egg whites
1 c. sugar
20 sm. saltine crackers, crushed
1 tsp. vinegar
2 1/2 tsp. vanilla
1 tsp. baking powder
1/2 c. chopped pecans
1 pkg. dessert topping mix
1/2 c. powdered sugar
1 8-oz. package softened cream cheese
1 can blueberry pie filling

Beat egg whites until stiff peaks form; add sugar gradually. Mix crackers, vinegar, 1 teaspoon vanilla, baking powder and pecans together; fold in egg whites. Spread mixture into buttered 9-inch pie pan. Bake at 325 degrees for 20 minutes. Cool. Prepare topping mix according to package directions; add powdered sugar, remaining vanilla and cream cheese. Spread over meringue. Chill for at least 5 hours. Spread cream cheese layer with pie filling. Yield: 12 servings.

PEACH MERINGUE PIE

3 egg whites, beaten
1 c. sugar
1/4 tsp. baking powder
12 soda crackers, finely crushed
1/2 c. pecans
1/2 tsp. vanilla
Sliced peaches
Whipped cream

Preheat oven to 325 degrees. Beat egg whites until stiff peaks form; add sugar gradually, mixing well. Mix baking powder with cracker crumbs; add crumb mixture, pecans and vanilla to egg whites. Spread in greased 9-inch pie pan. Bake for 30 minutes; cool. Refrigerate overnight. Top with peaches and whipped cream.

PECAN CRACKER PIE

3 egg whites
1/2 tsp. baking powder
1 c. sugar
1/2 c. broken pecans
1/2 tsp. vanilla
12 lge. unsalted soda crackers, crushed
Whipped cream

Beat egg whites with baking powder until stiff peaks form; add sugar. Beat thoroughly. Fold in pecans, vanilla and crackers, stirring well. Pour into 9-inch buttered pie plate. Bake at 375 degrees for 20 minutes. Chill. Cover with whipped cream; refrigerate for 2 hours before serving. Yield: 8 servings.

STRAWBERRY PARTY MERINGUE

Sifted powdered sugar
1/2 c. butter
3 egg yolks
1 tbsp. lemon juice
1 tsp. grated lemon peel
Meringue Shell
1 pt. fresh strawberries
1/2 c. whipping cream
1/2 tsp. vanilla

Cream 2 cups powdered sugar, butter and egg yolks until light and fluffy; beat in lemon juice and peel. Spread over bottom of Meringue Shell. Hull strawberries; arrange over creamy layer, pressing down lightly. Reserve several perfect berries for garnish. Whip cream, 2 tablespoons powdered sugar and vanilla together until stiff; spread over berries. Chill in refrigerator for several hours or overnight. Garnish with reserved berries.

Strawberry Party Meringue . . . Succulent fresh berries fill the center of a make-ahead meringue.

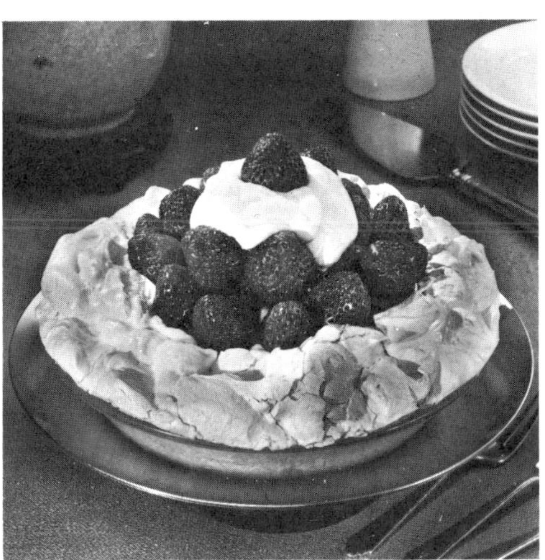

Meringue Shell

4 egg whites
1/2 tsp. cream of tartar
1/4 tsp. salt
1/2 tsp. vanilla
1 c. powdered sugar

Have egg whites at room temperature. Combine egg whites, cream of tartar, salt and vanilla in large bowl of mixer. Beat until foamy; add 1 cup powdered sugar gradually, beating until stiff peaks form. Spread meringue about 1 inch thick over bottom of greased 9-inch pie pan, building up high, fluffy border. Keep rim of pan free of meringue. Bake at 275 degrees for 1 hour. Meringue should be delicate cream color and feel dry and firm to the touch. Let meringue cool in pan.

Microwave

The microwave oven . . . possibly the newest cooking excitement in the kitchen in a generation! It is estimated by 1985 that the microwave oven will be as common to American households as the television set. That means if you don't already own one, you are probably considering the purchase of one very soon. For all the benefits of a microwave oven . . . its cool, clean and energy-saving operation, its extraordinary time savings and convenience . . . the more a homemaker knows about making the most of a microwave oven, the better her meals will be!

The microwave oven can create what might be called a "fast food line" for any kitchen. Yet, the home-cooked fast foods prepared in the microwave oven are likely to be far fresher, more nutritious, and less expensive than "fast foods" bought outside the home. Microwaving is versatile, too. It takes the place of baking, roasting, boiling, pan-frying, and it saves time and energy by reducing conventional cooking times up to 75%.

HOW DOES A MICROWAVE OVEN WORK? A conventional oven uses dry heat, first heating the air in the oven by convection, then slowly heating the food until it is cooked. Microwaves, which are a form of energy created by a magnetron inside the oven unit, are absorbed by foods, causing the food molecules to rotate rapidly. This rotation causes friction; heat results, and the food cooks. Absorbed by the water, fat, and sugar in foods, microwaves penetrate about 1 inch into the food, and the food molecules rub together about 2500 times per second. So, the heat moves from the outside of the food to the middle, and not from the inside out, as one popular microwave myth suggests. As the food cooks, the air inside the oven, the oven itself, and the cooking dish stay cool.

To dispel another microwave myth, microwave ovens DO NOT produce any dangerous radiation. As stated above, microwaves merely cause the food molecules to rub together rapidly, causing friction and heat, but no danger. X-rays and gamma rays, which are examples of dangerous radiation, cause molecules to break apart, and microwaves are nothing like these. Instead, microwaves are a form of electromagnetic or radiant energy having a certain wave length, as do infrared light or high frequency radio waves. Microwaves are common in the air, from TV and telephone towers, short wave radios, police and airline radars, any electric motor with brushes, and many other everyday items. As for persons with pacemakers, they should take only the same precautions around a microwave oven as they would any common appliance. If unsure, consult a physician. Because microwave ovens are manufactured under very strict regulations, they are as safe as any other home heating appliance.

So, enjoy your microwave oven! It can open a new and convenient world of cooking in your kitchen, yet with the same delicious results you've always had.

WHY USE A MICROWAVE OVEN? In addition to convenience, versatile use, time and energy savings, microwave cooking has a lot to offer today's busy homemaker. Foods can be prepared in the proper, even pretty, serving dishes. This means fewer messy pots and pans to wash up after mealtime. If dinner is delayed, the foods can be easily reheated without loss of flavor, moisture, and texture. This is also true for leftovers. And, many dishes can be prepared in advance and frozen for later use by busy moms, babysitters, hungry teenagers, and other reluctant cooks (like husbands!). A microwave oven is easy to clean, too. Spills don't burn or bake onto the oven surface and are easily cleaned with a damp cloth. Plus, a cooler oven means a cooler kitchen and a cooler cook!

Best of all, the microwave defrosts frozen foods in a matter of minutes. Even a large roast can go from freezer to microwave to table in a fraction of the usual time, with perfect results. You can use your own recipes for microwaving, too. Compare your favorites to similar recipes in this and any reliable microwave cookbook, and adapt yours to its cooking times and suggestions. Once you become familiar with cooking times for various foods, it becomes almost second nature to adapt your personal collection of conventional recipes to microwave cooking.

HOW FAVORITE FOODS RESPOND TO MICROWAVE COOKING: Think of it! In a matter of minutes you can prepare a full range of dishes for breakfast, lunch, or dinner menus that everyone in the family will love. This includes barbecued chicken, baked potatoes, lasagna, vegetable soup, baked fresh fish, appetizers, and desserts, and plenty more! So, most, but not all, foods can be deliciously prepared in the microwave oven. Foods that are conventionally prepared on the range surface respond the best.

The microwave oven cooks foods so quickly that those requiring overall browning tend to cook before they are browned. Their flavor will be perfectly delicious, only the browned appearance will be lacking. Cakes will rise high in the microwave oven and cook with a superb texture, although they will not brown. Nor will cookies. This is never noticed in cakes and cookies of a dark color, such as chocolate. Large roasts over 4 pounds, whole chickens, and bacon will brown nicely due to long cooking times in relation to their volume. Thinner cuts of meat will cook up flavorful and tender, but will not brown. Many recipes for these often include a suggestion to brush the meat with Kitchen Bouquet, soy sauce, or Worcestershire sauce to give the preferred brown finish. Many microwave oven manufacturers offer an optional browning dish or browning element with various oven models. Plus, the browning can be accomplished under the broiler of your conventional oven.

Studies tell us that there is no difference in the nutritional value of foods whether cooked in a conventional or microwave oven. However, many people say that foods cooked by microwave taste fresher and juicier. This is probably due to the speed and method of microwave cooking, which tends to retain the natural color, moisture, texture, and flavor of food. And, the more quickly a food can be cooked, the more water-soluble vitamins and minerals are preserved.

THE MICROWAVE OVEN IS NOT RECOMMENDED FOR HOME CANNING! Non-acid and low acid foods require certain periods of time in a pressure cooker for safe preparation. Even high acid foods that can be prepared by the water bath method of canning must be cooked at a high temperature and a certain amount of time that the microwave oven is not designed to provide. However, home-canned foods may be prepared for serving in the microwave oven just as any other food may be.

You can save time in some food preservation methods in the microwave oven. You can blanch vegetables for freezing, and prepare jams, jellies, and relishes in your microwave oven.

CHOOSE THE RIGHT MICROWAVE OVEN COOKWARE: Microwave energy is either absorbed, reflected or transmitted by different materials. Food must be able to absorb the microwave energy to cook. So, the cookware you use must be able to transmit the microwaves, not absorb or reflect them.

Ovenproof glass, most ceramics, and paper tableware transmit microwaves and are recommended for microwave use. Check these carefully for metal in the glaze composition or decoration. Do not use china with gold, silver, or platinum bands. Metal reflects the microwaves and will cause uneven and unsatisfactory cooking results. The use of metal ovenware may even cause damage to the oven unit. Follow the instructions provided by the manufacturer of your oven for proper use of shallow metal packaging used for some frozen dinners.

The well-known makers of quality ovenware now offer a full selection of ovenware for the microwave oven. Tableware manufacturers also produce dinnerware suitable for microwave use and clearly state which can and cannot be used. Most any plastic container can be used for thawing foods in the microwave oven. Only plastics designated "safe for microwave oven and dishwasher use" or "can be placed in boiling water" are suitable for actual microwave cooking. You can also use clay pots (such as Romertopf) in your microwave oven, with the same presoaking requirements used in conventional cooking methods. To test a utensil for the microwave, place it in the oven for 20 seconds on the "High" setting. If it is still cool when the time is up, it is probably safe for microwave use.

FINAL SUGGESTIONS: Follow your microwave recipes carefully. Measure food quantities accurately because the times relate to the quantity of foods. Generally, microwave timings are reduced by about half when the quantity is reduced, or almost doubled when the quantity is doubled.

Covering plates and containers of food during heating helps to shorten cooking times by keeping the steam near the food. Use plastic wrap or waxed paper when a heatproof cover is not provided with the cooking container. Provide vent holes for plastic wrap covers or a steam build-up may cause the plastic to burst and tear.

If heating only one container, place it in the center of the microwave oven. If heating several small containers, place them in a circle around the center for best results.

Check food as it cooks. To spread heat evenly during the cooking process, stir or turn the foods, or rotate the dish. Casseroles, gravies, and other very moist mixtures benefit most from stirring. Usually, it is best to stir from the center out.

Foods that are being thawed in the microwave oven need to be turned over, often several times, for even results.

In many ways, microwave cooking is no different from any other form of cooking. For confidence and best results, plan ahead and shop ahead. Read your recipes carefully and be sure you have all the necessary ingredients on hand. Cook the foods that take the longest first. Then, during their "standing time," microwave the foods that require the shorter amounts of time. You will notice that many recipes call for a "standing time" after cooking to allow the heat to distribute evenly throughout the foods.

Microwave cooking means that you can enjoy cooking like never before! It's fast, efficient, and the results are as delicious – if not more so – as you have always enjoyed. Here is a selection of microwave recipes to help you make the most of your microwave!

NIPPY NACHOS

20 lge. tortilla chips
1 jar taco sauce
5 oz. Monterey Jack cheese, shredded
Shredded Cheddar cheese
Sliced olives

Arrange chips on large waxed paper-lined glass plate. Sprinkle taco sauce over chips according to taste. Sprinkle cheeses over chips evenly. Top each chip with olive slice. Microwave on High for 1 minute. Rotate dish. Microwave on High for 1 to 2 minutes longer or until cheese melts. Serve hot. Yield: 20 nachos.

SNICK-SNACKS

2 c. Wheat Chex
2 c. Rice Chex
2 c. Corn Chex
6 oz. pretzel sticks
3/4 lb. red peanuts
3/4 c. butter
1 1/2 tsp. each garlic and onion salt
3 tbsp. Worcestershire sauce

Combine cereals, pretzels and peanuts in 3-quart glass casserole. Combine remaining ingredients in glass measuring cup. Heat butter mixture in microwave on High for 1 minute or until melted. Pour butter mixture over cereal mixture. Microwave on High for 8 to 10 minutes longer, stirring occasionally.

FACE-UP REUBENS

4 slices toasted rye bread
1/2 lb. corned beef, sliced
1/2 c. sauerkraut, drained
1/4 c. Thousand Island dressing
4 slices Swiss cheese

Place bread on paper towel-lined glass platter. Layer with beef, sauerkraut and dressing. Top with cheese slice. Cover with plastic wrap. Microwave on High for 1 to 2 minutes or until cheese melts. Let stand 2 minutes before serving.

BARBECUED ROUND STEAK

1 2-lb. round steak
1/2 c. minced onion
1/2 c. minced celery
2 tsp. garlic salt
1 10 1/2-oz. can tomato soup
2 tbsp. brown sugar
2 tbsp. Worcestershire sauce
2 tbsp. lemon juice
2 tsp. prepared mustard
1 tsp. Tabasco sauce

Cut round steak into serving pieces. Place in 3-quart glass casserole. Combine remaining ingredients; pour over steak. Refrigerate for several hours. Microwave, covered, on Simmer for 40 to 50 minutes.

ALL-AMERICAN MEAT LOAF

1 1/2 lb. ground beef
3/4 c. oatmeal
1 med. onion, chopped
1 c. catsup
1/4 c. milk
2 eggs, beaten
2 tbsp. horseradish
1 1/2 tsp. salt
1/4 tsp. pepper
2 tsp. prepared mustard
3 tbsp. brown sugar

Combine ground beef, oatmeal, onion, 1/2 cup catsup, milk, eggs, 1 tablespoon horseradish, salt and pepper in large mixing bowl; mix well. Spoon into 10-inch plastic ring mold. Microwave on Roast for 12 to 15 minutes. Let stand for 15 minutes. Combine mustard, 1 tablespoon horseradish, brown sugar and 1/2 cup catsup; mix well. Invert meat ring onto glass serving platter. Pour glaze over. Microwave on High for 3 minutes to heat glaze.

TRADITIONAL LASAGNA

1 8-oz. package lasagna noodles
1 tsp. salt
1 1/2 lb. ground beef
1/2 c. chopped onion
1/4 c. chopped green pepper
1 pkg. spaghetti sauce mix
2 c. tomato sauce
1/2 c. drained mushroom pieces
1 1/2 c. cottage cheese
6 to 8 oz. sliced mozzarella cheese
1/2 c. grated Parmesan cheese

Place noodles in 9 x 13-inch glass baking dish. Cover with water. Sprinkle with salt. Microwave on High, uncovered, for 15 minutes. Remove from oven. Let noodles stand in cooking water while preparing meat sauce. Crumble ground beef in 3-quart glass casserole. Add onion and green pepper. Microwave on High for 5 minutes, uncovered; stir well. Microwave for 3 minutes longer; drain off juices. Stir in spaghetti sauce mix, tomato sauce and mushrooms. Arrange layers of 1/3 of the noodles, 1/3 of the beef mixture, 1/2 of the cottage cheese and 1/2 of the mozzarella cheese in 9 x 13-inch glass baking dish. Repeat layers ending with noodles and ground beef mixture. Sprinkle with Parmesan cheese. Cover loosely with waxed paper. Microwave on High for 8 minutes; turn dish. Microwave on High for 7 minutes longer. Let stand, covered, for 5 minutes before serving.

PORK RIBS AND SAUERKRAUT

2 lb. pork ribs
1 16-oz. can sauerkraut, drained
1 c. applesauce
2 tbsp. brown sugar
1 sm. onion, finely chopped
1/4 tsp. caraway seed
1/4 tsp. garlic powder

Place ribs in glass baking dish with larger pieces toward sides of dish; cover loosely. Microwave on High for 13 to 15 minutes or until meat is no longer pink; drain. Turn and rearrange ribs. Combine remaining ingredients; mix well. Spoon over ribs; cover loosely. Microwave on High for 10 to 12 minutes longer or until sauerkraut mixture is hot and meat is done. Yield: 4-6 servings.

BASIC CHICKEN

1/3 c. margarine
1 tsp. garlic salt
3/4 c. bread crumbs
1 tbsp. parsley flakes
1 tsp. salt
Dash of pepper
1/4 tsp. poultry seasoning
1 2 1/2 to 3-lb. fryer, cut up
Paprika

Place margarine in 2-quart glass baking dish. Microwave on High for 1 minute or until margarine is melted. Combine garlic salt, bread crumbs, parsley flakes, salt, pepper and poultry seasoning in large mixing bowl; mix well. Roll chicken in melted margarine; dip in crumb mixture. Place chicken in 2-quart glass baking dish, skin side down. Microwave on High for 10 to 12 minutes; turn chicken pieces over. Microwave on High for 10 to 12 minutes longer. Sprinkle with paprika.

SPECIAL BARBECUED CHICKEN

1 2 1/2 to 3-lb. chicken, cut up
1 c. catsup
1/4 c. Worcestershire sauce
1/4 c. vinegar
1/4 c. (packed) brown sugar
1 lge. onion, chopped
2 tbsp. cornstarch
1 tbsp. lemon juice
1 tsp. salt
1 tsp. celery seed
1/4 tsp. liquid smoke
Dash of red pepper sauce

Arrange chicken, skin side up, in oblong glass baking dish. Combine remaining ingredients with 1/2 cup water in 4-cup glass measure; mix well. Microwave on High for 3 minutes; stir. Microwave on High for 2 to 3 minutes longer or until mixture boils and thickens. Pour sauce over chicken; cover loosely. Microwave on High for 10 minutes longer. Rearrange chicken. Baste; cover loosely. Microwave on High for 10 to 15 minutes longer or until chicken is tender, basting every 5 minutes. Yield: 6-8 servings.

QUICKIE CHICK

1 2 to 3-lb. chicken, disjointed
1/2 c. margarine, melted
3/4 c. crushed Ritz crackers
1 pkg. dry onion soup mix

Dip chicken pieces in melted margarine. Combine crushed crackers and onion soup mix in plastic bag; shake to mix well. Drop 2 pieces of chicken at a time in bag; shake bag to coat chicken. Arrange chicken pieces, skin side up, in a 12 x 8 x 2-inch glass baking dish. Cover with waxed paper. Microwave on High for 20 to 22 minutes or until chicken is tender.

SEVEN-CAN SEAFOOD CASSEROLE

1 12-oz. package med. noodles, cooked
1 can tuna, drained
1 can shrimp, drained
1 can lobster, drained
1 can mushroom soup
1 can cream of celery soup
1 soup can milk
1 can French-fried onion rings

Combine all ingredients except onion rings; blend well. Place in 3-quart glass casserole; cover. Microwave on High for 10 to 12 minutes or until heated through. Top with onion rings. Microwave on High for 1 to 2 minutes longer. Yield: 6 servings.

FILLETS AMANDINE

1 lb. fish fillets
Lemon juice to taste
Salt to taste
1/2 c. slivered almonds
1/2 c. margarine

Rub fillets with lemon juice and salt. Place in 2-quart glass casserole; cover. Microwave on High for 5 to 6 minutes or until fish flakes easily. Combine almonds and margarine in small glass bowl. Microwave on High for 5 to 6 minutes or until lightly browned. Pour over fillets. Yield: 4 servings.

TWICE-BAKED POTATOES

4 med. potatoes, cleaned and dried
1/4 c. margarine
1/2 c. grated Cheddar cheese
1 tbsp. grated onion
1/2 tsp. salt
Pepper to taste
3/4 c. milk
Paprika

Prick potato skins with fork. Microwave on High for 8 minutes; turn potatoes over. Microwave on High for 8 minutes longer. Slice hot potatoes lengthwise; scoop out insides, saving shells. Whip potatoes, margarine, cheese, onion, salt and pepper together. Blend in milk gradually. Spoon potato mixture into shells. Microwave on High for 5 minutes longer. Sprinkle with paprika.

SCALLOPED CORN

2 c. cooked corn
2 eggs, beaten
1 tsp. salt
Pepper to taste
3/4 c. evaporated milk
1/2 c. cracker crumbs
2 tbsp. margarine
1/4 c. sliced green pepper

Combine corn, eggs, salt, pepper and milk in 1 1/2-quart glass casserole. Sprinkle with cracker crumbs. Dot with margarine. Top with green pepper strips. Microwave on High for 8 to 10 minutes, rotating 1/4 turn halfway through cooking. Let stand for 10 minutes. Yield: 4-6 servings.

BUTTERED CABBAGE WEDGES

1/2 med. cabbage, cut into 4 to 6 wedges
1/2 tsp. caraway seed
2 tbsp. butter
Salt

Arrange cabbage wedges in glass baking dish. Add 2 tablespoons water. Sprinkle with caraway seed; cover. Microwave on High for 7 minutes; rotate dish. Microwave on high for 5 to 6 minutes longer or until cabbage is tender. Place butter in small glass bowl. Microwave on High for 30 seconds or until butter is melted; drizzle over cabbage. Sprinkle with salt. Yield: 4-6 servings.

CHEEZY BROCCOLI-RICE CASSEROLE

1 tbsp. dried onion flakes
1 c. cooked rice
1 can cream of mushroom soup
1 pkg. frozen chopped broccoli
Salt and pepper to taste
1 8-oz. jar Cheez Whiz

Add onion flakes to rice before cooking rice. Add cream of mushroom soup to cooked rice. Microwave broccoli using package instructions. Add broccoli to rice mixture. Season with salt and pepper. Top with Cheez Whiz; cover. Microwave on High for 10 minutes or until cheese bubbles. Yield: 6 servings.

BAKED BROWN RICE

1 egg, beaten
1 c. milk
1/2 c. finely chopped parsley
1 clove of garlic, finely chopped
1 sm. onion, minced
2 c. cooked brown rice
1/2 c. sharp grated cheese
Curry powder to taste
Salt to taste

Combine all ingredients; mix well. Pour into greased 7-inch glass ring mold. Microwave on High for 6 to 8 minutes. Let stand for 5 minutes before serving. Yield: 4 servings.

NANCY'S VEGETABLE SOUP

2 cans beef broth
1 1-lb. can mixed vegetables
1 tsp. salt
1 tsp. celery flakes
1/2 tsp. pepper
1 bay leaf

Combine all ingredients with 1 1/2 cups water in 2 1/2-quart glass casserole. Microwave on High for 10 to 12 minutes or until piping hot. Yield: 4-6 servings.

SAVORY CHEESE BREAD

2 3/4 c. flour
2 tbsp. sugar
1/2 tsp. salt
1/2 c. butter
1 pkg. dry yeast
1 c. milk
1 egg, beaten
1 pkg. dry onion soup mix
1 c. shredded Cheddar cheese

Combine flour, sugar, salt and butter in large mixing bowl. Cut through mixture with pastry blender until mixture resembles coarse meal. Dissolve yeast in 1/4 cup warm water. Add dissolved yeast, milk and egg to crumbly mixture. Beat with spoon until well blended. Combine 2 tablespoons soup mix and 1/4 cup cheese; mix well. Set aside. Add remaining soup mix and cheese to batter; stir well. Pour batter into 2 greased 8 x 4 x 3-inch glass loaf dishes. Sprinkle with reserved soup mix mixture. Cover lightly. Let rise in warm place for 1 1/2 to 2 hours or until dough is slightly puffy. Microwave 1 loaf at a time on Low for 10 to 12 minutes, rotating dish 1/2 turn after 5 minutes. Let stand 5 minutes. Place on cooling rack.

ZUCCHINI BREAD

2 c. sugar
3 eggs, beaten
1 c. oil
2 c. grated zucchini
2 c. flour
1/2 tsp. ground cloves
1 tbsp. cinnamon
1/4 tsp. nutmeg
1 tsp. salt
1/4 tsp. baking powder
1 1/2 tsp. soda
2 tsp. vanilla extract
1 c. chopped walnuts

Combine sugar and eggs in large mixing bowl. Add oil and zucchini; mix well. Add remaining ingredients; blend well. Pour into large microwave bundt pan. Microwave on High for 4 minutes; rotate dish. Microwave on High for 4 to 6 minutes longer or until bread begins to pull away from sides. Let stand for 10 to 15 minutes before turning out of pan. Frost if desired.

PEANUT BRITTLE

1 c. fresh peanuts
1 c. sugar
1/2 c. light corn syrup
Pinch of salt
1 tsp. butter
1 tsp. vanilla extract
1 tsp. soda

Combine peanuts, sugar, corn syrup and salt in 1 1/2-quart glass casserole. Microwave on High for 7 to 8 minutes, stirring well after 4 minutes. Add butter and vanilla to syrup, blending well. Microwave on High for 1 to 2 minutes longer. Peanuts will be lightly browned and syrup very hot. Add soda; stir gently until light and foamy. Pour mixture onto lightly greased cookie sheet. Let cool for 30 minutes to 1 hour. Break into small pieces. Store in airtight container. Roasted, salted peanuts may be used but omit salt and add peanuts after first 4 mintues of cooking.

PECAN PIE SUPREME

1 c. dark corn syrup
1/4 c. margarine
1/2 c. (packed) brown sugar
3 eggs, beaten
1/4 tsp. salt
1/2 tsp. cinnamon
1 tsp. vanilla extract
1 c. quick-cooking oats
1/3 c. chopped pecans
1 baked 9-in. pie shell

Combine corn syrup, margarine and brown sugar in 4-cup glass measure. Microwave on High for 3 1/2 minutes or until mixture boils, stirring once. Combine eggs, salt, cinnamon and vanilla in large bowl; beat well. Slowly beat in hot syrup mixture. Stir in oats and pecans. Pour into pie shell. Microwave on High for 3 minutes or until center is puffed, rotating plate twice. Place pie 3 inches from broiler element. Broil for 2 to 3 minutes or until top is slightly browned.

ALL-AMERICAN APPLE CAKE

1 1/2 c. flour
3/4 tsp. soda
3/4 tsp. cinnamon
1/2 tsp. salt
1/4 c. salad oil
3/4 c. sugar
1 egg, beaten
3 tbsp. buttermilk
1 1/2 c. diced apples, peeled
3 tbsp. butter
2 tbsp. milk
1/3 c. (packed) brown sugar
1/4 tsp. vanilla extract
1/2 c. shredded coconut

Sift first 4 ingredients in bowl; set aside. Combine salad oil and sugar; beat until light and fluffy. Add egg; mix well. Add buttermilk and dry ingredients alternately to sugar mixture, beating well after each addition. Beat for 2 minutes or until smooth. Fold in apples. Pour into buttered 8-inch square glass baking dish. Microwave on High for 3 minutes; turn dish. Microwave on High for 3 to 4 minutes longer. Let stand for 5 minutes. Microwave butter in 2-cup glass measure on High until melted. Add remaining ingredients; mix well. Spread over top of hot cake. Place under broiler for 1 to 2 minutes or until mixture bubbles. Serve warm.

GERMAN CHOCOLATE CAKE

1/2 c. butter
1/2 c. milk
1 pkg. coconut-almond or pecan frosting mix
1 pkg. German chocolate cake mix
2 eggs

Place 1/4 cup butter in two 8-inch round glass or plastic cake pans. Microwave each on Roast for 2 minutes or until butter is melted. Stir 1/4 cup milk and 1/2 package frosting mix into each. Set aside. Prepare cake mix with eggs and 1 1/2 cups water according to package directions. Pour half the batter into each prepared pan. Let batter stand for 10 minutes. Microwave one layer at a time on Low for 7 minutes. Microwave on High for 6 minutes or until toothpick comes out clean. Cool for 5 minutes. Loosen edges; invert to cool. Frosting may stick to pan; remove with spatula and spread on cake. Cool to handle; stack layers.

Mincemeat

Mincemeat is an elaborate, zesty-flavored compound of chopped or ground fruits; spices; sugar; and sometimes chopped or ground meat or suet. It is used as an ingredient in baked goods. Packaged mincemeat is commercially available in retail grocery stores.

INGREDIENTS: Dried fruits such as raisins and currants and citrus fruits and rinds are common ingredients, as are sweetly pungent spices like cinnamon, cloves, and nutmeg. When meat is used, it is usually beef. Brandy, rum, or other spirits may be poured over the mixture, which is then allowed to ripen. Favorite variations to classic mincemeat are green tomato mincemeat and pear mincemeat. These derive their names and distinctive flavors from the addition of either green tomatoes or pears.

PREPARATION: Ingredients are combined and mixed well. The mixture is simmered, with frequent stirring, for 1/2 hour. Meat broth may be added as needed. Mincemeat is packed into sterilized jars and sealed.

STORING: Store jars in cool place. Mincemeat packed in jars suitable for freezing may be frozen up to 3 months.

USES: Use in pie fillings, cakes, cookies, tarts, and turnovers.

PEAR MINCEMEAT

7 1/2 lb. pears
1 apple
1 orange
1 lemon
3 lb. sugar
1 tsp. salt
2 lb. raisins
1 c. vinegar
1 tsp. allspice
1 tsp. cloves
1 tsp. cinnamon
1 2 1/2-lb. can crushed pineapple

Peel and core pears and apple; peel and section orange and lemon. Grind pears, apple, orange and lemon; combine with sugar, salt, raisins, vinegar, spices and pineapple. Blend thoroughly. Simmer, stirring occasionally, for 2 hours or until thickened. Pour into hot sterilized jars; seal.

CLASSIC MINCEMEAT

4 lb. cooked ground beef
2 lb. suet, ground
4 lb. seeded raisins
4 lb. whole currants
4 lb. brown sugar
1 lb. ground citron
8 lb. apples, chopped
4 lemons, ground
4 oranges, ground
1 qt. strong coffee
1 tsp. cloves
1 tsp. cinnamon
1 tsp. mace
1 tsp. nutmeg
1/2 tsp. allspice
1 gal. cider
Salt to taste
Meat broth

Combine all ingredients except meat broth; mix well. Simmer, stirring frequently, for 30 minutes; add meat broth to mixture as needed. Pour into sterilized jars; seal. Yield: 14 quarts.

GREEN TOMATO MINCEMEAT

1 peck green tomatoes, coarsely ground
1/2 peck sour apples, coarsely ground
5 lb. brown sugar
1 lb. raisins, coarsely ground
1 lb. currants, coarsely ground
1/2 lb. citron, finely chopped
Juice and rind of 2 lemons
1 tbsp. cinnamon
1 1/2 tsp. cloves
1 1/2 tsp. nutmeg
1 tbsp. salt

Add water to green tomatoes to cover. Bring to a boil; drain. Repeat three times; drain. Add remaining ingredients; mix well. Simmer, stirring frequently, for 1 hour. Pour into sterilized jars; seal.

HOLIDAY CAKE

2 1/2 c. flour
1 1/2 tsp. baking powder
1/2 tsp. soda
1/2 tsp. salt
1 1-lb. jar mincemeat
1 c. white raisins
1 c. chopped nuts
1 c. sugar
1/2 c. melted butter
1 tsp. rum
2 eggs

Sift dry ingredients. Combine mincemeat with raisins, nuts, sugar, butter and rum; add to dry ingredients. Add eggs, one at a time, beating well after each addition. Pour into lightly greased, floured tube pan. Bake at 300 degrees for 1 hour and 30 minutes.

MINCEMEAT DROPS

1 c. shortening
1 1/2 c. sugar
3 eggs, well beaten
1 pkg. mincemeat
3 1/4 c. flour
1 tsp. soda
1/2 tsp. salt

Cream shortening and sugar. Add eggs; beat until mixture is smooth. Crumble mincemeat into egg mixture; mix well. Sift flour, soda and salt. Add to batter; mix well. Drop by teaspoonfuls 2 inches apart on lightly greased cookie sheet. Bake at 400 degrees for 10 to 12 minutes or until lightly browned. Yield: 4 dozen.

MINCEMEAT-APPLESAUCE CAKE

1 pkg. applesauce cake mix
1 1-lb. 12-oz. jar mincemeat
1 1/2 c. chopped nuts
5 eggs
Light corn syrup
1 c. butter
1 pkg. vanilla butter cream frosting mix
1 tbsp. rum flavoring

Combine cake mix, mincemeat, nuts, 3 eggs and 1/4 cup water; blend as cake package directs. Place in greased and floured tube pan. Bake at 350 degrees for 65 to 70 minutes, or until cake tests done. Cool for 15 minutes; remove from pan. Glaze with corn syrup. Blend butter with frosting mix; add remaining eggs and rum flavoring. Beat until fluffy. Refrigerate; form into balls. Refrigerate until serving time. Serve sauce balls on cake.

CHOCOLATE MINCEMEAT COOKIES

2 c. flour
2 tsp. baking soda
1/2 c. vegetable shortening
1/2 tsp. salt
1 c. sugar
3 eggs
1 9-oz. package mincemeat
1 12-oz. package chocolate morsels

Preheat oven to 375 degrees. Sift flour and soda. Blend shortening, salt and sugar; beat in eggs, one at a time, beating well after each addition. Stir in flour mixture, mincemeat and chocolate morsels. Drop by tablespoonfuls onto greased cookie sheet. Bake at 375 degrees for 10 minutes. Yield: 4 dozen cookies.

CREAMY MINCEMEAT PIE

Sifted flour
1/2 tsp. salt
1/3 c. shortening
1/2 c. oats
2 c. prepared mincemeat
1/3 c. (firmly packed) brown sugar
3/4 c. heavy cream, whipped
1/2 c. broken pecans

Sift 3/4 cup flour and salt together; cut in shortening until mixture resembles coarse crumbs. Stir in oats; sprinkle 3 tablespoons water by tablespoonfuls over mixture. Stir lightly with fork until just moistened; add additional water just to blend dough together, if necessary. Form into ball; roll out on lightly floured board to 13-inch circle. Fit loosely into 9-inch pie plate; trim and flute edges. Spoon mincemeat into pie shell. Combine brown sugar and 2 tablespoons flour with cream; blend well. Pour over mincemeat; sprinkle top with pecans. Bake at 425 degrees for 15 minutes; reduce heat to 325 degrees. Bake for 15 minutes longer or until filling is set. Yield: 6 servings.

HOLIDAY CREAM PIE

1 28-oz. jar mincemeat
1 unbaked 9-inch pie shell
3 tbsp. brown sugar
2 tbsp. flour
1 c. heavy cream
3/4 c. chopped pecans

Spread mincemeat in pie shell. Combine sugar and flour; stir in cream. Pour over mincemeat; sprinkle with nuts. Bake at 425 degrees for 40 to 45 minutes.

MINCEMEAT CHIFFON PIE

1 env. unflavored gelatin
1 1-lb. jar mincemeat
3 eggs, separated
2 tbsp. brandy
1 tbsp. grated orange rind
1/2 c. sugar
1 c. heavy cream
1 baked pastry shell

Sprinkle gelatin over 1/4 cup cold water. Combine mincemeat, egg yolks, brandy and orange rind in saucepan; cook, stirring constantly, until heated through. Stir in gelatin; refrigerate for 30 minutes.

Baked Mincemeat Pudding . . . Serve this popular holiday dessert accompanied by ice cream balls.

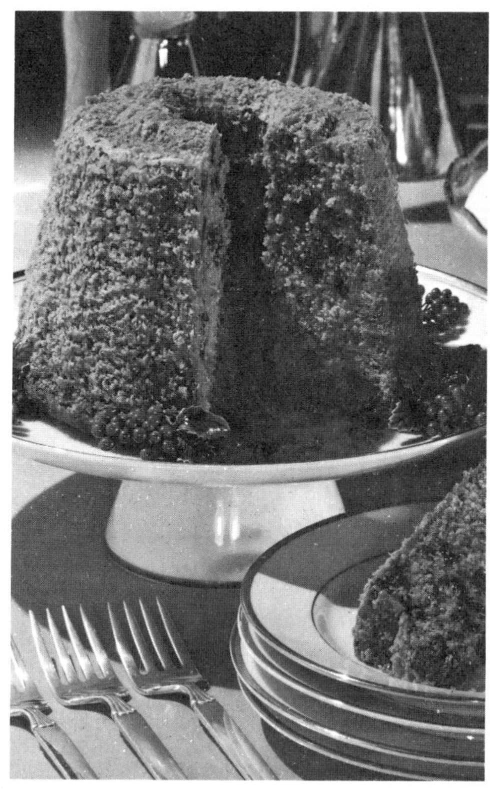

Beat egg whites and sugar until stiff peaks form; fold into mincemeat mixture. Whip cream until soft peaks form. Fold 1/2 of the whipped cream into mincemeat mixture. Pour into pastry shell. Refrigerate for 3 hours; garnish with remaining whipped cream.

BAKED MINCEMEAT PUDDING

2 1/4 c. sifted flour
2 1/2 tsp. baking powder
1 tsp. salt
1/2 c. butter
3/4 c. sugar
2 eggs
2 c. prepared mincemeat
1/4 c. milk

Sift flour with baking powder and salt. Cream butter; add sugar gradually, creaming well. Add eggs; beat until light and fluffy. Add dry ingredients alternately with mincemeat and milk, stirring after each addition to blend well. Pour into greased and floured 2-quart tube pudding mold. Bake at 325 degrees for 1 hour or until done. Let stand in mold for 10 minutes before turning out. Serve warm; top with vanilla ice cream if desired. Yield: 8-10 servings.

Mint

Mint is an aromatic herb with a fruit-like taste and a refreshing aftertaste. Peppermint, spearmint, apple, and pineapple mint are just some of the more than 40 varieties of mint.

AVAILABILITY: Mint is available year-round. Most of the supply is grown domestically. Fresh mint is a popular, perennial garden herb that will grow in almost any soil.

BUYING: Mint is processed and sold in a variety of forms; fresh, green *mint leaves; mint flakes* that are dried and crushed mint leaves; and *mint extract* which is the concentrate of essential oils.

STORING: Like all herbs, mint will retain its exceptional potency if stored in a cool, dry place.

USES: Processed forms of mint are used in numerous products including medicine. *Mint leaves* are used primarily as garnishes for platters and beverages. *Mint flakes* are added to vegetables, appetizers, and cold and hot soups. *Mint extract* is an important flavoring in baking and candy making, as well as in the ever-popular lamb accompaniment, mint jelly.

CANDIED MINT LEAVES

Mint leaves
1 egg white
1/2 c. sugar
6 drops of peppermint oil

Remove mint leaves from stems; coat both sides with slightly beaten egg white. Combine sugar and peppermint oil; dip leaves in sugar, coating well. Place on waxed paper-lined cookie sheet. Bake in 300-degree oven until dry. Use as garnish for fruit salads or cocktails.

AFTER DINNER MINTS

1 egg white
1 tbsp. cream
1 tsp. vanilla
3 drops of peppermint flavoring
Food coloring
1 box confectioners' sugar
1 tsp. (heaping) soft butter

Combine egg white, cream, vanilla, flavoring and food coloring. Add sugar all at once; mix well. Blend in butter; shape right consistency to roll into small balls, adding more sugar, if needed. Arrange balls on waxed paper-lined cookie sheet; press each ball with tines of fork dipped in powdered sugar. Let stand overnight to form crust; pack in tins with waxed paper between each layer. May be frozen and kept for several months.

MINT TAFFY

1 c. sugar
1/2 c. golden syrup
1/2 c. honey
Pinch of cream of tartar
1 tsp. vanilla
2 tbsp. butter
1 tsp. peppermint extract

Combine sugar, syrup and honey in saucepan; cook until sugar is dissolved, stirring constantly. Add cream of tartar; bring to a boil. Boil for about 20 minutes, stirring constantly. Add vanilla, butter and peppermint extract; return to a boil. Pour into buttered pan; let cook until able to handle. Pull until smooth; cut into cushions.

BUTTER MINTS

3 tbsp. soft butter
1/4 c. cream
1/4 tsp. salt
1 tsp. vanilla
2 tsp. peppermint flavoring
1 lb. powdered sugar
Food coloring

Combine butter and cream; stir in salt, vanilla and flavoring. Knead in sugar until mixture is smooth. Tint with food coloring as desired. Shape into small balls; place on cookie sheets. Press mints to flatten. Let stand for 24 hours to dry; store in airtight container.

NO-COOK MINTS

1/3 c. soft margarine
1/3 c. corn syrup
1 tsp. peppermint flavoring
1/2 tsp. salt
4 1/2 c. sifted powdered sugar
Food coloring

Combine margarine, corn syrup, flavoring and salt in large mixing bowl. Add sugar; mix with spoon and hands until smooth. Tint with food coloring, as desired. Shape as desired; store in cool place.

PULLED MINTS

2 c. sugar
1 stick butter
4 drops of food coloring
Several drops of oil of wintergreen

Combine sugar, butter and 1/2 cup water in heavy saucepan. Shake pan or stir lightly with a wooden spoon until sugar has dissolved enough to start cooking; do not stir again. Cook rapidly to 260 degrees on candy thermometer. Pour onto a cold buttered marble slab. Pour food coloring and wintergreen on top of candy; let cool for 2 minutes. Butter hands; pull mints while still hot. Pull until smooth; twist and cut with kitchen shears. Store in airtight container. Do not make on a rainy day.

FAIRY KISSES

2 egg whites
3/4 c. sugar
1 lb. chocolate mints

Preheat oven to 350 degrees. Beat egg whites until stiff, adding sugar gradually. Chop chocolate mints with sharp knife; fold into egg whites. Drop by spoonfuls onto brown paper-lined cookie sheet. Place in oven; turn off oven heat. Let stand until oven is cool. Yield: 60 small cookies.

GRASSHOPPER CREAM CORNUCOPIAS

1/4 c. butter
1/2 c. maple syrup
1/2 c. flour
1 c. heavy cream
2 tbsp. creme de menthe
1 tbsp. white creme de cacao

Combine butter and syrup in saucepan. Bring to a boil over high heat; boil hard for 30 seconds. Remove from heat. Add flour; beat until smooth. Drop batter by level tablespoonfuls about 2 inches apart onto warmed greased baking sheet. Bake at 300 degrees for 9 to 12 minhtes. Let cool slightly; remove each wafer and quickly lap over two edges to form cornucopia. Place on wire rack to cool. Wafers may be returned to oven to soften, if necessary. Beat cream, creme de menthe and creme de cacao together until stiff; do not overbeat. Spoon lightly into cornucopias; place on baking sheet without touching. Freeze until firm. Place in plastic bag until ready to serve. Do not thaw before serving. Cornucopias may be stored in tightly covered container and filled with grasshopper cream at serving time, if desired.

STARLIGHT MINT COOKIES

3 1/4 c. flour
1 tsp. soda
1/2 tsp. salt
1/2 c. butter
1/2 c. shortening
1/2 c. (packed) brown sugar
1 c. sugar
2 eggs
2 tbsp. water
1 tsp. vanilla
1 pkg. thin mint wafers
Walnut halves

Sift flour, soda and salt together. Cream butter and shortening; add sugars gradually. Mix well. Add eggs, water and vanilla; beat well. Blend in sifted ingredients; place in refrigerator to chill thoroughly. Enclose each wafer in 1 tablespoon dough; place 2 inches apart on greased baking sheet. Top with walnut half. Bake at 375 degrees for 10 to 12 minutes.

CREME DE MENTHE MOUSSE

1/2 gal. vanilla ice cream
1 bottle green maraschino cherries
3/4 c. creme de menthe
20 coconut macaroons, crushed
1/2 c. chopped toasted pecans

Soften ice cream slightly; drain and chop cherries. Combine all ingredients; mix well. Pack into covered container; store in freezer until ready to use. Mousse will keep indefinitely.

FROZEN MINT SUPREME

1 c. vanilla wafer crumbs
2/3 c. butter
2 c. powdered sugar
3 eggs, separated
1 tsp. vanilla
2 sq. unsweetened chocolate, melted
1/2 c. chopped nuts
1 qt. mint ice cream, softened

Line 2 ice cube trays with wafer crumbs. Cream butter and sugar until smooth; add egg yolks, vanilla and chocolate. Beat well. Add nuts; fold in stiffly beaten egg whites. Spread chocolate mixture over crumbs; freeze for 3 hours. Spread ice cream over frozen mixture; return to freezer until ready to serve.

MINT ICE CREAM CAKE

1 qt. vanilla ice cream
1 angel food cake
8 chocolate mint patties
1/2 c. chopped nuts
1/2 pt. whipping cream

Soften ice cream slightly; cut cake into 3 layers. Chop mint patties coarsely. Stir chopped patties and nuts into softened ice cream; spread between cake layers. Spread top and side of cake with whipped cream. Freeze until ready to serve.

MINT SQUARES

12 crushed graham crackers
1/4 lb. pillow mints
1 1/2 c. miniature marshmallows
1 c. heavy cream, whipped
2 tbsp. sugar
1 tsp. vanilla
1/3 c. chopped nuts

Place 2/3 of the graham crackers in lightly greased 9 x 9-inch pan. Crush pillow mints. Combine marshmallows, mints, whipped cream, sugar, vanilla and nuts; mix well. Pour over graham cracker crust; sprinkle with remaining crackers. Chill until ready to serve.

CREME DE MENTHE PIE

Color photograph for this recipe on page 491.

1 1/4 c. chocolate wafer crumbs
3/4 c. sugar
1/3 c. melted butter
1 env. unflavored gelatin
1/8 tsp. salt
3 eggs, separated
1/4 c. green creme de menthe
1/4 c. white creme de cacao
1 1/2 c. heavy cream
Chopped pistachio nuts
Chopped cherries

Mix wafer crumbs, 1/4 cup sugar and butter; press into 9-inch pie plate. Bake in 400-degree oven for 5 minutes; cool. Combine gelatin, 1/4 cup sugar and salt in medium saucepan. Beat egg yolks and 1/2 cup cold water together; stir into gelatin mixture. Cook over low heat, stirring constantly, for 3 to 5 minutes or until thickened and gelatin is dissolved. Remove from heat; stir in creme de menthe and creme de cacao. Chill, stirring occasionally, until mixture is consistency of unbeaten egg white. Beat egg whites until stiff but not dry. Add remaining sugar gradually; beat until stiff peaks form. Fold into gelatin mixture. Whip 1 cup cream until stiff; fold into gelatin mixture. Pour into chocolate crust; chill until firm. Whip remaining cream until stiff; arrange on pie in wreath shape. Sprinkle with nuts and cherries.

Mocha

Mocha is a distinctive, full-bodied flavoring that is created from coffee or a coffee and chocolate combination. Mocha may also mean flavored with coffee or coffee and chocolate.

Popular Mocha desserts are cake, pie, torte, mousse, ice cream, parfait, sundaes, tortoni, and pudding. Mocha icings and sauces are also familiar favorites.

Individual recipes for Mocha sweets may specify instant powdered coffee or brewed coffee. Chocolate may be added in the form of squares, chips, pieces, or cocoa powder.

DELICIOUS MOCHA CAKE

1 1/2 c. sugar
1/2 c. shortening
1 egg
1/2 c. cocoa
2 tsp. vanilla
2 c. flour
1 tsp. soda
1 tsp. baking powder
1/2 tsp. salt
1 1/2 c. coffee

Cream sugar and shortening; add egg, cocoa and vanilla. Beat well. Sift dry ingredients together; add to cocoa mixture. Add coffee; beat thoroughly. Pour into greased tube pan. Bake at 350 degrees for 45 minutes. Frost with chocolate frosting, if desired. Yield: 10-12 servings.

MYSTERY MOCHA CAKE

Sugar
1 c. sifted flour
2 tsp. baking powder
1/8 tsp. salt
1 sq. chocolate
2 tbsp. butter
1/2 c. milk
1 tsp. vanilla
1/2 c. (packed) brown sugar
4 tbsp. cocoa
1 c. cold coffee

Sift 3/4 cup sugar, flour, baking powder and salt together. Melt chocolate and butter in saucepan; add milk and vanilla. Add to flour mixture; mix well. Pour into greased pan. Combine 1/4 cup sugar, brown sugar and cocoa; sprinkle over batter. Pour coffee over top. Bake at 350 degrees for 40 minutes. Yield: 8 servings.

MOCHA CHOCOLATE MOLD

2 env. unflavored gelatin
2 tsp. instant coffee
1/2 c. boiling water
1 c. semisweet chocolate chips
1 tbsp. sugar
1/8 tsp. salt
1/2 tsp. vanilla extract
2 egg yolks
1 c. heavy cream
1 1/2 c. crushed ice, drained

Place 1/4 cup cold water, gelatin and instant coffee in blender; add 1/2 cup boiling water. Cover; blend at low speed for 1 minute or until gelatin is dissolved. Add chocolate chips, sugar, salt and vanilla. Blend at high speed until mixture is smooth. Add egg yolks, cream and crushed ice; blend until mixture begins to thicken. Pour into 1-quart mold immediately. Let stand for 10 minutes before serving. Yield: 6 servings.

MOCHA CHERRY DESSERT

24 lge. marshmallows
1/2 c. strong coffee
1 c. whipping cream
1 No. 2 can Bing cherries
4 tbsp. red wine

Melt marshmallows in coffee over low heat. Chill. Whip cream until stiff peaks form; blend into chilled mixture. Pour into eight dessert cups. Chill. Drain cherries, reserving juice. Pour juice in saucepan; simmer until liquid is reduced to slightly more than half. Combine cherries, juice and wine. Pour over dessert to serve. Yield: 8 servings.

MOCHA ICEBOX CAKE

1/2 c. butter
1 1/2 c. powdered sugar
4 egg yolks
1 tsp. vanilla
2 tbsp. instant coffee
1/4 c. rum
2 c. heavy cream, whipped
2 doz. ladyfingers
2 doz. crushed coconut macaroons
Toasted almonds

Cream butter, sugar, egg yolks, vanilla, instant coffee and rum. Add half the whipped cream. Line pan with ladyfingers. Pour half the creamed mixture over ladyfingers; top with macaroons. Cover with remaining creamed mixture. Refrigerate for 24 hours. Top with remaining whipped cream and almonds.

MOCHA ANGEL CAKE

1 angel food cake
1 pkg. instant chocolate pudding mix
1 c. heavy cream
1 c. cold milk
2 tsp. instant coffee

Cut angel food cake into 3 layers. Blend chocolate pudding mix, cream, milk and instant coffee; beat for 1 minute or until thick enough to spread. Fill cake layers; garnish with chocolate shot or curls. Freeze until ready to serve. Yield: 12 servings.

MOCHA CLOUD

2 tsp. vanilla
1/4 tsp. cream of tartar
Dash of salt
4 egg whites, at room temperature
1 1/4 c. sugar
2 6-oz. packages semisweet chocolate pieces
1 tbsp. powdered instant coffee
1 c. whipped cream

Add 1 teaspoon vanilla, cream of tartar and salt to egg whites; beat until frothy. Add sugar gradually; beat until stiff peaks form. Spread mixture on paper-covered baking sheets in four 7 1/2-inch circles. Bake at 275 degrees for 1 hour. Turn off oven; let circles dry in oven for 1 hour. Melt chocolate over hot water; stir in coffee and 1/4 cup boiling water. Beat until creamy and slightly cooled; fold in whipped cream and remaining vanilla. Stack meringue circles together with filling between each, spreading filling to edge. Chill; cut into wedges to serve. Yield: 6 servings.

MOCHA FROTH

1 env. unflavored gelatin
1/2 c. sugar
1 tbsp. instant coffee
1 tbsp. cocoa
1/8 tsp. salt
1 tsp. vanilla
2 egg whites

Soften gelatin in 2 tablespoons cold water; set aside. Combine sugar, coffee, cocoa and salt. Add 1 1/2 cups boiling water; add gelatin mixture. Stir to dissolve. Add vanilla. Refrigerate until slightly thickened; add egg whites. Beat cocoa mixture at high speed with electric mixer until thickened. Refrigerate. Serve with slightly sweetened whipped cream, if desired. Yield: 8 servings.

MOCHA ICE CREAM

1 lge. can evaporated milk
30 marshmallows
1 c. strong coffee
1 c. crushed vanilla wafers
1/2 c. chopped nuts

Chill milk in refrigerator tray until crystals form at edges. Whip thoroughly. Melt marshmallows in coffee over low heat; cool. Combine whipped milk and coffee mixture. Sprinkle half the crushed wafers in two refrigerator trays; pour in half the coffee mixture. Sprinkle remaining wafers on top; add remaining coffee mixture. Sprinkle top with chopped nuts; freeze.

MOCHA COFFEE PARFAIT

1/2 pt. whipping cream
1/4 c. sugar
1 tbsp. instant coffee
2 pt. chocolate ice cream

Combine cream, sugar and coffee; stir until coffee dissolves. Chill thoroughly. Beat until mixture holds soft peaks. Spoon alternate layers of ice cream and whipped cream into chilled parfait glasses. Serve at once or store in freezer. Yield: 4-6 servings.

MOCHA FREEZE

1 1/2 c. graham cracker crumbs
3/4 c. sugar
1/2 c. chopped walnuts
1/4 c. butter, softened
1 c. evaporated milk
3 egg whites, at room temperature
1/8 tsp. salt
3 tbsp. instant chocolate drink powder
1 tsp. instant coffee

Combine crumbs, 1/4 cup sugar and walnuts; add butter, mixing well. Sprinkle 2 cups crumb mixture in waxed paper-lined 9-inch square pan; press down well. Freeze. Chill evaporated milk in refrigerator tray until soft ice crystals form around edges. Beat egg whites and salt until frothy; beat in remaining sugar gradually. Whip chilled milk in chilled bowl until stiff peaks form; add chocolate drink powder and coffee. Fold into meringue. Spread over crumb mixture lightly; sprinkle remaining crumbs on top. Freeze overnight. Cut into squares.

MOCHA-NUT TORTONI

2 egg whites
1/2 c. sugar
2 c. heavy cream
2 tbsp. instant coffee
2 egg yolks, slightly beaten
2 tsp. vanilla
1/4 c. semisweet chocolate pieces
1/2 c. finely chopped nuts

Beat egg whites until stiff peaks form; add 1/4 cup sugar gradually, beating well. Whip cream with remaining sugar and coffee until stiff peaks form; add egg yolks and vanilla. Fold into egg whites. Melt chocolate over hot, not boiling water; cool slightly. Fold chocolate and nuts into egg white mixture. Pour into freezer trays. Freeze. Remove from freezer; serve immediately. Yield: 12-14 servings.

MOCHA PEANUT CLUSTERS

1/3 c. butter
1 c. chocolate pieces
16 marshmallows
1 tbsp. instant coffee
2 c. chopped, salted peanuts

Melt butter, chocolate pieces and marshmallows in double boiler. Stir occasionally; cook until mixture is creamy. Add instant coffee. Remove from heat; stir in peanuts. Drop by teaspoonfuls onto waxed paper or cookie sheet. Cool. Yield: 48 clusters.

PARTY MOCHA TORTE

4 oz. sweet cooking chocolate
1 tbsp. strong coffee
1/4 c. butter
1/2 c. sugar
6 eggs, separated
1/2 tsp. baking powder
Pinch of salt
3 tbsp. sifted flour

Melt chocolate in coffee. Cream butter and sugar; add egg yolks, one at a time, beating constantly. Add cooled chocolate. Sift dry ingredients; add alternately with beaten egg whites to chocolate mixture. Bake in 2 buttered and floured cake pans at 350 degrees for 25 minutes. Cool; turn out carefully.

Frosting

5 oz. chocolate	*3 beaten egg yolks*
3 tbsp. sugar	*3/4 pt. whipped cream*
Pinch of salt	

Combine chocolate, sugar, salt and 3 tablespoons water; cook until smooth. Cool slightly; add egg yolks, one at a time. Cool thoroughly; add whipped cream. Spread between layers and on top of torte. Chill for 4 to 8 hours. Yield: 6-8 servings.

MOCHA SUPREME

1 12-oz. package chocolate chips	*7 eggs, separated*
2 tbsp. instant coffee	*1 tsp. vanilla*
2 tbsp. sugar	*1 8 1/2-oz. package chocolate wafers, crushed*
1/8 tsp. salt	

Combine chips, coffee, sugar, salt and 2 tablespoons water in saucepan; melt over low heat. Remove from heat; add egg yolks and vanilla. Mix together thoroughly. Beat egg whites until stiff peaks form; fold into chocolate mixture. Place 1/3 of crumbs in buttered 8-inch baking pan; spread half the chocolate mixture on top. Place 1/3 of the crumbs over chocolate mixture; freeze for 1 hour. Remove from freezer; add remaining chocolate mixture and remaining crumbs. Chill in freezer for 1 hour longer. Garnish with whipped cream before serving. Yield: 9 servings.

Mocha Coffee Parfait . . . Chocolate ice cream and coffee whipped cream in alternate layers.

MOCHA CHIFFON PIE

1 1/2 c. flour	*1 1/4 c. milk*
3/4 c. (scant) shortening	*3 eggs, separated*
1 env. unflavored gelatin	*2 tbsp. instant coffee*
Sugar	*1/2 c. heavy cream, whipped*

Place flour in bowl; cut in shortening. Add 1/4 cup cold water; mix. Roll dough out; fit into 9-inch pie plate. Bake at 425 degrees for about 12 minutes. Cool. Soften gelatin in 1/4 cup cold water; set aside. Combine 1/3 cup sugar, milk, egg yolks and coffee in saucepan; cook, stirring constantly, until thick. Stir in gelatin mixture. Cool. Beat egg whites with 3/4 cup sugar until stiff peaks form. Fold whipped cream and egg whites into cooled mixture. Pour filling into crust. Let stand for 4 hours before serving. Yield: 6 servings.

Molasses

Molasses is a thick, rich syrup separated from raw sugar during refining. It contains calcium and iron. (3 1/2 ounces light molasses = 252 calories; 3 1/2 ounces dark molasses = 232 calories)

KINDS: There are four primary types of molasses. *Light molasses* and *dark molasses,* derived from different stages of sugar refining, are most commonly used in cookery. Light molasses is the mildest of all types. Dark molasses is heavier and less sweet. *Blackstrap molasses* is a bitter, unpalatable waste product of sugar manufacturing. It is rarely used in cooking. *Unsulphured molasses* is not a byproduct of sugar refining. It is specially manufactured from the juice of sun-ripened sugar cane. Unlike light and dark molasses, it contains no sulphur dioxide.

AVAILABILITY: *Light and dark*–Sold year-round, bottled and canned, in retail grocery stores. *Blackstrap*–Sold in some health food stores. *Unsulphured*–Sold year-round in large-mouthed jars in retail grocery stores.

STORING: Keep unopened bottles, cans, and jars 1 to 2 months.

PREPARATION: *To substitute molasses for sugar*–Because molasses is richer than sugar it should replace no more than 1/2 the amount of sugar specified in recipe. In baked products, substitute 1 cup molasses for 1 cup sugar. Add 1/2 teaspoon baking soda for each cup molasses to neutralize acidity of syrup. If recipe specifies baking powder, omit it or reduce quantity. Because molasses contains liquid, reduce water, milk, or other liquid specified in recipe by 1/4 cup for 1 cup molasses. *To measure* molasses–Grease measuring container. Pour syrup into container, or spoon it into container to level mark. Scrape out all syrup from cup when adding molasses to mixture.

USES: Use as sugar substitute. Serve *light* molasses as table syrup. Use *light, dark, and unsulphured* molasses in biscuits, breads, cakes, pies, cookies, doughnuts, candies, puddings, and curried fruits.

ARABIAN RIBBON CAKE

3 c. sifted cake flour
3 tsp. baking powder
1/2 tsp. salt
2/3 c. butter
1 1/2 c. sugar
3 eggs, separated
1 1/4 c. milk
1 tsp. vanilla
1 1/2 tsp. cinnamon
1/4 tsp. cloves
1/2 tsp. mace
1/2 tsp. nutmeg
3 tbsp. molasses

Sift flour with baking powder and salt 3 times. Cream butter. Add sugar; cream until fluffy. Add egg yolks one at a time, beating well after each addition. Add flour mixture alternately with milk, beating after each addition, until smooth. Add vanilla. Beat egg whites until soft peaks form. Stir into batter quickly. Fill 1 greased 9-inch layer pan with 1/3 of the batter. Add spices and molasses to remaining batter; blend well. Pour into 2 greased 9-inch layer pans. Bake at 375 degrees for 20 to 25 minutes. Cool.

Raisin-Orange Filling

3 tbsp. flour
1 tbsp. orange rind
3/4 c. water
2 c. seeded raisins, ground
1/2 c. sugar
1/2 c. orange juice
Pinch of salt
2/3 c. chopped nuts, toasted

Combine all ingredients except nuts in saucepan. Simmer for 5 minutes or until thickened, stirring constantly. Add nuts; cool. Spread filling between cake layers, placing white layer between spice layers.

Tart Lemon Frosting

4 tbsp. butter
1 tsp. lemon rind
3 c. confectioners' sugar
3 tbsp. lemon juice
Pinch of salt

Cream butter and lemon rind. Add some of the sugar gradually, blending after each addition. Add remaining sugar alternately with lemon juice, mixing well. Add salt. Spread on top and side of cake. Yield: 6-10 servings.

NEW ORLEANS MOLASSES CAKE

1/4 lb. butter, melted
1/2 c. sugar
1 c. dark molasses
1 tsp. cinnamon
1 tsp. ginger
1 tsp. cloves
2 tsp. soda
2 1/2 c. flour
2 eggs, beaten

Cream butter and sugar; add molasses and spices. Dissolve soda in 1 cup boiling water; stir into creamed mixture. Stir in flour; add eggs, blending well. Spoon batter into 2 greased and floured layer cake pans. Bake at 350 degrees for about 30 minutes. Frost if desired.

SHOOFLY CAKE

3 c. flour
1 c. shortening
1 c. sugar
1 tsp. soda
1 c. molasses

Mix first 3 ingredients until crumbly; reserve 1/2 cup crumbs. Mix soda, molasses and 1 cup hot water; stir into remaining crumbs. Spoon batter into layer cake pan; sprinkle with reserved crumbs. Bake at 350 degrees for 40 minutes. Serve warm or cold.

MOLASSES-PEANUT BRITTLE

2 c. sugar
1 c. light corn syrup
1/4 c. dark molasses
2 tbsp. butter
2 c. salted peanuts
1 tbsp. soda

Combine sugar, syrup and 1/2 cup water in 3-quart saucepan. Bring to a boil, stirring until sugar is dissolved. Cook to hard-crack stage or to 290 degrees on candy thermometer. Stir in molasses and butter; cook for 30 seconds. Remove from heat; stir in peanuts and soda quickly. Mix thoroughly; pour onto large greased cookie sheet immediately. Cool; break into pieces. Yield: 2 pounds.

MOLASSES BAR COOKIES

6 tbsp. shortening
1 c. sugar
2 eggs, beaten
1/3 c. molasses
1 tsp. cinnamon
1/2 tsp. nutmeg
1/2 tsp. ginger
1/4 tsp. salt
3/4 tsp. soda
2 c. flour
Jelly

Cream shortening and sugar; add eggs, reserving 2 tablespoons egg. Add remaining ingredients except jelly. Place on floured board; divide into 4 parts. Roll up each part; place on greased baking sheet. Flatten each roll; spread reserved egg over top. Bake at 350 degrees for 15 to 20 minutes. Cool; cut into bars. Make depressions in center of warm cookies. Fill depressions with jelly. Yield: 3 dozen.

OLD-FASHIONED MOLASSES DROP COOKIES

1 c. butter
1 c. sugar
3 eggs, beaten
1/2 c. molasses
3 c. flour
1 tsp. soda
1 tsp. cinnamon
1 tsp. cloves
1 tsp. nutmeg
1/2 c. sour milk
1/2 c. raisins
1/2 c. chopped walnuts

Cream butter and sugar; add eggs and molasses. Combine flour, soda and spices. Add flour mixture and sour milk to molasses mixture alternately. Fold in raisins and walnuts. Drop by spoonfuls on greased baking sheet. Bake at 350 degrees for 15 to 20 minutes.

SOFT MOLASSES COOKIES

2/3 c. shortening
1 1/2 c. (packed) brown sugar
1 egg, beaten
1/2 c. molasses
1 tsp. vanilla
3 1/2 c. flour
1 tsp. soda
1 tsp. baking powder
2 tsp. cinnamon
1 tsp. ground cloves
1/2 tsp. ginger
1 tsp. salt
2/3 c. sour milk

Cream shortening; add sugar gradually, beating until light. Add egg, molasses and vanilla; blend well. Sift dry ingredients together; add to creamed mixture alternately with milk. Drop by teaspoonfuls onto greased baking sheet. Bake at 375 degrees for 10 to 12 minutes. Yield: 8 dozen cookies.

MOLASSES-SUGAR COOKIES

3/4 c. shortening
1 c. sugar
1 egg
2 tsp. soda
1/4 c. molasses
2 c. flour
1/2 tsp. salt
1/2 tsp. cloves
1 tsp. cinnamon

Cream shortening and sugar; add egg. Add soda to molasses; add to creamed mixture. Sift flour, salt, cloves and cinnamon together; stir into molasses mixture. Form into small balls; place on greased baking sheet. Flatten with glass dipped in additional sugar. Bake at 375 degrees for 8 to 10 minutes. Yield: 40-45 cookies.

HOLIDAY HERMITS

3/4 c. soft butter
1 1/2 c. (packed) light brown sugar
1/2 c. light molasses
3 eggs
4 c. sifted cake flour
1 tsp. salt
1 tsp. cinnamon
1 tsp. nutmeg
1/2 tsp. cloves
1/2 tsp. allspice
1/2 tsp. mace
1/4 c. strong coffee
1 c. chopped nuts
1 c. raisins
1 c. currants

Cream butter and sugar until fluffy. Beat in molasses. Add eggs, one at a time, beating well after each addition. Sift flour, salt and spices together. Add to creamed mixture alternately with coffee, beating until smooth. Fold in nuts and fruit carefully. Line 15 x 10 x 1-inch pan with waxed paper. Pour batter into prepared pan, smoothing carefully into corners. Bake in 350-degree oven for about 20 minutes. Turn out on rack; remove waxed paper. Cut loaf into squares. Yield: 3 dozen bars.

MOLASSES CURRIED FRUIT

1 1-lb. can cling peach halves
1 1-lb. can pear halves
1 1-lb. can whole unpeeled apricots
1 20-oz. can pineapple slices
1/2 c. unsulphured molasses
1/4 c. vinegar
1 3-in. stick cinnamon
2 tsp. curry powder
6 maraschino cherries

Drain syrup from fruits into saucepan. Bring to a boil; boil rapidly until reduced to 3/4 cup liquid. Add molasses, vinegar, cinnamon and curry powder; bring to a boil. Add drained fruits; simmer for 5 minutes. Spoon into serving bowl; garnish with cherries. Yield: 12 servings.

MOLASSES CRUMB PIES

3 c. flour
1 c. sugar
1 c. margarine
1 tsp. soda
1 c. molasses
3 8-in. baked pie shells

Combine flour, sugar and margarine until of crumb consistency. Reserve 1 cup crumbs for topping. Stir soda into 1 cup hot water. Add molasses; stir until mixture foams. Pour into remaining flour mixture; mix well. Pour filling into pie shells. Bake at 325 degrees for 8 minutes. Sprinkle reserved crumbs over pies; bake for about 17 minutes longer.

OLD-FASHIONED MOLASSES PIE

1 1/4 c. molasses
2 tbsp. butter
4 eggs
2 tbsp. flour
2/3 c. sugar
1 unbaked pastry shell

Bring molasses and butter to a boil in saucepan. Beat eggs until light and fluffy. Mix flour and sugar with eggs; add to molasses mixture. Pour filling into pie shell. Bake at 350 degrees for 30 minutes or until set. Yield: 8 servings.

SPICY MOLASSES PIE

3/4 c. flour
1/2 c. (packed) brown sugar
1/8 tsp. nutmeg
1/8 tsp. ginger
1/8 tsp. cloves
1/2 tsp. cinnamon
1/4 tsp. salt
2 tbsp. shortening
1/2 tbsp. soda
1/2 c. molasses
1 egg yolk, beaten
1 unbaked 9-in. pastry shell

Combine flour, sugar, spices and salt; blend in shortening until crumbly. Dissolve soda in 3/4 cup boiling water; combine soda mixture, molasses and egg yolk. Alternate layers of crumb mixture and egg mixture in pastry shell; ending with crumb mixture on top. Bake at 450 degrees until crust edges start to brown. Reduce oven temperature to 350 degrees; bake for 20 minutes longer. Yield: 8 servings.

PENNSYLVANIA DUTCH SHOOFLY PIES

1 tsp. soda
1 1/2 c. dark molasses
3 c. flour
1 c. (packed) brown sugar
1/2 c. shortening
1 tsp. salt
2 unbaked 9-in. pie crusts

Dissolve soda in 1 1/2 cups boiling water; add molasses. Blend flour, sugar, shortening and salt until of cornmeal consistency. Spoon molasses mixture into pie crusts; top with crumb mixture. Bake at 350 degrees for 45 minutes.

HOLIDAY MOLASSES STEAMED PUDDING

1 c. buttermilk
1 tsp. (heaping) soda
1/2 c. sugar
1/4 tsp. salt
4 tbsp. molasses
1 egg, beaten
1 3/4 c. vegetable shortening, melted
1 c. scalded raisins, cooled
2 c. flour
2 egg yolks
1 1/2 c. confectioners' sugar
Juice of 1 lemon
1/2 pt. cream, whipped

Mix buttermilk and soda together until foaming. Add sugar, salt, molasses, egg, shortening, raisins and flour, stirring gently. Pour into greased angel food cake pan. Place on rack in steamer over water. Steam for 2 hours. Beat egg yolks until lemon colored; add confectioners' sugar gradually, beating well. Stir in lemon juice; fold in cream. Serve sauce with pudding. Yield: 8 servings.

SPICY MOLASSES PUDDING

3 c. flour
1 c. raisins
2/3 c. molasses
1 c. (scant) milk
1/3 c. butter, melted
1/2 tsp. cinnamon
1/4 tsp. cloves
1/4 tsp. nutmeg
1 tsp. salt
1 tsp. soda

Combine flour, raisins, molasses, milk, butter, spices, salt and soda. Spoon into greased mold. Place mold on rack in steamer over enough boiling water to come 1/2 of the way up side of mold. Steam for 3 hours. Serve with cream if desired.

STEAMED MOLASSES PUDDING

3/4 c. seedless raisins
1 1/2 c. sifted flour
3/4 tsp. soda
3/4 tsp. cinnamon
3/4 tsp. ginger
3/4 tsp. salt
2 tbsp. butter
3/4 c. molasses
1 egg, beaten

Cover raisins with hot water in saucepan; cook for 5 minutes or until plump. Drain and chop. Sift flour, soda, cinnamon, ginger and salt together. Combine 1/3 cup boiling water and butter; let stand until butter is melted. Stir in molasses and egg. Resift dry ingredients; add to molasses mixture. Add raisins; beat until blended. Pour into 6 greased 8-ounce molds, filling each mold 1/2 full. Cover tightly with double thickness of waxed paper. Place molds on rack in large kettle; pour enough water into kettle to come halfway up sides of molds. Cover kettle. Steam for 1 hour over boiling water, adding additional water if needed. Cool molds for 5 minutes; loosen around edges with knife. Unmold onto heated serving plate. Yield: 6 servings.

Mushroom

Mushrooms are fleshy fungi that are classified as vegetables in cookery. Relative newcomers to America, mushrooms have been cultivated in this country for only 100 years. They are high in the B vitamins, protein, iron, and other trace minerals but are low in calories. (1 pound fresh mushrooms = 60 calories)

AVAILABILITY: Fresh mushrooms are available year-round with the greatest supplies marketed from September to June. Canned mushrooms are available year-round whole, sliced, chopped, and in stems and pieces, as are frozen and dried mushrooms.

BUYING: Look for firm dry mushrooms. Tiny brown spots or opened caps are indications of ripeness.

STORING: Fresh mushrooms store well for 2-3 days. Do not wash. Place on a tray and cover with dampened paper towel. Place tray in refrigerator so that air can circulate completely around mushrooms. Remoisten the towel each day of storage. Cooked mushrooms can be refrigerated in a covered dish for several days. *To freeze* mushrooms, place unopened container of fresh mushrooms in freezer without any precleaning or preparation. Whole fresh mushrooms may also be frozen in plastic bags or freezer containers. Freeze for one month. Or, broil or saute mushrooms until half-cooked. Cool and place round side down in freezer container. Seal, label, and freeze. To prepare later, thaw and complete broiling or sauteeing.

PREPARATION: Wipe fresh mushrooms clean with a moistened cloth or wash them quickly in cold running water to remove sand and soil. Never soak or peel mushrooms. Either slice lengthwise, from the cap through the stem, or separate stem from cap. Prepare only those mushrooms to be cooked immediately, and do not let them stand. *To saute*—Slice mushrooms in half lengthwise. Heat enough butter to prevent sticking in a heavy skillet. Add mushrooms and reduce heat; cook 5-10 minutes. *To broil*—Wash mushrooms, remove stems, and rub caps with butter. Set caps round side up in a baking pan and place in preheated broiler for 4 minutes. Remove, place round side down, and return to broiler for 5 minutes. Just before serving, add butter, salt, pepper, and lemon juice and heat under broiler.

USES: Mushrooms are used in soups, sauces, gravies, or in meat, poultry, seafood, vegetable, and egg dishes. They are served in omelets, casseroles, sandwiches, and with shish kabobs. Mushrooms caps can be stuffed or served on toast.

MUSHROOM APPETIZER

Color photograph for this recipe on page 306.

3/4 lb. small fresh mushrooms
6 tbsp. olive oil
3 tbsp. white vinegar
1 tsp. oregano leaves
1 tsp. salt
1/2 tsp. sugar
1/4 tsp. pepper
1/4 c. finely chopped onion
2 tbsp. diced pimento
1/2 clove of garlic, minced

Trim stems from mushrooms. Cover with boiling water; let stand for 1 minute. Drain. Immerse in ice water until completely chilled; drain thoroughly. Combine oil, vinegar, oregano, salt, sugar and pepper in small bowl; mix well. Stir in onion, pimento and garlic. Place alternate layers of mushrooms and vinegar mixture into 1 quart jar, cover. Chill thoroughly. Serve as appetizer or side dish. Mushrooms keep for several weeks in refrigerator. Two 6 or 8-ounce cans whole mushrooms, drained, may be substituted for fresh mushrooms.

CAPERED MUSHROOMS

1 3-oz. can sliced mushrooms
1 tbsp. chopped onion
1 clove garlic, minced
3 tbsp. Italian dressing
1 tsp. capers

Drain mushrooms. Combine mushrooms, onion, garlic, Italian dressing and capers in a small covered container. Marinate for 1 to 2 days in refrigerator.

PICKLED MUSHROOMS

2 6-oz. cans broiled mushrooms
1 c. vinegar
2 tsp. pickling spice
3/4 c. (packed) dark brown sugar

Drain mushrooms; reserve 1/2 cup liquid. Place mushrooms in quart jar. Combine vinegar, pickling spice, reserved liquid and brown sugar in saucepan; bring to a boil. Reduce heat; simmer for 5 minutes. Pour over mushrooms. Refrigerate for 2 days.

MARINATED MUSHROOMS

1/4 c. vinegar
1 clove of garlic, split
2 tbsp. lemon juice
1 sm. bay leaf
1/4 tsp. salt
Freshly ground pepper
3 tbsp. olive oil
1 tbsp. catsup
1 4-oz. can mushroom caps, drained

Combine vinegar, garlic, lemon juice, bay leaf, salt and pepper; boil for 15 minutes. Cool. Add olive oil and catsup; pour over mushrooms. Cover; refrigerate for at least 12 hours.

PIQUANT MUSHROOMS

1 lb. fresh mushrooms
1 clove of garlic, crushed
3 tsp. Italian seasoning
1 tsp. salt
1/2 tsp. pepper
1 c. red wine vinegar
Salad oil

Slice mushrooms; place in 2-quart jar. Add garlic, Italian seasoning, salt, pepper and vinegar. Fill jar with oil; place lid on jar. Shake well. Refrigerate overnight. Jar may be inverted several times before serving.

MUSHROOM-CHEESE CANAPÉS

1/4 lb. fresh mushrooms, sliced thin
1 tbsp. butter
1 8-oz. package cream cheese
1 tsp. minced onion
Salt and pepper to taste
Cream
Sm. bread rounds

Saute mushrooms in butter for 5 to 10 minutes or until crisp-tender; mix with cream cheese and onion. Add salt, pepper and enough cream to soften. Toast bread rounds on one side; spread untoasted side with mushroom mixture. Refrigerate until ready to use. Arrange on baking sheets; broil 3 to 4 inches from source of heat until puffy and lightly browned. Serve immediately.

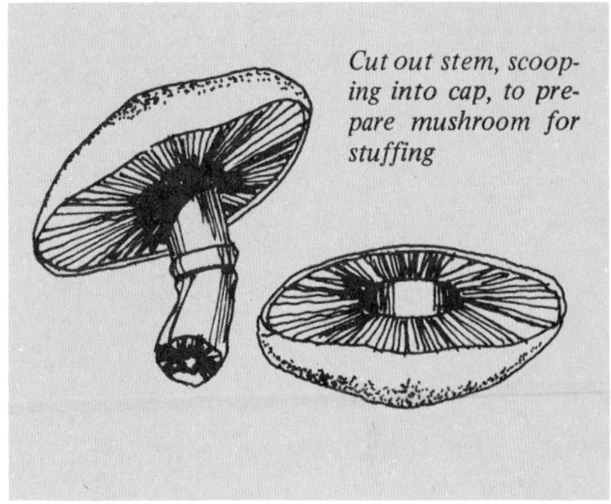

Cut out stem, scooping into cap, to prepare mushroom for stuffing

MUSHROOM MITES

24 lge. mushrooms
1/4 lb. hot bulk sausage
1/4 lb. mild bulk sausage

Remove stems from mushrooms; wash thoroughly. Combine sausages; blend well. Stuff tops of mushrooms. Broil 3 to 4 inches from source of heat until sausage is cooked and tops are lightly browned. Serve immediately.

MUSHROOM ROLL-UPS

1 lb. mushrooms
1/4 c. finely chopped celery
1 med. onion, finely chopped
Butter
1 tbsp. Worcestershire sauce
1/2 tsp. salt
12 slices bread

Chop mushrooms coarsely; saute mushrooms, celery and onion in 2 tablespoons butter until mushrooms are tender. Add Worcestershire sauce and salt. Remove crusts from bread; roll slices thin. Spread mushroom mixture on bread; roll up diagonally. Cut slices in half; brush with butter. Bake at 400 degrees until lightly browned. Serve immediately.

SPICED MUSHROOM AND CELERY SALAD

1/2 lb. fresh mushrooms
2 c. sliced celery
2 1/2 tbsp. olive oil
2 tbsp. lemon juice
3/4 tsp. salt
1/4 tsp. sugar
1/8 tsp. ground white pepper
1/8 tsp. onion salt
1/8 tsp. instant garlic powder

Slice mushrooms. Combine mushrooms and celery in salad bowl. Mix oil, lemon juice, salt, sugar, white pepper, onion salt and garlic powder together, blending well. Pour dressing over mushrooms and celery, coating well. Serve on lettuce-lined salad plates. Yield: 6 servings.

Spiced Mushroom and Celery Salad . . . An onion and garlic dressing accompanies this salad.

MUSHROOM SANDWICHES

Fresh mushrooms
Thinly sliced bread
Butter
Mayonnaise
Grated onion to taste

Chop mushrooms fine; remove crusts from bread. Saute mushrooms in small amount of butter for 10 minutes; cool. Add mayonnaise to moisten and onion. Spread bread with butter; spread with mushroom mixture. Roll; toast. Serve hot.

MUSHROOM SOUP

1 lb. fresh mushrooms
3 slices bacon, diced
2 tbsp. flour
1 sm. onion, chopped
1 can sauerkraut juice
Salt and pepper to taste

Cook mushrooms in 1 quart water until tender. Drain; reserve liquid. Fry bacon until partially done. Add flour; cook until lightly browned. Add onion; saute, stirring constantly, for 5 minutes. Combine sauerkraut juice with reserved liquid; season with salt and pepper. Bring to a boil; add 1/2 cup sauerkraut juice mixture to bacon mixture gradually. Simmer, stirring constantly, until mixture is smooth. Add remaining sauerkraut liquid gradually. Add mushrooms; simmer, stirring constantly, until well blended and heated through.

MUSHROOM SOUP WITH WHIPPED CREAM

1 lb. mushrooms, chopped
1/4 lb. butter
3 tbsp. flour
Pinch of salt
1 qt. milk, warmed
1 bay leaf
1/2 pt. heavy cream, whipped

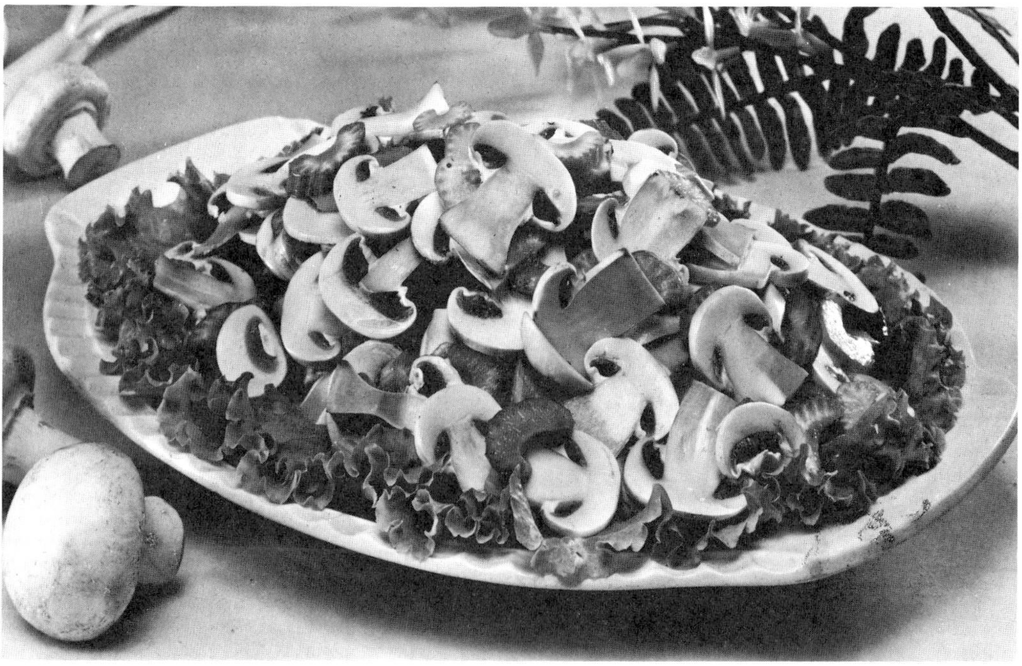

Saute mushrooms in butter over low heat until tender and golden brown. Add flour and salt; stir until smooth. Stir in milk; add bay leaf. Simmer, stirring constantly, until thickened; remove bay leaf. Fold in whipped cream. Garnish with chopped parsley.

CLUB MUSHROOM CASSEROLE

1 lb. fresh mushrooms, sliced
1/2 c. butter
1/3 c. flour
3 c. milk
2 tsp. Worcestershire sauce
1 1/2 tsp. salt
1/4 tsp. pepper
4 hard-cooked eggs, sliced
1/2 c. diced green pepper
1 4-oz. can pimento, diced
2 c. shredded process cheese

Saute mushrooms in butter; remove from pan. Add flour to remaining butter in pan; add milk gradually. Cook, stirring constantly, until thickened; add mushrooms and remaining ingredients except cheese. Place in greased 2-quart casserole. Bake at 350 degrees for 30 minutes or until browned; top with cheese. May be served over hot rice or toast. Yield: 6-8 servings.

MUSHROOMS AND EGGS IN CHEESE SAUCE

Color photograph for this recipe on page 73.

1 1/2 c. sliced mushrooms
1 tbsp. lemon juice
1/4 c. butter
1/2 c. chopped celery
1/2 c. chopped green pepper
1/4 c. chopped onion
2 tbsp. all-purpose flour
1/2 tsp. salt
Dash of pepper
1 c. milk
1 c. shredded Cheddar cheese
1/4 tsp. Worcestershire sauce
3 hard-cooked eggs
Rice
Chow mein noodles

Toss mushrooms with lemon juice. Melt butter in chafing dish blazer pan. Add mushrooms, celery, green pepper and onion; saute until almost tender. Stir in flour, salt and pepper; remove from heat. Stir in milk gradually; cook over medium heat, stirring constantly, until thickened. Cook for 2 minutes longer; remove from heat. Add cheese and Worcestershire sauce; stir until cheese is melted. Reserve 1 egg yolk; chop remaining eggs. Add to sauce; heat to serving temperature. Do not boil. Sieve remaining egg yolk; sprinkle on mushroom mixture. Garnish with parsley. Place blazer pan over burner. Serve mushroom mixture over rice and chow mein noodles. Yield: 6 servings.

GOLDEN MUSHROOM CASSEROLE

1/2 lb. mushrooms, sliced
1 tbsp. grated onion
4 tbsp. butter
1/2 tsp. salt
1/4 tsp. pepper
1/4 tsp. dried tarragon
1 tbsp. flour
2 tbsp. grated Swiss cheese
2 egg yolks
1 c. heavy cream
3 tbsp. fine bread crumbs

Combine mushrooms, onion and 2 tablespoons butter in small heavy saucepan; cover. Simmer, stirring frequently, over low heat for 3 to 5 minutes or until mushrooms are just tender. Season with salt, pepper and tarragon. Add flour and cheese; stir until smooth. Pour into buttered 1-quart baking dish. Beat egg yolks with cream; pour over mushroom mixture. Sprinkle with bread crumbs. Melt remaining butter; drizzle over crumbs. Bake in 400-degree oven for 10 minutes or until golden brown and set.

MUSHROOMS FLORENTINE

2 pkg. frozen chopped spinach
1 lb. fresh mushrooms
Butter
1 tsp. salt
1/4 c. chopped onion
1 c. grated Cheddar cheese
Garlic salt to taste

Prepare spinach according to package directions; drain well. Cut stems from mushrooms; saute stems and caps in small amount of butter until browned. Melt 1/4 cup butter. Line shallow 10-inch casserole with spinach; add salt, onion and melted butter. Sprinkle with 1/2 cup cheese. Arrange mushrooms over spinach; season with garlic salt. Sprinkle with remaining cheese. Bake for 20 minutes at 350 degrees or until cheese is melted and lightly browned. Yield: 6-8 servings.

MUSHROOMS WITH BLEU CHEESE

2 lb. large fresh mushrooms
1/2 c. crumbled bleu cheese
1 c. dry bread crumbs
1/8 tsp. minced chives
2 tbsp. butter
1/4 c. sherry
1/2 c. heavy cream

Remove stems from mushrooms; place 1 piece of cheese in each cavity. Saute crumbs and chives in butter lightly; add remaining cheese. Place layer of crumb mixture in buttered casserole; add mushrooms, cavity side up. Sprinkle with sherry and remaining crumb mixture; cover with cream. Bake, covered, at 375 degrees for 25 minutes. Yield: 6 servings.

SCALLOPED MUSHROOMS AND ALMONDS

3 lb. small mushrooms
1/3 c. butter
2 c. light cream
4 tbsp. flour
1/3 c. toasted almonds
Salt and pepper to taste
Chopped parsley
Paprika

Saute mushrooms in butter in skillet for 5 minutes; add cream. Bring to a boil. Mix flour with enough water to form a paste; add to mushroom mixture. Simmer, stirring constantly, until smooth and thickened. Add almonds; season with salt and pepper. Place in greased baking dish. Bake in 350-degree oven for 20 minutes or until heated through. Sprinkle with parsley and paprika. Yield: 6-8 servings.

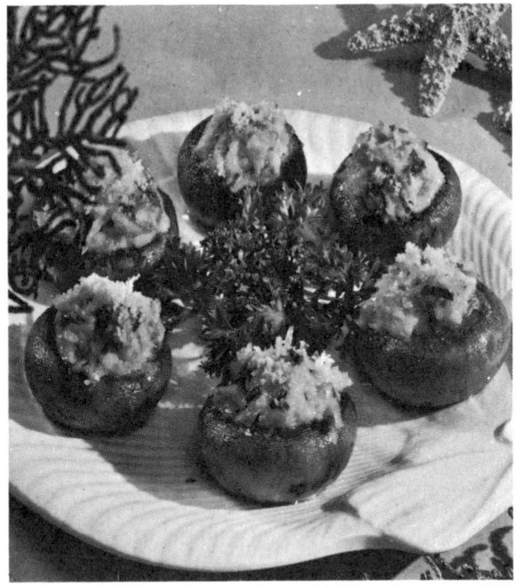

Crab Meat Stuffed Mushrooms . . . Crab meat flavored with lemon and onion fills mushroom caps.

CRAB MEAT-STUFFED MUSHROOMS

3/4 lb. medium fresh mushrooms
Melted butter
1 7 1/2-oz. can crab meat
4 tbsp. soft bread crumbs
2 eggs, lightly beaten
2 tbsp. mayonnaise
2 tbsp. chopped chives
1 tsp. lemon juice
1/8 tsp. ground white pepper

Preheat oven to 375 degrees. Remove stems from mushrooms; brush caps with melted butter. Arrange in greased baking dish. Drain and flake crab meat. Combine crab meat, 2 tablespoons crumbs, eggs, mayonnaise, chives, lemon juice, pepper and 2 tablespoons butter in small bowl. Fill each mushroom cap with some of the crab mixture. Combine 2 tablespoons butter and remaining bread crumbs; sprinkle over crab stuffing. Bake for 15 minutes; serve hot.

BORDELAISE MUSHROOMS

1/2 lb. mushrooms
1/2 tsp. salt
1/4 tsp. pepper
1 clove of garlic, crushed
1/4 c. olive oil
2 shallots, minced
1 tsp. minced parsley

Clean mushrooms; cut off stems 1/2 inch from caps. Slice through stems; season with salt and pepper. Saute caps, stems and garlic in oil in skillet; simmer, stirring gently, for 5 minutes. Add shallots immediately; saute, stirring constantly, for 5 minutes longer. Sprinkle with parsley. Serve immediately.

FRENCH-FRIED MUSHROOMS

1 lb. fresh mushrooms
1/4 c. milk
3/4 c. pancake mix

Dip mushrooms into milk; dip into pancake mix. Fry in deep fat at 375 degrees for 2 minutes or until golden brown; drain on absorbent toweling.

HOT AND TANGY MUSHROOMS

3 lb. mushrooms
2 cloves of garlic, minced
1/4 c. olive oil
1 tbsp. oregano
1 tsp. crushed hot red pepper
3 oz. cooking wine

Boil mushrooms for 5 minutes; drain. Brown garlic in oil with oregano. Add mushrooms, hot pepper and wine. Simmer for 1 hour or until mushrooms are tender.

MUSHROOM PATTIES

2 c. cooked mushrooms
1 egg, beaten
1/2 tsp. salt
Pinch of pepper
1 sm. onion, grated
Cracker meal

Grind mushrooms; add egg, seasonings and onion. Mix well; shape into patties. Coat patties with cracker meal; fry in small amount of hot fat until golden brown.

MUSHROOM PUDDING

2 c. small bread cubes, toasted
1/4 c. Parmesan cheese
1/2 c. chopped green onions
5 c. fresh mushrooms, coarsely chopped
1/2 c. chopped celery
3 tbsp. butter
2 tbsp. lemon juice
4 eggs
2 c. milk
1 tsp. salt
1/4 tsp. thyme

Mix bread cubes, cheese and onions. Saute mushrooms and celery in butter; add lemon juice. Cook, stirring, until juice evaporates. Stir into bread mixture. Spoon into a 6-cup baking dish. Beat eggs with milk, salt and thyme; pour over mushroom mixture. Place in pan of hot water. Bake at 325 degrees for 45 minutes.

MUSHROOM RING

1 lb. fresh mushrooms, finely chopped
1 c. finely chopped celery
2/3 c. margarine
8 eggs, beaten
1 1/3 c. milk
5 c. soft bread crumbs
1 tbsp. chopped pimento
2 tsp. salt

Saute mushrooms and celery in margarine. Blend eggs, milk, bread crumbs, pimento and salt; fold in vegetables. Pour into 2-quart buttered ring mold; set in pan of hot water. Bake at 350 degrees for 40 minutes; turn onto hot serving dish. Center may be filled with cream sauce.

MUSHROOMS À LA KING

3 stalks celery, finely chopped
1 lb. mushrooms
3 tbsp. butter
2 tbsp. flour
2 c. milk
Salt and pepper to taste

Paprika
3 hard-cooked eggs, thinly sliced
1/4 c. sliced ripe olives
2 tbsp. sherry
Dry toast

Cook celery until tender in small amount of water; drain. Slice mushrooms; saute in butter. Stir in flour and milk; cook, stirring constantly, until thickened. Season with salt, pepper and paprika; add celery, eggs and olives. Simmer until heated through; add sherry just before serving. Serve over toast.

MUSHROOMS IN FRESH TOMATO SAUCE

1 clove of garlic, crushed
3/4 c. sliced onion
2 tbsp. vegetable oil
3 c. diced fresh tomatoes
1 1/2 tsp. salt
1/4 tsp. pepper
1/2 tsp. crumbled oregano
1 1/2 lb. sliced mushrooms

Saute garlic and onion in oil until onion is tender; add tomatoes and seasonings. Simmer until tomatoes are tender; add mushrooms. Simmer, covered, for 10 minutes longer. Yield: 6 servings.

MUSHROOMS IN SOUR CREAM

2 c. canned mushrooms
1 tbsp. chopped onion
1 tbsp. margarine
2 tsp. flour
1/2 c. sour cream

Combine undrained mushrooms and onion in saucepan; simmer for 10 minutes. Melt margarine in skillet; blend in flour. Cook, stirring, until lightly browned; add to mushrooms. Cook, stirring constantly, until thickened. Stir in sour cream; heat through. Yield: 4 servings.

EASY MUSHROOM PIE

1 recipe pie pastry
1 lb. mushrooms
Salt and pepper to taste
1 tbsp. flour
Dash of onion juice
1/2 tsp. Worcestershire sauce
1 1/2 tbsp. melted butter
3 tbsp. light cream

Line small pie pan with pastry. Bake at 400 degrees for 7 minutes. Remove from oven; cool. Slice mushrooms; place in pastry shell. Sprinkle with salt, pepper and flour; add onion juice, Worcestershire sauce, butter and cream. Cover with strips of pastry. Bake in 400-degree oven for 20 minutes or until mushrooms are tender and pastry is browned. Yield: 4 servings.

MUSHROOM-CHEESE PIE

1 1/2 lb. mushrooms, sliced
1 c. thinly sliced onions
4 tbsp. butter
1/3 c. flour
1 8-oz. carton cottage cheese
1/4 c. chopped parsley
1/4 c. dry sherry
2 tsp. salt
1/8 tsp. pepper
2 c. sifted flour
2/3 c. shortening
4 to 5 tbsp. ice water

Saute mushrooms and onions in butter until tender. Add flour; mix well. Add cottage cheese, parsley, sherry, 1 teaspoon salt and pepper; mix thoroughly. Preheat oven to 425 degrees. Sift flour and remaining salt together; cut into shortening. Add ice water gradually, stirring with fork, to form dough. Roll out half of dough to form 12-inch circle; line 9-inch pie pan. Roll out remaining dough; cut into strips. Pour filling into pastry-lined pie pan. Arrange lattice strips on top. Flute edge. Bake on bottom rack of oven for 40 to 45 minutes until lightly browned. Cool 5 minutes. Yield: 6-8 servings.

SAVORY CREAMED MUSHROOMS

1/4 c. butter
1 tbsp. chopped onion
1/4 c. chopped green pepper
1/4 c. flour
2 c. milk
1/2 lb. American cheese, shredded
2 cans mushrooms
3 hard-cooked eggs, sliced
3 tbsp. minced pimento
1/4 c. sliced stuffed green olives
2 5-oz. cans chow mein noodles

Melt butter in saucepan over low heat; cook onion and green pepper until tender. Blend in flour; add milk gradually. Cook, stirring constantly, until sauce is smooth and thickened. Add cheese and drained mushrooms; simmer until cheese is melted. Add eggs, pimento and olives; heat through. Serve over chow mein noodles. Yield: 6 servings.

BACON-STUFFED MUSHROOMS

16 lge. fresh mushroom
6 slices bacon, cut into pieces
1/4 c. minced onion
1/4 c. fine bread crumbs
1/2 tsp. salt
1/8 tsp. pepper
1/4 tsp. paprika
1 c. sour cream
1/4 tsp. Worcestershire sauce

Remove stems from mushrooms; chop stems. Place caps in greased shallow baking dish. Brown bacon in skillet; remove. Saute mushroom stems and onion in bacon drippings until onion is tender; drain. Combine onion mixture with remaining ingredients; mix thoroughly. Spoon mixture into mushroom caps. Bake at 350 degrees for 20 minutes. Yield: 4 servings.

STUFFED MUSHROOMS IN CREAM

1 lb. medium mushrooms
3 tbsp. chopped parsley
1/4 c. butter, softened
1 c. finely chopped nuts
1 clove of garlic, crushed
1/4 tsp. thyme
1/2 tsp. salt
1/8 to 1/2 tsp. pepper
1/2 c. heavy cream

Remove stems from mushrooms; chop stems. Arrange mushrooms caps in shallow baking dish, hollow-side up. Combine all remaining ingredients except cream; fill mushroom caps. Pour cream over mushrooms. Bake at 350 degrees for 20 minutes. Baste occasionally with sauce. Yield: 6-8 servings.

GOURMET STUFFED MUSHROOMS

3 slices bread, crusts removed
1 lb. large fresh mushrooms
1 tbsp. butter
3/4 c. finely chopped onions
Salad oil
Seasoned salt to taste
1 tbsp. parsley flakes
1/2 tsp. salt
1/8 tsp. pepper
1/4 tsp. marjoram
1/4 tsp. thyme
1 tsp. Worcestershire sauce
3 tbsp. sherry
1 egg, slightly beaten
1/4 c. toasted slivered almonds

Cut bread slices into cubes. Remove stems from mushrooms; chop stems finely. Melt butter; add mushroom stems and onions. Saute until onions are transparent; remove from heat. Brush outsides of mushroom caps with oil; arrange, hollow side up, in shallow baking dish. Sprinkle insides of caps with seasoned salt. Combine onion mixture, bread cubes and remaining ingredients; fill caps. Bake at 425 degrees for 15 minutes or until mushrooms are tender. Yield: 6-10 servings.

WALNUT-STUFFED MUSHROOMS

12 lge. mushrooms
4 sm. mushrooms
2 stalks celery, chopped
1 onion, chopped
1/2 green pepper, chopped
1 c. cracker crumbs
1/4 c. walnuts, chopped
Salt and pepper to taste
1/2 tsp. soy sauce
Butter

Wash mushrooms; scoop out stems and as much of large mushrooms as possible, leaving shell. Saute celery, onion and green pepper. Chop up small mushrooms and centers of large mushrooms and stems. Add cracker crumbs, walnuts, salt, pepper and soy sauce. Combine mushroom and onion mixtures. Place pat of butter in bottom of each large mushroom; stuff with filling. Place mushrooms in flat pan. Bake at 350 degrees for 20 minutes. Yield: 4 servings.

Mustard

MUSTARD DIP

1 c. dry mustard
1 c. wine vinegar
3 eggs
1 c. sugar

Mix mustard and vinegar; let stand overnight. Mix eggs and sugar in double boiler; add mustard mixture. Cook, stirring constantly, over boiling water until smooth and thickened. Refrigerate until ready to use; keeps indefinitely. Yield: 1 2/3 pints.

MUSTARD RING

1 env. unflavored gelatin
4 eggs
3/4 c. sugar
2 tbsp. dry mustard
1/2 tsp. salt
1 c. vinegar
1/2 pt. heavy cream, whipped

Soften gelatin in 1/4 cup water. Beat eggs until thick and lemony; pour over gelatin in top of double boiler. Add sugar, mustard, salt and vinegar; mix well. Cook, stirring constantly, until smooth and thickened. Cool; fold in whipped cream. Pour into ring mold; chill until set. Freezes well.

Noodles

Noodles are usually a dry dough or pasta, made from flour, water, and eggs. The inclusion of eggs, which increases food value, distinguishes noodles from macaroni. Often prepared types are fine, medium, and wide noodles, bows, and squares. Spinach, or green noodles, contain 3 percent spinach solids. Noodles contain carbohydrates and some protein. However, most types are enriched with thiamine, iron, riboflavin, and niacin to meet federal standards. (3 1/2 ounces cooked noodles = 125 calories)

AVAILABILITY: Sold year-round in retail grocery stores in boxes and cellophane packages.

STORING: Uncooked noodles may be stored in a cool dry place for 3 to 6 months. Store cooked noodles, covered, in the refrigerator for 4 to 5 days.

PREPARATION: Noodles and macaroni are prepared exactly alike. (See MACARONI.) 1 pound noodles = 5 1/2 cups uncooked = 10 cups cooked.

SERVING: Serve with butter and grated Parmesan cheese for a main dish accompaniment. Use in soups and casseroles.

BAKED NOODLE RING

1/2 c. butter, creamed
1 carton creamed cottage cheese
4 eggs, lightly beaten
1 lb. noodles, cooked

Mix half the butter with cheese and eggs; mix with noodles. Press into well greased ring mold. Dot with remaining butter. Bake at 350 degrees for 40 minutes. Center may be filled with creamed meats or vegetables. Yield: 8 servings.

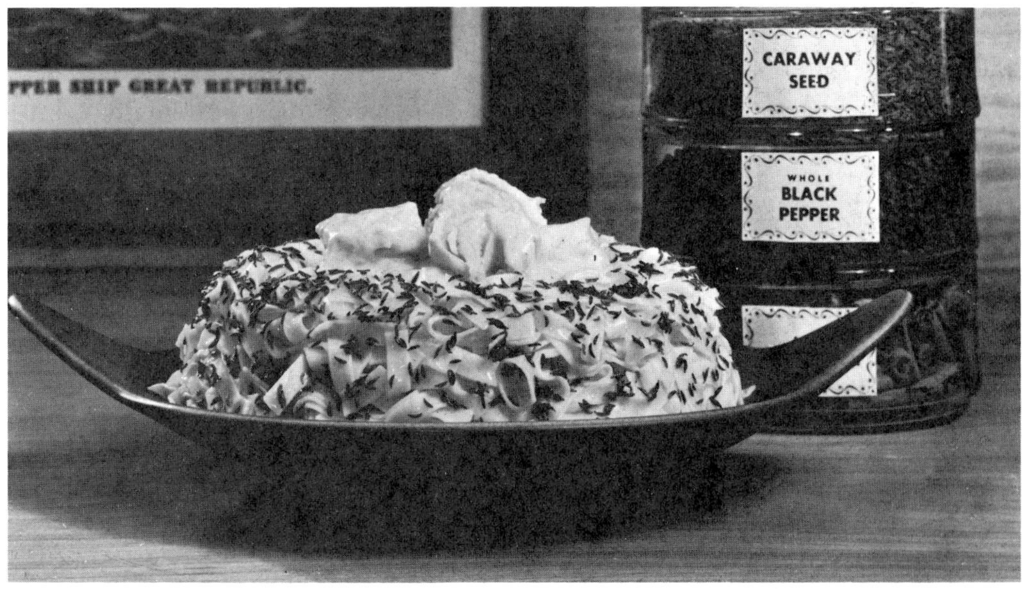

Noodle Ring with Caraway Seed . . . Seasoned creamed tuna heaped in the center of a mold.

NOODLE RING WITH CARAWAY SEED

1/2 lb. noodles
1 tbsp. caraway seed
4 tbsp. butter
3 tbsp. flour
1 1/2 c. milk
2 6-oz. cans tuna
3/4 tsp. salt
1/4 tsp. ground thyme
1/8 tsp. ground pepper

Cook noodles according to package directions. Drain and rinse. Add caraway seed and 1 tablespoon butter. Toss lightly; turn into greased 1 1/2-quart ring mold. Place in pan of hot water to keep warm. Melt remaining butter in saucepan. Blend in flour; stir in milk. Cook until thick, stirring constantly. Drain and flake tuna; add to white sauce. Add seasonings. Mix well. Heat, stirring as little as possible. Turn noodle ring out on hot platter. Fill center with creamed tuna. Yield: 6 servings.

ORANGE-FILBERT NOODLES

Photograph for this recipe on page 428.

Salt
1 lb. wide egg noodles
2 c. chopped filberts
1/2 c. butter
2 tsp. grated orange peel
1 c. orange juice
1/2 tsp. pepper

Add 2 tablespoons salt to 6 quarts rapidly boiling water in large saucepan. Add noodles gradually so that water continues to boil. Cook, stirring occasionally, until tender. Drain in colander. Saute filberts in butter in saucepan for about 5 minutes; add orange peel and juice. Combine filbert mixture, noodles, 3/4 teaspoon salt and pepper in serving dish; toss lightly. Garnish with orange slices if desired. Yield: 8 servings.

BUSY DAY NOODLE CASSEROLE

2 c. noodles
8 slices bacon, halved
1 clove of garlic, halved
1/2 c. minced onions
1 No. 2 can tomatoes
1 c. soft bread crumbs
1 1/2 tsp. salt
1 tsp. sugar
1/4 c. grated Parmesan cheese

Preheat oven to 350 degrees. Cook noodles according to package directions; drain. Fry bacon in skillet until crisp; remove bacon. Pour off fat; return 1/4 cup drippings to skillet. Add garlic; cook for 3 minutes. Remove garlic. Add onions; cook until tender. Add tomatoes, crumbs, salt, sugar and cheese; cook for 8 to 10 minutes. Pour into 1 1/2-quart casserole. Add noodles and bacon; toss well. Bake, covered, for 30 minutes. Yield: 4 servings.

COTTAGE NOODLE CASSEROLE

Salt
8 oz. wide noodles
1 env. cream of leek soup
1/4 c. butter
1/4 tsp. pepper
1/4 tsp. dry mustard
2 c. milk
2 c. creamed cottage cheese
1 1-lb. can applesauce
1/4 c. raisins
1 c. grated sharp Cheddar cheese

Add 1 tablespoon salt to 3 quarts boiling water; add noodles gradually. Cook, stirring occasionally, until noodles are tender; drain. Combine soup mix, butter, 1/4 teaspoon salt, pepper, mustard and milk in saucepan; cook over medium heat, stirring constantly, until thickened. Combine sauce, cottage cheese, applesauce, raisins and 1/2 cup cheese; toss sauce mixture with noodles lightly. Turn into 2 1/2-quart baking dish. Sprinkle with remaining cheese. Bake at 350 degrees for 30 minutes or until bubbling hot. Yield: 6 servings.

BLUE-NOODLE CASSEROLE

3 c. noodles
3 tbsp. butter
3 tbsp. flour
Salt and pepper to taste
1 c. milk
3/4 c. blue cheese
3 tbsp. chopped green pepper
3 tbsp. chopped pimento

Cook noodles according to package directions. Rinse well; drain. Melt butter in small saucepan; blend in flour, salt and pepper. Stir in milk; cook, stirring constantly, until thick. Add cheese; stir until melted. Combine sauce, noodles, green pepper and pimento in greased casserole. Bake at 350 degrees for 30 minutes. Yield: 4-6 servings.

CHEESE-NOODLE RING

2 c. cooked fine noodles
1 c. grated Cheddar cheese
1 c. bread cubes
1 med. onion, chopped
2 tbsp. chopped parsley
1 sm. can pimentos, chopped
1/2 c. cream
1/4 c. melted butter

Mix all ingredients well; spoon into buttered ring mold. Place mold in pan of water. Bake at 300 degrees for 40 to 45 minutes. Serve with creamed crab, chicken or ham, if desired. Yield: 6 servings.

CHICKEN-NOODLE CASSEROLE

1 8-oz. package noodles
1 can chicken
1 can asparagus, drained
1 can mushroom soup
1/4 c. chopped green pepper
1 2-oz. can pimento
1 c. grated cheese
2 c. white sauce

Cook noodles according to package directions; drain. Combine all ingredients except white sauce; place in buttered casserole. Pour white sauce over top. Bake at 350 degrees for 30 minutes. Yield: 6 servings.

GOURMET NOODLES

1 6-oz. package thin noodles
1 c. cottage cheese
1 c. sour cream
1/4 c. minced onion
1 clove of garlic, minced
Dash of hot sauce
2 tsp. Worcestershire sauce
1/4 tsp. salt
Dash of pepper
2 eggs, well beaten
3 tbsp. grated American cheese

Cook noodles according to package directions; drain well. Stir in all remaining ingredients except cheese; pour into greased 1 1/2-quart casserole. Place casserole in pan of hot water. Bake at 350 degrees for 30 minutes. Sprinkle with cheese. Bake for 10 minutes longer. Yield: 6 servings.

GREEN NOODLE CASSEROLE

2 tbsp. chopped onion
Butter
2 tsp. Worcestershire sauce
3/4 c. white wine
2 cans mushroom soup
1 c. sour cream
1/2 tsp. curry powder
1 tbsp. chopped parsley
1/4 tsp. salt
1/4 tsp. pepper
1/4 tsp. oregano
1/4 tsp. paprika
1 can mushrooms
2 cans minced clams
1/2 lb. green noodles, cooked
4 oz. grated sharp cheese

Brown onion in small amount of butter in large skillet. Add Worcestershire sauce, wine, soup, sour cream, curry powder, parsley, salt, pepper, oregano, paprika, mushrooms and clams. Place noodles in buttered casserole; add layer of clam mixture. Repeat layers. Top with cheese, reserving small amount. Bake at 350 degrees for 35 minutes. Remove from oven; sprinkle with reserved cheese. Bake for 10 minutes longer. Yield: 8 servings.

NAPLES NOODLES

2 cloves of garlic, minced
2 tbsp. olive oil
2 1-lb. cans tomatoes
1 6-oz. can tomato paste
1 1/2 tsp. salt
1/4 tsp. basil
1/8 tsp. oregano
1 8-oz. package wide noodles
8 oz. Cheddar cheese, sliced

Saute garlic in hot oil in large saucepan over low heat for 10 minutes, until tender. Add tomatoes, tomato paste, salt, basil and oregano. Stir to blend; bring to a boil. Reduce heat; cover. Simmer for 1 hour and 30 minutes or until mixture is the consistency of chili sauce. Cook noodles according to package directions; drain. Arrange noodles, tomato sauce and cheese slices in 2 alternate layers in greased 2-quart baking dish. Bake at 350 degrees for 30 minutes or until sauce is bubbly and cheese melts. Yield: 4 servings.

NOODLE CASSEROLE

1 lb. wide noodles
1 8-oz. package cream cheese, softened
1/4 c. soft butter
3 c. sour cream
1 lge. onion, finely chopped
4 eggs, well beaten
1 tsp. salt
1/4 tsp. pepper

Preheat oven to 350 degrees. Cook noodles in boiling salted water according to package directions; drain well. Combine cream cheese and butter; beat until creamy. Stir in sour cream and onion; fold mixture into noodles. Combine eggs, salt and pepper; stir into noodles gently. Pour into greased 2-quart casserole. Bake for 45 minutes or until top is golden brown. Yield: 6-8 servings.

NOODLE KUGEL

1/2 lb. medium noodles, cooked
1 egg
Sugar to taste
1/3 c. sour cream
1 3-oz. package cream cheese, softened
1/2 c. raisins
3 tbsp. butter

Combine all ingredients; mix thoroughly. Place in buttered 8-inch round casserole. Bake in 350-degree oven for 45 minutes or until brown. Yield: 4-6 servings.

NOODLE LAYER PUDDING

1 lb. cottage cheese, drained
4 egg yolks
1/2 c. heavy cream
2 tbsp. sugar
1 tsp. salt
1 lb. wide noodles, cooked
1/4 c. bread crumbs
1/4 c. melted butter

Combine cottage cheese, egg yolks, cream, sugar and salt; beat until smooth. Alternate layers of noodles and cottage cheese mixture in buttered baking dish, starting and ending with noodles. Sprinkle with bread crumbs; pour butter over crumbs. Bake at 375 degrees for 30 minutes. Yield: 4-6 servings.

NOODLE PUDDING

1 lb. thin egg noodles
1 egg, slightly beaten
1 c. sour cream
1 1/4 c. sugar
1 tsp. cinnamon
4 pared apples, sliced
1 c. raisins
1/2 c. chopped nuts

Preheat oven to 325 degrees. Cook noodles until partially tender in boiling salted water. Drain; rinse well. Place noodles in large bowl; add egg and sour cream. Add sugar and cinnamon. Mix well; fold in apples and raisins. Turn into buttered baking dish; sprinkle with nuts. Bake at 325 degrees for 1 hour or until pudding is firm and apples are tender. Serve with additional sour cream. Yield: 6 servings.

MAIN DISH NOODLE PUDDING

Color photograph for this recipe on page 74.

Salt
6 c. fine egg noodles
2 tbsp. salad oil
1 1/4 c. chopped onion
1/2 c. chopped parsley
1/4 tsp. freshly ground pepper
1/4 tsp. ground nutmeg
1 12-oz. can luncheon meat, diced
4 eggs
2 c. reliquified nonfat dry milk
1/3 c. grated Parmesan cheese

Add 1 1/2 tablespoons salt to 5 quarts boiling water; add noodles gradually so that water continues to boil. Cook, stirring occasionally, until just tender; drain in colander. Heat oil in large skillet over medium heat. Add onion; saute until golden. Stir in parsley; cook just until wilted. Remove from heat; stir in 1 1/2 teaspoons salt, pepper, nutmeg and luncheon meat. Alternate 3 layers of noodles with 3 layers of meat mixture in greased 2 1/2-quart casserole, beginning with noodles and ending with meat mixture. Beat eggs, milk and cheese together in bowl; pour over noodle mixture. Cover. Bake in 350-degree oven for 35 minutes. Uncover; bake for 20 minutes longer.

NOODLES FLAMBOYANT

1 lb. med. noodles
8 eggs, beaten
1 1/4 c. sugar
1 c. chopped apples
1 c. raisins
Juice of 1 lemon
Juice of 1 orange
Grated lemon rind to taste
Grated orange rind to taste
1 tsp. cinnamon
3 tbsp. cooking oil
Salt to taste

Cook noodles for 6 minutes in boiling salted water; drain. Combine noodles, eggs, sugar, apples, raisins, lemon juice, orange juice and rinds. Pour into 2 large baking dishes; stir in all remaining ingredients. Bake at 325 degrees for 1 hour and 30 minutes. Yield: 12 servings.

NOODLE SEAFOOD CASSEROLE

1 12-oz. package med. noodles
1 can tuna, drained
1 can shrimp, drained
1 can lobster, drained
1 can mushroom soup
1 can cream of celery soup
1 soup can milk
1 can French-fried onion rings

Cook noodles according to package directions; drain. Combine all ingredients except onion rings; blend well. Place in large casserole. Top with onion rings; seal with aluminum foil. Bake in 350-degree oven for 30 minutes. Yield: 6 servings.

NOODLES WITH FRUIT

1 lb. wide noodles
2 eggs, beaten
Dash of salt
1/4 c. sugar
1 tsp. vanilla
1 lge. can fruit cocktail
1 c. milk
2 tbsp. chopped nuts
2 tbsp. raisins
Cinnamon
Crushed cornflakes
2 tbsp. butter

Cook noodles in boiling salted water until tender; drain. Place eggs in mixing bowl; add salt, sugar and vanilla, stirring well. Drain fruit; reserve juice. Combine juice and milk; add to egg mixture. Alternate layers of noodles, fruit cocktail, nuts and raisins, ending with fruits and nuts in buttered 9 x 13-inch baking pan; pour egg mixture over noodles. Sprinkle with cinnamon lightly; sprinkle with cornflake crumbs. Dot with butter. Bake at 350 degrees for 1 hour and 10 minutes. Yield: 6-8 servings.

NOODLE SOUFFLÉ

3 eggs, separated
1/2 c. butter, melted
2 tbsp. sugar
1 c. sour cream
1 lb. creamed cottage cheese
8 oz. cooked noodles
Corn flake crumbs

Beat egg yolks until yellow; add butter and sugar. Beat well. Add sour cream, cottage cheese and noodles; mix well. Beat egg whites until stiff peaks form; fold into noodle mixture. Pour into greased casserole. Cover with crumbs; dot with additional butter. Bake at 375 degrees for 45 minutes. Yield: 8 servings.

PIQUANT NOODLE CASSEROLE

1/2 lb. sliced bacon
1 1-lb. package fine noodles
3 c. cottage cheese
3 c. sour cream
2 cloves of garlic, crushed
2 onions, minced
2 tbsp. Worcestershire sauce
Dash of hot sauce
4 tsp. salt
3 tbsp. prepared horseradish
1 c. grated Parmesan cheese

Fry bacon in skillet until crisp. Drain on absorbent paper. Cook noodles in boiling salted water until tender; drain well. Mix all remaining ingredients except Parmesan cheese in large bowl. Add noodles and bacon; toss with 2 forks until well mixed. Turn into buttered, deep 3 1/2-quart casserole. Bake, covered, at 350 degrees for 30 minutes or until heated through. Sprinkle with 1/4 cup Parmesan cheese. Broil 4 inches from source of heat until golden. Top with remaining Parmesan cheese and additional sour cream to serve. Yield: 12 servings.

POPPY SEED CASSEROLE

1 12-oz. package med. noodles
2 c. creamed cottage cheese
1 c. sour cream
1 sm. box poppy seed
Freshly ground pepper to taste

Cook noodles according to package directions; drain. Place noodles in greased casserole dish, alternating with layers of cottage cheese and sour cream. Sprinkle each layer with 1 teaspoon poppy seed and pepper. Bake at 350 degrees for 45 minutes or until crust forms on top. Yield: 8 servings.

SPANISH NOODLES

1/2 lb. ground beef
2 tbsp. bacon drippings
1 8-oz. package noodles, cooked
1 tsp. salt
1 green pepper, chopped
1 onion, diced
1 No. 2 1/2 can tomatoes
1/2 c. chili sauce

Brown beef in bacon drippings in large skillet. Add all remaining ingredients; cook, covered, over high heat until steaming. Reduce heat; simmer for 40 minutes. Yield: 6 servings.

SPICY NOODLE DISH

1 lb. wide egg noodles
3 eggs, beaten
1 lb. cottage cheese
1 tsp. cinnamon
3 tbsp. sugar

Cook noodles for 5 minutes in boiling salted water. Drain; rinse well. Combine noodles and all remaining ingredients; pour into buttered baking dish. Bake at 350 degrees for 1 hour. Yield: 6 servings.

SPINACH NOODLES

1 pkg. spinach noodles
1/2 c. butter
1/2 c. Parmesan cheese

Cook noodles in boiling salted water until just tender. Drain well; place in large bowl. Add butter and cheese; mix gently by tumbling with two forks until butter and cheese have been absorbed by noodles. Serve with additional grated cheese sprinkled over top. Yield: 6 servings.

WATERCRESS-NOODLE CASSEROLE

1/4 c. margarine
2 tbsp. minced onion
3 tbsp. flour
1/2 tsp. salt
1/4 tsp. white pepper
2 c. cream
2 tbsp. wine vinegar
1/2 c. shredded Parmesan cheese
1/2 c. sliced ripe olives
1 c. chopped watercress
8 oz. noodles, cooked and drained
Buttered bread crumbs

Melt margarine in saucepan; add onion. Cook for 3 minutes or until soft. Combine flour, salt and pepper, blending well; heat until bubbling, stirring constantly. Remove pan from heat; add cream gradually, blending well. Return to heat; bring to a boil rapidly. Cook for 1 to 2 minutes longer. Remove from heat; stir in vinegar. Blend in cheese, stirring until melted. Blend in olives and watercress; toss sauce with noodles gently. Turn into buttered casserole; top with buttered bread crumbs. Bake in 350-degree oven until slightly brown. Yield: 8-10 servings.

Nutmeg

Nutmeg is an aromatic sweet spice produced from the seed of an apricot-like fruit. The fruit is grown on a huge tropical evergreen. The nutmeg seed is separated from the fruit and dried either in the sun or over charcoal fires.

AVAILABILITY: Nutmeg is available year-round in the United States through import from Indonesia, Brazil, and the West Indies.

BUYING: Nutmeg is processed and sold in two forms: *whole* and *ground nutmeg.*

STORING: Keep nutmeg in a tightly closed container in a cool, dry place.

PREPARATION: *To grind* whole nutmeg—use kitchen or nutmeg grater (available in hardware stores). One nutmeg seed = 3 teaspoons ground nutmeg.

USES: Nutmeg is an important cooking spice in preparing cakes, breads, doughnuts; puddings and custards; beverages, especially eggnog; and creamed meat and vegetable dishes. Its flavor is prominent in such commercially prepared blends as Apple Pie Spice and Pumpkin Pie Spice.

INDIAN NUTMEG CAKE

2 c. sugar
3/4 c. bacon drippings
1 c. raisins
1 tsp. ground cloves
1 tsp. nutmeg
1 tsp. allspice
1/2 tsp. salt
3 1/2 c. all-purpose flour
1 tsp. soda
2 tsp. baking powder
1 c. chopped walnuts

Combine sugar, bacon drippings, 2 cups water, raisins, spices and salt in 1-quart saucepan; boil for 5 minutes, stirring occasionally. Cool. Sift flour, soda and baking powder together; add to raisin mixture. Add walnuts; beat well. Pour batter into greased and floured 12 x 14-inch pan. Bake at 350 degrees for about 40 minutes. Cool cake. Frost with brown sugar frosting or powdered sugar frosting if desired.

NUTMEG FEATHER CAKE

1/4 c. butter
1/4 c. shortening
1 1/2 c. sugar
1/2 tsp. vanilla
3 beaten eggs
2 c. sifted all-purpose flour
2 tsp. nutmeg
1 tsp. soda
1 tsp. baking powder
1/4 tsp. salt
1 c. buttermilk
Confectioners' sugar

Cream butter and shortening; add sugar gradually, creaming until light. Add vanilla and eggs; beat until light and fluffy. Sift dry ingredients together; add to creamed mixture alternately with buttermilk, beating well after each addition. Pour into greased 13 x 9 x 2-inch pan. Bake in 350-degree oven for 35 to 40 minutes or until cake tests done. Sift confectioners' sugar over cake.

NUTMEG BUTTERBALLS

1 c. blanched almonds
1 c. butter
1/2 c. sugar
1 tsp. vanilla
2 c. all-purpose flour
1/2 c. confectioners' sugar
2 tsp. nutmeg

Grind almonds coarsely with food grinder. Cream butter and sugar thoroughly; blend in ground almonds and vanilla. Work in flour. Shape into small 1 1/2-inch balls; chill. Place on greased baking sheet. Bake in 300-degree oven for 15 to 20 minutes or until light golden brown. Combine confectioners' sugar and nutmeg. Roll cookies in sugar mixture while still warm. Yield: 6 dozen cookies.

NUTMEG COOKIES

Color photograph for this recipe on page 492.

1/2 c. butter
1/2 c. sugar
6 tbsp. cream
Grated rind of 1 orange
3 tbsp. orange juice
1 1/2 c. flour
2 c. potato flour
1 1/2 tsp. nutmeg
1/2 tsp. salt

Cream butter and sugar in bowl. Combine cream, orange rind and orange juice. Sift flours, nutmeg and salt together; add to creamed mixture alternately with orange juice mixture. Shape into roll; wrap in waxed paper. Refrigerate overnight. Slice cookies; cut holes in 1 side of each cookie. Place on greased baking sheet. Prick cookies with fork. Bake at 375 degrees for 8 to 10 minutes.

NUTMEG JUMBLES

2/3 c. shortening
1 1/2 c. sugar
2 eggs
3 tsp. baking powder
2 tbsp. nutmeg
3 c. sifted flour
1 tsp. salt
1 c. milk

Cream shortening; add sugar and eggs, mixing until fluffy. Sift baking powder, nutmeg, flour and salt together. Add dry ingredients and milk alternately to creamed mixture. Drop by spoonfuls onto greased and floured cookie sheets; sprinkle tops with additional nutmeg. Bake in 375-degree oven for 12 minutes.

BAKED NUTMEG CUSTARD

3 slightly beaten eggs
1/4 c. sugar
1/4 tsp. salt
2 c. milk, scalded
1 tsp. vanilla
Nutmeg to taste

Combine eggs, sugar and salt. Cool milk slightly. Stir milk and vanilla into egg mixture gradually. Set six 5-ounce custard cups in shallow pan on oven rack. Pour hot water 1 inch deep around cups. Pour in custard; sprinkle with nutmeg. Bake in 325-degree oven for 45 minutes to 1 hour or until knife inserted into center comes out clean. Serve warm or chilled. Yield: 6 servings.

RICH NUTMEG CUSTARD

3 eggs
1 qt. milk
1/2 c. sugar
1/2 tsp. vanilla
1 tsp. nutmeg
1/2 pt. whipping cream, whipped

Beat eggs until lemon colored. Combine eggs, milk and sugar in top of double boiler. Cook, stirring, over boiling water until thickened. Remove from heat; add vanilla and nutmeg. Add whipped cream to custard; chill. Serve cold in small glasses. Yield: 4-6 servings.

NUTMEG BREAD

1/2 c. shortening
1 c. sugar
1 egg
2 c. sifted flour
1/2 tsp. baking powder
1/2 tsp. salt
1/2 tsp. soda
2 tsp. nutmeg
1 c. sour milk

Cream shortening and sugar. Add egg; mix well. Sift flour, baking powder, salt, soda and nutmeg together; add to creamed mixture alternately with sour milk. Pour into greased 9 x 5 x 3-inch loaf pan. Let stand for 20 minutes. Bake at 350 degrees for 1 hour to 1 hour and 10 minutes. Cool for 5 minutes; remove from pan.

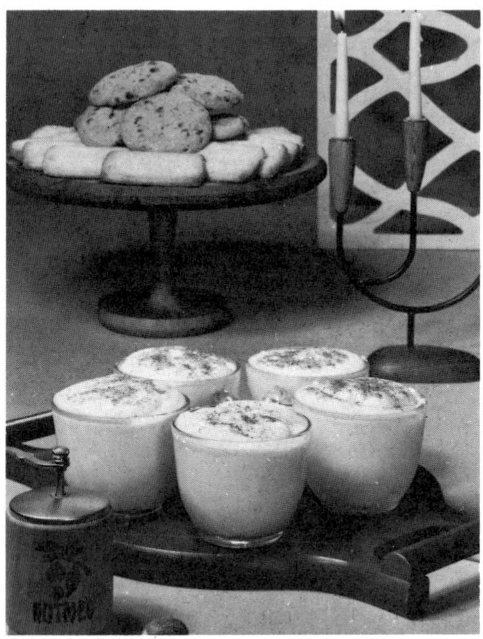

Spicy Nutmeg Mousse . . . Pineapple juice brings tartness to this creamy frozen dessert.

SPICY NUTMEG MOUSSE

1 6-oz. can frozen pineapple drink
Ground nutmeg
1 tsp. vanilla
1/2 c. sugar
1 c. heavy cream, whipped
2 egg whites

Thaw pineapple drink enough to stir. Turn into mixing bowl. Add 1 teaspoon nutmeg, vanilla and sugar. Mix well. Fold in whipped cream. Beat egg whites until stiff peaks form; fold into pineapple mixture. Spoon mousse into punch cups; freeze until firm. Sprinkle with nutmeg just before serving. Yield: 6 servings.

Oatmeal

Oatmeal is a ground cereal grain processed from the interior, edible portion of hulled oats. It is most often cooked and served as a breakfast porridge or cereal. Oatmeal may be coarsely or finely ground. Oats ground to the finest possible texture are marketed as *oat flour.* Oatmeal is sometimes called "rolled oats," although the two products are technically different. Rolled oats are flakes made from hulled, softened, and roller-flattened oats. Oatmeal contains protein, carbohydrate, calcium, iron, and some B vitamins. (1 cup cooked oatmeal, regular or quick-cooking = 150 calories)

AVAILABILITY: *Oatmeal* is available year-round in retail grocery stores. Both regular and quick-cooking oatmeal is sold in cylindrical cardboard containers; instant oatmeal is sold in packages. *Oat flour* is available year-round in many specialty and health food stores.

STORING: Store oatmeal or oat flour in original container on kitchen shelf 3 months. Cooked oatmeal may be refrigerated for up to 4 days.

PREPARATION: *Oatmeal breakfast cereal*—Place 3 to 4 1/2 cups water and 1 teaspoon salt in top of double boiler. Bring water to rapid boil over direct heat. Gradually add 1 1/2 cups oatmeal. Boil gently 3 to 5 minutes, stirring occasionally. Remove from heat and cover. Place over bottom part of double boiler that contains simmering water. Cook regular oatmeal in double boiler 15-30 minutes, the quick-cooking variety 5-10 minutes. Makes 4 servings. Always refer to instructions on container for alternate method of preparation, special directions, and specific cooking times. Follow label directions on packages of instant oatmeal. (1 pound = 5 cups uncooked = 10 cups cooked)

SERVING: Serve oatmeal breakfast cereal hot with milk and sugar. Use oatmeal in breads, loaves, cakes, cookies, muffins, and pancakes. When used in breads, oatmeal is usually combined with flour to obtain desired texture.

OATMEAL-PEANUT LOAF

2/3 c. cooked oatmeal
1/4 c. chopped green pepper
3 tbsp. minced onion
1 tsp. salt
2 tsp. lemon juice
1 c. chopped salted peanuts
1 egg
1/3 c. milk
2/3 c. fine crumbs
1/4 lb. cheese, grated

Combine oatmeal, green pepper, onion, salt, lemon juice and peanuts. Beat egg and milk together. Pour over oatmeal mixture, blending well. Spoon into greased casserole. Sprinkle with crumbs and cheese. Bake at 350 degrees for about 45 minutes to 1 hour or until done. May serve with mushroom sauce if desired. Yield: 4 servings.

OATMEAL AND COTTAGE CHEESE LOAF

1 c. cottage cheese
1 c. cold cooked oats
1 c. milk
1 egg, slightly beaten
1 tbsp. shortening, melted
1/2 tsp. salt
Dash of pepper
1 tsp. poultry seasoning
Dash of Worcestershire sauce
1 tbsp. chopped onions

Combine cottage cheese, oats, milk and egg; stir in shortening, seasonings and onions. Spoon oat mixture into greased casserole. Bake at 350 degrees for about 30 minutes or until heated through and lightly browned on top.

Tomato Sauce

1 lge. can tomatoes
1 sliced onion
8 whole cloves
3 tbsp. butter
3 tbsp. flour
Salt and pepper to taste

Cook tomatoes, onion and cloves for 20 minutes in saucepan. Remove cloves. Brown butter in frying pan; add flour. Cook until smooth and brown, stirring constantly. Season to taste. Add tomato mixture, blending well until smooth. Serve sauce over oatmeal loaf.

DUTCH OATMEAL CAKE

1 c. quick-cooking oatmeal
1 c. (packed) brown sugar
1 c. sugar
1/2 c. shortening
2 beaten eggs
1 1/2 c. flour
1 tsp. soda
1 tsp. cinnamon
1/2 tsp. salt
Frosting

Pour 1 1/2 cups boiling water over oatmeal; let cool. Cream brown sugar, sugar, shortening and eggs until fluffy. Add flour, soda, cinnamon and salt. Add oatmeal mixture. Pour batter into 9 x 13 x 2-inch loaf pan. Spoon Frosting over cake. Bake at 350 degrees for 40 to 45 minutes.

Frosting

6 tbsp. margarine
1/2 c. (packed) brown sugar
1/2 tsp. vanilla
1 c. shredded coconut
1/2 c. chopped nuts

Melt margarine in skillet; add remaining ingredients, mixing well.

OATMEAL-ORANGE CAKE

3/4 c. butter
1 c. sugar
2 eggs
1 1/2 c. flour
2 tsp. baking powder
1/2 tsp. cinnamon
1/2 tsp. salt
1 c. quick-cooking oats
1 c. milk
1/2 c. (packed) brown sugar
1/2 c. chopped nuts
3 tbsp. orange juice

Cream 1/2 cup butter and sugar together in mixing bowl. Beat in eggs one at a time, beating well after each addition. Sift flour, baking powder, cinnamon and salt together. Add sifted dry ingredients, oats and milk to creamed mixture alternately, blending well. Spoon batter into 9-inch square pan. Bake at 350 degrees for 35 to 40 minutes. Melt remaining butter; add brown sugar, nuts and orange juice. Spread glaze over warm cake. Place under broiler until bubbly. Yield: 6-8 servings.

APPLE-FILLED OATMEAL COOKIES

1 c. butter
1 c. (packed) brown sugar
2 eggs
2 c. flour
2 tsp. baking powder
1/2 tsp. salt
1 tsp. cinnamon
1/2 tsp. cloves
1/2 c. milk
2 c. quick-cooking oats
Apple Filling

Cream butter and sugar together; beat until fluffy. Beat in eggs. Sift flour, baking powder, salt, cinnamon and cloves together; add to creamed mixture alternately with milk. Stir in oats. Reserve about 3/4 cup of dough. Drop remaining dough from teaspoon onto greased cookie sheet. Make small depression in center of each cookie; fill with Apple Filling. Cover filling with small amount of reserved dough. Bake at 375 degrees for 10 to 12 minutes. Yield: 3 dozen.

Apple Filling

1 c. unpared diced apples
1/4 c. raisins
1/4 c. chopped pecans
1/2 c. sugar

Combine all ingredients and 2 tablespoons water in saucepan; cook, stirring constantly, for 10 minutes or until mixture is thick and apples are tender. Cool.

LACE COOKIES

Color photograph for this recipe on page 489.

1/2 c. butter
1/2 c. sugar
1/3 c. sifted all-purpose flour
1/4 tsp. salt
1 c. quick-cooking oats
2 tbsp. milk

Preheat oven to 375 degrees. Melt butter in saucepan. Stir in remaining ingredients, mixing well. Drop by teaspoonfuls about 3 inches apart onto greased and floured cookie sheets. Spread thin with spatula. Bake for 5 to 7 minutes or until edges are brown. Remove from oven; let stand for 1 minute. Remove cookies from cookie sheet carefully with wide spatula. Cookies will be thin and lacy. Cool thoroughly. Yield: 3 1/2 dozen.

OATMEAL-CHOCOLATE CHIP COOKIES

1 c. sifted flour
1 tsp. baking powder
1/2 tsp. salt
1 tsp. cinnamon
1/4 tsp. nutmeg
3/4 c. shortening
1 c. brown sugar
2 eggs
1/3 c. milk
1 c. chocolate chips
3 c. quick cooking oatmeal
1 c. chopped walnuts

Sift flour, baking powder, salt and spices together into mixing bowl. Add shortening, brown sugar, eggs and half the milk. Beat for about 2 minutes or until smooth. Fold in remaining milk, chocolate chips, oatmeal and walnuts. Drop from teaspoon onto greased cookie sheet. Bake in 375-degree oven for 12 to 15 minutes. Yield: 5 dozen cookies.

OAT COOKIES

Color photograph for this recipe on page 492.

1 1/4 c. rolled oats
1 5/8 c. flour
1/2 tsp. salt
1/2 tsp. baking powder
5/8 c. margarine
6 tbsp. milk
Butter
Marmalade

Mix all ingredients except butter and marmalade in bowl. Drop by spoonfuls onto greased baking sheet; flatten with glass dipped in flour. Bake at 400 degrees for about 5 minutes. Serve warm with butter and marmalade.

OATMEAL ROLL-OUTS

3 c. rolled oats
3 c. flour
2 c. shortening
1 tbsp. salt
1 c. (packed) brown sugar

Combine oats and flour; blend in shortening, creaming well. Add salt, brown sugar and 1/4 cup cold water; mix well. Roll out to 1/4-inch thickness on lightly floured surface. Cut with cookie cutter. Place 1 inch apart on ungreased cookie sheet. Bake at 350 degrees for about 15 to 20 minutes or until lightly browned. Yield: 3-4 dozen cookies.

WAFER-THIN OATMEAL CAKES

Color photograph for this recipe on page 483.

1 1/4 c. oatmeal
3/4 c. sugar
1/4 c. light molasses
1/4 c. milk
5/8 c. melted margarine
1 c. flour, sifted
1/2 tsp. baking powder

Combine all ingredients in mixing bowl, blending well. Drop batter from teaspoon about 3 inches apart onto greased baking sheet. Bake at 350 degrees for about 8 minutes or until light brown. Let stand for 1 minute, remove from baking sheet with spatula. Shape around rolling pin or large glass; cool. Yield: 5 dozen cookies.

OATMEAL MUFFINS

1 egg
2/3 c. cold cooked oatmeal
2 tbsp. salad oil
1 c. milk
2 c. sifted flour
3 tsp. baking powder
2 tbsp. sugar
1/2 tsp. salt

Beat egg; add oatmeal and salad oil, mixing well. Stir in milk. Sift flour, baking powder, sugar and salt together; add to oatmeal mixture. Mix only enough to combine. Fill greased muffin cups 2/3 full. Bake at 425 degrees for 25 minutes. Yield: 12 muffins.

OATMEAL-MOLASSES BREAD

6 c. unsifted flour
2 c. rolled oats
1 tsp. salt
2 pkg. dry yeast
1/2 c. milk
1/2 c. molasses
1/2 c. margarine
2 eggs, at room temperature

Mix 1 cup flour, oats, salt and undissolved dry yeast in large bowl. Combine 1 cup water, milk, molasses and margarine in saucepan. Heat until liquids are warm. Margarine does not need to melt. Add to dry ingredients gradually; beat for 2 minutes at medium speed with electric mixer, scraping bowl occasionally. Add eggs and enough flour to make thick batter. Beat at high speed for 2 minutes, scraping bowl occasionally. Stir in enough additional flour to make soft dough. Turn out onto lightly floured board; knead for about 8 to 10 minutes or until smooth and elastic. Place in greased bowl, turning to grease top. Cover; let rise in warm place, free from draft, for

Oatmeal-Molasses Bread . . . Eggs and molasses give this bread unusual richness.

about 1 hour or until doubled in bulk. Punch dough down; turn out onto lightly floured board. Divide dough into 4 equal parts; set 2 pieces aside. Roll 2 pieces into 12-inch long ropes. Twist together; turn ends under to seal. Place in greased loaf pan. Repeat with remaining 2 pieces of dough to form second loaf. Cover; let rise in warm place, free from draft, for about 1 hour or until doubled in bulk. Bake in 400-degree oven for 30 minutes or until bread tests done. Remove from pans; cool on wire racks.

OATMEAL BROWN BREAD

1 c. rolled oats
2 tsp. salt
3 tbsp. butter
1 tsp. sugar
1 pkg. yeast
1/2 c. molasses
1 c. whole wheat flour
4 1/2 c. all-purpose flour

Combine oats, salt and butter. Pour 2 cups boiling water over oats mixture; cool. Combine sugar and yeast in 1/2 cup lukewarm water; let stand for 15 minutes. Stir into cooled oatmeal mixture. Add molasses; beat in whole wheat flour and 2 cups flour. Beat well; work in remaining flour. Place in greased bowl. Cover; let rise in warm place until doubled in bulk. Divide dough into 3 equal parts. Shape into loaves; place in greased loaf pans. Let rise until nearly doubled in bulk. Bake in 350-degree oven for 50 minutes. Yield: 3 loaves.

OATMEAL-RAISIN BREAD

1 c. evaporated milk
1 c. quick-cooking rolled oats
1 egg
1/2 c. (packed) brown sugar
1 tsp. salt
1 c. sifted, fine whole wheat flour
3 tsp. baking powder
1 c. raisins, chopped
2 tbsp. shortening, melted

Pour milk over oats; let stand. Beat egg until light; add brown sugar gradually, beating until fluffy. Add oat mixture; mix well. Sift salt, flour and baking powder together; stir into oat mixture until blended. Stir in raisins and shortening. Pour into greased 8 1/2 x 4 1/2 x 2 1/2-inch loaf pan. Bake at 350 degrees for about 50 minutes to 1 hour. Yield: 1 loaf.

Okra

Okra is an edible green seed pod. The plant producing okra is native to Africa but today grows extensively in the American South. Okra is especially associated with southern cuisine as a favorite vegetable and Creole gumbo thickener. Okra contains Vitamins A and C, carbohydrate, and calcium. (8 medium 3-inch cooked okra pods = 30 calories)

AVAILABILITY: Fresh okra is available year-round but supplies are comparatively small. It is most plentiful from June-October, with the peak months from July-August. Canned and frozen small, whole pods and pods cut into rings are sold year-round. Canned okra fermented in salt brine and small, pickled pods are also sold year-round.

BUYING: Choose tender, bright green, fresh okra of short to medium length (2-4 inches). Tips should bend slightly under pressure. Avoid dull, dry, hard, shriveled, or discolored pods that will be flavorless or tough when cooked. 1 pound okra serves 2 people.

STORING: Wash fresh okra and place in covered container. Refrigerate 4 days. Store unopened cans 1 to 2 months on kitchen shelf. Refrigerate opened cans 4 days. Fresh frozen and commercially frozen okra keeps 1 month in refrigerator freezer and 1 year in home freezer. *To freeze*—Choose young, tender pods. Wash. Cut off stems. Separate into small and large sizes. Blanch small pods in boiling water 2-3 minutes, large pods 3-4 minutes. Chill in ice water 3-5 minutes. Drain. Pack by size in freezer containers, leaving 1/2 inch head space. Seal, label, and freeze. *To can*—Choose tender pods. Wash. Remove stems. Cover with boiling water in saucepan. Bring water to boil. Remove from heat. Pack hot okra into canning jars. Cover with boiling liquid. Process 40 minutes at 10 pounds pressure. (See CANNING.)

PREPARATION: Okra may be boiled, steamed, fried, baked, scalloped, stewed, and sauteed. See individual recipe instructions. *To boil*—Scrub pods well. Cut off stems. Leave small pods whole. Cut large pods into 1/2 inch slices. Add 1/2 cup salted water to 1 1/4 pounds okra in saucepan. Cook uncovered until barely tender, 10-15 minutes. Drain. Makes 4 servings. *To steam*—Prepare okra for cooking as above. Steam pods in colander over hot water until just tender. Do not overcook boiled or steamed okra as it tends to become gummy and unappetizing. *To fry*—Wash pods. Cut off stems. Cut into 1/4 inch slices. Dip into beaten egg and fine bread crumbs or cornmeal. Fry in deep or shallow hot fat till browned. Drain.

SERVING: Serve boiled or steamed okra as a side dish vegetable with melted butter; hollandaise sauce; butter, salt, pepper, and vinegar or lemon juice; minced onion; or minced garlic. Use okra in salads, soups, gumbos, and casseroles.

CREAMY OKRA SOUP

6 okra pods
1 onion, shredded
3 lge. tomatoes, chopped
Salt to taste
Dash of red pepper
Dash of pepper
2 tbsp. butter
3 c. half and half

Slice okra pods crosswise; combine okra, onion, tomatoes, seasonings, butter and 2 cups water in kettle. Cook until vegetables are tender. Stir in half and half; heat just to boiling point. Serve immediately.

HEARTY OKRA SOUP

1 egg, beaten
1 lb. cut okra
1 1/4 c. cornmeal
1/4 c. bacon drippings
2 1/2 c. canned tomatoes
1 tbsp. sugar
1/2 c. catsup
1 med. onion, chopped
1 med. bell pepper, chopped
Salt and pepper to taste

Combine egg and okra in bowl; coat with cornmeal. Fry in drippings over medium heat until browned. Add tomatoes, sugar, catsup, onion and bell pepper. Cover; simmer until vegetables are tender. Season with salt and pepper; serve at once.

BOILED OKRA

1 qt. okra with 1/2-inch stems
1 tbsp. cider vinegar
1 tbsp. bacon drippings
Salt to taste

Place okra in pan with cold water to just cover. Add vinegar; cook until fork tender. Do not stir okra while cooking. Add bacon drippings; season with salt. Lift okra from pan carefully to serve.

DUTCH OVEN OKRA

1 qt. sliced okra
1/2 c. minced onion
Salt to taste
3 tbsp. cooking oil

Combine all ingredients in greased Dutch oven; cover. Bake at 400 degrees for about 40 minutes or until tender, stirring occasionally.

FRITTER-FRIED OKRA

1 c. flour
3 tsp. baking powder
1/2 tsp. salt
2 eggs, well beaten
1/3 c. milk
5 c. thinly sliced okra

Sift flour with baking powder and salt. Add eggs and milk; stir until smooth. Add okra; mix well. Drop by spoonfuls into deep hot fat; fry until golden. Yield: 6-8 servings.

OKRA AND CHEESE CASSEROLE

1/2 lb. okra
4 tomatoes, sliced
1 onion, minced
1 lb. American cheese, cubed
Salt and pepper

Preheat oven to 325 degrees. Cut tips and ends from okra; slice crosswise. Arrange tomatoes, onion, okra and cheese in layers in buttered casserole; add seasonings to each layer. Bake, covered, for 40 minutes. Yield: 4 servings.

OKRA CASSEROLE

1/4 c. rice
1 qt. sliced okra
1 qt. cooked tomatoes
1/2 tsp. salt
Pepper to taste
1/4 tsp. curry powder
1 tbsp. butter

Place rice in buttered baking dish; add okra and tomatoes. Season with salt, pepper and curry powder; dot with butter. Bake, covered, in 325-degree oven for 45 minutes or until rice is tender. Remove cover. Bake until top is browned. Yield: 6 servings.

OKRA CREOLE

1/4 c. chopped onion
1 green pepper, chopped
2 c. sliced okra
1 c. canned corn
3/4 c. chopped tomatoes
1 tsp. salt
1/8 tsp. pepper

Cook onion and green pepper in hot fat until onion is golden, stirring frequently. Add okra; cook for 5 minutes, stirring occasionally. Add remaining ingredients; cover and simmer for 15 to 20 minutes.

OKRA CROQUETTES

1/2 c. shortening
1 egg, beaten
1 tbsp. flour
3 tbsp. cornmeal
1/2 tsp. salt
1/4 tsp. pepper
2 c. minced okra
1/4 c. minced onion

Heat shortening in 10-inch skillet. Combine egg, flour, cornmeal, salt and pepper; mix well. Stir in okra and onion. Drop from tablespoon into hot fat; cook for 3 minutes or until golden brown, turning once and flattening with spatula. Yield: 4 servings.

OKRA ETOUFFE

3 c. sliced okra
1/4 c. cooking oil
1 c. canned tomatoes
1 onion, chopped
1 green pepper, chopped
Salt and pepper to taste
Red pepper to taste
1/4 c. cracker or potato chip crumbs (opt.)

Spread okra in greased casserole; cover with oil, tomatoes, onion, green pepper and seasonings. Cover loosely with foil. Bake at 400 degrees for 1 hour or until tender, stirring occasionally. Uncover; top with crumbs. Bake until browned.

OKRA PATTIES

1 1/2 c. sliced okra
2 tbsp. buttermilk
3 tbsp. flour
2 tbsp. cornmeal
1 tsp. salt
1/8 tsp. pepper
1 egg, beaten
Cooking oil

Boil okra in a small amount of water until tender; drain well. Combine okra, buttermilk, flour, cornmeal, salt, pepper and egg. Drop by tablespoonfuls into heated oil; fry until brown.

OKRA PILAU

4 bacon slices, chopped
2 c. sliced okra
1 c. long grain rice
Salt and pepper to taste

Fry bacon in saucepan until almost crisp. Add okra; fry until tender. Add 1 1/2 cups water, rice, salt and pepper; cover. Cook over low heat, for about 1 hour and 30 minutes or until rice is dry, stirring occasionally. Yield: 4-6 servings.

SCALLOPED OKRA

1 sm. onion, chopped
1/4 tsp. salt
1/2 tsp. pepper
2 tbsp. melted butter
2 c. cooked okra
1/2 c. grated cheese
1 egg, beaten
3/4 c. bread crumbs
Buttered crumbs

Combine onion, salt, pepper, butter and okra. Arrange half the okra mixture in small buttered baking dish; top with half the cheese. Spoon the egg over cheese; sprinkle with the bread crumbs. Repeat layers; top with buttered crumbs. Bake at 350 degrees for 30 minutes.

SPANISH OKRA

1/4 lb. okra
2 lge. fresh tomatoes
4 tbsp. butter
3 tbsp. chopped onion
1 tsp. salt
2 tbsp. chili powder
3 drops of hot sauce

Cut okra in 1/4-inch slices; dice tomatoes. Melt butter in skillet. Add okra, tomatoes, and onion; saute for 5 minutes. Stir in salt, chili powder, hot sauce and 1 cup water; simmer, covered, until vegetables are tender and mixture has thickened.

Olive

Olives are small, oval, tender-fleshed fruit that contains a hard pit. They grow on exquisitely gnarled evergreens in subtropical climates. There are three types of olives: the Spanish-style or *green olives* that are stored in unheated brine for 6 to 12 months until they have fermented; the smooth, black *ripe olives* that are placed in boiling brine, then exposed to the air until the characteristic black color develops; and the jet black *Greek* or *Italian olives* that are dried or salt-cured, thus acquiring their wrinkled or shriveled appearance. (1 extra large green olive = 7 calories; 1 extra large ripe olive = 11 calories; 1 extra large Greek olive = 20 calories)

AVAILABILITY: Olives are available year-round in jars, cans, or by the pound. Leading olive-producing areas are California and Mediterranian countries. Also commercially available is olive oil that is extracted from the flesh of ripe olives.

BUYING: Olives are graded according to the following sizes: small, medium, large. Dependably high quality olives are such established varieties as Kalamata, Ascalano, Manzanillo, and Mission. Buy green olives packed in weak salt brine, pitted, unpitted, or stuffed. Buy ripe olives pickled, dried, and oil-packed, pitted or unpitted, whole, sliced, and chopped. Buy Greek olives dried or packed in oil.

STORING: Unopened cans or jars of olives will keep indefinitely at room temperature. Store opened containers indefinitely in refrigerator. Olives should always be firm.

USES: Olives are universally enjoyed as accompaniments and appetizers. They also add zest to salads, sandwiches, soups and stews, and casseroles.

BROILED OLIVES

1/2 pkg. sliced bacon
1 jar lge. olives

Cut bacon slices in half. Wrap each olive in bacon slice; secure with wooden pick. Broil 5 inches from source of heat until bacon is crisp; turn to broil evenly. Yield: 4-6 servings.

CURRIED OLIVE APPETIZERS

1 4 1/2-oz. can chopped ripe olives
3/4 c. grated Cheddar cheese
1/4 c. sliced green onions
4 tbsp. mayonnaise
1/4 tsp. curry powder
Pinch of salt
10 slices thinly sliced bread
2 tbsp. minced parsley

Combine olives, cheese, onions, mayonnaise, curry powder and salt; mix well. Remove crusts from bread slices; toast under broiler. Spread olive mixture on toast. Place on cookie sheet; cut each slice into 6 small squares. Broil 4 inches from source of heat until bubbly; sprinkle with parsley. Serve hot.

OLIVE CANAPES

2 hard-cooked eggs, minced
Mayonnaise
1 tsp. chopped parsley
6 stuffed olives, chopped
Dash of paprika
Dash of onion salt
Bread slices
Butter

Combine eggs, 2 tablespoons mayonnaise, parsley, olives, paprika and onion salt; mix thoroughly. Cover egg mixture; set aside for 30 minutes. Toast bread slices on one side in small amount of butter in hot skillet. Spread untoasted side of bread slice with mayonnaise. Spread with egg mixture. Cut into small squares, triangles or stars. Garnish with pickle or olive. Yield: 2 dozen.

OLIVE-CHEESE BALLS

1 15-oz. jar bacon and cheese spread
5 tbsp. butter
3/4 c. flour
Dash of Worcestershire sauce
1 sm. jar olives

Combine spread, butter, flour and Worcestershire sauce; blend well. Shape dough around olives. Place on ungreased pan. Bake at 400 degrees for 12 minutes. Yield: 10-12 servings.

OLIVE-HAM APPETIZERS

3/4 c. cooked ground ham
1/2 c. chopped olives
1 tbsp. sour cream
1 tsp. mustard
1 tsp. Worcestershire sauce
1 recipe pastry dough
1 tbsp. caraway seed

Combine all ingredients except pastry and caraway seed. Divide pastry dough into 6 parts. Roll each part into 5 x 3-inch rectangle. Sprinkle 1/2 teaspoon caraway seed over each portion: spread olive mixture over top. Roll rectangles, starting at long ends; pinch to seal. Do not close ends of rolls. Place on baking sheet. Bake at 450 degrees for 12 minutes. Slice to serve. Yield: 20 servings.

OLIVE-ONION DIP

1 pt. sour cream with chives
1 4-oz. jar stuffed olives, chopped
1 pkg. onion soup mix
1/4 tsp. celery salt
Dash of Worcestershire sauce
1/4 tsp. garlic salt
Salt and pepper to taste

Combine all ingredients; mix well. Yield: 6 servings.

RIPE OLIVE APPETIZERS

25 pitted ripe olives
3 tbsp. minced green onions
1/2 c. flour
1/4 tsp. salt
Dash of dry mustard
1 c. shredded sharp Cheddar cheese
2 tbsp. butter, melted and cooled
1 tsp. milk
2 drops of hot sauce

Stuff olives with onions. Blend flour, salt and mustard; mix in cheese. Stir in all remaining ingredients; shape 1 teaspoon cheese mixture around each olive. Place on baking sheet. Bake at 400 degrees for 12 minutes; may be refrigerated before baking.

RIPE OLIVE CHILI

Color photograph for this recipe on page 734.

2 1-lb. cans kidney beans
1/2 lb. lean ground beef
1 tbsp. cooking oil
1 1 5/8-oz. package chili seasoning mix
1 1-lb. can stewed tomatoes
1 8-oz. can tomato sauce
1/2 tsp. salt
1 1/2 c. canned pitted ripe olives

Drain and rinse kidney beans. Cook beef in oil in skillet until lightly browned. Add kidney beans, chili seasoning mix, tomatoes, tomato sauce and salt; simmer for 10 minutes. Drain olives; add to beef mixture. Heat for several minutes longer. Serve as dip with tortillas. Yield: 6 servings.

AL FRESCO OLIVE SALAD

Color photograph for this recipe on page 312.

1 qt. diced carrots
1 pt. diced potatoes
1 1/2 c. canned pitted ripe olives
1/4 c. chopped green onions
1 sm. clove of garlic, minced
1 tbsp. butter
1/2 c. California Dressing

Cook carrots and potatoes in boiling, salted water for about 7 minutes or until just tender. Do not overcook. Drain and cool. Cut olives into quarters. Cook onions and garlic in butter in saucepan until soft but not browned. Combine carrot mixture, olives and onion mixture with California Dressing; mix lightly. Spoon into oiled 6-cup mold; press down lightly. Cover; refrigerate overnight. Unmold; garnish with ripe olives, carrot curls and watercress.

California Dressing

2/3 c. salad oil
1/3 c. garlic wine vinegar
1 1/2 tsp. seasoned salt
1/4 tsp. seasoned pepper
1/2 tsp. paprika
1/2 tsp. sugar
2 tbsp. crumbled blue cheese
2 canned pimentos, mashed

Combine first 6 ingredients; add cheese and pimentos. Beat well or process in blender. Yield: 6-8 servings.

CABBAGE-OLIVE SALAD

1 med. cabbage, chopped
1 green pepper, chopped
12 stuffed olives, sliced
1 sm. can pimento, chopped
1 sm. onion, grated
1/2 c. sugar
1/2 c. vinegar
1/2 c. salad oil
1 tsp. salt
1 tsp. prepared mustard
1 tsp. celery seed

Combine cabbage, green pepper, olives, pimento and onion; mix well. Place in 2-quart casserole. Add sugar; mix well. Combine vinegar, salad oil, salt, prepared mustard and celery seed in saucepan. Bring to a boil; pour over cabbage mixture. Cover; refrigerate for 24 hours before serving. Yield: 6-8 servings.

OLIVE-CHEESE SALAD

1 lge. head lettuce
1 sm. can pimentos, drained
2 sm. cans anchovies
1 med. can ripe olives
1 med. can stuffed olives
1/2 lb. bleu cheese, cubed
1/2 lb. Cheddar cheese, cut into strips
1/2 lb. sliced hard salami, cut in wedges
2 lge. onions, sliced
Vinegar
Oil

Break lettuce into small pieces; add pimentos, anchovies, ripe olives and stuffed olives. Add bleu cheese, Cheddar cheese, salami wedges and onion slices. Toss with enough vinegar and oil to coat. Yield: 8-10 servings.

OLIVE SALAD PLATE

Crisp salad greens
6 chilled oranges, peeled
2/3 c. chopped ripe olives
1/3 c. finely chopped leeks
1/2 c. olive oil
2 tbsp. red wine vinegar
1 tsp. ground coriander
1/4 tsp. salt
1/4 tsp. pepper
1/4 tsp. sugar
1/4 tsp. dry mustard

Line chilled salad platter with greens. Cut oranges into thin crosswise slices. Arrange orange slices on greens. Sprinkle with chopped olives and leeks. Garnish with whole olives. Shake olive oil, vinegar, coriander, salt, pepper, sugar and mustard in covered jar until blended well. Pour over oranges.

OLIVE-CORNED BEEF SALAD

1 pkg. lemon gelatin
1 can corned beef, chopped
1 c. chopped celery
1/2 c. chopped stuffed olives
1 c. salad dressing

Dissolve gelatin in 1 1/2 cups boiling water. Cool; refrigerate until partially set. Add all remaining ingredients; mix well. Pour into 8-inch square pan. Chill until firm. Yield: 9 servings.

OLIVE RING

1 c. thinly sliced ripe olives
2 env. plain gelatin
3 tbsp. vinegar
Lemon juice to taste
1/2 tsp. salt
1/4 tsp. hot sauce
2 c. cottage cheese
1/3 c. mayonnaise
1 c. cucumber
1/4 c. sliced spring onions
1/2 c. diced green pepper
Salad greens
Radishes

Arrange center olive slices in circle in 6-cup ring mold. Soften gelatin in 1 cup cold water; stir over low heat until gelatin is dissolved. Remove from heat; stir in 1 1/2 cups water, vinegar, lemon juice, salt and hot sauce. Chill until mixture mounds from spoon. Fold in cottage cheese, mayonnaise, cucumber, onions, green pepper and remaining olives. Spoon into mold; chill until firm. Unmold on salad greens; fill center with radishes. Yield: 6 servings.

OLIVE-NUT SPREAD

1 c. pimento-stuffed olives
1 c. walnuts
Mayonnaise

Grind olives and walnuts together. Stir in enough mayonnaise until mixture is of spreading consistency.

GOURMET RIPE OLIVE POULET

6 boned double chicken breasts
Chopped chives
1 1/2 c. canned pitted California ripe olives
Garlic salt
2 tbsp. butter
2 tsp. cornstarch
2 tbsp. lemon juice
2 4 3/4-oz. jars strained apricots
3 tbsp. brandy

Preheat oven to 400 degrees. Place chicken breasts skin sides down; sprinkle each breast with 1 teaspoon chives. Arrange 4 olives on center of each breast; fold meat around olives. Cut remaining olives in half; set aside. Fasten breasts with small skewers. Sprinkle with garlic salt. Place, skin sides down, in melted butter in baking dish. Bake for 30 minutes. Mix cornstarch, lemon juice and apricots. Heat to boiling point, stirring frequently. Stir brandy into apricot sauce. Remove chicken from oven; turn, skin sides up. Spoon sauce over chicken breasts. Bake for 20 minutes longer, adding remaining halved olives for last 5 minutes of cooking. Garnish with parsley.

OLIVES AND CHEESE

4 pkg. lime gelatin
1 med. can crushed pineapple
1 sm. carton cottage cheese
2 stalks celery, chopped
1 sm. bottle stuffed olives, sliced
1 sm. package cream cheese
1/4 c. mayonnaise

Dissolve gelatin in 7 cups boiling water; cool. Drain pineapple; reserve juice. Combine cottage cheese, pineapple, celery and olives; stir into gelatin mixture. Shape cream cheese into small balls; add to mixture. Pour into large mold; chill until firm. Thin mayonnaise with reserved juice; top gelatin mold with mayonnaise mixture to serve. Yield: 12 servings.

RIPE OLIVE CHOP-CHOP

3 sm. cans chopped ripe olives
1 1/2 c. finely chopped celery
1 c. chopped dill pickles
1/2 c. finely chopped onion
1 clove of garlic, minced
1 2-oz. can anchovy fillets
1/2 c. salad oil
1/4 c. wine vinegar
1/4 tsp. pepper

Combine olives, celery, dill pickles, onion and garlic in large bowl; toss lightly to mix. Drain oil from anchovies; add oil to olive mixture. Cut anchovies into tiny pieces; stir into olive mixture. Combine salad oil, wine vinegar and pepper; toss with olive mixture. Yield: 5 cups.

Gourmet Ripe Olive Poulet . . . Olive-stuffed chicken breasts are glazed with a tart mixture.

RIPE OLIVE SOUP

2 4-oz. cans ripe olives, minced
1 sm. clove of garlic
3 c. chicken stock
2 eggs
1 c. cream
Salt and pepper to taste

Simmer olives and garlic in chicken stock for 15 minutes. Discard garlic; reserve stock. Beat eggs with cream; add 1 cup reserved stock. Mix well; add to remaining stock gradually. Place over low heat, stirring constantly, until thickened slightly; do not boil. Add salt and pepper. Serve hot, garnished with minced dill. Yield: 6 servings.

OLIVE-NUT BREAD

2 1/2 c. flour
4 tsp. baking powder
1/3 c. sugar
1/2 tsp. salt
1 c. milk
1 egg, beaten
1 c. stuffed green olives, sliced
1 c. chopped walnuts
2 tbsp. chopped pimento
Cream cheese

Sift flour, baking powder, sugar and salt together. Combine milk and egg; add to dry ingredients. Stir in olives, walnuts and pimento. Place in greased loaf pan. Bake at 350 degrees for 1 hour. Cool for 10 minutes before removing from pan. Slice thin; spread with cream cheese before serving.

RIPE OLIVE AND CHEESE CUSTARD

1 c. rice
1 c. pitted ripe olives
2 eggs
1 8-oz. carton sour cream
1 c. milk
1 tbsp. minced onion
Salt and pepper
6 oz. white American cheese, grated

Prepare rice according to package directions; cool. Quarter olives, reserving 3 whole olives for garnish. Beat eggs thoroughly; blend in sour cream and milk. Add onion, 1/2 teaspoon salt and 1/4 teaspoon pepper. Grease sides and bottom of greased 1 1/2-quart baking dish. Place layer of half the rice in dish. Add layer of half the olives and half the cheese. Pour half the egg mixture over cheese. Repeat layers. Cut reserved olives in half; spread over cheese. Bake at 350 degrees for 35 minutes or until set and golden.

Omelet

An omelet is a mixture of eggs and seasonings that is cooked in a well-buttered and well-heated pan or skillet until firm and delicately browned. Liquid such as cream, milk, or water is sometimes added. There are two basic kinds of omelets: the *French omelet,* in which the whole egg is beaten; and the *puffy omelet,* in which egg whites are beaten separately from egg yolks. The latter method produces a fluffier, soufflelike omelet. All omelets are varieties of the two kinds. French omelets may be folded over ham, cheese, onions, mushrooms, jam, or a more elaborate filling. Plain or fancy, all omelets make tantalizing breakfast dishes, luncheon specials, and entrees.

PREPARATION: *French omelet*—Bring eggs to room temperature. Beat with a whisk until fluffy. Add seasonings and liquid (if specified in recipe). Pour into heated butter in omelet pan or skillet. Cook slowly over low heat, moving the pan back and forth. As undersurface sets, gently lift omelet from sides of pan with spatula to allow uncooked egg to flow underneath. When whole omelet is firm, loosen from sides of pan. Add to center of omelet ingredients which melt easily, such as cheese and creamed foods. Carefully fold one side of omelet over filling. Or roll omelet over filling. *Puffy omelet*—Bring eggs to room temperature. Beat egg whites until stiff. Beat egg yolks with a whisk until thick and lemon-colored. Add seasonings and liquid (if specified in recipe) to egg yolk. Fold yolk into whites. Pour mixture into heated butter in pan or skillet. Cook slowly over low heat until bottom is light brown. Remove from heat. Place skillet in moderately hot oven. Bake omelet until light brown on top. Remove from oven. Fold in half. Slide onto platter. Serve immediately. Accompany with sauce if desired.

BANANA OMELET

6 eggs, at room temperature
Butter
1 banana, chopped

Beat eggs slightly. Melt butter in skillet; add banana. Pour in eggs. Cook over low heat until eggs are set; fold over. Brown slightly. Do not overcook. Yield: 6 servings.

BASIC FRENCH OMELET

4 eggs
Salt and pepper
1 tbsp. butter

Beat eggs with 2 tablespoons water. Add salt and pepper to taste. Heat butter in omelet pan over medium heat until butter is hot and bubbly. Add egg mixture, cooking until set around edge. Pull omelet away from side of pan with fork, rolling pan to allow uncooked egg to seep down underneath. Fold omelet over when set but not dry. Place on heated serving platter. Serve immediately. Yield: 1-2 servings.

FLAMING STRAWBERRY OMELET

Color photograph for this recipe on page 487.

4 eggs, separated
1/4 tsp. salt
1 tbsp. sugar
4 tbsp. rum
1 tbsp. butter
2 c. sliced sweetened strawberries

Beat egg yolks with salt in mixing bowl until light. Add sugar and 1 tablespoon rum, mixing well. Beat egg whites until stiff; fold into egg yolk mixture. Melt butter in chafing dish. Pour egg mixture into pan; cook over medium heat, spooning egg mixture from sides into middle until set. Fold omelet in half; sprinkle with additional sugar. Spoon strawberries over omelet. Ignite remaining rum in a ladle; pour over omelet slowly. Serve flaming.

OMELET CREOLE

2/3 c. instant nonfat dry milk powder
6 eggs, separated
1 1/2 tsp. salt
1/2 tsp. white pepper
5 tbsp. butter
1 med. green pepper
1 med. onion, chopped
1 c. chopped mushrooms
3 med. peeled tomatoes, chopped
1/2 tsp. Worcestershire sauce
1/4 tsp. dried sweet basil

Beat 2/3 cup water and dry milk powder together until thick. Add egg yolks, 1 teaspoon salt and white pepper; blend until smooth. Beat egg whites until stiff but not dry. Fold into dry milk mixture. Melt 3 tablespoons butter in skillet. Add egg mixture. Cover; cook over medium heat for about 20 minutes or until omelet is slightly dry on top. Place green pepper, onion and mushrooms in saucepan with remaining butter. Cook until tender. Add tomatoes, remaining salt and seasonings. Cook until tomatoes are tender. Place omelet on heated platter, browned side down, spoon sauce over 1/2 of the omelet. Fold over. Garnish with parsley.

Omelet Creole . . . An omelet folded around seasoned onion, pepper, mushrooms and tomatoes.

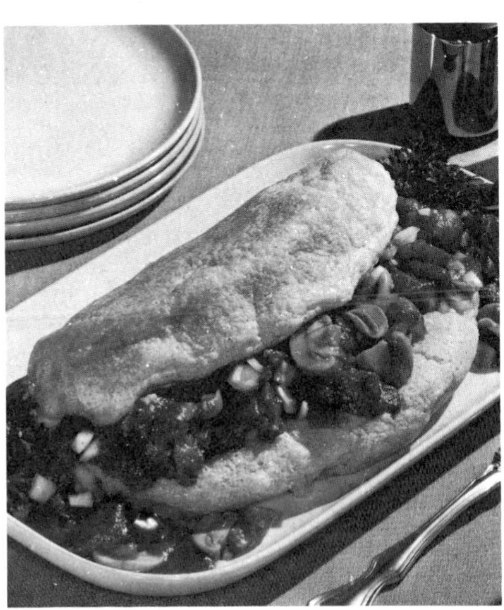

OMELET WITH SAUCE

4 eggs, separated
1/4 c. milk
1/2 tsp. salt
Dash of white pepper
1 tbsp. butter
Sauce

Beat egg whites until stiff but not dry. Beat egg yolks until thick and lemon colored; blend in milk, salt and pepper. Fold in egg whites gently. Heat butter in skillet until moderately hot; add egg mixture. Cook over low heat for 3 to 5 minutes or until omelet puffs up and is firm and lightly browned on bottom. Bake in 325-degree oven until top is dry. Loosen omelet from pan gently. Cut halfway down across the center. Spread with half the Sauce; fold in half carefully. Spread remaining Sauce on top; serve hot.

Sauce

2 tbsp. bacon fat
2/3 c. onion, finely chopped
2 tbsp. chopped green pepper
1/2 clove of garlic
2 tbsp. chopped celery
1 tbsp. sugar
1/4 c. chopped stuffed olives
1 sm. bay leaf
6 whole cloves
1 tsp. salt
1/4 tsp. white pepper
2 1/2 c. stewed tomatoes

Melt fat in heavy skillet; add onion, green pepper, garlic and celery. Saute for 5 minutes; remove garlic. Add remaining ingredients; simmer over low heat with cover ajar for 20 to 30 minutes. Remove cover; cook until thick. Remove bay leaf and cloves.

ITALIAN CHEESE OMELET

8 eggs
1 tsp. salt
1 tbsp. parsley, chopped
1/2 c. cubed Parmesan cheese
Pepper to taste
1/2 tbsp. corn oil

Break eggs into medium bowl. Beat with rotary beater until mixed but not foamy. Add salt, parsley, cheese and pepper. Heat oil in frying pan over medium heat. Pour egg mixture into pan; lower heat slightly. Cook until omelet is set around edges, loosening omelet occasionally with spatula. Fold omelet over; brown slightly. Yield: 4 servings.

SWISS CHEESE OMELET

1 4-oz. can sliced mushrooms
3 tbsp. butter
1 sm. onion, minced
6 eggs
1/4 c. Italian dressing
1/2 c. shredded Swiss cheese

Drain mushrooms. Melt 2 tablespoons butter in skillet; saute onion and mushrooms until golden. Beat eggs, dressing, 2 tablespoons water and cheese together; pour egg mixture over mushroom mixture in skillet. Omelet should set at edge at once. Reduce heat slightly; lift cooked portions at edge so uncooked egg mixture flows underneath. Add remaining butter; slide pan back and forth over moderate heat rapidly until mixture is set but surface is still moist. Increase heat to brown bottom quickly. Fold omelet in half; roll out onto heated platter. Yield: 4-6 servings.

SOUTHERN CHEESE OMELET

4 eggs
1/4 c. minced onion
1/8 tsp. salt
1/8 tsp. pepper
1 tbsp. ham gravy
2 slices American cheese

Beat eggs slightly; add onion, salt and pepper. Place ham gravy in skillet over low heat; pour egg mixture into skillet. Do not stir. Cover; cook for 5 minutes or until mixture is firm. Remove from heat; cut in half. Place cheese on 1 half; top cheese with remaining half. Leave omelet in skillet until cheese melts. Serve hot. Yield: 4 servings.

BACON-EGG FOO YUNG

1/2 lb. bacon, chopped
3/4 c. chopped celery
1/2 c. peas
1 can water chestnuts
1/2 c. chopped onion
1 can bean sprouts, drained
1/2 c. sliced mushrooms
8 eggs, beaten
1 1/2 tsp. soy sauce
1 1/2 tsp. salt
1/2 tsp. pepper
2 tsp. cornstarch
1/2 tsp. sugar
1 tsp. oil

Cook bacon bits in skillet until crisp; drain on paper toweling. Combine bacon, celery, peas, water chestnuts, onion, bean sprouts, mushrooms, eggs, 1/2 teaspoon soy sauce, 1 teaspoon salt and pepper in bowl; mix thoroughly. Pour about 1/4 cup egg mixture for each omelet onto hot greased griddle. Bake on each side over medium heat until set but not dry. Place omelets on heated serving platter. Combine remaining soy sauce and salt in saucepan. Add cornstarch, sugar, oil and 1/2 cup water. Boil for 5 minutes, stirring constantly, until thickened. Serve sauce with Egg Foo Yung. Yield: 6 servings.

CHICKEN-EGG FOO YUNG

6 eggs, beaten
2/3 c. finely sliced onion
1/4 c. finely chopped celery
1 c. bean sprouts, drained
1 1/2 c. cubed cooked chicken

Combine eggs, onion, celery, bean sprouts and chicken. Pour about 1/4 cup egg mixture on hot greased griddle for each omelet. Cook over medium heat until set but not dry on each side.

Hot Soy Sauce

5 tsp. soy sauce
2 tsp. cornstarch
2 tsp. sugar
2 tsp. vinegar
3/4 tsp. salt

Combine soy sauce, cornstarch, sugar, vinegar, salt and 1 cup cold water in saucepan. Boil for 5 minutes. Serve sauce with Egg Foo Yung.

SHRIMP-EGG FOO YUNG

1/2 c. chopped onion
1 clove of garlic, minced
Cooking oil
1 c. canned shrimp
6 eggs, slightly beaten
1/2 tsp. salt
Dash of pepper
Soy sauce

Saute onion and garlic in 1 tablespoon hot oil in skillet until soft. Add shrimp; cook over low heat for about 2 to 3 minutes or until lightly browned. Remove shrimp mixture; cool. Combine eggs, salt and pepper; add shrimp mixture. Heat 2 tablespoons oil in skillet; pour in egg mixture. Reduce heat. Cover; cook slowly for about 10 minutes or until eggs are set. Fold over in center; turn out on hot platter. Serve immediately with soy sauce. Yield: 4 servings.

MEXICALI OMELET

5 eggs
1 sm. can mushrooms, drained
18 stuffed olives, chopped
1 med. green pepper, chopped
1 med. onion, chopped
6 strips bacon, diced
1 1/2 tsp. oregano
1 tsp. garlic powder
Salt and pepper to taste
4 slices cheese
1 sm. can taco sauce

Beat eggs slightly; add mushrooms and olives. Saute green pepper, onion and bacon in skillet. Add egg mixture and seasonings. Cook over medium heat until omelet is partially set; top with cheese. Cook until cheese is slightly melted; pour taco sauce over top. Cook until cheese has melted. Yield: 6 servings.

NEVER-FAIL FLUFFY OMELET

2 tbsp. quick-cooking tapioca
3/4 tsp. salt
1/8 tsp. pepper
3/4 c. milk
1 tbsp. butter
4 eggs, separated

Combine tapioca, salt, pepper and milk in saucepan. Place over low heat; bring to a boil, stirring constantly. Add butter; remove from heat. Cool slightly. Beat egg yolks until thick and lemon colored. Add milk mixture; mix well. Fold mixture into stiffly beaten egg whites. Turn into hot greased 10-inch skillet. Cook over low heat for 3 minutes. Place in oven. Bake at 350 degrees for 15 minutes or until knife inserted in center comes out clean. Cut across omelet crosswise 1/2 of the way through. Fold over carefully; serve on hot platter. Yield: 4 servings.

PUFFY OMELET

8 eggs, separated
3 tbsp. milk
1 tsp. salt
1/2 tsp. hot sauce
3 tbsp. soft margarine

Beat egg whites with electric mixer until stiff and shiny but still moist. Add milk, salt and hot sauce to egg yolks. Beat egg yolk mixture until light and lemon-colored. Fold egg yolk mixture into egg whites. Melt margarine in 10 or 12-inch oven-proof skillet over low heat. Tilt pan to coat sides. Pour in omelet mixture. Cook for 5 to 6 minutes or until bottom is lightly browned. Bake in 325-degree oven for 15 to 18 minutes until center is cooked. Cut partway through center at right angle. Fold over with spatula; press down gently. Slip onto heated serving platter. Yield: 3-4 servings.

SIMPLE SIMON OMELET

5 eggs
1/3 c. milk
1/4 tsp. salt
1/4 tsp. pepper
Butter
1 can sliced mushrooms
3 slices Cheddar cheese
1 sm. can spaghetti sauce

Break eggs in medium mixing bowl; add milk, salt and pepper. Beat until well mixed and light in color. Place small amount of butter in heavy skillet; heat over low heat. Add eggs; cook, covered, for about 5 minutes until eggs are set. Bottom should be lightly browned. Drain mushrooms; cut cheese into triangles. Heat sauce and mushrooms in saucepan. Run spatula around side of omelet; pour half the sauce over omelet. Fold omelet over with pancake turner. Place on ovenproof platter; pour remaining sauce on top of omelet. Top with cheese. Place under broiler for about 3 minutes to melt cheese. Serve immediately. Yield: 6 servings.

SPANISH OMELET

1 sm. onion, chopped
2 tbsp. bacon drippings
1 1/2 c. tomatoes
Salt
Pepper to taste
1/4 tsp. oregano
1/4 tsp. cumin
1 med. new potato, boiled
6 eggs
1/4 c. light cream

Saute onion in 1 tablespoon bacon drippings. Add tomatoes, salt to taste, pepper, oregano and cumin. Sliver potato; add to sauce. Simmer for about 15 minutes. Beat eggs well; add cream and 1/4 teaspoon salt, beating thoroughly. Place remaining bacon drippings in heavy skillet; heat slightly. Add egg mixture; cook over low heat without stirring until eggs are set. Lift omelet in places to allow egg to run under omelet. Spoon half the sauce onto omelet; fold over. Cook for about 3 minutes longer. Pour remaining sauce over omelet before serving. Serve hot. Yield: 6 servings.

SPINACH OMELET

3 eggs
1/4 tsp. salt
1/4 tsp. pepper
6 tbsp. Parmesan cheese
1 c. chopped cooked spinach
1/4 c. oil

Beat eggs well in deep bowl; add salt, pepper and cheese. Add spinach to egg mixture. Heat oil in large frying pan; add egg mixture. Cook over medium heat until bottom is browned. Turn over; brown other side. Serve immediately. Yield: 2 servings.

VALENCIANA OMELET

1 sm. can tomato sauce
1 sm. onion, chopped
1/2 green pepper, chopped
1 stalk celery, chopped
Salt and pepper to taste
1 sm. can English peas
6 eggs, beaten
8 slices fried bacon, crumbled
1 sm. can pimentos

Combine tomato sauce, onion and green pepper in skillet; add celery, salt and pepper. Simmer until vegetables are tender. Add peas. Pour half the eggs into greased omelet pan; cook over medium heat until edge is set. Bake in 325-degree oven until top is browned. Repeat with remaining eggs. Place omelets in heated serving dish. Fill 1/2 of each omelet with bacon; add some of the sauce and pimento. Fold omelets over; pour remaining sauce over both omelets. Garnish with remaining pimento. Yield: 6 servings.

Onions

Onions are edible bulb-shaped herbs with a pungent odor and flavor caused by their high sulphur content. There are two kinds of onions: mature *dried onions* that are yellow, white, or red in color; and *green onions* that have very little or no bulb formation. Dried onions include: mild-flavored varieties such as Spanish, Bermuda, Early Gano, Italian, and Pearl; and strong-flavored varieties such as Globe, Creole, Australian Brown, and Ebenezer. Leeks, shallots, and scallions comprise the green onion family. Onions contain Vitamin C and other vitamins and minerals. (1 medium onion, raw = 50 calories; 6 green onions without tops = 25 calories)

AVAILABILITY: Dried onions are available year-round. Frozen and canned whole onions, as well as French-fried onion rings, are available year-round. Green onions, too, are available year-round with peak months from May through August.

BUYING: *Dried onions*—Look for bright, clean, firm, well-shaped specimens with dry, paper-thin skins and small necks. Avoid onions with green sunburned patches, blemishes, or fresh sprouts. *Green onions* are usually sold in bunches. Select fresh, crisp onions with green tops, firm 2- to 3-inch white portions, and medium-sized roots. Avoid onions with yellowed, wilted, and discolored tops.

STORING: Store dried onions at room temperature in a cool, dry, well ventilated place for 1 to 4 weeks. Before storing green onions, snip wilted parts with kitchen shears. Wrap in plastic bag. Store in refrigerator crisper 1 to 4 months.

PREPARATION: *For dried onions—To peel,* slit skin with knife from stem to root. Peel onion under running water to avoid teary eyes. Or pour boiling water over onions and allow them to stand several minutes. Then remove several layers of skin. Leave whole, quarter, or slice and separate into rings. *To*

boil—Drop peeled onions into boiling salted water. Cook covered 15 to 30 minutes or until skin becomes transparent. Onion slices cook in about 10 minutes. Drain and season to taste. Onions may also be baked, broiled, sauteed, and French-fried (rings). For detailed instructions, see specific recipes. *For green onions—To boil*—Wash onions and remove loose layers of skin. Cut tops, leaving 3 inch stems. Cook covered in boiling salted water 8 to 10 minutes.
USES: Dried onions are exceptionally versatile foods. They may be used as a seasoning with other foods, as garnishes for platters, or as a main-dish vegetable. Use green onions raw in salads, and for flavoring in soups, stews, and other hot dishes.
(See VEGETABLES.)

DILLED ONIONS

1 lge. Bermuda onion
1/2 c. sugar
2 tsp. salt
1/2 tsp. dillweed
1/2 c. white vinegar

Slice onion thin; separate into rings. Pack onion into 1-pint container. Mix remaining ingredients with 1/4 cup water; bring to a boil. Pour over onion; cover tightly. Chill overnight.

FRENCH ONION SOUP

3 to 4 lge. Spanish onions
Butter
1/2 tsp. salt
1/4 tsp. coarsely ground pepper
6 c. rich beef stock
1 tsp. Worcestershire sauce
French bread
Grated Parmesan cheese

Slice onions thin; saute, stirring gently, in 1/2 cup butter until just tender. Add seasonings and beef stock; simmer for 15 to 20 minutes. Add Worcestershire sauce just before serving. Cut French bread in 1/4-inch slices; toast 1 side. Spread untoasted side with butter; place on baking sheet. Sprinkle with cheese; toast until lightly browned. Float toast on each portion of soup; sprinkle with additional cheese. Yield: 4-6 servings.

BOUNTIFUL VEGETABLE PLATTER

Color photograph for this recipe on page 310.

8 lge. Bermuda onions
2 8-oz. packages frozen green peas with cream sauce
2 strips bacon, diced
2 slices bread, diced
2 16-oz. cans baby whole carrots
1/4 c. finely chopped parsley
1/4 c. melted butter

Peel onions; scoop out centers, leaving 3/4-inch thick shell. Place in boiling, salted water; simmer until onions are tender but still hold shape. Leave in hot water. Heat peas according to package directions. Fry bacon in skillet until crisp. Remove from skillet; drain. Add bread cubes to bacon drippings in skillet. Fry until brown and crisp. Heat carrots in saucepan; drain and toss with parsley and butter. Place onions on platter. Fill with peas; top with bacon and croutons. Surround onions with carrots. Serve at once.

CHARCOALED ONIONS

6 med. onions, peeled
6 bouillon cubes
3 tsp. butter
Salt and pepper to taste

Scoop out small hole in top of each onion; fill with bouillon cube, butter, salt and pepper. Wrap separately in aluminum foil. Place on hot coals for about 30 minutes; turn frequently. Serve immediately. Yield: 6 servings.

BATTER-FRIED ONIONS

1 lge. Bermuda onion
1 c. beer
Flour
Salt to taste

Peel and thinly slice onion; separate into rings. Combine beer with enough flour to make a thin batter. Dip onion rings into batter; drain off excess batter. Fry in deep fat at 375 degrees until golden brown and crisp; drain on absorbent towels. Sprinkle with salt.

FRENCH-FRIED ONION RINGS

2 to 3 lge. onions
1 c. sifted flour
1/2 tsp. baking powder
1/2 tsp. salt
1 tsp. sugar
3/4 c. milk
1 egg
2 tbsp. melted fat

Cut onions into 1/4-inch slices; separate into rings. Sift flour with baking powder, salt and sugar. Combine milk, egg and fat; add to dry ingredients all at once, beating until smooth. Dip onion rings into batter; drain off excess batter. Fry in deep fat at 375 degrees until golden brown and crisp. Drain on absorbent paper; sprinkle with salt. Yield: 4 servings.

GLAZED ONIONS

3 lb. small white onions
4 tsp. sugar
1 tsp. dry mustard
1/2 tsp. salt
6 tbsp. melted butter
1/4 tsp. paprika

Peel onions; cook in boiling salted water to cover for 15 minutes. Drain. Arrange onions in shallow pan. Combine sugar, mustard, salt and butter; pour over onions. Sprinkle with paprika. Bake at 350 degrees for 20 minutes or until tender and glazed. Yield: 6 servings.

PECAN-SHERRIED ONIONS

1 lb. small white onions
2 tbsp. butter
2 tbsp. flour
1/2 tsp. salt
1 1/2 c. milk
1 tbsp. dry sherry
1/4 c. chopped pecans

Cook onions in boiling salted water for 15 to 20 minutes or until tender; drain. Melt butter in large saucepan; blend in flour and salt. Add milk all at once; cook, stirring constantly, over high heat until mixture is smooth and thickened. Blend in sherry. Add onions; heat through. Serve topped with pecans. Yield: 5-6 servings.

GERMAN ONION CAKE

1 pkg. hot roll mix
4 lge. yellow onions
1/4 c. butter
2 c. sour cream
3 eggs
1/2 tsp. salt
1/2 tsp. caraway seed

Prepare hot roll mix according to package directions; let dough rise until doubled in bulk. Peel and thinly slice onions; saute in butter in large skillet, stirring occasionally, for 30 minutes or until onions are limp and golden. Cool slightly. Beat sour cream, eggs and salt until blended; stir in onion mixture. Punch dough down; let rest for 10 minutes. Roll dough to 11 x 15-inch rectangle. Line greased 13 x 9-inch pan carefully with dough; turn up 1-inch edge on all sides. Pour onion filling into dough-lined pan; sprinkle caraway seed over top. Bake at 350 degrees for 55 minutes or until crust is browned and custard is set. Serve warm.

GOURMET ONION DISH

1 qt. 1/2-in. onion slices
1/2 can bean sprouts,
1 pkg. slivered almonds
1 can cream of mushroom soup
Salt to taste
Monosodium glutamate
1/2 c. corn flake crumbs
2 tbsp. butter, melted

Cook onion slices in boiling salted water until tender; drain. Rinse bean sprouts thoroughly; drain well. Arrange layers of onions, almonds, bean sprouts and soup in casserole; sprinkle each layer with salt and monosodium glutamate. Toss crumbs in butter; sprinkle over top. Bake in 350-degree oven for 30 minutes or until heated through.

AMBER ONIONS

12 sm. onions
2 tbsp. butter
2 tbsp. honey
2 tbsp. tomato soup
1/2 tsp. paprika
1/2 tsp. salt

Peel onions; crosscut each end. Cover with boiling salted water in saucepan; boil for 5 minutes. Drain; place in greased baking dish. Combine remaining ingredients; pour over onions. Bake at 350 degrees for 30 minutes or until tender. Yield: 4 servings.

PIQUANT GLAZED ONIONS

8 sm. white onions
2 tbsp. butter
1 tbsp. (packed) brown sugar
1 tsp. lemon juice
1/4 tsp. salt
1/8 tsp. ground ginger

Boil onions in salted water in small saucepan for 15 minutes; drain. Melt butter in small skillet; stir in brown sugar, lemon juice, salt and ginger. Add onions; simmer, turning frequently, for 15 minutes or until lightly glazed. Yield: 4 servings.

SCALLOPED ONIONS WITH PEANUTS

2 lb. medium onions
4 tbsp. margarine
2 tbsp. flour
1 c. milk
1/4 c. chopped peanuts
Salt and pepper to taste
3/4 c. dry bread crumbs or cubes
Paprika

Boil onions in lightly salted water until tender; drain. Melt 2 tablespoons margarine; stir in flour. Add milk gradually; cook, stirring constantly, until thickened. Layer onions, white sauce and peanuts in casserole; season to taste. Mix crumbs with remaining margarine; sprinkle over onion mixture. Sprinkle with paprika. Bake at 325 degrees for 25 minutes or until heated through. Yield: 6-8 servings.

BAKED ONIONS WITH CREAMED FRESH PEAS

6 med. onions
3 tbsp. butter
3 tbsp. flour
1 1/2 c. milk
1 c. grated Cheddar cheese
1/2 teaspoon salt
Pepper to taste
1/8 tsp. paprika
1/2 tsp. dry mustard
1 tsp. Worcestershire sauce
1 lb. fresh green peas

Clean and peel onions, leaving blossom ends intact. Drop onions into boiling salted water to cover; cook until soft. Cool; remove centers by pushing through one end, leaving shell of 3 to 4 layers of onion. Melt butter in saucepan; blend in flour. Add milk gradually, stirring constantly. Cook over low heat until sauce thickens and is smooth. Add cheese, salt, pepper, paprika, dry mustard and Worcestershire sauce; heat until cheese melts. Hull peas. Cook, covered, in boiling salted water for 8 to 12 minutes. Drain; fold into cheese sauce. Place onions in baking dish; fill cavities with cheese mixture. Cover dish. Bake at 350 degrees for 15 to 20 minutes or until heated through. Yield: 6 servings.

Baked Onions with Creamed Fresh Peas . . . Onion surrounds peas in a savory cheese sauce.

ONION-APPLE SCALLOP

9 med. onions
6 med. cooking apples
12 slices bacon, cut up
3/4 tsp. salt
1/2 c. buttered crumbs

Peel onions and apples; slice 1/8 inch thick. Fry bacon in skillet until crisp; drain. Alternate layers of onions, apples and bacon in greased baking dish. Sprinkle each layer with salt. Add 1 cup water; top with crumbs. Bake, covered, in 375-degree oven for about 45 minutes. Remove cover; bake until browned. Yield: 6 servings.

ONIONS VIENNESE

2 1/2 lb. med. Bermuda onions
2 tbsp. sherry
1/2 c. chopped celery
1/4 c. chopped pimentos
1 c. mushrooms
1/2 tsp. marjoram
Pinch of thyme
1 tbsp. seasoned salt
2 c. medium white sauce
Cracker crumbs
1 c. diced Cheddar cheese
Paprika to taste

Peel and quarter onions; cover with water in saucepan. Bring to a boil; drain. Combine sherry, celery, pimentos, mushrooms and seasonings in bowl; add white sauce. Blend well. Combine sauce mixture with onions. Place layer of onion mixture in buttered casserole. Sprinkle with crumbs; dot with cheese. Repeat layers; sprinkle with paprika. Bake in 325-degree oven for 1 hour. Yield: 10 servings.

FILLED ONION SHELLS

8 onions, peeled
1/4 tsp. salt
1 can cream of mushroom soup
1/4 c. milk
3/4 c. buttered bread crumbs

Combine onions, salt and 1 quart water in saucepan. Bring to a boil; simmer for 12 minutes. Drain; cool. Cut thin slice from tops of onions; hollow out center of each onion, leaving 1/2-inch shell. Chop onion centers; combine with soup. Blend in milk. Fill onion shells with soup mixture. Place in 2 1/2-quart casserole; pour remaining soup mixture over onions. Cover with bread crumbs. Bake at 350 degrees for 1 hour. Yield: 6-8 servings.

GOURMET STUFFED ONIONS

8 med. onions, peeled
Chicken livers
2 strips bacon
1 tbsp. sherry
2 c. thick white sauce
Sliced mushrooms
Seasoned bread crumbs
1 can mushroom soup
Butter
Parsley

Boil onions in lightly salted water to cover until just tender; drain well. Remove centers from onions; chop fine. Saute livers and bacon; chop fine. Add sherry to white sauce; combine with mushrooms, chopped ingredients and bread crumbs. Stuff onion shells with mixture; place in shallow greased casserole. Remaining stuffing may be spooned around onions. Pour mushroom soup over onions. Dot with butter; sprinkle with parsley. Bake at 250 degrees for 1 hour. Yield: 8 servings.

STUFFED ONIONS

8 lge. onions
2 tbsp. chopped cooked ham
3 tbsp. crumbs
2 tbsp. butter
2 tbsp. milk
1 tbsp. chopped parsley
1 egg, beaten
Salt and pepper to taste
Buttered bread crumbs

Cook onions in boiling salted water until tender; drain. Cut slice from top of each onion; remove center, leaving 1/4-inch shell. Chop onion centers; combine with remaining ingredients except bread crumbs. Stuff onions; place in well-greased baking dish. Sprinkle with bread crumbs. Bake for 45 minutes to 1 hour at 350 degrees. Yield: 6-8 servings.

ONION PIE

1 c. round buttery cracker crumbs
Margarine
2 c. sliced onions
1 c. scalded milk
2 eggs, lightly beaten
1 tsp. salt
1 1/2 c. grated sharp cheese

Preheat oven to 300 degrees. Combine cracker crumbs and 1/3 cup melted margarine; pat crumb mixture against bottom and side of pie plate. Bake for 10 minutes. Saute onions lightly in 2 tablespoons margarine; add milk. Cook, stirring, until blended. Stir small amount of hot mixture into eggs; stir egg mixture into hot mixture. Add salt; turn into cracker crust. Top with cheese. Bake for about 20 minutes. Yield: 6-8 servings.

ONIONS IN RICH PASTRY

Flour
1 tsp. salt
1 1/4 c. margarine
1 egg, slightly beaten
Milk
4 c. chopped onions
1 c. sliced mushrooms
1 3-oz. package cream cheese
1/2 c. grated Parmesan cheese

Sift 1 1/2 cups flour and 1/2 teaspoon salt into bowl; cut in 1/2 cup margarine. Blend egg with 1 tablespoon milk; add to flour mixture. Stir with fork until dough clings together; roll out to 1/8-inch thickness. Cut with 2 1/2-inch round cutter. Arrange pastry circles in large pie pan, lining side and bottom. Reserve 6 to 8 circles. Place onions in saucepan; cover with water. Add remaining salt. Boil for 10 minutes; drain. Place remaining margarine, mushrooms and onions in skillet; saute lightly for 10 minutes. Add cream cheese, stirring until cheese is melted; add Parmesan cheese. Combine 1 cup milk and 2 tablespoons flour; stir into cheese mixture. Pour into baking dish; top with reserved pastry circles. Bake at 400 degrees for 20 to 25 minutes. Yield: 6 servings.

SWEET AND SOUR ONIONS

4 lge. onions, sliced
1/4 c. cider vinegar
1/4 c. melted butter
1/4 c. sugar

Arrange onions in 1-quart baking dish. Combine vinegar, butter and sugar with 1/4 cup boiling water; pour over onions. Bake at 300 degrees for 1 hour. Yield: 4-6 servings.

Orange

Oranges are citrus fruit with a tough, oily, reddish-yellow outer rind and edible juicy pulp. Spanish colonists brought oranges to the United States, and they are now grown in California, Arizona, and Florida. There are three species of orange: sweet, sour, and mandarin. *Sour orange* production on a commercial scale is limited to southern Spain. These oranges are too bitter and acid for eating and are used instead in the manufacture of marmalade and in certain beverages. *Sweet oranges* are usually round in shape but may be elongated, flattened, or have conical protuberances. *Mandarin oranges* are somewhat flattened at either end. They have a thin, loose peel and when ripe are bright orange in color. The popular tangerine is a variety of mandarin orange. Sweet and mandarin oranges are the most commonly produced oranges in the United States. Two varieties of sweet orange, the Washington Naval and the Valencia, spurred commercial orange-growing in the United States.

AVAILABILITY: Oranges are available year-round. *Sweet oranges:* Washington Naval oranges, the principal winter oranges, are available from November to May. Valencias, the principal summer oranges, are available from May to November (California crop) and February to June (Florida crop). *Tangerines* are available in greatest supply from November to March.

BUYING: Choose firm, heavy oranges that have finely textured skins. Surface blemishes are superficial and do not indicate inferior quality. Color does not indicate maturity: green oranges are as ripe as reddish-yellow ones. Avoid oranges that are light colored, puffy, or spongy as they are probably lacking in juiciness.

STORING: To store sweet oranges, keep uncovered in cold room or refrigerator for 1-2 weeks. Some oranges may keep longer. Tangerines should be stored covered and will keep about 1 week in the refrigerator.

MANDARIN SALAD

1 can mandarin orange slices
1/2 jar pineapple cheese spread
1/3 c. chopped pecans
1 c. miniature marshmallows
2 tbsp. mayonnaise

Drain orange slices. Combine spread, pecans, marshmallows and mayonnaise; mix thoroughly. Stir orange slices into marshmallow mixture, blending well. Serve on lettuce leaf. Yield: 6 servings.

HOLIDAY ORANGE MOLD

1 11-oz. can mandarin oranges
2 7-oz. bottles ginger ale
1 pkg. orange gelatin
1 tsp. lemon juice
1/2 tsp. vanilla
Dash of salt
1/2 c. whipping cream, whipped
2 med. bananas, sliced
Shredded coconut

Drain oranges. Pour 1 bottle ginger ale into saucepan; bring to a boil. Add gelatin; stir until dissolved. Add remaining ginger ale, lemon juice, vanilla and salt, blending well. Refrigerate until partially set. Fold in whipped cream, bananas and oranges; place in 1-quart mold. Chill until firm. Top with coconut. Yield: 8-9 servings.

ORANGE AND AVOCADO SALAD

Color photograph for this recipe on page 319.

2 avocados
3 fresh oranges
3/4 c. salad dressing
1/4 c. fresh orange juice
1/2 tsp. paprika
1/2 tsp. salt
Iceberg lettuce

Peel, seed and slice avocados. Peel, seed and slice oranges. Mix salad dressing, orange juice, paprika and salt well. Place alternate slices of avocado and orange on lettuce leaves; drizzle with dressing. Yield: 6 servings.

ORANGE-PEANUT BUTTER SALAD

8 oranges
1/4 c. mayonnaise
1/4 c. peanut butter
1 1/2 c. sliced celery
1/2 c. peanuts
2 bananas, sliced

Cut slices from tops of oranges; cut off peel, spiral fashion. Remove remaining white membrane. Slice oranges 1/4 inch thick; reserve 6 orange slices. Dice remaining orange slices coarsely. Blend mayonnaise and peanut butter until smooth. Combine diced oranges, celery, peanuts and banana slices; add peanut butter mixture. Toss lightly. Serve on crisp greens; garnish with cream cheese balls and reserved orange slices. Yield: 6 servings.

SPICY ORANGE SALAD

1 13-oz. can mandarin oranges
1 6-in. stick cinnamon
1/2 tsp. whole cloves
1/4 tsp. salt
2 3-oz. packages orange gelatin
3 tbsp. lemon juice
1/2 c. chopped walnuts

Drain oranges, reserving juice; combine juice and enough water to make 1 3/4 cups liquid. Place in saucepan. Add spices and salt; simmer for 10 minutes. Let steep for 10 minutes. Strain. Dissolve gelatin in hot mixture; add 2 cups cold water and lemon juice. Chill until partially set. Fold in oranges and walnuts. Place in mold; chill until firm.

BRAZILIAN ORANGE CAKE

5 eggs, separated
1 c. orange juice
2 c. flour
2 c. sugar
1 tsp. baking powder
1/2 tsp. vanilla

Combine egg yolks and orange juice. Mix flour, sugar and baking powder together; add to egg yolk mixture gradually. Beat for 2 minutes. Add vanilla; fold in beaten egg whites. Pour in well-greased pan. Bake at 350 degrees for 25 minutes. Yield: 6 servings.

GLAZED ORANGE CAKE

1 1/4 c. butter
2 2/3 c. sugar
1/2 tsp. vanilla
2 tbsp. grated orange rind
5 eggs
3 c. cake flour
1 tbsp. baking powder
Pinch of salt
3/4 c. milk
1/3 c. orange juice

Cream 1 cup butter and 2 cups sugar until light and fluffy; stir in vanilla and orange rind. Add eggs, one at a time, beating well after each addition. Sift flour, baking powder and salt together; add to creamed mixture alternately with milk. Spoon into buttered and floured 10-inch tube pan. Bake at 350 degrees for 1 hour or until top of cake springs back when touched. Cool on wire rack for 2 minutes. Combine remaining butter and sugar and orange juice; place in saucepan over low heat, stirring until sugar is dissolved. Pour evenly over hot cake in pan; cool thoroughly before removing from pan. Yield: 10-15 servings.

ORANGE AMBROSIA ROLL

4 eggs, separated
3/4 c. sugar
1/4 tsp. almond extract
1 c. sifted self-rising flour
Confectioners' sugar
1 pkg. orange-flavored pudding mix
1 11-oz. can mandarin oranges
1 c. coconut
1 c. heavy cream, whipped

Beat egg whites until foamy; beat in sugar, 2 tablespoons at a time, until shiny peaks form. Beat egg yolks until thick and lemon-colored; blend in almond extract. Fold into beaten egg whites; sift flour, 1/4 cup at a time, over egg mixture, folding in gently after each addition. Turn into waxed paper-lined 10 x 15-inch jelly roll pan. Bake at 375 degrees for 12 minutes or until cake tests done. Loosen edges. Turn out onto towel dusted with confectioners' sugar; remove waxed paper. Beginning at narrow end, roll up cake and towel, jelly roll fashion. Cool on wire rack. Prepare pudding mix according to package directions; refrigerate. Drain oranges, reserve 12 segments. Combine pudding, orange segments, and coconut. Unroll cake; remove towel. Spread with pudding mixture; reroll. Garnish with whipped cream and reserved orange segments. Chill until ready to serve.

ORANGE MARMALADE CAKE

3/4 c. orange juice
1 pkg. orange gelatin
4 eggs
1 box yellow cake mix
3/4 c. cooking oil
Grated rind of 2 oranges
Orange marmalade

Combine juice and gelatin; beat well. Add eggs, cake mix and oil; mix thoroughly. Stir in orange rind. Pour into 2 greased layer cake pans. Bake at 350 degrees for 45 minutes. Turn out on wire racks. Spread marmalade between layers and on top of warm cake.

ORANGE CHIFFON CAKE

2 1/4 c. sifted cake flour
1 1/2 c. sugar
3 tsp. baking powder
1 tsp. salt
1/2 c. salad oil
5 egg yolks
Grated rind and juice of 2 oranges
1 c. egg whites
1/2 tsp. cream of tartar

Sift flour, sugar, baking powder and salt together into mixing bowl. Make well in center of flour mixture; add oil, egg yolks and orange rind. Add enough water to orange juice to make 3/4 cup liquid; add to yolk mixture. Beat with spoon until smooth. Pour egg whites into large mixing bowl with cream of tartar; whip egg whites until stiff peaks form. Pour egg yolk mixture over egg whites gradually; fold gently until just blended. Do not stir. Pour into ungreased 10-inch tube pan. Bake at 325 degrees for 65 minutes. Turn pan upside down; place tube on funnel. Let stand until cooled. Yield: 12-15 servings.

ORANGE SLICE CAKE

1 lb. candy orange slices
1 8-oz. package chopped dates
1 c. chopped nuts
3 1/2 c. sifted flour
1 c. margarine
2 c. sugar
4 eggs
1/2 c. buttermilk
1 tsp. soda
1 can shredded coconut
2 c. confectioners' sugar
1 c. orange juice

Cut candy slices into small pieces. Coat dates, candy and nuts in 1/2 cup flour; set aside. Cream margarine with sugar; add eggs, one at a time, blending well after each addition. Add buttermilk. Sift remaining flour with soda; add to buttermilk mixture. Fold in candy mixture, stirring well; add coconut. Place in greased and floured 9-inch tube pan. Bake for 3 hours at 250 degrees. Leave cake in pan. Mix sugar and juice well; pour over hot cake. Leave cake in tube pan until cooled thoroughly.

ORANGE LOVER'S CAKE

1 lge. orange
1 c. raisins
1/3 c. walnuts
2 c. sifted flour
1 tsp. soda
1 tsp. salt
1 1/3 c. sugar
1/2 c. cooking oil
1 c. milk
2 eggs
1 tsp. cinnamon

Squeeze juice from orange, reserving juice. Grind orange pulp, rind, raisins and walnuts together. Sift flour, soda, salt and 1 cup sugar together; add oil and 3/4 cup milk, mixing well. Beat eggs with remaining milk; stir into batter. Fold in ground mixture. Pour batter into greased, lightly floured 12 x 8 x 2-inch pan. Bake at 350 degrees for 40 minutes. Pour reserved orange juice over warm cake. Combine remaining sugar and cinnamon; sprinkle over cake.

CANDY ORANGE SQUARES

2 tbsp. butter
1 c. (packed) brown sugar
2 eggs, beaten
1 c. flour
1/2 tsp. baking powder
1 1/2 c. chopped orange candy slices
1 tsp. vanilla
1 c. chopped nuts

Cream butter and sugar together. Add eggs; beat well. Combine flour, baking powder and orange slices; add to creamed mixture. Add vanilla and 1 tablespoon water; stir well. Stir in nuts; spread in greased and floured 9-inch square pan. Bake at 325 degrees for 35 minutes. Cut while warm. Yield: 24 cookies.

MANDARIN ORANGE SOUFFLE

2 sm. packages orange gelatin
1 c. orange juice
1 pt. orange sherbet
1 c. sour cream
2 c. mandarin oranges, drained
1 c. crushed pineapple, drained
1 c. flaked coconut

Dissolve gelatin in 1 cup hot water; add orange juice. Cool slightly. Stir in sherbet and sour cream; chill until slightly thickened. Add fruits and 1/2 cup coconut. Pour into 2-quart mold or 12 individual molds; sprinkle remaining coconut on top. Chill until set. Yield: 12 servings.

ORANGE BLOSSOM CAKE

2 c. milk
1 tbsp. cornstarch
1 c. sugar
4 egg yolks
2 tbsp. gelatin
3/4 c. orange juice
1 tsp. grated orange rind
1 pt. heavy cream, whipped
1 1/2 doz. ladyfingers

Pour milk into double boiler; place over low heat until heated through. Combine cornstarch, sugar and egg yolks; mix well. Stir hot milk into yolk mixture; return to double boiler. Cook, stirring frequently, until thickened; cool. Soften gelatin in 1/4 cup cold water; add to orange juice and rind. Combine gelatin mixture and milk mixture; blend thoroughly. Refrigerate until thickened. Fold whipped cream into gelatin mixture. Split ladyfingers; cut 3/4 inch from end of each half. Stand ladyfingers around edge of springform pan; line pan with cut pieces. Pour whipped cream mixture into pan; refrigerate overnight.

ORANGE FROMAGE

Color photograph for this recipe on page 486.

1 pkg. lemon pudding mix
1 c. whipped cream
6 sm. oranges

Prepare pudding mix according to package directions; cool. Fold in whipped cream. Cut through peel of each orange to orange pulp in 6 equal parts, cutting 3/4 of the way to bottom. Remove orange from rind, leaving rind whole. Cut orange rinds in petal shape. Fill each orange rind with pudding; place on serving dish. Chill. Separate orange into sections and place orange sections on top of pudding. Garnish with slivered almonds if desired.

FRESH ORANGE CUSTARD BRULEE

2 c. light cream
1 c. milk
5 lge. egg yolks, lightly beaten
1/4 c. sugar
1 tsp. vanilla
1 env. unflavored gelatin
2 tbsp. fresh orange juice
Candied Orange Slices

Combine cream and milk in double boiler; heat to scalding. Combine egg yolks and sugar in mixing bowl; beat until blended and sugar is dissolved. Add scalded milk mixture to egg yolks mixture gradually, beating constantly. Return mixture to double boiler. Cook over hot water, stirring constantly, until thickened to heavy cream consistency. Stir in vanilla. Soften gelatin in orange juice; add to hot custard, stirring until gelatin is dissolved. Pour into 1 1/2-quart shallow baking dish. Chill until set. Arrange Candied Orange Slices on custard.

Candied Orange Slices

3/4 c. sugar
2 med. oranges

Combine sugar and 1/2 cup water in small saucepan. Cook, without stirring, to 240 degrees on candy thermometer or soft-ball stage. Cut each orange in half lengthwise; cut each half in thin slices, removing seeds. Cook orange slices, several at a time, in boiling syrup for 5 minutes. Remove from syrup with slotted spoon. Pour remaining syrup over oranges. Cool thoroughly.

Fresh Orange Custard Brulee . . . Candied orange slices top this egg-rich chilled dessert.

ORANGE CUSTARD PUDDING

2 oranges
Sugar
1 qt. milk
3 tbsp. flour
3 egg yolks
1 tsp. vanilla
3 egg whites

Section oranges; marinate segments in small amount of sugar. Set aside. Place milk in saucepan over low heat. Simmer; do not boil. Combine flour, egg yolks and 1 cup sugar; add to milk gradually, stirring constantly. Cook to desired thickness. Pour into glass casserole; add vanilla. Stir in orange segments. Beat egg whites until stiff peaks form; top custard mixture with egg whites. Bake in 450-degree oven until browned lightly. Chill.

ORANGE ICEBOX PUDDING

1 lge. can evaporated milk
1 sm. sponge cake
2 c. orange juice
Sugar
Grated rind of 2 oranges
1 pkg. lemon gelatin
Juice of 1 lemon
1/2 pt. whipping cream

Pour milk into refrigerator tray; chill until ice crystals form around edges. Chill mixing bowl and beaters. Cut sponge cake into 3 layers. Combine 1 cup orange juice, 1/4 cup sugar, orange rind and gelatin in saucepan. Place over low heat, stirring constantly, until gelatin is dissolved. Add remaining orange juice and lemon juice; cool. Pour milk into chilled bowl; beat until stiff peaks form. Fold whipped milk into gelatin mixture. Layer gelatin mixture and cake layers in oblong pan, beginning and ending with gelatin mixture. Refrigerate overnight. Whip cream until stiff peaks form, adding sugar to taste. Serve pudding topped with whipped cream. Yield: 8-10 servings.

BAKED STUFFED ORANGES

6 navel oranges
Miniature marshmallows
1/2 c. chopped dried figs
Shredded coconut
1 c. chopped walnuts

Cut off tops of oranges; discard. Scoop out pulp; place in bowl. Remove membranes and small amount of juice. Add 1/2 cup marshmallows, figs, 1/2 cup coconut and walnuts; mix. Fill orange shells with fruit mixture. Place 2 marshmallows on each orange; sprinkle with small amount of coconut. Place oranges in glass baking dish. Bake at 350 degrees for 30 minutes. Yield: 6 servings.

BRANDIED ORANGES

6 lge. oranges
1/2 c. shredded almonds
2/3 c. chopped dates
1/3 c. brandy
2/3 c. orange juice

Peel oranges; cut into thin slices. Combine oranges, almonds and dates; mix lightly. Combine brandy and orange juice; pour over top. Chill before serving. Yield: 6 servings.

BUTTER-BAKED ORANGES

8 lge. oranges
1/2 c. sugar
8 tsp. butter

Wash oranges; grate skins slightly. Cover oranges with water Bring to a boil; simmer for 30 minutes. Drain; cool. Cut off small slice at blossom end; remove core. Place 1 tablespoon sugar and 1 teaspoon butter in center of each orange. Place in buttered baking dish; fill 2/3 full with water. Bake, covered, in 350-degree oven for 2 hours. Yield: 8 servings.

CANDIED ORANGE PEEL

6 oranges
1 1/2 c. sugar

Cut peel from oranges in 1/4-inch strips; remove white membrane. Cover with cold water. Bring to a boil; drain. Repeat twice, reserving 1 1/2 cups liquid from last draining. Combine peel with sugar; add reserved liquid. Cook for 45 minutes or until just dry, stirring frequently. Roll in additional sugar. Place strips on waxed paper to dry.

FRUIT-FILLED ORANGES

Large oranges
Diced bananas
Diced plums
Mint sprigs
1/2 c. jellied cranberry sauce
1/4 c. honey
1 tsp. lemon juice

Slice tops from oranges; remove orange sections. Combine orange sections, bananas and plums; fill orange shells with fruit mixture. Garnish with mint. Beat cranberry sauce until smooth; stir in honey and lemon juice. Serve over orange mixture.

ORANGE FLUFF

24 lge. marshmallows
1/2 c. orange juice concentrate
3/4 c. (about) crushed graham crackers
1/4 c. finely chopped nuts
1/4 c. melted butter
1 c. whipping cream
Sugar to taste

Combine marshmallows and orange juice concentrate in double boiler; cook over low heat until marshmallows are melted. Chill thoroughly. Mix crumbs, nuts and butter; press into 9-inch square pan. Chill. Whip cream until stiff peaks form; fold in sugar. Fold in orange mixture; turn into crust. Sprinkle with additional graham cracker crumbs. Chill. Yield: 6-9 servings.

ORANGE GOBLINS

4 med. oranges
1 1/2 qt. lime sherbet
Licorice jelly beans
4 stemmed maraschino cherries

Cut thin slice of peel from one end of each orange to serve as base. Slice top off oranges 1/4 to 1/3 down; reserve slices. Scoop out orange pulp with spoon. Fill orange cups with sherbet, rounding top as for ice cream cone. Make eyes, nose and mouth with jelly beans. Place reserved orange slices on sherbet at angle as hat; secure with toothpicks. Place cherries on toothpicks. Freeze until ready to serve. Yield: 4 servings.

SLICED ORANGES WITH GRAND MARNIER

6 oranges
2 c. sugar
Grand Marnier to taste

Cut peel from oranges in julienne strips, leaving white pulp on oranges. Combine sugar and 1 cup water; bring to a boil. Cook for 8 minutes. Add strips of orange peel; cook until tender. Combine syrup and Grand Marnier. Peel white pulp from oranges; cut in halves. Seed oranges; place, cut side down, in serving dish. Spoon hot orange peel syrup over oranges; chill. Garnish with candied violets.

ORANGE TREAT

4 sm. peeled oranges
1 c. flaked coconut
1 peeled apple, diced
1/4 c. orange juice

Section oranges. Combine orange sections and all remaining ingredients in salad bowl; mix well. Chill until ready to serve. Yield: 4-6 servings.

ORANGE HONEY CUBES

1 loaf unsliced day-old white bread
1/4 c. (packed) light brown sugar
3/4 tsp. cinnamon
2 tbsp. honey
2 tbsp. frozen Florida orange juice
1/4 c. melted butter
1/4 c. coarsely chopped nuts

Cut crusts from top and sides of bread. Cut bread lengthwise almost through to bottom crust; cut crosswise to form 8 cubes. Combine sugar, cinnamon, honey, orange juice, melted butter and nuts; stir until blended. Pour mixture over bread, letting mixture run down into cubes and over top. Tie loosely with string. Place on cookie sheet. Bake in 350-degree oven for 10 to 15 minutes. Remove string; serve warm. Yield: 6 servings.

Orange Honey Cubes . . . Orange juice concentrate transforms bread into coffee cake.

DELICIOUS ORANGE MUFFINS

Color photograph for this recipe on page 734.

2 c. sifted flour
1 tsp. soda
1 tsp. salt
1/2 c. shortening
Grated rind of 1 orange
1 sq. unsweetened chocolate, grated
1 1/2 c. (about) buttermilk

Sift flour, soda and salt together into bowl. Cut in shortening until mixture is consistency of cornmeal. Add grated rind and chocolate; stir in enough buttermilk to make soft dough. Spoon dough into paper baking cups in muffin tins. Bake at 425 degrees for about 15 minutes.

ORANGE ROLLS

1 1/4 c. warm milk
1/2 c. shortening
1 tsp. salt
1/3 c. sugar
1 cake yeast
2 well-beaten eggs
Grated orange peel
3/8 c. orange juice
5 c. flour
1 c. sifted powdered sugar

Combine milk, shortening, salt and sugar; dissolve yeast in milk mixture. Add eggs, 2 tablespoons orange peel and 1/4 cup orange juice; mix thoroughly. Add flour; mix to form soft dough. Cover; let stand for 10 minutes. Turn out on lightly floured surface; knead until dough is elastic. Place in greased bowl; let rise in warm place for about 2 hours or until doubled in bulk. Punch down; roll out dough 1/2 inch thick. Cut into 6-inch strips, 1/2 inch wide. Knot each strip; arrange on baking sheet. Cover; let rise until doubled in bulk. Bake at 400 degrees for 15 minutes. Combine remaining orange juice, 1 teaspoon orange peel and powdered sugar; blend well. Spread rolls with orange topping. Yield: 24 servings.

LITTLE ORANGE LOAVES

1 pkg. orange muffin mix
1 c. chopped walnuts
3/4 c. whole cranberry sauce

Prepare muffin mix according to package directions; stir in walnuts and cranberry sauce, blending well. Spoon into 6 greased 6-ounce orange juice cans. Bake at 375 degrees for 30 minutes or until bread tests done; cool for 5 minutes. Cut end out of can, ease loaves out of cans with spatula. Store overnight.

ORANGE BREAD

3/4 c. sliced orange peel
3 c. sifted flour
5 tsp. baking powder
1 tsp. salt
1 c. sugar
1 c. sliced Brazil nuts
2 eggs, beaten
1 1/4 c. milk
2 tbsp. melted butter

Cook orange peel in boiling water to cover until tender. Drain; let dry. Sift flour, baking powder and salt together; add sugar, nuts and orange peel. Mix well. Combine eggs, milk and butter. Add to dry ingredients; mix well. Pour into well-greased loaf pan. Bake at 350 degrees for 1 hour or until bread tests done.

ORANGE-NUT BREAD

2 tbsp. shortening
1 c. honey
1 egg, beaten
1 1/2 tbsp. grated orange rind
2 1/4 c. flour
2 1/2 tsp. baking powder
1/2 tsp. salt
1/8 tsp. soda
3/4 c. orange juice
3/4 c. chopped nuts

Cream shortening and honey. Add beaten egg and orange rind. Sift dry ingredients together; add alternately with orange juice to honey mixture. Add chopped nuts. Pour into waxed paper-lined greased loaf pan. Bake in 325-degree oven for 1 hour and 10 minutes or until browned. Yield: 1 loaf.

ORANGE SLICE BREAD

3/4 c. shortening
2 c. sugar
1 egg, beaten
1 tsp. salt
1 c. cold coffee
1 c. sour milk
1 tsp. soda
4 c. flour, sifted
2 c. dates, finely chopped
1 lb. orange slices, diced
1 c. chopped nuts
1 tsp. cinnamon and nutmeg
1 tsp. nutmeg

Cream shortening and sugar together; add egg, salt and coffee. Combine sour milk and soda; add to creamed mixture. Add sifted flour, dates, diced orange slices, nuts and spices; mix well. Pour into 2 well-greased loaf pans. Bake at 325 degrees for 1 hour to 1 hour and 30 minutes. Yield: 2 loaves.

SPICED ORANGE WEDGES

4 oranges
2 c. sugar
1/2 c. vinegar
12 whole cloves
3 pieces stick cinnamon

Place whole oranges in saucepan; add 1 quart water. Bring to a boil; boil for 20 minutes. Drain oranges; cut into eighths. Combine sugar, 1 1/4 cups water, vinegar, cloves and cinnamon in saucepan; stir over low heat until sugar is dissolved. Bring to a boil; add oranges. Reduce heat; simmer for 20 minutes. Cool; store, covered, in refrigerator. Remove cloves and cinnamon before serving.

ORANGE PASTRY SQUARES

1 3-oz. package lemon gelatin
1 3-oz. package orange gelatin
1 can evaporated milk,
3/4 c. sugar
Juice of 1 orange
1 c. graham cracker crumbs

Add gelatins to 1 cup boiling water; stir until dissolved. Refrigerate until thickened. Whip chilled milk until soft peaks form; add sugar and orange juice. Beat until blended well; stir in gelatin mixture. Beat thoroughly. Sprinkle crumbs in waxed paper-lined 9 x 14 x 2-inch cake pan. Pour gelatin mixture into pan. Refrigerate until firm. Cut in squares to serve. Yield: 12 servings.

Oxtail

Oxtails are the skinned tails of cattle. They contain a great deal of bone and gristle but when cooked by simmering for a long period of time, they provide a richly flavored meat. Allow 1-1 1/2 pounds oxtails for two servings. Oxtails are also used to prepare a hearty stew-like soup.

BRAISED OXTAILS

2 to 3 lb. oxtail, disjointed
1 to 2 tbsp. flour
Salt and pepper
3 bay leaves
6 peppercorns
1 med. onion, chopped
6 med. carrots, cut in strips
1 10-oz. package frozen peas
6 med. potatoes, halved

Roll oxtail in flour; season with salt and pepper. Brown oxtail in 2 tablespoons fat in heavy skillet; add 1 cup water, bay leaves, peppercorns and onion. Simmer, covered, for 3 hours and 30 minutes or until oxtail is tender; add water as needed. Add carrots, peas and potatoes; cook for 40 minutes or until vegetables are tender. Transfer oxtail to hot platter; surround with vegetables. Mix additional flour and water to form paste. Add paste to remaining liquid; stir until gravy is thickened. Season to taste. Yield: 6 servings.

OXTAILS IN SAVORY SAUCE

3 lb. oxtails, disjointed
2 tbsp. butter
1/4 c. instant minced onion
1 tbsp. dry mustard
1 tbsp. arrowroot
1 tbsp. dried mushrooms
1 can beef bouillon
1 c. red wine
2 tbsp. tomato paste
1 tsp. seasoned salt
1 tsp. salt
1 tsp. monosodium glutamate
Dash of cayenne pepper
1/2 c. sour cream
Chopped parsley

Saute oxtails in butter in skillet until browned; remove from skillet. Soak onion in 1/4 cup water for 5 minutes; stir into pan drippings. Add mustard, arrowroot, mushrooms, bouillon and wine. Simmer, stirring constantly, until thickened and smooth. Stir in tomato paste, seasoned salt, salt, monosodium glutamate and cayenne pepper. Arrange oxtails in baking dish; pour sauce over oxtails. Bake, covered, at 250 degrees for 3 hours or until oxtails are tender. Stir in sour cream; sprinkle with parsley. Heat through; serve with noodles or rice if desired.

LOUISIANA-STYLE OXTAILS

2 oxtails
1 1/2 tsp. salt
2 tbsp. flour
1 tbsp. butter
2 bouillon cubes
1/2 tsp. Tabasco
1 c. dry red wine
1 1-lb. can tomatoes
4 sm. carrots, finely diced
1 med. onion, finely chopped
2 stalks celery, chopped
1 bay leaf
1/2 tsp. bottled brown gravy sauce
3 med. peeled potatoes, quartered

Cut oxtails into 2-inch pieces. Blend salt and flour together; roll oxtails in flour mixture. Brown oxtails in butter in heavy kettle. Dissolve bouillon cubes in 1 cup hot water. Add bouillon, Tabasco, wine, tomatoes, carrots, onion, celery, bay leaf and brown gravy sauce to oxtails. Add additional water if necessary. Cover; simmer for about 4 hours or until oxtails are tender. Skim off fat; add potatoes. Cover; cook for 30 minutes longer. Yield: 4 servings.

Louisiana-Style Oxtails . . . A tasty ragout that combines oxtails with vegetables in a sauce.

OXTAIL RAGOUT

2 oxtails, disjointed
1/4 c. flour
1 tsp. salt
1 lge. onion, chopped
1 clove of garlic, chopped
1 tsp. paprika
1 c. canned tomatoes
12 sm. white onions
12 lge. mushrooms
1 c. diced potatoes

Coat oxtails with flour; sprinkle with salt. Brown in large skillet in hot fat; stir in chopped onion, garlic, paprika and tomatoes. Simmer, covered, for 2 hours or until oxtails are tender; add water as needed. Arrange onions, mushrooms and potatoes around meat; add enough water to make 1 cup liquid. Simmer, covered, for 30 minutes or until vegetables are tender.

ROASTED OXTAIL JOINTS

24 2-in. diameter oxtail joints
1 can tomatoes
1 can consomme
1 soup can Burgundy
1 1/2 tsp. salt
3 bay leaves
1/2 tsp. garlic, crushed
2 tsp. whole oregano
1 tsp. whole basil

Arrange joints cut side up in roaster. Combine remaining ingredients; pour over oxtails. Bake, covered, at 350 degrees for 2 hours and 30 minutes or until tender.

OXTAIL SOUP

2 to 3 lb. oxtails
1 med. onion
2 to 3 carrots
1 c. celery
Salt and pepper to taste
1/4 c. parsley flakes
1/3 c. barley

Simmer oxtails in 6 cups water in large saucepan for 1 hour or until oxtails are tender. Remove bones from oxtails and broth. Chop onion, carrots and celery coarsely; add to broth. Season with salt and pepper; add parsley and barley. Simmer, covered, for 40 minutes longer or until vegetables are tender.

Oyster

Oysters are mollusks with two rough, irregularly-shaped shells that enclose succulent, dark gray meat. Oysters grow in shallow inshore waters the world over. In the United States, oysters are found on the Atlantic Coast from Massachusetts south, west along the Gulf coast to Texas, and on the Pacific Coast. Large Pacific oysters are cultivated from oysters originally imported from Japan. Small, delicate, and tender Olympia oysters are native to the West Coast. Oysters contain protein, carbohydrate, calcium, iron, phosphorus, Vitamin A, thiamine, niacin, and riboflavin. (1 cup raw meat = 160 calories)

AVAILABILITY: Best season for fresh oysters is September through April. They are sold in shell by the dozen or as shucked oysters (meat and liquid only) in pint or quart containers. Whole oysters or pieces canned in water and bottled oyster juice are sold year-round. Frozen and smoked oysters sold year-round.

BUYING: *In-shell*–Look for tightly closed shells, indicating oysters are alive. *Shucked*–Look for plump, gray, fresh-smelling meat with clear juice. 1 quart undrained shucked oysters serves 6 people.

STORING: *In-shell*–Refrigerate at 39 degrees. Keep dry. *Shucked*–Place in closed container. Cover with juice. Refrigerate at 39 degrees. Container may be placed in crushed ice if desired. Use in-shell and shucked oysters as soon as possible. *Canned*–Refrigerate opened cans 1 to 2 days. Keep unopened cans on kitchen shelf 1 year. *Frozen*–Store in refrigerator freezer 2 months or in home freezer 1 year.

PREPARATION: To prepare fresh, live oysters, scrub well and rinse in cold water. Hold in hand with deeper shell down. Work over strainer and bowl to catch juice. Insert edge of oyster knife into back hinge of shell. Pry gently and lift top shell. Insert knife enough to sever back hinge muscle. Run knife between shells to open. Discard top shell if oysters are to be served raw (see below). Or, to prepare for use in cooking, remove oysters from shell. Examine carefully for pieces of shell adhering to meat and remove any particles. Put oysters in strainer. Rinse in cold water if sandy. Dry oysters to be fried or used in a cream dish.

SERVING: Serve raw oyster meat with juice on half shell atop crushed ice. Accompany with cocktail sauce or lemon wedges. Oysters may also be sauteed, broiled, baked, fried, stewed, roasted, spiced, and pickled. Or they can be used in loaves, fritters, souffles, omelets, chowders, bisques, pies, and sandwiches. (See SEAFOOD.)

ANGELS ON HORSEBACK

1 pt. oysters, drained
2 tbsp. chopped parsley
1/2 tsp. salt
Dash of paprika
Dash of pepper
10 slices bacon, cut in thirds

Sprinkle oysters with parsley and seasonings. Place oyster on each piece of bacon; wrap bacon around oyster, securing with toothpick. Grill until bacon is crisp. Turn carefully. Grill for several minutes longer or until bacon is crisp.

OYSTERS A LA ROCKEFELLER

5 tbsp. butter
1/2 c. strained spinach
2 tbsp. minced onion
2 tsp. minced celery
3 tbsp. fine dry crumbs
1/4 tsp. herb blend for fish
1/4 tsp. anchovy paste
1/4 tsp. salt
Few grains of pepper
24 oysters in shells

Melt butter in saucepan. Add spinach, onion, celery, crumbs, herb blend, anchovy paste, salt and pepper; mix well. Remove oysters from shells; set aside. Scrub 24 half shells; arrange shells on 4 pie plates holding hot rock salt. Place 1 oyster in each shell; place pie plates under broiler. Broil for 5 minutes. Place spoonful of spinach mixture on each oyster; broil until thoroughly heated. Serve immediately. Yield: 4 servings.

OYSTER COCKTAIL

2 tsp. horseradish
3 tbsp. catsup
1 tsp. salt
2 tbsp. vinegar
4 tbsp. lemon juice
1/4 tsp. hot sauce
Oysters, chilled

Combine all ingredients except oysters; mix well. Place in refrigerator to chill thoroughly. Arrang oysters in chilled cocktail dishes; spoon sauce ovei top. Serve with crackers or potato chips.

OYSTERS ERNIE

Melted butter
1/3 c. fresh lemon juice
1 c. steak sauce
1/3 c. Worcestershire sauce
2 jiggers sherry
24 oysters
Salt and pepper to taste
Flour

Combine 3 tablespoons butter, lemon juice, steak sauce, Worcestershire sauce and sherry in saucepan; heat thoroughly. Season oysters with salt and pepper; dredge in flour. Saute in butter in heavy skillet until lightly browned; add sauce. Serve on hot plate with frilled toothpicks. Sauce may be strained and used again.

OYSTER PICKUPS

1 pt. oysters
Salt to taste
Pepper to taste
Parsley, chopped fine
Bacon slices

Sprinkle each oyster with salt, pepper and parsley. Cut bacon slices into thirds; wrap each oyster in bacon piece, securing with toothpick. Place on cookie sheet. Bake in 450-degree oven for 12 to 15 minutes or until bacon is crisp. Serve hot.

OYSTER SALAD

2 cans oysters, minced
8 crackers, ground
5 hard-boiled eggs, minced
6 sweet pickles, chopped
1 egg, beaten
1 tsp. dry mustard
1 tsp. pepper
3/4 c. vinegar

Combine oysters, crackers, eggs and pickles; mix well. Mix remaining ingredients together in saucepan; cook until mixture begins to thicken. Pour over oyster mixture; let stand for at least 12 hours before serving. Yield: 6 servings.

CREAM OF OYSTER SOUP

1/4 c. butter
2 tbsp. flour
1 qt. milk
1 tsp. salt
1/4 tsp. celery salt
Dash of pepper
1 pt. oysters

Melt butter in saucepan over low heat; blend in flour. Add milk; cook, stirring constantly, until sauce boils and thickens. Add seasonings; stir in oysters and liquor. Heat thoroughly until oysters plump and edges begin to curl. Serve hot with crackers or buttered toast strips.

EASY OYSTER STEW

1/2 c. minced celery
2 tbsp. butter
1/4 tsp. Worcestershire sauce
1 8-oz. can oysters
2 c. hot milk
Dash of salt and pepper

Saute celery in butter in saucepan until tender. Add Worcestershire sauce and oysters with liquor; heat slowly for about 3 to 5 minutes or until oysters begin to curl. Add hot milk and seasonings; heat just to boiling point. Do not boil. Serve in bowls; garnish with paprika.

OYSTER BISQUE

1 pt. fresh oysters
3 c. milk
1 bay leaf
1 tsp. garlic salt
2 tsp. Worcestershire sauce
Dash of nutmeg
2 tbsp. butter
1/4 c. instant mashed potato granules
1 can tomato soup

Pour oysters and liquor in heavy saucepan; cook slowly until edges begin to curl. Drain and chop oysters. Scald milk in kettle; add seasonings and butter. Stir in potato granules. Add small amount of milk mixture to slightly beaten egg yolk; combine with remaining milk mixture. Stir in tomato soup; blend well. Add chopped oysters; return to low heat. Beat egg white until stiff; fold into bisque. Garnish with parsley flakes or paprika; serve immediately.

PARSLIED OYSTER STEW

2 doz. oysters
4 tbsp. butter
1 qt. half and half
Juice of 1 sm. onion
Pinch of thyme
1 bay leaf
1 tsp. salt
1/2 tsp. pepper
Finely chopped parsley

Combine oysters, liquor and butter in saucepan; simmer gently until edges of oysters curl. Add half and half, onion, thyme and bay leaf; season with salt and pepper. Bring just to boiling point. Sprinkle each bowl with parsley; ladle in stew and serve immediately.

Tabasco Oyster Stew . . . A flavorful stew topped with butter and tiny oyster crackers.

TABASCO OYSTER STEW

1 tsp. celery salt
1 tbsp. Worcestershire sauce
2 doz. oysters with liquid
1/2 tsp. paprika
1 qt. milk
1/2 tsp. Tabasco
Butter

Combine celery salt, Worcestershire sauce, oysters and liquid and paprika in deep kettle. Heat until edges of oysters curl slightly. Add milk; bring to a boil. Remove from heat; stir in Tabasco. Serve with lump of butter in each bowl. Yield: 4 servings.

RICH OYSTER STEW

2 c. milk
2 c. light cream
2 doz. oysters
2 tbsp. butter
Dash of Worcestershire sauce
Salt and pepper to taste
Celery salt to taste

Heat milk and cream together in kettle until a film forms over top; do not boil. Drain oysters; reserve liquor. Place oysters in saucepan; add 2 tablespoons reserved liquor, butter and Worcestershire sauce. Heat until oysters plump and edges begin to curl. Bring remaining reserved oyster liquor to a boil; stir into cream mixture. Add oyster mixture; season with salt, pepper and celery salt. Serve immediately.

FRIED OYSTERS

3 eggs
3 tbsp. heavy cream
48 oysters
Flour
Coarse cracker crumbs
Butter
Salt and pepper to taste

Beat eggs lightly; stir in cream. Dredge oysters in flour; dip in egg mixture. Roll in cracker crumbs. Let oysters stand for several minutes. Melt butter in frypan; saute oysters quickly on both sides until lightly browned. Season with salt and pepper; serve on hot platter. Garnish with lemon wedges.

OYSTER FRITTERS

1 c. flour
1/2 tsp. salt
1 tbsp. melted butter
1 egg, lightly beaten
1/2 c. beer
1 egg white
Vegetable shortening
24 oysters
Lemon wedges

Sift 1/2 cup flour and salt into mixing bowl; stir in butter and egg, using wooden spoon. Add beer gradually; mix until batter is almost smooth. Do not overmix. Let batter rest at room temperature for about 1 hour. Beat egg white until stiff; fold into batter gently, blending well. Heat shortening in deep fat fryer to 375 degrees. Dip oysters into remaining flour; shake off excess flour. Dip into batter; let excess batter drain off. Fry oysters, five or six at a time, for 3 to 4 minutes or until puffed and golden brown. Drain on paper towel. Serve with lemon wedges. Yield: 4-6 servings.

SOUTHERN-FRIED OYSTERS

1 egg
1/4 c. milk
1/4 c. flour
1/4 tsp. salt
1 pt. oysters
1 c. self-rising cornmeal

Combine egg, milk, flour and salt; beat until smooth. Dip oysters in batter then roll in cornmeal. Fry in hot deep fat until golden brown.

GOURMET OYSTER LOAF

1 long loaf sourdough French bread
Butter
1 tsp. garlic powder
6 tbsp. flour
1/2 tsp. salt
1/4 tsp. pepper
2 jars sm. oysters, drained
4 tbsp. olive oil

Cut a slice off top of loaf; scoop out inside, leaving a shell. Mix 1/4 cup butter with garlic powder; rub inside of lid and shell with the garlic butter. Combine flour, salt and pepper; dredge oysters in flour mixture. Fry in oil and 2 tablespoons butter until golden brown. Place in buttered shell.

Sauce

1/2 stick butter
3 tbsp. flour
1 c. half and half
1/2 tsp. salt
1/4 tsp. pepper
1 tbsp. Worcestershire sauce
1/2 tsp. paprika
1/4 tsp. thyme
1/4 tsp. mace
Dash of hot sauce
Dash of cayenne pepper
1/3 c. sauterne
1/2 c. chopped ripe olives

Melt butter in saucepan; blend in flour. Add half and half gradually; cook until thick, stirring constantly. Stir in seasonings; add sauterne. Pour over oysters; sprinkle with olives. Place lid on shell; wrap loaf in a damp cloth. Place on baking sheet. Bake at 300 degrees for 20 to 30 minutes. Cut into 2 to 3-inch slices; garnish with parsley, if desired.

SOURDOUGH OYSTER LOAF

1 round loaf sourdough French bread
1 stick butter
24 standard oysters
Fine dry bread crumbs
Salt to taste
Freshly ground pepper
Minced parsley
Lemon juice

Cut off 1/3 top of loaf; scoop out center and top, leaving 1-inch crust all around. Melt butter; paint inside of loaf. Place on cookie sheet. Bake in 400-degree oven for 10 minutes. Drain oysters; coat with crumbs. Season with salt and pepper. Saute in melted butter for about 4 or 5 minutes or until golden and plump. Arrange layer of oysters in toasted loaf; sprinkle with parsley and lemon juice. Repeat layers until all oysters are used. Place top on loaf; paint outside with butter. Place on baking sheet. Bake in 400-degree oven for 8 to 10 minutes. Slice and serve immediately.

NORFOLK OYSTERS

1 1/2 c. hot boiled rice
1 pt. oysters, drained
2 tbsp. flour
1 can oyster stew
Butter
Salt and pepper
1 c. buttered cracker crumbs

Spread half the rice in greased baking dish; cover with half the oysters. Add flour to oyster stew; mixing well. Pour half the stew over rice and oysters. Dot with butter; sprinkle with salt and pepper. Repeat, using remaining ingredients. Cover with crumbs. Bake in 375-degree oven for 30 minutes.

OYSTER PAN ROAST

1 pat butter
1 tsp. Worcestershire sauce
1 tsp. paprika
1 tsp. celery salt
1/4 c. clam juice
8 oysters
1 tbsp. chili sauce
1/2 c. cream

Melt butter in heavy saucepan; add Worcestershire sauce, paprika, celery salt and clam juice, stirring well. Add oysters; cook over low to medium heat until edges are curled. Add chili sauce and cream; heat through. Serve over toast. Yield: 2 servings.

OYSTERS TETRAZZINI

1/2 c. butter
1/2 c. flour
2 c. milk
2 c. cream
Salt and pepper to taste
2 tbsp. dry mustard
1/2 c. oyster liquid
2 pkg. frozen oysters, thawed
Paprika
Chopped parsley to taste
Dash of hot sauce
1 lb. sliced bacon
1 8-oz. package spaghetti, cooked
1 1/2 c. grated sharp cheese

Melt butter in large saucepan; stir in flour until smooth. Add milk and cream gradually, stirring until blended. Add seasonings and oyster liquid. Cook over low heat, stirring constantly, until thickened. Sprinkle oysters with paprika, parsley and hot sauce. Wrap each oyster in bacon strip; secure bacon strips with wooden picks. Place oysters on baking pan. Bake at 325 degrees until bacon is crisp. Remove wooden picks. Arrange layers of spaghetti, oysters, sauce and cheese in large casserole, ending with cheese on top. Bake at 350 degrees for 30 minutes. Yield: 6 servings.

OYSTERS EN BROCHETTE

16 oysters
2 tsp. lemon juice
Salt and pepper to taste
16 mushroom caps
4 strips bacon
Melted butter

Sprinkle oysters with lemon juice, salt and pepper. Place 1 mushroom cap on skewer; run skewer through end of bacon strip. Add 1 oyster; loop bacon around oyster and back onto skewer. Repeat procedure until 4 mushroom caps and 4 oysters have been placed on each skewer. Brush with melted butter; place in broiling pan under broiler. Broil until bacon is done, turning several times. Serve with parsley and lemon wedges. All ingredients may be placed on 1 skewer, if desired. Yield: 2 servings.

BREADED OYSTERS

1 qt. oysters
8 c. soft bread crumbs
1 c. melted butter
Salt and pepper to taste

Drain oysters, reserving liquor. Arrange layers of bread crumbs and oysters in greased baking dish; pour melted butter over each layer. Add salt and pepper. End with bread crumbs on top. Pour reserved oyster liquor over layers. Bake in 350-degree oven for 45 minutes. Yield: 12 servings.

NEW ENGLAND SCALLOPED OYSTERS

14 common crackers
1 pt. oysters
1 1/2 c. milk
Salt and pepper to taste
Dash of hot sauce
Butter

Crush crackers finely; cover bottom of greased shallow casserole with 1/3 of the cracker crumbs. Cover crackers with 1/2 of the oysters. Moisten well with milk; add salt and pepper. Repeat layer of crackers, oysters, milk and seasonings; add remaining crumbs and milk. Dot top well with butter. Bake in 350-degree oven for 50 minutes. Yield: 4 servings.

OYSTER BLAIZE

1 pt. oysters
2 c. cracker crumbs
1/4 c. butter, melted
3 eggs, beaten
1 pt. milk, scalded

Combine oysters, crumbs, butter, eggs and milk; place in greased casserole. Bake in 450-degree oven for 30 minutes. Serve immediately. Yield: 6 servings.

SHERRIED SCALLOPED OYSTERS

3 doz. oysters
1/2 tsp. salt
1/4 tsp. pepper
3 tbsp. cream
5 tbsp. sherry
2 tsp. Worcestershire sauce
3 c. coarse toast crumbs
1/3 c. melted butter

Drain oysters, reserving 1/2 cup liquor. Combine reserved liquor, salt, pepper, cream sherry and Worcestershire sauce. Blend toast crumbs with butter, mixing well. Arrange layers of crumb mixture and oysters in 2-quart casserole, beginning and ending with crumb mixture. Pour oyster liquor mixture over each layer of oysters. Bake at 425 degrees for 30 minutes. Yield: 4 servings.

SPECIAL SCALLOPED OYSTERS

2 tsp. chopped parsley
1/3 c. butter
1 pt. oysters with liquor
1 c. cracker crumbs
1 egg, beaten
1/2 c. cream
1 tsp. lemon juice
1/8 tsp. cayenne pepper
1/8 tsp. mustard
1/2 c. buttered bread crumbs

Saute parsley in butter in skillet. Mix oysters, cracker crumbs, egg, cream, lemon juice, cayenne pepper and mustard together. Pour into greased casserole. Top with bread crumbs. Bake at 350 degrees for about 30 minutes or until browned on top. Yield: 4 servings.

Palm, Hearts of

Heart of palm is the end bud of the cabbage palm. This bud looks like a miniature cabbage. Heart of palm is available fresh in subtropical areas where it grows; in other parts of the country, it is available canned.

HEARTS OF PALM-AVOCADO SALAD

3 heads Bibb lettuce
3 14-oz. cans hearts of palm
3 lge. avocados, diced
1/4 c. vinegar
3/4 c. olive oil
1 tsp. salt
1 tsp. cayenne pepper

Tear lettuce into bite-sized pieces into salad bowl. Drain hearts of palm; slice 1/4 inch thick. Combine hearts of palm and avocados with lettuce. Blend vinegar with olive oil, salt and cayenne pepper; mix thoroughly. Pour over salad; toss lightly.

HEARTS OF PALM-OKRA SALAD

1 can okra, drained
1 can hearts of palm, drained
French dressing
Romaine lettuce
Lemon juice
Mayonnaise

Cover okra and hearts of palm with French dressing; chill for several hours. Drain okra mixture; arrange on lettuce. Sprinkle with lemon juice; serve with mayonnaise. Garnish with pimento or green peppers, if desired.

HEARTS OF PALM SALAD SUPREME

1 c. finely diced pineapple
4 c. sliced hearts of palm
1/4 c. chopped dates
1/4 c. chopped candied ginger
4 tbsp. vanilla ice cream
2 tbsp. crunchy peanut butter
2 tbsp. mayonnaise
Green food coloring
Pineapple juice

Combine pineapple, hearts of palm, dates and ginger in salad bowl. Blend ice cream, peanut butter, mayonnaise and enough food coloring to tint pale green; thin with pineapple juice to desired consistency. Pour dressing over salad; toss lightly.

Pancake

Pancakes, round, flat members of the quick bread family, are light, tender cakes that are browned on a griddle over direct heat. Sometimes they are referred to as griddlecakes or flapjacks. They are customarily served with a sweetened sauce or syrup for breakfast or with meat or seafood for luncheon or dinner.

INGREDIENTS: Pancake batter usually consists of flour, eggs, milk, shortening, and leavening. Such fruits as apples, blueberries, bananas, and strawberries may be mixed with the ingredients or used as fillings. Cornmeal, potato, and buckwheat pancakes are also tasty variations.

PREPARATION: Follow specific recipe instructions. For thinner pancakes, add more liquid; for thicker pancakes, add flour. To test griddle–sprinkle with a few drops of water; when water sizzles, griddle is ready. Brush griddle with small amount of shortening and pour on batter. When top surface is puffy and covered with bubbles, turn pancakes. Serve pancakes hot from the griddle or cover them with a towel and keep them warm in a slow oven.

STORING: *To freeze* pancake batter, store in freezer container. *To freeze* cooked pancakes –Cool thoroughly. Cut a cardboard bottom slightly larger than the pancake. Cover with clear plastic wrap. Stack pancakes about 2 inches high, alternating pancakes with double layers of plastic wrap. Top with more cardboard. Secure stack with freezer tape and place in clear plastic. Freeze. To thaw–Remove pancake stack from plastic bag and thaw at room temperature. Place thawed pancakes on cookie sheet in warm oven to heat.

APPLE PANCAKES

2 c. flour
2 tbsp. sugar
4 tsp. baking powder
1 tsp. salt
2 eggs, separated
2 c. milk
2 tbsp. melted butter
1 c. grated peeled apple

Combine flour, sugar, baking powder and salt in mixing bowl. Beat egg yolks until thick and lemony; beat egg whites until stiff peaks form. Combine milk, egg yolks and butter in small bowl; mix well. Add to flour mixture; beat until smooth. Stir in apple; fold in egg whites. Pour batter by 1/2 cupfuls onto hot ungreased griddle; cook until puffy and bubbly. Turn; brown other side. Serve with syrup.

BANANA PANCAKES

2 to 3 ripe bananas
1 1/2 c. buttermilk
2 eggs
2 tbsp. sugar
2 c. self-rising flour
1/4 tsp. soda
2 tbsp. melted butter

Mash bananas. Add buttermilk, eggs and sugar; blend well. Add flour and soda; beat thoroughly. Add melted butter. Pour onto greased hot griddle; cook on both sides until brown. Serve with butter and powdered sugar. Yield: 8-10 servings.

BASIC PANCAKES

2 c. sifted flour
3 tsp. baking powder
1/4 c. sugar
1 tsp. salt
2 eggs
2 c. milk
1/3 c. salad oil

Sift flour, baking powder, sugar and salt. Beat eggs; stir in milk and oil. Add dry ingredients; beat to a smooth batter. Drop by tablespoonfuls onto hot ungreased griddle. Bake until underside is golden brown and bubbles appear over surface; turn. Bake other side. Repeat procedure until all batter is used.

BLUEBERRY PANCAKES

1 c. sifted flour
1 1/2 tsp. baking powder
1 tbsp. sugar
1/2 tsp. salt
1/4 tsp. cinnamon
1 egg, separated
2 tbsp. melted butter
3/4 c. milk
3/4 c. drained blueberries

Sift flour, baking powder, sugar, salt and cinnamon. Beat egg yolk until thick and lemony; beat egg white until stiff peaks form. Add butter to egg yolk; stir in milk. Add to dry ingredients; mix just to moisten. Fold in stiffly beaten egg white. Add blueberries; mix lightly. Pour batter on hot greased griddle. Bake on both sides until lightly browned. Serve with butter. Yield: 8 pancakes.

DOUBLE BLUEBERRY PANCAKES

Color photograph for this recipe on page 735.

1 c. milk
2 tbsp. light corn syrup
1 tbsp. corn oil
1 egg

1 c. pancake mix	*1/3 c. cottage cheese*
3/4 c. blueberries	*Blueberry syrup*

Combine milk, corn syrup, corn oil and egg in mixing bowl. Add pancake mix; stir until dry ingredients are moistened. Batter will be lumpy. Stir in blueberries and cottage cheese carefully. Pour 1/4 cup batter for each pancake on hot griddle; cook until brown, turning once. Serve with blueberry syrup. Yield: 8 pancakes.

BUTTERMILK PANCAKES

2 c. sifted flour	*2 tbsp. sugar*
2 tsp. baking powder	*2 eggs*
1 tsp. soda	*1/2 c. oil*
1/2 tsp. salt	*1 3/4 c. buttermilk*

Sift dry ingredients. Beat eggs slightly; add oil and buttermilk. Combine egg mixture with dry ingredients; stir just to moisten. Bake on hot griddle on both sides until lightly browned.

CORN BREAD GRIDDLE CAKES

1 pkg. corn bread mix	*3/4 c. confectioners' sugar*
2 tbsp. cooking oil	
1 c. berry jam	

Prepare corn bread mix according to package directions; add 1/4 cup additional liquid and 2 tablespoons oil. Mix only until moistened. Pour small amount batter onto hot greased griddle. Bake on both sides until lightly browned. Place about 1 tablespoon jam in center of each griddle cake; roll. Sprinkle with confectioners' sugar; serve hot.

COTTAGE CHEESE-FRUIT PANCAKES

3 well-beaten eggs	*1/4 c. sifted flour*
1 c. cream-style cottage cheese	*1/4 tsp. salt*
	Strawberry jam
2 tbsp. salad oil	*Confectioners' sugar*

Preheat griddle. Combine eggs, cheese and salad oil. Sift flour and salt together; add to egg mixture. Stir just to moisten. Bake cakes on lightly greased griddle. Place 1 tablespoon jam in center of each cake; bring edges of pancake together and roll under. Sprinkle with confectioners' sugar. Serve immediately.

DESSERT PANCAKES

4 eggs, separated	*Dash of salt*
1 tbsp. sugar	*1 pt. vanilla ice cream*
1 c. sifted flour	
1 1/2 c. milk	*1 c. sliced strawberries*
Grated rind of 1 lemon	
	1 recipe meringue
Butter	

Beat egg yolks until thick and lemony; beat egg whites until stiff peaks form. Combine egg yolks and sugar; beat until sugar is dissolved. Add flour and milk alternately to egg mixture, beating well after each addition. Stir in lemon rind, 2 tablespoons melted butter and salt. Fold in egg whites. Pour 1 cup batter onto hot buttered griddle; tilt griddle to spread batter evenly. Cook on both sides until lightly browned; stack and keep warm. Spoon ice cream and strawberries down center of pancakes. Roll; place 2 inches apart in ovenproof dish. Cover each pancake with meringue. Bake at 550 degrees for 2 minutes or until meringue is lightly browned.

FRENCH PANCAKES

3 eggs	*1/2 c. cream*
1/2 c. flour	*1/4 tsp. salt*

Combine all ingredients; blend thoroughly. Pour small quantity of batter into hot well-buttered skillet and spread over bottom in thin sheet. Cook on both sides until golden brown. Spread with a tart jelly; roll up. Garnish with slices of lemon and sprigs of parsley.

FRENCH POTATO PANCAKES

2 lge. potatoes	*Nutmeg*
1 med. onion	*1/2 tsp. chopped parsley*
2 tbsp. flour	
1/4 tsp. salt	*2 eggs, separated*
Pepper	*Butter*

Peel and grate potatoes and onion. Combine potatoes, onion and flour with seasonings and parsley; blend well. Beat egg yolks slightly; stir into potato mixture. Beat egg whites until stiff peaks form; fold into potato mixture. Drop by tablespoonfuls onto greased hot griddle; cook on both sides until lightly browned.

ICELANDIC PANCAKES

1 c. flour	*1 tsp. vanilla*
1 tbsp. sugar	*1 c. milk*
1/4 tsp. baking powder	*Confectioners' sugar*
Dash of salt	*Strawberry preserves*
1 egg, well beaten	*Whipped cream*
1 tbsp. butter, melted	

Sift dry ingredients; add egg, butter, vanilla and milk. Beat until smooth. Pour small quantity of batter onto hot griddle; tilt griddle to spread batter thinly. Cook on both sides until lightly browned; remove. Cover lightly with confectioners' sugar. Stack next pancake on top; sprinkle with sugar. Place strawberry preserves in center of pancake; roll. Top with whipped cream.

JOHNNYCAKE

3/4 c. cornmeal	*1 tsp. baking powder*
1/4 c. flour	*1/2 c. milk*
3/4 tsp. salt	*1 tbsp. cooking oil*
1/2 tsp. sugar	*1 egg, slightly beaten*

Sift dry ingredients into bowl; stir in milk, oil and egg. Drop by tablespoonfuls onto lightly greased hot skillet; cook on both sides until lightly browned. Yield: 6 to 8 servings.

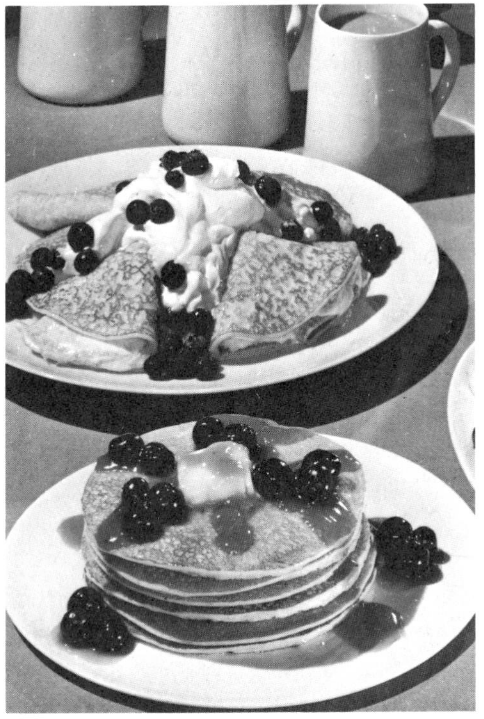

Norwegian Pancakes . . . Sour cream pancakes filled with whipped cream.

NORWEGIAN PANCAKES

1 c. sour cream
1 c. small curd cottage cheese
4 eggs, slightly beaten
3/4 c. sifted flour
1 tbsp. sugar
3/4 tsp. salt
Softened butter
Frozen blueberries, thawed

Blend sour cream and cottage cheese; add eggs and dry ingredients. Beat with electric mixer until mixed well. Drop batter by 1/2 cupfuls onto hot greased griddle; bake until bubbles break on surface. Turn; bake until browned. Spread pancakes with butter; stack as high as desired. Top with blueberries. May spread pancakes with sweetened whipped cream, fold in half and fold in half again, dusting with confectioners' sugar. Arrange 4 pancakes on each serving plate. Top with sweetened whipped cream and blueberries if desired.

NORWEGIAN POTATO PANCAKES

1 c. flour
1 qt. mashed potatoes
Salt
Butter
Brown sugar

Add enough flour to mashed potatoes to make dough easy to handle. Add small amount salt. Knead dough on floured board just enough to mix. Roll small portions of dough very thin, using enough flour to prevent dough from sticking. Bake on ungreased griddle until lightly browned on both sides. Spread pancakes with butter and sugar.

POLISH PANCAKES

3 eggs
2 tbsp. sugar
1/2 tsp. salt
6 tbsp. flour
3/4 c. milk
Mashed cooked prunes
Confectioners' sugar

Beat eggs well. Combine sugar, salt and flour; stir into eggs all at once. Add milk; beat until blended. Pour just enough batter into hot greased skillet to cover bottom; tilt skillet to spread batter evenly. Cook, shaking skillet, until cake is lightly browned on bottom and dry and firm on top. Repeat with remaining batter. Allow cakes to cool. Spread cakes with prunes; roll. Stack on serving dish; sprinkle with confectioners' sugar.

POTATO PANCAKES

6 lge. potatoes, finely grated
2 eggs
1 sm. onion, finely cut
1/2 c. flour
Salt and pepper to taste

Combine all ingredients; blend well. Drop by tablespoonfuls onto greased hot griddle; cook on both sides until lightly browned.

PUFF PANCAKES WITH STRAWBERRIES AND SOUR CREAM

2 eggs
1 c. milk
2 1/3 c. prepared biscuit mix
2 tbsp. sugar
1/4 c. cooking oil
1 c. sour cream
1 10-oz. package frozen strawberries

Beat eggs until thick and lemony; blend in milk. Add biscuit mix and sugar; mix just until moistened. Fold in cooking oil. Drop by spoonfuls onto hot griddle. Bake until underside is golden brown and bubbles appear on surface. Turn; bake other side. Repeat procedure until all batter is used. Arrange on large platter; spoon sour cream and strawberries over pancakes.

RICE PANCAKES

2 c. cooked rice
2 eggs, well beaten
1/4 c. chopped almonds
1/2 tsp. grated lemon rind
2 tbsp. flour

Combine rice, eggs, almonds, lemon rind and flour, blend lightly. Drop by spoonfuls onto hot lightly greased griddle; cook on both sides until lightly browned. Serve with jam, syrup or honey.

RUSSIAN PANCAKES

3 tbsp. flour
Sugar
1/2 tsp. baking powder
2 eggs
Milk
1 carton cottage cheese, drained
1 tsp. nutmeg
1 tsp. vanilla
Butter

Combine flour, 1 tablespoon sugar and baking powder; add eggs. Blend in milk to form thin batter; beat well. Pour just enough batter into hot greased skillet to cover bottom; tilt skillet to spread batter evenly. Cook, shaking skillet, until cake is lightly browned and dry on top. Repeat with remaining batter. Allow cakes to cool. Blend cottage cheese, 3/4 cup sugar, nutmeg and vanilla; mix well. Place 1 tablespoon cheese filling down center of browned side of each pancake. Roll; tuck in ends. Brown in hot butter; serve immediately. Garnish with sour cream, jam or fresh fruit as desired.

STRAWBERRY PANCAKES

1 c. cake flour
1/2 tsp. salt
Confectioners' sugar
3 eggs
3/4 c. milk
5 tbsp. melted butter
2 boxes strawberries, sliced

Sift flour, salt and 2 tablespoons sugar. Beat eggs until light; stir in milk. Blend egg and flour mixtures until just moistened. Stir in butter. Drop by spoonfuls onto hot griddle. Bake until underside is golden brown and bubbles appear on surface. Turn; bake other side. Remove pancakes to large plate; heap with strawberries. Roll pancakes; sprinkle with additional confectioners' sugar. Garnish with crisp bacon and whole strawberries.

SUGARPLUM STRAWBERRY PANCAKES

1 egg
2 c. packaged layer or pound cake mix
1/3 c. flour
1/3 c. chopped nuts

Add egg and 1/2 cup water to cake mix; beat until smooth. Stir in flour and nuts. Drop by spoonfuls onto hot greased griddle. Bake until underside is golden brown and bubbles appear on surface. Turn; bake other side. Serve hot with sweetened strawberries and whipped cream spooned over cakes shortcake-fashion.

SUNDAY MORNING PANCAKES

1/2 c. self-rising flour
1/2 tsp. sugar
1 egg, beaten
1/2 c. sour cream
1/4 tsp. soda

Combine all ingredients; beat until batter is smooth. Pour small amount of batter onto hot ungreased griddle. Bake until underside is golden brown and bubbles appear on surface. Turn; bake other side. Repeat procedure until all batter is used.

Papaya

The papaya is a melon-like fruit with a thin, smooth skin, oblong shape, and a center cavity that is full of seeds. Ripe papayas have a yellow-orange rind and are soft to the touch. In flavor, they resemble cantaloupes. Papayas are available year-round.

FLORIDA FRUIT SALAD

1 papaya
1 mango
1 cantaloupe
1 c. sour cream
1/4 tsp. salt

Cube fruits; combine in large bowl. Refrigerate for 1 hour. Pour sour cream over mixture. Sprinkle salt over fruits; fold cream into fruits gently. Serve on crisp lettuce. Yield: 8 servings.

HAWAIIAN PAPAYA SALAD

1 med. peeled papaya, diced
1 ripe peeled pineapple, diced
3 bananas, diced
2 peeled oranges, diced
3 red apples, diced
1/4 c. chopped walnuts
1 c. diced marshmallows
1/4 c. grated fresh coconut
4 tbsp. honey

Combine all ingredients; chill thoroughly. Serve on lettuce or ti leaves topped with additional coconut. Yield: 8 servings.

PAPAYA SALAD

1 med. papaya
4 c. shredded lettuce
1/3 c. tarragon vinegar
1/4 c. sugar
1 tbsp. lime juice
1/2 tsp. salt
1/2 tsp. dry mustard
1/2 tsp. minced onion
1/4 tsp. paprika

Peel papaya; cut into cubes, reserving seeds. Combine papaya with lettuce. Place all remaining ingredients in electric blender; cover. Blend thoroughly. Add 1 1/2 tablespoons reserved seeds; blend until seeds are size of coarsely ground pepper. Chill. Toss papaya and lettuce with dressing. Yield: 6 servings.

PAPAYA SAUCE CAKE

1/4 c. shortening
1 c. sugar
1 egg, beaten
1/2 c. cooked raisins
2 tsp. lemon juice
1 c. mashed ripe papaya
1 3/4 c. self-rising flour
1/2 tsp. cinnamon
1/2 tsp. nutmeg
1/4 tsp. ginger

Cream shortening and sugar; add beaten egg, raisins and lemon juice. Mix papaya pulp with 3 tablespoons water; stir into raisin mixture. Sift dry ingredients together; add to papaya mixture. Pour into greased 8 x 8-inch pan. Bake at 350 degrees for 50 minutes or until cake tests done.

PAPAYA SHERBET

1 c. sieved papaya pulp
Juice of 1 orange
Juice of 1 lemon
1/2 c. sugar
1 c. milk

Combine papaya pulp and juices. Combine sugar and milk; stir thoroughly. Add to fruit mixture. Pour into 2 ice trays; freeze. Remove from freezer; beat until soft and fluffy. Return to freezer. Remove from freezer; beat until fluffy just before serving. Yield: 6 servings.

Parsnip

A parsnip is a white root vegetable that is available year-round. Look for smooth, firm, well-shaped small parsnips. Allow 1 1/2 pound parsnips to serve 4.
(See VEGETABLES.)

BAKED PARSNIPS

1 pkg. parsnips, peeled
1 egg, beaten
1 tbsp. flour
1 tbsp. milk
1/4 lb. cracker crumbs
1/2 c. butter, melted

Cook parsnips in boiling water until tender; drain. Combine egg, flour and milk; blend well. Dip parsnips into flour mixture; roll in crumbs. Pour butter into baking dish; place parsnips over butter in single layer. Bake at 350 degrees for 30 minutes or until brown, turning once. Yield: 8 servings.

PARSNIPS AU GRATIN

1/4 c. butter
1/4 c. flour
2 c. milk
1 tsp. salt
1/4 tsp. pepper
6 med. parsnips, peeled and cooked
1/2 c. grated American cheese

Melt butter; blend in flour. Add milk; cook, stirring constantly, until thickened. Add salt and pepper. Slice parsnips; place in greased baking dish. Pour sauce over top. Sprinkle with cheese. Bake in 350-degree oven for 30 minutes. Yield: 6-8 servings.

PARSNIPS IN ORANGE SAUCE

12 sm. parsnips, peeled and cooked
1/2 c. orange juice
2 tbsp. brown sugar
1/2 tsp. salt
2 tbsp. light corn syrup
1/8 tsp. paprika
2 tbsp. butter
Grated orange peel

Place parsnips in shallow 8 x 12-inch casserole. Combine orange juice, sugar, salt, syrup and paprika; pour over parsnips. Dot with butter; sprinkle with orange peel. Bake at 400 degrees for 20 minutes. Yield: 6 servings.

ROSEMARY-PARSNIP CASSEROLE

12 parsnips
6 tbsp. butter
1/4 tsp. rosemary
2 tbsp. flour
1/4 c. grated Parmesan cheese
2 c. half and half
1/2 c. cracker crumbs

Peel parsnips; cook in boiling, salted water for 30 minutes or until tender. Drain; cut in half lengthwise. Arrange half the parsnips in greased 2-quart baking dish. Dot with 1 tablespoon butter; sprinkle with half the rosemary, flour and cheese. Drizzle with half the half and half. Repeat, making second layer. Melt remaining butter; toss with cracker crumbs. Sprinkle over top of casserole. Bake at 400 degrees for 20 minutes. Yield: 6 servings.

Fresh Parsnip Cakes . . . Sauteed, seasoned mashed parsnip cakes accompanies meat or fish.

FRESH PARSNIP CAKES

2 c. mashed cooked parsnips
1 1/2 tsp. salt
1/4 tsp. ground pepper
1 tsp. sugar
1 tsp. paprika
1 egg, slightly beaten
1 tsp. fresh lemon juice
1/2 c. fine dry bread crumbs
Flour
Bacon drippings

Combine parsnips, salt, pepper, sugar, paprika, egg, lemon juice and dry bread crumbs; mix well. Shape into 2 1/2-inch patties, 1/2-inch thick. Dip in flour. Saute in bacon dripping in skillet, turning to brown both sides. Serve hot with beef, ham, pork or lamb. Yield: 4 to 5 servings.

FRIED PARSNIPS

3 med. parsnips, peeled
Salt
1/4 c. flour
1/4 c. cornmeal
1 tsp. pepper
1 c. salad oil

Cut parsnips in half lengthwise. Cook parsnips in boiling salted water until tender; drain. Mix flour, cornmeal, 1 teaspoon salt and pepper; roll parsnips in flour mixture. Fry in hot oil in skillet until golden brown. Yield: 6 servings.

PARSNIP PATTIES

6 cooked parsnips, mashed
2 eggs
1 tsp. salt
3 tbsp. sugar
1/4 c. flour
Cooking oil

Mix parsnips, eggs, salt and sugar; add flour, blending well. Shape into patties; saute in skillet in small amount of oil until browned, turning once. Yield: 4-5 servings.

PARSNIP SALAD

2 c. grated parsnips
1 c. thinly sliced celery
1 tbsp. grated onion
2 c. chopped pickle
Salt and pepper to taste
1 hard-boiled egg, chopped
1/2 c. mayonnaise

Mix parsnips, celery, onion and pickle; sprinkle with salt and pepper. Stir in egg; mix with mayonnaise. Serve on lettuce. Yield: 6 servings.

PARSNIPS IN TOMATO SAUCE

1 No. 2 1/2 can tomatoes
1 1/2 tsp. salt
1 bay leaf
1/2 c. diced celery
1 tsp. sugar
1/8 tsp. pepper
1 med. onion, diced
3 whole cloves
2 lb. parsnips, peeled

Combine tomatoes, salt, bay leaf, celery, sugar, pepper, onion and cloves; simmer, covered, for 30 minutes. Cut parsnips crosswise into 3/8-inch thick slices; cook in small amount of water for 30 minutes or until tender. Drain thoroughly. Add parsnips to tomato mixture; simmer for 10 minutes. Yield: 6 servings.

Pastry, Pie

HOW TO MAKE PASTRY

The correct preparation of pastry is the key to successful pie making. Pie crusts should be a delight to the eye as well as to the palate. They should be pale golden brown and flaky. Often they are fluted or decorated in some way.

EQUIPMENT: There are a few pieces of equipment essential to preparing pastry. Foremost among these is a *pastry blender.* This utensil has a wooden handle and several thin metal rings that arc from one side of the handle to the other. When preparing pastry, use a blender to cut in shortening with the dry ingredients and to blend water with the shortening-flour mixture. A *cloth-covered rolling pin* and *board* are two more important pieces of equipment. These, too, help ensure a flaky crust. When rolling pie crust dough, if too much flour (used to keep the dough from sticking to either the pin or the rolling surface) gets into the dough, it may toughen the dough. A cloth covering on the rolling pin and board absorbs most of the flour and releases it as needed to prevent sticking. You can make your own cloth covering for a rolling pin with a child's clean white-ribbed cotton sock. Cut off and discard the sock's foot and slip the remaining ribbed part over the rolling pin. A coarsely-textured dish towel doubles as a cloth covering for your rolling surface. To give pies a finished professional look, consider investing in a *pastry wheel.* This tool cuts out pie crust with a distinctive scalloped edge, giving an attractive look to lattice-topped pies. A *pastry brush* helps distribute egg white or milk evenly over the top crust for a shiny, appetizing appearance. *Pie tape* in varying widths is available in many grocery and hardware stores. Wrapped around the outer edge of the pie, it prevents burning and helps the edge develop a pale golden brown color that is appetizing to behold. *Pie pans* come in many materials. Most are 8 or 9 inches in diameter. Dull-finished pans give the most evenly browned bottom crusts. Glass or enamelware pans reduce baking time by 1/5 to 1/4 of specified recipe time.

PREPARATION: Before beginning to mix pie crust, preheat the oven and chill the ingredients: the shortening, the water, even the flour. Also chill utensils, such as the pastry blender (see above) and the bowl. Chilling helps prevent the shortening from breaking down and blending with the flour before baking. During baking, small particles of chilled shortening melt quickly under great heat and blend with the flour that surrounds them, producing flakes. The result is layer upon layer of flakes with intervening air spaces. But if the shortening breaks down before baking, the result is a hard and brittle pie crust. *To mix the dough*—Cut the shortening into the flour until the blend is similar in appearance to cornmeal. Sprinkle the liquid, a tablespoon at a time, onto the shortening-flour mixture. Mix the liquid and dry ingredients with a tossing motion. Dough is ready for rolling when it cleans the bowl. Before rolling out the dough it is sometimes recommended that the dough be stored in a closed container in the refrigerator for at least 12 hours. This tenderizes it, helps prevent shrinkage during baking, and makes it easier to handle. Chilled dough should be removed from the refrigerator at least 1 hour before being rolled out. Handle dough quickly and lightly. Form it into a ball and roll from the center of that ball outward. Avoid pressing down hard or rolling in a to-and-fro motion—both may break down shortening particles and result in a tough crust. If the dough tears as it is being rolled, patch it immediately. Never reroll the dough: rerolling increases the possibility of tough pie crust. *To prepare for baking*—One-crust pies—Pie shells for one-crust pies are usually baked at very high temperatures. To keep the shell from shrinking, do not stretch the crust when you are putting it in the pan. To prevent the shell from puffing up, prick it at half-inch intervals with a fork or fill it with uncooked rice, dried beans, macaroni, or pieces of bread. Two-crust pies—Roll the bottom crust about 1/8-inch thick. Ease it into the pie plate, avoiding stretching. Fill the crust. Roll out top crust, cut slits as desired, then pick up one edge of the crust dough on your rolling pin. Roll to wrap loosely around the pin; roll across the filled pie in the reverse direction to form the top crust. *Some information to help create successful pies follows:* When pie juices spill into the oven, sprinkle the spill with salt to prevent smoke and smell. To prevent a soggy bottom crust if the pie has a juicy filling, brush the crust with an egg white or melted butter before adding the filling. Be sure that the filling is very hot when put into the shell. To avoid spills when carrying custard pie to the oven, place the crust-filled pie plate on the oven rack and pour the filling into it.

ALMOND TART SHELLS

1 c. butter
3/4 c. sugar
2 1/3 c. flour
1 c. ground blanched almonds
1 egg

Combine all ingredients; blend thoroughly. Roll dough thin. Line buttered tart tins with dough. Bake at 350 degrees for 20 minutes; cool. Fill with desired filling.

EXTRA-RICH PIE CRUST

2 c. flour
1 tsp. baking powder
1/2 tsp. salt
1 tbsp. sugar
1/4 lb. soft butter
1 egg, separated
3 tbsp. sour cream
Milk

Sift first 4 ingredients together; cut in butter. Add egg yolk and sour cream; blend well. Divide into 2 parts; roll out on floured surface. Press half the pastry into pie pan. Add desired filling; cover with remaining pastry. Brush top with egg white; sprinkle with milk and additional sugar. Bake in 350-degree oven.

BEST-EVER PIE CRUST

2 c. lard, melted
4 c. flour
1 c. milk
2 tsp. salt

Combine lard, flour, milk and salt; blend thoroughly. Dough will be soft. Place in covered bowl; chill overnight. Will keep for 2 weeks.

PASTRY FOR APPLE PIE

2 c. sifted flour
1/2 tsp. salt
1 c. grated sharp Cheddar cheese
1/2 c. vegetable shortening
3 to 4 tbsp. cold water

Sift flour with salt into a medium-sized bowl. Add cheese; toss to mix thoroughly with flour. Cut in shortening until mixture resembles coarse meal. Sprinkle water over pastry mixture, 1 tablespoon at a time; mix until dough will hold together. Shape into a ball; roll out.

PENNSYLVANIA DUTCH PASTRY

3 c. flour
1 tsp. salt
1 1/4 c. shortening
5 tbsp. water
1 egg
1 tsp. vinegar

Sift flour and salt; cut in shortening until mixture resembles coarse cornmeal. Beat water, egg and vinegar together; stir into flour mixture. Shape into ball. Chill until ready to use.

SALAD OIL PASTRY

2 c. flour, sifted
1 tsp. salt
1/2 c. salad oil
5 tbsp. ice water

Sift flour with salt. Stir in oil until thoroughly blended; add water to moisten. Handle as little as possible.

ORANGE PASTRY

2 c. sifted flour
1/2 tsp. salt
3/4 c. butter
2 tbsp. confectioners' sugar
1 egg, separated
2 tsp. grated orange rind
1/4 c. orange juice

Combine flour and salt. Cream butter with confectioners' sugar and egg yolk; blend in orange rind and dry ingredients. Add orange juice; mix until stiff dough forms.

SPECIAL PIE CRUST

1 egg
1 tbsp. vinegar
5 1/2 c. flour
1 lb. lard
2 tbsp. brown sugar
1 tbsp. salt
1 tsp. baking powder

Beat egg in measuring cup. Fill measuring cup to 3/4 full with cold water; add vinegar. Rub flour, lard, brown sugar, salt and baking powder together with hands. Add liquid all at once and work until smooth. Store, covered, in refrigerator until ready to use.

SPICED PASTRY

4 c. flour
2 c. sugar
1/2 tsp. cinnamon
1/2 tsp. baking powder
1/4 tsp. cloves
1 lb. unblanched almonds, ground
1 lb. butter
1 egg, lightly beaten

Sift first 5 ingredients together into large bowl; add almonds. Cut in butter until mixture resembles meal; add egg. Knead lightly; form into ball.

WALNUT PASTRY

1 c. shortening
2 c. flour
1/2 tsp. salt
1/2 c. finely chopped nuts

Cut shortening into flour; add salt, nuts and 1/2 cup water. Mix lightly; shape into ball.

Peach

Peaches are round, sweet, juicy, velvet-skinned orange-yellow fruit with a single pit. They are from a tree of the rose family widely grown in America's temperate regions. There are hundreds of peach varieties. All, however, are either yellow-fleshed or white-fleshed and belong to one of two categories: clingstone or freestone. The single pit or seed of *clingstone* peaches adheres firmly to the fruit flesh; the single pit of *freestone* peaches separates easily from the flesh. Firmer, smoother clingstone peaches are used primarily in commercial canning. They are the most popular of all canned fruit. Tastier freestone peaches are enjoyed as a raw fresh fruit. Yellow-fleshed peaches supply Vitamin A; yellow-fleshed and white-fleshed peaches contain protein, carbohydrate, calcium, niacin, and Vitamin C. (1 whole medium raw peach = 35 calories)

AVAILABILITY: Fresh peaches are marketed from late May to mid-October. Peak supply is in July and August. Canned peaches, halved or sliced, water-packed or syrup-packed, are sold year-round. Commercially frozen, dried, pickled, and spiced peaches are available year-round.

BUYING: Look for firm, blemish-free. fresh fruit. Skin should be fine-grained. Deep red cheeks are not a sign or ripeness. Greenish fruit is immature and flavorless. Soft fruit is overripe and should be purchased only for immediate use. 1 pound fruit or 3 medium-sized peaches = 2 cups sliced fruit or 1 cup pulp. 1 1/4 pounds = 1 pint frozen or 1 pint canned fruit.

STORING: Refrigerate fresh, ripe fruit 3 to 5 days. Do not wash and do not cover. If you have bought underripe fruit, allow to ripen within 3 to 4 days at room temperature. Store unopened cans on kitchen shelf 1 year. Refrigerate opened cans up to 5 days. Store dried fruit on kitchen shelf up to 8 months. *To freeze*—Prepare sugar syrup by dissolving 3 cups sugar in 4 cups water. Pour into liquid-tight containers. Chill until ready to use. Just before adding fruit, stir in 1/2 teaspoon ascorbic acid for each cup of syrup used. Peel firm and ripe fruit. Slice or halve directly into cold syrup. Press fruit into container. Add syrup to cover. Leave 1/2-inch head space for pint containers, 1-inch head space for quart containers. To hold fruit under syrup, crumble freezer paper and place on top of fruit. Seal, label, and freeze. Keep fresh frozen and commercially frozen fruit in refrigerator's freezer up to 3 months or in home freezer 1 year.

PREPARATION: *To peel*—Dip fruit in boiling water about 30 seconds. Plunge immediately into iced water. Skin will slip off easily. *To can*—Select firm, ripe peaches. Proceed according to directions under CANNING.

SERVING: Enjoy peaches as a fresh, raw fruit. Pickled or spiced peaches can be used for an accompaniment. Peaches are also used in chutneys, jams, preserves, conserves; in salads; in desserts such as tortes, cobblers, cakes, pies, puddings, ice cream, bombes, parfaits, and milk shakes.

FROZEN PEACHES

9 c. sugar
3 cans frozen orange juice concentrate
1 crate fresh peaches, blanched and peeled

Combine sugar and orange juice concentrate; stir. Slice peaches into sugar and orange mixture; mix lightly. Place in freezer containers. Freeze.

SPICED CANNED PEACHES

1 No. 2 1/2 can peach halves
3 tbsp. vinegar
1 stick cinnamon, broken
5 or 6 whole cloves

Drain liquid from peaches into saucepan. Add vinegar and spices; bring to a boil. May add small amount of sugar, if needed. Add peaches; simmer for 5 to 10 minutes. Yield: 4-5 servings.

PERSIAN PEACHES

4 c. sliced peaches
1/2 c. orange juice
3 tbsp. honey
2 tbsp. finely chopped candied ginger

Combine all ingredients; blend gently. Cover; chill well. Spoon into chilled sherbet dishes.

PEACH PLEASER

1 can peach halves
Maple syrup
Butter
Whipped cream

Drain peaches; reserve syrup. Pour reserved syrup into shallow baking dish; arrange peaches in syrup, cut side up. Fill peaches with maple syrup; dot with butter. Bake at 375 degrees for 15 minutes; serve warm with whipped cream.

PEACH-BLUE CHEESE SALAD

1 1-lb. 13-oz. can peach halves
1/4 c. sour cream
1/4 c. mayonnaise
1/2 c. crumbled blue cheese
1 8 3/4-oz. can crushed pineapple
1 11-oz. can mandarin oranges
Lettuce cups

Drain peaches; reserve syrup. Blend syrup, sour cream, mayonnaise and blue cheese well. Drain pineapple and oranges; fold into cheese mixture. Place peach halves, cup side up, in lettuce cups on salad plates. Fill each peach with 1/4 cup fruit mixture.

PICKLED PEACHES

3 lb. sugar
9 lb. peaches, peeled
1 c. vinegar

Pour sugar over peaches; let stand for several hours. Add vinegar; cook until syrup thickens, stirring occasionally. Place in sterilized jars; seal.

PEACHES SUPREME

8 fresh peach halves
2 tbsp. melted butter
1/2 c. mincemeat
Sour cream

Arrange peach halves in greased baking dish; brush with melted butter. Spoon rounded tablespoons of mincemeat into each half. Spoon any remaining mincemeat around peach halves. Bake in 350-degree oven for 15 to 20 minutes or until peaches are lightly browned. Top with sour cream; serve.

Peaches Supreme . . . Prepared mincemeat fills the center of peach halves for a quick dessert.

Peach Romanoff . . . This chilled dessert combines fresh peaches with ice cream.

PEACH ROMANOFF

1 c. sliced sweetened fresh peaches
1/3 c. Cointreau
1/2 c. evaporated milk
2 tbsp. lemon juice
1 qt. peach ice cream, softened

Mix peaches and Cointreau; let stand until ready to use. Chill evaporated milk in freezer tray until icy crystals form. Chill small mixer bowl and beaters. Pour milk into bowl; whip with mixer at high speed until fluffy. Add lemon juice; whip until stiff peaks form. Beat ice cream in large bowl until creamy; fold in peach and milk mixtures. Beat just until blended. May be stored in freezer for 1 hour. Serve in chilled dessert dishes.

QUICK PICKLED PEACHES

1 lge. can peach halves
1/2 c. sugar
1/3 c. vinegar
1/2 c. cinnamon candies

Drain peaches; mix juice with sugar, vinegar and candies. Bring to a boil. Add peach halves; boil for 3 minutes.

FROZEN PEACH SALAD

1 sm. package orange gelatin
3 c. fresh peaches, crushed
2 c. miniature marshmallows
1 sm. can crushed pineapple
1/2 c. chopped nuts
1 sm. bottle maraschino cherries, quartered
2 c. sour cream
1 c. frozen whipped topping

Dissolve gelatin in 1 cup boiling water; ch.l until partially set. Mix all remaining ingredients in bowl; stir in gelatin. Pour into paper liners in muffin cups; freeze. Remove from freezer 15 minutes before serving; peel liners from salad. Serve on salad greens.

PEACH PICKLE SALAD MOLD

2 lge. jars spiced peaches
2 pkg. orange gelatin
2 cans white seedless grapes, drained
1 No. 2 can pineapple tidbits
1 c. almonds or pecans, chopped

Drain peaches, reserving juice; cut into small cubes. Pour 2 1/2 cups reserved juice into saucepan; bring to a boil. Remove from heat; add gelatin, stirring to dissolve. Let stand until cool. Drain grapes and pineapple. Combine peaches, grapes, pineapple and nuts; stir into gelatin. Chill until firm.

PEACHES BEAUJOLAIS

2 c. peaches
1/2 c. blackberry jelly
3/4 c. rose wine
1 3-oz. package black cherry gelatin
1 3-oz. package orange gelatin
1/4 c. lemon juice
1 c. Beaujolais

Drain peaches, reserving 3/4 cup syrup. Combine peach syrup, jelly and wine in saucepan; bring to a boil. Remove from heat. Add gelatin, one package at a time, stirring until dissolved; add peaches, lemon juice and Beaujolais. Pour into mold; chill until set. Unmold; serve on fresh salad greens. Yield: 6 servings.

SPICY PEACH SALAD

1 lge. can sliced peaches
1/4 c. vinegar
12 whole cloves
3 sticks cinnamon
1 pkg. orange gelatin

Drain peaches; reserve syrup. Add enough water to reserved syrup to make 1 1/2 cups liquid. Mix liquid with vinegar and spices; bring to a boil. Reduce heat; cook slowly for 10 minutes. Remove spices; add gelatin to hot liquid. Stir to dissolve; cool. Add peaches to gelatin mixture. Pour into mold; chill until firm. Yield: 6 servings.

BAKED PEACHES

6 peaches, drained
1 banana, sliced
1/3 c. (packed) brown sugar
1 1/3 c. orange juice
1/4 c. shredded coconut
1/4 c. fine dry bread crumbs

Place peaches in shallow baking dish; place banana over peaches. Mix brown sugar and orange juice; place over low heat, stirring until sugar is dissolved. Pour over banana. Mix coconut and bread crumbs; sprinkle over top. Bake in 375-degree oven for 15 minutes or until coconut is browned lightly. Yield: 6 servings.

ALMOND-PEACH TORTE

2 1/2 c. flour
1/2 c. chopped toasted almonds
Sugar
1/2 tsp. salt
3/4 c. butter
3 1/2 c. chilled sliced peaches
2 c. whipping cream
1/4 tsp. almond extract
1 c. chilled crushed pineapple

Combine flour, almonds, 1/3 cup sugar and salt; cut in butter. Add 1/2 cup cold water gradually; toss with fork until moistened. Form into ball; divide into 3 parts. Roll each part to 8-inch circle, 1/8 inch thick; place on baking sheet. Bake at 375 degrees for 10 minutes or until browned lightly; cool. Drain peaches. Reserve 8 peach slices; chop remaining peaches. Whip cream with 1/4 cup sugar and almond extract until stiff peaks form; reserve 1 cup. Drain pineapple. Fold chopped peaches and pineapple into whipped cream. Spread half the fruit mixture on pastry circle; top with second circle and remaining fruit mixture.Top with circle; spread with reserved whipped cream. Garnish with reserved peach slices; chill for 3 hours. Yield: 10-12 servings.

BRANDY PEACHES

4 tbsp. butter
1/2 c. sugar
4 fresh peaches, peeled
3 oz. brandy

Place butter and sugar in double boiler; cook over boiling water until melted. Stir in 1/4 cup water; add peaches. Cook for 35 minutes, turning peaches several times. Add brandy; serve. Yield: 4 servings.

CREAMY PEACH DESSERT

1/2 tsp. salt
1 1/4 c. flour
1/2 c. margarine
1/2 c. sour cream
1 c. sugar
3 egg yolks, slightly beaten
4 c. fresh peach slices

Mix salt and 1 1/8 cups flour; cut in margarine until size of small peas. Blend in 2 tablespoons sour cream, forming dough. Pat on bottom and sides of 10 x 6-inch baking dish. Bake at 425 degrees for 10 minutes. Mix sugar, egg yolks, remaining flour and remaining sour cream until blended well. Arrange peaches in hot crust; pour sour cream mixture over top. Cover with foil. Bake at 350 degrees for 35 minutes. Remove foil. Bake for 10 minutes or until custard is set. Serve warm.

DEEP-DISH PEACH COBBLER

1/2 c. butter, melted
1 c. sugar
1 c. self-rising flour
1 c. milk
1 qt. sliced peaches

Combine butter, sugar, flour and milk in blender; blend. Pour into buttered casserole. Add peaches; do not stir. Bake at 350 degrees until golden brown. Yield: 8 servings.

FRESH PEACH COFFEE CAKE

3 tbsp. shortening
3/4 c. sugar
1 1/2 tsp. salt
1/2 c. warm milk
1 pkg. yeast
1 egg, beaten
3 c. flour
Fresh ripe peaches, peeled
1/4 c. margarine, melted
1 tsp. cinnamon

Combine shortening, 3 tablespoons sugar, salt, milk and 1/2 cup warm water. Add yeast and egg; mix thoroughly. Add flour; mix until blended well. Let rise until doubled in bulk. Divide dough into 3 parts; pat into greased 9-inch cake pans, pressing dough down in each pan. Let rise for 1 hour or until doubled in bulk. Quarter enough peaches to cover cakes; place on cakes. Drizzle margarine over cakes. Mix remaining sugar and cinnamon; sprinkle over tops. Bake at 375 degrees for 40 minutes. Yield: 18 servings.

FRIED PEACH PIES

1 1-lb. can sliced peaches
3 tbsp. honey
2 tbsp. butter
1 tsp. shredded lemon peel
1 tsp. lemon juice
1/4 tsp. cinnamon
1 pkg. refrigerator biscuits
Confectioners' sugar

Drain peaches thoroughly. Combine peaches, honey, butter, peel, juice and cinnamon. Cook over medium heat for 15 minutes, stirring frequently, until thick and glossy. Separate biscuits; roll each to an oval shape, 5 inches long. Place rounded tablespoon filling just off center, lengthwise of each biscuit. Fold dough over; seal edges with tines of fork. Fry in deep fat at 375 degrees for 1 minute, turning once. Drain; sprinkle with confectioners' sugar. Yield: 10 servings.

PEACHY PARFAITS

Color photograph for this recipe on page 482.

1 env. unflavored gelatin
1 1/4 c. buttermilk
1 tbsp. lemon juice
1/2 c. sugar
3/4 tsp. almond extract
Yellow food coloring
3 peaches, sliced

Soften gelatin in 1/4 cup cold water in saucepan. Place over low heat; stir until gelatin is dissolved. Remove from heat; add buttermilk, lemon juice, sugar, almond extract and several drops of food coloring. Chill until mixture is consistency of unbeaten egg whites. Layer gelatin mixture and peaches in 3 tall glasses, using about 2/3 cup gelatin mixture in each glass. Chill until firm. 3 servings.

FROZEN PEACHES AND CREAM

1 1/2 c. crushed vanilla wafers
1/4 c. melted butter
2 tbsp. orange juice
1 tbsp. lemon juice
1/2 lb. marshmallows
1 c. fresh peaches, drained
1 c. whipping cream, whipped

Combine vanilla wafers with butter, blending well; pat evenly over sides and bottom of 8-inch baking dish. Chill. Mix orange juice and lemon juice; bring to a boil. Add marshmallows. Reduce heat; cook, stirring, until marshmallows are dissolved. Cool slightly; stir in peaches. Fold in whipped cream. Pour into wafer crust; freeze for 4 hours. Yield: 6-8 servings.

FROZEN PEACH PIE

1 box strawberry gelatin
1 lge. can evaporated milk, chilled
1 c. sugar
1 c. fresh peach slices
2 vanilla wafer pie crusts

Prepare gelatin according to package directions; set aside to cool. Whip milk; add gelatin, sugar and peaches. Pour into crusts; freeze. Remove from freezer just before serving. Yield: 2 pies.

PEACH CUSTARD ICE CREAM

6 to 8 peaches, peeled
2 3/4 c. sugar
3 eggs
3 tbsp. flour
Pinch of salt
1 qt. milk
2 qt. heavy cream

Sprinkle peaches with 3/4 cup sugar; let stand for 30 minutes. Beat until mushy. Beat eggs until light and fluffy; add flour, salt and remaining sugar. Beat well. Scald milk; add egg mixture. Stir mixture thoroughly. Place in double boiler; cook, stirring constantly, until smooth. Cool. Pour into freezer; blend in cream and peach mixture. Freeze.

PEACHY CUSTARD HIGH HATS

2 c. milk
3 eggs, separated
1 egg
2/3 c. sugar
Salt
1/2 tsp. vanilla
1/2 tsp. rum extract
2 drops almond extract
1 1-lb. 13-oz. can cling peach slices
Apricot jam

Peachy Custard High Hats . . . Peach slices sandwiched between custard and tender meringue.

Beat milk, egg yolks, egg, 1/3 cup sugar, 1/4 teaspoon salt and flavorings together. Pour into 6 ungreased custard cups. Set cups in pan of 1/2-inch deep water. Bake at 350 degrees for 45 to 55 minutes or until knife inserted in center comes out clean. Cool. Drain peaches; arrange peach slices in each custard cup, reserving some slices for garnish. Drizzle 1 tablespoon jam over peach slices in each cup. Beat egg whites with pinch of salt until soft peaks form. Add remaining sugar gradually, beating until stiff peaks form. Spread meringue over custard cups. Bake at 400 degrees for 5 minutes or until meringue is lightly browned. Cool; garnish with reserved peach slices.

PEACH MELBA

1 10-oz. package frozen red raspberries
2/3 c. sugar
Pinch cream of tartar
2 pt. vanilla ice cream
1 1-lb. can cling peach halves, drained

Thaw raspberries. Press raspberries through sieve into small saucepan, discarding seeds; stir in sugar and cream of tartar. Bring to a boil, stirring constantly. Cook, stirring constantly, for 3 minutes. Pour into small bowl. Scoop ice cream into dessert dishes; top each with peach half. Spoon raspberry sauce over each, dividing evenly.

GERMAN PEACH KUCHEN

2 c. sifted flour
3/4 c. sugar
1/4 tsp. baking powder
1 tsp. salt
1/2 c. butter
1 lge. can peach slices, drained
1 tsp. cinnamon
2 egg yolks, beaten
1 c. sour cream

Sift flour, 1/4 cup sugar, baking powder and salt together; cut in butter until mixture resembles fine crumbs. Press firmly against bottom and side of lightly greased 9-inch springform pan. Arrange peaches evenly over crumbs. Combine remaining sugar and cinnamon; sprinkle over peaches. Bake at 400 degrees for 15 minutes. Blend egg yolks and sour cream. Spoon over peaches. Bake for 20 minutes longer or until golden brown. Serve warm or chilled. Yield: 8 servings.

PEACH CUSTARD PIE

1 1/2 c. flour
1/2 tsp. salt
1/2 c. soft margarine
1 lge. can sliced peaches
1/2 c. sugar
1/2 tsp. cinnamon
1 egg, slightly beaten
1 c. evaporated milk

Mix flour and salt; cut in margarine until mixture resembles coarse crumbs. Add water to hold dough together. Roll out on floured board; place in 8-inch pan. Drain peaches; reserve 1/2 cup syrup. Arrange peaches on crust; sprinkle sugar and cinnamon over peaches. Bake at 375 degrees for 20 minutes. Mix reserved syrup, egg and milk; pour over peaches. Bake for 30 minutes longer. Serve warm.

PEACH BLANC MANGE

3/8 c. cornstarch
Pinch of salt
1 qt. light cream
Sugar
1 c. light rum
Sweetened sliced peaches

Mix cornstarch, salt and cream, stirring until smooth. Add sugar to taste. Bring to a boil in heavy saucepan. Cook for several minutes, stirring constantly, until thick. Remove from heat; add rum. Chill. Serve with peaches. Yield: 8 servings.

PEACH CORDIAL

1/4 c. light corn syrup
5 tsp. frozen orange juice concentrate
4 drops of aromatic bitters
4 med. peaches

Mix corn syrup, orange juice, 1 tablespoon water and bitters in cup; chill. Peel peaches; pit and slice. Place in dessert dishes; top with orange syrup. Garnish with mint, if desired. Yield: 4 servings.

PEACH DUMPLINGS

5 c. sliced peaches
1 c. sugar
2 tbsp. lemon juice
1/4 c. (packed) brown sugar
1 c. pancake mix
1/4 tsp. nutmeg
1/2 c. milk
2 tbsp. melted margarine

Combine peaches, 2 cups water, sugar and lemon juice in large saucepan; bring to a boil. Combine all remaining ingredients, stirring lightly; drop from tablespoon into hot peach mixture. Reduce heat. Cook, covered, for 15 minutes without lifting cover; serve warm with cream or ice cream. Yield: 6-8 servings.

PEACHES BRULOT

3 pkg. frozen peaches
3 egg yolks
1 c. light cream
Maple syrup
3 oz. brandy

Thaw peaches; drain. Place in chafing dish. Beat egg yolks in top of double boiler. Scald cream; pour into egg yolks slowly, stirring to blend. Cook, stirring constantly, for 6 minutes or until thickened. Cover peaches with maple syrup. Heat brandy; pour over peaches. Ignite; let flames subside. Serve peaches topped with cooked custard. Yield: 6 servings.

PEACHES AND CREAM ROLL

3 eggs
1/4 tsp. salt
1 1/4 c. sugar
1/4 tsp. almond flavoring
3/4 c. pancake mix
Confectioners' sugar
1 c. whipping cream
1 tbsp. Cointreau
2 lge. peaches, peeled and sliced

Grease bottom and sides of jelly roll pan; line bottom with greased waxed paper. Have eggs at room temperature. Beat eggs and salt in large mixer bowl until light and lemony. Add 3/4 cup sugar, a small amount at a time, beating constantly. Add almond flavoring and pancake mix, stirring until blended. Spread evenly in pan. Bake at 400 degrees for 7 to 8 minutes or until lightly browned. Sift confectioners' sugar on towel. Remove cake from oven; turn out onto towel immediately. Peel off paper. Roll cake and towel jelly roll fashion; cool on wire racks. Whip cream with remaining sugar and Cointreau. Unroll cake; spread cream mixture to within 1-inch of long sides. Cover with peach slices; reroll. Place, seam side down, on serving plate. Chill for at least 2 hours. Sprinkle with confectioners' sugar. Garnish with additional peach slices. Yield: 12 servings.

PEACHES SUPREME

1/4 c. (packed) brown sugar
1/2 c. light corn syrup
1/3 c. sherry
2 tbsp. butter
1 lge. can cling peach halves
Flaked coconut, toasted

Combine brown sugar, corn syrup, sherry and butter; simmer for 5 minutes. Drain peaches. Pour syrup mixture over peaches; let stand until ready to serve. Fill peaches with coconut. Serve warm. Yield: 5-6 servings.

PEACH FRITTERS

1 1/3 c. sifted flour
1/4 tsp. salt
2 tsp. baking powder
Sugar
1 egg
2 3/4 c. milk
Fresh peaches, peeled
Confectioners' sugar

Sift flour, salt, baking powder and 2 tablespoons sugar together. Beat egg; add egg and milk to flour mixture. Stir well. Cut peaches in half; sweeten to taste. Dip peaches in batter. Fry in deep fat heated to 365 degrees for 2 minutes. Sprinkle with confectioners' sugar.

PEACH MERINGUE TORTE

1 c. flour, sifted
1 tsp. baking powder
1/2 tsp. salt
3 1/2 c. peach slices
1/2 tsp. vanilla
1 tsp. grated lemon rind
1/2 c. butter
3/4 c. powdered sugar, sifted
4 eggs, separated
Sugar
1 c. heavy cream

Sift flour, baking powder and salt together. Drain peaches; reserve syrup. Combine vanilla, lemon rind and 1/4 cup syrup. Chill remaining syrup and peaches. Cream butter and powdered sugar. Beat in egg yolks gradually. Add flour mixture alternately with syrup mixture; beat thoroughly after each addition. Spread batter in 2 greased and floured 9 x 1 1/2-inch cake pans. Beat egg whites until foamy. Add 3/4 cups sugar gradually to egg whites. Beat until stiff peaks form. Spread meringue over cake batter; sprinkle with 2 tablespoons sugar. Bake at 325 degrees for 30 minutes. Cool for 10 minutes; remove from pans. Allow to cool on racks. Place 1 layer, meringue side down, on cake plate. Whip cream until stiff peaks form; sweeten with sugar to taste. Top with half the whipped cream and 1 cup peaches. Add second layer, meringue side up; top with remaining cream and peaches. Yield: 8 servings.

PEACH PRESERVE CAKE

1 c. butter
2 c. sugar
4 eggs
3 c. flour
1 tsp. cinnamon
1/3 tsp. cloves
1 tsp. soda
1 c. sour milk
1 c. chopped pecans
1 c. peach preserves

Cream butter and sugar; beat in eggs. Sift flour with cinnamon and cloves. Dissolve soda in milk; add alternately with flour mixture to creamed mixture. Stir in pecans and preserves. Pour into greased sheet cake pan. Bake at 350 degrees for 1 hour.

PEACH SHORTCAKE

1 lge. can sliced peaches
1 egg, beaten
1 c. prepared biscuit mix
1 tsp. lemon juice
Cinnamon
3 tbsp. flour
3 tbsp. sugar
2 tbsp. soft margarine
1/3 c. currant jelly

Drain peaches, reserving 1/4 cup syrup. Combine egg and reserved syrup; add biscuit mix. Beat well for 1 minute; spread in greased 10 x 6 x 1 1/2-inch baking dish. Arrange peaches on batter; sprinkle with lemon juice. Sprinkle with cinnamon. Combine flour, sugar, 1 teaspoon cinnamon and margarine; mix until crumbly. Sprinkle on peaches. Bake at 375 degrees for 25 minutes. Stir jelly until smooth; spoon over hot cake. Cut in squares; serve warm with whipped cream, if desired. Yield: 8 servings.

PEACH SYLLABUB

1 c. mashed peaches
1 tbsp. lemon juice
5/8 c. powdered sugar
1 c. whipping cream
1 egg white
2 tbsp. sherry

Combine peaches, lemon juice and 2 tablespoons sugar; set aside. Whip cream with 1/4 cup sugar. Beat egg white with 1/4 cup sugar until stiff peaks form. Combine whipped cream and egg white, blending lightly. Add wine; fold wine mixture into peaches. Yield: 4 servings.

PEACH UPSIDE-DOWN CUPCAKES

2 c. cake flour
1/2 c. sugar
3 tsp. baking powder
1/2 tsp. salt
1/4 c. melted shortening
2 eggs
1 c. milk
Butter
Brown sugar
Cooked dried peach halves

Sift flour, sugar, baking powder and salt together 3 times; add shortening, eggs and milk. Beat until batter is smooth and light. Place 1 teaspoon butter and 1 tablespoon brown sugar in each muffin cup; place over low heat until melted, blending thoroughly. Cut peach halves in 3 sections to resemble petals; place in muffin cups with cut side up. Fill cups half full with batter. Bake at 375 degrees for 25 minutes. Serve with vanilla ice cream, if desired.

PARISIAN PEACHES

4 c. sliced peaches
1/2 c. pineapple juice
3 tbsp. maple syrup
3/4 c. finely chopped walnuts

Mix all ingredients gently; cover. Refrigerate to chill. Spoon mixture into chilled sherbet dishes or over ice cream, if desired.

GLAZED PEACH PIE

4 c. sliced fresh peaches
3/4 c. sugar
1 pkg. orange gelatin
Dash of salt
4 tsp. lemon juice
1 baked 9-in. pie shell

Combine peaches and sugar; let stand for 10 minutes. Dissolve gelatin and salt in 1 cup hot water; add 1/2 cup cold water and lemon juice. Add peaches; chill until slightly thickened. Turn into cold pie shell, arranging peaches as desired. Chill until firm; garnish with whipped cream, if desired. Yield: 6 servings.

PEACH DELIGHT PIE

3 egg yolks
3/4 c. sugar
1 can evaporated milk
1 tsp. vanilla
1/2 tsp. almond flavoring
2 c. cooked dried peaches
Sugar
1 unbaked 9-inch pie shell
3 egg whites
Pinch of cream of tartar

Beat egg yolks thoroughly; add sugar and milk, beating well. Add flavorings. Mash peaches; add sugar to taste. Stir into milk mixture. Pour into pie shell. Bake at 400 degrees for 15 minutes; reduce heat to 350 degrees. Bake until brown and firm. Beat egg whites until soft peaks form; add 2 tablespoons sugar and cream of tartar. Beat until mixture stands in stiff peaks; spread on pie. Return pie to oven. Bake until lightly browned.

PEACHES AND CREAM PIE

1 No. 2 1/2 can sliced peaches
1 3-oz. package lemon gelatin
1 pt. vanilla ice cream
1/8 tsp. almond flavoring
1 9-in. pastry shell

Drain peaches, reserving syrup. Bring 1 cup peach syrup to a boil; add gelatin, stirring until dissolved. Add 1/2 cup cold water. Cut ice cream into pieces; add to hot liquid. Stir until melted; add flavoring. Chill until mixture begins to thicken. Reserve several peach slices for garnish; fold remaining peaches into mixture. Pour mixture into pie shell. Chill for 4 hours or until firm. Yield: 6 servings.

PEACH PAN PIE

4 c. sliced canned peaches	*Rind of 1 orange, grated*
2 c. sifted flour	*5/8 c. shortening*
3 tsp. baking powder	*1/2 tsp. cinnamon*
2 tsp. salt	*2 tbsp. butter*
5/8 c. sugar	

Drain peaches; reserve syrup. Set peaches aside. Sift flour, baking powder, 1 teaspoon salt and 2 tablespoons sugar together. Mix in orange rind. Cut in shortening with pastry blender. Stir in 2/3 cup reserved peach syrup to make soft dough. Turn onto lightly floured board. Knead lightly. Roll out to 1/8-inch thickness. Pat into 10-inch skillet; allow extra dough to hang over edge of pan. Place peaches on dough in pan. Combine remaining sugar, cinnamon and remaining salt; sprinkle over peaches. Dot with butter; pour 1 tablespoon reserved peach syrup over top. Fold extra dough toward center of pan, leaving center uncovered. Bake at 350 degrees for 35 to 40 minutes.

POACHED PEACHES WITH RUM

3 c. sugar	*1 tbsp. butter*
Salt	*1/2 c. dark rum*
1 tbsp. fresh lemon juice	*1 c. whipping cream, whipped*
12 lge. peaches, peeled	

Combine 3 1/2 cups boiling water, sugar and 1/8 teaspoon salt in saucepan; bring to a boil. Cook for 5 minutes or until syrupy. Stir in lemon juice; add peaches. Reduce heat; simmer for 20 minutes, turning peaches occasionally. Transfer peaches to serving bowl. Add butter and pinch of salt to hot syrup; stir until butter is melted. Stir in rum; pour over peaches. Refrigerate until ready to serve. Serve with whipped cream. Yield: 4-6 servings.

SKILLET PEACH DELIGHT

1 c. margarine	*1/8 tsp. salt*
1 c. flour	*1 tsp. baking powder*
1 c. sugar	*1 No. 3 can sliced peaches*
1 c. milk	

Melt margarine in 10-inch iron skillet. Mix flour, sugar, milk, salt and baking powder at medium speed with electric mixer for 2 minutes. Pour batter into center of skillet; top with peaches. Bake at 450 degrees until golden brown. Yield: 8 servings.

STUFFED PEACHES

6 ripe peaches	*1/2 tbsp. finely chopped citron*
1/2 c. chopped blanched almonds	*3 ladyfingers, finely chopped*
1/2 tbsp. sugar	*White wine to taste*
1/2 tbsp. minced candied orange peel	*3 oz. peach brandy*
1/2 peach, mashed	*3 oz. brandy*

Scald peaches in boiling water; slip off skins. Cut in half lengthwise; remove pits. Pound almonds in bowl with sugar, adding several drops of cold water. Mix in orange peel, mashed peach, citron and ladyfingers. Pack into peach cavities; place halves together. Secure with toothpicks; place in baking dish. Moisten peaches with wine; sprinkle with additional sugar. Heat brandies; pour over peaches. Ignite; serve immediately. Yield: 6 servings.

Peanut

Peanuts are not really nuts at all, but are pale brown, nutritious legumes that usually contain two edible seeds. They are harvested from a vine whose branches grow underground. Of the two types of peanuts, the Virginia and the Spanish, the Virginia has larger and longer kernels, a lower fat content, and a more distinctive flavor. The list of nutrients contained in both varieties of peanuts is impressive: protein, calcium, sodium, potassium, iron, niacin, riboflavin, and thiamine. (1 cup shelled peanuts = 840 calories)

AVAILABILITY: Fresh peanuts are available year-round chiefly from the southeastern United States and are sold in the shell or unshelled, roasted, and salted. Peanut oil and especially peanut butter are other important peanut products.

BUYING: In buying fresh peanuts, look for clean, uncracked shells; kernels should not rattle when shaken.

STORING: Store peanuts in shell in cool, dry, dark place for 9 months. Refrigeration is preferred. Refrigerate kernels in air-tight container for 3 months. Store vacuum-packed jars of peanuts indefinitely on kitchen shelf.

PREPARATION: *To shell*–Crack shell between fingers and remove whole kernels. *To chop* shelled peanuts–Use wooden board and straight-edged knife or chopping bowl and food chopper. *To roast*–Spread shelled kernels one layer deep in shallow pan. Roast in 300 degree oven for 30 to 45 minutes. Stir often. If desired, butter or margarine and salt may be added after roasting. *For "redskins"*–Remove peanuts from oven and add 1 teaspoon butter or margarine per cup peanuts. Stir until coated. Spread on absorbent paper and sprinkle with salt. *For plain salted nuts*–Cool roasted peanuts. Slip skins off by pressing kernels between thumb and forefinger. Place in skillet and add 1 teaspoon butter or margarine per cup peanuts. Stir constantly over low heat until coated and warm. Spread peanuts on absorbent paper and sprinkle with salt.

USES: Eat whole peanuts for snacks or in casseroles and salads. Use chopped peanuts and peanut butter in candies, souffles, cakes, cookies, and tortes.

PEANUT BUTTER AND CHUTNEY CANAPÉS

1 8-oz. package cream cheese
1/2 lb. crunchy peanut butter
4 oz. chutney, finely chopped
1/4 tsp. Worcestershire sauce
1/4 tsp. seasoned salt
Dry red wine
Crackers or party rye bread

Blend cream cheese, peanut butter, chutney, Worcestershire sauce and salt together; moisten with enough red wine to spread easily. Spread on crackers. May be stored in covered jar in refrigerator for weeks.

PEANUT BUTTER DIP

1 3-oz. package cream cheese
1/3 c. peanut butter
Milk

Combine cream cheese and peanut butter in electric mixer bowl; beat until smooth, adding enough milk to make of dipping consistency. Serve with potato chips or assorted crackers.

PEANUT BUTTER-ORANGE SALAD

8 oranges
1/4 c. mayonnaise
1/4 c. peanut butter
1/2 c. peanuts
1 1/2 c. thinly sliced celery
2 bananas, sliced

Cut slices from tops of oranges; cut off peel, spiral fashion. Remove remaining white membrane. Slice oranges 1/4 inch thick; reserve several orange slices. Dice remaining orange slices coarsely. Blend mayonnaise and peanut butter together until smooth. Combine diced oranges, peanuts, celery and banana slices; add peanut butter mixture. Toss lightly. Serve on crisp greens; garnish with reserved orange slices. Yield: 6 servings.

PEANUT BUTTER STEW

1 cut-up pig's foot
Salt and pepper to taste
1 2-lb. frying chicken
1/2 c. onion, sliced
2 hot chili peppers
1/2 c. chopped green pepper
1/2 tsp. thyme
1 c. peanut butter
1/2 c. tomato paste

Season pig's foot with salt and pepper. Cut chicken into serving pieces; season. Steam pig's foot in enough water to cover in kettle for 20 minutes. Add chicken pieces. Cover; cook for 15 minutes. Add onion, chili peppers, green pepper and thyme. Mix peanut butter in bowl with small amount of hot water; stir into stew. Add tomato paste; cook, stirring occasionally, until chicken is tender. Serve over hot rice. Yield: 6 servings.

ALL-AMERICAN SANDWICHES

1/4 c. figs
1/4 c. raisins
1/2 tsp. salt
1/2 c. peanut butter
2 tbsp. lemon juice
2 tbsp. corn syrup
Thin bread slices

Grind figs and raisins together; add salt, peanut butter, lemon juice and corn syrup. Mix well. Spread between bread slices.

PEANUT-APPLE SANDWICHES

6 slices bacon
1/2 c. peanut butter
2 tbsp. mayonnaise
2 tsp. lemon juice
1/2 c. finely diced tart apple
Buttered bread slices

Fry bacon; crumble. Blend peanut butter, mayonnaise and lemon juice together. Stir in apple and bacon. Spread filling between bread slices.

PEANUT BUTTER SANDWICH

12 bread slices
Butter
3 bananas, sliced
1/2 c. peanut butter

Spread half the bread slices with butter; cover with bananas. Spread remaining bread slices with peanut butter. Top bananas with peanut butter-covered bread. Yield: 6 sandwiches.

PEANUT BUTTER SUPREME

1/3 c. peanut butter
1/4 c. cream cheese
2 tbsp. honey
Bread slices

Mix peanut butter, cream cheese and honey together until blended. Trim crusts from bread; cut slices into animal shapes, using cookie cutters. Spread peanut butter mixture carefully on half the bread; top with remaining bread. May be covered and refrigerated until ready to serve.

PEANUT SANDWICH FILLING

1 sm. bottle olives
1 sm. bottle sweet pickles
4 hard-boiled eggs
1/2 lb. salted peanuts
1 tsp. salt
6 tsp. sugar
2 tsp. cornstarch
Dash of pepper
1 tsp. dry mustard
1 egg
1/2 c. vinegar
1 c. milk
1 tbsp. butter
Bread slices

Process olives, pickles, eggs and peanuts through food chopper. Combine salt, sugar, cornstarch, pepper and mustard, blending well. Beat in egg; add vinegar and milk. Place vinegar mixture in saucepan over low heat. Cook, stirring constantly, until thickened. Stir in butter until melted. Add peanut mixture, blending well. Spread filling between bread slices.

Peanut Casserole . . . Chopped peanuts bring exciting contrast to a popular macaroni dish.

PEANUT CASSEROLE

1 8-oz. package shell macaroni
2 c. chopped onions
1/2 c. chopped green pepper
2 tbsp. salad oil
2 lb. ground beef
2 tsp. salt
1/4 tsp. pepper
1 10-oz. can cream of tomato soup
1 c. evaporated milk
1 c. shredded Cheddar cheese
2 tbsp. Worcestershire sauce
1 c. coarsely chopped peanuts

Cook macaroni according to package directions until barely tender; drain. Combine onions, green pepper, salad oil and beef in large kettle. Cook over medium heat until beef has browned, breaking beef up with fork. Season with salt and pepper. Stir in soup, milk, 2/3 cup cheese and Worcestershire sauce. Add macaroni. Cover; simmer for 20 minutes, stirring occasionally. Turn into 2 1/2-quart greased casserole. Sprinkle with remaining cheese and peanuts. Bake in 350-degree oven for 30 minutes. Yield: 8-10 servings.

PEANUT BUTTER BREAD

2 c. all-purpose flour
3 tsp. baking powder
1/2 tsp. salt
1/2 c. sugar
1/2 c. peanut butter
2 eggs, beaten
1 c. milk
1 tsp. grated lemon rind
1/2 c. chopped salted peanuts
Melted butter

Sift dry ingredients together; rub in peanut butter until mixture is crumbly. Combine eggs, milk and lemon rind; add to flour mixture. Pour into greased 9 x 5-inch loaf pan; sprinkle with peanuts. Bake for about 1 hour at 350 degrees. Brush hot bread with melted butter. Let set overnight; remove from pan and slice.

PEANUT BUTTER MUFFINS

1/8 c. peanut butter
1/4 c. sugar
1 egg, beaten
1 1/2 c. flour
4 tsp. baking powder
1/2 tsp. salt
3/4 c. milk

Cream peanut butter and sugar; add egg. Sift dry ingredients together; add to creamed mixture alternately with milk. Fill greased muffin pans 2/3 full. Bake for 25 minutes at 350 degrees.

PEANUTTY TEA RING

1 10-count pkg. refrigerator biscuits
1/4 cup melted butter
1 c. finely chopped peanuts
1/2 c. powdered sugar

Separate biscuits; dip both sides in melted butter. Coat with peanuts. Arrange biscuits in overlapping circle on greased baking sheet. Bake at 425 degrees for 10 to 15 minutes or until golden brown. Mix powdered sugar and 1 tablespoon water; drizzle icing over hot tea ring. Slide ring onto serving plate. Serve warm. Yield: 6-8 servings.

PEANUT BUTTER CAKE

1 1-lb. 2 1/2-oz. package yellow cake mix
3 eggs, slightly beaten
Peanut butter
1/2 c. salad oil
1 c. margarine
3 1/2 c. confectioners' sugar
1 tsp. vanilla
1/2 c. evaporated milk
Pineapple juice to taste

Combine cake mix, eggs, 1 1/3 cups water, 1/2 cup peanut butter and oil, blending well. Spoon batter into greased 9-inch tube pan. Bake at 350 degrees for 1 hour or until cake tests done. Cool in pan for 10 minutes; remove from pan. Cool well on wire rack. Beat margarine until soft; beat in 1 cup confectioners' sugar. Add vanilla; beat until smooth. Add remaining confectioners' sugar, milk, pineapple juice and peanut butter to taste alternately; beat until smooth. Spread frosting over cake.

PEANUT BUTTER AND JELLY CAKE

2 c. sifted all-purpose flour
1 1/2 c. sugar
3 tsp. baking powder
1 tsp. salt
1/2 c. shortening
1/2 c. peanut butter
1 c. milk
2 eggs
1 10-oz. jar currant jelly
1 pkg. fluffy white frosting mix
1/2 c. chopped peanuts

Sift flour, sugar, baking powder and salt together in electric mixer bowl. Add shortening, peanut butter and milk. Beat for 2 minutes at medium speed. Add eggs; beat for 2 minutes longer. Pour batter into greased and lightly floured 13 x 9 x 2-inch pan. Bake at 350 degrees for 45 to 50 minutes. Cool. Break up jelly with fork; spread evenly over cake. Prepare frosting mix according to package directions. Spread frosting carefully over jelly on cake; sprinkle with peanuts. Cut into squares to serve. Yield: 16-20 servings.

PEANUT BUTTER CANDY

2 c. sugar
1/2 c. white syrup
1/2 c. water
2 egg whites, stiffly beaten
1 c. peanut butter

Combine sugar, syrup and 1/2 cup water in 1-quart saucepan. Bring to a boil, stirring constantly; reduce heat. Cook to hard-ball stage. Pour hot syrup over beaten egg whites in thin stream, beating until candy loses gloss and holds shape. Toss on floured board; pat and roll lightly to 1/4-inch thickness. Spread with peanut butter; roll up as for jelly roll. Cut in 1-inch slices. Yield: 60 pieces.

TEMPTING PEANUT BRITTLE

Color photograph for this recipe on page 488.

2 c. sugar
1 c. light corn syrup
1 1/2 c. salted peanuts
3 tbsp. butter
1 tsp. vanilla
2 tsp. soda

Combine sugar, corn syrup and 1/4 cup water in 3-quart heavy saucepan; mix well. Cook over medium heat, stirring constantly, until sugar dissolves. Cook, stirring frequently, until candy thermometer registers 285 degrees. Remove from heat; stir in peanuts and butter. Cook, stirring constantly, to 295 degrees. Remove from heat. Add vanilla and soda; stir quickly to blend. Mixture will foam. Pour onto greased marble slab or 2 large greased baking sheets; spread out thin. Cool for 5 minutes or just enough to handle. Turn candy over; pull to stretch as thin as possible. Cool thoroughly; break into pieces. Yield: About 2 pounds.

PEANUT BUTTER-COCONUT ROLL

Color photograph for this recipe on page 495.

1/4 c. creamy peanut butter
1/4 c. dark corn syrup
2 c. sifted confectioners' sugar
1/4 c. instant nonfat dry milk
1/4 tsp. salt
1 c. flaked coconut, chopped

Blend peanut butter and corn syrup in bowl; stir in 2 teaspoons water. Sift confectioners' sugar, dry milk and salt together; mix into peanut butter mixture. Add coconut; knead until well blended. Shape into roll; wrap in waxed paper. Chill for several hours or until firm. Cut into 1/4-inch slices with sharp knife. May tint with food coloring if desired. Yield: About 3/4 pound.

PEANUT BUTTER CRUNCH

2 c. sugar
1/2 c. evaporated milk
1/2 c. butter
1 c. crunchy peanut butter
2 c. quick-cooking oats
2 c. miniature marshmallows
1 tsp. vanilla

Bring sugar, milk, butter and peanut butter to a boil over medium heat in saucepan. Boil for 2 minutes, stirring constantly. Remove from heat; add oats, marshmallows and vanilla. Stir until blended and slightly thickened. Drop by spoonfuls onto waxed paper. Let cool. Yield: 50 servings.

PEANUT BUTTER LOGS

1 c. crunchy peanut butter
1 c. confectioners' sugar
2 c. oven-toasted rice cereal
1/2 c. chopped nuts
2 tbsp. butter
1 6-oz. package chocolate chips
2 tbsp. paraffin

Combine peanut butter, sugar, cereal, nuts and butter, blending well. Chill well. Roll into 2-inch logs. Melt chocolate and paraffin together over boiling water until thin. Dip logs into chocolate mixture. Place on waxed paper to harden. May be frozen.

PEANUT-BUTTERSCOTCH DROPS

1 pkg. butterscotch morsels
3 tbsp. peanut butter
3 c. corn flakes

Combine butterscotch morsels and peanut butter in double boiler; cook over boiling water until melted. Pour in corn flakes; stir until coated. Drop candy by spoonfuls onto waxed paper. Let harden.

PEANUT BLOSSOMS

1/2 c. butter
1/2 c. peanut butter
Sugar
1/2 c. (packed) brown sugar
1 egg
1 tsp. vanilla
1 3/4 c. sifted self-rising flour
Chocolate candy kisses

Cream butter, peanut butter, 1/2 cup sugar and brown sugar together. Add egg and vanilla, beating well. Blend in flour gradually; mix thoroughly. Shape dough into balls, using rounded teaspoon for each ball. Roll balls in sugar; place on ungreased cookie sheets. Bake at 375 degrees for 8 minutes; remove from oven. Place candy kiss on top of each cookie, pressing down firmly until cookie cracks. Return to oven. Bake for 2 to 5 minutes longer. Yield: 3 dozen cookies.

PEANUT BUTTER DROP COOKIES

2 c. (packed) brown sugar
2 eggs
1 1/4 c. shortening
1 tsp. vanilla
4 c. flour, sifted
1 tsp. soda
1 tsp. salt
Crunchy peanut butter

Cream brown sugar, eggs and shortening until fluffy; add vanilla and 1/2 cup water. Sift flour, soda and salt together; add to creamed mixture, blending well. Drop by spoonfuls onto greased cookie sheet. Place 1/2 teaspoon peanut butter on top of each cookie. Cover with 1/2 teaspoon remaining cookie dough. Bake at 350 degrees for about 12 to 15 minutes or until cookies are lightly browned. Yield: 5 dozen cookies.

EASY PEANUT BUTTER COOKIES

2 egg whites
1 c. crunchy peanut butter
1 c. sugar
1/2 tsp. almond extract

Beat egg whites until stiff; fold in peanut butter, sugar and almond extract. Drop by spoonfuls onto greased cookie sheet. Bake for 15 minutes at 350 degrees.

PEANUT BUTTER MOUNTAIN COOKIES

2 c. sugar
1 1/2 c. milk
1/2 c. margarine
2 1/2 c. oats
2 tsp. vanilla
3/4 c. peanut butter
3/4 c. raisins
1/2 c. chopped pecans
Food coloring

Combine sugar, milk and margarine in saucepan; bring to a boil. Boil for 1 minute and 30 seconds; remove from heat. Stir in oats, vanilla, peanut butter, raisins and pecans; add enough food coloring to tint desired color. Mix well. Drop by spoonfuls onto waxed paper. Yield: About 2 dozen.

PEANUT BUTTER SUPREMES

1 c. shortening
1 1/4 c. peanut butter
1 c. sugar
1 c. (packed) brown sugar
2 eggs
2 1/2 c. flour
1/4 tsp. salt
1/2 tsp. soda

Blend shortening and peanut butter together; add sugar and brown sugar, blending well. Beat in eggs until fluffy. Sift flour, salt and soda together; stir into peanut butter mixture, blending well. Shape dough into small balls; place on cookie sheets. Flatten each ball with fork. Bake at 375 degrees for 10 to 15 minutes. Yield: 4-5 dozen cookies.

PEANUT MOUNDS

1 c. butter
1/2 c. sugar
2 c. sifted flour
2 tsp. vanilla
1 3/4 c. chopped salted peanuts

Preheat oven to 350 degrees. Cream butter; add sugar gradually. Blend in flour, vanilla and peanuts. Pinch off 1-inch balls of dough. Place on ungreased cookie sheet. Bake at 325 degrees for 20 minutes. Roll in additional sugar while warm.

SPANISH PEANUT COOKIES

1 c. butter
2 c. (packed) brown sugar
2 eggs
2 c. flour
1 tsp. soda
1 tsp. cream of tartar
1 tsp. vanilla
1 7 1/4-oz. can salted Spanish peanuts
2 c. oatmeal
1 c. corn flakes

Cream butter and brown sugar; add eggs, beating well. Sift flour, soda and cream of tartar together; blend into creamed mixture gradually, mixing well. Stir in vanilla, peanuts, oatmeal and corn flakes. Drop by spoonfuls onto greased cookie sheets. Bake at 325 degrees for 12 minutes or until light brown. Do not overbake.

PEANUT BUTTER PARFAIT

1 c. (packed) brown sugar
1/3 c. milk
1/4 c. white corn syrup
1 tbsp. butter
1/4 c. peanut butter
Vanilla ice cream
Peanuts

Combine brown sugar, milk, syrup and butter in medium saucepan. Cook over medium heat until sugar dissolves and butter melts, stirring constantly. Remove from heat; add peanut butter. Beat with rotary beater or mixer until smooth; cool. Alternate layers of peanut butter sauce and ice cream in parfait glasses, beginning and ending with ice cream. Top with peanuts. Yield: 4 servings.

PEANUT BUTTER PIE

1 c. instant nonfat dry milk powder
Sugar
3 tbsp. (heaping) cornstarch
4 eggs, separated
3 tbsp. butter
1 tbsp. (heaping) peanut butter
1 baked 9-in. pie crust
1/2 tsp. cream of tartar

Combine milk powder, 1 cup sugar and cornstarch in saucepan; add slightly beaten egg yolks and 3 cups water. Mix until smooth. Cook over low heat, stirring constantly, until thick; remove from heat. Add butter and peanut butter; stir until melted. Pour filling into pie crust. Beat egg whites until stiff, adding 4 tablespoons sugar and cream of tartar. Spread meringue over pie. Bake in 400-degree oven for 10 to 12 minutes. Yield: 8 servings.

Pear

The pear is a smooth-skinned fruit with fine-grained, juicy, and sweet flesh. All major American varieties of pears are generally classified as summer or winter types, depending on their marketing season. Major American pear producing states are California, Oregon, and Washington. Pears supply protein, carbohydrate, calcium, and Vitamins A and C. (1 raw 3 inch x 2 1/2 inch pear = 100 calories)

KINDS: *Summer*—The Bartlett pear is the most familiar variety. Bell-shaped and yellow with a red blush, it is eaten raw or canned. When firm enough, it may be used in baking. *Winter*—Primary varieties include: Anjou, Bosc, Comice, Seckel, and Winter Neils. The *Anjou* pear is large and firm. Its thick skin varies in color from green to red. The Anjou's firmness makes it excellent for baking. It can also be canned. Fully ripened, soft Anjous may be eaten raw. The *Bosc* pear is large with a tapering neck. Slightly acidic, it is greenish brown to golden russet. It can be cooked or eaten raw. The *Comice* pear is large and round with greenish skin often tinged with red. The delicate melting flesh of this pear makes delicious eating. The *Seckel* pear is small, firm, fleshy, and sweet. Its color is yellowish brown. It is eaten raw and used in canning and pickling. The *Winter Neils* are sweet and yellowish green with russet dots. They are eaten raw and used in cooking and canning.

AVAILABILITY: With so many seasonal varieties, fresh pears are available in late summer and fall. The peak season is September and October. Supplies are imported (mainly from Argentina) in March through May when domestic quantity is small. Canned and dried pears are also available year-round. Canned fruit may be whole, quartered, sliced; packed in water, syrup, or juice. Halved dried fruit is packaged. Pears are also marketed spiced and pickled.

BUYING: Look for fairly firm, blemish-free fresh fruit with stems attached. Fruit is ripe if stem base yields readily to gentle pressure. Avoid misshapen, wilted, or shriveled fruit. Desirable color and shape depend on variety (see **KINDS** above). 1 pound, or 3 or 4 pears, yields 3 cups sliced fruit.

STORING: Refrigerate ripe fruit and use within a few days. Allow underripe fruit to ripen at room temperature. Store unopened cans on kitchen shelf 1 year. Refrigerate opened cans up to 5 days. Keep dried fruit on kitchen shelf up to 8 months. *To freeze* pears—Prepare a sugar syrup (see PEACHES). Select tender, juicy, fine-fleshed fruit. Peel, halve, and core. Slice, 1 1/2 inch thick, lengthwise directly into cold syrup. Leave 1/2-inch head space for pint containers and 1-inch head space for quart containers. To keep fruit covered with syrup, crumble freezer paper over top of fruit. Seal, label, and freeze.

USES: Wash and eat raw. Use in salads and jams. Pears can be spiced, pickled, and cooked in many ways. See individual recipes. Cook firm, slightly underripe fruit for best success. (See CANNING.)

PARTY PEAR SALAD

8 3-oz. packages lime gelatin
1/4 c. lemon juice
2 lb. cottage cheese
2 c. finely chopped celery
2 c. chopped pecans
2 c. mayonnaise
4 c. evaporated milk
4 1-lb. cans pears
Pecan halves

Dissolve 4 packages gelatin in 3 cups boiling water; cool. Add lemon juice. Fold in cottage cheese, celery, pecans and mayonnaise; mix well. Stir in milk; blend thoroughly. Ladle into lightly oiled 19 1/2 x 11 1/2 x 2 1/4-inch pan; chill until partially congealed. Drain pears; reserve syrup. Add water to reserved syrup to make 3 1/2 cups liquid. Bring to a boil. Add remaining gelatin; stir until dissolved. Chill until partially congealed. Arrange pear halves, cut side up, in gelatin layer. Place 1 pecan in each pear half. Ladle partially congealed gelatin over pears. Chill for 3 hours or until firm. Yield: 25 servings.

PEARADISE MINT SALAD

1 1-lb. 14-oz. can Bartlett pears
1 8 3/4-oz. can white grapes
1/3 c. lemon juice
1 6-oz. package lime gelatin
1/8 tsp. salt
1 c. sour cream
1/4 tsp. peppermint flavoring
1/2 c. toasted slivered almonds
Bunches white grapes, frosted

Drain pears and grapes; reserve syrups. Reserve 6 pear halves; chop remaining pears. Combine pear and grape syrups with lemon juice; heat to boiling. Dissolve gelatin in hot mixture; add 3/4 cup cold water and salt. Chill until partially set. Add sour cream and peppermint flavoring; mix until smooth. Add canned grapes, pears and nuts. Pour into 1-quart mold; chill until firm. Unmold onto a bed of lettuce. Garnish with reserved pear halves and bunches of grapes.

SEAFOAM SALAD WITH PEARS

1 No. 2 1/2 can pears
1 pkg. lime gelatin
1 8-oz. package cream cheese
2 tbsp. cream
1 c. whipping cream, whipped

Drain pears; reserve 1 cup syrup. Mash pears. Heat reserved syrup; dissolve gelatin in hot syrup. Blend cream cheese with cream; add to hot gelatin, stirring until cheese is dissolved. Cool until thickened. Fold in pears and whipped cream; pour into glass dish. Refrigerate for at least 12 hours. Cut into squares.

PEAR AND GRAPE SALAD

1 8-oz. package cream cheese
Milk
2 lge. ripe pears
Lettuce
Halved seedless green grapes

Soften cream cheese; add enough milk to make of spreading consistency. Peel and halve pears; arrange pears, cut side down, on bed of lettuce. Frost pears with cream cheese mixture. Press grapes, cut side down, onto pears, covering pears completely.

FROZEN FRUIT SALAD WITH PEARS

1 can pineapple tidbits
1 egg, beaten
1/4 c. sugar
2 1/2 tbsp. flour
1/2 tsp. salt
2 tbsp. vinegar
1 c. whipped cream
1 can pears
3 bananas, mashed
12 cherries

Drain pineapple; reserve 3/4 cup juice. Mix egg, sugar, flour, salt, vinegar and reserved pineapple juice; cook until thickened, stirring constantly. Cool. Drain pears; dice. Fold in whipped cream; add pineapple, pears, bananas and cherries. Place in mold; freeze.

FROZEN PEAR AND CREAM CHEESE SALAD

1 1-lb. can pears
2 3-oz. packages cream cheese
6 tbsp. French dressing
Salad greens
Mayonnaise

Drain pears; reserve juice. Cut pears into thin lengthwise slices. Mash cream cheese; add pear juice and 6 tablespoons French dressing. Beat until smooth. Arrange pear slices in refrigerator tray. Pour cheese mixture over pears. Freeze until firm; slice into squares. Arrange on salad greens; serve with mayonnaise or additional French dressing.

MARINATED PEAR SALAD

3 Bartlett pears, peeled
1 c. salad oil
1/4 c. white wine vinegar
1/2 tsp. salt
2 tbsp. chopped parsley
4 tsp. chopped pimento
1/2 tsp. basil
6 pitted dates
1/4 c. tangy cheese spread
Lettuce

Halve pears; core. Combine oil, vinegar, salt, parsley, pimento and basil in jar. Cover; shake well. Place pear halves, cut side down, in shallow bowl; pour oil dressing over pears. Chill, covered, for 1 hour to 1 hour and 30 minutes. Stuff dates with cheese spread. Arrange pears, cut side up, on lettuce-lined serving plate; garnish with dates. Spoon remaining dressing over pears.

PEAR SALAD BOWL

3 Anjou pears, peeled
1 avocado
Crisp lettuce
1/4 c. pecan halves
2 tbsp. frozen orange juice concentrate
1/4 c. lemon juice
1/4 c. sugar
3/4 c. salad oil
3/4 tsp. salt
1 tsp. paprika
1 tsp. prepared mustard
1 tsp. grated onion
1/2 tsp. celery seed

Core pears and slice into wedges; cut avocado in half and remove seed. Peel avocado; cut into wedges. Line salad bowl with crisp lettuce. Arrange pear and avocado wedges in in bowl; sprinkle with pecans. Combine remaining ingredients in pint jar. Cover; shake well. Add to salad; toss gently.

STUFFED PEAR SALAD

2 3-oz. packages cream cheese
2 c. creamed cottage cheese
1 c. snipped pitted dates
1 c. diced toasted almonds
8 fresh pears
Lemon juice
Salad greens

Soften cream cheese; blend with cottage cheese. Add dates and almonds; refrigerate for 3 hours. Pare, halve and scoop out centers of pears. Sprinkle pear halves generously with lemon juice. Arrange 2 pear halves on salad greens on individual salad plates. Fill each pear half with cheese mixture.

BARTLETT PEAR COFFEE CAKE

1 can Bartlett pear halves
1/4 c. sugar
1/2 tsp. salt
3 tbsp. butter
1/2 c. milk, scalded
1 pkg. yeast
1 egg, well beaten
1 1/2 c. sifted flour
2 tbsp. brown sugar
1/4 tsp. cinnamon
1/4 tsp. nutmeg
Confectioners' sugar

Drain and slice pears, reserving syrup. Add sugar, salt and 2 tablespoons butter to milk; cool to lukewarm. Dissolve yeast in 1/4 cup warm water in large mixing bowl; add milk mixture, egg and flour. Beat with electric mixer on high speed or by hand until smooth. Spread dough evenly in greased 8-inch square pan; arrange pears over top. Combine brown sugar, cinnamon and nutmeg; sprinkle over top. Dot with remaining butter. Cover; let rise in warm place until double in bulk. Bake at 400 degrees for 10 minutes. Reduce temperature to 350 degrees; bake for 20 to 25 minutes longer. Combine small amount of confectioners' sugar with enough reserved syrup for glaze; heat in saucepan, stirring until smooth. Drizzle over warm coffee cake. Yield: 9 servings.

BRANDIED PEARS

12 pears
1 c. light brown sugar
Sugar
1 tsp. cinnamon
1/2 tsp. nutmeg
Brandy
2 sticks butter
1 egg yolk

Remove skin from pears, leaving stems attached. Combine brown sugar, 2 tablespoons sugar, cinnamon and nutmeg; mix well. Roll pears in mixture. Place in large casserole; pour 1 tablespoon brandy over each pear. Bake in 350-degree oven for 20 minutes or until pears are tender. Cover pears, if necessary. Cream butter till fluffy; add 1 cup sugar slowly, beating constantly. Beat in egg yolk; pour in 4 tablespoons brandy slowly. Serve over pears.

CARAMEL PEARS

6 pears
3/4 c. sugar
2 tbsp. butter
1 c. heavy cream

Preheat oven to 475 degrees. Peel, quarter and core pears; arrange in 1 layer in buttered cake pan. Sprinkle with sugar; dot with butter. Bake for 15 minutes, basting once. Pour cream over pears; bake for 2 minutes longer. Serve hot. Yield: 6 servings.

COMPANY PEAR DESSERT

Butter
1 c. (firmly packed) brown sugar
1 1/3 c. sifted flour
1/2 c. flaked coconut
1/4 tsp. salt
3/4 c. pear juice
3/4 c. milk
2 eggs, slightly beaten
1/2 tsp. vanilla
3/4 c. whipping cream
1/4 c. sugar
1 tsp. cinnamon
6 canned pear halves, drained

Combine 1/2 cup butter, 1/2 cup brown sugar, 1 cup flour and coconut; mix well. Spread in 13 x 9 x 2-inch pan. Bake at 400 degrees foı 15 minutes. Remove from oven; stir to mix well. Press 2 cups hot coconut mixture against bottom and side of 9-inch round pan; cool. Combine remaining brown sugar and flour in saucepan; add salt. Blend in pear juice and milk; stir until smooth. Bring to a boil over medium heat; boil for 1 minute. Remove from heat; stir small amount of hot mixture into eggs gradually. Return to hot mixture; cook for 1 minute longer. Blend in 2 tablespoons butter and vanilla. Pour into crust; chill. Whip cream; spread on chilled mixture. Combine sugar and cinnamon. Dip pear halves into cinnamon mixture; arrange on whipped cream. Sprinkle remaining coconut mixture over top; serve at once. Yield: 6 servings.

POACHED PEARS WITH SOFT CUSTARD

Sugar
2 tsp. vanilla
8 firm pears
3/4 c. instant nonfat dry milk powder
4 eggs
1/4 tsp. salt
1 tbsp. butter
1/4 tsp. grated lemon peel

Combine 1 quart water and 1 1/2 cups sugar in large saucepan. Heat, stirring, until sugar is dissolved. Boil for 5 minutes. Add 1 teaspoon vanilla. Peel pears, leaving stems; place in syrup. Simmer for 30 minutes or until pears are tender, turning occasionally. Chill in syrup; drain. Stir milk powder into 2 cups water. Beat eggs, 1/4 cup sugar and salt together in saucepan. Add milk gradually. Cook, stirring, over medium heat until custard coats spoon. Stir in butter, lemon peel and remaining vanilla; chill well. Spoon custard into serving dish; add pears.

Poached Pears with Soft Custard . . . Grated lemon peel gives this dessert unusual flavor.

PEAR WHIP

1 No. 303 can pears
1 pkg. lemon gelatin
2 c. whipped cream
1 tsp. vanilla

Drain pears; reserve juice. Add enough water to reserved juice to measure 2 cups liquid. Combine gelatin and 1 cup liquid in saucepan; cook over low heat until gelatin is dissolved, stirring constantly. Stir in remaining liquid; chill until partially congealed. Whip gelatin mixture until fluffy. Add whipped cream. Mash pears; fold into gelatin mixture. Add vanilla; chill until firm. Spoon into sherbet glasses; serve with additional whipped cream, if desired.

CHOCOLATE PEARS

3/4 c. sugar
1 tbsp. cornstarch
1/4 tsp. cloves
1 tsp. cinnamon
1 1/2 tsp. cocoa
1 tbsp. butter
Pear halves

Combine sugar, cornstarch, cloves, cinnamon, cocoa and 1 cup water in saucepan; simmer until syrupy. Add butter and pear halves; simmer until pears are soft. Serve topped with whipped cream, if desired.

CURRIED PEARS

6 canned pears halves
1 tbsp. curry powder
3/4 c. brown sugar

Place pear halves on broiler pan rack, cut side up. Combine curry powder and brown sugar; place in hollows of pears. Broil until sugar is bubbly. Serve immediately.

FRESH PEAR CRUNCH

6 med. pears
1/2 c. sugar
1 tsp. cinnamon
1 c. flour
1/2 c. brown sugar
1 tsp. baking powder
1/2 tsp. salt
6 tbsp. shortening

Peel and halve pears; arrange in baking dish. Mix sugar, 1 cup water and cinnamon together; pour over pears. Mix flour, brown sugar, baking powder, salt and shortening together until crumbly; sprinkle over pears. Bake at 350 degrees for 30 minutes or until pears are tender and top is golden brown. Serve with ice cream or whipped cream, if desired. Yield: 6 servings.

PEAR CRISP

1 qt. sliced fresh pears
1 c. sifted flour
1/8 tsp. salt
1 c. brown sugar
1/2 c. butter
1/2 tsp. vanilla

Place pears in buttered baking pan. Combine flour, salt and brown sugar; cut in butter with fork or pastry blender. Add vanilla; sprinkle sugar mixture over fruit. Bake in 350-degree oven for about 25 to 30 minutes or until pears are tender and top is golden brown. Serve warm with cream, if desired.

PEAR DROPS

1/2 c. butter
3/4 c. brown sugar
1/2 c. sour cream
1 egg
1/2 tsp. peppermint flavoring
1 1/3 c. sifted flour
1 tsp. soda
1/2 tsp. salt
1 c. chopped canned pears
1 c. walnuts
1/4 c. chopped maraschino cherries

Cream butter and brown sugar together; blend in sour cream, egg and flavoring. Sift dry ingredients together; blend into sour cream mixture. Drain pears; stir pears, walnuts and cherries into batter. Drop from a teaspoon onto greased cookie sheets. Bake at 375 degrees for 15 to 18 minutes. Yield: 2 1/2 dozen cookies.

PEARS ARMENONVILLE

1 c. sugar
1/4 c. lemon juice
2 tbsp. butter
8 ripe pears
2 pkg. frozen raspberries, thawed
1/4 c. port
Sour cream

Combine sugar, lemon juice, butter and 2 cups boiling water in saucepan; simmer for 5 minutes. Remove skin from pears, leaving stems attached; arrange in 3-quart casserole. Add lemon mixture. Bake, covered, at 350 degrees for 45 minutes. Cool in liquid; drain. Sieve raspberries into large bowl; stir in port. Arrange pears in mixture; refrigerate for several hours or overnight, turning occasionally and basting with sauce. Serve pears with sauce and sour cream.

PEARS WITH DUMPLINGS

1 No. 2 1/2 can pears
2 sticks cinnamon
2 c. biscuit mix
1 tbsp. sugar
3/4 c. milk

Drain pears; reserve juice. Combine reserved juice and cinnamon in skillet; bring to a boil. Boil until liquid is reduced by half. Place pears in boiling syrup. Combine biscuit mix, sugar and milk; toss gently with fork. Drop by tablespoonfuls on top of pears; cover and simmer for 15 minutes or until dumplings are done.

PEARS MACAROON

3 lge. pears
1 tbsp. melted butter
1/3 c. apricot preserves
1/2 c. vermouth
4 macaroons, crumbled

Remove skin from pears; cut each pear into 8 sections. Place pears in shallow baking dish. Combine remaining ingredients; spread over pears. Bake at 425 degrees for 25 minutes. Serve with ice cream or whipped cream, if desired. Yield: 4 servings.

PEARS AU VIN

1 1-lb. can Bartlett pear halves
1/3 c. golden raisins
1/2 c. dried apricot halves
1/4 c. white wine

Combine pear halves and syrup with raisins and apricot halves. Add white wine; stir lightly, until all fruits are well covered. Chill for several hours. Serve cold.

CALIFORNIA PEAR PIE

6 lge. fresh California Bartlett pears
1/2 c. dried apricots
1/4 c. butter, softened
1/3 c. sugar
1/4 tsp. salt
2 tbsp. lemon juice
8 whole cloves
1/4 c. (packed) brown sugar
1 1/2 tbsp. cornstarch
1 baked 9-in. pie shell

Pare, halve and core pears; stuff with apricots. Spread butter over bottom of 10-inch skillet; sprinkle with half the sugar. Place pears in skillet; sprinkle with remaining sugar, salt, lemon juice and cloves. Add 1 cup water. Cover; bring to a boil. Reduce heat; simmer for about 20 minutes or until just tender. Remove pears from pan with slotted spoon; drain well, reserving liquid. Discard cloves. Add enough water to reserved liquid to make 1 1/4 cups liquid. Blend brown sugar and cornstarch; add to pear liquid. Cook, stirring, over medium heat until mixture comes to a boil and is thickened. Spoon half the sauce into pie shell; arrange pears in shell. Spoon remaining sauce over pears. Cool before cutting. Yield: 6-8 servings.

California Pear Pie . . . Fill a baked shell with apricot-stuffed pears in a seasoned sauce.

CREAMY PEAR PIE

3/4 c. sugar
1 tbsp. cornstarch
1/8 tsp. nutmeg
Dash of salt
1/2 c. cream
2 tbsp. lemon juice
1 No. 2 1/2 can Bartlett pears
Pastry for 2-crust pie

Sift sugar, cornstarch, nutmeg and salt together. Combine cream and lemon juice. Stir into dry ingredients; mix well. Drain and slice pears; add to cream mixture. Line pie plate with half the pastry; pour in pear filling. Cover with lattice crust. Bake at 425 degrees for 30 to 35 minutes. Pie may be sprinkled with nutmeg and top crust omitted, if desired.

DEEP-DISH PEAR PIE

1 c. sifted all-purpose flour
1/2 tsp. salt
1/3 c. shortening
1/4 c. grated Cheddar cheese

Sift flour and salt together; cut in shortening until mixture resembles coarse meal. Mix in cheese; stir in 1 tablespoon water at a time until pastry holds together. Chill in refrigerator until ready to use. Preheat oven to 350 degrees.

Pear Filling

2 lb. pears
1 tbsp. lemon juice
3 tbsp. flour
1 c. sugar
Dash of salt
1/2 tsp. cinnamon
1/2 tsp. nutmeg
1 tbsp. butter

Peel pears; cut in halves and core. Arrange in deep pie plate. Sprinkle with lemon juice. Mix flour, sugar, salt, cinnamon and nutmeg together; sprinkle over pears. Dot with butter. Roll pastry in a circle to fit over pie plate. Place over pears; crimp pastry to edge of pie plate. Slash in several places. Bake for 30 to 40 minutes. Serve with cream, if desired. Yield: 6 servings.

MONTANA PEAR PIE

4 lge. fresh pears
3 tbsp. frozen orange concentrate
1 unbaked 9-in. pie shell
1/2 c. sugar
Dash of salt
3/4 c. flour
1/2 c. butter or margarine
1 tsp. cinnamon

Pare and core pears; slice thinly. Mix with orange concentrate; arrange in pie shell. Blend sugar, salt, flour, butter and cinnamon together; sprinkle over pears. Bake at 400 degrees for about 40 minutes or until pears are tender. Yield: 8 servings.

PEAR-NUT PIE

4 c. diced fresh pears
1/2 c. sugar
Pinch of salt
2 tbsp. instant tapioca
1 tbsp. lemon juice
1/2 c. flour
1/4 c. (packed) brown sugar
4 tbsp. butter
1 c. chopped pecans
1 unbaked 9-in. pastry shell
1/2 pt. heavy cream

Mix diced pears with sugar, salt, tapioca and lemon juice; let stand for 10 minutes. Mix flour, brown sugar, butter and nuts until crumbly. Sprinkle one-half of crumb mixture into bottom of pastry-lined pan. Spoon in pears; top with remaining crumb mixture. Bake at 425 degrees for 40 minutes or until pears are tender when pierced with fork. Serve with sweetened whipped cream, if desired.

QUICK PEAR PIE

2 c. chopped pears
Sugar
1 egg, beaten
1 c. cream
Flour
1 tsp. vanilla
1/8 tsp. salt
1 unbaked pastry shell
1/4 c. butter

Combine pears, 1/2 cup sugar, egg, cream, 1 tablespoon flour, vanilla and salt; pour into pastry shell. Bake at 350 degrees for 15 minutes. Combine 2/3 cup flour, 1/3 cup sugar and butter; sprinkle over top of pie. Return to oven; bake for 30 minutes longer or until browned on top.

STREUSEL PEAR PIE

1/2 c. sugar
1 tsp. cinnamon
2 tbsp. lemon juice
1 1/2 tbsp. quick-cooking tapioca
6 c. sliced Bartlett pears
1 unbaked 9-in. pastry shell
1/2 c. (packed) brown sugar
1 c. flour
1/2 c. butter

Combine sugar, cinnamon, lemon juice, tapioca and pears; let stand for 15 minutes. Pour into pastry shell. Combine brown sugar and flour; cut in butter until mixture is crumbly. Pat evenly over pears. Bake at 375 degrees for 45 minutes or until crust is browned.

ROSY PEARS

6 pears
1/2 c. sugar
1/4 c. lemon juice
2 tbsp. butter
Few drops of red food coloring

Remove skin from pears, leaving stems attached. Place in 9-inch baking dish. Combine sugar, 1/2 cup water, lemon juice, butter and food coloring in saucepan; bring to a boil. Pour over pears. Bake at 350 degrees for about 1 hour or until tender, basting frequently.

SPICED PEARS

1 can pears
1/4 c. wine vinegar
1/4 tsp. cinnamon
1/8 tsp. cloves
1/8 tsp. nutmeg
3 tbsp. brown sugar
1 tbsp. butter
1/2 lemon, thinly sliced

Drain pears; reserve syrup. Place pears in saucepan. Combine reserved syrup, vinegar, spices, sugar, butter and lemon slices; add to pears. Simmer for 30 minutes.

STUFFED PEARS

12 lge. fresh pears
2 oz. blanched almonds
1/2 c. confectioners' sugar
1 tbsp. chopped glazed orange peel
1/2 c. dry sherry

Peel pears; cut in half and remove cores. Place in baking dish. Grind almonds; blend with half the sugar and orange peel. Spoon into pear halves; sprinkle with remaining sugar and sherry. Bake at 350 degrees for 10 minutes. Serve warm. Yield: 6 servings.

UPSIDE-DOWN PEAR CAKE

1 1-lb. 13-oz. can pears
1/4 c. melted butter
1/4 c. sugar
1 tsp. nutmeg
12 walnut halves
10 maraschino cherries
1 pkg. white cake mix
1 pkg. lemon gelatin
3/4 c. oil
4 eggs, slightly beaten
Lemon extract to taste

Preheat oven to 350 degrees. Drain pears; reserve 3/4 cup pear juice. Pour butter into 9 x 13-inch pan. Combine sugar and nutmeg; sprinkle over butter in pan. Arrange pears, cut sides down, in pan. Arrange walnuts and cherries between pears. Combine cake mix, gelatin, oil, eggs, reserved juice and lemon extract. Beat with mixer for 4 minutes. Pour batter over pear mixture in pan. Bake for 55 minutes or until cake tests done. Serve with whipped cream if desired.

Peas

The round, emerald-green pea is a leguminous vegetable that grows in a pod. There are two varieties of peas: garden or green peas and stock or field peas. *Green peas* are of two kinds: the smooth-skinned early June pea; and the wrinkled-skinned sweet pea. The small, hard *field pea* is most often dried and marketed with other dried legumes such as kidney or navy beans. Usually considered to be in the pea family, *black-eyed peas* or cowpeas are actually related to the bean family. (See BEANS.) Peas are wholesome sources of carbohydrates, Vitamins A and C, niacin, calcium, iron, and protein. (1 cup fresh or frozen cooked green peas = 115 calories; 1 cup canned peas, including liquid = 165 calories; 1 cup split or whole field peas = 240 calories)

AVAILABILITY: Fresh green peas are available year-round in certain areas, with peak production from April through July. Canned and frozen green peas constitute the bulk of the annual supply. Also available year-round are whole or split field peas.

BUYING: *Fresh green peas*—Choose bright green, well-filled pods that are velvety to the touch. Avoid swollen, yellowed, and gray-flecked pods. Wilted and flattened pods indicate immature peas. *Field peas*—Look for packages of dehulled dried peas.

STORING: Refrigerate fresh green peas, unshelled for 3 to 5 days. Store frozen peas 1 year in home freezer; canned peas 1 year on kitchen shelf. Field peas will keep 6 to 8 months on kitchen shelf. *To freeze* green peas—Shell peas and blanch in boiling water 1 1/2-minutes. Cool in cold water and drain. Pack peas into freezer container, leaving 1/2-inch head space. Seal and freeze up to 1 year.

PREPARATION: *To boil* green peas—Shell before cooking. Cook peas covered in 1 inch boiling salted water for 8 to 10 minutes. Drain and season to taste. To boil field peas and black-eyed peas—see BEANS. For other cooking methods, consult specific recipes.

SERVING: Serve cooked peas with butter or margarine; in cream sauce; in vegetable salads or in soups, stews, and other dishes. For flavor, add mint, grated lemon peel, marjoram, or oregano.

(See VEGETABLES.)

CREOLE BLACK-EYED PEAS

6 strips bacon
1 c. chopped celery
1 c. chopped green peppers
1 c. chopped onions
1 No. 303 can black-eyed peas
1 No. 303 can tomatoes
Salt and pepper to taste

Fry bacon until crisp; drain. Simmer celery, green peppers and onions in drippings until tender. Crumble bacon; combine with peas and tomatoes. Blend tomato mixture with onion mixture; season with salt and pepper. Simmer, covered, for 20 minutes longer.

HOPPING JOHN

1 c. dried black-eyed peas
1 ham hock
1 sm. onion, chopped
1 tsp. salt
1/4 tsp. pepper
1 c. instant rice
1 1-lb. can tomatoes

Cover peas with boiling water; add ham hock, onion, salt and pepper. Simmer, covered, for 1 hour and 15 minutes. Remove ham hock; remove rind, bone and excess fat. Shred ham; return to peas. Place rice over peas; add enough water to cover rice. Bring to a boil; remove from heat. Let stand, covered, until rice is fluffy; add tomatoes. Heat through. Yield: 6 servings.

COWBOY BLACK-EYED PEAS

1 No. 303 can black-eyed peas
1 med. sweet onion, sliced
1/2 tsp. Worcestershire sauce
2 tbsp. butter

Drain half the liquid from peas. Combine peas and remaining liquid, onion, Worcestershire sauce and butter in saucepan; simmer, covered, for 15 minutes or until heated through. Yield: 5 servings.

HOT BOLLOS

1 lb. black-eyed peas
1 clove of garlic, minced
1 fresh red pepper, minced
1 tsp. salt

Soak peas in water overnight; drain. Puree peas in blender container, small amount at a time, with garlic red pepper, salt and enough water to make thick paste. Beat, adding water gradually, until of batter consistency. Drop by heaping teaspoonfuls into deep medium-hot fat; brown, turning to brown evenly. Serve hot as appetizer or with seafood. Yield: 6-8 servings.

PICKLED BLACK-EYED PEAS

2 cans black-eyed peas
1 onion, chopped
1 c. salad oil
1/2 c. vinegar
1 tsp. salt
Pepper to taste
Hot sauce to taste
1 clove of garlic, crushed
1/4 c. chopped green pepper
1 can chopped mushrooms drained

Drain black-eyed peas; rinse well. Drain thoroughly Combine all ingredients. Refrigerate for at least 4 days before serving.

TEXAS CAVIAR

2 No. 2 cans black-eyed peas, drained
1/3 c. peanut oil
1/3 c. wine vinegar
1 clove of garlic
1/4 c. finely chopped onion
1/2 tsp. salt
Cracked pepper

Place peas in bowl with remaining ingredients; mix well. Store in refrigerator for 24 hours; remove garlic. Store for 2 days to 2 weeks before serving.

GREEN PEA-CUCUMBER SALAD

2 No. 2 cans green peas, drained
2 med. cucumbers, chopped
1 c. cubed American cheese
1 med. onion, chopped
2 hard-cooked eggs, sliced
1 tsp. salt
2 tbsp. salad dressing
Dash of pepper

Combine all ingredients in large salad bowl; chill until ready to serve. May be served on salad greens.

CONGEALED GREEN PEA SALAD

1 pkg. lemon gelatin
1/2 c. nuts
1 c. small green peas, drained
1 c. chopped celery
1 c. sliced olives
2 tbsp. lemon juice

Dissolve gelatin in 1 3/4 cup hot water; chill until partially set. Add remaining ingredients; pour into mold. Chill until set. Serve on lettuce with mayonnaise.

GREEN PEA-ONION SALAD

3 10-oz. packages frozen green peas
1 20-oz. package frozen onions
1/2 c. whipping cream, whipped
3/4 c. mayonnaise
1 head Boston lettuce
1 sm. celery heart, thinly sliced
2 tbsp. sweet pickle relish, drained

Cook frozen vegetables according to package directions; drain. Cool thoroughly. Combine whipped cream and mayonnaise. Line salad bowl with large outer leaves of lettuce. Break remaining lettuce in bite-sized pieces; add peas, onions, celery and pickle relish. Pour whipped cream mixture over salad. Toss lightly. Serve in salad bowl. Yield: 8-10 servings.

CREAM OF PEA SOUP WITH RIVVELS

2 lb. fresh peas
Salt to taste
1 c. cream
1 c. milk
2 eggs
2 c. flour
1/2 tsp. baking powder

Cook peas in 2 quarts salted water until crisp-tender; blend in cream and milk. Combine eggs, flour, baking powder and salt to taste. Rub mixture through hands, letting mixture fall into boiling soup in flakes. Simmer slowly for 20 minutes, stirring occasionally.

DELICIOUS SPLIT PEA SOUP

1 lb. green split peas
1 meaty hambone
1 1/2 c. sliced onion
1/2 tsp. pepper
1/4 tsp. garlic salt
1/4 tsp. marjoram
Salt to taste
1 c. diced celery
1 c. sliced carrots
1 tsp. parsley flakes

Soak peas overnight; drain. Combine 2 1/2 quarts water, peas, hambone, onion and seasonings in soup kettle. Simmer, covered, for 2 hours, stirring occasionally. Remove bone; cut off meat. Return meat to soup; add celery, carrots and parsley. Simmer, covered, for 45 minutes longer.

SWEDISH PEA SOUP

2 c. dried yellow peas
1 lb. salt pork
1 onion, chopped
Salt to taste
1/2 tsp. ground ginger

Soak peas overnight in 2 1/2 quarts water. Bring to a boil; reduce heat. Skim. Add salt pork and onion; simmer, covered, for 2 hours or until peas and salt pork are tender. Add salt, if needed. Stir in ginger and additional water, if necessary. Remove salt pork; slice. Serve separately with mustard, if desired.

Souper Peas . . . Mushroom soup, cheese, and herbs make onions and peas a gourmet's treat.

SOUPER PEAS

1 10 1/2-oz. can cream of mushroom soup
1 c. shredded Cheddar cheese
1 tbsp. chopped parsley
Dash of crushed tarragon
2 pkg. frozen green peas
12 whole onions, cooked

Stir soup in saucepan over low heat until smooth. Blend in 1/3 cup water, cheese, parsley and tarragon gradually. Heat until cheese is melted, stirring occasionally. Cook peas according to package directions; drain. Combine peas and onions in casserole. Pour sauce over vegetables. Bake in 350-degree oven for about 5 minutes or until heated through.

SPLIT YELLOW PEA SOUP WITH DUMPLINGS

1 lb. split yellow peas
1 meaty hambone
1 1/2 c. sliced onion
1 1/2 c. shredded cabbage
1 1/2 c. sliced carrots
1 c. chopped celery
Salt and pepper to taste
1 egg, beaten
1/2 c. milk
Flour

Soak peas overnight in water to cover; drain. Combine 2 1/2 quarts water, peas, hambone and onion. Simmer, covered, for 3 hours. Remove bone; cut off meat. Return meat to soup; add cabbage, carrots and celery. Season with salt and pepper. Simmer, covered, for 20 minutes or until vegetables are tender. Mix egg, milk and salt; add enough flour to form soft dough. Drop by teaspoonfuls into soup. Simmer, covered, for 7 to 10 minutes.

CHEESE-HERB PEAS

1 pkg. frozen peas
1 tbsp. butter
1/2 tsp. salt
1/2 tsp. basil
1/4 tsp. marjoram
1/2 6-oz. roll smoky cheese, cubed
1/3 c. sliced stuffed olives

Combine peas, 2 tablespoons water, butter, salt, basil and marjoram; cover tightly. Cook over low heat for 5 to 8 minutes or until peas are tender. Fold in cheese and olives. Yield: 4 servings.

FRENCH GREEN PEAS

5 or 6 outer lettuce leaves
3 lb. fresh peas
12 sm. onions
2 sprigs of parsley
1/2 c. butter, softened
2 1/2 tsp. sugar
2 tsp. salt

Arrange lettuce leaves in heavy saucepan. Combine peas with onions, parsley, butter, sugar and salt. Spoon mixture onto lettuce; sprinkle with 3 tablespoons water. Simmer, covered, for 15 minutes or until peas are tender; remove from heat. Shred lettuce; mix with peas.

ORANGE-MINT PEAS

2 tbsp. butter
1 can peas, drained
1/4 c. orange juice
2 tsp. sugar
1/2 grated orange rind
1/3 tsp. salt
2 tbsp. crushed mint

Melt butter in saucepan; add peas. Simmer for 5 minutes. Add orange juice, sugar, rind and salt. Simmer for 5 minutes longer. Add mint.

PARTY-PERFECT PEAS

3 pkg. frozen peas
2 cans water chestnuts
2 cans bean sprouts
1 lb. mushrooms
Butter
2 cans mushroom soup
2 cans French-fried onion rings

Cook peas according to package directions. Drain. Drain water chestnuts and bean sprouts; slice water chestnuts. Slice mushrooms; saute lightly in small amount of butter. Combine peas, water chestnuts, bean sprouts and mushrooms; stir in soup. Spoon into casserole. Bake at 350 degrees for 40 minutes. Cover with onion rings; bake for 5 minutes longer.

PEAS WITH BREADSTICKS

1 can peas
1 can asparagus
1 can cream of mushroom soup
1/2 c. grated cheese
8 thin bread strips
1/2 c. melted margarine

Drain peas and asparagus; place in shallow greased casserole. Spoon soup over vegetables; cover with cheese. Dip bread strips into margarine; arrange over cheese. Bake at 350 degrees for 45 minutes.

PEAS-CHESTNUT CASSEROLE

1 stick butter
1 sm. onion, minced
2 tbsp. chopped green pepper
1 c. diced celery
1 can water chestnuts, sliced
2 cans peas, drained
1 can cream of mushroom soup
2 pimentos, diced
Buttered cracker crumbs

Melt butter in heavy skillet. Add onion, green pepper and celery. Saute over moderate heat, stirring frequently, until tender. Remove from heat; add water chestnuts, peas, soup and pimentos. Place in casserole. Sprinkle with crumbs. Bake at 350 degrees until heated through and top is lightly browned.

PEAS OREGANO

1/2 c. butter
2 10-oz. packages frozen peas
1 tsp. salt
2 tbsp. lemon juice
2 tbsp. dried onion flakes
1 tsp. dried oregano
1 tsp. monosodium glutamate

Melt butter in medium skillet; add remaining ingredients. Simmer, covered, until peas are separated and tender. Yield: 8 servings.

PEAS CONTINENTAL

1 bunch green onions
Butter
1 tsp. flour
1/3 c. light cream
Salt and pepper
1 pkg. frozen green peas
1 tsp. sugar

Cut onions into 1-inch lengths; saute in 1 teaspoon butter for 3 to 4 minutes, stirring constantly. Blend in flour and cream; cook until thickened, stirring constantly. Add dash of salt and pepper. Combine peas, 1 tablespoon butter, 2 tablespoons water, 1/2 teaspoon salt and sugar. Bring to a boil; reduce heat. Simmer, covered, for 3 minutes; combine with onion mixture. Simmer, covered, until heated through.

PEAS AU GRATIN

2 tbsp. chopped onion
2 tbsp. butter
2 tbsp. flour
3/4 c. milk
1/4 lb. American cheese, cubed
1 sm. can button mushrooms, drained
2 boxes frozen peas, thawed
Bread or cracker crumbs

Brown onion in butter in skillet; stir in flour. Add milk gradually, stirring constantly, until smooth and thickened. Add cheese; stir until melted. Add mushrooms and peas. Pour into baking dish. Top with crumbs. Bake at 325 degrees for 30 minutes or until peas are tender. Yield: 8 servings.

PEAS WITH PEARL ONIONS

1 10-oz. package frozen peas
1 c. diagonally cut celery
1/2 c. slivered almonds
1/2 c. melted butter
1 sm. can onions
Salt and pepper to taste

Cook peas according to package directions; drain. Cook celery in boiling salted water until crisp-tender; drain. Brown almonds lightly in butter. Add onions, peas and celery; season with salt and pepper. Serve hot.

Pecan

Pecans are native American nuts produced by trees of the hickory family that are widely cultivated throughout the south central United States. They are used in cooking, especially in the South, and are the primary ingredient in the famous southern pecan pie. Their smooth brown mottled shells vary in thickness and shape. Pecan shells may be short and round or long and cylindrical. Texas, Oklahoma, Georgia, Alabama, and Mississippi are important pecan producers. Pecans are sources of fat, protein, carbohydrate, calcium, and Vitamin A. They are perhaps higher in fat than any other edible American nut. (1 cup pecan halves = 740 calories)

AVAILABILITY: Pecans are available year-round in shells and shelled. Pecans in shell are usually sold in bulk. Shelled pecans are sold

halved, chopped, or broken in a variety of containers, including film bags, cans, and jars.
BUYING: *In shell*—Look for clean shells free from scars, cracks, or holes. The heavier the nut, the meatier and more desirable the kernel. In a well-filled nut, the kernel does not rattle when nut is shaken. *Shelled*—Look for plump, meaty, crisp kernels. Broken or chopped kernels should not appear yellowish or oily. 1 pound in shell pecans = 2 1/4-cups shelled pecans.
STORING: Keep nuts in shell in cool, dark, dry place for 4 months. Or refrigerate nuts in shell 1 year. Keep shelled nuts in unopened packages 2 months on kitchen shelf; unopened cans keep indefinitely. Refrigerate shelled nuts 6 months or more in sealed packages or tightly closed containers. Nuts in shell and shelled may be frozen. *To freeze,* seal in plastic bag or place in tightly closed container. Store at 0 degree or below for 2 years.
PREPARATION: *To roast or toast*—Spread nutmeats in shallow pan. Add 1 teaspoon oil or melted butter per 1 cup kernels for richer flavor and deeper browning. Bake at 350 degrees, stirring occasionally, until lightly browned. Remove from heat and salt if desired. A small amount of fat added to nuts will make salt cling.
USES: Salt, spice, or sugar pecans for snacking. Add toasted nuts to creamed dishes, meat dishes, and vegetables. Use in salads, fruit cups, confections, biscuits, muffins, buns, waffles, cakes, pies, rolls, tortes, cookies, ice cream, stuffings, and loaves.

CREAMY BARBECUED PECANS

1/2 c. butter, melted
2 tbsp. Worcestershire sauce
2 tsp. garlic salt
10 drops of hot sauce
2 qt. pecan halves
Cream cheese, softened

Blend butter, Worcestershire sauce, garlic salt and hot sauce. Coat pecans with mixture. Place in baking pan. Bake at 250 degrees for 45 minutes; stir every 15 minutes gently. Spread cream cheese between 2 pecan halves to serve.

OVEN-TOASTED PECANS

1 qt. pecan halves
1/4 c. Worcestershire sauce
2 dashes of hot sauce
1/4 c. butter
Salt to taste

Combine all ingredients except salt; mix well. Spread in baking pan. Bake at 250 degrees for 30 minutes, stirring frequently. Drain on paper towels. Sprinkle with salt.

SPICED PECANS

1 c. sugar
1 tsp. (scant) syrup
1 tsp. cinnamon
Butter to taste
3 c. pecans

Combine sugar, 1/3 cup water, syrup and cinnamon in saucepan; cook to soft-ball stage. Add butter and pecans. Stir until white.

SUGARY PECANS

1 egg white
1 lb. pecan halves
1 c. sugar
1 tsp. salt
1/8 tsp. cinnamon

Beat egg white and 1 tablespoon water to froth; add pecans, moistening each. Mix sugar, salt and cinnamon. Roll pecans in sugar mixture. Spread in pan. Bake at 300 degrees for 45 minutes.

HARVEST PECAN CAKE

2 c. margarine, softened
2 1/4 c. (packed) brown sugar
6 eggs, separated
4 1/2 c. flour
1 tsp. baking powder
1 tsp. salt
3 tbsp. instant coffee
1/2 c. milk
1 tsp. vanilla
4 c. chopped pecans

Cream margarine; add sugar, blending well. Beat egg yolks until fluffy; stir into creamed mixture. Sift flour 3 times with baking powder and salt. Combine coffee and 3 tablespoons hot water. Combine milk, vanilla and coffee mixture. Add milk mixture alternately with flour mixture to creamed mixture. Beat egg whites until stiff peaks form; fold egg whites and nuts into flour mixture. Pour into greased tube pan. Bake at 325 degrees for 1 hour and 30 minutes. Cool in pan for 10 minutes. Cool on rack. Frost cake, if desired.

PECAN POUND CAKE

1 c. shortening
1 1/2 c. sugar
2 tbsp. milk
5 eggs
2 c. flour
1/2 tsp. mace
1 tsp. salt
3/4 c. broken pecans, toasted
2 tsp. lemon juice
1 tsp. grated lemon rind

Cream shortening with sugar; add milk. Mix well. Add one egg at a time, beating after each addition. Sift flour with mace and salt; add to creamed mixture. Add 1/2 cup pecans to batter. Add lemon juice and rind. Pour into greased 9-inch tube pan; sprinkle with remaining pecans. Bake at 325 degrees for 1 hour and 25 minutes. Cool for 5 minutes. Remove cake from pan; cool on wire rack.

PECAN ROLL

6 eggs, separated
Sugar
1 tsp. baking powder
1 1/2 c. grated pecans
Powdered sugar
2 c. heavy cream
1 1/2 tsp. sugar
1 tsp. almond extract
1/2 tsp. vanilla

Beat egg yolks and 1 3/4 cups sugar until thick and lemony. Mix baking powder and pecans; fold into yolks. Beat egg whites until stiff peaks form; fold into egg mixture. Spread in greased 16 x 11 3/4-inch jelly roll pan lined with greased waxed paper. Bake at 350 degrees for 20 minutes. Cover with damp towel; chill. Turn cake out on towel sprinkled with powdered sugar; remove paper. Whip heavy cream until stiff; add 1 1/2 teaspoons sugar, almond extract and vanilla. Spread on cake. Roll jelly roll fashion; chill until ready to serve. Sprinkle with powdered sugar. Serve with additional whipped cream. Yield: 10 servings.

TEXAS PECAN CAKE

3 tsp. baking powder
3 c. sifted flour
1 tsp. vanilla
1 1/3 c. milk
1 c. butter
2 c. sugar
8 egg yolks, beaten
1 c. chopped pecans

Combine baking powder and 2 3/4 cups flour; sift 3 times. Add vanilla to milk. Cream butter until soft and light. Add sugar gradually; continue creaming until fluffy. Add egg yolks; beat vigorously. Add milk and dry ingredients alternately to creamed mixture. Add pecans to remaining 1/4 cup flour; beat into batter. Pour into 3 greased and floured layer cake pans. Bake at 350 degrees for 30 minutes. Cool; ice with favorite frosting. Top with pecans, if desired.

TOASTED BUTTER-PECAN CAKE

2 c. chopped pecans
1 1/4 c. butter
2 c. sugar
4 eggs
3 c. sifted flour
2 tsp. baking powder
1/2 tsp. salt
1 c. milk
1 tsp. butter flavoring
3 tsp. vanilla
1 box confectioners' sugar
8 tbsp. evaporated milk

Combine pecans and 1/4 cup butter; place on cookie sheet. Bake at 350 degrees for 20 minutes, stirring frequently. Combine remaining butter and sugar; blend in eggs. Sift dry ingredients together; add to creamed mixture alternately with milk. Stir in butter flavoring, 2 teaspoons vanilla and 1 1/3 cups toasted pecans. Pour into three 9-inch greased and floured layer cake pans. Bake at 350 degrees for 25 minutes. Cool. Combine remaining toasted pecans with confectioners' sugar, evaporated milk and remaining vanilla. Spread on top and side of cake. Yield: 20 servings.

PECAN PATTIES

2 1/4 c. (packed) brown sugar
2 tbsp. dark corn syrup
1/4 c. cream
1/2 c. margarine
1 tsp. vanilla
1/8 tsp. salt
2 c. pecan halves

Combine all ingredients except pecans in saucepan. Place over low heat, stirring just until butter is melted; cook to soft-ball stage. Remove from heat; add pecans. Set pan in cold water until mixture is cool enough to touch. Beat until thick and creamy; drop into patties on waxed paper. Yield: 2 pounds.

CREOLE DROPS

3 c. sugar
1 tsp. vinegar
1 tbsp. margarine
3 c. chopped pecans

Combine sugar, 1 cup water and vinegar. Cook to soft-ball stage or to 236 degrees on candy thermometer. Add margarine and pecans. Remove from heat. Beat until mixture begins to thicken. Drop from teaspoon onto waxed paper.

MEXICAN PECAN CANDY

2 1/4 c. (packed) brown sugar
2 c. pecan halves
1/2 c. half and half
1 tbsp. (heaping) butter
1 tsp. vanilla

Combine sugar, pecans, half and half and butter in saucepan; cook to hard-ball stage. Remove from heat. Add vanilla; beat until creamy. Drop from teaspoon onto waxed paper. Yield: 2 dozen pieces.

PECAN DELIGHTS

2 c. sugar
1 tsp. soda
1 c. buttermilk
1/2 tsp. salt
2 tbsp. butter
2 1/2 c. pecan halves

Combine sugar, soda, buttermilk and salt. Cook over high heat for 5 minutes or to 210 degrees on candy thermometer. Stir frequently, scraping bottom of pan. Add butter and pecans. Cook, stirring constantly and scraping bottom and side of pan, until candy reaches soft-ball stage. Remove from heat. Cool slightly. Beat until thick and creamy. Drop from tablespoon onto waxed paper. Cool.

TEXAS MILLIONAIRES

1 c. sugar
1 c. (packed) brown sugar
1 c. dark corn syrup
1 c. margarine
2 c. evaporated milk
1 tsp. vanilla
1 lb. pecan halves
3 lge. milk chocolate bars
1/3 lb. paraffin

Combine sugar, brown sugar, syrup, margarine and 1 cup milk in saucepan; bring to a hard boil, stirring constantly. Add remaining milk gradually, allowing mixture to continue boiling. Cook to soft-ball stage. Remove from heat; stir gradually. Add vanilla and pecans. Pour into buttered 9 x 15-inch pan. Chill overnight. Cut into squares. Melt chocolate and paraffin in double boiler; dip candy squares into mixture. Cool on waxed paper.

PECAN-ORANGE DAINTIES

1 c. butter
1/2 c. sugar
2 c. flour
2 c. finely chopped pecans
2 tbsp. grated orange rind
1 tsp. vanilla
Sifted confectioners' sugar

Cream butter and sugar; stir in flour, pecans, orange rind and vanilla. Shape into small balls; place on cookie sheet. Bake at 300 degrees for 35 minutes. Cool slightly; roll in confectioners' sugar. Yield: 32 balls.

PECAN-BUTTER BALLS

1 c. butter
1/2 c. sugar
2 c. chopped pecans
1 tsp. vanilla
2 c. sifted flour
Flaked coconut

Cream butter and sugar until fluffy; mix in pecans, vanilla and flour thoroughly. Shape into balls; place on cookie sheet. Bake at 300 degrees for 20 minutes. Cool. Roll in coconut to coat. Yield: 2 dozen. dozen.

PECAN-RUM BALLS

1 c. crushed vanilla wafer crumbs
1 c. finely chopped pecans
Confectioners' sugar
2 tbsp. cocoa
1 1/2 tbsp. light corn syrup
1/4 c. rum

Combine crumbs, pecans, 1 cup confectioners' sugar and cocoa; blend in syrup and rum. Shape into small balls; roll in sugar.

PECAN LEBKUCHEN

3 1/2 c. flour
2 tbsp. cocoa
1 tsp. salt
1 tsp. soda
1 tsp. cinnamon
1 tsp. cloves
1 tsp. allspice
1/4 lb. citron, diced
1/4 lb. candied lemon rind, diced
1/4 lb. candied orange rind, diced
1 1/2 c. chopped pecans
1/2 c. shortening
1 c. (packed) brown sugar
2 eggs
1 c. molasses
1 c. black coffee

Sift dry ingredients together. Mix half the dry ingredients with fruits and nuts. Cream shortening with brown sugar; beat in one egg at a time. Add molasses; add dry ingredients alternately with coffee. Add fruit and nut mixture; beat well. Spread 3/8 inch thick on oiled and floured cookie sheet. Bake at 350 degrees for 25 minutes.

Icing

2 tbsp. lemon juice
2 c. confectioners' sugar
1/2 tsp. grated lemon rind

Blend juice and 2 tablespoons water into sugar and rind; spread over hot cake. Cut into 2-inch pieces. Store, tightly covered, for at least 1 week.

PECAN LOGS

5 tbsp. evaporated milk
3/4 tsp. rum flavoring
2 1/2 c. confectioners' sugar, sifted
1 c. coarsely chopped candied cherries
24 caramels
1 1/2 c. chopped pecans

Combine 2 tablespoons milk and rum flavoring in bowl; blend in confectioners' sugar. Knead until smooth and shiny; knead in cherries, adding additional confectioners' sugar, if necessary. Shape into 6-inch logs; roll in waxed paper. Chill until firm. Combine caramels with remaining milk; heat over boiling water until melted, stirring frequently. Turn into flat pan. Roll logs quickly in caramel mixture; coat with pecans. Roll in waxed paper. Chill until firm.

DUTCH PECAN PIE

5 egg whites
1 c. sugar
1/4 tsp. salt
1 tsp. vinegar
1 tsp. vanilla
1 c. crushed vanilla wafers
2 c. chopped pecans

Beat egg whites until stiff peaks form; add sugar gradually. Beat until glossy. Add salt, vinegar and vanilla; fold in crumbs and pecans. Pour into greased and floured 9-inch pie pan. Bake at 325 degrees for 1 hour. Yield: 6 servings.

GOLDEN PECAN PIE

3 eggs
1 c. light corn syrup
1 c. (packed) brown sugar
1 9-in. pie shell, unbaked
1 c. pecan halves

Beat eggs; add syrup and brown sugar. Mix well. Pour into pie shell. Sprinkle with pecans. Bake at 325 degrees for 1 hour.

PECAN TASSIES

1 3-oz. package cream cheese
Butter, softened
1 c. sifted flour
1 c. broken pecans
1 egg
3/4 c. (packed) brown sugar
1 tsp. vanilla
Dash of salt

Preheat oven to 325 degrees. Soften cream cheese; blend in 1/2 cup butter. Stir in flour; blend thoroughly. Chill for 1 hour. Shape into 2 dozen 1-inch balls. Place in small muffin cups; press on bottoms and sides of muffin cups. Sprinkle pecans in crusts. Beat egg, brown sugar, 1 tablespoon butter, vanilla and salt together; pour over pecans. Bake for 25 minutes. Cool. Remove from pans. Yield: 24 tarts.

SOUTHERN PECAN PIE

1 tbsp. butter
1 c. sugar
3 eggs, slightly beaten
1 c. dark corn syrup
1 tsp. vanilla
1 c. chopped pecans
1 pastry shell, unbaked
1/2 c. pecan halves

Cream butter and sugar thoroughly; add eggs, syrup, vanilla and chopped nuts. Mix well. Turn into pastry shell. Arrange pecan halves on top of pie. Place on lower rack of oven. Bake at 300 degrees for 45 minutes or until firm in center. Yield: 8 servings.

RICH PECAN PIE

3/4 c. sugar
2 tbsp. flour
1 tsp. salt
1 c. dark corn syrup
2 eggs
1/2 c. evaporated milk
1 c. broken pecans
3/4 tsp. vanilla
1 9-in. pie shell

Mix sugar, flour and salt in 1 1/2-quart bowl; stir in syrup. Beat in one egg at a time. Mix in evaporated milk, pecans and vanilla. Pour filling into pie shell. Bake at 350 degrees for 50 minutes or until firm. Cool before serving. Yield: 8 servings.

DELICIOUS PECAN TORTE

4 eggs, separated
1 c. sugar
2 tbsp. flour
Salt
1/2 tsp. baking powder
1 tbsp. dark rum
2 c. grated pecans
1/2 c. heavy cream
2 tsp. grated orange rind
1 6-oz. package semisweet chocolate bits
1/2 c. sour cream

Beat egg yolks until thick and light; beat in sugar. Mix flour, 1/2 teaspoon salt and baking powder; stir into egg mixture. Add rum and pecans. Beat egg whites until stiff peaks form; fold into rum mixture. Turn into 2 well-greased waxed paper-lined 8-inch layer cake pans. Bake at 350 degrees for 25 minutes or until cake tests done. Cool. Remove from pans. Whip cream until stiff peaks form; fold in orange rind. Spread 1 cake layer with flavored whipped cream; top with remaining layer. Melt chocolate bits over hot water; stir in sour cream and dash of salt. Spread on torte. Yield: 12 servings.

PARTY PECAN TORTE

6 eggs, separated
1 1/2 c. sugar
2 tbsp. flour
2 tsp. baking powder
1/4 tsp. salt
3 c. finely chopped pecans
Whipped cream

Beat egg yolks until thick and lemon colored; beat in half the sugar gradually. Mix flour, baking powder, salt and pecans. Beat into egg yolk mixture. Beat egg whites until stiff peaks form; beat in remaining sugar gradually. Fold egg white mixture into egg yolk mixture. Pour into two greased, paper-lined round 9-inch layer cake pans. Bake at 350 degrees for 25 minutes. Cool. Spread whipped cream between layers and over top and side of cake. Garnish with chocolate curls and pecan halves. Yield: 16 servings.

NUT TWISTS

1/2 c. scalded milk
1/2 c. shortening
Sugar
1/2 tsp. salt
1 tsp. vanilla
2 pkg. yeast
3 c. flour
3 eggs, at room temperature
1 tsp. cinnamon
3/4 c. chopped pecans

Combine milk, shortening, 3 tablespoons sugar, salt and vanilla. Dissolve yeast in 1/4 cup warm water; add to milk mixture. Add 1 1/2 cups flour; beat until smooth. Cover; let rise for 15 minutes. Add eggs, one at a time, beating well after each addition. Add remaining flour, beating until dough is smooth. Cover; let rise in warm place for 30 minutes. Combine 1 1/2 cups sugar, cinnamon and pecans in bowl. Place yeast mixture, 1 tablespoon at a time, in sugar mixture; coat well. Shape into strips; twist. Place on greased baking sheet; let stand for 5 minutes. Bake in 350-degree oven for 15 minutes.

ORANGE-PECAN MUFFINS

1 1/3 c. sifted flour
1 tsp. baking powder
1/2 tsp. soda
1/2 tsp. salt
3 tbsp. sugar
1 tbsp. butter
1 tbsp. grated orange rind
1 egg
1 c. sour cream
1/2 c. chopped pecans

Preheat oven to 375 degrees. Grease muffin cups. Sift flour, baking powder, soda and salt together. Combine sugar, butter, orange rind and egg in mixing bowl; stir in sour cream, dry ingredients and pecans. Fill muffin cups 2/3 full. Bake for 35 to 40 minutes. Yield: 1 dozen.

FLUFFY PECAN DESSERT

3 egg whites
1 c. sugar
1 tsp. baking powder
Dash of salt
1 tsp. vanilla
1 c. chopped pecans
1 c. crushed Corn Chex
Whipped cream

Preheat oven to 350 degrees. Beat egg whites until soft peaks form; add sugar, baking powder and salt. Beat until sugar is dissolved and meringue is stiff. Stir in vanilla, pecans and cereal crumbs. Spread filling evenly on greased 9-inch pie plate. Bake for 30 minutes or until lightly browned; cool. Top with whipped cream; sprinkle with additional chopped pecans.

Fluffy Pecan Dessert . . . A quick-and-easy dessert fancy enough for a special dinner party.

Penuche

Penuche, pronounced pah-NOO-chee, is a type of fudge that is based on brown sugar instead of white granulated sugar. The name is derived from the Mexican-Spanish word *panocha*, or raw sugar. It is also spelled penuchi. (See FUDGE.)

DELICIOUS PENUCHE CANDY

2 lb. (packed) dark brown sugar
1 lb. sugar
1 lge. can evaporated milk
1 c. milk
1/2 lb. butter
2 sm. packages caramel bits
1 c. chopped pecans
1 jar marshmallow creme

Combine brown sugar, sugar, evaporated milk, milk and butter in saucepan. Boil over low heat to soft-ball stage or to 238 degrees on candy thermometer. Remove from heat; stir in caramel bits until melted. Add pecans and marshmallow creme. Pour onto greased pan. Let harden; cut in squares.

PENUCHE BAR COOKIES

1/2 c. shortening
1/2 tsp. salt
1 1/2 c. (packed) brown sugar
Sifted flour
1 tsp. vanilla
2 beaten eggs
1/2 tsp. baking powder
1 1/2 c. shredded coconut
1 c. chopped nuts

Combine shortening and 1/4 teaspoon salt; add 1/2 cup sugar. Cream thoroughly. Add 1 cup flour; blend. Spread mixture in 8 x 12 x 2-inch greased pan. Bake at 325 degrees for 15 minutes or until lightly browned. Combine vanilla and remaining sugar; add to eggs. Beat until thick and foamy. Add remaining salt, baking powder, coconut, nuts and 2 tablespoons flour. Blend well. Spread over baked mixture. Return to oven; bake for about 15 minutes or until topping is firm and lightly browned. Cool; cut in small bars. Yield: 3 dozen bars.

CREAMY PENUCHE SQUARES

2 c. (packed) light brown sugar
1/2 c. evaporated milk
4 tbsp. butter
Pinch of salt
1 tsp. vanilla
Chopped nuts

Combine brown sugar, milk, butter and salt in saucepan. Boil over low heat to soft-ball stage or to 238 degrees on candy thermometer. Remove from heat; let stand for about 3 minutes. Beat until candy thickens; stir in vanilla and nuts. Pour into greased dish. Let harden; cut into squares. Yield: 20-25 servings.

PENUCHE ICING

1/2 c. butter
1 c. (packed) brown sugar
1/4 c. milk
2 c. sifted powdered sugar

Melt butter in saucepan; add brown sugar. Bring to a boil. Boil over low heat for 2 minutes, stirring constantly. Stir in milk; bring to a boil again, stirring constantly. Cool to lukewarm. Add powdered sugar gradually; beat until thick enough to spread. May add small amount of hot water if icing becomes too soft. Yield: Icing for one 2-layer cake.

PENUCHE-NUT FROSTING

1 stick butter
1 c. (packed) light brown sugar
1/4 c. milk
2 c. sifted confectioners' sugar
1 c. chopped pecans

Melt butter in saucepan; add sugar. Boil for 2 minutes, stirring constantly; add milk. Bring to a boil; remove from heat. Cool to lukewarm. Beat in confectioners' sugar until of spreading consistency. fold in nuts.

Peppermint

PEPPERMINT DAZZLER

2 c. vanilla wafer crumbs
3/4 c. melted butter
1 1/2 c. powdered sugar
3 eggs
3 sq. melted chocolate
1 1/2 c. heavy cream
2 c. miniature marshmallows
1/2 c. crushed peppermint candy

Combine wafer crumbs and 1/4 cup melted butter; line bottom of 8 x 12-inch pan with crumbs. Blend remaining butter and powdered sugar with electric mixer; add eggs and chocolate. Beat until fluffy. Pour over crumbs in pan. Whip cream; fold in marshmallows. Spread over chocolate mixture; sprinkle with candy. Freeze.

PEPPERMINT SPECIAL

2/3 c. softened butter
2 c. powdered sugar
3 eggs, separated
2 sq. melted chocolate
1 tsp. vanilla
1/2 c. crushed pecans
1 1/2 c. crushed vanilla wafers
1 qt. peppermint stick ice cream

Cream butter and sugar with electric mixer; add beaten egg yolks, chocolate and vanilla. Mix well. Add pecans. Fold in stiffly beaten egg whites. Line 9-inch square pan with crumbs. Spoon creamed mixture into pan. Freeze for 3 hours. Spread ice cream over creamed mixture; sprinkle with additional crumbs. May serve topped with whipped cream and cherries if desired. Yield: 8 servings.

PEPPERMINT PUDDING

1/4 lb. peppermint candy
1 1/2 env. unflavored gelatin

1 med. angel food cake
1/2 c. light cream
1 pt. heavy cream

Crush candy to fine powder. Soften gelatin in 1/2 cup cold water. Tear cake into bite-sized pieces. Combine candy and light cream in double boiler; heat until candy is dissolved. Add gelatin, stirring until dissolved. Cool. Whip heavy cream; fold into candy mixture. Arrange layers of cake pieces and candy mixture in serving bowl. Chill for 12 hours. Cut into squares; serve with additional whipped cream.

PEPPERMINT CREAM

24 marshmallows
1/2 c. milk
3 drops of peppermint flavoring
1 tsp. vanilla
1/8 tsp. salt
Green food coloring
1 c. heavy cream, whipped

Melt marshmallows in milk over hot water. Remove from heat; cool slightly. Stir in peppermint flavoring, vanilla, salt and desired amount of food coloring. Chill until mixture mounds slightly when dropped from spoon; fold in whipped cream. Spoon into parfait glasses; chill until firm. Garnish with green maraschino cherries and fresh mint leaves. Yield: 4 servings.

PEPPERMINT MELON BALLS

1 pkg. lime gelatin
1 c. hot water
1 c. cold water
Dash of peppermint extract
Assorted melon balls

Dissolve gealtin in 1 cup hot water. Add 1 cup cold water and peppermint extract. Chill until thickened. Beat with egg beater until frothy and thick. Pour into wet ring mold; chill until firm. Unmold; fill center with melon balls; garnish with fresh mint.

PEPPERMINT SUPREME

1 c. flour
1/4 c. (packed) brown sugar
1/2 c. butter
1/2 c. chopped walnuts
1 1-lb. 4-oz. can crushed pineapple
1 pkg. lime gelatin
1 c. cream cheese
1 c. sugar
2/3 c. evaporated milk
1/8 tsp. peppermint extract

Combine flour, brown sugar, butter and walnuts, blending to fine crumbs. Press into greased 12 x 8 x 2-inch pan. Bake at 400 degrees for 10 minutes; cool. Drain pineapple juice into saucepan; bring to a boil. Add gelatin, stirring to dissolve; cool. Blend cream cheese and sugar together until fluffy; blend in gelatin mixture. Add pineapple; chill until thickened. Combine milk and peppermint extract; freeze until ice crystals form. Beat milk mixture until thick; fold into pineapple mixture. Spoon filling into baked crust; chill until set.

Chocolate-Mint Glaze

1/2 c. chocolate bits
1/3 c. evaporated milk
1 tbsp. butter
1 tsp. peppermint extract

Combine all ingredients in saucepan over low heat, stirring until chocolate and butter are melted. Spoon glaze over chilled dessert, spreading evenly. Chill for 4 hours longer.

PEPPERMINT PUFFS

3/4 c. margarine
3/4 c. sugar
1 egg, separated
1 tsp. vanilla
2 c. sifted flour
1/2 c. crushed peppermint candy
Chocolate morsels

Cream margarine and 1/4 cup sugar thoroughly; stir in beaten egg yolk and vanilla. Add flour gradually, 1/2 cup at a time. Stir in crushed candy; roll into 1-inch balls. Beat egg white slightly. Dip balls into egg white; roll in remaining sugar. Place 1 chocolate morsel in center of each cookie. Place on ungreased baking sheet. Bake in 350-degree oven for 15 minutes. Remove from baking sheet immediately. Place on rack; cool. Yield: 4 1/2 dozen cookies.

PEPPERMINT WHIP

1 16-oz. package peppermint candy
2 c. whipped cream
1/2 pkg. miniature marshmallows

Crush candy into fine powder; set aside. Whip cream. Stir in crushed candy and marshmallows. Refrigerate for 2 hours; serve in dessert dishes. Yield: 8-12 servings.

PEPPERMINT STICK DESSERT

1 1/2 lb. peppermint candy
1 lb. vanilla wafers
6 c. whipped cream
1 c. miniature marshmallows
1 c. chopped walnuts

Crush peppermint candy and vanilla wafers separately until fine. Line 13 x 9 x 2 1/4-inch cake pan with half the wafer crumbs. Combine whipped cream, marshmallows, walnuts and peppermint candy. Pour whipped cream mixture over crumbs. Cover with remaining wafer crumbs. Chill overnight. Serve with additional whipped cream. Yield: 16-20 servings.

MINT-CHIP PIE

1 c. whipping cream
1 tbsp. powdered sugar
1 c. cold milk
1/2 tsp. peppermint extract
3 drops of green food coloring
1 pkg. instant vanilla pudding
1/2 c. chopped semisweet chocolate bits
1 baked 8-in. pie crust

Whip cream until soft peaks form, adding sugar gradually; set aside. Combine milk, peppermint extract and food coloring in bowl. Add pudding; beat with rotary beater for about 1 minute or until blended. Fold whipped cream mixture and chocolate into pudding. Pour into crust; chill until firm. Yield: 5-6 servings.

Candy Cane Pie . . . Crushed peppermint candy gives this chocolate chiffon pie zesty flavor.

CANDY CANE PIE

1 2/3 c. graham cracker crumbs
1/4 c. softened butter
Sugar
1 env. unflavored gelatin
2 sq. unsweetened chocolate
1 c. milk
2 eggs, separated
1/4 tsp. salt
1 c. heavy cream
1 c. crushed peppermint candy canes

Blend cracker crumbs, butter and 1/4 cup sugar together; press firmly against bottom and side of 9-inch pie plate. Bake at 375 degrees for 8 minutes. Cool. Soften gelatin in 1/2 cup cold water. Combine chocolate, 1/2 cup sugar and milk in top of double boiler. Heat over boiling water until chocolate melts. Beat until smooth. Beat egg yolks; stir into chocolate mixture gradually. Cook, stirring constantly, for 3 minutes. Add gelatin; stir until dissolved. Chill until thickened. Add salt to egg whites; beat until stiff but not dry. Beat in 1/4 cup sugar gradually. Whip cream. Fold egg whites and half the cream into chocolate mixture. Fold in 1/2 cup crushed peppermint candy canes. Spoon filling into crumb crust. Chill for about 2 hours and 30 minutes or until firm. Garnish pie with remaining whipped cream and crushed peppermint. Yield: 6-8 servings.

PEPPERMINT-FUDGE PIE

24 chocolate sandwich cookies
1/4 c. melted butter
4 c. miniature marshmallows
1/2 c. milk
1 c. heavy cream, whipped
1/2 c. crushed peppermint candy

Crush cookies to fine crumb consistency. Combine crumbs and butter; press into 9-inch pie pan. Chill. Combine 3 cups marshmallows and milk in double boiler. Heat, stirring, until marshmallows are melted. Chill until slightly thickened. Fold in whipped cream, remaining marshmallows and candy. Pour into crust. Chill until firm. Freezes well. Yield: 8 servings.

FRENCH MINT PIE

1/2 c. butter
1 c. powdered sugar
3 egg yolks
2 sq. unsweetened chocolate
1/4 tsp. peppermint flavoring
1 graham cracker crust
Whipped cream

Cream butter and sugar together. Add egg yolks, one at a time, beating well after each addition. Melt chocolate; add to creamed mixture. Stir in peppermint flavoring. Pour into graham cracker crust; top with whipped cream. Chill well.

Peppers

The pepper is the many-seeded fruit of a large woody plant family native to the Americas. There are many kinds of peppers, including familiar *bell or sweet peppers* and smaller, pungent *hot peppers* such as the chili and cayenne peppers. The large, mild-flavored sweet pepper is used in salads and prepared dishes, is cooked as a vegetable, or stuffed. Hot peppers are used in pickling, canning, and the production of paprika, chili powder, cayenne pepper, and other seasonings. The term "red pepper" refers to either the mature sweet pepper or the mature hot pepper, both of which turn bright red when fully ripe. Sweet peppers contain protein, carbohydrate, calcium, and Vitamins A and C. (1 raw medium sweet pepper without seeds and stem = 15 calories)

AVAILABILITY: Fresh sweet peppers are available year-round. Greatest supplies are available from July to August; smallest supplies from December to April. Frozen and canned sweet peppers sold year-round. Frozen peppers are marketed whole, halved, sliced, or diced.

BUYING: Look for heavy, thick-fleshed sweet peppers with crisp walls or sides and a glossy sheen. They should be medium to dark green unless fully ripe, in which case they may be red. Choose wide and chunky peppers for stuffing. Avoid peppers with thin, flimsy walls or peppers that are wilted, cut, or punctured. Immature peppers are soft, pliable, and pale. Buy 1 pepper per serving.

STORING: Store covered fresh sweet peppers in refrigerator crisper or other cool, moist place 1 week. Refrigerate covered cooked peppers 1 to 2 days. Keep frozen peppers in refrigerator freezer up to 3 months, or in home freezer 1 year. *To freeze*–Peppers lose crispness when frozen. Frozen peppers, however, can be used satisfactorily in cooking. Choose firm, crisp, bright peppers. Wash and cut off stems. Remove seeds and inner membranes. Leave whole, halve, dice, or cut into strips or rings. Scald whole peppers or halves in boiling water 3 minutes, sliced or diced peppers 2 minutes. Chill in ice water. Drain. Pack in freezer containers or bags, leaving 1/2-inch head space. Seal and freeze. *To can*–Wash peppers and remove stems. Remove seeds and inside membranes. Peel (see below). Proceed according to instructions under CANNING. Raw pack is not recommended for peppers.

PREPARATION: Always remove seeds and membranes from fresh peppers, as they irritate the eyes and lips. Peppers to be canned or used in certain dishes must be peeled. *To peel,* cook in hot water about 3 minutes, until skins slip off easily. Or, roast at 450 degrees about 3 minutes, or until skin is blistered and dark. Cool in cold water and rub off skins. *To stuff,* wash peppers. Cut off top or stem end to remove seeds and membranes. Wash inside and out. Leave whole. Parboil 5 minutes in boiling salted water. Drain before stuffing. *To boil,* drop slices, rings, or strips into boiling salted water to cover. If desired, season water with oregano for extra flavor. Cook 3 to 5 minutes. Drain. Season with salt, pepper, and butter and serve.

(See VEGETABLES).

PICKLED PEPPER

12 green peppers
3 c. vinegar
1 c. salad oil
1 tbsp. salt
1 c. pickling onions

Wash peppers; remove seeds and centers. Cut peppers into serving pieces. Bring vinegar, oil and salt to a boil. Add small amount of peppers and onions at a time, turning in boiling liquid until peppers change color. Cook until just crisp-tender. Cool; refrigerate to serve.

HARVARD PEPPER SALAD

3 lge. green peppers
1 lb. cheese, grated
1 c. broken pecans
1/2 c. mayonnaise
Salt to taste
Paprika to taste
8 pineapple slices
8 lettuce cups

Remove stem end from peppers; let stand for several minutes in cold water. Combine cheese, pecans, mayonnaise, salt and paprika; blend thoroughly. Drain and dry peppers; fill with cheese mixture. Chill. Place pineapple slice on each lettuce cup. Slice stuffed peppers; arrange on pineapple. Garnish with mayonnaise or parsley. Yield: 8 servings.

JELLIED GREEN PEPPER RINGS

4 lge. green peppers
1 pkg. lemon gelatin
1 c. chopped celery
1 c. chopped carrots
1 c. chopped cucumbers

Cut stem ends from green peppers; remove seeds. Dissolve gelatin in 2 cups boiling water; chill until slightly thickened. Add all remaining ingredients; spoon mixture into pepper shells. Chill until firm; cut each pepper crosswise into 6 slices. May be served on salad greens and garnished with radish roses and mayonnaise. Yield: 6 servings.

GREEN PEPPER STEW

1 onion, chopped
1/4 c. shortening
2 green peppers, chopped
2 tomatoes, chopped
1 tsp. salt
1/2 tsp. (scant) pepper
4 potatoes, diced
2 tbsp. flour

Brown onion in shortening in skillet. Add 2 cups water, peppers, tomatoes, salt and pepper; cook over low heat for 20 minutes. Add potatoes; cook until potatoes are just tender. Mix flour with a small amount of water; add flour mixture to vegetables, stirring constantly, until thickened. Yield: 4 servings.

CREOLE PEPPER CASSEROLE

8 lge. green peppers
1 1/2 tbsp. butter
1 1/2 tbsp. flour
1 c. milk
Salt to taste
1 can mushroom soup
1 1/2 c. cheese, grated
1 c. bread crumbs

Grind peppers coarsely. Cook in 3/4 cup water until tender; drain well. Combine butter and flour in saucepan, blending well; add milk and salt gradually, stirring constantly, until smooth and thickened. Mix sauce with mushroom soup and peppers. Pour mixture into buttered casserole. Sprinkle cheese over pepper mixture; top with bread crumbs. Bake at 300 degrees for 30 minutes. Yield: 6-8 servings.

GREEN PEPPER CASSEROLE

1 1/2 c. milk
1 c. cooked chopped green peppers
1 c. cracker crumbs
2 tbsp. butter
1 c. shredded Cheddar cheese
Salt and pepper to taste

Combine all ingredients in casserole; blend thoroughly. Bake at 350 degrees for 30 minutes. Yield: 6-8 servings.

ORIENTAL GREEN PEPPERS

2 green peppers
1/2 c. white raisins
1/3 c. slivered almonds
2 tbsp. butter

Cut green peppers into strips. Cook peppers in boiling salted water for 3 minutes; drain. Saute raisins and almonds in butter; mix with peppers. Serve immediately. Yield: 4-6 servings.

FRIED GREEN PEPPERS

4 green peppers, quartered
2 c. catsup
Salt and pepper to taste

Brown green peppers in 1 tablespoon hot fat in skillet. Pour off excess fat; add 2 cups water. Simmer, covered, until peppers are tender; add additional water, if necessary. Add catsup, salt and pepper. Cook for 15 minutes longer. Yield: 4 servings.

FRIED PEPPERS WITH EGGS

6 green peppers, sliced
1 onion, sliced
1/4 c. olive oil
4 eggs, beaten

Brown green peppers and onion in hot olive oil in skillet; stir in eggs. Cook over low heat until set and peppers are tender. Yield: 4 servings.

STEWED PEPPERS

3 slices bacon, diced
6 green peppers
1/2 bottle chili sauce
2 tbsp. catsup
1/4 tsp. salt
1/4 tsp. monosodium glutamate
Dash of pepper

Fry bacon in 1-quart pan until crisp; pour off excess fat. Cut peppers into 1/4-inch strips. Add peppers to bacon; stir in 1/3 cup water. Cover; simmer gently for 15 minutes. Add chili sauce, catsup, salt, monosodium glutamate and pepper. Simmer for 5 minutes longer. Yield: 4 servings.

BARBECUE-STUFFED PEPPERS

4 lge. green peppers
1 lb. ground beef
2/3 c. instant nonfat dry milk
2 tbsp. catsup
2 tsp. salt
1/8 tsp. pepper
1 egg
1 slice day-old bread, cubed
1/4 tsp. dry mustard
1/4 c. finely cut onion
3 tsp. Worcestershire sauce
1 8-oz. can tomato sauce
1 tbsp. vinegar
1/2 tsp. chili powder
2 tbsp. (packed) brown sugar

Remove stems and seeds from peppers. Combine beef, milk, catsup, 1 1/2 teaspoons salt, pepper, egg, bread, mustard, onion and 2 teaspoons Worcestershire sauce. Mix well. Combine all remaining ingredients; blend well. Place peppers in baking dish; place 1 tablespoon sauce in each. Fill with beef mixture. Spoon 1 tablespoon sauce over peppers. Bake, covered, at 350 degrees for 1 hour. Heat remaining sauce; serve with peppers. Yield: 4 servings.

CARROT-STUFFED GREEN PEPPERS

2 onions, chopped
3/4 c. olive oil
1 lb. carrots, grated
Salt
Sugar
1/2 tsp. minced parsley
8 green peppers
4 tomatoes, peeled

Saute onions in 2/3 cup olive oil; add carrots to onions with 1/2 teaspoon salt and 1 teaspoon sugar. Simmer, covered, for 5 minutes. Add parsley; stir occasionally. Stuff peppers loosely with carrot mixture. Place in large baking pan; add 1 cup water. Bake at 350 degrees until water is absorbed; cool in pan. Cut tomatoes into small pieces; cook in remaining olive oil. Mixture will be like paste; add sugar and salt to taste. Pour over cooled peppers; serve cool. Yield: 6-8 servings.

CHEESE-STUFFED PEPPERS

6 med. green peppers
6 bacon
1/3 c. chopped onion
3 c. cooked rice
3 c. shredded Cheddar cheese
2 tbsp. chopped pimento
1/2 tsp. salt
1/2 c. bread crumbs
Bacon curls
1 can green beans

Cut off tops of green peppers; remove seeds and membranes. Cook for 5 minutes in boiling salted water; drain. Cut bacon in small pieces; saute with onion until crisp and brown. Drain on absorbent toweling. Combine bacon, onion, rice, cheese, pimento and salt in mixing bowl; toss to blend. Spoon into green pepper cups, packing lightly. Place peppers in baking dish. Bake at 375 degrees for 30 minutes. Top with crumbs and bacon curls, if desired. Place green beans around peppers to serve. Yield: 6 servings.

CORN-STUFFED PEPPERS

6 green peppers
1 1/4 tsp. salt
3 c. corn
1 c. diced fresh tomato
1/4 tsp. pepper
1 1/2 tsp. minced dried onion
1/8 tsp. garlic powder
1 tsp. chili powder
3 tbsp. flour
2 tbsp. butter, melted

Slice tops from green peppers; remove seeds and membranes. Cook peppers in boiling salted water to cover for 5 minutes; drain. Combine all remaining ingredients; spoon into peppers. Place peppers in baking pan. Bake at 375 degrees for 35 minutes or until tender. Yield: 6 servings.

POTATO-STUFFED PEPPERS

6 green peppers
1 tsp. salt
1 tsp. monosodium glutamate
3 c. thick mashed potatoes
2 tbsp. minced onion
1 c. grated, sharp Cheddar cheese
1/3 c. milk
1/2 c. minced parsley
1/2 c. chopped salted peanuts

Remove blossom end of peppers; discard seeds. Bring 4 cups of water to a boil; add salt and monosodium glutamate. Drop peppers in water; reduce heat. Simmer for 3 minutes; drain. Combine all remaining ingredients except peanuts; blend well. Fill peppers; sprinkle peanuts over top of each pepper. Place upright in buttered casserole. Bake at 350 degrees for 25 minutes or until heated through. Yield: 6 servings.

CURRY-STUFFED GREEN PEPPERS

1/4 lb. ground beef
1/2 c. rice
1/2 c. peas
2 tsp. curry
Salt and pepper
1 sm. onion, chopped
4 lge. green peppers, cored
Stuffed green olives

Saute beef in small amount of fat in skillet; add all ingredients except green peppers and olives. Stuff peppers with beef mixture; top with olives. Place in shallow pan; add 1 cup water. Bake at 350 degrees for 45 minutes.

DEVILED HAM-STUFFED PEPPERS

3 c. crumbled corn bread
1 sm. tomato, chopped
1 4 1/2-oz. can deviled ham
2 tbsp. catsup
1/4 c. diced celery
2 tbsp. chopped celery leaves
1/2 tsp. pepper
1/4 tsp. red pepper
6 sm. green peppers, halved

Soften corn bread in small amount of warm water; combine with all remaining ingredients except peppers. Spoon mixture into pepper halves; place in deep baking dish. Add 2 cups hot water. Bake at 400 degrees for 45 minutes or until peppers are tender. Yield: 12 servings.

MACARONI-STUFFED PEPPERS

6 green peppers
1 c. cooked elbow macaroni
1/2 lb. American cheese, grated
1 c. cooked tomatoes
1 c. soft bread crumbs
1/4 tsp. Worcestershire sauce
1/4 tsp. salt
Dash of pepper
1/2 lb. American cheese, grated

Cut slice from top of each pepper; remove seeds. Cook in boiling salted water for 5 minutes; drain. Mix all remaining ingredients, except 1/3 of the cheese; fill peppers with mixture. Stand peppers upright in pan; sprinkle reserved cheese on top. Bake at 350 degrees for 30 minutes. Yield: 6 servings.

GERMAN-STYLE PEPPERS

2 hard rolls
6 green peppers
1 1/2 lb. ground beef
1 med. onion, chopped
2 eggs
Salt and pepper
3 drops of Worcestershire sauce
1 tbsp. parsley flakes
2 tbsp. flour
1 bouillon cube

Soften rolls in 1/2 cup water. Cut off tops of peppers; remove seeds. Combine beef, onion, eggs, salt, pepper, rolls, Worcestershire sauce, parsley flakes and 2 cups water. Mix well. Stuff peppers with mixture; replace tops of peppers. Fry peppers in hot fat for 5 minutes; add small amount of water. Cook, covered, for 45 minutes or until peppers are tender. Remove peppers to warm oven. Blend flour and 1 cup water in saucepan; place over medium heat, stirring constantly, until thickened. Add bouillon cube; stir until dissolved. Pour bouillon mixture over peppers. Yield: 3-6 servings.

NO-BAKE STUFFED PEPPERS

4 lge. green peppers
1 lb. ground beef
1 8-oz. can tomato sauce
2/3 c. grated Cheddar cheese
Salt and pepper to taste
1/4 tsp. garlic salt
1 c. cooked packaged precooked rice

Remove stems, seeds and membranes from peppers. Place peppers in boiling water; cook for 15 minutes or until fork-tender. Cook beef in skillet until tender; drain off excess fat. Stir in tomato sauce, cheese, seasonings and rice; simmer, stirring until cheese is melted and mixture is heated through. Spoon into hot cooked peppers. Yield: 4 servings.

SAVORY GREEN PEPPERS

6 green peppers, seeded
2 lb. ground beef
2 tbsp. cooking oil
1 sm. onion, chopped
1/8 tsp. pepper
1/8 tsp. garlic powder
1/8 tsp. cumin
2 tbsp. flour
1 med. can whole tomatoes

Place peppers in boiling water; let stand for 1 minute. Place in cold water; remove skins. Brown beef in oil; add onion, pepper, garlic powder and cumin. Cook until onion is browned. Stir in flour; mix in tomatoes and 1 cup water. Cook, stirring constantly, until thickened. Stuff beef mixture into peppers. Place peppers in baking dish. Bake at 375 degrees for 45 minutes. Yield: 6 servings.

SHRIMP-STUFFED PEPPERS

6 med. green peppers
2 tbsp. chopped onion
2 c. diced cooked shrimp
2 c. cooked rice
1 c. salad dressing
Dash of hot sauce
Pepper
Salt to taste
1 8-oz. can seasoned tomato sauce

Cut off tops of green peppers; remove seeds and membranes. Place in boiling salted water. Cook for 5 minutes; drain. Sprinkle insides with salt. Combine all remaining ingredients except sauce; fill peppers. Place upright in 10 x 6 x 1 1/2-inch baking dish; cover with tomato sauce. Bake at 350 degrees for 30 minutes. Spoon tomato sauce over filling before serving. Yield: 6 servings.

STUFFED BELL PEPPERS

Color photograph for this recipe on page 310.

6 fresh green peppers
6 ears of fresh corn
1 lb. ground beef
1/4 c. chopped fresh onion
Salt and pepper

Cut tops from green peppers; remove seeds and membranes. Cook in boiling, salted water until partially done; drain. Cut corn from cobs; place in skillet. Add 1/2 cup water; cook over low heat, stirring frequently, until water has evaporated. Add ground beef, onion, salt and pepper; cook until beef is brown, stirring occasionally. Stuff green peppers with corn mixture; place in baking pan. Bake at 350 degrees for about 30 minutes. Garnish as desired.

PEPPERS IN MUSHROOM SAUCE

1/2 c. chopped celery
1 c. chopped onions
2 tbsp. flour
1 lb. cooked ground beef
1 can tomatoes
Chopped pimento
4 green peppers
1 can cream of mushroom soup

Saute celery and onions in a small amount of fat in skillet until tender. Stir in flour. Add beef, tomatoes and pimento; simmer over low heat for several minutes. Cut peppers in half; remove pulp and seeds. Pour boiling water over peppers; let stand for 5 minutes. Remove peppers from water; drain. Fill peppers with beef mixture. Place peppers in baking dish; pour soup over. Bake at 300 degrees until bubbly.

PEPPERS IN TOMATO SAUCE

6 green peppers
6 slices bread
Salt and pepper
1 tbsp. parsley
1 tbsp. thyme
1 tsp. garlic salt
1/2 c. grated Italian cheese
2 eggs, beaten
1/4 c. salad oil
1 sm. can tomato sauce

Slice peppers into halves; discard seeds. Set 10 halved peppers aside; chop remaining halves. Remove crust from bread; crumble bread into bowl. Add chopped peppers, salt, pepper, parsley, thyme, garlic salt, cheese and eggs. Mix well; stuff peppers with mixture. Pour oil in baking dish; place peppers in dish. Bake, covered, at 350 degrees for 45 minutes. Add tomato sauce. Bake, uncovered, for 15 minutes longer or until peppers are slightly browned. Yield: 6-8 servings.

BEEF-STUFFED GREEN PEPPERS

Color photograph for this recipe on page 66.

3 green peppers
1 tsp. salt
1/8 tsp. pepper
1 tbsp. Worcestershire sauce
1/3 c. oats
1 egg, beaten
Catsup
1/4 c. finely chopped onion
1 1/2 lb. ground beef

Cut green peppers in half lengthwise; remove seeds. Cook in boiling, salted water for 5 minutes; invert and drain thoroughly. Combine salt, pepper, Worcestershire sauce, oats, egg, 1/3 cup catsup, onion and ground beef, mixing thoroughly. Pack about 1/2 cup of the beef mixture into each green pepper half; place peppers in 12 x 8-inch baking dish. Top each stuffed pepper with 2 teaspoons catsup. Bake at 350 degrees for 30 to 35 minutes. Yield: 6 servings.

Perch

The term perch refers to several varieties of lean, spiny-finned fresh- and salt-water fishes. *Freshwater perch,* known also as yellow or ring perch, are olive green to golden yellow in color with 6 to 8 vertical bands on their sides. *Ocean perch,* otherwise known as perch or rosefish, are actually related to the sea bass or rockfish family. Both fresh- and salt-water perch have light and flaky, though somewhat coarse, textures. Perch is rich in protein and mineral salts, especially iodine, iron, and copper. (3 1/2 ounces raw perch = 100 calories)

AVAILABILITY: Freshwater perch are available year-round, fresh or frozen, whole or filleted. Ocean perch, also in constant supply, is usually filleted and frozen. Market weight for perch averages 2 pounds.

BUYING: Select whole, fresh perch that has bright, clear bulging eyes; reddish pink gills; tight, shiny scales; firm, elastic flesh; and a fresh odor. Allow 1 pound cleaned and scaled fish for 2 people, 1 pound fish fillet for 3.

STORING: Wrap fresh perch in moistureproof paper. Refrigerate and use within 2 days. *To freeze* perch—Remove scales, head, and tail from fish. Eviscerate. Wash perch thoroughly and drain. Dip briefly in light brine solution. Wrap in moisture- and vapor-proof paper and seal. Frozen perch (freshwater and ocean varieties) keeps in refrigerator frozen food compartment 2 to 3 weeks; in home freezer 1 year. Keep fish frozen until ready to use.

PREPARATION: Frozen perch will thaw in the refrigerator overnight or at room temperature in 3 to 4 hours. Never refreeze perch after thawing; use as soon as possible to prevent spoilage. Perch may be fried, sauteed, broiled, baked, poached, or steamed. Refer to specific recipes for more detailed cooking instructions.

SERVING: Perch is often prepared in casseroles, served with tasty sauces or lemon, and garnished with parsley.

(See SEAFOOD.)

PERCH FLORENTINE

1 lb. perch fillets
1 10-oz. package frozen chopped spinach
1/4 c. flour
1/2 tsp. salt
1/8 tsp. pepper
Dash of nutmeg
1 1/2 c. milk
1/2 c. grated Parmesan cheese
1/2 tsp. Worcestershire sauce
Paprika

Skin fillets. Cook spinach according to package directions. Drain thoroughly. Blend flour, salt, pepper and nutmeg into 1/4 cup fat in skillet. Add milk gradually; cook until thick and smooth, stirring constantly. Add cheese and Worcestershire sauce; stir until blended. Arrange half the fish in well-greased 10 x 6 x 2-inch baking dish. Combine spinach with 1/2 cup sauce; spread over fish. Arrange remaining fish over spinach; top with remaining sauce. Sprinkle with paprika. Bake at 350 degrees for 25 minutes or until fish flakes easily. Yield: 6servings.

PERCH AU GRATIN

1 1-lb. package frozen perch fillets
2 tbsp. fine cracker crumbs
1 c. canned tomatoes
2 tbsp. chopped onion
1/4 tsp. salt
1/8 tsp. pepper
1 tbsp. butter
1/4 c. grated Cheddar cheese

Thaw fillets. Sprinkle cracker crumbs in greased 1-quart shallow baking dish; place fillets on crumbs. Combine tomatoes, onion, salt and pepper; pour over fillets. Dot with butter; sprinkle with cheese. Bake at 350 degrees for 35 minutes or until fish flakes easily with fork.

PERCH-POTATO CASSEROLE

1/4 c. butter, melted
2 tbsp. flour
2 c. milk
2 c. soft bread crumbs
3 lb. boiled perch, boned and flaked
2 c. sliced cooked potatoes
2 med. onions, sliced
Salt and pepper to taste

Blend 2 tablespoons butter with flour; add milk, stirring constantly, until thickened. Reserve small amount of crumbs for topping. Place 1/2 of the perch, potatoes, onions and remaining crumbs in layers in greased 2-quart casserole. Add seasonings and 1 cup white sauce. Repeat. Top with reserved crumbs; dot with remaining butter. Bake in 325-degree oven for 1 hour. Yield: 6 servings.

FILLET TURBANS

1 tbsp. chopped onion
1 tbsp. chopped celery
1/4 c. melted butter
1/2 c. chopped watercress
1/4 tsp. salt
1/8 tsp. pepper
1 c. fine dry bread crumbs
4 perch fillets

Saute onion and celery in 2 tablespoons butter until tender; add watercress, seasonings and bread crumbs. Roll fillets around inside of 4 greased custard cups or muffin tins; spoon stuffing into centers. Brush tops with remaining butter. Bake in 375-degree oven for 20 minutes or until fish flakes easily with fork. Turn out onto serving dish; garnish with additional watercress. Yield: 4 servings.

PERCH FILLETS WITH CHIVES

1 1/2 lb. perch fillets
Salt and pepper
2 tbsp. snipped fresh chives
2 eggs, beaten
2 c. crushed potato chips
6 tbsp. butter
Lemon slices

Sprinkle fillets on both sides with salt and pepper to taste. Sprinkle chives evenly over one side of half the fillets. Top each chive-covered fillet with another. Secure with toothpicks, if necessary. Dip fillet sandwiches into beaten egg carefully; coat with chips. Melt butter in large frying pan until bubbly. Add fillets; saute over medium heat for 6 minutes on each side or until golden brown and crisp on outside and flaky at center. Turn only once. Serve with lemon slices. Yield: 6 servings.

OVEN-FRIED PERCH

2 lb. frozen perch fillets
1/2 c. milk
2 tsp. salt
1/2 c. cornmeal
1/2 c. flour
2 tbsp. chopped parsley
2 tbsp. melted butter
2 tbsp. lemon juice

Thaw frozen fillets; remove skin. Combine milk and salt; combine cornmeal, flour and parsley. Dip fillets in milk. Put 2 fillets together, sandwich fashion; roll in cornmeal mixture. Place in well-greased 12 x 15-inch casserole; sprinkle remaining cornmeal mixture over fillets. Combine butter and lemon juice; drizzle over fillets. Bake at 500 degrees for 12 minutes or until fish flakes. Serve with lemon wedges and parsley. Yield: 6 servings.

BATTER-FRIED PERCH

2 lb. ocean perch fillets
1 tsp. lemon juice
1 1/2 tsp. salt
1 c. flour
1 tbsp. paprika
1 10-oz. can beer

Skin fillets; cut into 3-inch pieces. Sprinkle fillets with lemon juice and 1/2 teaspoon salt. Combine flour, paprika and remaining salt. Add beer gradually; beat until batter is thin and smooth. Dip fillets in batter; fry in deep 350-degree fat for 3 to 4 minutes or until fillets are brown and flake easily. Drain on absorbent paper. Garnish with lemon wedges and parsley. Serve with french-fried potatoes if desired. Yield: 6 servings.

Batter-Fried Perch . . . Frozen fillets are dipped in a beer-flavored batter and deep fat fried.

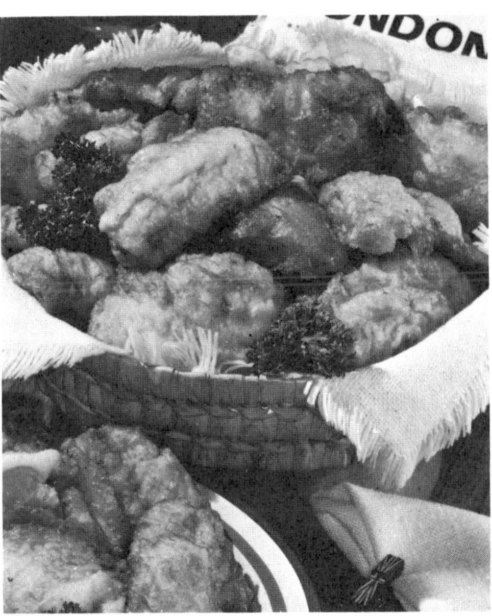

DEEP-FRIED PERCH

2 lb. frozen perch fillets
Salt
1 c. pancake flour
1 egg
1/2 c. milk
1 lb. shortening

Thaw perch; wash and drain. Season to taste. Combine flour, egg and milk, blending well. Dip fillets in batter; drain. Heat shortening in skillet; place fillets in skillet. Cook for 10 minutes or until golden brown. Drain on paper towels. Yield: 6 servings.

SOUTHERN PAN-FRIED PERCH

2 to 3 lb. perch
1 c. shortening
2 tbsp. salt
1/2 c. cornmeal

Cut perch into serving pieces. Heat shortening in skillet over medium heat. Mix salt and cornmeal; roll perch in cornmeal mixture. Place in skillet; fry for 3 minutes or until browned delicately. Yield: 4 servings.

MEDITERRANEAN PERCH

2 lb. perch fillets
Juice of 1 lemon
Salt and pepper
1/4 c. chopped onion
1 clove of garlic, minced
2 tbsp. oil
1 6-oz. can tomato paste
1/2 tsp. oregano
1/4 c. dry white wine
1 2-oz. can mushrooms, drained
2 tbsp. dry bread crumbs
3 tbsp. Parmesan cheese
1 tbsp. chopped parsley

Cut fillets into serving pieces; sprinkle with lemon juice, salt and pepper to taste. Place fillets in greased shallow baking dish. Saute onion and garlic in oil until tender. Combine tomato paste, 1 1/2 cups water, 1/2 teaspoon salt, 1/4 teaspoon pepper and oregano; add to onion mixture. Simmer for 20 minutes; stir in wine. Pour sauce over fillets. Combine mushrooms, crumbs, cheese and parsley. Place topping over each fillet. Bake at 375 degrees for 35 minutes. Yield: 4-6 servings.

OCEAN PERCH AMANDINE

1 pkg. frozen perch fillets
1/4 c. almonds
3 tbsp. soft butter
Grated rind of 1 lemon
1/2 tsp. paprika
1/4 tsp. salt
1/4 tsp. pepper

Let fillets thaw in refrigerator. Blanch almonds in boiling water; remove skins. Chop almonds coarsely. Mix with all remaining ingredients. Separate fillets; arrange, skin side down, in baking dish. Spread top of perch with almond mixture. Bake at 350 degrees for 12 minutes or until fish flakes easily.

PERCH FILLETS WITH BLEU CHEESE

Perch fillets
1/2 c. butter
1 c. bleu cheese, crumbled
3 tsp. lemon juice
1 tbsp. salt
1/8 tsp. pepper

Bake fillets at 350 degrees until opaque but not flaky. Combine all remaining ingredients. Stir over low heat until blended and thickened slightly. Pour cheese over fillets. Broil 6 minutes, 4 inches from source of heat, until browned slightly. Yield: 6-8 servings.

PERCH POACHED IN TOMATO SAUCE

2 c. tomatoes
1/2 tsp. salt
1 bay leaf
1 tbsp. minced onion
1/2 tsp. peppercorns
2 lb. perch fillets
1 tbsp. butter

Cook tomatoes, salt, bay leaf, onion and peppercorns in greased skillet until reduced by one-half. Add perch; simmer for 5 minutes. Turn perch carefully; simmer for 5 minutes longer. Remove perch to hot platter. Strain tomato sauce; add butter. Pour over fish. Yield: 6 servings.

POACHED PERCH

4 perch
Salt to taste
1/2 c. mild vinegar
1/2 c. melted butter
1/4 c. minced parsley
1/4 tsp. pepper

Place perch in skillet; add boiling water to just cover perch. Add salt and vinegar. Bring to a boil; cover. Reduce heat; simmer for 12 minutes. Place perch on platter. Mix butter, parsley and pepper; pour over perch. Yield: 4 servings.

QUICK-BAKED PERCH

1/2 c. milk
2 tsp. salt
Perch
Fine dry bread crumbs
Cooking oil

Preheat oven to 500 degrees. Combine milk and salt; dip perch into mixture. Roll in bread crumbs. Place in oiled shallow baking pan, drizzling each piece lightly with oil. Bake for 12 minutes or until brown and crisp.

ROLL-UPS SUPREME

6 perch fillets
1 No. 303 can long green beans
1 can celery soup
1 tbsp. lemon juice
1 tbsp. Worcestershire sauce
1/4 c. slivered almonds
1/4 c. grated Parmesan cheese

Roll each fillet around several beans; place in 8 x 10-inch baking dish. Mix soup with lemon juice and Worcestershire sauce; pour over roll-ups. Sprinkle with almonds and cheese. Bake at 350 degrees for 30 minutes. Yield: 5-6 servings.

SHERRY PERCH FILLETS

Milk
1 lb. perch fillets
1/4 to 1/2 c. sherry
1 c. buttered bread crumbs

Pour milk into baking dish to 1/4-inch depth. Arrange perch in dish; pour sherry over perch. Cover with bread crumbs. Bake at 350 degrees for 45 minutes or until perch is flaky and brown. Serve with tartar sauce or lemon butter and parsley flakes.

Persimmon

The persimmon is a conical, light or deep orange fruit. It is similar to the plum in taste and texture. When fully ripe, persimmons are delightfully rich and sweet. The most commonly marketed seedless persimmons are cultivated primarily in California from varieties native to the Orient. Some varieties grow wild in eastern, southern, and southeastern United States. These, however, are all used locally, are smaller than cultivated persimmons, and have seeds. Persimmons contain protein, carbohydrate, calcium, and Vitamins A and C. (1 raw 2 1/2-inch persimmon = 75 calories)

AVAILABILITY: Persimmons are available three months out of the year: October, November, and December. Peak month is November.

BUYING: Look for plump, smooth fruit with stems attached. Skins should be unbroken. Ripe fruit at its flavor peak is soft.

STORING: Allow immature fruit to ripen in a cool, dark, dry place. Refrigerate ripe fruit and use as soon as possible. Store frozen fruit puree in refrigerator's freezer up to 3 months or in home freezer 1 year.

PREPARATION: *To puree*—Choose soft, ripe fruit. Wash. Peel. Cut into sections. Press sections through sieve. Or, mash fruit, removing seeds from native varieties. If pulp is not used immediately, add 1 tablespoon lemon juice to 2 cups pulp to prevent darkening. *To freeze* puree—Press pulp as above. To each 4 cups pulp, add 1/8 teaspoon ascorbic acid to help prevent darkening and flavor loss. Native varieties of fruit need no addition of sugar. Cultivated varieties may be packed with or without sugar. If you use sugar, add 1 cup sugar to each 4 cups pulp. Pack into containers, leaving 1/2-inch head space. Seal, label, and freeze.

USES: Wash and chill fresh fruit. Serve whole or halved. May be served with cream, lemon or lime, or ice cream. Use fresh or frozen puree in cakes, pies, puddings, custards, ice cream, and sherbets.

PERFECT PERSIMMON COOKIES

1 c. sugar
1/2 c. shortening
1 egg, beaten
1 tsp. soda
1 c. persimmon pulp
2 c. flour
1 tsp. salt
1/2 tsp. cinnamon
1/8 tsp. cloves
1/8 tsp. nutmeg
1 c. chopped nuts

Cream 1/2 cup sugar with shortening. Mix remaining sugar with egg; add to creamed mixture. Dissolve soda in persimmon pulp; beat into sugar mixture. Combine dry ingredients; add to persimmon mixture. Mix in nuts. Drop from spoon onto baking sheet. Bake at 375 degrees for 10 to 15 minutes.

HOLIDAY PERSIMMON CAKE

2 1/2 c. flour
2 c. sugar
1/2 tsp. salt
2 tsp. baking powder
2 tsp. soda
1 c. nuts
1 c. raisins
1 c. glazed fruit
1 c. milk
2 eggs, beaten
2 c. persimmon pulp
3 tbsp. butter
2 tsp. vanilla

Sift dry ingredients together; sift over mixture of nuts and fruits. Mix thoroughly, separating nuts and fruits. Add remaining ingredients; mix well. Pour into bine all remaining ingredients; mix well. Pour into well-greased tube pan. Bake in 300-degree oven for 1 hour or until cake tests done. Yield: 16 servings.

SPICY PERSIMMON CAKE

2 c. sugar
2 tbsp. shortening
2 c. persimmon pulp
2 c. flour
1 tsp. cinnamon
1 tsp. nutmeg
1 tsp. soda
2 tsp. baking powder
1/2 tsp. salt
1 c. raisins
1 c. chopped dates
2 c. chopped walnuts
1 tsp. vanilla

Cream sugar and shortening; stir in persimmon pulp. Sift dry ingredients together; add to creamed mixture. Fold in fruits and walnuts; add vanilla. Place batter in greased and floured tube pan. Bake at 350 degrees for 1 hour and 15 minutes.

INDIANA PERSIMMON DESSERT

1 c. persimmon pulp
1 c. milk
2 eggs
1/2 c. butter
1 tsp. cinnamon
1 tsp. nutmeg
1/2 tsp. cloves
1 tsp. baking powder
1 c. flour
2 1/2 c. sugar

Mix pulp, milk, eggs, butter, cinnamon, nutmeg, cloves, baking powder and flour; add 1 1/2 cups sugar. Mix thoroughly; pour into well-oiled loaf pan. Bake at 375 degrees for 20 minutes. Mix remaining sugar and 1/2 cup water thoroughly; pour over pudding. Bake for 10 minutes longer. Yield: 8-10 servings.

PRIZE PERSIMMON PUDDING

1/4 c. butter
1 c. milk
1 egg
1 c. sugar
1/4 tsp. salt
1 tsp. soda
2 c. persimmon pulp
2 c. flour
1 c. chopped dates
1/2 c. chopped nuts

Cream butter. Add milk, egg, sugar, salt and soda; mix well. Stir in persimmon pulp; add flour. Blend in dates and nuts. Turn into greased 9-inch square pan. Bake at 325 degrees for 45 minutes. Serve with whipped cream. Yield: 9 servings.

PERSIMMON-NUT PUDDING

3 eggs, beaten
2 c. persimmon pulp
1 1/2 c. sugar
1/2 tsp. cinnamon
1/2 tsp. nutmeg
1 tsp. salt
1/2 tsp. baking soda
2 c. sifted flour
1 3/4 c. milk
3 tbsp. melted butter
1 c. chopped nuts

Combine eggs and pulp; beat well. Add sugar and spices; beat until blended. Combine dry ingredients. Stir into persimmon mixture with milk and butter; mix thoroughly. Blend in nuts. Pour into greased loaf pan. Bake at 320 degrees for 1 hour and 15 minutes or until set. Serve with whipped cream.

Pickle

Pickles are vegetables that have been preserved in a brine or vinegar solution. The most common and popular pickles are made from cucumbers—dill, sweet, bread-and-butter, and Polish-style.

INGREDIENTS: In selecting vegetables for pickling, choose only fresh, firm, unblemished, and slightly underripe specimens of small to medium size. They should have been harvested no more than 24 hours in advance. Most vegetables are pickled by the addition of some or all of the following ingredients. *Salt*—Use only pure, pickling or dairy salt that contains no additives. Granulated and flake forms are also satisfactory. You may purchase these salts at feed-supply stores. *Vinegar*—Use a good quality, sediment-free vinegar of 4 to 6 percent acidity. Distilled white vinegar preserves the color of the produce and ensures crispness. Cider or herb vinegars, while more flavorful, may darken the pickles. *Water*—Use soft, distilled, or rain water if possible, because the minerals in hard water interfere with curing. If only hard water is available, boil it, skim the scum, and allow it to stand 24 hours before using. *Spices*—Use fresh and whole spices. Old spices may have lost the desired pungency. Ground spices may darken the produce. Tie spices in a thin, cloth bag so that they can be easily removed after cooking. *Sugar*—Either brown or white sugar may be used. Brown sugar gives a richer flavor, white sugar a clearer color.

EQUIPMENT: For heating pickling liquids use *kettles* of enamel, glass, aluminum, or stainless steel. *Do not use* zinc, copper, brass, galvanized, or iron utensils. Wooden, stainless steel, or aluminum *spoons* are best for stirring. Seal pickles in standard glass canning *jars* with enamel-lined or glass *lids*.

METHODS OF PREPARATION: There are two basic methods employed in curing pickles: the 24-hour or short-brine pickling and the long-brine or sour pickling. In *short-brine pickling*, the vegetables are soaked in a salt solution for 24 hours and then processed in a seasoned vinegar solution. Little or no fermentation occurs. In *long-brine* and *sour pickling*, the vegetables are soaked in brine for 2 to 6 weeks until the desired stage of curing is reached. During this time the natural sugar from the vegetables combines with the salt to form an acid bath. For detailed instructions on pickling, consult specific recipes.

(See CUCUMBER.)

DIFFERENT BREAD AND BUTTER PICKLES

1 gal. cucumbers
1 red sweet pepper
1 green sweet pepper
12 med. onions
1 sm. cauliflower
1/2 c. salt
Cracked ice
5 c. sugar
5 c. white vinegar
1 1/2 tsp. turmeric
2 tsp. celery seed
1 tsp. mustard seed
1 tsp. pickling spice
2 cloves of garlic, split

Slice cucumbers, peppers and onions paper thin; break cauliflower into flowerets. Layer vegetables, salt and ice in crock; let stand, covered, for 3 hours. Drain thoroughly. Combine sugar, vinegar, spices and garlic in large kettle. Bring to a boil; boil for 3 minutes. Add vegetables; stir well. Bring to a boil; boil for 3 minutes longer. Seal in hot sterilized jars.

BREAD AND BUTTER PICKLES

1 gal. fresh cucumbers, thinly sliced
12 sm. onions, thinly sliced
1/2 c. salt
Cracked ice
4 c. sugar
4 c. vinegar
2 tsp. turmeric powder
1/2 tsp. cloves
1 tsp. celery seed
2 tsp. mustard seed (opt.)

Alternate layers of cucumbers, onions, salt and cracked ice in crock; let stand, covered, for 3 hours. Drain thoroughly. Combine sugar, vinegar and spices; bring to a boil. Add cucumbers, mix well. Simmer, stirring frequently, until mixture comes just to a boil; remove from heat. Seal in hot sterilized jars.

CHERRY DILL PICKLES

Small cucumbers
Cherry leaves
Dill
Salt
Pickling spice
Sugar
Vinegar

Layer cucumbers, cherry leaves and dill in crock; cover with brine made in proportions of 1 cup salt to 5 quarts water. Weight down; cover with cloth. Let stand at room temperature for 10 days. Remove cucumbers from brine; rinse well. Drain thoroughly. Slice cucumbers 1/2 inch thick. Pack into hot sterilized quart jars; add 1 teaspoon pickling spices to each jar. Make a syrup in proportions of 3 cups sugar to 1 cup vinegar; cook until slightly thickened. Pour over pickles; fill jars to within 1/2 inch from top. Seal. Let stand for four to six weeks.

DILL DANDIES

24 lge. cucumbers
Powdered alum
Cloves of garlic
Fresh dill
Hot red pepper
4 c. cider vinegar
1/2 to 1 c. salt
4 c. water
Grape leaves

Let cucumbers stand overnight in water to cover; drain thoroughly. Pack cucumbers in sterilized jars; to each jar add 1/8 teaspoon powdered alum, 1 clove of garlic, 2 sprigs of dill and 1 hot red pepper. Combine vinegar, salt and water; bring to a boil. Fill jars with brine; top each with fresh grape leaf. Seal immediately. Store in cool place for six weeks before using.

GARLIC-DILL PICKLES

10 cucumbers
Garlic cloves, split
Dill heads
1 c. sugar
1 c. salt
8 qt. water
1 qt. white vinegar

Cut ends off cucumbers; pack in sterilized quart jars. Place 2 to 3 garlic cloves in each quart; stuff one head of dill in each quart. Bring sugar, salt, water and vinegar to a boil; pour over cucumbers filling to top. Cap loosely; use hot water pack. Tighten caps.

KOSHER DILL PICKLES

Cucumbers
1 clove of garlic
1 dried red pepper
1/2 tsp. celery seed
2 slices onion
2 slices green pepper
Fresh dill
1 1/2 c. salt
1 qt. cider vinegar

Pack cucumbers in sterilized quart jars; add garlic, red pepper, celery seed, onion, green pepper and 1 to 2 sprigs of dill to each jar, Combine salt, vinegar and 4 quarts water. Bring to a boil; pour over cucumbers to within 1/2 inch of jar top. Seal immediately. Let stand 4 to 6 weeks before serving.

ARISTOCRAT PICKLES

24 med. cucumbers
Salt
2 tbsp. alum
2 tbsp. ginger
6 c. sugar
1 qt. vinegar
1 tsp. cloves
1 tsp. allspice
1 tsp. cinnamon

Slice cucumbers paper thin. Make brine, using 1/4 cup salt to 1 gallon water; pour over cucumbers in crock. Let stand for 7 days; stir daily. On eighth day, drain off brine; wash cucumbers. Cover cucumbers with water in kettle; add alum. Bring to a boil; boil for 10 minutes. Drain. Repeat process using ginger. Combine sugar, vinegar, cloves, allspice and cinnamon in kettle. Add cucumbers; bring to a boil. Boil for 30 minutes. Pack in hot sterilized jars; seal. Yield: 6 pints.

GARLIC CUCUMBER PICKLES

10 7-in. firm cucumbers
Salt
5 c. cider vinegar
1/4 c. sweet pepper flakes
3/4 c. sugar
3 tbsp. instant minced onion
2 tbsp. garlic powder
1 tsp. ground pepper

Slice cucumbers lengthwise into eighths. Combine cucumbers and 1/4 cup salt. Cover with cold water in large container; let stand for 2 hours. Drain; rinse well with cold water. Combine 1 cup water, vinegar, pepper flakes, sugar, onion, garlic powder, pepper and 1 teaspoon salt in large pot. Bring to boiling point; add cucumbers. Return to boiling point; reduce heat. Simmer for 8 minutes. Pack in hot, sterilized jars; seal at once.

Garlic Cucumber Pickles . . . Old-fashioned pickles with a tangy flavor.

MILLION DOLLAR PICKLES

6 qt. cucumbers, sliced
1/2 c. salt
12 sm. onions, quartered
3 red or green peppers, cut into strips
1 sm. can pimento, cut into strips
5 c. vinegar
6 c. sugar
2 tbsp. mustard seed
1 tsp. turmeric seed

Soak cucumbers in salted water to cover for 3 hours; drain well. Combine remaining ingredients with 1 cup water; bring to a boil, stirring to dissolve sugar. Add cucumbers. Bring to a boil; boil for 5 minutes. Pack into sterilized jars; seal.

SOUR PICKLES

12 lb. cucumbers
1 gal. cider vinegar
1 c. salt
1 c. sugar
1 c. white mustard seeds

Pack cucumbers into sterilized jars. Combine vinegar, 1 quart water, salt, sugar and mustard seeds in large kettle. Bring to a boil. Pour hot syrup over cucumbers to within 1/2 inch of top of jar. Seal immediately.

CRISP SWEET PICKLES

5 qt. thinly sliced cucumbers
6 med. onions, thinly sliced
3 cloves of garlic, split
1/2 c. salt
Crushed ice
5 c. sugar
2 tsp. turmeric
1 1/2 tsp. celery seed
2 tbsp. mustard seed
3 c. vinegar

Place cucumbers, onions and garlic cloves in a large pan; add salt. Cover with crushed ice and mix thoroughly; let stand for 3 hours. Drain thoroughly. Combine sugar, turmeric, celery seed, mustard seed and vinegar in large kettle; bring just to a boil. Add cucumbers and onions. Bring just to a boil; heat through. Seal in hot, sterilized jars.

ICICLE PICKLES

7 lb. cucumbers
1 c. slaked lime
2 qt. vinegar
4 lb. sugar
3 tbsp. pickling spice

Slice cucumbers into finger-sized strips; remove seeds. Mix lime with 1 gallon water in crock. Add cucumbers; stir well. Let stand for 24 hours; drain. Wash until water is clear; drain thoroughly. Combine vinegar, sugar and pickling spice in large kettle; add cucumbers. Let stand for 2 hours. Bring to a boil; simmer, stirring occasionally, for 1 hour or until cucumbers are transparent. Pack in hot sterilized jars; seal.

CRISPY CHUNKS

8 med. cucumbers
Salt
2 c. vinegar
2 tsp. alum
4 c. sugar
2 c. white vinegar
1 tbsp. pickling spice

Place cucumbers in a gallon crock; cover with brine, using 1/2 cup salt per quart of water. Let stand for three days. Drain; cover with cold water. Let stand for three days; change water each day. Cut cucumbers in chunks; add vinegar, 4 cups water and alum. Bring to a boil; remove from heat. Let stand for two days. Drain cucumbers. Combine sugar, 2 cups white vinegar and pickling spice; bring to a boil. Pour over cucumbers; let stand overnight. Repeat process for 2 additional days. Bring cucumbers and syrup to a boil. Pack in hot sterilized jars. Seal.

SLICED SWEET PICKLES

4 qt. small cucumbers
2 green peppers
6 onions
3 cloves of garlic
1/3 c. salt
Cracked ice
5 c. sugar
3 c. vinegar
2 tbsp. mustard seed
1 1/2 tsp. turmeric
1 1/2 tsp. celery salt

Slice cucumbers, green peppers, onions and garlic paper thin. Layer vegetables, salt and ice in crock; let stand, covered, for 3 hours. Drain thoroughly. Combine sugar, vinegar, mustard seed, turmeric and celery salt in large kettle; bring to a boil, stirring until sugar is dissolved. Add vegetables to syrup; mix well. Bring to a boil, stirring frequently. Pack in hot sterilized jars; seal.

SWEET STICKLES

7 lb. cucumbers
1 c. slaked lime
1 1/2 qt. white vinegar
7 1/2 c. sugar
1 1/2 tbsp. celery seed
1 1/2 tbsp. salt
Green food coloring

Peel cucumbers and cut lengthwise; remove seeds. Slice in finger-sized strips; cut in desired lengths. Dissolve lime in 1 gallon water; pour over cucumbers in crock. Soak overnight. Drain; wash well until water is clear. Soak in clear water for 3 to 4 hours; drain. Combine vinegar, sugar, celery seed, salt and food coloring, as desired, in large kettle; bring to a boil. Add cucumbers; stir gently just to coat cucumbers. Remove from heat; let stand overnight. Bring to a boil; reduce heat. Simmer, stirring occasionally, for 30 minutes or until cucumbers are transparent. Pack in hot sterilized jars; seal.

BEST WATERMELON PICKLES

10 lb. watermelon rind
1 qt. white vinegar
12 lb. sugar
3/4 tsp. oil of cloves
3/4 tsp. oil of cinnamon

Peel and slice rind into small pieces; cover with cold water. Let stand in cool place for 24 hours. Rinse thoroughly; drain well. Cover with cold water; bring to a boil. Simmer for 10 minutes; drain. Rinse thoroughly; drain completely. Bring vinegar, sugar and oils to a boil, stirring until sugar is dissolved; pour over rind in large kettle. Stir well until all rind is covered. Let stand for 24 hours. Boil for 7 to 10 minutes or until rind is tender. Pour into crock; stir each day for 5 days. Return to kettle; bring to a boil. Remove from heat; seal in hot sterilized jars.

EASY WATERMELON PICKLES

1 1/2 qt. watermelon rind, peeled
3 tbsp. salt
8 c. sugar
1 pt. cider vinegar
2 tbsp. whole cloves
2 tbsp. whole allspice
6 3-in. cinnamon sticks

Cut rind in 1-inch cubes. Soak rind overnight in salt and 1 quart water; drain. Cover with water; cook until tender. Drain. Boil 2 cups water, sugar and vinegar for 5 minutes. Tie spices in cheesecloth bag; add to liquid. Add rind; simmer, stirring frequently, for 45 minutes or until transparent. Remove bag; seal in hot sterilized jars.

Pineapple

Native to South America, the pineapple is a heavy fruit with a leafy crown that is shaped like a pine cone. It has succulent, fragrant flesh and refreshingly sweet juice. Color of the tough, horny rind may be deep yellow, brownish green, or mottled green and brown. The fibrous flesh may be white or deep yellow. Pineapples grow on low, cactus-like plants. Hawaii, Puerto Rico, and Mexico are major pineapple suppliers to the United States. The most widely grown variety of pineapple is the large, orange-yellow Smooth Cayenne or Cayenna from Hawaii and Mexico. Another important variety is the Red Spanish pineapple from Puerto Rico. Pineapples contain protein, calcium, and Vitamins A and C. (1 cup raw diced pineapple = 75 calories; 1 cup canned pineapple juice = 120 calories)

AVAILABILITY: Fresh pineapples are available year-round with greatest supplies from March to June. Smallest supplies are available in September. Canned pineapple and canned pineapple juice are sold year-round. Canned pineapple slices, chunks, tidbits, or spears and canned crushed pineapple usually packed in syrup are available year-round as are frozen pineapple chunks and frozen pineapple juice concentrate.

BUYING: Choose heavy, fragrant pineapples with flat, almost hollow eyes and small, compact crowns. Ripe pineapples are often, but not always, deep yellow. To test for ripeness, pull out one of the inner crown leaves. In desirably ripe fruit, the leaf will come out easily. Or, snap your thumb and forefinger against the fruit. Ripe fruit will sound dull and solid; immature fruit will have a hollow thud. Avoid discolored fruit or fruit with soft watery spots.

STORING: Allow immature fruit to ripen at room temperature. Do not expose to heat or sunlight. Refrigerate fresh ripe fruit and use within 2 days. Wrap to prevent other foods from absorbing odor. Keep unopened cans on kitchen shelf 1 year. Refrigerate opened cans up to 5 days. *To freeze*–Select fully ripe, firm fruit. Pare. Remove core and eyes. Slice, dice, crush or cut into cubes, wedges, or sticks. For unsweetened pack, fit fruit tightly in containers without sugar syrup. Leave 1/2-inch head space. For syrup pack, fit fruit tightly in containers. Cover with cold sugar syrup, leaving 1/2-inch head space for pint containers or 1-inch head space for quart containers. Seal, label, and freeze. For syrup, dissolve 7 cups sugar in 4 cups water. You may replace all or part of the water with pineapple juice. Freeze pineapple in refrigerator's freezer 3 months or in home freezer 1 year.

PREPARATION: *To peel*–Cut whole fruit in 4 to 6 wedges, depending on size, by slicing through from top to bottom. Leave crown attached to wedges. Remove flesh from each wedge by running a narrow bladed knife between rind and flesh. Don't try to come too close to rind, as eyes will be left in flesh. This procedure eliminates having to take out the eyes later. *To can*–Slice fruit. Pare, core, and remove eyes. Shred or cut into cubes. Pack, cover, and process according to instructions under CANNING.

SERVING: Serve fresh pineapple as is or with other fruits. Use in salads, conserves, preserves, and a variety of desserts. Pineapple juice makes an excellent iced drink and can also be used in fruit punches. Fresh pineapple and frozen pineapple juice cannot be added to gelatin salads without being cooked (brought to a boil) as they both contain a substance that inhibits gelling. Canned pineapple may be used as is.

FRIED PINEAPPLE

1 tsp. sugar
4 tbsp. flour
1 egg, slightly beaten
1/4 tsp. salt
2 tbsp. milk
6 slices pineapple, drained
1/2 c. bread crumbs

Combine sugar and flour. Combine egg, salt and milk. Dredge pineapple with flour mixture; dip in egg mixture. Cover with crumbs. Brown in small amount of hot fat. Yield: 6 servings.

SKEWERED PINEAPPLE SANDWICHES

Color photograph for this recipe on page 733.

1 8 1/4-oz. can pineapple slices
4 3-in. thick slices sourdough bread
1/3 c. butter
1/4 tsp. mixed Italian herbs
Dash of garlic powder
8 slices salami
8 slices mozzarella cheese
1 egg
1/3 c. milk
1/2 c. grated Parmesan cheese

Preheat oven to 400 degrees. Drain pineapple. Make 2 slits, 1 inch apart, in each bread slice from top to bottom, leaving bottom crust intact. Mix butter, Italian herbs and garlic powder; spread in slits. Wrap 1 salami slice around each mozzarella cheese slice. Place 1 pineapple slice in 1 slit and 2 salami-wrapped cheese slices in other slit in each slice of bread. Secure each sandwich with 2 bamboo skewers. Beat egg with milk in shallow dish; roll skewered sandwiches in egg mixture to lightly moisten surfaces. Place on buttered baking sheet; sprinkle with Parmesan cheese. Bake for about 15 minutes or until browned. Yield: 4 sandwiches.

PINEAPPLE-ON-A-SPIT

1 med. pineapple
15 to 20 whole cloves
1/2 c. maple syrup
1/2 tsp. cinnamon

Pare pineapple, leaving leafy crown intact. Remove pineapple eyes; replace with whole cloves. Center pineapple on spit. Mix syrup and cinnamon. Secure pineapple with holding fork. Wrap leafy end in foil. Let rotate over hot coals 4 inches from source of heat for 45 minutes, basting frequently with maple syrup mixture. Slice; serve hot.

LAYERED PINEAPPLE SALAD

1 pkg. lime gelatin
3/4 c. canned pineapple juice
1 c. crushed pineapple, drained
1 pkg. lemon gelatin
1/2 c. whipped cream
1 3-oz. package cream cheese

Dissolve lime gelatin in 1 cup hot water. Add pineapple juice and pineapple. Chill until firm. Dissolve lemon gelatin in 1 cup hot water. Add 3/4 cup cold water; chill until thickened slightly. Place bowl of lemon gelatin in larger bowl of ice and water. Whip gelatin until fluffy and thick. Add whipped cream to cream cheese gradually; whip until thick and smooth. Fold cheese mixture into whipped gelatin mixture; pour over the firm lime-pineapple layer. Chill until firm. Yield: 9 servings.

PINEAPPLE BLIZZARD

1 3-oz. package cream cheese
1/4 c. mayonnaise
15 marshmallows, quartered
2 tbsp. lemon juice
1 c. pineapple, drained and diced
1/4 c. dates, diced
1 c. whipped cream

Combine cheese and mayonnaise; mix until smooth. Add marshmallows, lemon juice, pineapple and dates; stir thoroughly. Fold in whipped cream. Pour into freezer tray. Freeze.

PINK PINEAPPLE SALAD

1 med. can crushed pineapple
2 c. sugar
2 tbsp. lemon juice
2 pkg. cherry gelatin
2 c. grated American cheese
1/2 pt. cream, whipped

Combine pineapple, sugar and lemon juice; bring to a boil. Pour over gelatin; stir until dissolved. Add 1 cup cold water; chill until partially set. Add cheese; fold in whipped cream. Chill until firm. Yield: 10-12 servings.

GOLDEN PINEAPPLE SALAD MOLD

1 1-lb. 4 1/2-oz. can pineapple tidbits
1/4 c. lemon juice
1/2 tsp. dry mustard
1 tsp. seasoned salt
1 egg, beaten
1 12-oz. can apricot-pineapple nectar
2 env. unflavored gelatin
2 tbsp. mayonnaise
2 c. whipped cream

Drain pineapple, reserving syrup. Combine reserved syrup, lemon juice, mustard, salt and egg. Combine nectar and 1/2 cup water in saucepan; sprinkle gelatin over liquid. Heat until gelatin dissolves. Add egg mixture gradually. Cook over low heat for several minutes, stirring constantly, until mixture begins to thicken. Remove from heat, blend in mayonnaise. Chill until thickened. Fold in whipped cream and pineapple tidbits. Turn into 5-cup mold; chill until firm. Turn out on serving plate. Garnish with additional pineapple tidbits and mint sprigs. Yield: 6 servings.

Golden Pineapple Salad Mold . . . Apricot nectar combines with pineapple in an elegant salad.

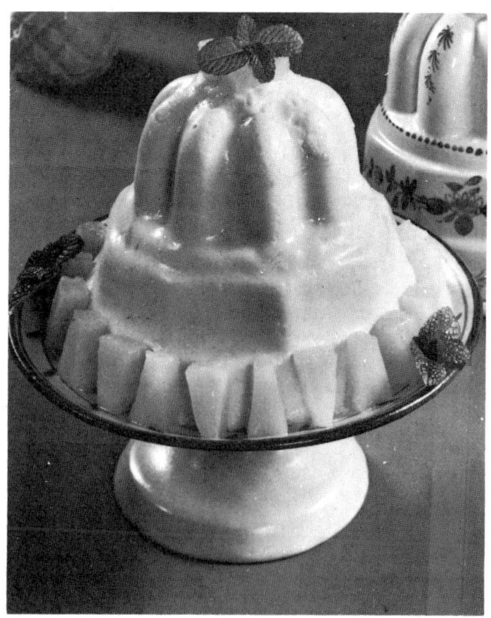

PINEAPPLE SURPRISE

1 pkg. lemon gelatin
1 sm. can crushed pineapple
Juice of 1/2 lemon
1/2 c. sugar
1/2 c. chopped pimento
3/4 c. grated mild cheese
1/2 c. heavy cream, whipped
Mayonnaise
Dash of paprika

Dissolve gelatin in 1 cup boiling water. Mix pineapple, lemon juice and sugar in pan; bring to a boil. Cook for 3 minutes. Stir pineapple mixture into gelatin. Refrigerate until partially set. Add pimento, cheese and whipped cream; fold together. Pour into individual molds or 1 large mold; chill until firm. Top with mayonnaise and paprika.

PINEAPPLE-ORANGE SALAD

2 tbsp. flour
1 c. pineapple juice
1/4 c. butter
1/8 c. sugar
Pinch of salt
1 egg, well beaten
4 slices pineapple, finely cut
2 tbsp. lemon juice
2 orange sections, finely cut
1/4 c. chopped nuts
10 marshmallows, diced
8 maraschino cherries
1 pt. whipped cream

Make paste of flour and 1/4 cup pineapple juice. Add remaining juice gradually, stirring constantly. Add butter, sugar and salt. Cook in double boiler for 10 minutes. Add egg; cook for several minutes longer, stirring constantly. Cool. Add pineapple, lemon juice, oranges, nuts, marshmallows and cherries; fold in whipped cream. Pour in refrigerator tray; freeze. Yield: 8 servings.

PINEAPPLE-WINE SUPREME

1 No. 2 can pineapple chunks
2 tbsp. gelatin
1/2 c. sugar
1/4 c. lemon juice
3/4 c. pecans, broken
1 1/4 c. sherry

Drain pineapple; reserve juice. Soften gelatin in 1/2 cup cold water. Add enough water to reserved juice to make 1 1/4 cups liquid. Bring juice mixture to a boil; add softened gelatin. Stir until dissolved. Combine pineapple chunks, sugar, lemon juice, pecans and sherry; pour into mold. Pour enough gelatin over to hold in place. Chill until firm. Pour in remaining gelatin mixture. Chill until firm. Yield: 6-8 servings.

RED AND WHITE SALAD

1 pkg. lemon gelatin
10 marshmallows, diced
1 sm. can crushed pineapple
1 sm. package cream cheese, softened
1/4 c. salad dressing
1 c. whipping cream, whipped
1/4 c. chopped nuts
1 pkg. strawberry gelatin

Prepare lemon gelatin according to package directions; add marshmallows to hot gelatin. Stir well; cool. Add pineapple, cream cheese, salad dressing, cream, and nuts. Pour into mold; chill until firm. Prepare strawberry gelatin according to package directions; pour over top of firm gelatin. Chill until firm. Yield: 9-12 servings.

PINEAPPLE-OATMEAL MUFFINS

1 sm. can crushed pineapple
1 c. quick-cooking oats
1/2 c. sour cream
1/3 c. shortening
1/3 c. (packed) brown sugar
1 tsp. grated orange peel
1 egg, beaten
1 1/4 c. sifted flour
1 tsp. baking powder
1/2 tsp. soda
1 tsp. salt

Combine pineapple, oats and sour cream; let stand for 15 minutes. Cream shortening, sugar and orange peel together thoroughly; beat in egg. Sift flour with baking powder, soda and salt. Add to creamed mixture alternately with oatmeal mixture. Spoon into well-greased large muffin pans. Bake at 400 degrees for 25 minutes. Yield: 1 dozen.

HAWAIIAN CAKE

1 c. margarine
2 c. sugar
4 eggs, beaten
1/2 tsp. salt
2 tsp. baking powder
1 sm. can crushed pineapple
1 can flaked coconut
1 c. chopped pecans
2 tsp. vanilla
2 tsp. rum flavoring
4 c. graham cracker crumbs

Cream margarine, sugar and eggs thoroughly. Add salt and baking powder. Drain 1/4 cup juice from pineapple; reserve juice. Add pineapple, coconut, pecans, vanilla, flavoring and crumbs; mix well. Pour into waxed paper-lined tube pan. Bake at 350 degrees for 1 hour and 30 minutes or until cake tests done. Remove from pan; pour reserved juice over cake while warm.

PINEAPPLE UPSIDE-DOWN CAKE

1 c. (packed) brown sugar
2 tbsp. butter, melted
1 can sliced pineapple
2 c. sugar
Flour
2 eggs
2 tsp. baking powder
2 c. cream
1 tsp. vanilla

Sprinkle brown sugar and butter in bottom of iron skillet or pan. Drain pineapple; reserve juice. Layer pineapple over brown sugar. Mix 1 cup sugar, 2 cups flour, 1 egg, baking powder, 1 cup cream and vanilla thoroughly; pour over pineapple. Bake at 350 degrees for 20 minutes or until cake tests done. Invert on plate. Combine remaining sugar and 2 tablespoons flour; mix well. Heat remaining cream and reserved juice in saucepan; stir in sugar mixture until blended. Cook until slightly thickened. Beat egg well; add small amount of cream mixture to egg, stirring constantly. Return egg mixture to saucepan; cook, stirring constantly, until thickened. Serve sauce with cake.

PINEAPPLE-TOPPED CAKE

4 c. sugar
Butter
3 eggs
2 1/2 c. flour
3 tsp. baking powder
1/2 c. pineapple juice
2 tsp. vanilla
1 No. 2 can crushed pineapple
1 c. milk
1/4 tsp. salt

Cream 1 1/2 cups sugar and 3/4 cup butter; add eggs, one at a time, beating thoroughly after each addition. Combine flour and baking powder; add to creamed mixture alternately with pineapple juice, 1/2 cup water and vanilla. Mix well. Pour into 13 x 9 x 2-inch pan. Bake at 325 degrees for 35 minutes. Drain pineapple; reserve juice. Combine remaining sugar, milk, 1 teaspoon butter and salt in saucepan; cook, stirring frequently, until sugar is dissolved. Remove from heat; beat until cooled slightly. Add pineapple. Pour small amount of reserved juice over cake. Cover top and sides of cake with topping.

PINEAPPLE-COCONUT CAKE

2 1/2 c. crushed pineapple
3 c. sugar
2 1/2 c. sifted flour
2 tsp. soda
1/2 tsp. salt
2 lge. eggs
1 c. margarine
1 c. evaporated milk
1 c. flaked coconut
1/2 c. chopped nuts

Preheat oven to 350 degrees. Combine pineapple with juice, 1 1/2 cups sugar, flour, soda, salt and eggs in large bowl; mix for 3 minutes with spoon. Grease and line 8 x 12-inch pan with 2 thicknesses waxed paper. Pour batter into pan. Bake for 30 minutes. Cool in pan for 15 minutes; turn out on rack. Combine remaining sugar, margarine and milk in heavy saucepan; bring to a boil. Stir once; boil for 4 minutes without stirring. Remove from heat; stir in coconut and nuts. Let cool; beat until of desired spreading consistency. Frost cake; chill. Yield: 12-15 servings.

PINEAPPLE ROLL

1 c. sifted cake flour
1 1/2 tsp. baking powder
1/4 tsp. salt
3 eggs
1 c. sugar
1 tsp. grated lemon rind
1/2 tsp. vanilla
Confectioners' sugar
Pineapple jam

Sift flour, baking powder and salt. Have eggs at room temperature. Beat eggs in large mixer bowl for 10 minutes or until light and lemony. Add sugar gradually, beating constantly. Add lemon rind and vanilla. Fold in dry ingredients, 1/4 cup at a time. Add water in thin steady stream, folding into batter. Line 10 x 15-inch jelly roll pan with greased waxed paper. Pour batter into pan. Bake at 375 degrees for 12 to 15 minutes. Cut crusty edges from cake; turn cake out on towel sprinkled with confectioners' sugar. Remove paper; roll cake in towel. Cool. Unroll; spread with pineapple jam. Reroll. Sprinkle with confectioners' sugar. Yield: 12 servings.

DELICIOUS PINEAPPLE SQUARES

4 eggs, separated
1 c. sugar
1 c. grated pineapple
1/2 pkg. lemon gelatin
1 c. crushed vanilla wafers
1/2 c. melted butter

Beat egg yolks until lemon colored. Add 1/2 cup sugar and pineapple. Place in saucepan over low heat, stirring constantly, until thickened. Remove from heat; add gelatin. Stir until gelatin is dissolved. Set in pan of cold water or ice cubes to cool. Beat egg whites until stiff peaks form. Add remaining sugar; fold into pineapple mixture. Cool. Combine crumbs and butter; place 2/3 of the crumbs in 9 x 9-inch pan. Pour in pudding mixture; sprinkle remaining crumbs on top. Chill; cut in squares. Yield: 12-15 servings.

FRENCH PINEAPPLE

1 lb. vanilla wafers, crushed
1/2 c. butter
2 c. powdered sugar
4 eggs
1 c. heavy cream
1 c. crushed pineapple
1 sm. bottle maraschino cherries, chopped
1 1/2 c. broken pecans

Line shallow pan with half the wafer crumbs. Beat butter until light; add sugar gradually, beating constantly. Beat eggs until light; add to sugar mixture, beating until smooth. Spread sugar mixture over crumbs. Whip cream until stiff peaks form; fold in pineapple, maraschino cherries and pecans. Pour pineapple mixture over sugar mixture; top with remaining crumbs. Refrigerate for 24 hours. Yield: 8-10 servings.

FROSTED DELIGHT

1 lge. can crushed pineapple
1 env. unflavored gelatin
1/3 c. mint-flavored apple jelly
1 c. whipping cream
1 tsp. powdered sugar

Drain pineapple, reserving 1/2 cup juice. Blend gelatin and pineapple juice; bring to a boil, stirring constantly. Add jelly; stir over medium heat until melted. Mix in pineapple; cool. Whip cream with confectioners' sugar until stiff peaks form. Fold whipped cream into jelly mixture. Pour into freezer tray; refrigerate until firm or freeze until firm but not solid. Garnish with mint. Yield: 8 servings.

FROZEN PINEAPPLE DESSERT

1 whole pineapple
Brown sugar
Raisins
Dates
Maraschino cherries chopped
Nuts
Pineapple sherbet

Remove top from pineapple. Hollow out shell. Place shell in freezer; reserve top. Remove hard core from pineapple pieces; chop in small pieces. Add enough brown sugar to sweeten pineapple slightly; add fruits and nuts. Let mixture stand for 1 hour. Layer pineapple mixture with sherbet in frozen shell. Return to freezer immediately. Freeze until firm; place top on pineapple. Serve whole pineapple on bed of crushed ice.

PINEAPPLE-COCONUT FLUFF

1 pkg. orange gelatin
1 4-oz. package cream cheese, softened
1 sm. can crushed pineapple
3/4 c. flaked coconut

Dissolve gelatin in 1 1/3 cups hot water. Add cream cheese. Whip until blended and bubbly. Stir in pineapple and coconut. Pour into greased mold; chill until firm. Yield: 4-6 servings.

DREAMY PINEAPPLE PIE

1 c. sugar
1/2 c. flour
1 sm. can crushed pineapple
Salt to taste
3 eggs, separated
1 baked 9-in. pie shell
Frozen dessert topping

Mix sugar, flour, pineapple, salt and egg yolks, blending well; add 1 1/2 cups boiling water gradually, stirring constantly. Place in double boiler; cook until thickened. Cool. Beat egg whites until stiff peaks form; fold into pineapple mixture. Pour into pie shell; spread topping over filling. Yield: 6-8 servings.

RICH PINEAPPLE PIE

2 c. sugar
1/2 c. margarine
6 eggs
1 tbsp. flour
1 c. flaked coconut
1 c. crushed pineapple, drained
1 unbaked 9-in. pie shell

Cream sugar and margarine together. Add one egg at a time, beating well after each addition. Add flour. Mix in coconut and pineapple gradually. Pour into pie shell. Bake at 350 degrees for 35 minutes. Yield: 8 servings.

PINEAPPLE DROP COOKIES

2/3 c. shortening
1 1/4 c. (packed) brown sugar
2 eggs
1 tsp. vanilla
3/4 c. crushed pineapple
2 c. flour
1 1/2 tsp. baking powder
1/4 tsp. soda
1 tsp. salt

Cream shortening, sugar, eggs and vanilla together. Add pineapple. Add dry ingredients. Drop by teaspoonfuls onto greased cookie sheet. Bake at 375 degrees for 10 minutes. Yield: 4 dozen.

PINEAPPLE PARFAIT

1 20-oz. can pineapple chunks
1 3-oz. package lemon gelatin
1 c. evaporated milk
2 tbsp. lemon juice
1 c. chopped celery
1/2 c. chopped nuts
1/3 c. mayonnaise

Drain pineapple; reserve syrup. Bring 1 cup pineapple syrup to a boil; pour over gelatin. Stir to dissolve. Chill until thickened. Chill milk in freezer until crystals form; whip until stiff peaks form. Add lemon juice; whip until stiff peaks form. Add all remaining ingredients to gelatin; fold into whipped milk mixture with pineapple chunks. Place in tall glasses; chill until firm. Yield: 6 servings.

PINEAPPLE POLYNESIAN TORTE

2 13 1/4-oz. cans pineapple tidbits
1 1-lb. 1-oz. package pound cake mix
1/2 c. sugar
3 tbsp. cornstarch
1/8 tsp. salt
1 egg, beaten
1 tbsp. butter
1/4 tsp. grated lemon peel
1 tbsp. lemon juice
2 2-oz. envelopes whipped topping mix

Drain pineapple, reserving syrup. Prepare cake batter according to package directions. Turn into greased 9-inch springform pan. Bake in 325-degree oven for about 50 minutes or until cake tests done. Cool. Split into 3 layers. Combine reserved pineapple syrup with sugar, cornstarch and salt. Cook, stirring constantly, until mixture boils and thickens. Stir small amount of hot mixture into egg; return to remaining cooked mixture. Stir briskly; cook for 60 seconds longer over low heat. Remove from heat. Blend in butter, lemon peel, lemon juice and pineapple tidbits. Cool. Prepare topping mix according to package directions. Place cake layers together, spreading pineapple mixture and topping mixture on each layer.

Pineapple Polynesian Torte . . . Prepare this spectacular dessert with mixes and canned pineapple.

PINEAPPLE-RAISIN COOKIES

Color photograph for this recipe on page 490.

1 c. (packed) golden brown sugar
1/2 c. soft butter
1 egg
1 tsp. vanilla
3/4 c. undrained crushed pineapple
1/2 c. raisins
2 c. sifted all-purpose flour
1 tsp. baking powder
1/2 tsp. soda
1/2 tsp. salt
1/2 c. chopped walnuts

Combine brown sugar, butter, egg and vanilla in bowl; beat until fluffy. Add pineapple and raisins. Sift flour with baking powder, soda and salt. Add to pineapple mixture; mix well. Stir in walnuts. Drop by spoonfuls 2 inches apart on greased cookie sheet. Bake in 375-degree oven for 12 to 15 minutes or until lightly browned. Yield: 4 dozen.

PINEAPPLE SPONGE

1 can crushed pineapple
1 pkg. lemon gelatin
6 marshmallows, cut up
1/2 pt. cream, whipped

Drain pineapple; reserve juice. Add enough water to reserved juice to make 1 cup liquid. Bring to a boil; add pineapple, gelatin and marshmallows, blending well. Chill until partially set; beat with rotary beater. Fold in whipped cream; chill until firm.

PINEAPPLE SURPRISE

6 eggs, beaten
3 tbsp. vinegar
1 tbsp. sugar
1 tsp. salt
1 tsp. mustard
4 c. whipped cream
2 lge. cans crushed pineapple, drained
1 lb. marshmallows, diced

Combine eggs with 3 tablespoons water, vinegar, sugar, salt and mustard in double boiler. Cook until thick, stirring constantly. Cool slightly. Fold in whipped cream, pineapple and marshmallows. Pour into 9 x 12-inch glass pan. Chill overnight. Yield: 14 servings.

PINEAPPLE TURNOVERS

1 c. butter, softened
1 c. cream cheese, softened
2 c. flour
1 can pineapple pie filling

Mix butter, cream cheese and flour; blend well. Chill for overnight. Roll pastry 1/8 inch thick. Cut into rounds. Place 1 tablespoon pie filling on 1 round; cover with round. Brush edge with small amount of water. Seal edges. Prick holes in top with fork. Place in baking pan. Bake at 350 degrees for 30 minutes. Yield: 18 servings.

CHILLED PINEAPPLE PUDDING

1 c. powdered sugar
2/3 c. butter, melted
2 eggs
1 lb. vanilla wafers, crushed
1 No. 2 1/2 can crushed pineapple, drained
1 c. chopped pecans
1 pt. whipping cream

Mix sugar, butter and eggs. Pat layer of crumbs into baking dish; pour sugar mixture over crumbs. Spread pineapple over sugar mixture. Sprinkle pecans over pineapple. Spoon whipped cream over pecans; top with crumbs. Chill for several hours.

PINEAPPLE-WALNUT PUDDING

1 sm. package vanilla pudding mix
1 1/2 c. unsweetened pineapple juice
1 c. heavy cream, whipped
1/2 c. broken walnuts

Prepare pudding mix according to package directions, using 1 1/2 cups pineapple juice instead of milk. Cool thoroughly. Beat until smooth; fold in whipped cream and walnuts. Chill. Garnish pudding with walnut halves. Yield: 4 servings.

SCALLOPED PINEAPPLE

1 c. margarine
2 c. sugar
3 eggs
4 c. large soft bread cubes
1 No. 2 1/2 can crushed pineapple
1/4 c. milk

Cream margarine and sugar; add eggs, bread cubes, pineapple and milk, blending well. Place in greased oblong baking dish. Bake at 325 degrees for 1 hour. Yield: 10-12 servings.

Pistachio

QUESILLO

3 c. pineapple juice
3 c. sugar
12 eggs
1/2 c. raisins

Bring pineapple juice and sugar to a boil, stirring until sugar is dissolved; cook until mixture is reduced to 2 cups. Reserve 1 cup syrup. Beat eggs until light and fluffy; add to syrup. Stir in raisins. Pour into 2-quart mold. Place the mold in pan of water. Bake at 350 degrees for 1 hour or until set. Cool. Place on platter; pour reserved syrup over custard. Garnish with pineapple.

SOUR CREAM NUTS

1 c. sugar
1/3 c. sour cream
1 tsp. light corn syrup
2 tbsp. butter
1 tsp. vanilla
2 c. pistachio nuts

Combine sugar, sour cream and syrup in saucepan; cover. Bring to a boil over low heat; cook to soft-ball stage. Add butter and vanilla; cool to lukewarm. Beat until mixture loses gloss. Add nuts; stir until coated. Spread on foil. Break apart when cool. Yield: 16 servings.

GERMAN NUT CAKE

1 c. sugar
5 eggs, separated
1 whole egg
1 c. pistachios, ground
1 tsp. vanilla
1/2 tsp. cinnamon
Pinch of salt
1/3 c. butter
2 c. confectioners' sugar
Sherry

Beat sugar, egg yolks and whole egg; add pistachios, vanilla, cinnamon and salt, mixing well. Beat egg whites until stiff peaks form; fold into batter. Pour into greased waxed paper-lined 10-inch pan. Bake at 350 degrees for 35 minutes. Cool slightly; remove from pan to cake plate. Cream butter and confectioners' sugar together; add enough sherry to make smooth icing. Fill and frost cake. Yield: 16 servings.

PISTACHIO BUNDT CAKE

1 pkg. yellow cake mix
4 eggs
1 c. orange juice
1/2 c. cooking oil
1 box instant pistachio pudding mix
3/4 c. chocolate syrup

Place cake mix, eggs, orange juice, oil and pudding mix in mixing bowl. Mix at low speed with electric mixer for 1 minute; mix at high speed for 3 minutes or until well-blended. Pour 2/3 of the batter into well-greased bundt pan. Mix chocolate syrup into remaining batter; pour batter in pan. Run knife through batter to marbleize. Bake at 350 degrees for 1 hour; cool in pan for 10 minutes. Invert on cake plate. Yield: 10 servings.

PISTACHIO NUT ROLL

3/4 c. sifted flour
1/2 tsp. baking powder
1/2 tsp. salt
2 sq. unsweetened chocolate
5 eggs, at room temperature
Sugar
1/4 tsp. soda
2 tbsp. confectioners' sugar
Pistachio Filling
Chocolate Frosting
3 tbsp. chopped pistachio nuts

Sift flour with baking powder and salt. Melt chocolate over hot water. Beat eggs until thick and light in color. Add 3/4 cup sugar gradually, 1 tablespoon at a time, beating well after each addition. Add flour mixture all at once; blend in with wire whip. Add 1/4 cup cold water, soda and 2 tablespoons sugar. Stir until thick and smooth. Stir quickly into batter. Pour into greased, waxed paper-lined 15 1/2 x 10 1/2 x 1-inch pan. Bake at 350 degrees for 20 minutes. Turn cake out immediately on towel sprinkled with confectioners' sugar. Remove waxed paper; trim off edges. Roll up at once, rolling towel with cake to keep cake from sticking together. Cool on cake rack for 30 minutes. Unroll carefully. Fill roll with Pistacio Filling; reroll. Spread with Chocolate Frosting; sprinkle with pistachio nuts. Freeze. Remove from freezer 30 minutes before serving.

Pistachio Filling

1 1/4 c. whipped cream
1 tsp. vanilla
8 drops green food coloring
1/2 tsp. almond extract
2 tbsp. confectioners' sugar
4 drops yellow food coloring

Combine ingredients and beat until just thick enough to spread, but still glossy.

Chocolate Frosting

2 sq. unsweetened chocolate
1/4 c. soft butter
1 c. sifted confectioners' sugar
1 egg yolk, slightly beaten
2 tbsp. milk
1/2 tsp. vanilla

Melt chocolate over hot water. Remove from heat; cool to lukewarm. Cream butter. Add chocolate, blending well. Blend in 1/2 cup of the sugar. Add egg yolk gradually, creaming well. Add remaining confectioners' sugar alternately with milk, beating after each addition until smooth. Blend in vanilla.

CHINESE CANDY

1 6-oz. package chocolate chips
1 6-oz. package butterscotch chips
1 can Chinese noodles
1 c. salted pistachio nuts

Melt chocolate and butterscotch chips over hot water. Pour over noodles and nuts. Drop from teaspoon onto waxed paper; cool. Yield: 1 pound.

PISTACHIO BUTTER COOKIES

1 c. sifted flour
1/3 c. sugar
2/3 c. pistachio nuts, ground
Soft butter
1 sq. chocolate
1/3 c. sifted confectioners' sugar
1 egg yolk

Sift together flour and sugar into large bowl; add pistachios. Blend in 1/2 cup butter with pastry blender to form dough. Chill for 2 hours. Roll out on floured pastry cloth to 1/8-inch thickness. Cut into rounds with floured 2 1/4-inch cutter. Place on baking sheet. Bake at 375 degrees for 7 minutes or until light golden brown. Melt chocolate over hot water; cool. Cream 1 tablespoon butter and sugar. Add egg yolk and chocolate; blend well. Spread cookies with chocolate frosting; sprinkle with slivered nuts, if desired. Yield: 3 dozen.

PISTACHIO CRISPS

2 eggs
2 1/4 c. (packed) brown sugar
2 c. sifted cake flour
1/2 tsp. baking powder
1/8 tsp. salt
1 1/2 c. coarsely chopped pistachio nuts
1 tsp. vanilla

Beat eggs until light; Add sugar gradually. Sift flour, baking powder and salt together; add sugar mixture, beating well. Add pistachios and vanilla. Chill for several hours or until dough is easy to handle. Dust hands with powdered sugar. Roll dough in hands to make sticks 2 1/2 inches long. Place on greased cookie sheet 2 inches apart. Bake at 350 degrees for 15 minutes. Remove from cookie sheet immediately; place on wire racks to cool. Yield: 60 cookies.

HUNGARIAN PISTACHIO BARS

1 3/4 c. (packed) brown sugar
1/2 c. butter
1 tsp. vanilla
1 1/4 c. flour
1 1/2 tsp. baking powder
Chopped nuts
2 egg whites

Combine 3/4 cup brown sugar, butter, vanilla, flour and baking powder; mix well. Press into 9 x 13-inch pan. Sprinkle with nuts. Beat egg whites until stiff peaks form; add remaining brown sugar. Beat until mixed thoroughly. Spread over crumb mixture. Bake at 350 degrees for 30 minutes. Yield: 12-16 servings.

PISTACHIO CREAM TARTS

6 egg yolks
1 c. sugar
1 env. unflavored gelatin
2 c. heavy cream, whipped
Chopped pistachio nuts
1/2 c. dark rum
16 baked tart shells
Bittersweet chocolate

Beat egg yolks until light; beat in sugar. Soften gelatin in 1/2 cup cold water; dissolve over low heat. Cool. Stir gelatin mixture into egg mixture; fold in whipped cream and nuts. Blend in rum. Chill until partially thickened; spoon into tart shells. Chill until firm. Sprinkle with chocolate and additional nuts.

SUGARED PISTACHIO BALLS

2 1/2 c. vanilla wafer crumbs
2 tbsp. cocoa
1 1/2 c. confectioners' sugar
1 c. finely chopped pistachio nuts
1/3 c. bourbon
3 tbsp. light corn syrup

Combine crumbs, cocoa, 1 cup confectioners' sugar and pistachios in medium bowl. Add bourbon and corn syrup; mix well. Shape into 1-inch balls; roll in remaining confectioners' sugar. Store in loosely covered container for 2 days. Yield: 3 1/2 dozen.

Pizza

Pizza, the famed dish that originated in Naples, Italy, is an open-faced pie that has become extremely popular throughout the United States. A thin layer of yeast dough is rolled to fit a large, round pizza pan or other shallow baking pan. The dough/crust is topped or spread with various tasty mixtures and baked until crisp. Individual pizzas can be made by using flattened biscuits, biscuit halves, or English muffins as the crust.

INGREDIENTS: The dough for pizza crust consists of flour, water, yeast, and shortening. Toppings include combinations of tomatoes and tomato sauce; herbs and seasonings; mozzarella, Parmesan, and Romano cheese; anchovies, sausage, pepperoni, and ground beef; mushrooms, olives, and onions.

SERVING: Cut into wedge-shaped serving pieces. Always serve pizza piping hot.

ENGLISH MUFFIN PIZZA

3 English muffins
3/4 c. tomatoes, drained
6 slices American cheese
Salt
Cayenne pepper
Grated Parmesan cheese
Oregano
Vegetable oil

Pull muffins apart; toast lightly. Place in shallow baking pan. Chop tomatoes; spread on muffins. Top with cheese. Sprinkle with salt, cayenne pepper, grated cheese and oregano. Place one teaspoon oil over each muffin. Bake approximately 15 minutes at 400 degrees.

JIFFY PIZZAS

1 c. catsup
1/2 tsp. salt
1/2 tsp. Worcestershire sauce
1/2 tsp. garlic salt
2 drops of hot sauce
1/2 tsp. thyme
1 can refrigerator biscuits
1/2 lb. ground beef, cooked
3/4 c. grated cheese

Combine catsup, salt, Worcestershire sauce, garlic salt, hot sauce and thyme; mix for sauce. Roll each biscuit to 4-inch circle. Cover circles with ground beef; spread with sauce. Sprinkle with cheese. Place on baking sheet. Bake at 425 degrees for 10 minutes.

LITTLE PIZZAS

1 can refrigerator biscuits
1 sm. can tomato sauce
1 lb. ground beef, cooked
1 tsp.salt
1/2 tsp. pepper
1/2 c. chopped onions
1/2 c. Parmesan cheese

Preheat oven to 475 degrees. Roll biscuits out to 1/4-inch thickness. Spread half the tomato sauce over biscuits. Cover with a layer of beef; sprinkle seasonings and onions and cheese over beef. Top with remaining tomato sauce. Place on greased cookie sheet. Bake for 20 to 25 minutes.

NO-CRUST PIZZA

1 lb. ground sirloin
1 tsp. salt
1/2 tsp. pepper
2 tbsp. A-1 sauce
1 8-oz. can tomato sauce
1/2 c. finely diced onion
2-oz. grated Parmesan cheese
1/2 tsp. oregano

Mix sirloin, salt, pepper and A-1 sauce. Pack lightly into a greased 9-inch pie pan. Pour tomato sauce over sirloin; sprinkle with onion, cheese and oregano. Bake 25 minutes at 350 degrees.

Cheese and Sausage Pizza . . . Canned biscuits make the crust of this all-time favorite pizza.

CHEESE AND SAUSAGE PIZZA

2 c. diced salami
1 8-oz. can tomato sauce
1 6-oz. can tomato paste
1/3 c. finely chopped onion
1 1/2 tsp. oregano
1 tsp. basil
1 tsp. garlic salt
1/2 tsp. sugar
2 8-oz. cans refrigerator biscuits
2 6-oz. packages mozzarella cheese
2/3 c. shredded Parmesan cheese

Combine salami, tomato sauce, tomato paste, onion, oregano, basil, garlic salt and sugar; mix well. Roll biscuits on floured surface into 5-inch rounds. Fit rolled biscuits over bottom and sides of two 12-inch pizza pans. Bake in 400-degree oven for about 5 minutes or until slightly browned. Cover crusts with 1/2 of the mozzarella cheese. Spread tomato mixture over cheese. Top with remaining mozzarella cheese; sprinkle with Parmesan cheese. Return to oven; bake for about 15 minutes or until crust is done and cheese is melted. Garnish with parsley if desired.

MINI PIZZAS

Refrigerator biscuits
Tomato paste
Anchovy fillets
Oregano
Mozzarella cheese, cut into sm. squares

Flatten each biscuit to 1/4-inch thickness. Place on cookie sheets. Spread with tomato paste; top with anchovy fillets. Sprinkle with oregano. Top with cheese. Bake at 400 degrees for 6 to 8 minutes or until lightly browned. Pepperoni, small shrimp, onion slices, sliced olives, sliced frankfurters, pimentos and chopped green pepper may be used as toppings instead of anchovy fillets.

PIE PAN PIZZA

1 tbsp. prepared mustard
2/3 c. milk
2 c. prepared biscuit mix
2 No. 2 cans tomatoes
1 tsp. oregano
1 tsp. garlic powder
3 med. green peppers
2 lb. hot pork sausage
2 c. Cheddar cheese, cubed
1 tbsp. grated Parmesan cheese

Stir mustard into milk; blend with biscuit mix. Knead for 1 minute; divide dough into four parts. Line 9-inch pie pans with dough. Combine tomatoes, oregano and garlic in saucepan. Slice green peppers thin; add to tomato mixture. Simmer, covered, until peppers are tender. Crumble pork sausage into skillet; saute, stirring frequently, until thoroughly cooked and browned. Drain off excess fat. Combine sausage with tomato mixture; spoon into prepared crusts. Top with Cheddar cheese; sprinkle with Parmesan cheese. Bake in 375-degree oven 25 to 30 minutes or until crust is golden brown.

PIZZA BITES

1 lb. bulk pork sausage
1/4 c. catsup
Oregano to taste
Party rye bread slices
1 lb. mozzarella cheese, grated

Saute sausage in skillet until thoroughly cooked and browned; drain off excess fat. Combine sausage, catsup and oregano; spread over bread slices. Sprinkle cheese over sausage mixture. Broil 3 to 4 inches from source of heat for 5 minutes or until cheese is melted and lightly browned. Serve immediately.

PIZZA FROM SCRATCH

1/2 c. tomato paste
1 c. canned tomatoes
2 tbsp. chopped onion
1/8 tsp. celery seed
1/2 tsp. oregano
1 tbsp. chili powder
1/4 tsp. ground cumin
1 pkg. yeast
2 tbsp. shortening
2 tbsp. sugar
2 tsp. salt
1 beaten egg
Flour
Cornmeal
Melted butter
1 lb. ground beef
10 slices mozzarella cheese
1 tsp. sweet basil

Combine first 7 ingredients for sauce; cook until thickened. Strain; cool. Dissolve yeast in 1/4 cup warm water. Pour 1 cup boiling water over shortening, sugar and 1 teaspoon salt. Cool to lukewarm. Add egg and yeast mixture. Mix in enough flour to form soft dough. Let rise until doubled in bulk. Roll out thin; place on cornmeal-covered baking sheet. Brush with melted butter. Brown ground beef; add remaining salt. Spread sauce over dough; add ground beef. Top with cheese; sprinkle with sweet basil. Bake pizza at 400 degrees for 15 minutes or until cheese is melted and crust lightly browned.

PIZZA SPECIAL

1 c. biscuit mix
1/4 lb. sausage
1/2 lb. ground beef
3 oz. pepperoni
1 8-oz. can tomato sauce
1 tbsp. sugar
1 tbsp. mustard
1/2 tsp. salt
Dash of pepper
1/4 tsp. oregano
1/4 tsp. anise
1/4 tsp. fennel seed
1 tbsp. dried onion
1/4 c. grated Cheddar cheese
3 tbsp. Parmesan cheese

Preheat oven to 425 degrees. Combine biscuit mix and 1/3 cup water to form dough. Spread dough thinly in 12-inch round pizza pan. Prick with fork. Bake 5 to 7 minutes. Remove from oven. Reduce heat to 375 degrees. Brown sausage and ground beef; drain. Combine meats with tomato sauce, sugar, mustard, salt, pepper, herbs and onion. Bring to a boil; simmer for 10 minutes. Spread meat mixture over dough; sprinkle with Cheddar cheese. Top with Parmesan cheese. Bake for 10 minutes.

Plum

Plums are round smooth-skinned, reddish-purple to yellowish-green fruit that contain a single, flattened pit. The flesh is thick and juicy with either a sweet or tart taste. Plums grow on a tree in the rose family that can thrive in most areas of the United States. All plums belong to one of two categories: clingstone or freestone. The single pit of *clingstone* plums adheres to the flesh; that of *freestone* plums separates easily from the flesh. Clingstone plums are usually enjoyed as a raw, fresh fruit. Freestone plums are also known as fresh prunes or prune-plums. They are suitable for drying because of their firm flesh and high sugar and acid content. They can be dried without fermenting when the pit is left in. Plums supply Vitamins A and C, calcium and carbohydrates. (1 2-inch raw plum = 25 calories)

KINDS: There are three main varieties of plums: European, Japanese, and American. European varieties may be red, yellow, blue, or purple. They include Damson, Mirabelle, Greengage and the Agen and Italian prune-plums that may be dried. Japanese plums are usually red or yellow in color and somewhat oval in shape. Included in this group are the Santa Rosa, Duarte, Kelsey, and Wickson. American plums usually grow wild and may be too sour to eat raw. A familiar variety found along the Atlantic seaboard is the beach plum that is made into jelly.

AVAILABILITY: Fresh clingstone plums are available from May through September with peak supplies during July and August. Fresh freestone prune-plums are available from July through October with September the peak month. Canned plums in sugar- and water-pack are sold year-round, as are plum preserves, plum butter, and wild beach plum jelly.

BUYING: Select plump, clean, smooth, fresh plums and prune-plums that yield gently to pressure. They should be firm but not hard. The fruit should be full-colored but color alone is not an index of ripeness. Look for a softening at the tip to indicate mature fruit. Avoid cracked, shriveled, softened, leaky, or sunburned (brownish) fruit.

STORING: Allow underripe plums to ripen at room temperature. Then refrigerate the fruit for 3 to 5 days. Store unopened cans of plums on the kitchen shelf 1 year. *To freeze*—Use firm, ripe, unblemished fruit. Halve or quarter. Remove pits. Pack plums into freezer containers. Mix 5 cups sugar in 4 cups water and add 1/4 teaspoon ascorbic acid per cup of syrup. Heat until sugar is dissolved. Cool. Cover fruit with cooled syrup, leaving 1/2-inch head space. Seal, label, and freeze. Keep fresh frozen plums in refrigerator's freezer 2 to 3 months, in home freezer 1 year.

PREPARATION: *To peel*—See PEACHES. *To can*—Select firm, ripe plums. Follow general directions given under CANNING.

SERVING: Enjoy whole or halved raw, fresh plums and prune-plums as snacks or light desserts. For cooking and baking pies, tortes, pastries, breads, and compotes, fresh or canned prune-plums are preferred because the pits are so easily removed.

GREENGAGE PLUM SALAD

1 1-lb. 4-oz. can greengage plums
1 3-oz. package lemon gelatin
Lemon juice
1/2 tsp. salt
3/4 c. slivered toasted almonds

Drain juice from plums; add enough water to make 2 cups liquid. Heat to boiling; pour over gelatin. Add small amount of lemon juice and salt; stir until dissolved. Cool until thickened. Pour 2 tablespoons gelatin into each of 6 baking cups or individual molds. Chill until firm. Chill remaining gelatin until syrupy. Pit plums and chop; fold plums and almonds into gelatin. Spoon over firm gelatin in molds. Chill until firm. Serve in lettuce cups with salad dressing. Yield: 6 servings.

PLUM KUCHEN

1/2 c. soft butter
1/2 c. sugar
3 eggs
1/2 tsp. almond extract
1 c. all-purpose flour
14 to 16 fresh Italian plums or purple plums
Confectioners' sugar

Cream butter with sugar in small bowl until smoothly blended. Add eggs, one at a time, beating well after each addition. Stir in almond extract and flour; mix well. Spread batter evenly in buttered floured 10-inch round pan. Cut plums in half and remove pits; arrange halves, cut side up, over batter. Sprinkle plums with additional sugar. Bake at 375 degrees for 40 minutes; cool for 30 minutes before serving. Sprinkle with confectioners' sugar.

PURPLE PLUM COFFEE CAKE

2 pkg. yeast
3/4 c. warm milk
1 3/4 c. sugar
1 tsp. vanilla
1/2 c. margarine
5 c. flour
2 eggs, lightly beaten
4 lb. fresh purple plums

Dissolve yeast in 1/4 cup lukewarm water; stir in milk, 3/4 cup sugar, vanilla, margarine and half the flour. Beat well. Stir in eggs and remaining flour; place in greased bowl. Cover; let rise until doubled in bulk. Punch dough down; pat into two 10-inch springform pans, building up rims. Quarter plums lengthwise; stick into dough in rows, letting ends protrude. Let rise for 1 hour. Bake at 350 degrees for 25 minutes. Remove from oven; sprinkle with remaining sugar.

SOUTHERN PLUM ROLL

2 1/4 c. prepared biscuit mix
5 tbsp. sugar
Milk
1 No. 2 1/2 can plums
2 tbsp. butter
1 tbsp. flour

Combine biscuit mix and 2 tablespoons sugar; moisten with enough milk to form a stiff dough. Roll into oblong shape on slightly floured board; sprinkle with 2 tablespoons sugar. Drain plums, reserving juice; remove seeds. Press through food mill. Spread plums evenly on rolled dough; dot with butter. Roll as for jelly roll; cut into 1-inch slices. Place in buttered baking dish, cut side up. Blend flour and 1 tablespoon sugar with reserved plum juice; pour over rolls. Bake at 400 degrees for 25 to 30 minutes. Serve warm.

DELICIOUS PLUM CAKE

3/4 c. butter
1 c. sugar
3 eggs
2 c. flour
1 tsp. soda
3 tbsp. plum juice
1 c. chopped purple plums
2 tsp. cinnamon
1 tsp. nutmeg
1/4 tsp. salt
1 c. chopped pecans

Cream butter and sugar together. Add eggs; mix well. Combine flour and soda; add to butter mixture alternately with plum juice and plums. Add spices and salt; fold in pecans. Pour into two 9-inch pans. Bake at 350 degrees for 30 to 35 minutes. Let cake cool.

Icing

1 c. sugar
1 tbsp. flour
2 eggs
1/2 c. plum juice
1 c. chopped plums
Pinch of salt
2 tbsp. butter

Combine sugar and flour in saucepan. Add eggs and plum juice; mix well. Add plums and salt; bring to a slow boil. Cook until mixture is of spreading consistency. Remove from heat. Add butter; beat until cool enough to spread. Frost cooled cake.

PLUM CAKE WITH WALNUTS

1 jar jr. baby food plums
1 1/2 c. flour
1 c. sugar
1 tsp. soda
1 tsp. baking powder
1/2 tsp. salt
1/2 c. cold water
1 c. chopped walnuts
1/3 c. raisins
1/3 c. cooking oil
1 tbsp. vinegar
1 tsp. vanilla
1 egg

Reserve 1 heaping tablespoon plums for Frosting. Combine remaining ingredients; beat by hand for 1 minute. Pour into greased 9-inch square cake pan. Bake in 350-degree oven for 30 to 35 minutes. Cool cake slightly; remove from pan. Finish cooling in cake rack.

Frosting

2 c. confectioners' sugar
1/4 c. butter
1/2 tsp. vanilla
1 tbsp. (heaping) plums

Cream sugar and butter together; stir in vanilla and reserved plums. Spread Frosting on cake.

EASY PLUM CAKE

2 c. self-rising flour
1/2 tsp. salt
1 tsp. cloves
1 tsp. cinnamon
1 c. salad oil
2 c. sugar
3 eggs
2 jars baby food plums
1/2 c. chopped nuts

Sift flour, salt, cloves and cinnamon together. Combine oil, sugar and eggs; beat until blended. Beat in plums. Add flour mixture; mix well. Fold in nuts. Turn batter into greased and floured tube pan or bundt pan. Bake at 325 degrees for 1 hour to 1 hour and 15 minutes.

DAMSON PLUM TARTS

1 qt. fresh damson plums
4 c. sugar
Unbaked tart shells

Seed plums; combine plums and sugar in saucepan. Cook until plums are tender, stirring frequently. Spoon into tart shells. Bake at 450 degrees until tart shells are brown and done.

PLUM WONDERFUL

1 can purple plums
2 eggs
1 c. chopped almonds or walnuts
1/4 c. sugar
Dash of salt
1 tbsp. confectioners' sugar

Preheat oven to 325 degrees. Drain plums; reserve 1/2 cup juice. Remove pits. Arrange plums in casserole; add reserved juice. Beat eggs lightly; beat in almonds, sugar and salt. Spoon over plums. Bake for 30 minutes. Sprinkle with confectioners' sugar. Serve warm or cool. Yield: 4 servings.

WILD PLUM DELIGHT

1 qt. large ripe wild plums
1 1/2 c. coffee cream
1 1/2 c. sugar
2 tbsp. cornstarch
1 tsp. almond extract

Cook plums in 2 cups water until skins split; remove from heat. Drain plums; remove pits. Combine plum pulp, cream, sugar and cornstarch in saucepan; cook over medium heat until thick. Remove from heat; add almond extract. Spoon into 8 sherbet glasses; chill. Top with whipped cream or ice cream, if desired.

Plum Pudding

Plum pudding is a steamed or boiled pudding frequently served at holiday times. Originally, it was prepared with plums but gradually raisins, currants, dried fruits, and even almonds replaced the plums as ingredients. However, the name remained unchanged.

DELICIOUS PLUM PUDDING

1 tsp. soda
1 c. molasses
2 c. flour
1 tsp. baking powder
1 tsp. salt
1 tsp. cinnamon
1/4 tsp. cloves
1/4 tsp. nutmeg
1 c. soft bread crumbs
1 c. chopped suet
1 c. chopped dates
1 c. chopped raisins
1/2 c. chopped nuts
1 c. milk
2 eggs
1/2 c. melted butter
1 c. sifted confectioners' sugar
1 tsp. vanilla
1 c. heavy cream, whipped

Stir soda into molasses. Combine flour, baking powder, salt, spices, bread crumbs, suet, dates, raisins and nuts in large bowl. Add molasses mixture and milk; mix well. Pour into 2 greased 1-pound molds; cover tightly. Steam for 1 hour and 30 minutes. Beat eggs until thick and foamy; beat in butter, confectioners' sugar and vanilla. Fold in whipped cream. Serve sauce over pudding.

ENGLISH PLUM PUDDING

Sifted flour
1 1/2 tsp. salt
3/4 tsp. soda
1 tsp. cinnamon
1/4 tsp. nutmeg
1/2 tsp. mace
1 1/4 c. raisins, chopped
1 1/4 c. currants
4 oz. citron
2 oz. orange peel, chopped
1/2 c. nuts, chopped
1/2 c. bread crumbs
3/4 c. hot milk
1 1/8 c. (packed) brown sugar
5 eggs, separated
1/2 lb. suet, chopped
1/4 c. fruit juice
1/2 c. apricot jam
1 1/2 c. sugar
1/4 c. butter
1 tsp. vanilla

Sift 3/4 cup flour, 1 teaspoon salt, soda and spices together; stir in fruits and nuts. Soften crumbs in milk for 10 minutes. Beat brown sugar and egg yolks together; add suet and crumb mixture. Stir into fruit mixture. Add juice and jam. Beat egg whites until stiff peaks form; fold into batter. Turn into greased mold. Steam, tightly covered, for 3 hours and 30 minutes. Mix 2 tablespoons flour, sugar and remaining salt together well; add all remaining ingredients and 4 cups water. Place in saucepan over low heat; cook until thickened. Serve with pudding.

FROZEN PLUM PUDDING

1 tbsp. gelatin
1 c. sugar
3 egg yolks, beaten
2 c. whipped cream
1/2 c. raisins
1 c. chopped nuts
4 oz. red and green candied cherries
4 oz. candied pineapple

Dissolve gelatin in 1/4 cup boiling water; set aside. Cook sugar and 1 cup cold water together until thread forms. Add syrup to egg yolks; beat until cool. Add gelatin. Fold in whipped cream; add raisins, nuts and fruits. Place in 2 refrigerator trays or paper baking cups. Freeze. Yield: 16 servings.

Old-Fashioned Plum Pudding . . . Make holidays important with this steamed pudding.

OLD-FASHIONED PLUM PUDDING

1 tsp. cinnamon
1 tsp. allspice
1/4 tsp. ground cloves
1 tsp. baking powder
1/2 tsp. soda
1/2 tsp. salt
2 c. fine dry bread crumbs
1 c. ground suet
2 eggs
3/4 c. Grandma's West Indies molasses
3/4 c. orange juice
3/4 c. evaporated milk
1 tbsp. flour
1 c. diced glazed mixed fruit
1 15-oz. package raisins

Mix spices, baking powder, soda, salt and bread crumbs together. Add suet, eggs, molasses, orange juice and milk. Sprinkle flour over glazed fruit and raisins; toss lightly. Add to molasses mixture, stirring well. Turn into greased 2-quart pudding mold. Place mold on rack in deep kettle; pour in boiling water to half the depth of mold. Steam for 5 hours, adding additional boiling water during steaming if necessary. Garnish with confectioners' sugar icing if desired. Serve warm. Yield: 12 servings.

Pompano

BAKED POMPANO CREOLE

1 5-lb. pompano
2 tsp. salt
1/8 tsp. pepper
2 tsp. flour
1/4 c. cooking oil
1 c. chopped onion
1 c. chopped celery
1/8 tsp. hot sauce
1/4 tsp. garlic salt
2 1/2 c. strained canned tomatoes
8 capers
2 tbsp. chopped parsley
1 lemon, sliced

Place pompano in pan; sprinkle 1 teaspoon salt, pepper, flour and 2 tablespoons oil over top. Add 1/2 cup hot water. Bake at 350 degrees for 30 minutes. Cook onion and celery in remaining oil over low heat for 5 minutes. Add hot sauce, remaining salt, garlic salt, tomatoes, capers and 4 cups hot water. Simmer for 10 minutes; pour over pompano. Bake at 325 degrees for 30 minutes longer, basting several times with sauce. Serve on platter; top with parsley and lemon slices. Yield: 6 servings.

POMPANO EN PAPILLOTE

1 onion, finely chopped
Butter, melted
1 c. flour
2 c. milk, scalded
2 eggs, beaten
Dash of nutmeg
Dash of hot sauce
1 oz. sauterne
1/2 lb. cooked shrimp, chopped
1/2 lb. cooked crawfish, chopped
Salt
2 pompano steak slices, skinned

Saute onion for 5 minutes in butter in skillet. Add flour gradually to form paste; cook until dry. Add milk gradually, stirring constantly; cook until thickened. Beat eggs with nutmeg, hot sauce and sauterne; fold into cream sauce. Add shrimp and crawfish; salt to taste. Spread small amount of cream sauce over buttered French paper; place 1 pompano steak over sauce. Top with additional cream sauce and remaining pompano. Spread remaining sauce over top. Fold paper to form bag with crimped edges. Brush with additional melted butter. Bake for 30 minutes at 350 degrees. Yield: 4 servings.

Popcorn

HEAVENLY HASH POPCORN

2 qt. popped popcorn
1 c. miniature marshmallows
1/2 c. salted peanuts
9 3/4-oz. milk chocolate bars

Preheat oven to 300 degrees. Spread popcorn in buttered jelly roll pan; sprinkle with marshmallows and peanuts. Arrange chocolate bars over top. Place in oven. Bake for 5 minutes. Cool slightly; toss.

KRAZY KRUNCH

2 qt. popped popcorn
1 c. pecans
2/3 c. almonds or peanuts
1 1/3 c. sugar
1 c. margarine
1/2 c. light corn syrup
1 tsp. vanilla

Mix popcorn and nuts on large cookie sheet. Combine sugar, margarine and syrup in 1 1/2-quart saucepan; bring to a boil over medium heat, stirring constantly. Cook, stirring occasionally, for 10 minutes or until mixture turns light caramel color. Remove from heat; stir in vanilla. Pour over popcorn and nuts; coat well. Spread out to dry. Break apart; store in tightly covered container. Yield: About 2 pounds.

NEVER-FAIL POPCORN BALLS

1/2 c. margarine | *1 gal. popped popcorn*
32 lge. marshmallows

Melt margarine and marshmallows together; pour over popcorn. Shape into balls; serve. Yield: 24 balls.

CARAMEL POPCORN

Color photograph for this recipe on page 495.

1/4 c. corn oil | *1 c. dark corn syrup*
1/2 c. popcorn | *1 c. sugar*
1 c. salted peanuts | *1/4 c. margarine*

Heat oil in 4-quart kettle over medium heat for 3 minutes. Add popcorn; cover, leaving small air space at edge of cover. Shake frequently over medium heat until popping stops. Place popcorn into large, greased heat-resistant bowl; add peanuts. Heat in 300-degree oven until syrup is prepared. Combine corn syrup, sugar, 1/4 cup water and margarine in heavy 2-quart saucepan. Bring to a boil over medium heat, stirring constantly. Cook, stirring occasionally, to 280 degrees on candy thermometer or until small amount of syrup dropped into cold water separates into hard but not brittle threads. Remove popcorn mixture from oven; pour syrup over popcorn mixture gradually, stirring quickly until kernels are evenly coated. Spread on 2 greased baking sheets; spread out into thin layer with greased hands. Cool; separate into clusters. Store in tightly covered container. Yield: 1 1/2 pounds.

OVEN CARAMEL CORN

2 c. (packed) brown sugar | *1 tsp. salt*
1 c. margarine | *1 tsp. butter flavoring*
1/2 c. light corn syrup | *1/2 tsp. soda*
8 qt. popped popcorn

Combine sugar, margarine, syrup, salt and flavoring; bring to a boil. Cook for 5 minutes. Remove from heat; add soda. Pour mixture over popcorn; mix well. Scatter in large shallow pan. Bake at 250 degrees for 1 hour; stirring frequently.

PEANUT BUTTER POPCORN

1/4 c. popcorn | *1/2 c. light corn syrup*
2 tbsp. shortening | *1/2 c. peanut butter*
1/2 c. sugar | *1/2 tsp. vanilla*

Pop popcorn in shortening. Place in bowl. Combine sugar and syrup in saucepan over low heat; bring to a boil, stirring constantly. Remove from heat; stir in peanut butter and vanilla. Pour over popcorn; mix well. Pour onto cookie sheet; cool.

POPCORN BALLS

1 c. sugar | *2 tbsp. butter*
1 c. light corn syrup | *1/4 tsp. soda*
1 tbsp. vinegar | *1 tsp. cream of tartar*
1/2 tsp. salt | *9 qt. popped popcorn, warm*
1 tsp. vanilla

Combine sugar, syrup, vinegar and salt in saucepan; place over low heat. Cook until mixture reaches soft-ball stage on candy thermometer. Remove from heat. Add vanilla, butter, soda and cream of tartar. Beat with egg beater until foamy. Pour over popcorn; form into balls, lightly. Yield: 26-30 balls.

Popover

Popovers are a muffin-like quick bread usually made from eggs, milk, butter, flour, and seasonings. Since steam is the leavening agent, neither baking soda nor baking powder is used. There are many variations to standard popover recipes. Whole wheat flour, cheese, or blanched almonds are just a few familiar choices for flavor excitement. Popovers are so named because the lightness of the batter causes it to "pop over" the sides of the cooking pan when baking. Perfect popovers are tender, moist, and hollow on the inside; well-browned and puffy on the top; flaky, crisp, and firm on the sides.

PREPARATION: Sift flour before measuring. Combine ingredients according to specific recipe directions. Beat until smooth. Batter is seldom heavier than whipping cream. If small eggs are used and cause a thick batter, add a little milk. Heat pans before greasing them to promote rising of batter. Muffin cups, custard cups, oven-glass cups, or other similar baking utensils may be used. Fill pan 2/3 full or less; popovers double in bulk when baked. Place pans in hot oven and bake according to recipe. A too-hot oven causes popovers to brown before popping; a too-cold oven causes popovers to flop when they should rise. Many recipes will instruct you to reduce heat and continue baking once popovers have risen. Whatever the specific directions, always allow *full baking time* indicated in recipe. To test for doneness, you may remove a popover and check firmness of walls. Insufficient cooking time causes popovers to collapse. To permit steam to escape after you remove popovers from heat, insert sharp paring knife gently into popovers. Never cover hot baked popovers; they become soggy.

SERVING: Serve hot with butter for breakfast, lunch, dinner or tea. They are often served with roast beef.

BASIC POPOVERS

1 c. flour
1/2 tsp. salt
1 c. milk
2 eggs
1 tbsp. melted butter

Preheat oven to 400 degrees. Sift flour and salt into bowl; add milk, eggs and butter. Beat with mixer until smooth. Fill greased popover pans 1/2 full. Bake for 30 minutes or until well-puffed and golden; pierce during last 5 minutes of baking to allow steam to escape.

BLENDER POPOVERS

1 c. milk
2 eggs
1 c. sifted flour
1/4 tsp. salt

Place all ingredients into blender container; cover. Blend on high speed for 15 seconds; pour into hot greased popover pans. Bake at 450 degrees for 15 minutes; reduce heat to 350 degrees. Bake for 15 minutes longer.

DELUXE POPOVERS

1 2/3 c. sifted flour
1/2 tsp. salt
2 tbsp. butter
1 1/3 c. milk
4 eggs
1 egg white

Combine flour, salt, butter and milk in a blender container; mix on high speed until smooth. Add eggs and egg white; blend until smooth. Pour into hot greased popover pans. Bake at 450 degrees for 10 minutes; reduce temperature to 350 degrees. Bake for 15 to 20 minutes longer.

EASY POPOVERS

1 c. sifted flour
1/4 tsp. salt
2 eggs, beaten
1 c. milk
2 tbsp. melted shortening

Sift flour and salt. Combine eggs, milk and shortening; add to flour mixture gradually, beating for 1 minute or until smooth. Fill greased hot popover pans 3/4 full. Bake at 450 degrees for 20 minutes. Reduce oven temperature to 350 degrees and bake for 15 to 20 minutes longer.

Poppy Seed

Poppy seeds are the herbaceous seeds of a poppy that thrives in northern Europe and the Middle East. They are available only in whole form and are used with baked products such as rolls, breads, cakes, cookies, and pastries; over noodles, rice, and broiled fish; and with green beans, boiled onions, and new potatoes.

POPPY SEED LOAF

2 eggs
1 1/2 c. sugar
3/4 c. cooking oil
1 tsp. vanilla
1/4 c. poppy seed
2 c. flour
1 tsp. baking powder
1 tsp. salt
1 c. evaporated milk

Beat eggs; add sugar and oil. Mix well; add vanilla and poppy seed. Sift flour, baking powder and salt; add to poppy seed mixture alternately with milk. Pour into loaf pan. Bake at 350 degrees for 1 hour or until cake tests done.

EASY POPPY SEED CAKE

1/2 c. butter
1/2 c. margarine
1 1/2 c. sugar
4 eggs, separated
1 c. sour cream
1 tsp. soda
2 c. flour
3 tsp. vanilla
1 2-oz. can poppy seed
Confectioners' sugar

Cream butter, margarine, sugar and egg yolks in large mixing bowl. Combine sour cream and soda. Add sour cream mixture, flour, vanilla and poppy seed; mix well. Beat egg whites until stiff peaks form. Fold egg whites into batter; pour into ungreased tube pan. Bake at 350 degrees for 1 hour. Cool inverted over cake plate; cake will drop. Sprinkle with sifted confectioners' sugar.

POPPY SEED CHIFFON CAKE

Color photograph for this recipe on page 482.

1/2 c. poppy seed
1 pkg. lemon chiffon cake mix
1 tsp. grated lemon peel
1 4-oz. package lemon pie filling mix
1/2 c. heavy cream

Soften poppy seed in 1/4 cup water for 1 to 2 hours. Prepare cake mix according to package directions; stir in poppy seed. Pour into 2 ungreased 9-inch loaf pans. Bake according to package directions; cool. Prepare pie filling mix according to package directions, reducing water by 1/2 cup and adding lemon peel. Cool. Cut 1 loaf horizontally into thirds. Remaining loaf may be used in favorite recipe or frozen. Whip cream; fold into lemon filling. Spread on each layer; place layers together. Spread filling on top of cake; chill before serving.

POPPY SEED DELIGHT

1/2 lb. margarine
2 c. sugar
1 c. mashed potatoes
4 eggs
1/2 c. milk
1 c. flour
3 tsp. baking powder
1/2 tsp. cinnamon
1/2 lb. ground poppy seed
1 tsp. vanilla
1/4 c. chopped nuts

Cream margarine and sugar; add potatoes, eggs and milk. Sift flour, baking powder and cinnamon; add to egg mixture. Fold in poppy seed, vanilla and nuts; mix well. Pour into greased tube pan. Bake at 350 degrees for 1 hour. Cool. May be sprinkled with sifted powdered sugar.

Pork

Pork is a favorite American meat second only to beef in popularity. Pork is the flesh of a pig or hog. It is available fresh and cured. *Fresh pork* cuts include jowl, shoulder, loin, belly, leg, shanks, hocks, knuckles, feet, and tail. *Cured pork* includes smoked shoulder butt, picnic, loin, loin chops, and salt pork; cooked picnics; and canned smoked picnics and loins. Both fresh and cured pork are excellent sources of high quality protein, iron, niacin, riboflavin, and thiamine. (3 1/2 ounces fresh or cured pork = approximately 400 calories, depending on the cut)

AVAILABILITY: Fresh pork is available year-round, with the greatest supply from October to January. Cured pork is available year-round. Canned fresh pork and frozen processed pork are available year-round.

BUYING: Allow 1/4-1/3 pound boneless pork or 1/2-3/4 pound bone-in pork per serving. *Fresh pork*—Look for a firm, white layer of external fat and meat that is grayish pink or pale rose in color. Meat should be firm, fine-grained, and well-marbled with fat. *Tender cuts* of fresh pork include the jowl, shoulder, loin, belly, and leg. *Less tender cuts* include the shanks, hocks, knuckles, feet, and tail. *Ground pork* is also available. *Cured pork*—Depend upon a packer's label for quality as there are wide variances in the flavor of cured pork products.

STORING: *Fresh pork*—Loosen wrapper and store fresh pork in the coldest part of the refrigerator. Chops and spareribs keep 3 days; roasts 5-6 days. Unopened canned pork products keep 1 year on the kitchen shelf; if opened, 2-3 days in the refrigerator. *To freeze fresh pork,* wrap in moisture- and vapor-proof paper. Do not salt meat before freezing. Fresh pork keeps in the refrigerator freezer compart-

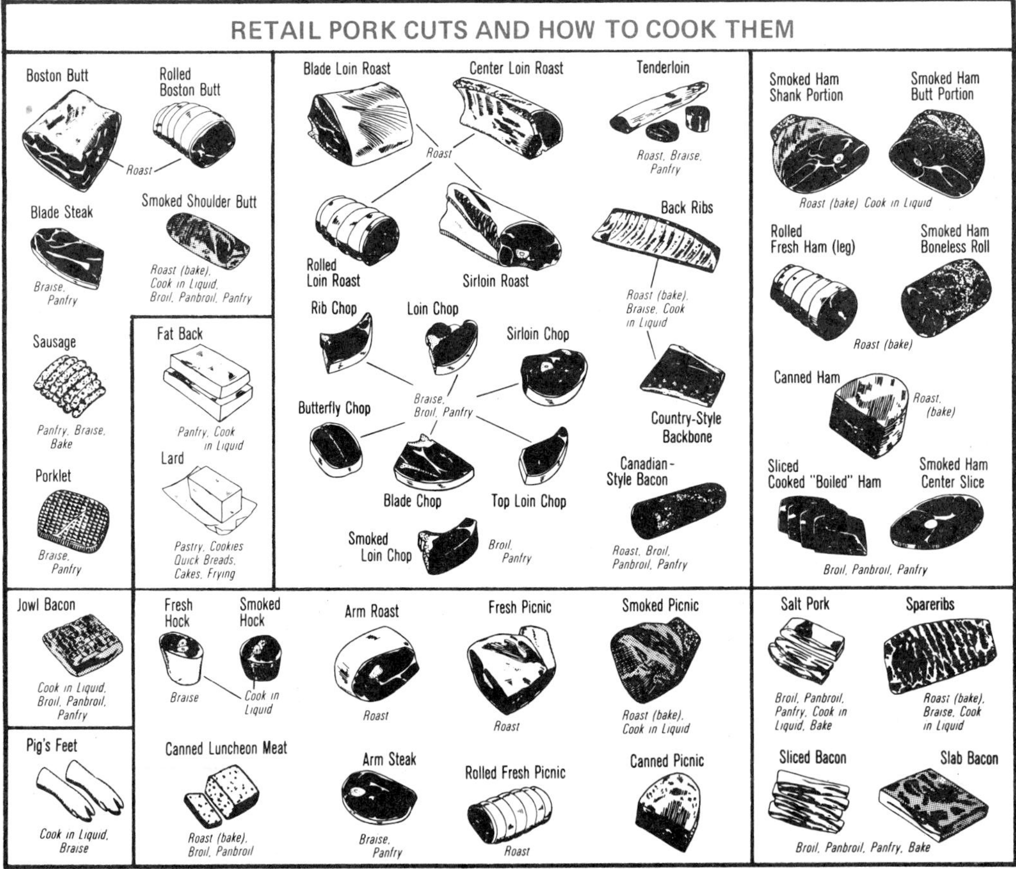

TIMETABLE FOR COOKING PORK				
	ROASTED AT 300 - 350 F. OVEN TEMPERATURE		BROILED	BRAISED
CUT	Meat Thermometer Reading Degrees F.	Time Minutes Per lb.	Total Time Minutes	Total Time Hours
FRESH				
Loin				
Center	185	35 to 40		
Ends	185	45 to 50		
Shoulder				
Rolled	185	40 to 45		
Boston Butt	185	45 to 50		
Leg or Ham	185	30 to 35		
Chops				3/4 to1
Spareribs				1 1/2
SMOKED				
Ham				
Whole	160	18 to 20		
Half	160	22 to 25		
Shank portion	160	35 to 40		
Butt portion	160	35 to 40		
Ham Slice				
(1/2 inch)			10 to 12	
(1 inch)			16 to 20	
Picnic	170	35		
Shoulder Butt	170	35		
Bacon			4 to 5	

ment 2-3 weeks. Uncooked cuts keep 3-4 months in the home freezer; cooked cuts keep 2-3 months in the home freezer. Ground pork keeps 1-3 months in home freezer. *Cured pork*—Canned cured pork should generally be stored in the refrigerator where it keeps up to 1 year. Cured cuts keep 1 week in the refrigerator; salt pork keeps 2-3 weeks. *Do not freeze cured pork.*

PREPARATION: The kind of pork you buy determines how it is to be prepared. *Fresh pork*—Tender cuts are cooked by dry heat methods (broiling, roasting, grilling) while the less tender cuts are cooked by moist heat methods (braising, stewing, boiling). *Always cook pork until it is well done and no trace of pink remains* as pork may contain some parasites that must be destroyed. *Cured pork*—Canned cured pork is often heated before serving. Follow package instructions. Cuts of cured pork are baked, cooked in liquid, or pan-broiled. See chart that follows for recommended times and temperatures.

(See BACON, CARVING, and HAM.)

LOIN BARBECUE

1 4-lb. pork loin roast
Salt to taste
2 tbsp. flour
1 c. catsup
2 tsp. prepared mustard
1/4 tsp. red pepper
1 tsp. Worcestershire sauce
1 tsp. vinegar
1 clove of garlic, chopped

Brown roast in small amount of fat in Dutch oven; sprinkle with salt. Add a small amount of water; cook, covered, over low heat, until tender. Remove roast from liquid. Combine flour and all remaining ingredients. Stir into hot liquid; blend well. Dice roast; combine with sauce. Simmer in sauce for 10 minutes. Serve on hamburger buns. Yield: 8 servings.

PORK ON A BUN

1 med. onion, chopped
1/2 c. chopped celery
1/3 c. chopped green pepper
1 c. catsup
1/4 c. (packed) brown sugar
2 tbsp. vinegar
2 tbsp. Worcestershire sauce
1 tsp. salt
1 tsp. chili powder
4 c. cooked pork roast
Hamburger buns

Combine all ingredients except buns in medium pan; simmer until vegetables and pork are tender. Serve on buns. Yield: 6 servings.

PORK BARBECUE

1 med. onion, diced
2 tbsp. butter
2 tbsp. vinegar
2 tbsp. (packed) brown sugar
1/4 c. lemon juice
1 c. chili sauce
1 tsp. minced parsley
1/2 tsp. prepared mustard
3 tbsp. Worcestershire sauce
1 tsp. salt
Dash of pepper
1 4-lb. pork roast

Brown onion in butter in saucepan. Add all remaining ingredients except pork roast; simmer for 30 minutes. Place roast in small amount of water in Dutch oven; simmer, covered, for 2 hours or until tender. Shred roast; mix with sauce. Serve on hamburger buns. Yield: 4 servings.

BAKED STUFFED PORK TENDERLOIN

3 pork tenderloins
3/8 c. melted butter
2 c. toasted bread crumbs
1 egg, slightly beaten
1/2 sm. onion, minced
1/2 tsp. minced parsley
1/2 tsp. salt
1/4 tsp. celery salt
1/8 tsp. powdered sage
Dash of pepper

Wipe tenderloins with damp cloth; split open. Lay flat; rub with 2 tablespoons melted butter. Combine bread crumbs, 1/3 cup boiling water, egg, onion, parsley, salt, celery salt, sage, pepper and remaining butter. Beat until light; spread on tenderloin. Roll up tenderloin; tie with string. Arrange in baking pan; sprinkle with salt lightly. Pour 2/3 cup boiling water in pan. Bake at 400 degrees for 1 hour or until tenderloins are tender. Cut and remove strings. Gravy may be made from drippings in pan, if desired. Yield: 6 servings.

CABBAGE ROLL WITH PORK

1 lge. cabbage
2 lb. ground pork
1 c. rice
1 1/2 tsp. salt
1/2 tsp. pepper
2 No. 2 1/2 cans sauerkraut
2 tbsp. butter
2 tbsp. flour

Steam cabbage in small amount of water in saucepan to soften; separate leaves. Combine pork, rice, salt and pepper. Place small amount of pork mixture on cabbage leaf; roll up leaf. Spread sauerkraut in Dutch oven; add layer of cabbage rolls. Repeat layers until all rolls are used. Cover with water; simmer for 2 hours. Brown butter and flour in skillet; add 1 cup water, stirring constantly, to make thin sauce. Pour over rolls to serve. Yield: 8 servings.

CALABACITA

2 lb. pork
1 lge. onion, diced
Margarine
2 No. 2 cans whole kernel corn
1/2 lb. yellow squash, chopped
2 No. 2 cans tomatoes
1 tsp. red pepper
1 tsp. coarsely ground pepper
Salt to taste
1/4 c. chili powder
2 c. rice

Cut pork into bite-sized cubes; brown in small amount of fat in Dutch oven. Saute onion in margarine in small skillet; add to pork. Add corn, squash and tomatoes; mix thoroughly. Add peppers, salt and chili powder. Cook, over low heat for 1 hour; stir frequently. Prepare rice according to package directions. Serve pork over rice. Yield: 8 servings.

PORK MILANI CASSEROLE

1 lb. boneless pork loin
2 tbsp. salad oil
1/2 c. chopped onion
1/2 c. chopped celery
1 med. green pepper, chopped
1 can sliced mushrooms
1 tbsp. Worcestershire sauce
1 tsp. salt
1/8 tsp. pepper
1/2 tsp. basil
1 can mushroom soup
1/2 c. milk
1 8-oz. package spaghetti
1 tomato, peeled and sliced
1 1/2 c. croutons
2 tbsp. butter, melted
1 c. grated sharp Cheddar cheese

Cut pork into 1-inch cubes. Brown pork in oil in skillet on all sides. Add onion, celery and green pepper. Saute until tender; mix in mushrooms, Worcestershire sauce, salt, pepper and basil. Simmer, covered, for 25 minutes. Blend in soup and milk; simmer, covered, for 5 minutes. Preheat oven to 350 degrees. Cook spaghetti in 3 quarts boiling salted water for 8 minutes; drain. Combine pork mixture with spaghetti in casserole. Overlap tomatoes around edge of casserole. Toss croutons in melted butter; sprinkle over spaghetti mixture and tomatoes. Sprinkle grated cheese over top. Bake for 30 minutes or until cheese melts. Yield: 8 servings.

PORK SAVORY

3 lb. pork, cubed
4 1/2 tsp. salt
1/2 tsp. pepper
2 1/2 c. sliced carrots
1 c. sifted flour
3 c. sour cream
2 1/2 c. diced potatoes
1 tbsp. minced onion
1 1/2 c. green lima beans

Sprinkle pork with 1 1/2 teaspoons salt and pepper. Brown in small amount of fat in skillet; add 3 cups water. Simmer, covered, until pork is tender. Cook carrots in small amount of water until crisp-tender. Combine flour and sour cream; beat until smooth. Combine with pork and broth. Add all vegetables; blend well. Bake, covered, at 375 degrees for 1 hour. Bake, uncovered, for 30 minutes longer or until brown on top.

PORK STEAK CASSEROLE

1 1/2 lb. pork steak, cubed
1 c. chopped celery
1 c. chopped onions
1 can mushroom pieces
1 can mushroom soup
1 can tomato soup
1 8-oz. package wide noodles, cooked
2 tbsp. butter

Brown steak in small amount of fat in skillet; add celery and onions with 1/2 cup water. Simmer for 12 minutes or until celery is tender. Add mushrooms and soups. Rinse cans with 1 cup water; add to mixture. Drain noodles; add to pork mixture. Pour into casserole; top with butter. Bake at 350 degrees for 45 minutes. Yield: 4 servings.

PORK STEAK WITH MUSHROOM SAUCE

1 2-lb. pork steak
1/2 c. flour
1 tbsp. butter
1 sm. onion, sliced
Salt and pepper
2 cans cream of mushroom soup

Cut pork into serving pieces; dredge in flour. Melt butter in skillet; brown pork on both sides. Place pork in deep baking dish. Place onion on pork; sprinkle with salt and pepper. Heat soup and 1 1/2 soup cans water in skillet; pour over pork. Bake, covered, at 300 degrees for 1 hour and 30 minutes or until tender. Yield: 6 servings.

SWEET AND SOUR PORK

3 lb. pork butt, cut in cubes
4 tsp. soy sauce
1 tsp. monosodium glutamate
1 tsp. ginger
Dash of garlic salt
2 eggs
1/2 c. flour
1/4 c. cornstarch
1/4 c. salad oil
1 c. pineapple syrup
1 c. vinegar
1 c. sugar
1 can pineapple chunks, drained
1 green pepper, chopped
2 tbsp. chopped candied ginger
2 ripe tomatoes, cubed

Mix pork cubes, 2 tablespoons soy sauce, monosodium glutamate, ginger and garlic salt; let stand for 30 minutes. Combine eggs, flour and 2 tablespoons cornstarch; beat until smooth. Pour over pork, mixing well. Mixture will be thick and sticky. Heat oil in skillet; saute pork until well-browned on all sides. Drain off fat. Place pork mixture in greased baking dish. Bake in 350-degree oven until tender. Combine pineapple syrup, vinegar, sugar and remaining soy sauce; bring to a boil. Combine remaining cornstarch and small amount of water to form a paste; stir into syrup mixture. Cook until thickened. Add pineapple, green pepper and ginger. Add tomatoes, just before serving. Pour over hot drained pork.

ALL-IN-ONE PORK CHOPS

Salt and pepper to taste
Flour
6 pork chops
1/4 c. cooking oil
3 med. carrots, sliced
4 med. potatoes, sliced

Combine salt, pepper and flour; dredge chops in seasoned flour. Brown in oil in heavy skillet. Add 1 1/2 cups water; simmer, covered, for 30 minutes. Add carrots; cook, covered, for 15 minutes. Add potatoes; cook, covered, until potatoes are tender. Add water, if necessary. Yield: 4 servings.

APPLE-STUFFED PORK CHOPS

4 pork chops, 1 in. thick
Salt and pepper to taste
1 tart apple, sliced
2 tsp. (packed) brown sugar
1 egg, slightly beaten
1/2 c. crushed corn flakes

Cut chops along bone to form pocket; season with salt and pepper. Fill with mixture of apple slices and brown sugar. Dip chops into mixture of egg and 1 tablespoon water. Roll chops in corn flakes; brown in hot fat in skillet. Add 1 cup water. Bake, covered, at 350 degrees for 45 minutes or until tender, adding water, if necessary. Yield: 4 servings.

BAKED CHOPS WITH HERB GRAVY

6 center-cut pork chops
1 lge. onion, chopped
1 tbsp. melted margarine
3 tbsp. flour
2 c. milk
1/4 tsp. salt
1/2 tsp. oregano
1/4 tsp. marjoram
1/4 tsp. thyme
1/3 c. chopped parsley

Brown chops quickly in hot skillet; place in 2-quart casserole. Saute onion in margarine and pan drippings until brown; stir in flour, blending well. Add milk, stirring constantly, until smooth. Add all remaining ingredients. Pour over chops. Bake, covered, at 300 degrees for 2 hours or until tender, stirring twice. Yield: 6 servings.

BAKED PORK CHOPS AND RICE

Salt and pepper to taste
8 center-cut pork chops
2 tbsp. salad oil
1 sm. can mushrooms
1 1/2 c. long grain rice
1 can beef consomme
1 green pepper, sliced
1 onion, sliced
1 tomato, sliced

Season pork; saute in oil until browned well. Combine mushrooms, rice, consomme and 1 1/2 soup cans water; place in lightly-greased casserole. Arrange chops on top. Place slice of pepper, onion and tomato on each chop. Cover tightly. Bake at 350 degrees for 1 hour and 30 minutes. Yield: 4 servings.

CHOPS AND RICE WITH WHITE WINE

4 pork chops
2 tbsp. fat
1 med. onion
1/4 c. chopped green pepper
1 c. long grain rice
1 c. cream of celery soup
1/2 c. white wine
1/4 tsp. rosemary
1 tsp. salt
1/8 tsp. pepper

Brown pork chops on both sides in fat in skillet. Remove chops. Add onion and green pepper; cook until tender. Add rice; cook until brown. Add 1/2 cup boiling water; cook for 5 minutes. Combine soup, 1 cup cold water, wine, rosemary, salt and pepper; stir into rice mixture. Turn into greased 2-quart casserole. Place chops on top. Cover. Bake at 350 degrees for 30 minutes. Uncover; turn chops. Add small amount of hot water, if dry. Bake, uncovered, until rice has absorbed liquid and chops are tender. Yield: 4 servings.

California Pork Chops . . . Pork chops simmered in herb-seasoned fruit cocktail are an unusual dish.

CALIFORNIA PORK CHOPS

6 lge. loin pork chops
1 1-lb. 14-oz. can fruit cocktail
1/2 tsp. grated lemon rind
1/3 c. lemon juice
1/4 tsp. crushed tarragon
1 tsp. salt
1/8 tsp. pepper
1 tbsp. cornstarch

Trim excess fat from pork chops; rub large skillet with scraps of fat. Brown chops in hot skillet. Drain fruit cocktail, reserving syrup. Combine reserved syrup, lemon rind, lemon juice, tarragon, salt and pepper; pour over chops. Simmer for 55 to 60 minutes, until chops are tender. Remove chops to heated serving platter. Combine cornstarch and 2 tablespoons cold water. Stir into pan juices; cook, stirring constantly, until thickened and clear. Add fruit; heat for 2 to 3 minutes. Pour sauce over chops; serve. Yield: 6 servings.

BARBECUED PORK CHOPS

1/4 c. vinegar
2 tbsp. sugar
1 tbsp. prepared mustard
1 1/2 tsp. salt
1/2 tsp. pepper
1/4 tsp. cayenne pepper
1 slice lemon
1 med. onion, sliced
2 tbsp. Worcestershire sauce
1/2 c. catsup
1 tsp. liquid smoke
6 rib pork chops, 1/2 in. thick

Mix 1/2 cup water, vinegar, sugar, mustard, salt, pepper and cayenne pepper together in saucepan. Add lemon and onion; simmer for 20 minutes. Add Worcestershire sauce, catsup and liquid smoke; bring to a boil. Place chops in 11 1/2 x 7 1/2 x 1 1/2-inch baking dish; pour sauce over chops. Bake, uncovered, at 350 degrees for 1 hour and 25 minutes, turning chops once. Yield: 6 servings.

STUFFED PORK CHOPS

Color photograph for this recipe on page 69.

6 1 1/2 in.-thick pork chops
1 c. cooked rice
2 tbsp. chopped green pepper
2 tbsp. chopped onion
1/2 tsp. salt
1/4 tsp. poultry seasoning
2 tbsp. shortening
1 can complete cooking sauce for pork chops

Cut pocket in pork chops. Mix rice, green pepper, onion, salt and poultry seasoning in 2-quart bowl. Stuff pork chops. Brown chops in hot shortening in 10-inch skillet; place in shallow 2-quart baking dish. Add cooking sauce; cover. Bake in 350-degree oven for 45 minutes or until chops are tender. Yield: 6 servings.

BLUE CHEESE-STUFFED PORK CHOPS

3 tbsp. butter
1 tsp. minced onion
1/4 c. finely sliced fresh mushrooms
1/2 c. crumbled blue cheese
3/4 c. fine dry bread crumbs
Pinch of salt
6 thick pork chops with pockets

Melt butter in skillet; cook onion and mushrooms for 5 minutes. Remove from heat; stir in blue cheese, bread crumbs and salt. Stuff pockets in chops with dressing; secure with toothpicks. Place in shallow baking dish. Bake at 325 degrees for 1 hour or until tender. Yield: 6 servings.

BRAISED LEMON PORK CHOPS

6 pork chops, 1 in. thick
Salt and pepper to taste
1/2 c. catsup
2 tbsp. (packed) brown sugar
6 lemon slices

Brown chops in heavy frying pan; season with salt and pepper. Combine catsup, 1/2 cup water and brown sugar; pour over chops. Place lemon slice on each chop. Bake, covered, at 350 degrees for 45 minutes or until pork is tender. Yield: 6 servings.

BURGUNDY PORK CHOPS

8 pork chops, 1 in. thick
Salt and pepper to taste
Oregano
2 tbsp. shortening
1 c. Burgundy
1 lemon, cut in wedges

Sprinkle chops with salt, pepper and oregano. Refrigerate overnight. Brown chops in hot shortening in heavy skillet. Pour Burgundy over chops; cover. Cook over medium heat until tender and Burgundy has evaporated, turning occasionally. Serve with lemon wedges. Yield: 8 servings.

DELUXE STUFFED PORK CHOPS

3 c. diced unpeeled tart apples
3/4 c. diced celery
2 tbsp. sugar
1/3 c. butter
6 c. cubed raisin bread
1 tsp. poultry seasoning
2 tsp. salt
1/4 tsp. marjoram
2 1/2 c. chicken broth
1 egg, beaten
6 loin pork chops 1 1/2 in. thick
1/8 tsp. pepper
4 tbsp. flour

Combine apples, celery, sugar, butter and 1/3 cup water in saucepan. Bring to a boil. Cover; cook for 5 minutes. Combine bread, poultry seasoning, 1 1/2 teaspoons salt and marjoram. Combine 1/2 cup chicken broth and egg; add to bread mixture. Add hot apple mixture; toss with fork to mix. Turn into buttered 1 1/2 quart casserole. Bake, uncovered, in 350-degree oven for 35 minutes. Cut pocket next to bone on inside of chops. Fill pocket with dressing. Spread remaining dressing in greased baking dish. Secure openings in chops with toothpick. Sprinkle chops with 1/2 teaspoon salt and pepper. Place in baking pan, add 1 cup broth. Bake, covered, at 350 degrees for 1 hour. Uncover; bake for 30 minutes longer or until brown. Remove chops to hot platter. Pour off excess fat. Add flour to pan drippings, stirring to blend. Add remaining chicken broth and 1 cup water to mixture; cook for 5 minutes.

FRUIT-GLAZED PORK CHOPS

6 double-rib pork chops
Salt and pepper to taste
2 c. (packed) brown sugar
1/2 c. pineapple juice
1/2 c. honey
2 tsp. dry mustard
6 whole cloves
6 whole coriander seeds, crushed
Orange slices
Lemon slices
Lime slices
Maraschino cherries
6 bananas, peeled
Lemon juice
2 tbsp. butter
1/4 c. honey

Brown chops in fat in skillet. Sprinkle with salt and pepper. Place in shallow baking dish. Combine brown sugar, juice, honey, mustard, cloves and coriander, mixing well. Spoon 3 tablespoons mixture over each chop. Bake at 350 degrees for 1 hour and 15 minutes or until chops are tender, basting occasionally with remaining juice mixture. Secure orange, lemon and lime slices to each chop with toothpick. Top each chop with cherry. Baste fruit with remaining juice mixture. Bake for 10 minutes longer. Dip bananas in lemon juice. Melt butter in skillet; stir in honey. Add bananas. Cook over low heat, turning gently, until bananas are hot and glazed. Do not overcook. Serve with glazed pork chops. Yield: 6 servings.

GLAZED PORK CHOPS

6 1-in. loin pork chops, trimmed
1 tsp. salt
3 tbsp. vinegar
1 1/2 c. (packed) brown sugar
1 tsp. dry mustard

Arrange chops in 13 x 9 1/2 x 2-inch baking dish. Sprinkle with salt. Combine all remaining ingredients; spread over chops. Bake, uncovered, at 350 degrees for 1 hour and 30 minutes. Turn over to serve. Yield: 6 servings.

NEAPOLITAN PORK CHOPS

6 pork chops, 1 in. thick
2 tbsp. vegetable oil
1 c. sliced onion
1 lb. fresh button mushrooms
1 c. thinly sliced green pepper
1 can tomatoes
1/2 tsp. oregano
1 tsp. salt
1/8 tsp. pepper

Trim fat from chops. Brown chops on both sides in hot oil in skillet. Remove chops. Saute onion, mushrooms and green pepper in oil until tender. Add tomatoes, oregano, salt and pepper; simmer for 5 minutes. Add pork chops; cover. Simmer for 1 hour or until tender. Uncover; simmer for 15 minutes longer if thicker sauce is desired. Yield: 6 servings.

GOURMET PORK CHOPS

6 pork chops
Salt
1/2 c. (packed) brown sugar
1/2 c. creme de cassis
2 red apples
1 tbsp. butter
1/4 c. dry white wine
1/2 c. pistachio nuts
1/2 c. preserved ginger

Flatten pork chops to 3/4-inch thickness. Broil on one side at 400 degrees 4 inches from source of heat until browned. Reduce oven temperature to 350 degrees. Turn chops; sprinkle with salt. Cook brown sugar in small skillet over low heat until sugar melts; add creme de cassis. Cook for several minutes or until mixture becomes red. Pour over chops. Bake in 350-degree oven for 20 minutes longer. Core apples but do not peel; cut into thick slices. Cook slices in butter and wine until just tender but still retain shape. Arrange chops in overlapping row on warm platter; sprinkle pistachio nuts over chops. Fill centers of apple slices with preserved ginger. Arrange apple slices to one side of platter or encircling chops. Yield: 6 servings.

HERBED PORK CHOPS

6 loin pork chops
2 tbsp. flour
1 tsp. salt
Dash of pepper
1 can cream of mushroom soup
1/4 tsp. rosemary, crushed
1 can French-fried onion rings
1/2 c. sour cream

Trim excess fat from chops. Place excess fat in skillet; render until 2 tablespoons fat collects in skillet. Remove trimmings. Mix flour, salt and pepper. Dredge chops in seasoned flour. Brown in hot fat; place in shallow baking dish. Combine soup, 3/4 cup water and rosemary; pour over chops. Sprinkle with half the onion rings. Cover. Bake at 350 degrees for 50 minutes or until pork is tender. Uncover; sprinkle with remaining onion rings. Bake for 10 minutes longer. Remove pork to platter. Blend sour cream into soup mixture in saucepan; heat through. Serve gravy with pork. Yield: 6 servings.

ORIENTAL PORK CHOPS

6 pork chops
1/2 c. soy sauce
1 clove of garlic, minced

Score fat edges of chops; place in shallow baking dish. Combine all remaining ingredients and 1/2 cup water; pour over chops. Refrigerate overnight. Arrange marinated chops on broiler pan rack. Broil 3 inches from source of heat for 10 minutes on each side. Yield: 6 servings.

PORK CHOP DINNER

6 pork chops
Salt and pepper to taste
3 lge. sweet potatoes
Lemon juice
6 slices pineapple
12 large prunes
12 whole cloves
1/2 c. pineapple juice

Season pork chops with salt and pepper; brown in small amount of fat in skillet. Peel sweet potatoes; cut in half. Rub with lemon juice. Place over chops; add pineapple slices. Remove pits from prunes; insert cloves. Add prunes and pineapple juice. Cover; cook over high heat until steaming. Reduce heat to low. Simmer for 45 minutes. Serve hot.

PORK CHOPS AND SAUERKRAUT

1 can sauerkraut
1 tsp. pepper
1/2 tsp. salt
4 thick pork chops

Place sauerkraut in casserole; season pork chops. Place chops over sauerkraut. Bake, covered, at 350 degrees for 1 hour. Bake, uncovered, for 20 minutes longer or until pork chops brown. Yield: 4 servings.

PORK CHOPS CREOLE

6 thick pork chops
1/4 c. cooking oil
1 clove of garlic, finely chopped
1/2 c. green pepper, chopped
1 sm. onion, chopped
4 med. fresh peeled tomatoes, chopped
1/2 tsp. thyme
1 tsp. salt
Pepper

Brown pork chops lightly in 2 tablespoons oil in large skillet. Saute garlic, green pepper and onion in 2 tablespoons oil in small skillet. Add tomatoes, thyme, salt and pepper. Add pork chops to sauce. Steam, covered, for 30 minutes or until tender. Yield: 6 servings.

PORK CHOPS DUCHESSE

Salt to taste
4 thick pork chops
Flour
1 onion, sliced
2 1/2 c. sauerkraut
Mashed potatoes

Salt pork chops; dredge in flour. Brown chops in 3 tablespoons hot fat in skillet. Pour fat into baking dish; add onion. Cover onion with sauerkraut. Place chops on top of sauerkraut. Bake, covered, at 300 degrees for 1 hour and 30 minutes. Cover chops with layer of mashed potatoes. Bake at 400 degrees until potatoes are browned lightly. Yield: 4 servings.

PORK CHOPS IN ORANGE SAUCE

Flour
1 tsp. salt
6 pork chops
1 tbsp. oil
1 c. orange juice
1 tbsp. grated orange rind
1 tsp. sugar

Mix 1/4 cup flour with salt. Dredge chops with flour mixture; brown in hot oil in heavy skillet. Pour off all fat. Add 1/2 cup orange juice; cook for 30 minutes. Remove chops from pan; keep hot in oven. Blend rind, sugar, 1 teaspoon flour and remaining orange juice in skillet. Cook, stirring constantly, until thickened. Pour over chops to serve. Yield: 6 servings.

PORK CHOPS IN PRUNE SAUCE

1/2 c. chili sauce
1 1/2 tbsp. lemon juice
1 tbsp. grated onion
1/4 tbsp. dry mustard
1/2 c. prune juice
1/2 tsp. salt
1/2 tsp. paprika
2 tsp. Worcestershire sauce
1/2 c. chopped celery
6 thick pork chops
6 cooked prunes

Combine all ingredients except chops and prunes; marinate chops in mixture for 1 hour. Place in baking dish; pour marinade around chops. Bake, covered, at 350 degrees for 45 minutes. Remove cover; place cooked prune on top of each chop. Bake, uncovered, until chops are tender and glazed. Serve with sauce. Yield: 4-6 servings.

PORK CHOPS STUFFED WITH MUSHROOMS

1 med. onion, minced
3 tbsp. butter
1/3 c. mushrooms, minced
Thyme
2 tbsp. chopped parsley
1/2 c. toasted bread crumbs
Salt and pepper
1 egg, lightly beaten
4 thick loin chops with pockets

Saute onion in butter until transparent; add mushrooms, several leaves of thyme, parsley and crumbs. Mix well; remove from heat. Season to taste; stir in egg. Stuff chops; brown in small amount of fat in skillet. Place in greased casserole. Bake at 350 degrees for 1 hour. Yield: 4 servings.

SOUTHERN-STYLE PORK WITH RICE

6 thick pork chops
2/3 c. rice
1 c. water
2 tsp. salt
1/2 c. chopped onion
1 1-lb. can tomatoes, chopped
1 c. whole kernel corn
1/4 tsp. pepper

Trim fat from pork chops; render in large skillet. Brown chops in fat gradually; remove from skillet. Pour off excess fat. Spread rice in skillet; add water. Sprinkle with 1 teaspoon salt. Arrange chops over rice. Sprinkle with remaining salt. Add onion and tomatoes; spoon on corn. Sprinkle with pepper; bring to a boil. Reduce heat; simmer, covered, for 35 minutes. Add water, if necessary. Yield: 6 servings.

STUFFED PORK CHOPS

2 c. dried bread cubes
1 c. cracker crumbs
Pepper
1/2 tsp. poultry seasoning
Sage to taste
1 tbsp. onion
3 tbsp. melted butter
Salt to taste
4 thick pork chops, with pockets
Flour
1/4 c. cooking oil
1 can mushroom soup

Combine bread, crackers, 1/8 teaspoon pepper, poultry seasoning and sage. Cook onion in small amount of butter until tender. Add onion and remaining butter to bread mixture; toss gently until mixed thoroughly. Add enough water to moisten. Sprinkle salt and pepper to taste on outside and inside pockets of chops. Fill pockets with stuffing; fasten with toothpicks. Flour both sides; brown in oil gradually. Add mushroom soup. Bake covered, in 350-degree oven for 60 minutes or until tender.

WILD RICE AND PORK CHOPS

1 c. wild rice
8 slices bacon
1 med. onion, minced
1 tsp. salt
1/4 tsp. pepper
1/2 tsp. oregano
6 pork chops, 1 1/2 in. thick
Poultry seasoning to taste

Wash rice well. Cover with hot water; bring to a boil. Cook for 5 minutes. Drain; rinse with hot water. Cover rice with hot salted water. Bring to a boil; cook, stirring occasionally, for 20 minutes or until rice is tender. Drain well. Dice bacon; saute with onion until the bacon is crisp and onion is tender. Add rice, salt, pepper and oregano; toss to blend well. Place mixture in large baking dish. Brown chops well on both sides in skillet; sprinkle with additional salt, pepper, and poultry seasoning. Place over rice. Cover; set casserole in pan of hot water. Bake at 325 degrees for 1 hour and 30 minutes or until chops are tender. Make gravy in pan in which chops were browned, if desired.

GELATIN PORK LOAF

3 lb. pork
1 1/2 tsp. salt
1/4 tsp. pepper
1/2 tsp. celery seed
1/2 c. crushed crackers
1/2 tsp. dry mustard
Hard-boiled eggs, chopped
2 tbsp. unflavored gelatin

Simmer pork in 1 cup water until tender; cool and grind. Add salt, pepper, celery seed, crackers, mustard and eggs. Soften gelatin in 3 tablespoons warm water; add to pork mixture. Pack in loaf pan. Refrigerate for several hours. Yield: 8-10 servings.

CROWN ROAST OF PORK

1 8-lb. crown pork roast
Salt and pepper
2/3 c. butter
1/2 c. finely minced onion
1 c. chopped celery
8 c. bread crumbs
2 tsp. sage, thyme or marjoram
Poultry seasoning to taste
1 8-oz. can sliced mushrooms
Crab apples

Season roast to taste with salt and pepper. Place in roasting pan, bone ends up; wrap bone ends in foil. Bake, uncovered, in 325-degree oven for 2 hours and 20 minutes. Melt butter in skillet; add onion. Cook until transparent. Stir in celery; heat through. Turn into deep bowl; add all remaining ingredients, 2 teaspoons salt and 1/2 teaspoon pepper. Moisten with water, if necessary. Place in center of crown. Bake for 1 hour longer. Replace foil wraps on bone end with crab apples to serve. Yield: 10 servings.

CHINESE ROAST PORK

1 3-lb. lean pork roast
1 tsp. salt
1/3 c. soy sauce
3 tbsp. lemon juice
2 tbsp. sugar
1/8 tsp. red food coloring
3 cloves of garlic, minced
1/4 tsp. ginger
4 sm. green onions
1 sm. onion, sliced

Wipe pork with damp cloth. Combine salt, soy sauce, lemon juice, sugar, red food coloring, garlic and ginger; rub onto pork. Cut green onions into 1-inch lengths. Place pork in roasting pan; add onion, green onions and 1/2 cup water. Bake at 325 degrees for 2 hours. Slice into 1/4-inch slices.

ISLAND PORK AMBROSIA

1 jar strained apricots
5 tbsp. honey
1/4 c. lemon juice
1/4 c. soya sauce
1/2 clove of garlic, minced
1/2 sm. onion, minced
1/3 c. ginger ale
1/8 tsp. ginger
1/8 tsp. pepper
1 5-lb. loin pork roast

Combine first 9 ingredients; pour over roast. Marinate in refrigerator overnight, turning roast frequently. Bake at 325 degrees for 3 hours and 30 minutes, basting frequently. Make gravy with remaining liquids, if desired. Yield: 6 servings.

LUAU PORK AMBROSIA

1 5-lb. pork roast
4 jars strained apricots
1/3 c. honey
1/4 c. fresh lemon juice
1/4 c. soy sauce
1/2 clove of garlic, minced
1 sm. onion, minced
1 c. ginger ale
1/8 tsp. ginger
1/8 tsp. pepper
1 No. 2 can whole unpeeled apricots
1 tbsp. grated lemon rind
1/4 c. grated coconut
Parsley sprigs

Place pork in large bowl. Combine 2 jars strained apricots, honey, lemon juice, soy sauce, garlic, onion, ginger ale, ginger and pepper; pour over pork. Marinate for 5 hours, turning occasionally. Remove pork from sauce, reserving marinade. Place roast on spit. Cook over low coals 6 inches from source of heat for 3 hours. Cook for 25 minutes longer, basting with marinade frequently. Spread 1 jar strained apricots over roast; cook for 5 minutes. Heat remaining marinade with 1 jar apricots; serve over pork. Heat whole apricots and lemon rind together. Place roast on hot serving platter. Surround with whole apricots; sprinkle with coconut and parsley sprigs. Yield: 6-8 servings.

MARINATED PORK ROAST

1 5-lb. pork roast, boned and rolled
1/2 c. soy sauce
1/2 c. dry sherry
1 tbsp. dry mustard
1 tsp. thyme
1 tsp. ginger
2 cloves of garlic, minced

Place roast in large plastic bag; place in deep bowl. Combine remaining ingredients. Pour over roast; close bag tightly. Let stand overnight in refrigerator. Remove from marinade. Place on rack in shallow roasting pan. Bake at 325 degrees for 3 hours or to 175 degrees on meat thermometer, basting with marinade occasionally. Yield: 10 servings.

ORANGE PORK

1 3-lb. pork loin roast
Cracked pepper
Orange marmalade

Place pork on cooking rack, fat side up. Coat fat with pepper. Bake at 350 degrees for 1 hour. Remove from oven; coat with marmalade. Return to oven. Bake until tender. Yield: 4-6 servings.

POLYNESIAN PORK

1 3-lb. pork shoulder roast
1 c. rice, cooked
1/2 c. chopped green pepper
1/2 c. chopped pimento
2 tbsp. parsley flakes
3 tbsp. vegetable oil
2 tbsp. lemon juice
2 tsp. sugar
1 tsp. salt
2 c. diced celery
1 c. mayonnaise
1 tsp. curry powder
2 tsp. soy sauce

Bake roast at 350 degrees for 2 hours and 30 minutes; cool thoroughly. Combine rice, green pepper, pimento and parsley in large bowl; toss lightly with oil, lemon juice, sugar and salt. Chill in mold for 2 hours. Trim fat from pork; cut into cubes. Combine with celery in large bowl; mix in mayonnaise, curry powder and soy sauce. Toss lightly; chill. Unmold rice mixture onto platter; place pork mixture in center. Yield: 6 servings.

PORK LOIN IN RED WINE

1 3-lb. pork loin
Salt and pepper
Sage to taste
Nutmeg to taste
1 clove of garlic, crushed
1/4 c. chopped parsley
1/4 c. chopped onion
1 bay leaf
2 c. red wine
1 c. canned consomme

Rub pork loin with salt, pepper, sage and nutmeg. Place roast in small amount of fat in large skillet with crushed garlic; brown on all sides. Reserve pan drippings. Place roast in baking dish; add parsley, onion, bay leaf and wine. Bake at 350 degrees for 2 hours or until tender, turning twice. Add consomme. Bake for 20 minutes longer. Place on platter; stir reserved drippings into wine mixture in roasting pan. Serve with pork. Yield: 4-6 servings.

PORK LOIN WITH APPLESAUCE

1 tbsp. flour
1 tsp. salt
1 tsp. dry mustard
1/4 tsp. pepper
1 4-lb. pork loin roast
1 lb. can applesauce
1/4 c. (packed) brown sugar
1/4 tsp. cinnamon
1/4 tsp. cloves

Combine flour, salt, mustard and pepper; rub over roast. Place fat side up in roasting pan. Bake at 325 degrees for 1 hour. Combine applesauce and all remaining ingredients; spread over roast. Bake for 1 hour longer. Yield: 8 servings.

PORK ROAST WITH VEGETABLES

1 4-lb. pork roast
Salt
2 c. chopped onions
6 lge. potatoes
2 No. 2 cans lima beans
2 No. 2 cans peas
1 lge. can green beans
Pepper to taste
1 c. barbecue sauce

Rub roast with salt; place in large pan on bottom rack of oven. Bake at 350 degrees for 3 hours. Combine onions, potatoes, beans, peas, green beans, salt to taste and pepper; cook until potatoes are tender. Slice roast into 1/2-inch slices. Cover evenly with vegetables. Pour sauce over vegetables; spread out evenly. Bake for 30 minutes longer. Yield: 12 servings.

ROAST PORK WITH APRICOT GLAZE

1 pork roast
Salt and pepper
Whole cloves
1 c. dried apricots
1/2 c. (packed) brown sugar
1 tbsp. cornstarch
Cooked green beans

Score fat on roast with knife to form squares; rub with salt and pepper. Stick with cloves. Place on rack in roasting pan, fat side up. Bake at 350 degrees for 35 minutes per pound or to 185 degrees on meat thermometer. Simmer apricots in 2 cups water until tender. Drain apricots; reserve 1 cup juice. Combine brown sugar, cornstarch and half the apricot juice; spoon over pork 30 minutes before end of baking time. Baste frequently with mixture and drippings until pork is glazed and golden. Place roast on platter. Season beans with 1/4 cup drippings and reserved juice. Circle pork with green beans and apricots.

ROAST PORK DINNER

1 4-lb. roast loin of pork
1 1/2 tsp. salt
1/2 tsp. caraway seed
1/8 tsp. pepper
1/2 c. chopped fresh onions
Butter
2 1/2 lb. small potatoes

Sprinkle pork with salt, caraway seed and pepper; place in shallow baking pan. Bake in 325-degree oven for about 1 hour. Pour off excess drippings. Saute onions in butter in skillet; add to roast. Add small amount of water; bake for 30 minutes longer. Pare potatoes; cook in boiling salted water in covered saucepan for 8 minutes. Drain. Place potatoes around roast; bake for 1 hour, turning occasionally. Place pork and potatoes on heated serving platter; garnish with parsley. Yield: 4-6 servings.

Roast Pork Dinner . . . Small potatoes roasted with pork and seasoned with herbs.

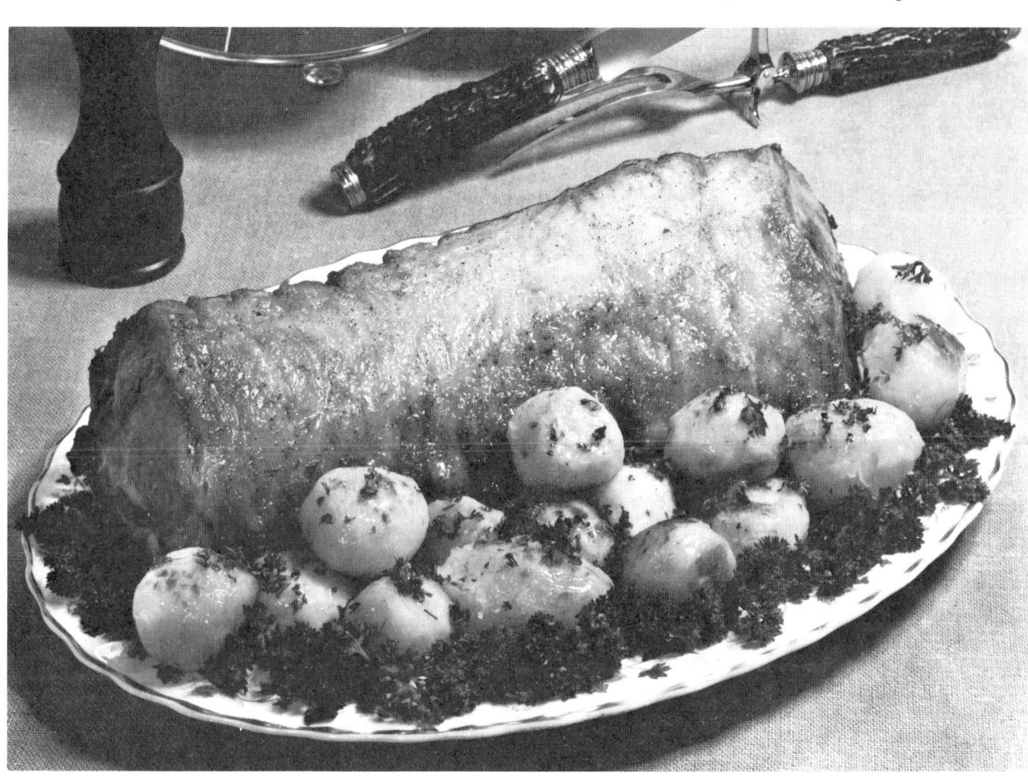

Pork Roast Maraschino . . . A sweet and sour fruit and pickle glaze bastes this roast pork.

PORK ROAST MARASCHINO

1 tbsp. salad oil
2 cloves of garlic
1 29-1/2-oz. can pineapple chunks
1 c. undrained sweet mixed pickles
1 16-oz. jar red maraschino cherries
5 tsp. cornstarch
1 tbsp. soy sauce
2 tsp. salt
1 5-lb. pork loin roast

Heat oil in saucepan; saute garlic. Remove garlic. Drain pineapple, pickles and cherries, reserving liquids. Set fruits and pickles aside. Blend cornstarch with 2 tablespoons cold water; add reserved liquid, soy sauce and salt. Add cornstarch mixture to oil in saucepan; cook, stirring, until thickened. Set glaze aside. Place roast on rack in shallow roasting pan. Bake in 325-degree oven for 35 to 45 minutes per pound or until meat thermometer registers 170 degrees. Baste roast with some of the glaze during last hour and 30 minutes of baking time. Add fruits and pickles to remaining glaze; heat through. Spoon over and around roast on serving platter.

HERBED PORK ROAST

Color photograph for this recipe on page 65.

1 5-lb. pork loin
Salt and pepper
Crushed thyme leaves to taste
Crushed marjoram leaves to taste
1/2 c. apple jelly
2 tbsp. dry sauterne
3 tbsp. flour
1/2 c. milk

Trim fat on pork loin to 1/8 inch; sprinkle loin with seasonings. Place in shallow baking pan. Bake in 325-degree oven for 1 hour and 45 minutes. Simmer apple jelly and sauterne in small saucepan over medium heat for 3 minutes, stirring frequently. Brush loin with some of the jelly mixture. Bake for 1 hour and 15 minutes longer, basting occasionally with remaining jelly mixture. Remove loin to heated serving platter. Pour off drippings from baking pan; skim off fat. Return 1/2 cup drippings to baking pan; place over low heat. Blend in flour; add 1 1/2 cups water and milk. Cook for 2 minutes, stirring frequently; season with salt and pepper. Yield: 8-10 servings. Serve gravy with loin.

SAUERKRAUT AND PORK WITH DUMPLINGS

1 3-lb. pork roast
1 No. 2 1/2 can sauerkraut
1 med. onion, chopped
6 med. potatoes, pared
2 c. prepared biscuit mix
3/4 c. milk

Place roast in Dutch oven; arrange sauerkraut and onion around roast. Fill with water until sauerkraut is covered. Bake, covered, in 325-degree oven for 3 hours. Cook potatoes in boiling salted water until tender. Mix all remaining ingredients well with fork. Place roast in Dutch oven on top of stove over low heat. Spoon biscuit mixture onto boiling sauerkraut.

Cover. Cook for 10 minutes over low heat. Uncover; cook for 10 minutes longer. Drain potatoes; mash. Place mashed potatoes in serving dish; arrange sauerkraut and dumplings over top. Remove roast to platter; serve with potatoes, sauerkraut and dumplings. Yield: 6 servings.

TASTY BARBECUED PORK

1/2 tsp. salt
1/4 tsp. pepper
1 4-lb. pork roast
1 sm. onion, chopped
2 c. tomato juice
2 tbsp. Worcestershire sauce
2 tbsp. flour

Salt and pepper roast; brown in small amount of fat in large skillet. Bake at 400 degrees until tender. Cool thoroughly. Slice roast. Place 2 cups water in skillet; add onion, tomato juice and Worcestershire sauce. Combine flour and 1/4 cup water, blending well. Add flour mixture to tomato mixture, stirring constantly, until thickened. Place sliced pork in gravy; simmer until heated through. Yield: 6 servings.

VIRGINIA ROAST PORK

1 3 to 4-lb. pork loin roast
Cloves
2 tsp. salt
1/2 tsp. pepper
2 c. cider
Flour
3/4 c. chicken broth

Score fat on pork; stud with cloves. Mix 1 teaspoon salt and 1/4 teaspoon pepper; sprinkle over roast. Bake, uncovered, at 350 degrees, allowing 35 minutes per pound. Baste with cider, adding small amount at a time. Drain off fat. Stir 2 tablespoons flour into pan drippings, blending well. Add broth, stirring constantly, until thickened. Stir in remaining salt and pepper. Yield: 8 servings.

ROAST SUCKLING PIG

1 10-lb. suckling pig
1 lge. onion, minced
3/4 c. butter, melted
2 18-oz. loaves bread
1 tbsp. sage
1 1/2 tsp. salt
1/8 tsp. pepper
1 sm. red apple
Cranberries

Rinse inside of prepared pig; pat dry. Saute onion in 1/2 cup butter; soak bread in 3 cups water. Combine onion, bread, sage, salt and pepper. Fill pig lightly with dressing; secure opening. Tie legs in place; put piece of wood in mouth and place pig in kneeling position in roasting pan. Sprinkle with additional salt. Pour 1 cup hot water in pan. Place foil over ears and tail. Bake at 325 degrees for 3 hours and 30 minutes, basting frequently with remaining butter. Remove foil; bake for 30 minutes longer or until pig is tender. Place pig in kneeling position on hot platter. Remove block; place apple in mouth and cranberries in eye sockets. Yield: 10-12 servings.

SAVORY PORK PIE

1 1/2 lb. pork butt cubes
3 tbsp. flour
2 tbsp. butter
1/3 c. chopped celery
3/4 c. chopped onion
1 tsp. salt
1/8 tsp. pepper
1/2 c. half and half
Prepared biscuit mix

Cut pork into 1-inch cubes; dredge in flour. Brown cubes in butter; add celery, onion, salt, pepper and 1 1/2 cups boiling water. Simmer, covered, for 1 hour and 30 minutes. Add water, if necessary. Stir in half and half; bring back to simmer. Place in baking dish. Preheat oven to 450 degrees. Prepare biscuit mix according to package directions for biscuits. Top hot mixture with biscuits. Bake for 10 to 12 minutes. Yield: 6-8 servings.

BARBECUED COUNTRY-STYLE SPARERIBS

4 lb. country-style spareribs
1 lge. onion, sliced
1 tsp. salt
1 tsp. paprika
1/2 tsp. celery salt
1/4 c. (packed) brown sugar
1/4 c. vinegar
1 tbsp. Worcestershire sauce
1 c. catsup

Preheat oven to 450 degrees. Cut spareribs into strips; lay in roasting pan, fat side up. Arrange onion slices over spareribs. Place in oven. Bake for 25 minutes or until spareribs begin to brown. Combine all remaining ingredients into small saucepan; mix well. Bring to a boil. Reduce oven to 350 degrees. Pour sauce over spareribs; turn, coating with sauce. Bake for 1 hour or until tender, basting every 15 minutes with sauce. Yield: 4 servings.

COUNTRY-STYLE RIBS

3 lb. spareribs
1 c. catsup
1/3 c. cider vinegar
2 tbsp. dark corn syrup
1 env. onion soup mix
1 clove of garlic, minced
1/8 tsp. chili powder
Dash of pepper

Place spareribs in broiler pan without rack. Bake in 450-degree oven for 30 minutes. Reduce heat to 350 degrees; continue cooking ribs for 30 minutes longer. Combine catsup, vinegar, corn syrup, soup mix, garlic, chili powder and pepper in quart jar. Add 1 1/4 cups hot water. Cover, shake well. Remove spareribs from oven; drain off fat. Pour sauce over ribs. Bake, basting occasionally, for 35 minutes or until ribs are tender and brown and sauce is thickened. Yield: 4-6 servings.

SPARERIBS AND SAUERKRAUT

3 lb. spareribs, cut in 2-rib pieces
1 1-lb. 11-oz. can sauerkraut
1/2 c. chopped onions
1/4 tsp. marjoram
2 tsp. sugar
1 tsp. salt
1/4 tsp. pepper

Arrange ribs, rib ends down, in 13 x 9-inch baking dish. Bake, covered, at 325 degrees for 1 hour and 30 minutes; pour off drippings. Remove spareribs; combine sauerkraut, onions, marjoram and sugar in baking dish. Arrange spareribs, browned side up, on top of sauerkraut mixture; season with salt and pepper. Bake, uncovered, for 45 minutes or until spareribs are tender. Yield: 4-6 servings.

BARBECUED SPARERIBS

8 lb. spareribs
1 c. catsup
1 c. claret
1/4 c. vinegar
2 tbsp. (packed) brown sugar
2 tbsp. Worcestershire sauce
1 tsp. English mustard
1/2 tsp. smoked salt
1 tsp. chili powder
1 grated clove of garlic
1 tbsp. soy sauce
1/4 tsp. cayenne pepper
1 med. onion, grated
1 tbsp. celery seed

Bake ribs in 400-degree oven for 5 minutes. Combine all remaining ingredients except celery seed; pour over ribs. Reduce heat to 350 degrees. Bake for 45 minutes, basting occasionally. Sprinkle with additional smoked salt and celery seed. Bake for 15 minutes longer or until hot and almost dry. Cut ribs apart; serve. Yield: 4-6 servings.

FRESH PORK AND CORN DUMPLINGS

3 lb. fresh pork backbone
1 sm. hot red pepper
1 tsp. sage
1 1/2 tsp. salt
2 c. cornmeal
1/4 c. flour
1 tsp. baking powder

Place pork in 4-quart kettle; add 2 quarts water, red pepper, sage and 1 teaspoon salt. Cover; bring to boil. Simmer for 3 hours or until pork is tender. Remove pork from kettle; reserve liquid in kettle, keeping hot. Brown pork in 350-degree oven. Combine cornmeal, flour, remaining salt and baking powder; stir in 1 cup boiling water and 1 cup reserved liquid. Form into egg-sized dumplings; drop into remaining hot liquid in kettle. Cover; simmer for 45 minutes.

OUTRIGGER RIBS WITH GINGER SAUCE

1/2 c. soy sauce
1/2 c. catsup
3 tbsp. (packed) brown sugar
2 tsp. ginger
3 lb. spareribs
1 tsp. monosodium glutamate
1/4 c. sugar
1 tsp. salt

Combine soy sauce, catsup, brown sugar and ginger. Let mixture stand overnight. Rub ribs on both sides with monosodium glutamate, sugar and salt; let stand for 3 hours. Brush with ginger sauce; let stand for 1 hour. Place ribs on rack in shallow baking pan. Bake at 450 degrees for 15 minutes; pour off fat. Reduce temperature to 350 degrees. Bake for 1 hour longer or until tender, turning ribs and brushing with sauce several times. Yield: 4-5 servings.

SKILLET SPARERIBS

1 1/2 lb. pork ribs, cut in serving pieces
Salt and pepper to taste
1 lge. onion, chopped
1 sm. green pepper, chopped
3 stalks celery, chopped
2 cloves of garlic, chopped
1 c. rice
1 tsp. salt
Pepper and red pepper to taste
2 tbsp. chopped parsley
2 tbsp. chopped green onion tops

Turn electric skillet control to 350 degrees. Season ribs; brown, covered, in skillet. Remove ribs; pour off excess drippings, reserving 3 tablespoons in skillet. Add onion, green pepper, celery and garlic to drippings; simmer until transparent, stirring frequently. Add rice, salt, peppers and 1 1/4 cups water; stir well. Top mixture with ribs; cover. Reduce heat to 300 degrees. Cook for 20 minutes or until rice is tender. Add parsley and green onion tops; cook for 5 minutes. Yield: 8 servings.

SPARERIBS IN CHERRY SAUCE

2 pieces loin ribs
1 tbsp. fat
1 No. 2 can sour cherries
1/4 tsp. cloves
1 clove of garlic, crushed
1/4 c. (packed) brown sugar
1/4 tsp. dry mustard
1/2 tsp. salt
2 tbsp. flour
3 tbsp. vinegar

Cut spareribs into 3-rib portions. Brown in hot fat in skillet. Remove from skillet; keep hot. Drain cherries; reserve juice. Add reserved juice, cloves, garlic, brown sugar, mustard, salt, flour, vinegar, and 1 cup water to skillet. Cook, stirring constantly, until sauce is thick and smooth. Return ribs to skillet; add cherries. Cook, covered, on top of stove gradually for 1 1/2 hours. Baste frequently with sauce.

SWEET AND SOUR SPARERIBS

Salt and pepper to taste
1 1/2 lb. pork spareribs
1 tbsp. oil
1 c. pineapple juice
3 tbsp. cornstarch
1/2 c. sugar
1 tbsp. soy sauce
3 tbsp. vinegar
4 slices pineapple, cut into chunks
1 green pepper, cut into strips

Salt and pepper spareribs; brown on both sides. Place in baking dish. Heat oil and pineapple juice in saucepan over low heat. Combine cornstarch, sugar, soy sauce, vinegar and 3/8 cup water. Add hot juice, stirring constantly, until thick. Add pineapple and green pepper; pour over meat. Bake at 350 degrees for 1 hour. Serve over steamed rice or Chinese noodles. Yield: 4 servings.

TEXAS-BARBECUED SPARERIBS

3 lb. spareribs
Lemon slices
1/2 c. chopped onion
2 tbsp. brown sugar
1 tbsp. paprika
1 tsp. salt
1 tsp. dry mustard
1/4 tsp. chili powder
1/8 tsp. cayenne pepper
2 tbsp. Worcestershire sauce
1/4 c. vinegar
1 c. tomato juice
1/4 c. catsup
1/2 c. water

Cut spareribs into serving pieces; place in roasting pan. Arrange 1 lemon slice on each serving. Sprinkle with onion. Bake in 450-degree oven for 30 minutes. Mix all remaining ingredients in saucepan. Simmer for 15 minutes or until thickened slightly. Pour over ribs; reduce oven temperature to 350 degrees. Bake for 1 hour, basting every 15 minutes with sauce. Add water, if necessary. Bake covered, for 30 minutes longer.

SPICY PORK STEAKS

4 pork steaks, cut 1/2 in. thick	*1 tbsp. vinegar*
2 tbsp. shortening	*1/8 tsp. cinnamon*
1 tsp. salt	*1/8 tsp. allspice*
1/8 tsp. pepper	*1/8 tsp. cloves*
2 tbsp. (packed) brown sugar	*12 prunes*
	16 dried apricot halves

Brown steaks in shortening; pour off pan drippings. Season steaks with salt and pepper. Mix 1/2 cup water with brown sugar, vinegar, cinnamon, allspice and cloves; pour over steaks. Add prunes and apricots. Simmer, covered, for 45 minutes or until steaks are tender. Thicken liquid for gravy, if desired. Yield: 4 servings.

TOMATO SWEET AND SOUR PORK

3 lb. pork shoulder, cubed	*1/3 c. (packed) brown sugar*
3 tbsp. oil	*3 tbsp. soy sauce*
2 8 1/4-oz. cans pineapple tidbits	*1 clove of garlic, minced*
2 8-oz. cans tomato sauce	*1/4 tsp. ginger*
1/3 c. vinegar	*1/2 green pepper, diced*

Saute pork in hot oil in skillet until golden brown on all sides. Drain pineapple, reserving syrup. Combine reserved syrup, tomato sauce, vinegar, brown sugar and soy sauce; add to pork. Stir in garlic and ginger. Simmer, covered, for 1 hour and 30 minutes or until pork is tender. Add pineapple and green pepper; simmer until green pepper is crisp-tender. Serve over hot rice. Yield: 8-10 servings.

Potato

Economical, nutritious, plentiful, and versatile, potatoes are a staple of American diet. These root vegetables or tubers may be elongated or round; large, medium, or small; red, russet, or white. Generally, all potatoes can be classified as either early new potatoes or late mature potatoes. New potatoes, marketed during the spring and summer, are not fully mature when harvested. They have thin, feathery red or white skins and sometimes skinned areas. They are best boiled or used in salads. Mature potatoes are harvested when fully grown. They are marketed the greater part of the year. Mature potatoes include familiar varieties like Idaho, Maine, and Long Island potatoes, mealy types excellent for baking and mashing, and varieties like Early Rose, Green Mountain, and Cobbler potatoes, waxy types good for scalloping, frying, creaming, and for use in salads. Potatoes are grown commercially in every mainland state, but Idaho leads production. Potatoes are outstanding sources of Vitamin C. They also supply Vitamin A, thiamine, riboflavin, niacin, iron, calcium, and protein. Potatoes are not, as popularly believed, fattening. Only when fried or served with butter or gravy do potatoes become calorically high. (1 medium baked and peeled potato = 90 calories; 1 medium boiled and peeled potato = 105 calories; 10 deep fat French-fries = 155 calories; 1 cup mashed potatoes with milk = 125 calories; 10 potato chips = 110 calories)

AVAILABILITY: Fresh year-round with minimum monthly fluctuation. Usually sold loose or in consumer-sized packages of 5, 10, 15, 20, or 25 pounds. Packaged, canned, frozen, and dehydrated potatoes and/or potato products processed and sold year-round. Packaged potato chips, frozen French-fries, and dehydrated flakes or granules for mashed potatoes are among the most commonly marketed processed potato products.

BUYING: Choose firm, well-shaped potatoes with shallow eyes. Mature potatoes with thick, dry skins store well. Early new potatoes should have thin, feathery skins. Some skinned surface is normal. Avoid potatoes with cuts, bruises, decay, or green portions (green indicates bitterness). Also avoid wilted potatoes or potatoes that have sprouts.

STORING: Keep fresh potatoes in a cool, dark place, preferably between 45 and 50 degrees. Never store in an airtight container; pack loosely in bag or bin to premit air circulation. Don't place storage bag on damp cellar floor. New potatoes keep one week to ten days; mature potatoes keep several months. Store frozen products in refrigerator freezer up to 3 months or in home freezer 1 year. Keep unopened canned products on kitchen shelf 1 year. *Freezing fresh potatoes is not recommended.* However, cooked potatoes may be frozen satisfactorily. Pack mashed potatoes, French-fried potatoes, and potato chips in freezer containers, leaving 1/2-inch head space. Wrap baked stuffed potatoes individually, excluding as much air as possible. Freeze for time indicated above. *To can new potatoes*—Wash, scrape, and rinse. Boil in water 10 minutes. Drain. Hot pack only. Proceed according to instructions under CANNING.

PREPARATION: Versatile potatoes may be boiled, baked, stuffed, mashed, French-fried, scalloped, or creamed. They are used in main dishes like hash, New England boiled dinners, and casseroles; in salads; and in soups and chowders. Potatoes are also used in breads and desserts like custard pie and cake. Some information or tips on cooking potatoes follow. *Boiled new potatoes*—Prepare just before cooking by scraping, not peeling. Don't soak before boiling. Cook in minimum amount of water, just enough to keep potatoes from sticking. Start potatoes in boiling salted water, bring to quick boil, reduce heat to just keep water bubbling. Prevent overcooking by testing for tenderness with fork. *Baked potatoes*—Never soak potatoes to be baked. For tender skin, brush with melted butter before baking. Baked potatoes pricked with fork before cooking will be mealy, as steam escapes easily. *French-fried potatoes*—For light color soak potatoes to be French-fried in water. Limit soaking time to 15 minutes to minimize vitamin loss. Fry just before serving; left standing, French-fried potatoes become soft and soggy. *Mashed potatoes*—Dry potatoes to be mashed by draining and then placing pan over gentle flame. Add a teaspoon of baking powder to mashed potatoes for light and fluffy texture. Scald cream or milk to be added to mashed potatoes for smooth texture. To avoid watery mashed potatoes, mash over low heat, stir occasionally to prevent scorching.

SERVING: Serve baked potatoes with butter or sour cream. Serve boiled potatoes with butter. Complementary seasonings for potatoes include chopped green onions, chives, minced parsley, caraway seeds, chopped dill, crumbled fried bacon, and so on.

(See VEGETABLES.)

POTATO CHIPS

6 potatoes, peeled
Salt to taste

Slice potatoes paper thin; soak in cold water for 1 hour. Drain; pat dry between paper toweling. Place just enough potato slices in frying basket to cover bottom. Fry in hot deep fat for 3 minutes or until lightly browned, shaking basket frequently. Drain on paper toweling; sprinkle with salt.

TINY POTATO APPETIZER

2 tbsp. butter
Chicken stock base
1 No. 303 can tiny potatoes, drained
1 tbsp. chopped chives
1 c. sour cream
Paprika

Melt butter in chafing dish; add 1 teaspoon stock base. Add potatoes; stir to coat well. Simmer, covered, until heated through. Sprinkle potatoes with paprika; serve with wooden picks. Stir chives into sour cream. Garnish with additional chives, if desired.

BAVARIAN POTATO SOUP

4 slices bacon, diced
6 leeks, sliced thin
1/4 c. chopped onion
2 tbsp. flour
4 c. bouillon
3 lge. potatoes, sliced
2 egg yolks, beaten
1 c. sour cream
1 tbsp. minced parsley
1 tbsp. minced chervil

Saute bacon in deep saucepan for 5 minutes. Add leeks and onion; saute for 5 minutes. Stir in flour. Add bouillon slowly, stirring constantly. Add potatoes; simmer for 1 hour. Combine egg yolks and cream; stir into potato mixture. Simmer for 10 minutes, stirring constantly. Add parsley and chervil.

BROWN POTATO SOUP

2 1/2 c. potatoes
1 tbsp. salt
1/4 tsp. pepper
1/4 tsp. onion salt
1/4 tsp. celery salt
4 c. milk
2 tbsp. butter
3/4 c. flour

Peel and dice potatoes. Combine potatoes, salt, pepper, onion and celery salt in saucepan in 2 cups water. Simmer, covered, until potatoes are tender. Drain potatoes, reserving liquid. Combine milk, reserved liquid and 2 cups water; bring to a boil. Reduce heat; simmer. Cut butter into flour until mixture resembles coarse crumbs. Brown crumbs in small skillet, stirring constantly. Stir crumbs into milk mixture; cook, stirring constantly, for 5 minutes. Add potatoes; simmer for 5 minutes or until heated through. Yield: 6-8 servings.

CREAM OF POTATO SOUP

2 c. diced potatoes
1 c. milk
1 onion, thickly sliced
2 tbsp. butter
1 tbsp. chopped parsley
1 tbsp. flour
1/2 tsp. salt
Dash of pepper

Cook potatoes in 2 cups water until tender. Scald milk with onion in top of double boiler. Melt butter in small skillet; add parsley. Cook until wilted; stir in flour and seasonings. Remove onion from milk; add butter mixture. Cook, stirring constantly, until slightly thickened. Drain potatoes; reserve liquid. Rice potatoes; return to potato liquid. Combine with white sauce in double boiler; stir until well blended. May be garnished with additional chopped parsley.

CURRIED POTATO SOUP

2/3 c. chopped onion
1 tsp. curry powder
2 tbsp. butter
3 c. diced potatoes
2 tsp. salt
2 1/2 c. milk

Cook onion with curry powder in butter in large saucepan until tender. Add potatoes, 2 cups boiling water and salt; cook until potatoes are tender. Mash potatoes; add milk. Heat through.

PENNSYLVANIA DUTCH POTATO SOUP

2 c. diced potatoes
2 tbsp. onion
2 tbsp. margarine
2 tbsp. flour
2 c. milk
1/8 tsp. celery salt
Salt and pepper to taste
1 hard-cooked egg, chopped

Boil potatoes in 1 cup water for 15 minutes or until tender. Brown onion in margarine; blend in flour. Add 1/2 cup milk. Simmer, stirring constantly, until thickened. Add flour mixture, seasonings and remaining milk to potatoes. Cook, stirring occasionally, until thickened. Garnish with egg.

POTATO-MUSHROOM SOUP

3 c. coarsely chopped mushrooms
1 med. onion, chopped
1/4 c. butter
1 c. 1/2-in. potato cubes
1 c. boiling water
2 c. milk
2 egg yolks
2 c. sour cream
2 tsp. salt
1/4 tsp. pepper
1/4 tsp. leaf thyme
1/8 tsp. mace
1/8 tsp. nutmeg
Chopped parsley

Cook mushrooms and onion in butter in heavy saucepan for 3 minutes. Add potatoes and water; bring to a boil. Simmer, covered, for 10 minutes or until potatoes are tender; remove from heat. Beat milk and egg yolks together with fork. Combine with cream, salt, pepper, thyme, mace and nutmeg. Stir into hot mixture gradually; bring just to a boil, stirring constantly. Serve immediately. Sprinkle with parsley. Yield: 6 servings.

SWISS CREAM OF POTATO SOUP

4 med. potatoes
2 bacon slices, diced
1/4 c. minced onion
2 tbsp. butter
1 tbsp. snipped parsley
2 tsp. salt
1/2 tsp. nutmeg
Dash of pepper
1/4 tsp. dry mustard
1 tsp. Worcestershire sauce
3 c. milk
1/2 c. grated Swiss cheese

Cook potatoes in small amount of water until tender; drain. Peel potatoes; mash. Saute bacon and onion over low heat, stirring, until brown. Add bacon mixture, butter, parsley, salt, nutmeg, pepper, mustard and Worcestershire sauce to potatoes. Stir in milk; simmer, stirring constantly, until heated through. Sprinkle with cheese; serve at once.

EASY POTATO SALAD

6 baked potatoes, thinly sliced
Wine vinegar
1/3 c. chopped pickles
1/2 c. chopped celery
1/3 c. chopped red onion
1/2 c. mayonnaise
1/2 c. sour cream
Celery salt
Hard-cooked eggs, sliced
Tomato wedges

Marinate potatoes, covered, in 1/4 cup wine vinegar for 2 hours; stir occasionally. Add pickles, celery and onion. Mix mayonnaise and sour cream; add dash of wine vinegar. Pour over salad; mix thoroughly. Chill until ready to serve. Sprinkle with celery salt. Garnish with hard-cooked eggs and tomato wedges.

RIPE OLIVE POTATO SALAD

2 to 3 tbsp. salad oil
1 tbsp. vinegar
1 tsp. salt
1/8 tsp. pepper
2 c. hot diced potatoes
1 c. pitted chopped ripe olives
2 hard-cooked eggs, diced
1 c. sliced celery
1/4 c. diced dill pickles
1/4 c. diced pimento
1/3 c. mayonnaise
1 tsp. grated onion

Blend oil, vinegar, salt and pepper; mix thoroughly. Pour over potatoes; toss lightly. Chill for at least 1 hour. Add olives, eggs, celery, pickles and pimento. Blend mayonnaise and onion; mix lightly with salad. Chill until ready to serve.

HOT GERMAN POTATO SALAD

6 lge. potatoes
1/2 lb. bacon
1 onion, diced
1 tbsp. flour
1/2 c. vinegar
1 tsp. salt
1/2 tsp. pepper
1 tbsp. sugar
2 tsp. angostura bitters

Boil potatoes in salted water to cover; peel and cube. Dice bacon; fry in large skillet until brown and crisp. Remove bacon bits; drain on absorbent paper. Saute onion in bacon drippings until soft. Stir flour into onion mixture. Mix vinegar, 1/2 cup water, salt, pepper and sugar together. Add to flour mixture gradually, stirring constantly, over low heat until thickened. Add bitters; cook until sauce is smooth and glossy. Add potatoes; heat through. Add bacon bits; mix well. Serve warm. Garnish with parsley. Yield: 6 servings.

Hot German Potato Salad . . . This hearty salad goes well with ham, pork, or other dishes.

DILLWEED-POTATO SALAD

7 med. potatoes
1/2 c. salad oil
2 tbsp. vinegar
1 tsp. salt
Dash of pepper
1 tsp. garlic powder
1 tsp. onion powder
1 c. mayonnaise
4 hard-cooked eggs, chopped
1/2 c. sour cream
1/3 c. sliced green onions and tops
2 tsp. chopped dillweed
3/4 c. diced celery

Cook potatoes in water to cover; drain. Peel; slice while warm. Combine oil, vinegar, salt, pepper, garlic powder and onion powder; blend thoroughly. Pour 1/3 of the dressing over potatoes. Let stand for at least 1 hour. Add mayonnaise, eggs, sour cream, onions, dillweed and celery to remaining dressing; combine with potato mixture. Chill until ready to serve.

GOLDEN HOT POTATO SALAD

6 lge. potatoes
2 tbsp. pickle relish
1 onion, chopped
4 stalks celery, chopped
Salt and pepper
2 or 3 eggs, beaten
1/2 c. sugar
1 tsp. dry mustard
2 tbsp. flour
1/2 c. vinegar
2 tbsp. butter
4 hard-boiled eggs

Cook potatoes; cool. Peel; dice. Mix potatoes, pickle relish, onion and celery; season with salt and pepper to taste. Cream eggs and sugar; add mustard, 1 teaspoon salt and flour. Blend; add vinegar, 1 1/2 cups water and butter. Cook until thickened; add 1/2 cup water if needed. Pour over potato mixture. Slice hard-boiled eggs; add to salad.

MOLDED POTATO-TOMATO SALAD

1 env. unflavored gelatin
1 1/2 c. hot chicken broth
1/4 tsp. pepper
1 tsp. salt
1 hard-cooked egg, sliced
1 c. sliced tomatoes
1 c. diced cooked potatoes
1 c. diced celery
1 tsp. minced onion
1 c. cottage cheese
Radishes

Soften gelatin in 1/4 cup water; stir into chicken broth. Add pepper and salt, stirring until gelatin is dissolved. Pour 1/8 of the mixture into loaf pan; chill until firm. Arrange egg and tomatoes in pattern over congealed layer. Combine potatoes, celery, onion, cottage cheese and remaining gelatin mixture; pour carefully over egg and tomatoes. Chill until set. Garnish with radishes and additional tomatoes.

PATIO HOT POTATO SALAD

6 slices bacon, finely cut
6 med. potatoes
1 1/2 tsp. salt
1/8 tsp. pepper
1/2 tsp. celery seed
1 tbsp. sugar
1 tbsp. flour
2 tbsp. chopped onion
1/4 c. vinegar
1/4 c. water
2 tbsp. parsley
Several sliced radishes

Saute bacon in skillet until crisp; remove from skillet. Reserve 1/4 cup bacon drippings. Peel potatoes and dice. Place potatoes in center of 24 x 18-inch rectangle of heavy-duty foil. Combine salt, pepper, celery seed, sugar, flour and onion; sprinkle over potatoes. Pour vinegar, water and reserved bacon drippings over potatoes; sprinkle bacon over top. Bring sides of foil together; fold ends. Seal securely. Grill for 20 minutes. Turn package over; grill for 20 minutes longer. May be baked at 425 degrees for 1 hour, if desired. Garnish with parsley and radishes.

PICNIC POTATO SALAD

2 lb. potatoes
1 c. chopped celery with tops
2 onions, finely chopped
1 green pepper, finely chopped
4 pimentos, chopped
3 tbsp. chopped parsley
3 tbsp. pickle juice
2 c. mayonnaise
1/4 c. capers
12 stuffed olives, thinly sliced
1 c. diced cucumbers
8 sweet pickles, diced
Salt and pepper
Paprika

Cook potatoes in water to cover; drain. Peel potatoes; cut into cubes. Combine celery, onions, green pepper, pimentos, parsley, pickle juice and mayonnaise; mix thoroughly. Chill for at least 2 hours. Combine capers, olives, cucumbers, pickles and potatoes; add dressing. Add salt and pepper to taste; toss lightly. Sprinkle with paprika.

POTATO SALAD WITH COOKED DRESSING

5 or 6 med. potatoes
1/3 c. finely chopped onion
1/2 c. finely chopped celery
1 egg, slightly beaten
2 tbsp. sugar
2 tbsp. vinegar
1/2 tsp. dry mustard
1/8 to 1/4 tsp. red pepper
1 c. mayonnaise
Paprika
Fresh parsley

Combine potatoes, onion and celery. Place egg, sugar, vinegar, mustard and pepper in top of double boiler. Cook over hot water, stirring constantly, until thickened. Remove from heat; cool slightly. Blend in mayonnaise; mix well. Pour over potato mixture. Toss lightly. Garnish with paprika and parsley.

SOUR CREAM-POTATO SALAD

6 c. cooked diced potatoes
1/4 c. melted butter
1 bunch green onions
4 hard-cooked eggs, separated
1 c. chopped celery
1 1/2 tsp. salt
1/2 tsp. pepper
1 c. sour cream
1/2 c. mayonnaise
1 tbsp. prepared mustard
2 tbsp. sugar

Toss potatoes lightly in butter. Chop onions and tops; reserve small amount of tops. Add onions to potatoes. Chop egg whites; add to potato mixture. Add celery, salt and pepper; toss lightly. Mash egg yolks; add sour cream, mayonnaise, mustard and sugar. Mix well. Pour over potato mixture; toss. Garnish with reserved onion tops and radish roses or strips of pimento.

BLUE CHEESE-BACON POTATOES

4 med. baking potatoes
Shortening
1/2 c. sour cream
1 oz. blue cheese, crumbled
1/4 c. milk
4 tbsp. butter
3/4 tsp. salt
Dash of pepper
4 slices bacon, crisp-cooked, drained and crumbled

Rub potatoes with shortening; bake in 400-degree oven for 1 hour or until potatoes are tender. Remove from oven; cut lengthwise slices from potatoes. Scoop out centers; mash. Add sour cream, blue cheese, milk, butter, salt and pepper to mashed potatoes; beat with mixer until fluffy. Spoon mixture lightly into potato shells. Place on baking sheet; bake at 400 degrees for 15 minutes or until heated through. Fry bacon until crisp; drain. Crumble. Sprinkle each with crumbled bacon.

CREOLE-STUFFED POTATOES

6 lge. baking potatoes
1 c. chopped onions
1/2 c. chopped green pepper
4 tbsp. butter
1 c. diced tomatoes
2 tbsp. milk
2 tsp. salt
1/4 tsp. pepper
Paprika

Bake potatoes at 400 degrees for 1 hour or until tender. Saute onions and green pepper in butter until onions are transparent; add tomatoes. Cook for 2 minutes. Halve potatoes lengthwise. Scoop out centers; reserve shells. Whip milk and seasonings into potatoes; fold in onion mixture. Fill shells; dot with additional butter. Sprinkle with paprika. Bake at 400 degrees for 20 minutes. Serve immediately.

PARTY-STUFFED BAKED POTATOES

4 lge. baking potatoes
1/2 c. cream
1/4 c. butter
1/2 tsp. salt
Dash of pepper
2 eggs
1 tbsp. chopped chives
1/4 c. grated sharp cheese

Bake potatoes at 425 degrees for 45 minutes to 1 hour or until tender. Cut potatoes into halves lengthwise; scoop out centers. Mash potatoes; add cream, butter, salt, pepper, eggs and chives. Whip until light and fluffy. Pile into shells; sprinkle with cheese. Bake at 425 degrees for 10 minutes longer or until tops are lightly browned.

TWICE-BAKED POTATOES WITH ONION

6 med. potatoes
2 sm. onions, chopped
3 tbsp. butter
Grated Parmesan cheese
Paprika

Bake potatoes; halve lengthwise. Scoop out centers; mash. Saute onions in butter until tender. Combine potatoes, onions and cheese; mix well. Fill potato shells; sprinkle with paprika. Drizzle with additional melted butter. Chill until ready to use. Bake at 350 degrees for 20 minutes or until heated through.

TWICE-BAKED POTATOES WITH ROQUEFORT

4 med. baking potatoes
Shortening
1/2 c. sour cream
1 oz. Roquefort cheese, crumbled
1/4 c. milk
4 tbsp. butter
3/4 tsp. salt
Dash of pepper
4 slices bacon

Rub potatoes with shortening. Bake in 400-degree oven for 1 hour or until potatoes are tender. Remove from oven; cut lengthwise slices from each potato. Scoop out centers; mash. Stir in sour cream, Roquefort cheese, milk, butter, salt and pepper; beat with mixer until fluffy. Spoon mixture lightly into potato shells. Place on baking sheet; return to oven for 15 minutes or until heated through. Fry bacon until crisp; drain well. Crumble; sprinkle over potatoes. Serve immediately.

TABASCO-BAKED STUFFED POTATOES

6 med. baking potatoes
4 tbsp. butter
1/2 c. hot milk
1/2 tsp. Tabasco
Salt
Paprika to taste

Place potatoes in baking pan. Bake in 450-degree oven for about 1 hour. Cut lengthwise slice from top of each potato. Scoop out centers, taking care not to break skin. Mash potato pulp; add butter, blending well. Combine milk and Tabasco; add to potato mixture, beating until light and fluffy. Add additional milk if necessary. Season with salt to taste. Pile filling lightly into shells, rounding up slightly. Dot with additional butter; sprinkle with paprika. Bake in 425-degree oven 15 minutes or until lightly browned. May add grated cheese, deviled ham, diced cooked chicken, shredded beef or oysters to basic potato mixture if desired. Reheat to serve. Yield: 6 servings.

Tabasco-Baked Stuffed Potatoes . . . Potato shells are refilled with highly seasoned mashed potatoes.

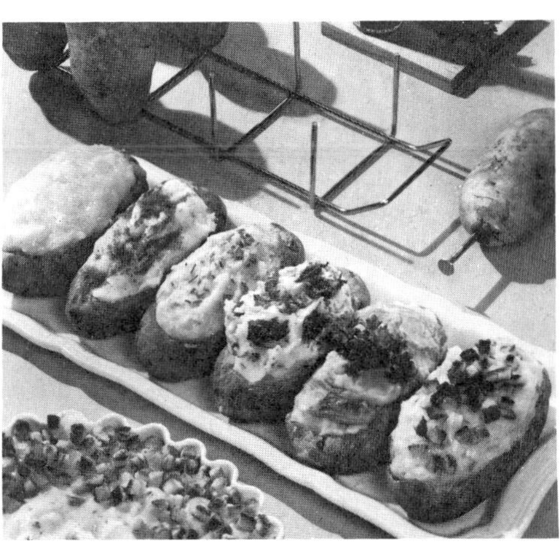

MODESTO POTATOES

1 tbsp. flour
3 tbsp. butter
4 med. potatoes, peeled and sliced
1 med. onion, sliced
1 clove of garlic, minced
Salt and pepper to taste
1/3 c. sauterne
1/3 c. chicken or beef broth
1/2 tsp. minced thyme
1 tbsp. minced parsley

Brown flour in butter in heavy skillet. Add potatoes, onion, garlic, salt and pepper; fry, turning often, until slightly browned. Add sauterne, broth and thyme. Simmer, covered, until potatoes are tender and liquid is absorbed. Sprinkle with parsley.

EASY POTATO BALLS

Potatoes
Salt and pepper
Butter
Cream
Chopped green onion tops

Bake potatoes; scoop out insides. Mash with salt, pepper and butter to taste. Moisten with cream; form balls with ice cream scoop. Place in shallow greased baking dish. Brush with melted butter. Sprinkle with onion. Bake at 350 degrees until heated through and lightly browned. Yield: 4 servings.

GERMAN-STYLE POTATO BALLS

8 med.-sized potatoes
1 tbsp. salt
2 eggs
1 1/4 c. flour
3 tbsp. cream of wheat
1/2 c. bread crumbs
1/4 tsp. nutmeg

Boil potatoes until tender; peel. Rice potatoes; spread on towel to remove excess moisture. Place potatoes in large bowl; sprinkle with salt. Make well in center; add eggs, flour, cream of wheat, bread crumbs and nutmeg. Work together until dry; add more flour if needed. Roll into balls 2 inches in diameter. Drop into boiling, salted water; boil, covered, for about 8 minutes after balls rise to top of water until center tests done. Yield: 8 to 10 servings.

POTATO-CHEESE BALLS

1/2 c. grated American cheese
2 c. cooked mashed potatoes
Salt to taste
1/2 c. bread crumbs
1 egg, beaten
1 tbsp. milk

Combine cheese, potatoes and salt; form into balls. Roll in bread crumbs; dip in egg blended with milk. Place on baking sheet. Bake at 450 degrees for 15 minutes.

DELMONICO POTATOES

2 c. boiled sliced potatoes
2 hard-boiled eggs, sliced
1/2 c. grated cheese
1/2 c. buttered crumbs
2 c. white sauce

Layer potatoes, eggs, cheese and crumbs in baking dish, ending with crumbs. Pour white sauce over top. Bake in 400-degree oven for 15 minutes or until heated through.

BARBECUED CHEESE POTATOES

4 lge. potatoes, sliced thin
1/4 c. chopped onion
1 1/2 c. milk
1 tbsp. butter
1/2 tsp. salt
1 tbsp. chopped parsley
1/8 tsp. pepper
1 tbsp. catsup
1/2 tsp. Worcestershire sauce
Dash of hot sauce
3/4 c. finely diced American cheese

Mix all ingredients in heavy skillet. Cover. Cook over low heat for about 1 hour or until potatoes are tender. Yield: 6-8 servings.

DELUXE HASHED BROWNS

1 lge. package frozen hashed browns
1 can cream of celery soup
1 can cream of potato soup
1 c. sour cream
2 tbsp. chopped onion
3 tbsp. chopped green pepper
1 tsp. salt
1/4 tsp. pepper
Chopped parsley
Paprika

Thaw hashed browns. Combine all ingredients except paprika in large bowl. Pour into greased 9 x 13-inch baking pan. Sprinkle with paprika. Bake at 300 degrees for 1 hour and 30 minutes.

PATRICIAN POTATOES

3 c. creamed cottage cheese
4 c. cooked mashed potatoes
3/4 c. sour cream
4 1/2 tsp. salt
1 1/2 tbsp. finely grated onion
1/8 tsp. white pepper
Melted butter
1/2 c. chopped toasted almonds

Beat cottage cheese until smooth; blend in potatoes. Add cream, salt, onion and pepper; mix well. Spoon into well-buttered, shallow 2-quart casserole. Brush potato mixture with melted butter. Bake in 350-degree oven for 30 minutes. Remove from oven; place under broiler until lightly browned. Sprinkle with almonds. This dish may be prepared ahead and baked when ready to serve.

POTATO PUFF

2 c. instant mashed potatoes
3 eggs, separated
1/4 c. chopped pimento
1/4 c. chopped green onions
1 tsp. salt
1 clove of garlic, minced
2 c. cream-style cottage cheese
1 c. sour cream
2 tbsp. butter

Prepare potatoes according to package directions. Beat egg yolks until thick and lemony. Beat egg whites until stiff peaks form. Combine potatoes with pimento, onions, salt, garlic, cottage cheese, sour cream and beaten egg yolks; mix well. Fold in stiffly beaten egg whites. Pour into greased 2 1/2-quart casserole; dot with butter. Bake at 325 degrees for 1 hour.

HASHED BROWN POTATOES

Color photograph for this recipe on page 314.

3 c. cubed cooked potatoes
1 tsp. salt
1/8 tsp. pepper
1 tbsp. minced onion
1/4 c. margarine

Sprinkle potatoes with salt, pepper and onion. Heat margarine in skillet. Add potatoes; cook until brown, stirring frequently. Place in serving dish; garnish with chopped parsley.

SWEDISH GREEN POTATOES

8 lge. boiled potatoes
3/4 c. milk
1 tsp. sugar
1/2 c. melted butter
2 tsp. salt
1/4 tsp. pepper
1 pkg. frozen chopped spinach
2 tbsp. chopped chives

Mash potatoes; add milk, sugar, butter, salt and pepper. Beat until light and fluffy. Cook spinach according to package directions; drain well. Blend chives and spinach into potato mixture; spoon into greased casserole. Bake at 375 degrees for 20 minutes or until heated through.

POTATOES AU GRATIN

Color photograph for this recipe on page 314.

4 c. sliced potatoes
6 tbsp. butter
6 tbsp. flour
1 c. milk
1 c. cream
1 c. chicken broth
Salt and pepper to taste

Cook potatoes in boiling, salted water until partially done; drain. Place in casserole. Melt butter in saucepan; add flour, mixing well. Add milk, cream and chicken broth; cook, stirring, until thickened. Add salt and pepper; pour over potatoes. Bake at 350 degrees for 45 minutes or until lightly browned.

DRESDEN POTATOES

1/2 lb. salt pork, sliced thin
1 c. sliced onions
1 tbsp. flour
3/4 c. vinegar
2 tsp. salt
1/8 tsp. pepper
6 c. sliced boiled potatoes

Brown salt pork in skillet until crisp; remove. Add onions; cook until transparent. Add flour, stirring constantly until browned; add 1/4 cup water, vinegar, salt and pepper. Stir in potatoes gently; simmer, covered, until heated through.

HERB-BUTTERED HASH-BROWNS

1 pkg. frozen hash-brown potatoes
1/4 c. melted butter
1 tsp. chopped parsley
1 tsp. chopped chives
1 tsp. dillseed
1/4 tsp. monosodium glutamate
1/2 tsp. salt

Prepare potatoes according to package directions. Combine butter with herbs; add to potatoes. Blend lightly; beat through.

CRUNCH-TOP POTATOES

4 lge. baking potatoes, peeled
1/3 c. butter
3/4 c. crushed corn flakes
1 1/2 c. shredded sharp cheese
1 1/2 tsp. salt
1 1/2 tsp. paprika

Cut potatoes crosswise into 1/2-inch slices. Melt butter in jelly roll pan in 375-degree oven. Add single layer of potatoes; turn slices once in butter. Mix remaining ingredients; sprinkle over potatoes. Bake at 375 degrees for 30 minutes or until crisp.

OVEN-BROWNED POTATO FANS

Potatoes
Salt and pepper
Melted butter

Peel potatoes and cut into lengthwise slices 1/4 inch thick through 2/3 of each potato to resemble fans. Place in shallow baking dish; sprinkle with salt, pepper and melted butter. Bake at 400 degrees for 45 minutes or until tender. Baste occasionally with pan drippings.

OVEN-FRIED GARLIC-POTATOES

4 med. potatoes, quartered
2 tbsp. cooking oil
Salt and pepper
Garlic salt
Parsley flakes

Dip potatoes in oil; sprinkle lightly with salt, pepper, garlic salt and parsley. Place in foil-lined pan. Bake at 350 degrees for 45 minutes, or until browned. Yield: 4-6 servings.

OVEN-FRIED POTATO WAFERS

Potatoes
Butter
Salt and pepper
Minced parsley

Rub potatoes with butter. Cut into rounds 1/4 inch thick. Place in buttered shallow baking dish; sprinkle with salt and pepper. Bake in 375-degree oven for 20 minutes or until tender. Garnish with parsley.

WHIPPED POTATOES PAPRIKA

Color photograph for this recipe on page 314.

6 med. potatoes, cubed
1 3-oz. package cream cheese
1/4 c. butter
Salt and pepper to taste
Milk
Paprika

Cook potatoes in boiling, salted water until tender; drain. Add cream cheese, butter, salt, pepper and enough milk for desired consistency; beat with electric mixer until smooth and fluffy. Place in serving dish; sprinkle with paprika.

BOILED POTATOES WITH CHEESE SAUCE

Color photograph for this recipe on page 314.

10 sm. new potatoes
1/4 c. margarine
1/4 c. flour
2 c. milk
1 c. grated cheese
Salt and pepper to taste

Peel potatoes. Cook in boiling, salted water until tender; drain. Keep warm. Melt margarine in saucepan. Add flour; mix well. Add milk; cook, stirring constantly, until thickened. Remove from heat. Add cheese, stirring until melted. Stir in salt and pepper. Place potatoes in serving dish; pour cheese sauce over potatoes.

NEW POTATOES WITH HERBS

1/3 c. flour
1/2 tsp. thyme
1/2 tsp. marjoram
3/4 tsp. salt
1/8 tsp. pepper
1 lb. new potatoes, peeled
1 clove of garlic, split
1 bay leaf
3 tbsp. butter

Preheat oven to 450 degrees. Mix flour, thyme, marjoram, salt and pepper; roll potatoes in flour mixture. Place in greased baking dish; add garlic clove and bay leaf. Dot with butter; cover tightly. Bake for 40 minutes or until potatoes are tender inside and crisp outside.

POTATO CANDY

2 sm. baked potatoes
1 1/2 to 2 boxes confectioners' sugar
1 tsp. vanilla
Crunchy peanut butter

Peel potatoes; mash in large mixing bowl. Add sugar and vanilla gradually until mixture is of consistency of dough; roll out on waxed paper. Spread generously with peanut butter; roll into log. Chill for several hours or overnight. Slice; store in refrigerator. Rolls may be frozen.

Poultry

Poultry refers to a number of edible domestic and wild birds. Throughout this encyclopedia, entries such as CHICKEN, CAPON, CORNISH HEN, GAME BIRDS, and TURKEY describe in detail how to buy, store, prepare, and serve these birds. The tables that follow give approximate roasting times and temperatures for poultry; illustrated instructions on stuffing and trussing poultry also follow.

(See CARVING.)

HOW TO STUFF AND TRUSS POULTRY

Never stuff a bird until just before roasting. Stuffing that is allowed to sit inside a bird may become spoiled by bacterial contamination. Follow the step-by-step instructions below to stuff and truss poultry.

1. Place stuffing in the stomach and neck cavities, filling them loosely. Fill the bird only about 3/4 full as stuffings expand during cooking.

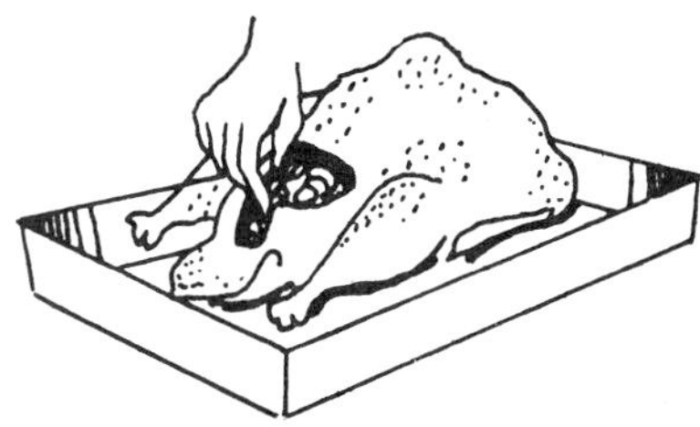

2. Place small skewers at 1- to 2-inch intervals across the stuffed cavities and crisscross a string on the skewers to close the cavity. Tie the legs together close to the body.

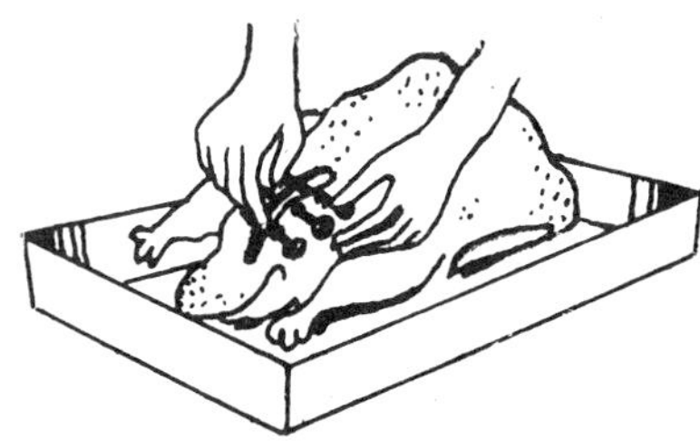

3. Tie a string around the bird's neck skin, leaving two long ends. Turn the wings back, as shown above, and secure them with the ends of the neck string.

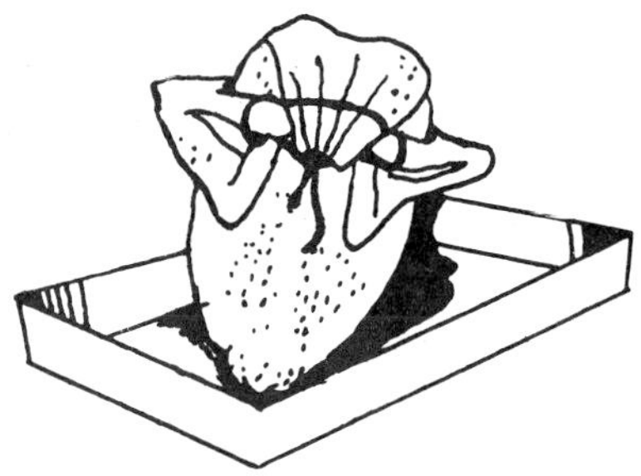

GAME BIRDS

GAME BIRDS	READY-TO-COOK WEIGHT	OVEN TEMP.	ROASTING TIME	AMOUNT PER SERVING
Wild Duck	1-2 lbs.	350°	1 hr.	1-1 1/2 lbs.
Wild Goose	2-4 lbs. 4-6 lbs.	325°	1-1 1/2 hrs. 1 1/2-2 1/2 hrs.	1-1 1/2 lbs.
Partridge	1/2-1 lb.	350°	30-45 min.	1/2-1 lb.
Pheasant	1-3 lbs.	350°	1-2 1/2 hrs.	1-1 1/2 lbs.
Quail	4-6 oz.	375°	15-20 min.	1/2-1 lb.
Squab	12-14 oz.	350°	30-50 min.	12-14 oz.

DOMESTIC BIRDS

DOMESTIC BIRDS	READY-TO-COOK WEIGHT	OVEN TEMP.	ROASTING TIME	
			UNSTUFFED	STUFFED
Chicken	1 1/2-2 lbs. 2-2 1/2 lbs. 2 1/2-3 lbs. 3-4 lbs.	400° 375° 375° 375°	3/4 hr. 1 hr. 1 1/4 hrs. 1 1/2 hrs.	1 1/2 hr. 1 1/4 hrs. 1 1/2 hrs. 2 hrs.
Capon	5-8 lbs.	325°	2 1/2 hrs.	3 1/2 hrs.
Turkey	6-8 lbs. 8-12 lbs. 12-16 lbs. 16-20 lbs. 20-24 lbs.	325° 325° 325° 325° 325°	3 hrs. 3 1/2 hrs. 4 1/2 hrs. 5 1/2 hrs. 6 1/2 hrs.	3 1/2 hrs. 4 1/2 hrs. 5 1/2 hrs. 6 1/2 hrs. 7 hrs.
Foil-Wrapped Turkey	8-10 lbs. 10-12 lbs. 14-16 lbs. 18-20 lbs. 22-24 lbs.	450° 450° 450° 450° 450°	2 1/4 hrs. 2 1/2 hrs. 3 hrs. 3 1/4 hrs. 3 1/2 hrs.	2 1/2 hrs. 3 hrs. 3 1/4 hrs. 3 1/2 hrs. 3 3/4 hrs.
Domestic Duck	3-5 lbs.	375° then 425°	1 1/2 hrs. 15 min .	2 hrs. 15 min.
Domestic Goose	4-6 lbs. 6-8 lbs. 8-10 lbs. 10-12 lbs. 12-14 lbs.	325° 325° 325° 325° 325°	2 3/4 hrs. 3 hrs. 3 1/2 hrs. 3 3/4 hrs. 4 1/4 hrs.	3 hrs. 3 1/2 hrs. 3 3/4 hrs. 4 1/4 hrs. 4 3/4 hrs.
Cornish Game Hen	1-1 1/2 lbs.	350°	3/4 hr.	1 hr.

Pound Cake

A pound cake is rich in egg and butter or shortening. It has a simple flavor and a firm, compact texture. Originally the principal ingredients were measured in pounds thus giving it its name. It is baked either in a tube pan or a paper-lined loaf pan.

INGREDIENTS: Traditional pound cakes still contain 1 pound each of butter, sugar, flour, and about 8 to 10 eggs. More modern recipes vary the amounts of the basic ingredients and may add milk and chemical leavening. Other variations of ingredients include vanilla, chocolate, brandy, rosewater; candied fruit, raisins, nuts, coconut; and sour cream. A tasty glaze may also be applied to a cooling pound cake.

STORING: Pound cakes have excellent keeping qualities. *To freeze*—Wrap cooled pound cake in moisture- and vapor-proof paper and freeze. Or slice cooled cake and place double thicknesses of plastic wrap between each slice. Double wrap entire stack to prevent drying out and freeze. Slices will thaw in 10 minutes or they can be toasted until warm.

PREPARATION: Have all ingredients at room temperature. Follow specific recipe directions for combining ingredients. Beat mixture until silky and smooth, preferably with an electric mixer.

SERVING: Pound cakes are versatile. Serve pound cake slices with butter and jam, ice cream and sauce topping, or fruit. Cover with pudding or make dainty pound cake sandwiches.

(See CAKE.)

BRANDY POUND CAKE

1/2 lb. butter
1 2/3 c. sugar
5 eggs
1/2 tsp. mace
2 c. sifted cake flour
2 oz. brandy

Cream butter and sugar until light and fluffy. Add eggs, one at a time, beating well after each addition. Add mace, flour and brandy; mix well. Pour into greased and floured tube pan. Bake for 1 hour and 15 minutes at 325 degrees. Let cool for 10 minutes before removing from pan. Cool thoroughly.

Brandy Frosting

2 tbsp. butter
1 pkg. confectioners' sugar
Milk
3/4 oz. brandy

Combine butter with sugar; add enough milk for thick spreading consistency. Stir in brandy; spread frosting over cake.

APPLE POUND CAKE

2 c. sugar
3 c. chopped apples
1 1/2 c. cooking oil
2 eggs
3 c. flour
1 1/2 tsp. soda
1 tsp. salt
2 tbsp. vanilla
1 c. nuts

Pour sugar over apples; let stand for 20 minutes. Beat oil and eggs together; sift flour, soda and salt together. Add apples to oil mixture; beat until sugar is dissolved. Stir in flour mixture slowly; add vanilla and nuts. Pour into greased and floured tube pan. Bake for 1 hour at 350 degrees. Let cool in pan for about 10 minutes before turning out on cake rack.

BUTTERMILK POUND CAKE

3 c. sugar
1 stick soft butter
1/2 c. shortening
5 eggs
3 c. flour
1 c. buttermilk
1/2 tsp. soda
1 tsp. vanilla
1 tsp. lemon flavoring

Combine sugar, butter and shortening; beat until smooth. Beat in eggs, one at a time, beating well after each addition. Add flour and buttermilk alternately; mix well. Dissolve soda in 1 tablespoon water; stir into batter. Add flavorings; pour into greased tube pan. Bake at 350 degrees for 1 hour and 15 minutes. Let cool for 10 minutes before removing from pan; invert onto cake rack to cool completely.

Buttermilk Icing

1 tsp. soda
1 c. buttermilk
2 c. sugar
3/4 c. butter
1 tsp. vanilla

Stir soda into buttermilk; combine all ingredients except vanilla in saucepan. Cook until icing forms soft ball; cool. Add vanilla; beat slightly. Spread over side and top of cake.

CHERRY POUND CAKE

1 c. shortening
1 c. sugar
1 tsp. grated lemon rind
1 tbsp. lemon juice
5 eggs
1 c. candied cherries
1/2 c. mixed candied peel
2 1/2 c. sifted flour
1/2 tsp. salt
1 tsp. baking powder

Cream shortening, sugar, lemon rind and juice; add eggs, one at a time, beating well after each addition. Combine cherries and peel with 1/2 cup flour. Sift remaining flour with salt and baking powder; add to batter by thirds, beating well after each addition. Stir in floured fruit; pour batter into greased and floured tube pan. Bake at 300 degrees for about 1 hour and 45 minutes or until cake tests done. Cool cake for 10 minutes before removing from pan. Cool; wrap in waxed paper and let stand for 1 week before using.

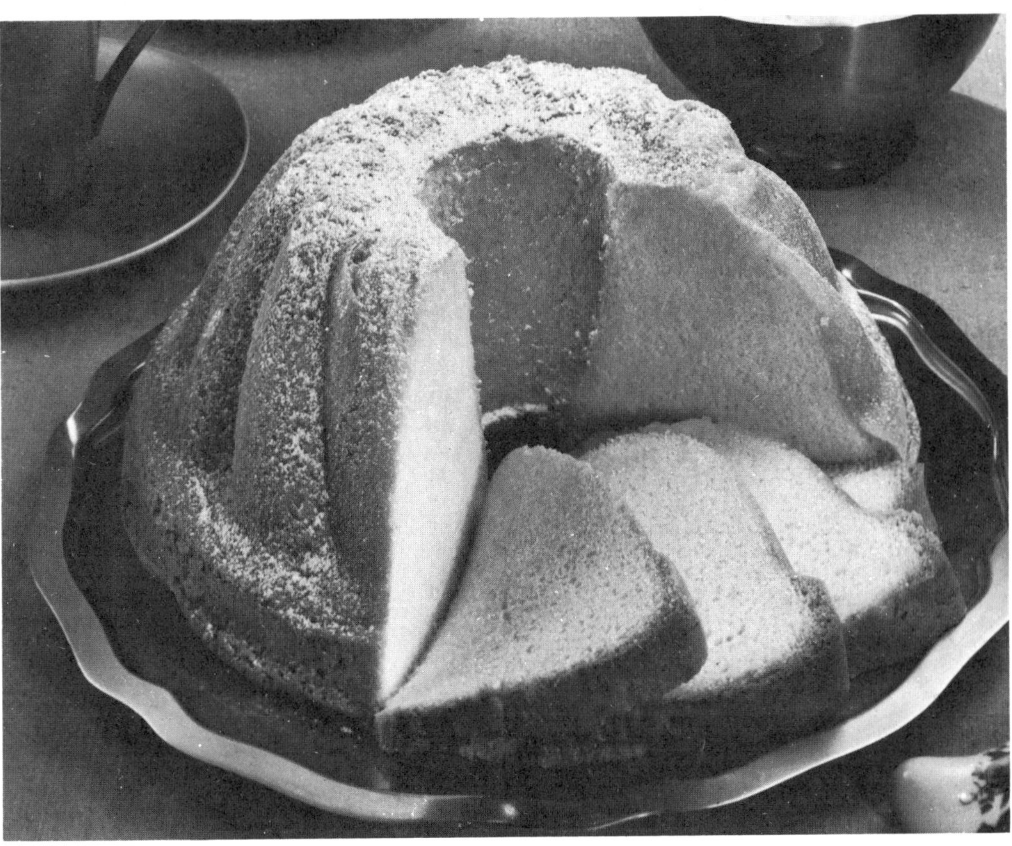

Pound Cake . . . Serve this favorite topped with jam, whipped cream, sauce, or ice cream.

POUND CAKE

3 1/2 c. cake flour, sifted
1 tsp. baking powder
1/2 tsp. salt
1/4 tsp. mace
1 3/4 c. butter
2 c. confectioners' sugar
8 eggs
1 tsp. vanilla
1/2 tsp. almond extract
1/2 tsp. lemon extract

Preheat oven to 325 degrees. Sift flour twice with baking powder, salt and mace. Cream butter until light and fluffy. Add sugar gradually; beat well until sugar mixture resembles whipped cream. Add eggs, one at a time, beating well after each addition. Stir in about half the flour mixutre. Add extracts and remaining flour mixture. Mix at lowest speed with electric mixer. Pour batter into 10 x 4-inch greased tube cake pan. Cut through batter several times with knife to break air bubbles. Bake for 1 hour to 1 hour and 10 minutes. Remove from pan immediately; let cool on cake rack.

CINNAMON-NUT POUND CAKE

1 pkg. white cake mix
1 sm. carton sour cream
3/4 c. butter-flavored oil
1/2 c. sugar
4 eggs
1 c. chopped pecans
1 tsp. cinnamon
2 tbsp. (packed) brown sugar
Juice of 1 lge. lemon
1 c. confectioners' sugar

Combine cake mix, sour cream, oil and sugar; beat in eggs, one at a time, beating well after each addition. Beat for at least 5 minutes. Mix pecans, cinnamon and brown sugar. Place 1/2 of nut mixture in well-buttered and floured bundt pan; add batter. Sprinkle remaining mixture over top. Bake at 325 degrees for 55 minutes or until cake tests done. Let cake stand for 15 minutes before removing from pan. Mix lemon juice and powdered sugar; pour over warm cake.

EASY POUND CAKE

1 lb. butter
3 c. sugar
9 eggs
4 c. flour, sifted
1 tsp. baking powder
1/2 tsp. salt
1 c. milk
1 tsp. vanilla
1 tsp. almond flavoring

Cream butter and sugar together until light and fluffy. Add eggs, one at a time, beating well after each addition. Sift flour, baking powder and salt together; add to butter mixture alternately with milk. Mix well. Stir in flavorings; pour batter into 2 small greased and floured tube pans. Bake at 350 degrees for about 45 minutes or until cakes test done. Let cool for 10 minutes before removing from pans.

CHOCOLATE POUND CAKE

1 4-oz. package sweet cooking chocolate
2 c. sugar
1 c. shortening
4 eggs
2 tsp. vanilla
2 tsp. butter flavoring
1 c. buttermilk
3 c. sifted flour
1/2 tsp. soda
1 tsp. salt

Partially melt chocolate in double boiler over hot water. Remove from hot water; stir rapidly until entirely melted. Let cool. Cream sugar and shortening. Add eggs, flavorings and buttermilk; mix well. Sift dry ingredients together; add to shortening. Mix well. Stir in chocolate until blended; pour batter into well-greased and floured 9-inch tube pan. Bake at 300 degrees for 1 hour and 30 minutes. Remove from pan; place tight-fitting cover over hot cake. Let stand until thoroughly cooled.

COCONUT POUND CAKE

1 can coconut
1 c. shortening
2 c. sugar
4 eggs
3 c. flour
1/2 tsp. salt
1/2 tsp. soda
1/2 tsp. baking powder
1 c. buttermilk
2 tbsp. coconut flavoring
Icing

Reserve 1/2 cup coconut for Icing; combine remaining coconut, shortening, sugar and eggs. Mix well. Sift flour, salt, soda and baking powder together; add to coconut mixture alternately with buttermilk and flavoring. Pour into greased and floured tube pan. Bake at 325 degrees for 1 hour and 15 minutes. Pour Icing over cake; let stand for 2 hours before removing from pan.

Icing

2 c. sugar
3 tbsp. margarine
2 tbsp. white corn syrup
1 1/2 tbsp. coconut flavoring

Combine sugar, 1 cup water, margarine, syrup and flavoring in saucepan; bring to a boil. Cook for 5 minutes. Add reserved coconut.

CRANBERRY POUND CAKE

3 c. sifted flour
2 tsp. baking powder
3/4 tsp. salt
1 c. butter
2 1/2 c. sugar
3 eggs
1 egg yolk
3/4 c. milk
1 tsp. orange flavoring
3/4 c. chopped cranberries
1/2 c. chopped pecans
2 c. confectioners' sugar
Juice from 1/2 orange
Juice from 1/2 lemon

Sift flour, baking powder and salt together. Cream butter; add sugar gradually, creaming until light and fluffy. Add eggs and yolk, one at a time, beating well after each addition. Add flour mixture to butter mixture alternately with milk; mix well. Stir in flavoring, cranberries and nuts; mix well. Pour into greased and floured tube pan. Bake at 375 degrees for 1 hour. Cook for 10 minutes; remove from pan and cool completely. Combine remaining ingredients; mix well. Spread over side and top of cake.

LEMON POUND CAKE

1 c. butter
1/2 c. soft shortening
2 c. sugar
5 eggs
1/4 tsp. salt
1 tsp. vanilla
1 tsp. lemon extract
3 c. sifted flour
1 7-oz. bottle lemon-flavored carbonated drink
Confectioners' sugar, sifted

Preheat oven to 325 degrees. Combine butter and shortening in large bowl; beat until creamy. Add sugar gradually, beating constantly until fluffy. Add eggs, one at a time, beating well after each addition. Stir in salt and flavorings. Add flour alternately with lemon-flavored drink; mix well. Pour into greased tube pan. Bake for about 1 hour and 30 minutes. Cool on wire rack for 10 minutes before removing from pan. Cut around side and tube carefully with thin spatula; invert onto cake rack. Cool completely; sprinkle top with confectioners' sugar.

POPPY SEED POUND CAKE

Poppy seed
1 pkg. pound cake mix
2 tsp. vanilla
Grated lemon rind
6 tbsp. butter
3 c. sifted confectioners' sugar
1 1/2 tsp. milk
1 1/2 tsp. lemon juice
Yellow food coloring

Preheat oven to 325 degrees. Toast 1/3 cup poppy seed in pie pan for 15 minutes, stirring occasionally. Remove from oven; cool. Prepare cake mix according to package directions. Fold in poppy seed; reserve 1 tablespoon for icing. Add 1/2 teaspoon vanilla and 1 tablespoon lemon rind. Bake in greased 10 x 5 x 3-inch pan for 1 hour or until cake tests done. Cool for 20 minutes. Cream butter in bowl; gradually beat in 1 cup sugar, remaining vanilla, milk and lemon juice. Beat in remaining sugar gradually until light and fluffy. Tint with food coloring as desired. Spread on cake. Sprinkle with lemon rind and poppy seed. Refrigerate for 4 hours or overnight.

SOUR CREAM POUND CAKE

1/2 lb. butter
3 c. sugar
6 eggs, separated
3 c. sifted flour
1/4 tsp. soda
1/2 pt. sour cream
1 tsp. vanilla

Cream butter and sugar together until light and fluffy. Add egg yolks, one at a time, beating well after each addition. Sift flour with soda; add to butter mixture alternately with sour cream and vanilla. Blend until smooth. Fold in stiffly beaten egg whites; pour into greased and floured tube pan. Bake at 300 degrees for 1 hour and 30 minutes or until cake tests done. Let cool for 10 minutes; remove from pan and cool thoroughly.

Cream Cheese-Pineapple Icing

1 No. 2 can crushed pineapple
1/4 stick butter
1/4 c. sugar
Juice of 1 lemon
1 3-oz. package cream cheese
1 pkg. confectioners' sugar

Combine pineapple, butter and sugar in saucepan; cook until mixture is thickened and transparent, stirring constantly. Let stand until cool. Combine lemon juice and cream cheese; blend in confectioners' sugar. Add pineapple mixture; beat well. Spread on cake.

Praline

Pralines are silky-smooth confections that are similar in both taste and texture to penuche (See PENUCHE). They are reknowned throughout the South and especially in New Orleans. Most recipes for pralines specify the following basic ingredients: white or brown sugar, corn syrup, nutmeats (especially pecans), evaporated milk or cream, and flavoring. Sometimes raisins or coconut are added in place of nuts.

PREPARATION: Combine ingredients and cook as directed in recipe. Pralines are usually cooked to the soft-ball stage (that is, a drop of the mixture forms a soft, pliable ball when dropped into very cold water and when it registers from 234 to 240 degrees on a candy thermometer). Beat the candy with a wooden spoon until thickened and slightly changed in color. Drop from a tablespoon to form patties. Waxed paper or a marble slab provide the best surface. If the candy hardens before you finish dropping it from the spoon, add a few drops of cream or water and blend thoroughly. Allow pralines to harden before removing from surface.

STORING: Pralines do not keep well unless they have been properly prepared for storage. Wrap the candy in aluminum foil or clear plastic, place in airtight containers and store in a cool, dry place.

(See CANDY.)

QUICK PRALINE ROLLS

1 pkg. yeast
2 1/4 c. sifted flour
2 tbsp. sugar
2 tsp. baking powder
1/2 tsp. salt
2/3 c. butter
1/3 c. scalded milk, cooled
1 egg
3/4 c. (packed) brown sugar
1/2 c. chopped nuts

Soften yeast in 1/4 cup warm water. Sift flour, sugar, baking powder and salt together into mixing bowl; cut in 1/3 cup butter until mixture resembles fine crumbs. Stir in scalded milk, egg and yeast mixture; beat well. May be stored in refrigerator overnight. Knead on well-floured surface; roll out to 15 x 10-inch rectangle. Cream remaining butter and brown sugar until fluffy; spread half the sugar mixture over dough. Sprinkle chopped nuts over sugar mixture; roll up. Cut into 1-inch slices; place on greased cookie sheets. Flatten; spread with remaining sugar mixture. Let rise in warm place until doubled in bulk. Bake at 425 degrees for 12 minutes.

BEST PRALINES

1 c. (packed) brown sugar
1 c. sugar
2 c. pecan halves
1/2 c. evaporated milk

Mix all ingredients thoroughly. Cook over medium heat to soft-ball stage, stirring constantly. Cool slightly. Beat until mixture starts to thicken. Drop candy rapidly from a spoon onto greased waxed paper to form patties. Stir in small amount of hot water, if necessary, to thin.

BROWN SUGAR PRALINES

2 c. sugar
1 c. (packed) brown sugar
1/2 c. milk
1/2 c. evaporated milk
1/4 c. butter
1/4 tsp. salt
3 c. broken pecans

Combine sugars and milks with butter and salt in heavy saucepan. Bring to a boil gradually over medium heat. Add pecans. Cook until candy reaches soft-ball stage, 234 degrees on the candy thermometer. Remove from heat; stir just enough to give creamy look. Drop from spoon onto waxed paper. Yield: 6 dozen.

BUTTERMILK PRALINES

3 c. sugar
1 tsp. soda
1/8 tsp. salt
1 c. buttermilk
3/4 c. light corn syrup
2 tbsp. butter
2 c. pecan halves

Combine all ingredients except pecans. Cook to soft-ball stage. Add pecans; beat until mixture loses gloss. Drop onto waxed paper. Yield: 3 dozen.

LOUISIANA CREAM PRALINES

1 box light brown sugar
1/8 tsp. salt
3/4 c. evaporated milk
1 tbsp. butter
2 c. pecan halves

Mix brown sugar, salt, evaporated milk and butter in 2-quart saucepan. Cook, stirring over low heat until sugar is dissolved. Add pecans; cook over medium heat to soft-ball stage or to 234 degrees on candy thermometer, stirring constantly. Remove from heat; cool for 5 minutes. Stir rapidly until mixture begins to thicken and coats pecans lightly. Drop rapidly from tablespoon onto lightly greased cookie sheet to form patties. Stir several drops of hot water if mixture is too thick. Let patties stand until cool and set. Yield: 20 servings.

CREAM PRALINES

2 1/4 c. (packed) brown sugar
3/4 c. evaporated milk
2 c. pecan halves
1 1/2 tsp. rum flavoring

Cook sugar, milk and pecans over low heat, stirring constantly, until sugar is dissolved. Cook to 236 degrees on candy thermometer, stirring constantly. Cool candy slightly; add rum flavoring. Beat until mixture begins to thicken; drop from teaspoon onto waxed paper. Yield: 30 pieces.

CREAMY PRALINES

3 c. sugar
1 c. evaporated milk
Pinch of salt
1 tbsp. butter
1 1/2 c. pecan halves

Dissolve 1 cup sugar in skillet over low heat, stirring constantly. Place remaining sugar, milk and salt in heavy kettle; bring to a boil. Add butter. Add dissolved sugar. Cook to soft-ball stage. Remove from heat; beat well. Add pecans. Drop from spoon onto waxed paper. Pralines may be flattened or left in mounds.

CREOLE PRALINES

3/4 c. (packed) brown sugar
3/4 c. sugar
1/2 c. evaporated milk
1 tbsp. butter
1 c. pecan halves
1/4 tsp. vanilla

Combine brown sugar, sugar, milk and butter in saucepan; bring to a boil. Reduce heat; cook to soft-ball stage. Remove from heat; beat until creamy. Add pecans and vanilla. Drop by spoonfuls onto buttered dish.

EASY PRALINES

1 pkg. instant butterscotch pudding mix
1/2 c. (packed) brown sugar
1 c. sugar
1/2 c. evaporated milk
1 tbsp. butter
1 1/2 c. chopped pecans

Mix all ingredients except pecans in heavy 1 1/2-quart saucepan; bring to a full boil, stirring constantly. Cook for 3 minutes gradually, stirring often, until candy reaches soft-ball stage. Remove from heat; add chopped pecans. Beat until candy begins to thicken but looks shiny. Drop mixture quickly onto waxed paper to form 2-inch patties. Yield: 15 servings.

MAPLE PRALINE LOUISIANE

3 c. sugar
1 tsp. maple extract
1 1/2 c. small pecans
1/4 tsp. cream of tartar

Combine all ingredients and 1 1/2 cups hot water in saucepan; place over medium heat. Cook to 234 degrees on candy thermometer, stirring occasionally. Remove from heat. Stir with wooden spoon for 5 minutes or until mixture begins to lose gloss and appears slightly granular. Spoon onto buttered pan. Reheat mixture gradually if too thick. Yield: 2 pounds.

PRALINE PATTIES

2 c. sugar
3/4 tsp. soda
1 c. half and half
1 1/2 tbsp. butter
2 c. pecan halves

Combine sugar and soda; stir in half and half gradually. Bring to a boil over medium heat, stirring occasionally. Reduce heat; cook, stirring constantly, to soft-ball stage or to 234 degrees on candy thermometer. Remove from heat; add butter immediately. Add pecans. Beat mixture for 3 minutes or until thick. Drop from metal spoon onto waxed paper. Add small amount of hot water, if necessary. Yield: 24-30 patties.

SHERRY PRALINES

2 1/2 c. sugar
1/8 tsp. soda
1/4 c. light corn syrup
1/2 c. milk
2 tbsp. sherry
2 c. pecan halves
1 tbsp. butter

Combine sugar, soda, syrup and milk; cook over medium heat, stirring until sugar is completely dissolved. Continue cooking until small amount of mixture forms soft ball in cold water or to 236 degrees on candy thermometer. Do not stir while cooking. Add sherry, pecans and butter; stir lightly until mixture becomes creamy. Drop by spoonfuls on waxed paper. Yield: 24 patties.

Preserves

Preserves are fruits that are canned whole or in uniformly sized pieces in sugar syrup about the consistency of honey. Characteristically, preserves have clear color and retain both the shape and flavor of the fruits they contain.

INGREDIENTS: Fruit is the principal ingredient in preserves. Fruit should be at the firm-ripe stage and without blemishes. If it is to be left whole, the pieces should be of uniform size.

PREPARATION: Preserves are generally prepared by boiling sugar and fruit until the fruit is tender and the syrup thick and at a temperature 9 degrees above the boiling temperature for water. *To prepare fruit*—Firm fruits, such as peaches or citrus fruits, should be cooked in water until they are slightly tender. Small soft fruits, such as pears and berries, should be allowed to sit overnight in the sugar in which they will be cooked. As they sit, they will absorb this sugar and become firmer; during the preserving process, they will hold their shapes better. *To cook fruit and sugar*—For less tart fruit, allow 3/4 pound sugar to 1 pound fruit. Cook fruits in small batches, using not more than 4 pounds of fruit at one time. Use a fairly wide pan to cook the fruit and sugar so that the mixture will not boil over. Cook over medium heat; too high a temperature causes the sugar to caramelize. If the syrup becomes too thick before the fruit is tender and transluscent, add boiling water 1/4 cup at a time. If the fruit is clear and tender but the syrup is still too thin, remove the fruit and continue to cook syrup to desired consistency or temperature.

PROCESSING: When preserves have been cooked, there are two methods of canning them. (1) Place fruit in scalded jars to within 3/4 inch of top; add syrup to within 1/2 inch of top. Remove air by sliding a table knife down the inside of the jar against the glass surface on each side. Wipe the jar mouth; adjust lid; process by waterbath method. (2) Let fruit/syrup mixture stand for 12-24 hours to improve the color and texture of the fruit. Place cool fruit in scalded jars to within 3/4 inch of top; add syrup to within 1/2 inch. Proceed as above.

STORING: (See JAM.)

SERVING: (See JAM.)

(See CANNING.)

BLUE PLUM PRESERVES

3 lb. blue plums
1 sm. box frozen raspberries
7 c. sugar
1 pkg. powdered pectin

Pit plums; grind. Cook plums in large kettle for 3 minutes; add raspberries. Bring to a boil; stir in sugar. Boil rapidly for 3 minutes. Remove from heat; stir in pectin until dissolved. Skim. Pour into hot sterilized jars; seal with paraffin.

EASY FIG PRESERVES

2 c. sugar
2 c. figs
1/2 lemon, thinly sliced

Pour sugar and 1 cup water into heavy kettle; bring to a rolling boil. Place figs and lemon in syrup; cook for 20 minutes or until syrup is as thick as desired. Pour into sterilized jars; seal with paraffin.

FIG PRESERVES WITH GELATIN

3 c. peeled figs
3 c. sugar
1 6-oz. box strawberry gelatin

Mix all ingredients in heavy kettle; cook for 10 minutes over medium-high heat. Pour into sterilized jars; seal with paraffin.

PERFECT FIG PRESERVES

1 c. soda
6 qt. figs
6 lb. sugar

Sprinkle soda over figs; cover with 6 quarts boiling water. Let stand for 10 minutes. Drain; rinse well in cold water. Combine sugar with 4 quarts water; bring to a boil, stirring until sugar is dissolved. Add figs gradually; bring to a boil. Reduce heat. Simmer, stirring occasionally, until figs are tender and transparent. Lift figs out carefully; place in shallow pan. Boil syrup until thick as honey; cover figs completely with syrup. Let stand overnight. Pack figs in sterilized jars; fill with syrup to within 1/2 inch of jar top. Seal; process for 25 minutes at simmering temperature.

GRAPE PRESERVES

2 gal. grapes
4 c. sugar
1 tbsp. lemon juice

Place grapes in large kettle; cover with water. Cook until grape skins pop. Pour into colander over pan; drain for 30 minutes. Place colander over another pan; mash pulp and remaining juice into pan. Measure 4 cups pulp; combine pulp, sugar and lemon juice in kettle. Place pulp, sugar and lemon juice in kettle or saucepan. Cook, stirring constantly, for 30 minutes or until thickened. Pour into hot sterilized jars; seal with paraffin.

MIXED FRUIT PRESERVES

1 lb. apples, peeled and sliced
1 lb. peaches, peeled and sliced
1 lb. pears, peeled and sliced
1 lb. quinces, peeled and sliced
7 c. sugar
4 tbsp. lemon juice
Paraffin

Cover fruits with water; cook until tender. Drain fruits; reserve 3 cups liquid. Add sugar to reserved liquid; boil for 10 minutes. Add cooked fruits and lemon juice; cook until fruits are transparent. Let stand for several hours. Pack fruits into hot sterilized jars. Boil syrup until as thick as honey. Pour over fruits; seal immediately with paraffin.

OVEN PEAR PRESERVES

2 lb. pears
1 lemon, finely chopped
4 c. sugar
2 tbsp. chopped candied ginger

Mix pears, lemon, sugar and ginger. Cover; let stand overnight. Bring to a boil. Bake at 350 degrees for 10 minutes. Reduce oven temperature to 300 degrees; bake for 1 hour or until thick and amber-colored. Pour into hot sterilized jars; seal.

PEAR PRESERVES

3 lb. peeled pears, cored and ground or diced
2 tbsp. lemon juice
1 3-oz. package lemon gelatin
5 1/2 c. sugar
1 pkg. powdered pectin

Peel, core and dice pears. Mix pears and lemon juice in large kettle. Add gelatin; bring to a rolling boil, stirring occasionally. Add sugar; return to a full rolling boil. Boil for 1 minute, stirring constantly. Remove from heat; add pectin. Stir and skim. Ladle into sterilized jars to within 1/2 inch of jar top; seal with paraffin. Yield: Nine 6-ounce jars.

STRAWBERRY PRESERVES

2 qt. fresh strawberries
6 c. sugar

Stem strawberries. Place in kettle; cover with boiling water. Let stand for 3 minutes; drain. Pour strawberries into kettle; bring to a boil over medium heat. Boil for 3 minutes. Add 3 cups sugar; boil for 3 minutes. Stir in remaining sugar; boil for 3 minutes longer. Remove from heat; stir with wooden spoon until foam subsides and strawberries are cool. Skim. Ladle into sterilized jars; seal with paraffin.

SUN-COOKED STRAWBERRY PRESERVES

2 qt. ripe strawberries
Sugar

Stem strawberries; weigh. Measure amount of sugar to equal weight of strawberries. Place strawberries in preserving kettle; pour sugar over top. Let stand for several hours. Place over low heat; cook, stirring gently. Increase heat gradually as sugar dissolves, stirring carefully. Bring to a boil; boil for 10 minutes. Skim; pour into shallow pan. Cover with cheesecloth; place outdoors on table each sunny day for 3 to 5 days until juice is thickened. Stir each afternoon when preserves are brought inside. Place in sterilized jars; cover with paraffin.

GREEN TOMATO PRESERVES

6 c. sugar
6 c. thinly sliced green tomatoes
3 lemons, thinly sliced

Add 2 cups sugar to tomatoes; let stand until juice forms. Cover lemons with water; cook until just tender. Combine tomatoes, lemons and remaining sugar; simmer until thickened and clear. Seal in hot sterilized jars.

OLD-TIME TOMATO PRESERVES

5 lb. firm ripe tomatoes, peeled and quartered
8 c. sugar
1 orange, thinly sliced
1 lemon, thinly sliced

Peel and quarter tomatoes; cover with sugar. Let stand overnight. Drain; reserve syrup. Heat syrup to a boil; cook until syrup spins thread. Add tomatoes, orange and lemon; cook over low heat until tomatoes are transparent. Place in hot sterilized glasses; seal. Yield: Twelve 6-ounce glasses.

TOMATO PRESERVES

2 1/2 lb. ripe tomatoes
1 1/2 tsp. grated lemon rind
1/4 c. lemon juice
6 1/2 c. sugar
1 bottle liquid pectin

Scald tomatoes; peel. Chop tomatoes; bring to a boil in preserving kettle. Reduce heat; simmer for 10 minutes. Measure 3 cups tomato pulp into kettle; add lemon rind, juice and sugar. Mix well; bring to a full rolling boil over high heat. Boil for 1 minute, stirring constantly. Remove from heat; stir in pectin. Pack into sterilized jars; seal.

WATERMELON RIND PRESERVES

4 lb. watermelon rind
1/2 c. salt
4 tsp. stick cinnamon
4 tsp. whole cloves
9 c. sugar
4 lemons, sliced

Remove outer green rind and any pink flesh from watermelon rind; cut into cubes. Soak watermelon rind overnight in 1 gallon salted water. Drain; cover with fresh water. Cook for 30 minutes or until tender; drain well. Tie spices in small cloth bag. Place sugar, 2 quarts water, lemons and spices in large kettle; boil for 5 minutes. Add watermelon rind; cook for 30 minutes or until transparent. Remove spice bag. Pour into sterilized jars; seal.

Pretzels

SUGAR PRETZELS

1 1/4 c. sugar
1 c. butter
4 egg yolks, slightly beaten
Grated rind of 2 lemons
3 1/2 c. flour

Cream sugar and butter; add egg yolks, stirring well. Add lemon rind and flour; mix thoroughly. Pinch off dough; roll into small pieces. Twist into pretzel shapes; place on lightly greased cookie sheet. Bake at

350 degrees for 15 minutes. Cool before removing from cookie sheet. Yield: 24-30 servings.

BUTTERSCOTCH PRETZELS

1 6-oz. package butterscotch pieces
2 tbsp. vegetable oil
12 thin pretzels

Melt butterscotch pieces with oil in double boiler. Dip pretzels, one at a time, into mixture. Place on waxed paper; chill until firm. Yield: 12 servings.

CHOCOLATE PRETZELS

1 6-oz. package chocolate pieces
2 tbsp. vegetable oil
12 thin pretzels

Melt chocolate pieces with oil in double boiler. Dip pretzels, one at a time, into mixture. Place on waxed paper; chill until firm. Yield: 12 servings.

GERMAN PRETZELS

3/4 c. soft shortening
1/2 c. sugar
4 c. milk, scalded
2 pkg. yeast
12 c. flour
1 1/2 tsp. baking powder
1 1/2 tsp. salt
2 tbsp. household lye
3 tbsp. coarse salt

Stir shortening and sugar into milk until shortening is melted. Pour milk mixture into large bowl; cool until lukewarm. Soften yeast in 1/4 cup warm water. Combine yeast mixture and 6 cups flour; stir until smooth. Cover; let rise in warm place for 30 minutes or until light and bubbly. Sift remaining flour with baking powder and salt. Stir dough down; beat in flour mixture gradually until dough is blended. Let rise in greased large bowl until doubled in bulk. Punch down; divide into 6 equal pieces. Let stand for 10 minutes. Divide each piece into 10 portions of equal size. Using palms of hands, roll each into strand, 1/2 inch in diameter and 18 inches long. Twist into pretzel shape, tucking ends under. Cover shaped pretzels lightly; let rise until doubled in size. Add lye to 2 quarts cold water in large pan; heat until solution is steaming but not boiling. Place pretzels, one at a time, right side down, on wide-slotted turner. Lower pretzel into lye solution for 2 seconds; remove. Drain. Place right side up on greased baking sheet; sprinkle with coarse salt. Bake at 400 degrees for 15 minutes or until browned well. Yield: 5 dozen.

SOFT PRETZELS

1 pkg. yeast
1 tsp. salt
1 1/2 tsp. sugar
4 c. flour
1 egg, beaten
Coarse salt

Soften yeast in 1 1/2 cups lukewarm water in large bowl; add salt and sugar. Mix in flour with hands; knead to form soft dough. Do not allow dough to rise. Cut immediately into small pieces. Roll into ropes; form into pretzel shapes. Cover cookie sheet with foil; dust with flour. Place pretzels on sheet. Brush with egg; sprinkle with coarse salt. Bake at 400 degrees for 15 minutes. Yield: 2-4 dozen.

Prune

Prunes are the dried fruit of several varieties of bluish-purple freestone plums. Only the plums that can be dried with the pit in without fermenting such as the Petite d'Agen, Robe de Sergeant, Imperial, and Sugar become dried prunes. Dried prunes are tree-ripened and usually dried by dehydration to control the loss of moisture from the fruit. They are excellent sources of quick energy, Vitamin A, calcium, iron, thiamine, and riboflavin. (4 uncooked prunes = 70 calories)

AVAILABILITY: Prunes are marketed year-round in small, medium, large, and extra-large sizes. They are sold pitted and unpitted in plastic bags, cartons, or by the pound. Cans and jars of prune juice and pre-cooked prunes are also available.

STORING: Keep prunes in a cool, dry place. During the summer, refrigeration is recommended. Store unopened packages of prunes on the kitchen shelf 6 to 8 months. *To freeze* —See PLUM.

PREPARATION: Prunes are usually plumped before being prepared for eating or baking. Refer to the specific recipe directions or use either of the following methods: (1) Place prunes in saucepan with cold water to cover. Simmer 10 to 20 minutes until tender. Cool in liquid. (2) Cover prunes with water. Soak, covered, for 24 hours in the refrigerator. You may want to add lemon or orange slices or rind; brown sugar, maple syrup, or honey; and spices. Or plump prunes in citrus juice, tea, or port wine for a mellower flavor.

USES: Prunes are a nutritious, energy-supplying breakfast food or snack. They may also be used in meat and poultry dressings; as accompaniments for main dishes; in salads and compotes; and in many baked products.

(See PLUM.)

FROZEN PRUNE SALAD

1 can prunes, drained, chopped and juice reserved
2 pkg. cream cheese
1 c. pecans
1 pt. whipping cream, whipped

Drain prunes; reserve juice. Chop prunes; mix with cream cheese. Blend in pecans. Spread mixture in freezer tray. Pour reserved juice over top; add cream. Freeze. Cut into squares; serve on lettuce. Yield: 16 servings.

PRUNE MOLD

1 pkg. lemon gelatin
1 c. prune juice
1 tbsp. lemon juice
3/4 c. chopped cooked prunes
1/4 c. chopped nuts

Dissolve gelatin in 1 cup boiling water; stir in juices. Pour into 8 x 8-inch glass pan; refrigerate until partially set. Mix in prunes and nuts; chill until firm.

STUFFED PRUNE SALAD

18 cooked prunes
1 3-oz. package cream cheese
1/4 tsp. grated orange peel
2 tbsp. orange juice
6 pineapple slices, drained
1/3 c. flaked coconut
French dressing

Drain prunes. Slit down 1 side; remove pit. Soften cheese; blend in orange peel and juice. Fill prunes with cheese mixture. Arrange pineapple slices and prunes on lettuce; sprinkle with coconut. Serve with French dressing. Yield: 6 servings.

FILLED PRUNE CAKE

3/4 c. butter
1 c. sugar
3 eggs, separated
1 tsp. soda
3 tbsp. sour cream
1 tsp. cinnamon
1 tsp. allspice
1 tsp. nutmeg
1 c. finely chopped dried or canned prunes
1 1/2 c. flour
Creamy Filling

Cream butter and sugar; beat in egg yolks. Dissolve soda in 2 tablespoons hot water. Add soda, sour cream, cinnamon, allspice, nutmeg, prunes and flour, blending well. Fold in stiffly beaten egg whites. Pour batter into 2 large layer cake pans. Bake at 325 degrees for 30 minutes or until cake tests done. Remove from pans. Spread hot Creamy Filling between layers and on top of hot cake immediately.

Creamy Filling

1 egg, beaten
1 c. sugar
1/3 c. sour cream
1/2 c. finely cut prunes
1/2 c. light raisins
1/4 c. butter
1/2 c. pecans
1 tsp. vanilla

Combine egg, sugar, sour cream, prunes, raisins and butter in saucepan, blending well. Bring to a boil; cook for 3 minutes. Add pecans and vanilla.

PRUNE CUPCAKES

1/2 c. butter
1 c. sugar
1 egg
2 egg yolks
2 c. cake flour
1 tsp. soda
1/8 tsp. cloves
1 tsp. cinnamon
1/4 tsp. allspice
1/4 tsp. nutmeg
1/4 tsp. salt
3/4 c. buttermilk
1 c. chopped cooked prunes

Cream butter and sugar thoroughly. Add egg and egg yolks, mixing well. Sift dry ingredients together; add to creamed mixture alternately with buttermilk. Drain prunes; stir in batter. Fill cupcake tins 3/4 full. Bake at 350 degrees for 25 minutes. Yield: About 24 cupcakes.

PRUNE PIE

1/2 c. (packed) brown sugar
2 tbsp. cornstarch
1 c. prune juice
2 tbsp. butter
1 c. cooked dried prunes, chopped
1 orange, peeled and diced
1 baked 9-in. pie shell
2 egg whites
1/4 c. sugar

Mix brown sugar, cornstarch and juice in saucepan; place over low heat. Cook, until thickened. Add butter, prunes and orange; cook over low heat for 5 minutes. Pour into pie shell. Beat egg whites and sugar until stiff peaks form. Cover filling with meringue. Bake at 350 degrees for 20 minutes. Cool; serve with whipped cream on top.

PRUNE FLUFF

1/2 lb. prunes
1/8 tsp. cinnamon
1 c. sugar
1/3 c. cornstarch
1 tsp. lemon juice
2 egg whites, stiffly beaten
1/2 c. chopped nuts

Cook prunes in 2 cups water until tender; drain. Remove pits; cut prunes into small pieces. Combine prunes, cinnamon, sugar and 1 1/2 cups boiling water in saucepan; simmer for 10 minutes. Blend cornstarch with small amount of cold water; stir into prune mixture. Cook for 5 minutes, stirring constantly. Let cool. Fold in lemon juice, egg whites and nuts. Pour into serving dishes; chill.

PRUNE TORTE

1 box spice cake mix
2 c. heavy cream
1 jar strained prunes
1 c. pecans

Prepare cake mix according to package directions for two-layer cake. Split cooled layers into halves, making 4 layers. Beat cream until stiff peaks form; fold in strained prunes. Spread between layers and on top of torte; sprinkle with nuts. Chill until serving time. Yield: 12-16 servings.

Pudding, Bread

APPLE-TOPPED BREAD PUDDING

4 c. milk
1 tbsp. butter
1/4 tsp. salt
3/4 c. sugar
2 c. small dry bread cubes
4 slightly beaten eggs
1 tsp. vanilla
Juice of 1 orange
Grated rind of 1 orange
3 to 4 apples
Cinnamon

Scald milk; add butter, salt and sugar. Stir bread cubes into milk mixture; add eggs, vanilla, orange juice and rind. Blend thoroughly; pour mixture into well-greased 8 x 11 1/2-inch baking dish. Pare and core apples; arrange in rows over top of pudding. Sprinkle apples with cinnamon; place baking dish in pan of hot water. Bake at 325 degrees for 1 hour to 1 hour and 30 minutes or until inserted knife comes out clean.

BROWN SUGAR BREAD PUDDING

2 c. bread cubes
1/2 c. brown sugar
1/4 tsp. salt
1 tsp. cinnamon
1 tsp. vanilla
2 1/2 c. milk
1/2 c. raisins
2 slightly beaten eggs
1/2 c. chopped walnuts
2 tbsp. butter

Combine bread cubes with brown sugar, salt and cinnamon; add vanilla, milk, raisins, eggs and walnuts. Pour mixture into well-greased 1-quart baking dish; dot with butter. Bake at 325 degrees for 45 minutes or until inserted knife comes out clean.

STEAMED BREAD PUDDING

1 c. sugar
1 tsp. cinnamon
1/2 tsp. cloves
1 tsp. soda
4 tsp. butter
1 egg, beaten
2 c. bread crumbs
1 c. nuts
1 c. raisins

Combine sugar, cinnamon, cloves, soda, butter and egg with 1 cup water; stir in bread crumbs, nuts and raisins. Place pudding into mold; seal tightly. Steam for 1 hour. Serve with Brown Sugar Sauce.

Brown Sugar Sauce

1/2 stick butter
1/4 tsp. salt
1 c. brown sugar
1 1/2 c. evaporated milk
1 tsp. cornstarch

Combine all ingredients in saucepan; bring to a boil. Boil 1 minute. Serve sauce over pudding.

CHOCOLATE BREAD PUDDING

2 c. dry bread crumbs
2 c. scalded milk
1/4 tsp. salt
3/4 c. sugar
1/2 c. cocoa
2 eggs, slightly beaten
1 tsp. vanilla
2 tbsp. melted butter

Soak bread crumbs in milk for 30 minutes. Stir salt, sugar and cocoa together; add eggs, vanilla and butter. Pour into well-greased casserole; place casserole in shallow pan of hot water. Bake at 350 degrees for 1 hour.

COCONUT BREAD PUDDING

8 slices bread
4 c. scalded milk
4 eggs, separated
1 sm. can evaporated milk
2 tbsp. almond extract
Sugar
1 1/2 c. coconut
1/2 stick butter, melted

Soak bread in milk. Beat egg yolks and 1 egg white; add evaporated milk, 1 tablespoon almond extract and 1 1/2 cups sugar gradually. Add mixture to bread and milk; add coconut and butter. Bake at 300 degrees for 40 to 45 minutes or until inserted knife comes out clean. Beat remaining egg whites until soft peaks form. Add remaining sugar and almond extract gradually; beat until egg whites are glossy. Spoon meringue over pudding. Sprinkle with additional coconut. Bake at 325 degrees for 5 to 7 minutes or until lightly browned.

DATE BREAD PUDDINGS

1 c. sugar
2 eggs
1 c. bread crumbs
1 c. milk
1 c. dates, chopped fine
1 c. pecans
1 tsp. baking powder
1 tsp. vanilla
1 tsp. cinnamon
1 tsp. nutmeg
Pinch of salt

Beat sugar and eggs until light. Soak bread in milk; add to egg mixture. Stir in remaining ingredients; pour into greased custard cups. Bake at 350 degrees for 30 minutes.

DELICIOUS BREAD PUDDING

2 c. dry bread crumbs
4 c. hot milk
1/2 c. sugar
3 eggs, beaten
4 tbsp. melted margarine
1/2 tsp. salt
1 tsp. vanilla
3/4 c. raisins
1/4 tsp. nutmeg
1/4 tsp. cinnamon

Add bread crumbs to hot milk; cool. Combine sugar, eggs, margarine, salt, vanilla, raisins, nutmeg and cinnamon with bread mixture. Pour into buttered baking dish; place dish in pan of hot water. Bake at 350 degrees for 1 hour or until knife inserted comes out clean.

ORANGE MERINGUE BREAD PUDDING

1/3 c. butter
1 1/4 c. sugar
2 eggs, separated
1/4 c. orange juice
1 1/2 tsp. grated orange rind
2 c. soft bread crumbs

Cream butter and 1 cup sugar; beat in egg yolks. Add 1/2 cup water, orange juice and rind; mix well. Combine bread with egg mixture. Bake in a 1 1/2-quart greased casserole at 350 degrees for 30 to 35 minutes. Beat egg whites until soft peaks form; add remaining sugar gradually. Beat until egg whites are glossy; spread meringue over pudding. Bake for 5 to 10 minutes longer or until lightly browned.

SPICED BREAD CRUMB PUDDING

1 c. bread crumbs
1 c. sour milk
1/4 c. shortening
1 c. (packed) brown sugar
2 tbsp. molasses
1/2 c. flour
1 tsp. soda
1/2 tsp. cinnamon
1/4 tsp. cloves
3/4 c. raisins

Soak bread crumbs in milk for 30 minutes. Cream shortening and sugar; add molasses. Sift flour with soda and spices; add to sugar mixture. Add raisins; stir in bread crumb mixture. Pour into buttered baking dish. Bake at 350 degrees for 45 minutes. Serve with Vanilla Sauce.

Vanilla Sauce

1 c. sugar
1/2 c. butter
1 egg, well beaten
Vanilla to taste

Mix sugar, butter and egg in saucepan; add 4 to 5 teaspoons water. Beat slightly. Bring to a boil; remove from heat. Cool; add vanilla.

CARAMEL-TOPPED BREAD PUDDING

3 slices stale bread, cut in cubes
2/3 c. raisins
2 eggs, beaten
1/3 c. sugar
1/4 tsp. salt
2 c. milk
1/2 tsp. vanilla
1/3 c. brown sugar
1 tbsp. soft butter
1 tbsp. cream
1/3 c. chopped nuts

Combine bread cubes and 1/3 cup raisins; beat eggs with sugar and salt. Add milk and vanilla to egg mixture; blend well. Pour egg mixture over bread mixture; blend well. Pour into 8-inch square baking dish; place dish in pan of hot water. Bake at 350 degrees for 1 hour or until inserted knife comes out clean. Combine brown sugar, butter, cream, nuts and remaining raisins; spread over pudding. Return to oven; bake for 10 minutes longer or until topping bubbles.

Pumpkin

Large, round, bright orange pumpkins are sweet-fleshed fruit of a trailing vine. They belong to the gourd family and are thus related to such other familiar gourds as squash, cucumbers, and melons. North American Indians relied on native pumpkins for food long before colonists settled our country. Pumpkins soon became a staple in the colonial diet, too. Today they are traditionally associated with Thanksgiving and bountiful harvests. Pumpkins supply Vitamin A and iron. (1/2 cup cooked pumpkin = 35 calories)

AVAILABILITY: Fresh pumpkins are sold primarily in October, with small supplies available in September and November. Canned and pureed pumpkin are available year-round. Frozen pumpkin pies are also sold.

BUYING: Look for fairly firm, heavy, bright orange pumpkins that are blemish-free. Buy 1/2 pound per serving if pumpkin is to be cooked as a vegetable.

STORING: Keep fresh whole pumpkin on kitchen shelf about 1 month or in refrigerator for up to 4 months. Store unopened cans on kitchen shelf 1 year or opened cans in refrigerator 4 days. Freeze pumpkins in refrigerator freezer up to 3 months or in home freezer 1 year. *To freeze*—Wash pumpkin. Cut into uniform pieces, removing seeds. Bake at 350 degrees or steam until tender. Cool. Scoop flesh from skins and discard skins. Mash flesh or put through a food grinder. Pack in freezer containers, leaving 1/2-inch head space. Label, date, and freeze. Or make pie filling according to recipe, package, and freeze. *To can*—Peel pumpkin. Cut into 1-inch cubes. Remove seeds. Cook with enough water to prevent sticking or steam until tender. Mash. Pack hot in jars and process according to instructions under CANNING.

PREPARATION: 3 pounds raw pumpkin yields approximately 3 cups cooked and mashed pumpkin. To cook for pie filling, cut pumpkin in half. Remove seeds. Cut into small pieces. Peel. Cook, covered, in 1 inch boiling salted water 25 to 30 minutes or until tender. Drain. Mash. Season and proceed as directed in specific pie recipe.

SERVING: Use in spicy pumpkin pie and pumpkin soup. Also use in breads, rolls, souffles, cakes, tarts, custards, preserves, ice cream, and so on. Pumpkins can be cooked like winter squash and served as a vegetable. They may also be substituted for winter squash in many recipes.

SPICED PUMPKIN

4 c. pumpkin, cubed
3 c. cider vinegar
1 1/2 lb. sugar
1 tbsp. whole cloves
1/2 oz. stick cinnamon

Place pumpkin in colander; pour boiling water over pumpkin until pieces are hot. Chill pumpkin in ice water; drain. Combine vinegar, 3/4 cup water, sugar and spices in saucepan; simmer until sugar is dissolved. Add pumpkin; simmer until pumpkin is transparent and syrup has thickened. Let stand for 24 hours; drain, reserving syrup. Bring syrup to a boil; add pumpkin. Pickles may be immediately poured into sterilized jars and sealed or set aside for 24 hours longer for immediate use.

PUMPKIN SOUP

1 1/2 lb. soup meat	*1/2 med. onion*
3/4 lb. pig's tails	*1 sprig of thyme*
2 lb. pumpkin	*1 hot pepper*
1 clove of garlic	*Salt to taste*
2 green onions	

Place soup meat, pig's tails and 4 quarts of hot water in large kettle. Bring to a boil; cook until meats are tender. Add all remaining ingredients except salt. Cook until pumpkin is tender. Remove meats from kettle; force pumpkin through strainer. Return meats; add salt to taste. Serve. Yield: 16 servings.

CHRISTMAS PUMPKIN BREAD

1/2 c. vegetable oil	*1/2 tsp. cinnamon*
2 eggs	*1/2 tsp. nutmeg*
1 c. canned pumpkin	*1/4 tsp. salt*
1 2/3 c. sifted flour	*1/2 c. candied cherries, cut up*
1 1/4 c. sugar	*1/2 c. chopped nuts*
1 tsp. baking soda	

Combine oil, eggs, 1/3 cup water and pumpkin in large bowl. Sift flour, sugar, baking soda, cinnamon, nutmeg and salt together. Beat into pumpkin mixture gradually. Stir in cherries and nuts. Pour into greased and floured 9 x 5 x 3-inch loaf pan Bake in 350-degree oven for 1 hour or until loaf tests done.

FIESTA PUMPKIN BREAD

1 lge. can pumpkin pie mix	*2 1-lb. 1-oz. packages nut bread mix*
1 egg, beaten	

Combine all ingredients thoroughly, stirring until smooth. Pour into 2 large loaf pans. Bake at 350 degrees for 50 minutes.

OLD-FASHIONED PUMPKIN BREAD

3 c. sugar	*1 tsp. nutmeg*
3 1/2 c. flour	*1 c. chopped pecans*
2 tsp. soda	*1 c. salad oil*
1 1/2 tsp. salt	*4 eggs, beaten*
1 tsp. cinnamon	*1 No. 303 can pumpkin*

Sift sugar, flour, soda, salt and spices into large mixing bowl. Make well in center; add nuts, oil, eggs, 2/3 cup water and pumpkin. Blend well; pour into large greased and floured angel food cake pan or two small loaf pans. Bake at 325 degrees for 1 hour and 10 minutes.

SIMPLE PUMPKIN BREAD

1 c. canned or cooked pumpkin	*1 egg*
2 tbsp. butter	*2 c. flour*
1 c. sugar	*3 tsp. baking powder*
	1/2 tsp. salt

Strain all liquid from pumpkin. Cream butter and sugar; beat in egg. Sift all remaining ingredients together; add to creamed mixture alternately with pumpkin. Pour into greased 8 x 4 x 2 1/2-inch pan; let rise in warm place for 20 minutes. Bake in 350-degree oven for 45 minutes or until loaf tests done. Yield: 1 loaf.

PUMPKIN BISCUITS

1/2 c. strained cooked pumpkin	*1/4 c. butter*
1/4 c. sugar	*1/2 c. scalded milk*
1/2 tsp. salt	*1/4 yeast cake*
	2 1/2 c. flour

Combine pumpkin, sugar, salt, butter and milk; cool to lukewarm. Dissolve yeast in 1/4 cup lukewarm water. Add yeast and flour to pumpkin mixture; cover. Let rise overnight. Roll out on floured surface; shape into biscuits. Let rise until doubled in bulk. Bake at 375 degrees until browned. Yield: 12-18 biscuits.

PUMPKIN MUFFINS

1 egg	*1/2 tsp. cinnamon*
3/4 c. milk	*1/4 tsp. nutmeg*
2 tbsp. cooking oil	*1/4 tsp. cloves*
1/2 c. pumpkin	*2 c. prepared biscuit mix*
1/2 c. sugar	

Mix egg, milk, oil and pumpkin thoroughly; add all remaining ingredients. Fill muffin tins or baking cups half full. Bake at 400 degrees for 20 minutes. Yield: 12-18 muffins.

FROZEN PUMPKIN SQUARES

1/4 lb. marshmallows, chopped	*1/8 tsp. ginger*
1 c. cooked or canned pumpkin	*1/8 tsp. salt*
1/4 tsp. cinnamon	*1 pt. vanilla ice cream*
	Ginger cookie crumbs

Place marshmallows, pumpkin, cinnamon, ginger and salt in double boiler over hot water. Heat, stirring occasionally, until marshmallows are melted. Cool slightly; stir in ice cream. Line refrigerator tray with cookie crumbs, reserving 1/4 of the crumbs for top. Pour pumpkin mixture over crumbs. Sprinkle remaining crumbs on top. Freeze. Remove from freezer 10 minutes before serving. Cut in squares. Yield: 8 servings.

PUMPKIN DELIGHT

16 gingersnaps, crushed	*1/2 c. sugar*
1 c. pumpkin	*1/2 tsp. salt*
1 qt. vanilla ice cream, softened	*1/4 tsp. cinnamon*
	1/8 tsp. nutmeg
	1/2 c. chopped nuts

Place gingersnap crumbs in greased 8-inch pan; reserve 1/4 cup crumbs for top. Combine all remaining ingredients; mix thoroughly. Pour into pan. Sprinkle reserved crumbs over top. Freeze until firm. Cut into squares to serve. Yield: 6 servings.

PUMPKIN CAKE

1/2 c. chopped dates
1/2 c. chopped walnuts
Flour, sifted
1/4 c. butter
1 c. (packed) brown sugar
2/3 c. cooked pumpkin
1 tsp. vanilla
2 eggs
1/2 tsp. baking powder
1/2 tsp. cinnamon
1/2 tsp. nutmeg
1/4 tsp. ginger
1/4 tsp. soda

Mix dates, nuts and 2 tablespoons flour; set aside. Melt butter over low heat; blend in brown sugar. Remove from heat; stir in pumpkin and vanilla. Beat in eggs, one at a time. Sift 1/2 cup flour with all remaining dry ingredients; add to pumpkin mixture, mixing thoroughly. Stir in dates and nuts; turn into greased 9 x 1 1/2-inch round baking pan. Bake in 350-degree oven for 25 minutes. Serve warm with whipped cream. Yield: 8 servings.

PUMPKIN COOKIES

2 1/4 c. sugar
3/4 c. shortening
2 eggs, well beaten
1 lge. can pumpkin
1 1/4 tsp. soda
4 c. flour, sifted
4 tsp. baking powder
2 c. raisins
1 c. chopped nuts
1/2 tsp. ginger
1/2 tsp. cinnamon
1/2 tsp. allspice
1/4 tsp. cloves
1 tsp. salt
2 tsp. vanilla

Cream together sugar and shortening. Add eggs, pumpkin and soda. Mix in all remaining ingredients; stir well. Drop from teaspoon onto cookie sheet. Sprinkle with cinnamon sugar. Bake at 375 degrees for 8 to 10 minutes. Yield: 9 dozen.

CRUNCHY PUMPKIN CREAM PIE

1/2 c. butter
1/4 c. (packed) brown sugar
1/2 c. chopped walnuts
1 1/3 c. sifted flour
3/4 c. sugar
1 c. pumpkin
1/4 tsp. cinnamon
1/4 tsp. nutmeg
1/4 tsp. allspice
1/4 tsp. salt
2 eggs, well beaten

Mix butter, brown sugar, walnuts and 1 cup flour with hands; spread in 13 x 9 x 2-inch pan. Bake in 400-degree oven for 15 minutes. Stir; reserve 3/4 cup mixture for topping. Press remaining mixture into 9-inch pie pan; cool. Combine remaining flour, sugar, pumpkin, spices, salt and eggs in saucepan; cook until thick, stirring constantly. Pour into pie shell; sprinkle with reserved topping. Yield: 6 servings.

DIFFERENT PUMPKIN PIE

3/4 c. (packed) brown sugar
1 env. unflavored gelatin
1 tsp. cinnamon
1/2 tsp. cloves
1/2 tsp. nutmeg
1/2 tsp. salt
3 eggs, separated
1/2 c. milk
1 1-lb. can pumpkin
1 c. sour cream
1/4 c. sugar
1 baked 10-in. pie shell

Combine brown sugar, gelatin, spices and salt in saucepan; add beaten egg yolks, milk and pumpkin. Mix well. Cook over medium heat, stirring constantly, until gelatin dissolves. Remove from heat; cool slightly. Add sour cream; mix well. Beat egg whites until slightly stiff; add sugar gradually, one tablespoon at a time, beating after each addition. Continue beating until stiff peaks form. Fold in pumpkin mixture. Pour into pie shell. Chill for 4 hours before serving. Yield: 6 servings.

GRAND CHAMPION PUMPKIN PIE

2 c. pumpkin
1/2 c. sugar
1/2 c. (packed) brown sugar
1 tsp. cinnamon
1/2 tsp. nutmeg
1/4 tsp. ginger
1 tsp. salt
1 tbsp. flour
3 eggs, beaten
1/2 c. cream
1 c. milk
1 unbaked 9-in. pie shell

Mix all ingredients except pie shell together. Pour mixture into pie shell. Bake in 425-degree oven for 10 minutes. Reduce temperature to 375 degrees; bake 45 minutes or until knife inserted in center comes out clean.

PUMPKIN CHIFFON PIE

Color photograph for this recipe on page 484.

1 c. sifted all-purpose flour
1/4 tsp. salt
3 tbsp. butter
2 tbsp. shortening
Milk
1 c. sugar
1 tbsp. unflavored gelatin
1/2 tsp. ginger
1/2 tsp. cinnamon
1/2 tsp. nutmeg
3 eggs, separated
1 1/4 c. mashed cooked pumpkin
1 tsp. grated orange rind
1/4 c. orange juice
Sweetened whipped cream

Preheat oven to 450 degrees. Sift flour and salt together into mixing bowl. Cut in butter and shortening until mixture resembles small peas. Sprinkle 3 tablespoons milk over flour mixture, 1 tablespoon at a time, mixing lightly with fork after each addition. Shape into ball. Flatten dough slightly on lightly floured board; roll out 1/8 inch thick in circle 1 inch larger than 9-inch pie plate. Place in pie plate. Fold extra dough under and flute edge. Prick bottom and sides well with fork. Bake for 10 minutes or until lightly browned; cool. Mix 1/2 cup sugar, gelatin, ginger, cinnamon and nutmeg in 2-quart saucepan. Beat egg yolks in a bowl; stir in 1/2 cup milk. Add to gelatin mixture; cook over medium heat, stirring constantly, until mixture comes to a boil. Stir in pumpkin, orange rind and orange juice; chill until partially set. Beat egg whites until frothy. Add remaining sugar gradually; beat until stiff peaks form. Fold into pumpkin mixture; place filling in pie crust. Chill for at least 6 hours or until firm. Serve with whipped cream; garnish with additional grated orange rind.

PUMPKIN CUSTARD PIE

1 c. canned pumpkin
3 lge. eggs, separated
1 c. sugar
3/4 c. milk

3/4 c. evaporated milk	*1/4 tsp. nutmeg*
1/4 tsp. cinnamon	*1 9-in. pastry shell*

Beat pumpkin and egg yolks together; mix in sugar and milks. Stir in cinnamon and nutmeg. Fold in stiffly beaten egg whites. Pour into pastry shell. Bake at 350 degrees for 1 hour. Yield: 6 servings.

PUMPKIN-NUT PIE

3 eggs, slightly beaten	*1 tsp. vanilla*
1 c. canned pumpkin	*1/2 tsp. cinnamon*
1/2 c. sugar	*1/4 tsp. salt*
1/2 c. (packed) brown sugar	*1 unbaked 9-in. pastry shell*
1/2 c. dark corn syrup	*1 c. chopped pecans*

Combine eggs, pumpkin, sugars, corn syrup, vanilla, cinnamon, and salt in mixing bowl; mix well. Pour into pastry shell; top with pecans. Bake in 350-degree oven for 40 minutes or until knife inserted in center tests clean. Cool. Serve with mound of whipped cream, if desired. Yield: 6 servings.

PUMPKIN-RUM PIE

3 eggs, separated	*1/2 c. milk*
3/4 c. (packed) brown sugar	*1 sm. can pumpkin*
	1 tsp. cinnamon
1/2 tsp. nutmeg	*Sugar*
1/4 tsp. cloves	*1 baked 9-in. pie shell*
1 env. unflavored gelatin	*1/2 pt. whipping cream*
Rum	

Beat egg yolks in double boiler; add brown sugar, milk, pumpkin, cinnamon, nutmeg and cloves. Cook over boiling water for 10 minutes or until slightly thickened, stirring constantly. Soften gelatin in 1/2 cup cold water; stir into hot pumpkin mixture until dissolved. Cool; add 3/4 cup rum. Beat egg whites until stiff peaks form, adding 1/2 cup sugar; fold into pumpkin mixture. Pour filling into pie crust; refrigerate overnight. Whip cream until stiff, adding rum and sugar to taste. Serve whipped cream mixture over pie. Yield: 8-10 servings.

PUMPKIN SURPRISE PIE

1/2 lb. marshmallows	*1/2 c. instant nonfat dry milk powder*
1 1/4 c. cooked pumpkin	*1 baked 9-in. pie shell*
1/2 tsp. salt	*Pecan halves*
1/2 tsp. cinnamon	
1/4 tsp. ginger	

Combine marshmallows, pumpkin and seasonings in top of double boiler. Heat over boiling water until marshmallows are melted; cool. Combine milk powder and 1/2 cup cold water; chill until icy crystals form. Whip milk mixture until stiff. Fold in pumpkin mixture. Turn filling into pie shell; chill well. Garnish with pecan halves.

Pumpkin Surprise Pie . . . Marshmallows and whipped milk powder give this pie lightness.

PUMPKIN SHERRY PIE

1 env. plain gelatin
3 eggs, separated
1 c. strained cooked or canned pumpkin
1/2 c. sherry
1 c. sugar
1/4 tsp. salt
1/2 tsp. cinnamon
1/4 tsp. nutmeg
1/4 tsp. ginger
1 baked 9-in. pastry shell
Whipped cream

Soften gelatin in 1/4 cup cold water. Beat egg yolks slightly in double boiler; stir in pumpkin, sherry, 1/4 cup sugar, salt, cinnamon, nutmeg and ginger. Cook over boiling water, stirring constantly, for 5 minutes. Remove from heat; add gelatin. Stir until dissolved; chill until mixture begins to thicken. Fold in stiffly beaten egg whites with remaining sugar. Pour into pie shell; chill for several hours. Top with whipped cream before serving.

PUMPKIN SPICE PIE

1 1-lb. can pumpkin
1/2 c. sugar
1/2 c. (packed) brown sugar
1 tbsp. molasses
Pinch of salt
1 tsp. cinnamon
1 lge. can evaporated milk
1 c. heavy cream
1 1/2 c. milk
1/2 tsp. ginger
1/4 tsp. nutmeg
1 tbsp. cornstarch
4 eggs
1 unbaked 9-in. pie shell

Preheat oven to 425 degrees. Mix pumpkin, sugars, molasses, salt, cinnamon, evaporated milk, cream, milk, ginger, nutmeg, cornstarch and eggs; pour into pie shell. Bake for 15 minutes. Reduce temperature to 350 degrees. Bake for 45 minutes or until knife inserted in center comes clean.

Quiche

Pronounced KEESH, this is the name applied to various French-born dishes consisting of either a pastry shell or pie crust with savory, unsweetened egg and cream custard or similar filling. Various ingredients such as meat, seafood, onions, and/or cheese are frequently either added to the filling itself or spread on the bottom of the pastry shell or pie crust before the filling is spooned on top. Quiches are baked and served warm as a brunch, luncheon, or supper dish. Smaller tart-like quiches make choice hors d'oeuvres.

Perhaps the most famous of all quiches is Quiche Lorraine, said to have originated in northeastern France. Quiche Lorraine is traditionally made with crumbled bacon and often with shredded Swiss cheese as well. Bacon and cheese are sprinkled on the bottom of the pastry shell before the unsweetened filling is added.

BACON-CHEESE PIE

1/2 c. chopped onion
2 tbsp. butter
1 baked 9-in. pie crust
1 c. grated sharp Cheddar cheese
1 c. milk, scalded
3 eggs, slightly beaten
1/2 tsp. salt
1/8 tsp. pepper
1/8 tsp. thyme
8 slices fried bacon

Saute onion in butter until golden; spoon into pie crust. Sprinkle onion with cheese. Combine milk and eggs; add salt, pepper and thyme. Pour into crust. Crumble 2 pieces bacon; sprinkle over pie. Bake at 350 degrees for 20 to 25 minutes or until knife inserted in center comes out clean. Garnish with remaining bacon slices arranged spoke-fashion over pie.

CANADIAN BACON QUICHE

1 c. diced Canadian bacon
1 tsp. butter
1 med. onion, grated
1/2 c. Swiss cheese, grated
1 unbaked pie shell
4 slightly beaten eggs
1 1/2 c. evaporated milk
1 c. milk
1 c. cream
1/2 tsp. salt
1/4 tsp. pepper
1 pinch of nutmeg

Saute bacon in butter in skillet until golden brown; remove bacon. Add onion; saute for 5 minutes. Place bacon, onion and cheese in pie shell. Combine remaining ingredients with 1/2 cup water; blend well. Pour egg mixture into shell. Bake at 450 degrees for 15 minutes. Reduce heat to 350 degrees; bake for 15 to 20 minutes or until custard is set.

CLASSIC QUICHE LORRAINE

1 lb. bacon, cooked and crumbled
1 1/2 c. Swiss cheese, grated
1 unbaked 10-in. pie shell
4 eggs, slightly beaten
1 tbsp. flour
3/4 tsp. salt
Dash of pepper
Dash of nutmeg
1 c. heavy cream
1 c. half and half

Place bacon and cheese in pie shell. Mix remaining ingredients well; pour over bacon and cheese. Bake in 375-degree oven for 50 minutes or until knife inserted in center comes out clean.

CHEESE FONDUE SAVANT
Recipe On Page 222.

NORWEGIAN COUNTRY LOAVES
Recipe For This Photograph On Page 152.

SEEDED WHITE BREAD
Recipe For This Photograph On Page 153.

INTERNATIONAL FONDUE
Recipe For This Photograph On Page 102.

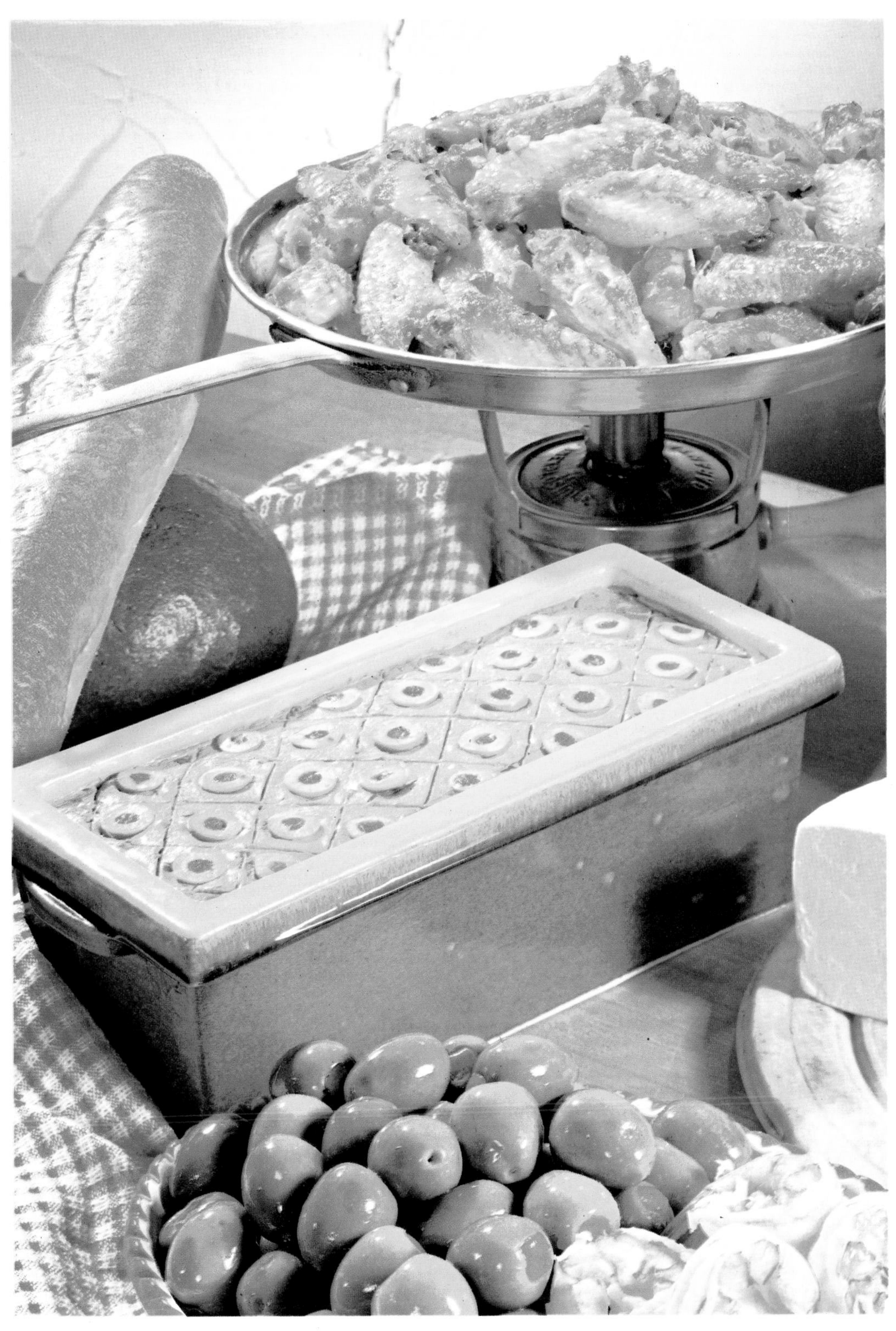

BARBECUED CHICKEN-LITTLE LEGS AND CHICKEN LIVER-OLIVE PATE
Recipes For This Photograph On Pages 246 and 252.

FRUIT BREAD
Recipe For This Photograph On Page 860.

SAFFRON COFFEE RING
Recipe For This Photograph On Page 298.

JET-SET CHICKEN FONDUE
Recipe For This Photograph On Page 240.

WAFFLE HEARTS
Recipe For This Photograph On Page 917.

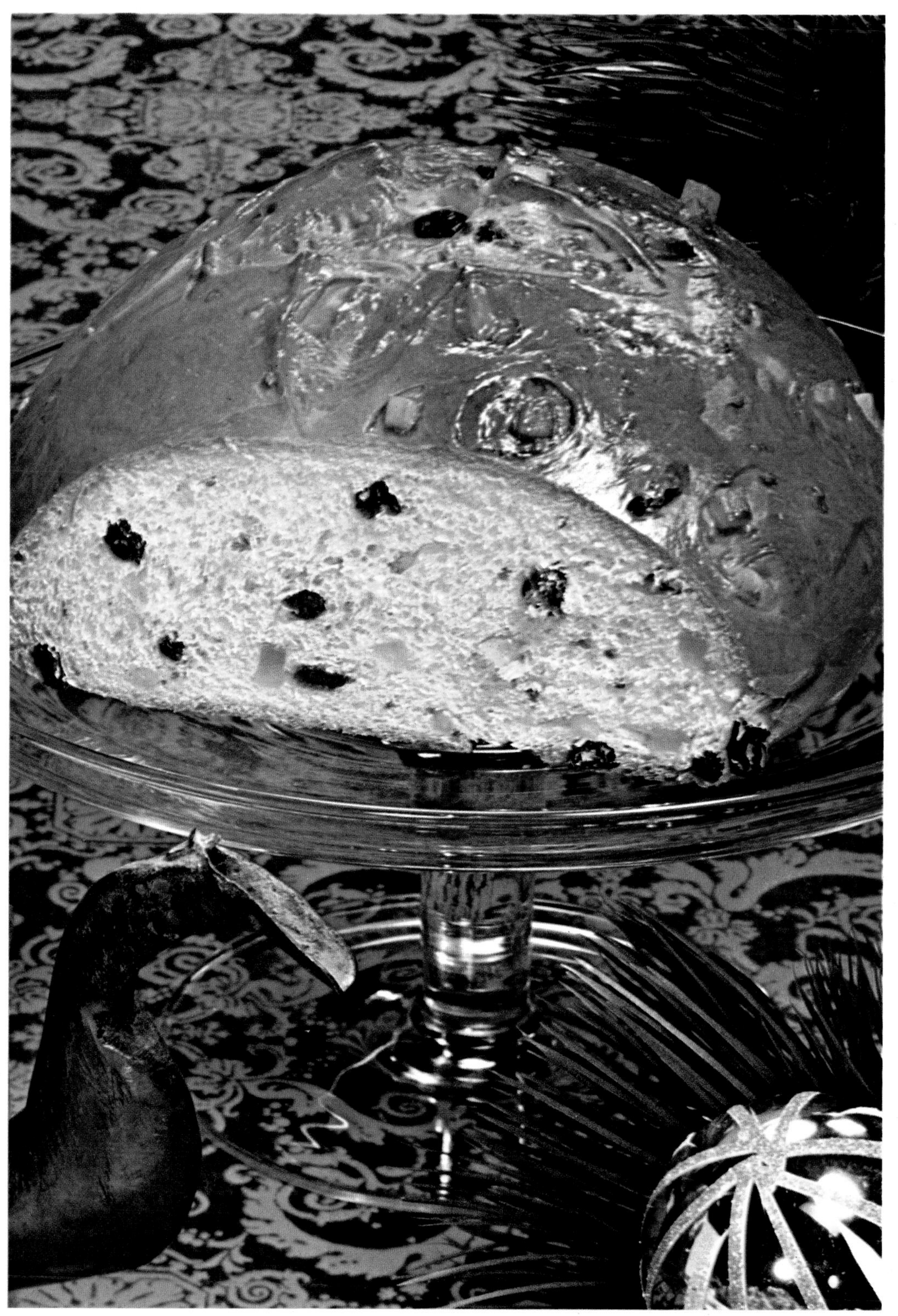

PANETTONE
Recipe For This Photograph On Page 860.

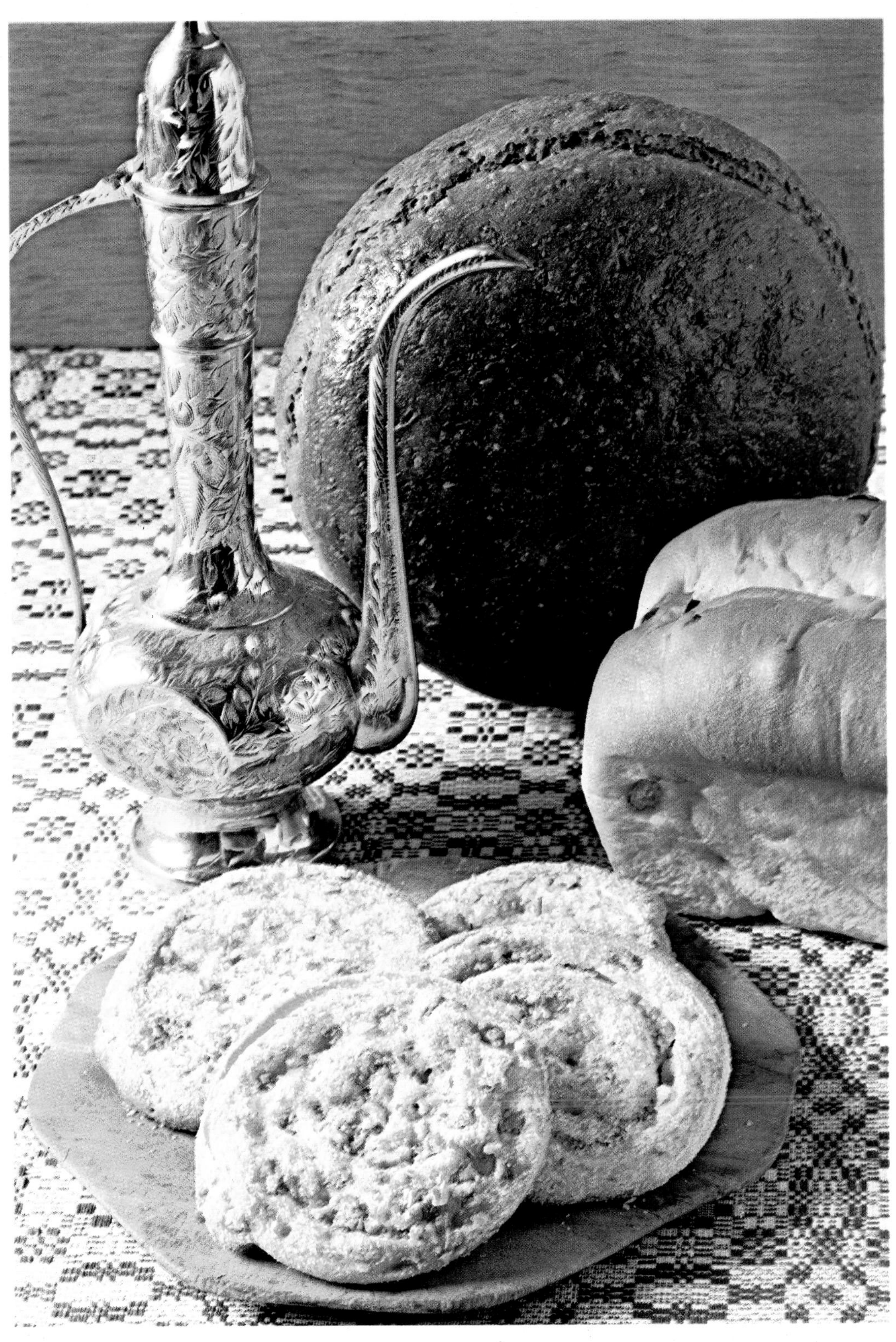

RUSSIAN BLACK BREAD, SUGAR-CRISP BALLS, AND IRISH FRECKLE BREAD
Recipes For This Photograph On Pages 153, 862 and 152.

TUNA-CHEESE FONDUE
Recipe For This Photograph On Page 887.

ARTICHOKES WITH AL PESTO BUTTER
Recipe For This Photograph On Page 38.

CREAMED COD ON WAFFLES
Recipe For This Photograph On Page 288.

FRESH POTATO ROLLS DELICIOUS ⇨
Recipe For This Photograph On Page 763.

FRESH POTATO-FRUIT COFFEECAKE ⇨
Recipe For This Photograph On Page 297.

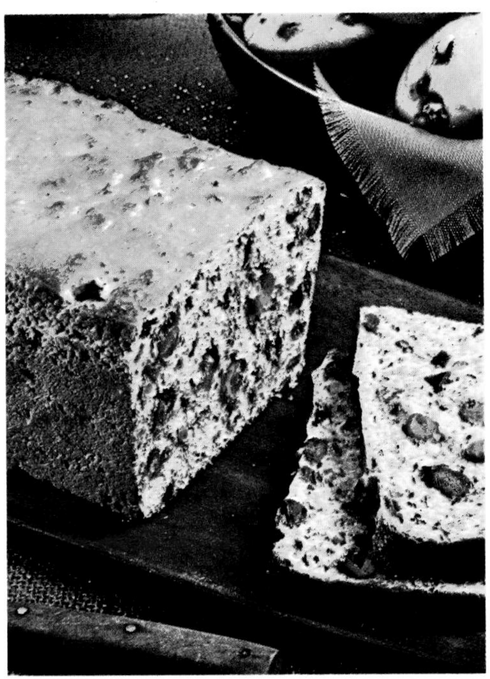

CRANBERRY FRUIT LOAF
Recipe For This Photograph On Page 341.

SUNDIAL CHEESE FRUIT PLATTER
Recipe For This Photograph On Page 222.

⇦

CHOCOLATE MARSHMALLOW FONDUE
Recipe For This Photograph On Page 265.

⇨

HEARTY BEEF FONDUE
Recipe For This Photograph On Page 102.

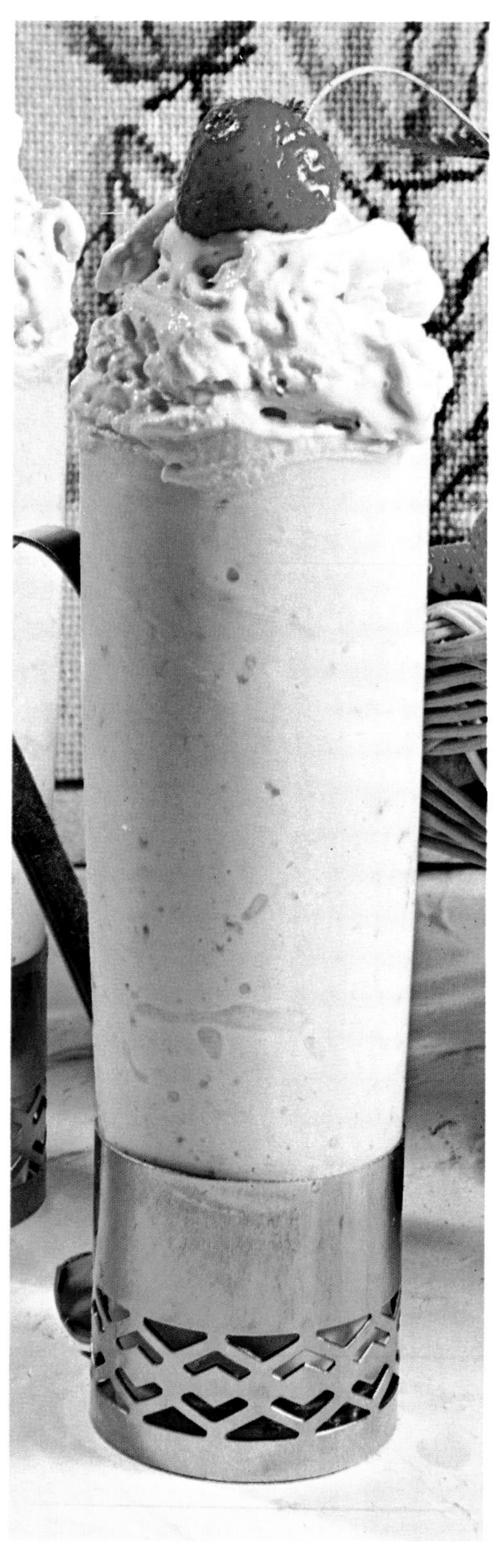

STRAWBERRY THICKSHAKES
Recipe For This Photograph On Page 125.

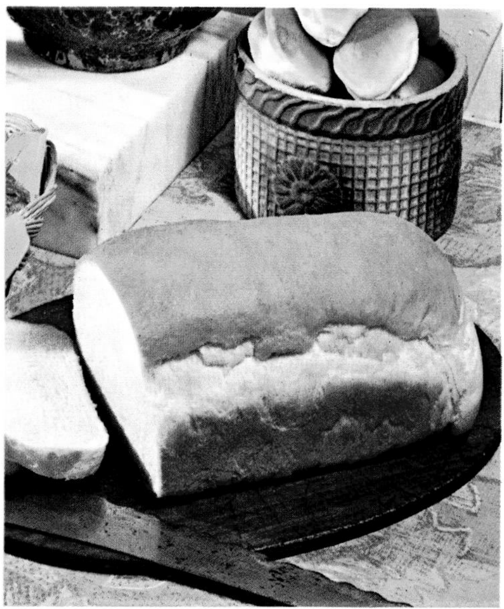

SOURDOUGH BREAD
Recipe For This Photograph On Page 154.

BRIOCHES
Recipe For This Photograph On Page 155.

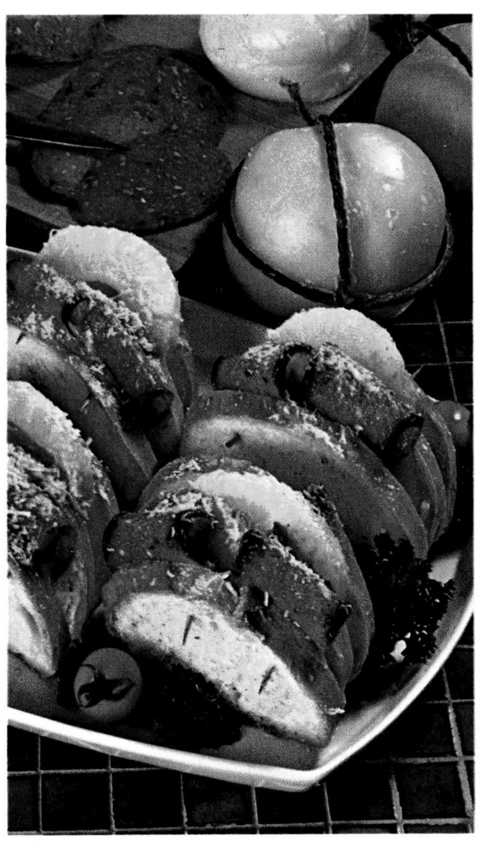

SKEWERED PINEAPPLE SANDWICHES
Recipe For This Photograph On Page 670.

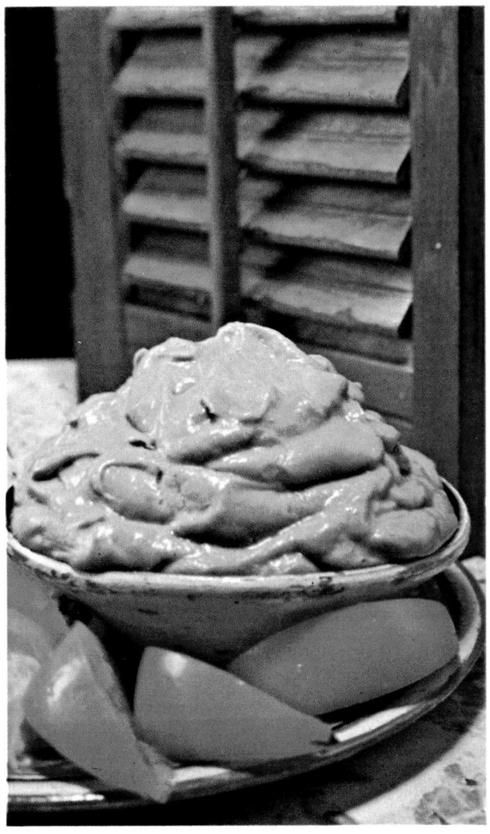

AVOCADO CREAM
Recipe For This Photograph On Page 53.

A TRIO OF CHEESE DIPS
Recipe For This Photograph On Page 218.

HOT CINNAMON SPICED WINE
Recipe For This Photograph On Page 126.

RIPE OLIVE CHILI
Recipe For This Photograph On Page 604.

⇨

DOUBLE BLUEBERRY PANCAKES
Recipe For This Photograph On Page 625.

⇦

DELICIOUS ORANGE MUFFINS
Recipe For This Photograph On Page 617.

BACON CUSTARD PIE

Pastry for 1 9-in pie
Egg white
1 tbsp. flour
1 1/2 c. Swiss cheese, grated
1/2 lb. lean bacon
1 lge. onion, sliced
2 tbsp. butter
3 eggs
1 c. light cream
1 c. milk
1/2 tsp. salt
1/2 tsp. chopped parsley
Dash of cayenne pepper
Dash of nutmeg

Preheat oven to 450 degrees. Line glass pie plate with pastry; brush with small amount of egg white. Bake for 5 minutes. Prick crust with fork, if necessary. Remove from oven. Mix flour with cheese. Fry bacon until crisp; drain on paper towel. Discard bacon fat. Separate onion into rings; cook in butter in same pan. Place cheese in pie shell; sprinkle with bacon and onion rings. Beat eggs lightly; add cream, milk and seasonings. Pour egg mixture over ingredients in pastry shell; shake pan to settle liquid. Bake for 15 minutes; reduce heat to 350 degrees. Bake for 10 to 15 minutes longer or until custard sets. Cool for 10 minutes before cutting.

CONTINENTAL CHEESE PIE

2 c. finely rolled soda cracker crumbs
3 tbsp. softened butter
8 slices bacon
3 c. thinly sliced onions
1 1/4 c. milk, scalded
3 eggs, slightly beaten
1/4 tsp. salt
1/4 lb. grated Cheddar cheese

Blend 1 cup cracker crumbs with softened butter; line bottom and sides of a 9-inch pie plate. Fry bacon until crisp; drain on paper towel. Drain off fat from pan. Add onions to pan; saute until lightly brown. Spread crumbled bacon and onions over crumb crust. Stir small amount of scalded milk into eggs; return to milk. Add salt. Mix in half the grated cheese; heat until melted, stirring constantly. Pour over onions. Combine remaining cheese with remaining cracker crumbs; sprinkle over custard mixture. Bake in 325-degree oven for 45 minutes or until knife inserted in center comes out clean. Garnish with additional crumbled bacon, if desired.

CORN QUICHE LORRAINE

6 strips bacon, diced
1 med. onion, minced
1 unbaked 10-in. pie shell
1/2 c. grated Swiss cheese
4 eggs, slightly beaten
1 c. milk
1 c. heavy cream
1 1-lb. 1-oz. can cream-style corn
Pinch of nutmeg
1/2 tsp. salt
1/4 tsp. pepper

Cook bacon in small skillet; drain on towel. Add onion to bacon fat; saute for 5 minutes or just until tender. Drain on paper towel. Cover pie crust with bacon, onion and 1/4 cup cheese. Combine remaining cheese, eggs, milk, cream, corn and seasonings in bowl; blend thoroughly. Pour over bacon mixture. Bake at 450 degrees for 18 minutes.

THE OLIVER
Recipe On Page 788.

CRAB MEAT QUICHE

1 8-in. unbaked pie shell
2 eggs
1 c. cream
1 tsp. monosodium glutamate
Salt
Dash of cayenne pepper
3 oz. grated Swiss cheese
3 oz. grated Gruyere cheese
1 tbsp. flour
1 6-oz. can crab meat, flaked

Prick bottom and sides of pie shell; bake for 10 minutes at 450 degrees. Beat eggs with cream, monosodium glutamate, salt and cayenne pepper. Combine cheeses, flour and crab meat. Sprinkle over pie shell; pour cream mixture over top. Bake at 325 degrees for 45 minutes to 1 hour or until knife inserted in center comes out clean.

PETITE CRAB QUICHES

1 3-oz. package cream cheese
1 stick margarine
1 c. flour
1 egg, beaten
3/4 c. cream
1 tsp. Parmesan cheese, grated
1/4 c. crab meat
1/2 tsp. salt

Soften cream cheese and margarine; add flour. Chill for 1 hour. Shape into twenty-four 1-inch balls. Press into small muffin tins. Bake for 5 minutes in 350-degree oven. Combine egg, cream, Parmesan cheese, crab meat and salt. Pour mixture into muffin tins. Reduce oven temperature to 325 degrees; bake for 15 minutes longer.

CHEDDAR QUICHE SUPREME

1 c. sifted flour
1/2 tsp. salt
1/2 stick butter
1/2 c. shredded Cheddar cheese
1/3 c. half and half
4 eggs, slightly beaten
1 1/2 c. milk
Dash of pepper
1 8-oz. package sharp cheese, shredded
Few drops of hot sauce
3/4 c. diced cooked ham
1/3 c. chopped green pepper
Parsley
Pimento strips

Sift flour and 1/4 teaspoon salt; cut in butter. Stir in Cheddar cheese. Add half and half; stir until dough holds together. Roll on lightly floured board; fit into large pie pan. Fold and flute edge to make standing rim. Combine remaining salt and next seven ingredients; mix well. Pour into pie shell. Bake at 350 degrees for 40 to 45 minutes or until knife inserted in center comes out clean. Garnish with parsley and pimento strips.

EASY QUICHE

1 pkg. pie crust mix
1/2 lb. Swiss cheese, grated
1 tbsp. flour
3 eggs
1 c. cream
Salt and pepper

Preheat oven to 400 degrees. Prepare 9-inch pie shell according to package directions. Combine cheese and flour; spread mixture evenly over crust. Beat eggs well; add cream, salt and pepper. Blend; pour over cheese. Bake for 15 minutes at 400 degrees. Reduce oven temperature to 325 degrees; bake for 30 minutes or until knife inserted in center comes out clean.

HAM QUICHE

1 unbaked 10-in. pastry shell
6 slices bacon
1 sm. onion, thinly sliced
4 eggs
1 1/2 c. light cream
1/4 tsp. dry mustard
1/2 tsp. basil
1/2 tsp. salt
1/2 lb. boiled ham, cut into thin strips
1/4 lb. Swiss cheese, grated

Place pastry shell in freezer until well chilled. Cook bacon until crisp; drain on paper towel. Cook onion in bacon drippings until transparent; drain. Beat eggs, cream, mustard, basil and salt until well blended. Crumble bacon; mix in onion. Sprinkle in pastry shell; add half the ham and half the cheese. Add remaining ham; top with cheese. Pour egg mixture over all. Bake at 425 degrees for 15 minutes; reduce oven temperature to 350 degrees. Bake for 30 minutes or until knife inserted in center comes out clean.

MUSHROOM QUICHE

4 tbsp. butter
2 tbsp. minced shallots
1 lb. mushrooms, diced
1 1/2 tsp. salt
1 tsp. lemon juice
4 eggs
1 c. heavy cream
1/8 tsp. pepper
1/8 tsp. nutmeg
1/2 c. grated Swiss cheese
1 baked pie shell

Melt 3 tablespoons butter; add shallots, mushrooms, 1 teaspoon salt and lemon juice. Simmer, covered, for 10 minutes or until liquid evaporates and mushrooms are tender. Beat eggs with cream; add remaining salt, pepper and nutmeg. Stir in mushroom mixture; pour into pie shell. Sprinkle with cheese; dot with remaining butter. Bake at 350 degrees for 35 minutes or until knife inserted in center comes out clean.

PARMESAN QUICHE

Recipe 2-crust pie pastry
4 oz. butter
1/2 lb. Swiss cheese
1/2 lb. Cheddar cheese
4 tbsp. flour
2 tbsp. grated Parmesan cheese
Dash of nutmeg
8 eggs
1 tbsp. salt
4 c. half and half

Divide pie dough in half; roll out and line 2 pie pans. Brown butter; cool to lukewarm. Grate Swiss and Cheddar cheeses coarsely; mix with 1 tablespoon flour, Parmesan cheese and nutmeg. Divide mixture evenly into pie crusts. Beat eggs with nutmeg, salt and 1 tablespoon flour; blend with half and half and remaining flour. Strain mixture; beat in butter vigorously. Divide mixture into pie shells. Bake at 375 degrees for 30 minutes; reduce oven temperature to 350 degrees. Bake for 20 minutes longer or until knife inserted in center comes out clean.

QUICHE MARRAKESH

1 recipe 2-crust pie pastry
2 c. shredded Swiss cheese
4 tsp. flour
2 c. diced cooked ham
6 eggs, slightly beaten
2 lge. cans evaporated milk
2 1 3/4-oz. package cream of leek soup

Roll out pastry to make two 9-inch pie shells; mix cheese with flour. Sprinkle half the mixture into pie shells; top with ham. Combine eggs with 2/3 cup water and milk. Add soup mix; blend well. Pour soup mixture over ham and cheese. Sprinkle with remaining cheese mixture. Bake at 400 degrees for 25 minutes or until knife inserted in center comes out clean.

SPINACH QUICHE

1/2 c. shortening
2 1/2 c. sifted flour
Egg white
4 c. chopped fresh spinach
4 eggs
4 c. milk
1 1/4 tsp. salt
1/2 c. chopped bacon

Cut shortening into flour; add enough water to make a firm dough. Roll out on floured board; line 10-inch pie pan with dough. Brush with egg white. Place spinach in pastry. Combine eggs, milk and salt; mix well. Pour custard over spinach; top with bacon. Bake at 450 degrees for 10 minutes; reduce oven temperature to 350 degrees. Bake for 15 minutes longer or until knife inserted in center comes out clean.

TASTY QUICHE LORRAINE

1 recipe pie pastry
1/2 tsp. dry mustard
1/4 tsp. paprika
1 1/2 tsp. beef bouillon
3 eggs
1/2 c. milk
2 tsp. flour
Dash of cayenne pepper
5 slices bacon, crisply fried
1/4 c. grated Cheddar cheese

Prepare pastry, adding mustard and paprika to dry mix. Roll out pastry to fit 8-inch pie plate. Bake in 375- degree oven for 10 minutes. Add bouillon to eggs; beat thoroughly. Slowly add milk, flour and seasoning. Crumble bacon; stir into egg mixture with cheese. Pour into pie shell. Bake at 350 degrees for 30 minutes or until knife inserted in center comes out clean.

Raisin

Raisins are grapes that have been vine-ripened and sun-dried. There are two types: seedless and seeded. The most important *seedless* variety, the Thompson Seedless, is dark, bluish-brown in color. The *seeded* Muscat raisin is reddish-brown in color. Raisins have a high sugar and iron content with lesser quantities of Vitamin A, thiamine, riboflavin, and copper. (1/4 cup raisins = 120 calories)
AVAILABILITY: Raisins are available year-round. They are usually sold in boxes; however, muscat raisins are sometimes sold in clusters. Also available are Golden Raisins, which, unlike the other types, have been dehydrated indoors and treated with sulphur to preserve the mellow golden color.
STORING: Keep unopened packages of raisins on the kitchen shelf for 5 months. Store contents of an opened package in an airtight container in a cool, dark place for 4 to 5 months.
PREPARATION: See CURRANTS.
USES: Raisins are both a healthful snack and an important baking ingredient. They are widely used in cakes, sweet breads, and cookies.
(See GRAPE.)

BOILED RAISIN CAKE

2 c. (packed) brown sugar
4 tbsp. (heaping) butter
1 tsp. cinnamon
1 tsp. cloves
1/2 tsp. allspice
1/2 tsp. nutmeg
1 tsp. salt
1 1/2 c. raisins
3 c. flour
2 tsp. soda
3/4 c. walnuts (opt.)

Combine sugar, 2 cups hot water, butter, spices, salt and raisins in large saucepan. Bring to a boil; cook for 5 minutes. Remove from heat; allow to cool thoroughly. Add flour, soda and walnuts; mix well. Pour into greased 9 x 13-inch pan. Bake at 350 degrees for 1 hour and 15 minutes.

RAISIN MINCEMEAT CAKE

1 sm. box mincemeat
1 box raisins
1 tsp. cinnamon
1 tsp. nutmeg
1 c. margarine
1 1/2 c. sugar
4 c. flour
2 tsp. soda
1 c. chopped nuts

Combine mincemeat, raisins, spices, margarine, sugar and 2 1/2 cups boiling water in saucepan; bring to a boil. Cook for 15 minutes; cool. Add flour, soda and nuts; pour into waxed paper-lined tube pan. Bake at 300 degrees for 1 hour and 30 minutes. Yield: 20 servings.

RAISIN-ORANGE CAKE

2 c. raisins
2 c. sugar
1 tsp. salt
2 tsp. soda
1 tsp. nutmeg
1 c. salad oil
2 tsp. vanilla
4 c. flour
1 1/2 c. chopped nuts
1/2 c. frozen orange juice concentrate
1 c. (packed) brown sugar
1/2 c. butter
1 c. coconut

Cover raisins with water; bring to a boil. Cook for 15 minutes; cool. Drain raisins, reserving liquid. Add enough water to raisin liquid to equal 2 cups. Combine sugar, salt, soda and nutmeg; add oil, vanilla, reserved liquid and flour. Add raisins and 1 cup nuts. Place mixture in greased 8 x 13-inch pan. Bake at 325 degrees for 1 hour. Combine orange juice concentrate, brown sugar and butter; cook until sugar is dissolved. Add coconut and remaining nuts; pour over cake. Broil until browned.

SPICED RAISIN CAKE

4 c. applesauce
1 tsp. soda
2 c. sugar
1/2 c. butter
2 tsp. cinnamon
2 tsp. nutmeg
1 tsp. allspice
1 tsp. cloves
1 box raisins
1 c. chopped black walnuts
4 c. flour

Combine applesauce and soda; stir well. Add all remaining ingredients except flour; mix well. Add flour; mix thoroughly. Pour into greased tube pan. Bake at 375 degrees for 1 hour.

RAISIN-HONEY DROPS

3/4 c. honey
3/4 c. sugar
3/4 c. butter
1 egg
2 c. sifted flour
1 tsp. salt
1 tsp. cinnamon
1/2 tsp. soda
2 c. oats
1 c. seedless raisins

Cream honey, sugar, butter and egg. Sift flour, salt, cinnamon and soda together; stir into creamed mixture. Add oats and raisins; drop by rounded teaspoonfuls onto greased cookie sheets. Place on upper shelf of oven. Bake in 375-degree oven for 12 minutes or until browned lightly. Cool on racks. Yield: 4 dozen.

RAISIN COOKIES

2 c. raisins
2 c. sugar
1 c. shortening
2 eggs
1 tsp. vanilla
1 c. nuts
4 c. flour
1 tsp. baking powder
1 tsp. soda
2 tsp. salt
1 tsp. cinnamon
1/4 tsp. nutmeg
1/4 tsp. allspice

Combine 1 cup water and raisins in saucepan; bring to a boil. Cook for 5 minutes; cool. Cream sugar, shortening and eggs. Add vanilla, raisin mixture and nuts. Sift dry ingredients together; blend into creamed mixture. Drop from spoon onto greased cookie sheet. Bake at 375 degrees for 12 to 15 minutes. Yield: 5 dozen.

RAISIN TARTS

1 recipe pie pastry
1/2 c. butter
1 c. sugar
3 egg yolks
1/2 c. milk
1 tsp. vanilla
1 c. chopped raisins
1 c. chopped nuts

Line muffin tins with pastry. Cream butter and sugar; add egg yolks. Beat well; add milk, vanilla, raisins and nuts. Mix well; pour mixture into lined muffin tins. Bake at 375 degrees for 30 minutes. Cover with meringue or whipped cream, if desired. Yield: 12 servings.

HARVEST MOON MUSCAT RAISIN PIE

1/3 c. seeded raisins
3 eggs, separated
Sugar
2 tbsp. flour
2 tbsp. vinegar
2 tbsp. butter
1 baked 9-in. pastry shell
1/4 tsp. cream of tartar

Simmer raisins in saucepan in 2 cups water for about 5 minutes. Combine egg yolks, 1 cup sugar, flour and vinegar; beat until light and creamy. Add to raisins gradually. Cook, stirring constantly, for about 4 to 5 minutes or until filling thickens. Remove from heat; blend in butter. Cool slightly. Pour filling into pastry shell. Cool. Beat egg whites and cream of tartar until foamy. Beat in 6 tablespoons sugar gradually; beat until stiff peaks form. Spread meringue over pie. Bake at 425 degrees for 4 to 5 minutes or until meringue is lightly browned.

Harvest Moon Muscat Raisin Pie . . . This raisin-filled, meringue-topped pie is easy to prepare.

RAISIN MERINGUE PIE

2 tbsp. cornstarch
1 c. sugar
1/4 tsp. salt
1 tsp. cinnamon
1/2 tsp. nutmeg
1/4 tsp. cloves
2 eggs, separated
1 c. sour cream
1 c. raisins
1 1/2 tsp. lemon juice
1/2 c. chopped walnuts
1 baked 9-in. pie shell
1/4 tsp. cream of tartar

Mix cornstarch, 3/4 cup sugar, salt and spices in double boiler; add egg yolks, mixing well. Add sour cream, raisins and lemon juice; cook over hot water until thick. Cool slightly; add walnuts, blending well. Pour into pie shell. Beat egg whites until frothy; add cream of tartar. Beat until stiff peaks form. Add remaining sugar gradually; beat until mixture becomes stiff and glossy. Top filling with meringue. Bake at 300 degrees for 15 to 20 minutes. Yield: 8 servings.

SOUR CREAM RAISIN PIE

1 unbaked 9-in. pie crust
1 c. sugar
1 c. sour cream
3 eggs, beaten
1 tsp. cinnamon
1/4 tsp. salt
1 c. cooked raisins, drained

Line pie plate with crust. Mix sugar and sour cream; add eggs. Combine cinnamon, salt and raisins; add to sugar mixture. Pour into crust. Bake at 450 degrees for 10 minutes; reduce heat to 350 degrees. Bake for 30 minutes longer. Yield: 6-8 servings.

HASTY PUDDING

1 c. flour
1 1/2 tsp. baking powder
1/2 tsp. salt
1/4 c. (packed) brown sugar
1/2 c. milk
1 tsp. vanilla
1/4 c. melted butter
1/4 c. seedless raisins
3/4 c. maple syrup

Sift flour, baking powder and salt; add brown sugar. Blend in milk, vanilla and butter; pour into 1-quart casserole. Sprinkle with raisins. Combine syrup and 1/3 cup water in saucepan; bring to a boil. Pour over batter. Bake at 350 degrees for 35 minutes. Yield: 6 servings.

RAISIN PUDDING

2 c. (packed) brown sugar
1/4 c. butter
1 c. sugar
1 tsp. cinnamon
1 tsp. nutmeg
2 c. flour
2 tsp. soda
2 c. sour milk
1 c. raisins
Whipped cream

Combine brown sugar, 4 cups hot water and 2 tablespoons butter in 9 x 13-inch pan; bring to a boil. Remove from heat. Cream sugar and remaining butter; add dry ingredients alternately with sour milk. Fold in raisins. Drop by teaspoonfuls into brown sugar mixture. Bake at 375 degrees for 30 minutes or until firm to touch. Serve warm with whipped cream. Yield: 12 servings.

BREAKFAST MUSCAT NUT BREAD

2/3 c. sugar
1/4 c. soft butter
1 tsp. grated lemon peel
2 eggs
2 c. sifted flour
3 tsp. baking powder
1/2 tsp. soda
1 tsp. salt
1 8 3/4-oz. can crushed pineapple
1 c. chopped raisins
1/2 c. chopped pecans

Cream sugar, butter and lemon peel until light and fluffy. Beat in eggs until blended well. Sift flour with baking powder, soda and salt. Add to creamed mixture alternately with pineapple, mixing until blended well. Stir in raisins and pecans. Spoon into greased and floured 9 x 5 x 3-inch loaf pan. Let stand for 15 minutes. Bake at 325 degrees for 1 hour or until loaf tests done. Let loaf stand in pan for 10 minutes; turn out on wire rack to cool thoroughly before storing. Sift powdered sugar over top of loaf before serving, if desired. Yield: 1 loaf.

RAISIN-OATMEAL BREAD

1 c. flour
1 tsp. soda
1/2 tsp. salt
1 c. oats
1 egg, slightly beaten
1/2 c. (packed) brown sugar
1 c. buttermilk
1 c. raisins
1/2 c. chopped walnuts

Sift flour, soda and salt together; add oats. Mix egg and sugar; beat until smooth. Add buttermilk; beat. Add to flour mixture; add raisins and walnuts. Pour into greased loaf pan. Bake at 350 degrees for 50 minutes or until bread tests done.

DATE AND RAISIN MUFFINS

1 egg, beaten
2 tbsp. (packed) brown sugar
1/4 tsp. salt
2 c. flour
2 tsp. baking powder
1 c. milk
2 tbsp. melted shortening
2 tbsp. chopped raisins
2 tbsp. chopped dates

Preheat oven to 400 degrees. Mix egg, brown sugar and salt. Sift flour with baking powder. Add milk alternately with flour mixture. Add shortening, raisins and dates; beat only until ingredients are blended. Pour into greased muffin pans. Bake for 25 minutes. Yield: 1 dozen.

RAISIN-ORANGE MUFFINS

3 c. sifted flour
4 tsp. baking powder
3 tbsp. sugar
2 tsp. salt
1/2 c. shortening
2 eggs, beaten
1 1/4 c. milk
2/3 c. chopped raisins
1 1/2 tsp. grated orange rind
1/2 c. chopped nuts

Sift flour, baking powder, sugar and salt together; cut in shortening. Combine eggs and milk; add to flour mixture. Stir enough just to dampen flour. Add raisins, orange rind and nuts; stir lightly. Place in greased muffin pans. Bake at 425 degrees for 25 minutes. Yield: 14 muffins.

ENGLISH TEA MUFFINS

1/2 c. shortening
3/4 c. sugar
1 egg
2 c. flour
2 tsp. baking powder
1/4 tsp. cinnamon
Pinch of salt
1 c. milk
2/3 c. raisins
Brown sugar
Pecans

Cream shortening and sugar; add egg. Sift dry ingredients together; add to creamed mixture alternately with milk. Mix in raisins; place in greased muffin tins. Sprinkle with mixture of brown sugar, additional cinnamon and pecans. Bake at 350 degrees for 15 to 20 minutes. Yield: 18 muffins.

RAISIN GRIDDLE CAKES

3 1/2 c. sifted flour
1 c. sugar
1 1/2 tsp. baking powder
1 tsp. salt
1/2 tsp. soda
1 tsp. nutmeg
1 c. shortening
1 egg
1/2 c. milk
1 1/4 c. raisins
Cooking oil

Sift dry ingredients together into bowl; cut in shortening until mixture is mealy. Beat egg; add milk. Blend; add egg mixture and raisins to flour mixture. Stir until all ingredients are moistened and dough holds together. Roll 1/4 inch thick on lightly floured board; cut with 2-inch round cookie cutter. Heat griddle until water scattered on griddle sizzles. Do not overheat griddle. Oil griddle lightly; place cakes on griddle. Tops become puffy as bottoms brown. Turn; brown other side. Serve warm. Cakes may be cut, stacked between layers of waxed paper and frozen until needed. Yield: 4 dozen.

RAISIN-BLACK WALNUT BREAD

2 c. raisins
2 1/2 tsp. soda
3 eggs
1 1/2 c. sugar
1 tbsp. shortening
4 c. sifted flour
1/4 tsp. salt
1 c. chopped black walnuts
1 to 1 1/2 tsp. vanilla

Mix raisins, 2 1/2 cups hot water and soda; let stand overnight. Beat eggs slightly; add sugar and shortening. Mix well. Drain raisins; reserve liquid. Sift flour and salt; add to egg mixture alternately with reserved raisin liquid. Add raisins, walnuts and vanilla. Place in 5 greased 1-pound coffee cans. Bake at 325 degrees for 1 hour.

ROUND RAISIN-NUT BREAD

2 c. raisins
2 tsp. soda
2 eggs, beaten
1 1/2 c. sugar
Dash of salt
1 1/2 tsp. vanilla
3 c. flour
1 c. chopped nuts

Combine raisins, 2 cups water and soda; bring to a boil. Remove from heat; cool. Mix eggs, sugar, salt and vanilla; add raisin mixture alternately with flour. Fold in nuts; place in 4 one-pound coffee cans. Bake at 350 degrees for 1 hour. Let set overnight before serving.

Raspberry

Raspberries are the sweet, juicy red, black, or purple fruit from a prickly brambled bush of the rose family. They are somewhat rounder and smaller than their close relatives, blackberries. Both red and black raspberries are native to the United States; purple raspberries are a hybrid of the red and black types. Raspberries supply Vitamins A and C, and calcium. (1/2 cup canned water-packed red raspberries = 66 calories; 1/2 cup canned water-packed black raspberries = 84 calories)

AVAILABILITY: Fresh raspberries, usually packed in pint or quart containers, are available in June and July. In some areas fresh berries are sold in May and from August to November. Canned and frozen raspberries are available year-round.

BUYING: Look for clean, plump fresh raspberries with bright solid color. Overripe berries are dull, soft, and drippy. Underripe berries have adhering caps. Desirable raspberries are free from dirt, moisture, mold, and decay.

STORING: Raspberries are among the most perishable of all fruits and should be bought for immediate use only. However, raspberries freeze well. *To freeze* raspberries, choose large ripe berries. Wash in ice water, a few at a time, to avoid bruising this fragile fruit. Drain. To pack, fill liquid-tight freezer container 1/4 full with berries. Add layer of sugar. Continue alternating layers of berries and layers of sugar until container is full. Allow 1 cup sugar for 4 cups berries. Raspberries make their own syrup once sugar is added. Seal, label, and freeze. Raspberries may also be packed dry by freezing berries in a shallow pan before packaging for freezer.

SERVING: Fresh chilled raspberries are delicious served with cream. They also make colorful and zesty additions to fruit cups but should be added last as they soften quickly in liquid. Raspberries are also used in pies, cakes, ice cream, sherbert, sauces, jams, jellies, and so on.

DOUBLE RASPBERRY SALAD

1 6-oz. package raspberry gelatin
1/4 c. red jelly
1 10-oz. package frozen red raspberries
1/2 c. sour cream

Dissolve gelatin and jelly in 3 cups boiling water; reserve half the mixture. Add frozen berries to remaining gelatin mixture; stir until berries are separated and mixture thickens. Chill in 1-quart ring mold at least 4 hours. Blend reserved gelatin mixture into sour cream and chill. Beat until smooth and creamy. Serve with salad.

RASPBERRY-APPLESAUCE SALAD

1 8-oz. package frozen raspberries
2 pkg. raspberry gelatin
1 c. finely chopped walnuts
1 c. applesauce
1 1/2 c. miniature marshmallows
1 12-oz. carton sour cream

Drain raspberries. Dissolve gelatin in 2 2/3 cups boiling water; chill until partially set. Add raspberries, walnuts and applesauce. Chill until firm. Dissolve marshmallows over hot water; remove from heat. Add sour cream; blend thoroughly. Serve over salad.

RASPBERRY-CRANBERRY SALAD

1 pkg. raspberry gelatin
1 pkg. frozen raspberries
1 c. whole cranberry sauce
1 tbsp. lemon juice
1/2 c. drained crushed pineapple
1 can mandarin orange sections
1/2 c. chopped nuts

Dissolve gelatin in boiling water; add frozen raspberries. Stir until separated; add 1/2 cup cold water, cranberry sauce, lemon juice, pineapple, oranges and nuts. Pour into 8 x 8-inch pan or mold. Chill until firm.

RASPBERRY PARTY SALAD

1 3-oz. package lemon gelatin
1 3-oz. package raspberry gelatin
1 pkg. frozen red raspberries
1 14-oz. jar cranberry-orange relish
1 c. lemon-lime carbonated beverage

Dissolve gelatins in 2 cups boiling water; add berries and relish. Stir well. Chill until partially set; add carbonated beverage slowly and carefully. Mix well; pour into mold. Chill until firm.

RASPBERRY-RHUBARB SALAD

1 pkg. frozen rhubarb
Sugar
2 c. pineapple juice
1 pkg. raspberry gelatin
2 c. tart apples, peeled and chopped
1 c. chopped pecans or walnuts

Cook rhubarb according to package directions; drain. Add sugar to taste; add pineapple juice. Bring to a boil; add gelatin, stirring until dissolved. Cool until partially set; add apples and pecans. Mix well; pour into molds. Refrigerate overnight.

RASPBERRY-PINEAPPLE SALAD

1 pkg. raspberry gelatin
1 c. vanilla ice cream
3 tbsp. orange juice
1 9-oz. can crushed pineapple, drained
1/2 c. chopped nuts

Dissolve gelatin in 1 cup hot water. Add ice cream gradually; stir until dissolved. Fold orange juice, pineapple and nuts into gelatin mixture. Chill until firm.

RASPBERRY CAKE

2 c. flour
1 1/2 tsp. baking powder
1/2 tsp. soda
1 tsp. salt
1 tsp. cinnamon
1/2 c. shortening
1 1/4 c. sugar
3 eggs
3/4 c. buttermilk
1 tsp. vanilla
1/2 c. nuts
1 c. raspberries

Sift flour, baking powder, soda, salt and cinnamon. Blend in shortening and sugar; cream well. Add eggs, one at a time, beating well after each addition. Combine buttermilk and vanilla. Add flour mixture and milk alternately to creamed mixture, ending with flour. Blend thoroughly. Stir in nuts; fold in raspberries. Pour batter into two round 8-inch cake pans. Bake at 350 degrees for 30 minutes or until cake tests done.

Raspberry Frosting

1/3 c. butter
1 tsp. salt
2 tbsp. mashed raspberries
2 tbsp. hot cream
1 tsp. vanilla
Confectioners' sugar

Cream butter, salt, mashed raspberries, cream and vanilla; add sugar until of desired spreading consistency. Frost cake.

RASPBERRY ROLL

4 eggs, at room temperature
3/4 c. sugar
3/4 c. sifted cake flour
1/4 tsp. salt
3/4 tsp. baking powder
1 tsp. vanilla
1 1/3 c. flaked coconut
Confectioners' sugar
1 pkg. raspberry gelatin
1 pkg. frozen raspberries
1 pkg. dessert topping mix

Beat eggs until light and lemon colored. Add sugar gradually; continue beating until glossy. Sift flour, salt and baking powder. Fold flour mixture into egg mixture; add vanilla. Spread batter into a greased, waxed paper-lined jelly roll pan; sprinkle coconut over batter. Bake at 400 degrees for 15 minutes. Turn cake out on a cloth sprinkled with confectioners' sugar. Remove paper from cake; roll cake with cloth. Cool thoroughly on cake rack. Dissolve gelatin in 1 cup boiling water. Add frozen fruit; stir until berries separate. Chill until partially set. Prepare dessert topping mix according to package directions. Unroll cake; spread with filling. Reroll; spread with topping mix. Chill until ready to serve.

RASPBERRY-RUM CAKE WITH CUSTARD SAUCE

1 10-oz. package frozen raspberries	*1 pkg. instant vanilla pudding mix*
1 pound cake	*2 c. milk*
Rum	*1 c. light cream*

Thaw raspberries. Pierce top of pound cake in several places with fork. Sprinkle with 1/3 cup rum; let stand for 30 minutes or longer. Combine pudding mix, milk, cream and 2 tablespoons rum; beat for about 2 minutes or until blended. Chill for 30 minutes. Slice cake into 3/4-inch slices; place on serving plates. Top with raspberries. Stir pudding; pour over raspberries.

RASPBERRY-SAUCED MELBA

1 1/4 c. sugar	*2 c. fresh raspberries*
1/4 tsp. salt	*1 qt. vanilla ice cream*
1 tsp. vanilla	
6 sm. fresh peaches	

Combine 1 cup sugar, 1 cup water and salt in saucepan. Bring to boiling point, stirring constantly. Cover; boil for 3 to 4 minutes. Remove from heat; stir in vanilla. Dip peaches into hot water; plunge into cold water. Slip skins off. Cut in half; remove stones. Return sugar syrup to heat; add 2 peach halves at a time. Simmer for 3 to 4 minutes or until peaches are tender when pierced with fork. Remove peaches from syrup with slotted spoon, draining excess syrup back into saucepan. Repeat process with remaining peaches. Chill. Process raspberries through sieve. Blend in remaining sugar; chill. Spoon ice cream into 6 serving dishes. Place chilled peaches, cut sides down, on ice cream. Top with raspberry sauce. Yield: 6 servings.

Raspberry-Sauced Melba . . . Fresh raspberry sauce tops succulent fresh peaches and ice cream.

AMBER PIE

1 c. buttermilk	*3 eggs, separated*
1 c. raspberries	*1 tbsp. butter*
1 c. sugar	*1 baked pie shell*
3 tbsp. flour	

Combine buttermilk, raspberries, sugar, flour, egg yolks and butter in double boiler over hot water. Cook, stirring constantly, until filling thickens. Remove from heat; turn into pie shell. Beat egg whites until stiff peaks form. Spread meringue over filling; seal edges. Bake at 350 degrees for 15 minutes or until lightly browned.

FRESH RASPBERRY PIE

1 c. water	*1/2 c. crushed raspberries*
1 c. sugar	*1 qt. raspberries*
3 tbsp. cornstarch	*1 baked pie shell*

Combine water, sugar and cornstarch; cook until thickened. Stir in crushed raspberries. Place whole raspberries in pie shell. Pour sugar mixture over berries. Bake at 350 degrees for 30 minutes or until crust is lightly browned. Serve with ice cream or whipped cream if desired.

RASPBERRY-ALMOND PASTRY

4 c. flour	*1 lb. almonds, ground*
2 c. sugar	*1 lb. butter*
1/2 tsp. cinnamon	*1 egg, lightly beaten*
1/2 tsp. baking powder	*Raspberry jam*
1/4 tsp. cloves	

Sift first 5 ingredients together into large bowl; add almonds. Cut in butter until mixture resembles meal; add egg. Knead lightly; form into ball. Press 2/3 of the dough into 10 x 16-inch baking pan; spread with raspberry jam. Roll remaining dough out; cut 4 long 1/2-inch wide strips. Place strips length of pan. Cut 6 shorter strips; place crosswise, making lattice top. Bake at 350 degrees for 45 minutes. Cool; serve with ice cream.

RASPBERRY CHIFFON PIE

1 10-oz. package frozen red raspberries	*1 env. dessert topping mix*
	Dash of salt
	2 egg whites
1 3-oz. package raspberry gelatin	*1/4 c. sugar*
2 tbsp. lemon juice	*1 baked 9-in. pastry shell*

Thaw raspberries; drain. Reserve liquid; add water to measure 2/3 cup liquid. Dissolve gelatin in 3/4 cup boiling water; add lemon juice and reserved syrup. Chill until partially set. Prepare topping mix according to package directions. Beat gelatin mixture until soft peaks form. Fold in raspberries and half the topping mix. Add salt to egg whites; beat until soft peaks form. Add sugar gradually; beat until stiff peaks form. Fold into raspberry mixture. Pile into cooled pastry shell; chill. Place remaining topping mix into a pastry bag. Form scrolls on top of chilled pie. Whole fresh or frozen raspberries may be used for additional garnish.

RASPBERRY MERINGUE PIE

1 1/4 c. sifted flour
1/4 tsp. soda
1/4 tsp. salt
1/2 c. margarine
Sugar
1 tsp. vanilla
2 eggs, separated
2 tbsp. cornstarch
1 10-oz. package frozen raspberries
1/2 c. walnuts, chopped

Sift flour, soda and salt together. Cream margarine and 1/3 cup sugar; add vanilla. Beat egg yolks; add to flour mixture. Add sifted ingredients; mix well. Press into 10-inch pie plate. Mix 1/4 cup sugar and cornstarch in saucepan; add raspberries. Cook over low heat until thickened; pour over mixture in pie plate. Top with walnuts. Beat egg whites until soft peaks form; add 2 tablespoons sugar gradually. Beat until stiff peaks form. Spread over walnuts. Bake at 350 degrees for 30 minutes.

RASPBERRY VELVET PIE

1 10-oz. package frozen raspberries
1 pkg. raspberry gelatin
1/4 lb. marshmallows
1 c. heavy cream, whipped
Vanilla wafers

Thaw raspberries; drain. Reserve syrup; add water to syrup to measure 1 cup liquid. Dissolve gelatin in 1 cup boiling water; stir in marshmallows until partially melted. Add raspberry liquid. Chill until partially congealed. Beat until fluffy; fold in raspberries and whipped cream. Line 9-inch pie plate with vanilla wafers; fill with raspberry mixture. Chill until set. Serve with additional whipped cream.

RASPBERRY-WALNUT SUPREME

1 10-oz. package frozen red raspberries
1 1/4 c. flour
1/3 c. confectioners' sugar
1/2 c. soft butter
3/4 c. walnuts
2 eggs
1 1/2 c. sugar
1/2 tsp. salt
1/2 tsp. baking powder
1 tsp. vanilla
2 tbsp. cornstarch
1 tbsp. lemon juice
Whipped cream

Thaw raspberries; drain. Reserve liquid. Combine 1 cup flour, confectioners' sugar and butter. Press mixture in bottom of 13 x 9-inch pan. Bake at 350 degrees for 15 minutes. Cool. Spoon raspberries over crust; sprinkle with walnuts. Beat eggs with 1 cup sugar in small mixing bowl until light and fluffy. Add salt, 1/4 cup flour, baking powder and vanilla; blend well. Pour over walnuts. Bake at 350 degrees for 30 to 35 minutes or until golden brown. Chill; cut into squares. Combine 1/2 cup water, reserved liquid, remaining sugar and cornstarch in saucepan. Cook, stirring constantly, until thickened and clear. Stir in lemon juice; cool. Serve sauce and whipped cream over squares.

RASPBERRY ANGEL DESSERT

2 tbsp. gelatin
3 eggs, separated
2 c. milk
1 c. sugar
1 c. raspberries
2 c. cream, whipped
1 c. miniature marshmallows
1/2 c. pecans
1 angel food cake

Soften gelatin in 1/2 cup cold water. Beat yolks; add milk and sugar. Mix well. Cook in top of double boiler over hot water until mixture coats spoon. Add gelatin; stir until dissolved. Cool; add raspberries. Fold in whipped cream, beaten egg whites, marshmallows and pecans. Line bottom of oiled tube pan with pieces of angel cake. Pour half the raspberry mixture over cake; add another layer of cake and remaining gelatin mixture. Chill until set. Garnish with whipped cream.

RASPBERRY FLUFF

20 graham wafers, crushed
1/4 c. (packed) brown sugar
1/4 c. melted butter
1/2 tsp. cinnamon
Juice of 1 lemon
1 3-oz. package raspberry gelatin
Juice of 1 orange
1 15-oz. can evaporated milk
3/4 c. sugar

Combine first 4 ingredients; press into 13 x 9-inch pan, reserving 1/4 of the mixture for topping. Chill. Combine juices with 3/4 cup boiling water. Stir in gelatin until dissolved; cool until partially set. Chill milk in refrigerator tray for 20 minutes or until ice crystals form. Whip milk to form peaks; beat in sugar. Fold gelatin mixture into whipped milk; pour over crumb mixture. Chill until firm. Sprinkle reserved crumbs over top.

RASPBERRY SWIRL

1 c. graham cracker crumbs
3 tbsp. sugar
1/4 c. melted butter
1 10-oz. package frozen raspberries
1 3-oz. package red raspberry gelatin
1/2 lb. marshmallows
1/2 c. milk
1/2 pt. heavy cream, whipped

Mix cracker crumbs, 1 tablespoon sugar and butter; press firmly against bottom of 9 x 9 x 2-inch pan. Chill. Sprinkle remaining sugar over raspberries; let stand for several minutes. Dissolve gelatin in 1 cup boiling water. Drain raspberries; reserve syrup. Add water to syrup to measure 1 cup liquid; stir liquid into gelatin. Chill until partially set. Combine marshmallows and milk in saucepan; heat until marshmallows are melted. Cool completely; fold in whipped cream. Add raspberries to gelatin; swirl in marshmallow mixture. Pour into crust; chill until set.

BLACK RASPBERRY TAPIOCA

1 box pearl tapioca
5 c. boiling water
1/4 tsp. salt
1 c. sugar
2 boxes raspberry gelatin
1 No. 2 can black raspberries

Place tapioca, 4 cups boiling water and salt in top of double boiler; cook, stirring occasionally, for 1 hour and 30 minutes. Stir in sugar. Dissolve gelatin in 1 cup boiling water; stir in 1 cup cold water, raspberries and tapioca. Chill for several hours or overnight. Serve with whipped cream or cream, if desired.

BERRY KUCHEN

2 c. flour
3/4 tsp. salt
3 tsp. baking powder
1/4 c. shortening
2 eggs
1/2 c. milk
2 c. raspberries
3/4 c. (packed) brown sugar
1 tbsp. cornstarch
1/2 c. sugar
2 tbsp. butter, melted
1/2 tsp. vanilla

Sift flour, 1/2 teaspoon salt and baking powder; cut in shortening. Beat in 1 egg and milk. Pat dough in greased 10 x 8-inch pan; push dough up edges. Arrange raspberries over dough; sprinkle raspberries with brown sugar. Combine remaining ingredients; beat well. Pour over raspberries. Bake at 350 degrees for 35 minutes.

MAIDS OF HONOR

1/2 c. shortening
2 eggs
3/4 c. sugar
2 c. sifted flour
1/4 tsp. salt
2 tsp. baking powder
1 1/2 c. seedless raspberry jam
1/2 c. blanched almonds

Cream shortening and eggs. Add sugar; beat until light and fluffy. Sift in flour, salt and baking powder. Shape into small balls; place in well-greased miniature muffin cups. Press around edges of cups. Mix jam and almonds; place in pastry. Bake at 425 degrees for 10 minutes; cool. Garnish with sweetened whipped cream or whipped topping.

RASPBERRY-COCONUT SQUARES

1 c. sifted flour
1 tsp. baking powder
3/4 c. butter
1 tbsp. milk
2 eggs
1/2 c. raspberry jam
1 c. sugar
1 4-oz. can coconut
1 tsp. vanilla

Sift flour and baking powder; cut in 1/2 cup butter until crumbly. Mix milk with 1 slightly beaten egg; stir into flour mixture. Blend well. Spread dough in 8-inch square pan. Spread with jam. Beat remaining egg until frothy; add remaining melted butter and sugar, beating well after each addition. Mix in coconut and vanilla. Spread mixture over jam. Bake at 350 degrees 30 minutes. Cool. Cut into squares with sharp knife. Yield: 16 squares.

BLUSHING TOP BAVARIAN

1 env. unflavored gelatin
3/4 c. sugar
Evaporated milk
1/2 tsp. salt
1 1/3 c. flaked coconut

Blushing Top Bavarian . . . Red raspberries contrast with coconut-rich Bavarian cream.

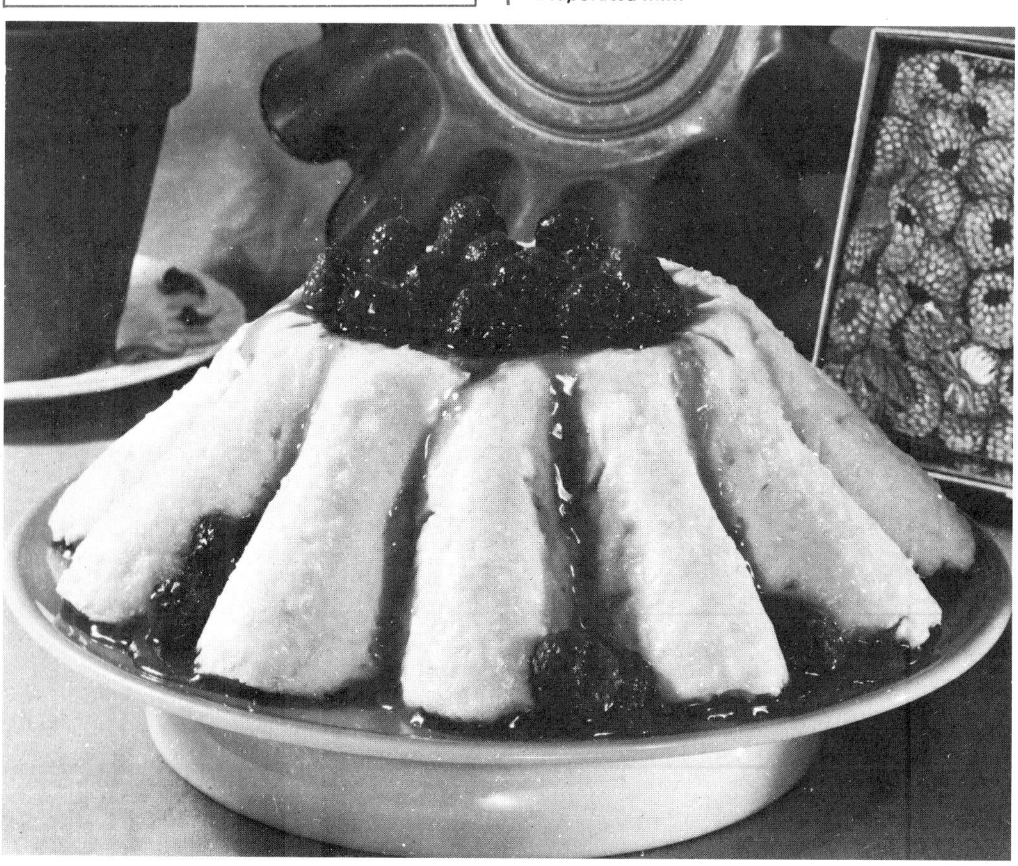

Soften gelatin in 1/3 cup cold water in 2-quart saucepan. Add sugar, 3/4 cup milk and salt. Cook, stirring, over medium heat until gelatin is dissolved. Chill until thickened. Chill 2/3 cup milk in ice tray until almost frozen at edges. Pour milk into chilled small bowl of electric mixer. Whip with electric mixer at high speed until stiff. Beat in coconut and gelatin mixture at low speed, scraping side of bowl frequently. Pour into six 1/2-cup molds. Chill until firm.

Blushing Sauce

2 10-oz. packages frozen raspberries, thawed
1/2 c. sugar
3 tbsp. cornstarch
2 tsp. lemon juice

Drain raspberries, reserving syrup. Mix sugar and cornstarch in 2-quart saucepan. Stir in reserved syrup and lemon juice gradually. Cook, stirring, over medium heat until mixture bubbles. Boil for about 1 minute, stirring constantly, until thick and clear. Remove from heat; stir in raspberries. Cool. Unmold bavarians on serving dishes; spoon sauce over tops.

RASPBERRY SUPREME

1 pt. red raspberries
1/4 c. sugar
1/8 tsp. salt
2 tbsp. cornstarch
4 egg whites, stiffly beaten

Crush raspberries in saucepan; bring to a boil. Mix sugar, salt and cornstarch; add to raspberries, a small amount at a time. Cook, stirring constantly, until thickened; cool. Fold in egg whites; pour into buttered baking dish. Place dish in pan of hot water. Bake at 325 degrees for 30 to 40 minutes. Serve with custard sauce or whipped topping, if desired.

RASPBERRY-LEMON MOUSSE

1 qt. vanilla ice cream
1 6-oz. can frozen raspberry-lemon punch
1 egg white
1/2 c. sugar
1 c. whipping cream
1 10-oz. package frozen raspberries

Let ice cream soften slightly at room temperature. Spread ice cream evenly in bottom of 9 x 9 x 2-inch pan; freeze until firm. Thaw punch; combine with 2 tablespoons water in cup. Beat egg white until soft peaks form. Add sugar gradually, beating until stiff peaks form. Fold punch into meringue slowly until completely blended. Beat cream until stiff peaks form. Thaw raspberries; fold into cream. Fold raspberry mixture into meringue mixture; spoon evenly over ice cream in pan. Freeze for 3 hours or until firm.

RED RASPBERRY ROLLS

1 c. flour
1 1/2 tsp. baking powder
Sugar
1/4 tsp. salt
3 tbsp. shortening
6 tbsp. milk
1 tbsp. butter, melted
1 10-oz. package frozen red raspberries
1 1/2 tsp. quick tapioca

Mix flour, baking powder, 1 1/2 teaspoons sugar and salt; cut in shortening. Stir in milk slowly to form soft dough. Turn dough on lightly floured board; roll into 12 x 8-inch rectangle. Brush with butter. Drain raspberries; reserve liquid. Spread raspberries over dough. Sprinkle with 1 tablespoon sugar; roll jelly roll fashion. Cut into 6 slices. Combine reserved syrup and tapioca; bring to a boil. Cook for 2 minutes, stirring frequently. Pour into 7 x 7 x 2-inch pan; place dough slices in hot juice mixture. Bake at 350 degrees for 25 minutes or until lightly browned. Yield: 6 servings.

Red Snapper

Red snapper is a colorful, lean-fleshed fish. It is found predominantly in Gulf Coast waters but is also caught off warm Atlantic shores. Red snapper is just one member of the large snapper family but is perhaps more commonly prepared than other types. Related to sea bass, red snapper varies from 2 to 3 feet long and weighs up to 30 pounds. Its choice flavor is as distinctive as its red scales, orange fins, and blue-streaked body. Like all fish, it is high in protein. (4 ounces = 95 calories)

AVAILABILITY: Fresh red snapper is available year-round where caught. It is sold whole, in steaks, and in fillets.

BUYING: Look for whole fresh fish that has bright, clear, bulging eyes; reddish pink gills; tight shiny scales; firm elastic flesh; and fresh odor.

STORING: Wrap fresh red snapper in moistureproof paper and refrigerate. Use as soon as possible, within 1 or 2 days. Red snapper may be frozen at 0 degree for up to 3 months (the sooner it is eaten, the better the flavor). *To freeze,* dip whole fish, steaks, or fillets in cold salted water for 20 seconds. Prepare water by dissolving 1 cup salt in 1 gallon ice water. Wrap whole fish individually in moistureproof and vaporproof paper. Or, pack fillets and steaks in layers in cartons. Place freezer paper between layers for easy separation when thawing. Wrap carton with moistureproof and vaporproof paper. Seal, label, and freeze.

PREPARATION: Red snapper may be cooked in almost any manner: baked, broiled, sauteed, poached, fried, boiled, and so on. When baked or broiled, the fish usually requires frequent basting or brushing with oil. Use as is as entree and also in salads, soups, and stews.

SERVING: Red snapper is usually served with a sauce. A rich, slightly tart sauce is complementary.
(See SEAFOOD.)

RED SNAPPER CASSEROLE

1 tsp. sugar
1 2-lb. red snapper
1/4 tsp. salt
Dash of pepper
1 clove of garlic
1 red pepper pod
1 med. onion, minced
2 1/2 c. cooked tomatoes
1 tbsp. Worcestershire sauce
1/2 c. olive oil
1 jigger claret
2 c. potato balls
1 c. mushroom buttons

Brown sugar in skillet, stirring constantly. Sprinkle red snapper with salt and pepper. Place garlic and pepper pod inside. Place onion in pan with sugar. Cover with tomatoes; add snapper, Worcestershire sauce, olive oil, claret and potato balls. Bake at 400 degrees for 15 minutes. Add mushrooms. Bake for 15 minutes longer or until snapper and potato balls are tender. Yield: 6 servings.

BAKED SNAPPER WITH STUFFING BALLS

2 1/2 lb. skinned red snapper fillets
Soft butter
2 tbsp. lemon juice
Salt and pepper
1/2 8-oz. package herb-seasoned stuffing mix
1 10-oz. can tomato juice
1/2 c. chopped parsley
1/4 c. chopped celery
1/4 c. chopped onion
4 lge. thin apple slices

Place fillets in greased shallow baking dish. Combine 2 tablespoons butter and lemon juice; brush over fillets. Season with salt and pepper. Bake at 375 degrees for 20 minutes. Combine stuffing mix and tomato juice. Saute parsley and vegetables in 3 tablespoons butter in skillet until just tender; add to stuffing mixture, tossing lightly with fork. Shape stuffing mixture lightly into 5 balls, using about 1/2 cup for each ball. Place stuffing balls on slices of apple; arrange around fillets. Bake for 15 minutes longer or until fish flakes easily and stuffing is browned on top. Garnish with parsley. Yield: 4 servings.

Baked Snapper with Stuffing Balls . . . Quick and easy herb-seasoned stuffing accompanies snapper.

RED SNAPPER PUDDING

3 lb. red snapper, baked and boned
3 eggs
1 c. milk
1/2 c. butter, melted
1/2 c. cracker crumbs
1 tbsp. chopped parsley
1 tbsp. scraped onion
Juice of 1 lemon
Salt and pepper to taste

Shred fish; place in bowl. Add eggs; beat well. Add milk and half the butter, cracker crumbs, parsley, onion, lemon juice, salt and pepper. Place in greased baking dish; top with cracker crumbs and remaining butter. Add additional milk if mixture is dry. Set baking dish in pan of hot water. Bake in 300-degree oven for 40 minutes. Serve with tartar sauce. Yield: 6-8 servings.

SHERRIED RED SNAPPER

2 cans mushrooms
1 onion, minced
1/4 c. butter
2 1/4 lb. snapper fillets
1/4 c. flour
3/4 c. sherry
Dash of Worcestershire sauce
3 c. milk
2 bouillon cubes
2 lge. cans grated Parmesan cheese
2 lb. cooked shrimp

Drain mushrooms, reserving liquid. Combine onion and butter in skillet; cook fillets in butter until white. Remove from skillet. Blend flour into skillet drippings; stir in sherry, Worcestershire sauce, reserved liquid and milk. Cook, stirring, until smooth; add bouillon cubes, cheese and shrimp. Layer fillets in greased casserole; top with mushrooms. Pour sauce over mushrooms. Bake at 325 degrees for 30 minutes. Yield: 8 servings.

SNAPPER WITH CREOLE SAUCE

6 slices bacon
1 6-lb. red snapper
Salt and pepper
4 stalks celery, chopped
4 med. onions, chopped
2 green peppers, finely chopped
4 cloves of garlic, finely chopped
3/8 c. cooking oil
3 lge. cans tomatoes
1/2 tsp. hot sauce
1/2 tsp. thyme
1/4 tsp. oregano

Fry bacon slices until crisp; remove from skillet. Grease snapper inside and out with small amount of bacon drippings; rub in salt and pepper. Bake at 350 degrees for 30 minutes. Saute celery, onions, green peppers and garlic in remaining bacon drippings and cooking oil. Add tomatoes, hot sauce, thyme and oregano. Pour over snapper; bake for 10 to 15 minutes longer. Garnish with lemon slices and parsley. Yield: 8 servings.

SNAPPER WITH POTATOES

3 med. red snapper
8 peeled potatoes
1 onion, sliced
4 pieces of bacon
Salt and pepper to taste

Place snapper in large baking dish; arrange potatoes around snapper. Place onion and bacon on top of snapper. Season with salt and pepper. Bake at 350 degrees until potatoes are tender. Yield: 6-8 servings.

DEEP-FRIED RED SNAPPER

3 lb. snapper, salted
1/2 c. flour
1 egg
1/4 c. milk
2 c. fine dry bread crumbs
Salt to taste

Roll snapper in flour. Combine egg and milk; beat well. Dip red snapper in egg mixture. Combine crumbs and salt; coat red snapper with bread crumbs. Fry in large skillet in deep hot fat for 15 minutes. Yield: 6 servings.

FRIED SNAPPER

2 lb. red snapper, filleted
1 bottle beer
Buttermilk pancake mix

Cut snapper into 3/4-inch slices. Combine beer and enough pancake mix to make batter. Dip snapper into batter; fry in deep fat until browned. Yield: 4-6 servings.

OVEN-FRIED SNAPPER

1 pkg. frozen red snapper fillets
1 egg
1/2 c. milk
Dash of salt
Bread crumbs
Butter

Thaw fillets. Combine egg, milk and salt; dip fillets into egg mixture. Coat with crumbs. Place in shallow buttered baking dish; dot with butter. Bake at 350 degrees for 35 minutes. Yield: 4 servings.

CORN-STUFFED SNAPPER

1/2 c. mayonnaise
1/2 c. Thousand Island dressing
1 sm. onion, chopped
3 tbsp. Worcestershire sauce
3 tbsp. lemon juice
3 tbsp. butter, melted
6 bread slices
1 egg, beaten
1 med. onion, grated
1/2 c. whole kernel corn
1/4 c. grated cheese
1 sm. tomato, cubed
8 red snapper

Combine mayonnaise, dressing, chopped onion, Worcestershire sauce, lemon juice and melted butter; mix well. Moisten bread with small amount of water; stir until bread is softened. Combine bread mixture, egg, grated onion, corn, cheese and tomato to make stuffing. Stuff snapper with corn mixture. Pour mayonnaise mixture over snapper. Bake at 350 degrees for 50 minutes.

SOUTHERN PAN-FRIED SNAPPER

2 to 3 lb. red snapper
1 c. shortening
2 tbsp. salt
1/2 c. cornmeal

Cut snapper into serving pieces. Heat shortening in frypan over medium heat. Mix salt and cornmeal; roll snapper in cornmeal mixture. Place in skillet; fry for 3 minutes or until delicately browned. Yield: 4 servings.

CHARCOAL-GRILLED SNAPPER STEAKS

1 lb. red snapper steaks
1/2 c. oil
1/4 c. lemon juice
2 tsp. salt
1/2 tsp. Worcestershire sauce
1/4 tsp. white pepper
Dash of hot sauce
Paprika

Cut snapper steaks into serving portions; place in greased, hinged wire grills. Combine remaining ingredients except paprika. Baste snapper with sauce; sprinkle with paprika. Cook 4 inches from source of heat for 8 minutes. Baste with sauce; sprinkle with paprika. Turn; cook for 7 to 10 minutes longer or until snapper flakes easily when tested with fork. Yield: 6 servings.

STUFFED SNAPPER

1 2 1/2-3-lb. red snapper
Salt
2 c. corn bread crumbs
2 slices white bread, crumbled
1 whole egg
1 onion, chopped
1/2 tsp. poultry seasoning
1/4 c. margarine, melted
2 slices bacon

Split snapper down 1 side of backbone. Rub cavity with salt. Combine remaining ingredients except margarine and bacon for stuffing. Add enough hot water to bind mixture together. Place stuffing inside cavity of snapper. Fasten with toothpicks. Pour margarine over snapper. Place bacon on top. Bake at 325 degrees for 30 minutes per pound. Serve with tartar sauce.

POACHED RED SNAPPER

1 red snapper
Salt to taste
1/2 c. mild vinegar
1/2 c. melted butter
1/4 c. minced parsley
1/4 tsp. pepper

Place snapper in skillet; add boiling water to just cover snapper. Add salt and vinegar. Bring to a boil; cover. Reduce heat; simmer for 12 minutes. Place snapper on platter. Mix butter, parsley and pepper; pour over snapper. Yield: 4 servings.

RED SNAPPER WITH VEGETABLES

1 6-lb. red snapper
Butter
Pepper
2 tbsp. lemon juice
1/2 c. chopped celery
1/2 c. chopped parsley
3/4 c. chopped green pepper
1 clove of garlic, minced
Cinnamon
1 c. chopped onions
1/4 c. flour
4 c. tomatoes
Salt

Prepare whole snapper for baking. Cut deep gashes in both sides crosswise of snapper, 1 1/2 inches apart. Rub well inside and out with butter. Rub pepper, 1 teaspoon butter and lemon juice into each gash. Combine celery, parsley, green pepper and garlic. Stuff gashes with celery mixture. Place snapper in greased paper-lined pan. Sprinkle lightly with cinnamon and any remaining vegetable mixture. Saute onions lightly in 1/2 cup butter; add flour and tomatoes, stirring constantly. Cook until thickened. Season with salt and pepper. Pour sauce over snapper. Bake at 325 degrees for 1 hour. Baste frequently with sauce. Yield: 6 servings.

SNAPPER A LA MARYLAND

1 8 to 10-lb. snapper
1/2 c. butter
3/4 c. flour
4 c. milk
2 c. cream
1 tsp. salt
1/4 tsp. white pepper
Dash of yellow food coloring
3 eggs
1 c. sherry

Cook the snapper in salted water until tender; cool. Bone and chop snapper. Melt butter; stir in flour. Cook until smooth. Heat milk and cream until warm; add to butter and flour, stirring constantly, until thickened. Add salt and pepper. Add several drops of food coloring and snapper; cook over low heat for 10 minutes. Remove from heat. Beat eggs with additional salt and pepper to taste; add small amount of snapper sauce to eggs, stirring constantly. Return egg mixture to remaining snapper sauce; stir well. Add sherry; keep on low heat until ready to serve. Serve in soup plates with toast.

Relish

A relish is a savory or pickled preserved food that is often served as an accompaniment to meat or main dishes. *Vegetable relishes* are prepared from chopped or small vegetables that are either sweet or sour, spiced or unspiced. Vegetable relishes are moist but not juicy; the vegetables are usually tender-crisp. *Fruit relishes* consist of chopped or small fruits usually preserved with sugar, spices, and vinegar. One type of fruit relish, chutney is highly seasoned with onion, garlic, ginger, hot peppers, and so on.
(See CHUTNEY.)

PROCESSING: Relishes are most often canned by the waterbath method because there is enough vinegar and salt in the ingredients to prevent spoilage or bacterial contamination. (See CANNING and PICKLE.)

MUSTARD RELISH MOLDS

1 env. unflavored gelatin
1/3 c. mayonnaise
1 c. mustard pickle relish
1/2 c. finely diced green pepper
2 tbsp. finely chopped onion
1 c. finely diced celery

Sprinkle gelatin on 1 cup cold water in saucepan to soften. Place over medium heat, stirring constantly, until dissolved. Stir into mayonnaise gradually. Chill to consistency of unbeaten egg white. Fold in pickle relish, green pepper, onion and celery. Turn into individual molds; chill until firm. May be served on sliced tomatoes if desired. Yield: 6-8 servings.

TANGY CRANBERRY RELISH MOLDS

2 c. fresh cranberries
1/2 c. sugar
1/4 tsp. salt
1 env. unflavored gelatin
2 peeled oranges, sectioned
1/4 c. finely diced celery

Process cranberries through food chopper; sprinkle with sugar and salt. Let stand for 10 minutes. Sprin-

Mustard Relish Molds and Tangy Cranberry Relish Molds . . . Serve at buffets or with meat or poultry.

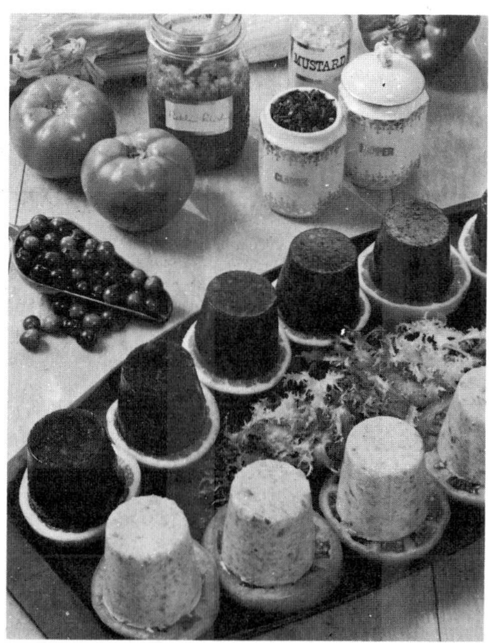

kle gelatin on 1/2 cup cold water in saucepan to soften. Place over medium heat, stirring constantly, until dissolved. Remove from heat. Dice orange sections; add cranberry mixture and celery. Stir into gelatin mixture. Turn into 6 individual molds; chill until firm. Unmold on orange slices if desired. Yield: 6 servings.

BEAN RELISH

2 c. chopped green tomatoes
2 c. chopped green or red peppers
2 c. peeled, diced cucumbers
2 c. chopped onions
1/2 c. salt
2 c. chopped celery
2 c. diced carrots
1 can lima beans
1 can red kidney beans
1 can wax beans
3 c. sugar
3/4 qt. vinegar
1 tbsp. dry mustard

Soak tomatoes, peppers, cucumbers and onions overnight in 2 quarts salted water; drain. Add celery, carrots and water to cover; bring to a boil. Cook 30 minutes; drain. Add all remaining ingredients; bring to a boil. Pour into sterilized jars; seal while hot. Yield: 10 pints.

BEET RELISH

6 c. beets
6 c. sugar
3 c. vinegar
1 tsp. cinnamon
1 tsp. cloves

Blanch beets; peel. Grind beets; add sugar, vinegar, cinnamon and cloves. Cook for 30 minutes or until tender.

CABBAGE RELISH

1 med. cabbage, ground
10 carrots, ground
4 lge. onions, ground
3 green peppers, ground
2 tsp. salt
2 tsp. mustard seed
2 tsp. celery seed
1 c. sugar
1 c. wine vinegar

Combine all ingredients and 1 cup water in large kettle. Cook, covered, over medium heat for 1 hour, stirring occasionally. Pour into sterilized jars; seal. Yield: 6 pints.

CORN RELISH

1/4 c. chopped prepared chutney, drained
1/2 c. sweet pickle relish
1/4 tsp. mustard seed
1 12-oz. can whole kernel corn, drained
1/4 tsp. salt
1 4-oz. jar pimentos, chopped

Combine all ingredients; mix well. Cover; refrigerate. Yield: 6 servings.

GREEN TOMATO RELISH

4 c. ground onions
4 c. ground cabbage
4 c. ground green tomatoes
12 green peppers, ground
6 red peppers, ground
1/2 c. salt
6 c. sugar
1 tbsp. celery seed
2 tbsp. mustard seed
1 1/2 tsp. turmeric
4 c. vinegar

Sprinkle vegetables with salt; let stand overnight. Drain; rinse with cold water. Combine remaining ingredients and 2 cups water; bring to a boil. Add vegetables; bring to a boil. Stir well; do not simmer longer than 2 minutes. Seal in sterilized jars. Yield: 8 pints.

CRISP MUSTARD MIX

6 med. chopped cucumbers
2 c. chopped onion
3 sweet peppers, chopped
1 med. head cauliflower, cut up
1 qt. pickling onions
1 c. pickling salt
4 c. sugar
4 c. vinegar
3/4 c. flour
1/4 c. dry mustard
1 1/2 tsp. turmeric
1 tbsp. celery salt

Layer vegetables and pickling salt in large bowl; cover with cold water. Let stand overnight. Drain; rinse with cold water. Combine sugar and vinegar; bring to a boil. Mix remaining ingredients; add small amount of vinegar mixture, stirring constantly, until blended. Cool. Add spice mixture to boiling vinegar mixture; stir well. Add drained vegetables; cook for 10 to 15 minutes. Seal in hot sterilized jars. Yield: 6 1/2 pints.

HOT DOG RELISH

3 carrots, peeled
3 sweet red peppers, cored and seeded
2 qt. sliced cucumbers
2 qt. sliced green tomatoes
2 qt. sliced onions
Sugar
Salt
2 tbsp. mixed pickling spices
1 1/2 c. vinegar
1/2 tsp. cayenne pepper

Grind carrots, peppers, cucumbers, tomatoes and onions; add 1/2 cup sugar, mixing well. Sprinkle with salt; let stand overnight. Tie pickling spices in cheesecloth bag. Drain vegetable mixture; combine with vinegar, cayenne pepper, spice bag and 1 1/2 pounds sugar. Simmer for 45 minutes. Remove spice bag. Pour into sterilized hot jars; seal. Yield: 6 pints.

RIPE TOMATO GARDEN RELISH

6 sweet peppers, chopped
1 qt. chopped celery
1 qt. sliced onions
3 tbsp. salt
2 tbsp. sugar
4 qt. peeled sliced ripe tomatoes

Combine peppers, celery, onions and 4 cups water; add salt and sugar. Bring to a boil; cook for 20 minutes. Add tomatoes. Bring back to a boil; pour into jars. Process in water bath, 30 minutes for quarts and 25 minutes for pints. Yield: 12 pints.

INDIAN RELISH

12 green tomatoes
6 red peppers
6 green peppers
4 lge. onions
1 tbsp. celery seed
2 tbsp. salt
1 1/2 lb. sugar
3 c. vinegar

Grind tomatoes, peppers and onions; drain. Mix all ingredients; bring to a boil. Cook for 25 minutes. Pour into hot pint jars; seal. Yield: 6-7 pints.

IOWA CORN RELISH

20 ears of sweet corn
1 c. chopped green pepper
1 c. chopped sweet red pepper
1 1/4 c. chopped onion
1 c. chopped celery
2 c. sugar
1 1/2 tbsp. mustard seed
2 tbsp. salt
1 tsp. celery seeds
1 tsp. turmeric
1 qt. white vinegar

Cook corn in boiling salted water for 5 minutes; plunge into cold water. Cut kernels from cobs; measure 2 1/2 quarts. Combine all ingredients; simmer for 20 minutes. Pack into hot sterilized pint jars, leaving 1 inch space. Vinegar solution must cover vegetables. Adjust lids. Process for 5 minutes at 5 pounds pressure in canner or for 15 minutes in boiling water bath. Yield: 6-7 pints.

PEPPER HASH

15 green sweet peppers
15 red sweet peppers
15 lge. white onions
1 1/2 c. sugar
2 1/2 tbsp. salt
1 pt. vinegar
1/4 tsp. cayenne pepper

Grind peppers and onions. Cover with boiling water; let stand for 10 minutes. Drain. Add all remaining ingredients; bring to boil. Pack into sterilized jars; seal.

PEPPER JAM

Red sweet peppers
2 tbsp. salt
6 c. sugar
4 c. vinegar

Remove seeds and midribs from peppers; chop fine. Mix 7 cups of peppers with salt. Let stand for 4 hours. Add sugar and vinegar. Bring to a boil; cook until thickened. Pour, boiling hot, into hot jar. Seal at once.

PICCALILLI

2 qt. sliced green tomatoes
1 pt. chopped onions
1 pt. sliced green peppers
1 qt. shredded cabbage
1 pt. sliced carrots
1 pt. chopped celery
2 oz. mustard seed
1 tsp. turmeric
4 tbsp. salt
2 lb. sugar
2 qt. white vinegar

Place all ingredients in large kettle; mix well. Cook for 1 hour gradually, stirring occasionally. Pour into hot sterilized jars; seal at once. Yield: 12 pints.

PICKLED GARDEN RELISH

1/2 sm. cauliflower
2 carrots
2 stalks celery
1 green pepper
1 4-oz. jar pimento
1 3-oz. jar pitted green olives
3/4 c. wine vinegar
1/2 c. olive oil
2 tbsp. sugar
1/2 tsp. oregano
1/4 tsp. pepper
1 tsp. salt

Break cauliflower into flowerets; slice. Pare carrots; cut in 2-inch strips. Cut celery in 1-inch pieces; cut green pepper in 2-inch strips. Drain pimento; cut in strips. Drain olives. Combine all ingredients with 1/4 cup water in large skillet; bring to a boil, stirring occasionally. Reduce heat; simmer, covered, for 5 minutes. Cool. Refrigerate for at least 24 hours. Drain well before serving. Yield: 6 servings.

QUICK MEAT RELISH

1 lge. can tomatoes
3/4 c. vinegar
1/2 tsp. cinnamon
1 tsp. salt
1 lge. onion, chopped
1 tbsp. sugar
1/3 tsp. cloves
Pinch of cayenne pepper

Mix all ingredients together; boil for 15 minutes. Serve cooled. Yield: 1 pint.

SAUERKRAUT RELISH

1 No. 2 can sauerkraut, drained
1 c. diced green pepper
1/2 c. chopped onion
1 pimento, chopped
1 c. sugar
1/2 c. salad oil
1/2 c. vinegar
1 tsp. salt

Chop sauerkraut; mix with pepper, onion and pimento. Add all remaining ingredients; mix well. Chill.

TOMATO-CUCUMBER RELISH

1 pkg. French dressing mix
1/2 c. vinegar
1/4 c. salad oil
2 onions, chopped
2 tomatoes, sliced into thin wedges
1 med. cucumber, peeled and sliced

Combine mix, 1/4 cup water, vinegar and oil in pint jar. Shake well. Place vegetables in shallow bowl; pour dressing over top. Mix lightly. Chill thoroughly. Yield: 2 cups.

ZUCCHINI RELISH

10 c. peeled, chopped zucchini
4 c. chopped onions
5 tbsp. salt
2 1/4 c. cider vinegar
6 c. sugar
1 tbsp. nutmeg
1 tbsp. turmeric
2 tbsp. cornstarch
2 tbsp. celery seed
1/2 tsp. pepper

Grind zucchini and onions; add salt. Let stand overnight. Drain; rinse in cold water. Drain thoroughly. Add remaining ingredients; cook for 30 minutes, stirring frequently. Seal in sterilized jars.

CRANBERRY RELISH

1 lb. cranberries
4 to 5 med. apples, quartered
Peel of 1/2 orange
2 oranges, peeled and sectioned
2 c. sugar

Rinse cranberries; drain. Grind fruits and orange peel. Add sugar. Store in refrigerator or freezer.

CRANBERRY-WALNUT RELISH

1 c. coarsely broken walnuts
1 c. orange marmalade
2 1-lb. cans cranberry sauce
1 tbsp. lemon juice

Place walnuts on baking sheet. Bake at 350 degrees for 12 minutes. Cool. Add remaining ingredients; chill. Serve with meat dishes. Yield: 12-16 servings.

PEAR RELISH

2 gal. whole pears
1 doz. sweet peppers
1 doz. red hot peppers
1 doz. medium onions
2 c. vinegar
2 c. prepared mustard
3 c. sugar
1 tbsp. salt
2 tsp. celery seed

Force pears, peppers and onions through food chopper. Combine all ingredients; cook for 25 minutes. Stir occasionally. Fill jars; seal well. Yield: 16-18 pints.

Rhubarb

Rhubarb, a member of the buckwheat family, is distinguished by large leaves and thick, succulent, edible stalks. Although it is by definition a vegetable, rhubarb is used mainly as a fruit. It has a pleasingly tart flavor and a delicate pinkish-red color. Supplies of Vitamins A and C, niacin, and iron are present in rhubarb. (1 cup rhubarb cooked with sugar = 385 calories)

AVAILABILITY: The marketing season for fresh rhubarb lasts from February through June. However, limited supplies are usually available year-round.

BUYING: Select fresh, crisp, tender stalks that are pink or red in color. The younger, pinker stalks are usually more tender than the older stalks. Rhubarb is usually marketed like fresh celery and in some areas may even be known as red celery.

STORING: Wrap rhubarb in foil or plastic. Store in vegetable crisper or on refrigerator shelf for 3 or 4 days. *To freeze*—Wash and trim rhubarb; cut into 1- or 2-inch blocks. If desired, blanch the vegetable in boiling water 1 minute; promptly cool in cold water. Pack pieces in moisture- and vapor-proof containers leaving 1/2-inch head space. Seal, label, and freeze. Or dissolve 3 cups sugar in 4 cups water and chill the syrup thoroughly. Pack rhubarb pieces into freezer containers. Cover with cold syrup leaving 1/2-inch head space. Seal, label, and freeze.

PREPARATION: Rhubarb may be eaten stewed, baked, or combined with many other foods. Refer to recipes for the various ways to prepare rhubarb. If the stalks are stringy and tough, peel like celery. *Never cook the leaves.* They contain a strong, harmful acid. *To stew*—Wash and cut 1 pound rhubarb into 1-inch blocks. Place in saucepan and add 3/4 to 1 cup sugar and a few tablespoons water. Cover and simmer 18 to 20 minutes until tender.

USES: Rhubarb is a versatile food. It is used in pies or salads or as a meat accompaniment.

OVEN-COOKED RHUBARB

3 c. diced rhubarb, cut into 1/2-in. pieces
1 c. sugar
1/2 c. raisins

Combine all ingredients; place in baking dish. Bake, covered, at 325 degrees until just bubbly. Remove from oven; serve. Yield: 6 servings.

RHUBARB SALAD

3 c. diced fresh rhubarb
1/2 c. sugar
1 3-oz. package lemon gelatin
1/4 c. lemon juice
2 c. thinly sliced celery
1 c. chopped nuts

Combine rhubarb, sugar and 1/2 cup boiling water; simmer until rhubarb is tender. Mix 2 cups hot rhubarb sauce with gelatin; stir until dissolved. Add 1 3/4 cups cold water, lemon juice, celery and nuts. Chill until firm. Yield: 8 servings.

TART RHUBARB SALAD

1 11-oz. can mandarin oranges
4 c. diced rhubarb
3/4 c. sugar
1/4 tsp. salt
1 3-oz. package strawberry gelatin
2 tbsp. lemon juice

Drain oranges; reserve juice. Combine rhubarb, 1 cup water, sugar and salt; bring to a boil. Reduce heat; simmer just until rhubarb loses crispness. Remove from heat; add gelatin. Stir until dissolved; add lemon juice. Add enough water to reserved juice to make 1 cup liquid; stir into rhubarb mixture. Chill until partially thickened; fold in oranges. Spoon into 8-inch square glass dish; chill until firm. Yield: 8 servings.

RHUBARB SAUCE

2 lb. rhubarb, diced
1 orange, ground
4 c. sugar
1 lge. can crushed pineapple

Mix rhubarb, orange, sugar and pineapple. Cook for 30 minutes or until thickened, stirring constantly. Pour into sterilized pint jars; seal.

RHUBARB BREAD

1 1/2 c. (packed) brown sugar
2/3 c. salad oil
1 egg
1 c. sour milk
1 tsp. salt
1 tsp. soda
1 tsp. vanilla
2 1/2 c. flour
1 1/2 c. diced rhubarb
1/2 c. chopped nuts
1/2 c. sugar
1/4 c. butter

Mix all ingredients except sugar and butter together; place in 2 greased loaf pans. Mix sugar and butter; sprinkle over loaves. Bake at 325 degrees for 1 hour and 15 minutes.

RHUBARB-BREAD PUDDING

2 c. dry bread cubes
4 c. scalded milk
1 tbsp. butter
1/4 tsp. salt
1 tbsp. artificial liquid sweetener
3/4 c. sugar
4 eggs, slightly beaten
1 tsp. vanilla
2 c. diced rhubarb

Soak bread in milk for 5 minutes; add butter, salt, sweetener and sugar. Pour over eggs gradually, stirring constantly. Add vanilla; mix. Place rhubarb in greased 8 x 11-inch baking dish; pour bread mixture over rhubarb. Place in pan of hot water. Bake at 350 degrees for 50 minutes. Yield: 6 servings.

RHUBARB COBBLER

1/4 c. butter
Sugar
1 c. flour
2 tsp. baking powder
1/4 tsp. salt
1/2 c. milk
3 c. diced rhubarb
1 c. fruit juice

Cream butter and 1/2 cup sugar until light and fluffy. Sift flour, baking powder and salt together; stir into butter mixture alternately with milk. Beat until smooth. Pour into loaf pan. Spoon rhubarb over batter; sprinkle 3/4 cup sugar over rhubarb. Pour fruit juice over top. Bake at 375 degrees for 45 to 50 minutes. Serve warm with cream, whipped cream or ice cream, if desired. Yield: 6 servings.

RHUBARB CRISP

1 c. flour
Dash of salt
1 c. sugar
2 eggs, beaten
3 c. diced rhubarb
3/4 c. (packed) brown sugar
1/4 c. butter

Mix 1/4 cup flour, salt, sugar, and eggs. Combine egg mixture and rhubarb; place in 8 x 8-inch baking pan. Pour flour mixture over rhubarb. Combine brown sugar, 3/4 cup flour and butter; blend until mixture resembles fine crumbs. Sprinkle over rhubarb mixture. Bake at 350 degrees for 45 minutes. Serve with vanilla ice cream. Yield: 9 servings.

RHUBARB CRUNCH

1 c. sifted flour
3/4 c. oats
1 c. (packed) brown sugar
1/2 c. melted butter
1 tsp. cinnamon
4 c. cut rhubarb
1 c. sugar
2 tbsp. cornstarch
1 tsp. vanilla

Combine flour, oats, brown sugar, butter and cinnamon; place half the crumb mixture in 9-inch square pan. Add rhubarb. Combine sugar, cornstarch, 1 cup water and vanilla; cook until thick and clear. Pour over rhubarb; cover with remaining crumb mixture. Bake at 350 degrees for 1 hour. Serve warm or cold with cream. Yield: 9 servings.

RHUBARB CUSTARD PIE

3 eggs, beaten
2 2/3 tbsp. milk
2 c. sugar
1/4 c. flour
3/4 tsp. nutmeg
3 1/2 c. coarsely chopped rhubarb
Pastry for 1 9-in. 2-crust pie
1 tbsp. butter

Beat eggs and milk; stir in sugar, flour, nutmeg and rhubarb. Pour into pie pan lined with crust. Dot with butter. Cover with top crust. Bake at 400 degrees for 60 minutes or until brown. Yield: 6 servings.

RHUBARB DELIGHT

4 c. chopped rhubarb
2 c. sugar
3 eggs
1 c. flour
1 tsp. baking powder
Pinch of salt

Place rhubarb in buttered 9-inch square cake pan; sprinkle with 1 cup sugar. Beat eggs until light and fluffy; add remaining sugar and 3 tablespoons water. Add sifted dry ingredients; stir until flour is blended. Pour over rhubarb. Bake at 350 degrees for 35 to 40 minutes. Cool; serve with whipped cream. Yield: 8 servings.

RHUBARB DUMPLINGS

2 c. sifted flour
3 tsp. baking powder
2 tbsp. sugar
1 tsp. salt
3 tbsp. shortening
1 egg, beaten
Milk
6 c. cooked sweetened rhubarb sauce

Sift flour, baking powder, sugar and salt together; cut in shortening. Place egg in measuring cup; add enough milk to make 3/4 cup liquid. Beat into flour mixture. Drop by tablespoonfuls into boiling rhubarb sauce. Cover; reduce heat to medium. Cook for 15 minutes; serve hot with cream. Yield: 6-8 servings.

RHUBARB DESSERT ROLLS

Sugar
3 c. flour
3 tsp. baking powder
1/2 tsp. salt

1/2 c. shortening
1 c. milk
Melted butter
3 c. diced rhubarb

Combine 1 1/2 cups sugar and 1 1/2 cups water; cook for 5 minutes. Pour syrup into 12 x 8-inch baking pan. Sift flour with baking powder, salt and 1/3 cup sugar; cut in shortening. Add milk; stir until blended. Roll dough into 1/8-inch thick square on floured board. Brush with melted butter. Spread rhubarb over dough; roll jelly roll fashion. Cut roll into slices; place slices in syrup. Bake at 400 degrees for 40 minutes. Yield: 10-12 servings.

RHUBARB-NUT CAKE

1 3/4 c. (packed) brown sugar
2/3 c. salad oil
1 egg
1 c. sour milk
1 tsp. salt
1 1/2 c. diced rhubarb
1 tsp. soda
1 tsp. vanilla
2 1/2 c. flour
1/2 c. chopped nuts
1 tsp. butter

Mix 1 1/2 cups brown sugar, oil, egg, milk, salt, rhubarb, soda, vanilla, flour and nuts; blend well. Pour into greased and floured tube pan. Mix remaining brown sugar and butter; sprinkle over cake mixture. Bake at 325 degrees for 1 hour.

RHUBARB DOWDY

1 3/4 c. sugar
1 tbsp. cornstarch
3 c. chopped fresh rhubarb
3/4 c. sifted flour
1 tsp. baking powder
1/8 tsp. salt
1 tbsp. butter
1 egg
1/2 tsp. vanilla
1 c. bran flakes

Rhubarb Dowdy . . . Feature this authentic New England-style dessert for family suppers.

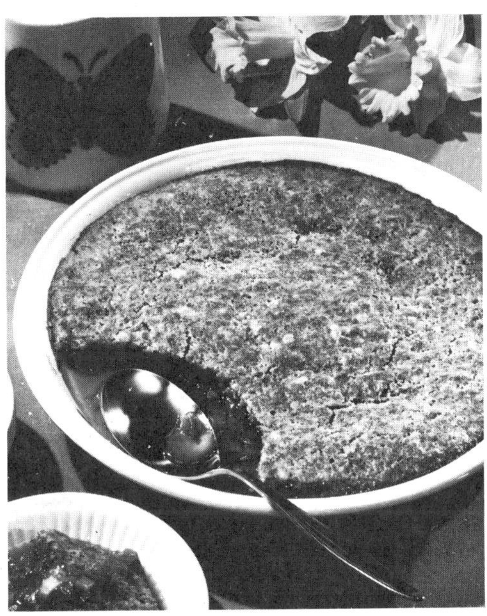

Mix 1 1/4 cups sugar and cornstarch together; add rhubarb and 1/3 cup water. Bring to a full rolling boil quickly, stirring constantly. Pour into 10 x 6 x 2-inch baking dish. Sift flour, baking powder and salt together. Add butter to 1/4 cup hot water, stirring until melted. Beat egg until thick. Add butter mixture, remaining sugar and vanilla, beating until blended. Crush cereal slightly; add cereal and sifted dry ingredients to egg mixture, stirring lightly until combined. Spread batter over rhubarb. Bake in 375-degree oven for about 25 minutes. Serve warm. Yield: 6-8 servings.

RHUBARB SHERBET

4 c. diced rhubarb
Sugar
1/4 c. light corn syrup
1/2 c. orange juice
1 tsp. lemon rind
2 tbsp. lemon juice
2 egg whites, stiffly beaten
1/4 tsp. salt

Cook rhubarb in 1/2 cup water for 5 minutes. Add 1 cup sugar, syrup, orange juice, lemon rind and juice. Bring to a boil. Cool; pour into refrigerator tray. Freeze for 1 hour. Turn mixture into chilled bowl; whip. Fold in egg whites combined with 2 teaspoons sugar and salt. Return to freezing tray; freeze, stirring occasionally. Yield: 6 servings.

RHUBARB-STRAWBERRY DESSERT

3 c. chopped rhubarb
1 pkg. strawberry gelatin
1 1/2 c. flour
Sugar
1/2 tsp. salt
2 tsp. baking powder
1/4 c. shortening
1 egg, beaten
1/4 c. milk
1/4 c. butter

Combine rhubarb and gelatin. Sift 1 cup flour, 2 tablespoons sugar, salt and baking powder together; cut in shortening. Combine egg and milk; add to flour mixture. Pat dough into 8 x 8-inch baking pan; bring dough up 3/4 inch on sides. Pour in rhubarb mixture. Combine 1 cup sugar and remaining flour; cut in butter until crumbly. Sprinkle over rhubarb. Bake at 375 degrees for 45 minutes. Yield: 8 servings.

Rice

The edible seed of a cereal grass, rice is perhaps the most important food in the world. It is economical, nutritious, plentiful, versatile, and easy-to-prepare. Rice supplies carbohydrates, protein, calcium, iron, and some B vitamins. (1 cup cooked white rice = 185 calories; 1 cup cooked brown rice = 200 calories; 1 cup cooked pre-cooked rice = 210 calories; 2/3 cup cooked wild rice = 205 calories)

KINDS: In the United States there are five

most commonly marketed kinds of rice: regular white milled rice, brown rice, parboiled rice, pre-cooked rice, and wild rice. *Regular white milled rice* makes up the bulk of consumer sales. The seed's hull and bran are removed and the grain is highly polished to produce white rice. It is ready to cook as bought. White rice may be short-grained, medium-grained, or long-grained. Short-grained rice is soft and "chalky." When cooked, it is slightly sticky. It is easily molded and thus ideal for rice rings, croquettes and puddings. Short-grained rice is usually the cheapest of the three grain sizes. Medium-grained rice is good quality, average priced rice. Medium-grained rice is more easily separated after cooking than is short-grained rice. Uncooked long-grained rice is hard and translucent. When cooked it is fluffy and easily separated. Because of its desirable appearance and texture, it is the best rice to serve with curries, stews, chicken, meat, and so on. *Brown rice* is the whole, unpolished rice grain without the outer inedible hull. It contains all natural vitamins, minerals, and oils of rice and is thus nutritionally better than regular white rice. Brown rice is chewy and nutlike when cooked. *Parboiled rice,* including converted rice, is rice that has been briefly boiled in water before the milling process. Parboiling aids in retention of natural nutrients. When cooked, parboiled rice is fluffy, easily separated, and plump. Flavor is somewhat nutlike. *Pre-cooked or quick-type rice* is completely cooked before being packaged and marketed. The homemaker merely steams it in boiling water before serving. *Wild rice,* from a native American grass, is probably the most expensive rice. It is considered a delicacy. The brownish-white grains are larger than those of ordinary white rice. The distinctive flavor of wild rice is complementary to game and poultry.

AVAILABILITY: All five types marketed year-round in convenient consumer-sized packages.

STORING: Store uncooked rice in original package on kitchen shelf. Properly sealed after usage, it keeps indefinitely. Refrigerate cooked white rice 1 week. Cover first to prevent rice from drying out or absorbing other food flavors. Cooked white rice freezes well at 0 degree or below for 6 to 8 months. *To freeze,* first cool before packing in freezer containers. Cooked white rice combined with other foods can also be satisfactorily frozen. Freezing time depends on nature of other foods.

PREPARATION: *To prepare regular white milled rice:* 3 cups uncooked rice yields approximately 3 cups boiled rice. There are many equally desirable ways to boil rice, of which the following is just one. Do not rinse rice; washing causes vitamin and mineral loss. Combine 2 cups water and 1 teaspoon salt in large saucepan with tightfitting lid. For hard water, add 1 teaspoon lemon juice, 1/2 teaspoon cream of a tartar, or 1 tablespoon vinegar to water to keep rice white while cooking. Bring water to boil. Add 1 cup rice to the boiling water. Let water return to vigorous boil. Adjust lid on saucepan and reduce heat to simmer. Allow rice to cook about 20 to 30 minutes. Do not stir rice or raise lid. Stirring rice after it has boiled mashes grains and creates a gummy product. Raising lid lets out steam and lowers temperature, thus lengthening cooking time. To test for doneness, press kernel with back of fork against side of pan. It will be soft throughout when desirably done. Do not leave cooked rice in cooking pan for more than 5 or 10 minutes; if allowed to rest in pan, rice packs. For extra-tender rice, measure 1/3 cup more water and increase cooking time 4 to 5 minutes. For drier rice, fluff cooked rice lightly with fork. Cover. Let stand no longer than 5 to 10 minutes to steam dry. For brown, parboiled, pre-cooked, and wild rice, follow package instructions or individual recipe directions. To reheat refrigerated or frozen rice, cover bottom of saucepan with liquid. Bring water to boil, add rice. Break frozen rice into small pieces before adding. Cover pan with tightfitting lid. Turn heat to simmer. Steam about 5 minutes. If frozen rice is not thoroughly heated, add a small amount of liquid and simmer 1 or 2 minutes longer.

SERVING: Rice can be served in innumerable ways and combined with many different foods. Serve boiled rice as a breakfast cereal with cream and sugar, molasses, syrup, or fruit. Or serve as a side dish vegetable with butter. Rice combines well with other vegetables. Accompany curries with rice. Use in casseroles, skillet meals, salads, molds, croquettes, soups, stuffings, and so on. Use also in desserts like custards and puddings.

FRUITED RICE SALAD

Color photograph for this recipe on page 312.

1/2 c. diced celery
1/4 c. minced onion
2 tbsp. butter
2 tsp. grated orange peel
1 c. orange juice
1/2 tsp. poultry seasoning
1 c. water
1 c. rice
6 fluted orange shells

Saute celery and onion in butter in saucepan until tender. Add remaining ingredients except orange shells; bring to a boil. Stir well. Reduce heat; cover. Simmer for about 25 minutes or until rice is tender and liquid absorbed. Chill. Spoon rice mixture into orange shells; serve. Yield: 6 servings.

AMBER RICE CASSEROLE

1/2 c. rice
1/2 c. orange juice
1 1/8 tsp. salt
3 med. carrots, grated
1 1/2 c. grated cheese
2 eggs, beaten
1/8 tsp. pepper
2 tbsp. chopped onion
1/3 c. milk
1 tsp. dried parsley flakes
Cayenne pepper to taste

Combine rice, orange juice, 1 cup water and salt in saucepan; cook for 20 minutes or until rice is tender. Place carrots in 1-quart casserole. Blend in rice mixture and all remaining ingredients. Bake at 350 degrees for 40 minutes.

ITALIAN RICE AND BEANS

1 c. dried navy beans
3 tbsp. onion flakes
1/4 tsp. instant minced garlic
1 tbsp. minced salt pork
2 tbsp. butter
2 tbsp. olive oil
1 c. canned tomatoes
2 tsp. salt
1 tsp. sugar
1 tsp. sage leaves
2 c. long-grained rice
4 c. beef broth
tbsp. parsley flakes
3 tbsp. grated Parmesan cheese

Soak beans overnight in 3 cups water. Soften onion flakes and garlic in 2 tablespoons water. Combine salt pork, 1 tablespoon butter and 1 tablespoon oil in 4-quart saucepan; saute onions and garlic until lightly browned. Add beans, tomatoes, salt, sugar and sage. Cover; simmer for 1 hour. Stir in rice and broth. Cover; simmer for 30 minutes or until rice is tender and has absorbed most of the broth. Add remaining butter and oil, parsley flakes and cheese. Mix lightly; serve hot.

Italian Rice and Beans . . . An economical main dish combining rice, dried beans, and tomatoes.

BROWNED RICE AND CHESTNUTS

1/4 c. olive oil
1 c. sliced onions
1 c. rice
1 can beef consomme
1/2 tsp. hot sauce
1/2 c. chopped parsley
Salt to taste
1 can water chestnuts, chopped

Heat olive oil in skillet. Brown onions lightly; add rice. Cook, stirring constantly, until brown. Add consomme, 1 can water and all remaining ingredients. Place in 1 1/2-quart casserole; cover. Bake at 350 degrees for 1 hour. Yield: 6 servings.

SHERRIED RICE

3 tbsp. salad oil
1 lge. onion, chopped
3 c. rice
2 1/2 cans consomme
1/2 consomme can sherry
2 1/2 tsp. salt
Pepper to taste
Marjoram to taste

Heat oil in large saucepan; add onion. Saute until yellow. Add rice; toss until lightly browned. Dilute consomme with 2 cans water and sherry; stir into rice. Add salt, pepper and marjoram. Bring to a quick boil. Pour into casserole; cover tightly. Bake in 350-degree oven for 45 minutes or until rice is tender. Yield: 12 servings.

SAVORY RICE

1 med. onion, chopped
1 med. green pepper, chopped
1/2 c. margarine
1 c. rice
1 can mushroom soup
1 can beef broth

Saute onion and pepper in margarine; stir in all remaining ingredients and 1 soup can water. Pour into casserole. Bake at 325 degrees for 1 hour. Let stand for several minutes before serving. Yield: 8 servings.

BROWN RICE CASSEROLE

1 1/2 c. long grain rice
1 c. chopped onion
1/2 c. butter
2 cans beef bouillon
1 2 1/2-oz. can mushrooms, chopped

Place rice, onion and butter in skillet; cook over medium heat, stirring constantly, until brown. Add bouillon and mushrooms. Place in 1 1/2-quart casserole; cover. Bake at 300 degrees for 1 hour and 20 minutes. Remove cover; bake for 10 minutes longer. Yield: 6-8 servings.

BUTTERED RICE

2 tsp. salt
1 c. long grain rice
1/3 c. butter
Dash of garlic salt
Dash of monosodium glutamate
1 14-oz. can chicken broth
1/2 c. minced parsley
1/4 c. toasted slivered almonds

Combine salt and 2 cups water in saucepan; bring to a boil. Pour over rice; let stand for 30 minutes. Rinse rice with cold water; drain well. Melt butter in skillet. Add rice; cook over medium heat, stirring frequently, for 5 minutes or until butter is almost absorbed. Turn rice into 1-quart casserole; sprinkle with garlic salt and monosodium glutamate. Pour chicken broth over top; cover. Bake in 325-degree oven for 45 minutes. Add parsley; fluff rice with fork. Sprinkle with almonds. Bake, uncovered, for 10 minutes longer. Yield: 6-8 servings.

CHEESE-RICE BAKE

1 c. scalded milk
1 1/2 c. soft bread crumbs
1/2 lb. sharp cheese, diced
2 tbsp. butter
1/2 tsp. salt
3 eggs, separated
1 1/2 c. cooked rice

Combine milk, bread crumbs, cheese, butter and salt in large bowl. Beat egg yolks well; add to cheese mixture. Add rice; stir to mix. Beat egg whites until stiff peaks form; fold into rice mixture. Pour into greased baking dish. Bake at 325 degrees for 30 minutes or until set.

CHINESE RICE

3/4 c. instant rice
1/4 c. butter
1/3 c. flour
1 tsp. dry mustard
1/2 tsp. salt
1 tsp. salad herbs
2 c. milk
3 lge. eggs, separated
3/4 c. diced cheese

Prepare rice according to package directions. Melt butter in double boiler; stir in flour, mustard, salt and salad herbs. Add milk gradually, stirring constantly. Stir in slightly beaten egg yolks; add cheese. Cook, stirring constantly, until thickened; fold in rice. Fold in well-beaten egg whites. Turn into baking dish. Bake at 375 degrees for 30 minutes or until browned. Yield: 4-6 servings.

COMPANY RICE CASSEROLE

2/3 c. butter
1 15-oz. package instant rice
2 8-oz. cans mushrooms
3/4 c. chopped onion
3 c. diced celery
1 tsp. salt
3/4 tsp. marjoram
1/8 tsp. sage
1/8 tsp. thyme
1 c. broken pecans

Melt butter in large pan; add all remaining ingredients and 3 1/2 cups water, stirring until thoroughly blended. Cover. Bring to a boil. Remove from heat. Let stand for 20 minutes. Fluff gently; spoon into buttered casserole. Bake at 350 degrees for 30 minutes. Yield: 8-10 servings.

COMPANY WILD RICE

1/2 c. wild rice
3/4 tsp. salt
2 tbsp. chopped onion
1 tbsp. chopped green pepper
1 4-oz. can sliced mushrooms
1 tbsp. butter
1/2 c. heavy cream
1 can cream of mushroom soup
1/8 tsp. dried marjoram
Dash of basil
Dash of tarragon
1/4 tsp. curry powder
1/8 tsp. pepper

Wash rice 3 times in cold water. Add 1/2 teaspoon salt to 1 1/2 cups boiling water; stir in rice. Cover; simmer for 30 minutes or until rice is tender and water absorbed. Saute onion, green pepper, drained mushrooms and butter in saucepan for 5 minutes. Stir in cream, soup, remaining salt and all remaining ingredients; simmer for 10 minutes. Add rice; heat until hot, stirring occasionally. Place in buttered casserole. Bake in 350-degree oven until brown. Yield: 6 servings.

GREEN RICE

2 c. cooked rice
2 eggs, beaten
1/2 lb. Cheddar cheese, grated
1 c. chopped fresh parsley
1/4 c. cooking oil
1 sm. onion, chopped
1 tsp. garlic salt
1 lge. can evaporated milk
Salt and pepper to taste

Combine all ingredients; mix well. Turn into greased baking dish. Place dish in pan of water. Bake at 350 degrees for 45 minutes.

HOLIDAY RICE

1 med. onion, chopped
1/2 c. butter
1/2 tsp. garlic salt
1 tsp. oregano
1 can consomme
1 c. rice
1 can mushrooms with butter

Saute onion in butter until tender; add garlic salt and oregano. Spoon onion mixture into 1 1/2-quart casserole; add all remaining ingredients and 1/2 soup can water. Bake, covered, at 350 degrees for 1 hour.

MEXICAN RICE

2 c. cooked rice
2 cartons sour cream
1 can green chilies, chopped
1 pkg. Monterey Jack cheese, cut in strips
Cheddar cheese, grated

Cook rice; add sour cream and chilies. Place in baking dish; cover with layer of cheese. Repeat layers, ending with layer of rice on top. Bake in 350-degree oven for 25 minutes; remove from oven. Top with Cheddar cheese; return to oven for 5 minutes longer. Yield: 4-6 servings.

WILD RICE SUPREME

1 onion, diced
1/3 c. butter
2 c. wild rice
4 1/2 c. chicken broth
1 c. sliced fresh mushrooms

2 tomatoes, diced
1/2 c. slivered almonds
1/4 c. diced cooked bacon
Pinch of saffron
1/4 tsp. thyme
1/4 tsp. oregano

Saute onion in butter. Add rice; toss to coat well. Place rice mixture in large casserole. Bring broth to a boil; pour over rice. Add all remaining ingredients; mix well. Cover. Bake at 325 degrees for 1 hour. Bake, uncovered, for 15 minutes longer. Yield: 8 servings.

ARROZ A LA MEXICANA

2 c. rice
1/4 c. shortening
1 c. peeled tomatoes, chopped
1/2 c. shelled tender peas
1 onion, finely chopped
1 clove of garlic, minced
1 sprig of parsley
4 1/2 c. warm broth
Salt to taste

Soak rice in hot water to cover for 30 minutes. Rinse well in strainer under cold water; drain. Heat shortening in large frying pan until smoking hot. Drop in rice; stir constantly until golden brown. Spoon rice into large saucepan; add remaining ingredients. Cook, covered, over low heat, without stirring, for 45 minutes or until rice is fluffy and moist. Yield: 6 servings.

CHILI-RICE PRONTO

1 med. onion, diced
1/4 c. oil
1 1/3 c. instant rice
1/2 tsp. salt
1 lge. can chili

Saute onion in oil; add rice. Cook, stirring, until golden; stir in 1 1/2 cups water, salt and chili. Bring to a boil; cover. Reduce heat; simmer for 5 minutes. Yield: 4 servings.

FRIED RICE

2 strips bacon
1/4 carrot, grated
1 med. onion, chopped
3/4 c. chopped ham
2 eggs
3 c. cold cooked rice
2 tbsp. soy sauce
Salt to taste
1/4 green pepper, chopped
Juice of 1 clove of garlic

Fry bacon until crisp; crumble. Cook carrot and onion in bacon drippings; remove from pan. Fry ham; remove from pan. Scramble eggs; remove from pan. Place rice in pan; add soy sauce, salt and green pepper. Stir until heated; return all ingredients to pan, adding garlic juice. Serve hot with additional soy sauce, if desired. Yield: 6 servings.

SPANISH RICE WITH CHEESE

3 slices bacon
1 sm. onion, chopped
1/4 c. chopped green pepper
1/4 c. chopped celery
1/2 tsp. salt
3/4 c. instant rice
2 c. canned tomatoes
1 tsp. sugar
1/4 tsp. Worcestershire sauce
1 c. shredded Cheddar cheese

Fry bacon in heavy 2-quart saucepan. Remove bacon from pan; drain. Remove all but 1 tablespoon bacon drippings from pan. Add onion, green pepper and celery to pan; brown lightly. Stir in 1 cup water and salt; bring to a boil. Stir in rice, tomatoes, sugar and Worcestershire sauce. Reduce heat; simmer for 5 to 10 minutes, until rice is tender but still in separate grains. Stir occasionally. Crumble bacon; stir into rice mixture. Sprinkle cheese over top. Cover; cook for 5 minutes longer or until cheese is melted. Yield: 6 servings.

SAUCY RICE LOAF

3 eggs, lightly beaten
1 1/2 c. cooked rice
1 1/2 c. grated American cheese
1/2 c. fine dry bread crumbs
1/4 c. chopped celery
1 tbsp. chopped onion
1 tbsp. chopped parsley
1 tbsp. chopped green pepper
1/4 c. chopped stuffed olives
3/4 tsp. salt
1/2 tsp. prepared mustard
1 c. milk
1/4 c. melted butter

Combine all ingredients; mix well. Place in greased, waxed paper-lined 9 x 5 x 3-inch pan. Place pan in container of hot water. Bake at 325 degrees for 1 hour or until loaf is set in center. Loosen loaf around edges with spatula; turn onto heated platter. Remove paper. Serve with Tomato-Mushroom Sauce.

Tomato-Mushroom Sauce

3 tbsp. butter
3 tbsp. flour
1/2 c. milk
1 8 oz. can tomato sauce
1/2 tsp. salt
1/8 tsp. pepper
1 can sliced mushrooms, undrained

Melt butter in saucepan; blend in flour. Stir in milk and tomato sauce gradually. Cook, stirring constantly, until smooth and thickened. Add seasonings and mushrooms; heat through gently. Yield: 6 servings.

STUFFED GRAPE LEAVES

1 lb. fresh tender grape leaves
1 1/4 c. rice, washed
1/2 c. chick peas
1/2 c. chopped parsley
1/2 c. chopped mint
1/2 c. minced scallions
1 1/2 tsp. salt
1/4 tsp. pepper
1/4 tsp. cinnamon
1/2 c. olive oil
4 cloves of garlic
1/2 c. lemon juice

Wash and drain grape leaves. Mix rice, peas, parsley, mint, scallions, salt, pepper, cinnamon and oil; stuff 1 leaf at a time using heaping teaspoon of stuffing. Roll up, folding bottom of leaf up over stuffing and folding in sides. Place garlic in bottom of 4-quart pan; add rolls side by side in layers. Sprinkle with additional salt and lemon juice; add 1 1/2 cups water. Cook gently, covered, for 45 minutes. Drain off sauce; arrange rolls on serving platter. Yield: 6-8 servings.

RAISIN RICE

1 c. rice
4 tbsp. butter
1/2 c. raisins
1/2 c. almonds
Sour cream

Cook rice in 2 cups water with 2 tablespoons butter. Place remaining butter, raisins and almonds in large skillet; cook until raisins are plumped. Stir in rice; mix well. Serve topped with sour cream. Yield: 4-6 servings.

RICE-PINEAPPLE PUDDING

1/2 c. rice
2 eggs, beaten
1 can crushed pineapple
1/2 c. raisins
1/2 c. sugar
1/2 tsp. salt
3 c. milk
Butter
Nutmeg

Pour rice into boiling salted water. Cook until tender; drain. Add eggs, pineapple, raisins, sugar, salt and milk. Pour into casserole. Dot with butter; sprinkle with nutmeg. Bake at 325 degrees for 50 minutes. Yield: 6 servings.

AROMATIC RICE PUDDING

4 tbsp. rice
1 qt. milk
4 tbsp. sugar
1 tsp. salt
2 tsp. angostura bitters
1/2 pt. heavy cream, whipped

Combine rice, milk, sugar and salt in saucepan. Bring to a boil; reduce heat. Place pan on asbestos pad over low flame; simmer very slowly, uncovered, for 1 hour to 1 hour and 30 minutes or until thick. Stir occasionally during cooking. Turn heat off; stir in bitters. Let pudding cool in pan. Chill in refrigerator.

Aromatic Rice Pudding . . . The unusual flavor of this creamy pudding comes from bitters.

Whip cream until stiff; fold into rice pudding mixture. Spoon pudding into individual dessert dishes. Garnish each serving with maraschino cherry if desired. Yield: 6-8 servings.

YANKEE RICE PUDDING

1 c. instant rice
1 1/2 c. milk
1/4 c. sugar
1/2 tsp. salt
1/2 tsp. cinnamon or nutmeg
1/4 c. seedless raisins

Combine all ingredients. Bring to a full boil, stirring constantly. Remove from heat; cover. Let stand for 15 minutes, stirring occasionally. Serve warm with cream. Yield: 6 servings.

KRIS KRINGLES

Color photograph for this recipe on page 490.

1 c. sugar
1 c. light corn syrup
1 c. peanut butter
6 c. oven-toasted rice cereal
1 6-oz. package semisweet chocolate morsels
1 6-oz. package butterscotch morsels

Mix sugar and corn syrup in 3-quart saucepan; bring to a boil over moderate heat. Remove from heat. Stir in peanut butter and cereal. Press into greased 13 x 9-inch pan. Let harden. Melt chocolate and butterscotch morsels over hot, not boiling, water, stirring until blended. Spread over cereal mixture; chill for about 5 minutes or until chocolate mixture is firm. Cut into diamonds, squares or bars. Yield: about 4 dozen.

Rolls

A roll is one of any variously shaped small breads prepared with yeast dough. Rolls are generally considered either *sweet rolls* or *dinner rolls*, depending upon their ingredients.

INGREDIENTS: Both sweet and dinner rolls are variations of basic yeast bread dough to which an egg or eggs and slightly more sugar and shortening than usual have been added. Sweet roll dough frequently includes flavorings among its ingredients.

PREPARATION: Follow directions for preparing dough and letting it rise. *Sweet rolls*—Shape and/or fill sweet rolls as recipe directs. *Dinner rolls*—Shape as cloverleafs, crescents or butterhorns, Parkerhouse, snails, or figure eights. Dinner rolls may also be twisted or braided. They are often sprinkled with poppy, celery, caraway, or sesame seeds. *To bake*—Bake rolls at high temperatures (400-450 degrees, depending upon recipe) as they are

small breads and tend to dry out at lower temperatures. For a soft crust, grease tops before baking. For a crisp crust, do not grease tops before or after baking. After baking, remove rolls from pan at once and cool on rack.
(See BREAD, CINNAMON, and COFFEE-CAKE.)

BASIC ROLL DOUGH

2 pkg. dry yeast
1/4 c. sugar
1 tsp. salt
3 tbsp. margarine
1 beaten egg
5 1/4 c. (about) flour

Dissolve yeast in 1 cup warm water. Combine 3/4 cup hot water, sugar, salt and margarine; cool to lukewarm. Add yeast mixture, egg and 2 1/2 cups flour; beat until smooth. Add enough remaining flour to make soft dough. Turn out on lightly floured board; knead until smooth and elastic. Place dough in greased bowl, turning to grease top; cover tightly. Store in refrigerator until doubled in bulk. Punch down; roll out on floured board. Shape into rolls; place on greased baking pan. Bake at 350 degrees until golden brown. Dough will keep for 4 to 5 days in refrigerator.

BRAN REFRIGERATOR ROLLS

1 c. shortening
3/4 c. sugar
1 c. whole bran cereal
1 1/2 tsp. salt
2 pkg. yeast
2 eggs, beaten
6 c. (or more) flour
Melted margarine

Combine shortening, 1 cup boiling water, sugar, bran cereal and salt; cool. Dissolve yeast in 1 cup lukewarm water; add to bran mixture. Stir in eggs; fold in flour. Roll out half the mixture at a time to 1/2-inch thick circle. Cut into pie-shaped wedges; brush with margarine. Roll up, starting at wide end. Place on baking sheet; let rise for about 1 hour and 30 minutes. Bake in 450-degree oven until golden brown. Unused dough may be stored in refrigerator. Yield: 36 rolls.

BUTTERHORNS

1 c. milk, scalded
1/2 c. shortening
1/2 c. sugar
1 tsp. salt
1 pkg. dry yeast
3 eggs, beaten
4 1/2 c. flour
Salad oil

Combine milk, shortening, sugar and salt; cool to lukewarm. Add yeast; stir well until dissolved. Beat in eggs. Add flour; mix to smooth soft dough. Knead lightly on floured surface. Place dough in greased bowl; cover. Let rise until doubled in bulk. Divide dough into 3 parts; roll each part on lightly floured surface to 9-inch circle. Brush with oil. Cut each circle into 12 to 16 wedge-shaped pieces. Roll each wedge, starting with wide end and rolling to point. Arrange in greased baking pan; shape in curve as for crescent rolls. Brush with oil. Cover; let rise until doubled in bulk. Bake at 425 degrees for 15 minutes. Yield: 36 rolls.

ANGEL ROLLS

1 pkg. yeast
5 1/2 c. sifted flour
1 tsp. soda
3 tsp. baking powder
4 tbsp. sugar
1 tsp. salt
1 c. shortening
2 c. buttermilk

Dissolve yeast in 2 tablespoons lukewarm water. Sift dry ingredients together; cut in shortening. Add yeast mixture and buttermilk; knead until dough holds together. Roll out to 1/2 to 3/4-inch thickness; cut with biscuit cutter. Fold in half as for Parker House rolls; place on baking sheet. Bake at 400 degrees for 15 to 20 minutes. Dough may be frozen or chilled for later use. Yield: 3 dozen.

BUTTERMILK-ONION BUNS

1 c. buttermilk
3 tbsp. sugar
1/2 tsp. soda
1 tsp. salt
1 pkg. yeast
4 tbsp. salad oil
3 c. flour
1 tsp. baking powder
1/2 c. chopped onions and tops

Combine buttermilk, sugar, soda and salt; mix well. Dissolve yeast in 1/2 cup lukewarm water; add yeast and salad oil to buttermilk mixture. Add flour, baking powder and onions; beat well. Place in greased bowl; let rise for 2 hours or until doubled in bulk. Shape into hamburger or hot dog buns. Place on cookie sheets; let rise until doubled in bulk. Bake at 400 degrees for 10 to 12 minutes or until golden.

ONE-HOUR BUTTERMILK ROLLS

2 pkg. yeast
1 1/2 c. lukewarm buttermilk
1/2 c. melted shortening
3 tbsp. sugar
4 1/2 c. flour
1/2 tsp. soda
1 tsp. salt

Sprinkle yeast in 1/4 cup lukewarm water; add buttermilk, shortening and sugar. Sift flour, soda and salt into liquid mixture; beat until smooth. Let stand for 10 minutes. Roll out; shape as desired. Place in baking pan; let rise for about 30 minutes in warm place. Bake at 400 degrees for 15 minutes or until lightly browned. Yield: 2 dozen rolls.

CANADIAN BUNS

3/4 c. salted potato water
Sugar
1/2 c. shortening
1 pkg. yeast
2 eggs, beaten
4 1/2 c. flour

Heat potato water in saucepan; stir in 1/2 cup sugar until dissolved. Add shortening; cool to lukewarm. Pour 1/2 cup lukewarm water into large bowl; stir in 1 teaspoon sugar. Sprinkle with yeast; let stand for 10 minutes. Stir well. Stir in potato water mixture, eggs and 2 1/4 cup flour; beat until smooth. Work in remaining flour to make soft dough. Knead lightly in bowl; let rise until doubled in bulk. Shape into buns; place on baking sheet. Let rise until nearly doubled in bulk. Bake at 375 degrees for 20 minutes.

AIRY CHEESE ROLLS

1 pkg. dry yeast
1 3/4 c. milk, scalded
1 c. shredded sharp American cheese
1/4 c. sugar
2 tbsp. shortening
1 tsp. salt
4 c. sifted all-purpose flour
1 egg, beaten
1/2 c. cornmeal

Dissolve yeast in 1/4 cup lukewarm water. Combine milk, cheese, sugar, shortening and salt in large bowl of electric mixer; stir until cheese melts. Cool to lukewarm. Add 2 cups flour; beat at medium speed with mixer for 2 minutes. Add egg, yeast, cornmeal and remaining flour; beat for 2 minutes. Cover; let rise in warm place for about 1 hour and 30 minutes or until doubled in bulk. Stir down. Fill greased 2 1/2-inch muffin pans 1/2 full. Cover; let rise for about 45 minutes or until doubled in bulk. Bake at 375 degrees for 15 to 20 minutes. Yield: 2 dozen.

CHEESE-PIMENTO ROLLS

1 pkg. yeast
1/3 c. milk
2 1/4 c. flour
1/2 c. soft shortening
2 tbsp. sugar
1/2 tsp. salt
1 egg
1/4 c. grated cheese
2 tbsp. chopped green pepper
1 tbsp. chopped pimento

Dissolve yeast in 1/4 cup lukewarm water. Scald milk; cool to lukewarm. Combine milk and yeast mixture in large mixer bowl; add 1 1/4 cups flour, shortening, sugar, salt and egg. Beat with electric mixer for 1 minute. Add cheese, green pepper, pimento and remaining flour; mix well. Beat for 1 minute longer. Spoon into greased muffin tins; let rise for about 1 hour or until doubled in bulk. Bake at 400 degrees for 15 to 20 minutes. Yield: 18 small rolls.

PUMPERNICKEL CLOVERLEAF ROLLS

5 c. unsifted flour
1 c. unsifted rye flour
1 tbsp. salt
1/2 c. whole bran cereal
1/3 c. yellow cornmeal
1 pkg. dry yeast
2 tbsp. dark molasses
1 1-oz. square unsweetened chocolate
Margarine
1 c. mashed potatoes, at room temperature
1 tsp. caraway seed
1/2 tsp. cornstarch

Combine flour and rye flour. Mix 1 cup flour mixture, salt, bran cereal, cornmeal and yeast thoroughly in a large bowl. Combine 1 3/4 cups water, molasses, chocolate and 1 tablespoon margarine in saucepan. Heat over low heat until liquids are warm. Margarine and chocolate do not need to melt. Add to dry ingredients gradually; beat for 2 minutes at medium speed with electric mixer, scraping bowl occasionally. Add mashed potatoes and enough flour mixture to make thick batter. Beat at high speed for 2 minutes, scraping bowl occasionally. Stir in caraway seed and enough additional flour mixture to make soft dough. Turn out onto lightly floured board. Cover dough with bowl; let rest for 15 minutes. Knead for about 12 minutes or until smooth and elastic. Place in greased bowl, turning to grease top. Cover; let rise in warm place, free from draft,

Pumpernickel Cloverleaf Rolls . . . These molasses and rye rolls complement ham, pork, and sausage.

for about 1 hour or until doubled in bulk. Punch dough down; let rise again for 30 minutes. Punch dough down; turn out onto lightly floured board. Divide dough into 4 equal parts. Form each part into 8-inch roll. Cut into 8 equal pieces. Divide each piece into 3 sections; form into small balls. Brush sides with melted margarine. Place 3 balls in each cup of greased medium muffin pans. Cover; let rise in warm place, free from draft, for about 45 minutes or until doubled in bulk. Bake in 375-degree oven for about 25 minutes or until rolls test done. Combine cornstarch and 1/2 cup water. Cook over medium heat, stirring constantly, until mixture starts to boil. Cook for 1 minute longer. Brush cornstarch mixture over tops of rolls. Return rolls to oven; bake for 2 to 3 minutes longer to set glaze. Remove from pans; cool on wire racks.

FRESH POTATO ROLLS DELICIOUS

Color photograph for this recipe on page 729.

1 pkg. dry yeast
2/3 c. scalded milk
1/2 c. shortening
1 c. fresh hot mashed potatoes
1/4 c. sugar
2 tsp. salt
3 lge. eggs, lightly beaten
8 1/2 c. (about) sifted flour
3 tbsp. melted butter

Sprinkle yeast over 1/2 cup warm water; stir until dissolved. Combine the milk, shortening, potatoes, sugar and salt in large bowl; cool to lukewarm. Add yeast and eggs, blending well. Add 1 1/2 cups flour; mix well. Cover; let rise in warm place for about 1 hour or until bubbly. Stir in enough remaining flour to make stiff dough. Turn onto lightly floured board; knead until smooth and elastic. Place in lightly greased bowl, turning to grease surface. Cover; refrigerate overnight. Shape into small balls. Place in greased and lightly floured muffin tins; brush with melted butter. Let rise in warm place for 1 hour and 15 minutes or until doubled in bulk. Bake at 425 degrees for 20 minutes. Yield: About 40 medium rolls.

CLOVERLEAF DINNER ROLLS

1/2 c. shortening
1 pkg. yeast
1 egg
1/3 c. sugar
1 tsp. salt
3 c. (heaping) flour
Butter

Melt shortening in 1/2 cup boiling water; let cool to lukewarm. Mix yeast and 3/4 cup lukewarm water; add to shortening mixture. Blend egg, sugar, salt and 1/2 cup water; add to yeast mixture. Mix in flour. Divide dough; place in 2 bowls. Cover; refrigerate overnight. Place 3 small balls of dough in each cup of greased and floured muffin pans. Let stand for 30 minutes. Dot with butter. Bake at 400 degrees for 10 minutes. Yield: 2 1/2 dozen rolls.

CRUSTY ROLLS

1 tbsp. sugar
1 1/2 tsp. salt
1 pkg. yeast
3 1/2 c. (about) all-purpose flour
2 tbsp. salad oil
2 egg whites
Sesame seed
1 egg yolk

Combine 1 cup lukewarm water, sugar, salt and yeast in large bowl; stir until yeast is dissolved. Add 1 cup flour; mix well. Add oil; beat until batter is smooth. Beat egg whites until stiff but not dry; fold into batter. Add remaining flour; mix to moderately stiff dough. Turn out onto lightly floured board; knead until smooth. Place in greased bowl. Cover; let rise until doubled in bulk. Punch down; let rise for 15 minutes. Punch down; shape into 18 rolls. Dip in sesame seed; place on greased baking sheet. Cover; let rise until doubled in bulk. Beat egg yolk with 1 tablespoon water; brush rolls with egg yolk mixture. Bake at 400 degrees for 15 minutes.

DRIED BEEF ROLLS

1 pkg. dry yeast
1/4 c. shortening
2 tbsp. sugar
1 tsp. salt
1 c. milk, scalded
1/2 c. bran cereal
3 oz. dry chipped beef, minced
1 egg, slightly beaten
3 1/4 c. (about) flour
Melted butter
1/4 c. grated onion

Soften yeast in 1/4 cup lukewarm water. Combine shortening, sugar, salt and milk in bowl; add cereal and beef. Cool to lukewarm; add egg and yeast mixture, mixing well. Add flour; mix well. Knead for 3 to 5 minutes; place in greased bowl. Cover. Let rise until doubled in bulk; roll out to 18 x 12-inch rectangle. Brush with butter; spread with onion. Roll up as for jelly roll; slice. Place slices on greased sheet. Let rise for 1 hour. Bake in 400-degree oven for 20 minutes.

EASY YEAST CRESCENT ROLLS

1/2 c. butter
1/2 c. sugar
1 c. milk, scalded
1 pkg. yeast
4 c. flour
1 tsp. salt
3 eggs, beaten

Add butter and sugar to milk; stir until dissolved. Cool to lukewarm. Sprinkle in yeast; let soak for 5 minutes. Combine flour and salt in mixing bowl; add yeast mixture, blending well. Add eggs; cover. Refrigerate overnight. Divide dough into 4 equal parts; roll out on floured board into circles as for pie. Cut each circle into 12 wedges; roll wedges up, beginning with larger end. Place on cookie sheet; let rise for 1 hour. Bake at 350 degrees for 10 to 15 minutes.

OVERNIGHT ROLLS

2 pkg. dry yeast
2 tsp. salt
3/4 c. sugar
3/4 c. butter
3 eggs, beaten
8 c. (about) flour

Dissolve yeast in 1/2 cup lukewarm water. Combine salt, sugar and butter in 1 cup boiling water; mix well until butter is melted. Add 1 cup cold water, eggs, yeast mixture and part of the flour; beat well. Add enough remaining flour to make soft dough; knead. Place dough in large bowl; refrigerate overnight. Shape as desired on baking sheet. Let rise for 2 hours or longer. Bake at 375 degrees for 15 to 20 minutes. Yield: 15 rolls.

PARKER HOUSE ROLLS

1 c. milk, scalded
1 pkg. yeast
4 tbsp. sugar
4 c. sifted flour
1 1/2 tsp. salt
1 egg, beaten
4 tbsp. melted shortening
Butter, melted

Cool milk to lukewarm. Sprinkle yeast into mixing bowl; add sugar. Add milk to yeast mixture; stir well. Add half the flour and salt; mix well. Add egg and shortening; beat thoroughly. Add remaining flour gradually; mix well. Let rise until doubled in bulk; roll dough out on floured board to 1/2-inch thickness. Cut into rounds with small biscuit cutter. Crease with dull side of knife just to sides of center. Brush with melted butter; fold smaller sides over wider sides. Place on greased baking pan. Let rise until doubled in bulk. Bake at 400 degrees for 15 to 20 minutes. Yield: 2 dozen rolls.

POTATO ROLLS

1 pkg. yeast
1 c. sugar
1 c. hot mashed potatoes
4 eggs, beaten
Salt to taste
1 c. (scant) shortening
Flour
Butter
Powdered sugar

Dissolve yeast in 1 cup lukewarm water. Add sugar to potatoes; cool. Add yeast; let stand overnight. Add eggs and salt; add shortening and enough flour to make batter. Let rise until light; add enough flour to make soft dough. Let rise in bowl until light; roll out about 1/2 inch thick. Cut with round cutter. Place rolls on cookie sheet; fold over as for Parker House rolls. Let rise until doubled in bulk. Bake at 350 degrees for about 15 minutes or until lightly browned. Mix small amount of flour and butter; rub over tops of hot rolls. Sprinkle with powdered sugar. Yield: 4 dozen rolls.

RYE ROLLS

2 c. milk
1/4 c. shortening
1/4 c. (packed) brown sugar
2 tsp. salt
2 tbsp. dark molasses
1/2 tsp. soda
1 pkg. yeast
2 beaten eggs
3 c. rye flour
Flour
Melted butter
2 tsp. caraway seed

Scald milk; add shortening, brown sugar, salt, molasses and soda. Cool to lukewarm. Sprinkle in yeast; stir until dissolved. Add eggs and rye flour; beat thoroughly. Add enough flour to make soft dough; beat well. Place in greased bowl; let rise until doubled in bulk. Punch down; let rise again until doubled in bulk. Turn out on floured board; roll out to desired thickness. Cut into wedges. Shape wedges into crescent rolls. Place on greased pans. Let rise until doubled in bulk. Bake in 375-degree oven for 12 to 15 minutes. Brush each roll with melted butter; sprinkle with additional salt and caraway seed. Yield: 3 1/2 dozen rolls.

SOUR CREAM AND CHIVE BUNS

3/4 c. sour cream
2 tbsp. sugar
1 tsp. salt
2 tbsp. soft shortening
1 pkg. yeast
2 1/4 c. flour
1 egg, slightly beaten
1 1/2 tbsp. chopped chives

Combine sour cream, sugar, salt and shortening in saucepan; bring to boiling point. Cool to lukewarm. Dissolve yeast in 1/4 cup warm water. Combine sour cream mixture, yeast and half the flour, beating until smooth. Add remaining flour, egg and chives; beat well. Scrape down side of bowl; cover with cloth. Let dough rise in warm place for about 30 minutes or until doubled in bulk. Spoon batter into 12 greased muffin cups, 1/2 full. Let rise in warm place for 20 to 30 minutes or until dough reaches top of muffin cups. Bake in preheated 400-degree oven for 15 to 20 minutes.

SOUR CREAM ROLLS

1 c. sour cream
1 1/2 pkg. yeast
1 c. margarine, softened
1/2 c. sugar
1/2 tsp. salt
4 c. flour
2 eggs, beaten

Heat sour cream in double boiler until slightly yellow around edge. Dissolve yeast in 1/3 cup lukewarm water. Combine margarine, sugar and salt; pour sour cream over margarine mixture. Cool to lukewarm. Blend in 1 cup flour. Add yeast and 1 cup flour. Beat in eggs and remaining flour. Cover; refrigerate for 6 hours or overnight. Divide dough into 4 portions. Roll each portion into 1/4-inch thick round. Cut each round into 12 wedge-shaped pieces.

Caraway-Rye Pan Rolls . . . Nut-like flavored rolls that highlight dinner, supper, or lunch.

Roll up, beginning at wide ends. Place on greased baking sheet; curve into crescents. Let rise for 1 hour. Bake for 15 minutes at 375 degrees. Yield: 8-10 servings.

PARKER HOUSE ROLLS

Color photograph for this recipe on page 732.

2 3/4 to 3 1/4 c. unsifted flour	*5 tbsp. margarine*
1/4 c. sugar	*2/3 c. hot tap water*
1/2 tsp. salt	*1 egg, at room temperature*
1 pkg. dry yeast	*Melted margarine*

Mix 3/4 cup flour, sugar, salt and undissolved yeast thoroughly in large bowl. Add softened margarine. Add hot water gradually; beat for 2 minutes with electric mixer at medium speed, scraping bowl occasionally. Add egg and 1/2 cup flour; beat at high speed for 2 minutes, scraping bowl occasionally. Stir in enough remaining flour to make soft dough. Turn out onto lightly floured board; knead for 8 to 10 minutes or until smooth and elastic. Place in greased bowl, turning to grease top. Cover; let rise in warm place, free trom draft, for about 1 hour or until doubled in bulk. Punch down. Turn out onto lightly floured board; divide in half. Roll each half into 1/4-inch thick circle; cut with a 2 1/2-inch biscuit cutter. Crease each round with dull edge of knife to 1 side of center; brush each round with melted margarine to within 1/4 inch of edge. Fold larger side over smaller so edges just meet; pinch well with fingers to seal. Place on greased baking sheets so rolls are almost touching. Cover; let rise in warm place, free from draft, for about 1 hour or until doubled in bulk. Brush rolls with melted margarine. Bake in 400-degree oven for 10 to 15 minutes or until done. Remove from baking sheets; cool on wire racks. Yield: 2-3 dozen.

CARAWAY-RYE PAN ROLLS

4 c. unsifted flour	*1 pkg. dry yeast*
1 c. unsifted rye flour	*1 c. milk*
1 tbsp. sugar	*2 tbsp. honey*
1 tbsp. salt	*1 tbsp. margarine*
1 tbsp. caraway seed	*1 egg white, slightly beaten*

Combine flour and rye flour. Mix 1 2/3 cups flour mixture, sugar, salt, caraway seed and yeast in large bowl. Combine milk, 3/4 cup water, honey and margarine in saucepan. Heat over low heat until liquids are warm. Margarine does not need to melt. Add to dry ingredients gradually; beat for 2 minutes at medium speed with electric mixer, scraping bowl occasionally. Add enough flour mixture to make thick batter. Beat at high speed for 2 minutes, scraping bowl occasionally. Stir in enough flour mixture to make soft dough. Turn dough out onto lightly floured board. Knead for about 8 to 10 minutes or until smooth and elastic. Place in greased bowl, turning to grease top. Cover; let rise in warm place, free from draft, for about 1 hour or until doubled in bulk. Punch dough down; turn out onto lightly floured board. Divide in half; form each half into smooth ball. Cover; let rest for 10 minutes. Form each piece into 12-inch long roll. Cut into 12 equal pieces; form into smooth balls. Place in 2 greased 9-inch round cake pans. Cover; let rise in warm place, free from draft, for about 1 hour or until doubled in bulk. Combine egg white and 2 tablespoons water; brush over rolls. Bake in 400-degree oven for about 25 minutes or until rolls test done. Remove from baking pans; cool on wire racks.

TOMATO JUICE ROLLS

1 pkg. dry yeast	*1 egg, beaten*
1 c. warm tomato juice	*3 tbsp. salad oil*
1 1/4 tsp. salt	*5 1/2 c. flour*
1/3 c. sugar	

Dissolve yeast in 1/2 cup lukewarm water; add remaining ingredients, stirring with spoon. Place dough in bowl; cover. Set in warm place; let rise until doubled in bulk. Place on floured board; roll out to 1/2 inch thickness. Cut with biscuit cutter; place rolls close together on cake roll pan. Cover; let rise until doubled in bulk. Bake at 400 degrees for 10 to 12 minutes. Yield: About 3 dozen rolls.

DELICIOUS WHOLE WHEAT ROLLS

2/3 c. shortening	*1 pkg. yeast*
Sugar	*2 eggs, beaten*
1 tbsp. salt	*3 c. whole wheat flour*
1 c. mashed cooked potatoes	*3 1/2 c. (about) flour*

Combine 1 cup hot water, shortening, 1/2 cup sugar, salt and potatoes; cool to lukewarm. Dissolve yeast and 1 teaspoon sugar in 1/2 cup lukewarm water. Add to potato mixture; add eggs, mixing well. Beat in whole wheat flour until smooth. Add enough flour to make soft dough; place in greased bowl. Refrigerate. Shape dough into rolls; place on baking sheet. Let rise for 3 hours or until doubled in bulk. Bake at 350 degrees until lightly browned.

CHOCOLATE ROLLS

1 pkg. yeast	*1/3 c. cocoa*
2 1/2 c. flour	*2 tbsp. butter*
1/4 c. shortening	*1 c. powdered sugar*
1/4 c. sugar	*3 tbsp. milk*
Salt	*1/2 tsp. vanilla*
1 egg, beaten	

Soften yeast in 1 cup lukewarm water; beat in 1 cup flour. Add shortening, sugar, 1 teaspoon salt, egg and cocoa; mix well. Add enough remaining flour to make soft dough; place in greased bowl. Grease top of dough; let rise for about 1 hour and 30 minutes. Roll out on floured board. Combine butter, powdered sugar, 1/8 teaspoon salt, milk and vanilla. Blend until smooth. Spread frosting over dough. Roll up as for jelly roll; cut into 1-inch slices. Place slices in greased 9 x 13-inch pan. Let rise until doubled in bulk. Bake at 375 degrees for about 25 minutes. Remove from pan; frost with any remaining frosting. Yield: 10 servings.

BASIC SWEET ROLL DOUGH

2 pkg. dry yeast
1 1/2 c. lukewarm milk
1/2 c. sugar
2 tsp. salt
2 eggs
1/2 c. soft shortening
7 1/2 c. flour

Dissolve yeast in 1/2 cup lukewarm water; add milk, sugar, salt, eggs, shortening and half the flour. Mix until smooth; add enough remaining flour to make easily handled dough. Turn onto lightly floured board; knead until smooth. Place in greased bowl, turning to grease top. Cover; let rise in warm place for about 1 hour and 30 minutes or until doubled in bulk. Punch down; let rise for about 30 minutes. Form into desired shapes; place on baking sheet. Bake at 400 degrees for 15 to 20 minutes. Yield: 2 dozen rolls.

CINNAMON-PECAN ROLLS

Melted butter
2 c. milk
1 1/2 c. sugar
2 tsp. salt
6 1/2 c. flour
2 pkg. dry yeast
2 eggs, at room temperature
4 tsp. cinnamon
2 sticks margarine
2 c. (packed) brown sugar
4 tbsp. white corn syrup
Pecan halves

Heat 1/2 cup melted butter, milk, 1/2 cup water, 1/2 cup sugar and salt together until warm. Add 4 cups flour, yeast and eggs. Beat with electric mixer at high speed for 3 to 4 minutes. Add remaining flour gradually, kneading as dough becomes too stiff to beat. Brush dough with butter; let rise until doubled in bulk. Punch down; divide into 4 portions. Roll each portion into 8 x 10 x 3/4-inch rectangle. Brush each rectangle with 2 tablespoons butter. Combine remaining sugar and cinnamon; sprinkle over rectangles. Roll up as for jelly roll. Cut each roll into 8 slices. Place 1/2 stick margarine, 1/2 cup brown sugar and 1 tablespoon corn syrup in each of 4 bread pans; heat in oven until melted. Mix well. Place pecan halves in bottom of each pan. Place 8 dough slices, cut side down, in each prepared pan. Let rise until doubled in bulk. Bake at 375 degrees for 25 minutes. Place pans on racks for 2 1/2 minutes. Invert pans; remove rolls.

COMPANY ROLLS

1 c. sour cream
1 pkg. yeast
2 tbsp. shortening
3 tbsp. sugar
1/8 tsp. soda
1 tsp. salt
1 lge. egg, beaten
3 c. flour
3 tbsp. butter
2/3 c. (packed) brown sugar
1/2 c. chopped nuts
1/2 c. raisins

Heat sour cream to lukewarm. Dissolve yeast in 1/4 cup lukewarm water. Mix shortening, sugar, soda, salt and egg in large bowl. Stir in sour cream and yeast mixture. Add flour. Knead for about 5 minutes. Cover; let stand for 5 minutes. Roll out to 1/4-inch thickness; spread with butter, brown sugar, nuts and raisins. Roll up as for jelly roll; cut into 1-inch thick slices. Let rise for 1 hour or until doubled in bulk. Place in greased pan. Bake at 375 degrees for 20 minutes. Yield: 3 dozen.

FRENCH BREAKFAST PUFFS

1/3 c. soft shortening
1/2 c. sugar
1 egg, slightly beaten
1 1/2 c. flour
1 1/2 tsp. baking powder
1/2 tsp. salt
1/4 tsp. nutmeg
1/2 c. milk
Melted butter
Cinnamon sugar

Mix shortening, sugar and egg thoroughly. Sift flour, baking powder, salt and nutmeg together; stir into shortening mixture alternately with milk. Fill muffin cups 2/3 full. Bake at 350 degrees for 25 minutes or until golden brown. Roll immediately in melted butter and cinnamon sugar. Yield: 12 puffs.

HOT CROSS BUNS

3 1/2 c. flour
1/2 tsp. salt
1/2 c. sugar
4 tbsp. margarine
1/2 c. milk
1 egg, beaten
1 pkg. yeast
1/2 tsp. grated lemon rind
2 oz. currants
Confectioners' sugar glaze

Sift 3 cups flour, salt and sugar together; work in margarine until of fine crumb consistency. Combine milk and 1/2 cup water; heat to scalding point. Cool to lukewarm; stir into egg. Dissolve yeast in lukewarm mixture. Form well in flour mixture; pour liquid into well. Stir until blended; add lemon rind and currants. Spread remaining flour on board; knead dough, working in flour until smooth. Place dough in greased bowl; cover. Let rise until doubled in bulk. Punch down; pull dough off in small pieces. Shape into buns; arrange on greased and floured pan. Let rise until doubled in bulk. Snip crosses on tops of buns with scissors. Bake at 400 degrees for about 15 minutes. Glaze hot buns with confectioners' sugar glaze. Yield: 3 dozen rolls.

LEMON-NUT ROLLS

1 pkg. yeast
1/3 c. shortening
Sugar
1/2 c. mashed potatoes
1 tsp. salt
1/2 c. scalded milk
1 egg
Grated lemon rind
1 tbsp. lemon juice
4 c. flour
Melted margarine
1/2 c. chopped pecans

Soften yeast in 1/4 cup lukewarm water. Combine shortening, 1/2 cup sugar, mashed potatoes, salt and milk. Blend well; cool to lukewarm. Stir in egg, 1 teaspoon grated lemon rind, lemon juice and yeast. Add enough flour to form easily handled dough. Knead well. Let rise for about 1 hour. Roll out to 16 x 12-inch rectangle; brush with margarine. Combine 3/4 cup sugar, pecans and 2 teaspoons grated lemon rind. Sprinkle on dough. Roll up as for jelly roll; cut into 16 slices. Place on baking sheet. Let rise for 30 to 45 minutes. Bake at 375 degrees for 30 to 45 minutes.

Lemon Glaze

1/2 c. powdered sugar
1 tsp. grated lemon rind
1 1/2 tsp. lemon juice
1 tsp. milk

Combine all ingredients; mix well. Drizzle glaze over rolls.

ORANGE BOWKNOTS

1 1/4 c. milk, scalded
1/2 c. butter
1/3 c. sugar
1 tsp. salt
1 pkg. yeast
2 eggs, beaten
1/4 c. orange juice
2 tbsp. grated orange rind
5 c. flour

Combine milk, butter, sugar and salt; cool to lukewarm. Add yeast, eggs, orange juice and rind; beat well. Mix in flour; let stand for 10 minutes. Knead on lightly floured board. Place in greased bowl; cover. Place in refrigerator until ready to use. Roll out to 1/2-inch thickness. Cut in long strips; tie in knots. Place on baking sheet. Let rise for about 4 hours or until doubled in bulk. Bake at 350 degrees for 10 to 12 minutes. Spread with orange topping if desired. Yield: 24 rolls.

PHILADELPHIA STICKY BUNS

3/4 c. milk
1/3 c. sugar
1 tsp. salt
9 tbsp. butter
2 pkg. dry yeast
1 egg, slightly beaten
4 c. (about) flour
1 1/2 c. (packed) dark brown sugar
1/2 c. currants, plumped
1/2 c. chopped pecans
1 tbsp. cinnamon
1 c. dark corn syrup

Scald milk; stir in sugar, salt and 4 tablespoons butter. Cool to lukewarm. Dissolve yeast in 1/3 cup warm water in large bowl; stir in milk mixture, egg and half the flour. Beat until smooth; stir in enough remaining flour to make soft dough. Turn onto lightly floured board; knead for about 8 minutes or until smooth and elastic. Place in greased bowl; turn to grease top. Cover; let rise in warm place for about 1 hour or until doubled in bulk. Mix 1/2 cup brown sugar with currants, pecans and cinnamon; set aside. Mix remaining brown sugar, 4 tablespoons butter and corn syrup; bring to a boil. Pour into two 9-inch square pans; cool. Punch dough down; divide in half. Roll each half on floured board to 9 x 14-inch rectangle; spread with remaining butter. Sprinkle each rectangle with half the pecan mixture. Roll up as for jelly roll from 9-inch side; seal edges. Cut into 1-inch slices; place, cut sides down, in syrup mixture in pan. Cover; let rise in warm place for about 45 minutes or until doubled in bulk. Bake at 350 degrees for about 25 minutes or until light brown. Invert on plate; cool. Yield: 18 servings.

QUICK OAT KOLACHES

1/3 c. butter
1 3/4 c. prepared biscuit mix
1 c. rolled oats
1/4 c. sugar
1 egg, beaten
1/4 c. milk
1 tsp. vanilla
8 tbsp. raspberry preserves
Confectioners' sugar

Cut butter into biscuit mix with pastry blender until mixture resembles coarse crumbs; stir in oats and sugar. Combine egg, milk and vanilla; add to oat mixture. Stir only until moistened. Turn onto lightly floured board; knead lightly several times. Roll out 1/2 inch thick; cut into 3-inch rounds with floured cookie cutter. Place on greased baking sheet. Make deep indentation in center of each round; fill with preserves. Bake at 400 degrees for 10 to 15 minutes; sprinkle with confectioners' sugar. Serve warm. Yield: About 12 servings.

QUICK PARTY ROLLS

2 pkg. yeast
1/4 c. melted butter
1 tsp. salt
1 box egg custard mix
3 1/2 c. flour

Dissolve yeast in 1 1/4 cups warm water. Stir in butter, salt and egg custard mix. Add flour gradually, blending well. Turn out on floured board; knead several times. Roll out; cut into 24 rounds with biscuit cutter. Fold over as for Parker House rolls. Place on cookie sheet; cover and let rise until doubled in bulk. Bake at 400 degrees until golden brown.

SAFFRON BUNS

1/4 tsp. powdered saffron
2 pkg. yeast
1/2 c. butter
1 c. hot milk
3 beaten eggs
5 c. unsifted flour
1/2 c. sugar
3/4 tbsp. salt
1 tsp. nutmeg
1 c. seedless raisins
1/2 c. candied chopped citron
1 tbsp. grated lemon rind

Soak powdered saffron in 2 tablespoons hot water. Dissolve yeast in 1/4 cup lukewarm water. Melt butter in hot milk; cool to lukewarm. Mix yeast, saffron, milk and eggs together. Sift 2 cups flour with sugar, salt and nutmeg; add egg mixture. Mix well. Add raisins, citron and grated lemon rind to remaining flour; add to egg mixture. Knead well; place in greased bowl. Cover; let rise in warm place for 1 hour and 30 minutes or until doubled in bulk. Form into buns; place on baking sheet. Let rise again until nearly doubled in bulk. Bake at 375 degrees for 15 to 20 minutes. Brush with additional butter. May frost with powdered sugar frosting if desired. Yield: 4 dozen buns.

SQUAW ROLLS

Flour
1 tbsp. baking powder
1 tsp. salt
1 c. milk

Sift 2 cups flour, baking powder and salt together; add milk gradually, making soft dough. Turn out dough on floured board; knead for several minutes, working in flour as needed. Cover with damp cloth; let dough rest for 5 minutes. Cut into small pieces with sharp knife or kitchen shears. Drop into deep hot fat; fry till golden brown. Serve immediately.

Romaine

CANLIS SALAD

2 heads romaine lettuce
2 tomatoes, cut into eighths
6 bacon slices, crumbled
1/2 c. grated Romano cheese
6 green onions, chopped
Pinch of oregano
2 1/2 oz. garlic olive oil
Juice of 1/2 lemon
1 tsp. freshly ground pepper
1/2 tsp. salt
1 coddled egg

Break romaine into bowl; add tomatoes, bacon, cheese, onions and oregano. Pour oil, lemon juice, pepper, salt, and coddled egg into separate bowl. Whip with beater; pour over salad. Add croutons; toss. Yield: 4-6 servings.

ROMAINE SALAD

1/2 c. olive oil
1/2 c. salad oil
1/4 c. red wine vinegar
1 1/2 tsp. salt
1/4 c. minced parsley
Freshly ground pepper
1/4 c. minced chives
1 tsp. tarragon
1 lge. head romaine, torn into pieces

Combine all ingredients except romaine. Pour over romaine; toss well. Yield: 6 servings.

WESTPORT SALAD

2 heads romaine lettuce
1 c. mayonnaise
1 tbsp. lemon juice
2 tbsp. grated Parmesan cheese
1 clove of garlic, crushed
Dash of monosodium glutamate
Salt and freshly ground pepper
1/2 head cauliflower, grated
1/2 c. grated bread crumbs

Tear romaine into bite-sized pieces. Mix mayonnaise, lemon juice, cheese, garlic, monosodium glutamate, salt and pepper. Toss romaine with dressing; top with cauliflower and bread crumbs.

WILTED SALAD GREENS

6 slices bacon, cut up
3 eggs
1/4 c. sugar
2/3 c. cream
1/4 c. chopped onion
1 tsp. salt
Dash of pepper
1 qt. romaine, shredded
1/4 c. vinegar

Fry bacon until crisp; set aside. Beat eggs and sugar together; add cream, blending well. Add egg mixture to bacon and drippings. Cook over low heat, stirring constantly, until thickened. Combine romaine, onion, salt and pepper; pour dressing over. Add vinegar; toss until blended well. Garnish with egg slices.

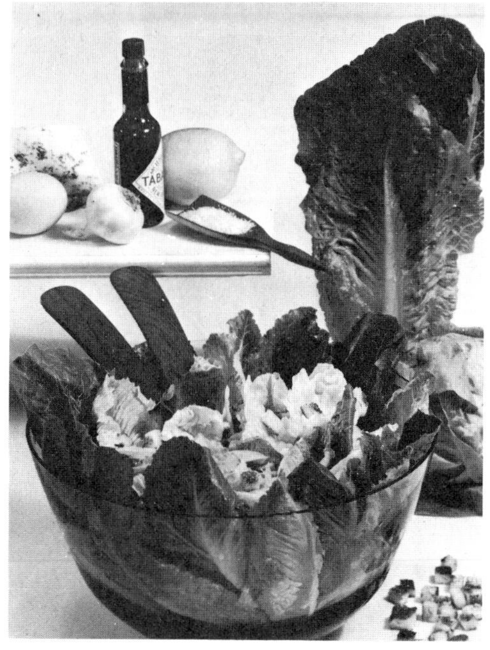

Romaine Caesar Salad . . . The classic main dish salad that features greens and a savory dressing.

ROMAINE CAESAR SALAD

Salad oil
1 garlic clove, minced
2 c. bread cubes
1 lge. head romaine
1 lge. head lettuce
1/4 c. grated Parmesan cheese
1/4 c. crumbled bleu cheese
1/4 c. lemon juice
1/4 tsp. Tabasco
3/4 tsp. salt
1/4 tsp. dry mustard
1 egg

Heat 2 tablespoons salad oil in skillet with garlic. Add bread cubes; heat until lightly browned. Tear crisp, chilled romaine and lettuce into bite-sized pieces into salad bowl; sprinkle with cheeses. Combine 1/2 cup oil, lemon juice, Tabasco, salt and dry mustard; shake to blend. Pour over salad greens; toss lightly. Break egg into salad; toss lightly until egg disappears. Add croutons, tossing well; serve immediately. Yield: 6 servings.

Rutabagas

Rutabagas are yellow-fleshed root vegetables that are members of the cabbage family. However, they are often known as yellow turnips. Rutabagas differ from white turnips in that their flavor is stronger, their shape is more elongated, and their flesh is denser. They are an excellent source of protein, carbohydrates, vitamins (A, C, niacin) and minerals (calcium, phosphorus, potassium). (4 ounces cooked rutabaga = 25 calories)

AVAILABILITY: Rutabagas are sold year-round with the most plentiful supplies available from October through March.

BUYING: Select smooth, firm, moderately elongated rutabagas that feel heavy for their size. There should be a minimum of leaf scars at the crown and of fibrous roots at the base. Avoid soft, shriveled, coarse, or light-weight specimens. Rutabagas are marketed without tops. They are often coated with a thin layer of paraffin to prevent the loss of moisture. To remove paraffin–Peel with a knife or food parer before cooking.

STORING: Keep rutabagas in a cool, moist, well-ventilated place for several months, ideally at 55 degrees; or refrigerate for 1 month. *To freeze*–Wash, peel and cut rutabagas into small pieces. Either parboil for 2 minutes, cool and drain; or boil until tender, drain, mash, and cool. Then pack rutabagas into freezer containers leaving 1/2-inch head space. Seal, label, and freeze.

PREPARATION: *To boil* rutabagas–Scrub; peel; and cut into larger pieces for mashing or dice. Cook covered in boiling salted water until tender. Cooking time ranges from 20 to 40 minutes, depending on the maturity of the vegetable and the size of the pieces. Drain, mash if desired, and season to taste. Or, follow the specific recipe directions for creaming, baking, or combining in stews, soups or casseroles.

(See VEGETABLES.)

BUTTERED RUTABAGAS

1 1/2 to 2 lb. rutabagas
1 1/2 tsp. Worcestershire sauce
1/4 tsp. onion powder
1/4 c. sugar
1 tsp. salt
3 to 4 drops of hot sauce
Butter to taste

Peel rutabagas; cut into small pieces. Place in saucepan. Add Worcestershire sauce, onion powder, sugar, salt and hot sauce. Cover with water; bring to a boil. Cook until tender. Add butter; mash with fork.

MASHED RUTABAGA

1 lge. rutabaga
1 tsp. salt
Pepper to taste
2 tbsp. butter
1/4 c. heavy cream

Peel rutabaga; cut into slices or cubes. Cook in boiling salted water for 15 to 20 minutes or until tender; drain thoroughly. Mash rutabaga with potato masher until smooth; add pepper and additional salt, if needed. Add butter and cream; heat and serve. Yield: 6 servings.

RUTABAGA SOUP

1 3-lb. meaty beef shank bone
2 tbsp. salt
4 qt. water
2 lb. rutabagas, cubed

Bring shank bone to a boil in salted water; cook until meat is tender. Add rutabagas. Cook until beef comes from bone and rutabagas are tender. Add water, if necessary. Yield: 6 servings.

SAUTEED RUTABAGA

2 slices bacon
1 lge. rutabaga, sliced

Cut bacon crosswise into small pieces; fry in skillet until crisp. Remove bacon. Place rutabaga in skillet. Cook, covered, over medium-high heat for 20 minutes or until tender, turning occasionally. Add bacon; heat through to serve. Yield: 3-4 servings.

FINNISH RUTABAGA PUDDING

2 lb. rutabagas
1 tsp. salt
4 tbsp. butter
2 tbsp. milk
1/2 tsp. sugar
1/8 tsp. ground nutmeg
1/8 tsp. ground pepper

Preheat oven to 375 degrees. Peel rutabagas; cut into quarters. Place in saucepan in 1 inch boiling water and salt. Bring to boiling point; cook, for 5 minutes. Cover; cook for 20 minutes longer or until rutabagas are soft. Mash and sieve. Add 2 tablespoons butter, milk, sugar, nutmeg and pepper. Mix well. Turn into greased 9-inch pie plate. Make indentations over top with tip of tablespoon. Pour remaining melted butter over surface. Bake for 40 to 45 minutes or until top is lightly browned. Garnish with sprig of parsley. Yield: 6 servings.

Finnish Rutabaga Pudding . . . A popular vegetable becomes an unusual and spicy dish.

RUTABAGA CASSEROLE

1 med. rutabaga
2 tbsp. butter
2 tbsp. white toast crumbs
1/2 c. milk
1 egg
White pepper to taste
1 tbsp. brown sugar
Salt to taste
Nutmeg to taste

Slice rutabaga. Cook until tender; mash. Mix in butter and 1 tablespoon crumbs. Add milk gradually. Add all remaining ingredients except nutmeg. Pour into well-greased mold or casserole; sprinkle remaining crumbs and nutmeg on top. Bake at 350 degrees for 30 minutes. Yield: 6-8 servings.

RUTABAGAS PARMESAN

2 tsp. brown sugar
1/4 c. finely grated Parmesan cheese
1/2 tsp. salt
1/4 tsp. pepper
1 lge. rutabaga
1 can beef consomme

Mix brown sugar, cheese, salt and pepper; set aside. Quarter rutabaga; slice sections into 1/4-inch slices. Place slices into greased deep casserole in layers, sprinkling each layer with cheese mixture. Pour beef consomme over top. Cover. Bake at 350 degrees for 1 hour. Bake, uncovered, for 30 minutes longer or until tender. Yield: 4-6 servings.

SWEET RUTABAGAS

1 No. 2 can rutabagas
2 tbsp. brown sugar
1 tbsp. dark corn syrup
2 tbsp. butter
Marshmallows

Mix rutabagas and brown sugar in casserole; pour corn syrup over top. Dot with butter; cover with marshmallows. Bake, covered, at 350 degrees for 20 to 30 minutes. Yield: 5-6 servings.

Rye

Rye is a type of cereal grain that is often finely ground into flour. Unlike wheat flour, its cell structure is delicate and its gluten content unstable. (Gluten is the protein substance that causes doughs to rise evenly.) Rye flour is always darker than wheat flour. Because of its properties rye flour tends to produce a baked product that is moist and compact. It contains carbohydrates, calcium, and some B vitamins.

AVAILABILITY: Rye flour is usually available year-round in many health food stores and some local retail stores.

STORING: Store rye flour at room temperature in a tightly covered container.

PREPARATION: Used alone in home-baked goods, rye flour yields a heavy, compact product. For pumpernickel bread this is the preferred texture. For rye breads, a combination of rye flour and whole wheat or white flour will produce a lighter, less crumbly loaf. To substitute rye flour—Allow 1 1/4 cup rye flour for 1 cup all-purpose flour. The following hints are suggested in the preparation of rye-based breads: 1) do not sift the flour; 2) do not allow the dough to rise too long; and 3) scald the milk specified in the recipe.

USES: Rye flour is used in the commercial production of rye and pumpernickel breads and crackers. It is also used to prepare home-baked yeast and quick breads, rolls, muffins and biscuits.

CASSEROLE RYE BATTER BREAD

1 c. milk
3 tbsp. sugar
1 tbsp. salt
1 1/2 tbsp. shortening
1 pkg. yeast
1 tsp. caraway seed
3 c. sifted flour
1 1/2 c. rye flour

Scald milk; stir in sugar, salt and shortening. Cool to lukewarm; turn into mixing bowl. Pour 1 cup warm water in small bowl; sprinkle in yeast, stirring until dissolved. Stir into milk mixture, adding caraway seed. Add flour and rye flour all at once to milk mixture; mix until blended well. Cover bowl; let rise in warm place for 50 minutes. Preheat oven to 400 degrees. Stir batter down; mix vigorously for 30 seconds. Turn batter into greased 1 1/2-quart casserole. Bake for about 50 minutes or until bread tests done. Turn out on wire rack. Yield: 1 loaf.

HEIDELBERG RYE BREAD

1 yeast cake
1 tbsp. shortening
1 tsp. salt
1 tsp. sugar
1 tbsp. caraway seed
1/2 c. molasses
1/4 c. cocoa
2 c. rye flour
White flour

Combine 2 cups warm water, yeast, shortening, salt and sugar, mixing well; let stand for several minutes. Add remaining ingredients to make stiff elastic dough. Let rise for 1 hour and 30 minutes. Shape into loaves; let rise until doubled in bulk. Bake at 350 degrees for 45 to 60 minutes. Yield: 2 loaves.

HONEY-RYE BREAD

1/4 c. shortening
2 c. milk, scalded
3/4 c. honey
1 tbsp. salt
3 eggs, slightly beaten
2 pkg. yeast
4 c. whole wheat flour
2 c. rye flour
2 1/2 to 3 c. flour

Melt shortening in milk in 6-quart bowl; mix in honey and salt. Cool to lukewarm. Add eggs; mix thoroughly. Dissolve yeast in 1 cup water; stir into egg mixture. Add whole wheat flour and rye flour; mix well. Add enough flour to make stiff dough; let rest for 30 minutes. Place on floured board; knead in remaining flour. Place in greased bowl; cover. Let rise in warm place until doubled in bulk. Divide into 3 parts; place in 9 x 5 x 3-inch loaf pans. Cover; let rise to tops of pans. Bake at 375 degrees for 30 minutes or until browned.

ITALIAN RYE BREAD

1 cake yeast
6 c. flour
4 c. rye flour
2 1/2 tbsp. caraway seed
1 tsp. salt
Cornmeal

Dissolve yeast in 3 cups warm water. Add flours, caraway seed and salt; mix well. Turn out onto floured surface; knead well. Place in greased bowl in warm area; let rise until doubled in bulk. Turn out onto floured surface; knead. Form into 8 small round loaves. Sprinkle cookie sheet with cornmeal; place loaves on cookie sheet. Do not put into bread pans. Bake at 400 degrees for 30 to 40 minutes.

RIESKA

2 c. rye flour
Salt
2 tsp. sugar
2 tsp. baking powder
1 c. evaporated milk
Butter

Mix flour, 3/4 teaspoon salt, sugar and baking powder in bowl; stir in milk and 2 tablespoons melted butter until smooth. Turn onto buttered cookie sheet; pat out to 14 x 1/2-inch circle. Prick with fork; sprinkle with salt. Bake at 450 degrees for 10 minutes or until browned lightly. Cut into wedges; spread with butter. Serve immediately. Yield: 8-10 servings.

RYE-BRAN BREAD

8 c. flour
4 c. rye flour
3 c. all-bran
2 yeast cakes
2 tbsp. salt
1/3 c. (packed) brown sugar
Bacon drippings

Mix flours together; make a well in center. Add all-bran to well. Dissolve yeast in 1/2 cup warm water. Stir 5 cups warm water, salt, brown sugar and yeast mixture together; add all at once to flour mixture. Knead until dough is smooth and elastic. Form into 3 loaves; grease each loaf with bacon drippings. Place in loaf pans. Let rise until doubled in bulk. Bake in 400-degree oven for 15 minutes; reduce temperature to 375 degrees. Bake for 40 minutes longer. Yield: 3 loaves.

RYE BREAD

2 pkg. yeast
1/3 c. dark molasses
4 1/2 c. flour
Vegetable oil
1 tbsp. salt
2 c. rye flour
1 tsp. caraway seed
2 tbsp. grated orange rind

Sprinkle yeast over 2 cups lukewarm water; let stand for several minutes. Add molasses and 2 cups flour; beat well. Add 1/4 cup oil, salt, rye flour, remaining flour, caraway seed and orange rind; knead well. Place in greased bowl; let rise for 45 minutes or until doubled in bulk. Punch down; divide into 4 portions. Place in loaf pans. Grease top of loaves; let rise for 1 hour. Bake at 375 degrees for 45 minutes. Oil tops. Turn out onto board to cool. Yield: 4 loaves.

RYE-RAISIN BREAD

1/2 c. shortening
1/2 c. molasses
1 pkg. yeast
1/4 c. sugar
2 tbsp. salt
4 c. rye flour
1 lb. raisins
6 c. white flour

Melt shortening. Add 4 cups water and molasses; heat to lukewarm. Soften yeast in 1/4 cup warm water; add sugar, salt and yeast mixture to molasses mixture. Stir in rye flour and raisins. Stir in flour gradually, using part of flour for kneading bread. Knead in enough flour so dough is not sticky. Let rise in warm place until doubled in bulk; punch down. Let rise until doubled in bulk again; form into loaves. Let rise until doubled in bulk. Bake at 350 degrees for 1 hour. Yield: 4 loaves.

SWEDISH SWEET RYE BREAD

1 pkg. yeast
1 1/2 c. sifted rye flour
1/2 c. sugar
1 tsp. salt
3 tbsp. soft butter
1 tsp. aniseed
1 tbsp. minced candied orange peel
5 1/2 c. sifted flour

Soften yeast in 1/4 cup lukewarm water. Sift rye flour, sugar and salt together. Add 2 cups boiling water gradually; blend well. Stir in butter; cool to lukewarm. Blend in yeast, aniseed and orange peel. Mix in flour gradually to make stiff dough. Turn out on floured board. Let dough stand for several minutes. Knead dough for 10 minutes or until smooth. Place in greased bowl. Let rise until doubled in bulk or for 1 hour. Shape into 4 long rolls; place side by side on greased baking sheet. Let rise for 30 minutes. Bake in 375-degree oven for 50 minutes. Bread may be brushed with slightly beaten egg white mixed with 1/4 cup water during baking for a high gloss. Yield: 4 loaves.

SWEDISH RYE BREAD

2 cakes yeast
1 tbsp. sugar
7 to 8 c. flour
2 c. rye flour
1/2 c. (packed) brown sugar
3/4 c. molasses
1 tbsp. salt
2 tbsp. shortening
1 tbsp. caraway seed
1 tbsp. aniseed
Salad oil

Soften yeast in 3 cups warm water. Add sugar; let stand for 5 minutes. Stir in enough flour to make sponge. Combine rye flour, brown sugar, molasses, salt, shortening, caraway seed and aniseed in large bowl; add enough boiling water to make paste. Stir in yeast mixture; add enough remaining flour to make smooth, easily handled dough. Let rise until doubled in bulk. Knead down; shape in 4 loaves. Place in pans; let rise until doubled in bulk. Bake at 350 degrees for 1 hour. Cool; brush tops with salad oil.

SWISS BEER-RYE BREAD

4 c. rye flour
4 c. (or more) flour
2 c. beer
1/2 c. warmed molasses
2 pkg. yeast
1/3 c. margarine
2 tsp. salt
1 1/4 tbsp. caraway seed

Place rye flour and 3 cups flour in large bowl; make well in center. Pour all remaining ingredients except caraway seed and remaining flour in well; let stand for several minutes. Mix well; add caraway seed. Knead in remaining flour; place in bowl. Let rise until doubled in bulk. Shape into 2 loaves; place in greased loaf pans. Let rise until doubled in bulk. Bake at 350 degrees for 35 to 45 minutes or until loaves test done. Yield: 2 loaves.

TRADITIONAL RYE BREAD

2 cakes yeast
1 c. sugar
5 tsp. salt
1/4 c. melted shortening
1/4 c. molasses
7 to 8 c. flour
4 c. medium rye flour

Dissolve yeast in 4 cups warm water; add sugar, salt, shortening and molasses. Add 1/2 of the flour and 1/2 of the rye flour; beat until smooth. Stir in remaining rye flour; add enough remaining flour to make soft dough. Knead until smooth; let rise in warm place until doubled in bulk. Punch down; let rise until doubled in bulk. Shape into 4 loaves; place in loaf pans. Cover; let rise until doubled in bulk. Bake at 375 degrees for 35 to 40 minutes. Remove from pans; cool.

Saffron

Saffron, the dried stamens of a crocus, is considered one of the most precious spices. It is mild flavored and gold colored. It is available only in whole form and is used with baked foods, casseroles, and rice.

SAFFRON BREAD

6 c. flour
1/2 c. sugar
1 tsp. salt
1/4 tsp. nutmeg
1/4 tsp. mace
1 c. currants
1/2 lb. margarine
2 pkg. yeast
1 pkg. powdered saffron
1 c. scalded milk

Combine flour, sugar, salt, nutmeg, mace, currants and margarine in large bowl until blended. Soften yeast in 1/2 cup warm water; steep saffron in 1/2 cup hot water. Make well in flour mixture; add saffron water, scalded milk and yeast, mixing well. Place in greased bowl, turning dough to grease top. Cover; let rise until doubled in bulk. Form into loaves; let rise again until doubled in bulk. Bake in 375-degree oven for 15 minutes. Reduce oven temperature to 350 degrees; bake for 30 minutes longer. Yield: 2 loaves.

CORNISH-FRUITED SAFFRON BREAD

1/2 tsp. saffron threads
1 1/2 tsp. brandy
1 pkg. yeast
2 eggs
1/2 c. butter, melted
1 c. lukewarm milk
4 c. sifted flour
3/4 c. sugar
1/2 tsp. nutmeg
1/4 tsp. mace
1/4 c. raisins
1/4 c. currants
1/3 c. diced mixed candied fruits

Soak saffron in brandy for 15 minutes. Strain; discard saffron. Dissolve yeast in 1/4 cup lukewarm water; mix 1 beaten egg, butter and milk. Sift dry ingredients together. Add raisins, currants and candied fruits; mix well. Add yeast, butter mixture and brandy; mix well. Place in greased bowl, turning dough to grease top. Cover; let rise for 2 hours. Place on floured board; roll lightly in flour. Roll out 1/2 inch thick into rectangle. Roll, jelly roll fashion; fold ends under. Place on greased baking pan, seam side down. Beat remaining egg with 1 tablespoon water; brush over top. Let rise until doubled in bulk. Bake at 400 degrees for 5 minutes. Reduce oven temperature to 375 degrees; bake for 25 minutes. Reduce oven temperature to 350 degrees; bake for 20 minutes longer. Turn out on cake rack; cool before slicing.

Sage

Sage is an herb belonging to the mint family. It is available whole, rubbed, ground, and in commercially prepared poultry seasonings. Use sage in dressings, stews, and chowders.

SAGE BREAD

1 pkg. yeast
1 c. lukewarm cottage cheese
2 tbsp. sugar
1 tbsp. minced onion
1 tbsp. butter
2 tsp. powdered sage
1 tsp. salt
1/4 tsp. soda
1 egg
2 1/4 to 2 1/2 c. flour

Soften yeast in 1/4 cup warm water. Combine cottage cheese, sugar, onion, butter, sage, salt, soda, egg and yeast mixture; add flour, forming stiff dough. Cover; let rise for 50 minutes or until doubled in bulk. Stir down; let rise for 30 to 40 minutes. Place in greased 8-inch round casserole. Bake at 350 degrees for 40 to 50 minutes. Brush crust with butter; sprinkle with salt if desired.

SAGE-CARAWAY BREADSTICKS

1 c. lukewarm milk
1 tbsp. sugar
1 1/2 tsp. salt
1/2 tsp. nutmeg
1 tsp. leaf sage, crumbled
2 tsp. caraway seed
1 pkg. yeast
1 egg
1 c. soft butter
3 to 3 1/4 c. sifted flour

Combine milk, sugar, salt, nutmeg, sage and caraway seed. Add yeast; stir until dissolved. Add egg and butter; stir in flour to make soft dough. Refrigerate overnight. Roll into 8-inch long sticks. Place 1 inch apart on greased baking sheet. Let rise until doubled in bulk. Bake at 350 degrees for 12 to 15 minutes. Yield: 3 dozen.

SAGE DINNER BREAD

4 c. prepared biscuit mix
1 tsp. ground sage
1/2 c. butter
1 1/3 c. milk
2 tsp. grated onion
1 egg, slightly beaten

Combine biscuit mix and sage in medium bowl; cut in butter until mixture is crumbly. Add milk and onion. Divide dough into 18 parts; roll each part into 12-inch long rope. Braid 3 ropes together, pinching at ends to hold in place to make 6 braids. Place 3 braids, side by side, on cookie sheet, shaping ends in oval. Top with 2 more braids for middle layer; place remaining braid on top. Brush with egg. Bake at 375 degrees for 1 hour or until golden. Serve warm. Yield: 6-8 servings.

Salad Dressings

A salad dressing is a sauce used to flavor a salad. There are two groups of salad dressings: cooked and uncooked. *Cooked* salad dressings are prepared over heat and resemble white sauce. *Uncooked* salad dressings may be creamy or clear and are prepared from a mixture of an acid such as lemon juice or vinegar and an oil. Both are seasoned to complement the salads they accompany.

INGREDIENTS: There are two principal ingredients in both cooked and uncooked salad dressings: an acid and oil. The acid is usually vinegar. *Vinegars* come as red, white, and cider; the latter are extremely acidic. There are also herb-flavored vinegars. Tarragon is one of the most popular herb-flavored vinegars used in salad dressings. There are two other acids used in salad dressings: *dry sherry* and *lemon juice.* Lemon juice is less acidic than vinegar and so more of it is needed in a dressing. *Oils* include olive, safflower, corn, or peanut. By itself, olive oil has a rather strong flavor. A combination of 2 parts vegetable oil to 1 part olive oil retains the smoothness of olive oil while keeping its flavor from becoming overwhelming.

PREPARATION: *Cooked dressings*—Follow recipe instructions, keeping the heat low as a high temperature tends to toughen eggs, which are important ingredients in cooked dressings. *Uncooked dressings*—Use a covered glass jar to prepare uncooked dressings. To thicken the oil and to mellow the acid, try adding an ice cube just before shaking the dressing. Both cooked and uncooked dressings should be seasoned to harmonize with the salads they accompany. Follow recipe instructions or see HERBS and SPICES.

BOILED DRESSING

1/4 c. sugar
1 tsp. dry mustard
1 tsp. salt
2 tbsp. cornstarch
2 tbsp. vinegar
2 tbsp. lemon juice
2 tbsp. butter
2 egg yolks, beaten

Mix dry ingredients in saucepan; stir in vinegar, lemon juice, 1 1/2 cups water and butter. Cook over low heat, stirring frequently, until thickened. Add small amount of hot mixture to egg yolks gradually, stirring constantly. Stir egg yolk mixture into lemon juice mixture gradually, stirring constantly; cook for 1 minute longer. Remove from heat; cool. Place in jar; cover. Keep refrigerated.

DRESSING FOR POTATO SALAD

2 eggs, beaten
1 c. cream
1 1/2 tbsp. salt
3 tbsp. vinegar

Combine eggs and cream in saucepan; bring to a boil over low heat, stirring constantly until thickened. Add salt and vinegar; cool. Refrigerate until ready to use.

FLUFFY HONEY DRESSING

2 eggs
1/2 c. honey
1/4 c. lemon juice
2 tbsp. frozen orange juice
1/8 tsp. salt
1/2 c. heavy cream, whipped
2 tsp. grated lemon rind

Beat eggs; stir in honey, lemon juice, orange juice and salt. Cook over low heat, stirring constantly, until thickened; cool. Fold in whipped cream and lemon rind. Serve with fresh fruit. Yield: 2 cups.

FRUIT SALAD DRESSING

3 tbsp. butter
2 tbsp. flour
1/2 c. milk
3 egg yolks, beaten
1 1/2 tbsp. lemon juice
1/4 c. orange juice
2 tbsp. sugar
1/4 tsp. salt
1/4 tsp. prepared mustard

Melt butter; blend in flour. Add milk; cook over low heat, stirring, until mixture thickens and is bubbly. Stir in egg yolks; cook for 1 minute longer, stirring constantly. Remove from heat; stir in fruit juices, sugar, salt and mustard. Chill thoroughly before using. Yield: 1 cup dressing.

HOT DUTCH DRESSING

4 strips bacon, diced
1 egg
1/4 c. sugar
1 tbsp. vinegar

Fry bacon in skillet until crisp; drain and crumble. Beat egg; beat in sugar. Stir in vinegar and 1 tablespoon water; stir into pan drippings in skillet. Cook until slightly thickened, stirring constantly; remove from heat. Add bacon; cool slightly before using.

SALAD DRESSING FOR COLESLAW

1/4 c. vinegar
1 tsp. salt
2 tbsp. sugar
1 egg, beaten
1/2 tsp. prepared mustard
1 tbsp. margarine

Mix vinegar, 1/2 cup water, salt, sugar, egg and mustard together. Place margarine in small saucepan; melt over low heat. Add vinegar mixture; cook until thickened, stirring constantly. Cool.

AVOCADO-BACON DRESSING

1/2 c. mashed ripe avocado
1 tbsp. lemon juice
1/2 c. sour cream
1/3 c. salad oil
1 clove of garlic, minced
1/2 tsp. sugar
1/2 tsp. chili powder
1/4 tsp. salt
1/4 tsp. hot sauce
4 slices chopped cooked bacon

Combine all ingredients in blender container; blend well. Chill until ready to serve.

AVOCADO SALAD DRESSING

1 egg, beaten
1/2 tsp. dry mustard
1/2 c. salad oil
1/4 tsp. hot sauce
Juice of 2 lemons
1 tbsp. Worcestershire sauce
2 avocados
2 fresh green onions, chopped
1/2 tsp. salt
1/2 tsp. pepper
Garlic salt to taste
1/2 c. mayonnaise

Blend egg and mustard together; add oil. Mix thoroughly; add hot sauce, lemon juice and Worcestershire sauce. Mash avocados; add onions, salt, pepper and garlic salt. Mix well; add mayonnaise. Chill for 2 hours. Serve over lettuce. Yield: 6-8 servings.

CELERY SEED DRESSING

1 1/4 c. sugar
2 tsp. dry mustard
2 tsp. salt
1 tbsp. onion juice
2/3 c. vinegar
2 c. salad oil
2 tbsp. celery seed

Mix sugar, mustard, salt, onion juice and half the vinegar; beat well. Add oil and remaining vinegar alternately; beat until mixture holds together. Stir in celery seed.

SWEET CELERY SEED DRESSING

10 tbsp. sugar
1/2 tsp. grated onion
1 tsp. salt
1 tsp. dry mustard
1/3 c. white vinegar
1 c. vegetable oil
1 tbsp. celery seed

Blend sugar, onion, salt and mustard in small electric mixer bowl. Add vinegar and oil alternately by spoonfuls, beating constantly with electric mixer. Add celery seed, stirring in by hand. Store in refrigerator.

BLEU CHEESE DRESSING

1 env. French salad dressing mix
1/2 c. sour cream
1/2 c. crumbled bleu cheese

Prepare salad dressing mix according to package directions. Add salad dressing to sour cream gradually, stirring constantly. Add bleu cheese; mix well. Yield: 1 3/4 cups.

CHEDDAR SALAD DRESSING

1/3 c. tarragon vinegar
1 c. salad oil
1/4 tsp. pepper
1/4 tsp. dry mustard
1 tsp. salt
1 tsp. sugar
Dash of cayenne pepper
1/2 c. grated sharp Cheddar cheese

Combine all ingredients except cheese in jar; shake thoroughly. Chill. Add cheese just before serving. Serve over orange, grapefruit or desired fruit salads.

COTTAGE CHEESE DRESSING

1 c. cottage cheese
2 tbsp. mayonnaise
1/4 tsp. paprika
1 tsp. Worcestershire sauce
Salt and pepper

Combine all ingredients; blend well. Yield: 1 cup.

DRESSING FOR CAESAR SALAD

1 egg
3/4 c. salad oil
1/4 c. lemon juice
1 tsp. salt
1/4 tsp. pepper
1 tbsp. Worcestershire sauce
1/4 c. grated Parmesan cheese

Place egg in boiling water for 1 minute. Break into bowl; beat until fluffy. Beat at high speed, adding oil gradually. Reduce speed; add all remaining ingredients. Yield: 12 servings.

FLUFFY CHEESE DRESSING

1 3-oz. package cream cheese
2 tbsp. mayonnaise
2 tbsp. maraschino cherry juice
1 tbsp. milk
2 tsp. lemon juice
1 2-oz. package dessert topping mix
1 tbsp. minced maraschino cherries

Combine cream cheese, mayonnaise, cherry juice, milk and lemon juice; beat until smooth. Prepare topping mix according to package directions; fold into cream cheese mixture. Stir in cherries; chill. Whip chilled mixture until fluffy. Serve over fruit salads.

ROQUEFORT-BUTTERMILK DRESSING

1 c. buttermilk
1/2 c. mayonnaise
Pinch of salt
4 oz. Roquefort cheese, crumbled

Combine buttermilk, mayonnaise and salt. Add cheese; stir well. Store in covered container in refrigerator. Yield: 2 cups.

ROQUEFORT-ANCHOVY DRESSING

1/3 c. chopped green onions
2 c. mayonnaise
2 cloves of garlic, pressed
1/2 c. chopped parsley
2 tbsp. anchovy paste
1/2 c. vinegar
2 tbsp. lemon juice
6 oz. Roquefort cheese, crumbled
Salt and pepper to taste

Combine onions, mayonnaise, garlic and parsley. Blend anchovy paste, vinegar and lemon juice; add to mayonnaise mixture. Beat cheese into dressing; season with salt and pepper. Chill well.

ROQUEFORT DRESSING

1 pt. sour cream
1 pt. mayonnaise
1/2 pt. salad dressing
2 tbsp. wine vinegar
1 tbsp. lemon juice
1 tbsp. sugar
1/2 tsp. salt
6 oz. Roquefort cheese, crumbled

Blend all ingredients together except cheese; blend well. Add cheese. Let stand overnight in refrigerator. Yield: 1 1/2 quarts.

CHEF'S SALAD DRESSING

1 tsp. sugar
1 tsp. salt
1/8 tsp. pepper
2 tsp. grated onion
Dash of paprika
1/3 c. salad oil
2 tbsp. vinegar
2 tbsp. catsup

Combine all ingredients in jar; cover. Shake well to mix. Yield: 6 servings.

FRENCH DRESSING

1 c. catsup
1 c. vegetable oil
Juice of 1 lemon
1/2 c. white vinegar
1/2 c. sugar
1 sm. onion, grated
1/2 tsp. salt

Place all ingredients in 1-quart jar; cover tightly. Shake vigorously. Refrigerate until ready to serve.

ROYAL FRENCH DRESSING

1/2 c. sugar
1/2 c. salad oil
2 tbsp. catsup
1 tsp. salt
1 tsp. paprika
1 sm. onion, grated
1/2 tsp. garlic powder
1/4 c. vinegar
1 tbsp. lemon juice

Place all ingredients except vinegar and lemon juice in bowl; beat until thick. Add vinegar and lemon juice, beating constantly.

TOMATO FRENCH DRESSING

1 10 3/4-oz. can tomato soup
1/2 soup can vinegar
1/2 soup can salad oil
2 tbsp. minced onion
2 tbsp. sugar
2 tsp. dry mustard
1 tsp. salt
1/4 tsp. pepper

Combine soup, vinegar, oil, onion and seasonings in 1-quart jar; shake well before using. May vary recipe by adding crumbled blue cheese, chopped hard-cooked egg, minced green pepper, minced garlic or curry powder. Yield: About 2 2/3 cups dressing.

Tomato French Dressing . . . Prepare this authentic French dressing easily by using tomato soup.

GARLIC DRESSING

1 1/3 c. olive oil
1/2 c. vinegar
1 tsp. sugar
1 1/2 tsp. salt
1/2 tsp. dry mustard
4 cloves of garlic, sliced

Combine all ingredients in jar; cover. Shake well. Yield: 2 cups.

GREEN GODDESS SALAD DRESSING

1 c. mayonnaise
1/2 c. sour cream
1/4 tsp. garlic powder
2 green onions and tops, chopped
1/4 c. chopped green pepper
2 tbsp. lemon juice
1/4 c. minced parsley
1/4 tsp. pepper
3 anchovy fillets
Dash of Worcestershire sauce

Place all ingredients in blender container; cover. Blend for 10 seconds at high speed or until pale green and smooth. Yield: 2 cups.

ITALIAN DRESSING

1/2 c. (packed) brown sugar
1/2 c. vinegar
1/2 c. catsup
1/2 c. salad oil
1 sm. onion, minced
1 clove of garlic, minced
Pinch of dry mustard
Salt and pepper to taste

Combine all ingredients. Blend thoroughly.

POPPY SEED DRESSING

2 tbsp. sugar
1 tsp. salt
1/3 c. honey
2 tbsp. prepared mustard
2 tbsp. vinegar
2/3 c. salad oil
1 tbsp. minced onion
3 tsp. poppy seed

Combine sugar, salt, honey, mustard and vinegar. Add oil gradually, beating with electric mixer; stir in onion and poppy seed. Chill. Shake well before using.

REMOULADE DRESSING

2 hard-cooked egg yolks, sieved
2 cloves of garlic, crushed
1 1/2 tbsp. prepared mustard
1 1/2 c. mayonnaise
2 tbsp. vinegar
1 tbsp. Worcestershire sauce
Dash of hot sauce
2 tbsp. (heaping) minced parsley
1 tbsp. paprika
Salt and pepper to taste

Combine all ingredients in bowl; mix well. Pour into jar; refrigerate for 2 hours before serving. Serve on green salad or chilled cooked shrimp. Yield: 1 pint.

RIM BAK DRESSING

1 clove of garlic, minced
1 c. mayonnaise
1/2 c. salad oil
1/2 tsp. salt
1 tbsp. vinegar
1 tbsp. Worcestershire sauce
1/4 c. chili sauce
1 tbsp. prepared French mustard
1 tsp. pepper
Dash of hot sauce
Dash of paprika
Juice of 1 med. onion

Combine all ingredients and 2 tablespoons water in jar; shake well. Serve on lettuce or green salad.

RUSSIAN DRESSING

1/2 tsp. salt
1/2 tsp. paprika
1 1/2 tsp. celery seed
Juice of 1 lemon
1 tbsp. vinegar
1 c. salad oil
1 tbsp. Worcestershire sauce
1/2 c. catsup
1/4 c. grated onion
1/4 c. light corn syrup

Combine all ingredients; beat well. Chill. Yield: 2 cups.

SOUR CREAM-ANCHOVY SALAD DRESSING

1/2 pt. sour cream
1 c. mayonnaise
1 sm. can anchovies, minced
3 tbsp. minced green onion
1/2 clove of garlic, pressed
2 tbsp. lemon juice
1 tsp. salt
1/2 tsp. pepper

Combine all ingredients in blender container; blend. Chill for 2 hours before serving. Yield: 2 cups.

SOUR CREAM DRESSING FOR CUCUMBER SALAD

1 c. sour cream
2 tbsp. lemon juice
2 tbsp. vinegar
1 tsp. prepared mustard
1/2 c. finely chopped cucumber
1 tbsp. sugar
1/4 tsp. paprika

Beat sour cream until smooth, thick and light. Mix all remaining ingredients together; add to sour cream gradually. Mix well. Yield: 2 cups.

PIQUANT THOUSAND ISLAND DRESSING

1/2 c. mayonnaise
2 tbsp. chili sauce
2 tbsp. chopped green pepper
1 chopped hard-boiled egg
Salt and pepper
12 stuffed olives, chopped
1 sm. sweet pickle, chopped
2 sm. green onions, chopped

Blend mayonnaise with chili sauce; add all remaining ingredients. Refrigerate until ready to use. Yield: 1 1/2 cups.

VINAIGRETTE SALAD DRESSING

1 1/2 c. salad oil
1/2 c. vinegar
1/4 sm. onion
1 1-in. strip green pepper
1 1/2-in. strip pimento

1 tsp. salt	*2 drops of hot sauce*
1 tsp. sugar	

Place all ingredients in blender container. Blend at low speed until vegetables are minced. Yield: 2 cups.

QUICK THOUSAND ISLAND DRESSING

2 hard-boiled eggs, mashed	*1 sm. bottle catsup*
1 pt. mayonnaise	*Salt and pepper to taste*

Blend ingredients together well. Chill.

VINEGAR AND OIL DRESSING

1/4 c. vinegar	*1 onion, chopped*
1 tsp. celery seed	*1/2 c. sugar*
1 tsp. mustard	*1 c. vegetable oil*

Place vinegar, celery seed, mustard, onion and sugar in mixer bowl; beat with electric mixer until blended. Beat in oil gradually. Yield: 6-8 servings.

Salmon

Salmon are perhaps one of the best-known and most popular of all fish. They annually provide one of the most awesome and intriguing spectacles in nature when, en masse, they leave their ocean home to go upriver, against the currents, and return to their birthplaces to spawn. There is only one variety ot Atlantic salmon. The five varieties of Pacific salmon include Sockeye or Red Salmon; Chinook or King Salmon that may weigh up to 100 pounds; Medium Red, Coho, or silver salmon; Chum or Keta Salmon; and Pink Salmon, the smallest of the five. Salmon are primarily a low calorie, high protein food that contains calcium and Vitamins A, B, and D. (3 ounces canned salmon = 173 calories; 1 1/3 ounces baked fresh salmon = 140 calories)

AVAILABILITY: Salmon are available year-round in fresh, frozen, canned, salted, and smoked forms. Peak season for fresh salmon is summer to early fall when the fish are spawning. Fresh salmon is sold whole or in fillets and steaks.

BUYING: In buying fresh salmon, look for bright, clear, bulging eyes; red or pink, clean, fresh-smelling gills; bright, shiny, tight scales; and firm flesh that springs back when pressed. There should be no odor. Allow 3/4 to 1 pound fresh salmon per serving.

STORING: Wrap fresh salmon in moisture-proof paper or place it in a covered dish. Store in refrigerator for 1-2 days. Canned salmon, unopened, keeps on the kitchen shelf for up to 1 year; opened, it keeps 3-4 days in the refrigerator. *To freeze* fresh or smoked salmon, wrap in moisture- and vapor-proof paper. Seal, label, and freeze. Salmon keeps in the refrigerator freezer 3-4 months, in the home freezer for up to 1 year.

PREPARATION: Thaw frozen fish in refrigerator, 24 hours for each 1 pound fish. For quicker thawing, place wrapped package under cold running water. Never thaw fish at room temperature or in warm water. Fresh and canned salmon can be baked, steamed, broiled, poached, grilled, or fried.

SERVING: Serve fresh or canned salmon as an entree or in a variety of hot and cold dishes such as casseroles, souffles, loaves, salads, and sandwiches. Serve smoked salmon cold as an appetizer or main dish.

(See SEAFOOD.)

HOT SALMON SANDWICHES

4 slices toasted bread	*1 pkg. dried cream of mushroom soup*
4 hard-boiled eggs, quartered	*1 can salmon, drained and flaked*
1/2 c. grated Cheddar cheese	*1/2 c. crushed potato chips*
2 c. cold milk	

Place toast in square shallow casserole. Arrange eggs on toast; sprinkle with cheese. Add milk to soup gradually; heat in saucepan, stirring, until soup comes to a boil. Reduce heat; stir in salmon. Pour over toast. Sprinkle with chips. Bake at 425 degrees for 10 to 15 minutes.

SALMON-COTTAGE CHEESE SANDWICH

Whole wheat bread slices, toasted	*Cottage cheese*
Butter	*Sliced tomato*
Flaked salmon	*Seasonings to taste*

Spread half the toast slices with butter. Add layer of salmon; cover with layer of cottage cheese. Add tomato slices and seasonings; top with remaining toast slices.

SALMON-POTATO SOUP

4 med. potatoes, diced	*1 stick butter*
1 qt. milk	*1 sm. onion, finely chopped*
1 pt. half and half cream	*Salt and pepper to taste*
1 No. 2 can salmon	

Cook potatoes in large saucepan in salted water to cover until just tender. Add milk, cream, salmon, butter and onion. Season with salt and pepper. Simmer for 20 to 30 minutes.

EASY SALMON SOUP

1 can pink salmon
1 qt. milk
1/4 c. butter
Salt and pepper
1/2 tsp. Worcestershire sauce

Drain and flake salmon; remove skin and bones. Scald milk in top of double boiler over boiling water. Stir in salmon, butter, salt, pepper and Worcestershire sauce. Simmer for 30 minutes or until heated through.

SALMON BISQUE

1 1-lb. can pink salmon
1 c. canned tomatoes
1/2 c. chopped onion
2 tbsp. chopped parsley
4 tbsp. butter
4 tbsp. flour
3 c. milk
1 1/2 tsp. salt
1/2 tsp. paprika

Simmer salmon, tomatoes, onion, parsley and 2 cups water for 20 minutes. Melt butter in large saucepan, blend in flour. Stir milk in gradually; add salt and paprika. Cook, stirring, until smooth and boiling; stir in salmon mixture gradually. Bring just to a boil; remove from heat. Serve immediately. Yield: 5 servings.

BASIC SALMON SALAD

1 head lettuce, coarsely shredded
1/3 c. chopped celery
1/3 c. slivered green pepper
1 tbsp. chopped parsley
1 tbsp. chopped chives
2/3 c. cubed cucumber
1/2 c. mayonnaise
1/8 tsp. hot sauce
1 tsp. lemon juice
2 hard-cooked eggs
2 tomatoes
1 1 lb. can salmon, coarsely flaked

Combine lettuce, celery, green pepper, parsley, chives and cucumber in wooden bowl. Mix mayonnaise with hot sauce and lemon juice; add to vegetable mixture and toss. Cut eggs and tomatoes into wedges; add to salad. Add salmon, tossing lightly.

CANADIAN SALMON MOLD

2 tbsp. unflavored gelatin
1 c. hot chicken bouillon
1 c. mayonnaise
3 tbsp. chili sauce
2 tbsp. lemon juice
1 tbsp. finely chopped onion
1/2 tsp. Worcestershire sauce
1/2 tsp. monosodium glutamate
Salt and pepper to taste
1 c. finely diced celery
1/2 c. sliced stuffed olives
1 c. cooked salmon, flaked

Soften gelatin in 1/2 cup cold water; dissolve in hot bouillon. Cool slightly; add to mayonnaise gradually, blending well after each addition. Add chili sauce, lemon juice, onion, Worcestershire sauce, monosodium glutamate, salt and pepper; chill until partially set. Combine celery, olives and salmon; add to chilled mixture. Turn into greased 5-cup mold; chill until firm.

MAGIC SALMON MOLD

2 c. canned salmon
2 pkg. lime gelatin
1/4 c. mild vinegar
3 tbsp. lemon juice
1 tsp. salt
2 c. finely shredded cabbage
3 hard-cooked eggs, sliced

Drain and flake salmon; remove skin and bones. Place salmon in bottom of mold. Dissolve gelatin in 1 1/2 cups boiling water; add 1 1/4 cups cold water, vinegar, lemon juice and salt. Pour half the gelatin over salmon; chill until set. Fill mold with alternating layers of cabbage and eggs; cover with remaining gelatin. Chill until set.

SALMON-CUCUMBER MOLD

1 pkg. unflavored gelatin
1 1/4 tsp. salt
1 tsp. sugar
2 tsp. lemon juice
1 tsp. vinegar
1/2 tsp. pepper
1 cucumber, finely grated
1 1-lb. can red salmon

Soften gelatin in 1/4 cup cold water for 5 minutes; add 1/2 cup boiling water, stirring until dissolved. Add salt, sugar, lemon juice, vinegar and pepper; cool. Add cucumber with juice. Chill until slightly congealed, stirring occasionally. Remove skin and bones from salmon; flake. Fold into gelatin mixture. Turn into lightly greased mold; chill until firm.

SALMON MOUSSE

2 env. unflavored gelatin
1/2 c. vinegar
4 c. flaked salmon
2 c. finely chopped celery
2 tbsp. sugar
2 tbsp. pickle relish
2 tsp. mustard
2 1/2 tsp. salt
1 c. heavy cream, whipped

Soften gelatin in 1/2 cup cold water and vinegar; dissolve over boiling water. Cool. Stir in salmon, celery, sugar, relish, mustard and salt; fold in whipped cream. Pour into fish-shaped mold; chill until set.

SALMON-AVOCADO YU SUNG

3 ripe halved avocados, seeded
1 tbsp. lemon juice
1 sm. can salmon
3 tbsp. sour cream
2 tbsp. mayonnaise
1 tsp. soy sauce
1 5-oz. can water chestnuts, slivered
1 tbsp. chopped preserved ginger
1/4 c. chopped ripe olives
2 tbsp. chopped green onions
Carrot curls
Parsley

Sprinkle cut surfaces of avocados with lemon juice. Drain and flake salmon, reserving liquid. Combine sour cream, mayonnaise, soy sauce and reserved liquid. Add salmon, water chestnuts, ginger, olives and onions; mix lightly. Pile salad into avocado halves; garnish with carrot curls and parsley. Serve on lettuce if desired.

BAKED SALMON WITH LEMON SAUCE

1 c. chopped celery
1/2 c. chopped green pepper
6 c. bread cubes
1/2 c. sliced stuffed olives
2 tbsp. chopped parsley
1/4 tsp. pepper
1 clove of garlic, minced
Salt
4 tbsp. lemon juice
Melted margarine
2 lb. salmon steak
Garlic salt to taste
Paprika to taste
2 egg yolks, beaten
1 1/2 c. medium white sauce

Combine first 7 ingredients with 1 cup hot water; add 1 tablespoon salt, 2 tablespoons lemon juice and 1/2 cup melted margarine. Place in shallow greased baking dish; place salmon on top. Brush with additional margarine; sprinkle with additional salt, garlic salt and paprika. Bake in 350-degree oven for 1 hour and 30 minutes. Combine egg yolks, remaining lemon juice and white sauce in double boiler. Cook over boiling water, stirring constantly, until heated through. Serve sauce over salmon. Garnish with parsley.

BAKED SALMON WITH SAUCE

1 1-lb. can salmon
1 c. cracker crumbs
5 tbsp. melted butter
1/2 c. light cream
4 eggs
2 tsp. flour
1 c. milk

Drain salmon, reserve liquid. Combine salmon, crumbs, 4 tablespoons butter and cream. Separate 3 eggs; add beaten egg yolks to salmon mixture. Fold in stiffly beaten egg whites. Turn into casserole. Bake at 350 degrees for 25 minutes. Beat remaining egg. Blend flour into remaining butter; add milk, reserved liquid and beaten egg. Cook, stirring, until thickened and bubbly. Serve sauce with salmon.

BAKED STUFFED SALMON

1 10-lb. salmon, dressed
Salt
3 tbsp. lemon juice
1 c. chopped celery
1 c. chopped celery leaves
2 onions, chopped
1/2 c. butter
1/2 lb. mushrooms, sliced
1 loaf whole wheat bread, crumbled
2 tsp. poultry seasoning
1/4 tsp. pepper
1 8-oz. bottle stuffed olives

Rub inside of salmon with 1 tablespoon salt; sprinkle with lemon juice. Saute celery, celery leaves and onions in butter in skillet; add mushrooms. Cook for 5 minutes. Combine celery mixture with crumbs; add seasonings. Chop olives; add to stuffing. Place stuffing in one side of salmon; sew sides together. Place salmon in greased baking dish; sprinkle with 1 teaspoon salt. Bake in 425-degree oven, allowing 10 minutes to the pound; baste frequently. May serve with rich white sauce and hard-cooked egg slices if desired. Yield: 15-20 servings.

FOIL-BAKED SALMON

1 10-lb. salmon, dressed
1/2 lb. butter
1 lge. onion, sliced

Split salmon in half lengthwise; arrange on large piece of aluminum foil, skin side down. Cover with thin slices of butter; top with onion slices. Wrap foil around salmon securely. Cook on grate over campfire or on charcoal broiler until fish flakes easily.

SURPRISE SALMON RING

1 California lemon
10 2-lb. thin fish fillets
Salt
Paprika to taste
2 tsp. grated fresh lemon peel
2 tbsp. fresh lemon juice
1 tbsp. instant minced onions
1 1-lb. can salmon
1/4 c. dry bread crumbs
1 tbsp. dry parsley flakes
1/8 tsp. pepper
2 tbsp. catsup

Cut lemon into 5 slices; arrange in bottom of greased 6-cup ring mold. Sprinkle fillets with salt to taste and paprika. Line mold with fillets, arranging fillets crosswise and overlapping. Leave tips of fillets extended outside of mold. Combine grated lemon peel, lemon juice and onions; let stand for 5 minutes. Drain and flake salmon. Combine lemon juice mixture, salmon, bread crumbs, 1/4 teaspoon salt, parsley, pepper and catsup. Pack salmon mixture into fish-lined mold. Fold tips of fillets over filling. Cover mold with aluminum foil, crimping around edges to seal tightly. Place in pan filled with 1 inch hot water. Bake at 400 degrees for 40 minutes. Remove foil; let cool for 5 minutes. Tilt pan slightly to drain off excess liquid. Loosen around edges with spatula; turn out onto serving plate. Fill center with creamed peas if desired.

Surprise Salmon Ring . . . Lemon, onion, salmon, and catsup combine in a mold perfect for buffets.

SALMON IN BARBECUE SAUCE

1 5-lb. salmon
Salt and pepper to taste
Butter
1 lge. onion, chopped
1 bottle catsup
1 tsp. soy sauce
1 tsp. mustard
1 tsp. Worcestershire sauce
Hot sauce

Cut salmon into serving pieces; place in foil-lined shallow baking dish. Sprinkle with salt and pepper. Melt small amount of butter; drizzle over salmon. Fold foil over salmon. Bake at 350 degrees for 30 minutes. Saute onion in 1/4 pound butter; add catsup, soy sauce, mustard, Worcestershire sauce and several drops of hot sauce. Simmer until thick; pour over salmon. Bake for 30 minutes or until salmon flakes easily, basting frequently with sauce. Yield: 8 servings.

SALMON MOUSSE WITH HOLLANDAISE SAUCE

2 16-oz. cans salmon
1 c. cream
6 eggs
2 tbsp. chopped green onion
1 tbsp. chopped parsley
1/2 tsp. salt
1/4 tsp. pepper
1 pkg. hollandaise sauce mix

Preheat oven to 400 degrees. Drain and flake salmon, removing skin and bones. Combine salmon, cream, eggs, onion, parsley, salt and pepper in large mixer bowl. Beat with electric mixer until smooth; pour into greased 6-cup ring mold. Place mold in large pan half filled with boiling water. Bake for 1 hour or until knife inserted in center comes out clean. Remove mold from pan of water. Bake for 20 minutes longer. Loosen mold; invert onto serving plate. Prepare sauce mix according to package directions. Serve sauce with mousse.

SALMON PUFF

1 tbsp. butter
2 tbsp. flour
3/4 c. milk
1 1-lb. can salmon
1 stalk celery, chopped
1 sm. onion, chopped
Chopped parsley to taste
Dash of pepper
1 tsp. salt
1 tbsp. dry mustard
2 eggs, separated

Preheat oven to 350 degrees. Melt butter in saucepan; stir in flour until smooth. Add milk gradually; cook over low heat, stirring constantly, until thickened. Drain salmon; flake. Add to white sauce; add celery, onion, parsley, pepper, salt and mustard. Stir in beaten egg yolks. Beat egg whites until stiff; fold into salmon mixture. Pour into greased 1 1/2-quart casserole. Bake for 35 minutes. Yield: 4-6 servings.

SALMON SUPREME

4 salmon steaks
Salt and pepper
2 tbsp. chopped onions
1 c. shredded Cheddar cheese
1/2 pt. sour cream
1 tbsp. chopped parsley
Paprika

Place salmon in greased shallow baking dish; sprinkle with salt, pepper and onions. Sprinkle with cheese; spoon sour cream over salmon. Sprinkle with parsley and paprika. Bake for 30 minutes in 350-degree oven or until salmon flakes easily.

SALMON WITH WATER CHESTNUT DRESSING

8 1/4-in. salmon steaks
1 1/4 c. dry white wine
2 eggs, slightly beaten
1 can cream of chicken soup
1 5-oz. can water chestnuts
1 pkg. frozen spinach, thawed
1 8-oz. package stuffing mix
2 tsp. powdered sage
2 tbsp. butter, melted

Marinate salmon in 1/2 cup wine for 30 minutes. Combine eggs, soup and remaining wine, beating until smooth. Drain and slice water chestnuts; add water chestnuts and remaining ingredients to wine mixture. Mix well. Arrange salmon in foil-lined shallow pan; top with dressing, patting down firmly. Bake at 350 degrees for 45 minutes.

COMPANY SALMON CASSEROLE

1 5-oz. package yellow rice mix
1 1-lb. can salmon
1 can cream of celery soup
1 3-oz. can sliced mushrooms
1/2 c. chopped walnuts
3/4 c. grated cheese

Cook rice according to package directions. Drain and flake salmon, remove skin and bones. Flake coarsely. Combine salmon, soup, 1/2 soup can water and mushrooms in large mixing bowl. Fold rice into salmon mixture gently. Pour into 3-quart greased casserole; sprinkle with walnuts and cheese. Bake in 350-degree oven for 30 minutes. Garnish with fresh parsley.

SAUCY SALMON WITH GREEN SAUCE

1 1-lb. can salmon
1 4-oz. jar pimento
1 1/2 c. minced cooked carrots
1 c. minced cooked potatoes
3/4 c. cooked corn
3/4 c. cooked peas
2 tbsp. minced onion
1 c. fine cracker crumbs
1/2 tsp. salt
1/8 tsp. pepper
1/8 tsp. thyme
1 1/2 c. milk
2 eggs, separated
1 vegetable bouillon cube
1/4 lb. fresh spinach
2 tbsp. butter
2 tbsp. flour
1/4 c. sour cream
1 tsp. lemon juice

Drain and flake salmon. Drain and mince pimento. Combine salmon, pimento, carrots, potatoes, corn, peas, onion, cracker crumbs and seasonings in large bowl. Stir in 1 cup milk and beaten egg yolks; mix well. Beat egg whites until stiff; fold into salmon mixture. Turn mixture into heavily greased 1 1/2-quart ring mold. Cover mold tightly with foil; set mold in pan containing 1 inch hot water. Bake at

375 degrees for 20 minutes. Remove foil; bake for 30 minutes longer. Combine bouillon cube and boiling water in saucepan, stirring until bouillon cube is dissolved. Add spinach; cook, covered, for 5 minutes or until spinach is wilted. Turn into blender container; process until spinach is pureed. Melt butter in saucepan; blend in flour. Stir in remaining milk gradually; add spinach puree. Cook, stirring constantly, for 3 minutes, or until thickened. Blend in sour cream and lemon juice, keep warm. Remove salmon ring from oven; let stand for 5 minutes. Invert ring onto serving platter. Serve sauce with salmon mold.

GOLDEN FISH CASSEROLE

2 med. thinly sliced onions
1 sm. green pepper, thinly sliced
1 tbsp. butter
4 tbsp. flour
3/4 tsp. salt
2 c. milk
1 1-lb. can salmon, flaked
1 tbsp. lemon juice
1 basic biscuit recipe
2 chopped pimentos
3/8 c. grated sharp cheese

Saute onions and green pepper in skillet in butter for 5 minutes; blend in flour and salt. Remove from heat; stir milk in gradually. Return to heat; bring to a boil, stirring constantly. Cook for 5 minutes; stir in salmon and lemon juice carefully. Pour salmon mixture into greased deep 8-inch baking dish. Bake in 400-degree oven for 10 minutes. Roll biscuit dough out 1/4 inch thick into rectangle; sprinkle with pimentos and cheese. Roll up tightly; cut into eight 1-inch slices. Place biscuits on hot salmon mixture. Bake for 30 minutes or until rolls are lightly browned. Yield: 8 servings.

SALMON AU GRATIN

1 1-lb. can salmon
1 c. chopped celery
1 sm. grated onion
1/3 c. butter
1/3 c. flour
1 tsp. salt
1/4 tsp. pepper
3 c. scalded milk
2 c. cooked rice
1 4-oz. can mushrooms, drained
1/2 lb. grated American cheese
1/4 c. minced parsley

Drain salmon; flake. Combine celery and onion in butter in saucepan; saute for 5 minutes. Blend in flour, salt and pepper; add milk gradually. Cook, stirring constantly, until thickened and smooth. Stir in salmon, rice, mushrooms and cheese; turn into casserole. Bake at 350 degrees for 20 minutes or until bubbly and heated through. Garnish with parsley. Yield: 6 servings.

CHARCOAL-BROILED SALMON

1 6-lb. whole silver salmon, dressed
Slivered almonds to taste
Melted butter
Paprika
Salt to taste
Pepper to taste

Cut salmon in half lengthwise. Combine almonds and 3 tablespoons butter; keep warm. Sprinkle paprika, salt and pepper on cut sides of salmon. Place salmon on charcoal grill, meat side down; sear for 3 to 4 minutes. Place enough aluminum foil over top of salmon to cover skin; turn foil-covered side over. Brush butter over seared meat; add almonds. Place aluminum foil quickly over salmon to hold in heat. Raise grill to 4 inches above coals; cook for about 20 minutes or until salmon flakes easily.

SALMON-NOODLE CASSEROLE

1/4 c. butter
1/4 c. flour
1/4 tsp. dry mustard
1/4 tsp. paprika
1 tsp. salt
1 2/3 c. evaporated milk
2 4-oz. cans sliced mushrooms
1 tsp. Worcestershire sauce
1 tbsp. lemon juice
1/4 c. grated Parmesan cheese
1 1-lb. can salmon
1 8-oz. package med. noodles
1/2 c. sliced stuffed olives
Buttered cheese cracker crumbs

Melt butter in medium saucepan; remove from heat. Blend in flour, mustard, paprika and salt. Stir in evaporated milk. Drain mushrooms, reserving liquid. Add enough water to reserved liquid to measure 1 cup. Add to flour mixture. Cook, stirring over medium heat until thickened. Stir in Worcestershire sauce, lemon juice and cheese. Drain and flake salmon. Cook noodles according to package directions; drain. Add salmon, noodles, olives and mushrooms to cream sauce. Spoon into greased 2-quart casserole. Top with cracker crumbs. Bake at 375 degrees for 30 minutes. Yield: 6-8 servings.

Salmon-Noodle Casserole . . . Canned salmon is the basis of this penny-pinching main dish.

Salmon Steaks with Creamed Macaroni . . . In less than an hour, you can prepare this flavorful dish.

SALMON STEAKS WITH CREAMED MACARONI

1/4 c. melted butter
4 1-in. thick salmon steaks
1 tbsp. salt
2 c. elbow macaroni
1 10 1/2-oz. can cream of celery soup
1/2 c. milk
2 tbsp. Chablis
1/4 c. slivered ripe olives
1 tsp. instant minced onion

Pour butter into large shallow baking dish; arrange salmon in butter. Bake at 425 degrees for 20 minutes, brushing frequently with butter drippings. Add salt to 3 quarts rapidly boiling water in large saucepan. Add macaroni gradually so that water continues to boil. Cook, stirring occasionally, until tender. Drain in colander. Combine macaroni, soup, milk, Chablis, olives and onion; spoon around salmon. Reduce oven temperature to 350-degrees; bake for 15 minutes longer or until bubbling. Brush salmon with additional butter as needed. Garnish with additional slivered olives, lemon slice and parsley. Yield: 4 servings.

SALMON CASSEROLE WITH CUCUMBER SAUCE

1 1/2 c. instant rice
2 tbsp. instant minced onion
1 1-lb. can salmon
2 tsp. salt
1/4 tsp. pepper
2 eggs, separated
1 egg, beaten
Butter
1/4 c. lemon juice
1/2 c. drained grated cucumber

Prepare rice according to package directions. Combine onion and 1/4 cup cold water, let stand for 5 minutes. Drain salmon; flake. Mix rice, onion, salmon, salt and pepper. Beat egg whites until stiff peaks form. Add egg whites and egg to salmon mixture, blending well. Turn into 1 1/2-quart casserole; brush with 2 tablespoons melted butter. Bake for 30 minutes at 375 degrees. Garnish with lemon wedges and parsley. Beat egg yolks slightly in small saucepan; add lemon juice and 1/4 cup butter. Stir over low heat until blended. Add 1/4 cup butter; cook, stirring constantly, until thickened. Stir in cucumber. Serve sauce with salmon casserole.

CREAM PUFFS WITH CREAMED SALMON

1 10-oz. package frozen peas
3/4 c. self-rising cornmeal
3/4 c. self-rising flour
1/2 c. butter
4 eggs
1 med. onion, sliced
1 can cream of mushroom soup
2/3 c. milk
1/4 tsp. dillweed
1 1-lb. can salmon, drained

Preheat oven to 400 degrees. Thaw peas. Combine cornmeal and flour. Combine 1 cup water and butter in saucepan; bring to a boil. Add flour mixture all at once; reduce heat. Cook, stirring constantly until mixture forms a soft ball. Remove from heat; cool slightly. Add eggs, one at a time, beating well after each addition. Drop batter from tablespoon onto greased baking sheet to make 8 shells. Bake for 30 minutes or until firm. Turn off oven; leave puffs in oven for 20 minutes. Remove shells to wire rack; cool slightly. Cut tops off shells and remove soft interior. Cook peas and onion in 1/4 cup water for about 5 minutes. Add soup, milk and dillweed; stir until smooth. Flake salmon; fold into soup mixture. Heat to serving temperature. Spoon filling into shells; replace tops.

SALMON TETRAZZINI

4 oz. spaghetti
1 1-lb. can salmon
Milk
2 tbsp. butter
2 tbsp. flour
1/4 tsp. salt
1/8 tsp. nutmeg
1/8 tsp. pepper
2 tbsp. dry sherry
1 3-oz. can sliced mushrooms
2 tbsp. bread crumbs
2 tbsp. grated Parmesan cheese

Cook spaghetti according to package directions; drain. Drain salmon, reserving liquid. Add enough milk to reserved salmon liquid to make 2 cups liquid. Break salmon into large pieces. Melt butter; blend in flour, salt, nutmeg and pepper. Add milk mixture all at once; cook over medium heat, stirring until thickened and bubbly. Add sherry and spaghetti. Drain mushrooms; add mushrooms and salmon to sauce. Pour into 1-quart casserole. Combine crumbs and cheese; sprinkle over top. Bake at 350 degrees for 35 minutes or until heated through. Yield: 6 servings.

DEEP-FRIED SALMON FRITTERS

1 1-lb. can red salmon
1 1/4 c. sifted flour
1 1/2 tsp. baking powder
1 tsp. salt
1/4 c. yellow cornmeal
1 egg, slightly beaten
3/4 c. milk

Drain salmon; break into bite-sized pieces. Sift flour with baking powder and salt; stir in cornmeal. Combine egg and milk; stir into dry ingredients. Fold in salmon. Drop by heaping spoonfuls into 375-degree deep fat. Fry until golden brown. Drain on paper towels.

QUICK SALMON CROQUETTES

1 can salmon
2 eggs, beaten
1 tsp. salt
Crushed corn flakes
1 tsp. baking powder

Drain salmon; reserve liquid. Flake salmon; remove skin and bones. Combine salmon, reserved liquid, eggs, salt and corn flake crumbs to make a firm mixture; blend in baking powder. Shape into croquettes; roll in additional crumbs. Fry in small amount of fat in skillet until lightly browned.

SALMON PATTIES WITH MUSHROOM TOPPING

2 c. canned salmon
Milk
1 egg, beaten
1 c. cracker crumbs
1 tbsp. lemon juice
1/4 c. chopped onion
Salt and pepper to taste
Cream of mushroom soup

Drain salmon; reserve liquid, adding enough milk to make 3/4 cup liquid. Combine salmon and egg in mixing bowl; mix well. Stir in milk mixture and remaining ingredients except soup; mix well. Shape into 6 patties; place in greased baking pan. Bake at 350 degrees for 30 minutes. Remove from oven; top with 2 tablespoons soup for each patty. Return to oven; bake for 10 minutes longer. Garnish with parsley. Yield: 4-6 servings.

SAUCY SALMON CROQUETTES

1 1-lb. can salmon
1 c. cracker crumbs
2 eggs
Cocktail sauce
1 tbsp. grated onion
1 tsp. lemon juice

Drain and flake salmon; remove bones and skin. Combine salmon, 1/4 cup cracker crumbs, 1 egg, 1/4 cup cocktail sauce, onion and lemon juice. Shape mixture into croquettes. Beat remaining egg lightly in shallow dish; stir in 2 tablespoons water. Coat croquettes with remaining crumbs; dip in egg mixture. Dip in crumbs again; pat coating firmly. Fry in deep hot fat until golden brown. Serve with additional cocktail sauce.

SALMON AND RICE PIE

1/3 c. cooked rice
4 tbsp. butter
4 tbsp. grated cheese
1 baked 9-in. pastry shell
1 1/2 c. canned salmon
2 tbsp. flour
1 c. milk
1 egg, lightly beaten

Combine rice, 2 tablespoons butter and 2 tablespoons cheese. Spread in pie shell; top with salmon. Melt remaining butter; blend in flour. Add milk gradually; cook, stirring until thickened. Remove from heat. Stir in egg; pour over salmon. Sprinkle with remaining cheese. Bake at 450 degrees for 10 minutes. Yield: 6 servings.

SALMON POACHED IN COURT BOUILLON

1 lge. onion, sliced
4 carrots, sliced
2 stalks celery, sliced
2 bay leaves
1 bouquet garni
1 6-lb. salmon, dressed
Lemon slices
Cucumber slices
Fresh parsley
1 c. mayonnaise
2 tbsp. finely chopped tarragon leaves
2 tbsp. finely chopped onion
Lemon juice
Salt and freshly ground pepper to taste

Combine sliced onion, carrots, celery, bay leaves and bouquet garni with 8 cups water in large kettle. Bring to a boil; skim. Reduce heat; simmer for 30 minutes. Cool slightly. Wrap salmon in cheesecloth; lower into bouillon. Add additional liquid if needed. Simmer for 45 minutes or until fish flakes easily with a fork. Remove salmon from liquid carefully; unwrap. Remove skin carefully. Arrange salmon on hot platter; garnish with lemon slices, cucumber and parsley. Combine mayonnaise with 4 tablespoons minced parsley, tarragon leaves, chopped onion, lemon juice, salt and pepper; blend well. Serve sauce with salmon.

SALMON-CELERY LOAF

1 1-lb. can salmon
1 can celery soup
2 eggs, beaten
2 1/2 c. soft bread crumbs
1 hard-cooked egg, chopped
3 tsp. pickle relish
1 c. thin white sauce, heated
1/4 tsp. seafood seasoning
1/4 tsp. onion powder

Drain and flake salmon; remove skin and bones. Add soup, eggs and crumbs; mix lightly. Turn into greased 8 1/2 x 4 1/2-inch loaf pan. Bake at 350 degrees for 1 hour. Mix remaining ingredients; serve sauce over loaf. Yield: 6 servings.

SAVORY SALMON BAKE

1 lge. can salmon, drained
1 lge. can corn niblets, drained
1 can cream of mushroom soup
2 eggs, beaten
1 c. crushed corn flakes
Salt and pepper to taste
Mashed potatoes
Paprika

Flake salmon; add corn. Mix in soup, eggs, corn flakes, salt and pepper; place in greased casserole. Top with mashed potatoes; sprinkle with paprika. Bake in 350-degree oven for 45 minutes or until golden brown.

SWEET AND SOUR SALMON

1 1-lb. can salmon
2 med. onions, sliced
1 tsp. salt
3 tbsp. sugar
1/2 c. vinegar
2 tbsp. flour
2 egg yolks, beaten

Drain salmon, reserving liquid; arrange on serving platter. Boil onions in small amount of water until tender. Drain; reserve liquid. Place onions on salmon. Mix reserved salmon and onion liquids with salt, sugar, vinegar and flour; bring to a boil. Cook, stirring, for several minutes. Add to egg yolks gradually, stirring constantly; pour over salmon mixture.

Sandwiches

AVOCADO-BACON SANDWICH

Color photograph for this recipe on page 736

1/2 c. soft butter
1 tbsp. crumbled basil
6 slices corn bread
6 slices bacon
1 ripe avocado, sliced
12 cherry tomatoes
12 canned pitted California ripe olives
Salt and pepper to taste
1 lime

Mix butter and basil; spread over corn bread. Cut bacon slices in half; fry until crisp. Arrange bacon strips, avocado, tomato halves and ripe olives on corn bread; sprinkle with salt and pepper. Cut lime into sixths; garnish each sandwich with lime wedge. Lime juice may be squeezed over all sandwich ingredients. Serve with knife and fork. Yield: 6 open-faced sandwiches.

BUCKAROO SANDWICHES

6 slices raisin bread, toasted
1/4 c. butter
1 egg, lightly beaten
1 4 1/2-oz. can deviled ham
1 c. shredded Cheddar cheese

Spread 1 side of each bread slice with butter. Mix egg, ham and cheese; spread on buttered side of each piece of toast. Place under broiler for 2 to 3 minutes. Yield: 6 servings.

LONG BOY SANDWICH

2 10-in. loaves French bread
Butter
Lettuce leaves
16 slices assorted luncheon meats
6 tomato slices
1 4 1/2-oz. can deviled ham
1 3-oz. package cream cheese
2 tbsp. pickle relish

Long Boy Sandwiches . . . Deviled ham, meat, and cream cheese contrast in these family favorites.

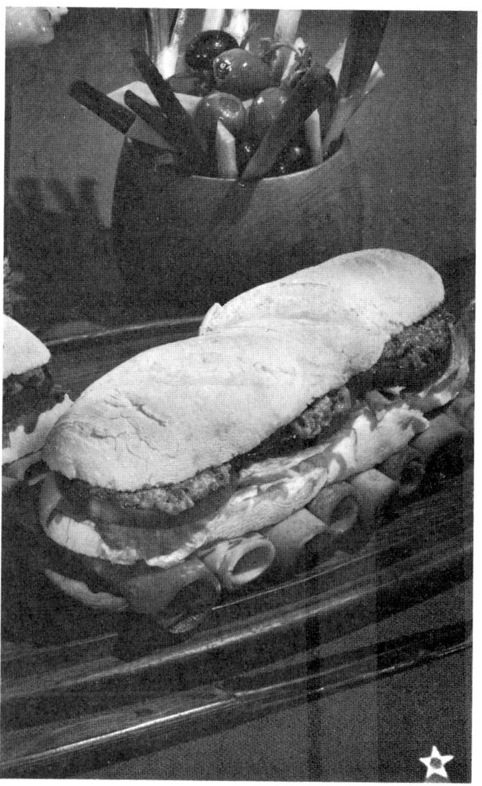

Cut bread, lengthwise, into thirds. Spread cut sides of bottom portions with butter. Top with lettuce leaves. Roll each slice of meat up as for jelly roll. Arrange 8 rolls crosswise on lettuce on each sandwich. Spread center portion of bread with butter; place over meat rolls. Top with lettuce leaves. Arrange 3 tomato slices on lettuce on each sandwich. Combine deviled ham, cream cheese and relish. Top tomato slices with deviled ham mixture; cover with top slices of bread.

BRIDGE CLUB SPECIAL

2 slices white bread
2 slices whole wheat bread
Butter
1 slice pineapple
Chopped cooked chicken
Mayonnaise
Sharp Cheddar cheese spread
Cream cheese, softened
Cream

Cut bread slices into rounds; butter on both sides. Place pineapple slice on 1 white slice. Moisten chicken with desired amount of mayonnaise; spread chicken mixture over 1 whole wheat slice. Place spread whole wheat slice over pineapple. Spread remaining whole wheat slice with cheese spread; place over chicken mixture. Top with remaining white bread slice. Combine cream cheese and enough cream to make of spreading consistency. Frost sandwich with cream cheese mixture. Garnish with stuffed olive or sprig of parsley.

BUNSTEADS

1 7-oz. can tuna
8 oz. American cheese, cubed
3 hard-cooked eggs, chopped
2 tbsp. chopped green pepper
1 tbsp. chopped stuffed olives
2 tbsp. chopped sweet pickles
1/2 c. salad dressing
6 frankfurter buns, split

Drain and flake tuna. Combine tuna, cheese, eggs, green pepper, olives, pickles and salad dressing; mix well. Spread filling in buns; wrap in foil. Place on baking sheet. Bake at 250 degrees for about 30 minutes or until filling is heated and cheese melts. Yield: 6 servings.

CLUB SANDWICHES

4 slices bacon
4 slices tomato
1/2 sm. cucumber, sliced
12 slices toasted bread, buttered
1/4 c. relish sandwich spread
4 slices cooked chicken
4 slices Muenster cheese

Saute bacon until crisp in skillet; drain. Place 1 tomato, cucumber and bacon slice on each of 4 toast slices. Cover each sandwich with bread slice. Spread sandwich relish over tops of bread slices; arrange chicken and cheese on spread tops of bread. Top with remaining bread. Place on cookie sheet. Bake at 450 degrees for 5 minutes or until cheese melts slightly. Press wooden picks into sandwiches to serve; cut into quarters. Garnish with olives and pickles. Yield: 4 servings.

CUCUMBER-EGG SANDWICH

Color photograph for this recipe on page 736.

2 cucumbers
1 1/2 tsp. salt
6 slices whole wheat bread
6 tbsp. soft butter
3 hard-cooked eggs
12 canned pitted California ripe olives, halved
Sour Cream Whip
Sliced green onion

Peel cucumbers; slice thinly and sprinkle with salt. Chill for at least 30 minutes; squeeze out excess moisture. Spread bread with butter; arrange cucumbers, sieved eggs and halved ripe olives on bread. Top with Sour Cream Whip; sprinkle with green onion.

Sour Cream Whip

3/4 c. sour cream
1 tbsp. lemon juice
1/2 tsp. salt
1 tbsp. thinly sliced green onion

Combine all ingredients; blend well. Yield: 6 open-faced sandwiches.

DENVER

4 slices bacon, diced
1 lge. onion, chopped
4 eggs, beaten
1/4 c. cream
Salt
Pepper
8 slices toasted bread

Fry bacon in skillet until crisp; remove from skillet. Drain off excess fat. Saute onion in pan drippings. Combine onion and bacon in skillet. Combine eggs, cream, salt and pepper; add to bacon mixture. Cook until eggs are set, but still moist. Spread between toast slices for sandwiches. Yield: 4 sandwiches.

DIABLO GRILL

1 4 1/2-oz. can deviled ham
1/4 c. pickle relish
12 slices white bread
Salad dressing
Cheese slices
6 tomato slices
Melted margarine

Blend ham and relish well. Spread 1 side of each bread slice with salad dressing. Cover half the spread bread slices with cheese, ham mixture and tomatoes. Top tomatoes with second slice of cheese. Cover with remaining bread, spread sides down. Brush with margarine; grill 4 inches from source of heat on both sides until lightly browned. Yield: 6 servings.

DUDE RANCHERS

8 slices rye bread
1 c. shredded cabbage
4 slices cooked turkey
4 slices tomato
4 slices cooked bacon
1/4 c. mayonnaise
1/2 c. grated Parmesan cheese
1 tsp. cream-style horseradish

Cover each slice rye bread with shredded cabbage, turkey slice, tomato slice and bacon strip. Combine mayonnaise, Parmesan cheese and horseradish. Spoon topping over sandwiches; place on baking sheet. Broil for 5 minutes or until topping is bubbly. Yield: 4 sandwiches.

FIRESIDE SANDWICH

8 oz. sharp cheese
1 lb. wieners, cut coarsely
2 hard-boiled eggs, chopped
4 green onions, sliced
1/2 c. sliced stuffed olives
1/2 can tomato paste
2 tbsp. mayonnaise
15 wiener buns

Cut cheese into 1/2-inch cubes; combine cheese, wieners, eggs, onions and olives. Blend tomato paste and mayonnaise together; add to wiener mixture. Split buns; spoon filling into buns. Wrap each bun in foil. Place on baking sheet. Bake at 350 degrees for 15 to 20 minutes. Yield: 15 servings.

HOT CRAB HERO

2 7 1/2-oz. cans crab meat
1/2 c. mayonnaise
1/4 c. chopped parsley
1/4 c. sour cream
1 tbsp. lemon juice
1/2 tsp. garlic salt
1 15 x 3-in. loaf French bread
Margarine
1/4 lb. thinly sliced Swiss cheese

Drain and flake crab meat. Combine crab meat, mayonnaise, parsley, sour cream, lemon juice and garlic salt. Cut bread in half lengthwise; place on baking sheet, cut side up. Spread with margarine; top with cheese. Trim cheese to fit bread. Use trimmed pieces to cover remaining bread. Cover cheese with crab mixture. Bake in 350-degree oven for 25 minutes or until lightly browned. Cut each half into 3 pieces.

OPEN-FACED HEROES

1 lge. onion, chopped
3 tbsp. salad oil
2 lb. ground beef
2 8-oz. cans tomato sauce with mushrooms
1 tsp. oregano
1 tsp. salt
4 split hero rolls, buttered
1 8-oz. package sliced mozzarella cheese
8 stuffed green olives, sliced

Cook onion in oil in large skillet until just tender; push to side. Shape beef into large patty; brown for 5 minutes. Break into chunks; stir in tomato sauce, oregano and salt. Simmer for 10 minutes. Place rolls in single layer in large shallow baking pan; spoon beef mixture over rolls. Cut cheese into triangles; cover sandwiches with cheese triangles and olives. Broil 4 to 6 inches from source of heat for 3 minutes or until cheese begins to melt and bubble. Yield: 8 servings.

ITALIAN SANDWICH

Butter
8 slices bread
4 slices mozzarella cheese
1/2 c. sour cream
Oregano to taste
2 tbsp. chopped onion
2 tomatoes, sliced
Seasoned salt
8 slices bacon, fried

Spread butter on 1 side of each bread slice. Top buttered side of each of 4 bread slices with 1 slice cheese, 2 tablespoons sour cream, dash of oregano, 1/2 tablespoon chopped onion and tomato slice. Sprinkle with seasoned salt. Place 2 slices bacon over each sandwich; top with remaining bread slices, buttered sides down. Place sandwiches, cheese sides down, in skillet. Cover; cook until bottom bread slice is browned. Turn; brown other side. Yield: 4 servings.

BAKED EGG SANDWICH LOAF

1 tbsp. prepared mustard
1 1/2 tsp. Worcestershire sauce
1 tsp. minced onion
1 tbsp. lemon juice
4 drops of hot sauce
1/2 tsp. salt
1/8 tsp. pepper
2/3 c. salad dressing
10 hard-boiled eggs, minced
4 slices crisp bacon, crumbled
1 1-lb. loaf day-old white bread
3 tbsp. melted butter
2 tbsp. grated Parmesan cheese

Combine seasonings and salad dressing; stir in eggs and bacon. Mix well. Trim crust from bread; cut into 4 lengthwise slices. Place 1 slice on greased baking sheet; spread with 1/3 of the egg mixture. Place second slice over egg mixture; spread with half the remaining egg mixture. Place third slice on top of egg mixture; spoon remaining egg mixture over slice. Top with remaining bread slice. Press 3-inch strip of foil around loaf lengthwise. Bake in 450-degree oven for 10 minutes. Brush top with butter; sprinkle with cheese. Bake for 8 minutes longer or until golden brown. Cut into slices to serve. Yield: 10-12 servings.

BUBBLE SANDWICH LOAF

3/4 c. chopped cooked chicken
1/4 c. snipped watercress
2 tbsp. minced celery
Mayonnaise
Salt and pepper
2 3-oz. packages softened cream cheese
1/4 c. chopped cucumber
1/4 tsp. dried dill
Red food coloring
3 hard-cooked eggs, chopped
1/4 c. chopped stuffed olives
1 tsp. prepared mustard
1 7-oz. pan butter rolls
Butter

Bubble Sandwich Loaf . . . This attractive sandwich loaf is topped with packaged biscuits.

Combine chicken, watercress, celery and enough mayonnaise to moisten. Season to taste with salt and pepper; chill. Blend cream cheese, cucumber, dill and desired amount of food coloring. Chill. Combine eggs, olives, mustard and enough mayonnaise to moisten; season to taste with salt and pepper. Remove rolls from pan in one piece. Slice connected rolls into 4 round layers with sharp knife. Spread bottom layer with softened butter; spread with chicken filling. Top with second layer; spread with cream cheese mixture. Top with third layer; spread with egg filling. Cover with top circle of rolls. Wrap in clear plastic wrap; chill for at least 2 hours. Cut into wedges to serve. Yield: 6 servings.

HOT SANDWICH LOAF

4 hard-cooked eggs, mashed
1/3 c. chopped ripe olives
3/8 c. mayonnaise
1 tsp. salt
1 c. chopped cooked ham
3 tbsp. diced dill pickles
1 1-lb. loaf unsliced bread
Butter
2 c. diced process cheese
1/2 c. milk

Mix eggs, olives, 2 tablespoons mayonnaise and salt. Mix ham, dill pickles and remaining mayonnaise. Cut bread into 3 lengthwise slices. Spread 1 slice bread with egg mixture; spread 1 slice bread with ham mixture. Place slices together to form loaf; spread outside with butter. Place on baking sheet. Bake at 375 degrees for 15 to 20 minutes. Melt cheese in milk in double boiler. Cut loaf into thick slices; serve with hot cheese mixture. Yield: 8 servings.

NIPPY SANDWICHES

1/2 c. finely shredded dried beef
1 3-oz. package cream cheese, softened
1 tbsp. horseradish
1 tbsp. minced onion
1 tbsp. salad dressing
Soft butter
12 whole wheat bread slices

Combine beef, cream cheese, horseradish, onion and salad dressing. Butter bread slices to edge on 1 side. Divide beef mixture into 6 parts. Place 1 part on buttered side of 6 bread slices, spreading to edges. Top with remaining bread slices, buttered sides down. Cut in half to serve. Freezes well. Yield: 6 servings.

PARTY SURPRISE LOAF

1/2 c. butter
1/2 c. shredded Parmesan cheese
3 anchovies, chopped
1/2 lb. cooked ham, diced
2 hard-cooked eggs, chopped
1/4 c. sweet pickle relish, drained
1 loaf French bread

Cream butter; add cheese, anchovies, ham, eggs and relish. Mix well. Cut lengthwise slice from top of bread; hollow out loaf. Fill with anchovy mixture; replace top slice. Wrap in foil; chill. Cut crosswise to serve.

Superb Sandwich Loaf . . . This elegant sandwich loaf can be prepared hours before serving.

SUPERB SANDWICH LOAF

1 1 1/2-lb. loaf unsliced bread
1/2 c. softened butter
8 oz. braunschweiger
1/2 c. chopped ripe olives
Mayonnaise
1/4 c. grated American cheese
1/4 c. drained sweet pickle relish
10 oz. assorted cold cuts
8 oz. baked ground ham
1/4 c. chopped celery
1/2 c. chopped pecans
1 tsp. grated onion
1 tsp. prepared horseradish
1/4 tsp. salt
3 8-oz. packages cream cheese
1/4 c. milk
Green food coloring
Pimento squares
Stuffed green olives, sliced
Green pepper strips
Sweet pickle relish, drained

Trim crusts from bread; cut loaf lengthwise into 4 slices. Spread butter on one side of bottom and top slices; spread both sides of remaining slices with butter. Combine braunschweiger, ripe olives and 1/4 cup mayonnaise. Spread on buttered side of bottom bread slice. Combine grated cheese, pickle relish and 2 tablespoons mayonnaise. Spread on second slice of bread; top with cold cuts. Combine ham, celery and pecans. Mix onion, horseradish and 1/2 cup mayonnaise together; add to ham mixture. Spread on third slice. Assemble slices in order, topping with fourth slice of bread, buttered side down. Wrap in waxed paper; place in refrigerator for several hours or overnight. Add salt to cream cheese; soften with milk, mixing well. Place sandwich loaf on serving plate. Frost with softened cream cheese mixture, reserving 3/4 cup for garnish. Add desired amount of green food coloring to reserved cream cheese mixture, blending well. Garnish loaf with reserved cream cheese mixture, pimento squares, sliced green olives, green pepper strips and pickle relish. Chill well before serving.

THE OLIVER

Color photograph for this recipe on page 736.

1 lge. round loaf French bread, split
Soft butter
12 thin slices mild cheese
18 slices dry salami
1 lge. green pepper, cut in rings
2 c. drained pitted California ripe olives

Hollow out a portion of soft crumbs from both bread halves; spread with butter. Cover bottom half with cheese, salami, green pepper and olives; top with remaining half of bread loaf. Wrap in waxed paper to crush olives and blend flavors. Cut into 6 or 8 wedges to serve.

SHRIMP-OLIVE SANDWICH

Color photograph for this recipe on page 736.

1/2 lb. fresh shrimp
Dry sherry
3 tbsp. lemon juice
4 slices light rye bread
3 tbsp. soft butter
4 oz. cream cheese
12 canned pitted California ripe olives
2 tbsp. chopped parsley
Pepper to taste

Cook shrimp; peel and devein. Toss shrimp in 3 tablespoons sherry and lemon juice; let stand for 30 minutes. Spread bread with butter. Soften cream cheese at room temperature; mix with 2 teaspoons sherry. Spread cream cheese mixture on buttered bread. Drain shrimp; cut ripe olives in half. Arrange shrimp and olives over cream cheese. Sprinkle parsley and pepper over top. 4 open sandwiches.

ORANGE-LEEK SANDWICH

Color photograph for this recipe on page 736.

6 tbsp. soft butter
2 1/2 tsp. ground coriander
3 slices dark unseeded rye bread
1 7-oz. can tuna, drained
9 canned pitted California ripe olives, quartered
1 peeled orange, thinly sliced
3 tbsp. thinly sliced leeks

Mix butter and coriander; spread over bread. Arrange flaked tuna, quartered olives, sliced orange and leeks on bread. Yield: 3 open-faced sandwiches.

PEANUT BUTTER-FRUIT SANDWICHES

1/4 c. figs
1/4 c. raisins
1/2 tsp. salt
1/2 c. peanut butter
2 tbsp. lemon juice
2 tbsp. light corn syrup
Thin bread slices

Grind figs and raisins together; add salt, peanut butter, lemon juice and corn syrup. Mix well. Spread between bread slices.

REUBEN'S DELUXE GRILL

1 pkg. sour cream sauce mix
Milk
2 tsp. prepared mustard
Sliced rye bread
Sliced Swiss cheese
Sliced corned beef
Drained sauerkraut
Melted margarine

Prepare sauce mix according to package directions, using 3/4 cup milk; stir in mustard. Spread bottom bread slice with sour cream sauce; cover with cheese, corned beef and sauerkraut. Top with cheese and top bread slices. Grill 4 inches from source of heat on both sides in small amount of melted margarine until lightly browned.

REUBEN ROLL-UPS

1 8-oz. can sauerkraut
2 slices Swiss cheese
1 pkg. refrigerator crescent rolls
1 tbsp. Thousand Island dressing
8 thin slices cooked corned beef

Drain and chop sauerkraut; cut cheese into 1/2-inch strips. Unroll dough; separate into 8 triangles. Mix sauerkraut and dressing. Place 1 slice corned beef across wide end of each dough triangle; spread 2 tablespoons sauerkraut mixture on corned beef. Top with 2 strips cheese. Roll up, beginning at wide ends of triangles. Place on ungreased baking sheet. Bake at 375 degrees for 10 to 15 minutes or until golden brown. Serve hot. Yield: 8 servings.

ROYAL TOMATO SANDWICHES

1/4 c. butter
4 oz. Roquefort cheese
1/4 c. Worcestershire sauce
6 slices bread
Thin tomato slices
Lettuce

Cream butter and cheese well; add Worcestershire sauce. Beat until smooth. Spread filling on 3 bread slices; top with tomato slices and lettuce. Place remaining bread slices over sandwiches. Cut into quarters to serve. Yield: 3 sandwiches.

SKILLET TOASTWICHES

1 can corned beef
1 c. grated American cheese
1/4 c. mayonnaise
1/2 c. chopped pickles
1 tbsp. grated onion
12 slices bread
2 tbsp. butter
2 eggs
3/4 c. evaporated milk

Mix corned beef, cheese, mayonnaise, pickles and onion together. Mixture will be thick. Spread evenly on 6 slices bread; top with remaining bread. Melt butter in skillet. Beat eggs lightly; stir in milk. Dip sandwiches into egg mixture. Brown on each side for 2 to 3 minutes. Cut in half diagonally to serve.

SWEET SANDWICH SPREAD

2/3 c. ground raisins
1/3 c. chopped pecans
1 c. sugar
1 egg
1 c. mayonnaise

Combine all ingredients in saucepan; cook, stirring frequently, for 10 minutes or until thickened. Cool before serving.

FAVORITE SPREAD

1/2 lb. bologna
1/2 lb. cheese
1 med. onion
3 med. sweet pickles
1/4 c. mayonnaise
1/4 c. tomato paste
2 tbsp. sugar

Grind bologna, cheese, onion and pickles together; mix well with mayonnaise, tomato paste and sugar. Yield: 12 servings.

HOT SUBMARINE SANDWICHES

1 loaf French bread
1 lb. ground beef, cooked
1/2 c. tomato soup
2 tbsp. minced onion
1/4 tsp. dry mustard
1/4 tsp. pepper
1 tsp. salt
1/2 tsp. garlic salt
1/8 tsp. oregano
American cheese slices
Tomato slices

Cut bread in half lengthwise. Combine beef, soup, onion, mustard, pepper, salt, garlic salt and oregano. Cover both halves with beef mixture. Place under broiler 6 inches from source of heat until heated through. Overlap cheese and tomato slices on beef mixture. Place under broiler until cheese melts.

SUBMARINE SANDWICH

1 loaf French bread
Smoked ham slices
Swiss cheese slices
1/4 c. chopped onion
1 tbsp. mustard
1 tsp. caraway seed
1/4 c. margarine, softened

Cut bread in half lengthwise. Cover 1 bread half with ham and cheese, overlapping cheese on ham. Combine onion, mustard, caraway seed and margarine; spread on remaining bread half. Press halves together; wrap in foil. Bake at 350 degrees for 20 minutes. Yield: 8-10 servings.

TEENAGER'S MAMMOTH SANDWICH

1 lge. loaf French bread
Butter
Mustard
Italian salad dressing
Mayonnaise
Salt and pepper to taste
8 lettuce leaves
4 slices Swiss cheese
6 slices salami
2 dill pickles, sliced
6 slices cooked ham
4 slices American cheese
4 slices bologna
1 lge. tomato, sliced
1 med. onion, sliced

Split bread in half lengthwise; spread generously with butter, mustard, salad dressing, mayonnaise, salt and pepper. Arrange layers of lettuce, Swiss cheese, salami, dill pickles, ham, American cheese, bologna, tomato and onion on bottom half. Replace top. Slice to serve. Yield: 6-8 servings.

TOUCHDOWNERS

2 c. ground cooked meat
2 tbsp. chopped pickle
2 tbsp. chopped onion
1/3 c. salad dressing
1 sm. apple, chopped
Salt and pepper to taste
12 slices buttered bread

Mix meat, pickle, onion, salad dressing, apple and salt and pepper together; spread over 6 slices bread. Top with remaining bread slices. Yield: 6 sandwiches.

TRIPLE TREAT SANDWICH

Hamburger buns
Swiss cheese slices, halved
Hot cooked Canadian bacon
Scrambled eggs

Split and toast buns; cover bottom bun halves with cheese. Broil 4 inches from source of heat until melted. Top with bacon, eggs and second slice cheese. Broil 4 inches from source of heat until cheese is melted. Cover with bun tops; serve.

VEGETABLE SANDWICHES

3/4 c. ground carrots
1/4 c. ground celery
1/4 c. ground green onions
1 lb. tomatoes, ground
1/4 c. ground cucumbers
Salt and pepper to taste
1/2 c. mayonnaise
1 8-oz. package cream cheese
Bread slices

Combine ground vegetables; add salt and pepper. Blend mayonnaise and cream cheese together; add to vegetable mixture. Refrigerate for 2 to 3 hours. Spread on bread slices; top with remaining bread.

VIENNA ROLL

Salt and pepper to taste
1 pt. ripe olives
12 hard-boiled eggs
1 green pepper, chopped
1 lb. sharp cheese
1 sm. onion, chopped
1 sm. can chicken
3 tbsp. salad oil
Chopped parsley
Mayonnaise
3 doz. rolls

Combine seasonings, olives, eggs, green pepper, cheese, onion, chicken, oil and parsley; add enough mayonnaise to moisten. Process sandwich mixture through food grinder. Cut rolls lengthwise; scoop out centers to make small hollow. Fill with sandwich mixture. Wrap in foil; twist ends. Heat in 300-degree oven for about 15 minutes. Serve in foil.

WALKING SANDWICH

1 tbsp. prepared mustard
1/2 c. salad dressing
3 tbsp. light cream
2 tbsp. vinegar
2 tbsp. minced onion
1/4 tsp. caraway seed
3 c. finely shredded cabbage
12 slices rye bread, buttered
6 slices Swiss cheese
12 thin slices cooked corned beef

Stir mustard into salad dressing; add cream and vinegar. Toss onion, caraway seed and cabbage together; add enough dressing to moisten. Toss well. Top half the bread with cheese, 2 slices corned beef and slaw. Cover with remaining bread. Serve remaining dressing with sandwiches. Yield: 6 servings.

WESTERN SANDWICH

1 tsp. butter
1 egg
1 tbsp. minced onion
1 tbsp. minced green pepper
2 tbsp. milk
2 tbsp. chopped cooked ham
1/8 tsp. salt
Dash of pepper
2 slices buttered bread

Heat butter in small skillet over medium heat. Blend egg, onion, green pepper, milk, ham, salt and pepper; pour into skillet. Cook, stirring, to cook evenly. Shape into flat round to fit bread while still moist. Place between bread; serve hot. Yield: 1 sandwich.

Sardine

SARDINE PIZZA SALAD

4 beefsteak tomatoes, sliced
3 4-oz. cans Maine sardines
1 lge. cucumber, sliced
4 hard-cooked eggs, chopped
1/4 lb. sharp cheese, cubed
French dressing

Arrange tomatoes on outer edge of round platter. Drain sardines; place in smaller circle on inner edge of tomatoes. Arrange cucumbers in smaller circle overlapping sardines. Spoon chopped eggs and cheese cubes in center of cucumber ring. Sprinkle well with dressing. Yield: 4-6 servings.

SARDINE PUFFS

2 3 1/4-oz. cans sardines, drained
48 round buttery crackers
3 egg whites
1 tsp. Worcestershire sauce
2 tsp. minced onion
3/4 c. grated Cheddar cheese

Cut sardines into bite-sized pieces. Place piece of sardine in center of each cracker. Place on baking sheet. Beat egg whites until stiff but not dry. Fold in Worcestershire sauce, onion and cheese. Drop egg mixture from teaspoon onto each sardine. Bake at 450 degrees for 8 minutes or until puffy and golden.

SARDINE SNACKS

8 slices bread, crusts removed
Melted butter
1/2 c. chili sauce
1/4 tsp. chili powder
Dash of garlic powder
1 can sardines, drained
2 tsp. lemon juice
1 c. grated process Cheddar cheese

Toast bread; brush with butter. Combine chili sauce, chili powder and garlic powder; spread on toast. Cut each slice into 4 strips; arrange on baking sheet. Place 1 sardine on each strip; sprinkle with lemon juice and cheese. Broil 4 inches from source of heat until cheese melts and is light brown. Yield: 32 snacks.

Sardine Pizza Salad . . . Circles of sardines, vegetables, and cheese make this dish look pizza-like.

BAKED SARDINES

3 eggs, separated
1 can sardines, minced
1/2 c. bread crumbs
3 tbsp. melted butter
1 tbsp. lemon juice
Salt
Pepper
3 stalks celery, chopped
2 med. onions, minced
1 green pepper, minced
1/2 tsp. minced parsley

Beat egg yolks until light; add sardines, bread crumbs, butter, lemon juice, salt, pepper, celery, onions, green pepper and parsley. Beat egg whites until stiff peaks form; add to sardine mixture. Place in greased baking dish. Bake at 350 degrees for 30 minutes. Yield: 4 servings.

SAVORY SARDINE PIE

1 pkg. pie crust mix
1 lge. can sardines in tomato sauce
1 med. onion, sliced
1/2 tsp. salt
1/2 tsp. pepper
1 1/2 tsp. parsley flakes
Milk

Prepare pie crust mix according to package directions. Line pie plate with crust. Add sardines; top with onion, salt, pepper and parsley. Moisten edge of pie crust with small amount of milk. Add top crust; seal edges. Cut vents in top crust; brush with small amount of milk. Bake at 425 degrees for 30 minutes.

SARDINES AND POTATOES AU GRATIN

2 tbsp. minced onion
2 tbsp. butter
2 tbsp. flour
2 c. milk
1 c. grated sharp Cheddar cheese
1 1/2 tsp. salt
2 tsp. Worcestershire sauce
1/2 tsp. pepper
5 c. sliced cooked potatoes
2 cans sardines

Saute onion in butter in skillet for 1 minute; remove from heat. Stir in flour. Add milk gradually, stirring constantly. Cook, stirring, until smooth and thickened. Add all remaining ingredients except potatoes and sardines. Place potatoes and 1 can chopped sardines in shallow 2-quart baking dish; cover with cheese sauce. Bake at 350 degrees for 15 minutes. Arrange remaining whole sardines on top. Bake for 15 minutes longer. Yield: 6 servings.

Sauces

Sauces are zesty and piquant toppings for many meats, vegetables, and appetizers. They usually consist of a liquid, a thickening agent, a basic flavor, and seasoning. There are two general groupings of sauces: savory and sweet. (See SAUCES, DESSERT.) Included in the group of savory sauces are: 1) flour-and-butter sauces (Roux, Bechamel, White Sauce); 2) egg-based sauces (Hollandaise, Bernaise); 3) wine, barbecue, and sweet-sour sauces.

STORING: Most sauces can be stored in the refrigerator for about 1 week. Pour into a container and cover tightly. Egg-based sauces do not store well.

PREPARATION: Follow specific recipe directions for preparing sauces. For flour-and-butter sauces–Cook flour and butter together to permit starch granules to swell evenly. Add remaining ingredients and cook until properly thickened. For egg-based sauces–Never add eggs directly to hot liquid or they might curdle. Do not allow the sauce to boil. For barbecue, wine, and sweet-sour sauces–Cornstarch is often used to thicken these sauces. It creates a translucent appearance. The specific recipe directions will provide the most detailed information for such sauces.

ALL-AMERICAN BARBECUE SAUCE

3 tbsp. margarine
1 onion, chopped
1 green pepper, chopped
1/2 c. chopped celery
3 tbsp. sugar
1 1/2 tsp. dry mustard
3 tbsp. vinegar
1/4 c. lemon juice
2 tbsp. Worcestershire sauce
2 tbsp. catsup

Melt margarine in saucepan. Cook onion, green pepper and celery slowly in margarine until tender. Blend in sugar and mustard. Add all remaining ingredients and 3/4 cup water; mix well. Simmer for 10 minutes or until heated through.

BECHAMEL SAUCE

1/4 c. butter
2 tbsp. chopped onion
1/2 c. flour
2 c. milk
2 c. stock
Pinch of thyme
Dash of white pepper
Pinch of freshly grated nutmeg

Melt butter in double boiler over low heat. Saute onion in butter until transparent. Blend in flour; add milk and stock gradually. Place over hot water; add thyme, pepper and nutmeg. Cook for 1 hour, stirring frequently. Strain sauce through fine sieve.

BLENDER HOLLANDAISE

4 egg yolks
Juice of 1/2 lemon
1/4 tsp. salt
1/2 c. butter

Combine egg yolks, lemon juice and salt in blender container. Heat butter until bubbling in saucepan. Blend egg yolk mixture on high speed until well mixed. Add bubbling butter gradually, blending on low speed. Pour over hot vegetable.

NO-COOK BERNAISE

4 egg yolks
1/2 tsp. salt
1/8 tsp. cayenne pepper
1 c. melted butter
2 tbsp. lemon juice
2 tsp. minced onion
2 tsp. minced parsley
1 tsp. dried tarragon

Beat egg yolks at high speed with electric mixer until thick. Beat in salt and cayenne pepper. Add 1/4 cup butter, 1 teaspoon at a time. Combine remaining butter, lemon juice, onion, parsley and tarragon. Beat into yolk mixture gradually. Serve sauce immediately. Yield: 6 servings.

BORDELAISE SAUCE

2 tbsp. chopped onion or shallots
3/4 c. red wine
1/2 bay leaf
Pinch of thyme
2 tbsp. butter
1/3 c. sliced mushrooms
1 1/2 tbsp. flour
1 c. beef broth
Salt and pepper to taste

Combine onion, wine, bay leaf and thyme in saucepan; simmer until wine is reduced to 1/4 cup. Strain liquid, rubbing onion through sieve. Saute mushrooms in butter; blend in flour. Add beef broth, stirring constantly. Cook until mixture is thickened; add salt, pepper and wine mixture. Simmer for 5 minutes.

CURRY FONDUE SAUCE

1 c. sour cream
1/2 c. mayonnaise
1 tbsp. chopped parsley
2 tsp. curry powder
1 tsp. lemon juice
1/2 tsp. Worcestershire sauce
1/4 tsp. salt

Combine all ingredients, mixing well. Cover; refrigerate for several hours before serving. Yield: 1 1/2 cups.

CHEESE SAUCE

3 tbsp. butter
3 tbsp. flour
1/2 tsp. salt
1/8 tsp. pepper
2 c. milk
1 1/2 c. grated American cheese

Melt butter in small saucepan; blend in flour, salt and pepper. Stir in milk gradually. Cook, stirring constantly, over low heat until sauce is thickened and bubbly. Add cheese; stir until melted. Yield: 6 servings.

CHERRY SAUCE

1 can tart red cherries
3/4 c. sugar
1/8 tsp. salt
1 tbsp. cornstarch
1 tsp. almond flavoring

Drain cherries, reserving syrup. Mix sugar, salt and cornstarch in small saucepan. Stir in reserved cherry syrup; cook over low heat until thickened and clear. Add cherries and almond flavoring; mix well. Cook only until cherries are heated through. Serve over ham.

CHESTNUT SAUCE

12 chestnuts
Salt and pepper to taste
2 tbsp. cream
1 c. boiling milk

Place chestnuts in boiling water; cook until tender. Remove skins; press through sieve. Add salt, pepper and cream. Pour milk into chestnut mixture gradually; place over low heat until heated through. Serve with chicken or turkey.

CREAMY SAUCE FOR VEGETABLES

1/2 c. butter
1/2 c. grated Parmesan cheese
1 tsp. salt
2 c. sour cream
1/4 c. chopped chives
1/3 c. chopped cucumber

Cream butter, cheese and salt together; blend in sour cream. Stir in chives and cucumber; mix well. Spoon sauce over hot vegetables just before serving. Yield: 3 cups.

CREOLE SHRIMP SAUCE

1/4 c. mayonnaise
1/4 c. Worcestershire sauce
1 tsp. prepared horseradish
1/4 c. catsup
1/4 tsp. garlic juice
1/2 tsp. salt
1/8 tsp. pepper

Combine all ingredients; mix well. Cover; refrigerate for several hours before serving. Yield: 3/4 cup.

CROQUETTE SAUCE

3 tbsp. butter
5 tbsp. sifted flour
1 c. milk
1/4 tsp. onion juice
1/4 tsp. celery salt
1/4 tsp. salt
1/8 tsp. pepper
1/4 tsp. lemon juice
1/2 tsp. Worcestershire sauce

Melt butter in small saucepan over low heat; blend in flour. Add milk gradually, stirring constantly. Add onion juice, celery salt, salt, pepper, lemon juice and Worcestershire sauce; cook, stirring constantly, until thickened.

CUCUMBER SAUCE

1 med. cucumber
1 tbsp. grated onion
1/4 c. mayonnaise
2 tsp. vinegar
1 tbsp. minced parsley
1/2 c. sour cream
Salt and pepper to taste

Cut cucumber in half lengthwise. Grate enough cucumber to measure 1 cup; drain. Combine onion, mayonnaise, vinegar, parsley, sour cream, salt and pepper; blend thoroughly. Stir in cucumber; chill until ready to use. Serve with seafood.

EASY MORNAY SAUCE

1/4 c. butter
1/4 c. flour
1 tsp. salt
1/2 tsp. paprika

2 c. chicken stock
2 egg yolks
2 tbsp. heavy cream
1 tsp. lemon juice
1 tbsp. minced parsley
2 tbsp. grated Swiss cheese

Melt butter in saucepan over low heat. Add flour, salt and paprika, stirring until smooth. Cook for about 1 minute, stirring constantly. Remove from heat; add chicken stock gradually, stirring constantly. Return to heat; stir until sauce is bubbly. Beat egg yolks lightly with cream; beat small amount of hot sauce into egg yolk mixture. Stir egg yolk mixture into remaining sauce; cook until smooth and thickened, stirring constantly. Add lemon juice, parsley and cheese; stir until cheese is melted. Serve.

HOLLANDAISE SAUCE

3 egg yolks
3 tbsp. lemon juice
1/4 tsp. salt
1/2 c. soft Chiffon margarine

Blend egg yolks, lemon juice and salt together in small saucepan. Add margarine. Cook, stirring constantly, over low heat until margarine melts and sauce thickens. Serve hot or at room temperature. Any leftover sauce may be stored in refrigerator. Stir in small amount of hot water to serve. Yield: About 3/4 cup sauce.

Hollandaise Sauce . . . An almost foolproof recipe for one of the most elegant of all sauces.

HORSERADISH DRESSING

1/2 tsp. mustard
1 1/2 tsp. salt
1 1/2 tsp. sugar
1 1/2 tbsp. flour
1/8 tsp. paprika
1 egg, beaten
1 c. milk
1/4 c. vinegar
1 1/2 tbsp. shortening
3 tbsp. prepared horseradish

Mix mustard, salt, sugar, flour and paprika in double boiler; stir in egg well. Add milk and vinegar; cook over hot water until thick, stirring frequently. Add shortening and horseradish; stir until shortening is melted. Yield: 8 servings.

MINT SAUCE

1 jar red currant or apple jelly
1 tbsp. minced fresh mint
1 tbsp. grated orange rind
1 tsp. grated lemon rind

Turn jelly into small saucepan; break into small pieces with fork. Stir in mint, orange rind and lemon rind. Stir sauce over low heat just until jelly is melted.

MUSHROOM SAUCE FOR STEAK

3 tbsp. butter
2 c. sliced mushrooms
1 tbsp. flour
1 tsp. soy sauce
3/4 c. light cream
Salt and pepper

Melt butter in small shallow saucepan. Add mushrooms to saucepan; sprinkle with flour. Cook over medium heat for 8 to 10 minutes or until mushrooms are lightly browned. Add soy sauce and cream gradually. Cook, stirring frequently, until sauce is thickened and bubbly; add salt and pepper.

NEWBURG SAUCE

1 tbsp. butter
2 tbsp. flour
1 c. cream
Salt to taste
Dash of cayenne pepper
2 egg yolks
2 tbsp. sherry

Melt butter in double boiler; add flour, stirring until smooth. Pour in cream gradually, stirring constantly. Cook, stirring, until smooth and thickened. Do not boil. Add salt and cayenne pepper. Beat egg yolks lightly; add small amount of hot sauce to egg yolks, stirring constantly. Stir egg yolk mixture into hot sauce, stirring constantly; cook for 3 minutes. Remove from heat; stir in sherry. Serve with seafood, especially lobster.

QUICK BARBECUE SAUCE

1/2 c. margarine
1/2 c. oil
1/4 c. vinegar
Juice of 1 lemon
1 tbsp. Worcestershire sauce
1 c. catsup
1 tbsp. prepared mustard
1/2 c. sugar
Dash of hot sauce

Melt margarine in saucepan. Add remaining ingredients; mix well. Cook over low heat, stirring, just until blended and heated through.

BASIC WHITE SAUCE

Thin

1 tbsp. butter
1 tbsp. flour
1/2 tsp. salt
1 c. milk

Medium

2 tbsp. butter
2 tbsp. flour
1/2 tsp. salt
1 c. milk

Thick

1/4 c. butter
1/4 c. flour
1/2 tsp. salt
1 c. milk

Melt butter in small saucepan over low heat. Add flour and salt, stirring until blended and smooth. Cook for about 1 minute; do not brown. Remove from heat. Add milk gradually, stirring constantly. Return saucepan to heat; cook just until bubbly, stirring constantly.

RAISIN SAUCE

1/2 c. (packed) light brown sugar
1 tsp. mustard
2 tbsp. flour
2 tbsp. vinegar
2 tbsp. lemon juice
1/4 tbsp. grated lemon rind
1/3 c. raisins

Mix brown sugar, mustard and flour in small saucepan. Add vinegar, lemon juice, lemon rind and 1 1/2 cups water; mix well. Cook over low heat, stirring constantly, until thickened. Add raisins; cook until raisins are plumped. Yield: 10 servings.

RED WINE SAUCE

3 tbsp. butter
3 tbsp. flour
1 c. beef bouillon
1 c. button mushrooms
1 clove of garlic, crushed
1/2 c. minced green onions
1/2 c. Burgundy
1 tbsp. chopped parsley

Melt butter in small saucepan; blend in flour. Add bouillon gradually, stirring. Cook until slightly thickened, stirring constantly. Add mushrooms, garlic, onions and Burgundy. Cook for about 5 minutes longer; stir in parsley. Yield: 4-6 servings.

ROCKEFELLER SAUCE

2 pkg. frozen spinach
1 sm. bunch green onions, chopped
6 stalks celery, finely chopped
1 bunch parsley, finely chopped
1 1/2 c. margarine, melted
Salt to taste
2 tbsp. Worcestershire sauce
1/2 tsp. red pepper

Cook spinach according to package directions; drain. Combine onions, celery and parsley in blender container; add small amount of margarine. Cover blender; process for 30 seconds. Add salt, Worcestershire sauce and red pepper. Pour mixture into large bowl. Blend spinach with remaining margarine; combine mixtures. Blend again if necessary to mix well. Serve on drained and heated oysters; sprinkle with bread crumbs if desired.

REMOULADE SAUCE

4 c. mayonnaise
6 hard-boiled egg yolks, sieved
3 tbsp. dark salad mustard
2 tbsp. Worcestershire sauce
2 tbsp. paprika
Dash of hot sauce
1/4 c. vinegar
1/4 c. minced parsley
Horseradish to taste
Salt and pepper to taste

Combine all ingredients; mix well. Refrigerate for 12 hours before serving. Serve over seafood or green salad.

SAUCE MEUNIERE

1/2 c. butter
1 tbsp. chopped parsley
1 tbsp. chopped green onion
2 tbsp. lemon juice
1/2 tsp. salt
1/2 tsp. pepper
Dash of hot sauce
Dash of Worcestershire sauce

Melt butter in small saucepan. Cook over low heat until butter is browned. Add all remaining ingredients; mix well. Cook only until heated through. Serve over fish. Yield: 6 servings.

SEAFOOD LOUIS SAUCE

1 c. mayonnaise
1 c. chili sauce
1/4 c. sweet pickle relish
1 1/2 tsp. prepared mustard
1 tbsp. chopped chives
2 hard-cooked eggs, chopped
1 c. minced celery
1 tsp. grated lemon rind
2 tbsp. lemon juice
Salt and pepper to taste

Combine all ingredients; mix well. Cover; refrigerate until ready to serve. Yield: 12 servings.

SEAFOOD SAUCE

1 tbsp. butter
2 tbsp. minced onion
1 c. tomato sauce
1/2 tsp. Worcestershire sauce
10 drops of hot sauce
2 tbsp. lemon juice
1/4 tsp. dry mustard
Dash of salt and pepper

Melt butter in small saucepan. Saute onion lightly in butter. Add all remaining ingredients; mix well. Simmer until heated through.

SPANISH SAUCE

2 tbsp. butter
2 tbsp. chopped onion
1 tbsp. flour
2 c. chopped canned tomatoes
1/2 c. chopped celery
3/4 c. chopped green pepper
2 tbsp. chopped parsley
1/2 tsp. salt
Pepper to taste

Melt butter in small saucepan. Saute onion in butter for 3 minutes. Sprinkle flour over onion; stir in tomatoes quickly. Add celery and green pepper; simmer for 20 minutes, stirring frequently. Add parsley, salt and pepper; mix well. Serve hot on meats or cold on salads. Add 1 tablespoon cider vinegar to sauce when serving on salads if desired.

SWEET AND SOUR SAUCE

1 can pineapple chunks
1 tbsp. cornstarch
1/2 c. brown sugar
1/3 c. vinegar
2 tsp. soy sauce

Drain pineapple, reserving 6 tablespoons syrup. Mix cornstarch and brown sugar in small saucepan; stir in vinegar, soy sauce and reserved pineapple syrup. Add pineapple; bring to a boil. Reduce heat; simmer for about 2 minutes. Serve over beef, pork or chicken. Yield: 4 servings.

TACO SAUCE

12 ripe tomatoes
8 hot cattail peppers, chopped
8 long med.-hot green peppers, chopped
3 green peppers, chopped
1 onion, chopped
1/2 c. vinegar
Dash of salt
1 tbsp. sugar

Steam tomatoes until tender; peel and mash. Combine tomatoes, peppers, onion, 1/2 cup water, vinegar, salt and sugar in saucepan. Cook for 10 to 15 minutes. Yield: 7 pints.

TARTAR SAUCE

1/2 c. mayonnaise
2 tbsp. heavy cream
1 tbsp. minced onion
1 tbsp. minced green pepper
1 tbsp. minced parsley
1 tbsp. minced dill pickle, drained
1 tbsp. chopped capers, drained
1 tsp. vinegar

Combine all ingredients; mix well. Cover; refrigerate until ready to serve.

VINAIGRETTE SAUCE

2 sour pickles, minced
1 tsp. chopped chives
1 tsp. chopped parsley
1 tbsp. chopped capers
2 tsp. chopped green onions
2 tbsp. vinegar
1/4 c. salad oil

Combine all ingredients; mix well.

ONION BUTTER

1 tbsp. onion flakes
1 c. soft butter

Blend onion flakes into butter. Cover; refrigerate for several hours. Bring to room temperature before serving. Serve on baked potatoes or French bread.

QUICK CHILE SALSA

1 4-oz. can green chilies
1 1-lb. can tomatoes
1 sm. onion, chopped
1 tsp. sugar
Salt and pepper to taste
2 tbsp. salad oil
1 tbsp. wine vinegar

Chop chilies into small pieces. Combine chilies and tomatoes in jar, mashing tomatoes well. Add remaining ingredients; shake well. Cover jar. Let stand overnight.

Sauces, Dessert

There are hundreds of dessert sauces all of which belong to the category of sweet sauces. They add a glamorous finishing touch to many desserts. Choose dessert sauces that complement not dominate the flavor of the dessert. Combine and contrast textures and flavors. For example, a colorful and zippy mint sauce enlivens both the taste and texture of vanilla ice cream.
(See SAUCES.)

CREAMY BANANA TOPPING

1 ripe banana
1/2 tsp. lemon juice
1 tbsp. milk
1 c. frozen dessert topping, thawed

Mash banana in small bowl with lemon juice. Add milk. Fold topping into banana mixture. Chill well. Keeps for 1 to 2 hours in refrigerator. Yield: 1 1/4 cups.

BANANA-ORANGE SAUCE

Juice of 2 oranges
Juice of 1 lemon
1 banana, mashed
1 c. sugar

Blend all ingredients together; chill for 1 hour. Spoon sauce over ice cream and cake if desired. Yield: 6-8 servings.

BLUEBERRY SAUCE

1/2 c. sugar
2 tsp. cornstarch
Dash of salt
1 pt. blueberries
1 tbsp. lemon juice
1 tsp. grated lemon rind

Combine sugar, cornstarch, salt and 1/2 cup water in saucepan. Add blueberries. Bring to a boil; simmer for 4 minutes or until clear and thickened. Remove from heat; add lemon juice and rind. Chill. Serve over desired dessert.

BROWN SUGAR SAUCE

1 c. (packed) brown sugar, sifted
1/3 c. heavy cream
5 tbsp. butter
1/2 tbsp. vanilla

Add sugar to cream gradually, stirring constantly. Cream butter; add to brown sugar mixture slowly, stirring. Add vanilla; beat thoroughly.

BOURBON EGGNOG SAUCE

1/4 lb. butter
1 c. sugar
1 egg
1/2 pt. cream
1/2 jigger bourbon

Cream butter and sugar. Add egg; beat well. Stir in cream; cook in double boiler over boiling water, stirring constantly, until smooth and thickened. Remove from heat; add bourbon.

BRANDY-CUSTARD SAUCE

1 egg, separated
Dash of salt
1 c. sifted confectioners' sugar
1/2 c. heavy cream, whipped
3 tbsp. brandy

Beat egg white with salt until foamy. Add 1/2 cup sugar gradually, beating well after each addition. Beat just until egg whites form soft peaks. Beat egg yolk until thick; add remaining sugar gradually, beating until thick and lemony. Fold egg yolk into egg white; add whipped cream and brandy. Blend lightly.

BRANDY TOPPING

2 c. (packed) light brown sugar
1/4 c. flour
1/4 c. butter
Pinch of salt
1 tbsp. lemon juice
1 tsp. vanilla
1/2 c. brandy

Combine sugar, flour, butter and salt in saucepan; blend well. Add 3 cups boiling water gradually; simmer, stirring constantly, until smooth and thickened. Remove from heat; stir in lemon juice and vanilla. Add brandy to warm sauce just before serving. Serve over date-nut pudding, steamed puddings or mincemeat pie.

BUTTERSCOTCH SAUCE

1 1/2 c. (packed) brown sugar
1/4 c. butter
2/3 c. white corn syrup
3/4 c. evaporated milk

Combine brown sugar, butter and corn syrup in heavy saucepan over medium heat; stir until butter melts and ingredients are blended. Bring to a boil; cook to soft-ball stage or 235 degrees on candy thermometer. Remove from heat; cool slightly. Add evaporated milk slowly, stirring until blended. Store in refrigerator. Serve over ice cream.

MARASCHINO CHERRY SAUCE

3/4 c. sugar
1 tbsp. cornstarch
1/4 c. light corn syrup
1/4 c. orange juice
1/4 c. maraschino cherry juice
Red food coloring
6 maraschino cherries, cut up

Mix sugar and cornstarch in saucepan; add corn syrup, juices and 1/2 cup water gradually, stirring until smooth. Cook for 5 minutes or until slightly thickened. Tint with desired amount of food coloring. Add cherries. Serve sauce on peaches or mixed fruits.

FLUFFY HONEY DRESSING

2 eggs
1/2 c. honey
1/4 c. lemon juice
2 tbsp. frozen orange juice concentrate
1/8 tsp. salt
1/2 c. heavy cream, whipped
2 tsp. grated lemon peel

Beat eggs; stir in honey, juices and salt. Cook, stirring, over low heat until thickened. Cool. Fold in cream and lemon peel. Serve over fruit.

CHERRIES VERMOUTH

1 can cherry pie filling
1 tsp. allspice
1/4 c. sweet vermouth

Combine pie filling, allspice and vermouth in saucepan; simmer until heated through. Serve over ice cream.

RED CHERRY SAUCE

1 can pitted dark cherries
1/2 c. sugar
2 tbsp. cornstarch
1 tsp. lemon rind
1 tbsp. lemon juice
1/2 c. port
2 tbsp. butter

Drain cherries; reserve juice. Combine sugar, cornstarch and reserved juice in saucepan; simmer, stirring constantly, until smooth and thickened. Add cherries, lemon rind, lemon juice, port and butter; heat through. Serve warm over ice cream.

CHOCOLATE-ALMOND SAUCE

3 1-oz. squares unsweetened chocolate
1 3/4 c. cream
1 c. sugar
1/4 c. flour
1/4 tsp. salt
1 tbsp. butter
1 tsp. vanilla
1/2 c. slivered almonds

Melt chocolate in cream in double boiler over hot water. Cook until smooth, stirring occasionally. Combine sugar, flour and salt; add enough chocolate mixture to make smooth paste. Add to remaining chocolate mixture. Cook until smooth and thickened. Add butter, vanilla and almonds; blend well. Serve over ice cream.

CHOCOLATE-NUT SAUCE

1 12-oz. package semisweet chocolate pieces
1 c. milk
1 c. salted peanuts, crushed
2 c. miniature marshmallows

Combine chocolate pieces and milk in top of double boiler; cook, stirring constantly, over hot water until chocolate is melted. Add peanuts and marshmallows; stir until marshmallows are partially dissolved. Serve hot or cold over ice cream. Yield: 1 quart.

EASY CHOCOLATE SYRUP

1 1/2 c. sugar
4 tbsp. cocoa
1 tbsp. flour
1 c. milk

Combine all ingredients in saucepan; cook, stirring, over medium heat until mixture comes to a boil. Remove from heat. Syrup may be served hot or cold. Mixture thickens as it cools.Serve over ice cream.

FUDGE SAUCE

1/2 c. butter
2 1/4 c. confectioners' sugar
2/3 c. evaporated milk
6 sq. unsweetened chocolate

Mix butter and sugar in top of double boiler. Add evaporated milk and chocolate; cook over hot water for 30 minutes. Remove from heat; beat well. Store in refrigerator.

CUSTARD SAUCE

1 tbsp. cornstarch
1/2 c. butter
1 c. sifted powdered sugar
Pinch of salt
1 tsp. vinegar
1 tsp. vanilla

Combine cornstarch and 1 cup cold water; simmer, stirring constantly, until clear. Add remaining ingredients; simmer, stirring constantly, until smooth and thickened. Serve warm over pound cake.

FLAMING FRUIT SAUCE

1 c. sugar
1/4 c. chopped maraschino cherries
1/4 c. chopped walnuts
1 c. prepared mincemeat
1 tbsp. brandy
1 tbsp. lemon juice
6 sugar cubes
Lemon extract

Combine sugar and 1/2 cup water in saucepan. Bring to a boil; boil for 5 minutes. Remove from heat; add cherries, walnuts, mincemeat, brandy and lemon juice. Cool. Dip sugar cubes into lemon extract when ready to serve; place over sauce. Ignite; serve flaming sauce over ice cream.

HARD SAUCE

1 stick butter
1 1/2 c. confectioners' sugar
1 tsp. brandy
Dash of nutmeg

Cream butter; beat in confectioners' sugar gradually. Add brandy, drop by drop. Place in serving dish; sprinkle with nutmeg. Refrigerate for at least 1 hour.

HAWAIIAN RHUBARB SAUCE

3 c. diced rhubarb
1 c. crushed pineapple
1/2 c. sugar
2 tbsp. cornstarch
1/4 tsp. salt
Juice of 1/2 lemon
2 tbsp. butter
Red food coloring

Combine rhubarb, pineapple, sugar and 1/2 cup water in saucepan. Bring to slow boil. Mix cornstarch with 2 tablespoons cold water; add to rhubarb mixture. Simmer, stirring constantly, for 5 minutes; remove from heat. Add salt, lemon juice, butter and desired amount of food coloring. Stir well.

FLAMING LEMON-NUTMEG SAUCE

1/2 c. sugar
1 tbsp. cornstarch
1/4 tsp. salt
1/2 tsp. nutmeg
2 tbsp. margarine
1 1/2 tbsp. lemon juice
Lemon slices
Sugar cubes
Lemon extract

Combine sugar, cornstarch, salt and nutmeg in saucepan with 1 cup boiling water; cook, stirring constantly, until clear and slightly thickened. Add margarine; stir until melted. Add lemon juice. Cut lemon slices into thirds. Float lemon pieces on hot sauce. Dip cubes of sugar into lemon extract; place one on each bit of lemon. Ignite sugar. Serve immediately. Serve on fruitcake or plum pudding.

LEMON SAUCE

1/2 c. sugar
1 1/2 tbsp. cornstarch
1/4 tsp. salt
1 1/2 tbsp. lemon juice
2 tbsp. butter
1/8 tsp. nutmeg

Mix sugar, cornstarch and salt together in saucepan; add 1 cup boiling water gradually, stirring constantly. Boil over low heat for 5 minutes. Add remaining ingredients; blend well. Serve hot on gingerbread or fruitcake.

KEY LIME FRUIT SAUCE

1 pkg. Key lime flavored pie filling
1/2 c. sugar
1 1-lb. 14-oz. can pineapple chunks
2 tbsp. margarine
Chopped fresh fruits

Place pie filling in saucepan; blend in sugar. Add 2 1/2 cups cold water gradually, stirring until smooth. Cook over medium heat, stirring constantly, until mixture comes to a full boil. Remove from heat. Drain pineapple chunks, reserving 1 cup liquid. Add reserved liquid and margarine to lime mixture, stirring until margarine is melted. Chill thoroughly. Combine pineapple chunks and fresh fruits in serving dish. Serve sauce with fruit mixture.

Key Lime Fruit Sauce . . . Transform pie filling into a sauce that tops cool fruit chunks.

LEMON-BUTTERSCOTCH SAUCE

1/2 c. butter
1/2 c. sugar
1/2 c. corn syrup
1/8 tsp. salt
1/2 c. evaporated milk
1 6-oz. can frozen lemonade

Combine butter, sugar, corn syrup and salt. Bring to a boil, stirring constantly, until sugar is dissolved. Reduce heat; boil for 2 minutes. Remove from heat; stir in evaporated milk and lemonade. Cool.

MACAROON ICE CREAM SAUCE

1/2 lb. marshmallows
1/2 c. bourbon
24 almond macaroons
1 pt. heavy cream, whipped

Cut marshmallows into quarters; soak in bourbon until dissolved. Crush macaroons; fold into whipped cream. Add marshmallow mixture. Chill. Serve over ice cream.

MINT MALLOW SAUCE

1/2 c. marshmallow creme
1/4 c. mint jelly
Green food coloring

Combine marshmallow creme and 3 tablespoons water; whip with electric mixer until fluffy. Add jelly; beat until smooth. Tint with food coloring. Serve over ice cream.

ORANGE SAUCE

1 egg, slightly beaten
Juice and rind of 1 lemon
1 c. sugar
Juice and rind of 1 orange

Combine all ingredients in saucepan; cook, stirring constantly, until clear. Refrigerate until ready to use.

EASY PINEAPPLE SAUCE

1 c. orange juice
2 tbsp. lemon juice
1 sm. can crushed pineapple
Dash of salt
1/2 c. sugar
4 tbsp. cornstarch
3/4 stick butter

Combine juices, pineapple, salt and sugar; mix well. Stir 1/2 cup water and cornstarch together; add to pineapple mixture. Bring to a boil; simmer, stirring constantly, for 5 minutes. Remove from heat; stir in butter. Serve on sliced angel food or pound cake.

FLUFFY PINEAPPLE TOPPER

1 9-oz. can crushed pineapple
2 eggs
1/4 c. lemon juice
1/2 c. sugar
1 c. heavy cream, whipped
Green food coloring

Drain pineapple; reserve syrup. Beat eggs with reserved syrup, lemon juice and sugar. Cook over medium heat, stirring, for about 5 minutes or until slightly thickened. Cool; fold in pineapple and whipped cream. Tint with food coloring as desired; chill.

POMEGRANATE SAUCE

4 pomegranates
2 c. sugar
2 tbsp. lemon juice

Crush seeds from 4 pomegranates to make 1 cup juice. Combine pomegranate juice, 1 cup water and sugar in saucepan. Bring to a boil; simmer, stirring constantly, for 10 minutes. Remove from heat; stir in lemon juice. Serve over ice cream.

PRALINE SAUCE

1 c. chopped pecans
2 c. dark corn syrup
1/2 c. sugar

Toast pecans in 400-degree oven for 15 minutes. Combine syrup, sugar and 1/3 cup boiling water in saucepan; bring to a boil over medium heat, stirring constantly. Remove from heat; stir in pecans. Serve sauce over ice cream or cake.

RAISIN-NUT SAUCE

6 tbsp. cornstarch
3 c. corn syrup
1 1/2 tsp. salt
2 tbsp. lemon juice
1 1/2 c. raisins
1 1/2 c. chopped walnuts

Combine cornstarch, syrup and salt in saucepan; add lemon juice and 6 cups water gradually. Bring to a boil; cook for 2 minutes, stirring, until clear and thickened. Remove from heat; add raisins and walnuts.

RASPBERRY SAUCE

1 10-oz. package frozen raspberries
1 1/2 tsp. cornstarch
1 tbsp. sugar

Thaw frozen berries; sieve. Measure 1 cup juice. Mix cornstarch and sugar with 1 tablespoon cold water; add raspberry juice. Cook, stirring constantly, until sauce is smooth and thickened; simmer for 10 minutes longer. Chill. Yield: 1 cup sauce.

RUBY STRAWBERRY SAUCE

1 pt. strawberries
2 c. sugar
2 tbsp. cornstarch

Slice half the strawberries; mash remaining strawberries in small bowl. Combine sugar, cornstarch, 1/2 cup water and mashed strawberries in medium saucepan. Cook, stirring constantly, until mixture thickens and boils for 3 minutes; strain into medium bowl. Fold in sliced strawberries. Serve warm or cold over cake, ice cream or pudding.

RUM SAUCE

1/4 c. rum
1 1/2 c. dry sherry
1 tbsp. lime juice
2 tbsp. melted butter
2 tbsp. flour
3/4 c. sugar

Combine all ingredients in saucepan; simmer, stirring constantly, until thickened. Serve hot over pancakes, cake or ice cream.

SHERRY CREAM SAUCE

3 egg yolks
3/4 c. sugar
1 c. white wine
1 c. heavy cream, whipped

Beat egg yolks with sugar; add wine. Cook in double boiler until thickened, stirring constantly. Chill. Fold in whipped cream 1 hour before using. Serve over cake or use as filling for cream puffs.

Sauerkraut

Sauerkraut is shredded cabbage that has been fermented in a brine of cabbage juice and salt. It is light straw in color and, when raw, has a full-bodied tangy flavor and crisp firm texture. Sauerkraut is often referred to simply as "kraut." It is erroneously believed to be German in origin because the Germans gave this much-loved food its name. Freely translated, "sauerkraut" is German for "sour cabbage." However, Chinese laborers of the third century B.C. ate cabbage fermented in wine, the earliest form of sauerkraut. They knew that the cabbage helped prevent diseases caused by an all-rice diet. Sauerkraut is an excellent source of Vitamin C. It also supplies Vitamins B_1 and B_2, iron, calcium, and phosphorus. (1 cup canned drained sauerkraut = 30 calories)

AVAILABILITY: Sauerkraut is sold year-round canned in a brine of sauerkraut juice and salt water. Sauerkraut juice available year-round canned.

STORING: Store unopened cans on kitchen shelf and opened cans in refrigerator. Sauerkraut can be packed into freezer containers and frozen.

PREPARATION: Sauerkraut that is raw or barely heated through has tangy natural flavor. For more mildly-flavored sauerkraut, cook it for a longer time or blend it with other foods. See specific recipes.

SERVING: Sauerkraut especially complements frankfurters, spareribs, sausages, ham, pork, and game birds. Use it also in appetizers, first course specialities, salads, sandwiches, soups, stews, stuffings, and casseroles. Combine sauerkraut with leftover meats, fish, or vegetables as a food extender.
(See CABBAGE.)

SAUERKRAUT BALLS

1 1-lb. can sauerkraut, drained
1 med. onion, chopped fine
4 tbsp. butter
1 1/2 c. ground ham
1 clove of garlic, crushed
Flour
1/2 c. chicken broth
1 tbsp. chopped parsley
1/2 c. milk
2 beaten eggs
Fine bread crumbs

Grind sauerkraut. Brown onion lightly in butter in skillet. Add ham, garlic and 1/3 cup flour. Mix well. Stir broth, sauerkraut and parsley into onion mixture. Cook, stirring, until thick. Spread in flat pan; chill. Shape sauerkraut mixture into 1-inch balls. Combine milk and eggs. Roll balls in flour; dip into egg mixture. Roll in crumbs. Fry in deep 365 degree fat until lightly browned. Yield: 50 balls.

EASY SAUERKRAUT RELISH

1 No. 2 can sauerkraut
1 c. tomato catsup
1 c. chili sauce
1 c. chopped celery
1 c. chopped onion
1 c. chopped green pepper
2 tsp. paprika
1 c. sugar

Combine all ingredients; mix well. Allow to stand for 24 hours. Yield: 6-8 servings.

SAUERKRAUT RELISH

1 No. 303 can sauerkraut, drained
1 c. chopped onions
1/2 c. chopped green pepper
1 c. sugar
1 c. vinegar
1 sm. can pimento, chopped

Combine all ingredients; mix well. Cover; store in refrigerator for 24 hours before serving. Yield: 10 servings.

CANNED SAUERKRAUT

Salt
Shredded cabbage
Sugar
Vinegar

Place 1 teaspoon salt in each sterilized quart jar; fill each jar with cabbage. Add 1 teaspoon salt, 1 teaspoon sugar and 1 teaspoon vinegar; cover with boiling water. Seal tightly. Let stand for several weeks. Sauerkraut will be white and crisp.

OVERNIGHT SAUERKRAUT SALAD

1 16-oz. can sauerkraut, drained
1/2 c. dry white wine
1 sm. onion, minced
1 med. red apple, chopped
1 tsp. celery seed

Combine sauerkraut and wine in saucepan; cover. Simmer for 15 minutes. Cool. Combine onion, apple, and celery seed with sauerkraut mixture; cover. Chill overnight. Serve with pork roast or chops. Yield: 4 servings.

Sauerkraut and Apple Supreme . . . Pork with tangy sauerkraut, apples, and brown sugar.

SAUERKRAUT AND APPLE SUPREME

4 c. drained sauerkraut
2 peeled apples, chopped
1/2 c. apple brandy
1 tbsp. light brown sugar
2 tbsp. butter

Combine sauerkraut, apples, brandy, brown sugar and butter in skillet. Simmer, covered, for 5 minutes or until apples are tender. Spoon sauerkraut mixture into serving dish. Garnish with additional apple slices and parsley. Serve with pork.

SAUERKRAUT-CARROT SALAD

1 No. 303 can shredded sauerkraut
1/4 c. sugar
1/2 c. chopped celery
1/2 c. shredded carrots
1/2 c. chopped green pepper
1/4 c. chopped onion

Drain sauerkraut; combine sauerkraut and sugar in bowl. Chill for 30 minutes. Add celery, carrots, green pepper and onion; refrigerate for 12 hours. Yield: 4-6 servings.

ALSATIAN SAUERKRAUT

Bacon strips
1 can sauerkraut
Polish sausage
4 smoked pork chops
Whole peeled potatoes
Juniper berries
1 bottle white wine

Place bacon strips in bottom of 2-quart casserole; arrange half the sauerkraut over bacon. Cut sausage into 2-inch pieces; place pork chops and sausages over sauerkraut layer. Place potatoes over pork chops and sausages. Top with remaining sauerkraut. Add additional bacon strips; sprinkle with juniper berries. Cover with wine. Bake at 350 degrees for 1 hour and 30 minutes to 2 hours. Yield: 4-6 servings.

SAUERKRAUT WITH APPLES

4 c. drained sauerkraut
2 red apples, thinly sliced
1/2 c. apple brandy
1 tbsp. brown sugar
2 tbsp. butter

Combine sauerkraut, apples, brandy, brown sugar and butter in skillet; cover. Simmer 5 minutes or until apples are tender. Garnish with additional apple slices and parsley if desired.

HUNGARIAN SAUERKRAUT CASSEROLE

1 lb. ground beef
1 lb. ground pork
1 tbsp. shortening
1/2 c. rice
1 lge. can sauerkraut
1 sm. onion, chopped
1 tsp. paprika
1/4 tsp. pepper
1/2 tsp. salt
1 pt. sour cream

Brown beef and pork in shortening in large skillet. Add 1/2 cup water; let simmer. Cook rice in boiling water for 15 to 20 minutes; drain. Cook sauerkraut in small amount of water for about 15 minutes; drain. Arrange layers of sauerkraut and rice in greased casserole, sprinkling each layer with small amount of onion and seasonings. Add 2 to 3 tablespoons sour cream to each layer. Repeat until all ingredients are used, ending with sauerkraut on top. Bake at 350 degrees for 35 to 40 minutes. Yield: 12 servings.

ORANGE SAUERKRAUT

1 1-lb. 12-oz. can sauerkraut
1 11-oz. can mandarin oranges
2 tsp. grated orange peel
1 tsp. caraway seed
1/2 c. raisins
Salt and pepper to taste
2 tbsp. melted butter

Drain sauerkraut and oranges, reserving juice from oranges. Combine sauerkraut, orange peel, caraway seed, raisins and reserved juice. Add salt and pepper. Place in greased 1 1/2-quart casserole; cover. Bake in 350-degree oven for 1 hour. Arrange orange segments on top; drizzle with melted butter. Return to oven for 10 minutes. Yield: 6 servings.

SAUERKRAUT-APPLESAUCE BAKE

3 c. cooked sauerkraut
1 c. applesauce
2 onions, grated
4 tbsp. brown sugar
1 tsp. caraway seed
2 tbsp. butter

Arrange layers of sauerkraut, applesauce and onions in 2-quart casserole; dot with brown sugar, caraway seed and butter. Bake in 300-degree oven for 2 hours. Yield: 6 servings.

SAUERKRAUT-PORK CASSEROLE

1 lge. onion
Margarine
3 tbsp. paprika
2 lb. lean boneless pork
3/4 c. rice
1 No. 2 1/2 can sauerkraut
1/2 pt. sour cream
Milk

Cut onion into small cubes; saute in margarine in frypan until transparent. Add paprika; stir well. Cut pork into 1-inch cubes; add to onion. Saute until browned. Add enough water to completely cover pork mixture. Simmer, covered, for 35 to 45 minutes or until tender. Cook rice according to package directions. Wash sauerkraut in strainer; drain thoroughly. Saute in margarine for several minutes. Place half the sauerkraut in 2-quart casserole. Spread rice over sauerkraut; top with pork mixture. Cover with remaining sauerkraut. Pour pan drippings over layers. Dilute sour cream with milk; spread over top. Bake at 350 degrees for 45 to 60 minutes. Broil for several minutes to brown top. May be prepared ahead and refrigerated before adding sour cream. Yield: 6 servings.

SAUERKRAUT SPECIAL

1 med. onion, chopped
1/4 c. chopped green pepper
2 tbsp. salad oil
2 7 1/2-oz. cans tomato sauce
1 can mushrooms, chopped
1 med. apple, chopped
1 lge. can sauerkraut
1/2 c. packaged precooked rice
3 tbsp. brown sugar
1/4 tsp. caraway seed
1 tbsp. chili powder
1 pkg. wieners, chopped
1 tbsp. salt

Cook onion and green pepper in oil in skillet until limp. Combine all ingredients; pour into greased baking dish. Bake for 1 hour at 350 degrees. Yield: 15 servings.

SPICY SAUERKRAUT

1/2 lb. bacon, diced
2 med. onions, chopped
1 No. 2 1/2 can sauerkraut
1 No. 2 1/2 can tomatoes
1 c. (packed) brown sugar

Brown bacon and onions in large skillet; drain. Add remaining ingredients; mix well. Pour into 2-quart casserole. Bake at 350 degrees for 1 hour. Yield: 8-10 servings.

PLANKED KRAUT DINNER

Color photograph for this recipe on page 311.

1 clove of garlic, minced
1/2 c. chopped onion
Butter
2 c. drained sauerkraut
3 tbsp. sugar
1/2 tsp. salt
Pepper to taste
1 4-oz. can pimentos
8 carrots
1/4 c. (packed) light brown sugar
1 tbsp. light corn syrup
2 tbsp. prepared mustard
8 frankfurters
4 servings mashed potatoes

Saute garlic and onion in 3 tablespoons butter in large skillet until tender. Add sauerkraut, sugar, 1/4 teaspoon salt and pepper. Drain pimentos; dice. Add to sauerkraut mixture; toss until well mixed. Cover; keep warm over low heat. Pare carrots; cut into 1-inch slices diagonally. Simmer in salted water for about 20 minutes or until tender; drain. Combine 2 tablespoons butter, brown sugar, corn syrup, mustard and remaining salt in small saucepan; heat until blended, stirring constantly. Pour over carrots; toss gently until coated. Place sauerkraut mixture in center of large heatproof plank. Cut 3 diagonal 1/2-inch deep slits in frankfurters; brush with melted butter. Arrange frankfurters, carrots and mashed potatoes around sauerkraut mixture; drizzle melted butter over potatoes. Broil 6 to 8 inches from heat until frankfurters and potatoes are lightly browned. Yield: 4 servings.

SAUERKRAUT CAKE

2/3 c. butter
1 1/2 c. sugar
3 eggs
1 tsp. vanilla
2 1/4 c. flour
1/2 c. cocoa
1 tsp. baking powder
1 tsp. soda
1/4 tsp. salt
2/3 c. sauerkraut

Cream butter, sugar, eggs and vanilla together. Sift dry ingredients together; add to creamed mixture alternately with 1 cup water. Rinse sauerkraut; drain well. Chop sauerkraut finely; add to batter. Spoon into greased and floured 9 x 13-inch pan. Bake at 350 degrees for 35 to 40 minutes.

Sausage

Sausages are processed meat products commonly made from finely chopped pork, beef, veal, or varying combinations of the three. The meat is highly flavored with seasonings such as salt, pepper, sage, mace, ginger, nutmeg, garlic, and so on. It is then stuffed into cleaned and prepared animal entrails or synthetic casings. There are many different kinds of sausages because of varying sausage meats, spices, and processing procedures. Generally, all sausages may be classified as fresh, requiring refrigeration; or dry, requiring no refrigeration. Fresh sausages may be smoked or smoked and precooked. Perhaps the two most familiar fresh sausages are all-pork sausage, made from selected fresh pork cuts and usually seasoned with thyme and sage; and smoked and precooked frankfurters (see FRANKFURTERS). Other fresh sausages include country style sausage; kielbasa or Polish sausage; bratwurst; blutwurst or blood sausage; braunschweiger; knockwurst; and bologna. Common dry sausages, which are dry cured and usually smoked, are salami; pepperoni; mortadella; Lebanon bologna; chorizo; and cervelat or cervelas. The latter sausages are also called "summer sausages" because they store well, requiring no refrigeration, even during this season. Pork sausage contains protein, fat, and calcium. (4 oz. canned pork sausage = 340 calories)

AVAILABILITY: Sausages are sold year-round in a variety of ways, including by the pound, canned, or packaged. Pork sausage may be marketed in patties or link form. A pound box contains 16 links; oblong patties are 12 to the pound.

BUYING: Always examine package label of all sausages. Federal regulations require the listing of sausage ingredients in order of predominance. If more than 3 1/2-percent cereal fillers or non-fat dry milk has been added, sausages are labeled "imitation." However, unless marked "pure" or "all meat," sausages probably contain some cereal fillers. Sausages may be marked "skinless"; this means that synthetic casings have been removed. Buy approximately 1 pound fresh sausage for 4 servings, slightly less for dry sausages.

STORING: Refrigerate fresh sausages. Freshly ground sausage meat and country style sausage should be used as soon as possible. Keep dry sausages in cool, dark, dry place indefinitely.

PREPARATION: Depending on variety, sausages may be broiled, pan broiled, baked, pan fried, or boiled. To broil or pan fry sausages, prick sausages to keep skins from bursting. This is unnecessary if you add a small amount of cold water to pan before cooking. If sausages swell anyway, prick lightly with fork before they burst. Cook link sausages slowly with frequent turning. Fried sausages are tender and less greasy if placed in cold frying pan with no added fat.

SERVING: Use sausages in hors d'oeuvres, snacks, salads, soups, sandwiches, casseroles, scrapple, stuffings, antipastos, pasta dishes, other main dishes, and so on.

ENGLISH SAUSAGE ROLLS

1 lb. pork sausage
2 c. flour
1/2 tsp. salt
2/3 c. shortening

Cook sausage in small skillet partially. Sift flour with salt; cut in shortening with pastry blender. Add 5 tablespoons ice water, 1 spoonful at a time using fork to combine water. Add only enough water to make ingredients' hold together. Divide dough into 2 equal parts. Roll 1 part on floured surface into 1/8-inch thick rectangle, cut into 8 equal pieces. Place small amount of sausage on each piece. Moisten edges of pastry; fold over, pressing edges together. Place on greased cookie sheet. Bake at 400 degrees for 20 minutes. Yield: 16 servings.

FROSTED BRAUNSCHWEIGER ROLL

1 lb. braunschweiger
1/2 c. catsup
1 tsp. Worcestershire sauce
1 3-oz. package cream cheese, softened
Snipped parsley
Paprika to taste

Skin braunschweiger; mash with fork. Beat in catsup and Worcestershire sauce. Place on waxed paper; shape into 9-inch long roll. Refrigerate until firm. Remove paper; place on tray. Frost entire surface with cream cheese, thinning cream cheese with small amount of milk if necessary. Sprinkle top with parsley and paprika. Serve with cocktail crackers.

SAUSAGE BALLS

1/2 tsp. salt
1 lb. pork sausage
1 lb. fresh ground pork
1/2 c. rice
3 tbsp. flour
2 c. milk
1 tsp. cinnamon
1/8 tsp. cloves

Combine salt, sausage, pork and rice; shape into 1-inch balls. Brown balls gradually in skillet. Add 1 cup water; simmer for about 1 hour or until water has evaporated. Remove balls from skillet; blend flour into pan drippings. Stir in milk and spices gradually. Cook over low heat, stirring constantly, until thickened. Return sausage ball to skillet; heat through. Serve in chafing dish with cocktail picks.

SAUSAGE BITES

1 lb. bulk sausage
1 egg, slightly beaten
1/2 c. fine cracker crumbs
1/3 c. milk
1/2 tsp. sage
1/2 tsp. salt
1/2 tsp. barbecue seasoning
1 sm. can tomato sauce
2 tbsp. brown sugar
1 tbsp. vinegar
1 tbsp. soy sauce

Combine sausage, egg, crumbs, milk, sage, salt and barbecue seasoning. Beat at high speed with electric mixer for 5 minutes. Shape into 3 dozen 1-inch balls. Place in electric skillet. Set temperature at 225 degrees; brown sausage balls. Pour off excess fat. Mix 1/2 cup water, tomato sauce, sugar, vinegar and soy sauce. Pour over sausages; cover. Reduce temperature to 200 degrees; simmer for 15 minutes. Serve from chafing dish with wooden picks.

SAUSAGE PINWHEELS

2 c. flour
1/3 c. cornmeal
2 tsp. baking powder
1/2 tsp. salt
1/4 c. shortening
Milk
1 lb. sausage

Combine dry ingredients; cut shortening into flour mixture until mixture resembles fine crumbs. Add milk, mixing thoroughly to form stiff dough. Roll into rectangle; cover with thin layer of sausage. Roll up as for jelly roll. Chill overnight. Cut in thin slices. Bake at 400 degrees for 10 to 12 minutes or until brown. Yield: 3 dozen.

SAUSAGE-CHEESE BALLS

8 oz. Cheddar cheese, grated
2 c. prepared biscuit mix
1 1-lb. package bulk sausage

Combine all ingredients; mix until blended well. Form into 1-inch balls. Place in large shallow baking pan. Bake at 350 degrees for 20 to 25 minutes. Serve hot.

SAUSAGE CASSEROLE

3 c. diced potatoes
3 c. chopped cabbage
1 lb. bulk sausage
1 1/2 tsp. salt
1/4 tsp. pepper

Mix all ingredients thoroughly. Pack into 2-quart casserole. Pour 1/2 cup water over top; cover. Bake at 325 degrees for 1 hour and 30 minutes. Yield: 8 servings.

SAUSAGE MOSTACCIOLI

1 lb. pork sausage links
1/2 c. chopped green peppers
1/2 c. chopped onions
1 1-lb. can tomatoes
1 6-oz. can tomato paste
1/2 tsp. salt
1/2 tsp. oregano
1/4 tsp. pepper
8 oz. mostaccioli
8 oz. Cheddar cheese, thinly sliced
Grated Parmesan cheese

Panfry sausage according to package directions. Drain off liquid; cut sausage links in half crosswise. Remove sausage from skillet. Add green peppers and onions; saute in fat until tender. Drain off excess fat. Add tomatoes, tomato paste, 1/2 cup water, salt, oregano and pepper to onion mixture. Layer mostaccioli, sausage, sauce and Cheddar cheese in 2-quart casserole. Repeat layers. Sprinkle with Parmesan cheese. Bake at 350 degrees for 30 minutes. Yield: 6-8 servings.

SOUTHERN SAUSAGE CASSEROLE

1/2 lb. pork sausage
1 c. chopped celery
1/4 c. chopped onions
1/4 c. chopped green pepper
1 c. cooked kidney beans
2 tbsp. minced parsley
3/4 tsp. salt
3/4 c. tomato paste
1 c. sifted flour
1 1/2 tsp. baking powder
2 tbsp. shortening
1/2 c. shredded American cheese
1/2 c. milk

Brown sausage in heavy skillet; add all vegetables except beans. Brown vegetables lightly; drain off excess fat. Season with 1/4 teaspoon salt. Combine tomato paste and 3/4 cup water; add to sausage mixture. Add beans; mix well. Cover; simmer for 10 minutes. Pour mixture into 1 1/2-quart casserole. Sift flour with baking powder and remaining salt. Cut in shortening until mixture is crumbly. Add cheese and milk, mixing only until dry ingredients are moistened. Drop cheese mixture by spoonfuls over top of sausage mixture. Bake at 425 degrees for 20 minutes. Yield: 6 servings.

Sausage-Sauerkraut Casserole . . . The perfect supper dish, sausages with apples in sauerkraut.

SAUSAGE-SAUERKRAUT CASSEROLE

1 1-lb. roll Polish sausage
4 Washington apples
1 tsp. caraway seed
2 1/2 c. sauerkraut
3 tbsp. bacon fat

Cut sausage into 1/2-inch thick slices; arrange half the sausage in bottom of greased casserole. Peel and core apples; cut into crosswise slices. Arrange half the apples over sausage. Add caraway seed to sauerkraut; spread over apple mixture. Arrange remaining sausage slices on sauerkraut; top with remaining apple slices. Pour bacon fat over top. Cover. Bake at 350 degrees for 35 to 40 minutes. Yield: 4 servings.

SAUSAGE-PEANUT PILAF

1 lb. pork sausage
1 c. finely sliced celery
1/2 c. chopped onions
1 c. cooked rice
1 can mushroom soup
1/4 c. chopped green pepper
1/3 c. chopped salted peanuts
6 to 8 stuffed green olives, sliced

Cook sausage until browned lightly. Add celery and onions; cook for 3 minutes. Pour off drippings; add rice, soup and green pepper to sausage mixture. Pour into 1-quart casserole; sprinkle with chopped peanuts. Bake at 350 degrees for 30 minutes. Top with sliced olives; serve. Yield: 4-6 servings.

HOMEMADE SAUSAGE WITH SAGE

2 lb. lean pork, ground
1 tsp. salt
1/2 tsp. sage
1/2 tsp. cumin
1/4 tsp. ginger
1 bay leaf
1/2 tsp. pepper

Mix pork thoroughly with remaining ingredients; shape into 12 to 15 patties. Fry in skillet for 8 minutes on each side, until browned. Yield: 8-12 servings.

GERMAN OATMEAL SAUSAGE

1 pork shoulder
Salt to taste
Quick-cooking oats
1 tbsp. thyme
Butter

Bring pork to a boil in 2 cups water with 2 teaspoons salt in Dutch oven; simmer until tender. Remove from broth; cool. Grind pork; return to broth. Heat to boiling; add oats. Cook, stirring, until oats drop from spoon. Add thyme and additional salt before mixture thickens. Pour into molds; let stand until firm. Remove; wrap in foil or freezer paper. Freeze; cut in thin slices. Fry in butter until crisp. Yield: 4-6 servings.

VENISON SAUSAGE

12 lb. lean venison
6 lb. pork fat
3 tbsp. sage
4 tsp. cloves
2 tsp. nutmeg
1/4 c. salt
1/4 c. pepper

Trim fat from venison; grind with medium blade of grinder. Grind pork fat; add to venison. Add sage, cloves, nutmeg, salt and pepper; mix well. Chill for 24 hours. Wrap in foil; freeze.

HUNGARIAN SAUSAGE LOAF

2 lb. pork sausage
4 c. bread crumbs
1 egg, slightly beaten
1 c. sour cream
Paprika to taste

Combine all ingredients; pack firmly into loaf pan. Bake in 350-degree oven for 1 hour and 30 minutes. Yield: 6 servings.

LEMON-SAUSAGE LOAF

1 lb. pork sausage
1 egg
3 slices bread, crumbled
Grated rind of 1 lemon
1 tsp. salt
1/4 tsp. allspice
1/4 tsp. paprika
2 slices bacon
2 slices tomato

Combine all ingredients except bacon and tomato; form into loaf. Place in baking pan; top with bacon and tomato. Bake at 350 degrees for 30 minutes. Yield: 6 servings.

BARBECUED SAUSAGE

1 lb. link sausage
1 onion, chopped
1/2 c. chopped celery
Butter
1/2 c. catsup
Salt and pepper to taste
1 tsp. Worcestershire sauce
1/4 c. vinegar
1/4 c. sugar
1 tbsp. prepared mustard
1 tsp. paprika

Bring sausage to a boil in small amount of water; cook for 2 minutes, browning slightly. Cut into bite-sized pieces. Cook onion and celery in small amount of butter until tender and transparent. Add sausage. Combine all remaining ingredients; pour over sausage mixture. Simmer for 30 minutes. Serve on buns. Yield: 6 servings.

PIGS IN BLANKETS

2 c. flour
1 tsp. salt
4 tsp. baking powder
4 tbsp. shortening
3/4 c. milk
8 pork sausages

Mix flour, salt and baking powder; sift twice. Cut in shortening; add milk. Roll out 1/4 inch thick on floured surface; cut into squares. Fry sausages partially; roll up in squares of dough, leaving ends open. Bake on greased baking sheet in 400-degree oven for 15 minutes. Yield: 8 servings.

HOT SAUSAGE AND APPLE SANDWICH

1 lb. sausage
3 apples, sliced
Buttered toast

Shape sausage into round patties, 1/2 inch thick. Fry until browned and tender; remove from pan. Keep sausage hot. Saute apple slices in small amount of sausage drippings. Place sausage patty and apple slice on each piece buttered toast. Garnish with bacon curls.Yield: 4 servings.

SAUSAGE CAKE

1 lb. raisins
1 1/2 tsp. soda
1 lb. mild sausage
3 c. flour
Juice and grated rind of 1 orange
2 c. sugar
1/2 tsp. salt
Cinnamon to taste
Allspice to taste
1 c. chopped nuts

Bring raisins to a boil in water to cover in saucepan. Drain, reserving 1 cup liquid. Dissolve soda in reserved liquid. Combine raisins, soda mixture, sausage, flour, orange juice, rind, sugar and seasonings. Stir in nuts. Spoon into baking dish. Bake at 350 degrees for 1 hour and 30 minutes.

SAUSAGE DUMPLINGS

1 lge. can tomatoes
Salt
Pepper to taste
2 c. flour
1 tsp. baking powder
1/2 lb. bulk sausage
1 egg, slightly beaten

Mash tomatoes in saucepan; season with salt to taste and pepper. Bring to a boil. Sift flour, baking powder and 1/2 teaspoon salt together; add sausage. Mix well; add egg. Drop by spoonfuls into tomato mixture; cook for 15 minutes. Yield: 4 servings.

SAUSAGE-NOODLE SPECIAL

3/4 lb. pork sausage
4 oz. wide noodles
1/2 c. chopped onion
1/2 c. sliced celery
1/2 tsp. salt
1/8 tsp. pepper
1 tsp. chili powder
1/2 tsp. dry mustard
1/2 tsp. sugar
1 20-oz. can tomatoes
1/2 c. grated cheese

Cut sausage into 1-inch pieces; brown well in skillet. Drain off all fat. Add noodles, onion and celery. Sprinkle with salt, pepper, chili powder, dry mustard and sugar. Combine tomatoes, 1/2 cup water and cheese. Pour over mixture in skillet. Simmer, covered, for 30 minutes, stirring occasionally. Add additional boiling water if necessary. Serve hot with additional grated cheese. Yield: 4-5 servings.

SAUSAGE-PEACH BALLS

1 lb. pork sausage
2 tbsp. minced onion
2 c. soft bread crumbs
1/4 tsp. salt
1/8 tsp. pepper
1 egg, beaten
8 canned peach halves
24 whole cloves
Hot peach syrup

Preheat oven to 350 degrees. Combine sausage, onion, crumbs, seasonings and egg; form into 8 balls. Arrange peach halves, cut sides up, in shallow baking dish. Stick 3 cloves around edge of each peach half; place sausage balls in peach centers. Bake for 45 minutes; drain off fat. Pour syrup over sausage balls. Yield: 4 servings.

SAUSAGE PIES

2 c. flour
4 tsp. baking powder
Salt
2 tbsp. shortening
1/4 c. milk
3/4 lb. sausage
4 tomatoes, halved crosswise

Sift flour with baking powder and 1/2 teaspoon salt; add shortening. Mix thoroughly with pastry blender. Add milk to make stiff dough; knead until smooth. Roll out 1/8 inch thick; cut into eight 4-inch squares. Divide sausage into 8 flat cakes; place on each square of dough. Fold up edges to resemble small pies. Crust should hold in liquids cooked from sausage but not cover sausage completely. Place tomato halves over sausage. Sprinkle each pie lightly with salt to taste. Bake at 400 degrees for 25 minutes or until crust is brown and crisp. Yield: 8 servings.

SAUCY SAUSAGE PINWHEELS

1 1/2 c. cornmeal
2 1/2 c. sifted flour
2 tbsp. baking powder
4 tsp. salt
1/2 c. shortening
1 1/3 c. milk
2 lb. bulk sausage, cooked
2 c. grated sharp cheese
2 6-oz. cans tomato paste
1/2 tsp. oregano
1/4 tsp. pepper
1/2 c. sliced stuffed olives

Sift cornmeal, flour, baking powder and 2 teaspoons salt together into bowl. Cut in shortening until mixture resembles coarse crumbs. Add milk; stir lightly until mixture is just moistened. Divide dough into 2 parts. Knead 1 part gently for several seconds on lightly floured board. Roll to form 10 x 16-inch rectangle. Spread half the sausage and half the cheese over dough. Roll lengthwise, jelly roll fashion. Cut into 12 slices, 1 3/8 inches wide. Repeat with second part of dough. Place in greased large muffin cups. Bake at 400 degrees for 15 to 28 minutes. Combine tomato paste, 2 cups water, oregano, remaining salt, pepper and olives; mix thoroughly. Bring to a boil. Serve over pinwheels.

SAUSAGE RING

1 lb. sausage
Bread crumbs
1 egg
1 c. milk
1/4 c. minced onions
1 c. shredded sharp Cheddar cheese
1/2 tsp. salt
1/4 tsp. monosodium glutamate

Break up sausage in large bowl; add all remaining ingredients. Stir, mixing well until blended thoroughly. Place in buttered foil-lined ring mold. Bake at 350 degrees for 1 hour. Drain off excess fat. Invert sausage ring onto round preheated platter. Strip off foil. Fill center of ring with mashed potatoes if desired. Yield: 4 servings.

SAUSAGE SPOON DISH

2 c. milk
1 c. cornmeal
1 tbsp. sugar
1/2 tsp. salt
1 tsp. baking powder
2 eggs, separated
1 lb. sausage
4 oz. grated cheese

Scald milk; add cornmeal, sugar, salt and baking powder. Let cool. Add beaten egg yolks; fold in stiffly beaten egg whites. Pour into greased 2-quart baking dish. Bake at 350 degrees. Saute sausage in skillet until all fat is rendered; drain on absorbent paper. Crumble sausage over cornmeal mixture. Sprinkle cheese over sausage. Bake for 20 minutes longer. Yield: 6 servings.

SAUSAGE SUNBURST

1 lb. pork sausage links
1 1/4 c. sifted flour
1 c. cornmeal
2 tbsp. baking powder
2 tbsp. sugar
1/2 tsp. soda
3/4 tsp. salt
1 c. buttermilk
1/2 c. chopped onions
2 c. milk

Brown sausage in large skillet; drain fat into measuring cup. Arrange half the links in skillet in sunburst fashion, radiating from center. Sift 1 cup flour and remaining dry ingredients together into bowl; stir in 3 tablespoons sausage drippings. Add buttermilk, stirring just enough to blend. Pour batter over links. Bake at 400 degrees for 25 minutes. Invert onto serving plate. Measure 1/4 cup drippings into separate skillet; brown onions in drippings. Blend in remaining flour; add milk all at once. Bring to a boil, stirring constantly; cook for 1 minute. Quarter remaining links; add to milk mixture. Serve gravy over sunburst. Yield: 5-6 servings.

STUFFED SAUSAGE ROLL

2 lb. bulk sausage
2 c. diced apples
2 c. bread crumbs
2 sm. onions, chopped

Pat sausage into rectangle, 1/2 inch thick, on waxed paper; chill for 1 hour. Mix apples, bread crumbs and onions together; spread over sausage. Roll, jelly roll fashion; tuck in edges to enclose filling. Place in shallow baking pan. Bake at 350 degrees for 45 minutes. Cut into 1-inch slices to serve.

SPANISH SAUSAGE

1 1/2 lb. bulk pork sausage
1 No. 2 can tomato juice
1/2 c. minced onions
1/2 c. minced green pepper
1/2 c. finely chopped celery
1/2 tsp. salt
Dash of pepper
1 1/2 tsp. sugar
2 tbsp. flour
Grated Parmesan cheese

Shape sausage into 10 patties; brown in hot skillet. Pour off half the fat; add tomato juice, onions, green pepper, celery and seasonings. Simmer, covered, for 1 hour. Remove sausage to hot platter. Blend flour and 1/4 cup water, making smooth paste; add to tomato juice mixture, stirring constantly, until mixture is bubbly and thickened. Pour sauce over sausage; sprinkle with cheese. Serve hot. Yield: 5 servings.

SURPRISE SAUSAGE STICKS

16 sausage links
1/2 c. milk
1/4 c. shortening
3 tbsp. sugar
1 pkg. yeast
2 3/4 c. sifted self-rising flour
1/2 lb. sharp Cheddar cheese
1 tbsp. melted butter

Cook sausages until lightly browned; set aside. Scald milk; add shortening, sugar and 1/4 cup cold water, mixing well. Cool to lukewarm. Dissolve yeast in 1/4 cup warm water; add to lukewarm milk mixture, mixing well. Add flour gradually, about 1/2 cup at a time; mix well to form dough. Turn out onto lightly floured board. Knead for 3 minutes or until smooth. Place in greased bowl; cover with towel. Let rise in warm place for 30 minutes or until doubled in bulk. Punch dough down; turn out on lightly floured board. Knead for 3 minutes. Roll dough into 16-inch square. Cut into sixteen 4-inch squares. Place sausage in center of each square. Cut cheese into 32 strips, 3 1/2 x 1/4 inches wide. Add two strips of cheese, 1 on each side of sausage. Fold dough over sausage and cheese; press edges together. Place, seam sides down, 1 inch apart on greased baking sheet. Cover lightly; let rise for 20 minutes. Bake in 425-degree oven for 12 minutes. Brush with melted butter; serve hot.

Scallop

Scallops are mollusks with two delicately ridged shells that are joined together by an edible muscle. The muscle is the portion of the scallop that is usually eaten. It is removed from the shells immediately after capture and preserved on ice. There are two types of scallops: the deep sea and bay varieties. *Sea scallops* contain large, coarse, 1- to 2-inch muscles. They are found in the icy waters of the North and Middle Atlantic. *Bay scallops* are small and tender with a maximum muscle width of 3/4-inch. They inhabit inshore bays and estuaries from Long Island Sound north to Nantucket. Scallops are rich in protein, B vitamins, and minerals. They are low in fat content. (3 1/2 ounces uncooked scallops = 80 calories)

AVAILABILITY: Scallops are most often shucked and cleaned before marketing. Fresh sea scallops are available year-round, fresh bay scallops from September through April. They are usually preserved on ice and sold by the pound. Frozen and canned sea and bay scallops are available year-round.

BUYING: Fresh scallops should be virtually free of liquid and should have a detectable sweet odor. Sea scallops are white, orange, or pink. The more expensive bay scallops are usually creamy white, light tan, or pink. Allow 1/3 to 1/2 pound scallops per serving.

STORING: For fresh scallops–Pack on ice and refrigerate at a temperature near 33 degrees. Use within 2 days. For frozen scallops –Keep frozen until ready to use. Thaw in refrigerator and use as soon as possible.

PREPARATION: Scallops lend themselves to various methods of preparation: broiling, baking, sauteing, frying, stewing, and so on. To shuck freshly caught scallops – Wash and scrub shells thoroughly. Place in a 300 degree oven until the shells have opened. Remove muscle, wash and pat dry. Leave bay scallops whole; halve or quarter sea scallops across grain. See specific recipe directions for more detailed preparation.

SERVING: Scallops are both tasty and versatile. They can be enjoyed raw as an appetizer or cooked in fish salads and stews and in creamed and casserole dishes. They can also be skewered with bacon pieces and grilled. (See SEAFOOD.)

BROILED SCALLOPS WITH PEACHES

1 lb. scallops
2 tbsp. melted butter
2 tbsp. lemon juice
1/2 tsp. salt
Dash of pepper
12 canned peach halves
1/4 tsp. cinnamon
1/4 tsp. cloves
1/4 tsp. mace
3 slices bacon

Cut scallops into 1/2-inch pieces; saute in butter until golden brown. Combine lemon juice, 1/4 teaspoon salt, pepper and scallops; place peach halves in 11 x 7 x 1-inch baking pan. Combine cinnamon, cloves, mace and remaining salt. Sprinkle over peaches. Place about 2 tablespoons scallop mixture in center of each peach. Cut bacon into fourths crosswise. Place slice on each peach. Broil about 4 inches from source of heat for 8 to 10 minutes or until bacon is crisp.

COQUILLE ST. JACQUES

6 tbsp. butter
3 tbsp. flour
1 tsp. salt
1/8 tsp. white pepper
2 c. light cream
1/4 c. finely chopped onions
1/2 lb. scallops, sliced
1/2 c. sliced mushrooms
3/4 lb. cooked shrimp
1/2 lb. crab meat
2 tbsp. sherry
5 tbsp. bread crumbs

Combine 4 tablespoons butter with flour, salt and white pepper in skillet; stir in cream gradually. Simmer, stirring constantly, until sauce is smooth and thickened. Saute onions in remaining butter in small skillet; add scallops. Saute for 5 minutes; remove onions and scallops. Add mushrooms; saute for 3 to 5 minutes. Combine shrimp, scallops, onions, crab meat, mushrooms and sherry with sauce; mix lightly. Place in individual baking dishes; sprinkle with crumbs. Bake at 400 degrees for 15 minutes or until heated through and crumbs are browned.

SCALLOPS WITH GRAPES

1 pt. sea scallops
Margarine
2 sm. onions, chopped
1 tbsp. cornstarch
1 c. seedless white grapes
1 tbsp. chopped parsley
1/2 tsp. salt
1/8 tsp. cayenne pepper
1/8 tsp. garlic powder
2 egg yolks
1/2 c. light cream

Cut scallops into 3/4-inch cubes. Saute scallops in 2 tablespoons margarine for 10 minutes; drain, reserving pan drippings. Add enough water to pan drippings to equal 1 cup liquid. Melt 2 tablespoons margarine in 2-quart saucepan over medium heat. Saute onions until golden; blend in cornstarch into onion mixture. Remove from heat; stir in pan drippings gradually. Cook over medium heat until mixture comes to a boil; boil for 1 minute, stirring constantly. Reduce heat to low; add scallops, grapes, parsley, salt, cayenne pepper and garlic powder. Beat egg yolks with cream; stir into scallop mixture gradually. Turn into shallow 2 1/2-quart baking dish. Sprinkle with 1 cup fine dry bread crumbs if desired. Bake at 400 degrees for 5 minutes. Yield: 6 servings.

OVEN-FRIED SCALLOPS

3 tbsp. butter
1 lb. scallops
1/2 c. crumbs
1/8 tsp. pepper
1/8 tsp. paprika

Melt butter in skillet. Roll scallops in butter. Mix crumbs, pepper and paprika; dredge scallops with seasoned crumbs. Place in baking pan. Bake for 15 minutes at 350 degrees. Broil for 10 to 15 minutes or until lightly browned.

Scallops with Grapes . . . An eye-catching dish simple enough for a quick but elegant meal.

CREAMED SCALLOPS

4 tbsp. butter
4 tbsp. flour
1 tsp. salt
1/4 tsp. pepper
1/2 tsp. dry mustard
1 1/2 pt. milk
1 onion, finely chopped
1 tbsp. chopped parsley
1 tbsp. lemon juice
1 1/2 pt. scallops

Melt butter in top of double boiler over boiling water; blend in flour, salt, pepper and mustard. Add milk; cook, stirring, until thickened. Stir in onion, parsley and lemon juice. Add scallops; blend well. Simmer for 10 minutes or until scallops are tender. Serve on toast.

SCALLOPS AU GRATIN

1 sm. green pepper
1 med. onion
4 stalks celery
1 pkg. frozen scallops
4 tbsp. butter
1 1/2 c. soft bread crumbs
1/2 c. grated Cheddar cheese
1/2 tsp. salt
Pepper to taste
1 c. light cream

Preheat oven to 350 degrees. Chop green pepper, onion and celery. Cover scallops with cold water in saucepan; bring to a boil. Drain immediately. Melt 2 tablespoons butter; mix with crumbs. Saute green pepper, onion and celery in remaining butter for about 5 minutes. Arrange layers of scallops, cheese and vegetables in greased casserole; season each layer with salt and pepper. Pour cream over top. Bake at 350 degrees for 30 minutes.

SAVORY SCALLOPS

1/2 c. chopped bacon
1/4 c. minced onion
1 tsp. salt
1/4 c. flour
1/8 tsp. hot sauce
1 pkg. frozen scallops
2 tbsp. Worcestershire sauce
1/4 c. lemon juice
1/2 c. fresh minced parsley

Fry bacon over low heat in heavy skillet. Add onion; cook until golden. Sprinkle with salt, flour and hot sauce; do not stir. Simmer until flour is absorbed in bacon fat. Partially thaw frozen scallops to separate; reserve scallop liquid. Add scallops to skillet; stir just to mix. Simmer, covered, for 15 minutes; stir after 5 minutes. Combine Worcestershire sauce, lemon juice and reserved scallop liquid. Add lemon juice mixture and parsley to scallop mixture. Stir well; turn off heat. Stir over warm burner until sauce covers each scallop.

SCALLOPS DELUXE

3/4 lb. scallops
1 sm. onion, finely chopped
1 tsp. salt
1 beef bouillon cube
2 cans cream of celery soup
1 pimento, diced
1 tsp. lemon juice
2 eggs, beaten
3 tbsp. grated cheese
2 c. finely crushed saltine crackers

Quarter scallops; place in saucepan. Add onion, salt, bouillon cube and 2 cups water. Cook for 15 minutes or until scallops are just tender. Mix soup, pimento, lemon juice, eggs and cheese together; add to scallop mixture. Stir in half the cracker crumbs; pour into 9-inch casserole. Sprinkle remaining crumbs over top. Bake at 350 degrees for 30 minutes.

SCALLOPS MORNAY

2 10-oz. packages frozen chopped broccoli
1 1/2 lb. scallops
1/2 c. dry white wine
Parsley
Milk
2 tbsp. instant minced onion
1/4 c. butter
1/4 c. flour
1/2 tsp. salt
Dash of cayenne pepper
1 c. grated Swiss cheese
2 tbsp. grated Parmesan cheese

Preheat oven to 450 degrees. Cook broccoli according to package directions; drain well. Turn into 6 individual casseroles. Combine scallops with wine and parsley; bring to a boil. Reduce heat; simmer for 5 minutes or until scallops are tender. Drain scallops; reserve liquid. Cut each scallop in half. Add enough milk to reserved liquid to measure 2 1/2 cups. Saute onion in butter in small saucepan, stirring constantly, until golden brown; remove from heat. Stir in flour, salt and cayenne pepper; stir in reserved liquid gradually. Bring to a boil, stirring. Add 3/4 cup Swiss cheese. Cook, stirring constantly, until cheese is melted; remove from heat. Stir in scallops; spoon over broccoli in casseroles. Combine remaining Swiss cheese with Parmesan cheese; sprinkle over scallop mixture. Bake for 10 to 15 minutes or until heated through and golden brown. Yield: 6 servings.

SCALLOPS MEUNIERE

2 lb. scallops
1/2 c. milk
1/2 c. flour
1 tsp. salt
1/4 tsp. freshly ground pepper
1/2 c. peanut oil
1/4 c. butter
2 tbsp. lemon juice
2 tbsp. dry white wine
1 tbsp. chopped parsley

Dice scallops coarsely. Cover with milk; let stand for 2 minutes. Drain scallops. Combine flour, salt and pepper; coat scallops with flour mixture. Combine oil and butter in skillet; saute scallops over medium heat, turning until lightly browned on all sides. Remove scallops to heated platter. Heat additional butter with lemon juice until frothy; add white wine and parsley. Pour over scallops.

SCALLOPS SAUTE

2 tbsp. butter
1 1/2 lb. scallops
2/3 c. chili sauce
1/3 c. catsup
1 tbsp. prepared horseradish
1 tbsp. lemon juice
1 tbsp. Worcestershire sauce
2 tsp. prepared mustard
1/8 tsp. garlic salt
Finely chopped parsley

Heat butter in medium skillet; add scallops. Saute over high heat, stirring, for 5 to 8 minutes or until browned and tender. Combine chili sauce, catsup, horseradish, lemon juice, Worcestershire sauce, mustard and garlic salt in small bowl; mix well. Pour sauce around scallops; heat just to boiling point. Sprinkle with parsley.

SCALLOP-SHRIMP KABOBS

Color photograph for this recipe on page 67.

Scallops
Shrimp
Cherry tomatoes
Green pepper cubes
Seafood seasoning
Melted butter
1 box Italian-style risotta rice

Place scallops, shrimp, tomatoes and green pepper cubes on skewers; sprinkle with seafood seasoning. Grill over charcoal or broil in oven until done, basting frequently with butter. Prepare rice according to package directions; place in serving dish. Place kabobs on rice; serve. Kabobs may be prepared a day ahead and refrigerated until ready to cook.

Scrapple

Pennsylvania Dutch housewives, practical utilizers of meat by-products, created scrapple from "scraps" of pork and cornmeal.

PREPARATION: A whole hog's head, pork shoulder, neck bones, or other boney pieces may be used to make scrapple. Pork is simmered in water until the meat separates easily from the bones. The meat is then removed from the broth and chopped. A cornmeal "mush" is then prepared by adding cornmeal to broth. Meat and seasonings are combined with the mush. Mixture is poured into loaf pans and chilled until firm. It is then sliced and quickly fried in hot fat until crisp and brown.

SERVING: Always serve scrapple hot. Arrange scrapple over vegetables, pastas, or fruits such as grilled pineapple. Or serve with brown sugar syrup, spiced cinnamon applesauce, or eggs and sausage. May be baked with scalloped potatoes, used to stuff green peppers, used to make croquettes, and so on.

OLD-FASHIONED SCRAPPLE

2 c. ground pork
2 c. ground beef
3 c. meat broth
2 tsp. salt
1/4 tsp. pepper
1 1/2 tsp. sage
Cayenne pepper to taste
1 c. cornmeal

Combine pork, beef and broth in saucepan; bring to a boil. Add seasonings. Sift cornmeal into meat mixture gradually, stirring constantly. Cook for 30 minutes. Pour into mold; chill until firm. Cut into thin slices; fry in lightly greased skillet until browned. Yield: 8 servings.

PENNSYLVANIA DUTCH SCRAPPLE

1 lge. beef soupbone with meat
1 lb. beef bones with marrow
2 lb. beef liver
2 lb. beef heart
1 1/2 c. cornmeal
1 c. buckwheat flour
Sausage seasoning
Garlic powder to taste
Salt and pepper to taste

Cook soup and marrow bones in 8 cups boiling salted water in heavy kettle until meat falls from bones. Remove fat from meat; discard bones. Boil liver and heart in stock until tender; remove, reserving 6 cups stock. Process meat through food grinder; return to stock. Stir cornmeal and flour into reserved stock gradually; add seasonings. Cook over low heat for 1 hour, stirring frequently. Pour into bread pans; chill until set. Wrap in waxed paper; store in refrigerator. Slice as needed; fry in lightly greased skillet.

BREAKFAST SCRAPPLE

1 lb. ground lean pork
2 beef bouillon cubes
Salt to taste
1 1/2 c. cornmeal
1/2 c. buckwheat flour
1 tsp. (heaping) ground sage

Combine pork, bouillon cubes and 1 quart water in large saucepan. Season with salt; bring to a boil. Mix cornmeal, flour and 2 cups water together; add to boiling mixture gradually, stirring well. Cook over low heat for 1 hour, stirring frequently. Add sage. Place in bread pan; refrigerate for at least 6 hours. Slice thin; fry until crisp. Yield: 6-8 servings.

HOOSIER COUNTRY SCRAPPLE

2 c. ground cooked pork
1 c. ground cooked beef
1 c. ground cooked liver
4 c. broth
1 1/2 c. cornmeal
2 tsp. salt
1/2 tsp. sage

Combine pork, beef, liver and broth in saucepan; bring just to boiling point. Dampen cornmeal with small amount of water; stir into pork mixture. Add salt and sage. Boil, stirring constantly, until thick. Pour into 2 loaf pans; chill for 12 hours. Slice; fry in lightly greased skillet. Yield: 20 servings.

CHICKEN SCRAPPLE

3 c. seasoned chicken broth
1 c. diced cooked chicken
1/2 tsp. salt
1 c. yellow cornmeal
2 tbsp. shortening

Combine broth, chicken and salt in 3-quart saucepan; bring to a boil. Stir in cornmeal; cook until thick, stirring constantly. Pour into loaf pan; chill until set. Cut into slices; fry until light brown on both sides in shortening. Yield: 8 servings.

Seafood

In this encyclopedia, the most popularly served fish and shellfish have been described in such individual entries as BASS, CRAB, HALIBUT, TROUT, and so on. Refer to pages 8-11 for a detailed description of the cooking methods suggested in these entries. In describing fish, reference has been made to their being available whole, drawn, dressed, and as steaks and fillets. The following illustrated descriptions will clarify each of these market forms.

WHOLE FISH are those marketed just as they come from the water. Almost all whole fish must be scaled before cooking. Many of them are small and are cooked whole with only the entrails removed. Larger whole fish are either baked or have the head, tail, and fins removed before being split or cut into serving-size pieces.

DRAWN FISH are marketed with only the entrails removed. These fish must generally be scaled before cooking. Small drawn fish are cooked whole. Larger ones are either baked whole or the head, tail, and fins are removed and the fish split into serving-size pieces.

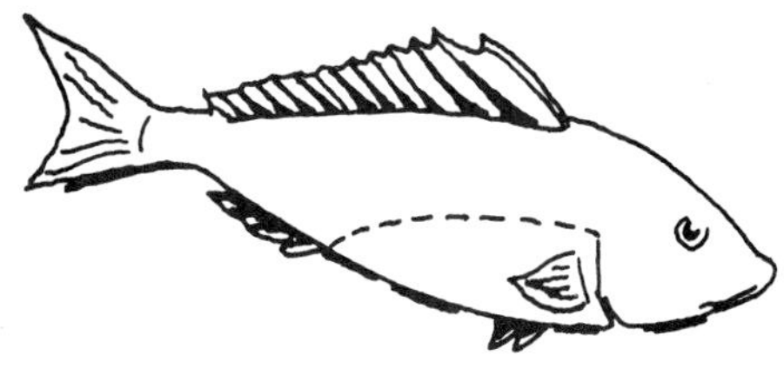

DRESSED FISH are scaled and have the entrails removed. The head, tail, and fins are often removed as well. Smaller fish are cooked as they are. Larger ones are baked as they are or are cut into serving-size pieces.

STEAKS are crosscut sections of larger dressed fish. They are ready to cook as purchased. Some of the largest steaks may be divided into serving-size portions before being cooked. A small piece of backbone is usually the only bone that remains in fish steaks.

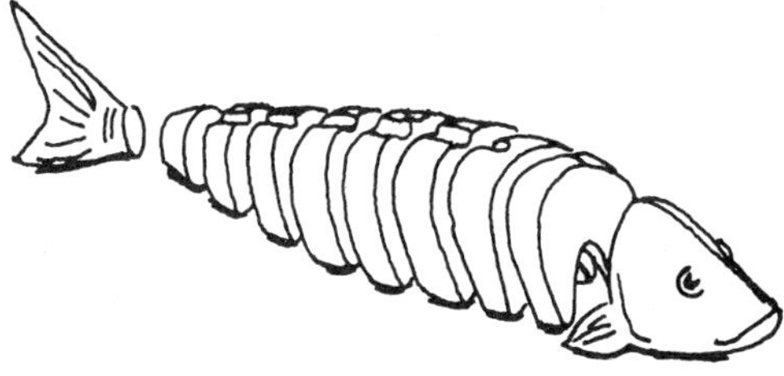

FILLETS are the sides of fish cut lengthwise away from the backbone. They are practically boneless and require no preparation before being cooked. Some fillets have the skin and scales on them; others are skinned. A *single fillet* is cut from only one side of the fish. *Butterfly fillets* are the two fillets, one from each side, held together by skin and uncut meat.

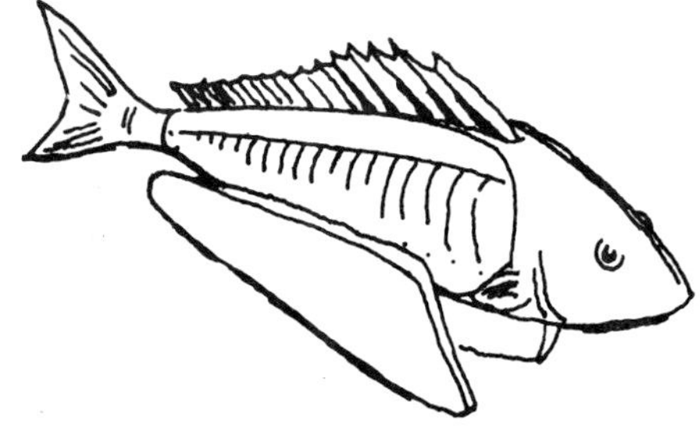

CLEANING AND DRESSING FISH: Because the method of cleaning and dressing shellfish differs from species to species, information on this subject is contained within individual entries on specific shellfish. However, virtually all fish are cleaned and dressed alike. Information on cleaning and dressing whole fish either bought in the market or caught by sport fishermen follows. Refer to the following illustration to determine the parts of fish referred to in the instructions.

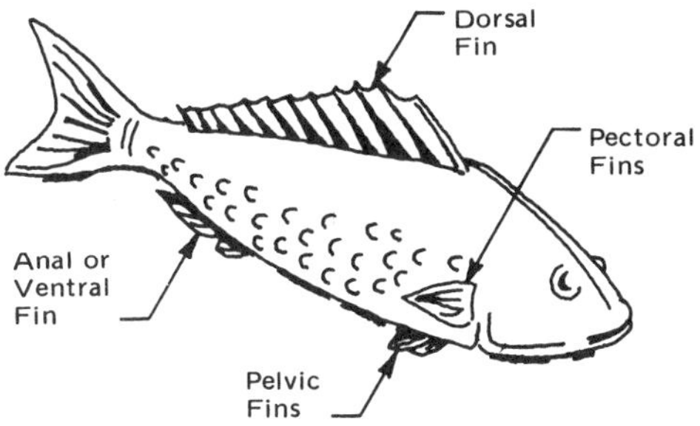

SCALING AND CLEANING: Scales are removed more easily from a wet fish than from a dry one, so it is recommended to soak fish in cold water for a few minutes before scaling. Lay the fish on a flat surface. With one hand, hold it firmly by the head. Holding a knife almost vertically, scrape off the scales, working from tail to head. Be especially careful to remove all the scales near the base of the fins and the head. With a sharp knife, cut the fish's belly from the anal or ventral fin to the head. Remove the intestines. Cut around the pelvic fins and remove them.

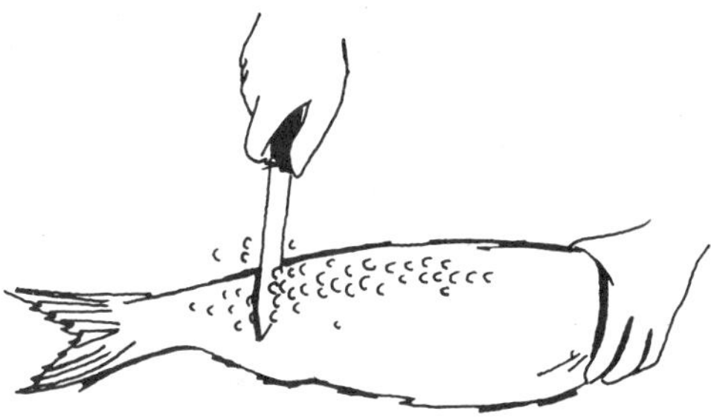

DRESSING: Remove the head, including the pectoral fins, by cutting above the collarbone. Cut off tail.

If the backbone is large, cut down to it on each side of the fish's head, then snap the bone by bending it over the edge of the working surface. Cut through any remaining flesh that holds the head to the body. Cut off tail.

Remove the dorsal or large back fin by cutting the fish along both sides of this fin.

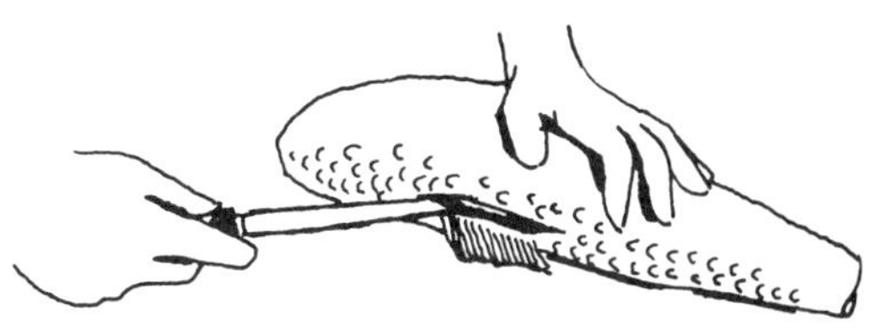

Pull the fin forward quickly toward the front of the fish, removing the fin and its root bones attached. Remove pelvic and anal or ventral fins in the same way. Never trim the fins off with shears or a knife since the bones at the base of the fins will be left in the fish. Wash fish in cold running water to rinse out blood, any remaining entrails, and membranes. Fish is now dressed and ready to be cooked. To cut fish into steaks or fillets, see below.

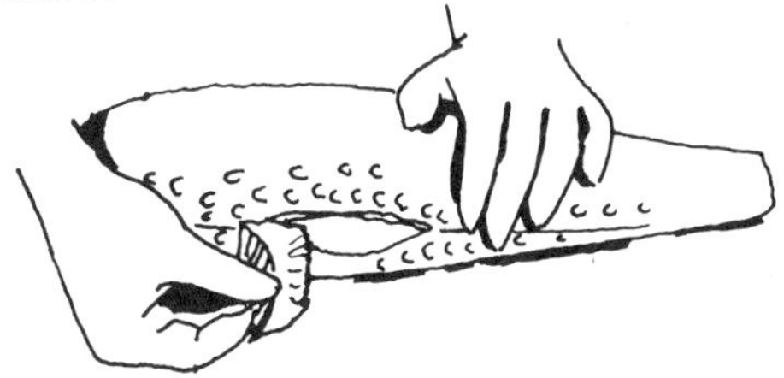

TO CUT STEAKS: Cut large dressed fish crosswise in slices about one inch-thick.

TO CUT A FILLET: With a sharp knife, cut through the fish along the back from the tail to head end. Then cut down to the backbone just above the collarbone.

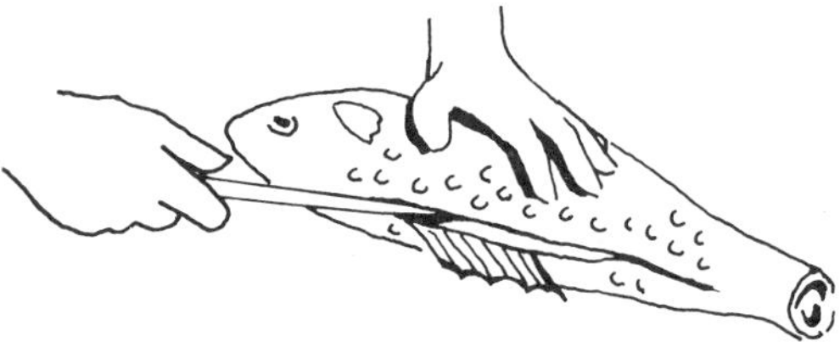

Turn the knife flat and cut the flesh along the backbone to the tail. Cut the flesh away from the rib bones.

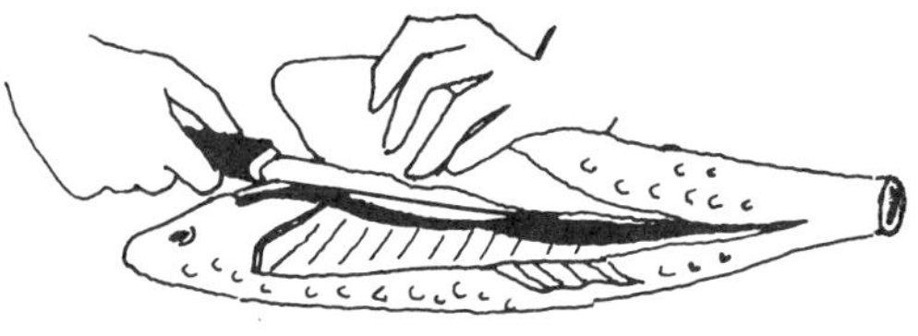

Lift the entire side of the fish in one piece. Repeat the operation on the other side, if desired.

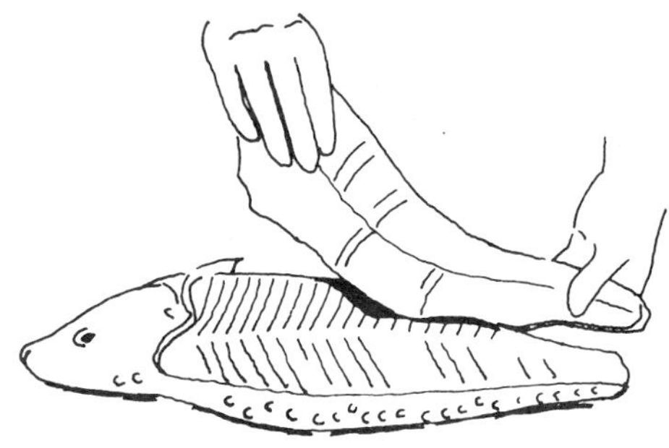

To skin fillets, lay them flat on a working surface, skin side down. Holding the tail end with your fingers, cut through the flesh to the skin about one-half inch from the fillet's end. Flatten knife on skin and cut the flesh away from skin by pushing knife forward while holding free end of skin firmly between fingers.

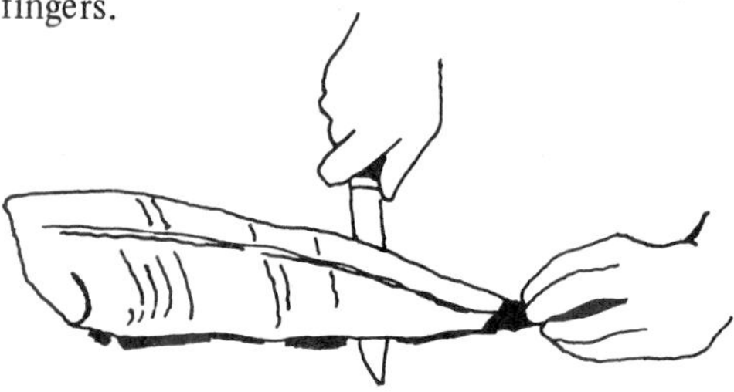

Sesame Seed

Sesame seeds are also known as "bene seeds", and are believed to bring good luck. They were introduced into American cookery by African slaves who had long used them in their native lands. Sesame seeds are an herb with a rich toasted-nut flavor. They are available only whole in either toasted or untoasted form. Use them as a topping for baked breads, cakes, cookies, and in candies.

SESAME SPIRALS

2 5 1/2-oz. packages cocktail frankfurters
32 2-in. strips Swiss cheese
1 8-oz. package refrigerator biscuits
2 tbsp. melted butter
2 tbsp. sesame seed

Cut lengthwise slit in each frankfurter; insert strip of cheese in each slit. Quarter 8 biscuits; shape each quarter in 4-inch strip. Wind, spiral fashion, around each frankfurter; place on baking sheet. Brush with butter; sprinkle with sesame seed. Bake at 400 degrees for 10 minutes or until heated through and lightly browned.

SESAME PASTRIES

2 c. flour
1/4 c. sugar
1 1/2 tsp. baking powder
1/4 tsp. salt
1/2 c. margarine
1 egg, slightly beaten
1/4 c. milk
1 c. sesame seed

Combine flour, sugar, baking powder and salt in mixing bowl; cut in margarine. Stir in egg and milk to form soft dough. Roll dough into balls by tablespoons. Flatten slightly; roll in sesame seed. Place on lightly greased cookie sheets. Bake at 375 degrees for 15 minutes or until lightly browned. Serve with wedges of cheese. Yield: About 2 1/2 dozen.

SESAME BRAID

1 pkg. yeast
1/4 c. sugar
4 1/2 c. sifted flour
2 tsp. salt
2 eggs
2 tbsp. oil
1 egg yolk, beaten
1/4 c. sesame seed

Mix yeast, sugar and 1/4 cup warm water; let stand for 5 minutes. Sift flour and salt into large bowl; make well in flour. Add eggs, oil, 1 cup lukewarm water and yeast mixture. Knead until smooth. Dough will be sticky. Place dough in large oiled bowl; cover. Let rise until doubled in bulk. Punch down; let rise again until almost doubled in bulk. Punch down; divide dough into 3 equal parts. Roll into strips; braid loosely. Place on greased cookie sheet. Cover; let rise until doubled in bulk. Brush carefully with egg yolk; sprinkle with sesame seed. Bake at 375 degrees for 30 minutes or until golden brown.

Sesame Seed Tossed Green Salad . . . A sharply-flavored salad with croutons for texture contrast.

SESAME SEED TOSSED GREEN SALAD

2 heads leaf lettuce
1 lb. spinach leaves
3 tomatoes, peeled
1/2 c. small sweet onion rings
3 tbsp. toasted sesame seed
1 tsp. salt
1/4 tsp. pepper
1/2 tsp. dry mustard
3 tbsp. vinegar
1 tbsp. honey
1/2 c. vegetable oil
2 c. herb-seasoned stuffing croutons

Trim salad greens; tear into bite-sized pieces. Cut tomatoes into wedges. Combine salad greens, tomato wedges, onion rings and sesame seed; toss well. Refrigerate. Combine salt, pepper and dry mustard in small mixing bowl; stir in vinegar and honey. Add oil gradually, beating with rotary beater. Chill well. Combine salad dressing and croutons with salad; toss well. Serve immediately. Yield: 8-10 servings.

SESAME-CHEESE BREAD

3 c. flour
2 tbsp. baking powder
1 1/2 tsp. salt
1 tbsp. minced onion
1 c. vegetable shortening
1 c. milk
1 beaten egg
1 c. grated sharp cheese
3 tbsp. butter, melted
2 tbsp. sesame seed

Preheat oven to 400 degrees. Sift flour, baking powder and salt into large bowl; add onion. Blend in shortening until mixture is texture of coarse meal. Combine milk and egg; mix well. Add half the cheese to flour mixture; add milk mixture. Blend well. Spread in greased 8 x 8-inch pan; sprinkle with remaining cheese, butter and sesame seed. Bake for 20 minutes or until golden brown.

SESAME STICKS

1 pkg. refrigerator biscuits
Milk
2 tbsp. sesame seed
1 1/2 c. oven-toasted rice cereal, crushed
2 tsp. salt

Cut biscuits in half. Roll each half into 4-inch long pencil-thin stick. Brush with milk. Combine sesame seed, crumbs and salt. Roll sticks in crumb mixture. Place on greased baking sheet. Bake at 450 degrees for 10 minutes or until lightly browned.

SESAME SEED THINS

1 stick butter
2 c. (packed) brown sugar
1 egg
1 c. flour
1/4 tsp. salt
1/2 tsp. baking powder
1 tsp. vanilla
3/4 c. toasted sesame seed

Cream butter and sugar. Add egg, flour, salt and baking powder; mix well. Add vanilla and sesame seed; blend. Drop, 1/2 teaspoon at a time, onto greased baking sheet. Bake at 325 degrees for 8 minutes or until lightly browned. Cool for 1 minute; remove from baking sheet. Yield: 8 1/2 dozen wafers.

SESAME-SWISS CHEESE LOAF

2 c. sifted flour	*1/3 c. toasted sesame seed*
3 tbsp. sugar	*2 eggs, beaten*
4 tsp. baking powder	*1 1/4 c. milk*
1 1/2 tsp. salt	*1/4 c. salad oil*
1 c. shredded Swiss cheese	

Sift flour, sugar, baking powder and salt together into bowl; stir in cheese and sesame seed. Blend eggs, milk and oil. Add all at once to flour mixture; stir just until moistened. Pour batter into greased 4 1/2 x 8 1/2-inch loaf pan. Bake at 375 degrees for 1 hour or until bread tests done. Cool for 15 minutes; remove from pan.

Shad

Saltwater shad is a white-fleshed edible fish prized for its sweet, delicate flavor. Firmly granulated shad roe is a delicacy. Shad varies from 2 to 2 1/2 feet long and usually weighs less than 5 pounds. Native to European waters and our Atlantic Coast, shad was successfully introduced to America's Pacific shores in the late 1800's. Each February silvery-blue shad migrate to warm freshwater rivers to spawn. As spring advances, many fish are netted in rivers of the eastern United States. High in fat content, shad supplies protein, calcium, Vitamin A, and niacin. (4 ounces shad = 190 calories; 4 ounces shad roe = 200 calories)

AVAILABILITY: Fresh shad is available almost year-round in those regions where caught. Best season is January to May. Shad is usually sold whole or drawn. Frozen shad and canned shad roe are also marketed.

BUYING: Look for whole fresh fish with clear, bright, bulging eyes; reddish pink gills; tight shiny scales; firm elastic flesh; and fresh odor.

STORING: Cover fresh shad with plastic wrap or aluminum foil. Store in coldest part of refrigerator 1 to 2 days. To freeze fresh shad, wrap whole fish individually in moistureproof and vaporproof paper. Seal. Freeze at 0 degree or below up to 6 weeks.

PREPARATION: Shad can be broiled, baked, planked, sauteed, steamed, grilled, or panfried. "Fatty" fish like shad are especially suited to broiling, baking, and planking because high oil content prevents the fish from drying out. Shad contains a lot of bones; remove as many as possible before cooking. Use tweezers if necessary. Shad roe can be baked, sauteed, broiled, or cooked according to special recipe instructions. Cook gently with slow heat. Do not overcook shad roe; it becomes dry and tasteless. 6 ounces shad roe makes 1 serving.

SERVING: Garnish shad colorfully with parsley, lemon slices, radish slices and so on. Serve shad roe as a luncheon dish or savory, or use it to garnish shad. Use shad roe in souffles, croquettes, and salads.

(See SEAFOOD.)

BAKED STUFFED SHAD

Milk	*Poultry seasoning to taste*
4 slices bread	*1 5 lb. shad*
1 sm. onion, chopped	*3 strips bacon*
Salt and pepper to taste	

Pour milk over bread in bowl just to moisten. Add onion, salt, pepper and poultry seasoning. Stuff shad; sew opening closed. Lay strips of bacon over shad. Place in shallow foil-lined pan. Cover bottom of pan with water; add water as necessary during baking. Bake at 200 degrees for 4 hours or until fish flakes easily with a fork.

BONELESS BAKED SHAD

1 5 lb. shad	*Salt and pepper to taste*
1 qt. water	*4 slices bacon*
1 tbsp. vinegar	

Remove roe from shad; reserve roe. Boil shad in saucepan in water with vinegar and seasonings for 20 minutes; drain. Place in heavy roaster; cover. Bake at 200 degrees for 4 hours and 30 minutes or until fish flakes easily. Add roe; bake for 30 minutes longer. Place bacon slices across shad; broil until bacon is browned.

EDGEWATER SHAD ROE AMANDINE

1 c. bouillon	*1/2 tbsp. butter*
2 tbsp. lemon juice	*1/2 c. toasted almonds, slivered*
1 pair shad roe	
4 strips bacon	

Combine bouillon and lemon juice; bring to a boil. Add roe; simmer for 5 minutes. Drain roe; discard liquid. Rinse roe in cold water; remove center vein. Cook bacon over low heat; drain on paper towels. Drain off fat from pan; reserve 2 tablespoons. Add butter to reserved fat in skillet; saute roe over low heat for about 15 minutes, turning to brown. Remove to hot platter. Add almonds to skillet; stir over high heat just to heat through. Pour almonds and butter over the roe; serve with lemon wedges and strips of bacon.

OGEECHEE BAKED SHAD

4 tbsp. salad oil
1 tbsp. monosodium glutamate
2 tbsp. salt
1 tbsp. pepper
2 tbsp. lemon juice
1 6-lb. shad, dressed
4 strips bacon
1 qt. milk

Mix oil, monosodium glutamate, salt, pepper and lemon juice; rub shad thoroughly. Place large piece heavy-duty foil in shallow baking pan; place strips of bacon on foil. Arrange shad on bacon strips. Pour milk around shad; close foil securely, tent fashion. Bake at 200 degrees for 6 hours.

Shortcake

Shortcakes are light, flaky biscuits or slices of sweet cake that are smothered with sweetened fruits (raspberries, strawberries, peaches, bananas, and pears) and plain or whipped heavy cream.

PREPARATION: There are three types of shortcake: large, individual, and sponge. For large shortcakes–Spread the biscuit dough in 2 layer pans. Dot with butter and bake until medium brown. Place a generous heaping of fruit between and on top of the shortcake layers. For individual shortcakes–Bake biscuits in 2- or 3-inch rounds. While still warm break apart and spread with butter. Spoon fruit over and between biscuit halves. For sponge shortcakes–Prepare slices of cake as for large shortcakes.

SERVING: Always serve shortcakes warm. (See BISCUITS.)

BLUEBERRY SHORTCAKE

1 recipe pie pastry
1 qt. blueberries
1 tbsp. lemon juice
Sugar
10 tbsp. butter
1/3 c. flour
3 eggs, beaten
1 qt. milk
1 tsp. vanilla
1 c. whipping cream

Roll pastry out; cut into 24 rounds with large cookie cutter. Place rounds on baking sheet. Bake at 400 degrees for 8 minutes or until lightly browned. Cool. Combine blueberries, lemon juice, sugar to taste, 1 cup water and 4 tablespoons butter in saucepan; bring to a boil. Reduce heat; cook, covered, for 5 minutes. Cool, covered. Blend 3/4 cup sugar and flour together; add remaining butter, eggs and milk. Cook, stirring constantly, until thickened. Stir in vanilla; cool. Place 12 pastry rounds on individual serving plates; cover with custard. Top with remaining rounds; spoon blueberry mixture over tops. Whip cream; sweeten slightly. Serve shortcake with whipped cream.

FAMILY FAVORITE STRAWBERRY SHORTCAKE

2 c. sifted flour
2 tbsp. sugar
3 tsp. baking powder
1/2 tsp. salt
Butter
1 egg, beaten
1/2 c. light cream
4 c. sweetened strawberries
1 c. heavy cream, whipped

Sift flour, sugar, baking powder and salt together into bowl; cut in 1/2 cup butter until mixture resembles coarse crumbs. Combine egg and light cream; add to flour mixture. Stir until dough clings together. Turn dough onto floured surface; knead lightly. Pat dough into 3/4-inch thick rectangle; cut with 2 1/2-inch cutter. Place on greased baking sheet. Bake at 450 degrees for 10 minutes. Split cakes while warm; spread with 3 tablespoons softened butter. Spoon strawberries between cake halves; top with whipped cream. Yield: 8 servings.

PEACH SHORTCAKE

3-lb. pared peaches, sliced
1 c. (packed) light brown sugar
1/2 c. lemon juice
1 1/2 tsp. salt
3 1/3 c. sifted all-purpose flour
1 1/4 c. shortening
Sugar
1 1/2 c. heavy cream

Combine peaches, brown sugar and lemon juice; chill for 1 hour. Mix salt and flour in bowl; cut in shortening with pastry blender until mixture resembles coarse meal. Sprinkle with 7 to 8 tablespoons water; toss with fork. Press into ball. Divide dough into 4 parts. Roll each part out on lightly floured surface into 8-inch circle, trimming edges evenly with 8-inch round cake pan. Place circles on baking sheets; sprinkle with sugar. Prick with fork. Bake in 425-degree oven for 15 minutes or until golden brown. Cool on racks. Whip cream with 1 tablespoon sugar until soft peaks form. Stack pastry circles on large serving plate, topping each circle with peach mixture and whipped cream. Yield: 10 servings.

Peach Shortcake . . . Fresh peaches, crisp pastry, and whipped cream form a summer dessert.

CHERRY SHORTCAKE

2 c. flour
3/4 c. sugar
4 tsp. baking powder
1/2 tsp. salt
1 tsp. nutmeg
1/3 c. margarine
1/3 c. shortening
1 egg, slightly beaten
2 tbsp. milk
1 can cherry pie filling

Preheat oven to 375 degrees. Grease 9-inch square pan. Sift flour with sugar, baking powder, salt and nutmeg; cut in margarine and shortening until mixture resembles fine meal. Combine egg and milk; add to flour mixture. Stir until liquid is absorbed. Press into pan. Bake for 20 minutes. Remove from oven; cover with cherry pie filling. Bake for 10 minutes longer. Serve warm with whipped topping if desired.

STRAWBERRY-GRAHAM SHORTCAKE

3/4 c. butter
1 1/4 c. (packed) dark brown sugar
1 1/2 tsp. vanilla
3 eggs
1 c. sifted all-purpose flour
3 1/2 tsp. baking powder
3/4 tsp. salt
1/2 c. chopped walnuts
2 c. graham cracker crumbs
1 c. milk
1 1/2 c. heavy cream
1/4 c. sugar
1 1/4 tsp. orange extract
2 pt. fresh California strawberries

Cream butter, brown sugar and vanilla together in bowl until fluffy; beat in eggs, one at a time, beating well after each addition. Sift flour, baking powder and salt together; blend in walnuts and cracker crumbs. Add crumb mixture to egg mixture alternately with milk, beating well after each addition. Spread batter in 2 greased waxed paper-lined 9-inch square cake pans. Bake in 375-degree oven for 30 to 35 minutes or until cakes test done. Cool slightly; remove from pans. Whip cream with sugar and orange extract until soft peaks form. Spread half the cream on 1 cake layer; slice half the strawberries over layer. Top layer with remaining cake. Spread with remaining cream; garnish with remaining whole strawberries.

MIXED FRUIT SHORTCAKE

1 c. chopped apples
1 c. chopped cranberries
1 c. crushed pineapple
1 c. sugar
Sweet biscuits or sponge cake
Whipped cream

Combine fruits and sugar; let stand for 5 to 6 hours. Serve on biscuits; top with whipped cream.

Strawberry-Graham Shortcake . . . Graham crackers and walnuts gives this dessert unusual flavor.

ROYAL STRAWBERRY CAKE

1 c. sugar
4 tbsp. shortening
1 egg, beaten
2 c. flour
3 tsp. baking powder
1/8 tsp. salt
1 c. milk
1 tsp. vanilla
1 qt. strawberries
1/2 pt. heavy cream whipped

Cream sugar and shortening together; add egg. Sift flour, baking powder and salt together; add to creamed mixture, small amount at a time. Add half the milk; mix in remaining milk and vanilla. Spoon batter into shallow greased pan. Bake at 350 degrees for 20 minutes or until cake tests done. Cool; split in half. Reserve several whole strawberries; crush remaining berries. Sweeten crushed strawberries to taste with additional sugar; spread whipped cream and crushed strawberries between cake layers. Cover top with whipped cream and reserved whole strawberries.

OLD-FASHIONED SHORTCAKE

2 c. sifted all-purpose flour
1 c. sugar
3 tsp. baking powder
1/2 tsp. salt
1/2 c. butter
3/4 c. milk
3 1-pt. boxes fresh strawberries
1 c. heavy cream
2 tbsp. confectioners' sugar

Preheat oven to 450 degrees. Sift flour, 1/4 cup sugar, baking powder and salt into large bowl. Cut butter into flour mixture until mixture resembles coarse cornmeal. Make well in center of mixture; pour in milk all at once. Mix quickly with fork just to moisten flour. Turn into lightly greased 8 x 8 x 2-inch baking pan. Press dough lightly to fit into pan evenly. Bake for 12 to 15 minutes or until golden. Reserve several whole strawberries for garnish; remove hulls from remaining strawberries. Slice into bowl. Add remaining sugar; mix well. Whip cream just until stiff; stir in confectioners' sugar gently. Cut shortcake in half crosswise; place, cut side up, on serving plate. Spoon on half the strawberry slices. Set top of cake in place, cut side down; spoon remaining sliced strawberries over top of cake. Mound whipped cream lightly in center; garnish with reserved strawberries. Serve at once.

Shrimp

Shrimp are palatable shellfish that have been savored as delicacies for thousands of years. Common varieties include the common or white shrimp that is greenish grey when uncooked; brown or Brazilian that is brownish red when uncooked; Gulf pink or coral shrimp, Alaskan, and Californian shrimp that all vary in color and size. When cooked, all shrimp have a pink or coral color. Shrimp are rich in protein and low in both calories and fat. They are an excellent source of iron, copper, and Vitamins A, B, and D. (3 1/2 ounces fresh shrimp = 91 calories; 3 1/2 ounces fried shrimp = 225 calories; 3 1/2 ounces canned shrimp = 80 calories)

AVAILABILITY: Whereas shrimp were once available only in coastal regions, modern packaging and refrigeration and fishing techniques have made them available nationally. Fresh shrimp are available year-round as are frozen, canned, and dried shrimp. The latter are usually available only in specialty food stores.

BUYING: Look for shrimp that are firm and sweet smelling. Fresh shrimp are graded according to size: Jumbo have about 15 shrimp to the pound; Large have about 25 to the pound; Medium have about 35 to the pound; and Small have about 50 to the pound. About 1 1/2 pounds uncooked shrimp yields 3/4 pounds peeled, cooked, cleaned shrimp. Frozen shrimp are available cleaned and ready-to-cook; pre-cooked and ready for use; and peeled, cleaned, breaded, and ready to fry. Canned shrimp is available in brine or dry packed.

STORING: Wrap fresh shrimp in moisture-proof and vaporproof paper and store in the coldest part of the refrigerator for 1-2 days. Freshly cooked or canned opened shrimp keep in the refrigerator for 3-4 days. Canned shrimp, unopened, keep on the kitchen shelf for 1 year. *To freeze* shrimp—Wash and pack closely together, a few at a time. Wrap in small packages then surround the packages with moistureproof and vaporproof paper. Frozen shrimp keep in the refrigerator freezer compartment up to 2 months or in the home freezer for 4 months.

PREPARATION: Shrimp served cold are usually prepared by boiling. *To boil peeled and deveined* shrimp—Place shrimp in boiling salted water to cover. Adjust lid; allow water to return to boiling point and remove from heat. Let stand 2-4 minutes. Drain and chill. Or cover shrimp with cold water and add 1 tablespoon salt and 1 teaspoon sugar. Bring water to boil and let cook 8-10 minutes. Remove from heat and chill shrimp, still in cooking water. Drain and serve. *To boil unpeeled shrimp*—Wash and place in boiling salted water. Cover and let water return to boiling. Simmer 5 minutes, remove from heat, drain, peel, devein, wash, and chill. *To fry* shrimp—Shell and devein them. Coat with batter and fry in deep, hot fat 2-4 minutes.

SERVING: Shrimp are often served plain with salt, lemon slices, and cocktail sauce. They are also served in salads, sandwiches, casseroles, chowders, stews, gumbos, and so on.

(See SEAFOOD.)

PICKLED SHRIMP

2 1/2 lb. shrimp, cooked
3 med. onions, sliced
7 bay leaves
1 1/4 c. salad oil
3/4 c. white vinegar
1 1/2 tsp. salt
2 1/2 tsp. celery seed
2 1/2 tsp. juice of capers
Dash of hot sauce

Alternate layers of shrimp and onions in bowl; spread bay leaves over shrimp mixture. Mix all remaining ingredients; pour over shrimp mixture. Refrigerate for 24 hours, tossing occasionally. Add pepper, horseradish and paprika if desired. Yield: 6 servings.

SHRIMP MOLD

2 tbsp. unflavored gelatin
1 can tomato soup
1 8-oz. package cream cheese
1/2 c. chopped stuffed olives
1 c. finely diced celery
1 tsp. grated onion
1 c. mayonnaise
1 tbsp. Worcestershire sauce
2 tsp. hot sauce
Juice of 2 lemons
2 c. chopped cooked shrimp

Soften gelatin in 1/2 cup cold water; set aside. Heat soup in double boiler; add cream cheese. Beat until smooth. Add gelatin; stir until dissolved. Add all remaining ingredients; cool. Pour into slightly greased mold. Refrigerate overnight. Turn out onto serving tray. Garnish with parsley, celery leaves or watercress. Serve with round buttery crackers.

SWEET AND SOUR SHRIMP

1/4 c. butter
1 lb. shrimp, cooked
1/4 tsp. salt
1/4 tsp. pepper
1/4 c. vinegar
2 tbsp. soy sauce
6 whole cloves
1 bay leaf
1 16-oz. can pineapple chunks
1 1/2 tbsp. cornstarch
1 c. green pepper

Melt butter in large skillet; brown shrimp lightly. Season with salt and pepper. Add vinegar, soy sauce, 1/2 cup water, cloves and bay leaf. Simmer, covered, for 10 minutes. Drain pineapple; reserve syrup. Mix 2 tablespoons reserved syrup with cornstarch. Stir remaining reserved syrup into shrimp. Blend in cornstarch mixture. Bring to a boil gradually, stirring constantly. Cook for 5 minutes or until sauce is thick and clear, stirring occasionally. Add pineapple chunks. Cut green pepper into 3/4-inch squares; add to shrimp mixture. Cook until just tender. Bring to a boil. Serve in chafing dish with wooden picks. Yield: 12 servings.

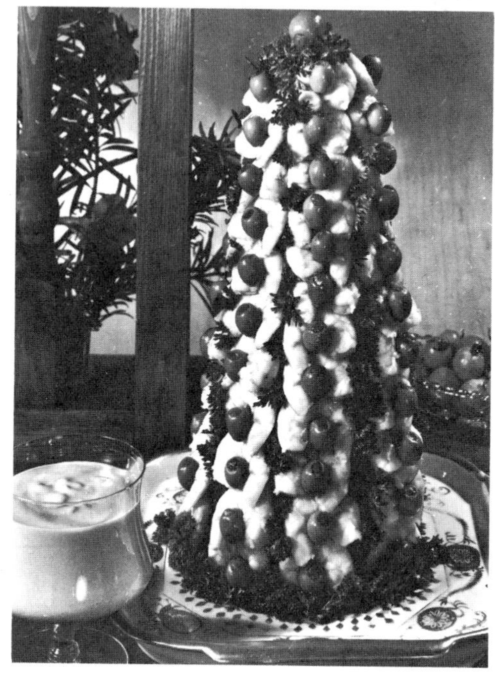

Olive-Shrimp Tree with Spanish Sauce . . . A colorful appetizer that features holiday colors.

OLIVE-SHRIMP TREE WITH SPANISH SAUCE

4 lb. medium shrimp
1 12-in. styrofoam cone
Wide-mesh screening
Pins or staples
2 bunches parsley
2 1/2 c. pimento-stuffed olives
Spanish Sauce

Cook shrimp in boiling salted water for about 3 to 5 minutes; peel and devein. Cover styrofoam cone with screening; fasten with pins or staples. Separate parsley into individual sprigs; insert stems in screening. Cover entire cone with parsley sprigs. Insert wooden picks in vertical rows in styrofoam cone, spacing picks about 1 inch apart. Place 1 shrimp, curved side up, on each pick. Place additional pick in curve of each shrimp; fasten olive on each pick. Top cone with additional stuffed olive; surround with parsley sprigs. Sprinkle or spray entire surface lightly with water; cover with plastic wrap. Chill until serving time. Serve with Spanish Sauce as a dip.

Spanish Sauce

1 c. mayonnaise
1/2 c. catsup
1/4 c. chili sauce
1/2 c. chopped pimento-stuffed olives
1 1/2 tbsp. brandy
1/2 tsp. Dijon mustard
1/2 tsp. Worcestershire sauce
1/2 tsp. curry powder
1/2 tsp. paprika
1/2 tsp. lemon juice
Dash of coarsely ground pepper

Blend mayonnaise, catsup, chili sauce and olives together; stir in brandy. Add remaining ingredients, blending well. Chill.

SHRIMP BOATS

1 can shrimp, chopped
2 hard-boiled eggs, diced
1/4 tsp. celery salt
Salt and pepper
3/4 c. mayonnaise
1/4 c. cream
16 bread slices, crusts removed

Combine shrimp, eggs, celery salt, salt and pepper. Combine mayonnaise with cream; fold into shrimp mixture. Spread shrimp mixture between bread slices. Cut into halves, diagonally; fasten corners with wooden picks. Place on cookie sheet; broil 4 inches from source of heat for 10 to 15 minutes or until bread is toasted. Yield: 8 servings.

SHRIMP REMOULADE

1 bunch green onions, chopped
1 celery stalk, chopped
2 cloves of garlic, chopped
1 sprig of parsley, chopped
5 tbsp. creole mustard
2 tbsp. paprika
Salt and pepper to taste
1/3 c. vinegar
2/3 c. olive oil
1 1/2 lb. cooked shrimp
Shredded lettuce
Tomato wedges

Combine onions, celery, garlic and parsley; add mustard, paprika, salt and pepper. Mix thoroughly with vinegar; add olive oil. Stir in shrimp; marinate for 3 hours. Serve on shredded lettuce; garnish with tomatoes. Yield: 6 servings.

CONGEALED SHRIMP SALAD

2 pkg. unflavored gelatin
3 c. tomato juice
1/4 c. lemon juice
1 tbsp. onion juice
1 tsp. Worcestershire sauce
Salt and pepper to taste
1 c. mayonnaise
2 lb. cooked chopped shrimp
1/2 c. chopped onion
1/4 c. chopped green pepper
1/4 c. chopped celery
Lettuce leaves
Paprika
Parsley

Soften gelatin in 1/4 cup water. Combine tomato juice, lemon juice, onion juice, Worcestershire sauce, salt and pepper; bring to a boil. Pour hot ingredients over gelatin; stir until gelatin is dissolved. Place in refrigerator; chill until mixture begins to thicken. Add mayonnaise. Beat with rotary beater until smooth. Add shrimp, onion, green pepper and celery. Pour into rectangular dish; chill until firm. Serve in squares on lettuce; garnish with additional mayonnaise, paprika and parsley. Yield: 8 servings.

FESTIVE SHRIMP SALAD

1/2 c. mayonnaise
2/3 c. catsup
Hot sauce to taste
1 lge. onion, chopped
2 med. pickles, diced
1 qt. cooked shrimp
Lettuce
2 stalks celery, diced
4 hard-boiled eggs, chopped
1 lge. tomato, chopped

Mix mayonnaise, catsup, hot sauce, onion and pickles together; pour over shrimp, coating well. Place shrimp mixture on lettuce leaves; cover with celery, eggs and tomato. Yield: 6 servings.

HOT SHRIMP SALAD

Butter
1 c. flour
1 qt. milk
1 tsp. salt
1/4 tsp. pepper
1/8 tsp. nutmeg
2 7 1/2-oz. cans shrimp
4 hard-cooked eggs, sliced
1 sm. green pepper, diced
1/2 c. almonds
2 slices toasted bread, cubed
Paprika to taste

Combine 1 cup butter and flour in saucepan; stir to make a paste. Add milk to flour mixture gradually. Cook, stirring constantly, until smooth and thickened; add salt, pepper and nutmeg. Pour sauce into greased 13 x 9 x 2-inch baking dish. Drain shrimp; chop coarsely. Add shrimp, eggs, green pepper and almonds to cream sauce. Cover with toast cubes; dot with butter. Sprinkle cubes with paprika. Bake at 350 degrees for 30 minutes. Yield: 8-10 servings.

ORIGINAL SHRIMP LOUIS

1 c. mayonnaise
1 tbsp. tarragon vinegar
3 tbsp. chili sauce
1 tsp. Worcestershire sauce
2 tbsp. chopped pimento
1 clove of garlic, crushed
1 tsp. salt
1 tsp. powdered sugar
1 tsp. paprika
1/4 tsp. mustard
Lettuce leaves
Shrimp, cooked
Tomatoes, quartered
Hard-cooked eggs, quartered

Combine mayonnaise, vinegar, chili sauce and Worcestershire sauce. Mix in pimento, garlic, salt, sugar, paprika and mustard. Mix well; refrigerate, covered. Arrange lettuce leaves on plate. Place desired number of shrimp in center. Circle with tomato and egg wedges. Pour sauce over shrimp.

SHRIMP-PINEAPPLE OUTRIGGER

1 lb. fresh shrimp
1 tbsp. seafood seasoning
1 tbsp. salt
1/4 c. vinegar
1 ripe pineapple
French dressing

Combine shrimp, seasoning, salt, vinegar and 4 cups water; mix well. Place in saucepan; bring to a boil. Simmer, covered, for about 5 minutes or until pink. Drain; remove shells. Devein. Cool. Cut pineapple, including crown, in half. Remove fruit, leaving shell about 1/4 inch thick. Remove core. Dice pineapple; mix with shrimp. Marinate with enough French dressing to coat. Spoon shrimp mixture into pineapple shell. Garnish with fresh flowers.

SHRIMP LUNCHEON SALAD

3 cans shrimp
2 c. cooked shell macaroni
1 c. chopped cauliflower
1 c. sliced celery
1/2 c. chopped parsley
1/4 c. chopped sweet pickle
1/2 c. mayonnaise
3 tbsp. garlic French dressing
1 tbsp. lemon juice
1 tsp. grated onion
1 tsp. celery seed
1 tsp. salt
1/4 tsp. pepper
Salad greens

Drain shrimp; cut into halves. Combine macaroni, cauliflower, celery, parsley, pickle and shrimp. Blend mayonnaise, French dressing, lemon juice, onion, celery seed, salt and pepper together; mix well. Add mayonnaise mixture to shrimp mixture; toss lightly. Chill. Serve on salad greens; garnish with egg slices. Yield: 6 servings.

SHRIMP SALAD ARNAUD

1/3 c. wine tarragon vinegar
1/3 c. red wine vinegar
4 tsp. salt
2 tsp. cracked pepper
1 tbsp. monosodium glutamate
Red pepper to taste
1/4 c. paprika
1 tbsp. sugar
4 drops of hot sauce
1 clove of garlic, slightly crushed
1 tsp. basil
2 tsp. celery seed
3/4 c. minced chives
1/2 c. minced parsley
3/4 c. minced celery
2 c. olive oil
3/4 c. horseradish mustard
5 lb. cooked shrimp

Combine vinegars, salt, pepper, monosodium glutamate, red pepper, paprika, sugar, hot sauce, garlic, basil, celery seed, chives, parsley and celery; mix thoroughly. Let stand for 30 minutes. Add olive oil, mustard and 1/3 cup ice water. Mix in bowl until blended well. Refrigerate for 24 hours; stir occasionally. Marinate shrimp in the dressing for 2 hours before serving. Place 12 shrimp per serving on bed of shredded lettuce; serve with remaining dressing.

SHRIMP SALAD NEW ORLEANS

1 c. cold cooked rice
1 lb. chopped cooked shrimp
3/4 tsp. salt
1 tbsp. lemon juice
1/4 c. chopped green pepper
1 tbsp. minced onion
1/3 c. mayonnaise
2 tbsp. French dressing
1 tbsp. chopped stuffed olives
3/4 c. diced cauliflower
Dash of freshly ground pepper

Combine all ingredients; toss lightly. Serve on fresh salad greens. Yield: 4 servings.

BAKED SHRIMP

1 1/2 lb. shrimp, shelled
3/4 c. toasted bread crumbs
3/4 c. round buttery cracker crumbs
1/2 tsp. garlic salt
1/2 tsp. celery salt
1/2 tsp. parsley flakes
Dash of lemon juice
1/2 c. melted butter

Place shrimp in single layer in baking pan. Mix all remaining ingredients; spread over shrimp. Bake at 400 degrees for 30 minutes. Yield: 4 servings.

BARBECUED SHRIMP KABOBS

12 slices bacon
1 lb. cooked shrimp
1 4-oz. can mushrooms, drained
1 can pineapple chunks, drained
1/4 c. soy sauce
1/4 c. salad oil
1/4 c. lemon juice
1/4 c. chopped parsley
1/2 tsp. salt
Dash of pepper

Fry bacon until cooked but not crisp; cut each slice in half. Alternate shrimp, mushrooms, pineapple and bacon on long skewers until skewers are filled. Combine all remaining ingredients. Brush kabobs generously with sauce; place on grill 4 inches from source of heat. Broil for 3 minutes; turn, brush with sauce. Broil for 3 minutes longer or until browned lightly. Yield: 4 servings.

BURMESE SHRIMP

1/4 c. oil
2 c. sliced onions
1 tsp. saffron
3/4 tbsp. chili powder
1/2 c. chopped onion
2 tbsp. minced garlic
1 tbsp. ginger
1 1/2 tsp. salt
2 lb. shelled shrimp, deveined
2 c. sour cream

Heat oil in skillet; sautè onions until browned lightly. Add saffron, chili powder, chopped onion, garlic, ginger, salt and shrimp; mix well. Cook over low heat for 6 minutes. Stir in sour cream; cook until heated through, but do not boil. Serve with rice. Yield: 4 servings.

BELMONT SEAFOOD

1 can artichoke hearts
2 lb. shrimp, cooked
2 tbsp. butter
3 tbsp. flour
1/4 tsp. red pepper
1/4 tsp. paprika
1 tsp. salt
1 pt. half and half
1 tsp. Worcestershire sauce
1 tbsp. catsup
1 tsp. lemon juice
2 tbsp. sherry

Cut artichoke hearts in thin slices; drain for 1 hour. Alternate layers of shrimp and artichoke hearts in casserole. Melt butter in saucepan; add flour, pepper, paprika and salt, stirring until blended. Add half and half gradually; cook, stirring constantly, until thickened. Add Worcestershire sauce, catsup, lemon juice and sherry; pour over shrimp and artichoke hearts. Bake at 325 degrees for about 30 minutes. Yield: 6 servings.

SHRIMP AU GRATIN

5 slices bread
1 lb. shrimp, shelled and diced
1/2 c. cottage cheese
1/4 c. butter
3 tbsp. flour
1 tsp. paprika
1 1/4 c. milk
1/2 c. shredded Cheddar cheese

Cut bread into 1/2-inch cubes. Combine half the bread cubes, shrimp and cottage cheese; spread in greased baking dish. Melt 2 tablespoons butter; blend in flour and paprika to make smooth paste. Add milk gradually; heat, stirring constantly, until mixture thickens. Add cheese; cook over low heat, stirring constantly, until cheese melts. Pour sauce over shrimp mixture. Top with remaining bread cubes; pour remaining melted butter over bread cubes. Bake at 350 degrees for 25 to 30 minutes. Yield: 4-6 servings.

SWEET AND PUNGENT SHRIMP

1 lb. fresh shrimp
1 sm. can sliced pineapple
1/2 c. (packed) brown sugar
1/2 c. vinegar
2 tbsp. soy sauce
3 tbsp. cornstarch
1 green pepper, cut in strips
1 tomato, cut into wedges

Cook shrimp in boiling salted water for 3 to 5 minutes or until done. Do not overcook. Shell and devein shrimp. Drain pineapple, reserving syrup in saucepan. Cut pineapple slices in half; set aside. Add brown sugar, vinegar, soy sauce and 1 cup water to reserved pineapple syrup. Bring to a boil. Combine cornstarch and 1/4 cup water. Add to syrup mixture. Cook, stirring constantly, until thickened. Add green pepper, pineapple and tomato wedges. Cook for 5 minutes. Add shrimp; heat through. Serve immediately. May serve over hot cooked rice. Yield: 4 servings.

Sweet and Pungent Shrimp . . . Shrimp, pineapple, peppers, and tomato in a sweet and sour sauce.

SHRIMP NEWBURG CASSEROLE

1 8-oz. package noodles
1 can frozen shrimp soup
1 sm. can evaporated milk
1/4 c. grated sharp cheese
1 pkg. frozen shrimp
1 c. salad dressing
1/4 c. sherry

Cook noodles according to package directions; drain. Place in greased baking dish. Combine soup, milk, cheese and shrimp in double boiler; cook, stirring frequently, until smooth. Stir in salad dressing and sherry. Pour over noodles. Bake at 325 degrees for 20 minutes. Yield: 6 servings.

Shrimp Creole . . . This famous New Orleans dish is yours with this easy-to-prepare recipe.

SHRIMP CREOLE

1/4 c. butter
1 c. coarsely chopped onion
1 c. diced celery
1 sm. clove of garlic, minced
2 tbsp. flour
1 tsp. salt
1 tsp. sugar
Dash of cayenne pepper
1 tsp. paprika
1/2 sm. bay leaf
4 drops of hot sauce
1/2 c. diced green pepper
1 1-lb. 3-oz. can tomatoes
2 c. cooked cleaned shrimp

Melt butter in frypan; saute onion, celery and garlic until tender but not brown. Add flour and seasonings; stir until blended. Stir in green pepper and tomatoes. Cook for 10 minutes over low heat, stirring occasionally. Add shrimp; heat through.

Cheese Rice

1 tbsp. butter
1 tsp. salt
1 1/2 c. rice
2 tbsp. minced onion
2 c. shredded American cheese
1 tsp. prepared mustard

Bring 3 cups water to boiling point in saucepan. Add butter, salt and rice; bring to a boil. Reduce heat to low; cook, covered, for about 20 to 25 minutes or until rice is tender. Stir onion, cheese and mustard into rice. Line hot 2-quart casserole with cheese mixture; fill center with shrimp mixture. Garnish with parsley. Yield: 6 servings.

CHARLESTON SHRIMP CREOLE

2 med. onions, diced
1 green pepper, diced
1 1/2 c. diced celery
1/4 c. bacon drippings
1 qt. canned tomatoes
3 tbsp. tomato paste
Hot sauce to taste
3 c. cooked shrimp, shelled

Saute onions, green pepper and celery in bacon drippings for 15 minutes or until tender and transparent but not brown. Add tomatoes and tomato paste. Simmer for 30 to 45 minutes longer or until thickened. Add hot sauce. Add shrimp; cook for 15 minutes before serving. Serve over cooked rice. Yield: 6 servings.

FRENCH-FRIED SHRIMP

2 lb. shrimp
1 tsp. salt
Juice of 1 lemon
2 tbsp. oil
1 c. flour
3 tsp. baking powder
1/3 tsp. cream of tartar
Pepper to taste
2 eggs, separated

Shell and devein shrimp. Combine 2 cups water, salt, lemon juice and 1 tablespoon oil in bowl; soak shrimp in mixture for 30 minutes. Drain shrimp. Mix flour, baking powder, cream of tartar, additional salt to taste and pepper. Add 1 cup ice water; mix well. Fold in beaten egg yolks and remaining oil. Fold in stiffly beaten egg whites. Dip shrimp into batter. Fry in deep fat, several at a time.

PENTAGON SHRIMP

1 c. salad oil
2 c. sliced green pepper
5 c. sliced onions
2 c. diced celery
1 c. chopped celery leaves
1 c. chili sauce
1 c. raisins
1 tsp. thyme
1 tsp. curry powder
1 tsp. salt
1 tsp. pepper
1 tsp. cayenne pepper
3 bay leaves
1/2 c. chopped parsley
1 2/3 c. chopped toasted almonds
2 No. 2 1/2 cans tomatoes
1 lge. can cocktail vegetable juice
5 lb. cooked shrimp

Heat oil in large skillet; add green pepper, onions, celery and celery leaves. Cook over low heat until onion is transparent but not brown. Add all remaining ingredients except shrimp. Simmer for 1 hour, stirring occasionally. Add shrimp; heat thoroughly. Serve over rice if desired. Yield: 20 servings.

SCAMPI

1 lb. large shrimp
1/2 c. butter
1/2 tsp. salt
6 cloves of garlic, crushed
2 tbsp. chopped parsley
1 tsp. grated lemon peel
1 tbsp. lemon juice

Preheat oven to 400 degrees. Shell shrimp; leave tails intact. Devein. Melt butter in 13 x 9 x 2-inch baking pan. Add salt, garlic and 1 tablespoon parsley; mix well. Arrange shrimp in single layer in baking dish. Bake for 5 minutes. Turn shrimp; sprinkle with lemon peel, lemon juice and remaining parsley. Bake for 8 to 10 minutes longer or until just tender. Arrange shrimp on heated platter. Pour butter mixture over. Garnish with lemon wedges. Serve immediately. Yield: 6 servings.

SHRIMP A LA JACQUES

1 lb. cooked shrimp
5 egg yolks
Thick white sauce
1 1/2 oz. white wine
Garlic butter
1 pkg. Gouda cheese

Cut shrimp into bite-sized pieces; place in ramekins or shells. Add egg yolks to warm white sauce, stirring quickly. Add wine; stir well. Pour over shrimp in shells. Add desired amount of garlic butter; top with cheese. Brown under broiler, 4 inches from source of heat; serve hot. Garnish with lemon wedges.

SHRIMP CAKES

1 lb. shelled shrimp
2 med. potatoes
1 med. onion
1 tsp. salt
1 tsp. pepper
1 egg, beaten

Grind shrimp, potatoes and onion in food chopper. Mix well; add seasonings. Shape into patties; dip into egg. Fry in deep hot fat until golden brown. Yield: 4 servings.

SHRIMP DELISH

1 c. butter
2 cloves of garlic, minced
1 tbsp. onion, minced
2 tbsp. fresh parsley, chopped
2 tbsp. bread crumbs
1 lb. frozen shrimp
1/2 c. fresh mushrooms, chopped
1 c. fresh tomatoes, chopped

Melt butter in heavy skillet; add garlic, onion, parsley and bread crumbs, blending well. Place in skillet. Bring to a boil gradually. Thaw shrimp; shell and devein. Add to butter mixture. Cook for 5 minutes. Add mushrooms and tomatoes; cook until shrimp is tender. Serve over rice. Yield: 4 servings.

SHRIMP ETOUFFE

1 med. onion, minced
2 green onions, minced
3 cloves of garlic, minced
1/4 c. finely chopped celery
1/2 c. butter
2 tbsp. flour
1 10 1/2-oz. can tomato puree
2 bay leaves
1 tbsp. Worcestershire sauce
4 drops of hot sauce
1 tsp. salt
1/2 tsp. sugar
1/2 tsp. whole thyme, crushed
1/8 tsp. pepper
1 lb. shrimp, shelled

Saute onion, green onions, garlic and celery in butter until tender. Add flour, stirring well; cook, stirring constantly, until browned lightly. Add 2 1/2 cups water, tomato puree, bay leaves, Worcestershire sauce and hot sauce, salt, sugar, thyme and pepper. Simmer, for 25 minutes, stirring occasionally, or until sauce is of desired consistency. Add shrimp; cook for 15 minutes. Garnish with quartered hard-cooked eggs. Yield: 4-6 servings.

SHRIMP STROGANOFF

Color photograph for this recipe on page 80.

3 tbsp. butter
1/2 c. chopped onion
1 sm. clove of garlic, minced
1/4 c. all-purpose flour
1 tsp. salt
1/2 tsp. dillweed
1 10 1/2-oz. can beef broth
1 2-oz. can sliced mushrooms
2 c. cooked shrimp
1 c. yogurt, at room temperature

Melt butter in chafing dish blazer pan. Add onion and garlic; saute until onion is tender. Stir in flour, salt and dillweed. Remove from heat; stir in beef broth and mushrooms with liquid gradually. Cook over medium heat, stirring constantly, until thickened. Add shrimp; cook over low heat for 5 to 10 minutes. Stir in yogurt; heat to serving temperature. Do not boil. Place blazer pan over hot water. Serve shrimp mixture over rice or noodles. Yield: 4-6 servings.

SHRIMP FLORENTINE

3 lge. shrimp
Salt and pepper to taste
Cracker crumbs
Oil
3 tbsp. cooked chopped spinach
3 1/2 slices bacon, fried
3 3-in. squares Muenster cheese

Butterfly shrimp; sprinkle with salt and pepper. Roll in cracker crumbs. Fry until brown in skillet in hot oil, 1 inch deep. Place shrimp on foil-lined cookie sheet. Top each shrimp with 1 tablespoon chopped spinach, 1/2 slice bacon and 1 square of cheese. Bake at 400 degrees for about 5 minutes. Yield: 1 serving.

SHRIMP DE JONGHE

2 c. butter
1 c. chopped parsley
1/2 c. sherry
2 c. bread crumbs
1 clove of garlic, crushed
5 lb. shrimp, shelled
2 tbsp. lemon juice

Cream butter, parsley, sherry, bread crumbs and garlic; shape into roll. Chill. Cook shrimp in boiling salted water to cover for 4 minutes; drain. Sprinkle lemon juice over shrimp; arrange in shallow baking dish. Slice chilled mixture; arrange over shrimp. Broil for 10 minutes 6 inches from source of heat. Yield: 12 servings.

SHRIMP LORRAINE

1 tbsp. chopped parsley
1 tbsp. minced green pepper
1 sm. onion, chopped
1/2 tsp. soy sauce
1 can mushroom soup
3/4 c. half and half
1/4 tsp. nutmeg
1 1/2 lb. shrimp, shelled
3 tbsp. apricot brandy
4 oz. mushroom buttons
1 c. grated cheese

Saute parsley, green pepper and onion in small amount of fat in skillet. Add soy sauce, mushroom soup and half and half; stir over low heat until smooth. Add nutmeg, shrimp, brandy and mushrooms. Add grated cheese just before serving. Serve hot over rice. Yield: 6 servings.

SHRIMP MARENGO

Bacon drippings
1 c. chopped onion
1 lb. fresh mushrooms, sliced
1 clove of garlic, minced
1 lge. can Italian-style plum tomatoes
1 6-oz. can tomato paste
1 can chicken broth
1 tsp. monosodium glutamate
1 1/4 tsp. oregano
1 1/4 tsp. crushed basil
1 bay leaf
1 tbsp. salt
1/4 tsp. pepper
1 tbsp. sugar
3 drops of hot sauce
2 lb. shelled shrimp, deveined

Heat bacon drippings in large skillet; saute onion, mushrooms and garlic until mushrooms are tender. Add tomatoes, tomato paste, chicken broth, monosodium glutamate, oregano, basil, bay leaf, salt, pepper, sugar and hot sauce; bring to a boil. Simmer, uncovered, for 20 minutes. Add shrimp; cook for 10 minutes longer or until shrimp are tender. Serve over rice. Yield: 6 servings.

SHRIMP MARINARA

2 tbsp. salad oil
1/4 c. chopped celery
1/4 tsp. garlic salt
1 tsp. oregano
1/4 tsp. salt
1/8 tsp. cayenne pepper
1/4 tsp. sugar
1/2 tsp. basil
2 tbsp. minced parsley
1 No. 2 1/2 can tomatoes
1 lb. shelled shrimp, deveined

Heat oil in large pan; add celery. Cook celery until tender. Add all remaining ingredients except shrimp; simmer until mixture is thickened slightly. Add shrimp; cook for 5 minutes. Serve over hot rice. Yield: 6 servings.

SHRIMP NEWBURG

2 tbsp. butter
1 3/4 tbsp. flour
1 c. cream
3 tbsp. catsup
3/4 tbsp. Worcestershire sauce
1 lb. cooked shrimp
Salt to taste
Paprika to taste
Dash of cayenne pepper
3 tbsp. sherry

Melt butter; stir in flour to make a paste. Add cream gradually; cook, stirring constantly, until thickened. Add catsup and Worcestershire sauce, stirring well. Add shrimp; stir until heated through. Season with salt, paprika and cayenne pepper. Add sherry just before serving. Yield: 4 servings.

SHRIMP ROCKEFELLER

Butter
Worcestershire sauce
1 1/2 tsp. salt
1/8 tsp. hot sauce
2 pkg. frozen chopped spinach
1/2 head lettuce, chopped
6 green onions, minced
2 tbsp. parsley
1 1/2 stalks celery, chopped
1/2 c. bread crumbs
2 lb. small shrimp, cooked
3 tbsp. flour
1 1/2 c. milk
1/2 c. Parmesan cheese
1/2 c. buttered bread crumbs

Heat 1/2 cup butter, 1 tablespoon Worcestershire sauce, salt and hot sauce in skillet; add spinach, lettuce, onions, parsley and celery. Simmer for 10 minutes. Add crumbs. Spread in greased casserole. Cover with shrimp. Melt 3 tablespoons butter; stir in flour. Add milk gradually; cook until thickened, stirring constantly. Add 1/4 teaspoon Worcestershire sauce and cheese, stirring until cheese is melted. Pour sauce over shrimp; top with buttered crumbs. Bake at 350 degrees for 20 minutes.

SWEET AND PUNGENT SHRIMP

1 No. 2 can pineapple chunks
1/4 c. (packed) brown sugar
2 tbsp. cornstarch
1/2 tsp. salt
1/3 c. vinegar
1 1/2 tbsp. soy sauce

1 green pepper, cut into strips
1 onion, sliced
1 lb. cooked shelled shrimp
Hot cooked rice

Drain pineapple; reserve juice. Combine brown sugar, cornstarch, salt, vinegar, soy sauce and reserved juice, blending well; cook until thickened slightly, stirring constantly. Add green pepper, onion and pineapple chunks; cook for 3 minutes. Remove from heat; add shrimp. Cover; let stand for 10 minutes. Bring mixture to a boil, stirring constantly. Serve with rice. Yield: 4 servings.

Sole

Sole (also called Dover or English sole) is a European flatfish that is related to the American flounder. It is found exclusively in North European waters and is flown to the United States frozen in fillets. The flesh is firm, white, digestible, and easily separated from the bone; the flavor is more delicate than that of flounder. However what is commonly regarded in the United States as fillet of sole is actually a number of fishes of the flounder family (Lemon sole, Gray sole). In most recipes flounder especially baby flounder can be successfully substituted for Dover sole.
(See FLOUNDER and SEAFOOD.)

FILLET OF SOLE PANE

1 4 1/2-oz. jar sliced mushrooms
3 tbsp. butter, melted
1/2 c. chopped pecans
Salt
Pepper to taste
1 1/2 lb. sole fillets
1 egg, beaten
1/4 c. milk
3/4 c. fine bread crumbs
2 c. cooked rice

Preheat oven to 400 degrees. Drain mushrooms; saute in butter in skillet until lightly browned. Stir in pecans; sprinkle lightly with salt and pepper. Spread mushroom mixture on fillets. Roll tightly; skewer with wooden picks. Combine egg, milk and 1/2 teaspoon salt. Dip fillets into egg mixture; roll in bread crumbs. Spoon rice into greased casserole. Arrange fillets over rice. Bake for about 20 minutes or until fish flakes easily. Garnish with parsley and lemon slices. Yield: 6 servings.

Fillet of Sole Pane . . . Breaded sole rolls are stuffed with a savory mushroom-pecan mixture.

BAKED SOLE IN LEMON MAYONNAISE

Juice of 1 lemon
1 c. mayonnaise
Salt to taste
White pepper to taste
1/4 c. minced parsley
2 lb. 1-in. thick fillets of sole
Paprika

Stir lemon juice into mayonnaise gradually; add salt, pepper and parsley. Arrange sole in greased baking pan. Cover sole with sauce. Bake at 350 degrees for about 35 minutes. Sprinkle with paprika; garnish with parsley. Yield: 5-6 servings.

FILLETS OF SOLE VERONIQUE

1 1/2 lb. sole fillets
1 tsp. salt
1/8 tsp. pepper
1 tbsp. butter
1/4 c. chopped fresh onion
1 clove of garlic
1/2 c. dry white wine
1 tsp. fresh lemon juice
1/4 c. light cream
1 egg yolk, slightly beaten
1 tsp. flour
2 c. fresh seedless grapes

Sprinkle fillets with salt and pepper; roll up and fasten with wooden picks. Set aside. Melt butter in 10-inch skillet; add onion. Saute until tender. Spear garlic on wooden pick; add to onion mixture. Pour in wine and lemon juice. Arrange fillets in skillet. Cover; simmer for 5 to 10 minutes or until fish flakes easily. Remove fillets to serving platter; keep warm. Discard garlic. Strain liquid in skillet; return to skillet. Combine cream and egg yolk; stir into liquid in skillet gradually. Sprinkle flour over mixture, stirring to blend. Cook over medium heat, stirring constantly, until thickened and smooth. Add grapes; cook until grapes are heated through. Pour sauce over fillets. Garnish with additional grape clusters if desired. Yield: 6 servings.

Fillet of Sole Veronique . . . This gourmet treat features sole and grapes with a delicate sauce.

BAKED SOLE WITH TOMATO SAUCE

1 1-lb. package fillets of sole, thawed
Salt and pepper to taste
3 tbsp. butter
1 med. onion, chopped
2 sm. green onions, chopped
1 clove of garlic, minced
1 1/2 tbsp. flour
1 c. dry white wine
1/2 c. cream
5 tomatoes, coarsely chopped
1 tsp. chopped parsley
Pinch of tarragon
Pinch of thyme
Pinch of basil
1/4 c. fine bread crumbs
2 tbsp. grated Parmesan cheese

Place fillets in greased baking dish; season with salt and pepper. Melt butter in saucepan. Add onion, green onions and garlic; saute for 5 minutes. Stir in flour; add wine gradually. Bring to a boil; add cream gradually, stirring constantly until thickened. Simmer for 5 minutes. Add tomatoes, parsley, tarragon, thyme and basil. Pour sauce over sole; sprinkle with bread crumbs and cheese. Bake at 350 degrees for 20 to 25 minutes. Yield: 4 servings.

BAKED SOLE IN WHITE WINE

2 lb. sole fillets
3 c. thinly sliced cooked potatoes
1 4-oz. can sliced mushrooms
1 tsp. paprika
1/2 tsp. salt
1/4 tsp. pepper
1 c. sour cream
1/2 c. dry white wine
2 tbsp. flour
1 tbsp. grated onion
Grated parsley

Skin fillets; cut into serving portions. Arrange potatoes in greased 12 x 8 x 2-inch baking dish. Drain mushrooms; spread over potatoes. Combine paprika, salt and pepper. Sprinkle half the seasoning over potatoes and mushrooms. Combine sour cream, wine, flour and onion. Spread half the sour cream mixture over mushrooms. Top with fillets. Sprinkle fillets with remaining seasoning; spread with remaining sour cream mixture. Bake at 350 degrees for 35 to 45 minutes or until fish flakes easily. Remove from oven; let stand for 10 minutes for easier serving. Sprinkle with parsley. Yield: 6 servings.

FILLETS DE SOLE BONNE FEMME

2 tbsp. melted butter
3 tbsp. lemon juice
1/4 c. finely chopped onion
1 lb. fillet of sole
1/2 c. cream of mushroom soup
1 1-oz. can sm. mushrooms, drained

Combine butter, lemon juice and onion; pour into 11 x 7-inch baking dish. Dip sole into butter mixture, turning to coat. Place sole, skin side up, in butter mixture. Bake at 350 degrees for 20 minutes. Add soup and mushrooms; bake for 10 minutes longer. Yield: 4 servings.

FILLETS OF SOLE CASSEROLE

1 lb. fillets of sole
1 sm. onion, thinly sliced
1/2 lemon, thinly sliced
2 tbsp. butter, diced
Salt and pepper to taste
Milk

Arrange layers of fillets, onion and lemon slices in greased casserole, dotting each layer with butter and sprinkling with salt and pepper. Pour enough milk over layers to cover. Bake at 325 degrees for about 25 minutes or until fish flakes easily.

FILLETS DE SOLE DUGLEREE

1 onion, minced
8 oz. sliced mushrooms
4 tbsp. butter
3 med. tomatoes, peeled
1 lb. sole fillets
1 c. dry white wine
Salt and pepper to taste
3 egg yolks, beaten
2 tbsp. sour cream
1 tsp. chopped parsley

Saute onion and mushrooms in 2 tablespoons butter in large skillet. Chop tomatoes coarsely; add to mushroom mixture. Arrange sole on tomato mixture; add wine. Sprinkle with salt and pepper; cover. Cook over low heat until sole is poached; do not boil. Remove from heat; transfer sole to heated platter. Boil tomato mixture over high heat until liquid has been reduced by half. Melt remaining butter. Combine egg yolks, sour cream and melted butter; stir small amount of egg mixture into tomato mixture. Return to pan. Cook, shaking pan, until boiling. Season with salt and pepper; add parsley. Pour sauce over sole. Yield: 4 servings.

FILLETS OF SOLE SAN JOAQUIN

Butter
1 onion, chopped
1/2 c. chopped parsley
1/2 c. seasoned cooked rice
Salt
1/8 tsp. pepper
2 eggs
3/4 c. milk
8 fillets of sole
Fine dry bread crumbs
1 can cream of mushroom soup
1 c. white wine

Melt 1/4 cup butter in skillet. Saute onion and parsley until onion is soft and transparent. Add rice, 1/2 teaspoon salt and pepper. Beat eggs with milk; season lightly with salt. Spread rice mixture evenly over each fillet; roll up. Fasten with skewers. Dip each roll into egg mixture; roll in bread crumbs. Refrigerate for 30 minutes or longer. Brown rolls lightly in melted butter; remove to shallow baking dish. Mix soup with wine. Simmer for 15 minutes, stirring frequently; pour sauce around sole. Broil until lightly browned.

FILLETS OF SOLE IN WINE SAUCE

1 tsp. parsley
1 tsp. chopped green onion
3 fresh mushrooms, chopped
1 stalk celery, chopped
2 tbsp. olive oil
1 bay leaf
1/2 c. consomme
1 c. white wine
8 med. fillets of sole
Grated Parmesan cheese

Brown parsley, onion, mushrooms and celery lightly in hot olive oil in saucepan. Add bay leaf, consomme and wine. Bring to a boil. Simmer for 10 minutes. Place fillets in greased casserole. Cook sauce until reduced to 1 cup liquid; pour over fillets. Sprinkle with cheese. Bake at 450 degrees for 10 minutes. Garnish with parsley and lemon slices if desired. Yield: 8 servings.

SOLE WITH ALMONDS AND GRAPES

6 sole fillets
Seasoned flour
2 tbsp. oil
Butter
1/2 c. green seedless grapes
1/2 c. blanched, slivered almonds
3 tbsp. consomme
Juice of 1/2 lemon
Dash of Worcestershire sauce

Dust fillets with seasoned flour. Heat oil and 2 tablespoons butter in skillet; saute fillets for 3 to 4 minutes on each side until lightly browned. Remove fillets to heated platter. Add 2 tablespoons butter to pan drippings in skillet; add grapes. Cook grapes for 2 to 3 minutes; spoon over fillets. Add 1 tablespoon butter to skillet; saute almonds until lightly browned. Stir in consomme, lemon juice and Worcestershire sauce. Heat sauce; pour over fillets. Yield: 6 servings.

SOLE IN BANANA LEAF

6 fillets of sole
Salt
1/4 grated fresh coconut
3 green chili peppers
1 tsp. coriander
1 tsp. caraway seed
1 tsp. fresh mint leaves
3 cloves of garlic
1 tsp. cumin
1 tbsp. sugar
Banana leaves
Oil

Season fillets with salt to taste. Process coconut, chili peppers, coriander, caraway seed, mint leaves and garlic through food grinder. Add cumin, 1/2 teaspoon salt and sugar. Coat fillets with paste. Cut banana leaves into pieces large enough to wrap around each fillet. Grease one side of each banana leaf piece. Place fillets on greased sides; wrap and fasten with thread. Fry fillets on each side in oil in skillet for 10 minutes. Place on baking sheet. Bake at 350 degrees for 15 minutes. Serve.

SOLE CANADIAN

2 pkg. frozen fillets of sole
1 pkg. herb seasoned stuffing mix
Butter
Salt and pepper to taste
2 c. dry vermouth

Preheat oven to 350 degrees. Place half the fillets in greased 8-inch square pan. Mix stuffing according to package directions; spoon over fillets. Arrange remaining fillets on stuffing; dot with butter. Sprinkle with salt and pepper; pour vermouth over fillets. Let stand for 1 to 2 minutes. Cover with foil. Bake for 30 to 35 minutes. Sole should be slightly moist. Yield: 6 servings.

SOLE IN CHAMPAGNE SAUCE

2 bay leaves
Celery leaves to taste
1 onion, sliced
5 peppercorns
2 sprigs of parsley
1 split champagne
6 sole fillets
3 tbsp. butter
3 tbsp. flour
1/2 c. heavy cream
Salt and white pepper to taste
1 egg yolk

Combine 1 1/2 cups water, bay leaves, celery leaves, onion, peppercorns and parsley in large saucepan. Simmer for 10 to 15 minutes. Strain; add half the champagne to bouillon. Poach sole gently in seasoned liquid. Do not overcook. Remove fillets to warm serving platter. Increase heat; boil stock until reduced to 1/2 cup liquid. Stir in remaining champagne. Melt butter in skillet; stir in flour. Add 1 cup champagne mixture and cream; cook, stirring constantly, until thickened. Cool slightly; season with salt and pepper. Add egg yolk; stir well. Pour sauce over sole; garnish with chopped parsley. Yield: 6 servings.

SOLE IN MUSHROOM SAUCE

1 pkg. mushroom soup mix
1/2 pt. sour cream
1/4 tsp. fines herbes
3 tbsp. white wine
1 tbsp. lemon juice
2 tbsp. butter
1 lb. fillets of sole
Salt and pepper to taste

Combine soup mix, sour cream, fines herbes, wine and lemon juice in small bowl. Melt butter in electric frypan; heat to 225 degrees. Add fillets. Pour sour cream mixture over sole; season with salt and pepper. Reduce heat; simmer, covered, for 7 minutes or until fish flakes easily. Sprinkle with chopped parsley or chives.

SOLE WITH SHELLFISH

4 1/2 lb. fillets of sole
Salt and pepper to taste
2/3 c. butter
5 tbsp. sifted flour
Cream
1/2 c. white wine
1/2 lb. small cooked shrimp
1/2 lb. cooked crab meat
Dash of cayenne pepper
2 tbsp. Worcestershire sauce
Paprika

Cut fillets into serving pieces; sprinkle with salt and pepper. Place in greased casserole. Bake at 350 degrees for 35 minutes. Melt 1/2 cup butter in skillet; brown slightly. Add flour; stir until smooth. Drain fish liquid from casserole; add enough cream to make 2 1/2 cups liquid. Stir liquid into butter mixture; cook over low heat, stirring constantly, until thickened and smooth. Add wine, shrimp, crab meat, cayenne pepper and Worcestershire sauce. Sprinkle paprika over fillets; dot with remaining butter. Spoon sauce over sole. Bake, covered, at 350 degrees until heated through.

WALNUT-STUFFED LEMON SOLE

1 1/2 c. chopped mushrooms
2 tbsp. chopped onions
2 tbsp. butter
1/2 c. finely chopped walnuts, toasted
1/4 c. chopped parsley
Salt
1/8 tsp. dillweed
6 fillets of sole
Juice of 1 lemon
Pepper

Brown mushrooms and onions in butter in saucepan. Mix in walnuts, parsley, salt to taste and dillweed. Drizzle sole with lemon juice; season with salt and pepper to taste. Place spoonful of mushroom mixture on skin side of each fillet; roll up as for jelly roll. Secure with wooden picks. Place fillets in greased baking dish. Brush with additional melted butter. Bake at 350 degrees for 25 to 30 minutes or until fish flakes easily.

Mornay Sauce

4 tbsp. butter
1 tbsp. finely chopped onion
3 tbsp. flour
3/4 c. chicken broth
1 c. cream
2 egg yolks, beaten
1/2 c. shredded Swiss cheese

Heat 3 tablespoons butter in heavy saucepan. Cook onion until tender. Blend in flour; heat until bubbly. Add broth and cream gradually, stirring constantly. Bring to a boil rapidly, stirring constantly; boil for 2 minutes. Blend small amount of hot mixture into egg yolks; return to hot mixture. Add cheese and remaining butter. Serve sauce over fillets.

Souffle

A souffle is a fluffy baked dish prepared with a thick sauce, flavoring, and eggs. Savory souffles have meat, fish, cheese, or vegetables as the flavoring and are served as main dishes. Sweet souffles add sugar to the sauce and use chocolate, vanilla, pureed fruits, jam, or nuts as the flavoring. They are served as desserts. There is a popular misconception that souffles are difficult to make. This may have been true years ago when oven temperatures could not be accurately regulated and the frequent shifts in temperature caused souffles to fall. But with today's modern ovens and automatic temperature controls, souffle-making is surprisingly easy—and satisfying.

EQUIPMENT: Souffle-making requires just a few pieces of special equipment. One is a *whisk,* a wooden- or metal-handled utensil designed for whipping eggs or egg whites to a great volume. Another is the *souffle dish,* an ovenproof utensil made of metal, porcelain, or glass. It is round with absolutely straight sides. Sometimes a souffle dish is not high enough to hold up the souffle. In such cases, a collar is tied around the dish. These collars can be made of buttered paper or oiled foil. For beating egg whites, use any large *bowl* except one made of aluminum. Aluminum may cause egg whites to become gray in color. Finally, you will need a utensil to puree the food used as flavoring. An *electric blender* is ideal, but a *food mill* or *strainer* works as well.

PREPARATION: Before beginning to mix the souffle, prepare both the dish and the flavoring. *To prepare the dish*–Grease the inside well with butter. Coat it with dried bread crumbs or grated cheese if you are making a savory souffle. For sweet souffles, the coating should be sugar. *To prepare the flavoring* –Cook it if necessary. Then put it through an electric blender, food mill, or strainer until all lumps are removed and it is very fine. *To mix the souffle*–Remove eggs from the refrigerator and separate them. Allow whites to come to room temperature before beating them to increase their volume. Following specific recipe instructions, prepare a thick sauce, being careful to cook it until any taste of raw flour is gone. Remove it from the heat and add egg yolks if specified in recipe. Add pureed flavoring and return the sauce to low heat, cooking for a minute or two, stirring constantly. Keep sauce warm while beating egg whites. The success of a souffle depends in large measure on how well the whites are beaten. As much air as possible should be incorporated into them since it is this air that expands under the oven's heat and gives the souffle its characteristic lightness. If using a whisk, beat the whites in an over-and-under motion. If using a rotary or electric beater, lift the beaters from the whites periodically to force more air into the mixture. Egg whites have been beaten enough if they hold peaks when dropped from a beater. Once they are this stiff, fold about one-third of them into the sauce. Add the remaining egg whites, still folding in. Do not overmix; if white streaks are in the mixture, it does not matter. Scrape the batter into the prepared souffle dish. Run your finger around the inside of the dish to about half an inch depth and when the souffle is cooked, it will have a slightly "top hat" appearance. Pop the dish into the oven, and don't open the door again for at least 20 minutes. If you prefer a souffle that is baked outside and still slightly runny inside, allow about 25 minutes baking time. If you prefer one that is well done throughout, allow 30 to 35 minutes. Souffles must be served immediately, or they collapse as the hot air in them escapes.

Soups, Vegetable

CREAMED VEGETABLE SOUP

Color photograph for this recipe on page 305.

1 c. diced carrots
1 c. cubed potatoes
1 green pepper, diced
1/2 c. sliced green onions
1 c. diced celery
1/2 lb. salt pork
1/2 c. flour
1 qt. milk
Salt to taste

Cook carrots, potatoes, green pepper, celery and green onions in boiling, salted water until tender; drain. Wash salt pork; cut into cubes. Cook in large saucepan over low heat until brown, stirring frequently. Add flour; mix well. Stir in milk; cook, stirring constantly, until thickened. Season with salt. Add vegetables; heat through.

LOW-CALORIE VEGETABLE SOUP

1 lge. onion, chopped
4 carrots, chopped
4 stalks celery, chopped
1/2 head cabbage, chopped
1 46-oz. can tomato juice
6 bouillon cubes
1 bay leaf
Salt and pepper to taste

Combine all ingredients with 3 cups water in kettle; blend well. Simmer for 1 hour or until vegetables are tender.

OLD-FASHIONED VEGETABLE SOUP

1 soupbone
1 lb. lean beef, diced
1 tbsp. salt
2 carrots, diced
1 onion, diced
1 1/2 c. peas
1 c. tomatoes
3 stalks celery, diced
1 c. sliced okra
1 4-oz. package noodles

Bring soupbone, beef and 3 quarts water to a boil; reduce heat. Simmer, covered, for 1 hour and 30 minutes. Add remaining ingredients; simmer, covered, for 30 minutes or until vegetables are tender. Serve sprinkled with chopped parsley if desired.

QUICK VEGETABLE SOUP

1 lb. ground beef
1 c. sliced onion
1/2 c. potatoes, diced
1 c. shredded cabbage
1 c. sliced carrots
1 c. cut up celery
1 46-oz. can tomato juice
1/4 c. rice
2 cans beef bouillon
1/2 tsp. basil
1/4 tsp. thyme
1 bay leaf
1 tsp. salt
1/2 tsp. pepper

Saute ground beef and onion in large kettle until browned. Add potatoes, cabbage, carrots, celery, tomato juice, rice and bouillon with 1 1/2 cups water to beef mixture; season with basil, thyme, bay leaf, salt and pepper. Bring to a boil; reduce heat. Simmer, covered, for 1 hour or until vegetables are tender.

STOCKLESS VEGETABLE SOUP

1/4 c. chopped celery
1/3 c. chopped string beans
1 c. chopped cabbage
1 sm. onion, chopped
1/3 c. diced carrots
1/3 c. peas
1 c. diced potatoes
1 1/2 tsp. salt
Dash of pepper
2 tbsp. butter
2 tbsp. flour
1 tbsp. catsup

Combine all vegetables except potatoes in kettle; add 3 1/2 cups water, salt and pepper. Bring to a boil; reduce heat. Simmer for 3 minutes. Add potatoes; cook for 15 minutes. Remove from heat. Combine butter and flour in small frypan; heat until golden brown, stirring constantly. Add to cooked soup. Stir in catsup. Yield: 4 servings.

VEGETABLE SOUP PAR EXCELLENCE

1 3-lb. meaty soupbone
1/4 c. pearl barley
1/4 c. dried split green peas
1/4 c. lentils
1/4 c. dried navy beans
1 1-lb. can tomatoes
1 med. potato, diced
3 carrots, thickly sliced
1 onion, chopped
1 10-oz. package beans
1 10-oz. package peas
1 sm. rutabaga, diced
1 1/2 tbsp. salt
1/4 tsp. pepper

Simmer soupbone in 3 quarts water in kettle for 2 hours. Add barley, split peas, lentils and navy beans; simmer for 1 hour longer. Remove soupbone; cut off meat. Return meat to stock. Refrigerate overnight. Remove fat. Add remaining ingredients. Add water if needed. Simmer for 1 hour or until vegetables are tender.

Sour Cream

Pleasantly tangy, thick, and smooth, sour cream is a commercial dairy product made from fresh sweet cream. The cream is pasteurized and homogenized for even fat distribution. It is then treated with lactic acid bacteria and held at a certain temperature for a specified time until properly "soured." The cream is chilled to stop chemical activity before being packaged. Sour cream contains Vitamin A and calcium. (1 tablespoon = 25 calories)

AVAILABILITY: Sour cream is sold year-round in most retail grocery stores. It is usually marketed in wax-coated containers of varying sizes.

STORING: Keep sour cream covered and refrigerated. Use while fresh, within 3 or 4 days. Do not freeze sour cream.

PREPARATION: Sour cream tends to curdle when exposed to high temperatures. It may also curdle when held for a long time at low temperature. In cooked dishes, add sour cream near the end and keep temperature low. If sour cream does curdle only the appearance—not the flavor—is affected.

SERVING: Use sour cream as a salad dressing for fruits and fruit molds; as a meat sauce for beef, lamb, and especially veal; as a dessert topping for pies, cobblers, gingerbread, spice cake, and so on. Float sour cream on chilled tomato juice or jellied consomme and spoon onto baked potatoes. Also use sour cream as an ingredient in dips, mayonnaise, soups, sauces, gravies, biscuits, rolls, cakes, cookies, pies, candies, main dishes, and vegetable dishes.

SOUR CREAM-HORSERADISH MOLD

2 env. unflavored gelatin
2 tbsp. lemon juice
1 5-oz. jar horseradish
1 c. mayonnaise
1 c. sour cream

Soften gelatin in 1/2 cup water; dissolve in 1/4 cup boiling water. Combine gelatin, lemon juice and horseradish; blend mayonnaise and sour cream thoroughly. Combine gelatin and sour cream mixtures; mix well. Pour into mold; chill until firm. May be served with ham or beef. Yield: 8 servings.

SOUR CREAM-DILL DIP

1 c. sour cream
1 c. mayonnaise
1 tsp. Beau Monde seasoning
1 tsp. dillweed
1 tbsp. dried parsley
1 tbsp. dried onion flakes

Combine sour cream and mayonnaise; blend thoroughly. Stir in remaining ingredients; mix well. Chill until ready to serve.

HERBED SOUR CREAM DIP

2 c. sour cream
2 tbsp. chopped parsley
1 tsp. Beau Monde seasoning
2 tbsp. chopped chives
1/8 tsp. curry powder
1/2 tsp. salt
1/4 tsp. paprika

Combine all ingredients; blend thoroughly. Serve in hollowed-out red cabbage, grapefruit, eggplant or pineapple if desired.

SOUR CREAM-GREEN CHILI DIP

1 sm. can chopped green chilies
1 c. sour cream
Garlic salt

Drain green chilies; stir into sour cream. Add garlic salt to taste; blend well. Chill until ready to serve.

PARMESAN-SOUR CREAM DIP

1 c. mayonnaise
1/2 c. sour cream
1 tsp. dry mustard
1/4 c. grated Parmesan cheese
Boiled ham slices

Combine mayonnaise, sour cream, mustard and cheese. Roll ham slices up as for jelly roll. Cut into 4 slices. Insert wooden picks into ham; dip in spread.

SNAPPY DIP

1 env. onion soup mix
1 pt. sour cream
1 4-oz. can chicken spread
1/2 tsp. parsley flakes
Dash of hot sauce
1 tsp. horseradish

Combine all ingredients; blend thoroughly. Chill until ready to serve.

SPICY SOUR CREAM DIP

1 green pepper
1 med. onion
6 slices bacon
1 pt. sour cream
1 pt. mayonnaise
3/4 c. buttermilk
1 tsp. dried parsley flakes
1/2 tsp. celery salt
1/2 tsp. garlic salt
1/2 tsp. onion salt

Grind green pepper and onion. Fry bacon until crisp; crumble into onion mixture. Add remaining ingredients; mix well. Chill until ready to serve. Yield: 1 quart.

ZIPPY DIP

1 3-oz. package cream cheese
1 c. sour cream
1 4-oz. package dried beef, diced
3/4 tsp. caraway seed
1/2 tsp. dried mustard
1/4 tsp. curry powder
1/4 c. minced onion

Bring cream cheese to room temperature. Combine cream cheese with sour cream; blend well. Stir in remaining ingredients; chill until ready to serve.

SOUR CREAM PUFFS

1 1/4 c. flour
2 tsp. baking powder
1/2 tsp. salt
1/4 c. shortening
3/4 c. sour cream
1 1/2 tsp. dillseed

Sift flour, baking powder and salt together; cut in shortening until of consistency of cornmeal. Add sour cream; blend well. Pat out on floured surface to 1/8-inch thickness; cut with 1-inch cutter. Place on ungreased cookie sheet. Sprinkle with dillseed. Bake in 475-degree oven for 10 minutes. May be served with ham spreads.

SOUR CREAM-AVOCADO SALAD

2 pkg. lime gelatin
1 c. sour cream
1 c. mayonnaise
1/2 tsp. salt
2 c. mashed ripe avocados
2 tsp. snipped parsley
1/4 c. diced sweet pickle
2 tbsp. chopped pimento
2/3 c. chopped salted almonds

Dissolve gelatin in 1 cup boiling water; cool until partially set. Combine sour cream, mayonnaise, salt and avocados; blend well. Add to gelatin; stir until smooth and blended. Fold in remaining ingredients; turn into 2-quart mold. Chill until firm. Serve on mixed greens surrounded with fresh fruits.

SOUR CREAM-CUCUMBER SALAD

1 pkg. lime gelatin
1 tsp. salt
2 tbsp. vinegar
1 tsp. onion juice
1/2 c. mayonnaise
1 c. sour cream
2 c. minced drained cucumbers

Dissolve gelatin and salt in 1 cup boiling water; add vinegar and onion juice. Chill until partially set. Fold in mayonnaise; blend thoroughly. Fold in sour cream and cucumbers; blend thoroughly. Pour into wet mold; chill until firm.

SOUR CREAM FRUIT MOLD

1 8-oz. can crushed pineapple
1 8-oz. can pear halves
2 pkg. lime gelatin
1 c. sour cream
Crisp salad greens
Honeydew melon balls
Cantaloupe balls

Drain pineapple and pears; reserve syrups. Dissolve gelatin in 1 1/2 cups boiling water; stir in 1 1/2 cups cold water. Combine reserved syrups; add 2/3 cup syrup to gelatin mixture. Chill until thickened. Dice pears; combine pears, pineapple and sour cream. Blend gelatin mixture with sour cream mixture. Pour into 5 1/2-cup wet ring mold. Chill until firm. Unmold onto salad greens; garnish with honeydew melon and cantaloupe balls.

SOUR CREAM-LIME GELATIN SALAD

1 pkg. lime gelatin
1 c. chopped pecans
1 c. sour cream
1 sm. can crushed pineapple, drained

Dissolve gelatin in 1 1/4 cups boiling water; chill until partially set. Add remaining ingredients, mix well. Pour into mold; chill until firm.

SOUR CREAM FRUIT MEDLEY

1 can fruit cocktail, drained
1 can mandarin orange slices, drained
1 c. sour cream
1 c. miniature marshmallows
1 can chunk pineapple, drained

Combine all ingredients in serving bowl; chill overnight.

SOUR CREAM SALAD RING

2 env. unflavored gelatin
4 chicken bouillon cubes
3 tbsp. lemon juice
1 tsp. dry mustard
2 1/2 tsp. curry powder
1 tsp. onion salt
2 c. sour cream
1 c. chopped celery
1/2 c. chopped green pepper
1/2 c. slivered toasted almonds

Soften gelatin in 1/2 cup cold water. Pour 2 cups boiling water over bouillon cubes; stir until dissolved. Add lemon juice, mustard, curry powder and onion salt; mix well. Pour bouillon mixture over gelatin; stir until gelatin is dissolved. Cool for 5 minutes. Stir in sour cream; mix well. Chill until partially set; add celery, green pepper and almonds. Pour into ring mold; chill until firm. Yield: 8 servings.

BLACK WALNUT-SOUR CREAM CAKE

4 c. sifted flour
2 tsp. soda
1 1/2 tsp. ground cardamom
1/2 tsp. mace
1 c. butter
2 c. sugar
2 eggs
1 1/2 c. sour cream
1 c. chopped black walnuts
Confectioners' sugar

Sift flour, soda, cardamom and mace together. Cream butter and sugar until fluffy. Add eggs; beat well. Add flour mixture and sour cream alternately to egg mixture. Add walnuts. Pour into greased and lightly floured bundt pan. Bake at 350 degrees for 1 hour or until cake tests done. Cool for 5 minutes. Remove from pan; cool on wire rack. Dust cake lightly with confectioners' sugar.

SOUR CREAM SURPRISE CAKE

1/2 c. butter
1 1/4 c. sugar
2 eggs
1 tsp. vanilla
1 c. sour cream
1/4 tsp. salt
2 c. flour
1 tsp. baking powder
1 tsp. soda
1/2 c. chopped walnuts
1 tsp. cinnamon

Cream butter and 1 cup sugar. Add eggs, vanilla and sour cream; beat well. Sift salt, flour, baking powder and soda together; add to creamed mixture. Combine walnuts, remaining sugar and cinnamon; mix well. Pour half the batter into greased tube pan; sprinkle half the nut mixture over batter in pan. Cover with remaining batter; sprinkle with remaining nut mixture. Bake at 350 degrees for 30 minutes or until cake tests done.

SOUR CREAM SPICE CAKE

1/2 c. margarine
1/2 tsp. salt
1 tsp. cinnamon
1/4 tsp. cloves
1/4 tsp. nutmeg
1/4 tsp. mace
1/2 tsp. allspice
1 1/2 c. brown sugar
3 eggs
2 tsp. baking powder
1/2 tsp. soda
2 1/2 c. sifted flour
1 c. sour cream
4 tbsp. butter
2 tbsp. milk
1 c. shredded coconut

Combine margarine, salt, spices and 1 cup brown sugar; cream until light and fluffy. Add eggs, one at a time, beating well after each addition. Add baking powder and soda to flour; sift three times. Add small amounts of flour to creamed mixture alternately with sour cream, beating after each addition until smooth. Pour batter into greased and floured 10 x 10 x 2-inch pan. Bake in 350-degree oven for 40 minutes or until cake tests done. Cool in pan. Combine butter, remaining brown sugar and milk in saucepan; bring to a boil. Remove from heat; add coconut. Pour on warm cake; spread evenly. Place cake under broiler 4 to 5 inches from source of heat; broil until coconut becomes golden brown.

TANGY WHITE CANDY

1 c. sour cream
2 c. sugar
2 tbsp. butter
1 c. chopped nuts
1 tsp. vanilla

Combine sour cream, sugar and butter in saucepan; cook until mixture reaches soft-ball stage. Remove from heat. Cool for 10 minutes. Add nuts and vanilla. Stir lightly; pour into greased pan. Cool completely; cut into squares.

SOUR CREAM NUTS

1 c. sugar
1/3 c. sour cream
1 tsp. light corn syrup
2 tbsp. butter
1 tsp. vanilla
2 c. chopped nuts

Combine sugar, sour cream and syrup in saucepan; cover. Cook to soft-ball stage over low heat. Add butter and vanilla; cool to lukewarm. Beat until mixture loses gloss. Add nuts; stir until coated. Spread on foil. Separate when cool.

SOUR CREAM-DATE DREAMS

1/4 c. shortening
3/4 c. (packed) brown sugar
1/2 tsp. vanilla
1 beaten egg
1 1/4 c. flour
1/2 tsp. soda
1/4 tsp. baking powder
1/4 tsp. salt
1/4 tsp. cinnamon
1/8 tsp. nutmeg
1/2 c. sour cream
2/3 c. chopped dates
Walnuts

Cream shortening, sugar and vanilla; add egg. Sift dry ingredients together; add alternately with sour cream to egg mixture. Add dates. Drop from teaspoon onto greased cookie sheet; top with walnuts. Bake at 400 degrees for 10 minutes or until lightly browned. Yield: 3 dozen cookies.

SOUR CREAM-RAISIN COOKIES

1/2 c. soft butter
1 c. (packed) brown sugar
1 egg
2 c. sifted cake flour
2 tsp. baking powder
1/2 tsp. salt
1/2 tsp. soda
1/2 tsp. nutmeg
1/2 c. sour cream
1/2 c. seedless raisins
3/4 c. chopped nuts

Cream butter and brown sugar until light; beat in egg. Sift dry ingredients together; add to creamed mixture alternately with sour cream, beating until smooth. Stir in raisins and nuts. Drop by spoonfuls onto lightly greased cookie sheets. Bake at 400 degrees for 10 minutes or until lightly browned. Yield: 4 dozen cookies.

SOUR CREAM-SUGAR COOKIES

1 1/2 c. butter
3 c. sugar
3 eggs
1 tbsp. vanilla
1 tsp. soda
1 c. sour cream
6 c. flour
1 tsp. salt

Cream butter with sugar and eggs; add vanilla. Mix soda with sour cream. Add flour and salt alternately with sour cream mixture to batter. Refrigerate overnight. Drop by spoonfuls onto greased cookie sheet. Bake at 375 degrees for 10 minutes. Yield: 6 dozen.

SOUR CREAM-CHERRY PIE

1 No. 2 can red cherries
1 unbaked 9-in. pie shell
2 egg yolks, beaten
1 c. sugar
2 tbsp. flour
1/8 tsp. salt
1 c. sour cream

Drain cherries; pour into pie shell. Mix egg yolks, sugar, flour, salt and sour cream thoroughly; pour over cherries. Bake for 40 minutes at 350 degrees or until filling is set. Yield: 6 servings.

SOUR CREAM MERINGUE PIE

3/4 c. sugar
1 c. sour cream
1/2 c. raisins
1/4 tsp. ground cloves
1/2 tsp. cinnamon
3 eggs, separated
1 baked 9-in. pie shell

Combine 1/2 cup sugar, sour cream, raisins, cloves, cinnamon and beaten egg yolks in top of double boiler; cook over hot water, stirring constantly, until mixture is smooth and thickened. Remove from heat; cool. Fold in 1 stiffly beaten egg white; pour into pie shell. Beat remaining egg whites until soft peaks form; add remaining sugar, 1 tablespoon at a time. Beat until stiff peaks form. Spread meringue over sour cream filling. Bake in 350-degree oven for 10 minutes or until lightly browned.

SOUR CREAM-RAISIN PIE

2 tbsp. cornstarch
1 c. sugar
1/4 tsp. salt
1 tsp. cinnamon
1/2 tsp. nutmeg
1/4 tsp. cloves
2 eggs, separated
1 c. sour cream
1 c. raisins
1 1/2 tsp. lemon juice
1/2 c. chopped walnuts
1 baked 9-in. pie shell
1/4 tsp. cream of tartar

Combine cornstarch, 3/4 cup sugar, salt and spices in top of double boiler; add beaten egg yolks. Mix well; add sour cream, raisins and lemon juice. Cook, stirring, over hot water until smooth and thickened; cool slightly. Add walnuts; blend well. Pour into pie shell. Beat egg whites until frothy; add cream of tartar. Beat until stiff peaks form. Add remaining sugar gradually; beat until glossy. Top pie with meringue. Bake at 300 degrees for 15 minutes or until lightly browned.

Spaghetti

Spaghetti is a rod- or string-like pasta that is made from water and semolina, the gritty residue of milled durum wheat. Tossed with tomato sauce and grated Parmesan or Romano cheese, spaghetti is a tasty and filling meal. There are several types of spaghetti: short and thick fusilli; thin spaghettini; and long slender vermicelli. Like other pastas spaghetti is usually enriched with iron, thiamine, riboflavin, and niacin. (1 cup cooked spaghetti = 155 calories)

(See MACARONI.)

ITALIAN SPAGHETTI SALAD

1 1-lb. package thin spaghetti
2 lge. onions, diced
2 cucumbers, diced
2 green peppers, diced
Salt and pepper to taste
3 tbsp. white vinegar
3 hard-boiled eggs, diced
Mayonnaise

Break spaghetti into small pieces; cook in boiling salted water until tender. Drain; chill in refrigerator. Place onions, cucumbers and green peppers in bowl; add salt, pepper and vinegar. Marinate for 1 hour; drain. Add spaghetti and eggs. Season to taste, stirring well. Add enough mayonnaise to moisten well about 1 hour before serving. Yield: About 12 servings.

SPAGHETTI-FRUIT SALAD

4 eggs, beaten
1/2 c. lemon juice
2 c. confectioners' sugar
Dash of salt
6 med. apples, diced
1 can crushed pineapple
2 c. spaghetti, cooked
2 bananas, diced
1/2 c. chopped nuts
1 c. orange sections, diced
2 c. sweetened cream, whipped

Combine eggs, lemon juice, sugar and salt in saucepan. Cook over low heat, stirring frequently, until thickened; cool. Add apples, spaghetti, pineapple, bananas, nuts and oranges. Refrigerate for 24 hours. Fold in whipped cream.

SPAGHETTI-BEAN SALAD

1 16-oz. package spaghetti
2 cans red kidney beans
1 small head cabbage, shredded
1 small onion, minced
1 stalk celery, diced
3 eggs, beaten
1 1/8 c. sugar
1 small jar prepared mustard
3 tbsp. butter

Cook spaghetti according to package directions; drain. Rinse kidney beans; drain. Combine vegetables and spaghetti. Combine all remaining ingredients in saucepan. Place over low heat; cook until mixture thickens slightly, stirring frequently. Cool; stir into salad.

SPAGHETTI SEA SALAD

1 1-lb. package spaghetti
1 lge. can tuna, drained
Mayonnaise
1 c. chopped celery

Cook spaghetti in boiling salted water in large kettle until tender; drain. Add tuna and enough mayonnaise to moisten. Add celery; mix well. Serve chilled. Yield: About 12 servings.

SPAGHETTI BROCCOLI

1 1/2 tbsp. salt
12-oz. spaghetti
2 10-oz. packages broccoli spears
1/3 c. olive oil
2 cloves of garlic, crushed
1/2 tsp. crushed thyme leaves
1/2 tsp. crushed marjoram leaves
1/2 c. dry sauterne
Pepper

Spaghetti Broccoli . . . Herbs season this unusual dish that complements almost every meat.

Add salt to 5 quarts rapidly boiling water in large saucepan. Add spaghetti gradually so that water continues to boil. Cook, stirring occasionally, until tender. Drain in colander. Cook broccoli according to package directions; drain and cut into 2-inch pieces. Heat olive oil in large pot over medium heat; add garlic, stirring until golden. Add thyme, marjoram, spaghetti and sauterne; toss until mixed. Cook for about 3 minutes over low heat. Add broccoli to spaghetti mixture; toss lightly. Season to taste with salt and pepper. Spoon into serving dish; serve immediately.

BUSY DAY SPAGHETTI

1 lb. ground beef
1/4 lb. sausage
1 onion, chopped
1 green pepper, chopped
1 c. sliced mushrooms
1 No. 2 can tomatoes
1 8-oz. can tomato sauce
1 tsp. salt
1/4 tsp. Worcestershire sauce
6 drops of hot sauce

Brown beef and sausage in skillet; add onion and green pepper. Cook for 5 minutes. Add all remaining ingredients; bring to a boil. Reduce heat to low. Cover; simmer for 30 to 35 minutes, stirring occasionally. Serve over cooked spaghetti; sprinkle with grated Parmesan cheese, if desired.

CHICKEN SPAGHETTI

1 lge. hen
1 lb. spaghetti
4 slices bacon
1 c. chopped onion
1/2 sm. bottle Worcestershire sauce
1 bottle catsup
Garlic salt to taste
Salt and pepper to taste
8 hard-boiled eggs, chopped
1 green pepper, chopped
1 c. chopped celery
Cheese

Cook hen in boiling salted water until tender; remove meat from bones. Cook spaghetti; drain. Fry bacon in skillet; remove and chop. Cook onion until tender, but not brown, in bacon drippings. Mix Worcestershire sauce and catsup; add garlic salt, salt and pepper, eggs, green pepper and celery. Combine chicken, spaghetti, bacon and catsup mixture; mix well. Place in greased baking dish. Bake at 325 degrees for 1 hour. Remove from oven; sprinkle cheese over top. Return to oven. Bake until cheese is melted. Yield: 8-10 servings.

BAKED SPAGHETTI

1 No. 2 can tomatoes
2 med. onions, coarsely ground
1 green pepper, coarsely ground
2 sm. cloves of garlic, coarsely ground
2 tbsp. bacon drippings
2 bay leaves
4 whole cloves
Salt and pepper to taste
1 lb. ground beef
1/2 lb. sharp cheese, grated
1 8-oz. package thin spaghetti, cooked
Parmesan cheese
1 c. sauted mushrooms

Simmer tomatoes in saucepan until tender. Fry onions, green pepper and garlic in bacon drippings until tender; combine onion mixture, tomatoes, bay leaves, cloves, salt and pepper. Cover with water; simmer for 30 minutes. Cook beef; do not brown. Add beef and cheese to tomato mixture. Heat, stirring frequently, until cheese melts. Alternate layers of sauce and spaghetti in deep casserole, topping with sauce. Bake at 250 degrees for 1 hour and 30 minutes. Serve with cheese and mushrooms. Yield: 6 servings.

CHICKEN SPAGHETTI WITH SHRIMP

3 lge. onions, sliced
1 clove of garlic, chopped
1 c. chopped celery
3 tbsp. shortening
2 tbsp. flour
2 c. chicken stock
2 c. strained tomatoes
2 tsp. chili powder
Salt and pepper to taste
Sugar to taste
Worcestershire sauce to taste
1 6-lb. chicken, roasted
1 lb. shrimp, cooked
1 lb. mushrooms
2 9-oz. packages spaghetti, cooked
Parmesan cheese, grated
Butter

Saute onions, garlic and celery in shortening in skillet until golden. Stir in flour, blending well; add chicken stock and tomatoes. Cook, stirring, until mixture thickens. Season with chili powder, salt, pepper, sugar and Worcestershire sauce. Cut chicken from bones in large pieces. Add chicken, shrimp, mushrooms and spaghetti. Place alternate layers of chicken mixture and cheese in buttered casserole. Dot with butter. Bake in 350-degree oven for 45 minutes. Yield: 12 servings.

SALMON-SPAGHETTI CASSEROLE

1/2 8-oz. package spaghetti
1 3/4 c. canned tomatoes
1 tsp. minced onion
1 tsp. salt
1 tsp. sugar
Dash of pepper
1 tbsp. flour
2 tbsp. butter, melted
1 7 3/4-oz. can salmon, flaked
1/2 c. soft bread crumbs

Cook spaghetti in boiling salted water until tender; drain. Combine tomatoes, onion, salt, sugar and pepper in saucepan; blend flour and 1 tablespoon butter. Stir into tomato mixture, blending well; simmer for 10 minutes. Arrange spaghetti, tomatoes and salmon in alternate layers in greased 1-quart casserole. Toss crumbs with remaining butter; sprinkle over salmon mixture. Bake in 400-degree oven for 30 minutes. Yield: 3-4 servings.

PARTY SPAGHETTI CASSEROLE

1/2 c. chopped onion
1/2 c. chopped green pepper
1 clove of garlic, minced
3 tbsp. shortening
1 lb. ground beef
1 1-lb. 12-oz. can tomatoes
1 c. grated sharp cheese
1 tsp. monosodium glutamate
1 1/2 tsp. salt
2 tsp. Worcestershire sauce
1 4-oz. can sliced mushrooms
1 can tomato soup
1 15 1/2-oz. can spaghetti sauce with meat
1/2 lb. spaghetti, cooked
Parmesan cheese

Saute onion, green pepper and garlic in shortening; add beef. Cook until beef begins to brown. Add tomatoes, cheese, monosodium glutamate, salt and Worcestershire sauce; cook over low heat for 35 minutes, stirring frequently. Drain mushrooms. Add mushrooms, soup and spaghetti sauce; cook for 15 minutes. Stir in spaghetti. Pour into casserole; top with cheese. Bake, covered, at 350 degrees for 1 hour. Yield: 6 servings.

CHICKEN SPAGHETTI DELUXE

1 5-6 lb. chicken, cooked
1 bunch celery, chopped
3 cloves of garlic, crushed
1 onion, chopped
1 green pepper, chopped
1/2 c. margarine, melted
1 lge. can tomatoes
2 cans mushrooms, chopped
1 sm. can pimento, finely chopped
Salt and pepper to taste
Dash of Worcestershire sauce
1 lge. package spaghetti
4 c. chicken broth
1 bottle stuffed olives
Parmesan cheese, grated

Remove chicken from bones; cut into large pieces. Saute celery, garlic, onion and green pepper in margarine in skillet for 30 minutes. Add tomatoes, mushrooms, pimento, salt, pepper and Worcestershire sauce. Simmer for 30 minutes. Add chicken. Cook spaghetti in broth until broth is absorbed. Mix with chicken mixture. Top with olives and cheese. Yield: 12 servings.

Spaghetti Dinner Athenian . . . Packaged spaghetti dinner is the basis of this main dish.

SPAGHETTI DINNER ATHENIAN

1 pkg. complete spaghetti dinner with mushrooms
1/8 tsp. cinnamon
3 whole cloves
2 tbsp. butter

Preheat oven to 425 degrees. Cook spaghetti according to package directions. Drain. Combine canned mushroom sauce, cinnamon and cloves in saucepan; simmer for about 10 minutes. Remove cloves from sauce. Add butter and canned cheese to spaghetti; toss well. Pack spaghetti mixture into greased 1-quart mold. Heat in oven for 5 minutes. Unmold onto heated platter. Pour half the sauce over mold. Serve remaining sauce with each serving. Yield: 4 servings.

CURRIED TUNA SPAGHETTI

2 cans cream of chicken soup
2 cans cream of mushroom soup
1 c. milk
1 lb. thin spaghetti
4 tsp. curry powder
1 6-oz. can whole mushrooms
1 tbsp. scraped onion
1/2 tsp. dried thyme
1/4 tsp. dried basil
1/4 tsp. oregano
2 cans tuna, flaked

Combine soups, milk and 1/2 cup water in saucepan; stir until blended. Simmer for 10 minutes, stirring. Cook spaghetti in 6 quarts boiling salted water until tender; drain. Combine 1/4 cup warm water and curry powder; add to hot soup mixture. Add mushrooms, onion, thyme, basil and oregano; simmer for 10 minutes, stirring. Add tuna; heat through. Place spaghetti on serving plates; pour tuna mixture over spaghetti. Yield: 10 servings.

FRICASSEED CHICKEN BREASTS WITH SPAGHETTI

3 chicken breasts, halved
Seasoned flour
3 tbsp. salad oil
2 chicken bouillon cubes
Salt and pepper to taste
1 can sliced mushrooms
1 10-oz. package spaghetti

Dredge chicken in seasoned flour, brown in hot oil in skillet. Dissolve bouillon cubes in 1 1/2 cups hot water; add to chicken. Season to taste. Add mushrooms and liquid. Cover; simmer until chicken is tender. Cook spaghetti according to package directions; drain. Place on serving platter; top with chicken. Add pan gravy. Yield: 6 servings.

ITALIAN SPAGHETTI

1 tbsp. salt
1 tbsp. pepper
1/4 c. butter
1/4 c. olive oil
2 tbsp. chopped parsley
4 med. onions, chopped fine
4 cloves of garlic
2 sm. cans tomato puree
2 cans tomato paste
2 tsp. Worcestershire sauce
2 lb. ground beef
Pinch of soda
2 lb. spaghetti
Parmesan cheese

Combine salt, pepper, butter, olive oil, parsley, onions, garlic and 1 cup water in saucepan. Cook until onions are tender. Add tomato puree, tomato paste and Worcestershire sauce. Bring to a boil. Fry ground beef in skillet until browned; add to tomato mixture. Simmer over low heat, being careful not to scorch, for 5 hours or longer. Add soda before removing from heat. Cook spaghetti in boiling, salted water until tender; rinse with hot water. Drain. Place spaghetti on warm plates; pour sauce over spaghetti. Sprinkle with Parmesan cheese. Yield: 8 servings.

ITALIAN MEATBALL SPAGHETTI

3/4 c. chopped onions
1 tsp. garlic salt
2 1-lb. cans tomatoes
2 6-oz. cans tomato paste
1 tbsp. sugar
1 1/2 tsp. salt
1/2 tsp. pepper
1 bay leaf
1 1/2 tsp. crushed oregano
Meatballs
1 lb. spaghetti, cooked

Cook onions with garlic salt in hot fat in skillet until tender, but not brown. Combine 1 cup water, tomatoes, tomato paste, sugar, salt, pepper, bay leaf and oregano; add to onions. Simmer for 45 minutes; remove bay leaf. Drop meatballs into simmering sauce; cook for 15 minutes. Serve sauce and meatballs over spaghetti.

Meatballs

1 lb. ground beef
1 c. dry bread crumbs
1/2 c. grated Parmesan cheese
1 tbsp. chopped parsley
1 tsp. garlic salt
1/2 c. milk
2 eggs, beaten
1/2 tsp. salt
Dash of pepper

Combine all ingredients; shape into balls. Brown in hot fat in skillet.

SPAGHETTI FOR A CROWD

10 lb. ground beef
6 c. fine dry bread crumbs
5 tsp. garlic salt
12 eggs
Salt
2 1/2 tsp. pepper
1 1/4 c. olive oil
5 c. tomato sauce
4 1/2 qt. canned tomatoes
3 cloves of garlic, minced
1 1/4 c. finely chopped onions
2 1/2 tsp. oregano
5 lb. spaghetti

Combine beef, bread crumbs, garlic salt, eggs, 5 teaspoons salt and 1 1/4 teaspoons pepper. Mix well; shape into 1-inch balls. Cook in oil until lightly browned on all sides. Place tomato sauce, tomatoes, garlic, onions, 4 teaspoons salt, remaining pepper and oregano in Dutch oven. Cook, covered, over low heat for 1 hour, stirring occasionally; add meatballs to sauce. Simmer for 30 minutes. Add spaghetti to 7 1/2 gallons rapidly boiling water in large kettle. Cook, covered, until tender, stirring occasionally; drain. Serve meatballs and sauce over spaghetti. Yield: 50 servings.

SPAGHETTI AND MEATBALLS

1 lb. Italian sweet sausage
2 No. 2 1/2 cans tomato puree
1 1/2 tsp. garlic salt
1 tbsp. basil
2 tbsp. dried parsley flakes
1 1/2 tsp. salt
Meatballs
1 lb. spaghetti

Brown sausage in large saucepan; do not drain off fat. Add puree, 2 puree cans water, garlic salt, basil, parsley and salt. Bring to a boil; simmer for 1 hour and 30 minutes, stirring every 20 minutes. Add Meatballs to sauce; simmer for 1 hour. Cook spaghetti according to package directions; drain. Serve with Meatballs and sauce; sprinkle with additional grated cheese.

Meatballs

1 lb. ground beef chuck
1/2 c. bread crumbs
1 egg
1 tbsp. parsley flakes
3/4 tsp. garlic salt
1 1/2 tbsp. grated Romano cheese
1/2 tsp. salt
Dash of pepper

Combine all ingredients and 1/8 cup water; shape into balls. Chill for several minutes.

ITALIAN MEAT SAUCE

1 1/2 lb. pork neck bones
2 lb. ground beef
3 med. onions, chopped
1 clove of garlic, minced
3 cans tomato paste
2 c. tomato puree
1 tbsp. vinegar
3 tsp. mustard
1 tbsp. Worcestershire sauce
1 tbsp. hot sauce
1 tbsp. chili powder
1/4 tsp. basil
1/4 tsp. rosemary
1/4 tsp. oregano
Salt and pepper to taste

Combine neck bones, beef, onions, garlic, tomato paste, 3 cans water, puree, vinegar, mustard, Worcestershire sauce and hot sauce, stirring well, in large kettle. Cook, stirring frequently, for 2 hours. Add chili powder, basil, rosemary and oregano, salt and pepper. Cook for 2 hours longer. Yield: 25 servings.

ITALIAN SPAGHETTI SAUCE

1 lge. onion, chopped
2 tbsp. salad oil
2 lb. ground beef
2 sm. cans tomato paste
1/4 c. oregano
1 sm. can stewed tomatoes
2 tbsp. thyme
1 lge. bay leaf
1 tbsp. salt
1 tbsp. pepper

Saute onion in oil until transparent. Brown beef in large saucepan; drain off excess fat. Add tomato paste, 2 paste cans water, oregano, tomatoes, thyme, onion and bay leaf. Sprinkle with salt and pepper. Bring to a boil; simmer until beef is tender and flavors are blended, stirring occasionally. Sauce may be frozen. Yield: 6-8 servings.

SPAGHETTI MEAT SAUCE

1 lb. pork links, cases removed
2 1/2 lb. ground beef
2 lb. ground round steak
1 tbsp. salt
3 green peppers, cut into thin strips
2 carrots, sliced
6 med. onions, chopped
3 stalks celery, thinly sliced
4 No. 303 cans whole tomatoes
1 can tomato soup
1 pkg. mushroom soup mix
1 lge. can button mushrooms, drained
2 12-oz. cans tomato paste
1/2 tsp. oregano
1/2 tsp. pepper
1/2 tsp. red pepper
1/2 tsp. celery salt
1/2 tsp. onion salt
1/2 tsp. rosemary
1/2 tsp. crushed bay leaf
2 cloves of garlic

Fry links in skillet until tender; drain off fat. Place links in large kettle. Brown beef and steak in skillet; add to links. Combine all remaining ingredients; mix with meats mixture, blending well. Simmer for 3 hours. Remove garlic. Serve over spaghetti. Yield: 6 quarts.

SPAGHETTI SAUCE FROM ITALY

1 lb. ground beef
1 lge. onion, chopped
1 sm. green pepper, chopped
1 tsp. salt
1/2 tsp. pepper
1 can tomato sauce
1 can whole tomatoes
1/4 c. Chianti
1 bay leaf
1/4 tsp. oregano
1 tsp. garlic salt
1 tsp. Italian seasoning
Cooked spaghetti
Parmesan cheese

Brown beef, onion and green pepper in Dutch oven. Add 2 cups water and all remaining ingredients except spaghetti and cheese; simmer for 3 hours, adding water occasionally as needed. Cook down to thick sauce. Mix spaghetti with sauce; let stand for 20 minutes before serving. Top with cheese. Yield: 6-8 servings.

SPAGHETTI SAUCE SUPREME

6 cloves of garlic, crushed
3 onions, chopped
2 green peppers, chopped
1 1/2 lb. ground beef
1/2 lb. sausage
2 lge. cans tomato paste
2 cans tomato sauce
4 c. beef stock
1/2 tsp. oregano
1 tbsp. dry mustard
1 tsp. basil
1 tbsp. sugar
1 tbsp. monosodium glutamate
Salt and pepper to taste

Brown garlic in 3/8 cup fat in skillet; discard. Add onions and green peppers; stir well. Cook until light brown. Crumble beef and sausage in skillet; cook, stirring, until browned. Set aside; pour off fat. Place beef mixture in large Dutch oven. Add tomato paste and sauce; stir thoroughly. Rinse skillet with small amount of stock; add to kettle. Add remaining stock to make soupy mixture. Add oregano, mustard, basil, sugar, monosodium glutamate, salt and pepper; stir well. Simmer, covered, for 2 hours, stirring occasionally. Correct seasoning. Yield: 8 servings.

SPAGHETTI LOAF WITH TOMATO SAUCE

1 8-oz. package spaghetti
1 1/2 c. milk
3 eggs, slightly beaten
1 tbsp. chopped parsley
1/3 c. chopped green pepper
1 tsp. salt
1/8 tsp. pepper
Sauce

Cook spaghetti according to package directions; drain. Combine milk, eggs, parsley, green pepper, salt and pepper; mix well. Add spaghetti. Pour into greased 9 x 5 x 2 3/4-inch loaf pan. Place in pan containing warm water up to level of loaf. Bake at 375 degrees for 45 minutes. Unmold loaf; serve with Sauce.

Sauce

3 tbsp. minced onion
3 tbsp. salad oil
2 tbsp. flour
3 c. canned tomatoes
1 tsp. sugar
1 tsp. salt
1/8 tsp. pepper
1/2 lb. frankfurters, sliced

Cook onion in oil until tender; blend in flour. Remove from heat; add tomatoes. Stir until blended; add sugar, salt and pepper. Add frankfurters to sauce; cook until slightly thickened.

SPAGHETTI WITH CLAM SAUCE

1/2 lb. spaghetti, cooked
Salt
1/3 c. olive oil
3 cloves of garlic, minced
1/8 tsp. pepper
2 sm. cans minced clams
1/2 c. minced parsley
1/2 c. grated Parmesan cheese

Cook spaghetti in 4 quarts boiling salted water until tender, stirring often; drain. Heat olive oil in heavy skillet over low heat. Add garlic; brown slightly. Add 1/3 teaspoon salt, pepper, clams and 2 cups water; cook for 15 minutes. Add parsley; cook for 5 minutes longer. Place spaghetti in deep bowl. Pour sauce over spaghetti. Top with Parmesan cheese. Add additional Parmesan cheese to individual servings, if desired. Yield: 4-6 servings.

Spinach

Strong-flavored, leafy spinach is a vegetable or salad "green" noted for its nutritional value. There are two kinds of spinach, crumpled-leaf and smooth-leaf. Crumpled-leaf spinach is usually marketed fresh; smooth-leafed spinach is generally canned. Spinach supplies protein, calcium, iron, and Vitamins A and C. (1 cup cooked spinach = 40 calories)

AVAILABILITY: Fresh spinach is sold year-round by the pound or washed, trimmed, and packaged in plastic bags. Peak supply is from March to June; smallest supply is from July to September. Canned and frozen spinach are also marketed. Frozen spinach may be whole leaf or chopped.

BUYING: In buying fresh spinach, look for healthy green, crisp, blemish-free spinach. Avoid spinach with coarse stems or yellow, wilted, or dried leaves. Examine spinach carefully for insects. Buy 2 pounds fresh spinach to serve 4 people.

STORING: Wash (see PREPARATION below) and drain fresh spinach. Place in container and cover. Refrigerate up to 4 days. Store commercially frozen and fresh frozen spinach in refrigerator's freezer 3 months or in home freezer 1 year. Keep unopened cans on kitchen shelf 1 year or opened cans in refrigerator about 4 days. *To freeze* fresh spinach—Remove tough stems and undesirable blemished leaves. Wash thoroughly (see PREPARATION below). Scald 1 1/2 minutes. Chill in ice water. Retain water that clings to leaves and package in freezer containers. Leave 1/2-inch head space. Label, date, freeze. *To can* fresh spinach—Wash thoroughly (see PREPARATION below). Remove tough stems and undesirable leaves. Place in cheesecloth and steam until wilted, about 10 minutes. Hot pack according to instructions under CANNING.

PREPARATION: Always wash spinach thoroughly. To wash, discard bruised, wilted, or yellowed leaves. Cut off tough or dried stem ends. Place leaves in large pan of warm water. Swish spinach around in water. Lift carefully out of water so that grit and sand remain on bottom of pan. Repeat procedure. Rinse under cold running water. *Cook spinach* in tightly covered pan. Spinach cooks with only the water that clings to leaves after washing. Butter or meat drippings (especially ham or bacon fat) may be added to spinach if desired. Cook slowly until just tender and still slightly crisp, about 3 to 10 minutes. Spinach can also be baked, scalloped, creamed, molded, and so on. See specific recipe directions. Frozen spinach should be partially thawed before cooking.

SERVING: Season cooked spinach with salt, pepper, butter; lemon juice; nutmeg and curry powder; or light cream and horseradish. Garnish with sliced hard-cooked egg or grated egg yolks. Use spinach also in omelets, souffles, loaves, and so on. Use uncooked spinach in fresh vegetable salads.

(See CANNING and VEGETABLES.)

SAVORY SPINACH SALAD

1 sm. package lemon gelatin
1/2 tsp. salt
3 tbsp. vinegar
1 1/2 c. chopped cooked spinach
2 tsp. grated onion

Dissolve gelatin and salt in 1 cup boiling water. Add 1/2 cup cold water and vinegar. Chill until thickened. Fold in spinach and onion; pour into 1-quart mold. Chill until firm.

SPINACH-COTTAGE CHEESE SALAD

1 pkg. lemon gelatin
1 1/2 tbsp. vinegar
1/2 c. mayonnaise
1/4 tsp. salt
1/8 tsp. pepper
1 c. chopped spinach
3/4 c. cottage cheese
1/3 c. celery, chopped
1 tbsp. chopped onion

Dissolve gelatin in 1 cup hot water; add 1/2 cup cold water, vinegar, mayonnaise, salt and pepper. Blend well. Chill for 15 minutes or until partially set. Turn mixture into bowl; whip until fluffy. Fold in spinach, cottage cheese, celery and chopped onion; pour into mold. Chill until firm.

SPINACH-ARTICHOKE SALAD

1/2 c. chopped pine nuts
1/4 c. salad oil
3 tbsp. tarragon vinegar
1/4 tsp. grated lemon peel
1/2 tsp. salt
1/8 tsp. nutmeg
1 1/2 qt. bite-sized pieces of spinach
1 sm. can artichokes, diced

Combine pine nuts, oil, vinegar, lemon peel, salt and nutmeg in small jar; shake well. Place spinach in salad bowl; chill. Toss spinach with dressing just before serving; add artichokes.

SPINACH-BACON SALAD

1/2 lb. bacon
1 c. salad oil
1/2 c. vinegar
3/4 c. sugar
2 tsp. salt
1/3 c. catsup
2 c. water chestnuts, diced
2 lb. spinach, torn
1 c. bean sprouts, drained
1 Bermuda onion, sliced
4 hard-cooked eggs, chopped

Cook bacon crisp; drain and crumble. Combine oil, vinegar, sugar, salt and catsup in blender container; blend well. Combine bacon and all remaining ingredients; toss with dressing.

TOSSED SPINACH SALAD

1 lb. fresh spinach
1 1/2 c. cored, diced Washington golden Delicious apples
1 sm. red onion, thinly sliced
2 tbsp. lemon juice
1 tsp. salad oil
1/4 tsp. seasoned salt
1/4 tsp. Worcestershire sauce
1 tsp. sugar

Remove stems and large ribs from spinach; tear up larger leaves. Wash and drain. Place in large covered saucepan; steam for 1 to 2 minutes or just until slightly wilted. Drain off any liquid. Combine spinach, apples and onion in salad bowl. Combine remaining ingredients. Pour over salad; toss lightly. Yield: 6 servings.

Tossed Spinach Salad . . . For new salad flavor, feature this blend of spinach, apples, and onions.

Spinach Slaw . . . A zesty slaw with carrots, radishes, spinach, onion, and cottage cheese.

SPINACH SLAW

1 1/2 c. canned pitted California ripe olives
4 c. shredded fresh spinach
1/4 c. thinly sliced radishes
2 tbsp. thinly sliced green onion
1 thinly-sliced carrot
1 c. cottage cheese
2 tbsp. salad oil
2 tbsp. cider vinegar
1 tsp. salt
1/4 tsp. dry mustard
Dash of liquid red pepper seasoning

Cut olives into pieces; combine olives, spinach, radishes, onion and carrot in salad bowl. Blend cottage cheese, oil, vinegar and seasonings together; pour dressing over salad, tossing well. Garnish with additional ripe olives. Yield: 6 servings.

SPINACH SALAD BOWL

4 c. bite-sized pieces of spinach
2 c. bite-sized pieces of lettuce
6 crisp-cooked bacon slices
6 green onions, thinly sliced
4 hard-cooked eggs, chopped
Lemon and oil dressing

Place spinach and lettuce in salad bowl; crumble bacon into small bits. Add onions, eggs and bacon to spinach mixture. Add desired amount of dressing; toss lightly just before serving.

BAKED SPINACH WITH CHIVES

2 pkg. frozen chopped spinach
2 3-oz. packages cream cheese with chives
Juice of 1 lemon
1 tbsp. Worcestershire sauce
1 4-oz. can sliced mushrooms
Cracker crumbs

Cook spinach according to package directions; drain well. Add cream cheese; stir until dissolved. Add lemon juice, Worcestershire sauce and mushrooms. Pour into buttered 2-quart casserole; top with cracker crumbs. Bake at 325 degrees for 30 minutes or until crumbs are browned.

GRECIAN SPINACH PIE

3 lb. spinach, chopped
1/2 c. chopped parsley
1/2 c. chopped dill
1 bunch scallions, chopped
Salt
1 lb. onions, chopped
1/2 c. olive oil
1/2 lb. feta cheese
Pepper
8 to 10 phylo

Mix spinach, parsley, dill and scallions in large bowl; sprinkle with salt. Drain; squeeze out moisture. Brown onions in oil; stir into spinach mixture. Stir in cheese; season to taste with salt and pepper. Stack 4 to 5 phylo in shallow oiled baking pan; brush each sheet with oil. Add spinach mixture. Cover with remaining pastry sheets; brush with oil. Cut steam vent. Bake at 325 degrees for 40 minutes.

SAVORY SPINACH SQUARES

2 pkg. frozen chopped spinach
2/3 c. milk
1/4 c. melted butter
1/2 c. minced onion
2 tbsp. dried parsley flakes
1 1/2 tsp. salt
1 tsp. Worcestershire sauce
1/2 tsp. thyme
1/2 tsp. nutmeg
4 eggs, beaten
2 c. cooked rice
2 c. shredded process American cheese

Prepare spinach according to package directions; drain well. Combine milk, butter, onion, parsley flakes, salt, Worcestershire sauce, thyme and nutmeg; mix well. Add to eggs. Combine egg mixture with spinach, rice and cheese; blend well. Pour into a greased shallow 2-quart baking dish. Bake in 350-degree oven for 40 minutes or until set. Cut into squares.

SESAME SPINACH

1 pkg. fresh spinach
1/2 c. soy sauce
1 tbsp. monosodium glutamate
3 tbsp. sugar
1 tsp. salt
1 tbsp. toasted sesame seed

Bring 4 cups water to a boil; add spinach. Bring to a boil again; turn off heat. Let spinach stand for 5 minutes; drain well. Arrange spinach evenly on large platter; refrigerate. Cut spinach into 2-inch sections. Combine all remaining ingredients; bring to a boil. Reduce heat; simmer for 5 minutes. Cool. Pour sauce over spinach.

SHERRIED SPINACH

1 pkg. frozen chopped spinach
2 tbsp. butter
Dash of nutmeg
Salt and pepper to taste
1/4 lb. sliced mushrooms
2 tbsp. dry sherry
1/4 c. heavy cream
Croutons

Cook spinach according to package directions; drain. Combine 1 tablespoon butter, nutmeg, salt and pepper with spinach in saucepan. Saute mushrooms in remaining butter; add mushrooms and sherry to spinach mixture. Fold in cream; simmer until heated through. Place in serving dish; sprinkle with croutons.

SPINACH-ARTICHOKE BAKE

2 pkg. frozen chopped spinach
1/2 lb. fresh mushrooms
3/8 c. butter
1 tbsp. flour
1/2 c. milk
1/2 tsp. salt
1/8 tsp. garlic powder
1 No. 2 can artichoke hearts, drained
1 c. sour cream
1 c. mayonnaise
1/4 c. lemon juice

Cook spinach according to package directions; drain. Reserve several whole mushrooms; slice remaining mushrooms. Saute sliced mushrooms in 4 tablespoons butter. Melt remaining butter in saucepan; blend in flour. Add milk; cook, stirring, until sauce is thickened. Add seasonings. Stir in sliced mushrooms and spinach. Arrange artichokes in baking dish; pour spinach mixture over artichokes. Blend sour cream, mayonnaise and lemon juice; stir over low heat until smooth and hot. Pour over spinach mixture; garnish with reserved mushrooms. Bake at 375 degrees for 15 minutes.

DELUXE SPINACH BAKE

2 pkg. frozen spinach
1/2 c. chopped onion
5 tbsp. butter
1 tbsp. flour
2 eggs, beaten
2 c. milk
1 c. soft bread crumbs
1 c. grated Cheddar cheese
1 can cream of mushroom soup
3 hard-cooked eggs, chopped

Prepare spinach according to package directions; drain. Saute onion in butter in saucepan until transparent; stir in flour. Combine eggs and milk; add to flour mixture, stirring constantly, until smooth and thickened. Fold bread crumbs and 1/2 cup cheese into cooked spinach. Combine spinach with hot mixture; place in buttered casserole. Bake at 350 degrees for 30 minutes. Combine mushroom soup, eggs and remaining cheese in saucepan. Heat through. Serve with spinach.

SPINACH MADELINE

2 pkg. frozen chopped spinach
1/4 c. butter
2 tbsp. flour
2 tbsp. chopped onion
1/2 c. evaporated milk
1/2 tsp. pepper
Red pepper to taste
3/4 tsp. celery salt
3/4 tsp. garlic salt
1/2 tsp. salt
1 tsp. Worcestershire sauce
1 6-oz. roll jalapeno pepper cheese, diced
Buttered bread crumbs

Cook spinach according to package directions; drain well. Reserve 1/2 cup liquid. Melt butter in saucepan; add flour, stirring until well blended and smooth. Add onion; cook until transparent. Add milk and spinach liquid slowly, stirring constantly. Cook until smooth and thickened. Add seasonings, Worcestershire sauce and cheese. Combine cream sauce with spinach. Place in greased baking dish; top with buttered crumbs. Bake at 350 degrees for 25 minutes.

SPINACH MASQUERADE

2 lb. fresh spinach
1/2 c. chopped onion
2 tbsp. butter
2/3 c. catsup
1 tbsp. lemon juice
1/2 tsp. chili powder
1/4 c. grated American cheese

Preheat oven to 350 degrees. Cook spinach in small amount of water until just tender; drain. Saute onion in butter; add spinach and all remaining ingredients except cheese. Place in 1-quart casserole; sprinkle with cheese. Bake for 20 minutes or until heated through.

SPINACH PUFF

1 tbsp. minced onion
1 tbsp. minced green pepper
1 tbsp. minced celery
4 tbsp. butter
3 tbsp. flour
1/2 tsp. salt
1/8 tsp. pepper
1 c. milk
4 eggs, separated
2 c. cooked spinach, drained

Saute onion, green pepper and celery in butter until tender. Blend in flour, salt and pepper; add milk gradually, stirring until thickened and smooth. Beat egg yolks until thick and lemon colored; stir slowly into white sauce. Add spinach. Beat egg whites until stiff; fold into spinach mixture. Turn into buttered 1-quart casserole; set in pan of hot water. Bake at 350 degrees for 50 minutes or until knife inserted comes out clean.

SPINACH-SOUR CREAM DISH

2 pkg. frozen chopped spinach
1 8-oz. package cream cheese, softened
2 tbsp. horseradish
1 c. sour cream
6 slices fried bacon, crumbled
Salt to taste
1 c. herb-seasoned stuffing mix
1/2 stick butter, melted

Cook spinach according to package directions; drain. Blend in cream cheese; add horseradish, sour cream, bacon and salt. Mix well; place in casserole. Blend stuffing mix with melted butter; sprinkle on top. Bake in 350-degree oven for 20 minutes or until heated through and lightly browned. Yield: 6 servings.

CHINESE-STYLE SPINACH

1 1/2 lb. fresh spinach
2 tbsp. corn oil
2 cloves of garlic, crushed
1 1/2 tsp. salt
1 tsp. sugar
1/4 tsp. monosodium glutamate

Wash and drain spinach; remove wilted leaves and heavy stems. Heat oil with garlic in skillet over high heat; add spinach. Stir until oil is thoroughly mixed with spinach. Add seasonings; mix well. Cook, covered, for 2 minutes longer. Place spinach mixture in serving dish; garnish with hard-cooked eggs and crumbled, crisp bacon, if desired.

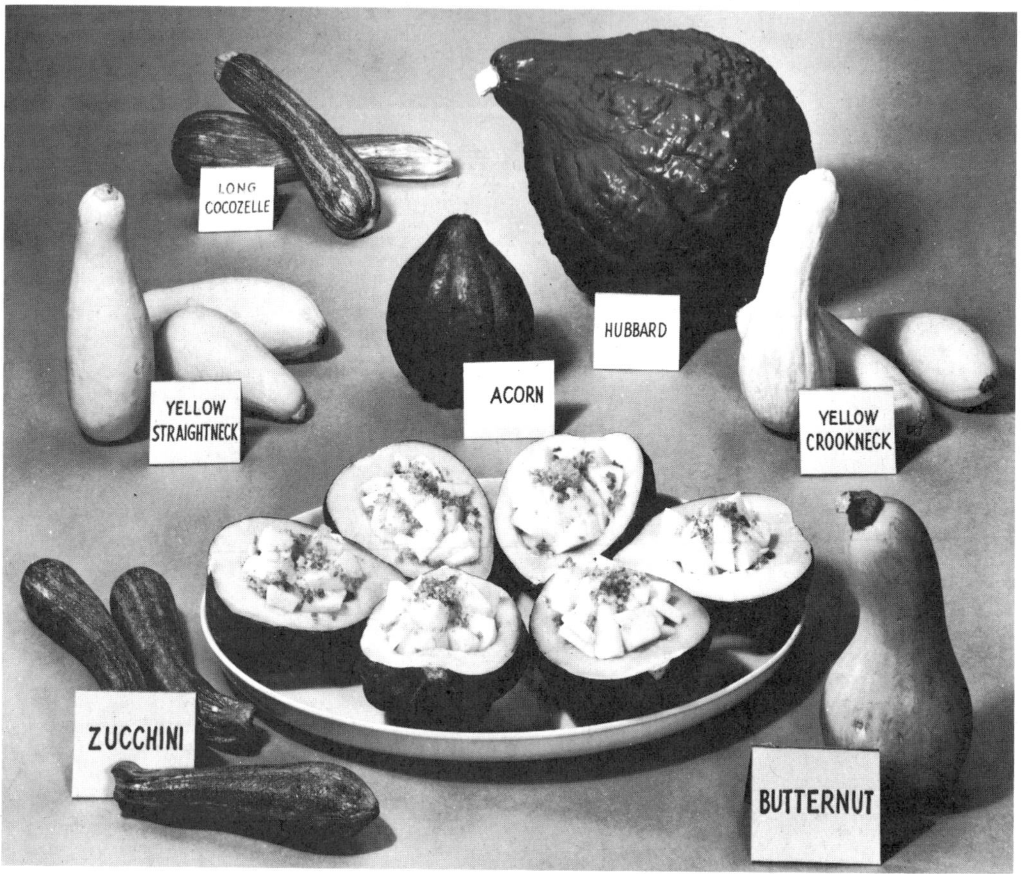

Squash

Squashes are varied fruits of the gourd family that are served as vegetables. The two main types of squash—summer and winter—differ principally in the maturity of the fruit at harvesting. *Summer squash* is immature fruit with light-colored flesh; tender, edible seeds; and a thin green, yellow or white rind. Some well-known varieties are Zucchini, Yellow Straightneck and Crookneck, Patty Pan, and Cocozelle. *Winter squash* is vine-ripened and usually has a thick, coarse dark green or orange rind. The seeds are hard, tough, and inedible. Butternut is the sole exception to this description. Some common market varieties are Acorn, Butternut, Buttercup or Turban, Golden Delicious, and Hubbard. Squash is rich in nutrients: Vitamins A, C, niacin, and calcium. (1 cup diced summer squash = 30 calories; 1 cup mashed winter squash = 130 calories)

AVAILABILITY: Summer squash is usually available year-round; the most abundant market supply is during May and June. Most varieties of winter squash are available from August through March, peak months being October and November. Acorn and Butternut, however, are usually available year-round. (See illustration.) Also commercially available are summer and winter canned and frozen squash.

BUYING: *For summer squash*—Look for firm, well-developed, glossy specimens that feel heavy for their size. Avoid summer squash with dried or blackened stems and a tough, hard rind. *For winter squash*—Select heavy, blemish-free squash with a coarse rind. Avoid water-spotted and tender-skinned specimens. Buy Butternut squash according to summer squash description.

STORING: *For summer squash*—Store in refrigerator vegetable crisper as soon as possible

CHARACTERISTICS OF COMMON SQUASH VARIETIES

SUMMER SQUASH	WINTER SQUASH
Yellow Straightneck and Yellow Crookneck Widely grown; available year round; color light yellow early, becoming deeper as it matures; moderately warted.	**Acorn** Widely grown; available year round; smooth skin, ribbed; color blackish-green changing to dull orange with some dull green.
Scallop or Patty Pan Widely grown; available year round; skin smooth; color pale green when young, white later.	**Butternut** Available year round; smooth skin; color light creamy brown or dark yellow.
Zucchini Widely grown; available year round; color dark green over pale yellow, heavily marked with greenish-black lace pattern forms dark green stripes.	**Buttercup or Turban** Available late summer through winter; color dark green to blackish-green, faintly striped with gray; turban is light gray.
Cocozelle Widely grown; available year round; color striped dark green or greenish-black with pale greenish-yellow.	**Hubbard** Available late August to March; warted and ridged; color dark bronze green or blue-gray or orange-red, depending on specific variety.

after purchasing. Use within 3 days. *For winter squash*–Store uncrowded in well ventilated area at 50 to 55 degrees for 1 to 4 weeks. *To freeze* summer squash–Wash thoroughly and slice into 1/2-inch pieces. Cook covered in a small amount boiling water for 5 minutes. Mash if desired. Chill immediately by setting saucepan containing squash over cracked ice. Pack squash into freezer containers leaving 1/2-inch head space. Seal, label, and freeze. *To freeze* winter squash–Halve or slice into serving pieces. Remove seeds. Place in shallow baking dish containing 1/2-inch water. Bake squash at 350 degrees for 40 minutes or until tender. Separate pulp from rind and mash if desired. Pack into freezer containers leaving 1/2-inch head space. Or wrap uncooked pieces in plastic or foil and store in plastic bag. Freeze squash 2 to 3 months in frozen foods compartment, 1 year in home freezer.

PREPARATION: *For summer squash*–Scrub rind, but do not pare. Cut into slices or cubes. *To boil*–Cook squash covered in small amount of water for 8 to 15 minutes. Do not overcook. Drain and season to taste. *For winter squash–To bake*–Cut squash into serving pieces and remove seeds. Bake in 400 degree oven for 30 to 60 minutes. Serve in the shell or scrape out pulp and mash. Season to taste. For further instructions see specific recipes.

USES: Squash is truly a year-round food. Cook summer squash with finely chopped onion or chive. Dot generously with butter or simmer gently in tomato sauce. Add butter, brown sugar or honey, salt and pepper to winter squash for a confection-like treat.

(See VEGETABLES and ZUCCHINI)

BAKED ACORN SQUASH

2 med. acorn squash
4 tbsp. butter
Salt to taste
4 tbsp. (packed) brown sugar
Pepper to taste

Cut squash into halves, lengthwise; remove seeds. Place halves, cut side down, in shallow pan. Bake at 400 degrees for 30 minutes. Turn cut side up; sprinkle with butter, salt, brown sugar and pepper. Bake at 400 degrees for 30 minutes or until tender.

BAKED SQUASH AND SAUSAGE

3 acorn squash
1 lb. bulk sausage
Salt and pepper to taste

Cut squash into halves; remove seeds. Arrange squash, cut side down, in shallow greased baking pan. Bake at 350 degrees for 20 minutes. Shape sausage into 6 flat patties; brown lightly in skillet. Turn squash; sprinkle with salt and pepper. Place sausage patty in each half. Bake for 20 minutes longer or until squash is tender and sausage is cooked through.

CANDIED SQUASH CRESCENTS

3 med. acorn squash
3/4 c. butter
3/4 c. (packed) light brown sugar
3 tbsp. lemon juice
1/2 tsp. ground ginger
1/2 tsp. salt

Halve squash lengthwise; scoop out seeds. Trim ends. Cut each half crosswise into 1/2-inch thick slices. Cook in small amount of boiling salted water in large skillet for 20 minutes or until tender; drain. Melt butter in skillet; stir in brown sugar, lemon juice, ginger and salt. Place squash in single layer in pan, turning to coat well with syrup. Cook, turning several times, for 5 minutes or until squash are glazed.

DILLED ACORN SQUASH

4 c. peeled cubed acorn squash
Salt
2 tbsp. sliced green onions and tops
1 tbsp. butter
1/2 c. sour cream
2 tbsp. milk
Dash of pepper
1/2 tsp. dillweed

Cook squash in boiling salted water for 10 minutes or until tender; drain well. Keep warm. Cook green onions in butter until tender; blend in sour cream, milk, 1/2 teaspoon salt and pepper. Bring just to a boil. Arrange squash on serving plate; top with sour cream mixture. Sprinkle with dillweed.

SAUSAGE AND APPLE-STUFFED SQUASH

3 lge. acorn squash
1 1/2 lb. sausage
3/4 c. oats
1/2 tsp. salt
1/2 c. chopped apple
1/4 c. chopped onion
1 tbsp. minced parsley
1/2 c. milk

Cut squash into halves; remove seeds. Place squash, cut side down, in baking pan. Pour small amount of water in pan. Bake in 350-degree oven for 30 minutes. Combine sausage, oats, salt, apple, onion, parsley and milk. Make 18 balls; brown in slightly greased skillet. Turn squash up; place 3 sausage balls in center of each squash. Bake for 40 minutes longer or until squash is tender.

FRUITED ACORN SQUASH

Photograph for this recipe on page 842.

3 1-lb. acorn squash
Butter
Salt to taste
Ground pepper to taste
1 lge. apple
1 lge. orange
1/2 c. toasted almonds
1/2 c. (packed) brown sugar

Preheat oven to 375 degrees. Cut squash in half lengthwise; remove seeds. Place 1 teaspoon butter in each half; sprinkle with salt and pepper. Peel and dice apple. Peel and section orange. Arrange apple and orange in squash cavities; sprinkle with almonds. Mix brown sugar with 2 tablespoons butter; sprinkle over tops. Bake for 1 hour and 20 minutes or until squash is tender. Yield: 6 servings.

GROUND BEEF-FILLED SQUASH

Color photograph for this recipe on page 71.

3 fresh acorn squash
1 lb. ground beef
1/2 c. herb-seasoned stuffing mix
1 tbsp. minced fresh parsley
1 tsp. salt
2 tbsp. minced fresh onion
1/2 tsp. pepper
3/4 c. beef bouillon
1/2 c. sliced fresh mushrooms
Butter

Cut squash in half lengthwise; remove seeds. Place, cut sides down, in baking pan; add 1/4 inch boiling water to pan. Bake at 350 degrees for 30 minutes or until almost tender. Saute ground beef until crumbly. Add stuffing mix, parsley, salt, onion, pepper and bouillon; toss lightly to combine. Turn squash, cut sides up; fill with beef mixture. Return to oven; bake for 20 to 30 minutes longer. Saute mushrooms in butter; arrange over stuffed squash. Yield: 6 servings.

BAKED CUSHAW

4 c. cooked cushaw
1 egg
1 c. sugar
1 tbsp. flour
1/2 tsp. vanilla
1/2 c. margarine
1/4 tsp. baking powder
Nutmeg to taste

Combine all ingredients in blender container; blend well. Place mixture in a greased baking dish. Bake at 350 degrees until heated through and browned.

CUSHAW PIE

1 1/2 c. cushaw
1 c. (packed) brown sugar
1 tsp. cinnamon
1/4 tsp. ginger
1/4 tsp. allspice
1/2 tsp. salt
1 tbsp. flour
2 eggs
1 c. milk
1/2 c. cream
1 tsp. vanilla
1 unbaked 9-in. pie shell

Combine cushaw, brown sugar, spices, salt and flour; mix well. Beat eggs; add milk, cream and vanilla. Blend egg mixture into cushaw mixture; pour into pie shell. Bake at 450 degrees for 10 minutes; reduce oven temperature to 325 degrees. Bake for 45 minutes longer or until filling is firm.

Stuffed Butternut Squash . . . Diced apples and ham and dry mustard stuff mild-flavored squash.

STUFFED BUTTERNUT SQUASH

3 sm. butternut squash
1/2 tsp. salt
1 c. diced tart cooking apples
2 c. diced cooked ham
1 tsp. dry mustard
1/4 tsp. ground black pepper

Preheat oven to 425 degrees. Wash and cut squash in halves lengthwise. Remove seeds. Sprinkle inside with salt. Place cut side down in a pan. Pour in 1/4-inch boiling water. Bake for 30 minutes or until almost tender. Turn squash halves cut side up. Combine remaining ingredients; spoon into squash cavities. Reduce oven temperature to 375 degrees and bake 20 minutes or until apples are tender. Serve hot. Yield: 6 servings.

FESTIVE SQUASH

1 1/2 lb. small yellow squash
1 sm. onion, grated
2 carrots, grated
1 sm. jar pimentos, chopped
Salt to taste
1 can cream of chicken soup
1/2 pt. sour cream
1/2 c. butter
1 8-oz. package herb-seasoned stuffing mix

Slice squash; cook in small amount of boiling salted water until almost tender. Drain; mash. Stir in onion, carrots, pimentos, salt, soup and sour cream. Melt butter; toss stuffing mix with butter. Reserve portion of stuffing; line 13 x 8 x 2-inch casserole with remaining stuffing. Pour squash mixture over stuffing; top with reserved stuffing. Bake at 350 degrees for 30 minutes or until heated through and browned. Yield: 8 servings.

CRUNCHY SQUASH BAKE

2 lb. small yellow squash
1/2 tsp. salt
Dash of white pepper
2 tbsp. butter
1 sm. onion, grated
1 c. heavy cream
1 c. Spanish peanuts
8 slices crisp bacon, crumbled
1/4 c. dry bread crumbs

Preheat oven to 350 degrees. Cook squash in small amount of salted boiling water until tender and water has evaporated. Mash squash. Add salt, pepper, butter, onion and cream, mixing well. Spoon into greased shallow 9-inch baking dish. Bake for 50 minutes. Sprinkle with peanuts, bacon and crumbs. Bake for 5 minutes longer or until top is browned.

FRIED SQUASH SURPRISE

4 med. squash
Cornmeal
1 med. onion, diced
1 to 2 sm. green peppers, diced

Slice squash into 1/2-inch pieces; coat well with cornmeal. Fry squash, onion and green peppers in skillet in hot fat until squash is golden brown.

GINGERED SQUASH

2 pkg. frozen squash
1/4 c. (packed) brown sugar
2 tsp. ginger
1 tsp. salt
Dash of pepper
2 tsp. butter

Place frozen squash in top of double boiler over boiling water. Cook, covered, until thawed. Stir in remaining ingredients; cook for 5 minutes longer.

LOUISIANA SQUASH

6 yellow summer squash
4 chopped green onions
1/4 c. butter
1 lb. cleaned shrimp
Salt and pepper to taste

Scrub squash and cut into 1/4-inch thick slices. Cook with onions in 3 tablespoons water in saucepan. Add 1 teaspoon butter. Cook, covered, chopping squash occasionally, until squash is just tender. Place shrimp in remaining hot butter in skillet. Saute quickly until pink. Add shrimp and drippings to squash. Cook until all liquid is absorbed. Season with salt and pepper. Serve over hot rice, if desired.

MEXICAN SQUASH WITH CHILIES

4 med. summer squash, diced
1/2 sm. onion, chopped
4 tbsp. cooking oil
1/2 c. chopped tomatoes
1/2 c. chopped canned green chili peppers
Salt and pepper to taste
1/2 c. grated American cheese

Saute squash and onion in oil until just tender. Drain off excess grease. Blend in tomatoes, chili peppers, salt and pepper. Cook over moderately low heat for 15 minutes. Remove from heat; blend in cheese.

SQUASH CASSEROLE

3 lb. yellow squash, sliced
2 onions, chopped
2 carrots, sliced
2 cans cream of chicken soup
1 carton sour cream
1 sm. jar pimento, chopped
1/2 c. butter
1 pkg. herb-seasoned stuffing mix

Cook squash, onions and carrots together in salted water to cover until tender; drain well. Add soup, sour cream and pimento. Melt butter; stir in stuffing mix. Spread half the stuffing mix in greased casserole. Pour in squash mixture; cover with remaining stuffing mix. Bake at 375 degrees for 45 minutes.

SQUASH PIQUANT

1 pkg. frozen squash
1 tbsp. butter
1 slice bacon
1/2 tsp. salt
1/4 tsp. pepper
1/4 tsp. sugar
1/4 c. chopped onion
1 tbsp. chopped green pepper
3/4 c. crushed cracker crumbs
1 egg, beaten

Cook squash in small amount of water in saucepan until tender. Add butter; mash squash. Fry bacon; reserve drippings. Chop bacon. Mix all ingredients with bacon drippings; place in baking dish. Bake at 350 degrees for 30 minutes or until heated through and lightly browned. Yield: 8 servings.

SQUASH RING

6 c. cubed yellow squash
1 med. onion, diced
1/2 med. green pepper, diced
1 clove of garlic, minced
1 tsp. salt
2 tbsp. sugar
1/4 c. butter
1 tbsp. Worcestershire sauce
1/2 tsp. pepper
1/2 tsp. hot sauce
1 c. bread crumbs
3 eggs, well beaten
1/2 c. milk

Cook squash, onion, green pepper and garlic in small amount of water in saucepan until tender; drain well. Add remaining ingredients; mix well. Place squash mixture in greased 1 1/2-quart ring mold; place mold in pan of water. Bake at 350 degrees for 40 minutes. Keep warm until ready to serve. Unmold; fill center of ring with buttered green lima beans or English peas, if desired. Garnish with small whole pickled beets.

STUFFED SQUASH

8 squash
1/2 tsp. salt
Pepper to taste
4 chicken livers, cooked
4 slices bacon, broiled
1 can cream of mushroom soup
2 c. buttered bread crumbs

Halve squash; scoop out seed. Cook in small amount of water for 10 minutes; drain. Sprinkle with salt and pepper. Mince chicken livers; crumble bacon. Combine chicken livers, bacon and mushroom soup. Fill squash cavities. Top with bread crumbs; place in shallow pan with water to cover bottom. Bake at 350 degrees for 10 minutes or until bread crumbs are brown.

STUFFED PATTY PAN SQUASH

2 3/4-lb. patty pan squash
4 ears cooked fresh corn
1 1/2 c. day-old bread crumbs
1/3 c. diced green pepper
3 tbsp. diced onion
3/4 c. diced fresh tomatoes
2 tsp. salt
1/8 tsp. ground pepper
3/4 c. grated American cheese

Stuffed Patty Pan Squash . . . Colorful corn, pepper, tomatoes, and cheese contrast in this dish.

Preheat oven to 350 degrees. Place whole squash in saucepan with boiling water to cover. Cover; parboil for 15 minutes or until about half done. Remove from water; cool. Cut slice from top of each squash; scoop out seeds. Cut corn kernels off cobs. Measure 1 1/2 cups cut corn; add bread crumbs, green pepper, onion, tomatoes, salt and pepper. Spoon filling into cavities of squash. Place in baking pan. Bake for 30 minutes. Sprinkle with cheese; bake for 10 minutes longer or until cheese has melted. Yield: 6 servings.

STUFFED SUMMER SQUASH

4 sm. summer squash
2 tbsp. chopped green pepper
2 tbsp. finely minced onion
2 tbsp. finely diced celery
1/3 c. butter
1 4-oz. can mushrooms, drained
1/2 tsp. salt
Pinch of pepper
1 tsp. sage
1 tbsp. parsley flakes
1/4 tsp. poultry seasoning
1 c. fine dry bread crumbs
Sherry

Cook squash in small amount of boiling water until just tender; drain. Saute green pepper, onion and celery in butter until onion is transparent. Mince mushrooms; add to onion mixture with seasonings. Stir in bread crumbs; heat through. Halve squash lengthwise; scoop out pulp. Add pulp to crumb mixture; blend well. Heap stuffing into squash shells; place in baking pan. Drizzle 1/4 to 1/2 teaspoon sherry over stuffing in each shell. Bake, covered, in 350-degree oven for 10 minutes.

SUMMER SQUASH

1 med. yellow squash
Salt
1 egg, beaten
1 1/2 c. tomatoes
1 sm. onion, chopped
1 1/2 c. bread crumbs
2 tbsp. melted butter
2 slices bread, crumbled

Cube squash; cook for 8 minutes in saucepan in small amount of salted water. Drain. Combine egg and tomatoes in bowl; add 1/4 teaspoon salt. Add remaining ingredients except bread. Place in buttered casserole; place crumbled bread over top. Bake at 350 degrees for 45 minutes.

TOMATO-FILLED SQUASH

8 yellow crookneck squash
1 lge. green pepper, chopped
3 tomatoes, diced
2 med. onions, diced
3 slices bacon, chopped
1/2 lb. American cheese, grated
1 tsp. salt
1/4 tsp. pepper
Fine dry bread crumbs
Butter

Cook squash in boiling salted water for 5 minutes or until just tender; drain. Halve squash lengthwise; scoop out pulp. Combine pulp with green pepper, tomatoes, onions, bacon, cheese, salt and pepper. Spoon filling into squash cavities. Top each with bread crumbs; dot with butter. Bake at 400 degrees for 20 minutes.

YELLOW CROOKNECK SQUASH PUFF

2 lb. yellow crookneck squash
1/2 c. milk
2 c. soft bread crumbs
1 tsp. salt
1 tsp. grated onion
1/4 tsp. pepper
1 c. grated sharp Cheddar cheese
2 eggs, separated

Slice squash; cook in small amount of water until tender. Drain. Mash. Mix all ingredients except egg whites; fold in beaten egg whites lightly. Turn into baking dish; set dish in pan of hot water. Bake at 350 degrees for 30 minutes or until set. Yield: 6 servings.

Strawberry

Plump, juicy bright red strawberries are the sweet edible fruit of a trailing bush. Wild strawberries grow in eastern United States but larger varieties are cultivated throughout the country. Strawberries are, in fact, among the most widely grown and most popular of all dessert and preserve fruits. They supply Vitamins A and C and calcium. (1 cup uncooked strawberries = 55 calories)

AVAILABILITY: In some areas fresh strawberries are available year-round. Supply is greatest from April to July; May and June are peak months. Fresh strawberries are commonly sold in pint and quart containers. Frozen strawberries are marketed year-round.

BUYING: Choose clean, bright red fresh strawberries that are free from moisture. Fresh green caps *should* be attached. (Unlike other mature berries, ripe strawberries have caps intact.) Avoid small misshapen or leaky berries or fruit with hard green areas.

STORING: Cover unwashed fresh strawberries and refrigerate. Do not crowd or press berries. Because strawberries are highly perishable use within 1 to 2 days. Store fresh frozen and commercially frozen berries in refrigerator's freezer up to 3 months or in home freezer 1 year. *To freeze* fresh strawberries–Choose firm, ripe berries. Wash a few berries at a time in pan of warm water. Lift gently from water and drain. Remove caps. Slice strawberries directly into bowl. Sprinkle berries with sugar, allowing 3/4 cup sugar for 1 quart berries. Turn berries over and over until sugar dissolves and juice forms. Pack mixture into freezer containers, leaving 1/2-inch head space for pint containers. Crumble small piece of parchment or freezer paper on top of berries to keep them under juice. Seal firmly, label, date, freeze. 2/3 quart fresh berries yields 1 pint frozen berries. To use prepared syrup pack, dissolve 4 3/4 cups sugar in 4 cups water. Place washed sliced berries in freezer containers. Cover with cold syrup. Leave 1/2-inch head space in pint containers.

SERVING: Serve chilled strawberries with cream. Large, perfect berries may be served with caps attached and dipped into powdered sugar. Use strawberries in jams, preserves, ice cream, sherbet, shortcakes, tarts, pies, fruit punches, fruit cups, salad molds, sauces, and so on.

FROZEN STRAWBERRY SALAD

2 c. sour cream
3/4 c. sugar
1 tbsp. lemon juice
1 c. crushed strawberries, sweetened

Combine all ingredients; stir well. Place in freezer tray; freeze. Cut into servings. Yield: 4 servings.

DELUXE STRAWBERRY-CREAM SALAD

2 3-oz. packages strawberry gelatin
2 10-oz. packages frozen sliced strawberries
1 ripe banana, diced
1 13 1/2-oz. can crushed pineapple
1 c. diced canned pears
1 c. sour cream

Add 2 cups hot water to gelatin; stir to dissolve. Add frozen strawberries; stir occasionally until thawed. Add remaining fruits; stir well. Pour half the mixture into 8 x 8 x 2-inch pan; chill until firm. Spread evenly with sour cream. Pour on remaining gelatin mixture; chill until firm. Top each serving with spoonful sour cream, if desired. Yield: 9 servings.

LAYERED STRAWBERRY-NUT SALAD

2 3-oz. packages strawberry gelatin
2 pkg. frozen strawberries
3 bananas, mashed
1 1-lb. 4-oz. can crushed pineapple
1 c. chopped walnuts
1 pt. sour cream

Combine gelatin and 1 cup boiling water; stir until dissolved. Thaw berries slightly. Add strawberries, bananas, drained pineapple and walnuts. Place half the mixture in 9 x 9-inch pan; chill until firm. Spread sour cream evenly over top; carefully spoon on remaining strawberry mixture. Chill until firm. Yield: 9 servings.

STRAWBERRY CREAM SALAD

1/2 c. mayonnaise
1 8-oz. package cream cheese, softened
1/4 c. orange juice
1 10-oz. package frozen strawberries
1 3-oz. package strawberry gelatin

Blend mayonnaise and cream cheese; mix well. Blend in orange juice gradually. Thaw strawberries; drain, reserving 1/2 cup syrup. Dissolve gelatin in 1 1/2 cups boiling water; add strawberry syrup. Stir gelatin into mayonnaise mixture; chill until slightly thickened. Fold in strawberries; pour into 1-quart mold. Chill until firm. Yield: 6 servings.

SWEETHEART SALAD

1 6-oz. package strawberry gelatin
1 10-oz. package frozen strawberries
1 c. crushed pineapple
1 c. chopped nuts
1 pkg. whipped topping mix
1 tbsp. milk
1 8-oz. package cream cheese

Dissolve gelatin in 2 1/2 cups boiling water; chill until partially set. Add strawberries, pineapple and nuts; pour into 9 x 13-inch pan. Chill until firm. Prepare topping mix according to package directions. Combine topping, milk and cream cheese; spread over chilled mixture. Refrigerate until serving time. Yield: 12 servings.

STRAWBERRY AUTUMN SOUP

2 pt. fresh California strawberries
1 c. sugar
1/8 tsp. salt
1 c. sour cream
3/4 c. claret
3 lemon slices
1 c. heavy cream, whipped

Remove hulls from strawberries. Liquefy 1 cup strawberries, 1/4 cup sugar and 1 cup water with electric blender or mixer. Pour into large saucepan. Repeat until all strawberries are used. Stir in salt, 1 cup sour cream, claret and lemon slices. Heat slowly

Strawberry Autumn Soup . . . Strawberries, wine, cream, and sour cream made into soup.

to serving temperature, gradually, stirring constantly. Fold 1/2 cup additional sour cream into whipped cream gently. Spoon over top of soup; garnish with additional fresh halved strawberries.

SALLY LUNN

Color photograph for this recipe on page 485.

1 c. scalded milk
1/2 c. sugar
2 tsp. salt
1/2 c. melted butter
1 pkg. dry yeast
3 eggs, beaten
5 c. sifted all-purpose flour
1/2 tsp. nutmeg
3 pt. fresh strawberries
Whipped cream

Combine milk, 1/4 cup sugar, salt and butter in a bowl; cool to lukewarm. Combine 1/2 cup warm water and yeast in large mixing bowl; stir until yeast is dissolved. Add milk mixture and eggs; mix well. Beat in flour gradually until smooth. Cover; let rise in warm place for 1 hour or until doubled in bulk. Stir down; turn into greased and sugared 10-inch tube pan. Cover; let rise for about 30 minutes or until doubled in bulk. Mix remaining sugar and nutmeg; sprinkle over top. Bake in 400-degree oven for 40 minutes. Remove from oven; cool for 5 minutes. Remove from pan; mound strawberries in center. Serve with whipped cream. 8-10 servings.

STRAWBERRY-MERINGUE TORTE

1/2 c. margarine
1 1/2 c. sugar
4 eggs, separated
1 1/3 c. cake flour
Pinch of salt
1 1/3 tsp. baking powder
1/3 c. milk
1/2 tsp. vanilla
1/8 tsp. cream of tartar
2 boxes frozen strawberries

Cream margarine with 1/2 cup sugar; add egg yolks. Beat until fluffy and blended well. Sift flour, salt and baking powder together; add alternately with milk to creamed mixture. Add vanilla; spread in two greased waxed paper-lined 8-inch layer cake pans. Do not push mixture to side of pan. Beat egg whites until stiff peaks form; add cream of tartar and remaining sugar gradually. Beat until stiff peaks form; pour over cakes. Bake at 300 degrees for 20 minutes. Increase temperature to 350 degrees. Bake for 15 minutes. Cool; remove from pans. Remove paper from cakes. Spoon half the berries over top of 1 cake; top with other cake. Spoon remaining berries over top. Add berries just before serving. Yield: 8 servings.

STRAWBERRY SUPREME CAKE

1 box white cake mix
1 3-oz. package strawberry gelatin
1/2 c. oil
4 eggs
1 pkg. frozen strawberries, thawed
1/4 c. butter
3/4 box powdered sugar

Combine cake mix, gelatin, oil, eggs, 3/4 of the package strawberries and 1/4 cup water in electric mixer bowl; mix until light and creamy. Pour into greased and floured 9 x 13-inch pan. Bake at 350 degrees for 50 minutes. Cool in pan. Combine remaining strawberries, butter and powdered sugar in bowl; beat until light and fluffy. Spread over cake. Yield: 15-18 servings.

STRAWBERRY DELIGHT

1 c. cake flour
1 1/2 c. sifted confectioners' sugar
1 1/2 c. egg whites
1 1/2 tsp. cream of tartar
1/4 tsp. salt
1 1/4 c. sugar
2 1/2 tsp. vanilla
1/2 tsp. almond flavoring
1/2 pt. whipped cream
1 10-oz. package frozen strawberries

Sift flour and confectioners' sugar together three times. Combine egg whites, cream of tartar and salt in large bowl; beat with electric mixer until foamy. Add 1 cup sugar, 2 tablespoons at a time, to egg whites; beat until meringue holds stiff peaks. Fold in 1 1/2 teaspoons vanilla and almond flavoring. Sift flour mixture over meringue gradually; fold in gently just until flour mixture disappears. Pour batter into ungreased 10-inch tube pan; cut through batter with knife gently. Bake at 375 degrees for 1 hour or until cake tests done. Invert on funnel; suspend until cold. Whip cream with remaining vanilla and sugar until mixture stands in soft peaks. Frost cold cake on top with whipped cream. Top with strawberries. Yield: 10 servings.

FINNISH STRAWBERRY CAKE

5 eggs, separated
3/4 c. sugar
3 c. crushed strawberries
1 c. cookie crumbs
1 tsp. almond extract
Whipped cream

Beat egg yolks until light; add sugar. Beat until mixture is stiff and lemon colored. Drain strawberries; stir into egg mixture. Add crumbs and almond extract. Beat egg whites until stiff peaks form; fold into strawberry mixture. Pour mixture into buttered 8 x 12-inch baking dish. Bake at 350 degrees for 35 minutes. Serve with whipped cream. Yield: 8 servings.

CREAM CHEESE HALO WITH STRAWBERRIES

1 env. unflavored gelatin
1 8-oz. package cream cheese, softened
1/2 c. sugar
Dash of salt
1/2 tsp. almond extract
1 1/4 c. milk
1 c. heavy cream, whipped
1 pt. strawberries

Soften gelatin in 1/4 cup cold water. Dissolve over hot water. Combine cream cheese, sugar, salt and extract; blend until smooth. Add milk and gelatin mixture gradually to cream cheese mixture. Chill until partially set. Fold in whipped cream. Pour into 1-quart ring mold. Chill until firm. Unmold; fill center with strawberries. Yield: 6-8 servings.

ANGEL DELIGHT

1 c. milk
1 tbsp. unflavored gelatin
1 c. sugar
3 eggs, separated
1 pt. whipping cream, whipped
Strawberries

Combine milk, gelatin and 1/2 cup sugar; let set for 30 minutes to soften gelatin. Beat egg yolks and remaining sugar together; add to gelatin mixture. Cook in double boiler for 15 minutes. Cool thoroughly. Stir cooked mixture, whipped cream and stiffly beaten egg whites together until blended well. Pour into 9 x 13-inch pan. Refrigerate until firm. Serve with strawberries. Yield: 8-10 servings.

COEUR A LA CRÈME

1 lb. cottage cheese
1 lb. cream cheese
2 c. heavy cream
Salt
Mint
Strawberries

Beat cottage cheese and cream cheese in bowl until smooth; add cream gradually. Season with salt. Line heart-shaped basket with cheesecloth; fill with cheese. Place basket on plate; refrigerate overnight. Unmold onto glass platter; remove cheesecloth. Arrange mint and strawberries on mold. Yield: 6 servings.

STRAWBERRIES AND CREAM

1 pkg. strawberry gelatin
1/2 pt. sour cream
1 pkg. frozen strawberries, thawed

Dissolve gelatin in 1 cup hot water; add 1/2 cup cold water. Pour into bowl; refrigerate until partially thickened. Mix sour cream with strawberries. Stir into gelatin mixture. Pour into 4-cup mold; chill until firm. Yield: 6 servings.

EASY STRAWBERRY MOLD

1 c. strawberries
1/2 c. sugar
1 pkg. strawberry gelatin
2 c. frozen whipped topping

Combine strawberries, sugar and 1 cup of water; bring to a boil. Cook until strawberries are tender. Add gelatin, stirring to dissolve. Add 1 cup cold water. Chill until partially thickened. Blend in frozen topping. Pour into individual molds or 1 large mold; chill until firm. Unmold; garnish with additional whipped topping and strawberries, if desired. Yield: 10-12 servings.

STRAWBERRY CHAMPAGNE RING

1 3-oz. package lemon gelatin
1 3-oz. package orange-pineapple gelatin
1 12-oz. bottle champagne, chilled
Strawberries, sweetened to taste

Combine lemon and orange-pineapple gelatins with 1 cup boiling water; stir over moderate heat until dissolved. Remove from heat; add 1 cup ice water, stirring vigorously to form bubbles. Chill until mixture thickens, stirring occasionally. Add champagne, stirring gently until mixture is no longer foamy. Turn into 6 1/2-cup ring mold; chill until firm. Unmold; fill center of ring with strawberries. Yield: 6 servings.

STRAWBERRY COMPANY DESSERT

1 3-oz. package strawberry gelatin
1 tbsp. sugar
1/2 tsp. salt
1/2 pt. heavy cream, whipped
1 10-oz. package frozen strawberries, thawed
1/2 10-in. angel food cake

Dissolve gelatin in 1 1/4 cups hot water; add sugar and salt. Cool until thickened but not set; fold in cream and strawberries. Tear cake into pieces. Place half the cake in 9 x 13-inch pan; add half the strawberry mixture. Repeat; refrigerate until firm. Yield: 10 servings.

STRAWBERRY-FILLED ANGEL CAKE

1 angel food cake mix
1 10-oz. box frozen strawberries
1 sm. package strawberry gelatin
1 pt. whipping cream

Bake cake according to package directions; cool. Heat strawberries in saucepan over low heat; add strawberry gelatin. Stir until dissolved. Chill until partially set. Whip cream until stiff peaks form. Beat gelatin mixture into whipped cream gradually. Cut 1-inch layer crosswise from top of cake. Remove center of cake, leaving 1-inch wall around cake. Fill cake with whipped cream mixture, reserving 1 cup for frosting. Return 1-inch layer to top of cake. Frost cake with reserved whipped cream mixture. Chill for 2 hours before serving. Garnish with strawberries. Yield: 12 servings.

STRAWBERRY FLANS

3/4 c. orange juice
6 sponge cake shells
3 c. strawberry halves
3 tbsp. sugar
1 1/2 c. heavy cream
4 1/2 tsp. Cointreau

Sprinkle 1 tablespoon orange juice in center of each shell; refrigerate, covered. Combine remaining juice with strawberries and sugar; mix gently. Chill, covered, for 1 hour. Divide strawberries equally into shells. Pour over any remaining liquid. Whip cream until stiff peaks form; fold in Cointreau. Spoon over strawberries. Serve immediately, garnished with whole berries. Yield: 6 servings.

STRAWBERRY MOUSSE

1 qt. strawberries
1/2 c. sugar
1/2 c. white wine
2 env. unflavored gelatin
2 c. heavy cream, whipped

Crush berries; add sugar and wine. Stir well; chill. Soften gelatin in 1/2 cup cold water; add 1/2 cup boiling water. Stir to dissolve; cool. Combine gelatin and chilled strawberry mixture; beat until thickened slightly. Fold in whipped cream; turn into 2-quart ring mold. Fill ring with additional strawberries and whipped cream to serve; garnish top with large berries. Yield: 10-12 servings.

STRAWBERRY COOKIES

1 lb. coconut, flaked
1/2 lb. walnuts
2 tbsp. sugar
2 tbsp. red food coloring
2 pkg. strawberry gelatin
1 can sweetened condensed milk
Powdered sugar frosting
Green food coloring

Grind coconut and walnuts in food chopper; add sugar, red coloring and gelatin. Blend well; reserve part of mixture. Add condensed milk, stirring well. Shape into strawberries by taking small amount and rolling by hand to form berry. Roll in reserved red sugar mixture. Add stems of powdered sugar frosting tinted with green food coloring. Store in refrigerator or freezer. Yield: 50-60 cookies.

FROSTY STRAWBERRY SQUARES

1 c. sifted flour
1/4 c. (packed) brown sugar
1/2 c. chopped nuts
1/2 c. butter, melted
2 egg whites
1 c. sugar
2 c. sliced strawberries
2 tbsp. lemon juice
1 c. whipping cream, whipped

Combine flour, brown sugar, nuts and butter, mixing well. Spread evenly in shallow baking pan. Bake at 350 degrees for 20 minutes, stirring occasionally. Sprinkle 2/3 of the crumbs in 13 x 9-inch baking pan. Combine egg whites, sugar, berries and lemon juice in large bowl; beat with electric mixer at high speed until stiff peaks form. Fold in whipped cream. Spoon over crumbs; top with remaining crumbs. Freeze. Cut into 12 squares. Garnish with whole strawberries. Yield: 12 servings.

FROZEN STRAWBERRY MOUSSE

1 16-oz. box frozen strawberries
1 pt. sour cream
1 c. sugar
1 tbsp. vanilla

Thaw strawberries. Combine with remaining ingredients. Beat well; pour into 2 freezer trays. Cover trays with foil; freeze. Allow to thaw for 10 minutes before serving. Yield: 8 servings.

STRAWBERRY ICE CREAM

1 c. sugar
1 pt. strawberries, mashed
1 egg, beaten
Juice of 1/2 lemon
1/4 tsp. vanilla
1/2 pt. whipping cream, whipped
2 tbsp. cream

Add sugar to berries, stirring well; add egg, lemon juice and vanilla. Mix well. Fold whipped cream into strawberry mixture. Pour into freezer tray; freeze for 30 minutes. Stir in cream; return to freezer for 30 minutes. Remove from freezer; stir well. Return to freezer until ready to serve. Yield: 8 servings.

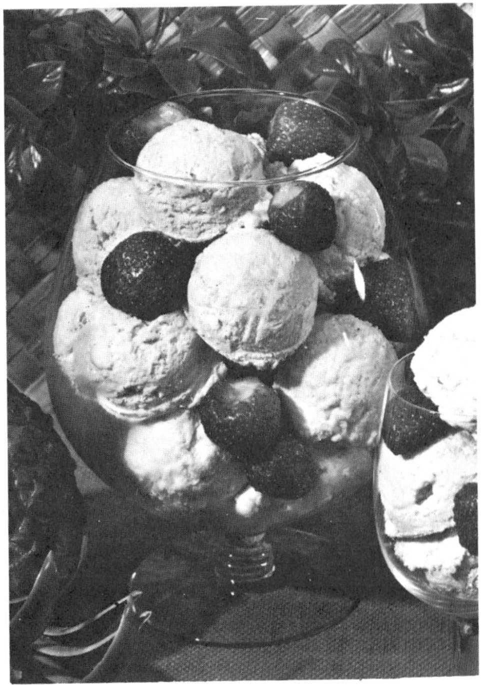

Tropical Sherbet . . . A pineapple-strawberry-lemon frozen dessert ideal for summertime meals.

TROPICAL SHERBET

1 6-oz. can frozen strawberry-lemon punch
1 2/3 c. evaporated milk
1 9-oz. can crushed pineapple
1 c. sugar

Thaw punch. Turn evaporated milk into ice cube tray; chill in freezer until partially frozen. Drain pineapple, reserving liquid. Whip milk in large bowl with electric mixer at highest speed until stiff. Blend in reserved pineapple liquid gradually. Add undiluted punch. Fold in pineapple and sugar. Turn into 2 ice cube trays; freeze for 2 to 3 hours or until firm. Scoop into dessert glasses; garnish with whole strawberries. Yield: About 10-12 servings.

GLAZED STRAWBERRY PIE

1 qt. strawberries
1 c. sugar
2 1/2 tbsp. cornstarch
1/8 tsp. salt
Several drops of red food coloring
1 baked 9-in. pie shell
Whipped cream

Combine 1 cup strawberries with 3/4 cup sugar and 1 cup water; place over heat. Cook for 5 minutes. Remove from heat; mash with spoon. Add cornstarch, remaining sugar and salt, stirring well. Cook until thickened, stirring constantly. Add food coloring; cool. Place remaining strawberries in pie shell; pour in strawberry glaze. Serve with whipped cream. Yield: 6-8 servings.

MILE-HIGH STRAWBERRY PIE

1 10-oz. package frozen strawberries
1 c. sugar
2 egg whites
1 tsp. lemon juice
1/8 tsp. salt
1 tsp. strawberry flavoring
1/2 c. whipping cream
1 tsp. vanilla
1 baked 9-in. pie shell

Thaw strawberries. Combine strawberries with sugar, egg whites, lemon juice, salt and strawberry flavoring; beat with electric mixer for 15 minutes. Whip cream until stiff peaks form; add vanilla. Fold into strawberry mixture; pour into pie shell. Freeze; top with additional strawberries to serve, if desired. Yield: 6 servings.

STRAWBERRY CREAM PIE

1/4 c. lemon juice
1 can sweetened condensed milk
3 eggs, separated
1 sm. package cream cheese, softened
1 c. strawberries
1 baked 9-in. pie shell
3 tbsp. sugar
1/8 tsp. vanilla
Pinch of salt

Mix lemon juice in milk until thickened. Beat egg yolks; add cream cheese, mixing well. Stir strawberries and cream cheese mixture into milk mixture. Pour into pie shell. Beat egg whites, sugar, vanilla and salt until stiff peaks form. Pour over pie. Bake at 350 degrees until browned lightly. Yield: 6 servings.

STRAWBERRY-ORANGE PIE

1 3-oz. package cream cheese
Sugar
1 tbsp. milk
1 tsp. vanilla
1 9-in. crumb crust
1 1/2 tbsp. cornstarch
1/2 c. orange juice
1/4 c. Cointreau
3 tbsp. light corn syrup
2 1/2 c. orange sections
1 pt. fresh California strawberries, halved

Soften cream cheese. Blend cream cheese, 2 tablespoons sugar, milk and 1/2 teaspoon vanilla together; spread in bottom of pie crust. Chill. Mix cornstarch with 3 tablespoons sugar in saucepan; blend in orange juice and Cointreau. Cook, stirring constantly, until thickened. Stir in remaining vanilla; cool well. Blend in corn syrup. Arrange orange sections in pie crust, reserving several for garnish; top with halved strawberries, cut sides up. Arrange reserved orange sections in center of pie. Spoon cooled orange glaze over fruit; chill for about 3 hours or until firm.

Strawberry-Orange Pie . . . Red berries and oranges in a crumb crust provide flavor and color.

STRAWBERRY DESSERT PIE

20 soda crackers, crushed fine
1/4 c. melted butter
4 egg whites
1 tsp. vinegar
1 c. sugar
1 tsp. vanilla
1 1/2 c. strawberries, sliced
Whipped cream
Crushed walnuts

Combine cracker crumbs and butter, blending thoroughly. Press mixture into 9-inch pie plate. Beat egg whites until stiff peaks form; add vinegar, sugar and vanilla gradually. Beat for 5 minutes. Pour into cracker crust. Bake at 450 degrees for 10 minutes. Remove from oven; cool. Place strawberries on top of pie; cover with whipped cream. Sprinkle walnuts over whipped cream. Garnish with whole strawberries. Chill for 24 hours. Yield: 8 servings.

STRAWBERRY MAGIC PIE

1 env. plain gelatin
1 c. strawberry preserves
2 tbsp. lemon juice
1 c. sour cream
1 baked 8-in. pie shell
Whipped cream

Soften gelatin in 1/2 cup water; place over low heat, stirring until dissolved. Add preserves and lemon juice; beat in sour cream. Pour into pie shell; chill. Top with whipped cream. Yield: 6 servings.

STRAWBERRY PARFAIT PIE

1 12-oz. box sliced frozen strawberries
1 pkg. strawberry gelatin
1 1/4 c. hot berry juice
1 pt. vanilla ice cream
1 baked 8-in. pie shell, cooled

Thaw strawberries; drain, reserving juice. Add enough hot water to reserved juice to equal 1 1/4 cups liquid. Place liquid in large saucepan over low heat; heat through. Remove from heat; add gelatin, stirring to dissolve. Add ice cream by spoonfuls, stirring until melted. Chill for 20 minutes or until thickened but not set; fold in strawberries. Turn into pie shell. Chill for 30 minutes or until firm. Garnish with whipped cream or whole berries. Yield: 6-8 servings.

STRAWBERRY SATIN PIE

3/4 c. sugar
Cornstarch
3 tbsp. flour
1/2 tsp. salt
2 c. milk
1 slightly beaten egg
1/2 c. cream, whipped
1 tsp. vanilla
1 baked 9-in. pie crust
3 c. strawberries
Several drops of red food coloring

Combine 1/2 cup sugar, 3 tablespoons cornstarch, flour and salt; stir in milk gradually. Bring to a boil, stirring constantly; cook, stirring, until thick. Stir small amount of hot mixture into egg; add to hot mixture. Bring to a boil; cool. Chill; fold in whipped cream and vanilla. Fill pie crust with creamy filling. Slice 2 1/2 cups berries over filling. Crush remaining berries; add 1/2 cup water. Cook for 2 minutes. Sieve strawberries. Mix remaining sugar and 2 teaspoons cornstarch; stir in strawberry juice gradually. Cook, stirring constantly, until thick and clear. Add coloring; cool slightly. Spoon over berries. Refrigerate until serving time. Top with additional whipped cream. Garnish with whole strawberries. Yield: 6-8 servings.

STRAWBERRY PIE SUPREME

2 qt. strawberries
2 c. sugar
1/4 c. cornstarch
Juice of 1 lemon
2 tbsp. butter
2 baked 8-in. pie shells
1/2 pt. heavy cream, whipped

Crush 1 quart strawberries; mix with sugar, cornstarch, lemon juice and butter. Place in saucepan; cook until thickened. Cool. Slice remaining strawberries; spread in pie shells. Spread cooked mixture on each pie; add whipped cream. Chill for several hours before serving. Yield: 12 servings.

STRAWBERRY-BREAD PUDDING

Color photograph for this recipe on page 491.

2 pt. fresh strawberries
1 c. sugar
1/4 tsp. cinnamon
Dash of cloves
12 slices day-old bread
1/3 c. melted butter
2 c. sweetened whipped cream

Reserve several strawberries for garnish. Cut remaining strawberries in half; place in saucepan. Add sugar, spices and 2 tablespoons water; bring to a boil, stirring constantly. Reduce heat; simmer for 3 to 4 minutes. Remove crusts from bread; brush bread slices on both sides with butter. Line bottom and sides of 1 1/2-quart baking dish with bread slices; brugh edges of bread with syrup from cooked strawberries. Alternate layers of cooked strawberries and remaining bread in baking dish; cover. Chill for several hours or overnight. Brush reserved strawberries with egg white; sprinkle lightly with additional sugar. Place on rack to dry. Garnish pudding with whipped cream and frosted strawberries.

STRAWBERRY TARTS

1 8-oz. package cream cheese, softened
1 1/2 c. sugar
1 tsp. grated lemon rind
2 tbsp. lemon juice
2 tbsp. cream
8 baked tart shells
Strawberries
3 tbsp. cornstarch

Combine cream cheese, 1/2 cup sugar, lemon rind, lemon juice and cream in bowl; mix until of the consistency of whipped cream. Line tart shells with cheese mixture; fill with strawberries.Mash 3 cups strawberries with remaining sugar; let stand for 30 minutes. Blend in cornstarch; cook until thick and clear. Strain and cool. Pour over strawberries; refrigerate. Garnish with whipped cream. Place glaze on tarts. Yield: 6-8 servings.

STRAWBERRY JAM CAKE

1 c. shortening
2 c. sugar
4 eggs
1 c. strawberry jam
3 c. flour
1 tsp. cinnamon
1/2 tsp. cloves
1/2 tsp. ginger
1/2 tsp. allspice
1 tsp. soda
1 c. buttermilk
2 c. (packed) brown sugar
1/4 c. butter
1 tsp. vanilla
3 tsp. cream

Cream shortening with sugar; add eggs, one at a time. Add jam. Sift flour with spices; dissolve soda in buttermilk. Add flour mixture and buttermilk mixture alternately to jam mixture; mix well. Pour into greased large tube pan. Bake at 325 degrees for 1 hour and 30 minutes or until cake pulls away from pan at edges. Bring brown sugar and 1/2 cup water to a boil until mixture spins thread. Combine butter, vanilla and cream in mixing bowl. Pour brown sugar mixture over butter mixture gradually; beat until thick enough to spread. Add more cream, if necessary. Spread on cake.

STRAWBERRY CAKE ROLL

1 c. flour
1 tsp. baking powder
1/2 tsp. salt
3 lge. eggs
1 c. sugar
1 tsp. vanilla
Powdered sugar
1/2 pt. whipping cream, whipped
1 qt. strawberries, sliced

Sift flour, baking powder and salt together. Beat eggs with electric mixer until thick; beat in sugar gradually. Blend in 1/3 cup water and vanilla at low speed. Fold in flour mixture by hand until batter is smooth. Turn into greased and paper-lined 15 x 10-inch baking pan. Bake at 350 degrees for 12 to 15 minutes. Turn out onto powdered sugar-sprinkled towel; peel off paper. Roll cake up in towel; cool. Unroll; spread with whipped cream and strawberries. Reroll; slice. Yield: 10 servings.

STEAMED STRAWBERRY PUDDING

Butter
Sugar
1 egg
1 c. milk
2 c. flour
2 tsp. baking powder
1/4 tsp. salt
1 qt. strawberries, sliced

Cream 1 tablespoon butter and 1 tablespoon sugar; add egg, blending thoroughly. Add milk and flour alternately to creamed mixture. Add baking powder and salt, stirring well. Pour into greased baking pan; place in pan of lukewarm water. Steam, covered, for 1 hour. Cream 1/2 cup sugar and 1/2 cup butter. Mix strawberries with 1/2 cup sugar. Combine strawberry mixture with creamed mixture. Slice pudding; pour sauce over hot pudding. Yield: 6-8 servings.

STRAWBERRY BREAD

1 c. butter
1 1/2 c. sugar
1 tsp. vanilla
1 tsp. salt
1 tsp. lemon juice
4 eggs
1/2 tsp. soda
1/2 c. sour cream
3 c. flour
1/2 c. chopped nuts
1 c. strawberry preserves
1 tbsp. red food coloring

Blend butter, sugar, vanilla, salt and juice; beat in eggs, one at a time. Dissolve soda in sour cream; add to egg mixture. Fold in flour, nuts, preserves and food coloring. Pour batter into 2 large or 4 small greased loaf pans. Bake at 350 degrees for 35 to 40 minutes or until bread pulls away from pans.

STRAWBERRIES ROMANOFF

5 egg yolks
1 c. sugar
1 c. sherry
1 pt. whipped cream
4 pt. strawberries

Beat egg yolks; add sugar and sherry. Cook in double boiler until velvety and smooth; cool. Fold in whipped cream; add strawberries. Yield: 12 servings.

STRAWBERRY ICE

2 c. sugar
1 qt. strawberries, sieved
Juice of 2 lemons

Combine sugar and 1 cup water; bring to a boil. Cook for 5 minutes. Cool slightly; add strawberries and lemon juice. Pour into freezer tray; freeze. Yield: 8-12 servings.

CALIFORNIA STRAWBERRY CREAM ICE (CHURN METHOD)

1 3/4 c. sugar
4 c. California strawberry puree
2 tbsp. lemon juice
4 egg whites, lightly beaten
1/2 tsp. salt
1 c. heavy cream

Combine sugar and 2/3 cup water in small saucepan. Bring to a boil; cook, stirring, until sugar is dissolved. Cool. Combine syrup with remaining ingredients. Pour into container of churn-type freezer; freeze according to manufacturers' instructions for sherbet. Yield: 7 1/2 quarts.

CALIFORNIA STRAWBERRY ICE CREAM (REFRIGERATOR METHOD)

2 c. sugar
4 pt. fresh California strawberries
2/3 c. orange juice
1/4 c. lemon juice
2 c. heavy cream, whipped

Combine sugar and 1 cup water in saucepan; bring to a boil. Cook for 5 minutes; cool. Puree strawberries with electric blender or sieve. Strain to remove seeds. Combine puree, juices and sugar syrup; fold in whipped cream. Pour into refrigerator trays; freeze until firm. Yield: 2 quarts.

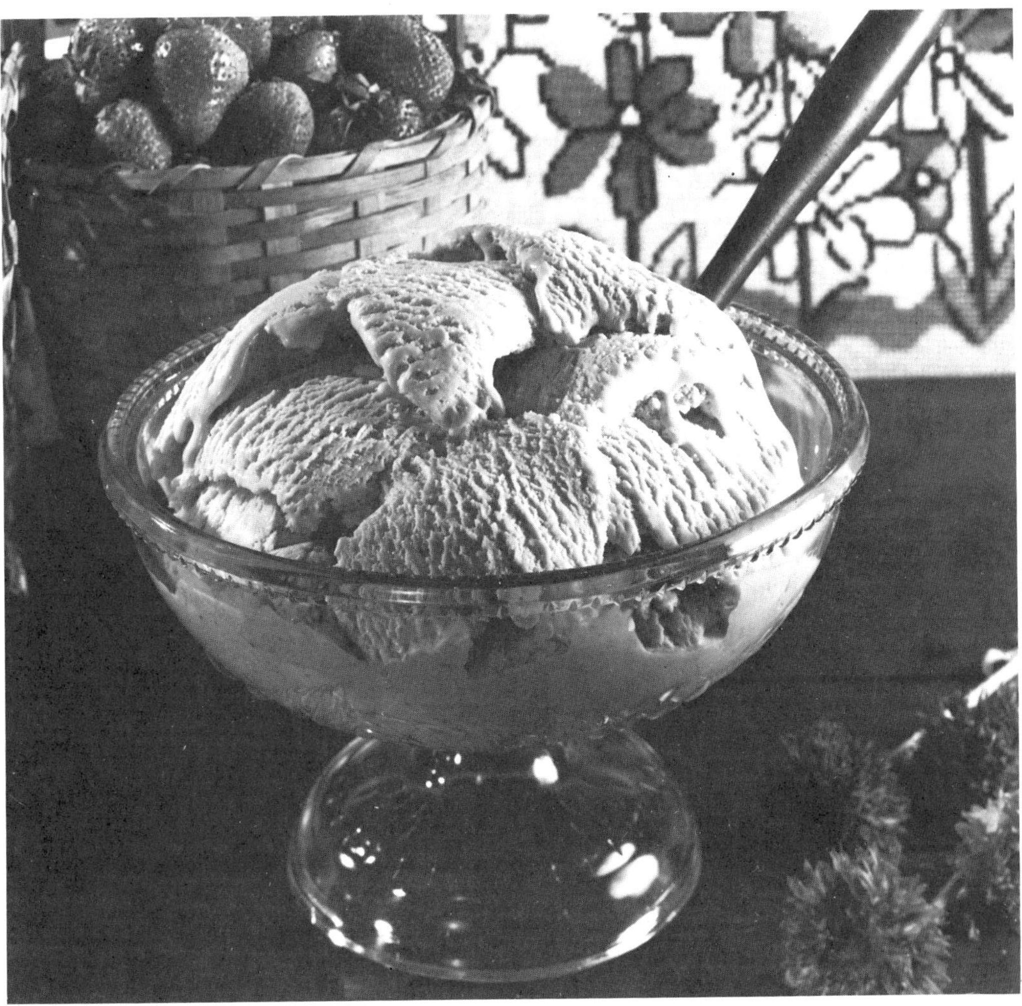

California Strawberry Cream Ices and Ice Creams . . . Both the churn and the refrigerator method.

CALIFORNIA STRAWBERRY ICE CREAM (CHURN METHOD)

6 egg yolks
2 c. sugar
1/2 tsp. salt
3 c. scalded milk
1 tbsp. vanilla
3 1/4 c. heavy cream
2 c. California strawberry puree
12 drops of red food coloring

Beat egg yolks, 1 cup sugar and salt together; stir in scalded milk gradually. Pour into medium saucepan; cook, stirring, over medium heat until mixture coats metal spoon. Remove from heat; add vanilla. Cool. Stir in cream; chill well. Stir remaining sugar into strawberry puree; let stand for several hours or until sugar is completely dissolved. Combine strawberry mixture with chilled custard. Add food coloring. Pour into container of churn-type freezer; freeze according to manufacturers instructions for ice cream. Yield: 4 quarts.

CALIFORNIA STRAWBERRY CREAM ICE (REFRIGERATOR METHOD)

4 pt. fresh California strawberries
1 1/2 c. sugar
2 tbsp. light corn syrup
2 tbsp. lemon juice
4 egg whites
1/2 tsp. salt
1 c. heavy cream, whipped

Puree strawberries with electric blender or food mill; strain to remove seeds. Combine sugar, corn syrup, 2/3 cup water and lemon juice in saucepan; cook, stirring, over medium heat until sugar is dissolved. Bring to a boil without stirring; boil until temperature on candy thermometer reaches 238 degrees. Beat egg whites with salt in large mixing bowl until stiff peaks form. Pour sugar syrup over egg whites, gradually, beating constantly. Beat until mixture is thick and shiny. Fold whipped cream into strawberry puree. Fold strawberry mixture into egg white mixture until blended. Pour into 4 freezer trays; freeze until firm. Remove from freezer; beat with electric mixer until smooth. Return to trays; freeze until firm. Yield: 2 quarts.

STRAWBERRY CROWN

1/2 c. butter
1/4 c. (packed) brown sugar
1 c. sifted flour
1/2 c. chopped pecans
1 env. unflavored gelatin
2 pt. halved strawberries
1 tsp. lemon juice
3/4 c. sugar
Several drops of red food coloring
1 c. whipping cream, whipped

Preheat oven to 400 degrees. Mix butter, brown sugar, flour and pecans with hands; spread in 13 x 9 1/2 x 2-inch pan. Bake for 15 minutes. Stir with spoon; cool. Soften gelatin in 1/2 cup cold water. Mash 1 cup strawberries in saucepan; add lemon juice and sugar. Bring to a boil, stirring occasionally; remove from heat. Stir in gelatin until dissolved; add food coloring. Pour thin layer of gelatin mixture in 1 1/2-quart mold; refrigerate until set. Arrange several uncooked berries in gelatin to form design. Chill remaining gelatin mixture until partially set; fold in remaining berries and whipped cream. Alternate layer of berry mixture and crumb mixture, starting with berry mixture and ending with crumb mixture. Make 4 layers of each. Chill; unmold. Garnish with berries. Yield: 8 servings.

STRAWBERRY STACK DESSERT

6 canned refrigerator biscuits
Cooking oil
Sweetened strawberries
Whipped cream

Roll biscuits very thin; stick several times with fork. Fry in oil in skillet until brown and crisp, turning once. Cool. Place one biscuit on shallow platter; cover with berries. Repeat until all biscuits are used, making top layer of berries. Serve with whipped cream.

Sugar Cookie

ANIMAL SUGAR COOKIES

1 c. sugar
1/2 c. shortening
2 eggs
2 tbsp. milk
1 tbsp. lemon extract
3 1/2 c. flour
2 tsp. baking powder

Cream sugar and shortening in bowl until light and fluffy. Add eggs, milk and lemon extract; beat well. Sift remaining ingredients together; add to creamed mixture. Cover and chill. Roll out on floured surface to 1/4-inch thickness; cut with animal cookie cutters. Place on lightly greased baking sheet. Bake at 375 degrees for 8 minutes or until lightly browned. Garnish cookies with colored icing if desired.

SUGAR COOKIES

Color photograph for this recipe on page 494.

2 c. sifted flour
1 1/4 tsp. baking powder
1/4 tsp. salt
1/3 c. corn oil
1 egg
Milk
3/4 c. sugar
1 tsp. vanilla

Sift flour, baking powder and salt together into mixing bowl. Add oil; blend well. Mixture will appear dry. Beat egg; add enough milk to equal 1/3 cup liquid. Stir in sugar and vanilla. Beat until light and fluffy; stir into flour mixture. Chill for about 1 hour. Roll out on floured board or cloth 1/8 to 1/4 inch thick. Cut with floured 2-inch round cutter or as desired. Place on ungreased cookie sheet. Bake in 400-degree oven for about 9 minutes or until lightly browned. May be sprinkled with colored sugar before baking, if desired. Yield: 3 dozen 2-inch cookies.

FILLED SUGAR COOKIES

1 c. shortening
2 1/2 c. sugar
2 eggs
1 1/2 c. orange juice
1/2 tsp. vanilla
Salt
3 c. flour
1 tsp. soda
1/2 tsp. baking powder
1 1/2 c. chopped raisins

Cream shortening with 2 cups sugar; beat eggs into sugar mixture thoroughly. Stir in 1 cup orange juice and vanilla; blend in 1/4 teaspoon salt, flour, soda and baking powder. Chill, covered, for 3 hours or overnight. Combine raisins, remaining sugar and orange juice and dash of salt in saucepan; simmer, stirring constantly until mixture thickens. Remove from heat; cool. Roll out dough on lightly floured board to 1/4-inch thickness; cut with 2 1/2-inch cutter. Place half the cookies on cookie sheet; spread filling over each. Cover with remaining cookies; seal edges. Prick each cookie top with fork. Bake in 425-degree oven for 10 minutes. Yield: 2 1/2 dozen.

Sweet Breads

APPLE BREAD

1/2 c. margarine
1 c. sugar
2 eggs
1 tsp. soda
2 tbsp. sour milk
2 c. flour
1/2 tsp. salt
2 c. chopped apples
1/2 c. chopped nuts
1 tsp. vanilla

Cream margarine and sugar. Add eggs, soda, sour milk, flour, salt, apples, nuts and vanilla; mix well. Pour into greased and floured 9 x 5-inch loaf pan.

Topping

2 tbsp. melted butter
1 tsp. cinnamon
2 tbsp. flour
2 tbsp. sugar

Combine all ingredients; mix well. Sprinkle over bread. Bake at 350 degrees for 1 hour and 10 minutes. Cool on wire rack.

APPLE-CHERRY-NUT BREAD

4 c. sifted flour
2 tsp. baking powder
1 tsp. salt
1 tsp. soda

1 1/4 c. sugar
2/3 c. shortening
3 eggs
1 can applesauce
1 c. chopped nuts
1/2 c. maraschino cherries, chopped
2 tbsp. grated lemon peel
1 c. powdered sugar
2 tbsp. evaporated milk
1 tsp. vanilla extract

Sift flour, baking powder, salt and soda. Beat sugar and shortening until fluffy. Add eggs; beat until smooth. Beat in flour mixture alternately with applesauce. Stir in nuts, cherries and lemon peel. Pour into 2 greased 9 x 5 x 3-inch loaf pans. Bake at 350 degrees for 50 minutes or until lightly browned. Remove bread from pans while warm; cool. Blend powdered sugar and milk until smooth; add vanilla. Spread on loaves.

APPLE-WALNUT BREAD

2 c. packaged biscuit mix
1 c. oats
3/4 c. sugar
1/4 tsp. salt
1 tsp. baking powder
1/2 c. broken walnuts
1/2 c. semisweet chocolate pieces
1/2 c. golden seedless raisins
1 egg, beaten
1/4 c. milk
1 c. canned applesauce

Combine biscuit mix, oats, sugar, salt and baking powder; add walnuts, chocolate pieces and raisins. Combine egg and milk; stir into chocolate mixture. Stir in applesauce; beat vigorously for 30 seconds. Spoon into greased loaf pan. Bake at 350 degrees for 50 minutes or until bread tests done. Cool in pan for 10 minutes; remove to rack. Cool.

Cottage Fruit Bread . . . Serve this fruit bread at breakfast, lunch, or for snacks.

COTTAGE FRUIT BREAD

2 c. sifted all-purpose flour
3 tsp. baking powder
3/4 tsp. salt
1 c. diced mixed candied fruits
1/2 c. whole candied cherries
1/3 c. butter
1/2 c. (packed) brown sugar
2 eggs
2 tsp. grated lemon rind
1 c. creamed cottage cheese

Combine flour, baking powder and salt; stir in candied fruits and cherries. Set aside. Combine butter and sugar in electric mixer bowl; beat with mixer until light and fluffy. Add eggs, one at a time, beating well after each addition. Blend in lemon rind and cottage cheese. Add fruit mixture; stir just until dry ingredients are moistened. Spoon into greased 9 x 5 x 3-inch loaf pan. Bake at 350 degrees for 1 hour or until bread tests done. Cool in pan for 10 minutes; remove from pan. Cool on wire rack.

ARABIAN NUT LOAF

3/4 c. hot coffee
1 c. chopped dates
1/3 c. shortening
1 c. sugar
2 eggs
1 3/4 c. flour
1 1/2 tsp. baking powder
1/2 tsp. salt
1/2 tsp. soda
1/2 tsp. vanilla
1/2 c. chopped nuts

Pour coffee over dates; cool. Cream shortening and sugar; add eggs one at a time, beating well after each addition. Sift dry ingredients together; add to creamed mixture alternately with coffee mixture. Stir in vanilla and nuts. Pour into greased waxed paper-lined loaf pan. Bake at 350 degrees for 1 hour or until bread tests done. Cool on wire rack.

BISHOP'S BREAD

2 1/2 c. flour
2 c. (packed) brown sugar
1/2 tsp. salt
1/2 c. shortening
1 tsp. baking powder
1/2 tsp. soda
1 tsp. cinnamon
1 egg
3/4 c. buttermilk

Blend flour, brown sugar, salt and shortening; mix until crumbly. Reserve 3/4 cup crumb mixture. Add baking powder, soda, cinnamon, egg and buttermilk to remaining crumb mixture; beat well until batter is smooth. Pour into 2 greased 8-inch round pans; sprinkle reserved crumb mixture over top. Bake at 400 degrees for 25 minutes. Bread freezes well.

BUBBLE LOAF

1 tsp. cinnamon
3/4 c. chopped pecans
3/4 c. sugar
1 pkg. hot roll mix
3/4 c. melted butter
1/2 c. dark corn syrup

Combine cinnamon, pecans and sugar. Prepare hot roll mix according to package directions; let rise until doubled in bulk. Shape into 1-inch balls. Dip into 1/2 cup melted butter; roll in cinnamon mixture. Place in greased tube pan in staggered layers. Let rise until doubled in bulk. Combine remaining butter and syrup; pour over balls. Bake at 400 degrees for 25 minutes. Cool slightly; turn out of pan. Break into pieces to serve. Yield: 12 servings.

CARDAMOM COFFEE BRAID

3 c. milk
2 pkg. dry yeast
1 c. sugar
4 eggs, slightly beaten
1/2 c. soft butter
1 tsp. salt
9 crushed cardamom seed
Flour

Heat milk in saucepan until warm; add yeast. Let stand for 5 minutes; stir until dissolved. Add sugar, eggs, butter, salt and cardamom seed. Add flour to make stiff dough; knead until smooth. Let rise until doubled in bulk. Divide into 3 equal portions; divide each portion into 3 sections. Roll into long rolls; braid 3 rolls together, making 3 braids. Place on baking sheet; let rise until doubled in bulk. Bake at 350 degrees for 30 minutes; frost with confectioners' sugar glaze if desired.

CHOCOLATE FRUIT BREAD

2 c. milk, scalded
5 tbsp. sugar
2 tbsp. salt
2 pkg. yeast
2 eggs, beaten
13 c. sifted flour
5 tbsp. melted butter
1 c. chopped candied fruit
1 c. chocolate chips
Confectioners' sugar

Mix milk, sugar and salt; cool to lukewarm. Dissolve yeast in 2 cups warm water; add to milk mixture. Add eggs. Add 6 cups flour; beat until smooth. Add butter, 6 cups flour, candied fruit and chocolate chips; mix well. Knead in remaining flour. Place in greased bowl; cover. Let rise for 1 hour and 30 minutes or until doubled in bulk. Shape into 8 loaves; place in greased loaf pans. Let rise for 1 hour or until doubled in bulk. Bake at 400 degrees for 15 minutes. Reduce oven temperature to 375 degrees; bake for 30 minutes longer. Sprinkle with confectioners' sugar while hot.

CINNAMON-NUT BREAD

1 1/2 c. raisins
1/4 c. shortening
1 c. sugar
1 tbsp. molasses
3 c. flour
1/2 tsp. salt
1 tsp. soda
2 tsp. baking powder
1/2 tsp. cinnamon
1 1/2 c. chopped nuts

Preheat oven to 350 degrees. Place raisins in 1/2 cup boiling water; cool. Drain raisins; reserve water. Cream shortening, sugar and molasses. Sift flour, salt, soda, baking powder and cinnamon together. Add flour mixture to creamed mixture alternately with reserved raisin water, mixing well. Fold in raisins and nuts. Spoon batter into 6 greased and floured soup cans. Bake for 30 minutes or until bread tests done.

COFFEE SPICE BREAD

1/4 c. shortening
3/4 c. sugar
2 eggs
2 c. flour
1 tbsp. baking powder
1 tsp. salt
1 tsp. cinnamon
1/4 tsp. ground cloves
1/4 tsp. allspice
3/4 c. strong coffee

Cream shortening and sugar until fluffy; beat in eggs. Sift dry ingredients together; add to creamed mixture alternately with coffee. Pour batter into greased loaf pan. Bake at 375 degrees for 40 minutes or until bread tests done.

FRUITED BROWN BREAD

4 c. raisins
2 c. chopped dates
4 tsp. soda
1/4 c. butter
4 c. (packed) brown sugar
4 eggs
4 tsp. cinnamon
2 tsp. ground cloves
6 c. flour
1/2 c. molasses
1 1/2 c. chopped nuts

Combine raisins, dates, soda and butter with 3 1/2 cups boiling water; cool. Add brown sugar, eggs, cinnamon, cloves, flour and molasses; beat well. Stir in nuts. Pour into 8 small loaf pans. Bake at 300 degrees for 1 hour. Garnish with walnut halves and maraschino cherries.

HOT CROSS BREAD

2 pkg. yeast	*2/3 c. sugar*
2/3 c. milk, scalded	*2/3 c. butter*
3 eggs, beaten lightly	*1 3/4 tsp. salt*
1 1/2 c. mashed potatoes	*6 c. flour*
	1 c. raisins

Dissolve yeast in 2/3 cup warm water. Cool milk to lukewarm; beat eggs with milk. Add potatoes, sugar, butter, yeast mixture and salt. Add flour and raisins; mix to soft dough. Place on floured board; knead for 10 minutes. Place in greased bowl; let rise until doubled in bulk. Knead well; place in 2 greased bread pans. Let rise until doubled in bulk. Bake in 400-degree oven for 45 minutes.

KING'S BREAD

1/2 c. milk, scalded	*1 c. currants*
2 pkg. dry yeast	*1/2 c. candied cherries*
2 3/4 c. flour	*1/2 c. chopped dried apricots*
1 stick butter	*1/2 tsp. cinnamon*
1 c. sugar	*1/2 tsp. nutmeg*
1/2 tsp. salt	*1/2 tsp. ground cloves*
3 eggs	
1 c. raisins	

Cool milk to lukewarm. Pour 1/2 cup warm water into large bowl; sprinkle yeast on water. Let stand for 10 minutes. Stir in milk and 1 1/2 cups flour; beat until smooth. Cover. Let rise in warm place for about 30 minutes or until doubled in bulk. Cream butter; add sugar and salt gradually. Stir into yeast mixture. Beat in eggs, one at a time. Add fruits, spices and remaining flour; beat until blended. Turn into 2 greased 9-inch loaf pans. Cover. Let rise in warm place for about 1 hour and 15 minutes or until just doubled in bulk. Bake in 350-degree oven for 1 hour or until loaves are golden brown. Cool. Spread with thin lemon confectioners' sugar frosting if desired.

NECTARINE-NUT LOAF

3 fresh nectarines	*2 1/2 c. sifted all-purpose flour*
1/2 c. shortening	*2 1/2 tsp. baking powder*
1 c. sugar	*1 tsp. salt*
2 eggs	*1/2 c. chopped pecans*
1 tsp. vanilla	

Blanch nectarines; remove peel. Mash enough nectarine pulp to measure 1 cup. Cream shortening with sugar; mix in eggs and vanilla. Sift flour with baking powder and salt; add to creamed mixture alternately with mashed nectarines, mixing well after each addition. Fold in pecans. Turn into greased and floured 9 x 5 x 3-inch loaf pan. Bake in 350-degree oven for about 1 hour. Cool in pan for 10 minutes; remove from pan. Cool on wire rack. Wrap well; store overnight.

Nectarine-Nut Loaf . . . This fruit and nut bread is ideal for holiday gift-giving.

FRUIT BREAD

Color photograph for this recipe on page 724.

1/2 c. seedless raisins
1/2 c. currants
1 c. butter
1 c. sugar
Grated rind of 1/2 lemon
Dash of nutmeg
4 eggs
1/4 c. citron
3 tbsp. brandy
1 1/2 c. flour
1/2 tsp. baking powder
Fine bread crumbs

Place raisins and currants in a bowl; cover with hot water. Let stand for about 30 minutes. Drain; place on absorbent paper. Cream butter in bowl. Add sugar gradually; mix well. Stir in grated rind and nutmeg. Add eggs, one at a time, beating well after each addition. Stir in raisins, currants, citron and brandy. Sift flour with baking powder into butter mixture; mix well. Sprinkle enough bread crumbs into a greased loaf pan to coat sides and bottom. Pour raisin mixture into pan. Bake at 325 degrees for 1 hour and 30 minutes or until bread tests done. Remove from pan; cool. Wrap in aluminum foil; store for 4 to 5 days before slicing.

KULICH

Color photograph for this recipe on page 482.

1/2 c. milk
1/4 c. sugar
1 tsp. salt
2 tbsp. margarine
1 pkg. yeast
1 egg
2 1/2 c. (about) unsifted flour
1 tsp. grated lemon peel
1/4 c. raisins
1/4 c. chopped almonds
Confectioners' sugar icing
Colored candies

Scald milk; pour into large bowl. Add sugar, salt and margarine. Cool to lukewarm. Measure 1/4 cup warm water into small warm bowl. Sprinkle in yeast; stir until dissolved. Add egg, yeast and 1 cup flour to lukewarm milk mixture; beat until smooth. Stir in lemon peel and enough additional flour to make soft dough. Turn out onto lightly floured board; knead for about 5 minutes or until smooth and elastic. Place in greased bowl, turning to grease top. Cover; let rise in warm place, free from draft, for about 1 hour or until doubled in bulk. Punch dough down; knead in raisins and almonds. Divide dough in half; shape each half in a ball. Press each ball into 2 greased 1-pint cans or two 1-pound coffee or shortening cans. Cover; let rise until doubled in bulk. Bake in 350-degree oven for 30 to 35 minutes or until cakes test done. Turn out of cans at once. Cool; frost tops with confectioners' sugar icing. Sprinkle with candies. Yield: 2 cakes.

ORANGE-RAISIN LOAF

1 c. sugar
2 tbsp. melted butter
1 egg, lightly beaten
2 tbsp. grated orange rind
1/3 c. orange juice
2 c. sifted flour
1 tsp. baking powder
1 tsp. soda
1/4 tsp. salt
1/4 c. raisins
1/2 c. coarsely chopped nuts
2 tbsp. vanilla

Combine sugar and butter; add egg, orange rind, orange juice and 1/2 cup boiling water. Mix lightly. Sift flour, baking powder, soda and salt together; add to orange mixture. Add raisins, nuts and vanilla; mix well. Place in greased loaf pan. Bake for 1 hour at 350 degrees.

PANETTONE

Color photograph for this recipe on page 726.

4 1/2 to 5 1/2 c. unsifted flour
1/2 c. sugar
1 tsp. salt
2 pkg. dry yeast
1/2 c. milk
1/2 c. margarine
4 eggs, at room temperature
1/2 c. chopped citron
1/2 c. seedless raisins
2 tbsp. pine nuts
1 tbsp. aniseed

Mix 1 1/2 cups flour, sugar, salt and undissolved yeast thoroughly in large bowl. Combine milk, 1/2 cup water and margarine in saucepan. Place over low heat until liquids are warm. Margarine does not need to melt. Add to dry ingredients gradually; beat for 2 minutes with electric mixer at medium speed, scraping bowl occasionally. Add 3 eggs and 1/2 cup flour; beat at high speed for 2 minutes, scraping bowl occasionally. Stir in citron, raisins, pine nuts and aniseed. Add enough remaining flour to make soft dough. Turn out onto lightly floured board; knead for 8 to 10 minutes or until smooth and elastic. Place in greased bowl, turning to grease top. Cover; let rise in warm place, free from draft, for about 1 hour or until doubled in bulk. Punch down. Cover; let rise again for 30 minutes or until almost doubled in bulk. Punch down. Turn out onto lightly floured board; divide in half. Form into round balls; place on opposite corners of greased baking sheet. Cut a cross 1/2 inch deep on top of each ball. Cover; let rise in warm place, free from draft, for about 1 hour or until doubled in bulk. Beat remaining egg with 1 tablespoon water; brush on loaves. Bake in 350-degree oven for 35 to 45 minutes or until done. Remove from baking sheet. Cool.

PINEAPPLE-DATE LOAF

1/4 c. soft butter
1/2 c. sugar
1 egg
1/4 tsp. lemon extract
1 8 1/2-oz. can crushed pineapple
1/4 c. chopped nuts
2 1/2 c. sifted flour
2 1/2 tsp. baking powder
1/4 tsp. soda
1 tsp. salt
1/2 c. finely chopped dates
1/4 c. chopped maraschino cherries

Cream butter and sugar; add egg and lemon extract. Drain pineapple, reserving liquid. Mix reserved liquid and 1/4 cup water. Add pineapple and nuts to creamed mixture. Sift dry ingredients together; add dates. Mix well; stir into creamed mixture alternately with pineapple liquid. Drain cherries; fold into batter. Pour into greased 9 x 5 x 3-inch pan. Bake at 375 degrees for 55 minutes. Cool in pan for 10 minutes; remove from pan. Let stand overnight before serving.

PINEAPPLE-NUT BREAD

1 c. raisins
1 3/4 c. flour
2 tsp. baking powder
1/2 tsp. salt

1/4 tsp. soda
3/4 c. chopped walnuts
3/4 c. (packed) brown sugar
3 tbsp. butter
2 eggs
1 c. crushed pineapple
2 tbsp. sugar
1/2 tsp. cinnamon

Cover raisins with hot water; drain. Sift flour, baking powder, salt and soda together; add walnuts and raisins. Combine brown sugar, butter and eggs; beat until fluffy. Stir in half the flour mixture; stir in pineapple. Add remaining flour mixture; beat until smooth. Pour into greased 9 x 5 x 3-inch loaf pan. Combine sugar and cinnamon; sprinkle over batter. Bake in 350-degree oven for about 1 hour or until bread tests done. Cool on wire rack.

PLUCKING BREAD

1 1/4 c. milk, scalded
1 1/4 c. sugar
2 tsp. cinnamon
1/2 tsp. nutmeg
1 pkg. dry yeast
4 1/2 c. flour
4 egg yolks
1 c. melted butter
1 tsp. salt
3/4 c. chopped pecans

Cool milk to lukewarm. Mix 3/4 cup sugar, cinnamon and nutmeg. Soften yeast in 1/4 cup warm water for 5 minutes; add milk and 1 cup flour. Beat well. Let stand for about 20 minutes or until bubbly and light. Blend egg yolks, remaining sugar, 1/2 cup butter and salt; add to yeast mixture. Work in remaining flour; knead until smooth and elastic. Place in greased bowl; cover. Let rise until doubled in bulk. Mix remaining butter, cinnamon mixture and pecans. Turn dough out onto floured surface; divide in half. Shape into 2 long rolls. Cut each roll into 24 pieces; roll pieces into balls. Dip balls into pecan mixture; place close together in large greased tube pan. Let stand in warm place for about 45 minutes or until doubled in bulk. Bake at 350 degrees for 45 minutes. Turn out onto rack. Cool.

SOUR CREAM-PRUNE BREAD

1 c. sour cream
1 c. chopped cooked prunes
1 1/2 c. sifted flour
1/2 tsp. salt
2 tsp. baking powder
1 tsp. soda
3/4 c. sugar
1 c. whole wheat flour
1/2 c. prune juice
1 egg, beaten
2 tbsp. melted butter

Mix sour cream and prunes. Sift flour, salt, baking powder, soda and sugar together; stir into sour cream mixture. Add whole wheat flour; mix well. Add prune juice, egg and butter; mix well. Pour into 2 greased 9 x 5 x 3-inch loaf pans. Bake in 350-degree oven for 50 minutes.

SPICY NUT DESSERT BREAD

1 tsp. soda
1/2 c. margarine
1 c. sugar
1 egg
1 c. raisins
1 c. sweetened applesauce
1/2 c. chopped walnuts
2 c. flour
1 tsp. cinnamon
1/2 tsp. allspice
1/2 tsp. nutmeg
1/2 tsp. salt

Dissolve soda in 2 tablespoons hot water. Cream margarine, sugar and egg well; stir in raisins, applesauce and walnuts. Sift flour, spices and salt together; stir into creamed mixture. Add soda mixture; beat well. Spread batter in 2 greased 8 x 5 x 3-inch pans. Bake at 350 degrees for 1 hour. Bread freezes well.

SWISS CREAM-NUT LOAF

1 c. heavy cream
1 egg
1 c. sugar
1 tsp. grated lemon peel
1 c. chopped walnuts
1 c. raisins
1 3/4 c. sifted flour
1 1/2 tsp. baking powder
1/4 tsp. salt

Beat cream until soft peaks form; beat in egg and sugar until blended. Mix in lemon peel, walnuts and raisins. Blend flour, baking powder and salt together; fold into cream mixture. Grease bottom of 9 1/2 x 5 x 3-inch pan; spoon batter into pan. Bake at 325 degrees for 1 hour and 10 minutes. Cool bread for 15 minutes in pan on wire rack. Remove from pan; cool completely.

TUTTI FRUTTI BREAD

1 pkg. yeast
Sugar
1/2 c. chopped candied cherries
1/2 c. chopped candied peel
1 c. raisins
6 c. flour
3/4 c. milk
1/2 c. shortening
1 1/2 tsp. salt
1 egg

Dissolve yeast and 1 teaspoon sugar in 1/2 cup warm water; let stand for 10 minutes. Combine cherries, peel and raisins; sprinkle with 1/4 cup flour. Scald milk. Combine shortening, salt and 1/4 cup sugar in large bowl; pour in hot milk. Cool to lukewarm beat in egg, yeast and 2 cups flour. Add fruits and enough remaining flour to make soft dough. Knead dough until elastic; place in greased bowl. Cover; let rise until doubled in bulk. Shape into 2 or 3 loaves; place in bread pans. Let rise until doubled in bulk. Bake at 375 degrees for 1 hour or until loaves test done.

WALNUT-HONEY LOAF

1 c. honey
1 c. milk
1/2 c. sugar
2 1/2 c. sifted flour
1 tsp. soda
1 tsp. salt
1/2 c. walnuts
1/4 c. shortening
1 egg

Combine honey, milk and sugar in 3-quart saucepan; warm over medium heat, stirring constantly, just until sugar is dissolved. Cool. Add remaining ingredients; beat for 2 minutes or until blended. Turn into well-greased, lightly floured loaf pan. Bake at 325 degrees for 1 hour and 15 minutes or until bread tests done. Cool for 15 minutes in pan. Remove from pan; cool thoroughly on wire racks.

SUGAR-CRISP ROLLS

Color photograph for this recipe on page 727.

2 to 2 1/2 c. unsifted flour
1 1/4 c. sugar
1/2 tsp. salt
1 pkg. dry yeast
1/4 c. milk
1/4 c. margarine
1 egg, at room temperature
1 c. chopped pecans
Melted margarine

Mix 3/4 cup flour, 1/4 cup sugar, salt and undissolved yeast thoroughly in large bowl. Combine milk, water and 1/4 cup margarine in saucepan; place over low heat until liquids are warm. Margarine does not need to melt. Add to dry ingredients gradually; beat for 2 minutes with electric mixer at medium speed, scraping bowl occasionally. Add egg and 1/4 cup flour; beat at high speed for 2 minutes, scraping bowl occasionally. Stir in enough remaining flour to make soft dough. Turn out onto lightly floured board; knead for 8 to 10 minutes or until smooth and elastic. Cover; let rise in warm place, free from draft, for about 1 hour or until doubled in bulk. Punch down; let rise for 30 minutes longer. Combine remaining sugar and pecans. Punch dough down. Turn out onto lightly floured board; roll out to 9 x 18-inch rectangle. Brush with melted margarine; sprinkle with half the sugar mixture. Roll up from long side as for jelly roll; seal edges. Cut into 1-inch slices. Roll each slice of dough into 4-inch circle, using remaining sugar mixture in place of flour on board, coating both sides with sugar mixture. Place on greased baking sheets. Cover; let rise in warm place, free from draft, for about 30 minutes or until doubled in bulk. Bake in 375-degree oven for 10 to 15 minutes or until done. Remove from baking sheets; cool on wire racks. Yield: 1 1/2 dozen.

Sweetbreads

Sweetbread is the term for certain glands of calves, lambs, and young steers that are used as food. They are considered a great delicacy. Each animal has two kinds of sweetbread, one in the throat, called throat or neck sweetbread; and one in the body proper, called stomach sweetbread. White and tender veal and lamb sweetbreads are probably the most preferred. Red, tough beef sweetbread is less desirable and is best when mixed with other meats in meat pies, meat patties, stews, pates, and so on. Sweetbread is rich in protein. (3 1/2 ounces uncooked veal sweetbread = 94 calories; 3 1/2 ounces uncooked lamb sweetbread = 94 calories; 3 1/2 ounces uncooked beef sweetbread = 207 calories)

AVAILABILITY: Sweetbreads are sold year-round fresh or frozen.

BUYING: When purchasing fresh sweetbreads look for firm and clear specimens.

STORING: Unless used immediately, sweetbreads are unfit to eat. Use fresh sweetbreads as soon as purchased. Do not refrigerate unless you first wash and precook sweetbreads according to directions under PREPARATION (below). Then, use sweetbreads within 24 hours. Keep frozen sweetbreads in freezer until ready to use.

PREPARATION: To prepare for refrigeration or for cooking—Place sweetbread in cold water to draw out blood. Let soak about 1 hour, changing water several times. Remove sweetbread from water. Place into pan of fresh cold water, enough to cover, with 1 teaspoon salt and 1 tablespoon vinegar or fresh lemon juice for 4 cups water. Slowly bring to a boil. Simmer gently about 10 to 20 minutes. Remove from heat and drain. Hold sweetbreads under cold running water. Slip off thin membrane with fingers. Cut out tubes, veins, and cartilage without tearing delicate tissues. Refrigerate or cook. Sweetbread may be baked, broiled, braised, sauteed, poached, fried, or so on. See specific recipe instructions. *To thaw* frozen sweetbreads—Drop sweetbreads into boiling water. Simmer gently. Use as for fresh sweetbreads (above).

SERVING: Serve sweetbreads as a main dish or in casserole.

FRENCH SWEETBREADS

2 pairs sweetbreads
1 tbsp. lemon juice
Salt
3/4 c. butter
1 tbsp. grated onion
2 tbsp. flour
1/2 pt. cream
1/4 tsp. celery salt
6 slices toast, cut into quarters

Plunge sweetbreads into cold water; let stand for 1 hour. Drain; place in boiling water with lemon juice and 2 teaspoons salt. Simmer for 20 minutes; drain. Plunge into cold water; remove coarse membranes. Heat butter in hot skillet; cook until butter is foamy. Add onion; cook until transparent. Add sweetbreads; saute until golden brown. Remove; drain on absorbent paper. Add flour to butter; stir until smooth. Add cream, salt to taste and celery salt; cook until thickened, stirring constantly. Add sweetbreads. Serve over toast. Yield: 6 servings.

FRIED SWEETBREADS

1 lb. sweetbreads
1/4 c. bread crumbs
1/2 tsp. salt
1/8 tsp. pepper
1/8 tsp. ginger
1 egg, beaten

Cook sweetbreads in boiling salted water for 20 minutes. Cut into bite-sized pieces. Roll in crumbs combined with salt, pepper and ginger. Dip in egg; coat with crumbs. Fry in deep hot fat until brown on all sides. Yield: 4 servings.

SPANISH SWEETBREAD

1 sweetbread
Salt and pepper to taste
Flour
1 sm. can tomatoes
1/2 med. onion, chopped
1 jalapeno pepper, chopped

Slice sweetbread; salt and pepper slices. Roll in flour; brown in small amount of fat in skillet. Combine tomatoes, onion and pepper in separate pan; add 1/2 cup water. Bring to a boil. Pour tomato mixture over browned sweetbread; simmer for 20 minutes. Yield: 6 servings.

SWEETBREAD-KIDNEY STEW

1 pair beef kidneys
1 lb. sweetbreads
2 med. onions, diced
Salt and pepper to taste
Flour

Skin kidneys; remove fat, blood vessels and connective tissue. Simmer in 1 quart water for 45 minutes or until tender. Add sweetbreads, onions, salt and pepper. Cook for 45 minutes or until kidneys are tender, adding water as needed. Do not stir. Combine 2 tablespoons flour and enough water to make a paste for each cup broth. Add flour mixture to kidney mixture, stirring constantly until thickened and bubbly. Serve with rice. Yield: About 6 servings.

SAUTEED SWEETBREADS

1 c. vinegar
2 pairs sweetbreads
1/2 c. cracker crumbs
1 tbsp. flour
1 egg, beaten
Salt and pepper to taste
Salad oil

Combine vinegar and 1 cup water; soak sweetbreads in mixture for 15 minutes. Remove membranes; separate sweetbreads. Combine crumbs and flour. Dip sweetbreads in egg; roll in crumb mixture. Sprinkle with salt and pepper. Heat small amount of salad oil in frying pan; saute sweetbreads until brown. Cover; cook for 30 to 40 minutes. Serve with Worcestershire sauce, if desired. Yield: 6 servings.

SWEETBREADS AND MUSHROOMS

1 1/2 lb. sweetbreads
Butter
1 tbsp. flour
6 sm. shallots, chopped
1 sprig of parsley, chopped
1/2 lb. fresh mushrooms
1/2 c. heavy cream
1 egg yolk
Fried ham slices
Toast

Soak sweetbreads in cold water; bring to a boil. Cook until tender. Remove skins from sweetbreads; reserve stock. Make roux with 2 teaspoons butter and flour; cook until golden brown, stirring constantly. Add sweetbreads, shallots and parsley. Add stock; simmer slowly until sauce is thick. Saute mushrooms in generous amount of butter in skillet. Combine cream and egg; heat well. Add mushrooms. Stir mushroom mixture into sweetbread mixture. Heat through; do not bring to a boil. Place ham slices on toast; top with mushroom mixture.

SWEETBREADS A LA KING

1 c. deveined sweetbreads
1 can cream of chicken soup
1 tbsp. dried minced onion
4 slices American cheese, diced
1 c. milk
2 tbsp. chopped pimento
2 tbsp. chopped green pepper
1 can refrigerator biscuits

Combine all ingredients except biscuits; cook over low heat for 15 minutes, stirring occasionally, until cheese melts. Serve sweetbread mixture over hot biscuits. Yield: 5-6 servings.

SWEETBREADS EN CASSEROLE

3 lb. sweetbreads
1 lge. onion
1 tbsp. shortening
Salt and pepper to taste
Paprika to taste
Parsley flakes
1 c. bouillon
1 lb. sliced calf liver
2 tbsp. cornstarch
1 lb. fresh mushrooms
8 patty shells

Plunge sweetbreads in boiling water; let stand for several minutes. Remove outer skin. Saute onion in shortening in skillet until tender; add salt and pepper, paprika and parsley flakes. Stir in bouillon. Add sweetbreads and liver; cook gradually for 30 minutes or until tender. Blend cornstarch with small amount of cold water; add to sweetbread mixture, stirring constantly, until thickened. Add mushrooms. Cook for 10 minutes longer; pour over warmed patty shells. Garnish with small pimentos. Yield: 8 servings.

SWEETBREADS MARSALA

2 pairs sweetbreads
1 tbsp. vinegar
1 egg, beaten
1/2 c. fine dry bread crumbs
1/2 tsp. salt
1/2 tsp. pepper
1/4 c. melted butter
Oil
1/2 c. cream sherry

Soak sweetbreads in cold water for 30 minutes, changing water twice. Drain. Plunge in boiling water to which vinegar has been added. Cook for 5 minutes. Place in ice water for 10 minutes. Wipe dry; remove membranes. Cut into thick slices. Dip into egg; roll in crumbs, seasoned with salt and pepper. Dip into butter. Dip in egg and crumbs a second time; cook in small amount of heated oil until golden brown. Pour sherry over sweetbreads. Cover; cook for 10 minutes longer. Yield: 4-5 servings.

SWEETBREADS IN MUSHROOM SAUCE

6 to 8 sweetbreads
1 tbsp. lemon juice
1 can mushrooms, drained
3 tbsp. butter
3 tbsp. flour
1 c. milk

Simmer sweetbreads for 20 minutes in boiling salted water and lemon juice; drain. Plunge sweetbreads into cold water. Remove membranes; cut into 1/2-inch slices. Saute mushrooms in butter in skillet until tender; add sweetbreads, browning lightly. Stir in flour until blended; add milk, stirring constantly, until mixture comes to a boil. Add additional milk to thin gravy, if necessary. Yield: 4 servings.

SWEETBREADS ON SKEWERS

1 pair calf sweetbreads
Thinly sliced lean bacon
Mushroom caps
Butter

Preheat oven to 400 degrees. Soak sweetbreads in water to cover for 10 minutes; trim. Break into 1-inch chunks. Cook bacon until partially tender; wrap sweetbreads with bacon. Spread mushroom caps lightly with butter. Place sweetbreads and mushrooms alternately on skewers; place skewers over edges of narrow baking pan. Bake for 10 minutes. Yield: 2 servings.

Sweet Potato

The sweet potato is a palatably sweet root vegetable. A native to the Americas, it thrives primarily in warm climates where the growing season is lengthy. Sweet potatoes are of two types: the dry-fleshed variety and moist-fleshed variety commonly marketed as yams. Genuine yams, grown only in the tropics, are entirely different than this variety of sweet potato. The *dry-fleshed* sweet potato has yellow fawn-colored skin and yellow-orange pulp. Some popular varieties are Big Stem, Yellow Jersey, and Maryland Golden. The *moist-fleshed yams* are sweeter and more popular. The skin is orange, pale rose, or copper red; the pulp is orange to red. Popular varieties are Porto Rican, Nancy Hall, and Nancy Gold. Sweet potatoes are a substantial source of food energy, Vitamins A and C, calcium, and iron. (1 baked sweet potato = 155 calories)

AVAILABILITY: Sweet potatoes are usually available year-round with marked seasonal variation. The greatest supply is from September through December with a gradual decline thereafter to a low point during June and July. Canned, frozen, and dehydrated sweet potato products are also available.

BUYING: Select smooth, well-shaped specimens whose skins are bright and uniformly colored. Avoid sweet potatoes with growth cracks or evidence of injury or decay. Allow 4 to 6 sweet potatoes for 4 average servings.

STORING: Sweet potatoes are quite perishable. Purchase a quantity that can be used in about 1 week. Store them in a cool, dry place at 55 to 60 degrees. *To freeze*—Boil sweet potatoes in jackets until nearly tender. Drain and cool at room temperature. Peel; halve, slice, or mash. Dip halves or slices in solution of 1 quart water and 1/2 cup lemon juice. Mix 2 tablespoons orange or lemon juice into mashed potatoes. Pack into freezer containers leaving 1/2-inch head space. Seal, label and freeze. Do not store frozen sweet potatoes more than 3 months.

PREPARATION: Sweet potatoes may be boiled, mashed, fried, baked, candied, and glazed. It is advisable whenever possible to cook sweet potatoes in their jackets in order to preserve the delicate sweetness. Consult specific recipes for further cooking information. *To boil*—Scrub skins well. Cook sweet potatoes in boiling salted water to cover for 30 to 55 minutes. Drain at once. Peel, mash if desired, and season to taste. *To bake*—Grease the skins of clean sweet potatoes. Bake in a 425 degree oven for 35 to 60 minutes.

USES: Sweet potatoes are a favorite main dish accompaniment in place of pasta or white potatoes. They can also be made into luscious dessert foods: pies, custards, cookies, and cakes.

(See VEGETABLES.)

FRUITED SWEET POTATOES

1 1-lb. 2-oz. can sweet potatoes
1/2 1-lb. can sliced peaches
1/2 1-lb. can apricots
1/2 c. miniature marshmallows
2 tbsp. brown sugar
1 tbsp. butter

Slice sweet potatoes. Drain peaches; reserve 1/2 cup syrup. Drain apricots; reserve 1/2 cup syrup. Alternate layers of potatoes and fruits in 1 1/2-quart casserole, mixing in several marshmallows. Blend brown sugar and reserved fruit syrups; pour over layers. Top with remaining marshmallows; dot with butter. Bake in 350-degree oven for 15 to 20 minutes or until golden brown. Yield: 6-8 servings.

GLAZED BAKED SWEET POTATOES

4 lge. sweet potatoes, peeled
3/4 c. (packed) brown sugar
6 tbsp. butter
1/2 tsp. salt
1/2 c. pecan halves

Cook sweet potatoes in water to cover in saucepan for 15 minutes or until nearly tender. Drain; halve potatoes lengthwise. Arrange in greased baking dish. Mix 3 tablespoons boiling water, brown sugar, butter and salt in saucepan; cook for 3 minutes. Pour over potatoes; top with pecans. Bake at 350 degrees for 30 minutes. Yield: 8-10 servings.

APPLE-YAM-PINEAPPLE TURBANS

4 3/4-in. peeled yam slices
8 3/4-in. cored Washington apple slices
4 lge. pineapple slices
4 1 1/2-in. squares of cabbage
French dressing
Parsley sprigs

Brush yam, apple, pineapple slices and cabbage squares with French dressing. Cut heavy-duty foil into eight 9-inch squares; arrange pineapple slices on half the foil squares. Place cabbage squares on remaining foil. Layer 1 yam slice and 1 apple slice on pineapple. Top cabbage with remaining apple slices. Double-fold foil across top; double-fold open ends toward center of each packet. Place foil packets in 1 inch boiling water in large saucepan. Cover; simmer for about 20 minutes. Remove from foil; place stacks on platter. Garnish with parsley. Yield: 8 servings.

Apple-Yam-Pineapple Turbans . . . A colorful fruit and vegetable dish of red, orange, and yellow.

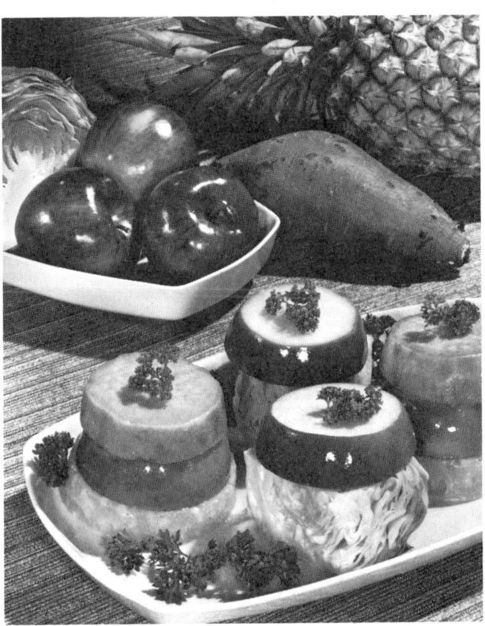

JAMAICAN YAM CASSEROLE

1 1-lb. can yams, drained
1/2 med. banana, sliced
1/4 c. orange juice
1/2 tsp. salt
1/8 tsp. pepper
2 tbsp. chopped pecans
2 tbsp. toasted flaked coconut

Preheat oven to 350 degrees. Place yams in greased 1-quart casserole; arrange banana slices over yams. Pour juice over layers. Sprinkle with salt and pepper. Top with pecans and coconut. Bake, covered, for 30 minutes. Yield: 2 servings.

MERINGUE-TOPPED YAMS

2 c. cooked whipped yams
1 egg, separated
2 tbsp. butter
2 tbsp. (about) sugar
1/2 tsp. salt
1 tsp. cinnamon

Preheat oven to 350 degrees. Mix yams and beaten egg yolk until smooth; blend in butter, sugar, salt and cinnamon. Place in greased pie pan. Beat egg white and additional sugar to taste together until stiff peaks form. Spread meringue on top of yam mixture. Bake for 30 minutes or until meringue is lightly browned. Yield: 4-5 servings.

PRALINE SWEET POTATO CASSEROLE

4 c. mashed sweet potatoes
Melted butter
Packed brown sugar
1/3 c. light cream
2 tsp. brandy extract
1 tsp. salt
1/8 tsp. pepper
1 tsp. grated orange peel
1/2 tsp. ginger
1 tsp. cinnamon
1/4 tsp. allspice
1/2 c. chopped pecans

Combine sweet potatoes, 3 tablespoons melted butter, 1/4 cup brown sugar, cream, brandy extract, salt, pepper, orange peel, ginger, 1/2 teaspoon cinnamon and allspice; mix well. Spoon into greased 2-quart shallow baking dish. Combine 1/3 cup brown sugar, pecans, 1/4 cup melted butter and remaining cinnamon. Stir until blended thoroughly. Spread brown sugar mixture over potato mixture. Bake in 350-degree oven for 30 minutes.

SWEET POTATO CASSEROLE

1 lge. can sweet potatoes
3 eggs, beaten
1 c. butter, melted
1/2 c. (packed) brown sugar
1 1/2 c. sugar
1/2 tsp. nutmeg
3 c. corn flakes, crumbled
1 c. chopped pecans

Drain potatoes; reserve 1/2 cup potato liquid. Combine potatoes, reserved liquid, eggs, 1/2 cup butter, brown sugar, sugar and nutmeg. Mix thoroughly; turn into greased baking dish. Bake at 300 degrees for 15 minutes. Combine corn flakes, remaining butter and pecans. Spread corn flake mixture over sweet potatoes. Bake for 15 minutes longer.

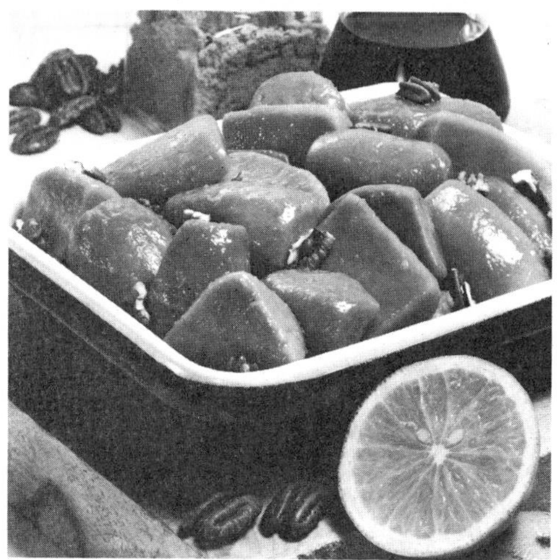

Louisiana Yams a La Francaise . . . Elegant sweet potatoes prepared in a traditional southern way.

LOUISIANA YAMS A LA FRANCAISE

1/2 c. (packed) light brown sugar
1 tbsp. cornstarch
1/4 tsp. salt
Grated rind and juice of 1 orange
3 tbsp. cream sherry
1/4 c. butter
4 med. cooked Louisiana yams
1/2 c. chopped pecans

Mix brown sugar, cornstarch, salt, orange rind and juice together in saucepan. Bring to a boil over medium heat, stirring constantly. Add sherry and butter, stirring until butter melts. Peel and quarter yams. Place yams in casserole; sprinkle with pecans. Pour orange syrup over yams, turning once to coat well. Bake in 350-degree oven for 15 to 20 minutes or until yams are heated through and glazed. Two drained 16-ounce cans Louisiana yams may be substituted for fresh yams if desired. Yield: 4-6 servings.

SWEET POTATOES DENISE

6 cooked sweet potatoes
1 1/2 c. whole cranberry sauce
3 tbsp. dry sherry
1/4 tsp. nutmeg
1/4 c. (packed) brown sugar
2 tbsp. butter
1/4 c. chopped pecans
1/4 c. raisins

Peel and slice sweet potatoes. Combine cranberry sauce, sherry, 1/2 cup water, nutmeg and brown sugar in saucepan. Bring to a boil; cook over low heat for 5 minutes. Stir in butter until melted. Arrange sweet potatoes, pecans and raisins in greased casserole; pour sauce over top. Bake in 350-degree oven for 25 minutes. Yield: 6-8 servings.

SWEET POTATO-ORANGE CASSEROLE

1 orange
3 c. cooked sweet potato slices
4 tsp. butter
1 c. miniature marshmallows

Cut unpeeled orange into slices; quarter each slice. Arrange layers of potatoes and orange in greased casserole. Dot with butter. Bake at 350 degrees for 20 minutes. Sprinkle with marshmallows. Bake until marshmallows are lightly browned and melted.

SWEET POTATO PONE

2 1/2 c. grated uncooked sweet potatoes
1 c. sugar
1 tbsp. grated orange rind
2 eggs, beaten
1 tsp. nutmeg
2 tbsp. butter, melted
1 c. chopped nuts
1/4 tsp. cinnamon
3/4 c. milk

Blend all ingredients together; place in greased casserole. Top with additional butter. Bake in 350-degree oven for 45 minutes or until golden brown. Yield: 6 servings.

SWEET POTATO SOUFFLÉ

1 No. 2 can crushed pineapple
2 uncooked sweet potatoes, grated
1 1/2 c. sugar
1 c. raisins
1 c. chopped nuts
3/8 c. butter
1 tsp. vanilla
1 c. milk
Marshmallows

Drain pineapple; combine pineapple and remaining ingredients except marshmallows. Pour into greased casserole. Bake at 350 degrees for 35 minutes. Top with marshmallows. Bake for 10 minutes longer. Yield: 8-10 servings.

SWEET POTATO SURPRISE

1 1-lb. can sweet potato halves
1 1/4 c. (packed) brown sugar
1/4 tsp. salt
1 tsp. shredded orange peel
1 1/2 tbsp. cornstarch
1/8 tsp. cinnamon
1 1-lb. can apricot halves
2 tbsp. margarine
1/2 c. chopped pecans

Place sweet potatoes in greased 10 x 6 x 1 1/2-inch dish. Combine brown sugar, salt, orange peel, cornstarch and cinnamon in saucepan. Drain apricots; reserve 1 cup syrup. Arrange apricots over sweet potatoes. Stir reserved syrup into brown sugar mixture; bring to a boil over medium heat, stirring constantly. Cook for 2 minutes; add margarine and pecans. Pour sauce over apricots. Bake at 375 degrees for 25 minutes. Yield: 6 servings.

SWEET POTATOES WITH ORANGE SAUCE

1 unpeeled orange, quartered
3/4 c. sugar
3/4 c. cinnamon candies
8 med. sweet potatoes
1 tsp. salt
1/2 tsp. cinnamon
2 tbsp. butter
1/2 c. shredded coconut

Grind orange sections; add sugar, candies and 3/4 cup water. Cook in saucepan, stirring frequently, until candies are dissolved. Bring potatoes to a boil in salted water; cook until tender. Drain, peel and halve sweet potatoes. Place potatoes in greased baking dish; sprinkle with salt and cinnamon. Dot with butter; cover with orange syrup. Bake at 350 degrees for 20 minutes, basting occasionally. Turn potatoes in syrup; sprinkle with coconut. Bake for 10 minutes longer. Yield: 8-10 servings.

SWEET POTATOES WITH SAUSAGE TOPPING

2 17-oz. cans sweet potatoes
1 8-oz. can pineapple tidbits
1 lb. pork sausage
1 tbsp. salt
1/4 c. raisins

Drain and mash potatoes; drain pineapple. Brown sausage in skillet; drain off fat. Mix potatoes, salt, raisins and pineapple; pour into 1 1/2-quart baking dish. Place sausage on top. Bake at 350 degrees for 20 to 25 minutes. Yield: 6 servings.

COCONUT-BROILED LOUISIANA YAMS

8 med. cooked yams
1 1/2 c. shredded coconut
1/2 c. (packed) brown sugar
1/4 c. butter
1/4 c. heavy cream
1/4 c. maraschino cherries

Peel and halve yams. Arrange in greased shallow 2-quart casserole; sprinkle with 1 cup coconut. Combine brown sugar, butter and cream; pour over yams. Top with remaining coconut and cherries. Broil 4 to 5 inches from source of heat for 4 minutes or until coconut is lightly browned. Yield: 8 servings.

FRENCH-FRIED SWEET POTATO CHIPS

3 sweet potatoes, peeled
Confectioners' sugar

Cut potatoes to 1-inch strips; cover with cold salted water. Soak for 30 minutes; drain and dry. Fry in hot deep fat. Sprinkle with sugar.

GLAZED SWEET POTATOES

2 1-lb. cans sweet potatoes
2 3-oz. packages orange gelatin
1/2 c. (packed) light brown sugar
Dash of salt
2 tbsp. butter

Drain sweet potatoes. Dissolve gelatin, brown sugar and salt in 2 cups boiling water in skillet. Add butter; bring to a full boil, stirring constantly. Add sweet potatoes; cook over medium heat for 15 minutes, basting frequently, until syrup is thick and glossy. Serve hot. Yield: 6-8 servings.

SWEET POTATO CRUMB BALLS

1 can sweet potatoes, drained
1 tsp. brown sugar
Melted butter
Salt and pepper
Bread crumbs

Mash sweet potatoes; add brown sugar, 1 tablespoon butter and seasonings. Chill well. Form into balls; roll in bread crumbs. Fry in butter in skillet until crumbs are browned. Yield: 6 servings.

SWEET POTATO ROLLS

1 c. cooked mashed sweet potatoes
Melted butter
1 pkg. dry yeast
1 egg
Salt
3 tbsp. sugar
5 c. sifted flour
1 c. powdered sugar
3 tbsp. orange juice
1 tbsp. grated orange rind

Mix sweet potatoes and 3 tablespoons butter. Dissolve yeast in 1/2 cup warm water; add to sweet potato mixture. Add egg, 1 teaspoon salt and sugar; blend well. Add flour alternately with 3/4 cup warm water. Turn onto floured board; knead well. Place in greased bowl; cover. Let rise for 2 hours or until doubled in bulk; roll out on floured board to desired thickness. Cut into desired shapes; brush with melted butter. Place on greased cookie sheet or in muffin pans; let rise for 1 hour or until doubled in bulk. Bake at 425 degrees for 15 minutes. Combine powdered sugar, orange juice, orange rind and dash of salt; spread on hot rolls. Yield: 10 servings.

LOUISIANA YAMS WITH GRAPES

1/4 c. butter
1/3 c. (packed) dark brown sugar
1/2 tsp. grated lemon peel
2 tbsp. lemon juice
4 med. cooked Louisiana yams
1 1/2 c. halved dark grapes, seeded

Melt butter in large skillet; stir in brown sugar, lemon peel and juice. Heat until blended and bubbling. Peel yams; cut into thick slices. Add yams and grapes to hot syrup. Cook, partially covered, over medium heat for 8 to 10 minutes, turning yams once.

Louisiana Yams with Grapes . . . For a party dish, feature these candied sweet potatoes and grapes.

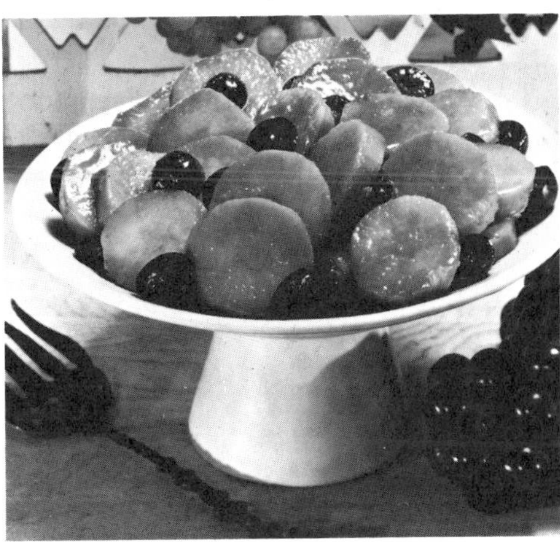

SWEET POTATO CROQUETTES

5 med. sweet potatoes, cooked
2 tbsp. sugar
2 tbsp. butter
1 tsp. lemon juice
6 marshmallows
2 egg whites, slightly beaten
2 c. crushed corn flakes

Peel potatoes; mash. Add sugar, butter and lemon juice, blending well. Shape some potato mixture around each marshmallow; chill for 1 hour. Dip into egg whites; roll in corn flakes. Fry in deep fat at 375 degrees until golden brown. Drain; serve at once. Yield: 6 servings.

SWEET POTATOES IN APPLE CUPS

4 sweet potatoes, cooked
3 tbsp. butter
1/4 tsp. salt
2 tbsp. sugar
4 red cooking apples
4 marshmallows

Mash potatoes; add butter, salt and sugar. Scoop out insides of apples, leaving 1/2-inch shell. Fill apple shells with mashed potatoes. Place in baking dish. Bake at 325 degrees for 15 minutes or until apples are tender. Place marshmallows on top; return to oven. Bake until brown. Yield: 4 servings.

SWEET POTATOES IN ORANGE BASKETS

12 oranges
10 med. sweet potatoes
1/2 c. butter
2 egg whites

Cut oranges in half, leaving strip of rind across top to form handle. Hollow out insides; reserve 1/2 cup juice. Cook potatoes in small amount of water until tender; drain. Peel and mash. Stir in butter and reserved orange juice. Beat egg whites until stiff peaks form; fold into potato mixture. Heap potato mixture in orange baskets; place in baking pan. Bake in 350-degree oven for about 10 minutes or until heated through. Yield: 12 servings.

TRADITIONAL CANDIED YAMS

10 sm. yams
1 c. butter, melted
1 pkg. brown sugar
1 c. chopped pecans

Place yams on baking sheet. Bake at 425 degrees for about 45 minutes or until tender; peel. Place half the butter in small mixing bowl; soak yams in butter for about 5 minutes. Combine brown sugar and pecans; roll yams in pecan mixture. Place yams in shallow casserole; pour remaining butter over yams. Sprinkle with remaining brown sugar mixture. Bake at 350 degrees until slightly brown and syrupy. Yield: 6 servings.

KENTUCKY BOURBON YAMS

2 No. 2 1/2 cans yams
1 c. (packed) brown sugar
2 tbsp. butter
2 tbsp. milk
1/4 c. bourbon
Marshmallows

Heat yams in yam liquid in saucepan over low heat; drain. Mash until light and fluffy; add all remaining ingredients except marshmallows. Turn into 1-quart casserole; top with marshmallows. Bake at 350 degrees for 15 minutes. Yield: 4-6 servings.

OLD-FASHIONED SWEET POTATO PUDDING

2 eggs, beaten
1/3 c. sugar
1/2 tsp. salt
3/4 tsp. allspice
1/4 tsp. cloves
1/4 c. dark syrup
2 c. milk, hot
2 c. grated sweet potatoes
1/3 c. butter

Combine eggs, sugar, salt, spices and syrup. Mix milk, sweet potatoes and butter; cook until sweet potatoes are heated through. Add to syrup mixture; blend well. Pour into greased baking dish. Bake at 300 degrees for 2 hours. Serve warm with light cream or whipped cream, if desired.

SWEET POTATO SALAD

1 lge. can sweet potatoes
4 hard-boiled eggs, chopped
1 med. onion, chopped fine
1 c. chopped celery
1 tsp. salt
1/8 tsp. pepper
1/4 salad dressing
1/4 c. Durkee's dressing

Drain sweet potatoes; mash. Mix sweet potatoes, eggs, onion, celery, salt, pepper, salad dressing and Durkee's dressing. Refrigerate for at least 6 hours or overnight.

SWEET POTATO DROP COOKIES

1 c. shortening
1 1/4 c. sugar
1 egg, beaten
2 c. mashed sweet potatoes
2 c. sifted flour
4 tsp. baking powder
1 tsp. salt
1 tsp. cinnamon
1 tsp. cloves
1/2 tsp. nutmeg
1/2 c. raisins

Cream shortening and sugar; add egg, sweet potatoes, dry ingredients and raisins. Drop from spoon onto lightly greased cookie sheet. Bake at 375 degrees for 15 minutes.

Table Settings and Service

An attractive, well-set table that is appropriate to the occasion helps greatly in making mealtimes relaxed, enjoyable occasions. In this section, table settings and service ranging from very formal to informal are described and illustrated. The information contained here has been developed over the years based on the principles of efficiency and consideration for others. Knowing what to do in any mealtime situation is an aid not only to your own well-being but to that of your fellow diners.

EQUIPMENT: Basic equipment for table setting and service includes linen, glasses, flatware, and dishes. Linen ranges from plastic mats to fine lace and damask tablecloths and napkins. Glasses may be made of plastic, crystal, or a variety of other materials. Flatware may be stainless steel or silver. Dishes may be made from translucent bone china, porcelain, pottery, or plastic as well as many other materials. The type and quantity of linen, glasses, flatware, and dishes you choose depend to a large extent on the kind of meals you serve and how much entertaining you do.

TABLE SETTINGS: Settings may range from formal to casual. The former are often used for special dinner or luncheon parties while the latter tend to be used for most other meals. A third method of setting is the buffet.

Formal dinner setting–The table is covered with a lace or linen cloth that hangs 9 to 15 inches over the table edge on all sides. Napkins are folded once the long way and twice the short way to form a rectangle as shown in the illustration below.

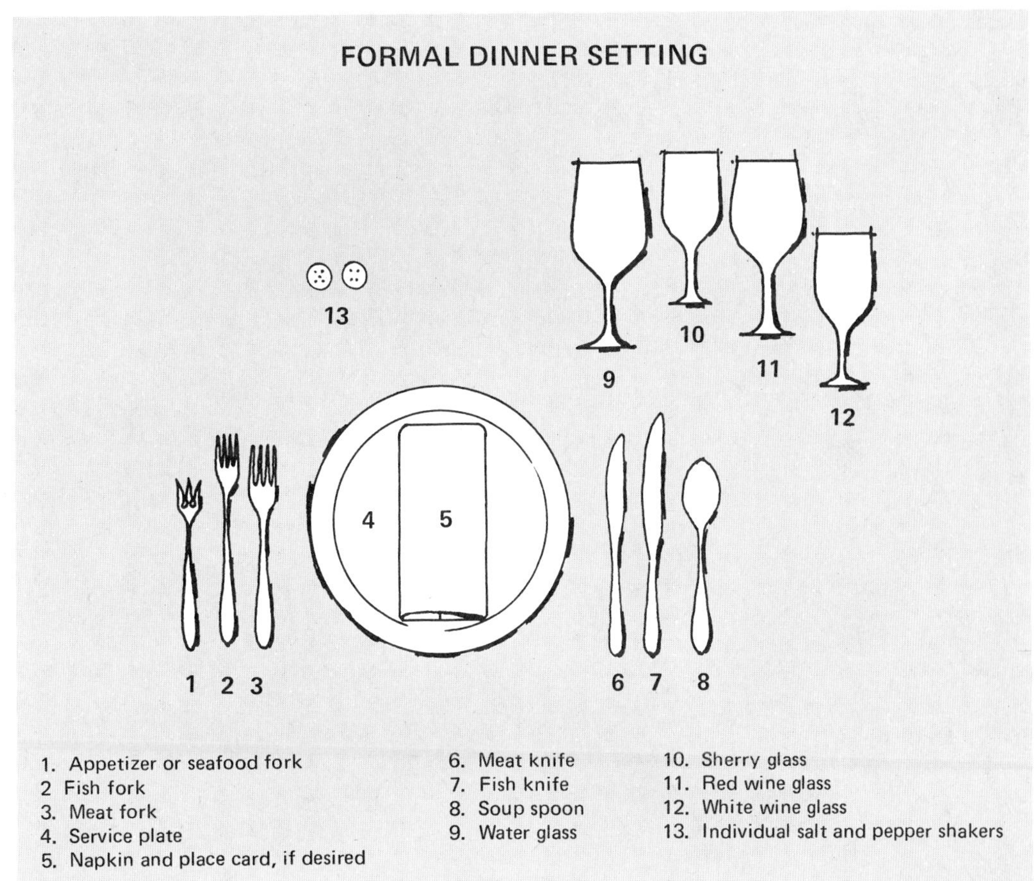

1. Appetizer or seafood fork
2 Fish fork
3. Meat fork
4. Service plate
5. Napkin and place card, if desired
6. Meat knife
7. Fish knife
8. Soup spoon
9. Water glass
10. Sherry glass
11. Red wine glass
12. White wine glass
13. Individual salt and pepper shakers

Silver is placed about one inch from the table edge, and about 18 to 24 inches of dining space is allowed each guest. Silver is always used for formal occasions; stainless steel is not appropriate. The diner uses the pieces on the outside first, working his way in as the meal progresses. As a general rule, not more than three pieces of silverware are set to each side of the service plate. In the above illustration, provision has been made for seafood appetizer, soup, fish, and meat courses. In some parts of the country, the salad course replaces one or the other of these courses. If it replaces the seafood appetizer, then the fork for that course is replaced by a salad fork. If it replaces the soup course, the seafood appetizer fork takes the place of the soup spoon, and the salad fork replaces the seafood fork. Formal dinners are served by servants who clear the utensils, plates, and glasses at the completion of each course. At the end of the meat course, only the water glass remains on the table. The table is cleared of crumbs and the dessert course laid as illustrated below.

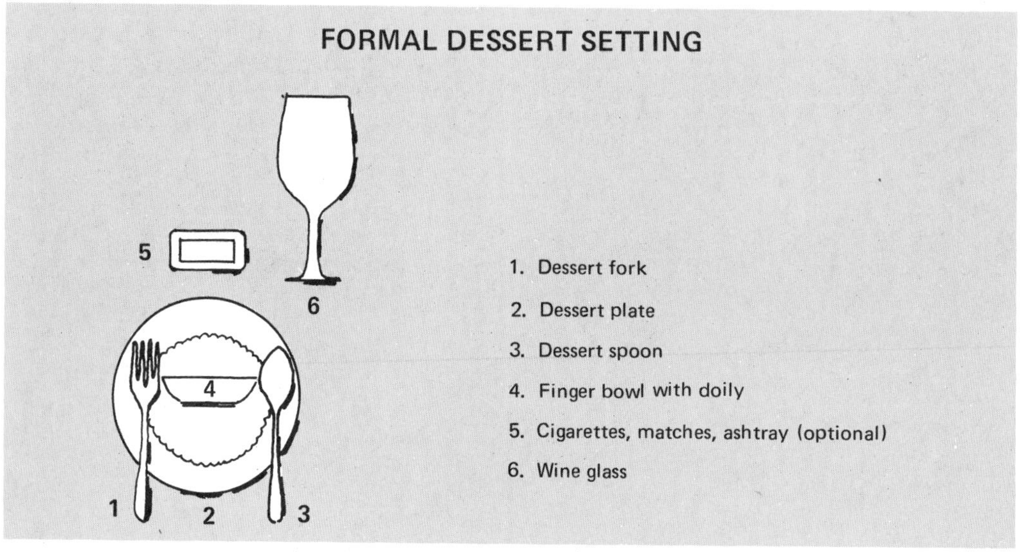

The guest uses the fingerbowl, then removes it and the doily beneath it to the upper left-hand corner of his place. He places the fork to the left of the dessert plate and the spoon to its right and awaits the serving of dessert. If coffee accompanies the dessert course, it is served demitasse with the spoon in place on the saucer and to the right of the cup handle. *Formal luncheon setting*—The setting is much the same as for a formal dinner with the silverware laid one inch in from the table's edge and about 18-24 inches of space allowed each diner. The silverware and dishes used vary, as shown in the illustration below.

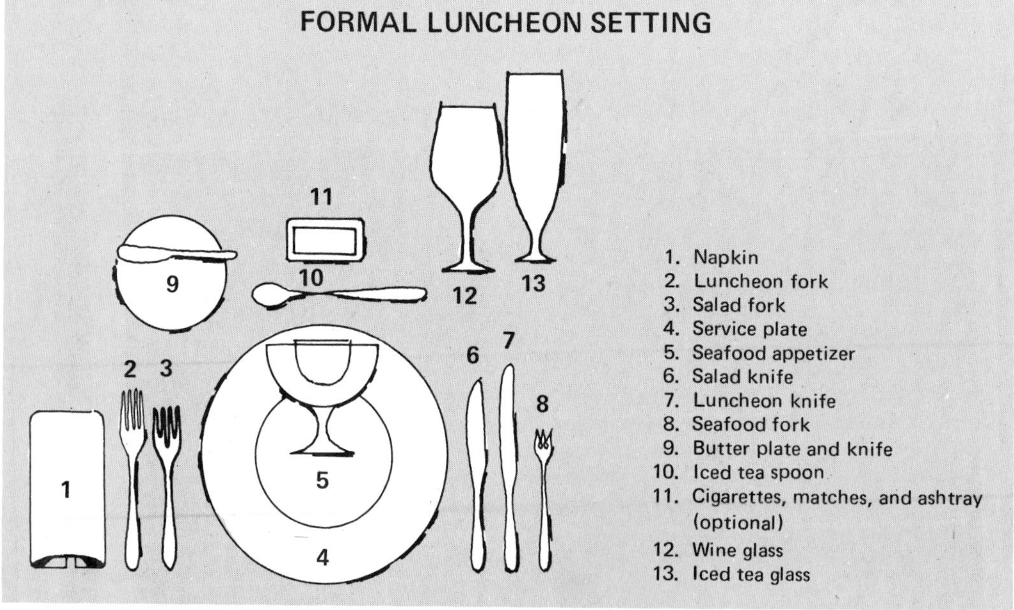

The salad knife and fork may be omitted if there is no salad course. If your local preference is for salads before the main course, reverse the positions of the salad and luncheon forks and knives. If dessert is served as a separate course, follow the serving instructions given under *formal dinner setting. Informal meal settings*—The dishes and silverware used in these settings will be determined by the meal being served and whether it is breakfast, luncheon, or dinner. As a general rule, set a breakfast table as shown below.

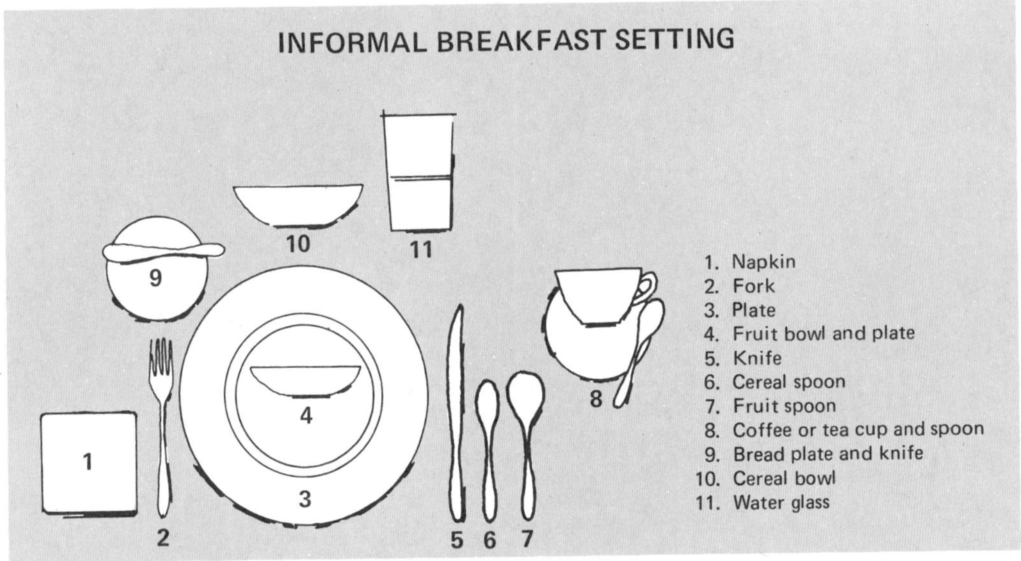

If there is fruit juice, the fruit bowl and plate (4) are replaced by a second glass placed to the right of the water glass (11). The cereal bowl (10) is on the table only if it contains cold cereal. Hot cereals are served directly from the kitchen. The informal luncheon setting is a combination of the breakfast and dinner settings, using dishes, glasses, and flatware appropriate to the foods being served. The informal dinner setting varies according to number and type of courses. The basic setting when the guests gather as illustrated below.

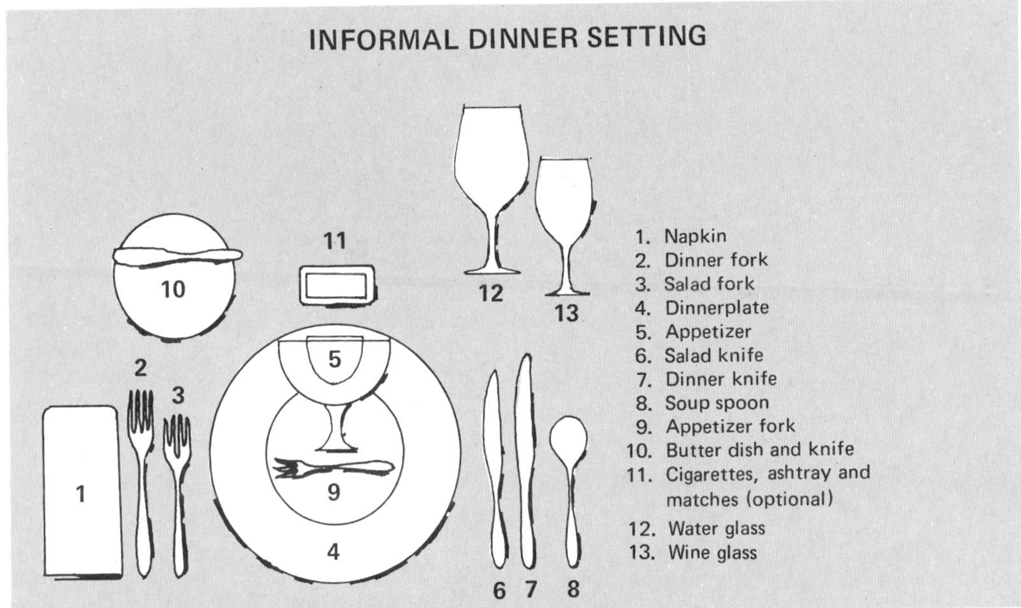

The positions of the salad knife and fork should be reversed if you prefer to serve the salad before dinner. If there are no soup or appetizer courses planned, implements for these courses would be removed. *Buffet setting*—For large parties, buffet service is best. It can range from very formal to casual. The linens, glasses, flatware, and dishes used as well as the table appointments determine the formality of the occasion. Buffet guests eat their meal seated at small tables, around a large table, or just scattered throughout the room or rooms in which the party is being given. Generally, when guests are seated the party is more formal than if they are scattered. As shown in the illustration below, food, dishes, silver, napkins, and coffee are spread on a large table. Each guest helps himself, beginning by picking up a plate and proceeding clockwise around the table, ultimately ending by selecting his silver and napkin. If the buffet table is against one wall, the coffee, cups, cream, sugar, silver, and napkins may be set up at a smaller table. Following the main course, guests return to the original or another buffet table that has been set up for dessert.

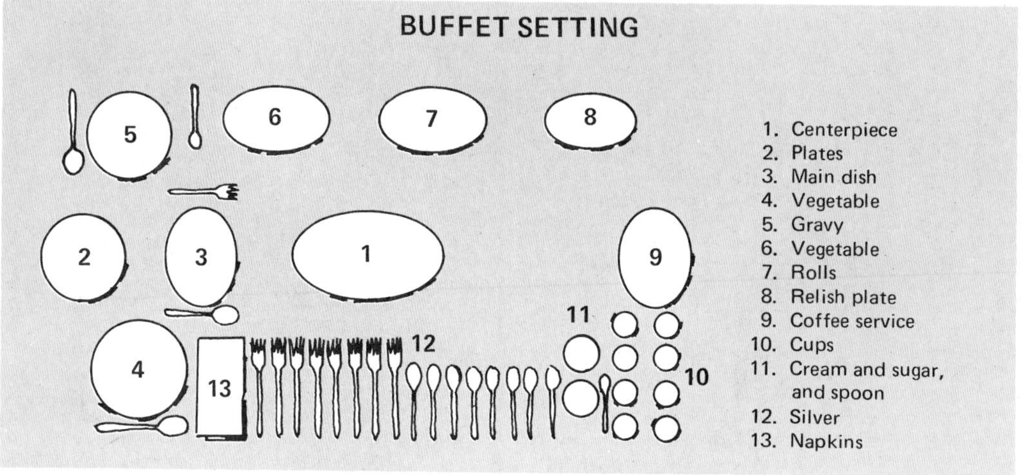

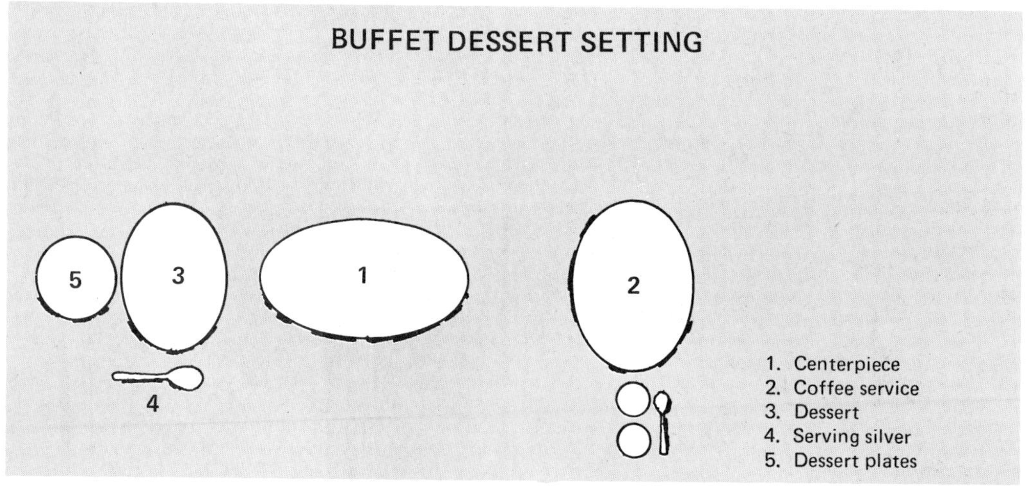

They begin by picking up a dessert plate and move around the table, helping themselves to dessert and to coffee or tea, if desired.

TABLE SERVICE: There are four basic ways of serving meals. One, *buffet,* has been included in **TABLE SETTINGS**, above. The other three are American or family style, English style, and Russian style. *American or family style*—This is the least formal way of serving meals. Foods are already on the table, either at an individual's place or in serving dishes. If serving dishes are used, they are passed to each person in turn. When using this type of service, it is customary to wait until everyone has been served before beginning to eat. *English Style*–In this slightly more formal way of serving, the host and hostess serve their guests. The host carves the meat, fish, or poultry, and fills each plate from a stack of plates he has close at hand. He then passes each plate to the hostess who fills it with vegetables and passes it to the guests, beginning with the first person on the hostess' right. When this style of serving is used, guests either wait until everyone has been served to begin eating or eat as soon as they have received their plates, whichever is the local custom. *Russian style*–This formal style of serving is used with the very formal table setting described in the first part of this section. You will need about one servant for every six people to be served. The servants serve the food from the left of each guest and remove the plates from his right. Servants should always be certain that the handles of any serving implement faces the guests. Wines are served during the various courses. Water glasses are kept about 3/4 full. Servants should keep a folded napkin in their left hands to catch drops when pouring. In Russian style service, a guest eats as soon as he is served.

Taffy

CREAMY TAFFY

2 c. sugar
2 c. cream
2 c. light corn syrup
1 env. unflavored gelatin
1/3 bar paraffin, finely cut
1/2 tsp. vanilla

Combine sugar, cream and syrup in heavy kettle; bring to a rolling boil. Dissolve gelatin in 1/4 cup water. Add to sugar mixture. Add paraffin; stir in vanilla. Cook to 250 degrees on candy thermometer, stirring constantly. Pour mixture into large well-greased shallow pan; cool until able to handle. Pull taffy with well-greased hands until cool and firm; shape into long pieces. Snip into bite-sized pieces.

JUST TAFFY

2 c. sugar
2 tbsp. butter
5 tbsp. vinegar

Combine sugar, 1/2 cup hot water and butter in saucepan; bring to a boil. Add vinegar; boil to hard-crack stage or 300 degrees on candy thermometer. Pour onto greased platter; cool enough to handle. Pull over and over; cut into 1-inch pieces with buttered scissors.

EASY TAFFY

2 c. sugar
1 tbsp. white vinegar

Combine sugar, vinegar and 1 cup water in saucepan. Stir until sugar dissolves. Cook to hard-crack stage or to 275 degrees on candy thermometer. Pour out on well-greased platter. Pull edges to center and centers out with well-greased hands. Pull until taffy is white; cut into bite-sized pieces.

MAPLE TAFFY

1 c. maple-blended syrup
1 3/4 c. corn syrup
2 tbsp. butter
1 tbsp. vinegar
1/4 tsp. soda
1 tsp. vanilla

Combine first 4 ingredients in saucepan; bring to a boil over medium heat, stirring until blended. Cook to hard-ball stage or 265 degrees on candy thermometer. Remove from heat; add soda and vanilla. Beat until smooth and creamy. Pour into shallow greased pan. Cool enough to handle. Pull strips 3/4 inch in diameter with lightly buttered hands; cut strips into 1-inch pieces with scissors. Wrap each piece in waxed paper.

MOLASSES TAFFY

1 1/8 c. (packed) light brown sugar
1/4 c. butter
1/4 c. molasses
1 tbsp. vinegar
1 c. chopped nuts

Combine sugar, butter, molasses, vinegar and 2 tablespoons water in a large pan. Cook quickly over high heat, without stirring, to hard-crack stage or 275 degrees on candy thermometer. Add nuts and quickly pour into buttered pan. Cool and break into pieces.

SALT WATER TAFFY

2 1/2 c. sugar
1 1/4 c. white corn syrup
1 tbsp. butter
2 tsp. salt
Food coloring
2 drops peppermint oil

Combine sugar, syrup and 2 cups water in saucepan; bring to a boil, stirring constantly. Boil without stirring, until temperature reaches 250 degrees on candy thermometer. Remove from heat; add butter and salt. Pour out onto buttered platters; cool enough to handle. Drop food coloring and flavoring on top; pull until candy glistens and hardens. Cut into bite-sized pieces; wrap in waxed paper.

Tangerine

TANGERINE-WALNUT TOSS

1 head lettuce, shredded
2 c. tangerine sections
1/2 onion, sliced
1/3 c. Italian dressing
1 tbsp. butter, melted
1/4 tsp. salt
1/2 c. walnut halves

Combine lettuce, tangerine, onion and dressing; toss together lightly. Combine butter, salt and walnut halves in skillet over low heat. Stir until walnuts are crisp. Top with walnuts.

TANGERINE CHIFFON CAKE

1 3/4 c. sugar
1 c. shortening
5 eggs
2 c. cake flour
5 tbsp. tangerine juice
1 tbsp. vanilla
1/4 tsp. salt

Cream sugar and shortening; add one egg at a time, beating well after each addition. Add 1 cup flour; beat for 2 minutes. Add tangerine juice, vanilla, salt and remaining flour; beat for 2 minutes longer. Pour into 10-inch greased and floured tube pan. Bake in 350-degree oven for 1 hour.

TANGERINE SNOW

1 pkg. low calorie orange flavored gelatin
3/4 c. tangerine juice
1/4 tsp. liquid sweetener
1 egg white, beaten

Dissolve gelatin in 1/4 cup hot water; add tangerine juice and sweetener. Chill until slightly thickened. Place bowl containing gelatin mixture in larger bowl of ice and water; whip until fluffy and thick. Fold in egg white; pour into 4 individual molds. Chill until firm; unmold.

TANGERINE CREME

1 can frozen tangerine juice concentrate
1 c. heavy cream, whipped
2 egg whites
1/2 c. sugar

Fold undiluted tangerine concentrate into whipped cream. Beat egg whites until soft peaks form; add sugar, gradually, beating until stiff peaks form. Fold into whipped cream mixture. Pour into 1-quart refrigerator tray; freeze until firm.

BAKED TANGERINES

6 Florida tangerines
2 tbsp. sugar
2 tbsp. butter
2/3 c. orange juice
Orange Cranberry Relish

Cut 8 vertical slits in tangerine skin from blossom end to about 1 inch from bottom. Pull peel down; turn pointed ends in. Remove white membrane. Loosen sections at center; pull apart slightly. Fill each center with 1 teaspoon sugar; dot with 1 teaspoon butter. Place tangerines in baking pan; pour orange juice over tangerines. Bake in 325-degree oven for 30 minutes. Spoon small amount of Orange Cranberry Relish in center of each tangerine. Yield: 6 servings.

Orange Cranberry Relish

2 Florida oranges
4 c. fresh cranberries
2 c. sugar

Quarter oranges; remove seeds. Process orange quarters with peel and cranberries through food chopper. Add sugar to mixture. Chill in refrigerator for several hours before serving. Yield: 1 quart.

TANGERINE CREAM MOUSSE

1 env. unflavored gelatin
1/4 c. sugar
1/8 tsp. salt
1 6-oz. can frozen Florida tangerine concentrate
1 c. heavy cream

Mix gelatin, sugar and salt in saucepan. Add 1/2 cup water; place over medium heat, stirring constantly, until gelatin, sugar and salt are dissolved. Remove from heat; stir in tangerine concentrate until melted. Chill to consistency of unbeaten egg white. Whip cream; fold into tangerine mixture. Turn into 4-cup mold; chill until firm. Unmold; garnish with tangerine sections.

Tangerine Orange Sauce

2 tsp. cornstarch
1/2 c. sugar
1/4 tsp. salt
1 c. Florida orange juice
2 Florida tangerines

Mix cornstarch, sugar and salt in saucepan. Stir in orange juice. Bring to a boil, stirring constantly until thickened. Cool. Section tangerines; remove seeds. Add tangerine sections to sauce. Serve sauce with mousse.

Tangerine Cream Mousse and Tangerine Orange Sauce . . . A tangy and light summer dessert.

TANGERINE SHERBET

1 c. sugar
Grated rind of 4 tangerines
4 c. tangerine juice
4 tbsp. lemon juice

Boil sugar and 1 1/2 cups water for 10 minutes. Add rind to hot syrup. Cool slightly; add tangerine and lemon juices. Add sugar if needed. Chill thoroughly; strain and freeze.

TANGERINE CUSTARD PUDDING

3 tangerines, peeled
Sugar
4 c. milk
3 tbsp. flour
3 eggs, separated
1 tsp. vanilla

Section tangerines; marinate in small amount of sugar. Let stand until ready to use. Simmer milk; do not boil. Mix flour, egg yolks and 1 cup sugar; add to milk gradually, stirring constantly. Cook to desired thickness. Pour into glass casserole; add vanilla. Stir in tangerine sections. Beat egg whites until stiff peaks form; use as topping. Brown in 450-degree oven quickly. Chill; serve cold.

TANGERINE PIE

1 3/8 c. sugar
1/4 c. cornstarch
1/4 tsp. salt
3 eggs, separated
2 tbsp. margarine
1/3 c. tangerine juice
1 1/2 tsp. grated tangerine rind
1 baked 9-in. pie shell

Combine 1/2 cup sugar, cornstarch and salt in double boiler; blend in water gradually. Cook over boiling water, stirring constantly, until thickened; cook, covered, for 10 minutes longer, stirring occasionally. Beat egg yolks and 1/2 cup sugar together; blend small amount of hot mixture into egg yolk mixture. Stir yolk mixture into remaining hot mixture in double boiler; cook over boiling water for 2 minutes, stirring constantly. Remove from heat; add margarine, juice and rind. Cool. Pour into pie shell. Beat egg whites and remaining sugar together until stiff peaks form; top filling with meringue. Bake at 350 degrees for 20 minutes. Yield: 6 servings.

Tomato

Botanically, tomatoes are large, pulpy red or yellow berries or fruit. In cooking they are prized as a colorful and nutritious vegetable. Tomatoes are believed to be native to Central or South America. They were not grown to any extent in the United States until the 1800's. Today tomatoes are produced in almost every state. Tomatoes are often described as "home-grown" or "beefsteak." Home-grown tomatoes are those that have been allowed to ripen fully on the vine; they are especially delicious. Beefsteak tomatoes are any exceptionally large, firm-fleshed tomatoes ideal for slicing, stuffing, and so on. Some familiar kinds of tomatoes are cherry, pear, and plum tomatoes. *Cherry tomatoes* are almost perfectly round and about the size of walnuts. *Pear tomatoes* are pear-shaped and usually considered sweeter than other types. *Plum tomatoes* are small and plum-shaped. Tomatoes contain significant amounts of Vitamins A and C. They also supply protein, iron, calcium, carbohydrates, thiamine, and niacin. (1 raw 7 ounce tomato = 40 calories; 1 cup canned tomato juice = 45 calories)

AVAILABILITY: Fresh tomatoes are available year-round. Greatest commercial supply is from May to October. July to September are peak months. From January to April, supplies are relatively low. Fresh tomatoes are usually sold by the pound, often in cellophane-wrapped cartons. Canned tomatoes and tomato juice, paste, and puree are sold year-round. Canned tomatoes are usually peeled and packed in their own juice. They may be whole or in pieces.

BUYING: Choose rich red, plump, smooth fresh tomatoes. Tomatoes that are less than fully ripe are firm and pink to light red in color. Select sizes and shapes of tomatoes depending on usage. Uniform, well-shaped, medium-sized tomatoes are good for slicing, stuffing, and halving and broiling. Rough or irregularly shaped tomatoes are satisfactory for use in beverages, casseroles, and so on but are not desirable for salads or stuffing. Avoid puffy or bruised tomatoes, or tomatoes with yellow areas or deep growth cracks. Tomatoes packed in cartons are difficult to examine. Check for moisture on bottom of carton, an indication of badly bruised or spoiled tomatoes. Buy 2 pounds or approximately 8 small tomatoes to serve 4 people.

STORING: Allow unripened tomatoes to mature at room temperature. To prevent bruising lay stem-end down on padded surface and do not stack. For quick ripening, place tomatoes in paper bag. Leave in dark, not damp, place 3 to 4 days. Do not ripen tomatoes in the sun; they will soften. Refrigerate fully ripened tomatoes for several days. Store unopened cans on kitchen shelf 1 year and opened cans in refrigerator about 4 days. *To freeze* fresh tomatoes—It is best to stew them first. Cool by placing saucepan in a larger pan filled with ice water. Package, label, date, and freeze. Use for cooking within 2 months. *To can* fresh tomatoes–Choose sound and ripe specimens. Wash. Cut out stem and peel (see PREPARATION below). Raw pack or hot pack according to instructions under CANNING.

PREPARATION: Tomatoes may be cooked in a variety of ways; see specific recipe directions for baking, broiling, frying, stewing, and so on. *To peel* tomatoes–Dip in boiling water 1/2 to 1 minute, until skins crack. Plunge into cold water. Cut out stem and slip off skins. Or hold tomato on fork over heat. Rotate until tomato wrinkles and splits. Pull off skin, cut out core. *To remove seeds*–Cut tomato crosswise and squeeze gently. *To remove juice*–Cut off stem end. Holding tomato in palm of hand with palm down over bowl, press tomato tightly to eject juice. Seeds will be ejected also. *To simmer* as a vegetable–Quarter tomatoes. Place in saucepan with finely chopped onion and sugar (1 to 2 teaspoons sugar for 6 to 8 tomatoes). Generally, no water is required. Cover saucepan. Simmer tomatoes 5 to 15 minutes.

SERVING: Serve tomatoes hot with celery salt, salt, pepper, butter. Or top with grated cheese. To juicy tomatoes add toasted bread cubes or buttered crumbs. Use raw tomatoes in salads and as garnishes. For salads, dress tomatoes separately and add as salad garnish to prevent tomato juice from thinning salad dressing. Or, slice tomatoes vertically for less bleeding. Use tomatoes also in canapes, aspics, catsup, relishes, soups, sauces, souffles, casseroles, main dishes, and so on. Pickle or fry unripe green tomatoes. Serve chilled tomato juice as an appetizer. Garnish with thin lemon slices or sprigs of fresh herbs such as parsley, basil, or thyme.

(See CANNING and VEGETABLES.)

HERBED TOMATOES

6 ripe tomatoes
2/3 c. vinegar
1/4 c. snipped parsley
1/4 c. sliced green onions
1 tsp. salt
1/4 tsp. pepper
1/2 tsp. thyme
1 clove of garlic, minced
2/3 c. salad oil

Peel tomatoes; place in deep bowl. Combine remaining ingredients in jar; cover. Shake well; pour over tomatoes. Chill, covered, overnight; spoon dressing over tomatoes occasionally.

FIRE AND ICE TOMATOES

6 lge. ripe tomatoes
1 lge. green pepper
1 red onion
3/4 c. vinegar
1 1/2 tsp. mustard seed
1 1/2 tsp. celery salt
1/2 tsp. salt
4 1/2 tsp. sugar
1/8 tsp. pepper
1 cucumber

Peel and quarter tomatoes; slice green pepper into strips. Slice onion; separate into rings. Place in bowl. Combine vinegar, mustard seed, celery salt, salt, sugar, pepper and 1/4 cup water in saucepan; bring to a boil. Boil for 1 minute. Pour over tomato mixture; cool. Peel and slice cucumber; add to tomato mixture. Serve as relish or side dish. Will keep refrigerated for several days.

TOMATO-CHEESE SPREAD

1 lb. sharp cheese
1 can tomato soup
1 can chopped mushrooms
1 med. onion, finely chopped
1 jar stuffed olives, sliced

Melt cheese in top of double boiler over boiling water; blend in soup, mushrooms and onion. Spread on small biscuits and top with olives. Broil 4 to 5 inches from source of heat just until cheese is lightly browned.

CREAM OF TOMATO SOUP

3 tbsp. butter
2 tbsp. flour
1 tsp. salt
1/8 tsp. pepper
2 c. strained tomatoes
1/4 tsp. soda
4 c. milk

Blend first 4 ingredients in heavy saucepan over low heat; add tomatoes. Cook for 5 minutes; add soda. Add milk; bring to a boil. Reduce heat; simmer for 5 minutes.

HOMEMADE TOMATO SOUP

7 qt. ripe tomatoes, chopped
7 stalks celery, chopped
7 sprigs of parsley, chopped
Green peppers to taste
5 med. onions, chopped
7 whole cloves
7 bay leaves
1 1/2 c. flour
1 1/2 c. sugar
4 tbsp. salt
2 tsp. paprika
3/4 c. butter

Combine first 7 ingredients in saucepan; cook until tender. Press through sieve. Bring to a boil. Combine remaining ingredients with 1 cup hot water; blend to a smooth paste. Add to tomato mixture; stir until well thickened. Pour into hot sterilized jars; seal.

OLD-FASHIONED TOMATO SOUP

2 c. spaghetti
1 qt. canned tomatoes
1/2 c. heavy cream
Salt and pepper to taste

Cook spaghetti according to package directions; drain. Add tomatoes; bring to a boil. Remove from heat; add cream, salt and pepper.

SPANISH GAZPACHO

1 clove of garlic, crushed
1/2 tsp. salt
2 tbsp. olive oil
5 ripe tomatoes, chopped
1 chopped onion
1/4 tsp. pepper
1/4 tsp. paprika
1 1/2 tbsp. vinegar
1 1/2 c. bouillon
1/4 c. dry bread crumbs

Mix all ingredients together except bread crumbs; refrigerate for at least 1 hour or overnight. Grind in food mill; add more salt, if needed. Add bread crumbs just before serving; pour into soup bowls. Place 1 ice cube in each bowl; serve with croutons, chopped green peppers and chopped cucumbers.

HORSERADISH-TOMATO ASPIC

1 pkg. lemon gelatin
1 c. hot tomato juice
2 tsp. prepared horseradish
1 c. cold tomato juice
2 tsp. grated onion
1 1/2 tsp. salt
Dash of cayenne
1/2 c. mayonnaise
1/2 c. sour cream
1/4 c. chili sauce

Dissolve gelatin in hot tomato juice; add remaining ingredients. Pour into shallow pan, 1/2-inch deep. Chill until firm. Cut into 1/2-inch cubes. Combine mayonnaise, sour cream and chili sauce; chill. Serve over salad.

TOMATO-VEGETABLE ASPIC

4 c. tomato juice
2 pkg. lemon gelatin
2 tbsp. lemon juice
1/8 tsp. hot sauce
1 tsp. Worcestershire sauce
1/4 tsp. salt
1/8 tsp. pepper
1 c. chopped celery
1/2 c. sliced stuffed green olives
1 c. sliced cucumber
1/4 c. chopped green onions

Heat 2 cups tomato juice in saucepan; stir in gelatin until dissolved. Stir in remaining tomato juice, lemon juice, hot sauce, Worcestershire sauce, salt and pepper; chill until partially congealed. Stir in celery, olives, cucumber and onions; turn into oiled mold. Chill until firm.

TOMATO ASPIC WITH CHEESE BALLS

2 tbsp. unflavored gelatin
3 1/2 c. canned tomatoes
2 tbsp. minced onion
1/2 bay leaf
1 stalk celery, minced
1/8 tsp. paprika
1/8 tsp. salt
2 tbsp. vinegar
1 lge. package cream cheese
Cream

Soften gelatin in 1/2 cup cold water for 5 minutes. Combine tomatoes, onion, bay leaf, celery, paprika and salt in saucepan. Bring to a boil; cook for 10 minutes. Add vinegar and gelatin; stir until gelatin is dissolved. Strain mixture into ring mold; chill until firm. Soften cream cheese with small amount of cream. Roll into balls; chill. Unmold aspic on lettuce; place cream cheese balls in center of ring.

TOMATO-CAVIAR SALAD

6 med. tomatoes, peeled
1 tsp. salt
Dash of pepper
1 3 1/2-oz. jar black caviar
1/4 c. mayonnaise

Hollow out tomatoes slightly at stem end. Sprinkle with salt and pepper; invert and drain well. Chill for 1 hour. Blend caviar with mayonnaise. Place tomatoes on lettuce; top with caviar mixture.

TOMATOES PIQUANT

6 ripe tomatoes, peeled
2/3 c. salad oil
1/4 c. tarragon vinegar
1/4 c. snipped parsley
1/4 c. sliced green onions
1/2 tsp. dried thyme
1 tsp. salt
1/4 tsp. pepper
1 garlic clove, minced

Place tomatoes in deep bowl. Combine remaining ingredients in jar; cover. Shake well; pour over tomatoes. Cover; chill for several hours or overnight. Spoon dressing over tomatoes occasionally; drain. Place tomatoes on lettuce shells; garnish with additional parsley.

FRESH STUFFED TOMATOES

Color photograph for this recipe on page 308.

6 fresh tomatoes
2 c. cottage cheese
1/4 c. chopped fresh chives
1/4 c. chopped fresh green onion
1/4 c. half and half
Salt to taste

Cut each tomato 3/4 of the way down into 6 wedges; separate wedges slightly. Mix cottage cheese, chives, green onion, half and half and salt. Spoon filling into center of each tomato. Garnish as desired with mayonnaise and fresh parsley strips.

TOMATOES STUFFED WITH GUACAMOLE

3 lge. ripe avocados
2 tsp. lemon juice
Salt and pepper to taste
1 pt. cottage cheese
1 green onion, chopped
1 1/2 tbsp. chili sauce
6 lge. tomatoes
Lettuce leaves
Paprika
6 pitted ripe olives

Peel and seed avocados; mash until creamy. Add lemon juice, salt, pepper, cottage cheese, green onion and chili sauce; blend well. Blanch tomatoes; remove skins. Place tomatoes on end; cut into eighths, slicing almost to bottom. Spread petals gently; arrange tomatoes on lettuce leaves. Fill each with guacamole; sprinkle paprika on top. Garnish with pitted ripe olives.

Tomato Stuffed with Pineapple-Chicken Salad . . . Zippy fruit dressing and a crunchy salad.

TOMATOES VINAIGRETTE

12 thick tomato slices
1 c. olive oil
1/3 c. vinegar
2 tsp. crushed oregano
1 tsp. salt
1/2 tsp. pepper
1/2 tsp. dry mustard
2 cloves of garlic, crushed
6 lettuce cups
Minced green onion
Minced parsley

Arrange tomato slices in 8 x 8 x 2-inch baking dish. Combine next 7 ingredients; spoon over tomatoes. Cover; chill for at least 2 hours. Spoon dressing over tomatoes occasionally. Arrange tomato slices in lettuce cups; sprinkle with green onion and parsley. Drizzle each salad with small amount of dressing.

SCALLOPED TOMATOES

2 tbsp. butter
1/4 c. chopped onion
4 slices day-old bread, cubed
4 lge. tomatoes, diced
1/4 c. chopped parsley
1/2 c. grated carrots
1 tsp. salt
1/8 tsp. pepper
1/2 tsp. dry mustard

Melt butter in skillet. Add onion and bread; saute until light brown. Reserve 1/2 cup for topping. Combine remaining bread mixture with remaining ingredients; blend thoroughly. Place in buttered baking dish; top with reserved bread mixture. Bake at 350 degrees for 30 minutes.

TOMATO STUFFED WITH PINEAPPLE-CHICKEN SALAD

4 c. cooked cubed chicken
2 c. pineapple chunks
1 c. sliced celery
1/2 c. slivered almonds
1/2 c. chopped green pepper
8 med. tomatoes
3 tbsp. sugar
1/4 c. flour
1/2 tsp. salt
3/4 c. pineapple juice
2 egg yolks
1/4 c. lemon juice
1/3 c. instant nonfat dry milk powder

Combine chicken, pineapple chunks, celery, almonds and green pepper, tossing well. Cut each tomato into 4 sections, cutting part way down; pull apart slightly. Stuff tomatoes with chicken salad; arrange on lettuce-lined serving dish. Chill. Combine sugar, flour and salt in saucepan; add pineapple juice gradually, mixing well. Cook over low heat, stirring, until thickened. Beat egg yolks; add small amount of cooked mixture to egg yolks. Return to remaining mixture in saucepan. Cook for 3 minutes, stirring constantly until smooth. Remove from heat; add lemon juice. Chill. Add dry milk powder to 1/3 cup ice water; whip until stiff. Fold into dressing; spoon dressing over stuffed tomatoes. Yield: 8 servings.

BAKED TOMATO RAREBIT

3 c. fresh bread cubes
1 1/2 c. grated cheese
2 eggs
1/2 tsp. mustard
1 1/2 tsp. salt
1 lge. can tomatoes

Arrange layers of bread cubes and cheese in greased casserole. Beat eggs; pour over bread and cheese.

Add seasonings; pour tomatoes over all. Let stand for 10 minutes. Bake at 350 degrees for 30 minutes. Serve with crisp bacon.

CHEESE TOMATOES

1/2 c. stuffing mix
1 No. 2 1/2 can tomatoes
1 tbsp. butter
1 tbsp. bacon drippings
1/4 tsp. garlic salt
1/2 tsp. seasoned salt
2 tsp. sugar
1 c. thinly sliced onion
3/4 c. grated Cheddar cheese
1/4 tsp. oregano

Place half the stuffing mix in buttered shallow baking dish. Combine tomatoes, butter, drippings, garlic salt, seasoned salt and sugar; pour half the mixture over stuffing mix. Add half the onion; add half the cheese. Repeat layers; sprinkle with oregano. Bake at 350 degrees for 30 minutes.

DANISH TOMATOES

Tomatoes
Sugar
Salt
Buttered croutons
Crumbled bleu cheese

Cut tops off tomatoes; cut tomatoes in wedges from top toward bottom as for petals. Spread; sprinkle with sugar and salt. Place in pan. Bake at 375 degrees for 10 minutes. Add croutons and cheese; bake until cheese bubbles.

DEEP-SOUTH CANDIED TOMATOES

1/4 c. chopped onion
2 tbsp. butter
1 qt. canned tomatoes
Brown sugar
1/4 tsp. chili powder
Salt and pepper to taste
1 1/2 c. buttered bread crumbs

Saute onion in butter in skillet until golden. Add tomatoes, 2/3 cup brown sugar and seasonings. Simmer, stirring occasionally until thickened. Spoon mixture into baking dish; sprinkle with 2 tablespoons brown sugar and crumbs. Bake at 350 degrees until crumbs are browned.

HERBED TOMATOES

3 ripe tomatoes, halved
Salt and pepper to taste
Sugar
1/2 c. dried bread crumbs
Butter
1 tsp. chopped parsley
2 garlic cloves, finely chopped
1 tsp. basil
2 mashed anchovies

Season tomatoes with salt and pepper; dust lightly with sugar. Place close together in baking dish. Combine bread crumbs, 2 tablespoons butter and remaining ingredients; mix well. Spread over tomatoes; dot with butter. Bake in 400-degree oven for 20 minutes. Two teaspoons anchovy paste may be substituted for anchovies.

TOMATOES PROVENCAL

4 slices bacon, diced
1 onion, sliced
1/4 lb. fresh mushrooms, sliced
1 tsp. seasoned salt
1 tbsp. flour
2 lb. tomatoes, cut in 1/2-in. slices
6 tbsp. Parmesan cheese
1 tbsp. butter

Saute bacon until crisp; add onion and mushrooms. Saute, stirring, until golden; stir in salt and flour. Arrange half the tomato slices in buttered 10 x 6 x 2-inch baking dish. Top with onion-mushroom mixture; sprinkle with 3 tablespoons cheese. Add remaining tomatoes; sprinkle with remaining cheese. Dot with butter. Bake at 350 degrees for 40 minutes or until heated through.

TOMATO-CHEESE CASSEROLE

1 7-oz. package elbow macaroni
6 slices bacon
3 tbsp. butter
3 tbsp. flour
1 1/2 tsp. salt
1/8 tsp. pepper
2 c. milk
2 c. shredded sharp American cheese
3 med. tomatoes, sliced
Paprika to taste

Cook macaroni in large saucepan in 2 quarts boiling salted water until tender. Drain. Fry bacon until crisp; drain. Cool and crumble. Melt butter in saucepan over low heat; blend in flour, salt and pepper. Add milk gradually, stirring constantly; cook until sauce is smooth and thickened. Remove from heat. Add 1 1/2 cups cheese, stirring until cheese is melted. Add bacon. Spoon half the macaroni into greased 2-quart baking dish. Arrange half the tomato slices over macaroni. Cover tomato slices with half the cheese sauce. Repeat layers ending with cheese sauce on top. Sprinkle with paprika. Garnish with additional tomato slices; sprinkle slices with additional shredded cheese. Bake in 350-degree oven for about 30 minutes or until hot and browned. Yield: 8 servings.

Tomato-Cheese Casserole . . . Macaroni and bacon alternate with tomato slices and cheese sauce.

EASY TOMATO PUDDING

1 10-oz. can tomato puree
1 c. (packed) light brown sugar
1/4 tsp. salt
1 c. bread, cut into 1-in. cubes
1/4 c. melted butter

Combine puree, brown sugar and salt with 1/4 cup boiling water in saucepan; boil for 5 minutes. Place bread cubes in casserole. Pour melted butter over bread cubes; add tomato mixture. Bake, covered, at 375 degrees for 30 minutes.

FRESH TOMATO CASSEROLE

Color photograph for this recipe on page 316.

6 med. fresh tomatoes
1/2 c. chopped celery
1/2 c. chopped fresh green pepper
1/2 c. chopped fresh onion
Salt to taste
2 c. fresh corn, cut from cob
3 hard-boiled eggs, sliced
2 c. medium white sauce

Peel and chop 5 tomatoes. Place in saucepan; add celery, green pepper and onion. Cook, stirring occasionally, for 15 minutes; stir in salt. Place half the mixture in casserole. Add half the corn. Add eggs and half the white sauce. Add remaining tomato mixture and remaining corn. Cover with remaining white sauce. Bake at 350 degrees for about 45 minutes. Slice remaining tomato; place on casserole. Garnish with parsley if desired.

MUSHROOM-STUFFED TOMATOES

Color photograph for this recipe on page 320.

6 fresh tomatoes
Salt
6 lge. fresh mushrooms
2 tbsp. melted butter

Preheat oven to 350 degrees. Cut slice from top of each tomato; scoop out some of the pulp carefully. Sprinkle lightly with salt to taste. Remove stems from mushrooms; place 1 mushroom in each tomato, cavity side up. Brush with butter. Arrange tomatoes in buttered casserole; cover with foil. Bake for about 20 minutes or until mushrooms are done. Garnish with chopped parsley if desired. Yield: 6 servings.

CREOLE-STUFFED TOMATOES

3 slices bacon
1/4 c. chopped onion
1/4 c. chopped green pepper
6 tomatoes
1 c. whole kernel corn
1 tsp. seasoned salt
1/4 tsp. oregano
6 slices cheese

Fry bacon until crisp; crumble. Saute onion and green pepper in 1 tablespoon bacon drippings in skillet. Remove slice from top and scoop pulp from each tomato. Add pulp, corn, salt and oregano to vegetables in skillet; heat through. Add bacon to vegetable mixture; reserve small amount for garnish. Fill tomato cups; top with cheese and reserved bacon. Place in shallow dish. Bake in 350-degree oven for 15 minutes or until heated through and cheese is melted.

BAKED DILL-STUFFED TOMATOES

6 med. tomatoes
Salt and pepper
1 1/2 c. coarse dry bread crumbs
1/2 tsp. dillseed
1 tbsp. finely chopped onion
1 tbsp. chopped parsley
1/4 c. butter, melted

Slice stem end from tomatoes; remove pulp. Sprinkle insides with salt and pepper; invert to drain. Combine remaining ingredients with tomato pulp; stuff tomatoes. Place in shallow baking dish. Bake at 350 degrees for 15 minutes or until heated through. Yield: 6 servings.

ITALIAN-STUFFED TOMATOES

6 tomatoes
1 pkg. frozen leaf spinach
Salt and pepper
1 1/2 tsp. margarine
1 3-oz. jar Romano cheese

Preheat oven to 350 degrees. Cut slices from stem end of tomatoes; scoop out pulp. Prepare spinach according to package directions; drain well. Sprinkle insides of tomatoes lightly with salt and pepper; stuff with spinach. Place 1/4 teaspoon margarine on top of each tomato; cover with cheese. Place in casserole. Bake for 30 minutes or until tender and heated through.

TOMATOES STUFFED WITH ZUCCHINI

8 tomatoes
1 lb. zucchini
Olive oil
1 tbsp. shallots, chopped
1 1/2 c. bread crumbs
Basil to taste
Garlic salt to taste
Salt and pepper to taste
1/2 c. Parmesan cheese
Butter

Scoop out centers of tomatoes; drain. Dice zucchini; saute in olive oil with shallots. Mix in 1 cup crumbs, basil, garlic salt, salt and pepper. Stuff tomatoes; sprinkle with mixture of remaining crumbs and Parmesan cheese. Dot with butter. Bake at 375 degrees for 15 minutes or until tender and heated through.

BROILED TOMATO CUPS

6 firm tomatoes
Garlic salt
Pepper
2 med. onions, chopped
1 green pepper, chopped
1 c. bread crumbs
Butter
Grated Cheddar cheese

Cut tops from tomatoes; remove pulp. Chop pulp; season to taste with garlic salt and pepper. Stir in onions and green pepper; spoon mixture into tomato shells. Top with bread crumbs; dot with butter. Place stuffed tomatoes in baking dish. Broil until tomato mixture is golden brown. Top with cheese; return to broiler. Broil until cheese is melted.

CURRIED TOMATOES

1 tbsp. chopped onion
2 tbsp. butter
6 tomatoes, sliced
1/2 c. evaporated milk

1 tbsp. flour
1 tsp. curry powder
Pinch of salt

Saute onion in butter in skillet until transparent; add tomatoes. Bring to a boil; reduce heat. Mix remaining ingredients; pour over tomato mixture. Cook, stirring constantly, until thickened. Serve over hot, buttered toast.

BROILED TOMATO NAPOLI

4 lge. tomatoes
1 c. fresh bread crumbs
1/4 c. melted butter
2 tbsp. grated Parmesan cheese
1/2 tsp. Italian seasoning

Slice tomatoes; place in baking pan. Blend bread crumbs, butter, cheese and seasoning; spoon over tomatoes. Broil 10 inches from source of heat for 5 minutes or until heated through and browned; serve at once.

DEVILED TOMATOES

4 tomatoes, halved
Salt and freshly ground pepper to taste
Cayenne pepper to taste
2 tbsp. buttered bread crumbs
2 tbsp. butter
1/2 tsp. prepared mustard
1/8 tsp. hot sauce
2 tsp. Worcestershire sauce
1 tsp. sugar
1 1/2 tbsp. vinegar
1 egg yolk

Place tomatoes on baking sheet, cut side up; sprinkle lightly with salt, pepper, cayenne pepper and bread crumbs. Melt butter in small saucepan; add mustard, hot sauce, Worcestershire sauce, sugar, vinegar and additional salt. Bring to a boil. Beat egg yolk; add small amount of vinegar mixture, stirring constantly. Stir egg yolk into vinegar mixture; simmer, stirring constantly, until thickened, Broil tomatoes until crumbs are browned. Place 1 spoonful sauce on each half; serve.

FRENCH-FRIED TOMATOES

1 egg, beaten
Milk
Flour
1/2 tsp. baking powder
1/2 tsp. salt
1 tbsp. sugar
Tomatoes, sliced 1/4 in. thick

Mix egg, 2 cups milk, 1 1/2 cups flour, baking powder, salt and sugar. Dip tomato slices in milk; dip in flour. Dip in egg mixture. Fry in 350-degree fat until browned.

FRIED GREEN TOMATOES

5 green tomatoes
1/3 c. flour
3/4 tsp. salt
1/4 tsp. of pep
1/4 c. shortening

Slice tomatoes 1/2 inch thick. Combine flour, salt and pepper; coat tomato slices with mixture. Heat shortening in skillet until sizzling hot. Add tomatoes; cook quickly until browned on one side. Turn tomatoes carefully; reduce heat. Cook until heated through.

TOMATO CROQUETTES

1/2 c. flour
1/2 tsp. baking powder
1/4 tsp. salt
1/8 tsp. pepper
1 tsp. melted butter
1 egg, beaten
1/4 c. milk
1 lge. can whole tomatoes

Combine first 7 ingredients; mix to a smooth batter. Drain tomatoes thoroughly. Dip into batter; fry in hot fat until browned. Drain on absorbent toweling.

Tongue

BEEF TONGUE SUPREME

1 lge. beef tongue
1 tbsp. salt
1 clove of garlic
1 sm. onion, finely chopped
1 c. tomato juice
1 tbsp. sugar
1 tbsp. butter
2 tsp. Worcestershire sauce
2 drops of hot sauce

Place tongue in saucepan; cover with water. Add salt and garlic. Boil, covered, for 2 hours or until tongue is tender; add additional water if needed. Remove from pan; reserve 1/2 cup liquid. Peel tongue; cut into 1-inch slices. Return tongue to pan; add reserved liquid and remaining ingredients. Simmer, covered, for 30 minutes.

BEEF TONGUE WITH GARLIC

1 tbsp. soda
1 3-lb. beef tongue
1 clove of garlic

Combine soda with 1 cup hot water; scrub beef tongue well with soda water. Place in pressure cooker with garlic; cook according to pressure cooker directions. Cool; skin and slice before serving.

PICKLED TONGUE

1 med. beef tongue
Salt and pepper to taste
2 tbsp. sugar
Vinegar

Place tongue in kettle; cover with cold water. Bring to a boil; boil for 20 minutes. Pour off water; cover with boiling water. Boil for 1 hour longer or until tongue is tender. Remove from liquid; reserve liquid. Cool tongue; peel and slice, return to kettle. Add salt, pepper, sugar and equal parts reserved liquid and vinegar. Boil for 20 minutes longer; cool in vinegar mixture.

Jellied Tongue Mold . . . An easy-to-prepare main dish of canned tongue and soup.

JELLIED TONGUE MOLD

1 env. unflavored gelatin
1 10 1/2-oz. can consomme
2 tbsp. lemon juice
1/2 c. diced cooked tongue
1/2 c. minced cucumber
1/4 c. sliced celery
2 tbsp. sliced stuffed olives
3 slices tongue
4 cucumber slices

Sprinkle gelatin on 1/2 cup cold water to soften. Place over low heat, stirring until dissolved. Remove from heat; blend in consomme and lemon juice. Chill until slightly thickened. Fold in diced tongue, cucumber, celery and olives. Arrange tongue and cucumber slices in bottom of loaf pan; pour gelatin mixture over slices. Chill until firm. Unmold on lettuce-lined serving platter. Yield: 4 servings.

GLAZED TONGUE

1 beef tongue
1 can jellied cranberry sauce
1/4 c. dried apricots
1/4 c. raisins
1/2 tsp. lemon juice

Place tongue in Dutch oven in water to cover; bring to a boil. Boil tongue slowly for 2 hours or until tender. Peel and slice; place in baking dish. Heat cranberry sauce in saucepan until dissolved; remove from heat. Add apricots, raisins, lemon juice and 1/4 cup water; blend well. Pour over tongue. Bake, covered, at 350 degrees for 1 hour.

SMOKED TONGUE RAREBIT

12 slices cooked tongue
2 tbsp. butter
2 tbsp. flour
1/4 tsp. paprika
1/4 tsp. dry mustard
1 c. milk
1 c. grated Cheddar cheese
1/2 tsp. Worcestershire sauce

Cut tongue into 3-inch strips. Melt butter in saucepan; stir in flour, paprika and mustard. Add milk; cook, stirring constantly, until thickened. Add cheese; simmer, stirring, until cheese is melted. Add Worcestershire sauce; fold in tongue. Simmer until heated through. Serve over rice.

SWEET-SOUR TONGUE

1 3-lb. beef tongue
4 1/2 tsp. pickling spice
2/3 c. (packed) brown sugar
1/3 c. lemon juice
1 15-oz. can tomato sauce

Place tongue in Dutch oven; cover with water. Simmer covered for 1 1/2 hours or until tender. Remove from liquid; peel and slice. Discard liquid; return meat to Dutch oven. Combine pickling spice tied in small bag, brown sugar, lemon juice, tomato sauce and 1/4 cup water; blend well. Pour over tongue. Bake at 350 degrees for 1 hour.

TONGUE WITH CHERRY SAUCE

1 4-lb. beef tongue
1 tsp. peppercorns
1 tbsp. salt
1 med. onion
6 cloves
1 bay leaf
1/2 c. (packed) brown sugar
1 tbsp. cornstarch
1/2 tsp. powdered cloves
1 c. pitted sour cherries
1 tbsp. lemon juice
2 tbsp. butter

Cover tongue with water in Dutch oven; add peppercorns, salt, onion, cloves and bay leaf. Bring to a boil; reduce heat. Simmer, covered, until tender. Remove tongue; strain and reserve 1 cup broth. Peel tongue; cut into 1/2-inch slices. Arrange in glass baking dish. Combine sugar, reserved broth, cornstarch and powdered cloves in saucepan; cook, stirring constantly, until thickened and clear. Add cherries, lemon juice and butter; pour over tongue. Bake at 350 degrees for 30 minutes.

Trout

Trout is an abundant species of fish related to the salmon family. They inhabit cool freshwater lakes and streams as well as deep sea regions. Trout are valued both as a game and food fish. They are practically scaleless with few bones and delicate tasty flesh. Most varieties average 8 to 12 inches in length. Trout is high in protein and B Vitamins. (5 ounces broiled brook trout = 145 calories; 5 ounces broiled lake trout = 240 calories)

KINDS: There are two main groupings of trout: freshwater and sea trout. *Freshwater trout* include: brook trout (rainbow and speckled) that probably derive their delicate flavor from their spring-water habitat; and lake trout that are found in most large Northern lakes. *Sea trout* include steelhead and salmon trout that live in the sea but return annually to nearby rivers to spawn.

AVAILABILITY: Most varieties of trout are available year-round. Freshwater brook trout are raised for commercial consumption in hatcheries. They are marketed whole either fresh, frozen, or smoked in sizes of 1/3 to 1/2 pound. Sea trout are usually available in steaks and fillets. Lake trout, the best known game variety, are usually in season from April to November.

BUYING: Select whole fresh fish with bright, clear, bulging eyes; reddish pink gills; tight shiny scales; firm elastic flesh; and fresh odor. Avoid fresh trout that are soft or flabby.

STORING: Wrap whole fresh trout in moisture- and vapor-proof paper and refrigerate for 1 to 2 days. Store commercially frozen fish in original packages and freeze until ready to use. *To freeze* fresh fish–Wrap whole fish individually in moistureproof paper. Seal, label, and freeze. Or stack fillets and steaks in cartons with freezer paper between layers. Wrap carton with moistureproof paper and freeze. Freeze whole fish, steaks, and fillets in home freezer for 6 weeks.

PREPARATION: Whole trout with head and tail intact may be grilled, broiled, baked, poached, panfried, or sauteed. *Truite au Bleu* is a true gourmet's delight. A live trout is killed with a blow to the head and immediately plunged into a court bouillon (See COURT BOUILLON) for 4 to 6 minutes. The trout will turn brilliant blue when done. See specific recipes for trout steaks or fillets or try trout in salmon recipes. (See SALMON)

SERVING: Garnish fresh-cooked trout with a sprinkling of paprika or snipped parsley and lemon wedges.

(See SEAFOOD.)

TROUT MARGUERY

1 lb. trout
1/2 pt. oysters
1/2 lb. shrimp
2 onions, minced
2 tbsp. chopped green pepper
1/4 lb. butter
1 c. medium white sauce
4 tbsp. sherry
3/4 c. sliced mushrooms
1/8 tsp. hot sauce
Salt and pepper to taste
2 c. seasoned hot mashed potatoes
1/8 lb. sharp cheese, grated

Poach trout, oysters and shrimp separately for 5 minutes. Drain well. Separate trout into large pieces; place in buttered casserole. Chop oysters and shrimp; spread over trout. Cook onions and green pepper in butter until transparent. Add white sauce, sherry, mushrooms and hot sauce; blend well. Season with salt and pepper. Pour sauce over shrimp mixture. Bake at 350 degrees for 20 minutes. Remove from oven; flute hot mashed potatoes around edge. Sprinkle with cheese. Return to oven for 10 minutes or until lightly browned and cheese is melted.

TROUT-POTATO CASSEROLE

Salt
3 lb. trout
1/2 c. flour
1/8 tsp. pepper
6 sm. onions, halved
6 med. potatoes, chopped
8 strips bacon
1 can tomato sauce

Salt trout lightly; mix flour with 1 teaspoon salt and pepper. Roll trout in flour mixture; place in 8 x 12 x 2-inch baking pan. Place onions and potatoes around trout. Arrange bacon over trout; pour tomato sauce mixed with 1/2 cup water over top. Bake at 350 degrees for 15 minutes or until bacon is browned. Bake, covered, for 1 hour longer or until fish flakes easily with a fork.

BAKED TROUT

2 12-oz. packages frozen trout, thawed
1/4 c. butter
1/4 c. finely chopped celery
1 tsp. salt
1/4 tsp. pepper
1 tbsp. lemon juice
1/4 c. chopped sweet mixed pickles

Arrange trout in greased 1 1/2-quart shallow baking dish. Melt butter over low heat; add celery. Saute until tender. Add seasonings, lemon juice and pickles. Pour sauce over trout. Bake in 350-degree oven for 20 to 25 minutes or until fish flakes easily. Garnish with lemon slices and parsley if desired.

Baked Trout . . . Flavorful trout is baked with a seasoned sauce of celery, lemon, and pickles.

BAKED TROUT WITH SPICY SAUCE

2 trout fillets
1 c. barbecue sauce
2 c. seasoned bread crumbs
2 c. (packed) brown sugar
2 c. catsup
2 tbsp. mustard

Dip fillets in barbecue sauce; coat well with bread crumbs. Bake at 325 degrees for 20 minutes or until browned. Combine sugar, catsup and mustard; simmer for 3 minutes. Serve over trout. Garnish with lemon slices and parsley.

BROILED MOUNTAIN TROUT

Mountain trout
Salt and pepper to taste
Lemon juice to taste
Butter
2 tbsp. melted butter
1/2 tsp. chopped parsley

Clean and bone trout; sprinkle with salt, pepper and lemon juice. Place in well-buttered shallow baking pan; spread with butter. Broil for 15 minutes. Combine melted butter and 2 tablespoons lemon juice; add parsley. Pour over trout.

CRISP TROUT FILLETS

Pancake mix
Lemon-lime carbonate beverage
8 trout fillets, salted
Corn oil

Make thick batter of pancake mix and beverage; dip fillets into batter. Fry in deep oil at 350 degrees for 10 minutes or until golden brown.

DEEP-FRIED TROUT

1/2 lb. sea trout, cut into 8 pieces
Salt to taste
1 1/2 c. pancake flour
1/2 c. crushed almonds
3 c. vegetable oil

Season trout with salt. Mix pancake flour with almonds; dredge trout in flour mixture. Cook, turning once, in hot oil until browned. Drain on absorbent toweling.

FRIED MOUNTAIN TROUT

1 stick butter
4 trout
Flour
1/2 c. slivered almonds
1 tsp. chopped chives
Juice of 1 lemon

Melt butter in heavy skillet; coat trout well with flour. Fry in hot butter until browned on both sides; remove. Reduce heat; add almonds, chives and lemon juice. Saute until almonds are golden. Pour over trout.

PAN-FRIED TROUT

1 trout
Bread crumbs
Salt to taste
1 tbsp. shortening

Roll trout in mixture of crumbs and salt. Heat shortening in skillet; fry trout, turning once, for 4 minutes or until browned and fish flakes easily with a fork.

SPECKLED TROUT

12 speckled trout
1 c. flour
Salt and pepper to taste

Coat trout well with flour. Fry trout in small amount of hot fat in skillet over low heat until trout are golden brown on both sides. Remove from skillet; sprinkle with salt and pepper. Drain on absorbent toweling.

TROUT AMANDINE

4 fillets of trout
1 c. milk
1 tsp. salt
1/8 tsp. black pepper
1/2 c. flour
1 c. butter
1/2 c. almonds, chopped

Dip fillets in milk. Season with salt and pepper; dredge in flour. Brown fillets on both sides in 1/4 cup butter in skillet. Remove fish from skillet; add remaining butter. Saute almonds until golden; serve over cooked fillets. Garnish with lemon slices and parsley.

CRISPY-FRIED RAINBOW TROUT

5 rainbow trout, cleaned
1/4 c. evaporated milk
1 1/2 tsp. salt
Dash of pepper
1/2 c. flour
1/4 c. yellow cornmeal
1 tsp. paprika

Wash trout; dry well. Blend milk, salt and pepper together. Combine flour, cornmeal and paprika Dip trout into milk mixture; roll in flour mixture. Fry in hot fat in skillet over medium heat for 4 to 5 minutes or until brown. Turn carefully; fry for 4 to 5 minutes longer or until brown and fish flakes easily when tested with fork. Drain on absorbent paper. Arrange trout on heated serving platter; garnish with parsley, lemon slices and pimento strips. Yield: 5 servings.

Crispy-Fried Rainbow Trout . . . Sportsman's catch rolled in seasoned cornmeal and fried.

FILLET OF TROUT SUPREME

Salt and pepper to taste
4 trout, dressed
Red pepper to taste
Softened butter
1 tsp. minced parsley
3 slices lemon

Salt and pepper trout; sprinkle with red pepper. Place on sheet of heavy-duty foil; spread with butter. Fold foil over; seal edges. Grill 5 inches from coals for 6 minutes; turn once. Arrange trout on heated platter. Sprinkle with parsley; garnish with lemon slices.

Caper Sauce

1 c. mayonnaise
1 1/2 tsp. hot sauce
2 tbsp. capers
2 tbsp. minced dill pickle
1/2 med. onion, grated
? tbsp. Worcestershire sauce
1 tbsp. garlic salt

Combine mayonnaise, hot sauce, capers, dill pickle and onion; blend well. Stir in Worcestershire sauce and garlic salt. Chill until ready to serve.

TROUT LORRAINE

Fresh med. trout
Flour
Butter
1/2 pt. heavy cream

Roll each trout lightly in flour. Fry trout in 1/4 cup butter in skillet over low heat until golden brown on each side; salt. Cook, covered, over very low heat for 8 minutes. Place trout on hot platter. Add 4 tablespoons butter to pan drippings; pour in cream. Simmer, stirring constantly until mixture is heated through. Pour over trout.

TROUT MEUNIERE

3/4 c. flour
Salt to taste
Freshly ground pepper to taste
1/8 tsp. thyme
4 brook trout
1/2 stick margarine
1/2 stick butter
1/2 c. chopped mushrooms
1 tbsp. lemon juice
4 tbsp. chopped parsley
1 tbsp. chopped chives

Combine flour, salt, pepper and thyme; roll trout in seasoned flour. Cook trout in margarine in skillet over low heat until browned on both sides. Place trout on heated platter; keep hot. Brown butter in saucepan. Add mushrooms; saute for 5 minutes. Add lemon juice, parsley, chives and salt. Simmer, stirring constantly, until heated through; pour over trout. Garnish with lemon slices dusted with paprika.

PATIO-GRILLED TROUT

Trout
Bacon

Wrap trout with desired amount of bacon; fasten with wooden picks. Place on rack; cook, turning once, over coals until bacon is crisp. Damp hickory chips may be placed on coals if hickory flavor is desired. Serve with melted butter sauce.

SAUCY GRILLED TROUT

1/4 c. French dressing
1 tbsp. lemon juice
1 tsp. salt
1/4 tsp. pepper
6 dressed trout

Combine French dressing, lemon juice, salt and pepper; mix well. Brush trout inside and out with sauce. Place trout on well-greased grill. Grill over moderately hot coals for 15 minutes. Turn; brush with sauce. Grill for 15 minutes longer or until fish flakes easily.

SOUTHERN-GRILLED TROUT

Salt and pepper to taste
4 lge. speckled trout
1/2 c. melted butter
1/3 c. lemon juice
5 tbsp. chopped parsley
1/2 c. grated onion
1/2 tsp. paprika
5 tbsp. Worcestershire sauce
1/8 tsp. cayenne pepper

Salt and pepper trout; place each trout on foil square. Mix remaining ingredients; pour over trout. Close foil securely. Grill over hot coals, turning occasionally for 30 minutes or until fish flakes easily.

TROUT AU BLEU

6 fresh trout
1/2 c. vinegar
1 chicken bouillon cube
1 sm. bay leaf
1/3 c. melted butter
1 tbsp. lemon juice
1/3 c. capers, drained

Split trout. Combine vinegar, bouillon cube and 1/2 cup hot water in skillet; heat, stirring, until bouillon cube is dissolved. Add bay leaf; simmer for 10 minutes. Add trout; simmer for 15 minutes or until fish flakes easily. Combine butter, lemon juice and capers; simmer until heated through. Serve with trout.

KETTLE TROUT

3 lge. stalks celery, chopped
1 carrot, sliced thin
4 sprigs of parsley, chopped
3 bay leaves
4 cloves
3 slices lemon
2 tbsp. vinegar
1 lb. trout, filleted

Place 2 quarts water in large kettle; add all ingredients except trout. Bring to a boil; simmer for 5 minutes. Cut trout into serving pieces; add to seasoned liquid. Simmer, covered, for 5 minutes or until fish flakes easily with a fork.

OVEN-POACHED TROUT

1 4-lb. trout
1 tbsp. finely chopped carrot
1 tbsp. finely chopped onion
1 tbsp. finely chopped celery
1 sprig of parsley
1 tbsp. butter
1 clove
1 bay leaf
1 tsp. salt
1 tbsp. vinegar
1/2 c. cream
1/2 c. catsup

Place trout in baking pan. Combine carrot, onion, celery, parsley, butter, clove, bay leaf, salt, vinegar and 1 quart water; blend well. Pour over trout. Bake at 375 degrees for 30 minutes. Remove trout to heated platter. Mix cream and catsup; heat through. Serve with trout.

BAKED STUFFED TROUT

1 2-lb. trout
2 c. soft bread crumbs
1 tsp. salt
1/4 c. chopped parsley
1/8 tsp. pepper
1/2 tsp. poultry seasoning
Melted butter
2 tbsp. lemon juice

Preheat oven to 400 degrees. Place trout in well-greased baking dish. Mix crumbs, salt, parsley, pepper, poultry seasoning, 1/4 cup butter and lemon juice; stuff fish. Fasten opening. Brush with additional butter. Bake for 20 minutes or until fish flakes easily with a fork. Garnish with additional parsley.

HERB-STUFFED TROUT

1/2 8-oz. package herb-seasoned stuffing mix
1 tbsp. minced onion
1/2 tsp. ground thyme
2 tbsp. melted butter
1 3-lb. trout
1 tsp. salt
Pepper to taste

Combine stuffing mix, onion, thyme, butter and 1/4 cup hot water; blend well. Rub cavity of trout with salt and pepper; fill with stuffing. Secure opening. Rub with additional butter; place on rack in baking pan. Bake at 350 degrees for 35 minutes or until trout flakes easily with a fork.

STUFFED TROUT WITH MUSHROOMS

1/4 c. chopped onions
6 tbsp. melted butter
1/2 c. cracker crumbs
1/2 c. bread crumbs
1/4 tsp. salt
1/2 tsp. sage
2 1-lb. trout
1/2 c. white wine
1/2 lb. small mushrooms

Saute onions in 3 tablespoons butter; add cracker crumbs, bread crumbs, salt and sage. Stuff trout; place in greased baking dish. Cut shallow slits in trout. Bake at 400 degrees for 10 minutes; baste with 2 tablespoons butter. Add wine; bake for 10 minutes longer or until fish flakes easily with a fork. Saute mushrooms in remaining butter. Remove trout to heated platter. Add drippings to mushrooms; blend well. Spoon over trout.

TROUT BARNEE

1 c. wild rice
6 boned rainbow trout
Salt to taste
White pepper to taste
Paprika to taste
6 lge. slices tomato
6 lge. mushroom caps
12 sm. strips King crab meat
Melted butter
1 c. macadamia nuts

Cook rice according to package directions; drain. Arrange trout in shallow well-buttered pan. Season lightly with salt, pepper and paprika. Spoon rice into opening of each trout; top each with tomato slice and 1 mushroom cap. Arrange 2 thin strips of crab meat on each. Brush lightly with melted butter. Bake, basting occasionally with butter, at 350 degrees for 20 minutes or until trout flakes easily with a fork. Brown macadamia nuts in 1/4 cup melted butter. Serve trout on shredded lettuce with macadamia nut sauce.

TROUT MARYLAND

1 c. herb-seasoned stuffing mix
1/2 c. walnuts
8 trout
Butter, melted
Lemon juice

Mix bread stuffing with walnuts; fill cavity of each trout with 3 tablespoons stuffing. Secure opening. Arrange in shallow baking pan. Brush trout with butter mixed with a small amount of lemon juice. Bake, basting frequently with butter mixture, at 350 degrees for 15 minutes, until fish flakes easily with a fork. Broil until lightly browned. Serve with lemon wedges.

SHRIMP-STUFFED TROUT

2 c. cooked shrimp
2 eggs
1 c. cream
1/2 c. mushrooms, chopped
2 tsp. chives
Butter, melted
1 tbsp. flour
1 4-lb. boned trout
Salt and pepper to taste
4 tbsp. sherry
2 limes, quartered

Mix shrimp, eggs and 1/2 cup cream. Add mushrooms and chives to butter in skillet; saute until tender. Add flour; cook until smooth. Add shrimp mixture; cook until thickened. Place trout in buttered baking dish; spread shrimp mixture in trout cavity. Secure opening. Add remaining cream; sprinkle with salt and pepper. Add sherry. Bake at 350 degrees for 45 minutes or until fish flakes easily with a fork. Serve with limes.

Tuna

Tuna is any one of several edible saltwater fishes related to mackerel. It is probably best-known and most often served in the form of commercially canned tuna fish. Found on both Atlantic and Pacific coasts, tuna is valued as a robust game fish as well as for its flaky, tender meat. Meat varies from white to purplish red, depending on the variety. True delicate white tuna meat comes from albacore and is used for the finest canned tuna fish. Tuna contains protein, calcium, Vitamin A, and niacin. (3 ounces tuna packed in oil, drained = 170 calories)

AVAILABILITY: Fresh, frozen, canned, smoked, salted tuna is sold year-round. Fresh tuna is marketed whole, in steaks, and in fillets. Canned tuna fish may be packed in oil or in water. Meat may be solid, chunk, flaked, or grated.

BUYING: Select whole fresh fish with clear, bulging eyes; reddish or pink gills; bright, shiny, tightly clinging scales; firm flesh that springs back when lightly pressed; and fresh, pleasant odor. Buy 1/3 to 1/2 pound edible fish or 1 pound whole fish per serving. Examine labels of canned tuna fish. "White meat" tuna comes from albacore only. "Light meat" tuna comes from other varieties and is not considered as fine as white meat tuna.

STORING: Wrap fresh fish in moistureproof paper or place in covered dish. Refrigerate and use within 1 to 2 days. Store commercially frozen fish in original packages and freeze until ready to use. Keep canned tuna on kitchen shelf 1 year or opened cans in refrigerator about 3 days. *To freeze* fresh fish–Wrap whole fish individually in moistureproof paper. Seal, label, and freeze. Or, stack fillets and steaks in cartons with freezer paper between layers for easy separation during thawing. Wrap carton with moistureproof paper; seal. Freeze both whole fish and steak and fillets at 0 degree or below for 6 weeks.

PREPARATION: Fresh tuna may be grilled, fried, baked, poached, sauteed, steamed, broiled, boiled, or pan-fried. Fillets and steaks may be cooked without thawing. Allow additional cooking time, however. Thaw whole fish in refrigerator, or for quicker thawing, hold under cold running water. Never thaw fish at room temperature; it will be limp and soggy.

SERVING: Garnish fresh-cooked fish colorfully. Use fresh and/or canned tuna fish in hors d'oeuvres, sauces, omelets, salads, soufles, pies, stews, croquettes, loaves, casseroles, and so on. See specific recipe instructions. (See SEAFOOD.)

BROILED TUNA APPETIZERS

1 can refrigerator biscuits
1 7-oz. can tuna
2 egg whites
1/2 tsp. salt
1/2 c. mayonnaise
1 tbsp. minced celery
1 tbsp. pickle relish

Preheat oven to 400 degrees. Separate each biscuit into thirds; place on ungreased cookie sheet. Bake for 8 to 10 minutes or until golden brown. Drain tuna; flake. Beat egg whites with salt until stiff peaks form; fold in tuna, mayonnaise, celery and relish. Spread 1 teaspoonful on each biscuit. Broil 6 inches from source of heat for 3 minutes or until golden brown; serve immediately. May be refrigerated before baking for 3 hours.

BIT OF PUFFS

1/2 c. butter
1 c. flour
1/4 tsp. salt
4 eggs
1 can tuna
3 tbsp. mayonnaise
2 tbsp. chopped sweet pickle

Combine butter with 1 cup boiling water. Add flour and salt all at once; stir rapidly. Cook, stirring, until mixture leaves side of pan and forms ball. Cool slightly; add eggs, one at a time, beating well after each addition. Drop from teaspoon onto greased baking sheet. Bake at 450 degrees for 15 minutes. Reduce heat to 325 degrees; bake for 25 minutes longer. Cool; cut in half horizontally. Combine tuna, mayonnaise and pickle; fill puffs. Place halves together.

TEMPTING TUNA DIP

1 3-oz. package cream cheese
1 c. sour cream
1 7-oz. can tuna
1/4 c. stuffed olives, chopped
2 tbsp. chopped chives
2 tsp. prepared horseradish
1 tsp. Worcestershire sauce
1/4 tsp. salt

Have cream cheese at room temperature. Blend cheese and sour cream until fluffy. Drain and flake tuna. Add tuna, olives, chives, horseradish, Worcestershire sauce and salt to cheese mixture; blend well. Chill for 2 hours. Serve with vegetable relishes, crackers or chips.

TUNA-CHEESE FONDUE

Color photograph for this recipe on page 728.

1 clove of garlic, halved
2 c. dry white wine
1/2 lb. Swiss cheese
1/2 lb. Gruyere cheese
1 1/2 tbsp. cornstarch
2 tbsp. kirsch
Dash of nutmeg
1 6 1/2-oz. can tuna
Cubes of French bread

Rub inside of fondue pot with garlic. Add wine; warm over medium heat. Do not boil. Dice cheese. Add cheese gradually, stirring until cheese melts and mixture begins to boil. Blend cornstarch, kirsch and nutmeg; stir into cheese mixture. Drain and flake tuna; add to cheese mixture. Cook, stirring constantly for 1 minute. Place over heating unit of pot; serve with bread cubes. Yield: 4 servings.

TUNA-ONION DIP

1 7-oz. can tuna
1 pkg. onion soup mix
1 c. sour cream
1/4 c. Chablis

Drain tuna; flake. Combine all ingredients; mix well. Chill for at least 1 hour. Serve as dip with crackers, potato chips or raw vegetable sticks.

TUNA AND CHEESE CANAPES

1 7-oz. can tuna
1 c. grated Cheddar cheese
2 tbsp. sherry
1/4 tsp. freshly ground pepper
4 slices buttered toast

Drain and flake tuna; combine tuna, cheese, sherry and pepper. Cut toast into quarters; spread with tuna mixture. Bake at 350 degrees for 5 minutes or until lightly browned.

TUNA MINIATURES

1 7-oz. can tuna
2 c. corn flakes, crushed
1/3 c. milk
1/4 c. mayonnaise
1 tbsp. chopped parsley
1/4 c. minced onion
1/2 tsp. Worcestershire sauce
1 tsp. lemon juice
1/4 tsp. salt
1/8 tsp. pepper

Drain tuna; flake. Mix half the cereal with milk; add mayonnaise, tuna, parsley, onion, Worcestershire sauce, juice, salt and pepper. Mix well. Form into 1-inch balls; roll in remaining cereal. Place on well-greased baking sheet. Bake in 425-degree oven for 15 minutes or until heated through. Serve immediately.

TUNA-STUFFED TOMATOES

1 pt. cherry tomatoes
1 can tuna
2 tbsp. sour cream
2 tbsp. horseradish
Parsley

Slice thin tops from tomatoes. Remove pulp; drain shells inverted on paper towels. Combine tuna, sour cream and horseradish in bowl; fill tomatoes with tuna mixture. Chill; garnish with parsley.

TUNA-TATER THINS

1 1/2 c. self-rising flour
1/2 c. instant potato flakes
1/2 c. tuna
2 tbsp. grated Cheddar cheese
1/2 c. butter

Combine flour, potato flakes, tuna and cheese; cut in butter until mixture resembles coarse meal. Sprinkle 2 tablespoons water over mixture; mix lightly until dough just holds together. Roll out on floured surface to 1/8-inch thickness; cut into rounds with 2-inch cutter. Place on ungreased cookie sheet. Bake at 375 degrees for 12 minutes or until golden brown.

TUNA TEASERS

1 7-oz. can tuna
1 c. sifted flour
1 1/2 tsp. baking powder
1 tsp. onion salt
1/2 tsp. curry powder
Dash of cayenne pepper
1/4 c. butter
1/2 c. milk
1 c. shredded Cheddar cheese
1 tbsp. finely minced green pepper

Drain tuna; flake. Mix flour, baking powder, onion salt, curry powder and cayenne pepper in mixing bowl; cut in butter until mixture resembles coarse meal. Add milk all at once; stir until well blended. Add tuna, cheese and green pepper; mix well. Drop by teaspoonfuls onto lightly greased cookie sheets. Bake at 450 degrees for 12 minutes or until golden and crusty.

TUNA BISQUE

1 7-oz. can tuna
2 1/2 c. milk
1 can cream of asparagus soup
1 can cream of mushroom soup
Sherry to taste

Drain tuna; flake. Combine 1 cup milk, soups and sherry in blender container. Cover; process on high speed until smooth. Pour into saucepan; add remaining milk and tuna. Simmer, stirring constantly, for 10 minutes or until heated through.

TUNA POTATO SOUP

2 7-oz. cans tuna
2 cans frozen cream of potato soup
2 tbsp. butter
1 med. onion, chopped
1 c. milk
1/4 tsp. pepper
12 sprigs of parsley, chopped fine

Drain tuna; flake. Thaw soup. Melt butter in saucepan; saute onion in butter until transparent. Stir in tuna; remove from heat. Add 1 cup water, soup, milk, pepper and parsley to tuna mixture; blend well. Return to heat; simmer, stirring occasionally, for 15 minutes.

HOT TUNA SANDWICHES

1 c. chunk tuna
1 c. cubed American cheese
3 hard-boiled eggs, chopped
2 tbsp. sweet relish
2 tbsp. chopped green pepper
2 tbsp. chopped onion
6 sandwich buns

Combine all ingredients except buns; fill buns with tuna mixture. Wrap in aluminum foil. Bake at 250 degrees for 30 minutes.

TUNA CHEESEBURGERS

2 cans tuna
1 egg
1 tbsp. finely chopped onion
Salt to taste
8 sandwich buns
8 slices cheese

Drain tuna; flake. Combine tuna, egg, onion and salt; mix well. Spread mixture on buns. Add slice of cheese to each bun; wrap in foil. Bake at 350 degrees for 20 minutes.

TUNABURGERS

2 7-oz. cans tuna
3 slices bread
2/3 c. evaporated milk
1 tbsp. prepared mustard
1 tbsp. catsup
1 tbsp. pickle relish
6 sandwich buns, halved

Drain tuna; flake. Remove crusts from bread; place in bowl. Pour milk over bread. Add mustard, catsup and relish; mix until blended. Add tuna; mix well. Spoon onto 6 bun halves. Broil 4 to 5 inches from source of heat for 8 minutes or until browned; top with remaining bun halves.

TUNA-CHEESE BROIL

1 can tuna
1 1/2 tsp. mustard
1/4 tsp. Worcestershire sauce

3/4 c. mayonnaise
1 1/2 tsp. grated onion
2 tbsp. chopped green pepper
3 sandwich rolls, split
6 tomato slices
1/4 c. shredded American cheese

Drain tuna; flake. Combine tuna, mustard, Worcestershire sauce, 1/4 cup mayonnaise, onion and green pepper; mix well. Spread tuna mixture on roll halves; top with tomato slices and remaining mayonnaise mixed with cheese. Broil 4 inches from source of heat for 2 minutes or until lightly browned and heated through.

TUNA SANDWICH SPREAD

1 loaf thin-sliced bread
1 can tuna
1 med. apple, chopped fine
1 hard-boiled egg, diced
1 sm. onion, chopped fine
2 sweet pickles, diced
1/2 c. finely chopped pecans
1/2 c. diced celery
Mayonnaise

Trim crusts from bread; flatten slices with rolling pin. Drain tuna; flake. Combine remaining ingredients, adding mayonnaise to desired spreading consistency. Spread tuna mixture between bread slices.

TUNA TREASURE CHEST

1 1-lb. loaf French bread
Melted butter
2 7-oz. cans tuna
1/2 c. pickle relish
1 1/2 c. chopped hard-cooked eggs
2 c. cubed cheese
1 c. mayonnaise

Cut bread in half lengthwise; scoop out centers. Brush insides with melted butter. Drain tuna; flake. Combine tuna, pickle relish, eggs, cheese and mayonnaise; spoon into bread shells. Place in shallow baking pan. Bake for 10 minutes at 400 degrees. Slice each loaf half in 5 sections; serve hot.

JELLIED TUNA SALAD

2 cans chunk-style tuna
2 hard-cooked eggs, chopped
1/2 c. chopped olives
2 tbsp. capers
1 tbsp. minced onion
1 env. unflavored gelatin
2 c. mayonnaise
Tomatoes
1 avocado

Drain tuna; flake. Combine tuna, eggs, olives, capers and onion; toss lightly. Soften gelatin in 1/4 cup water; dissolve over hot water. Stir gelatin into mayonnaise; combine with tuna mixture. Pour into ring mold; chill until firm. Peel and quarter tomatoes. Peel avocado; slice thin. Sprinkle tomatoes and avocado slices with French dressing. Serve in center of tuna ring.

MOLDED TUNA-EGG SALAD

3 cans tuna
2 sm. packages lemon gelatin
1 c. mayonnaise
1 c. heavy cream, whipped
2 c. chopped celery
2 tsp. salt
1 green pepper, diced
2 tbsp. grated onion
6 hard-cooked eggs, chopped
1 c. chopped pecans

Drain tuna; flake. Dissolve gelatin in 2 cups boiling water; chill until partially set. Whip. Blend mayonnaise and whipped cream; fold into gelatin. Add tuna, celery, salt, green pepper, onion, eggs and pecans; blend well. Turn into mold. Chill until firm.

EASY TUNA SALAD

1 7-oz. can tuna
4 hard-cooked eggs, chopped
2 lge. carrots, grated
3/4 c. diced celery
2 tsp. celery seed
2 tbsp. chopped chives
3 tbsp. mayonnaise
Salt and pepper to taste

Drain tuna; flake. Combine tuna with remaining ingredients in salad bowl. Blend in additional mayonnaise if needed. Serve on crisp greens; garnish as desired.

GERMAN TUNA-POTATO SALAD

2 7-oz. cans tuna
6 slices bacon, chopped
1/2 c. chopped celery
1/2 c. chopped onion
3 tbsp. sugar
1 tbsp. flour
1/2 tsp. paprika
1/4 tsp. salt
1/4 tsp. celery seed
1/2 c. vinegar
3 c. sliced cooked potatoes
Chopped parsley

Drain tuna; break into large pieces. Fry bacon in frypan until crisp; drain on absorbent paper. Saute celery and onion in bacon drippings in frypan until tender. Combine sugar, flour, paprika, salt and celery seed. Stir into onion mixture. Add 1 cup water and vinegar gradually; cook until thickened, stirring constantly. Add potatoes, bacon and tuna. Mix lightly. Cover; cook over low heat for 5 to 10 minutes or until hot and bubbly. Sprinkle with parsley. Serve in lettuce-lined salad bowl. Yield: 6 servings.

German Tuna-Potato Salad . . . A one meal dish of hot and seasoned potato and tuna salad.

MOLDED TUNA-TOMATO SALAD

1 env. unflavored gelatin
3/4 c. chili sauce
2 c. cottage cheese
1 c. sour cream
1/2 tsp. prepared mustard
1/2 tsp. sugar
1/4 tsp. salt
1 7-oz. can tuna
1/2 c. finely chopped celery
1/4 c. sliced green onions

Soften gelatin in 1/4 cup water. Bring chili sauce to a boil in saucepan; add gelatin. Stir until dissolved. Combine cottage cheese, sour cream, mustard, sugar and salt in large bowl; blend well. Drain tuna; flake. Fold in tuna, celery, onions and chili sauce; pour into 6-cup mold. Chill until firm.

MOLDED TUNA SALAD

2 env. unflavored gelatin
1 can tomato soup
2 sm. packages cream cheese
1 c. mayonnaise
1/2 c. finely chopped celery
1/4 c. finely chopped onion
1 clove of garlic, crushed
1 can tuna
Juice of 1/2 lemon
1/2 c. finely chopped green pepper
1/2 c. chopped olives
1/2 c. chopped nuts
4 chopped eggs

Soften gelatin in 1/2 cup cold water. Bring tomato soup to a boil in saucepan; stir in cream cheese until smooth. Add gelatin; stir until dissolved. Cool. Drain tuna; flake. Fold tuna and remaining ingredients into soup mixture; pour into mold. Chill until firm.

TUNA-CUCUMBER MOUSSE

1 env. unflavored gelatin
1 can cream of chicken soup
1 7-oz. can tuna
1/4 tsp. minced onion
1/8 tsp. salt
1 tbsp. lemon juice
1/4 c. mayonnaise
1 1/2 c. chopped cucumbers

Soften gelatin in 1/4 cup cold water. Bring soup to a boil in saucepan; add gelatin. Stir until dissolved. Drain tuna; flake. Fold tuna, onion, salt and lemon juice into soup mixture. Cool slightly; add mayonnaise and cucumbers. Mix well; pour into a 1-quart mold. Chill until firm.

CURRIED TUNA SALAD

1 can tuna
1 c. canned shrimp
1/2 c. chopped celery
1/4 c. chopped ripe olives
1/2 c. mayonnaise
2 tbsp. lemon juice
1 tsp. curry powder
3 c. cold cooked rice
2 tbsp. French dressing
1/2 c. snipped parsley

Drain tuna; break into pieces. Chill tuna and shrimp. Combine tuna, shrimp, celery and olives; add mayonnaise, lemon juice and curry powder. Toss lightly. Toss rice with French dressing and parsley; spoon onto serving platter. Heap salad on top.

TUNA GUMBO SALAD

1 pkg. lemon gelatin
1 can chicken gumbo soup
1 can tuna
1/2 c. diced celery
1/4 c. finely chopped onion
1/2 c. mayonnaise
1/2 c. cream, whipped

Dissolve gelatin in 1/2 cup boiling water; add soup. Chill until partially set. Drain tuna; flake. Add celery, onion and tuna; fold in mayonnaise and whipped cream. Pour into 6 individual molds or 1-quart mold; chill until firm.

SALAD NICOISE

1 lge. can tuna
1 head lettuce
1 onion, sliced
1 can red beets, chopped
1 can garbanzo beans
4 hard-cooked eggs, sliced
2 tomatoes, chopped
1/2 green pepper, chopped
Salt and pepper to taste
Whole dill seed to taste
1/8 tsp. garlic powder
Beau Monde seasoning to taste

Drain tuna; break into pieces. Tear lettuce into bite-sized pieces; separate onion into rings. Combine all ingredients in large salad bowl; toss lightly. Serve with desired dressing.

SUPER TUNA TOSS

1 clove of garlic, halved
2 7-oz. cans tuna
1/2 sm. head lettuce
1 c. thinly sliced celery
2 c. chopped spinach
1 c. bean sprouts, drained
1/4 c. chopped onion
1/2 c. French dressing
Tomato wedges

Rub inside of salad bowl with cut surface of garlic. Drain tuna; break into chunks. Tear lettuce into bite-sized pieces. Combine lettuce, tuna, celery, spinach, bean sprouts and onion in large salad bowl; add dressing. Toss lightly. Garnish with tomato wedges.

TUNA-ORANGE CUPS

1 7-oz. can tuna
6 oranges
1/2 c. sliced celery
2 tbsp. chopped pimento
1/2 c. cooked peas
2/3 c. French dressing
1 tbsp. Worcestershire sauce

Drain tuna; flake. Slice tops from oranges; remove pulp. Scallop edges of orange shells. Cut pulp into cubes; toss with tuna, celery, pimento, peas, French dressing and Worcestershire sauce. Fill orange shells.

TUNA SALAD IN TOMATOES

6 tomatoes
Lettuce
1 7-oz. can tuna
3 hard-cooked eggs
5 radishes, finely cut
1/4 c. finely cut celery
1/4 c. finely cut green pepper
1/2 tsp. garlic salt
1 tsp. pepper
Salad dressing

Arrange tomatoes on 6 lettuce-lined plates. Cut tomatoes into wedges almost to bottom. Spread wedges. Combine remaining ingredients except salad dressing; add salad dressing to moisten to desired consistency. Pile salad lightly into tomato cups.

TUNA SALAD WAIKIKI

2 7-oz. cans solid pack tuna
1/4 c. sour cream
1/4 c. mayonnaise
1 tbsp. white wine vinegar
1 tsp. monosodium glutamate
1 c. thinly sliced celery
2 tbsp. diced pimento
2 tbsp. chopped crystallized ginger
3/4 c. slivered toasted almonds
8 slices pineapple, chilled
Lettuce

Drain tuna; separate into bite-sized pieces. Blend sour cream, mayonnaise, vinegar and monosodium glutamate. Fold into tuna; mix well. Combine remaining ingredients except pineapple and lettuce; toss with tuna mixture. Arrange pineapple slices on lettuce on individual salad plates. Spoon tuna mixture over pineapple slices. Garnish with ripe olives if desired.

TUNA POLYNESIAN PLATTER

Color photograph for this recipe on page 312.

3/4 c. seedless raisins
3 7-oz. cans tuna in vegetable oil
1 c. chopped celery
3/4 c. flaked coconut
1/2 c. toasted slivered almonds
1/2 c. mayonnaise
2 tbsp. lemon juice
1 tsp. soy sauce
1/2 tsp. nutmeg
1/4 tsp. ginger
Salad greens
Pineapple slices
Peach halves
Pear halves
Figs
Apricots

Place raisins in saucepan; cover with water. Bring to a boil. Remove from heat; let stand for 5 minutes. Drain. Combine tuna, celery, coconut, raisins and almonds in bowl. Blend mayonnaise with lemon juice, soy sauce, nutmeg and ginger; toss lightly with tuna mixture. Chill. Pile tuna salad on greens in center of serving platter; arrange fruits around tuna salad. Garnish tuna salad with additional coconut and almonds if desired. Yield: 6-8 servings.

CREAMED TUNA WITH CHEESE ROLLS

1/2 c. sliced green pepper
2 slices onion
3 tbsp. butter
6 tbsp. flour
1 tsp. salt
3 1/2 c. milk
1 1-lb. can tuna, flaked
1 tbsp. lemon juice
1 1/2 c. flour
3 tsp. baking powder
Pepper to taste
3 tbsp. shortening
3/4 c. grated cheese
2 chopped pimentos

Saute green pepper and onion in butter in skillet until tender. Add flour and 1/2 teaspoon salt; stir until blended. Add 3 cups milk slowly; cook, stirring until thickened and smooth. Simmer for 2 minutes. Stir in tuna and lemon juice; pour into large shallow baking dish. Sift flour, baking powder, remaining salt and pepper; cut in shortening. Add remaining milk; stir until mixed. Knead lightly on floured board; roll out to 8 x 12-inch sheet. Sprinkle with cheese and pimentos. Roll up jelly roll fashion, starting at 8-inch side; cut into 8 slices. Flatten slightly; place on tuna mixture. Bake at 450 degrees for 30 minutes or until browned.

TUNA-CHEESE PIZZA ROLL-UPS

1 pkg. yeast
1 tbsp. sugar
1 tbsp. shortening
1 tsp. salt
3 c. (about) sifted flour
3 tbsp. butter
1 tbsp. oregano
1 1/2 tsp. garlic salt
1 c. milk
2 1/2 c. shredded mozzarella cheese
2 7-oz. cans tuna
1 med. green pepper

Dissolve yeast in 1/4 cup warm water. Heat 1 cup water in saucepan until almost simmering. Combine sugar, shortening and salt in mixing bowl. Stir in hot water until sugar is dissolved and shortening is melted. Cool to lukewarm. Stir in 1 cup flour; beat until smooth. Beat in yeast. Stir in enough flour to make moderately stiff dough. Turn out onto lightly floured board; knead for 5 to 8 minutes or until smooth and satiny. Shape into ball; place in lightly greased bowl, turning to grease sides. Cover; let rise in warm place for about 1 hour or until doubled in bulk. Punch down. Divide dough in half; shape each half into a ball. Let rest for 10 minutes. Melt butter in saucepan; stir in 1/4 cup flour, oregano and garlic salt. Blend in milk gradually. Bring to a boil, stirring constantly. Remove from heat; stir in 1 1/2 cups cheese. Cool. Roll out each half of dough into greased 13-inch pizza pan. Spread half the cheese mixture on each circle, leaving 1/2-inch border. Drain and flake tuna; spread half the tuna and 1/2 cup cheese over pizzas. Top with green pepper. Bake in 425-degree oven for 15 to 20 minutes or until edges are golden brown. Cut each circle into 6 equal wedges. Roll up wedges as for jelly roll beginning at narrow end. Secure with wooden picks. Serve warm.

Tuna-Cheese Pizza Roll-Ups . . . Cut pizza into wedges, roll up, and skewer with party picks.

CURRIED TUNA WITH ALMOND RICE

1/2 c. butter
4 tbsp. flour
1 1/2 tsp. curry powder
2 c. milk
1 7-oz. can tuna
1 tsp. salt
1/2 tsp. pepper
1 c. chopped blanched almonds
3 c. hot cooked rice
Paprika

Melt 4 tablespoons butter over low heat; blend in flour and curry powder. Add milk; cook, stirring constantly, until thickened. Drain tuna; flake. Stir tuna, salt and pepper into curry sauce. Simmer, covered, for 30 minutes. Saute almonds in 2 tablespoons butter in saucepan. Stir in rice and remaining butter. Serve tuna mixture over rice. Sprinkle with paprika.

CURRIED TUNA WITH MUSHROOMS

1 med. onion, minced
3 tbsp. butter
1 14-oz. can pineapple chunks
1 tbsp. cornstarch
1 tbsp. curry powder
1/2 tsp. ground cloves
1 3-oz. can sliced broiled mushrooms
1 7-oz. can solid-pack tuna
1 1/2 c. cooked rice
3 tbsp. orange peel, finely chopped

Saute onion in butter until soft. Drain pineapple; reserve liquid. Reserve 1/2 cup pineapple for garnish; add remaining pineapple to onion. Mix cornstarch with 2 tablespoons water; add curry and cloves. Cook, stirring, until thickened. Add water to reserved juice to measure 2 cups; combine with mushrooms and tuna. Simmer, stirring occasionally, until smooth and heated through. Serve over rice in chafing dish. Garnish with reserved pineapple chunks and orange peel.

PACIFIC TUNA SURPRISE

2 tbsp. butter
1 c. thinly sliced onion
1 c. thinly sliced celery
1 lge. green pepper, diced
1 13 1/2-oz. can pineapple chunks
2 tbsp. cornstarch
1 13 1/4-oz. can chicken broth
2 tsp. soy sauce
1/2 tsp. salt
2 7-oz. cans tuna, drained
1/2 c. sliced water chestnuts
1 3-oz. can chow mein noodles

Heat butter in large skillet; add onion, celery and green pepper. Cook just until tender. Drain pineapple; reserve syrup. Combine reserved syrup and cornstarch; add chicken broth, soy sauce and salt. Pour into skillet; cook over medium heat, stirring constantly, until thickened and smooth. Add tuna, water chestnuts and pineapple; simmer, covered, until heated through. Serve over noodles.

GOURMET TUNA PIE

2 hard-cooked eggs, sliced
1 8-in. pie shell
2 cans tuna
2 eggs, well beaten
1/4 c. butter, melted
4 tsp. minced parsley
Salt
1/4 tsp. sweet basil
1 tsp. grated onion
2/3 c. shredded cucumber
1/4 c. mayonnaise
2 tsp. vinegar
1/2 c. sour cream
1/8 tsp. pepper

Arrange eggs in pie shell. Drain tuna; flake. Combine flaked tuna, eggs, butter, 2 teaspoons parsley, 1/4 teaspoon salt and basil; mix well. Pour over sliced eggs. Bake at 425 degrees for 20 to 25 minutes or until golden brown. Press onion and cucumber in strainer to remove juice; combine with remaining ingredients and dash of salt. Chill; serve with pie.

TUNA-CHEESE PIE

2 7-oz. cans tuna
1 unbaked 9-in. pie shell
1 c. shredded Swiss cheese
1 tbsp. flour
3 eggs
1/2 tsp. salt
1/2 tsp. dry mustard
Dash of cayenne
1/2 c. ale
1 c. heavy cream

Drain tuna; flake. Bake pie shell at 375 degrees for 8 minutes or until lightly browned. Arrange layers of tuna and cheese in pie shell. Sprinkle flour over cheese. Beat eggs, salt, mustard and cayenne together. Beat in ale and cream; pour over tuna and cheese. Bake for 40 minutes or until center is firm.

TUNA-CHEESE PUFF

1 c. flour
1/2 tsp. salt
1/4 tsp. pepper
1/4 tsp. ground thyme
1/4 c. grated Parmesan cheese
1 14 1/2-oz. can evaporated milk
5 eggs, separated
2 tbsp. lemon juice
1 7-oz. can tuna
1 tbsp. sesame seed

Preheat oven to 325 degrees. Combine flour, salt, pepper, thyme and cheese in medium mixing bowl. Stir in evaporated milk, slightly beaten egg yolks and lemon juice. Add undrained tuna, flaking with fork and mixing until blended. Beat egg whites until stiff but not dry. Fold into tuna mixture lightly. Turn into greased 1 1/2-quart casserole. Sprinkle sesame

Tuna-Cheese Puff . . . A quick and easy souffle-like blend of canned tuna, cheese, and seasonings.

seed over top. Bake for 1 hour. Serve immediately with lemon butter. Yield: 4-6 servings.

SWEET AND SOUR TUNA

3 tbsp. butter
2 green peppers, cut in strips
1 1-lb. can pineapple chunks
1 1-lb. can onions, drained
1 chicken bouillon cube
8 maraschino cherries
2 7-oz. cans tuna
2 tbsp. sugar
1/3 c. vinegar
1/4 c. cornstarch
Cooked rice

Melt butter in skillet; cook green peppers in butter for 5 minutes or until crisp-tender. Drain pineapple, reserve syrup. Add 1 cup reserved syrup, pineapple, onions and bouillon cube to green peppers; bring to a boil. Reduce heat; simmer for 5 minutes. Drain and halve cherries. Drain tuna; break into pieces. Add tuna, cherries, sugar and vinegar to green pepper mixture; blend well. Blend remaining reserved pineapple syrup with cornstarch; stir into tuna mixture. Simmer, stirring constantly, until clear and thickened. Serve over rice.

TUNA CANTONESE

2 tbsp. flour
1/2 tsp. salt
2 tbsp. butter, melted
1 c. milk
1/4 lb. Cheddar cheese spread
1 can flaked tuna
3 hard-boiled eggs, diced
1 c. salad dressing
1/4 c. chopped sweet pickles
1/4 c. chopped pimento
2 tbsp. chopped onion
1/4 c. chopped celery
1 can chow mein noodles
Paprika

Combine flour and salt with butter in skillet over medium heat; stir until smooth. Add milk; stir constantly until smooth and thickened. Add cheese spread, tuna, eggs, salad dressing, pickles, pimento, onion and celery; mix well. Spread noodles in buttered 6 x 10 x 2-inch baking dish; pour tuna mixture over noodles. Sprinkle with paprika. Bake at 350 degrees for 30 minutes or until heated through.

TUNA LOAF WITH DILL SAUCE

3 c. milk
3 c. soft bread cubes
2 cans tuna
4 eggs, lightly beaten
1/4 c. minced onion
1 tbsp. lemon juice
1 tbsp. minced parsley
1 1/2 tsp. salt
1 1/4 tsp. paprika
2 tbsp. butter
2 tbsp. flour
1/3 c. minced dill pickle
2 tbsp. dill pickle liquid
1 tbsp. chopped pimento

Combine 2 cups milk and bread cubes in saucepan; bring just to a boil. Remove from heat; beat until smooth. Drain tuna; flake. Combine tuna, bread mixture, eggs, onion, lemon juice, parsley, 1 teaspoon salt and 1 teaspoon paprika. Mix well; turn into greased 9 x 5 x 3-inch pan. Bake at 325 degrees for 55 minutes or until firm. Cool in pan for 10 minutes. Invert onto platter; slice. Melt butter in saucepan; blend in flour, remaining salt and remaining paprika. Cook, stirring, until bubbly. Add remaining milk gradually; simmer, stirring constantly, until thickened. Add dill pickle, pickle liquid and pimento; mix well. Heat through. Serve sauce over loaf.

TUNA A LA PHILIPPINE

1 c. diagonally sliced celery
1 med. onion, sliced
1/2 c. green pepper strips
1 tbsp. cooking oil
3 c. cooked rice
1/4 tsp. salt
1/4 tsp. monosodium glutamate
Dash of pepper
1/4 tsp. garlic salt
1/8 tsp. ground ginger
2 7-oz. cans tuna, drained

Cook celery, onion and green pepper in hot oil in large skillet until crisp-tender. Remove vegetables from skillet. Add rice, seasonings and ginger to skillet; mix well. Add tuna; stir lightly. Cook, stirring occasionally, over high heat for 2 minutes. Stir in 3/4 cup water; add vegetable mixture. Mix carefully; bring to a boil. Reduce heat; simmer, covered, for 5 minutes. Turn into heated serving dish; garnish outer edge with thin omelet strips or scrambled eggs.

Sauce Oriental

1/4 c. (packed) brown sugar
2 tsp. cornstarch
1/2 tsp. dry mustard
1/4 c. tarragon vinegar
1 tbsp. soy sauce

Mix sugar, cornstarch and mustard in small saucepan. Stir in vinegar, soy sauce and 1/2 cup water. Bring rapidly to a boil, stirring constantly; boil for 3 minutes or until thickened. Serve with Tuna a la Philippine.

TUNA TETRAZZINI

2 7-oz. cans tuna
1/2 lb. spaghetti
1/2 lb. sliced mushrooms
2 tbsp. butter
2 cans cream of mushroom soup
1 c. milk
2 tbsp. sherry
1/4 tsp. ground nutmeg
1/2 c. grated Parmesan cheese

Preheat oven to 375 degrees. Drain tuna; flake. Break spaghetti into 3-inch pieces. Cook in salted water until tender; drain. Saute mushrooms in butter over medium heat for 2 minutes. Combine mushrooms with spaghetti and tuna in 2 1/2-quart casserole. Blend soup, milk, sherry and nutmeg; stir into spaghetti mixture. Sprinkle with cheese. Bake for 35 minutes or until heated through and cheese is lightly browned.

Turkey

Savored for plumpness and tenderness, turkeys have a long history as traditional holiday fare. They are members of the poultry family and are bred for their large amount of succulent white meat. Turkey is high in protein, niacin, and iron. (2 slices roast turkey = 190 calories)

AVAILABILITY: Turkeys are available year-round in a variety of forms. The peak season runs from October through January. Turkeys are marketed dressed and ready-to-cook. *Dressed turkeys* are sold fresh and undrawn with the feathers removed. Ask your butcher to draw the bird, pull the leg tendons, and cut the neck off close to the body. Weigh the bird after it has been drawn to determine roasting weight. *Ready-to-cook turkeys* are sold fresh and frozen. They are packaged with the neck and giblets in the stomach cavity. Also available are fresh or frozen turkey parts; smoked turkey; boned and rolled turkey roasts; and pre-cooked turkey rolls.

BUYING: Look for a processor's brand name and U.S. Government Grade A or B when buying fresh or frozen turkey. For fresh turkey, there should be layers of yellow fat under the skin. The skin should be creamy and free from pinfeathers. The breastbone and joints should be flexible; the cavities, fresh-smelling. For turkeys under 12 pounds, allow 3/4-1 pound per person; for birds over 12 pounds, 1/2 to 3/4 pound is sufficient.

STORING: *For fresh turkeys*—Remove original wrapping. Wash and pat dry. Wrap bird loosely in plastic. Use within 2-4 days. *For frozen turkey*—Keep frozen in original wrapping until ready to use. *For cooked turkey*—Remove stuffing to separate container. Refrigerate and use within 2-3 days. Cover cooked turkey with foil and refrigerate for 5-6 days. *To freeze fresh turkey*—For ready-to-cook birds, unwrap, wash turkey, and pat dry. Remove giblets and wrap in moistureproof paper. Truss turkey so that wings and legs lie close to body. Wrap in moistureproof and vaporproof material, forcing all air out. Seal and freeze turkey and giblets in refrigerator frozen foods compartment 2-3 weeks, in home freezer 3 months. *Never stuff turkey before freezing. To freeze cooked turkey*—Remove turkey meat from bones and wrap in aluminum foil. Seal, label, and freeze in home freezer for 2 months.

PREPARATION: *For fresh turkey*—Wash bird inside and out with cold running water. *For frozen turkey*—To thaw, place frozen turkey in original wrapping in shallow pan. Thaw in refrigerator for 2-3 days, depending on size of bird. As soon as turkey has thawed, remove market wrapping. *To stuff and truss turkey*—Allow 1 scant cup of stuffing per pound of ready-to-cook turkey. Extra stuffing may be baked in aluminum foil or in a casserole dish (see DRESSINGS). Fill neck cavity lightly and fasten skin with skewers or stitching. Pull wing tips onto back, pierce and tie together. Pack stomach cavity lightly with stuffing. Insert skewers and lace cavity closed with string. Tie leg bones together. Place turkey on rack in open roasting pan. Insert meat thermometer between thigh and body. Do not allow thermometer to touch bone. Roast turkey in a 325 degree oven for the time listed under POULTRY. Turkey should be cooked to an internal temperature of 180-185 degrees. For other ways to prepare fresh or cooked turkey, see specific recipes.

SERVING: Remove cooked turkey to serving platter. Let turkey set 20-30 minutes before serving to facilitate carving. Garnish with sprigs of parsley and/or watercress. And remember to pass cranberry sauce.

(See CARVING and POULTRY.)

BREAST OF TURKEY IN ASPIC

4 tbsp. unflavored gelatin
1 pt. turkey stock
1/4 c. sherry
1 egg white
1 sm. can truffles
1 c. ham, cut up
1 lb. sliced turkey breast
Salt and pepper to taste

Soften gelatin in small amount of stock in saucepan; add remaining stock, sherry and egg white. Bring to a boil; boil for 2 minutes, stirring constantly. Sieve through muslin cloth without pressing. Pour 1/3 of the stock mixture into mold; chill until set. Slice truffles. Arrange truffles and ham over congealed mixture; cover with turkey. Season with salt and pepper; add remaining stock mixture. Chill until set or overnight.

MOLDED TURKEY AND CRANBERRY SALAD

2 env. unflavored gelatin
2 c. whole cranberry sauce
1 c. crushed pineapple
1/2 c. coarsely chopped walnuts
4 tbsp. lemon juice
2 c. diced cooked turkey
1 c. chopped celery
2 tbsp. minced parsley
1 c. mayonnaise
3/4 tsp. salt

Soften 1 envelope gelatin in 1/4 cup water; stir over hot water until gelatin is dissolved. Combine cranberry sauce, pineapple, walnuts and 1 tablespoon lemon juice; blend in dissolved gelatin. Turn into 9 x 5-inch loaf pan. Chill until firm. Soften remaining gelatin in 1/4 cup water; dissolve, stirring, over hot water. Combine turkey, celery, parsley, mayonnaise, salt and remaining lemon juice; add gelatin. Stir until well blended. Pour over first gelatin layer. Chill until firm.

TURKEY SALAD RING

1 env. unflavored gelatin
1/2 c. cold water
1 c. hot turkey stock
1/4 tsp. onion salt
2/3 c. chilled evaporated milk
1 tbsp. lemon juice
1 1/2 c. diced cooked turkey

Soften gelatin in 1/2 cup cold water; dissolve in turkey stock. Add onion salt; chill until partially set. Beat milk until soft peaks form; beat gelatin mixture until fluffy. Combine milk, gelatin mixture and lemon juice; fold in turkey. Pour into ring mold; chill until firm.

CURRIED PINEAPPLE-TURKEY SALAD

2 tsp. curry powder
1/2 c. cider vinegar
1 tbsp. sugar
Garlic salt
1 1-lb. 4 1/2-oz. can pineapple chunks
4 c. diced cooked turkey
1 c. thinly sliced celery
1/3 c. finely chopped green onions
1/4 c. finely chopped green pepper
1 c. mayonnaise
2 tsp. butter
1 c. dark seedless raisins

Combine curry powder, vinegar, sugar and 1/2 teaspoon garlic salt in saucepan; heat to simmering. Cool. Drain pineapple; Combine pineapple, curry mixture and turkey, mixing lightly. Chill well. Add onions, celery, green pepper and mayonnaise, tossing gently. Melt butter in skillet; saute raisins for 2 to 3 minutes. Sprinkle raisins with garlic salt to taste.

Curried Pineapple-Turkey Salad . . . An unusual and delicious way to use leftover turkey.

Spoon salad into lettuce-lined salad bowl. Serve with garlic raisins, chopped macadamia nuts, chopped hard-cooked egg, toasted coconut chips and other desired condiments.

CURRIED TURKEY SALAD

1 c. golden raisins
1 c. pineapple tidbits
4 c. cooked turkey
2 diced apples
2 ripe tomatoes, diced
1/2 c. flaked coconut
1 tsp. monosodium glutamate
1 1/4 c. mayonnaise
2 tsp. curry powder
2 tsp. chopped chutney

Pour 1 cup boiling water over raisins. Let stand for 5 minutes; drain well. Drain pineapple; reserve 2 tablespoons syrup. Toss turkey with pineapple, raisins, apples, tomatoes and coconut. Sprinkle with monosodium glutamate; toss. Blend mayonnaise with reserved pineapple syrup, curry powder and chutney. Add to turkey mixture; toss until well coated. Chill thoroughly; sprinkle with crumbled crisp bacon, if desired.

HOLIDAY TURKEY SALAD

4 c. cooked turkey
1 c. pineapple tidbits
1/2 c. chopped cranberries
1 c. seedless grapes
1 c. chopped apple
1/2 c. seedless raisins
1 c. chopped walnuts
1 1/2 c. mayonnaise
1/2 c. sugar
Lettuce

Combine turkey, fruits and walnuts; chill for 1 hour. Blend mayonnaise with sugar; mix until sugar is dissolved. Toss salad with mayonnaise mixture. Arrange in lettuce-lined salad bowl; serve immediately.

POLYNESIAN TURKEY SALAD

1 13 1/2-oz. can pineapple tidbits
2 c. diced cooked turkey
1 c. sliced celery
1/4 c. diced pimento
1/2 c. sour cream
1/4 tsp. salt
2 tbsp. lemon juice
1/4 tsp. dillweed
Salad greens

Drain pineapple. Combine pineapple, turkey, celery and pimento in large bowl; chill. Mix sour cream, salt, lemon juice and dillweed; stir into turkey mixture. Serve on salad greens.

TURKEY-FRUIT SALAD

1 c. diced turkey
1 c. chopped pineapple
1 c. chopped apple
1/2 c. chopped orange
1 lge. banana, sliced
1/2 c. sliced grapes
1/2 c. chopped walnuts
1/2 c. mayonnaise
1/4 c. orange juice
2 tsp. sugar

Combine turkey, pineapple, apple, orange, banana, grapes and walnuts; chill. Combine remaining ingredients; chill. Mix dressing with turkey mixture.

Macaroni-Turkey Salad . . . An attractive blend of macaroni, turkey, beans, and artichoke hearts.

MACARONI-TURKEY SALAD

1 tbsp. salt
2 c. elbow macaroni
1 c. sour cream
1/3 c. mayonnaise
1/4 c. lemon juice
1 tsp. seasoned salt
1/2 tsp. dillweed
1/4 tsp. white pepper
2 c. slivered cooked turkey
1 c. cut cooked green beans
1/4 c. chopped sweet onion
1 4-oz. can drained pimentos, halved
1 6-oz. jar marinated artichoke hearts, drained
Crisp salad greens

Add 1 tablespoon salt to rapidly boiling water in large saucepan. Add macaroni gradually so that water continues to boil. Cook, stirring occasionally, until tender. Drain in colander. Rinse with cold water; drain again. Blend sour cream, mayonnaise, lemon juice, seasoned salt, dillweed and pepper in large bowl. Add macaroni; toss well. Arrange turkey, beans, onion, pimentos and artichoke hearts over macaroni; chill. Toss together just before serving. Serve on salad greens. Yield: 4-6 servinas.

HOT TURKEY BUNS

4 c. diced turkey
1 c. chopped ripe olives
1 c. chopped celery
1 c. grated Cheddar cheese
1 c. salad dressing
16 hamburger buns

Mix all ingredients except buns in large mixing bowl. Scoop centers out of buns; fill with turkey mixture. Wrap buns tightly in foil; place on baking sheet. Bake in 350-degree oven for 15 minutes. Serve hot.

TURKEY SANDWICHES DELUXE

Slices bread
Cold sliced turkey
Slices Swiss cheese
Lettuce
Thousand Island dressing

Layer bread slice with turkey, Swiss cheese and lettuce; repeat layers. Top with dressing. Serve immediately.

TURKEY SALAD SANDWICHES

2 c. diced turkey
1 c. diced celery
2 tbsp. diced onion
2 chopped hard-boiled eggs
1/2 c. grated cheese
1/2 tsp. salt
1/2 tsp. pepper
1 c. mayonnaise
Bread slices

Combine all ingredients except bread slices; blend well. Spread mixture on bread for sandwiches.

CURRIED TURKEY SOUP

1 c. diced celery
1 c. diced peeled apple
1/2 c. chopped onion
1/4 c. butter
1/4 c. flour
2 tsp. curry powder
1 1/2 tsp. salt
1/8 tsp. pepper
1 qt. milk
2 c. diced cooked turkey

Saute celery, apple and onion in butter in saucepan until tender; blend in flour, curry powder, salt and pepper. Add milk gradually; simmer, stirring constantly, until thickened. Add turkey; heat through.

SPECIAL TURKEY SOUP

Turkey carcass
Leftover gravy and turkey
1 tsp. salt
1/8 tsp. pepper
1 med. onion, chopped
1/4 c. sliced celery
1/4 c. sliced carrot
1 tbsp. butter
1 tbsp. flour
Alphabet noodles
1 c. heavy cream
Sherry to taste

Break carcass into pieces; place in large kettle. Add gravy and meat; cover with water. Bring to a boil slowly; simmer, covered, for 4 hours. Add seasonings and vegetables; cook for 30 minutes longer. Cool; remove bones and skin. Refrigerate; skim off fat. Blend butter and flour into smooth paste; blend into soup before reheating. Return soup to heat; bring to a boil. Add desired amount of noodles; cook for 10 minutes, or until noodles are tender. Add cream and sherry; simmer, stirring, until just heated through.

THRIFTY TURKEY SOUP

Turkey carcass
2 onions, finely chopped
6 stalks celery, finely chopped
6 carrots, finely chopped
2 chicken bouillon cubes
1 c. rice

Cover carcass with water in large kettle; simmer for 2 hours or until meat falls from bones. Remove carcass; pick meat from bones. Strain broth; return meat and broth to kettle. Add remaining ingredients; mix well. Simmer, stirring occasionally, for 45 minutes.

TURKEY SOUP

1 turkey carcass
Giblets
2 tsp. salt
3/4 tsp. hot sauce
2 sprigs of parsley
2 celery stalks with leaves
2 onions, sliced
1/2 tsp. basil leaves
1 bay leaf
1/2 c. precooked rice
1 c. carrot slices
1 c. leftover diced turkey
Chopped parsley

Break up turkey carcass; place in large cooking pot. Add any leftover gravy and giblets. Add 2 quarts cold water, salt, hot sauce, parsley, celery stalks, onions, basil and bay leaf. Cover; simmer for 3 hours. Strain; skim off fat. Reheat to boiling point; add rice and carrot slices. Cover; cook for about 15 minutes or until rice is tender. Add diced turkey. Pour into soup tureen; garnish with chopped parsley. Yield: About 1 1/2 quarts.

Turkey Soup . . . A delicious, old-fashioned soup prepared with leftover turkey and seasonings.

DEEP-DISH TURKEY SUPREME

2 c. diced cooked turkey
1 4-oz. can sliced mushrooms, drained
1/4 c. sliced stuffed green olives
1 1-oz. envelope onion gravy mix
1/2 tsp. poultry seasoning
1 c. packaged biscuit mix

Combine turkey, mushrooms and olives in 1 1/2-quart casserole. Stir in gravy mix, 1 cup water and poultry seasoning. Combine biscuit mix and 1/4 cup water; stir just until moistened. Drop batter by spoonfuls over turkey mixture. Bake at 450 degrees for 10 minutes. Reduce oven temperature to 350 degrees. Bake for 10 minutes longer or until heated through and topping is golden brown.

SPECIAL TURKEY CASSEROLE

5 tbsp. sifted flour
1 tsp. salt
1/4 tsp. onion salt
1/4 c. melted butter
2 1/2 c. light cream
1 1/3 c. packaged precooked rice
1 1/2 c. turkey broth
1 1/2 c. cooked asparagus
Sliced turkey
1/2 c. grated American cheese
2 tbsp. toasted slivered almonds

Sift flour, 1/2 teaspoon salt and onion salt; add to butter in top of double boiler over boiling water. Cook, stirring, until blended; add cream. Cook, stirring occasionally, until thickened. Place rice in 2-quart shallow baking dish. Combine broth and remaining salt; pour over rice. Add asparagus and turkey; cover with sauce. Sprinkle with cheese. Bake at 375 degrees for 20 minutes. Top with almonds.

TURKEY SQUARES

2 pkg. frozen artichoke hearts, thawed
1 1-lb. 12-oz. can tomatoes
1 1-pt. 2-oz. can tomato juice
1/4 c. cooking oil
1/4 c. chopped onion
1/4 c. chopped green pepper
1 tsp. salt
1 tsp. garlic salt
Dash of cayenne
1 c. long grain rice
3 c. diced cooked turkey
1/4 c. sliced stuffed green olives
1 can mushroom soup
1/2 soup can milk

Thaw artichoke hearts; drain. Combine all ingredients except mushroom soup and milk in large mixing bowl; stir well. Place in greased 9-inch square pan. Bake at 350 degrees for 1 hour; let stand for 5 minutes. Cut into squares. Combine mushroom soup with milk; blend well. Serve hot with turkey squares.

FESTIVE TURKEY DIVAN

2 pkg. frozen broccoli spears
Sliced cooked turkey
2 cans cream of chicken soup
2 tsp. Worcestershire sauce
1 c. grated Parmesan cheese
2 tsp. prepared mustard
2 tsp. onion powder
1/4 c. sherry

Cook broccoli according to package directions; drain. Arrange broccoli in greased 13 x 9-inch pan; cover with layer of turkey. Combine remaining ingredients in saucepan; stir over low heat until cheese is melted. Pour mixture over turkey and broccoli. Bake at 400 degrees for 30 minutes.

TURKEY AND WILD RICE CASSEROLE

1 c. wild rice
1 lb. mushrooms, sliced
1 onion, chopped
3 tbsp. butter
2 tsp. salt
1/4 tsp. pepper
3 c. diced cooked turkey
1/2 c. sliced blanched almonds
3 c. turkey broth
1 1/2 c. heavy cream

Wash rice; cover with boiling water. Let stand for 1 hour; drain well. Saute mushrooms and onion in butter in large skillet for 10 minutes. Combine rice, mushrooms, onion, salt, pepper, turkey and almonds; spoon into greased casserole. Pour in broth and cream. Bake, covered, at 350 degrees for 1 hour and 30 minutes.

TURKEY LOAF

1/4 c. shortening
1 c. hot milk
2 c. chopped cooked turkey
2 c. soft bread crumbs
1/2 tsp. salt
1/4 tsp. pepper
2 eggs, beaten
1/4 c. chopped celery
1/4 c. chopped onion

Melt shortening in milk in saucepan over low heat. Combine remaining ingredients. Add milk mixture; blend well. Pack lightly into greased loaf pan. Bake at 350 degrees for 45 minutes. Let stand for 5 minutes before slicing.

TURKEY PIE WITH CORN BREAD TOPPING

1 can cream of mushroom soup
1 3/4 c. milk
1 c. cooked peas
1 pimento, sliced
1 1/2 c. diced cooked turkey
3/4 c. sifted flour
3/4 c. yellow cornmeal
2 tsp. baking powder
3/4 tsp. salt
1/4 c. shortening
1 egg, lightly beaten

Combine soup, 1 cup milk, peas, pimento and turkey in saucepan; heat through. Pour into shallow 2-quart baking dish. Combine flour, cornmeal, baking powder and salt; cut in shortening. Mix egg and remaining milk; add to flour mixture. Mix well; pour over turkey mixture. Bake at 425 degrees for 25 minutes or until topping is golden brown.

TURKEY ROLL-UP

3 tbsp. butter
4 tbsp. flour
1 tsp. instant minced onion
1 c. milk
1 1/2 c. diced cooked turkey
1 tsp. diced pimento
1/4 c. chopped black olives
1 tsp. salt
1/8 tsp. pepper
1/4 tsp. paprika
2 c. biscuit mix
1 egg yolk

Melt butter in saucepan; blend in flour and onion. Add milk; stir over low heat until thickened. Add turkey, pimento, olives, salt, pepper and paprika; cool. Prepare biscuit dough according to package directions; roll out in 1/4-inch thick square. Spread dough with turkey mixture to within 1 inch of edge; roll as for jelly roll. Place, seam side down, on greased baking sheet; prick top with fork. Beat egg yolk with small amount of water; brush roll with egg yolk. Bake in 450-degree oven for 25 minutes or until golden brown. Serve with turkey gravy.

TURKEY IN STUFFING CRUST

6 c. stuffing mix
1/2 c. chopped onion
3 tbsp. butter
1/4 c. flour
2 1/2 c. evaporated milk
3 c. chopped cooked turkey
1/4 tsp. pepper
1/4 tsp. thyme
1/8 tsp. poultry seasoning

Combine stuffing mix and enough water to moisten; mix well. Press into greased 12 x 7 1/2 x 2-inch baking dish. Bake at 400 degrees for 10 minutes. Saute onion in butter; blend in flour. Stir in milk gradually; simmer, stirring constantly, until sauce is smooth and thickened. Add remaining ingredients; mix well. Place in stuffing crust. Reduce oven temperature to 350 degrees; bake for 30 minutes or until heated through.

TURKEY TETRAZZINI

1 6-oz. package noodles
6 tbsp. butter
6 tbsp. flour
1/4 tsp. pepper
1/2 tsp. celery salt
2 c. turkey stock
1 c. cream, scalded
1 6-oz. can mushrooms
1/3 c. almonds
3 tbsp. minced parsley
2 c. turkey
1/2 c. grated longhorn cheese

Cook noodles in boiling salted water until tender; drain. Melt butter in saucepan. Add flour; blend well. Add seasonings and stock; cook, stirring constantly, over low heat until thickened. Remove from heat; stir in cream, mushrooms, almonds and parsley. Alternate layers of noodles, turkey and mushroom sauce in greased 2-quart casserole; top with cheese. Bake in 350-degree oven for 1 hour.

TURKEY WALDORF

2 c. milk
8 c. turkey stock
1 c. butter
1 1/2 c. flour

1/8 tsp. nutmeg
1/4 tsp. celery salt
1/8 tsp. poultry seasoning
1/2 c. sauterne
10 c. cooked turkey
4 c. canned white grapes
4 c. slivered toasted almonds
4 c. fine bread crumbs

Combine milk and stock in saucepan; heat. Blend butter in flour in saucepan; add seasonings. Add hot liquid; simmer, stirring occasionally, until smooth and thickened. Add sauterne; blend well. Arrange layers of turkey, grapes, 3 1/2 cups almonds and bread crumbs in greased casserole; repeat until all are used. Cover with remaining almonds. Bake at 350 degrees for 20 minutes or until heated through and lightly browned.

ROAST TURKEY WITH ORANGE-RICE STUFFING

1 12-lb. turkey
1 c. butter
1 c. chopped onion
1 c. orange juice
3 tbsp. grated orange rind
4 c. chopped celery
1 tsp. poultry seasoning
5 1/3 c. packaged precooked rice
1/2 c. chopped parsley

Pat turkey cavity dry with paper toweling, leaving outside moist. Sprinkle cavity with salt to taste and pepper. Melt butter in large saucepan; add onion. Saute until onion is tender but not browned. Add 4 cups water, orange juice, orange rind, celery, 2 tablespoons salt and poultry seasoning. Bring to a boil; stir in rice. Cover; remove from heat. Let stand for 5 minutes; stir in parsley, fluffing rice with fork. Stuff rice mixture into neck and body cavity of turkey. Fasten neck skin to body with skewer. Push legs under band of skin at tail. Place turkey, breast side up, in shallow roasting pan. Cover with loose tent of aluminum foil if desired. Bake at 325 degrees for 4 hours and 30 minutes. Let stand for 15 to 20 minutes for easier carving.

BEST BARBECUED TURKEY

Color photograph for this recipe on page 75.

1/2 c. chopped onion
1 1/2 tbsp. butter
1 1/2 c. catsup
1/4 c. (packed) brown sugar
1 clove of garlic, minced
1 lemon, thinly sliced
1/4 c. Worcestershire sauce
2 tsp. prepared mustard
1 tsp. salt
1/4 tsp. pepper
1 6 to 12-lb. fresh or frozen turkey
Barbecue salt

Saute onion in butter in small saucepan until lightly browned. Add remaining ingredients, except turkey and barbecue salt; simmer for 20 minutes. Remove lemon slices. Store in covered jar in refrigerator if not used immediately. Thaw turkey, if frozen. Rinse turkey; pat dry. Start charcoal briquet fire 20 to 30 minutes before cooking turkey, allowing about 5 pounds charcoal for beginning fire. Push burning charcoal to center as turkey cooks and fire burns; add new briquettes as needed around edge. Sprinkle cavity of turkey generously with barbecue salt, using 2 to 3 tablespoons; prepare turkey for roasting, flattening wings over breast and tying securely. Insert spit rod in front of tail; run diagonally through breast bone. Fasten tightly with spit forks at both ends; tie legs together securely with twine. Test carefully for balance, readjusting spit rod until turkey is well balanced. Insert meat thermometer into thickest part of inside thigh, making sure thermometer does not touch bone or spit rod and that thermometer will clear charcoal as spit turns. Knock off gray ash from coals; push coals to back of firebox. Place drip pan made of heavy-duty foil directly under turkey in front of coals. Attach spit; start rotisserie. Cook for 25 minutes per pound or to 180 to 185 degrees on meat thermometer, basting generously and frequently with barbecue sauce during last 30 minutes of cooking.

ROAST TURKEY IN FOIL

1 12-lb. turkey
Salt to taste
Freshly ground pepper to taste
Butter
1 recipe stuffing
1/4 c. dry white wine
1/4 c. brandy
1 tsp. thyme
1 tsp. basil

Rub turkey cavity with salt and pepper; rub skin with butter. Fill turkey loosely with stuffing. Place turkey on large sheet of foil in roasting pan. Combine wine, brandy, thyme and basil; mix well. Pour over turkey; seal foil tightly. Bake at 400 degrees for 3 hours and 30 minutes; fold foil back. Bake for 30 minutes longer or until turkey is browned.

SMOKED TURKEY

1 7-lb. turkey
1/2 tsp. garlic salt
Salt and pepper
1/3 c. liquid smoke
1/4 c. butter

Rub turkey cavity and skin with garlic salt, salt and pepper. Brush turkey inside and out with 1/4 cup liquid smoke. Refrigerate overnight. Place turkey in shallow roasting pan. Bake in 500-degree oven for 15 minutes. Reduce oven temperature to 400 degrees. Combine 1 cup boiling water, butter and remaining liquid smoke; pour into baking pan. Bake turkey for 2 hours longer or until tender; baste with pan liquid. Serve cold.

TURKEY IN-A-BAG

1 12-lb. turkey
1 tsp. salt
1/2 c. melted butter
1 24-oz. loaf bread
Chopped onion to taste
Sage to taste
Pepper to taste
1 c. chopped celery tops
1 egg

Preheat oven to 325 degrees. Rub inside of turkey with salt; rub outside with butter. Tear bread in small pieces; add onion, sage, pepper, celery tops and egg. Mix well; stir in enough hot water to moisten. Stuff turkey cavity with part of the dressing. Place remaining dressing in casserole. Place turkey in brown paper bag with seam of bag on top; fasten securely with staples or paper clips. Place on broiler pan. Bake turkey and dressing for 3 hours. Tear bag open; use drippings for gravy.

EASY-BAKED TURKEY

1 12-lb. turkey
Butter

Preheat oven to 450 degrees. Pour 3 cups water into roasting pan. Rub breast of turkey well with butter. Place in roasting pan; cover. Bake for 1 hour and 10 minutes. Turn off oven heat; do not open oven door. Leave turkey in oven overnight.

ROAST TURKEY A LA BRISTOL

1 12-lb. turkey
Salt and pepper to taste
Paprika to taste
3/4 c. butter, softened
1 8-oz. can frozen orange juice concentrate

Preheat oven to 325 degrees. Season turkey inside and out with salt, pepper and paprika. Rub turkey inside and out with 1/4 cup butter; place in baking pan. Bake for 30 minutes. Pour orange juice concentrate over turkey; bake for 20 minutes longer. Mix remaining butter and 1/2 cup boiling water; baste turkey. Bake until turkey tests done; baste every 20 minutes with butter mixture. May prepare favorite dressing recipe and stuff turkey before baking, if desired.

TURKEY CROQUETTES

3 tbsp. butter
4 tbsp. flour
1 c. milk
2 c. diced cooked turkey
1/2 tsp. salt
1/8 tsp. paprika
1/8 tsp. celery salt
1 tsp. lemon juice
1/4 tsp. grated onion
2 c. crushed corn flakes
1 egg, beaten

Melt butter in saucepan; add flour. Cook, stirring, until smooth. Add milk; cook, stirring, until thickened. Combine turkey, 1/2 teaspoonful salt, paprika, celery salt, lemon juice, onion and milk mixture; mix well. Spread on plate. Chill for 6 hours or overnight. Shape as desired for croquettes; dip into crumbs. Mix egg with water; dip croquettes into egg mixture. Coat again with crumbs. Fry in deep fat until golden brown.

TURKEY CACCIATORE

3 c. chopped cooked turkey
1/4 c. cooking oil
1/2 c. chopped onions
1 2-lb. 3-oz. can tomatoes
1/2 c. dry white wine
1 tsp. salt
1/4 tsp. pepper
1/2 bay leaf
1/8 tsp. thyme
1/4 tsp. marjoram
Cooked spaghetti

Brown turkey lightly in oil. Add remaining ingredients except spaghetti; simmer, covered, for 1 hour. Remove cover; cook until thickened. Serve over spaghetti.

CREAMED TURKEY AND MUSHROOMS

2 3-oz. cans sliced broiled mushrooms
1/2 c. light cream
1 1/2 tsp. instant chicken bouillon
1/4 c. butter
1/3 c. flour
1/8 tsp. white pepper
1/8 tsp. grated nutmeg
2 c. diced cooked turkey
1 2-oz. jar pimentos, drained
2 tbsp. sherry
1/4 c. toasted slivered almonds

Drain mushrooms; reserve liquid. Add water to reserved liquid to measure 1 1/2 cups. Stir in cream and chicken bouillon. Melt butter in 10-inch skillet over moderate heat; blend in flour, pepper and nutmeg. Cook for 1 minute, stirring constantly. Stir in cream mixture; cook, stirring constantly, until thickened. Drain pimentos; slice. Stir in turkey, mushrooms and pimentos; heat through. Stir in sherry and half the almonds; sprinkle remaining almonds on top. Serve with hot scones.

TURKEY DELUXE

2 green peppers
1/2 c. butter
6 tbsp. flour
1/4 c. diced pimento
2 tbsp. Worcestershire sauce
1/2 tsp. onion salt
Salt to taste
2 7-oz. bottles lemon-lime carbonated drink
1 c. light cream
6 c. diced cooked turkey

Cut green peppers into thin strips; cook in butter over low heat for 5 minutes or until tender. Mix in flour; blend thoroughly. Add pimento, Worcestershire sauce, onion salt and salt. Stir in carbonated drink and cream; simmer, stirring constantly, until thickened and smooth. Add turkey; simmer, stirring constantly, until heated through. Serve over rice or noodles. Yield: 12 servings.

EAST INDIAN CURRIED TURKEY

6 tbsp. margarine
1 med. onion, minced
2 tbsp. diced green pepper
4 tbsp. flour
1 1/2 c. turkey stock
1 6-oz. can mushrooms
3 c. cubed cooked turkey
1 lge. apple, pared and diced
1 5-oz. can water chestnuts, drained and sliced
3 tbsp. chopped pimento
1 tbsp. finely chopped parsley
1 1/2 tsp. curry powder
Salt and pepper to taste

Melt margarine in large skillet; add onion and green pepper. Saute until tender; stir in flour until smooth. Add stock and mushrooms. Mix turkey, apple, water chestnuts, pimento, parsley, curry powder, salt and pepper. Add to flour mixture; stir well. Heat through.

Turnip

Turnips are root vegetables with a delicate white flesh and a vivid purple collar around the crown. They are slightly flattened in shape. The leafy turnip greens are also a tasty vegetable. Although turnips are members of the mustard family, they are usually associated with rutabagas. (See RUTABAGA.) Turnips and turnip greens are rich in nutrients: Vitamins A and C, calcium, iron, and riboflavin. (4 ounces cooked turnips = 25 calories; 4 ounces cooked turnip greens, including liquid = 23 calories)

AVAILABILITY: Fresh, frozen, and canned turnips and greens are available year-round. The peak months for fresh crops are from October through March.

BUYING: Turnips are sold in bunches with or without the tops. To select turnips–See RUTABAGA. To select greens–Look for young, tender, bright green leaves that are neither wilted or yellowed.

STORING: For turnips–See RUTABAGA. For greens–Remove turnip roots and damaged leaves. Rinse thoroughly in cold, running water. Follow specific recipe directions for cooking turnip greens.

USES: Both turnips and turnip greens are welcome main-dish accompaniments, especially with duck, mutton, or pork.

(See VEGETABLES.)

DOGPATCH TURNIPS

1 lb. turnips
4 tbsp. butter, melted
4 tbsp. flour
1 tbsp. minced onion
1/3 c. cream
Salt and pepper to taste
3 eggs, separated

Pare and slice turnips; cook in saucepan in small amount of salted water for 30 minutes or until tender. Drain; reserve 1/3 cup liquid. Mash turnips. Combine butter and flour in saucepan; add onion, reserved liquid and cream gradually. Simmer, stirring constantly, until smooth and thickened. Add mashed turnips and seasonings; stir small amount of hot mixture into well-beaten egg yolks. Blend egg yolk mixture with hot mixture in saucepan. Beat egg whites until stiff peaks form; fold into turnip mixture. Pour into buttered baking dish. Bake at 350 degrees for 25 minutes or until heated through. Yield: 6 servings.

FRIED TURNIPS

Turnips
Salt
Flour
1 egg, beaten
Finely ground bread crumbs
Shortening

Pare turnips; cut in 1/2-inch slices. Cook in boiling salted water until just tender; drain. Cool. Combine egg with 1 tablespoon water. Dip slices in flour; dip in egg mixture. Dip in bread crumbs. Fry turnip slices in small amount of hot shortening in skillet until golden brown on both sides.

GOLDEN TURNIP SCALLOP

1 apple
6 c. shredded yellow turnips
1 tsp. salt
2 tbsp. (packed) brown sugar
1/8 tsp. pepper
4 tbsp. butter

Pare, core and chop apple. Mix turnips, 3/4 of the apple, salt, brown sugar and pepper in 6-cup baking dish. Sprinkle remaining chopped apple in ring on top; dot with butter. Cover. Bake in 350-degree oven for 1 hour and 30 minutes or until turnips are tender.

STEAMED TURNIPS

1 lb. sliced young turnips
Salt and pepper
Butter
Lemon juice to taste
Vinegar to taste

Steam turnips in small amount of water in steamer for 20 minutes or until tender; drain. Season with salt and pepper; add butter, juice and vinegar. Toss lightly.

SCALLOPED TURNIPS

6 med. turnips
1 egg
1/2 c. cream
Grated cheese

Boil turnips in salted water until tender. Drain; slice. Place in baking dish. Beat egg and cream together; pour over turnips. Sprinkle cheese over turnips. Bake at 350 degrees for 20 minutes or until cheese melts.

SCALLOPED TURNIPS AND PEAS

2 c. cooked mashed turnips
1 c. cooked peas
4 tbsp. butter
4 tbsp. flour
2 c. milk
1 tsp. salt
1/4 tsp. pepper
1/2 c. bread crumbs
1/2 c. grated cheese

Place turnips and peas in 1-quart casserole. Melt butter in saucepan; add flour, stirring until well blended. Add milk; cook, stirring constantly, until thickened. Add salt and pepper. Pour sauce over vegetable mixture. Sprinkle with crumbs and cheese. Bake at 375 degrees for 25 minutes or until heated through.

TURNIP CUPS

6 sm. white turnips, pared
1 tbsp. lemon juice
3 cooked beets, diced
4 tsp. butter

Cook turnips in water with lemon juice until just tender; cool. Scoop out centers; stuff turnips with beets. Dot with butter; place in shallow baking dish. Bake at 325 degrees for 20 minutes or until heated through. Serve garnished with parsley.

STUFFED TURNIPS

8 med. turnips, peeled
1/2 lb. ground beef
2 tbsp. catsup
1 c. bread crumbs
1 tsp. finely chopped onion
Salt and pepper
Butter

Cook turnips in salted water until just tender; drain. Cool. Scoop out centers; reserve 2 tablespoons pulp. Mash reserved pulp. Mix beef, catsup, 1/2 cup bread crumbs, onion, reserved pulp, salt and pepper. Spoon filling into turnip cups. Cover with remaining bread crumbs; dot with butter. Bake at 350 degrees for 40 minutes.

TOP-OF-THE-STOVE TURNIPS

1 c. milk
1 tsp. salt
3 c. pared thinly sliced turnips
2 c. pared sliced carrots
1/2 c. sliced onion
1/4 c. diced celery
1/4 c. diced green pepper
1 tbsp. butter
1 c. grated American cheese
3 tbsp. fine cracker crumbs

Bring 1 cup water and milk to a boil in saucepan. Add salt, turnips, carrots, onion, celery and green pepper; simmer, covered, for 20 minutes or until just tender. Add butter, grated cheese and cracker crumbs. Simmer, covered, until cheese is melted.

TURNIP GREENS

1/2 lb. bacon
3 lb. turnip greens

Chop bacon. Wash greens; remove tough stems and bruised leaves. Combine bacon and greens in 1 quart water in a saucepan; bring to a boil. Reduce heat; simmer, covered, for 45 minutes or until greens are tender.

TURNIP GREENS WITH CORNMEAL DUMPLINGS

3 lb. turnip greens
1/2 lb. sliced bacon
1/2 c. sifted flour
1 tsp. baking powder
1/2 c. yellow corn meal
1/2 tsp. garlic salt
1/8 tsp. pepper
1 egg
1/4 c. milk
1 tbsp. melted butter

Wash greens; remove tough stems and bruised leaves. Chop bacon. Combine greens and bacon in saucepan in 1 1/2 quarts water; bring to a boil. Reduce heat; simmer, covered, for 45 minutes or until greens are tender. Sift dry ingredients into mixing bowl; add egg, milk and butter. Stir until batter is well mixed. Drop dumplings by teaspoonfuls into greens. Cover tightly; simmer for 15 minutes.

TURNIP PUFF

1 tbsp. finely minced onion
2 tbsp. butter
2 tbsp. flour
3 c. mashed turnips
1 tsp. salt
1 tbsp. sugar
1/8 tsp. pepper
2 eggs, separated

Cook onion in butter until just tender. Add flour; blend well. Add turnips, salt, sugar, pepper and beaten egg yolks; stir well. Beat egg whites until stiff but not dry; fold into turnip mixture. Pour into buttered casserole. Bake at 375 degrees for 40 minutes.

Vanilla

VANILLA OPERA CREAMS

1/4 lb. butter
1 lb. confectioners' sugar
2/3 c. milk
1 tsp. vanilla

Melt butter in saucepan; add sugar and milk. Bring to a boil; boil until mixture forms soft ball, or 234 degrees on candy thermometer. Remove from heat. Add vanilla; beat until creamy. Turn into buttered pan; cool slightly. Cut into squares.

CREAM LAYER CAKE

3 eggs, separated
1 c. sugar
1 c. sifted flour
1 tsp. baking powder
1 tsp. unflavored gelatin
1/2 c. milk
1/2 pt. cream
1/4 c. confectioners' sugar
1/2 tsp. vanilla

Beat egg yolks with sugar in large mixing bowl. Add 3 tablespoons water; mix well. Sift flour with baking powder; fold into egg mixture. Beat egg whites until stiff peaks form; fold into flour mixture. Pour batter into 3 layer cake pans. Bake at 400 degrees for 10 minutes or until cake tests done. Soften gelatin in milk; heat, stirring constantly, until gelatin is dissolved. Cool. Whip cream and confectioners' sugar; add vanilla. Add gelatin mixture; blend well. Refrigerate for at least 3 hours. Spread gelatin mixture between cake layers. Top with gelatin mixture.

VANILLA CHIFFON CAKE

2 c. flour
1 1/2 c. sugar
3 tsp. baking powder
1 tsp. salt
1/2 c. oil
7 egg yolks
2 tsp. vanilla
1/2 tsp. cream of tartar
1 c. egg whites

Sift flour, sugar, baking powder and salt into mixing bowl; make a well in dry ingredients. Add oil, egg yolks, 3/4 cup water and vanilla. Beat with mixer at medium speed for 2 minutes or until smooth. Add cream of tartar to egg whites in large bowl; beat with mixer at high speed until stiff peaks form. Pour batter over beaten egg whites gradually; fold gently just until blended. Pour into 10-inch tube pan. Bake at 325 degrees for 55 minutes. Increase oven temperature to 350 degrees. Bake for 10 minutes longer or until cake tests done. Invert to cool. Frost with desired frosting.

VANILLA WAFER CAKE

1 c. butter
2 c. sugar
6 eggs
1/2 c. milk
1 tsp. vanilla
1 c. chopped pecans
1 7-oz. can flaked coconut
1 12-oz. box vanilla wafers, crushed

Cream butter and sugar together; add eggs, one at a time, beating well after each addition. Add milk and vanilla; mix well. Add pecans, coconut and vanilla wafers; mix well. Pour into well-greased and floured tube pan. Bake at 350 degrees for 1 hour.

VANILLA-NUT COOKIES

1 1/2 tsp. baking powder
2 c. sifted flour
1/8 tsp. salt
6 tbsp. butter
1 c. sugar
1/4 c. (packed) brown sugar
1 egg, well beaten
1 c. chopped nuts
1 tbsp. milk
1 1/2 tsp. vanilla

Sift baking powder, flour and salt. Cream butter thoroughly in large mixing bowl; add sugars gradually. Cream until light and fluffy; stir in egg, nuts, milk and vanilla. Add dry ingredients gradually. Mix well. Shape into rolls, 1 1/2 inches in diameter; roll in waxed paper. Chill overnight or until firm enough to slice. Cut into 1/8-inch thick slices. Bake at 425 degrees for 5 minutes or until lightly browned.

VANILLA SPRITZ COOKIES

2 c. butter
1 c. confectioners' sugar
1/2 c. sugar
1 egg
3 1/2 c. flour
1 tsp. vanilla

Combine all ingredients in large mixing bowl; blend thoroughly. Force dough through cookie press onto chilled baking sheets. Bake at 375 degrees for 8 minutes or until set but not browned.

BAKED CUSTARD

4 c. milk
1/2 c. sugar
4 eggs
1/4 tsp. salt
1 tsp. vanilla
Mace to taste

Scald milk. Combine sugar, eggs, salt and vanilla in large mixing bowl; beat well. Add milk to egg mixture gradually; beat until smooth. Pour custard into eight 5-ounce custard cups; place cups in shallow pan in hot water 1 inch deep. Sprinkle custard with mace. Bake at 325 degrees for 45 minutes or until knife inserted in center comes out clean.

BLENDER CUSTARD

3 eggs
2 c. milk
1/2 c. powdered milk
1/4 c. sugar
1/8 tsp. salt
1 tsp. vanilla
Cinnamon to taste

Place all ingredients except cinnamon in blender container; blend thoroughly. Pour into greased baking dish. Sprinkle with cinnamon. Place baking dish in shallow pan in hot water 1 inch deep. Bake at 300 degrees for 40 minutes or until knife inserted in center comes out clean.

FLAN

4 tbsp. sugar
2 c. milk
4 eggs, beaten
2 tbsp. sugar
1/8 tsp. salt
1/2 tsp. vanilla

Caramelize sugar in small skillet until light brown syrup forms. Spread on sides and bottom of 6 custard cups immediately. Scald milk in large saucepan; stir in eggs, sugar, salt and vanilla gradually. Blend well. Pour into custard cups. Set cups in pan of hot water. Bake at 350 degrees for 30 minutes or until knife inserted in center comes out clean. Loosen custards; invert. Chill before serving.

CRÉME BRÛLÉE

1 pt. heavy cream
1 tbsp. sugar
4 egg yolks
1 tsp. vanilla
3/4 c. (packed) light brown sugar

Pour cream into top of double boiler; cook, covered, over hot water for 5 minutes or until just heated through. Remove from heat. Add sugar; stir until dissolved. Beat yolks well; beat into cream. Add vanilla; stir well. Pour into 8-inch square glass baking dish; set in pan of water. Bake at 300 degrees for 50 minutes or until set. Cool; chill well. Sprinkle brown sugar over custard. Broil 6 inches from source of heat just until sugar is melted. Cool; refrigerate. Tap caramel to break before serving.

DELUXE VANILLA ICE CREAM

2/3 c. sweetened condensed milk
1 1/2 tsp. vanilla
1 c. heavy cream

Combine milk and vanilla with 1/2 cup water; chill. Whip cream until soft peaks form. Fold whipped cream into chilled mixture. Pour into freezer trays; freeze until just firm. Place mixture in mixing bowl; beat just until smooth. Return to freezer trays; freeze until firm.

EASY VANILLA ICE CREAM

4 eggs
2 c. sugar
2 tbsp. vanilla
1 1/2 pt. cream
3 1/2 qt. milk

Beat eggs; add sugar gradually. Beat until sugar is dissolved. Stir in remaining ingredients; mix well. Pour into ice cream freezer container to 1 inch from top. Freeze according to freezer directions.

OLD-FASHIONED CREAM PIE

1 1/4 c. sugar
1/4 c. flour
1 2/3 c. cream
2 tbsp. butter
1 tsp. vanilla
Yellow food coloring
1 unbaked 9-in. pie shell
Nutmeg

Combine sugar and flour. Heat cream in saucepan. Add sugar mixture; cook, stirring constantly, until slightly thickened. Add butter and vanilla; mix well. Add food coloring to desired tint; pour into pie shell. Sprinkle lightly with nutmeg. Bake at 400 degrees for 20 minutes.

VANILLA GRAHAM CRACKER PIE

2 c. milk
3 tbsp. flour
1 3/4 tbsp. cornstarch
Sugar
1/4 tsp. salt
2 egg yolks, slightly beaten
Butter
1 tsp. vanilla
1 baked 8-in. pie shell
4 graham crackers, crushed fine
Meringue

Scald milk in top of double boiler. Combine flour, cornstarch, 1/2 cup sugar and salt; mix thoroughly. Add to scalded milk; cook, stirring constantly, for 15 minutes or until smooth and thickened. Add small amount of hot mixture to egg yolks; blend well. Stir egg yolk mixture into hot mixture; return to heat. Add 1 tablespoon butter; cook for 1 minute longer. Cool. Add vanilla; pour into pie shell. Combine cracker crumbs with 1 teaspoon butter and 1 teaspoon sugar; sprinkle half the mixture over filling. Pile meringue lightly over filling; sprinkle with remaining crumb mixture. Bake in 325-degree oven for 15 minutes or until firm and lightly browned.

VELVETY CUSTARD PIE

4 eggs, slightly beaten
1/2 c. sugar
1/4 tsp. salt
1 tsp. vanilla
2 1/2 c. milk, scalded
1 unbaked 9-in. pie shell
Nutmeg

Combine eggs, sugar, salt and vanilla in large bowl; mix thoroughly. Stir in milk slowly; blend well. Pour into pie shell immediately; sprinkle top with nutmeg. Bake in 475-degree oven for 5 minutes. Reduce oven temperature to 425 degrees. Bake for 10 minutes longer or until knife inserted in center comes out clean.

COTTAGE PUDDING

1/4 c. butter
2/3 c. sugar
1 egg, beaten
2 1/4 c. flour
4 tsp. baking powder
1/2 tsp. salt
1 c. milk
Vanilla Sauce

Cream butter and sugar. Add egg; blend well. Sift flour, baking powder and salt; add to creamed mixture alternately with milk. Spoon batter into greased muffin pans. Bake at 350 degrees for 35 minutes. Serve with Vanilla Sauce.

Vanilla Sauce

1/2 c. sugar
1 tbsp. cornstarch
2 tbsp. butter
1 tsp. vanilla
1/8 tsp. salt

Mix sugar and cornstarch in saucepan; add 1 cup boiling water gradually, stirring constantly. Boil, stirring constantly, for 5 minutes; remove from heat. Add butter, vanilla and salt; blend well.

RICH VANILLA PIE

1 c. (packed) brown sugar
1/2 c. dark molasses
Flour
1 egg
1 tsp. vanilla
1 unbaked 9-in. pie shell
1/2 tsp. soda
1/2 tsp. baking powder
1/4 c. shortening, melted

Combine 1/2 cup sugar, molasses, 1 cup flour, egg, 1 cup water and vanilla in saucepan; mix well. Cook, stirring constantly, until thickened; pour into pie shell. Combine remaining sugar, 1 tablespoon flour, soda, baking powder and shortening; blend until of consistency of coarse meal. Top pie with crumbs. Bake at 375 degrees for 40 minutes or until filling is set.

BLITZ TORTE

1/2 c. butter
1 1/2 c. sugar
4 eggs, separated
5 tbsp. milk
1 c. flour
1 tsp. baking powder
1 c. chopped nuts
Custard

Cream butter and 1/2 cup sugar; beat egg yolks until thick and lemony. Add egg yolks, milk, flour and baking powder to creamed mixture; blend well. Spread batter in 2 greased 9-inch pans. Beat egg whites until stiff peaks form. Add remaining sugar gradually. Beat until glossy. Spread over batter; sprinkle with nuts. Bake at 250 degrees for 25 minutes. Increase oven temperature to 350 degrees. Bake for 20 minutes longer. Place 1 layer on serving dish; cover with custard. Top with remaining layer.

Custard

1 egg
1/3 c. sugar
2 tsp. flour
1/8 tsp. salt
1 c. milk
Vanilla to taste

Blend egg, sugar, flour and salt in top of double boiler; stir in milk. Cook, stirring constantly, over hot water until thickened; stir in vanilla.

THUNDER AND LIGHTNING TORTE

1 1/2 c. sugar
1/2 c. butter
4 eggs, separated
7 tbsp. milk
1 c. flour
1 tbsp. baking powder
1 c. chopped nuts
Whipped cream

Cream 1/2 cup sugar with butter; add egg yolks. Blend thoroughly. Add milk, flour and baking powder; mix well. Pour batter into 2 greased 8-inch cake pans. Beat egg whites until stiff peaks form; add remaining sugar gradually. Beat until glossy. Spread meringue over cakes; sprinkle nuts over meringue. Bake at 350 degrees for 30 minutes. Cool. Spread whipped cream between layers and on top of cake.

Veal

Veal, calves' flesh used as food, is mild-flavored, succulent, and exceptionally tender. The finest lean veal is from milk-fed calves that are 6 to 12 weeks old. Veal supplies protein, calcium, iron, and niacin. (3 1/2 ounces broiled veal loin chop = 235 calories; 3 1/2 ounces broiled veal cutlet = 215 calories; 3 1/2 ounces veal rib roast = 270 calories)

AVAILABILITY: Veal is sold year-round. It is especially plentiful in late winter and spring. Veal is available in a variety of retail cuts to suit individual tastes and budgets. See chart.

BUYING: Always examine meat packer's brand and U. S. Department of Agriculture grades. Government grades, in order of meat excellence, are US Prime, US Choice, US Good, US Standard, US Utility. Appearance of meat depends on age of calf when butchered. The most desirable veal is grayish pink, fine-grained, velvety, and lean. There is no fat marbling but there may be some white exterior fat. Exterior fat should be firm and creamy. Bones are small, soft, and red. Meat from older animals is redder. Roasts should be deep pink, firm, and covered with a layer of yellowish fat. In buying roasts, allow 1/4 to 1/3 pound boneless or 1/3 to 1/2 pound bone-in per serving.

STORING: Remove meat from original package. Rewrap loosely and refrigerate. Use ground veal and stew meat within 2 days, all other meats within 2 to 3 days. Veal can be frozen 1 to 2 weeks in refrigerator's freezer or 6 to 7 months in home freezer. Ground veal, however, stores 2 to 3 months in home freezer.

PREPARATION: Veal is cooked in a variety of ways depending on retail cut. See chart. Veal needs extra-special handling since it has less fat and more connective tissues than other popular meats such as beef. For perfect tenderness and juiciness, lard veal with bacon, salt pork or fatback pork or place strips of fat over top of meat. For better flavor and color keep roasts uncovered while cooking. Do not uncover veal while braising. When preparing stews, brown veal first for added flavor.

SERVING: Do not serve strong-flavored vegetables with veal; choose complementary delicate vegetables. Use veal also in loaves, pies.

BREADED VEAL CHOPS

1/2 tsp. salt
1/8 tsp. pepper
2 tbsp. flour
4 veal chops, boned
1 egg, beaten
Fine bread crumbs
1/2 c. oil
1 c. light cream
2 tbsp. minced parsley
1/4 c. chopped onion

Combine salt, pepper and flour; dredge veal chops. Dip chops into egg; roll in bread crumbs. Cook slowly in oil until golden brown on both sides. Remove chops to hot platter. Add cream, parsley and onion to browned bits in pan; blend thoroughly. Simmer until heated through; serve with veal.

ORIENTAL VEAL CHOPS

1 c. rice
1 tsp. salt
1 can onion soup
1 tsp. thyme
4 thick veal chops
Salt and pepper
2 tbsp. shortening
2 tbsp. lemon juice
1 can mandarin oranges
3/4 c. pitted cooked prunes

Combine rice, salt, soup and thyme in shallow baking dish; blend well. Sprinkle chops with salt and pepper; brown in shortening in skillet. Place on rice mixture. Add 1/2 cup water to pan drippings; stir to blend thoroughly. Pour over veal chops; sprinkle with lemon juice. Bake, covered, in 350-degree oven for 30 minutes; remove from oven. Drain oranges; reserve liquid. Place prunes and oranges on chops; add reserved liquid. Bake, covered, for 20 minutes longer.

MARINATED VEAL CHOPS

4 3/4-in. thick veal chops
2 cloves of garlic, minced
1/3 c. salad oil
3 tbsp. soy sauce
2 tbsp. catsup
1 tbsp. vinegar
1/4 tsp. pepper

Trim veal. Combine garlic, salad oil, soy sauce, catsup, vinegar and pepper in shallow pan; blend thoroughly. Place veal in marinade; turn to coat well. Refrigerate, covered, for at least 3 hours or overnight. Saute veal in small amount of fat in skillet for 25 minutes or until browned on both sides and tender.

VEAL POLONAISE

4 veal loin chops
Salt and pepper
1/4 c. flour
1 lge. onion, sliced
3 tbsp. chopped parsley
1 tbsp. oil
1 8-oz. can tomato sauce
1/2 c. beef bouillon
1 4-oz. can mushrooms
1/2 c. sour cream
2 tbsp. sherry

Sprinkle chops on both sides with salt and pepper; flour lightly. Brown chops, onion and parsley in oil in large skillet; stir in tomato sauce, bouillon and mushrooms. Bring to a boil; reduce heat. Simmer, covered, for 30 minutes or until chops are tender. Arrange chops on platter. Stir sour cream and sherry into gravy. Bring just to a boil; pour over chops. Garnish with parsley. Serve with rice.

VEAL GOURMET

1 5-oz. can water chestnuts
1 3-oz. can sliced mushrooms
1/2 c. dry red wine
1/2 tsp. salt
1/8 tsp. marjoram
1/4 tsp. monosodium glutamate
4 3/4-in. thick veal chops
2 tbsp. shortening
2 tbsp. cornstarch
Paprika

Drain water chestnuts and mushrooms; reserve liquid. Slice water chestnuts paper thin. Combine wine, salt, marjoram and monosodium glutamate in shallow dish; marinate chops for at least 1 hour in mixture. Drain; reserve marinade. Brown chops in hot shortening in skillet; add marinade. Simmer, covered, for 30 minutes or until chops are tender. Combine reserved liquids and cornstarch; stir into veal mixture. Add water chestnuts and mushrooms; blend well. Simmer, stirring until thickened. Sprinkle with paprika before serving.

VEAL VERONICA

6 3/4-in. thick veal chops
2 tbsp. cooking oil
Salt and pepper
1 chicken bouillon cube
1/2 c. dry white wine
1 tbsp. cornstarch
1 tbsp. snipped parsley
1 tbsp. chopped green onion
1 c. halved grapes
2 tsp. lemon juice

Brown chops in oil in skillet; season with salt and pepper. Dissolve bouillon cube in 1/2 cup boiling water; add to chops. Pour in wine; simmer, covered, for 45 minutes or until chops are tender. Remove chops to warm platter. Skim fat from pan drippings. Combine cornstarch and 1/4 cup cold water; stir into pan drippings. Add parsley and onion. Cook over medium heat, stirring, until mixture is thickened. Stir in grapes and lemon juice; simmer until grapes are heated through. Pour sauce over chops.

LEMON VEAL SUPREME

3 eggs
1/2 c. lemon juice
6 thinly sliced veal cutlets
Bread crumbs
Cooking oil
1 lb. Gruyere cheese, sliced
2 pt. heavy cream

Beat eggs with lemon juice. Dip veal into egg mixture; dip into crumbs. Refrigerate for 1 hour. Brown veal on both sides in small amount of oil in skillet; place in shallow baking dish. Arrange cheese slices over veal; add cream. Bake at 350 degrees until cheese melts and cream bubbles.

VEAL CUTLET CORDON BLEU

Color photograph for this recipe on page 79.

12 thin slices veal
Salt and pepper to taste
6 thin slices Swiss cheese
6 thin slices boiled ham
Flour
3 eggs, beaten
3/4 c. bread crumbs
3/4 c. butter

Pound veal slices with meat hammer until flat; sprinkle with salt and pepper. Place 1 slice cheese and 1 slice ham on 6 veal slices; cover with remaining veal slices. Pound edges together. Dip in flour, then dip in crumbs. Fry in butter in skillet until brown on both sides. Place on platter; garnish with parsley, cherry tomatoes and onion rings. Yield: 6 servings.

VEAL CUTLET MONTMORENCY

Melted margarine
Olive oil
6 5-oz. breaded veal cutlets
1 lge. peeled tomato
1 lge. avocado
Sauce Mornay

Combine small amounts of margarine and olive oil in skillet; saute cutlets until golden. Place in shallow baking dish. Cut tomato and avocado into 6 wedges each; top each cutlet with 1 tomato and 1 avocado wedge. Top with 3 tablespoons Sauce Mornay; brown slightly under broiler. Serve with green noodles and tossed saled, if desired.

Sauce Mornay

3 tbsp. margarine
3 tbsp. flour
1 c. light cream, heated
1/2 c. Parmesan cheese
Salt and pepper
Nutmeg to taste
Hot sauce to taste

Combine margarine and flour in skillet; simmer, stirring, for 2 minutes or until smooth. Pour in cream gradually; stir until thickened. Add cheese; blend until smooth and cheese is melted. Season with salt, pepper, nutmeg and hot sauce.

VEAL JUBILEE

2 lb. veal cutlets
3 eggs, beaten
1 can Italian bread crumbs
Butter
1 1/3 c. light cream
1 can Queen Ann cherries

Dip veal into eggs. Coat with crumbs; refrigerate for 1 hour. Brown quickly in small amount of butter in skillet; place in baking dish. Combine cream, cherry juice, cherries and stock in saucepan; bring to a boil, stirring constantly. Pour over veal. Bake at 325 degrees for 1 hour or until veal is tender.

VEAL OREGANO

2 lb. veal cutlets, 1/4 in. thick
1/2 tsp. garlic salt
1/4 tsp. pepper
Flour
1/4 c. butter
1 med. onion, sliced thin
1/2 lb. fresh mushrooms, sliced
1 tsp. parsley flakes
1/4 tsp. oregano
1/2 tsp. salt
1 7-oz. bottle lemon-lime carbonated beverage

Season cutlets with garlic salt and pepper; dredge in flour. Pound lightly. Brown cutlets in butter in skillet on both sides; remove from skillet. Add onion and mushrooms to pan drippings; cook, stirring, until lightly browned. Stir in parsley flakes, oregano and salt; mix well. Add cutlets and beverage; simmer, covered, for 45 minutes or until cutlets are tender. Additional beverage may be added, if necessary.

Veal and Green Bean Casserole . . . Sour cream gives this seasoned main dish unusual smoothness.

VEAL AND GREEN BEAN CASSEROLE

1 1/2 lb. 1/2-in. thick veal steak
1/2 c. butter
1 tsp. salt
1/4 tsp. pepper
1 6-oz. can sliced mushrooms
1 c. coarsely chopped onion
1 tbsp. paprika
1 tbsp. flour
2 c. sour cream
1 9-oz. package frozen cross-cut green beans
2 tbsp. chopped parsley
1/3 c. fine corn flake crumbs
1/4 c. shredded Parmesan cheese

Cut veal into serving pieces; saute in 2 tablespoons butter in skillet. Sprinkle with half the salt and pepper. Drain mushrooms, reserving liquid. Add reserved liquid to veal; cover. Cook over low heat for 35 to 40 minutes or until veal is tender. Melt 1/4 cup butter; saute onion until tender. Blend in paprika, flour and remaining salt. Add mushrooms and sour cream. Cook over low heat, stirring constantly, until heated through. Cook beans according to package directions; drain. Add sour cream mixture, green beans and parsley to veal mixture. Pour into shallow 2-quart casserole. Melt remaining butter; stir in crumbs and cheese. Sprinkle around edge of casserole. Bake in 350-degree oven for about 20 minutes or until bubbling. Garnish with parsley; serve. Yield: 6 servings.

VENETIAN VEAL PIE

2 c. flour
1 1/2 tsp. garlic salt
1 tsp. leaf oregano
Grated Parmesan cheese
3/4 c. butter
1 1-lb. veal steak, cubed
2 c. tomatoes
1 c. tomato sauce
1/2 c. chopped onion
1 tbsp. sugar
1 tsp. sweet basil
1/2 tsp. salt
1/2 tsp. oregano
1/8 tsp. pepper
1/4 lb. Cheddar cheese

Sift 1 1/2 cups flour with garlic salt; add oregano and 1/4 cup cheese. Cut in 1/2 cup butter until of consistency of cornmeal. Sprinkle water over mixture just to moisten; stir until dough holds together. Roll out 2/3 of the dough on floured surface to 11-inch circle. Fit into pie pan. Flute edges. Coat veal with remaining flour; brown in remaining butter in skillet. Stir in tomatoes, tomato sauce, onion, remaining Parmesan cheese, sugar, basil, salt, remaining garlic salt, oregano and pepper. Simmer, covered, for 35 minutes or until veal is tender; turn into pastry-lined pan. Cut Cheddar cheese into 4 slices; place over veal mixture. Roll out remaining dough 1/8 inch thick; cut into 2-inch rounds. Place on cheese; overlap slightly. Bake at 400 degrees for 30 minutes or until crust is golden brown.

VEAL POT ROAST

1 4-lb. rump of veal
Corn oil
1 lge. onion, sliced
1/2 tsp. monosodium glutamate
1/4 tsp. rosemary leaves
Salt and pepper
1 sm. can mushrooms
Flour

Brown veal on all sides in small amount of oil in Dutch oven; add onion, monosodium glutamate and 1/4 cup water. Simmer, covered, for 2 hours or until tender; remove veal. Add seasonings and mushrooms to pan juices; thicken with flour, if desired. Serve over veal.

ROAST LOIN OF YOUNG VEAL

4 veal kidneys
1 6-lb. leg of veal, boned
1/4 lb. butter
2 tsp. salt
1/2 tsp. pepper
1/2 tsp. sage
1/2 tsp. mace
1/8 tsp. thyme
3 stalks celery, sliced
2 carrots, sliced
1 onion, sliced
2 shallots, chopped
1/2 c. dry white wine
1 1/2 c. beef bouillon
1/2 c. cream
2 tsp. tarragon

Preheat oven to 350 degrees. Roll kidneys inside veal roast; secure. Combine 2/3 stick butter with salt, pepper, sage, mace and thyme; spread mixture over veal. Spread remaining butter in roasting pan; place veal in pan. Arrange vegetables around veal; pour wine over veal. Bake, basting frequently, for 3 hours or until veal is tender. Remove veal to platter; keep warm. Pour bouillon into roasting pan; stir to loosen brown particles. Simmer for 5 minutes; strain into saucepan. Skim fat. Add cream and tarragon; blend well. Simmer, stirring, until heated through. Serve with veal.

VEAL SHOULDER WITH DILL SAUCE

1 3-lb. boned veal shoulder
1 tbsp. salt
4 whole allspice
6 peppercorns
1 bay leaf
Fresh dill
2 tbsp. butter
2 tbsp. flour
2 egg yolks
1/2 c. heavy cream

Roll veal as for jelly roll; tie. Place in 2 quarts boiling water in Dutch oven; add salt, allspice, peppercorns, bay leaf and 5 sprigs of dill. Simmer, covered, for 2 hours or until tender. Remove veal from stock; keep warm. Strain stock; reserve. Melt butter in Dutch oven; stir in flour. Stir in 2 1/2 cups reserved stock gradually; simmer, stirring, until thickened. Stir in 1/3 cup snipped dill. Mix egg yolks with cream; stir rapidly into sauce. Simmer just until heated through. Add salt, if needed. Serve sauce with veal.

NEW ORLEANS VEAL

1/4 tsp. thyme
1/4 tsp. marjoram
1/4 tsp. rosemary
1/2 tsp. fines herbes
1/2 sm. onion, minced
4 tbsp. lemon juice
1 sirloin of veal
Salt to taste
Cayenne pepper to taste
1 egg, beaten
3/4 c. bread crumbs
1 1/2 c. chicken bouillon

Combine thyme, marjoram, rosemary, fines herbes, onion and half the lemon juice. Rub veal with salt and cayenne pepper; place in lightly greased shallow baking dish. Bake at 450 degrees for 15 minutes. Reduce oven temperature to 300 degrees. Pour herb mixture over veal; cover with brown paper. Bake for 35 minutes per pound longer. Transfer veal to another baking dish; reserve drippings. Combine egg and bread crumbs; spread over veal. Bake until bread crumbs are browned and crusty. Combine bouillon and remaining lemon juice in saucepan; stir in reserved drippings. Heat through. Serve gravy with veal.

STUFFED BREAST OF VEAL

1 5-lb. breast of veal
2 10-oz. packages frozen spinach
1/2 c. minced onion
1/2 c. grated cheese
2 eggs, lightly beaten
1/2 tsp. dried basil
1 c. coarse bread crumbs
1/2 tsp. dried mint
1/2 tsp. pepper
1 tbsp. garlic salt
1/2 c. olive oil
1/2 c. lemon juice

Have pocket cut in veal. Prepare spinach according to package directions; drain thoroughly. Combine spinach with onion, cheese, eggs, basil, bread crumbs, mint, pepper and garlic salt in large bowl; mix well. Stuff veal with mixture; secure opening. Place veal in roasting pan; add 1 cup water. Bake at 350 degrees for 1 hour and 30 minutes or until veal is tender; baste frequently with mixture of olive oil and lemon juice.

SCALLOPINI

1 1 1/2-lb. veal steak, 1/2 in. thick
1 tsp. salt
1 tsp. paprika
1/2 c. salad oil
1/4 c. lemon juice
1 clove of garlic, split
1 tsp. prepared mustard
1/4 tsp. nutmeg
1/2 tsp. sugar
1/4 c. flour
1 med. onion, thinly sliced
1 green pepper, cut in strips
1 can chicken bouillon
1/4 lb. mushrooms, sliced
1 tbsp. butter
6 pimento-stuffed olives, sliced

Cut veal in serving pieces. Combine salt, paprika, oil, lemon juice, garlic, mustard, nutmeg and sugar; mix well. Place veal in 1 layer in baking pan; pour sauce over veal. Turn veal to coat well; let stand for 15 minutes. Remove garlic. Drain veal; reserve sauce. Dip veal into flour. Brown in small amount of hot fat in skillet; add onion and green pepper. Combine chicken bouillon with reserved sauce; pour over veal mixture. Simmer, covered, for 40 minutes or until tender. Brown mushrooms in butter in small skillet; add mushrooms and olives to veal mixture. Stir well; simmer for 5 minutes longer.

VEAL PARMIGIANA

3 veal steaks
1 c. bread crumbs
1/2 c. grated Parmesan cheese
Salt and pepper to taste
Garlic powder to taste
2 eggs
2 tbsp. milk
Olive oil
1 med. onion, chopped
1 lge. can whole tomatoes
1 12-oz. can tomato paste
1 tsp. oregano
1 tsp. sweet basil
6 slices mozzarella cheese

Halve steaks. Combine crumbs, Parmesan cheese, salt, pepper and garlic powder. Beat eggs lightly with milk. Dip steaks into egg mixture; coat with crumb mixture. Fry in oil in skillet until golden brown on both sides; place in baking dish. Saute onion in pan drippings until transparent; add tomatoes, tomato paste, 3/4 cup water, oregano, basil, salt, pepper and garlic powder. Blend thoroughly. Simmer, covered, for 30 minutes. Pour sauce over steaks. Bake, covered, at 350 degrees for 45 minutes. Place mozzarella cheese on steak. Bake until cheese is melted. Serve with spaghetti.

PEPPERY SCHNITZEL

1 1 1/2-lb. thin veal steak
1/2 c. chopped onion
1 clove of garlic, minced
Vegetable shortening
1/4 c. flour
1 1/2 tsp. salt
1/4 tsp. pepper
1 c. sour cream
1/3 c. beef consomme
1 tbsp. paprika
3 drops of hot sauce
1 2 1/2-oz. can sliced mushrooms
1 8 1/2-oz. can peas
1/3 c. chopped green pepper

Pound veal to 1/8-inch thickness. Saute onion and garlic in small amount of shortening in skillet until tender; remove from skillet. Mix flour with salt and pepper. Dip veal into seasoned flour; brown on both sides in remaining shortening in skillet. Add onion mixture; simmer, covered, for 25 minutes or until veal is tender. Combine sour cream, consomme, paprika and hot sauce; blend well. Pour over veal mixture. Drain mushrooms and peas; add with green pepper to veal mixture. Simmer, covered, just until heated through. Serve with buttered noodles; garnish with parsley.

ALMOND-VEAL IMPERIAL

2 lb. veal
2 tbsp. shortening
1 tsp. salt
2 c. chopped celery
1/4 c. chopped green pepper
1/2 c. chopped onion
1/4 c. pimento
1 4-oz. can mushrooms
1 can mushroom soup
1/4 c. soy sauce
1 8-oz. package noodles, cooked
1/2 c. sour cream
1/2 c. sliced almonds

Cut veal into 1-inch cubes; brown in shortening in skillet. Pour off excess grease. Add salt, celery, green pepper, onion, pimento, mushrooms, soup, soy sauce and 1/2 cup water; blend well. Simmer, covered, for 45 minutes. Combine noodles, sour cream and veal mixture; mix well. Pour into greased 2 1/2-quart casserole; top with almonds. Bake at 325 degrees for 30 minutes.

VENETIAN VEAL

1 1-lb. 1/2-in. thick veal steak
1/2 c. butter
1/2 c. chopped celery
1/4 c. chopped onion
1/4 c. chopped carrots
1 4-oz. can sliced mushrooms, drained
2 tbsp. flour
1/2 tsp. salt
1/8 tsp. pepper
1 c. milk
1/4 tsp. thyme
1/4 tsp. basil
1/8 tsp. marjoram
2 tbsp. chopped parsley
1 6-oz. can tomato paste

Preheat oven to 350 degrees. Cut veal into strips; remove bone. Brown veal in 1/4 cup butter in a skillet. Place in greased 1 1/4-quart casserole; set aside. Add remaining butter to drippings in skillet. Saute celery, onion, carrots and mushrooms. Remove with slotted spoon; place over veal in casserole. Reserve 2 tablespoons pan drippings in skillet; stir in flour, salt and pepper. Add milk gradually; Cook, stirring, until smooth and slightly thickened. Add remaining seasonings, parsley and tomato paste; stir until blended. Pour sauce over veal mixture in casserole. Bake for about 1 hour. Serve with buttered noodles if desired.

Venetian Veal . . . Serve this blend of veal, celery, onion, carrots, and mushrooms over noodles.

VEAL BIRDS WITH WILD RICE

3 green peppers, sliced
3 onions, sliced
1 stick butter
1 tsp. celery seed
1/8 tsp. hot sauce
2 tbsp. Worcestershire sauce
3 c. cooked wild rice
3 slices veal round steak
Salt and pepper to taste
Flour

Saute green peppers and onions in melted butter in skillet until tender; stir in celery seed, hot sauce, Worcestershire sauce and rice. Remove from heat; cool. Season veal with salt and pepper; cut steaks into halves. Place generous ball of rice stuffing on each veal steak. Roll up; fasten securely. Dust rolls with flour; brown on all sides in small amount of fat in large skillet. Remove veal from skillet; add 1 cup water to pan drippings. Stir to loosen browned particles; return veal to skillet. Simmer, covered, for 1 hour or until veal is tender.

ESCALOPE DE VEAU CHASSEUR

2 1/2 tsp. salt
1/2 tsp. freshly ground pepper
1/4 c. flour
12 thin slices veal
1/4 lb. mushrooms, sliced
1/2 c. chopped onion
3 tbsp. olive oil
1/2 c. dry white wine
1 1/2 c. canned tomatoes, drained
1/2 tsp. basil
3 tbsp. butter
1 tbsp. minced parsley

Combine half the salt and pepper with flour; dip veal into mixture. Saute mushrooms and onion in oil in saucepan for 10 minutes or until onions are transparent; add wine. Cook over high heat until reduced by half; stir in tomatoes, basil and remaining salt and pepper. Simmer, covered, for 30 minutes. Saute veal in butter in skillet for 5 minutes on each side. Arrange on hot platter. Pour tomato mixture into skillet. Cook over high heat for 1 minute; stir to loosen browned particles. Add parsley; pour sauce over veal.

HUNGARIAN PAPRIKA VEAL

1 lb. round veal steak, 1/2 in. thick
1/3 c. flour
1/2 tsp. salt
1/4 tsp. pepper
1 tbsp. paprika
2 med. onions, sliced
1 pt. sour cream

Cut veal into 1-inch squares; roll in flour seasoned with salt, pepper and paprika. Brown veal on all sides in small amount of hot fat in skillet. Add onions; saute lightly until just tender. Place veal and onions in 2-quart saucepan; add 1/2 cup water. Simmer, covered, for 30 minutes or until veal is tender. Stir in sour cream and additional water, if needed, to make gravy; heat through. Serve over rice.

VEAL ROLLS WITH BACON

4 thin slices veal
4 slices bacon
1 tbsp. butter
1 onion, sliced
1 tbsp. flour
1 tsp. salt
1/4 tsp. pepper

Pound veal to 1/8-inch thickness; place 1 slice bacon on each slice veal. Roll up; tie securely. Brown butter and onion in saucepan; add flour, stirring until browned. Place veal in saucepan; add 1 cup water and seasonings. Simmer, covered, for 45 minutes. Remove cover; let sauce cook down, if necessary.

VEAL TAORMINA

1 lge. eggplant
2 eggs, slightly beaten
1 c. fine dry bread crumbs
3/4 c. salad oil
1 lb. ground veal
3 8-oz. cans tomato sauce
2 tsp. sugar
1 tsp. oregano
1/2 tsp. basil
1/2 tsp. salt
1 8-oz. package sliced mozzarella cheese
1/2 c. grated Parmesan cheese

Peel eggplant; slice 1/4 inch thick. Dip eggplant into eggs; coat with crumbs. Brown eggplant in oil in large skillet; drain on paper toweling. Drain oil from skillet. Shape veal into large patty; place in skillet. Brown for 5 minutes on each side; break patty into chunks. Stir in tomato sauce, sugar, oregano, basil and salt; simmer for 10 minutes. Cut mozzarella cheese into triangles. Layer 1/3 of the eggplant slices, veal sauce, Parmesan and mozzarella cheeses in greased 13 x 9 x 2-inch baking dish. Repeat layers twice; arrange remaining mozzarella triangles in pattern on top. Bake at 350 degrees for 40 minutes or until heated through and cheese is melted. Garnish with ripe olive slices, if desired.

Vegetables

Vegetables are one of the homemaker's best friends. They are low in cost and calories, yet high in nutritional values and flavor. Vegetables can be used in a variety of ways: as a hot main dish accompaniment or a cool marinated salad; or in soups, stews, and casseroles. In the three charts that follow, information has been compiled in an easy-to-read form on cooking and seasoning vegetables, the months in which they are most available, and the nutrients they contain. For further information about specific vegetables, consult the individual entries and the accompanying recipes that appear in alphabetical order throughout this encyclopedia. Included in these sections are invaluable tips on buying, storing, preparing, and serving vegetables. Other entries that will also provide helpful information about vegetables are CANNING, HERBS and SPICES.

COOKING AND SEASONING VEGETABLES

VEGETABLE	MINUTES COOKING TIME IN BOILING WATER	SUGGESTED SEASONINGS
ARTICHOKE	10-15	Dill, French dressing, lemon butter
ASPARAGUS		Mustard seed, sesame seed, tarragon, lemon butter, nutmeg, dry mustard, caraway seed
spears	10-20	
tips, pieces	5-15	
BEANS (lima)	25-30	Savory, tarragon, thyme, marjoram, oregano, sage
BEANS (snap)	12-16	Basil, dill, marjoram, mint, mustard seed, oregano, savory, tarragon, thyme
BEETS		Allspice, bay leaves, caraway seed, cloves, dill, ginger, mustard seed, savory, thyme, orange, celery seed, nutmeg, vinegar
young, whole	30-45	
older, whole	45-90	
sliced	15-25	
BROCCOLI	10-15	Seasoned butters, dill, lemon butter, caraway seed, mustard seed, tarragon
BRUSSELS SPROUTS	15-20	Basil, caraway seed, dill, mustard seed, sage, thyme, lemon butter
CABBAGE		Caraway seed, celery seed, dill, mint, mustard seed, nutmeg, savory, tarragon, peppers
shredded	3-10	
wedges	10-15	
CARROTS		Allspice, bay leaves, caraway seed, dill, fennel, ginger, mace, marjoram, mint, nutmeg, thyme, cloves, curry powder, parsley flakes
young, whole	15-20	
older, whole	20-30	
sliced	10-15	
CAULIFLOWER		Caraway seed, celery salt, dill, mace, tarragon, seasoned butters, sesame seed, poppy seed
separated	8-15	
whole	15-25	
CELERY	15-18	Seasoned butters
CORN (on the cob)	5-15	Green pepper, paprika, garlic powder, onion salt
EGGPLANT	8-15	Marjoram, oregano, dill
GREENS	10-30	Meat drippings, peppers, onion
OKRA	10-15	Meat drippings
ONIONS	15-30	Caraway seed, mustard seed, nutmeg, oregano, sage, thyme
PARSNIPS		Parsley, onion, dill, lemon butter
whole	20-40	
quartered	8-15	

VEGETABLE	MINUTES COOKING TIME IN BOILING WATER	SUGGESTED SEASONINGS
PEAS	12-16	Basil, dill, marjoram, mint, oregano, poppy seed, rosemary, sage, savory
POTATOES		
whole, medium	25-40	Basil, bay leaves, caraway, celery seed, dill, chives, mustard seed, oregano, poppy seed, thyme
quartered	20-25	
diced	10-15	
SPINACH	3-10	Basil, mace, marjoram, nutmeg, oregano, vinegar
SQUASH		
summer, sliced	8-15	Allspice, basil, cinnamon, cloves, fennel, ginger, mustard seed, nutmeg, rosemary, garlic
winter, cut-up	15-20	
SWEET POTATOES	30-55	Allspice, cardamom, cinnamon, cloves, nutmeg
TOMATOES (cut-up)	7-15	Basil, bay leaves, celery seed, oregano, sage, sesame seed, tarragon, thyme
TURNIPS and RUTABAGAS		
whole	20-30	Cloves, ginger, onion, caraway seed
cut-up	10-20	

The chart below details which vitamins and minerals are available in the most frequently served vegetables. Some vegetables contain traces of nutrients other than those listed, but vitamins A, B_1, B_2, and C as well as calcium and iron are the primary nutrients found in almost all vegetables. By serving your family a wide range of fresh, frozen, and canned vegetables in the course of a week's meals, you can ensure that they receive all the vitamins and minerals they need to maintain strong, healthy bodies.

VEGETABLE NUTRITIONAL CHART

VEGETABLE	SIZE SERVING Equivalent To 100 Grams	NUTRIENTS PER 100 GRAMS Vitamins	Minerals
Asparagus	6 spears	A, C	
Beans (lima)	2/3 cup	C, B_1	iron
Beans (snap)	3/4 cup	A, C	iron
Beets	2 2¼-inch diam.	C	iron
Beet greens	¼ lb.	A*, C	iron*
Broccoli	¼ lb.	A*, C*, B_2	calcium, iron
Brussels sprouts	seven	C*	iron
Cabbage	¼ lb.	C*	
Carrots	2-4-inches long	A*	iron

VEGETABLE	SIZE SERVING Equivalent To 100 Grams	NUTRIENTS PER 100 GRAMS Vitamins	Minerals
Cauliflower	1/3 small head	C*	
Celery	6 stalks	C	
Chard	¼ lb.	A*, C	iron
Collard greens	¼ lb.	A*, C*, B_1, B_2	calcium*, iron
Corn	1 ear	C, B_1	
Cucumbers	14 slices	C	
Dandelion greens	¼ lb.	A*, C, B_1	calcium, iron*
Eggplant	1 4-inch slice		
Endive	¼ lb.	A*, C	iron
Kale	¼ lb.	A*, C*, B_2	calcium*, iron
Lettuce (iceberg)	1/3 head	A, C	
Lettuce (leaf)	10 lg. leaves	A, C	iron
Mustard greens	¼ lb.	A*, C*, B_2	calcium*, iron
Okra	5-10 pods	A, C*	calcium
Onions	2 medium	C	
Parsley	1 bunch	A*, C*	calcium, iron*
Parsnips	1 small	C	
Peas (green)	3/4 cup	A, C*, B_1	
Peppers	1 large	A, C*	
Potatoes	1 small	C	
Pumpkin	½ cup	A*, C	
Radishes	10 small	C	iron
Rutabagas	3/4 cup	C	
Spinach	¼ lb.	A*, C*, B_2	
Squash (summer)	3/4 cup	C	
Squash (winter)	½ cup	A*, C	
Sweet potatoes	2/3 medium	A*, C	
Tomatoes	1 small	A, C	
Turnips	3/4 cup	C	
Turnip greens	¼ lb.	A*, C*, B_2*	calcium*, iron
Watercress	1 bunch	A*, C*	calcium, iron

*Indicates excellent source of vitamin or mineral.

VEGETABLE GROWING SEASONS CHART

Month	Vegetables Available (*indicates peak of availability)
January	broccoli*, Brussels sprouts, cabbage, carrots, celeriac, celery, Chinese cabbage*, chives, collards*, endive-escarole*, kale*, leeks*, lettuce-romaine, mushrooms, mustard greens*, onions, parsley, parsnips, peppers, potatoes, shallots, spinach, squash, sweet potatoes, turnips-rutabagas
February	artichokes, broccoli*, cabbage, carrots, celeriac*, celery, Chinese cabbage, chives, collards, endive-escarole*, kale, leeks, lettuce-romaine, mushrooms, mustard greens, onions, parsley, parsnips, peppers, potatoes, shallots, spinach, squash, sweet potatoes, turnips-rutabagas
March	artichokes*, asparagus, broccoli, cabbage*, carrots*, celeriac, celery*, Chinese cabbage, chives*, collards, dandelion greens, endive-escarole*, garlic*, kale, leeks*, lettuce-romaine, mushrooms, onions, parsley, parsnips*, peas (green), peppers, potatoes, shallots*, spinach*, squash
April	artichokes*, asparagus*, broccoli*, cabbage*, carrots*, celery*, Chinese cabbage, chives, dandelion greens*, escarole-endive, garlic, leeks, lettuce-romaine, onions, parsley, peas (green)*, peppers, potatoes, spinach, squash, sweet potatoes, turnips-rutabagas,
May	asparagus*, beans (snap), cabbage*, carrots*, celery*, Chinese cabbage, chives, corn, cucumbers, dandelion greens, endive-escarole, lettuce-romaine, onions*, onions (green), parsley*, peas (green), peppers, potatoes, radishes*, spinach, squash, tomatoes*, turnips-rutabagas
June	asparagus, beans (lima), beans (snap)*, beets*, cabbage, carrots, celery, Chinese cabbage, chives, corn, cucumbers*, dandelion greens, endive-escarole, kohlrabi*, lettuce-romaine, okra, onions, onions (green)*, parsley*, peas (green), peppers, potatoes, radishes*, spinach, squash, tomatoes*, turnips-rutabagas
July	beans (lima)*, beans (snap)*, beets, cabbage, carrots, celery, Chinese cabbage, chives, corn*, cucumbers*, eggplant, endive-escarole, kohlrabi, lettuce-romaine, okra*, onions, onions (green)*, parsley, peppers*, potatoes, radishes, spinach, squash, tomatoes*, turnips-rutabagas
August	beans (lima)*, beans (snap), beets, cabbage, carrots, celery, Chinese cabbage, chives, corn*, cucumbers, eggplant*, endive-escarole, garlic*, lettuce-romaine, okra*, onions, onions (green), parsley, peppers*, potatoes, squash, tomatoes*, turnips-rutabagas
September	beans (lima), beans (snap), beets, Brussels sprouts, cabbage, carrots, cauliflower, celery, Chinese cabbage, chives, corn, eggplant, endive-escarole, garlic*, kohlrabi, lettuce-romaine, okra, onions, parsley, peppers, potatoes, spinach, squash, tomatoes*, turnips-rutabagas
October	beans (lima), beans (snap), broccoli, Brussels sprouts*, cabbage, cauliflower*, celery, Chinese cabbage, chives, eggplant, endive-escarole, kohlrabi, lettuce-romaine, okra, onions, parsley, peppers, potatoes, pumpkins*, spinach, squash, sweet potatoes, tomatoes, turnips-rutabagas
November	broccoli, Brussels sprouts*, carrots, celeriac, celery, Chinese cabbage, chives, endive-escarole, leeks, lettuce-romaine, mushrooms*, onions, parsley*, peppers, potatoes, shallots*, spinach, squash*, sweet potatoes*, turnips-rutabagas*
December	broccoli, Brussels sprouts, cabbage, carrots, celeriac*, celery, Chinese cabbage*, chives*, collards, endive-escarole, kale*, leeks, lettuce-romaine, mushrooms*, mustard greens, onions, parsley, peppers, potatoes, shallots, spinach, squash, sweet potatoes*, turnips-rutabagas*

Vichyssoise

VICHYSSOISE ROYALE

3 tbsp. butter
1 1/2 c. thinly sliced onions
3/4 c. diced celery
3 c. chicken stock
1 1/2 c. thinly sliced potatoes
1/2 tsp. salt
1 1/2 c. light cream
1/8 tsp. pepper
1/4 tsp. paprika
1 1/2 tbsp. minced chives

Melt butter in saucepan over low heat; add onions and celery. Saute until tender and transparent; add stock, potatoes and salt. Bring to a boil; reduce heat. Simmer, covered, for 20 minutes or until potatoes are tender. Force mixture through sieve; add cream, pepper and paprika. Blend well; chill thoroughly. Serve in chilled cups; sprinkle with chives. Yield: 8 servings.

VICHYSSOISE

1/4 c. butter
1 1/2 c. chopped leeks
3 c. thinly sliced potatoes
4 chicken bouillon cubes
3 c. milk
1 tsp. salt
1/8 tsp. white pepper
1/8 tsp. paprika
1 c. cream
2 tbsp. finely chopped chives

Melt butter in large, heavy saucepan; add leeks. Cook, stirring, until transparent but not brown. Add potato slices, 1 cup hot water and bouillon cubes; cover. Cook over medium heat until potato-slices are tender. Press through fine sieve. Return puree to saucepan; add milk, stirring rapidly to blend. Stir in salt, white pepper and paprika. Add cream; heat only to serving temperature. Chill quickly; serve cold. Garnish with chopped chives. Yield: 6 servings.

Vichyssoise . . . A cold soup prepared with milk, leeks, and potatoes, perfect for summer meals.

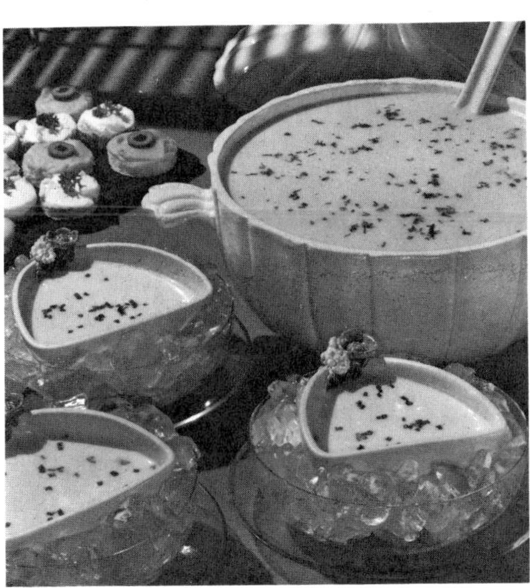

Waffles

Waffles are crisp, honeycombed cakes that are prepared from a yeast- or quick-leavened batter. They are cooked in a *waffle iron*—a utensil with two hinged metal sections that mold the waffle into a grid-like network.

INGREDIENTS: Most waffles are based on a mixture of butter, eggs, flour, sugar, leavening, and milk or cream. Cornmeal and whole wheat flour are popular ingredients as are cheese, bits of ham or bacon, chocolate, nuts, and fruit.

PREPARATION: Follow specific recipe directions for combining ingredients. Preheat waffle iron. It will not require greasing since the batter is so butter-rich. Make sure that the batter is thin enough to pour easily. Cover grid surface about 2/3 full. The batter will spread out to the edges by itself. Close lid. Wait until all the steam has emerged from the crack, about 4 minutes. Do not open lid too soon or the waffles will collapse and be heavy. Remove the waffle from iron. Before baking consecutive waffles, close lid and allow waffle iron to reheat to the proper temperature.

STORING: Waffles are best served warm from the waffle iron. However, they can be frozen for future use. *To freeze*—Cool cooked waffles thoroughly. Stack waffle sections or whole waffles with double thicknesses of waxed paper between each layer. Wrap entire stack in foil or plastic and freeze. Use within 3 weeks. Reheat sections in toaster; place whole waffles on rack in 450-degree oven for 3 to 5 minutes.

SERVING: Serve waffles morning, noon, and night. Enjoy piping hot waffles with syrup, honey, or jams. For lunch or supper feature waffles topped with creamed shrimp, crab, or tuna as the main dish. Or heap ice cream and a sweetened sauce on waffles for an unbeatable dessert treat. To clean waffle iron – brush out crumbs from the grid and wipe with a dry paper towel. Clean the outside with a dampened cloth.

GAUFRES

1 1/2 c. milk
2 tbsp. sugar
1 tsp. salt
1/4 c. margarine
1 pkg. yeast
2 1/2 c. unsifted flour
2 eggs, separated

Scald milk. Stir in sugar, salt and margarine; cool to lukewarm. Measure 1/2 cup warm water into large warm bowl; sprinkle in yeast, stirring until dissolved. Add lukewarm milk mixture. Stir in flour; beat until smooth. Beat in egg yolks. Let rise for about 1 hour in warm place, free from draft, until doubled in bulk. Stir down; add small amount additional liquid if necessary to make soft batter. Beat egg whites until stiff but not dry; fold into batter. Bake until brown in hot waffle iron. Serve with whole strawberries, powdered sugar or whipped cream if desired.

CHOCOLATE WAFFLES

2 c. flour
3 tsp. baking powder
1/2 tsp. salt
3 tbsp. cocoa
4 tbsp. sugar
2 eggs, separated
4 tbsp. butter, melted
1 1/4 c. milk
1 tsp. vanilla

Sift dry ingredients into large mixing bowl; add well-beaten egg yolks, butter, milk and vanilla. Beat egg whites until stiff peaks form. Fold egg whites into flour mixture. Pour batter into hot waffle iron. Bake until crisp. Serve with vanilla ice cream.

CORNMEAL WAFFLES

1 c. sifted flour
1 c. yellow cornmeal
3 tsp. baking powder
1 tsp. salt
3 eggs, well beaten
1 3/4 c. milk
1 tbsp. sugar
5 tbsp. melted shortening

Sift flour, cornmeal, baking powder and salt into large bowl. Combine well-beaten eggs, milk and sugar; add to flour mixture. Blend thoroughly; stir in shortening. Bake in hot waffle iron until golden brown.

Gaufres . . . These yeast-raised waffles are served with powdered sugar or whipped cream.

CHEESE WAFFLES

3 eggs, separated
2 c. milk
1/2 c. melted butter
3 c. sifted flour
3 tbsp. sugar
1 1/2 tbsp. baking powder
Salt and pepper
1 1/4 c. grated cheese

Beat egg yolks; add milk and melted butter. Mix well. Sift flour, sugar and baking powder; add to egg mixture. Blend thoroughly; season to taste with salt and pepper. Add cheese, stirring just to blend. Beat egg whites until stiff peaks form; fold into batter. Bake in hot waffle iron until golden brown.

CORN WAFFLES

2 c. sifted flour
3 tbsp. sugar
3 tbsp. baking powder
1 tsp. salt
2 eggs, separated
1 1/4 c. milk
1 No. 2 can cream-style corn
1/2 c. melted butter

Sift dry ingredients. Beat egg yolks; add milk, corn, and melted butter. Add egg mixture to dry ingredients; blend well. Beat egg whites until stiff peaks form; fold into batter. Bake in hot waffle iron until golden brown.

GINGER WAFFLES

1 1/2 c. flour
1/4 c. sugar
1/2 tsp. salt
1 tsp. soda
1 tsp. baking powder
3 eggs, beaten
1/2 c. molasses
1 c. buttermilk
1/2 c. shortening, melted

Sift dry ingredients together. Add eggs, molasses and buttermilk; beat until smooth. Stir in shortening. Bake in hot waffle iron until golden brown.

GRANDMA'S WAFFLES

2 c. flour
3 tsp. baking powder
1/2 tsp. salt
2 eggs, separated
1 3/4 c. milk
1/2 c. salad oil

Sift dry ingredients into large bowl; add well-beaten egg yolks and milk. Blend thoroughly; stir in oil. Beat egg whites until stiff peaks form; fold into batter. Bake in hot waffle iron until golden brown.

JAMES RIVER WAFFLES

3 eggs, separated
2 c. buttermilk
2 c. flour
2 tsp. baking powder
1/4 tsp. salt
1 tsp. soda
6 tbsp. butter, melted

Beat egg yolks; add 1 cup buttermilk. Sift dry ingredients; add to egg yolk mixture. Add remaining buttermilk and butter. Beat egg whites until stiff peaks form; fold into batter. Bake in hot waffle iron until golden brown.

SUNDAY NIGHT WAFFLES

2 eggs
3/4 c. salad oil
2 1/2 c. milk
2 1/2 c. flour
1 1/2 tbsp. sugar
3/4 tsp. salt
4 tsp. baking powder

Combine eggs, oil and milk in mixer bowl; blend thoroughly at medium speed. Sift dry ingredients; add to egg mixture. Beat for 2 minutes or until well blended. Bake until golden brown. Serve with favorite topping.

YEAST WAFFLES

1 1/2 c. milk
3 eggs, separated
1 c. oil
2 c. whole wheat flour
1 tsp. salt
1 tsp. sugar
1 pkg. yeast

Combine milk, egg yolks, oil, flour and salt in 2-quart mixer bowl; beat well. Mix 1/2 cup water, sugar and yeast together; stir until yeast and sugar are dissolved. Stir into flour mixture. Beat egg whites until stiff peaks form; fold into batter. Refrigerate overnight. Bake in hot waffle iron until crisp and golden brown. Let stand overnight. Yield: 24 servings.

WAFFLE HEARTS

Color photograph for this recipe on page 724.

2 c. sweetened whipped cream
1 c. fresh raspberries
3/4 c. strong brewed coffee
3/4 c. milk
1 c. sour cream
1 egg
1/4 c. salad oil
1 1/2 c. pancake mix

Mix whipped cream and raspberries; chill. Combine coffee, milk, sour cream, egg and oil in a bowl; blend well. Add pancake mix; beat with electric mixer until smooth. Pour enough batter into hot waffle iron to spread to 1 inch from edge. Bake until steaming stops. Cut waffles in heart-shaped size. Serve with whipped cream mixture. One-half cup raspberry jam may be substituted for fresh raspberries.

Walnut

FAVORITE WALNUT CAKE

3 c. sifted cake flour
2 tsp. baking powder
1 1/2 tsp. salt
1 3/4 c. sugar
1 c. soft shortening
4 eggs
3/4 c. milk
2 tsp. vanilla
1 c. finely chopped walnuts

Sift dry ingredients into large mixer bowl. Add shortening, 2 eggs, milk and vanilla. Beat for 2 minutes with mixer at medium speed. Add 2 eggs; beat 2 minutes longer. Fold in walnuts. Pour into greased 9-inch tube pan lined on bottom with waxed paper. Bake at 375 degrees for 1 hour or until cake tests done. Cool in pan on wire rack for 10 minutes. Remove from pan; peel off paper. Cool on rack.

BLACK WALNUT CAKE

Butter
1 c. sugar
1 3/4 c. flour
2 1/2 tsp. baking powder
1/2 c. coffee
3/4 c. black walnuts
5 egg whites, stiffly beaten
1 c. (packed) brown sugar
1/3 c. cream
1 c. coconut

Cream 1/2 cup butter and sugar. Sift flour and baking powder. Add sifted dry ingredients to sugar mixture alternately with coffee. Add walnuts. Fold in egg whites. Pour into 12 x 7-inch greased and floured pan. Bake at 350 degrees for 40 minutes or until cake tests done. Cream 1/3 cup butter and brown sugar; add cream and coconut. Blend thoroughly. Frost cake while still warm; broil until icing is golden brown.

WALNUT GLORY CAKE

3/4 c. flour
2 tsp. cinnamon
1 tsp. salt
9 eggs, separated
1 1/2 c. sugar
2 tsp. vanilla
2 c. finely chopped walnuts

Combine flour, cinnamon and salt. Beat egg whites in large mixing bowl until soft mounds form; add 3/4 cup sugar gradually. Beat until stiff peaks form. Combine egg yolks, vanilla and remaining sugar in mixing bowl; beat until thick and lemon-colored. Stir in dry ingredients. Fold batter gently into egg whites; fold in walnuts. Turn into ungreased 10-inch tube pan. Bake at 350 degrees for 55 minutes or until cake tests done. Invert pan immediately; cool completely. Remove from pan; sprinkle with confectioners' sugar, if desired.

WALNUT ROLL

4 eggs
3/4 c. sugar
1 c. finely minced walnuts
1/2 c. fine bread crumbs
Pinch of salt
1 tsp. vanilla
Confectioners' sugar
1 c. heavy cream, whipped

Beat eggs and sugar with mixer for 10 minutes or until thick and lemony. Fold in walnuts, crumbs, salt and vanilla. Pour into well-greased and floured 10 1/2 x 16-inch pan. Bake at 350 degrees for 18 minutes or until lightly browned. Loosen edges; turn cake out on towel coated with confectioners' sugar. Trim edges; roll cake and towel jelly roll fashion. Cool on wire rack. Unroll; spread with cream. Reroll; refrigerate until ready to serve. Walnuts may be minced finely in blender. Yield: 8 servings.

WALNUT WONDER CAKE

2 sticks butter
1 1/4 c. sugar
2 eggs
1 tsp. vanilla
2 c. flour
1 tsp. baking powder
1 tsp. soda
1 c. sour cream
1/3 c. (packed) brown sugar
1 tsp. cinnamon
1 c. walnuts

Cream butter and 1 cup sugar. Add eggs and vanilla; blend well. Add flour, baking powder, soda and sour cream; blend thoroughly. Pour half the batter into 9 x 12-inch pan. Combine brown sugar, remaining sugar, cinnamon and walnuts; sprinkle half the walnut mixture evenly over batter in pan. Cover with remaining batter; sprinkle remaining walnut mixture over top. Bake at 350 degrees for 35 minutes or until cake tests done.

WALNUT SPOON PUDDING

1 c. soft dried dark figs
1/4 c. soft butter
2/3 c. (packed) brown sugar
1/4 tsp. cinnamon
1/8 tsp. cloves
1/8 tsp. nutmeg
1 egg, beaten
3/4 c. sifted all-purpose flour
1/4 tsp. soda
1/2 tsp. salt
1 c. chopped California walnuts

Clip stems from figs; cut into small pieces. Cream butter, brown sugar, spices and egg together until blended and fluffy. Sift flour, soda and salt together; add to creamed mixture, blending well. Stir in figs and walnuts. Turn into greased 9-inch square pan.

Walnut Spoon Pudding . . . A richly seasoned fig and walnut pudding topped with bourbon sauce.

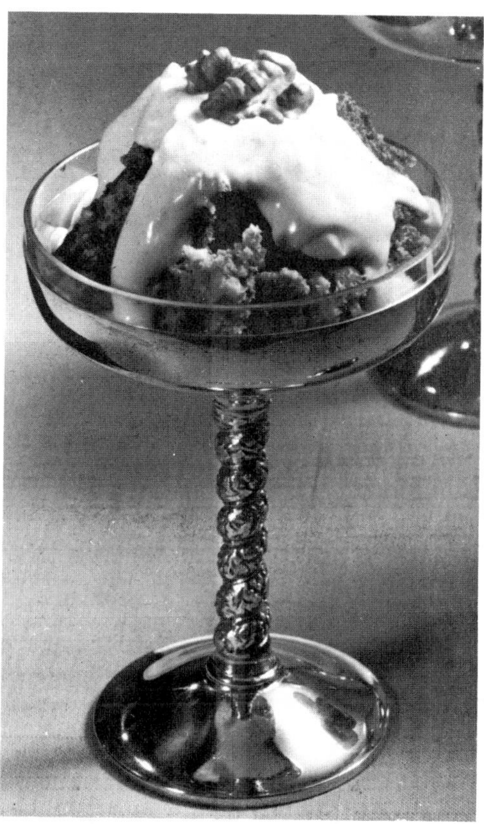

Bake at 350 degrees for 20 to 25 minutes. Spoon into serving dishes. Serve warm with Fluffy Bourbon Sauce.

Fluffy Bourbon Sauce

2 egg yolks
1 c. sifted powdered sugar
Pinch of salt
4 tbsp. bourbon
1 c. whipping cream, whipped

Beat egg yolks, sugar and salt together until thick and lemon colored; stir in bourbon gradually. Fold whipped cream into sauce. Chill until serving time. Spoon sauce over warm pudding. Yield: 8 servings.

CANDIED WALNUTS

2 c. (packed) brown sugar
1 c. milk
1 tbsp. margarine
1 tsp. vanilla
1/8 tsp. salt
2 qt. walnuts

Combine sugar, milk and margarine in heavy saucepan; cook to soft-ball stage or 238 degrees on candy thermometer. Add vanilla and salt. Beat until creamy; add walnuts. Mix until well coated. Spread on foil; separate walnuts.

CREAMY CANDIED WALNUTS

1 1/2 c. sugar
1/2 c. sour cream
2 tbsp. butter
1 tsp. vanilla
1 tsp. cinnamon
2 1/2 c. walnuts

Bring sugar, sour cream and butter to a boil in heavy saucepan; cook, stirring frequently, to soft-ball stage or 238 degrees on candy thermometer. Cool; add vanilla and cinnamon. Stir in walnuts. Spoon onto buttered foil; separate walnuts.

SPICED WALNUTS

1/3 c. strong coffee
1 c. sugar
1/2 tsp. cinnamon
1/2 tsp. salt
1 1/2 c. walnuts
1/2 tsp. vanilla

Mix coffee, sugar, cinnamon and salt; boil to 236 degrees on candy thermometer. Add walnuts and vanilla; stir until mixture is stiff. Turn onto waxed paper. Separate walnuts.

WALNUT BUTTER CRUNCH

1 lb. butter
2 c. sugar
2 tbsp. light corn syrup
2 c. coarsely chopped walnuts
1 6-oz. package semisweet chocolate pieces
1/2 c. finely chopped walnuts

Melt butter in heavy 2-quart saucepan over low heat. Add sugar, stirring constantly, until dissolved. Add 1/4 cup water and syrup. Cook over low heat until candy is brittle when tested in cold water or 290 degrees on candy thermometer. Remove from heat; stir in coarsely chopped walnuts. Spread in greased 15 x 10 x 1-inch jelly roll pan; cool until hardened. Melt chocolate over hot water; pour over crunch. Sprinkle with finely chopped walnuts; break into bite-sized pieces.

BLACK WALNUT-CHIP COOKIES

2/3 c. shortening
1 c. sugar
1/2 c. (packed) brown sugar
2 eggs
1 tsp. vanilla
2 c. flour
1 tsp. salt
1 tsp. soda
2 tbsp. milk
1/2 c. black walnuts
1/2 c. coconut
1 c. chocolate chips

Cream shortening, sugars, eggs and vanilla in large mixer bowl. Add dry ingredients and milk; blend well. Stir in walnuts, coconut and chips. Drop by teaspoonfuls onto greased cookie sheet. Bake at 375 degrees for 8 minutes or until lightly browned.

WALNUT COOKIES

4 eggs
2 c. (packed) brown sugar
1/4 tsp. salt
1/2 tsp. baking powder
1 c. flour
1 c. chopped walnuts
2 tsp. almond extract

Beat eggs until light; add sugar gradually. Mix in remaining dry ingredients and walnuts; stir in almond extract. Drop by teaspoonfuls onto greased and floured cookie sheet. Bake at 375 degrees until golden brown. Remove cookies immediately from cookie sheet; cool.

WALNUT MERINGUE BARS

1/2 lb. unsalted butter
1 1/2 c. sugar
1 egg yolk
1/2 tsp. salt
2 1/2 c. sifted flour
1 c. currant jelly
4 egg whites
1 tsp. lemon extract
Walnuts

Cream butter with 1/2 cup sugar. Add egg yolk and salt; mix well. Add flour; blend thoroughly. Pat mixture into 10 x 15-inch rectangle on cookie sheet. Spread jelly over dough to within 1/4 inch of edge. Beat egg whites until foamy; beat in remaining sugar gradually. Beat until stiff peaks form. Fold in lemon extract and 3/4 cup finely ground walnuts. Spread meringue over jelly layer; seal to edge of dough. Sprinkle 1 cup chopped walnuts over meringue. Bake at 350 degrees for 35 minutes or until browned. Cut into squares while warm.

FROZEN WALNUT MOUSSE

2 eggs, separated
1/2 c. sugar
1 pt. heavy cream
1 tsp. vanilla
1 c. ground walnuts

Beat egg whites until stiff peaks form; add 1/4 cup sugar gradually. Beat until glossy. Beat egg yolks with remaining sugar until thick and lemony. Whip cream; add vanilla. Combine egg yolks with whipped cream and walnuts; blend well. Fold into egg whites; spoon into mold. Freeze, covered, until ready to serve. Serve with rum sauce, if desired.

RICH WALNUT TORTE

16 eggs, separated
2 c. sugar
1 1/2 c. ground walnuts
1 tbsp. baking powder
3 tbsp. cracker meal
1 tbsp. whiskey
1/3 c. flour
1 c. coffee
1/2 c. butter
1 tsp. vanilla

Place egg yolks in mixer bowl; beat at highest speed for 10 minutes. Add 1 cup sugar, walnuts, baking powder, cracker meal and whiskey; mix well. Beat egg whites until stiff peaks form; fold into egg yolk mixture. Spread into 4 greased, floured and waxed paper-lined 8-inch layer pans. Bake at 350 degrees for 30 minutes. Cool for 5 minutes before removing from pan. Blend flour with small amount of coffee. Pour remaining coffee into saucepan; bring to a boil. Reduce heat; stir in flour mixture. Cook, stirring constantly, until thickened. Cool. Cream butter and remaining sugar until light and fluffy. Beat in coffee mixture, 1 tablespoon at a time. Add vanilla and spread between torte layers. Refrigerate until ready to serve.

WALNUT DELIGHT

1 1/3 c. graham cracker crumbs
1 c. sugar
1 tsp. baking powder
1/2 tsp. salt
1 tsp. vanilla
1/2 c. coarsely chopped walnuts
3 eggs, separated
1 c. heavy cream, whipped

Combine crumbs, sugar, baking powder, salt, vanilla and walnuts; stir in slightly beaten egg yolks. Beat egg whites until stiff peaks form; add to walnut mixture. Blend thoroughly. Pour into well-buttered and lightly floured pie pan. Bake at 350 degrees for 30 minutes. Serve warm with whipped cream.

WALNUT BREAD

1 1/4 c. sifted flour
2 tsp. baking powder
3/4 tsp. soda
1 1/4 tsp. salt
1 1/4 c. graham flour
1 c. chopped walnuts
1 egg
1/3 c. (packed) brown sugar
1/2 c. light molasses
3/4 c. buttermilk
3 tbsp. melted shortening

Sift flour with baking powder, soda and salt. Stir in graham flour and walnuts. Beat egg lightly; beat in brown sugar, molasses, buttermilk and shortening. Stir into dry mixture just until flour is moistened. Spoon into 3 greased 1-pound cans. Bake at 350 degrees for 45 minutes or until bread tests done. Let stand for 10 minutes; turn out onto wire rack.

WALNUT ROLL-UPS

2 pkg. yeast
Milk
2 tsp. salt
1/4 c. sugar
1/2 c. butter
4 eggs
5 c. flour
1 c. ground walnuts
1 c. (packed) light brown sugar
1/2 tsp. vanilla

Dissolve yeast in 1/3 cup lukewarm water. Scald 2/3 cup milk; stir in salt, sugar and butter. Cool. Stir in yeast mixture; beat in 2 eggs and 2 egg yolks. Add half the flour; beat with mixer at high speed. Knead in remaining flour until smooth and elastic. Place in greased bowl; cover. Let rise until doubled in bulk. Mix walnuts, brown sugar and vanilla with water to form smooth paste. Divide dough into 4 parts; roll out each part on floured board to 12-inch circle. Cut each circle into 12 parts. Place 1 scant teaspoon walnut filling on wide end of each triangle; roll up towards point. Place, point down, on greased cookie sheet; let rise until doubled in bulk. Beat remaining egg whites with 1/4 cup milk until frothy. Brush crescents with egg white mixture. Bake at 350 degrees for 20 minutes or until golden brown.

WALNUT STREUSEL LOAF

6 tbsp. butter
3/4 c. sugar
2 eggs
1 tsp. vanilla
2 c. flour
1 1/2 tsp. baking powder
1 tsp. salt
1/2 tsp. soda
1 tsp. cinnamon
1/4 tsp. nutmeg
1 c. sour cream
1/3 c. (packed) brown sugar
1 c. chopped walnuts

Cream 4 tablespoons butter and sugar until fluffy; beat in eggs, one at a time, beating well after each addition. Stir in vanilla. Sift flour, baking powder, salt, soda, 1/2 teaspoon cinnamon and nutmeg together; add to creamed mixture alternately with sour cream. Mix remaining butter and cinnamon with brown sugar and walnuts. Spoon 1/3 of the cake batter into greased loaf pan; sprinkle with half the walnut mixture. Repeat layers; top with remaining cake batter. Bake at 350 degrees for 55 minutes or until golden brown.

Watercress

COMPANY TOSSED SALAD

2 cloves of garlic
2 bunches watercress
1 sm. head lettuce
1/2 c. sliced almonds
1 c. cauliflowerets
1/2 avocado, diced
1 tomato, diced
1 tsp. salt
2 tbsp. lemon juice
1/4 tsp. sugar
1/4 tsp. pepper
1/8 tsp. celery seed
1/2 tsp. paprika
3/4 tsp. dry mustard
5 tbsp. salad oil

Split 1 clove of garlic; rub salad bowl with garlic. Remove coarse stems from watercress; tear watercress and lettuce into bite-sized pieces into salad bowl. Toast almonds in 350-degree oven until lightly browned; cool. Combine almonds, cauliflowerets, avocado and tomato with salad greens. Mince remaining clove of garlic; combine with salt, lemon juice, sugar, pepper, celery seed, paprika, mustard and salad oil. Blend thoroughly. Pour dressing over salad; toss lightly. Serve immediately.

TOSSED WATERCRESS SALAD

2 bunches watercress
1 head Bibb lettuce
1/2 head iceberg lettuce
1/2 lge. cucumber
1 c. halved cherry tomatoes
1/2 c. sliced green pepper
1/4 c. sliced ripe olives
3 slices bacon
1/4 c. grated Parmesan cheese
Creamy Garlic Dressing

Remove coarse stems from watercress; tear salad greens into bite-sized pieces. Arrange greens in large salad bowl. Pare and slice cucumber; add cucumber, tomatoes, green pepper and ripe olives to greens. Fry bacon until crisp; crumble coarsely. Sprinkle over salad; sprinkle with Parmesan cheese. Toss with Creamy Garlic Dressing; serve immediately.

Creamy Garlic Dressing

1 c. bottled Italian salad dressing
1 c. mayonnaise
1/4 c. shredded Cheddar cheese
1 tsp. anchovy paste

Combine all ingredients in jar; blend thoroughly. Chill until ready to use.

WATERCRESS SALAD BOWL

2 lge. bunches watercress
2 med. tomatoes, cut into wedges
1/2 c. pitted ripe olives
1/2 c. sliced celery
1/2 c. olive oil
1/4 c. fresh lemon juice
1/2 tsp. salt
1/8 tsp. pepper
2 cloves of garlic, split

Combine watercress, tomatoes, olives and celery in salad bowl; chill. Blend oil, lemon juice, seasonings and garlic in jar with tight-fitting lid. Shake well. Let dressing stand at room temperature for 1 hour. Remove garlic before serving. Yield: About 3/4 cup.

Watercress Salad Bowl . . . Peppery watercress complements tomatoes, celery, and olives.

SPECIAL WATERCRESS SALAD

3 bunches watercress
2 onions, sliced thin
4 slices bacon
2 eggs
2 c. salad oil
2 tbsp. horseradish
1/4 c. catsup
2 tbsp. grated onion
1 tsp. salt
1/3 c. vinegar
2 tbsp. paprika
1 tsp. Worcestershire sauce
1/8 tsp. hot sauce

Remove coarse stems from watercress; tear into bite-sized pieces into salad bowl. Separate onions into rings; add to watercress. Fry bacon until crisp; drain. Crumble bacon over onions. Combine eggs, oil, horseradish, catsup, onion, salt, vinegar, paprika, Worcestershire sauce and hot sauce in quart jar; blend thoroughly. Pour desired amount of dressing over salad; toss lightly. Serve immediately. Remaining dressing may be refrigerated until needed.

WATERCRESS-FRUIT SALAD

1 bunch watercress
2 oranges, sectioned
1 lge. avocado, diced
1/2 c. salad oil
1/4 c. lime juice
1/4 c. fruit-flavored punch
1/2 tsp. salt
1 tbsp. sugar

Remove coarse stems from watercress; tear into bite-sized pieces into salad bowl. Add oranges and avocado. Combine salad oil with lime juice, punch, salt and sugar in jar; blend thoroughly. Pour dressing over salad; toss lightly. Serve immediately.

WATERCRESS-ORANGE SALAD

2 bunches watercress
3 heads Belgian endive
2 oranges
2 shallots, finely chopped
1/3 c. olive oil
2 tbsp. lemon juice
Salt and pepper to taste

Wash, trim and cut watercress into small pieces; place in large bowl. Cut endive in 1/4-inch pieces. Peel and section oranges. Add endive and orange sections to watercress. Combine remaining ingredients in jar; blend well. Pour over salad; toss gently.

WATERCRESS SALAD SUPREME

2 bunches watercress
2 heads leaf lettuce
2 tart peeled apples, thinly sliced
1/2 c. chopped walnuts
1/8 tsp. salt
1/4 c. sugar
1/4 c. maple syrup
1 tbsp. dry mustard
1 tsp. sweet basil
1 clove of garlic, minced
3/4 c. olive oil

Remove coarse stems from watercress; tear watercress and lettuce into bite-sized pieces into salad bowl. Add apples and walnuts. Combine salt, sugar, syrup, mustard, basil, garlic and olive oil in small jar; blend thoroughly. Pour dressing over salad; toss lightly. Serve immediately.

WATERCRESS-GRAPE SALAD

1 bunch watercress
1 can mandarin orange slices, drained
1 c. seeded grapes
1/4 c. pecans, chopped
French dressing

Remove coarse stems from watercress; tear into bite-sized pieces into salad bowl. Add oranges, grapes and pecans. Pour dressing over salad; toss lightly. Serve immediately.

WATERCRESS SANDWICHES

1 3-oz. package cream cheese
1 loaf thin-sliced bread
1 c. slivered almonds, toasted
2 tbsp. finely chopped watercress
1/4 tsp. salt
Sprigs of watercress

Have cream cheese at room temperature. Trim crusts from bread; flatten slices with rolling pin. Beat cheese until fluffy; fold in almonds, watercress, and salt. Spread 1 teaspoonful cream cheese mixture on each bread slice. Roll, jelly roll fashion; place seam side down on cookie sheet. Cover with waxed paper; refrigerate until ready to serve. Tuck sprigs of watercress in ends of each sandwich.

HEAT WAVE WATERCRESS SOUP

1 cucumber
1 peeled avocado, sliced
1 7-oz. can green chile salsa
1/4 c. watercress
1/4 tsp. garlic salt
1 10 1/2-oz. can beef bouillon

Heat Wave Watercress Soup . . . A nutritious cold soup that hits the spot when temperatures rise.

Peel cucumber; cut into chunks. Place cucumber, avocado, chile salsa, watercress and garlic salt in blender container; process until vegetables are well blended. Pour in bouillon gradually, mixing well. Chill well; serve over ice in punch bowl. Garnish with cucumber slices and watercress sprigs. Yield: 6 servings.

Watermelon

MELON-BERRY BASKET

1 med. watermelon
1 honeydew melon
1 cantaloupe
2 c. sweetened raspberries

Cut watermelon in half lengthwise; leave part of top for handle. Scoop balls from center of melon with melon scoop. Scallop edge of watermelon. Cut honeydew and cantaloupe; scoop out balls. Mix melon balls and raspberries together; place in watermelon basket. Chill basket until ready to serve.

MINTED WATERMELON BALLS

1 c. sugar
1/4 c. (packed) mint leaves
4 tbsp. lemon juice
6 c. watermelon balls

Combine sugar, mint leaves and 2 cups water in small saucepan; bring to a boil, stirring until sugar is dissolved. Reduce heat; simmer for 5 minutes. Strain syrup; stir in lemon juice. Cool; chill well. Arrange watermelon balls in chilled sherbet glasses; add mint syrup. Chill until ready to serve.

WATERMELON FANTASY

1 watermelon
1 cantaloupe
2 bananas
1 can pineapple chunks
1 12-oz. bottle lemon-lime carbonated drink

Cut watermelon lengthwise; scoop balls from center with melon scoop. Halve cantaloupe; remove seeds. Scoop balls from cantaloupe. Cut bananas into bite-sized pieces. Drain pineapple chunks. Combine fruits in half the watermelon shell; toss lightly. Chill, covered, until ready to serve. Pour chilled lemon-lime drink over fruits; serve immediately.

WATERMELON SUPREME

1 watermelon
3 cantaloupes
4 peaches
4 pears
3 bananas
4 apples
1 20-oz. can pineapple chunks
2 lb. seedless grapes
1 pt. fresh strawberries
1 c. coconut

Cut watermelon in half lengthwise. Scoop melon balls from center with melon scoop. Cut cantaloupe in half; remove seeds. Scoop out small balls from cantaloupe. Peel peaches; cut peaches, pears, bananas and apples into chunks. Drain pineapple; reserve juice. Cover peaches, pears, bananas and apples with reserved juice. Combine fruits; place in half the watermelon shell. Sprinkle with coconut. Refrigerate, covered, for at least 8 hours.

MELON-MINT SALAD RING

1 pkg. lime gelatin
Mint extract
Watermelon and honeydew balls

Dissolve gelatin in 1 cup hot water; add 1 cup cold water and mint extract to desired flavor. Chill until partially set; beat until frothy. Fold in melon balls; pour in ring mold. Chill until firm.

SUMMER DAY SALAD

1 sm. bottle maraschino cherries
3 c. watermelon balls
1 c. honeydew melon balls
1 c. pineapple chunks
1 c. fresh strawberries
1/2 c. mayonnaise
1/2 tsp. poppy seed

Drain cherries; reserve 2 tablespoons juice. Combine melon balls and fruits in lettuce-lined bowl. Blend mayonnaise, reserved juice and poppy seed; mix well. Pour over fruits and melon balls; toss lightly. Serve immediately.

WATERMELON SALAD

Watermelon
Cottage cheese
Mayonnaise
Sugar
Nutmeg

Halve watermelon; scoop balls from center with melon scoop. Arrange balls on crisp lettuce on individual salad plates. Top melon balls with 2 tablespoons cottage cheese. Combine mayonnaise and sugar; blend well. Spoon mayonnaise over salads; sprinkle with nutmeg.

CRÉME DE MENTHE-MELON BALLS

Papaya balls
Watermelon balls
Cantaloupe balls
Creme de menthe

Place chilled melon balls in sherbet glasses; pour creme de menthe over fruit. Chill until ready to serve.

WATERMELON ICE

1/2 lge. watermelon
Juice of 4 oranges
Juice of 2 lemons
1 c. sugar
1 egg white

Scoop meat from melon. Strain melon through cheesecloth bag; squeeze to extract all juice. Combine watermelon, orange and lemon juices with sugar; stir until sugar is dissolved. Pour into freezer trays; freeze partially. Beat egg white until stiff peaks form. Turn juice mixture into large bowl; beat in egg white. Return to freezer trays; freeze until firm. Serve in scooped out melon rind; garnish with watermelon, honeydew or cantaloupe balls, cherries and seedless grapes.

WATERMELON PARTY SHERBET

1 6-oz. can frozen pink lemonade concentrate
2 c. diced watermelon
1 c. sugar
2 egg whites, stiffly beaten

Partially thaw lemonade concentrate; blend with watermelon and sugar. Pour into freezer tray; freeze until partially set. Turn out into large bowl; fold in egg whites. Return to freezer tray; chill until partially set. Stir well; freeze until firm.

WATERMELON PINK SHERBET

3/4 c. sugar
Salt to taste
2 tbsp. fresh lemon juice
1 tbsp. fresh lime juice
2 c. watermelon pulp, crushed

Boil sugar and 1/2 cup water until mixture spins fine thread or 230 degrees on candy thermometer; cool. Add salt, lemon and lime juices to watermelon pulp. Add syrup; stir to blend well. Pour into ice cube trays or loaf pan; freeze overnight.

WATERMELON-SPICE PIE

Watermelon rind
1 c. sugar
1 tsp. cinnamon
1/3 tsp. nutmeg
1/4 tsp. cloves
1/8 tsp. salt
2 tbsp. flour
1/4 c. vinegar
1/2 c. raisins
1 recipe 2-crust pie pastry

Cut green outer rind and most of pulp from watermelon rind; cut into 1/4-inch cubes. Combine 1 1/2 cups cubes with water to cover in saucepan; simmer until tender. Drain; add sugar, cinnamon, nutmeg, cloves, salt, flour, vinegar and raisins to watermelon cubes; blend well. Pour into pastry shell; cover with pastry. Cut steam vents. Bake at 450 degrees until crust is browned. Reduce temperature to 350 degrees; bake until filling is set.

Whitefish

Whitefish is an edible freshwater fish related to trout and salmon. It derives its name from its white color. The fish is found primarily in the Great Lakes but it also inhabits other cold North American inland waters. Whitefish flesh is fat, firm, and succulent. It is especially delicious and is considered a great delicacy when smoked. Whitefish roe is lightly salted and made into caviar (see CAVIAR).

Like all fish, whitefish is a rich source of protein. (3 1/2 ounces fresh uncooked whitefish = 155 calories; 3 1/2 ounces smoked whitefish = 155 calories)

AVAILABILITY: Fresh whitefish is sold year-round whole and in fillets. Frozen whitefish is available in fillets. Whole drawn smoked whitefish is widely marketed in the East and Midwest. Roe caviar is sold in some retail stores.

BUYING: Select whole fresh fish with clear, bulging eyes; reddish or pink gills; bright, shiny, tightly clinging scales; firm flesh that springs back when lightly pressed; and fresh, pleasant odor. Buy 1/3 to 1/2 pound edible fish or 1 pound whole fish per serving.

STORING: Wrap fresh fish in moistureproof paper or place in covered dish. Refrigerate and use within 1 to 2 days. Store commercially frozen fish in original package and freeze until ready to use. Refrigerate smoked whitefish up to 1 week.

PREPARATION: Whitefish can be prepared by almost every method for seafood cookery, including broiling, baking, poaching, planking, and so on. Fresh whitefish roe may be sauteed or poached.

SERVING: Serve whitefish with lemon butter, parsley butter or complementary sauce. Use whitefish in gefilte fish, cakes, fritters, and so on. Serve smoked whole or sectioned whitefish on a bed of watercress and garnish with lemon wedges, parsley, or chopped onion. Accompany with pumpernickel bread and perhaps caviar.
(See SEAFOOD.)

SEVICHE

1 1/2 lb. whitefish fillets
6 tbsp. lime juice
16 pitted green Spanish olives
3 peeled tomatoes, finely minced
3/4 c. catsup
2 tbsp. olive liquid
1/2 c. olive oil
1 tsp. dry oregano
2 tsp. salt
5/8 tsp. hot sauce

Cut whitefish fillets into bite-sized pieces; soak whitefish in lime juice for 1 hour and 30 minutes. Place fish in sieve. Rinse well with cold water. Combine whitefish with olives and tomatoes; toss lightly. Combine catsup, olive liquid, olive oil, oregano, salt and hot sauce; blend well. Pour sauce over whitefish; chill until ready to serve.

WHITEFISH FILLETS SUPREME

1 lb. whitefish fillets
1 tbsp. vinegar
3 tbsp. shortening
2 tbsp. flour
1/2 tsp. salt
1/8 tsp. pepper
1/4 tsp. paprika
1/8 tsp. celery salt
1/8 tsp. thyme
2 tsp. chopped parsley
1 c. milk
1/2 c. grated cheese
2 onions, sliced
1/2 c. soft bread crumbs

Cook whitefish for 5 minutes in boiling water to which vinegar has been added; drain. Melt 2 tablespoonfuls shortening in saucepan. Add flour, salt, pepper, paprika, celery salt, thyme and parsley; blend well. Stir in milk gradually; cook, stirring, over low heat until thickened. Blend in cheese, stirring constantly, until melted. Saute onions in remaining shortening in skillet until transparent. Place onions in greased 6 x 10-inch baking dish; add whitefish. Pour cheese sauce over fish; sprinkle with crumbs. Bake at 425 degrees for 25 minutes or until fish flakes easily with a fork.

BAKED FISH AU GRATIN

2 lb. whitefish fillets
8 slices Cheddar cheese
1 tsp. thyme
1/4 c. chopped parsley
1 c. chopped onions
2 tbsp. vegetable oil
2 tbsp. flour
1 tsp. salt
1/8 tsp. pepper
1 c. milk

Place half the fillets in greased 9 x 9 x 3/4-inch baking dish. Cover with 4 slices cheese; repeat layers. Sprinkle with thyme and parsley. Saute onions in oil in skillet over medium heat until transparent; blend in flour, salt and pepper. Stir in milk gradually. Bring to a boil over low heat, stirring constantly; boil, stirring, for 1 minute. Pour over whitefish mixture. Bake at 400 degrees for 20 minutes or until fish flakes easily with a fork.

BAKED WHITEFISH ON CELERY LEAVES

Celery leaves
4 tbsp. lemon juice
4 thick whitefish fillets
1/2 tsp. salt
1/4 tsp. white pepper
Paprika
1 1/2 c. mayonnaise
1/2 c. sweet relish
3 green onions, chopped
1 tbsp. chopped parsley
1/4 c. macadamia nuts, chopped

Cover bottom of shallow casserole dish with celery leaves. Sprinkle lemon juice over whitefish. Sprinkle with salt, pepper and paprika; let stand for 20 minutes. Place whitefish on celery leaves. Combine mayonnaise, relish, green onions and parsley; blend well. Spread over fish; sprinkle macadamia nuts over top. Bake in 350-degree oven for 25 minutes or until fish flakes easily with a fork.

LAWALU WHITEFISH

1 3 to 4-lb. whitefish
1/8 tsp. salt
2 slices bacon

Split whitefish in half; sprinkle with salt. Place bacon between whitefish halves. Wrap whitefish in foil. Cook over hot coals for 30 minutes or until fish flakes easily with a fork.

STUFFED WHITEFISH

1 lb. salmon steak, chopped
1 egg white
1 tsp. salt
1/2 c. cream
1 clove of garlic, minced
2 tbsp. chopped onion
2 tbsp. chopped mushrooms
1 tsp. thyme
Dash of pepper
1 3-lb. whitefish fillet
8 shrimp
Butter
Chopped chives
4 tomatoes, peeled
Bread crumbs
Chopped parsley
Grated cheese

Combine salmon, egg white, salt, cream, garlic, onion, mushrooms, thyme and pepper. Place whitefish, split butterfly fashion, skin side down on plank. Spread salmon mixture 1 inch thick over half the whitefish; fold other half over. Slash crosswise several times; secure opening. Split shrimp lengthwise half their length; dip into butter. Place on top of fish. Dot fish with butter; sprinkle shrimp with chopped chives. Cut tomatoes into halves; garnish with tomatoes sprinkled with crumbs, parsley, butter and cheese. Bake in 375-degree oven for 10 minutes. Broil 5 to 6 inches from source of heat for 20 minutes or until fish flakes easily with a fork. Serve immediately.

GEFILTE FISH

3 lb. whitefish
4 med. onions
3 eggs, well beaten
1 tbsp. salt
2 tsp. black pepper
1 tsp. sugar
1/2 c. cracker meal
2 carrots, peeled

Fillet fish; save heads, skin and bones. Grind whitefish; use small blade. Grind 2 onions; combine whitefish and onions in wooden chopping bowl. Stir in eggs, 2 teaspoons salt, pepper and sugar. Chop well; add cracker meal and 1/2 cup water gradually. Slice remaining onions and carrots. Place heads, skin and bones, 1 teaspoon salt, remaining onions and carrots in large kettle; add 2 quarts water. Bring to a boil; boil for 30 minutes. Form whitefish mixture into individual balls the size of small oranges. Place whitefish balls into liquid in kettle; add water, if necessary, to cover whitefish balls. Simmer for 2 hours and 30 minutes or until stock has been reduced by half. Remove from heat; carefully remove whitefish balls to serving platter. Top each ball with slice of cooked carrot. Strain fish stock into bowl; refrigerate fish and stock until stock jells. Serve cold with horseradish.

BATTER-FRIED WHITEFISH

2 lb. whitefish
1 c. flour
2 tsp. baking powder
1 tsp. salt
1 tsp. sugar
1 egg, separated
1 tsp. melted butter

Cut whitefish into serving pieces. Sift flour, baking powder, salt and sugar into bowl; add egg yolk. Add butter and water to make medium batter; mix well. Beat egg white until stiff peaks form; fold egg white into batter. Dip whitefish into batter. Fry in deep fat at 350 degrees for 6 minutes or until golden brown; drain on absorbent paper.

WHITEFISH AMANDINE

2 lb. whitefish fillets
2 tbsp. lemon juice
2 tsp. salt
1/8 tsp. pepper
1/2 c. flour
1/2 c. blanched slivered almonds
2 tbsp. chopped parsley

Cut fillets into serving portions. Sprinkle with lemon juice, salt and pepper; roll in flour. Fry in small amount of hot fat over medium heat for 10 minutes or until browned; turn once. Remove fillets to hot platter. Saute almonds in pan drippings until lightly browned; add parsley. Serve over fish.

GRILLED LAKE SUPERIOR WHITEFISH MAITRE D'HOTEL

1/4 c. margarine, melted
1/8 tsp. salt
Dash of ground pepper
1 2-lb. whitefish, boned and split
1 tbsp. chopped parsley
1 tsp. lemon juice
Parsley Sprigs
Lemon Wedges

Preheat broiler. Brush broiler rack lightly with some of the melted margarine. Stir salt and pepper into remaining margarine. Brush inside of whitefish with some of the margarine mixture. Place whitefish, skin sides up, on broiler rack. Brush skin with small amount of margarine mixture. Reserve remaining margarine mixture. Broil whitefish 3 to 4 inches away from source of heat for about 10 minutes or until fish flakes easily with fork. Place whitefish on serving platter. Stir chopped parsley and lemon juice into remaining margarine mixture; pour over whitefish. Garnish with parsley sprigs and lemon. Yield: 3 servings.

Grilled Lake Superior Whitefish Maitre d'Hotel . . . Garnish this fish with parsley and lemon.

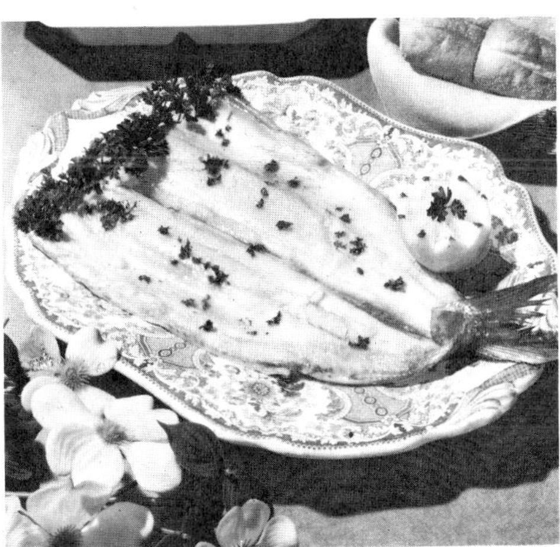

Wine

Wines add greatly to the pleasure of a meal. The selection of wine is often based on the foods that the wine will accompany. *Appetizer wines* are served chilled with or without food. *Red dinner wines* are served at room temperature as accompaniments to steak, roasts, chops, and cheeses. *Rose,* generally classed as a red dinner wine, is served chilled. *White dinner wines* are served well chilled and accompany seafoods, chicken, omelets, or other light foods. *Dessert wines* are served after dinner or alone as a refreshing beverage. They are served chilled or at cool room temperature (60 degrees) and accompany fruit, cookies, cheese, or nuts. *Sparkling wines* are served well chilled and are excellent.

TYPES OF WINE: Wines are described as being dry or sweet. The term "dry" is the direct opposite of "sweet" and means that the wine is almost tart in flavor. *Burgundy*–A dry, full-bodied red dinner wine. Pinot Noir, Red Pinot, and Gamay are burgundies that are named for the grapes from which they come. *Chablis*–A soft, dry, less tart and full-bodied white dinner wine. Pinots are the best-known types of Chablis. *Champagne*–Naturally sparkling wine that ranges from very dry or brut to semi-dry or sec to sweet. Pink Champagne is sometimes marketed as Sparkling Rose. Champagnes go well with every course. *Chianti*–A dry, slightly tart, full-bodied red dinner wine. *Claret*–A dry, tart, light- to medium-bodied brilliant red dinner wine. Cabernet, Zinfandel, and Grignolino are popular Clarets. *Cold Duck and Very Cold Duck*–Combinations of champagne and sparkling burgundy that go well with every course. *Muscatel*–A fruit-flavored sweet dessert wine with the distinctive flavor and aroma of the Muscat grapes from which it is produced. *Port*–A rich, sweet, full-bodied, fruit-flavored dessert wine. Port ranges in color from deep red to pale gold or white to tawny. *Rhine wine*–A very dry, tart, light-bodied white dinner wine. Among the types of Rhine wine are Reislings. *Rose*–A light pink, fruit-flavored, light-bodied

TYPE	WINES	SERVING GLASSES
Appetizer Wines	Sherry, Vermouth	Serve in a 2 1/2–4 ounce glass
Red Dinner Wines	Burgundy, Chianti, Claret, Rosé	Serve in a 6–9 ounce glass
White Dinner Wines	Chablis, Rhine Wine, Sauterne	Serve in a 6–9 ounce glass
Dessert Wines	Muscatel, Port, Sweet or Cream Sherry, Tokay	Serve in a 2 1/2–4 ounce glass
Sparkling Wines	Champagne, Cold or Very Cold Duck, Sparkling Burgundy	Serve in a 5–9 ounce glass

red dinner wine that ranges from dry to slightly sweet. *Sauterne*—A golden colored, full-bodied white dinner wine that ranges from dry to sweet. Types include Semillon, Sauvignon Blanc, and Haut Sauterne. The latter is so sweet it is often served as a dessert wine. *Sherry*—A rich, nut-flavored appetizer wine that ranges from dry to sweet and in color from pale to dark amber. There is also a cream sherry that is served as a dessert wine. *Sparkling Burgundy*—Bright red, sweet, fruit-flavored wine with natural effervescence similar to that of champagne. Sparkling Burgundy goes well with any food. *Tokay*—A pinkish amber dessert wine with a slightly nutlike flavor. It is less sweet than port but cannot be considered a dry wine. *Vermouth*—A spicy, aromatic, light-bodied appetizer wine that ranges from dry to sweet.

Yogurt

RASPBERRY YOGURT RING

2 c. sifted flour
1 tsp. soda
1/2 tsp. baking powder
1/4 tsp. salt
1 c. (packed) light brown sugar
1/2 c. butter
1 egg
1 tsp. vanilla
1 c. red raspberry yogurt
Confectioners' sugar

Sift flour, soda, baking powder and salt. Cream brown sugar and butter in mixer bowl until fluffy; beat in egg and vanilla. Stir in flour mixture alternately with yogurt just until blended. Spoon into greased 9-inch tube pan. Bake at 350 degrees for 50 minutes or until cake tests done. Cool cake in pan on wire rack for 10 minutes. Loosen edges and center with knife; turn onto rack. Cool completely. Sprinkle lightly with confectioners' sugar just before serving.

YOGURT-CUCUMBER SALAD

3 med. cucumbers
1/4 tsp. salt
1 clove of garlic, cut
1 tbsp. vinegar
1/2 tsp. dillweed
1 pt. yogurt
2 tbsp. olive oil
1 tbsp. chopped mint leaves

Peel and quarter cucumbers; slice paper thin. Add salt to cucumbers; mix well. Rub bowl with garlic; swish vinegar around bowl. Add dillweed, yogurt, oil and mint; stir until thickened and smooth. Add cucumbers; toss gently until well coated.

YOGURT COFFEE CAKE

1 c. powdered sugar
6 eggs
1 c. flour
1 tsp. soda
Lemon juice
1 c. yogurt
4 tbsp. butter, melted
2 c. sugar
Almonds

Beat sugar and eggs in large bowl for 5 minutes. Add sifted flour and soda. Combine 2 tablespoons lemon juice, yogurt and butter; add to egg mixture. Mix well; pour into greased and lightly floured 8 x 8-inch square baking dish. Bake at 375 degrees for 1 hour. Combine sugar, 2 cups water and 1 teaspoon lemon juice in a saucepan; cook, stirring, over low heat, until sugar is dissolved. Cool. Remove bread from oven; prick with wooden pick. Pour sugar mixture over top; allow to stand for at least 30 minutes before cutting in squares. Garnish with almonds.

Zabaglione

MARSALA ZABAGLIONE

4 egg yolks
4 tbsp. sugar
Dash of salt
Twist of lemon peel
6 tbsp. Marsala

Combine egg yolks, sugar, salt and lemon peel in top of double boiler; beat over simmering water. Add Marsala gradually; beat constantly until custard is fluffy, smooth and thickened. Serve warm or cold in stemmed glasses. Custard separates when cold; stir until smooth before serving.

Zucchini

Zucchini is a well-known variety of summer squash. It is also called Italian squash. Smooth, dark green, and cylindrical, zucchini resembles the cucumber. The flesh of zucchini is pale green and delicately flavored. For availability, buying, storing, preparation, and serving, see SQUASH.
(See VEGETABLES.)

Zucchini Salad . . . Zucchini, frozen peas and onions, and salad dressing mix in a quick salad.

ZUCCHINI SALAD

1 lb. small zucchini, thinly sliced
1 10-oz. package frozen green peas and pearl onions
1 env. Italian salad dressing mix
2 tbsp. cider vinegar
Crisp salad greens

Cook zucchini in 2 cups boiling salted water in saucepan for 1 minute; drain. Cook frozen peas and onions according to package directions. Drain. Prepare salad dressing mix according to package directions. Combine 1/2 cup dressing with cooked vegetables; add vinegar. Cover; chill for at least 4 hours, stirring occasionally. Line chilled salad bowl with salad greens; spoon in marinated vegetables. Yield: 8 servings.

BAKED ZUCCHINI WITH TOMATOES

1 tsp. chopped onion
1 clove of garlic, minced
1 tbsp. salad oil
1 No. 2 1/2 can tomatoes
2 lb. zucchini, sliced
2 c. bread crumbs

Brown onion and garlic in salad oil; add tomatoes. Place half the zucchini in buttered 2-quart baking dish. Add half the tomato mixture; add half the bread crumbs. Repeat layers. Bake in 400-degree oven for 1 hour.

FRIED ZUCCHINI

2 tbsp. flour
1/2 tsp. salt
Pepper to taste
1 egg, beaten
1 tbsp. lemon juice
4 zucchini squash, sliced
3/4 c. bread crumbs
1/4 c. shortening

Mix flour, salt and pepper; blend egg with lemon juice. Coat zucchini with flour mixture; dip into egg mixture. Coat with crumbs. Fry in shortening until tender and browned on both sides.

ITALIAN ZUCCHINI

2 lb. zucchini, sliced
1 onion, chopped fine
1 clove of garlic, crushed
1 tbsp. oil
1 can tomato paste
3/4 c. tomato juice
4 slices bread, cubed
1/4 c. buttered bread crumbs
1/4 c. grated Parmesan cheese

Cook squash in boiling, salted water until just tender; drain. Saute onion and garlic in oil until tender; add tomato paste and tomato juice. Place half the squash in lightly buttered casserole; add half the bread cubes. Add half the tomato mixture; repeat layers. Cover with buttered crumbs and cheese. Bake at 350 degrees for 30 minutes.

PANNED ZUCCHINI WITH DILL

1 sprig of fresh dill, chopped
1/2 sm. onion, chopped
1 qt. sliced zucchini
1/2 tsp. salt
Pepper to taste

Cook dill and onion in small amount of hot fat in large skillet until transparent; add zucchini, salt and pepper. Simmer, covered, for 10 minutes or until just tender. Add 1/4 cup of water, if needed.

STUFFED ZUCCHINI

3 zucchini
Salt
2 tbsp. minced onion
3 tbsp. butter
1 c. soft bread crumbs
1/2 c. cooked tomatoes
Pepper

Cook zucchini in boiling salted water for 10 minutes; drain. Halve zucchini lengthwise. Scoop out pulp; reserve shells. Mix pulp, onion, butter, bread crumbs and tomatoes; season to taste. Spoon mixture into zucchini shells; arrange on baking sheet. Bake at 350 degrees for 15 minutes or until tops are lightly browned.

ZUCCHINI-BROWN RICE BAKE

2 c. thinly sliced zucchini
3/4 c. packaged precooked brown rice
1/2 c. chopped parsley
1/4 c. chopped onion
1/2 tsp. salt
3 eggs, beaten
1/4 c. milk
1 c. grated cheese

Combine zucchini, rice, parsley, onion and salt with 3/4 cup boiling water in saucepan; cook, covered, for 15 minutes. Beat eggs, milk and cheese together; stir into zucchini mixture. Pour into baking dish. Bake at 350 degrees for 35 minutes or until set.

ZUCCHINI PIE

2 1/2 lb. zucchini
2 tbsp. butter
1 c. diced Velveeta cheese
Salt and pepper to taste
8 saltines, crumbled

Trim ends from zucchini; cut into small chunks. Boil in small amount of water for 10 minutes or until just tender; drain thoroughly. Add butter and cheese; stir until melted. Add salt and pepper. Turn into greased 10-inch pie plate; top with saltine crumbs. Bake at 400 degrees for 15 minutes.

Index

PHOTOGRAPHY CREDITS: Florida Citrus Commission; McIlhenny Company; The Nestle Company; United Fresh Fruit and Vegetable Association; Knox Gelatine, Inc.; National Broiler Council; Grandma's West Indies Molasses; Anderson, Clayton & Company: Chiffon Margarine, Seven Seas Dressing; Tuna Research Foundation; Keith Thomas Company; California Strawberry Advisory Board; California Artichoke Advisory Board; Spanish Green Olive Commission; Brussels Sprouts Marketing Program; R. C. Bigelow, Inc.; National Cherry Growers & Industries Foundation; National Macaroni Institute; International Tuna Fish Association; Pickle Packers International; California Dried Fig Advisory Board; Filbert/Hazelnut Institute; National Kraut Packers Association; Louisiana Yam Commission; Carnation Company; Procter & Gamble Company: Crisco Division; Apple Pantry: Washington State Apple Commission; Pet, Inc.; American Dry Milk Institute, Inc.; National Dairy Council; Standard Fruit & Steamship Company: Cabana Bananas; California Avocado Advisory Board; The R. T. French Company; Nabisco, Inc.; Corning Glass Works; General Foods Kitchens; Quaker Oats Company; Evaporated Milk Association; Best Foods: A Division of CPC International; Standard Brands Products: Fleischmann's Yeast, Fleischmann's Margarine, Planter's Nuts, Planter's Oil; Royal Puddings and Gelatins; Pineapple Growers Association; Olive Administrative Committee; National Association of Frozen Food Packers; Halibut Association of North America; Shrimp Association of the Americas; Processed Apples Institute; Rice Council; Angostura-Wuppermann Corporation; North American Blueberry Council; South African Rock Lobster Service Corporation; National Livestock and Meat Board; National Turkey Federation; California Beef Council; Pillsbury Company; American Dairy Association; DIAMOND Walnut Growers, Inc.; Kelloggs Company; California Raisin Advisory Board; American Honey Institute; National Meat Canners Association; Instant Potato Products Association; National Pecan Shellers & Processors Association; Pie Filling Institute; National Fisheries Institute; U. S. Department of Commerce: National Marine Fisheries Western Growers Association; The Borden Company; Sugar Information, Inc.; Ocean Spray Cranberries, Inc.; McCormick & Company, Inc.; Armour and Company; Sunkist Growers; Ball Corporation; American Lamb Council; Fishery Marketing Specialist; C & H Sugar Kitchen; The American Mushroom Institute; Florida Fruit and Vegetable Association; The American Spice Trade Association; Campbell Soup Company; Marine Sardine Council; American Home Foods: Chef-Boy-Ar-Dee; Wheat Flour Institute; Costal Valley Canning Company; Cling Peach Advisory Board; Ralston-Purina Company. COVER: Washington State Apple Commission.

Printed in the United States of America.